WORLD
COMPENDIUM

OF HEALTHCARE FACILITIES AND NONPROFIT ORGANIZATIONS

EDITED BY

Ebby Elahi, M.D., M.B.A.

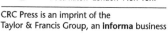

CRC Press
Taylor & Francis Group
Boca Raton London New York

CRC Press is an imprint of the
Taylor & Francis Group, an **informa** business

First edition published 2022
by CRC Press
6000 Broken Sound Parkway NW, Suite 300, Boca Raton, FL 33487-2742

and by CRC Press
2 Park Square, Milton Park, Abingdon, Oxon, OX14 4RN

CRC Press is an imprint of Taylor & Francis Group, LLC

© 2022 Virtue Foundation

ISBN: 9781032229522 (hbk)
ISBN: 9781032229461 (pbk)
ISBN: 9781003274872 (ebk)

DOI: 10.1201/9781003274872

This book is dedicated to all of our partners around the globe who work tirelessly to improve healthcare for all those in need.

Contents

Preface

The journey that has led to this compendium began nearly two decades ago, when a group of like-minded professionals came together to create the Virtue Foundation. Our idealism of wanting to serve those in need in resource-poor regions around the world was soon to be confronted with the challenging reality of making these interventions effective, ethical, and lasting. It was not long before I began questioning the long-term value of discrete missions and their potential harm to the communities they were intended to serve.

These concerns led me to reconsider the pursuit of short-term interventions in favor of complex yet sustainable training programs overseas. Such efforts would require the cooperation of governments, international and national stakeholders, professionals, and philanthropists. Yet I was confronted time and again with seemingly insurmountable obstacles to effecting sustainable change in dynamic socio-political environments. As it soon became apparent, many long-term projects remained too heavily dependent on a complex set of factors to remain truly sustainable. Beyond the cacophony of well-intentioned voices calling for lasting change was an unsettling landscape dotted with graveyards of unfinished buildings and abandoned projects. Without such critical factors as a stable government, sustained economic support, personal security, protection from corruption, and community buy-in, even the most laudable philanthropic efforts would be destined to encounter insurmountable headwinds. Perhaps this explained the uneven presence of non-governmental organizations in well-known metropolitan centers despite rural and at times large population areas with greater need.

This concern was the core impetus behind the present compendium. Collaborating with a group of academics and professionals in fields ranging from healthcare and economics to data science and analytics, we thus sought ways to help optimize our interventions and engagements around the globe. To our great surprise, we found a dearth of practical resources to provide satisfactory answers to our questions. The search for solutions led us on a decade-long journey, beginning with data mapping projects and culminating in the adoption of machine learning and artificial intelligence as a means to better define need and intervention opportunities worldwide. This compendium represents one of the first products of this Actionable Data Initiative and provides perhaps the world's most comprehensive compilation of healthcare facilities and nonprofits in low and lower-middle-income countries. The first volume of this compendium— *Insights in Global Health*—was published by Taylor & Francis and included 24 low-income countries as defined by the World Bank. This expanded edition includes an additional 48 lower-middle-income countries along with a companion digital platform, VFMatch.org.

This compendium offers a fresh perspective on global health interventions. Philanthropic interventions need not conform to an all-or-nothing model whereby they are considered either ineffective short-term neocolonial voluntourism, or complex, bureaucratic and inefficient undertakings marked by inertia and inflexibility. By making data accessible, the information age promises customizable and targeted matching of needs and resources at the individual and organizational levels, thereby reducing the inefficiencies that have historically plagued international healthcare philanthropy.

As a practicing physician for over two decades, I continue to believe that even a single life transformed reaffirms the inherent value of philanthropic medicine. Yet, by cooperating together and harnessing the power of data, we can exponentially expand our impact far beyond what any one individual can do alone. For me, this book is a testament to the power of collaboration in bringing about meaningful change.

Ebby Elahi

Editor Biography

Dr. Ebby Elahi is Clinical Professor of Ophthalmology, Otolaryngology and Public Health at the Icahn School of Medicine at Mount Sinai, and Director of Fifth Avenue Associates. An oculofacial surgeon, Dr. Elahi is a fellow of the American Academy of Ophthalmology, the American Society of Ophthalmic Plastic and Reconstructive Surgery, and past president of the New York Facial Plastic Surgery Society. Inducted into the Alpha Omega Alpha Medical Honor Society, he is actively involved in research and education, and holds several surgical device patents. He is the recipient of multiple awards for his academic teaching and contributions to the international community. Dr. Elahi completed his medical and postgraduate education at the Mount Sinai School of Medicine and earned his MBA from Columbia University.

For over twenty years, Dr. Elahi has been an advocate for issues surrounding global health and currently serves as Director of Global Affairs at the Virtue Foundation, an NGO in special consultative status to the United Nations Economic and Social Council. There he has led volunteer surgical expeditions in over 20 countries. He also leads the Actionable Data Initiative, a multi-disciplinary global health AI project, and is the Editor of *Insights in Global Health: A Compendium of Healthcare Facilities and Nonprofit Organizations*, an output of that initiative, published by Taylor & Francis.

Acknowledgments

World Compendium of Healthcare Facilities and Nonprofit Organizations is the product of a multi-year interdisciplinary collaboration and builds on the publication of *Insights in Global Health*. It should be noted that more than 20,000 work hours contributed by over 90 people were necessary to make this project a reality. We owe a deep debt of gratitude to all those who have graciously contributed to this project over the past several years, including the Actionable Data Initiative Steering Committee, especially Dr. Joan LaRovere, Kim Azzarelli, Dr. Omar Besbes, and Dr. Matthew Baker, as well as the Virtue Foundation staff, including Nicolas Douard, Allen Nasseri, Mohammed Bataglia, and former program director Anna Szczepanek, for their selfless and tireless dedication to this project and exemplary work ethic. Lastly, the visionary leadership of Drs. Joseph Salim and Joan LaRovere at the Virtue Foundation merits special recognition. While there is simply no way to individually thank the many selfless volunteers and other contributors, below we have sought to acknowledge the volunteers who have made a significant contribution to this project and without whom this compendium would not have become a reality.

Volunteer Contributors

Eliza Abrams	Student/Researcher, Massachusetts General Hospital/Harvard Medical School	Volunteer
Evan Afshin, M.D.	Clinical Research Fellow, Weill Cornell Medicine	Volunteer
Amine Allouah, Ph.D.	Data Scientist, Columbia University	Volunteer
Adam Ammar, M.D.	Resident, Montefiore Medical Center/Albert Einstein College of Medicine, Department of Neurosurgery; Harvard Medical School, Program in Global Surgery and Social Change	Volunteer
Kimberly Ashayeri, M.D.	Resident, New York University, Department of Neurosurgery	Volunteer
Kim Azzarelli, J.D.	CEO, Seneca Women; Chair, Cornell Law School's Center for Women and Justice	Senior Advisor/Editor
Matthew Baker, Ph.D.	Associate Professor of Economics, CUNY Hunter	Advisor
Rosie Balfour-Lynn, MBBS BSc	Paediatric Trainee, North Thames Training Program, London, UK	Volunteer
Alexander Barash, M.D.	Ophthalmologist, New York Eye and Ear Infirmary of Mount Sinai	Volunteer
Joshua Benton	Medical Student, Albert Einstein College of Medicine	Volunteer
Omar Besbes, Ph.D.	Vikram S. Pandit Professor of Business, Columbia Business School	Advisor
Nitin Chopra, M.D., MBA	Resident, New York Eye and Ear Infirmary of Mount Sinai, Department of Ophthalmology	Volunteer
Jared Dashevsky	Medical Student, Icahn School of Medicine at Mount Sinai	Volunteer
Maria del Rio Sanin, MS	Service Designer and Project Manager, Barcelona, Spain	Volunteer
Murray Echt, M.D.	Resident, Montefiore Medical Center/Albert Einstein College of Medicine, Department of Neurosurgery	Volunteer
Niki Elahi, MPH	Student, Columbia University, School of Dental Medicine	Volunteer
Mattia Filiaci, Ph.D.	Director, Risk Management, Credit Suisse	Volunteer
Adison Fortunel, M.D.	Resident, Montefiore Medical Center/Albert Einstein College of Medicine, Department of Neurosurgery	Volunteer
Nysa Gandhi	Student, Roland Park Country School	Volunteer
Saadi Ghatan, M.D.	Associate Professor of Neurosurgery, Mount Sinai Health System	Volunteer

Yvonne Jones	Surgical Technician, Mount Sinai Medical Center	Volunteer
Ellen Kampinsky	Editorial Director, Seneca Women	Volunteer
Joan LaRovere, M.D., MSc, MBA	Assistant Professor of Pediatrics, Boston Children's Hospital/Harvard Medical School	Contributor/Senior Editor
Michaela Leone	Data Scientist, Icahn School of Medicine	Volunteer
Zidong Liu	Data Scientist, University of Cambridge	Virtue Foundation Staff (former)
Michael Longo, M.D.	Resident, Vanderbilt University Medical Center, Department of Neurosurgery	Volunteer
Qingchen Meng	Master of Science in Actuarial Science, University of Iowa	Volunteer
Hannah Oblak	Research Intern, Yale University	Volunteer
Aleka Scoco, M.D.	Resident, Montefiore Medical Center/Albert Einstein College of Medicine, Department of Neurosurgery	Volunteer
Janak Shah, M.D.	Ophthalmologist, Netrapuja Research Centre/Netrapuja Eye Care	Volunteer
Preeti Shah, M.D.	Ophthalmologist, Netrapuja Research Centre/Netrapuja Eye Care	Volunteer
Noah Shohet *(1996-2021)*	Office Administrator, Sea Surgery Center	Volunteer
Reza Yassari, M.D.	Professor of Neurosurgery, Montefiore Medical Center/Albert Einstein College of Medicine	Volunteer

Institutional Contributors

Columbia Business School

DataRobot

Dun & Bradstreet

Goldman Sachs Gives

Harvard University Center for Geographic Analysis

Icahn School of Medicine at Mount Sinai

Massachusetts Institute of Technology

Procter & Gamble

Wolfram Alpha

Specialty Abbreviations

Specialty	Abbreviation
Allergy and Immunology	All-Immu
Anesthesiology	Anesth
Cardiothoracic Surgery	CT Surg
Cardiovascular Medicine	CV Med
Critical Care Medicine	Crit-Care
Dentistry & Maxillofacial Surgery	Dent-OMFS
Dermatology	Derm
Emergency/Disaster Medicine	ER Med
Endocrinology	Endo
Family Medicine/General Practice	General
Gastroenterology	GI
Geriatric Medicine	Geri
Hematology & Oncology	Heme-Onc
Infectious & Tropical Diseases	Infect Dis
Internal Medicine	Medicine
Logistics and Operations	Logist-Op
Maternal–Fetal Medicine	MF Med
Medical Genetics and Genomics	Genetics
Neonatology and Perinatology	Neonat
Nephrology	Nephro
Neurological Surgery	Neurosurg
Neurology	Neuro
Nutrition	Nutr
Ophthalmology/Optometry	Ophth-Opt
Orthopaedic Medicine & Surgery	Ortho
Otolaryngology	ENT
Palliative Medicine	Palliative
Pathology & Laboratory Medicine	Path
Pediatric Surgery	Ped Surg
Pediatrics	Peds
Physical Medicine and Rehabilitation	Rehab
Plastic Surgery	Plast
Podiatry	Pod
Psychiatry	Psych
Public Health	Pub Health
Pulmonology and Critical Care Medicine	Pulm-Critic
Radiation Oncology	Rad-Onc
Radiology & Nuclear Medicine	Radiol
Rheumatology	Rheum
Surgery	Surg
Urology	Urol
Vascular Surgery	Vasc Surg
Women's Health, Obstetrics and Gynecology	OB-GYN

Introduction

Today the global marketplace for delivery of targeted healthcare in resource-poor regions presents challenging barriers. That is to say, while human and capital resources available to care for underserved populations have increased, these resources remain unevenly distributed. The people and institutions that wish to deliver healthcare—volunteers, nonprofits, governments, the private sector—lack ready access to the granular, local data necessary to identify those most in need. *World Compendium of Healthcare Facilities and Nonprofit Organizations* seeks to address this information asymmetry and thereby reduce the frictions that lead to inefficient delivery of services or disengagement.

Among the most comprehensive resources of its kind, *World Compendium* presents a curated directory of nonprofits, non-governmental organizations (NGOs), hospitals, and healthcare facilities in 72 low and lower-middle-income countries as classified by the World Bank. Access to such data highlights areas that are underserved or in need of additional assistance. The content is listed by country and enhanced with custom maps and country overviews.

World Compendium was born out of Virtue Foundation's considerable experience providing direct healthcare in resource-poor regions. For nearly 20 years, Virtue Foundation volunteers, working in collaboration with local healthcare professionals, have been providing surgical and medical services worldwide. During this time, much has been learned about the necessity for access to reliable targeted data as a means to provide efficient healthcare delivery.

World Compendium is also an outgrowth of the *Virtue Foundation Actionable Data Initiative,* a multi-year interdisciplinary journey of research and experimentation in applying AI and data science to global health. Harnessing advancements in technology and machine learning, the Foundation has created a first-of-its-kind mapping-and-matching global health platform for local nonprofits and healthcare organizations that can be found at VFMatch.org. This compendium represents one of the first products of this initiative, providing a curated view of demand-side data and enabling volunteer medical professionals, governments, and other stakeholders to better identify where healthcare services are available and where additional resources are needed.

The first volume of this compendium—*Insights in Global Health*—was published by Taylor & Francis and included 24 low-income countries. This expanded edition includes an additional 48 lower-middle-income countries. Each of the 72 chapters presents a brief country overview, a map depicting the locations of healthcare facilities, and a curated list of nonprofit organizations and healthcare facilities. QR codes associated with each country listing link back to the web platform, providing access to further information about the organizations as well as the ability to interact with the data in a customizable manner. It should be noted that, with respect to India, only nonprofits have been included in *World Compendium* due to limitations on the size of this print edition. The web platform, however, also includes a comprehensive listing of Indian healthcare facilities.

Approach and Methodology

Nonprofit Data Collection and Curation

Using specific keywords and medical specialty descriptors, a pipeline for querying and identifying nonprofit websites was created for targeted regions. Forty-three separate medical specialties, 7 generic terms, and 4 nonprofit keywords were applied to produce a total of 14,288 unique query combinations and executed on various search engines and social media platforms. This resulted in 2,734,535 candidate nonprofit web pages that were subsequently indexed using custom crawlers built with open-source Python libraries as a distributed Spark application, running on parallel workers on Amazon Web Services. This list was complemented with known public resources, such as the United Nations database for NGOs.

A decision-tree script extracted the domains, deduplicated web pages, and created a recursive multilevel indexing tree, identifying 167,457 unique candidate nonprofit websites. Further data including contact information, donation links, and other metadata, were captured using regular expressions and pattern matching techniques. To minimize the likelihood of collected websites not representing an actual healthcare nonprofit organization and to minimize noise, machine learning methods were employed to filter the data. A training set of 11,877 websites was thus manually labeled by the Virtue Foundation volunteer team. An auto-tuned word N-Gram text modeler, using token occurrences, and optimized for sensitivity over precision, achieved best performance on this training set. In addition to being able to predict whether or not a website represents a nonprofit, the classifier was also able to determine whether the organization's activities were concentrated on healthcare. The inference process applied to the 167,457 candidate websites returned 11,119 organizations as healthcare nonprofits. Predicting whether a nonprofit was involved in healthcare proved challenging, as numerous healthcare-related websites belonging to educational organizations, publications and for-profit entities have a high likelihood of being incorrectly classified as providing healthcare. Therefore, all 11,119 organizations underwent further manual review to establish legitimacy, identify healthcare services provided, confirm countries of activity, and find additional relevant information. At completion, the total number of nonprofit organizations was narrowed down to 3,174. Due to space constraints, only 2,292 nonprofit organizations were ultimately included in the book, based on their quality and relevance. The companion online platform provides a more comprehensive and regularly updated dataset.

Healthcare Facility Data Collection and Curation

Healthcare facility data was primarily sourced from the OpenStreetMap humanitarian data layer. Given the abundant, and at times outdated, hospital listings in the OpenStreetMap dataset, uniform filtering based on building footprint, facility name, and online presence was applied to limit the data to hospitals and facilities with the highest impact and capacity. Area-based filtering was employed to exclude buildings too small to be a hospital based on square footage. Keyword filtering was then used to exclude non-hospitals on name (e.g., "health post"), factoring for linguistic differences. Lastly, to establish activity, a scoring system was derived for each candidate facility by searching for related websites, local directories, government reports, social media posts, and more. Public APIs, including Bing Maps, OpenStreetMap Nominatim, and Geonames were called to capture and externally validate additional details. The purpose of these integrations was to (1) reverse-geocode hospital coordinates to return missing addresses, and (2) validate the location of the hospitals with close proximity to country borders. This approach was premised on the assumption that principal hospitals are more likely to be referenced online, whether by individuals, governments, or nonprofits. Filtering was complemented by several rounds of manual curation and review.

Future Directions

Data contained in this compendium presents only the first steps in improving the nonprofit and healthcare facility landscape in low and lower-middle-income countries. Much work remains to be done to better our understanding of the granularity specific to each region and healthcare system. The Foundations's development of a vulnerability index based on macro-level health statistics, bed capacity, and population mobility in targeted regions is a step in this direction. VFMatch. org, the digital tool, will continue to be developed, adding new geographies along with additional insights from multiple, disparate sources of data. Additionally, data from social media activity can help identify acute medical conditions in real time and facilitate rapid assistance where needed. Information sources such as public satellite data and ground images obtained from online user activity can be further used in conjunction with machine-learning algorithms to validate the location of hospitals, estimate facility area, and even predict the number of beds needed. Together, these and other features will enhance the global marketplace for the exchange of healthcare services.

A Final Word

World Compendium presents comprehensive healthcare data for 72 low and lower-middle-income countries in an accessible single-source format. In addition to the printed volume, Virtue Foundation is providing access to this compendium free of charge in digital format through the Taylor & Francis Open Access program. *World Compendium* and its related digital tool, VFMatch.org, are the result of over 20,000 hours of work by over 90 volunteers and other contributors across healthcare, data science, and other professions. Yet, it marks only the beginning of the journey. In due course, demand-side data—the healthcare facilities and NGOs that comprise the healthcare ecosystem—will be expanded to include more countries and regions. At the same time, machine-learning algorithms will provide the supply-side data—healthcare professionals and organizations delivering services. The combined data will be available to stakeholders on VFMatch.org, a platform that will continue to be optimized to best match needs to particular skill sets and resources.

It should be noted that *World Compendium* represents a snapshot in time of countries and organizations and is by no means exhaustive. The nature of the project has several limitations, including the lack of readily available information in certain resource-poor regions. In many instances, organizations do not have a digital presence and up-to-date health data is often not available on a granular or regional level. In addition, the query pipeline was constructed in English and, as a result,

some candidate websites in non-English languages have not been included. Furthermore, the methodology applied here is subject to the technological limitations of capturing and processing large swaths of data, a limitation compounded by the unpredictable political, economic, and social changes that are often at play in low and lower-middle-income countries. Finally, *World Compendium* should not be viewed as a specific recommendation or endorsement of organizations or volunteer opportunities. Rather, in combination with the digital product, VFMatch.org, it is meant to serve as a starting point for those interested in researching and engaging in meaningful healthcare interventions.

Today, advancements in technology and big data allow us to leverage information to improve decision-making and provide opportunities to effect change beyond isolated interventions. It is hoped that this compendium and its related digital platform will help improve health outcomes for individuals, communities, and countries around the world.

About Virtue Foundation

Virtue Foundation is a nonprofit organization with special consultative status to the United Nations Economic and Social Council. The Foundation's mission is to increase awareness, inspire action, and render assistance through healthcare, education, and empowerment initiatives. Virtue Foundation is guided by the principle that true global change must begin within each of us—one person at a time, one act at a time.

Country Directory

Healthcare Facility

Algeria

The People's Democratic Republic of Algeria is located in the Maghreb region of North Africa; by total land area, Algeria is the largest country in Africa. It is bordered by Tunisia, Libya, Niger, Mali, Mauritania, Western Sahara, Morocco, and the Mediterranean Sea. As much as 90 percent of Algeria's total area is covered by the Sahara Desert, leaving the population of 43.6 million to reside predominantly in the more fertile and habitable north. The capital, Algiers, is also located in the north, close to the Mediterranean coast. The population is 99 percent Arab-Berber in ethnic makeup and speaks mostly Arabic, French, Berber, or Tamazight, and several other dialects. Ninety-nine percent of the population identifies as Muslim.

Algeria is considered a regional power in North Africa, having the highest human development index of all continental (non-island) countries in Africa. It also has one of the largest economies on the African continent, based mostly on the export of energy resources. Algeria supplies large quantities of natural gas to Europe, in addition to petroleum. These commodities make up one-third of Algeria's gross domestic product. As such, the country quickly industrialized after gaining independence from France in 1962. As a result of its rapid industrialization and growth, Algeria cleared all of its debt and invested heavily in infrastructure and social policies.

As the country developed over time, its health indicators improved as well. Life expectancy has increased to about 77 years. As the population lives to older ages, non-communicable diseases contribute most to death in Algeria. These include ischemic heart disease, stroke, hypertensive heart disease, chronic kidney disease, congenital defects, diabetes, and COPD. Notably, death due to diabetes and Alzheimer's disease increased by over 60 percent between 2009 and 2019. Other leading causes of death include road injuries, neonatal disorders, and lower respiratory infections. The risk factors driving these leading causes of death include high blood pressure, high body-mass index, high fasting plasma glucose, malnutrition, dietary risks, tobacco use, air pollution, high LDL, kidney dysfunction, and occupational risks.

43.6M
Population

$3,310
GDP Per Capita

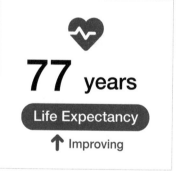

77 years
Life Expectancy
↑ Improving

172
Doctors/100k

Physician Density

190
Beds/100k

Hospital Bed Density

112
Deaths/100k

Maternal Mortality

Algeria
Nonprofit Organizations

Africa CDC
Aims to strengthen the capacity and capability of Africa's public health institutions and partnerships to detect and respond quickly and effectively to disease threats and outbreaks, based on data-driven interventions and programs.
Infect Dis, Logist-Op, Pub Health
⊕ https://vfmat.ch/339c

Africa Health Organisation
Leads collaborative efforts among countries in Africa and other partners to promote health equity, combat disease, and improve quality of life.
Logist-Op, Pub Health
⊕ https://vfmat.ch/b1c5

Africa Humanitarian Action (AHA)
Responds to crises, conflicts, and disasters in Africa, while informing and advising the international community, governments, civil society, and the private sector on humanitarian issues of concern to Africa. Supports institutional and organizational development efforts.
General, Infect Dis, MF Med, Nutr, OB-GYN
⊕ https://vfmat.ch/3ca2

Association of Medical Doctors of Asia (AMDA)
Strives to support people affected by disasters and economic distress on their road to recovery, establishing a true partnership with special emphasis on local initiative.
ER Med, Logist-Op, Pub Health
⊕ https://vfmat.ch/e3d4

Carter Center, The
Seeks to prevent and resolve conflicts, enhance freedom and democracy, and improve health, while remaining committed to human rights and the alleviation of human suffering.
Infect Dis, MF Med, Ophth-Opt
⊕ https://vfmat.ch/6556

Christian Aid Ministries
Strives to be a trustworthy and efficient channel for Amish, Mennonite, and other conservative Anabaptist groups and individuals to minister to physical and spiritual needs around the world.
CT Surg, ER Med, Logist-Op, Ortho, Pub Health
⊕ https://vfmat.ch/7b33

Global Oncology (GO)
Brings the best in cancer care to underserved patients around the world and collaborates across geographic, professional, and academic borders to improve cancer care, research, and education.
Heme-Onc, Path, Rad-Onc
⊕ https://vfmat.ch/fcb8

Globus Relief
Aims to improve the delivery of healthcare worldwide by gathering, processing, and distributing surplus medical supplies to charities at home and abroad.
Logist-Op
⊕ https://vfmat.ch/a2b7

Humanity & Inclusion
Works alongside people with disabilities and vulnerable populations, taking action and bearing witness in order to respond to their essential needs, improve their living conditions and health, and promote respect for their dignity and fundamental rights.
General, Infect Dis, MF Med, Medicine, Ortho, Peds, Psych, Pub Health, Rehab
⊕ https://vfmat.ch/16b7

International Council of Ophthalmology
Works with ophthalmologic societies and others to enhance ophthalmic education and improve access to the highest-quality eye care in order to preserve and restore vision for people of the world.
Ophth-Opt
⊕ https://vfmat.ch/ffd2

International Federation of Gynecology and Obstetrics (FIGO)
Implements global projects on specific women's health issues.
MF Med, Medicine, Neonat, OB-GYN, Surg, Urol
⊕ https://vfmat.ch/c4b4

International Federation of Red Cross and Red Crescent Societies (IFRC)
Coordinates and directs international assistance following natural and manmade disasters in nonconflict situations through the world's largest humanitarian and development network. Provides disaster-preparedness programs, healthcare activities, and promotes humanitarian values.
ER Med, General, Infect Dis, Nutr
⊕ https://vfmat.ch/b4ee

International Organization for Migration (IOM) – The UN Migration Agency
Promotes evidence-informed policies and holistic, preventive, and curative health programs that are beneficial, accessible, and equitable for vulnerable migrants.
General, Infect Dis, OB-GYN
⊕ https://vfmat.ch/621a

International Planned Parenthood Federation (IPPF)
Leads a locally owned, globally connected civil society movement that provides and enables services and champions sexual and reproductive health and rights for all, especially the underserved.
Infect Dis, MF Med, OB-GYN
⊕ https://vfmat.ch/dc97

InterSurgeon
Fosters collaborative partnerships in the field of global surgery that will advance clinical care, teaching, training, research, and the provision and maintenance of medical equipment.
ENT, Neurosurg, Ortho, Ped Surg, Plast, Surg, Urol
⊕ https://vfmat.ch/6f8a

Maghreb-American Health Foundation
Promotes education around health equity, the prevention of birth defects, and improvement in quality of life for people of the Maghreb region of North Africa.
Anesth, CV Med, Neurosurg, Ped Surg, Radiol, Surg, Urol
⊕ https://vfmat.ch/b3bd

Management Sciences for Health (MSH)
Works with countries and communities to save lives and improve the health of the world's poorest and most vulnerable people by building strong, resilient, sustainable health systems.
Infect Dis, Logist-Op, Pub Health
⊕ https://vfmat.ch/6aa2

Médecins du Monde/Doctors of the World
Provides care, bears witness, and supports social change worldwide with innovative medical programs and evidence-based advocacy initiatives.
ER Med, General, Infect Dis, MF Med, Neonat, OB-GYN, Peds, Pub Health
⊕ https://vfmat.ch/a43d

Rotary International
Provides service to others, improves lives, and advances world understanding, goodwill, and peace through its fellowship of business, professional, and community leaders.
ER Med, General, Infect Dis, MF Med, OB-GYN
⊕ https://vfmat.ch/8fb5

Sanofi Espoir Foundation
Contributes to reducing health inequalities among populations that need it most by applying a socially responsible approach focused on fighting childhood cancers in low-income countries, improving maternal and newborn health, and improving access to care.
ER Med, OB-GYN, Peds
⊕ https://vfmat.ch/943b

Swiss Tropical and Public Health Institute
Contributes to the improvement of the health of populations internationally, nationally, and locally through excellence in research, education, and services.
Infect Dis, Pub Health
⊕ https://vfmat.ch/2ee4

Union for International Cancer Control (UICC)
Unites and supports the cancer community to reduce the global cancer burden, promote greater equity, and ensure that cancer control continues to be a priority in the world health and development agenda.
Heme-Onc, Pub Health
⊕ https://vfmat.ch/88b1

United Nations Children's Fund (UNICEF)
Works in over 190 countries and territories to save children's lives, defend their rights, and help them fulfill their potential, from early childhood through adolescence.
All-Immu, Infect Dis, MF Med, Neonat, Nutr, OB-GYN, Ped Surg, Peds, Pub Health
⊕ https://vfmat.ch/42d7

United Nations Development Programme (UNDP)
Helps countries achieve the simultaneous eradication of extreme poverty and significant reduction of inequalities and exclusion using a sustainable human development approach.
Infect Dis, Logist-Op, Pub Health
⊕ https://vfmat.ch/935c

United Nations High Commissioner for Refugees (UNHCR)
Safeguards the rights and well-being of people who have been forced to flee, ensuring that everybody has the right to seek asylum and find safe refuge in another country, with the goal of seeking lasting solutions.

General, MF Med, Medicine, OB-GYN, Peds, Psych, Pub Health
⊕ https://vfmat.ch/6636

United Nations Population Fund (UNFPA)
Supports reproductive healthcare for women and youth in more than 150 countries, focusing on delivering a world in which every pregnancy is wanted, every childbirth is safe, and every young person's potential is fulfilled.
Infect Dis, MF Med, Neonat, OB-GYN, Peds, Pub Health
⊕ https://vfmat.ch/c969

World Federation of Hemophilia (WFH)
Aims to improve and sustain care for people with inherited bleeding disorders by pursuing long-term relationships with individuals and organizations who share the values of WFH's development model.
Heme-Onc
⊕ https://vfmat.ch/5121

World Health Organization, The (WHO)
The United Nations' agency for health provides leadership on global health matters, shapes the health research agenda, sets norms and standards, articulates evidence-based policy options, provides technical support and monitoring to countries, and assesses health trends.
ER Med, General, Infect Dis, Logist-Op, MF Med, OB-GYN, Peds, Psych, Pub Health
⊕ https://vfmat.ch/c476

Algeria

Healthcare Facilities

Ahmed Ouroua
Zighout Youcef, Papeterie Khennouf, Algeria
🌐 https://vfmat.ch/2d6e

Al Azhar Clinic
Chéraga, Algeria
https://vfmat.ch/z2d7

Al-Quds District Hospital Public Corporation
Teniet Safra, Djelfa, Algeria
🌐 https://vfmat.ch/686a

Aïn Naadja Military Hospital
Kobua, Kobua, Algeria
🌐 https://vfmat.ch/gain

CHU Annaba Ibn Rochd University Hospital
Annaba, Annaba, Algeria
🌐 https://vfmat.ch/syxp

CHU Béjaïa, Khelil Amrane Hospital
Béjaïa, Béjaïa, Algeria
🌐 https://vfmat.ch/2mdt

CHU/EPSP Zéralda Belkacemi Tayeb
Zeralda, Algiers, Algeria
🌐 https://vfmat.ch/d24y

Dr. Ben Zarjab Hospital
Douar Moulay Mostafa, Aïn Témouchent, Algeria
🌐 https://vfmat.ch/2998

EPH Akloul Ali
Akbou, Akbou, Algeria
🌐 https://vfmat.ch/7rkj

Eph Bachir Ben Nacer Biskra
Biskra, Biskra, Algeria
🌐 https://vfmat.ch/ewqu

EPH Taibet
Taibet, Algeria
🌐 https://vfmat.ch/a43a

Hakim Sadanne Hospital
Biskra, Biskra, Algeria
🌐 https://vfmat.ch/ekrr

Hospital in Sidi Khaled
Sidi Khaled, Biskra, Algeria
🌐 https://vfmat.ch/b3f1

Hospital Makour Hamou
Ain Delfa, Algeria
🌐 https://vfmat.ch/mgiq

Houari Boumediene Kasr El Hiran Public Hospital
Sedrata, Souk Ahras, Algeria
🌐 https://vfmat.ch/5193

Hôpital Ahmed Medeghri
Aïn Témouchent, Aïn Témouchent, Algeria
🌐 https://vfmat.ch/3c51

Hôpital de Beni Messous
Beni Messous, Algiers, Algeria
🌐 https://vfmat.ch/8956

Hôpital de Bormadia
Douar el Messabhia, Relizane, Algeria
🌐 https://vfmat.ch/c7f6

Hôpital de Maghnia
Maghnia, Tlemcen, Algeria
🌐 https://vfmat.ch/267c

Hôpital des Sœurs Bedj Chlef
Bensouna, Chlef, Algeria
🌐 https://vfmat.ch/fb1f

Hôpital Mohamed Boudiaf
Bouïra, Bouïra, Algeria
🌐 https://vfmat.ch/f5ef

Hôpital Saadaoui Mokhtar
Aïn Oussera, Djelfa, Algeria
🌐 https://vfmat.ch/5836

Ibn Sina Hospital
Oum El Bouaghi, Oum el Bouaghi, Algeria
🌐 https://vfmat.ch/7b39

New Hospital of Bordj Badji Mokhtar, The
Bordj Badji Mokhtar, Algeria
🌐 https://vfmat.ch/2b71

Mustapha University Hospital Center
Sidi M'Hamed, Algiers, Algeria
🌐 https://vfmat.ch/2d72

Saej Yahya Public Facility
Télagh, Sidi Bel Abbès, Algeria
🌐 https://vfmat.ch/b6f9

Sidi Bel Abbès General Hospital
Sidi Bel Abbès, Sidi Bel Abbès wilaya, Algeria
🌐 https://vfmat.ch/ae3b

University Hospital Abdelhamid Ben Badis
Constantine, Algeria
🌐 https://vfmat.ch/1wyr

University Hospital: Benflis Al-Tohamy
Batna, Batna, Algeria
🌐 https://vfmat.ch/j6nf

Urgences Cité Aatya
Cité Aatya, Relizane, Algeria
🌐 https://vfmat.ch/8d8c

Healthcare Facility

Angola

The second largest and most populous Portuguese-speaking country in the world, behind only Brazil, the Republic of Angola lies on the southwestern coast of Africa, along the Atlantic Ocean. Angola's neighbors include Namibia, the Democratic Republic of the Congo, and Zambia. The country also includes a small province called Cabinda, which is geographically separated from Angola by a small area of the Democratic Republic of the Congo. The Angolan population of 33.6 million people is made up of several ethnic groups such as the Ovimbundu, Kimbundu, Bakongo, and Mestico. Languages spoken include Portuguese, the official language, as well as Umbundu, Kikongo, Kimbundu, Chokwe, Nhaneca, Ngaguela, Fiote, Kwanhama, Muhumbi, and Luvale. The majority of Angolans live in urban areas, and in the western half of the country, near the capital of Luanda.

Angola achieved independence from Portugal in 1975, after a long and difficult anti-colonial struggle. Post-independence, Angola experienced several decades of conflict and instability, including a civil war that ended in 2002. Despite remaining stable since then, the country still has high rates of poverty, with about 40 percent of the population living below the poverty line. In addition, unemployment is high and literacy levels are low. Angola's economy is one of the fastest growing in the region due to oil production and other mineral resources, but this growth has not benefited the majority of the population.

High levels of poverty have contributed to lacking health indicators in the country. Angola suffers from high rates of child and maternal mortality, and life expectancy is among the lowest in the world, at 61 years. Leading causes of death include neonatal disorders, HIV/AIDS, diarrheal diseases, lower respiratory infections, tuberculosis, malaria, stroke, ischemic heart disease, road injuries, cirrhosis, and protein-energy malnutrition. The risk factors that contribute most to death and disability include malnutrition, unsafe sex, air pollution, alcohol and tobacco use, high blood pressure, high fasting plasma glucose, high body-mass index, dietary risks, occupational risks, and insufficient sanitation and clean water.

33.6M

Population

$1,896

GDP Per Capita

61 years

Life Expectancy

↑ Improving

22
Doctors/100k

Physician Density

80
Beds/100k

Hospital Bed Density

241
Deaths/100k

Maternal Mortality

Angola

Nonprofit Organizations

Abt Associates
Seeks to improve the quality of life and economic well-being of people worldwide, while striving to meet and exceed the highest professional standards.
General, Logist-Op, MF Med, OB-GYN, Peds
⊕ https://vfmat.ch/cec2

Aceso Global
Provides strategic healthcare advisory services in low- and middle-income countries to design and deliver highly customized, evidence-based solutions that address the complex nature of healthcare systems, with a goal to strengthen and provide affordable, high-quality care to all.
Logist-Op, Pub Health
⊕ https://vfmat.ch/b3b7

Adventist Health International
Focuses on upgrading and managing mission hospitals by providing governance, consultation, and technical assistance to a number of affiliated Seventh-Day Adventist hospitals throughout Africa, Asia, and the Americas.
Dent-OMFS, General, Pub Health
⊕ https://vfmat.ch/16aa

Africa CDC
Aims to strengthen the capacity and capability of Africa's public health institutions and partnerships to detect and respond quickly and effectively to disease threats and outbreaks, based on data-driven interventions and programs.
Infect Dis, Logist-Op, Pub Health
⊕ https://vfmat.ch/339c

Africa Health Organisation
Leads collaborative efforts among countries in Africa and other partners to promote health equity, combat disease, and improve quality of life.
Logist-Op, Pub Health
⊕ https://vfmat.ch/b1c5

Africa Indoor Residual Spraying Project (AIRS)
Aims to protect millions of people in Africa from malaria by spraying insecticide on walls, ceilings, and other indoor resting places of mosquitoes that transmit malaria.
Infect Dis
⊕ https://vfmat.ch/9bd1

Africa Inland Mission International
Seeks to establish churches and community development programs including healthcare projects, based in Christian ministry.
Anesth, Dent-OMFS, ER Med, General, MF Med, Medicine, OB-GYN, OB-GYN, Ophth-Opt, Ped Surg, Peds, Rehab
⊕ https://vfmat.ch/f2f6

Africa Relief and Community Development
Provides comprehensive relief and developmental aid to people of the African continent regardless of gender, race, or religion.
Nutr, Pub Health
⊕ https://vfmat.ch/6cd2

African Field Epidemiology Network (AFENET)
Strengthens field epidemiology and public health laboratory capacity to contribute effectively to addressing epidemics and other major public health problems in Africa.
All-Immu, Infect Dis, Path, Pub Health
⊕ https://vfmat.ch/df2e

Amref Health Africa
Serves millions of people across 35 countries in Sub-Saharan Africa, strengthening health systems, and training African health workers to respond to the continent's most critical health issues.
All-Immu, General, Infect Dis, Logist-Op, MF Med, OB-GYN, Path, Pub Health, Surg
⊕ https://vfmat.ch/6985

Baylor International Pediatric AIDS Initiative (BIPAI) at Texas Children's Hospital
Provides high-quality, high-impact, highly ethical pediatric and family-centered healthcare, health professional training, and clinical research focused on HIV/AIDS, tuberculosis, malaria, malnutrition, and other conditions impacting the health of children worldwide.
Infect Dis, Medicine, OB-GYN, Peds, Pub Health, Surg
⊕ https://vfmat.ch/e6ba

CARE
Works around the globe to save lives, defeat poverty, and achieve social justice.
ER Med, General
⊕ https://vfmat.ch/7232

Caritas Pro Vitae Gradu Charitable Trust
Supports Catholic charitable projects with social and humanitarian efforts, and aims to assist people in need including children, the elderly, sick, and disabled through healthcare, poverty relief, and education.
ER Med, General, Logist-Op, Medicine, OB-GYN, Ophth-Opt, Path, Peds, Pub Health, Radiol, Rehab, Surg
⊕ https://vfmat.ch/b2ca

Carter Center, The
Seeks to prevent and resolve conflicts, enhance freedom and democracy, and improve health, while remaining committed to human rights and the alleviation of human suffering.
Infect Dis, MF Med, Ophth-Opt
⊕ https://vfmat.ch/6556

Centro Evangelico de Medicina do Lubango (CEML)
Inspired by the Christian faith, seeks to restore health and offer hope by providing

medical, surgical, and dental services for an estimated 50% of Angolans who have no alternative coverage.

Anesth, ER Med, General, Medicine, OB-GYN, Ophth-Opt, Path, Radiol, Surg

⊕ https://vfmat.ch/61d6

Christian Health Service Corps
Brings Christian doctors, health professionals, and health educators committed to serving the poor to places that otherwise have little or no access to healthcare.

Anesth, Dent-OMFS, General, Medicine, Peds, Surg

⊕ https://vfmat.ch/da57

Christian Medical & Dental Associations
Based in Christian ministry, deploys medical and dental teams to underserved communities to provide vital healthcare.

Anesth, Dent-OMFS, ER Med, General, Medicine, OB-GYN, Ophth-Opt, Peds, Pub Health, Radiol, Rehab, Surg

⊕ https://vfmat.ch/921c

Core Group
Aims to improve and expand community health practices for underserved populations, especially women and children, through collaborative action and learning.

General, Infect Dis, MF Med, Medicine, OB-GYN, Peds, Pub Health

⊕ https://vfmat.ch/9de3

COVID-19 Clinical Research Coalition
Advocates and collaborates for the advancement of COVID-19 research driven by the needs of low-resource settings, and works for equitable access to solutions to the pandemic.

All-Immu, Infect-Dis, MF Med, Path, Pub Health

⊕ https://vfmat.ch/d1f4

CURE
Operates charitable hospitals and programs in underserved countries worldwide, where patients receive surgical treatment, based in Christian ministry.

Anesth, Neurosurg, Ortho, Ped Surg, Peds, Rehab, Surg

⊕ https://vfmat.ch/aa16

Direct Relief
Improves the health and lives of people affected by poverty or emergency situations by mobilizing and providing essential medical resources needed for their care.

ER Med, Logist-Op

⊕ https://vfmat.ch/58e5

Doctors with Africa (CUAMM)
Advocates for the universal right to health and promotes the values of international solidarity, justice, and peace. Works to protect and improve the well-being and health of vulnerable communities in Africa with a long-term development perspective.

ER Med, Infect Dis, MF Med, Neonat, OB-GYN, Peds

⊕ https://vfmat.ch/d2fb

Doctors Without Borders/Médecins Sans Frontières (MSF)
Responds to emergencies and provides lifesaving medical care where needed most, including during disasters, conflicts, and epidemics.

Anesth, Crit-Care, ER Med, General, Infect Dis, Nutr, OB-GYN, Ped Surg, Peds, Psych, Pub Health, Surg

⊕ https://vfmat.ch/f363

Elizabeth Glaser Pediatric AIDS Foundation
Seeks to end global pediatric HIV/AIDS through prevention and treatment programs, research, and advocacy.

Infect Dis, Nutr, OB-GYN, Peds

⊕ https://vfmat.ch/d6ec

END Fund, The
Aims to control and eliminate the most prevalent neglected diseases among the world's poorest and most vulnerable people.

Infect Dis

⊕ https://vfmat.ch/2614

Episcopal Relief & Development
Provides relief in times of disaster and promotes sustainable development by identifying and addressing the root causes of suffering.

Infect Dis, MF Med, Neonat, Nutr, Peds

⊕ https://vfmat.ch/7cfa

eRanger
Provides sustainable solutions to transportation and medical provision such as ambulances and mobile clinics in developing countries.

ER Med, General, Logist-Op

⊕ https://vfmat.ch/4c18

Fistula Foundation
Aims to engage the support of people worldwide who are eager to see the day that no woman suffers from obstetric fistula. Raises and directs funds to doctors and hospitals providing life-transforming surgery to women in need.

OB-GYN

⊕ https://vfmat.ch/e958

Global Ministries – The United Methodist Church
As the worldwide mission and development agency of The United Methodist Church, Global Ministries works with more than 300 hospitals and clinics around the world through its Global Health Unit.

Anesth, CT Surg, CV Med, Crit-Care, Dent-OMFS, Derm, ER Med, GI, General, Infect Dis, Logist-Op, MF Med, Medicine, Neonat, Nephro, Nutr, OB-GYN, Ophth-Opt, Ortho, Palliative, Peds, Pod, Psych, Pub Health, Rehab, Rheum, Surg, Urol

⊕ https://vfmat.ch/1723

Global Oncology (GO)
Brings the best in cancer care to underserved patients around the world and collaborates across geographic, professional, and academic borders to improve cancer care, research, and education.

Heme-Onc, Path, Rad-Onc

⊕ https://vfmat.ch/fcb8

Global Vision 2020
Provides prescription eyeglasses to people who live in parts of the world lacking necessary infrastructure for obtaining affordable corrective eyewear.

Logist-Op, Ophth-Opt

⊕ https://vfmat.ch/7373

Globus Relief
Aims to improve the delivery of healthcare worldwide by gathering, processing, and distributing surplus medical supplies to charities at home and abroad.

Logist-Op

⊕ https://vfmat.ch/a2b7

Good Shepard International Foundation
Strives to promote inclusive and sustainable development for the most marginalized and vulnerable people, with a special focus on women, girls, and children, inspired by the Christian faith.

ER Med

⊕ https://vfmat.ch/ad9a

Health Volunteers Overseas (HVO)
Improves the availability and quality of healthcare through the education, training, and professional development of the health workforce in resource-scarce countries.

All-Immu, Anesth, CV Med, Dent-OMFS, Derm, ENT, ER Med, Endo, GI, Heme-Onc, Infect Dis, Medicine, Medicine, Nephro, Neuro, OB-GYN, Ophth-Opt, Ortho, Peds, Plast, Psych, Pulm-Critic, Rehab, Rheum, Surg

⊕ https://vfmat.ch/42b2

ICAP at Columbia University
Serves as global leader in supporting the scale-up of multidisciplinary HIV/AIDS prevention, care, and treatment programs based on a family-focused approach.

General, Infect Dis, MF Med, Medicine, OB-GYN, Pub Health

⊕ https://vfmat.ch/a8ef

IMA World Health
Works to build healthier communities by collaborating with key partners to serve vulnerable people with a focus on health, healing, and well-being for all.

Infect Dis, MF Med, Nutr, OB-GYN, Pub Health
⊕ https://vfmat.ch/8316

International Federation of Red Cross and Red Crescent Societies (IFRC)

Coordinates and directs international assistance following natural and manmade disasters in nonconflict situations through the world's largest humanitarian and development network. Provides disaster-preparedness programs, healthcare activities, and promotes humanitarian values.
ER Med, General, Infect Dis, Nutr
⊕ https://vfmat.ch/b4ee

International Organization for Migration (IOM) – The UN Migration Agency

Promotes evidence-informed policies and holistic, preventive, and curative health programs that are beneficial, accessible, and equitable for vulnerable migrants.
General, Infect Dis, OB-GYN
⊕ https://vfmat.ch/621a

John Snow, Inc. (JSI)

Aims to improve the health and well-being of underserved and vulnerable people and communities throughout the world.
General, Infect Dis, Logist-Op, MF Med, OB-GYN, Peds, Psych, Pub Health
⊕ https://vfmat.ch/ba78

Johns Hopkins Center for Communication Programs

Believes in the power of communication to save lives by empowering people to adopt healthy behaviors for themselves, their families, and their communities.
General, Infect Dis, Logist-Op, OB-GYN, Pub Health
⊕ https://vfmat.ch/1bf9

Joint Aid Management (JAM)

Provides food security, nutrition, water, and sanitation to vulnerable African communities in dignified and sustainable ways.
ER Med, Nutr
⊕ https://vfmat.ch/dcac

Joint Aid Management (JAM) Canada

Strives to provide food security, nutrition, water, and sanitation to vulnerable African communities in dignified and sustainable ways.
Nutr, Pub Health
⊕ https://vfmat.ch/8756

Joint United Nations Programme on HIV/AIDS (UNAIDS)

Aims to place people living with HIV and people affected by the virus at the decision-making table and at the center of designing, delivering, and monitoring the AIDS response.
Infect Dis
⊕ https://vfmat.ch/464a

Management Sciences for Health (MSH)

Works with countries and communities to save lives and improve the health of the world's poorest and most vulnerable people by building strong, resilient, sustainable health systems.
Infect Dis, Logist-Op, Pub Health
⊕ https://vfmat.ch/6aa2

MAP International

Provides medicines and health supplies to those in need around the world so they might experience life to the fullest.
Logist-Op
⊕ https://vfmat.ch/deed

Medical Care Development International

Works to improve the health of vulnerable populations through integrated, sustainable, and locally driven interventions.
Infect Dis, OB-GYN, Peds, Pub Health
⊕ https://vfmat.ch/da87

MedShare

Aims to improve the quality of life of people, communities, and the planet by sourcing and directly delivering surplus medical supplies and equipment to communities in need around the world.

Logist-Op
⊕ https://vfmat.ch/c8bc

MENTOR Initiative

Saves lives in emergencies through tropical disease control, and helps people recover from crisis with dignity, working side by side with communities, health workers, and health authorities to leave a lasting impact.
ER Med, Infect Dis
⊕ https://vfmat.ch/3bd5

Mercy and Love Foundation

Aims to provide orphaned and vulnerable children with basic human needs such as food, clothing, and shelter, enabling them to thrive.
General, Peds
⊕ https://vfmat.ch/649a

mothers2mothers (m2m)

Employs and trains local women living with HIV as community health workers called Mentor Mothers to support women, children, and adolescents with vital medical services, education, and support.
Infect Dis, MF Med, OB-GYN, Peds, Pub Health
⊕ https://vfmat.ch/6557

Médecins du Monde/Doctors of the World

Provides care, bears witness, and supports social change worldwide with innovative medical programs and evidence-based advocacy initiatives.
ER Med, General, Infect Dis, MF Med, Neonat, OB-GYN, Peds, Pub Health
⊕ https://vfmat.ch/a43d

Norwegian People's Aid

Aims to improve living conditions, to create a democratic, just, and safe society.
ER Med, Logist-Op
⊕ https://vfmat.ch/2d8e

Order of Malta

Supports forgotten or excluded people, especially those living in conflict zones or amid natural disasters, by providing medical assistance, caring for refugees, and distributing medicines and necessities.
ER Med, General, Infect Dis, MF Med, Nephro, OB-GYN, Ortho, Psych
⊕ https://vfmat.ch/1fab

Organization for the Prevention of Blindness, The (OPC)

Provides research, and treatments and cures for people affected by blindness and blinding diseases in Francophone Africa.
Infect Dis, Ophth-Opt
⊕ https://vfmat.ch/86d6

Partners for Development (PfD)

Works to improve quality of life for vulnerable people in underserved communities through local and international partnerships.
Infect Dis, MF Med, Neonat, Peds
⊕ https://vfmat.ch/d2f6

Project SOAR

Conducts HIV operations research around the world to identify practical solutions to improve HIV prevention, care, and treatment services.
ER Med, General, MF Med, OB-GYN, Psych
⊕ https://vfmat.ch/1a77

PSI – Population Services International

Aims to improve the health of people in the developing world by focusing on challenges such as a lack of family planning, HIV/AIDS, barriers to maternal health, and the greatest threats to children under the age of 5, including malaria, diarrhea, pneumonia, and malnutrition.
Infect Dis, MF Med, OB-GYN, Peds
⊕ https://vfmat.ch/ffe3

Rotary International

Provides service to others, improves lives, and advances world understanding, goodwill, and peace through its fellowship of business, professional, and community leaders.
ER Med, General, Infect Dis, MF Med, OB-GYN
⊕ https://vfmat.ch/8fb5

Saham Foundation
Aims to create lasting change among the most vulnerable populations in Morocco and Sub-Saharan Africa through healthcare, youth engagement, and social inclusion.
Anesth, Dent-OMFS, ENT, OB-GYN, Ophth-Opt, Ped Surg, Peds, Pub Health, Radiol, Surg, Urol
⊕ https://vfmat.ch/54d6

Salvation Army International, The
Seeks to meet human needs through services in education, healthcare, community support, emergency response, and ministry development, inspired by the Christian faith.
Dent-OMFS, Derm, ER Med, Infect Dis, MF Med, Medicine, Nutr, OB-GYN, Ophth-Opt, Palliative, Psych, Rehab, Surg
⊕ https://vfmat.ch/8eb3

Saving Moses
Aims to save babies, up to age 5, by meeting the most intense and urgent survival needs, where help is least available.
MF Med, Neonat, Nutr, OB-GYN, Peds
⊕ https://vfmat.ch/6a88

SIGN Fracture Care International
Builds orthopedic capacity around the world and provides the injured poor access to fracture surgery by donating orthopedic education and implant systems to surgeons in developing countries.
Ortho, Rehab, Surg
⊕ https://vfmat.ch/123d

SOS Children's Villages International
Supports children through alternative care and family strengthening.
ER Med, Peds
⊕ https://vfmat.ch/aca1

Swiss Tropical and Public Health Institute
Contributes to the improvement of the health of populations internationally, nationally, and locally through excellence in research, education, and services.
Infect Dis, Pub Health
⊕ https://vfmat.ch/2ee4

Task Force for Global Health, The
Consists of programs and focus areas that cover a range of global health issues including neglected tropical diseases, infectious diseases, vaccines, field epidemiology, public health informatics, health workforce development, and global health ethics.
Infect Dis, Logist-Op, Medicine, Ophth-Opt, Peds
⊕ https://vfmat.ch/714c

Tearfund
Responds to crisis and partners with local churches to bring restoration to those living in poverty, inspired by the Christian faith.
ER Med, Logist-Op
⊕ https://vfmat.ch/f6cf

Texas Children's Global Health
Addresses healthcare needs in resource-limited settings locally and globally by improving maternal and child health through the implementation of innovative, sustainable, in-country programs to train health professionals and build functional healthcare infrastructure.
Anesth, ER Med, Heme-Onc, Infect Dis, MF Med, Nutr, OB-GYN, Peds, Pub Health, Surg
⊕ https://vfmat.ch/4a1d

U.S. President's Malaria Initiative (PMI)
Supports low-income countries to help control and eliminate malaria through cost-effective, lifesaving malaria interventions.
Infect Dis, MF Med, OB-GYN
⊕ https://vfmat.ch/dc8b

United Methodist Volunteers in Mission (UMVIM)
Engages in short-term missions each year in ministries as varied as disaster response, community development, pastor training, microenterprise, agriculture, Vacation Bible School, building repair and construction, and medical/

dental services.
Dent-OMFS, ER Med, General
⊕ https://vfmat.ch/1ee6

United Nations Children's Fund (UNICEF)
Works in over 190 countries and territories to save children's lives, defend their rights, and help them fulfill their potential, from early childhood through adolescence.
All-Immu, Infect Dis, MF Med, Neonat, Nutr, OB-GYN, Ped Surg, Peds, Pub Health
⊕ https://vfmat.ch/42d7

United Nations Development Programme (UNDP)
Helps countries achieve the simultaneous eradication of extreme poverty and significant reduction of inequalities and exclusion using a sustainable human development approach.
Infect Dis, Logist-Op, Pub Health
⊕ https://vfmat.ch/935c

United Nations High Commissioner for Refugees (UNHCR)
Safeguards the rights and well-being of people who have been forced to flee, ensuring that everybody has the right to seek asylum and find safe refuge in another country, with the goal of seeking lasting solutions.
General, MF Med, Medicine, OB-GYN, Peds, Psych, Pub Health
⊕ https://vfmat.ch/6636

United Nations Population Fund (UNFPA)
Supports reproductive healthcare for women and youth in more than 150 countries, focusing on delivering a world in which every pregnancy is wanted, every childbirth is safe, and every young person's potential is fulfilled.
Infect Dis, MF Med, Neonat, OB-GYN, Peds, Pub Health
⊕ https://vfmat.ch/c969

United States Agency for International Development (USAID)
Promotes and demonstrates democratic values abroad and advances a free, peaceful, and prosperous world. Leads the U.S. government's international development and disaster assistance through partnerships and investments that save lives.
ER Med, Infect Dis, MF Med, OB-GYN, Peds
⊕ https://vfmat.ch/9a99

United States President's Emergency Plan for AIDS Relief (PEPFAR)
The U.S. global HIV/AIDS response works to prevent new HIV infections and accelerate progress to control the global epidemic in more than 50 countries, by partnering with governments to support sustainable, integrated, and country-led responses to HIV/AIDS.
Infect Dis, Pub Health
⊕ https://vfmat.ch/a57c

University of California, Berkeley: Bixby Center for Population, Health & Sustainability
Aims to help manage population growth, improve maternal health, and address the unmet need for family planning within a human rights framework.
OB-GYN
⊕ https://vfmat.ch/ff2b

University of California: Global Health Institute
Mobilizes people and resources across the University of California to advance global health research, education, and collaboration.
General, OB-GYN, Pub Health
⊕ https://vfmat.ch/ee7f

USAID: Health Finance and Governance Project
Uses research to implement strategies to help countries develop robust governance systems, increase their domestic resources for health, manage those resources more effectively, and make wise purchasing decisions.
Logist-Op
⊕ https://vfmat.ch/8652

Vitamin Angels
Helps at-risk populations in need—specifically pregnant women, new mothers, and children under age 5—to gain access to life-changing vitamins and minerals.

General, Nutr
⊕ https://vfmat.ch/7da1

Women's Refugee Commission
Seeks to improve lives by protecting the rights of women, children, and youth displaced by conflict and crisis through researching their needs, identifying solutions, and advocating for programs and policies to strengthen their resilience.
General, MF Med, Neonat, OB-GYN, Peds, Psych
⊕ https://vfmat.ch/3d8f

World Blind Union (WBU)
Represents those experiencing blindness, speaking to governments and international bodies on issues concerning visual impairments.
Ophth-Opt
⊕ https://vfmat.ch/2bd3

World Federation of Hemophilia (WFH)
Aims to improve and sustain care for people with inherited bleeding disorders by pursuing long-term relationships with individuals and organizations who share the values of WFH's development model.
Heme-Onc
⊕ https://vfmat.ch/5121

World Health Organization, The (WHO)
The United Nations' agency for health provides leadership on global health matters, shapes the health research agenda, sets norms and standards, articulates evidence-based policy options, provides technical support and monitoring to countries, and assesses health trends.
ER Med, General, Infect Dis, Logist-Op, MF Med, OB-GYN, Peds, Psych, Pub Health
⊕ https://vfmat.ch/c476

World Medical Relief
Facilitates the distribution of surplus medical resources where they are needed.
Logist-Op
⊕ https://vfmat.ch/72dc

World Vision International
Works with vulnerable communities around the world to overcome poverty and injustice with child-focused programs in disaster management, health, nutrition, economic development, education, clean water, sanitation, and hygiene.
ER Med, General, Infect Dis, MF Med, Nutr, OB-GYN, Peds
⊕ https://vfmat.ch/2642

 **Angola**

Healthcare Facilities

CEML Hospital (Centro Evangelico de Medicina do Lubango)
Lubango, Huíla, Angola
🌐 https://vfmat.ch/njvv

Centro Auditivo Internacional de Angola (CAINA)
Luanda, Angola
https://vfmat.ch/4314

Centro de Saude do Machiqueira
João Caldeira, Huíla, Angola
🌐 https://vfmat.ch/1724

Clínica do Hospital Municipal do Namacunde
Namacunde, Cunene, Angola
🌐 https://vfmat.ch/41a1

Clínica Multiperfil
Luanda, Angola
https://vfmat.ch/5sak

Hospital Américo Boavida (HAB)
Muceques, Luanda, Angola
🌐 https://vfmat.ch/f259

Hospital Central do Lobito
Lobito, Benguela, Angola
🌐 https://vfmat.ch/d9ed

Hospital Central do Lubango
Lubango, Huíla, Angola
🌐 https://vfmat.ch/e68d

Hospital da Missão Católica do Chiulo
Ondjiva, Cunene, Angola
🌐 https://vfmat.ch/5621

Hospital das 500 Casas
Viana, Luanda, Angola
🌐 https://vfmat.ch/47d1

Hospital de Kalukembe
Camucua, Huíla, Angola
🌐 https://vfmat.ch/3a63

Hospital de Menongue
Bairro Saúde, Cuando Cobango, Angola
🌐 https://vfmat.ch/c4ec

Hospital do Caminho de Ferro
Lobito, Benguela, Angola
🌐 https://vfmat.ch/b697

Hospital do Prenda
Arguelles, Luanda, Angola
🌐 https://vfmat.ch/e8ff

Hospital do Sumbe
Chingo, Kwanza Sul, Angola
🌐 https://vfmat.ch/798f

Hospital dos Cajueiros
Luanda, Luanda, Angola
🌐 https://vfmat.ch/xlp5

Hospital General da Barra do Dande
Barra do Dande, Bengo, Angola
🌐 https://vfmat.ch/3aa1

Hospital General de Benguela
Columbulaco, Benguela, Angola
🌐 https://vfmat.ch/6a72

Hospital Geral 17 de Setembro
Sumbe, Kwanza Sul, Angola
🌐 https://vfmat.ch/888c

Hospital Geral de Luanda
Luanda, Luanda, Angola
🌐 https://vfmat.ch/5c93

Hospital Josina Machel
Salinas da Samba, Luanda, Angola
🌐 https://vfmat.ch/def8

Hospital Militar Aviação
Aviação, Huambo, Angola
🌐 https://vfmat.ch/5f92

Hospital Militar Central
Salinas da Samba, Luanda, Angola
🌐 https://vfmat.ch/be6a

Hospital Militar da Catumbela
Lobito, Angola
🌐 https://vfmat.ch/4bc3

Hospital Militar do Lubango
Lubango, Huíla, Angola
🌐 https://vfmat.ch/2fbd

Hospital Municipal de Cacuaco
Cacuaco, Luanda, Angola
🌐 https://vfmat.ch/17da

Hospital Municipal de Chipindo
Chipindo, Huíla, Angola
🌐 https://vfmat.ch/1317

Hospital Municipal de Viana Kapalanga
Viana, Luanda, Angola
🌐 https://vfmat.ch/6e94

Hospital Municipal do Sambizanga
Muceques, Luanda, Angola
🌐 https://vfmat.ch/c792

Hospital Neves Bendinha
Kilamba Kiaxi, Luanda, Angola
🌐 https://vfmat.ch/da18

Hospital Nossa Senhora da Paz
Cubal, Angola
🌐 https://vfmat.ch/7qsd

Hospital Pediatrico David Bernardino
Luanda, Angola
🌐 https://vfmat.ch/tmmz

Hospital Pediátrico Pioneiro Zeca
Lubango, Huíla, Angola
⊕ https://vfmat.ch/f96b

Hospital Provincial do Cunene
Omupanda, Cunene, Angola
⊕ https://vfmat.ch/52fc

Hospital Provincial do Uíge
Uíge, Uíge, Angola
⊕ https://vfmat.ch/6kya

Hospital Provincial Ngola Kimbanda
Namibe, Namibe, Angola
⊕ https://vfmat.ch/d961

Hospital Psiquiátrico de Luanda
Salinas da Samba, Luanda, Angola
⊕ https://vfmat.ch/32f1

Hospital Regional do Huambo
Maia, Huambo, Angola
⊕ https://vfmat.ch/278b

Hospital Sanatório de Luanda
Van-Dúnem Loy, Luanda, Angola
⊕ https://vfmat.ch/64d1

Lucrécia Paím Maternity
Luanda, Angola
⊕ https://vfmat.ch/rbxe

Maternidade Augusto N'Gangula
Muceques, Luanda, Angola
⊕ https://vfmat.ch/6f9a

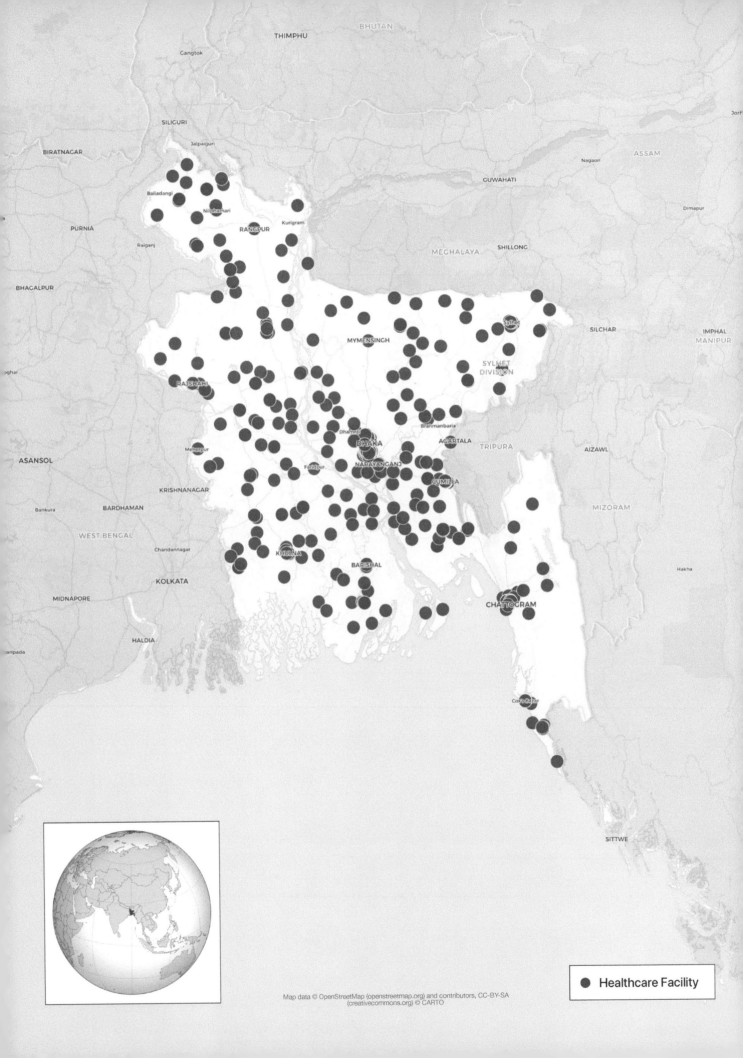

Healthcare Facility

Bangladesh

The People's Republic of Bangladesh, in South Asia, shares borders with India, Myanmar, and the Bay of Bengal. It is the eighth most populous country in the world, home to 164.1 million people, and is one of the most densely populated countries in the world. The capital, Dhaka, its largest city, is also the economic and political center of Bangladesh. The population is ethnically homogeneous, with 98 percent identifying as Bengali, and linguistically homogeneous, with 98.8 percent speaking Bangla (Bengali). Islam is the most commonly practiced religion, making Bangladesh the third largest Muslim-majority country in the world. Bangladesh is known for its famed mangrove forests, home to some of the most fertile soils in the world, and a vibrant ecosystem.

Bangladesh partitioned from India in 1947 to become East Pakistan. A movement based in Bengali nationalism and self-determination led to Bangladesh's independence as a sovereign nation in 1971. Despite ongoing challenges of corruption, political unrest, a refugee crisis, and the negative effects of climate change, Bangladesh has continued to grow and develop. It is considered an emerging market and has one of the fastest-growing economies, particularly compared to the rest of Asia. Since 2005, the economy has grown about six percent annually. About half of Bangladeshis work in agriculture, with rice the largest crop. In addition, the industrial sector features heavily in the economy, and Bangladesh is one of the largest garment exporters in the world. In all, poverty rates decreased from 44 percent in 1991 to 15 percent in 2016, marking a significant improvement.

As economic and development indicators have improved over time, so have Bangladesh's health indicators. Child mortality in under-five and under-one age groups decreased significantly between 1990 and 2019. Life expectancy has also steadily increased. However, both communicable and non-communicable diseases continue to be leading causes of death, including stroke, ischemic heart disease, COPD, neonatal disorders, lower respiratory infections, diabetes, diarrheal diseases, tuberculosis, cirrhosis, and malignant neoplasms. The risk factors that contribute most to death and disability include malnutrition, air pollution, high blood pressure, tobacco use, dietary risks, high fasting plasma glucose, high body-mass index, high LDL, drowning, and insufficient water, sanitation, and hygiene.

164.1M

Population

$1,969

GDP Per Capita

73 years

Life Expectancy

↑ Improving

64
Doctors/100k

Physician Density

80
Beds/100k

Hospital Bed Density

173
Deaths/100k

Maternal Mortality

Bangladesh

Nonprofit Organizations

A Leg To Stand On (ALTSO)
Provides free, high-quality prosthetic limbs, orthotic devices, and wheelchairs to children with untreated limb disabilities in the developing world.
Logist-Op, Ortho
⊕ https://vfmat.ch/a48d

A Stitch in Time
Seeks to address socially crippling but readily treatable conditions, such as genital prolapse in women who lack access, by providing technically advanced pelvic reconstructive surgery, free of charge, to restore women's bodies in geographically or access remote areas of the world.
Anesth, OB-GYN
⊕ https://vfmat.ch/6474

Aastha Foundation
Provides quality and compassionate care, including pain management and emotional and spiritual support, to patients and their family members.
Geri, Heme-Onc, Palliative, Pub Health
⊕ https://vfmat.ch/feeb

Abt Associates
Seeks to improve the quality of life and economic well-being of people worldwide, while striving to meet and exceed the highest professional standards.
General, Logist-Op, MF Med, OB-GYN, Peds
⊕ https://vfmat.ch/cec2

Aceso Global
Provides strategic healthcare advisory services in low- and middle-income countries to design and deliver highly customized, evidence-based solutions that address the complex nature of healthcare systems, with a goal to strengthen and provide affordable, high-quality care to all.
Logist-Op, Pub Health
⊕ https://vfmat.ch/b3b7

Acid Survivors Foundation
Works to prevent acid and burn violence and empower survivors, especially women and children, and provides free care for burn violence patients at its hospital.
Nutr, Surg
⊕ https://vfmat.ch/fc33

Action Against Hunger
Aims to end life-threatening hunger for good through treating and preventing malnutrition across more than 45 countries.
Nutr
⊕ https://vfmat.ch/2dbc

Advance Family Planning
Aims to achieve global expansion and access to quality contraceptive information, services, and supplies through financial investment and political commitment.

General, MF Med, Pub Health
⊕ https://vfmat.ch/7478

Aga Khan Foundation Canada
Tackles the root causes of poverty, with a special focus on marginalized groups such as women and girls. Programs provide access to education and healthcare, food, and opportunity.
Pub Health
⊕ https://vfmat.ch/7f8b

Age International
Helps older people living in some of the world's poorest places to have improved well-being and be treated with dignity through a variety of programs, including emergency relief and cataract surgery.
ER Med, Geri, Logist-Op, Nutr, Ophth-Opt, Palliative, Pub Health
⊕ https://vfmat.ch/c7e2

Al Basar International Foundation
Works with local partners to treat preventable blindness, and helps set up sustainable infrastructure so local teams can save sight in their communities.
Ophth-Opt
⊕ https://vfmat.ch/a8b5

Al-Khair Foundation
Provides emergency relief and developmental support in some of the world's most impoverished areas.
Dent-OMFS, General, MF Med, Nutr, Peds
⊕ https://vfmat.ch/921d

Al-Mustafa Welfare Trust
Seeks to alleviate poverty and provides medical and social development assistance to the poor and vulnerable around the world.
General, Ophth-Opt
⊕ https://vfmat.ch/c5f4

Alliance for Smiles
Improves the lives of children and communities impacted by cleft by providing free comprehensive treatment while building local capacity for long-term care.
Dent-OMFS, Ped Surg, Plast, Surg
⊕ https://vfmat.ch/bb32

Aloha Medical Mission
Brings hope and changes the lives of people; serves overseas and in Hawai'i.
Anesth, Crit-Care, Dent-OMFS, ENT, ER Med, General, Medicine, OB-GYN, Ophth-Opt, Ortho, Ped Surg, Peds, Plast, Surg, Urol
⊕ https://vfmat.ch/72ac

Amal Foundation
Works to end the cycle of poverty through programs in education, healthcare,

emergency response, and women's empowerment.
Dent-OMFS, General, Nutr
⊕ https://vfmat.ch/ac74

American Heart Association (AHA)
Fights heart disease and stroke, striving to save and improve lives.
CV Med, Crit-Care, General, Heme-Onc, Medicine, Peds
⊕ https://vfmat.ch/4747

American Stroke Association
Works to prevent, treat, and beat stroke by funding innovative research, fighting for stronger public health policies, and providing lifesaving tools and information.
CV Med, Crit-Care, Heme-Onc, Medicine, Neuro, Pub Health, Pulm-Critic, Vasc Surg
⊕ https://vfmat.ch/746f

Americares
Saves lives and improves health for people affected by poverty or disaster and responds with life-changing medicine, medical supplies, and health programs including domestic and global medical clinics.
All-Immu, ER Med, General, Infect Dis, MF Med, Nutr
⊕ https://vfmat.ch/e567

Amsterdam Institute for Global Health and Development (AIGHD)
Provides sustainable solutions to major health problems across our planet by forging synergies among disciplines, healthcare delivery, research, and education.
Infect Dis
⊕ https://vfmat.ch/d73d

AO Alliance
Builds solutions to lessen the burden of injuries in low- and middle-income countries, while enhancing the care of the injured to reduce human suffering, disability, and poverty.
Ortho, Surg
⊕ https://vfmat.ch/8cd5

ARC The Australian Respiratory Council
Fosters research to promote respiratory health and works to improve lung health in communities of disadvantaged and Indigenous people.
Infect Dis
⊕ https://vfmat.ch/69f2

ASHIC Foundation
Aims to ensure proper care, treatment, and quality of life for children with cancer and their families.
Heme-Onc, Palliative
⊕ https://vfmat.ch/f594

Association of Baptists - AOB
Aims to provide medical care and training for southern Bangladesh, and promote the physical, spiritual, social, and educational development of all Bangladeshis.
General, MF Med, OB-GYN, Ortho, Path, Pub Health, Rehab, Surg
⊕ https://vfmat.ch/bfb7

Association of Medical Doctors of Asia (AMDA)
Strives to support people affected by disasters and economic distress on their road to recovery, establishing a true partnership with special emphasis on local initiative.
ER Med, Logist-Op, Pub Health
⊕ https://vfmat.ch/e3d4

Austrian Doctors
Stands for a life in dignity and takes care of the health of disadvantaged people. Helps all people regardless of gender, skin color, religion and sexual orientation.
General, Infect Dis, Medicine
⊕ https://vfmat.ch/e929

Backpacker Medics
Aims to bring effective medical care to those who need it most through a platform for paramedics and other pre-hospital workers to engage in humanitarian work and travel to remote areas of the world to deliver healthcare, establish healthcare facilities, and provide education.

Crit-Care, ER Med, OB-GYN
⊕ https://vfmat.ch/c4e5

BanglaCare Foundation - BCF
Aims to provide better access to healthcare to people in Bangladesh through the implementation of telehealth centers.
General
⊕ https://vfmat.ch/7f4f

Bangladesh Health Development Initiative (BHDI)
Aims to support and standardize village medical network practices.
General, Peds, Pub Health
⊕ https://vfmat.ch/4b1a

Bangladesh Lions Foundation
Promotes and funds human healthcare services and human welfare, including services in physiotherapy, education, dentistry, and advanced eye care.
Dent-OMFS, ENT, Ophth-Opt, Rehab
⊕ https://vfmat.ch/416f

Bangladesh Medical Relief Foundation
Provides targeted and effective medical aid and assistance to poor areas of Bangladesh.
ER Med, General, Pub Health
⊕ https://vfmat.ch/ed11

Barzani Charity Foundation (BCF)
Provides humanitarian aid without discrimination to vulnerable populations in the pursuit of peace and sustainability for humanity and nature.
CT Surg, General
⊕ https://vfmat.ch/b192

BDesh Foundation
Provides poverty alleviation, disaster relief, health and sanitation, and educational projects.
General, Ophth-Opt
⊕ https://vfmat.ch/85c1

Beani Bazar Cancer and General Hospital
Aims to create awareness and provides medical treatment for disadvantaged cancer patients in Bangladesh.
CV Med, General, OB-GYN, Ped Surg, Peds, Pub Health, Rad-Onc, Rad-Onc, Surg, Surg
⊕ https://vfmat.ch/44f3

BFIRST – British Foundation for International Reconstructive Surgery & Training
Supports projects across the developing world to train surgeons in their local environment to effectively manage devastating injuries.
Anesth, Plast, Surg
⊕ https://vfmat.ch/ad4f

Boston Children's Hospital: Global Health Program
Helps solve pediatric global healthcare challenges by transferring expertise through long-term partnerships with scalable impact, while working in the field to strengthen healthcare systems, advocate, research, and provide care delivery or education as a way of sustainably improving the health of children worldwide.
Anesth, CV Med, Crit-Care, ER Med, Heme-Onc, Infect Dis, Medicine, Nutr, Palliative, Ped Surg, Peds
⊕ https://vfmat.ch/f9f8

BRAC USA
Seeks to empower people and communities in situations of poverty, illiteracy, disease, and social injustice. Interventions aim to achieve large-scale, positive changes through economic and social programs that enable everyone to realize their potential.
ER Med, General, Infect Dis, Logist-Op, MF Med, OB-GYN
⊕ https://vfmat.ch/9d9e

Breast Cancer Support
Aims to save lives and end breast cancer forever in women and men through education, treatment, emotional assistance, and financial support.

Heme-Onc, Logist-Op, Pub Health, Rad-Onc, Radiol
⊕ https://vfmat.ch/cb78

Bridge of Life
Aims to strengthen healthcare globally through sustainable programs that prevent and treat chronic disease.
Logist-Op, Nephro, OB-GYN, Peds, Surg
⊕ https://vfmat.ch/5b68

British Council for Prevention of Blindness (BCPB)
Funds research into blindness prevention and sight restoration in children and adults in low- and lower-middle-income countries.
Ophth-Opt
⊕ https://vfmat.ch/eaf4

Canadian Medical Assistance Teams (CMAT)
Provides relief and medical aid to the victims of natural and man-made disasters around the world.
Anesth, ER Med, Medicine, OB-GYN, Peds, Psych, Rehab, Surg
⊕ https://vfmat.ch/5232

Canadian Reconstructive Surgery Foundation, The
Develops, organizes, and manages, in participation with developing countries, the delivery of reconstructive medical-care programs, technologies, and education to those who cannot otherwise obtain the care they need.
Anesth, Dent-OMFS, Plast
⊕ https://vfmat.ch/15f4

CARE
Works around the globe to save lives, defeat poverty, and achieve social justice.
ER Med, General
⊕ https://vfmat.ch/7232

Care Channels International
We engage communities through a variety of education, health, and livelihood programs.
Dent-OMFS, General, Surg
⊕ https://vfmat.ch/fc48

Carter Center, The
Seeks to prevent and resolve conflicts, enhance freedom and democracy, and improve health, while remaining committed to human rights and the alleviation of human suffering.
Infect Dis, MF Med, Ophth-Opt
⊕ https://vfmat.ch/6556

Catholic World Mission
Works to rebuild communities worldwide by helping to alleviate poverty and empower underserved areas, while spreading the message of the Catholic Church.
ER Med, General, Nutr, Peds
⊕ https://vfmat.ch/7b5f

cbm New Zealand
Inspired by the Christian faith, aims to improve the quality of life for those living with the double disadvantage of poverty and disability.
Crit-Care, Infect Dis, Logist-Op, Nutr, OB-GYN, Ophth-Opt, Ortho, Psych, Rehab, Surg
⊕ https://vfmat.ch/c14b

Centre for the Rehabilitation of the Paralysed - CRP
Provides medical treatment, rehabilitation, and support services to individuals with disabilities, with a focus on physical, emotional, social, psychological, and economic support.
Neuro, Ortho, Path, Radiol, Rehab, Rheum, Surg
⊕ https://vfmat.ch/79c4

Chain of Hope (La Chaîne de l'Espoir)
Helps underprivileged children around the world by providing them with access to healthcare.
Anesth, CT Surg, Crit-Care, ER Med, Neurosurg, Ortho, Ped Surg, Surg, Vasc Surg
⊕ https://vfmat.ch/e871

Child Health Awareness Foundation (CHAF)
Aims to address basic health needs, disease, and illiteracy of underprivileged populations, focusing on mother and child health.
CV Med, Dent-OMFS, General, MF Med, Nutr, Plast, Pub Health
⊕ https://vfmat.ch/d7ce

Children Without Worms
Enhances the health and development of children by reducing intestinal worm infections.
Infect Dis, Pub Health
⊕ https://vfmat.ch/6bee

Children's Surgery International
Provides free medical and surgical services to children in need around the world, and instructs and trains local surgeons and other medical providers such as doctors, anesthesiologists, nurses, and technicians.
Anesth, Dent-OMFS, Ortho, Ped Surg, Peds, Plast, Surg
⊕ https://vfmat.ch/26d3

Christian Aid Ministries
Strives to be a trustworthy and efficient channel for Amish, Mennonite, and other conservative Anabaptist groups and individuals to minister to physical and spiritual needs around the world.
CT Surg, ER Med, Logist-Op, Ortho, Pub Health
⊕ https://vfmat.ch/7b33

Christian Blind Mission (CBM)
Aims to improve the quality of life of persons with disabilities in the poorest countries, addressing poverty as a cause and a consequence of disability, and working in partnership to create a society for all.
ENT, General, Infect Dis, OB-GYN, Ophth-Opt, Ortho, Peds, Psych, Rehab, Surg
⊕ https://vfmat.ch/3824

Christian Connections for International Health (CCIH)
Promotes global health and wholeness from a Christian perspective.
All-Immu, General, Infect Dis, MF Med, Neonat, OB-GYN, Psych
⊕ https://vfmat.ch/fa5d

Christian Medical & Dental Associations
Based in Christian ministry, deploys medical and dental teams to underserved communities to provide vital healthcare.
Anesth, Dent-OMFS, ER Med, General, Medicine, OB-GYN, Ophth-Opt, Peds, Pub Health, Radiol, Rehab, Surg
⊕ https://vfmat.ch/921c

Columbia University: Global Mental Health Programs
Pioneers research initiatives, promotes mental health, and aims to reduce the burden of mental illness worldwide.
Psych
⊕ https://vfmat.ch/c5cd

Concern Worldwide
Seeks to permanently transform the lives of people living in extreme poverty, tackling its root causes, and building resilience.
Logist-Op, MF Med, Nutr, OB-GYN
⊕ https://vfmat.ch/77e9

Core Group
Aims to improve and expand community health practices for underserved populations, especially women and children, through collaborative action and learning.
General, Infect Dis, MF Med, Medicine, OB-GYN, Peds, Pub Health
⊕ https://vfmat.ch/9de3

COVID-19 Clinical Research Coalition
Advocates and collaborates for the advancement of COVID-19 research driven by the needs of low-resource settings, and works for equitable access to solutions to the pandemic.
All-Immu, Infect-Dis, MF Med, Path, Pub Health
⊕ https://vfmat.ch/d1f4

CURE
Operates charitable hospitals and programs in underserved countries worldwide,

where patients receive surgical treatment, based in Christian ministry.
Anesth, Neurosurg, Ortho, Ped Surg, Peds, Rehab, Surg
⊕ https://vfmat.ch/aa16

Dianova
Works in prevention and treatment of addiction, while promoting social progress in international forums.
Psych, Pub Health
⊕ https://vfmat.ch/1998

Direct Relief
Improves the health and lives of people affected by poverty or emergency situations by mobilizing and providing essential medical resources needed for their care.
ER Med, Logist-Op
⊕ https://vfmat.ch/58e5

Doctors Without Borders/Médecins Sans Frontières (MSF)
Responds to emergencies and provides lifesaving medical care where needed most, including during disasters, conflicts, and epidemics.
Anesth, Crit-Care, ER Med, General, Infect Dis, Nutr, OB-GYN, Ped Surg, Peds, Psych, Pub Health, Surg
⊕ https://vfmat.ch/f363

Doctors Worldwide
Focuses on health access, health improvement, and health emergencies to serve communities in need so they can build healthier and happier futures.
Dent-OMFS, ER Med, General, MF Med, Palliative, Peds
⊕ https://vfmat.ch/99cd

Dream Poverty Eradication Foundation - DPEF
Aims to alleviate poverty among the ultra-poor in remote areas of Bangladesh and inspire people to take action to reshape local communities.
ENT, ER Med, General, Infect Dis, MF Med, Neonat, OB-GYN, Ophth-Opt, Ortho, Peds, Surg
⊕ https://vfmat.ch/43a9

Drugs for Neglected Diseases Initiative
Develops lifesaving medicines for people with neglected diseases around the world, having developed eight treatments for five deadly diseases and saved millions of lives since 2003.
Infect Dis, Pub Health
⊕ https://vfmat.ch/969c

Duke University: Global Health Institute
Sparks innovation in global health research and education, and brings together knowledge and resources to address the most important global health issues of our time.
All-Immu, Infect Dis, MF Med, OB-GYN, Pub Health
⊕ https://vfmat.ch/c4cd

Effect: Hope (The Leprosy Mission Canada)
Connects like-minded Canadians to people suffering in isolation from debilitating, neglected tropical diseases such as leprosy, lymphatic filariasis, and Buruli ulcer.
General, Infect Dis
⊕ https://vfmat.ch/f12a

Ending Eclampsia
Seeks to expand access to proven, underutilized interventions and commodities for the prevention, early detection, and treatment of pre-eclampsia and eclampsia and to strengthen global partnerships.
MF Med, Neonat, OB-GYN
⊕ https://vfmat.ch/8589

EngenderHealth
Works to implement high-quality, gender-equitable programs that advance sexual and reproductive health and rights.
General, MF Med, OB-GYN, Peds
⊕ https://vfmat.ch/1cb2

Evidence Project, The
Improves family-planning policies, programs, and practices through the strategic generation, translation, and use of evidence.

General, MF Med
⊕ https://vfmat.ch/f9e7

Eye Foundation of America
Works toward a world without childhood blindness.
Ophth-Opt
⊕ https://vfmat.ch/a7eb

Firefly Mission
Organizes humanitarian missions to help people in less fortunate situations while serving as a vehicle for the spiritual development of members and the beneficiaries of its missions.
Logist-Op, Ophth-Opt, Pub Health
⊕ https://vfmat.ch/d215

Fistula Foundation
Aims to engage the support of people worldwide who are eager to see the day that no woman suffers from obstetric fistula. Raises and directs funds to doctors and hospitals providing life-transforming surgery to women in need.
OB-GYN
⊕ https://vfmat.ch/e958

Foundation for Special Surgery
Provides high-quality, complex surgical care by increasing surgical expertise in Africa through the participation of surgeons across various specialties to provide premium care and skills transfer/education to benefit patients.
Anesth, CT Surg, ENT, Endo, Neurosurg, Plast, Surg, Urol
⊕ https://vfmat.ch/53db

Fred Hollows Foundation, The
Works toward a world in which no person is needlessly blind or vision impaired.
Ophth-Opt, Pub Health, Surg
⊕ https://vfmat.ch/73e5

Friends for Asia Foundation, The
Develops international volunteer projects that assist local communities in overcoming challenges, and provides volunteers with the experience of contributing to those communities as a valued participant.
General
⊕ https://vfmat.ch/f8a9

Friends In Village Development Bangladesh - FIVDB
Aims to give disadvantaged women, men and children a greater voice, reduce their vulnerability and increase their use of citizenship rights.
General, OB-GYN, Ophth-Opt, Pub Health
⊕ https://vfmat.ch/5f54

Friends of UNFPA
Promotes the health, dignity, and rights of women and girls around the world by supporting the lifesaving work of UNFPA, the United Nations' reproductive health and rights agency, through education, advocacy, and fundraising.
MF Med, OB-GYN
⊕ https://vfmat.ch/2a3a

German Doctors
Conducts voluntary medical work in developing countries and brings help where misery is part of everyday life.
General, Infect Dis, Medicine
⊕ https://vfmat.ch/21ad

GFA World
Based in Christian ministry, sponsors medical camps for the sick, provides disaster relief to vulnerable populations, and empowers impoverished communities with basic necessities such as clean water, vocational training, and education.
General, Infect Dis
⊕ https://vfmat.ch/63ee

Gift of Life International
Provides lifesaving cardiac treatment to children in developing countries while developing sustainable pediatric cardiac programs by implementing screening, surgical, and training missions.

Anesth, CT Surg, CV Med, Crit-Care, Ped Surg, Peds, Pulm-Critic
⊕ https://vfmat.ch/f2f9

Global Alliance to Prevent Prematurity And Stillbirth (GAPPS)
Seeks to improve birth outcomes worldwide by reducing the burden of premature birth and stillbirth.
All-Immu, Infect Dis, MF Med, Neonat, Neonat, OB-GYN
⊕ https://vfmat.ch/3f74

Global Clinic
Seeks to ensure that any effort to provide medical services is accompanied by a long-term program to improve the health of residents of its partner communities.
Dent-OMFS, ER Med, General, OB-GYN, OB-GYN, Ophth-Opt, Surg
⊕ https://vfmat.ch/9e48

Global Force for Healing
Works to end preventable maternal and newborn deaths by supporting the scaling of effective grassroots, community-led, culturally respectful care and education in underserved areas around the globe using the midwifery model of care.
Neonat, OB-GYN
⊕ https://vfmat.ch/deb2

Global Medical Foundation Australia
Provides medical, surgical, dental, and educational welfare to underprivileged communities and gives them access to basics that are often taken for granted.
Dent-OMFS, ER Med, General, OB-GYN, Ortho, Surg
⊕ https://vfmat.ch/fa56

Global Ministries – The United Methodist Church
As the worldwide mission and development agency of The United Methodist Church, Global Ministries works with more than 300 hospitals and clinics around the world through its Global Health Unit.
Anesth, CT Surg, CV Med, Crit-Care, Dent-OMFS, Derm, ER Med, GI, General, Infect Dis, Logist-Op, MF Med, Medicine, Neonat, Nephro, Nutr, OB-GYN, Ophth-Opt, Ortho, Palliative, Peds, Pod, Psych, Pub Health, Rehab, Rheum, Surg, Urol
⊕ https://vfmat.ch/1723

Global Network for Women and Children's Health Research
Aims to improve maternal and child health outcomes and building health research capacity in resource-poor settings by testing cost-effective, sustainable interventions that provide guidance for the practice of evidence-based medicine. Scientists from developing countries, together with peers in the United States, lead teams that address priority research needs through randomized clinical trials and implementation research conducted in low-resource areas.
MF Med, OB-GYN
⊕ https://vfmat.ch/a187

Global Oncology (GO)
Brings the best in cancer care to underserved patients around the world and collaborates across geographic, professional, and academic borders to improve cancer care, research, and education.
Heme-Onc, Path, Rad-Onc
⊕ https://vfmat.ch/fcb8

Global Outreach Doctors
Provides global health medical services in developing countries affected by famine, infant mortality, and chronic health issues.
All-Immu, Anesth, ER Med, General, Infect Dis, MF Med, Peds, Surg
⊕ https://vfmat.ch/8514

Global Vision 2020
Provides prescription eyeglasses to people who live in parts of the world lacking necessary infrastructure for obtaining affordable corrective eyewear.
Logist-Op, Ophth-Opt
⊕ https://vfmat.ch/7373

GlobalMedic
Provides disaster relief and lifesaving humanitarian aid.
ER Med, Pub Health
⊕ https://vfmat.ch/dfe6

Globus Relief
Aims to improve the delivery of healthcare worldwide by gathering, processing,

and distributing surplus medical supplies to charities at home and abroad.
Logist-Op
⊕ https://vfmat.ch/a2b7

Healing Little Hearts
Sends specialist medical teams to perform free lifesaving heart surgery on babies and children in developing parts of the world.
Anesth, CT Surg, CV Med, Ped Surg, Peds, Surg
⊕ https://vfmat.ch/ffc1

Health and Education For All - HAEFA
Aims to empower global disadvantaged and displaced populations through education and free, essential healthcare services.
General
⊕ https://vfmat.ch/c54a

Health Volunteers Overseas (HVO)
Improves the availability and quality of healthcare through the education, training, and professional development of the health workforce in resource-scarce countries.
All-Immu, Anesth, CV Med, Dent-OMFS, Derm, ENT, ER Med, Endo, GI, Heme-Onc, Infect Dis, Medicine, Medicine, Nephro, Neuro, OB-GYN, Ophth-Opt, Ortho, Peds, Plast, Psych, Pulm-Critic, Rehab, Rheum, Surg
⊕ https://vfmat.ch/42b2

HealthServe Australia
Develops sustainable health programs that improve health and well-being and partners with community groups to build community capacity to meet health needs.
Infect Dis, Logist-Op, OB-GYN, Psych, Pub Health
⊕ https://vfmat.ch/7276

Healthy DEvelopments
Provides Germany-supported health and social protection programs around the globe in a collaborative knowledge management process.
All-Immu, General, Infect Dis, Logist-Op, MF Med
⊕ https://vfmat.ch/dc31

Helen Keller International
Seeks to eliminate preventable vision loss, malnutrition, and diseases of poverty.
Infect Dis, Nutr, OB-GYN, Ophth-Opt, Peds
⊕ https://vfmat.ch/b654

HelpAge International
Works to ensure that people everywhere understand how much older people contribute to society and that they must enjoy their right to healthcare, social services, economic, and physical security.
General, Geri, Infect Dis, Medicine, Pub Health
⊕ https://vfmat.ch/5d91

Hernia International
Aims to provide relief from sickness, and protection and preservation of health, for persons affected by groin and abdominal hernias and residing in low- and middle-income countries.
Surg
⊕ https://vfmat.ch/e98e

HOPE Foundation for Women and Children of Bangladesh
HOPE's mission is to provide quality health services to the most marginalized population in rural Bangladesh using education, community outreach, and the provision of compassionate healthcare.
Anesth, Dent-OMFS, MF Med, Neonat, OB-GYN, Ped Surg, Plast
⊕ https://vfmat.ch/dbdc

HumaniTerra
Helps countries and populations emerging from economic and human crisis to rebuild their healthcare system in a sustainable way. Committed to three fundamental and complementary actions: operating, training, and rebuilding.
Anesth, ENT, ER Med, MF Med, OB-GYN, Ortho, Plast, Surg
⊕ https://vfmat.ch/b371

Humanity First
Provides aid and assistance to those in need, offering sustainable development

solutions to society while providing and empowering local communities with the resources to help themselves.
ER Med, General, MF Med, Ophth-Opt
⊕ https://vfmat.ch/13cc

Hunger Project, The
Aims to end hunger and poverty by pioneering sustainable, grassroots, women-centered strategies and advocating for their widespread adoption in countries throughout the world.
Infect Dis, Nutr, OB-GYN, Pub Health
⊕ https://vfmat.ch/3a49

IMPACT Foundation
Works to prevent and alleviate needless disability by restoring sight, mobility, and hearing.
ENT, MF Med, OB-GYN, Ophth-Opt, Ortho, Peds, Surg
⊕ https://vfmat.ch/ba28

Institute for Healthcare Improvement (IHI)
Aims to improve health and healthcare worldwide by working with health professionals to strengthen systems.
Crit-Care, Infect Dis, MF Med, Medicine, Neonat, OB-GYN, Pub Health
⊕ https://vfmat.ch/ecae

International Agency for the Prevention of Blindness (IAPB), The
Leads international efforts in blindness-prevention activities, works toward a world where no one is needlessly visually impaired, and ensures that everyone has access to the best possible standard of eye health.
Infect Dis, Ophth-Opt, Pub Health
⊕ https://vfmat.ch/87a2

International Campaign for Women's Right to Safe Abortion
Works to build an international network and campaign that brings together organizations with an interest in promoting and providing safe abortion to create a shared platform for advocacy, debate, and dialogue and the sharing of skills and experience.
OB-GYN, Pub Health, Surg
⊕ https://vfmat.ch/f341

International Council of Ophthalmology
Works with ophthalmologic societies and others to enhance ophthalmic education and improve access to the highest-quality eye care in order to preserve and restore vision for people of the world.
Ophth-Opt
⊕ https://vfmat.ch/ffd2

International Eye Foundation (IEF)
Eliminates preventable and treatable blindness by making quality sustainable eye care services accessible and affordable worldwide.
Infect Dis, Logist-Op, Ophth-Opt
⊕ https://vfmat.ch/e839

International Federation of Gynecology and Obstetrics (FIGO)
Implements global projects on specific women's health issues.
MF Med, Medicine, Neonat, OB-GYN, Surg, Urol
⊕ https://vfmat.ch/c4b4

International Federation of Red Cross and Red Crescent Societies (IFRC)
Coordinates and directs international assistance following natural and manmade disasters in nonconflict situations through the world's largest humanitarian and development network. Provides disaster-preparedness programs, healthcare activities, and promotes humanitarian values.
ER Med, General, Infect Dis, Nutr
⊕ https://vfmat.ch/b4ee

International Learning Movement (ILM UK)
Supports some of the world's poorest people in developing countries with core projects in education, safe drinking water, and healthcare.
General, Ophth-Opt
⊕ https://vfmat.ch/b974

International Organization for Migration (IOM) – The UN Migration Agency
Promotes evidence-informed policies and holistic, preventive, and curative health programs that are beneficial, accessible, and equitable for vulnerable migrants.
General, Infect Dis, OB-GYN
⊕ https://vfmat.ch/621a

International Planned Parenthood Federation (IPPF)
Leads a locally owned, globally connected civil society movement that provides and enables services and champions sexual and reproductive health and rights for all, especially the underserved.
Infect Dis, MF Med, OB-GYN
⊕ https://vfmat.ch/dc97

International Relief Teams
Helps families survive and recover after a disaster by delivering timely and effective assistance through programs that improve their health and well-being while also providing a hopeful future for underserved communities.
Dent-OMFS, ER Med, General, Nutr, Ophth-Opt
⊕ https://vfmat.ch/ffd5

International Rescue Committee (IRC)
Responds to the world's worst humanitarian crises and helps people whose lives and livelihoods are shattered by conflict and disaster to survive, recover, and gain control of their future.
ER Med, General, Infect Dis, MF Med, Peds
⊕ https://vfmat.ch/5d24

InterSurgeon
Fosters collaborative partnerships in the field of global surgery that will advance clinical care, teaching, training, research, and the provision and maintenance of medical equipment.
ENT, Neurosurg, Ortho, Ped Surg, Plast, Surg, Urol
⊕ https://vfmat.ch/6f8a

IntraHealth International
Improves the performance of health workers and strengthens the systems in which they work.
CV Med, Endo, General, Infect Dis, MF Med, Neonat, Nutr, OB-GYN
⊕ https://vfmat.ch/ddc8

Ipas
Focuses efforts on women and girls who want contraception or abortion, and builds programs around their needs and how best to support them.
OB-GYN
⊕ https://vfmat.ch/8e39

iQra International
Provides medical aid to disabled people globally, and raises awareness of the neglect and discrimination they face in developing countries.
General, Logist-Op, Ophth-Opt
⊕ https://vfmat.ch/9282

Iranian Red Crescent
Aims to provide effective relief services in the wake of crises, to alleviate human suffering, and to empower the affected community.
ER Med, General, Infect Dis, Logist-Op, Nutr, OB-GYN, Psych, Rehab
⊕ https://vfmat.ch/c352

Islamic Medical Association of North America
Fosters health promotion, disease prevention, and health maintenance in communities around the world through direct patient care and health programs.
Anesth, Dent-OMFS, ER Med, General, Logist-Op, Ophth-Opt, Peds, Plast, Surg
⊕ https://vfmat.ch/a157

Ispahani Islamia Eye Institute and Hospital (IIEI&H)
Strives to make high-quality ophthalmic care accessible to all people at an affordable price.
Ophth-Opt
⊕ https://vfmat.ch/21d3

Jhpiego
Creates and delivers transformative healthcare solutions that save lives, in

partnership with national governments, health experts, and local communities.
General, Infect Dis, OB-GYN, Surg
⊕ https://vfmat.ch/45b8

John Snow, Inc. (JSI)
Aims to improve the health and well-being of underserved and vulnerable people and communities throughout the world.
General, Infect Dis, Logist-Op, MF Med, OB-GYN, Peds, Psych, Pub Health
⊕ https://vfmat.ch/ba78

Johns Hopkins Center for Communication Programs
Believes in the power of communication to save lives by empowering people to adopt healthy behaviors for themselves, their families, and their communities.
General, Infect Dis, Logist-Op, OB-GYN, Pub Health
⊕ https://vfmat.ch/1bf9

Johns Hopkins Center for Global Health
Facilitates and focuses the extensive expertise and resources of the Johns Hopkins institutions, together with global collaborators, to effectively address and ameliorate the world's most pressing health issues.
General, Genetics, Logist-Op, MF Med, Peds, Psych, Pub Health, Pulm-Critic
⊕ https://vfmat.ch/54ce

Joint United Nations Programme on HIV/AIDS (UNAIDS)
Aims to place people living with HIV and people affected by the virus at the decision-making table and at the center of designing, delivering, and monitoring the AIDS response.
Infect Dis
⊕ https://vfmat.ch/464a

Kind Cuts for Kids
Aims to improve medical services for children in developing countries through education, demonstration, and skills transfer to local healthcare professionals.
Anesth, Medicine, Ped Surg, Surg
⊕ https://vfmat.ch/e3d7

LAMB
Provides healthcare and development services for vulnerable people of North West Bangladesh, inspired by the Christian faith.
Dent-OMFS, General, Infect Dis, MF Med, OB-GYN, Ophth-Opt, Surg
⊕ https://vfmat.ch/f145

Last Mile Health
Links community health workers with frontline health workers—nurses, doctors, and midwives at community clinics—and supports them to bring lifesaving services to the doorsteps of people living far from care.
General, Logist-Op, OB-GYN, Pub Health
⊕ https://vfmat.ch/37da

Lepra
Works directly with communities in Bangladesh, India, Mozambique, and Zimbabwe to find, treat, and rehabilitate people affected by leprosy.
Infect Dis, Pub Health, Rehab
⊕ https://vfmat.ch/5d1c

Leprosy Mission England and Wales, The
Leads the fight against leprosy by supporting people living with leprosy today and serving future generations by working to end transmission of the disease.
Infect Dis, Pub Health
⊕ https://vfmat.ch/4c67

Leprosy Mission International
Seeks to empower people with leprosy to attain healing, dignity, and life in all its fullness.
Infect Dis
⊕ https://vfmat.ch/95a9

Leprosy Mission: Northern Ireland, The
Leads the fight against leprosy by supporting people living with leprosy today and serving future generations by working to end the transmission of the disease.
General, Infect Dis
⊕ https://vfmat.ch/e265

Life for a Child
Supports the provision of the best possible healthcare, given local circumstances, to all children and youth with diabetes in less-resourced countries, through the strengthening of existing diabetes services.
Endo, Medicine, Peds
⊕ https://vfmat.ch/d712

Lifebox
Seeks to provide safer surgery and anesthesia in low-resource countries by investing in tools, training, and partnerships for safe surgery.
Anesth, Crit-Care, Surg
⊕ https://vfmat.ch/2d4d

Light for the World
Contributes to a world in which persons with disabilities fully exercise their rights, and assists persons with disabilities living in poverty.
Ophth-Opt, Rehab
⊕ https://vfmat.ch/3ff6

Limbs International
Engages communities and transforms lives through affordable, sustainable prosthetic solutions and rehabilitation services in developing countries.
Logist-Op, Ortho, Pod, Rehab
⊕ https://vfmat.ch/dc84

London School of Hygiene & Tropical Medicine: Health in Humanitarian Crises Centre
Advances health and health equity in crisis-affected countries through research, education, and translation of knowledge into policy and practice.
ER Med, Infect Dis, Pub Health
⊕ https://vfmat.ch/96ad

London School of Hygiene & Tropical Medicine: International Centre for Eye Health
Works to improve eye health and eliminate avoidable visual impairment and blindness with a focus on low-income populations.
Logist-Op, Ophth-Opt, Pub Health
⊕ https://vfmat.ch/6f5f

Management Sciences for Health (MSH)
Works with countries and communities to save lives and improve the health of the world's poorest and most vulnerable people by building strong, resilient, sustainable health systems.
Infect Dis, Logist-Op, Pub Health
⊕ https://vfmat.ch/6aa2

MAP International
Provides medicines and health supplies to those in need around the world so they might experience life to the fullest.
Logist-Op
⊕ https://vfmat.ch/deed

Marie Stopes International
Provides the contraception and safe abortion services that enable women all over the world to choose their own futures.
Infect Dis, MF Med, Neonat, OB-GYN, Pub Health
⊕ https://vfmat.ch/9525

Massachusetts General Hospital Global Surgery Initiative
Aims to improve surgical education and access to advanced surgical care in resource-limited settings around the world by performing surgical operations as visitors, training local surgeons, and sharing medical technology through international partnerships across disciplines.
Anesth, Crit-Care, ER Med, Heme-Onc, Peds, Surg
⊕ https://vfmat.ch/31b1

Maternity Foundation
Works to ensure safer childbirth for women and newborns everywhere through innovative mobile health solutions such as the Safe Delivery App, a mobile training tool for skilled birth attendants.
MF Med, OB-GYN, Pub Health
⊕ https://vfmat.ch/ff4f

Medair
Works to relieve human suffering in some of the world's most remote and devastated places, saving lives in emergencies and helping people in crises survive and recover, inspired by the Christian faith.
ER Med, General, Logist-Op, MF Med, Pub Health
⊕ https://vfmat.ch/5b33

Medical Teams International
Seeks to restore health as the first step to restoring hope, working to bring basic but lifesaving medical care to those in need.
Dent-OMFS, ER Med, General, MF Med, Pub Health
⊕ https://vfmat.ch/8d1c

MedShare
Aims to improve the quality of life of people, communities, and the planet by sourcing and directly delivering surplus medical supplies and equipment to communities in need around the world.
Logist-Op
⊕ https://vfmat.ch/c8bc

Mercy Malaysia
Provides medical relief, sustainable health-related development, and risk reduction activities for vulnerable communities, in both crisis and non-crisis situations.
ER Med, General, OB-GYN, Peds
⊕ https://vfmat.ch/f678

Mercy Without Limits
Educates and empowers women and children by enabling them to have an effective and positive role in constructing a better society.
ER Med
⊕ https://vfmat.ch/c3b6

Midland International Aid Trust
Provides food, goods, clothing, and equipment to those in financial need or who are suffering as a result of a disaster.
CT Surg, Dent-OMFS, ENT, Logist-Op, OB-GYN, Ophth-Opt, Ortho, Ped Surg, Plast, Pub Health, Rehab
⊕ https://vfmat.ch/7eb2

MiracleFeet
Brings low-cost treatment to every child on the planet born with clubfoot, a leading cause of physical disability.
Ortho, Peds, Rehab
⊕ https://vfmat.ch/bda8

Mission Bambini
Helps to support children living in poverty and sickness, and lacking education, giving them the opportunity for and hope of a better life.
CT Surg, CV Med, Crit-Care, ER Med, Ped Surg, Peds
⊕ https://vfmat.ch/dc1a

MSI Reproductive Choices (Marie Stopes International)
Seeks to deliver quality family planning and reproductive healthcare to women around the world.
MF Med
⊕ https://vfmat.ch/5c82

Multi-Agency International Training and Support (MAITS)
Improves the lives of some of the world's poorest people living with disabilities through better access to quality health and education services and support.
Neuro, Psych, Rehab
⊕ https://vfmat.ch/9dcd

Muslim Aid
Aims to improve the lives of those in need, and to address the underlying structural and systemic causes of poverty in their communities, inspired by the Muslim faith.
ER Med, Infect Dis, MF Med, Nutr
⊕ https://vfmat.ch/a8ed

Muslim Welfare Canada
Serves vulnerable populations by supporting healthcare clinics, food security

programs, and other humanitarian projects.
Logist-Op, Nutr
⊕ https://vfmat.ch/a227

Médecins du Monde/Doctors of the World
Provides care, bears witness, and supports social change worldwide with innovative medical programs and evidence-based advocacy initiatives.
ER Med, General, Infect Dis, MF Med, Neonat, OB-GYN, Peds, Pub Health
⊕ https://vfmat.ch/a43d

Mérieux Foundation
Committed to fighting infectious diseases that affect developing countries by capacity building, particularly in clinical laboratories, and focusing on diagnosis.
Logist-Op, Path
⊕ https://vfmat.ch/a23a

Nalta Hospital and Community Health Foundation (NHCHF)
Works to improve village healthcare through delivering cost-effective service, strengthening community capacity, and connecting with similar programs nationally and internationally.
Dent-OMFS, Derm, ENT, ER Med, General, Infect Dis, Nutr, OB-GYN, Ophth-Opt, Ortho, Path, Peds, Pub Health
⊕ https://vfmat.ch/cd93

NCD Alliance
Unites and strengthens civil society to stimulate collaborative advocacy, action, and accountability for NCD (noncommunicable disease) prevention and control.
All-Immu, CV Med, General, Heme-Onc, Medicine, Peds, Psych
⊕ https://vfmat.ch/abdd

Network for Improving Critical Care Systems and Training (NICST)
Provides critical-care training for staff in developing countries.
Crit-Care, General, Pulm-Critic
⊕ https://vfmat.ch/71f8

OneSight
Brings eye exams and glasses to people who lack access to vision care.
Ophth-Opt
⊕ https://vfmat.ch/3ecc

Operation Cleft
Provides free cleft repair surgery to those in need in Bangladesh.
Dent-OMFS, ENT, Ped Surg, Plast, Surg
⊕ https://vfmat.ch/8971

Operation Eyesight Universal
Aims to prevent blindness, restore sight, and eliminate avoidable blindness.
Ophth-Opt
⊕ https://vfmat.ch/f629

Options
Believes in a world in which women and children can access the high-quality health services they need, without financial burden.
Logist-Op, MF Med, Neonat, OB-GYN
⊕ https://vfmat.ch/3a48

Optometry Giving Sight
Delivers eye exams and low or no-cost glasses, provides training for local eye care professionals, and establishes optometry schools, vision centers and optical labs.
Ophth-Opt
⊕ https://vfmat.ch/33ea

Orbis International
Works to prevent and treat blindness through hands-on training and improved access to quality eye care.
Anesth, Ophth-Opt, Surg
⊕ https://vfmat.ch/f2b2

Oxford University Global Surgery Group (OUGSG)
Aims to contribute to the provision of high-quality surgical care globally, particularly in low- and middle-income countries (LMICs), while bringing

together students, researchers, and clinicians with an interest in global surgery, anesthesia, and obstetrics and gynecology.

Anesth, MF Med, OB-GYN, Ortho, Surg

🌐 https://vfmat.ch/c624

Partners for World Health

Sorts, evaluates, repackages, and prepares supplies and equipment for distribution to individuals, communities, and healthcare facilities in need, both locally and internationally.

ER Med, General, Logist-Op

🌐 https://vfmat.ch/982e

Pathfinder International

Champions sexual and reproductive health and rights worldwide, mobilizing communities most in need to break through barriers and forge paths to a healthier future.

OB-GYN

🌐 https://vfmat.ch/a7b3

PEDSI Global Health

Promotes medical educational activities in the U.S., Bangladesh, and developing countries, including training for BLS and PALS.

CV Med, Neonat, Peds

🌐 https://vfmat.ch/fe76

Physicians Across Continents

Provides high-quality medical care to people affected by crises and disasters.

CV Med, Dent-OMFS, Heme-Onc, MF Med, Nephro, Nephro, OB-GYN, Ped Surg, Plast, Surg

🌐 https://vfmat.ch/fe5d

Population Council

Conducts research to address critical health and development issues, helping deliver solutions to improve lives around the world.

Logist-Op, Pub Health

🌐 https://vfmat.ch/1777

Première Urgence International

Helps civilians who are marginalized or excluded as a result of natural disasters, war, or economic collapse.

ER Med, General, MF Med, Peds, Psych

🌐 https://vfmat.ch/62ba

PSI – Population Services International

Aims to improve the health of people in the developing world by focusing on challenges such as a lack of family planning, HIV/AIDS, barriers to maternal health, and the greatest threats to children under the age of 5, including malaria, diarrhea, pneumonia, and malnutrition.

Infect Dis, MF Med, OB-GYN, Peds

🌐 https://vfmat.ch/ffe3

Quasem Foundation

Dedicated to improving the lives of the impoverished people of Northern Bangladesh.

MF Med, OB-GYN, Ophth-Opt

🌐 https://vfmat.ch/6fd9

RAD-AID International

Improves and optimizes access to medical imaging and radiology in low-resource regions of the world.

Rad-Onc, Radiol

🌐 https://vfmat.ch/537f

Reach Beyond

Aims to reach and impact underserved communities with medical care and community development, based in Christian ministry.

ER Med, General

🌐 https://vfmat.ch/cc5c

Reconstructing Women International

Treats patients in their local communities through groups of international volunteers made up of female plastic surgeons using local medical facilities, in cooperation with local medical professionals.

Anesth, Plast, Rehab, Surg

🌐 https://vfmat.ch/924a

Relief International

Helps people in fragile settings achieve good health and nutrition by delivering primary healthcare and emergency treatment, and builds local capacity to ensure that communities in vulnerable situations have the access to the quality care they need to live healthy lives.

ER Med, General, MF Med, Neonat, OB-GYN, Peds, Psych

🌐 https://vfmat.ch/1522

RestoringVision

Empowers lives by restoring vision for millions of people in need.

Ophth-Opt

🌐 https://vfmat.ch/e121

ReSurge International

Provides reconstructive surgical care and builds surgical capacity in developing countries.

Anesth, Dent-OMFS, Ped Surg, Plast, Surg

🌐 https://vfmat.ch/9937

Rotaplast International

Helps children and families worldwide by eliminating the burden of cleft lip and/or palate, burn scarring, and other deformities by sending medical teams to provide free reconstructive surgery, ancillary treatment, and training.

Anesth, Dent-OMFS, ENT, Ped Surg, Plast, Surg

🌐 https://vfmat.ch/78b3

Rotary Action Group for Family Health & AIDS Prevention (RFHA)

Works to save and improve the lives of children and families who lack access to preventive healthcare and education.

Dent-OMFS, Infect Dis, OB-GYN, Ophth-Opt, Peds

🌐 https://vfmat.ch/6563

Rotary International

Provides service to others, improves lives, and advances world understanding, goodwill, and peace through its fellowship of business, professional, and community leaders.

ER Med, General, Infect Dis, MF Med, OB-GYN

🌐 https://vfmat.ch/8fb5

Rutgers New Jersey Medical School

Seeks to support and promote the global health efforts of the faculty, staff, and students in the areas of education, research, and service through the Rutgers New Jersey Medical School's Office of Global Health.

Anesth, CV Med, Crit-Care, Neurosurg, OB-GYN, Psych

🌐 https://vfmat.ch/8e67

SAJIDA Foundation

Strives to improve the quality of life in communities in Bangladesh through sustainable and effective interventions, such as those in healthcare, women's empowerment, microfinance, business, and education.

Dent-OMFS, Derm, ER Med, General, Nutr, OB-GYN, Ophth-Opt, Ortho, Peds, Pub Health, Rehab, Surg

🌐 https://vfmat.ch/a769

Salvation Army International, The

Seeks to meet human needs through services in education, healthcare, community support, emergency response, and ministry development, inspired by the Christian faith.

Dent-OMFS, Derm, ER Med, Infect Dis, MF Med, Medicine, Nutr, OB-GYN, Ophth-Opt, Palliative, Psych, Rehab, Surg

🌐 https://vfmat.ch/8eb3

Samaritan's Purse International Disaster Relief

Provides spiritual and physical aid to hurting people around the world, such as victims of war, poverty, natural disasters, disease, and famine, based in Christian ministry.

Anesth, CT Surg, Crit-Care, Dent-OMFS, Derm, ENT, ER Med, Endo, GI, General, Heme-Onc, Infect Dis, MF Med, Neonat, Nephro, Neuro, Neurosurg, Nutr, OB-GYN, Ophth-Opt, Ortho, Path, Ped Surg, Peds, Plast, Psych, Pulm-Critic, Radiol,

Rehab, Rheum, Surg, Urol, Vasc Surg
⊕ https://vfmat.ch/87e3

Sanofi Espoir Foundation
Contributes to reducing health inequalities among populations that need it most by applying a socially responsible approach focused on fighting childhood cancers in low-income countries, improving maternal and newborn health, and improving access to care.
ER Med, OB-GYN, Peds
⊕ https://vfmat.ch/943b

SATMED
Serves nongovernmental organizations, hospitals, medical universities, and other healthcare providers active in resource-poor areas, by providing open-access e-health services for the health community.
Logist-Op
⊕ https://vfmat.ch/b8d5

Save the Children
Gives children around the world a healthy start in life, the opportunity to learn, and protection from harm.
All-Immu, Crit-Care, ER Med, General, Infect Dis, MF Med, Medicine, Neonat, OB-GYN, Peds, Psych, Pub Health
⊕ https://vfmat.ch/2e73

SEE International
Provides sustainable medical, surgical, and educational services through volunteer ophthalmic surgeons, with the objectives of restoring sight and preventing blindness to disadvantaged individuals worldwide.
Ophth-Opt, Surg
⊕ https://vfmat.ch/6e1b

Serve Humanity Foundation (SHF)
Provides education, job training, community creation, and empowerment, and access to medical care to underserved and underprivileged communities.
General
⊕ https://vfmat.ch/d2f5

SEVA
Delivers vital eye care services to the world's most vulnerable, including women, children, and Indigenous peoples.
Ophth-Opt, Surg
⊕ https://vfmat.ch/1e87

Shongi Global
Inspired by the Christian faith, works to improve lives and opportunities, especially for women and children, through education, nutrition, food supply, health, safety, environmental intervention, and entrepreneurism.
Dent-OMFS, Infect Dis, Nutr, Ophth-Opt
⊕ https://vfmat.ch/7828

Sight for All
Empowers communities to deliver comprehensive, evidence-based, high-quality eye healthcare through the provision of research, education, and equipment.
Logist-Op, Ophth-Opt, Surg
⊕ https://vfmat.ch/e34b

Sightsavers
Works with partners in developing countries to help eliminate avoidable blindness and advocates for equal opportunity for the disabled.
Infect Dis, Ophth-Opt, Surg
⊕ https://vfmat.ch/aa52

SIGN Fracture Care International
Builds orthopedic capacity around the world and provides the injured poor access to fracture surgery by donating orthopedic education and implant systems to surgeons in developing countries.
Ortho, Rehab, Surg
⊕ https://vfmat.ch/123d

Simavi
Strives for a world in which all women and girls are socially and economically empowered and pursue their rights to live a healthy life, free from discrimination,

coercion, and violence.
MF Med, OB-GYN
⊕ https://vfmat.ch/b57b

Smile Asia
Delivers free surgical care, through medical missions and outreach centers, to children with facial deformities such as cleft lip and cleft palate, and aims to raise standards of medical care by creating opportunities for collaborative learning and exchange of best practices.
Anesth, Dent-OMFS, Ped Surg, Peds, Plast
⊕ https://vfmat.ch/d674

Smile Train, Inc.
Treats children with cleft lip through a sustainable and local model that supports surgery and other forms of essential care.
Logist-Op, Pub Health
⊕ https://vfmat.ch/822c

Sonar Bangla Foundation (SBF)
Aims to combat kidney disease in Bangladesh by providing dialysis, screening and treatment, laboratory services, training, and development.
Nephro
⊕ https://vfmat.ch/6f1a

SOS Children's Villages International
Supports children through alternative care and family strengthening.
ER Med, Peds
⊕ https://vfmat.ch/aca1

Spreeha Bangladesh Foundation
Strives to break the cycle of poverty for underprivileged people by providing healthcare, education, and skills training.
General, Infect Dis, MF Med, Nutr, Ophth-Opt, Pub Health
⊕ https://vfmat.ch/52da

Sri Sathya Sai International Organization
Inspired by spiritual teachings, carries out efforts in global healthcare, education, humanitarian relief, and youth engagement.
Dent-OMFS, General, Logist-Op, Nutr, Ophth-Opt, Pub Health
⊕ https://vfmat.ch/9bda

Surgeons for Smiles
Brings first-class medical and dental care to those in need, in developing countries around the world.
Anesth, Dent-OMFS, OB-GYN, Ped Surg, Plast, Surg
⊕ https://vfmat.ch/3427

Swasti
Aims to transform the lives of marginalized communities by ensuring their access to quality healthcare and thereby contributing to poverty alleviation.
Pub Health
⊕ https://vfmat.ch/be8b

Swiss Doctors
Aims to improve the health of populations in developing countries through medical-aid projects and training.
General, Infect Dis, Medicine
⊕ https://vfmat.ch/311a

Swiss Tropical and Public Health Institute
Contributes to the improvement of the health of populations internationally, nationally, and locally through excellence in research, education, and services.
Infect Dis, Pub Health
⊕ https://vfmat.ch/2ee4

Symbiosis
Aims to empower the poor and marginalized in Bangladesh through group formation, education and training, collective savings, and peer lending.
MF Med, Ophth-Opt
⊕ https://vfmat.ch/441a

Syrian American Medical Society (SAMS)
Provides medical professionals with continued training, networking, and

opportunities to participate in humanitarian efforts affecting conflict-impacted populations.

CT Surg, CV Med, Crit-Care, Dent-OMFS, Endo, GI, General, Logist-Op, Medicine, Nephro, OB-GYN, Ophth-Opt, Path, Peds, Plast, Psych, Pulm-Critic, Radiol, Rehab, Surg, Urol

⊕ https://vfmat.ch/5dbf

Task Force for Global Health, The

Consists of programs and focus areas that cover a range of global health issues including neglected tropical diseases, infectious diseases, vaccines, field epidemiology, public health informatics, health workforce development, and global health ethics.

Infect Dis, Logist-Op, Medicine, Ophth-Opt, Peds

⊕ https://vfmat.ch/714c

Team Broken Earth

Brings medical relief and education to those who need it most by sending volunteer teams of healthcare professionals to areas of wide-ranging relief response.

Medicine, OB-GYN, Ophth-Opt, Rehab, Surg

⊕ https://vfmat.ch/bfcd

Tearfund

Responds to crisis and partners with local churches to bring restoration to those living in poverty, inspired by the Christian faith.

ER Med, Logist-Op

⊕ https://vfmat.ch/f6cf

Terre des hommes (Tdh) Foundation

Works to improve the daily life of children and their relatives in the areas of health, protection and emergency, in Europe, Africa, Asia, Latin America, and the Near and Middle East.

CT Surg, CV Med, OB-GYN, Ped Surg, Pub Health

⊕ https://vfmat.ch/5c26

Tilganga Institute of Ophthalmology (TIO)

Supports the prevention and control of blindness in Nepal and the region.

Ophth-Opt

⊕ https://vfmat.ch/ff5d

Two Worlds Cancer Collaboration

Collaborates with local care professionals in lesser-resourced countries to help reduce the burden of cancer and other life-limiting illnesses.

Heme-Onc, Palliative, Peds, Pub Health, Rad-Onc

⊕ https://vfmat.ch/fbdd

Unforgotten Fund, The (UNFF)

Provides lifesaving humanitarian relief to UN Field Operations and projects such as water supply, sanitation and hygiene (WASH), food security, health, and shelter.

ER Med, MF Med, Nutr, OB-GYN, Peds

⊕ https://vfmat.ch/928f

Union for International Cancer Control (UICC)

Unites and supports the cancer community to reduce the global cancer burden, promote greater equity, and ensure that cancer control continues to be a priority in the world health and development agenda.

Heme-Onc, Pub Health

⊕ https://vfmat.ch/88b1

Union of Medical Care and Relief Organizations-USA - UOSSM USA

Aims to provide lifesaving support, medical relief, and access to quality healthcare and mental health services to people affected by crises.

Dent-OMFS, ER Med, General, Nutr, Psych, Rehab

⊕ https://vfmat.ch/a8e2

United Hands Relief & Development

Works to funnel efforts toward alleviating and immediately responding to the sufferings of others around the globe, regardless of nationality, race, religion, or social status.

ER Med, General, Infect Dis, Ophth-Opt, Surg

⊕ https://vfmat.ch/2771

United Nations Children's Fund (UNICEF)

Works in over 190 countries and territories to save children's lives, defend their rights, and help them fulfill their potential, from early childhood through adolescence.

All-Immu, Infect Dis, MF Med, Neonat, Nutr, OB-GYN, Ped Surg, Peds, Pub Health

⊕ https://vfmat.ch/42d7

United Nations Development Programme (UNDP)

Helps countries achieve the simultaneous eradication of extreme poverty and significant reduction of inequalities and exclusion using a sustainable human development approach.

Infect Dis, Logist-Op, Pub Health

⊕ https://vfmat.ch/935c

United Nations High Commissioner for Refugees (UNHCR)

Safeguards the rights and well-being of people who have been forced to flee, ensuring that everybody has the right to seek asylum and find safe refuge in another country, with the goal of seeking lasting solutions.

General, MF Med, Medicine, OB-GYN, Peds, Psych, Pub Health

⊕ https://vfmat.ch/6636

United Nations Population Fund (UNFPA)

Supports reproductive healthcare for women and youth in more than 150 countries, focusing on delivering a world in which every pregnancy is wanted, every childbirth is safe, and every young person's potential is fulfilled.

Infect Dis, MF Med, Neonat, OB-GYN, Peds, Pub Health

⊕ https://vfmat.ch/c969

United States Agency for International Development (USAID)

Promotes and demonstrates democratic values abroad and advances a free, peaceful, and prosperous world. Leads the U.S. government's international development and disaster assistance through partnerships and investments that save lives.

ER Med, Infect Dis, MF Med, OB-GYN, Peds

⊕ https://vfmat.ch/9a99

University of Pennsylvania Perelman School of Medicine Center for Global Health

Aims to improve health equity worldwide through enhanced public health awareness and access to care, discovery, and outcomes-based research, and comprehensive educational programs grounded in partnership.

Heme-Onc, Infect Dis, OB-GYN

⊕ https://vfmat.ch/cb57

University of Toronto: Global Surgery

Focuses on excellent clinical care, outstanding research productivity, and the delivery of state-of-the-art educational programs.

Surg

⊕ https://vfmat.ch/1ad5

USA for United Nations High Commissioner for Refugees (UNHCR)

Serves and protects refugees and displaced people through emergency relief, cash assistance, education, resettlement, and the rebuilding of livelihoods.

ER Med, General, Logist-Op, Nutr, Pub Health

⊕ https://vfmat.ch/293c

USAID: Fistula Care Plus

Builds on, enhances, and expands the work undertaken by the previous Fistula Care project (2007–2013), with attention to prevention, detection, treatment, reintegration and new areas of focus so that obstetric fistula can become a rare event for future generations.

MF Med, OB-GYN, Surg

⊕ https://vfmat.ch/a7cd

USAID: Health Finance and Governance Project

Uses research to implement strategies to help countries develop robust governance systems, increase their domestic resources for health, manage those resources more effectively, and make wise purchasing decisions.

Logist-Op

⊕ https://vfmat.ch/8652

USAID: Maternal and Child Health Integrated Program

Works to improve the health of women and their families, including programs for maternal, newborn, and child health, immunization, family planning, nutrition, malaria, and HIV/AIDS.

All-Immu, General, Infect Dis, MF Med

⊕ https://vfmat.ch/4415

USAID: TB Care II

Focuses on tuberculosis care and treatment.

Infect Dis

⊕ https://vfmat.ch/57d4

Vision Care

Restores sight and helps patients get regular treatment at short-term eye camps and long-term base clinics by having doctors, missionaries, volunteers, and sponsors work together.

Ophth-Opt

⊕ https://vfmat.ch/9d7c

Vital Strategies

Helps governments strengthen their public health systems to contend with the most important and difficult health challenges, while accelerating progress on the world's most pressing health problems.

CV Med, Infect Dis, Peds

⊕ https://vfmat.ch/fe25

Vitamin Angels

Helps at-risk populations in need—specifically pregnant women, new mothers, and children under age 5—to gain access to life-changing vitamins and minerals.

General, Nutr

⊕ https://vfmat.ch/7da1

Voluntary Service Overseas (VSO)

Works with health workers, communities, and governments to improve health services and rights for women, babies, youth, people with disabilities, and prisoners.

General, MF Med, OB-GYN

⊕ https://vfmat.ch/213d

Walk for Life

Enables children born with clubfoot in Bangladesh the opportunity to walk, run, jump, and play by providing life-changing treatment for the deformity.

Ortho, Ped Surg, Pod, Surg

⊕ https://vfmat.ch/1866

We Care for Humanity (WCH)

Promotes sustainable social change and the sustainable development goals developed by the United Nations, including: no poverty, good health and well-being, gender equality, human rights, climate action, and strong institutions.

General, Logist-Op, Pub Health

⊕ https://vfmat.ch/8b4e

WF AID

Seeks to build capacity and provide emergency aid, human assistance, and international development, where required in the world.

CT Surg, Dent-OMFS, ENT, ER Med, General, Infect Dis, Logist-Op, Nutr, Ophth-Opt, Ortho, Path, Radiol, Rehab, Surg

⊕ https://vfmat.ch/ebd7

White Ribbon Alliance, The

Leads a movement for reproductive, maternal, and newborn health and accelerates progress by putting citizens at the center of global, national, and local health efforts.

MF Med, OB-GYN

⊕ https://vfmat.ch/496b

Women and Children First

Pioneers approaches that support communities to solve problems themselves.

MF Med, Neonat, OB-GYN, Peds

⊕ https://vfmat.ch/cdc9

Women's Refugee Commission

Seeks to improve lives by protecting the rights of women, children, and youth displaced by conflict and crisis through researching their needs, identifying solutions, and advocating for programs and policies to strengthen their resilience.

General, MF Med, Neonat, OB-GYN, Peds, Psych

⊕ https://vfmat.ch/3d8f

World Blind Union (WBU)

Represents those experiencing blindness, speaking to governments and international bodies on issues concerning visual impairments.

Ophth-Opt

⊕ https://vfmat.ch/2bd3

World Care Foundation

Encourages humanitarian efforts to help those in need anywhere in the world, regardless of their faith, color, gender, and ethnicity. Projects include orphanages, orphan sponsorship, medical centers, refugee crisis work, and education.

ER Med, General, Pub Health

⊕ https://vfmat.ch/987a

World Child Cancer

Works to improve diagnosis, treatment, and support for children with cancer, and their families, in low- and middle-income parts of the world.

Heme-Onc, Ped Surg, Rad-Onc

⊕ https://vfmat.ch/fbbc

World Council of Optometry

Facilitates the development of optometry worldwide and promotes eye health and vision care through advocacy, education, policy development, and humanitarian outreach.

Ophth-Opt, Pub Health

⊕ https://vfmat.ch/c92e

World Federation of Hemophilia (WFH)

Aims to improve and sustain care for people with inherited bleeding disorders by pursuing long-term relationships with individuals and organizations who share the values of WFH's development model.

Heme-Onc

⊕ https://vfmat.ch/5121

World Health Organization, The (WHO)

The United Nations' agency for health provides leadership on global health matters, shapes the health research agenda, sets norms and standards, articulates evidence-based policy options, provides technical support and monitoring to countries, and assesses health trends.

ER Med, General, Infect Dis, Logist-Op, MF Med, OB-GYN, Peds, Psych, Pub Health

⊕ https://vfmat.ch/c476

World Medical Relief

Facilitates the distribution of surplus medical resources where they are needed.

Logist-Op

⊕ https://vfmat.ch/72dc

World Parkinson's Program

Seeks to improve the quality of life of those affected by Parkinson's disease through education and advocacy, and provides free medication and support services.

Logist-Op, Neuro, Pub Health

⊕ https://vfmat.ch/c96d

World Telehealth Initiative
Provides medical expertise to the world's most vulnerable communities to build local capacity and deliver core health services through a network of volunteer healthcare professionals supported with state-of-the-art technology.
Derm, Infect Dis, MF Med, Medicine, Neuro, OB-GYN, Peds, Pulm-Critic
⊕ https://vfmat.ch/fa91

World Vision International
Works with vulnerable communities around the world to overcome poverty and injustice with child-focused programs in disaster management, health, nutrition, economic development, education, clean water, sanitation, and hygiene.
ER Med, General, Infect Dis, MF Med, Nutr, OB-GYN, Peds
⊕ https://vfmat.ch/2642

Bangladesh

Healthcare Facilities

Abedin Hospital Pvt.
Jagannathpur, Dhaka, Bangladesh
⊕ https://vfmat.ch/535a

Ad-din Akij Medical College Hospital
Khulna, Bangladesh
⊕ https://vfmat.ch/aa87

Ad-Din Women's Medical College Hospital
Bāgunbāri, Dhaka, Bangladesh
⊕ https://vfmat.ch/baa6

Adamdighi Upazila Health Complex
Kaikuri, Rajshahi Division, Bangladesh
⊕ https://vfmat.ch/154d

AIMS Hospital Ltd.
Merul Badda, Dhaka, Bangladesh
⊕ https://vfmat.ch/6749

AITAM Hospital-Adabar
Adāba Chak, Dhaka, Bangladesh
⊕ https://vfmat.ch/6275

Al Amin Dental College And General Hospital
Debpur, Sylhet, Bangladesh
⊕ https://vfmat.ch/fa6e

Al-Helal Specialized Hospital Limited
Senpāra Parbata, Dhaka, Bangladesh
⊕ https://vfmat.ch/c114

Al-Manar Hospital Ltd.
Sarāi Jāfrābād, Dhaka, Bangladesh
⊕ https://vfmat.ch/1a47

Al-Raji Hospital
Tejgaon, Dhaka, Bangladesh
⊕ https://vfmat.ch/dc44

Ambia Memorial Hospital
Bāghia, Barisāl, Bangladesh
⊕ https://vfmat.ch/52be

America Australia Bangladesh Friendship Hospital
Birāmpur, Rangpur Division, Bangladesh
⊕ https://vfmat.ch/749b

Amtali Upazila Health Complex
Amtali, Barisāl, Bangladesh
⊕ https://vfmat.ch/14d2

Ark Hospital Limited
Purākar, Dhaka, Bangladesh
⊕ https://vfmat.ch/da76

Asgar Ali Hospital
Dhaka, Dhaka, Bangladesh
⊕ https://vfmat.ch/3dac

Ashuganj Upazila Health Complex
Char Chārtala, Chittagong, Bangladesh
⊕ https://vfmat.ch/a2c6

Atpara Upazila Health Complex
Ātpāra, Mymensingh Division, Bangladesh
⊕ https://vfmat.ch/32b9

Atwari Upazila Health Complex
Atwāri, Rangpur Division, Bangladesh
⊕ https://vfmat.ch/f462

Avicenna Hospital
Sirajganj, Bangladesh
⊕ https://vfmat.ch/98zi

Aysha Memorial Specialised Hospital (Pvt.) Ltd.
Mahākhāli, Dhaka, Bangladesh
⊕ https://vfmat.ch/7e6b

Badda General Hospital Pvt.
Bādda, Dhaka, Bangladesh
⊕ https://vfmat.ch/b7ee

Bakerganj Upazila Health Complex
Bakerganj, Barishal, Bangladesh
⊕ https://vfmat.ch/8ec5

Balaganj Upazila Health Complex
Balaganj, Sylhet, Bangladesh
⊕ https://vfmat.ch/54b4

Baliakandi Upazila Health Complex
Iliskol, Dhaka, Bangladesh
⊕ https://vfmat.ch/ca1d

Balukhali Medecins Sans Frontieres (MSF) Hospital
Balukhali, Chattogram, Bangladesh
⊕ https://vfmat.ch/cf2a

Bancharampur Upazila Health Complex
Āchhādnagar, Chittagong, Bangladesh
⊕ https://vfmat.ch/271c

Bangabandhu Sheikh Mujib Medical College Hospital, Faridpur
Faridpur, Dhaka, Bangladesh
⊕ https://vfmat.ch/e5ee

Bangabandhu Sheikh Mujib Medical University (BSMMU)
Shahbag, Dhaka, Bangladesh
⊕ https://vfmat.ch/sy8e

Bangabandhu Sheikh Mujib Medical University (BSMMU) Hospital
Dhaka, Bangladesh
⊕ https://vfmat.ch/c8jk

Banghabondhu Memorial Hospital
Chattogram, Chattogram, Bangladesh
⊕ https://vfmat.ch/dfda

Bangladesh ENT Hospital LTD.
Dhaka, Bangladesh
⊕ https://vfmat.ch/db39

Bangladesh Korea Friendship Hospital
Paschim Pānisāil, Dhaka, Bangladesh
⊕ https://vfmat.ch/2b1c

Bangladesh Medical College Hospital
Dhanmondi, Dhaka, Bangladesh
⊕ https://vfmat.ch/b55c

Baniachang Upazila Health Complex
Baniachang, Sylhet, Bangladesh
⊕ https://vfmat.ch/17df

Barisal General Hospital
Gāwāsār, Barisāl, Bangladesh
⊕ https://vfmat.ch/e63d

Barisal Heart Foundation
Barishal, Bangladesh
⊕ https://vfmat.ch/2472

Barura Upazila Health Complex
Barura, Chattogram, Bangladesh
⊕ https://vfmat.ch/ad8f

Basail Upazila Health Complex
Basail, Dhaka, Bangladesh
⊕ https://vfmat.ch/d446

Barakah General Hospital Limited, The
Shahar Khilgaon, Dhaka, Bangladesh
⊕ https://vfmat.ch/54ac

Beani Bazar Cancer Hospital & Healthcare Centre
Beani Bazar, Sylhet, Bangladesh
⊕ https://vfmat.ch/afb2

Beanibazar Upazila Health Complex
Māligrām, Sylhet, Bangladesh
⊕ https://vfmat.ch/86b6

Begumganj Upazila Health Complex
Chhangrām, Chittagong, Bangladesh
⊕ https://vfmat.ch/a9a6

Bellevue Hospital
Nasirābād, Chittagong, Bangladesh
⊕ https://vfmat.ch/249c

Bera Upazila Health Complex
Bera, Rajshahi Division, Bangladesh
⊕ https://vfmat.ch/f9b7

Bhanga Upazila Health Complex
Hāsāmdia, Dhaka, Bangladesh
⊕ https://vfmat.ch/bf28

Bhangura Health Care Ltd Hospital
Pār Chaubaria, Rajshahi Division, Bangladesh
⊕ https://vfmat.ch/ca7f

Bhangura Upazila Health Complex
Pār Chaubaria, Rajshahi Division, Bangladesh
⊕ https://vfmat.ch/d9d6

Bhedarganj Upazila Health Complex
Surjyadighāl, Dhaka, Bangladesh
⊕ https://vfmat.ch/8dd2

Bhuapur Eye Hospital
Bhuapur, Dhaka, Bangladesh
⊕ https://vfmat.ch/ju6w

BIHS General Hospital
Bara Sayek, Dhaka, Bangladesh
⊕ https://vfmat.ch/624f

Birampur Upazila Health Complex
Beldānga, Rangpur Division, Bangladesh
⊕ https://vfmat.ch/edbf

BIRDEM General Hospital
Dhaka, Bangladesh
⊕ https://vfmat.ch/cf51

BIRDEM General Hospital 2
Dhaka South City Corporation, Dhaka, Bangladesh
⊕ https://vfmat.ch/d6dc

Birsrestha Nur Mohammad Hospital
Sardah, Rajshahi, Bangladesh
⊕ https://vfmat.ch/a145

Biswanath Upazila Health Complex
Kdapur, Sylhet, Bangladesh
⊕ https://vfmat.ch/23a2

BNSB Eye Hospital Patuakhali
Patuakhali, Barishal, Bangladesh
⊕ https://vfmat.ch/a374

Bogra Chest Disease Hospital
Bogra, Rajshahi, Bangladesh
⊕ https://vfmat.ch/eee9

Bogra Diabetic Somity
Bogra, Rajshahi, Bangladesh
⊕ https://vfmat.ch/41b6

BRAC Hospital
Habiganj, Sylhet, Bangladesh
⊕ https://vfmat.ch/af5d

Brahmanpara Upazila Health Complex
Dīrghābhūmi, Chittagong, Bangladesh
⊕ https://vfmat.ch/ad9b

BUET Medical Center
Azimpur, Dhaka, Bangladesh
⊕ https://vfmat.ch/16b9

Cantonment General Hospital
Chittagong, Chittagong, Bangladesh
⊕ https://vfmat.ch/c3c9

CARe Medical College Hospital
Mohammadpur, Dhaka, Bangladesh
⊕ https://vfmat.ch/12c3

CARe Medical College Hospital Ltd
Barāba, Dhaka, Bangladesh
⊕ https://vfmat.ch/e616

Center for Specialized Care & Research (CSCR) Hospital & Diagnostic Center
Chattogram, Bangladesh
⊕ https://vfmat.ch/587d

Central Bashabo General Hospital
Dhaka, Dhaka, Bangladesh
⊕ https://vfmat.ch/47ef

Central Hospital Cox's Bazar
Choca Pāra, Chittagong, Bangladesh
⊕ https://vfmat.ch/cdf9

Central Hospital Dhaka
Dhaka, Dhaka, Bangladesh
⊕ https://vfmat.ch/pnyg

Central Hospital Sylhet
Sylhet, Sylhet, Bangladesh
⊕ https://vfmat.ch/22cb

Centre for the Rehabilitation of the Paralysed (CRP)
Nayābāri, Dhaka, Bangladesh
⊕ https://vfmat.ch/555d

Centre Point Hospital Limited
Nasirābād, Chittagong, Bangladesh
⊕ https://vfmat.ch/fde3

Chandina General Hospital
Chandina, Chittagong, Bangladesh
⊕ https://vfmat.ch/8e8c

Chandina Upazila Health Complex
Bāgur, Chittagong, Bangladesh
⊕ https://vfmat.ch/6e39

Chandpur General Hospital
Chandpur, Chattogram, Bangladesh
⊕ https://vfmat.ch/d958

Chapai Nawabganj Abhunik Sadar Hospital
Chāinpara, Rajshahi Division, Bangladesh
⊕ https://vfmat.ch/28c8

Char Rajibpur Upazila Health Complex
Launchghat, Mymensingh Division, Bangladesh
⊕ https://vfmat.ch/7b26

Charghat Upazila Health Complex
Chārghāt, Rajshahi Division, Bangladesh
⊕ https://vfmat.ch/95ed

Chatkhil Upazila Health Complex
Dhāmālia, Chittagong, Bangladesh
⊕ https://vfmat.ch/63c1

Chattogram Maa-O-Shishu Hospital
Agrabad, Chattogram, Bangladesh
⊕ https://vfmat.ch/94fc

Chattogram Port Authority Hospital
Chattogram, Bangladesh
⊕ https://vfmat.ch/8b5e

Checkup Diagnostic Center
Nasirābād, Chittagong, Bangladesh
⊕ https://vfmat.ch/e489

ChildCare Hospital
Chattogram, Bangladesh
⊕ https://vfmat.ch/ff35

Chitalmari Upazila Health Complex
Kurmani, Khulna, Bangladesh
⊕ https://vfmat.ch/af58

Chittagong General Hospital
Nasirābād, Chittagong, Bangladesh
⊕ https://vfmat.ch/eea8

Chittagong Medical College Hospital
Nasirābād, Chittagong, Bangladesh
⊕ https://vfmat.ch/3e75

Chittagong Metropolitan Hospital Limited
Nasirābād, Chittagong, Bangladesh
⊕ https://vfmat.ch/4892

City Corporation General Hospital
Chattogram, Bangladesh
⊕ https://vfmat.ch/cc8c

City Hospital Ltd.
Mohammadpur, Dhaka, Bangladesh
⊕ https://vfmat.ch/7446

City Hospital, Jashore
Jashore, Bangladesh
⊕ https://vfmat.ch/gp1v

Combined Military Hospital (CMH)
Dhāmālkot, Bangladesh
⊕ https://vfmat.ch/de9e

Comfort Diagnostic Centre Pvt. Ltd.
Rāja Bāzār, Dhaka, Bangladesh
⊕ https://vfmat.ch/fc46

Cox's Bazar District Sadar Hospital
Cox's Bazar, Chattogram, Bangladesh
⊕ https://vfmat.ch/2e34

Cumilla General Hospital
Asrafpur, Chittagong, Bangladesh
⊕ https://vfmat.ch/8524

Cumilla Medical Center
Cumilla, Bangladesh
⊕ https://vfmat.ch/cbwn

Cumilla Medical College Hospital
Cumilla, Chattogram, Bangladesh
⊕ https://vfmat.ch/ad1d

Dacope Upazila Health Complex
Chālna, Khulna, Bangladesh
⊕ https://vfmat.ch/4c28

Daganbhuiya Upazila Health Complex
Daganbhuiya, Chattogram, Bangladesh
⊕ https://vfmat.ch/4649

Dalit Hospital
Chuknagar, Dumuria, Bangladesh
⊕ https://vfmat.ch/zvzv

Damurhuda Upazila Health Complex
Damurhuda, Khulna, Bangladesh
⊕ https://vfmat.ch/de73

Danish Bangladesh Leprosy Mission Hospital (DBLM)
Nilphamari, Rangpur, Bangladesh
⊕ https://vfmat.ch/huxb

Dar-Us Shefa Private Hospital
Kushtia, Khulna, Bangladesh
⊕ https://vfmat.ch/356f

Dashmina Upazila Health Complex
Dashmina, Barishal, Bangladesh
⊕ https://vfmat.ch/ff68

Daudkandi Upazila Health Complex
Ichhāpura, Chittagong, Bangladesh
⊕ https://vfmat.ch/2c4c

Daulatpur Upazila Health Complex
Sumidpur Chak, Dhaka, Bangladesh
⊕ https://vfmat.ch/571a

Debidwar Upazila Health Complex
Bijalipānjar, Chittagong, Bangladesh
⊕ https://vfmat.ch/44c8

Debiganj Upazila Health Complex
Debiganj, Rangpur, Bangladesh
⊕ https://vfmat.ch/a651

Delduar Upazila Health Complex
Delduār, Dhaka, Bangladesh
⊕ https://vfmat.ch/7e25

Delta Health Care, Chattogram Ltd.
Chattogram, Bangladesh
⊕ https://vfmat.ch/2ec7

Dhaka Central International Medical College & Hospital
Dhaka, Bangladesh
⊕ https://vfmat.ch/a5be

Dhaka Children's Hospital
Sekerkalsi, Dhaka, Bangladesh
⊕ https://vfmat.ch/ed19

Dhaka General Hospital and Orthopaedic Hospital
Barāba, Dhaka, Bangladesh
⊕ https://vfmat.ch/4fb6

Dhaka Health Care Hospital
Shahbag, Dhaka, Bangladesh
⊕ https://vfmat.ch/8abb

Dhaka Infectious Diseases Hospital
Dhaka, Dhaka, Bangladesh
⊕ https://vfmat.ch/41gt

Dhaka Medical College Hospital
Dhaka, Dhaka, Bangladesh
⊕ https://vfmat.ch/5ed8

Dhaka National Medical Institute Hospital
Kāliganj, Dhaka, Bangladesh
⊕ https://vfmat.ch/6562

DHAKA SHISHU (CHILDREN) HOSPITAL
Barāba, Dhaka, Bangladesh
⊕ https://vfmat.ch/d5c8

Dhamoirhat Upazila Health Complex
Dhamoirhat, Rajshahi, Bangladesh
⊕ https://vfmat.ch/54d7

Dighinala Upazila Health Complex
Boalkhāli Bāzār, Chittagong, Bangladesh
⊕ https://vfmat.ch/41ed

Dimla Upazila Health Complex
Titpāra, Rangpur Division, Bangladesh
⊕ https://vfmat.ch/55ae

Dinajpur Diabetes O Swasthoseba Hospital
Rangpur, Bangladesh
⊕ https://vfmat.ch/siwj

Dinajpur General Hospital
Dinājpur, Rangpur Division, Bangladesh
⊕ https://vfmat.ch/9eb3

Doctors Without Borders Bangladesh
Nawāb Char, Dhaka, Bangladesh
⊕ https://vfmat.ch/b6c8

Dohar General Hospital
Duhār, Dhaka, Bangladesh
⊕ https://vfmat.ch/6aab

DPRC Hospital & Diagnostic Lab
Dhaka, Dhaka, Bangladesh
⊕ https://vfmat.ch/fb76

DR. AZMAL HOSPITAL LTD.
Senpāra Parbata, Dhaka, Bangladesh
⊕ https://vfmat.ch/143f

Dr. M R Khan Shishu Hospital & Institute of Child Health
Dhaka, Bangladesh
⊕ https://vfmat.ch/91ze

Durgapur Upazila Health Complex
Durgāpur, Mymensingh Division, Bangladesh
⊕ https://vfmat.ch/c458

East West Medical College and Hospital
Rasādia, Dhaka, Bangladesh
⊕ https://vfmat.ch/fc34

Eden Multicare Hospital
Taleperbāg, Dhaka, Bangladesh
⊕ https://vfmat.ch/67b8

Enam Medical College & Hospital
Savar, Dhaka, Bangladesh
⊕ https://vfmat.ch/f6bb

ENT And Head-Neck Cancer Hospital And Institute, The
Barāba, Dhaka, Bangladesh
⊕ https://vfmat.ch/9cc5

Euro-Bangla Heart Hospital
Dhaka, Bangladesh
⊕ https://vfmat.ch/cad1

Evercare Hospital Dhaka
Dhaka, Dhaka, Bangladesh
⊕ https://vfmat.ch/5dfb

Fakirhat Upazila Health Complex
Fakirhāt, Khulna, Bangladesh
⊕ https://vfmat.ch/fbe2

Faridganj Upazila Health Complex
Farīdganj, Chittagong, Bangladesh
⊕ https://vfmat.ch/e668

Feni Diabetic Hospital
Feni, Chittagong, Bangladesh
⊕ https://vfmat.ch/c2f4

Feni General Hospital
Feni, Chattogram, Bangladesh
⊕ https://vfmat.ch/8cd9

Fouad Al-Khateeb Hospital, Cox's Bazar
Choca Pāra, Chittagong, Bangladesh
⊕ https://vfmat.ch/db1e

Fulbari Upazila Health Complex
Fulbari, Rangpur Division, Bangladesh
⊕ https://vfmat.ch/a21f

Gaibandha District Hospital
Gaibandha, Rangpur Division, Bangladesh
⊕ https://vfmat.ch/9dca

Galachipa Upazila Health Complex
Ratnadi, Khulna, Bangladesh
⊕ https://vfmat.ch/fe88

Gausul Azam BNSB Eye Hospital
Newtown, Rangpur Division, Bangladesh
⊕ https://vfmat.ch/b1d3

Gazaria Upazila Health Complex
Bhaberchar, Dhaka, Bangladesh
⊕ https://vfmat.ch/7d3c

Gazi Medical College and Hospital
Baniakhāmār, Khulna, Bangladesh
⊕ https://vfmat.ch/433b

Godagari Upazila Health Complex
Lālbāgh, Rajshahi Division, Bangladesh
⊕ https://vfmat.ch/e66a

Gonoshastha Nagar Hospital
Sukrābād, Dhaka, Bangladesh
⊕ https://vfmat.ch/aae3

Good Heal Hospital
Maijdee, Chattogram, Bangladesh
⊕ https://vfmat.ch/h8ck

Good Health Hospital, Rangpur
Rangpur, Bangladesh
⊕ https://vfmat.ch/gg1p

Goshairhat Upazila Health Complex
Dhipur, Dhaka, Bangladesh
⊕ https://vfmat.ch/6de5

Government Unani and Ayurvedic Medical College and Hospital
Ibrāhimpur, Dhaka, Bangladesh
⊕ https://vfmat.ch/72fb

Green Life Medical College Hospital
Dhaka, Dhaka, Bangladesh
⊕ https://vfmat.ch/4e9c

Green View Hospital
Patuakhali, Barishal, Bangladesh
⊕ https://vfmat.ch/9f4a

Gurudaspur Eye Hospital
Gurudaspur, Rajshahi, Bangladesh
⊕ https://vfmat.ch/miff

Gurudaspur Upazila Health Complex
Gurudaspur, Rajshahi, Bangladesh
⊕ https://vfmat.ch/1a11

Haimchar Upazila Health Complex
Muzzampur, Chittagong, Bangladesh
⊕ https://vfmat.ch/e41a

Hajiganj Upazila Health Complex
Haziganj, Chattogram, Bangladesh
⊕ https://vfmat.ch/82c5

Hakimpur Upazila Health Complex
Chandipur, Rangpur Division, Bangladesh
⊕ https://vfmat.ch/8836

Harirampur Upazila Health Complex
Piyāj Char, Dhaka, Bangladesh
⊕ https://vfmat.ch/4971

Hatiya Upazila Health Complex
Char King, Chittagong, Bangladesh
⊕ https://vfmat.ch/c7de

Health City Specialized Hospital
Bogra, Rajshahi Division, Bangladesh
⊕ https://vfmat.ch/bff5

Health Complex, Santosh
Tangail, Dhaka, Bangladesh
⊕ https://vfmat.ch/7633

Hikmah Eye Hospital
Shahar Khilgaon, Dhaka, Bangladesh
⊕ https://vfmat.ch/fc97

Holy Health Hospital Ltd.
Chattogram, Bangladesh
⊕ https://vfmat.ch/efec

Homna Upazila Health Complex
West Baidyerkāndi, Chittagong, Bangladesh
⊕ https://vfmat.ch/8812

HOPE Hospital
Ramu, Chattogram, Bangladesh
⊕ https://vfmat.ch/uknx

Hossainpur Upazila Health Complex
Hossainpur, Dhaka, Bangladesh
⊕ https://vfmat.ch/bc6b

Ibn Sina Hospital Sylhet Limited
Debpur, Sylhet, Bangladesh
⊕ https://vfmat.ch/e1ea

Ibn Sina Medical College Hospital
Dhaka, Bangladesh
⊕ https://vfmat.ch/421c

Ibn Sina Specialized Hospital, Dhanmondi
Dhanmondi, Dhaka, Bangladesh
⊕ https://vfmat.ch/a67b

Ibrahim Cardiac Hospital & Research Institute
Dhaka, Bangladesh
⊕ https://vfmat.ch/iegc

Ibrahim General Hospital
Bārikābād, Dhaka, Bangladesh
⊕ https://vfmat.ch/ec7c

Ibrahim Iqbal Memorial Hospital
Chattogram, Bangladesh
⊕ https://vfmat.ch/4961

Imperial Hospital Limited
Pahartali, Chittagong, Bangladesh
⊕ https://vfmat.ch/44f9

Impulse Hospital
Tejgaon, Dhaka, Bangladesh
⊕ https://vfmat.ch/3f23

Inani Union Sub Center
Inani, Chattogram, Bangladesh
⊕ https://vfmat.ch/e741

IOM LifeCare Medical Center
Mahākhāli, Dhaka, Bangladesh
⊕ https://vfmat.ch/2827

iQra Disabled Children's Hospital (IDCH)
Sylhet, Bangladesh
⊕ https://vfmat.ch/p5ck

Ishwardi Eye Hospital
Ishwardi, Rajshahi, Bangladesh
⊕ https://vfmat.ch/ijbx

Ishwardi Upazila Health Complex
Ishurdi, Rajshahi Division, Bangladesh
⊕ https://vfmat.ch/76bd

Islami Bank Central Hospital
Paltan, Dhaka, Bangladesh
⊕ https://vfmat.ch/6ce7

Islami Bank Hospital – Barisal
Char Āicha, Barisāl, Bangladesh
⊕ https://vfmat.ch/bd12

Islami Bank Hospital – Mirpur
Sekerkalsi, Dhaka, Bangladesh
⊕ https://vfmat.ch/2e2f

Islami Bank Hospital – Motijheel
Shahar Khilgaon, Dhaka, Bangladesh
⊕ https://vfmat.ch/d3c9

Islami Bank Medical College & Hospital, Rajshahi
Rajshahi, Bangladesh
⊕ https://vfmat.ch/6iyz

Ispahani Islamia Eye Institute and Hospital
Tejteri Bāzār, Dhaka, Bangladesh
⊕ https://vfmat.ch/aaab

Jagannathpur Upazila Health Complex
Jagannāthpur, Rajshahi Division, Bangladesh
⊕ https://vfmat.ch/7ee1

Jaintapur Upazila Health Complex
Jaintiāpur, Rajshahi Division, Bangladesh
⊕ https://vfmat.ch/2cf1

Jessore General Hospital
Jessore, Khulna, Bangladesh
⊕ https://vfmat.ch/c773

Jhenaidah Diabetes Hospital
Bara Kāmārkunda, Khulna, Bangladesh
⊕ https://vfmat.ch/f62f

Jhenaidah District Hospital
Jhenaidah, Khulna, Bangladesh
⊕ https://vfmat.ch/11d2

Jhenaidah Shishu Hospital
Jhenaidah, Khulna, Bangladesh
⊕ https://vfmat.ch/72bd

Jhilmil Hospital
Dākpāra, Dhaka, Bangladesh
⊕ https://vfmat.ch/e53a

Kachua Upazila Health Complex
Kachua, Chattogram, Bangladesh
⊕ https://vfmat.ch/b842

Kalaroa Upazila Health Complex
Kālāroa, Khulna, Bangladesh
⊕ https://vfmat.ch/71ce

Kaliganj Upazila Health Complex
Helāi, Khulna, Bangladesh
⊕ https://vfmat.ch/7af5

Kalihati Upazila Health Complex
Kālihāti, Rajshahi Division, Bangladesh
⊕ https://vfmat.ch/ada8

Kalkini Upazila Health Complex
Kalkini, Dhaka, Bangladesh
⊕ https://vfmat.ch/3528

Kalmakanda Upazila Health Complex
Mantala, Mymensingh Division, Bangladesh
⊕ https://vfmat.ch/1132

Kamrangirchar Hospital
Jangalbāri, Dhaka, Bangladesh
⊕ https://vfmat.ch/cb9b

Kanaighat Upazila Health Complex
Bishanpur, Sylhet, Bangladesh
⊕ https://vfmat.ch/adf8

Kashipur Al-Habib Hospital
Sonaimuri, Chittagong, Bangladesh
⊕ https://vfmat.ch/bccf

Kaukhali Upazila Health Complex
Kaukhaki, Barishal, Bangladesh
⊕ https://vfmat.ch/5b3e

KC Hospital & Diagnostic Center
Dakshin Khān, Dhaka, Bangladesh
⊕ https://vfmat.ch/6f4a

Kendua Upazila Health Complex
Ghorāil, Mymensingh Division, Bangladesh
⊕ https://vfmat.ch/8c2e

Keraniganj Upazila Health Complex
Keraniganj, Dhaka, Bangladesh
⊕ https://vfmat.ch/2d33

Keshabpur Upazila Health Complex
Kesabpur, Khulna, Bangladesh
⊕ https://vfmat.ch/1855

Khoksha Upazila Health Complex
Hilālpur, Khulna, Bangladesh
⊕ https://vfmat.ch/da7f

Khulna City Medical College Hospital
Khulna, Bangladesh
⊕ https://vfmat.ch/9ceb

Khulna Shishu Hospital
Khulna, Khulna, Bangladesh
⊕ https://vfmat.ch/1479

Kidney Foundation Hospital And Research Centre
Rasūlpur, Rajshahi Division, Bangladesh
⊕ https://vfmat.ch/a396

Kishoreganj General Hospital
Kishorganj, Dhaka, Bangladesh
⊕ https://vfmat.ch/74f6

Kotalipara Upazila Health Complex
Kotalipara, Dhaka, Bangladesh
⊕ https://vfmat.ch/4a7f

Kuliarchar Upazila Health Complex
Kuliār Char, Dhaka, Bangladesh
⊕ https://vfmat.ch/38b5

Kumudini Hospital
Mirzāpur, Dhaka, Bangladesh
⊕ https://vfmat.ch/7df4

Kurmitola General Hospital
Kurmitola, Dhaka, Bangladesh
⊕ https://vfmat.ch/d31c

Kushtia General Hospital
Kushtia, Khulna, Bangladesh
⊕ https://vfmat.ch/bb28

Kutupalong Hospital
Kutupālong, Chittagong, Bangladesh
⊕ https://vfmat.ch/a5f1

Kuwait Bangladesh Friendship Government Hospital
Dhaka, Bangladesh
⊕ https://vfmat.ch/92fa

Lab One Diagnostic Center
Nasirābād, Chittagong, Bangladesh
⊕ https://vfmat.ch/4c93

LABAID Diagnostic Chattogram
Nasirābād, Chittagong, Bangladesh
⊕ https://vfmat.ch/8154

LABAID Specialized Hospital
Gulshan, Dhaka, Bangladesh
⊕ https://vfmat.ch/8577

Labaid Specialized Hospital
Dhaka, Dhaka, Bangladesh
⊕ https://vfmat.ch/4abc

Labaid Specialized Hospital – Malibag
Bara Magbāzār, Dhaka, Bangladesh
⊕ https://vfmat.ch/b38b

Laksham Upazila Health Complex
Lākshām, Chittagong, Bangladesh
⊕ https://vfmat.ch/cacf

Lakshmipur Sadar Hospital
Shamsirābād, Chittagong, Bangladesh
⊕ https://vfmat.ch/d953

Lalon Shah Diagnostic Center & Hospital
Kushtia, Khulna, Bangladesh
⊕ https://vfmat.ch/tmwt

LAMB Hospital
Dinajpur, Rangpur, Bangladesh
⊕ https://vfmat.ch/i6hl

Life Line Hospital and Cardiac Center
Moulvibazar, Bangladesh
⊕ https://vfmat.ch/dc1d

Log Gate Hospital
Kaptai, Chittagong, Bangladesh
⊕ https://vfmat.ch/6d3d

Lohagara Upazila Health Complex
Lohāgara, Khulna, Bangladesh
⊕ https://vfmat.ch/ee45

M Abdur Rahim Medical College Hospital
Dinajpur, Rangpur, Bangladesh
⊕ https://vfmat.ch/c56c

Ma-Moni Hospital
Chattogram, Bangladesh
⊕ https://vfmat.ch/3eb2

Madan Upazila Health Complex
Madan, Bangladesh
⊕ https://vfmat.ch/6162

Madaripur Sadar Hospital
Madaripur, Dhaka, Bangladesh
⊕ https://vfmat.ch/2d98

Madhabpur Upazila Health Complex
Madhabpur, Sylhet, Bangladesh
⊕ https://vfmat.ch/cac1

Madhukhali Upazila Health Complex
Gārākhola Madhukhāli, Dhaka, Bangladesh
⊕ https://vfmat.ch/6894

Magura General Hospital
Pār Nandoali, Khulna, Bangladesh
⊕ https://vfmat.ch/522f

Mainamati Cantonment General Hospital
Comilla, Chittagong, Bangladesh
⊕ https://vfmat.ch/84f3

Mamun Private Hospital
Maulavi Bāzār, Sylhet, Bangladesh
⊕ https://vfmat.ch/faaf

Manikchari Upazila Health Complex
Manikchari, Chattogram, Bangladesh
⊕ https://vfmat.ch/9953

Manikganj District Hospital
Uttar Seota, Dhaka, Bangladesh
⊕ https://vfmat.ch/baf4

Manirampur Upazila Health Complex
Manirampur, Khulna, Bangladesh
⊕ https://vfmat.ch/5461

Manpura Upazila Health Complex
Manpura, Barisāl, Bangladesh
⊕ https://vfmat.ch/7844

Marie Stopes Bangladesh
Char Kāmrāngi, Dhaka, Bangladesh
⊕ https://vfmat.ch/5bb8

MARKS Medical College & Hospital
Mirpur, Dhaka, Bangladesh
⊕ https://vfmat.ch/2187

Maternal and Child Health Training Institute
Azimpur, Dhaka, Bangladesh
⊕ https://vfmat.ch/afb7

Mathbaria Upazila Health Complex
Mathba, Barisāl, Bangladesh
⊕ https://vfmat.ch/59f6

Matiranga Upazila Health Complex
Matiranga, Chattogram, Bangladesh
⊕ https://vfmat.ch/aec5

Matlab Upazila Health Complex
Matlab Bāzār, Chittagong, Bangladesh
⊕ https://vfmat.ch/1f8a

Maula Buksh Sardar Datobbo Chokkhu Hospital
Kāliganj, Dhaka, Bangladesh
⊕ https://vfmat.ch/4c7c

Max Hospital & Diagnostic Ltd.
Nasirābād, Chittagong, Bangladesh
⊕ https://vfmat.ch/5812

Medecins Sans Frontieres (MSF) Hospital IPD
Balukhali, Chattogram, Bangladesh
⊕ https://vfmat.ch/b6db

Meherpur General Hospital
Meherpur, Khulna, Bangladesh
⊕ https://vfmat.ch/f67f

Memorial Christian Hospital
Malumghat, Bangladesh
⊕ https://vfmat.ch/p26b

Metro Diagnostic Center Ltd.
Nasirābād, Chittagong, Bangladesh
⊕ https://vfmat.ch/48a1

Mirpur Adhunik Hospital & Diagnostic Center
Chākuli, Dhaka, Bangladesh
⊕ https://vfmat.ch/acba

Mirror Hospital
Panchlaish, Chattogram, Bangladesh
⊕ https://vfmat.ch/d51d

Mirzaganj Upazila Health Complex
Uttar Subidkhali, Barisāl, Bangladesh
🌐 https://vfmat.ch/fd61

Mohanpur Upazila Health Complex
Mohanpur, Rajshahi, Bangladesh
🌐 https://vfmat.ch/29c4

Mollahat Upazila Health Complex
Mollahat, Khulna, Bangladesh
🌐 https://vfmat.ch/811b

Momtaz Uddin General Hospital
Ashulia, Dhaka, Bangladesh
🌐 https://vfmat.ch/2c95

Monowara Hospital
Shahbag, Dhaka, Bangladesh
🌐 https://vfmat.ch/daea

Monu Miya Hospital
Barogaon, Chittagong, Bangladesh
🌐 https://vfmat.ch/75bb

Moon Hospital
Cumilla, Chittagong, Bangladesh
🌐 https://vfmat.ch/c3de

Mother Care Hospital
Taleperbāg, Dhaka, Bangladesh
🌐 https://vfmat.ch/8ec2

Mount Adora Hospital – Akhalia
Mollāgaon, Sylhet, Bangladesh
🌐 https://vfmat.ch/7e9a

Mugda Medical College and Hospital
Purātan Paltanerlāin, Dhaka, Bangladesh
🌐 https://vfmat.ch/c39b

Munshiganj District Hospital
Munshiganj, Dhaka, Bangladesh
🌐 https://vfmat.ch/3718

Muradnagar Upazila Health Complex
Noākāndi, Chittagong, Bangladesh
🌐 https://vfmat.ch/1b1e

Mustafiz Glaucoma Research & Eye Hospital
Mirpur, Dhaka, Bangladesh
🌐 https://vfmat.ch/8c91

Nachole Upazila Health Complex
Nachole, Rajshahi, Bangladesh
🌐 https://vfmat.ch/c55e

Nageswari Upazila Health Complex
Nageswari, Rangpur, Bangladesh
🌐 Htrps://vfmat.ch/63b5

Nagorik Hospital
Khalisha, Rangpur Division, Bangladesh
🌐 https://vfmat.ch/3796

Nalitabari Upazila Health Complex
Nalitābāri, Mymensingh Division, Bangladesh
🌐 https://vfmat.ch/343d

Naogaon Eye Hospital
Naogaon, Rajshahi, Bangladesh
🌐 https://vfmat.ch/2w6g

Narail District Hospital
Uttar Pankabila, Khulna, Bangladesh
🌐 https://vfmat.ch/214b

Narayanganj General Hospital
Talla, Dhaka, Bangladesh
🌐 https://vfmat.ch/243a

Nargis Memorial Hospital (Pvt) Ltd.
Rupsa, Khulna, Bangladesh
🌐 https://vfmat.ch/485c

Nari Maitree
Khilgaon, Dhaka, Bangladesh
🌐 https://vfmat.ch/f239

Naria Upazila Health Complex
Naria, Dhaka, Bangladesh
🌐 https://vfmat.ch/d32d

National Center for Hearing and Speech for Children
Dhaka, Bangladesh
🌐 https://vfmat.ch/9246

National Center For Prevention Of Rheumatic Fever & Heart Disease (NCCRF)
Barāba, Dhaka, Bangladesh
🌐 https://vfmat.ch/f6bc

National Heart Foundation Hospital of Bangladesh
Dhaka, Bangladesh
🌐 https://vfmat.ch/42cb

National Hospital
Daganbhuiya, Chattogram, Bangladesh
🌐 https://vfmat.ch/c3ce

National Hospital Pvt. Ltd.
Nasirābād, Chittagong, Bangladesh
🌐 https://vfmat.ch/28b5

National Institute of Cancer Research & Hospital
Dhaka, Bangladesh
🌐 https://vfmat.ch/guyu

National Institute of Cardiovascular Diseases (NICVD)
Dhaka, Bangladesh
🌐 https://vfmat.ch/1kcr

National Institute of Diseases of the Chest and Hospital
Dhaka, Bangladesh
🌐 https://vfmat.ch/bl9i

National Institute of Neurosciences & Hospital
Dhaka, Bangladesh
🌐 https://vfmat.ch/xcxx

National Institution of Ophthalmology & Hospital
Dhaka, Bangladesh
🌐 https://vfmat.ch/3g6e

Natore District Hospital
Natore, Rajshahi Division, Bangladesh
🌐 https://vfmat.ch/1abf

Nawabganj Upazila Health Complex
Nawabganj, Dhaka, Bangladesh
🌐 https://vfmat.ch/28b7

Netrakona Ideal Hospital Private, Ltd.
Netrakona, Bangladesh
🌐 https://vfmat.ch/akyb

Netrokona District Hospital
Netrokona, Mymensingh, Bangladesh
🌐 https://vfmat.ch/cea2

Nibedita Shishu Hospital Ltd.
Dhaka South City Corporation, Dhaka, Bangladesh
🌐 https://vfmat.ch/f7ba

North East Medical College & Hospital
South Surma, Sylhet, Bangladesh
🌐 https://vfmat.ch/8875

Northern Medical College & Hospital
Shibpur, Dhaka, Bangladesh
🌐 https://vfmat.ch/c12f

Pabna Sadar Hospital
Pābna, Rajshahi Division, Bangladesh
🌐 https://vfmat.ch/b744

Padma General Hospital
Dhaka, Bangladesh
🌐 https://vfmat.ch/c96f

Pan Pacific Hospital, Training & Research Institute Ltd.
Paltan, Dhaka, Bangladesh
🌐 https://vfmat.ch/c8ae

Panchagarh General Hospital
Islāmbāg, Rangpur Division, Bangladesh
🌐 https://vfmat.ch/d576

Panchbibi Upazila Health Complex
Goneshpur, Rajshahi Division, Bangladesh
⊕ https://vfmat.ch/4465

Pangsha Upazila Health Complex
Pangsha, Dhaka, Bangladesh
⊕ https://vfmat.ch/7a6e

Patenga Naval Hospital
Dhangar Char, Chittagong, Bangladesh
⊕ https://vfmat.ch/8843

Patuakhali Medical College Hospital
Kālikāpur, Khulna, Bangladesh
⊕ https://vfmat.ch/b19b

Patuakhali Sadar Hospital
Kālikāpur, Khulna, Bangladesh
⊕ https://vfmat.ch/f1d9

People's Hospital Ltd., Chattogram
Chattogram, Bangladesh
⊕ https://vfmat.ch/d54b

Phulpur Upazila Health Complex
Diu, Mymensingh, Bangladesh
⊕ https://vfmat.ch/4abb

Pioneer Hospital and Diagnostic Center Ltd.
Raozan, Chattogram, Bangladesh
⊕ https://vfmat.ch/8dde

Police Lines Hospital
Sylhet, Bangladesh
⊕ https://vfmat.ch/29d2

Popular Medical College Hospital
Idga, Dhaka, Bangladesh
⊕ https://vfmat.ch/1176

Popular Medicine Center Ltd.
Dhaka, Dhaka, Bangladesh
⊕ https://vfmat.ch/8415

Popular Medicine Corner
Nilkāntha, Rangpur Division, Bangladesh
⊕ https://vfmat.ch/662a

Pranto Specialized Hospital
Mymensingh, Bangladesh
⊕ https://vfmat.ch/xht2

Prime Bank Eye Hospital
Dhanmondi, Dhaka, Bangladesh
⊕ https://vfmat.ch/21b2

Prime Hospital Ltd
Maijdi, Chittagong, Bangladesh
⊕ https://vfmat.ch/2a1f

Probin Hospital
Kāfrul, Dhaka, Bangladesh
⊕ https://vfmat.ch/1a32

Prof .M. A. Matin Memorial BNSB Base Eye Hospital
Sirajganj, Rajshahi, Bangladesh
⊕ https://vfmat.ch/1mkn

Puratan Hospital
Daulatdia, Khulna, Bangladesh
⊕ https://vfmat.ch/6426

Puraton Hospital Jame Masjid
Nilphamari, Rangpur, Bangladesh
⊕ https://vfmat.ch/319e

Queens Hospital Pvt. Ltd
Jessore, Khulna, Bangladesh
⊕ https://vfmat.ch/b19d

Rafatullah Community Hospital
Bogura, Rajshahi Division, Bangladesh
⊕ https://vfmat.ch/kwlq

Railway General Hospital
Paltan, Dhaka, Bangladesh
⊕ https://vfmat.ch/b596

Raipur Upazila Health Complex
Raipur, Chattogram, Bangladesh
⊕ https://vfmat.ch/d5ab

Rajapur Upazila Health Complex
Manoharpur, Barisāl, Bangladesh
⊕ https://vfmat.ch/de79

Rajoir Upazila Health Complex
Rājair, Dhaka, Bangladesh
⊕ https://vfmat.ch/3642

Rajshahi Cancer Hospital and Research Center Trust
Natore, Rajshahi, Bangladesh
⊕ https://vfmat.ch/a868

Rajshahi Eye Hospital
Rajshahi, Bangladesh
⊕ https://vfmat.ch/h1uu

Rajshahi Shishu Hospital
Pipacipara, Rajshahi Division, Bangladesh
⊕ https://vfmat.ch/a622

Rangamati General Hospital
Rangamati, Chittagong, Bangladesh
⊕ https://vfmat.ch/e8db

Rangpur Medical College Hospital
Nilkāntha, Rangpur Division, Bangladesh
⊕ https://vfmat.ch/e467

Regent Hospital Ltd.
Dhaka, Dhaka, Bangladesh
⊕ https://vfmat.ch/6f54

Rezaul Haque Trust Hospital
Monohardi, Dhaka, Bangladesh
⊕ https://vfmat.ch/9553

Riverside Hospital
Nawāb Char, Dhaka, Bangladesh
⊕ https://vfmat.ch/9748

Royal Care and Surgical Hospital
Taleperbāg, Dhaka, Bangladesh
⊕ https://vfmat.ch/d4cf

Royal Hospital Limited
Nasirābād, Chittagong, Bangladesh
⊕ https://vfmat.ch/3afe

Saghatta Upazila Health Complex
Shāghātta, Rajshahi Division, Bangladesh
⊕ https://vfmat.ch/b6e8

Salauddin Specialized Hospital
Tikatuli, Dhaka, Bangladesh
⊕ https://vfmat.ch/211c

Samorita Hospital Limited
Rāja Bāzār, Dhaka, Bangladesh
⊕ https://vfmat.ch/41ac

Sarail Upazila Health Complex
Sarail, Chattogram, Bangladesh
⊕ https://vfmat.ch/2ccf

Sariakandi Upazila Health Complex
Shāriākāndi, Rajshahi Division, Bangladesh
⊕ https://vfmat.ch/299a

Sarishabari Upazila Health Complex
Sarishābāri, Mymensingh, Bangladesh
⊕ https://vfmat.ch/b123

Sarkari Karmachari Hospital
Dhaka, Bangladesh
⊕ https://vfmat.ch/d7te

Sathitun Nesa Eye Hospital
Narayanganj, Dhaka, Bangladesh
⊕ https://vfmat.ch/web9

Satkhira District Hospital
Satkhira, Khulna, Bangladesh
⊕ https://vfmat.ch/3b59

Satkhira Medical College Hospital
Satkhira, Khulna, Bangladesh
⊕ https://vfmat.ch/513a

Saturia Upazila Health Complex
Nāndeswari, Dhaka, Bangladesh
⊕ https://vfmat.ch/e6d1

Senbag Upazila Health Complex
Senbag, Chattogram, Bangladesh
⊕ https://vfmat.ch/2e93

Sensiv Pvt. Ltd.
Nasirābād, Chittagong, Bangladesh
⊕ https://vfmat.ch/5df4

Serajdikhan Upazila Health Complex
Ichhāpur, Dhaka, Bangladesh
⊕ https://vfmat.ch/9499

Shaheed Sheikh Abu Naser Specialized Hospital
Goālkhāli, Khulna, Bangladesh
⊕ https://vfmat.ch/2ffb

Shaheed Suhrawardy Medical College & Hospital (ShSMC)
Dhaka, Bangladesh
⊕ https://vfmat.ch/ta8x

Shaheed Ziaur Rahman Medical College Hospital (SZMCH)
Sakpāla, Rajshahi Division, Bangladesh
⊕ https://vfmat.ch/6f5c

Shahjadpur Eye Hospital
Shahjadpur, Dhaka, Bangladesh
⊕ https://vfmat.ch/l8nd

Shahrasti Upazila Health Complex
Shahrasti, Chattogram, Bangladesh
⊕ https://vfmat.ch/3a88

Shariatpur Sadar Hospital
Shariatpur District, Dhaka, Bangladesh
⊕ https://vfmat.ch/ddff

Sher-E-Bangla Medical College Hospital
Barishal, Barishal, Bangladesh
⊕ https://vfmat.ch/99fa

Sherpur District Hospital
Sherpur, Mymensingh, Bangladesh
⊕ https://vfmat.ch/e7a4

Shibchar Upazila Health Complex
Kānchikāta, Dhaka, Bangladesh
⊕ https://vfmat.ch/88eb

Shibganj Upazila Health Complex
Lāldaha, Rajshahi Division, Bangladesh
⊕ https://vfmat.ch/f718

Shibpur Upazila Health Complex
Bāniādi, Dhaka, Bangladesh
⊕ https://vfmat.ch/891d

Singra Upazila Health Complex
Singra, Rajshahi, Bangladesh
⊕ https://vfmat.ch/43c7

Sono Hospital
Kushtia, Khulna, Bangladesh
⊕ https://vfmat.ch/faab

SQUARE HOSPITALS LTD.
Sukrābād, Dhaka, Bangladesh
⊕ https://vfmat.ch/39d7

Sreemangal Upazila Health Complex
Sreemangal, Sylhet, Bangladesh
⊕ https://vfmat.ch/5564

Sreenagar Upazila Health Complex
Harpāra, Dhaka, Bangladesh
⊕ https://vfmat.ch/f1bb

Sunamganj Sadar Hospital
Sunāmganj, Sylhet, Bangladesh
⊕ https://vfmat.ch/27ae

Sundarganj Upazila Health Complex
Dakshin Bāmanjol, Rangpur, Bangladesh
⊕ https://vfmat.ch/36bb

Surgiscope Hospital – Unit 1
Chattogram, Bangladesh
⊕ https://vfmat.ch/9fa3

Surgiscope Hospital – Unit 2
Chattogram, Bangladesh
⊕ https://vfmat.ch/24c1

Sylhet MAG Osmani Medical College Hospital
Kajolshah, Sylhet, Bangladesh
⊕ https://vfmat.ch/ef3f

Sylhet Women's Medical College Hospital
Sylhet, Bangladesh
⊕ https://vfmat.ch/4b4e

T.B. Hospital Jessore
Jashore, Khulna, Bangladesh
⊕ https://vfmat.ch/e5d6

Tahirpur Upazila Health Complex
Tākātukia, Sylhet, Bangladesh
⊕ https://vfmat.ch/338c

Tarail Upazila Health Complex
Tārāil, Dhaka, Bangladesh
⊕ https://vfmat.ch/223f

Tarash Eye Hospital
Tarash, Rajshahi, Bangladesh
⊕ https://vfmat.ch/zd5u

TB Hospital
Salimpur, Chattogram, Bangladesh
⊕ https://vfmat.ch/6c31

Teknaf Upazila Health Complex
Teknaf, Chattogram, Bangladesh
⊕ https://vfmat.ch/1bba

Terokhada Upazila Health Complex
Dasbhāla, Khulna, Bangladesh
⊕ https://vfmat.ch/d62a

Thakurgaon District Hospital
Thakurgaon, Rangpur Division, Bangladesh
⊕ https://vfmat.ch/95ea

Thakurgoan BGB Hospital
Nichintapur, Rangpur Division, Bangladesh
⊕ https://vfmat.ch/8784

Tongibari Upazila Health Complex
Tangibāri, Dhaka, Bangladesh
⊕ https://vfmat.ch/967c

Ulipur Upazila Health Complex
Ulipur, Rangpur, Bangladesh
⊕ https://vfmat.ch/e1f3

Ultra Assay Center
Ziānagar, Chittagong, Bangladesh
⊕ https://vfmat.ch/b3f3

United Hospital Limited
Sāmāir, Dhaka, Bangladesh
⊕ https://vfmat.ch/5abf

Universal Medical College Hospital
Mahākhāli, Dhaka, Bangladesh
⊕ https://vfmat.ch/994f

Uttara Adhunik Medical College Hospital (BMSRI)
Ābdullāpur, Dhaka, Bangladesh
⊕ https://vfmat.ch/7884

Uttara Central Hospital & Diagnostic Center
Dhaka, Bangladesh
⊕ https://vfmat.ch/77dc

Uttara Crescent Hospital
Dhaka, Bangladesh
⊕ https://vfmat.ch/2dc4

Uttara Ma-O-Shishu Hospital LTD
Uttara, Dhaka, Bangladesh
⊕ https://vfmat.ch/ff83

Welcare Hospital Limited
Rāmchandrapur, Dhaka, Bangladesh
⊕ https://vfmat.ch/a6d4

Z.H. Sikder Women's Medical College & Hospital
Dhaka, Bangladesh
⊕ https://vfmat.ch/da91

Z.H. Sikder Women's Medical College General and Cardiac Hospital
Dhaka, Bangladesh
⊕ https://vfmat.ch/2fe8

Healthcare Facility

Benin

The Republic of Benin, in West Africa, lies between Togo, Nigeria, Burkina Faso, and Niger. Referred to as the birthplace of Vodou and home to centuries-old palaces in Abomey, Benin has a small, young population of 13.3 million. The country comprises several ethnic groups including the Fon, Adja, Yoruba, Bariba and Fulani, who speak their namesake languages as well as the country's official language, French.

Benin gained independence from France in 1960. Since establishing its democratic system of government more than 20 years ago, Benin has become one of Africa's most stable democracies. Its farm-based economy, which employs about 70 percent of the country's population, has grown significantly from decade to decade. Benin has also invested in infrastructure, including renovating its port. Today, Benin has an economic growth rate of about 5 percent. Despite this growth, poverty remains a pressing issue faced by roughly 40 percent of the population. Benin is particularly vulnerable to climate hazards, as well as to the effect of economic and political changes in Nigeria, its largest trading partner.

Life expectancy continues to rise, nearing 62 years of age. Despite some improvements in health indicators, the health challenges that contribute most to death and disability in the country are communicable and non-communicable diseases. Significant causes of death include malaria, neonatal disorders, lower respiratory infections, diarrheal disease, stroke, ischemic heart disease, congenital defects, tuberculosis, HIV/AIDS, and measles. Stroke, ischemic heart disease, and measles have significantly increased in recent years. Of note, trauma from road injuries is a major cause of disability.

13.3M
Population

$1,291
GDP Per Capita

62 years
Life Expectancy
↑ Improving

7	**50**	**397**
Doctors/100k	**Beds**/100k	**Deaths**/100k
Physician Density	Hospital Bed Density	Maternal Mortality

Benin

Nonprofit Organizations

Abt Associates
Seeks to improve the quality of life and economic well-being of people worldwide, while striving to meet and exceed the highest professional standards.
General, Logist-Op, MF Med, OB-GYN, Peds
⊕ https://vfmat.ch/cec2

Advance Family Planning
Aims to achieve global expansion and access to quality contraceptive information, services, and supplies through financial investment and political commitment.
General, MF Med, Pub Health
⊕ https://vfmat.ch/7478

Africa CDC
Aims to strengthen the capacity and capability of Africa's public health institutions and partnerships to detect and respond quickly and effectively to disease threats and outbreaks, based on data-driven interventions and programs.
Infect Dis, Logist-Op, Pub Health
⊕ https://vfmat.ch/339c

Africa Health Organisation
Leads collaborative efforts among countries in Africa and other partners to promote health equity, combat disease, and improve quality of life.
Logist-Op, Pub Health
⊕ https://vfmat.ch/b1c5

Africa Indoor Residual Spraying Project (AIRS)
Aims to protect millions of people in Africa from malaria by spraying insecticide on walls, ceilings, and other indoor resting places of mosquitoes that transmit malaria.
Infect Dis
⊕ https://vfmat.ch/9bd1

Africa Relief and Community Development
Provides comprehensive relief and developmental aid to people of the African continent regardless of gender, race, or religion.
Nutr, Pub Health
⊕ https://vfmat.ch/6cd2

African Field Epidemiology Network (AFENET)
Strengthens field epidemiology and public health laboratory capacity to contribute effectively to addressing epidemics and other major public health problems in Africa.
All-Immu, Infect Dis, Path, Pub Health
⊕ https://vfmat.ch/df2e

African Health Now
Promotes and provides information and access to sustainable primary healthcare to women, children, and families living across Sub-Saharan Africa.
Dent-OMFS, Endo, General, Infect Dis, MF Med, OB-GYN
⊕ https://vfmat.ch/c766

Al Basar International Foundation
Works with local partners to treat preventable blindness, and helps set up sustainable infrastructure so local teams can save sight in their communities.
Ophth-Opt
⊕ https://vfmat.ch/a8b5

Amref Health Africa
Serves millions of people across 35 countries in Sub-Saharan Africa, strengthening health systems, and training African health workers to respond to the continent's most critical health issues.
All-Immu, General, Infect Dis, Logist-Op, MF Med, OB-GYN, Path, Pub Health, Surg
⊕ https://vfmat.ch/6985

AO Alliance
Builds solutions to lessen the burden of injuries in low- and middle-income countries, while enhancing the care of the injured to reduce human suffering, disability, and poverty.
Ortho, Surg
⊕ https://vfmat.ch/8cd5

Asclepius Snakebite Foundation
Seeks to reverse the cycle of tragic snakebite outcomes through a combination of innovative research, clinical medicine, and education-based public health initiatives.
Infect Dis, Pub Health
⊕ https://vfmat.ch/d37d

BroadReach
Collaborates with governments, multinational health organizations, donors, and private-sector companies to effect healthcare reform and solve the world's biggest health challenges.
Logist-Op
⊕ https://vfmat.ch/7812

Canada-Africa Community Health Alliance
Sends Canadian volunteer teams on two- to three-week missions to African communities to work hand-in-hand with local partners.
General, Infect Dis, MF Med, OB-GYN, Peds, Surg
⊕ https://vfmat.ch/4c94

CARE
Works around the globe to save lives, defeat poverty, and achieve social justice.
ER Med, General
⊕ https://vfmat.ch/7232

Caritas Pro Vitae Gradu Charitable Trust
Supports Catholic charitable projects with social and humanitarian efforts, and aims to assist people in need including children, the elderly, sick, and disabled through healthcare, poverty relief, and education.

ER Med, General, Logist-Op, Medicine, OB-GYN, Ophth-Opt, Path, Peds, Pub Health, Radiol, Rehab, Surg
⊕ https://vfmat.ch/b2ca

Carter Center, The
Seeks to prevent and resolve conflicts, enhance freedom and democracy, and improve health, while remaining committed to human rights and the alleviation of human suffering.
Infect Dis, MF Med, Ophth-Opt
⊕ https://vfmat.ch/6556

Chain of Hope (La Chaîne de l'Espoir)
Helps underprivileged children around the world by providing them with access to healthcare.
Anesth, CT Surg, Crit-Care, ER Med, Neurosurg, Ortho, Ped Surg, Surg, Vasc Surg
⊕ https://vfmat.ch/e871

Challenge Initiative, The
Seeks to rapidly and sustainably scale up proven reproductive health solutions among the urban poor.
MF Med, OB-GYN, Peds
⊕ https://vfmat.ch/2f77

Children's Lifeline International
Provides medical teams and surgical assistance to underprivileged children in developing countries through missions in partnership with local hospitals.
CV Med, Dent-OMFS, General, MF Med, Neurosurg, Peds, Rehab
⊕ https://vfmat.ch/6fea

Christian Blind Mission (CBM)
Aims to improve the quality of life of persons with disabilities in the poorest countries, addressing poverty as a cause and a consequence of disability, and working in partnership to create a society for all.
ENT, General, Infect Dis, OB-GYN, Ophth-Opt, Ortho, Peds, Psych, Rehab, Surg
⊕ https://vfmat.ch/3824

Christian Connections for International Health (CCIH)
Promotes global health and wholeness from a Christian perspective.
All-Immu, General, Infect Dis, MF Med, Neonat, OB-GYN, Psych
⊕ https://vfmat.ch/fa5d

Core Group
Aims to improve and expand community health practices for underserved populations, especially women and children, through collaborative action and learning.
General, Infect Dis, MF Med, Medicine, OB-GYN, Peds, Pub Health
⊕ https://vfmat.ch/9de3

COVID-19 Clinical Research Coalition
Advocates and collaborates for the advancement of COVID-19 research driven by the needs of low-resource settings, and works for equitable access to solutions to the pandemic.
All-Immu, Infect-Dis, MF Med, Path, Pub Health
⊕ https://vfmat.ch/d1f4

Developing Country NGO Delegation: Global Fund to Fight AIDS, TB & Malaria
Works to strengthen the engagement of civil society actors and organizations in developing countries to build a world in which AIDS, TB, and malaria are no longer global, public health, and human rights threats.
Infect Dis, Pub Health
⊕ https://vfmat.ch/3149

Direct Relief
Improves the health and lives of people affected by poverty or emergency situations by mobilizing and providing essential medical resources needed for their care.
ER Med, Logist-Op
⊕ https://vfmat.ch/58e5

Enabel
As the development agency of the Belgian federal government, charged with

implementing Belgium's international development policy, carries out public service assignments in Belgium and abroad pursuant to the 2030 Agenda for Sustainable Development.
General, Infect Dis, Logist-Op, MF Med, OB-GYN, Peds, Pub Health
⊕ https://vfmat.ch/5af7

EngenderHealth
Works to implement high-quality, gender-equitable programs that advance sexual and reproductive health and rights.
General, MF Med, OB-GYN, Peds
⊕ https://vfmat.ch/1cb2

Fistula Foundation
Aims to engage the support of people worldwide who are eager to see the day that no woman suffers from obstetric fistula. Raises and directs funds to doctors and hospitals providing life-transforming surgery to women in need.
OB-GYN
⊕ https://vfmat.ch/e958

Fondation Follereau
Promotes the quality of life of the most vulnerable African communities. Alongside trusted partners, the foundation supports local initiatives in healthcare and education.
General, Infect Dis, OB-GYN
⊕ https://vfmat.ch/bcc7

Foundation for Healthcare for Humanity
Provide assistance in the development and implementation of medical programs in the United States, Africa, South America, Eastern Europe, and the Caribbean.
General
⊕ https://vfmat.ch/ba7f

Global Aid Network (GAiN) Australia
Inspired by the Christian faith, provides support to people living in crisis through programs in healthcare, humanitarian aid, disaster response, clean water, and sanitation.
Dent-OMFS, Ophth-Opt
⊕ https://vfmat.ch/6cb8

Global Clubfoot Initiative (GCI)
Promotes and resources the treatment of children with clubfoot in developing countries using the Ponseti technique.
Ortho, Ped Surg
⊕ https://vfmat.ch/f229

Global Oncology (GO)
Brings the best in cancer care to underserved patients around the world and collaborates across geographic, professional, and academic borders to improve cancer care, research, and education.
Heme-Onc, Path, Rad-Onc
⊕ https://vfmat.ch/fcb8

Global Reconstructive Surgery Outreach
Supports surgeons, doctors, and nurses financially to enable them to provide critically needed plastic and reconstructive surgeries to the poor.
Logist-Op, Surg
⊕ https://vfmat.ch/f262

Globus Relief
Aims to improve the delivery of healthcare worldwide by gathering, processing, and distributing surplus medical supplies to charities at home and abroad.
Logist-Op
⊕ https://vfmat.ch/a2b7

Grace Dental and Medical (GDM) Missions
Sends and supports dental and medical missions based in Christian ministry with the aim of church planting.
Dent-OMFS, ER Med, General
⊕ https://vfmat.ch/bdea

Grassroot Soccer
Leverages the power of soccer to educate, inspire, and mobilize at-risk youth in developing countries to overcome their greatest health challenges, live healthier

and more productive lives, and be agents for change in their communities.

Infect Dis

⊕ https://vfmat.ch/3521

Health Equity Initiative

Aims to build and sustain a global community that engages across sectors and disciplines to advance health equity.

Pub Health

⊕ https://vfmat.ch/e2e2

Health Volunteers Overseas (HVO)

Improves the availability and quality of healthcare through the education, training, and professional development of the health workforce in resource-scarce countries.

All-Immu, Anesth, CV Med, Dent-OMFS, Derm, ENT, ER Med, Endo, GI, Heme-Onc, Infect Dis, Medicine, Medicine, Nephro, Neuro, OB-GYN, Ophth-Opt, Ortho, Peds, Plast, Psych, Pulm-Critic, Rehab, Rheum, Surg

⊕ https://vfmat.ch/42b2

Hernia Help

Provides free hernia surgery to underserved children and adults in the Western Hemisphere, practicing the preferential option for the poor. Trains, mentors, develops, and supports local general surgeons who will serve as trainers and future leaders to create self-sustaining teams.

Anesth, Surg

⊕ https://vfmat.ch/6319

Hernia International

Aims to provide relief from sickness, and protection and preservation of health, for persons affected by groin and abdominal hernias and residing in low- and middle-income countries.

Surg

⊕ https://vfmat.ch/e98e

Hope Walks

Frees children, families, and communities from the burden of clubfoot, inspired by the Christian faith.

Ortho, Ped Surg, Peds, Rehab

⊕ https://vfmat.ch/f6d4

Hospice Africa

Aims to provide a holistic and culturally sensitive palliative care service through accurate treatment of pain.

Palliative

⊕ https://vfmat.ch/9f86

Humanity & Inclusion

Works alongside people with disabilities and vulnerable populations, taking action and bearing witness in order to respond to their essential needs, improve their living conditions and health, and promote respect for their dignity and fundamental rights.

General, Infect Dis, MF Med, Medicine, Ortho, Peds, Psych, Pub Health, Rehab

⊕ https://vfmat.ch/16b7

Humanity First

Provides aid and assistance to those in need, offering sustainable development solutions to society while providing and empowering local communities with the resources to help themselves.

ER Med, General, MF Med, Ophth-Opt

⊕ https://vfmat.ch/13cc

Hunger Project, The

Aims to end hunger and poverty by pioneering sustainable, grassroots, women-centered strategies and advocating for their widespread adoption in countries throughout the world.

Infect Dis, Nutr, OB-GYN, Pub Health

⊕ https://vfmat.ch/3a49

International Agency for the Prevention of Blindness (IAPB), The

Leads international efforts in blindness-prevention activities, works toward a world where no one is needlessly visually impaired, and ensures that everyone has access to the best possible standard of eye health.

Infect Dis, Ophth-Opt, Pub Health

⊕ https://vfmat.ch/87a2

International Council of Ophthalmology

Works with ophthalmologic societies and others to enhance ophthalmic education and improve access to the highest-quality eye care in order to preserve and restore vision for people of the world.

Ophth-Opt

⊕ https://vfmat.ch/ffd2

International Federation of Gynecology and Obstetrics (FIGO)

Implements global projects on specific women's health issues.

MF Med, Medicine, Neonat, OB-GYN, Surg, Urol

⊕ https://vfmat.ch/c4b4

International Federation of Red Cross and Red Crescent Societies (IFRC)

Coordinates and directs international assistance following natural and manmade disasters in nonconflict situations through the world's largest humanitarian and development network. Provides disaster-preparedness programs, healthcare activities, and promotes humanitarian values.

ER Med, General, Infect Dis, Nutr

⊕ https://vfmat.ch/b4ee

International Organization for Migration (IOM) – The UN Migration Agency

Promotes evidence-informed policies and holistic, preventive, and curative health programs that are beneficial, accessible, and equitable for vulnerable migrants.

General, Infect Dis, OB-GYN

⊕ https://vfmat.ch/621a

International Pediatric Nephrology Association (IPNA)

Leads global efforts to successfully address the care for all children with kidney disease through advocacy, education, and training.

Medicine, Nephro, Peds

⊕ https://vfmat.ch/b59d

International Planned Parenthood Federation (IPPF)

Leads a locally owned, globally connected civil society movement that provides and enables services and champions sexual and reproductive health and rights for all, especially the underserved.

Infect Dis, MF Med, OB-GYN

⊕ https://vfmat.ch/dc97

International Trachoma Initiative (iTi)

Works toward a world free from trachoma, a preventable cause of blindness, and provides comprehensive support to national ministries of health and governmental and nongovernmental organizations to implement a comprehensive approach to fight trachoma.

Infect Dis, Ophth-Opt

⊕ https://vfmat.ch/3278

International Union Against Tuberculosis and Lung Disease

Develops, implements, and assesses anti-tuberculosis, lung health, and noncommunicable disease programs.

Infect Dis, Pub Health, Pulm-Critic

⊕ https://vfmat.ch/3e82

IntraHealth International

Improves the performance of health workers and strengthens the systems in which they work.

CV Med, Endo, General, Infect Dis, MF Med, Neonat, Nutr, OB-GYN

⊕ https://vfmat.ch/ddc8

Ipas

Focuses efforts on women and girls who want contraception or abortion, and builds programs around their needs and how best to support them.

OB-GYN

⊕ https://vfmat.ch/8e39

Iris Mundial

Aims to improve the ocular health of underserved people in developing countries by giving them access to high-quality preventive and curative eye care services.

Ophth-Opt
⊕ https://vfmat.ch/4f85

Jhpiego
Creates and delivers transformative healthcare solutions that save lives, in partnership with national governments, health experts, and local communities.
General, Infect Dis, OB-GYN, Surg
⊕ https://vfmat.ch/45b8

John Snow, Inc. (JSI)
Aims to improve the health and well-being of underserved and vulnerable people and communities throughout the world.
General, Infect Dis, Logist-Op, MF Med, OB-GYN, Peds, Psych, Pub Health
⊕ https://vfmat.ch/ba78

Johns Hopkins Center for Communication Programs
Believes in the power of communication to save lives by empowering people to adopt healthy behaviors for themselves, their families, and their communities.
General, Infect Dis, Logist-Op, OB-GYN, Pub Health
⊕ https://vfmat.ch/1bf9

Joint United Nations Programme on HIV/AIDS (UNAIDS)
Aims to place people living with HIV and people affected by the virus at the decision-making table and at the center of designing, delivering, and monitoring the AIDS response.
Infect Dis
⊕ https://vfmat.ch/464a

Light House Medical Missions
Inspired by the Christian faith, provides programs in healthcare provision, nutrition, emergency relief and response, and water, sanitation, and hygiene (WASH).
ER Med, General, Surg
⊕ https://vfmat.ch/cecd

Lions Clubs International
Empowers volunteers to serve their communities, meet humanitarian needs, encourage peace, and promote international understanding through Lions Clubs.
Heme-Onc, Medicine, Nutr, Ophth-Opt
⊕ https://vfmat.ch/7b12

Management Sciences for Health (MSH)
Works with countries and communities to save lives and improve the health of the world's poorest and most vulnerable people by building strong, resilient, sustainable health systems.
Infect Dis, Logist-Op, Pub Health
⊕ https://vfmat.ch/6aa2

MAP International
Provides medicines and health supplies to those in need around the world so they might experience life to the fullest.
Logist-Op
⊕ https://vfmat.ch/deed

Maternity Foundation
Works to ensure safer childbirth for women and newborns everywhere through innovative mobile health solutions such as the Safe Delivery App, a mobile training tool for skilled birth attendants.
MF Med, OB-GYN, Pub Health
⊕ https://vfmat.ch/ff4f

Medical Care Development International (MCD International)
Works to strengthen health systems through innovative, sustainable interventions.
Infect Dis, Logist-Op, OB-GYN, Pub Health
⊕ https://vfmat.ch/dc5c

Medical Care Development Interntional
Works to improve the health of vulnerable populations through integrated, sustainable, and locally driven interventions.
Infect Dis, OB-GYN, Peds, Pub Health
⊕ https://vfmat.ch/da87

MedShare
Aims to improve the quality of life of people, communities, and the planet by sourcing and directly delivering surplus medical supplies and equipment to communities in need around the world.
Logist-Op
⊕ https://vfmat.ch/c8bc

Mercy and Love Foundation
Aims to provide orphaned and vulnerable children with basic human needs such as food, clothing, and shelter, enabling them to thrive.
General, Peds
⊕ https://vfmat.ch/649a

Mercy Ships
Operates hospital ships staffed by volunteers to bring hope, healing, and healthcare to underserved communities worldwide.
Anesth, Dent-OMFS, Logist-Op, Neonat, OB-GYN, Ophth-Opt, Ortho, Palliative, Plast, Psych, Surg
⊕ https://vfmat.ch/2e99

Mission Partners for Christ
Provides medication, treatment, screenings, and health education in underserved communities around the world, inspired by the Christian faith.
Dent-OMFS, General, Ophth-Opt
⊕ https://vfmat.ch/eb25

Médecins du Monde/Doctors of the World
Provides care, bears witness, and supports social change worldwide with innovative medical programs and evidence-based advocacy initiatives.
ER Med, General, Infect Dis, MF Med, Neonat, OB-GYN, Peds, Pub Health
⊕ https://vfmat.ch/a43d

Mérieux Foundation
Committed to fighting infectious diseases that affect developing countries by capacity building, particularly in clinical laboratories, and focusing on diagnosis.
Logist-Op, Path
⊕ https://vfmat.ch/a23a

Order of Malta
Supports forgotten or excluded people, especially those living in conflict zones or amid natural disasters, by providing medical assistance, caring for refugees, and distributing medicines and necessities.
ER Med, General, Infect Dis, MF Med, Nephro, OB-GYN, Ortho, Psych
⊕ https://vfmat.ch/1fab

Organization for the Prevention of Blindness, The (OPC)
Provides research, and treatments and cures for people affected by blindness and blinding diseases in Francophone Africa.
Infect Dis, Ophth-Opt
⊕ https://vfmat.ch/86d6

Partners for Development (PfD)
Works to improve quality of life for vulnerable people in underserved communities through local and international partnerships.
Infect Dis, MF Med, Neonat, Peds
⊕ https://vfmat.ch/d2f6

PINCC Preventing Cervical Cancer
Seeks to prevent female-specific diseases in developing countries by utilizing low-cost and low-technology methods to create sustainable programs through patient education, medical personnel training, and facility outfitting.
OB-GYN
⊕ https://vfmat.ch/9666

PSI – Population Services International
Aims to improve the health of people in the developing world by focusing on challenges such as a lack of family planning, HIV/AIDS, barriers to maternal health, and the greatest threats to children under the age of 5, including malaria, diarrhea, pneumonia, and malnutrition.
Infect Dis, MF Med, OB-GYN, Peds
⊕ https://vfmat.ch/ffe3

RestoringVision
Empowers lives by restoring vision for millions of people in need.
Ophth-Opt
⊕ https://vfmat.ch/e121

Rockefeller Foundation, The
Works to promote the well-being of humanity.
Logist-Op, Nutr, Pub Health
⊕ https://vfmat.ch/5424

Rotary Action Group for Family Health & AIDS Prevention (RFHA)
Works to save and improve the lives of children and families who lack access to preventive healthcare and education.
Dent-OMFS, Infect Dis, OB-GYN, Ophth-Opt, Peds
⊕ https://vfmat.ch/6563

Rotary International
Provides service to others, improves lives, and advances world understanding, goodwill, and peace through its fellowship of business, professional, and community leaders.
ER Med, General, Infect Dis, MF Med, OB-GYN
⊕ https://vfmat.ch/8fb5

Sanofi Espoir Foundation
Contributes to reducing health inequalities among populations that need it most by applying a socially responsible approach focused on fighting childhood cancers in low-income countries, improving maternal and newborn health, and improving access to care.
ER Med, OB-GYN, Peds
⊕ https://vfmat.ch/943b

SATMED
Serves nongovernmental organizations, hospitals, medical universities, and other healthcare providers active in resource-poor areas, by providing open-access e-health services for the health community.
Logist-Op
⊕ https://vfmat.ch/b8d5

Shammesh – Vers un Monde Meilleur
Aims to transfer skills, knowledge, financial means, and resources to populations in distress or in situations of extreme poverty, in France and abroad.
Dent-OMFS, General, Peds, Pub Health
⊕ https://vfmat.ch/9aed

Sightsavers
Works with partners in developing countries to help eliminate avoidable blindness and advocates for equal opportunity for the disabled.
Infect Dis, Ophth-Opt, Surg
⊕ https://vfmat.ch/aa52

SINA Health
Aims to improve the health and educational status of the population in low- and middle-income countries.
General, Logist-Op
⊕ https://vfmat.ch/9ad3

Sisters of the Immaculate Heart of Mary, Mother of Christ
Based in Chrisitan ministry, seeks to motivate people, especially the poor and the less privileged, to live venerable and dignified lives through credibility-structured programs, education, various medical and humanitarian services, along with self-realization and self-empowerment opportunities.
Infect Dis, Logist-Op, Nutr, Pub Health
⊕ https://vfmat.ch/5774

Smile Train, Inc.
Treats children with cleft lip through a sustainable and local model that supports surgery and other forms of essential care.
Logist-Op, Pub Health
⊕ https://vfmat.ch/822c

Solthis
Improves disease prevention and access to quality care by strengthening the health systems and services of the countries served.
General, Infect Dis, Logist-Op, MF Med, Neonat, Path
⊕ https://vfmat.ch/a71d

SOS Children's Villages International
Supports children through alternative care and family strengthening.
ER Med, Peds
⊕ https://vfmat.ch/aca1

Sri Sathya Sai International Organization
Inspired by spiritual teachings, carries out efforts in global healthcare, education, humanitarian relief, and youth engagement.
Dent-OMFS, General, Logist-Op, Nutr, Ophth-Opt, Pub Health
⊕ https://vfmat.ch/9bda

Sustainable Kidney Care Foundation (SKCF)
Works to provide treatment for kidney injury where none exists, and aims to reduce mortality from treatable acute kidney injury (AKI).
Infect Dis, Medicine, Nephro
⊕ https://vfmat.ch/1926

Swiss Tropical and Public Health Institute
Contributes to the improvement of the health of populations internationally, nationally, and locally through excellence in research, education, and services.
Infect Dis, Pub Health
⊕ https://vfmat.ch/2ee4

Task Force for Global Health, The
Consists of programs and focus areas that cover a range of global health issues including neglected tropical diseases, infectious diseases, vaccines, field epidemiology, public health informatics, health workforce development, and global health ethics.
Infect Dis, Logist-Op, Medicine, Ophth-Opt, Peds
⊕ https://vfmat.ch/714c

Terre des hommes (Tdh) Foundation
Works to improve the daily life of children and their relatives in the areas of health, protection and emergency, in Europe, Africa, Asia, Latin America, and the Near and Middle East.
CT Surg, CV Med, OB-GYN, Ped Surg, Pub Health
⊕ https://vfmat.ch/5c26

Turing Foundation
Aims to contribute toward a better world and a better society by focusing on efforts such as health, art, education, and nature.
Infect Dis
⊕ https://vfmat.ch/6bcc

U.S. President's Malaria Initiative (PMI)
Supports low-income countries to help control and eliminate malaria through cost-effective, lifesaving malaria interventions.
Infect Dis, MF Med, OB-GYN
⊕ https://vfmat.ch/dc8b

Union for International Cancer Control (UICC)
Unites and supports the cancer community to reduce the global cancer burden, promote greater equity, and ensure that cancer control continues to be a priority in the world health and development agenda.
Heme-Onc, Pub Health
⊕ https://vfmat.ch/88b1

United Nations Children's Fund (UNICEF)
Works in over 190 countries and territories to save children's lives, defend their rights, and help them fulfill their potential, from early childhood through adolescence.
All-Immu, Infect Dis, MF Med, Neonat, Nutr, OB-GYN, Ped Surg, Peds, Pub Health
⊕ https://vfmat.ch/42d7

United Nations Development Programme (UNDP)
Helps countries achieve the simultaneous eradication of extreme poverty and significant reduction of inequalities and exclusion using a sustainable human development approach.

Infect Dis, Logist-Op, Pub Health
⊕ https://vfmat.ch/935c

Logist-Op
⊕ https://vfmat.ch/72dc

United Nations High Commissioner for Refugees (UNHCR)
Safeguards the rights and well-being of people who have been forced to flee, ensuring that everybody has the right to seek asylum and find safe refuge in another country, with the goal of seeking lasting solutions.
General, MF Med, Medicine, OB-GYN, Peds, Psych, Pub Health
⊕ https://vfmat.ch/6636

United Nations Population Fund (UNFPA)
Supports reproductive healthcare for women and youth in more than 150 countries, focusing on delivering a world in which every pregnancy is wanted, every childbirth is safe, and every young person's potential is fulfilled.
Infect Dis, MF Med, Neonat, OB-GYN, Peds, Pub Health
⊕ https://vfmat.ch/c969

United Surgeons for Children (USFC)
Pursues greater health and opportunity for children in the most neglected pockets of the world, with a specific focus on and expertise in surgery.
Anesth, CT Surg, Neonat, Neurosurg, OB-GYN, Peds, Radiol, Surg
⊕ https://vfmat.ch/3b4c

USAID: African Strategies for Health
Identifies and advocates for best practices, enhancing technical capacity of African regional institutions, and engaging African stakeholders to address health issues in a sustainable manner.
All-Immu, Infect Dis, OB-GYN, Peds
⊕ https://vfmat.ch/c272

USAID: Global Health Supply Chain Program
Combines 8 complementary projects working globally to achieve stronger, more resilient health supply chains.
Infect Dis, Logist-Op, Pub Health
⊕ https://vfmat.ch/115f

USAID: Health Finance and Governance Project
Uses research to implement strategies to help countries develop robust governance systems, increase their domestic resources for health, manage those resources more effectively, and make wise purchasing decisions.
Logist-Op
⊕ https://vfmat.ch/8652

USAID: Leadership, Management and Governance Project
Improves leadership, management, and governance practices to strengthen health systems and improve health for all, including vulnerable populations worldwide.
Logist-Op
⊕ https://vfmat.ch/d35e

World Blind Union (WBU)
Represents those experiencing blindness, speaking to governments and international bodies on issues concerning visual impairments.
Ophth-Opt
⊕ https://vfmat.ch/2bd3

World Federation of Hemophilia (WFH)
Aims to improve and sustain care for people with inherited bleeding disorders by pursuing long-term relationships with individuals and organizations who share the values of WFH's development model.
Heme-Onc
⊕ https://vfmat.ch/5121

World Health Organization, The (WHO)
The United Nations' agency for health provides leadership on global health matters, shapes the health research agenda, sets norms and standards, articulates evidence-based policy options, provides technical support and monitoring to countries, and assesses health trends.
ER Med, General, Infect Dis, Logist-Op, MF Med, OB-GYN, Peds, Psych, Pub Health
⊕ https://vfmat.ch/c476

World Medical Relief
Facilitates the distribution of surplus medical resources where they are needed.

 # Benin

Healthcare Facilities

Centre de Santé de Tika
RN 4, Adjohoun, Ouémé, Benin
⊕ https://vfmat.ch/acc9

Centre de Santé Oganla de Ketou
RNIE 4, Oke Ola, Plateau, Benin
⊕ https://vfmat.ch/f66c

Centre Hospitalier Départemental de Borgou-Alibori
Parakou, Benin
⊕ https://vfmat.ch/5921

Centre Hospitalier Départemental de Mono
RN 23, Possotomè, Mono, Benin
⊕ https://vfmat.ch/a728

Centre Hospitalier Départemental de Natitingou (CHD)
RNIE 3; RN 7, Natitingou, Atakora, Benin
⊕ https://vfmat.ch/832e

Centre Hospitalier Universitaire Départemental de l'Ouémé-Plateau
Rue l`Inspection, Porto-Novo, Benin
⊕ https://vfmat.ch/a4f4

CHD Centre Hospitalier du Zou
Hospital, RNIE 4, Abomey, Benin
⊕ https://vfmat.ch/e916

CNHU Centre National Hospitalier Universitaire
Littoral, Cotonou, Benin
⊕ https://vfmat.ch/c889

Enfant du Bénin
117 RNIE 1, Abomey-Calavi, Atlantique, Benin
⊕ https://vfmat.ch/3665

Hospital Area Bembérékè-Sinendé
Bembéréké, Benin
⊕ https://vfmat.ch/5dba

Hospital Dogbo
Dogbo, Benin
⊕ https://vfmat.ch/7c74

Hospital Malanville Karimama
Malanville, Benin
⊕ https://vfmat.ch/9d11

Hospital Zone de Kandi
RNIE 2, Kandi, Benin
⊕ https://vfmat.ch/e176

Hospital Zone de Tchaourou
Tchaourou, Benin
⊕ https://vfmat.ch/ee9a

HZ Allada
Allada, Benin
⊕ https://vfmat.ch/243c

HZ Saint-Jean de Dieu Parakou
Parakou, Benin
⊕ https://vfmat.ch/3691

Hôpital Ahmadiyya
Parakou, Benin
⊕ https://vfmat.ch/2bda

Hôpital Avlékété
Avlékété, Benin
⊕ https://vfmat.ch/b81c

Hôpital Bethesda
Avenue du Renouveau, Sainte Rita, Littoral, Benin
⊕ https://vfmat.ch/dc72

Hôpital Cent Lits
Boulevard de Comè, Akodéha Kpodji, Akodeha, Comé, Mono, Benin
⊕ https://vfmat.ch/1ead

Hôpital d'Instructions des Armées de Cotonou
Rue 238, Cotonou, Benin
⊕ https://vfmat.ch/1676

Hôpital de Grand-Popo
Grand-Popo, Benin
⊕ https://vfmat.ch/9d51

Hôpital de Karimama
Karimama, Benin
⊕ https://vfmat.ch/c4b2

Hôpital de l'Enfant et de la Mère Lagune
Rue des Dako Donou, Cotonou, Benin
⊕ https://vfmat.ch/e394

Hôpital de l'Ordre de Malte
RN 6, Djougou, Donga, Benin
⊕ https://vfmat.ch/ee77

Hôpital de la Zone Sanitaire Djidja-Abomey-Agbangnizoun
Djidja, Benin
⊕ https://vfmat.ch/fa92

Hôpital de Liboussou
RNIE 7, Liboussou, Alibori, Benin
⊕ https://vfmat.ch/c788

Hôpital de Menontin
Rue 9.224, Kindonou, Littoral, Benin
⊕ https://vfmat.ch/7568

Hôpital de Tchikandou
RNIE 6, Tchikandou, Borgou, Benin
⊕ https://vfmat.ch/34d9

Hôpital de Zone Ayélawadjè
2ème Arrondissement, Cotonou, Benin
⊕ https://vfmat.ch/7326

Hôpital de Zone Bassila
Rue 043, Bassila, Donga, Benin
🌐 https://vfmat.ch/2ecd

Hôpital de Zone Comè
Comè, Benin
🌐 https://vfmat.ch/d8cd

Hôpital de Zone d'Adjohoun
RN4, Akpro-Misserete, Benin
🌐 https://vfmat.ch/1e4f

Hôpital de Zone d'Èkpè
Ekpè, Ouémé, Benin
🌐 https://vfmat.ch/e66c

Hôpital de Zone de Aplahoué
RNIE 4, Aplahoué, Kouffo, Benin
🌐 https://vfmat.ch/6213

Hôpital de Zone de Banikouara
RN 8, Banikoara, Benin
🌐 https://vfmat.ch/c8df

Hôpital de Zone de Covè
RNIE 4, Flessa, Loko Alankpé, Zangnanado, Zou,
Benin
🌐 https://vfmat.ch/e4d6

Hôpital de Zone de Dassa-Zoumé
Dassa-Zoumé, Benin
🌐 https://vfmat.ch/29b8

Hôpital de Zone de Glazoué
Glazoué, Benin
🌐 https://vfmat.ch/49f7

Hôpital de Zone de Kouandé
Kouandé, Benin
🌐 https://vfmat.ch/566e

Hôpital de Zone de Lokossa
Colodo, Lokossa, Mono, Benin
🌐 https://vfmat.ch/1389

Hôpital de Zone de Natitingou
RNIE 3; RN 7, Natitingou, Atakora, Benin
🌐 https://vfmat.ch/4152

Hôpital de Zone de Ouidah
Ouidah, Benin
🌐 https://vfmat.ch/ca1c

Hôpital de Zone de Pobè
RN 3, Pobè, Plateau, Benin
🌐 https://vfmat.ch/e74c

Hôpital de Zone de Sakété
Sakété, Benin
🌐 https://vfmat.ch/9923

Hôpital de Zone de Savalou
Savalou, Benin
🌐 https://vfmat.ch/c8a2

Hôpital de Zone de Suru Lere
Rue 1647, Cotonou, Benin
🌐 https://vfmat.ch/5f13

Hôpital de Zone d'Abomey-Calavi
RNIE 2, Abomey-Calavi, Atlantique, Benin
🌐 https://vfmat.ch/f92f

Hôpital de Zone KTL
Ayahohoué, Benin
🌐 https://vfmat.ch/7988

Hôpital de Zone Savè
Savè, Benin
🌐 https://vfmat.ch/b94c

Hôpital Djougou
Djougou, Benin
🌐 https://vfmat.ch/8cc8

Hôpital du Militaire
RNIE 2, Parakou, Borgou, Benin
🌐 https://vfmat.ch/8cd2

Hôpital Evangélique de Bembéréké
Bembéréké, Benin
🌐 https://vfmat.ch/2393

Hôpital La Croix de Zinvié
RN 31, Zinvié, Atlantique, Benin
🌐 https://vfmat.ch/8339

Hôpital Padre Pio N'Dali
N'Dali, Benin
🌐 https://vfmat.ch/9b6f

Hôpital Saint Jean de Dieu Tanguiéta
RNIE 3, Tanguiéta, Atakora, Benin
🌐 https://vfmat.ch/9362

Hôpital Saint Luc de Cotonou
Cotonou, Benin
🌐 https://vfmat.ch/4c84

Hôpital Saint-Martin à Papané
Papané, Benin
🌐 https://vfmat.ch/893d

Hôpital Sainte Bakhita
Natitingou, Benin
🌐 https://vfmat.ch/ed13

Hôpital Sanitaire de N'Dali
RNIE 2, N'Dali, Borgou, Benin
🌐 https://vfmat.ch/4594

Hôpital Sunon Séro
RN 10, TÈPA, Borgou, Benin
🌐 https://vfmat.ch/edf1

Islamic Hospital
Porto-Novo, Benin
🌐 https://vfmat.ch/b9f8

Médecins d'Afrique
RN 3, Idenan, Kétou, Plateau, Benin
🌐 https://vfmat.ch/6fba

Nikki-Hospital
Nikki, Benin
🌐 https://vfmat.ch/ca69

SAM Hospital
Sam, Benin
🌐 https://vfmat.ch/8e62

● Healthcare Facility

Bhutan

The Kingdom of Bhutan, in the Himalayas of south-central Asia, is well known for its unique development philosophy. It measures Gross National Happiness (GNH), in which the progress of the country is guided by the well-being and happiness of its population. Bordered by China and India, Bhutan is also close to Nepal and Bangladesh. It holds a strategic location in the region, controlling several major mountain passes into the Himalayas. Ethnically, the population of 857,423 is 50 percent Ngalop; other groups include Nepali and Lhotshampas. Languages spoken include Dzongkha (the official language), Sharchokpa, and Lhotshamkha, as well as other foreign languages. The Bhutanese are predominantly Lamaistic Buddhist; there are also Indian and Nepali-influenced Hindus. As much as 43 percent of the population lives in urban areas, including about 200,000 in the capital of Thimphu.

Bhutan was historically a remote kingdom, isolated from the world by the vast mountains in which it is located. However, in the second half of the 20th century, the country became more connected to the global community. In the 1990s, Bhutan moved away from its status as an absolute monarchy, and in 2008 the country became a multiparty parliamentary democracy. Bhutan has since enjoyed economic stability and development, due in large part to its significant water resources and hydropower revenues. Overall, the country has made significant progress, reducing poverty from 36 percent of the population to 12 percent between 2007 and 2017. Bhutan's GDP has increased about 7.5 percent annually since the early 1980s, making it one of the fastest-growing economies in the world.

In addition to boosting economic development, Bhutan has improved many of its healthcare indicators. Average life expectancy increased from 60 years in 1990 to 72 years in 2019. Nonetheless, non-communicable diseases have increased over time as leading causes of death. These include ischemic heart disease, COPD, stroke, cirrhosis, diabetes, and chronic kidney disease. Communicable diseases also contribute to deaths in Bhutan, including lower respiratory infections, neonatal disorders, diarrheal diseases, and tuberculosis. The risk factors that contribute most to death and disability include malnutrition, air pollution, high blood pressure, dietary risks, high fasting plasma glucose, high body-mass index, tobacco use, occupational risks, high LDL levels, kidney dysfunction, and lack of sanitation and clean water.

0.86M

Population

$3,122

GDP Per Capita

72 years

Life Expectancy

↑ Improving

46
Doctors/100k

Physician Density

174
Beds/100k

Hospital Bed Density

183
Deaths/100k

Maternal Mortality

Bhutan

Nonprofit Organizations

Ability Bhutan Society
Provides direct interventions for the empowerment of individuals with diverse abilities to enhance the capabilities of people living with disabilities in Bhutan, and also develops core groups of trained social workers and caregivers to provide services.
Dent-OMFS, General, Pub Health
⊕ https://vfmat.ch/c67c

Americas Association for the Care of Children (AACC)
Reduces the impact of poverty in marginalized and underserved populations by empowering communities through compassionate and holistic education.
Dent-OMFS, MF Med, OB-GYN, Pub Health
⊕ https://vfmat.ch/19c5

Association of Medical Doctors of Asia (AMDA)
Strives to support people affected by disasters and economic distress on their road to recovery, establishing a true partnership with special emphasis on local initiative.
ER Med, Logist-Op, Pub Health
⊕ https://vfmat.ch/e3d4

Australian Himalayan Foundation
Works in partnership with people of the remote Himalaya to improve living standards through better education and training, improved health services, and environmental sustainability.
General, MF Med, OB-GYN, Peds
⊕ https://vfmat.ch/3428

Bhutan Kidney Foundation
Aims to reduce chronic kidney disease through education, prevention and treatment and to improve access to timely diagnosis in order to improve patients' quality of life.
Nephro, Pub Health
⊕ https://vfmat.ch/82c6

Firefly Mission
Organizes humanitarian missions to help people in less fortunate situations while serving as a vehicle for the spiritual development of members and the beneficiaries of its missions.
Logist-Op, Ophth-Opt, Pub Health
⊕ https://vfmat.ch/d215

Global Foundation For Children With Hearing Loss
Aims to help babies and young children who are deaf or hard of hearing and living in low- and middle-income countries by providing access to early identification, hearing technology, and locally based professional expertise.
Ortho, Peds, Plast
⊕ https://vfmat.ch/d1d1

Global Oncology (GO)
Brings the best in cancer care to underserved patients around the world and collaborates across geographic, professional, and academic borders to improve cancer care, research, and education.
Heme-Onc, Path, Rad-Onc
⊕ https://vfmat.ch/fcb8

Globus Relief
Aims to improve the delivery of healthcare worldwide by gathering, processing, and distributing surplus medical supplies to charities at home and abroad.
Logist-Op
⊕ https://vfmat.ch/a2b7

Health Volunteers Overseas (HVO)
Improves the availability and quality of healthcare through the education, training, and professional development of the health workforce in resource-scarce countries.
All-Immu, Anesth, CV Med, Dent-OMFS, Derm, ENT, ER Med, Endo, GI, Heme-Onc, Infect Dis, Medicine, Medicine, Nephro, Neuro, OB-GYN, Ophth-Opt, Ortho, Peds, Plast, Psych, Pulm-Critic, Rehab, Rheum, Surg
⊕ https://vfmat.ch/42b2

Helping Hands Health Education
Provides sustainable health and education services to children and adults throughout the world.
Dent-OMFS, General, Logist-Op, OB-GYN, Ophth-Opt, Peds
⊕ https://vfmat.ch/36da

Himalayan Cataract Project
Works to cure needless blindness with the highest quality care at the lowest cost.
Anesth, Ophth-Opt, Surg
⊕ https://vfmat.ch/3b3d

International Federation of Red Cross and Red Crescent Societies (IFRC)
Coordinates and directs international assistance following natural and manmade disasters in nonconflict situations through the world's largest humanitarian and development network. Provides disaster-preparedness programs, healthcare activities, and promotes humanitarian values.
ER Med, General, Infect Dis, Nutr
⊕ https://vfmat.ch/b4ee

International Pediatric Nephrology Association (IPNA)
Leads global efforts to successfully address the care for all children with kidney disease through advocacy, education, and training.
Medicine, Nephro, Peds
⊕ https://vfmat.ch/b59d

International Planned Parenthood Federation (IPPF)
Leads a locally owned, globally connected civil society movement that provides and enables services and champions sexual and reproductive health and rights for all, especially the underserved.
Infect Dis, MF Med, OB-GYN
🌐 https://vfmat.ch/dc97

Joint United Nations Programme on HIV/AIDS (UNAIDS)
Aims to place people living with HIV and people affected by the virus at the decision-making table and at the center of designing, delivering, and monitoring the AIDS response.
Infect Dis
🌐 https://vfmat.ch/464a

Kids Care Everywhere
Seeks to empower physicians in under-resourced environments with multimedia, state-of-the-art medical software, and to inspire young professionals to become future global healthcare leaders.
Logist-Op, Ped Surg, Peds
🌐 https://vfmat.ch/bc23

MAP International
Provides medicines and health supplies to those in need around the world so they might experience life to the fullest.
Logist-Op
🌐 https://vfmat.ch/deed

MedShare
Aims to improve the quality of life of people, communities, and the planet by sourcing and directly delivering surplus medical supplies and equipment to communities in need around the world.
Logist-Op
🌐 https://vfmat.ch/c8bc

Mission Regan
Collects supplies, medication, and medical equipment and provides them to those who are in desperate need, both locally and globally.
Logist-Op
🌐 https://vfmat.ch/2bc1

RAD-AID International
Improves and optimizes access to medical imaging and radiology in low-resource regions of the world.
Rad-Onc, Radiol
🌐 https://vfmat.ch/537f

RENEW
Enables survivors of gender-based violence to be financially and emotionally independent; expands partnerships to ensure effective delivery of services.
General, Logist-Op, OB-GYN
🌐 https://vfmat.ch/eb2d

RestoringVision
Empowers lives by restoring vision for millions of people in need.
Ophth-Opt
🌐 https://vfmat.ch/e121

ReSurge International
Provides reconstructive surgical care and builds surgical capacity in developing countries.
Anesth, Dent-OMFS, Ped Surg, Plast, Surg
🌐 https://vfmat.ch/9937

Rotary International
Provides service to others, improves lives, and advances world understanding, goodwill, and peace through its fellowship of business, professional, and community leaders.
ER Med, General, Infect Dis, MF Med, OB-GYN
🌐 https://vfmat.ch/8fb5

Save the Children
Gives children around the world a healthy start in life, the opportunity to learn, and protection from harm.

All-Immu, Crit-Care, ER Med, General, Infect Dis, MF Med, Medicine, Neonat, OB-GYN, Peds, Psych, Pub Health
🌐 https://vfmat.ch/2e73

SEVA
Delivers vital eye care services to the world's most vulnerable, including women, children, and Indigenous peoples.
Ophth-Opt, Surg
🌐 https://vfmat.ch/1e87

Sight for All
Empowers communities to deliver comprehensive, evidence-based, high-quality eye healthcare through the provision of research, education, and equipment.
Logist-Op, Ophth-Opt, Surg
🌐 https://vfmat.ch/e34b

SIGN Fracture Care International
Builds orthopedic capacity around the world and provides the injured poor access to fracture surgery by donating orthopedic education and implant systems to surgeons in developing countries.
Ortho, Rehab, Surg
🌐 https://vfmat.ch/123d

Smile Asia
Delivers free surgical care, through medical missions and outreach centers, to children with facial deformities such as cleft lip and cleft palate, and aims to raise standards of medical care by creating opportunities for collaborative learning and exchange of best practices.
Anesth, Dent-OMFS, Ped Surg, Peds, Plast
🌐 https://vfmat.ch/d674

SoundMind Project, The
Creates innovative solutions to pressing healthcare needs in the areas of neuroscience and mental health, by harnessing the knowledge and cultural assets of communities worldwide toward improving understanding of the mind.
Genetics, Neuro, Psych, Rehab
🌐 https://vfmat.ch/21a5

Sri Sathya Sai International Organization
Inspired by spiritual teachings, carries out efforts in global healthcare, education, humanitarian relief, and youth engagement.
Dent-OMFS, General, Logist-Op, Nutr, Ophth-Opt, Pub Health
🌐 https://vfmat.ch/9bda

Swasti
Aims to transform the lives of marginalized communities by ensuring their access to quality healthcare and thereby contributing to poverty alleviation.
Pub Health
🌐 https://vfmat.ch/be8b

Task Force for Global Health, The
Consists of programs and focus areas that cover a range of global health issues including neglected tropical diseases, infectious diseases, vaccines, field epidemiology, public health informatics, health workforce development, and global health ethics.
Infect Dis, Logist-Op, Medicine, Ophth-Opt, Peds
🌐 https://vfmat.ch/714c

Tilganga Institute of Ophthalmology (TIO)
Supports the prevention and control of blindness in Nepal and the region.
Ophth-Opt
🌐 https://vfmat.ch/ff5d

Union for International Cancer Control (UICC)
Unites and supports the cancer community to reduce the global cancer burden, promote greater equity, and ensure that cancer control continues to be a priority in the world health and development agenda.
Heme-Onc, Pub Health
🌐 https://vfmat.ch/88b1

United Nations Children's Fund (UNICEF)
Works in over 190 countries and territories to save children's lives, defend their rights, and help them fulfill their potential, from early childhood

through adolescence.

All-Immu, Infect Dis, MF Med, Neonat, Nutr, OB-GYN, Ped Surg, Peds, Pub Health

⊕ https://vfmat.ch/42d7

United Nations Development Programme (UNDP)
Helps countries achieve the simultaneous eradication of extreme poverty and significant reduction of inequalities and exclusion using a sustainable human development approach.

Infect Dis, Logist-Op, Pub Health

⊕ https://vfmat.ch/935c

United Nations High Commissioner for Refugees (UNHCR)
Safeguards the rights and well-being of people who have been forced to flee, ensuring that everybody has the right to seek asylum and find safe refuge in another country, with the goal of seeking lasting solutions.

General, MF Med, Medicine, OB-GYN, Peds, Psych, Pub Health

⊕ https://vfmat.ch/6636

United Nations Population Fund (UNFPA)
Supports reproductive healthcare for women and youth in more than 150 countries, focusing on delivering a world in which every pregnancy is wanted, every childbirth is safe, and every young person's potential is fulfilled.

Infect Dis, MF Med, Neonat, OB-GYN, Peds, Pub Health

⊕ https://vfmat.ch/c969

USAID: Leadership, Management and Governance Project
Improves leadership, management, and governance practices to strengthen health systems and improve health for all, including vulnerable populations worldwide.

Logist-Op

⊕ https://vfmat.ch/d35e

World Health Organization, The (WHO)
The United Nations' agency for health provides leadership on global health matters, shapes the health research agenda, sets norms and standards, articulates evidence-based policy options, provides technical support and monitoring to countries, and assesses health trends.

ER Med, General, Infect Dis, Logist-Op, MF Med, OB-GYN, Peds, Psych, Pub Health

⊕ https://vfmat.ch/c476

Bhutan

Healthcare Facilities

Central Regional Referral Hospital, Gelephu
Gelephu, Geylegphug, Bhutan
⊕ https://vfmat.ch/327a

Dagapela Hospital
Dagana, Bhutan
⊕ https://vfmat.ch/jfap

Dzongkhag Hospital
Paro Populated3, Paro, Bhutan
⊕ https://vfmat.ch/3289

Imtrat Hospital
Thimphu, Thimphu, Bhutan
⊕ https://vfmat.ch/cbd6

Jigme Dorji Wangchuck National Referral Hospital
Tashi Chho Dzong, Thimphu, Bhutan
⊕ https://vfmat.ch/76f8

Menjong Diagnostic Centre Private Limited
Thimphu, Bhutan
⊕ https://vfmat.ch/txxi

Paro District Hospital
Paro, Bhutan
https://vfmat.ch/xz28

Phuntsholing Hospital
Phuentsholing, Chukha, Bhutan
⊕ https://vfmat.ch/41ef

Royal Bhutan Army Hospital
Thimphu, Bhutan
https://vfmat.ch/cyel

Samdrup Jongkhar General Hospital
Darranga, Assam, Bhutan
⊕ https://vfmat.ch/2cde

Sarpang Hospital
Saralpāra, Assam, Bhutan
⊕ https://vfmat.ch/236f

Wangdicholing Hospital
Wangchukling, Bhutan
⊕ https://vfmat.ch/gbeh

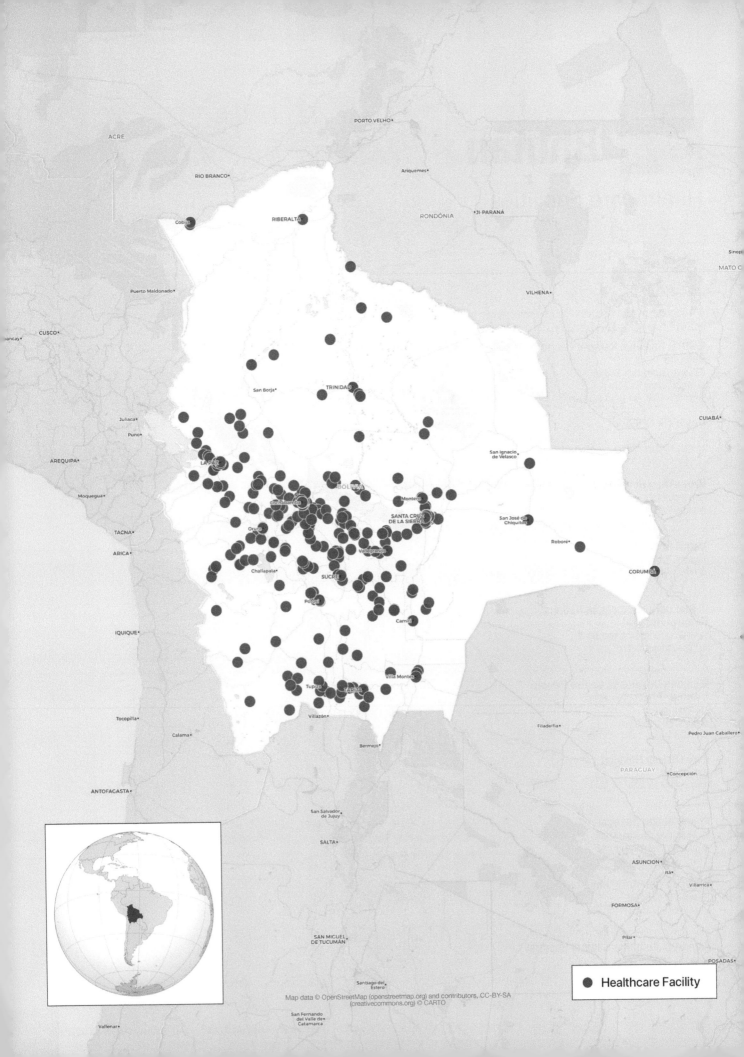

Healthcare Facility

Bolivia

The Plurinational State of Bolivia, in South America, is landlocked by its neighbors Brazil, Paraguay, Argentina, Chile, and Peru. About one-third of Bolivia's area is located within the Andean Mountains. Bolivia's 11.8 million people are distributed around the country, with a high-altitude plain in the west the most densely populated. Other population hubs include the city of Santa Cruz and the capital, La Paz. The Bolivian population is ethnically diverse, with a majority being Mestizo. There are several languages that are considered the official language of Bolivia, including Spanish, Quechua, Aymara, and Guarani. At least 36 other indigenous languages are spoken throughout the country. Almost 80 percent of the population identifies as Roman Catholic, with smaller proportions of evangelicals and Pentecostals, as well as Protestants. Lake Titicaca, the lake with the highest elevation above sea level (12,507 feet), is located there, as is the world's largest salt flat, which contains 50 percent to 70 percent of the world's lithium.

A former colony of Spain, Bolivia gained independence in 1825 after a 16-year war. Modern-day Bolivia has significantly decreased poverty rates; however, it is still considered the second poorest country in South America. Education is low quality, and access to educational opportunities is unevenly distributed among the rural and indigenous populations. Bolivia is rich in natural resources and mineral deposits, such as petroleum, natural gas, tin, silver, lithium, and copper. Other economic sectors include agriculture, forestry, fishing, and manufacturing.

In addition to a high rate of poverty, Bolivia also ranks poorly in health metrics. The risk of major infectious diseases is considered high, with high incidence rates of bacterial diarrhea, hepatitis A, dengue fever, and malaria. Leading causes of death in Bolivia include ischemic heart disease, lower respiratory infections, stroke, chronic kidney disease, neonatal disorders, diabetes, cirrhosis, stomach cancer, COPD, road injuries, congenital defects, and tuberculosis. The risk factors that contribute most to death and disability include malnutrition, high body-mass index, high fasting plasma glucose, air pollution, high blood pressure, dietary risks, kidney dysfunction, alcohol and tobacco use, high LDL, and a lack of water, sanitation, and hygiene.

11.8M

Population

$3,143

GDP Per Capita

72 years

Life Expectancy

↑ Improving

103
Doctors/100k

Physician Density

129
Beds/100k

Hospital Bed Density

155
Deaths/100k

Maternal Mortality

Bolivia

Nonprofit Organizations

A Broader View Volunteers
Provides developing countries around the world with significant volunteer programs that aid the neediest communities and forge a lasting bond between those volunteering and those they have helped.
Dent-OMFS, ER Med, Infect Dis, MF Med
🌐 https://vfmat.ch/3bec

Americares
Saves lives and improves health for people affected by poverty or disaster and responds with life-changing medicine, medical supplies, and health programs including domestic and global medical clinics.
All-Immu, ER Med, General, Infect Dis, MF Med, Nutr
🌐 https://vfmat.ch/e567

Anba Abraam Charity
Aims to improve the lives of underprivileged and vulnerable people with a focus on funding healthcare and surgical programs, programs for the physically and mentally disabled, and support for people without speech, inspired by the Christian faith.
Dent-OMFS, Logist-Op, Nutr, Rehab
🌐 https://vfmat.ch/b62d

Andean Medical Mission
Aims to provide high-quality eye care, advice and treatment through surgical trips to Bolivia's rural areas.
Logist-Op, Ophth-Opt
🌐 https://vfmat.ch/3ef2

Association of Medical Doctors of Asia (AMDA)
Strives to support people affected by disasters and economic distress on their road to recovery, establishing a true partnership with special emphasis on local initiative.
ER Med, Logist-Op, Pub Health
🌐 https://vfmat.ch/e3d4

Bridge of Life
Aims to strengthen healthcare globally through sustainable programs that prevent and treat chronic disease.
Logist-Op, Nephro, OB-GYN, Peds, Surg
🌐 https://vfmat.ch/5b68

Buddhist Tzu Chi Medical Foundation
Provides healthcare to the poor, operates six hospitals in Taiwan and mobile medical and dental clinics in the U.S., manages a bone marrow bank, and organizes over 8,600 physicians who provide free medical services to more than 2 million people globally.
Crit-Care, Dent-OMFS, ER Med, General
🌐 https://vfmat.ch/ff61

Burn Care International
Seeks to improve the lives of burn survivors around the world through effective rehabilitation.
Derm, Nutr, Psych, Surg
🌐 https://vfmat.ch/78d1

Canadian Dental Relief International
Provides free dental services to marginalized people and trains local health workers to provide dental care for their communities.
Dent-OMFS
🌐 https://vfmat.ch/3c64

Canadian Reconstructive Surgery Foundation, The
Develops, organizes, and manages, in participation with developing countries, the delivery of reconstructive medical-care programs, technologies, and education to those who cannot otherwise obtain the care they need.
Anesth, Dent-OMFS, Plast
🌐 https://vfmat.ch/15f4

CARE
Works around the globe to save lives, defeat poverty, and achieve social justice.
ER Med, General
🌐 https://vfmat.ch/7232

Carter Center, The
Seeks to prevent and resolve conflicts, enhance freedom and democracy, and improve health, while remaining committed to human rights and the alleviation of human suffering.
Infect Dis, MF Med, Ophth-Opt
🌐 https://vfmat.ch/6556

Centro Medico Susan Hou
Seeks to improve the health and quality of life of communities surrounding its medical clinic in Bolivia by providing continuous, free healthcare.
Dent-OMFS, General, Ophth-Opt
🌐 https://vfmat.ch/d741

Chain of Hope
Provides lifesaving heart operations for children around the world and supports the development of cardiac services in numerous developing and war-torn countries.
Anesth, CT Surg, CV Med, Crit-Care, Ped Surg, Peds, Pulm-Critic, Surg
🌐 https://vfmat.ch/1b1b

CharityVision International
Focuses on restoring curable sight impairment worldwide by empowering local physicians and creating sustainable solutions.
Logist-Op, Ophth-Opt, Surg
🌐 https://vfmat.ch/6231

Child Family Health International (CFHI)
Connects students with local health professionals and community leaders transforming perspectives about self, global health, and healing.
General, Infect Dis, OB-GYN, Ophth-Opt, Palliative, Peds
⊕ https://vfmat.ch/729e

ChildFund Australia
Works to reduce poverty for children in many of the world's most disadvantaged communities.
ER Med, General, Peds
⊕ https://vfmat.ch/13df

Children Without Worms
Enhances the health and development of children by reducing intestinal worm infections.
Infect Dis, Pub Health
⊕ https://vfmat.ch/6bee

Christian Aid Ministries
Strives to be a trustworthy and efficient channel for Amish, Mennonite, and other conservative Anabaptist groups and individuals to minister to physical and spiritual needs around the world.
CT Surg, ER Med, Logist-Op, Ortho, Pub Health
⊕ https://vfmat.ch/7b33

Christian Blind Mission (CBM)
Aims to improve the quality of life of persons with disabilities in the poorest countries, addressing poverty as a cause and a consequence of disability, and working in partnership to create a society for all.
ENT, General, Infect Dis, OB-GYN, Ophth-Opt, Ortho, Peds, Psych, Rehab, Surg
⊕ https://vfmat.ch/3824

Christian Medical & Dental Associations
Based in Christian ministry, deploys medical and dental teams to underserved communities to provide vital healthcare.
Anesth, Dent-OMFS, ER Med, General, Medicine, OB-GYN, Ophth-Opt, Peds, Pub Health, Radiol, Rehab, Surg
⊕ https://vfmat.ch/921c

Columbia University: Global Mental Health Programs
Pioneers research initiatives, promotes mental health, and aims to reduce the burden of mental illness worldwide.
Psych
⊕ https://vfmat.ch/c5cd

Core Group
Aims to improve and expand community health practices for underserved populations, especially women and children, through collaborative action and learning.
General, Infect Dis, MF Med, Medicine, OB-GYN, Peds, Pub Health
⊕ https://vfmat.ch/9de3

COVID-19 Clinical Research Coalition
Advocates and collaborates for the advancement of COVID-19 research driven by the needs of low-resource settings, and works for equitable access to solutions to the pandemic.
All-Immu, Infect-Dis, MF Med, Path, Pub Health
⊕ https://vfmat.ch/d1f4

Cross Catholic Outreach
Mobilizes the global Catholic Church to transform impoverished communities through the provision of food, water, housing, education, orphan support, medical care, microenterprise, and disaster relief.
All-Immu, General, Nutr, OB-GYN, Rehab
⊕ https://vfmat.ch/22f4

Curamericas Global
Partners with communities abroad to save the lives of mothers and children by providing health services and education.
General, Infect Dis, MF Med, OB-GYN, Peds, Pub Health
⊕ https://vfmat.ch/286b

Direct Relief
Improves the health and lives of people affected by poverty or emergency situations by mobilizing and providing essential medical resources needed for their care.
ER Med, Logist-Op
⊕ https://vfmat.ch/58e5

Doctors on Mission
Provides sustainable medical healthcare to needy countries, including those having experienced recent disasters and areas where minority groups are persecuted.
General, Logist-Op, Medicine, Nutr
⊕ https://vfmat.ch/5244

Drugs for Neglected Diseases Initiative
Develops lifesaving medicines for people with neglected diseases around the world, having developed eight treatments for five deadly diseases and saved millions of lives since 2003.
Infect Dis, Pub Health
⊕ https://vfmat.ch/969c

Duke University: Global Health Institute
Sparks innovation in global health research and education, and brings together knowledge and resources to address the most important global health issues of our time.
All-Immu, Infect Dis, MF Med, OB-GYN, Pub Health
⊕ https://vfmat.ch/c4cd

Emergency Response Team Search And Rescue, The (ERTSAR)
Provides technical rescue and medical response in the immediate aftermath of a disaster while providing strategic, smart, and sustainable solutions.
ER Med, Logist-Op
⊕ https://vfmat.ch/c599

Emory University School of Medicine: Global Surgery Program
A leading institution with the highest standards in education, biomedical research, and patient care.
Anesth, Dent-OMFS, ER Med, Pub Health, Surg, Urol
⊕ https://vfmat.ch/2b26

Esperança
Works to improve health and provide hope through disease prevention, education, and medical/surgical treatment.
Anesth, Dent-OMFS, ENT, General, Neurosurg, Nutr, OB-GYN, Ophth-Opt, Ortho, Ped Surg, Peds, Plast, Pub Health, Surg, Urol, Vasc Surg
⊕ https://vfmat.ch/5cf3

Foundation for Healthcare for Humanity
Provide assistance in the development and implementation of medical programs in the United States, Africa, South America, Eastern Europe, and the Caribbean.
General
⊕ https://vfmat.ch/ba7f

Fundación Totaí
Seeks to provide free or affordable services in the areas of health, sport, education, and community aid, inspired by the Christian faith.
Dent-OMFS, ENT, General, Peds
⊕ https://vfmat.ch/dc5a

Gift of Life International
Provides lifesaving cardiac treatment to children in developing countries while developing sustainable pediatric cardiac programs by implementing screening, surgical, and training missions.
Anesth, CT Surg, CV Med, Crit-Care, Ped Surg, Peds, Pulm-Critic
⊕ https://vfmat.ch/f2f9

Global ENT Outreach
Saves lives and prevents avoidable deafness from ear disease for those affected by poverty and lack of care so they can reach their full human potential.
ENT, Surg
⊕ https://vfmat.ch/ef5c

Global Legacy

Supports and initiates projects with a high impact on health, education, and the advancement of women in rural communities.

Ophth-Opt

⊕ https://vfmat.ch/ff92

Global Ministries – The United Methodist Church

As the worldwide mission and development agency of The United Methodist Church, Global Ministries works with more than 300 hospitals and clinics around the world through its Global Health Unit.

Anesth, CT Surg, CV Med, Crit-Care, Dent-OMFS, Derm, ER Med, GI, General, Infect Dis, Logist-Op, MF Med, Medicine, Neonat, Nephro, Nutr, OB-GYN, Ophth-Opt, Ortho, Palliative, Peds, Pod, Psych, Pub Health, Rehab, Rheum, Surg, Urol

⊕ https://vfmat.ch/1723

Global Oncology (GO)

Brings the best in cancer care to underserved patients around the world and collaborates across geographic, professional, and academic borders to improve cancer care, research, and education.

Heme-Onc, Path, Rad-Onc

⊕ https://vfmat.ch/fcb8

Globus Relief

Aims to improve the delivery of healthcare worldwide by gathering, processing, and distributing surplus medical supplies to charities at home and abroad.

Logist-Op

⊕ https://vfmat.ch/a2b7

Good Shepard International Foundation

Strives to promote inclusive and sustainable development for the most marginalized and vulnerable people, with a special focus on women, girls, and children, inspired by the Christian faith.

ER Med

⊕ https://vfmat.ch/ad9a

Hancock County Medical Mission

Serves as an information, coordination, and funding agency for medical missions that provide medical, surgical, and nursing services.

Anesth, General, Logist-Op, Medicine, Surg

⊕ https://vfmat.ch/8313

Healing Hands Foundation, The

Provides high-quality surgical procedures, medical treatment, dental care, and educational support in under-resourced areas worldwide.

Anesth, Dent-OMFS, General, Ped Surg, Peds, Surg

⊕ https://vfmat.ch/4bfc

Healing the Children

Helps underserved children around the world secure the medical care they need to lead more fulfilling lives.

Anesth, Dent-OMFS, ENT, General, Medicine, Ophth-Opt, Ped Surg, Peds, Plast, Surg

⊕ https://vfmat.ch/d4ee

Health Equity Initiative

Aims to build and sustain a global community that engages across sectors and disciplines to advance health equity.

Pub Health

⊕ https://vfmat.ch/e2e2

Health Volunteers Overseas (HVO)

Improves the availability and quality of healthcare through the education, training, and professional development of the health workforce in resource-scarce countries.

All-Immu, Anesth, CV Med, Dent-OMFS, Derm, ENT, ER Med, Endo, GI, Heme-Onc, Infect Dis, Medicine, Medicine, Nephro, Neuro, OB-GYN, Ophth-Opt, Ortho, Peds, Plast, Psych, Pulm-Critic, Rehab, Rheum, Surg

⊕ https://vfmat.ch/42b2

Heineman Medical Outreach

Provides medical and educational assistance globally to promote sustainable healthcare and enhanced living standards in underserved communities through the International Medical Outreach (IMO) program, a collaborative partnership between Heineman Medical Outreach and Atrium Health.

Anesth, CT Surg, CV Med, ER Med, General, Heme-Onc, Logist-Op, Medicine, Neonat, OB-GYN, Ped Surg, Peds, Surg, Vasc Surg

⊕ https://vfmat.ch/389b

HelpAge International

Works to ensure that people everywhere understand how much older people contribute to society and that they must enjoy their right to healthcare, social services, economic, and physical security.

General, Geri, Infect Dis, Medicine, Pub Health

⊕ https://vfmat.ch/5d91

Hope Worldwide

Changes lives through the compassion and commitment of dedicated staff and volunteers delivering sustainable, high-impact, community-based services to the poor and underserved.

Dent-OMFS, General, OB-GYN, Ophth-Opt, Peds

⊕ https://vfmat.ch/89b3

House of Hope International

Inspired by the Christian faith, provides rehabilitation for women and children leaving the world of prostitution and human trafficking and helps integrate them into society.

Dent-OMFS, General, OB-GYN

⊕ https://vfmat.ch/2dbb

Humanity & Inclusion

Works alongside people with disabilities and vulnerable populations, taking action and bearing witness in order to respond to their essential needs, improve their living conditions and health, and promote respect for their dignity and fundamental rights.

General, Infect Dis, MF Med, Medicine, Ortho, Peds, Psych, Pub Health, Rehab

⊕ https://vfmat.ch/16b7

International Campaign for Women's Right to Safe Abortion

Works to build an international network and campaign that brings together organizations with an interest in promoting and providing safe abortion to create a shared platform for advocacy, debate, and dialogue and the sharing of skills and experience.

OB-GYN, Pub Health, Surg

⊕ https://vfmat.ch/f341

International Children's Heart Foundation

Provides free surgical care, medical training, and technology to save the lives of children with congenital heart disease in developing countries.

Anesth, CT Surg, CV Med, Crit-Care, Ped Surg, Peds, Pulm-Critic

⊕ https://vfmat.ch/86c1

International Council of Ophthalmology

Works with ophthalmologic societies and others to enhance ophthalmic education and improve access to the highest-quality eye care in order to preserve and restore vision for people of the world.

Ophth-Opt

⊕ https://vfmat.ch/ffd2

International Federation of Gynecology and Obstetrics (FIGO)

Implements global projects on specific women's health issues.

MF Med, Medicine, Neonat, OB-GYN, Surg, Urol

⊕ https://vfmat.ch/c4b4

International Federation of Red Cross and Red Crescent Societies (IFRC)

Coordinates and directs international assistance following natural and manmade disasters in nonconflict situations through the world's largest humanitarian and development network. Provides disaster-preparedness programs, healthcare activities, and promotes humanitarian values.

ER Med, General, Infect Dis, Nutr

⊕ https://vfmat.ch/b4ee

International Medical Relief

Provides sustainable education, training, medical and dental care, and disaster relief and response in vulnerable communities worldwide.

Dent-OMFS, General, Infect Dis, Medicine, OB-GYN
⊕ https://vfmat.ch/b3ed

International Organization for Migration (IOM) – The UN Migration Agency
Promotes evidence-informed policies and holistic, preventive, and curative health programs that are beneficial, accessible, and equitable for vulnerable migrants.
General, Infect Dis, OB-GYN
⊕ https://vfmat.ch/621a

International Planned Parenthood Federation (IPPF)
Leads a locally owned, globally connected civil society movement that provides and enables services and champions sexual and reproductive health and rights for all, especially the underserved.
Infect Dis, MF Med, OB-GYN
⊕ https://vfmat.ch/dc97

International Smile Power
Partners with people to improve and sustain dental health and build bridges of friendship around the world.
Dent-OMFS
⊕ https://vfmat.ch/ba69

International Society of Nephrology
Aims to advance worldwide kidney health.
Nephro
⊕ https://vfmat.ch/1bae

Ipas
Focuses efforts on women and girls who want contraception or abortion, and builds programs around their needs and how best to support them.
OB-GYN
⊕ https://vfmat.ch/8e39

Iris Global
Serves the poor, the destitute, the lost, and the forgotten by providing adoration, outreach, family, education, relief, development, healing, and the arts.
General, Infect Dis, Nutr, Pub Health
⊕ https://vfmat.ch/37f8

iSight Missions
To empower local eye care providers to establish self-supporting eye clinics to offer permanent care to impoverished persons.
Ophth-Opt
⊕ https://vfmat.ch/9739

Izumi Foundation
Develops and supports programs that improve health and healthcare in neglected regions of Africa and Latin America.
⊕ https://vfmat.ch/f29a

Joint United Nations Programme on HIV/AIDS (UNAIDS)
Aims to place people living with HIV and people affected by the virus at the decision-making table and at the center of designing, delivering, and monitoring the AIDS response.
Infect Dis
⊕ https://vfmat.ch/464a

Kaya Responsible Travel
Promotes sustainable social, environmental, and economic development, empowers communities, and cultivates educated, compassionate global citizens through responsible travel.
All-Immu, Crit-Care, Dent-OMFS, ER Med, General, Geri, Infect Dis, MF Med, Medicine, Nutr, OB-GYN, Peds, Psych, Pub Health, Rehab
⊕ https://vfmat.ch/b2cf

Kybele Incorporated
Aims to create healthcare partnerships across borders to improve childbirth safety.
Anesth, Neonat, OB-GYN, Pub Health
⊕ https://vfmat.ch/5fc9

Light for the World
Contributes to a world in which persons with disabilities fully exercise their rights, and assists persons with disabilities living in poverty.
Ophth-Opt, Rehab
⊕ https://vfmat.ch/3ff6

Limbs International
Engages communities and transforms lives through affordable, sustainable prosthetic solutions and rehabilitation services in developing countries.
Logist-Op, Ortho, Pod, Rehab
⊕ https://vfmat.ch/dc84

Maestro Cares Foundation
Aims to provide the highest living conditions for vulnerable children through educational programs, housing and nutritional programs.
Logist-Op, Nutr
⊕ https://vfmat.ch/4de6

Management Sciences for Health (MSH)
Works with countries and communities to save lives and improve the health of the world's poorest and most vulnerable people by building strong, resilient, sustainable health systems.
Infect Dis, Logist-Op, Pub Health
⊕ https://vfmat.ch/6aa2

MAP International
Provides medicines and health supplies to those in need around the world so they might experience life to the fullest.
Logist-Op
⊕ https://vfmat.ch/deed

Marie Stopes International
Provides the contraception and safe abortion services that enable women all over the world to choose their own futures.
Infect Dis, MF Med, Neonat, OB-GYN, Pub Health
⊕ https://vfmat.ch/9525

Maryknoll Lay Missioners
Based in Christian ministry, aims to collaborate with poor communities in Africa, Asia, and the Americas in order to respond to basic needs, including heathcare, and to help create a more compassionate world.
Logist-Op, Nutr
⊕ https://vfmat.ch/2ce6

Massachusetts General Hospital Global Surgery Initiative
Aims to improve surgical education and access to advanced surgical care in resource-limited settings around the world by performing surgical operations as visitors, training local surgeons, and sharing medical technology through international partnerships across disciplines.
Anesth, Crit-Care, ER Med, Heme-Onc, Peds, Surg
⊕ https://vfmat.ch/31b1

Medical Care Development International
Works to improve the health of vulnerable populations through integrated, sustainable, and locally driven interventions.
Infect Dis, OB-GYN, Peds, Pub Health
⊕ https://vfmat.ch/da87

Medical Ministry International
Provides compassionate healthcare in areas of need, inspired by the Christian faith.
CT Surg, Dent-OMFS, ENT, General, OB-GYN, Ophth-Opt, Ortho, Plast, Rehab, Surg, Urol, Vasc Surg
⊕ https://vfmat.ch/5da6

Medicus Mundi Italia
Carries out programs in basic community health, health education, maternal and child health, nutrition, and infectious disease.
General, Infect Dis, Logist-Op, MF Med, Nutr, Peds, Pub Health, Rehab
⊕ https://vfmat.ch/4413

MedSend
Funds qualified healthcare professionals to serve the physical and spiritual needs

of people around the world, enabling healthcare providers to work where they have been called.

General

🌐 https://vfmat.ch/661c

MedShare

Aims to improve the quality of life of people, communities, and the planet by sourcing and directly delivering surplus medical supplies and equipment to communities in need around the world.

Logist-Op

🌐 https://vfmat.ch/c8bc

Mending Kids

Provides free, lifesaving surgical care to sick children worldwide by deploying volunteer medical teams and teaching communities to become medically self-sustaining through the education of local medical staff.

Anesth, CT Surg, ENT, Ortho, Ortho, Ped Surg, Plast, Surg

🌐 https://vfmat.ch/4d61

Mercy Ships

Operates hospital ships staffed by volunteers to bring hope, healing, and healthcare to underserved communities worldwide.

Anesth, Dent-OMFS, Logist-Op, Neonat, OB-GYN, Ophth-Opt, Ortho, Palliative, Plast, Psych, Surg

🌐 https://vfmat.ch/2e99

MiracleFeet

Brings low-cost treatment to every child on the planet born with clubfoot, a leading cause of physical disability.

Ortho, Peds, Rehab

🌐 https://vfmat.ch/bda8

Mission Bambini

Helps to support children living in poverty and sickness, and lacking education, giving them the opportunity for and hope of a better life.

CT Surg, CV Med, Crit-Care, ER Med, Ped Surg, Peds

🌐 https://vfmat.ch/dc1a

Mission Regan

Collects supplies, medication, and medical equipment and provides them to those who are in desperate need, both locally and globally.

Logist-Op

🌐 https://vfmat.ch/2bc1

MSI Reproductive Choices (Marie Stopes International)

Seeks to deliver quality family planning and reproductive healthcare to women around the world.

MF Med

🌐 https://vfmat.ch/5c82

Médecins du Monde/Doctors of the World

Provides care, bears witness, and supports social change worldwide with innovative medical programs and evidence-based advocacy initiatives.

ER Med, General, Infect Dis, MF Med, Neonat, OB-GYN, Peds, Pub Health

🌐 https://vfmat.ch/a43d

Northwestern University Feinberg School of Medicine: Institute for Global Health

Aims to improve access to essential surgical care by addressing the barriers to care, with multidisciplinary and bidirectional partnerships, through innovation, research, education, policy, and advocacy. Goals also include training of the next generation of global health leaders, and building sustainable capacity in regions with health inequities.

Anesth, ER Med, Heme-Onc, Logist-Op, MF Med, OB-GYN, Ped Surg, Surg

🌐 https://vfmat.ch/24f3

Norwegian People's Aid

Aims to improve living conditions, to create a democratic, just, and safe society.

ER Med, Logist-Op

🌐 https://vfmat.ch/2d8e

Nuestros Pequeños Hermanos (NPH)

Strives to create a loving and safe family environment for vulnerable children

living in extreme conditions.

Psych, Rehab

🌐 https://vfmat.ch/57c4

Nuestros Pequeños Hermanos (Our Little Brothers and Sisters) New Zealand

Helps vulnerable children and families break the cycle of poverty with assistance through its pediatric hospital, healthcare clinics, day care centers, and scholarship programs.

CT Surg, Heme-Onc, Infect Dis, Nutr, OB-GYN, Peds, Rehab

🌐 https://vfmat.ch/e9cc

Open Heart International

Provides surgical interventions and best practices to the most disadvantaged communities on the planet.

CT Surg, MF Med, OB-GYN, Ophth-Opt, Plast, Surg

🌐 https://vfmat.ch/dab2

Operation Smile

Treats patients with cleft lip and cleft palate, and creates solutions that deliver safe surgery to people where it's needed most.

Anesth, Dent-OMFS, ENT, Ped Surg, Plast

🌐 https://vfmat.ch/5c29

Orbis International

Works to prevent and treat blindness through hands-on training and improved access to quality eye care.

Anesth, Ophth-Opt, Surg

🌐 https://vfmat.ch/f2b2

Order of Malta

Supports forgotten or excluded people, especially those living in conflict zones or amid natural disasters, by providing medical assistance, caring for refugees, and distributing medicines and necessities.

ER Med, General, Infect Dis, MF Med, Nephro, OB-GYN, Ortho, Psych

🌐 https://vfmat.ch/1fab

Ponseti International

Provides global leadership in building high-quality, locally directed, and sustainable capacity to deliver the Ponseti clubfoot care pathway at the country level.

Ortho, Ped Surg, Peds, Rehab

🌐 https://vfmat.ch/476b

Project Concern International (PCI)

Drives innovation from the ground up to enhance health, end hunger, overcome hardship, and advance women and girls—resulting in meaningful and measurable change in people's lives.

Infect Dis, MF Med, Nutr, OB-GYN, Peds

🌐 https://vfmat.ch/5ed7

Project Pacer International

Provides modern cardiac therapy to indigent patients in the developing world.

CT Surg, CV Med

🌐 https://vfmat.ch/f812

RestoringVision

Empowers lives by restoring vision for millions of people in need.

Ophth-Opt

🌐 https://vfmat.ch/e121

ReSurge International

Provides reconstructive surgical care and builds surgical capacity in developing countries.

Anesth, Dent-OMFS, Ped Surg, Plast, Surg

🌐 https://vfmat.ch/9937

Rockefeller Foundation, The

Works to promote the well-being of humanity.

Logist-Op, Nutr, Pub Health

🌐 https://vfmat.ch/5424

Rosa Vera Fund, The
Seeks to facilitate preventive health and social interventions for children and healthcare workers in and around Monter, Bolivia.
Nutr, Palliative, Peds, Rehab, Surg
⊕ https://vfmat.ch/67c7

Rotary International
Provides service to others, improves lives, and advances world understanding, goodwill, and peace through its fellowship of business, professional, and community leaders.
ER Med, General, Infect Dis, MF Med, OB-GYN
⊕ https://vfmat.ch/8fb5

ROW Foundation
Works to improve the quality of training for healthcare providers, and the diagnosis and treatment available to people with epilepsy and associated psychiatric disorders in under-resourced areas of the world.
Neuro, Psych
⊕ https://vfmat.ch/25eb

Rutgers New Jersey Medical School
Seeks to support and promote the global health efforts of the faculty, staff, and students in the areas of education, research, and service through the Rutgers New Jersey Medical School's Office of Global Health.
Anesth, CV Med, Crit-Care, Neurosurg, OB-GYN, Psych
⊕ https://vfmat.ch/8e67

Salvation Army International, The
Seeks to meet human needs through services in education, healthcare, community support, emergency response, and ministry development, inspired by the Christian faith.
Dent-OMFS, Derm, ER Med, Infect Dis, MF Med, Medicine, Nutr, OB-GYN, Ophth-Opt, Palliative, Psych, Rehab, Surg
⊕ https://vfmat.ch/8eb3

Samaritan's Purse International Disaster Relief
Provides spiritual and physical aid to hurting people around the world, such as victims of war, poverty, natural disasters, disease, and famine, based in Christian ministry.
Anesth, CT Surg, Crit-Care, Dent-OMFS, Derm, ENT, ER Med, Endo, GI, General, Heme-Onc, Infect Dis, MF Med, Neonat, Nephro, Neuro, Neurosurg, Nutr, OB-GYN, Ophth-Opt, Ortho, Path, Ped Surg, Peds, Plast, Psych, Pulm-Critic, Radiol, Rehab, Rheum, Surg, Urol, Vasc Surg
⊕ https://vfmat.ch/87e3

Save the Children
Gives children around the world a healthy start in life, the opportunity to learn, and protection from harm.
All-Immu, Crit-Care, ER Med, General, Infect Dis, MF Med, Medicine, Neonat, OB-GYN, Peds, Psych, Pub Health
⊕ https://vfmat.ch/2e73

SEE International
Provides sustainable medical, surgical, and educational services through volunteer ophthalmic surgeons, with the objectives of restoring sight and preventing blindness to disadvantaged individuals worldwide.
Ophth-Opt, Surg
⊕ https://vfmat.ch/6e1b

Smile Train, Inc.
Treats children with cleft lip through a sustainable and local model that supports surgery and other forms of essential care.
Logist-Op, Pub Health
⊕ https://vfmat.ch/822c

Smiles Forever
Aims to improve the quality of life for impoverished children through free preventive and restorative dentistry.
Dent-OMFS
⊕ https://vfmat.ch/1272

Soddo Christian Hospital
Mobilizes volunteers to help transform communities through healthcare and education, based in Christian ministry.
ER Med, General
⊕ https://vfmat.ch/efa4

Solidarity Bridge
Seeks to increase access to safe, affordable surgery and other essential healthcare by partnering in a spirit of solidarity with communities in Bolivia and Paraguay.
CT Surg, Dent-OMFS, Derm, General, Neurosurg, OB-GYN, Ped Surg, Surg
⊕ https://vfmat.ch/9984

SOS Children's Villages International
Supports children through alternative care and family strengthening.
ER Med, Peds
⊕ https://vfmat.ch/aca1

Sri Sathya Sai International Organization
Inspired by spiritual teachings, carries out efforts in global healthcare, education, humanitarian relief, and youth engagement.
Dent-OMFS, General, Logist-Op, Nutr, Ophth-Opt, Pub Health
⊕ https://vfmat.ch/9bda

Surgical Friends Foundation
Provides reconstructive surgery and post-operative care to individuals living with physical deformities and lacking access to quality medical care.
Dent-OMFS, ENT, Plast, Surg
⊕ https://vfmat.ch/8286

Swiss Tropical and Public Health Institute
Contributes to the improvement of the health of populations internationally, nationally, and locally through excellence in research, education, and services.
Infect Dis, Pub Health
⊕ https://vfmat.ch/2ee4

Task Force for Global Health, The
Consists of programs and focus areas that cover a range of global health issues including neglected tropical diseases, infectious diseases, vaccines, field epidemiology, public health informatics, health workforce development, and global health ethics.
Infect Dis, Logist-Op, Medicine, Ophth-Opt, Peds
⊕ https://vfmat.ch/714c

Tearfund
Responds to crisis and partners with local churches to bring restoration to those living in poverty, inspired by the Christian faith.
ER Med, Logist-Op
⊕ https://vfmat.ch/f6cf

Union for International Cancer Control (UICC)
Unites and supports the cancer community to reduce the global cancer burden, promote greater equity, and ensure that cancer control continues to be a priority in the world health and development agenda.
Heme-Onc, Pub Health
⊕ https://vfmat.ch/88b1

United Nations Children's Fund (UNICEF)
Works in over 190 countries and territories to save children's lives, defend their rights, and help them fulfill their potential, from early childhood through adolescence.
All-Immu, Infect Dis, MF Med, Neonat, Nutr, OB-GYN, Ped Surg, Peds, Pub Health
⊕ https://vfmat.ch/42d7

United Nations Development Programme (UNDP)
Helps countries achieve the simultaneous eradication of extreme poverty and significant reduction of inequalities and exclusion using a sustainable human development approach.
Infect Dis, Logist-Op, Pub Health
⊕ https://vfmat.ch/935c

United Nations High Commissioner for Refugees (UNHCR)
Safeguards the rights and well-being of people who have been forced to flee, ensuring that everybody has the right to seek asylum and find safe refuge in

another country, with the goal of seeking lasting solutions.
General, MF Med, Medicine, OB-GYN, Peds, Psych, Pub Health
⊕ https://vfmat.ch/6636

United Nations Office for the Coordination of Humanitarian Affairs (OCHA)

Contributes to principled and effective humanitarian response through coordination, advocacy, policy, information management, and humanitarian financing tools and services, by leveraging functional expertise throughout the organization.
Logist-Op
⊕ https://vfmat.ch/22b8

United Nations Population Fund (UNFPA)

Supports reproductive healthcare for women and youth in more than 150 countries, focusing on delivering a world in which every pregnancy is wanted, every childbirth is safe, and every young person's potential is fulfilled.
Infect Dis, MF Med, Neonat, OB-GYN, Peds, Pub Health
⊕ https://vfmat.ch/c969

United States Agency for International Development (USAID)

Promotes and demonstrates democratic values abroad and advances a free, peaceful, and prosperous world. Leads the U.S. government's international development and disaster assistance through partnerships and investments that save lives.
ER Med, Infect Dis, MF Med, OB-GYN, Peds
⊕ https://vfmat.ch/9a99

University of Illinois at Chicago: Center for Global Health

Aims to improve the health of populations around the world and reduce health disparities by collaboratively conducting trans-disciplinary research, training the next generations of global health leaders, and building the capacities of global and local partners.
Pub Health
⊕ https://vfmat.ch/b749

University of Virginia: Anesthesiology Department Global Health Initiatives

Educates and trains physicians to help people achieve healthy productive lives, and advances knowledge in the medical sciences.
Anesth, Pub Health
⊕ https://vfmat.ch/1b8b

USAID: Leadership, Management and Governance Project

Improves leadership, management, and governance practices to strengthen health systems and improve health for all, including vulnerable populations worldwide.
Logist-Op
⊕ https://vfmat.ch/d35e

USAID: Maternal and Child Health Integrated Program

Works to improve the health of women and their families, including programs for maternal, newborn, and child health, immunization, family planning, nutrition, malaria, and HIV/AIDS.
All-Immu, General, Infect Dis, MF Med
⊕ https://vfmat.ch/4415

Vanderbilt University Medical Center: Global Surgery

Aims to improve the healthcare of individuals and communities regionally, nationally, and internationally, combining transformative learning programs and compelling discoveries to provide distinctive personalized care.
CT Surg, CV Med, Neurosurg, Ophth-Opt, Ortho, Ped Surg, Surg, Urol
⊕ https://vfmat.ch/ee28

Vision Care

Restores sight and helps patients get regular treatment at short-term eye camps and long-term base clinics by having doctors, missionaries, volunteers, and sponsors work together.
Ophth-Opt
⊕ https://vfmat.ch/9d7c

Vision Outreach International

Advocates for helping the blind in underserved regions of the world and empowers the poor through sight restoration.

Ophth-Opt
⊕ https://vfmat.ch/9721

Vitamin Angels

Helps at-risk populations in need—specifically pregnant women, new mothers, and children under age 5—to gain access to life-changing vitamins and minerals.
General, Nutr
⊕ https://vfmat.ch/7da1

Women Orthopaedist Global Outreach (WOGO)

Provides free, life-altering orthopedic surgery that eliminates debilitating arthritis and restores disabled joints so that women can reclaim their ability to care for themselves, their families, and their communities.
Anesth, Ortho, Rehab, Surg
⊕ https://vfmat.ch/6386

World Council of Optometry

Facilitates the development of optometry worldwide and promotes eye health and vision care through advocacy, education, policy development, and humanitarian outreach.
Ophth-Opt, Pub Health
⊕ https://vfmat.ch/c92e

World Federation of Hemophilia (WFH)

Aims to improve and sustain care for people with inherited bleeding disorders by pursuing long-term relationships with individuals and organizations who share the values of WFH's development model.
Heme-Onc
⊕ https://vfmat.ch/5121

World Health Organization, The (WHO)

The United Nations' agency for health provides leadership on global health matters, shapes the health research agenda, sets norms and standards, articulates evidence-based policy options, provides technical support and monitoring to countries, and assesses health trends.
ER Med, General, Infect Dis, Logist-Op, MF Med, OB-GYN, Peds, Psych, Pub Health
⊕ https://vfmat.ch/c476

World Medical Relief

Facilitates the distribution of surplus medical resources where they are needed.
Logist-Op
⊕ https://vfmat.ch/72dc

World Rehabilitation Fund

Enables individuals around the world with functional limitations and participation restrictions to achieve community and social integration through physical and socioeconomic rehabilitation and advocacy.
Ortho, Rehab
⊕ https://vfmat.ch/a5bc

World Vision International

Works with vulnerable communities around the world to overcome poverty and injustice with child-focused programs in disaster management, health, nutrition, economic development, education, clean water, sanitation, and hygiene.
ER Med, General, Infect Dis, MF Med, Nutr, OB-GYN, Peds
⊕ https://vfmat.ch/2642

Bolivia

Healthcare Facilities

Centro de Trauma Hospital Corazón de Jesús
El Alto, La Paz, Bolivia
⊕ https://vfmat.ch/37dc

Clinica Saint Jude
Potosí, Potosí, Bolivia
⊕ https://vfmat.ch/126e

Hospital Agramont
El Alto, La Paz, Bolivia
⊕ https://vfmat.ch/285c

Hospital Arco Iris
La Paz, La Paz, Bolivia
⊕ https://vfmat.ch/81d3

Hospital Aurelio Melean
Totora, Cochabamba, Bolivia
⊕ https://vfmat.ch/4ed9

Hospital Belga
Cochabamba, Cochabamba, Bolivia
⊕ https://vfmat.ch/f38f

Hospital Boliviano Canadiense Santa Maria Magdalena
Magdalena, Beni, Bolivia
⊕ https://vfmat.ch/3558

Hospital Boliviano Espanol de Patacamaya
Patacamaya, La Paz, Bolivia
⊕ https://vfmat.ch/9aee

Hospital Central Ivirgarzama
Ivirgarzama, Cochabamba, Bolivia
⊕ https://vfmat.ch/d97b

Hospital Clinico Viedma
Cochabamba, Cochabamba, Bolivia
⊕ https://vfmat.ch/5261

Hospital Cochabamba
Cochabamba, Cochabamba, Bolivia
⊕ https://vfmat.ch/bf7d

Hospital COMBASE (Comision Boliviana de Accion Social Evangelica)
Cochabamba, Cochabamba, Bolivia
⊕ https://vfmat.ch/4a54

Hospital Comunitario Valle Hermoso
Cochabamba, Cochabamba, Bolivia
⊕ https://vfmat.ch/c6c2

Hospital COSSMIL (La Paz)
La Paz, La Paz, Bolivia
⊕ https://vfmat.ch/9a7e

Hospital COSSMIL (Tarija)
Tarija, Tarija, Bolivia
⊕ https://vfmat.ch/3ec1

Hospital Cristo de las Americas
Sucre, Chuquisaca, Bolivia
⊕ https://vfmat.ch/644c

Hospital Cubano Chacaltaya
La Paz, La Paz, Bolivia
⊕ https://vfmat.ch/145f

Hospital Daniel Bracamonte
Potosí, Potosí, Bolivia
⊕ https://vfmat.ch/9291

Hospital de Capinota
Capinota, Cochabamba, Bolivia
⊕ https://vfmat.ch/c492

Hospital de Huachacalla
Huachacalla, Oruro, Bolivia
⊕ https://vfmat.ch/d9ec

Hospital de la Mujer
La Paz, La Paz, Bolivia
⊕ https://vfmat.ch/f487

Hospital de la Republica de Iran
El Alto, La Paz, Bolivia
⊕ https://vfmat.ch/cba2

Hospital de Niños
Catavi, Potosí, Bolivia
⊕ https://vfmat.ch/5f88

Hospital de Niños René Balderas Lopez
Montero, Santa Cruz, Bolivia
⊕ https://vfmat.ch/547b

Hospital de Psiquiatría
La Paz, La Paz, Bolivia
⊕ https://vfmat.ch/844a

Hospital de Reyes
Reyes, El Beni, Bolivia
⊕ https://vfmat.ch/3efa

Hospital de Santa Bárbara
Sucre, Chuquisaca, Bolivia
⊕ https://vfmat.ch/f953

Hospital de Tiquipaya
Tiquipaya, Cochabamba, Bolivia
⊕ https://vfmat.ch/b37c

Hospital de Vacas
Vacas, Cochabamba, Bolivia
⊕ https://vfmat.ch/14d1

Hospital del Niño Manuel Ascencio Villarroel
Cochabamba, Cochabamba, Bolivia
⊕ https://vfmat.ch/efd3

Hospital del Norte (Cochabamba)
Cochabamba, Cochabamba, Bolivia
⊕ https://vfmat.ch/9317

Hospital del Norte (El Alto)
El Alto, La Paz, Bolivia
⊕ https://vfmat.ch/e6a2

Hospital del Sud
Cochabamba, Cochabamba, Bolivia
⊕ https://vfmat.ch/41e9

Hospital Edgar Montano
Cochabamba, Cochabamba, Bolivia
⊕ https://vfmat.ch/48ca

Hospital El Alto Sur
El Alto, La Paz, Bolivia
⊕ https://vfmat.ch/234b

Hospital Elizabeth Seton
Cochabamba, Cochabamba, Bolivia
⊕ https://vfmat.ch/e2bc

Hospital Florida
Samaipata, Santa Cruz, Bolivia
⊕ https://vfmat.ch/c2ea

Hospital General San Juan de Dios
Oruro, Oruro, Bolivia
⊕ https://vfmat.ch/c117

Hospital Gineco Obstetrico y Neonatal Dr. Jaime Sanchez Porcel
Sucre, Chuquisaca, Bolivia
⊕ https://vfmat.ch/3a53

Hospital Harry Williams
Cochabamba, Cochabamba, Bolivia
⊕ https://vfmat.ch/92fc

Hospital Inmaculada Concepcion
Potosí, Potosí, Bolivia
⊕ https://vfmat.ch/de8c

Hospital Jacobo Abularach
Santa Ana de Yacuma, El Beni, Bolivia
⊕ https://vfmat.ch/e975

Hospital Jaime Mendoza
Sucre, Chuquisaca, Bolivia
⊕ https://vfmat.ch/bf53

Hospital Japonés
Santa Cruz de la Sierra, Santa Cruz, Bolivia
⊕ https://vfmat.ch/5bb5

Hospital Juan XXIII
La Paz, La Paz, Bolivia
⊕ https://vfmat.ch/c178

Hospital Kolping
Warnes, Santa Cruz de la Sierra, Bolivia
⊕ https://vfmat.ch/dbb7

Hospital La Merced
La Paz, La Paz, Bolivia
⊕ https://vfmat.ch/a231

Hospital La Paz
La Paz, La Paz, Bolivia
⊕ https://vfmat.ch/be9f

Hospital Luis Espinal
Sucre, Chuquisaca, Bolivia
⊕ https://vfmat.ch/8974

Hospital Luis Uria de la Oliva
La Paz, La Paz, Bolivia
⊕ https://vfmat.ch/8972

Hospital Madre Teresa de Calcuta
Cantumarca, Potosí, Bolivia
⊕ https://vfmat.ch/c5b8

Hospital Mamerto Eguez
Charagua, Santa Cruz, Bolivia
⊕ https://vfmat.ch/d97e

Hospital Metodista
Obrajes, La Paz, Bolivia
⊕ https://vfmat.ch/8ef6

Hospital Municipal 3 De Noviembre
San Ignacio de Moxos, Beni, Bolivia
⊕ https://vfmat.ch/238b

Hospital Municipal Achacachi Capitán Juan Uriona
Achacachi, La Paz, Bolivia
⊕ https://vfmat.ch/42ac

Hospital Municipal Alfonso Gumucio R.
Montero, Santa Cruz, Bolivia
⊕ https://vfmat.ch/e8cd

Hospital Municipal Andres Cuschieri
Colcapirhua, Cochabamba, Bolivia
⊕ https://vfmat.ch/f2d8

Hospital Municipal Bajío del Oriente
Santa Cruz, Santa Cruz, Bolivia
⊕ https://vfmat.ch/f448

Hospital Municipal Barrios Mineros
Oruro, Oruro, Bolivia
⊕ https://vfmat.ch/7b32

Hospital Municipal Bernardino Gil Julio
San Jose de Chiquitos, Santa Cruz, Bolivia
⊕ https://vfmat.ch/db7c

Hospital Municipal Boliviano Holandes
La Paz, La Paz, Bolivia
⊕ https://vfmat.ch/f7fa

Hospital Municipal Camiri
Camiri, Santa Cruz, Bolivia
⊕ https://vfmat.ch/5731

Hospital Municipal Carmen Lopez
Aiquile, Cochabamba, Bolivia
⊕ https://vfmat.ch/4e8b

Hospital Municipal Cotahuma
La Paz, La Paz, Bolivia
⊕ https://vfmat.ch/4dc4

Hospital Municipal Cuatro Canadas
Cuatro Cañadas, Santa Cruz, Bolivia
⊕ https://vfmat.ch/e6ff

Hospital Municipal de Ascensión de Guarayos
Ascencion de Guarayos, Santa Cruz, Bolivia
⊕ https://vfmat.ch/11d1

Hospital Municipal de Caranavi
Caranavi, La Paz, Bolivia
⊕ https://vfmat.ch/79bb

Hospital Municipal Distrital Pampa de la Isla
Santa Cruz, Santa Cruz, Bolivia
⊕ https://vfmat.ch/446e

Hospital Municipal DM7 El Tatu
Santa Cruz, Santa Cruz, Bolivia
⊕ https://vfmat.ch/b282

Hospital Municipal El Torno
El Torno, Santa Cruz, Bolivia
⊕ https://vfmat.ch/61c1

Hospital Municipal Francés
Santa Cruz, Santa Cruz, Bolivia
⊕ https://vfmat.ch/iat2

Hospital Municipal Los Andes
El Alto, La Paz, Bolivia
⊕ https://vfmat.ch/8625

Hospital Municipal Los Negros
Los Negros, Santa Cruz, Bolivia
⊕ https://vfmat.ch/f2d2

Hospital Municipal Los Pinos
La Paz, La Paz, Bolivia
⊕ https://vfmat.ch/3af2

Hospital Municipal Modelo Corea
El Alto, La Paz, Bolivia
⊕ https://vfmat.ch/a4bc

Hospital Municipal Nuestra Señora del Rosario
Warnes, Santa Cruz, Bolivia
⊕ https://vfmat.ch/9aaa

Hospital Municipal Principe de Paz
Puerto Quijarro, Santa Cruz, Bolivia
⊕ https://vfmat.ch/98f2

Hospital Municipal Señor de Malta
Vallegrande, Santa Cruz, Bolivia
⊕ https://vfmat.ch/81f3

Hospital Municipal Viacha
Viacha, La Paz, Bolivia
⊕ https://vfmat.ch/6671

Hospital Municipal Virgen de Cotoca
Cotoca, Santa Cruz, Bolivia
⊕ https://vfmat.ch/3a21

Hospital Obrero No.1 (La Paz)
La Paz, La Paz, Bolivia
⊕ https://vfmat.ch/152a

Hospital Obrero No.4 (Oruro)
Oruro, Oruro, Bolivia
⊕ https://vfmat.ch/caca

Hospital Obrero No.6 Dr. Jaime Mendoza (Sucre)
Sucre, Chuquisaca, Bolivia
⊕ https://vfmat.ch/895a

Hospital Obrero No.7 (Tarija)
Tarija, Tarija, Bolivia
⊕ https://vfmat.ch/3dce

Hospital Obrero No.8 (Trinidad)
Trinidad, Beni, Bolivia
⊕ https://vfmat.ch/b727

Hospital Obrero Villa 1 de Mayo (Santa Cruz)
Santa Cruz, Santa Cruz, Bolivia
⊕ https://vfmat.ch/eeb2

Hospital Oruro-Corea
Oruro, Oruro, Bolivia
⊕ https://vfmat.ch/c81e

Hospital Otorrino-Oftalmologico
La Paz, La Paz, Bolivia
⊕ https://vfmat.ch/df2c

Hospital Padilla Dr. Marco Rojas Zurita
Padilla, Chuquisaca, Bolivia
⊕ https://vfmat.ch/12e4

Hospital Psiquiatrico San Benito Menni
Santa Cruz, Santa Cruz, Bolivia
⊕ https://vfmat.ch/f6b8

Hospital Regional San Juan de Dios
Tarija, Tarija, Bolivia
⊕ https://vfmat.ch/7385

Hospital Renato Castro
Arampampa, Potosí, Bolivia
⊕ https://vfmat.ch/b5b9

Hospital San Francisco de Asís
La Paz, La Paz, Bolivia
⊕ https://vfmat.ch/398d

Hospital San Gabriel
La Paz, La Paz, Bolivia
⊕ https://vfmat.ch/97f2

Hospital San Juan de Dios (Camargo)
Camargo, Chuquisaca, Bolivia
⊕ https://vfmat.ch/755d

Hospital San Juan de Dios (Cliza)
Cliza, Cochabamba, Bolivia
⊕ https://vfmat.ch/a861

Hospital San Juan de Dios (Santa Cruz)
Santa Cruz, Santa Cruz, Bolivia
⊕ https://vfmat.ch/34a2

Hospital San Martin de Porres (Huanuni)
Huanuni, Oruro, Bolivia
⊕ https://vfmat.ch/8b53

Hospital San Martin de Porres (Tiraque)
Tiraque, Cochabamba, Bolivia
⊕ https://vfmat.ch/1643

Hospital San Pedro Claver
Tiraque, Chuquisaca, Bolivia
⊕ https://vfmat.ch/d661

Hospital San Roque Padcaya
Padcaya, Tarija, Bolivia
⊕ https://vfmat.ch/e2e4

Hospital Santa Maria
Huanuni, Oruro, Bolivia
⊕ https://vfmat.ch/6581

Hospital Seguro Social Universitario (Cobija)
Cobija, Pando, Bolivia
⊕ https://vfmat.ch/e167

Hospital Seguro Social Universitario (Cochabamba)
Cochabamba, Cochabamba, Bolivia
⊕ https://vfmat.ch/7253

Hospital Seguro Social Universitario (La Paz)
La Paz, La Paz, Bolivia
⊕ https://vfmat.ch/cfbe

Hospital Seguro Social Universitario (Potosí)
Potosí, Potosí, Bolivia
⊕ https://vfmat.ch/ff7f

Hospital Seguro Social Universitario (Sucre)
Sucre, Chuquisaca, Bolivia
⊕ https://vfmat.ch/e521

Hospital Solomon Klein Sacaba
Cochabamba, Cochabamba, Bolivia
⊕ https://vfmat.ch/293f

Hospital Trinidad
Trinidad, Beni, Bolivia
⊕ https://vfmat.ch/b7aa

Hospital Univalle
Cochabamba, Cochabamba, Bolivia
⊕ https://vfmat.ch/5947

Hospital Univalle de Norte
Cochabamba, Cochabamba, Bolivia
⊕ https://vfmat.ch/c333

Hospital Universitario Hernández Vera
Santa Cruz, Santa Cruz, Bolivia
⊕ https://vfmat.ch/48fc

Hospital Universitario Nuestra Señora de La Paz
La Paz, La Paz, Bolivia
⊕ https://vfmat.ch/3a32

Hospital Universitario San Franciso Xavier
Sucre, Chuquisaca, Bolivia
⊕ https://vfmat.ch/7599

Hospital Villa Yunguyo
El Alto, La Paz, Bolivia
⊕ https://vfmat.ch/7723

Hospital Virgen de las Angustias
Tiraque, Cochabamba, Bolivia
⊕ https://vfmat.ch/229a

Hospital Virgen Milagrosa
Santa Cruz, Santa Cruz, Bolivia
⊕ https://vfmat.ch/5c47

Hospital Vladimir Bejarano
Gutiérrez, Santa Cruz, Bolivia
⊕ https://vfmat.ch/83a8

Instituto de Gastroenterología Boliviano-Japonés
Sucre, Chuquisaca, Bolivia
⊕ https://vfmat.ch/61f6

Micro Hospital Gran Paititi
Warnes, Santa Cruz, Bolivia
⊕ https://vfmat.ch/f7c3

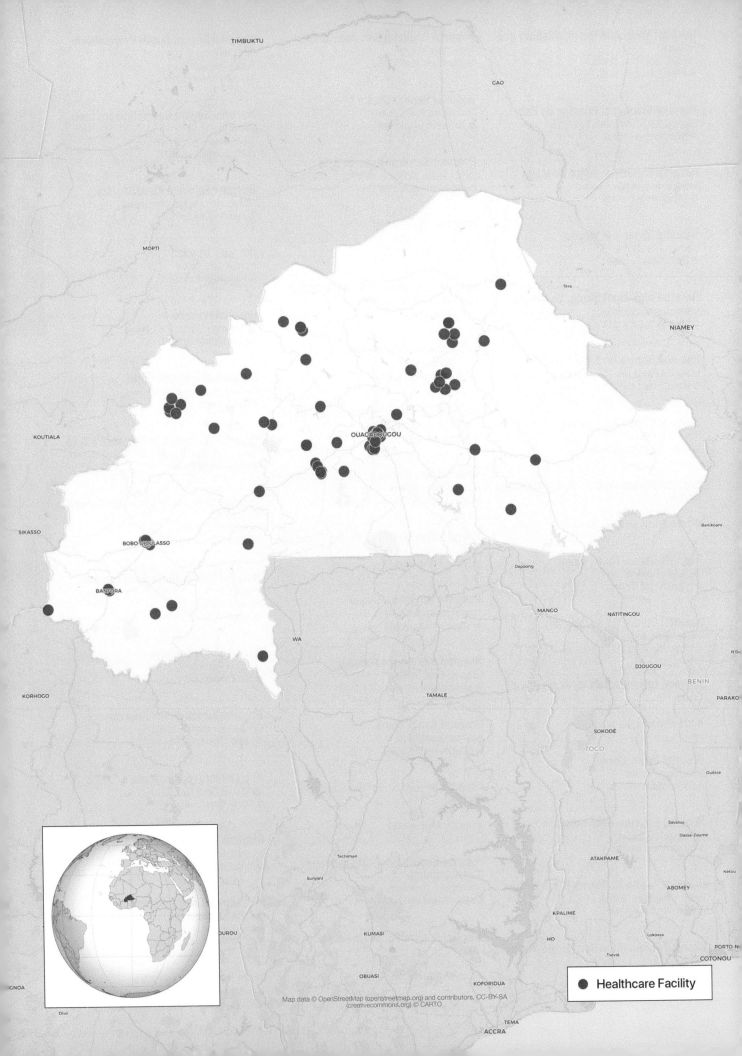

Healthcare Facility

Burkina Faso

Burkina Faso is a country located in West Africa, landlocked by Mali, Niger, Benin, Togo, Ghana, and Ivory Coast. The population is unevenly distributed, with most people living in the center and southern portions of the country. About 32 percent of the population lives in urban areas, including Ouagadougou, the capital, which is home to nearly 3 million people and geographically located in the center of the country. The country's population of 21.4 million is ethnically diverse, including groups such as Mossi, Fulani, Gurma, Bobo, Gurunsi, Senufo, Bissa, Lobi, and Dagara. French is the official and most commonly spoken language, while about 90 percent of the population also speaks one of many recognized local African dialects. About 64 percent of the population identifies as Muslim, and 25 percent identifies as Roman Catholic. Burkina Faso has one of the highest fertility rates in the world, with 5.1 children being born per woman. This has resulted in a rapidly growing, and proportionally young, population, with 65 percent of people under the age of 25.

Burkina Faso was a French colony and achieved independence in 1960. For several decades after, governmental instability prevailed, with several military coups taking place. The country overall faces many challenges in security and deteriorating stability, with terrorist activity and attacks contributing to what has become a humanitarian crisis with large numbers of internally displaced persons. This ongoing conflict and insecurity has contributed to significant development challenges in the areas of health and education. Unemployment is widespread, only one-third of the population is literate, and more than 40 percent of people live below the national poverty line. The largest portion of the economy is based in agriculture, with 80 percent of the population involved in subsistence farming. The economy is also supplemented by revenues in gold exports, albeit minimally.

Burkina Faso faces several health challenges. The population has a life expectancy of 62 years, one of the lowest in the world. Residents and visitors face a high risk of infectious diseases, such as hepatitis A, typhoid fever, dengue fever, malaria, schistosomiasis, and more. Leading causes of death include several communicable and non-communicable diseases, including malaria, lower respiratory infections, neonatal disorders, diarrheal diseases, ischemic heart disease, congenital defects, tuberculosis, stroke, hemoglobinopathies, road injuries, HIV/AIDS, and meningitis. The risk factors that contribute most to death and disability include malnutrition, air pollution, insufficient clean water and sanitation, high blood pressure, high fasting plasma glucose, dietary risks, high body-mass index, alcohol and tobacco use, unsafe sex, and non-optimal temperature.

21.4M

Population

$831

GDP Per Capita

62 years

Life Expectancy

↑ Improving

9
Doctors/100k

Physician Density

40
Beds/100k

Hospital Bed Density

320
Deaths/100k

Maternal Mortality

Burkina Faso

Nonprofit Organizations

Abt Associates
Seeks to improve the quality of life and economic well-being of people worldwide, while striving to meet and exceed the highest professional standards.
General, Logist-Op, MF Med, OB-GYN, Peds
🌐 https://vfmat.ch/cec2

Action Against Hunger
Aims to end life-threatening hunger for good through treating and preventing malnutrition across more than 45 countries.
Nutr
🌐 https://vfmat.ch/2dbc

Advance Family Planning
Aims to achieve global expansion and access to quality contraceptive information, services, and supplies through financial investment and political commitment.
General, MF Med, Pub Health
🌐 https://vfmat.ch/7478

Africa CDC
Aims to strengthen the capacity and capability of Africa's public health institutions and partnerships to detect and respond quickly and effectively to disease threats and outbreaks, based on data-driven interventions and programs.
Infect Dis, Logist-Op, Pub Health
🌐 https://vfmat.ch/339c

Africa Health Organisation
Leads collaborative efforts among countries in Africa and other partners to promote health equity, combat disease, and improve quality of life.
Logist-Op, Pub Health
🌐 https://vfmat.ch/b1c5

Africa Indoor Residual Spraying Project (AIRS)
Aims to protect millions of people in Africa from malaria by spraying insecticide on walls, ceilings, and other indoor resting places of mosquitoes that transmit malaria.
Infect Dis
🌐 https://vfmat.ch/9bd1

Africa Relief and Community Development
Provides comprehensive relief and developmental aid to people of the African continent regardless of gender, race, or religion.
Nutr, Pub Health
🌐 https://vfmat.ch/6cd2

African Field Epidemiology Network (AFENET)
Strengthens field epidemiology and public health laboratory capacity to contribute effectively to addressing epidemics and other major public health problems in Africa.
All-Immu, Infect Dis, Path, Pub Health
🌐 https://vfmat.ch/df2e

Against Malaria Foundation
Helps protect people from malaria. Funds anti-malaria nets, specifically long-lasting insecticidal nets (LLINs), and works with distribution partners to ensure they are used. Tracks and reports on net use and malaria case data.
Infect Dis
🌐 https://vfmat.ch/337d

Al Basar International Foundation
Works with local partners to treat preventable blindness, and helps set up sustainable infrastructure so local teams can save sight in their communities.
Ophth-Opt
🌐 https://vfmat.ch/a8b5

Alliance for International Medical Action, The (ALIMA)
Provides quality medical care to vulnerable populations, partnering with and developing national medical organizations and conducting medical research to bring innovation to 12 African countries where ALIMA works.
ER Med, General, Infect Dis, Logist-Op, MF Med, OB-GYN, Path, Peds, Psych, Pub Health
🌐 https://vfmat.ch/1c11

American Academy of Pediatrics
Seeks to attain optimal physical, mental, and social health and well-being for all infants, children, adolescents, and young adults.
Anesth, Crit-Care, Neonat, Ped Surg
🌐 https://vfmat.ch/9633

AO Alliance
Builds solutions to lessen the burden of injuries in low- and middle-income countries, while enhancing the care of the injured to reduce human suffering, disability, and poverty.
Ortho, Surg
🌐 https://vfmat.ch/8cd5

ASAP Foundation
Helps to relieve poverty in villages in Burkina Faso.
Infect Dis, Pub Health
🌐 https://vfmat.ch/mszm

Barka Foundation, The
Provides sustainable access to clean water, promotes sanitation and hygiene, seeks gender equality, and offers food security programs.
OB-GYN
🌐 https://vfmat.ch/suh3

BroadReach
Collaborates with governments, multinational health organizations, donors, and private-sector companies to effect healthcare reform and solve the world's biggest health challenges.

Logist-Op
⊕ https://vfmat.ch/7812

Burkina Health Foundation
Works in partnership with the local community and others to create sustainable medical resources.
CV Med, Dent-OMFS, GI, Ophth-Opt, Radiol
⊕ https://vfmat.ch/8wsu

Carter Center, The
Seeks to prevent and resolve conflicts, enhance freedom and democracy, and improve health, while remaining committed to human rights and the alleviation of human suffering.
Infect Dis, MF Med, Ophth-Opt
⊕ https://vfmat.ch/6556

cbm New Zealand
Inspired by the Christian faith, aims to improve the quality of life for those living with the double disadvantage of poverty and disability.
Crit-Care, Infect Dis, Logist-Op, Nutr, OB-GYN, Ophth-Opt, Ortho, Psych, Rehab, Surg
⊕ https://vfmat.ch/c14b

Chain of Hope (La Chaîne de l'Espoir)
Helps underprivileged children around the world by providing them with access to healthcare.
Anesth, CT Surg, Crit-Care, ER Med, Neurosurg, Ortho, Ped Surg, Surg, Vasc Surg
⊕ https://vfmat.ch/e871

Challenge Initiative, The
Seeks to rapidly and sustainably scale up proven reproductive health solutions among the urban poor.
MF Med, OB-GYN, Peds
⊕ https://vfmat.ch/2f77

Children's Lifeline International
Provides medical teams and surgical assistance to underprivileged children in developing countries through missions in partnership with local hospitals.
CV Med, Dent-OMFS, General, MF Med, Neurosurg, Peds, Rehab
⊕ https://vfmat.ch/6fea

Christian Blind Mission (CBM)
Aims to improve the quality of life of persons with disabilities in the poorest countries, addressing poverty as a cause and a consequence of disability, and working in partnership to create a society for all.
ENT, General, Infect Dis, OB-GYN, Ophth-Opt, Ortho, Peds, Psych, Rehab, Surg
⊕ https://vfmat.ch/3824

Christian Connections for International Health (CCIH)
Promotes global health and wholeness from a Christian perspective.
All-Immu, General, Infect Dis, MF Med, Neonat, OB-GYN, Psych
⊕ https://vfmat.ch/fa5d

COVID-19 Clinical Research Coalition
Advocates and collaborates for the advancement of COVID-19 research driven by the needs of low-resource settings, and works for equitable access to solutions to the pandemic.
All-Immu, Infect-Dis, MF Med, Path, Pub Health
⊕ https://vfmat.ch/d1f4

DEAR Foundation, The
Provides support for people in need, particularly women and children, by supporting humanitarian projects administered by NGOs, primarily in the areas of health and education.
Dent-OMFS, OB-GYN
⊕ https://vfmat.ch/a747

Direct Relief
Improves the health and lives of people affected by poverty or emergency situations by mobilizing and providing essential medical resources needed for their care.

ER Med, Logist-Op
⊕ https://vfmat.ch/58e5

Doctors Without Borders/Médecins Sans Frontières (MSF)
Responds to emergencies and provides lifesaving medical care where needed most, including during disasters, conflicts, and epidemics.
Anesth, Crit-Care, ER Med, General, Infect Dis, Nutr, OB-GYN, Ped Surg, Peds, Psych, Pub Health, Surg
⊕ https://vfmat.ch/f363

Enabel
As the development agency of the Belgian federal government, charged with implementing Belgium's international development policy, carries out public service assignments in Belgium and abroad pursuant to the 2030 Agenda for Sustainable Development.
General, Infect Dis, Logist-Op, MF Med, OB-GYN, Peds, Pub Health
⊕ https://vfmat.ch/5af7

EngenderHealth
Works to implement high-quality, gender-equitable programs that advance sexual and reproductive health and rights.
General, MF Med, OB-GYN, Peds
⊕ https://vfmat.ch/1cb2

Evidence Project, The
Improves family-planning policies, programs, and practices through the strategic generation, translation, and use of evidence.
General, MF Med
⊕ https://vfmat.ch/f9e7

Fondation Follereau
Promotes the quality of life of the most vulnerable African communities. Alongside trusted partners, the foundation supports local initiatives in healthcare and education.
General, Infect Dis, OB-GYN
⊕ https://vfmat.ch/bcc7

Foundation for Healthcare for Humanity
Provide assistance in the development and implementation of medical programs in the United States, Africa, South America, Eastern Europe, and the Caribbean.
General
⊕ https://vfmat.ch/ba7f

Frontline Aids
Acts as the UK-based secretariat of a global partnership of national organizations working to support community action on HIV/AIDS.
Infect Dis
⊕ https://vfmat.ch/gqcx

Gift of Life International
Provides lifesaving cardiac treatment to children in developing countries while developing sustainable pediatric cardiac programs by implementing screening, surgical, and training missions.
Anesth, CT Surg, CV Med, Crit-Care, Ped Surg, Peds, Pulm-Critic
⊕ https://vfmat.ch/f2f9

Global Clubfoot Initiative (GCI)
Promotes and resources the treatment of children with clubfoot in developing countries using the Ponseti technique.
Ortho, Ped Surg
⊕ https://vfmat.ch/f229

Global Oncology (GO)
Brings the best in cancer care to underserved patients around the world and collaborates across geographic, professional, and academic borders to improve cancer care, research, and education.
Heme-Onc, Path, Rad-Onc
⊕ https://vfmat.ch/fcb8

Globus Relief
Aims to improve the delivery of healthcare worldwide by gathering, processing, and distributing surplus medical supplies to charities at home and abroad.

Logist-Op
⊕ https://vfmat.ch/a2b7

Good Shepard International Foundation

Strives to promote inclusive and sustainable development for the most marginalized and vulnerable people, with a special focus on women, girls, and children, inspired by the Christian faith.

ER Med
⊕ https://vfmat.ch/ad9a

Grace for Impact

Provides high-quality healthcare and education to the rural poor, where it is needed most, in Sub-Saharan Africa and Southeast Asia.

Dent-OMFS, General, Ophth-Opt
⊕ https://vfmat.ch/3ed1

Grassroot Soccer

Leverages the power of soccer to educate, inspire, and mobilize at-risk youth in developing countries to overcome their greatest health challenges, live healthier and more productive lives, and be agents for change in their communities.

Infect Dis
⊕ https://vfmat.ch/3521

Health Equity Initiative

Aims to build and sustain a global community that engages across sectors and disciplines to advance health equity.

Pub Health
⊕ https://vfmat.ch/e2e2

Health Volunteers Overseas (HVO)

Improves the availability and quality of healthcare through the education, training, and professional development of the health workforce in resource-scarce countries.

All-Immu, Anesth, CV Med, Dent-OMFS, Derm, ENT, ER Med, Endo, GI, Heme-Onc, Infect Dis, Medicine, Medicine, Nephro, Neuro, OB-GYN, Ophth-Opt, Ortho, Peds, Plast, Psych, Pulm-Critic, Rehab, Rheum, Surg
⊕ https://vfmat.ch/42b2

Helen Keller International

Seeks to eliminate preventable vision loss, malnutrition, and diseases of poverty.

Infect Dis, Nutr, OB-GYN, Ophth-Opt, Peds
⊕ https://vfmat.ch/b654

Hope Walks

Frees children, families, and communities from the burden of clubfoot, inspired by the Christian faith.

Ortho, Ped Surg, Peds, Rehab
⊕ https://vfmat.ch/f6d4

Hospice Africa

Aims to provide a holistic and culturally sensitive palliative care service through accurate treatment of pain.

Palliative
⊕ https://vfmat.ch/9f86

HumaniTerra

Helps countries and populations emerging from economic and human crisis to rebuild their healthcare system in a sustainable way. Committed to three fundamental and complementary actions: operating, training, and rebuilding.

Anesth, ENT, ER Med, MF Med, OB-GYN, Ortho, Plast, Surg
⊕ https://vfmat.ch/b371

Humanity & Inclusion

Works alongside people with disabilities and vulnerable populations, taking action and bearing witness in order to respond to their essential needs, improve their living conditions and health, and promote respect for their dignity and fundamental rights.

General, Infect Dis, MF Med, Medicine, Ortho, Peds, Psych, Pub Health, Rehab
⊕ https://vfmat.ch/16b7

Humanity First

Provides aid and assistance to those in need, offering sustainable development solutions to society while providing and empowering local communities with the resources to help themselves.

ER Med, General, MF Med, Ophth-Opt
⊕ https://vfmat.ch/13cc

Hunger Project, The

Aims to end hunger and poverty by pioneering sustainable, grassroots, women-centered strategies and advocating for their widespread adoption in countries throughout the world.

Infect Dis, Nutr, OB-GYN, Pub Health
⊕ https://vfmat.ch/3a49

IMA World Health

Works to build healthier communities by collaborating with key partners to serve vulnerable people with a focus on health, healing, and well-being for all.

Infect Dis, MF Med, Nutr, OB-GYN, Pub Health
⊕ https://vfmat.ch/8316

International Federation of Gynecology and Obstetrics (FIGO)

Implements global projects on specific women's health issues.

MF Med, Medicine, Neonat, OB-GYN, Surg, Urol
⊕ https://vfmat.ch/c4b4

International Federation of Red Cross and Red Crescent Societies (IFRC)

Coordinates and directs international assistance following natural and manmade disasters in nonconflict situations through the world's largest humanitarian and development network. Provides disaster-preparedness programs, healthcare activities, and promotes humanitarian values.

ER Med, General, Infect Dis, Nutr
⊕ https://vfmat.ch/b4ee

International Organization for Migration (IOM) – The UN Migration Agency

Promotes evidence-informed policies and holistic, preventive, and curative health programs that are beneficial, accessible, and equitable for vulnerable migrants.

General, Infect Dis, OB-GYN
⊕ https://vfmat.ch/621a

International Planned Parenthood Federation (IPPF)

Leads a locally owned, globally connected civil society movement that provides and enables services and champions sexual and reproductive health and rights for all, especially the underserved.

Infect Dis, MF Med, OB-GYN
⊕ https://vfmat.ch/dc97

International Rescue Committee (IRC)

Responds to the world's worst humanitarian crises and helps people whose lives and livelihoods are shattered by conflict and disaster to survive, recover, and gain control of their future.

ER Med, General, Infect Dis, MF Med, Peds
⊕ https://vfmat.ch/5d24

International Trachoma Initiative (iTi)

Works toward a world free from trachoma, a preventable cause of blindness, and provides comprehensive support to national ministries of health and governmental and nongovernmental organizations to implement a comprehensive approach to fight trachoma.

Infect Dis, Ophth-Opt
⊕ https://vfmat.ch/3278

Intersos

Provides emergency medical assistance to victims of armed conflicts, natural disasters, and extreme exclusion, with particular attention to the protection of the most vulnerable people.

ER Med, General, Nutr
⊕ https://vfmat.ch/dbac

IntraHealth International

Improves the performance of health workers and strengthens the systems in which they work.

CV Med, Endo, General, Infect Dis, MF Med, Neonat, Nutr, OB-GYN
⊕ https://vfmat.ch/ddc8

Ipas

Focuses efforts on women and girls who want contraception or abortion, and builds programs around their needs and how best to support them.
OB-GYN
⊕ https://vfmat.ch/8e39

Izumi Foundation

Develops and supports programs that improve health and healthcare in neglected regions of Africa and Latin America.
⊕ https://vfmat.ch/f29a

Jhpiego

Creates and delivers transformative healthcare solutions that save lives, in partnership with national governments, health experts, and local communities.
General, Infect Dis, OB-GYN, Surg
⊕ https://vfmat.ch/45b8

John Snow, Inc. (JSI)

Aims to improve the health and well-being of underserved and vulnerable people and communities throughout the world.
General, Infect Dis, Logist-Op, MF Med, OB-GYN, Peds, Psych, Pub Health
⊕ https://vfmat.ch/ba78

Johns Hopkins Center for Communication Programs

Believes in the power of communication to save lives by empowering people to adopt healthy behaviors for themselves, their families, and their communities.
General, Infect Dis, Logist-Op, OB-GYN, Pub Health
⊕ https://vfmat.ch/1bf9

Joint United Nations Programme on HIV/AIDS (UNAIDS)

Aims to place people living with HIV and people affected by the virus at the decision-making table and at the center of designing, delivering, and monitoring the AIDS response.
Infect Dis
⊕ https://vfmat.ch/464a

Lay Volunteers International Association (LVIA)

Fosters local and global change to help overcome extreme poverty, reinforce equitable and sustainable development, and enhance dialogue between Italian and African communities.
ER Med, Logist-Op, MF Med, Neonat, Nutr, OB-GYN, Peds
⊕ https://vfmat.ch/ecd4

Life for a Child

Supports the provision of the best possible healthcare, given local circumstances, to all children and youth with diabetes in less-resourced countries, through the strengthening of existing diabetes services.
Endo, Medicine, Peds
⊕ https://vfmat.ch/d712

Light for the World

Contributes to a world in which persons with disabilities fully exercise their rights, and assists persons with disabilities living in poverty.
Ophth-Opt, Rehab
⊕ https://vfmat.ch/3ff6

Light House Medical Missions

Inspired by the Christian faith, provides programs in healthcare provision, nutrition, emergency relief and response, and water, sanitation, and hygiene (WASH).
ER Med, General, Surg
⊕ https://vfmat.ch/cecd

Lutherans in Medical Missions (LIMM)

Works with local and global partners to promote healing in medically underserved communities.
General, Logist-Op, Pub Health
⊕ https://vfmat.ch/c5aa

Management Sciences for Health (MSH)

Works with countries and communities to save lives and improve the health of the world's poorest and most vulnerable people by building strong, resilient, sustainable health systems.

Infect Dis, Logist-Op, Pub Health
⊕ https://vfmat.ch/6aa2

Marie Stopes International

Provides the contraception and safe abortion services that enable women all over the world to choose their own futures.
Infect Dis, MF Med, Neonat, OB-GYN, Pub Health
⊕ https://vfmat.ch/9525

Medical Care Development International

Works to improve the health of vulnerable populations through integrated, sustainable, and locally driven interventions.
Infect Dis, OB-GYN, Peds, Pub Health
⊕ https://vfmat.ch/da87

Medicus Mundi Italia

Carries out programs in basic community health, health education, maternal and child health, nutrition, and infectious disease.
General, Infect Dis, Logist-Op, MF Med, Nutr, Peds, Pub Health, Rehab
⊕ https://vfmat.ch/4413

MedShare

Aims to improve the quality of life of people, communities, and the planet by sourcing and directly delivering surplus medical supplies and equipment to communities in need around the world.
Logist-Op
⊕ https://vfmat.ch/c8bc

Mercy and Love Foundation

Aims to provide orphaned and vulnerable children with basic human needs such as food, clothing, and shelter, enabling them to thrive.
General, Peds
⊕ https://vfmat.ch/649a

Mission Africa

Brings medical care, training, and compassion to underserved communities in Africa, based in Christian ministry.
Dent-OMFS, General, Infect Dis
⊕ https://vfmat.ch/df4d

Mission Regan

Collects supplies, medication, and medical equipment and provides them to those who are in desperate need, both locally and globally.
Logist-Op
⊕ https://vfmat.ch/2bc1

Morbidity Management and Disability Prevention Project (MMPD)

Helps countries provide high-quality treatment and care for people suffering from the debilitating effects of trachoma and lymphatic filariasis, complementing other major initiatives supporting disease elimination through mass drug administration.
Heme-Onc, Infect Dis, Ophth-Opt
⊕ https://vfmat.ch/387e

MSI Reproductive Choices (Marie Stopes International)

Seeks to deliver quality family planning and reproductive healthcare to women around the world.
MF Med
⊕ https://vfmat.ch/5c82

Médecins du Monde/Doctors of the World

Provides care, bears witness, and supports social change worldwide with innovative medical programs and evidence-based advocacy initiatives.
ER Med, General, Infect Dis, MF Med, Neonat, OB-GYN, Peds, Pub Health
⊕ https://vfmat.ch/a43d

Mérieux Foundation

Committed to fighting infectious diseases that affect developing countries by capacity building, particularly in clinical laboratories, and focusing on diagnosis.
Logist-Op, Path
⊕ https://vfmat.ch/a23a

Options

Believes in a world in which women and children can access the high-quality health services they need, without financial burden.

Logist-Op, MF Med, Neonat, OB-GYN

⊕ https://vfmat.ch/3a48

Order of Malta

Supports forgotten or excluded people, especially those living in conflict zones or amid natural disasters, by providing medical assistance, caring for refugees, and distributing medicines and necessities.

ER Med, General, Infect Dis, MF Med, Nephro, OB-GYN, Ortho, Psych

⊕ https://vfmat.ch/1fab

Orphan Life Foundation

Advocates for orphaned children in Burkina Faso by providing educational, health, and foster home and shelter services, while facilitating adoption processes.

Infect Dis, Logist-Op, Nutr, Pub Health

⊕ https://vfmat.ch/14ea

PATH

Advances health equity through innovation and partnerships so people, communities, and economies can thrive.

All-Immu, CV Med, Endo, Heme-Onc, Infect Dis, MF Med, Neonat, Nutr, OB-GYN, Path, Peds, Pulm-Critic

⊕ https://vfmat.ch/b4db

Pathfinder International

Champions sexual and reproductive health and rights worldwide, mobilizing communities most in need to break through barriers and forge paths to a healthier future.

OB-GYN

⊕ https://vfmat.ch/a7b3

Pharmacists Without Borders Canada

Provides pharmaceutical and technical assistance in the implementation or improvement of community and hospital pharmacies internationally.

⊕ https://vfmat.ch/7658

Première Urgence International

Helps civilians who are marginalized or excluded as a result of natural disasters, war, or economic collapse.

ER Med, General, MF Med, Peds, Psych

⊕ https://vfmat.ch/62ba

RestoringVision

Empowers lives by restoring vision for millions of people in need.

Ophth-Opt

⊕ https://vfmat.ch/e121

Rockefeller Foundation, The

Works to promote the well-being of humanity.

Logist-Op, Nutr, Pub Health

⊕ https://vfmat.ch/5424

Rotary International

Provides service to others, improves lives, and advances world understanding, goodwill, and peace through its fellowship of business, professional, and community leaders.

ER Med, General, Infect Dis, MF Med, OB-GYN

⊕ https://vfmat.ch/8fb5

Salvation Army International, The

Seeks to meet human needs through services in education, healthcare, community support, emergency response, and ministry development, inspired by the Christian faith.

Dent-OMFS, Derm, ER Med, Infect Dis, MF Med, Medicine, Nutr, OB-GYN, Ophth-Opt, Palliative, Psych, Rehab, Surg

⊕ https://vfmat.ch/8eb3

Sanofi Espoir Foundation

Contributes to reducing health inequalities among populations that need it most by applying a socially responsible approach focused on fighting childhood cancers in low-income countries, improving maternal and newborn health, and improving access to care.

ER Med, OB-GYN, Peds

⊕ https://vfmat.ch/943b

Santé Diabète

Addresses the lack of access to care for people with diabetes in Africa, with the mission of saving lives through disease prevention and management and improving quality of life through care delivery.

Endo, Medicine, Vasc Surg

⊕ https://vfmat.ch/7652

Save the Children

Gives children around the world a healthy start in life, the opportunity to learn, and protection from harm.

All-Immu, Crit-Care, ER Med, General, Infect Dis, MF Med, Medicine, Neonat, OB-GYN, Peds, Psych, Pub Health

⊕ https://vfmat.ch/2e73

Sightsavers

Works with partners in developing countries to help eliminate avoidable blindness and advocates for equal opportunity for the disabled.

Infect Dis, Ophth-Opt, Surg

⊕ https://vfmat.ch/aa52

SINA Health

Aims to improve the health and educational status of the population in low- and middle-income countries.

General, Logist-Op

⊕ https://vfmat.ch/9ad3

Smile Train, Inc.

Treats children with cleft lip through a sustainable and local model that supports surgery and other forms of essential care.

Logist-Op, Pub Health

⊕ https://vfmat.ch/822c

Solthis

Improves disease prevention and access to quality care by strengthening the health systems and services of the countries served.

General, Infect Dis, Logist-Op, MF Med, Neonat, Path

⊕ https://vfmat.ch/a71d

Swiss Tropical and Public Health Institute

Contributes to the improvement of the health of populations internationally, nationally, and locally through excellence in research, education, and services.

Infect Dis, Pub Health

⊕ https://vfmat.ch/2ee4

Task Force for Global Health, The

Consists of programs and focus areas that cover a range of global health issues including neglected tropical diseases, infectious diseases, vaccines, field epidemiology, public health informatics, health workforce development, and global health ethics.

Infect Dis, Logist-Op, Medicine, Ophth-Opt, Peds

⊕ https://vfmat.ch/714c

Tearfund

Responds to crisis and partners with local churches to bring restoration to those living in poverty, inspired by the Christian faith.

ER Med, Logist-Op

⊕ https://vfmat.ch/f6cf

Terre des hommes (Tdh) Foundation

Works to improve the daily life of children and their relatives in the areas of health, protection and emergency, in Europe, Africa, Asia, Latin America, and the Near and Middle East.

CT Surg, CV Med, OB-GYN, Ped Surg, Pub Health

⊕ https://vfmat.ch/5c26

Turing Foundation

Aims to contribute toward a better world and a better society by focusing on efforts such as health, art, education, and nature.

Infect Dis
⊕ https://vfmat.ch/6bcc

U.S. President's Malaria Initiative (PMI)
Supports low-income countries to help control and eliminate malaria through cost-effective, lifesaving malaria interventions.
Infect Dis, MF Med, OB-GYN
⊕ https://vfmat.ch/dc8b

Union for International Cancer Control (UICC)
Unites and supports the cancer community to reduce the global cancer burden, promote greater equity, and ensure that cancer control continues to be a priority in the world health and development agenda.
Heme-Onc, Pub Health
⊕ https://vfmat.ch/88b1

United Nations Children's Fund (UNICEF)
Works in over 190 countries and territories to save children's lives, defend their rights, and help them fulfill their potential, from early childhood through adolescence.
All-Immu, Infect Dis, MF Med, Neonat, Nutr, OB-GYN, Ped Surg, Peds, Pub Health
⊕ https://vfmat.ch/42d7

United Nations Development Programme (UNDP)
Helps countries achieve the simultaneous eradication of extreme poverty and significant reduction of inequalities and exclusion using a sustainable human development approach.
Infect Dis, Logist-Op, Pub Health
⊕ https://vfmat.ch/935c

United Nations High Commissioner for Refugees (UNHCR)
Safeguards the rights and well-being of people who have been forced to flee, ensuring that everybody has the right to seek asylum and find safe refuge in another country, with the goal of seeking lasting solutions.
General, MF Med, Medicine, OB-GYN, Peds, Psych, Pub Health
⊕ https://vfmat.ch/6636

United Nations Office for the Coordination of Humanitarian Affairs (OCHA)
Contributes to principled and effective humanitarian response through coordination, advocacy, policy, information management, and humanitarian financing tools and services, by leveraging functional expertise throughout the organization.
Logist-Op
⊕ https://vfmat.ch/22b8

United Nations Population Fund (UNFPA)
Supports reproductive healthcare for women and youth in more than 150 countries, focusing on delivering a world in which every pregnancy is wanted, every childbirth is safe, and every young person's potential is fulfilled.
Infect Dis, MF Med, Neonat, OB-GYN, Peds, Pub Health
⊕ https://vfmat.ch/c969

USA for United Nations High Commissioner for Refugees (UNHCR)
Serves and protects refugees and displaced people through emergency relief, cash assistance, education, resettlement, and the rebuilding of livelihoods.
ER Med, General, Logist-Op, Nutr, Pub Health
⊕ https://vfmat.ch/293c

USAID: Leadership, Management and Governance Project
Improves leadership, management, and governance practices to strengthen health systems and improve health for all, including vulnerable populations worldwide.
Logist-Op
⊕ https://vfmat.ch/d35e

USAID: Maternal and Child Health Integrated Program
Works to improve the health of women and their families, including programs for maternal, newborn, and child health, immunization, family planning, nutrition, malaria, and HIV/AIDS.
All-Immu, General, Infect Dis, MF Med
⊕ https://vfmat.ch/4415

USAID: Maternal and Child Survival Program
Works to prevent child and maternal deaths.
Infect Dis, MF Med, Neonat, OB-GYN, Peds
⊕ https://vfmat.ch/6fcf

Vitamin Angels
Helps at-risk populations in need—specifically pregnant women, new mothers, and children under age 5—to gain access to life-changing vitamins and minerals.
General, Nutr
⊕ https://vfmat.ch/7da1

West African Health Organization
Aims to attain high standards and protection of health of the people in West Africa through harmonization of policies of the member states to combat health problems.
Infect Dis, MF Med, OB-GYN
⊕ https://vfmat.ch/7363

Willing and Abel
Seeks to provide connections between children in developing nations and specialist centers, helping with visas, passports, transportation, and finances.
Anesth, Dent-OMFS, Ped Surg
⊕ https://vfmat.ch/9dc7

World Children's Fund
Commits to helping children worldwide who are suffering the effects of poverty, disease, natural disaster, famine, abuse, civil strife, and war.
General, Logist-Op, MF Med, Nutr, OB-GYN, Pub Health
⊕ https://vfmat.ch/9cd8

World Federation of Hemophilia (WFH)
Aims to improve and sustain care for people with inherited bleeding disorders by pursuing long-term relationships with individuals and organizations who share the values of WFH's development model.
Heme-Onc
⊕ https://vfmat.ch/5121

World Health Organization, The (WHO)
The United Nations' agency for health provides leadership on global health matters, shapes the health research agenda, sets norms and standards, articulates evidence-based policy options, provides technical support and monitoring to countries, and assesses health trends.
ER Med, General, Infect Dis, Logist-Op, MF Med, OB-GYN, Peds, Psych, Pub Health
⊕ https://vfmat.ch/c476

World Hope International
Empowers the poorest individuals around the world so they can become agents of change within their communities, by offering resources and knowledge.
Infect Dis, Logist-Op, MF Med, OB-GYN, Peds
⊕ https://vfmat.ch/a4b8

World Medical Relief
Facilitates the distribution of surplus medical resources where they are needed.
Logist-Op
⊕ https://vfmat.ch/72dc

Worldwide Fistula Fund
Protects and restores the health and dignity of the world's most vulnerable women by preventing and treating devastating childbirth injuries.
OB-GYN
⊕ https://vfmat.ch/8813

Burkina Faso

Healthcare Facilities

Bassiyam Wenatip la Yolse
Bassiyam, Kadiogo, Burkina Faso
🌐 https://vfmat.ch/i5fd

Centre Abel Sanou
Bobo-Dioulasso, Hauts-Bassins, Burkina Faso
🌐 https://vfmat.ch/nci3

Centre Hospitalier régional de Koudougou
Koudougou, BF, Burkina Faso
🌐 https://vfmat.ch/klbi

Centre Hospitalier Régional de Kaya
Sanmatenga, Centre-Nord, Burkina Faso
🌐 https://vfmat.ch/mb2j

Centre Hospitalier Universitaire de Ouahigouya
Ouahigouya, Nord, Burkina Faso
🌐 https://vfmat.ch/9dyg

Centre Hospitalier Universitaire de Tingandogo
Ouagadougou, Centre Region, Burkina Faso
🌐 https://vfmat.ch/8mxu

Centre Hospitalier Universitaire Yalgado Ouédraogo
Ouagadougou, Centre, Burkina Faso
🌐 https://vfmat.ch/edu5

Centre Hôspitalier Régional de Banfora
Banfora, Cascades, Burkina Faso
🌐 https://vfmat.ch/ughc

Centre Hôspitalier Régional de Dori
Dori, Sahel, Burkina Faso
🌐 https://vfmat.ch/hqxr

Centre Médical de Nagrin
Ouagadougou, Centre Region, Burkina Faso
🌐 https://vfmat.ch/a8jk

Centre Médical de Nouna
Nouna, Boucle du Mouhoun, Burkina Faso
🌐 https://vfmat.ch/gbqj

Centre Médical Paul VI
Ouagadougou, Centre, Burkina Faso
🌐 https://vfmat.ch/me3l

CHR de Ziniaré
Ziniare, Plateau-Central, Burkina Faso
🌐 https://vfmat.ch/zavs

CHR Fada
Fada N'Gourma, Est, Burkina Faso
🌐 https://vfmat.ch/quaj

Clinical El Fateh Suka
Ouagadougou, Burkina Faso
🌐 https://vfmat.ch/w3dv

Clinique La Grace Marie
Ouagadougou, Centre Region, Burkina Faso
🌐 https://vfmat.ch/6lmi

CM1 (Hospital) de Tougan
Tougan, Boucle du Mouhoun, Burkina Faso
🌐 https://vfmat.ch/xgip

CMA de Batié
Butie, Sud-Ouest, Burkina Faso
🌐 https://vfmat.ch/n4w1

CMA de Boromo
Boromo, Boucle du Mouhoun, Burkina Faso
🌐 https://vfmat.ch/ndb2

CMA de Gourcy
Gourcy, Nord, Burkina Faso
🌐 https://vfmat.ch/2rsj

CMA de Ouargaye
Ouargaye, Centre-Est, Burkina Faso
🌐 https://vfmat.ch/iwv5

CMA de Pissy
Ouagadougou, Centre, Burkina Faso
🌐 https://vfmat.ch/njad

CMA de Sabou
Sabou, Centre-Ouest, Burkina Faso
🌐 https://vfmat.ch/tpkb

CMA de Sanogho
Sanogho, Centre-Est, Burkina Faso
🌐 https://vfmat.ch/fdn9

CREN – Centro Recupero e Educazione alla Nutrizione
Koudougou, Boulkiemde, Burkina Faso
🌐 https://vfmat.ch/jyz1

Hospital at Dédougou
Dedougou, Boucle du Mouhoun, Burkina Faso
🌐 https://vfmat.ch/bh7a

Hôpital de District de Bogodogo
Ouagadougou, Centre Region, Burkina Faso
🌐 https://vfmat.ch/m1vm

Hôpital de l'Amitié
Koudougou, Centre-West, Burkina Faso
🌐 https://vfmat.ch/e4j6

Hôpital de Ouahigouya
Ouahigouya, Nord, Burkina Faso
🌐 https://vfmat.ch/t7pb

Hôpital Saint Camille de Nanoro
Nanoro, Centre-Ouest, Burkina Faso
🌐 https://vfmat.ch/6u7d

Hôpital Saint Camille de Ouagadougou
Ouagadougou, Centre Region, Burkina Faso
🌐 https://vfmat.ch/yu3r

Institut Médico Psycho Educatif
Ouagadougou, Centre Region, Burkina Faso
⊕ https://vfmat.ch/tj3n

Koupéla District Hospital
Koupéla, Centre-Est, Burkina Faso
⊕ https://vfmat.ch/jwmc

Polyclinic International Du Coeur
Ouagadougou, Burkina Faso
⊕ https://vfmat.ch/w5tq

Saint Joseph Hospital
Bobo-Dioulasso, Hauts-Bassins, Burkina Faso
⊕ https://vfmat.ch/3ykm

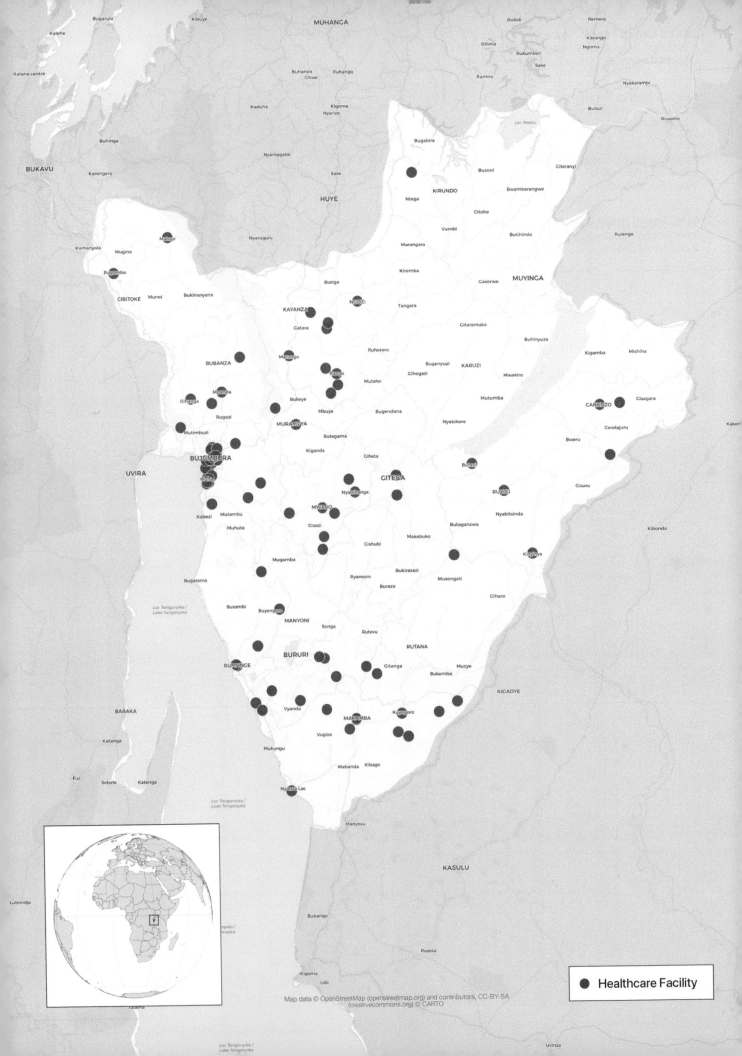

Healthcare Facility

Burundi

Landlocked in the middle of Central-East Africa, the Republic of Burundi lies between Tanzania, Uganda, and the Democratic Republic of the Congo, and shares a long border with Lake Tanganyika. One of the last-standing African monarchies, whose kingship fell in 1966, Burundi has a population of 12.2 million. While small, Burundi is one of the most densely populated countries in Africa, with 470 inhabitants per square kilometer. The nation is 75 percent Christian and is unique for its linguistic homogeneity; nearly the entire population speaks Kirundi.

Formerly a colony of Germany and Belgium, Burundi achieved independence in 1962, followed by decades of ethnic tension. The country has experienced both a civil war and a string of contentious elections. Ethnic friction between the usually-dominant Tutsi minority and the Hutu majority has further damaged the country's political stability and ability to control corruption. The majority of the population continues to live in poverty, with economic instability disproportionately affecting rural areas, where only 2 percent of households have access to electricity. In addition, food insecurity in Burundi is nearly double the average for sub-Saharan countries.

While life expectancy has increased and under-five mortality has decreased over time, communicable and non-communicable diseases continue to contribute to poor health indicators and a large burden of disease in the population. Illnesses causing the most deaths include diarrheal diseases, neonatal disorders, tuberculosis, malaria, lower respiratory infections, stroke, ischemic heart disease, congenital defects, HIV/AIDS, and protein-energy malnutrition, with significant increases in stroke and ischemic heart disease in recent years. Road injuries have also increased significantly in recent years and are a main contributor to disability.

12.2M
Population

$274
GDP Per Capita

62 years
Life Expectancy
↑ Improving

10
Doctors/100k

Physician Density

79
Beds/100k

Hospital Bed Density

548
Deaths/100k

Maternal Mortality

Burundi

Nonprofit Organizations

143 LIFE Foundation
Seeks to educate and empower individuals living with malaria, TB, HIV/AIDS, STDs and other health disparities related to sexual health.
Infect Dis, MF Med
🌐 https://vfmat.ch/d59b

Abt Associates
Seeks to improve the quality of life and economic well-being of people worldwide, while striving to meet and exceed the highest professional standards.
General, Logist-Op, MF Med, OB-GYN, Peds
🌐 https://vfmat.ch/cec2

Africa CDC
Aims to strengthen the capacity and capability of Africa's public health institutions and partnerships to detect and respond quickly and effectively to disease threats and outbreaks, based on data-driven interventions and programs.
Infect Dis, Logist-Op, Pub Health
🌐 https://vfmat.ch/339c

Africa Health Organisation
Leads collaborative efforts among countries in Africa and other partners to promote health equity, combat disease, and improve quality of life.
Logist-Op, Pub Health
🌐 https://vfmat.ch/b1c5

Africa Humanitarian Action (AHA)
Responds to crises, conflicts, and disasters in Africa, while informing and advising the international community, governments, civil society, and the private sector on humanitarian issues of concern to Africa. Supports institutional and organizational development efforts.
General, Infect Dis, MF Med, Nutr, OB-GYN
🌐 https://vfmat.ch/3ca2

Africa Indoor Residual Spraying Project (AIRS)
Aims to protect millions of people in Africa from malaria by spraying insecticide on walls, ceilings, and other indoor resting places of mosquitoes that transmit malaria.
Infect Dis
🌐 https://vfmat.ch/9bd1

Africa Relief and Community Development
Provides comprehensive relief and developmental aid to people of the African continent regardless of gender, race, or religion.
Nutr, Pub Health
🌐 https://vfmat.ch/6cd2

African Health Now
Promotes and provides information and access to sustainable primary healthcare to women, children, and families living across Sub-Saharan Africa.

Dent-OMFS, Endo, General, Infect Dis, MF Med, OB-GYN
🌐 https://vfmat.ch/c766

African Mission Health Foundation
Aims to strengthen African mission hospitals by providing quality, compassionate care for the hurting and forgotten and helping improve Sub-Saharan Africa's health system.
Infect Dis, Neonat, OB-GYN, Peds, Surg
🌐 https://vfmat.ch/5b14

Against Malaria Foundation
Helps protect people from malaria. Funds anti-malaria nets, specifically long-lasting insecticidal nets (LLINs), and works with distribution partners to ensure they are used. Tracks and reports on net use and malaria case data.
Infect Dis
🌐 https://vfmat.ch/337d

American Academy of Ophthalmology
Protects sight and empowers lives by serving as an advocate for patients and the public, leading ophthalmic education, and advancing the profession of ophthalmology.
Ophth-Opt
🌐 https://vfmat.ch/89a2

Amref Health Africa
Serves millions of people across 35 countries in Sub-Saharan Africa, strengthening health systems, and training African health workers to respond to the continent's most critical health issues.
All-Immu, General, Infect Dis, Logist-Op, MF Med, OB-GYN, Path, Pub Health, Surg
🌐 https://vfmat.ch/6985

AO Alliance
Builds solutions to lessen the burden of injuries in low- and middle-income countries, while enhancing the care of the injured to reduce human suffering, disability, and poverty.
Ortho, Surg
🌐 https://vfmat.ch/8cd5

Association for the Promotion of Human Health (APSH), Burundi
Promotes good health, education, and hope for children and underprivileged populations in Burundi.
CV Med, General, Infect Dis, OB-GYN
🌐 https://vfmat.ch/1e7c

Beta Humanitarian Help
Provides plastic surgery in underserved areas of the world.
Anesth, Plast
🌐 https://vfmat.ch/7221

Bread and Water for Africa UK
Aims to create better access to education, nutrition, and healthcare for some of Africa's most vulnerable children and their communities.
General, MF Med, Nutr
⊕ https://vfmat.ch/c855

Canadian Foundation for Women's Health
Seeks to advance the health of women in Canada and around the world through research, education, and advocacy in obstetrics and gynecology.
MF Med, OB-GYN
⊕ https://vfmat.ch/f41e

CARE
Works around the globe to save lives, defeat poverty, and achieve social justice.
ER Med, General
⊕ https://vfmat.ch/7232

Carter Center, The
Seeks to prevent and resolve conflicts, enhance freedom and democracy, and improve health, while remaining committed to human rights and the alleviation of human suffering.
Infect Dis, MF Med, Ophth-Opt
⊕ https://vfmat.ch/6556

Catholic Organization for Relief & Development Aid (CORDAID)
Provides humanitarian assistance and creates opportunities to improve security, healthcare, education, and inclusive economic growth in fragile and conflict-affected areas.
ER Med, Infect Dis, MF Med, OB-GYN, Peds, Psych
⊕ https://vfmat.ch/8ae5

Center for Strategic and International Studies (CSIS) Commission on Strengthening America's Health Security
Brings together a distinguished and diverse group of high-level opinion leaders bridging security and health, with the core aim to chart a bold vision for the future of U.S. leadership in global health.
ER Med, Infect Dis, MF Med, Pub Health
⊕ https://vfmat.ch/6d7f

Chain of Hope
Provides lifesaving heart operations for children around the world and supports the development of cardiac services in numerous developing and war-torn countries.
Anesth, CT Surg, CV Med, Crit-Care, Ped Surg, Peds, Pulm-Critic, Surg
⊕ https://vfmat.ch/1b1b

Christian Blind Mission (CBM)
Aims to improve the quality of life of persons with disabilities in the poorest countries, addressing poverty as a cause and a consequence of disability, and working in partnership to create a society for all.
ENT, General, Infect Dis, OB-GYN, Ophth-Opt, Ortho, Peds, Psych, Rehab, Surg
⊕ https://vfmat.ch/3824

Cleft Africa
Strives to provide underserved Africans with cleft lips and palates with access to the best possible treatment for their condition, so that they can live a life free of the health problems caused by cleft.
Anesth, Dent-OMFS, Ped Surg, Surg
⊕ https://vfmat.ch/8298

Comitato Collaborazione Medica (CCM)
Supports development processes that safeguard and promote the right to health with a global approach, working on health needs and influencing socio-economic factors, identifying poverty as the main cause for the lack of health.
All-Immu, General, Infect Dis, MF Med, OB-GYN
⊕ https://vfmat.ch/4272

Concern Worldwide
Seeks to permanently transform the lives of people living in extreme poverty, tackling its root causes, and building resilience.
Logist-Op, MF Med, Nutr, OB-GYN
⊕ https://vfmat.ch/77e9

Core Group
Aims to improve and expand community health practices for underserved populations, especially women and children, through collaborative action and learning.
General, Infect Dis, MF Med, Medicine, OB-GYN, Peds, Pub Health
⊕ https://vfmat.ch/9de3

Developing Country NGO Delegation: Global Fund to Fight AIDS, TB & Malaria
Works to strengthen the engagement of civil society actors and organizations in developing countries to build a world in which AIDS, TB, and malaria are no longer global, public health, and human rights threats.
Infect Dis, Pub Health
⊕ https://vfmat.ch/3149

Direct Relief
Improves the health and lives of people affected by poverty or emergency situations by mobilizing and providing essential medical resources needed for their care.
ER Med, Logist-Op
⊕ https://vfmat.ch/58e5

Doctors Without Borders/Médecins Sans Frontières (MSF)
Responds to emergencies and provides lifesaving medical care where needed most, including during disasters, conflicts, and epidemics.
Anesth, Crit-Care, ER Med, General, Infect Dis, Nutr, OB-GYN, Ped Surg, Peds, Psych, Pub Health, Surg
⊕ https://vfmat.ch/f363

Enabel
As the development agency of the Belgian federal government, charged with implementing Belgium's international development policy, carries out public service assignments in Belgium and abroad pursuant to the 2030 Agenda for Sustainable Development.
General, Infect Dis, Logist-Op, MF Med, OB-GYN, Peds, Pub Health
⊕ https://vfmat.ch/5af7

END Fund, The
Aims to control and eliminate the most prevalent neglected diseases among the world's poorest and most vulnerable people.
Infect Dis
⊕ https://vfmat.ch/2614

EngenderHealth
Works to implement high-quality, gender-equitable programs that advance sexual and reproductive health and rights.
General, MF Med, OB-GYN, Peds
⊕ https://vfmat.ch/1cb2

Episcopal Relief & Development
Provides relief in times of disaster and promotes sustainable development by identifying and addressing the root causes of suffering.
Infect Dis, MF Med, Neonat, Nutr, Peds
⊕ https://vfmat.ch/7cfa

Fracarita International
Provides support and services in the fields of mental healthcare, care for people with a disability, and education.
Psych, Rehab
⊕ https://vfmat.ch/8d3c

Fred Hollows Foundation, The
Works toward a world in which no person is needlessly blind or vision impaired.
Ophth-Opt, Pub Health, Surg
⊕ https://vfmat.ch/73e5

Global Clubfoot Initiative (GCI)
Promotes and resources the treatment of children with clubfoot in developing countries using the Ponseti technique.
Ortho, Ped Surg
⊕ https://vfmat.ch/f229

Global Ministries – The United Methodist Church

As the worldwide mission and development agency of The United Methodist Church, Global Ministries works with more than 300 hospitals and clinics around the world through its Global Health Unit.

Anesth, CT Surg, CV Med, Crit-Care, Dent-OMFS, Derm, ER Med, GI, General, Infect Dis, Logist-Op, MF Med, Medicine, Neonat, Nephro, Nutr, OB-GYN, Ophth-Opt, Ortho, Palliative, Peds, Pod, Psych, Pub Health, Rehab, Rheum, Surg, Urol

⊕ https://vfmat.ch/1723

Global Oncology (GO)

Brings the best in cancer care to underserved patients around the world and collaborates across geographic, professional, and academic borders to improve cancer care, research, and education.

Heme-Onc, Path, Rad-Onc

⊕ https://vfmat.ch/fcb8

Globus Relief

Aims to improve the delivery of healthcare worldwide by gathering, processing, and distributing surplus medical supplies to charities at home and abroad.

Logist-Op

⊕ https://vfmat.ch/a2b7

Health Equity Initiative

Aims to build and sustain a global community that engages across sectors and disciplines to advance health equity.

Pub Health

⊕ https://vfmat.ch/e2e2

HealthNet TPO

Aims to facilitate and strengthen communities and help them to regain control and maintain their health and well-being, believing that even the most vulnerable people have the inner strength to build a better future for themselves.

Crit-Care, General, Infect Dis, Logist-Op, Medicine, OB-GYN, Ophth-Opt, Peds, Psych, Pub Health, Surg

⊕ https://vfmat.ch/67d6

Healthy DEvelopments

Provides Germany-supported health and social protection programs around the globe in a collaborative knowledge management process.

All-Immu, General, Infect Dis, Logist-Op, MF Med

⊕ https://vfmat.ch/dc31

Hope and Healing International

Gives hope and healing to children and families trapped by poverty and disability.

General, Nutr, Ophth-Opt, Peds, Rehab

⊕ https://vfmat.ch/c638

Hope Walks

Frees children, families, and communities from the burden of clubfoot, inspired by the Christian faith.

Ortho, Ped Surg, Peds, Rehab

⊕ https://vfmat.ch/f6d4

Hospice Africa

Aims to provide a holistic and culturally sensitive palliative care service through accurate treatment of pain.

Palliative

⊕ https://vfmat.ch/9f86

ICAP at Columbia University

Serves as global leader in supporting the scale-up of multidisciplinary HIV/AIDS prevention, care, and treatment programs based on a family-focused approach.

General, Infect Dis, MF Med, Medicine, OB-GYN, Pub Health

⊕ https://vfmat.ch/a8ef

International Agency for the Prevention of Blindness (IAPB), The

Leads international efforts in blindness-prevention activities, works toward a world where no one is needlessly visually impaired, and ensures that everyone has access to the best possible standard of eye health.

Infect Dis, Ophth-Opt, Pub Health

⊕ https://vfmat.ch/87a2

International Council of Ophthalmology

Works with ophthalmologic societies and others to enhance ophthalmic education and improve access to the highest-quality eye care in order to preserve and restore vision for people of the world.

Ophth-Opt

⊕ https://vfmat.ch/ffd2

International Federation of Red Cross and Red Crescent Societies (IFRC)

Coordinates and directs international assistance following natural and manmade disasters in nonconflict situations through the world's largest humanitarian and development network. Provides disaster-preparedness programs, healthcare activities, and promotes humanitarian values.

ER Med, General, Infect Dis, Nutr

⊕ https://vfmat.ch/b4ee

International Medical and Surgical Aid (IMSA)

Aims to save lives and alleviate suffering through education, healthcare, surgical camps, and quality medical programs.

Anesth, General, Ped Surg, Surg

⊕ https://vfmat.ch/2561

International Medical Corps

Seeks to improve quality of life through health interventions and related activities that strengthen underserved communities worldwide, with the flexibility to respond rapidly to emergencies and offer medical services and training to people at the highest risk.

ER Med, General, Infect Dis, Nutr, OB-GYN, Peds, Pub Health, Surg

⊕ https://vfmat.ch/a8a5

International Organization for Migration (IOM) – The UN Migration Agency

Promotes evidence-informed policies and holistic, preventive, and curative health programs that are beneficial, accessible, and equitable for vulnerable migrants.

General, Infect Dis, OB-GYN

⊕ https://vfmat.ch/621a

International Planned Parenthood Federation (IPPF)

Leads a locally owned, globally connected civil society movement that provides and enables services and champions sexual and reproductive health and rights for all, especially the underserved.

Infect Dis, MF Med, OB-GYN

⊕ https://vfmat.ch/dc97

International Rescue Committee (IRC)

Responds to the world's worst humanitarian crises and helps people whose lives and livelihoods are shattered by conflict and disaster to survive, recover, and gain control of their future.

ER Med, General, Infect Dis, MF Med, Peds

⊕ https://vfmat.ch/5d24

International Trachoma Initiative (iTi)

Works toward a world free from trachoma, a preventable cause of blindness, and provides comprehensive support to national ministries of health and governmental and nongovernmental organizations to implement a comprehensive approach to fight trachoma.

Infect Dis, Ophth-Opt

⊕ https://vfmat.ch/3278

John Snow, Inc. (JSI)

Aims to improve the health and well-being of underserved and vulnerable people and communities throughout the world.

General, Infect Dis, Logist-Op, MF Med, OB-GYN, Peds, Psych, Pub Health

⊕ https://vfmat.ch/ba78

Johns Hopkins Center for Global Health

Facilitates and focuses the extensive expertise and resources of the Johns Hopkins institutions, together with global collaborators, to effectively address and ameliorate the world's most pressing health issues.

General, Genetics, Logist-Op, MF Med, Peds, Psych, Pub Health, Pulm-Critic

⊕ https://vfmat.ch/54ce

Joint United Nations Programme on HIV/AIDS (UNAIDS)

Aims to place people living with HIV and people affected by the virus at the decision-making table and at the center of designing, delivering, and monitoring the AIDS response.

Infect Dis

🌐 https://vfmat.ch/464a

Kibuye Hope Hospital (KHH)

Serves and treats surrounding communities through high-quality specialist doctors, a robust medical school, government support, and an expanding campus, inspired by the Christian faith.

Anesth, ER Med, Medicine, Ophth-Opt, Ophth-Opt, Path, Peds, Radiol, Surg

🌐 https://vfmat.ch/bdf8

Lay Volunteers International Association (LVIA)

Fosters local and global change to help overcome extreme poverty, reinforce equitable and sustainable development, and enhance dialogue between Italian and African communities.

ER Med, Logist-Op, MF Med, Neonat, Nutr, OB-GYN, Peds

🌐 https://vfmat.ch/ecd4

Life for a Child

Supports the provision of the best possible healthcare, given local circumstances, to all children and youth with diabetes in less-resourced countries, through the strengthening of existing diabetes services.

Endo, Medicine, Peds

🌐 https://vfmat.ch/d712

LifeNet International

Transforms African healthcare by equipping and empowering existing local health centers to provide quality, sustainable, and lifesaving care to patients.

General, Infect Dis, MF Med, Neonat, OB-GYN, Pub Health

🌐 https://vfmat.ch/e5d2

Light House Medical Missions

Inspired by the Christian faith, provides programs in healthcare provision, nutrition, emergency relief and response, and water, sanitation, and hygiene (WASH).

ER Med, General, Surg

🌐 https://vfmat.ch/cecd

Limbs International

Engages communities and transforms lives through affordable, sustainable prosthetic solutions and rehabilitation services in developing countries.

Logist-Op, Ortho, Pod, Rehab

🌐 https://vfmat.ch/dc84

Lions Clubs International

Empowers volunteers to serve their communities, meet humanitarian needs, encourage peace, and promote international understanding through Lions Clubs.

Heme-Onc, Medicine, Nutr, Ophth-Opt

🌐 https://vfmat.ch/7b12

Management Sciences for Health (MSH)

Works with countries and communities to save lives and improve the health of the world's poorest and most vulnerable people by building strong, resilient, sustainable health systems.

Infect Dis, Logist-Op, Pub Health

🌐 https://vfmat.ch/6aa2

MAP International

Provides medicines and health supplies to those in need around the world so they might experience life to the fullest.

Logist-Op

🌐 https://vfmat.ch/deed

Medical Care Development International

Works to improve the health of vulnerable populations through integrated, sustainable, and locally driven interventions.

Infect Dis, OB-GYN, Peds, Pub Health

🌐 https://vfmat.ch/da87

Medical Mission Trips

Provides medical aid, welfare assistance, and educational opportunities in Brazil, Honduras, Guatemala, Kenya, Burundi, and Ethiopia.

General

🌐 https://vfmat.ch/9117

Medicus Mundi Italia

Carries out programs in basic community health, health education, maternal and child health, nutrition, and infectious disease.

General, Infect Dis, Logist-Op, MF Med, Nutr, Peds, Pub Health, Rehab

🌐 https://vfmat.ch/4413

MedShare

Aims to improve the quality of life of people, communities, and the planet by sourcing and directly delivering surplus medical supplies and equipment to communities in need around the world.

Logist-Op

🌐 https://vfmat.ch/c8bc

Mercy and Love Foundation

Aims to provide orphaned and vulnerable children with basic human needs such as food, clothing, and shelter, enabling them to thrive.

General, Peds

🌐 https://vfmat.ch/649a

Mercy Ships

Operates hospital ships staffed by volunteers to bring hope, healing, and healthcare to underserved communities worldwide.

Anesth, Dent-OMFS, Logist-Op, Neonat, OB-GYN, Ophth-Opt, Ortho, Palliative, Plast, Psych, Surg

🌐 https://vfmat.ch/2e99

Mission Partners for Christ

Provides medication, treatment, screenings, and health education in underserved communities around the world, inspired by the Christian faith.

Dent-OMFS, General, Ophth-Opt

🌐 https://vfmat.ch/eb25

NCD Alliance

Unites and strengthens civil society to stimulate collaborative advocacy, action, and accountability for NCD (noncommunicable disease) prevention and control.

All-Immu, CV Med, General, Heme-Onc, Medicine, Peds, Psych

🌐 https://vfmat.ch/abdd

Operation Fistula

Exists to end obstetric fistula by building models of care that serve every woman, everywhere.

MF Med, OB-GYN, Surg

🌐 https://vfmat.ch/ce8e

Pact

Works on the ground to improve the lives of those who are challenged by poverty and marginalization, striving for a world in which all people are heard, capable, and vibrant.

Infect Dis, Logist-Op, MF Med, Pub Health

🌐 https://vfmat.ch/9a6c

Pan-African Academy of Christian Surgeons (PAACS)

Exists to train and support African surgeons to provide excellent, compassionate care to those most in need, inspired by the Christian faith.

Anesth, CT Surg, Neurosurg, OB-GYN, Ortho, Ped Surg, Plast, Surg

🌐 https://vfmat.ch/85ba

Partners in Health

Responds to the moral imperative to provide high-quality healthcare globally to those who need it most, while striving to ease suffering by providing a comprehensive model of care that includes access to food, transportation, housing, and other key components of healing.

CT Surg, General, Heme-Onc, Infect Dis, MF Med, Neurosurg, OB-GYN, Ortho, Plast, Psych, Urol

🌐 https://vfmat.ch/dc9c

Pathfinder International
Champions sexual and reproductive health and rights worldwide, mobilizing communities most in need to break through barriers and forge paths to a healthier future.
OB-GYN
⊕ https://vfmat.ch/a7b3

PINCC Preventing Cervical Cancer
Seeks to prevent female-specific diseases in developing countries by utilizing low-cost and low-technology methods to create sustainable programs through patient education, medical personnel training, and facility outfitting.
OB-GYN
⊕ https://vfmat.ch/9666

Project Concern International (PCI)
Drives innovation from the ground up to enhance health, end hunger, overcome hardship, and advance women and girls—resulting in meaningful and measurable change in people's lives.
Infect Dis, MF Med, Nutr, OB-GYN, Peds
⊕ https://vfmat.ch/5ed7

PSI – Population Services International
Aims to improve the health of people in the developing world by focusing on challenges such as a lack of family planning, HIV/AIDS, barriers to maternal health, and the greatest threats to children under the age of 5, including malaria, diarrhea, pneumonia, and malnutrition.
Infect Dis, MF Med, OB-GYN, Peds
⊕ https://vfmat.ch/ffe3

RestoringVision
Empowers lives by restoring vision for millions of people in need.
Ophth-Opt
⊕ https://vfmat.ch/e121

Rockefeller Foundation, The
Works to promote the well-being of humanity.
Logist-Op, Nutr, Pub Health
⊕ https://vfmat.ch/5424

Rotary International
Provides service to others, improves lives, and advances world understanding, goodwill, and peace through its fellowship of business, professional, and community leaders.
ER Med, General, Infect Dis, MF Med, OB-GYN
⊕ https://vfmat.ch/8fb5

Salvation Army International, The
Seeks to meet human needs through services in education, healthcare, community support, emergency response, and ministry development, inspired by the Christian faith.
Dent-OMFS, Derm, ER Med, Infect Dis, MF Med, Medicine, Nutr, OB-GYN, Ophth-Opt, Palliative, Psych, Rehab, Surg
⊕ https://vfmat.ch/8eb3

Samaritan's Purse International Disaster Relief
Provides spiritual and physical aid to hurting people around the world, such as victims of war, poverty, natural disasters, disease, and famine, based in Christian ministry.
Anesth, CT Surg, Crit-Care, Dent-OMFS, Derm, ENT, ER Med, Endo, GI, General, Heme-Onc, Infect Dis, MF Med, Neonat, Nephro, Neuro, Neurosurg, Nutr, OB-GYN, Ophth-Opt, Ortho, Path, Ped Surg, Peds, Plast, Psych, Pulm-Critic, Radiol, Rehab, Rheum, Surg, Urol, Vasc Surg
⊕ https://vfmat.ch/87e3

Santé Communauté Développement
Promotes the health of communities in Burundi through information, education, and promotion of good practices leading to health and development.
General, OB-GYN
⊕ https://vfmat.ch/62d4

Save the Children
Gives children around the world a healthy start in life, the opportunity to learn, and protection from harm.

All-Immu, Crit-Care, ER Med, General, Infect Dis, MF Med, Medicine, Neonat, OB-GYN, Peds, Psych, Pub Health
⊕ https://vfmat.ch/2e73

SCI Foundation
Seeks to prevent and treat neglected infectious diseases, with a focus on eliminating parasitic worm infections through strengthening impactful and comprehensive health programs across Sub-Saharan Africa.
Infect Dis, Pub Health
⊕ https://vfmat.ch/5444

SEE International
Provides sustainable medical, surgical, and educational services through volunteer ophthalmic surgeons, with the objectives of restoring sight and preventing blindness to disadvantaged individuals worldwide.
Ophth-Opt, Surg
⊕ https://vfmat.ch/6e1b

SIGN Fracture Care International
Builds orthopedic capacity around the world and provides the injured poor access to fracture surgery by donating orthopedic education and implant systems to surgeons in developing countries.
Ortho, Rehab, Surg
⊕ https://vfmat.ch/123d

SINA Health
Aims to improve the health and educational status of the population in low- and middle-income countries.
General, Logist-Op
⊕ https://vfmat.ch/9ad3

Smile Train, Inc.
Treats children with cleft lip through a sustainable and local model that supports surgery and other forms of essential care.
Logist-Op, Pub Health
⊕ https://vfmat.ch/822c

Soddo Christian Hospital
Mobilizes volunteers to help transform communities through healthcare and education, based in Christian ministry.
ER Med, General
⊕ https://vfmat.ch/efa4

Solthis
Improves disease prevention and access to quality care by strengthening the health systems and services of the countries served.
General, Infect Dis, Logist-Op, MF Med, Neonat, Path
⊕ https://vfmat.ch/a71d

Swiss Tropical and Public Health Institute
Contributes to the improvement of the health of populations internationally, nationally, and locally through excellence in research, education, and services.
Infect Dis, Pub Health
⊕ https://vfmat.ch/2ee4

Task Force for Global Health, The
Consists of programs and focus areas that cover a range of global health issues including neglected tropical diseases, infectious diseases, vaccines, field epidemiology, public health informatics, health workforce development, and global health ethics.
Infect Dis, Logist-Op, Medicine, Ophth-Opt, Peds
⊕ https://vfmat.ch/714c

Tearfund
Responds to crisis and partners with local churches to bring restoration to those living in poverty, inspired by the Christian faith.
ER Med, Logist-Op
⊕ https://vfmat.ch/f6cf

Terre des hommes (Tdh) Foundation
Works to improve the daily life of children and their relatives in the areas of health, protection and emergency, in Europe, Africa, Asia, Latin America, and the Near and Middle East.

CT Surg, CV Med, OB-GYN, Ped Surg, Pub Health
⊕ https://vfmat.ch/5c26

Union for International Cancer Control (UICC)
Unites and supports the cancer community to reduce the global cancer burden, promote greater equity, and ensure that cancer control continues to be a priority in the world health and development agenda.
Heme-Onc, Pub Health
⊕ https://vfmat.ch/88b1

United MegaCare
Seeks to deliver high-caliber services and programming across its areas of focus: education, health and wellness, secure families, and disaster resiliency.
ER Med, General, Infect Dis, Nutr, Ophth-Opt, Peds
⊕ https://vfmat.ch/ea18

United Nations Children's Fund (UNICEF)
Works in over 190 countries and territories to save children's lives, defend their rights, and help them fulfill their potential, from early childhood through adolescence.
All-Immu, Infect Dis, MF Med, Neonat, Nutr, OB-GYN, Ped Surg, Peds, Pub Health
⊕ https://vfmat.ch/42d7

United Nations Development Programme (UNDP)
Helps countries achieve the simultaneous eradication of extreme poverty and significant reduction of inequalities and exclusion using a sustainable human development approach.
Infect Dis, Logist-Op, Pub Health
⊕ https://vfmat.ch/935c

United Nations High Commissioner for Refugees (UNHCR)
Safeguards the rights and well-being of people who have been forced to flee, ensuring that everybody has the right to seek asylum and find safe refuge in another country, with the goal of seeking lasting solutions.
General, MF Med, Medicine, OB-GYN, Peds, Psych, Pub Health
⊕ https://vfmat.ch/6636

United Nations Office for the Coordination of Humanitarian Affairs (OCHA)
Contributes to principled and effective humanitarian response through coordination, advocacy, policy, information management, and humanitarian financing tools and services, by leveraging functional expertise throughout the organization.
Logist-Op
⊕ https://vfmat.ch/22b8

United Nations Population Fund (UNFPA)
Supports reproductive healthcare for women and youth in more than 150 countries, focusing on delivering a world in which every pregnancy is wanted, every childbirth is safe, and every young person's potential is fulfilled.
Infect Dis, MF Med, Neonat, OB-GYN, Peds, Pub Health
⊕ https://vfmat.ch/c969

United States Agency for International Development (USAID)
Promotes and demonstrates democratic values abroad and advances a free, peaceful, and prosperous world. Leads the U.S. government's international development and disaster assistance through partnerships and investments that save lives.
ER Med, Infect Dis, MF Med, OB-GYN, Peds
⊕ https://vfmat.ch/9a99

USA for United Nations High Commissioner for Refugees (UNHCR)
Serves and protects refugees and displaced people through emergency relief, cash assistance, education, resettlement, and the rebuilding of livelihoods.
ER Med, General, Logist-Op, Nutr, Pub Health
⊕ https://vfmat.ch/293c

USAID: EQUIP Health
Exists as an effective, efficient response mechanism to achieving global HIV epidemic control by delivering the right intervention at the right place and in the right way.

Infect Dis
⊕ https://vfmat.ch/d76a

USAID: Health Finance and Governance Project
Uses research to implement strategies to help countries develop robust governance systems, increase their domestic resources for health, manage those resources more effectively, and make wise purchasing decisions.
Logist-Op
⊕ https://vfmat.ch/8652

USAID: Human Resources for Health 2030 (HRH2030)
Helps low- and middle-income countries develop the health workforce needed to prevent maternal and child deaths, support the goals of Family Planning 2020, control the HIV/AIDS epidemic, and protect communities from infectious diseases.
Logist-Op
⊕ https://vfmat.ch/9ea8

Village Health Works
Provides quality, compassionate healthcare in a dignified environment while also addressing the root causes of illness, poverty, violence, and neglect.
Anesth, General, Infect Dis, MF Med, Medicine, OB-GYN, Peds, Psych, Surg
⊕ https://vfmat.ch/56b5

Vision for the Poor
Reduces human suffering and improves quality of life through the recovery of sight by building sustainable eye hospitals in developing countries, empowering local eye specialists, funding essential ophthalmic infrastructure, and partnering with like-minded agencies.
Ophth-Opt
⊕ https://vfmat.ch/528e

Vision Outreach International
Advocates for helping the blind in underserved regions of the world and empowers the poor through sight restoration.
Ophth-Opt
⊕ https://vfmat.ch/9721

Vitamin Angels
Helps at-risk populations in need—specifically pregnant women, new mothers, and children under age 5—to gain access to life-changing vitamins and minerals.
General, Nutr
⊕ https://vfmat.ch/7da1

Wings of Hope for Africa Foundation
Aims to support family welfare, empowers communities, and develops self-sufficiency programs to end poverty in Burundi and Rwanda, East Africa, and in Calgary, Canada.
Infect Dis, Medicine, Peds
⊕ https://vfmat.ch/8d4e

Women's Refugee Commission
Seeks to improve lives by protecting the rights of women, children, and youth displaced by conflict and crisis through researching their needs, identifying solutions, and advocating for programs and policies to strengthen their resilience.
General, MF Med, Neonat, OB-GYN, Peds, Psych
⊕ https://vfmat.ch/3d8f

World Anaesthesia Society (WAS)
Aims to support anesthesiologists with an interest in working in low-income regions of the world.
Anesth
⊕ https://vfmat.ch/37fe

World Health Organization, The (WHO)
The United Nations' agency for health provides leadership on global health matters, shapes the health research agenda, sets norms and standards, articulates evidence-based policy options, provides technical support and monitoring to countries, and assesses health trends.
ER Med, General, Infect Dis, Logist-Op, MF Med, OB-GYN, Peds, Psych, Pub Health
⊕ https://vfmat.ch/c476

World Relief

Brings sustainable solutions to the world's greatest problems: disasters, extreme poverty, violence, oppression, and mass displacement.

ER Med, Nutr, Psych, Pub Health

⊕ https://vfmat.ch/fbcd

World Vision International

Works with vulnerable communities around the world to overcome poverty and injustice with child-focused programs in disaster management, health, nutrition, economic development, education, clean water, sanitation, and hygiene.

ER Med, General, Infect Dis, MF Med, Nutr, OB-GYN, Peds

⊕ https://vfmat.ch/2642

Burundi

Healthcare Facilities

Aluma
Boulevard de l'Unité, Bujumbura, Bujumbura Mairie, Burundi
⊕ https://vfmat.ch/22a7

Banyagihugu 2
Avenue du Marche Kanyosha, Kanyosha, Bujumbura Mairie, Burundi
⊕ https://vfmat.ch/2635

Bethel
7ème Avenue, Kanyosha, Bujumbura Mairie, Burundi
⊕ https://vfmat.ch/b33f

Bukiriro
RN 3, Kanyosha, Bujumbura Mairie, Burundi
⊕ https://vfmat.ch/a2f1

Bumerec
Avenue Ririkumutima, Bujumbura, Bujumbura Mairie, Burundi
⊕ https://vfmat.ch/e57a

Cabara
RN 3, Kigwena, Rumonge, Burundi
⊕ https://vfmat.ch/8f3f

Cankuzo Hospital
RN 11, Cankuzo, Burundi
⊕ https://vfmat.ch/28af

Cemadif
Rue Mugamba, Bujumbura, Bujumbura Mairie, Burundi
⊕ https://vfmat.ch/a4bd

Centre Medico Chirurgical de Kinindo (CMCK)
RN 3, Muha, Bujumbura Mairie, Burundi
⊕ https://vfmat.ch/7e17

Centre Médico-technique de Ngozi
Ngozi, Burundi
⊕ https://vfmat.ch/146c

Cibitoke District Hospital
RN 5, Cibitoke, Cibitoke, Burundi
⊕ https://vfmat.ch/b264

Croix Rouge Mwaro
RP 31, Mwaro, Mwaro, Burundi
⊕ https://vfmat.ch/11ac

Dunga
RN 11, Makamba, Makamba, Burundi
⊕ https://vfmat.ch/d54f

Enfant Soleil
Chaussée du Peuple Murundi, Bujumbura, Bujumbura Mairie, Burundi
⊕ https://vfmat.ch/4ec8

Gasenyi I
Rango, Kayanza, Burundi
⊕ https://vfmat.ch/86d9

Gisenyi
Buyagira, Makamba, Burundi
⊕ https://vfmat.ch/8984

Horizon
7ème Avenue, Kanyosha, Bujumbura Mairie, Burundi
⊕ https://vfmat.ch/4579

Hospital at Bisoro
Bisoro, Mwaro, Burundi
⊕ https://vfmat.ch/22a9

Hospital at Bubera
Bubera, Rumonge, Burundi
⊕ https://vfmat.ch/9e2f

Hospital at Buta
RN 17, Buta, Bururi, Burundi
⊕ https://vfmat.ch/6abf

Hospital at Bwatemba
Bwatemba, Bururi, Burundi
⊕ https://vfmat.ch/b964

Hospital at Gashirwe
Gashirwe, Cankuzo, Burundi
⊕ https://vfmat.ch/c7f4

Hospital at Gatabo
Gatabo, Makamba, Burundi
⊕ https://vfmat.ch/cfd5

Hospital at Gatakazi
Gatakazi, Musongati, Rutana, Burundi
⊕ https://vfmat.ch/32fb

Hospital at Gihanga
Gihanga, Burundi
⊕ https://vfmat.ch/5b3c

Hospital at Gishiha
Gishiha, Makamba, Burundi
⊕ https://vfmat.ch/2825

Hospital at Kanyosha
8ème Avenue, Kanyosha, Bujumbura Mairie, Burundi
⊕ https://vfmat.ch/1a4a

Hospital at Kigwena
RN 3, Kigwena, Rumonge, Burundi
⊕ https://vfmat.ch/4a92

Hospital at Makamba
Makamba, Burundi
⊕ https://vfmat.ch/37d1

Hospital at Matara
RN7, Matara, Bujumbura Rural, Burundi
⊕ https://vfmat.ch/34c7

Hospital at Matongo
RN 1, Matongo, Kayanza, Burundi
⊕ https://vfmat.ch/5184

Hospital at Mugeni
Mugeni, Makamba, Burundi
⊕ https://vfmat.ch/a8da

Hospital at Muhama
Muhama, Makamba, Burundi
⊕ https://vfmat.ch/bb42

Hospital at Munini
RN 17, Munini, Bururi, Burundi
⊕ https://vfmat.ch/ba6f

Hospital at Muramvya
RN 2, Muramvya, Muramvya, Burundi
⊕ https://vfmat.ch/89b6

Hospital at Musenyi
Ngozi, Musenyi, Burundi
⊕ https://vfmat.ch/b6c9

Hospital at Nyabihanga
Nyabihanga, Burundi
⊕ https://vfmat.ch/cd2b

Hospital at Nyakararo
RN 18, Nyakararo, Mwaro, Burundi
⊕ https://vfmat.ch/361f

Hospital at Nyakuguma
Nyakuguma, Rutana, Burundi
⊕ https://vfmat.ch/83ab

Hospital at Nyarurama
Nyarurama, Burundi
⊕ https://vfmat.ch/a976

Hospital at Rorero
Rorero, Burundi
⊕ https://vfmat.ch/692d

Hospital at Rukago
RP 51, Rukago, Kayanza, Burundi
⊕ https://vfmat.ch/34b9

Hospital Bwiza Jabe
Boulevard Ouest, Bujumbura, Bujumbura Mairie, Burundi
⊕ https://vfmat.ch/7d61

Hospital Gaheta
Muramvya, Mbuye, Burundi
⊕ https://vfmat.ch/3b1c

Hospital Gahombo
Kayanza, Gahombo, Burundi
⊕ https://vfmat.ch/fc9b

Hospital Kankima
Bujumbura Rural, Mugongomanga, Burundi
⊕ https://vfmat.ch/3195

Hospital Karehe
Muramvya, Mbuye, Burundi
⊕ https://vfmat.ch/9176

Hospital Muramvya
Muramvya, Burundi
⊕ https://vfmat.ch/3aeb

Hospital Mutaho
Mutaho, Muramvya, Burundi
⊕ https://vfmat.ch/3b77

Hôpital de Kinyinya
RP 72, Kinyinya, Ruyigi, Burundi
⊕ https://vfmat.ch/12b9

Hôpital de Rumonge
RN 3, Rumonge, Rumonge, Burundi
⊕ https://vfmat.ch/addd

Hôpital Général de Mpanda
RN 9, Mpanda, Burundi
⊕ https://vfmat.ch/529a

Hôpital Kibumbu
RN 18, Kibumbu, Mwaro, Burundi
⊕ https://vfmat.ch/3968

Hôpital Mabayi
RN 10, Mabayi, Cibitoke, Burundi
⊕ https://vfmat.ch/8421

Hôpital Militaire de Kamenge
Boulevard du 28 Novembre, Bujumbura, Burundi
⊕ https://vfmat.ch/5e8e

Hôpital MSF de l'Arche
Avenue Kibezi, Bujumbura, Bujumbura Mairie, Burundi
⊕ https://vfmat.ch/74e5

Hôpital Nyanzalac
RN 3, Nyanza Lac, Makamba, Burundi
⊕ https://vfmat.ch/1895

Hôpital Prince Régent Charles (HPRC)
9 Avenue de l'Hôpital, Bujumbura, Burundi
⊕ https://vfmat.ch/7519

Hôpital Roi Khaled
Vers ETS Kamenge, Bujumbura, Bujumbura Mairie, Burundi
⊕ https://vfmat.ch/7dfe

Hôpital Régional de Gitega
Gitega, Burundi
⊕ https://vfmat.ch/6d2c

Ibitalo ya Butezi
RP 201, Butezi, Ruyigi, Burundi
⊕ https://vfmat.ch/68ea

Izere
RN 11, Makamba, Makamba, Burundi
⊕ https://vfmat.ch/8e46

Kayogoro
RN 11, Makamba, Makamba, Burundi
⊕ https://vfmat.ch/51ce

Kibezi
Bururi, Mugamba, Burundi
⊕ https://vfmat.ch/b88c

Kibuye Hope Hospital (KHH)
Songa, Gitega, Burundi
⊕ https://vfmat.ch/216c

Kigutu Hospital
Kirungu, Burundi
⊕ https://vfmat.ch/afc3

Kinima
RN 3, Mena, Bujumbura Rural, Burundi
⊕ https://vfmat.ch/7dcd

Kira Hospital
Boulevard de la Liberté, Bujumbura, Bujumbura Mairie, Burundi
⊕ https://vfmat.ch/f933

La Charité
Boulevard Général Adolphe Nshimirimana, Bujumbura, Bujumbura Mairie, Burundi
⊕ https://vfmat.ch/1752

Misericorde
Rue Gitaramuka, Bujumbura, Bujumbura Mairie, Burundi
⊕ https://vfmat.ch/941d

Muberure
RN 1, Mirango, Bujumbura Mairie, Burundi
⊕ https://vfmat.ch/75cf

Mugendo
Nyange, Kirundo, Burundi
⊕ https://vfmat.ch/e17e

Muhweza
Rubimba, Bururi, Burundi
⊕ https://vfmat.ch/18d1

Murengeza
RP 105, Murira, Bubanza, Burundi
⊕ https://vfmat.ch/c2e8

Musigati
RN 9, Bubanza, Bubanza, Burundi
⊕ https://vfmat.ch/a161

Muzenga I
RN 17, Kiremba, Bururi, Burundi
⊕ https://vfmat.ch/a211

Muzenga II
Buyengero, Burundi
⊕ https://vfmat.ch/24ca

Nyabiraba
RP 108, Vugizo, Bujumbura Rural, Burundi
⊕ https://vfmat.ch/bc18

Nyakaraye
RP 32, Kavumu, Mwaro, Burundi
⊕ https://vfmat.ch/147f

Parable
3ème Avenue, Muha, Bujumbura Mairie, Burundi
⊕ https://vfmat.ch/4c2b

REMA Hospital
RN 13, Nyamutobo, Ruyigi, Burundi
⊕ https://vfmat.ch/9cd4

Saint David
Boulevard Général Adolphe Nshimirimana,
Bujumbura, Bujumbura Mairie, Burundi
⊕ https://vfmat.ch/8d14

Saint Sauveur
RN 3, Rumonge, Rumonge, Burundi
⊕ https://vfmat.ch/46a5

Santé Pour Tous
23e Avenue, Bujumbura, Bujumbura Mairie, Burundi
⊕ https://vfmat.ch/15ca

Solidarité
22e Avenue, Bujumbura, Bujumbura Mairie, Burundi
⊕ https://vfmat.ch/688b

Swaa-Burundi
Boulevard Mwambutsa, Bujumbura, Bujumbura
Mairie, Burundi
⊕ https://vfmat.ch/f283

Umuvyeyi
RN 3, Muha, Bujumbura Mairie, Burundi
⊕ https://vfmat.ch/7f39

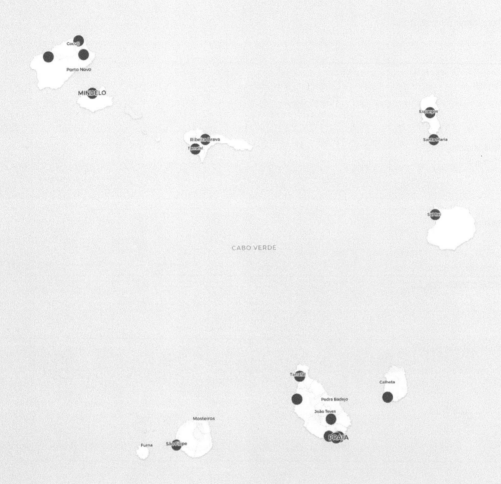

Cocui
Porto Novo
MINDELO
Ribeira Brava
Tarrafal
Espargos
Santa Maria

CABO VERDE

Tarrafal
Calheta
Pedra Badejo
João Teves
Mosteiros
PRAIA
Furna
São Filipe

● Healthcare Facility

Cabo Verde

Located in the Atlantic Ocean 500 kilometers off the western coast of Africa, Cabo Verde is an archipelago consisting of 10 volcanic islands. These islands were entirely uninhabited until the 15th century, when the Portuguese discovered and colonized them. Also known as Cape Verde, the Republic of Cabo Verde is home to 590,000 people distributed throughout the islands, with more than half living on Sao Tiago Island, site of the capital, Praia. About 67 percent of Cape Verdeans are urban dwellers. The population identifies mostly as ethnically Creole, with other ethnic groups including African and European. Portuguese is the official language, while Krioulo is also widely spoken throughout the country and diaspora.

Since gaining independence from Portugal in 1975, Cabo Verde has maintained one of the most stable democratic governments in Africa, as well as one of the continent's most stable economies. Only about 10 percent of Cabo Verde's land is arable, and there are few mineral resources. Instead, much of the economy is grounded in tourism, drawing visitors with its pleasant climate, attractive beaches, stable economy, and close proximity to Europe. Tourism contributed substantially to the country's rapid economic and social progress between 1990 and 2008. Much of the population is employed in the service industry, and also commerce, trade, transport, and public services.

Non-communicable diseases have increased since 2009 to become the leading cause of death in Cabo Verde. Death due to ischemic heart disease, stroke, diabetes, prostate cancer, stomach cancer, and chronic kidney disease all increased by 50 percent or more between 2009 and 2019. Other leading causes of death include lower respiratory infections, cirrhosis, Alzheimer's disease, self-harm, and interpersonal violence. While neonatal disorders and HIV/AIDS continue to contribute substantially to death in Cabo Verde, these decreased by nearly 50 percent between 2009 and 2019, indicating substantial progress. Risk factors that contribute most to death and disability include high blood pressure, malnutrition, air pollution, high body-mass index, high fasting plasma glucose, dietary risks, alcohol and tobacco use, high LDL, kidney dysfunction, insufficient sanitation and clean water, and unsafe sex.

0.59M
Population

$3,064
GDP Per Capita

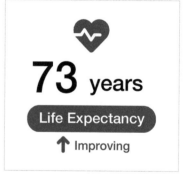

73 years
Life Expectancy
↑ Improving

78
Doctors/100k

Physician Density

210
Beds/100k

Hospital Bed Density

58
Deaths/100k

Maternal Mortality

Cabo Verde

Nonprofit Organizations

Africa CDC
Aims to strengthen the capacity and capability of Africa's public health institutions and partnerships to detect and respond quickly and effectively to disease threats and outbreaks, based on data-driven interventions and programs.
Infect Dis, Logist-Op, Pub Health
⊕ https://vfmat.ch/339c

Africa Health Organisation
Leads collaborative efforts among countries in Africa and other partners to promote health equity, combat disease, and improve quality of life.
Logist-Op, Pub Health
⊕ https://vfmat.ch/b1c5

Africa Relief and Community Development
Provides comprehensive relief and developmental aid to people of the African continent regardless of gender, race, or religion.
Nutr, Pub Health
⊕ https://vfmat.ch/6cd2

Children Without Worms
Enhances the health and development of children by reducing intestinal worm infections.
Infect Dis, Pub Health
⊕ https://vfmat.ch/6bee

Global Oncology (GO)
Brings the best in cancer care to underserved patients around the world and collaborates across geographic, professional, and academic borders to improve cancer care, research, and education.
Heme-Onc, Path, Rad-Onc
⊕ https://vfmat.ch/fcb8

Globus Relief
Aims to improve the delivery of healthcare worldwide by gathering, processing, and distributing surplus medical supplies to charities at home and abroad.
Logist-Op
⊕ https://vfmat.ch/a2b7

Healing the Children
Helps underserved children around the world secure the medical care they need to lead more fulfilling lives.
Anesth, Dent-OMFS, ENT, General, Medicine, Ophth-Opt, Ped Surg, Peds, Plast, Surg
⊕ https://vfmat.ch/d4ee

Humanity & Inclusion
Works alongside people with disabilities and vulnerable populations, taking action and bearing witness in order to respond to their essential needs, improve their living conditions and health, and promote respect for their dignity and fundamental rights.

General, Infect Dis, MF Med, Medicine, Ortho, Peds, Psych, Pub Health, Rehab
⊕ https://vfmat.ch/16b7

International Federation of Red Cross and Red Crescent Societies (IFRC)
Coordinates and directs international assistance following natural and manmade disasters in nonconflict situations through the world's largest humanitarian and development network. Provides disaster-preparedness programs, healthcare activities, and promotes humanitarian values.
ER Med, General, Infect Dis, Nutr
⊕ https://vfmat.ch/b4ee

International Organization for Migration (IOM) – The UN Migration Agency
Promotes evidence-informed policies and holistic, preventive, and curative health programs that are beneficial, accessible, and equitable for vulnerable migrants.
General, Infect Dis, OB-GYN
⊕ https://vfmat.ch/621a

International Planned Parenthood Federation (IPPF)
Leads a locally owned, globally connected civil society movement that provides and enables services and champions sexual and reproductive health and rights for all, especially the underserved.
Infect Dis, MF Med, OB-GYN
⊕ https://vfmat.ch/dc97

Joint United Nations Programme on HIV/AIDS (UNAIDS)
Aims to place people living with HIV and people affected by the virus at the decision-making table and at the center of designing, delivering, and monitoring the AIDS response.
Infect Dis
⊕ https://vfmat.ch/464a

MedShare
Aims to improve the quality of life of people, communities, and the planet by sourcing and directly delivering surplus medical supplies and equipment to communities in need around the world.
Logist-Op
⊕ https://vfmat.ch/c8bc

Mercy and Love Foundation
Aims to provide orphaned and vulnerable children with basic human needs such as food, clothing, and shelter, enabling them to thrive.
General, Peds
⊕ https://vfmat.ch/649a

Order of Malta
Supports forgotten or excluded people, especially those living in conflict zones or amid natural disasters, by providing medical assistance, caring for refugees, and distributing medicines and necessities.

ER Med, General, Infect Dis, MF Med, Nephro, OB-GYN, Ortho, Psych
🌐 https://vfmat.ch/1fab

Organization for the Prevention of Blindness, The (OPC)
Provides research, and treatments and cures for people affected by blindness and blinding diseases in Francophone Africa.
Infect Dis, Ophth-Opt
🌐 https://vfmat.ch/86d6

Project Health CV Inc.
Facilitates and assists healthcare providers to develop and implement individual healthcare programs within Cape Verde's healthcare system and to provide those without access to quality healthcare within Cape Verde's healthcare system.
Heme-Onc, Logist-Op, Ortho, Surg, Urol
🌐 https://vfmat.ch/47fa

RAD-AID International
Improves and optimizes access to medical imaging and radiology in low-resource regions of the world.
Rad-Onc, Radiol
🌐 https://vfmat.ch/537f

Rotary International
Provides service to others, improves lives, and advances world understanding, goodwill, and peace through its fellowship of business, professional, and community leaders.
ER Med, General, Infect Dis, MF Med, OB-GYN
🌐 https://vfmat.ch/8fb5

SOS Children's Villages International
Supports children through alternative care and family strengthening.
ER Med, Peds
🌐 https://vfmat.ch/aca1

Task Force for Global Health, The
Consists of programs and focus areas that cover a range of global health issues including neglected tropical diseases, infectious diseases, vaccines, field epidemiology, public health informatics, health workforce development, and global health ethics.
Infect Dis, Logist-Op, Medicine, Ophth-Opt, Peds
🌐 https://vfmat.ch/714c

United Nations Children's Fund (UNICEF)
Works in over 190 countries and territories to save children's lives, defend their rights, and help them fulfill their potential, from early childhood through adolescence.
All-Immu, Infect Dis, MF Med, Neonat, Nutr, OB-GYN, Ped Surg, Peds, Pub Health
🌐 https://vfmat.ch/42d7

United Nations Development Programme (UNDP)
Helps countries achieve the simultaneous eradication of extreme poverty and significant reduction of inequalities and exclusion using a sustainable human development approach.
Infect Dis, Logist-Op, Pub Health
🌐 https://vfmat.ch/935c

United Nations High Commissioner for Refugees (UNHCR)
Safeguards the rights and well-being of people who have been forced to flee, ensuring that everybody has the right to seek asylum and find safe refuge in another country, with the goal of seeking lasting solutions.
General, MF Med, Medicine, OB-GYN, Peds, Psych, Pub Health
🌐 https://vfmat.ch/6636

United Nations Population Fund (UNFPA)
Supports reproductive healthcare for women and youth in more than 150 countries, focusing on delivering a world in which every pregnancy is wanted, every childbirth is safe, and every young person's potential is fulfilled.
Infect Dis, MF Med, Neonat, OB-GYN, Peds, Pub Health
🌐 https://vfmat.ch/c969

World Health Organization, The (WHO)
The United Nations' agency for health provides leadership on global health matters, shapes the health research agenda, sets norms and standards, articulates evidence-based policy options, provides technical support and monitoring to countries, and assesses health trends.
ER Med, General, Infect Dis, Logist-Op, MF Med, OB-GYN, Peds, Psych, Pub Health
🌐 https://vfmat.ch/c476

Cabo Verde

Healthcare Facilities

Centro de Saúde da Boa Vista
Sal Rei, Cabo Verde
⊕ https://vfmat.ch/u3sx

Centro de Saúde de Tarrafal de São Nicolau
Praia Branca, Tarrafal de São Nicolau, Cabo Verde
⊕ https://vfmat.ch/367b

Clinitur
Santa Maria, Sal Island, Cabo Verde
⊕ https://vfmat.ch/e2es

Hospital Cutelo de Acucar
Monte Tabor, Sao Felipe, Cabo Verde
⊕ https://vfmat.ch/53c6

Hospital de Ribeira Brava
Calejão, Tarrafal de São Nicolau, Cabo Verde
⊕ https://vfmat.ch/df24

Hospital de São Domingos
Nora, São Domingos, Cabo Verde
⊕ https://vfmat.ch/623a

Hospital do Maio
Morro, Maio, Cabo Verde
⊕ https://vfmat.ch/dd5a

Hospital do Sal
Preguiça, Sal, Cabo Verde
⊕ https://vfmat.ch/b76e

Hospital Dr. Agostinho Neto
Beach City, Santiago Island, Cabo Verde
⊕ https://vfmat.ch/a919

Hospital Dr. Baptista de Sousa
Casa do Cabo Submarino, São Vicente, Cabo Verde
⊕ https://vfmat.ch/a194

Hospital in São Martinho Ribeira Grande de Santiago
São Martinho, Ribeira Grande de Santiago, Cabo Verde
⊕ https://vfmat.ch/6492

Hospital Regional Dr. João Morais
Mão para Trás, Ribeira Grande, Cabo Verde
⊕ https://vfmat.ch/fe2a

Hospital Regional Santiago Norte
Tras-os-Montes, Tarrafal, Cabo Verde
⊕ https://vfmat.ch/994b

Iramar Clinic
Praia, Cabo Verde
⊕ https://vfmat.ch/mjqp

Montanha
Perdia, Porto Novo, Cabo Verde
⊕ https://vfmat.ch/b46a

PMI
Fazenda, Cabo Verde
⊕ https://vfmat.ch/9bcd

Healthcare Facility

Cambodia

Known for its scenic and natural beauty, featuring forests and rice paddies, the Kingdom of Cambodia is bordered by Thailand, Vietnam, and Laos. Predominantly Buddhist, Cambodia has a population of approximately 17.3 million, mostly from the Khmer ethnic group and speaking the Khmer language. Other ethnicities include Cham, Chinese, and Vietnamese. Most of the population is concentrated in the southeast, around the capital, Phnom Penh, with other large populations near the Tonle Sap lake—Southeast Asia's largest freshwater lake—and the Mekong River.

A former colony of France, Cambodia won its independence in 1953. Over the past two decades, Cambodia has experienced significant economic expansion, with an average 8 percent annual growth between 1998 and 2018, fueled primarily by a robust tourism industry, in addition to garment exports. As a result, poverty decreased from 48 percent in 2007 to 14 percent in 2014. While this is a significant improvement, the quality of health and education remain challenged as a whole.

Economic growth has yielded overall improvements in the health status of the population. Life expectancy has increased to 70 years of age, and maternal mortality has decreased. However, there remains room for improvement. The most common causes of death include stroke, lower respiratory infections, cirrhosis, tuberculosis, neonatal disorders, diabetes, COPD, lung cancer, road injuries, and HIV/AIDS. Risk factors such as malnutrition, air pollution, alcohol and tobacco use, high blood sugar, and diet contribute to the heavy burden of non-communicable disease.

17.3M

Population

$1,513

GDP Per Capita

70 years

Life Expectancy

↑ Improving

19
Doctors/100k

Physician Density

90
Beds/100k

Hospital Bed Density

160
Deaths/100k

Maternal Mortality

Cambodia

Nonprofit Organizations

A Broader View Volunteers
Provides developing countries around the world with significant volunteer programs that aid the neediest communities and forge a lasting bond between those volunteering and those they have helped.
Dent-OMFS, ER Med, Infect Dis, MF Med
⊕ https://vfmat.ch/3bec

A Leg To Stand On (ALTSO)
Provides free, high-quality prosthetic limbs, orthotic devices, and wheelchairs to children with untreated limb disabilities in the developing world.
Logist-Op, Ortho
⊕ https://vfmat.ch/a48d

A World of Difference
Aids women and children in southeast Asia, with a focus on art education, literacy, and health.
Dent-OMFS
⊕ https://vfmat.ch/8682

Abt Associates
Seeks to improve the quality of life and economic well-being of people worldwide, while striving to meet and exceed the highest professional standards.
General, Logist-Op, MF Med, OB-GYN, Peds
⊕ https://vfmat.ch/cec2

Action Against Hunger
Aims to end life-threatening hunger for good through treating and preventing malnutrition across more than 45 countries.
Nutr
⊕ https://vfmat.ch/2dbc

Against Malaria Foundation
Helps protect people from malaria. Funds anti-malaria nets, specifically long-lasting insecticidal nets (LLINs), and works with distribution partners to ensure they are used. Tracks and reports on net use and malaria case data.
Infect Dis
⊕ https://vfmat.ch/337d

Age International
Helps older people living in some of the world's poorest places to have improved well-being and be treated with dignity through a variety of programs, including emergency relief and cataract surgery.
ER Med, Geri, Logist-Op, Nutr, Ophth-Opt, Palliative, Pub Health
⊕ https://vfmat.ch/c7e2

AIDS Healthcare Foundation
Provides cutting-edge HIV/AIDS medical care and advocacy to over one million people in 43 countries.
Infect Dis
⊕ https://vfmat.ch/b27c

Al Basar International Foundation
Works with local partners to treat preventable blindness, and helps set up sustainable infrastructure so local teams can save sight in their communities.
Ophth-Opt
⊕ https://vfmat.ch/a8b5

Aloha Medical Mission
Brings hope and changes the lives of people; serves overseas and in Hawai'i.
Anesth, Crit-Care, Dent-OMFS, ENT, ER Med, General, Medicine, OB-GYN, Ophth-Opt, Ortho, Ped Surg, Peds, Plast, Surg, Urol
⊕ https://vfmat.ch/72ac

American International Health Alliance (AIHA)
Strengthens health systems and workforce capacity worldwide through locally driven, peer-to-peer institutional partnerships.
CV Med, ER Med, Infect Dis, Medicine, OB-GYN
⊕ https://vfmat.ch/69fd

Americares
Saves lives and improves health for people affected by poverty or disaster and responds with life-changing medicine, medical supplies, and health programs including domestic and global medical clinics.
All-Immu, ER Med, General, Infect Dis, MF Med, Nutr
⊕ https://vfmat.ch/e567

AO Alliance
Builds solutions to lessen the burden of injuries in low- and middle-income countries, while enhancing the care of the injured to reduce human suffering, disability, and poverty.
Ortho, Surg
⊕ https://vfmat.ch/8cd5

ARC The Australian Respiratory Council
Fosters research to promote respiratory health and works to improve lung health in communities of disadvantaged and Indigenous people.
Infect Dis
⊕ https://vfmat.ch/69f2

ASAP Ministries
Provides education and healthcare to refugees and the poor, based in Christian ministry.
Dent-OMFS, General
⊕ https://vfmat.ch/266e

Assist International
Designs and implements humanitarian programs that build capacity, develop opportunities, and save lives around the world.
Infect Dis, Ped Surg, Peds
⊕ https://vfmat.ch/9a3b

Association of Medical Doctors of Asia (AMDA)

Strives to support people affected by disasters and economic distress on their road to recovery, establishing a true partnership with special emphasis on local initiative.

ER Med, Logist-Op, Pub Health

⊕ https://vfmat.ch/e3d4

Australian Health Humanitarian Aid (AHHA)

Provides free eye surgery, eye care, and medical and dental treatment to the underprivileged, along with training to local students and doctors.

Dent-OMFS, Ophth-Opt, Surg

⊕ https://vfmat.ch/dffc

Aziza's Place

Supports vulnerable children in close collaboration with their families and communities by providing a range of educational and developmental services.

General, Peds

⊕ https://vfmat.ch/d771

Benjamin H. Josephson, MD Fund

Provides healthcare professionals with the financial resources necessary to deliver medical services for those in need throughout the world.

General, OB-GYN

⊕ https://vfmat.ch/6acc

BFIRST – British Foundation for International Reconstructive Surgery & Training

Supports projects across the developing world to train surgeons in their local environment to effectively manage devastating injuries.

Anesth, Plast, Surg

⊕ https://vfmat.ch/ad4f

Bureau of International Health Cooperation

Seeks to improve healthcare around the world, including developing countries, using expertise, and contribute to healthier lives of Japanese people by bringing these experiences back to Japan.

ER Med, Heme-Onc, Infect Dis, Peds, Pub Health

⊕ https://vfmat.ch/947d

Cambodia Vision Foundation

Aims to work with small provincial towns in Cambodia, focusing on blindness prevention and basic medical healthcare, giving the gift of sight to the poor of rural Cambodia who suffer from debilitating eye disease.

General, Ophth-Opt, Surg

⊕ https://vfmat.ch/b388

Cambodia World Family

Aims to provide free dental care to every child in need in Cambodia.

Dent-OMFS

⊕ https://vfmat.ch/993e

Cambodia-Dutch Foundation, The

Supports the Cambodian population, especially rural residents living below the poverty line, by raising funds for programs in education, water and sanitation, healthcare, and employment.

General, MF Med, Ophth-Opt

⊕ https://vfmat.ch/4ce2

Cambodian Buddhism Association for Vulnerable Children

Aims to improve access to education and health services for the most vulnerable Cambodian children, women, and disabled people in society.

General, Nutr

⊕ https://vfmat.ch/e955

Cambodian Diabetes Association Siem Reap

Strives to enable hundreds of thousands of Cambodians living with diabetes to successfully manage their diabetes and delay the onset of associated complications.

Endo, Pub Health

⊕ https://vfmat.ch/c992

Cambodian Health Professionals Association of America

Works to promote health and social well-being through ongoing service and education to medically underserved Cambodians living in both the United States and Cambodia.

Dent-OMFS, General, Neonat, Ophth-Opt, Ortho, Rehab, Surg

⊕ https://vfmat.ch/d76f

Canadian Vision Care

Consists of eye healthcare professionals who donate time and resources to the development of vision care in the developing world.

Ophth-Opt

⊕ https://vfmat.ch/3a38

CARE

Works around the globe to save lives, defeat poverty, and achieve social justice.

ER Med, General

⊕ https://vfmat.ch/7232

Chain of Hope (La Chaîne de l'Espoir)

Helps underprivileged children around the world by providing them with access to healthcare.

Anesth, CT Surg, Crit-Care, ER Med, Neurosurg, Ortho, Ped Surg, Surg, Vasc Surg

⊕ https://vfmat.ch/e871

CharityVision International

Focuses on restoring curable sight impairment worldwide by empowering local physicians and creating sustainable solutions.

Logist-Op, Ophth-Opt, Surg

⊕ https://vfmat.ch/6231

Chhlat Health

Aims to give high-quality care for happier, longer lives, and to give purpose and longevity to Cambodian seniors.

⊕ https://vfmat.ch/3ffd

ChildFund Australia

Works to reduce poverty for children in many of the world's most disadvantaged communities.

ER Med, General, Peds

⊕ https://vfmat.ch/13df

Children of War Foundation

Delivers access to global health and education to communities affected by poverty, war, natural disaster, climate change, and migration challenges.

ER Med, General, Logist-Op, Peds, Surg

⊕ https://vfmat.ch/de51

Children Without Worms

Enhances the health and development of children by reducing intestinal worm infections.

Infect Dis, Pub Health

⊕ https://vfmat.ch/6bee

Children's Lifeline International

Provides medical teams and surgical assistance to underprivileged children in developing countries through missions in partnership with local hospitals.

CV Med, Dent-OMFS, General, MF Med, Neurosurg, Peds, Rehab

⊕ https://vfmat.ch/6fea

Christian Aid Ministries

Strives to be a trustworthy and efficient channel for Amish, Mennonite, and other conservative Anabaptist groups and individuals to minister to physical and spiritual needs around the world.

CT Surg, ER Med, Logist-Op, Ortho, Pub Health

⊕ https://vfmat.ch/7b33

Christian Connections for International Health (CCIH)

Promotes global health and wholeness from a Christian perspective.

All-Immu, General, Infect Dis, MF Med, Neonat, OB-GYN, Psych

⊕ https://vfmat.ch/fa5d

Christian Health Service Corps

Brings Christian doctors, health professionals, and health educators committed to serving the poor to places that otherwise have little or no access to healthcare.

Anesth, Dent-OMFS, General, Medicine, Peds, Surg
⊕ https://vfmat.ch/da57

Christian Medical Ministry to Cambodia/Jeremiah's Hope
Aims to provide excellent medical care to the poor and quality medical education to the healthcare community of Cambodia.
CT Surg, Neurosurg, OB-GYN, Ortho, Surg
⊕ https://vfmat.ch/7cc5

Clinton Health Access Initiative (CHAI)
Aims to save lives and reduce the burden of disease in low- and middle-income countries. Works with partners to strengthen the capabilities of governments and the private sector to create and sustain high-quality health systems.
General, Heme-Onc, Infect Dis, Logist-Op, MF Med, Medicine, Neonat, Nutr, OB-GYN, Path, Peds, Rad-Onc
⊕ https://vfmat.ch/9ed7

Compassionate Eye
Aims to support the social good by supplying infrastructure and personnel for sanitation, education, medical care, small business, and job training.
General, Infect Dis, MF Med, OB-GYN, Peds
⊕ https://vfmat.ch/1915

Connect with Cambodia
Aims to improve the lives of Cambodians living in poverty through medical care and attention.
General, Peds
⊕ https://vfmat.ch/9149

Cornerstone Education and Research
Seeks to provide the local and global community with medical research and education in orthopedic care, expand medical research in the development of innovative technologies, and provide physician and community education.
Ortho
⊕ https://vfmat.ch/f549

Covenant Medicine Outreach
Inspired by the Christian faith, provides medical care for those less fortunate.
General
⊕ https://vfmat.ch/769a

COVID-19 Clinical Research Coalition
Advocates and collaborates for the advancement of COVID-19 research driven by the needs of low-resource settings, and works for equitable access to solutions to the pandemic.
All-Immu, Infect-Dis, MF Med, Path, Pub Health
⊕ https://vfmat.ch/d1f4

Dentaid
Seeks to treat, equip, train, and educate people in need of dental care.
Dent-OMFS
⊕ https://vfmat.ch/a183

Direct Relief
Improves the health and lives of people affected by poverty or emergency situations by mobilizing and providing essential medical resources needed for their care.
ER Med, Logist-Op
⊕ https://vfmat.ch/58e5

Doctors Without Borders/Médecins Sans Frontières (MSF)
Responds to emergencies and provides lifesaving medical care where needed most, including during disasters, conflicts, and epidemics.
Anesth, Crit-Care, ER Med, General, Infect Dis, Nutr, OB-GYN, Ped Surg, Peds, Psych, Pub Health, Surg
⊕ https://vfmat.ch/f363

Douleurs Sans Frontières (Pain Without Borders)
Supports local actors in taking charge of the assessment and treatment of pain and suffering, in an integrated manner and adapted to the realities of each country.
Anesth, Palliative, Psych, Rehab
⊕ https://vfmat.ch/324c

Duke University: Global Health Institute
Sparks innovation in global health research and education, and brings together knowledge and resources to address the most important global health issues of our time.
All-Immu, Infect Dis, MF Med, OB-GYN, Pub Health
⊕ https://vfmat.ch/c4cd

Evidence Project, The
Improves family-planning policies, programs, and practices through the strategic generation, translation, and use of evidence.
General, MF Med
⊕ https://vfmat.ch/f9e7

Exceed Worldwide
Supports people with disabilities living in poverty by providing free prosthetic and orthotic services in South and Southeast Asia.
Ortho, Peds
⊕ https://vfmat.ch/dd24

Eye Care Foundation
Helps prevent and cure avoidable blindness and visual impairment in low-income countries.
Ophth-Opt, Surg
⊕ https://vfmat.ch/c8f9

Eye Foundation of America
Works toward a world without childhood blindness.
Ophth-Opt
⊕ https://vfmat.ch/a7eb

Finn Church Aid
Supports people in the most vulnerable situations within fragile and disaster-affected regions in three thematic priority areas: right to peace, livelihood, and education.
ER Med, Psych, Pub Health
⊕ https://vfmat.ch/9623

Firefly Mission
Organizes humanitarian missions to help people in less fortunate situations while serving as a vehicle for the spiritual development of members and the beneficiaries of its missions.
Logist-Op, Ophth-Opt, Pub Health
⊕ https://vfmat.ch/d215

Flame
Provides support, medical aid, housing, and training for children and their families so they can become the future leaders of Cambodia.
General, Pub Health
⊕ https://vfmat.ch/1f7e

Flying Doctors of America
Brings together teams of physicians, dentists, nurses, and other healthcare professionals to care for people who would not otherwise receive medical care.
Dent-OMFS, GI, General, Surg
⊕ https://vfmat.ch/58b6

Forgotten International, The
Develops programs that alleviate poverty and the suffering of impoverished women and children in both the United States and worldwide.
Logist-Op, Nutr, OB-GYN, Peds, Pub Health
⊕ https://vfmat.ch/26f3

Foundation for International Development Relief (FIDR)
Implements assistance projects in developing countries to improve the living environment of residents, while promoting regional development centered on the welfare of children.
Pub Health
⊕ https://vfmat.ch/7356

Fred Hollows Foundation, The
Works toward a world in which no person is needlessly blind or vision impaired.
Ophth-Opt, Pub Health, Surg
⊕ https://vfmat.ch/73e5

Free to Smile Foundation
Serves impoverished and underserved children suffering from cleft lip/palate deformities around the world.
Anesth, Dent-OMFS, ENT, Ped Surg, Plast
⊕ https://vfmat.ch/218b

Friends Without A Border
Provides free, high-quality healthcare to children of areas of dire need in Southeast Asia, by developing infrastructure, providing care, creating health education programs, and training local healthcare professionals at Lao Friends Hospital for Children, Angkor Hospital for Children, and The Lake Clinic in Cambodia.
Anesth, ER Med, Infect Dis, Logist-Op, Neonat, Nutr, Ortho, Ped Surg, Peds, Radiol, Surg
⊕ https://vfmat.ch/58b9

Gift of Life International
Provides lifesaving cardiac treatment to children in developing countries while developing sustainable pediatric cardiac programs by implementing screening, surgical, and training missions.
Anesth, CT Surg, CV Med, Crit-Care, Ped Surg, Peds, Pulm-Critic
⊕ https://vfmat.ch/f2f9

Gift of Vision Foundation
Promotes and provides medical assistance to the poor and vocational skills to the uneducated in local communities and abroad.
Dent-OMFS, General, Ophth-Opt
⊕ https://vfmat.ch/d985

Global Aid Network (GAiN) Australia
Inspired by the Christian faith, provides support to people living in crisis through programs in healthcare, humanitarian aid, disaster response, clean water, and sanitation.
Dent-OMFS, Ophth-Opt
⊕ https://vfmat.ch/6cb8

Global Blood Fund
Delivers grants, equipment, and training to over 50 countries in Africa, Asia, Eastern Europe, the Middle East, Latin America and the Caribbean.
Pub Health
⊕ https://vfmat.ch/6377

Global Clinic
Seeks to ensure that any effort to provide medical services is accompanied by a long-term program to improve the health of residents of its partner communities.
Dent-OMFS, ER Med, General, OB-GYN, OB-GYN, Ophth-Opt, Surg
⊕ https://vfmat.ch/9e48

Global Dental Relief
Brings free dental care to impoverished children in partnership with local organizations, and delivers treatment and preventive care in dental clinics that serve children in schools and remote villages.
Dent-OMFS
⊕ https://vfmat.ch/29b6

Global Legacy
Supports and initiates projects with a high impact on health, education, and the advancement of women in rural communities.
Ophth-Opt
⊕ https://vfmat.ch/ff92

Global Medical Foundation Australia
Provides medical, surgical, dental, and educational welfare to underprivileged communities and gives them access to basics that are often taken for granted.
Dent-OMFS, ER Med, General, OB-GYN, Ortho, Surg
⊕ https://vfmat.ch/fa56

Global Medical Missions Alliance
Brings and promotes Christian-centered missionary life to the body of healthcare professionals and its partners.
Dent-OMFS, ER Med, Pub Health, Rehab, Surg
⊕ https://vfmat.ch/29c7

Global Medical Volunteers
Aims to advance medical services and education in developing nations around the world.
GI, Surg, Urol
⊕ https://vfmat.ch/dfec

Global Ministries – The United Methodist Church
As the worldwide mission and development agency of The United Methodist Church, Global Ministries works with more than 300 hospitals and clinics around the world through its Global Health Unit.
Anesth, CT Surg, CV Med, Crit-Care, Dent-OMFS, Derm, ER Med, GI, General, Infect Dis, Logist-Op, MF Med, Medicine, Neonat, Nephro, Nutr, OB-GYN, Ophth-Opt, Ortho, Palliative, Peds, Pod, Psych, Pub Health, Rehab, Rheum, Surg, Urol
⊕ https://vfmat.ch/1723

Global Oncology (GO)
Brings the best in cancer care to underserved patients around the world and collaborates across geographic, professional, and academic borders to improve cancer care, research, and education.
Heme-Onc, Path, Rad-Onc
⊕ https://vfmat.ch/fcb8

Global Primary Care
Aims to promote and support individuals and organizations that increase access to primary care through sustainable efforts for people living in the poorest places of the world.
General, Logist-Op, Medicine
⊕ https://vfmat.ch/742b

Global Vision 2020
Provides prescription eyeglasses to people who live in parts of the world lacking necessary infrastructure for obtaining affordable corrective eyewear.
Logist-Op, Ophth-Opt
⊕ https://vfmat.ch/7373

Globus Relief
Aims to improve the delivery of healthcare worldwide by gathering, processing, and distributing surplus medical supplies to charities at home and abroad.
Logist-Op
⊕ https://vfmat.ch/a2b7

Handa Foundation, The
Builds hospitals and schools in Southeast Asia.
Anesth, Infect Dis, Psych, Surg
⊕ https://vfmat.ch/eacf

Health Care Volunteers International
Provides direct patient care, capacity building, and educational projects in developing countries, and specializes in leveraging technology in order to provide low-cost solutions, drive better outcomes, and expand care to far more individuals in need around the globe.
General, OB-GYN, Peds, Plast, Rehab
⊕ https://vfmat.ch/69a6

Health Poverty Action
Works in partnership with people around the world who are pursuing change in their own communities to demand health justice and challenge power imbalances.
ER Med, General, Infect Dis, Psych, Pub Health
⊕ https://vfmat.ch/ee58

HealthServe Australia
Develops sustainable health programs that improve health and well-being and partners with community groups to build community capacity to meet health needs.
Infect Dis, Logist-Op, OB-GYN, Psych, Pub Health
⊕ https://vfmat.ch/7276

Healthy DEvelopments
Provides Germany-supported health and social protection programs around the globe in a collaborative knowledge management process.
All-Immu, General, Infect Dis, Logist-Op, MF Med
⊕ https://vfmat.ch/dc31

Hear the World (Entendre le Monde)
Aims to operate on as many patients as possible, train surgeons, assess the causes of deafness, and improve the diagnosis and treatment of deafness.
ENT, Peds
⊕ https://vfmat.ch/9c15

Hear the World Foundation
Advocates worldwide for equal opportunities and improved quality of life for people in need with hearing loss.
ENT, Peds
⊕ https://vfmat.ch/122c

Hearing Health Foundation
Prevents and cures hearing loss and tinnitus through groundbreaking research and promotes hearing health.
Surg
⊕ https://vfmat.ch/2e71

Hebron Medical Center (HMC)
Promotes and contributes to the well-being of the Cambodian community and the cultivation of local medical professionals, through the provision of top-quality medical services.
Dent-OMFS, General, Ophth-Opt, Palliative, Path
⊕ https://vfmat.ch/2d9c

Helen Keller International
Seeks to eliminate preventable vision loss, malnutrition, and diseases of poverty.
Infect Dis, Nutr, OB-GYN, Ophth-Opt, Peds
⊕ https://vfmat.ch/b654

HELP CODE ITALIA ONLUS
Seeks to improve life conditions of children in the communities where they live, through direct and indirect projects designed to support their well-being, education, and development.
General, Nutr, Pub Health
⊕ https://vfmat.ch/1dd9

HelpAge International
Works to ensure that people everywhere understand how much older people contribute to society and that they must enjoy their right to healthcare, social services, economic, and physical security.
General, Geri, Infect Dis, Medicine, Pub Health
⊕ https://vfmat.ch/5d91

Hernia International
Aims to provide relief from sickness, and protection and preservation of health, for persons affected by groin and abdominal hernias and residing in low- and middle-income countries.
Surg
⊕ https://vfmat.ch/e98e

HumaniTerra
Helps countries and populations emerging from economic and human crisis to rebuild their healthcare system in a sustainable way. Committed to three fundamental and complementary actions: operating, training, and rebuilding.
Anesth, ENT, ER Med, MF Med, OB-GYN, Ortho, Plast, Surg
⊕ https://vfmat.ch/b371

Humanity & Inclusion
Works alongside people with disabilities and vulnerable populations, taking action and bearing witness in order to respond to their essential needs, improve their living conditions and health, and promote respect for their dignity and fundamental rights.
General, Infect Dis, MF Med, Medicine, Ortho, Peds, Psych, Pub Health, Rehab
⊕ https://vfmat.ch/16b7

IMPACT Foundation
Works to prevent and alleviate needless disability by restoring sight, mobility, and hearing.
ENT, MF Med, OB-GYN, Ophth-Opt, Ortho, Peds, Surg
⊕ https://vfmat.ch/ba28

Institute of Applied Dermatology
Aims to alleviate difficult-to-treat skin ailments by combining biomedicine with Ayurveda, homeopathy, yoga, and other traditional Indian medicine.
All-Immu, Derm, Infect Dis, Nutr, Pod, Pub Health
⊕ https://vfmat.ch/c6eb

International Agency for the Prevention of Blindness (IAPB), The
Leads international efforts in blindness-prevention activities, works toward a world where no one is needlessly visually impaired, and ensures that everyone has access to the best possible standard of eye health.
Infect Dis, Ophth-Opt, Pub Health
⊕ https://vfmat.ch/87a2

International Council of Ophthalmology
Works with ophthalmologic societies and others to enhance ophthalmic education and improve access to the highest-quality eye care in order to preserve and restore vision for people of the world.
Ophth-Opt
⊕ https://vfmat.ch/ffd2

International Federation of Gynecology and Obstetrics (FIGO)
Implements global projects on specific women's health issues.
MF Med, Medicine, Neonat, OB-GYN, Surg, Urol
⊕ https://vfmat.ch/c4b4

International Federation of Red Cross and Red Crescent Societies (IFRC)
Coordinates and directs international assistance following natural and manmade disasters in nonconflict situations through the world's largest humanitarian and development network. Provides disaster-preparedness programs, healthcare activities, and promotes humanitarian values.
ER Med, General, Infect Dis, Nutr
⊕ https://vfmat.ch/b4ee

International Hearing Foundation
Supports hearing-related service, education, and research.
ENT, Surg
⊕ https://vfmat.ch/3ee2

International League of Dermatological Socieities
Strives to promote high-quality education, clinical care, research and innovation that will improve skin health globally.
Derm, Infect Dis
⊕ https://vfmat.ch/7388

International Medical Relief
Provides sustainable education, training, medical and dental care, and disaster relief and response in vulnerable communities worldwide.
Dent-OMFS, General, Infect Dis, Medicine, OB-GYN
⊕ https://vfmat.ch/b3ed

International Organization for Migration (IOM) – The UN Migration Agency
Promotes evidence-informed policies and holistic, preventive, and curative health programs that are beneficial, accessible, and equitable for vulnerable migrants.
General, Infect Dis, OB-GYN
⊕ https://vfmat.ch/621a

International Pediatric Nephrology Association (IPNA)
Leads global efforts to successfully address the care for all children with kidney disease through advocacy, education, and training.
Medicine, Nephro, Peds
⊕ https://vfmat.ch/b59d

International Planned Parenthood Federation (IPPF)
Leads a locally owned, globally connected civil society movement that provides and enables services and champions sexual and reproductive health and rights for all, especially the underserved.
Infect Dis, MF Med, OB-GYN
⊕ https://vfmat.ch/dc97

InterSurgeon

Fosters collaborative partnerships in the field of global surgery that will advance clinical care, teaching, training, research, and the provision and maintenance of medical equipment.

ENT, Neurosurg, Ortho, Ped Surg, Plast, Surg, Urol

⊕ https://vfmat.ch/6f8a

Iris Global

Serves the poor, the destitute, the lost, and the forgotten by providing adoration, outreach, family, education, relief, development, healing, and the arts.

General, Infect Dis, Nutr, Pub Health

⊕ https://vfmat.ch/37f8

Japan Heart

Provides medical care in areas where it is currently out of reach, wherever that may be.

Heme-Onc, Medicine, OB-GYN, Ped Surg, Peds, Plast, Surg

⊕ https://vfmat.ch/1cd3

John Snow, Inc. (JSI)

Aims to improve the health and well-being of underserved and vulnerable people and communities throughout the world.

General, Infect Dis, Logist-Op, MF Med, OB-GYN, Peds, Psych, Pub Health

⊕ https://vfmat.ch/ba78

Johns Hopkins Center for Communication Programs

Believes in the power of communication to save lives by empowering people to adopt healthy behaviors for themselves, their families, and their communities.

General, Infect Dis, Logist-Op, OB-GYN, Pub Health

⊕ https://vfmat.ch/1bf9

Joint United Nations Programme on HIV/AIDS (UNAIDS)

Aims to place people living with HIV and people affected by the virus at the decision-making table and at the center of designing, delivering, and monitoring the AIDS response.

Infect Dis

⊕ https://vfmat.ch/464a

Kaya Responsible Travel

Promotes sustainable social, environmental, and economic development, empowers communities, and cultivates educated, compassionate global citizens through responsible travel.

All-Immu, Crit-Care, Dent-OMFS, ER Med, General, Geri, Infect Dis, MF Med, Medicine, Nutr, OB-GYN, Peds, Psych, Pub Health, Rehab

⊕ https://vfmat.ch/b2cf

Khmer HIV/AIDS NGO Alliance (KHANA)

Leads in the HIV response while addressing wider health and development needs.

Infect Dis, OB-GYN, Pub Health

⊕ https://vfmat.ch/51ee

Kids Care Everywhere

Seeks to empower physicians in under-resourced environments with multimedia, state-of-the-art medical software, and to inspire young professionals to become future global healthcare leaders.

Logist-Op, Ped Surg, Peds

⊕ https://vfmat.ch/bc23

Kind Cuts for Kids

Aims to improve medical services for children in developing countries through education, demonstration, and skills transfer to local healthcare professionals.

Anesth, Medicine, Ped Surg, Surg

⊕ https://vfmat.ch/e3d7

Kindred Hearts

Provides accessible and affordable medical care and education in Cambodia, with the goal of improving the overall quality of life and health of Cambodians.

General

⊕ https://vfmat.ch/752e

Kindred House

Works to empower people to fight global poverty and associated health conditions through sustainable, life-changing health and development programs.

Dent-OMFS, MF Med

⊕ https://vfmat.ch/28c4

Light for the World

Contributes to a world in which persons with disabilities fully exercise their rights, and assists persons with disabilities living in poverty.

Ophth-Opt, Rehab

⊕ https://vfmat.ch/3ff6

Limbs International

Engages communities and transforms lives through affordable, sustainable prosthetic solutions and rehabilitation services in developing countries.

Logist-Op, Ortho, Pod, Rehab

⊕ https://vfmat.ch/dc84

London School of Hygiene & Tropical Medicine: Health in Humanitarian Crises Centre

Advances health and health equity in crisis-affected countries through research, education, and translation of knowledge into policy and practice.

ER Med, Infect Dis, Pub Health

⊕ https://vfmat.ch/96ad

Love Without Boundaries

Provides healing, education, and refuge to vulnerable children worldwide.

CT Surg, Dent-OMFS, Nutr, Ortho, Ped Surg, Peds, Rehab, Surg

⊕ https://vfmat.ch/d1fc

Lutherans in Medical Missions (LIMM)

Works with local and global partners to promote healing in medically underserved communities.

General, Logist-Op, Pub Health

⊕ https://vfmat.ch/c5aa

MAGNA International

Helps those who are suffering or recovering from conflicts and disasters by reducing the risks of diseases and treating them immediately.

ER Med, General, Infect Dis, Peds, Surg

⊕ https://vfmat.ch/58f4

MAP International

Provides medicines and health supplies to those in need around the world so they might experience life to the fullest.

Logist-Op

⊕ https://vfmat.ch/deed

Marie Stopes International

Provides the contraception and safe abortion services that enable women all over the world to choose their own futures.

Infect Dis, MF Med, Neonat, OB-GYN, Pub Health

⊕ https://vfmat.ch/9525

Maryknoll Lay Missioners

Based in Christian ministry, aims to collaborate with poor communities in Africa, Asia, and the Americas in order to respond to basic needs, including heathcare, and to help create a more compassionate world.

Logist-Op, Nutr

⊕ https://vfmat.ch/2ce6

Medical Ministry International

Provides compassionate healthcare in areas of need, inspired by the Christian faith.

CT Surg, Dent-OMFS, ENT, General, OB-GYN, Ophth-Opt, Ortho, Plast, Rehab, Surg, Urol, Vasc Surg

⊕ https://vfmat.ch/5da6

Medical Missions for Children (MMFC)

Provides quality surgical and dental services to poor and underprivileged children and young adults in various countries throughout the world, and facilitates the transfer of education, knowledge, and recent innovations to the local medical communities.

Dent-OMFS, ENT, Endo, Ortho, Ped Surg, Peds, Plast

⊕ https://vfmat.ch/1631

Medical Relief International
Exists to provide dental, medical, humanitarian aid, and other services deemed necessary for the benefit of people in need.
Dent-OMFS, General
⊕ https://vfmat.ch/192b

Medical Teams International
Seeks to restore health as the first step to restoring hope, working to bring basic but lifesaving medical care to those in need.
Dent-OMFS, ER Med, General, MF Med, Pub Health
⊕ https://vfmat.ch/8d1c

MedShare
Aims to improve the quality of life of people, communities, and the planet by sourcing and directly delivering surplus medical supplies and equipment to communities in need around the world.
Logist-Op
⊕ https://vfmat.ch/c8bc

Mercy in Action
Inspired by the Christian faith, carries out programs in maternal and newborn health, primary healthcare for children under 5, and midwifery education.
General, MF Med, Neonat, OB-GYN, Peds, Pub Health
⊕ https://vfmat.ch/cc88

Mercy Medical Center Cambodia
Based in Christian ministry, seeks to provide high-quality, evidence-based, cost-effective care, while taking a comprehensive and holistic approach to health.
OB-GYN, Ophth-Opt, Path, Surg
⊕ https://vfmat.ch/d126

Mini Molars Cambodia
Helps children in need in Cambodia with free dental care.
Dent-OMFS
⊕ https://vfmat.ch/d935

MiracleFeet
Brings low-cost treatment to every child on the planet born with clubfoot, a leading cause of physical disability.
Ortho, Peds, Rehab
⊕ https://vfmat.ch/bda8

Mission Bambini
Helps to support children living in poverty and sickness, and lacking education, giving them the opportunity for and hope of a better life.
CT Surg, CV Med, Crit-Care, ER Med, Ped Surg, Peds
⊕ https://vfmat.ch/dc1a

Mission Plasticos
Provides reconstructive plastic surgical care to those in need, and generates sustainable outcomes through training, education, and research.
Plast
⊕ https://vfmat.ch/97cb

MSD for Mothers
Designs scalable solutions that help end preventable maternal deaths.
MF Med, OB-GYN, Pub Health
⊕ https://vfmat.ch/9f99

MSI Reproductive Choices (Marie Stopes International)
Seeks to deliver quality family planning and reproductive healthcare to women around the world.
MF Med
⊕ https://vfmat.ch/5c82

Multi-Agency International Training and Support (MAITS)
Improves the lives of some of the world's poorest people living with disabilities through better access to quality health and education services and support.
Neuro, Psych, Rehab
⊕ https://vfmat.ch/9dcd

Médecins du Monde/Doctors of the World
Provides care, bears witness, and supports social change worldwide with innovative medical programs and evidence-based advocacy initiatives.
ER Med, General, Infect Dis, MF Med, Neonat, OB-GYN, Peds, Pub Health
⊕ https://vfmat.ch/a43d

Mérieux Foundation
Committed to fighting infectious diseases that affect developing countries by capacity building, particularly in clinical laboratories, and focusing on diagnosis.
Logist-Op, Path
⊕ https://vfmat.ch/a23a

NextSteps Cambodia
Seeks to provide treatment and support to Cambodian children with physical impairment and disability.
Plast
⊕ https://vfmat.ch/4b57

Nokor Tep Foundation
Seeks to develop a women's hospital (Nokor Tep Women's Hospital) that is focused on gynecological issues and women's cancers, thereby alleviating the silent suffering of women in Cambodia.
General, Heme-Onc, OB-GYN, Palliative, Path, Pub Health
⊕ https://vfmat.ch/4b4c

Northwest Medical Volunteers
Provides medical training and assistance in plastic and reconstructive surgery to underserved communities.
Anesth, Ped Surg, Plast
⊕ https://vfmat.ch/72b4

Northwestern University Feinberg School of Medicine: Institute for Global Health
Aims to improve access to essential surgical care by addressing the barriers to care, with multidisciplinary and bidirectional partnerships, through innovation, research, education, policy, and advocacy. Goals also include training of the next generation of global health leaders, and building sustainable capacity in regions with health inequities.
Anesth, ER Med, Heme-Onc, Logist-Op, MF Med, OB-GYN, Ped Surg, Surg
⊕ https://vfmat.ch/24f3

Norwegian People's Aid
Aims to improve living conditions, to create a democratic, just, and safe society.
ER Med, Logist-Op
⊕ https://vfmat.ch/2d8e

Nursing Beyond Borders
Provides healthcare and education to children and communities, and focuses as well on disease prevention by providing nurses to serve in orphanages, shelters, schools, and clinics.
Logist-Op, MF Med, Peds
⊕ https://vfmat.ch/71e6

One Good Turn
Provides practical medical education and culturally sensitive medical care to neglected communities worldwide.
Dent-OMFS, General
⊕ https://vfmat.ch/545f

One-2-One Charitable Trust
Aims to support dental, medical, educational, vocational, and physical needs, regardless of ethnicity, gender, and religion.
Dent-OMFS, General, Logist-Op, MF Med, Nutr
⊕ https://vfmat.ch/6aaf

Open Heart International
Provides surgical interventions and best practices to the most disadvantaged communities on the planet.
CT Surg, MF Med, OB-GYN, Ophth-Opt, Plast, Surg
⊕ https://vfmat.ch/dab2

Operation Corazón
Offers support to individuals and families in need by delivering humanitarian aid, relief, support services, equipment, clothing, medicine, and food.

General, Nutr
⊕ https://vfmat.ch/5f76

Operation Rainbow Canada
Provides free reconstructive surgery and related healthcare for cleft lip
and cleft palate deformities to impoverished children and young adults in
developing countries.
Surg
⊕ https://vfmat.ch/7f25

Options
Believes in a world in which women and children can access the high-quality
health services they need, without financial burden.
Logist-Op, MF Med, Neonat, OB-GYN
⊕ https://vfmat.ch/3a48

Optometry Giving Sight
Delivers eye exams and low or no-cost glasses, provides training for local
eye care professionals, and establishes optometry schools, vision centers and
optical labs.
Ophth-Opt
⊕ https://vfmat.ch/33ea

Order of Malta
Supports forgotten or excluded people, especially those living in conflict zones or
amid natural disasters, by providing medical assistance, caring for refugees, and
distributing medicines and necessities.
ER Med, General, Infect Dis, MF Med, Nephro, OB-GYN, Ortho, Psych
⊕ https://vfmat.ch/1fab

Pact
Works on the ground to improve the lives of those who are challenged by poverty
and marginalization, striving for a world in which all people are heard, capable,
and vibrant.
Infect Dis, Logist-Op, MF Med, Pub Health
⊕ https://vfmat.ch/9a6c

Partners for Development (PfD)
Works to improve quality of life for vulnerable people in underserved communities
through local and international partnerships.
Infect Dis, MF Med, Neonat, Peds
⊕ https://vfmat.ch/d2f6

Partners for World Health
Sorts, evaluates, repackages, and prepares supplies and equipment for
distribution to individuals, communities, and healthcare facilities in need, both
locally and internationally.
ER Med, General, Logist-Op
⊕ https://vfmat.ch/982e

PATH
Advances health equity through innovation and partnerships so people,
communities, and economies can thrive.
*All-Immu, CV Med, Endo, Heme-Onc, Infect Dis, MF Med, Neonat, Nutr, OB-GYN,
Path, Peds, Pulm-Critic*
⊕ https://vfmat.ch/b4db

Pharmacists Without Borders Canada
Provides pharmaceutical and technical assistance in the implementation or
improvement of community and hospital pharmacies internationally.
⊕ https://vfmat.ch/7658

Phoenix International Foundation, Inc.
Aims to improve quality of life by providing medical care to underserved
populations, inspired by the Christian faith.
General, Ophth-Opt
⊕ https://vfmat.ch/b464

Physicians Across Continents
Provides high-quality medical care to people affected by crises and disasters.
*CV Med, Dent-OMFS, Heme-Onc, MF Med, Nephro, Nephro, OB-GYN, Ped Surg,
Plast, Surg*
⊕ https://vfmat.ch/fe5d

PINCC Preventing Cervical Cancer
Seeks to prevent female-specific diseases in developing countries by utilizing
low-cost and low-technology methods to create sustainable programs through
patient education, medical personnel training, and facility outfitting.
OB-GYN
⊕ https://vfmat.ch/9666

Population Council
Conducts research to address critical health and development issues, helping
deliver solutions to improve lives around the world.
Logist-Op, Pub Health
⊕ https://vfmat.ch/1777

Project Angkor
Works to enhance the health of the underserved by providing free healthcare;
building lasting relationships with local doctors, nurses, clinics and hospitals;
and providing free education and training to local health-care professionals
and students.
Dent-OMFS, ER Med, General, Medicine, Ophth-Opt, Peds
⊕ https://vfmat.ch/a91a

Project Sothea
Improves outcomes of people who suffer from illnesses (both acute and chronic)
and increases their access to quality healthcare.
General
⊕ https://vfmat.ch/f954

PSI – Population Services International
Aims to improve the health of people in the developing world by focusing on
challenges such as a lack of family planning, HIV/AIDS, barriers to maternal
health, and the greatest threats to children under the age of 5, including malaria,
diarrhea, pneumonia, and malnutrition.
Infect Dis, MF Med, OB-GYN, Peds
⊕ https://vfmat.ch/ffe3

Raise and Support The Poor (RSP)
Aims to bring health, education and opportunity to marginalized children in the
Cambodian countryside.
Dent-OMFS, ER Med, General, MF Med
⊕ https://vfmat.ch/d726

RestoringVision
Empowers lives by restoring vision for millions of people in need.
Ophth-Opt
⊕ https://vfmat.ch/e121

ReSurge International
Provides reconstructive surgical care and builds surgical capacity in
developing countries.
Anesth, Dent-OMFS, Ped Surg, Plast, Surg
⊕ https://vfmat.ch/9937

Right to Sight and Health
Seeks to reduce the prevalence of blindness and visual impairment, especially
among low-income communities in Northern Ghana.
Ophth-Opt
⊕ https://vfmat.ch/7ff1

Rockefeller Foundation, The
Works to promote the well-being of humanity.
Logist-Op, Nutr, Pub Health
⊕ https://vfmat.ch/5424

Rose Charities International
Aims to support communities to improve quality of life and reduce the effects of
poverty through innovative, self-sustaining projects, and partnerships.
*ENT, ER Med, General, Infect Dis, Neonat, OB-GYN, Ophth-Opt, Ped Surg, Peds,
Rehab, Urol*
⊕ https://vfmat.ch/53df

Rotary International
Provides service to others, improves lives, and advances world understanding,
goodwill, and peace through its fellowship of business, professional, and

community leaders.
ER Med, General, Infect Dis, MF Med, OB-GYN
⊕ https://vfmat.ch/8fb5

Rutgers New Jersey Medical School
Seeks to support and promote the global health efforts of the faculty, staff, and students in the areas of education, research, and service through the Rutgers New Jersey Medical School's Office of Global Health.
Anesth, CV Med, Crit-Care, Neurosurg, OB-GYN, Psych
⊕ https://vfmat.ch/8e67

Salvation Army International, The
Seeks to meet human needs through services in education, healthcare, community support, emergency response, and ministry development, inspired by the Christian faith.
Dent-OMFS, Derm, ER Med, Infect Dis, MF Med, Medicine, Nutr, OB-GYN, Ophth-Opt, Palliative, Psych, Rehab, Surg
⊕ https://vfmat.ch/8eb3

SEE International
Provides sustainable medical, surgical, and educational services through volunteer ophthalmic surgeons, with the objectives of restoring sight and preventing blindness to disadvantaged individuals worldwide.
Ophth-Opt, Surg
⊕ https://vfmat.ch/6e1b

Seeing is Believing
Provides vision screening and eyeglasses to underprivileged people throughout the world.
Logist-Op, OB-GYN, Ophth-Opt
⊕ https://vfmat.ch/b6be

SEVA
Delivers vital eye care services to the world's most vulnerable, including women, children, and Indigenous peoples.
Ophth-Opt, Surg
⊕ https://vfmat.ch/1e87

Sharing Foundation, The
Aims to meet the physical, emotional, educational and medical needs of orphaned and seriously disadvantaged children in Cambodia.
All-Immu, General
⊕ https://vfmat.ch/46eb

Sight for All
Empowers communities to deliver comprehensive, evidence-based, high-quality eye healthcare through the provision of research, education, and equipment.
Logist-Op, Ophth-Opt, Surg
⊕ https://vfmat.ch/e34b

SIGN Fracture Care International
Builds orthopedic capacity around the world and provides the injured poor access to fracture surgery by donating orthopedic education and implant systems to surgeons in developing countries.
Ortho, Rehab, Surg
⊕ https://vfmat.ch/123d

SINA Health
Aims to improve the health and educational status of the population in low- and middle-income countries.
General, Logist-Op
⊕ https://vfmat.ch/9ad3

SladeChild Foundation
Provides food, clothing, shelter, education, and medical care to some of the world's most impoverished children.
Dent-OMFS, General, Logist-Op, Ophth-Opt
⊕ https://vfmat.ch/14c5

Smile Asia
Delivers free surgical care, through medical missions and outreach centers, to children with facial deformities such as cleft lip and cleft palate, and aims to raise standards of medical care by creating opportunities for collaborative learning and exchange of best practices.
Anesth, Dent-OMFS, Ped Surg, Peds, Plast
⊕ https://vfmat.ch/d674

Smile Train, Inc.
Treats children with cleft lip through a sustainable and local model that supports surgery and other forms of essential care.
Logist-Op, Pub Health
⊕ https://vfmat.ch/822c

SmileOnU
Empowers dental professionals to help and educate those who may not have adequate dental knowledge and access to oral health services.
Dent-OMFS, Surg
⊕ https://vfmat.ch/cb6d

Soddo Christian Hospital
Mobilizes volunteers to help transform communities through healthcare and education, based in Christian ministry.
ER Med, General
⊕ https://vfmat.ch/efa4

Sonja Kill Memorial Hospital
Aims to improve the health situation of Cambodians, especially children and expectant mothers, regardless of their ability to pay, through healthcare at a charity hospital.
Anesth, ER Med, MF Med, MF Med, Neonat, OB-GYN, Path, Peds, Radiol, Rehab, Surg
⊕ https://vfmat.ch/61e3

SOS Children's Villages International
Supports children through alternative care and family strengthening.
ER Med, Peds
⊕ https://vfmat.ch/aca1

Speech & Hearing Project
Aims to collaborate with organizations in developing countries and to connect them with Australian speech pathologists and audiologists to improve speech and hearing services abroad.
Ophth-Opt
⊕ https://vfmat.ch/574e

Spine Care International
Extends spine care to the underprivileged and provides life-changing treatment to those who may otherwise be constrained to living with chronic pain.
Neurosurg, Ortho, Rehab, Surg
⊕ https://vfmat.ch/a867

Sri Sathya Sai International Organization
Inspired by spiritual teachings, carries out efforts in global healthcare, education, humanitarian relief, and youth engagement.
Dent-OMFS, General, Logist-Op, Nutr, Ophth-Opt, Pub Health
⊕ https://vfmat.ch/9bda

Stanford University School of Medicine: Weiser Lab Global Surgery
Integrates research, education, patient care, and community service.
Logist-Op, Pub Health, Surg
⊕ https://vfmat.ch/9153

Stop TB Partnership Korea
Fights against tuberculosis, one of the most dangerous infectious killers in the world.
Infect Dis
⊕ https://vfmat.ch/3e3b

Students for Kids International Projects (SKIP)
Strives to educate and empower students to initiate and maintain sustainable community projects for the health, welfare, and education of children.
Dent-OMFS, General, Nutr, Peds, Pub Health
⊕ https://vfmat.ch/de4e

Surgical Friends Foundation
Provides reconstructive surgery and post-operative care to individuals living with physical deformities and lacking access to quality medical care.
Dent-OMFS, ENT, Plast, Surg
🌐 https://vfmat.ch/8286

Sustainable Health Empowerment (SHE)
Harnesses the power of education, local resources and cross-cultural collaboration to foster equitable healthcare in underserved communities around the world.
Dent-OMFS, General, OB-GYN, Ophth-Opt, Pub Health, Rehab
🌐 https://vfmat.ch/31ef

Sustainable Kidney Care Foundation (SKCF)
Works to provide treatment for kidney injury where none exists, and aims to reduce mortality from treatable acute kidney injury (AKI).
Infect Dis, Medicine, Nephro
🌐 https://vfmat.ch/1926

Swasti
Aims to transform the lives of marginalized communities by ensuring their access to quality healthcare and thereby contributing to poverty alleviation.
Pub Health
🌐 https://vfmat.ch/be8b

Swiss Tropical and Public Health Institute
Contributes to the improvement of the health of populations internationally, nationally, and locally through excellence in research, education, and services.
Infect Dis, Pub Health
🌐 https://vfmat.ch/2ee4

Task Force for Global Health, The
Consists of programs and focus areas that cover a range of global health issues including neglected tropical diseases, infectious diseases, vaccines, field epidemiology, public health informatics, health workforce development, and global health ethics.
Infect Dis, Logist-Op, Medicine, Ophth-Opt, Peds
🌐 https://vfmat.ch/714c

Team 5 Medical Foundation
Provides medical care in the most overlooked remote areas of the world supported by sponsorships, donations, and the dedication of its volunteers.
ER Med, General, Peds, Plast, Pulm-Critic
🌐 https://vfmat.ch/f267

Tearfund
Responds to crisis and partners with local churches to bring restoration to those living in poverty, inspired by the Christian faith.
ER Med, Logist-Op
🌐 https://vfmat.ch/f6cf

Transparent Fish Fund
Inspires others to join in alleviating poverty in East Asia by empowering small but high-impact NGOs to be sustainable and transparent in their programs.
CV Med, General, MF Med, Nutr, Peds
🌐 https://vfmat.ch/7714

U.S. President's Malaria Initiative (PMI)
Supports low-income countries to help control and eliminate malaria through cost-effective, lifesaving malaria interventions.
Infect Dis, MF Med, OB-GYN
🌐 https://vfmat.ch/dc8b

UNC Health Foundation
Secures resources and supports empathy and expertise in patient care, research, education, and advocacy in underserved communities around the world.
Heme-Onc, Infect Dis, Neuro, Peds, Pub Health
🌐 https://vfmat.ch/7129

Union for International Cancer Control (UICC)
Unites and supports the cancer community to reduce the global cancer burden, promote greater equity, and ensure that cancer control continues to be a priority in the world health and development agenda.

Heme-Onc, Pub Health
🌐 https://vfmat.ch/88b1

United Nations Children's Fund (UNICEF)
Works in over 190 countries and territories to save children's lives, defend their rights, and help them fulfill their potential, from early childhood through adolescence.
All-Immu, Infect Dis, MF Med, Neonat, Nutr, OB-GYN, Ped Surg, Peds, Pub Health
🌐 https://vfmat.ch/42d7

United Nations Development Programme (UNDP)
Helps countries achieve the simultaneous eradication of extreme poverty and significant reduction of inequalities and exclusion using a sustainable human development approach.
Infect Dis, Logist-Op, Pub Health
🌐 https://vfmat.ch/935c

United Nations High Commissioner for Refugees (UNHCR)
Safeguards the rights and well-being of people who have been forced to flee, ensuring that everybody has the right to seek asylum and find safe refuge in another country, with the goal of seeking lasting solutions.
General, MF Med, Medicine, OB-GYN, Peds, Psych, Pub Health
🌐 https://vfmat.ch/6636

United Nations Population Fund (UNFPA)
Supports reproductive healthcare for women and youth in more than 150 countries, focusing on delivering a world in which every pregnancy is wanted, every childbirth is safe, and every young person's potential is fulfilled.
Infect Dis, MF Med, Neonat, OB-GYN, Peds, Pub Health
🌐 https://vfmat.ch/c969

University of California Los Angeles: David Geffen School of Medicine Global Health Program
Catalyzes opportunities to improve health globally by engaging in multi-disciplinary and innovative education programs, research initiatives, and bilateral partnerships that provide opportunities for trainees, faculty, and staff to contribute to sustainable health initiatives and to address health inequities facing the world today.
All-Immu, Infect Dis, Logist-Op, MF Med, Medicine, Neonat, OB-GYN, Ortho, Ped Surg, Peds, Radiol
🌐 https://vfmat.ch/f1a4

University of Michigan: Department of Surgery Global Health
Improves the health of patients, populations and communities through excellence in education, patient care, community service, research and technology development, and through leadership activities.
Anesth, Ortho, Surg
🌐 https://vfmat.ch/2fd8

University of Washington: The International Training and Education Center for Health (I-TECH)
Works with local partners to develop skilled healthcare workers and strong national health systems in resource-limited countries.
Infect Dis, Pub Health
🌐 https://vfmat.ch/642f

USAID: A2Z The Micronutrient and Child Blindness Project
Aims to increase the use of key micronutrient and blindness interventions to improve child and maternal health.
MF Med, Neonat, Nutr, Ophth-Opt, Surg
🌐 https://vfmat.ch/c5f1

USAID: Health Finance and Governance Project
Uses research to implement strategies to help countries develop robust governance systems, increase their domestic resources for health, manage those resources more effectively, and make wise purchasing decisions.
Logist-Op
🌐 https://vfmat.ch/8652

USAID: Leadership, Management and Governance Project
Improves leadership, management, and governance practices to strengthen health systems and improve health for all, including vulnerable populations worldwide.

Logist-Op
⊕ https://vfmat.ch/d35e

Ventura Global Health Project (VGHP)
Aims to encourage and facilitate a lifelong interest in global health by providing grants to support local medical professionals providing care to underserved populations.
Dent-OMFS, ER Med, General, Infect Dis, Logist-Op, OB-GYN, Ophth-Opt, Ortho, Peds, Plast, Surg, Urol
⊕ https://vfmat.ch/a746

Virtue Foundation
Increases awareness, inspires action and renders assistance through healthcare, education, and empowerment initiatives.
Anesth, Crit-Care, Dent-OMFS, ENT, ER Med, Heme-Onc, Logist-Op, Neurosurg, OB-GYN, Ophth-Opt, Ortho, Path, Ped Surg, Peds, Plast, Radiol, Rehab, Surg
⊕ https://vfmat.ch/6481

Vision Care
Restores sight and helps patients get regular treatment at short-term eye camps and long-term base clinics by having doctors, missionaries, volunteers, and sponsors work together.
Ophth-Opt
⊕ https://vfmat.ch/9d7c

Vitamin Angels
Helps at-risk populations in need—specifically pregnant women, new mothers, and children under age 5—to gain access to life-changing vitamins and minerals.
General, Nutr
⊕ https://vfmat.ch/7da1

Voluntary Service Overseas (VSO)
Works with health workers, communities, and governments to improve health services and rights for women, babies, youth, people with disabilities, and prisoners.
General, MF Med, OB-GYN
⊕ https://vfmat.ch/213d

VOSH (Volunteer Optometric Services to Humanity) International
Facilitates the provision and the sustainability of vision care worldwide for people who can neither afford nor obtain such care.
Ophth-Opt
⊕ https://vfmat.ch/a149

Water and Healthcare Foundation (WAH)
Aims to improve the lives and conditions of rural communities in Cambodia, through dedication to sustainable clean water, health, and education projects.
ER Med, MF Med, Ophth-Opt, Peds
⊕ https://vfmat.ch/7ed3

Watsi
Uses technology to make healthcare a reality for those who might not otherwise be able to afford it.
Pub Health, Surg
⊕ https://vfmat.ch/41a3

Wealth By Health Steps For Change Foundation
Aims to improve the health and well-being of underserved populations by providing accessible resources that support the attainment of greater quality of life.
All-Immu, CV Med, Dent-OMFS, General, Medicine, Ophth-Opt, Palliative, Peds, Pub Health
⊕ https://vfmat.ch/153a

World Federation of Hemophilia (WFH)
Aims to improve and sustain care for people with inherited bleeding disorders by pursuing long-term relationships with individuals and organizations who share the values of WFH's development model.
Heme-Onc
⊕ https://vfmat.ch/5121

World Health Organization, The (WHO)
The United Nations' agency for health provides leadership on global health matters, shapes the health research agenda, sets norms and standards, articulates evidence-based policy options, provides technical support and monitoring to countries, and assesses health trends.
ER Med, General, Infect Dis, Logist-Op, MF Med, OB-GYN, Peds, Psych, Pub Health
⊕ https://vfmat.ch/c476

World Hope International
Empowers the poorest individuals around the world so they can become agents of change within their communities, by offering resources and knowledge.
Infect Dis, Logist-Op, MF Med, OB-GYN, Peds
⊕ https://vfmat.ch/a4b8

World Medical Relief
Facilitates the distribution of surplus medical resources where they are needed.
Logist-Op
⊕ https://vfmat.ch/72dc

World Rehabilitation Fund
Enables individuals around the world with functional limitations and participation restrictions to achieve community and social integration through physical and socioeconomic rehabilitation and advocacy.
Ortho, Rehab
⊕ https://vfmat.ch/a5bc

World Relief
Brings sustainable solutions to the world's greatest problems: disasters, extreme poverty, violence, oppression, and mass displacement.
ER Med, Nutr, Psych, Pub Health
⊕ https://vfmat.ch/fbcd

World Telehealth Initiative
Provides medical expertise to the world's most vulnerable communities to build local capacity and deliver core health services through a network of volunteer healthcare professionals supported with state-of-the-art technology.
Derm, Infect Dis, MF Med, Medicine, Neuro, OB-GYN, Peds, Pulm-Critic
⊕ https://vfmat.ch/fa91

World Vision International
Works with vulnerable communities around the world to overcome poverty and injustice with child-focused programs in disaster management, health, nutrition, economic development, education, clean water, sanitation, and hygiene.
ER Med, General, Infect Dis, MF Med, Nutr, OB-GYN, Peds
⊕ https://vfmat.ch/2642

Worldwide Healing Hands
Works to improve the quality of healthcare for women and children in the most underserved areas of the world and to stop the preventable deaths of mothers.
General, MF Med, Neonat, OB-GYN
⊕ https://vfmat.ch/b331

Your Aid We Deliver
Strives to improve Cambodian children's lives through providing safe water supplies, education, and dental care.
Dent-OMFS
⊕ https://vfmat.ch/94b5

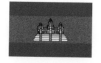

Cambodia

Healthcare Facilities

Ang Snoul Referral Hospital
Phnom Penh, Cambodia
⊕ https://vfmat.ch/ipxv

Angkor Chum Referral Hospital
Angkor Chum, Cambodia
⊕ https://vfmat.ch/e9fc

Angkor Hospital for Children
Svay Dangkum, Siem Reap, Cambodia
⊕ https://vfmat.ch/6ffc

Baray District Referral Hospital
Trapeang Svay, Kampong Thom, Cambodia
⊕ https://vfmat.ch/5bcf

Bati Referral Hospital
Phumĭ Châmbák, Takeo, Cambodia
⊕ https://vfmat.ch/42f8

Battambang Provincial Hospital
Battamburg, Cambodia
⊕ https://vfmat.ch/yd1g

Calmette Hospital
Phnom Penh, Cambodia
⊕ https://vfmat.ch/dc27

Cambodia-China Friendship Preah Kossamak Hospital
Phnom Penh, Cambodia
⊕ https://vfmat.ch/fd19

Central Hospital Phnom Penh
Phnom Penh, Cambodia
⊕ https://vfmat.ch/yd7u

Chamkor Morn Referral Hospital
Phnom Penh, Cambodia
⊕ https://vfmat.ch/3d5h

Cheung Prey Referral Hospital
Phnom Penh, Cambodia
⊕ https://vfmat.ch/fpy6

Cho Ray Phnom Penh Hospital
Phnom Penh, Phnom Penh, Cambodia
⊕ https://vfmat.ch/ser3

Dangkor Referral Hospital
Phumĭ Khva, Phnom Penh, Cambodia
⊕ https://vfmat.ch/d49b

Institute Pasteur du Cambodge
Phnom Penh, Cambodia
⊕ https://vfmat.ch/pkfy

Kamchaymear Referral Hospital
Kâmchay Méa, Prey Veng, Cambodia
⊕ https://vfmat.ch/b14b

Kampong Cham Provincial Hospital
Kampong, Cambodia
⊕ https://vfmat.ch/5uyh

Kampong Chhnang Hospital
Krong, Kampong Chhnang, Cambodia
⊕ https://vfmat.ch/2634

Kampong Speu Referral Hospital
Phumĭ Snaôr, Kampong Speu, Cambodia
⊕ https://vfmat.ch/49ed

Kampong Thom Provincial Hospital
Kampong Thom, Cambodia
⊕ https://vfmat.ch/7b4f

Kampong Trach Referral Hospital
Kampong Trach, Cambodia
⊕ https://vfmat.ch/5ebe

Kampot Referral Hospital
Krong Kampot, Cambodia
⊕ https://vfmat.ch/7c38

Kantha Bopha IV Children's Hospital
Phnom Penh, Cambodia
⊕ https://vfmat.ch/28b2

Kantha Bopha Jayavarmann VII Hospital
Krong Siem Reap, Siem Reap, Cambodia
⊕ https://vfmat.ch/b84c

Katha Bopha I Children's Hospital
Phnom Penh, Cambodia
⊕ https://vfmat.ch/iqcg

Katha Bopha II Children's Hospital
Phnom Penh, Cambodia
⊕ https://vfmat.ch/jxp6

Khmer Soviet Friendship Hospital
Phnom Penh, Cambodia
⊕ https://vfmat.ch/dbf3

Kien Svay Referral Hospital
Kien Svay, Cambodia
⊕ https://vfmat.ch/41e1

Kirivong Referral Hospital
Ta Ou, Takeo, Cambodia
⊕ https://vfmat.ch/f46a

Koh Kong Provincial Referral Hospital
Krong Khemara, Phoumin, Cambodia
⊕ https://vfmat.ch/1dcb

Kratie Referral Hospital
Kracheh, Cambodia
⊕ https://vfmat.ch/224f

Makara Provincial Referral Hospital
Mlouprey Kompong, Pranak, Cambodia
⊕ https://vfmat.ch/abbe

Maliya Hospital
Phnom Penh, Cambodia
⊕ https://vfmat.ch/clcx

Mean Chey Referral Hospital
Phnom Penh, Cambodia
⊕ https://vfmat.ch/bjfi

Military Hospital
Russey, Preah Vihear, Cambodia
⊕ https://vfmat.ch/2c3b

Military Region II Hospital
Phumĭ Âmpĭl Leu, Kampong Cham, Cambodia
⊕ https://vfmat.ch/5b71

National Pediatric Hospital
Khan Toul Kork, Phnom Penh, Cambodia
⊕ https://vfmat.ch/3377

Nokor Tep Women's Hospital
Dangkor District, Phnom Penh, Cambodia
⊕ https://vfmat.ch/b564

Ouksaphea Hospital
Khan Meanchey, Phnom Penh, Cambodia
⊕ https://vfmat.ch/a99c

Pacific Phnom Penh Hospital
Phnom Penh, Cambodia
⊕ https://vfmat.ch/tjvc

Phnom Penh Referral Hospital
Phnom Penh, Cambodia
⊕ https://vfmat.ch/6c48

Ponhea Leu Referral Hospital
Thommeak Treiy, Kandal, Cambodia
⊕ https://vfmat.ch/8432

Preah Ang Duong Hospital
Phnom Penh, Cambodia
⊕ https://vfmat.ch/cb9a

Preah Ket Mealea Hospital
Chrouy Changva, Phnom Penh, Cambodia
⊕ https://vfmat.ch/c3df

Preah Kossamak National Hospital
Phnom Penh, Cambodia
⊕ https://vfmat.ch/ndtz

Preah Sihanouk Province Referral Hospital
Sangkat 4, Preah Sihanouk, Cambodia
⊕ https://vfmat.ch/b3fd

Prestige Hospital, The
Phnom Penh, Cambodia
⊕ https://vfmat.ch/7cab

Ratanakiri Provincial Referral Hospital
Banlung, Cambodia
⊕ https://vfmat.ch/4544

Royal Angkor International Hospital
Krong, Siem Reap, Cambodia
⊕ https://vfmat.ch/9fbb

Royal Hospital – Phnom Penh
Phnom Penh, Cambodia
⊕ https://vfmat.ch/a371

Samdech Ov Referral Hospital
Kiloumaetr Lekh Prammuoy, Phnom Penh, Cambodia
⊕ https://vfmat.ch/86b9

Sen Mororom Hospital
Sen Monorom, Cambodia
⊕ https://vfmat.ch/e3d9

Sen Sok International University Hospital
Phnom Penh, Cambodia
⊕ https://vfmat.ch/4f12

Siem Reap Referral Hospital
Siem Reap, Cambodia
⊕ https://vfmat.ch/7164

Sihanouk Hospital Center of HOPE (SHCH)
Phnom Penh, Cambodia
⊕ https://vfmat.ch/f2wu

Stung Treng Referral Hospital
Stung Treng, Krong Stung Treng, Cambodia
⊕ https://vfmat.ch/2f17

Sunrise Japan Hospital – Phnom Penh
Chrouy Changva, Phnom Penh, Cambodia
⊕ https://vfmat.ch/7fcb

Svay Rieng Provincial Referral Hospital
Phumĭ Taléan, Svay Rieng, Cambodia
⊕ https://vfmat.ch/8874

Takeo Referral Hospital
Krong Doun Kaev, Takeo, Cambodia
⊕ https://vfmat.ch/dd63

Thmor Koul District Referral Hospital
Thmor Koul, Battambang, Cambodia
⊕ https://vfmat.ch/c61c

Victory Hospital
Phumĭ Dei Lo, Kandal, Cambodia
⊕ https://vfmat.ch/7cf8

World Mate Emergency Hospital
Romchek IV, Rattanak Battambang, Cambodia
⊕ https://vfmat.ch/n6ab

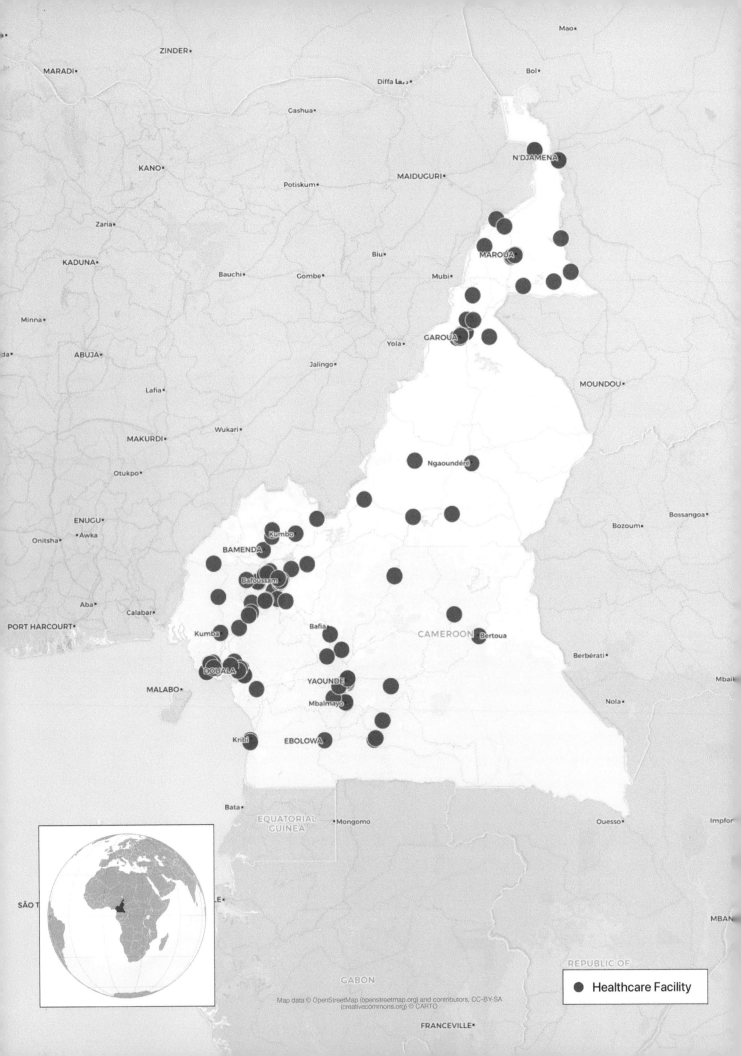

● Healthcare Facility

Cameroon

The Republic of Cameroon, in Central Africa, is neighbored by Nigeria, Chad, Central African Republic, Republic of the Congo, Gabon, and Equatorial Guinea. Cameroon's population of 28.5 million comprises several different ethnic groups including Bamileke-Bamu, Beti/Bassa, Mbam, Biu-Mandara, Arab-Choa/Hausa/Kanuri, Adamawa-Ubangi, Grassfields, Kako, Meka/Pygmy, Cotier/Ngoe/Oroko, and Southwestern Bantu. Cameroon's ethnic diversity is represented by as many as 24 major languages spoken throughout the country, while English and French are the official languages. In addition to ethnic and linguistic diversity, Cameroon is also religiously diverse, with Roman Catholic, Protestant, Christian, Muslim, and animist populations. Also known as the "hinge of Africa," Cameroon exhibits all the major climates and vegetative features that can be found in Africa: coast, desert, mountains, rainforest, and savanna. As a result, it is also sometimes referred to as Africa in miniature.

Prior to its independence in 1960, Cameroon was a French colony. A formerly British portion of the country merged with French Cameroon in 1961 to form the country's modern borders. Since then, Cameroon has continued to suffer from high rates of poverty, with a lack of investment in public programs and insufficient social safety nets. In addition, food insecurity in the north has worsened due to the activities of armed groups and insurgencies. Rural areas of Cameroon especially suffer from a lack of job opportunities, poor educational systems, a deficient healthcare infrastructure, and insufficient sanitation and clean water.

The population of Cameroon is proportionately young, with more than 60 percent of the population under 25 years of age. Cameroon also has one of the highest maternal mortality rates in the world. The most common causes of death include HIV/AIDS, malaria, diarrheal diseases, lower respiratory infections, neonatal disorders, stroke, ischemic heart disease, tuberculosis, road injuries, and diabetes. Notably, death due to measles has decreased by nearly 62 percent; however, it is still considered one of the main causes of mortality.

28.5M
Population

$1,499
GDP Per Capita

59 years
Life Expectancy
↑ Improving

9
Doctors/100k
Physician Density

130
Beds/100k
Hospital Bed Density

529
Deaths/100k
Maternal Mortality

Cameroon

Nonprofit Organizations

A Broader View Volunteers
Provides developing countries around the world with significant volunteer programs that aid the neediest communities and forge a lasting bond between those volunteering and those they have helped.

Dent-OMFS, ER Med, Infect Dis, MF Med

⊕ https://vfmat.ch/3bec

Abt Associates
Seeks to improve the quality of life and economic well-being of people worldwide, while striving to meet and exceed the highest professional standards.

General, Logist-Op, MF Med, OB-GYN, Peds

⊕ https://vfmat.ch/cec2

Action Against Hunger
Aims to end life-threatening hunger for good through treating and preventing malnutrition across more than 45 countries.

Nutr

⊕ https://vfmat.ch/2dbc

Addis Clinic, The
Uses telemedicine to care for people living in medically underserved areas, connects volunteer physicians with global health challenges, and provides support to local partner organizations and frontline health workers.

General, Infect Dis

⊕ https://vfmat.ch/f82f

Africa CDC
Aims to strengthen the capacity and capability of Africa's public health institutions and partnerships to detect and respond quickly and effectively to disease threats and outbreaks, based on data-driven interventions and programs.

Infect Dis, Logist-Op, Pub Health

⊕ https://vfmat.ch/339c

Africa Health Organisation
Leads collaborative efforts among countries in Africa and other partners to promote health equity, combat disease, and improve quality of life.

Logist-Op, Pub Health

⊕ https://vfmat.ch/b1c5

Africa Humanitarian Action (AHA)
Responds to crises, conflicts, and disasters in Africa, while informing and advising the international community, governments, civil society, and the private sector on humanitarian issues of concern to Africa. Supports institutional and organizational development efforts.

General, Infect Dis, MF Med, Nutr, OB-GYN

⊕ https://vfmat.ch/3ca2

Africa Relief and Community Development
Provides comprehensive relief and developmental aid to people of the African continent regardless of gender, race, or religion.

Nutr, Pub Health

⊕ https://vfmat.ch/6cd2

African Field Epidemiology Network (AFENET)
Strengthens field epidemiology and public health laboratory capacity to contribute effectively to addressing epidemics and other major public health problems in Africa.

All-Immu, Infect Dis, Path, Pub Health

⊕ https://vfmat.ch/df2e

African Mission Health Foundation
Aims to strengthen African mission hospitals by providing quality, compassionate care for the hurting and forgotten and helping improve Sub-Saharan Africa's health system.

Infect Dis, Neonat, OB-GYN, Peds, Surg

⊕ https://vfmat.ch/5b14

Against Malaria Foundation
Helps protect people from malaria. Funds anti-malaria nets, specifically long-lasting insecticidal nets (LLINs), and works with distribution partners to ensure they are used. Tracks and reports on net use and malaria case data.

Infect Dis

⊕ https://vfmat.ch/337d

Agatha Foundation, The
Seeks to end poverty and hunger, promote universal education, promote gender equality, reduce child mortality, improve maternal health, and combat HIV/AIDS, malaria, and other diseases.

Infect Dis, Logist-Op, Medicine, OB-GYN, Peds

⊕ https://vfmat.ch/9b26

Al Basar International Foundation
Works with local partners to treat preventable blindness, and helps set up sustainable infrastructure so local teams can save sight in their communities.

Ophth-Opt

⊕ https://vfmat.ch/a8b5

Alliance for International Medical Action, The (ALIMA)
Provides quality medical care to vulnerable populations, partnering with and developing national medical organizations and conducting medical research to bring innovation to 12 African countries where ALIMA works.

ER Med, General, Infect Dis, Logist-Op, MF Med, OB-GYN, Path, Peds, Psych, Pub Health

⊕ https://vfmat.ch/1c11

Amref Health Africa
Serves millions of people across 35 countries in Sub-Saharan Africa, strengthening health systems, and training African health workers to respond to the continent's most critical health issues.

All-Immu, General, Infect Dis, Logist-Op, MF Med, OB-GYN, Path, Pub Health, Surg
⊕ https://vfmat.ch/6985

Amsterdam Institute for Global Health and Development (AIGHD)
Provides sustainable solutions to major health problems across our planet by forging synergies among disciplines, healthcare delivery, research, and education.
Infect Dis
⊕ https://vfmat.ch/d73d

Angel of Mercy
Relieves suffering and loneliness of people living with HIV/AIDS, diabetes, or heart disease, along with orphans and underprivileged children in the community.
Infect Dis, Pub Health
⊕ https://vfmat.ch/f67a

AO Alliance
Builds solutions to lessen the burden of injuries in low- and middle-income countries, while enhancing the care of the injured to reduce human suffering, disability, and poverty.
Ortho, Surg
⊕ https://vfmat.ch/8cd5

Benjamin H. Josephson, MD Fund
Provides healthcare professionals with the financial resources necessary to deliver medical services for those in need throughout the world.
General, OB-GYN
⊕ https://vfmat.ch/6acc

BethanyKids
Transforms the lives of African children with surgical conditions and disabilities through pediatric surgery, rehabilitation, public education, spiritual ministry, and the training of health professionals.
Neurosurg, Nutr, Ortho, Ped Surg, Peds, Rehab, Surg
⊕ https://vfmat.ch/db4e

Brain Project Africa
Provides the highest level of medical care, facilitates knowledge transfer, and donates the necessary medical equipment where it's most impactful.
Neuro, Neurosurg, Ortho
⊕ https://vfmat.ch/d4fd

Bridge of Life
Aims to strengthen healthcare globally through sustainable programs that prevent and treat chronic disease.
Logist-Op, Nephro, OB-GYN, Peds, Surg
⊕ https://vfmat.ch/5b68

Cameroon Baptist Convention (CBC) Health Services
Seeks to provide comprehensive healthcare, child care, education and social services to the poorest and most vulnerable, inspired by the Christian faith.
CV Med, Crit-Care, Dent-OMFS, Derm, ENT, Endo, General, Heme-Onc, Infect Dis, MF Med, Neonat, Nutr, OB-GYN, Ophth-Opt, Ortho, Palliative, Path, Peds, Psych, Pub Health, Radiol, Rehab, Surg
⊕ https://vfmat.ch/faf3

CARE
Works around the globe to save lives, defeat poverty, and achieve social justice.
ER Med, General
⊕ https://vfmat.ch/7232

Carter Center, The
Seeks to prevent and resolve conflicts, enhance freedom and democracy, and improve health, while remaining committed to human rights and the alleviation of human suffering.
Infect Dis, MF Med, Ophth-Opt
⊕ https://vfmat.ch/6556

Catholic Organization for Relief & Development Aid (CORDAID)
Provides humanitarian assistance and creates opportunities to improve security, healthcare, education, and inclusive economic growth in fragile and conflict-affected areas.

ER Med, Infect Dis, MF Med, OB-GYN, Peds, Psych
⊕ https://vfmat.ch/8ae5

Catholic World Mission
Works to rebuild communities worldwide by helping to alleviate poverty and empower underserved areas, while spreading the message of the Catholic Church.
ER Med, General, Nutr, Peds
⊕ https://vfmat.ch/7b5f

Chain of Hope
Provides lifesaving heart operations for children around the world and supports the development of cardiac services in numerous developing and war-torn countries.
Anesth, CT Surg, CV Med, Crit-Care, Ped Surg, Peds, Pulm-Critic, Surg
⊕ https://vfmat.ch/1b1b

Children Without Worms
Enhances the health and development of children by reducing intestinal worm infections.
Infect Dis, Pub Health
⊕ https://vfmat.ch/6bee

Christian Blind Mission (CBM)
Aims to improve the quality of life of persons with disabilities in the poorest countries, addressing poverty as a cause and a consequence of disability, and working in partnership to create a society for all.
ENT, General, Infect Dis, OB-GYN, Ophth-Opt, Ortho, Peds, Psych, Rehab, Surg
⊕ https://vfmat.ch/3824

Christian Connections for International Health (CCIH)
Promotes global health and wholeness from a Christian perspective.
All-Immu, General, Infect Dis, MF Med, Neonat, OB-GYN, Psych
⊕ https://vfmat.ch/fa5d

Christian Medical & Dental Associations
Based in Christian ministry, deploys medical and dental teams to underserved communities to provide vital healthcare.
Anesth, Dent-OMFS, ER Med, General, Medicine, OB-GYN, Ophth-Opt, Peds, Pub Health, Radiol, Rehab, Surg
⊕ https://vfmat.ch/921c

Clinton Health Access Initiative (CHAI)
Aims to save lives and reduce the burden of disease in low- and middle-income countries. Works with partners to strengthen the capabilities of governments and the private sector to create and sustain high-quality health systems.
General, Heme-Onc, Infect Dis, Logist-Op, MF Med, Medicine, Neonat, Nutr, OB-GYN, Path, Peds, Rad-Onc
⊕ https://vfmat.ch/9ed7

Columbia Vagelos College of Physicians and Surgeons Programs in Global Health
Harnesses the expertise of the medical school to improve health worldwide by training global health leaders, building capacity through interdisciplinary education and training programs, and addressing unmet health needs through research and application.
CV Med, Derm, Genetics, Heme-Onc, Infect Dis, Medicine, OB-GYN, Ophth-Opt, Peds, Psych, Pub Health, Pulm-Critic, Surg
⊕ https://vfmat.ch/a9e5

COVID-19 Clinical Research Coalition
Advocates and collaborates for the advancement of COVID-19 research driven by the needs of low-resource settings, and works for equitable access to solutions to the pandemic.
All-Immu, Infect-Dis, MF Med, Path, Pub Health
⊕ https://vfmat.ch/d1f4

Cry Cameroon
Provides education, health, shelter, and nutritional care to children, along with spiritual guidance inspired by the Christian faith.
Peds
⊕ https://vfmat.ch/25ab

Dental Helping Hands
Provides dental health services to underserved communities in developing countries.
Dent-OMFS
⊕ https://vfmat.ch/7ba5

Direct Relief
Improves the health and lives of people affected by poverty or emergency situations by mobilizing and providing essential medical resources needed for their care.
ER Med, Logist-Op
⊕ https://vfmat.ch/58e5

DKT INTERNATIONAL INC
Seeks to provide couples with affordable and safe options for family planning and HIV/AIDS prevention through dynamic social marketing.
General, Surg
⊕ https://vfmat.ch/b3a7

Doctors Without Borders/Médecins Sans Frontières (MSF)
Responds to emergencies and provides lifesaving medical care where needed most, including during disasters, conflicts, and epidemics.
Anesth, Crit-Care, ER Med, General, Infect Dis, Nutr, OB-GYN, Ped Surg, Peds, Psych, Pub Health, Surg
⊕ https://vfmat.ch/f363

Dream Sant'Egidio
Seeks to counter HIV/AIDS in Africa by eliminating the transmission of HIV from mother to child, with a focus on women because of the importance of their role in the community.
Infect Dis, MF Med, Neonat, OB-GYN, Path, Peds
⊕ https://vfmat.ch/f466

Duke University: Global Health Institute
Sparks innovation in global health research and education, and brings together knowledge and resources to address the most important global health issues of our time.
All-Immu, Infect Dis, MF Med, OB-GYN, Pub Health
⊕ https://vfmat.ch/c4cd

eHealth Africa
Builds stronger health systems in Africa through the design and implementation of data-driven solutions, responding to local needs and providing underserved communities with the necessary tools to lead healthier lives.
Logist-Op, Path
⊕ https://vfmat.ch/db6a

Elizabeth Glaser Pediatric AIDS Foundation
Seeks to end global pediatric HIV/AIDS through prevention and treatment programs, research, and advocacy.
Infect Dis, Nutr, OB-GYN, Peds
⊕ https://vfmat.ch/d6ec

eRanger
Provides sustainable solutions to transportation and medical provision such as ambulances and mobile clinics in developing countries.
ER Med, General, Logist-Op
⊕ https://vfmat.ch/4c18

Essential Medical Technology Foundation, The
Develops and deploys effective, high-quality, and affordable medical devices adapted to the needs of impoverished communities across the globe.
Logist-Op, Pub Health
⊕ https://vfmat.ch/bbb4

FAIRMED Sri Lanka
Aims to improve the circumstances of all people at risk for or affected by leprosy and other neglected tropical diseases in Sri Lanka.
Infect Dis
⊕ https://vfmat.ch/c463

Favour Low-Cost Healthcare (FALCOH) Foundation
Provides essential, sustainable healthcare services to underprivileged groups in

African communities.
ER Med, Geri, Infect Dis, OB-GYN, Pub Health, Surg
⊕ https://vfmat.ch/5b6d

Foundation for Special Surgery
Provides high-quality, complex surgical care by increasing surgical expertise in Africa through the participation of surgeons across various specialties to provide premium care and skills transfer/education to benefit patients.
Anesth, CT Surg, ENT, Endo, Neurosurg, Plast, Surg, Urol
⊕ https://vfmat.ch/53db

Global Blood Fund
Delivers grants, equipment, and training to over 50 countries in Africa, Asia, Eastern Europe, the Middle East, Latin America and the Caribbean.
Pub Health
⊕ https://vfmat.ch/6377

Global Force for Healing
Works to end preventable maternal and newborn deaths by supporting the scaling of effective grassroots, community-led, culturally respectful care and education in underserved areas around the globe using the midwifery model of care.
Neonat, OB-GYN
⊕ https://vfmat.ch/deb2

Global Ministries – The United Methodist Church
As the worldwide mission and development agency of The United Methodist Church, Global Ministries works with more than 300 hospitals and clinics around the world through its Global Health Unit.
Anesth, CT Surg, CV Med, Crit-Care, Dent-OMFS, Derm, ER Med, GI, General, Infect Dis, Logist-Op, MF Med, Medicine, Neonat, Nephro, Nutr, OB-GYN, Ophth-Opt, Ortho, Palliative, Peds, Pod, Psych, Pub Health, Rehab, Rheum, Surg, Urol
⊕ https://vfmat.ch/1723

Global Oncology (GO)
Brings the best in cancer care to underserved patients around the world and collaborates across geographic, professional, and academic borders to improve cancer care, research, and education.
Heme-Onc, Path, Rad-Onc
⊕ https://vfmat.ch/fcb8

Global Reconstructive Surgery Outreach
Supports surgeons, doctors, and nurses financially to enable them to provide critically needed plastic and reconstructive surgeries to the poor.
Logist-Op, Surg
⊕ https://vfmat.ch/f262

Global Vision 2020
Provides prescription eyeglasses to people who live in parts of the world lacking necessary infrastructure for obtaining affordable corrective eyewear.
Logist-Op, Ophth-Opt
⊕ https://vfmat.ch/7373

Globus Relief
Aims to improve the delivery of healthcare worldwide by gathering, processing, and distributing surplus medical supplies to charities at home and abroad.
Logist-Op
⊕ https://vfmat.ch/a2b7

Grace Dental and Medical (GDM) Missions
Sends and supports dental and medical missions based in Christian ministry with the aim of church planting.
Dent-OMFS, ER Med, General
⊕ https://vfmat.ch/bdea

Grassroot Soccer
Leverages the power of soccer to educate, inspire, and mobilize at-risk youth in developing countries to overcome their greatest health challenges, live healthier and more productive lives, and be agents for change in their communities.
Infect Dis
⊕ https://vfmat.ch/3521

Healing Little Hearts
Sends specialist medical teams to perform free lifesaving heart surgery on babies

and children in developing parts of the world.
Anesth, CT Surg, CV Med, Ped Surg, Peds, Surg
🌐 https://vfmat.ch/ffc1

Health For All Mission
Promotes health and wellness in the following areas: healthcare, education, economic development, and the environment.
Dent-OMFS, General, Pub Health
🌐 https://vfmat.ch/fe1a

Healthy DEvelopments
Provides Germany-supported health and social protection programs around the globe in a collaborative knowledge management process.
All-Immu, General, Infect Dis, Logist-Op, MF Med
🌐 https://vfmat.ch/dc31

Heineman Medical Outreach
Provides medical and educational assistance globally to promote sustainable healthcare and enhanced living standards in underserved communities through the International Medical Outreach (IMO) program, a collaborative partnership between Heineman Medical Outreach and Atrium Health.
Anesth, CT Surg, CV Med, ER Med, General, Heme-Onc, Logist-Op, Medicine, Neonat, OB-GYN, Ped Surg, Peds, Surg, Vasc Surg
🌐 https://vfmat.ch/389b

Helen Keller International
Seeks to eliminate preventable vision loss, malnutrition, and diseases of poverty.
Infect Dis, Nutr, OB-GYN, Ophth-Opt, Peds
🌐 https://vfmat.ch/b654

HelpMeSee
Trains local cataract specialists in Manual Small Incision Cataract Surgery (MSICS) in significant numbers, to meet the increasing demand for surgical services in the communities most impacted by cataract blindness.
Anesth, Ophth-Opt, Surg
🌐 https://vfmat.ch/973c

Hope and Healing International
Gives hope and healing to children and families trapped by poverty and disability.
General, Nutr, Ophth-Opt, Peds, Rehab
🌐 https://vfmat.ch/c638

Hope For A Better Future (H4BF)
Provides humanitarian assistance in crisis situations and contributes to sustainable development within communities in Cameroon.
MF Med, Pub Health
🌐 https://vfmat.ch/9b3a

Hospice Africa
Aims to provide a holistic and culturally sensitive palliative care service through accurate treatment of pain.
Palliative
🌐 https://vfmat.ch/9f86

HumaniTerra
Helps countries and populations emerging from economic and human crisis to rebuild their healthcare system in a sustainable way. Committed to three fundamental and complementary actions: operating, training, and rebuilding.
Anesth, ENT, ER Med, MF Med, OB-GYN, Ortho, Plast, Surg
🌐 https://vfmat.ch/b371

Humanity First
Provides aid and assistance to those in need, offering sustainable development solutions to society while providing and empowering local communities with the resources to help themselves.
ER Med, General, MF Med, Ophth-Opt
🌐 https://vfmat.ch/13cc

ICAP at Columbia University
Serves as global leader in supporting the scale-up of multidisciplinary HIV/AIDS prevention, care, and treatment programs based on a family-focused approach.
General, Infect Dis, MF Med, Medicine, OB-GYN, Pub Health
🌐 https://vfmat.ch/a8ef

IHSAN Foundation for West Africa
Seeks to improve the social and economic lives of the people of West Africa through educational, humanitarian, and healthcare projects.
Dent-OMFS, ER Med, General, Infect Dis
🌐 https://vfmat.ch/c719

International Agency for the Prevention of Blindness (IAPB), The
Leads international efforts in blindness-prevention activities, works toward a world where no one is needlessly visually impaired, and ensures that everyone has access to the best possible standard of eye health.
Infect Dis, Ophth-Opt, Pub Health
🌐 https://vfmat.ch/87a2

International Council of Ophthalmology
Works with ophthalmologic societies and others to enhance ophthalmic education and improve access to the highest-quality eye care in order to preserve and restore vision for people of the world.
Ophth-Opt
🌐 https://vfmat.ch/ffd2

International Federation of Gynecology and Obstetrics (FIGO)
Implements global projects on specific women's health issues.
MF Med, Medicine, Neonat, OB-GYN, Surg, Urol
🌐 https://vfmat.ch/c4b4

International Federation of Red Cross and Red Crescent Societies (IFRC)
Coordinates and directs international assistance following natural and manmade disasters in nonconflict situations through the world's largest humanitarian and development network. Provides disaster-preparedness programs, healthcare activities, and promotes humanitarian values.
ER Med, General, Infect Dis, Nutr
🌐 https://vfmat.ch/b4ee

International Medical Corps
Seeks to improve quality of life through health interventions and related activities that strengthen underserved communities worldwide, with the flexibility to respond rapidly to emergencies and offer medical services and training to people at the highest risk.
ER Med, General, Infect Dis, Nutr, OB-GYN, Peds, Pub Health, Surg
🌐 https://vfmat.ch/a8a5

International Organization for Migration (IOM) – The UN Migration Agency
Promotes evidence-informed policies and holistic, preventive, and curative health programs that are beneficial, accessible, and equitable for vulnerable migrants.
General, Infect Dis, OB-GYN
🌐 https://vfmat.ch/621a

International Pediatric Nephrology Association (IPNA)
Leads global efforts to successfully address the care for all children with kidney disease through advocacy, education, and training.
Medicine, Nephro, Peds
🌐 https://vfmat.ch/b59d

International Planned Parenthood Federation (IPPF)
Leads a locally owned, globally connected civil society movement that provides and enables services and champions sexual and reproductive health and rights for all, especially the underserved.
Infect Dis, MF Med, OB-GYN
🌐 https://vfmat.ch/dc97

International Rescue Committee (IRC)
Responds to the world's worst humanitarian crises and helps people whose lives and livelihoods are shattered by conflict and disaster to survive, recover, and gain control of their future.
ER Med, General, Infect Dis, MF Med, Peds
🌐 https://vfmat.ch/5d24

International Trachoma Initiative (iTi)
Works toward a world free from trachoma, a preventable cause of blindness, and provides comprehensive support to national ministries of health and governmental

and nongovernmental organizations to implement a comprehensive approach to fight trachoma.

Infect Dis, Ophth-Opt

⊕ https://vfmat.ch/3278

Intersos

Provides emergency medical assistance to victims of armed conflicts, natural disasters, and extreme exclusion, with particular attention to the protection of the most vulnerable people.

ER Med, General, Nutr

⊕ https://vfmat.ch/dbac

InterSurgeon

Fosters collaborative partnerships in the field of global surgery that will advance clinical care, teaching, training, research, and the provision and maintenance of medical equipment.

ENT, Neurosurg, Ortho, Ped Surg, Plast, Surg, Urol

⊕ https://vfmat.ch/6f8a

Ipas

Focuses efforts on women and girls who want contraception or abortion, and builds programs around their needs and how best to support them.

OB-GYN

⊕ https://vfmat.ch/8e39

IVUmed

Aims to make quality urological care available worldwide by providing medical and surgical education for physicians and nurses, and treatment for thousands of children and adults.

Anesth, OB-GYN, Ped Surg, Surg, Urol

⊕ https://vfmat.ch/e619

Jhpiego

Creates and delivers transformative healthcare solutions that save lives, in partnership with national governments, health experts, and local communities.

General, Infect Dis, OB-GYN, Surg

⊕ https://vfmat.ch/45b8

John Snow, Inc. (JSI)

Aims to improve the health and well-being of underserved and vulnerable people and communities throughout the world.

General, Infect Dis, Logist-Op, MF Med, OB-GYN, Peds, Psych, Pub Health

⊕ https://vfmat.ch/ba78

Johns Hopkins Center for Communication Programs

Believes in the power of communication to save lives by empowering people to adopt healthy behaviors for themselves, their families, and their communities.

General, Infect Dis, Logist-Op, OB-GYN, Pub Health

⊕ https://vfmat.ch/1bf9

Johns Hopkins Center for Global Health

Facilitates and focuses the extensive expertise and resources of the Johns Hopkins institutions, together with global collaborators, to effectively address and ameliorate the world's most pressing health issues.

General, Genetics, Logist-Op, MF Med, Peds, Psych, Pub Health, Pulm-Critic

⊕ https://vfmat.ch/54ce

Joint United Nations Programme on HIV/AIDS (UNAIDS)

Aims to place people living with HIV and people affected by the virus at the decision-making table and at the center of designing, delivering, and monitoring the AIDS response.

Infect Dis

⊕ https://vfmat.ch/464a

Life for African Mothers

Aims to save the lives of pregnant women in Sub-Saharan Africa.

MF Med, Neonat, OB-GYN

⊕ https://vfmat.ch/fce2

Management Sciences for Health (MSH)

Works with countries and communities to save lives and improve the health of the world's poorest and most vulnerable people by building strong, resilient, sustainable health systems.

Infect Dis, Logist-Op, Pub Health

⊕ https://vfmat.ch/6aa2

MAP International

Provides medicines and health supplies to those in need around the world so they might experience life to the fullest.

Logist-Op

⊕ https://vfmat.ch/deed

Massachusetts General Hospital Global Surgery Initiative

Aims to improve surgical education and access to advanced surgical care in resource-limited settings around the world by performing surgical operations as visitors, training local surgeons, and sharing medical technology through international partnerships across disciplines.

Anesth, Crit-Care, ER Med, Heme-Onc, Peds, Surg

⊕ https://vfmat.ch/31b1

Mbingo Baptist Hospital

Based in Christian ministry, aims to provide exemplary healthcare with genuine compassion.

Dent-OMFS, ENT, Medicine, OB-GYN, Ophth-Opt, Ortho, Path, Peds, Surg

⊕ https://vfmat.ch/1eca

Medical Care Development International (MCD International)

Works to strengthen health systems through innovative, sustainable interventions.

Infect Dis, Logist-Op, OB-GYN, Pub Health

⊕ https://vfmat.ch/dc5c

Medical Care Development International

Works to improve the health of vulnerable populations through integrated, sustainable, and locally driven interventions.

Infect Dis, OB-GYN, Peds, Pub Health

⊕ https://vfmat.ch/da87

Medicines for Humanity

Aims to save the lives of vulnerable children by strengthening systems of maternal and child health in the communities served.

Infect Dis, MF Med, OB-GYN

⊕ https://vfmat.ch/8d13

MedShare

Aims to improve the quality of life of people, communities, and the planet by sourcing and directly delivering surplus medical supplies and equipment to communities in need around the world.

Logist-Op

⊕ https://vfmat.ch/c8bc

MENTOR Initiative

Saves lives in emergencies through tropical disease control, and helps people recover from crisis with dignity, working side by side with communities, health workers, and health authorities to leave a lasting impact.

ER Med, Infect Dis

⊕ https://vfmat.ch/3bd5

Mercy and Love Foundation

Aims to provide orphaned and vulnerable children with basic human needs such as food, clothing, and shelter, enabling them to thrive.

General, Peds

⊕ https://vfmat.ch/649a

Mercy Ships

Operates hospital ships staffed by volunteers to bring hope, healing, and healthcare to underserved communities worldwide.

Anesth, Dent-OMFS, Logist-Op, Neonat, OB-GYN, Ophth-Opt, Ortho, Palliative, Plast, Psych, Surg

⊕ https://vfmat.ch/2e99

Mission Bambini

Helps to support children living in poverty and sickness, and lacking education, giving them the opportunity for and hope of a better life.

CT Surg, CV Med, Crit-Care, ER Med, Ped Surg, Peds

⊕ https://vfmat.ch/dc1a

Mission Doctors Association

Provides life-saving medical care for the poor and training for local healthcare professionals around the world.

CV Med, Dent-OMFS, General, Logist-Op, Medicine, OB-GYN, Ophth-Opt, Peds, Surg

⊕ https://vfmat.ch/6c18

Morbidity Management and Disability Prevention Project (MMPD)

Helps countries provide high-quality treatment and care for people suffering from the debilitating effects of trachoma and lymphatic filariasis, complementing other major initiatives supporting disease elimination through mass drug administration.

Heme-Onc, Infect Dis, Ophth-Opt

⊕ https://vfmat.ch/387e

Médecins du Monde/Doctors of the World

Provides care, bears witness, and supports social change worldwide with innovative medical programs and evidence-based advocacy initiatives.

ER Med, General, Infect Dis, MF Med, Neonat, OB-GYN, Peds, Pub Health

⊕ https://vfmat.ch/a43d

Mérieux Foundation

Committed to fighting infectious diseases that affect developing countries by capacity building, particularly in clinical laboratories, and focusing on diagnosis.

Logist-Op, Path

⊕ https://vfmat.ch/a23a

New Horizons Collaborative

Advances a holistic, integrated approach to high-quality pediatric HIV care and treatment with a specific focus on those in need of advanced treatment.

Infect Dis, Peds, Pub Health

⊕ https://vfmat.ch/a76a

Newborn, Infant, and Child Health International (NICHE)

Aims to make outstanding care of newborn babies commonplace in poorly resourced areas of the world.

Crit-Care, General, Neonat, Peds

⊕ https://vfmat.ch/8817

Noma Fund

Aims to raise awareness of noma disease, prevents its occurrence, and manage cases of complications in Africa.

Dent-OMFS, Infect Dis, Logist-Op, Plast, Pub Health, Surg

⊕ https://vfmat.ch/4693

Ophtalmo Sans Frontières

Fights against blindness and low vision in French-speaking Africa.

Anesth, Ophth-Opt, Surg

⊕ https://vfmat.ch/7643

Optometry Giving Sight

Delivers eye exams and low or no-cost glasses, provides training for local eye care professionals, and establishes optometry schools, vision centers and optical labs.

Ophth-Opt

⊕ https://vfmat.ch/33ea

Orbis International

Works to prevent and treat blindness through hands-on training and improved access to quality eye care.

Anesth, Ophth-Opt, Surg

⊕ https://vfmat.ch/f2b2

Order of Malta

Supports forgotten or excluded people, especially those living in conflict zones or amid natural disasters, by providing medical assistance, caring for refugees, and distributing medicines and necessities.

ER Med, General, Infect Dis, MF Med, Nephro, OB-GYN, Ortho, Psych

⊕ https://vfmat.ch/1fab

Pan African Thoracic Society (PATS)

Aims to promote lung health in Africa, the continent most afflicted by morbidity and death from respiratory diseases, by promoting education, research, advocacy,

optimal care, and the development of African capacity to address respiratory challenges in the continent.

CV Med, Crit-Care, Pulm-Critic

⊕ https://vfmat.ch/5457

Pan-African Academy of Christian Surgeons (PAACS)

Aims to train and disciple African surgeons and related specialists to become leaders and servants, providing excellent and compassionate care to those most in need, based in Christian ministry.

Anesth, CT Surg, OB-GYN, Ortho, Ped Surg, Plast, Surg

⊕ https://vfmat.ch/b444

Pan-African Academy of Christian Surgeons (PAACS)

Exists to train and support African surgeons to provide excellent, compassionate care to those most in need, inspired by the Christian faith.

Anesth, CT Surg, Neurosurg, OB-GYN, Ortho, Ped Surg, Plast, Surg

⊕ https://vfmat.ch/85ba

Partners for World Health

Sorts, evaluates, repackages, and prepares supplies and equipment for distribution to individuals, communities, and healthcare facilities in need, both locally and internationally.

ER Med, General, Logist-Op

⊕ https://vfmat.ch/982e

Patcha Foundation

Aims to support and provide the latest and most innovative approaches to diagnosis and treatment of cancer and other chronic diseases in limited-resource settings in Africa.

ER Med, General, Logist-Op, Nutr, Palliative, Peds, Surg

⊕ https://vfmat.ch/ea4a

Première Urgence International

Helps civilians who are marginalized or excluded as a result of natural disasters, war, or economic collapse.

ER Med, General, MF Med, Peds, Psych

⊕ https://vfmat.ch/62ba

Project SOAR

Conducts HIV operations research around the world to identify practical solutions to improve HIV prevention, care, and treatment services.

ER Med, General, MF Med, OB-GYN, Psych

⊕ https://vfmat.ch/1a77

PSI – Population Services International

Aims to improve the health of people in the developing world by focusing on challenges such as a lack of family planning, HIV/AIDS, barriers to maternal health, and the greatest threats to children under the age of 5, including malaria, diarrhea, pneumonia, and malnutrition.

Infect Dis, MF Med, OB-GYN, Peds

⊕ https://vfmat.ch/ffe3

Purpose Medical Mission

Strives to achieve long-term and self-sustaining healthy communities where extreme poverty and lack of basic healthcare and education are a problem.

General, Logist-Op, Medicine, Pub Health, Surg

⊕ https://vfmat.ch/3fe7

RAD-AID International

Improves and optimizes access to medical imaging and radiology in low-resource regions of the world.

Rad-Onc, Radiol

⊕ https://vfmat.ch/537f

RestoringVision

Empowers lives by restoring vision for millions of people in need.

Ophth-Opt

⊕ https://vfmat.ch/e121

Right to Sight and Health

Seeks to reduce the prevalence of blindness and visual impairment, especially among low-income communities in Northern Ghana.

Ophth-Opt
⊕ https://vfmat.ch/7ff1

Rockefeller Foundation, The
Works to promote the well-being of humanity.
Logist-Op, Nutr, Pub Health
⊕ https://vfmat.ch/5424

Rotary International
Provides service to others, improves lives, and advances world understanding, goodwill, and peace through its fellowship of business, professional, and community leaders.
ER Med, General, Infect Dis, MF Med, OB-GYN
⊕ https://vfmat.ch/8fb5

Sanofi Espoir Foundation
Contributes to reducing health inequalities among populations that need it most by applying a socially responsible approach focused on fighting childhood cancers in low-income countries, improving maternal and newborn health, and improving access to care.
ER Med, OB-GYN, Peds
⊕ https://vfmat.ch/943b

Save A Child's Heart
Provides lifesaving cardiac treatment to children in developing countries, and trains healthcare professionals from these countries to deliver quality care in their communities.
CT Surg, CV Med, Crit-Care, Ped Surg, Peds
⊕ https://vfmat.ch/1bef

SEE International
Provides sustainable medical, surgical, and educational services through volunteer ophthalmic surgeons, with the objectives of restoring sight and preventing blindness to disadvantaged individuals worldwide.
Ophth-Opt, Surg
⊕ https://vfmat.ch/6e1b

Sightsavers
Works with partners in developing countries to help eliminate avoidable blindness and advocates for equal opportunity for the disabled.
Infect Dis, Ophth-Opt, Surg
⊕ https://vfmat.ch/aa52

SIGN Fracture Care International
Builds orthopedic capacity around the world and provides the injured poor access to fracture surgery by donating orthopedic education and implant systems to surgeons in developing countries.
Ortho, Rehab, Surg
⊕ https://vfmat.ch/123d

SINA Health
Aims to improve the health and educational status of the population in low- and middle-income countries.
General, Logist-Op
⊕ https://vfmat.ch/9ad3

Sisters of the Immaculate Heart of Mary, Mother of Christ
Based in Chrisitan ministry, seeks to motivate people, especially the poor and the less privileged, to live venerable and dignified lives through credibility-structured programs, education, various medical and humanitarian services, along with self-realization and self-empowerment opportunities.
Infect Dis, Logist-Op, Nutr, Pub Health
⊕ https://vfmat.ch/5774

Smile Train, Inc.
Treats children with cleft lip through a sustainable and local model that supports surgery and other forms of essential care.
Logist-Op, Pub Health
⊕ https://vfmat.ch/822c

Society of Gynecologists Obstetricians of Cameroon
Optimizes the level of practice of obstetric-gynecological medicine by collaborating with relevant stakeholders.

Logist-Op, OB-GYN, Pub Health
⊕ https://vfmat.ch/2a2c

Sofia Global
Inspired by the Christian faith, promotes an equitable and sustainable society through education, healthcare, pastoral work, and community capacity-building.
General, Heme-Onc, Infect Dis, MF Med, OB-GYN, Peds
⊕ https://vfmat.ch/263c

Solthis
Improves disease prevention and access to quality care by strengthening the health systems and services of the countries served.
General, Infect Dis, Logist-Op, MF Med, Neonat, Path
⊕ https://vfmat.ch/a71d

Sound Seekers
Supports people with hearing loss by enabling access to healthcare and education.
ENT
⊕ https://vfmat.ch/ef1c

Sri Sathya Sai International Organization
Inspired by spiritual teachings, carries out efforts in global healthcare, education, humanitarian relief, and youth engagement.
Dent-OMFS, General, Logist-Op, Nutr, Ophth-Opt, Pub Health
⊕ https://vfmat.ch/9bda

Sustainable Kidney Care Foundation (SKCF)
Works to provide treatment for kidney injury where none exists, and aims to reduce mortality from treatable acute kidney injury (AKI).
Infect Dis, Medicine, Nephro
⊕ https://vfmat.ch/1926

Swiss Tropical and Public Health Institute
Contributes to the improvement of the health of populations internationally, nationally, and locally through excellence in research, education, and services.
Infect Dis, Pub Health
⊕ https://vfmat.ch/2ee4

Task Force for Global Health, The
Consists of programs and focus areas that cover a range of global health issues including neglected tropical diseases, infectious diseases, vaccines, field epidemiology, public health informatics, health workforce development, and global health ethics.
Infect Dis, Logist-Op, Medicine, Ophth-Opt, Peds
⊕ https://vfmat.ch/714c

U.S. President's Malaria Initiative (PMI)
Supports low-income countries to help control and eliminate malaria through cost-effective, lifesaving malaria interventions.
Infect Dis, MF Med, OB-GYN
⊕ https://vfmat.ch/dc8b

Union for International Cancer Control (UICC)
Unites and supports the cancer community to reduce the global cancer burden, promote greater equity, and ensure that cancer control continues to be a priority in the world health and development agenda.
Heme-Onc, Pub Health
⊕ https://vfmat.ch/88b1

United Methodist Volunteers in Mission (UMVIM)
Engages in short-term missions each year in ministries as varied as disaster response, community development, pastor training, microenterprise, agriculture, Vacation Bible School, building repair and construction, and medical/dental services.
Dent-OMFS, ER Med, General
⊕ https://vfmat.ch/1ee6

United Nations Children's Fund (UNICEF)
Works in over 190 countries and territories to save children's lives, defend their rights, and help them fulfill their potential, from early childhood through adolescence.
All-Immu, Infect Dis, MF Med, Neonat, Nutr, OB-GYN, Ped Surg, Peds, Pub

Health
⊕ https://vfmat.ch/42d7

United Nations Development Programme (UNDP)
Helps countries achieve the simultaneous eradication of extreme poverty and significant reduction of inequalities and exclusion using a sustainable human development approach.
Infect Dis, Logist-Op, Pub Health
⊕ https://vfmat.ch/935c

United Nations High Commissioner for Refugees (UNHCR)
Safeguards the rights and well-being of people who have been forced to flee, ensuring that everybody has the right to seek asylum and find safe refuge in another country, with the goal of seeking lasting solutions.
General, MF Med, Medicine, OB-GYN, Peds, Psych, Pub Health
⊕ https://vfmat.ch/6636

United Nations Office for the Coordination of Humanitarian Affairs (OCHA)
Contributes to principled and effective humanitarian response through coordination, advocacy, policy, information management, and humanitarian financing tools and services, by leveraging functional expertise throughout the organization.
Logist-Op
⊕ https://vfmat.ch/22b8

United Nations Population Fund (UNFPA)
Supports reproductive healthcare for women and youth in more than 150 countries, focusing on delivering a world in which every pregnancy is wanted, every childbirth is safe, and every young person's potential is fulfilled.
Infect Dis, MF Med, Neonat, OB-GYN, Peds, Pub Health
⊕ https://vfmat.ch/c969

United States Agency for International Development (USAID)
Promotes and demonstrates democratic values abroad and advances a free, peaceful, and prosperous world. Leads the U.S. government's international development and disaster assistance through partnerships and investments that save lives.
ER Med, Infect Dis, MF Med, OB-GYN, Peds
⊕ https://vfmat.ch/9a99

United States President's Emergency Plan for AIDS Relief (PEPFAR)
The U.S. global HIV/AIDS response works to prevent new HIV infections and accelerate progress to control the global epidemic in more than 50 countries, by partnering with governments to support sustainable, integrated, and country-led responses to HIV/AIDS.
Infect Dis, Pub Health
⊕ https://vfmat.ch/a57c

United Surgeons for Children (USFC)
Pursues greater health and opportunity for children in the most neglected pockets of the world, with a specific focus on and expertise in surgery.
Anesth, CT Surg, Neonat, Neurosurg, OB-GYN, Peds, Radiol, Surg
⊕ https://vfmat.ch/3b4c

University of California Los Angeles: David Geffen School of Medicine Global Health Program
Catalyzes opportunities to improve health globally by engaging in multi-disciplinary and innovative education programs, research initiatives, and bilateral partnerships that provide opportunities for trainees, faculty, and staff to contribute to sustainable health initiatives and to address health inequities facing the world today.
All-Immu, Infect Dis, Logist-Op, MF Med, Medicine, Neonat, OB-GYN, Ortho, Ped Surg, Peds, Radiol
⊕ https://vfmat.ch/f1a4

University of California, San Francisco: Center for Global Surgery and Health Equity
Leads and supports academic global surgery, while strengthening surgical-care systems in low-resource settings through research and education.
Anesth, OB-GYN, Surg
⊕ https://vfmat.ch/564f

University of New Mexico School of Medicine: Project Echo
Seeks to improve health outcomes worldwide through the use of a technology called telementoring, a guided-practice model in which the participating clinician retains responsibility for managing the patient.
General, Infect Dis, MF Med, OB-GYN, Path, Peds
⊕ https://vfmat.ch/6c9a

University of Pennsylvania Perelman School of Medicine Center for Global Health
Aims to improve health equity worldwide through enhanced public health awareness and access to care, discovery, and outcomes-based research, and comprehensive educational programs grounded in partnership.
Heme-Onc, Infect Dis, OB-GYN
⊕ https://vfmat.ch/cb57

University of Washington: Department of Global Health
Improves health for all through research, education, training, and service, addresses the causes of disease and health inequities at multiple levels, and collaborates with partners to develop and sustain locally led, quality health systems, programs, and policies.
Infect Dis, Logist-Op, Pub Health
⊕ https://vfmat.ch/f543

USA for United Nations High Commissioner for Refugees (UNHCR)
Serves and protects refugees and displaced people through emergency relief, cash assistance, education, resettlement, and the rebuilding of livelihoods.
ER Med, General, Logist-Op, Nutr, Pub Health
⊕ https://vfmat.ch/293c

USAID: Health Policy Initiative
Provides field-level programming in health policy development and implementation.
General, Infect Dis, MF Med, OB-GYN, Peds
⊕ https://vfmat.ch/8f84

USAID: Human Resources for Health 2030 (HRH2030)
Helps low- and middle-income countries develop the health workforce needed to prevent maternal and child deaths, support the goals of Family Planning 2020, control the HIV/AIDS epidemic, and protect communities from infectious diseases.
Logist-Op
⊕ https://vfmat.ch/9ea8

USAID: Leadership, Management and Governance Project
Improves leadership, management, and governance practices to strengthen health systems and improve health for all, including vulnerable populations worldwide.
Logist-Op
⊕ https://vfmat.ch/d35e

Value Health Africa
Aims to alleviate human suffering by improving health and well-being for all irrespective of age, gender, or race in Cameroon and Africa at large.
General, Infect Dis, OB-GYN, Pub Health
⊕ https://vfmat.ch/4a8f

Ventura Global Health Project (VGHP)
Aims to encourage and facilitate a lifelong interest in global health by providing grants to support local medical professionals providing care to underserved populations.
Dent-OMFS, ER Med, General, Infect Dis, Logist-Op, OB-GYN, Ophth-Opt, Ortho, Peds, Plast, Surg, Urol
⊕ https://vfmat.ch/a746

Vision for All Foundation
Implements ophthalmic healthcare projects; aims to create and support ophthalmic centers and existing structures in order to support the training of medical and paramedical personnel in the ophthalmology; and seeks to promote prevention, diagnosis, and treatment of ophthalmic pathologies.
Dent-OMFS, Ophth-Opt, Pub Health
⊕ https://vfmat.ch/dd72

Vitamin Angels
Helps at-risk populations in need—specifically pregnant women, new mothers,

and children under age 5—to gain access to life-changing vitamins and minerals.
General, Nutr
⊕ https://vfmat.ch/7da1

Watsi
Uses technology to make healthcare a reality for those who might not otherwise be able to afford it.
Pub Health, Surg
⊕ https://vfmat.ch/41a3

Willing and Abel
Seeks to provide connections between children in developing nations and specialist centers, helping with visas, passports, transportation, and finances.
Anesth, Dent-OMFS, Ped Surg
⊕ https://vfmat.ch/9dc7

World Child Cancer
Works to improve diagnosis, treatment, and support for children with cancer, and their families, in low- and middle-income parts of the world.
Heme-Onc, Ped Surg, Rad-Onc
⊕ https://vfmat.ch/fbbc

World Council of Optometry
Facilitates the development of optometry worldwide and promotes eye health and vision care through advocacy, education, policy development, and humanitarian outreach.
Ophth-Opt, Pub Health
⊕ https://vfmat.ch/c92e

World Federation of Hemophilia (WFH)
Aims to improve and sustain care for people with inherited bleeding disorders by pursuing long-term relationships with individuals and organizations who share the values of WFH's development model.
Heme-Onc
⊕ https://vfmat.ch/5121

World Health Organization, The (WHO)
The United Nations' agency for health provides leadership on global health matters, shapes the health research agenda, sets norms and standards, articulates evidence-based policy options, provides technical support and monitoring to countries, and assesses health trends.
ER Med, General, Infect Dis, Logist-Op, MF Med, OB-GYN, Peds, Psych, Pub Health
⊕ https://vfmat.ch/c476

World Heart Federation
Leads the global fight against heart disease and stroke, with a focus on low- and middle-income countries.
CV Med, Crit-Care, Heme-Onc, Medicine, Peds
⊕ https://vfmat.ch/ea51

World Medical Relief
Facilitates the distribution of surplus medical resources where they are needed.
Logist-Op
⊕ https://vfmat.ch/72dc

Cameroon

Healthcare Facilities

Banso Baptist Hospital – Kumbo
Bamenda, North-West, Cameroon
⊕ https://vfmat.ch/5cc2

Baptist Hospital Banyo
Banyo, Adamaoua, Cameroon
⊕ https://vfmat.ch/1e1f

Baptist Hospital Mutengene
Mutengene, South-West, Cameroon
⊕ https://vfmat.ch/c1c5

Belabo Centre Médical d'Arrondissement (CMA)
Belabo, East, Cameroon
⊕ https://vfmat.ch/c1ef

Buea Seventh-day Adventist Hospital
Buea, Cameroon
⊕ https://vfmat.ch/pud4

Cameroon Oncology Center
Douala, Cameroon
⊕ https://vfmat.ch/nmqv

Cardiac Center Shisong-Kumbo
Kumbo, Littoral, Cameroon
⊕ https://vfmat.ch/aeea

CDC Cottage Hospital
Tiko, South-West, Cameroon
⊕ https://vfmat.ch/6bb9

Centre Hospitalier de Recherche et d'Application en Chirurgie Endoscopique et Reproduction Humaine
Ngousso, Yaoundé, Cameroon
⊕ https://vfmat.ch/9da4

Centre Médical de TYO-Ville
Njisse, West, Cameroon
⊕ https://vfmat.ch/f45c

CSI de Zokok
Maroua, Far North, Cameroon
⊕ https://vfmat.ch/3d5c

CSI King Place
Bafoussam, West, Cameroon
⊕ https://vfmat.ch/ee84

Dunger Baptist Hospital
Mbem, North-West, Cameroon
⊕ https://vfmat.ch/4b54

EPC Djoungolo
Etoa-meki, Yaoundé, Cameroon
⊕ https://vfmat.ch/649e

Health Foundation Ad-Lucem
Douala, Littoral, Cameroon
⊕ https://vfmat.ch/ce1d

Hôpital Ad Lucem de Bangang
Letia, West, Cameroon
⊕ https://vfmat.ch/f999

Hôpital Ad Lucem de Dizangué
Dizangué, Littoral, Cameroon
⊕ https://vfmat.ch/affb

Hôpital Ad Lucem de Mbouda
Mbouda, West, Cameroon
⊕ https://vfmat.ch/1b9e

Hôpital Adlucem de Mbouda
Bafang, West, Cameroon
⊕ https://vfmat.ch/3b79

Hôpital Catholique de Saint Dominique de Djunang
Bafoussam, Mifi, West, Cameroon
⊕ https://vfmat.ch/a9a3

Hôpital Cemao de Meskine
Miskine, Far North, Cameroon
⊕ https://vfmat.ch/5cac

Hôpital Central de Dschang
Dschang, West, Cameroon
⊕ https://vfmat.ch/d57a

Hôpital Central de Yaoundé
Yaoundé, Centre, Cameroon
⊕ https://vfmat.ch/8bc8

Hôpital d'Ebome
Kribi, South, Cameroon
⊕ https://vfmat.ch/aedc

Hôpital d'Ombessa
Ombésa, Centre, Cameroon
⊕ https://vfmat.ch/98de

Hôpital de Bangou Carrefour
Dengniep, West, Cameroon
⊕ https://vfmat.ch/413d

Hôpital de District d'Akonolinga
Akonolinga, Centre, Cameroon
⊕ https://vfmat.ch/4ed8

Hôpital de District d'Efoulan
Yaoundé, Centre, Cameroon
⊕ https://vfmat.ch/4f81

Hôpital de District de Bafang
Bafang, West, Cameroon
⊕ https://vfmat.ch/53dd

Hôpital de District de Bangangté
Bangangté, West, Cameroon
⊕ https://vfmat.ch/5a5d

Hôpital de District de Batcham
Batcham, Bamboutos, West, Cameroon
⊕ https://vfmat.ch/4df6

Hôpital de District de Bibemi
Bibemi, North, Cameroon
⊕ https://vfmat.ch/de2b

Hôpital de District de Biyem-Assi
Yaoundé, Centre, Cameroon
⊕ https://vfmat.ch/a37f

Hôpital de District de Bonamoussadi
Douala, Littoral, Cameroon
⊕ https://vfmat.ch/b62e

Hôpital de District de Bonassama
Bonabéri, Littoral, Cameroon
⊕ https://vfmat.ch/a22c

Hôpital de District de Bota
Limbe, South-West, Cameroon
⊕ https://vfmat.ch/5c6b

Hôpital de District de Deido
Douala, Littoral, Cameroon
⊕ https://vfmat.ch/18d2

Hôpital de District de Dibombari - MINSANTE
Dibombari, Littoral, Cameroon
⊕ https://vfmat.ch/2af6

Hôpital de District de Foumban
Foumban, West, Cameroon
⊕ https://vfmat.ch/a375

Hôpital de District de Kaélé
Kaélé, Far North, Cameroon
⊕ https://vfmat.ch/5c2b

Hôpital de District de Kolofata
Kolofata, Far North, Cameroon
⊕ https://vfmat.ch/fb8c

Hôpital de District de Kouoptamo
Kouoptamo, West, Cameroon
⊕ https://vfmat.ch/6b9c

Hôpital de District de Kumba
Kumba, South-West, Cameroon
⊕ https://vfmat.ch/51cc

Hôpital de District de Logbaba
Douala, Littoral, Cameroon
⊕ https://vfmat.ch/a4a4

Hôpital de District de Loum
Loum, Littoral, Cameroon
⊕ https://vfmat.ch/3143

Hôpital de District de Mamfe
Mamfe, South-West, Cameroon
⊕ https://vfmat.ch/9914

Hôpital de District de Mayo Oulo
Baléré, North, Cameroon
⊕ https://vfmat.ch/5191

Hôpital de District de Mbankomo
Zoatoupsi, Centre, Cameroon
⊕ https://vfmat.ch/a5e1

Hôpital de District de Melong
New Melong, Littoral, Cameroon
⊕ https://vfmat.ch/b714

Hôpital de District de Mokolo
Mokolo, Far North, Cameroon
⊕ https://vfmat.ch/8bf9

Hôpital de District de Monatele
Mvomékak, Centre, Cameroon
⊕ https://vfmat.ch/1c1d

Hôpital de District de Mora
Mora, Far North, Cameroon
⊕ https://vfmat.ch/a383

Hôpital de District de Newbell
Douala, Littoral, Cameroon
⊕ https://vfmat.ch/fa47

Hôpital de District de Ngoumou
Ngoumou, Centre, Cameroon
⊕ https://vfmat.ch/d714

Hôpital de District de Nylon
Douala, Littoral, Cameroon
⊕ https://vfmat.ch/21c2

Hôpital de District de Pitoa
Pitoa, North, Cameroon
⊕ https://vfmat.ch/1af4

Hôpital de District de Sa'a
Sa'a, Lekié, Centre, Cameroon
⊕ https://vfmat.ch/e6b4

Hôpital de District de Sangmelima
Sangmélima, South, Cameroon
⊕ https://vfmat.ch/8ada

Hôpital de District de Tignère
Tignère, Adamaoua, Cameroon
⊕ https://vfmat.ch/e3e2

Hôpital de District de Yoko
Yoko, Centre, Cameroon
⊕ https://vfmat.ch/71cf

Hôpital de la Cass
Biting, Centre, Cameroon
⊕ https://vfmat.ch/68d7

Hôpital de la CNPS
Garoua, Bénoué, North, Cameroon
⊕ https://vfmat.ch/217d

Hôpital de la Garnison de Garoua
Garoua, Bénoué, North, Cameroon
⊕ https://vfmat.ch/abda

Hôpital de la Police de Bafoussam
Bafoussam, West, Cameroon
⊕ https://vfmat.ch/728a

Hôpital de Ndoungué
Ndoungué, Littoral, Cameroon
⊕ https://vfmat.ch/edff

Hôpital de Tchomso
Baham, West, Cameroon
⊕ https://vfmat.ch/1ef4

Hôpital des Soeurs
Douala, Cameroon
⊕ https://vfmat.ch/bbaf

Hôpital du Bien
Melen, Centre, Cameroon
⊕ https://vfmat.ch/7273

Hôpital Esperance (Agréé Profam) Djamboutou
Ouro Labo, North, Cameroon
⊕ https://vfmat.ch/397b

Hôpital Famla
Fou-sap, West, Cameroon
⊕ https://vfmat.ch/3dc5

Hôpital Genyco Obstetrique de Douala (HGOPED) (Hôpital Gynéco-Obstétrique et Pédiatrique de Douala (HGOPED))
Douala, Littoral, Cameroon
⊕ https://vfmat.ch/57b4

Hôpital Général de Douala
Douala, Wouri, Littoral, Cameroon
⊕ https://vfmat.ch/7338

Hôpital Général de Yaoundé
Yaoundé, Centre, Cameroon
⊕ https://vfmat.ch/8b56

Hôpital Jésus Sauve et Guérit Full Gospel Mission
Poumpoumré, North, Cameroon
⊕ https://vfmat.ch/f729

Hôpital Laquintinie
Douala, Littoral, Cameroon
⊕ https://vfmat.ch/48e2

Hôpital Leproserie de la Dibamba
Yasika, Littoral, Cameroon
⊕ https://vfmat.ch/1154

Hôpital Militaire de Buea
Bokoko, Buea, Fako, South-West, Cameroon
⊕ https://vfmat.ch/732e

Hôpital Militaire de Camp Yeyap 2
Melen, Center, Cameroon
⊕ https://vfmat.ch/4654

Hôpital Militaire de Douala
Bonanjo, Douala, Wouri, Littoral, Cameroon
⊕ https://vfmat.ch/63ab

Hôpital Militaire de Garoua
Garoua, North, Cameroon
⊕ https://vfmat.ch/3f59

Hôpital Militaire de Yaounde
Yaounde, Mfoundi, Centre, Cameroon
⊕ https://vfmat.ch/e5a7

Hôpital Militaire Up Station Bamenda
Bamenda, North West, Cameroon
⊕ https://vfmat.ch/8128

Hôpital Muea
Muea, South-West, Cameroon
⊕ https://vfmat.ch/914c

Hôpital Palia
Pouss, Cameroon
⊕ https://vfmat.ch/5787

Hôpital Privé Islamique de Bamaré
Pallar, Far North, Cameroon
⊕ https://vfmat.ch/547c

Hôpital Protestant Bonaberi CEBEC
Bonabéri, Littoral, Cameroon
⊕ https://vfmat.ch/eccb

Hôpital Protestant Cité Sic
Douala, Littoral, Cameroon
⊕ https://vfmat.ch/12d1

Hôpital Protestant Mbouo
MBouo, Bafoussam, Cameroon
⊕ https://vfmat.ch/4233

Hôpital Référence de Sangmelima
Sangmélima, South, Cameroon
⊕ https://vfmat.ch/4f4a

Hôpital Régional de Bafoussam
Mundum, West, Cameroon
⊕ https://vfmat.ch/3525

Hôpital Régional de Bamenda
Bamenda, North-West, Cameroon
⊕ https://vfmat.ch/a3df

Hôpital Régional de Bertoua
Bertoua, East, Cameroon
⊕ https://vfmat.ch/ba16

Hôpital Régional de Buea
Buea, Fako, South-West, Cameroon
⊕ https://vfmat.ch/baae

Hôpital Régional de Ebolowa
Ebolowa, South, Cameroon
⊕ https://vfmat.ch/cf78

Hôpital Régional de Garoua
Garoua, North, Cameroon
⊕ https://vfmat.ch/48ed

Hôpital Régional de Limbe
Limbe, South-West, Cameroon
⊕ https://vfmat.ch/c1e2

Hôpital Régional de Ngaoundéré
Béka, Adamaoua, Cameroon
⊕ https://vfmat.ch/441f

Hôpital Régional de Nkongsamba
Nkongsamba, Littoral, Cameroon
⊕ https://vfmat.ch/85cb

Hôpital Régional de Yagoua
Yagoua, Far North, Cameroon
⊕ https://vfmat.ch/218f

Hôpital Saint-Luc
Mbalmayo, Centre, Cameroon
⊕ https://vfmat.ch/2edd

Hôpital Saint-Rosaire
Mbalmayo, Centre, Cameroon
⊕ https://vfmat.ch/9d49

Hôpital Sainte Jeanne-Antide Thouret
Ngaoundal, Adamaoua, Cameroon
⊕ https://vfmat.ch/f5db

Hôpital Santa Helena PK11
Douala, Littoral, Cameroon
⊕ https://vfmat.ch/6aa3

Hôpital St Vincent de Paul
Dschang, West, Cameroon
⊕ https://vfmat.ch/3368

Hôpital St. Martin de Porres
Bamenda, Njinikom, Cameroon
⊕ https://vfmat.ch/jrzg

Hôpital St.Thérèse de Nomayos
Nomayos, Centre, Cameroon
⊕ https://vfmat.ch/f833

Insolafrica
Kribi, Cameroon
⊕ https://vfmat.ch/98ed

Mary Health of Africa General Hospital
Fontem, South-West, Cameroon
⊕ https://vfmat.ch/c47e

Mbingo Baptist Hospital
Mbengo, North-West, Cameroon
⊕ https://vfmat.ch/bc53

Mboppi Baptist Hospital
Bassa, Littoral, Cameroon
⊕ https://vfmat.ch/9c91

Medical Center Le Jourdain
Yaoundé, Cameroon
⊕ https://vfmat.ch/z5a6

NSIF Hospital
Yaoundé, Centre, Cameroon
⊕ https://vfmat.ch/f3bb

Polyclinique du Palais
Yaoundé, Cameroon
⊕ https://vfmat.ch/yqan

Presbyterian Health Services in Cameroon
Manyemen, South-West, Cameroon
⊕ https://vfmat.ch/4b43

Tibati Baptist Health Center
Tibati, Adamaoua, Cameroon
⊕ https://vfmat.ch/ad56

Tienschinecam
Hérazaya, Far North, Cameroon
⊕ https://vfmat.ch/4b84

Healthcare Facility

Central African Republic

Located in the middle of the African continent is the Central African Republic (CAR), whose neighbors include Chad, Sudan, South Sudan, the Democratic Republic of the Congo, the Republic of the Congo, and Cameroon. Known for its exceptional natural beauty and wildlife, the CAR is home to a young population of 5.4 million people living primarily in the western and central areas of the country and around the capital city of Bangui. The majority of the population is Christian and culturally falls into several ethnic groups including the Baya, Banda, Mandjia, Sara, and M'Baka-bantu. The national language is Sangho, but French is also spoken in an official capacity.

The Central African Republic achieved independence from France in 1960 and has since experienced decades of misrule, military coups, contentious elections, and rebellion. The country's most recent state of turmoil was the result of a violent takeover of power in 2013 and an uprising that displaced 25 percent of the population. In February 2018, progress was made when the country signed an African Union–mediated peace agreement with 14 armed groups; however, fighting between rebel groups continues. Today the CAR is one of the world's poorest and least developed countries. About 71 percent of the population lives below the international poverty line.

As a result of conflict and economic turmoil, more than half the country requires humanitarian assistance, with over one million in acute need. Health indicators include an alarming maternal mortality rate and an average life expectancy of 53 years. Leading causes of death include tuberculosis, diarrheal diseases, lower respiratory infections, HIV/AIDS, neonatal disorders, and malaria. In recent years, congenital defects and stroke have also become more significant contributors to death, as have road injuries.

5.4M
Population

$477
GDP Per Capita

53 years
Life Expectancy
↑ Improving

7
Doctors/100k
Physician Density

100
Beds/100k
Hospital Bed Density

829
Deaths/100k
Maternal Mortality

Central African Republic

Nonprofit Organizations

Action Against Hunger
Aims to end life-threatening hunger for good through treating and preventing malnutrition across more than 45 countries.
Nutr
🌐 https://vfmat.ch/2dbc

Africa CDC
Aims to strengthen the capacity and capability of Africa's public health institutions and partnerships to detect and respond quickly and effectively to disease threats and outbreaks, based on data-driven interventions and programs.
Infect Dis, Logist-Op, Pub Health
🌐 https://vfmat.ch/339c

Africa Health Organisation
Leads collaborative efforts among countries in Africa and other partners to promote health equity, combat disease, and improve quality of life.
Logist-Op, Pub Health
🌐 https://vfmat.ch/b1c5

Africa Inland Mission International
Seeks to establish churches and community development programs including healthcare projects, based in Christian ministry.
Anesth, Dent-OMFS, ER Med, General, MF Med, Medicine, OB-GYN, OB-GYN, Ophth-Opt, Ped Surg, Peds, Rehab
🌐 https://vfmat.ch/f2f6

Africa Relief and Community Development
Provides comprehensive relief and developmental aid to people of the African continent regardless of gender, race, or religion.
Nutr, Pub Health
🌐 https://vfmat.ch/6cd2

Al Basar International Foundation
Works with local partners to treat preventable blindness, and helps set up sustainable infrastructure so local teams can save sight in their communities.
Ophth-Opt
🌐 https://vfmat.ch/a8b5

Alliance for International Medical Action, The (ALIMA)
Provides quality medical care to vulnerable populations, partnering with and developing national medical organizations and conducting medical research to bring innovation to 12 African countries where ALIMA works.
ER Med, General, Infect Dis, Logist-Op, MF Med, OB-GYN, Path, Peds, Psych, Pub Health
🌐 https://vfmat.ch/1c11

American Academy of Pediatrics
Seeks to attain optimal physical, mental, and social health and well-being for all infants, children, adolescents, and young adults.

Anesth, Crit-Care, Neonat, Ped Surg
🌐 https://vfmat.ch/9633

Carter Center, The
Seeks to prevent and resolve conflicts, enhance freedom and democracy, and improve health, while remaining committed to human rights and the alleviation of human suffering.
Infect Dis, MF Med, Ophth-Opt
🌐 https://vfmat.ch/6556

Catholic Organization for Relief & Development Aid (CORDAID)
Provides humanitarian assistance and creates opportunities to improve security, healthcare, education, and inclusive economic growth in fragile and conflict-affected areas.
ER Med, Infect Dis, MF Med, OB-GYN, Peds, Psych
🌐 https://vfmat.ch/8ae5

Children's Emergency Relief International
Works with children, families, communities, and governments to provide a family environment as the first and best option for children to grow in.
General, Pub Health
🌐 https://vfmat.ch/92ae

Christian Medical & Dental Associations
Based in Christian ministry, deploys medical and dental teams to underserved communities to provide vital healthcare.
Anesth, Dent-OMFS, ER Med, General, Medicine, OB-GYN, Ophth-Opt, Peds, Pub Health, Radiol, Rehab, Surg
🌐 https://vfmat.ch/921c

Concern Worldwide
Seeks to permanently transform the lives of people living in extreme poverty, tackling its root causes, and building resilience.
Logist-Op, MF Med, Nutr, OB-GYN
🌐 https://vfmat.ch/77e9

Dental Hope for Children
Seeks to provide dental services to children in underserved areas, based in Christian ministry.
Dent-OMFS
🌐 https://vfmat.ch/1426

Doctors with Africa (CUAMM)
Advocates for the universal right to health and promotes the values of international solidarity, justice, and peace. Works to protect and improve the well-being and health of vulnerable communities in Africa with a long-term development perspective.
ER Med, Infect Dis, MF Med, Neonat, OB-GYN, Peds
🌐 https://vfmat.ch/d2fb

Doctors Without Borders/Médecins Sans Frontières (MSF)
Responds to emergencies and provides lifesaving medical care where needed most, including during disasters, conflicts, and epidemics.
Anesth, Crit-Care, ER Med, General, Infect Dis, Nutr, OB-GYN, Ped Surg, Peds, Psych, Pub Health, Surg
⊕ https://vfmat.ch/f363

Dream Sant'Egidio
Seeks to counter HIV/AIDS in Africa by eliminating the transmission of HIV from mother to child, with a focus on women because of the importance of their role in the community.
Infect Dis, MF Med, Neonat, OB-GYN, Path, Peds
⊕ https://vfmat.ch/f466

EMERGENCY
Provides free, high-quality healthcare to victims of war, poverty, and landmines. Also builds hospitals and trains local staff, while pursuing medicine based on human rights.
ER Med, Neonat, OB-GYN, Ophth-Opt, Ped Surg
⊕ https://vfmat.ch/c361

Enabel
As the development agency of the Belgian federal government, charged with implementing Belgium's international development policy, carries out public service assignments in Belgium and abroad pursuant to the 2030 Agenda for Sustainable Development.
General, Infect Dis, Logist-Op, MF Med, OB-GYN, Peds, Pub Health
⊕ https://vfmat.ch/5af7

END Fund, The
Aims to control and eliminate the most prevalent neglected diseases among the world's poorest and most vulnerable people.
Infect Dis
⊕ https://vfmat.ch/2614

Finn Church Aid
Supports people in the most vulnerable situations within fragile and disaster-affected regions in three thematic priority areas: right to peace, livelihood, and education.
ER Med, Psych, Pub Health
⊕ https://vfmat.ch/9623

Fondation Follereau
Promotes the quality of life of the most vulnerable African communities. Alongside trusted partners, the foundation supports local initiatives in healthcare and education.
General, Infect Dis, OB-GYN
⊕ https://vfmat.ch/bcc7

Fracarita International
Provides support and services in the fields of mental healthcare, care for people with a disability, and education.
Psych, Rehab
⊕ https://vfmat.ch/8d3c

Global Ministries – The United Methodist Church
As the worldwide mission and development agency of The United Methodist Church, Global Ministries works with more than 300 hospitals and clinics around the world through its Global Health Unit.
Anesth, CT Surg, CV Med, Crit-Care, Dent-OMFS, Derm, ER Med, GI, General, Infect Dis, Logist-Op, MF Med, Medicine, Neonat, Nephro, Nutr, OB-GYN, Ophth-Opt, Ortho, Palliative, Peds, Pod, Psych, Pub Health, Rehab, Rheum, Surg, Urol
⊕ https://vfmat.ch/1723

Global Oncology (GO)
Brings the best in cancer care to underserved patients around the world and collaborates across geographic, professional, and academic borders to improve cancer care, research, and education.
Heme-Onc, Path, Rad-Onc
⊕ https://vfmat.ch/fcb8

Globus Relief
Aims to improve the delivery of healthcare worldwide by gathering, processing,

and distributing surplus medical supplies to charities at home and abroad.
Logist-Op
⊕ https://vfmat.ch/a2b7

Grassroot Soccer
Leverages the power of soccer to educate, inspire, and mobilize at-risk youth in developing countries to overcome their greatest health challenges, live healthier and more productive lives, and be agents for change in their communities.
Infect Dis
⊕ https://vfmat.ch/3521

HumaniTerra
Helps countries and populations emerging from economic and human crisis to rebuild their healthcare system in a sustainable way. Committed to three fundamental and complementary actions: operating, training, and rebuilding.
Anesth, ENT, ER Med, MF Med, OB-GYN, Ortho, Plast, Surg
⊕ https://vfmat.ch/b371

IHSAN Foundation for West Africa
Seeks to improve the social and economic lives of the people of West Africa through educational, humanitarian, and healthcare projects.
Dent-OMFS, ER Med, General, Infect Dis
⊕ https://vfmat.ch/c719

International Agency for the Prevention of Blindness (IAPB), The
Leads international efforts in blindness-prevention activities, works toward a world where no one is needlessly visually impaired, and ensures that everyone has access to the best possible standard of eye health.
Infect Dis, Ophth-Opt, Pub Health
⊕ https://vfmat.ch/87a2

International Federation of Red Cross and Red Crescent Societies (IFRC)
Coordinates and directs international assistance following natural and manmade disasters in nonconflict situations through the world's largest humanitarian and development network. Provides disaster-preparedness programs, healthcare activities, and promotes humanitarian values.
ER Med, General, Infect Dis, Nutr
⊕ https://vfmat.ch/b4ee

International Medical Corps
Seeks to improve quality of life through health interventions and related activities that strengthen underserved communities worldwide, with the flexibility to respond rapidly to emergencies and offer medical services and training to people at the highest risk.
ER Med, General, Infect Dis, Nutr, OB-GYN, Peds, Pub Health, Surg
⊕ https://vfmat.ch/a8a5

International Organization for Migration (IOM) – The UN Migration Agency
Promotes evidence-informed policies and holistic, preventive, and curative health programs that are beneficial, accessible, and equitable for vulnerable migrants.
General, Infect Dis, OB-GYN
⊕ https://vfmat.ch/621a

International Planned Parenthood Federation (IPPF)
Leads a locally owned, globally connected civil society movement that provides and enables services and champions sexual and reproductive health and rights for all, especially the underserved.
Infect Dis, MF Med, OB-GYN
⊕ https://vfmat.ch/dc97

International Rescue Committee (IRC)
Responds to the world's worst humanitarian crises and helps people whose lives and livelihoods are shattered by conflict and disaster to survive, recover, and gain control of their future.
ER Med, General, Infect Dis, MF Med, Peds
⊕ https://vfmat.ch/5d24

International Trachoma Initiative (iTi)
Works toward a world free from trachoma, a preventable cause of blindness, and provides comprehensive support to national ministries of health and governmental and nongovernmental organizations to implement a comprehensive approach to

fight trachoma.
Infect Dis, Ophth-Opt
⊕ https://vfmat.ch/3278

Islamic Medical Association of North America
Fosters health promotion, disease prevention, and health maintenance in communities around the world through direct patient care and health programs.
Anesth, Dent-OMFS, ER Med, General, Logist-Op, Ophth-Opt, Peds, Plast, Surg
⊕ https://vfmat.ch/a157

Joint United Nations Programme on HIV/AIDS (UNAIDS)
Aims to place people living with HIV and people affected by the virus at the decision-making table and at the center of designing, delivering, and monitoring the AIDS response.
Infect Dis
⊕ https://vfmat.ch/464a

Life for a Child
Supports the provision of the best possible healthcare, given local circumstances, to all children and youth with diabetes in less-resourced countries, through the strengthening of existing diabetes services.
Endo, Medicine, Peds
⊕ https://vfmat.ch/d712

Lions Clubs International
Empowers volunteers to serve their communities, meet humanitarian needs, encourage peace, and promote international understanding through Lions Clubs.
Heme-Onc, Medicine, Nutr, Ophth-Opt
⊕ https://vfmat.ch/7b12

London School of Hygiene & Tropical Medicine: Health in Humanitarian Crises Centre
Advances health and health equity in crisis-affected countries through research, education, and translation of knowledge into policy and practice.
ER Med, Infect Dis, Pub Health
⊕ https://vfmat.ch/96ad

MAP International
Provides medicines and health supplies to those in need around the world so they might experience life to the fullest.
Logist-Op
⊕ https://vfmat.ch/deed

Massachusetts General Hospital Global Surgery Initiative
Aims to improve surgical education and access to advanced surgical care in resource-limited settings around the world by performing surgical operations as visitors, training local surgeons, and sharing medical technology through international partnerships across disciplines.
Anesth, Crit-Care, ER Med, Heme-Onc, Peds, Surg
⊕ https://vfmat.ch/31b1

Medical Care Development International
Works to improve the health of vulnerable populations through integrated, sustainable, and locally driven interventions.
Infect Dis, OB-GYN, Peds, Pub Health
⊕ https://vfmat.ch/da87

MENTOR Initiative
Saves lives in emergencies through tropical disease control, and helps people recover from crisis with dignity, working side by side with communities, health workers, and health authorities to leave a lasting impact.
ER Med, Infect Dis
⊕ https://vfmat.ch/3bd5

Mercy and Love Foundation
Aims to provide orphaned and vulnerable children with basic human needs such as food, clothing, and shelter, enabling them to thrive.
General, Peds
⊕ https://vfmat.ch/649a

Mercy Ships
Operates hospital ships staffed by volunteers to bring hope, healing, and healthcare to underserved communities worldwide.

Anesth, Dent-OMFS, Logist-Op, Neonat, OB-GYN, Ophth-Opt, Ortho, Palliative, Plast, Psych, Surg
⊕ https://vfmat.ch/2e99

Médecins du Monde/Doctors of the World
Provides care, bears witness, and supports social change worldwide with innovative medical programs and evidence-based advocacy initiatives.
ER Med, General, Infect Dis, MF Med, Neonat, OB-GYN, Peds, Pub Health
⊕ https://vfmat.ch/a43d

Order of Malta
Supports forgotten or excluded people, especially those living in conflict zones or amid natural disasters, by providing medical assistance, caring for refugees, and distributing medicines and necessities.
ER Med, General, Infect Dis, MF Med, Nephro, OB-GYN, Ortho, Psych
⊕ https://vfmat.ch/1fab

Organization for the Prevention of Blindness, The (OPC)
Provides research, and treatments and cures for people affected by blindness and blinding diseases in Francophone Africa.
Infect Dis, Ophth-Opt
⊕ https://vfmat.ch/86d6

Philia Foundation
Seeks to invest sustainably in people and marginalized communities in order to improve health and education in Africa.
Anesth, ER Med, General, Heme-Onc, MF Med, Neurosurg, OB-GYN, Ophth-Opt, Ortho, Pub Health, Surg, Urol
⊕ https://vfmat.ch/a352

Première Urgence International
Helps civilians who are marginalized or excluded as a result of natural disasters, war, or economic collapse.
ER Med, General, MF Med, Peds, Psych
⊕ https://vfmat.ch/62ba

RestoringVision
Empowers lives by restoring vision for millions of people in need.
Ophth-Opt
⊕ https://vfmat.ch/e121

Rotary International
Provides service to others, improves lives, and advances world understanding, goodwill, and peace through its fellowship of business, professional, and community leaders.
ER Med, General, Infect Dis, MF Med, OB-GYN
⊕ https://vfmat.ch/8fb5

Sanofi Espoir Foundation
Contributes to reducing health inequalities among populations that need it most by applying a socially responsible approach focused on fighting childhood cancers in low-income countries, improving maternal and newborn health, and improving access to care.
ER Med, OB-GYN, Peds
⊕ https://vfmat.ch/943b

SINA Health
Aims to improve the health and educational status of the population in low- and middle-income countries.
General, Logist-Op
⊕ https://vfmat.ch/9ad3

Smile Train, Inc.
Treats children with cleft lip through a sustainable and local model that supports surgery and other forms of essential care.
Logist-Op, Pub Health
⊕ https://vfmat.ch/822c

Swiss Tropical and Public Health Institute
Contributes to the improvement of the health of populations internationally, nationally, and locally through excellence in research, education, and services.
Infect Dis, Pub Health
⊕ https://vfmat.ch/2ee4

Task Force for Global Health, The

Consists of programs and focus areas that cover a range of global health issues including neglected tropical diseases, infectious diseases, vaccines, field epidemiology, public health informatics, health workforce development, and global health ethics.

Infect Dis, Logist-Op, Medicine, Ophth-Opt, Peds

⊕ https://vfmat.ch/714c

Tearfund

Responds to crisis and partners with local churches to bring restoration to those living in poverty, inspired by the Christian faith.

ER Med, Logist-Op

⊕ https://vfmat.ch/f6cf

United Nations Children's Fund (UNICEF)

Works in over 190 countries and territories to save children's lives, defend their rights, and help them fulfill their potential, from early childhood through adolescence.

All-Immu, Infect Dis, MF Med, Neonat, Nutr, OB-GYN, Ped Surg, Peds, Pub Health

⊕ https://vfmat.ch/42d7

United Nations Development Programme (UNDP)

Helps countries achieve the simultaneous eradication of extreme poverty and significant reduction of inequalities and exclusion using a sustainable human development approach.

Infect Dis, Logist-Op, Pub Health

⊕ https://vfmat.ch/935c

United Nations High Commissioner for Refugees (UNHCR)

Safeguards the rights and well-being of people who have been forced to flee, ensuring that everybody has the right to seek asylum and find safe refuge in another country, with the goal of seeking lasting solutions.

General, MF Med, Medicine, OB-GYN, Peds, Psych, Pub Health

⊕ https://vfmat.ch/6636

United Nations Office for the Coordination of Humanitarian Affairs (OCHA)

Contributes to principled and effective humanitarian response through coordination, advocacy, policy, information management, and humanitarian financing tools and services, by leveraging functional expertise throughout the organization.

Logist-Op

⊕ https://vfmat.ch/22b8

United Nations Population Fund (UNFPA)

Supports reproductive healthcare for women and youth in more than 150 countries, focusing on delivering a world in which every pregnancy is wanted, every childbirth is safe, and every young person's potential is fulfilled.

Infect Dis, MF Med, Neonat, OB-GYN, Peds, Pub Health

⊕ https://vfmat.ch/c969

United States Agency for International Development (USAID)

Promotes and demonstrates democratic values abroad and advances a free, peaceful, and prosperous world. Leads the U.S. government's international development and disaster assistance through partnerships and investments that save lives.

ER Med, Infect Dis, MF Med, OB-GYN, Peds

⊕ https://vfmat.ch/9a99

University of Virginia: Anesthesiology Department Global Health Initiatives

Educates and trains physicians to help people achieve healthy productive lives, and advances knowledge in the medical sciences.

Anesth, Pub Health

⊕ https://vfmat.ch/1b8b

USA for United Nations High Commissioner for Refugees (UNHCR)

Serves and protects refugees and displaced people through emergency relief, cash assistance, education, resettlement, and the rebuilding of livelihoods.

ER Med, General, Logist-Op, Nutr, Pub Health

⊕ https://vfmat.ch/293c

Vitamin Angels

Helps at-risk populations in need—specifically pregnant women, new mothers, and children under age 5—to gain access to life-changing vitamins and minerals.

General, Nutr

⊕ https://vfmat.ch/7da1

World Health Organization, The (WHO)

The United Nations' agency for health provides leadership on global health matters, shapes the health research agenda, sets norms and standards, articulates evidence-based policy options, provides technical support and monitoring to countries, and assesses health trends.

ER Med, General, Infect Dis, Logist-Op, MF Med, OB-GYN, Peds, Psych, Pub Health

⊕ https://vfmat.ch/c476

World Vision International

Works with vulnerable communities around the world to overcome poverty and injustice with child-focused programs in disaster management, health, nutrition, economic development, education, clean water, sanitation, and hygiene.

ER Med, General, Infect Dis, MF Med, Nutr, OB-GYN, Peds

⊕ https://vfmat.ch/2642

Central African Republic

Healthcare Facilities

ACABEF Antenne Ouaka
Ouaka, Bambari, Centre Ville, Central African
Republic
⊕ https://vfmat.ch/e851

Hospital at Batangafo
Batangafo, Central African Republic
⊕ https://vfmat.ch/5bd8

Hospital at Dohiya
Nana-Mambere, Bouar, Niem-Yelewa, Dohiya, Central
African Republic
⊕ https://vfmat.ch/fcb7

Hospital at Kella Moelle
Ouham-Pende, Koui, Kella Moelle, Central African
Republic
⊕ https://vfmat.ch/6fcc

Hospital at Kokol
RR 6, Bétara, Ouham-Pendé, Central African Republic
⊕ https://vfmat.ch/613c

Hospital at Kounpala
Ouham-Pende, Bocaranga, Loura, Kounpala, Central
African Republic
⊕ https://vfmat.ch/869e

Hospital at Kounpo
Kounpo, Ouham-Pendé, Central African Republic
⊕ https://vfmat.ch/d822

Hospital at Yelewa
Nana-Mambere, Bouar, Niem-Yelewa, Yelewa, Central
African Republic
⊕ https://vfmat.ch/546b

Hôpital Communautaire
Avenue des Martyrs, Bangui, Central African Republic
⊕ https://vfmat.ch/25ef

Hôpital de Bimbo
Bimbo, Central African Republic
⊕ https://vfmat.ch/2f15

Hôpital de l'Amitié
1359 RN 2, Bangî – Bangui, Central African Republic
⊕ https://vfmat.ch/c52e

Hôpital Préfectoral
RN 3, Bouar, Nana-Mambéré, Central African
Republic
⊕ https://vfmat.ch/af1b

Hôpital Préfectoral
RN 8, N'Délé, Bamingui-Bangoran, Central African
Republic
⊕ https://vfmat.ch/7cef

Hôpital Préfectoral de Kaga-Bandoro
Nana-Gribizi, Kaga-Bandoro, Centreville, Central
African Republic
⊕ https://vfmat.ch/eb73

Hôpital Régional de Berbérati
RN 6, Berbérati, Mambéré-Kadéï, Central African
Republic
⊕ https://vfmat.ch/9e55

Hôpital Régional de Bria
RN 5, Bria, Haute-Kotto, Central African Republic
⊕ https://vfmat.ch/d69c

**Hôpital Universitaire Régional de
Bambari**
RN2, Bambari, Central African Republic
⊕ https://vfmat.ch/5517

PS Bodouk
RN 1, Bokongo 1, Ouham, Central African Republic
⊕ https://vfmat.ch/a48c

PS de Boyali Yaho
Boyali Yaho, Ouham-Pendé, Central African Republic
⊕ https://vfmat.ch/2dd3

PS de Oda-Kete
Oda-Kota, Ouham, Central African Republic
⊕ https://vfmat.ch/2fbb

PS de Patcho
RR 10, Boumbala 2, Nana-Grébizi, Central African
Republic
⊕ https://vfmat.ch/eaf8

PS de Tolle
RR 4, Gouni, Ouham-Pendé, Central African Republic
⊕ https://vfmat.ch/ac99

PS Gbade
Route Gbade – Bobili, Boyongo, Ouham, Central
African Republic
⊕ https://vfmat.ch/ea1b

PS Pendé
RR 4, Kalandao, Ouham-Pendé, Central African
Republic
⊕ https://vfmat.ch/1c35

Sanguere Lim
Ouham-Pende, Koui, Koui, Sanguere Lim, Central
African Republic
⊕ https://vfmat.ch/f737

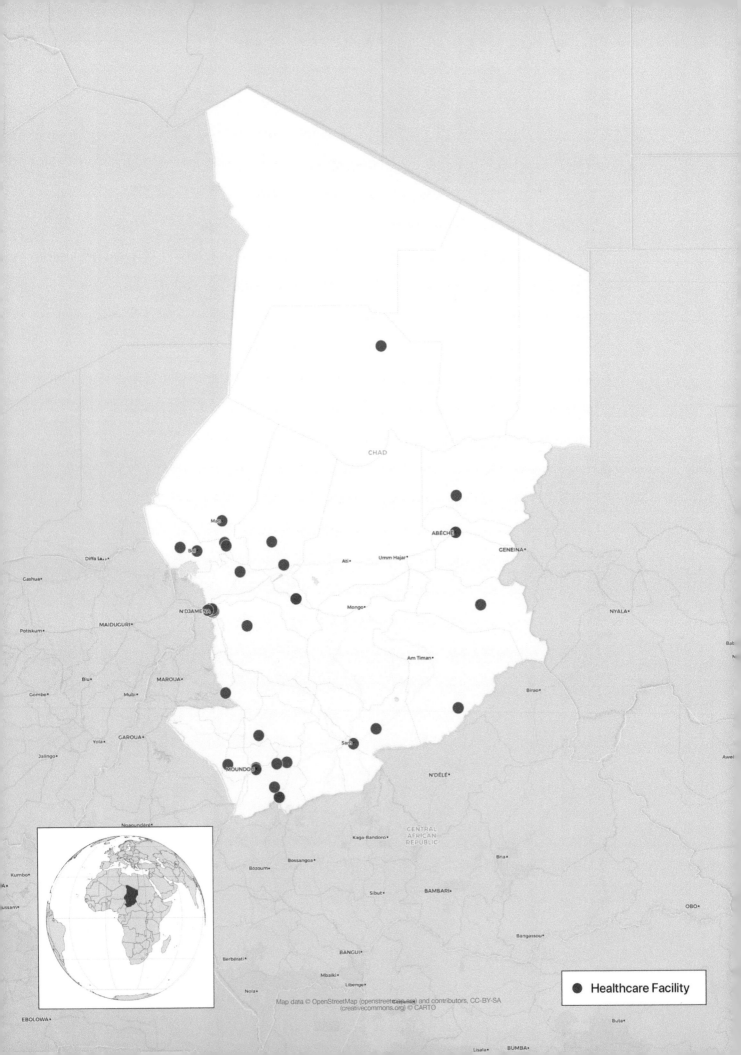

CHAD

ABÉCHÉ

GENEINA

Diffa La...•

Gashua•

Ati•   Umm Hajar•

NYALA•

Potiskum•   N'DJAMENA

MAIDUGURI•   Mongo•

Biu•   Am Timan•

Mubi•
MAROUA•

Birao•

Yola•   GAROUA•

Jalingo•   Sa...

N'DÉLÉ•   Awei

MOUNDOU•

Ngaoundéré•

CENTRAL
AFRICAN
REPUBLIC

Kumbo•   Kaga-Bandoro•   Bria•

...ssam•   Bozoum•   Bossangoa•

Sibut•   BAMBARI•

OBO•

Bangassou•

Berbérati•   BANGUI•

Mbaiki•

Libenge•

Nola•

● Healthcare Facility

EBOLOWA•   Buta•

Map data © OpenStreetMap (openstreetmap.org) and contributors, CC-BY-SA
(creativecommons.org) © CARTO

Lisala•   BUMBA•

Chad

The Republic of Chad, a landlocked country in central Africa, is home to more than 17.4 million people. Its capital city, N'Djamena, is known for a blend of modern and historical architecture and culture. Apart from its capital, Chad is largely rural. With about 200 ethnic groups, Chad has a diverse cultural history and population; upward of 120 languages and dialects are spoken, with French, Arabic, and Sara recognized as the official languages.

Chad gained its independence in 1960, and has since experienced conflict with bordering countries, invasions, civil warfare, and recurring rebellions. Decades of instability have left much of the population struggling: 66 percent of Chadians live in extreme poverty. Chad's limited resources and poor infrastructure must also accommodate more than 450,000 refugees from Sudan, the Central African Republic, and Nigeria. Previously a primarily agrarian economy, Chad became heavily dependent on oil after its discovery in 2013. Compounding an already dangerous socioeconomic situation is the impact of climate change and rapid desertification of Lake Chad.

Poverty, conflict, and instability have in turn affected the health of the Chadian population, many of whom experience food insecurity and hunger. About 43 percent of children under five are stunted, and 2.2 million are malnourished. Chad has one of the highest maternal mortality rates in central Africa due to inadequate access to health services. In addition to high maternal mortality, diarrheal diseases, lower respiratory infections, malaria, tuberculosis, stroke, ischemic heart disease, congenital defects, HIV/AIDS, and meningitis contribute most to deaths in the country. Death caused by neonatal disorders is also of notable significance and has increased substantially in recent years. The majority of physicians are concentrated in one region, near N'Djamena; the entire country urgently needs a larger and more evenly distributed healthcare workforce and a more developed healthcare infrastructure. The average life expectancy at birth is 54.

17.4M
Population

$615
GDP Per Capita

54 years
Life Expectancy

↑ Improving

5	40	1,140
Doctors/100k	**Beds**/100k	**Deaths**/100k
Physician Density	Hospital Bed Density	Maternal Mortality

Chad

Nonprofit Organizations

Action Against Hunger
Aims to end life-threatening hunger for good through treating and preventing malnutrition across more than 45 countries.
Nutr
⊕ https://vfmat.ch/2dbc

Adventist Health International
Focuses on upgrading and managing mission hospitals by providing governance, consultation, and technical assistance to a number of affiliated Seventh-Day Adventist hospitals throughout Africa, Asia, and the Americas.
Dent-OMFS, General, Pub Health
⊕ https://vfmat.ch/16aa

Africa CDC
Aims to strengthen the capacity and capability of Africa's public health institutions and partnerships to detect and respond quickly and effectively to disease threats and outbreaks, based on data-driven interventions and programs.
Infect Dis, Logist-Op, Pub Health
⊕ https://vfmat.ch/339c

Africa Health Organisation
Leads collaborative efforts among countries in Africa and other partners to promote health equity, combat disease, and improve quality of life.
Logist-Op, Pub Health
⊕ https://vfmat.ch/b1c5

Africa Humanitarian Action (AHA)
Responds to crises, conflicts, and disasters in Africa, while informing and advising the international community, governments, civil society, and the private sector on humanitarian issues of concern to Africa. Supports institutional and organizational development efforts.
General, Infect Dis, MF Med, Nutr, OB-GYN
⊕ https://vfmat.ch/3ca2

Africa Inland Mission International
Seeks to establish churches and community development programs including healthcare projects, based in Christian ministry.
Anesth, Dent-OMFS, ER Med, General, MF Med, Medicine, OB-GYN, OB-GYN, Ophth-Opt, Ped Surg, Peds, Rehab
⊕ https://vfmat.ch/f2f6

Africa Relief and Community Development
Provides comprehensive relief and developmental aid to people of the African continent regardless of gender, race, or religion.
Nutr, Pub Health
⊕ https://vfmat.ch/6cd2

Al Basar International Foundation
Works with local partners to treat preventable blindness, and helps set up sustainable infrastructure so local teams can save sight in their communities.
Ophth-Opt
⊕ https://vfmat.ch/a8b5

Alliance for International Medical Action, The (ALIMA)
Provides quality medical care to vulnerable populations, partnering with and developing national medical organizations and conducting medical research to bring innovation to 12 African countries where ALIMA works.
ER Med, General, Infect Dis, Logist-Op, MF Med, OB-GYN, Path, Peds, Psych, Pub Health
⊕ https://vfmat.ch/1c11

Americares
Saves lives and improves health for people affected by poverty or disaster and responds with life-changing medicine, medical supplies, and health programs including domestic and global medical clinics.
All-Immu, ER Med, General, Infect Dis, MF Med, Nutr
⊕ https://vfmat.ch/e567

AO Alliance
Builds solutions to lessen the burden of injuries in low- and middle-income countries, while enhancing the care of the injured to reduce human suffering, disability, and poverty.
Ortho, Surg
⊕ https://vfmat.ch/8cd5

CARE
Works around the globe to save lives, defeat poverty, and achieve social justice.
ER Med, General
⊕ https://vfmat.ch/7232

Carter Center, The
Seeks to prevent and resolve conflicts, enhance freedom and democracy, and improve health, while remaining committed to human rights and the alleviation of human suffering.
Infect Dis, MF Med, Ophth-Opt
⊕ https://vfmat.ch/6556

Children of War Foundation
Delivers access to global health and education to communities affected by poverty, war, natural disaster, climate change, and migration challenges.
ER Med, General, Logist-Op, Peds, Surg
⊕ https://vfmat.ch/de51

Christian Aid Ministries
Strives to be a trustworthy and efficient channel for Amish, Mennonite, and other conservative Anabaptist groups and individuals to minister to physical and spiritual needs around the world.
CT Surg, ER Med, Logist-Op, Ortho, Pub Health
⊕ https://vfmat.ch/7b33

Christian Blind Mission (CBM)

Aims to improve the quality of life of persons with disabilities in the poorest countries, addressing poverty as a cause and a consequence of disability, and working in partnership to create a society for all.

ENT, General, Infect Dis, OB-GYN, Ophth-Opt, Ortho, Peds, Psych, Rehab, Surg

⊕ https://vfmat.ch/3824

Christian Connections for International Health (CCIH)

Promotes global health and wholeness from a Christian perspective.

All-Immu, General, Infect Dis, MF Med, Neonat, OB-GYN, Psych

⊕ https://vfmat.ch/fa5d

Christian Health Service Corps

Brings Christian doctors, health professionals, and health educators committed to serving the poor to places that otherwise have little or no access to healthcare.

Anesth, Dent-OMFS, General, Medicine, Peds, Surg

⊕ https://vfmat.ch/da57

Concern Worldwide

Seeks to permanently transform the lives of people living in extreme poverty, tackling its root causes, and building resilience.

Logist-Op, MF Med, Nutr, OB-GYN

⊕ https://vfmat.ch/77e9

Direct Relief

Improves the health and lives of people affected by poverty or emergency situations by mobilizing and providing essential medical resources needed for their care.

ER Med, Logist-Op

⊕ https://vfmat.ch/58e5

Doctors Without Borders/Médecins Sans Frontières (MSF)

Responds to emergencies and provides lifesaving medical care where needed most, including during disasters, conflicts, and epidemics.

Anesth, Crit-Care, ER Med, General, Infect Dis, Nutr, OB-GYN, Ped Surg, Peds, Psych, Pub Health, Surg

⊕ https://vfmat.ch/f363

eHealth Africa

Builds stronger health systems in Africa through the design and implementation of data-driven solutions, responding to local needs and providing underserved communities with the necessary tools to lead healthier lives.

Logist-Op, Path

⊕ https://vfmat.ch/db6a

END Fund, The

Aims to control and eliminate the most prevalent neglected diseases among the world's poorest and most vulnerable people.

Infect Dis

⊕ https://vfmat.ch/2614

eRanger

Provides sustainable solutions to transportation and medical provision such as ambulances and mobile clinics in developing countries.

ER Med, General, Logist-Op

⊕ https://vfmat.ch/4c18

Evangelical Alliance Mission, The (TEAM)

Provides services in the areas of church planting, community development, healthcare, social justice, business as mission, and more.

Dent-OMFS, General, Ophth-Opt

⊕ https://vfmat.ch/9faa

Fistula Foundation

Aims to engage the support of people worldwide who are eager to see the day that no woman suffers from obstetric fistula. Raises and directs funds to doctors and hospitals providing life-transforming surgery to women in need.

OB-GYN

⊕ https://vfmat.ch/e958

Global Oncology (GO)

Brings the best in cancer care to underserved patients around the world and collaborates across geographic, professional, and academic borders to improve

cancer care, research, and education.

Heme-Onc, Path, Rad-Onc

⊕ https://vfmat.ch/fcb8

Globus Relief

Aims to improve the delivery of healthcare worldwide by gathering, processing, and distributing surplus medical supplies to charities at home and abroad.

Logist-Op

⊕ https://vfmat.ch/a2b7

Health Equity Initiative

Aims to build and sustain a global community that engages across sectors and disciplines to advance health equity.

Pub Health

⊕ https://vfmat.ch/e2e2

Hear the World Foundation

Advocates worldwide for equal opportunities and improved quality of life for people in need with hearing loss.

ENT, Peds

⊕ https://vfmat.ch/122c

Hope and Healing International

Gives hope and healing to children and families trapped by poverty and disability.

General, Nutr, Ophth-Opt, Peds, Rehab

⊕ https://vfmat.ch/c638

Humanity & Inclusion

Works alongside people with disabilities and vulnerable populations, taking action and bearing witness in order to respond to their essential needs, improve their living conditions and health, and promote respect for their dignity and fundamental rights.

General, Infect Dis, MF Med, Medicine, Ortho, Peds, Psych, Pub Health, Rehab

⊕ https://vfmat.ch/16b7

Humanity First

Provides aid and assistance to those in need, offering sustainable development solutions to society while providing and empowering local communities with the resources to help themselves.

ER Med, General, MF Med, Ophth-Opt

⊕ https://vfmat.ch/13cc

International Agency for the Prevention of Blindness (IAPB), The

Leads international efforts in blindness-prevention activities, works toward a world where no one is needlessly visually impaired, and ensures that everyone has access to the best possible standard of eye health.

Infect Dis, Ophth-Opt, Pub Health

⊕ https://vfmat.ch/87a2

International Federation of Red Cross and Red Crescent Societies (IFRC)

Coordinates and directs international assistance following natural and manmade disasters in nonconflict situations through the world's largest humanitarian and development network. Provides disaster-preparedness programs, healthcare activities, and promotes humanitarian values.

ER Med, General, Infect Dis, Nutr

⊕ https://vfmat.ch/b4ee

International Medical and Surgical Aid (IMSA)

Aims to save lives and alleviate suffering through education, healthcare, surgical camps, and quality medical programs.

Anesth, General, Ped Surg, Surg

⊕ https://vfmat.ch/2561

International Organization for Migration (IOM) – The UN Migration Agency

Promotes evidence-informed policies and holistic, preventive, and curative health programs that are beneficial, accessible, and equitable for vulnerable migrants.

General, Infect Dis, OB-GYN

⊕ https://vfmat.ch/621a

International Planned Parenthood Federation (IPPF)

Leads a locally owned, globally connected civil society movement that provides and enables services and champions sexual and reproductive health and rights for all, especially the underserved.

Infect Dis, MF Med, OB-GYN

⊕ https://vfmat.ch/dc97

International Rescue Committee (IRC)

Responds to the world's worst humanitarian crises and helps people whose lives and livelihoods are shattered by conflict and disaster to survive, recover, and gain control of their future.

ER Med, General, Infect Dis, MF Med, Peds

⊕ https://vfmat.ch/5d24

International Trachoma Initiative (iTi)

Works toward a world free from trachoma, a preventable cause of blindness, and provides comprehensive support to national ministries of health and governmental and nongovernmental organizations to implement a comprehensive approach to fight trachoma.

Infect Dis, Ophth-Opt

⊕ https://vfmat.ch/3278

International Union Against Tuberculosis and Lung Disease

Develops, implements, and assesses anti-tuberculosis, lung health, and noncommunicable disease programs.

Infect Dis, Pub Health, Pulm-Critic

⊕ https://vfmat.ch/3e82

Intersos

Provides emergency medical assistance to victims of armed conflicts, natural disasters, and extreme exclusion, with particular attention to the protection of the most vulnerable people.

ER Med, General, Nutr

⊕ https://vfmat.ch/dbac

Islamic Medical Association of North America

Fosters health promotion, disease prevention, and health maintenance in communities around the world through direct patient care and health programs.

Anesth, Dent-OMFS, ER Med, General, Logist-Op, Ophth-Opt, Peds, Plast, Surg

⊕ https://vfmat.ch/a157

Jhpiego

Creates and delivers transformative healthcare solutions that save lives, in partnership with national governments, health experts, and local communities.

General, Infect Dis, OB-GYN, Surg

⊕ https://vfmat.ch/45b8

Joint United Nations Programme on HIV/AIDS (UNAIDS)

Aims to place people living with HIV and people affected by the virus at the decision-making table and at the center of designing, delivering, and monitoring the AIDS response.

Infect Dis

⊕ https://vfmat.ch/464a

Leprosy Mission International

Seeks to empower people with leprosy to attain healing, dignity, and life in all its fullness.

Infect Dis

⊕ https://vfmat.ch/95a9

Lions Clubs International

Empowers volunteers to serve their communities, meet humanitarian needs, encourage peace, and promote international understanding through Lions Clubs.

Heme-Onc, Medicine, Nutr, Ophth-Opt

⊕ https://vfmat.ch/7b12

Management Sciences for Health (MSH)

Works with countries and communities to save lives and improve the health of the world's poorest and most vulnerable people by building strong, resilient, sustainable health systems.

Infect Dis, Logist-Op, Pub Health

⊕ https://vfmat.ch/6aa2

MAP International

Provides medicines and health supplies to those in need around the world so they might experience life to the fullest.

Logist-Op

⊕ https://vfmat.ch/deed

Medical Care Development International

Works to improve the health of vulnerable populations through integrated, sustainable, and locally driven interventions.

Infect Dis, OB-GYN, Peds, Pub Health

⊕ https://vfmat.ch/da87

MENTOR Initiative

Saves lives in emergencies through tropical disease control, and helps people recover from crisis with dignity, working side by side with communities, health workers, and health authorities to leave a lasting impact.

ER Med, Infect Dis

⊕ https://vfmat.ch/3bd5

Mercy and Love Foundation

Aims to provide orphaned and vulnerable children with basic human needs such as food, clothing, and shelter, enabling them to thrive.

General, Peds

⊕ https://vfmat.ch/649a

Mission Africa

Brings medical care, training, and compassion to underserved communities in Africa, based in Christian ministry.

Dent-OMFS, General, Infect Dis

⊕ https://vfmat.ch/df4d

Operation Fistula

Exists to end obstetric fistula by building models of care that serve every woman, everywhere.

MF Med, OB-GYN, Surg

⊕ https://vfmat.ch/ce8e

Order of Malta

Supports forgotten or excluded people, especially those living in conflict zones or amid natural disasters, by providing medical assistance, caring for refugees, and distributing medicines and necessities.

ER Med, General, Infect Dis, MF Med, Nephro, OB-GYN, Ortho, Psych

⊕ https://vfmat.ch/1fab

Organization for the Prevention of Blindness, The (OPC)

Provides research, and treatments and cures for people affected by blindness and blinding diseases in Francophone Africa.

Infect Dis, Ophth-Opt

⊕ https://vfmat.ch/86d6

Première Urgence International

Helps civilians who are marginalized or excluded as a result of natural disasters, war, or economic collapse.

ER Med, General, MF Med, Peds, Psych

⊕ https://vfmat.ch/62ba

RestoringVision

Empowers lives by restoring vision for millions of people in need.

Ophth-Opt

⊕ https://vfmat.ch/e121

Rockefeller Foundation, The

Works to promote the well-being of humanity.

Logist-Op, Nutr, Pub Health

⊕ https://vfmat.ch/5424

Rotary International

Provides service to others, improves lives, and advances world understanding, goodwill, and peace through its fellowship of business, professional, and community leaders.

ER Med, General, Infect Dis, MF Med, OB-GYN

⊕ https://vfmat.ch/8fb5

Sightsavers
Works with partners in developing countries to help eliminate avoidable blindness and advocates for equal opportunity for the disabled.
Infect Dis, Ophth-Opt, Surg
⊕ https://vfmat.ch/aa52

SIGN Fracture Care International
Builds orthopedic capacity around the world and provides the injured poor access to fracture surgery by donating orthopedic education and implant systems to surgeons in developing countries.
Ortho, Rehab, Surg
⊕ https://vfmat.ch/123d

SINA Health
Aims to improve the health and educational status of the population in low- and middle-income countries.
General, Logist-Op
⊕ https://vfmat.ch/9ad3

Sisters of the Immaculate Heart of Mary, Mother of Christ
Based in Chrisitan ministry, seeks to motivate people, especially the poor and the less privileged, to live venerable and dignified lives through credibility-structured programs, education, various medical and humanitarian services, along with self-realization and self-empowerment opportunities.
Infect Dis, Logist-Op, Nutr, Pub Health
⊕ https://vfmat.ch/5774

Smile Train, Inc.
Treats children with cleft lip through a sustainable and local model that supports surgery and other forms of essential care.
Logist-Op, Pub Health
⊕ https://vfmat.ch/822c

Solthis
Improves disease prevention and access to quality care by strengthening the health systems and services of the countries served.
General, Infect Dis, Logist-Op, MF Med, Neonat, Path
⊕ https://vfmat.ch/a71d

Swiss Tropical and Public Health Institute
Contributes to the improvement of the health of populations internationally, nationally, and locally through excellence in research, education, and services.
Infect Dis, Pub Health
⊕ https://vfmat.ch/2ee4

Task Force for Global Health, The
Consists of programs and focus areas that cover a range of global health issues including neglected tropical diseases, infectious diseases, vaccines, field epidemiology, public health informatics, health workforce development, and global health ethics.
Infect Dis, Logist-Op, Medicine, Ophth-Opt, Peds
⊕ https://vfmat.ch/714c

Tearfund
Responds to crisis and partners with local churches to bring restoration to those living in poverty, inspired by the Christian faith.
ER Med, Logist-Op
⊕ https://vfmat.ch/f6cf

Union for International Cancer Control (UICC)
Unites and supports the cancer community to reduce the global cancer burden, promote greater equity, and ensure that cancer control continues to be a priority in the world health and development agenda.
Heme-Onc, Pub Health
⊕ https://vfmat.ch/88b1

United Nations Children's Fund (UNICEF)
Works in over 190 countries and territories to save children's lives, defend their rights, and help them fulfill their potential, from early childhood through adolescence.
All-Immu, Infect Dis, MF Med, Neonat, Nutr, OB-GYN, Ped Surg, Peds, Pub Health
⊕ https://vfmat.ch/42d7

United Nations Development Programme (UNDP)
Helps countries achieve the simultaneous eradication of extreme poverty and significant reduction of inequalities and exclusion using a sustainable human development approach.
Infect Dis, Logist-Op, Pub Health
⊕ https://vfmat.ch/935c

United Nations High Commissioner for Refugees (UNHCR)
Safeguards the rights and well-being of people who have been forced to flee, ensuring that everybody has the right to seek asylum and find safe refuge in another country, with the goal of seeking lasting solutions.
General, MF Med, Medicine, OB-GYN, Peds, Psych, Pub Health
⊕ https://vfmat.ch/6636

United Nations Office for the Coordination of Humanitarian Affairs (OCHA)
Contributes to principled and effective humanitarian response through coordination, advocacy, policy, information management, and humanitarian financing tools and services, by leveraging functional expertise throughout the organization.
Logist-Op
⊕ https://vfmat.ch/22b8

United Nations Population Fund (UNFPA)
Supports reproductive healthcare for women and youth in more than 150 countries, focusing on delivering a world in which every pregnancy is wanted, every childbirth is safe, and every young person's potential is fulfilled.
Infect Dis, MF Med, Neonat, OB-GYN, Peds, Pub Health
⊕ https://vfmat.ch/c969

United States Agency for International Development (USAID)
Promotes and demonstrates democratic values abroad and advances a free, peaceful, and prosperous world. Leads the U.S. government's international development and disaster assistance through partnerships and investments that save lives.
ER Med, Infect Dis, MF Med, OB-GYN, Peds
⊕ https://vfmat.ch/9a99

United Surgeons for Children (USFC)
Pursues greater health and opportunity for children in the most neglected pockets of the world, with a specific focus on and expertise in surgery.
Anesth, CT Surg, Neonat, Neurosurg, OB-GYN, Peds, Radiol, Surg
⊕ https://vfmat.ch/3b4c

USA for United Nations High Commissioner for Refugees (UNHCR)
Serves and protects refugees and displaced people through emergency relief, cash assistance, education, resettlement, and the rebuilding of livelihoods.
ER Med, General, Logist-Op, Nutr, Pub Health
⊕ https://vfmat.ch/293c

Ventura Global Health Project (VGHP)
Aims to encourage and facilitate a lifelong interest in global health by providing grants to support local medical professionals providing care to underserved populations.
Dent-OMFS, ER Med, General, Infect Dis, Logist-Op, OB-GYN, Ophth-Opt, Ortho, Peds, Plast, Surg, Urol
⊕ https://vfmat.ch/a746

Women's Refugee Commission
Seeks to improve lives by protecting the rights of women, children, and youth displaced by conflict and crisis through researching their needs, identifying solutions, and advocating for programs and policies to strengthen their resilience.
General, MF Med, Neonat, OB-GYN, Peds, Psych
⊕ https://vfmat.ch/3d8f

World Anaesthesia Society (WAS)
Aims to support anesthesiologists with an interest in working in low-income regions of the world.
Anesth
⊕ https://vfmat.ch/37fe

World Health Organization, The (WHO)

The United Nations' agency for health provides leadership on global health matters, shapes the health research agenda, sets norms and standards, articulates evidence-based policy options, provides technical support and monitoring to countries, and assesses health trends.

ER Med, General, Infect Dis, Logist-Op, MF Med, OB-GYN, Peds, Psych, Pub Health

⊕ https://vfmat.ch/c476

World Vision International

Works with vulnerable communities around the world to overcome poverty and injustice with child-focused programs in disaster management, health, nutrition, economic development, education, clean water, sanitation, and hygiene.

ER Med, General, Infect Dis, MF Med, Nutr, OB-GYN, Peds

⊕ https://vfmat.ch/2642

Worldwide Healing Hands

Works to improve the quality of healthcare for women and children in the most underserved areas of the world and to stop the preventable deaths of mothers.

General, MF Med, Neonat, OB-GYN

⊕ https://vfmat.ch/b331

Chad

Healthcare Facilities

Adventist Hospital at Moundou
Moundou, Chad
🌐 https://vfmat.ch/3284

Ancien Hôpital de Goré
Yanmodo, Logone Oriental, Chad
🌐 https://vfmat.ch/9d71

Bere Adventist Hospital
Bere, Chad
🌐 https://vfmat.ch/db32

Bokoro Hospital
Bokoro, Chad
🌐 https://vfmat.ch/2371

Centre de Sante Roi Fayca
N'Djamena, Chad
🌐 https://vfmat.ch/713f

Health District Administration
Sarh – Kyabe – Am Timan, كيابي Kyabé, Moyen-
Chari شاري الأوسط, Chad / تشاد
🌐 https://vfmat.ch/513d

Hôpital Chinois
Rond Point Gaoui دوار غاوي, N'Djaména انجمينا,
N'Djaména انجمينا, Chad / تشاد
🌐 https://vfmat.ch/4ceb

Hospital Alima
Ngouri, Chad
🌐 https://vfmat.ch/eded

Hospital at Abéché
Abéché, Chad
🌐 https://vfmat.ch/a2ab

Hospital at Dourbali
Dourbali/Abouguerne, Chad
🌐 https://vfmat.ch/d37c

Hospital at Kochan
Kochan, Biltine, Chad
🌐 https://vfmat.ch/3efe

Hospital at Timberi
Timberi, Chad
🌐 https://vfmat.ch/ef85

Hospital Bokoro
RN N'Djamena-Bokoro, Bokoro-Hadjer-Lamis, Chad
🌐 https://vfmat.ch/2461

Hospital District de Massakory
Ndjamena – Massakory – Faya Largeau National
Road, Massakory ماساكوري, Hadjer-Lamis حجر
لميس, Chad / تشاد
🌐 https://vfmat.ch/1ca5

Hospital Kouga
Kouga-Chad, Chad
🌐 https://vfmat.ch/b1b2

Hospital Moussoro
Moussoro, Chad
🌐 https://vfmat.ch/7968

Hôpital Central
زنقة العقيد مول Rue du Colonel Moll, Djambal Bor
جامبال بحر, N'Djaména انجمينا, Chad / تشاد
🌐 https://vfmat.ch/5b67

Hôpital Central de Sarh
Sarh, Chad
🌐 https://vfmat.ch/4efd

Hôpital de District de Beinamar
Palagamian, لوقون الغربية Logone Occidental, Chad
/ تشاد
🌐 https://vfmat.ch/bb4a

Hôpital de Farcha Zarafa
1er Arrondissement طريق فارشا/ الدائرة الأولى,
N'Djamena, 1er Arrondissement / الدائرة الأولى,

BP41, Chad / تشاد
🌐 https://vfmat.ch/d1bc

Hôpital de Faya
Chari Chifini شارع شيفيني, Faya-Largeau فايا لارجو,
Borkou بوركو, Chad / تشاد
🌐 https://vfmat.ch/9d9b

Hôpital de Goré
Yanmodo يانمودو, Logone Oriental لوقون الشرقية,
Chad / تشاد
🌐 https://vfmat.ch/aab3

Hôpital de Gozator
N'Djamena, Chad
🌐 https://vfmat.ch/68e1

Hôpital de Guinebor II
شارع أبو رتشا, N'Djaména انجمينا, N'Djaména
انجمينا, Chad / تشاد
🌐 https://vfmat.ch/d632

Hôpital de Kindjiria
Massakory-N'Gouri-Bol-Niger Border, Délékerie
Kangara, Hadjer-Lamis حجر لميس, Chad / تشاد
🌐 https://vfmat.ch/48c4

Hôpital de l'Union
N'Djamena – Moundou, N'Djaména انجمينا,
N'Djaména انجمينا, Chad / تشاد
🌐 https://vfmat.ch/82b4

Hôpital de la Paix
N'Djamena, Chad
🌐 https://vfmat.ch/ed6d

Hôpital de la Renaissance
شارع بيرميل, N'Djaména انجمينا, N'Djaména انجمينا,
Chad / تشاد
🌐 https://vfmat.ch/2cea

Hôpital de Mao
Mao ماو, Kanem كانم, Chad / تشاد
🌐 https://vfmat.ch/dbc5

Hôpital du Distric Sanitaire de Baga Sola
Baga Sola, Chad
⊕ https://vfmat.ch/b178

Hôpital Garnison
3015 زنقة, N'Djaména انجمينا, N'Djaména انجمينا,
Chad / تشاد
⊕ https://vfmat.ch/7f44

Hôpital Général de Doba
Moundou – Doba National Road, Ndoubeu Aeroport,
Logone Oriental لوقون الشرقية, Chad / تشاد
⊕ https://vfmat.ch/4851

Hôpital Mère et Enfant
Rue du Cherif شارع الشريف, N'Djaména انجمينا,
N'Djaména انجمينا, Chad / تشاد
⊕ https://vfmat.ch/63aa

Hôpital Provincial de Moussoro
Ndjamena – Massakory – Faya Largeau National
Road, Moussoro موسورو, Barh el Gazel بحر الغزال,
Chad / تشاد
⊕ https://vfmat.ch/bd69

Hôpital Régional d'Abéché
Abéché, Chad
⊕ https://vfmat.ch/678a

Hôpital Régional de Bol
Bol بول, Lac البحيرة, Chad / تشاد
⊕ https://vfmat.ch/be1c

Hôpital Régional de Bongor
Djamena-Moundou, Bongor, Chad
⊕ https://vfmat.ch/da14

Hôpital Régional de Goz Beida
مسار جبل, Goz Beïda قوز بيضة, Sila سيلا, Chad / تشاد
⊕ https://vfmat.ch/414d

Hôpital Saint Joseph
Bébédja, Chad
⊕ https://vfmat.ch/66f7

Le Bon Samaritain Hospital
Pont de Chagoua, N'Djaména انجمينا, N'Djaména
انجمينا, Chad / تشاد
⊕ https://vfmat.ch/283d

National General Reference Hospital
Rond Point Mairie دوار دار البلدية, N'Djaména انجمينا,
N'Djaména انجمينا, Chad / تشاد
⊕ https://vfmat.ch/1bb1

Ordre de Malte
Chari-mongo شارع شاري-مونقو, N'Djaména
انجمينا, N'Djaména انجمينا, Chad / تشاد
⊕ https://vfmat.ch/378d

Singamong
Avenue Tombalbaye, Doumbeur 1, Logone
Occidental, Chad
⊕ https://vfmat.ch/bd98

Hahaia هاهايا

MORONI

Foumbouni فومبوني

Hajoho هاجوهو

MUTSAMUDU

Bambao

COMOROS

Domoni

Hoani

FOMBONI
Djoiezi

Pomoni

B
Acoua

Ts

S

Bouc

Ka

● Healthcare Facility

Comoros

Nicknamed the "Perfumed Islands" thanks to its fragrant plant life and natural beauty, the Comoros archipelago, formally known as Union of the Comoros, is a small, mountainous island country in the Indian Ocean, off the coast of Eastern Africa. The population of 865,000 people is composed of several ethnic groups including Antalote, Cafre, Makoa, Oimatsaha, and Sakalava; the overwhelming majority are Sunni Muslim. Three official languages are spoken throughout the country: Arabic, French, and Shikomoro, a blend of Swahili and Arabic. Of the three islands that make up the Comoros, Anjouan is the most densely populated, with the capital, Maroni, also being fairly dense. Despite these high-density areas, as much as two-thirds of the population live in rural areas.

Comoros is considered one of the world's poorest countries, with much of its population relying on subsistence agriculture and fishing. One fourth of the population is considered to be extremely poor, living below the national poverty line. A limited number of job opportunities, no universities, a lack of advanced healthcare, and widespread poverty have resulted in a steady migration of Comorans moving abroad (mainly to France) in search of a better life. The diaspora has grown to such an extent that 25 percent of Comoros' 2013 GDP was attributed to remittances.

The most common causes of death in Comoros include stroke, lower respiratory infections, ischemic heart disease, neonatal disorders, tuberculosis, diarrheal diseases, malaria, diabetes, cirrhosis, and hypertensive heart disease. Death due to malaria has decreased by over 50 percent in the past 10 years, however it still causes substantial mortality in the country. The risk factors that contribute most to death and disability include malnutrition, air pollution, high blood pressure, dietary risks, high body-mass index, high fasting plasma glucose, tobacco use, and insufficient water, sanitation, and hygiene.

0.86M
Population

$1,403
GDP Per Capita

64 years
Life Expectancy
↑ Improving

17
Doctors/100k

Physician Density

216
Beds/100k

Hospital Bed Density

273
Deaths/100k

Maternal Mortality

Comoros

Nonprofit Organizations

Africa Health Organisation
Leads collaborative efforts among countries in Africa and other partners to promote health equity, combat disease, and improve quality of life.
Logist-Op, Pub Health
🌐 https://vfmat.ch/b1c5

Africa Relief and Community Development
Provides comprehensive relief and developmental aid to people of the African continent regardless of gender, race, or religion.
Nutr, Pub Health
🌐 https://vfmat.ch/6cd2

African Health Now
Promotes and provides information and access to sustainable primary healthcare to women, children, and families living across Sub-Saharan Africa.
Dent-OMFS, Endo, General, Infect Dis, MF Med, OB-GYN
🌐 https://vfmat.ch/c766

Al Basar International Foundation
Works with local partners to treat preventable blindness, and helps set up sustainable infrastructure so local teams can save sight in their communities.
Ophth-Opt
🌐 https://vfmat.ch/a8b5

Australian Doctors for Africa
Develops healthier environments and builds capacity through the provision of voluntary medical assistance, while training and teaching doctors, nurses, and allied health workers; improving infrastructure; and providing medical equipment.
Anesth, ENT, GI, Logist-Op, MF Med, OB-GYN, Ortho, Ped Surg, Peds, Urol
🌐 https://vfmat.ch/f769

Center for Strategic and International Studies (CSIS) Commission on Strengthening America's Health Security
Brings together a distinguished and diverse group of high-level opinion leaders bridging security and health, with the core aim to chart a bold vision for the future of U.S. leadership in global health.
ER Med, Infect Dis, MF Med, Pub Health
🌐 https://vfmat.ch/6d7f

Developing Country NGO Delegation: Global Fund to Fight AIDS, TB & Malaria
Works to strengthen the engagement of civil society actors and organizations in developing countries to build a world in which AIDS, TB, and malaria are no longer global, public health, and human rights threats.
Infect Dis, Pub Health
🌐 https://vfmat.ch/3149

Global Oncology (GO)
Brings the best in cancer care to underserved patients around the world and collaborates across geographic, professional, and academic borders to improve cancer care, research, and education.
Heme-Onc, Path, Rad-Onc
🌐 https://vfmat.ch/fcb8

Health Equity Initiative
Aims to build and sustain a global community that engages across sectors and disciplines to advance health equity.
Pub Health
🌐 https://vfmat.ch/e2e2

International Federation of Red Cross and Red Crescent Societies (IFRC)
Coordinates and directs international assistance following natural and manmade disasters in nonconflict situations through the world's largest humanitarian and development network. Provides disaster-preparedness programs, healthcare activities, and promotes humanitarian values.
ER Med, General, Infect Dis, Nutr
🌐 https://vfmat.ch/b4ee

International Medical and Surgical Aid (IMSA)
Aims to save lives and alleviate suffering through education, healthcare, surgical camps, and quality medical programs.
Anesth, General, Ped Surg, Surg
🌐 https://vfmat.ch/2561

International Organization for Migration (IOM) – The UN Migration Agency
Promotes evidence-informed policies and holistic, preventive, and curative health programs that are beneficial, accessible, and equitable for vulnerable migrants.
General, Infect Dis, OB-GYN
🌐 https://vfmat.ch/621a

Joint United Nations Programme on HIV/AIDS (UNAIDS)
Aims to place people living with HIV and people affected by the virus at the decision-making table and at the center of designing, delivering, and monitoring the AIDS response.
Infect Dis
🌐 https://vfmat.ch/464a

Management Sciences for Health (MSH)
Works with countries and communities to save lives and improve the health of the world's poorest and most vulnerable people by building strong, resilient, sustainable health systems.
Infect Dis, Logist-Op, Pub Health
🌐 https://vfmat.ch/6aa2

Mercy and Love Foundation
Aims to provide orphaned and vulnerable children with basic human needs such as food, clothing, and shelter, enabling them to thrive.

General, Peds
⊕ https://vfmat.ch/649a

Mercy Ships
Operates hospital ships staffed by volunteers to bring hope, healing, and healthcare to underserved communities worldwide.
Anesth, Dent-OMFS, Logist-Op, Neonat, OB-GYN, Ophth-Opt, Ortho, Palliative, Plast, Psych, Surg
⊕ https://vfmat.ch/2e99

NCD Alliance
Unites and strengthens civil society to stimulate collaborative advocacy, action, and accountability for NCD (noncommunicable disease) prevention and control.
All-Immu, CV Med, General, Heme-Onc, Medicine, Peds, Psych
⊕ https://vfmat.ch/abdd

Order of Malta
Supports forgotten or excluded people, especially those living in conflict zones or amid natural disasters, by providing medical assistance, caring for refugees, and distributing medicines and necessities.
ER Med, General, Infect Dis, MF Med, Nephro, OB-GYN, Ortho, Psych
⊕ https://vfmat.ch/1fab

RestoringVision
Empowers lives by restoring vision for millions of people in need.
Ophth-Opt
⊕ https://vfmat.ch/e121

Rockefeller Foundation, The
Works to promote the well-being of humanity.
Logist-Op, Nutr, Pub Health
⊕ https://vfmat.ch/5424

Rotary International
Provides service to others, improves lives, and advances world understanding, goodwill, and peace through its fellowship of business, professional, and community leaders.
ER Med, General, Infect Dis, MF Med, OB-GYN
⊕ https://vfmat.ch/8fb5

Sanofi Espoir Foundation
Contributes to reducing health inequalities among populations that need it most by applying a socially responsible approach focused on fighting childhood cancers in low-income countries, improving maternal and newborn health, and improving access to care.
ER Med, OB-GYN, Peds
⊕ https://vfmat.ch/943b

Santé Diabète
Addresses the lack of access to care for people with diabetes in Africa, with the mission of saving lives through disease prevention and management and improving quality of life through care delivery.
Endo, Medicine, Vasc Surg
⊕ https://vfmat.ch/7652

SINA Health
Aims to improve the health and educational status of the population in low- and middle-income countries.
General, Logist-Op
⊕ https://vfmat.ch/9ad3

Sofia Global
Inspired by the Christian faith, promotes an equitable and sustainable society through education, healthcare, pastoral work, and community capacity-building.
General, Heme-Onc, Infect Dis, MF Med, OB-GYN, Peds
⊕ https://vfmat.ch/263c

Union for International Cancer Control (UICC)
Unites and supports the cancer community to reduce the global cancer burden, promote greater equity, and ensure that cancer control continues to be a priority in the world health and development agenda.
Heme-Onc, Pub Health
⊕ https://vfmat.ch/88b1

United Nations Children's Fund (UNICEF)
Works in over 190 countries and territories to save children's lives, defend their rights, and help them fulfill their potential, from early childhood through adolescence.
All-Immu, Infect Dis, MF Med, Neonat, Nutr, OB-GYN, Ped Surg, Peds, Pub Health
⊕ https://vfmat.ch/42d7

United Nations Development Programme (UNDP)
Helps countries achieve the simultaneous eradication of extreme poverty and significant reduction of inequalities and exclusion using a sustainable human development approach.
Infect Dis, Logist-Op, Pub Health
⊕ https://vfmat.ch/935c

United Nations High Commissioner for Refugees (UNHCR)
Safeguards the rights and well-being of people who have been forced to flee, ensuring that everybody has the right to seek asylum and find safe refuge in another country, with the goal of seeking lasting solutions.
General, MF Med, Medicine, OB-GYN, Peds, Psych, Pub Health
⊕ https://vfmat.ch/6636

United Nations Population Fund (UNFPA)
Supports reproductive healthcare for women and youth in more than 150 countries, focusing on delivering a world in which every pregnancy is wanted, every childbirth is safe, and every young person's potential is fulfilled.
Infect Dis, MF Med, Neonat, OB-GYN, Peds, Pub Health
⊕ https://vfmat.ch/c969

United States Agency for International Development (USAID)
Promotes and demonstrates democratic values abroad and advances a free, peaceful, and prosperous world. Leads the U.S. government's international development and disaster assistance through partnerships and investments that save lives.
ER Med, Infect Dis, MF Med, OB-GYN, Peds
⊕ https://vfmat.ch/9a99

World Health Organization, The (WHO)
The United Nations' agency for health provides leadership on global health matters, shapes the health research agenda, sets norms and standards, articulates evidence-based policy options, provides technical support and monitoring to countries, and assesses health trends.
ER Med, General, Infect Dis, Logist-Op, MF Med, OB-GYN, Peds, Psych, Pub Health
⊕ https://vfmat.ch/c476

Comoros

Healthcare Facilities

Centre d'Imagerie Médicale
Moroni, Grand Comore, Comoros
🌐 https://vfmat.ch/fr1a

Centre Hospitalier de Fomboni
Mohéli, Comoros
🌐 https://vfmat.ch/lpam

Centre Hospitalier National El Maarouf
Moroni, Grande Comore, Comoros
🌐 https://vfmat.ch/4d1c

CMC Mitsamiouli
Mitsamiouli, Ouhozi, Nkourani, Grande Comore,
Comoros
🌐 https://vfmat.ch/b873

Hombo Centre Hospitalier Regional
Mutsamudu, Anjouan, Comoros
🌐 https://vfmat.ch/kenn

Hospital de Hombo
Mutsamudu, Hombo, Anjouan, Comoros
🌐 https://vfmat.ch/7ff4

Hôpital de Bambao Anjouan Comores
Domoney, Anjouan, Comoros
🌐 https://vfmat.ch/wi26

Hôpital de Domoni
Domoney, Anjouan, Comoros
🌐 https://vfmat.ch/pjxl

Hôpital de Hombo
Mutsamudu, Comoros
🌐 https://vfmat.ch/gbdt

Hôpital de Moidja Hamahamet
Mouadja, Grand Comore, Comoros
🌐 https://vfmat.ch/skuz

Hôpital de Sambakouni
Samba-Kouni, Grande Comore, Comoros
🌐 https://vfmat.ch/ldid

Hôpital de Tsembehu
Tsembehou, Anjouan, Comoros
🌐 https://vfmat.ch/vrhw

Mkazi Hospital
Mkazi, Grande Comore, Comoros
🌐 https://vfmat.ch/ehtw

YAOUNDE

MBALMAYO

EBOLOWA   Sangmelima

Ebebiyin

MONGOMO

MBAÏKI

NOLA

Mouale

LIBENGE

OUÉSSO

IMPFONDO

MBANDAKA

Liranga

FRANCEVILLE

BOLOBO

BANDUNDU

DOLISIE

KINSHASA

KENGE   Masi Manimba

KIKWIT

POINTE-NOIRE

TSHELA

MBANZA-NGUNGU

BOMA   MATADI

M'BANZA CONGO

● Healthcare Facility

Congo

Filled with incredible wildlife and known for its variety of national parks, the Republic of the Congo is located on the western coast of Central Africa, bordered by Angola, Gabon, Cameroon, Central African Republic, and the Democratic Republic of the Congo. The population of 5.4 million resides mostly in the southern regions of the country, especially in the coastal area of Pointe-Noire, the second largest city after the capital, Brazzaville. Nearly 70 percent of the population lives in these two cities and along the railroad that connects them; the rest of the country is sparsely inhabited by contrast.The population comprises a variety of ethnic groups, including Kongo, Teke, Mbochi, Sangha, Mbere/Mbeti/Kele, Punu, Pygmy, Oubanguiens, Duma, and Makaa. About three-fourths of the population is Christian. Interestingly, about one-sixth of the land in the Congo is set aside for conservation.

Formerly a French colony, Middle Congo became the Republic of the Congo in 1960 when the country gained its independence. While poverty rates have decreased over time, they are still quite high: 41 percent in 2011 compared to 51 percent in 2005. Extreme poverty rates have increased due to a drop in the price of oil, a key Congolese export. Health and education remain underdeveloped and lacking throughout the country.

The high poverty rate is reflected in the health of the population. Maternal and infant mortality are high: approximately 5 percent of children do not live to their fifth birthday. Chronic malnutrition affects 21 percent of children. Leading causes of death include HIV/AIDS, ischemic heart disease, stroke, malaria, lower respiratory infections, neonatal disorders, tuberculosis, diarrheal diseases, road injuries, diabetes, and cirrhosis. In addition to malnutrition, the risk factors that contribute most to death and disability include unsafe sex, air pollution, high blood pressure, high body-mass index, high fasting plasma glucose, dietary risks, alcohol and tobacco use, and insufficient water, sanitation, and hygiene.

5.4M
Population

$1973
GDP Per Capita

65 years
Life Expectancy
↑ Improving

11
Doctors/100k

Physician Density

160
Beds/100k

Hospital Bed Density

378
Deaths/100k

Maternal Mortality

Congo

Nonprofit Organizations

Africa CDC
Aims to strengthen the capacity and capability of Africa's public health institutions and partnerships to detect and respond quickly and effectively to disease threats and outbreaks, based on data-driven interventions and programs.
Infect Dis, Logist-Op, Pub Health
⊕ https://vfmat.ch/339c

Africa Health Organisation
Leads collaborative efforts among countries in Africa and other partners to promote health equity, combat disease, and improve quality of life.
Logist-Op, Pub Health
⊕ https://vfmat.ch/b1c5

Africa Relief and Community Development
Provides comprehensive relief and developmental aid to people of the African continent regardless of gender, race, or religion.
Nutr, Pub Health
⊕ https://vfmat.ch/6cd2

Al Basar International Foundation
Works with local partners to treat preventable blindness, and helps set up sustainable infrastructure so local teams can save sight in their communities.
Ophth-Opt
⊕ https://vfmat.ch/a8b5

Amref Health Africa
Serves millions of people across 35 countries in Sub-Saharan Africa, strengthening health systems, and training African health workers to respond to the continent's most critical health issues.
All-Immu, General, Infect Dis, Logist-Op, MF Med, OB-GYN, Path, Pub Health, Surg
⊕ https://vfmat.ch/6985

AO Alliance
Builds solutions to lessen the burden of injuries in low- and middle-income countries, while enhancing the care of the injured to reduce human suffering, disability, and poverty.
Ortho, Surg
⊕ https://vfmat.ch/8cd5

Christian Medical & Dental Associations
Based in Christian ministry, deploys medical and dental teams to underserved communities to provide vital healthcare.
Anesth, Dent-OMFS, ER Med, General, Medicine, OB-GYN, Ophth-Opt, Peds, Pub Health, Radiol, Rehab, Surg
⊕ https://vfmat.ch/921c

DKT INTERNATIONAL INC
Seeks to provide couples with affordable and safe options for family planning and HIV/AIDS prevention through dynamic social marketing.

General, Surg
⊕ https://vfmat.ch/b3a7

Dream Sant'Egidio
Seeks to counter HIV/AIDS in Africa by eliminating the transmission of HIV from mother to child, with a focus on women because of the importance of their role in the community.
Infect Dis, MF Med, Neonat, OB-GYN, Path, Peds
⊕ https://vfmat.ch/f466

Global Oncology (GO)
Brings the best in cancer care to underserved patients around the world and collaborates across geographic, professional, and academic borders to improve cancer care, research, and education.
Heme-Onc, Path, Rad-Onc
⊕ https://vfmat.ch/fcb8

Globus Relief
Aims to improve the delivery of healthcare worldwide by gathering, processing, and distributing surplus medical supplies to charities at home and abroad.
Logist-Op
⊕ https://vfmat.ch/a2b7

Healthcare Relief (Health for Africa)
Works toward relief of poverty and sickness, supporting causes including healthcare services, healthy campaigns for those in poverty, and research.
Logist-Op, Pub Health
⊕ https://vfmat.ch/da5a

HELP CODE ITALIA ONLUS
Seeks to improve life conditions of children in the communities where they live, through direct and indirect projects designed to support their well-being, education, and development.
General, Nutr, Pub Health
⊕ https://vfmat.ch/1dd9

International Federation of Red Cross and Red Crescent Societies (IFRC)
Coordinates and directs international assistance following natural and manmade disasters in nonconflict situations through the world's largest humanitarian and development network. Provides disaster-preparedness programs, healthcare activities, and promotes humanitarian values.
ER Med, General, Infect Dis, Nutr
⊕ https://vfmat.ch/b4ee

International Organization for Migration (IOM) – The UN Migration Agency
Promotes evidence-informed policies and holistic, preventive, and curative health programs that are beneficial, accessible, and equitable for vulnerable migrants.

General, Infect Dis, OB-GYN
⊕ https://vfmat.ch/621a

International Planned Parenthood Federation (IPPF)
Leads a locally owned, globally connected civil society movement that provides and enables services and champions sexual and reproductive health and rights for all, especially the underserved.
Infect Dis, MF Med, OB-GYN
⊕ https://vfmat.ch/dc97

Life for a Child
Supports the provision of the best possible healthcare, given local circumstances, to all children and youth with diabetes in less-resourced countries, through the strengthening of existing diabetes services.
Endo, Medicine, Peds
⊕ https://vfmat.ch/d712

Medical Care Development International
Works to improve the health of vulnerable populations through integrated, sustainable, and locally driven interventions.
Infect Dis, OB-GYN, Peds, Pub Health
⊕ https://vfmat.ch/da87

Mercy and Love Foundation
Aims to provide orphaned and vulnerable children with basic human needs such as food, clothing, and shelter, enabling them to thrive.
General, Peds
⊕ https://vfmat.ch/649a

New Sight Eye Care
Works to provide hope to the blind and their loved ones in Africa, particularly in Northern Congo.
Ophth-Opt
⊕ https://vfmat.ch/c132

Order of Malta
Supports forgotten or excluded people, especially those living in conflict zones or amid natural disasters, by providing medical assistance, caring for refugees, and distributing medicines and necessities.
ER Med, General, Infect Dis, MF Med, Nephro, OB-GYN, Ortho, Psych
⊕ https://vfmat.ch/1fab

Organization for the Prevention of Blindness, The (OPC)
Provides research, and treatments and cures for people affected by blindness and blinding diseases in Francophone Africa.
Infect Dis, Ophth-Opt
⊕ https://vfmat.ch/86d6

Partners for Development (PfD)
Works to improve quality of life for vulnerable people in underserved communities through local and international partnerships.
Infect Dis, MF Med, Neonat, Peds
⊕ https://vfmat.ch/d2f6

Philia Foundation
Seeks to invest sustainably in people and marginalized communities in order to improve health and education in Africa.
Anesth, ER Med, General, Heme-Onc, MF Med, Neurosurg, OB-GYN, Ophth-Opt, Ortho, Pub Health, Surg, Urol
⊕ https://vfmat.ch/a352

Physicians Across Continents
Provides high-quality medical care to people affected by crises and disasters.
CV Med, Dent-OMFS, Heme-Onc, MF Med, Nephro, Nephro, OB-GYN, Ped Surg, Plast, Surg
⊕ https://vfmat.ch/fe5d

Pioneer Christian Hospital
Seeks to serve the medically underserved in Central Africa, inspired by the Christian faith.
Infect Dis, Medicine, OB-GYN, Path, Peds, Radiol, Surg
⊕ https://vfmat.ch/f26f

RestoringVision
Empowers lives by restoring vision for millions of people in need.
Ophth-Opt
⊕ https://vfmat.ch/e121

Rotary International
Provides service to others, improves lives, and advances world understanding, goodwill, and peace through its fellowship of business, professional, and community leaders.
ER Med, General, Infect Dis, MF Med, OB-GYN
⊕ https://vfmat.ch/8fb5

Salvation Army International, The
Seeks to meet human needs through services in education, healthcare, community support, emergency response, and ministry development, inspired by the Christian faith.
Dent-OMFS, Derm, ER Med, Infect Dis, MF Med, Medicine, Nutr, OB-GYN, Ophth-Opt, Palliative, Psych, Rehab, Surg
⊕ https://vfmat.ch/8eb3

Serving Others Worldwide
Aims to provide aid to the poor, distressed, and underprivileged by providing healthcare and dental services, and by building schools, orphanages, libraries, and medical clinics in undeveloped countries.
Dent-OMFS, General
⊕ https://vfmat.ch/69cb

Sightsavers
Works with partners in developing countries to help eliminate avoidable blindness and advocates for equal opportunity for the disabled.
Infect Dis, Ophth-Opt, Surg
⊕ https://vfmat.ch/aa52

SINA Health
Aims to improve the health and educational status of the population in low- and middle-income countries.
General, Logist-Op
⊕ https://vfmat.ch/9ad3

Smile Train, Inc.
Treats children with cleft lip through a sustainable and local model that supports surgery and other forms of essential care.
Logist-Op, Pub Health
⊕ https://vfmat.ch/822c

Sri Sathya Sai International Organization
Inspired by spiritual teachings, carries out efforts in global healthcare, education, humanitarian relief, and youth engagement.
Dent-OMFS, General, Logist-Op, Nutr, Ophth-Opt, Pub Health
⊕ https://vfmat.ch/9bda

Task Force for Global Health, The
Consists of programs and focus areas that cover a range of global health issues including neglected tropical diseases, infectious diseases, vaccines, field epidemiology, public health informatics, health workforce development, and global health ethics.
Infect Dis, Logist-Op, Medicine, Ophth-Opt, Peds
⊕ https://vfmat.ch/714c

Union for International Cancer Control (UICC)
Unites and supports the cancer community to reduce the global cancer burden, promote greater equity, and ensure that cancer control continues to be a priority in the world health and development agenda.
Heme-Onc, Pub Health
⊕ https://vfmat.ch/88b1

United Nations Children's Fund (UNICEF)
Works in over 190 countries and territories to save children's lives, defend their rights, and help them fulfill their potential, from early childhood through adolescence.
All-Immu, Infect Dis, MF Med, Neonat, Nutr, OB-GYN, Ped Surg, Peds, Pub Health
⊕ https://vfmat.ch/42d7

United Nations Development Programme (UNDP)

Helps countries achieve the simultaneous eradication of extreme poverty and significant reduction of inequalities and exclusion using a sustainable human development approach.

Infect Dis, Logist-Op, Pub Health

⊕ https://vfmat.ch/935c

United Nations Population Fund (UNFPA)

Supports reproductive healthcare for women and youth in more than 150 countries, focusing on delivering a world in which every pregnancy is wanted, every childbirth is safe, and every young person's potential is fulfilled.

Infect Dis, MF Med, Neonat, OB-GYN, Peds, Pub Health

⊕ https://vfmat.ch/c969

United States Agency for International Development (USAID)

Promotes and demonstrates democratic values abroad and advances a free, peaceful, and prosperous world. Leads the U.S. government's international development and disaster assistance through partnerships and investments that save lives.

ER Med, Infect Dis, MF Med, OB-GYN, Peds

⊕ https://vfmat.ch/9a99

United Surgeons for Children (USFC)

Pursues greater health and opportunity for children in the most neglected pockets of the world, with a specific focus on and expertise in surgery.

Anesth, CT Surg, Neonat, Neurosurg, OB-GYN, Peds, Radiol, Surg

⊕ https://vfmat.ch/3b4c

World Federation of Hemophilia (WFH)

Aims to improve and sustain care for people with inherited bleeding disorders by pursuing long-term relationships with individuals and organizations who share the values of WFH's development model.

Heme-Onc

⊕ https://vfmat.ch/5121

World Health Organization, The (WHO)

The United Nations' agency for health provides leadership on global health matters, shapes the health research agenda, sets norms and standards, articulates evidence-based policy options, provides technical support and monitoring to countries, and assesses health trends.

ER Med, General, Infect Dis, Logist-Op, MF Med, OB-GYN, Peds, Psych, Pub Health

⊕ https://vfmat.ch/c476

World Medical Relief

Facilitates the distribution of surplus medical resources where they are needed.

Logist-Op

⊕ https://vfmat.ch/72dc

Congo

Healthcare Facilities

Centre Hospitalier Universitaire de Brazzaville (CHU-BZV)
Poto-Poto, Brazzaville, Republic of the Congo
🌐 https://vfmat.ch/d8fb

Centre National de Sécurité Sociale
Brazzaville, Republic of the Congo
🌐 https://vfmat.ch/ba2d

Clinical Louise Michel
Pointe-Noire, Republic of the Congo
🌐 https://vfmat.ch/4zqy

Clinical Medico-Chirurgicale Cogemo
Brazzaville, Republic of the Congo
🌐 https://vfmat.ch/clyd

Clinique Securex
Brazzaville, Republic of the Congo
🌐 https://vfmat.ch/dlmb

Hôpital Central des Armées Pierre Mobengo
Poto-Poto, Brazzaville, Republic of the Congo
🌐 https://vfmat.ch/439f

Hôpital de Base de Bacongo
Bacongo, Brazzaville, Republic of the Congo
🌐 https://vfmat.ch/718d

Hôpital de Campagne de Nkombo
Djiri, Brazzaville, Republic of the Congo
🌐 https://vfmat.ch/4596

Hôpital de Loandjili
Pointe-Noire, Kouilou, Republic of the Congo
🌐 https://vfmat.ch/66a4

Hôpital de Makélékélé
Makélékélé, Brazzaville, Republic of the Congo
🌐 https://vfmat.ch/1d93

Hôpital de Mossendjo
Mossendjo, Niari, Republic of the Congo
🌐 https://vfmat.ch/7fff

Hôpital de Référence de Dolisie
Dolisie, Niari, Republic of the Congo
🌐 https://vfmat.ch/577a

Hôpital de Talangaï
Talangaï, Brazzaville, Republic of the Congo
🌐 https://vfmat.ch/227f

Hôpital Général Adolphe Sicé
Pointe-Noire, Kouilou, Republic of the Congo
🌐 https://vfmat.ch/8af8

Hôpital Général de Dolisie
Dolisie, Niari, Republic of the Congo
🌐 https://vfmat.ch/3bcb

Hôpital Général de Nkombo
Djiri, Brazzaville, Republic of the Congo
🌐 https://vfmat.ch/c5b9

Hôpital Général de Patra
Pointe-Noire, Kouilou, Republic of the Congo
🌐 https://vfmat.ch/8be4

Hôpital Général Edith Lucie Bongo Ondimba
Oyo, Cuvette, Republic of the Congo
🌐 https://vfmat.ch/eb7d

Hôpital Militaire de Dolisie
Dolisie, Niari, Republic of the Congo
🌐 https://vfmat.ch/684a

Hôpital Mère-Enfant Blanche Gomez
Poto-Poto, Brazzaville, Republic of the Congo
🌐 https://vfmat.ch/5169

Hôpital Régional des Armées de Pointe-Noire
Pointe-Noire, Kouilou, Republic of the Congo
🌐 https://vfmat.ch/9d3d

Hôpital Sino-Congolaise de Mfilou
Brazzaville, Republic of the Congo
🌐 https://vfmat.ch/bb5e

Pioneer Christian Hospital
Impfondo, Likouala, Republic of the Congo
🌐 https://vfmat.ch/nt4e

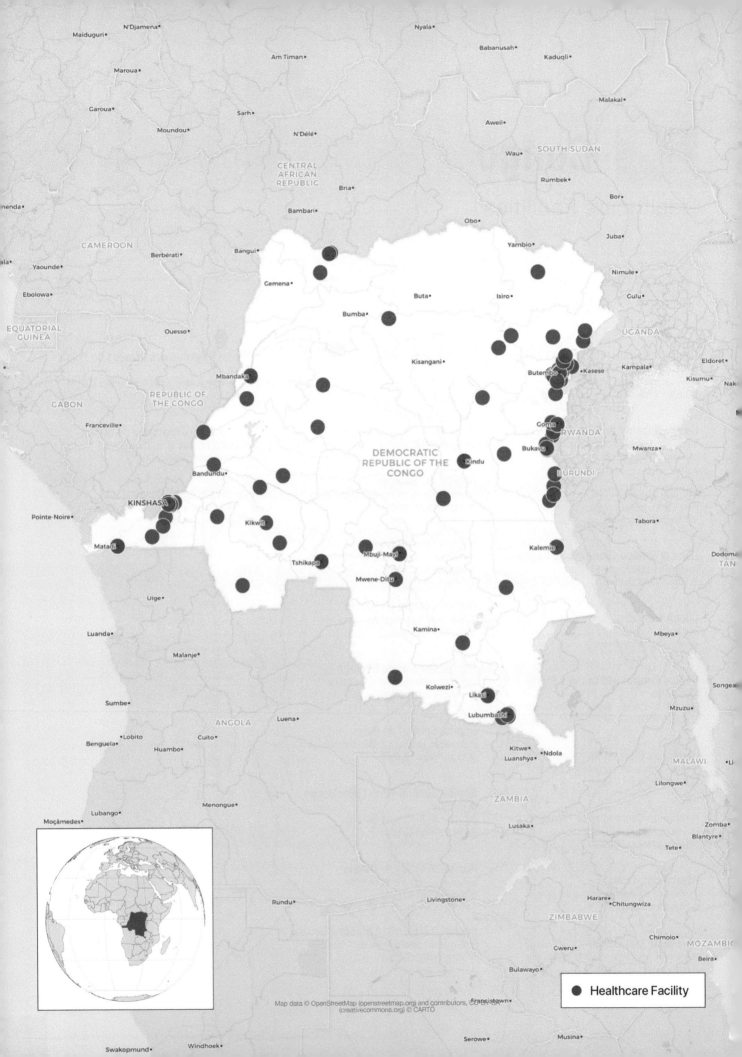

Healthcare Facility

Democratic Republic of the Congo (DRC)

The Democratic Republic of the Congo (DRC) is the largest country in sub-Saharan Africa, with an area equivalent to Western Europe. A beautiful country, the DRC is home to vast reserves of resources ranging from diamonds to hydroelectric potential. The population of more than 105 million comprises more than 200 ethnic groups, most of which are Bantu. As much as 45 percent of the population lives in urban areas, predominantly in the cities in the northeast and in the capital, Kinshasa. French is the official language of the DRC; many people communicate using Lingala, the lingua franca.

The Democratic Republic of the Congo won its independence from Belgium in 1960, followed by years of political and social instability. The country has experienced conflict stemming from decades of civil war and corruption, which still exists today. And while the economic situation in the DRC has improved over the past two decades, in 2018 about 72 percent of the population lived in extreme poverty. Less than half of the population has access to clean drinking water, and only 20 percent has access to sanitation.

The country's largely rural population faces a high burden of communicable and non-communicable diseases, as well as injuries. Significant causes of death include malaria, tuberculosis, lower respiratory infections, neonatal disorders, diarrheal diseases, stroke, ischemic heart disease, road injuries, hypertensive heart disease, cirrhosis, congenital defects, and HIV/AIDS. A number of Ebola outbreaks has also burdened the DRC. Fears of epidemic coupled with violence across the country has contributed to a growing public health challenge: poor mental health and depressive disorders. Unfortunately, maternal and child health indicators have not improved significantly since the beginning of the century.

105M
Population

$557
GDP Per Capita

61 years
Life Expectancy
↑ Improving

9
Doctors/100k
Physician Density

80
Beds/100k
Hospital Bed Density

473
Deaths/100k
Maternal Mortality

Democratic Republic of the Congo (DRC)

Nonprofit Organizations

143 LIFE Foundation
Seeks to educate and empower individuals living with malaria, TB, HIV/AIDS, STDs and other health disparities related to sexual health.
Infect Dis, MF Med
🌐 https://vfmat.ch/d59b

A.F.R.I.C.A.N. Foundation
Aims to improve cardiovascular health in Sub-Saharan Africa.
CV Med, Crit-Care
🌐 https://vfmat.ch/517e

Abt Associates
Seeks to improve the quality of life and economic well-being of people worldwide, while striving to meet and exceed the highest professional standards.
General, Logist-Op, MF Med, OB-GYN, Peds
🌐 https://vfmat.ch/cec2

Accomplish Children's Trust
Provides education and medical care to children with disabilities. Also addresses the financial implications of caring for a child with disabilities by helping families to earn an income.
Neuro, Peds, Rehab
🌐 https://vfmat.ch/de84

Action Against Hunger
Aims to end life-threatening hunger for good through treating and preventing malnutrition across more than 45 countries.
Nutr
🌐 https://vfmat.ch/2dbc

Advance Family Planning
Aims to achieve global expansion and access to quality contraceptive information, services, and supplies through financial investment and political commitment.
General, MF Med, Pub Health
🌐 https://vfmat.ch/7478

Africa CDC
Aims to strengthen the capacity and capability of Africa's public health institutions and partnerships to detect and respond quickly and effectively to disease threats and outbreaks, based on data-driven interventions and programs.
Infect Dis, Logist-Op, Pub Health
🌐 https://vfmat.ch/339c

Africa Health Organisation
Leads collaborative efforts among countries in Africa and other partners to promote health equity, combat disease, and improve quality of life.
Logist-Op, Pub Health
🌐 https://vfmat.ch/b1c5

Africa Humanitarian Action (AHA)
Responds to crises, conflicts, and disasters in Africa, while informing and advising the international community, governments, civil society, and the private sector on humanitarian issues of concern to Africa. Supports institutional and organizational development efforts.
General, Infect Dis, MF Med, Nutr, OB-GYN
🌐 https://vfmat.ch/3ca2

Africa Indoor Residual Spraying Project (AIRS)
Aims to protect millions of people in Africa from malaria by spraying insecticide on walls, ceilings, and other indoor resting places of mosquitoes that transmit malaria.
Infect Dis
🌐 https://vfmat.ch/9bd1

Africa Inland Mission International
Seeks to establish churches and community development programs including healthcare projects, based in Christian ministry.
Anesth, Dent-OMFS, ER Med, General, MF Med, Medicine, OB-GYN, OB-GYN, Ophth-Opt, Ped Surg, Peds, Rehab
🌐 https://vfmat.ch/f2f6

Africa Relief and Community Development
Provides comprehensive relief and developmental aid to people of the African continent regardless of gender, race, or religion.
Nutr, Pub Health
🌐 https://vfmat.ch/6cd2

African Field Epidemiology Network (AFENET)
Strengthens field epidemiology and public health laboratory capacity to contribute effectively to addressing epidemics and other major public health problems in Africa.
All-Immu, Infect Dis, Path, Pub Health
🌐 https://vfmat.ch/df2e

Against Malaria Foundation
Helps protect people from malaria. Funds anti-malaria nets, specifically long-lasting insecticidal nets (LLINs), and works with distribution partners to ensure they are used. Tracks and reports on net use and malaria case data.
Infect Dis
🌐 https://vfmat.ch/337d

AISPO
Implements international initiatives in the healthcare sector and remains involved in various projects to combat poverty, social injustice, and disease around the world.
All-Immu, ER Med, GI, General, Infect Dis, Logist-Op, MF Med, Neonat, OB-GYN, Peds, Psych, Pub Health, Radiol
🌐 https://vfmat.ch/c9e6

Al Basar International Foundation
Works with local partners to treat preventable blindness, and helps set up sustainable infrastructure so local teams can save sight in their communities.
Ophth-Opt
⊕ https://vfmat.ch/a8b5

Alight
Works closely with refugees, trafficked persons, economic migrants, and other displaced persons to co-design solutions that help them build full and fulfilling lives, with healthcare, clean water, shelter protection, and economic opportunity.
ER Med, General, Infect Dis, MF Med, Neonat, Peds
⊕ https://vfmat.ch/5993

Alliance for International Medical Action, The (ALIMA)
Provides quality medical care to vulnerable populations, partnering with and developing national medical organizations and conducting medical research to bring innovation to 12 African countries where ALIMA works.
ER Med, General, Infect Dis, Logist-Op, MF Med, OB-GYN, Path, Peds, Psych, Pub Health
⊕ https://vfmat.ch/1c11

Alliance for Smiles
Improves the lives of children and communities impacted by cleft by providing free comprehensive treatment while building local capacity for long-term care.
Dent-OMFS, Ped Surg, Plast, Surg
⊕ https://vfmat.ch/bb32

American Academy of Pediatrics
Seeks to attain optimal physical, mental, and social health and well-being for all infants, children, adolescents, and young adults.
Anesth, Crit-Care, Neonat, Ped Surg
⊕ https://vfmat.ch/9633

American Foundation for Children with AIDS
Provides critical comprehensive services to infected and affected HIV-positive children and their caregivers.
Infect Dis, Nutr, Pub Health
⊕ https://vfmat.ch/6258

Americares
Saves lives and improves health for people affected by poverty or disaster and responds with life-changing medicine, medical supplies, and health programs including domestic and global medical clinics.
All-Immu, ER Med, General, Infect Dis, MF Med, Nutr
⊕ https://vfmat.ch/e567

Amref Health Africa
Serves millions of people across 35 countries in Sub-Saharan Africa, strengthening health systems, and training African health workers to respond to the continent's most critical health issues.
All-Immu, General, Infect Dis, Logist-Op, MF Med, OB-GYN, Path, Pub Health, Surg
⊕ https://vfmat.ch/6985

AO Alliance
Builds solutions to lessen the burden of injuries in low- and middle-income countries, while enhancing the care of the injured to reduce human suffering, disability, and poverty.
Ortho, Surg
⊕ https://vfmat.ch/8cd5

Association of Medical Doctors of Asia (AMDA)
Strives to support people affected by disasters and economic distress on their road to recovery, establishing a true partnership with special emphasis on local initiative.
ER Med, Logist-Op, Pub Health
⊕ https://vfmat.ch/e3d4

Bureau of International Health Cooperation
Seeks to improve healthcare around the world, including developing countries, using expertise, and contribute to healthier lives of Japanese people by bringing these experiences back to Japan.
ER Med, Heme-Onc, Infect Dis, Peds, Pub Health
⊕ https://vfmat.ch/947d

Canada-Africa Community Health Alliance
Sends Canadian volunteer teams on two- to three-week missions to African communities to work hand-in-hand with local partners.
General, Infect Dis, MF Med, OB-GYN, Peds, Surg
⊕ https://vfmat.ch/4c94

Canadian Foundation for Women's Health
Seeks to advance the health of women in Canada and around the world through research, education, and advocacy in obstetrics and gynecology.
MF Med, OB-GYN
⊕ https://vfmat.ch/f41e

CARE
Works around the globe to save lives, defeat poverty, and achieve social justice.
ER Med, General
⊕ https://vfmat.ch/7232

Carter Center, The
Seeks to prevent and resolve conflicts, enhance freedom and democracy, and improve health, while remaining committed to human rights and the alleviation of human suffering.
Infect Dis, MF Med, Ophth-Opt
⊕ https://vfmat.ch/6556

Catholic Organization for Relief & Development Aid (CORDAID)
Provides humanitarian assistance and creates opportunities to improve security, healthcare, education, and inclusive economic growth in fragile and conflict-affected areas.
ER Med, Infect Dis, MF Med, OB-GYN, Peds, Psych
⊕ https://vfmat.ch/8ae5

Catholic World Mission
Works to rebuild communities worldwide by helping to alleviate poverty and empower underserved areas, while spreading the message of the Catholic Church.
ER Med, General, Nutr, Peds
⊕ https://vfmat.ch/7b5f

Center for Strategic and International Studies (CSIS) Commission on Strengthening America's Health Security
Brings together a distinguished and diverse group of high-level opinion leaders bridging security and health, with the core aim to chart a bold vision for the future of U.S. leadership in global health.
ER Med, Infect Dis, MF Med, Pub Health
⊕ https://vfmat.ch/6d7f

Central Congo Partnership
Collaborates with Partners in Mission to work with other clinical leadership in the Congo, providing assessment of the medical needs of underserved communities toward developing strategic responses.
General, Ophth-Opt, Surg
⊕ https://vfmat.ch/2eb4

Chain of Hope (La Chaîne de l'Espoir)
Helps underprivileged children around the world by providing them with access to healthcare.
Anesth, CT Surg, Crit-Care, ER Med, Neurosurg, Ortho, Ped Surg, Surg, Vasc Surg
⊕ https://vfmat.ch/e871

Christian Blind Mission (CBM)
Aims to improve the quality of life of persons with disabilities in the poorest countries, addressing poverty as a cause and a consequence of disability, and working in partnership to create a society for all.
ENT, General, Infect Dis, OB-GYN, Ophth-Opt, Ortho, Peds, Psych, Rehab, Surg
⊕ https://vfmat.ch/3824

Christian Connections for International Health (CCIH)
Promotes global health and wholeness from a Christian perspective.
All-Immu, General, Infect Dis, MF Med, Neonat, OB-GYN, Psych
⊕ https://vfmat.ch/fa5d

Christian Health Service Corps

Brings Christian doctors, health professionals, and health educators committed to serving the poor to places that otherwise have little or no access to healthcare.

Anesth, Dent-OMFS, General, Medicine, Peds, Surg

⊕ https://vfmat.ch/da57

Clinton Health Access Initiative (CHAI)

Aims to save lives and reduce the burden of disease in low- and middle-income countries. Works with partners to strengthen the capabilities of governments and the private sector to create and sustain high-quality health systems.

General, Heme-Onc, Infect Dis, Logist-Op, MF Med, Medicine, Neonat, Nutr, OB-GYN, Path, Peds, Rad-Onc

⊕ https://vfmat.ch/9ed7

Concern Worldwide

Seeks to permanently transform the lives of people living in extreme poverty, tackling its root causes, and building resilience.

Logist-Op, MF Med, Nutr, OB-GYN

⊕ https://vfmat.ch/77e9

CONDADA Congolese Doctors and Dentists Association UK

Strives to improve and advance healthcare provision through a growing network of medical and dental professionals.

Infect Dis, Logist-Op, OB-GYN, Peds

⊕ https://vfmat.ch/38da

Congo River Journey

Aims to make a difference in the healthcare of thousands of people in Lukolela, Democratic Republic of the Congo, through its hospital, St. Vincent the Servant.

General, Infect Dis, OB-GYN, Psych, Surg

⊕ https://vfmat.ch/e4da

Core Group

Aims to improve and expand community health practices for underserved populations, especially women and children, through collaborative action and learning.

General, Infect Dis, MF Med, Medicine, OB-GYN, Peds, Pub Health

⊕ https://vfmat.ch/9de3

COVID-19 Clinical Research Coalition

Advocates and collaborates for the advancement of COVID-19 research driven by the needs of low-resource settings, and works for equitable access to solutions to the pandemic.

All-Immu, Infect-Dis, MF Med, Path, Pub Health

⊕ https://vfmat.ch/d1f4

Cura for the World

Seeks to heal, nourish, and embrace the neglected by building medical clinics in remote communities in dire need of medical care.

ER Med, General, Peds

⊕ https://vfmat.ch/c55f

Dikembe Mutombo Foundation

Strives to improve the health, education, and quality of life for the people of the Democratic Republic of the Congo through an emphasis on primary healthcare and disease prevention, the promotion of health policy, health research, and increased access to healthcare education.

All-Immu, Dent-OMFS, OB-GYN, Ophth-Opt, Ortho, Ped Surg, Surg

⊕ https://vfmat.ch/85d4

Direct Relief

Improves the health and lives of people affected by poverty or emergency situations by mobilizing and providing essential medical resources needed for their care.

ER Med, Logist-Op

⊕ https://vfmat.ch/58e5

Doctors Without Borders/Médecins Sans Frontières (MSF)

Responds to emergencies and provides lifesaving medical care where needed most, including during disasters, conflicts, and epidemics.

Anesth, Crit-Care, ER Med, General, Infect Dis, Nutr, OB-GYN, Ped Surg, Peds, Psych, Pub Health, Surg

⊕ https://vfmat.ch/f363

Drugs for Neglected Diseases Initiative

Develops lifesaving medicines for people with neglected diseases around the world, having developed eight treatments for five deadly diseases and saved millions of lives since 2003.

Infect Dis, Pub Health

⊕ https://vfmat.ch/969c

Effect: Hope (The Leprosy Mission Canada)

Connects like-minded Canadians to people suffering in isolation from debilitating, neglected tropical diseases such as leprosy, lymphatic filariasis, and Buruli ulcer.

General, Infect Dis

⊕ https://vfmat.ch/f12a

eHealth Africa

Builds stronger health systems in Africa through the design and implementation of data-driven solutions, responding to local needs and providing underserved communities with the necessary tools to lead healthier lives.

Logist-Op, Path

⊕ https://vfmat.ch/db6a

Elizabeth Glaser Pediatric AIDS Foundation

Seeks to end global pediatric HIV/AIDS through prevention and treatment programs, research, and advocacy.

Infect Dis, Nutr, OB-GYN, Peds

⊕ https://vfmat.ch/d6ec

Enabel

As the development agency of the Belgian federal government, charged with implementing Belgium's international development policy, carries out public service assignments in Belgium and abroad pursuant to the 2030 Agenda for Sustainable Development.

General, Infect Dis, Logist-Op, MF Med, OB-GYN, Peds, Pub Health

⊕ https://vfmat.ch/5af7

END Fund, The

Aims to control and eliminate the most prevalent neglected diseases among the world's poorest and most vulnerable people.

Infect Dis

⊕ https://vfmat.ch/2614

EngenderHealth

Works to implement high-quality, gender-equitable programs that advance sexual and reproductive health and rights.

General, MF Med, OB-GYN, Peds

⊕ https://vfmat.ch/1cb2

Episcopal Relief & Development

Provides relief in times of disaster and promotes sustainable development by identifying and addressing the root causes of suffering.

Infect Dis, MF Med, Neonat, Nutr, Peds

⊕ https://vfmat.ch/7cfa

eRanger

Provides sustainable solutions to transportation and medical provision such as ambulances and mobile clinics in developing countries.

ER Med, General, Logist-Op

⊕ https://vfmat.ch/4c18

Fistula Foundation

Aims to engage the support of people worldwide who are eager to see the day that no woman suffers from obstetric fistula. Raises and directs funds to doctors and hospitals providing life-transforming surgery to women in need.

OB-GYN

⊕ https://vfmat.ch/e958

Fondation Follereau

Promotes the quality of life of the most vulnerable African communities. Alongside trusted partners, the foundation supports local initiatives in healthcare and education.

General, Infect Dis, OB-GYN

⊕ https://vfmat.ch/bcc7

Fracarita International

Provides support and services in the fields of mental healthcare, care for people with a disability, and education.

Psych, Rehab

⊕ https://vfmat.ch/8d3c

Friends of Butoke

Supports the community of Butoke in the West Kasai Province of the Democratic Republic of the Congo by ministering to victims of poverty, oppression, and abuse in areas of food security and nutrition, education, access to healthcare, malnutrition, care of those with disabilities, and human rights.

ER Med, General, Nutr, OB-GYN, Peds, Surg

⊕ https://vfmat.ch/1518

Gift of Life International

Provides lifesaving cardiac treatment to children in developing countries while developing sustainable pediatric cardiac programs by implementing screening, surgical, and training missions.

Anesth, CT Surg, CV Med, Crit-Care, Ped Surg, Peds, Pulm-Critic

⊕ https://vfmat.ch/f2f9

Global Alliance to Prevent Prematurity And Stillbirth (GAPPS)

Seeks to improve birth outcomes worldwide by reducing the burden of premature birth and stillbirth.

All-Immu, Infect Dis, MF Med, Neonat, Neonat, OB-GYN

⊕ https://vfmat.ch/3f74

Global Clubfoot Initiative (GCI)

Promotes and resources the treatment of children with clubfoot in developing countries using the Ponseti technique.

Ortho, Ped Surg

⊕ https://vfmat.ch/f229

Global Ministries – The United Methodist Church

As the worldwide mission and development agency of The United Methodist Church, Global Ministries works with more than 300 hospitals and clinics around the world through its Global Health Unit.

Anesth, CT Surg, CV Med, Crit-Care, Dent-OMFS, Derm, ER Med, GI, General, Infect Dis, Logist-Op, MF Med, Medicine, Neonat, Nephro, Nutr, OB-GYN, Ophth-Opt, Ortho, Palliative, Peds, Pod, Psych, Pub Health, Rehab, Rheum, Surg, Urol

⊕ https://vfmat.ch/1723

Global Network for Women and Children's Health Research

Aims to improve maternal and child health outcomes and building health research capacity in resource-poor settings by testing cost-effective, sustainable interventions that provide guidance for the practice of evidence-based medicine. Scientists from developing countries, together with peers in the United States, lead teams that address priority research needs through randomized clinical trials and implementation research conducted in low-resource areas.

MF Med, OB-GYN

⊕ https://vfmat.ch/a187

Global Offsite Care

Aims to be a catalyst for increased access to specialized healthcare for all, and provides technology platforms to doctors and clinics around the world through Rotary Club-sponsored telemedicine projects.

Crit-Care, ER Med, General, Pulm-Critic

⊕ https://vfmat.ch/61b5

Global Oncology (GO)

Brings the best in cancer care to underserved patients around the world and collaborates across geographic, professional, and academic borders to improve cancer care, research, and education.

Heme-Onc, Path, Rad-Onc

⊕ https://vfmat.ch/fcb8

Global Outreach Doctors

Provides global health medical services in developing countries affected by famine, infant mortality, and chronic health issues.

All-Immu, Anesth, ER Med, General, Infect Dis, MF Med, Peds, Surg

⊕ https://vfmat.ch/8514

Global Strategies

Empowers communities in the most neglected areas of the world to improve the lives of women and children through healthcare.

MF Med, Neonat, OB-GYN, Peds

⊕ https://vfmat.ch/ef92

Globus Relief

Aims to improve the delivery of healthcare worldwide by gathering, processing, and distributing surplus medical supplies to charities at home and abroad.

Logist-Op

⊕ https://vfmat.ch/a2b7

Good Shepard International Foundation

Strives to promote inclusive and sustainable development for the most marginalized and vulnerable people, with a special focus on women, girls, and children, inspired by the Christian faith.

ER Med

⊕ https://vfmat.ch/ad9a

Grassroot Soccer

Leverages the power of soccer to educate, inspire, and mobilize at-risk youth in developing countries to overcome their greatest health challenges, live healthier and more productive lives, and be agents for change in their communities.

Infect Dis

⊕ https://vfmat.ch/3521

Hands At Work

Based in Christian ministry, supports those in need through its community intervention model with a focus on food security, education, and basic healthcare.

General, Infect Dis, Nutr, Pub Health

⊕ https://vfmat.ch/7274

HandUp Congo

Responds to community requests by providing the tools and training to help Congolese communities generate income to improve education, health, and well-being.

Crit-Care, ER Med, General, MF Med, Ophth-Opt, Pub Health

⊕ https://vfmat.ch/7a8b

HEAL Africa

Compassionately serves vulnerable people and communities in the Democratic Republic of the Congo through a holistic approach to healthcare, education, community action, and leadership development in response to changing needs.

Medicine, OB-GYN, Ortho, Peds, Surg

⊕ https://vfmat.ch/cf5d

Heineman Medical Outreach

Provides medical and educational assistance globally to promote sustainable healthcare and enhanced living standards in underserved communities through the International Medical Outreach (IMO) program, a collaborative partnership between Heineman Medical Outreach and Atrium Health.

Anesth, CT Surg, CV Med, ER Med, General, Heme-Onc, Logist-Op, Medicine, Neonat, OB-GYN, Ped Surg, Peds, Surg, Vasc Surg

⊕ https://vfmat.ch/389b

Hope and Healing International

Gives hope and healing to children and families trapped by poverty and disability.

General, Nutr, Ophth-Opt, Peds, Rehab

⊕ https://vfmat.ch/c638

Hope Walks

Frees children, families, and communities from the burden of clubfoot, inspired by the Christian faith.

Ortho, Ped Surg, Peds, Rehab

⊕ https://vfmat.ch/f6d4

Hospice Africa

Aims to provide a holistic and culturally sensitive palliative care service through accurate treatment of pain.

Palliative

⊕ https://vfmat.ch/9f86

Humanity First

Provides aid and assistance to those in need, offering sustainable development solutions to society while providing and empowering local communities with the resources to help themselves.

ER Med, General, MF Med, Ophth-Opt

⊕ https://vfmat.ch/13cc

ICAP at Columbia University

Serves as global leader in supporting the scale-up of multidisciplinary HIV/AIDS prevention, care, and treatment programs based on a family-focused approach.

General, Infect Dis, MF Med, Medicine, OB-GYN, Pub Health

⊕ https://vfmat.ch/a8ef

IMA World Health

Works to build healthier communities by collaborating with key partners to serve vulnerable people with a focus on health, healing, and well-being for all.

Infect Dis, MF Med, Nutr, OB-GYN, Pub Health

⊕ https://vfmat.ch/8316

Imaging the World

Develops sustainable models for ultrasound imaging in the world's lowest resource settings and uses a technology-enabled solution to improve healthcare access, integrating lifesaving ultrasound and training programs in rural communities.

Logist-Op, OB-GYN, Radiol

⊕ https://vfmat.ch/59e4

International Agency for the Prevention of Blindness (IAPB), The

Leads international efforts in blindness-prevention activities, works toward a world where no one is needlessly visually impaired, and ensures that everyone has access to the best possible standard of eye health.

Infect Dis, Ophth-Opt, Pub Health

⊕ https://vfmat.ch/87a2

International Council of Ophthalmology

Works with ophthalmologic societies and others to enhance ophthalmic education and improve access to the highest-quality eye care in order to preserve and restore vision for people of the world.

Ophth-Opt

⊕ https://vfmat.ch/ffd2

International Federation of Red Cross and Red Crescent Societies (IFRC)

Coordinates and directs international assistance following natural and manmade disasters in nonconflict situations through the world's largest humanitarian and development network. Provides disaster-preparedness programs, healthcare activities, and promotes humanitarian values.

ER Med, General, Infect Dis, Nutr

⊕ https://vfmat.ch/b4ee

International Medical Corps

Seeks to improve quality of life through health interventions and related activities that strengthen underserved communities worldwide, with the flexibility to respond rapidly to emergencies and offer medical services and training to people at the highest risk.

ER Med, General, Infect Dis, Nutr, OB-GYN, Peds, Pub Health, Surg

⊕ https://vfmat.ch/a8a5

International Organization for Migration (IOM) – The UN Migration Agency

Promotes evidence-informed policies and holistic, preventive, and curative health programs that are beneficial, accessible, and equitable for vulnerable migrants.

General, Infect Dis, OB-GYN

⊕ https://vfmat.ch/621a

International Pediatric Nephrology Association (IPNA)

Leads global efforts to successfully address the care for all children with kidney disease through advocacy, education, and training.

Medicine, Nephro, Peds

⊕ https://vfmat.ch/b59d

International Planned Parenthood Federation (IPPF)

Leads a locally owned, globally connected civil society movement that provides and enables services and champions sexual and reproductive health and rights for all, especially the underserved.

Infect Dis, MF Med, OB-GYN

⊕ https://vfmat.ch/dc97

International Rescue Committee (IRC)

Responds to the world's worst humanitarian crises and helps people whose lives and livelihoods are shattered by conflict and disaster to survive, recover, and gain control of their future.

ER Med, General, Infect Dis, MF Med, Peds

⊕ https://vfmat.ch/5d24

International Trachoma Initiative (iTi)

Works toward a world free from trachoma, a preventable cause of blindness, and provides comprehensive support to national ministries of health and governmental and nongovernmental organizations to implement a comprehensive approach to fight trachoma.

Infect Dis, Ophth-Opt

⊕ https://vfmat.ch/3278

International Union Against Tuberculosis and Lung Disease

Develops, implements, and assesses anti-tuberculosis, lung health, and noncommunicable disease programs.

Infect Dis, Pub Health, Pulm-Critic

⊕ https://vfmat.ch/3e82

Intersos

Provides emergency medical assistance to victims of armed conflicts, natural disasters, and extreme exclusion, with particular attention to the protection of the most vulnerable people.

ER Med, General, Nutr

⊕ https://vfmat.ch/dbac

InterSurgeon

Fosters collaborative partnerships in the field of global surgery that will advance clinical care, teaching, training, research, and the provision and maintenance of medical equipment.

ENT, Neurosurg, Ortho, Ped Surg, Plast, Surg, Urol

⊕ https://vfmat.ch/6f8a

IntraHealth International

Improves the performance of health workers and strengthens the systems in which they work.

CV Med, Endo, General, Infect Dis, MF Med, Neonat, Nutr, OB-GYN

⊕ https://vfmat.ch/ddc8

Ipas

Focuses efforts on women and girls who want contraception or abortion, and builds programs around their needs and how best to support them.

OB-GYN

⊕ https://vfmat.ch/8e39

Izumi Foundation

Develops and supports programs that improve health and healthcare in neglected regions of Africa and Latin America.

⊕ https://vfmat.ch/f29a

Jericho Road Community Health Center

Provides holistic healthcare for underserved and marginalized communities around the world, inspired by the Christian faith.

Anesth, General, Heme-Onc, Infect Dis, Medicine, OB-GYN, Ped Surg, Peds, Psych, Surg

⊕ https://vfmat.ch/3d6b

Jewish World Watch

Brings help and healing to survivors of mass atrocities around the globe and seeks to inspire people of all faiths and cultures to join the ongoing fight against genocide.

ER Med, Logist-Op, OB-GYN, Peds

⊕ https://vfmat.ch/8c92

Jhpiego

Creates and delivers transformative healthcare solutions that save lives, in partnership with national governments, health experts, and local communities.

General, Infect Dis, OB-GYN, Surg

⊕ https://vfmat.ch/45b8

John Snow, Inc. (JSI)

Aims to improve the health and well-being of underserved and vulnerable people and communities throughout the world.

General, Infect Dis, Logist-Op, MF Med, OB-GYN, Peds, Psych, Pub Health

⊕ https://vfmat.ch/ba78

Johns Hopkins Center for Communication Programs

Believes in the power of communication to save lives by empowering people to adopt healthy behaviors for themselves, their families, and their communities.

General, Infect Dis, Logist-Op, OB-GYN, Pub Health

⊕ https://vfmat.ch/1bf9

Johns Hopkins Center for Global Health

Facilitates and focuses the extensive expertise and resources of the Johns Hopkins institutions, together with global collaborators, to effectively address and ameliorate the world's most pressing health issues.

General, Genetics, Logist-Op, MF Med, Peds, Psych, Pub Health, Pulm-Critic

⊕ https://vfmat.ch/54ce

Joint United Nations Programme on HIV/AIDS (UNAIDS)

Aims to place people living with HIV and people affected by the virus at the decision-making table and at the center of designing, delivering, and monitoring the AIDS response.

Infect Dis

⊕ https://vfmat.ch/464a

Kids Care Everywhere

Seeks to empower physicians in under-resourced environments with multimedia, state-of-the-art medical software, and to inspire young professionals to become future global healthcare leaders.

Logist-Op, Ped Surg, Peds

⊕ https://vfmat.ch/bc23

Last Mile Health

Links community health workers with frontline health workers—nurses, doctors, and midwives at community clinics—and supports them to bring lifesaving services to the doorsteps of people living far from care.

General, Logist-Op, OB-GYN, Pub Health

⊕ https://vfmat.ch/37da

Leja Bulela

Supports internally displaced persons living in Tshibombo Tshimuangi, Democratic Republic of the Congo, and the residents of Kasai-Oriental Province with initiatives that promote adequate healthcare, educational opportunities, and agricultural opportunities.

General, OB-GYN, Peds

⊕ https://vfmat.ch/afee

Leprosy Mission International

Seeks to empower people with leprosy to attain healing, dignity, and life in all its fullness.

Infect Dis

⊕ https://vfmat.ch/95a9

Life for a Child

Supports the provision of the best possible healthcare, given local circumstances, to all children and youth with diabetes in less-resourced countries, through the strengthening of existing diabetes services.

Endo, Medicine, Peds

⊕ https://vfmat.ch/d712

LifeNet International

Transforms African healthcare by equipping and empowering existing local health centers to provide quality, sustainable, and lifesaving care to patients.

General, Infect Dis, MF Med, Neonat, OB-GYN, Pub Health

⊕ https://vfmat.ch/e5d2

Light for the World

Contributes to a world in which persons with disabilities fully exercise their rights, and assists persons with disabilities living in poverty.

Ophth-Opt, Rehab

⊕ https://vfmat.ch/3ff6

Light House Medical Missions

Inspired by the Christian faith, provides programs in healthcare provision, nutrition, emergency relief and response, and water, sanitation, and hygiene (WASH).

ER Med, General, Surg

⊕ https://vfmat.ch/cecd

Limbs International

Engages communities and transforms lives through affordable, sustainable prosthetic solutions and rehabilitation services in developing countries.

Logist-Op, Ortho, Pod, Rehab

⊕ https://vfmat.ch/dc84

London School of Hygiene & Tropical Medicine: Health in Humanitarian Crises Centre

Advances health and health equity in crisis-affected countries through research, education, and translation of knowledge into policy and practice.

ER Med, Infect Dis, Pub Health

⊕ https://vfmat.ch/96ad

MAGNA International

Helps those who are suffering or recovering from conflicts and disasters by reducing the risks of diseases and treating them immediately.

ER Med, General, Infect Dis, Peds, Surg

⊕ https://vfmat.ch/58f4

Malaika

Operates in the Democratic Republic of Congo with the mission of empowering girls and their communities through education and health.

General, Infect Dis

⊕ https://vfmat.ch/94ad

Management Sciences for Health (MSH)

Works with countries and communities to save lives and improve the health of the world's poorest and most vulnerable people by building strong, resilient, sustainable health systems.

Infect Dis, Logist-Op, Pub Health

⊕ https://vfmat.ch/6aa2

MAP International

Provides medicines and health supplies to those in need around the world so they might experience life to the fullest.

Logist-Op

⊕ https://vfmat.ch/deed

Marie Stopes International

Provides the contraception and safe abortion services that enable women all over the world to choose their own futures.

Infect Dis, MF Med, Neonat, OB-GYN, Pub Health

⊕ https://vfmat.ch/9525

Medair

Works to relieve human suffering in some of the world's most remote and devastated places, saving lives in emergencies and helping people in crises survive and recover, inspired by the Christian faith.

ER Med, General, Logist-Op, MF Med, Pub Health

⊕ https://vfmat.ch/5b33

Medical Benevolence Foundation (MBF)

Works with partners in developing countries to build sustainable healthcare for those most in need through faith-based global medical missions.

General, Logist-Op, MF Med, OB-GYN, Surg

⊕ https://vfmat.ch/c3e8

Medical Care Development International (MCD International)

Works to strengthen health systems through innovative, sustainable interventions.

Infect Dis, Logist-Op, OB-GYN, Pub Health
⊕ https://vfmat.ch/dc5c

Medical Care Development International
Works to improve the health of vulnerable populations through integrated, sustainable, and locally driven interventions.
Infect Dis, OB-GYN, Peds, Pub Health
⊕ https://vfmat.ch/da87

Medical Mission Aid Inc
Advances effective healthcare in disadvantaged communities through medical scholarships, grants for supplies and support for local health initiatives.
Infect Dis, Logist-Op, OB-GYN, Pub Health, Rehab
⊕ https://vfmat.ch/8b83

MedShare
Aims to improve the quality of life of people, communities, and the planet by sourcing and directly delivering surplus medical supplies and equipment to communities in need around the world.
Logist-Op
⊕ https://vfmat.ch/c8bc

MENTOR Initiative
Saves lives in emergencies through tropical disease control, and helps people recover from crisis with dignity, working side by side with communities, health workers, and health authorities to leave a lasting impact.
ER Med, Infect Dis
⊕ https://vfmat.ch/3bd5

Mercy and Love Foundation
Aims to provide orphaned and vulnerable children with basic human needs such as food, clothing, and shelter, enabling them to thrive.
General, Peds
⊕ https://vfmat.ch/649a

Mercy Ships
Operates hospital ships staffed by volunteers to bring hope, healing, and healthcare to underserved communities worldwide.
Anesth, Dent-OMFS, Logist-Op, Neonat, OB-GYN, Ophth-Opt, Ortho, Palliative, Plast, Psych, Surg
⊕ https://vfmat.ch/2e99

MiracleFeet
Brings low-cost treatment to every child on the planet born with clubfoot, a leading cause of physical disability.
Ortho, Peds, Rehab
⊕ https://vfmat.ch/bda8

Mission Bambini
Helps to support children living in poverty and sickness, and lacking education, giving them the opportunity for and hope of a better life.
CT Surg, CV Med, Crit-Care, ER Med, Ped Surg, Peds
⊕ https://vfmat.ch/dc1a

Mission Regan
Collects supplies, medication, and medical equipment and provides them to those who are in desperate need, both locally and globally.
Logist-Op
⊕ https://vfmat.ch/2bc1

MPACT for Mankind
Transforms communities by improving health outcomes, enhancing knowledge, and providing hope while promoting sustainable growth.
ER Med, General
⊕ https://vfmat.ch/1c61

MSD for Mothers
Designs scalable solutions that help end preventable maternal deaths.
MF Med, OB-GYN, Pub Health
⊕ https://vfmat.ch/9f99

MSI Reproductive Choices (Marie Stopes International)
Seeks to deliver quality family planning and reproductive healthcare to women

around the world.
MF Med
⊕ https://vfmat.ch/5c82

Médecins du Monde/Doctors of the World
Provides care, bears witness, and supports social change worldwide with innovative medical programs and evidence-based advocacy initiatives.
ER Med, General, Infect Dis, MF Med, Neonat, OB-GYN, Peds, Pub Health
⊕ https://vfmat.ch/a43d

New Horizons Collaborative
Advances a holistic, integrated approach to high-quality pediatric HIV care and treatment with a specific focus on those in need of advanced treatment.
Infect Dis, Peds, Pub Health
⊕ https://vfmat.ch/a76a

Norwegian People's Aid
Aims to improve living conditions, to create a democratic, just, and safe society.
ER Med, Logist-Op
⊕ https://vfmat.ch/2d8e

Nurses with Purpose
Supports nurses who have a passion to serve in their communities and abroad through medical mission trips in several different medical specialties.
General
⊕ https://vfmat.ch/384a

Operation Fistula
Exists to end obstetric fistula by building models of care that serve every woman, everywhere.
MF Med, OB-GYN, Surg
⊕ https://vfmat.ch/ce8e

Operation Smile
Treats patients with cleft lip and cleft palate, and creates solutions that deliver safe surgery to people where it's needed most.
Anesth, Dent-OMFS, ENT, Ped Surg, Plast
⊕ https://vfmat.ch/5c29

Operation Walk
Provides the gift of mobility through life-changing joint replacement surgeries, at no cost for those in need in the U.S. and globally.
Anesth, Ortho, Rehab, Surg
⊕ https://vfmat.ch/bafe

Options
Believes in a world in which women and children can access the high-quality health services they need, without financial burden.
Logist-Op, MF Med, Neonat, OB-GYN
⊕ https://vfmat.ch/3a48

Order of Malta
Supports forgotten or excluded people, especially those living in conflict zones or amid natural disasters, by providing medical assistance, caring for refugees, and distributing medicines and necessities.
ER Med, General, Infect Dis, MF Med, Nephro, OB-GYN, Ortho, Psych
⊕ https://vfmat.ch/1fab

Organization for the Prevention of Blindness, The (OPC)
Provides research, and treatments and cures for people affected by blindness and blinding diseases in Francophone Africa.
Infect Dis, Ophth-Opt
⊕ https://vfmat.ch/86d6

Pact
Works on the ground to improve the lives of those who are challenged by poverty and marginalization, striving for a world in which all people are heard, capable, and vibrant.
Infect Dis, Logist-Op, MF Med, Pub Health
⊕ https://vfmat.ch/9a6c

Panzi Hospital and Foundations
Creates a safe space that supports women's physical healing, fosters their

emotional recovery, and helps rebuild livelihoods and communities for survivors of sexual violence.

Derm, ENT, GI, Infect Dis, Medicine, OB-GYN, Ophth-Opt, Peds, Rehab, Rheum, Urol

⊕ https://vfmat.ch/1686

PATH
Advances health equity through innovation and partnerships so people, communities, and economies can thrive.

All-Immu, CV Med, Endo, Heme-Onc, Infect Dis, MF Med, Neonat, Nutr, OB-GYN, Path, Peds, Pulm-Critic

⊕ https://vfmat.ch/b4db

Pathfinder International
Champions sexual and reproductive health and rights worldwide, mobilizing communities most in need to break through barriers and forge paths to a healthier future.

OB-GYN

⊕ https://vfmat.ch/a7b3

Paul Carlson Partnership
Works together with partners in Africa to invest in local efforts in medical and economic development.

ER Med, General

⊕ https://vfmat.ch/cef2

Philips Foundation
Aims to reduce healthcare inequality by providing access to quality healthcare for disadvantaged communities.

CV Med, OB-GYN, Ped Surg, Peds, Surg, Urol

⊕ https://vfmat.ch/bacb

Praesens
Provides solutions that improve surveillance and rapid deployment in case of disease outbreaks in areas regularly affected by epidemic and endemic diseases, while driving change and making countries safe from epidemics by working for and with local partners.

Logist-Op, Path, Pub Health

⊕ https://vfmat.ch/ab96

Première Urgence International
Helps civilians who are marginalized or excluded as a result of natural disasters, war, or economic collapse.

ER Med, General, MF Med, Peds, Psych

⊕ https://vfmat.ch/62ba

Project SOAR
Conducts HIV operations research around the world to identify practical solutions to improve HIV prevention, care, and treatment services.

ER Med, General, MF Med, OB-GYN, Psych

⊕ https://vfmat.ch/1a77

Purpose Medical Mission
Strives to achieve long-term and self-sustaining healthy communities where extreme poverty and lack of basic healthcare and education are a problem.

General, Logist-Op, Medicine, Pub Health, Surg

⊕ https://vfmat.ch/3fe7

RestoringVision
Empowers lives by restoring vision for millions of people in need.

Ophth-Opt

⊕ https://vfmat.ch/e121

Rockefeller Foundation, The
Works to promote the well-being of humanity.

Logist-Op, Nutr, Pub Health

⊕ https://vfmat.ch/5424

Rotary International
Provides service to others, improves lives, and advances world understanding, goodwill, and peace through its fellowship of business, professional, and community leaders.

ER Med, General, Infect Dis, MF Med, OB-GYN

⊕ https://vfmat.ch/8fb5

ROW Foundation
Works to improve the quality of training for healthcare providers, and the diagnosis and treatment available to people with epilepsy and associated psychiatric disorders in under-resourced areas of the world.

Neuro, Psych

⊕ https://vfmat.ch/25eb

Salvation Army International, The
Seeks to meet human needs through services in education, healthcare, community support, emergency response, and ministry development, inspired by the Christian faith.

Dent-OMFS, Derm, ER Med, Infect Dis, MF Med, Medicine, Nutr, OB-GYN, Ophth-Opt, Palliative, Psych, Rehab, Surg

⊕ https://vfmat.ch/8eb3

Sanofi Espoir Foundation
Contributes to reducing health inequalities among populations that need it most by applying a socially responsible approach focused on fighting childhood cancers in low-income countries, improving maternal and newborn health, and improving access to care.

ER Med, OB-GYN, Peds

⊕ https://vfmat.ch/943b

Save the Children
Gives children around the world a healthy start in life, the opportunity to learn, and protection from harm.

All-Immu, Crit-Care, ER Med, General, Infect Dis, MF Med, Medicine, Neonat, OB-GYN, Peds, Psych, Pub Health

⊕ https://vfmat.ch/2e73

Saving Moses
Aims to save babies, up to age 5, by meeting the most intense and urgent survival needs, where help is least available.

MF Med, Neonat, Nutr, OB-GYN, Peds

⊕ https://vfmat.ch/6a88

SCI Foundation
Seeks to prevent and treat neglected infectious diseases, with a focus on eliminating parasitic worm infections through strengthening impactful and comprehensive health programs across Sub-Saharan Africa.

Infect Dis, Pub Health

⊕ https://vfmat.ch/5444

SEE International
Provides sustainable medical, surgical, and educational services through volunteer ophthalmic surgeons, with the objectives of restoring sight and preventing blindness to disadvantaged individuals worldwide.

Ophth-Opt, Surg

⊕ https://vfmat.ch/6e1b

Sightsavers
Works with partners in developing countries to help eliminate avoidable blindness and advocates for equal opportunity for the disabled.

Infect Dis, Ophth-Opt, Surg

⊕ https://vfmat.ch/aa52

SIGN Fracture Care International
Builds orthopedic capacity around the world and provides the injured poor access to fracture surgery by donating orthopedic education and implant systems to surgeons in developing countries.

Ortho, Rehab, Surg

⊕ https://vfmat.ch/123d

SINA Health
Aims to improve the health and educational status of the population in low- and middle-income countries.

General, Logist-Op

⊕ https://vfmat.ch/9ad3

Smile Train, Inc.
Treats children with cleft lip through a sustainable and local model that supports surgery and other forms of essential care.
Logist-Op, Pub Health
⊕ https://vfmat.ch/822c

Sofia Global
Inspired by the Christian faith, promotes an equitable and sustainable society through education, healthcare, pastoral work, and community capacity-building.
General, Heme-Onc, Infect Dis, MF Med, OB-GYN, Peds
⊕ https://vfmat.ch/263c

Solthis
Improves disease prevention and access to quality care by strengthening the health systems and services of the countries served.
General, Infect Dis, Logist-Op, MF Med, Neonat, Path
⊕ https://vfmat.ch/a71d

Sri Sathya Sai International Organization
Inspired by spiritual teachings, carries out efforts in global healthcare, education, humanitarian relief, and youth engagement.
Dent-OMFS, General, Logist-Op, Nutr, Ophth-Opt, Pub Health
⊕ https://vfmat.ch/9bda

Surgical Healing of Africa's Youth Foundation, The (S.H.A.Y.)
Provides volunteer reconstructive surgery to children in need, including treating congenital anomalies such as cleft lip/palate and general reconstruction.
Anesth, Dent-OMFS, Peds, Plast
⊕ https://vfmat.ch/41a7

Sustainable Cardiovascular Health Equity Development Alliance
Fights cardiovascular disease in underserved populations globally via education, training, and increasing interventional capacity.
CV Med, Pub Health, Radiol
⊕ https://vfmat.ch/799c

Sustainable Kidney Care Foundation (SKCF)
Works to provide treatment for kidney injury where none exists, and aims to reduce mortality from treatable acute kidney injury (AKI).
Infect Dis, Medicine, Nephro
⊕ https://vfmat.ch/1926

Sustainable Medical Missions
Trains and supports Indigenous healthcare and faith leaders in underdeveloped communities to treat neglected tropical diseases (NTDs) and other endemic conditions affecting the poorest community members, by pairing faith-based solutions with best practices.
Infect Dis, Pub Health
⊕ https://vfmat.ch/9165

Swiss Tropical and Public Health Institute
Contributes to the improvement of the health of populations internationally, nationally, and locally through excellence in research, education, and services.
Infect Dis, Pub Health
⊕ https://vfmat.ch/2ee4

T1International
Supports local communities with the tools needed to stand up for the right to better access to insulin and diabetes supplies.
Endo, General, Medicine, Pub Health
⊕ https://vfmat.ch/d7d4

Task Force for Global Health, The
Consists of programs and focus areas that cover a range of global health issues including neglected tropical diseases, infectious diseases, vaccines, field epidemiology, public health informatics, health workforce development, and global health ethics.
Infect Dis, Logist-Op, Medicine, Ophth-Opt, Peds
⊕ https://vfmat.ch/714c

Tearfund
Responds to crisis and partners with local churches to bring restoration to those living in poverty, inspired by the Christian faith.
ER Med, Logist-Op
⊕ https://vfmat.ch/f6cf

Turing Foundation
Aims to contribute toward a better world and a better society by focusing on efforts such as health, art, education, and nature.
Infect Dis
⊕ https://vfmat.ch/6bcc

U.S. President's Malaria Initiative (PMI)
Supports low-income countries to help control and eliminate malaria through cost-effective, lifesaving malaria interventions.
Infect Dis, MF Med, OB-GYN
⊕ https://vfmat.ch/dc8b

UNC Health Foundation
Secures resources and supports empathy and expertise in patient care, research, education, and advocacy in underserved communities around the world.
Heme-Onc, Infect Dis, Neuro, Peds, Pub Health
⊕ https://vfmat.ch/7129

Union for International Cancer Control (UICC)
Unites and supports the cancer community to reduce the global cancer burden, promote greater equity, and ensure that cancer control continues to be a priority in the world health and development agenda.
Heme-Onc, Pub Health
⊕ https://vfmat.ch/88b1

United Nations Children's Fund (UNICEF)
Works in over 190 countries and territories to save children's lives, defend their rights, and help them fulfill their potential, from early childhood through adolescence.
All-Immu, Infect Dis, MF Med, Neonat, Nutr, OB-GYN, Ped Surg, Peds, Pub Health
⊕ https://vfmat.ch/42d7

United Nations Development Programme (UNDP)
Helps countries achieve the simultaneous eradication of extreme poverty and significant reduction of inequalities and exclusion using a sustainable human development approach.
Infect Dis, Logist-Op, Pub Health
⊕ https://vfmat.ch/935c

United Nations High Commissioner for Refugees (UNHCR)
Safeguards the rights and well-being of people who have been forced to flee, ensuring that everybody has the right to seek asylum and find safe refuge in another country, with the goal of seeking lasting solutions.
General, MF Med, Medicine, OB-GYN, Peds, Psych, Pub Health
⊕ https://vfmat.ch/6636

United Nations Office for the Coordination of Humanitarian Affairs (OCHA)
Contributes to principled and effective humanitarian response through coordination, advocacy, policy, information management, and humanitarian financing tools and services, by leveraging functional expertise throughout the organization.
Logist-Op
⊕ https://vfmat.ch/22b8

United Nations Population Fund (UNFPA)
Supports reproductive healthcare for women and youth in more than 150 countries, focusing on delivering a world in which every pregnancy is wanted, every childbirth is safe, and every young person's potential is fulfilled.
Infect Dis, MF Med, Neonat, OB-GYN, Peds, Pub Health
⊕ https://vfmat.ch/c969

United States Agency for International Development (USAID)
Promotes and demonstrates democratic values abroad and advances a free, peaceful, and prosperous world. Leads the U.S. government's international development and disaster assistance through partnerships and investments that save lives.

ER Med, Infect Dis, MF Med, OB-GYN, Peds
⊕ https://vfmat.ch/9a99

United States President's Emergency Plan for AIDS Relief (PEPFAR)
The U.S. global HIV/AIDS response works to prevent new HIV infections and accelerate progress to control the global epidemic in more than 50 countries, by partnering with governments to support sustainable, integrated, and country-led responses to HIV/AIDS.
Infect Dis, Pub Health
⊕ https://vfmat.ch/a57c

University of California, Los Angeles: UCLA-DRC Health Research and Training Program
Aims to strengthen local and international capacity to rapidly identify and respond to disease outbreaks, conduct critical infectious disease research, and develop innovative prevention and control strategies.
All-Immu, Infect Dis, MF Med, Path, Pub Health
⊕ https://vfmat.ch/84ab

University of California: Global Health Institute
Mobilizes people and resources across the University of California to advance global health research, education, and collaboration.
General, OB-GYN, Pub Health
⊕ https://vfmat.ch/ee7f

Upright Africa
Empowers the people of the Democratic Republic of Congo to build a sustainable future for themselves by sharing practical procedures and techniques with Congolese medical professionals. Also provides daily necessities to those without access.
General, Infect Dis, Nutr, Ped Surg, Surg
⊕ https://vfmat.ch/74cd

USA for United Nations High Commissioner for Refugees (UNHCR)
Serves and protects refugees and displaced people through emergency relief, cash assistance, education, resettlement, and the rebuilding of livelihoods.
ER Med, General, Logist-Op, Nutr, Pub Health
⊕ https://vfmat.ch/293c

USAID: EQUIP Health
Exists as an effective, efficient response mechanism to achieving global HIV epidemic control by delivering the right intervention at the right place and in the right way.
Infect Dis
⊕ https://vfmat.ch/d76a

USAID: Fistula Care Plus
Builds on, enhances, and expands the work undertaken by the previous Fistula Care project (2007–2013), with attention to prevention, detection, treatment, reintegration and new areas of focus so that obstetric fistula can become a rare event for future generations.
MF Med, OB-GYN, Surg
⊕ https://vfmat.ch/a7cd

USAID: Global Health Supply Chain Program
Combines 8 complementary projects working globally to achieve stronger, more resilient health supply chains.
Infect Dis, Logist-Op, Pub Health
⊕ https://vfmat.ch/115f

USAID: Health Finance and Governance Project
Uses research to implement strategies to help countries develop robust governance systems, increase their domestic resources for health, manage those resources more effectively, and make wise purchasing decisions.
Logist-Op
⊕ https://vfmat.ch/8652

USAID: Health Policy Initiative
Provides field-level programming in health policy development and implementation.

General, Infect Dis, MF Med, OB-GYN, Peds
⊕ https://vfmat.ch/8f84

USAID: Leadership, Management and Governance Project
Improves leadership, management, and governance practices to strengthen health systems and improve health for all, including vulnerable populations worldwide.
Logist-Op
⊕ https://vfmat.ch/d35e

USAID: Maternal and Child Health Integrated Program
Works to improve the health of women and their families, including programs for maternal, newborn, and child health, immunization, family planning, nutrition, malaria, and HIV/AIDS.
All-Immu, General, Infect Dis, MF Med
⊕ https://vfmat.ch/4415

USAID: Maternal and Child Survival Program
Works to prevent child and maternal deaths.
Infect Dis, MF Med, Neonat, OB-GYN, Peds
⊕ https://vfmat.ch/6fcf

Vision for All Foundation
Implements ophthalmic healthcare projects; aims to create and support ophthalmic centers and existing structures in order to support the training of medical and paramedical personnel in the ophthalmology; and seeks to promote prevention, diagnosis, and treatment of ophthalmic pathologies.
Dent-OMFS, Ophth-Opt, Pub Health
⊕ https://vfmat.ch/dd72

Vitamin Angels
Helps at-risk populations in need—specifically pregnant women, new mothers, and children under age 5—to gain access to life-changing vitamins and minerals.
General, Nutr
⊕ https://vfmat.ch/7da1

Vodacom Foundation
Brings people together to maximize impact in three key areas: health, education, and safety and security.
Logist-Op
⊕ https://vfmat.ch/f116

Watsi
Uses technology to make healthcare a reality for those who might not otherwise be able to afford it.
Pub Health, Surg
⊕ https://vfmat.ch/41a3

Women for Women International
Supports the most marginalized women to earn and save money, improve health and well-being, influence decisions in their home and community, and connect to networks for support.
MF Med, OB-GYN
⊕ https://vfmat.ch/768c

Women Orthopaedist Global Outreach (WOGO)
Provides free, life-altering orthopedic surgery that eliminates debilitating arthritis and restores disabled joints so that women can reclaim their ability to care for themselves, their families, and their communities.
Anesth, Ortho, Rehab, Surg
⊕ https://vfmat.ch/6386

Women's Refugee Commission
Seeks to improve lives by protecting the rights of women, children, and youth displaced by conflict and crisis through researching their needs, identifying solutions, and advocating for programs and policies to strengthen their resilience.
General, MF Med, Neonat, OB-GYN, Peds, Psych
⊕ https://vfmat.ch/3d8f

World Children's Fund
Commits to helping children worldwide who are suffering the effects of poverty, disease, natural disaster, famine, abuse, civil strife, and war.
General, Logist-Op, MF Med, Nutr, OB-GYN, Pub Health
⊕ https://vfmat.ch/9cd8

World Federation of Hemophilia (WFH)

Aims to improve and sustain care for people with inherited bleeding disorders by pursuing long-term relationships with individuals and organizations who share the values of WFH's development model.

Heme-Onc

⊕ https://vfmat.ch/5121

World Health Organization, The (WHO)

The United Nations' agency for health provides leadership on global health matters, shapes the health research agenda, sets norms and standards, articulates evidence-based policy options, provides technical support and monitoring to countries, and assesses health trends.

ER Med, General, Infect Dis, Logist-Op, MF Med, OB-GYN, Peds, Psych, Pub Health

⊕ https://vfmat.ch/c476

World Hope International

Empowers the poorest individuals around the world so they can become agents of change within their communities, by offering resources and knowledge.

Infect Dis, Logist-Op, MF Med, OB-GYN, Peds

⊕ https://vfmat.ch/a4b8

World Relief

Brings sustainable solutions to the world's greatest problems: disasters, extreme poverty, violence, oppression, and mass displacement.

ER Med, Nutr, Psych, Pub Health

⊕ https://vfmat.ch/fbcd

World Vision International

Works with vulnerable communities around the world to overcome poverty and injustice with child-focused programs in disaster management, health, nutrition, economic development, education, clean water, sanitation, and hygiene.

ER Med, General, Infect Dis, MF Med, Nutr, OB-GYN, Peds

⊕ https://vfmat.ch/2642

WorldShare

Connects faith-based groups in the UK with their counterparts in underdeveloped countries to promote community development and holistic support for children.

Dent-OMFS, ER Med, General, Peds, Pub Health, Surg

⊕ https://vfmat.ch/9eae

Democratic Republic of the Congo (DRC)

Healthcare Facilities

Bribano Médical
Avenue Tumba, Kingabwa, Kinshasa, Democratic Republic of the Congo
⊕ https://vfapp.org/2925

Bugarula
Bugarula, Sud-Kivu, Democratic Republic of the Congo
⊕ https://vfapp.org/363a

CH Anuarite
RN4, Paida, Nord-Kivu, Democratic Republic of the Congo
⊕ https://vfapp.org/4792

CH Baraka
Route Kitulu, Butembo, Nord-Kivu, Democratic Republic of the Congo
⊕ https://vfapp.org/83cc

CH Butuhe
RS534, Butuhe, Nord-Kivu, Democratic Republic of the Congo
⊕ https://vfapp.org/f659

CH Cbca
Avenue des Martyrs, Butembo, Nord-Kivu, Democratic Republic of the Congo
⊕ https://vfapp.org/cc62

CH Cemebu
RS1032, Katwa, Nord-Kivu, Democratic Republic of the Congo
⊕ https://vfapp.org/e819

CH de Gloria
RN44, Beni, Nord-Kivu, Democratic Republic of the Congo
⊕ https://vfapp.org/aae6

CH Dieu Merci
Route Kitulu, Butembo, Nord-Kivu, Democratic Republic of the Congo
⊕ https://vfapp.org/ecfb

CH Don Beni
RN2, Butembo, Nord-Kivu, Democratic Republic of the Congo
⊕ https://vfapp.org/a53a

Ch Fepsi
Avenue du Centre, Butembo, Nord-Kivu, Democratic Republic of the Congo
⊕ https://vfapp.org/1d45

CH Kasinga
RS534, Butuhe, Nord-Kivu, Democratic Republic of the Congo
⊕ https://vfapp.org/3953

CH Maboya
RN2, Maboya, Nord-Kivu, Democratic Republic of the Congo
⊕ https://vfapp.org/76cc

CH Mahamba
RN2, Butembo, Nord-Kivu, Democratic Republic of the Congo
⊕ https://vfapp.org/654e

CH Makasi
RN2, Butembo, Nord-Kivu, Democratic Republic of the Congo
⊕ https://vfapp.org/ffd9

CH Mama Muyisa
Avenue du Marché, Butembo, Nord-Kivu, Democratic Republic of the Congo
⊕ https://vfapp.org/6e72

CH Matanda
RN2, Butembo, Nord-Kivu, Democratic Republic of the Congo
⊕ https://vfapp.org/61d2

CH Muchanga
RN2, Butembo, Nord-Kivu, Democratic Republic of the Congo
⊕ https://vfapp.org/bbcc

CH Mukongo
Butembo, Nord-Kivu, Democratic Republic of the Congo
⊕ https://vfapp.org/5188

CH Mukuna
Route Kitulu, Butembo, Nord-Kivu, Democratic Republic of the Congo
⊕ https://vfapp.org/5566

CH Rughenda
Route Kitulu, Butembo, Nord-Kivu, Democratic Republic of the Congo
⊕ https://vfapp.org/e857

CH Rwenzori
RN2, Butembo, Nord-Kivu, Democratic Republic of the Congo
⊕ https://vfapp.org/49f9

CH Saint Luc
Route Kitulu, Butembo, Nord-Kivu, Democratic Republic of the Congo
⊕ https://vfapp.org/2e77

CH Sainte Famille
Route Kitulu, Butembo, Nord-Kivu, Democratic Republic of the Congo
⊕ https://vfapp.org/9dea

CH Sainte Stella
RN2, Lubero, Nord-Kivu, Democratic Republic of the Congo
⊕ https://vfapp.org/34ca

CH Tumaini
Butembo, Nord-Kivu, Democratic Republic of the Congo
⊕ https://vfapp.org/69f5

CH Uor
RN2, Butembo, Nord-Kivu, Democratic Republic of the Congo
⊕ https://vfapp.org/9bed

CH Vighole
RS1032, Katwa, Nord-Kivu, Democratic Republic of the Congo
⊕ https://vfapp.org/7b48

CHU de Mbandaka
Avenue Cimetière, Mbandaka, Équateur, Democratic Republic of the Congo
⊕ https://vfapp.org/1cf2

CHU de Ruwenzori
Route Kitulu, Butembo, Nord-Kivu, Democratic Republic of the Congo
⊕ https://vfapp.org/312e

Clinique Ngaliema
Avenue des Cliniques, Cliniques, Kinshasa, Democratic Republic of the Congo
⊕ https://vfapp.org/e9c4

CPN Espoir
Avenue de l'Est, Kingabwa, Kinshasa, Democratic Republic of the Congo
⊕ https://vfapp.org/3653

HGR Beni
RN2, Beni, Nord-Kivu, Democratic Republic of the Congo
⊕ https://vfapp.org/ca65

HGR Bukama
Avenue de la Prison, Bukama, Haut-Lomami, Democratic Republic of the Congo
⊕ https://vfapp.org/b4c3

HGR Charite Maternelle
Goma, Democratic Republic of the Congo
⊕ https://vfapp.org/68bd

HGR de Kasaji
RN39, Kasaji, Lualaba, Democratic Republic of the Congo
⊕ https://vfapp.org/3678

HGR de Vuhovi
Vuhovi, Nord-Kivu, Democratic Republic of the Congo
⊕ https://vfapp.org/b1ec

HGR Katwa
RS1032, Katwa, Nord-Kivu, Democratic Republic of the Congo
⊕ https://vfapp.org/b5d9

HGR Kitatumba
29756, Butembo, Nord-Kivu, Democratic Republic of the Congo
⊕ https://vfapp.org/4a7e

HGR Le Roi
RN2, Butembo, Nord-Kivu, Democratic Republic of the Congo
⊕ https://vfapp.org/14f2

HGR Lubero
RN2, Lubero, Nord-Kivu, Democratic Republic of the

Congo
⊕ https://vfapp.org/4bd2

HGR Masereka
Butembo, Nord-Kivu, Democratic Republic of the Congo
⊕ https://vfapp.org/b1d6

HJ Hospital
Petit Boulevard Industriel, Industriel, Kinshasa, Democratic Republic of the Congo
⊕ https://vfapp.org/9546

Hospital at Beni
Beni, Democratic Republic of the Congo
⊕ https://vfapp.org/cff2

Hospital at Monkole
Kasangulu, Democratic Republic of the Congo
⊕ https://vfapp.org/8de8

Hospital Gecamines Kambove
Kambove-Likasi, Democratic Republic of the Congo
⊕ https://vfapp.org/4a74

Hospital General de Mukongola
Kabare, Democratic Republic of the Congo
⊕ https://vfapp.org/1db9

Hospital Mtaa Wa Kivu Kusini
Mtaa Wa Kivu Kusini, Goma, Democratic Republic of the Congo
⊕ https://vfapp.org/2a93

Hospital Saint Joseph
N1, Kinshasa, Democratic Republic of the Congo
⊕ https://vfapp.org/c959

Hôpital Catholique Tonga
Avenue Etonga, Bahumbu, Kinshasa, Democratic Republic of the Congo
⊕ https://vfapp.org/927a

Hôpital de Baraka
Piste d'aviation, Baraka, Sud-Kivu, Democratic Republic of the Congo
⊕ https://vfapp.org/e564

Hôpital de Dungu
RP420, Dungu, Haut-Uele, Democratic Republic of the Congo
⊕ https://vfapp.org/c9ef

Hôpital de Gungu
RP231, Gungu, Kwilu, Democratic Republic of the Congo
⊕ https://vfapp.org/32a3

Hôpital de Kayna
RN2, Kayna, Nord-Kivu, Democratic Republic of the Congo
⊕ https://vfapp.org/1d7e

Hôpital de Kenge
RP242, Kenge, Kwango, Democratic Republic of the Congo
⊕ https://vfapp.org/e5f6

Hôpital de Kirotshe
RN2, Kalehe, Democratic Republic of the Congo
⊕ https://vfapp.org/8dbe

Hôpital de la Rive
Avenue des Touristes, Kinshasa, Kinshasa, Democratic Republic of the Congo
⊕ https://vfapp.org/5b6c

Hôpital de Référence de Kiamvu
Matadi, Kongo-Central, Democratic Republic of the Congo
⊕ https://vfapp.org/1187

Hôpital de Référence de Makala
Rue Dua, Selembao, Kinshasa, Democratic Republic of the Congo
⊕ https://vfapp.org/e87c

Hôpital de Référence de Matete
Avenue Diwaz, Vivi, Kinshasa, Democratic Republic of the Congo
⊕ https://vfapp.org/2365

Hôpital du Cinquantenaire
Avenue de la Libération, ONL, Kinshasa, Democratic Republic of the Congo
⊕ https://vfapp.org/f685

Hôpital General de Reference de Lubutu
RN3, Lubutu, Maniema, Democratic Republic of the Congo
⊕ https://vfapp.org/e1ce

Hôpital General de Référence de Bafwasende
Bafwasende, Democratic Republic of the Congo
⊕ https://vfapp.org/fead

Hôpital General de Référence de Kalemie
59, Avenue Lumumba, District du Tanganyika, Province du Katanga, Democratic Republic of the Congo
⊕ https://vfapp.org/55ad

Hôpital Gécamines de Kipushi
Kipushi, Democratic Republic of the Congo
⊕ https://vfapp.org/42eb

Hôpital Gécamines Sud
Route de Kipushi, Mampala, Haut-Katanga, Democratic Republic of the Congo
⊕ https://vfapp.org/16a4

Hôpital Général de Shabunda
Avenue Aeroport, Shabunda, Sud-Kivu, Democratic Republic of the Congo
⊕ https://vfapp.org/e798

Hôpital Général de Bikoro
RN21, Bikoro, Équateur, Democratic Republic of the Congo
🌐 https://vfapp.org/4462

Hôpital Général de Dipumba
Avenue de la Kanshi, Nzaba, Bipemba, Democratic Republic of the Congo
🌐 https://vfapp.org/f792

Hôpital Général de Fizi
RP527, Rtnc, Sud-Kivu, Democratic Republic of the Congo
🌐 https://vfapp.org/be33

Hôpital Général de Mandima
N4, Mambasa, Democratic Republic of the Congo
🌐 https://vfapp.org/93c2

Hôpital Général de Nia-Nia
RN4, Nia-Nia, Ituri, Democratic Republic of the Congo
🌐 https://vfapp.org/9cbb

Hôpital Général de Référence
RP628, Manono, Tanganyika, Democratic Republic of the Congo
🌐 https://vfapp.org/c65e

Hôpital Général de Référence d'Oshwe
RS212, Oshwe, Mai-Ndombe, Democratic Republic of the Congo
🌐 https://vfapp.org/f63f

Hôpital Général de Référence d'Uvira
RN5, Shishi, Sud-Kivu, Democratic Republic of the Congo
🌐 https://vfapp.org/ec76

Hôpital Général de Référence de Geti
Gety, Ituri, Democratic Republic of the Congo
🌐 https://vfapp.org/4477

Hôpital Général de Référence de Kikwit
Avenue Lukengo, Kikwit, Kwilu, Democratic Republic of the Congo
🌐 https://vfapp.org/636a

Hôpital Général de Référence de Kindu/ HGR
Avenue de l'Hopital, CAMP SNCC/KINDU, Maniema, Democratic Republic of the Congo
🌐 https://vfapp.org/7f6b

Hôpital Général de Référence de Mbandaka
Avenue Mundji, Mbandaka, Équateur, Democratic Republic of the Congo
🌐 https://vfapp.org/ff53

Hôpital Général de Référence de Monkoto
RS315, Monkoto, Tshuapa, Democratic Republic of the Congo
🌐 https://vfapp.org/2ed6

Hôpital Général de Référence de Mushie
Rue Mahenge, Mushie, Mai-Ndombe, Democratic Republic of the Congo
🌐 https://vfapp.org/6337

Hôpital Général de Référence de Mutwanga
Mutwanga, Nord-Kivu, Democratic Republic of the Congo
🌐 https://vfapp.org/d5eb

Hôpital Général de Référence de Nundu
RN5, Mboko, Sud-Kivu, Democratic Republic of the Congo
🌐 https://vfapp.org/af92

Hôpital Général de Référence de Panzi
Bukavu, Democratic Republic of the Congo
🌐 https://vfapp.org/862b

Hôpital Général de Référence de Sia
RP219, Sia, Kwilu, Democratic Republic of the Congo
🌐 https://vfapp.org/1815

Hôpital Général de Référence de Tshikapa
RN1, Tshikapa, Kasaï, Democratic Republic of the Congo
🌐 https://vfapp.org/7fd5

Hôpital Général de Référence du Nord Kivu
RN2, Les Volcans, Nord-Kivu, Democratic Republic of the Congo
🌐 https://vfapp.org/a2a1

Hôpital Général de Référence Tunda
RP511, Djele, Maniema, Democratic Republic of the Congo
🌐 https://vfapp.org/45f1

Hôpital Général de Référence Wangata
Wangata, Équateur, Democratic Republic of the Congo
🌐 https://vfapp.org/514b

Hôpital Général de Référence Yalimbongo
RP405, Yalimbongo, Tshopo, Democratic Republic of the Congo
🌐 https://vfapp.org/c156

Hôpital Général de Yumbi
Avenue Martyr, Yumbi, Mai-Ndombe, Democratic Republic of the Congo
🌐 https://vfapp.org/2379

Hôpital Général du Cinquantenaire
Avenue Muela, Munua, Haut-Katanga, Democratic Republic of the Congo
🌐 https://vfapp.org/491a

Hôpital Géréral de Référence de Panzi
RP239, Panzi, Kwango, Democratic Republic of the Congo
🌐 https://vfapp.org/e63f

Hôpital Kimbanguiste
Avenue de la IIème République, Kutu, Kinshasa, Democratic Republic of the Congo
🌐 https://vfapp.org/4675

Hôpital Militaire Régional de Kinshasa Camp Kokolo
Avenue de la Libération, La Voix du Peuple, Kinshasa, Democratic Republic of the Congo
🌐 https://vfapp.org/6915

Hôpital Moderne – Lopitálo ya motindo mwa sika
RN8, Boende, Tshuapa, Democratic Republic of the Congo
🌐 https://vfapp.org/5896

Hôpital Monkole 3
Avenue Monkole, Kinshasa, Kinshasa, Democratic Republic of the Congo
🌐 https://vfapp.org/915c

Hôpital Mutombo
Boulevard Lumumba, Sans Fil, Kinshasa, Democratic Republic of the Congo
🌐 https://vfapp.org/5893

Hôpital PNC/Camp Soyo
Matadi – Ango Ango, Matadi, Kongo-Central, Democratic Republic of the Congo
🌐 https://vfapp.org/9571

Hôpital Provincial Général de Reférence de Bukavu
Bukavu, Democratic Republic of the Congo
🌐 https://vfapp.org/8bca

Hôpital Provincial Général de Référence de Kinshasa
Avenue de l'Hôpital, Golf, Kinshasa, Democratic Republic of the Congo
🌐 https://vfapp.org/82e1

Hôpital Pédiatrique de Kalembelembe
Avenue Kalembelembe, Lokole, Kinshasa, Democratic Republic of the Congo
🌐 https://vfapp.org/32b3

Hôpital Radem
Avenue Changalele III, Gambela 1, Haut-Katanga, Democratic Republic of the Congo
🌐 https://vfapp.org/9899

Hôpital Saint Luc de Kisantu
RN16, Kisantu, Kongo-Central, Democratic Republic of the Congo
🌐 https://vfapp.org/bc83

Hôpital Saint-Jean-Baptiste de Bonzola
Mbuji-Mayi, Democratic Republic of the Congo
🌐 https://vfapp.org/21cb

Hôpital SNCC/KINDU
Avenue Industrielle, CAMP SNCC/KINDU, Maniema, Democratic Republic of the Congo
🌐 https://vfapp.org/f4ba

Hôpital SS Mabanga
Rue Lubaya, Yolo-Sud 1, Kinshasa, Democratic
Republic of the Congo
⊕ https://vfapp.org/dd6b

Hôpital Tshiamala
RN1, Mwene-Ditu, Lomami, Democratic Republic of
the Congo
⊕ https://vfapp.org/9bfb

IME Loko
Lisala-Gbadolite, Wodzo, Nord-Ubangi, Democratic
Republic of the Congo
⊕ https://vfapp.org/4634

Jukayi
Kabuluanda, Kananga, Kasaï-Central, Democratic
Republic of the Congo
⊕ https://vfapp.org/2942

Kawembe General Referral Hospital
Mbuji-Mayi, Democratic Republic of the Congo
⊕ https://vfapp.org/ccfd

Kihumba
Kihumba, Sud-Kivu, Democratic Republic of the
Congo
⊕ https://vfapp.org/e238

Kinshasa General Hospital
Avenue de l'Hopital, Kinshasa, Democratic Republic
of the Congo
⊕ https://vfapp.org/e2ca

Kitumaini
Avenue de Kambove, Kiwele, Haut-Katanga,
Democratic Republic of the Congo
⊕ https://vfapp.org/4922

Les Aiglons
3ème Rue, Malemba, Kinshasa, Democratic Republic
of the Congo
⊕ https://vfapp.org/fc99

Ma Famille
20 Boulevard Lumumba, Quartier 12, Kinshasa,
Democratic Republic of the Congo
⊕ https://vfapp.org/f34b

Mbanza-Ngungu Hospital
R115, Mbanza-Ngungu, Democratic Republic of the
Congo
⊕ https://vfapp.org/fb2a

**Mobayi Mbongo General Reference
Hospital**
RN24, Beseli, Nord-Ubangi, Democratic Republic of
the Congo
⊕ https://vfapp.org/e2e9

MSF – Bon Marché
Bigo, Bunia, Ituri, Democratic Republic of the Congo
⊕ https://vfapp.org/26ca

ORT Foyer
Avenue Upemba, Kisale, Haut-Katanga, Democratic
Republic of the Congo
⊕ https://vfapp.org/9958

Panzi Hospital
Mushununu, Q. Panzi, Bukavu 266, Democratic
Republic of the Congo
⊕ https://vfapp.org/b627

Railroad Hospital
Avenue De Lukafu, SNCC, Haut-Katanga, Democratic
Republic of the Congo
⊕ https://vfapp.org/42ef

TVC Medical
77 Kenge, Diomi, Kinshasa, Democratic Republic of
the Congo
⊕ https://vfapp.org/eebf

TVC Medical Mobayi
Mobayi-Mbongo, Democratic Republic of the Congo
⊕ https://vfapp.org/6961

Vanga Evangelical Hospital
Tshikapa, Democratic Republic of the Congo
⊕ https://vfapp.org/2445

Yolo Medical
Avenue Yolo, Mososo, Kinshasa, Democratic Republic
of the Congo
⊕ https://vfapp.org/2211

Healthcare Facility

Djibouti

The Republic of Djibouti is located in the Horn of Africa, bordered by Somaliland, Eritrea, the Red Sea, and the Gulf of Aden. While small in geographical size, Djibouti benefits from a particularly strategic location, jutting out into the Gulf of Aden. Its modern port serves important traffic coming across the Red Sea and the Indian Ocean. Djibouti is home to the lowest point in Africa, the saline Lake Assal, which is 509 feet below sea level. The population of about 940,000 is composed of 60 percent Somali and 35 percent Afar people, speaking the official languages of French and Arabic, in addition to Somali and Afar. The vast majority of the population is Sunni Muslim, with a small portion, mostly foreigners, identifying as Christian. More than 78 percent of Djiboutians live in cities. The capital of Djibouti, also named Djibouti, is home to 600,000 people. Other cities throughout the country have significantly lower populations, none exceeding 50,000.

Formerly known as French Somaliland and the French Territory of the Afars and Issas, Djibouti adopted its modern name after it gained independence from France in 1977. Due to Djibouti's harsh climate and limited arable land, agriculture is not a key economic sector. Rural areas are known for raising sheep and goats in small herds for meat, milk, and skins. Overall, Djibouti faces high levels of unemployment because there are few natural resources, agriculture is not a viable industry, and there is limited development in the manufacturing and industrial sectors. Therefore, the country focuses primarily on the service sector, which accounts for the majority of its GDP. Many Djiboutians struggle with unemployment, and poor housing and insufficient water and sanitation facilities contribute to poor overall living conditions.

Chewing khat, a practice that dates back thousands of years in the Horn of Africa, is widespread in Djibouti, and can lead to adverse health effects, such as depression. In addition to pervasive khat chewing, other factors that contribute to poor health include: malnutrition, unsafe sex, air pollution, high blood pressure, tobacco, dietary risks, high fasting plasma glucose, high body-mass index, kidney dysfunction, non-optimal temperature, and a lack of water, sanitation, and hygiene. The causes of most deaths in the country include HIV/AIDS, neonatal disorders, lower respiratory infections, ischemic heart disease, stroke, tuberculosis, diarrheal diseases, cirrhosis, diabetes, protein-energy malnutrition, and congenital defects. Notably, deaths due to non-communicable diseases such as ischemic heart disease, stroke, cirrhosis, and diabetes have all increased by at least 48 percent or more over the past decade.

0.94M
Population

$3,426
GDP Per Capita

67 years
Life Expectancy
↑ Improving

22
Doctors/100k
Physician Density

140
Beds/100k
Hospital Bed Density

248
Deaths/100k
Maternal Mortality

Djibouti

Nonprofit Organizations

143 LIFE Foundation
Seeks to educate and empower individuals living with malaria, TB, HIV/AIDS, STDs and other health disparities related to sexual health.
Infect Dis, MF Med
⊕ https://vfmat.ch/d59b

Action For East African People
Acts on the needs of women and children living in East Africa while promoting the grassroots advancement of the East African community of Bloomington, Minnesota.
Dent-OMFS, General, OB-GYN, Pub Health
⊕ https://vfmat.ch/4db7

Africa Health Organisation
Leads collaborative efforts among countries in Africa and other partners to promote health equity, combat disease, and improve quality of life.
Logist-Op, Pub Health
⊕ https://vfmat.ch/b1c5

Africa Humanitarian Action (AHA)
Responds to crises, conflicts, and disasters in Africa, while informing and advising the international community, governments, civil society, and the private sector on humanitarian issues of concern to Africa. Supports institutional and organizational development efforts.
General, Infect Dis, MF Med, Nutr, OB-GYN
⊕ https://vfmat.ch/3ca2

Association of Medical Doctors of Asia (AMDA)
Strives to support people affected by disasters and economic distress on their road to recovery, establishing a true partnership with special emphasis on local initiative.
ER Med, Logist-Op, Pub Health
⊕ https://vfmat.ch/e3d4

BroadReach
Collaborates with governments, multinational health organizations, donors, and private-sector companies to effect healthcare reform and solve the world's biggest health challenges.
Logist-Op
⊕ https://vfmat.ch/7812

CARE
Works around the globe to save lives, defeat poverty, and achieve social justice.
ER Med, General
⊕ https://vfmat.ch/7232

Direct Relief
Improves the health and lives of people affected by poverty or emergency situations by mobilizing and providing essential medical resources needed for their care.

ER Med, Logist-Op
⊕ https://vfmat.ch/58e5

Global Oncology (GO)
Brings the best in cancer care to underserved patients around the world and collaborates across geographic, professional, and academic borders to improve cancer care, research, and education.
Heme-Onc, Path, Rad-Onc
⊕ https://vfmat.ch/fcb8

Globus Relief
Aims to improve the delivery of healthcare worldwide by gathering, processing, and distributing surplus medical supplies to charities at home and abroad.
Logist-Op
⊕ https://vfmat.ch/a2b7

IMA World Health
Works to build healthier communities by collaborating with key partners to serve vulnerable people with a focus on health, healing, and well-being for all.
Infect Dis, MF Med, Nutr, OB-GYN, Pub Health
⊕ https://vfmat.ch/8316

International Federation of Red Cross and Red Crescent Societies (IFRC)
Coordinates and directs international assistance following natural and manmade disasters in nonconflict situations through the world's largest humanitarian and development network. Provides disaster-preparedness programs, healthcare activities, and promotes humanitarian values.
ER Med, General, Infect Dis, Nutr
⊕ https://vfmat.ch/b4ee

International Organization for Migration (IOM) – The UN Migration Agency
Promotes evidence-informed policies and holistic, preventive, and curative health programs that are beneficial, accessible, and equitable for vulnerable migrants.
General, Infect Dis, OB-GYN
⊕ https://vfmat.ch/621a

International Planned Parenthood Federation (IPPF)
Leads a locally owned, globally connected civil society movement that provides and enables services and champions sexual and reproductive health and rights for all, especially the underserved.
Infect Dis, MF Med, OB-GYN
⊕ https://vfmat.ch/dc97

Local Initiatives for Education (L.I.F.E.)
Provides potable water, food, agricultural support, educational resources, and medical care in Africa, while working alongside community leaders to accomplish these goals.

Logist-Op, Pub Health
⊕ https://vfmat.ch/dd91

Medical Care Development International
Works to improve the health of vulnerable populations through integrated, sustainable, and locally driven interventions.
Infect Dis, OB-GYN, Peds, Pub Health
⊕ https://vfmat.ch/da87

Organization for the Prevention of Blindness, The (OPC)
Provides research, and treatments and cures for people affected by blindness and blinding diseases in Francophone Africa.
Infect Dis, Ophth-Opt
⊕ https://vfmat.ch/86d6

Philips Foundation
Aims to reduce healthcare inequality by providing access to quality healthcare for disadvantaged communities.
CV Med, OB-GYN, Ped Surg, Peds, Surg, Urol
⊕ https://vfmat.ch/bacb

Resource Exchange International
Provides holistic education and training to improve knowledge and skills and build human capacity within communities in emerging nations.
Derm, ENT, Ortho
⊕ https://vfmat.ch/6d49

Resource Exchange International
Sends long-term staff and short-term professionals in areas of education, medicine, and business to train leaders in emerging nations so that they can train others.
General
⊕ https://vfmat.ch/6863

RestoringVision
Empowers lives by restoring vision for millions of people in need.
Ophth-Opt
⊕ https://vfmat.ch/e121

Rotary International
Provides service to others, improves lives, and advances world understanding, goodwill, and peace through its fellowship of business, professional, and community leaders.
ER Med, General, Infect Dis, MF Med, OB-GYN
⊕ https://vfmat.ch/8fb5

United Nations Children's Fund (UNICEF)
Works in over 190 countries and territories to save children's lives, defend their rights, and help them fulfill their potential, from early childhood through adolescence.
All-Immu, Infect Dis, MF Med, Neonat, Nutr, OB-GYN, Ped Surg, Peds, Pub Health
⊕ https://vfmat.ch/42d7

United Nations Development Programme (UNDP)
Helps countries achieve the simultaneous eradication of extreme poverty and significant reduction of inequalities and exclusion using a sustainable human development approach.
Infect Dis, Logist-Op, Pub Health
⊕ https://vfmat.ch/935c

United Nations High Commissioner for Refugees (UNHCR)
Safeguards the rights and well-being of people who have been forced to flee, ensuring that everybody has the right to seek asylum and find safe refuge in another country, with the goal of seeking lasting solutions.
General, MF Med, Medicine, OB-GYN, Peds, Psych, Pub Health
⊕ https://vfmat.ch/6636

United Nations Population Fund (UNFPA)
Supports reproductive healthcare for women and youth in more than 150 countries, focusing on delivering a world in which every pregnancy is wanted, every childbirth is safe, and every young person's potential is fulfilled.

Infect Dis, MF Med, Neonat, OB-GYN, Peds, Pub Health
⊕ https://vfmat.ch/c969

United States Agency for International Development (USAID)
Promotes and demonstrates democratic values abroad and advances a free, peaceful, and prosperous world. Leads the U.S. government's international development and disaster assistance through partnerships and investments that save lives.
ER Med, Infect Dis, MF Med, OB-GYN, Peds
⊕ https://vfmat.ch/9a99

Women's Refugee Commission
Seeks to improve lives by protecting the rights of women, children, and youth displaced by conflict and crisis through researching their needs, identifying solutions, and advocating for programs and policies to strengthen their resilience.
General, MF Med, Neonat, OB-GYN, Peds, Psych
⊕ https://vfmat.ch/3d8f

World Federation of Hemophilia (WFH)
Aims to improve and sustain care for people with inherited bleeding disorders by pursuing long-term relationships with individuals and organizations who share the values of WFH's development model.
Heme-Onc
⊕ https://vfmat.ch/5121

World Health Organization, The (WHO)
The United Nations' agency for health provides leadership on global health matters, shapes the health research agenda, sets norms and standards, articulates evidence-based policy options, provides technical support and monitoring to countries, and assesses health trends.
ER Med, General, Infect Dis, Logist-Op, MF Med, OB-GYN, Peds, Psych, Pub Health
⊕ https://vfmat.ch/c476

 # Djibouti

Healthcare Facilities

Al Rahma Hospital
Ville, Balbala, Djibouti
⊕ https://vfmat.ch/klii

Centre Yonis Toussaint Hospital
Ville, Djibouti
⊕ https://vfmat.ch/gw1u

Dar Al Hanan
Grande Mosquée de Djibouti, Seventh District, Djibouti
⊕ https://vfmat.ch/b2vf

Dikhil District Hospital
Dikhil, Djibouti
⊕ https://vfmat.ch/ules

Djibouti Medical Center
Djibouti City, Djibouti Region, Djibouti
⊕ https://vfmat.ch/sxsh

Djibouti Military Hospital (Hospital Militaire de Djibouti)
Djibouti City, Djibouti Region, Djibouti
⊕ https://vfmat.ch/c8v7

FK Medical
Djibouti City, Djibouti Region, Djibouti
⊕ https://vfmat.ch/4w2n

French Military Hospital, Djibouti
GMC Bouffard, Djibouti
⊕ https://vfmat.ch/78dt

Halas Hospital
Djibouti (city)., Djibouti
⊕ https://vfmat.ch/bvfc

Hospital General Peltier
Jibuti, Djibouti
⊕ https://vfmat.ch/argu

Hôpital Bouffard
Djibouti, Djibouti, Djibouti
⊕ https://vfmat.ch/dtfd

Hopital De Balbala "Cheiko"
Balbala, Djibouti City, Djibouti
⊕ https://vfmat.ch/enz6

Hôpital Militaire Djibouti-Soudan
Ambouli, Djibouti, Djibouti
⊕ https://vfmat.ch/5819

Hôpital Pneumo-Phtisiologique Chakib Saad Omar
Djibouti City, Djibouti, Djibouti
⊕ https://vfmat.ch/utuu

Hôpital Regional D'Ali Sabieh Dr. Ahmed Absieh Warsama
Guelile, Djibouti
⊕ https://vfmat.ch/7dfc

Service de Santé des Armées
Ambouli, Djibouti, Djibouti
⊕ https://vfmat.ch/225d

Sovereign Djibouti Medical Services – SDMS
Djibouti City, Djibouti, Djibouti
⊕ https://vfmat.ch/jpqd

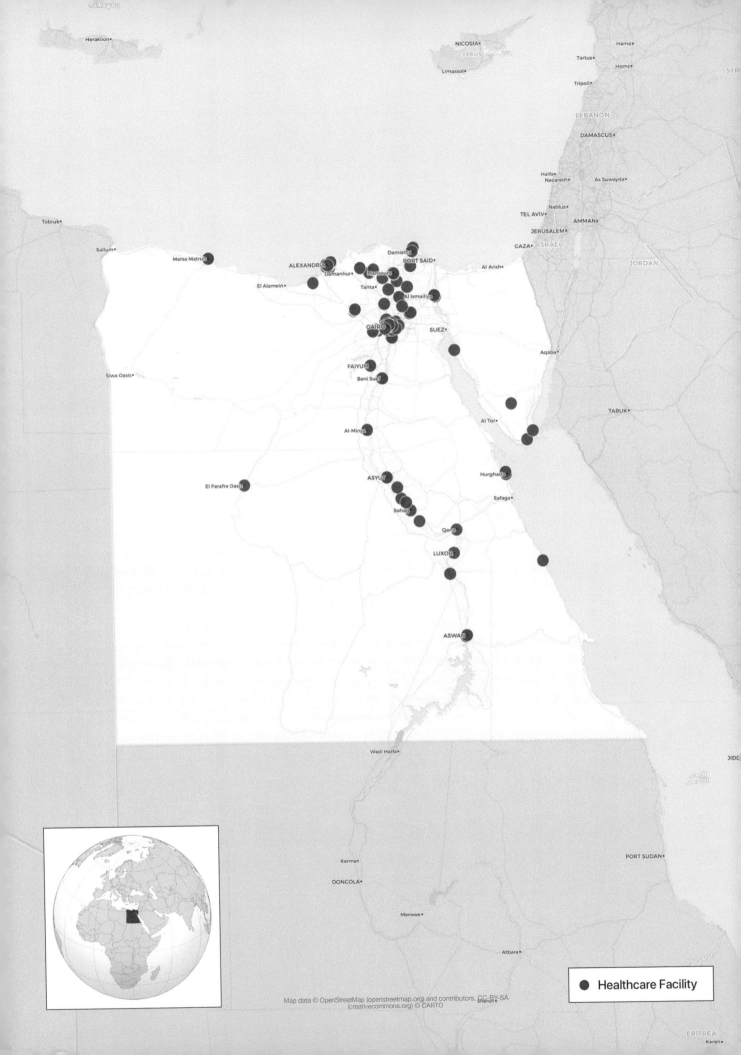

Healthcare Facility

Egypt

The Arab Republic of Egypt officially spans two continents: the northeast corner of Africa and the southwest corner of Asia, bordered by the Gaza Strip (Palestine), Israel, the Gulf of Aqaba, the Red Sea, Sudan, and Libya. Several other countries are located in close proximity to Egypt on the other side of the Gulf of Aqaba. Its population of 106.4 million is ethnically homogenous, identifies as overwhelmingly Egyptian, and speaks mostly Arabic, the country's official language. In some instances, English and French are spoken as well. As much as 90 percent of the population is Sunni Muslim. Much of the population lives within 20 kilometers of the Nile River and the Nile River Delta, leaving large swaths of the country completely uninhabited. About 43 percent of the population lives in cities, with 21 million people living in Cairo, the capital. Egypt is unique in that it has one of the longest documented histories of any country, going as far back as the 6th millennium BC.

The history of modern-day Egypt is commonly noted as beginning in 1922, when it gained independence from the British Empire. Since then, Egypt has experienced decades of social and religious upheaval and political unrest, in addition to a social revolution in 2011. As a result, local terrorism continues to be a problem, and economic underdevelopment is pervasive. Rapid population growth of 46 percent between 1994 and 2014 has put considerable strain on the country, affecting jobs, housing, education, sanitation, and healthcare. Unemployment of youth ages 15–24 is particularly high, with males experiencing unemployment rates of 25 percent and women 38 percent.

Since the 1990s, the Egyptian Ministry of Health has increased its expenditure on public health programs, and as a result the number of government health centers, beds in hospitals, doctors, and dentists has increased. In addition to the public health system, there is also a system of Islamic healthcare centers and private clinics, which together have been able to serve most of the population. Most deaths in Egypt are caused by ischemic heart disease, cirrhosis, stroke, road injuries, chronic kidney disease, hypertensive heart disease, lower respiratory infection, diabetes, COPD, and liver cancer. Notably, non-communicable diseases such as diabetes, ischemic heart disease, and cirrhosis have all increased between 2009 and 2019. In addition, while diarrheal diseases and neonatal disorders have decreased substantially over the same period, they are still considered to be the top causes of death in Egypt. About 32 percent of the population is considered obese, and infectious diseases such as hepatitis A, typhoid fever, and schistosomiasis are prevalent.

106.4M
Population

$3,548
GDP Per Capita

72 years
Life Expectancy
↑ Improving

75
Doctors/100k

Physician Density

143
Beds/100k

Hospital Bed Density

37
Deaths/100k

Maternal Mortality

Egypt

Nonprofit Organizations

5 Rivers Heart Association
Works to help underserved populations by creating innovative ways to deliver cost-effective medicine while optimizing resource utilization.
CT Surg, GI, General
🌐 https://vfmat.ch/2deb

A Broader View Volunteers
Provides developing countries around the world with significant volunteer programs that aid the neediest communities and forge a lasting bond between those volunteering and those they have helped.
Dent-OMFS, ER Med, Infect Dis, MF Med
🌐 https://vfmat.ch/3bec

Abt Associates
Seeks to improve the quality of life and economic well-being of people worldwide, while striving to meet and exceed the highest professional standards.
General, Logist-Op, MF Med, OB-GYN, Peds
🌐 https://vfmat.ch/cec2

Africa CDC
Aims to strengthen the capacity and capability of Africa's public health institutions and partnerships to detect and respond quickly and effectively to disease threats and outbreaks, based on data-driven interventions and programs.
Infect Dis, Logist-Op, Pub Health
🌐 https://vfmat.ch/339c

Africa Health Organisation
Leads collaborative efforts among countries in Africa and other partners to promote health equity, combat disease, and improve quality of life.
Logist-Op, Pub Health
🌐 https://vfmat.ch/b1c5

Aga Khan Foundation Canada
Tackles the root causes of poverty, with a special focus on marginalized groups such as women and girls. Programs provide access to education and healthcare, food, and opportunity.
Pub Health
🌐 https://vfmat.ch/7f8b

AISPO
Implements international initiatives in the healthcare sector and remains involved in various projects to combat poverty, social injustice, and disease around the world.
All-Immu, ER Med, GI, General, Infect Dis, Logist-Op, MF Med, Neonat, OB-GYN, Peds, Psych, Pub Health, Radiol
🌐 https://vfmat.ch/c9e6

Alexandria Pediatric Oncology Charity
Ensures that all children with cancer are receiving unconditioned medical care and service for free.

Heme-Onc, Peds, Rad-Onc
🌐 https://vfmat.ch/e116

Alliance for Smiles
Improves the lives of children and communities impacted by cleft by providing free comprehensive treatment while building local capacity for long-term care.
Dent-OMFS, Ped Surg, Plast, Surg
🌐 https://vfmat.ch/bb32

American Heart Association (AHA)
Fights heart disease and stroke, striving to save and improve lives.
CV Med, Crit-Care, General, Heme-Onc, Medicine, Peds
🌐 https://vfmat.ch/4747

American Stroke Association
Works to prevent, treat, and beat stroke by funding innovative research, fighting for stronger public health policies, and providing lifesaving tools and information.
CV Med, Crit-Care, Heme-Onc, Medicine, Neuro, Pub Health, Pulm-Critic, Vasc Surg
🌐 https://vfmat.ch/746f

Anba Abraam Charity
Aims to improve the lives of underprivileged and vulnerable people with a focus on funding healthcare and surgical programs, programs for the physically and mentally disabled, and support for people without speech, inspired by the Christian faith.
Dent-OMFS, Logist-Op, Nutr, Rehab
🌐 https://vfmat.ch/b62d

Baylor College of Medicine: Global Surgery
Trains leaders in academic global surgery and remains dedicated to advancements in the areas of patient care, biomedical research, and medical education.
ENT, Infect Dis, OB-GYN, Ortho, Ped Surg, Plast, Pub Health, Radiol, Surg, Urol
🌐 https://vfmat.ch/21f5

Benjamin H. Josephson, MD Fund
Provides healthcare professionals with the financial resources necessary to deliver medical services for those in need throughout the world.
General, OB-GYN
🌐 https://vfmat.ch/6acc

Big Heart Foundation
Aims to safeguard the rights and improve the lives of vulnerable children and families worldwide, particularly in the Arab region, through advocacy, humanitarian, and development efforts.
ER Med, Nutr, Ophth-Opt, Plast, Rad-Onc
🌐 https://vfmat.ch/fff4

Breast Cancer Support
Aims to save lives and end breast cancer forever in women and men through education, treatment, emotional assistance, and financial support.
Heme-Onc, Logist-Op, Pub Health, Rad-Onc, Radiol
⊕ https://vfmat.ch/cb78

Brigham and Women's Hospital Global Health Hub
Cares for patients in underserved settings, provides education to staff who work in those areas to create sustainable change, and conducts research designed to improve health in such settings.
General, Infect Dis
⊕ https://vfmat.ch/a8a3

CARE
Works around the globe to save lives, defeat poverty, and achieve social justice.
ER Med, General
⊕ https://vfmat.ch/7232

Carter Center, The
Seeks to prevent and resolve conflicts, enhance freedom and democracy, and improve health, while remaining committed to human rights and the alleviation of human suffering.
Infect Dis, MF Med, Ophth-Opt
⊕ https://vfmat.ch/6556

Chain of Hope
Provides lifesaving heart operations for children around the world and supports the development of cardiac services in numerous developing and war-torn countries.
Anesth, CT Surg, CV Med, Crit-Care, Ped Surg, Peds, Pulm-Critic, Surg
⊕ https://vfmat.ch/1b1b

CharityVision International
Focuses on restoring curable sight impairment worldwide by empowering local physicians and creating sustainable solutions.
Logist-Op, Ophth-Opt, Surg
⊕ https://vfmat.ch/6231

Children of War Foundation
Delivers access to global health and education to communities affected by poverty, war, natural disaster, climate change, and migration challenges.
ER Med, General, Logist-Op, Peds, Surg
⊕ https://vfmat.ch/de51

Children's Lifeline International
Provides medical teams and surgical assistance to underprivileged children in developing countries through missions in partnership with local hospitals.
CV Med, Dent-OMFS, General, MF Med, Neurosurg, Peds, Rehab
⊕ https://vfmat.ch/6fea

Children's Cancer Hospital Foundation Egypt
Prevents and combats cancer through research, education, and healthcare, provided free of charge with passion and justice.
Anesth, ER Med, Heme-Onc, Infect Dis, Path, Peds, Radiol
⊕ https://vfmat.ch/e28b

Christian Aid Ministries
Strives to be a trustworthy and efficient channel for Amish, Mennonite, and other conservative Anabaptist groups and individuals to minister to physical and spiritual needs around the world.
CT Surg, ER Med, Logist-Op, Ortho, Pub Health
⊕ https://vfmat.ch/7b33

Columbia Vagelos College of Physicians and Surgeons Programs in Global Health
Harnesses the expertise of the medical school to improve health worldwide by training global health leaders, building capacity through interdisciplinary education and training programs, and addressing unmet health needs through research and application.
CV Med, Derm, Genetics, Heme-Onc, Infect Dis, Medicine, OB-GYN, Ophth-Opt, Peds, Psych, Pub Health, Pulm-Critic, Surg
⊕ https://vfmat.ch/a9e5

Covenant Medicine Outreach
Inspired by the Christian faith, provides medical care for those less fortunate.
General
⊕ https://vfmat.ch/769a

COVID-19 Clinical Research Coalition
Advocates and collaborates for the advancement of COVID-19 research driven by the needs of low-resource settings, and works for equitable access to solutions to the pandemic.
All-Immu, Infect-Dis, MF Med, Path, Pub Health
⊕ https://vfmat.ch/d1f4

Direct Relief
Improves the health and lives of people affected by poverty or emergency situations by mobilizing and providing essential medical resources needed for their care.
ER Med, Logist-Op
⊕ https://vfmat.ch/58e5

DKT INTERNATIONAL INC
Seeks to provide couples with affordable and safe options for family planning and HIV/AIDS prevention through dynamic social marketing.
General, Surg
⊕ https://vfmat.ch/b3a7

Doctors Without Borders/Médecins Sans Frontières (MSF)
Responds to emergencies and provides lifesaving medical care where needed most, including during disasters, conflicts, and epidemics.
Anesth, Crit-Care, ER Med, General, Infect Dis, Nutr, OB-GYN, Ped Surg, Peds, Psych, Pub Health, Surg
⊕ https://vfmat.ch/f363

Duke University: Global Health Institute
Sparks innovation in global health research and education, and brings together knowledge and resources to address the most important global health issues of our time.
All-Immu, Infect Dis, MF Med, OB-GYN, Pub Health
⊕ https://vfmat.ch/c4cd

Egypt Cancer Network 57357 USA
Provides resources to Egyptian hospitals and nonprofit organizations focused on cancer in the areas of patient care, scientific advancement, and education.
Pub Health
⊕ https://vfmat.ch/c14e

Evidence Project, The
Improves family-planning policies, programs, and practices through the strategic generation, translation, and use of evidence.
General, MF Med
⊕ https://vfmat.ch/f9e7

Eye Foundation of America
Works toward a world without childhood blindness.
Ophth-Opt
⊕ https://vfmat.ch/a7eb

Gift of Life International
Provides lifesaving cardiac treatment to children in developing countries while developing sustainable pediatric cardiac programs by implementing screening, surgical, and training missions.
Anesth, CT Surg, CV Med, Crit-Care, Ped Surg, Peds, Pulm-Critic
⊕ https://vfmat.ch/f2f9

Global Ministries – The United Methodist Church
As the worldwide mission and development agency of The United Methodist Church, Global Ministries works with more than 300 hospitals and clinics around the world through its Global Health Unit.
Anesth, CT Surg, CV Med, Crit-Care, Dent-OMFS, Derm, ER Med, GI, General, Infect Dis, Logist-Op, MF Med, Medicine, Neonat, Nephro, Nutr, OB-GYN, Ophth-Opt, Ortho, Palliative, Peds, Pod, Psych, Pub Health, Rehab, Rheum, Surg, Urol
⊕ https://vfmat.ch/1723

Global Oncology (GO)
Brings the best in cancer care to underserved patients around the world and collaborates across geographic, professional, and academic borders to improve cancer care, research, and education.
Heme-Onc, Path, Rad-Onc
⊕ https://vfmat.ch/fcb8

Globus Relief
Aims to improve the delivery of healthcare worldwide by gathering, processing, and distributing surplus medical supplies to charities at home and abroad.
Logist-Op
⊕ https://vfmat.ch/a2b7

Great Faith Vision
Partners with like-minded organizations to bring physical and spiritual sight to the communities served, inspired by the Christian faith.
Ophth-Opt
⊕ https://vfmat.ch/21e2

Health Outreach to the Middle East (H.O.M.E.)
Offers physical and Christian-inspired spiritual healing to people in need in the Middle East, providing medical care and education.
Anesth, Dent-OMFS, ER Med, General, Geri, Infect Dis, MF Med, Medicine, OB-GYN, Path, Peds, Psych, Surg
⊕ https://vfmat.ch/134e

Hospice Egypt
Seeks to support adult (18+) terminally ill patients, regardless of their socio-economic class, gender, or religion, completely free of charge.
Palliative
⊕ https://vfmat.ch/22a3

Humanity & Inclusion
Works alongside people with disabilities and vulnerable populations, taking action and bearing witness in order to respond to their essential needs, improve their living conditions and health, and promote respect for their dignity and fundamental rights.
General, Infect Dis, MF Med, Medicine, Ortho, Peds, Psych, Pub Health, Rehab
⊕ https://vfmat.ch/16b7

Institute for Healthcare Improvement (IHI)
Aims to improve health and healthcare worldwide by working with health professionals to strengthen systems.
Crit-Care, Infect Dis, MF Med, Medicine, Neonat, OB-GYN, Pub Health
⊕ https://vfmat.ch/ecae

International Children's Heart Foundation
Provides free surgical care, medical training, and technology to save the lives of children with congenital heart disease in developing countries.
Anesth, CT Surg, CV Med, Crit-Care, Ped Surg, Peds, Pulm-Critic
⊕ https://vfmat.ch/86c1

International Council of Ophthalmology
Works with ophthalmologic societies and others to enhance ophthalmic education and improve access to the highest-quality eye care in order to preserve and restore vision for people of the world.
Ophth-Opt
⊕ https://vfmat.ch/ffd2

International Eye Foundation (IEF)
Eliminates preventable and treatable blindness by making quality sustainable eye care services accessible and affordable worldwide.
Infect Dis, Logist-Op, Ophth-Opt
⊕ https://vfmat.ch/e839

International Federation of Gynecology and Obstetrics (FIGO)
Implements global projects on specific women's health issues.
MF Med, Medicine, Neonat, OB-GYN, Surg, Urol
⊕ https://vfmat.ch/c4b4

International Federation of Red Cross and Red Crescent Societies (IFRC)
Coordinates and directs international assistance following natural and manmade disasters in nonconflict situations through the world's largest humanitarian and development network. Provides disaster-preparedness programs, healthcare activities, and promotes humanitarian values.
ER Med, General, Infect Dis, Nutr
⊕ https://vfmat.ch/b4ee

International Learning Movement (ILM UK)
Supports some of the world's poorest people in developing countries with core projects in education, safe drinking water, and healthcare.
General, Ophth-Opt
⊕ https://vfmat.ch/b974

International Organization for Migration (IOM) – The UN Migration Agency
Promotes evidence-informed policies and holistic, preventive, and curative health programs that are beneficial, accessible, and equitable for vulnerable migrants.
General, Infect Dis, OB-GYN
⊕ https://vfmat.ch/621a

International Planned Parenthood Federation (IPPF)
Leads a locally owned, globally connected civil society movement that provides and enables services and champions sexual and reproductive health and rights for all, especially the underserved.
Infect Dis, MF Med, OB-GYN
⊕ https://vfmat.ch/dc97

International Trachoma Initiative (iTi)
Works toward a world free from trachoma, a preventable cause of blindness, and provides comprehensive support to national ministries of health and governmental and nongovernmental organizations to implement a comprehensive approach to fight trachoma.
Infect Dis, Ophth-Opt
⊕ https://vfmat.ch/3278

InterSurgeon
Fosters collaborative partnerships in the field of global surgery that will advance clinical care, teaching, training, research, and the provision and maintenance of medical equipment.
ENT, Neurosurg, Ortho, Ped Surg, Plast, Surg, Urol
⊕ https://vfmat.ch/6f8a

IOF – International Osteoporosis Foundation
Aims to fight against osteoporosis and promote bone and musculoskeletal health worldwide.
Endo, OB-GYN, Ortho
⊕ https://vfmat.ch/89d8

Islamic Medical Association of North America
Fosters health promotion, disease prevention, and health maintenance in communities around the world through direct patient care and health programs.
Anesth, Dent-OMFS, ER Med, General, Logist-Op, Ophth-Opt, Peds, Plast, Surg
⊕ https://vfmat.ch/a157

John Snow, Inc. (JSI)
Aims to improve the health and well-being of underserved and vulnerable people and communities throughout the world.
General, Infect Dis, Logist-Op, MF Med, OB-GYN, Peds, Psych, Pub Health
⊕ https://vfmat.ch/ba78

Johns Hopkins Center for Communication Programs
Believes in the power of communication to save lives by empowering people to adopt healthy behaviors for themselves, their families, and their communities.
General, Infect Dis, Logist-Op, OB-GYN, Pub Health
⊕ https://vfmat.ch/1bf9

Kybele Incorporated
Aims to create healthcare partnerships across borders to improve childbirth safety.
Anesth, Neonat, OB-GYN, Pub Health
⊕ https://vfmat.ch/5fc9

La Salle International Foundation
Provides support for educational, health, and human services, along with

humanitarian relief to people in developed and underdeveloped areas.
General
⊕ https://vfmat.ch/5891

Light for Sight 21
Aims to eliminate severe visual impairment among all children and adolescents with keratoconus.
Ophth-Opt
⊕ https://vfmat.ch/ef55

Limbs International
Engages communities and transforms lives through affordable, sustainable prosthetic solutions and rehabilitation services in developing countries.
Logist-Op, Ortho, Pod, Rehab
⊕ https://vfmat.ch/dc84

Magdi Yacoub Global Heart Foundation
Works to change the health outcomes of the most vulnerable, particularly children, by improving comprehensive, advanced cardiac care available to all people in need.
CT Surg, CV Med, Medicine, Vasc Surg
⊕ https://vfmat.ch/2f6c

Management Sciences for Health (MSH)
Works with countries and communities to save lives and improve the health of the world's poorest and most vulnerable people by building strong, resilient, sustainable health systems.
Infect Dis, Logist-Op, Pub Health
⊕ https://vfmat.ch/6aa2

MAP International
Provides medicines and health supplies to those in need around the world so they might experience life to the fullest.
Logist-Op
⊕ https://vfmat.ch/deed

Medical Mission Aid Inc
Advances effective healthcare in disadvantaged communities through medical scholarships, grants for supplies and support for local health initiatives.
Infect Dis, Logist-Op, OB-GYN, Pub Health, Rehab
⊕ https://vfmat.ch/8b83

Medici Per I Diritti Umani (MEDU)
Treats and brings medical aid to the most vulnerable populations, and—starting from medical practice—denounces violations of human rights and, in particular, exclusion from access to treatment.
ER Med, General, Psych, Pub Health
⊕ https://vfmat.ch/5384

MedShare
Aims to improve the quality of life of people, communities, and the planet by sourcing and directly delivering surplus medical supplies and equipment to communities in need around the world.
Logist-Op
⊕ https://vfmat.ch/c8bc

MSD for Mothers
Designs scalable solutions that help end preventable maternal deaths.
MF Med, OB-GYN, Pub Health
⊕ https://vfmat.ch/9f99

Médecins du Monde/Doctors of the World
Provides care, bears witness, and supports social change worldwide with innovative medical programs and evidence-based advocacy initiatives.
ER Med, General, Infect Dis, MF Med, Neonat, OB-GYN, Peds, Pub Health
⊕ https://vfmat.ch/a43d

NCD Alliance
Unites and strengthens civil society to stimulate collaborative advocacy, action, and accountability for NCD (noncommunicable disease) prevention and control.
All-Immu, CV Med, General, Heme-Onc, Medicine, Peds, Psych
⊕ https://vfmat.ch/abdd

Operation International
Offers medical aid to adults and children suffering from lack of quality healthcare in impoverished countries.
Dent-OMFS, ER Med, Heme-Onc, OB-GYN, Ophth-Opt, Ortho, Ped Surg, Plast, Surg
⊕ https://vfmat.ch/b52a

Operation Smile
Treats patients with cleft lip and cleft palate, and creates solutions that deliver safe surgery to people where it's needed most.
Anesth, Dent-OMFS, ENT, Ped Surg, Plast
⊕ https://vfmat.ch/5c29

Options
Believes in a world in which women and children can access the high-quality health services they need, without financial burden.
Logist-Op, MF Med, Neonat, OB-GYN
⊕ https://vfmat.ch/3a48

Order of Malta
Supports forgotten or excluded people, especially those living in conflict zones or amid natural disasters, by providing medical assistance, caring for refugees, and distributing medicines and necessities.
ER Med, General, Infect Dis, MF Med, Nephro, OB-GYN, Ortho, Psych
⊕ https://vfmat.ch/1fab

Pan-African Academy of Christian Surgeons (PAACS)
Aims to train and disciple African surgeons and related specialists to become leaders and servants, providing excellent and compassionate care to those most in need, based in Christian ministry.
Anesth, CT Surg, OB-GYN, Ortho, Ped Surg, Plast, Surg
⊕ https://vfmat.ch/b444

Pan-African Academy of Christian Surgeons (PAACS)
Exists to train and support African surgeons to provide excellent, compassionate care to those most in need, inspired by the Christian faith.
Anesth, CT Surg, Neurosurg, OB-GYN, Ortho, Ped Surg, Plast, Surg
⊕ https://vfmat.ch/85ba

Pathfinder International
Champions sexual and reproductive health and rights worldwide, mobilizing communities most in need to break through barriers and forge paths to a healthier future.
OB-GYN
⊕ https://vfmat.ch/a7b3

PEACE
Aims to offer children a higher quality of life by providing access to life-changing medical procedures through volunteer doctors, hospitals, and community members.
Peds
⊕ https://vfmat.ch/f8c5

Ponseti International
Provides global leadership in building high-quality, locally directed, and sustainable capacity to deliver the Ponseti clubfoot care pathway at the country level.
Ortho, Ped Surg, Peds, Rehab
⊕ https://vfmat.ch/476b

Population Council
Conducts research to address critical health and development issues, helping deliver solutions to improve lives around the world.
Logist-Op, Pub Health
⊕ https://vfmat.ch/1777

Project HOPE
Works on the front lines of the world's health challenges, partnering hand-in-hand with communities, healthcare workers, and public health systems to ensure sustainable change.
CV Med, ER Med, Endo, General, Infect Dis, MF Med, Peds
⊕ https://vfmat.ch/2bd7

Reach

Promotes the health of vulnerable populations through technical support to local, regional, and global efforts to prevent and control rheumatic fever and rheumatic heart disease (RF/RHD).

CV Med, Medicine, Pub Health

⊕ https://vfmat.ch/3f52

Real Medicine Foundation (RMF)

Provides humanitarian support to people living in disaster- and poverty-stricken areas, focusing on the person as a whole by providing medical/physical, emotional, economic, and social support.

ER Med, General, Infect Dis, Nutr, Peds, Psych

⊕ https://vfmat.ch/d45a

Refuge Egypt

Serves refugees, migrants, and asylum-seekers living in Egypt who have fled their original country of nationality. Provides programs in humanitarian assistance and youth outreach, along with capacity and livelihoods programs, education, and medical services.

General, Infect Dis, Medicine, OB-GYN, Peds, Psych

⊕ https://vfmat.ch/fb9f

Resource Exchange International

Provides holistic education and training to improve knowledge and skills and build human capacity within communities in emerging nations.

Derm, ENT, Ortho

⊕ https://vfmat.ch/6d49

Resource Exchange International

Sends long-term staff and short-term professionals in areas of education, medicine, and business to train leaders in emerging nations so that they can train others.

General

⊕ https://vfmat.ch/6863

RestoringVision

Empowers lives by restoring vision for millions of people in need.

Ophth-Opt

⊕ https://vfmat.ch/e121

Rotaplast International

Helps children and families worldwide by eliminating the burden of cleft lip and/or palate, burn scarring, and other deformities by sending medical teams to provide free reconstructive surgery, ancillary treatment, and training.

Anesth, Dent-OMFS, ENT, Ped Surg, Plast, Surg

⊕ https://vfmat.ch/78b3

Rotary International

Provides service to others, improves lives, and advances world understanding, goodwill, and peace through its fellowship of business, professional, and community leaders.

ER Med, General, Infect Dis, MF Med, OB-GYN

⊕ https://vfmat.ch/8fb5

Save the Children

Gives children around the world a healthy start in life, the opportunity to learn, and protection from harm.

All-Immu, Crit-Care, ER Med, General, Infect Dis, MF Med, Medicine, Neonat, OB-GYN, Peds, Psych, Pub Health

⊕ https://vfmat.ch/2e73

SEVA

Delivers vital eye care services to the world's most vulnerable, including women, children, and Indigenous peoples.

Ophth-Opt, Surg

⊕ https://vfmat.ch/1e87

Smile Train, Inc.

Treats children with cleft lip through a sustainable and local model that supports surgery and other forms of essential care.

Logist-Op, Pub Health

⊕ https://vfmat.ch/822c

Solthis

Improves disease prevention and access to quality care by strengthening the health systems and services of the countries served.

General, Infect Dis, Logist-Op, MF Med, Neonat, Path

⊕ https://vfmat.ch/a71d

Syrian American Medical Society (SAMS)

Provides medical professionals with continued training, networking, and opportunities to participate in humanitarian efforts affecting conflict-impacted populations.

CT Surg, CV Med, Crit-Care, Dent-OMFS, Endo, GI, General, Logist-Op, Medicine, Nephro, OB-GYN, Ophth-Opt, Path, Peds, Plast, Psych, Pulm-Critic, Radiol, Rehab, Surg, Urol

⊕ https://vfmat.ch/5dbf

Task Force for Global Health, The

Consists of programs and focus areas that cover a range of global health issues including neglected tropical diseases, infectious diseases, vaccines, field epidemiology, public health informatics, health workforce development, and global health ethics.

Infect Dis, Logist-Op, Medicine, Ophth-Opt, Peds

⊕ https://vfmat.ch/714c

Team 5 Medical Foundation

Provides medical care in the most overlooked remote areas of the world supported by sponsorships, donations, and the dedication of its volunteers.

ER Med, General, Peds, Plast, Pulm-Critic

⊕ https://vfmat.ch/f267

Tearfund

Responds to crisis and partners with local churches to bring restoration to those living in poverty, inspired by the Christian faith.

ER Med, Logist-Op

⊕ https://vfmat.ch/f6cf

Terre des hommes (Tdh) Foundation

Works to improve the daily life of children and their relatives in the areas of health, protection and emergency, in Europe, Africa, Asia, Latin America, and the Near and Middle East.

CT Surg, CV Med, OB-GYN, Ped Surg, Pub Health

⊕ https://vfmat.ch/5c26

Transplant Links Community (TLC)

Provides hands-on training in kidney transplantation for surgeons, doctors, and nurses in low- and middle-income countries.

Nephro, Surg, Urol

⊕ https://vfmat.ch/bb46

Union for International Cancer Control (UICC)

Unites and supports the cancer community to reduce the global cancer burden, promote greater equity, and ensure that cancer control continues to be a priority in the world health and development agenda.

Heme-Onc, Pub Health

⊕ https://vfmat.ch/88b1

Unite 4 Humanity

Aims to provide emergency aid and support for Muslim communities across the world.

General, Nutr, OB-GYN, Ophth-Opt, Plast, Psych, Rehab

⊕ https://vfmat.ch/fbe7

United Nations Children's Fund (UNICEF)

Works in over 190 countries and territories to save children's lives, defend their rights, and help them fulfill their potential, from early childhood through adolescence.

All-Immu, Infect Dis, MF Med, Neonat, Nutr, OB-GYN, Ped Surg, Peds, Pub Health

⊕ https://vfmat.ch/42d7

United Nations Development Programme (UNDP)

Helps countries achieve the simultaneous eradication of extreme poverty and significant reduction of inequalities and exclusion using a sustainable human development approach.

Infect Dis, Logist-Op, Pub Health
🌐 https://vfmat.ch/935c

United Nations High Commissioner for Refugees (UNHCR)
Safeguards the rights and well-being of people who have been forced to flee, ensuring that everybody has the right to seek asylum and find safe refuge in another country, with the goal of seeking lasting solutions.
General, MF Med, Medicine, OB-GYN, Peds, Psych, Pub Health
🌐 https://vfmat.ch/6636

United Nations Population Fund (UNFPA)
Supports reproductive healthcare for women and youth in more than 150 countries, focusing on delivering a world in which every pregnancy is wanted, every childbirth is safe, and every young person's potential is fulfilled.
Infect Dis, MF Med, Neonat, OB-GYN, Peds, Pub Health
🌐 https://vfmat.ch/c969

University of New Mexico School of Medicine: Project Echo
Seeks to improve health outcomes worldwide through the use of a technology called telementoring, a guided-practice model in which the participating clinician retains responsibility for managing the patient.
General, Infect Dis, MF Med, OB-GYN, Path, Peds
🌐 https://vfmat.ch/6c9a

USAID: Maternal and Child Health Integrated Program
Works to improve the health of women and their families, including programs for maternal, newborn, and child health, immunization, family planning, nutrition, malaria, and HIV/AIDS.
All-Immu, General, Infect Dis, MF Med
🌐 https://vfmat.ch/4415

USAID: Maternal and Child Survival Program
Works to prevent child and maternal deaths.
Infect Dis, MF Med, Neonat, OB-GYN, Peds
🌐 https://vfmat.ch/6fcf

Vision Care
Restores sight and helps patients get regular treatment at short-term eye camps and long-term base clinics by having doctors, missionaries, volunteers, and sponsors work together.
Ophth-Opt
🌐 https://vfmat.ch/9d7c

Vision for All Foundation
Implements ophthalmic healthcare projects; aims to create and support ophthalmic centers and existing structures in order to support the training of medical and paramedical personnel in the ophthalmology; and seeks to promote prevention, diagnosis, and treatment of ophthalmic pathologies.
Dent-OMFS, Ophth-Opt, Pub Health
🌐 https://vfmat.ch/dd72

Vision Outreach International
Advocates for helping the blind in underserved regions of the world and empowers the poor through sight restoration.
Ophth-Opt
🌐 https://vfmat.ch/9721

Visionaries International
Works toward reducing the burden of corneal blindness in the developing world by assessing and addressing what limits corneal surgeons in each locale.
Anesth, Ophth-Opt, Pub Health, Surg
🌐 https://vfmat.ch/3d2e

We Care for Humanity (WCH)
Promotes sustainable social change and the sustainable development goals developed by the United Nations, including: no poverty, good health and well-being, gender equality, human rights, climate action, and strong institutions.
General, Logist-Op, Pub Health
🌐 https://vfmat.ch/8b4e

Wings of Healing
Provides medical aid and education to African countries through medical mission programs and long-term educational partnerships.

Anesth, MF Med, Neonat, OB-GYN, Surg
🌐 https://vfmat.ch/f1e4

World Federation of Hemophilia (WFH)
Aims to improve and sustain care for people with inherited bleeding disorders by pursuing long-term relationships with individuals and organizations who share the values of WFH's development model.
Heme-Onc
🌐 https://vfmat.ch/5121

World Health Organization, The (WHO)
The United Nations' agency for health provides leadership on global health matters, shapes the health research agenda, sets norms and standards, articulates evidence-based policy options, provides technical support and monitoring to countries, and assesses health trends.
ER Med, General, Infect Dis, Logist-Op, MF Med, OB-GYN, Peds, Psych, Pub Health
🌐 https://vfmat.ch/c476

World Medical Relief
Facilitates the distribution of surplus medical resources where they are needed.
Logist-Op
🌐 https://vfmat.ch/72dc

World Parkinson's Program
Seeks to improve the quality of life of those affected by Parkinson's disease through education and advocacy, and provides free medication and support services.
Logist-Op, Neuro, Pub Health
🌐 https://vfmat.ch/c96d

Egypt

Healthcare Facilities

10th of Ramadan Central Hospital
Tenth of Ramadan, Sharqia, Egypt
⊕ https://vfmat.ch/63be

6th of October City Central Hospital
Sixth of October, Giza, Egypt
⊕ https://vfmat.ch/ab5a

6th of October Hospital for Health Insurance
Dokki, Giza, Egypt
⊕ https://vfmat.ch/fca5

Abbasiya Mental Health Hospital
Nasr City, Cairo, Egypt
⊕ https://vfmat.ch/1774

Adam International Hospital (Giza Branch)
Agouza, Giza, Egypt
⊕ https://vfmat.ch/9293

Adam International Hospital (Nasr City Branch)
Nasr City, Cairo, Egypt
⊕ https://vfmat.ch/7xve

Adam International Hospital (Tanta Branch)
Tanta, Gharbia, Egypt
⊕ https://vfmat.ch/ja1q

Agouza Police Hospital
Giza, Giza, Egypt
⊕ https://vfmat.ch/3443

Ahmed Galal Military Hospital
El Nozha, Cairo Governorate, Egypt
⊕ https://vfmat.ch/87ef

Ahmed Maher Teaching Hospital
Ābdīn, Cairo, Egypt
⊕ https://vfmat.ch/6d8d

Air Force Hospital (Aviation Hospital)
Abbasseya, Cairo, Egypt
⊕ https://vfmat.ch/3fe5

Al Agouza Hospital
Agouza, Giza, Egypt
⊕ https://vfmat.ch/91db

Al Amal Hospital
Mīt 'Uqbah, Giza, Egypt
⊕ https://vfmat.ch/4f8b

Al Azhar University Hospital
Nasr City, Cairo Governorate, Egypt
⊕ https://vfmat.ch/7ebc

Al Bank Al Ahly Hospital
Al Basātīn, Cairo, Egypt
⊕ https://vfmat.ch/8ec9

Al Delta Hospital
Ras El Bar, Damietta, Egypt
⊕ https://vfmat.ch/7256

Al Fath Islamic Hospital
Maadi, Cairo Governorate, Egypt
⊕ https://vfmat.ch/42f1

Al Hayat Hospital
Al Walideyah Al Qebleyah, Assiut Governorate, Egypt
⊕ https://vfmat.ch/ade4

Al Helal Hospital
Abdeen, Cairo, Egypt
⊕ https://vfmat.ch/32c1

Al Nas Hospital
Shubra El Kheima 2, Qalyubiyya, Egypt
⊕ https://vfmat.ch/rqwd

Al Rawda Hospital
Manial Alrawda, Cairo, Egypt
⊕ https://vfmat.ch/6f41

Al Safwa Hospital
Sixth of October, Giza Governorate, Egypt
⊕ https://vfmat.ch/7514

Al Salam Eye Hospital
Asyut, Asyut Governorate, Egypt
⊕ https://vfmat.ch/c637

Al Salam Hospital
Agouza, Giza Governorate, Egypt
⊕ https://vfmat.ch/5534

Al Shorouk Hospital
Mohandeseen, Giza Governorate, Egypt
⊕ https://vfmat.ch/342e

Al Wadi Hospital
Sixth of October, Giza, Egypt
⊕ https://vfmat.ch/48e8

Al Watany Eye Hospital (WEH)
El Nozha, Cairo, Egypt
⊕ https://vfmat.ch/5b64

Alexandria International Hospital
Alexandria, Alexandria, Egypt
⊕ https://vfmat.ch/e4d8

Alexandria University Hospital For Students
Bab Sharqi, Alexandria, Egypt
⊕ https://vfmat.ch/7cea

Alsalam Hospital – El Mohandessin
Agouza, Giza, Egypt
⊕ https://vfmat.ch/gfp1

Andalusia Hospital Maadi
Cairo, Egypt
⊕ https://vfmat.ch/t6xf

Arab Contractors Medical Center
Nasr City, Cairo, Egypt
⊕ https://vfmat.ch/77b9

Armed Forces Hospital Kobry El Kobba
Heliopolis, Cairo, Egypt
⊕ https://vfmat.ch/2be1

As-Salam International Hospital
New Cairo, Cairo, Egypt
⊕ https://vfmat.ch/ecbc

Aswan Chest Diseases Hospital
Aswan, Aswan Governorate, Egypt
⊕ https://vfmat.ch/8c24

Aswan Military Hospital
Aswan, Aswan, Egypt
⊕ https://vfmat.ch/3b9e

Asyut University Hospital
Asyut 2, Asyut, Egypt
⊕ https://vfmat.ch/4acb

Badran Hospital
Dokki, Giza, Egypt
⊕ https://vfmat.ch/ae21

Badrawi Hospital
Agouza, Giza, Egypt
⊕ https://vfmat.ch/7fc9

Baheya Hospital
Minya El Qamh, Giza, Egypt
⊕ https://vfmat.ch/5vjs

Banha University Hospital
Banha, Qalyubiyya, Egypt
⊕ https://vfmat.ch/d36d

Beni Suef General Hospital
Beni Suef, Beni Suef, Egypt
⊕ https://vfmat.ch/424e

Beni Suef University Hospital
Beni Suef, Beni Suef, Egypt
⊕ https://vfmat.ch/4a17

Borg El Arab University Hospital Pediatric Oncology Center
Borg El Arab, Alexandria, Egypt
⊕ https://vfmat.ch/g6qt

Borg El Zahraa Hospital
Beni Suef, Beni Suef, Egypt
⊕ https://vfmat.ch/35bd

Cairo University Hospitals
Old Cairo, Cairo, Egypt
⊕ https://vfmat.ch/kvi1

Children's Cancer Hospital Egypt 57357
Cairo, Egypt
⊕ https://vfmat.ch/kaiw

Cleopatra Hospitals – Nile Badrawi Hospital
Maadi, Cairo, Egypt
⊕ https://vfmat.ch/fd1f

Coptic Hospital
Cairo, Cairo, Egypt
⊕ https://vfmat.ch/d836

Damascus Hospital Cairo
Giza, Giza Governorate, Egypt
⊕ https://vfmat.ch/32b7

Damietta Cancer Institute
Damietta, Damietta Governorate, Egypt
⊕ https://vfmat.ch/d1e3

Dar Al Fouad Hospital (Cairo Branch)
Nasr City, Cairo, Egypt
⊕ https://vfmat.ch/bf82

Dar Al Fouad Hospital (Giza Branch, Main)
Sixth of October, Giza, Egypt
⊕ https://vfmat.ch/1e73

Dar Al Shifa Hospital
Sadat City, Monufia, Egypt
⊕ https://vfmat.ch/a946

Dar Alhekma Hospital
Nasr City, Cairo, Egypt
⊕ https://vfmat.ch/6ab2

Demerdash Hospital
El Weili, Cairo, Egypt
⊕ https://vfmat.ch/e76f

Desouk General Hospital
Desouk, Kafr El Sheikh, Egypt
⊕ https://vfmat.ch/986f

Dr. Abou El Azayem Hospital (Nasr City Branch)
Nasr City, Cairo, Egypt
⊕ https://vfmat.ch/41dc

Dr. Mohamed Shabrawichy Hospital
Dokki, Giza, Egypt
⊕ https://vfmat.ch/cb63

Dr. Yosri Gohar Gohar Hospital
Old Cairo, Cairo, Egypt
⊕ https://vfmat.ch/596f

Dream Hospital
Sixth of October, Giza, Egypt
⊕ https://vfmat.ch/819b

Egyptair Hospital
El Nozha, Cairo, Egypt
⊕ https://vfmat.ch/ebaa

El Badari Central Hospital
El Badari, Asyut, Egypt
⊕ https://vfmat.ch/a3bc

El Badrawy Hospital
Montaza 2, Alexandria, Egypt
⊕ https://vfmat.ch/7c92

EL Demerdash Hospital
El Weili, Cairo, Egypt
⊕ https://vfmat.ch/f4he

El Doaah Hospital (The Preachers Hospital)
Heliopolis, Cairo, Egypt
⊕ https://vfmat.ch/4859

El Farafra Central Hospital
Farafra, New Valley, Egypt
⊕ https://vfmat.ch/9b5b

El Fath Hospital
Alexandria, Alexandria, Egypt
⊕ https://vfmat.ch/672d

El Galaa Teaching Hospital
Azbakeya, Cairo, Egypt
⊕ https://vfmat.ch/48af

El Ghandour Hospital (10th of Ramadan City Branch)
Tenth of Ramadan, Sharqia, Egypt
⊕ https://vfmat.ch/a245

El Ghandour Hospital (Bilbeis Branch)
Bilbeis, Sharqia, Egypt
⊕ https://vfmat.ch/b61d

El Helmeya Military Hospital
Zeitoun, Cairo, Egypt
⊕ https://vfmat.ch/72a5

El Hussein University Hospital
El Darb El Ahmar, Cairo, Egypt
⊕ https://vfmat.ch/rryy

El Khalifa General Hospital
El-Darb El-Ahmar, Cairo, Egypt
⊕ https://vfmat.ch/e796

El Kurdi Central Hospital
El Kurdi, Dakahlia, Egypt
⊕ https://vfmat.ch/d2fd

El Mabarra Hospital Assiut
Assiut, Assiut, Egypt
⊕ https://vfmat.ch/3c57

El Mabarra Hospital Maadi
Maadi, Cairo, Egypt
⊕ https://vfmat.ch/5cf4

El Mabarra Hospital Minya
Minya, Minya, Egypt
⊕ https://vfmat.ch/c4ba

El Maragha Central Hospital
El Maragha, Sohag, Egypt
⊕ https://vfmat.ch/9638

El Merghany Hospital
Nasr City, Cairo, Egypt
⊕ https://vfmat.ch/ac12

El Nada Hospital (El Manial Branch)
Old Cairo, Cairo, Egypt
⊕ https://vfmat.ch/eb9e

El Nozha International Hospital
El Nozha, Cairo, Egypt
⊕ https://vfmat.ch/c15a

El Obour Health Insurance Hospital
Kafr El Sheikh 1, Kafr El Sheikh, Egypt
⊕ https://vfmat.ch/d6d3

El Qabbary General Hospital
Port al-Basal, Alexandria, Egypt
⊕ https://vfmat.ch/d324

El Rakhawy Hospital (El Mokattam branch)
El Mokattam, Cairo, Egypt
⊕ https://vfmat.ch/4132

El Rayyan Hospital
Maadi, Cairo, Egypt
⊕ https://vfmat.ch/4e31

El Sadat Central Hospital
Sadat City, Monufia, Egypt
⊕ https://vfmat.ch/ef93

El Safa Hospital
Agouza, Giza, Egypt
⊕ https://vfmat.ch/3b17

El Senbellawein General Hospital
El Senbellawein, Dakhalia, Egypt
⊕ https://vfmat.ch/5133

El Shatby University Hospital for Obstetricians & Gynecologists
Bab Sharqi, Alexandria, Egypt
⊕ https://vfmat.ch/748a

El Zaqaziq General Hospital
Zagazig, Sharqia, Egypt
⊕ https://vfmat.ch/5cde

El Zawya El Hamra General Hospital
El Zawya El Hamra, Cairo, Egypt
⊕ https://vfmat.ch/ab64

El Zohour Hospital
Sixth of October, Giza, Egypt
⊕ https://vfmat.ch/7fbe

Elaj Hospital (Nasr City Branch)
Nasr City, Cairo, Egypt
⊕ https://vfmat.ch/p4mn

Elite Hospital
Alexandria, Alexandria, Egypt
⊕ https://vfmat.ch/caln

Eye Hospital, The
Bab Sharqi, Alexandria, Egypt
⊕ https://vfmat.ch/7ea7

Faiyum General Hospital
Faiyum, Faiyum, Egypt
⊕ https://vfmat.ch/93dd

Fever Hospital Mahalla
El Mahalla El Kubra, Gharbia, Egypt
⊕ https://vfmat.ch/ae2d

Forsan Elsahraa Orabi Specialist Hospital
Marsa Matrouh, Matrouh, Egypt
⊕ https://vfmat.ch/bac5

Gamal Abdel Nasser Hospital
Bab Sharqi, Alexandria, Egypt
⊕ https://vfmat.ch/ce37

Ganzouri Specialized Hospital
Zeitoun, Cairo, Egypt
⊕ https://vfmat.ch/4yeh

General Military Hospital for Families
El Sharabiya, Cairo, Egypt
⊕ https://vfmat.ch/ba3e

Gezeera International Hospital – El Sallab
El Mansoura 1, Dakhlia, Egypt
⊕ https://vfmat.ch/c5ce

Green Crescent Hospital (10th of Ramadan City)
Tenth of Ramadan City, Sharqia, Egypt
⊕ https://vfmat.ch/e82f

Hassabo International Hospital
Nasr City, Cairo, Egypt
⊕ https://vfmat.ch/7edf

Health Insurance Hospital Beni Suef
Beni Suef, Beni Suef, Egypt
⊕ https://vfmat.ch/efd7

Heliopolis Hospital
El Nozha, Cairo, Egypt
⊕ https://vfmat.ch/cf97

Helwan General Hospital
Helwan, Cairo, Egypt
⊕ https://vfmat.ch/d2a2

Helwan Mental Health Hospital
Helwan, Cairo, Egypt
⊕ https://vfmat.ch/eef8

Hurghada Fever Hospital
Hurghada 1, Red Sea, Egypt
⊕ https://vfmat.ch/73cf

Hurghada General Hospital
Hurghada 2, Red Sea, Egypt
⊕ https://vfmat.ch/7d95

Hurghada Military Hospital
Hurghada 2, Red Sea, Egypt
⊕ https://vfmat.ch/e4ca

Ibn Sina Hospital
Tenth of Ramadan, Sharqia, Egypt
⊕ https://vfmat.ch/29e4

Internal Medicine Hospital Kasr Alainy
El Sayeda Zeinab, Cairo, Egypt
⊕ https://vfmat.ch/b6ed

Islamic Call Hospital
Beni Suef, Beni Suef, Egypt
⊕ https://vfmat.ch/3e43

Ismailia General Hospital
Ismailia, Ismailia, Egypt
⊕ https://vfmat.ch/a84f

Italian Hospital Umberto I Cairo
El Weili, Cairo, Egypt
⊕ https://vfmat.ch/c1a5

Khamis Specialized Hospital
Tenth of Ramadan, Sharqia, Egypt
⊕ https://vfmat.ch/ea3c

Luxor General Hospital
Luxor, Luxor, Egypt
⊕ https://vfmat.ch/5baf

Maadi Armed Forces Hospital
Maadi, Cairo, Egypt
⊕ https://vfmat.ch/4eab

Madina Women's Hospital
Sidi Gaber, Alexandria, Egypt
⊕ https://vfmat.ch/8549

Magrabi Eye Hospital Cairo
El Khalifa, Cairo, Egypt
⊕ https://vfmat.ch/e1f2

Mansheyet El Bakry General Hospital
Heliopolis, Cairo, Egypt
⊕ https://vfmat.ch/7115

Mansoura International Hospital
Mansoura, Dakahlia, Egypt
⊕ https://vfmat.ch/5fee

Mansoura Military Hospital
El Mansoura, Dakahlia, Egypt
⊕ https://vfmat.ch/cb99

Mansoura University Hospital
El Mansoura, Dakahlia, Egypt
⊕ https://vfmat.ch/89c7

Matrouh General Hospital
Mersa Matruh, Matrouh, Egypt
⊕ https://vfmat.ch/78bd

Minya General Hospital
Minya, Minya, Egypt
⊕ https://vfmat.ch/26e7

Minya University Hospital
Minya, Minya, Egypt
⊕ https://vfmat.ch/2256

Misr Al Gadida Military Hospital
Ain Shams, Cairo, Egypt
⊕ https://vfmat.ch/a812

Misr International Hospital (Dokki Branch)
Dokki, Giza, Egypt
⊕ https://vfmat.ch/73aa

Mokattam Specialized Hospital
El Mokattam, Cairo, Egypt
⊕ https://vfmat.ch/b2da

Mostafa Kamel Hospital for Armed Forces
Sidi Gaber, Alexandria, Egypt
⊕ https://vfmat.ch/a8ae

Nasaaem Hospital
New Cairo 1, Cairo, Egypt
⊕ https://vfmat.ch/eed4

Nasr City Health Insurance Hospital
Nasr City, Cairo, Egypt
⊕ https://vfmat.ch/fd1e

Nasr Hospital Helwan
Helwan, Cairo, Egypt
⊕ https://vfmat.ch/a89c

Nasser Institute For Research and Treatment
El Sahel, Cairo, Egypt
⊕ https://vfmat.ch/be8e

National Cancer Institute
Cairo, Cairo, Egypt
⊕ https://vfmat.ch/97d8

National Heart Institute
Agouza, Giza, Egypt
⊕ https://vfmat.ch/d3a7

Naval Military Hospital, The
Gomrok, Alexandria, Egypt
⊕ https://vfmat.ch/d869

New University Hospital
Sidi Gaber, Alexandria, Egypt
⊕ https://vfmat.ch/316c

Nile Health Insurance Hospital
Shubra El Kheima 1, Qalyubiyya, Egypt
⊕ https://vfmat.ch/be2b

Nile Hospital
Hurghada 1, Red Sea, Egypt
⊕ https://vfmat.ch/jpku

Noor Mohammadi Specialist Hospital
El Warraq, Giza, Egypt
⊕ https://vfmat.ch/593d

October 6 University Hospital (O6U Hospital)
Sixth of October, Giza, Egypt
⊕ https://vfmat.ch/eiam

Om El Nour Hospital
Heliopolis, Cairo, Egypt
⊕ https://vfmat.ch/3836

One Day Surgeries Hospital (El Zawya El Hamra Branch)
El Zawya El Hamra, Cairo, Egypt
⊕ https://vfmat.ch/75ae

One Day Surgeries Hospital (Maadi Branch)
Maadi, Cairo, Egypt
⊕ https://vfmat.ch/8dc8

One Day Surgeries Hospital (Ras El Bar Branch)
Ras El Bar, Damietta, Egypt
⊕ https://vfmat.ch/bab9

Palestine Hospital
Heliopolis, Cairo, Egypt
⊕ https://vfmat.ch/5fe1

Petroleum Gas – Petrogas Hospital
Heliopolis, Cairo, Egypt
⊕ https://vfmat.ch/ee96

Petroleum Hospital
Alexandria, Alexandria, Egypt
⊕ https://vfmat.ch/6cd7

Police Hospital 6th of October City
Sixth of October, Giza Governorate, Egypt
⊕ https://vfmat.ch/22aa

Police Hospital Alexandria
Amreya 1, Alexandria, Egypt
⊕ https://vfmat.ch/2dfd

Police Hospital Asyut
Asyut 2, Asyut, Egypt
⊕ https://vfmat.ch/cb36

Police Hospital Nasr City
Nasr City, Cairo, Egypt
⊕ https://vfmat.ch/ac4e

Port Ghalib Hospital
Marsa Alam, Red Sea, Egypt
⊕ https://vfmat.ch/a6cc

Qalin Central Hospital
Qallin, Kafr El Sheikh, Egypt
⊕ https://vfmat.ch/8d15

Qalioub Specialized Hospital (Qalioub Central Hospital)
Qalyub, Qalyubiyya, Egypt
⊕ https://vfmat.ch/dbe3

Qena General Hospital
Qena, Qena, Egypt
⊕ https://vfmat.ch/527e

Rabaa El Adaweya Medical Center
Nasr City, Cairo, Egypt
⊕ https://vfmat.ch/9a95

Ras El Bar Central Hospital
Ras El Bar, Damietta, Egypt
⊕ https://vfmat.ch/c641

Ras Sidr General Hospital
Ras Sidr, South Sinai, Egypt
⊕ https://vfmat.ch/b86e

Research Institute of Ophthalmology
Giza, Giza, Egypt
⊕ https://vfmat.ch/4815

Royal Hospital
Maadi, Cairo, Egypt
⊕ https://vfmat.ch/9d4c

Sadr Esna Hospital
Esna, Luxor, Egypt
⊕ https://vfmat.ch/c9c6

Safwat Al Golf Hospital
Nasr City, Cairo, Egypt
⊕ https://vfmat.ch/88c6

Sahla Hospital
Moharam Bek, Alexandria, Egypt
⊕ https://vfmat.ch/7713

Saint Catherine Hospital
Saint Catherine, South Sinai, Egypt
⊕ https://vfmat.ch/481e

Sandoub Health Insurance Hospital
El Mansoura, Dakahlia, Egypt
⊕ https://vfmat.ch/acbc

Saudi German Hospital – Cairo
El Nozha, Cairo, Egypt
⊕ https://vfmat.ch/a2wb

Shaker Hospital
Heliopolis, Cairo Governorate, Egypt
⊕ https://vfmat.ch/39d9

Sharm International Hospital
Sharm El Sheikh 1, South Sinai, Egypt
⊕ https://vfmat.ch/4a97

Sharq El Madina Hospital
Montaza 2, Alexandria, Egypt
⊕ https://vfmat.ch/a1bb

Sidi Gaber Specialized Hospital
Sidi Gaber, Alexandria, Egypt
⊕ https://vfmat.ch/f249

Suez Canal Authority Hospital
Ismailia, Ismailia, Egypt
⊕ https://vfmat.ch/ae8d

Tabarak Maternity and Children Hospital (Golf Ground Branch)
Mansoura, Dakahlia Governorate, Egypt
⊕ https://vfmat.ch/3882

Tabarak Maternity and Children Hospital (New Cairo Branch)
New Cairo, Cairo, Egypt
⊕ https://vfmat.ch/43e5

Tahta General Hospital
Tahta, Sohag, Egypt
⊕ https://vfmat.ch/37bd

Teachers Hospital
Zamalek, Giza, Egypt
⊕ https://vfmat.ch/fb3c

University Children's Hospital Abu El-Rish Al-Munira
El Sayeda Zeinab, Cairo, Egypt
⊕ https://vfmat.ch/qtrh

Zamzam Hospital
Moharam Bek, Alexandria, Egypt
⊕ https://vfmat.ch/346e

Zohairy Hospital
Old Cairo, Cairo, Egypt
⊕ https://vfmat.ch/7d88

Fatma El Zahraa Hospital
Dekhela, Alexandria, Egypt
⊕ https://vfmat.ch/f399

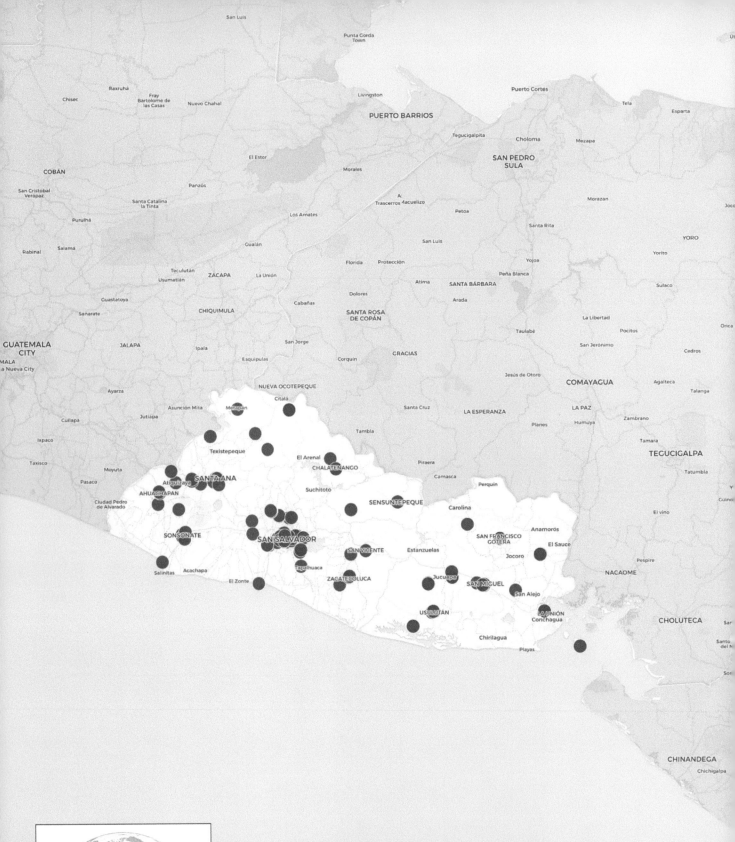

Healthcare Facility

El Salvador

Nicknamed the "Land of Volcanoes," the Republic of El Salvador is bordered by Honduras, Guatemala, and the Pacific Ocean. It is the smallest country in Central America. The population of 6.5 million is overwhelmingly ethnically Mestizo. Languages spoken include Spanish, the official language, and Nawat. About half the population is Roman Catholic, while the rest is Protestant. The country is densely populated throughout, with many people living in and around San Salvador, the capital. Overall, nearly 75 percent of the population lives in urban areas. About 20 percent of Salvadorans live abroad due to a combination of poor economic conditions, civil war, natural disasters, and violence. The geography of El Salvador is unique, with dozens of volcanoes—many of them active—throughout the landscape.

El Salvador is a former colony of Spain; it achieved independence in 1821, and then again from the Central American Federation in 1839. A civil war ended in 1992, which led to political reforms, but the country has struggled with stability ever since. El Salvador suffers from low economic growth rates and persistent poverty, inequality, and violent gang-related crime. It is afflicted with some of the highest homicide rates in the world. Because so much of the population lives outside El Salvador, remittances account for a large portion of the Salvadoran economy—they make up nearly 20 percent of the GDP surpassed only by exports.

El Salvador faces many challenges when it comes to health. Many of the country's doctors work only in urban areas, resulting in unequal access to healthcare services. Moreover, malnutrition is prevalent throughout the country, while communicable diseases such as dengue fever, malaria, and cholera have re-emerged. Interpersonal violence decreased slightly between 2009 and 2019, but it still continues to be a leading cause of mortality in El Salvador. Other leading causes of death include ischemic heart disease, chronic kidney disease, lower respiratory infections, diabetes, stroke, Alzheimer's disease, cirrhosis, road injuries, and COPD. The risk factors that contribute most to death and disability include high fasting plasma glucose, high body-mass index, high blood pressure, kidney dysfunction, dietary risks, malnutrition, air pollution, high LDL, alcohol and tobacco use, and unsafe sex.

6.5M

Population

$3,799

GDP Per Capita

73 years

Life Expectancy

↑ Improving

287
Doctors/100k

Physician Density

120
Beds/100k

Hospital Bed Density

46
Deaths/100k

Maternal Mortality

El Salvador

Nonprofit Organizations

A Broader View Volunteers
Provides developing countries around the world with significant volunteer programs that aid the neediest communities and forge a lasting bond between those volunteering and those they have helped.
Dent-OMFS, ER Med, Infect Dis, MF Med
⊕ https://vfmat.ch/3bec

Abt Associates
Seeks to improve the quality of life and economic well-being of people worldwide, while striving to meet and exceed the highest professional standards.
General, Logist-Op, MF Med, OB-GYN, Peds
⊕ https://vfmat.ch/cec2

AID FOR AIDS International
Aims to empower communities at risk of HIV and the population at large with comprehensive prevention through treatment, advocacy, education, and training.
Infect Dis, Logist-Op, Nutr, Psych, Pub Health
⊕ https://vfmat.ch/c43e

AIDS Healthcare Foundation
Provides cutting-edge HIV/AIDS medical care and advocacy to over one million people in 43 countries.
Infect Dis
⊕ https://vfmat.ch/b27c

Alight
Works closely with refugees, trafficked persons, economic migrants, and other displaced persons to co-design solutions that help them build full and fulfilling lives, with healthcare, clean water, shelter protection, and economic opportunity.
ER Med, General, Infect Dis, MF Med, Neonat, Peds
⊕ https://vfmat.ch/5993

American Academy of Pediatrics
Seeks to attain optimal physical, mental, and social health and well-being for all infants, children, adolescents, and young adults.
Anesth, Crit-Care, Neonat, Ped Surg
⊕ https://vfmat.ch/9633

Americares
Saves lives and improves health for people affected by poverty or disaster and responds with life-changing medicine, medical supplies, and health programs including domestic and global medical clinics.
All-Immu, ER Med, General, Infect Dis, MF Med, Nutr
⊕ https://vfmat.ch/e567

Basic Health International
Seeks to eliminate cervical cancer by conducting cutting-edge research on early prevention and treatment, and implementing sustainable strategies that can be scaled in limited-resource settings.
Infect Dis, OB-GYN
⊕ https://vfmat.ch/24c9

Buddhist Tzu Chi Medical Foundation
Provides healthcare to the poor, operates six hospitals in Taiwan and mobile medical and dental clinics in the U.S., manages a bone marrow bank, and organizes over 8,600 physicians who provide free medical services to more than 2 million people globally.
Crit-Care, Dent-OMFS, ER Med, General
⊕ https://vfmat.ch/ff61

Cambridge Global Health Partnerships (CGHP)
Works in partnership to inspire and enable people to improve healthcare globally.
Crit-Care, Dent-OMFS, ER Med, Heme-Onc, Infect Dis, MF Med, Ophth-Opt, Ortho
⊕ https://vfmat.ch/1599

CARE
Works around the globe to save lives, defeat poverty, and achieve social justice.
ER Med, General
⊕ https://vfmat.ch/7232

Carter Center, The
Seeks to prevent and resolve conflicts, enhance freedom and democracy, and improve health, while remaining committed to human rights and the alleviation of human suffering.
Infect Dis, MF Med, Ophth-Opt
⊕ https://vfmat.ch/6556

Catholic World Mission
Works to rebuild communities worldwide by helping to alleviate poverty and empower underserved areas, while spreading the message of the Catholic Church.
ER Med, General, Nutr, Peds
⊕ https://vfmat.ch/7b5f

Central American Eye Clinics (CAEC)
Aims to restore vision through high-quality eye care services and educational training programs for communities.
Logist-Op, Ophth-Opt
⊕ https://vfmat.ch/ff23

Chain of Hope
Provides lifesaving heart operations for children around the world and supports the development of cardiac services in numerous developing and war-torn countries.
Anesth, CT Surg, CV Med, Crit-Care, Ped Surg, Peds, Pulm-Critic, Surg
⊕ https://vfmat.ch/1b1b

CharityVision International
Focuses on restoring curable sight impairment worldwide by empowering local physicians and creating sustainable solutions.
Logist-Op, Ophth-Opt, Surg
🌐 https://vfmat.ch/6231

Childspring International
Provides life-changing surgeries for children from developing countries and transforms communities.
CT Surg, Medicine, Ophth-Opt, Ortho, Ped Surg, Peds, Surg
🌐 https://vfmat.ch/f939

Christian Aid Ministries
Strives to be a trustworthy and efficient channel for Amish, Mennonite, and other conservative Anabaptist groups and individuals to minister to physical and spiritual needs around the world.
CT Surg, ER Med, Logist-Op, Ortho, Pub Health
🌐 https://vfmat.ch/7b33

Christian Medical & Dental Associations
Based in Christian ministry, deploys medical and dental teams to underserved communities to provide vital healthcare.
Anesth, Dent-OMFS, ER Med, General, Medicine, OB-GYN, Ophth-Opt, Peds, Pub Health, Radiol, Rehab, Surg
🌐 https://vfmat.ch/921c

COAR Peace Mission
Provides foster care, education, pharmacy needs, and medical care for children, while also providing social services to the broader community.
Dent-OMFS, General, Nutr, Peds, Psych, Pub Health
🌐 https://vfmat.ch/756a

Columbia Vagelos College of Physicians and Surgeons Programs in Global Health
Harnesses the expertise of the medical school to improve health worldwide by training global health leaders, building capacity through interdisciplinary education and training programs, and addressing unmet health needs through research and application.
CV Med, Derm, Genetics, Heme-Onc, Infect Dis, Medicine, OB-GYN, Ophth-Opt, Peds, Psych, Pub Health, Pulm-Critic, Surg
🌐 https://vfmat.ch/a9e5

Core Group
Aims to improve and expand community health practices for underserved populations, especially women and children, through collaborative action and learning.
General, Infect Dis, MF Med, Medicine, OB-GYN, Peds, Pub Health
🌐 https://vfmat.ch/9de3

Cross Catholic Outreach
Mobilizes the global Catholic Church to transform impoverished communities through the provision of food, water, housing, education, orphan support, medical care, microenterprise, and disaster relief.
All-Immu, General, Nutr, OB-GYN, Rehab
🌐 https://vfmat.ch/22f4

Direct Relief
Improves the health and lives of people affected by poverty or emergency situations by mobilizing and providing essential medical resources needed for their care.
ER Med, Logist-Op
🌐 https://vfmat.ch/58e5

Doctors Without Borders/Médecins Sans Frontières (MSF)
Responds to emergencies and provides lifesaving medical care where needed most, including during disasters, conflicts, and epidemics.
Anesth, Crit-Care, ER Med, General, Infect Dis, Nutr, OB-GYN, Ped Surg, Peds, Psych, Pub Health, Surg
🌐 https://vfmat.ch/f363

Duke University: Global Health Institute
Sparks innovation in global health research and education, and brings together knowledge and resources to address the most important global health issues of our time.
All-Immu, Infect Dis, MF Med, OB-GYN, Pub Health
🌐 https://vfmat.ch/c4cd

Epilogos Charities
Works in solidarity with the people of San José Villanueva to improve their quality of life while transforming the lives of volunteers.
Dent-OMFS, General, Ophth-Opt, Pub Health
🌐 https://vfmat.ch/b8a2

Episcopal Relief & Development
Provides relief in times of disaster and promotes sustainable development by identifying and addressing the root causes of suffering.
Infect Dis, MF Med, Neonat, Nutr, Peds
🌐 https://vfmat.ch/7cfa

Eyes for the World
Aims to create awareness to prevent blindness and an opportunity for every person with treatable blindness to see a doctor.
Ophth-Opt
🌐 https://vfmat.ch/83c9

Foundation for International Medical Relief of Children (FIMRC)
Provides access to healthcare for low-resource and medically underserved families around the world.
General, Infect Dis, Peds, Pub Health
🌐 https://vfmat.ch/78b9

Fourteen Angels Co. El Salvador
Provides economic support to children with disabilities or terminal diseases through medicine, equipment, and transportation to help improve their quality of life.
Logist-Op
🌐 https://vfmat.ch/996f

Gift of Life International
Provides lifesaving cardiac treatment to children in developing countries while developing sustainable pediatric cardiac programs by implementing screening, surgical, and training missions.
Anesth, CT Surg, CV Med, Crit-Care, Ped Surg, Peds, Pulm-Critic
🌐 https://vfmat.ch/f2f9

Global Ministries – The United Methodist Church
As the worldwide mission and development agency of The United Methodist Church, Global Ministries works with more than 300 hospitals and clinics around the world through its Global Health Unit.
Anesth, CT Surg, CV Med, Crit-Care, Dent-OMFS, Derm, ER Med, GI, General, Infect Dis, Logist-Op, MF Med, Medicine, Neonat, Nephro, Nutr, OB-GYN, Ophth-Opt, Ortho, Palliative, Peds, Pod, Psych, Pub Health, Rehab, Rheum, Surg, Urol
🌐 https://vfmat.ch/1723

Global Oncology (GO)
Brings the best in cancer care to underserved patients around the world and collaborates across geographic, professional, and academic borders to improve cancer care, research, and education.
Heme-Onc, Path, Rad-Onc
🌐 https://vfmat.ch/fcb8

Global Smile Foundation
Provides comprehensive/interdisciplinary cleft care for patients born with cleft lip and palate in underserved communities throughout the world.
Anesth, Dent-OMFS, ENT, Logist-Op, Nutr, Ped Surg, Peds, Plast, Pub Health, Surg
🌐 https://vfmat.ch/7f6c

Globus Relief
Aims to improve the delivery of healthcare worldwide by gathering, processing, and distributing surplus medical supplies to charities at home and abroad.
Logist-Op
🌐 https://vfmat.ch/a2b7

Good Shepard International Foundation
Strives to promote inclusive and sustainable development for the most marginalized and vulnerable people, with a special focus on women, girls, and children, inspired by the Christian faith.
ER Med
⊕ https://vfmat.ch/ad9a

Grassroot Soccer
Leverages the power of soccer to educate, inspire, and mobilize at-risk youth in developing countries to overcome their greatest health challenges, live healthier and more productive lives, and be agents for change in their communities.
Infect Dis
⊕ https://vfmat.ch/3521

Harvesting in Spanish
Provides training, resources, and opportunities to serve, inspired by the Christian faith.
Dent-OMFS, ER Med, General, Nutr, Peds, Pub Health
⊕ https://vfmat.ch/3f55

Healing the Children
Helps underserved children around the world secure the medical care they need to lead more fulfilling lives.
Anesth, Dent-OMFS, ENT, General, Medicine, Ophth-Opt, Ped Surg, Peds, Plast, Surg
⊕ https://vfmat.ch/d4ee

Heartbeat International
Saves lives globally by providing cardiovascular implantable devices to needy people of the world.
CV Med
⊕ https://vfmat.ch/eb38

Heineman Medical Outreach
Provides medical and educational assistance globally to promote sustainable healthcare and enhanced living standards in underserved communities through the International Medical Outreach (IMO) program, a collaborative partnership between Heineman Medical Outreach and Atrium Health.
Anesth, CT Surg, CV Med, ER Med, General, Heme-Onc, Logist-Op, Medicine, Neonat, OB-GYN, Ped Surg, Peds, Surg, Vasc Surg
⊕ https://vfmat.ch/389b

HelpAge International
Works to ensure that people everywhere understand how much older people contribute to society and that they must enjoy their right to healthcare, social services, economic, and physical security.
General, Geri, Infect Dis, Medicine, Pub Health
⊕ https://vfmat.ch/5d91

Helping Hands Medical Missions
Delivers compassionate healthcare by hosting medical missions and treating patients in underserved communities around the world, based in Christian ministry.
Anesth, Dent-OMFS, ER Med, General, OB-GYN, Ophth-Opt, Surg
⊕ https://vfmat.ch/8efd

Hope Worldwide
Changes lives through the compassion and commitment of dedicated staff and volunteers delivering sustainable, high-impact, community-based services to the poor and underserved.
Dent-OMFS, General, OB-GYN, Ophth-Opt, Peds
⊕ https://vfmat.ch/89b3

IMA World Health
Works to build healthier communities by collaborating with key partners to serve vulnerable people with a focus on health, healing, and well-being for all.
Infect Dis, MF Med, Nutr, OB-GYN, Pub Health
⊕ https://vfmat.ch/8316

IMAHelps
Organizes medical humanitarian missions that provide some of the world's most underserved people with everything from general medical and dental care to life-changing surgeries, prosthetics, and other specialized services that reflect the expertise of our volunteers.
Anesth, CV Med, Dent-OMFS, Neuro, OB-GYN, Ophth-Opt, Ortho, Ped Surg, Peds, Plast, Rehab, Surg
⊕ https://vfmat.ch/d56b

International Eye Foundation (IEF)
Eliminates preventable and treatable blindness by making quality sustainable eye care services accessible and affordable worldwide.
Infect Dis, Logist-Op, Ophth-Opt
⊕ https://vfmat.ch/e839

International Federation of Gynecology and Obstetrics (FIGO)
Implements global projects on specific women's health issues.
MF Med, Medicine, Neonat, OB-GYN, Surg, Urol
⊕ https://vfmat.ch/c4b4

International Federation of Red Cross and Red Crescent Societies (IFRC)
Coordinates and directs international assistance following natural and manmade disasters in nonconflict situations through the world's largest humanitarian and development network. Provides disaster-preparedness programs, healthcare activities, and promotes humanitarian values.
ER Med, General, Infect Dis, Nutr
⊕ https://vfmat.ch/b4ee

International HELP
Works alongside churches, organizations, and community groups to help educate and empower local people in sustainable and effective ways for the improvement of health, while also providing health education and health services related to first aid, nutrition, water, sanitation, and hygiene.
General, MF Med
⊕ https://vfmat.ch/ccf5

International Organization for Migration (IOM) – The UN Migration Agency
Promotes evidence-informed policies and holistic, preventive, and curative health programs that are beneficial, accessible, and equitable for vulnerable migrants.
General, Infect Dis, OB-GYN
⊕ https://vfmat.ch/621a

International Planned Parenthood Federation (IPPF)
Leads a locally owned, globally connected civil society movement that provides and enables services and champions sexual and reproductive health and rights for all, especially the underserved.
Infect Dis, MF Med, OB-GYN
⊕ https://vfmat.ch/dc97

International Rescue Committee (IRC)
Responds to the world's worst humanitarian crises and helps people whose lives and livelihoods are shattered by conflict and disaster to survive, recover, and gain control of their future.
ER Med, General, Infect Dis, MF Med, Peds
⊕ https://vfmat.ch/5d24

International Union Against Tuberculosis and Lung Disease
Develops, implements, and assesses anti-tuberculosis, lung health, and noncommunicable disease programs.
Infect Dis, Pub Health, Pulm-Critic
⊕ https://vfmat.ch/3e82

InterSurgeon
Fosters collaborative partnerships in the field of global surgery that will advance clinical care, teaching, training, research, and the provision and maintenance of medical equipment.
ENT, Neurosurg, Ortho, Ped Surg, Plast, Surg, Urol
⊕ https://vfmat.ch/6f8a

Ipas
Focuses efforts on women and girls who want contraception or abortion, and builds programs around their needs and how best to support them.
OB-GYN
⊕ https://vfmat.ch/8e39

Izote

Creates sustainable projects that improve literacy, increase access to healthcare, and promote ecological conservation in El Salvador.

Ophth-Opt

⊕ https://vfmat.ch/979d

Izumi Foundation

Develops and supports programs that improve health and healthcare in neglected regions of Africa and Latin America.

⊕ https://vfmat.ch/f29a

John Snow, Inc. (JSI)

Aims to improve the health and well-being of underserved and vulnerable people and communities throughout the world.

General, Infect Dis, Logist-Op, MF Med, OB-GYN, Peds, Psych, Pub Health

⊕ https://vfmat.ch/ba78

Johns Hopkins Center for Communication Programs

Believes in the power of communication to save lives by empowering people to adopt healthy behaviors for themselves, their families, and their communities.

General, Infect Dis, Logist-Op, OB-GYN, Pub Health

⊕ https://vfmat.ch/1bf9

Joint United Nations Programme on HIV/AIDS (UNAIDS)

Aims to place people living with HIV and people affected by the virus at the decision-making table and at the center of designing, delivering, and monitoring the AIDS response.

Infect Dis

⊕ https://vfmat.ch/464a

Leadership in Medicine for the Underserved Program at MSU, The

Provides medical students the knowledge and skills necessary to address the varied medical needs of urban, rural, and international underserved populations.

Dent-OMFS, ER Med, Medicine, Nutr, OB-GYN, Peds, Pub Health, Radiol, Surg

⊕ https://vfmat.ch/84f1

Leland Dental Charities (LDC)

Supports the efforts of volunteers providing free dental care to the indigent people of El Salvador who cannot afford dental care in their communities.

Dent-OMFS

⊕ https://vfmat.ch/dee7

Lifebox

Seeks to provide safer surgery and anesthesia in low-resource countries by investing in tools, training, and partnerships for safe surgery.

Anesth, Crit-Care, Surg

⊕ https://vfmat.ch/2d4d

Limbs International

Engages communities and transforms lives through affordable, sustainable prosthetic solutions and rehabilitation services in developing countries.

Logist-Op, Ortho, Pod, Rehab

⊕ https://vfmat.ch/dc84

Los Medicos Voladores – The Flying Doctors

Aims to build and strengthen underserved communities through healthcare, education, and volunteerism.

Dent-OMFS, General

⊕ https://vfmat.ch/4411

Maestro Cares Foundation

Aims to provide the highest living conditions for vulnerable children through educational programs, housing and nutritional programs.

Logist-Op, Nutr

⊕ https://vfmat.ch/4de6

Management Sciences for Health (MSH)

Works with countries and communities to save lives and improve the health of the world's poorest and most vulnerable people by building strong, resilient, sustainable health systems.

Infect Dis, Logist-Op, Pub Health

⊕ https://vfmat.ch/6aa2

MAP International

Provides medicines and health supplies to those in need around the world so they might experience life to the fullest.

Logist-Op

⊕ https://vfmat.ch/deed

Maryknoll Lay Missioners

Based in Christian ministry, aims to collaborate with poor communities in Africa, Asia, and the Americas in order to respond to basic needs, including heathcare, and to help create a more compassionate world.

Logist-Op, Nutr

⊕ https://vfmat.ch/2ce6

Massachusetts Eye and Ear: Operation Airway

The global surgery program of Massachusetts Eye and Ear cares for children in developing countries who cannot breathe or speak due to airway complications.

Anesth, Crit-Care, ENT, Ped Surg, Pulm-Critic

⊕ https://vfmat.ch/3eb3

Massachusetts General Hospital Global Surgery Initiative

Aims to improve surgical education and access to advanced surgical care in resource-limited settings around the world by performing surgical operations as visitors, training local surgeons, and sharing medical technology through international partnerships across disciplines.

Anesth, Crit-Care, ER Med, Heme-Onc, Peds, Surg

⊕ https://vfmat.ch/31b1

Maverick Collective

Aims to build a global community of strategic philanthropists and informed advocates who use their intellectual and financial resources to create change.

Infect Dis, MF Med, OB-GYN

⊕ https://vfmat.ch/ea49

Medical Care Development International (MCD International)

Works to strengthen health systems through innovative, sustainable interventions.

Infect Dis, Logist-Op, OB-GYN, Pub Health

⊕ https://vfmat.ch/dc5c

Medical Care Development International

Works to improve the health of vulnerable populations through integrated, sustainable, and locally driven interventions.

Infect Dis, OB-GYN, Peds, Pub Health

⊕ https://vfmat.ch/da87

Medical Equipment Modernization Opportunity (MEMO)

Based in Christian ministry, works with churches and organizations to collect and send hospital equipment and supplies to healthcare facilities in need around the world.

Logist-Op

⊕ https://vfmat.ch/1c78

Medical Ministry International

Provides compassionate healthcare in areas of need, inspired by the Christian faith.

CT Surg, Dent-OMFS, ENT, General, OB-GYN, Ophth-Opt, Ortho, Plast, Rehab, Surg, Urol, Vasc Surg

⊕ https://vfmat.ch/5da6

Medical Missions Outreach

Visits developing countries to provide quality, ethical healthcare and outreach to those in need, based in Christian ministry.

Dent-OMFS, Ophth-Opt, Ortho, Surg

⊕ https://vfmat.ch/1197

Medical Teams International

Seeks to restore health as the first step to restoring hope, working to bring basic but lifesaving medical care to those in need.

Dent-OMFS, ER Med, General, MF Med, Pub Health

⊕ https://vfmat.ch/8d1c

MedShare

Aims to improve the quality of life of people, communities, and the planet by sourcing and directly delivering surplus medical supplies and equipment to

communities in need around the world.
Logist-Op
⊕ https://vfmat.ch/c8bc

Mending Faces
Restores hope and provides a brighter future to those whose lives are burdened by cleft lip, cleft palate, and other deformities.
Dent-OMFS, General, Nutr, Ped Surg, Peds
⊕ https://vfmat.ch/41a9

Mission Bambini
Helps to support children living in poverty and sickness, and lacking education, giving them the opportunity for and hope of a better life.
CT Surg, CV Med, Crit-Care, ER Med, Ped Surg, Peds
⊕ https://vfmat.ch/dc1a

Médecins du Monde/Doctors of the World
Provides care, bears witness, and supports social change worldwide with innovative medical programs and evidence-based advocacy initiatives.
ER Med, General, Infect Dis, MF Med, Neonat, OB-GYN, Peds, Pub Health
⊕ https://vfmat.ch/a43d

Northeast VOSH
Provides quality healthcare to those with limited means or access, both internationally and abroad.
Dent-OMFS, General, Nutr, Ophth-Opt, Rehab
⊕ https://vfmat.ch/f7b3

Norwegian People's Aid
Aims to improve living conditions, to create a democratic, just, and safe society.
ER Med, Logist-Op
⊕ https://vfmat.ch/2d8e

Nuestros Pequeños Hermanos (NPH)
Strives to create a loving and safe family environment for vulnerable children living in extreme conditions.
Psych, Rehab
⊕ https://vfmat.ch/57c4

Nuestros Pequeños Hermanos (Our Little Brothers and Sisters) New Zealand
Helps vulnerable children and families break the cycle of poverty with assistance through its pediatric hospital, healthcare clinics, day care centers, and scholarship programs.
CT Surg, Heme-Onc, Infect Dis, Nutr, OB-GYN, Peds, Rehab
⊕ https://vfmat.ch/e9cc

NYC Medics
Deploys mobile medical teams to remote areas of disaster zones and humanitarian emergencies, providing the highest level of medical care to those who otherwise would not have access to aid and relief efforts.
All-Immu, ER Med, Infect Dis, Surg
⊕ https://vfmat.ch/aeee

Operation Airway
Cares for children in developing countries with airway complications, teaches local healthcare providers, and researches how to improve this care around the world.
Anesth, ENT, Ped Surg, Pulm-Critic
⊕ https://vfmat.ch/2d48

Operation Footprint
Provides free surgical care to underserved children with genetic or acquired foot and ankle conditions, and trains local surgeons to manage and treat them.
Pod
⊕ https://vfmat.ch/6868

Operation Rainbow
Performs free orthopedic surgery, in developing countries, for children and young adults who do not otherwise have access to related medical procedures or equipment.
Anesth, Ortho, Ped Surg, Peds, Rehab, Surg
⊕ https://vfmat.ch/5dad

Operation Walk
Provides the gift of mobility through life-changing joint replacement surgeries, at no cost for those in need in the U.S. and globally.
Anesth, Ortho, Rehab, Surg
⊕ https://vfmat.ch/bafe

Order of Malta
Supports forgotten or excluded people, especially those living in conflict zones or amid natural disasters, by providing medical assistance, caring for refugees, and distributing medicines and necessities.
ER Med, General, Infect Dis, MF Med, Nephro, OB-GYN, Ortho, Psych
⊕ https://vfmat.ch/1fab

Partners for Visual Health
Provides vital, no cost eye care services to low-income residents of El Salvador.
Ophth-Opt
⊕ https://vfmat.ch/fa15

PATH
Advances health equity through innovation and partnerships so people, communities, and economies can thrive.
All-Immu, CV Med, Endo, Heme-Onc, Infect Dis, MF Med, Neonat, Nutr, OB-GYN, Path, Peds, Pulm-Critic
⊕ https://vfmat.ch/b4db

Physicians for Peace
Educates and empowers local providers of surgical care to alleviate suffering and transform lives in under-resourced communities around the world.
Crit-Care, Ped Surg, Plast, Psych, Surg, Urol
⊕ https://vfmat.ch/6a65

PSI – Population Services International
Aims to improve the health of people in the developing world by focusing on challenges such as a lack of family planning, HIV/AIDS, barriers to maternal health, and the greatest threats to children under the age of 5, including malaria, diarrhea, pneumonia, and malnutrition.
Infect Dis, MF Med, OB-GYN, Peds
⊕ https://vfmat.ch/ffe3

Restore Sight
Provides surgical and medical vision care to people in need around the world.
Ophth-Opt
⊕ https://vfmat.ch/f41c

RestoringVision
Empowers lives by restoring vision for millions of people in need.
Ophth-Opt
⊕ https://vfmat.ch/e121

Rotaplast International
Helps children and families worldwide by eliminating the burden of cleft lip and/or palate, burn scarring, and other deformities by sending medical teams to provide free reconstructive surgery, ancillary treatment, and training.
Anesth, Dent-OMFS, ENT, Ped Surg, Plast, Surg
⊕ https://vfmat.ch/78b3

Rotary International
Provides service to others, improves lives, and advances world understanding, goodwill, and peace through its fellowship of business, professional, and community leaders.
ER Med, General, Infect Dis, MF Med, OB-GYN
⊕ https://vfmat.ch/8fb5

Salvation Army International, The
Seeks to meet human needs through services in education, healthcare, community support, emergency response, and ministry development, inspired by the Christian faith.
Dent-OMFS, Derm, ER Med, Infect Dis, MF Med, Medicine, Nutr, OB-GYN, Ophth-Opt, Palliative, Psych, Rehab, Surg
⊕ https://vfmat.ch/8eb3

Samaritan's Purse International Disaster Relief
Provides spiritual and physical aid to hurting people around the world, such

as victims of war, poverty, natural disasters, disease, and famine, based in Christian ministry.

Anesth, CT Surg, Crit-Care, Dent-OMFS, Derm, ENT, ER Med, Endo, GI, General, Heme-Onc, Infect Dis, MF Med, Neonat, Nephro, Neuro, Neurosurg, Nutr, OB-GYN, Ophth-Opt, Ortho, Path, Ped Surg, Peds, Plast, Psych, Pulm-Critic, Radiol, Rehab, Rheum, Surg, Urol, Vasc Surg

⊕ https://vfmat.ch/87e3

Save the Children
Gives children around the world a healthy start in life, the opportunity to learn, and protection from harm.

All-Immu, Crit-Care, ER Med, General, Infect Dis, MF Med, Medicine, Neonat, OB-GYN, Peds, Psych, Pub Health

⊕ https://vfmat.ch/2e73

SEE International
Provides sustainable medical, surgical, and educational services through volunteer ophthalmic surgeons, with the objectives of restoring sight and preventing blindness to disadvantaged individuals worldwide.

Ophth-Opt, Surg

⊕ https://vfmat.ch/6e1b

Sight Surgery International
Recruits, coordinates, and deploys teams of volunteer medical professionals to perform free sight-restoring surgery throughout the emerging world.

Logist-Op, Ophth-Opt

⊕ https://vfmat.ch/fb9d

Smile Train, Inc.
Treats children with cleft lip through a sustainable and local model that supports surgery and other forms of essential care.

Logist-Op, Pub Health

⊕ https://vfmat.ch/822c

SOS Children's Villages International
Supports children through alternative care and family strengthening.

ER Med, Peds

⊕ https://vfmat.ch/aca1

Sri Sathya Sai International Organization
Inspired by spiritual teachings, carries out efforts in global healthcare, education, humanitarian relief, and youth engagement.

Dent-OMFS, General, Logist-Op, Nutr, Ophth-Opt, Pub Health

⊕ https://vfmat.ch/9bda

Surgeons of Service
Seeks to inspire humanitarian efforts, locally and globally, to create poverty awareness, instill education, and provide medical assistance.

Surg

⊕ https://vfmat.ch/9d4b

Swiss Tropical and Public Health Institute
Contributes to the improvement of the health of populations internationally, nationally, and locally through excellence in research, education, and services.

Infect Dis, Pub Health

⊕ https://vfmat.ch/2ee4

Task Force for Global Health, The
Consists of programs and focus areas that cover a range of global health issues including neglected tropical diseases, infectious diseases, vaccines, field epidemiology, public health informatics, health workforce development, and global health ethics.

Infect Dis, Logist-Op, Medicine, Ophth-Opt, Peds

⊕ https://vfmat.ch/714c

Team Nuestra Familia
Sets up clinics in rural El Salvador to help underserved communities gain access to quality medical and dental care.

General

⊕ https://vfmat.ch/82a1

Union for International Cancer Control (UICC)
Unites and supports the cancer community to reduce the global cancer burden,

promote greater equity, and ensure that cancer control continues to be a priority in the world health and development agenda.

Heme-Onc, Pub Health

⊕ https://vfmat.ch/88b1

United Methodist Volunteers in Mission (UMVIM)
Engages in short-term missions each year in ministries as varied as disaster response, community development, pastor training, microenterprise, agriculture, Vacation Bible School, building repair and construction, and medical/dental services.

Dent-OMFS, ER Med, General

⊕ https://vfmat.ch/1ee6

United Nations Children's Fund (UNICEF)
Works in over 190 countries and territories to save children's lives, defend their rights, and help them fulfill their potential, from early childhood through adolescence.

All-Immu, Infect Dis, MF Med, Neonat, Nutr, OB-GYN, Ped Surg, Peds, Pub Health

⊕ https://vfmat.ch/42d7

United Nations Development Programme (UNDP)
Helps countries achieve the simultaneous eradication of extreme poverty and significant reduction of inequalities and exclusion using a sustainable human development approach.

Infect Dis, Logist-Op, Pub Health

⊕ https://vfmat.ch/935c

United Nations High Commissioner for Refugees (UNHCR)
Safeguards the rights and well-being of people who have been forced to flee, ensuring that everybody has the right to seek asylum and find safe refuge in another country, with the goal of seeking lasting solutions.

General, MF Med, Medicine, OB-GYN, Peds, Psych, Pub Health

⊕ https://vfmat.ch/6636

United Nations Population Fund (UNFPA)
Supports reproductive healthcare for women and youth in more than 150 countries, focusing on delivering a world in which every pregnancy is wanted, every childbirth is safe, and every young person's potential is fulfilled.

Infect Dis, MF Med, Neonat, OB-GYN, Peds, Pub Health

⊕ https://vfmat.ch/c969

United States Agency for International Development (USAID)
Promotes and demonstrates democratic values abroad and advances a free, peaceful, and prosperous world. Leads the U.S. government's international development and disaster assistance through partnerships and investments that save lives.

ER Med, Infect Dis, MF Med, OB-GYN, Peds

⊕ https://vfmat.ch/9a99

University of New Mexico School of Medicine: Project Echo
Seeks to improve health outcomes worldwide through the use of a technology called telementoring, a guided-practice model in which the participating clinician retains responsibility for managing the patient.

General, Infect Dis, MF Med, OB-GYN, Path, Peds

⊕ https://vfmat.ch/6c9a

University of Virginia: Anesthesiology Department Global Health Initiatives
Educates and trains physicians to help people achieve healthy productive lives, and advances knowledge in the medical sciences.

Anesth, Pub Health

⊕ https://vfmat.ch/1b8b

USAID: Leadership, Management and Governance Project
Improves leadership, management, and governance practices to strengthen health systems and improve health for all, including vulnerable populations worldwide.

Logist-Op

⊕ https://vfmat.ch/d35e

Vision Care
Restores sight and helps patients get regular treatment at short-term eye camps and long-term base clinics by having doctors, missionaries, volunteers, and sponsors work together.

Ophth-Opt
⊕ https://vfmat.ch/9d7c

Vitamin Angels
Helps at-risk populations in need—specifically pregnant women, new mothers, and children under age 5—to gain access to life-changing vitamins and minerals.
General, Nutr
⊕ https://vfmat.ch/7da1

VOSH (Volunteer Optometric Services to Humanity) International
Facilitates the provision and the sustainability of vision care worldwide for people who can neither afford nor obtain such care.
Ophth-Opt
⊕ https://vfmat.ch/a149

Walkabout Foundation
Provides wheelchairs and rehabilitation in the developing world and funds research to find a cure for paralysis.
Logist-Op, Rehab
⊕ https://vfmat.ch/5582

Women and Children First
Pioneers approaches that support communities to solve problems themselves.
MF Med, Neonat, OB-GYN, Peds
⊕ https://vfmat.ch/cdc9

Women's Refugee Commission
Seeks to improve lives by protecting the rights of women, children, and youth displaced by conflict and crisis through researching their needs, identifying solutions, and advocating for programs and policies to strengthen their resilience.
General, MF Med, Neonat, OB-GYN, Peds, Psych
⊕ https://vfmat.ch/3d8f

World Federation of Hemophilia (WFH)
Aims to improve and sustain care for people with inherited bleeding disorders by pursuing long-term relationships with individuals and organizations who share the values of WFH's development model.
Heme-Onc
⊕ https://vfmat.ch/5121

World Health Organization, The (WHO)
The United Nations' agency for health provides leadership on global health matters, shapes the health research agenda, sets norms and standards, articulates evidence-based policy options, provides technical support and monitoring to countries, and assesses health trends.
ER Med, General, Infect Dis, Logist-Op, MF Med, OB-GYN, Peds, Psych, Pub Health
⊕ https://vfmat.ch/c476

World Medical Relief
Facilitates the distribution of surplus medical resources where they are needed.
Logist-Op
⊕ https://vfmat.ch/72dc

World Missions Possible
Provides EMS capacity-building, along with medical and vision care, to under-developed and rural areas.
ER Med, General, Heme-Onc, Neonat, Ophth-Opt, Surg
⊕ https://vfmat.ch/d6a5

World Vision International
Works with vulnerable communities around the world to overcome poverty and injustice with child-focused programs in disaster management, health, nutrition, economic development, education, clean water, sanitation, and hygiene.
ER Med, General, Infect Dis, MF Med, Nutr, OB-GYN, Peds
⊕ https://vfmat.ch/2642

El Salvador

Healthcare Facilities

Escalon Medical Center
San Salvador, El Salvador
https://vfmat.ch/qttv

Hospital Amatepec
El Cacao, San Salvador, El Salvador
⊕ https://vfmat.ch/b7d2

Hospital Bautista de El Salvador
San Salvador, El Salvador
⊕ https://vfmat.ch/a2c4

Hospital Cader
Santa Ana, Santa Ana, El Salvador
⊕ https://vfmat.ch/39df

Hospital Central Privado San Salvador
San Salvador, San Salvador, El Salvador
⊕ https://vfmat.ch/d6fc

Hospital Centro de Diagnóstico Colonia Medical
Mejicanos, San Salvador, El Salvador
⊕ https://vfmat.ch/4b45

Hospital Centro Ginecológico
Mejicanos, San Salvador, El Salvador
⊕ https://vfmat.ch/54d8

Hospital Centro Pediátrico
Mejicanos, San Salvador, El Salvador
⊕ https://vfmat.ch/9476

Hospital Climesa
Santa Ana, Santa Ana, El Salvador
⊕ https://vfmat.ch/5e4d

Hospital Climosal
Santa Tecla, El Salvador
⊕ https://vfmat.ch/bb43

Hospital de Diagnostico
San Salvador, San Salvador, El Salvador
⊕ https://vfmat.ch/jm2s

Hospital de Emergencias
Mejicanos, San Salvador, El Salvador
⊕ https://vfmat.ch/5f62

Hospital de Especialidades Metropol
El Ujushte, Usulután, El Salvador
⊕ https://vfmat.ch/9b7d

Hospital de Especialidades Nuestra Señora de la Paz
San Miguel, El Salvador
⊕ https://vfmat.ch/612e

Hospital de Especialidades Santa Rosa de Lima
Santa Rosa de Lima, La Unión, El Salvador
⊕ https://vfmat.ch/142c

Hospital de la Mujer
San Antonio Abad, San Salvador, El Salvador
⊕ https://vfmat.ch/bd7b

Hospital de Maternidad la Divina Providencia in Texacuangos
Santiago Texacuangos, San Salvador, El Salvador
⊕ https://vfmat.ch/jkwx

Hospital de Oncología
Mejicanos, San Salvador, El Salvador
⊕ https://vfmat.ch/a958

Hospital Divina Providencia
San Salvador, El Salvador
⊕ https://vfmat.ch/ae53

Hospital El Salvador
Ceiba de Guadalupe, La Libertad, El Salvador
⊕ https://vfmat.ch/9549

Hospital General del ISSS
Mejicanos, San Salvador, El Salvador
⊕ https://vfmat.ch/a3ac

Hospital Instituto del Cáncer
San Antonio Abad, San Salvador, El Salvador
⊕ https://vfmat.ch/334b

Hospital Josefino Vilaseca
El Amate, San Miguel, El Salvador
⊕ https://vfmat.ch/8cc5

Hospital La Ceiba
Ceiba de Guadalupe, La Libertad, El Salvador
⊕ https://vfmat.ch/3344

Hospital Merliot
Santa Tecla, El Salvador
⊕ https://vfmat.ch/6fbc

Hospital Militar
Zacamil, San Salvador, El Salvador
⊕ https://vfmat.ch/8c3b

Hospital Médico Quirúrgico del Instituto Salvadoreño Del Seguro Social
Mejicanos, San Salvador, El Salvador
⊕ https://vfmat.ch/e1b1

Hospital Médico Quirúrgico Sonsonate
Sonzacate, Sonsonate, El Salvador
⊕ https://vfmat.ch/b688

Hospital Nacional de Chalchuapa
Chalchuapa, Santa Ana, El Salvador
⊕ https://vfmat.ch/147b

Hospital Nacional de Ciudad Barrios Monseñor Oscar Arnulfo Romero
Ciudad Barrios, San Miguel, El Salvador
⊕ https://vfmat.ch/47f7

Hospital Nacional de Ilobasco
Ilobasco, Cabañas, El Salvador
⊕ https://vfmat.ch/3766

Hospital Nacional de la Unión
Conchagua, La Unión, El Salvador
⊕ https://vfmat.ch/4574

Hospital Nacional de Metapán
Metapán, Santa Ana, El Salvador
⊕ https://vfmat.ch/8c64

Hospital Nacional de Ninos Benjamin Bloom
San Salvador, El Salvador
⊕ https://vfmat.ch/7d1c

Hospital Nacional de Nueva Concepción
Nueva Concepción, Chalatenango, El Salvador
⊕ https://vfmat.ch/bfc1

Hospital Nacional de San Francisco Gotera
Hacienda Vieja, Morazán, El Salvador
⊕ https://vfmat.ch/c5ba

Hospital Nacional de Sensuntepeque
Tronalagua, Cabañas, El Salvador
⊕ https://vfmat.ch/9269

Hospital Nacional Dr. Jorge Arturo Mena
Santiago de María, Usulután, El Salvador
⊕ https://vfmat.ch/1673

Hospital Nacional Dr. Jorge Mazzini Villacorte Sonsonate
Río Las Monjas, Sonsonate, El Salvador
⊕ https://vfmat.ch/cf3b

Hospital Nacional Dr. Juan José Fernández Zacamil
Mejicanos, San Salvador, El Salvador
⊕ https://vfmat.ch/84c4

Hospital Nacional Dr. Luis Edmundo Vásquez
Chalatenango, Chalatenango, El Salvador
⊕ https://vfmat.ch/cfe4

Hospital Nacional General
San Salvador, El Salvador
⊕ https://vfmat.ch/6d19

Hospital Nacional General Francisco Menéndez
Los Huatales, Ahuachapán, El Salvador
⊕ https://vfmat.ch/bc22

Hospital Nacional Psiquiátrico
Soyapango, San Salvador, El Salvador
⊕ https://vfmat.ch/86e9

Hospital Nacional Rosales
El Tejar, San Salvador, El Salvador
⊕ https://vfmat.ch/7bea

Hospital Nacional San Bartolo
Ilopango, San Salvador, El Salvador
⊕ https://vfmat.ch/f33f

Hospital Nacional San Juan de Dios
La Cruz, San Miguel, El Salvador
⊕ https://vfmat.ch/f9c6

Hospital Nacional San Rafael
Santa Tecla, La Libertad, El Salvador
⊕ https://vfmat.ch/1fd6

Hospital Nacional Santa Gertrudis
San Antonio Tras El Cerro, San Vicente, El Salvador
⊕ https://vfmat.ch/48bc

Hospital Nacional Santa Rosa de Lima
Santa Rosa de Lima, La Unión, El Salvador
⊕ https://vfmat.ch/2184

Hospital Nacional Santa Teresa
Zacatecoluca, La Paz, El Salvador
⊕ https://vfmat.ch/e366

Hospital Nacional Santiago de María
Santiago de María, Usulután, El Salvador
⊕ https://vfmat.ch/1877

Hospital National San Pedro Usulutan
El Ujushte, Usulután, El Salvador
⊕ https://vfmat.ch/e21c

Hospital Paravida
San Salvador, San Salvador, El Salvador
⊕ https://vfmat.ch/pfte

Hospital Primero de Mayo ISSS
San Salvador, El Salvador
⊕ https://vfmat.ch/b19c

Hospital Regional de Sonsonate
San Ramón, Sonsonate, El Salvador
⊕ https://vfmat.ch/e8ae

Hospital San Francisco El Salvador
San Miguel, San Miguel, El Salvador
⊕ https://vfmat.ch/jqky

Hospital San Juan de Dios Santa Ana
Aldea San Antonio, Santa Ana, El Salvador
⊕ https://vfmat.ch/6592

Hospital San Mateo
Lourdes, El Salvador
⊕ https://vfmat.ch/8e11

National Women's Hospital
El Tejar, San Salvador, El Salvador
⊕ https://vfmat.ch/826d

New National Hospital Guadalupe
Nueva Guadalupe, San Miguel, El Salvador
⊕ https://vfmat.ch/4f84

Seguro Social de Usulután
El Ujushte, Usulután, El Salvador
⊕ https://vfmat.ch/998e

PORT SUDAN

Sawakin

Jubayt

ABHA

JIZAN

KEREN

KASSALA

ASMARA

HODEIDAH

المنصورة

MEK'ELÊ

ASSAB

GONDER

DJIBOUTI

DJIBOUTI

BAHIR DAR

DESSIE

DIRE DAWA

DEBRE BIRHAN

JIJIGA

HARAR

● Healthcare Facility

Eritrea

A small country in the Horn of Africa, the State of Eritrea is bordered by Sudan to the north and west, and Ethiopia and Djibouti to the south. Home to a historically important trade route, Eritrea was at times colonized by Italy and Ethiopia. As such, the country's cultural legacies are still apparent and interesting to experience. The majority of Eritrea's 6.1 million people belong to the Tigrinya and Tigre ethnic groups. Most of the population live in the middle of the country around urban centers like Asmara, the capital, and cities such as Keren. Overall, around 40 percent of the population is urban.

After a 30-year war for liberation from Ethiopia, Eritrea became independent in 1993. A brief period of stability was followed by a border war with Ethiopia in 1998, which ended in 2000. Since then, Eritrea has been in a state of transitional political arrangements. The highly militarized one-party state has been ranked by the Committee to Protect Journalists as the most censored country in the world. Eritrea's contentious history has left it as one of the poorest countries in Africa, facing economic and political strife.

Eritrea's political struggles have affected the overall health of the population, with preventable diseases making up around 70 percent of all disease. The country's impoverished population faces significant levels of death due to tuberculosis, lower respiratory infections, diarrheal diseases, neonatal disorders, HIV/AIDS, road injuries, protein-energy malnutrition, and measles. In recent years, death due to non-communicable diseases such as stroke, ischemic heart disease, cirrhosis, and diabetes has also increased significantly.

6.1M

Population

$643

GDP Per Capita

66 years

Life Expectancy

↑ Improving

8
Doctors/100k

Physician Density

70
Beds/100k

Hospital Bed Density

480
Deaths/100k

Maternal Mortality

Eritrea

Nonprofit Organizations

Africa CDC
Aims to strengthen the capacity and capability of Africa's public health institutions and partnerships to detect and respond quickly and effectively to disease threats and outbreaks, based on data-driven interventions and programs.
Infect Dis, Logist-Op, Pub Health
🌐 https://vfmat.ch/339c

Africa Health Organisation
Leads collaborative efforts among countries in Africa and other partners to promote health equity, combat disease, and improve quality of life.
Logist-Op, Pub Health
🌐 https://vfmat.ch/b1c5

Africa Relief and Community Development
Provides comprehensive relief and developmental aid to people of the African continent regardless of gender, race, or religion.
Nutr, Pub Health
🌐 https://vfmat.ch/6cd2

Al Basar International Foundation
Works with local partners to treat preventable blindness, and helps set up sustainable infrastructure so local teams can save sight in their communities.
Ophth-Opt
🌐 https://vfmat.ch/a8b5

Americares
Saves lives and improves health for people affected by poverty or disaster and responds with life-changing medicine, medical supplies, and health programs including domestic and global medical clinics.
All-Immu, ER Med, General, Infect Dis, MF Med, Nutr
🌐 https://vfmat.ch/e567

Amref Health Africa
Serves millions of people across 35 countries in Sub-Saharan Africa, strengthening health systems, and training African health workers to respond to the continent's most critical health issues.
All-Immu, General, Infect Dis, Logist-Op, MF Med, OB-GYN, Path, Pub Health, Surg
🌐 https://vfmat.ch/6985

Caritas Pro Vitae Gradu Charitable Trust
Supports Catholic charitable projects with social and humanitarian efforts, and aims to assist people in need including children, the elderly, sick, and disabled through healthcare, poverty relief, and education.
ER Med, General, Logist-Op, Medicine, OB-GYN, Ophth-Opt, Path, Peds, Pub Health, Radiol, Rehab, Surg
🌐 https://vfmat.ch/b2ca

Carter Center, The
Seeks to prevent and resolve conflicts, enhance freedom and democracy, and improve health, while remaining committed to human rights and the alleviation of human suffering.
Infect Dis, MF Med, Ophth-Opt
🌐 https://vfmat.ch/6556

Center for Strategic and International Studies (CSIS) Commission on Strengthening America's Health Security
Brings together a distinguished and diverse group of high-level opinion leaders bridging security and health, with the core aim to chart a bold vision for the future of U.S. leadership in global health.
ER Med, Infect Dis, MF Med, Pub Health
🌐 https://vfmat.ch/6d7f

Chain of Hope
Provides lifesaving heart operations for children around the world and supports the development of cardiac services in numerous developing and war-torn countries.
Anesth, CT Surg, CV Med, Crit-Care, Ped Surg, Peds, Pulm-Critic, Surg
🌐 https://vfmat.ch/1b1b

Christian Aid Ministries
Strives to be a trustworthy and efficient channel for Amish, Mennonite, and other conservative Anabaptist groups and individuals to minister to physical and spiritual needs around the world.
CT Surg, ER Med, Logist-Op, Ortho, Pub Health
🌐 https://vfmat.ch/7b33

Developing Country NGO Delegation: Global Fund to Fight AIDS, TB & Malaria
Works to strengthen the engagement of civil society actors and organizations in developing countries to build a world in which AIDS, TB, and malaria are no longer global, public health, and human rights threats.
Infect Dis, Pub Health
🌐 https://vfmat.ch/3149

Direct Relief
Improves the health and lives of people affected by poverty or emergency situations by mobilizing and providing essential medical resources needed for their care.
ER Med, Logist-Op
🌐 https://vfmat.ch/58e5

EMERGENCY
Provides free, high-quality healthcare to victims of war, poverty, and landmines. Also builds hospitals and trains local staff, while pursuing medicine based on human rights.
ER Med, Neonat, OB-GYN, Ophth-Opt, Ped Surg
🌐 https://vfmat.ch/c361

END Fund, The
Aims to control and eliminate the most prevalent neglected diseases among the world's poorest and most vulnerable people.
Infect Dis
⊕ https://vfmat.ch/2614

Finn Church Aid
Supports people in the most vulnerable situations within fragile and disaster-affected regions in three thematic priority areas: right to peace, livelihood, and education.
ER Med, Psych, Pub Health
⊕ https://vfmat.ch/9623

Fred Hollows Foundation, The
Works toward a world in which no person is needlessly blind or vision impaired.
Ophth-Opt, Pub Health, Surg
⊕ https://vfmat.ch/73e5

Global Oncology (GO)
Brings the best in cancer care to underserved patients around the world and collaborates across geographic, professional, and academic borders to improve cancer care, research, and education.
Heme-Onc, Path, Rad-Onc
⊕ https://vfmat.ch/fcb8

Globus Relief
Aims to improve the delivery of healthcare worldwide by gathering, processing, and distributing surplus medical supplies to charities at home and abroad.
Logist-Op
⊕ https://vfmat.ch/a2b7

Health Equity Initiative
Aims to build and sustain a global community that engages across sectors and disciplines to advance health equity.
Pub Health
⊕ https://vfmat.ch/e2e2

International Agency for the Prevention of Blindness (IAPB), The
Leads international efforts in blindness-prevention activities, works toward a world where no one is needlessly visually impaired, and ensures that everyone has access to the best possible standard of eye health.
Infect Dis, Ophth-Opt, Pub Health
⊕ https://vfmat.ch/87a2

International Federation of Gynecology and Obstetrics (FIGO)
Implements global projects on specific women's health issues.
MF Med, Medicine, Neonat, OB-GYN, Surg, Urol
⊕ https://vfmat.ch/c4b4

International Federation of Red Cross and Red Crescent Societies (IFRC)
Coordinates and directs international assistance following natural and manmade disasters in nonconflict situations through the world's largest humanitarian and development network. Provides disaster-preparedness programs, healthcare activities, and promotes humanitarian values.
ER Med, General, Infect Dis, Nutr
⊕ https://vfmat.ch/b4ee

International Trachoma Initiative (iTi)
Works toward a world free from trachoma, a preventable cause of blindness, and provides comprehensive support to national ministries of health and governmental and nongovernmental organizations to implement a comprehensive approach to fight trachoma.
Infect Dis, Ophth-Opt
⊕ https://vfmat.ch/3278

Joint United Nations Programme on HIV/AIDS (UNAIDS)
Aims to place people living with HIV and people affected by the virus at the decision-making table and at the center of designing, delivering, and monitoring the AIDS response.
Infect Dis
⊕ https://vfmat.ch/464a

Life for a Child
Supports the provision of the best possible healthcare, given local circumstances, to all children and youth with diabetes in less-resourced countries, through the strengthening of existing diabetes services.
Endo, Medicine, Peds
⊕ https://vfmat.ch/d712

Maternal Fetal Care International
Helps mothers and children survive and enjoy better health in the poorest regions of the world.
MF Med, Neonat, OB-GYN
⊕ https://vfmat.ch/7e72

MedShare
Aims to improve the quality of life of people, communities, and the planet by sourcing and directly delivering surplus medical supplies and equipment to communities in need around the world.
Logist-Op
⊕ https://vfmat.ch/c8bc

Mercy and Love Foundation
Aims to provide orphaned and vulnerable children with basic human needs such as food, clothing, and shelter, enabling them to thrive.
General, Peds
⊕ https://vfmat.ch/649a

Mercy Ships
Operates hospital ships staffed by volunteers to bring hope, healing, and healthcare to underserved communities worldwide.
Anesth, Dent-OMFS, Logist-Op, Neonat, OB-GYN, Ophth-Opt, Ortho, Palliative, Plast, Psych, Surg
⊕ https://vfmat.ch/2e99

Mission Bambini
Helps to support children living in poverty and sickness, and lacking education, giving them the opportunity for and hope of a better life.
CT Surg, CV Med, Crit-Care, ER Med, Ped Surg, Peds
⊕ https://vfmat.ch/dc1a

Operation Fistula
Exists to end obstetric fistula by building models of care that serve every woman, everywhere.
MF Med, OB-GYN, Surg
⊕ https://vfmat.ch/ce8e

Optometry Giving Sight
Delivers eye exams and low or no-cost glasses, provides training for local eye care professionals, and establishes optometry schools, vision centers and optical labs.
Ophth-Opt
⊕ https://vfmat.ch/33ea

Order of Malta
Supports forgotten or excluded people, especially those living in conflict zones or amid natural disasters, by providing medical assistance, caring for refugees, and distributing medicines and necessities.
ER Med, General, Infect Dis, MF Med, Nephro, OB-GYN, Ortho, Psych
⊕ https://vfmat.ch/1fab

People to People Canada (P2P)
Contributes to the fight against preventable diseases and addresses the full range of determinants of health (physical, social, economic, and cultural) affecting vulnerable communities.
Infect Dis, Psych, Pub Health
⊕ https://vfmat.ch/67d8

RestoringVision
Empowers lives by restoring vision for millions of people in need.
Ophth-Opt
⊕ https://vfmat.ch/e121

Rockefeller Foundation, The
Works to promote the well-being of humanity.

Logist-Op, Nutr, Pub Health
⊕ https://vfmat.ch/5424

Rotary International
Provides service to others, improves lives, and advances world understanding, goodwill, and peace through its fellowship of business, professional, and community leaders.
ER Med, General, Infect Dis, MF Med, OB-GYN
⊕ https://vfmat.ch/8fb5

SATMED
Serves nongovernmental organizations, hospitals, medical universities, and other healthcare providers active in resource-poor areas, by providing open-access e-health services for the health community.
Logist-Op
⊕ https://vfmat.ch/b8d5

Save A Child's Heart
Provides lifesaving cardiac treatment to children in developing countries, and trains healthcare professionals from these countries to deliver quality care in their communities.
CT Surg, CV Med, Crit-Care, Ped Surg, Peds
⊕ https://vfmat.ch/1bef

Surgeons for Smiles
Brings first-class medical and dental care to those in need, in developing countries around the world.
Anesth, Dent-OMFS, OB-GYN, Ped Surg, Plast, Surg
⊕ https://vfmat.ch/3427

Task Force for Global Health, The
Consists of programs and focus areas that cover a range of global health issues including neglected tropical diseases, infectious diseases, vaccines, field epidemiology, public health informatics, health workforce development, and global health ethics.
Infect Dis, Logist-Op, Medicine, Ophth-Opt, Peds
⊕ https://vfmat.ch/714c

United Nations Children's Fund (UNICEF)
Works in over 190 countries and territories to save children's lives, defend their rights, and help them fulfill their potential, from early childhood through adolescence.
All-Immu, Infect Dis, MF Med, Neonat, Nutr, OB-GYN, Ped Surg, Peds, Pub Health
⊕ https://vfmat.ch/42d7

United Nations Development Programme (UNDP)
Helps countries achieve the simultaneous eradication of extreme poverty and significant reduction of inequalities and exclusion using a sustainable human development approach.
Infect Dis, Logist-Op, Pub Health
⊕ https://vfmat.ch/935c

United Nations High Commissioner for Refugees (UNHCR)
Safeguards the rights and well-being of people who have been forced to flee, ensuring that everybody has the right to seek asylum and find safe refuge in another country, with the goal of seeking lasting solutions.
General, MF Med, Medicine, OB-GYN, Peds, Psych, Pub Health
⊕ https://vfmat.ch/6636

United Nations Office for the Coordination of Humanitarian Affairs (OCHA)
Contributes to principled and effective humanitarian response through coordination, advocacy, policy, information management, and humanitarian financing tools and services, by leveraging functional expertise throughout the organization.
Logist-Op
⊕ https://vfmat.ch/22b8

United Nations Population Fund (UNFPA)
Supports reproductive healthcare for women and youth in more than 150 countries, focusing on delivering a world in which every pregnancy is wanted, every childbirth is safe, and every young person's potential is fulfilled.

Infect Dis, MF Med, Neonat, OB-GYN, Peds, Pub Health
⊕ https://vfmat.ch/c969

University of Pennsylvania Perelman School of Medicine Center for Global Health
Aims to improve health equity worldwide through enhanced public health awareness and access to care, discovery, and outcomes-based research, and comprehensive educational programs grounded in partnership.
Heme-Onc, Infect Dis, OB-GYN
⊕ https://vfmat.ch/cb57

Women's Refugee Commission
Seeks to improve lives by protecting the rights of women, children, and youth displaced by conflict and crisis through researching their needs, identifying solutions, and advocating for programs and policies to strengthen their resilience.
General, MF Med, Neonat, OB-GYN, Peds, Psych
⊕ https://vfmat.ch/3d8f

World Federation of Hemophilia (WFH)
Aims to improve and sustain care for people with inherited bleeding disorders by pursuing long-term relationships with individuals and organizations who share the values of WFH's development model.
Heme-Onc
⊕ https://vfmat.ch/5121

World Health Organization, The (WHO)
The United Nations' agency for health provides leadership on global health matters, shapes the health research agenda, sets norms and standards, articulates evidence-based policy options, provides technical support and monitoring to countries, and assesses health trends.
ER Med, General, Infect Dis, Logist-Op, MF Med, OB-GYN, Peds, Psych, Pub Health
⊕ https://vfmat.ch/c476

 # Eritrea

Healthcare Facilities

Adi Quala Hospital
Adi Quala, Eritrea
🌐 https://vfmat.ch/dcff

Adikeyh Hospital
Adi Keyh, Eritrea
🌐 https://vfmat.ch/a1f9

Āssab Hospital
Āssab, Eritrea
🌐 https://vfmat.ch/75c2

Halibet Referral Hospital
ጎደና ሳሕል, ኣስመራ Asmara أسمرة, ዞባ
ማእከል المنطقة المركزية, Eritrea
🌐 https://vfmat.ch/c883

Keren Hospital
طريق أغوردات – كرن ጽርግያ ከረን ኣቋርዳት,
ከረን Keren كرن, ዞባ ዓንሰባ Anseba عنسبا, Eritrea
🌐 https://vfmat.ch/74c7

Massawa Hospital
ጽርግያ ኣስመራ ምጽዋዕ Asmara Massawa Road
طريق أسمرة – مصوع, ምጽዋዕ Massawa, ዞባ
ሰሜናዊ ቀይሕ ባሕሪ Northern Red Sea Zone
شمال البحر الأحمر, Eritrea
🌐 https://vfmat.ch/6d74

Mekane Hiwot Hospital
172-2 Street, Asmara, Zoba Center Central District,
Eritrea
🌐 https://vfmat.ch/9edf

Mendefera Referral Hospital
Mendefera, Eritrea
🌐 https://vfmat.ch/239f

Mini Hospital
P-4, Adewuhi, Adi Awhi, Eritrea
🌐 https://vfmat.ch/465a

Sanafi Hospital
Asmara Zalambesa Road, Adi Qiih/Adi Keyh, Eritrea
🌐 https://vfmat.ch/1a4e

Sembel Hospital
Asmara, Eritrea
🌐 https://vfmat.ch/34dd

St. Mary's Psychiatric Hospital Sembel
Zoba Center Street, Asmara, Asmara, Eritrea
🌐 https://vfmat.ch/3bf7

Tessenei Hospital
Teseney, Eritrea
🌐 https://vfmat.ch/97b1

Zonal Referral Hospital Ghinda
Asmara-Massawa Road, Dengolo, Northern Red Sea
Zone, Eritrea
🌐 https://vfmat.ch/fa46

Āk'ordat Hospital
Barentu – Ak'ordat Road / طريق بارنتو – أغوردات,
ኣቋርዳት Akordat أغوردات, ጋሽ-ባርካ Gash Barka
القاش ويركة, Eritrea
🌐 https://vfmat.ch/4451

Healthcare Facility

Eswatini

The Kingdom of Eswatini, formerly known as Swaziland, is a mountainous, landlocked country in Southern Africa, with neighbors that include Mozambique and South Africa. It is one of the smallest countries in Africa, but despite its small size, it is home to a diverse geography and climate. Because of Eswatini's mountainous geography, the population is unevenly distributed, with most people living in homestead settlements called imithi located in valleys and plains. About 25 percent of the population lives in urban areas, including Mbabane, the capital, home to 68,000 people. The country's population of 1.1 million are majority ethnically Swazi, with English and siSwati as both the common and official languages. About 90 percent of the population identifies as Christian.

Eswatini is governed by an absolute monarchy. Formerly a protectorate of Britain, Eswatini gained independence in 1968. Since then, the country has suffered from high rates of poverty, with nearly 60 percent of the population living below the poverty line as of 2017. Poverty is exacerbated by weak economic growth, high rates of unemployment, inequality, extreme weather events, and one of the world's highest rates of HIV/AIDS.

Eswatini faces several health challenges. The population has a life expectancy of 60 years, one of the lowest in the world. Contributing to this alarmingly low life expectancy is a high burden of infectious disease. While death due to HIV/AIDS decreased by over 60 percent between 2009 and 2019, it remains the top cause of death in the country. Other leading causes of death in Eswatini include lower respiratory infections, diabetes, tuberculosis, stroke, ischemic heart disease, diarrheal diseases, neonatal disorders, road injuries, and chronic kidney disease. The risk factors that contribute most to death and disability include unsafe sex, malnutrition, high body-mass index, insufficient clean water and sanitation, high fasting plasma glucose, air pollution, high blood pressure, alcohol use, dietary risks, and intimate partner violence.

1.1M

Population

$3,416

GDP Per Capita

60 years

Life Expectancy

↑ Improving

10
Doctors/100k

Physician Density

210
Beds/100k

Hospital Bed Density

437
Deaths/100k

Maternal Mortality

Eswatini

Nonprofit Organizations

143 LIFE Foundation
Seeks to educate and empower individuals living with malaria, TB, HIV/AIDS, STDs and other health disparities related to sexual health.
Infect Dis, MF Med
🌐 https://vfmat.ch/d59b

Aceso Global
Provides strategic healthcare advisory services in low- and middle-income countries to design and deliver highly customized, evidence-based solutions that address the complex nature of healthcare systems, with a goal to strengthen and provide affordable, high-quality care to all.
Logist-Op, Pub Health
🌐 https://vfmat.ch/b3b7

Africa CDC
Aims to strengthen the capacity and capability of Africa's public health institutions and partnerships to detect and respond quickly and effectively to disease threats and outbreaks, based on data-driven interventions and programs.
Infect Dis, Logist-Op, Pub Health
🌐 https://vfmat.ch/339c

Africa Health Organisation
Leads collaborative efforts among countries in Africa and other partners to promote health equity, combat disease, and improve quality of life.
Logist-Op, Pub Health
🌐 https://vfmat.ch/b1c5

Africa Relief and Community Development
Provides comprehensive relief and developmental aid to people of the African continent regardless of gender, race, or religion.
Nutr, Pub Health
🌐 https://vfmat.ch/6cd2

AIDS Healthcare Foundation
Provides cutting-edge HIV/AIDS medical care and advocacy to over one million people in 43 countries.
Infect Dis
🌐 https://vfmat.ch/b27c

American Academy of Ophthalmology
Protects sight and empowers lives by serving as an advocate for patients and the public, leading ophthalmic education, and advancing the profession of ophthalmology.
Ophth-Opt
🌐 https://vfmat.ch/89a2

Amref Health Africa
Serves millions of people across 35 countries in Sub-Saharan Africa, strengthening health systems, and training African health workers to respond to the continent's most critical health issues.

All-Immu, General, Infect Dis, Logist-Op, MF Med, OB-GYN, Path, Pub Health, Surg
🌐 https://vfmat.ch/6985

Arms Around Africa Foundation
Supports children, empowers women, and helps young people to overcome poverty through talent promotion, education, good health, life skills development, entrepreneurship, and enhanced access to other resources for social and economic development.
General, Infect Dis, OB-GYN, Peds
🌐 https://vfmat.ch/ad98

Baylor International Pediatric AIDS Initiative (BIPAI) at Texas Children's Hospital
Provides high-quality, high-impact, highly ethical pediatric and family-centered healthcare, health professional training, and clinical research focused on HIV/AIDS, tuberculosis, malaria, malnutrition, and other conditions impacting the health of children worldwide.
Infect Dis, Medicine, OB-GYN, Peds, Pub Health, Surg
🌐 https://vfmat.ch/e6ba

Bulembu Ministries Swaziland
Seeks to provide homes, education, and healthcare for orphans, inspired by the Christian faith.
ER Med, General, Ophth-Opt
🌐 https://vfmat.ch/f755

Cabrini Ministries Swaziland
Seeks to provide comprehensive healthcare, child care, education and social services to the poorest and most vulnerable, inspired by the Christian faith.
General, Infect Dis
🌐 https://vfmat.ch/fcb1

Catholic Healthcare Association of Southern Africa, The
Inspired by the Catholic faith, works to provide universal access to healthcare, eradicate gender-based violence, eliminate HIV/AIDS and tuberculosis, and provide mental healthcare.
General, Infect Dis, Logist-Op, Psych
🌐 https://vfmat.ch/715b

Centre for HIV-AIDS Prevention Studies, The (CHAPS)
Provides comprehensive HIV/AIDS care and infectious disease response, primary healthcare services, and training.
Infect Dis, Logist-Op, Medicine, Pub Health
🌐 https://vfmat.ch/1755

Challenge Ministries Swaziland
Provides healthcare, education, childcare, addiction rehabilitation, and other social services to impoverished communities, based in Christian ministry.
General, Infect Dis, Logist-Op, Nutr
🌐 https://vfmat.ch/66c2

Clinton Health Access Initiative (CHAI)
Aims to save lives and reduce the burden of disease in low- and middle-income countries. Works with partners to strengthen the capabilities of governments and the private sector to create and sustain high-quality health systems.
General, Heme-Onc, Infect Dis, Logist-Op, MF Med, Medicine, Neonat, Nutr, OB-GYN, Path, Peds, Rad-Onc
⊕ https://vfmat.ch/9ed7

Covenant Medicine Outreach
Inspired by the Christian faith, provides medical care for those less fortunate.
General
⊕ https://vfmat.ch/769a

Direct Relief
Improves the health and lives of people affected by poverty or emergency situations by mobilizing and providing essential medical resources needed for their care.
ER Med, Logist-Op
⊕ https://vfmat.ch/58e5

Doctors Without Borders/Médecins Sans Frontières (MSF)
Responds to emergencies and provides lifesaving medical care where needed most, including during disasters, conflicts, and epidemics.
Anesth, Crit-Care, ER Med, General, Infect Dis, Nutr, OB-GYN, Ped Surg, Peds, Psych, Pub Health, Surg
⊕ https://vfmat.ch/f363

Dream Sant'Egidio
Seeks to counter HIV/AIDS in Africa by eliminating the transmission of HIV from mother to child, with a focus on women because of the importance of their role in the community.
Infect Dis, MF Med, Neonat, OB-GYN, Path, Peds
⊕ https://vfmat.ch/f466

Elizabeth Glaser Pediatric AIDS Foundation
Seeks to end global pediatric HIV/AIDS through prevention and treatment programs, research, and advocacy.
Infect Dis, Nutr, OB-GYN, Peds
⊕ https://vfmat.ch/d6ec

Global Ministries – The United Methodist Church
As the worldwide mission and development agency of The United Methodist Church, Global Ministries works with more than 300 hospitals and clinics around the world through its Global Health Unit.
Anesth, CT Surg, CV Med, Crit-Care, Dent-OMFS, Derm, ER Med, GI, General, Infect Dis, Logist-Op, MF Med, Medicine, Neonat, Nephro, Nutr, OB-GYN, Ophth-Opt, Ortho, Palliative, Peds, Pod, Psych, Pub Health, Rehab, Rheum, Surg, Urol
⊕ https://vfmat.ch/1723

Global Oncology (GO)
Brings the best in cancer care to underserved patients around the world and collaborates across geographic, professional, and academic borders to improve cancer care, research, and education.
Heme-Onc, Path, Rad-Onc
⊕ https://vfmat.ch/fcb8

Globus Relief
Aims to improve the delivery of healthcare worldwide by gathering, processing, and distributing surplus medical supplies to charities at home and abroad.
Logist-Op
⊕ https://vfmat.ch/a2b7

Good Shepherd Hospital Eye Clinic
Aims to provide eye care to the people of Eswatini and neighboring countries.
Ophth-Opt, Pub Health, Surg
⊕ https://vfmat.ch/85fe

Grassroot Soccer
Leverages the power of soccer to educate, inspire, and mobilize at-risk youth in developing countries to overcome their greatest health challenges, live healthier and more productive lives, and be agents for change in their communities.
Infect Dis
⊕ https://vfmat.ch/3521

Hands At Work
Based in Christian ministry, supports those in need through its community intervention model with a focus on food security, education, and basic healthcare.
General, Infect Dis, Nutr, Pub Health
⊕ https://vfmat.ch/7274

Healthy Smiles Society
Seeks to provide and promote mobile dental services in rural developing countries.
Dent-OMFS
⊕ https://vfmat.ch/5d8e

Hope and Healing International
Gives hope and healing to children and families trapped by poverty and disability.
General, Nutr, Ophth-Opt, Peds, Rehab
⊕ https://vfmat.ch/c638

ICAP at Columbia University
Serves as global leader in supporting the scale-up of multidisciplinary HIV/AIDS prevention, care, and treatment programs based on a family-focused approach.
General, Infect Dis, MF Med, Medicine, OB-GYN, Pub Health
⊕ https://vfmat.ch/a8ef

Imaging the World
Develops sustainable models for ultrasound imaging in the world's lowest resource settings and uses a technology-enabled solution to improve healthcare access, integrating lifesaving ultrasound and training programs in rural communities.
Logist-Op, OB-GYN, Radiol
⊕ https://vfmat.ch/59e4

International Federation of Red Cross and Red Crescent Societies (IFRC)
Coordinates and directs international assistance following natural and manmade disasters in nonconflict situations through the world's largest humanitarian and development network. Provides disaster-preparedness programs, healthcare activities, and promotes humanitarian values.
ER Med, General, Infect Dis, Nutr
⊕ https://vfmat.ch/b4ee

International Planned Parenthood Federation (IPPF)
Leads a locally owned, globally connected civil society movement that provides and enables services and champions sexual and reproductive health and rights for all, especially the underserved.
Infect Dis, MF Med, OB-GYN
⊕ https://vfmat.ch/dc97

IVUmed
Aims to make quality urological care available worldwide by providing medical and surgical education for physicians and nurses, and treatment for thousands of children and adults.
Anesth, OB-GYN, Ped Surg, Surg, Urol
⊕ https://vfmat.ch/e619

Izumi Foundation
Develops and supports programs that improve health and healthcare in neglected regions of Africa and Latin America.
⊕ https://vfmat.ch/f29a

Jhpiego
Creates and delivers transformative healthcare solutions that save lives, in partnership with national governments, health experts, and local communities.
General, Infect Dis, OB-GYN, Surg
⊕ https://vfmat.ch/45b8

John Snow, Inc. (JSI)
Aims to improve the health and well-being of underserved and vulnerable people and communities throughout the world.
General, Infect Dis, Logist-Op, MF Med, OB-GYN, Peds, Psych, Pub Health
⊕ https://vfmat.ch/ba78

Johns Hopkins Center for Global Health
Facilitates and focuses the extensive expertise and resources of the Johns

Hopkins institutions, together with global collaborators, to effectively address and ameliorate the world's most pressing health issues.

General, Genetics, Logist-Op, MF Med, Peds, Psych, Pub Health, Pulm-Critic

⊕ https://vfmat.ch/54ce

Kaya Responsible Travel

Promotes sustainable social, environmental, and economic development, empowers communities, and cultivates educated, compassionate global citizens through responsible travel.

All-Immu, Crit-Care, Dent-OMFS, ER Med, General, Geri, Infect Dis, MF Med, Medicine, Nutr, OB-GYN, Peds, Psych, Pub Health, Rehab

⊕ https://vfmat.ch/b2cf

Kudvumisa Foundation

Provides quality healthcare and empowers the disenfranchised to escape poverty in the impoverished and marginalized communities of Eswatini.

Dent-OMFS, General, Infect Dis, Nutr, OB-GYN, Pub Health

⊕ https://vfmat.ch/8bdc

Management Sciences for Health (MSH)

Works with countries and communities to save lives and improve the health of the world's poorest and most vulnerable people by building strong, resilient, sustainable health systems.

Infect Dis, Logist-Op, Pub Health

⊕ https://vfmat.ch/6aa2

MAP International

Provides medicines and health supplies to those in need around the world so they might experience life to the fullest.

Logist-Op

⊕ https://vfmat.ch/deed

Medical Care Development International

Works to improve the health of vulnerable populations through integrated, sustainable, and locally driven interventions.

Infect Dis, OB-GYN, Peds, Pub Health

⊕ https://vfmat.ch/da87

MedShare

Aims to improve the quality of life of people, communities, and the planet by sourcing and directly delivering surplus medical supplies and equipment to communities in need around the world.

Logist-Op

⊕ https://vfmat.ch/c8bc

New Horizons Collaborative

Advances a holistic, integrated approach to high-quality pediatric HIV care and treatment with a specific focus on those in need of advanced treatment.

Infect Dis, Peds, Pub Health

⊕ https://vfmat.ch/a76a

Pact

Works on the ground to improve the lives of those who are challenged by poverty and marginalization, striving for a world in which all people are heard, capable, and vibrant.

Infect Dis, Logist-Op, MF Med, Pub Health

⊕ https://vfmat.ch/9a6c

Philani Maswati Charity

Works to develop projects such as building orphanages, houses for old people, care centers for the elderly and needy, and health rehabilitation programs.

General, Infect Dis, Palliative

⊕ https://vfmat.ch/216b

RestoringVision

Empowers lives by restoring vision for millions of people in need.

Ophth-Opt

⊕ https://vfmat.ch/e121

ReSurge International

Provides reconstructive surgical care and builds surgical capacity in developing countries.

Anesth, Dent-OMFS, Ped Surg, Plast, Surg

⊕ https://vfmat.ch/9937

Rotary International

Provides service to others, improves lives, and advances world understanding, goodwill, and peace through its fellowship of business, professional, and community leaders.

ER Med, General, Infect Dis, MF Med, OB-GYN

⊕ https://vfmat.ch/8fb5

Salvation Army International, The

Seeks to meet human needs through services in education, healthcare, community support, emergency response, and ministry development, inspired by the Christian faith.

Dent-OMFS, Derm, ER Med, Infect Dis, MF Med, Medicine, Nutr, OB-GYN, Ophth-Opt, Palliative, Psych, Rehab, Surg

⊕ https://vfmat.ch/8eb3

Sanofi Espoir Foundation

Contributes to reducing health inequalities among populations that need it most by applying a socially responsible approach focused on fighting childhood cancers in low-income countries, improving maternal and newborn health, and improving access to care.

ER Med, OB-GYN, Peds

⊕ https://vfmat.ch/943b

Saving Orphans Through Healthcare and Outreach (SOHO)

Works to transform the lives of orphans and vulnerable children through programs addressing health, education, and empowerment, inspired by the Christian faith.

General, Infect Dis, Nutr, Peds, Psych

⊕ https://vfmat.ch/e5ed

SEE International

Provides sustainable medical, surgical, and educational services through volunteer ophthalmic surgeons, with the objectives of restoring sight and preventing blindness to disadvantaged individuals worldwide.

Ophth-Opt, Surg

⊕ https://vfmat.ch/6e1b

Seed Global Health

Focuses on human resources for health capacity building at the individual, institutional, and national level through sustained collaborative engagement with partners.

Logist-Op

⊕ https://vfmat.ch/d12e

SOS Children's Villages International

Supports children through alternative care and family strengthening.

ER Med, Peds

⊕ https://vfmat.ch/aca1

STEPS

Works with partners, donors, doctors and parents towards a clear vision of a sustainable and effective solution to the disability caused by untreated clubfoot.

Logist-Op, Ortho, Pod

⊕ https://vfmat.ch/784d

Sustainabililty for Agriculture, Health, Education and Environment (Sahee)

Aims to sustainably improve the living conditions of underprivileged people in Eswatini and Peru through projects in agriculture, childhood development, farming, and health.

Infect Dis, Pub Health

⊕ https://vfmat.ch/d93a

Swasti

Aims to transform the lives of marginalized communities by ensuring their access to quality healthcare and thereby contributing to poverty alleviation.

Pub Health

⊕ https://vfmat.ch/be8b

Task Force for Global Health, The

Consists of programs and focus areas that cover a range of global health issues including neglected tropical diseases, infectious diseases, vaccines, field epidemiology, public health informatics, health workforce development, and global health ethics.

Infect Dis, Logist-Op, Medicine, Ophth-Opt, Peds
⊕ https://vfmat.ch/714c

Texas Children's Global Health

Addresses healthcare needs in resource-limited settings locally and globally by improving maternal and child health through the implementation of innovative, sustainable, in-country programs to train health professionals and build functional healthcare infrastructure.

Anesth, ER Med, Heme-Onc, Infect Dis, MF Med, Nutr, OB-GYN, Peds, Pub Health, Surg
⊕ https://vfmat.ch/4a1d

United MegaCare

Seeks to deliver high-caliber services and programming across its areas of focus: education, health and wellness, secure families, and disaster resiliency.

ER Med, General, Infect Dis, Nutr, Ophth-Opt, Peds
⊕ https://vfmat.ch/ea18

United Nations High Commissioner for Refugees (UNHCR)

Safeguards the rights and well-being of people who have been forced to flee, ensuring that everybody has the right to seek asylum and find safe refuge in another country, with the goal of seeking lasting solutions.

General, MF Med, Medicine, OB-GYN, Peds, Psych, Pub Health
⊕ https://vfmat.ch/6636

United Nations Population Fund (UNFPA)

Supports reproductive healthcare for women and youth in more than 150 countries, focusing on delivering a world in which every pregnancy is wanted, every childbirth is safe, and every young person's potential is fulfilled.

Infect Dis, MF Med, Neonat, OB-GYN, Peds, Pub Health
⊕ https://vfmat.ch/c969

United States Agency for International Development (USAID)

Promotes and demonstrates democratic values abroad and advances a free, peaceful, and prosperous world. Leads the U.S. government's international development and disaster assistance through partnerships and investments that save lives.

ER Med, Infect Dis, MF Med, OB-GYN, Peds
⊕ https://vfmat.ch/9a99

USAID: A2Z The Micronutrient and Child Blindness Project

Aims to increase the use of key micronutrient and blindness interventions to improve child and maternal health.

MF Med, Neonat, Nutr, Ophth-Opt, Surg
⊕ https://vfmat.ch/c5f1

USAID: Health Finance and Governance Project

Uses research to implement strategies to help countries develop robust governance systems, increase their domestic resources for health, manage those resources more effectively, and make wise purchasing decisions.

Logist-Op
⊕ https://vfmat.ch/8652

USAID: Health Policy Initiative

Provides field-level programming in health policy development and implementation.

General, Infect Dis, MF Med, OB-GYN, Peds
⊕ https://vfmat.ch/8f84

USAID: Maternal and Child Health Integrated Program

Works to improve the health of women and their families, including programs for maternal, newborn, and child health, immunization, family planning, nutrition, malaria, and HIV/AIDS.

All-Immu, General, Infect Dis, MF Med
⊕ https://vfmat.ch/4415

USAID: TB Care II

Focuses on tuberculosis care and treatment.

Infect Dis
⊕ https://vfmat.ch/57d4

Vision Care

Restores sight and helps patients get regular treatment at short-term eye camps and long-term base clinics by having doctors, missionaries, volunteers, and sponsors work together.

Ophth-Opt
⊕ https://vfmat.ch/9d7c

Vision Outreach International

Advocates for helping the blind in underserved regions of the world and empowers the poor through sight restoration.

Ophth-Opt
⊕ https://vfmat.ch/9721

Voluntary Service Overseas (VSO)

Works with health workers, communities, and governments to improve health services and rights for women, babies, youth, people with disabilities, and prisoners.

General, MF Med, OB-GYN
⊕ https://vfmat.ch/213d

World Federation of Hemophilia (WFH)

Aims to improve and sustain care for people with inherited bleeding disorders by pursuing long-term relationships with individuals and organizations who share the values of WFH's development model.

Heme-Onc
⊕ https://vfmat.ch/5121

World Health Organization, The (WHO)

The United Nations' agency for health provides leadership on global health matters, shapes the health research agenda, sets norms and standards, articulates evidence-based policy options, provides technical support and monitoring to countries, and assesses health trends.

ER Med, General, Infect Dis, Logist-Op, MF Med, OB-GYN, Peds, Psych, Pub Health
⊕ https://vfmat.ch/c476

World Vision International

Works with vulnerable communities around the world to overcome poverty and injustice with child-focused programs in disaster management, health, nutrition, economic development, education, clean water, sanitation, and hygiene.

ER Med, General, Infect Dis, MF Med, Nutr, OB-GYN, Peds
⊕ https://vfmat.ch/2642

Eswatini

Healthcare Facilities

Good Shepherd Mission Hospital
Siteki, Eswatani, Eswatini
⊕ https://vfmat.ch/6b34

Hlatikhulu General Hospital
Hlatsi, Shiselweni, Eswatini
⊕ https://vfmat.ch/6dee

Lubombo Referral Hospital
Siteki, Eswatini
⊕ https://vfmat.ch/xypm

Mankayane Government Hospital
Mankayane, Manzini, Eswatini
⊕ https://vfmat.ch/u7mi

Mathangeni Clinic
Matsapha, Eswatini
⊕ https://vfmat.ch/4eih

Mbabane Clinic
Mbabane, Eswatini
⊕ https://vfmat.ch/1cpg

Mbabane Government Hospital
Mbabane, Eswatini
⊕ https://vfmat.ch/541a

Mkhiwa Clinic
Manzini, Eswatini
⊕ https://vfmat.ch/9fk3

National Tuberculosis Hospital
Hhelehhele, Manzini, Eswatini
⊕ https://vfmat.ch/821e

Piggs Peak Government Hospital
Piggs Peak, Eswatini
⊕ https://vfmat.ch/13be

Raleigh Fitkin Memorial Hospital
Manzini, Eswatini
⊕ https://vfmat.ch/f82c

Women and Children's Hospital
Manzini, Manzini Region, Eswatini
⊕ https://vfmat.ch/e5b4

Healthcare Facility

Ethiopia

Located in the Horn of Africa, the Federal Democratic Republic of Ethiopia has a population of 110.9 million that is 44 percent Ethiopian Orthodox, 31 percent Muslim, and 23 percent Protestant. Eighty different ethnic groups, speaking 200 different native dialects, live there. Most of Ethiopia's population can be found in the highlands of the north and middle geographies of the country, particularly around the capital city of Addis Ababa. Ethiopia is often called the "Cradle of Mankind." Fossils of some of humankind's earliest ancestors can be found in Ethiopia, as well as nine UNESCO World Heritage Sites, more than any other country in Africa.

Ethiopia is the only country in sub-Saharan Africa to never be colonized, although it did experience Italian occupation from 1936–1941. But the country has faced decades of conflict with neighbors, environmental disasters, famine, forced population resettlement due to overworked land, and political instability. As a result, Ethiopia remains in a vulnerable state and has been ranked as one of the poorest countries in the world.

Poverty has resulted in poor health and a weak healthcare system that can't keep up with the population's needs. Maternal mortality, malaria, tuberculosis, and HIV/AIDS are all areas of concern. Significant malnutrition results in 50 percent of children having stunted growth by age five. The largest contributors to death include neonatal disorders, diarrheal disease, lower respiratory infections, HIV/AIDS, malaria, meningitis, and measles. Additional significant causes of death include non-communicable diseases, such as congenital defects as well as stroke, ischemic heart disease, and cirrhosis, which have increased substantially in recent years.

110.9M
Population

$936
GDP Per Capita

67 years
Life Expectancy
↑ Improving

8
Doctors/100k
Physician Density

33
Beds/100k
Hospital Bed Density

401
Deaths/100k
Maternal Mortality

Ethiopia

Nonprofit Organizations

143 LIFE Foundation
Seeks to educate and empower individuals living with malaria, TB, HIV/AIDS, STDs and other health disparities related to sexual health.
Infect Dis, MF Med
⊕ https://vfmat.ch/d59b

Abt Associates
Seeks to improve the quality of life and economic well-being of people worldwide, while striving to meet and exceed the highest professional standards.
General, Logist-Op, MF Med, OB-GYN, Peds
⊕ https://vfmat.ch/cec2

Aceso Global
Provides strategic healthcare advisory services in low- and middle-income countries to design and deliver highly customized, evidence-based solutions that address the complex nature of healthcare systems, with a goal to strengthen and provide affordable, high-quality care to all.
Logist-Op, Pub Health
⊕ https://vfmat.ch/b3b7

Action Against Hunger
Aims to end life-threatening hunger for good through treating and preventing malnutrition across more than 45 countries.
Nutr
⊕ https://vfmat.ch/2dbc

Action For East African People
Acts on the needs of women and children living in East Africa while promoting the grassroots advancement of the East African community of Bloomington, Minnesota.
Dent-OMFS, General, OB-GYN, Pub Health
⊕ https://vfmat.ch/4db7

Addis Clinic, The
Uses telemedicine to care for people living in medically underserved areas, connects volunteer physicians with global health challenges, and provides support to local partner organizations and frontline health workers.
General, Infect Dis
⊕ https://vfmat.ch/f82f

Advance Family Planning
Aims to achieve global expansion and access to quality contraceptive information, services, and supplies through financial investment and political commitment.
General, MF Med, Pub Health
⊕ https://vfmat.ch/7478

Adventist Health International
Focuses on upgrading and managing mission hospitals by providing governance, consultation, and technical assistance to a number of affiliated Seventh-Day Adventist hospitals throughout Africa, Asia, and the Americas.

Dent-OMFS, General, Pub Health
⊕ https://vfmat.ch/16aa

Africa CDC
Aims to strengthen the capacity and capability of Africa's public health institutions and partnerships to detect and respond quickly and effectively to disease threats and outbreaks, based on data-driven interventions and programs.
Infect Dis, Logist-Op, Pub Health
⊕ https://vfmat.ch/339c

Africa Health Organisation
Leads collaborative efforts among countries in Africa and other partners to promote health equity, combat disease, and improve quality of life.
Logist-Op, Pub Health
⊕ https://vfmat.ch/b1c5

Africa Humanitarian Action (AHA)
Responds to crises, conflicts, and disasters in Africa, while informing and advising the international community, governments, civil society, and the private sector on humanitarian issues of concern to Africa. Supports institutional and organizational development efforts.
General, Infect Dis, MF Med, Nutr, OB-GYN
⊕ https://vfmat.ch/3ca2

Africa Indoor Residual Spraying Project (AIRS)
Aims to protect millions of people in Africa from malaria by spraying insecticide on walls, ceilings, and other indoor resting places of mosquitoes that transmit malaria.
Infect Dis
⊕ https://vfmat.ch/9bd1

Africa Relief and Community Development
Provides comprehensive relief and developmental aid to people of the African continent regardless of gender, race, or religion.
Nutr, Pub Health
⊕ https://vfmat.ch/6cd2

African Field Epidemiology Network (AFENET)
Strengthens field epidemiology and public health laboratory capacity to contribute effectively to addressing epidemics and other major public health problems in Africa.
All-Immu, Infect Dis, Path, Pub Health
⊕ https://vfmat.ch/df2e

African Mission Health Foundation
Aims to strengthen African mission hospitals by providing quality, compassionate care for the hurting and forgotten and helping improve Sub-Saharan Africa's health system.
Infect Dis, Neonat, OB-GYN, Peds, Surg
⊕ https://vfmat.ch/5b14

Against Malaria Foundation

Helps protect people from malaria. Funds anti-malaria nets, specifically long-lasting insecticidal nets (LLINs), and works with distribution partners to ensure they are used. Tracks and reports on net use and malaria case data.

Infect Dis

⊕ https://vfmat.ch/337d

Age International

Helps older people living in some of the world's poorest places to have improved well-being and be treated with dignity through a variety of programs, including emergency relief and cataract surgery.

ER Med, Geri, Logist-Op, Nutr, Ophth-Opt, Palliative, Pub Health

⊕ https://vfmat.ch/c7e2

AHOPE for Children

Aims to help children orphaned by AIDS, especially those infected with HIV. Provides medical care to children, including administering lifesaving antiretroviral medication.

General, Infect Dis

⊕ https://vfmat.ch/8538

AIDS Healthcare Foundation

Provides cutting-edge HIV/AIDS medical care and advocacy to over one million people in 43 countries.

Infect Dis

⊕ https://vfmat.ch/b27c

Al Basar International Foundation

Works with local partners to treat preventable blindness, and helps set up sustainable infrastructure so local teams can save sight in their communities.

Ophth-Opt

⊕ https://vfmat.ch/a8b5

Al-Ihsan Foundation

Aims to establish and maintain a global society that serves and empowers all those in need.

ER Med, General, MF Med, Nutr, Ophth-Opt, Peds, Surg

⊕ https://vfmat.ch/fff2

AMARI (African Mental Health Research Initiative)

Seeks to build an Africa-led network of future leaders in mental, neurological, and substance use (MNS) research in Ethiopia, Malawi, South Africa, and Zimbabwe.

Neuro, Psych

⊕ https://vfmat.ch/5e9d

American Academy of Ophthalmology

Protects sight and empowers lives by serving as an advocate for patients and the public, leading ophthalmic education, and advancing the profession of ophthalmology.

Ophth-Opt

⊕ https://vfmat.ch/89a2

American Academy of Pediatrics

Seeks to attain optimal physical, mental, and social health and well-being for all infants, children, adolescents, and young adults.

Anesth, Crit-Care, Neonat, Ped Surg

⊕ https://vfmat.ch/9633

American International Health Alliance (AIHA)

Strengthens health systems and workforce capacity worldwide through locally driven, peer-to-peer institutional partnerships.

CV Med, ER Med, Infect Dis, Medicine, OB-GYN

⊕ https://vfmat.ch/69fd

Americares

Saves lives and improves health for people affected by poverty or disaster and responds with life-changing medicine, medical supplies, and health programs including domestic and global medical clinics.

All-Immu, ER Med, General, Infect Dis, MF Med, Nutr

⊕ https://vfmat.ch/e567

AMREF Flying Doctors

Aims to deliver medical air transport and health services using the latest aviation

and medical technology to ensure patients receive unrivaled care.

ER Med, Logist-Op

⊕ https://vfmat.ch/5d5e

Amref Health Africa

Serves millions of people across 35 countries in Sub-Saharan Africa, strengthening health systems, and training African health workers to respond to the continent's most critical health issues.

All-Immu, General, Infect Dis, Logist-Op, MF Med, OB-GYN, Path, Pub Health, Surg

⊕ https://vfmat.ch/6985

Amsterdam Institute for Global Health and Development (AIGHD)

Provides sustainable solutions to major health problems across our planet by forging synergies among disciplines, healthcare delivery, research, and education.

Infect Dis

⊕ https://vfmat.ch/d73d

Anania Mothers and Children Specialized Medical Center

Provides comprehensive and compassionate women's healthcare for mothers and children in Addis Ababa and surrounding cities.

ER Med, General, OB-GYN, Peds

⊕ https://vfmat.ch/a13e

AO Alliance

Builds solutions to lessen the burden of injuries in low- and middle-income countries, while enhancing the care of the injured to reduce human suffering, disability, and poverty.

Ortho, Surg

⊕ https://vfmat.ch/8cd5

Aslan Project, The

Seeks to elevate standards of pediatric cancer care and increase survival rates in limited-resource countries.

Anesth, Heme-Onc, Ped Surg, Peds, Psych, Rad-Onc, Rehab

⊕ https://vfmat.ch/e633

Assist International

Designs and implements humanitarian programs that build capacity, develop opportunities, and save lives around the world.

Infect Dis, Ped Surg, Peds

⊕ https://vfmat.ch/9a3b

Australian Doctors for Africa

Develops healthier environments and builds capacity through the provision of voluntary medical assistance, while training and teaching doctors, nurses, and allied health workers; improving infrastructure; and providing medical equipment.

Anesth, ENT, GI, Logist-Op, MF Med, OB-GYN, Ortho, Ped Surg, Peds, Urol

⊕ https://vfmat.ch/f769

Benjamin H. Josephson, MD Fund

Provides healthcare professionals with the financial resources necessary to deliver medical services for those in need throughout the world.

General, OB-GYN

⊕ https://vfmat.ch/6acc

BethanyKids

Transforms the lives of African children with surgical conditions and disabilities through pediatric surgery, rehabilitation, public education, spiritual ministry, and the training of health professionals.

Neurosurg, Nutr, Ortho, Ped Surg, Peds, Rehab, Surg

⊕ https://vfmat.ch/db4e

BFIRST – British Foundation for International Reconstructive Surgery & Training

Supports projects across the developing world to train surgeons in their local environment to effectively manage devastating injuries.

Anesth, Plast, Surg

⊕ https://vfmat.ch/ad4f

Bill & Melinda Gates Foundation

Focuses on global issues, such as poverty, health, and education, offering the opportunity to dramatically improve the quality of life for billions of people by building partnerships that bring together resources, expertise, and vision to identify issues, find answers, and drive change.

All-Immu, General, Infect Dis, MF Med, Neonat, OB-GYN, Pub Health

⊕ https://vfmat.ch/7cf2

Boston Cardiac Foundation, The

Provides advanced medical technologies and cardiac care, such as pacemaker implantation, to patients around the world who would otherwise have no access to these services.

Anesth, CT Surg, CV Med, Crit-Care

⊕ https://vfmat.ch/8fd3

Boston Children's Hospital: Global Health Program

Helps solve pediatric global healthcare challenges by transferring expertise through long-term partnerships with scalable impact, while working in the field to strengthen healthcare systems, advocate, research, and provide care delivery or education as a way of sustainably improving the health of children worldwide.

Anesth, CV Med, Crit-Care, ER Med, Heme-Onc, Infect Dis, Medicine, Nutr, Palliative, Ped Surg, Peds

⊕ https://vfmat.ch/f9f8

Bridge to Health Medical and Dental

Seeks to provide healthcare to those who need it most, based on a philosophy of partnership, education, and community development. Strives to bring solutions to global health issues in underserved communities through clinical outreach and medical and dental training.

Dent-OMFS, General, Infect Dis, MF Med, OB-GYN, Ophth-Opt, Ortho, Pub Health, Radiol

⊕ https://vfmat.ch/bb2c

BroadReach

Collaborates with governments, multinational health organizations, donors, and private-sector companies to effect healthcare reform and solve the world's biggest health challenges.

Logist-Op

⊕ https://vfmat.ch/7812

Burn Care International

Seeks to improve the lives of burn survivors around the world through effective rehabilitation.

Derm, Nutr, Psych, Surg

⊕ https://vfmat.ch/78d1

Canadian Network for International Surgery, The

Aims to improve maternal health, increase safety, and build local capacity in low-income countries by creating and providing surgical and midwifery courses, training domestically, and transferring skills.

Logist-Op, Surg

⊕ https://vfmat.ch/86ff

Cancer Care Ethiopia

Aims to provide a quality and standardized system of cancer care in Ethiopia for poor cancer patients by helping them get appropriate treatment; making their lives more comfortable; improving prevention, early detection, treatment, and palliative care; and raising awareness in society.

Heme-Onc, Nutr, Palliative

⊕ https://vfmat.ch/ad6f

CARE

Works around the globe to save lives, defeat poverty, and achieve social justice.

ER Med, General

⊕ https://vfmat.ch/7232

Caritas Pro Vitae Gradu Charitable Trust

Supports Catholic charitable projects with social and humanitarian efforts, and aims to assist people in need including children, the elderly, sick, and disabled through healthcare, poverty relief, and education.

ER Med, General, Logist-Op, Medicine, OB-GYN, Ophth-Opt, Path, Peds, Pub Health, Radiol, Rehab, Surg

⊕ https://vfmat.ch/b2ca

Carter Center, The

Seeks to prevent and resolve conflicts, enhance freedom and democracy, and

improve health, while remaining committed to human rights and the alleviation of human suffering.

Infect Dis, MF Med, Ophth-Opt

⊕ https://vfmat.ch/6556

Catherine Hamlin Fistula Foundation

Works to eradicate obstetric fistula by holistically treating women with obstetric fistulas in Ethiopia, as the global reference organization and leader in this effort.

MF Med, OB-GYN, Rehab, Surg

⊕ https://vfmat.ch/ab72

Catholic Organization for Relief & Development Aid (CORDAID)

Provides humanitarian assistance and creates opportunities to improve security, healthcare, education, and inclusive economic growth in fragile and conflict-affected areas.

ER Med, Infect Dis, MF Med, OB-GYN, Peds, Psych

⊕ https://vfmat.ch/8ae5

cbm New Zealand

Inspired by the Christian faith, aims to improve the quality of life for those living with the double disadvantage of poverty and disability.

Crit-Care, Infect Dis, Logist-Op, Nutr, OB-GYN, Ophth-Opt, Ortho, Psych, Rehab, Surg

⊕ https://vfmat.ch/c14b

Centre for Global Mental Health

Closes the care gap and reduces human rights abuses experienced by people living with mental, neurological, and substance use conditions, particularly in low-resource settings.

Neuro, OB-GYN, Palliative, Peds, Psych

⊕ https://vfmat.ch/a96d

Chain of Hope

Provides lifesaving heart operations for children around the world and supports the development of cardiac services in numerous developing and war-torn countries.

Anesth, CT Surg, CV Med, Crit-Care, Ped Surg, Peds, Pulm-Critic, Surg

⊕ https://vfmat.ch/1b1b

CharityVision International

Focuses on restoring curable sight impairment worldwide by empowering local physicians and creating sustainable solutions.

Logist-Op, Ophth-Opt, Surg

⊕ https://vfmat.ch/6231

ChildFund Australia

Works to reduce poverty for children in many of the world's most disadvantaged communities.

ER Med, General, Peds

⊕ https://vfmat.ch/13df

Children's Bridge Foundation

Supports health and education programs for orphaned and abandoned children in the developing world.

Infect Dis, Nutr, Peds, Surg

⊕ https://vfmat.ch/6486

Children's Lifeline International

Provides medical teams and surgical assistance to underprivileged children in developing countries through missions in partnership with local hospitals.

CV Med, Dent-OMFS, General, MF Med, Neurosurg, Peds, Rehab

⊕ https://vfmat.ch/6fea

Children's Surgery International

Provides free medical and surgical services to children in need around the world, and instructs and trains local surgeons and other medical providers such as doctors, anesthesiologists, nurses, and technicians.

Anesth, Dent-OMFS, Ortho, Ped Surg, Peds, Plast, Surg

⊕ https://vfmat.ch/26d3

Christian Aid Ministries

Strives to be a trustworthy and efficient channel for Amish, Mennonite, and

other conservative Anabaptist groups and individuals to minister to physical and spiritual needs around the world.
CT Surg, ER Med, Logist-Op, Ortho, Pub Health
⊕ https://vfmat.ch/7b33

Christian Blind Mission (CBM)
Aims to improve the quality of life of persons with disabilities in the poorest countries, addressing poverty as a cause and a consequence of disability, and working in partnership to create a society for all.
ENT, General, Infect Dis, OB-GYN, Ophth-Opt, Ortho, Peds, Psych, Rehab, Surg
⊕ https://vfmat.ch/3824

Christian Health Service Corps
Brings Christian doctors, health professionals, and health educators committed to serving the poor to places that otherwise have little or no access to healthcare.
Anesth, Dent-OMFS, General, Medicine, Peds, Surg
⊕ https://vfmat.ch/da57

Christian Medical & Dental Associations
Based in Christian ministry, deploys medical and dental teams to underserved communities to provide vital healthcare.
Anesth, Dent-OMFS, ER Med, General, Medicine, OB-GYN, Ophth-Opt, Peds, Pub Health, Radiol, Rehab, Surg
⊕ https://vfmat.ch/921c

Clinton Health Access Initiative (CHAI)
Aims to save lives and reduce the burden of disease in low- and middle-income countries. Works with partners to strengthen the capabilities of governments and the private sector to create and sustain high-quality health systems.
General, Heme-Onc, Infect Dis, Logist-Op, MF Med, Medicine, Neonat, Nutr, OB-GYN, Path, Peds, Rad-Onc
⊕ https://vfmat.ch/9ed7

Columbia University: Columbia Office of Global Surgery (COGS)
Helps to increase access to safe and affordable surgical care, as a means to reduce health disparities and the global burden of disease.
Anesth, CT Surg, Crit-Care, Dent-OMFS, ENT, ER Med, Infect Dis, MF Med, Neurosurg, OB-GYN, Ophth-Opt, Ortho, Ped Surg, Plast, Plast, Pub Health, Surg, Urol
⊕ https://vfmat.ch/4349

Columbia University: Global Mental Health Programs
Pioneers research initiatives, promotes mental health, and aims to reduce the burden of mental illness worldwide.
Psych
⊕ https://vfmat.ch/c5cd

Columbia Vagelos College of Physicians and Surgeons Programs in Global Health
Harnesses the expertise of the medical school to improve health worldwide by training global health leaders, building capacity through interdisciplinary education and training programs, and addressing unmet health needs through research and application.
CV Med, Derm, Genetics, Heme-Onc, Infect Dis, Medicine, OB-GYN, Ophth-Opt, Peds, Psych, Pub Health, Pulm-Critic, Surg
⊕ https://vfmat.ch/a9e5

Comitato Collaborazione Medica (CCM)
Supports development processes that safeguard and promote the right to health with a global approach, working on health needs and influencing socio-economic factors, identifying poverty as the main cause for the lack of health.
All-Immu, General, Infect Dis, MF Med, OB-GYN
⊕ https://vfmat.ch/4272

Compassionate Eye
Aims to support the social good by supplying infrastructure and personnel for sanitation, education, medical care, small business, and job training.
General, Infect Dis, MF Med, OB-GYN, Peds
⊕ https://vfmat.ch/1915

Concern Worldwide
Seeks to permanently transform the lives of people living in extreme poverty, tackling its root causes, and building resilience.

Logist-Op, MF Med, Nutr, OB-GYN
⊕ https://vfmat.ch/77e9

Core Group
Aims to improve and expand community health practices for underserved populations, especially women and children, through collaborative action and learning.
General, Infect Dis, MF Med, Medicine, OB-GYN, Peds, Pub Health
⊕ https://vfmat.ch/9de3

COVID-19 Clinical Research Coalition
Advocates and collaborates for the advancement of COVID-19 research driven by the needs of low-resource settings, and works for equitable access to solutions to the pandemic.
All-Immu, Infect-Dis, MF Med, Path, Pub Health
⊕ https://vfmat.ch/d1f4

Cross Catholic Outreach
Mobilizes the global Catholic Church to transform impoverished communities through the provision of food, water, housing, education, orphan support, medical care, microenterprise, and disaster relief.
All-Immu, General, Nutr, OB-GYN, Rehab
⊕ https://vfmat.ch/22f4

CURE
Operates charitable hospitals and programs in underserved countries worldwide, where patients receive surgical treatment, based in Christian ministry.
Anesth, Neurosurg, Ortho, Ped Surg, Peds, Rehab, Surg
⊕ https://vfmat.ch/aa16

CURE Children's Hospital of Zimbabwe
Heals children living with disabilities such as clubfoot, bowed legs, cleft lips, untreated burns, and hydrocephalus.
ENT, Neurosurg, Ortho, Peds, Plast
⊕ https://vfmat.ch/473c

CureCervicalCancer
Focuses on the early detection and prevention of cervical cancer around the globe for the women who need it most.
Heme-Onc, OB-GYN
⊕ https://vfmat.ch/ace1

D-tree Digital Global Health
Demonstrates and advocates for the potential of digital technology to transform health systems and improve health and well-being for all.
Logist-Op, MF Med, OB-GYN, Peds, Pub Health
⊕ https://vfmat.ch/1f79

Dentaid
Seeks to treat, equip, train, and educate people in need of dental care.
Dent-OMFS
⊕ https://vfmat.ch/a183

Direct Relief
Improves the health and lives of people affected by poverty or emergency situations by mobilizing and providing essential medical resources needed for their care.
ER Med, Logist-Op
⊕ https://vfmat.ch/58e5

DKT INTERNATIONAL INC
Seeks to provide couples with affordable and safe options for family planning and HIV/AIDS prevention through dynamic social marketing.
General, Surg
⊕ https://vfmat.ch/b3a7

Doctors with Africa (CUAMM)
Advocates for the universal right to health and promotes the values of international solidarity, justice, and peace. Works to protect and improve the well-being and health of vulnerable communities in Africa with a long-term development perspective.
ER Med, Infect Dis, MF Med, Neonat, OB-GYN, Peds
⊕ https://vfmat.ch/d2fb

Doctors Without Borders/Médecins Sans Frontières (MSF)
Responds to emergencies and provides lifesaving medical care where needed most, including during disasters, conflicts, and epidemics.
Anesth, Crit-Care, ER Med, General, Infect Dis, Nutr, OB-GYN, Ped Surg, Peds, Psych, Pub Health, Surg
⊕ https://vfmat.ch/f363

Drugs for Neglected Diseases Initiative
Develops lifesaving medicines for people with neglected diseases around the world, having developed eight treatments for five deadly diseases and saved millions of lives since 2003.
Infect Dis, Pub Health
⊕ https://vfmat.ch/969c

Duke University: Global Health Institute
Sparks innovation in global health research and education, and brings together knowledge and resources to address the most important global health issues of our time.
All-Immu, Infect Dis, MF Med, OB-GYN, Pub Health
⊕ https://vfmat.ch/c4cd

Elton John AIDS Foundation
Seeks to address and overcome the stigma, discrimination, and neglect that prevents ending AIDS by funding local experts to challenge discrimination, prevent infections, and provide treatment.
Infect Dis, Pub Health
⊕ https://vfmat.ch/9d31

Emory University School of Medicine
Aims to provide residents/fellows from clinical departments with knowledge and practical experience in global health by building ongoing collaborations between Emory University and academic institutions abroad.
Anesth, CV Med, General, Infect Dis, Pulm-Critic, Rheum, Surg
⊕ https://vfmat.ch/a6f7

Emory University School of Medicine: Global Surgery Program
A leading institution with the highest standards in education, biomedical research, and patient care.
Anesth, Dent-OMFS, ER Med, Pub Health, Surg, Urol
⊕ https://vfmat.ch/2b26

END Fund, The
Aims to control and eliminate the most prevalent neglected diseases among the world's poorest and most vulnerable people.
Infect Dis
⊕ https://vfmat.ch/2614

Engage Now Africa
Works to heal, rescue, and lift vulnerable individuals, families and communities of Africa out of extreme poverty and into self-reliance.
General, Ophth-Opt, Peds, Pub Health
⊕ https://vfmat.ch/16cd

EngenderHealth
Works to implement high-quality, gender-equitable programs that advance sexual and reproductive health and rights.
General, MF Med, OB-GYN, Peds
⊕ https://vfmat.ch/1cb2

eRanger
Provides sustainable solutions to transportation and medical provision such as ambulances and mobile clinics in developing countries.
ER Med, General, Logist-Op
⊕ https://vfmat.ch/4c18

Ethiopia Act
Aims to help those who suffer from diseases such as HIV/AIDS, cervical cancer, and tuberculosis. Based in Christian ministry, also aims to establish gospel-centered churches to serve people in need.
General, Infect Dis, Medicine, OB-GYN
⊕ https://vfmat.ch/945a

Ethiopia Healthcare Network
Provides healthcare to women and children in Ethiopia without access to services.
General, Infect Dis, MF Med, OB-GYN, Peds
⊕ https://vfmat.ch/b892

Ethiopia Medical Project (EMP)
Supports Buccama Health Centre in rural Ethiopia and focuses on preventing, raising awareness of, and treating podoconiosis and uterine prolapse.
Derm, General, OB-GYN, Ortho, Pod, Rehab
⊕ https://vfmat.ch/d9a1

Ethiopia Mission Trip
Aspires to create sustainable change that brings hope, health, opportunity, progress, and education.
General, Ophth-Opt
⊕ https://vfmat.ch/a7ba

Ethiopia Urban Health Extension Program (USAID)
Aims to support at scale the implementation and monitoring of the Government of Ethiopia's UHEP (GoE/UHEP), and to improve access to and demand for health services.
Infect Dis, MF Med, Pub Health
⊕ https://vfmat.ch/2f2a

Ethiopiaid
Aims to transform lives in Ethiopia and break the cycle of poverty by enabling the poorest and most vulnerable and their communities to live with dignity, to build resilience, and achieve real and sustainable solutions to the challenges they face.
ER Med, MF Med, Nutr, OB-GYN, Ortho, Palliative, Peds, Pub Health
⊕ https://vfmat.ch/5e59

Ethiopian Children's Fund, The
Works to uplift children and adolescents in extreme poverty, and to do so sustainably through education, nutrition, and primary healthcare.
General, Peds
⊕ https://vfmat.ch/4ea5

Evidence Project, The
Improves family-planning policies, programs, and practices through the strategic generation, translation, and use of evidence.
General, MF Med
⊕ https://vfmat.ch/f9e7

Eye Foundation of America
Works toward a world without childhood blindness.
Ophth-Opt
⊕ https://vfmat.ch/a7eb

Eyes for Africa
Works to make a difference by treating preventable blindness and restoring sight, resulting in improved lives and livelihoods.
Anesth, Ophth-Opt
⊕ https://vfmat.ch/9223

Facing Africa – NOMA
Helps Ethiopian children with noma (cancrum oris) and other severe facial deformities to get surgical treatment and start new lives.
Anesth, Dent-OMFS, Ped Surg, Plast, Surg
⊕ https://vfmat.ch/82d7

Fistula Foundation
Aims to engage the support of people worldwide who are eager to see the day that no woman suffers from obstetric fistula. Raises and directs funds to doctors and hospitals providing life-transforming surgery to women in need.
OB-GYN
⊕ https://vfmat.ch/e958

Flying Doctors of America
Brings together teams of physicians, dentists, nurses, and other healthcare professionals to care for people who would not otherwise receive medical care.
Dent-OMFS, GI, General, Surg
⊕ https://vfmat.ch/58b6

Foundation For International Education In Neurological Surgery (FIENS), The

Provides hands-on training and education to neurosurgeons around the world.

Neuro, Neurosurg, Surg

⊕ https://vfmat.ch/bab8

Foundation for Special Surgery

Provides high-quality, complex surgical care by increasing surgical expertise in Africa through the participation of surgeons across various specialties to provide premium care and skills transfer/education to benefit patients.

Anesth, CT Surg, ENT, Endo, Neurosurg, Plast, Surg, Urol

⊕ https://vfmat.ch/53db

Fracarita International

Provides support and services in the fields of mental healthcare, care for people with a disability, and education.

Psych, Rehab

⊕ https://vfmat.ch/8d3c

Fred Hollows Foundation, The

Works toward a world in which no person is needlessly blind or vision impaired.

Ophth-Opt, Pub Health, Surg

⊕ https://vfmat.ch/73e5

Free to Smile Foundation

Serves impoverished and underserved children suffering from cleft lip/palate deformities around the world.

Anesth, Dent-OMFS, ENT, Ped Surg, Plast

⊕ https://vfmat.ch/218b

Friends of UNFPA

Promotes the health, dignity, and rights of women and girls around the world by supporting the lifesaving work of UNFPA, the United Nations' reproductive health and rights agency, through education, advocacy, and fundraising.

MF Med, OB-GYN

⊕ https://vfmat.ch/2a3a

Gift of Life International

Provides lifesaving cardiac treatment to children in developing countries while developing sustainable pediatric cardiac programs by implementing screening, surgical, and training missions.

Anesth, CT Surg, CV Med, Crit-Care, Ped Surg, Peds, Pulm-Critic

⊕ https://vfmat.ch/f2f9

Global Alliance to Prevent Prematurity And Stillbirth (GAPPS)

Seeks to improve birth outcomes worldwide by reducing the burden of premature birth and stillbirth.

All-Immu, Infect Dis, MF Med, Neonat, Neonat, OB-GYN

⊕ https://vfmat.ch/3f74

Global Blood Fund

Delivers grants, equipment, and training to over 50 countries in Africa, Asia, Eastern Europe, the Middle East, Latin America and the Caribbean.

Pub Health

⊕ https://vfmat.ch/6377

Global Civic Sharing

Aims to support our neighbors' self-reliance and realize the sustainable development.

Nutr, Peds, Pub Health

⊕ https://vfmat.ch/d7ab

Global Clubfoot Initiative (GCI)

Promotes and resources the treatment of children with clubfoot in developing countries using the Ponseti technique.

Ortho, Ped Surg

⊕ https://vfmat.ch/f229

Global ENT Outreach

Saves lives and prevents avoidable deafness from ear disease for those affected by poverty and lack of care so they can reach their full human potential.

ENT, Surg

⊕ https://vfmat.ch/ef5c

Global Eye Mission

Strives to bring hope and healing to the lives of those living in underserved regions of the world by providing high-quality eye care to help the blind see, and improving the quality of life for individuals and entire communities.

Ophth-Opt, Surg

⊕ https://vfmat.ch/197e

Global Medical Foundation Australia

Provides medical, surgical, dental, and educational welfare to underprivileged communities and gives them access to basics that are often taken for granted.

Dent-OMFS, ER Med, General, OB-GYN, Ortho, Surg

⊕ https://vfmat.ch/fa56

Global Medical Missions Alliance

Brings and promotes Christian-centered missionary life to the body of healthcare professionals and its partners.

Dent-OMFS, ER Med, Pub Health, Rehab, Surg

⊕ https://vfmat.ch/29c7

Global NeuroCare

Aims to improve neurological care in developing countries by working with local partners to improve patient care, train physicians, and advance medical research.

Neuro, Neurosurg

⊕ https://vfmat.ch/d76c

Global Oncology (GO)

Brings the best in cancer care to underserved patients around the world and collaborates across geographic, professional, and academic borders to improve cancer care, research, and education.

Heme-Onc, Path, Rad-Onc

⊕ https://vfmat.ch/fcb8

Global Outreach Doctors

Provides global health medical services in developing countries affected by famine, infant mortality, and chronic health issues.

All-Immu, Anesth, ER Med, General, Infect Dis, MF Med, Peds, Surg

⊕ https://vfmat.ch/8514

Global Reconstructive Surgery Outreach

Supports surgeons, doctors, and nurses financially to enable them to provide critically needed plastic and reconstructive surgeries to the poor.

Logist-Op, Surg

⊕ https://vfmat.ch/f262

Globus Relief

Aims to improve the delivery of healthcare worldwide by gathering, processing, and distributing surplus medical supplies to charities at home and abroad.

Logist-Op

⊕ https://vfmat.ch/a2b7

GOAL

Works with the most vulnerable communities to help them respond to and recover from humanitarian crises, and to assist them in building transcendent solutions to mitigate poverty and vulnerability.

ER Med, General, Pub Health

⊕ https://vfmat.ch/bbea

Grace for Impact

Provides high-quality healthcare and education to the rural poor, where it is needed most, in Sub-Saharan Africa and Southeast Asia.

Dent-OMFS, General, Ophth-Opt

⊕ https://vfmat.ch/3ed1

Grassroot Soccer

Leverages the power of soccer to educate, inspire, and mobilize at-risk youth in developing countries to overcome their greatest health challenges, live healthier and more productive lives, and be agents for change in their communities.

Infect Dis

⊕ https://vfmat.ch/3521

Hamlin Fistula Ethiopia

Focuses on free treatment and prevention of childbirth injuries such as obstetric fistulas in the main hospital in Addis and the five outreach centers (Bahir Dar,

Mekele, Yirgalem, Harar, and Mutu). Also supports prevention through training at Hamlin College of Midwives, along with rehabilitation.
MF Med, OB-GYN, Path, Surg
⊕ https://vfmat.ch/3e56

Healing the Children
Helps underserved children around the world secure the medical care they need to lead more fulfilling lives.
Anesth, Dent-OMFS, ENT, General, Medicine, Ophth-Opt, Ped Surg, Peds, Plast, Surg
⊕ https://vfmat.ch/d4ee

Health Equity Initiative
Aims to build and sustain a global community that engages across sectors and disciplines to advance health equity.
Pub Health
⊕ https://vfmat.ch/e2e2

Health For All Mission
Promotes health and wellness in the following areas: healthcare, education, economic development, and the environment.
Dent-OMFS, General, Pub Health
⊕ https://vfmat.ch/fe1a

Health Poverty Action
Works in partnership with people around the world who are pursuing change in their own communities to demand health justice and challenge power imbalances.
ER Med, General, Infect Dis, Psych, Pub Health
⊕ https://vfmat.ch/ee58

Health[e] Foundation
Supports health professionals and community workers in the world's most vulnerable societies to ensure quality health for everyone in need by providing digital education and information, using e-learning and m-health.
Logist-Op
⊕ https://vfmat.ch/b73b

Healthy DEvelopments
Provides Germany-supported health and social protection programs around the globe in a collaborative knowledge management process.
All-Immu, General, Infect Dis, Logist-Op, MF Med
⊕ https://vfmat.ch/dc31

HelpAge Canada
Works in partnerships to improve and maintain the quality of life of vulnerable older persons and their communities in Canada and around the world.
ER Med, Geri
⊕ https://vfmat.ch/9945

HelpAge International
Works to ensure that people everywhere understand how much older people contribute to society and that they must enjoy their right to healthcare, social services, economic, and physical security.
General, Geri, Infect Dis, Medicine, Pub Health
⊕ https://vfmat.ch/5d91

Hernia International
Aims to provide relief from sickness, and protection and preservation of health, for persons affected by groin and abdominal hernias and residing in low- and middle-income countries.
Surg
⊕ https://vfmat.ch/e98e

Himalayan Cataract Project
Works to cure needless blindness with the highest quality care at the lowest cost.
Anesth, Ophth-Opt, Surg
⊕ https://vfmat.ch/3b3d

His Healing Hands
Seeks to provide disease treatment and prevention in partnership with indigenous evangelical Christian organizations that help guide activities.

General
⊕ https://vfmat.ch/ce38

Hope and Healing International
Gives hope and healing to children and families trapped by poverty and disability.
General, Nutr, Ophth-Opt, Peds, Rehab
⊕ https://vfmat.ch/c638

Hope Walks
Frees children, families, and communities from the burden of clubfoot, inspired by the Christian faith.
Ortho, Ped Surg, Peds, Rehab
⊕ https://vfmat.ch/f6d4

Horn of Africa Neonatal Development Services (HANDS)
Focuses on saving infants' lives in Ethiopia by facilitating the implementation of skilled medical care by local medical professionals.
MF Med, Neonat, Peds
⊕ https://vfmat.ch/8f47

Hospice Africa
Aims to provide a holistic and culturally sensitive palliative care service through accurate treatment of pain.
Palliative
⊕ https://vfmat.ch/9f86

Humanity & Inclusion
Works alongside people with disabilities and vulnerable populations, taking action and bearing witness in order to respond to their essential needs, improve their living conditions and health, and promote respect for their dignity and fundamental rights.
General, Infect Dis, MF Med, Medicine, Ortho, Peds, Psych, Pub Health, Rehab
⊕ https://vfmat.ch/16b7

Hunger Project, The
Aims to end hunger and poverty by pioneering sustainable, grassroots, women-centered strategies and advocating for their widespread adoption in countries throughout the world.
Infect Dis, Nutr, OB-GYN, Pub Health
⊕ https://vfmat.ch/3a49

Hunt Foundation, The
Organizes teams of medical professionals to travel to countries around the globe with the goal of healing individuals in need, while educating, training, and demonstrating proper medical and surgical techniques.
Neurosurg, Ortho, Surg
⊕ https://vfmat.ch/cee2

ICAP at Columbia University
Serves as global leader in supporting the scale-up of multidisciplinary HIV/AIDS prevention, care, and treatment programs based on a family-focused approach.
General, Infect Dis, MF Med, Medicine, OB-GYN, Pub Health
⊕ https://vfmat.ch/a8ef

Institute for Healthcare Improvement (IHI)
Aims to improve health and healthcare worldwide by working with health professionals to strengthen systems.
Crit-Care, Infect Dis, MF Med, Medicine, Neonat, OB-GYN, Pub Health
⊕ https://vfmat.ch/ecae

International Agency for the Prevention of Blindness (IAPB), The
Leads international efforts in blindness-prevention activities, works toward a world where no one is needlessly visually impaired, and ensures that everyone has access to the best possible standard of eye health.
Infect Dis, Ophth-Opt, Pub Health
⊕ https://vfmat.ch/87a2

International Children's Heart Foundation
Provides free surgical care, medical training, and technology to save the lives of children with congenital heart disease in developing countries.
Anesth, CT Surg, CV Med, Crit-Care, Ped Surg, Peds, Pulm-Critic
⊕ https://vfmat.ch/86c1

International Children's Heart Fund

Aims to promote the international growth and quality of cardiac surgery, particularly in children and young adults.

CT Surg, Ped Surg

⊕ https://vfmat.ch/33fb

International Council of Ophthalmology

Works with ophthalmologic societies and others to enhance ophthalmic education and improve access to the highest-quality eye care in order to preserve and restore vision for people of the world.

Ophth-Opt

⊕ https://vfmat.ch/ffd2

International Eye Foundation (IEF)

Eliminates preventable and treatable blindness by making quality sustainable eye care services accessible and affordable worldwide.

Infect Dis, Logist-Op, Ophth-Opt

⊕ https://vfmat.ch/e839

International Federation of Gynecology and Obstetrics (FIGO)

Implements global projects on specific women's health issues.

MF Med, Medicine, Neonat, OB-GYN, Surg, Urol

⊕ https://vfmat.ch/c4b4

International Federation of Red Cross and Red Crescent Societies (IFRC)

Coordinates and directs international assistance following natural and manmade disasters in nonconflict situations through the world's largest humanitarian and development network. Provides disaster-preparedness programs, healthcare activities, and promotes humanitarian values.

ER Med, General, Infect Dis, Nutr

⊕ https://vfmat.ch/b4ee

International Hearing Foundation

Supports hearing-related service, education, and research.

ENT, Surg

⊕ https://vfmat.ch/3ee2

International League of Dermatological Socieities

Strives to promote high-quality education, clinical care, research and innovation that will improve skin health globally.

Derm, Infect Dis

⊕ https://vfmat.ch/7388

International Learning Movement (ILM UK)

Supports some of the world's poorest people in developing countries with core projects in education, safe drinking water, and healthcare.

General, Ophth-Opt

⊕ https://vfmat.ch/b974

International Medical and Surgical Aid (IMSA)

Aims to save lives and alleviate suffering through education, healthcare, surgical camps, and quality medical programs.

Anesth, General, Ped Surg, Surg

⊕ https://vfmat.ch/2561

International Medical Corps

Seeks to improve quality of life through health interventions and related activities that strengthen underserved communities worldwide, with the flexibility to respond rapidly to emergencies and offer medical services and training to people at the highest risk.

ER Med, General, Infect Dis, Nutr, OB-GYN, Peds, Pub Health, Surg

⊕ https://vfmat.ch/a8a5

International Organization for Migration (IOM) – The UN Migration Agency

Promotes evidence-informed policies and holistic, preventive, and curative health programs that are beneficial, accessible, and equitable for vulnerable migrants.

General, Infect Dis, OB-GYN

⊕ https://vfmat.ch/621a

International Pediatric Nephrology Association (IPNA)

Leads global efforts to successfully address the care for all children with kidney disease through advocacy, education, and training.

Medicine, Nephro, Peds

⊕ https://vfmat.ch/b59d

International Planned Parenthood Federation (IPPF)

Leads a locally owned, globally connected civil society movement that provides and enables services and champions sexual and reproductive health and rights for all, especially the underserved.

Infect Dis, MF Med, OB-GYN

⊕ https://vfmat.ch/dc97

International Rescue Committee (IRC)

Responds to the world's worst humanitarian crises and helps people whose lives and livelihoods are shattered by conflict and disaster to survive, recover, and gain control of their future.

ER Med, General, Infect Dis, MF Med, Peds

⊕ https://vfmat.ch/5d24

International Trachoma Initiative (iTi)

Works toward a world free from trachoma, a preventable cause of blindness, and provides comprehensive support to national ministries of health and governmental and nongovernmental organizations to implement a comprehensive approach to fight trachoma.

Infect Dis, Ophth-Opt

⊕ https://vfmat.ch/3278

InterSurgeon

Fosters collaborative partnerships in the field of global surgery that will advance clinical care, teaching, training, research, and the provision and maintenance of medical equipment.

ENT, Neurosurg, Ortho, Ped Surg, Plast, Surg, Urol

⊕ https://vfmat.ch/6f8a

IntraHealth International

Improves the performance of health workers and strengthens the systems in which they work.

CV Med, Endo, General, Infect Dis, MF Med, Neonat, Nutr, OB-GYN

⊕ https://vfmat.ch/ddc8

Ipas

Focuses efforts on women and girls who want contraception or abortion, and builds programs around their needs and how best to support them.

OB-GYN

⊕ https://vfmat.ch/8e39

iSight Missions

To empower local eye care providers to establish self-supporting eye clinics to offer permanent care to impoverished persons.

Ophth-Opt

⊕ https://vfmat.ch/9739

Izumi Foundation

Develops and supports programs that improve health and healthcare in neglected regions of Africa and Latin America.

⊕ https://vfmat.ch/f29a

Jackson Hill Taye Foundation

Provides healthcare services for women and children in Ethiopia using state-of-the-art innovations, techniques, and equipment.

General, MF Med, OB-GYN, Peds

⊕ https://vfmat.ch/c289

JDC

Oversees and delivers comprehensive spine, heart, and cancer services in Ethiopia and beyond.

Ortho, Rehab, Surg

⊕ https://vfmat.ch/d85e

Jhpiego

Creates and delivers transformative healthcare solutions that save lives, in partnership with national governments, health experts, and local communities.

General, Infect Dis, OB-GYN, Surg

⊕ https://vfmat.ch/45b8

John Snow, Inc. (JSI)
Aims to improve the health and well-being of underserved and vulnerable people and communities throughout the world.
General, Infect Dis, Logist-Op, MF Med, OB-GYN, Peds, Psych, Pub Health
⊕ https://vfmat.ch/ba78

Johns Hopkins Center for Communication Programs
Believes in the power of communication to save lives by empowering people to adopt healthy behaviors for themselves, their families, and their communities.
General, Infect Dis, Logist-Op, OB-GYN, Pub Health
⊕ https://vfmat.ch/1bf9

Johns Hopkins Center for Global Health
Facilitates and focuses the extensive expertise and resources of the Johns Hopkins institutions, together with global collaborators, to effectively address and ameliorate the world's most pressing health issues.
General, Genetics, Logist-Op, MF Med, Peds, Psych, Pub Health, Pulm-Critic
⊕ https://vfmat.ch/54ce

Joint United Nations Programme on HIV/AIDS (UNAIDS)
Aims to place people living with HIV and people affected by the virus at the decision-making table and at the center of designing, delivering, and monitoring the AIDS response.
Infect Dis
⊕ https://vfmat.ch/464a

Kids Care Everywhere
Seeks to empower physicians in under-resourced environments with multimedia, state-of-the-art medical software, and to inspire young professionals to become future global healthcare leaders.
Logist-Op, Ped Surg, Peds
⊕ https://vfmat.ch/bc23

Kind Cuts for Kids
Aims to improve medical services for children in developing countries through education, demonstration, and skills transfer to local healthcare professionals.
Anesth, Medicine, Ped Surg, Surg
⊕ https://vfmat.ch/e3d7

Kletjian Foundation
Works toward a world in which all people have access to safe, sustainable, and high-quality medical care, building collaborative networks and supporting entrepreneurial leaders that promote global health equity.
CT Surg, ENT, General, Ortho, Surg
⊕ https://vfmat.ch/12c2

KNCV Tuberculosis Foundation
Aims to end human suffering through the global elimination of tuberculosis.
Pulm-Critic
⊕ https://vfmat.ch/98bf

La Salle International Foundation
Provides support for educational, health, and human services, along with humanitarian relief to people in developed and underdeveloped areas.
General
⊕ https://vfmat.ch/5891

Last Mile Health
Links community health workers with frontline health workers—nurses, doctors, and midwives at community clinics—and supports them to bring lifesaving services to the doorsteps of people living far from care.
General, Logist-Op, OB-GYN, Pub Health
⊕ https://vfmat.ch/37da

Lay Volunteers International Association (LVIA)
Fosters local and global change to help overcome extreme poverty, reinforce equitable and sustainable development, and enhance dialogue between Italian and African communities.
ER Med, Logist-Op, MF Med, Neonat, Nutr, OB-GYN, Peds
⊕ https://vfmat.ch/ecd4

Leprosy Mission England and Wales, The
Leads the fight against leprosy by supporting people living with leprosy today and serving future generations by working to end transmission of the disease.
Infect Dis, Pub Health
⊕ https://vfmat.ch/4c67

Leprosy Mission International
Seeks to empower people with leprosy to attain healing, dignity, and life in all its fullness.
Infect Dis
⊕ https://vfmat.ch/95a9

Leprosy Mission: Northern Ireland, The
Leads the fight against leprosy by supporting people living with leprosy today and serving future generations by working to end the transmission of the disease.
General, Infect Dis
⊕ https://vfmat.ch/e265

Life for a Child
Supports the provision of the best possible healthcare, given local circumstances, to all children and youth with diabetes in less-resourced countries, through the strengthening of existing diabetes services.
Endo, Medicine, Peds
⊕ https://vfmat.ch/d712

Lifebox
Seeks to provide safer surgery and anesthesia in low-resource countries by investing in tools, training, and partnerships for safe surgery.
Anesth, Crit-Care, Surg
⊕ https://vfmat.ch/2d4d

Light for the World
Contributes to a world in which persons with disabilities fully exercise their rights, and assists persons with disabilities living in poverty.
Ophth-Opt, Rehab
⊕ https://vfmat.ch/3ff6

Limbs International
Engages communities and transforms lives through affordable, sustainable prosthetic solutions and rehabilitation services in developing countries.
Logist-Op, Ortho, Pod, Rehab
⊕ https://vfmat.ch/dc84

Lions Clubs International
Empowers volunteers to serve their communities, meet humanitarian needs, encourage peace, and promote international understanding through Lions Clubs.
Heme-Onc, Medicine, Nutr, Ophth-Opt
⊕ https://vfmat.ch/7b12

Loma Linda University Health
Faith-based organization that aims to provide a stimulating clinical and research environment for the delivery of healthcare and the education of physicians, nurses, and other health professionals.
All-Immu, Anesth, CT Surg, CV Med, Crit-Care, Dent-OMFS, Derm, ENT, ER Med, Endo, GI, General, Genetics, Geri, Heme-Onc, Infect Dis, Logist-Op, MF Med, Medicine, Neonat, Nephro, Neuro, Neurosurg, Nutr, OB-GYN, Ophth-Opt, Ortho, Palliative, Path, Ped Surg, Peds, Plast, Pod, Psych, Pub Health, Pulm-Critic, Rad-Onc, Radiol, Rehab, Rheum, Surg, Urol, Vasc Surg
⊕ https://vfmat.ch/f5cb

London School of Hygiene & Tropical Medicine: International Centre for Eye Health
Works to improve eye health and eliminate avoidable visual impairment and blindness with a focus on low-income populations.
Logist-Op, Ophth-Opt, Pub Health
⊕ https://vfmat.ch/6f5f

Management Sciences for Health (MSH)
Works with countries and communities to save lives and improve the health of the world's poorest and most vulnerable people by building strong, resilient, sustainable health systems.
Infect Dis, Logist-Op, Pub Health
⊕ https://vfmat.ch/6aa2

MAP International
Provides medicines and health supplies to those in need around the world so they might experience life to the fullest.
Logist-Op
🌐 https://vfmat.ch/deed

Marie Stopes International
Provides the contraception and safe abortion services that enable women all over the world to choose their own futures.
Infect Dis, MF Med, Neonat, OB-GYN, Pub Health
🌐 https://vfmat.ch/9525

Massachusetts General Hospital Global Surgery Initiative
Aims to improve surgical education and access to advanced surgical care in resource-limited settings around the world by performing surgical operations as visitors, training local surgeons, and sharing medical technology through international partnerships across disciplines.
Anesth, Crit-Care, ER Med, Heme-Onc, Peds, Surg
🌐 https://vfmat.ch/31b1

Maternity Foundation
Works to ensure safer childbirth for women and newborns everywhere through innovative mobile health solutions such as the Safe Delivery App, a mobile training tool for skilled birth attendants.
MF Med, OB-GYN, Pub Health
🌐 https://vfmat.ch/ff4f

Maternity Worldwide
Works with communities and partners to identify and develop appropriate and effective ways to reduce maternal and newborn mortality and morbidity, facilitate communities to access quality skilled maternity care, and support the provision of quality skilled care.
MF Med, OB-GYN
🌐 https://vfmat.ch/822b

Maverick Collective
Aims to build a global community of strategic philanthropists and informed advocates who use their intellectual and financial resources to create change.
Infect Dis, MF Med, OB-GYN
🌐 https://vfmat.ch/ea49

Max Foundation, The
Seeks to increase global access to treatment, care, and support for people living with cancer.
General, Heme-Onc, Pub Health
🌐 https://vfmat.ch/8c7d

McGill University Health Centre: Centre for Global Surgery
Works to reduce the impact of injury by advancing surgical care through research and education in resource-limited settings.
ER Med, Logist-Op, Ped Surg, Surg
🌐 https://vfmat.ch/7246

MCM General Hospital
Provides advanced medical services to Ethiopians unable to get proper medical care, inspired by the Christian faith.
Anesth, Dent-OMFS, Medicine, Neurosurg, Nutr, OB-GYN, Ophth-Opt, Ortho, Peds, Radiol, Surg
🌐 https://vfmat.ch/6283

Medical Care Development International
Works to improve the health of vulnerable populations through integrated, sustainable, and locally driven interventions.
Infect Dis, OB-GYN, Peds, Pub Health
🌐 https://vfmat.ch/da87

Medical Ministry International
Provides compassionate healthcare in areas of need, inspired by the Christian faith.
CT Surg, Dent-OMFS, ENT, General, OB-GYN, Ophth-Opt, Ortho, Plast, Rehab, Surg, Urol, Vasc Surg
🌐 https://vfmat.ch/5da6

Medical Mission Trips
Provides medical aid, welfare assistance, and educational opportunities in Brazil, Honduras, Guatemala, Kenya, Burundi, and Ethiopia.
General
🌐 https://vfmat.ch/9117

Medical Missions Outreach
Visits developing countries to provide quality, ethical healthcare and outreach to those in need, based in Christian ministry.
Dent-OMFS, Ophth-Opt, Ortho, Surg
🌐 https://vfmat.ch/1197

Medical Relief Foundation
Provides quality education and comprehensive healthcare partnerships that are responsive to the needs of the patients, the host country, and the community.
CT Surg, ER Med, General, Infect Dis, Vasc Surg
🌐 https://vfmat.ch/9add

Medical Teams International
Seeks to restore health as the first step to restoring hope, working to bring basic but lifesaving medical care to those in need.
Dent-OMFS, ER Med, General, MF Med, Pub Health
🌐 https://vfmat.ch/8d1c

MedShare
Aims to improve the quality of life of people, communities, and the planet by sourcing and directly delivering surplus medical supplies and equipment to communities in need around the world.
Logist-Op
🌐 https://vfmat.ch/c8bc

Mercy and Love Foundation
Aims to provide orphaned and vulnerable children with basic human needs such as food, clothing, and shelter, enabling them to thrive.
General, Peds
🌐 https://vfmat.ch/649a

MicroResearch: Africa/Asia
Seeks to improve health outcomes in Africa by training, mentoring, and supporting local multidisciplinary health professional researchers.
Infect Dis, Nutr, OB-GYN, Psych
🌐 https://vfmat.ch/13e7

Mission Bambini
Helps to support children living in poverty and sickness, and lacking education, giving them the opportunity for and hope of a better life.
CT Surg, CV Med, Crit-Care, ER Med, Ped Surg, Peds
🌐 https://vfmat.ch/dc1a

Mission Regan
Collects supplies, medication, and medical equipment and provides them to those who are in desperate need, both locally and globally.
Logist-Op
🌐 https://vfmat.ch/2bc1

Mission Vision
Seeks to decrease blindness and other eye-related disabilities, and to increase academic performance and general quality of life.
Ophth-Opt
🌐 https://vfmat.ch/83d8

Morbidity Management and Disability Prevention Project (MMPD)
Helps countries provide high-quality treatment and care for people suffering from the debilitating effects of trachoma and lymphatic filariasis, complementing other major initiatives supporting disease elimination through mass drug administration.
Heme-Onc, Infect Dis, Ophth-Opt
🌐 https://vfmat.ch/387e

Mossy Foot Project, The
Works to provide mossy foot patients in Ethiopia with life-changing support through education, prevention, medical treatment, vocational training, and a message of hope.

Heme-Onc, Infect Dis, Ortho, Rehab
⊕ https://vfmat.ch/2f5c

MSD for Mothers
Designs scalable solutions that help end preventable maternal deaths.
MF Med, OB-GYN, Pub Health
⊕ https://vfmat.ch/9f99

MSI Reproductive Choices (Marie Stopes International)
Seeks to deliver quality family planning and reproductive healthcare to women around the world.
MF Med
⊕ https://vfmat.ch/5c82

Multi-Agency International Training and Support (MAITS)
Improves the lives of some of the world's poorest people living with disabilities through better access to quality health and education services and support.
Neuro, Psych, Rehab
⊕ https://vfmat.ch/9dcd

Médecins du Monde/Doctors of the World
Provides care, bears witness, and supports social change worldwide with innovative medical programs and evidence-based advocacy initiatives.
ER Med, General, Infect Dis, MF Med, Neonat, OB-GYN, Peds, Pub Health
⊕ https://vfmat.ch/a43d

NCD Alliance
Unites and strengthens civil society to stimulate collaborative advocacy, action, and accountability for NCD (noncommunicable disease) prevention and control.
All-Immu, CV Med, General, Heme-Onc, Medicine, Peds, Psych
⊕ https://vfmat.ch/abdd

New Horizons Collaborative
Advances a holistic, integrated approach to high-quality pediatric HIV care and treatment with a specific focus on those in need of advanced treatment.
Infect Dis, Peds, Pub Health
⊕ https://vfmat.ch/a76a

Nordic Medical Centre (NMC)
Contributes to health and well-being by providing high-level care to all patients through integrated clinical practice and health education.
ER Med, General, Medicine, Surg
⊕ https://vfmat.ch/7919

NTD Advocacy Learning Action (NALA)
Breaks the poverty cycle by eradicating neglected tropical diseases (NTDs) and other diseases of poverty.
Infect Dis, Pub Health
⊕ https://vfmat.ch/be81

NuVasive Spine Foundation (NSF)
Partners with leading spine surgeons, nonprofits, and in-country medical professionals/facilities to bring life-changing spine surgery to under-resourced communities around the world.
Logist-Op, Ortho, Ped Surg, Rehab, Surg
⊕ https://vfmat.ch/6ccc

Operation Eyesight Universal
Aims to prevent blindness, restore sight, and eliminate avoidable blindness.
Ophth-Opt
⊕ https://vfmat.ch/f629

Operation Fistula
Exists to end obstetric fistula by building models of care that serve every woman, everywhere.
MF Med, OB-GYN, Surg
⊕ https://vfmat.ch/ce8e

Operation Smile
Treats patients with cleft lip and cleft palate, and creates solutions that deliver safe surgery to people where it's needed most.
Anesth, Dent-OMFS, ENT, Ped Surg, Plast
⊕ https://vfmat.ch/5c29

Options
Believes in a world in which women and children can access the high-quality health services they need, without financial burden.
Logist-Op, MF Med, Neonat, OB-GYN
⊕ https://vfmat.ch/3a48

Optometry Giving Sight
Delivers eye exams and low or no-cost glasses, provides training for local eye care professionals, and establishes optometry schools, vision centers and optical labs.
Ophth-Opt
⊕ https://vfmat.ch/33ea

Orbis International
Works to prevent and treat blindness through hands-on training and improved access to quality eye care.
Anesth, Ophth-Opt, Surg
⊕ https://vfmat.ch/f2b2

Order of Malta
Supports forgotten or excluded people, especially those living in conflict zones or amid natural disasters, by providing medical assistance, caring for refugees, and distributing medicines and necessities.
ER Med, General, Infect Dis, MF Med, Nephro, OB-GYN, Ortho, Psych
⊕ https://vfmat.ch/1fab

Oromo Relief Association (ORA)
Works for all human beings affected by famine, armed conflicts, and other disasters, man-made or otherwise, without prejudice.
General, Geri
⊕ https://vfmat.ch/bff1

Oxford University Global Surgery Group (OUGSG)
Aims to contribute to the provision of high-quality surgical care globally, particularly in low- and middle-income countries (LMICs), while bringing together students, researchers, and clinicians with an interest in global surgery, anesthesia, and obstetrics and gynecology.
Anesth, MF Med, OB-GYN, Ortho, Surg
⊕ https://vfmat.ch/c624

Pact
Works on the ground to improve the lives of those who are challenged by poverty and marginalization, striving for a world in which all people are heard, capable, and vibrant.
Infect Dis, Logist-Op, MF Med, Pub Health
⊕ https://vfmat.ch/9a6c

Pan-African Academy of Christian Surgeons (PAACS)
Aims to train and disciple African surgeons and related specialists to become leaders and servants, providing excellent and compassionate care to those most in need, based in Christian ministry.
Anesth, CT Surg, OB-GYN, Ortho, Ped Surg, Plast, Surg
⊕ https://vfmat.ch/b444

Pan-African Academy of Christian Surgeons (PAACS)
Exists to train and support African surgeons to provide excellent, compassionate care to those most in need, inspired by the Christian faith.
Anesth, CT Surg, Neurosurg, OB-GYN, Ortho, Ped Surg, Plast, Surg
⊕ https://vfmat.ch/85ba

PATH
Advances health equity through innovation and partnerships so people, communities, and economies can thrive.
All-Immu, CV Med, Endo, Heme-Onc, Infect Dis, MF Med, Neonat, Nutr, OB-GYN, Path, Peds, Pulm-Critic
⊕ https://vfmat.ch/b4db

Pathfinder International
Champions sexual and reproductive health and rights worldwide, mobilizing communities most in need to break through barriers and forge paths to a healthier future.
OB-GYN
⊕ https://vfmat.ch/a7b3

People to People

Aims to build a bridge linking the diaspora with Ethiopian institutions for effective human resource development, healthcare, and education.
Crit-Care, ENT, ER Med, Infect Dis, Logist-Op, MF Med, Medicine, Neonat, Neuro, OB-GYN, Ophth-Opt, Peds, Pub Health, Urol
⊕ https://vfmat.ch/2431

People to People Canada (P2P)

Contributes to the fight against preventable diseases and addresses the full range of determinants of health (physical, social, economic, and cultural) affecting vulnerable communities.
Infect Dis, Psych, Pub Health
⊕ https://vfmat.ch/67d8

Population Council

Conducts research to address critical health and development issues, helping deliver solutions to improve lives around the world.
Logist-Op, Pub Health
⊕ https://vfmat.ch/1777

Project Concern International (PCI)

Drives innovation from the ground up to enhance health, end hunger, overcome hardship, and advance women and girls—resulting in meaningful and measurable change in people's lives.
Infect Dis, MF Med, Nutr, OB-GYN, Peds
⊕ https://vfmat.ch/5ed7

Project HOPE

Works on the front lines of the world's health challenges, partnering hand-in-hand with communities, healthcare workers, and public health systems to ensure sustainable change.
CV Med, ER Med, Endo, General, Infect Dis, MF Med, Peds
⊕ https://vfmat.ch/2bd7

Project Mercy

Provides community development and famine relief in Ethiopia.
MF Med, Medicine, OB-GYN, Peds, Surg
⊕ https://vfmat.ch/23ea

Project Pacer International

Provides modern cardiac therapy to indigent patients in the developing world.
CT Surg, CV Med
⊕ https://vfmat.ch/f812

Project SOAR

Conducts HIV operations research around the world to identify practical solutions to improve HIV prevention, care, and treatment services.
ER Med, General, MF Med, OB-GYN, Psych
⊕ https://vfmat.ch/1a77

PSI – Population Services International

Aims to improve the health of people in the developing world by focusing on challenges such as a lack of family planning, HIV/AIDS, barriers to maternal health, and the greatest threats to children under the age of 5, including malaria, diarrhea, pneumonia, and malnutrition.
Infect Dis, MF Med, OB-GYN, Peds
⊕ https://vfmat.ch/ffe3

RAD-AID International

Improves and optimizes access to medical imaging and radiology in low-resource regions of the world.
Rad-Onc, Radiol
⊕ https://vfmat.ch/537f

Rainbow Humanitarian Caretaker Foundation

Provides support for the urban poor and homeless women and children in Addis Ababa and for the rural community of Debre Musa, Ethiopia.
General, Peds
⊕ https://vfmat.ch/155f

Resolute Health Outreach

Builds the capacity of Ethiopian healthcare workers through training, equipment, and outcomes research.

Anesth, ENT, Endo, Logist-Op, Neuro, Ortho, Path, Plast, Surg, Vasc Surg
⊕ https://vfmat.ch/a811

RestoringVision

Empowers lives by restoring vision for millions of people in need.
Ophth-Opt
⊕ https://vfmat.ch/e121

Rheumatology for All

Increases access to rheumatology care in under-resourced regions through the creation of self-sustaining rheumatology training programs, by funding the education of local physicians to become rheumatologists and providing educational programs for local physicians.
Rheum
⊕ https://vfmat.ch/71ff

Rockefeller Foundation, The

Works to promote the well-being of humanity.
Logist-Op, Nutr, Pub Health
⊕ https://vfmat.ch/5424

Rose Charities International

Aims to support communities to improve quality of life and reduce the effects of poverty through innovative, self-sustaining projects, and partnerships.
ENT, ER Med, General, Infect Dis, Neonat, OB-GYN, Ophth-Opt, Ped Surg, Peds, Rehab, Urol
⊕ https://vfmat.ch/53df

Rotaplast International

Helps children and families worldwide by eliminating the burden of cleft lip and/or palate, burn scarring, and other deformities by sending medical teams to provide free reconstructive surgery, ancillary treatment, and training.
Anesth, Dent-OMFS, ENT, Ped Surg, Plast, Surg
⊕ https://vfmat.ch/78b3

Rotary International

Provides service to others, improves lives, and advances world understanding, goodwill, and peace through its fellowship of business, professional, and community leaders.
ER Med, General, Infect Dis, MF Med, OB-GYN
⊕ https://vfmat.ch/8fb5

ROW Foundation

Works to improve the quality of training for healthcare providers, and the diagnosis and treatment available to people with epilepsy and associated psychiatric disorders in under-resourced areas of the world.
Neuro, Psych
⊕ https://vfmat.ch/25eb

Rutgers New Jersey Medical School

Seeks to support and promote the global health efforts of the faculty, staff, and students in the areas of education, research, and service through the Rutgers New Jersey Medical School's Office of Global Health.
Anesth, CV Med, Crit-Care, Neurosurg, OB-GYN, Psych
⊕ https://vfmat.ch/8e67

Samaritan's Purse International Disaster Relief

Provides spiritual and physical aid to hurting people around the world, such as victims of war, poverty, natural disasters, disease, and famine, based in Christian ministry.
Anesth, CT Surg, Crit-Care, Dent-OMFS, Derm, ENT, ER Med, Endo, GI, General, Heme-Onc, Infect Dis, MF Med, Neonat, Nephro, Neuro, Neurosurg, Nutr, OB-GYN, Ophth-Opt, Ortho, Path, Ped Surg, Peds, Plast, Psych, Pulm-Critic, Radiol, Rehab, Rheum, Surg, Urol, Vasc Surg
⊕ https://vfmat.ch/87e3

Save A Child's Heart

Provides lifesaving cardiac treatment to children in developing countries, and trains healthcare professionals from these countries to deliver quality care in their communities.
CT Surg, CV Med, Crit-Care, Ped Surg, Peds
⊕ https://vfmat.ch/1bef

Save the Children
Gives children around the world a healthy start in life, the opportunity to learn, and protection from harm.
All-Immu, Crit-Care, ER Med, General, Infect Dis, MF Med, Medicine, Neonat, OB-GYN, Peds, Psych, Pub Health
⊕ https://vfmat.ch/2e73

SCI Foundation
Seeks to prevent and treat neglected infectious diseases, with a focus on eliminating parasitic worm infections through strengthening impactful and comprehensive health programs across Sub-Saharan Africa.
Infect Dis, Pub Health
⊕ https://vfmat.ch/5444

Serving Others Worldwide
Aims to provide aid to the poor, distressed, and underprivileged by providing healthcare and dental services, and by building schools, orphanages, libraries, and medical clinics in undeveloped countries.
Dent-OMFS, General
⊕ https://vfmat.ch/69cb

SEVA
Delivers vital eye care services to the world's most vulnerable, including women, children, and Indigenous peoples.
Ophth-Opt, Surg
⊕ https://vfmat.ch/1e87

Sightsavers
Works with partners in developing countries to help eliminate avoidable blindness and advocates for equal opportunity for the disabled.
Infect Dis, Ophth-Opt, Surg
⊕ https://vfmat.ch/aa52

SIGN Fracture Care International
Builds orthopedic capacity around the world and provides the injured poor access to fracture surgery by donating orthopedic education and implant systems to surgeons in developing countries.
Ortho, Rehab, Surg
⊕ https://vfmat.ch/123d

Simavi
Strives for a world in which all women and girls are socially and economically empowered and pursue their rights to live a healthy life, free from discrimination, coercion, and violence.
MF Med, OB-GYN
⊕ https://vfmat.ch/b57b

Simien Mountains Mobile Medical Service
Aims to deliver free, essential medical care to remote villages in Ethiopia's Simien Mountains.
General, Infect Dis, OB-GYN, Peds
⊕ https://vfmat.ch/3d48

SINA Health
Aims to improve the health and educational status of the population in low- and middle-income countries.
General, Logist-Op
⊕ https://vfmat.ch/9ad3

Smile Train, Inc.
Treats children with cleft lip through a sustainable and local model that supports surgery and other forms of essential care.
Logist-Op, Pub Health
⊕ https://vfmat.ch/822c

Soddo Christian Hospital
Mobilizes volunteers to help transform communities through healthcare and education, based in Christian ministry.
ER Med, General
⊕ https://vfmat.ch/efa4

SOS Children's Villages International
Supports children through alternative care and family strengthening.

ER Med, Peds
⊕ https://vfmat.ch/aca1

Stand By Me
Helps children facing terrible circumstances and provides the care, love, and attention they need to thrive through children's homes and schools.
Peds
⊕ https://vfmat.ch/a224

Stanford University School of Medicine: Weiser Lab Global Surgery
Integrates research, education, patient care, and community service.
Logist-Op, Pub Health, Surg
⊕ https://vfmat.ch/9153

Sustainable Cardiovascular Health Equity Development Alliance
Fights cardiovascular disease in underserved populations globally via education, training, and increasing interventional capacity.
CV Med, Pub Health, Radiol
⊕ https://vfmat.ch/799c

Sustainable Kidney Care Foundation (SKCF)
Works to provide treatment for kidney injury where none exists, and aims to reduce mortality from treatable acute kidney injury (AKI).
Infect Dis, Medicine, Nephro
⊕ https://vfmat.ch/1926

Swasti
Aims to transform the lives of marginalized communities by ensuring their access to quality healthcare and thereby contributing to poverty alleviation.
Pub Health
⊕ https://vfmat.ch/be8b

Swiss Tropical and Public Health Institute
Contributes to the improvement of the health of populations internationally, nationally, and locally through excellence in research, education, and services.
Infect Dis, Pub Health
⊕ https://vfmat.ch/2ee4

Task Force for Global Health, The
Consists of programs and focus areas that cover a range of global health issues including neglected tropical diseases, infectious diseases, vaccines, field epidemiology, public health informatics, health workforce development, and global health ethics.
Infect Dis, Logist-Op, Medicine, Ophth-Opt, Peds
⊕ https://vfmat.ch/714c

Tearfund
Responds to crisis and partners with local churches to bring restoration to those living in poverty, inspired by the Christian faith.
ER Med, Logist-Op
⊕ https://vfmat.ch/f6cf

THET Partnerships for Global Health
Trains and educates health workers in Africa and Asia, working in partnership with organizations and volunteers from across the UK.
General
⊕ https://vfmat.ch/f937

Third World Eye Care Society (TWECS)
Collects old, unused eyeglasses and distributes them in conjunction with eye exams given by properly trained individuals.
Logist-Op, Ophth-Opt
⊕ https://vfmat.ch/8618

Three Roots International
Cultivates community development and economic capacity by empowering families through education, health, and income-generating activities.
General, Infect Dis, Peds
⊕ https://vfmat.ch/bb33

Tilganga Institute of Ophthalmology (TIO)
Supports the prevention and control of blindness in Nepal and the region.
Ophth-Opt
⊕ https://vfmat.ch/ff5d

Tomorrow Come Foundation
Helps provide a safe home, support a healthy life, and foster growth through education for children in and around the New Hope Center for Children and Handicapped.
General, Rehab, Surg
⊕ https://vfmat.ch/1123

U.S. President's Malaria Initiative (PMI)
Supports low-income countries to help control and eliminate malaria through cost-effective, lifesaving malaria interventions.
Infect Dis, MF Med, OB-GYN
⊕ https://vfmat.ch/dc8b

Union for International Cancer Control (UICC)
Unites and supports the cancer community to reduce the global cancer burden, promote greater equity, and ensure that cancer control continues to be a priority in the world health and development agenda.
Heme-Onc, Pub Health
⊕ https://vfmat.ch/88b1

United Nations Children's Fund (UNICEF)
Works in over 190 countries and territories to save children's lives, defend their rights, and help them fulfill their potential, from early childhood through adolescence.
All-Immu, Infect Dis, MF Med, Neonat, Nutr, OB-GYN, Ped Surg, Peds, Pub Health
⊕ https://vfmat.ch/42d7

United Nations Development Programme (UNDP)
Helps countries achieve the simultaneous eradication of extreme poverty and significant reduction of inequalities and exclusion using a sustainable human development approach.
Infect Dis, Logist-Op, Pub Health
⊕ https://vfmat.ch/935c

United Nations High Commissioner for Refugees (UNHCR)
Safeguards the rights and well-being of people who have been forced to flee, ensuring that everybody has the right to seek asylum and find safe refuge in another country, with the goal of seeking lasting solutions.
General, MF Med, Medicine, OB-GYN, Peds, Psych, Pub Health
⊕ https://vfmat.ch/6636

United Nations Office for the Coordination of Humanitarian Affairs (OCHA)
Contributes to principled and effective humanitarian response through coordination, advocacy, policy, information management, and humanitarian financing tools and services, by leveraging functional expertise throughout the organization.
Logist-Op
⊕ https://vfmat.ch/22b8

United Nations Population Fund (UNFPA)
Supports reproductive healthcare for women and youth in more than 150 countries, focusing on delivering a world in which every pregnancy is wanted, every childbirth is safe, and every young person's potential is fulfilled.
Infect Dis, MF Med, Neonat, OB-GYN, Peds, Pub Health
⊕ https://vfmat.ch/c969

United States Agency for International Development (USAID)
Promotes and demonstrates democratic values abroad and advances a free, peaceful, and prosperous world. Leads the U.S. government's international development and disaster assistance through partnerships and investments that save lives.
ER Med, Infect Dis, MF Med, OB-GYN, Peds
⊕ https://vfmat.ch/9a99

United States President's Emergency Plan for AIDS Relief (PEPFAR)
The U.S. global HIV/AIDS response works to prevent new HIV infections and accelerate progress to control the global epidemic in more than 50 countries, by partnering with governments to support sustainable, integrated, and country-led responses to HIV/AIDS.
Infect Dis, Pub Health
⊕ https://vfmat.ch/a57c

University of British Columbia – Faculty of Medicine: Branch for International Surgical Care
Aims to advance sustainable improvements in the delivery of surgical care in the world's most underserved countries, by building capacity within the field of surgery through the provision of care in low-resource settings.
Anesth, ER Med, Neurosurg, Surg, Urol
⊕ https://vfmat.ch/4164

University of California Los Angeles: David Geffen School of Medicine Global Health Program
Catalyzes opportunities to improve health globally by engaging in multi-disciplinary and innovative education programs, research initiatives, and bilateral partnerships that provide opportunities for trainees, faculty, and staff to contribute to sustainable health initiatives and to address health inequities facing the world today.
All-Immu, Infect Dis, Logist-Op, MF Med, Medicine, Neonat, OB-GYN, Ortho, Ped Surg, Peds, Radiol
⊕ https://vfmat.ch/f1a4

University of California San Francisco: Francis I. Proctor Foundation for Ophthalmology
Aims to prevent blindness worldwide through research and teaching focused on infectious and inflammatory eye disease.
Ophth-Opt, Pub Health
⊕ https://vfmat.ch/cf47

University of California, Berkeley: Bixby Center for Population, Health & Sustainability
Aims to help manage population growth, improve maternal health, and address the unmet need for family planning within a human rights framework.
OB-GYN
⊕ https://vfmat.ch/ff2b

University of California: Global Health Institute
Mobilizes people and resources across the University of California to advance global health research, education, and collaboration.
General, OB-GYN, Pub Health
⊕ https://vfmat.ch/ee7f

University of Colorado: Global Emergency Care Initiative
Strives to sustainably improve emergency care outcomes in low- and middle-income communities worldwide by linking cutting-edge academics with excellent on-the-ground implementation.
ER Med
⊕ https://vfmat.ch/417a

University of Illinois at Chicago: Center for Global Health
Aims to improve the health of populations around the world and reduce health disparities by collaboratively conducting trans-disciplinary research, training the next generations of global health leaders, and building the capacities of global and local partners.
Pub Health
⊕ https://vfmat.ch/b749

University of Michigan Medical School Global REACH
Aims to facilitate health research, education, and collaboration among Michigan Medicine learners and faculty with our global partners to reduce health disparities for the benefit of communities worldwide.
ENT, General, Ophth-Opt, Peds, Psych, Pub Health, Urol
⊕ https://vfmat.ch/5f19

University of Michigan: Department of Surgery Global Health
Improves the health of patients, populations and communities through excellence in education, patient care, community service, research and technology development, and through leadership activities.

Anesth, Ortho, Surg
⊕ https://vfmat.ch/2fd8

University of New Mexico School of Medicine: Project Echo
Seeks to improve health outcomes worldwide through the use of a technology called telementoring, a guided-practice model in which the participating clinician retains responsibility for managing the patient.
General, Infect Dis, MF Med, OB-GYN, Path, Peds
⊕ https://vfmat.ch/6c9a

University of Pennsylvania Perelman School of Medicine Center for Global Health
Aims to improve health equity worldwide through enhanced public health awareness and access to care, discovery, and outcomes-based research, and comprehensive educational programs grounded in partnership.
Heme-Onc, Infect Dis, OB-GYN
⊕ https://vfmat.ch/cb57

University of Toledo: Global Health Program
Aims to be a transformative force in medical education, biomedical research, and healthcare delivery.
CV Med, CV Med, ER Med, Infect Dis, Medicine, Neuro, Neurosurg, OB-GYN, Ophth-Opt, Ortho, Peds, Plast, Psych, Surg
⊕ https://vfmat.ch/71f2

University of Toronto: Global Surgery
Focuses on excellent clinical care, outstanding research productivity, and the delivery of state-of-the-art educational programs.
Surg
⊕ https://vfmat.ch/1ad5

University of Virginia: Anesthesiology Department Global Health Initiatives
Educates and trains physicians to help people achieve healthy productive lives, and advances knowledge in the medical sciences.
Anesth, Pub Health
⊕ https://vfmat.ch/1b8b

University of Wisconsin-Madison: Department of Surgery
Provides comprehensive educational experiences, groundbreaking research, and superb patient care.
Anesth, ENT, ER Med, Endo, Peds, Plast, Pub Health, Surg
⊕ https://vfmat.ch/64c2

USA for United Nations High Commissioner for Refugees (UNHCR)
Serves and protects refugees and displaced people through emergency relief, cash assistance, education, resettlement, and the rebuilding of livelihoods.
ER Med, General, Logist-Op, Nutr, Pub Health
⊕ https://vfmat.ch/293c

USAID: Deliver Project
Builds a global supply chain to deliver lifesaving health products to people in order to enable countries to provide family planning, protect against malaria, and limit the spread of pandemic threats.
Infect Dis, Logist-Op, MF Med
⊕ https://vfmat.ch/374e

USAID: Health Finance and Governance Project
Uses research to implement strategies to help countries develop robust governance systems, increase their domestic resources for health, manage those resources more effectively, and make wise purchasing decisions.
Logist-Op
⊕ https://vfmat.ch/8652

USAID: Leadership, Management and Governance Project
Improves leadership, management, and governance practices to strengthen health systems and improve health for all, including vulnerable populations worldwide.
Logist-Op
⊕ https://vfmat.ch/d35e

USAID: Maternal and Child Health Integrated Program
Works to improve the health of women and their families, including programs for

maternal, newborn, and child health, immunization, family planning, nutrition, malaria, and HIV/AIDS.
All-Immu, General, Infect Dis, MF Med
⊕ https://vfmat.ch/4415

USAID: Maternal and Child Survival Program
Works to prevent child and maternal deaths.
Infect Dis, MF Med, Neonat, OB-GYN, Peds
⊕ https://vfmat.ch/6fcf

Vision Aid Overseas
Enables people living in poverty to access affordable glasses and eye care.
Ophth-Opt
⊕ https://vfmat.ch/c695

Vision Outreach International
Advocates for helping the blind in underserved regions of the world and empowers the poor through sight restoration.
Ophth-Opt
⊕ https://vfmat.ch/9721

Visionaries International
Works toward reducing the burden of corneal blindness in the developing world by assessing and addressing what limits corneal surgeons in each locale.
Anesth, Ophth-Opt, Pub Health, Surg
⊕ https://vfmat.ch/3d2e

Vital Strategies
Helps governments strengthen their public health systems to contend with the most important and difficult health challenges, while accelerating progress on the world's most pressing health problems.
CV Med, Infect Dis, Peds
⊕ https://vfmat.ch/fe25

Vitamin Angels
Helps at-risk populations in need—specifically pregnant women, new mothers, and children under age 5—to gain access to life-changing vitamins and minerals.
General, Nutr
⊕ https://vfmat.ch/7da1

Voluntary Service Overseas (VSO)
Works with health workers, communities, and governments to improve health services and rights for women, babies, youth, people with disabilities, and prisoners.
General, MF Med, OB-GYN
⊕ https://vfmat.ch/213d

Watsi
Uses technology to make healthcare a reality for those who might not otherwise be able to afford it.
Pub Health, Surg
⊕ https://vfmat.ch/41a3

Wax and Gold
Develops and implements scalable education programs capable of being duplicated in facilities nationwide.
MF Med, Neonat, Peds
⊕ https://vfmat.ch/dbd8

WEEMA International
Partners with rural communities in southwestern Ethiopia to provide safe water, lifesaving healthcare, quality education, and economic opportunities.
MF Med, Ophth-Opt, Peds, Pub Health
⊕ https://vfmat.ch/974c

Wings of Healing
Provides medical aid and education to African countries through medical mission programs and long-term educational partnerships.
Anesth, MF Med, Neonat, OB-GYN, Surg
⊕ https://vfmat.ch/f1e4

Women and Children First
Pioneers approaches that support communities to solve problems themselves.

MF Med, Neonat, OB-GYN, Peds
⊕ https://vfmat.ch/cdc9

Women's Refugee Commission
Seeks to improve lives by protecting the rights of women, children, and youth displaced by conflict and crisis through researching their needs, identifying solutions, and advocating for programs and policies to strengthen their resilience.
General, MF Med, Neonat, OB-GYN, Peds, Psych
⊕ https://vfmat.ch/3d8f

World Anaesthesia Society (WAS)
Aims to support anesthesiologists with an interest in working in low-income regions of the world.
Anesth
⊕ https://vfmat.ch/37fe

World Blind Union (WBU)
Represents those experiencing blindness, speaking to governments and international bodies on issues concerning visual impairments.
Ophth-Opt
⊕ https://vfmat.ch/2bd3

World Children's Fund
Commits to helping children worldwide who are suffering the effects of poverty, disease, natural disaster, famine, abuse, civil strife, and war.
General, Logist-Op, MF Med, Nutr, OB-GYN, Pub Health
⊕ https://vfmat.ch/9cd8

World Council of Optometry
Facilitates the development of optometry worldwide and promotes eye health and vision care through advocacy, education, policy development, and humanitarian outreach.
Ophth-Opt, Pub Health
⊕ https://vfmat.ch/c92e

World Federation of Hemophilia (WFH)
Aims to improve and sustain care for people with inherited bleeding disorders by pursuing long-term relationships with individuals and organizations who share the values of WFH's development model.
Heme-Onc
⊕ https://vfmat.ch/5121

World Health Organization, The (WHO)
The United Nations' agency for health provides leadership on global health matters, shapes the health research agenda, sets norms and standards, articulates evidence-based policy options, provides technical support and monitoring to countries, and assesses health trends.
ER Med, General, Infect Dis, Logist-Op, MF Med, OB-GYN, Peds, Psych, Pub Health
⊕ https://vfmat.ch/c476

World Medical Relief
Facilitates the distribution of surplus medical resources where they are needed.
Logist-Op
⊕ https://vfmat.ch/72dc

World Missions Possible
Provides EMS capacity-building, along with medical and vision care, to under-developed and rural areas.
ER Med, General, Heme-Onc, Neonat, Ophth-Opt, Surg
⊕ https://vfmat.ch/d6a5

World Parkinson's Program
Seeks to improve the quality of life of those affected by Parkinson's disease through education and advocacy, and provides free medication and support services.
Logist-Op, Neuro, Pub Health
⊕ https://vfmat.ch/c96d

World Surgical Foundation
Provides charitable surgical healthcare to the world's poor and underserved in developing nations.

Ped Surg, Surg
⊕ https://vfmat.ch/c162

World Telehealth Initiative
Provides medical expertise to the world's most vulnerable communities to build local capacity and deliver core health services through a network of volunteer healthcare professionals supported with state-of-the-art technology.
Derm, Infect Dis, MF Med, Medicine, Neuro, OB-GYN, Peds, Pulm-Critic
⊕ https://vfmat.ch/fa91

World Vision International
Works with vulnerable communities around the world to overcome poverty and injustice with child-focused programs in disaster management, health, nutrition, economic development, education, clean water, sanitation, and hygiene.
ER Med, General, Infect Dis, MF Med, Nutr, OB-GYN, Peds
⊕ https://vfmat.ch/2642

Worldwide Fistula Fund
Protects and restores the health and dignity of the world's most vulnerable women by preventing and treating devastating childbirth injuries.
OB-GYN
⊕ https://vfmat.ch/8813

WorldWide Orphans (WWO)
Seeks to transform the lives of vulnerable children, families, and communities through trauma-informed, evidence-based programming.
General, Peds, Pub Health
⊕ https://vfmat.ch/2538

Ethiopia

Healthcare Facilities

AaBET Hospital
1271 Dej. Zewdu Aba Koran Street, Addis Ababa, Ethiopia
⊕ https://vfmat.ch/d59c

Adama Referral Hospital
Adama, Ethiopia
⊕ https://vfmat.ch/1aa5

Addis Ababa Fistula Hospital
Addis Ababa, Ethiopia
⊕ https://vfmat.ch/7fa3

Addis Cardiac Hospital
Ring Road, Addis Ababa, Ethiopia
⊕ https://vfmat.ch/87b4

Addis Hiwot General Hospital
Addis Ababa, Ethiopia
⊕ https://vfmat.ch/a981

Adigrat Ras Sibhat Hospital
Adigrat, Ethiopia
⊕ https://vfmat.ch/fd4c

Aflagat General Hospital
Route 3, Bahir Dar, Ethiopia
⊕ https://vfmat.ch/ea43

Āksum K'idist Maryam Hospital
Bole Road, Axum, Tigray, Ethiopia
⊕ https://vfmat.ch/bdd3

Alert Hospital
Ring Road, Addis Ababa, Ethiopia
⊕ https://vfmat.ch/bb78

Amanuel Hospital
Congo Street, Addis Ababa, Ethiopia
⊕ https://vfmat.ch/8782

Amdework Hospital
Amdework, Ethiopia
⊕ https://vfmat.ch/8c8c

Amin General Hospital
Dejazmach Balcha Aba Nefso Street, Addis Ababa, Ethiopia
⊕ https://vfmat.ch/b8c7

Arba Minch Hospital
Arba Minch, Ethiopia
⊕ https://vfmat.ch/c762

Art Hospital
Dire Dawa, Ethiopia
⊕ https://vfmat.ch/f92e

Asaita Referral Hospital
Asaita, Afar, Ethiopia
⊕ https://vfmat.ch/461f

Asella Hospital
09, Assela, Ethiopia
⊕ https://vfmat.ch/659c

Assosa Hospital
Asosa – Kurmuk/Guba Road, Benishngul-Gumuz, Ethiopia
⊕ https://vfmat.ch/4bac

Atsbi Hospital
Tigray, Adigrat, Ethiopia
⊕ https://vfmat.ch/67cc

Attat Hospital
Welkite Gurage, Emdibir, Southern Nations Nationalities Peoples, Ethiopia
⊕ https://vfmat.ch/2e88

Ayder Referral Hospital
Mek'ele-Weldiya Road, Adi Gura, Tigray, Ethiopia
⊕ https://vfmat.ch/1c2b

B.G.M. Hospital
Addis Ababa, Ethiopia
⊕ https://vfmat.ch/6f27

Balcha Hospital
Liberia Street, Addis Ababa, Ethiopia
⊕ https://vfmat.ch/ef86

Bekoji Hospital
Bekoji, Ethiopia
⊕ https://vfmat.ch/731f

Bethel 2 Hospital
Addis Ababa, Ethiopia
⊕ https://vfmat.ch/3cc4

Bethel Teaching General Hospital
Addis Ababa, Ethiopia
⊕ https://vfmat.ch/535f

Bethezata Hospital
Ras Mekonnen Avenue, Addis Ababa, Addis Ababa, Ethiopia
⊕ https://vfmat.ch/4d33

Betsegah Obstetrics and Gynecology Special Hospital
Ghana Street, Addis Ababa, Ethiopia
⊕ https://vfmat.ch/6877

Bilal Hospital
Dire Dawa, Ethiopia
⊕ https://vfmat.ch/fdd4

Bishoftu
Bishoftu, Oromia, Ethiopia
⊕ https://vfmat.ch/ea6b

Black Lion Hospital Cancer Center
Burundi Street, Addis Ababa, Ethiopia
⊕ https://vfmat.ch/4e89

Bona General Hospital
Bona Qabelanka, Ethiopia
⊕ https://vfmat.ch/3183

Brass MCH Hospital
Ring Road, Addis Ababa, Ethiopia
⊕ https://vfmat.ch/27a1

Brooke Hospital
South Africa Street, Addis Ababa, Addis Ababa, Ethiopia
⊕ https://vfmat.ch/19a8

Butajira General Hospital
Butajira, Ethiopia
⊕ https://vfmat.ch/faa8

Chencha Hospital
Chencha, Ethiopia
⊕ https://vfmat.ch/7772

CURE Ethiopia Children's Hospital
Hamle 19 Public Park, Addis Ababa, Ethiopia
⊕ https://vfmat.ch/5b13

Debre Berhan Referral Hospital
ደብረ ብርሃን / Debre Birhan, Ethiopia
⊕ https://vfmat.ch/1ebb

Debre Birhan Referral Hospital
Debre Birhan, Ethiopia
⊕ https://vfmat.ch/6f3e

Debre Markos Referral Hospital
Debre Markos, Ethiopia
⊕ https://vfmat.ch/9f27

Dembecha Hospital
Dembecha, Ethiopia
⊕ https://vfmat.ch/c1d1

Dessie Hospital
ደሴ / Dessie, Ethiopia
⊕ https://vfmat.ch/63e1

Dilla Referral Hospital
Addis Ababa to Nairobi Road, ዲላ / Dilla, ኦሮሚያ ክልል / Oromia, Ethiopia
⊕ https://vfmat.ch/a646

Effesson Regional Hospital
Ataye, Ethiopia
⊕ https://vfmat.ch/135f

Eka Kotebe General Hospital
Fikre Mariam Aba Techan Street, Addis Ababa, Ethiopia
⊕ https://vfmat.ch/b49c

Ethio Wise Hospital
Fitawrari Habte Giorgis Street, Addis Ababa, Ethiopia
⊕ https://vfmat.ch/63bf

Ethio-Tebebe MCH Hospital
Sefere Selam, Addis Ababa, Ethiopia
⊕ https://vfmat.ch/c59a

Ethiopian Federal Police Commission Referral Hospital
Chad Street, Addis Ababa, Ethiopia
⊕ https://vfmat.ch/aac4

Fatsi Hospital
Fatsi/Tigray, Ethiopia
⊕ https://vfmat.ch/1a84

Felege Hiwot Referral Hospital
Bahir Dar Zuria, Ethiopia
⊕ https://vfmat.ch/d678

Gambella Hospital
Gambela – Gore, ጋምቤላ / Gambela, ጋምቤላ ሕዝቦች ክልል / Gambela, Ethiopia
⊕ https://vfmat.ch/931a

Gambi General Hospital
Haile Silase Road, Grass Village, Ethiopia
⊕ https://vfmat.ch/fc68

Harar General Hospital
Harar, Ethiopia
⊕ https://vfmat.ch/3335

Genet General Hospital
Genet General Hospital PLC, Addis Ababa, Ethiopia
⊕ https://vfmat.ch/9a9a

Gesund
Addis Ababa, Ethiopia
⊕ https://vfmat.ch/89c1

Ghandi Hospital
Ras Desta Damtew Street, Addis Ababa, Ethiopia
⊕ https://vfmat.ch/13c6

Gindeberet Hospital
Kachise, Oromia, Ethiopia
⊕ https://vfmat.ch/9155

Girawa
Girawa, Ethiopia
⊕ https://vfmat.ch/c9f4

Girum General Hospital
Addis Ketema Sub City, Addis Ababa, Ethiopia
⊕ https://vfmat.ch/37f2

Goba Hospital
Goba, Ethiopia
⊕ https://vfmat.ch/be1b

Gode Hospital
Gode – Walakhere Highway, ጎዴ / Gode, ሶማሌ ክልል / Somali, Ethiopia
⊕ https://vfmat.ch/13a9

Gonder University Hospital
Bahir Dar – Gonder Road, ጎንደር / Gonder, Ethiopia
⊕ https://vfmat.ch/b136

Haleluya General Hospital
Debre Zeit Road, Addis Ababa, Ethiopia
⊕ https://vfmat.ch/377c

Hamlin Fistula Hospital
Ring Road, Addis Ababa, Ethiopia
⊕ https://vfmat.ch/b548

Hiwot Fana Referral Hospital
Harar, Ethiopia
⊕ https://vfmat.ch/f68d

Haro Miriam Hospital
Cheliya, Ethiopia
⊕ https://vfmat.ch/6cb9

Hawaria H.C.
Ezhana Welene, Ethiopia
⊕ https://vfmat.ch/d197

Hawassa University Referral Hospital
Addis Ababa to Nairobi Road, Afarara, ኦሮሚያ ክልል / Oromia, Ethiopia
⊕ https://vfmat.ch/e931

Hayat Hospital
Addis Ababa, Ethiopia
⊕ https://vfmat.ch/cadd

Hoospitaala Rifti Vaalii
Oromia Street, ኣዳማ / Nazret, ኦሮሚያ ክልል / Oromia, Ethiopia
⊕ https://vfmat.ch/deb1

Hospital at Bahir Dar
Bezavit Road, Bete Mengistu Road ባሕር-ዳር / Bahir Dar, Ethiopia
⊕ https://vfmat.ch/ce3b

Hospital at Denan
Denan, ሶማሌ ክልል / Somali, Ethiopia
⊕ https://vfmat.ch/59a7

Hospital at Edaga Hamus Town
Saesi Tsaedaemba, Ethiopia
⊕ https://vfmat.ch/6bfc

Hospital at Hawassa
Addis Ababa to Nairobi Road, Afarara, ኦሮሚያ ክልል / Oromia, Ethiopia
⊕ https://vfmat.ch/1d56

Hospital at Jinka
Jinka, Gazer, Ethiopia
⊕ https://vfmat.ch/27a3

Hospital at Kembolcha
Kombosha, Oromia, Ethiopia
⊕ https://vfmat.ch/7dc7

Hospital at Kemse
Kemse, Ethiopia
⊕ https://vfmat.ch/1e67

Hospital at Mekele
Mekele, Ethiopia
⊕ https://vfmat.ch/5cba

Hospital at Metu
Metu, Ethiopia
⊕ https://vfmat.ch/e828

Hospital at Nazret
College Road, ኣዳማ /Nazret, ኦሮሚያ ክልል /
Oromia, Ethiopia
⊕ https://vfmat.ch/e832

Hospital at Sanja
Sanja, Ethiopia
⊕ https://vfmat.ch/67a1

Hospital at Shashamene
Shashemene, Ethiopia
⊕ https://vfmat.ch/f639

Hospital at Shoa Robit
Shoa Robit, Ethiopia
⊕ https://vfmat.ch/8b99

Hospital at Tigray
Godena Eyassu Street, Mek'elē, Tigray, Ethiopia
⊕ https://vfmat.ch/bc42

Hospital at Weldiya
Weldiya, Ethiopia
⊕ https://vfmat.ch/a4be

Hospital at Wukro Maray
3, ኣክሱም / Axum, Tigray, Ethiopia
⊕ https://vfmat.ch/582b

Hospital Emmanuel Cathedrale of Robe
8, Robe, Oromia, Ethiopia
⊕ https://vfmat.ch/a1ee

Hospital Sheik Hussein
Sheikh Hussein, Gololcha, Ethiopia
⊕ https://vfmat.ch/7775

Hospital Wacha
Tepi – Shishinda, Tepi, Southern Nations Nationalities
Peoples, Ethiopia
⊕ https://vfmat.ch/f47c

Hulsehet Referral Hospital
Churchill Avenue, Addis Ababa, Ethiopia
⊕ https://vfmat.ch/cd87

Ibex Hospital
Yohannis Church, Gonder, Ethiopia
⊕ https://vfmat.ch/e899

ICMC Hospital
Addis Ababa, Ethiopia
⊕ https://vfmat.ch/644a

JJU Meles Zenawi Memorial Referral Hospital
Jijiga, Ethiopia
⊕ https://vfmat.ch/4625

Jugal Hospital
Amir Uga, ሐረር / Harar, ሀረሪ ሁነኒ / Harar,
Ethiopia
⊕ https://vfmat.ch/bab6

Kadisco General Hospital
Road to Gergi Giorgis, Addis Ababa / አዲስ አበባ,
አዲስ አበባ / Addis Ababa, Ethiopia
⊕ https://vfmat.ch/3b8e

Karamara General Hospital
4, Jijiga, Somali Region, Ethiopia
⊕ https://vfmat.ch/d75b

Kidus Gebriel Hospital
Addis Ababa, Ethiopia
⊕ https://vfmat.ch/35ad

Kindo Koyisha Hospital
Chida-Sodo, Bale, ደቡብ ብሔሮች ብሔረሰቦችና
ሕዝቦች ክልል / Southern Nations Nationalities
Peoples, Ethiopia
⊕ https://vfmat.ch/4fd5

Kobo Hospital
Mek'ele-Weldiya Road, Kobo, Ethiopia
⊕ https://vfmat.ch/428d

Kuyi Hospital
Geter Kuy Road, Kuyi, Ethiopia
⊕ https://vfmat.ch/3f43

Kwante
Zizencio Guakepece, Zizencio, ደቡብ ብሔሮች
ብሔረሰቦችና ሕዝቦች ክልል / Southern Nations
Nationalities Peoples, Ethiopia
⊕ https://vfmat.ch/9458

Lalibela Hospital
Lalibela-Geshena-Road, Akotola, Ethiopia
⊕ https://vfmat.ch/692e

Land Mark Hospital
Mozambique Street, Addis Ababa, Ethiopia
⊕ https://vfmat.ch/d169

Lena Carl Hospital
Mek'ele-Weldiya Road, Maychew, Tigray, Ethiopia
⊕ https://vfmat.ch/bb38

Machew Hospital
Endamehoni, Ethiopia
⊕ https://vfmat.ch/69bd

Markos Hospital
Old Italian Road, መቐለ / Mek'elē, ትግራይ / Tigray,
Ethiopia
⊕ https://vfmat.ch/d233

MCM
Egzabheraab To Mebrathail, Addis Ababa, Ethiopia
⊕ https://vfmat.ch/d414

Mekelle Hospital
Witten Germany Street, Mek'elē, Tigray, Ethiopia
⊕ https://vfmat.ch/6aea

Meles Zenawi Memorial Referral Hospital
Jijiga, Ethiopia
⊕ https://vfmat.ch/9f2b

Menelik II Referral Hospital
Yeka, Addis Ababa, Ethiopia
⊕ https://vfmat.ch/68f9

Mizan-Aman Teaching Hospital
Mizan – Maji, Greater Aman, ደቡብ ብሔሮች
ብሔረሰቦችና ሕዝቦች ክልል / Southern Nations
Nationalities Peoples, Ethiopia
⊕ https://vfmat.ch/5745

Nain Specialized Maternal and Child Hospital
Mauritius Street, Addis Ababa / አዲስ አበባ, አዲስ
አበባ / Addis Ababa, Ethiopia
⊕ https://vfmat.ch/79f6

NEMMG Hospital Hossana
Welkite Gurage, Hossana, ደቡብ ብሔሮች
ብሔረሰቦችና ሕዝቦች ክልል / Southern Nations
Nationalities Peoples, Ethiopia
⊕ https://vfmat.ch/3d3f

Number One Health Station
Awash – Assab, Awragoda, Dire Dawa, Ethiopia
⊕ https://vfmat.ch/151f

Ras Desta Hospital
Addis Ababa, Ethiopia
⊕ https://vfmat.ch/d62e

Rim and Men's Hospital
Witten Germany Street, Mek'elē, Tigray, Ethiopia
⊕ https://vfmat.ch/73ce

Shanan Gibe General Hospital
Jimma, Ethiopia
⊕ https://vfmat.ch/e9f2

Shashamane Hospital
Kuyera Dedeba, Ethiopia
⊕ https://vfmat.ch/d8de

Shiek Hassan Referral Hospital
Jijiga, Ethiopia
⊕ https://vfmat.ch/f618

Shinshiro Primary Hospital
Shinshicho, Southern Nations Nationalities Peoples, Ethiopia
⊕ https://vfmat.ch/a1cb

Shone Hospital
41, ሾኔ / Shone, ደቡብ ብሔሮች ብሔረሰቦችና ሕዝቦች ክልል / Southern Nations Nationalities Peoples, Ethiopia
⊕ https://vfmat.ch/a3e3

Silk Road Hospital
Egypt Street, Addis Ababa, Addis Ababa, Ethiopia
⊕ https://vfmat.ch/bb16

Sister Aquila Hospital
Darartu Tulu Street, Adama, Nazret, Oromia, Ethiopia
⊕ https://vfmat.ch/667b

Soddo Christian Hospital
Sodo to Arba Minch, Sodo, Southern Nations Nationalities Peoples, Ethiopia
⊕ https://vfmat.ch/8ceb

St. Petros Specialized TB Hospital
Intoto Road, Addis Ababa, Ethiopia
⊕ https://vfmat.ch/d142

St. Paul's Hospital
Swaziland St, Addis Ababa, Ethiopia
⊕ https://vfmat.ch/638a

St. Yared Hospital
Fikre Mariam Aba Techan Street, Addis Ababa, Ethiopia
⊕ https://vfmat.ch/6cf9

Suhul Referral Hospital
3, Shire, Tigray, Ethiopia
⊕ https://vfmat.ch/221c

Tefera Hailu Memorial Hospital
Sekota, Ethiopia
⊕ https://vfmat.ch/e7e1

Tekelehaymanot Hospital
Gobena Aba Tigu Street, Addis Ababa, Ethiopia
⊕ https://vfmat.ch/9bbc

Tepi General Hospital
Tepi – Shishinda, Southern Nations Nationalities Peoples Region, Ethiopia
⊕ https://vfmat.ch/d11a

Tezena
Ring Road, Addis Ababa, Ethiopia
⊕ https://vfmat.ch/a54d

Tikur Anbass General Specialized Hospital
Wereda 03, Ethiopia
⊕ https://vfmat.ch/a797

Tirunesh Dibaba Hospital
Addis Ababa, Ethiopia
⊕ https://vfmat.ch/df54

Tor Hailoch
Smuts Av, Addis Ababa, Ethiopia
⊕ https://vfmat.ch/c75d

Tuber Clouses
Fitawrari Habte Giorgis Street, Addis Ababa, Ethiopia
⊕ https://vfmat.ch/c528

TZNA Hospital
TZNA General Hospital, Addis Ababa, Ethiopia
⊕ https://vfmat.ch/e5e1

Wanted Life Hospital
Belay Zeleke, Bahir Dar, Ethiopia
⊕ https://vfmat.ch/6a82

Wolayita Sodo University Hospital
Hawassa Sodo, Southern Nations Nationalities Peoples Region, Ethiopia
⊕ https://vfmat.ch/8811

Wukro General Hospital
Wukro, Tigray, Ethiopia
⊕ https://vfmat.ch/ae5d

Yekatit 12 Hospital
Weatherall Street, Addis Ababa, Ethiopia
⊕ https://vfmat.ch/d5aa

Yemariam Work Hospital
Awash – Assab Awragoda, Dire Dawa, Ethiopia
⊕ https://vfmat.ch/76ee

Yerer Hospital
Road to Gergi Giorgis, Addis Ababa, Ethiopia
⊕ https://vfmat.ch/add9

Yirga Alem Hospital
Yirgalem General Hospital, Sidama Zone, Southern Ethiopia
⊕ https://vfmat.ch/9941

Yordanos Orthopaedic Hospital
Tesema Aba Kemaw Street, Addis Ababa, Ethiopia
⊕ https://vfmat.ch/d112

Zewditu Memorial Hospital
Wendimeneh Street, Addis Ababa, Ethiopia
⊕ https://vfmat.ch/63e8

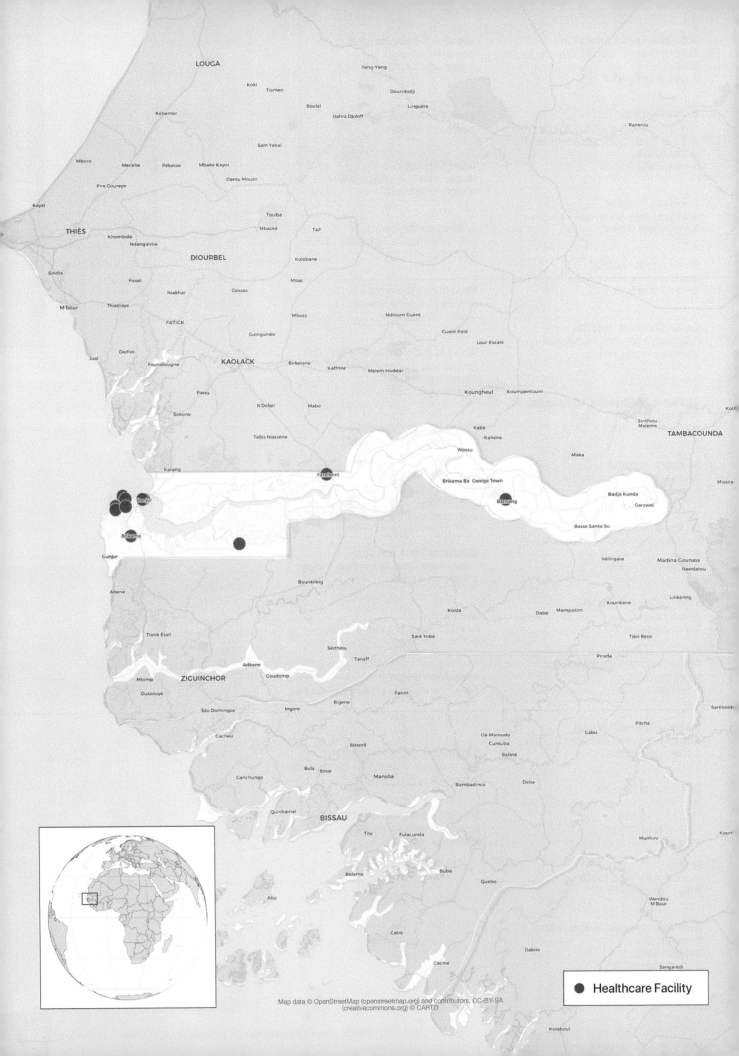

LOUGA

Yang-Yang

Koki
Tiamen
Doundodji

Kébemer
Boulal
Linguère

Dahra Djoloff

Mboro
Meckhe
Pékesse
Mbake Kayor

Darou Mousti

Ranérou

Pire Goureye

Sam Yabal

Kayar

Touba

THIÈS
Khombole
Mbacké
Taif

Ndangalma

Sindia
DIOURBEL
Kolobane

Fissel

Niakhar
Gossas
Mbar

M'bour
Thiadiaye

FATICK
Mboss
Ndioum Guènt

Joal
Diofior

Guinguinéo
Guent Paté

Foundiougne
KAOLACK
Lour-Escale

Birkelane

Sokone
Passy
Kaffrine
Malem Hoddar

N'Dofan
Mabo

Koungheul
Koumpentoum

Sinthiou
Maleme

Taïba Niassène

Kaba

TAMBACOUNDA

Karang
Kahène

Koti

Wassu
Maka

Farafenni

Missira

Brikama Ba George Town
Badja Kunda

Bandul
Bansang
Garowol

Brikama
Basse Santa Su

Gunjur
Velingara
Madina Gounass

Bounkiling
Rawdatou

Abene
Koïda
Dabo
Mampatim
Linkéring

Tionk Essil
Kounkané

Saré Yoba
Tiévi Bessi

Sédhiou

Adéane
Tanaff
Pirada

ZIGUINCHOR
Goudomp

Mlomp
Farim

Oussouye
Bigene
Saréboide

São Domingos
Ingoré

Cacheu
Pitche

Bissorã
Gabú

Bula
Câ-Mamudo

Canchungo
Binar
Mansôa
Cuntuba

Bafatá

Bambadinca
Deba

Quinhámel

Quinhámel
BISSAU

Tite
Fulacunda
Munhini

Bolama
Buba

Abu
Quebo

Wendou
M'Bour

Catió

Dabiss

Cacine
Sangarédi

Kolaboui

● Healthcare Facility

The Gambia

The Republic of The Gambia is a small West African country surrounded by Senegal on all sides except along its short coast. Referred to as the "smiling coast of Africa," The Gambia's long and winding shape was determined by British and French territory divisions established in the 19th century and follows the outline of the Gambia River. The majority of its more than 2.2 million person population is Muslim. It is one of the most densely populated countries in Africa, with about 57 percent of The Gambia's population concentrated in urban and peri-urban centers. The most commonly spoken language is English, in addition to several local languages representative of a variety of Gambian ethnic groups.

Since the country's independence from Britain in 1965, The Gambia has remained politically stable. Stability has not directly translated into prosperity, as nearly half of the population lives in poverty and almost 10 percent faces food insecurity. Two-thirds of the population earns their livelihood from the agricultural sector, but the overall output of the sector is low relative to the amount of arable land.

The poor socioeconomic situation in The Gambia is reflected in the health indicators of the country as well. Poverty in addition to a deteriorating infrastructure, a shortage of healthcare personnel, and an inadequate referral system contribute to a population in poor health. The top causes of death include lower respiratory infections, neonatal disorders, HIV/AIDS, tuberculosis, malaria, diarrheal diseases, maternal disorders, and increasingly, non-communicable diseases such as ischemic heart disease, stroke, liver cancer, and cirrhosis. Despite a precarious health situation in the country, some progress has been made: Life expectancy has continued to improve over the past few decades, as well as the under-five mortality rate, which is now nearly half of what it was in 1990.

2.2M
Population

$787
GDP Per Capita

62 years
Life Expectancy
↑ Improving

11
Doctors/100k
Physician Density

110
Beds/100k
Hospital Bed Density

597
Deaths/100k
Maternal Mortality

The Gambia

Nonprofit Organizations

Africa CDC
Aims to strengthen the capacity and capability of Africa's public health institutions and partnerships to detect and respond quickly and effectively to disease threats and outbreaks, based on data-driven interventions and programs.
Infect Dis, Logist-Op, Pub Health
⊕ https://vfmat.ch/339c

Africa Health Organisation
Leads collaborative efforts among countries in Africa and other partners to promote health equity, combat disease, and improve quality of life.
Logist-Op, Pub Health
⊕ https://vfmat.ch/b1c5

Africa Relief and Community Development
Provides comprehensive relief and developmental aid to people of the African continent regardless of gender, race, or religion.
Nutr, Pub Health
⊕ https://vfmat.ch/6cd2

African Cultural Exchange, Inc., The
Enriches lives through humanitarian programs in culture, development, education, and healthcare.
General
⊕ https://vfmat.ch/f238

African Field Epidemiology Network (AFENET)
Strengthens field epidemiology and public health laboratory capacity to contribute effectively to addressing epidemics and other major public health problems in Africa.
All-Immu, Infect Dis, Path, Pub Health
⊕ https://vfmat.ch/df2e

Against Malaria Foundation
Helps protect people from malaria. Funds anti-malaria nets, specifically long-lasting insecticidal nets (LLINs), and works with distribution partners to ensure they are used. Tracks and reports on net use and malaria case data.
Infect Dis
⊕ https://vfmat.ch/337d

Al Basar International Foundation
Works with local partners to treat preventable blindness, and helps set up sustainable infrastructure so local teams can save sight in their communities.
Ophth-Opt
⊕ https://vfmat.ch/a8b5

Al-Mustafa Welfare Trust
Seeks to alleviate poverty and provides medical and social development assistance to the poor and vulnerable around the world.
General, Ophth-Opt
⊕ https://vfmat.ch/c5f4

AO Alliance
Builds solutions to lessen the burden of injuries in low- and middle-income countries, while enhancing the care of the injured to reduce human suffering, disability, and poverty.
Ortho, Surg
⊕ https://vfmat.ch/8cd5

Arbeiter Samariter Bund (Workers' Samaritan Federation)
Engages in areas such as civil protection, rescue services, and social welfare, while operating a network of welcome centers to help refugees.
ER Med, General, Infect Dis, Logist-Op, Rehab
⊕ https://vfmat.ch/8a5b

Basic Foundations
Supports local projects and organizations that seek to meet the basic human needs of others in their community.
ER Med, General, Peds, Rehab, Surg
⊕ https://vfmat.ch/c4be

Bijilo Medical Center/Hospital (BMC)
Provides comprehensive and affordable quality medical services to all in the Gambia.
General, OB-GYN, Path, Peds, Radiol, Rehab, Surg
⊕ https://vfmat.ch/776d

Bill & Melinda Gates Foundation
Focuses on global issues, such as poverty, health, and education, offering the opportunity to dramatically improve the quality of life for billions of people by building partnerships that bring together resources, expertise, and vision to identify issues, find answers, and drive change.
All-Immu, General, Infect Dis, MF Med, Neonat, OB-GYN, Pub Health
⊕ https://vfmat.ch/7cf2

Breast Cancer Support
Aims to save lives and end breast cancer forever in women and men through education, treatment, emotional assistance, and financial support.
Heme-Onc, Logist-Op, Pub Health, Rad-Onc, Radiol
⊕ https://vfmat.ch/cb78

BroadReach
Collaborates with governments, multinational health organizations, donors, and private-sector companies to effect healthcare reform and solve the world's biggest health challenges.
Logist-Op
⊕ https://vfmat.ch/7812

Center for Strategic and International Studies (CSIS) Commission on Strengthening America's Health Security
Brings together a distinguished and diverse group of high-level opinion leaders bridging security and health, with the core aim to chart a bold vision for the future

of U.S. leadership in global health.
ER Med, Infect Dis, MF Med, Pub Health
⊕ https://vfmat.ch/6d7f

Chain of Hope
Provides lifesaving heart operations for children around the world and supports the development of cardiac services in numerous developing and war-torn countries.
Anesth, CT Surg, CV Med, Crit-Care, Ped Surg, Peds, Pulm-Critic, Surg
⊕ https://vfmat.ch/1b1b

Child Aid Gambia
Alleviates poverty among children and their families living in The Gambia and Senegal, and works to improve quality of life for children through specific projects for nutrition, education, and health.
Logist-Op, Nutr, OB-GYN, Peds
⊕ https://vfmat.ch/77a1

Children's Lifeline International
Provides medical teams and surgical assistance to underprivileged children in developing countries through missions in partnership with local hospitals.
CV Med, Dent-OMFS, General, MF Med, Neurosurg, Peds, Rehab
⊕ https://vfmat.ch/6fea

Developing Country NGO Delegation: Global Fund to Fight AIDS, TB & Malaria
Works to strengthen the engagement of civil society actors and organizations in developing countries to build a world in which AIDS, TB, and malaria are no longer global, public health, and human rights threats.
Infect Dis, Pub Health
⊕ https://vfmat.ch/3149

Dimbayaa Fertility for Africa
Provides infertility support through counseling, diagnosis, and treatment using artificial reproductive technology.
MF Med, OB-GYN
⊕ https://vfmat.ch/d2c5

Direct Relief
Improves the health and lives of people affected by poverty or emergency situations by mobilizing and providing essential medical resources needed for their care.
ER Med, Logist-Op
⊕ https://vfmat.ch/58e5

Gift of Life International
Provides lifesaving cardiac treatment to children in developing countries while developing sustainable pediatric cardiac programs by implementing screening, surgical, and training missions.
Anesth, CT Surg, CV Med, Crit-Care, Ped Surg, Peds, Pulm-Critic
⊕ https://vfmat.ch/f2f9

Global Blood Fund
Delivers grants, equipment, and training to over 50 countries in Africa, Asia, Eastern Europe, the Middle East, Latin America and the Caribbean.
Pub Health
⊕ https://vfmat.ch/6377

Global Oncology (GO)
Brings the best in cancer care to underserved patients around the world and collaborates across geographic, professional, and academic borders to improve cancer care, research, and education.
Heme-Onc, Path, Rad-Onc
⊕ https://vfmat.ch/fcb8

Globus Relief
Aims to improve the delivery of healthcare worldwide by gathering, processing, and distributing surplus medical supplies to charities at home and abroad.
Logist-Op
⊕ https://vfmat.ch/a2b7

Health Equity Initiative
Aims to build and sustain a global community that engages across sectors and

disciplines to advance health equity.
Pub Health
⊕ https://vfmat.ch/e2e2

Heart to Heart International
Strengthens communities through improving health access, providing humanitarian development, and administering crisis relief worldwide. Engages volunteers, collaborates with partners, and deploys resources to achieve this mission.
Anesth, ER Med, General, Logist-Op, Medicine, Path, Path, Peds, Psych, Pub Health, Surg
⊕ https://vfmat.ch/aacb

HelpMeSee
Trains local cataract specialists in Manual Small Incision Cataract Surgery (MSICS) in significant numbers, to meet the increasing demand for surgical services in the communities most impacted by cataract blindness.
Anesth, Ophth-Opt, Surg
⊕ https://vfmat.ch/973c

Hernia International
Aims to provide relief from sickness, and protection and preservation of health, for persons affected by groin and abdominal hernias and residing in low- and middle-income countries.
Surg
⊕ https://vfmat.ch/e98e

Horizons Trust UK
Provides quality healthcare for those who desperately need it but have no financial means, and aims to build and manage a high-quality medical facility for those who can afford private treatment.
General, Infect Dis, MF Med
⊕ https://vfmat.ch/12ef

Humanity First
Provides aid and assistance to those in need, offering sustainable development solutions to society while providing and empowering local communities with the resources to help themselves.
ER Med, General, MF Med, Ophth-Opt
⊕ https://vfmat.ch/13cc

International Agency for the Prevention of Blindness (IAPB), The
Leads international efforts in blindness-prevention activities, works toward a world where no one is needlessly visually impaired, and ensures that everyone has access to the best possible standard of eye health.
Infect Dis, Ophth-Opt, Pub Health
⊕ https://vfmat.ch/87a2

International Federation of Red Cross and Red Crescent Societies (IFRC)
Coordinates and directs international assistance following natural and manmade disasters in nonconflict situations through the world's largest humanitarian and development network. Provides disaster-preparedness programs, healthcare activities, and promotes humanitarian values.
ER Med, General, Infect Dis, Nutr
⊕ https://vfmat.ch/b4ee

International Learning Movement (ILM UK)
Supports some of the world's poorest people in developing countries with core projects in education, safe drinking water, and healthcare.
General, Ophth-Opt
⊕ https://vfmat.ch/b974

International Medical Relief
Provides sustainable education, training, medical and dental care, and disaster relief and response in vulnerable communities worldwide.
Dent-OMFS, General, Infect Dis, Medicine, OB-GYN
⊕ https://vfmat.ch/b3ed

International Mental Health Collaborating Network
Promotes and advocates for the human rights of people with mental health issues and gathers and shares the experiences and knowledge of good practices in community mental health from its membership network.

Psych
⊕ https://vfmat.ch/1551

International Organization for Migration (IOM) – The UN Migration Agency
Promotes evidence-informed policies and holistic, preventive, and curative health programs that are beneficial, accessible, and equitable for vulnerable migrants.
General, Infect Dis, OB-GYN
⊕ https://vfmat.ch/621a

International Trachoma Initiative (iTi)
Works toward a world free from trachoma, a preventable cause of blindness, and provides comprehensive support to national ministries of health and governmental and nongovernmental organizations to implement a comprehensive approach to fight trachoma.
Infect Dis, Ophth-Opt
⊕ https://vfmat.ch/3278

iQra International
Provides medical aid to disabled people globally, and raises awareness of the neglect and discrimination they face in developing countries.
General, Logist-Op, Ophth-Opt
⊕ https://vfmat.ch/9282

Islamic Medical Association of North America
Fosters health promotion, disease prevention, and health maintenance in communities around the world through direct patient care and health programs.
Anesth, Dent-OMFS, ER Med, General, Logist-Op, Ophth-Opt, Peds, Plast, Surg
⊕ https://vfmat.ch/a157

John Snow, Inc. (JSI)
Aims to improve the health and well-being of underserved and vulnerable people and communities throughout the world.
General, Infect Dis, Logist-Op, MF Med, OB-GYN, Peds, Psych, Pub Health
⊕ https://vfmat.ch/ba78

Light House Medical Missions
Inspired by the Christian faith, provides programs in healthcare provision, nutrition, emergency relief and response, and water, sanitation, and hygiene (WASH).
ER Med, General, Surg
⊕ https://vfmat.ch/cecd

Lions Clubs International
Empowers volunteers to serve their communities, meet humanitarian needs, encourage peace, and promote international understanding through Lions Clubs.
Heme-Onc, Medicine, Nutr, Ophth-Opt
⊕ https://vfmat.ch/7b12

London School of Hygiene & Tropical Medicine
Seeks to improve health and health equity in the UK and worldwide, working in partnership to achieve excellence in public and global health research, education, and translation of knowledge into policy and practice.
Infect Dis, Pub Health
⊕ https://vfmat.ch/349a

Lutherans in Medical Missions (LIMM)
Works with local and global partners to promote healing in medically underserved communities.
General, Logist-Op, Pub Health
⊕ https://vfmat.ch/c5aa

Management Sciences for Health (MSH)
Works with countries and communities to save lives and improve the health of the world's poorest and most vulnerable people by building strong, resilient, sustainable health systems.
Infect Dis, Logist-Op, Pub Health
⊕ https://vfmat.ch/6aa2

MAP International
Provides medicines and health supplies to those in need around the world so they might experience life to the fullest.

Logist-Op
⊕ https://vfmat.ch/deed

Maternal & Childhealth Advocacy International
Seeks to save and improve the lives of babies, children, and pregnant women in areas of extreme poverty by empowering and enabling in-country partners to strengthen emergency healthcare.
MF Med, Neonat, OB-GYN, Peds
⊕ https://vfmat.ch/ea67

Maternity Worldwide
Works with communities and partners to identify and develop appropriate and effective ways to reduce maternal and newborn mortality and morbidity, facilitate communities to access quality skilled maternity care, and support the provision of quality skilled care.
MF Med, OB-GYN
⊕ https://vfmat.ch/822b

Medical Care Development International
Works to improve the health of vulnerable populations through integrated, sustainable, and locally driven interventions.
Infect Dis, OB-GYN, Peds, Pub Health
⊕ https://vfmat.ch/da87

Medics for Humanity
Advocates the universal right to health and promotes the values of international solidarity, justice, and peace.
Endo, General, Medicine, Nephro
⊕ https://vfmat.ch/91f6

MedShare
Aims to improve the quality of life of people, communities, and the planet by sourcing and directly delivering surplus medical supplies and equipment to communities in need around the world.
Logist-Op
⊕ https://vfmat.ch/c8bc

Mercy and Love Foundation
Aims to provide orphaned and vulnerable children with basic human needs such as food, clothing, and shelter, enabling them to thrive.
General, Peds
⊕ https://vfmat.ch/649a

Mercy Ships
Operates hospital ships staffed by volunteers to bring hope, healing, and healthcare to underserved communities worldwide.
Anesth, Dent-OMFS, Logist-Op, Neonat, OB-GYN, Ophth-Opt, Ortho, Palliative, Plast, Psych, Surg
⊕ https://vfmat.ch/2e99

MiracleFeet
Brings low-cost treatment to every child on the planet born with clubfoot, a leading cause of physical disability.
Ortho, Peds, Rehab
⊕ https://vfmat.ch/bda8

OneSight
Brings eye exams and glasses to people who lack access to vision care.
Ophth-Opt
⊕ https://vfmat.ch/3ecc

Operation Fistula
Exists to end obstetric fistula by building models of care that serve every woman, everywhere.
MF Med, OB-GYN, Surg
⊕ https://vfmat.ch/ce8e

Options
Believes in a world in which women and children can access the high-quality health services they need, without financial burden.
Logist-Op, MF Med, Neonat, OB-GYN
⊕ https://vfmat.ch/3a48

PATH
Advances health equity through innovation and partnerships so people, communities, and economies can thrive.
All-Immu, CV Med, Endo, Heme-Onc, Infect Dis, MF Med, Neonat, Nutr, OB-GYN, Path, Peds, Pulm-Critic
⊕ https://vfmat.ch/b4db

People for Change
Helps to eliminate the scarcity of access to basic healthcare, improve children's educational prospects in underdeveloped areas, and improve communities' sustainable access to wholesome food.
General, Infect Dis, Nutr, Peds
⊕ https://vfmat.ch/7499

Power Up Gambia
Hopes to improve healthcare delivery in The Gambia by providing proven, reliable, and sustainable electricity through solar energy.
General
⊕ https://vfmat.ch/a671

Practical Tools Initiative
Provides or assists in the provision of education, training, healthcare projects, and all the necessary support designed to enable individuals to generate a sustainable income.
General, Logist-Op, MF Med
⊕ https://vfmat.ch/16b6

Project Aid the Gambia
Provides development efforts in areas of education, health, and agriculture in targeted rural communities, including the operation of Jahaly Health Centre, a kindergarten, and support of the Ministry of Health, with medical equipment and advice for rural healthcare.
General, Infect Dis, Logist-Op, MF Med, OB-GYN, Peds
⊕ https://vfmat.ch/96bd

RAD-AID International
Improves and optimizes access to medical imaging and radiology in low-resource regions of the world.
Rad-Onc, Radiol
⊕ https://vfmat.ch/537f

RestoringVision
Empowers lives by restoring vision for millions of people in need.
Ophth-Opt
⊕ https://vfmat.ch/e121

Riders for Health
Strives to ensure that reliable transport is available for healthcare services.
Logist-Op
⊕ https://vfmat.ch/7353

Riders for Health International
Aids in the last mile of healthcare delivery, by ensuring that healthcare reaches everyone, everywhere.
ER Med, Infect Dis, Logist-Op, Pub Health
⊕ https://vfmat.ch/85aa

Rockefeller Foundation, The
Works to promote the well-being of humanity.
Logist-Op, Nutr, Pub Health
⊕ https://vfmat.ch/5424

Rotary International
Provides service to others, improves lives, and advances world understanding, goodwill, and peace through its fellowship of business, professional, and community leaders.
ER Med, General, Infect Dis, MF Med, OB-GYN
⊕ https://vfmat.ch/8fb5

Safe Anaesthesia Worldwide
Provides anesthesia to those in need in low-income countries to enable lifesaving surgery.

Anesth, Plast
⊕ https://vfmat.ch/134a

Save A Child's Heart
Provides lifesaving cardiac treatment to children in developing countries, and trains healthcare professionals from these countries to deliver quality care in their communities.
CT Surg, CV Med, Crit-Care, Ped Surg, Peds
⊕ https://vfmat.ch/1bef

Save an orphan
Transforms the lives of children by providing them with medical aid, education, shelter, employment opportunities, and the means for a better tomorrow.
General, Infect Dis, MF Med
⊕ https://vfmat.ch/5742

Sightsavers
Works with partners in developing countries to help eliminate avoidable blindness and advocates for equal opportunity for the disabled.
Infect Dis, Ophth-Opt, Surg
⊕ https://vfmat.ch/aa52

SIGN Fracture Care International
Builds orthopedic capacity around the world and provides the injured poor access to fracture surgery by donating orthopedic education and implant systems to surgeons in developing countries.
Ortho, Rehab, Surg
⊕ https://vfmat.ch/123d

SINA Health
Aims to improve the health and educational status of the population in low- and middle-income countries.
General, Logist-Op
⊕ https://vfmat.ch/9ad3

Smile Train, Inc.
Treats children with cleft lip through a sustainable and local model that supports surgery and other forms of essential care.
Logist-Op, Pub Health
⊕ https://vfmat.ch/822c

Sound Seekers
Supports people with hearing loss by enabling access to healthcare and education.
ENT
⊕ https://vfmat.ch/ef1c

Students for Kids International Projects (SKIP)
Strives to educate and empower students to initiate and maintain sustainable community projects for the health, welfare, and education of children.
Dent-OMFS, General, Nutr, Peds, Pub Health
⊕ https://vfmat.ch/de4e

Sustainable Cardiovascular Health Equity Development Alliance
Fights cardiovascular disease in underserved populations globally via education, training, and increasing interventional capacity.
CV Med, Pub Health, Radiol
⊕ https://vfmat.ch/799c

Swiss Tropical and Public Health Institute
Contributes to the improvement of the health of populations internationally, nationally, and locally through excellence in research, education, and services.
Infect Dis, Pub Health
⊕ https://vfmat.ch/2ee4

T1International
Supports local communities with the tools needed to stand up for the right to better access to insulin and diabetes supplies.
Endo, General, Medicine, Pub Health
⊕ https://vfmat.ch/d7d4

Task Force for Global Health, The

Consists of programs and focus areas that cover a range of global health issues including neglected tropical diseases, infectious diseases, vaccines, field epidemiology, public health informatics, health workforce development, and global health ethics.

Infect Dis, Logist-Op, Medicine, Ophth-Opt, Peds

⊕ https://vfmat.ch/714c

United Nations Children's Fund (UNICEF)

Works in over 190 countries and territories to save children's lives, defend their rights, and help them fulfill their potential, from early childhood through adolescence.

All-Immu, Infect Dis, MF Med, Neonat, Nutr, OB-GYN, Ped Surg, Peds, Pub Health

⊕ https://vfmat.ch/42d7

United Nations Development Programme (UNDP)

Helps countries achieve the simultaneous eradication of extreme poverty and significant reduction of inequalities and exclusion using a sustainable human development approach.

Infect Dis, Logist-Op, Pub Health

⊕ https://vfmat.ch/935c

United Nations High Commissioner for Refugees (UNHCR)

Safeguards the rights and well-being of people who have been forced to flee, ensuring that everybody has the right to seek asylum and find safe refuge in another country, with the goal of seeking lasting solutions.

General, MF Med, Medicine, OB-GYN, Peds, Psych, Pub Health

⊕ https://vfmat.ch/6636

United Nations Population Fund (UNFPA)

Supports reproductive healthcare for women and youth in more than 150 countries, focusing on delivering a world in which every pregnancy is wanted, every childbirth is safe, and every young person's potential is fulfilled.

Infect Dis, MF Med, Neonat, OB-GYN, Peds, Pub Health

⊕ https://vfmat.ch/c969

USAID: Human Resources for Health 2030 (HRH2030)

Helps low- and middle-income countries develop the health workforce needed to prevent maternal and child deaths, support the goals of Family Planning 2020, control the HIV/AIDS epidemic, and protect communities from infectious diseases.

Logist-Op

⊕ https://vfmat.ch/9ea8

Vision Care

Restores sight and helps patients get regular treatment at short-term eye camps and long-term base clinics by having doctors, missionaries, volunteers, and sponsors work together.

Ophth-Opt

⊕ https://vfmat.ch/9d7c

Vitamin Angels

Helps at-risk populations in need—specifically pregnant women, new mothers, and children under age 5—to gain access to life-changing vitamins and minerals.

General, Nutr

⊕ https://vfmat.ch/7da1

Wisconsin Medical Project

Provides humanitarian aid, including donated medical equipment and supplies, to hospitals and clinics in areas of great need.

Logist-Op

⊕ https://vfmat.ch/ef3b

World Health Organization, The (WHO)

The United Nations' agency for health provides leadership on global health matters, shapes the health research agenda, sets norms and standards, articulates evidence-based policy options, provides technical support and monitoring to countries, and assesses health trends.

ER Med, General, Infect Dis, Logist-Op, MF Med, OB-GYN, Peds, Psych, Pub Health

⊕ https://vfmat.ch/c476

World Medical Relief

Facilitates the distribution of surplus medical resources where they are needed.

Logist-Op

⊕ https://vfmat.ch/72dc

 # The Gambia

Healthcare Facilities

Africmed
AU Summit Highway, Sukuta, West Coast,
The Gambia
⊕ https://vfmat.ch/dd3a

Ahmadiyya Hospital
Kombo Sillah Drive, Serrekunda, The Gambia
⊕ https://vfmat.ch/e7f8

Bansang Hospital Appeal
South Bank Road, Manneh Kunda, Upper River,
The Gambia
⊕ https://vfmat.ch/bcb6

Bijilo Medical Center/Hospital BMC
Bijilo, Serrekunda, The Gambia
⊕ https://vfmat.ch/6da4

Brikama District Hospital
Kombo Central, The Gambia
⊕ https://vfmat.ch/93b2

Bwiam General Hospital
South Bank Road, Bwiam, West Coast, The Gambia
⊕ https://vfmat.ch/b8c9

**Edward Francis Small Teaching
Hospital (EFSTH)**
Marina Parade, Banjul, Banjul, The Gambia
⊕ https://vfmat.ch/caeb

Farafenni Hospital
North Bank Road, Yallal Tankonjala, North Bank,
The Gambia
⊕ https://vfmat.ch/17f6

Medical Research Council
Garba Jahumpa Road, Serrekunda, Kanifing,
The Gambia
⊕ https://vfmat.ch/75e6

Psychiatric Hospital
Miniru Savage Road, Banjul, Banjul, The Gambia
⊕ https://vfmat.ch/1aa8

Serekunda General Hospital
Jimpex Road, Kanifing, Kanifing, The Gambia
⊕ https://vfmat.ch/54e1

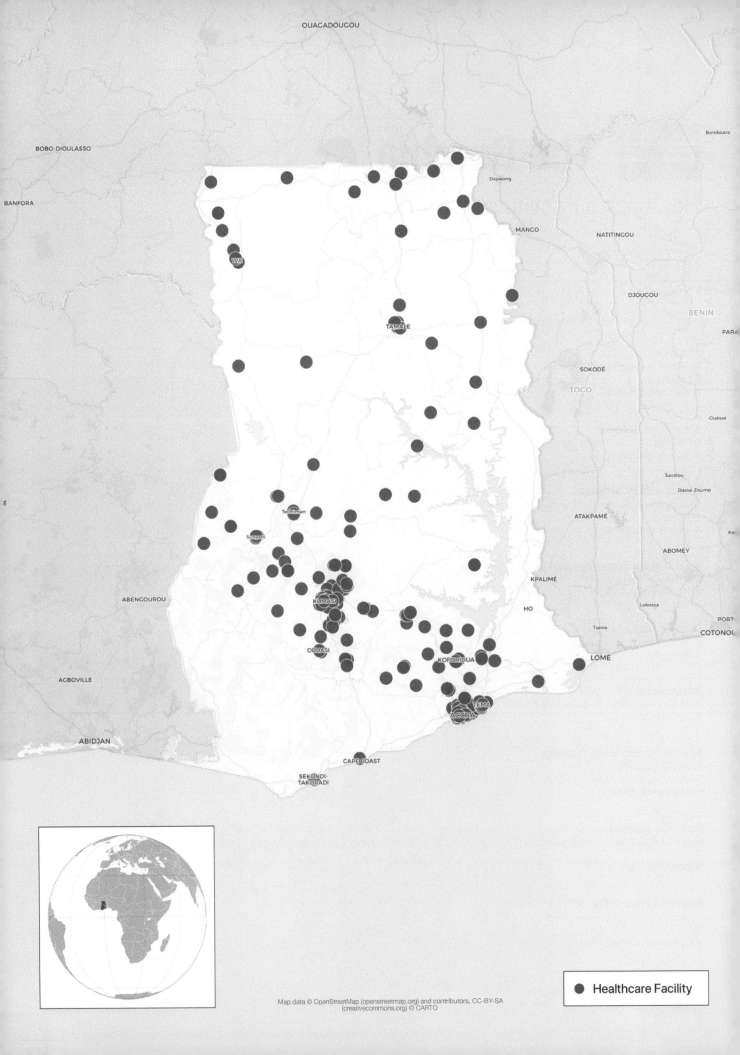

Healthcare Facility

Ghana

Dubbed "the gateway to West Africa," Ghana is blessed with stunning natural landscapes and tourist attractions that include waterfalls, palm-lined sandy beaches, rivers, reservoirs, lakes, caves, mountains, forests, and national parks. Dozens of forts and castles, and two UNESCO World Heritage sites, round out the offerings. Officially known as the Republic of Ghana, this West African country has a coastline along the Gulf of Guinea and shares borders with Ivory Coast to the west, Burkina Faso to the north, and Togo to the east. Ghana's population of roughly 32.4 million comprises multiple languages and ethnic groups. About 80 Ghanaian languages are spoken, with many people speaking at least one of the 10 major Ghanaian languages: Asante, Ewe, Fante, Brong, Dagomba, Dangme, Dagaare, Kokomba, Akyem, and Ga. Ghana inherited English from Great Britain during its colonial past, and it remains the official language and lingua franca.

Carved from the British colony of the Gold Coast and the Togoland Trust Territory, in 1957 Ghana became the first sub-Saharan country in colonial Africa to gain independence from British rule. Ghana was subsequently proclaimed a republic on July 1, 1960. Post-independence, the country faced political instability following a number of coup d'etats. Ghana returned to constitutional democracy in 1992, and since then the country has been one of the most stable political environments and democracies in Africa. As Africa's largest producer of gold, and the second largest producer of cocoa (after the Ivory Coast), Ghana is also rich in other mineral resources such as diamonds, bauxite, manganese ore, and oil. The economy is fairly agrarian, with about 54 percent of Ghana's total labor force employed in agriculture. However, high government debt, spending, and corruption, coupled with a fall in oil prices, have resulted in economic hardship.

Life expectancy in Ghana increased significantly, from age 57 to 64, between 2000 and 2019. Similarly, under-five mortality rates decreased from 99 to 46 deaths per 1,000 live births. Nonetheless, the population is still vulnerable to poor health. Both communicable and non-communicable diseases contribute to the most deaths, including malaria, stroke, lower respiratory infections, neonatal disorders, ischemic heart disease, HIV/AIDS, tuberculosis, diarrheal diseases, diabetes, and cirrhosis. Trauma, preterm birth complications, birth asphyxia, and mortality from road injuries are also significant.

32.4M

Population

$2,329

GDP Per Capita

64 years

Life Expectancy

↑ Improving

11
Doctors/100k

Physician Density

90
Beds/100k

Hospital Bed Density

308
Deaths/100k

Maternal Mortality

Ghana

Nonprofit Organizations

143 LIFE Foundation
Seeks to educate and empower individuals living with malaria, TB, HIV/AIDS, STDs and other health disparities related to sexual health.
Infect Dis, MF Med
🌐 https://vfmat.ch/d59b

5 Rivers Heart Association
Works to help underserved populations by creating innovative ways to deliver cost-effective medicine while optimizing resource utilization.
CT Surg, GI, General
🌐 https://vfmat.ch/2deb

A Broader View Volunteers
Provides developing countries around the world with significant volunteer programs that aid the neediest communities and forge a lasting bond between those volunteering and those they have helped.
Dent-OMFS, ER Med, Infect Dis, MF Med
🌐 https://vfmat.ch/3bec

Abt Associates
Seeks to improve the quality of life and economic well-being of people worldwide, while striving to meet and exceed the highest professional standards.
General, Logist-Op, MF Med, OB-GYN, Peds
🌐 https://vfmat.ch/cec2

Aceso Global
Provides strategic healthcare advisory services in low- and middle-income countries to design and deliver highly customized, evidence-based solutions that address the complex nature of healthcare systems, with a goal to strengthen and provide affordable, high-quality care to all.
Logist-Op, Pub Health
🌐 https://vfmat.ch/b3b7

Advance Family Planning
Aims to achieve global expansion and access to quality contraceptive information, services, and supplies through financial investment and political commitment.
General, MF Med, Pub Health
🌐 https://vfmat.ch/7478

Adventist Health International
Focuses on upgrading and managing mission hospitals by providing governance, consultation, and technical assistance to a number of affiliated Seventh-Day Adventist hospitals throughout Africa, Asia, and the Americas.
Dent-OMFS, General, Pub Health
🌐 https://vfmat.ch/16aa

Africa CDC
Aims to strengthen the capacity and capability of Africa's public health institutions and partnerships to detect and respond quickly and effectively to disease threats and outbreaks, based on data-driven interventions and programs.

Infect Dis, Logist-Op, Pub Health
🌐 https://vfmat.ch/339c

Africa Health Organisation
Leads collaborative efforts among countries in Africa and other partners to promote health equity, combat disease, and improve quality of life.
Logist-Op, Pub Health
🌐 https://vfmat.ch/b1c5

Africa Indoor Residual Spraying Project (AIRS)
Aims to protect millions of people in Africa from malaria by spraying insecticide on walls, ceilings, and other indoor resting places of mosquitoes that transmit malaria.
Infect Dis
🌐 https://vfmat.ch/9bd1

Africa Partners Medical
Works to improve the quality of medical services in Ghana and West Africa though education and equipment-related partnerships.
General, Infect Dis, Logist-Op, OB-GYN, Peds, Pub Health, Surg
🌐 https://vfmat.ch/2755

Africa Relief and Community Development
Provides comprehensive relief and developmental aid to people of the African continent regardless of gender, race, or religion.
Nutr, Pub Health
🌐 https://vfmat.ch/6cd2

African Christian Hospitals
Aims to provide excellent healthcare services to all in Nigeria, Ghana, and Tanzania, and equips and empowers African healthcare workers through medical scholarships and investments in hospitals.
General, Surg
🌐 https://vfmat.ch/5ff9

African Field Epidemiology Network (AFENET)
Strengthens field epidemiology and public health laboratory capacity to contribute effectively to addressing epidemics and other major public health problems in Africa.
All-Immu, Infect Dis, Path, Pub Health
🌐 https://vfmat.ch/df2e

African Health Now
Promotes and provides information and access to sustainable primary healthcare to women, children, and families living across Sub-Saharan Africa.
Dent-OMFS, Endo, General, Infect Dis, MF Med, OB-GYN
🌐 https://vfmat.ch/c766

AG Care – Ghana
Works to eliminate poverty by addressing the material and social needs of the poor, vulnerable, and marginalized in society.
General, Pub Health
⊕ https://vfmat.ch/5992

Against Malaria Foundation
Helps protect people from malaria. Funds anti-malaria nets, specifically long-lasting insecticidal nets (LLINs), and works with distribution partners to ensure they are used. Tracks and reports on net use and malaria case data.
Infect Dis
⊕ https://vfmat.ch/337d

Agyeman Eye Foundation
Aims to support blind and partially sighted people to lead independent and fulfilling lives by providing education about proper eye care, fundraising for those in need of eye treatment, and counseling those who have lost their sight.
Ophth-Opt
⊕ https://vfmat.ch/b312

Al Basar International Foundation
Works with local partners to treat preventable blindness, and helps set up sustainable infrastructure so local teams can save sight in their communities.
Ophth-Opt
⊕ https://vfmat.ch/a8b5

American Academy of Ophthalmology
Protects sight and empowers lives by serving as an advocate for patients and the public, leading ophthalmic education, and advancing the profession of ophthalmology.
Ophth-Opt
⊕ https://vfmat.ch/89a2

American Heart Association (AHA)
Fights heart disease and stroke, striving to save and improve lives.
CV Med, Crit-Care, General, Heme-Onc, Medicine, Peds
⊕ https://vfmat.ch/4747

American Stroke Association
Works to prevent, treat, and beat stroke by funding innovative research, fighting for stronger public health policies, and providing lifesaving tools and information.
CV Med, Crit-Care, Heme-Onc, Medicine, Neuro, Pub Health, Pulm-Critic, Vasc Surg
⊕ https://vfmat.ch/746f

Americares
Saves lives and improves health for people affected by poverty or disaster and responds with life-changing medicine, medical supplies, and health programs including domestic and global medical clinics.
All-Immu, ER Med, General, Infect Dis, MF Med, Nutr
⊕ https://vfmat.ch/e567

Amicus Onulus
Aims to provide quality and affordable healthcare to all clients while bridging the equity gaps in geographical access to health services.
General, Infect Dis
⊕ https://vfmat.ch/d831

Amref Health Africa
Serves millions of people across 35 countries in Sub-Saharan Africa, strengthening health systems, and training African health workers to respond to the continent's most critical health issues.
All-Immu, General, Infect Dis, Logist-Op, MF Med, OB-GYN, Path, Pub Health, Surg
⊕ https://vfmat.ch/6985

Amsterdam Institute for Global Health and Development (AIGHD)
Provides sustainable solutions to major health problems across our planet by forging synergies among disciplines, healthcare delivery, research, and education.
Infect Dis
⊕ https://vfmat.ch/d73d

AO Alliance
Builds solutions to lessen the burden of injuries in low- and middle-income countries, while enhancing the care of the injured to reduce human suffering, disability, and poverty.
Ortho, Surg
⊕ https://vfmat.ch/8cd5

Asamang SDA Hospital
Provides holistic health services with dedicated staff to ensure efficiency, effectiveness, and client satisfaction.
Dent-OMFS, OB-GYN, Pub Health, Surg
⊕ https://vfmat.ch/c6f9

Aspen Management Partnership for Health (AMP Health)
Works to improve health systems and outcomes by collaborating with governments to strengthen leadership and management capabilities through public-private partnership.
Logist-Op
⊕ https://vfmat.ch/ea78

Assist Africa
Believes that through education, entrepreneurial support, and access to healthcare, quality of life for many people can be improved dramatically and that sustainable economic growth and overall well-being are attainable through a focus on these three cornerstones.
Dent-OMFS, General, Surg
⊕ https://vfmat.ch/37fd

Aurum Institute, The
Seeks to impact global health by designing and delivering high-quality care and treatment to people in developing countries.
Infect Dis, Pub Health
⊕ https://vfmat.ch/ae2a

Benjamin H. Josephson, MD Fund
Provides healthcare professionals with the financial resources necessary to deliver medical services for those in need throughout the world.
General, OB-GYN
⊕ https://vfmat.ch/6acc

Bill & Melinda Gates Foundation
Focuses on global issues, such as poverty, health, and education, offering the opportunity to dramatically improve the quality of life for billions of people by building partnerships that bring together resources, expertise, and vision to identify issues, find answers, and drive change.
All-Immu, General, Infect Dis, MF Med, Neonat, OB-GYN, Pub Health
⊕ https://vfmat.ch/7cf2

Blueprints For Pangaea (B4P)
Aims to reallocate unused medical supplies from areas of excess to areas in need.
⊕ https://vfmat.ch/faba

BMT Ghana Foundation
Provides quality and comprehensive services through diagnostic testing, counseling and support, including a cure by bone marrow transplantation (BMT) for individuals and families at risk of sickle cell diseases, pediatric cancers, and blood disorders.
Heme-Onc, Ped Surg, Peds
⊕ https://vfmat.ch/f935

Boston Children's Hospital: Global Health Program
Helps solve pediatric global healthcare challenges by transferring expertise through long-term partnerships with scalable impact, while working in the field to strengthen healthcare systems, advocate, research, and provide care delivery or education as a way of sustainably improving the health of children worldwide.
Anesth, CV Med, Crit-Care, ER Med, Heme-Onc, Infect Dis, Medicine, Nutr, Palliative, Ped Surg, Peds
⊕ https://vfmat.ch/f9f8

Brain Project Africa
Provides the highest level of medical care, facilitates knowledge transfer, and donates the necessary medical equipment where it's most impactful.

Neuro, Neurosurg, Ortho

⊕ https://vfmat.ch/d4fd

Bridge of Life

Aims to strengthen healthcare globally through sustainable programs that prevent and treat chronic disease.

Logist-Op, Nephro, OB-GYN, Peds, Surg

⊕ https://vfmat.ch/5b68

Bright Sight Mission

Aims to prevent blindness from treatable eye conditions.

Ophth-Opt

⊕ https://vfmat.ch/c172

British Council for Prevention of Blindness (BCPB)

Funds research into blindness prevention and sight restoration in children and adults in low- and lower-middle-income countries.

Ophth-Opt

⊕ https://vfmat.ch/eaf4

BroadReach

Collaborates with governments, multinational health organizations, donors, and private-sector companies to effect healthcare reform and solve the world's biggest health challenges.

Logist-Op

⊕ https://vfmat.ch/7812

Bureau of International Health Cooperation

Seeks to improve healthcare around the world, including developing countries, using expertise, and contribute to healthier lives of Japanese people by bringing these experiences back to Japan.

ER Med, Heme-Onc, Infect Dis, Peds, Pub Health

⊕ https://vfmat.ch/947d

Cairdeas International Palliative Care Trust

Promotes and facilitates the provision of high-quality palliative care in the developing world, where such care is limited.

Palliative

⊕ https://vfmat.ch/35c4

CardioStart International

Provides free heart surgery and associated medical care to children and adults living in underserved regions of the world, irrespective of political or religious affiliation, through the collective skills of healthcare experts.

Anesth, CT Surg, CV Med, Crit-Care, Pub Health, Pulm-Critic

⊕ https://vfmat.ch/85ef

CARE

Works around the globe to save lives, defeat poverty, and achieve social justice.

ER Med, General

⊕ https://vfmat.ch/7232

Carter Center, The

Seeks to prevent and resolve conflicts, enhance freedom and democracy, and improve health, while remaining committed to human rights and the alleviation of human suffering.

Infect Dis, MF Med, Ophth-Opt

⊕ https://vfmat.ch/6556

Catholic World Mission

Works to rebuild communities worldwide by helping to alleviate poverty and empower underserved areas, while spreading the message of the Catholic Church.

ER Med, General, Nutr, Peds

⊕ https://vfmat.ch/7b5f

Changing Lives Together

Conducts humanitarian projects in healthcare, education, water, and sanitation in rural Ghana to help alleviate poverty and suffering.

General, Logist-Op, Neonat, Ophth-Opt, Pub Health

⊕ https://vfmat.ch/614d

Cheerful Hearts Foundation

Aims to stop child labor and trafficking by educating and empowering rural citizens through human rights, public health, and education initiatives.

Infect Dis, Pub Health

⊕ https://vfmat.ch/9c65

Child Family Health International (CFHI)

Connects students with local health professionals and community leaders transforming perspectives about self, global health, and healing.

General, Infect Dis, OB-GYN, Ophth-Opt, Palliative, Peds

⊕ https://vfmat.ch/729e

Children & Charity International

Puts people first by providing education, leadership, and nutrition programs along with mentoring and healthcare support services to children, youth, and families.

Nutr, Peds

⊕ https://vfmat.ch/6538

Children of War Foundation

Delivers access to global health and education to communities affected by poverty, war, natural disaster, climate change, and migration challenges.

ER Med, General, Logist-Op, Peds, Surg

⊕ https://vfmat.ch/de51

Children's Cardiac Foundation of Africa, The

Saves lives and improves the health of children with congenital heart disease in Africa.

CT Surg, Ped Surg, Surg

⊕ https://vfmat.ch/bbe9

Children's Lifeline International

Provides medical teams and surgical assistance to underprivileged children in developing countries through missions in partnership with local hospitals.

CV Med, Dent-OMFS, General, MF Med, Neurosurg, Peds, Rehab

⊕ https://vfmat.ch/6fea

Children's of Alabama: Global Surgery Program

Provides the finest pediatric health services to all children in an environment that fosters excellence in research and medical education.

CT Surg, CV Med, Crit-Care, Heme-Onc, Neurosurg, Ortho, Ped Surg, Peds, Surg, Urol

⊕ https://vfmat.ch/ff58

Children's Surgery International

Provides free medical and surgical services to children in need around the world, and instructs and trains local surgeons and other medical providers such as doctors, anesthesiologists, nurses, and technicians.

Anesth, Dent-OMFS, Ortho, Ped Surg, Peds, Plast, Surg

⊕ https://vfmat.ch/26d3

Christian Aid Ministries

Strives to be a trustworthy and efficient channel for Amish, Mennonite, and other conservative Anabaptist groups and individuals to minister to physical and spiritual needs around the world.

CT Surg, ER Med, Logist-Op, Ortho, Pub Health

⊕ https://vfmat.ch/7b33

Christian Blind Mission (CBM)

Aims to improve the quality of life of persons with disabilities in the poorest countries, addressing poverty as a cause and a consequence of disability, and working in partnership to create a society for all.

ENT, General, Infect Dis, OB-GYN, Ophth-Opt, Ortho, Peds, Psych, Rehab, Surg

⊕ https://vfmat.ch/3824

Christian Connections for International Health (CCIH)

Promotes global health and wholeness from a Christian perspective.

All-Immu, General, Infect Dis, MF Med, Neonat, OB-GYN, Psych

⊕ https://vfmat.ch/fa5d

Christian Eye Ministry

Aims to eliminate unnecessary blindness by establishing and supporting low-cost, locally managed eye centers to offer the world's poorest communities modern eye care.

Ophth-Opt
⊕ https://vfmat.ch/58f6

Christian Health Association of Ghana (CHAG)
Provides healthcare to the most vulnerable and underprivileged population groups in Ghana, particularly in remote areas, through its network of health facilities and health training institutions, based in Christian ministry.
General, Logist-Op, MF Med, Psych, Pub Health
⊕ https://vfmat.ch/f5fc

Christian Health Service Corps
Brings Christian doctors, health professionals, and health educators committed to serving the poor to places that otherwise have little or no access to healthcare.
Anesth, Dent-OMFS, General, Medicine, Peds, Surg
⊕ https://vfmat.ch/da57

Christian Medical & Dental Associations
Based in Christian ministry, deploys medical and dental teams to underserved communities to provide vital healthcare.
Anesth, Dent-OMFS, ER Med, General, Medicine, OB-GYN, Ophth-Opt, Peds, Pub Health, Radiol, Rehab, Surg
⊕ https://vfmat.ch/921c

Columbia Vagelos College of Physicians and Surgeons Programs in Global Health
Harnesses the expertise of the medical school to improve health worldwide by training global health leaders, building capacity through interdisciplinary education and training programs, and addressing unmet health needs through research and application.
CV Med, Derm, Genetics, Heme-Onc, Infect Dis, Medicine, OB-GYN, Ophth-Opt, Peds, Psych, Pub Health, Pulm-Critic, Surg
⊕ https://vfmat.ch/a9e5

Core Group
Aims to improve and expand community health practices for underserved populations, especially women and children, through collaborative action and learning.
General, Infect Dis, MF Med, Medicine, OB-GYN, Peds, Pub Health
⊕ https://vfmat.ch/9de3

COVID-19 Clinical Research Coalition
Advocates and collaborates for the advancement of COVID-19 research driven by the needs of low-resource settings, and works for equitable access to solutions to the pandemic.
All-Immu, Infect-Dis, MF Med, Path, Pub Health
⊕ https://vfmat.ch/d1f4

Cross Catholic Outreach
Mobilizes the global Catholic Church to transform impoverished communities through the provision of food, water, housing, education, orphan support, medical care, microenterprise, and disaster relief.
All-Immu, General, Nutr, OB-GYN, Rehab
⊕ https://vfmat.ch/22f4

CURE
Operates charitable hospitals and programs in underserved countries worldwide, where patients receive surgical treatment, based in Christian ministry.
Anesth, Neurosurg, Ortho, Ped Surg, Peds, Rehab, Surg
⊕ https://vfmat.ch/aa16

DEAR Foundation, The
Provides support for people in need, particularly women and children, by supporting humanitarian projects administered by NGOs, primarily in the areas of health and education.
Dent-OMFS, OB-GYN
⊕ https://vfmat.ch/a747

Dental Helping Hands
Provides dental health services to underserved communities in developing countries.
Dent-OMFS
⊕ https://vfmat.ch/7ba5

Diabetes Youth Care
Provides education and medical support to encourage personal growth, knowledge acquisition, and independence.
Endo, General
⊕ https://vfmat.ch/3291

Direct Relief
Improves the health and lives of people affected by poverty or emergency situations by mobilizing and providing essential medical resources needed for their care.
ER Med, Logist-Op
⊕ https://vfmat.ch/58e5

Divine Mother and Child Foundation - DMAC
Offers a community in which all mothers have access to skilled attendance before and during pregnancy, childbirth, and postpartum, and provides preventive health education, affordable quality healthcare services, and protection from all forms of violence.
General, Infect Dis, MF Med, OB-GYN
⊕ https://vfmat.ch/6572

DKT INTERNATIONAL INC
Seeks to provide couples with affordable and safe options for family planning and HIV/AIDS prevention through dynamic social marketing.
General, Surg
⊕ https://vfmat.ch/b3a7

Doctors for Africa/Ärzte für Afrika
Seeks to support the medical care system in West African Ghana and improve the desperately needed urological care.
Urol
⊕ https://vfmat.ch/deb6

Duke University: Global Health Institute
Sparks innovation in global health research and education, and brings together knowledge and resources to address the most important global health issues of our time.
All-Immu, Infect Dis, MF Med, OB-GYN, Pub Health
⊕ https://vfmat.ch/c4cd

Emofra Africa
Provides children affected by pediatric cancer with access to affordable quality healthcare regardless of their social/economic status.
Heme-Onc, Ped Surg, Peds
⊕ https://vfmat.ch/923f

Engage Now Africa
Works to heal, rescue, and lift vulnerable individuals, families and communities of Africa out of extreme poverty and into self-reliance.
General, Ophth-Opt, Peds, Pub Health
⊕ https://vfmat.ch/16cd

Episcopal Relief & Development
Provides relief in times of disaster and promotes sustainable development by identifying and addressing the root causes of suffering.
Infect Dis, MF Med, Neonat, Nutr, Peds
⊕ https://vfmat.ch/7cfa

eRanger
Provides sustainable solutions to transportation and medical provision such as ambulances and mobile clinics in developing countries.
ER Med, General, Logist-Op
⊕ https://vfmat.ch/4c18

Eugène Gasana Jr. Foundation
Provides the opportunity for compassionate and quality cancer care for children in developing nations.
Anesth, Heme-Onc, Ped Surg, Peds
⊕ https://vfmat.ch/27cb

Evidence Project, The
Improves family-planning policies, programs, and practices through the strategic generation, translation, and use of evidence.

General, MF Med
⊕ https://vfmat.ch/f9e7

Eye Foundation of America
Works toward a world without childhood blindness.
Ophth-Opt
⊕ https://vfmat.ch/a7eb

Eyes for the World
Aims to create awareness to prevent blindness and an opportunity for every person with treatable blindness to see a doctor.
Ophth-Opt
⊕ https://vfmat.ch/83c9

Fondation d'Harcourt
Promotes national and international projects and partnerships in the fields of mental health and psychosocial support; provides grants to organizations with specific expertise in mental health or psychosocial support to implement projects; and provides direct services.
Psych, Pub Health
⊕ https://vfmat.ch/4a8a

Foundation For International Education In Neurological Surgery (FIENS), The
Provides hands-on training and education to neurosurgeons around the world.
Neuro, Neurosurg, Surg
⊕ https://vfmat.ch/bab8

Foundation for International Urogynecological Assistance (FIUGA)
Supports urogynecological education, research, and care around the world.
OB-GYN, Pub Health, Urol
⊕ https://vfmat.ch/f95a

Foundation for Special Surgery
Provides high-quality, complex surgical care by increasing surgical expertise in Africa through the participation of surgeons across various specialties to provide premium care and skills transfer/education to benefit patients.
Anesth, CT Surg, ENT, Endo, Neurosurg, Plast, Surg, Urol
⊕ https://vfmat.ch/53db

Foundation Human Nature (FHN)
Helps marginalized communities by providing technical, human, and financial resources to sustainably strengthen primary healthcare and public health in Ecuador, Ghana, and Nepal.
ER Med, General, Infect Dis, OB-GYN, Peds, Pub Health
⊕ https://vfmat.ch/6e8c

Foundation of Orthopedics and Complex Spine (FOCOS)
Provides access to optimum orthopedic care to improve the quality of life in Ghana and other countries.
Ortho, Radiol, Rehab
⊕ https://vfmat.ch/c5ef

Ghana Association For Medical Aid (GAMA)
Provides services that promote a healthier lifestyle in the Ghanaian community.
Dent-OMFS, General, Geri, Pub Health
⊕ https://vfmat.ch/9888

Ghana Cleft Foundation
Provides support for cleft lip and palate services in Ghana and the West African sub-region through awareness creation, advocacy, resource mobilization, service provision, capacity building, and research.
Dent-OMFS, ENT
⊕ https://vfmat.ch/b4fa

Ghana Heart Foundation
Saves lives and improves health by informing the public about diseases of the heart and circulation, assisting people with cardiovascular disease, funding cardiovascular research, and training health workers involved in cardiovascular care.
CT Surg, CV Med
⊕ https://vfmat.ch/be6c

Ghana Hernia Society
Reduces the burden of disease from an inguinal hernia in Ghana through increasing access to high-quality care.
General, Rehab, Surg
⊕ https://vfmat.ch/2e83

Ghana Medical Relief
Collaborates with hospitals, churches, and organizations in the United States to provide supplies, medical equipment, and medical missions based on preventative healthcare and education.
Dent-OMFS, General, Logist-Op, OB-GYN, Ophth-Opt, Peds, Urol
⊕ https://vfmat.ch/ef56

Ghana Prostate Cancer Diagnostic Charity
Raises awareness of prostate cancer through education and seminars, and encourages wider recognition of the disease and swifter action in seeking medical treatment. Also, funds the acquisition of state-of-the-art equipment for early detection.
Logist-Op, Pub Health, Urol
⊕ https://vfmat.ch/9627

Ghana, W. Africa Medical Mission
Provides medical care to the outlying areas of Accra, Ghana.
General, Peds, Pub Health
⊕ https://vfmat.ch/a156

GHASPA
Advocates for professionalism and competency within the sterile processing industry in Ghana and Africa.
Logist-Op, Pub Health
⊕ https://vfmat.ch/ee43

Gift of Life International
Provides lifesaving cardiac treatment to children in developing countries while developing sustainable pediatric cardiac programs by implementing screening, surgical, and training missions.
Anesth, CT Surg, CV Med, Crit-Care, Ped Surg, Peds, Pulm-Critic
⊕ https://vfmat.ch/f2f9

Global Alliance to Prevent Prematurity And Stillbirth (GAPPS)
Seeks to improve birth outcomes worldwide by reducing the burden of premature birth and stillbirth.
All-Immu, Infect Dis, MF Med, Neonat, Neonat, OB-GYN
⊕ https://vfmat.ch/3f74

Global Blood Fund
Delivers grants, equipment, and training to over 50 countries in Africa, Asia, Eastern Europe, the Middle East, Latin America and the Caribbean.
Pub Health
⊕ https://vfmat.ch/6377

Global Brigades
Aims to inspire, mobilize, and collaborate with communities to implement their own healthcare and economic goals.
Dent-OMFS, General, Medicine, OB-GYN, Peds
⊕ https://vfmat.ch/78b2

Global Brigades Michigan State University
Aims to empower volunteers and under-resourced communities to resolve global health and economic disparities and inspire all involved to work collaboratively towards an equal world.
Dent-OMFS, General
⊕ https://vfmat.ch/dc9d

Global Emergency Care Skills
Aims to provide high-quality emergency medical training to healthcare professionals in countries where emergency medicine is a developing specialty.
ER Med
⊕ https://vfmat.ch/1827

Global Ministries – The United Methodist Church
As the worldwide mission and development agency of The United Methodist Church, Global Ministries works with more than 300 hospitals and clinics around

the world through its Global Health Unit.

Anesth, CT Surg, CV Med, Crit-Care, Dent-OMFS, Derm, ER Med, GI, General, Infect Dis, Logist-Op, MF Med, Medicine, Neonat, Nephro, Nutr, OB-GYN, Ophth-Opt, Ortho, Palliative, Peds, Pod, Psych, Pub Health, Rehab, Rheum, Surg, Urol
* https://vfmat.ch/1723

Global Oncology (GO)
Brings the best in cancer care to underserved patients around the world and collaborates across geographic, professional, and academic borders to improve cancer care, research, and education.

Heme-Onc, Path, Rad-Onc
* https://vfmat.ch/fcb8

Global Partnership for Zero Leprosy
Facilitates alignment of the leprosy community and accelerates effective collaborative action toward the goal of zero leprosy.

Infect Dis
* https://vfmat.ch/ec7b

Global Vision 2020
Provides prescription eyeglasses to people who live in parts of the world lacking necessary infrastructure for obtaining affordable corrective eyewear.

Logist-Op, Ophth-Opt
* https://vfmat.ch/7373

Globus Relief
Aims to improve the delivery of healthcare worldwide by gathering, processing, and distributing surplus medical supplies to charities at home and abroad.

Logist-Op
* https://vfmat.ch/a2b7

Grassroot Soccer
Leverages the power of soccer to educate, inspire, and mobilize at-risk youth in developing countries to overcome their greatest health challenges, live healthier and more productive lives, and be agents for change in their communities.

Infect Dis
* https://vfmat.ch/3521

Great Faith Vision
Partners with like-minded organizations to bring physical and spiritual sight to the communities served, inspired by the Christian faith.

Ophth-Opt
* https://vfmat.ch/21e2

Gye Nyame Mobile Clinic
Delivers professional psychiatric services and surgical treatments to children and adults in the Western and Ashanti regions of Ghana.

Ped Surg, Peds, Psych
* https://vfmat.ch/fa8c

HCDP GHANA
Seeks to partner and collaborate with local and international communities to empower community development based on self-determination needs and developmental agendas.

General, Surg
* https://vfmat.ch/1cca

Health & Development International (HDI)
Aims to prevent obstetric fistula and deaths from obstructed labor, preventing postpartum hemorrhage, and eradicating Guinea worm disease and lymphatic filariasis in Africa and elsewhere. Goal is to advance world public health, human dignity, and socioeconomics.

Infect Dis, OB-GYN
* https://vfmat.ch/25cd

Health Volunteers Overseas (HVO)
Improves the availability and quality of healthcare through the education, training, and professional development of the health workforce in resource-scarce countries.

All-Immu, Anesth, CV Med, Dent-OMFS, Derm, ENT, ER Med, Endo, GI, Heme-Onc, Infect Dis, Medicine, Medicine, Nephro, Neuro, OB-GYN, Ophth-Opt, Ortho, Peds, Plast, Psych, Pulm-Critic, Rehab, Rheum, Surg
* https://vfmat.ch/42b2

Healthcare Relief (Health for Africa)
Works toward relief of poverty and sickness, supporting causes including healthcare services, healthy campaigns for those in poverty, and research.

Logist-Op, Pub Health
* https://vfmat.ch/da5a

Hear the World Foundation
Advocates worldwide for equal opportunities and improved quality of life for people in need with hearing loss.

ENT, Peds
* https://vfmat.ch/122c

Heart to Heart International
Strengthens communities through improving health access, providing humanitarian development, and administering crisis relief worldwide. Engages volunteers, collaborates with partners, and deploys resources to achieve this mission.

Anesth, ER Med, General, Logist-Op, Medicine, Path, Path, Peds, Psych, Pub Health, Surg
* https://vfmat.ch/aacb

Heineman Medical Outreach
Provides medical and educational assistance globally to promote sustainable healthcare and enhanced living standards in underserved communities through the International Medical Outreach (IMO) program, a collaborative partnership between Heineman Medical Outreach and Atrium Health.

Anesth, CT Surg, CV Med, ER Med, General, Heme-Onc, Logist-Op, Medicine, Neonat, OB-GYN, Ped Surg, Peds, Surg, Vasc Surg
* https://vfmat.ch/389b

Help Is On The Way Ministries
Provides physical, spiritual, infrastructure, and financial help to developing areas of the world.

Ophth-Opt
* https://vfmat.ch/6eac

Helping Hands Medical Missions
Delivers compassionate healthcare by hosting medical missions and treating patients in underserved communities around the world, based in Christian ministry.

Anesth, Dent-OMFS, ER Med, General, OB-GYN, Ophth-Opt, Surg
* https://vfmat.ch/8efd

Himalayan Cataract Project
Works to cure needless blindness with the highest quality care at the lowest cost.

Anesth, Ophth-Opt, Surg
* https://vfmat.ch/3b3d

Hope and Healing International
Gives hope and healing to children and families trapped by poverty and disability.

General, Nutr, Ophth-Opt, Peds, Rehab
* https://vfmat.ch/c638

Hope Walks
Frees children, families, and communities from the burden of clubfoot, inspired by the Christian faith.

Ortho, Ped Surg, Peds, Rehab
* https://vfmat.ch/f6d4

HopeXchange Medical Centers
Provides innovative, high-quality, and cost-effective patient care, research, medical education, and service to communities through the collaboration of local and international expertise.

General, Heme-Onc, MF Med, Ophth-Opt, Peds
* https://vfmat.ch/3881

Hospice Africa
Aims to provide a holistic and culturally sensitive palliative care service through accurate treatment of pain.

Palliative
* https://vfmat.ch/9f86

Humanitas

Provides long-term, professional support to individuals in areas of devastating poverty around the world by building schools, treating illness, and creating lasting families for children without a home.

ER Med, General, Pub Health

⊕ https://vfmat.ch/5b5a

Humanity First

Provides aid and assistance to those in need, offering sustainable development solutions to society while providing and empowering local communities with the resources to help themselves.

ER Med, General, MF Med, Ophth-Opt

⊕ https://vfmat.ch/13cc

Hunger Project, The

Aims to end hunger and poverty by pioneering sustainable, grassroots, women-centered strategies and advocating for their widespread adoption in countries throughout the world.

Infect Dis, Nutr, OB-GYN, Pub Health

⊕ https://vfmat.ch/3a49

Icahn School of Medicine at Mount Sinai Arnhold Institute for Global Health

Specializes in global health systems and implementation research, working toward a world in which vulnerable people in every community have access to healthcare.

CV Med, Endo, General, Infect Dis, Logist-Op, MF Med, Medicine, Neonat, OB-GYN, Ophth-Opt, Peds, Plast, Pub Health

⊕ https://vfmat.ch/a327

IHSAN Foundation for West Africa

Seeks to improve the social and economic lives of the people of West Africa through educational, humanitarian, and healthcare projects.

Dent-OMFS, ER Med, General, Infect Dis

⊕ https://vfmat.ch/c719

Institute for Healthcare Improvement (IHI)

Aims to improve health and healthcare worldwide by working with health professionals to strengthen systems.

Crit-Care, Infect Dis, MF Med, Medicine, Neonat, OB-GYN, Pub Health

⊕ https://vfmat.ch/ecae

Inter Care Medical and for Africa

Provides targeted medical aid to rural health units in some of the poorest parts of Africa.

Logist-Op

⊕ https://vfmat.ch/64fb

International Agency for the Prevention of Blindness (IAPB), The

Leads international efforts in blindness-prevention activities, works toward a world where no one is needlessly visually impaired, and ensures that everyone has access to the best possible standard of eye health.

Infect Dis, Ophth-Opt, Pub Health

⊕ https://vfmat.ch/87a2

International Council of Ophthalmology

Works with ophthalmologic societies and others to enhance ophthalmic education and improve access to the highest-quality eye care in order to preserve and restore vision for people of the world.

Ophth-Opt

⊕ https://vfmat.ch/ffd2

International Eye Foundation (IEF)

Eliminates preventable and treatable blindness by making quality sustainable eye care services accessible and affordable worldwide.

Infect Dis, Logist-Op, Ophth-Opt

⊕ https://vfmat.ch/e839

International Federation of Gynecology and Obstetrics (FIGO)

Implements global projects on specific women's health issues.

MF Med, Medicine, Neonat, OB-GYN, Surg, Urol

⊕ https://vfmat.ch/c4b4

International Federation of Red Cross and Red Crescent Societies (IFRC)

Coordinates and directs international assistance following natural and manmade disasters in nonconflict situations through the world's largest humanitarian and development network. Provides disaster-preparedness programs, healthcare activities, and promotes humanitarian values.

ER Med, General, Infect Dis, Nutr

⊕ https://vfmat.ch/b4ee

International Health & Development Network (IHDN)

Seeks to develop effective and sustainable primary healthcare programs in small towns and villages in developing countries.

ER Med, General, Infect Dis, Surg

⊕ https://vfmat.ch/aff9

International Organization for Migration (IOM) – The UN Migration Agency

Promotes evidence-informed policies and holistic, preventive, and curative health programs that are beneficial, accessible, and equitable for vulnerable migrants.

General, Infect Dis, OB-GYN

⊕ https://vfmat.ch/621a

International Pediatric Nephrology Association (IPNA)

Leads global efforts to successfully address the care for all children with kidney disease through advocacy, education, and training.

Medicine, Nephro, Peds

⊕ https://vfmat.ch/b59d

International Planned Parenthood Federation (IPPF)

Leads a locally owned, globally connected civil society movement that provides and enables services and champions sexual and reproductive health and rights for all, especially the underserved.

Infect Dis, MF Med, OB-GYN

⊕ https://vfmat.ch/dc97

International Surgical Health Initiative (ISHI)

Provides free surgical care to underserved communities worldwide, regardless of race, religion, politics, geography, or financial considerations.

Anesth, ER Med, Logist-Op, Ped Surg, Surg, Urol

⊕ https://vfmat.ch/2374

International Trachoma Initiative (iTi)

Works toward a world free from trachoma, a preventable cause of blindness, and provides comprehensive support to national ministries of health and governmental and nongovernmental organizations to implement a comprehensive approach to fight trachoma.

Infect Dis, Ophth-Opt

⊕ https://vfmat.ch/3278

InterSurgeon

Fosters collaborative partnerships in the field of global surgery that will advance clinical care, teaching, training, research, and the provision and maintenance of medical equipment.

ENT, Neurosurg, Ortho, Ped Surg, Plast, Surg, Urol

⊕ https://vfmat.ch/6f8a

IntraHealth International

Improves the performance of health workers and strengthens the systems in which they work.

CV Med, Endo, General, Infect Dis, MF Med, Neonat, Nutr, OB-GYN

⊕ https://vfmat.ch/ddc8

Ipas

Focuses efforts on women and girls who want contraception or abortion, and builds programs around their needs and how best to support them.

OB-GYN

⊕ https://vfmat.ch/8e39

IVUmed

Aims to make quality urological care available worldwide by providing medical and surgical education for physicians and nurses, and treatment for thousands of children and adults.

Anesth, OB-GYN, Ped Surg, Surg, Urol
⊕ https://vfmat.ch/e619

Izumi Foundation
Develops and supports programs that improve health and healthcare in neglected regions of Africa and Latin America.

⊕ https://vfmat.ch/f29a

Jachie Eye Hospital
Seeks to provide first-class treatment of eye conditions to all patients regardless of color or creed.
Ophth-Opt
⊕ https://vfmat.ch/b614

JDC
Oversees and delivers comprehensive spine, heart, and cancer services in Ethiopia and beyond.
Ortho, Rehab, Surg
⊕ https://vfmat.ch/d85e

Jhpiego
Creates and delivers transformative healthcare solutions that save lives, in partnership with national governments, health experts, and local communities.
General, Infect Dis, OB-GYN, Surg
⊕ https://vfmat.ch/45b8

John Snow, Inc. (JSI)
Aims to improve the health and well-being of underserved and vulnerable people and communities throughout the world.
General, Infect Dis, Logist-Op, MF Med, OB-GYN, Peds, Psych, Pub Health
⊕ https://vfmat.ch/ba78

Johns Hopkins Center for Communication Programs
Believes in the power of communication to save lives by empowering people to adopt healthy behaviors for themselves, their families, and their communities.
General, Infect Dis, Logist-Op, OB-GYN, Pub Health
⊕ https://vfmat.ch/1bf9

Johns Hopkins Center for Global Health
Facilitates and focuses the extensive expertise and resources of the Johns Hopkins institutions, together with global collaborators, to effectively address and ameliorate the world's most pressing health issues.
General, Genetics, Logist-Op, MF Med, Peds, Psych, Pub Health, Pulm-Critic
⊕ https://vfmat.ch/54ce

Kaya Responsible Travel
Promotes sustainable social, environmental, and economic development, empowers communities, and cultivates educated, compassionate global citizens through responsible travel.
All-Immu, Crit-Care, Dent-OMFS, ER Med, General, Geri, Infect Dis, MF Med, Medicine, Nutr, OB-GYN, Peds, Psych, Pub Health, Rehab
⊕ https://vfmat.ch/b2cf

Kids Care Everywhere
Seeks to empower physicians in under-resourced environments with multimedia, state-of-the-art medical software, and to inspire young professionals to become future global healthcare leaders.
Logist-Op, Ped Surg, Peds
⊕ https://vfmat.ch/bc23

Kind Cuts for Kids
Aims to improve medical services for children in developing countries through education, demonstration, and skills transfer to local healthcare professionals.
Anesth, Medicine, Ped Surg, Surg
⊕ https://vfmat.ch/e3d7

King's Village Ghana, The
Provides healthcare, education, and community development to the country's poorest communities.
General, MF Med, Nutr, OB-GYN
⊕ https://vfmat.ch/c4a8

Korle-Bu Neuroscience Foundation
Committed to providing medical support for brain and spinal injuries and disease to the people of Ghana and West Africa.
Anesth, Logist-Op, Neuro, Neurosurg, Rehab
⊕ https://vfmat.ch/6695

Kybele Incorporated
Aims to create healthcare partnerships across borders to improve childbirth safety.
Anesth, Neonat, OB-GYN, Pub Health
⊕ https://vfmat.ch/5fc9

Le Mete Ghana
Promotes health and provides direct medical assistance to needy and vulnerable groups, such as children and women, while supporting the education of needy children and young health professionals.
Surg, Urol
⊕ https://vfmat.ch/caa1

Less Privileged Ghana Foundation
Aims to support women and youth in underprivileged areas of Ghana by providing education and health programs, while also helping individuals and communities develop vocational and entrepreneurial skills.
ENT, Ophth-Opt
⊕ https://vfmat.ch/4de7

Life for a Child
Supports the provision of the best possible healthcare, given local circumstances, to all children and youth with diabetes in less-resourced countries, through the strengthening of existing diabetes services.
Endo, Medicine, Peds
⊕ https://vfmat.ch/d712

Limbs International
Engages communities and transforms lives through affordable, sustainable prosthetic solutions and rehabilitation services in developing countries.
Logist-Op, Ortho, Pod, Rehab
⊕ https://vfmat.ch/dc84

Little Big Souls
Provides necessary support to premature and sick babies in less privileged parts of Africa through equipment donation, medical training, parental support, emergency transportation, and advocacy.
ER Med, Logist-Op, Neonat, Peds
⊕ https://vfmat.ch/2f43

Luke Society Missions Ghana
Provides medical care for the sick and comfort for the dying and, when appropriate, helps initiate economic development projects to assist people in providing for their families.
General, OB-GYN, Ophth-Opt, Peds
⊕ https://vfmat.ch/d752

LynnCare Foundation
Channels resources in support of health, education, and sanitation across Ghana.
General, Ophth-Opt, Pub Health
⊕ https://vfmat.ch/48eb

Making A Difference Foundation
Sponsors and organizes medical missions for medical providers to provide care to underserved communities around the world.
CV Med, Dent-OMFS, ER Med, General, Infect Dis, Logist-Op, MF Med, Neonat, Nutr, OB-GYN, Ophth-Opt, Ortho, Pub Health, Pulm-Critic, Rehab, Surg
⊕ https://vfmat.ch/5556

Management Sciences for Health (MSH)
Works with countries and communities to save lives and improve the health of the world's poorest and most vulnerable people by building strong, resilient, sustainable health systems.
Infect Dis, Logist-Op, Pub Health
⊕ https://vfmat.ch/6aa2

MAP International
Provides medicines and health supplies to those in need around the world so they might experience life to the fullest.
Logist-Op
🌐 https://vfmat.ch/deed

Marie Stopes International
Provides the contraception and safe abortion services that enable women all over the world to choose their own futures.
Infect Dis, MF Med, Neonat, OB-GYN, Pub Health
🌐 https://vfmat.ch/9525

Massachusetts General Hospital Global Surgery Initiative
Aims to improve surgical education and access to advanced surgical care in resource-limited settings around the world by performing surgical operations as visitors, training local surgeons, and sharing medical technology through international partnerships across disciplines.
Anesth, Crit-Care, ER Med, Heme-Onc, Peds, Surg
🌐 https://vfmat.ch/31b1

MaterCare International (MCI) (Canada)
Works to improve the lives and health of mothers and babies through programs in healthcare provision, training, research, and advocacy, with the aim to address maternal and perinatal mortality and morbidity in developing countries.
OB-GYN
🌐 https://vfmat.ch/a92e

Maternal Fetal Care International
Helps mothers and children survive and enjoy better health in the poorest regions of the world.
MF Med, Neonat, OB-GYN
🌐 https://vfmat.ch/7e72

Maternal Rights Ghana
Improves maternal and infant/child health and women's reproductive and sexual health, while educating and empowering women to make informed health decisions.
General, MF Med, Neonat, OB-GYN, Peds, Pub Health
🌐 https://vfmat.ch/4b2e

Maternity Foundation
Works to ensure safer childbirth for women and newborns everywhere through innovative mobile health solutions such as the Safe Delivery App, a mobile training tool for skilled birth attendants.
MF Med, OB-GYN, Pub Health
🌐 https://vfmat.ch/ff4f

McGill University Health Centre: Centre for Global Surgery
Works to reduce the impact of injury by advancing surgical care through research and education in resource-limited settings.
ER Med, Logist-Op, Ped Surg, Surg
🌐 https://vfmat.ch/7246

Medical Care Development International (MCD International)
Works to strengthen health systems through innovative, sustainable interventions.
Infect Dis, Logist-Op, OB-GYN, Pub Health
🌐 https://vfmat.ch/dc5c

Medical Care Development International
Works to improve the health of vulnerable populations through integrated, sustainable, and locally driven interventions.
Infect Dis, OB-GYN, Peds, Pub Health
🌐 https://vfmat.ch/da87

Medical Ministry International
Provides compassionate healthcare in areas of need, inspired by the Christian faith.
CT Surg, Dent-OMFS, ENT, General, OB-GYN, Ophth-Opt, Ortho, Plast, Rehab, Surg, Urol, Vasc Surg
🌐 https://vfmat.ch/5da6

Medical Missions Abroad Corp
Sponsors missions that provide healthcare, build houses, and care for children.

General, Logist-Op
🌐 https://vfmat.ch/a8ff

MedSend
Funds qualified healthcare professionals to serve the physical and spiritual needs of people around the world, enabling healthcare providers to work where they have been called.
General
🌐 https://vfmat.ch/661c

MedShare
Aims to improve the quality of life of people, communities, and the planet by sourcing and directly delivering surplus medical supplies and equipment to communities in need around the world.
Logist-Op
🌐 https://vfmat.ch/c8bc

Mercy Without Limits
Educates and empowers women and children by enabling them to have an effective and positive role in constructing a better society.
ER Med
🌐 https://vfmat.ch/c3b6

Methodist Faith Healing Hospital Ankaase
Works to make life whole by delivering holistic quality healthcare in the Ashanti region of Ghana.
CT Surg, ER Med, MF Med, Psych, Pub Health, Surg
🌐 https://vfmat.ch/21e9

Mission Doctors Association
Provides life-saving medical care for the poor and training for local healthcare professionals around the world.
CV Med, Dent-OMFS, General, Logist-Op, Medicine, OB-GYN, Ophth-Opt, Peds, Surg
🌐 https://vfmat.ch/6c18

Mission Regan
Collects supplies, medication, and medical equipment and provides them to those who are in desperate need, both locally and globally.
Logist-Op
🌐 https://vfmat.ch/2bc1

Mission to Heal
Aims to heal underserved people and train local practitioners in the most remote areas of the world through global healthcare missions.
Anesth, Infect Dis, OB-GYN, Surg
🌐 https://vfmat.ch/4718

Mission Vision
Seeks to decrease blindness and other eye-related disabilities, and to increase academic performance and general quality of life.
Ophth-Opt
🌐 https://vfmat.ch/83d8

Missions Medical Relief
Provides free medical care, professional advice, and health-related services to underprivileged communities while networking with other agencies to help fulfill this vision.
CT Surg, Dent-OMFS, ENT, General, Infect Dis, Ophth-Opt, Ped Surg, Peds, Pub Health, Surg
🌐 https://vfmat.ch/2acf

Motech Life-UK
Provides education, training, and healthcare services to the underprivileged people of the West African subcontinent, especially Ghana.
Anesth, Heme-Onc, Infect Dis, Logist-Op, OB-GYN, Ortho, Plast, Rehab, Surg
🌐 https://vfmat.ch/1491

mothers2mothers (m2m)
Employs and trains local women living with HIV as community health workers called Mentor Mothers to support women, children, and adolescents with vital medical services, education, and support.

Infect Dis, MF Med, OB-GYN, Peds, Pub Health
⊕ https://vfmat.ch/6557

MSI Reproductive Choices (Marie Stopes International)
Seeks to deliver quality family planning and reproductive healthcare to women around the world.
MF Med
⊕ https://vfmat.ch/5c82

Multi-Agency International Training and Support (MAITS)
Improves the lives of some of the world's poorest people living with disabilities through better access to quality health and education services and support.
Neuro, Psych, Rehab
⊕ https://vfmat.ch/9dcd

Nazarene Compassionate Ministries
Partners with local churches around the world to clothe, shelter, feed, heal, educate, and live in solidarity with those in need.
General, Infect Dis, OB-GYN
⊕ https://vfmat.ch/6b4d

Nursing Beyond Borders
Provides healthcare and education to children and communities, and focuses as well on disease prevention by providing nurses to serve in orphanages, shelters, schools, and clinics.
Logist-Op, MF Med, Peds
⊕ https://vfmat.ch/71e6

Nyarko Cleft Care
Aims to develop a comprehensive, self-sufficient, accessible, and affordable cleft lip and palate treatment center in Ghana to give hope to people affected by this condition.
Dent-OMFS, ENT, Plast, Surg
⊕ https://vfmat.ch/8aae

Okoa Project, The / Moving Health
Designs motorcycle ambulances, creates jobs, and saves lives one ride at a time.
ER Med, Logist-Op
⊕ https://vfmat.ch/1f6c

Olive Health Community Clinic
Aims to increase access to healthcare in less fortunate communities in Ghana by bringing doctors and healthcare personnel to underserved areas.
General
⊕ https://vfmat.ch/eda5

One World Brigades
Assists international communities with dental care and education.
Dent-OMFS, General
⊕ https://vfmat.ch/7933

Operation Eyesight
Works to eliminate blindness in partnership with governments, hospitals, medical professionals, corporations, and community development teams.
Ophth-Opt, Surg
⊕ https://vfmat.ch/b95d

Operation Eyesight Universal
Aims to prevent blindness, restore sight, and eliminate avoidable blindness.
Ophth-Opt
⊕ https://vfmat.ch/f629

Operation Hernia
Provides high-quality surgery at minimal cost to patients who otherwise would not receive it.
Anesth, Ortho, Surg
⊕ https://vfmat.ch/6e9a

Operation International
Offers medical aid to adults and children suffering from lack of quality healthcare in impoverished countries.
Dent-OMFS, ER Med, Heme-Onc, OB-GYN, Ophth-Opt, Ortho, Ped Surg, Plast, Surg
⊕ https://vfmat.ch/b52a

Operation Smile
Treats patients with cleft lip and cleft palate, and creates solutions that deliver safe surgery to people where it's needed most.
Anesth, Dent-OMFS, ENT, Ped Surg, Plast
⊕ https://vfmat.ch/5c29

Operation Walk
Provides the gift of mobility through life-changing joint replacement surgeries, at no cost for those in need in the U.S. and globally.
Anesth, Ortho, Rehab, Surg
⊕ https://vfmat.ch/bafe

Options
Believes in a world in which women and children can access the high-quality health services they need, without financial burden.
Logist-Op, MF Med, Neonat, OB-GYN
⊕ https://vfmat.ch/3a48

Orbis International
Works to prevent and treat blindness through hands-on training and improved access to quality eye care.
Anesth, Ophth-Opt, Surg
⊕ https://vfmat.ch/f2b2

Otumfuo Osei Tutu II Foundation
Works to improve the quality of life of Ghanaians by enhancing access to quality education, health and sustainable infrastructure, while promoting programs in ICT, tourism and socio-economic empowerment.
Dent-OMFS, General
⊕ https://vfmat.ch/8182

Pact
Works on the ground to improve the lives of those who are challenged by poverty and marginalization, striving for a world in which all people are heard, capable, and vibrant.
Infect Dis, Logist-Op, MF Med, Pub Health
⊕ https://vfmat.ch/9a6c

Palav
Provides support equipment for newborns with breathing difficulties and trains healthcare providers.
Peds
⊕ https://vfmat.ch/86bd

PANAHF – Pan Africa Heart Foundation
Targets primary prevention and specialized treatment of cardiovascular disease.
CV Med, Surg
⊕ https://vfmat.ch/8f25

PATH
Advances health equity through innovation and partnerships so people, communities, and economies can thrive.
All-Immu, CV Med, Endo, Heme-Onc, Infect Dis, MF Med, Neonat, Nutr, OB-GYN, Path, Peds, Pulm-Critic
⊕ https://vfmat.ch/b4db

Penn State College of Medicine: Global Health Center
An interdisciplinary center that provides organization and oversight for the medical center's educational, service, community research, and clinical care activities in global health.
CV Med, General, Pub Health, Surg
⊕ https://vfmat.ch/6f37

Philips Foundation
Aims to reduce healthcare inequality by providing access to quality healthcare for disadvantaged communities.
CV Med, OB-GYN, Ped Surg, Peds, Surg, Urol
⊕ https://vfmat.ch/bacb

PINCC Preventing Cervical Cancer
Seeks to prevent female-specific diseases in developing countries by utilizing low-cost and low-technology methods to create sustainable programs through patient education, medical personnel training, and facility outfitting.

OB-GYN
⊕ https://vfmat.ch/9666

Population Council
Conducts research to address critical health and development issues, helping deliver solutions to improve lives around the world.
Logist-Op, Pub Health
⊕ https://vfmat.ch/1777

Profer Aid International Foundation
Aims to create and share solutions for achieving truly equitable healthcare, with a focus on last-mile delivery of healthcare.
General, OB-GYN
⊕ https://vfmat.ch/ee14

Project Theia
Provides medical and surgical care to the underserved global community in the areas of oculoplastic, reconstructive, orbital, and facial surgery.
Anesth, General, Ophth-Opt, Plast
⊕ https://vfmat.ch/9d5a

Project HEAL
Aims to develop a system to classify hospitals based on their available resources, which emergency medical (ambulance) services can use to transport patients to the appropriate hospital based on their medical needs.
CV Med, Crit-Care, ER Med, Heme-Onc, Logist-Op, Medicine, OB-GYN, Peds
⊕ https://vfmat.ch/15fb

PSI – Population Services International
Aims to improve the health of people in the developing world by focusing on challenges such as a lack of family planning, HIV/AIDS, barriers to maternal health, and the greatest threats to children under the age of 5, including malaria, diarrhea, pneumonia, and malnutrition.
Infect Dis, MF Med, OB-GYN, Peds
⊕ https://vfmat.ch/ffe3

Public Health Initiative Ghana
Seeks to promote public health and its related activities in Ghana and beyond.
Infect Dis, Pub Health
⊕ https://vfmat.ch/9b17

RAD-AID International
Improves and optimizes access to medical imaging and radiology in low-resource regions of the world.
Rad-Onc, Radiol
⊕ https://vfmat.ch/537f

Rare Disease Ghana Initiative
Works to improve the well-being and quality of life of families affected by undiagnosed and rare diseases in Ghana.
Genetics
⊕ https://vfmat.ch/5bd5

Rebecca Foundation, The
Identifies and implements initiatives that support government efforts to improve the lives of Ghanaians, especially women and children.
Infect Dis, Logist-Op, OB-GYN, Pub Health
⊕ https://vfmat.ch/bb27

Relief International
Helps people in fragile settings achieve good health and nutrition by delivering primary healthcare and emergency treatment, and builds local capacity to ensure that communities in vulnerable situations have the access to the quality care they need to live healthy lives.
ER Med, General, MF Med, Neonat, OB-GYN, Peds, Psych
⊕ https://vfmat.ch/1522

RestoringVision
Empowers lives by restoring vision for millions of people in need.
Ophth-Opt
⊕ https://vfmat.ch/e121

Right to Sight and Health
Seeks to reduce the prevalence of blindness and visual impairment, especially among low-income communities in Northern Ghana.
Ophth-Opt
⊕ https://vfmat.ch/7ff1

Rotary Action Group for Family Health & AIDS Prevention (RFHA)
Works to save and improve the lives of children and families who lack access to preventive healthcare and education.
Dent-OMFS, Infect Dis, OB-GYN, Ophth-Opt, Peds
⊕ https://vfmat.ch/6563

Rotary International
Provides service to others, improves lives, and advances world understanding, goodwill, and peace through its fellowship of business, professional, and community leaders.
ER Med, General, Infect Dis, MF Med, OB-GYN
⊕ https://vfmat.ch/8fb5

Rutgers New Jersey Medical School
Seeks to support and promote the global health efforts of the faculty, staff, and students in the areas of education, research, and service through the Rutgers New Jersey Medical School's Office of Global Health.
Anesth, CV Med, Crit-Care, Neurosurg, OB-GYN, Psych
⊕ https://vfmat.ch/8e67

Salvation Army International, The
Seeks to meet human needs through services in education, healthcare, community support, emergency response, and ministry development, inspired by the Christian faith.
Dent-OMFS, Derm, ER Med, Infect Dis, MF Med, Medicine, Nutr, OB-GYN, Ophth-Opt, Palliative, Psych, Rehab, Surg
⊕ https://vfmat.ch/8eb3

Samaritan's Purse International Disaster Relief
Provides spiritual and physical aid to hurting people around the world, such as victims of war, poverty, natural disasters, disease, and famine, based in Christian ministry.
Anesth, CT Surg, Crit-Care, Dent-OMFS, Derm, ENT, ER Med, Endo, GI, General, Heme-Onc, Infect Dis, MF Med, Neonat, Nephro, Neuro, Neurosurg, Nutr, OB-GYN, Ophth-Opt, Ortho, Path, Ped Surg, Peds, Plast, Psych, Pulm-Critic, Radiol, Rehab, Rheum, Surg, Urol, Vasc Surg
⊕ https://vfmat.ch/87e3

Save A Child's Heart
Provides lifesaving cardiac treatment to children in developing countries, and trains healthcare professionals from these countries to deliver quality care in their communities.
CT Surg, CV Med, Crit-Care, Ped Surg, Peds
⊕ https://vfmat.ch/1bef

Second Chance Smile Global Dental Outreach Foundation
Provides acute dental care with regular follow-ups and training for local oral health educators, and advocates for sustainable government oral health policy.
Dent-OMFS, Infect Dis, Logist-Op
⊕ https://vfmat.ch/daaf

SEE International
Provides sustainable medical, surgical, and educational services through volunteer ophthalmic surgeons, with the objectives of restoring sight and preventing blindness to disadvantaged individuals worldwide.
Ophth-Opt, Surg
⊕ https://vfmat.ch/6e1b

Sightsavers
Works with partners in developing countries to help eliminate avoidable blindness and advocates for equal opportunity for the disabled.
Infect Dis, Ophth-Opt, Surg
⊕ https://vfmat.ch/aa52

SIGN Fracture Care International
Builds orthopedic capacity around the world and provides the injured poor access

to fracture surgery by donating orthopedic education and implant systems to surgeons in developing countries.
Ortho, Rehab, Surg
⊕ https://vfmat.ch/123d

Simavi
Strives for a world in which all women and girls are socially and economically empowered and pursue their rights to live a healthy life, free from discrimination, coercion, and violence.
MF Med, OB-GYN
⊕ https://vfmat.ch/b57b

SINA Health
Aims to improve the health and educational status of the population in low- and middle-income countries.
General, Logist-Op
⊕ https://vfmat.ch/9ad3

Sisters of the Immaculate Heart of Mary, Mother of Christ
Based in Chrisitan ministry, seeks to motivate people, especially the poor and the less privileged, to live venerable and dignified lives through credibility-structured programs, education, various medical and humanitarian services, along with self-realization and self-empowerment opportunities.
Infect Dis, Logist-Op, Nutr, Pub Health
⊕ https://vfmat.ch/5774

Smile Train, Inc.
Treats children with cleft lip through a sustainable and local model that supports surgery and other forms of essential care.
Logist-Op, Pub Health
⊕ https://vfmat.ch/822c

SOS Children's Villages International
Supports children through alternative care and family strengthening.
ER Med, Peds
⊕ https://vfmat.ch/aca1

Squads Abroad
Empowers volunteers and under-resourced communities to resolve global health, education, and economic disparities and inspire all involved to collaboratively work towards an equal world.
General
⊕ https://vfmat.ch/93e3

Sri Sathya Sai International Organization
Inspired by spiritual teachings, carries out efforts in global healthcare, education, humanitarian relief, and youth engagement.
Dent-OMFS, General, Logist-Op, Nutr, Ophth-Opt, Pub Health
⊕ https://vfmat.ch/9bda

St. John of God Hospital Ghana
Works to improve the health and living conditions of young orthopedic patients.
Ortho
⊕ https://vfmat.ch/eabd

St. Martin De Porres Hospital- Agomanya
Provides and sustains healthcare services for the poor, neglected, and marginalized segments of society.
Derm, General, OB-GYN, Peds, Surg
⊕ https://vfmat.ch/3593

Sustainable Kidney Care Foundation (SKCF)
Works to provide treatment for kidney injury where none exists, and aims to reduce mortality from treatable acute kidney injury (AKI).
Infect Dis, Medicine, Nephro
⊕ https://vfmat.ch/1926

Sustainable Medical Missions
Trains and supports Indigenous healthcare and faith leaders in underdeveloped communities to treat neglected tropical diseases (NTDs) and other endemic conditions affecting the poorest community members, by pairing faith-based solutions with best practices.

Infect Dis, Pub Health
⊕ https://vfmat.ch/9165

SVG Africa (Salormey Volunteers Group)
Provides community development information and services in the areas of health, education, environment, and ICTs.
General, Pub Health, Surg
⊕ https://vfmat.ch/e85a

Swiss Tropical and Public Health Institute
Contributes to the improvement of the health of populations internationally, nationally, and locally through excellence in research, education, and services.
Infect Dis, Pub Health
⊕ https://vfmat.ch/2ee4

Task Force for Global Health, The
Consists of programs and focus areas that cover a range of global health issues including neglected tropical diseases, infectious diseases, vaccines, field epidemiology, public health informatics, health workforce development, and global health ethics.
Infect Dis, Logist-Op, Medicine, Ophth-Opt, Peds
⊕ https://vfmat.ch/714c

Thyroid Ghana Foundation
Creates opportunities and awareness for early detection of thyroid problems, and supports thyroid research and institutions involved in thyroid disease management and affordable treatment.
Endo
⊕ https://vfmat.ch/4614

Tilganga Institute of Ophthalmology (TIO)
Supports the prevention and control of blindness in Nepal and the region.
Ophth-Opt
⊕ https://vfmat.ch/ff5d

Together for Ghana
Promotes public health in the Afram Plains North District of Ghana's Eastern Region.
General, Logist-Op, Pub Health
⊕ https://vfmat.ch/5af4

Transplant Links Community (TLC)
Provides hands-on training in kidney transplantation for surgeons, doctors, and nurses in low- and middle-income countries.
Nephro, Surg, Urol
⊕ https://vfmat.ch/bb46

TwinEpidemic
Works to quell the epidemic of diabetes and heart disease among ethnic communities worldwide.
CV Med, Endo, General, Logist-Op, Pub Health
⊕ https://vfmat.ch/e859

U.S. President's Malaria Initiative (PMI)
Supports low-income countries to help control and eliminate malaria through cost-effective, lifesaving malaria interventions.
Infect Dis, MF Med, OB-GYN
⊕ https://vfmat.ch/dc8b

Union for International Cancer Control (UICC)
Unites and supports the cancer community to reduce the global cancer burden, promote greater equity, and ensure that cancer control continues to be a priority in the world health and development agenda.
Heme-Onc, Pub Health
⊕ https://vfmat.ch/88b1

Unite 4 Humanity
Aims to provide emergency aid and support for Muslim communities across the world.
General, Nutr, OB-GYN, Ophth-Opt, Plast, Psych, Rehab
⊕ https://vfmat.ch/fbe7

Unite for Sight

Supports eye clinics worldwide by investing human and financial resources to eliminate patient barriers to eye care. Applies best practices in eye care, public health, volunteerism, and social entrepreneurship to achieve our goal of high-quality eye care for all.

Ophth-Opt, Surg

⊕ https://vfmat.ch/4fe7

United Nations Children's Fund (UNICEF)

Works in over 190 countries and territories to save children's lives, defend their rights, and help them fulfill their potential, from early childhood through adolescence.

All-Immu, Infect Dis, MF Med, Neonat, Nutr, OB-GYN, Ped Surg, Peds, Pub Health

⊕ https://vfmat.ch/42d7

United Nations Development Programme (UNDP)

Helps countries achieve the simultaneous eradication of extreme poverty and significant reduction of inequalities and exclusion using a sustainable human development approach.

Infect Dis, Logist-Op, Pub Health

⊕ https://vfmat.ch/935c

United Nations High Commissioner for Refugees (UNHCR)

Safeguards the rights and well-being of people who have been forced to flee, ensuring that everybody has the right to seek asylum and find safe refuge in another country, with the goal of seeking lasting solutions.

General, MF Med, Medicine, OB-GYN, Peds, Psych, Pub Health

⊕ https://vfmat.ch/6636

United Nations Population Fund (UNFPA)

Supports reproductive healthcare for women and youth in more than 150 countries, focusing on delivering a world in which every pregnancy is wanted, every childbirth is safe, and every young person's potential is fulfilled.

Infect Dis, MF Med, Neonat, OB-GYN, Peds, Pub Health

⊕ https://vfmat.ch/c969

United Service To Africa (USTA)

Aims to support whole-person care to meet the social, emotional, and spiritual needs of communities in Africa.

General, Nephro, Pub Health

⊕ https://vfmat.ch/bbb3

Universal Care for Africa Foundation (UCAF)

Aims to provide access to healthcare services and resources to people in Africa regardless of age, sex, or demographic area.

Infect Dis, OB-GYN

⊕ https://vfmat.ch/d83e

University of California Los Angeles: David Geffen School of Medicine Global Health Program

Catalyzes opportunities to improve health globally by engaging in multi-disciplinary and innovative education programs, research initiatives, and bilateral partnerships that provide opportunities for trainees, faculty, and staff to contribute to sustainable health initiatives and to address health inequities facing the world today.

All-Immu, Infect Dis, Logist-Op, MF Med, Medicine, Neonat, OB-GYN, Ortho, Ped Surg, Peds, Radiol

⊕ https://vfmat.ch/f1a4

University of California San Diego School of Medicine: Global Surgery

Aims to improve access to and maintain the quality of surgical care not only in the U.S. but also around the world—especially for the underserved.

Logist-Op, Ped Surg, Plast, Surg

⊕ https://vfmat.ch/4c9e

University of Colorado: Global Emergency Care Initiative

Strives to sustainably improve emergency care outcomes in low- and middle-income communities worldwide by linking cutting-edge academics with excellent on-the-ground implementation.

ER Med

⊕ https://vfmat.ch/417a

University of Michigan Medical School Global REACH

Aims to facilitate health research, education, and collaboration among Michigan Medicine learners and faculty with our global partners to reduce health disparities for the benefit of communities worldwide.

ENT, General, Ophth-Opt, Peds, Psych, Pub Health, Urol

⊕ https://vfmat.ch/5f19

University of Michigan: Department of Surgery Global Health

Improves the health of patients, populations and communities through excellence in education, patient care, community service, research and technology development, and through leadership activities.

Anesth, Ortho, Surg

⊕ https://vfmat.ch/2fd8

University of Pennsylvania Perelman School of Medicine Center for Global Health

Aims to improve health equity worldwide through enhanced public health awareness and access to care, discovery, and outcomes-based research, and comprehensive educational programs grounded in partnership.

Heme-Onc, Infect Dis, OB-GYN

⊕ https://vfmat.ch/cb57

University of Utah Global Health

Supports local organizations in their quest to improve quality of life in their communities all over the world.

Anesth, CT Surg, CV Med, Crit-Care, Dent-OMFS, ENT, ER Med, Infect Dis, OB-GYN, Ophth-Opt, Ped Surg, Ped Surg, Peds, Plast, Pub Health, Surg, Urol

⊕ https://vfmat.ch/bacd

University of Utah School of Medicine: Center for Global Surgery

Advocates for improved access to surgery worldwide, creates innovative solutions with measurable impact, and trains leaders to solve the most vexing problems in global health.

CT Surg, CV Med, ENT, ER Med, Plast, Surg, Urol

⊕ https://vfmat.ch/7c88

University of Washington: Department of Global Health

Improves health for all through research, education, training, and service, addresses the causes of disease and health inequities at multiple levels, and collaborates with partners to develop and sustain locally led, quality health systems, programs, and policies.

Infect Dis, Logist-Op, Pub Health

⊕ https://vfmat.ch/f543

USAID's Health Research Program

Funds maternal and child health implementation research and translates findings into effective health interventions that can be adapted globally.

Infect Dis, MF Med, OB-GYN, Peds

⊕ https://vfmat.ch/5991

USAID: Deliver Project

Builds a global supply chain to deliver lifesaving health products to people in order to enable countries to provide family planning, protect against malaria, and limit the spread of pandemic threats.

Infect Dis, Logist-Op, MF Med

⊕ https://vfmat.ch/374e

USAID: EQUIP Health

Exists as an effective, efficient response mechanism to achieving global HIV epidemic control by delivering the right intervention at the right place and in the right way.

Infect Dis

⊕ https://vfmat.ch/d76a

USAID: Health Finance and Governance Project

Uses research to implement strategies to help countries develop robust governance systems, increase their domestic resources for health, manage those resources more effectively, and make wise purchasing decisions.

Logist-Op

⊕ https://vfmat.ch/8652

USAID: Health Policy Initiative
Provides field-level programming in health policy development and implementation.
General, Infect Dis, MF Med, OB-GYN, Peds
🌐 https://vfmat.ch/8f84

USAID: Leadership, Management and Governance Project
Improves leadership, management, and governance practices to strengthen health systems and improve health for all, including vulnerable populations worldwide.
Logist-Op
🌐 https://vfmat.ch/d35e

USAID: Maternal and Child Health Integrated Program
Works to improve the health of women and their families, including programs for maternal, newborn, and child health, immunization, family planning, nutrition, malaria, and HIV/AIDS.
All-Immu, General, Infect Dis, MF Med
🌐 https://vfmat.ch/4415

USAID: Maternal and Child Survival Program
Works to prevent child and maternal deaths.
Infect Dis, MF Med, Neonat, OB-GYN, Peds
🌐 https://vfmat.ch/6fcf

Virtue Foundation
Increases awareness, inspires action and renders assistance through healthcare, education, and empowerment initiatives.
Anesth, Crit-Care, Dent-OMFS, ENT, ER Med, Heme-Onc, Logist-Op, Neurosurg, OB-GYN, Ophth-Opt, Ortho, Path, Ped Surg, Peds, Plast, Radiol, Rehab, Surg
🌐 https://vfmat.ch/6481

Vision Aid Overseas
Enables people living in poverty to access affordable glasses and eye care.
Ophth-Opt
🌐 https://vfmat.ch/c695

Vision Care
Restores sight and helps patients get regular treatment at short-term eye camps and long-term base clinics by having doctors, missionaries, volunteers, and sponsors work together.
Ophth-Opt
🌐 https://vfmat.ch/9d7c

Vision for a Nation
Makes eye care accessible and aims to unlock economic growth and human potential in the world's poorest communities.
Ophth-Opt
🌐 https://vfmat.ch/9c2c

Vision for the Poor
Reduces human suffering and improves quality of life through the recovery of sight by building sustainable eye hospitals in developing countries, empowering local eye specialists, funding essential ophthalmic infrastructure, and partnering with like-minded agencies.
Ophth-Opt
🌐 https://vfmat.ch/528e

Vision Outreach International
Advocates for helping the blind in underserved regions of the world and empowers the poor through sight restoration.
Ophth-Opt
🌐 https://vfmat.ch/9721

Vitamin Angels
Helps at-risk populations in need—specifically pregnant women, new mothers, and children under age 5—to gain access to life-changing vitamins and minerals.
General, Nutr
🌐 https://vfmat.ch/7da1

Voices for a Malaria-Free Future
Seeks to expand national movements of private- and public-sector leaders to mobilize political and popular support for malaria control.

Infect Dis, Path
🌐 https://vfmat.ch/4213

Voluntary Service Overseas (VSO)
Works with health workers, communities, and governments to improve health services and rights for women, babies, youth, people with disabilities, and prisoners.
General, MF Med, OB-GYN
🌐 https://vfmat.ch/213d

VOSH (Volunteer Optometric Services to Humanity) International
Facilitates the provision and the sustainability of vision care worldwide for people who can neither afford nor obtain such care.
Ophth-Opt
🌐 https://vfmat.ch/a149

Walkabout Foundation
Provides wheelchairs and rehabilitation in the developing world and funds research to find a cure for paralysis.
Logist-Op, Rehab
🌐 https://vfmat.ch/5582

Watsi
Uses technology to make healthcare a reality for those who might not otherwise be able to afford it.
Pub Health, Surg
🌐 https://vfmat.ch/41a3

West African AIDS Foundation
Provides comprehensive care to those living with HIV, tuberculosis, and related medical conditions, while contributing to the global agenda of ending AIDS by 2030.
Infect Dis, Pub Health
🌐 https://vfmat.ch/eb45

Willing and Abel
Seeks to provide connections between children in developing nations and specialist centers, helping with visas, passports, transportation, and finances.
Anesth, Dent-OMFS, Ped Surg
🌐 https://vfmat.ch/9dc7

Wipe-Away Foundation
Focuses on assisting people with serious health conditions who otherwise would not be able to raise needed funds, and works to ensure a crime-free society and overall well-being of the population.
Heme-Onc, Ophth-Opt, Pub Health, Surg
🌐 https://vfmat.ch/978d

Wisconsin Medical Project
Provides humanitarian aid, including donated medical equipment and supplies, to hospitals and clinics in areas of great need.
Logist-Op
🌐 https://vfmat.ch/ef3b

Women's Health to Wealth (WHW)
Works to engender healthier and empowered women for the progress and development of the Ashanti region of Ghana.
MF Med, Neonat, Peds, Pub Health
🌐 https://vfmat.ch/f9d7

World Child Cancer
Works to improve diagnosis, treatment, and support for children with cancer, and their families, in low- and middle-income parts of the world.
Heme-Onc, Ped Surg, Rad-Onc
🌐 https://vfmat.ch/fbbc

World Council of Optometry
Facilitates the development of optometry worldwide and promotes eye health and vision care through advocacy, education, policy development, and humanitarian outreach.
Ophth-Opt, Pub Health
🌐 https://vfmat.ch/c92e

World Federation of Hemophilia (WFH)

Aims to improve and sustain care for people with inherited bleeding disorders by pursuing long-term relationships with individuals and organizations who share the values of WFH's development model.

Heme-Onc

⊕ https://vfmat.ch/5121

World Health Organization, The (WHO)

The United Nations' agency for health provides leadership on global health matters, shapes the health research agenda, sets norms and standards, articulates evidence-based policy options, provides technical support and monitoring to countries, and assesses health trends.

ER Med, General, Infect Dis, Logist-Op, MF Med, OB-GYN, Peds, Psych, Pub Health

⊕ https://vfmat.ch/c476

World Heart Federation

Leads the global fight against heart disease and stroke, with a focus on low- and middle-income countries.

CV Med, Crit-Care, Heme-Onc, Medicine, Peds

⊕ https://vfmat.ch/ea51

World Hope International

Empowers the poorest individuals around the world so they can become agents of change within their communities, by offering resources and knowledge.

Infect Dis, Logist-Op, MF Med, OB-GYN, Peds

⊕ https://vfmat.ch/a4b8

World Medical Relief

Facilitates the distribution of surplus medical resources where they are needed.

Logist-Op

⊕ https://vfmat.ch/72dc

World Missions Possible

Provides EMS capacity-building, along with medical and vision care, to under-developed and rural areas.

ER Med, General, Heme-Onc, Neonat, Ophth-Opt, Surg

⊕ https://vfmat.ch/d6a5

World Vision International

Works with vulnerable communities around the world to overcome poverty and injustice with child-focused programs in disaster management, health, nutrition, economic development, education, clean water, sanitation, and hygiene.

ER Med, General, Infect Dis, MF Med, Nutr, OB-GYN, Peds

⊕ https://vfmat.ch/2642

Yonkofa Project, The

Aims to build and equip medical clinics in rural Western Ghana, staffed with Ghanaian medical professionals, establishing a sustainable medical care system.

General, Logist-Op, Pub Health

⊕ https://vfmat.ch/5f8e

You & Ghana Foundation

Organizes health outreach programs, builds projects to improve healthcare delivery, and collaborates with other organizations to improve health systems in order to provide quality care for maternal, newborn, and child health.

General, MF Med, Neonat, OB-GYN

⊕ https://vfmat.ch/ef64

Ghana

Healthcare Facilities

37 Military Hospital
Accra, Greater Accra, Ghana
🌐 https://vfmat.ch/1a6f

Abrafi Memorial Hospital
Kumasi, Dichemso, Ashanti, Ghana
🌐 https://vfmat.ch/b215

Accra Psychiatric Hospital
Adabraka, Accra, Greater Accra, Ghana
🌐 https://vfmat.ch/d123

Achimota Hospital
Achimota, Accra, Greater Accra, Ghana
🌐 https://vfmat.ch/7c93

Adabie Hospital
Atonsu – Mamponteng, Ashanti, Ghana
🌐 https://vfmat.ch/4b7f

Adoagire Hospital
Adoagire, Eastern Region, Ghana
🌐 https://vfmat.ch/b23a

Adom Hospital
Akratiebesa, Ashanti, Ghana
🌐 https://vfmat.ch/9e83

Adwoa Boatemaa Memorial Hospital
Korlegonno, Accra, Greater Accra, Ghana
🌐 https://vfmat.ch/5b47

Afenyo Memorial Hospital
Ashaiman Municipal District, Greater Accra, Ghana
🌐 https://vfmat.ch/45e7

Agyakwa Hospital Ltd.
Domeabra, Nkawkaw, Eastern Region, Ghana
🌐 https://vfmat.ch/1c8b

Ahmadiya Mission Hospital
Kaleo, Upper West, Ghana
🌐 https://vfmat.ch/3f2e

Ahmadiya Muslim Mission Hospital
Asokori, Ashanti, Ghana
🌐 https://vfmat.ch/11bd

Ahmadiya Mission Hospital
Kokofu, Ashanti, Ghana
🌐 https://vfmat.ch/65e3

Ahmadiya Muslim Hospital Techiman
Takofiano, Bono East, Ghana
🌐 https://vfmat.ch/23ec

Ahwene Memorial Hospital
Bekwai, Ashanti, Ghana
🌐 https://vfmat.ch/2a6b

Akim Oda Government Hospital
Akim Oda, Eastern, Ghana
🌐 https://vfmat.ch/d58d

Akomaa Memorial Aventist Hospital
Bekwai, Ashanti, Ghana
🌐 https://vfmat.ch/431a

Akuse Government Hospital
Akuse, Eastern, Ghana
🌐 https://vfmat.ch/b176

Amoah Memorial Hospital
Accra, Greater Accra, Ghana
🌐 https://vfmat.ch/1494

AngloGold Ashanti Hospital
Obuasi, Ashanti, Ghana
🌐 https://vfmat.ch/aac3

Arch Bishop Dery Memorial Hospital
Konta-Wa, Upper West, Ghana
🌐 https://vfmat.ch/a29b

Asamankese Government Hospital
Asamankese, Eastern, Ghana
🌐 https://vfmat.ch/d9de

Asare Odei Hospital
East Legon- Accra, Greater Accra, Ghana
🌐 https://vfmat.ch/8b38

Asesewa Government Hospital
Asesewa, Eastern Region, Ghana
🌐 https://vfmat.ch/e7f6

Assemblies of God Hospital Saboba
Saboba, Northern Region, Ghana
🌐 https://vfmat.ch/65f1

Atasomanso Hospital
Atasomanso, Ashanti, Ghana
🌐 https://vfmat.ch/e7f4

Atebubu Government Hospital
Atebubu, Bono East, Ghana
🌐 https://vfmat.ch/1121

Atibie Government Hospital
Atibie, Eastern, Ghana
🌐 https://vfmat.ch/bb7e

Atsyor Hospital Complex
Pankrono, Ashanti, Ghana
🌐 https://vfmat.ch/69c3

Atua Government Hospital
Yokunya, Eastern, Ghana
🌐 https://vfmat.ch/db61

Barnor Memorial Hospital
Accra, Greater Accra, Ghana
🌐 https://vfmat.ch/3jrs

Bawku Presbyterian Hospital
Bawku, Upper East, Ghana
🌐 https://vfmat.ch/f388

Bechem Government Hospital
Yawniakrom, Ahafo, Ghana
🌐 https://vfmat.ch/4d73

Begoro Hospital
Begoro, Eastern, Ghana
⊕ https://vfmat.ch/4f1c

Bekwai Government Hospital
Bekwai, Ashanti, Ghana
⊕ https://vfmat.ch/1117

Bengali Hospital
Tema, Greater Accra, Ghana
⊕ https://vfmat.ch/a76d

Bimbilla Hospital
Bimbilla, Northern Region, Ghana
⊕ https://vfmat.ch/64f4

Bole District Hospital
Bole, Savanna Region, Ghana
⊕ https://vfmat.ch/276a

Bolgatanga Regional Hospital
Bolgatanga, Upper East, Ghana
⊕ https://vfmat.ch/d997

Bomso Specialist Hospital
Bomso, Ashanti, Ghana
⊕ https://vfmat.ch/77c3

Bongo Hospital
Bongo, Upper East, Ghana
⊕ https://vfmat.ch/ae56

Bre Nye Kwa Hospital
Berekum, Bono Region, Ghana
⊕ https://vfmat.ch/568c

Bryant Mission Hospital
Boete-Obuasi, Ashanti Region, Ghana
⊕ https://vfmat.ch/4bbc

Bukom Ellphkwei Hospital
Ashaiman, Greater Accra, Ghana
⊕ https://vfmat.ch/d3e9

Caiquo Hospital
Tema, Greater Accra, Ghana
⊕ https://vfmat.ch/c362

Cape Coast Teaching Hospital
Cape Coast, Central Region, Ghana
⊕ https://vfmat.ch/2834

Charity Hospital
Kropo, Ashanti, Ghana
⊕ https://vfmat.ch/c72c

City Hospital
Amakom-Kumasi, Ashanti, Ghana
⊕ https://vfmat.ch/5ac6

Complex Hospital
Nsawam, Eastern, Ghana
⊕ https://vfmat.ch/c2c1

County Hospital
Kumasi, Ashanti, Ghana
⊕ https://vfmat.ch/547a

Dakopon Hospital
Kwamo- Kumasi, Ashanti, Ghana
⊕ https://vfmat.ch/edc1

Damongo Hospital
Damongo, Savanna Region, Ghana
⊕ https://vfmat.ch/ed3d

Dangme East District Hospital
Faithkope, Greater Accra, Ghana
⊕ https://vfmat.ch/51ff

Deseret Hospital
Sotuom, Greater Accra, Ghana
⊕ https://vfmat.ch/4785

Donkorkrom Presbyterian Hospital
Donkorkrom, Eastern Region, Ghana
⊕ https://vfmat.ch/b526

Dormaa Presbyterian Hospital
Domaa-Ahenkro, Bono, Ghana
⊕ https://vfmat.ch/8198

Eden Specialist Hospital
North Kaneshiei, Greater Accra, Ghana
⊕ https://vfmat.ch/d314

Effia Nkwanta Regional Hospital
Asamang, Western, Ghana
⊕ https://vfmat.ch/4a86

Effiduase District Hospital
Effiduase, Ashanti, Ghana
⊕ https://vfmat.ch/a3f3

Ejura District Hospital
Ejura, Ashanti Region, Ghana
⊕ https://vfmat.ch/8bf2

Emil Memorial Hospital
Wenkyi, Bono Region, Ghana
⊕ https://vfmat.ch/b673

Enyiresi Hospital
Enyiresi, Eastern Region, Ghana
⊕ https://vfmat.ch/44c1

Everest Hospital
Nsuta, Ashanti, Ghana
⊕ https://vfmat.ch/f18f

Family Care Hospital
Kodie-mowire, Ashanti, Ghana
⊕ https://vfmat.ch/3cf4

Family Health Hospital
Teshie, Accra, Greater Accra, Ghana
⊕ https://vfmat.ch/b946

FOCOS Orthopedic Hospital
Pantang, Accra, Greater Accra, Ghana
⊕ https://vfmat.ch/76ad

Ga East Municipal Hospital
Kwabenya-Accra, Greater Accra, Ghana
⊕ https://vfmat.ch/3ab1

GCD Hospital
Akwatia, Eastern, Ghana
⊕ https://vfmat.ch/b991

Ghana-Canada Medical Centre
Accra, Ghana
⊕ https://vfmat.ch/wwku

Global Evangelical Mission Hospital
Aprumasi, Ashanti, Ghana
⊕ https://vfmat.ch/cca3

Gloria Memorial Hospital
Akwatialine-Kumasi, Ashanti, Ghana
⊕ https://vfmat.ch/467c

Goaso Hospital
Goaso, Brong Ahafo, Ghana
⊕ https://vfmat.ch/dd6c

Greater Grace Hospital
Adenta-Accra, Greater Accra, Ghana
⊕ https://vfmat.ch/a814

Havan Millennium Hospital
Accra, Greater accra, Ghana
⊕ https://vfmat.ch/1e16

Hebrona Hospital
Sintreso, Ashanti, Ghana
⊕ https://vfmat.ch/dd44

Holy Family Hospital
Nkwakwa, Easten Region, Ghana
⊕ https://vfmat.ch/b137

Holy Family Hospital Berekum
Berekum, Bono, Ghana
⊕ https://vfmat.ch/49ab

Holy Family Hospital Techiman
Techiman, Bono East, Ghana
⊕ https://vfmat.ch/8c1c

International Mission Hospital (IHDN Mission Hospital)
Asaklobo, Volta, Ghana
⊕ https://vfmat.ch/f72d

Jamiatu Islamic Hospital
Wa, Upper West Region, Ghana
⊕ https://vfmat.ch/874c

Johpat Hospital
Dzorwulu, Accra, Greater Accra, Ghana
🌐 https://vfmat.ch/db3a

Juaben Government Hospital
Juaben, Ashanti Region, Ghana
🌐 https://vfmat.ch/7941

Juaso District Hospital
Juaso, Ashanti Region, Ghana
🌐 https://vfmat.ch/9425

Jubail Specialist Hospital
Sakumona, Greater Accra, Ghana
🌐 https://vfmat.ch/e4ea

Karikari Brobbery Hospital
Gbegbeyise-Accra, Greater Accra, Ghana
🌐 https://vfmat.ch/5d75

Keffam Hospital
Buahwini, Ashanti, Ghana
🌐 https://vfmat.ch/15a9

King David Hospital
Kotobabi-Accra, Greater Accra, Ghana
🌐 https://vfmat.ch/318c

Kintampo District Hospital
Kintampo, Bono East, Ghana
🌐 https://vfmat.ch/26bf

KNUST Hospital
Ayija-Kumasi, Ashanti Region, Ghana
🌐 https://vfmat.ch/b573

Koforidua Regional Hospital
Koforidua, Eastern, Ghana
🌐 https://vfmat.ch/844f

Kokofu General Hospital
Kokofu, Ashanti, Ghana
🌐 https://vfmat.ch/ce44

Komfo Anokye Teaching Hospital
Bantama-Kumasi, Ashanti, Ghana
🌐 https://vfmat.ch/6dd4

Konongo-Odumasi Government Hospital
Konongo, Ashanti Region, Ghana
🌐 https://vfmat.ch/7a29

Korle-bu Teaching Hospital
Korle-Bu-Accra, Greater Accra, Ghana
🌐 https://vfmat.ch/d748

Kumasi South Hospital
Atonsu-Agogo Kumasi, Ashanti Region, Ghana
🌐 https://vfmat.ch/a539

Kumorji Hospital
Cantonments-Accra, Greater Accra, Ghana
🌐 https://vfmat.ch/a525

Kuntenase Government Hospital
Kuntanasi, Ashanti Region, Ghana
🌐 https://vfmat.ch/b455

Kwabre District Hospital
Asonomaso, Kenyase, Ashanti Region, Ghana
🌐 https://vfmat.ch/8555

Kwahu Government Hospital
Nkawkaw, Atibie, Eastern Region, Ghana
🌐 https://vfmat.ch/b355

Kyebi Government Hospital
Kyebi, Adadientem, Eastern, Ghana
🌐 https://vfmat.ch/7964

Kyei Memorial Hospital
Akwatialine, Kumasi, Ashanti, Ghana
🌐 https://vfmat.ch/a6c6

La General Hospital
La, Greater Accra, Ghana
🌐 https://vfmat.ch/d85b

Lister Hospital And Fertility Centre
Accra, Ghana
🌐 https://vfmat.ch/q6jk

Mampong District Hospital
Mampong, Ashanti, Ghana
🌐 https://vfmat.ch/c5f3

Manhyia Hospital
Manhyia, Kumasi, Ashanti, Ghana
🌐 https://vfmat.ch/a7e7

Mankranso Government Hospital
Mankranso, Kumasi, Ashanti, Ghana
🌐 https://vfmat.ch/acfb

Manna Mission Hospital
Greda Estate, Teshie, Accra, Greater Accra, Ghana
🌐 https://vfmat.ch/9a77

Martin Memorial Hospital
Dzorwulu Accra, Greater Accra, Ghana
🌐 https://vfmat.ch/2366

Maternal and Child Health Hospital
Bantama, Kumasi, Ashanti, Ghana
🌐 https://vfmat.ch/8ea1

Mathias Hospital
Yegyi, Bono East, Ghana
🌐 https://vfmat.ch/d1c8

Mbrom Hospital
Mbrom Dichemso, Kumasi, Ashanti, Ghana
🌐 https://vfmat.ch/ba25

Medicas Hospital
Akuapem Mampong, Easten Region, Ghana
🌐 https://vfmat.ch/dc73

Medifem Hospital
Westlands, Accra, Greater Accra, Ghana
🌐 https://vfmat.ch/7b44

Methodist Faith Healing Hospital
Adum, Kumasi, Ashanti, Ghana
🌐 https://vfmat.ch/a3e6

Nadowli District Hospital
Nadowli, Upper West, Ghana
🌐 https://vfmat.ch/d26a

Naka and St. Ama Hospital
Kumasi, Buokrom, Ashanti, Ghana
🌐 https://vfmat.ch/b866

Nandom Hospital
Nandom, Upper West, Ghana
🌐 https://vfmat.ch/419e

Narh – Bita Hospital
Tema, Greater Accra, Ghana
🌐 https://vfmat.ch/f88b

New Edubiase Government Hospital
New Edubiase, Ashanti Region, Ghana
🌐 https://vfmat.ch/3fde

New Town Hospital
Ashanti-Town, Kumasi, Ashanti, Ghana
🌐 https://vfmat.ch/8bee

New Wa Regional Hospital
Wa, Upper West Region, Ghana
🌐 https://vfmat.ch/pcsb

Newlife Hospital
Adoagire, Eastern Region, Ghana
🌐 https://vfmat.ch/31fa

Nkawie-Toase Government Hospital
Nkawie-Toase, Ashanti Region, Ghana
🌐 https://vfmat.ch/e13a

Nkawkaw Holy Family Hospital
Nkawkaw, Easten Region, Ghana
🌐 https://vfmat.ch/e9c2

Nkenkaasu District Government Hospital
Nkenkaasu, Ashanti Region, Ghana
🌐 https://vfmat.ch/1171

Nkwabeng Hospital
Sunyani, Bono, Ghana
🌐 https://vfmat.ch/b456

North Legon Hospital
North Legon, Greater Accra, Ghana
🌐 https://vfmat.ch/2d29

Northern Community Eye Hospital
Tamale, Northern Region, Ghana
⊕ https://vfmat.ch/611e

Nsawam Hospital
Nsawam, Eastern, Ghana
⊕ https://vfmat.ch/2226

Nyinahin District Hospital
Nyinahin, Ashanti, Ghana
⊕ https://vfmat.ch/e1e9

Obuasi Government Hospital
Obuasi, Ashanti Region, Ghana
⊕ https://vfmat.ch/d2cd

Opoku Agyeman Hospital
Techiman, Bono East, Ghana
⊕ https://vfmat.ch/c47f

Owusu Memorial Hospital
Asufufu, Sunyani, Bono, Ghana
⊕ https://vfmat.ch/4fc7

Pantang Hospital
Pantang, Greater Accra, Ghana
⊕ https://vfmat.ch/6b85

Peace and Love Hospital
Duom, Ashanti, Ghana
⊕ https://vfmat.ch/7695

Poku Transport Hospital
Amakom, Kumasi, Ashanti Region, Ghana
⊕ https://vfmat.ch/9891

Police Hospital
Cantonment, Accra, Greater Accra, Ghana
⊕ https://vfmat.ch/a61c

Princess Marie Louise Children's Hospital
Accra, Greater Accra, Ghana
⊕ https://vfmat.ch/283f

Provita Specialist Hospital
Tema, Greater Accra, Ghana
⊕ https://vfmat.ch/b839

Queens Hospital
Atonsu Dompoase, Kumasi, Ashanti, Ghana
⊕ https://vfmat.ch/6ef5

Ridge Hospital
Ridge, Accra, Greater Accra, Ghana
⊕ https://vfmat.ch/dee4

Rophi Hospital
Baatsona, Accra, Greater Accra, Ghana
⊕ https://vfmat.ch/7f3a

Royal Ash Hospital
Aburaso, Kumasi, Ashanti Region, Ghana
⊕ https://vfmat.ch/3dca

Sabs Hospital
Achiase Nsuta, Eastern Region, Ghana
⊕ https://vfmat.ch/926a

Salaga Hospital
Salaga, Savanna Region, Ghana
⊕ https://vfmat.ch/f528

Sampa Hospital
Sampa, Bono, Ghana
⊕ https://vfmat.ch/77ca

Sandema Hospital
Sandema, Upper East, Ghana
⊕ https://vfmat.ch/4aa1

Sape Agbo Memorial Hospital
Kotobabi, Greater Accra, Ghana
⊕ https://vfmat.ch/4d5d

Savelugu Hospital
Savelugu, Northern, Ghana
⊕ https://vfmat.ch/eae6

SDA Hospital Asamang
Agona Akrofonso, Ashanti Region, Ghana
⊕ https://vfmat.ch/dcd7

SDA Hospital Boadi
Boadi, Ashanti, Ghana
⊕ https://vfmat.ch/b4f4

SDA Hospital Fwereso
Fwereso, Ashanti, Ghana
⊕ https://vfmat.ch/8d29

SDA Hospital Tamale
Tamale, Northern Region, Ghana
⊕ https://vfmat.ch/b8b8

SDA Hospital Wiamoase
Wiamoase, Ashanti Region, Ghana
⊕ https://vfmat.ch/c431

Sene District Hospital
Kwame Danso, Bono East, Ghana
⊕ https://vfmat.ch/6123

Siaw Larbi Memorial Hospital
Old Tafo, Kumasi, Ashanti Region, Ghana
⊕ https://vfmat.ch/4969

Siloam Hospital
North Kwadaso, Kumasi, Ashanti Region, Ghana
⊕ https://vfmat.ch/a677

Sissala West District Hospital
Gwollu, Upper West region, Ghana
⊕ https://vfmat.ch/7p8x

St. Anthony's Homeopathic Hospital
Abrepo, Kumasi, Ashanti, Ghana
⊕ https://vfmat.ch/54f1

St. Dominic Hospital
Akwatia, Eastern Region, Ghana
⊕ https://vfmat.ch/5d4d

St. Elizabeth Hospital
Hwidiem, Ahafo, Ghana
⊕ https://vfmat.ch/25d1

St. John of God Hospital
Duayaw-Nkwanta, Ahafo, Ghana
⊕ https://vfmat.ch/1efa

St. John's Hospital & Fertility Centre
Accra, Ghana
⊕ https://vfmat.ch/ufxz

St. Joseph's Hospital Jirapa
Jirapa, Upper West, Ghana
⊕ https://vfmat.ch/8161

St. Josephs Hospital
Koforidua-Nsutam Road, Eastern Region, Ghana
⊕ https://vfmat.ch/67b2

St. Jude Hospital Ltd.
Bidieso, Obuasi, Ashanti. Region, Ghana
⊕ https://vfmat.ch/6574

St. Luke Hospital Kasei
Kasei, Ashanti, Ghana
⊕ https://vfmat.ch/c3f7

St. Marku's Hospital
Asokwa Kumasi, Ashanti, Ghana
⊕ https://vfmat.ch/567f

St. Martin's Hospital
Agrosum, Ashanti, Ghana
⊕ https://vfmat.ch/45db

St. Martins Hospital
Asiti, Eastern, Ghana
⊕ https://vfmat.ch/2ba4

St. Mary's Hospital
Drobo, Bono, Ghana
⊕ https://vfmat.ch/e5c5

St. Michael's Hospital – Pramso
Jachie, Ghana
⊕ https://vfmat.ch/a735

St. Nicholas Hospital
Tema, Greater Accra, Ghana
⊕ https://vfmat.ch/c572

St. Patricks Hospital
Maase-Offinso, Ashanti, Ghana
⊕ https://vfmat.ch/7496

St. Peter's Hospital
Patabo, Ashanti, Ghana
⊕ https://vfmat.ch/fc78

St. Theresa's Hospital
Nkoranza, Bono East, Ghana
⊕ https://vfmat.ch/da79

Suhum Government Hospital
Suhum, Eastern Region, Ghana
⊕ https://vfmat.ch/ca79

Sulemana Memorial Hospital Ltd
Maamobi, Accra, Greater Accra, Ghana
⊕ https://vfmat.ch/7bc3

Suntreso Government Hospital
Suntreso, Kumasi, Ashanti, Ghana
⊕ https://vfmat.ch/579c

Sunyani Municipal Hospital
Sunyani, Bono, Ghana
⊕ https://vfmat.ch/9681

Sunyani Regional Hospital
Eje- Sunyani, Bono, Ghana
⊕ https://vfmat.ch/155c

Super Care Hospital
Ejisu, Ashanti Region, Ghana
⊕ https://vfmat.ch/d4f3

Tafo Government Hospital
Tafo, Eastern, Ghana
⊕ https://vfmat.ch/17a4

Tafo Hospital
Tafo, Ashanti Region, Ghana
⊕ https://vfmat.ch/9a4f

Tamale Central Hospital
Zobogu,-Tamale, Northern, Ghana
⊕ https://vfmat.ch/1d61

Tamale Teaching Hospital
Bulpiela- Tamale, Northern, Ghana
⊕ https://vfmat.ch/dfc9

Tamale West Hospital
Bulpiela, Tamale, Northern Region, Ghana
⊕ https://vfmat.ch/33d1

Tania Specialist Hospital
North Kanvilli, Tamale, Northern Region, Ghana
⊕ https://vfmat.ch/b4c5

Tema General Hospital
Tema Community 12, Greater Accra, Ghana
⊕ https://vfmat.ch/3f7f

Tema Women's Hospital
Tema, Greater Accra, Ghana
⊕ https://vfmat.ch/ad99

Tepa District Hospital
Tepa, Ashanti, Ghana
⊕ https://vfmat.ch/ce36

Tetteh Quarshie Memorial Hospital
Mampong Akuapem, Eastern Region, Ghana
⊕ https://vfmat.ch/bddc

The Bank Hospital
Cantonments, Greater Accra, Ghana
⊕ https://vfmat.ch/1v1m

The Rock Hospital
Odorkor, Accra, Greater Accra, Ghana
⊕ https://vfmat.ch/8573

The Trust Hospital (SSNIT)
Osu, Accra, Greater Accra, Ghana
⊕ https://vfmat.ch/2c38

Trust Care Specialist Hospital
South Suntreso, Kumasi, Ashanti Region, Ghana
⊕ https://vfmat.ch/e5b5

Tumu Municipal Hospital
Tumu, Upper West Region, Ghana
⊕ https://vfmat.ch/6a8f

Twumasi Memorial Hospital
Asokwa, Kumasi, Ashanti Region, Ghana
⊕ https://vfmat.ch/e829

University Hospital (Legon Hospital)
Legon, Accra, Greater Accra, Ghana
⊕ https://vfmat.ch/a7e4

Valco Hospital
Tema New Town, Greater Accra, Ghana
⊕ https://vfmat.ch/dcdf

Vicon Specialist Hospital
Dansoman, Accra, Greater Accra, Ghana
⊕ https://vfmat.ch/a73b

Volta Regional Hospital (Ho Teaching Hospital)
Ho, Ghana
⊕ https://vfmat.ch/vtzu

VRA Hospital
Kwamikuma, Eastern Region, Ghana
⊕ https://vfmat.ch/71de

Wa Municipal Hospital
Kpaguri, Wa, Upper West Region, Ghana
⊕ https://vfmat.ch/5f8f

Walewale Hospital
Walewale, North-East Region, Ghana
⊕ https://vfmat.ch/c9b6

War Memorial Hospital
Nogsenia, Navrongo, Upper East Region, Ghana
⊕ https://vfmat.ch/e624

Washie Hospital
Ahodwo, Kumasi, Ashanti Region, Ghana
⊕ https://vfmat.ch/2af2

Wenchi Methodist Hospital
Wenkyi, Bono Region, Ghana
⊕ https://vfmat.ch/7761

Westphalian Hospital Complex
Oyoko, Ashanti Region, Ghana
⊕ https://vfmat.ch/d84d

Wisdom Hospital
Dichemso, Kumasi, Ashanti, Ghana
⊕ https://vfmat.ch/2ca2

Yendi Hospital
Yendi, Northern, Ghana
⊕ https://vfmat.ch/6662

Zebilla Hospital
Zebilla, Upper East Region, Ghana
⊕ https://vfmat.ch/7ee9

Healthcare Facility

Guinea

The Republic of Guinea is a West African country bordered by Guinea-Bissau, Senegal, and Mali to the north, and Sierra Leone, Liberia, and Ivory Coast to the south. Home to the Gambia, the Niger, and the Sénégal rivers, Guinea is known for its lovely landscapes and captivating waterfalls. The country has a predominantly Muslim population of over 12.9 million, with the highest density in the south and west of the country. As many as 40 different languages are spoken throughout the country, although French is the most widely used.

Formerly part of both the Ghana Empire and the Mali Empire, Guinea achieved independence from French West Africa in 1958. What followed was a period of political instability as rival groups fought for political power. Guinea is rich in resources including gold, diamonds, and a large portion of the world's bauxite. Agriculture is the nation's primary source of employment and income, but this way of life is threatened by climate change, as annual rainfall totals decline and temperatures rise. About half of the population lives in poverty.

Widespread poverty is reflected in the population's overall health. In addition to poor healthcare infrastructure, the country was also the origin of the 2014 Ebola outbreak, which devastated Guinea and spread to neighboring nations. Leading causes of death include lower respiratory infections, malaria, neonatal disorders, diarrheal diseases, stroke, ischemic heart disease, tuberculosis, HIV/AIDS, meningitis, congenital defects, and measles. Death from measles has decreased substantially, but it still remains a significant health threat and a top cause of death.

12.9M
Population

$1,194
GDP Per Capita

62 years
Life Expectancy
↑ Improving

8
Doctors/100k
Physician Density

30
Beds/100k
Hospital Bed Density

576
Deaths/100k
Maternal Mortality

Guinea

Nonprofit Organizations

Abt Associates
Seeks to improve the quality of life and economic well-being of people worldwide, while striving to meet and exceed the highest professional standards.
General, Logist-Op, MF Med, OB-GYN, Peds
🌐 https://vfmat.ch/cec2

Advance Family Planning
Aims to achieve global expansion and access to quality contraceptive information, services, and supplies through financial investment and political commitment.
General, MF Med, Pub Health
🌐 https://vfmat.ch/7478

Africa CDC
Aims to strengthen the capacity and capability of Africa's public health institutions and partnerships to detect and respond quickly and effectively to disease threats and outbreaks, based on data-driven interventions and programs.
Infect Dis, Logist-Op, Pub Health
🌐 https://vfmat.ch/339c

Africa Health Organisation
Leads collaborative efforts among countries in Africa and other partners to promote health equity, combat disease, and improve quality of life.
Logist-Op, Pub Health
🌐 https://vfmat.ch/b1c5

Africa Humanitarian Action (AHA)
Responds to crises, conflicts, and disasters in Africa, while informing and advising the international community, governments, civil society, and the private sector on humanitarian issues of concern to Africa. Supports institutional and organizational development efforts.
General, Infect Dis, MF Med, Nutr, OB-GYN
🌐 https://vfmat.ch/3ca2

Africa Relief and Community Development
Provides comprehensive relief and developmental aid to people of the African continent regardless of gender, race, or religion.
Nutr, Pub Health
🌐 https://vfmat.ch/6cd2

African Aid International
Works to improve the lives of those most in need in practical and sustainable ways.
Dent-OMFS, Logist-Op
🌐 https://vfmat.ch/9372

Against Malaria Foundation
Helps protect people from malaria. Funds anti-malaria nets, specifically long-lasting insecticidal nets (LLINs), and works with distribution partners to ensure they are used. Tracks and reports on net use and malaria case data.

Infect Dis
🌐 https://vfmat.ch/337d

Al Basar International Foundation
Works with local partners to treat preventable blindness, and helps set up sustainable infrastructure so local teams can save sight in their communities.
Ophth-Opt
🌐 https://vfmat.ch/a8b5

Alliance for International Medical Action, The (ALIMA)
Provides quality medical care to vulnerable populations, partnering with and developing national medical organizations and conducting medical research to bring innovation to 12 African countries where ALIMA works.
ER Med, General, Infect Dis, Logist-Op, MF Med, OB-GYN, Path, Peds, Psych, Pub Health
🌐 https://vfmat.ch/1c11

Amref Health Africa
Serves millions of people across 35 countries in Sub-Saharan Africa, strengthening health systems, and training African health workers to respond to the continent's most critical health issues.
All-Immu, General, Infect Dis, Logist-Op, MF Med, OB-GYN, Path, Pub Health, Surg
🌐 https://vfmat.ch/6985

AO Alliance
Builds solutions to lessen the burden of injuries in low- and middle-income countries, while enhancing the care of the injured to reduce human suffering, disability, and poverty.
Ortho, Surg
🌐 https://vfmat.ch/8cd5

Asclepius Snakebite Foundation
Seeks to reverse the cycle of tragic snakebite outcomes through a combination of innovative research, clinical medicine, and education-based public health initiatives.
Infect Dis, Pub Health
🌐 https://vfmat.ch/d37d

BroadReach
Collaborates with governments, multinational health organizations, donors, and private-sector companies to effect healthcare reform and solve the world's biggest health challenges.
Logist-Op
🌐 https://vfmat.ch/7812

Carter Center, The
Seeks to prevent and resolve conflicts, enhance freedom and democracy, and improve health, while remaining committed to human rights and the alleviation of human suffering.

Infect Dis, MF Med, Ophth-Opt
⊕ https://vfmat.ch/6556

ChildFund Australia
Works to reduce poverty for children in many of the world's most disadvantaged communities.
ER Med, General, Peds
⊕ https://vfmat.ch/13df

Christian Blind Mission (CBM)
Aims to improve the quality of life of persons with disabilities in the poorest countries, addressing poverty as a cause and a consequence of disability, and working in partnership to create a society for all.
ENT, General, Infect Dis, OB-GYN, Ophth-Opt, Ortho, Peds, Psych, Rehab, Surg
⊕ https://vfmat.ch/3824

Christian Medical & Dental Associations
Based in Christian ministry, deploys medical and dental teams to underserved communities to provide vital healthcare.
Anesth, Dent-OMFS, ER Med, General, Medicine, OB-GYN, Ophth-Opt, Peds, Pub Health, Radiol, Rehab, Surg
⊕ https://vfmat.ch/921c

Core Group
Aims to improve and expand community health practices for underserved populations, especially women and children, through collaborative action and learning.
General, Infect Dis, MF Med, Medicine, OB-GYN, Peds, Pub Health
⊕ https://vfmat.ch/9de3

COVID-19 Clinical Research Coalition
Advocates and collaborates for the advancement of COVID-19 research driven by the needs of low-resource settings, and works for equitable access to solutions to the pandemic.
All-Immu, Infect-Dis, MF Med, Path, Pub Health
⊕ https://vfmat.ch/d1f4

Dentaid
Seeks to treat, equip, train, and educate people in need of dental care.
Dent-OMFS
⊕ https://vfmat.ch/a183

Direct Relief
Improves the health and lives of people affected by poverty or emergency situations by mobilizing and providing essential medical resources needed for their care.
ER Med, Logist-Op
⊕ https://vfmat.ch/58e5

Doctors Without Borders/Médecins Sans Frontières (MSF)
Responds to emergencies and provides lifesaving medical care where needed most, including during disasters, conflicts, and epidemics.
Anesth, Crit-Care, ER Med, General, Infect Dis, Nutr, OB-GYN, Ped Surg, Peds, Psych, Pub Health, Surg
⊕ https://vfmat.ch/f363

Dream Sant'Egidio
Seeks to counter HIV/AIDS in Africa by eliminating the transmission of HIV from mother to child, with a focus on women because of the importance of their role in the community.
Infect Dis, MF Med, Neonat, OB-GYN, Path, Peds
⊕ https://vfmat.ch/f466

Drugs for Neglected Diseases Initiative
Develops lifesaving medicines for people with neglected diseases around the world, having developed eight treatments for five deadly diseases and saved millions of lives since 2003.
Infect Dis, Pub Health
⊕ https://vfmat.ch/969c

Enabel
As the development agency of the Belgian federal government, charged with implementing Belgium's international development policy, carries out public service assignments in Belgium and abroad pursuant to the 2030 Agenda for Sustainable Development.
General, Infect Dis, Logist-Op, MF Med, OB-GYN, Peds, Pub Health
⊕ https://vfmat.ch/5af7

Episcopal Relief & Development
Provides relief in times of disaster and promotes sustainable development by identifying and addressing the root causes of suffering.
Infect Dis, MF Med, Neonat, Nutr, Peds
⊕ https://vfmat.ch/7cfa

eRanger
Provides sustainable solutions to transportation and medical provision such as ambulances and mobile clinics in developing countries.
ER Med, General, Logist-Op
⊕ https://vfmat.ch/4c18

Fistula Foundation
Aims to engage the support of people worldwide who are eager to see the day that no woman suffers from obstetric fistula. Raises and directs funds to doctors and hospitals providing life-transforming surgery to women in need.
OB-GYN
⊕ https://vfmat.ch/e958

Fondation Follereau
Promotes the quality of life of the most vulnerable African communities. Alongside trusted partners, the foundation supports local initiatives in healthcare and education.
General, Infect Dis, OB-GYN
⊕ https://vfmat.ch/bcc7

Gift of Life International
Provides lifesaving cardiac treatment to children in developing countries while developing sustainable pediatric cardiac programs by implementing screening, surgical, and training missions.
Anesth, CT Surg, CV Med, Crit-Care, Ped Surg, Peds, Pulm-Critic
⊕ https://vfmat.ch/f2f9

Global Ministries – The United Methodist Church
As the worldwide mission and development agency of The United Methodist Church, Global Ministries works with more than 300 hospitals and clinics around the world through its Global Health Unit.
Anesth, CT Surg, CV Med, Crit-Care, Dent-OMFS, Derm, ER Med, GI, General, Infect Dis, Logist-Op, MF Med, Medicine, Neonat, Nephro, Nutr, OB-GYN, Ophth-Opt, Ortho, Palliative, Peds, Pod, Psych, Pub Health, Rehab, Rheum, Surg, Urol
⊕ https://vfmat.ch/1723

Global Oncology (GO)
Brings the best in cancer care to underserved patients around the world and collaborates across geographic, professional, and academic borders to improve cancer care, research, and education.
Heme-Onc, Path, Rad-Onc
⊕ https://vfmat.ch/fcb8

Global Polio Eradication Initiative
Aims to eradicate polio worldwide.
All-Immu, Infect-Dis, Logist-Op, Pub Health
⊕ https://vfmat.ch/7e2c

Global Reconstructive Surgery Outreach
Supports surgeons, doctors, and nurses financially to enable them to provide critically needed plastic and reconstructive surgeries to the poor.
Logist-Op, Surg
⊕ https://vfmat.ch/f262

Globus Relief
Aims to improve the delivery of healthcare worldwide by gathering, processing, and distributing surplus medical supplies to charities at home and abroad.
Logist-Op
⊕ https://vfmat.ch/a2b7

Grassroot Soccer
Leverages the power of soccer to educate, inspire, and mobilize at-risk youth in

developing countries to overcome their greatest health challenges, live healthier and more productive lives, and be agents for change in their communities.
Infect Dis
⊕ https://vfmat.ch/3521

Health Equity Initiative
Aims to build and sustain a global community that engages across sectors and disciplines to advance health equity.
Pub Health
⊕ https://vfmat.ch/e2e2

Helen Keller International
Seeks to eliminate preventable vision loss, malnutrition, and diseases of poverty.
Infect Dis, Nutr, OB-GYN, Ophth-Opt, Peds
⊕ https://vfmat.ch/b654

Hospice Africa
Aims to provide a holistic and culturally sensitive palliative care service through accurate treatment of pain.
Palliative
⊕ https://vfmat.ch/9f86

Humanity First
Provides aid and assistance to those in need, offering sustainable development solutions to society while providing and empowering local communities with the resources to help themselves.
ER Med, General, MF Med, Ophth-Opt
⊕ https://vfmat.ch/13cc

IHSAN Foundation for West Africa
Seeks to improve the social and economic lives of the people of West Africa through educational, humanitarian, and healthcare projects.
Dent-OMFS, ER Med, General, Infect Dis
⊕ https://vfmat.ch/c719

International Agency for the Prevention of Blindness (IAPB), The
Leads international efforts in blindness-prevention activities, works toward a world where no one is needlessly visually impaired, and ensures that everyone has access to the best possible standard of eye health.
Infect Dis, Ophth-Opt, Pub Health
⊕ https://vfmat.ch/87a2

International Federation of Gynecology and Obstetrics (FIGO)
Implements global projects on specific women's health issues.
MF Med, Medicine, Neonat, OB-GYN, Surg, Urol
⊕ https://vfmat.ch/c4b4

International Federation of Red Cross and Red Crescent Societies (IFRC)
Coordinates and directs international assistance following natural and manmade disasters in nonconflict situations through the world's largest humanitarian and development network. Provides disaster-preparedness programs, healthcare activities, and promotes humanitarian values.
ER Med, General, Infect Dis, Nutr
⊕ https://vfmat.ch/b4ee

International Organization for Migration (IOM) – The UN Migration Agency
Promotes evidence-informed policies and holistic, preventive, and curative health programs that are beneficial, accessible, and equitable for vulnerable migrants.
General, Infect Dis, OB-GYN
⊕ https://vfmat.ch/621a

International Planned Parenthood Federation (IPPF)
Leads a locally owned, globally connected civil society movement that provides and enables services and champions sexual and reproductive health and rights for all, especially the underserved.
Infect Dis, MF Med, OB-GYN
⊕ https://vfmat.ch/dc97

International Trachoma Initiative (iTi)
Works toward a world free from trachoma, a preventable cause of blindness, and

provides comprehensive support to national ministries of health and governmental and nongovernmental organizations to implement a comprehensive approach to fight trachoma.
Infect Dis, Ophth-Opt
⊕ https://vfmat.ch/3278

Iris Global
Serves the poor, the destitute, the lost, and the forgotten by providing adoration, outreach, family, education, relief, development, healing, and the arts.
General, Infect Dis, Nutr, Pub Health
⊕ https://vfmat.ch/37f8

Jhpiego
Creates and delivers transformative healthcare solutions that save lives, in partnership with national governments, health experts, and local communities.
General, Infect Dis, OB-GYN, Surg
⊕ https://vfmat.ch/45b8

John Snow, Inc. (JSI)
Aims to improve the health and well-being of underserved and vulnerable people and communities throughout the world.
General, Infect Dis, Logist-Op, MF Med, OB-GYN, Peds, Psych, Pub Health
⊕ https://vfmat.ch/ba78

Johns Hopkins Center for Communication Programs
Believes in the power of communication to save lives by empowering people to adopt healthy behaviors for themselves, their families, and their communities.
General, Infect Dis, Logist-Op, OB-GYN, Pub Health
⊕ https://vfmat.ch/1bf9

Joint United Nations Programme on HIV/AIDS (UNAIDS)
Aims to place people living with HIV and people affected by the virus at the decision-making table and at the center of designing, delivering, and monitoring the AIDS response.
Infect Dis
⊕ https://vfmat.ch/464a

Lay Volunteers International Association (LVIA)
Fosters local and global change to help overcome extreme poverty, reinforce equitable and sustainable development, and enhance dialogue between Italian and African communities.
ER Med, Logist-Op, MF Med, Neonat, Nutr, OB-GYN, Peds
⊕ https://vfmat.ch/ecd4

Lifebox
Seeks to provide safer surgery and anesthesia in low-resource countries by investing in tools, training, and partnerships for safe surgery.
Anesth, Crit-Care, Surg
⊕ https://vfmat.ch/2d4d

Light for the World
Contributes to a world in which persons with disabilities fully exercise their rights, and assists persons with disabilities living in poverty.
Ophth-Opt, Rehab
⊕ https://vfmat.ch/3ff6

Lions Clubs International
Empowers volunteers to serve their communities, meet humanitarian needs, encourage peace, and promote international understanding through Lions Clubs.
Heme-Onc, Medicine, Nutr, Ophth-Opt
⊕ https://vfmat.ch/7b12

London School of Hygiene & Tropical Medicine: Health in Humanitarian Crises Centre
Advances health and health equity in crisis-affected countries through research, education, and translation of knowledge into policy and practice.
ER Med, Infect Dis, Pub Health
⊕ https://vfmat.ch/96ad

Lutherans in Medical Missions (LIMM)
Works with local and global partners to promote healing in medically underserved communities.

General, Logist-Op, Pub Health
⊕ https://vfmat.ch/c5aa

Management Sciences for Health (MSH)
Works with countries and communities to save lives and improve the health of the world's poorest and most vulnerable people by building strong, resilient, sustainable health systems.
Infect Dis, Logist-Op, Pub Health
⊕ https://vfmat.ch/6aa2

MAP International
Provides medicines and health supplies to those in need around the world so they might experience life to the fullest.
Logist-Op
⊕ https://vfmat.ch/deed

Medical Care Development International (MCD International)
Works to strengthen health systems through innovative, sustainable interventions.
Infect Dis, Logist-Op, OB-GYN, Pub Health
⊕ https://vfmat.ch/dc5c

Medical Care Development International
Works to improve the health of vulnerable populations through integrated, sustainable, and locally driven interventions.
Infect Dis, OB-GYN, Peds, Pub Health
⊕ https://vfmat.ch/da87

MedShare
Aims to improve the quality of life of people, communities, and the planet by sourcing and directly delivering surplus medical supplies and equipment to communities in need around the world.
Logist-Op
⊕ https://vfmat.ch/c8bc

MENTOR Initiative
Saves lives in emergencies through tropical disease control, and helps people recover from crisis with dignity, working side by side with communities, health workers, and health authorities to leave a lasting impact.
ER Med, Infect Dis
⊕ https://vfmat.ch/3bd5

Mercy and Love Foundation
Aims to provide orphaned and vulnerable children with basic human needs such as food, clothing, and shelter, enabling them to thrive.
General, Peds
⊕ https://vfmat.ch/649a

Mercy Ships
Operates hospital ships staffed by volunteers to bring hope, healing, and healthcare to underserved communities worldwide.
Anesth, Dent-OMFS, Logist-Op, Neonat, OB-GYN, Ophth-Opt, Ortho, Palliative, Plast, Psych, Surg
⊕ https://vfmat.ch/2e99

MiracleFeet
Brings low-cost treatment to every child on the planet born with clubfoot, a leading cause of physical disability.
Ortho, Peds, Rehab
⊕ https://vfmat.ch/bda8

Mérieux Foundation
Committed to fighting infectious diseases that affect developing countries by capacity building, particularly in clinical laboratories, and focusing on diagnosis.
Logist-Op, Path
⊕ https://vfmat.ch/a23a

Operation Fistula
Exists to end obstetric fistula by building models of care that serve every woman, everywhere.
MF Med, OB-GYN, Surg
⊕ https://vfmat.ch/ce8e

Order of Malta
Supports forgotten or excluded people, especially those living in conflict zones or amid natural disasters, by providing medical assistance, caring for refugees, and distributing medicines and necessities.
ER Med, General, Infect Dis, MF Med, Nephro, OB-GYN, Ortho, Psych
⊕ https://vfmat.ch/1fab

Organization for the Prevention of Blindness, The (OPC)
Provides research, and treatments and cures for people affected by blindness and blinding diseases in Francophone Africa.
Infect Dis, Ophth-Opt
⊕ https://vfmat.ch/86d6

Pact
Works on the ground to improve the lives of those who are challenged by poverty and marginalization, striving for a world in which all people are heard, capable, and vibrant.
Infect Dis, Logist-Op, MF Med, Pub Health
⊕ https://vfmat.ch/9a6c

RestoringVision
Empowers lives by restoring vision for millions of people in need.
Ophth-Opt
⊕ https://vfmat.ch/e121

Rockefeller Foundation, The
Works to promote the well-being of humanity.
Logist-Op, Nutr, Pub Health
⊕ https://vfmat.ch/5424

Rotary International
Provides service to others, improves lives, and advances world understanding, goodwill, and peace through its fellowship of business, professional, and community leaders.
ER Med, General, Infect Dis, MF Med, OB-GYN
⊕ https://vfmat.ch/8fb5

ROW Foundation
Works to improve the quality of training for healthcare providers, and the diagnosis and treatment available to people with epilepsy and associated psychiatric disorders in under-resourced areas of the world.
Neuro, Psych
⊕ https://vfmat.ch/25eb

Sanofi Espoir Foundation
Contributes to reducing health inequalities among populations that need it most by applying a socially responsible approach focused on fighting childhood cancers in low-income countries, improving maternal and newborn health, and improving access to care.
ER Med, OB-GYN, Peds
⊕ https://vfmat.ch/943b

Save the Children
Gives children around the world a healthy start in life, the opportunity to learn, and protection from harm.
All-Immu, Crit-Care, ER Med, General, Infect Dis, MF Med, Medicine, Neonat, OB-GYN, Peds, Psych, Pub Health
⊕ https://vfmat.ch/2e73

Sightsavers
Works with partners in developing countries to help eliminate avoidable blindness and advocates for equal opportunity for the disabled.
Infect Dis, Ophth-Opt, Surg
⊕ https://vfmat.ch/aa52

SIGN Fracture Care International
Builds orthopedic capacity around the world and provides the injured poor access to fracture surgery by donating orthopedic education and implant systems to surgeons in developing countries.
Ortho, Rehab, Surg
⊕ https://vfmat.ch/123d

Smile Train, Inc.
Treats children with cleft lip through a sustainable and local model that supports surgery and other forms of essential care.
Logist-Op, Pub Health
⊕ https://vfmat.ch/822c

Solthis
Improves disease prevention and access to quality care by strengthening the health systems and services of the countries served.
General, Infect Dis, Logist-Op, MF Med, Neonat, Path
⊕ https://vfmat.ch/a71d

Swiss Tropical and Public Health Institute
Contributes to the improvement of the health of populations internationally, nationally, and locally through excellence in research, education, and services.
Infect Dis, Pub Health
⊕ https://vfmat.ch/2ee4

Task Force for Global Health, The
Consists of programs and focus areas that cover a range of global health issues including neglected tropical diseases, infectious diseases, vaccines, field epidemiology, public health informatics, health workforce development, and global health ethics.
Infect Dis, Logist-Op, Medicine, Ophth-Opt, Peds
⊕ https://vfmat.ch/714c

Terre des hommes (Tdh) Foundation
Works to improve the daily life of children and their relatives in the areas of health, protection and emergency, in Europe, Africa, Asia, Latin America, and the Near and Middle East.
CT Surg, CV Med, OB-GYN, Ped Surg, Pub Health
⊕ https://vfmat.ch/5c26

U.S. President's Malaria Initiative (PMI)
Supports low-income countries to help control and eliminate malaria through cost-effective, lifesaving malaria interventions.
Infect Dis, MF Med, OB-GYN
⊕ https://vfmat.ch/dc8b

Union for International Cancer Control (UICC)
Unites and supports the cancer community to reduce the global cancer burden, promote greater equity, and ensure that cancer control continues to be a priority in the world health and development agenda.
Heme-Onc, Pub Health
⊕ https://vfmat.ch/88b1

United Nations Children's Fund (UNICEF)
Works in over 190 countries and territories to save children's lives, defend their rights, and help them fulfill their potential, from early childhood through adolescence.
All-Immu, Infect Dis, MF Med, Neonat, Nutr, OB-GYN, Ped Surg, Peds, Pub Health
⊕ https://vfmat.ch/42d7

United Nations Development Programme (UNDP)
Helps countries achieve the simultaneous eradication of extreme poverty and significant reduction of inequalities and exclusion using a sustainable human development approach.
Infect Dis, Logist-Op, Pub Health
⊕ https://vfmat.ch/935c

United Nations High Commissioner for Refugees (UNHCR)
Safeguards the rights and well-being of people who have been forced to flee, ensuring that everybody has the right to seek asylum and find safe refuge in another country, with the goal of seeking lasting solutions.
General, MF Med, Medicine, OB-GYN, Peds, Psych, Pub Health
⊕ https://vfmat.ch/6636

United Nations Population Fund (UNFPA)
Supports reproductive healthcare for women and youth in more than 150 countries, focusing on delivering a world in which every pregnancy is wanted, every childbirth is safe, and every young person's potential is fulfilled.

Infect Dis, MF Med, Neonat, OB-GYN, Peds, Pub Health
⊕ https://vfmat.ch/c969

United Surgeons for Children (USFC)
Pursues greater health and opportunity for children in the most neglected pockets of the world, with a specific focus on and expertise in surgery.
Anesth, CT Surg, Neonat, Neurosurg, OB-GYN, Peds, Radiol, Surg
⊕ https://vfmat.ch/3b4c

USAID: A2Z The Micronutrient and Child Blindness Project
Aims to increase the use of key micronutrient and blindness interventions to improve child and maternal health.
MF Med, Neonat, Nutr, Ophth-Opt, Surg
⊕ https://vfmat.ch/c5f1

USAID: Deliver Project
Builds a global supply chain to deliver lifesaving health products to people in order to enable countries to provide family planning, protect against malaria, and limit the spread of pandemic threats.
Infect Dis, Logist-Op, MF Med
⊕ https://vfmat.ch/374e

USAID: Health Finance and Governance Project
Uses research to implement strategies to help countries develop robust governance systems, increase their domestic resources for health, manage those resources more effectively, and make wise purchasing decisions.
Logist-Op
⊕ https://vfmat.ch/8652

USAID: Human Resources for Health 2030 (HRH2030)
Helps low- and middle-income countries develop the health workforce needed to prevent maternal and child deaths, support the goals of Family Planning 2020, control the HIV/AIDS epidemic, and protect communities from infectious diseases.
Logist-Op
⊕ https://vfmat.ch/9ea8

USAID: Maternal and Child Health Integrated Program
Works to improve the health of women and their families, including programs for maternal, newborn, and child health, immunization, family planning, nutrition, malaria, and HIV/AIDS.
All-Immu, General, Infect Dis, MF Med
⊕ https://vfmat.ch/4415

USAID: Maternal and Child Survival Program
Works to prevent child and maternal deaths.
Infect Dis, MF Med, Neonat, OB-GYN, Peds
⊕ https://vfmat.ch/6fcf

Vitamin Angels
Helps at-risk populations in need—specifically pregnant women, new mothers, and children under age 5—to gain access to life-changing vitamins and minerals.
General, Nutr
⊕ https://vfmat.ch/7da1

Walkabout Foundation
Provides wheelchairs and rehabilitation in the developing world and funds research to find a cure for paralysis.
Logist-Op, Rehab
⊕ https://vfmat.ch/5582

Willing and Abel
Seeks to provide connections between children in developing nations and specialist centers, helping with visas, passports, transportation, and finances.
Anesth, Dent-OMFS, Ped Surg
⊕ https://vfmat.ch/9dc7

Wisconsin Medical Project
Provides humanitarian aid, including donated medical equipment and supplies, to hospitals and clinics in areas of great need.
Logist-Op
⊕ https://vfmat.ch/ef3b

World Anaesthesia Society (WAS)
Aims to support anesthesiologists with an interest in working in low-income regions of the world.
Anesth
⊕ https://vfmat.ch/37fe

World Health Organization, The (WHO)
The United Nations' agency for health provides leadership on global health matters, shapes the health research agenda, sets norms and standards, articulates evidence-based policy options, provides technical support and monitoring to countries, and assesses health trends.
ER Med, General, Infect Dis, Logist-Op, MF Med, OB-GYN, Peds, Psych, Pub Health
⊕ https://vfmat.ch/c476

Guinea

Healthcare Facilities

CHU de Donka
Route Donka, Dixinn, Conakry, Guinea
⊕ https://vfmat.ch/5d71

CHU Ignace Deen
5e Avenue, Kaloum, Conakry, Guinea
⊕ https://vfmat.ch/5513

CMC Bernard Kouchner de Coronthie
10e Boulevard, Kaloum, Conakry, Guinea
⊕ https://vfmat.ch/755a

Hospital Prefectural de Dalaba
N5, Dalaba, Mamou, Guinea
⊕ https://vfmat.ch/36fe

Hôpital de Gaoual Prefectoral
N24, Gaoual, Boké, Guinea
⊕ https://vfmat.ch/3a2a

Hôpital de Kissidougou
N2, Kissidougou, Faranah, Guinea
⊕ https://vfmat.ch/3baa

Hôpital de l'Amitié Sino-Guinéenne
Rue RO. 209, Ratoma, Conakry, Guinea
⊕ https://vfmat.ch/9e85

Hôpital de Mandiana
Mandiana, Kankan, Guinea
⊕ https://vfmat.ch/3283

Hôpital Indo Guinéen
Rue MO.258, Matoto, Conakry, Guinea
⊕ https://vfmat.ch/154e

Hôpital Jean-Paul 2
Rue RO. 095, Ratoma, Conakry, Guinea
⊕ https://vfmat.ch/69ca

Hôpital Karakoro
Forecariah, Guinea
⊕ https://vfmat.ch/fad5

Hôpital Préfectoral de Koubia
Koubia, Labé, Guinea
⊕ https://vfmat.ch/4af2

Hôpital Préfectoral de Mandiana
Mandiana, Kankan, Guinea
⊕ https://vfmat.ch/f11e

Hôpital Préfectoral de Siguiri
N30, Siguiri, Kankan, Guinea
⊕ https://vfmat.ch/9614

Hôpital Préfectorale de Coyah
N1, Coyah, Kindia, Guinea
⊕ https://vfmat.ch/4629

Hôpital Régional Alpha Oumar Diallo
Place des Martyrs, Kindia, Kindia, Guinea
⊕ https://vfmat.ch/e775

Hôpital Régional de Boké
N3, Boké-Centre, Boké, Guinea
⊕ https://vfmat.ch/d95c

Hôpital Régional de Kankan
N1, Kankan-Centre, Kankan, Guinea
⊕ https://vfmat.ch/bd5a

Hôpital Régional de Labé
N8, Labé-Centre, Labé, Guinea
⊕ https://vfmat.ch/3e97

Regional Hospital at Nzérékoré
Nzérékoré, Guinea
⊕ https://vfmat.ch/9312

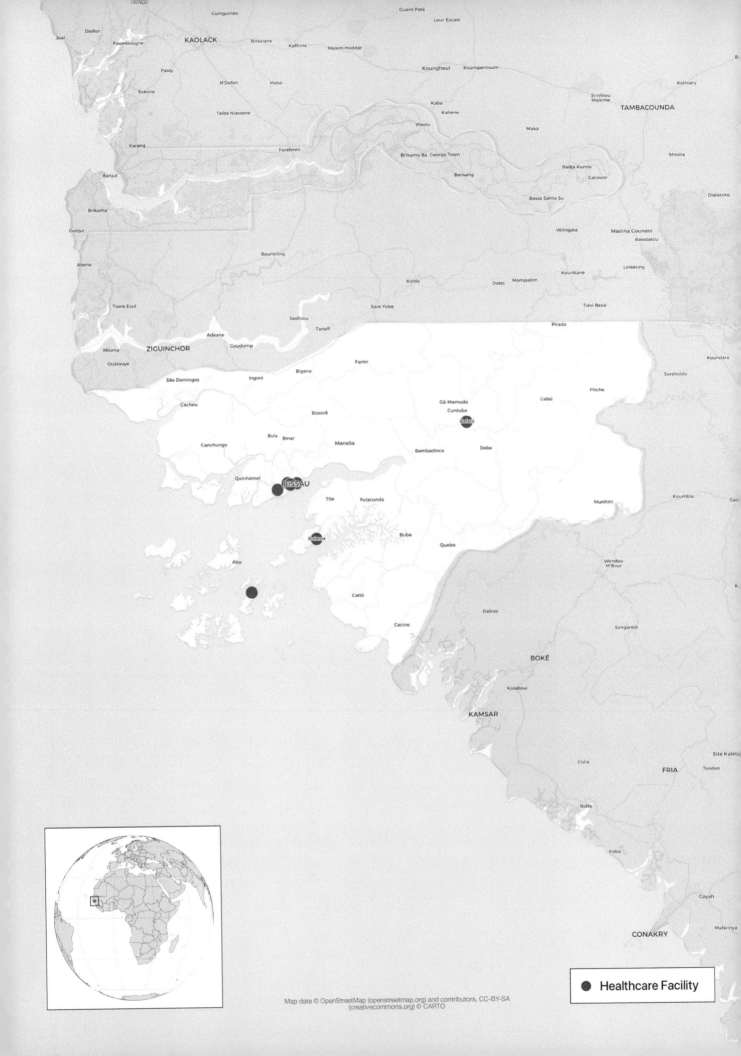

● Healthcare Facility

Guinea-Bissau

Located on the coast of West Africa, the Republic of Guinea-Bissau has a small, young population of 2 million people, two-thirds of whom are under age 30. About one-fifth of the population lives in the capital of Bissau and along the coast. As a coastal country, Guinea-Bissau has countless islands dotting the shoreline, with unique natural features and wildlife. Predominantly Muslim and Christian, Guinea-Bissau's population comprises several ethnic groups such as Fulani, Balanta, Mandinga, Papel, and Manjaco. Crioulo is the lingua franca, while Portuguese is the official language.

Guinea-Bissau was ruled by Portugal until 1974, and since independence, the country has experienced decades of political instability marked by a civil war and several coups. The result is a fragile country with high levels of unemployment, a weak economy, widespread corruption, and endemic poverty. Several public institutions are challenged, including an underdeveloped education infrastructure.

Despite its many economic and political challenges, Guinea-Bissau has seen improvements in recent decades; the under-five mortality rate has declined significantly since 1990, from over 200 deaths per 1,000 live births to under 80. Similarly, life expectancy continues to improve—but it still ranks among the lowest in the world. Despite some improvements in overall population health, top causes of death include neonatal disorders, diarrheal diseases, lower respiratory infections, HIV/AIDS, ischemic heart disease, stroke, tuberculosis, malaria, road injuries, and meningitis. Additionally, cases of measles have been increasing annually, posing a significant public health challenge.

2.0M
Population

$728
GDP Per Capita

58 years
Life Expectancy
↑ Improving

13
Doctors/100k
Physician Density

100
Beds/100k
Hospital Bed Density

667
Deaths/100k
Maternal Mortality

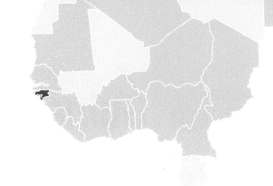

Guinea-Bissau

Nonprofit Organizations

Africa CDC
Aims to strengthen the capacity and capability of Africa's public health institutions and partnerships to detect and respond quickly and effectively to disease threats and outbreaks, based on data-driven interventions and programs.
Infect Dis, Logist-Op, Pub Health
⊕ https://vfmat.ch/339c

Africa Health Organisation
Leads collaborative efforts among countries in Africa and other partners to promote health equity, combat disease, and improve quality of life.
Logist-Op, Pub Health
⊕ https://vfmat.ch/b1c5

Africa Relief and Community Development
Provides comprehensive relief and developmental aid to people of the African continent regardless of gender, race, or religion.
Nutr, Pub Health
⊕ https://vfmat.ch/6cd2

African Field Epidemiology Network (AFENET)
Strengthens field epidemiology and public health laboratory capacity to contribute effectively to addressing epidemics and other major public health problems in Africa.
All-Immu, Infect Dis, Path, Pub Health
⊕ https://vfmat.ch/df2e

African Health Now
Promotes and provides information and access to sustainable primary healthcare to women, children, and families living across Sub-Saharan Africa.
Dent-OMFS, Endo, General, Infect Dis, MF Med, OB-GYN
⊕ https://vfmat.ch/c766

Al Basar International Foundation
Works with local partners to treat preventable blindness, and helps set up sustainable infrastructure so local teams can save sight in their communities.
Ophth-Opt
⊕ https://vfmat.ch/a8b5

BroadReach
Collaborates with governments, multinational health organizations, donors, and private-sector companies to effect healthcare reform and solve the world's biggest health challenges.
Logist-Op
⊕ https://vfmat.ch/7812

Center for Strategic and International Studies (CSIS) Commission on Strengthening America's Health Security
Brings together a distinguished and diverse group of high-level opinion leaders bridging security and health, with the core aim to chart a bold vision for the future of U.S. leadership in global health.

ER Med, Infect Dis, MF Med, Pub Health
⊕ https://vfmat.ch/6d7f

Developing Country NGO Delegation: Global Fund to Fight AIDS, TB & Malaria
Works to strengthen the engagement of civil society actors and organizations in developing countries to build a world in which AIDS, TB, and malaria are no longer global, public health, and human rights threats.
Infect Dis, Pub Health
⊕ https://vfmat.ch/3149

Doctors Without Borders/Médecins Sans Frontières (MSF)
Responds to emergencies and provides lifesaving medical care where needed most, including during disasters, conflicts, and epidemics.
Anesth, Crit-Care, ER Med, General, Infect Dis, Nutr, OB-GYN, Ped Surg, Peds, Psych, Pub Health, Surg
⊕ https://vfmat.ch/f363

Global Oncology (GO)
Brings the best in cancer care to underserved patients around the world and collaborates across geographic, professional, and academic borders to improve cancer care, research, and education.
Heme-Onc, Path, Rad-Onc
⊕ https://vfmat.ch/fcb8

Globus Relief
Aims to improve the delivery of healthcare worldwide by gathering, processing, and distributing surplus medical supplies to charities at home and abroad.
Logist-Op
⊕ https://vfmat.ch/a2b7

Humanity & Inclusion
Works alongside people with disabilities and vulnerable populations, taking action and bearing witness in order to respond to their essential needs, improve their living conditions and health, and promote respect for their dignity and fundamental rights.
General, Infect Dis, MF Med, Medicine, Ortho, Peds, Psych, Pub Health, Rehab
⊕ https://vfmat.ch/16b7

Humanity First
Provides aid and assistance to those in need, offering sustainable development solutions to society while providing and empowering local communities with the resources to help themselves.
ER Med, General, MF Med, Ophth-Opt
⊕ https://vfmat.ch/13cc

International Agency for the Prevention of Blindness (IAPB), The
Leads international efforts in blindness-prevention activities, works toward a world where no one is needlessly visually impaired, and ensures that everyone

has access to the best possible standard of eye health.
Infect Dis, Ophth-Opt, Pub Health
⊕ https://vfmat.ch/87a2

International Federation of Red Cross and Red Crescent Societies (IFRC)
Coordinates and directs international assistance following natural and manmade disasters in nonconflict situations through the world's largest humanitarian and development network. Provides disaster-preparedness programs, healthcare activities, and promotes humanitarian values.
ER Med, General, Infect Dis, Nutr
⊕ https://vfmat.ch/b4ee

International Organization for Migration (IOM) – The UN Migration Agency
Promotes evidence-informed policies and holistic, preventive, and curative health programs that are beneficial, accessible, and equitable for vulnerable migrants.
General, Infect Dis, OB-GYN
⊕ https://vfmat.ch/621a

International Trachoma Initiative (iTi)
Works toward a world free from trachoma, a preventable cause of blindness, and provides comprehensive support to national ministries of health and governmental and nongovernmental organizations to implement a comprehensive approach to fight trachoma.
Infect Dis, Ophth-Opt
⊕ https://vfmat.ch/3278

Johns Hopkins Center for Communication Programs
Believes in the power of communication to save lives by empowering people to adopt healthy behaviors for themselves, their families, and their communities.
General, Infect Dis, Logist-Op, OB-GYN, Pub Health
⊕ https://vfmat.ch/1bf9

Joint United Nations Programme on HIV/AIDS (UNAIDS)
Aims to place people living with HIV and people affected by the virus at the decision-making table and at the center of designing, delivering, and monitoring the AIDS response.
Infect Dis
⊕ https://vfmat.ch/464a

Lay Volunteers International Association (LVIA)
Fosters local and global change to help overcome extreme poverty, reinforce equitable and sustainable development, and enhance dialogue between Italian and African communities.
ER Med, Logist-Op, MF Med, Neonat, Nutr, OB-GYN, Peds
⊕ https://vfmat.ch/ecd4

Light House Medical Missions
Inspired by the Christian faith, provides programs in healthcare provision, nutrition, emergency relief and response, and water, sanitation, and hygiene (WASH).
ER Med, General, Surg
⊕ https://vfmat.ch/cecd

Lions Clubs International
Empowers volunteers to serve their communities, meet humanitarian needs, encourage peace, and promote international understanding through Lions Clubs.
Heme-Onc, Medicine, Nutr, Ophth-Opt
⊕ https://vfmat.ch/7b12

Medical Care Development International
Works to improve the health of vulnerable populations through integrated, sustainable, and locally driven interventions.
Infect Dis, OB-GYN, Peds, Pub Health
⊕ https://vfmat.ch/da87

MedShare
Aims to improve the quality of life of people, communities, and the planet by sourcing and directly delivering surplus medical supplies and equipment to communities in need around the world.
Logist-Op
⊕ https://vfmat.ch/c8bc

Mercy and Love Foundation
Aims to provide orphaned and vulnerable children with basic human needs such as food, clothing, and shelter, enabling them to thrive.
General, Peds
⊕ https://vfmat.ch/649a

Mercy Ships
Operates hospital ships staffed by volunteers to bring hope, healing, and healthcare to underserved communities worldwide.
Anesth, Dent-OMFS, Logist-Op, Neonat, OB-GYN, Ophth-Opt, Ortho, Palliative, Plast, Psych, Surg
⊕ https://vfmat.ch/2e99

Mission Bambini
Helps to support children living in poverty and sickness, and lacking education, giving them the opportunity for and hope of a better life.
CT Surg, CV Med, Crit-Care, ER Med, Ped Surg, Peds
⊕ https://vfmat.ch/dc1a

Order of Malta
Supports forgotten or excluded people, especially those living in conflict zones or amid natural disasters, by providing medical assistance, caring for refugees, and distributing medicines and necessities.
ER Med, General, Infect Dis, MF Med, Nephro, OB-GYN, Ortho, Psych
⊕ https://vfmat.ch/1fab

Organization for the Prevention of Blindness, The (OPC)
Provides research, and treatments and cures for people affected by blindness and blinding diseases in Francophone Africa.
Infect Dis, Ophth-Opt
⊕ https://vfmat.ch/86d6

Rockefeller Foundation, The
Works to promote the well-being of humanity.
Logist-Op, Nutr, Pub Health
⊕ https://vfmat.ch/5424

Rotary International
Provides service to others, improves lives, and advances world understanding, goodwill, and peace through its fellowship of business, professional, and community leaders.
ER Med, General, Infect Dis, MF Med, OB-GYN
⊕ https://vfmat.ch/8fb5

Sightsavers
Works with partners in developing countries to help eliminate avoidable blindness and advocates for equal opportunity for the disabled.
Infect Dis, Ophth-Opt, Surg
⊕ https://vfmat.ch/aa52

Sustainable Cardiovascular Health Equity Development Alliance
Fights cardiovascular disease in underserved populations globally via education, training, and increasing interventional capacity.
CV Med, Pub Health, Radiol
⊕ https://vfmat.ch/799c

Swiss Tropical and Public Health Institute
Contributes to the improvement of the health of populations internationally, nationally, and locally through excellence in research, education, and services.
Infect Dis, Pub Health
⊕ https://vfmat.ch/2ee4

Task Force for Global Health, The
Consists of programs and focus areas that cover a range of global health issues including neglected tropical diseases, infectious diseases, vaccines, field epidemiology, public health informatics, health workforce development, and global health ethics.
Infect Dis, Logist-Op, Medicine, Ophth-Opt, Peds
⊕ https://vfmat.ch/714c

United Nations Children's Fund (UNICEF)
Works in over 190 countries and territories to save children's lives, defend

their rights, and help them fulfill their potential, from early childhood
through adolescence.

All-Immu, Infect Dis, MF Med, Neonat, Nutr, OB-GYN, Ped Surg, Peds, Pub Health

⊕ https://vfmat.ch/42d7

United Nations Development Programme (UNDP)
Helps countries achieve the simultaneous eradication of extreme poverty and
significant reduction of inequalities and exclusion using a sustainable human
development approach.

Infect Dis, Logist-Op, Pub Health

⊕ https://vfmat.ch/935c

United Nations High Commissioner for Refugees (UNHCR)
Safeguards the rights and well-being of people who have been forced to flee,
ensuring that everybody has the right to seek asylum and find safe refuge in
another country, with the goal of seeking lasting solutions.

General, MF Med, Medicine, OB-GYN, Peds, Psych, Pub Health

⊕ https://vfmat.ch/6636

United Nations Population Fund (UNFPA)
Supports reproductive healthcare for women and youth in more than 150
countries, focusing on delivering a world in which every pregnancy is wanted,
every childbirth is safe, and every young person's potential is fulfilled.

Infect Dis, MF Med, Neonat, OB-GYN, Peds, Pub Health

⊕ https://vfmat.ch/c969

World Health Organization, The (WHO)
The United Nations' agency for health provides leadership on global health
matters, shapes the health research agenda, sets norms and standards,
articulates evidence-based policy options, provides technical support and
monitoring to countries, and assesses health trends.

ER Med, General, Infect Dis, Logist-Op, MF Med, OB-GYN, Peds, Psych, Pub Health

⊕ https://vfmat.ch/c476

 # Guinea-Bissau

Healthcare Facilities

Bafatá Hospital
Avenida Principal, Bafatá, Região de Bafatá, Guinea-Bissau
⊕ https://vfmat.ch/ce8c

Hospital 3 de Agosto
Avenida dos Combatentes da Liberdade da Pátria, Bissau, Sector autónomo de Bissau, Guinea-Bissau
⊕ https://vfmat.ch/325b

Hospital Marcelino Banca
Bubaque, Região de Bolama, Guinea-Bissau
⊕ https://vfmat.ch/d439

Hospital Militar de Bissau
Avenida dos Combatentes da Liberdade da Pátria, Bissau, Sector Autónomo de Bissau, Guinea-Bissau
⊕ https://vfmat.ch/aad4

Hospital Militar e Civil
Avenida Amílcar Cabral, Bolama, Região de Bolama, Guinea-Bissau
⊕ https://vfmat.ch/7c9f

Hospital Nacional Simão Mendes
Bissau, Guinea-Bissau
⊕ https://vfmat.ch/bffc

Hospital Raoul Follereau
Bissau, Guinea-Bissau
⊕ https://vfmat.ch/e9d5

Hospital Solidariedade de Bolama
Bolama, Guinea-Bissau
⊕ https://vfmat.ch/369d

Hôpital de Cumura
Prábis, Guinea-Bissau
⊕ https://vfmat.ch/28a6

● Healthcare Facility

Haiti

The Republic of Haiti is a tropical Caribbean country located south of Cuba and west of the Dominican Republic. The most mountainous country in the Caribbean, Haiti has stunning landscapes and views, along with natural coasts and beaches. The population is young, with 50 percent of Haiti's 11.2 million people under the age of 23. Haitians predominantly speak French and Creole, and are largely Roman Catholic and Protestant while practicing some elements of locally recognized Vodou.

Known for its revolutionary spirit, Haiti won independence from France in a slave-led revolution in 1804. Today, Haiti is the poorest country in the Western Hemisphere and grapples with ongoing political instability and natural disasters. In 2010, an earthquake hit Haiti, devastating its economy and killing more than 300,000 people. In 2016, Hurricane Matthew struck the country, causing losses totaling 32 percent of its GDP. Haiti remains particularly vulnerable to natural disasters, with 96 percent of the population at risk.

With about 65 percent of the population living in poverty, one-quarter of Haitians are unable to cover basic food requirements, and more than 40 percent lack access to clean water. Non-communicable diseases such as ischemic heart disease, stroke, diabetes, congenital defects, and chronic kidney disease have notably increased in recent years as the cause of most deaths in Haiti. While some communicable diseases have decreased on average, lower respiratory infections, HIV/AIDS, neonatal disorders, and diarrheal diseases continue to be significant contributors to deaths in the country.

11.2M

Population

$1,177

GDP Per Capita

64 years

Life Expectancy

↑ Improving

23
Doctors/100k

Physician Density

71
Beds/100k

Hospital Bed Density

480
Deaths/100k

Maternal Mortality

Haiti

Nonprofit Organizations

100X Development Foundation
Empowers children and families for a more hopeful and productive future through the support and care of orphaned children, education and job training for those in need, help for vulnerable youth to escape trafficking, and healthy nutrition and medical care for mothers to enable a safe birth.
ER Med, Infect Dis, OB-GYN, Peds, Psych
⊕ https://vfmat.ch/b629

Abt Associates
Seeks to improve the quality of life and economic well-being of people worldwide, while striving to meet and exceed the highest professional standards.
General, Logist-Op, MF Med, OB-GYN, Peds
⊕ https://vfmat.ch/cec2

Action Against Hunger
Aims to end life-threatening hunger for good through treating and preventing malnutrition across more than 45 countries.
Nutr
⊕ https://vfmat.ch/2dbc

Adventist Health International
Focuses on upgrading and managing mission hospitals by providing governance, consultation, and technical assistance to a number of affiliated Seventh-Day Adventist hospitals throughout Africa, Asia, and the Americas.
Dent-OMFS, General, Pub Health
⊕ https://vfmat.ch/16aa

Agape Global Health for Haiti
Seeks to provide direct medical care, public health education, water filtration kits, and prenatal care to people in La Gonave, Haiti, by deploying a team of volunteers who are dedicated, knowledgeable, and caring professionals with diverse experience.
General, MF Med, OB-GYN, Peds, Pub Health
⊕ https://vfmat.ch/5139

AID FOR AIDS International
Aims to empower communities at risk of HIV and the population at large with comprehensive prevention through treatment, advocacy, education, and training.
Infect Dis, Logist-Op, Nutr, Psych, Pub Health
⊕ https://vfmat.ch/c43e

Aid for Haiti
Seeks to share Christian faith with the people of Haiti through compassionate healthcare, spiritual ministry, and training for service.
ER Med, General, Nutr, OB-GYN, Pub Health
⊕ https://vfmat.ch/96f3

AIDS Healthcare Foundation
Provides cutting-edge HIV/AIDS medical care and advocacy to over one million people in 43 countries.

Infect Dis
⊕ https://vfmat.ch/b27c

Albert Schweitzer Hospital
Seeks to collaborate with people of the Artibonite Valley, Haiti, as they strive to improve their health and quality of life. Operates a 131-bed hospital with full, 24/7 service and provides access to healthcare for people living in remote areas.
Anesth, Crit-Care, ER Med, Infect Dis, MF Med, Medicine, OB-GYN, Path, Ped Surg, Peds, Radiol, Rehab, Surg
⊕ https://vfmat.ch/c554

Alliance for Children Foundation
Seeks to improve the lives of orphaned and at-risk children and their families ,where the need is greatest worldwide, by working with local partners to provide food, shelter, medical care, and educational programs.
General, Nutr, Ped Surg, Peds
⊕ https://vfmat.ch/7acb

American Academy of Ophthalmology
Protects sight and empowers lives by serving as an advocate for patients and the public, leading ophthalmic education, and advancing the profession of ophthalmology.
Ophth-Opt
⊕ https://vfmat.ch/89a2

American Academy of Pediatrics
Seeks to attain optimal physical, mental, and social health and well-being for all infants, children, adolescents, and young adults.
Anesth, Crit-Care, Neonat, Ped Surg
⊕ https://vfmat.ch/9633

Americares
Saves lives and improves health for people affected by poverty or disaster and responds with life-changing medicine, medical supplies, and health programs including domestic and global medical clinics.
All-Immu, ER Med, General, Infect Dis, MF Med, Nutr
⊕ https://vfmat.ch/e567

Americas Association for the Care of Children (AACC)
Reduces the impact of poverty in marginalized and underserved populations by empowering communities through compassionate and holistic education.
Dent-OMFS, MF Med, OB-GYN, Pub Health
⊕ https://vfmat.ch/19c5

AMG International
Inspired by theChristian faith, provides children with both food and care in youth development centers and medical help in hospitals, clinics and leprosy centers.
General, Geri, Medicine, Nutr, OB-GYN, Peds, Pub Health
⊕ https://vfmat.ch/cf71

Amurtel
Aims to alleviate suffering and provide immediate and long-term relief to women and children in need, and to improve their overall quality of life.
⊕ https://vfmat.ch/2b19

Angel Wings International
Provides compassionate and comprehensive medical care to underserved people of Haiti by developing local medical professions and skill sets of the local population.
ER Med, General, OB-GYN, Peds
⊕ https://vfmat.ch/f6c7

Arbeiter Samariter Bund (Workers' Samaritan Federation)
Engages in areas such as civil protection, rescue services, and social welfare, while operating a network of welcome centers to help refugees.
ER Med, General, Infect Dis, Logist-Op, Rehab
⊕ https://vfmat.ch/8a5b

Association Haïtienne de Développement Humain (AHDH)
Promotes the welfare of Haitians by contributing to or instituting humanitarian programs in health, education, culture, and development in Haiti and Louisiana.
ENT, General, MF Med, OB-GYN, Ophth-Opt, Peds, Pub Health, Surg
⊕ https://vfmat.ch/e462

Association of Haitian Physicians Abroad (AMHE)
Provides professional members a conduit to address the medical needs and concerns of the Haitian community at home and abroad.
General, Medicine, OB-GYN, Ophth-Opt, Peds, Surg
⊕ https://vfmat.ch/4599

Association of Medical Doctors of Asia (AMDA)
Strives to support people affected by disasters and economic distress on their road to recovery, establishing a true partnership with special emphasis on local initiative.
ER Med, Logist-Op, Pub Health
⊕ https://vfmat.ch/e3d4

Barco's Nightingales Foundation
Aims to honor the women and men who embrace the profession of nursing for their selfless contributions, dedication, and professionalism by focusing its philanthropic efforts on helping children.
General, Heme-Onc, Peds, Plast
⊕ https://vfmat.ch/a82d

Basic Foundations
Supports local projects and organizations that seek to meet the basic human needs of others in their community.
ER Med, General, Peds, Rehab, Surg
⊕ https://vfmat.ch/c4be

Basic Health International
Seeks to eliminate cervical cancer by conducting cutting-edge research on early prevention and treatment, and implementing sustainable strategies that can be scaled in limited-resource settings.
Infect Dis, OB-GYN
⊕ https://vfmat.ch/24c9

Batey Relief Alliance
Addresses socio-economic and health needs of children and their families severely affected by poverty, disease, and hunger in the Caribbean, through health, agricultural/cooperative, and development programs.
General
⊕ https://vfmat.ch/773b

Benjamin H. Josephson, MD Fund
Provides healthcare professionals with the financial resources necessary to deliver medical services for those in need throughout the world.
General, OB-GYN
⊕ https://vfmat.ch/6acc

Bethesda Evangelical Mission (BEM)
Provides essential medicines, lifesaving baby formula, training, and education for women and children, while working toward the prevention and eradication of disease, and promoting better health in some of the most neglected areas of southern Haiti.
General, MF Med, OB-GYN, Peds
⊕ https://vfmat.ch/45a7

Bicol Clinic Foundation Inc.
Treats patients primarily in the Philippines, Nepal, Haiti, and locally in the USA, while constructing a permanent outpatient clinic in the Bicol region of the Philippines and establishing a disaster-relief fund.
Crit-Care, Derm, ENT, ER Med, Endo, General, Infect Dis, MF Med, Medicine, Nutr, OB-GYN, Ophth-Opt, Pub Health, Surg, Urol
⊕ https://vfmat.ch/3f9e

Bless Back Worldwide
Collaborates with local partners in communities in Haiti and Nicaragua to enhance healthcare, empower businesses and enrich education.
Dent-OMFS, General, Logist-Op, OB-GYN, Peds, Pub Health
⊕ https://vfmat.ch/763d

Boston Children's Hospital: Global Health Program
Helps solve pediatric global healthcare challenges by transferring expertise through long-term partnerships with scalable impact, while working in the field to strengthen healthcare systems, advocate, research, and provide care delivery or education as a way of sustainably improving the health of children worldwide.
Anesth, CV Med, Crit-Care, ER Med, Heme-Onc, Infect Dis, Medicine, Nutr, Palliative, Ped Surg, Peds
⊕ https://vfmat.ch/f9f8

Bridge of Life
Aims to strengthen healthcare globally through sustainable programs that prevent and treat chronic disease.
Logist-Op, Nephro, OB-GYN, Peds, Surg
⊕ https://vfmat.ch/5b68

Bridges Global Missions
Deploys medical teams to Haiti and the Philippines in the aftermath of disasters to address prevailing needs and manage healthcare issues.
Dent-OMFS, ER Med, General, Infect Dis, Logist-Op, Medicine, Nutr, Nutr, Peds, Pub Health
⊕ https://vfmat.ch/c8d5

Brigham and Women's Center for Surgery and Public Health
Advances the science of surgical care delivery by studying effectiveness, quality, equity, and value at the population level, and develops surgeon-scientists committed to excellence in these areas.
Anesth, ER Med, Infect Dis, Pub Health, Surg
⊕ https://vfmat.ch/5d64

Brigham and Women's Hospital Global Health Hub
Cares for patients in underserved settings, provides education to staff who work in those areas to create sustainable change, and conducts research designed to improve health in such settings.
General, Infect Dis
⊕ https://vfmat.ch/a8a3

Brothers Keepers of Haiti
Cultivates empathy and compassion, serves the less fortunate, and cares for the tridimensional well-being of people (mind, body, and spirit) in rural Southeast Haiti (specifically in Jacmel, Cayes-Jacmel, and Orangers), inspired by the Christian faith.
General, Nutr
⊕ https://vfmat.ch/6345

Buddhist Tzu Chi Medical Foundation
Provides healthcare to the poor, operates six hospitals in Taiwan and mobile medical and dental clinics in the U.S., manages a bone marrow bank, and organizes over 8,600 physicians who provide free medical services to more than 2 million people globally.
Crit-Care, Dent-OMFS, ER Med, General
⊕ https://vfmat.ch/ff61

Bureau of International Health Cooperation
Seeks to improve healthcare around the world, including developing countries, using expertise, and contribute to healthier lives of Japanese people by bringing these experiences back to Japan.

ER Med, Heme-Onc, Infect Dis, Peds, Pub Health
⊕ https://vfmat.ch/947d

Burn Advocates
Supports burn survivors as they face the challenges of recovery, rehabilitation, and reintegration.
Anesth, Crit-Care, Derm, Ped Surg, Plast, Rehab, Rehab
⊕ https://vfmat.ch/9327

Camillian Disaster Service (CADIS) International
Promotes the development of locally based health programs for disaster-stricken communities through compassionate and coordinated interventions.
General, Logist-Op, MF Med
⊕ https://vfmat.ch/5281

Canadian Medical Assistance Teams (CMAT)
Provides relief and medical aid to the victims of natural and man-made disasters around the world.
Anesth, ER Med, Medicine, OB-GYN, Peds, Psych, Rehab, Surg
⊕ https://vfmat.ch/5232

Cap Haitien Dental Institute
Provides oral healthcare in Haiti, serves as a base clinic for outreach mobile dentistry, and provides service opportunities for visiting dentists and non-healthcare workers.
Dent-OMFS
⊕ https://vfmat.ch/2b9c

CapraCare
Provides access to medical care, preventive healthcare, mental health services, and health and nutrition education regardless of ability to pay for women, children, families, and the community to combat the physical, psychosocial, and environmental needs of those living in Fronfrede, Haiti.
ER Med, General, Medicine, OB-GYN, Peds, Psych
⊕ https://vfmat.ch/6c94

CardioStart International
Provides free heart surgery and associated medical care to children and adults living in underserved regions of the world, irrespective of political or religious affiliation, through the collective skills of healthcare experts.
Anesth, CT Surg, CV Med, Crit-Care, Pub Health, Pulm-Critic
⊕ https://vfmat.ch/85ef

CARE
Works around the globe to save lives, defeat poverty, and achieve social justice.
ER Med, General
⊕ https://vfmat.ch/7232

Care 2 Communities (C2C)
Provides vulnerable families access to sustainable, high-quality healthcare services.
General, Logist-Op, MF Med, Neonat
⊕ https://vfmat.ch/cb1d

Carter Center, The
Seeks to prevent and resolve conflicts, enhance freedom and democracy, and improve health, while remaining committed to human rights and the alleviation of human suffering.
Infect Dis, MF Med, Ophth-Opt
⊕ https://vfmat.ch/6556

Catholic Medical Mission Board (CMMB)
Works in partnership globally to deliver locally sustainable, quality health solutions to women, children, and their communities.
General, MF Med, Peds
⊕ https://vfmat.ch/9498

Catholic World Mission
Works to rebuild communities worldwide by helping to alleviate poverty and empower underserved areas, while spreading the message of the Catholic Church.
ER Med, General, Nutr, Peds
⊕ https://vfmat.ch/7b5f

Centre Médical Béraca (CMB)
Provides compassionate and quality care, inspired by the Christian faith.
Anesth, CV Med, Endo, Infect Dis, Logist-Op, Medicine, Nephro, Neuro, OB-GYN, Ortho, Path, Ped Surg, Peds, Pub Health, Pulm-Critic, Radiol, Surg
⊕ https://vfmat.ch/dc1c

Chain of Hope
Provides lifesaving heart operations for children around the world and supports the development of cardiac services in numerous developing and war-torn countries.
Anesth, CT Surg, CV Med, Crit-Care, Ped Surg, Peds, Pulm-Critic, Surg
⊕ https://vfmat.ch/1b1b

Chain of Hope (La Chaîne de l'Espoir)
Helps underprivileged children around the world by providing them with access to healthcare.
Anesth, CT Surg, Crit-Care, ER Med, Neurosurg, Ortho, Ped Surg, Surg, Vasc Surg
⊕ https://vfmat.ch/e871

Chances for Children
Aims to return children to good health through medical attention and good nutrition in a supportive, faith-based environment that is conducive to their emotional and physical development.
Dent-OMFS, General, Path, Peds
⊕ https://vfmat.ch/4f75

CharityVision International
Focuses on restoring curable sight impairment worldwide by empowering local physicians and creating sustainable solutions.
Logist-Op, Ophth-Opt, Surg
⊕ https://vfmat.ch/6231

Cheerful Heart Mission
Aims to improve the lives of underprivileged people living on the border of the Dominican Republic and Haiti by funding and managing programs focused on health, education, and economic development.
Dent-OMFS, General, Infect Dis, Peds
⊕ https://vfmat.ch/ff1e

Children & Charity International
Puts people first by providing education, leadership, and nutrition programs along with mentoring and healthcare support services to children, youth, and families.
Nutr, Peds
⊕ https://vfmat.ch/6538

Children of the Nations
Aims to raise children out of poverty and hopelessness so they can become leaders who transform their nations. Emphasizes caring for the whole child—physically, mentally, socially, and spiritually.
Anesth, Dent-OMFS, General, Surg
⊕ https://vfmat.ch/cc52

Children of War Foundation
Delivers access to global health and education to communities affected by poverty, war, natural disaster, climate change, and migration challenges.
ER Med, General, Logist-Op, Peds, Surg
⊕ https://vfmat.ch/de51

Children's Health Ministries
Fights to eliminate preventable infant and child deaths due to malnutrition, prematurity, and treatable diseases.
Crit-Care, General, MF Med, Neonat, Nutr, OB-GYN, Peds
⊕ https://vfmat.ch/8d86

Children's Lifeline International
Provides medical teams and surgical assistance to underprivileged children in developing countries through missions in partnership with local hospitals.
CV Med, Dent-OMFS, General, MF Med, Neurosurg, Peds, Rehab
⊕ https://vfmat.ch/6fea

Children's Surgery International
Provides free medical and surgical services to children in need around the world,

and instructs and trains local surgeons and other medical providers such as doctors, anesthesiologists, nurses, and technicians.
Anesth, Dent-OMFS, Ortho, Ped Surg, Peds, Plast, Surg
⊕ https://vfmat.ch/26d3

Childspring International
Provides life-changing surgeries for children from developing countries and transforms communities.
CT Surg, Medicine, Ophth-Opt, Ortho, Ped Surg, Peds, Surg
⊕ https://vfmat.ch/f939

Christian Aid Ministries
Strives to be a trustworthy and efficient channel for Amish, Mennonite, and other conservative Anabaptist groups and individuals to minister to physical and spiritual needs around the world.
CT Surg, ER Med, Logist-Op, Ortho, Pub Health
⊕ https://vfmat.ch/7b33

Christian Blind Mission (CBM)
Aims to improve the quality of life of persons with disabilities in the poorest countries, addressing poverty as a cause and a consequence of disability, and working in partnership to create a society for all.
ENT, General, Infect Dis, OB-GYN, Ophth-Opt, Ortho, Peds, Psych, Rehab, Surg
⊕ https://vfmat.ch/3824

Christian Health Service Corps
Brings Christian doctors, health professionals, and health educators committed to serving the poor to places that otherwise have little or no access to healthcare.
Anesth, Dent-OMFS, General, Medicine, Peds, Surg
⊕ https://vfmat.ch/da57

Christian Medical & Dental Associations
Based in Christian ministry, deploys medical and dental teams to underserved communities to provide vital healthcare.
Anesth, Dent-OMFS, ER Med, General, Medicine, OB-GYN, Ophth-Opt, Peds, Pub Health, Radiol, Rehab, Surg
⊕ https://vfmat.ch/921c

Christie's Heart Samaritan Care Foundation
Addresses the negative impacts of a lack of available outreach services for the underserved populations of Haiti, Dominican Republic, and the United States through medical services and basic needs support.
All-Immu, General, Nutr, Ophth-Opt, Peds
⊕ https://vfmat.ch/522e

Chronic Care International
Seeks to prevent and treat chronic illnesses through program design, education, information technology, medical equipment and supplies, and funding.
General, Logist-Op, Pub Health
⊕ https://vfmat.ch/425d

Circle of Health International (COHI)
Aligns with local, community-based organizations led and powered by women to help respond to the needs of the women and children that they serve. Helps with the provision of professional volunteers, capacity training, and procurement of requested and appropriate supplies and equipment. Raises funds for the organizations to provide the services required.
ER Med, Logist-Op, MF Med, Neonat, OB-GYN, Psych
⊕ https://vfmat.ch/8b63

Clinton Health Access Initiative (CHAI)
Aims to save lives and reduce the burden of disease in low- and middle-income countries. Works with partners to strengthen the capabilities of governments and the private sector to create and sustain high-quality health systems.
General, Heme-Onc, Infect Dis, Logist-Op, MF Med, Medicine, Neonat, Nutr, OB-GYN, Path, Peds, Rad-Onc
⊕ https://vfmat.ch/9ed7

Cloud Foundation
Provides access to healthcare for medically underserved communities in the Haitian countryside.
ER Med, General, Logist-Op, Peds
⊕ https://vfmat.ch/a467

Columbia University: Columbia Office of Global Surgery (COGS)
Helps to increase access to safe and affordable surgical care, as a means to reduce health disparities and the global burden of disease.
Anesth, CT Surg, Crit-Care, Dent-OMFS, ENT, ER Med, Infect Dis, MF Med, Neurosurg, OB-GYN, Ophth-Opt, Ortho, Ped Surg, Plast, Plast, Pub Health, Surg, Urol
⊕ https://vfmat.ch/4349

Columbia University: Global Mental Health Programs
Pioneers research initiatives, promotes mental health, and aims to reduce the burden of mental illness worldwide.
Psych
⊕ https://vfmat.ch/c5cd

Columbia Vagelos College of Physicians and Surgeons Programs in Global Health
Harnesses the expertise of the medical school to improve health worldwide by training global health leaders, building capacity through interdisciplinary education and training programs, and addressing unmet health needs through research and application.
CV Med, Derm, Genetics, Heme-Onc, Infect Dis, Medicine, OB-GYN, Ophth-Opt, Peds, Psych, Pub Health, Pulm-Critic, Surg
⊕ https://vfmat.ch/a9e5

Combat Blindness International
Works to eliminate preventable blindness worldwide by providing sustainable, equitable solutions for sight through partnerships and innovation.
Ophth-Opt
⊕ https://vfmat.ch/28ad

Community Coalition for Haiti (CCH)
Transforms lives through long-term and community-driven solutions in healthcare, education, and community development.
Anesth, General, Surg
⊕ https://vfmat.ch/96dc

Community Health Initiative Haiti
Works to create healthy, empowered, and self-directed communities in Haiti.
General, Logist-Op, Nutr, Peds, Surg
⊕ https://vfmat.ch/418a

Community Organized Relief Effort (CORE)
Saves lives and strengthens communities impacted by or vulnerable to crisis.
ER Med
⊕ https://vfmat.ch/36dd

Concern Worldwide
Seeks to permanently transform the lives of people living in extreme poverty, tackling its root causes, and building resilience.
Logist-Op, MF Med, Nutr, OB-GYN
⊕ https://vfmat.ch/77e9

Concerned Haitian Americans of Illinois – C.H.A.I.
Provides education, healthcare, and clothing to children on the northern coast of Haiti.
General, Logist-Op, Nutr
⊕ https://vfmat.ch/684c

Consider Haiti
Works to support grassroot efforts to create sustainable nutrition and medical support.
General, Nutr, Peds
⊕ https://vfmat.ch/52c8

Core Group
Aims to improve and expand community health practices for underserved populations, especially women and children, through collaborative action and learning.
General, Infect Dis, MF Med, Medicine, OB-GYN, Peds, Pub Health
⊕ https://vfmat.ch/9de3

Critical Care Disaster Foundation
Seeks to educate in-country healthcare providers from developing countries in

disaster and crisis medical management, and to develop an infrastructure of critical care services.

Anesth, Crit-Care, ER Med, Logist-Op, Pulm-Critic

⊕ https://vfmat.ch/a445

Cross Catholic Outreach
Mobilizes the global Catholic Church to transform impoverished communities through the provision of food, water, housing, education, orphan support, medical care, microenterprise, and disaster relief.

All-Immu, General, Nutr, OB-GYN, Rehab

⊕ https://vfmat.ch/22f4

CRUDEM Foundation, The
Provides quality healthcare to the sick and the poor in the Haitian community.

All-Immu, General, Heme-Onc, Infect Dis, Nutr, Peds

⊕ https://vfmat.ch/8c93

Curamericas Global
Partners with communities abroad to save the lives of mothers and children by providing health services and education.

General, Infect Dis, MF Med, OB-GYN, Peds, Pub Health

⊕ https://vfmat.ch/286b

CureCervicalCancer
Focuses on the early detection and prevention of cervical cancer around the globe for the women who need it most.

Heme-Onc, OB-GYN

⊕ https://vfmat.ch/ace1

Danita's Children
Strives to care for orphans and impoverished children in Haiti by providing education, nutrition, medical, and dental care, along with a nurturing environment, to the children and families served.

Dent-OMFS, Peds, Surg

⊕ https://vfmat.ch/e889

DEAR Foundation, The
Provides support for people in need, particularly women and children, by supporting humanitarian projects administered by NGOs, primarily in the areas of health and education.

Dent-OMFS, OB-GYN

⊕ https://vfmat.ch/a747

Dental Care for Children
Strives to provide high-quality dental services for disadvantaged children around the world who lack access to adequate dental care.

Dent-OMFS

⊕ https://vfmat.ch/25ca

Dental Helping Hands
Provides dental health services to underserved communities in developing countries.

Dent-OMFS

⊕ https://vfmat.ch/7ba5

Direct Relief
Improves the health and lives of people affected by poverty or emergency situations by mobilizing and providing essential medical resources needed for their care.

ER Med, Logist-Op

⊕ https://vfmat.ch/58e5

Doctors on Mission
Provides sustainable medical healthcare to needy countries, including those having experienced recent disasters and areas where minority groups are persecuted.

General, Logist-Op, Medicine, Nutr

⊕ https://vfmat.ch/5244

Doctors Without Borders/Médecins Sans Frontières (MSF)
Responds to emergencies and provides lifesaving medical care where needed most, including during disasters, conflicts, and epidemics.

Anesth, Crit-Care, ER Med, General, Infect Dis, Nutr, OB-GYN, Ped Surg, Peds,

Psych, Pub Health, Surg

⊕ https://vfmat.ch/f363

Dorsainvil Foundation
Provides free medical treatment and healthcare education at the Complexe Medical Sainte Philomene De L'Arcahaie, Haiti.

General, Pub Health

⊕ https://vfmat.ch/799f

Douleurs Sans Frontières (Pain Without Borders)
Supports local actors in taking charge of the assessment and treatment of pain and suffering, in an integrated manner and adapted to the realities of each country.

Anesth, Palliative, Psych, Rehab

⊕ https://vfmat.ch/324c

Duke University: Global Health Institute
Sparks innovation in global health research and education, and brings together knowledge and resources to address the most important global health issues of our time.

All-Immu, Infect Dis, MF Med, OB-GYN, Pub Health

⊕ https://vfmat.ch/c4cd

Edwards Lifesciences
Provides innovative solutions for people fighting cardiovascular disease, as a global leader in patient-focused medical innovations for structural heart disease, along with critical care and surgical monitoring.

Anesth, CT Surg, CV Med, Crit-Care, Ped Surg, Peds, Pulm-Critic, Surg, Vasc Surg

⊕ https://vfmat.ch/d671

Eleos Healing Global Mission
Based in Christian ministry, provides medical care to the sick, meeting their physical needs through medical and dental short-term missions.

Dent-OMFS, General, Nutr, Peds, Pub Health

⊕ https://vfmat.ch/61a4

Emergency Response Team Search And Rescue, The (ERTSAR)
Provides technical rescue and medical response in the immediate aftermath of a disaster while providing strategic, smart, and sustainable solutions.

ER Med, Logist-Op

⊕ https://vfmat.ch/c599

Emory Haiti Alliance
Provides essential surgical services to improve patient quality of life, engages in collaborative educational efforts with local healthcare staff, and assists in local healthcare infrastructure in the town of Pignon within the Central Plateau of Haiti.

Anesth, General, Surg, Urol

⊕ https://vfmat.ch/8c8f

Emory University School of Medicine
Aims to provide residents/fellows from clinical departments with knowledge and practical experience in global health by building ongoing collaborations between Emory University and academic institutions abroad.

Anesth, CV Med, General, Infect Dis, Pulm-Critic, Rheum, Surg

⊕ https://vfmat.ch/a6f7

Emory University School of Medicine: Global Surgery Program
A leading institution with the highest standards in education, biomedical research, and patient care.

Anesth, Dent-OMFS, ER Med, Pub Health, Surg, Urol

⊕ https://vfmat.ch/2b26

Episcopal Relief & Development
Provides relief in times of disaster and promotes sustainable development by identifying and addressing the root causes of suffering.

Infect Dis, MF Med, Neonat, Nutr, Peds

⊕ https://vfmat.ch/7cfa

eRanger
Provides sustainable solutions to transportation and medical provision such as

ambulances and mobile clinics in developing countries.
ER Med, General, Logist-Op
⊕ https://vfmat.ch/4c18

Espwa Foundation, The
Develops projects that empower the people of Haiti, alleviate poverty, build relationships, and ultimately encourage hope, inspired by the Christian faith.
General, Infect Dis, Nutr, Peds
⊕ https://vfmat.ch/3252

Evidence Project, The
Improves family-planning policies, programs, and practices through the strategic generation, translation, and use of evidence.
General, MF Med
⊕ https://vfmat.ch/f9e7

Eye Foundation of America
Works toward a world without childhood blindness.
Ophth-Opt
⊕ https://vfmat.ch/a7eb

F-M Haiti Medical Mission
Aims to provide surgery and improve the healthcare and lives of people in the village of Pignon, Haiti.
General, Ped Surg, Surg
⊕ https://vfmat.ch/5fef

Fondation Hôpital Bon Samaritain (HBS)
Provides healthcare services and outreach for the greater population of Haiti's Limbé Valley, located in the Département du Nord.
General, MF Med, OB-GYN, Peds
⊕ https://vfmat.ch/258e

Forward in Health
Provides medical aid to the people of Fonfred, Haiti, by bringing quality healthcare to the region—one patient at a time.
General, Infect Dis, MF Med, Ortho
⊕ https://vfmat.ch/ed32

Foundation for Healthcare for Humanity
Provide assistance in the development and implementation of medical programs in the United States, Africa, South America, Eastern Europe, and the Caribbean.
General
⊕ https://vfmat.ch/ba7f

Foundation for Hope and Health in Haiti (FHHH), The
Provides underserved areas in Haiti with access to quality medical care.
General, MF Med, OB-GYN, Peds
⊕ https://vfmat.ch/c8c6

Foundation for Peace
Works with local communities to build schools, medical clinics, water purification facilities, churches, and more.
General, Infect Dis
⊕ https://vfmat.ch/e9f7

Friends for Health in Haiti
Aims to improve the health of the people of Haiti in a caring, compassionate manner and seeks to develop a medical facility that will provide primary healthcare to people of all ages.
ER Med, General
⊕ https://vfmat.ch/c7ed

Friends of Haiti
Combines mutual efforts to improve health, education, and economic development in four sections of Thomazeau, Haiti.
Anesth, Dent-OMFS, Ophth-Opt, Surg
⊕ https://vfmat.ch/eb17

Friends of Hope International
Works with vulnerable and at-risk youth in Latin America and the Caribbean by providing food assistance, creating self-sustainable animal husbandry, agriculture and technical projects, and empowering communities towards self-sufficiency.

General, Nutr
⊕ https://vfmat.ch/6e9f

Friends of the Children Medical Mission
Provides medical care and education to the people of LaMontagne, Haiti, during mission trips throughout the year.
General, MF Med, Medicine, Peds, Psych, Rehab
⊕ https://vfmat.ch/2377

Friends of the Children of Haiti (FOTCOH)
Provides healthcare and hope to the children of Haiti.
Dent-OMFS, General, Nutr, OB-GYN, Surg
⊕ https://vfmat.ch/9424

Friends of UNFPA
Promotes the health, dignity, and rights of women and girls around the world by supporting the lifesaving work of UNFPA, the United Nations' reproductive health and rights agency, through education, advocacy, and fundraising.
MF Med, OB-GYN
⊕ https://vfmat.ch/2a3a

Functional Literacy Ministry of Haiti: Educational & Medical Mission
Provides healthcare, education, trade skills, and employment to improve the quality of life in Haitian communities.
Dent-OMFS, MF Med, Nutr, OB-GYN, Ophth-Opt, Peds
⊕ https://vfmat.ch/f44c

G3 Foundation
Provides basic and advanced dental services to needy populations throughout the Dominican Republic.
Dent-OMFS, General
⊕ https://vfmat.ch/bf4d

Gaskov Clergé Foundation (GCF)
Promotes health, sports, education, and sciences in both the United States and Haiti through scholarship programs for students.
CV Med, Dent-OMFS, Neuro, OB-GYN, Peds, Psych
⊕ https://vfmat.ch/a75e

Gift of Life International
Provides lifesaving cardiac treatment to children in developing countries while developing sustainable pediatric cardiac programs by implementing screening, surgical, and training missions.
Anesth, CT Surg, CV Med, Crit-Care, Ped Surg, Peds, Pulm-Critic
⊕ https://vfmat.ch/f2f9

Gift of Sight
Works to eradicate preventable blindness by fostering sustainable healthcare delivery in underserved global communities.
Ophth-Opt
⊕ https://vfmat.ch/fdd7

Global Alliance to Prevent Prematurity And Stillbirth (GAPPS)
Seeks to improve birth outcomes worldwide by reducing the burden of premature birth and stillbirth.
All-Immu, Infect Dis, MF Med, Neonat, Neonat, OB-GYN
⊕ https://vfmat.ch/3f74

Global Blood Fund
Delivers grants, equipment, and training to over 50 countries in Africa, Asia, Eastern Europe, the Middle East, Latin America and the Caribbean.
Pub Health
⊕ https://vfmat.ch/6377

Global Eye Project
Empowers local communities by building locally managed, sustainable eye clinics through education initiatives and volunteer-run professional training services.
Anesth, Ophth-Opt, Surg
⊕ https://vfmat.ch/cdba

Global First Responder (GFR)
Acts as a centralized network for individuals and agencies involved in relief work

worldwide and organizes and executes mission trips to areas in need, focusing not only on healthcare delivery but also on health education and improvements.

ER Med

⊕ https://vfmat.ch/a3e1

Global Force for Healing

Works to end preventable maternal and newborn deaths by supporting the scaling of effective grassroots, community-led, culturally respectful care and education in underserved areas around the globe using the midwifery model of care.

Neonat, OB-GYN

⊕ https://vfmat.ch/deb2

Global Healing

Improves access to high-quality healthcare in underserved countries by training medical professionals across the globe to improve pediatric healthcare using sustainable resources.

ER Med, General, Heme-Onc, Path

⊕ https://vfmat.ch/a787

Global Health Coalition

Integrates modern health technology into our world's poorest communities in partnership with international health organizations using an end-to-end, data-driven approach to improving healthcare delivery with the mission of improving health outcomes.

⊕ https://vfmat.ch/97d2

Global Health Teams

Provides quality medical care and services to people in great need, supporting medical clinics in rural Southwestern Haiti and providing critical medical services in impoverished, remote areas.

General, Infect Dis, MF Med, Medicine, OB-GYN, Peds

⊕ https://vfmat.ch/1f33

Global Health Volunteers

In partnership with in-country partners, aims to provide a transforming healing presence to the poor and underserved within communities in the developing world.

ER Med, General, Ophth-Opt, Rehab

⊕ https://vfmat.ch/a3f1

Global Legacy

Supports and initiates projects with a high impact on health, education, and the advancement of women in rural communities.

Ophth-Opt

⊕ https://vfmat.ch/ff92

Global Medical Missions Alliance

Brings and promotes Christian-centered missionary life to the body of healthcare professionals and its partners.

Dent-OMFS, ER Med, Pub Health, Rehab, Surg

⊕ https://vfmat.ch/29c7

Global Medical Volunteers

Aims to advance medical services and education in developing nations around the world.

GI, Surg, Urol

⊕ https://vfmat.ch/dfec

Global Ministries – The United Methodist Church

As the worldwide mission and development agency of The United Methodist Church, Global Ministries works with more than 300 hospitals and clinics around the world through its Global Health Unit.

Anesth, CT Surg, CV Med, Crit-Care, Dent-OMFS, Derm, ER Med, GI, General, Infect Dis, Logist-Op, MF Med, Medicine, Neonat, Nephro, Nutr, OB-GYN, Ophth-Opt, Ortho, Palliative, Peds, Pod, Psych, Pub Health, Rehab, Rheum, Surg, Urol

⊕ https://vfmat.ch/1723

Global Offsite Care

Aims to be a catalyst for increased access to specialized healthcare for all, and provides technology platforms to doctors and clinics around the world through Rotary Club-sponsored telemedicine projects.

Crit-Care, ER Med, General, Pulm-Critic

⊕ https://vfmat.ch/61b5

Global Oncology (GO)

Brings the best in cancer care to underserved patients around the world and collaborates across geographic, professional, and academic borders to improve cancer care, research, and education.

Heme-Onc, Path, Rad-Onc

⊕ https://vfmat.ch/fcb8

Global Surgical Access Foundation

Partners with underserved communities to provide competent, safe, and sustainable surgical care.

Anesth, Surg

⊕ https://vfmat.ch/ea5f

Global Therapy Group

Strives to provide rehabilitation services and sustainable therapy to the people of Haiti.

ER Med, General, Ortho, Rehab

⊕ https://vfmat.ch/6bcb

Global Vision 2020

Provides prescription eyeglasses to people who live in parts of the world lacking necessary infrastructure for obtaining affordable corrective eyewear.

Logist-Op, Ophth-Opt

⊕ https://vfmat.ch/7373

Globus Relief

Aims to improve the delivery of healthcare worldwide by gathering, processing, and distributing surplus medical supplies to charities at home and abroad.

Logist-Op

⊕ https://vfmat.ch/a2b7

GOAL

Works with the most vulnerable communities to help them respond to and recover from humanitarian crises, and to assist them in building transcendent solutions to mitigate poverty and vulnerability.

ER Med, General, Pub Health

⊕ https://vfmat.ch/bbea

God's Littlest Angels (GLA)

Provides exceptional neonatal care and a safe haven to the smallest, sickest, and most vulnerable children of Haiti.

MF Med, Neonat, OB-GYN, Peds

⊕ https://vfmat.ch/a49e

Grand Anse Surgery Project

Works to holistically and passionately fulfill society's obligation to provide quality surgical care for all by providing surgical care for the residents of Jeremie, Haiti.

Anesth, CT Surg, Endo, Ortho, Plast, Surg

⊕ https://vfmat.ch/bcf3

Grassroot Soccer

Leverages the power of soccer to educate, inspire, and mobilize at-risk youth in developing countries to overcome their greatest health challenges, live healthier and more productive lives, and be agents for change in their communities.

Infect Dis

⊕ https://vfmat.ch/3521

Haiti Cardiac Alliance

Works with partners to scale up the availability of lifesaving cardiac surgery to all Haitian children who need it.

Anesth, CT Surg, CV Med, Crit-Care, Peds

⊕ https://vfmat.ch/ee78

Haiti Clinic

Works to improve healthcare and health education in the impoverished nation of Haiti.

Dent-OMFS, General, Infect Dis, MF Med

⊕ https://vfmat.ch/183c

Haiti Companions

Provides medical, dental, and eye care to three communities in Gressier, Haiti. Except for occasional visits by American providers, all of the medical providers are Haitian and honored to be serving members of their own community.

Dent-OMFS, General, Ophth-Opt
⊕ https://vfmat.ch/85ea

Haiti Eye Mission
Seeks to provide eye care in Pignon, one of Haiti's most severely impoverished communities; to fight preventable and curable blindness through annual medical mission trips; and to build awareness and support networks.
Anesth, Ophth-Opt
⊕ https://vfmat.ch/a1d1

Haiti Health & Rehabilitation
Seeks to improve the quality of life in Haiti through healthcare, education, rehabilitation, and nutrition, and aims to improve the health and well-being of the sick and the disabled.
Nutr, Peds, Pub Health
⊕ https://vfmat.ch/d8d2

Haiti Health Initiative
Aims to improve the overall health and well-being of rural Haitians, one community at a time, by providing education and services in primary healthcare, dental care, public health, and nutrition.
Dent-OMFS, General, Infect Dis, Nutr, Ophth-Opt
⊕ https://vfmat.ch/2f29

Haiti Health Ministries
Provides medical care and ministry through an outpatient medical clinic in Gressier, Haiti.
General, Infect Dis, MF Med, Peds, Radiol, Surg
⊕ https://vfmat.ch/11e2

Haiti Health Trust, The
Provides high-quality health and disability care to the most vulnerable in Haiti.
General, Infect Dis, MF Med, Peds, Rehab
⊕ https://vfmat.ch/e346

Haiti Medical Mission of Wisconsin
Serves the people of rural and remote southeast Haiti by improving access to healthcare through a partnership with Centre de Santé Sacré-Cœur de Thiotte.
Crit-Care, Dent-OMFS, ER Med, General, Ophth-Opt, Ped Surg, Surg
⊕ https://vfmat.ch/fdee

Haiti Mobile Medical Mission
Works with Haitian health officials to set up medical clinics in the most underserved communities of Leogane, Haiti.
Dent-OMFS, General
⊕ https://vfmat.ch/24ae

Haiti Neurosurgery Initiative (HNI)
Strives to develop and support a sustainable model of clinical neurosurgical coverage in Haiti.
Neurosurg
⊕ https://vfmat.ch/955c

Haiti Now
Works to improve the lives of more than 700 impoverished children in Haiti, with a goal of empowering former Restavek girls to achieve a lifetime of emotional and economic self-reliance.
General, Genetics, OB-GYN, Psych
⊕ https://vfmat.ch/a7ce

Haiti Outreach Ministries
Based in Christian ministry, provides education and healthcare in partnership with the Haitian-led Mission Communautaire de l'Eglise Chretienne des Cites (MICECC).
Dent-OMFS, General, Peds
⊕ https://vfmat.ch/2e58

Haiti Outreach Program
Strengthens the spirit, mind, and body of the Haitian community by sending three to four medical teams to Haiti each year, with a focus on providing accessible healthcare and support for construction of a hospital and clinic.
General, Peds
⊕ https://vfmat.ch/3e2b

Haiti Outreach-Pwoje Espwa
Partners with the people of Borgne, Haiti, to promote and sustain community well-being through health, education, and economic initiatives.
General
⊕ https://vfmat.ch/2645

Haitian Global Health Alliance
Provides financial support for Les Centres GHESKIO in Port-au-Prince and its network of clinics, throughout Haiti, that provide clinical service, training, and research in HIV/AIDS and related diseases.
Crit-Care, Heme-Onc, Infect Dis, MF Med, MF Med, OB-GYN, Path, Pulm-Critic
⊕ https://vfmat.ch/f513

Haitian Health Foundation
Strives to improve the health and well-being of women, children, families, and communities living in the greater Jérémie region of Haiti, serving over 225,000 people in over 100 rural mountain villages, through healthcare, education, and community development.
Dent-OMFS, Endo, General, Infect Dis, OB-GYN, Path, Peds, Radiol
⊕ https://vfmat.ch/7fb3

Hands Up for Haiti
Seeks to deliver lifesaving healthcare to the underserved people of northern Haiti through Sante Kominote (community-based healthcare).
ER Med, Nutr, OB-GYN, Ophth-Opt, Peds, Pub Health
⊕ https://vfmat.ch/ab83

Harvard Medical School: Blavatnik Institute Global Health & Social Medicine
Applies social science and humanities research to constantly improve the practice of medicine, the delivery of treatment, and the development of healthcare policies, local and worldwide.
General, Infect Dis, Logist-Op, MF Med, Medicine, Neonat, Palliative, Psych, Surg
⊕ https://vfmat.ch/9bf1

Headwaters Relief Organization
Addresses public health issues for the most underserved populations of the world, providing psychosocial and medical support along with disaster debris cleanup and rebuilding in partnership with other organizations.
ER Med, Infect Dis, Logist-Op, Psych, Pub Health
⊕ https://vfmat.ch/e511

Healing Art Missions
Aims to provide resources and funding to rural communities in Haiti that lack access to basic resources, such as healthcare, education, employment, and clean drinking water.
Anesth, General, Nutr, OB-GYN, Ophth-Opt, Path, Peds, Surg
⊕ https://vfmat.ch/6f58

Health and Education for Haiti
Works collaboratively with the Haitian people to address their critical needs, especially those related to health and education, in four program areas: medical missions, education, infrastructure, and basic needs.
Anesth, ER Med, General, Heme-Onc, OB-GYN, Ophth-Opt, Ortho, Ped Surg, Peds
⊕ https://vfmat.ch/f9dc

Health and Educational Relief Organization (HERO)
Strives to improve the health and well-being of communities in need through medical and educational outreach programs.
Dent-OMFS, General, Ophth-Opt, Ped Surg, Surg
⊕ https://vfmat.ch/db98

Health Corps Haiti: Medical Student Missions
Fosters professional and academic medical education opportunities in Haiti with a "Learning Through Service" model. Designed for medical students, field operations also involve physicians, nurses, paramedics, and lay volunteers to care for the citizens of Artibonite, Haiti.
Dent-OMFS, ER Med, General, Infect Dis, Medicine, OB-GYN, Ophth-Opt, Peds, Surg
⊕ https://vfmat.ch/77c8

Health Equity Initiative

Aims to build and sustain a global community that engages across sectors and disciplines to advance health equity.

Pub Health

⊕ https://vfmat.ch/e2e2

Health Equity International

Provides essential health services to the most vulnerable people of southern Haiti, while building a comprehensive, efficient, and resilient health system that provides high-quality care.

Anesth, Dent-OMFS, ER Med, General, Geri, Infect Dis, Logist-Op, MF Med, Medicine, Neonat, OB-GYN, Ped Surg, Peds, Plast, Pub Health, Rehab, Surg, Vasc Surg

⊕ https://vfmat.ch/9bd7

Health Frontiers

Provides volunteer support to international health and child development efforts.

ER Med, Medicine, Peds

⊕ https://vfmat.ch/aa14

Health Volunteers Overseas (HVO)

Improves the availability and quality of healthcare through the education, training, and professional development of the health workforce in resource-scarce countries.

All-Immu, Anesth, CV Med, Dent-OMFS, Derm, ENT, ER Med, Endo, GI, Heme-Onc, Infect Dis, Medicine, Medicine, Nephro, Neuro, OB-GYN, Ophth-Opt, Ortho, Peds, Plast, Psych, Pulm-Critic, Rehab, Rheum, Surg

⊕ https://vfmat.ch/42b2

Hear the World Foundation

Advocates worldwide for equal opportunities and improved quality of life for people in need with hearing loss.

ENT, Peds

⊕ https://vfmat.ch/122c

Heart Fund, The

Aims to save the lives of children suffering from heart disease by developing innovative solutions that revolutionize access to cardiac care in developing countries.

Anesth, CV Med, Ped Surg, Peds, Surg

⊕ https://vfmat.ch/7e67

Heart to Heart International

Strengthens communities through improving health access, providing humanitarian development, and administering crisis relief worldwide. Engages volunteers, collaborates with partners, and deploys resources to achieve this mission.

Anesth, ER Med, General, Logist-Op, Medicine, Path, Path, Peds, Psych, Pub Health, Surg

⊕ https://vfmat.ch/aacb

Heineman Medical Outreach

Provides medical and educational assistance globally to promote sustainable healthcare and enhanced living standards in underserved communities through the International Medical Outreach (IMO) program, a collaborative partnership between Heineman Medical Outreach and Atrium Health.

Anesth, CT Surg, CV Med, ER Med, General, Heme-Onc, Logist-Op, Medicine, Neonat, OB-GYN, Ped Surg, Peds, Surg, Vasc Surg

⊕ https://vfmat.ch/389b

HelpAge International

Works to ensure that people everywhere understand how much older people contribute to society and that they must enjoy their right to healthcare, social services, economic, and physical security.

General, Geri, Infect Dis, Medicine, Pub Health

⊕ https://vfmat.ch/5d91

Hernia Help

Provides free hernia surgery to underserved children and adults in the Western Hemisphere, practicing the preferential option for the poor. Trains, mentors, develops, and supports local general surgeons who will serve as trainers and future leaders to create self-sustaining teams.

Anesth, Surg

⊕ https://vfmat.ch/6319

Hernia International

Aims to provide relief from sickness, and protection and preservation of health, for persons affected by groin and abdominal hernias and residing in low- and middle-income countries.

Surg

⊕ https://vfmat.ch/e98e

HERO Foundation USA

Matches veterans, EMS, and civilian medical volunteers with a permanent EMS program in Haiti.

ER Med, Pub Health

⊕ https://vfmat.ch/f54c

Higgins Brothers Surgicenter for Hope

Aims to address the critical shortage of surgical facilities and trained surgeons in Haiti through the volunteer efforts of surgeons and others, and by raising financial resources to develop a long-term solution serving all Haitians in Fonds-Parisien.

Anesth, Dent-OMFS, Heme-Onc, Medicine, OB-GYN, Path, Peds, Pod, Radiol, Surg, Urol, Vasc Surg

⊕ https://vfmat.ch/a959

His Healing Hands

Seeks to provide disease treatment and prevention in partnership with indigenous evangelical Christian organizations that help guide activities.

General

⊕ https://vfmat.ch/ce38

Hope for Haiti

Improves the quality of life for the Haitian people, particularly children, by taking an integrated approach to sustainability that focuses on education, healthcare, water, infrastructure, and economy.

Dent-OMFS, General, Logist-Op, Medicine, Nutr

⊕ https://vfmat.ch/92a7

Hope for Haiti (The Catholic Church of Saint Monica)

Provides medical, dental, and financial assistance to the poor and underserved of Haiti.

Dent-OMFS, General

⊕ https://vfmat.ch/edb2

Hope for Haitians

Provides housing, reliable food sources, clean water, medical care, education, and economic opportunity as part of a comprehensive approach to aid development in Haiti.

General

⊕ https://vfmat.ch/318b

Hope for the Children of Haiti

Seeks to empower Haitian children with the tools they need to succeed, including healthcare, and gives them the opportunity to become well-rounded, self-sufficient adults with a foundation in Christianity.

General, Peds

⊕ https://vfmat.ch/fe73

H.O.P.E. Haiti Outreach

Aims to help the Borgne, Haiti, community create a safe place where every child can count on food, clean water, healthcare, learning, and livelihood.

General, Infect Dis, Surg

⊕ https://vfmat.ch/df32

Hope Health Action

Facilitates sustainable, lifesaving health, and disability care for the world's most vulnerable, without any discrimination.

ER Med, MF Med, Neonat, Nutr, OB-GYN, Peds, Rehab

⊕ https://vfmat.ch/86f7

Hope Smiles

Develops and empowers healthcare leaders to restore hope and transform lives by mobilizing and equipping sustainable dental teams in unreached communities.

Dent-OMFS, Pub Health, Surg

⊕ https://vfmat.ch/8a76

Hope Walks
Frees children, families, and communities from the burden of clubfoot, inspired by the Christian faith.
Ortho, Ped Surg, Peds, Rehab
⊕ https://vfmat.ch/f6d4

Hope Worldwide
Changes lives through the compassion and commitment of dedicated staff and volunteers delivering sustainable, high-impact, community-based services to the poor and underserved.
Dent-OMFS, General, OB-GYN, Ophth-Opt, Peds
⊕ https://vfmat.ch/89b3

HumaniTerra
Helps countries and populations emerging from economic and human crisis to rebuild their healthcare system in a sustainable way. Committed to three fundamental and complementary actions: operating, training, and rebuilding.
Anesth, ENT, ER Med, MF Med, OB-GYN, Ortho, Plast, Surg
⊕ https://vfmat.ch/b371

Humanity & Inclusion
Works alongside people with disabilities and vulnerable populations, taking action and bearing witness in order to respond to their essential needs, improve their living conditions and health, and promote respect for their dignity and fundamental rights.
General, Infect Dis, MF Med, Medicine, Ortho, Peds, Psych, Pub Health, Rehab
⊕ https://vfmat.ch/16b7

Hunger Relief International
Works to fight hunger and increase self-sufficiency of children and families impacted by extreme poverty, natural disasters and civil conflicts.
Pub Health
⊕ https://vfmat.ch/4f7e

Hôpital Alma Mater
Provides quality preventive and curative care 24 hours a day to patients in Gros Morne, a rural region in northwest Haiti.
Dent-OMFS, General, Infect Dis, MF Med, Medicine, OB-GYN, Path, Peds, Radiol
⊕ https://vfmat.ch/65d4

ICAP at Columbia University
Serves as global leader in supporting the scale-up of multidisciplinary HIV/AIDS prevention, care, and treatment programs based on a family-focused approach.
General, Infect Dis, MF Med, Medicine, OB-GYN, Pub Health
⊕ https://vfmat.ch/a8ef

IMA World Health
Works to build healthier communities by collaborating with key partners to serve vulnerable people with a focus on health, healing, and well-being for all.
Infect Dis, MF Med, Nutr, OB-GYN, Pub Health
⊕ https://vfmat.ch/8316

Innovating Health International (IHI)
Treats chronic diseases and addresses women's health issues in Haiti, Somaliland, and Malawi.
ER Med, Heme-Onc, Medicine, OB-GYN, Path, Plast, Pub Health
⊕ https://vfmat.ch/e712

International Allied Missions (IAM), Haiti
Envisions a dynamic healthcare community that will aid the growth of Haitian doctors and nurses, and provide year-round support for medical professionals from around the world to care for, teach, and help facilitate a sustainable healthcare system in Haiti.
Anesth, Dent-OMFS, General, Peds, Surg
⊕ https://vfmat.ch/edcf

International Children's Heart Foundation
Provides free surgical care, medical training, and technology to save the lives of children with congenital heart disease in developing countries.
Anesth, CT Surg, CV Med, Crit-Care, Ped Surg, Peds, Pulm-Critic
⊕ https://vfmat.ch/86c1

International Children's Heart Fund
Aims to promote the international growth and quality of cardiac surgery, particularly in children and young adults.
CT Surg, Ped Surg
⊕ https://vfmat.ch/33fb

International Community Initiatives
Supports the charity and development projects of underserved communities by engaging volunteers, professionals and students in collaborative work with our partnering organizations.
ER Med, Peds, Pub Health
⊕ https://vfmat.ch/d54d

International Council of Ophthalmology
Works with ophthalmologic societies and others to enhance ophthalmic education and improve access to the highest-quality eye care in order to preserve and restore vision for people of the world.
Ophth-Opt
⊕ https://vfmat.ch/ffd2

International Eye Foundation (IEF)
Eliminates preventable and treatable blindness by making quality sustainable eye care services accessible and affordable worldwide.
Infect Dis, Logist-Op, Ophth-Opt
⊕ https://vfmat.ch/e839

International Federation of Gynecology and Obstetrics (FIGO)
Implements global projects on specific women's health issues.
MF Med, Medicine, Neonat, OB-GYN, Surg, Urol
⊕ https://vfmat.ch/c4b4

International Federation of Red Cross and Red Crescent Societies (IFRC)
Coordinates and directs international assistance following natural and manmade disasters in nonconflict situations through the world's largest humanitarian and development network. Provides disaster-preparedness programs, healthcare activities, and promotes humanitarian values.
ER Med, General, Infect Dis, Nutr
⊕ https://vfmat.ch/b4ee

International HELP
Works alongside churches, organizations, and community groups to help educate and empower local people in sustainable and effective ways for the improvement of health, while also providing health education and health services related to first aid, nutrition, water, sanitation, and hygiene.
General, MF Med
⊕ https://vfmat.ch/ccf5

International Learning Movement (ILM UK)
Supports some of the world's poorest people in developing countries with core projects in education, safe drinking water, and healthcare.
General, Ophth-Opt
⊕ https://vfmat.ch/b974

International Medical Alliance
Provides access to medical, vision, and dental care in underserved and vulnerable communities around the world, to improve health, wellness, and the quality of life for populations most in need.
Dent-OMFS, General, Infect Dis, OB-GYN, Ophth-Opt, Peds, Surg
⊕ https://vfmat.ch/2e7d

International Medical Relief
Provides sustainable education, training, medical and dental care, and disaster relief and response in vulnerable communities worldwide.
Dent-OMFS, General, Infect Dis, Medicine, OB-GYN
⊕ https://vfmat.ch/b3ed

International Medical Response
Supplements, supports, and enhances healthcare systems in communities across the world that have been incapacitated by natural disaster, extreme poverty, and/or regional conflict by sending a multidisciplinary team of healthcare professionals.

Anesth, General, OB-GYN, Surg
⊕ https://vfmat.ch/9ccd

International Missionary Fellowship
Serves a Northwestern community in Haiti by meeting basic needs such as medical care, education, and water, inspired by the Christian faith.
Dent-OMFS, General, OB-GYN, Ophth-Opt
⊕ https://vfmat.ch/f62c

International Organization for Migration (IOM) – The UN Migration Agency
Promotes evidence-informed policies and holistic, preventive, and curative health programs that are beneficial, accessible, and equitable for vulnerable migrants.
General, Infect Dis, OB-GYN
⊕ https://vfmat.ch/621a

International Outreach Program of St. Joseph's Health System
Works to save lives in developing countries by training doctors through partnerships with universities, medical schools, and teaching hospitals in countries that need more doctors.
Logist-Op
⊕ https://vfmat.ch/a751

International Planned Parenthood Federation (IPPF)
Leads a locally owned, globally connected civil society movement that provides and enables services and champions sexual and reproductive health and rights for all, especially the underserved.
Infect Dis, MF Med, OB-GYN
⊕ https://vfmat.ch/dc97

International Smile Power
Partners with people to improve and sustain dental health and build bridges of friendship around the world.
Dent-OMFS
⊕ https://vfmat.ch/ba69

International Women & Infant Sustainable Healthcare (IWISH Foundation)
Provides training to local medical care providers in Haiti to sustain quality care for women and children in local communities.
Logist-Op, MF Med, Neonat, OB-GYN, Peds
⊕ https://vfmat.ch/db52

Iranian Red Crescent
Aims to provide effective relief services in the wake of crises, to alleviate human suffering, and to empower the affected community.
ER Med, General, Infect Dis, Logist-Op, Nutr, OB-GYN, Psych, Rehab
⊕ https://vfmat.ch/c352

Iris Global
Serves the poor, the destitute, the lost, and the forgotten by providing adoration, outreach, family, education, relief, development, healing, and the arts.
General, Infect Dis, Nutr, Pub Health
⊕ https://vfmat.ch/37f8

Iris Mundial
Aims to improve the ocular health of underserved people in developing countries by giving them access to high-quality preventive and curative eye care services.
Ophth-Opt
⊕ https://vfmat.ch/4f85

Islamic Medical Association of North America
Fosters health promotion, disease prevention, and health maintenance in communities around the world through direct patient care and health programs.
Anesth, Dent-OMFS, ER Med, General, Logist-Op, Ophth-Opt, Peds, Plast, Surg
⊕ https://vfmat.ch/a157

IsraAID
Supports people affected by humanitarian crisis and partners with local communities around the world to provide urgent aid, assist recovery, and reduce the risk of future disasters.
ER Med, Infect Dis, Psych, Rehab
⊕ https://vfmat.ch/de96

IVUmed
Aims to make quality urological care available worldwide by providing medical and surgical education for physicians and nurses, and treatment for thousands of children and adults.
Anesth, OB-GYN, Ped Surg, Surg, Urol
⊕ https://vfmat.ch/e619

Izumi Foundation
Develops and supports programs that improve health and healthcare in neglected regions of Africa and Latin America.
⊕ https://vfmat.ch/f29a

John Snow, Inc. (JSI)
Aims to improve the health and well-being of underserved and vulnerable people and communities throughout the world.
General, Infect Dis, Logist-Op, MF Med, OB-GYN, Peds, Psych, Pub Health
⊕ https://vfmat.ch/ba78

Joint United Nations Programme on HIV/AIDS (UNAIDS)
Aims to place people living with HIV and people affected by the virus at the decision-making table and at the center of designing, delivering, and monitoring the AIDS response.
Infect Dis
⊕ https://vfmat.ch/464a

Kay Mackenson Clinic for Children with Chronic Diseases
Works to improve the health of Haitian children suffering from chronic illnesses by providing high-quality, compassionate, and family-centered care, in addition to education and solidarity.
General, Medicine, Peds
⊕ https://vfmat.ch/84e5

Kidejapa Surgical Missions
Provide plastic and reconstructive services to children of developing countries.
Ped Surg, Plast
⊕ https://vfmat.ch/a98f

Kletjian Foundation
Works toward a world in which all people have access to safe, sustainable, and high-quality medical care, building collaborative networks and supporting entrepreneurial leaders that promote global health equity.
CT Surg, ENT, General, Ortho, Surg
⊕ https://vfmat.ch/12c2

Konbit Sante Cap-Haitien Health Partnership
Supports the development of a sustainable health system to meet the needs of the Cap-Haitien community, with maximum local direction and support.
General, OB-GYN, Peds, Pub Health
⊕ https://vfmat.ch/16f2

La Salle International Foundation
Provides support for educational, health, and human services, along with humanitarian relief to people in developed and underdeveloped areas.
General
⊕ https://vfmat.ch/5891

Labakcare
Aims to improve the health of underserved communities by providing no-cost preventive healthcare services.
General, MF Med, Ophth-Opt
⊕ https://vfmat.ch/1e61

Lamp for Haiti
Works with and for the people of Haiti to improve the lives of some of the most marginalized persons in Haitian society.
ER Med, General, Infect Dis, Nutr, OB-GYN, Peds
⊕ https://vfmat.ch/8788

Last Mile Health
Links community health workers with frontline health workers—nurses, doctors, and midwives at community clinics—and supports them to bring lifesaving services to the doorsteps of people living far from care.

General, Logist-Op, OB-GYN, Pub Health
⊕ https://vfmat.ch/37da

Lavi Project
Provides medical care in Haiti by mobilizing medical missions/volunteers and collecting monetary donations and supplies to support clinics and programs.
General
⊕ https://vfmat.ch/e1aa

LEAP Global Missions
Provides specialized surgical services to underserved populations around the world.
Anesth, Dent-OMFS, ENT, Ped Surg, Peds, Plast, Surg
⊕ https://vfmat.ch/b447

Lespwa Lavi
Supports the community of Verrettes, Haiti, with a school and other programs such as healthcare and nutrition, based in Christian ministry.
ER Med, General, Nutr
⊕ https://vfmat.ch/dad3

Life for a Child
Supports the provision of the best possible healthcare, given local circumstances, to all children and youth with diabetes in less-resourced countries, through the strengthening of existing diabetes services.
Endo, Medicine, Peds
⊕ https://vfmat.ch/d712

Limbs International
Engages communities and transforms lives through affordable, sustainable prosthetic solutions and rehabilitation services in developing countries.
Logist-Op, Ortho, Pod, Rehab
⊕ https://vfmat.ch/dc84

Lions Clubs International
Empowers volunteers to serve their communities, meet humanitarian needs, encourage peace, and promote international understanding through Lions Clubs.
Heme-Onc, Medicine, Nutr, Ophth-Opt
⊕ https://vfmat.ch/7b12

Los Medicos Voladores – The Flying Doctors
Aims to build and strengthen underserved communities through healthcare, education, and volunteerism.
Dent-OMFS, General
⊕ https://vfmat.ch/4411

Love Takes Root
Aims to improve the lives of children by providing shelter, education, and healthcare.
Dent-OMFS, General, Logist-Op, Surg
⊕ https://vfmat.ch/832d

Lutherans in Medical Missions (LIMM)
Works with local and global partners to promote healing in medically underserved communities.
General, Logist-Op, Pub Health
⊕ https://vfmat.ch/c5aa

MAGNA International
Helps those who are suffering or recovering from conflicts and disasters by reducing the risks of diseases and treating them immediately.
ER Med, General, Infect Dis, Peds, Surg
⊕ https://vfmat.ch/58f4

Maison de Naissance: Global Birthing Home Foundation
Aims to significantly reduce maternal and infant mortality rates in impoverished communities by sponsoring Maison de Naissance ("Home of Birth"), a modern maternal health center supporting healthy mothers and healthy babies in Haiti.
General, MF Med, Neonat, OB-GYN
⊕ https://vfmat.ch/e959

Making A Difference Foundation
Sponsors and organizes medical missions for medical providers to provide care to

underserved communities around the world.
CV Med, Dent-OMFS, ER Med, General, Infect Dis, Logist-Op, MF Med, Neonat, Nutr, OB-GYN, Ophth-Opt, Ortho, Pub Health, Pulm-Critic, Rehab, Surg
⊕ https://vfmat.ch/5556

Management Sciences for Health (MSH)
Works with countries and communities to save lives and improve the health of the world's poorest and most vulnerable people by building strong, resilient, sustainable health systems.
Infect Dis, Logist-Op, Pub Health
⊕ https://vfmat.ch/6aa2

Maryknoll Lay Missioners
Based in Christian ministry, aims to collaborate with poor communities in Africa, Asia, and the Americas in order to respond to basic needs, including heathcare, and to help create a more compassionate world.
Logist-Op, Nutr
⊕ https://vfmat.ch/2ce6

Massachusetts General Hospital Global Surgery Initiative
Aims to improve surgical education and access to advanced surgical care in resource-limited settings around the world by performing surgical operations as visitors, training local surgeons, and sharing medical technology through international partnerships across disciplines.
Anesth, Crit-Care, ER Med, Heme-Onc, Peds, Surg
⊕ https://vfmat.ch/31b1

MaterCare International (MCI) (Canada)
Works to improve the lives and health of mothers and babies through programs in healthcare provision, training, research, and advocacy, with the aim to address maternal and perinatal mortality and morbidity in developing countries.
OB-GYN
⊕ https://vfmat.ch/a92e

Maternity Foundation
Works to ensure safer childbirth for women and newborns everywhere through innovative mobile health solutions such as the Safe Delivery App, a mobile training tool for skilled birth attendants.
MF Med, OB-GYN, Pub Health
⊕ https://vfmat.ch/ff4f

Maternity Worldwide
Works with communities and partners to identify and develop appropriate and effective ways to reduce maternal and newborn mortality and morbidity, facilitate communities to access quality skilled maternity care, and support the provision of quality skilled care.
MF Med, OB-GYN
⊕ https://vfmat.ch/822b

Maverick Collective
Aims to build a global community of strategic philanthropists and informed advocates who use their intellectual and financial resources to create change.
Infect Dis, MF Med, OB-GYN
⊕ https://vfmat.ch/ea49

McGill University Health Centre: Centre for Global Surgery
Works to reduce the impact of injury by advancing surgical care through research and education in resource-limited settings.
ER Med, Logist-Op, Ped Surg, Surg
⊕ https://vfmat.ch/7246

Medical Aid to Haiti (MATH)
Sponsors medical missions to Haiti and sponsors a Haitian-staffed mobile medical clinic in the Port-au-Prince area.
Anesth, MF Med, OB-GYN, Surg
⊕ https://vfmat.ch/e3f4

Medical Ambassadors International
Equipping communities through Christ-centered health and development.
Nutr, OB-GYN, Pub Health
⊕ https://vfmat.ch/8e76

Medical Benevolence Foundation (MBF)
Works with partners in developing countries to build sustainable healthcare for those most in need through faith-based global medical missions.
General, Logist-Op, MF Med, OB-GYN, Surg
⊕ https://vfmat.ch/c3e8

Medical Care Development International
Works to improve the health of vulnerable populations through integrated, sustainable, and locally driven interventions.
Infect Dis, OB-GYN, Peds, Pub Health
⊕ https://vfmat.ch/da87

Medical Evacuation Disaster Intervention Corps (Medic Corps)
Provides emergency response and medical care during times of catastrophic disaster, based in Christian ministry.
ER Med
⊕ https://vfmat.ch/c8cf

Medical Ministry International
Provides compassionate healthcare in areas of need, inspired by the Christian faith.
CT Surg, Dent-OMFS, ENT, General, OB-GYN, Ophth-Opt, Ortho, Plast, Rehab, Surg, Urol, Vasc Surg
⊕ https://vfmat.ch/5da6

Medical Mission Exchange (MMEX)
Gives medical mission organizations a way to share information among one another so they can capitalize on each other's strengths and better serve their patients.
All-Immu, Anesth, CT Surg, CV Med, Dent-OMFS, Derm, ER Med, General, OB-GYN, Ophth-Opt, Ortho, Path, Ped Surg, Plast, Psych, Radiol, Rehab, Surg, Urol
⊕ https://vfmat.ch/bc8c

Medical Mission Trips
Provides medical aid, welfare assistance, and educational opportunities in Brazil, Honduras, Guatemala, Kenya, Burundi, and Ethiopia.
General
⊕ https://vfmat.ch/9117

Medical Missionaries
Provides medical care, medicine, medical supplies, medical equipment, clothing, food, and other supplies to the poorest of the poor throughout the world.
ER Med, Logist-Op
⊕ https://vfmat.ch/5f15

Medical Relief International
Exists to provide dental, medical, humanitarian aid, and other services deemed necessary for the benefit of people in need.
Dent-OMFS, General
⊕ https://vfmat.ch/192b

Medical Teams International
Seeks to restore health as the first step to restoring hope, working to bring basic but lifesaving medical care to those in need.
Dent-OMFS, ER Med, General, MF Med, Pub Health
⊕ https://vfmat.ch/8d1c

Medicines for Humanity
Aims to save the lives of vulnerable children by strengthening systems of maternal and child health in the communities served.
Infect Dis, MF Med, OB-GYN
⊕ https://vfmat.ch/8d13

MedShare
Aims to improve the quality of life of people, communities, and the planet by sourcing and directly delivering surplus medical supplies and equipment to communities in need around the world.
Logist-Op
⊕ https://vfmat.ch/c8bc

Middle Ground
Works to fight against malnutrition in Haiti.
Nutr, Peds
⊕ https://vfmat.ch/e687

Midwives for Haiti
Increases access to skilled maternity care in Haiti by direct healthcare intervention and training programs through partnerships with Haiti's Ministry of Public Health and Population and other organizations.
MF Med, Neonat, OB-GYN
⊕ https://vfmat.ch/2c57

Mission of Hope
Partners with local churches to transform lives through church advancement, nutrition, education, and medical care to bring life transformation to every man, woman, and child.
General
⊕ https://vfmat.ch/d3c5

Mission of Love
Strives to identify community needs and supports initiatives and resources for healthcare facilities, education facilities, nutritional programs, and survival programs.
General, Pub Health, Surg
⊕ https://vfmat.ch/bb3d

Mission Regan
Collects supplies, medication, and medical equipment and provides them to those who are in desperate need, both locally and globally.
Logist-Op
⊕ https://vfmat.ch/2bc1

Mission Vision
Seeks to decrease blindness and other eye-related disabilities, and to increase academic performance and general quality of life.
Ophth-Opt
⊕ https://vfmat.ch/83d8

Mission-Haiti
Provides medical, educational, and child-focused programs to communities in need, inspired by the Christian faith.
General, Geri
⊕ https://vfmat.ch/4a6a

Mission: Haiti
Seeks to reach out to individuals, organizations, and congregations that wish to understand, encourage, love, and serve the people of Haiti through service teams.
General
⊕ https://vfmat.ch/b1b7

Mission: Restore
Trains medical professionals abroad in complex reconstructive surgery in order to create a sustainable infrastructure in which long-term relationships are forged and permanent change comes to pass.
Plast, Surg
⊕ https://vfmat.ch/3f5f

MIVO Foundation
Operates an orthopedic clinic in L'estere, Haiti, and brings orthopedic care and services to underserved communities through medical missions, based in Christian ministry.
Anesth, Ortho, Rehab
⊕ https://vfmat.ch/85a1

Mobility Outreach International
Enables mobility for children and adults in under-resourced areas of the world, and creates a sustainable orthopedic surgery model using local resources.
Ortho, Rehab
⊕ https://vfmat.ch/9376

More Than Medicine
Provides ENT head/neck care while supporting local doctors to grow the quality of medicine abroad.
Anesth, ENT, Heme-Onc, Surg
⊕ https://vfmat.ch/c4e8

MPACT for Mankind
Transforms communities by improving health outcomes, enhancing knowledge, and providing hope while promoting sustainable growth.
ER Med, General
🌐 https://vfmat.ch/1c61

MSD for Mothers
Designs scalable solutions that help end preventable maternal deaths.
MF Med, OB-GYN, Pub Health
🌐 https://vfmat.ch/9f99

Médecins du Monde/Doctors of the World
Provides care, bears witness, and supports social change worldwide with innovative medical programs and evidence-based advocacy initiatives.
ER Med, General, Infect Dis, MF Med, Neonat, OB-GYN, Peds, Pub Health
🌐 https://vfmat.ch/a43d

Mérieux Foundation
Committed to fighting infectious diseases that affect developing countries by capacity building, particularly in clinical laboratories, and focusing on diagnosis.
Logist-Op, Path
🌐 https://vfmat.ch/a23a

Northeast Hope for Haiti
Works to improve the health of people living in the greater Petite Rivière de l'Artibonite region of Haiti.
General, Surg
🌐 https://vfmat.ch/d145

Northwest Haiti Christian Mission (NWHCM)
Facilitates engagement in NWHCM's efforts, Based in Christian ministry, in fostering diverse programs that include primary and secondary schools, nutrition programs, medical clinics, orphanages, and the empowerment of indigenous churches.
Dent-OMFS, ER Med, General, MF Med, Nutr, Ophth-Opt, Surg
🌐 https://vfmat.ch/2438

Nuestros Pequeños Hermanos (NPH)
Strives to create a loving and safe family environment for vulnerable children living in extreme conditions.
Psych, Rehab
🌐 https://vfmat.ch/57c4

Nuestros Pequeños Hermanos (Our Little Brothers and Sisters) New Zealand
Helps vulnerable children and families break the cycle of poverty with assistance through its pediatric hospital, healthcare clinics, day care centers, and scholarship programs.
CT Surg, Heme-Onc, Infect Dis, Nutr, OB-GYN, Peds, Rehab
🌐 https://vfmat.ch/e9cc

Nyagi
Empowers local healthcare workers in resource-poor areas to diagnose life-threatening health conditions through accelerated, low-cost ultrasound skills training.
Logist-Op, Pub Health
🌐 https://vfmat.ch/5de5

NYC Medics
Deploys mobile medical teams to remote areas of disaster zones and humanitarian emergencies, providing the highest level of medical care to those who otherwise would not have access to aid and relief efforts.
All-Immu, ER Med, Infect Dis, Surg
🌐 https://vfmat.ch/aeee

One Good Turn
Provides practical medical education and culturally sensitive medical care to neglected communities worldwide.
Dent-OMFS, General
🌐 https://vfmat.ch/545f

One Spirit Medical Missions
Seeks to encourage and facilitate self-sufficiency in community health by training and supporting local community health workers, based in Christian ministry.
ER Med, General, Medicine
🌐 https://vfmat.ch/d271

Operation Endeavor M99+
Provides direct support for public health and safety, EMS system development, and disaster response in developing and underserved regions, both domestic and abroad, while providing training in rescue, emergency medicine, and trauma care.
Dent-OMFS, ER Med, Infect Dis, Logist-Op, OB-GYN, Peds, Surg
🌐 https://vfmat.ch/d83a

Operation International
Offers medical aid to adults and children suffering from lack of quality healthcare in impoverished countries.
Dent-OMFS, ER Med, Heme-Onc, OB-GYN, Ophth-Opt, Ortho, Ped Surg, Plast, Surg
🌐 https://vfmat.ch/b52a

Operation Medical
Commits efforts to promoting and providing high-quality medical care and education to communities that do not have adequate access.
Anesth, ENT, Logist-Op, OB-GYN, Ped Surg, Plast, Surg, Urol
🌐 https://vfmat.ch/7e1b

Operation Rainbow
Performs free orthopedic surgery, in developing countries, for children and young adults who do not otherwise have access to related medical procedures or equipment.
Anesth, Ortho, Ped Surg, Peds, Rehab, Surg
🌐 https://vfmat.ch/5dad

Operation Smile
Treats patients with cleft lip and cleft palate, and creates solutions that deliver safe surgery to people where it's needed most.
Anesth, Dent-OMFS, ENT, Ped Surg, Plast
🌐 https://vfmat.ch/5c29

Optivest Foundation
Funds strategic opportunities that are holistic and collaborative, inspired by the Christian faith.
General, Nutr
🌐 https://vfmat.ch/f1e6

Optometry Giving Sight
Delivers eye exams and low or no-cost glasses, provides training for local eye care professionals, and establishes optometry schools, vision centers and optical labs.
Ophth-Opt
🌐 https://vfmat.ch/33ea

Order of Malta
Supports forgotten or excluded people, especially those living in conflict zones or amid natural disasters, by providing medical assistance, caring for refugees, and distributing medicines and necessities.
ER Med, General, Infect Dis, MF Med, Nephro, OB-GYN, Ortho, Psych
🌐 https://vfmat.ch/1fab

Oregon Health Sciences University: Global Health Advocacy Program in Surgery
Contributes to the care of patients across the globe and advances OHSU's strategic plan to become an international leader in health and science.
General, Medicine, Peds, Pub Health, Surg
🌐 https://vfmat.ch/77a4

Organization for Renal Care in Haiti, The (TORCH)
Brings lifesaving medical care to patients with kidney disease in Haiti that is not otherwise available to them, while providing education, medical equipment, training, and resources to medical professionals and facilities in Haiti.
Medicine, Nephro
🌐 https://vfmat.ch/bda4

Orthopaedic Relief Services International
Provides increased clinical, educational, and infrastructural support for Hopital de

l'Universite d'Etat d'Haiti orthopedic surgical services and its residency program.
ER Med, General, Ortho
⊕ https://vfmat.ch/e9b3

Partners in Health
Responds to the moral imperative to provide high-quality healthcare globally to those who need it most, while striving to ease suffering by providing a comprehensive model of care that includes access to food, transportation, housing, and other key components of healing.
CT Surg, General, Heme-Onc, Infect Dis, MF Med, Neurosurg, OB-GYN, Ortho, Plast, Psych, Urol
⊕ https://vfmat.ch/dc9c

Paul Chester Children's Hope Foundation, The
Aims to improve the health and well-being of children and young adults in developing countries by providing early intervention where services are otherwise unavailable.
Anesth, Dent-OMFS, ENT, General, Logist-Op, Logist-Op, Ophth-Opt, Ped Surg, Peds, Surg
⊕ https://vfmat.ch/83e2

Pediatric Universal Life-Saving Effort, Inc. (PULSE)
Aims to increase access to acute- and intensive-care services for children, recognizing that a significant amount of childhood mortality is preventable. Utilizes time, talents, and resources and seeks to persuade others to share their gifts to enrich the lives of children worldwide.
Crit-Care, Logist-Op, Neonat, Ped Surg, Peds
⊕ https://vfmat.ch/f6b9

Peterborough Paramedics & Beyond (PPAB)
Provides opportunities for healthcare professionals and lay people to offer hands-on, sustainable medical and humanitarian services in impoverished communities.
General, Logist-Op
⊕ https://vfmat.ch/3ba6

Pharmacists Without Borders Canada
Provides pharmaceutical and technical assistance in the implementation or improvement of community and hospital pharmacies internationally.
⊕ https://vfmat.ch/7658

Phoenix Rising for Haiti
Creates networks of sustainable rehabilitation clinics throughout rural Haiti run by Haitian professionals and locally trained staff.
ER Med, General, OB-GYN, Ortho, Rehab
⊕ https://vfmat.ch/67ee

Picture of Health Foundation
Provides communities with health education and empowers people to alter unhealthy lifestyles, thus increasing both life expectancy and quality.
General, Pub Health
⊕ https://vfmat.ch/83e3

Project Concern International (PCI)
Drives innovation from the ground up to enhance health, end hunger, overcome hardship, and advance women and girls—resulting in meaningful and measurable change in people's lives.
Infect Dis, MF Med, Nutr, OB-GYN, Peds
⊕ https://vfmat.ch/5ed7

Project H.O.P.E., Inc.
Mobilizes volunteers to serve in Nicaragua and Haiti, building homes and conducting medical clinics, inspired by the Christian faith.
Dent-OMFS, General, Nutr, Ophth-Opt
⊕ https://vfmat.ch/99af

Project Haiti
Provides medical care and education in Haiti.
Anesth, General, Medicine, Radiol, Surg, Urol
⊕ https://vfmat.ch/f95b

Project Medishare for Haiti
Empowers Haitians to provide and receive access to quality healthcare, improves health infrastructure, and strengthen the skills of medical professionals.

General, MF Med, Nutr, OB-GYN, Peds
⊕ https://vfmat.ch/5f59

Project SOAR
Conducts HIV operations research around the world to identify practical solutions to improve HIV prevention, care, and treatment services.
ER Med, General, MF Med, OB-GYN, Psych
⊕ https://vfmat.ch/1a77

Promise for Haiti
Provides healthcare, education, evangelism, economic development, and safe water in Pignon, Haiti.
Dent-OMFS, General, Infect Dis, MF Med, OB-GYN, Ophth-Opt, Rehab
⊕ https://vfmat.ch/79b2

PSI – Population Services International
Aims to improve the health of people in the developing world by focusing on challenges such as a lack of family planning, HIV/AIDS, barriers to maternal health, and the greatest threats to children under the age of 5, including malaria, diarrhea, pneumonia, and malnutrition.
Infect Dis, MF Med, OB-GYN, Peds
⊕ https://vfmat.ch/ffe3

Queensland Foundation for Children, Health and Education (QFCHE)
Works for children, higher education, and scientific research, health, education, environment, public hygiene, population, and development, contributing to the development of the Haitian community.
General
⊕ https://vfmat.ch/8e4f

RAD-AID International
Improves and optimizes access to medical imaging and radiology in low-resource regions of the world.
Rad-Onc, Radiol
⊕ https://vfmat.ch/537f

Real Love Ministries International
Supports the people of Haiti by ministering to the needs of the total person—physical, emotional, and spiritual—based in Christian ministry.
General, MF Med, Nutr, Peds
⊕ https://vfmat.ch/c7d2

Real Medicine Foundation (RMF)
Provides humanitarian support to people living in disaster- and poverty-stricken areas, focusing on the person as a whole by providing medical/physical, emotional, economic, and social support.
ER Med, General, Infect Dis, Nutr, Peds, Psych
⊕ https://vfmat.ch/d45a

Reconstructing Women International
Treats patients in their local communities through groups of international volunteers made up of female plastic surgeons using local medical facilities, in cooperation with local medical professionals.
Anesth, Plast, Rehab, Surg
⊕ https://vfmat.ch/924a

Remote Area Medical Volunteer Corps
Brings free high-quality medical, vision, dental, and veterinary care to those in need.
Dent-OMFS, ER Med, General, Heme-Onc, MF Med, OB-GYN, Ophth-Opt
⊕ https://vfmat.ch/7669

RestoringVision
Empowers lives by restoring vision for millions of people in need.
Ophth-Opt
⊕ https://vfmat.ch/e121

Right to Sight and Health
Seeks to reduce the prevalence of blindness and visual impairment, especially among low-income communities in Northern Ghana.
Ophth-Opt
⊕ https://vfmat.ch/7ff1

Rose Charities International

Aims to support communities to improve quality of life and reduce the effects of poverty through innovative, self-sustaining projects, and partnerships.

ENT, ER Med, General, Infect Dis, Neonat, OB-GYN, Ophth-Opt, Ped Surg, Peds, Rehab, Urol

⊕ https://vfmat.ch/53df

Rotary International

Provides service to others, improves lives, and advances world understanding, goodwill, and peace through its fellowship of business, professional, and community leaders.

ER Med, General, Infect Dis, MF Med, OB-GYN

⊕ https://vfmat.ch/8fb5

ROW Foundation

Works to improve the quality of training for healthcare providers, and the diagnosis and treatment available to people with epilepsy and associated psychiatric disorders in under-resourced areas of the world.

Neuro, Psych

⊕ https://vfmat.ch/25eb

Rutgers New Jersey Medical School

Seeks to support and promote the global health efforts of the faculty, staff, and students in the areas of education, research, and service through the Rutgers New Jersey Medical School's Office of Global Health.

Anesth, CV Med, Crit-Care, Neurosurg, OB-GYN, Psych

⊕ https://vfmat.ch/8e67

Saint Rock Haiti Foundation

Provides quality primary healthcare, helps children and young adults access valuable education opportunities, institutes community outreach programs that support economic sustainability, and invests in infrastructure to support overall health.

Dent-OMFS, General, Infect Dis, MF Med, Nutr, OB-GYN, Path, Peds

⊕ https://vfmat.ch/5aa8

Salvation Army International, The

Seeks to meet human needs through services in education, healthcare, community support, emergency response, and ministry development, inspired by the Christian faith.

Dent-OMFS, Derm, ER Med, Infect Dis, MF Med, Medicine, Nutr, OB-GYN, Ophth-Opt, Palliative, Psych, Rehab, Surg

⊕ https://vfmat.ch/8eb3

SAMU Foundation

Provides medical first response and reconstruction when severe international emergencies occur.

ER Med, Infect Dis, Logist-Op, Psych, Pub Health

⊕ https://vfmat.ch/3196

Sante Haiti

Ensures that men, women, and children of Haiti are able to enjoy health as a human right, by providing services in education and empowerment.

General, Pub Health

⊕ https://vfmat.ch/c6e7

Save the Children

Gives children around the world a healthy start in life, the opportunity to learn, and protection from harm.

All-Immu, Crit-Care, ER Med, General, Infect Dis, MF Med, Medicine, Neonat, OB-GYN, Peds, Psych, Pub Health

⊕ https://vfmat.ch/2e73

Second Chance Haiti

Aims to empower families and leave a legacy through child sponsorship, family empowerment, and medical care programs.

Dent-OMFS, ER Med, General, Ophth-Opt, Psych

⊕ https://vfmat.ch/35d9

Second Chance Smile Global Dental Outreach Foundation

Provides acute dental care with regular follow-ups and training for local oral health educators, and advocates for sustainable government oral health policy.

Dent-OMFS, Infect Dis, Logist-Op

⊕ https://vfmat.ch/daaf

SEE International

Provides sustainable medical, surgical, and educational services through volunteer ophthalmic surgeons, with the objectives of restoring sight and preventing blindness to disadvantaged individuals worldwide.

Ophth-Opt, Surg

⊕ https://vfmat.ch/6e1b

Serve Humanity Foundation (SHF)

Provides education, job training, community creation, and empowerment, and access to medical care to underserved and underprivileged communities.

General

⊕ https://vfmat.ch/d2f5

ServeHAITI

Fosters health and development opportunities for the people of Grand-Bois, Haiti.

General, Neonat, OB-GYN, Peds

⊕ https://vfmat.ch/1193

SEVA

Delivers vital eye care services to the world's most vulnerable, including women, children, and Indigenous peoples.

Ophth-Opt, Surg

⊕ https://vfmat.ch/1e87

SIGN Fracture Care International

Builds orthopedic capacity around the world and provides the injured poor access to fracture surgery by donating orthopedic education and implant systems to surgeons in developing countries.

Ortho, Rehab, Surg

⊕ https://vfmat.ch/123d

SINA Health

Aims to improve the health and educational status of the population in low- and middle-income countries.

General, Logist-Op

⊕ https://vfmat.ch/9ad3

SladeChild Foundation

Provides food, clothing, shelter, education, and medical care to some of the world's most impoverished children.

Dent-OMFS, General, Logist-Op, Ophth-Opt

⊕ https://vfmat.ch/14c5

Smile Train, Inc.

Treats children with cleft lip through a sustainable and local model that supports surgery and other forms of essential care.

Logist-Op, Pub Health

⊕ https://vfmat.ch/822c

Soaring Unlimited

Works in partnership with the people of the greater Cap Haitien community to enhance quality of life in the areas of medical services, education, and community development.

General, MF Med, OB-GYN

⊕ https://vfmat.ch/c5ac

Soddo Christian Hospital

Mobilizes volunteers to help transform communities through healthcare and education, based in Christian ministry.

ER Med, General

⊕ https://vfmat.ch/efa4

Spine Care International

Extends spine care to the underprivileged and provides life-changing treatment to those who may otherwise be constrained to living with chronic pain.

Neurosurg, Ortho, Rehab, Surg

⊕ https://vfmat.ch/a867

Sri Sathya Sai International Organization

Inspired by spiritual teachings, carries out efforts in global healthcare, education,

humanitarian relief, and youth engagement.
Dent-OMFS, General, Logist-Op, Nutr, Ophth-Opt, Pub Health
⊕ https://vfmat.ch/9bda

St. Luke Foundation for Haiti
Provides comprehensive medical, educational, and social support services to some of the most marginalized groups in Haiti.
ER Med, Infect Dis, Logist-Op, MF Med, Nutr, OB-GYN, Peds, Peds, Pub Health
⊕ https://vfmat.ch/f6c5

Surgical Friends Foundation
Provides reconstructive surgery and post-operative care to individuals living with physical deformities and lacking access to quality medical care.
Dent-OMFS, ENT, Plast, Surg
⊕ https://vfmat.ch/8286

Sustainable Kidney Care Foundation (SKCF)
Works to provide treatment for kidney injury where none exists, and aims to reduce mortality from treatable acute kidney injury (AKI).
Infect Dis, Medicine, Nephro
⊕ https://vfmat.ch/1926

Sustainable Therapy And New Development (STAND): The Haiti Project
Works to establish permanent access to orthopedic rehabilitative services in the country of Haiti through direct patient care and clinical training of Haitian citizens.
General, Ortho, Rehab
⊕ https://vfmat.ch/8bea

Task Force for Global Health, The
Consists of programs and focus areas that cover a range of global health issues including neglected tropical diseases, infectious diseases, vaccines, field epidemiology, public health informatics, health workforce development, and global health ethics.
Infect Dis, Logist-Op, Medicine, Ophth-Opt, Peds
⊕ https://vfmat.ch/714c

Team Broken Earth
Brings medical relief and education to those who need it most by sending volunteer teams of healthcare professionals to areas of wide-ranging relief response.
Medicine, OB-GYN, Ophth-Opt, Rehab, Surg
⊕ https://vfmat.ch/bfcd

Team Canada Healing Hands
Provides and develops interdisciplinary rehabilitation treatment, education, and training in areas of need.
ENT, Neuro, Psych, Rehab
⊕ https://vfmat.ch/2eaf

Tearfund
Responds to crisis and partners with local churches to bring restoration to those living in poverty, inspired by the Christian faith.
ER Med, Logist-Op
⊕ https://vfmat.ch/f6cf

Terre des hommes (Tdh) Foundation
Works to improve the daily life of children and their relatives in the areas of health, protection and emergency, in Europe, Africa, Asia, Latin America, and the Near and Middle East.
CT Surg, CV Med, OB-GYN, Ped Surg, Pub Health
⊕ https://vfmat.ch/5c26

Tzu Chi Medical Foundation
Organizes medical missions through a global network of licensed doctors and nurses who provide medical care to impoverished communities and respond to disasters around the world.
Dent-OMFS, ER Med, Nutr, OB-GYN, Ophth-Opt, Peds, Pub Health
⊕ https://vfmat.ch/81a3

Union for International Cancer Control (UICC)
Unites and supports the cancer community to reduce the global cancer burden, promote greater equity, and ensure that cancer control continues to be a priority

in the world health and development agenda.
Heme-Onc, Pub Health
⊕ https://vfmat.ch/88b1

United MegaCare
Seeks to deliver high-caliber services and programming across its areas of focus: education, health and wellness, secure families, and disaster resiliency.
ER Med, General, Infect Dis, Nutr, Ophth-Opt, Peds
⊕ https://vfmat.ch/ea18

United Nations Children's Fund (UNICEF)
Works in over 190 countries and territories to save children's lives, defend their rights, and help them fulfill their potential, from early childhood through adolescence.
All-Immu, Infect Dis, MF Med, Neonat, Nutr, OB-GYN, Ped Surg, Peds, Pub Health
⊕ https://vfmat.ch/42d7

United Nations Development Programme (UNDP)
Helps countries achieve the simultaneous eradication of extreme poverty and significant reduction of inequalities and exclusion using a sustainable human development approach.
Infect Dis, Logist-Op, Pub Health
⊕ https://vfmat.ch/935c

United Nations High Commissioner for Refugees (UNHCR)
Safeguards the rights and well-being of people who have been forced to flee, ensuring that everybody has the right to seek asylum and find safe refuge in another country, with the goal of seeking lasting solutions.
General, MF Med, Medicine, OB-GYN, Peds, Psych, Pub Health
⊕ https://vfmat.ch/6636

United Nations Office for the Coordination of Humanitarian Affairs (OCHA)
Contributes to principled and effective humanitarian response through coordination, advocacy, policy, information management, and humanitarian financing tools and services, by leveraging functional expertise throughout the organization.
Logist-Op
⊕ https://vfmat.ch/22b8

United Nations Population Fund (UNFPA)
Supports reproductive healthcare for women and youth in more than 150 countries, focusing on delivering a world in which every pregnancy is wanted, every childbirth is safe, and every young person's potential is fulfilled.
Infect Dis, MF Med, Neonat, OB-GYN, Peds, Pub Health
⊕ https://vfmat.ch/c969

United States Agency for International Development (USAID)
Promotes and demonstrates democratic values abroad and advances a free, peaceful, and prosperous world. Leads the U.S. government's international development and disaster assistance through partnerships and investments that save lives.
ER Med, Infect Dis, MF Med, OB-GYN, Peds
⊕ https://vfmat.ch/9a99

United States President's Emergency Plan for AIDS Relief (PEPFAR)
The U.S. global HIV/AIDS response works to prevent new HIV infections and accelerate progress to control the global epidemic in more than 50 countries, by partnering with governments to support sustainable, integrated, and country-led responses to HIV/AIDS.
Infect Dis, Pub Health
⊕ https://vfmat.ch/a57c

University of Chicago: Center for Global Health
Collaborates with communities locally and globally to democratize education, increase service learning opportunities, and advance sustainable solutions to improve health and well-being while reducing global health inequities.
Genetics, MF Med, Peds, Pub Health
⊕ https://vfmat.ch/4f8f

University of Florida College of Medicine (Global Health Education Program)

Strives to improve individual and community health through discovery and clinical and translational science, and through technology, education, and patient-centered healthcare.

Anesth, Dent-OMFS, General, Ophth-Opt, Pub Health, Surg

⊕ https://vfmat.ch/aee1

University of Illinois at Chicago: Center for Global Health

Aims to improve the health of populations around the world and reduce health disparities by collaboratively conducting trans-disciplinary research, training the next generations of global health leaders, and building the capacities of global and local partners.

Pub Health

⊕ https://vfmat.ch/b749

University of Massachusetts Medical School: Department of Surgery Global Scholars

Provides state-of-the-art surgical care to patients and serves communities worldwide through education, research, and public service.

Anesth, ER Med, Surg

⊕ https://vfmat.ch/3e8e

University of Notre Dame – Haiti Program Neglected Tropical Diseases Initiative

Supports efforts by Hopital Sainte Croix (HSCC) in Leogane, Haiti, to eliminate lymphatic filariasis (LF) through mass drug administration and ease the suffering of Haitians afflicted with the disease through clinical therapies.

Infect Dis, Logist-Op, Pub Health

⊕ https://vfmat.ch/3cb8

University of Pennsylvania Perelman School of Medicine Center for Global Health

Aims to improve health equity worldwide through enhanced public health awareness and access to care, discovery, and outcomes-based research, and comprehensive educational programs grounded in partnership.

Heme-Onc, Infect Dis, OB-GYN

⊕ https://vfmat.ch/cb57

University of Virginia: Anesthesiology Department Global Health Initiatives

Educates and trains physicians to help people achieve healthy productive lives, and advances knowledge in the medical sciences.

Anesth, Pub Health

⊕ https://vfmat.ch/1b8b

University of Washington: The International Training and Education Center for Health (I-TECH)

Works with local partners to develop skilled healthcare workers and strong national health systems in resource-limited countries.

Infect Dis, Pub Health

⊕ https://vfmat.ch/642f

USA for United Nations High Commissioner for Refugees (UNHCR)

Serves and protects refugees and displaced people through emergency relief, cash assistance, education, resettlement, and the rebuilding of livelihoods.

ER Med, General, Logist-Op, Nutr, Pub Health

⊕ https://vfmat.ch/293c

USAID: EQUIP Health

Exists as an effective, efficient response mechanism to achieving global HIV epidemic control by delivering the right intervention at the right place and in the right way.

Infect Dis

⊕ https://vfmat.ch/d76a

USAID: Global Health Supply Chain Program

Combines 8 complementary projects working globally to achieve stronger, more resilient health supply chains.

Infect Dis, Logist-Op, Pub Health

⊕ https://vfmat.ch/115f

USAID: Health Finance and Governance Project

Uses research to implement strategies to help countries develop robust governance systems, increase their domestic resources for health, manage those resources more effectively, and make wise purchasing decisions.

Logist-Op

⊕ https://vfmat.ch/8652

USAID: Health Policy Initiative

Provides field-level programming in health policy development and implementation.

General, Infect Dis, MF Med, OB-GYN, Peds

⊕ https://vfmat.ch/8f84

USAID: Leadership, Management and Governance Project

Improves leadership, management, and governance practices to strengthen health systems and improve health for all, including vulnerable populations worldwide.

Logist-Op

⊕ https://vfmat.ch/d35e

USAID: Maternal and Child Survival Program

Works to prevent child and maternal deaths.

Infect Dis, MF Med, Neonat, OB-GYN, Peds

⊕ https://vfmat.ch/6fcf

Vanderbilt University Medical Center: Global Surgery

Aims to improve the healthcare of individuals and communities regionally, nationally, and internationally, combining transformative learning programs and compelling discoveries to provide distinctive personalized care.

CT Surg, CV Med, Neurosurg, Ophth-Opt, Ortho, Ped Surg, Surg, Urol

⊕ https://vfmat.ch/ee28

Variety – The Children's Charity International

Funds and delivers programs that focus on multiple unmet needs of children who are sick or disadvantaged, or live with disabilities and other special needs. Works at a local, national and international level, including the delivery of critical healthcare and medical equipment.

General, Infect Dis, Logist-Op

⊕ https://vfmat.ch/41f5

Vision Care

Restores sight and helps patients get regular treatment at short-term eye camps and long-term base clinics by having doctors, missionaries, volunteers, and sponsors work together.

Ophth-Opt

⊕ https://vfmat.ch/9d7c

Vision for the Poor

Reduces human suffering and improves quality of life through the recovery of sight by building sustainable eye hospitals in developing countries, empowering local eye specialists, funding essential ophthalmic infrastructure, and partnering with like-minded agencies.

Ophth-Opt

⊕ https://vfmat.ch/528e

Vision Outreach International

Advocates for helping the blind in underserved regions of the world and empowers the poor through sight restoration.

Ophth-Opt

⊕ https://vfmat.ch/9721

Visitation Hospital Foundation

Provides competent and compassionate healthcare to the people of southwest Haiti by empowering them with resources to pursue their basic right to health and health education.

All-Immu, General, Infect Dis, MF Med

⊕ https://vfmat.ch/aa2b

Vitamin Angels

Helps at-risk populations in need—specifically pregnant women, new mothers, and children under age 5—to gain access to life-changing vitamins and minerals.

General, Nutr

⊕ https://vfmat.ch/7da1

VOSH (Volunteer Optometric Services to Humanity) International

Facilitates the provision and the sustainability of vision care worldwide for people who can neither afford nor obtain such care.

Ophth-Opt

⊕ https://vfmat.ch/a149

Walkabout Foundation

Provides wheelchairs and rehabilitation in the developing world and funds research to find a cure for paralysis.

Logist-Op, Rehab

⊕ https://vfmat.ch/5582

Watsi

Uses technology to make healthcare a reality for those who might not otherwise be able to afford it.

Pub Health, Surg

⊕ https://vfmat.ch/41a3

Weill Cornell Medicine: Center for Global Health

Collaborates with international partners to improve the health of people in resource-poor countries through research, training, and service.

General, Infect Dis, OB-GYN

⊕ https://vfmat.ch/1813

Wichita County Medical Alliance

Mobilizes volunteers to assist in public health efforts in the U.S. and abroad, including medical missions and disaster relief.

General, Geri, Nutr, OB-GYN, Pub Health

⊕ https://vfmat.ch/fa55

Women's Refugee Commission

Seeks to improve lives by protecting the rights of women, children, and youth displaced by conflict and crisis through researching their needs, identifying solutions, and advocating for programs and policies to strengthen their resilience.

General, MF Med, Neonat, OB-GYN, Peds, Psych

⊕ https://vfmat.ch/3d8f

World Children's Fund

Commits to helping children worldwide who are suffering the effects of poverty, disease, natural disaster, famine, abuse, civil strife, and war.

General, Logist-Op, MF Med, Nutr, OB-GYN, Pub Health

⊕ https://vfmat.ch/9cd8

World Compassion Fellowship (WCF)

Serves the global poor and persecuted through relief, medical care, development, and training.

CV Med, ER Med, Endo, GI, General, Infect Dis, Medicine, Nutr, OB-GYN, Ortho, Peds, Psych, Pub Health, Rehab

⊕ https://vfmat.ch/7b97

World Council of Optometry

Facilitates the development of optometry worldwide and promotes eye health and vision care through advocacy, education, policy development, and humanitarian outreach.

Ophth-Opt, Pub Health

⊕ https://vfmat.ch/c92e

World Health Organization, The (WHO)

The United Nations' agency for health provides leadership on global health matters, shapes the health research agenda, sets norms and standards, articulates evidence-based policy options, provides technical support and monitoring to countries, and assesses health trends.

ER Med, General, Infect Dis, Logist-Op, MF Med, OB-GYN, Peds, Psych, Pub Health

⊕ https://vfmat.ch/c476

World Health Partnerships

Provides medical care and mental health education to allow people in underserved countries the foundation for improved physical, mental, and spiritual lives.

Anesth, OB-GYN, Psych, Surg

⊕ https://vfmat.ch/5d34

World Hope International

Empowers the poorest individuals around the world so they can become agents of change within their communities, by offering resources and knowledge.

Infect Dis, Logist-Op, MF Med, OB-GYN, Peds

⊕ https://vfmat.ch/a4b8

World Medical Relief

Facilitates the distribution of surplus medical resources where they are needed.

Logist-Op

⊕ https://vfmat.ch/72dc

World Rehabilitation Fund

Enables individuals around the world with functional limitations and participation restrictions to achieve community and social integration through physical and socioeconomic rehabilitation and advocacy.

Ortho, Rehab

⊕ https://vfmat.ch/a5bc

World Relief

Brings sustainable solutions to the world's greatest problems: disasters, extreme poverty, violence, oppression, and mass displacement.

ER Med, Nutr, Psych, Pub Health

⊕ https://vfmat.ch/fbcd

World Surgical Foundation

Provides charitable surgical healthcare to the world's poor and underserved in developing nations.

Ped Surg, Surg

⊕ https://vfmat.ch/c162

World Telehealth Initiative

Provides medical expertise to the world's most vulnerable communities to build local capacity and deliver core health services through a network of volunteer healthcare professionals supported with state-of-the-art technology.

Derm, Infect Dis, MF Med, Medicine, Neuro, OB-GYN, Peds, Pulm-Critic

⊕ https://vfmat.ch/fa91

World Vision International

Works with vulnerable communities around the world to overcome poverty and injustice with child-focused programs in disaster management, health, nutrition, economic development, education, clean water, sanitation, and hygiene.

ER Med, General, Infect Dis, MF Med, Nutr, OB-GYN, Peds

⊕ https://vfmat.ch/2642

Worldwide Healing Hands

Works to improve the quality of healthcare for women and children in the most underserved areas of the world and to stop the preventable deaths of mothers.

General, MF Med, Neonat, OB-GYN

⊕ https://vfmat.ch/b331

WorldWide Orphans (WWO)

Seeks to transform the lives of vulnerable children, families, and communities through trauma-informed, evidence-based programming.

General, Peds, Pub Health

⊕ https://vfmat.ch/2538

Yale School of Medicine: Global Surgery Division

Addresses the rising worldwide surgical disease burden in low-resource settings, both domestically and internationally, by mobilizing a community of surgical leaders to engage in international partnerships and implement quality improvement and training protocols.

ER Med, Infect Dis, Medicine, Peds

⊕ https://vfmat.ch/2bf7

Haiti

Healthcare Facilities

Alma Mater
Rue Balmir, Commune Gros Morne, Département de l'Artibonite, Haiti
🌐 https://vfmat.ch/4644

Anse Rouge Hospital Anse Rouge (AFME)
Rue St. Joseph, Commune Anse Rouge, Département de l'Artibonite, Haiti
🌐 https://vfmat.ch/eb93

Arcahaie Hospital Saint Joseph de Galilée
Rue Michel Lafrague, Commune Arcahaie, Département de l'Ouest, Haiti
🌐 https://vfmat.ch/dd8f

AVSI
Boulevard des Americains, Port-au-Prince, Haiti
🌐 https://vfmat.ch/f4f8

Baie de Henne
RD 102, Commune Bombardopolis, Département du Nord-Ouest, Haiti
🌐 https://vfmat.ch/a2cb

Bishop Joseph M. Sullivan Hospital
Plaine Marion, Haiti
🌐 https://vfmat.ch/32e3

Bon Samaritain des Roseaux
Commune Roseaux, Département de la Grande-Anse, Haiti
🌐 https://vfmat.ch/5981

Cal de Madian
RD 201, Commune Petite Rivière de Nippes, Département des Nippes, Haiti
🌐 https://vfmat.ch/48ec

CAL de Mont Organise
RD 602, Commune Mont Organisé, Département du Nord-Est, Haiti
🌐 https://vfmat.ch/c982

Care SOS France
Rue du Calvaire, Commune Môle-Saint-Nicolas, Département du Nord-Ouest, Haiti
🌐 https://vfmat.ch/6267

Carrefour Joute
RC 205C, Commune Saint-Jean-du-Sud, Département du Sud, Haiti
🌐 https://vfmat.ch/f445

CBP St. Raphael
RD 103, Commune Saint-Raphaël, Département du Nord, Haiti
🌐 https://vfmat.ch/39e4

Centre Ambulancier National
Delmas, Haiti
🌐 https://vfmat.ch/4cb7

Centre Hospitalier Christian Martinez
1 Rue Beaudrouin, Commune Jacmel, Département du Sud-Est, Haiti
🌐 https://vfmat.ch/5967

Centre Hospitalier de Lamardelle
RD 111, Commune Ganthier, Département de l'Ouest, Haiti
🌐 https://vfmat.ch/f15f

Centre Hospitalier Fontaine
Cité Soleil, Port-au-Prince, Haiti
🌐 https://vfmat.ch/ac3c

Com. Bonne Fin
RD 204, Commune Cavaillon, Département du Sud, Haiti
🌐 https://vfmat.ch/79d5

Corail Hospital
Route Départementale #703, Commune Corail, Département de la Grande-Anse, Haiti
🌐 https://vfmat.ch/1e65

Croix Rouge Haitienne
Impasse Saint Joseph, Commune Arcahaie, Département de l'Ouest, Haiti
🌐 https://vfmat.ch/ec89

Croix-Rouge at Fort-Liberté
Rue Sainte-Anne, Commune Fort-Liberté, Département du Nord-Est, Haiti
🌐 https://vfmat.ch/eed6

Fonfred
Route la Fresiliere, Commune Torbeck, Département du Sud, Haiti
🌐 https://vfmat.ch/ff54

French Hospital/Hôpital Français d'Haiti
Ruelle Nemour, Pòtoprens, Département de l'Ouest, Haiti
🌐 https://vfmat.ch/7ba8

German Red Cross Basic Care Unit
Delmas 52, Commune de Delmas, Département de l'Ouest, Haiti
🌐 https://vfmat.ch/343a

Gheskio
33 Boulevard Harry Truman, Pòtoprens, Département de l'Ouest, Haiti
🌐 https://vfmat.ch/c282

Grace Children's Hospital
Delmas 31, Port-au-Prince, Haiti
🌐 https://vfmat.ch/4e9f

Help Hospital
Rue Saint Laurent, Commune Léogâne, Département de l'Ouest, Haiti
🌐 https://vfmat.ch/4aeb

Hospital Bethel Fonds-des-Nègres/ Armée du Salut
RN 2, Commune Fonds-des-Nègres, Département des Nippes, Haiti
🌐 https://vfmat.ch/4f73

Hospital Bonneau St. Joseph
Duval 37, Commune Croix-des-Bouquets,
Département de l'Ouest, Haiti
⊕ https://vfmat.ch/9188

Hospital Finca
Rue Simone Duvalier, Les Cayes, Haiti
⊕ https://vfmat.ch/45aa

Hospital Fosref/Lakay Saint Marc
Saint-Marc, Haiti
⊕ https://vfmat.ch/8c95

Hospital La Sainte Famille
Jedo, Jacmel, Département du Sud-Est, Haiti
⊕ https://vfmat.ch/6583

Hospital Raboteau
16 Rue Frères Simmonds, Cité Militaire, Port-au-
Prince, Haiti
⊕ https://vfmat.ch/1912

Hôpital Adventiste d'Haïti
Diquini 63, Route de la Mairie de Carrefour, Kafou,
Port-au-Prince Département de l'Ouest, Haiti
⊕ https://vfmat.ch/13b5

Hôpital Albert Schweitzer (HAS)
Desjardines, Haiti
⊕ https://vfmat.ch/be8a

Hôpital Alma Mater
RN 5, Commune Gros Morne, Département de
l'Artibonite, Haiti
⊕ https://vfmat.ch/d47b

Hôpital Beraca la Pointe
Rue Monfort, Commune de Port-de-Paix,
Département du Nord-Ouest, Haiti
⊕ https://vfmat.ch/7fe4

Hôpital Bienfaisance de Pignon
Rue Hôpital de Bienfaisance, Commune Pignon,
Département du Nord, Haiti
⊕ https://vfmat.ch/1c97

Hôpital Borgne
Rue des Pecheurs, Commune Borgne, Département
du Nord, Haiti
⊕ https://vfmat.ch/93e7

Hôpital Charles Colimon
Petite Rivière de l'Artibonite, Haiti
⊕ https://vfmat.ch/5ce8

Hôpital Christ du Nord
Rues K et 17, Cap Haïtien, Haiti
⊕ https://vfmat.ch/ac93

**Hôpital Communautaire Autrichien-
Haïtien**
RC 102A, Commune Jean Rabel, Département du
Nord-Ouest, Haiti
⊕ https://vfmat.ch/bc11

**Hôpital Communautaire de Référence
Dr. Raoul Pierre-Louis**
Carrefour, Haiti
⊕ https://vfmat.ch/e348

Hôpital de Beudet
Rue Rigaud, Commune Croix-des-Bouquets,
Département de l'Ouest, Haiti
⊕ https://vfmat.ch/cfe7

**Hôpital de la Communauté Dame-
Marienne**
220, Commune Dame-Marie, Département de la
Grande-Anse, Haiti
⊕ https://vfmat.ch/5f89

Hôpital de la Nativite
Grand Rue, Commune Belladère, Département du
Centre, Haiti
⊕ https://vfmat.ch/efc8

Hôpital de Petit Trou de Nippes
Boulevard de la Liberté, Commune Petit Trou de
Nippes, Département des Nippes, Haiti
⊕ https://vfmat.ch/72cd

Hôpital de Port-à-Piment
Port-à-Piment, Haiti
⊕ https://vfmat.ch/435f

Hôpital de Robillard
Road to Citadelle, Commune de Milot, Département
du Nord, Haiti
⊕ https://vfmat.ch/9de6

Hôpital Dessalines Claire Heureuse
La Colline, Commune d'Aquin, Département du Sud,
Haiti
⊕ https://vfmat.ch/a65b

Hôpital Département de l'Ouest
Rue Haut Timo, Commune Léogâne, Département de
l'Ouest, Haiti
⊕ https://vfmat.ch/8975

Hôpital Espoir
Avenue Fragneauville, Commune de Delmas,
Département de l'Ouest, Haiti
⊕ https://vfmat.ch/eb3e

Hôpital Espérance
Route Grande-Savane, Commune Pilate,
Département du Nord, Haiti
⊕ https://vfmat.ch/9c82

Hôpital Français
378 Rue du Centre, Pòtoprens, Département de
l'Ouest, Haiti
⊕ https://vfmat.ch/66cd

Hôpital Glacis Courreaux
Château, Haiti
⊕ https://vfmat.ch/6fb6

Hôpital Immaculée Conception
Rue Monseigneur Maurice, Commune Les Cayes,
Département du Sud, Haiti
⊕ https://vfmat.ch/ed4a

Hôpital Justinien
Rue 17 Q, Cap Haitien, Haiti
⊕ https://vfmat.ch/f5cf

Hôpital La Providence des Gonaives
Gonaives, Haiti
⊕ https://vfmat.ch/3566

Hôpital L'Eglise de Dieu Réformé
Saintard, Haiti
⊕ https://vfmat.ch/ae26

Hôpital Notre Dame
32 RN 2, Arrondissement des Cayes, Haiti
⊕ https://vfmat.ch/9e31

**Hôpital Notre Dame de La Paix de Jean-
Rabel**
15, Rue Notre Dame, Jean-Rabel, Nord-Ouest, Haiti
⊕ https://vfmat.ch/775f

Hôpital Notre Dame des Palmistes
Île de La Tortue, Département du Nord-Ouest, Haiti
⊕ https://vfmat.ch/8873

Hôpital Saint Antoine
RC 205C, Commune Saint-Jean-du-Sud,
Département du Sud, Haiti
⊕ https://vfmat.ch/7131

Hôpital Saint Boniface
Fond-des-Blancs, Haiti
⊕ https://vfmat.ch/5fcb

Hôpital Saint Landy
Rue Aubrant, Pétion-Ville, Haiti
⊕ https://vfmat.ch/b889

Hôpital Saint Nicolas
Rue Savannah, Saint-Marc, Haiti
⊕ https://vfmat.ch/835d

Hôpital Saint-Jean de Limbé
RN 1, Commune Limbé, Département du Nord, Haiti
⊕ https://vfmat.ch/a676

Hôpital Saint-Pierre
RD 703, Commune Corail, Département de la
Grande-Anse, Haiti
⊕ https://vfmat.ch/5ca3

Hôpital Sainte Catherine
Avenue Soleil, Cité Soleil, Département de l'Ouest,
Haiti
⊕ https://vfmat.ch/48a2

Hôpital Sainte Croix
1 Rue La Croix, Commune Léogâne, Département de l'Ouest, Haiti
⊕ https://vfmat.ch/e6b9

Hôpital Sainte Marie Etoile de Mer
Cite Soleil, Ojapon Bas Ti Ayiti, Haiti
⊕ https://vfmat.ch/8422

Hôpital Sainte Thérèse de Hinche
Rue Paul Eugene Magloire, Commune Hinche, Département du Centre, Haiti
⊕ https://vfmat.ch/5855

Hôpital Sainte Thérèse de Miragoâne
RD 201, Commune Miragoane, Département des Nippes, Haiti
⊕ https://vfmat.ch/d96c

Hôpital Sainte-Anne
HT-7, Camp Perrin, Haiti
⊕ https://vfmat.ch/a125

Hôpital Universitaire de la Paix
Delmas 33, Delmas, Haiti
⊕ https://vfmat.ch/887c

Hôpital Universitaire de Mirebalais
RD 11, Arrondissement de Mirebalais, Haiti
⊕ https://vfmat.ch/71b2

Institut Fame Pereo
Pòtoprens, Département de l'Ouest, Haiti
⊕ https://vfmat.ch/e873

Jeremie Hôpital la Source
Rue Source Dommage, Commune de Jérémie, Département de la Grande-Anse, Haiti
⊕ https://vfmat.ch/ee83

Kay Sante Pa' W
Rue Jean Baptiste Point du Sable, Commune de Saint-Marc, Département de l'Artibonite, Haiti
⊕ https://vfmat.ch/3bbb

King's Hospital
Route Petite Place Cazeau, Caradeux, Haiti
⊕ https://vfmat.ch/3d4d

Medimax Hospital
Avenue Christophe, Pòtoprens, Département de l'Ouest, Haiti
⊕ https://vfmat.ch/3f19

Miragoane District Hospital
RN 2, Commune Miragoane, Département des Nippes, Haiti
⊕ https://vfmat.ch/bec1

Miragoane Hospital Paillant
RD 201, Commune Miragoane, Département des Nippes, Haiti
⊕ https://vfmat.ch/fb63

Mombin Crochu Hospital
Rue Salomon, Commune La Victoire, Département du Nord, Haiti
⊕ https://vfmat.ch/fa75

Mont Organisé Hospital
RD 602, Commune Mont Organisé, Département du Nord-Est, Haiti
⊕ https://vfmat.ch/e174

Notre Dame des Pins d'Orianie
RD 112, Commune Fonds-Verettes, Département du Sud-Est, Haiti
⊕ https://vfmat.ch/3498

Ouanaminthe Hospital
RN 6, Commune Ouanaminthe, Département du Nord-Est, Haiti
⊕ https://vfmat.ch/b95c

Port Au Prince Hospital Minustah
Boulevard Toussaint Louverture, Commune de Tabarre, Département de l'Ouest, Haiti
⊕ https://vfmat.ch/a546

Presidente Néstor C. Kirchner Hospital
Corail, Haiti
⊕ https://vfmat.ch/e47f

Saint Luke Hospital Croix de Bouquets
Croix-des-Bouquets, Haiti
⊕ https://vfmat.ch/dbad

Sainte Claire de Corail
RN 7, Commune Beaumont, Département de la Grande-Anse, Haiti
⊕ https://vfmat.ch/da44

Santé Pour Tous
Impasse Colas, Kafou, Département de l'Ouest, Haiti
⊕ https://vfmat.ch/f347

Savanne à Roche
Commune Petite Rivière de l'Artibonite, Département de l'Artibonite, Haiti
⊕ https://vfmat.ch/4f79

SKS Petite Rivière de Dame Marie
RD 702, Commune Dame-Marie, Département de la Grande-Anse, Haiti
⊕ https://vfmat.ch/5d4a

St. Damien's Pediatric Hospital
Port-au-Prince, Haiti
⊕ https://vfmat.ch/6eb2

State University of Haiti Hospital
Avenue Monseigneur Guilloux, Pòtoprens, Département de l'Ouest, Haiti
⊕ https://vfmat.ch/3182

Wesleyan Hospital
Anse-à-Galets, La Gonave, Haiti
⊕ https://vfmat.ch/5549

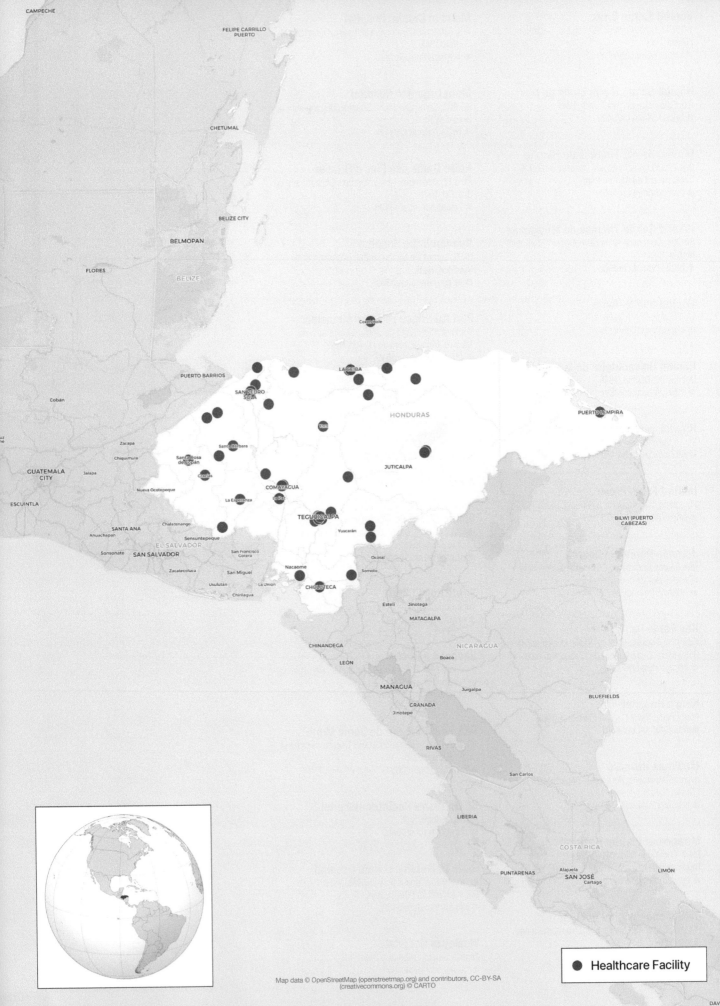

Healthcare Facility

Honduras

The Republic of Honduras, in Central America, is bordered by Guatemala, El Salvador, Nicaragua, the Pacific Ocean, and the Gulf of Honduras. The population of 9.3 million is overwhelmingly ethnically Mestizo, with smaller portions of the population identifying as Amerindian. The official language is Spanish, with Amerindian dialects spoken throughout the country. About 60 percent of the population lives in urban areas, predominantly in two major metropolitan centers: Tegucigalpa (the capital) and San Pedro Sula. About 46 percent of the population identifies as Roman Catholic, while 41 percent is Protestant. The name Honduras translates into "great depths," which is an accurate description of the deep waters off the coast of the country, home to the second largest coral reef system in the world.

Honduras has a long, rich history of Mesoamerican cultures, including Mayan. Colonized by Spain in the 16th century, Honduras gained independence in 1821 and has since experienced extended periods of political and social instability. Honduras has recently benefited from high levels of economic growth, the second highest in Central America and above average for the Latin American and Caribbean regions. Despite economic progress, Honduras is still challenged with high levels of poverty and inequality. The poverty rate is the second highest in the region, with more than half the population living in poverty. While enrollment in primary school is nearly universal, the quality of education is low, with poor school accountability and high dropout rates.

While life expectancy has increased, death rates remain high among those in lower economic demographics. Malnutrition and malaria remain persistent problems among the population's poorest. Leading causes of death include ischemic heart disease, stroke, interpersonal violence, chronic kidney disease, cirrhosis, COPD, neonatal disorders, lung cancer, diarrheal diseases, road injuries, and lower respiratory infections. The risk factors that contribute most to death and disability include high blood pressure, high fasting plasma glucose, malnutrition, high body-mass index, air pollution, dietary risks, kidney dysfunction, alcohol and tobacco use, high LDL, and insufficient water, sanitation, and hygiene.

9.3M

Population

$2,406

GDP Per Capita

75 years

Life Expectancy

↑ Improving

31
Doctors/100k

Physician Density

64
Beds/100k

Hospital Bed Density

65
Deaths/100k

Maternal Mortality

Honduras

Nonprofit Organizations

100X Development Foundation
Empowers children and families for a more hopeful and productive future through the support and care of orphaned children, education and job training for those in need, help for vulnerable youth to escape trafficking, and healthy nutrition and medical care for mothers to enable a safe birth.
ER Med, Infect Dis, OB-GYN, Peds, Psych
⊕ https://vfmat.ch/b629

A Broader View Volunteers
Provides developing countries around the world with significant volunteer programs that aid the neediest communities and forge a lasting bond between those volunteering and those they have helped.
Dent-OMFS, ER Med, Infect Dis, MF Med
⊕ https://vfmat.ch/3bec

Abt Associates
Seeks to improve the quality of life and economic well-being of people worldwide, while striving to meet and exceed the highest professional standards.
General, Logist-Op, MF Med, OB-GYN, Peds
⊕ https://vfmat.ch/cec2

Action for Education, Inc.
Aims to open schools and deliver medical care to communities in Honduras.
General, Ophth-Opt
⊕ https://vfmat.ch/2d6f

Adventist Health International
Focuses on upgrading and managing mission hospitals by providing governance, consultation, and technical assistance to a number of affiliated Seventh-Day Adventist hospitals throughout Africa, Asia, and the Americas.
Dent-OMFS, General, Pub Health
⊕ https://vfmat.ch/16aa

AID FOR AIDS International
Aims to empower communities at risk of HIV and the population at large with comprehensive prevention through treatment, advocacy, education, and training.
Infect Dis, Logist-Op, Nutr, Psych, Pub Health
⊕ https://vfmat.ch/c43e

Alliance for Smiles
Improves the lives of children and communities impacted by cleft by providing free comprehensive treatment while building local capacity for long-term care.
Dent-OMFS, Ped Surg, Plast, Surg
⊕ https://vfmat.ch/bb32

Aloha Medical Mission
Brings hope and changes the lives of people; serves overseas and in Hawai'i.
Anesth, Crit-Care, Dent-OMFS, ENT, ER Med, General, Medicine, OB-GYN, Ophth-Opt, Ortho, Ped Surg, Peds, Plast, Surg, Urol
⊕ https://vfmat.ch/72ac

American Academy of Pediatrics
Seeks to attain optimal physical, mental, and social health and well-being for all infants, children, adolescents, and young adults.
Anesth, Crit-Care, Neonat, Ped Surg
⊕ https://vfmat.ch/9633

American Cancer Society
Saves lives, celebrates lives, and leads the fight for a world without cancer.
Heme-Onc, Logist-Op, Medicine, Rad-Onc, Radiol
⊕ https://vfmat.ch/f996

Americans Caring Teaching Serving (ACTS) Honduras
Partners with local organizations on programs for health, education, agriculture and economic development.
Dent-OMFS, General, Ophth-Opt
⊕ https://vfmat.ch/de41

Americares
Saves lives and improves health for people affected by poverty or disaster and responds with life-changing medicine, medical supplies, and health programs including domestic and global medical clinics.
All-Immu, ER Med, General, Infect Dis, MF Med, Nutr
⊕ https://vfmat.ch/e567

Association of Medical Doctors of Asia (AMDA)
Strives to support people affected by disasters and economic distress on their road to recovery, establishing a true partnership with special emphasis on local initiative.
ER Med, Logist-Op, Pub Health
⊕ https://vfmat.ch/e3d4

Bay Island Community Healthcare Association
Supports quality medical care in the Bay Islands of Honduras and the work of Clinica Esperanza on the island of Roatan.
Dent-OMFS, General, OB-GYN, Path
⊕ https://vfmat.ch/8e49

Baylor College of Medicine: Global Surgery
Trains leaders in academic global surgery and remains dedicated to advancements in the areas of patient care, biomedical research, and medical education.
ENT, Infect Dis, OB-GYN, Ortho, Ped Surg, Plast, Pub Health, Radiol, Surg, Urol
⊕ https://vfmat.ch/21f5

Be The Light Medical Missions
Faith-based orgabization that seeks to provide access to basic human necessities, including clean water, food, shelter, clothing, and medical care.
ER Med, General, MF Med, Nutr, OB-GYN, Peds
⊕ https://vfmat.ch/1b3f

Benjamin H. Josephson, MD Fund
Provides healthcare professionals with the financial resources necessary to deliver medical services for those in need throughout the world.
General, OB-GYN
⊕ https://vfmat.ch/6acc

Bless The Children
Aims to help abandoned and impoverished children by empowering them with health, shelter, and nutritional and educational support.
CT Surg, Dent-OMFS, General, Logist-Op, Nutr, Pub Health, Surg
⊕ https://vfmat.ch/f19d

Brother's Brother Foundation
Seeks to promote international health and education through the efficient and effective distribution and provision of donated medical, educational, agricultural, and other resources.
Logist-Op
⊕ https://vfmat.ch/acb8

Buddhist Tzu Chi Medical Foundation
Provides healthcare to the poor, operates six hospitals in Taiwan and mobile medical and dental clinics in the U.S., manages a bone marrow bank, and organizes over 8,600 physicians who provide free medical services to more than 2 million people globally.
Crit-Care, Dent-OMFS, ER Med, General
⊕ https://vfmat.ch/ff61

Cape CARES Central American Relief Efforts
Delivers community-based care to rural Honduras, including primary care, medical and dental treatment, preventive care, and health education and training.
Dent-OMFS, General, Ophth-Opt, Peds
⊕ https://vfmat.ch/2c63

CardioStart International
Provides free heart surgery and associated medical care to children and adults living in underserved regions of the world, irrespective of political or religious affiliation, through the collective skills of healthcare experts.
Anesth, CT Surg, CV Med, Crit-Care, Pub Health, Pulm-Critic
⊕ https://vfmat.ch/85ef

CARE
Works around the globe to save lives, defeat poverty, and achieve social justice.
ER Med, General
⊕ https://vfmat.ch/7232

Carter Center, The
Seeks to prevent and resolve conflicts, enhance freedom and democracy, and improve health, while remaining committed to human rights and the alleviation of human suffering.
Infect Dis, MF Med, Ophth-Opt
⊕ https://vfmat.ch/6556

Catholic World Mission
Works to rebuild communities worldwide by helping to alleviate poverty and empower underserved areas, while spreading the message of the Catholic Church.
ER Med, General, Nutr, Peds
⊕ https://vfmat.ch/7b5f

CAUSE Canada
Strives to be a catalyst for global justice as a faith-based organization that aims to provide sustainable, integrated community development in rural West Africa and Central America through authentic, collaborative long-term relationships.
General, MF Med, Neonat, OB-GYN, Peds
⊕ https://vfmat.ch/6fc1

Center for Strategic and International Studies (CSIS) Commission on Strengthening America's Health Security
Brings together a distinguished and diverse group of high-level opinion leaders bridging security and health, with the core aim to chart a bold vision for the future of U.S. leadership in global health.
ER Med, Infect Dis, MF Med, Pub Health
⊕ https://vfmat.ch/6d7f

Central American Eye Clinics (CAEC)
Aims to restore vision through high-quality eye care services and educational training programs for communities.
Logist-Op, Ophth-Opt
⊕ https://vfmat.ch/ff23

Central American Medical Outreach (CAMO) Nutrition Program
Seeks to improve the quality of life for people of Central America by strengthening healthcare systems, including providing medical, surgical, and dental care and promoting sustainable community development.
Dent-OMFS, Derm, GI, General, Neuro, Neurosurg, Nutr, OB-GYN, Ophth-Opt, Plast, Surg, Urol
⊕ https://vfmat.ch/65bb

Central American Relief Efforts
Supports the healthcare and well-being of impoverished populations in Honduras by providing medical and dental healthcare through volunteer medical missions, and by targeting hunger and providing resources.
Dent-OMFS, ER Med, General
⊕ https://vfmat.ch/5d6c

Children's Lifeline International
Provides medical teams and surgical assistance to underprivileged children in developing countries through missions in partnership with local hospitals.
CV Med, Dent-OMFS, General, MF Med, Neurosurg, Peds, Rehab
⊕ https://vfmat.ch/6fea

Childspring International
Provides life-changing surgeries for children from developing countries and transforms communities.
CT Surg, Medicine, Ophth-Opt, Ortho, Ped Surg, Peds, Surg
⊕ https://vfmat.ch/f939

Christian Aid Ministries
Strives to be a trustworthy and efficient channel for Amish, Mennonite, and other conservative Anabaptist groups and individuals to minister to physical and spiritual needs around the world.
CT Surg, ER Med, Logist-Op, Ortho, Pub Health
⊕ https://vfmat.ch/7b33

Christian Blind Mission (CBM)
Aims to improve the quality of life of persons with disabilities in the poorest countries, addressing poverty as a cause and a consequence of disability, and working in partnership to create a society for all.
ENT, General, Infect Dis, OB-GYN, Ophth-Opt, Ortho, Peds, Psych, Rehab, Surg
⊕ https://vfmat.ch/3824

Christian Eye Ministry
Aims to eliminate unnecessary blindness by establishing and supporting low-cost, locally managed eye centers to offer the world's poorest communities modern eye care.
Ophth-Opt
⊕ https://vfmat.ch/58f6

Christian Health Service Corps
Brings Christian doctors, health professionals, and health educators committed to serving the poor to places that otherwise have little or no access to healthcare.
Anesth, Dent-OMFS, General, Medicine, Peds, Surg
⊕ https://vfmat.ch/da57

Christian Medical & Dental Associations
Based in Christian ministry, deploys medical and dental teams to underserved communities to provide vital healthcare.
Anesth, Dent-OMFS, ER Med, General, Medicine, OB-GYN, Ophth-Opt, Peds, Pub Health, Radiol, Rehab, Surg
⊕ https://vfmat.ch/921c

Circle of Health International (COHI)
Aligns with local, community-based organizations led and powered by women to help respond to the needs of the women and children that they serve. Helps with the provision of professional volunteers, capacity training, and procurement of requested and appropriate supplies and equipment. Raises funds for the

organizations to provide the services required.
ER Med, Logist-Op, MF Med, Neonat, OB-GYN, Psych
⊕ https://vfmat.ch/8b63

Clinton Health Access Initiative (CHAI)
Aims to save lives and reduce the burden of disease in low- and middle-income countries. Works with partners to strengthen the capabilities of governments and the private sector to create and sustain high-quality health systems.
General, Heme-Onc, Infect Dis, Logist-Op, MF Med, Medicine, Neonat, Nutr, OB-GYN, Path, Peds, Rad-Onc
⊕ https://vfmat.ch/9ed7

Compassion Med International
Supports medical relief missions worldwide, inspired by the Christian faith.
ER Med, General
⊕ https://vfmat.ch/2615

Core Group
Aims to improve and expand community health practices for underserved populations, especially women and children, through collaborative action and learning.
General, Infect Dis, MF Med, Medicine, OB-GYN, Peds, Pub Health
⊕ https://vfmat.ch/9de3

Cornerstone Education and Research
Seeks to provide the local and global community with medical research and education in orthopedic care, expand medical research in the development of innovative technologies, and provide physician and community education.
Ortho
⊕ https://vfmat.ch/f549

COVID-19 Clinical Research Coalition
Advocates and collaborates for the advancement of COVID-19 research driven by the needs of low-resource settings, and works for equitable access to solutions to the pandemic.
All-Immu, Infect-Dis, MF Med, Path, Pub Health
⊕ https://vfmat.ch/d1f4

Cross Catholic Outreach
Mobilizes the global Catholic Church to transform impoverished communities through the provision of food, water, housing, education, orphan support, medical care, microenterprise, and disaster relief.
All-Immu, General, Nutr, OB-GYN, Rehab
⊕ https://vfmat.ch/22f4

Developing Country NGO Delegation: Global Fund to Fight AIDS, TB & Malaria
Works to strengthen the engagement of civil society actors and organizations in developing countries to build a world in which AIDS, TB, and malaria are no longer global, public health, and human rights threats.
Infect Dis, Pub Health
⊕ https://vfmat.ch/3149

Direct Relief
Improves the health and lives of people affected by poverty or emergency situations by mobilizing and providing essential medical resources needed for their care.
ER Med, Logist-Op
⊕ https://vfmat.ch/58e5

Doctors Without Borders/Médecins Sans Frontières (MSF)
Responds to emergencies and provides lifesaving medical care where needed most, including during disasters, conflicts, and epidemics.
Anesth, Crit-Care, ER Med, General, Infect Dis, Nutr, OB-GYN, Ped Surg, Peds, Psych, Pub Health, Surg
⊕ https://vfmat.ch/f363

Duke University: Global Health Institute
Sparks innovation in global health research and education, and brings together knowledge and resources to address the most important global health issues of our time.
All-Immu, Infect Dis, MF Med, OB-GYN, Pub Health
⊕ https://vfmat.ch/c4cd

Episcopal Relief & Development
Provides relief in times of disaster and promotes sustainable development by identifying and addressing the root causes of suffering.
Infect Dis, MF Med, Neonat, Nutr, Peds
⊕ https://vfmat.ch/7cfa

Eyes for the World
Aims to create awareness to prevent blindness and an opportunity for every person with treatable blindness to see a doctor.
Ophth-Opt
⊕ https://vfmat.ch/83c9

Family Health & Development (FHD) Missions Honduras
Provides access to physical therapy, advanced education opportunities, and personal development for families in rural communities, inspired by the Christian faith.
Dent-OMFS, General
⊕ https://vfmat.ch/2ed3

Farm of the Child (Finca del Niño)
Cares for needy children and adolescents in a group home environment while providing education and healthcare, inspired by the Christian faith.
Dent-OMFS, Derm, GI, General, Path, Peds, Psych, Pulm-Critic
⊕ https://vfmat.ch/2ea5

Foundation For International Education In Neurological Surgery (FIENS), The
Provides hands-on training and education to neurosurgeons around the world.
Neuro, Neurosurg, Surg
⊕ https://vfmat.ch/bab8

Gift of Life International
Provides lifesaving cardiac treatment to children in developing countries while developing sustainable pediatric cardiac programs by implementing screening, surgical, and training missions.
Anesth, CT Surg, CV Med, Crit-Care, Ped Surg, Peds, Pulm-Critic
⊕ https://vfmat.ch/f2f9

Glo Foundation, The
Implements health, economic, and education initiatives to strategically meet community development goals.
Dent-OMFS, General, Nutr, Pub Health
⊕ https://vfmat.ch/812b

Global Brigades
Aims to inspire, mobilize, and collaborate with communities to implement their own healthcare and economic goals.
Dent-OMFS, General, Medicine, OB-GYN, Peds
⊕ https://vfmat.ch/78b2

Global Brigades Michigan State University
Aims to empower volunteers and under-resourced communities to resolve global health and economic disparities and inspire all involved to work collaboratively towards an equal world.
Dent-OMFS, General
⊕ https://vfmat.ch/dc9d

Global Eye Project
Empowers local communities by building locally managed, sustainable eye clinics through education initiatives and volunteer-run professional training services.
Anesth, Ophth-Opt, Surg
⊕ https://vfmat.ch/cdba

Global Healing
Improves access to high-quality healthcare in underserved countries by training medical professionals across the globe to improve pediatric healthcare using sustainable resources.
ER Med, General, Heme-Onc, Path
⊕ https://vfmat.ch/a787

Global Medical Missions
Organizes medical missions and partners with local medical organizations, usually hospitals or health systems, in fulfilling their mission of reaching their

community's health needs in developing countries by providing needed medical care and screening to those underserved.
General
🌐 https://vfmat.ch/8d73

Global Medical Missions Alliance
Brings and promotes Christian-centered missionary life to the body of healthcare professionals and its partners.
Dent-OMFS, ER Med, Pub Health, Rehab, Surg
🌐 https://vfmat.ch/29c7

Global Ministries – The United Methodist Church
As the worldwide mission and development agency of The United Methodist Church, Global Ministries works with more than 300 hospitals and clinics around the world through its Global Health Unit.
Anesth, CT Surg, CV Med, Crit-Care, Dent-OMFS, Derm, ER Med, GI, General, Infect Dis, Logist-Op, MF Med, Medicine, Neonat, Nephro, Nutr, OB-GYN, Ophth-Opt, Ortho, Palliative, Peds, Pod, Psych, Pub Health, Rehab, Rheum, Surg, Urol
🌐 https://vfmat.ch/1723

Global Oncology (GO)
Brings the best in cancer care to underserved patients around the world and collaborates across geographic, professional, and academic borders to improve cancer care, research, and education.
Heme-Onc, Path, Rad-Onc
🌐 https://vfmat.ch/fcb8

Global Vision 2020
Provides prescription eyeglasses to people who live in parts of the world lacking necessary infrastructure for obtaining affordable corrective eyewear.
Logist-Op, Ophth-Opt
🌐 https://vfmat.ch/7373

GlobalMedic
Provides disaster relief and lifesaving humanitarian aid.
ER Med, Pub Health
🌐 https://vfmat.ch/dfe6

Globus Relief
Aims to improve the delivery of healthcare worldwide by gathering, processing, and distributing surplus medical supplies to charities at home and abroad.
Logist-Op
🌐 https://vfmat.ch/a2b7

GOAL
Works with the most vulnerable communities to help them respond to and recover from humanitarian crises, and to assist them in building transcendent solutions to mitigate poverty and vulnerability.
ER Med, General, Pub Health
🌐 https://vfmat.ch/bbea

Good Shepard International Foundation
Strives to promote inclusive and sustainable development for the most marginalized and vulnerable people, with a special focus on women, girls, and children, inspired by the Christian faith.
ER Med
🌐 https://vfmat.ch/ad9a

Hands of Mercy Global Ministries
Aims to conduct international missions and partners with Mission Honduras to make free healthcare available to the people of Honduras, based in Christian ministry.
General, OB-GYN
🌐 https://vfmat.ch/68a9

Harvard Global Health Institute
Devoted to improving global health and pioneering the next generation of global health research, education, policy, and practice, with an evidence-based, innovative, integrative, and collaborative approach, harnessing the unique breadth of excellence within Harvard.
General, Infect Dis, Logist-Op
🌐 https://vfmat.ch/5867

Healing the Children
Helps underserved children around the world secure the medical care they need to lead more fulfilling lives.
Anesth, Dent-OMFS, ENT, General, Medicine, Ophth-Opt, Ped Surg, Peds, Plast, Surg
🌐 https://vfmat.ch/d4ee

Health Caring Services
Provides year-round quality healthcare for people in Honduras.
Dent-OMFS, ENT, GI, OB-GYN, Ophth-Opt, Ortho, Surg, Urol
🌐 https://vfmat.ch/8f4e

Health Equity Initiative
Aims to build and sustain a global community that engages across sectors and disciplines to advance health equity.
Pub Health
🌐 https://vfmat.ch/e2e2

Health Outreach
Aims to provide health and public health services, with a focus on dental care, to impoverished people in remote areas of developing countries.
Dent-OMFS, Pub Health
🌐 https://vfmat.ch/93d6

Heart to Heart International
Strengthens communities through improving health access, providing humanitarian development, and administering crisis relief worldwide. Engages volunteers, collaborates with partners, and deploys resources to achieve this mission.
Anesth, ER Med, General, Logist-Op, Medicine, Path, Path, Peds, Psych, Pub Health, Surg
🌐 https://vfmat.ch/aacb

Heartbeat International
Saves lives globally by providing cardiovascular implantable devices to needy people of the world.
CV Med
🌐 https://vfmat.ch/eb38

Heineman Medical Outreach
Provides medical and educational assistance globally to promote sustainable healthcare and enhanced living standards in underserved communities through the International Medical Outreach (IMO) program, a collaborative partnership between Heineman Medical Outreach and Atrium Health.
Anesth, CT Surg, CV Med, ER Med, General, Heme-Onc, Logist-Op, Medicine, Neonat, OB-GYN, Ped Surg, Peds, Surg, Vasc Surg
🌐 https://vfmat.ch/389b

Helping Hands for Honduras
Helps children and young adults with congenital heart defects.
CT Surg, CV Med, Ped Surg
🌐 https://vfmat.ch/4217

Honduraide
Provides comprehensive medical care to Honduran patients in need.
General, Surg
🌐 https://vfmat.ch/58bf

Honduran Children's Rescue Fund (HCRF)
Provides humanitarian aid services and medical equipment to children and young adults.
Dent-OMFS, ER Med, General, MF Med, Nutr
🌐 https://vfmat.ch/6db2

Honduras Compassion Partners
Partners with the people of La Paz to help achieve self-sufficiency, healthy living, and dignity by providing clean water, safe houses, and education.
Dent-OMFS, General
🌐 https://vfmat.ch/c3eb

Honduras Hope
Supports the economically and politically marginalized poor rural communities of Honduras through health, education, and self-sufficiency.

General, Nutr
⊕ https://vfmat.ch/6be4

Hope Walks
Frees children, families, and communities from the burden of clubfoot, inspired by the Christian faith.
Ortho, Ped Surg, Peds, Rehab
⊕ https://vfmat.ch/f6d4

Hope Worldwide
Changes lives through the compassion and commitment of dedicated staff and volunteers delivering sustainable, high-impact, community-based services to the poor and underserved.
Dent-OMFS, General, OB-GYN, Ophth-Opt, Peds
⊕ https://vfmat.ch/89b3

House of Hope International
Inspired by the Christian faith, provides rehabilitation for women and children leaving the world of prostitution and human trafficking and helps integrate them into society.
Dent-OMFS, General, OB-GYN
⊕ https://vfmat.ch/2dbb

Houston Shoulder to Shoulder Foundation
Aims to improve health services, promotes self-sufficiency at a grassroots level, and educates students, residents, and faculty on ongoing healthcare needs and daily challenges faced by people in rural, resource-poor areas.
Dent-OMFS, General, Ophth-Opt
⊕ https://vfmat.ch/c4c5

I Care International
Helps others improve their quality of life by providing the gift of better vision and health.
Ophth-Opt
⊕ https://vfmat.ch/9ba3

IMA World Health
Works to build healthier communities by collaborating with key partners to serve vulnerable people with a focus on health, healing, and well-being for all.
Infect Dis, MF Med, Nutr, OB-GYN, Pub Health
⊕ https://vfmat.ch/8316

InterAmerican Restoration Corporation, The
Seeks to facilitate the distribution of critical resources from the United States to impoverished communities in Central and South America.
Dent-OMFS, General, Pub Health
⊕ https://vfmat.ch/b6d7

International Campaign for Women's Right to Safe Abortion
Works to build an international network and campaign that brings together organizations with an interest in promoting and providing safe abortion to create a shared platform for advocacy, debate, and dialogue and the sharing of skills and experience.
OB-GYN, Pub Health, Surg
⊕ https://vfmat.ch/f341

International Children's Heart Foundation
Provides free surgical care, medical training, and technology to save the lives of children with congenital heart disease in developing countries.
Anesth, CT Surg, CV Med, Crit-Care, Ped Surg, Peds, Pulm-Critic
⊕ https://vfmat.ch/86c1

International Council of Ophthalmology
Works with ophthalmologic societies and others to enhance ophthalmic education and improve access to the highest-quality eye care in order to preserve and restore vision for people of the world.
Ophth-Opt
⊕ https://vfmat.ch/ffd2

International Eye Foundation (IEF)
Eliminates preventable and treatable blindness by making quality sustainable eye care services accessible and affordable worldwide.

Infect Dis, Logist-Op, Ophth-Opt
⊕ https://vfmat.ch/e839

International Eye Institute, Inc.
Provides adult and pediatric medical and surgical eye care to people with little access to these services.
Ophth-Opt
⊕ https://vfmat.ch/6242

International Federation of Gynecology and Obstetrics (FIGO)
Implements global projects on specific women's health issues.
MF Med, Medicine, Neonat, OB-GYN, Surg, Urol
⊕ https://vfmat.ch/c4b4

International Federation of Red Cross and Red Crescent Societies (IFRC)
Coordinates and directs international assistance following natural and manmade disasters in nonconflict situations through the world's largest humanitarian and development network. Provides disaster-preparedness programs, healthcare activities, and promotes humanitarian values.
ER Med, General, Infect Dis, Nutr
⊕ https://vfmat.ch/b4ee

International Health Services Group
Aims to improve access to quality health services in underserved areas of the world.
General, OB-GYN, Pub Health
⊕ https://vfmat.ch/d71a

International HELP
Works alongside churches, organizations, and community groups to help educate and empower local people in sustainable and effective ways for the improvement of health, while also providing health education and health services related to first aid, nutrition, water, sanitation, and hygiene.
General, MF Med
⊕ https://vfmat.ch/ccf5

International Medical Assistance Foundation
Provides quality medical and surgical care to indigent populations in the poorest regions of the world.
Anesth, CV Med, Neuro, OB-GYN, Path, Pulm-Critic
⊕ https://vfmat.ch/d8d5

International Medical Relief
Provides sustainable education, training, medical and dental care, and disaster relief and response in vulnerable communities worldwide.
Dent-OMFS, General, Infect Dis, Medicine, OB-GYN
⊕ https://vfmat.ch/b3ed

International Organization for Migration (IOM) – The UN Migration Agency
Promotes evidence-informed policies and holistic, preventive, and curative health programs that are beneficial, accessible, and equitable for vulnerable migrants.
General, Infect Dis, OB-GYN
⊕ https://vfmat.ch/621a

International Planned Parenthood Federation (IPPF)
Leads a locally owned, globally connected civil society movement that provides and enables services and champions sexual and reproductive health and rights for all, especially the underserved.
Infect Dis, MF Med, OB-GYN
⊕ https://vfmat.ch/dc97

International Relief Teams
Helps families survive and recover after a disaster by delivering timely and effective assistance through programs that improve their health and well-being while also providing a hopeful future for underserved communities.
Dent-OMFS, ER Med, General, Nutr, Ophth-Opt
⊕ https://vfmat.ch/ffd5

InterSurgeon
Fosters collaborative partnerships in the field of global surgery that will advance clinical care, teaching, training, research, and the provision and maintenance of

medical equipment.

ENT, Neurosurg, Ortho, Ped Surg, Plast, Surg, Urol

⊕ https://vfmat.ch/6f8a

Ipas
Focuses efforts on women and girls who want contraception or abortion, and builds programs around their needs and how best to support them.

OB-GYN

⊕ https://vfmat.ch/8e39

IVUmed
Aims to make quality urological care available worldwide by providing medical and surgical education for physicians and nurses, and treatment for thousands of children and adults.

Anesth, OB-GYN, Ped Surg, Surg, Urol

⊕ https://vfmat.ch/e619

Izumi Foundation
Develops and supports programs that improve health and healthcare in neglected regions of Africa and Latin America.

⊕ https://vfmat.ch/f29a

Johns Hopkins Center for Communication Programs
Believes in the power of communication to save lives by empowering people to adopt healthy behaviors for themselves, their families, and their communities.

General, Infect Dis, Logist-Op, OB-GYN, Pub Health

⊕ https://vfmat.ch/1bf9

Joint United Nations Programme on HIV/AIDS (UNAIDS)
Aims to place people living with HIV and people affected by the virus at the decision-making table and at the center of designing, delivering, and monitoring the AIDS response.

Infect Dis

⊕ https://vfmat.ch/464a

Lifebox
Seeks to provide safer surgery and anesthesia in low-resource countries by investing in tools, training, and partnerships for safe surgery.

Anesth, Crit-Care, Surg

⊕ https://vfmat.ch/2d4d

Little Angels of Honduras
Aims to reduce infant mortality in Honduras by assisting in the provision of optimal conditions for pregnancy, birth, and newborn care.

Logist-Op, MF Med, Neonat, Nutr, Peds

⊕ https://vfmat.ch/2649

Luke 9:2 Ministries
Provides medical and dental services for the poor, based in Christian ministry.

Dent-OMFS, General

⊕ https://vfmat.ch/b159

Lutherans in Medical Missions (LIMM)
Works with local and global partners to promote healing in medically underserved communities.

General, Logist-Op, Pub Health

⊕ https://vfmat.ch/c5aa

Making A Difference Foundation
Sponsors and organizes medical missions for medical providers to provide care to underserved communities around the world.

CV Med, Dent-OMFS, ER Med, General, Infect Dis, Logist-Op, MF Med, Neonat, Nutr, OB-GYN, Ophth-Opt, Ortho, Pub Health, Pulm-Critic, Rehab, Surg

⊕ https://vfmat.ch/5556

Management Sciences for Health (MSH)
Works with countries and communities to save lives and improve the health of the world's poorest and most vulnerable people by building strong, resilient, sustainable health systems.

Infect Dis, Logist-Op, Pub Health

⊕ https://vfmat.ch/6aa2

MAP International
Provides medicines and health supplies to those in need around the world so they might experience life to the fullest.

Logist-Op

⊕ https://vfmat.ch/deed

Massachusetts General Hospital Global Surgery Initiative
Aims to improve surgical education and access to advanced surgical care in resource-limited settings around the world by performing surgical operations as visitors, training local surgeons, and sharing medical technology through international partnerships across disciplines.

Anesth, Crit-Care, ER Med, Heme-Onc, Peds, Surg

⊕ https://vfmat.ch/31b1

Maverick Collective
Aims to build a global community of strategic philanthropists and informed advocates who use their intellectual and financial resources to create change.

Infect Dis, MF Med, OB-GYN

⊕ https://vfmat.ch/ea49

Medical Ministry International
Provides compassionate healthcare in areas of need, inspired by the Christian faith.

CT Surg, Dent-OMFS, ENT, General, OB-GYN, Ophth-Opt, Ortho, Plast, Rehab, Surg, Urol, Vasc Surg

⊕ https://vfmat.ch/5da6

Medical Mission Exchange (MMEX)
Gives medical mission organizations a way to share information among one another so they can capitalize on each other's strengths and better serve their patients.

All-Immu, Anesth, CT Surg, CV Med, Dent-OMFS, Derm, ER Med, General, OB-GYN, Ophth-Opt, Ortho, Path, Ped Surg, Plast, Psych, Radiol, Rehab, Surg, Urol

⊕ https://vfmat.ch/bc8c

Medical Mission Trips
Provides medical aid, welfare assistance, and educational opportunities in Brazil, Honduras, Guatemala, Kenya, Burundi, and Ethiopia.

General

⊕ https://vfmat.ch/9117

Medical Missions for Children (MMFC)
Provides quality surgical and dental services to poor and underprivileged children and young adults in various countries throughout the world, and facilitates the transfer of education, knowledge, and recent innovations to the local medical communities.

Dent-OMFS, ENT, Endo, Ortho, Ped Surg, Peds, Plast

⊕ https://vfmat.ch/1631

Medical Missions Outreach
Visits developing countries to provide quality, ethical healthcare and outreach to those in need, based in Christian ministry.

Dent-OMFS, Ophth-Opt, Ortho, Surg

⊕ https://vfmat.ch/1197

MedShare
Aims to improve the quality of life of people, communities, and the planet by sourcing and directly delivering surplus medical supplies and equipment to communities in need around the world.

Logist-Op

⊕ https://vfmat.ch/c8bc

Mending Kids
Provides free, lifesaving surgical care to sick children worldwide by deploying volunteer medical teams and teaching communities to become medically self-sustaining through the education of local medical staff.

Anesth, CT Surg, ENT, Ortho, Ortho, Ped Surg, Plast, Surg

⊕ https://vfmat.ch/4d61

Mercy Ships
Operates hospital ships staffed by volunteers to bring hope, healing, and healthcare to underserved communities worldwide.

Anesth, Dent-OMFS, Logist-Op, Neonat, OB-GYN, Ophth-Opt, Ortho, Palliative,

Plast, Psych, Surg
⊕ https://vfmat.ch/2e99

Mission Doctors Association
Provides life-saving medical care for the poor and training for local healthcare professionals around the world.
CV Med, Dent-OMFS, General, Logist-Op, Medicine, OB-GYN, Ophth-Opt, Peds, Surg
⊕ https://vfmat.ch/6c18

Mission of Love
Strives to identify community needs and supports initiatives and resources for healthcare facilities, education facilities, nutritional programs, and survival programs.
General, Pub Health, Surg
⊕ https://vfmat.ch/bb3d

Mission Regan
Collects supplies, medication, and medical equipment and provides them to those who are in desperate need, both locally and globally.
Logist-Op
⊕ https://vfmat.ch/2bc1

Mission UpReach
Focuses on educational services and leadership training based in communities, transforming them spiritually, economically and physically, including through organizing medical outreach programs and surgical missions.
Dent-OMFS, Logist-Op, Ophth-Opt, Ortho, Surg
⊕ https://vfmat.ch/38cc

Mission Vision
Seeks to decrease blindness and other eye-related disabilities, and to increase academic performance and general quality of life.
Ophth-Opt
⊕ https://vfmat.ch/83d8

Missions for Humanity
Inspired by the Christian faith, aims to break the cycle of poverty and reduce the number of families living in critical economic conditions by creating multifaceted programs such as those in humanitarian aid, nutrition, and health.
Dent-OMFS, General, Ophth-Opt
⊕ https://vfmat.ch/5bca

Missions Honduras
Provides assistance through education, prevention, community building, medical teams, and the arts to improve the lives of children and youth in Honduras.
Dent-OMFS
⊕ https://vfmat.ch/8df8

Missoula Medical Aid
Works with rural and impoverished communities in Honduras to improve health and access to healthcare.
General, Ophth-Opt
⊕ https://vfmat.ch/da28

Mitral Foundation
Committed to advancing the care of patients with mitral valve disease on a global scale.
CT Surg, CV Med, Crit-Care
⊕ https://vfmat.ch/a421

Médecins du Monde/Doctors of the World
Provides care, bears witness, and supports social change worldwide with innovative medical programs and evidence-based advocacy initiatives.
ER Med, General, Infect Dis, MF Med, Neonat, OB-GYN, Peds, Pub Health
⊕ https://vfmat.ch/a43d

NCD Alliance
Unites and strengthens civil society to stimulate collaborative advocacy, action, and accountability for NCD (noncommunicable disease) prevention and control.
All-Immu, CV Med, General, Heme-Onc, Medicine, Peds, Psych
⊕ https://vfmat.ch/abdd

New Orleans Medical Mission Services, Inc.
Provides free medical treatment, consultation, education, equipment, and supplies to needy people in foreign countries.
Dent-OMFS, Ophth-Opt, Rehab, Surg
⊕ https://vfmat.ch/e342

Northeast VOSH
Provides quality healthcare to those with limited means or access, both internationally and abroad.
Dent-OMFS, General, Nutr, Ophth-Opt, Rehab
⊕ https://vfmat.ch/f7b3

Norwegian People's Aid
Aims to improve living conditions, to create a democratic, just, and safe society.
ER Med, Logist-Op
⊕ https://vfmat.ch/2d8e

Nuestros Pequeños Hermanos (NPH)
Strives to create a loving and safe family environment for vulnerable children living in extreme conditions.
Psych, Rehab
⊕ https://vfmat.ch/57c4

Nuestros Pequeños Hermanos (Our Little Brothers and Sisters) New Zealand
Helps vulnerable children and families break the cycle of poverty with assistance through its pediatric hospital, healthcare clinics, day care centers, and scholarship programs.
CT Surg, Heme-Onc, Infect Dis, Nutr, OB-GYN, Peds, Rehab
⊕ https://vfmat.ch/e9cc

Nurse on a Mission
Helps fund nurses for medical mission trips and teams with underserved communities to access surgical and primary care globally.
Pub Health
⊕ https://vfmat.ch/ae61

NuVasive Spine Foundation (NSF)
Partners with leading spine surgeons, nonprofits, and in-country medical professionals/facilities to bring life-changing spine surgery to under-resourced communities around the world.
Logist-Op, Ortho, Ped Surg, Rehab, Surg
⊕ https://vfmat.ch/6ccc

Ohana One International Surgical Aid & Education
Provides surgical care for the global family through technology and training.
Anesth, Logist-Op, Ped Surg, Peds, Plast, Surg
⊕ https://vfmat.ch/86b8

One World Brigades
Assists international communities with dental care and education.
Dent-OMFS, General
⊕ https://vfmat.ch/7933

One World Surgery
Ignites the spirit of service and transforms lives by globally providing high-quality surgical care that is safe, timely, and accessible.
Anesth, Dent-OMFS, ENT, General, Heme-Onc, Medicine, OB-GYN, Ortho, Surg
⊕ https://vfmat.ch/a83c

OneWorld Health
Provides quality, affordable healthcare to communities in need and empowers them to achieve long-term improvements in health and quality of life.
Dent-OMFS, General, Infect Dis, Ortho, Peds, Rehab, Surg
⊕ https://vfmat.ch/71d7

Operation Footprint
Provides free surgical care to underserved children with genetic or acquired foot and ankle conditions, and trains local surgeons to manage and treat them.
Pod
⊕ https://vfmat.ch/6868

Operation International

Offers medical aid to adults and children suffering from lack of quality healthcare in impoverished countries.

Dent-OMFS, ER Med, Heme-Onc, OB-GYN, Ophth-Opt, Ortho, Ped Surg, Plast, Surg

⊕ https://vfmat.ch/b52a

Operation Smile

Treats patients with cleft lip and cleft palate, and creates solutions that deliver safe surgery to people where it's needed most.

Anesth, Dent-OMFS, ENT, Ped Surg, Plast

⊕ https://vfmat.ch/5c29

Operation Walk

Provides the gift of mobility through life-changing joint replacement surgeries, at no cost for those in need in the U.S. and globally.

Anesth, Ortho, Rehab, Surg

⊕ https://vfmat.ch/bafe

Order of Malta

Supports forgotten or excluded people, especially those living in conflict zones or amid natural disasters, by providing medical assistance, caring for refugees, and distributing medicines and necessities.

ER Med, General, Infect Dis, MF Med, Nephro, OB-GYN, Ortho, Psych

⊕ https://vfmat.ch/1fab

Orphan World Relief

Helps children in crisis, including orphans and refugees, by providing committed and compassionate support for their needs.

Logist-Op, Nutr

⊕ https://vfmat.ch/b841

PATH

Advances health equity through innovation and partnerships so people, communities, and economies can thrive.

All-Immu, CV Med, Endo, Heme-Onc, Infect Dis, MF Med, Neonat, Nutr, OB-GYN, Path, Peds, Pulm-Critic

⊕ https://vfmat.ch/b4db

Pediatric Universal Life-Saving Effort, Inc. (PULSE)

Aims to increase access to acute- and intensive-care services for children, recognizing that a significant amount of childhood mortality is preventable. Utilizes time, talents, and resources and seeks to persuade others to share their gifts to enrich the lives of children worldwide.

Crit-Care, Logist-Op, Neonat, Ped Surg, Peds

⊕ https://vfmat.ch/f6b9

Pella Area Teams to Honduras (PATTH)

Deploys medical, dental, and construction missions to underserved mountain villages in Honduras, based in Christian ministry.

Anesth, Dent-OMFS, General, Ophth-Opt, Rehab, Surg

⊕ https://vfmat.ch/c59c

Pharmacists Without Borders Canada

Provides pharmaceutical and technical assistance in the implementation or improvement of community and hospital pharmacies internationally.

⊕ https://vfmat.ch/7658

Physicians for Peace

Educates and empowers local providers of surgical care to alleviate suffering and transform lives in under-resourced communities around the world.

Crit-Care, Ped Surg, Plast, Psych, Surg, Urol

⊕ https://vfmat.ch/6a65

PINCC Preventing Cervical Cancer

Seeks to prevent female-specific diseases in developing countries by utilizing low-cost and low-technology methods to create sustainable programs through patient education, medical personnel training, and facility outfitting.

OB-GYN

⊕ https://vfmat.ch/9666

Point Honduras

Provides families in Tegucigalpa with facilities focused on physical needs, spiritual growth, educational support, and social connection, based in Christian ministry.

⊕ https://vfmat.ch/ac77

Ponseti International

Provides global leadership in building high-quality, locally directed, and sustainable capacity to deliver the Ponseti clubfoot care pathway at the country level.

Ortho, Ped Surg, Peds, Rehab

⊕ https://vfmat.ch/476b

Predisan Health Ministries

Delivers free or low-cost healthcare, substance-abuse rehabilitation, family counseling, and youth drug-prevention activities, inspired by the Christian faith.

Dent-OMFS, OB-GYN, Plast, Surg, Urol

⊕ https://vfmat.ch/cf26

Project Stretch

Provides dental services to disadvantaged children, funds projects for special-needs children and adults, and develops educational materials for training dental staff.

Dent-OMFS

⊕ https://vfmat.ch/766b

Project Theia

Provides medical and surgical care to the underserved global community in the areas of oculoplastic, reconstructive, orbital, and facial surgery.

Anesth, General, Ophth-Opt, Plast

⊕ https://vfmat.ch/9d5a

ProPapa Missions America

Supports efforts to improve health, education, and housing for those in need, particularly in the province of Yoro, Honduras.

Ortho

⊕ https://vfmat.ch/8e82

PSI – Population Services International

Aims to improve the health of people in the developing world by focusing on challenges such as a lack of family planning, HIV/AIDS, barriers to maternal health, and the greatest threats to children under the age of 5, including malaria, diarrhea, pneumonia, and malnutrition.

Infect Dis, MF Med, OB-GYN, Peds

⊕ https://vfmat.ch/ffe3

Rescue Hope

Connects medical professionals with opportunities to serve around the world and bring physical and spiritual healing to nations abroad.

ER Med, General

⊕ https://vfmat.ch/1428

Restore Sight

Provides surgical and medical vision care to people in need around the world.

Ophth-Opt

⊕ https://vfmat.ch/f41c

RestoringVision

Empowers lives by restoring vision for millions of people in need.

Ophth-Opt

⊕ https://vfmat.ch/e121

ReSurge International

Provides reconstructive surgical care and builds surgical capacity in developing countries.

Anesth, Dent-OMFS, Ped Surg, Plast, Surg

⊕ https://vfmat.ch/9937

Rice Foundation

Serves the poor by providing education, leadership training, medical and dental treatment, clean water, housing and food, inspired by the Christian faith.

Dent-OMFS

⊕ https://vfmat.ch/2966

Rockefeller Foundation, The

Works to promote the well-being of humanity.

Logist-Op, Nutr, Pub Health

⊕ https://vfmat.ch/5424

Rotary International
Provides service to others, improves lives, and advances world understanding, goodwill, and peace through its fellowship of business, professional, and community leaders.

ER Med, General, Infect Dis, MF Med, OB-GYN

⊕ https://vfmat.ch/8fb5

Ruth Paz Foundation
Provides medical care to poor and wounded Honduran boys and girls, complementing the healing process with kindness and dignity in a family-centered environment.

CV Med, Dent-OMFS, Derm, ENT, GI, Neuro, Neurosurg, Ophth-Opt, Ortho, Ortho, Path, Peds, Plast, Surg

⊕ https://vfmat.ch/315c

Saint Francis International Medical Mission
Brings first-class medical services to those in need.

Anesth, Derm, OB-GYN, Ophth-Opt, Peds, Surg

⊕ https://vfmat.ch/6335

Salvation Army International, The
Seeks to meet human needs through services in education, healthcare, community support, emergency response, and ministry development, inspired by the Christian faith.

Dent-OMFS, Derm, ER Med, Infect Dis, MF Med, Medicine, Nutr, OB-GYN, Ophth-Opt, Palliative, Psych, Rehab, Surg

⊕ https://vfmat.ch/8eb3

Samaritan's Purse International Disaster Relief
Provides spiritual and physical aid to hurting people around the world, such as victims of war, poverty, natural disasters, disease, and famine, based in Christian ministry.

Anesth, CT Surg, Crit-Care, Dent-OMFS, Derm, ENT, ER Med, Endo, GI, General, Heme-Onc, Infect Dis, MF Med, Neonat, Nephro, Neuro, Neurosurg, Nutr, OB-GYN, Ophth-Opt, Ortho, Path, Ped Surg, Peds, Plast, Psych, Pulm-Critic, Radiol, Rehab, Rheum, Surg, Urol, Vasc Surg

⊕ https://vfmat.ch/87e3

Sanofi Espoir Foundation
Contributes to reducing health inequalities among populations that need it most by applying a socially responsible approach focused on fighting childhood cancers in low-income countries, improving maternal and newborn health, and improving access to care.

ER Med, OB-GYN, Peds

⊕ https://vfmat.ch/943b

Save the Children
Gives children around the world a healthy start in life, the opportunity to learn, and protection from harm.

All-Immu, Crit-Care, ER Med, General, Infect Dis, MF Med, Medicine, Neonat, OB-GYN, Peds, Psych, Pub Health

⊕ https://vfmat.ch/2e73

SEE International
Provides sustainable medical, surgical, and educational services through volunteer ophthalmic surgeons, with the objectives of restoring sight and preventing blindness to disadvantaged individuals worldwide.

Ophth-Opt, Surg

⊕ https://vfmat.ch/6e1b

SEVA
Delivers vital eye care services to the world's most vulnerable, including women, children, and Indigenous peoples.

Ophth-Opt, Surg

⊕ https://vfmat.ch/1e87

Siempre Unidos
Works in close partnership with Honduran Episcopal Diocese and Ministry of Health to contain the HIV/AIDS epidemic in Honduras and minimize its impact.

⊕ https://vfmat.ch/b764

SIGN Fracture Care International
Builds orthopedic capacity around the world and provides the injured poor access to fracture surgery by donating orthopedic education and implant systems to surgeons in developing countries.

Ortho, Rehab, Surg

⊕ https://vfmat.ch/123d

Smile Train, Inc.
Treats children with cleft lip through a sustainable and local model that supports surgery and other forms of essential care.

Logist-Op, Pub Health

⊕ https://vfmat.ch/822c

Soddo Christian Hospital
Mobilizes volunteers to help transform communities through healthcare and education, based in Christian ministry.

ER Med, General

⊕ https://vfmat.ch/efa4

SOS Children's Villages International
Supports children through alternative care and family strengthening.

ER Med, Peds

⊕ https://vfmat.ch/aca1

Squads Abroad
Empowers volunteers and under-resourced communities to resolve global health, education, and economic disparities and inspire all involved to collaboratively work towards an equal world.

General

⊕ https://vfmat.ch/93e3

Sri Sathya Sai International Organization
Inspired by spiritual teachings, carries out efforts in global healthcare, education, humanitarian relief, and youth engagement.

Dent-OMFS, General, Logist-Op, Nutr, Ophth-Opt, Pub Health

⊕ https://vfmat.ch/9bda

St. Benedict Joseph Medical Center
Provides free medical, surgical, dental care, pre-natal and post-natal care, and arranges for surgical missions to Honduras.

ENT, OB-GYN, Ophth-Opt, Ortho, Plast, Pod, Surg, Urol

⊕ https://vfmat.ch/73ab

Summit in Honduras
Conducts medical and educational outreach to impoverished families and children in rural northwestern Honduras and supports medical, education, literacy, clean water, food support, and construction projects.

Dent-OMFS, General, Ophth-Opt, Surg

⊕ https://vfmat.ch/b334

Surgeons of Service
Seeks to inspire humanitarian efforts, locally and globally, to create poverty awareness, instill education, and provide medical assistance.

Surg

⊕ https://vfmat.ch/9d4b

Swiss Tropical and Public Health Institute
Contributes to the improvement of the health of populations internationally, nationally, and locally through excellence in research, education, and services.

Infect Dis, Pub Health

⊕ https://vfmat.ch/2ee4

Task Force for Global Health, The
Consists of programs and focus areas that cover a range of global health issues including neglected tropical diseases, infectious diseases, vaccines, field epidemiology, public health informatics, health workforce development, and global health ethics.

Infect Dis, Logist-Op, Medicine, Ophth-Opt, Peds

⊕ https://vfmat.ch/714c

Tearfund
Responds to crisis and partners with local churches to bring restoration to those living in poverty, inspired by the Christian faith.

ER Med, Logist-Op
⊕ https://vfmat.ch/f6cf

Tzu Chi Medical Foundation
Organizes medical missions through a global network of licensed doctors and nurses who provide medical care to impoverished communities and respond to disasters around the world.
Dent-OMFS, ER Med, Nutr, OB-GYN, Ophth-Opt, Peds, Pub Health
⊕ https://vfmat.ch/81a3

Unidad Hospitalaria Movil Latinoamerica (Latin America Mobile Hospital Unit)
Aims to bring healthcare to underserved areas of Latin America by delivering medical and surgical care.
Surg
⊕ https://vfmat.ch/2b1d

Union for International Cancer Control (UICC)
Unites and supports the cancer community to reduce the global cancer burden, promote greater equity, and ensure that cancer control continues to be a priority in the world health and development agenda.
Heme-Onc, Pub Health
⊕ https://vfmat.ch/88b1

Unite for Sight
Supports eye clinics worldwide by investing human and financial resources to eliminate patient barriers to eye care. Applies best practices in eye care, public health, volunteerism, and social entrepreneurship to achieve our goal of high-quality eye care for all.
Ophth-Opt, Surg
⊕ https://vfmat.ch/4fe7

United Methodist Volunteers in Mission (UMVIM)
Engages in short-term missions each year in ministries as varied as disaster response, community development, pastor training, microenterprise, agriculture, Vacation Bible School, building repair and construction, and medical/dental services.
Dent-OMFS, ER Med, General
⊕ https://vfmat.ch/1ee6

United Nations Children's Fund (UNICEF)
Works in over 190 countries and territories to save children's lives, defend their rights, and help them fulfill their potential, from early childhood through adolescence.
All-Immu, Infect Dis, MF Med, Neonat, Nutr, OB-GYN, Ped Surg, Peds, Pub Health
⊕ https://vfmat.ch/42d7

United Nations Development Programme (UNDP)
Helps countries achieve the simultaneous eradication of extreme poverty and significant reduction of inequalities and exclusion using a sustainable human development approach.
Infect Dis, Logist-Op, Pub Health
⊕ https://vfmat.ch/935c

United Nations High Commissioner for Refugees (UNHCR)
Safeguards the rights and well-being of people who have been forced to flee, ensuring that everybody has the right to seek asylum and find safe refuge in another country, with the goal of seeking lasting solutions.
General, MF Med, Medicine, OB-GYN, Peds, Psych, Pub Health
⊕ https://vfmat.ch/6636

United Nations Population Fund (UNFPA)
Supports reproductive healthcare for women and youth in more than 150 countries, focusing on delivering a world in which every pregnancy is wanted, every childbirth is safe, and every young person's potential is fulfilled.
Infect Dis, MF Med, Neonat, OB-GYN, Peds, Pub Health
⊕ https://vfmat.ch/c969

University of California Los Angeles: David Geffen School of Medicine Global Health Program
Catalyzes opportunities to improve health globally by engaging in multi-disciplinary and innovative education programs, research initiatives, and bilateral partnerships that provide opportunities for trainees, faculty, and staff to contribute to sustainable health initiatives and to address health inequities facing the world today.
All-Immu, Infect Dis, Logist-Op, MF Med, Medicine, Neonat, OB-GYN, Ortho, Ped Surg, Peds, Radiol
⊕ https://vfmat.ch/f1a4

University of Massachusetts Medical School: Department of Surgery Global Scholars
Provides state-of-the-art surgical care to patients and serves communities worldwide through education, research, and public service.
Anesth, ER Med, Surg
⊕ https://vfmat.ch/3e8e

University of Michigan: Department of Surgery Global Health
Improves the health of patients, populations and communities through excellence in education, patient care, community service, research and technology development, and through leadership activities.
Anesth, Ortho, Surg
⊕ https://vfmat.ch/2fd8

University of Minnesota: Global Surgery & Disparities Program
Works to understand and improve surgical, anesthesia, and OB/GYN care in underserved areas through partnerships with local providers, while training the next generation of academic global surgery leaders.
All-Immu, Dent-OMFS, ER Med, Heme-Onc, MF Med, Neurosurg, OB-GYN, Ophth-Opt, Path, Ped Surg, Plast, Surg, Urol
⊕ https://vfmat.ch/e59a

University of Wisconsin-Madison: Department of Surgery
Provides comprehensive educational experiences, groundbreaking research, and superb patient care.
Anesth, ENT, ER Med, Endo, Peds, Plast, Pub Health, Surg
⊕ https://vfmat.ch/64c2

USAID: Leadership, Management and Governance Project
Improves leadership, management, and governance practices to strengthen health systems and improve health for all, including vulnerable populations worldwide.
Logist-Op
⊕ https://vfmat.ch/d35e

Ventura Global Health Project (VGHP)
Aims to encourage and facilitate a lifelong interest in global health by providing grants to support local medical professionals providing care to underserved populations.
Dent-OMFS, ER Med, General, Infect Dis, Logist-Op, OB-GYN, Ophth-Opt, Ortho, Peds, Plast, Surg, Urol
⊕ https://vfmat.ch/a746

VHP (Voluntary Health Program)
Focuses on primary medical and surgical eye care to underserved rural areas in Central America and the Dominican Republic.
General, Ophth-Opt, Surg
⊕ https://vfmat.ch/3d63

Virginia Commonwealth University: Family Medicine & Epidemiology Global Health Program
Aims to build relationships with communities, develop sustainable medical services, and better appreciate the importance of health disparities and barriers to care.
General, MF Med, Medicine, Nutr, OB-GYN, Peds, Pub Health, Surg
⊕ https://vfmat.ch/a591

Virginia Hospital Center Medical Brigade
Seeks to bring expert care and hope to the Honduran poor to eliminate the health disparities they experience.
Dent-OMFS, ER Med, General, Nutr, Surg
⊕ https://vfmat.ch/ecca

Virtue Foundation
Increases awareness, inspires action and renders assistance through healthcare, education, and empowerment initiatives.
Anesth, Crit-Care, Dent-OMFS, ENT, ER Med, Heme-Onc, Logist-Op, Neurosurg,

OB-GYN, Ophth-Opt, Ortho, Path, Ped Surg, Peds, Plast, Radiol, Rehab, Surg
⊕ https://vfmat.ch/6481

Vision Health International
Brings high-quality eye care to underserved communities around the world.
Ophth-Opt
⊕ https://vfmat.ch/e97f

Vision Outreach International
Advocates for helping the blind in underserved regions of the world and empowers the poor through sight restoration.
Ophth-Opt
⊕ https://vfmat.ch/9721

Vitamin Angels
Helps at-risk populations in need—specifically pregnant women, new mothers, and children under age 5—to gain access to life-changing vitamins and minerals.
General, Nutr
⊕ https://vfmat.ch/7da1

Volunteers in Medical Missions (VIMM)
Ministers to the physical, medical, and spiritual needs of children and adults in developing countries throughout the world and provides opportunities for Christian medical professionals and other volunteers to experience missions first-hand.
General, Peds
⊕ https://vfmat.ch/9754

VOSH (Volunteer Optometric Services to Humanity) International
Facilitates the provision and the sustainability of vision care worldwide for people who can neither afford nor obtain such care.
Ophth-Opt
⊕ https://vfmat.ch/a149

Women and Children First
Pioneers approaches that support communities to solve problems themselves.
MF Med, Neonat, OB-GYN, Peds
⊕ https://vfmat.ch/cdc9

Women's Refugee Commission
Seeks to improve lives by protecting the rights of women, children, and youth displaced by conflict and crisis through researching their needs, identifying solutions, and advocating for programs and policies to strengthen their resilience.
General, MF Med, Neonat, OB-GYN, Peds, Psych
⊕ https://vfmat.ch/3d8f

World Federation of Hemophilia (WFH)
Aims to improve and sustain care for people with inherited bleeding disorders by pursuing long-term relationships with individuals and organizations who share the values of WFH's development model.
Heme-Onc
⊕ https://vfmat.ch/5121

World Health Organization, The (WHO)
The United Nations' agency for health provides leadership on global health matters, shapes the health research agenda, sets norms and standards, articulates evidence-based policy options, provides technical support and monitoring to countries, and assesses health trends.
ER Med, General, Infect Dis, Logist-Op, MF Med, OB-GYN, Peds, Psych, Pub Health
⊕ https://vfmat.ch/c476

World Hope International
Empowers the poorest individuals around the world so they can become agents of change within their communities, by offering resources and knowledge.
Infect Dis, Logist-Op, MF Med, OB-GYN, Peds
⊕ https://vfmat.ch/a4b8

World Medical Relief
Facilitates the distribution of surplus medical resources where they are needed.
Logist-Op
⊕ https://vfmat.ch/72dc

World Surgical Foundation
Provides charitable surgical healthcare to the world's poor and underserved in developing nations.
Ped Surg, Surg
⊕ https://vfmat.ch/c162

World Vision International
Works with vulnerable communities around the world to overcome poverty and injustice with child-focused programs in disaster management, health, nutrition, economic development, education, clean water, sanitation, and hygiene.
ER Med, General, Infect Dis, MF Med, Nutr, OB-GYN, Peds
⊕ https://vfmat.ch/2642

York County Medical Foundation
Provides medical care and humanitarian relief to the poor, the distressed, and the underprivileged, both locally and internationally.
OB-GYN, Plast, Surg
⊕ https://vfmat.ch/a55d

 # Honduras

Healthcare Facilities

Clinica de Especialidades Salud Integral
Siguatepeque, Honduras
https://vfmat.ch/3ca9

Dyer Rural Hospital (Jungle Hospital)
Los Planes, Atlántida, Honduras
⊕ https://vfmat.ch/vkrq

Fundación por la Vida del Niño Quemado
Nueva Suyapa, Francisco Morazán, Honduras
⊕ https://vfmat.ch/3c25

General Hospital of Tocoa
Tocoa, Colón, Honduras
⊕ https://vfmat.ch/56d2

Hospital Adventista
Valle de Ángeles, Francisco Morazán, Honduras
⊕ https://vfmat.ch/67c5

Hospital Alivio del Sufrimiento
San Isidro, El Paraíso, Honduras
⊕ https://vfmat.ch/1a83

Hospital and Clinic Ferraro
San Pedro Sula, Cortes Department, Honduras
⊕ https://vfmat.ch/qg5i

Hospital Anibal Murillo Escobar
Olanchito, Yoro, Honduras
⊕ https://vfmat.ch/cb6c

Hospital Bautista BMDMI Guaimaca
Los Jobos, Francisco Morazán, Honduras
⊕ https://vfmat.ch/53e8

Hospital Bendaña
Río Blanco Cortes, San Pedro Sula, Honduras
⊕ https://vfmat.ch/1736

Hospital Católico San Pío de Pietrelcina
San Pío de Pietrelcina, Tegucigalpa, Honduras
⊕ https://vfmat.ch/b891

Hospital CEMESA
San Pedro Sula, Cortes Department, Honduras
⊕ https://vfmat.ch/qcfv

Hospital de Especialidades San Felipe
Las Pilitas Tegucigalpa, Francisco Morazán, Honduras
⊕ https://vfmat.ch/8cf8

Hospital de Occidente
Santa Rosa de Copan, Honduras
⊕ https://vfmat.ch/5691

Hospital de Oriente Gabriela Alvarado
Danlí, El Paraíso, Honduras
⊕ https://vfmat.ch/9c98

Hospital de Puerto Cortés
Puerto Cortes, Cortes, Honduras
⊕ https://vfmat.ch/f3da

Hospital del Caribe
Puerto Cortes, Honduras
⊕ https://vfmat.ch/cc7f

Hospital del Valle
San Pedro Sula, Cortés, Honduras
⊕ https://vfmat.ch/e58b

Hospital DIME
Tegucigalpa, Francisco Morazán, Honduras
⊕ https://vfmat.ch/6792

Hospital Dr. Enrique Aguilar Cerrato
Intibucá, Honduras
⊕ https://vfmat.ch/9ah9

Hospital Dr. Juan Manuel Galvez
Gracias, Lempira, Honduras
⊕ https://vfmat.ch/d45e

Hospital El Carmen
Comayaguela, Francisco Morazán, Honduras
⊕ https://vfmat.ch/5d4b

Hospital Escuela
La Guillen, Francisco Morazán, Honduras
⊕ https://vfmat.ch/5d15

Hospital Evangélico
Siguatepeque, Comayagua, Honduras
⊕ https://vfmat.ch/38d1

Hospital Ferguson
Hacienda Galiqueme, Choluteca, Honduras
⊕ https://vfmat.ch/6934

Hospital General Atlántida
La Ceiba, Atlántida, Honduras
⊕ https://vfmat.ch/a794

Hospital Hermano Pedro
Villa Linda, Olancho, Honduras
⊕ https://vfmat.ch/5dc5

Hospital Honduras Medical Center
Tegucigalpa, Municipality of the Central District, Honduras
⊕ https://vfmat.ch/t2u3

Hospital Integrado Santa Bárbara
La Finca, Santa Bárbara, Honduras
⊕ https://vfmat.ch/845e

Hospital La Policlínica
Tegucigalpa, Honduras
⊕ https://vfmat.ch/8igd

Hospital Leonardo Martinez
Río Blanco, Cortés, Honduras
⊕ https://vfmat.ch/97d9

Hospital Loma de Luz
Balfate, Colón, Honduras
⊕ https://vfmat.ch/69dc

Hospital Manuel de Jesús Subirana
El Cerrito, Yoro, Honduras
⊕ https://vfmat.ch/126f

Hospital María Especialidades Pediátricas
Tegucigalpa, Francisco Morazán, Honduras
⊕ https://vfmat.ch/7225

Hospital Militar
San Pedro Sula, Cortés, Honduras
⊕ https://vfmat.ch/ff3d

Hospital Montecillos
La Paz, La Paz, Honduras
⊕ https://vfmat.ch/af34

Hospital Nacional Nor-Occidental Dr. Mario Catarino Rivas
San Pedro Sula, Cortes Department, Honduras
⊕ https://vfmat.ch/kaqs

Hospital Neuropsiquiátrico Mario Mendoza
Tegucigalpa, Francisco Morazán, Honduras
⊕ https://vfmat.ch/c2da

Hospital Oftálmologico Ponce
La Ceiba, Atlántida, Honduras
⊕ https://vfmat.ch/dc48

Hospital Puerto Lempira
Puerto Lempira, Gracias a Dios, Honduras
⊕ https://vfmat.ch/915f

Hospital Regional Atlantida
Le Ceiba, Atlántida, Honduras
⊕ https://vfmat.ch/a361

Hospital Regional del Sur
Hacienda Galiqueme, Choluteca, Honduras
⊕ https://vfmat.ch/e2af

Hospital Roatán
Roatán, Honduras
⊕ https://vfmat.ch/34b5

Hospital Roberto Suazo Córdova
Piedra Chata, La Paz, Honduras
⊕ https://vfmat.ch/124b

Hospital San Felipe
Tegucigalpa, Municipality of the Central District, Honduras
⊕ https://vfmat.ch/1rbc

Hospital San Lorenzo
San Lorenzo, Valle, Honduras
⊕ https://vfmat.ch/f765

Hospital Santo Hermano Pedro
Catacamas, Olancho, Honduras
⊕ https://vfmat.ch/phpq

Hospital Sula Socorro de lo Alto
Macuelizo, Santa Barbara, Honduras
⊕ https://vfmat.ch/5thr

Hospital Tela Integrado
Tela, Atlántida, Honduras
⊕ https://vfmat.ch/634a

Hospital Vicente D'Antoni
La Ceiba, Atlántida, Honduras
⊕ https://vfmat.ch/fec1

Maria Hospital, Pediatric Specialties
Tegucigalpa, Honduras
⊕ https://vfmat.ch/ullm

Red Descentralizada de Salud La Unión La Iguala
La Union, Lempira, Honduras
⊕ https://vfmat.ch/44cd

Viera
Tegucigalpa, Municipality of the Central District, Honduras
⊕ https://vfmat.ch/vtwp

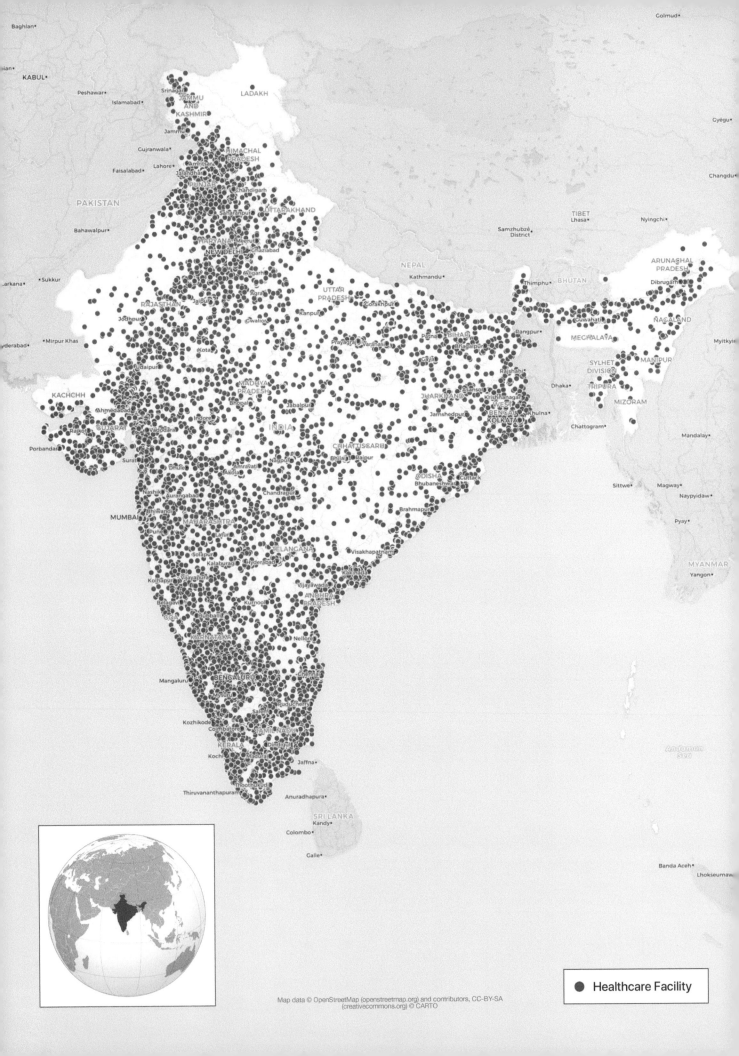

● Healthcare Facility

India

The Republic of India is bordered by the Indian Ocean, the Arabian Sea, the Bay of Bengal, Pakistan, China, Nepal, Bhutan, Bangladesh, and Myanmar. With 1.3 billion people, India is the second most populous country in the world and the seventh largest country by geographical size. About 40 percent of Indians live in urban areas, such as New Delhi (the capital), Mumbai, Kolkata, Bangalore, Chennai, and Hyderabad. The population is ethnically Indo-Aryan, Dravidian, and Mongoloid, while identifying religiously as predominantly Hindu, and also Muslim, Christian, and Sikh. The most common languages spoken include Hindi, Bengali, Marathi, Telugu, Tamil, Gujarati, Urdu, Kannada, Odia, Malayalam, Punjabi, Assamese, and Maithili. English is one of the official languages, along with 22 other recognized languages.

India gained independence from Britain in 1947, at which point the British Indian Empire split into two independent countries: Hindu-majority India and Muslim-majority Pakistan. Since the 2000s, India has made immense progress on poverty-alleviation efforts, lifting 90 million people out of poverty between 2011 and 2015. Other improvements include bringing 20 million children into primary school, increasing upper primary school enrollment by 10 percent, and improving rural water supply and sanitation. Gains have also been made in the healthcare sector, which has tackled issues such as maternal mortality, infectious disease, and quality of healthcare services.

Improvements in medical and public healthcare services since independence has increased life expectancy by 25 years. Smallpox was eradicated in 1977 and malaria is nearly so. Social services and quality of life continue to improve, with more deaths naturally resulting from non-communicable, rather than communicable, disease. Deaths due to ischemic heart disease, COPD, stroke, and diabetes increased by about 30–50 percent between 2009 and 2019. Other main causes of death include diarrheal diseases, neonatal disorders, lower respiratory infections, tuberculosis, cirrhosis, falls, road injuries, and self-harm. Common risk factors include malnutrition, air pollution, high blood pressure, high fasting plasma glucose, dietary risks, high body-mass index, high LDL, alcohol and tobacco use, and insufficient water, sanitation, and hygiene.

1,339.3M
Population

$1,901
GDP Per Capita

70 years
Life Expectancy
↑ Improving

93
Doctors/100k
Physician Density

53
Beds/100k
Hospital Bed Density

145
Deaths/100k
Maternal Mortality

India

Nonprofit Organizations

100X Development Foundation
Empowers children and families for a more hopeful and productive future through the support and care of orphaned children, education and job training for those in need, help for vulnerable youth to escape trafficking, and healthy nutrition and medical care for mothers to enable a safe birth.
ER Med, Infect Dis, OB-GYN, Peds, Psych
⊕ https://vfmat.ch/b629

5 Rivers Heart Association
Works to help underserved populations by creating innovative ways to deliver cost-effective medicine while optimizing resource utilization.
CT Surg, GI, General
⊕ https://vfmat.ch/2deb

A Broader View Volunteers
Provides developing countries around the world with significant volunteer programs that aid the neediest communities and forge a lasting bond between those volunteering and those they have helped.
Dent-OMFS, ER Med, Infect Dis, MF Med
⊕ https://vfmat.ch/3bec

A Leg To Stand On (ALTSO)
Provides free, high-quality prosthetic limbs, orthotic devices, and wheelchairs to children with untreated limb disabilities in the developing world.
Logist-Op, Ortho
⊕ https://vfmat.ch/a48d

A World of Difference
Aids women and children in southeast Asia, with a focus on art education, literacy, and health.
Dent-OMFS
⊕ https://vfmat.ch/8682

Aagya Foundation
Dedicates efforts to improving the lives of senior citizens by protecting their rights and keeping them both socially involved and mentally and physically healthy.
Geri, Palliative, Psych
⊕ https://vfmat.ch/2888

Aahwahan
Aims to make a positive impact on the lives of marginalized communities by developing programs and providing services in areas of education, health, women's empowerment, and agriculture.
General, Infect Dis
⊕ https://vfmat.ch/322e

Abha Seva Sadan Multitherapy Charitable Health Centre
Provides holistic care, including services in healthcare, education, nutrition, hygiene, and rehabilitation, to impoverished communities.

Rehab
⊕ https://vfmat.ch/771f

Abt Associates
Seeks to improve the quality of life and economic well-being of people worldwide, while striving to meet and exceed the highest professional standards.
General, Logist-Op, MF Med, OB-GYN, Peds
⊕ https://vfmat.ch/cec2

ACCESS Health International
Aims to improve access to high-quality and affordable healthcare for people everywhere, no matter what their age, in low-, middle- and high-income countries.
Logist-Op
⊕ https://vfmat.ch/6613

Aceso Global
Provides strategic healthcare advisory services in low- and middle-income countries to design and deliver highly customized, evidence-based solutions that address the complex nature of healthcare systems, with a goal to strengthen and provide affordable, high-quality care to all.
Logist-Op, Pub Health
⊕ https://vfmat.ch/b3b7

Action Against Hunger
Aims to end life-threatening hunger for good through treating and preventing malnutrition across more than 45 countries.
Nutr
⊕ https://vfmat.ch/2dbc

Action Service Hope for AIDS
Provides counseling, testing, treatment, support and rehabilitation to people infected and affected by HIV/AIDS and their communities.
Infect Dis
⊕ https://vfmat.ch/e7fe

Advance Family Planning
Aims to achieve global expansion and access to quality contraceptive information, services, and supplies through financial investment and political commitment.
General, MF Med, Pub Health
⊕ https://vfmat.ch/7478

Adventist Health International
Focuses on upgrading and managing mission hospitals by providing governance, consultation, and technical assistance to a number of affiliated Seventh-Day Adventist hospitals throughout Africa, Asia, and the Americas.
Dent-OMFS, General, Pub Health
⊕ https://vfmat.ch/16aa

Aga Khan Foundation Canada
Tackles the root causes of poverty, with a special focus on marginalized groups such as women and girls. Programs provide access to education and healthcare, food, and opportunity.
Pub Health
⊕ https://vfmat.ch/7f8b

Against Malaria Foundation
Helps protect people from malaria. Funds anti-malaria nets, specifically long-lasting insecticidal nets (LLINs), and works with distribution partners to ensure they are used. Tracks and reports on net use and malaria case data.
Infect Dis
⊕ https://vfmat.ch/337d

Age International
Helps older people living in some of the world's poorest places to have improved well-being and be treated with dignity through a variety of programs, including emergency relief and cataract surgery.
ER Med, Geri, Logist-Op, Nutr, Ophth-Opt, Palliative, Pub Health
⊕ https://vfmat.ch/c7e2

AIDS Healthcare Foundation
Provides cutting-edge HIV/AIDS medical care and advocacy to over one million people in 43 countries.
Infect Dis
⊕ https://vfmat.ch/b27c

Al Basar International Foundation
Works with local partners to treat preventable blindness, and helps set up sustainable infrastructure so local teams can save sight in their communities.
Ophth-Opt
⊕ https://vfmat.ch/a8b5

Aloha Medical Mission
Brings hope and changes the lives of people; serves overseas and in Hawai'i.
Anesth, Crit-Care, Dent-OMFS, ENT, ER Med, General, Medicine, OB-GYN, Ophth-Opt, Ortho, Ped Surg, Peds, Plast, Surg, Urol
⊕ https://vfmat.ch/72ac

Amar Gandhi Foundation (AGF)
Aims to spread awareness about organ donation and works toward prevention and control of kidney disease.
Nephro
⊕ https://vfmat.ch/6dfb

American Academy of Ophthalmology
Protects sight and empowers lives by serving as an advocate for patients and the public, leading ophthalmic education, and advancing the profession of ophthalmology.
Ophth-Opt
⊕ https://vfmat.ch/89a2

American Cancer Society
Saves lives, celebrates lives, and leads the fight for a world without cancer.
Heme-Onc, Logist-Op, Medicine, Rad-Onc, Radiol
⊕ https://vfmat.ch/f996

American Heart Association (AHA)
Fights heart disease and stroke, striving to save and improve lives.
CV Med, Crit-Care, General, Heme-Onc, Medicine, Peds
⊕ https://vfmat.ch/4747

American Stroke Association
Works to prevent, treat, and beat stroke by funding innovative research, fighting for stronger public health policies, and providing lifesaving tools and information.
CV Med, Crit-Care, Heme-Onc, Medicine, Neuro, Pub Health, Pulm-Critic, Vasc Surg
⊕ https://vfmat.ch/746f

American Tamil Medical Association (ATMA)
Provides medical missions to the needy in the U.S. and abroad during both peacetime and disasters.
Logist-Op, Pub Health
⊕ https://vfmat.ch/6cbe

Americares
Saves lives and improves health for people affected by poverty or disaster and responds with life-changing medicine, medical supplies, and health programs including domestic and global medical clinics.
All-Immu, ER Med, General, Infect Dis, MF Med, Nutr
⊕ https://vfmat.ch/e567

Americas Association for the Care of Children (AACC)
Reduces the impact of poverty in marginalized and underserved populations by empowering communities through compassionate and holistic education.
Dent-OMFS, MF Med, OB-GYN, Pub Health
⊕ https://vfmat.ch/19c5

AMG International
Inspired by theChristian faith, provides children with both food and care in youth development centers and medical help in hospitals, clinics and leprosy centers.
General, Geri, Medicine, Nutr, OB-GYN, Peds, Pub Health
⊕ https://vfmat.ch/cf71

Amrita Hospital
Aims to provide affordable care that meets the highest standards of medical treatment.
Anesth, CT Surg, CV Med, Derm, ENT, ER Med, Endo, GI, Geri, Heme-Onc, MF Med, Medicine, Nephro, Neuro, Neurosurg, OB-GYN, Ophth-Opt, Ortho, Ped Surg, Peds, Plast, Pulm-Critic, Radiol, Rehab, Rheum, Surg, Urol, Vasc Surg
⊕ https://vfmat.ch/87f5

Amsterdam Institute for Global Health and Development (AIGHD)
Provides sustainable solutions to major health problems across our planet by forging synergies among disciplines, healthcare delivery, research, and education.
Infect Dis
⊕ https://vfmat.ch/d73d

Amurtel
Aims to alleviate suffering and provide immediate and long-term relief to women and children in need, and to improve their overall quality of life.
⊕ https://vfmat.ch/2b19

Apnalaya: Empowering the Urban Poor
Aims to empower the urban poor, enabling access to basic services, healthcare, education and livelihoods and through advocacy with the government.
OB-GYN
⊕ https://vfmat.ch/126b

Aravind Eye Foundation
Founded to support the Aravind Eye Care System in its mission to eliminate needless blindness and spread Aravind's sustainable model of high-quality, patient-centric healthcare throughout the world.
Ophth-Opt
⊕ https://vfmat.ch/6ac8

Arogya World
Strives to prevent noncommunicable diseases through health education and lifestyle change.
Pub Health
⊕ https://vfmat.ch/6edf

Arthritis Foundation of Asia
Empowers people with arthritis through help, support ,and information, ensuring their voices are heard and their conditions more effectively managed.
Rheum
⊕ https://vfmat.ch/5f12

Arunodaya Charitable Trust
Strives to provide comprehensive eye care to individuals in need, with a focus on the prevention of eye disease.
General, Ophth-Opt, Peds, Pub Health
⊕ https://vfmat.ch/2db6

ASE Foundation
Provides support for education and research to the community of healthcare providers and patients for whom cardiovascular ultrasound is essential.

CT Surg, CV Med, Radiol
⊕ https://vfmat.ch/bb57

Ashraya Initiative for Children
Helps vulnerable children in Pune, India, with educational opportunities and holistic development, and by building healthy, empowered communities.
All-Immu, ER Med, General, MF Med, Nutr, Peds, Surg
⊕ https://vfmat.ch/692c

Association of Medical Doctors of Asia (AMDA)
Strives to support people affected by disasters and economic distress on their road to recovery, establishing a true partnership with special emphasis on local initiative.
ER Med, Logist-Op, Pub Health
⊕ https://vfmat.ch/e3d4

Australian Himalayan Foundation
Works in partnership with people of the remote Himalaya to improve living standards through better education and training, improved health services, and environmental sustainability.
General, MF Med, OB-GYN, Peds
⊕ https://vfmat.ch/3428

Austrian Doctors
Stands for a life in dignity and takes care of the health of disadvantaged people. Helps all people regardless of gender, skin color, religion and sexual orientation.
General, Infect Dis, Medicine
⊕ https://vfmat.ch/e929

Bal Umang Drishya Sanstha (BUDS)
Creates lasting change by building healthy communities, through efforts in disease prevention, child healthcare, education, and sustainable development.
ER Med, GI, Infect Dis, Nutr, OB-GYN, Peds, Psych
⊕ https://vfmat.ch/c358

BALCO Medical Centre
Aims to provide affordable, world-class cancer care to all.
Heme-Onc, Palliative, Path, Rad-Onc, Surg
⊕ https://vfmat.ch/c8fc

Bangalore Hospice Trust (BHT) Karunashraya
Provides compassionate care for people with terminal illnesses, and for their loved ones, through medical, emotional, spiritual, and social support.
Palliative, Rehab
⊕ https://vfmat.ch/f7c4

Basic Foundations
Supports local projects and organizations that seek to meet the basic human needs of others in their community.
ER Med, General, Peds, Rehab, Surg
⊕ https://vfmat.ch/c4be

Benjamin H. Josephson, MD Fund
Provides healthcare professionals with the financial resources necessary to deliver medical services for those in need throughout the world.
General, OB-GYN
⊕ https://vfmat.ch/6acc

BFIRST – British Foundation for International Reconstructive Surgery & Training
Supports projects across the developing world to train surgeons in their local environment to effectively manage devastating injuries.
Anesth, Plast, Surg
⊕ https://vfmat.ch/ad4f

Bhagat Hari Singh Charitable Hospital
Seeks to ensure that anyone in need, particularly those unable to afford basic medical care, can access treatment in a safe, clean hospital.
Dent-OMFS, ER Med, General, OB-GYN, Ophth-Opt, Ortho
⊕ https://vfmat.ch/46e6

Bhagia Heart Foundation
Aims to fund diagnosis, treatment, and prevention of heart and circulatory disease

for the underprivileged.
CT Surg, CV Med, Vasc Surg
⊕ https://vfmat.ch/5591

Bhagwan Mahaveer Cancer Hospital & Research Centre (BMCHRC)
Provides services in cancer prevention, treatment, education, and research, while providing affordable care to all, regardless of economic considerations.
Anesth, Heme-Onc, Neurosurg, Path, Plast, Rad-Onc, Radiol
⊕ https://vfmat.ch/68bf

Bharti Charitable Foundation
Seeks to provide treatment and rehabilitation for patients with impaired hearing.
ENT
⊕ https://vfmat.ch/335a

Bhoomika Group of Eye Hospitals
Brings free and affordable healthcare to the poor and elderly through service delivery, education, training, and research.
Ophth-Opt
⊕ https://vfmat.ch/e915

Bidada International Foundation
Provides medical and surgical treatment for patients of all ages, castes, and races.
All-Immu, CV Med, Dent-OMFS, Derm, ENT, Endo, GI, General, Heme-Onc, Nephro, Neuro, OB-GYN, Ophth-Opt, Ortho, Path, Ped Surg, Peds, Peds, Plast, Pod, Psych, Pulm-Critic, Radiol, Rehab, Rheum, Surg, Urol
⊕ https://vfmat.ch/71ae

Bill & Melinda Gates Foundation
Focuses on global issues, such as poverty, health, and education, offering the opportunity to dramatically improve the quality of life for billions of people by building partnerships that bring together resources, expertise, and vision to identify issues, find answers, and drive change.
All-Immu, General, Infect Dis, MF Med, Neonat, OB-GYN, Pub Health
⊕ https://vfmat.ch/7cf2

Boston Cardiac Foundation, The
Provides advanced medical technologies and cardiac care, such as pacemaker implantation, to patients around the world who would otherwise have no access to these services.
Anesth, CT Surg, CV Med, Crit-Care
⊕ https://vfmat.ch/8fd3

Boston Children's Hospital: Global Health Program
Helps solve pediatric global healthcare challenges by transferring expertise through long-term partnerships with scalable impact, while working in the field to strengthen healthcare systems, advocate, research, and provide care delivery or education as a way of sustainably improving the health of children worldwide.
Anesth, CV Med, Crit-Care, ER Med, Heme-Onc, Infect Dis, Medicine, Nutr, Palliative, Ped Surg, Peds
⊕ https://vfmat.ch/f9f8

Breakfast Revolution, The
Aims to combat malnutrition among children in India through holistic nutrition programs.
Logist-Op, Nutr, Pub Health
⊕ https://vfmat.ch/9995

Breast Cancer Support
Aims to save lives and end breast cancer forever in women and men through education, treatment, emotional assistance, and financial support.
Heme-Onc, Logist-Op, Pub Health, Rad-Onc, Radiol
⊕ https://vfmat.ch/cb78

Bridge of Life
Aims to strengthen healthcare globally through sustainable programs that prevent and treat chronic disease.
Logist-Op, Nephro, OB-GYN, Peds, Surg
⊕ https://vfmat.ch/5b68

Bridge Trust Ltd., The
Engages in relief, education, training, and development in India and Zambia, along with the U.K. and other developed nations.
General, Infect Dis, OB-GYN
⊕ https://vfmat.ch/e463

British Council for Prevention of Blindness (BCPB)
Funds research into blindness prevention and sight restoration in children and adults in low- and lower-middle-income countries.
Ophth-Opt
⊕ https://vfmat.ch/eaf4

BroadReach
Collaborates with governments, multinational health organizations, donors, and private-sector companies to effect healthcare reform and solve the world's biggest health challenges.
Logist-Op
⊕ https://vfmat.ch/7812

Bucket List
Offers a welcoming environment and diverse programs to underprivileged children and adolescents that support their academic, physical, mental and emotional growth, through efforts such as health camps, groups, and sports.
General, Logist-Op, Nutr, Peds
⊕ https://vfmat.ch/e56b

Burn Advocates
Supports burn survivors as they face the challenges of recovery, rehabilitation, and reintegration.
Anesth, Crit-Care, Derm, Ped Surg, Plast, Rehab, Rehab
⊕ https://vfmat.ch/9327

Cairdeas International Palliative Care Trust
Promotes and facilitates the provision of high-quality palliative care in the developing world, where such care is limited.
Palliative
⊕ https://vfmat.ch/35c4

Camillian Disaster Service (CADIS) International
Promotes the development of locally based health programs for disaster-stricken communities through compassionate and coordinated interventions.
General, Logist-Op, MF Med
⊕ https://vfmat.ch/5281

Can Protect Foundation
Provides free prevention, training, and awareness facilities to prevent breast and cervical cancer.
Heme-Onc, MF Med
⊕ https://vfmat.ch/f644

Canadian Reconstructive Surgery Foundation, The
Develops, organizes, and manages, in participation with developing countries, the delivery of reconstructive medical-care programs, technologies, and education to those who cannot otherwise obtain the care they need.
Anesth, Dent-OMFS, Plast
⊕ https://vfmat.ch/15f4

CanKids KidsCan
Partners with cancer centers for better standards of treatment and care for children with cancer through funding, needs assessment, social support staff, and more.
Heme-Onc, Nutr, Palliative, Pub Health
⊕ https://vfmat.ch/cdf4

Canwinn Foundation
Dedicates efforts to HIV/AIDS and cancer treatment and prevention, while providing the most reliable and affordable treatment referrals to those in need.
CV Med, Dent-OMFS, Derm, ENT, Endo, General, Logist-Op, OB-GYN, Ortho, Path, Peds, Pub Health, Rehab, Surg
⊕ https://vfmat.ch/92d8

CardioStart International
Provides free heart surgery and associated medical care to children and adults

living in underserved regions of the world, irrespective of political or religious affiliation, through the collective skills of healthcare experts.
Anesth, CT Surg, CV Med, Crit-Care, Pub Health, Pulm-Critic
⊕ https://vfmat.ch/85ef

CARE
Works around the globe to save lives, defeat poverty, and achieve social justice.
ER Med, General
⊕ https://vfmat.ch/7232

CARE Bihar
Focuses on reducing maternal, newborn, and child mortality and malnutrition, and on improving immunization rates and reproductive health services.
Pub Health
⊕ https://vfmat.ch/7b3d

Caring Souls Foundation (CASOF)
Prevents and helps treat cancer and HIV/AIDS through education, communication, research, and collaboration to create systems to financially aid patients.
Heme-Onc, Infect Dis, Logist-Op, Pub Health
⊕ https://vfmat.ch/de44

Caritas Hospital & Institute of Health Sciences
Provides quality healthcare services with the ultimate aim of relieving human beings from pain and suffering.
Anesth, Crit-Care, Dent-OMFS, Derm, ENT, ER Med, Endo, GI, General, Neonat, Nephro, OB-GYN, Ortho, Path, Peds, Plast, Psych, Pulm-Critic, Radiol, Rehab, Rheum, Urol
⊕ https://vfmat.ch/5243

Carter Center, The
Seeks to prevent and resolve conflicts, enhance freedom and democracy, and improve health, while remaining committed to human rights and the alleviation of human suffering.
Infect Dis, MF Med, Ophth-Opt
⊕ https://vfmat.ch/6556

Catholic Health Association of India
Promotes community health, enables the poor and marginalized to be collectively responsible for their health, and ensures the availability of reasonably priced healthcare.
General, Geri, OB-GYN, Palliative, Peds, Psych
⊕ https://vfmat.ch/b459

Catholic World Mission
Works to rebuild communities worldwide by helping to alleviate poverty and empower underserved areas, while spreading the message of the Catholic Church.
ER Med, General, Nutr, Peds
⊕ https://vfmat.ch/7b5f

cbm New Zealand
Inspired by the Christian faith, aims to improve the quality of life for those living with the double disadvantage of poverty and disability.
Crit-Care, Infect Dis, Logist-Op, Nutr, OB-GYN, Ophth-Opt, Ortho, Psych, Rehab, Surg
⊕ https://vfmat.ch/c14b

Center for Health and Hope
Supports and advocates for persons infected and affected by HIV/AIDS with programs of education, prevention, care, and treatment.
Pub Health
⊕ https://vfmat.ch/a52e

Center for Private Sector Health Initiatives
Aims to improve the health and well-being of people in developing countries by facilitating partnerships between the public and private sectors.
Infect Dis, Nutr, Peds
⊕ https://vfmat.ch/b198

Chain of Hope (La Chaîne de l'Espoir)
Helps underprivileged children around the world by providing them with access to healthcare.

Anesth, CT Surg, Crit-Care, ER Med, Neurosurg, Ortho, Ped Surg, Surg, Vasc Surg
⊕ https://vfmat.ch/e871

Challenge Initiative, The
Seeks to rapidly and sustainably scale up proven reproductive health solutions among the urban poor.
MF Med, OB-GYN, Peds
⊕ https://vfmat.ch/2f77

CharityVision International
Focuses on restoring curable sight impairment worldwide by empowering local physicians and creating sustainable solutions.
Logist-Op, Ophth-Opt, Surg
⊕ https://vfmat.ch/6231

Chennai Liver Foundation
Aims to reduce the incidence and impact of liver disease.
⊕ https://vfmat.ch/45da

Child Family Health International (CFHI)
Connects students with local health professionals and community leaders transforming perspectives about self, global health, and healing.
General, Infect Dis, OB-GYN, Ophth-Opt, Palliative, Peds
⊕ https://vfmat.ch/729e

Child Help Foundation
Carries out child-focused programs in education, health, food, and shelter.
ER Med
⊕ https://vfmat.ch/b5fe

Child in Need Institute (CINI)
Partners with governments, organizations, donors and communities to strengthen the capacity of children and women to ensure they achieve their rights to health, nutrition, education, and protection.
Logist-Op, Nutr, OB-GYN, Peds, Pub Health
⊕ https://vfmat.ch/8a37

ChildFund Australia
Works to reduce poverty for children in many of the world's most disadvantaged communities.
ER Med, General, Peds
⊕ https://vfmat.ch/13df

Children of War Foundation
Delivers access to global health and education to communities affected by poverty, war, natural disaster, climate change, and migration challenges.
ER Med, General, Logist-Op, Peds, Surg
⊕ https://vfmat.ch/de51

Children's Emergency Relief International
Works with children, families, communities, and governments to provide a family environment as the first and best option for children to grow in.
General, Pub Health
⊕ https://vfmat.ch/92ae

Children's HeartLink
Aims to save children's lives by transforming pediatric cardiac care in underserved parts of the world through long-term educational partnerships and robust monitoring.
⊕ https://vfmat.ch/24b3

Children's Hope India
Aims to lift children from poverty by nurturing the whole child and providing education, nutrition, medical care, and career building.
General, Logist-Op, Nutr, Ophth-Opt
⊕ https://vfmat.ch/7d2c

Children's Lifeline International
Provides medical teams and surgical assistance to underprivileged children in developing countries through missions in partnership with local hospitals.
CV Med, Dent-OMFS, General, MF Med, Neurosurg, Peds, Rehab
⊕ https://vfmat.ch/6fea

Childspring International
Provides life-changing surgeries for children from developing countries and transforms communities.
CT Surg, Medicine, Ophth-Opt, Ortho, Ped Surg, Peds, Surg
⊕ https://vfmat.ch/f939

Christian Aid Ministries
Strives to be a trustworthy and efficient channel for Amish, Mennonite, and other conservative Anabaptist groups and individuals to minister to physical and spiritual needs around the world.
CT Surg, ER Med, Logist-Op, Ortho, Pub Health
⊕ https://vfmat.ch/7b33

Christian Blind Mission (CBM)
Aims to improve the quality of life of persons with disabilities in the poorest countries, addressing poverty as a cause and a consequence of disability, and working in partnership to create a society for all.
ENT, General, Infect Dis, OB-GYN, Ophth-Opt, Ortho, Peds, Psych, Rehab, Surg
⊕ https://vfmat.ch/3824

Christian Connections for International Health (CCIH)
Promotes global health and wholeness from a Christian perspective.
All-Immu, General, Infect Dis, MF Med, Neonat, OB-GYN, Psych
⊕ https://vfmat.ch/fa5d

Cipla Foundation
Works with communities, NGO partners and institutions to create access to health, education, and livelihoods for underserved communities.
Geri, Infect Dis, Logist-Op, MF Med, OB-GYN, Palliative, Pub Health
⊕ https://vfmat.ch/769b

Clinton Health Access Initiative (CHAI)
Aims to save lives and reduce the burden of disease in low- and middle-income countries. Works with partners to strengthen the capabilities of governments and the private sector to create and sustain high-quality health systems.
General, Heme-Onc, Infect Dis, Logist-Op, MF Med, Medicine, Neonat, Nutr, OB-GYN, Path, Peds, Rad-Onc
⊕ https://vfmat.ch/9ed7

Clubfoot India Initiative Trust
Aims to support children with clubfoot and their families by providing treatment and to inspire action to eradicate disabilities caused by clubfoot.
Logist-Op, Ortho, Pod
⊕ https://vfmat.ch/5b1e

Coimbatore Cancer Foundation (CCF)
Seeks to educate, support, and enhance the well-being of people with cancer and their caregivers, and to improve cancer awareness among the public.
Palliative
⊕ https://vfmat.ch/4b8f

Columbia University: Columbia Office of Global Surgery (COGS)
Helps to increase access to safe and affordable surgical care, as a means to reduce health disparities and the global burden of disease.
Anesth, CT Surg, Crit-Care, Dent-OMFS, ENT, ER Med, Infect Dis, MF Med, Neurosurg, OB-GYN, Ophth-Opt, Ortho, Ped Surg, Plast, Plast, Pub Health, Surg, Urol
⊕ https://vfmat.ch/4349

Columbia University: Global Mental Health Programs
Pioneers research initiatives, promotes mental health, and aims to reduce the burden of mental illness worldwide.
Psych
⊕ https://vfmat.ch/c5cd

Columbia Vagelos College of Physicians and Surgeons Programs in Global Health
Harnesses the expertise of the medical school to improve health worldwide by training global health leaders, building capacity through interdisciplinary education and training programs, and addressing unmet health needs through research and application.
CV Med, Derm, Genetics, Heme-Onc, Infect Dis, Medicine, OB-GYN, Ophth-Opt,

Peds, Psych, Pub Health, Pulm-Critic, Surg
⊕ https://vfmat.ch/a9e5

Combat Blindness International
Works to eliminate preventable blindness worldwide by providing sustainable, equitable solutions for sight through partnerships and innovation.
Ophth-Opt
⊕ https://vfmat.ch/28ad

Concern India Foundation
Aims to make the disadvantaged self-reliant and to enable them to lead a life of dignity through education, health, and community development programs.
Logist-Op, Nutr, Pub Health, Rehab
⊕ https://vfmat.ch/784f

Core Group
Aims to improve and expand community health practices for underserved populations, especially women and children, through collaborative action and learning.
General, Infect Dis, MF Med, Medicine, OB-GYN, Peds, Pub Health
⊕ https://vfmat.ch/9de3

COVID-19 Clinical Research Coalition
Advocates and collaborates for the advancement of COVID-19 research driven by the needs of low-resource settings, and works for equitable access to solutions to the pandemic.
All-Immu, Infect-Dis, MF Med, Path, Pub Health
⊕ https://vfmat.ch/d1f4

Cura for the World
Seeks to heal, nourish, and embrace the neglected by building medical clinics in remote communities in dire need of medical care.
ER Med, General, Peds
⊕ https://vfmat.ch/c55f

Cure Spinal Muscular Atrophy (SMA) India
Brings treatment for SMA to India, making healthcare accessible, inclusive, and affordable for all; also creates awareness about SMA and the importance of genetic screening.
Genetics, Neuro
⊕ https://vfmat.ch/161c

Deenanath Mangeshkar Hospital and Research Center
Delivers competent, ethical, tertiary healthcare services to patients through a multi-speciality charitable hospital.
CT Surg, CV Med, Dent-OMFS, Derm, ENT, ER Med, GI, General, Heme-Onc, Medicine, Nephro, Neuro, Neurosurg, OB-GYN, Ophth-Opt, Ortho, Peds, Plast, Psych, Rad-Onc, Rehab, Urol
⊕ https://vfmat.ch/7d3b

Deesha Education Foundation
Seeks to provide quality healthcare and education affordable for everyone.
Ophth-Opt
⊕ https://vfmat.ch/b8c3

DESIRE Society: Caring for Special Children
Improves the lives of children struggling with the impact of the HIV/AIDS pandemic in India by providing services such as shelter, food, healthcare treatment, education, and psychosocial support.
General, Infect Dis, Peds
⊕ https://vfmat.ch/e4c8

Deva Foundation - Mission for Mankind
Seeks to promote mental well-being, education, research, and women's empowerment, to enable individuals and to support victims of natural disasters.
General, Psych, Rehab
⊕ https://vfmat.ch/23f3

Developing Indigenous Resources (DIR)
Aims to help all citizens achieve a level of health that empowers them to participate fully in social and economic development.
Dent-OMFS, Infect Dis, Logist-Op, Nutr, Ophth-Opt
⊕ https://vfmat.ch/422b

Dianova
Works in prevention and treatment of addiction, while promoting social progress in international forums.
Psych, Pub Health
⊕ https://vfmat.ch/1998

Direct Relief
Improves the health and lives of people affected by poverty or emergency situations by mobilizing and providing essential medical resources needed for their care.
ER Med, Logist-Op
⊕ https://vfmat.ch/58e5

Divine Onkar Mission
Seeks to create lasting change in people's lives by building sustainable communities through long-term projects, education, and medical assistance.
CV Med, Endo, Geri, Ophth-Opt
⊕ https://vfmat.ch/1c6a

Divine Shakti Foundation, The
Provides programs for holistic healthcare and supports research intended for the advancement of women and children's healthcare concerns.
Dent-OMFS, ENT, ER Med, General, OB-GYN, Ophth-Opt, Pub Health, Rehab
⊕ https://vfmat.ch/dc66

Divine Will Foundation
Funds educational, medical, nutritional, sustainable energy, and water purification projects.
CT Surg, CV Med, Ped Surg, Peds
⊕ https://vfmat.ch/6f1e

DKT INTERNATIONAL INC
Seeks to provide couples with affordable and safe options for family planning and HIV/AIDS prevention through dynamic social marketing.
General, Surg
⊕ https://vfmat.ch/b3a7

Doctors Without Borders/Médecins Sans Frontières (MSF)
Responds to emergencies and provides lifesaving medical care where needed most, including during disasters, conflicts, and epidemics.
Anesth, Crit-Care, ER Med, General, Infect Dis, Nutr, OB-GYN, Ped Surg, Peds, Psych, Pub Health, Surg
⊕ https://vfmat.ch/f363

Dr Ghosh Charitable Trust (DGCT)
Aims to ensure that everyone, regardless of socioeconomic background, has access to medical treatment, particularly for neurological disorders.
CV Med, Dent-OMFS, ER Med, General, Logist-Op, Neuro, Neurosurg, OB-GYN, Ophth-Opt, Ortho, Path, Peds, Radiol
⊕ https://vfmat.ch/f52d

Dr. GMP Foundation
Aims to promote public health, education, and upbringing of the local population with an emphasis on hygiene and medicine in the Himalayan region, especially India and Nepal.
ER Med, General, Surg
⊕ https://vfmat.ch/aa9b

Dr. VSN Geriatric Foundation
Provides services for the elderly such as home visits from doctors, advocates for policy changes, supports caregivers, educates medical professionals, and conducts research.
Geri
⊕ https://vfmat.ch/bfe3

Dr.Mohan's Diabetes Specialities Centre
Promotes diabetes awareness and provides education, screenings, medical care, supplies, and other support at low to no cost.
Endo, Logist-Op, Ophth-Opt, Pod
⊕ https://vfmat.ch/3ba9

Drugs for Neglected Diseases Initiative
Develops lifesaving medicines for people with neglected diseases around the

world, having developed eight treatments for five deadly diseases and saved millions of lives since 2003.
Infect Dis, Pub Health
⊕ https://vfmat.ch/969c

Duke University: Global Health Institute
Sparks innovation in global health research and education, and brings together knowledge and resources to address the most important global health issues of our time.
All-Immu, Infect Dis, MF Med, OB-GYN, Pub Health
⊕ https://vfmat.ch/c4cd

East Meets West Children's Foundation
Provides medical treatment and educational training for abandoned and destitute children.
General, Logist-Op
⊕ https://vfmat.ch/d6c5

Edwards Lifesciences
Provides innovative solutions for people fighting cardiovascular disease, as a global leader in patient-focused medical innovations for structural heart disease, along with critical care and surgical monitoring.
Anesth, CT Surg, CV Med, Crit-Care, Ped Surg, Peds, Pulm-Critic, Surg, Vasc Surg
⊕ https://vfmat.ch/d671

Effect: Hope (The Leprosy Mission Canada)
Connects like-minded Canadians to people suffering in isolation from debilitating, neglected tropical diseases such as leprosy, lymphatic filariasis, and Buruli ulcer.
General, Infect Dis
⊕ https://vfmat.ch/f12a

Ekam Foundation
Aims to improve health by providing reproductive, maternal, newborn, child, and adolescent healthcare and by facilitating lifesaving medical treatment for children.
Logist-Op, Path, Pub Health
⊕ https://vfmat.ch/c6fb

Ekjut
Works towards the improvement of maternal, newborn, and child health and nutrition of individuals in underserved and marginalized communities.
Infect Dis, Logist-Op, MF Med, Neonat
⊕ https://vfmat.ch/36c3

Elizabeth Glaser Pediatric AIDS Foundation
Seeks to end global pediatric HIV/AIDS through prevention and treatment programs, research, and advocacy.
Infect Dis, Nutr, OB-GYN, Peds
⊕ https://vfmat.ch/d6ec

Elton John AIDS Foundation
Seeks to address and overcome the stigma, discrimination, and neglect that prevents ending AIDS by funding local experts to challenge discrimination, prevent infections, and provide treatment.
Infect Dis, Pub Health
⊕ https://vfmat.ch/9d31

Enable Health Society
Aims to improve the health and well-being of individuals and communities with an emphasis on disease prevention, care, and management.
Endo, Infect Dis, Pub Health
⊕ https://vfmat.ch/be41

END Fund, The
Aims to control and eliminate the most prevalent neglected diseases among the world's poorest and most vulnerable people.
Infect Dis
⊕ https://vfmat.ch/2614

EngenderHealth
Works to implement high-quality, gender-equitable programs that advance sexual and reproductive health and rights.

General, MF Med, OB-GYN, Peds
⊕ https://vfmat.ch/1cb2

ESCO (Educational Social Cultural Organization)
Funds educational, social welfare, cultural, and healthcare programs in underserved areas, with a focus on projects that promote self-employment.
General, Nutr, Peds, Pub Health
⊕ https://vfmat.ch/ac2a

Every Infant matters
Focuses on the health of infants, girls, and women, including nutrition, blindness prevention, vaccination, and gender discrimination, in marginalized and poor communities.
Ophth-Opt, Peds, Pub Health
⊕ https://vfmat.ch/4d6a

Evidence Action
Aims to be a world leader in scaling evidence-based and cost-effective programs to reduce the burden of poverty.
General, Infect Dis
⊕ https://vfmat.ch/94b6

Evidence Project, The
Improves family-planning policies, programs, and practices through the strategic generation, translation, and use of evidence.
General, MF Med
⊕ https://vfmat.ch/f9e7

Eye Foundation of America
Works toward a world without childhood blindness.
Ophth-Opt
⊕ https://vfmat.ch/a7eb

Eye Mantra Foundation / Charitable Hospital
Provides affordable eye care and treatment for people living in poverty.
Ophth-Opt, Surg
⊕ https://vfmat.ch/48d2

Eyes for the World
Aims to create awareness to prevent blindness and an opportunity for every person with treatable blindness to see a doctor.
Ophth-Opt
⊕ https://vfmat.ch/83c9

Family Planning Association of India
Delivers essential health services focusing on sexual and reproductive health in 18 states.
Infect Dis, Pub Health
⊕ https://vfmat.ch/ef57

Firefly Mission
Organizes humanitarian missions to help people in less fortunate situations while serving as a vehicle for the spiritual development of members and the beneficiaries of its missions.
Logist-Op, Ophth-Opt, Pub Health
⊕ https://vfmat.ch/d215

First Hand Foundation
Brings together Cerner associates, Cerner technology, and the community to help children and families around the world achieve their full health potential and improve the health of individuals through innovative models.
⊕ https://vfmat.ch/188b

Forgotten International, The
Develops programs that alleviate poverty and the suffering of impoverished women and children in both the United States and worldwide.
Logist-Op, Nutr, OB-GYN, Peds, Pub Health
⊕ https://vfmat.ch/26f3

Foundation for International Medical Relief of Children (FIMRC)
Provides access to healthcare for low-resource and medically underserved families around the world.

General, Infect Dis, Peds, Pub Health
 ⊕ https://vfmat.ch/78b9

Fracarita International
Provides support and services in the fields of mental healthcare, care for people with a disability, and education.
Psych, Rehab
 ⊕ https://vfmat.ch/8d3c

Friends of UNFPA
Promotes the health, dignity, and rights of women and girls around the world by supporting the lifesaving work of UNFPA, the United Nations' reproductive health and rights agency, through education, advocacy, and fundraising.
MF Med, OB-GYN
 ⊕ https://vfmat.ch/2a3a

George Foundation, The
Helps alleviate poverty, promotes health and a clean environment, and strengthens democratic institutions and values in developing countries.
ER Med, General
 ⊕ https://vfmat.ch/43b9

George Institute for Global Health India, The
Seeks to improve the health of millions of people in India through the generation of high-quality evidence using discovery and implementation research.
General, Nephro, Peds
 ⊕ https://vfmat.ch/88d2

German Doctors
Conducts voluntary medical work in developing countries and brings help where misery is part of everyday life.
General, Infect Dis, Medicine
 ⊕ https://vfmat.ch/21ad

GFA World
Based in Christian ministry, sponsors medical camps for the sick, provides disaster relief to vulnerable populations, and empowers impoverished communities with basic necessities such as clean water, vocational training, and education.
General, Infect Dis
 ⊕ https://vfmat.ch/63ee

Gift of Life International
Provides lifesaving cardiac treatment to children in developing countries while developing sustainable pediatric cardiac programs by implementing screening, surgical, and training missions.
Anesth, CT Surg, CV Med, Crit-Care, Ped Surg, Peds, Pulm-Critic
 ⊕ https://vfmat.ch/f2f9

Give Sight Global
Provides vision care to underserved communities around the world by providing treatment for curable blindness and other preventable eye conditions.
Ophth-Opt, Pub Health
 ⊕ https://vfmat.ch/5c4d

Global Aid Network (GAiN) Australia
Inspired by the Christian faith, provides support to people living in crisis through programs in healthcare, humanitarian aid, disaster response, clean water, and sanitation.
Dent-OMFS, Ophth-Opt
 ⊕ https://vfmat.ch/6cb8

Global Alliance to Prevent Prematurity And Stillbirth (GAPPS)
Seeks to improve birth outcomes worldwide by reducing the burden of premature birth and stillbirth.
All-Immu, Infect Dis, MF Med, Neonat, Neonat, OB-GYN
 ⊕ https://vfmat.ch/3f74

Global Clinic
Seeks to ensure that any effort to provide medical services is accompanied by a long-term program to improve the health of residents of its partner communities.
Dent-OMFS, ER Med, General, OB-GYN, OB-GYN, Ophth-Opt, Surg
 ⊕ https://vfmat.ch/9e48

Global Dental Relief
Brings free dental care to impoverished children in partnership with local organizations, and delivers treatment and preventive care in dental clinics that serve children in schools and remote villages.
Dent-OMFS
 ⊕ https://vfmat.ch/29b6

Global Eye Project
Empowers local communities by building locally managed, sustainable eye clinics through education initiatives and volunteer-run professional training services.
Anesth, Ophth-Opt, Surg
 ⊕ https://vfmat.ch/cdba

Global First Responder (GFR)
Acts as a centralized network for individuals and agencies involved in relief work worldwide and organizes and executes mission trips to areas in need, focusing not only on healthcare delivery but also on health education and improvements.
ER Med
 ⊕ https://vfmat.ch/a3e1

Global Force for Healing
Works to end preventable maternal and newborn deaths by supporting the scaling of effective grassroots, community-led, culturally respectful care and education in underserved areas around the globe using the midwifery model of care.
Neonat, OB-GYN
 ⊕ https://vfmat.ch/deb2

Global Hospital and Research Centre
Aims to provide world-class, complete healthcare services responsibly and with a human touch at affordable prices.
Dent-OMFS, Derm, ENT, General, Neuro, OB-GYN, Ophth-Opt, Ortho, Path, Peds, Plast, Rad-Onc, Rehab, Surg
 ⊕ https://vfmat.ch/782b

Global Medical Foundation Australia
Provides medical, surgical, dental, and educational welfare to underprivileged communities and gives them access to basics that are often taken for granted.
Dent-OMFS, ER Med, General, OB-GYN, Ortho, Surg
 ⊕ https://vfmat.ch/fa56

Global Medical Training
Provides free medical and dental services to communities in Central America, and allows medical students, professionals, and others to expand their medical and cultural awareness.
Dent-OMFS, General, Logist-Op, Pub Health
 ⊕ https://vfmat.ch/3449

Global Ministries – The United Methodist Church
As the worldwide mission and development agency of The United Methodist Church, Global Ministries works with more than 300 hospitals and clinics around the world through its Global Health Unit.
Anesth, CT Surg, CV Med, Crit-Care, Dent-OMFS, Derm, ER Med, GI, General, Infect Dis, Logist-Op, MF Med, Medicine, Neonat, Nephro, Nutr, OB-GYN, Ophth-Opt, Ortho, Palliative, Peds, Pod, Psych, Pub Health, Rehab, Rheum, Surg, Urol
 ⊕ https://vfmat.ch/1723

Global Mission Partners, Inc.
Provides opportunities for short-term global medical mission opportunities, along with evangelism and construction missions, to serve persons who have little or no access to healthcare, adequate housing, and community outreach.
Dent-OMFS, General, Geri, Palliative, Psych
 ⊕ https://vfmat.ch/7db4

Global Network for Women and Children's Health Research
Aims to improve maternal and child health outcomes and building health research capacity in resource-poor settings by testing cost-effective, sustainable interventions that provide guidance for the practice of evidence-based medicine. Scientists from developing countries, together with peers in the United States, lead teams that address priority research needs through randomized clinical trials and implementation research conducted in low-resource areas.
MF Med, OB-GYN
 ⊕ https://vfmat.ch/a187

Global Offsite Care

Aims to be a catalyst for increased access to specialized healthcare for all, and provides technology platforms to doctors and clinics around the world through Rotary Club-sponsored telemedicine projects.

Crit-Care, ER Med, General, Pulm-Critic

⊕ https://vfmat.ch/61b5

Global Oncology (GO)

Brings the best in cancer care to underserved patients around the world and collaborates across geographic, professional, and academic borders to improve cancer care, research, and education.

Heme-Onc, Path, Rad-Onc

⊕ https://vfmat.ch/fcb8

Global Partnership for Zero Leprosy

Facilitates alignment of the leprosy community and accelerates effective collaborative action toward the goal of zero leprosy.

Infect Dis

⊕ https://vfmat.ch/ec7b

Global Pragathi

Aims to achieve sustainable development in communities through education, women and youth empowerment, and preventive healthcare.

All-Immu, Dent-OMFS, General, Logist-Op, MF Med, Nutr, Ophth-Opt, Pub Health

⊕ https://vfmat.ch/6a46

Global Strategies

Empowers communities in the most neglected areas of the world to improve the lives of women and children through healthcare.

MF Med, Neonat, OB-GYN, Peds

⊕ https://vfmat.ch/ef92

GlobalMedic

Provides disaster relief and lifesaving humanitarian aid.

ER Med, Pub Health

⊕ https://vfmat.ch/dfe6

Globe Eye Foundation

Provides affordable, up-to-date eye care regardless of caste, creed, or religion.

Ophth-Opt, Pub Health

⊕ https://vfmat.ch/c618

Globus Relief

Aims to improve the delivery of healthcare worldwide by gathering, processing, and distributing surplus medical supplies to charities at home and abroad.

Logist-Op

⊕ https://vfmat.ch/a2b7

Good Shepard International Foundation

Strives to promote inclusive and sustainable development for the most marginalized and vulnerable people, with a special focus on women, girls, and children, inspired by the Christian faith.

ER Med

⊕ https://vfmat.ch/ad9a

Grace for Impact

Provides high-quality healthcare and education to the rural poor, where it is needed most, in Sub-Saharan Africa and Southeast Asia.

Dent-OMFS, General, Ophth-Opt

⊕ https://vfmat.ch/3ed1

Grassroot Soccer

Leverages the power of soccer to educate, inspire, and mobilize at-risk youth in developing countries to overcome their greatest health challenges, live healthier and more productive lives, and be agents for change in their communities.

Infect Dis

⊕ https://vfmat.ch/3521

Hand In Hand USA

Provides free medical and dental care to impoverished communities, educates poor children, and supports and funds emergency relief groups in natural disasters.

Dent-OMFS, OB-GYN, Peds, Radiol

⊕ https://vfmat.ch/a2b8

Handi-Care Intl

Provides services for impoverished individuals and those with special needs, including care, education, rehabilitation, and vocational training.

General, Neuro, Neurosurg, Nutr, Peds, Rehab, Surg

⊕ https://vfmat.ch/5a27

Hans Foundation, The

Identifies and implements social development projects in areas of health, education, livelihoods, and disabilities in underprivileged communities of India.

Dent-OMFS, Derm, ER Med, OB-GYN, Ophth-Opt, Ortho, Palliative, Peds, Radiol, Surg

⊕ https://vfmat.ch/ccc4

Harvard Global Health Institute

Devoted to improving global health and pioneering the next generation of global health research, education, policy, and practice, with an evidence-based, innovative, integrative, and collaborative approach, harnessing the unique breadth of excellence within Harvard.

General, Infect Dis, Logist-Op

⊕ https://vfmat.ch/5867

Healing Little Hearts

Sends specialist medical teams to perform free lifesaving heart surgery on babies and children in developing parts of the world.

Anesth, CT Surg, CV Med, Ped Surg, Peds, Surg

⊕ https://vfmat.ch/ffc1

Healing the Children

Helps underserved children around the world secure the medical care they need to lead more fulfilling lives.

Anesth, Dent-OMFS, ENT, General, Medicine, Ophth-Opt, Ped Surg, Peds, Plast, Surg

⊕ https://vfmat.ch/d4ee

Health Poverty Action

Works in partnership with people around the world who are pursuing change in their own communities to demand health justice and challenge power imbalances.

ER Med, General, Infect Dis, Psych, Pub Health

⊕ https://vfmat.ch/ee58

Health Volunteers Overseas (HVO)

Improves the availability and quality of healthcare through the education, training, and professional development of the health workforce in resource-scarce countries.

All-Immu, Anesth, CV Med, Dent-OMFS, Derm, ENT, ER Med, Endo, GI, Heme-Onc, Infect Dis, Medicine, Medicine, Nephro, Neuro, OB-GYN, Ophth-Opt, Ortho, Peds, Plast, Psych, Pulm-Critic, Rehab, Rheum, Surg

⊕ https://vfmat.ch/42b2

Healthy DEvelopments

Provides Germany-supported health and social protection programs around the globe in a collaborative knowledge management process.

All-Immu, General, Infect Dis, Logist-Op, MF Med

⊕ https://vfmat.ch/dc31

Hear the World Foundation

Advocates worldwide for equal opportunities and improved quality of life for people in need with hearing loss.

ENT, Peds

⊕ https://vfmat.ch/122c

Hearing Health Foundation

Prevents and cures hearing loss and tinnitus through groundbreaking research and promotes hearing health.

Surg

⊕ https://vfmat.ch/2e71

Heart Fund, The

Aims to save the lives of children suffering from heart disease by

developing innovative solutions that revolutionize access to cardiac care in developing countries.
Anesth, CV Med, Ped Surg, Peds, Surg
⊕ https://vfmat.ch/7e67

Heart to Heart International
Strengthens communities through improving health access, providing humanitarian development, and administering crisis relief worldwide. Engages volunteers, collaborates with partners, and deploys resources to achieve this mission.
Anesth, ER Med, General, Logist-Op, Medicine, Path, Path, Peds, Psych, Pub Health, Surg
⊕ https://vfmat.ch/aacb

HelpAge India
Serves the elderly through the provision of services such as livelihood support, eye care, and physiotherapy.
General, Geri, Heme-Onc
⊕ https://vfmat.ch/cd85

HelpAge International
Works to ensure that people everywhere understand how much older people contribute to society and that they must enjoy their right to healthcare, social services, economic, and physical security.
General, Geri, Infect Dis, Medicine, Pub Health
⊕ https://vfmat.ch/5d91

HelpMeSee
Trains local cataract specialists in Manual Small Incision Cataract Surgery (MSICS) in significant numbers, to meet the increasing demand for surgical services in the communities most impacted by cataract blindness.
Anesth, Ophth-Opt, Surg
⊕ https://vfmat.ch/973c

Hernia International
Aims to provide relief from sickness, and protection and preservation of health, for persons affected by groin and abdominal hernias and residing in low- and middle-income countries.
Surg
⊕ https://vfmat.ch/e98e

Himalayan Cataract Project
Works to cure needless blindness with the highest quality care at the lowest cost.
Anesth, Ophth-Opt, Surg
⊕ https://vfmat.ch/3b3d

Himalayan Health Exchange
Brings healthcare services to remote, underserved areas and provides hands-on clinical experience for students and professionals pursuing a career in global health.
Dent-OMFS, ER Med, Infect Dis, Nutr, OB-GYN, Pub Health
⊕ https://vfmat.ch/5b76

Himalayan Health Project
Aims to elevate the overall oral health, vision and women's healthcare of people of the remote Himalayan region.
Dent-OMFS, OB-GYN, Ophth-Opt
⊕ https://vfmat.ch/daff

His Healing Hands
Seeks to provide disease treatment and prevention in partnership with indigenous evangelical Christian organizations that help guide activities.
General
⊕ https://vfmat.ch/ce38

Hope and Healing International
Gives hope and healing to children and families trapped by poverty and disability.
General, Nutr, Ophth-Opt, Peds, Rehab
⊕ https://vfmat.ch/c638

Hope for the Children Foundation India
Seeks to empower socially and economically challenged women and children to lead a life of dignity and self-reliance.

Logist-Op, Nutr, Pub Health
⊕ https://vfmat.ch/1a94

Hope Foundation India, The
Funds and support projects that help homeless children in Calcutta, specifically through programs in health, nutrition, child protection, and education.
Dent-OMFS, ENT, General, Infect Dis, Neurosurg, OB-GYN, Ortho, Path, Ped Surg, Plast, Surg
⊕ https://vfmat.ch/4bbb

HumaniTerra
Helps countries and populations emerging from economic and human crisis to rebuild their healthcare system in a sustainable way. Committed to three fundamental and complementary actions: operating, training, and rebuilding.
Anesth, ENT, ER Med, MF Med, OB-GYN, Ortho, Plast, Surg
⊕ https://vfmat.ch/b371

Humanity & Inclusion
Works alongside people with disabilities and vulnerable populations, taking action and bearing witness in order to respond to their essential needs, improve their living conditions and health, and promote respect for their dignity and fundamental rights.
General, Infect Dis, MF Med, Medicine, Ortho, Peds, Psych, Pub Health, Rehab
⊕ https://vfmat.ch/16b7

Humanity First
Provides aid and assistance to those in need, offering sustainable development solutions to society while providing and empowering local communities with the resources to help themselves.
ER Med, General, MF Med, Ophth-Opt
⊕ https://vfmat.ch/13cc

Hunger Project, The
Aims to end hunger and poverty by pioneering sustainable, grassroots, women-centered strategies and advocating for their widespread adoption in countries throughout the world.
Infect Dis, Nutr, OB-GYN, Pub Health
⊕ https://vfmat.ch/3a49

I-India
Aims to provide care and support for children and communities living on the streets of Jaipur; focuses on those in most urgent need.
All-Immu, ER Med, General, Logist-Op, Nutr, Path, Peds
⊕ https://vfmat.ch/e6d9

IMA World Health
Works to build healthier communities by collaborating with key partners to serve vulnerable people with a focus on health, healing, and well-being for all.
Infect Dis, MF Med, Nutr, OB-GYN, Pub Health
⊕ https://vfmat.ch/8316

IMAHelps
Organizes medical humanitarian missions that provide some of the world's most underserved people with everything from general medical and dental care to life-changing surgeries, prosthetics, and other specialized services that reflect the expertise of our volunteers.
Anesth, CV Med, Dent-OMFS, Neuro, OB-GYN, Ophth-Opt, Ortho, Ped Surg, Peds, Plast, Rehab, Surg
⊕ https://vfmat.ch/d56b

Imamia Medics International
Provides health education and healthcare services to underserved populations around the world, while giving Muslim health and science professionals an opportunity for career development.
Logist-Op, Medicine
⊕ https://vfmat.ch/dc22

ImPaCCT Foundation
Seeks to ensure that every child with cancer coming to Tata Memorial Hospital receives treatment and other support, regardless of family background.
Heme-Onc
⊕ https://vfmat.ch/6214

IMPACT Foundation

Works to prevent and alleviate needless disability by restoring sight, mobility, and hearing.

ENT, MF Med, OB-GYN, Ophth-Opt, Ortho, Peds, Surg

⊕ https://vfmat.ch/ba28

Impact India Foundation

Works to act as a catalyst to bring together the government, the corporate sector, and existing NGOs to develop mass health programs of national priority and to treat millions of people who are disabled by curable blindness, deafness, and physical handicaps and deformities.

Dent-OMFS, Infect Dis, Ophth-Opt, Peds, Rehab

⊕ https://vfmat.ch/c9f6

India Gospel League

Aims to bring sustainable transformation to rural villages throughout South Asia by building partnerships and caring for children, the poor and the sick.

Dent-OMFS, General, Logist-Op, Nutr, OB-GYN, Ophth-Opt, Palliative, Pub Health

⊕ https://vfmat.ch/56f6

India Tribal Care Trust (ITCT)

Works to uplift the physical, social and cultural well-being of tribal communities throughout India while ensuring the preservation of traditional and religious values.

ER Med, General, Pub Health

⊕ https://vfmat.ch/4143

India Vision Institute (IVI)

Provides access to primary eye care for underprivileged and rural Indians, creates awareness and practices advocacy.

Logist-Op, Ophth-Opt

⊕ https://vfmat.ch/af27

Indian Cancer Society

Aims to raise awareness that cancer is preventable and curable, facilitate early detection, offer support and medical aid, and facilitate advocacy and research.

Rad-Onc

⊕ https://vfmat.ch/d6fd

Indian Renal Foundation (IRF)

Works toward prevention, treatment, rehabilitation, education, and research in the area of kidney diseases.

Nephro, Rehab

⊕ https://vfmat.ch/d31b

Inga Health Foundation

Intends to set up dedicated multidisciplinary centres across India over the next 5 years and train surgeons and allied professionals in line with the highest international standards to man them.

Dent-OMFS, General

⊕ https://vfmat.ch/9e1e

Institute for Healthcare Improvement (IHI)

Aims to improve health and healthcare worldwide by working with health professionals to strengthen systems.

Crit-Care, Infect Dis, MF Med, Medicine, Neonat, OB-GYN, Pub Health

⊕ https://vfmat.ch/ecae

International Agency for the Prevention of Blindness (IAPB), The

Leads international efforts in blindness-prevention activities, works toward a world where no one is needlessly visually impaired, and ensures that everyone has access to the best possible standard of eye health.

Infect Dis, Ophth-Opt, Pub Health

⊕ https://vfmat.ch/87a2

International Campaign for Women's Right to Safe Abortion

Works to build an international network and campaign that brings together organizations with an interest in promoting and providing safe abortion to create a shared platform for advocacy, debate, and dialogue and the sharing of skills and experience.

OB-GYN, Pub Health, Surg

⊕ https://vfmat.ch/f341

International Children's Heart Foundation

Provides free surgical care, medical training, and technology to save the lives of children with congenital heart disease in developing countries.

Anesth, CT Surg, CV Med, Crit-Care, Ped Surg, Peds, Pulm-Critic

⊕ https://vfmat.ch/86c1

International Children's Heart Fund

Aims to promote the international growth and quality of cardiac surgery, particularly in children and young adults.

CT Surg, Ped Surg

⊕ https://vfmat.ch/33fb

International Council of Ophthalmology

Works with ophthalmologic societies and others to enhance ophthalmic education and improve access to the highest-quality eye care in order to preserve and restore vision for people of the world.

Ophth-Opt

⊕ https://vfmat.ch/ffd2

International Eye Foundation (IEF)

Eliminates preventable and treatable blindness by making quality sustainable eye care services accessible and affordable worldwide.

Infect Dis, Logist-Op, Ophth-Opt

⊕ https://vfmat.ch/e839

International Federation of Gynecology and Obstetrics (FIGO)

Implements global projects on specific women's health issues.

MF Med, Medicine, Neonat, OB-GYN, Surg, Urol

⊕ https://vfmat.ch/c4b4

International Federation of Red Cross and Red Crescent Societies (IFRC)

Coordinates and directs international assistance following natural and manmade disasters in nonconflict situations through the world's largest humanitarian and development network. Provides disaster-preparedness programs, healthcare activities, and promotes humanitarian values.

ER Med, General, Infect Dis, Nutr

⊕ https://vfmat.ch/b4ee

International Learning Movement (ILM UK)

Supports some of the world's poorest people in developing countries with core projects in education, safe drinking water, and healthcare.

General, Ophth-Opt

⊕ https://vfmat.ch/b974

International Medical Relief

Provides sustainable education, training, medical and dental care, and disaster relief and response in vulnerable communities worldwide.

Dent-OMFS, General, Infect Dis, Medicine, OB-GYN

⊕ https://vfmat.ch/b3ed

International Mental Health Collaborating Network

Promotes and advocates for the human rights of people with mental health issues and gathers and shares the experiences and knowledge of good practices in community mental health from its membership network.

Psych

⊕ https://vfmat.ch/1551

International Organization for Migration (IOM) – The UN Migration Agency

Promotes evidence-informed policies and holistic, preventive, and curative health programs that are beneficial, accessible, and equitable for vulnerable migrants.

General, Infect Dis, OB-GYN

⊕ https://vfmat.ch/621a

International Pediatric Nephrology Association (IPNA)

Leads global efforts to successfully address the care for all children with kidney disease through advocacy, education, and training.

Medicine, Nephro, Peds

⊕ https://vfmat.ch/b59d

International Planned Parenthood Federation (IPPF)
Leads a locally owned, globally connected civil society movement that provides and enables services and champions sexual and reproductive health and rights for all, especially the underserved.
Infect Dis, MF Med, OB-GYN
⊕ https://vfmat.ch/dc97

International Society of Nephrology
Aims to advance worldwide kidney health.
Nephro
⊕ https://vfmat.ch/1bae

International Union Against Tuberculosis and Lung Disease
Develops, implements, and assesses anti-tuberculosis, lung health, and noncommunicable disease programs.
Infect Dis, Pub Health, Pulm-Critic
⊕ https://vfmat.ch/3e82

International Village Clinic(IVC)
Brings health and medical services to impoverished villages in India.
General, Infect Dis, MF Med, Nutr, OB-GYN, Ophth-Opt, Path, Peds
⊕ https://vfmat.ch/27b1

International XLH Alliance
Amplifies the patient voice of X-linked hypophosphatemia (XLH) and related disorders by connecting groups worldwide to set a global multi-disciplinary standard of care and research that could not otherwise be achieved independently, to ensure that all patients' management is the same.
Genetics, Ortho, Peds
⊕ https://vfmat.ch/4f93

InterSurgeon
Fosters collaborative partnerships in the field of global surgery that will advance clinical care, teaching, training, research, and the provision and maintenance of medical equipment.
ENT, Neurosurg, Ortho, Ped Surg, Plast, Surg, Urol
⊕ https://vfmat.ch/6f8a

IntraHealth International
Improves the performance of health workers and strengthens the systems in which they work.
CV Med, Endo, General, Infect Dis, MF Med, Neonat, Nutr, OB-GYN
⊕ https://vfmat.ch/ddc8

Ipas
Focuses efforts on women and girls who want contraception or abortion, and builds programs around their needs and how best to support them.
OB-GYN
⊕ https://vfmat.ch/8e39

Iris Global
Serves the poor, the destitute, the lost, and the forgotten by providing adoration, outreach, family, education, relief, development, healing, and the arts.
General, Infect Dis, Nutr, Pub Health
⊕ https://vfmat.ch/37f8

Iris Mundial
Aims to improve the ocular health of underserved people in developing countries by giving them access to high-quality preventive and curative eye care services.
Ophth-Opt
⊕ https://vfmat.ch/4f85

Irish Red Cross
Delivers a wide range of services to some of the most vulnerable people at home and abroad, including heathcare services and relief to those affected by natural disasters and conflict.
ER Med, Infect Dis, Logist-Op, Nutr, Pub Health
⊕ https://vfmat.ch/e35f

Islamic Medical Association of North America
Fosters health promotion, disease prevention, and health maintenance in communities around the world through direct patient care and health programs.

Anesth, Dent-OMFS, ER Med, General, Logist-Op, Ophth-Opt, Peds, Plast, Surg
⊕ https://vfmat.ch/a157

IVUmed
Aims to make quality urological care available worldwide by providing medical and surgical education for physicians and nurses, and treatment for thousands of children and adults.
Anesth, OB-GYN, Ped Surg, Surg, Urol
⊕ https://vfmat.ch/e619

JDC
Oversees and delivers comprehensive spine, heart, and cancer services in Ethiopia and beyond.
Ortho, Rehab, Surg
⊕ https://vfmat.ch/d85e

Jeevika Trust
Seeks to promote economic development and social change by revitalizing rural communities through sustainable development.
Logist-Op, Nutr, Pub Health
⊕ https://vfmat.ch/474a

Jhpiego
Creates and delivers transformative healthcare solutions that save lives, in partnership with national governments, health experts, and local communities.
General, Infect Dis, OB-GYN, Surg
⊕ https://vfmat.ch/45b8

Jivan Foundation
Aids disabled people around the world in achieving independence in their lives.
Dent-OMFS, General, Heme-Onc, Ophth-Opt, Pub Health
⊕ https://vfmat.ch/cbda

John Snow, Inc. (JSI)
Aims to improve the health and well-being of underserved and vulnerable people and communities throughout the world.
General, Infect Dis, Logist-Op, MF Med, OB-GYN, Peds, Psych, Pub Health
⊕ https://vfmat.ch/ba78

Johns Hopkins Center for Communication Programs
Believes in the power of communication to save lives by empowering people to adopt healthy behaviors for themselves, their families, and their communities.
General, Infect Dis, Logist-Op, OB-GYN, Pub Health
⊕ https://vfmat.ch/1bf9

Johns Hopkins Center for Global Health
Facilitates and focuses the extensive expertise and resources of the Johns Hopkins institutions, together with global collaborators, to effectively address and ameliorate the world's most pressing health issues.
General, Genetics, Logist-Op, MF Med, Peds, Psych, Pub Health, Pulm-Critic
⊕ https://vfmat.ch/54ce

Joint United Nations Programme on HIV/AIDS (UNAIDS)
Aims to place people living with HIV and people affected by the virus at the decision-making table and at the center of designing, delivering, and monitoring the AIDS response.
Infect Dis
⊕ https://vfmat.ch/464a

Kailash Medical Foundation
Aims to improve the health and well-being of those in need around the world by going on missions to developing countries and providing medical, dental, and vision services to the underprivileged.
Dent-OMFS, General, Ophth-Opt
⊕ https://vfmat.ch/db41

Kaya Responsible Travel
Promotes sustainable social, environmental, and economic development, empowers communities, and cultivates educated, compassionate global citizens through responsible travel.
All-Immu, Crit-Care, Dent-OMFS, ER Med, General, Geri, Infect Dis, MF Med, Medicine, Nutr, OB-GYN, Peds, Psych, Pub Health, Rehab
⊕ https://vfmat.ch/b2cf

Keep a Child Alive
Committed to improving the health and well-being of vulnerable children, young people, adults, and families around the world, with a focus on combating the physical, social, and economic impacts of HIV/AIDS.
Infect Dis, MF Med, Neonat, OB-GYN
⊕ https://vfmat.ch/7f2f

KEM Hospital Pune
Seeks to provide good quality, ethical medical care, without discrimination and with compassion, dedication and a smile.
Anesth, CT Surg, CV Med, Crit-Care, Dent-OMFS, Derm, ENT, Endo, GI, General, Genetics, Heme-Onc, Infect Dis, MF Med, Medicine, Neonat, Nephro, Neuro, Neurosurg, OB-GYN, Ophth-Opt, Ortho, Palliative, Path, Ped Surg, Peds, Plast, Psych, Pub Health, Pulm-Critic, Rad-Onc, Radiol, Rehab, Rheum, Surg, Urol, Vasc Surg
⊕ https://vfmat.ch/76d2

Khambhati Charity International
Brings healthcare within the reach of every individual and commits to the achievement and sustenance of excellence in healthcare for the benefit of mankind.
CT Surg, CV Med, Crit-Care, ER Med, Endo, Heme-Onc, Logist-Op, Medicine, Nephro, Path, Radiol, Vasc Surg
⊕ https://vfmat.ch/71d4

Kidney Warriors Foundation
Advocates for policies that improve access to healthcare and that strengthen the quality of care for patients with kidney disease.
Endo, Nephro, Ped Surg, Peds, Surg
⊕ https://vfmat.ch/1672

Kids Care Everywhere
Seeks to empower physicians in under-resourced environments with multimedia, state-of-the-art medical software, and to inspire young professionals to become future global healthcare leaders.
Logist-Op, Ped Surg, Peds
⊕ https://vfmat.ch/bc23

Kind Cuts for Kids
Aims to improve medical services for children in developing countries through education, demonstration, and skills transfer to local healthcare professionals.
Anesth, Medicine, Ped Surg, Surg
⊕ https://vfmat.ch/e3d7

Kletjian Foundation
Works toward a world in which all people have access to safe, sustainable, and high-quality medical care, building collaborative networks and supporting entrepreneurial leaders that promote global health equity.
CT Surg, ENT, General, Ortho, Surg
⊕ https://vfmat.ch/12c2

Koshish Milap Trust
Serves the slum population in Vadodara by providing them with highly subsidized quality primary education and basic healthcare.
General
⊕ https://vfmat.ch/68e8

Ladakh Heart Foundation
Seeks to give people the opportunity to have access to proper healthcare, free of charge.
CT Surg, CV Med, Pub Health
⊕ https://vfmat.ch/b5ee

Leadership in Medicine for the Underserved Program at MSU, The
Provides medical students the knowledge and skills necessary to address the varied medical needs of urban, rural, and international underserved populations.
Dent-OMFS, ER Med, Medicine, Nutr, OB-GYN, Peds, Pub Health, Radiol, Surg
⊕ https://vfmat.ch/84f1

LEAP Global Missions
Provides specialized surgical services to underserved populations around the world.
Anesth, Dent-OMFS, ENT, Ped Surg, Peds, Plast, Surg
⊕ https://vfmat.ch/b447

Lepra
Works directly with communities in Bangladesh, India, Mozambique, and Zimbabwe to find, treat, and rehabilitate people affected by leprosy.
Infect Dis, Pub Health, Rehab
⊕ https://vfmat.ch/5d1c

Leprosy Mission Australia, The
Provides support to people with leprosy including screening, medical treatment and job opportunities, inspired by the Christian faith.
Infect Dis
⊕ https://vfmat.ch/9e4b

Leprosy Mission England and Wales, The
Leads the fight against leprosy by supporting people living with leprosy today and serving future generations by working to end transmission of the disease.
Infect Dis, Pub Health
⊕ https://vfmat.ch/4c67

Leprosy Mission International
Seeks to empower people with leprosy to attain healing, dignity, and life in all its fullness.
Infect Dis
⊕ https://vfmat.ch/95a9

Leprosy Mission: Northern Ireland, The
Leads the fight against leprosy by supporting people living with leprosy today and serving future generations by working to end the transmission of the disease.
General, Infect Dis
⊕ https://vfmat.ch/e265

Life for a Child
Supports the provision of the best possible healthcare, given local circumstances, to all children and youth with diabetes in less-resourced countries, through the strengthening of existing diabetes services.
Endo, Medicine, Peds
⊕ https://vfmat.ch/d712

Lifebox
Seeks to provide safer surgery and anesthesia in low-resource countries by investing in tools, training, and partnerships for safe surgery.
Anesth, Crit-Care, Surg
⊕ https://vfmat.ch/2d4d

Light for Sight 21
Aims to eliminate severe visual impairment among all children and adolescents with keratoconus.
Ophth-Opt
⊕ https://vfmat.ch/ef55

Light for the World
Contributes to a world in which persons with disabilities fully exercise their rights, and assists persons with disabilities living in poverty.
Ophth-Opt, Rehab
⊕ https://vfmat.ch/3ff6

Limbs International
Engages communities and transforms lives through affordable, sustainable prosthetic solutions and rehabilitation services in developing countries.
Logist-Op, Ortho, Pod, Rehab
⊕ https://vfmat.ch/dc84

Lions Clubs International
Empowers volunteers to serve their communities, meet humanitarian needs, encourage peace, and promote international understanding through Lions Clubs.
Heme-Onc, Medicine, Nutr, Ophth-Opt
⊕ https://vfmat.ch/7b12

Little Moppet Heart Foundation
Provides financial and medical support for treatment of children with congenital heart diseases.
⊕ https://vfmat.ch/1153

Lotus Life Foundation
Empowers organizations and people fighting the stigma against disability through medical intervention and education.
Logist-Op, Rehab
⊕ https://vfmat.ch/94dc

Lotus Medical Foundation
Works with people who are infected, affected, and at risk of HIV to provide education, support, advocacy and effective prevention programs, and delivers compassionate, comprehensive, and quality care services to those affected by HIV.
ER Med, General, Medicine, Nutr
⊕ https://vfmat.ch/6fd4

Love Without Boundaries
Provides healing, education, and refuge to vulnerable children worldwide.
CT Surg, Dent-OMFS, Nutr, Ortho, Ped Surg, Peds, Rehab, Surg
⊕ https://vfmat.ch/d1fc

Lung Care Foundation
Aims to prevent lung diseases through education and research, and to provide state-of-the-art clinical care, accessible to all.
Heme-Onc, Infect Dis, Pub Health, Pulm-Critic, Surg
⊕ https://vfmat.ch/a956

Madurai Health and Leprosy Relief Centre
Aims to provide voluntary health promotion and preventive services of general health education, leprosy awareness classes, case detection, treatment, and rehabilitation services for the leprosy-disabled in the Madurai District of Tamil Nadu, India.
Infect Dis, Rehab
⊕ https://vfmat.ch/a689

MAGNA International
Helps those who are suffering or recovering from conflicts and disasters by reducing the risks of diseases and treating them immediately.
ER Med, General, Infect Dis, Peds, Surg
⊕ https://vfmat.ch/58f4

Mahelerecen
Raises awareness and provides general health education, case detection, treatment, and rehabilitation for the leprosy-disabled.
Infect Dis
⊕ https://vfmat.ch/64d8

Making A Difference Foundation
Sponsors and organizes medical missions for medical providers to provide care to underserved communities around the world.
CV Med, Dent-OMFS, ER Med, General, Infect Dis, Logist-Op, MF Med, Neonat, Nutr, OB-GYN, Ophth-Opt, Ortho, Pub Health, Pulm-Critic, Rehab, Surg
⊕ https://vfmat.ch/5556

Manav Sadhna
Inspired by Mahatma Gandhi, humbly serves to strengthen underprivileged communities in Ahmedabad through programs in holistic education, nutrition, health and hygiene, youth and women's empowerment, senior care, livelihood, and more.
General, Geri, Medicine, Peds
⊕ https://vfmat.ch/96b7

Manthan Eye Healthcare Foundation
Provides screening and medical services to communities with limited access to eye care due to low income, disability or other restrictions, inspired by the Hindu faith.
Ophth-Opt
⊕ https://vfmat.ch/e9fb

MAP International
Provides medicines and health supplies to those in need around the world so they might experience life to the fullest.
Logist-Op
⊕ https://vfmat.ch/deed

Marie Stopes International
Provides the contraception and safe abortion services that enable women all over the world to choose their own futures.
Infect Dis, MF Med, Neonat, OB-GYN, Pub Health
⊕ https://vfmat.ch/9525

Maternal Fetal Care International
Helps mothers and children survive and enjoy better health in the poorest regions of the world.
MF Med, Neonat, OB-GYN
⊕ https://vfmat.ch/7e72

Maternity Foundation
Works to ensure safer childbirth for women and newborns everywhere through innovative mobile health solutions such as the Safe Delivery App, a mobile training tool for skilled birth attendants.
MF Med, OB-GYN, Pub Health
⊕ https://vfmat.ch/ff4f

Maverick Collective
Aims to build a global community of strategic philanthropists and informed advocates who use their intellectual and financial resources to create change.
Infect Dis, MF Med, OB-GYN
⊕ https://vfmat.ch/ea49

Max Foundation, The
Seeks to increase global access to treatment, care, and support for people living with cancer.
General, Heme-Onc, Pub Health
⊕ https://vfmat.ch/8c7d

Medical Mercy Canada
Seeks to improve the quality of life in impoverished areas through humanitarian projects with local participation, and provides funding for orphanages, geriatric and childcare centers, remote health clinics, medical aid centers, hospitals, rural schools, and health programs.
General
⊕ https://vfmat.ch/81dc

Medical Ministry International
Provides compassionate healthcare in areas of need, inspired by the Christian faith.
CT Surg, Dent-OMFS, ENT, General, OB-GYN, Ophth-Opt, Ortho, Plast, Rehab, Surg, Urol, Vasc Surg
⊕ https://vfmat.ch/5da6

Medical Missions for Children (MMFC)
Provides quality surgical and dental services to poor and underprivileged children and young adults in various countries throughout the world, and facilitates the transfer of education, knowledge, and recent innovations to the local medical communities.
Dent-OMFS, ENT, Endo, Ortho, Ped Surg, Peds, Plast
⊕ https://vfmat.ch/1631

Medical Missions Foundation
Provides surgical and medical care in underserved communities throughout the world and hopes to positively impact the lives of children and their families.
Anesth, Ped Surg, Surg
⊕ https://vfmat.ch/f385

Medical Relief for India
Provides free medical care to the poor and needy in India.
Ortho, Surg
⊕ https://vfmat.ch/ba64

Medicus Mundi Italia
Carries out programs in basic community health, health education, maternal and child health, nutrition, and infectious disease.
General, Infect Dis, Logist-Op, MF Med, Nutr, Peds, Pub Health, Rehab
⊕ https://vfmat.ch/4413

MedShare
Aims to improve the quality of life of people, communities, and the planet by

sourcing and directly delivering surplus medical supplies and equipment to communities in need around the world.
Logist-Op
⊕ https://vfmat.ch/c8bc

Mending Kids
Provides free, lifesaving surgical care to sick children worldwide by deploying volunteer medical teams and teaching communities to become medically self-sustaining through the education of local medical staff.
Anesth, CT Surg, ENT, Ortho, Ortho, Ped Surg, Plast, Surg
⊕ https://vfmat.ch/4d61

Merck for Mothers
Hopes to create a world where no woman has to die giving life by collaborating with partners to improve the health and well-being of women during pregnancy, childbirth, and the postpartum period.
MF Med, OB-GYN
⊕ https://vfmat.ch/5b51

Mercy in Action
Inspired by the Christian faith, carries out programs in maternal and newborn health, primary healthcare for children under 5, and midwifery education.
General, MF Med, Neonat, OB-GYN, Peds, Pub Health
⊕ https://vfmat.ch/cc88

MGM Eye Institute
Provides high-quality, comprehensive eye care services to all.
Ophth-Opt
⊕ https://vfmat.ch/3bea

Midland International Aid Trust
Provides food, goods, clothing, and equipment to those in financial need or who are suffering as a result of a disaster.
CT Surg, Dent-OMFS, ENT, Logist-Op, OB-GYN, Ophth-Opt, Ortho, Ped Surg, Plast, Pub Health, Rehab
⊕ https://vfmat.ch/7eb2

MiracleFeet
Brings low-cost treatment to every child on the planet born with clubfoot, a leading cause of physical disability.
Ortho, Peds, Rehab
⊕ https://vfmat.ch/bda8

Mission Bambini
Helps to support children living in poverty and sickness, and lacking education, giving them the opportunity for and hope of a better life.
CT Surg, CV Med, Crit-Care, ER Med, Ped Surg, Peds
⊕ https://vfmat.ch/dc1a

Mission: Restore
Trains medical professionals abroad in complex reconstructive surgery in order to create a sustainable infrastructure in which long-term relationships are forged and permanent change comes to pass.
Plast, Surg
⊕ https://vfmat.ch/3f5f

Mother Teresa Foundation
Inculcates the core values of St. Mother Teresa to create a healthy, compassionate, and responsive world.
CV Med, ER Med, Endo, General, OB-GYN, Peds, Pulm-Critic, Surg
⊕ https://vfmat.ch/139b

MSD for Mothers
Designs scalable solutions that help end preventable maternal deaths.
MF Med, OB-GYN, Pub Health
⊕ https://vfmat.ch/9f99

MSI Reproductive Choices (Marie Stopes International)
Seeks to deliver quality family planning and reproductive healthcare to women around the world.
MF Med
⊕ https://vfmat.ch/5c82

Multi-Agency International Training and Support (MAITS)
Improves the lives of some of the world's poorest people living with disabilities through better access to quality health and education services and support.
Neuro, Psych, Rehab
⊕ https://vfmat.ch/9dcd

Mumbai Cancer Care
Provides high-class, evidence-based oncology services to patients of all strata at an affordable price.
ENT, GI, OB-GYN, Palliative, Rad-Onc
⊕ https://vfmat.ch/ba62

Muslim Welfare Canada
Serves vulnerable populations by supporting healthcare clinics, food security programs, and other humanitarian projects.
Logist-Op, Nutr
⊕ https://vfmat.ch/a227

Mérieux Foundation
Committed to fighting infectious diseases that affect developing countries by capacity building, particularly in clinical laboratories, and focusing on diagnosis.
Logist-Op, Path
⊕ https://vfmat.ch/a23a

Narmada Health Group NHG
Aims to provide the highest standards of healthcare to all and to achieve professional excellence in education and community service.
Anesth, CT Surg, CV Med, Crit-Care, Derm, ENT, ER Med, Endo, GI, GI, General, General, Medicine, Nephro, Neuro, Neurosurg, OB-GYN, Ortho, Path, Peds, Plast, Psych, Pulm-Critic, Radiol, Rehab, Rheum, Surg, Urol
⊕ https://vfmat.ch/c53c

National Health Mission (NHM)
Provides accessible, affordable universal healthcare, both preventive and curative, and responds to the needs of the community.
CV Med, Dent-OMFS, Endo, Heme-Onc, Logist-Op, MF Med, Nutr, Ophth-Opt, Peds
⊕ https://vfmat.ch/868d

Native Medicare Charitable Trust
Provides education to underprivileged children and works to improve livelihoods through programs in education, health, and female empowerment.
Infect Dis
⊕ https://vfmat.ch/edb6

Nayonika Eye Care Charitable Trust
Provides comprehensive, low- or no-cost eye care to the neediest, including screening, treatment, vision aids and glasses.
Ophth-Opt
⊕ https://vfmat.ch/e275

Netra Jyoti Charitable Trust
Aims to provide the best in every subspecialty of eye healthcare, to advance knowledge and technology, and to educate and promote eye care.
ER Med, Ophth-Opt, Peds
⊕ https://vfmat.ch/a817

New Delhi Children's Hospital & Research Centre (NDCHRC)
Provides help to needy children, women, and elderly people through initiatives in healthcare, education, and environmental safety.
ER Med, General, Peds
⊕ https://vfmat.ch/14bb

Nidhi Foundation
Promotes the importance of nutrition and education, while providing holistic nutrition services to children and giving them a healthy start and opportunity to improve their health.
Dent-OMFS, Nutr, Ophth-Opt, Pub Health
⊕ https://vfmat.ch/d3d8

NLR International
Promotes and supports the prevention and treatment of leprosy, prevention of disabilities, social inclusion, and stigma reduction of people affected by leprosy.

Infect Dis, Pub Health
⊕ https://vfmat.ch/d7bd

NRI SEVA Foundation
Provides programs such as health services, education, senior day care, and women's empowerment.
Heme-Onc, Neuro, Ortho, Peds, Rheum
⊕ https://vfmat.ch/d3f4

OB Foundation
Works in partnership globally to deliver locally sustainable, quality healthcare, health education, and health solutions to medically underserved, rural communities.
General
⊕ https://vfmat.ch/91d7

Omashram Trust Old Age Care
Provides residential medical care for the elderly.
Geri, Palliative, Rehab
⊕ https://vfmat.ch/2acb

OneSight
Brings eye exams and glasses to people who lack access to vision care.
Ophth-Opt
⊕ https://vfmat.ch/3ecc

Open Door Foundation, The
Works on behalf of children in child-care homes and orphanages, focusing on academic sustainability, healthcare, child development, and infrastructure.
Dent-OMFS, General, Peds
⊕ https://vfmat.ch/1142

Open Heart International
Provides surgical interventions and best practices to the most disadvantaged communities on the planet.
CT Surg, MF Med, OB-GYN, Ophth-Opt, Plast, Surg
⊕ https://vfmat.ch/dab2

Operation Corazón
Offers support to individuals and families in need by delivering humanitarian aid, relief, support services, equipment, clothing, medicine, and food.
General, Nutr
⊕ https://vfmat.ch/5f76

Operation Eyesight
Works to eliminate blindness in partnership with governments, hospitals, medical professionals, corporations, and community development teams.
Ophth-Opt, Surg
⊕ https://vfmat.ch/b95d

Operation Eyesight Universal
Aims to prevent blindness, restore sight, and eliminate avoidable blindness.
Ophth-Opt
⊕ https://vfmat.ch/f629

Operation Fistula
Exists to end obstetric fistula by building models of care that serve every woman, everywhere.
MF Med, OB-GYN, Surg
⊕ https://vfmat.ch/ce8e

Operation Footprint
Provides free surgical care to underserved children with genetic or acquired foot and ankle conditions, and trains local surgeons to manage and treat them.
Pod
⊕ https://vfmat.ch/6868

Operation Hernia
Provides high-quality surgery at minimal cost to patients who otherwise would not receive it.
Anesth, Ortho, Surg
⊕ https://vfmat.ch/6e9a

Operation International
Offers medical aid to adults and children suffering from lack of quality healthcare in impoverished countries.
Dent-OMFS, ER Med, Heme-Onc, OB-GYN, Ophth-Opt, Ortho, Ped Surg, Plast, Surg
⊕ https://vfmat.ch/b52a

Operation Medical
Commits efforts to promoting and providing high-quality medical care and education to communities that do not have adequate access.
Anesth, ENT, Logist-Op, OB-GYN, Ped Surg, Plast, Surg, Urol
⊕ https://vfmat.ch/7e1b

Operation Rainbow Canada
Provides free reconstructive surgery and related healthcare for cleft lip and cleft palate deformities to impoverished children and young adults in developing countries.
Surg
⊕ https://vfmat.ch/7f25

Operation Smile
Treats patients with cleft lip and cleft palate, and creates solutions that deliver safe surgery to people where it's needed most.
Anesth, Dent-OMFS, ENT, Ped Surg, Plast
⊕ https://vfmat.ch/5c29

Operation Walk
Provides the gift of mobility through life-changing joint replacement surgeries, at no cost for those in need in the U.S. and globally.
Anesth, Ortho, Rehab, Surg
⊕ https://vfmat.ch/bafe

Options
Believes in a world in which women and children can access the high-quality health services they need, without financial burden.
Logist-Op, MF Med, Neonat, OB-GYN
⊕ https://vfmat.ch/3a48

Optometry Giving Sight
Delivers eye exams and low or no-cost glasses, provides training for local eye care professionals, and establishes optometry schools, vision centers and optical labs.
Ophth-Opt
⊕ https://vfmat.ch/33ea

Orbis International
Works to prevent and treat blindness through hands-on training and improved access to quality eye care.
Anesth, Ophth-Opt, Surg
⊕ https://vfmat.ch/f2b2

Orphan Life Foundation
Advocates for orphaned children in Burkina Faso by providing educational, health, and foster home and shelter services, while facilitating adoption processes.
Infect Dis, Logist-Op, Nutr, Pub Health
⊕ https://vfmat.ch/14ea

Orphan World Relief
Helps children in crisis, including orphans and refugees, by providing committed and compassionate support for their needs.
Logist-Op, Nutr
⊕ https://vfmat.ch/b841

Oxford University Global Surgery Group (OUGSG)
Aims to contribute to the provision of high-quality surgical care globally, particularly in low- and middle-income countries (LMICs), while bringing together students, researchers, and clinicians with an interest in global surgery, anesthesia, and obstetrics and gynecology.
Anesth, MF Med, OB-GYN, Ortho, Surg
⊕ https://vfmat.ch/c624

P. D. Hinduja Hospital and Medical Research Centre
Delivers medical care to all patients, and undertakes continuing education and

training for medical staff and research focused on community needs.
CV Med, ENT, Endo, GI, General, Logist-Op, OB-GYN, Ophth-Opt, Ortho, Path, Peds, Pub Health, Radiol, Rehab, Surg
⊕ https://vfmat.ch/183a

P. S. Mission Hospital
Works to create a healthcare system aimed at holistic healing through a professional, innovative and scientific approach, inspired by the Christian faith.
Anesth, CV Med, Dent-OMFS, Derm, ER Med, Endo, GI, General, Geri, Nephro, Neuro, OB-GYN, Ophth-Opt, Ortho, Path, Peds, Psych, Radiol, Rehab, Surg, Urol
⊕ https://vfmat.ch/efb3

Pain Relief and Palliative Care Society Hyderabad
Aims to increase availability and access to palliative and end-of-life care for those with advanced and terminal illness.
Palliative
⊕ https://vfmat.ch/988a

Palav
Provides support equipment for newborns with breathing difficulties and trains healthcare providers.
Peds
⊕ https://vfmat.ch/86bd

Palcare: The Jimmy S Bilimoria Foundation
Provides home-based, multidisciplinary palliative care service for patients, primarily those with stage 3 or stage 4 cancer.
Palliative
⊕ https://vfmat.ch/1e93

Pallium India
Aims to catalyze the development of effective pain relief and quality palliative care services, and their integration in healthcare across India, through delivery of services.
Palliative
⊕ https://vfmat.ch/45d3

Palms Care foundation
Seeks to meet all needs of orphans to give them an opportunity for a better life.
General, Peds, Pub Health
⊕ https://vfmat.ch/47e8

PATH
Advances health equity through innovation and partnerships so people, communities, and economies can thrive.
All-Immu, CV Med, Endo, Heme-Onc, Infect Dis, MF Med, Neonat, Nutr, OB-GYN, Path, Peds, Pulm-Critic
⊕ https://vfmat.ch/b4db

Pathfinder International
Champions sexual and reproductive health and rights worldwide, mobilizing communities most in need to break through barriers and forge paths to a healthier future.
OB-GYN
⊕ https://vfmat.ch/a7b3

Peedh Parai International
Aims to deliver advances in surgical sciences to deprived parts of the world, especially benefiting children with treatable surgical conditions.
Dent-OMFS, Ped Surg, Plast, Surg
⊕ https://vfmat.ch/77b8

Pepal
Brings together NGOs, global corporations, and the public sector to co-create solutions to big social issues, creating immediate and scalable solutions, and developing leaders who are capable of driving change in their communities.
Heme-Onc, Infect Dis, Pub Health
⊕ https://vfmat.ch/6dc5

Philips Foundation
Aims to reduce healthcare inequality by providing access to quality healthcare for disadvantaged communities.

CV Med, OB-GYN, Ped Surg, Peds, Surg, Urol
⊕ https://vfmat.ch/bacb

Phillips Renner Foundation
Works to reduce inequities in nutrition, dental care, and education by delivering high-impact health services and products to children in the poorest communities.
Dent-OMFS, Nutr
⊕ https://vfmat.ch/bce6

PINCC Preventing Cervical Cancer
Seeks to prevent female-specific diseases in developing countries by utilizing low-cost and low-technology methods to create sustainable programs through patient education, medical personnel training, and facility outfitting.
OB-GYN
⊕ https://vfmat.ch/9666

Population Council
Conducts research to address critical health and development issues, helping deliver solutions to improve lives around the world.
Logist-Op, Pub Health
⊕ https://vfmat.ch/1777

Power of Love Foundation
Aims to build strong and vibrant communities by ensuring that no child is born with HIV and to care for HIV-positive infants and children.
Infect Dis, Peds
⊕ https://vfmat.ch/72c6

PRASAD Chikitsa
Strives to benefit children and communities in need, and implements innovative solutions that respond to local conditions and cultures.
CV Med, Dent-OMFS, ENT, Endo, General, Infect Dis, Logist-Op, Nutr, OB-GYN, Ophth-Opt, Ortho, Plast, Psych, Pub Health, Surg
⊕ https://vfmat.ch/df8d

Prayas Social Welfare Society
Provides free education and vocational training to children and to marginalized girls and women.
General, Ophth-Opt
⊕ https://vfmat.ch/dc7a

Progressive Familial Intrahepatic Cholestasis Advocacy and Resource Network, Inc. (PFIC Network, Inc.)
Improves the lives of patients and families worldwide affected by progressive familial intrahepatic cholestasis (PFIC).
Crit-Care, ER Med, General, Medicine, Path, Ped Surg, Peds, Pub Health, Surg
⊕ https://vfmat.ch/43f6

Project 'Life'
Contributes to health, well-being, education, and livelihood of people by mobilizing the power of volunteers and generosity of donors through humanitarian activities and implementation of sustainable programs.
Heme-Onc, Neonat, OB-GYN, Peds, Pub Health
⊕ https://vfmat.ch/d499

Project Concern International (PCI)
Drives innovation from the ground up to enhance health, end hunger, overcome hardship, and advance women and girls—resulting in meaningful and measurable change in people's lives.
Infect Dis, MF Med, Nutr, OB-GYN, Peds
⊕ https://vfmat.ch/5ed7

Project HOPE
Works on the front lines of the world's health challenges, partnering hand-in-hand with communities, healthcare workers, and public health systems to ensure sustainable change.
CV Med, ER Med, Endo, General, Infect Dis, MF Med, Peds
⊕ https://vfmat.ch/2bd7

Project Pacer International
Provides modern cardiac therapy to indigent patients in the developing world.
CT Surg, CV Med
⊕ https://vfmat.ch/f812

Project Starfish

Aims to provide general healthcare services along with diabetic screening and treatment clinics in Southern India.

General

⊕ https://vfmat.ch/214c

Project Theia

Provides medical and surgical care to the underserved global community in the areas of oculoplastic, reconstructive, orbital, and facial surgery.

Anesth, General, Ophth-Opt, Plast

⊕ https://vfmat.ch/9d5a

PSI – Population Services International

Aims to improve the health of people in the developing world by focusing on challenges such as a lack of family planning, HIV/AIDS, barriers to maternal health, and the greatest threats to children under the age of 5, including malaria, diarrhea, pneumonia, and malnutrition.

Infect Dis, MF Med, OB-GYN, Peds

⊕ https://vfmat.ch/ffe3

RAD-AID International

Improves and optimizes access to medical imaging and radiology in low-resource regions of the world.

Rad-Onc, Radiol

⊕ https://vfmat.ch/537f

Rahbar Foundation

Supports educational, hunger, healthcare, and emergency relief programs; focuses on projects that promote employment and sustainable growth.

Dent-OMFS, General, Logist-Op, OB-GYN, Peds

⊕ https://vfmat.ch/1e21

Raindrops Children's Foundation

Provides medical aid and subsidized treatment to underprivileged children with life-threatening conditions.

Peds

⊕ https://vfmat.ch/1648

Rajiv Gandhi Mahila Vikas Pariyojana (RGMVP)

Strives for an equitable and just society by opening the doors of opportunity for the self-advancement of the poor and the deprived.

MF Med, Nutr, Ophth-Opt, Pub Health

⊕ https://vfmat.ch/1b4a

Rapid Response

Aims to provide immediate, effective, and sustainable support, such as food packets, relief kits, and medical camps, for victims of natural disasters in India.

Logist-Op, Nutr

⊕ https://vfmat.ch/ebc9

Ratna Nidhi Charitable Trust

Aims to tackle the problems of poverty in Mumbai, especially among children and people from the most underprivileged strata of society.

Dent-OMFS, General, Nutr, Ophth-Opt, Ortho, Peds, Rehab

⊕ https://vfmat.ch/79ff

Real Medicine Foundation (RMF)

Provides humanitarian support to people living in disaster- and poverty-stricken areas, focusing on the person as a whole by providing medical/physical, emotional, economic, and social support.

ER Med, General, Infect Dis, Nutr, Peds, Psych

⊕ https://vfmat.ch/d45a

Reconstructing Women International

Treats patients in their local communities through groups of international volunteers made up of female plastic surgeons using local medical facilities, in cooperation with local medical professionals.

Anesth, Plast, Rehab, Surg

⊕ https://vfmat.ch/924a

Reliance Foundation

Aims to build an inclusive India by pioneering a holistic model to address our nation's multifaceted development challenges, and contribute to its

collective aspirations.

CV Med, Heme-Onc, MF Med, Nephro, Neuro, OB-GYN, Ophth-Opt, Ortho, Peds

⊕ https://vfmat.ch/cd37

RestoringVision

Empowers lives by restoring vision for millions of people in need.

Ophth-Opt

⊕ https://vfmat.ch/e121

ReSurge International

Provides reconstructive surgical care and builds surgical capacity in developing countries.

Anesth, Dent-OMFS, Ped Surg, Plast, Surg

⊕ https://vfmat.ch/9937

RHD Action

Seeks to reduce the burden of rheumatic heart disease in vulnerable populations throughout the world.

CV Med, Medicine, Pub Health

⊕ https://vfmat.ch/f5d9

Riddhi Siddhi Charitable Trust

Provides educational opportunities and promotes health and social rights for the poor and marginalized.

MF Med, OB-GYN, Pub Health

⊕ https://vfmat.ch/de6a

Rising Star Outreach

Empowers individuals and families of those with leprosy to live healthy, productive lives through education, medical care, and community development.

Derm, Pub Health

⊕ https://vfmat.ch/6af7

Rotaplast International

Helps children and families worldwide by eliminating the burden of cleft lip and/or palate, burn scarring, and other deformities by sending medical teams to provide free reconstructive surgery, ancillary treatment, and training.

Anesth, Dent-OMFS, ENT, Ped Surg, Plast, Surg

⊕ https://vfmat.ch/78b3

Rotary Action Group for Family Health & AIDS Prevention (RFHA)

Works to save and improve the lives of children and families who lack access to preventive healthcare and education.

Dent-OMFS, Infect Dis, OB-GYN, Ophth-Opt, Peds

⊕ https://vfmat.ch/6563

Rotary International

Provides service to others, improves lives, and advances world understanding, goodwill, and peace through its fellowship of business, professional, and community leaders.

ER Med, General, Infect Dis, MF Med, OB-GYN

⊕ https://vfmat.ch/8fb5

ROW Foundation

Works to improve the quality of training for healthcare providers, and the diagnosis and treatment available to people with epilepsy and associated psychiatric disorders in under-resourced areas of the world.

Neuro, Psych

⊕ https://vfmat.ch/25eb

Rural Development Trust

Aims to empower rural areas in their struggle to eradicate poverty, suffering, and injustice, while ensuring that communities remain the main actors of development.

Anesth, Dent-OMFS, ER Med, Infect Dis, Medicine, Nutr, OB-GYN, Ophth-Opt, Ortho, Palliative, Path, Peds, Radiol, Surg, Urol

⊕ https://vfmat.ch/4ab4

Rutgers New Jersey Medical School

Seeks to support and promote the global health efforts of the faculty, staff, and students in the areas of education, research, and service through the Rutgers New Jersey Medical School's Office of Global Health.

Anesth, CV Med, Crit-Care, Neurosurg, OB-GYN, Psych
⊕ https://vfmat.ch/8e67

SAAR Foundation
Supports patients with Parkinson's and other neurological diseases by promoting early diagnosis, awareness and education, holistic care, and medical access for patients in need.
Neuro
⊕ https://vfmat.ch/3b58

Sahyog Foundation
Aims to address poverty, social inequality, and access to basic services such as healthcare and education through projects and programs at local, state, and national levels.
Dent-OMFS, Heme-Onc, Infect Dis, Ophth-Opt, Pub Health
⊕ https://vfmat.ch/ebe9

Salaam Baalak Trust
Provides care to children experiencing homelessness through services in health and nutrition, mental health, quality education & vocational training, and support for the arts.
Psych, Pub Health
⊕ https://vfmat.ch/93ae

Salvation Army International, The
Seeks to meet human needs through services in education, healthcare, community support, emergency response, and ministry development, inspired by the Christian faith.
Dent-OMFS, Derm, ER Med, Infect Dis, MF Med, Medicine, Nutr, OB-GYN, Ophth-Opt, Palliative, Psych, Rehab, Surg
⊕ https://vfmat.ch/8eb3

Sanjeevani
Aims to eliminate poverty, unemployment, poor health, and illiteracy in Uttarakhand, India.
Infect Dis, Nutr
⊕ https://vfmat.ch/5d85

Sankar Foundation Eye Institute
Strives to eradicate avoidable blindness and deafness by extending services to impoverished individuals and communities.
Ophth-Opt
⊕ https://vfmat.ch/7278

Sanman
Augments the efforts of palliative and other healthcare organizations, to empower and provide support to patients and their families.
⊕ https://vfmat.ch/5997

Sanofi Espoir Foundation
Contributes to reducing health inequalities among populations that need it most by applying a socially responsible approach focused on fighting childhood cancers in low-income countries, improving maternal and newborn health, and improving access to care.
ER Med, OB-GYN, Peds
⊕ https://vfmat.ch/943b

Save an orphan
Transforms the lives of children by providing them with medical aid, education, shelter, employment opportunities, and the means for a better tomorrow.
General, Infect Dis, MF Med
⊕ https://vfmat.ch/5742

Save the Children
Gives children around the world a healthy start in life, the opportunity to learn, and protection from harm.
All-Immu, Crit-Care, ER Med, General, Infect Dis, MF Med, Medicine, Neonat, OB-GYN, Peds, Psych, Pub Health
⊕ https://vfmat.ch/2e73

SEE International
Provides sustainable medical, surgical, and educational services through volunteer ophthalmic surgeons, with the objectives of restoring sight and preventing blindness to disadvantaged individuals worldwide.
Ophth-Opt, Surg
⊕ https://vfmat.ch/6e1b

Serve Humanity Foundation (SHF)
Provides education, job training, community creation, and empowerment, and access to medical care to underserved and underprivileged communities.
General
⊕ https://vfmat.ch/d2f5

Serving Others Worldwide
Aims to provide aid to the poor, distressed, and underprivileged by providing healthcare and dental services, and by building schools, orphanages, libraries, and medical clinics in undeveloped countries.
Dent-OMFS, General
⊕ https://vfmat.ch/69cb

Set Free Alliance
Works with in-country partners to rescue children, provide clean water, host medical clinics, and plant churches, based in Christian ministry.
General, Peds
⊕ https://vfmat.ch/bdb8

SEVA
Delivers vital eye care services to the world's most vulnerable, including women, children, and Indigenous peoples.
Ophth-Opt, Surg
⊕ https://vfmat.ch/1e87

Shanthi Bhavan Palliative Hospital
Aims to improve the quality of life of people with life-limiting or disabling diseases, by treating pain and by providing medical care and emotional, mental, and social support.
ER Med, Logist-Op, Nephro, Palliative, Path, Rehab
⊕ https://vfmat.ch/8f27

Sharon Palliative Care Center
Provides patient-centered and family-oriented palliative care and support.
Palliative
⊕ https://vfmat.ch/abc9

Shyam Oncology Foundation
Aims to improve all aspects of cancer care, primarily in India—including prevention, early diagnosis, treatment, and quality of life for all.
Palliative
⊕ https://vfmat.ch/5a12

Sightsavers
Works with partners in developing countries to help eliminate avoidable blindness and advocates for equal opportunity for the disabled.
Infect Dis, Ophth-Opt, Surg
⊕ https://vfmat.ch/aa52

SIGN Fracture Care International
Builds orthopedic capacity around the world and provides the injured poor access to fracture surgery by donating orthopedic education and implant systems to surgeons in developing countries.
Ortho, Rehab, Surg
⊕ https://vfmat.ch/123d

Simavi
Strives for a world in which all women and girls are socially and economically empowered and pursue their rights to live a healthy life, free from discrimination, coercion, and violence.
MF Med, OB-GYN
⊕ https://vfmat.ch/b57b

Singapore Red Cross
Responds to emergencies with a dedication to relieving human suffering and protecting human lives and dignity.
ER Med, General, Logist-Op, Pub Health, Surg
⊕ https://vfmat.ch/4d7c

Sitapur Eye Hospital
Aims to eradicate blindness and provide eye care to all at minimal cost, regardless of economic class, caste, sex, or religion.
Ophth-Opt
⊕ https://vfmat.ch/4fb7

Smile Asia
Delivers free surgical care, through medical missions and outreach centers, to children with facial deformities such as cleft lip and cleft palate, and aims to raise standards of medical care by creating opportunities for collaborative learning and exchange of best practices.
Anesth, Dent-OMFS, Ped Surg, Peds, Plast
⊕ https://vfmat.ch/d674

Smile Train, Inc.
Treats children with cleft lip through a sustainable and local model that supports surgery and other forms of essential care.
Logist-Op, Pub Health
⊕ https://vfmat.ch/822c

SmileOnU
Empowers dental professionals to help and educate those who may not have adequate dental knowledge and access to oral health services.
Dent-OMFS, Surg
⊕ https://vfmat.ch/cb6d

SmileStar
Provides free, quality dental care to disadvantaged communities in African countries and India.
Dent-OMFS
⊕ https://vfmat.ch/ade3

SNEH Foundation
Aims to ensure excellent early childhood education, nutrition, and health for every child in India.
Logist-Op, Nutr, OB-GYN, Pub Health
⊕ https://vfmat.ch/31b6

Society for Nutrition, Education & Health Action (SNEHA)
Aims to break the intergenerational cycle of poor health among women and children living in vulnerable settlements.
MF Med, Neonat, Nutr, OB-GYN
⊕ https://vfmat.ch/17d2

Soddo Christian Hospital
Mobilizes volunteers to help transform communities through healthcare and education, based in Christian ministry.
ER Med, General
⊕ https://vfmat.ch/efa4

Solace Charities
Provides financial, medical, moral and social support for families with children suffering from terminal illnesses.
General, Nutr, Peds, Pub Health
⊕ https://vfmat.ch/f68e

SOS Children's Villages International
Supports children through alternative care and family strengthening.
ER Med, Peds
⊕ https://vfmat.ch/aca1

Sri Shankara Cancer Foundation
Aims to be a pioneer in cancer cure and research asnd also to provide comprehensive cancer treatment to all cancer patients, particularly the poor.
Anesth, CV Med, Endo, GI, Heme-Onc, Medicine, Nephro, Nutr, Palliative, Path, Psych, Pulm-Critic, Radiol, Rehab
⊕ https://vfmat.ch/bfdb

Stand By Me
Helps children facing terrible circumstances and provides the care, love, and attention they need to thrive through children's homes and schools.
Peds
⊕ https://vfmat.ch/a224

Stanford University School of Medicine: Weiser Lab Global Surgery
Integrates research, education, patient care, and community service.
Logist-Op, Pub Health, Surg
⊕ https://vfmat.ch/9153

Students for Kids International Projects (SKIP)
Strives to educate and empower students to initiate and maintain sustainable community projects for the health, welfare, and education of children.
Dent-OMFS, General, Nutr, Peds, Pub Health
⊕ https://vfmat.ch/de4e

Sundaram Medical Foundation
Seeks to provide cost-effective, community-centered healthcare in an environment that is clean, caring and responsive to the needs of the patient.
CV Med, CV Med, Dent-OMFS, Derm, ER Med, Endo, GI, General, Heme-Onc, Medicine, Nephro, Neuro, OB-GYN, Ophth-Opt, Ortho, Peds, Psych, Pulm-Critic, Rheum, Surg
⊕ https://vfmat.ch/21d1

Suraj Eye Institute
Aims to provide eye care for all, supporting medical training, research and public health efforts, and partnering to develop innovative solutions.
Ophth-Opt, Peds
⊕ https://vfmat.ch/f85d

Sustainable Medical Missions
Trains and supports Indigenous healthcare and faith leaders in underdeveloped communities to treat neglected tropical diseases (NTDs) and other endemic conditions affecting the poorest community members, by pairing faith-based solutions with best practices.
Infect Dis, Pub Health
⊕ https://vfmat.ch/9165

Swadhar Institute for Development of Women and Children (Swadhar IDWC)
Provides services to women and children to ensure protection of rights, leading to self-reliance and empowerment.
Dent-OMFS, Derm, Infect Dis, Peds, Psych
⊕ https://vfmat.ch/68fc

Swasti
Aims to transform the lives of marginalized communities by ensuring their access to quality healthcare and thereby contributing to poverty alleviation.
Pub Health
⊕ https://vfmat.ch/be8b

Swiss Doctors
Aims to improve the health of populations in developing countries through medical-aid projects and training.
General, Infect Dis, Medicine
⊕ https://vfmat.ch/311a

Swiss Tropical and Public Health Institute
Contributes to the improvement of the health of populations internationally, nationally, and locally through excellence in research, education, and services.
Infect Dis, Pub Health
⊕ https://vfmat.ch/2ee4

Tamil Nadu Foundation
Empowers the underserved in Tamil Nadu through education, women's empowerment, rural development, and health and hygiene.
General, Infect Dis, Logist-Op
⊕ https://vfmat.ch/181e

Tara Foundation
Aims to enable hearing-impaired children to listen and speak like their hearing peers.
⊕ https://vfmat.ch/929a

Task Force for Global Health, The
Consists of programs and focus areas that cover a range of global health issues including neglected tropical diseases, infectious diseases, vaccines, field

epidemiology, public health informatics, health workforce development, and global health ethics.

Infect Dis, Logist-Op, Medicine, Ophth-Opt, Peds

⊕ https://vfmat.ch/714c

TB Alert

Offers a range of programmatic, advisory, technical, and training services around tuberculosis, and is active in international advocacy initiatives.

Infect Dis, Pub Health, Pulm-Critic

⊕ https://vfmat.ch/1d5e

Tearfund

Responds to crisis and partners with local churches to bring restoration to those living in poverty, inspired by the Christian faith.

ER Med, Logist-Op

⊕ https://vfmat.ch/f6cf

Terre des hommes (Tdh) Foundation

Works to improve the daily life of children and their relatives in the areas of health, protection and emergency, in Europe, Africa, Asia, Latin America, and the Near and Middle East.

CT Surg, CV Med, OB-GYN, Ped Surg, Pub Health

⊕ https://vfmat.ch/5c26

Texas Children's Global Health

Addresses healthcare needs in resource-limited settings locally and globally by improving maternal and child health through the implementation of innovative, sustainable, in-country programs to train health professionals and build functional healthcare infrastructure.

Anesth, ER Med, Heme-Onc, Infect Dis, MF Med, Nutr, OB-GYN, Peds, Pub Health, Surg

⊕ https://vfmat.ch/4a1d

Third World Eye Care Society (TWECS)

Collects old, unused eyeglasses and distributes them in conjunction with eye exams given by properly trained individuals.

Logist-Op, Ophth-Opt

⊕ https://vfmat.ch/8618

Thirumalai Charity Trust - TCT

Develops and delivers a unique model of accessible, affordable primary and secondary healthcare.

CV Med, Dent-OMFS, ENT, ER Med, Endo, General, MF Med, OB-GYN, Ophth-Opt, Ortho, Peds, Rehab, Surg

⊕ https://vfmat.ch/55b6

Tilganga Institute of Ophthalmology (TIO)

Supports the prevention and control of blindness in Nepal and the region.

Ophth-Opt

⊕ https://vfmat.ch/ff5d

Tulsi Chanrai foundation

Aims to establish high-quality sustainable and replicable models in primary healthcare, provision of safe drinking water, and eye care.

General, Infect Dis, MF Med, Nutr, OB-GYN, Ophth-Opt, Peds

⊕ https://vfmat.ch/3cc2

TwinEpidemic

Works to quell the epidemic of diabetes and heart disease among ethnic communities worldwide.

CV Med, Endo, General, Logist-Op, Pub Health

⊕ https://vfmat.ch/e859

Two Worlds Cancer Collaboration

Collaborates with local care professionals in lesser-resourced countries to help reduce the burden of cancer and other life-limiting illnesses.

Heme-Onc, Palliative, Peds, Pub Health, Rad-Onc

⊕ https://vfmat.ch/fbdd

Uday Foundation

Works on health, humanitarian assistance, and disaster relief.

ER Med, General, MF Med, OB-GYN, Peds, Pub Health

⊕ https://vfmat.ch/8ba9

Unforgotten Fund, The (UNFF)

Provides lifesaving humanitarian relief to UN Field Operations and projects such as water supply, sanitation and hygiene (WASH), food security, health, and shelter.

ER Med, MF Med, Nutr, OB-GYN, Peds

⊕ https://vfmat.ch/928f

Union for International Cancer Control (UICC)

Unites and supports the cancer community to reduce the global cancer burden, promote greater equity, and ensure that cancer control continues to be a priority in the world health and development agenda.

Heme-Onc, Pub Health

⊕ https://vfmat.ch/88b1

Unite 4 Humanity

Aims to provide emergency aid and support for Muslim communities across the world.

General, Nutr, OB-GYN, Ophth-Opt, Plast, Psych, Rehab

⊕ https://vfmat.ch/fbe7

Unite for Sight

Supports eye clinics worldwide by investing human and financial resources to eliminate patient barriers to eye care. Applies best practices in eye care, public health, volunteerism, and social entrepreneurship to achieve our goal of high-quality eye care for all.

Ophth-Opt, Surg

⊕ https://vfmat.ch/4fe7

United Hands Relief & Development

Works to funnel efforts toward alleviating and immediately responding to the sufferings of others around the globe, regardless of nationality, race, religion, or social status.

ER Med, General, Infect Dis, Ophth-Opt, Surg

⊕ https://vfmat.ch/2771

United Nations Children's Fund (UNICEF)

Works in over 190 countries and territories to save children's lives, defend their rights, and help them fulfill their potential, from early childhood through adolescence.

All-Immu, Infect Dis, MF Med, Neonat, Nutr, OB-GYN, Ped Surg, Peds, Pub Health

⊕ https://vfmat.ch/42d7

United Nations Development Programme (UNDP)

Helps countries achieve the simultaneous eradication of extreme poverty and significant reduction of inequalities and exclusion using a sustainable human development approach.

Infect Dis, Logist-Op, Pub Health

⊕ https://vfmat.ch/935c

United Nations High Commissioner for Refugees (UNHCR)

Safeguards the rights and well-being of people who have been forced to flee, ensuring that everybody has the right to seek asylum and find safe refuge in another country, with the goal of seeking lasting solutions.

General, MF Med, Medicine, OB-GYN, Peds, Psych, Pub Health

⊕ https://vfmat.ch/6636

United Nations Population Fund (UNFPA)

Supports reproductive healthcare for women and youth in more than 150 countries, focusing on delivering a world in which every pregnancy is wanted, every childbirth is safe, and every young person's potential is fulfilled.

Infect Dis, MF Med, Neonat, OB-GYN, Peds, Pub Health

⊕ https://vfmat.ch/c969

United Surgeons for Children (USFC)

Pursues greater health and opportunity for children in the most neglected pockets of the world, with a specific focus on and expertise in surgery.

Anesth, CT Surg, Neonat, Neurosurg, OB-GYN, Peds, Radiol, Surg

⊕ https://vfmat.ch/3b4c

United Way

Aims to improve lives by mobilizing the caring power of communities around the world to advance the common good by fighting for the health, education, and financial stability of every person.

General, Infect Dis, Pub Health
⊕ https://vfmat.ch/c812

University of British Columbia – Faculty of Medicine: Branch for International Surgical Care
Aims to advance sustainable improvements in the delivery of surgical care in the world's most underserved countries, by building capacity within the field of surgery through the provision of care in low-resource settings.
Anesth, ER Med, Neurosurg, Surg, Urol
⊕ https://vfmat.ch/4164

University of California Los Angeles: David Geffen School of Medicine Global Health Program
Catalyzes opportunities to improve health globally by engaging in multi-disciplinary and innovative education programs, research initiatives, and bilateral partnerships that provide opportunities for trainees, faculty, and staff to contribute to sustainable health initiatives and to address health inequities facing the world today.
All-Immu, Infect Dis, Logist-Op, MF Med, Medicine, Neonat, OB-GYN, Ortho, Ped Surg, Peds, Radiol
⊕ https://vfmat.ch/f1a4

University of California San Diego School of Medicine: Global Surgery
Aims to improve access to and maintain the quality of surgical care not only in the U.S. but also around the world–especially for the underserved.
Logist-Op, Ped Surg, Plast, Surg
⊕ https://vfmat.ch/4c9e

University of California San Francisco: Francis I. Proctor Foundation for Ophthalmology
Aims to prevent blindness worldwide through research and teaching focused on infectious and inflammatory eye disease.
Ophth-Opt, Pub Health
⊕ https://vfmat.ch/cf47

University of California San Francisco: Institute for Global Health Sciences
Dedicates its efforts to improving health and reducing the burden of disease in the world's most vulnerable populations by integrating expertise in the health, social, and biological sciences, training global health leaders, and developing solutions to the most pressing health challenges.
Infect Dis, OB-GYN, Pub Health
⊕ https://vfmat.ch/6587

University of California: Global Health Institute
Mobilizes people and resources across the University of California to advance global health research, education, and collaboration.
General, OB-GYN, Pub Health
⊕ https://vfmat.ch/ee7f

University of Chicago: Center for Global Health
Collaborates with communities locally and globally to democratize education, increase service learning opportunities, and advance sustainable solutions to improve health and well-being while reducing global health inequities.
Genetics, MF Med, Peds, Pub Health
⊕ https://vfmat.ch/4f8f

University of Chicago: Global Surgery
Aims to improve and sustain the surgical health of people and communities throughout the world with quality and ethical surgical policy and practice, while facilitating the education of the next generation of surgical leaders around the world to participate in the development of high-quality, ethical surgical programs.
CT Surg, ER Med, Neurosurg, Neurosurg, Ortho, Ped Surg, Plast, Surg, Vasc Surg
⊕ https://vfmat.ch/8b4f

University of Illinois at Chicago: Center for Global Health
Aims to improve the health of populations around the world and reduce health disparities by collaboratively conducting trans-disciplinary research, training the next generations of global health leaders, and building the capacities of global and local partners.
Pub Health
⊕ https://vfmat.ch/b749

University of Michigan Medical School Global REACH
Aims to facilitate health research, education, and collaboration among Michigan Medicine learners and faculty with our global partners to reduce health disparities for the benefit of communities worldwide.
ENT, General, Ophth-Opt, Peds, Psych, Pub Health, Urol
⊕ https://vfmat.ch/5f19

University of Michigan: Department of Surgery Global Health
Improves the health of patients, populations and communities through excellence in education, patient care, community service, research and technology development, and through leadership activities.
Anesth, Ortho, Surg
⊕ https://vfmat.ch/2fd8

University of Minnesota: Global Surgery & Disparities Program
Works to understand and improve surgical, anesthesia, and OB/GYN care in underserved areas through partnerships with local providers, while training the next generation of academic global surgery leaders.
All-Immu, Dent-OMFS, ER Med, Heme-Onc, MF Med, Neurosurg, OB-GYN, Ophth-Opt, Path, Ped Surg, Plast, Surg, Urol
⊕ https://vfmat.ch/e59a

University of New Mexico School of Medicine: Project Echo
Seeks to improve health outcomes worldwide through the use of a technology called telementoring, a guided-practice model in which the participating clinician retains responsibility for managing the patient.
General, Infect Dis, MF Med, OB-GYN, Path, Peds
⊕ https://vfmat.ch/6c9a

University of Pennsylvania Perelman School of Medicine Center for Global Health
Aims to improve health equity worldwide through enhanced public health awareness and access to care, discovery, and outcomes-based research, and comprehensive educational programs grounded in partnership.
Heme-Onc, Infect Dis, OB-GYN
⊕ https://vfmat.ch/cb57

University of Toledo: Global Health Program
Aims to be a transformative force in medical education, biomedical research, and healthcare delivery.
CV Med, CV Med, ER Med, Infect Dis, Medicine, Neuro, Neurosurg, OB-GYN, Ophth-Opt, Ortho, Peds, Plast, Psych, Surg
⊕ https://vfmat.ch/71f2

University of Toronto: Global Surgery
Focuses on excellent clinical care, outstanding research productivity, and the delivery of state-of-the-art educational programs.
Surg
⊕ https://vfmat.ch/1ad5

University of Utah Global Health
Supports local organizations in their quest to improve quality of life in their communities all over the world.
Anesth, CT Surg, CV Med, Crit-Care, Dent-OMFS, ENT, ER Med, Infect Dis, OB-GYN, Ophth-Opt, Ped Surg, Ped Surg, Peds, Plast, Pub Health, Surg, Urol
⊕ https://vfmat.ch/bacd

University of Virginia: Anesthesiology Department Global Health Initiatives
Educates and trains physicians to help people achieve healthy productive lives, and advances knowledge in the medical sciences.
Anesth, Pub Health
⊕ https://vfmat.ch/1b8b

University of Washington: The International Training and Education Center for Health (I-TECH)
Works with local partners to develop skilled healthcare workers and strong national health systems in resource-limited countries.
Infect Dis, Pub Health
⊕ https://vfmat.ch/642f

Unstoppable Foundation
Brings sustainable education to children and communities in developing countries.
Pub Health
⊕ https://vfmat.ch/f73c

USA for United Nations High Commissioner for Refugees (UNHCR)
Serves and protects refugees and displaced people through emergency relief, cash assistance, education, resettlement, and the rebuilding of livelihoods.
ER Med, General, Logist-Op, Nutr, Pub Health
⊕ https://vfmat.ch/293c

USAID: A2Z The Micronutrient and Child Blindness Project
Aims to increase the use of key micronutrient and blindness interventions to improve child and maternal health.
MF Med, Neonat, Nutr, Ophth-Opt, Surg
⊕ https://vfmat.ch/c5f1

USAID: Deliver Project
Builds a global supply chain to deliver lifesaving health products to people in order to enable countries to provide family planning, protect against malaria, and limit the spread of pandemic threats.
Infect Dis, Logist-Op, MF Med
⊕ https://vfmat.ch/374e

USAID: Health Finance and Governance Project
Uses research to implement strategies to help countries develop robust governance systems, increase their domestic resources for health, manage those resources more effectively, and make wise purchasing decisions.
Logist-Op
⊕ https://vfmat.ch/8652

USAID: Health Policy Initiative
Provides field-level programming in health policy development and implementation.
General, Infect Dis, MF Med, OB-GYN, Peds
⊕ https://vfmat.ch/8f84

USAID: Maternal and Child Health Integrated Program
Works to improve the health of women and their families, including programs for maternal, newborn, and child health, immunization, family planning, nutrition, malaria, and HIV/AIDS.
All-Immu, General, Infect Dis, MF Med
⊕ https://vfmat.ch/4415

USAID: Maternal and Child Survival Program
Works to prevent child and maternal deaths.
Infect Dis, MF Med, Neonat, OB-GYN, Peds
⊕ https://vfmat.ch/6fcf

USAID: TB Care II
Focuses on tuberculosis care and treatment.
Infect Dis
⊕ https://vfmat.ch/57d4

Ushalakshmi Breast Cancer Foundation
Aims to provide high-quality, innovative, and responsive breast cancer services and campaigns for excellence in breast cancer treatment and care.
OB-GYN
⊕ https://vfmat.ch/84cf

Variety – The Children's Charity International
Funds and delivers programs that focus on multiple unmet needs of children who are sick or disadvantaged, or live with disabilities and other special needs. Works at a local, national and international level, including the delivery of critical healthcare and medical equipment.
General, Infect Dis, Logist-Op
⊕ https://vfmat.ch/41f5

Vascular Birthmarks Foundation
Connects families affected by vascular birthmarks, anomalies, and related syndromes with evaluation and treatment, and supports physician education, medical mission trips, and research.

Dent-OMFS, Derm, Logist-Op
⊕ https://vfmat.ch/86d8

Vision Care
Restores sight and helps patients get regular treatment at short-term eye camps and long-term base clinics by having doctors, missionaries, volunteers, and sponsors work together.
Ophth-Opt
⊕ https://vfmat.ch/9d7c

Vision for All Foundation
Implements ophthalmic healthcare projects; aims to create and support ophthalmic centers and existing structures in order to support the training of medical and paramedical personnel in the ophthalmology; and seeks to promote prevention, diagnosis, and treatment of ophthalmic pathologies.
Dent-OMFS, Ophth-Opt, Pub Health
⊕ https://vfmat.ch/dd72

Vision Outreach International
Advocates for helping the blind in underserved regions of the world and empowers the poor through sight restoration.
Ophth-Opt
⊕ https://vfmat.ch/9721

Visionaries International
Works toward reducing the burden of corneal blindness in the developing world by assessing and addressing what limits corneal surgeons in each locale.
Anesth, Ophth-Opt, Pub Health, Surg
⊕ https://vfmat.ch/3d2e

Vitamin Angels
Helps at-risk populations in need—specifically pregnant women, new mothers, and children under age 5—to gain access to life-changing vitamins and minerals.
General, Nutr
⊕ https://vfmat.ch/7da1

Voluntary Health Services (VHS)
Provides patient-focused, affordable healthcare for all through a sustainable model and strives to integrate healthcare delivery, training, and research.
CV Med, Crit-Care, Dent-OMFS, ENT, ER Med, Endo, General, Geri, Heme-Onc, Infect Dis, MF Med, Medicine, Neonat, Nephro, Neuro, Neurosurg, Ophth-Opt, Ortho, Path, Pulm-Critic, Radiol, Rehab, Surg
⊕ https://vfmat.ch/23b9

Voluntary Service Overseas (VSO)
Works with health workers, communities, and governments to improve health services and rights for women, babies, youth, people with disabilities, and prisoners.
General, MF Med, OB-GYN
⊕ https://vfmat.ch/213d

VT SEVA: Volunteering Together for Service
To help rebuild and restructure the underprivileged and underserved communities.
Heme-Onc, OB-GYN
⊕ https://vfmat.ch/f7f1

Walkabout Foundation
Provides wheelchairs and rehabilitation in the developing world and funds research to find a cure for paralysis.
Logist-Op, Rehab
⊕ https://vfmat.ch/5582

Wealth By Health Steps For Change Foundation
Aims to improve the health and well-being of underserved populations by providing accessible resources that support the attainment of greater quality of life.
All-Immu, CV Med, Dent-OMFS, General, Medicine, Ophth-Opt, Palliative, Peds, Pub Health
⊕ https://vfmat.ch/153a

Weill Cornell Medicine: Center for Global Health
Collaborates with international partners to improve the health of people in resource-poor countries through research, training, and service.

General, Infect Dis, OB-GYN
⊕ https://vfmat.ch/1813

West Bengal Charity Foundation
Supports and assists communities in West Bengal with nutrition education, clothing, and employment.
Ophth-Opt
⊕ https://vfmat.ch/e9ee

WF AID
Seeks to build capacity and provide emergency aid, human assistance, and international development, where required in the world.
CT Surg, Dent-OMFS, ENT, ER Med, General, Infect Dis, Logist-Op, Nutr, Ophth-Opt, Ortho, Path, Radiol, Rehab, Surg
⊕ https://vfmat.ch/ebd7

White Ribbon Alliance, The
Leads a movement for reproductive, maternal, and newborn health and accelerates progress by putting citizens at the center of global, national, and local health efforts.
MF Med, OB-GYN
⊕ https://vfmat.ch/496b

Women's Refugee Commission
Seeks to improve lives by protecting the rights of women, children, and youth displaced by conflict and crisis through researching their needs, identifying solutions, and advocating for programs and policies to strengthen their resilience.
General, MF Med, Neonat, OB-GYN, Peds, Psych
⊕ https://vfmat.ch/3d8f

World Anaesthesia Society (WAS)
Aims to support anesthesiologists with an interest in working in low-income regions of the world.
Anesth
⊕ https://vfmat.ch/37fe

World Cancer Care Charitable Society
Aims to promote awareness and early detection of cancer.
Heme-Onc
⊕ https://vfmat.ch/b81f

World Care Foundation
Encourages humanitarian efforts to help those in need anywhere in the world, regardless of their faith, color, gender, and ethnicity. Projects include orphanages, orphan sponsorship, medical centers, refugee crisis work, and education.
ER Med, General, Pub Health
⊕ https://vfmat.ch/987a

World CF
Helps provide access to innovative surgical care for children and adults with abnormalities of the head and/or face.
Dent-OMFS, Neurosurg, Ped Surg, Plast, Surg
⊕ https://vfmat.ch/3df1

World Children's Fund
Commits to helping children worldwide who are suffering the effects of poverty, disease, natural disaster, famine, abuse, civil strife, and war.
General, Logist-Op, MF Med, Nutr, OB-GYN, Pub Health
⊕ https://vfmat.ch/9cd8

World Compassion Fellowship (WCF)
Serves the global poor and persecuted through relief, medical care, development, and training.
CV Med, ER Med, Endo, GI, General, Infect Dis, Medicine, Nutr, OB-GYN, Ortho, Peds, Psych, Pub Health, Rehab
⊕ https://vfmat.ch/7b97

World Council of Optometry
Facilitates the development of optometry worldwide and promotes eye health and vision care through advocacy, education, policy development, and humanitarian outreach.
Ophth-Opt, Pub Health
⊕ https://vfmat.ch/c92e

World Federation of Hemophilia (WFH)
Aims to improve and sustain care for people with inherited bleeding disorders by pursuing long-term relationships with individuals and organizations who share the values of WFH's development model.
Heme-Onc
⊕ https://vfmat.ch/5121

World Health Organization, The (WHO)
The United Nations' agency for health provides leadership on global health matters, shapes the health research agenda, sets norms and standards, articulates evidence-based policy options, provides technical support and monitoring to countries, and assesses health trends.
ER Med, General, Infect Dis, Logist-Op, MF Med, OB-GYN, Peds, Psych, Pub Health
⊕ https://vfmat.ch/c476

World Heart Federation
Leads the global fight against heart disease and stroke, with a focus on low- and middle-income countries.
CV Med, Crit-Care, Heme-Onc, Medicine, Peds
⊕ https://vfmat.ch/ea51

World Hope International
Empowers the poorest individuals around the world so they can become agents of change within their communities, by offering resources and knowledge.
Infect Dis, Logist-Op, MF Med, OB-GYN, Peds
⊕ https://vfmat.ch/a4b8

World Medical Relief
Facilitates the distribution of surplus medical resources where they are needed.
Logist-Op
⊕ https://vfmat.ch/72dc

World Missions Possible
Provides EMS capacity-building, along with medical and vision care, to under-developed and rural areas.
ER Med, General, Heme-Onc, Neonat, Ophth-Opt, Surg
⊕ https://vfmat.ch/d6a5

World Sight Foundation
Strives to deliver sustainable solutions for the alleviation of blindness, and for preserving sight, everywhere in the world.
Ophth-Opt
⊕ https://vfmat.ch/5af2

World Surgical Foundation
Provides charitable surgical healthcare to the world's poor and underserved in developing nations.
Ped Surg, Surg
⊕ https://vfmat.ch/c162

World Vision International
Works with vulnerable communities around the world to overcome poverty and injustice with child-focused programs in disaster management, health, nutrition, economic development, education, clean water, sanitation, and hygiene.
ER Med, General, Infect Dis, MF Med, Nutr, OB-GYN, Peds
⊕ https://vfmat.ch/2642

WorldShare
Connects faith-based groups in the UK with their counterparts in underdeveloped countries to promote community development and holistic support for children.
Dent-OMFS, ER Med, General, Peds, Pub Health, Surg
⊕ https://vfmat.ch/9eae

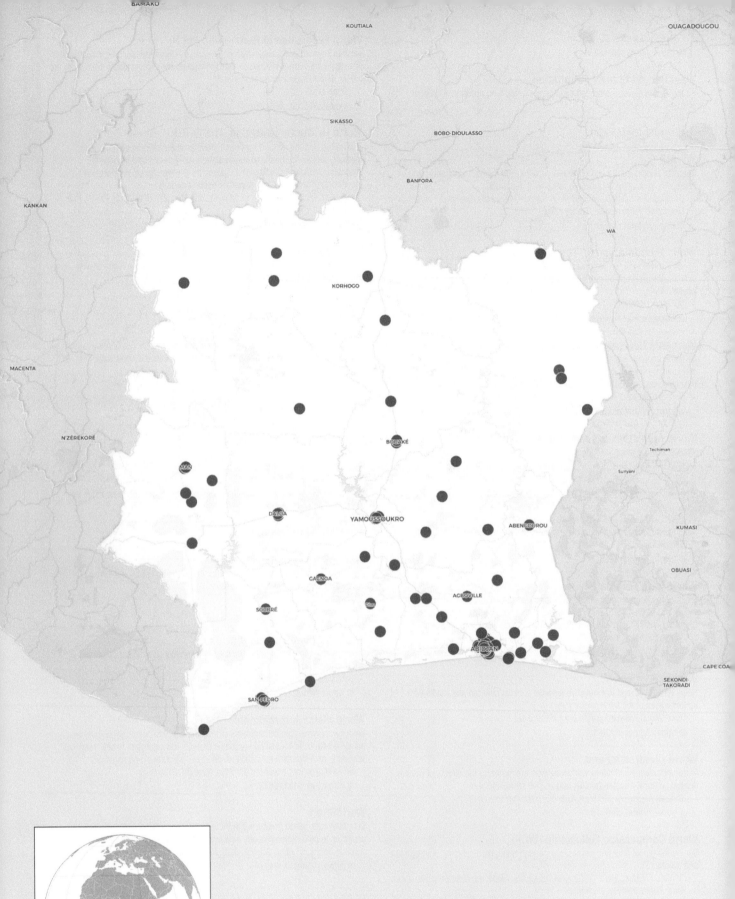

● Healthcare Facility

Ivory Coast

The Ivory Coast is located on the south coast of West Africa, bordered by Guinea, Liberia, Mali, Burkina Faso, Ghana, and the Gulf of Guinea. The Ivory Coast has a growing population of 28.1 million people, the majority of which live on the southern coast, in cities along the Atlantic Ocean. Much of the country's northern areas remain more sparsely populated. The population comprises several ethnic groups, including Akan, Voltaique/Gur, Northern Mande, Kru, Southern Mande, and some groups that are non-Ivorian. The population is equally religiously diverse: the majority are Muslim, followed by Catholic, Evangelical, Methodist, Christian, and animist. French is the official language and is most commonly spoken; there are also 60-plus native dialects. Music is an important part of the culture in the Ivory Coast, and various instruments and songs are used to share historical stories.

After the Ivory Coast gained independence from France in 1960, its economy grew due to its cocoa and coffee industries. However, during the 1980s, the economy declined, followed by political unrest, civil war, and the internal displacement of large portions of the population. Recently, the country has experienced rapid economic growth, with a robust agricultural sector based primarily on the production and export of cocoa beans, coffee, and palm oil. About two-thirds of the population is involved in agriculture or activities related to agriculture. Despite the growing economy, approximately 46 percent of the population lives below the poverty line, and the country has one of the highest gender inequality rates in the world.

A 2002 civil war disrupted the delivery of healthcare services to the population, and caused many healthcare practitioners to leave the country. In addition, with a large portion of the population living below the poverty line, health is overall poor. A pressing health challenge in the Ivory Coast is HIV/AIDS, one of the leading causes of death. Other leading causes of death include malaria, neonatal disorders, lower respiratory infections, ischemic heart disease, stroke, diarrheal diseases, tuberculosis, congenital defects, and cirrhosis. The risk factors that contribute most to death and disability in the Ivory Coast include malnutrition, air pollution, unsafe sex, high blood pressure, high body-mass index, alcohol and tobacco use, high fasting plasma glucose, dietary risks, and insufficient water, sanitation, and hygiene.

28.1M
Population

$2,326
GDP Per Capita

58 years
Life Expectancy
↑ Improving

16
Doctors/100k
Physician Density

40
Beds/100k
Hospital Bed Density

617
Deaths/100k
Maternal Mortality

Ivory Coast

Nonprofit Organizations

1040i
Works to provide safe drinking water, medical care, and education to the most vulnerable in West Africa.
Dent-OMFS, General, OB-GYN, Ophth-Opt, Ortho, Surg
⊕ https://vfmat.ch/9bba

143 LIFE Foundation
Seeks to educate and empower individuals living with malaria, TB, HIV/AIDS, STDs and other health disparities related to sexual health.
Infect Dis, MF Med
⊕ https://vfmat.ch/d59b

Abt Associates
Seeks to improve the quality of life and economic well-being of people worldwide, while striving to meet and exceed the highest professional standards.
General, Logist-Op, MF Med, OB-GYN, Peds
⊕ https://vfmat.ch/cec2

Access Ivory Coast
Aims to provide patient care and medical services to those in need in Ivory Coast, based in Christian ministry.
General, Peds
⊕ https://vfmat.ch/575b

Action Against Hunger
Aims to end life-threatening hunger for good through treating and preventing malnutrition across more than 45 countries.
Nutr
⊕ https://vfmat.ch/2dbc

Advance Family Planning
Aims to achieve global expansion and access to quality contraceptive information, services, and supplies through financial investment and political commitment.
General, MF Med, Pub Health
⊕ https://vfmat.ch/7478

Africa CDC
Aims to strengthen the capacity and capability of Africa's public health institutions and partnerships to detect and respond quickly and effectively to disease threats and outbreaks, based on data-driven interventions and programs.
Infect Dis, Logist-Op, Pub Health
⊕ https://vfmat.ch/339c

Africa Health Organisation
Leads collaborative efforts among countries in Africa and other partners to promote health equity, combat disease, and improve quality of life.
Logist-Op, Pub Health
⊕ https://vfmat.ch/b1c5

African Field Epidemiology Network (AFENET)
Strengthens field epidemiology and public health laboratory capacity to contribute effectively to addressing epidemics and other major public health problems in Africa.
All-Immu, Infect Dis, Path, Pub Health
⊕ https://vfmat.ch/df2e

American Academy of Pediatrics
Seeks to attain optimal physical, mental, and social health and well-being for all infants, children, adolescents, and young adults.
Anesth, Crit-Care, Neonat, Ped Surg
⊕ https://vfmat.ch/9633

American International Health Alliance (AIHA)
Strengthens health systems and workforce capacity worldwide through locally driven, peer-to-peer institutional partnerships.
CV Med, ER Med, Infect Dis, Medicine, OB-GYN
⊕ https://vfmat.ch/69fd

Amref Health Africa
Serves millions of people across 35 countries in Sub-Saharan Africa, strengthening health systems, and training African health workers to respond to the continent's most critical health issues.
All-Immu, General, Infect Dis, Logist-Op, MF Med, OB-GYN, Path, Pub Health, Surg
⊕ https://vfmat.ch/6985

AO Alliance
Builds solutions to lessen the burden of injuries in low- and middle-income countries, while enhancing the care of the injured to reduce human suffering, disability, and poverty.
Ortho, Surg
⊕ https://vfmat.ch/8cd5

Aya Project
Seeks to improve the health and education of rural communities in Ivory Coast through short-term mission trips and programs that work with local agencies.
General, OB-GYN
⊕ https://vfmat.ch/7aa9

BroadReach
Collaborates with governments, multinational health organizations, donors, and private-sector companies to effect healthcare reform and solve the world's biggest health challenges.
Logist-Op
⊕ https://vfmat.ch/7812

CARE
Works around the globe to save lives, defeat poverty, and achieve social justice.

ER Med, General
⊕ https://vfmat.ch/7232

Carter Center, The
Seeks to prevent and resolve conflicts, enhance freedom and democracy, and improve health, while remaining committed to human rights and the alleviation of human suffering.
Infect Dis, MF Med, Ophth-Opt
⊕ https://vfmat.ch/6556

Chain of Hope (La Chaîne de l'Espoir)
Helps underprivileged children around the world by providing them with access to healthcare.
Anesth, CT Surg, Crit-Care, ER Med, Neurosurg, Ortho, Ped Surg, Surg, Vasc Surg
⊕ https://vfmat.ch/e871

Challenge Initiative, The
Seeks to rapidly and sustainably scale up proven reproductive health solutions among the urban poor.
MF Med, OB-GYN, Peds
⊕ https://vfmat.ch/2f77

Christian Blind Mission (CBM)
Aims to improve the quality of life of persons with disabilities in the poorest countries, addressing poverty as a cause and a consequence of disability, and working in partnership to create a society for all.
ENT, General, Infect Dis, OB-GYN, Ophth-Opt, Ortho, Peds, Psych, Rehab, Surg
⊕ https://vfmat.ch/3824

Christian Health Service Corps
Brings Christian doctors, health professionals, and health educators committed to serving the poor to places that otherwise have little or no access to healthcare.
Anesth, Dent-OMFS, General, Medicine, Peds, Surg
⊕ https://vfmat.ch/da57

COVID-19 Clinical Research Coalition
Advocates and collaborates for the advancement of COVID-19 research driven by the needs of low-resource settings, and works for equitable access to solutions to the pandemic.
All-Immu, Infect-Dis, MF Med, Path, Pub Health
⊕ https://vfmat.ch/d1f4

Direct Relief
Improves the health and lives of people affected by poverty or emergency situations by mobilizing and providing essential medical resources needed for their care.
ER Med, Logist-Op
⊕ https://vfmat.ch/58e5

Doctors Without Borders/Médecins Sans Frontières (MSF)
Responds to emergencies and provides lifesaving medical care where needed most, including during disasters, conflicts, and epidemics.
Anesth, Crit-Care, ER Med, General, Infect Dis, Nutr, OB-GYN, Ped Surg, Peds, Psych, Pub Health, Surg
⊕ https://vfmat.ch/f363

Effect: Hope (The Leprosy Mission Canada)
Connects like-minded Canadians to people suffering in isolation from debilitating, neglected tropical diseases such as leprosy, lymphatic filariasis, and Buruli ulcer.
General, Infect Dis
⊕ https://vfmat.ch/f12a

Elizabeth Glaser Pediatric AIDS Foundation
Seeks to end global pediatric HIV/AIDS through prevention and treatment programs, research, and advocacy.
Infect Dis, Nutr, OB-GYN, Peds
⊕ https://vfmat.ch/d6ec

Elton John AIDS Foundation
Seeks to address and overcome the stigma, discrimination, and neglect that prevents ending AIDS by funding local experts to challenge discrimination, prevent infections, and provide treatment.

Infect Dis, Pub Health
⊕ https://vfmat.ch/9d31

END Fund, The
Aims to control and eliminate the most prevalent neglected diseases among the world's poorest and most vulnerable people.
Infect Dis
⊕ https://vfmat.ch/2614

EngenderHealth
Works to implement high-quality, gender-equitable programs that advance sexual and reproductive health and rights.
General, MF Med, OB-GYN, Peds
⊕ https://vfmat.ch/1cb2

Fondation Follereau
Promotes the quality of life of the most vulnerable African communities. Alongside trusted partners, the foundation supports local initiatives in healthcare and education.
General, Infect Dis, OB-GYN
⊕ https://vfmat.ch/bcc7

Foundation for Healthcare for Humanity
Provide assistance in the development and implementation of medical programs in the United States, Africa, South America, Eastern Europe, and the Caribbean.
General
⊕ https://vfmat.ch/ba7f

Fracarita International
Provides support and services in the fields of mental healthcare, care for people with a disability, and education.
Psych, Rehab
⊕ https://vfmat.ch/8d3c

Gift of Life International
Provides lifesaving cardiac treatment to children in developing countries while developing sustainable pediatric cardiac programs by implementing screening, surgical, and training missions.
Anesth, CT Surg, CV Med, Crit-Care, Ped Surg, Peds, Pulm-Critic
⊕ https://vfmat.ch/f2f9

Global Partnership for Zero Leprosy
Facilitates alignment of the leprosy community and accelerates effective collaborative action toward the goal of zero leprosy.
Infect Dis
⊕ https://vfmat.ch/ec7b

Global Vision 2020
Provides prescription eyeglasses to people who live in parts of the world lacking necessary infrastructure for obtaining affordable corrective eyewear.
Logist-Op, Ophth-Opt
⊕ https://vfmat.ch/7373

Globus Relief
Aims to improve the delivery of healthcare worldwide by gathering, processing, and distributing surplus medical supplies to charities at home and abroad.
Logist-Op
⊕ https://vfmat.ch/a2b7

Grassroot Soccer
Leverages the power of soccer to educate, inspire, and mobilize at-risk youth in developing countries to overcome their greatest health challenges, live healthier and more productive lives, and be agents for change in their communities.
Infect Dis
⊕ https://vfmat.ch/3521

Health Alliance International
Promotes policies and support programs that strengthen government primary healthcare and foster social, economic, and health equity for all.
General, Infect Dis, Logist-Op, MF Med, Neonat, OB-GYN, Psych
⊕ https://vfmat.ch/6f2d

Healthy Heart Medical Ministries

Seeks to decrease death and disability from cardiovascular disease in Ivory Coast by providing free medical care, medication, and education, inspired by the Christian faith.

CV Med, Endo, General

🌐 https://vfmat.ch/dee5

Heart Fund, The

Aims to save the lives of children suffering from heart disease by developing innovative solutions that revolutionize access to cardiac care in developing countries.

Anesth, CV Med, Ped Surg, Peds, Surg

🌐 https://vfmat.ch/7e67

Helen Keller International

Seeks to eliminate preventable vision loss, malnutrition, and diseases of poverty.

Infect Dis, Nutr, OB-GYN, Ophth-Opt, Peds

🌐 https://vfmat.ch/b654

Hernia International

Aims to provide relief from sickness, and protection and preservation of health, for persons affected by groin and abdominal hernias and residing in low- and middle-income countries.

Surg

🌐 https://vfmat.ch/e98e

Hospice Africa

Aims to provide a holistic and culturally sensitive palliative care service through accurate treatment of pain.

Palliative

🌐 https://vfmat.ch/9f86

Humanity First

Provides aid and assistance to those in need, offering sustainable development solutions to society while providing and empowering local communities with the resources to help themselves.

ER Med, General, MF Med, Ophth-Opt

🌐 https://vfmat.ch/13cc

ICAP at Columbia University

Serves as global leader in supporting the scale-up of multidisciplinary HIV/AIDS prevention, care, and treatment programs based on a family-focused approach.

General, Infect Dis, MF Med, Medicine, OB-GYN, Pub Health

🌐 https://vfmat.ch/a8ef

International Agency for the Prevention of Blindness (IAPB), The

Leads international efforts in blindness-prevention activities, works toward a world where no one is needlessly visually impaired, and ensures that everyone has access to the best possible standard of eye health.

Infect Dis, Ophth-Opt, Pub Health

🌐 https://vfmat.ch/87a2

International Council of Ophthalmology

Works with ophthalmologic societies and others to enhance ophthalmic education and improve access to the highest-quality eye care in order to preserve and restore vision for people of the world.

Ophth-Opt

🌐 https://vfmat.ch/ffd2

International Federation of Red Cross and Red Crescent Societies (IFRC)

Coordinates and directs international assistance following natural and manmade disasters in nonconflict situations through the world's largest humanitarian and development network. Provides disaster-preparedness programs, healthcare activities, and promotes humanitarian values.

ER Med, General, Infect Dis, Nutr

🌐 https://vfmat.ch/b4ee

International Organization for Migration (IOM) – The UN Migration Agency

Promotes evidence-informed policies and holistic, preventive, and curative health programs that are beneficial, accessible, and equitable for vulnerable migrants.

General, Infect Dis, OB-GYN

🌐 https://vfmat.ch/621a

International Pediatric Nephrology Association (IPNA)

Leads global efforts to successfully address the care for all children with kidney disease through advocacy, education, and training.

Medicine, Nephro, Peds

🌐 https://vfmat.ch/b59d

International Planned Parenthood Federation (IPPF)

Leads a locally owned, globally connected civil society movement that provides and enables services and champions sexual and reproductive health and rights for all, especially the underserved.

Infect Dis, MF Med, OB-GYN

🌐 https://vfmat.ch/dc97

International Rescue Committee (IRC)

Responds to the world's worst humanitarian crises and helps people whose lives and livelihoods are shattered by conflict and disaster to survive, recover, and gain control of their future.

ER Med, General, Infect Dis, MF Med, Peds

🌐 https://vfmat.ch/5d24

International Trachoma Initiative (iTi)

Works toward a world free from trachoma, a preventable cause of blindness, and provides comprehensive support to national ministries of health and governmental and nongovernmental organizations to implement a comprehensive approach to fight trachoma.

Infect Dis, Ophth-Opt

🌐 https://vfmat.ch/3278

IntraHealth International

Improves the performance of health workers and strengthens the systems in which they work.

CV Med, Endo, General, Infect Dis, MF Med, Neonat, Nutr, OB-GYN

🌐 https://vfmat.ch/ddc8

Ipas

Focuses efforts on women and girls who want contraception or abortion, and builds programs around their needs and how best to support them.

OB-GYN

🌐 https://vfmat.ch/8e39

Ivory Coast Medical Relief Team

Aims to empower impoverished populations in Ivory Coast with medical supplies, education, and disease control.

General

🌐 https://vfmat.ch/ccb7

IVUmed

Aims to make quality urological care available worldwide by providing medical and surgical education for physicians and nurses, and treatment for thousands of children and adults.

Anesth, OB-GYN, Ped Surg, Surg, Urol

🌐 https://vfmat.ch/e619

Jhpiego

Creates and delivers transformative healthcare solutions that save lives, in partnership with national governments, health experts, and local communities.

General, Infect Dis, OB-GYN, Surg

🌐 https://vfmat.ch/45b8

John Snow, Inc. (JSI)

Aims to improve the health and well-being of underserved and vulnerable people and communities throughout the world.

General, Infect Dis, Logist-Op, MF Med, OB-GYN, Peds, Psych, Pub Health

🌐 https://vfmat.ch/ba78

Johns Hopkins Center for Communication Programs

Believes in the power of communication to save lives by empowering people to adopt healthy behaviors for themselves, their families, and their communities.

General, Infect Dis, Logist-Op, OB-GYN, Pub Health

🌐 https://vfmat.ch/1bf9

Johns Hopkins Center for Global Health

Facilitates and focuses the extensive expertise and resources of the Johns Hopkins institutions, together with global collaborators, to effectively address and ameliorate the world's most pressing health issues.

General, Genetics, Logist-Op, MF Med, Peds, Psych, Pub Health, Pulm-Critic

⊕ https://vfmat.ch/54ce

Joint United Nations Programme on HIV/AIDS (UNAIDS)

Aims to place people living with HIV and people affected by the virus at the decision-making table and at the center of designing, delivering, and monitoring the AIDS response.

Infect Dis

⊕ https://vfmat.ch/464a

La Salle International Foundation

Provides support for educational, health, and human services, along with humanitarian relief to people in developed and underdeveloped areas.

General

⊕ https://vfmat.ch/5891

Management Sciences for Health (MSH)

Works with countries and communities to save lives and improve the health of the world's poorest and most vulnerable people by building strong, resilient, sustainable health systems.

Infect Dis, Logist-Op, Pub Health

⊕ https://vfmat.ch/6aa2

MAP International

Provides medicines and health supplies to those in need around the world so they might experience life to the fullest.

Logist-Op

⊕ https://vfmat.ch/deed

Maverick Collective

Aims to build a global community of strategic philanthropists and informed advocates who use their intellectual and financial resources to create change.

Infect Dis, MF Med, OB-GYN

⊕ https://vfmat.ch/ea49

Medical Care Development International (MCD International)

Works to strengthen health systems through innovative, sustainable interventions.

Infect Dis, Logist-Op, OB-GYN, Pub Health

⊕ https://vfmat.ch/dc5c

Medical Care Development International

Works to improve the health of vulnerable populations through integrated, sustainable, and locally driven interventions.

Infect Dis, OB-GYN, Peds, Pub Health

⊕ https://vfmat.ch/da87

MedShare

Aims to improve the quality of life of people, communities, and the planet by sourcing and directly delivering surplus medical supplies and equipment to communities in need around the world.

Logist-Op

⊕ https://vfmat.ch/c8bc

MENTOR Initiative

Saves lives in emergencies through tropical disease control, and helps people recover from crisis with dignity, working side by side with communities, health workers, and health authorities to leave a lasting impact.

ER Med, Infect Dis

⊕ https://vfmat.ch/3bd5

Mercy and Love Foundation

Aims to provide orphaned and vulnerable children with basic human needs such as food, clothing, and shelter, enabling them to thrive.

General, Peds

⊕ https://vfmat.ch/649a

Médecins du Monde/Doctors of the World

Provides care, bears witness, and supports social change worldwide with innovative medical programs and evidence-based advocacy initiatives.

ER Med, General, Infect Dis, MF Med, Neonat, OB-GYN, Peds, Pub Health

⊕ https://vfmat.ch/a43d

Operation Fistula

Exists to end obstetric fistula by building models of care that serve every woman, everywhere.

MF Med, OB-GYN, Surg

⊕ https://vfmat.ch/ce8e

Order of Malta

Supports forgotten or excluded people, especially those living in conflict zones or amid natural disasters, by providing medical assistance, caring for refugees, and distributing medicines and necessities.

ER Med, General, Infect Dis, MF Med, Nephro, OB-GYN, Ortho, Psych

⊕ https://vfmat.ch/1fab

Organization for the Prevention of Blindness, The (OPC)

Provides research, and treatments and cures for people affected by blindness and blinding diseases in Francophone Africa.

Infect Dis, Ophth-Opt

⊕ https://vfmat.ch/86d6

Pact

Works on the ground to improve the lives of those who are challenged by poverty and marginalization, striving for a world in which all people are heard, capable, and vibrant.

Infect Dis, Logist-Op, MF Med, Pub Health

⊕ https://vfmat.ch/9a6c

Pathfinder International

Champions sexual and reproductive health and rights worldwide, mobilizing communities most in need to break through barriers and forge paths to a healthier future.

OB-GYN

⊕ https://vfmat.ch/a7b3

PSI – Population Services International

Aims to improve the health of people in the developing world by focusing on challenges such as a lack of family planning, HIV/AIDS, barriers to maternal health, and the greatest threats to children under the age of 5, including malaria, diarrhea, pneumonia, and malnutrition.

Infect Dis, MF Med, OB-GYN, Peds

⊕ https://vfmat.ch/ffe3

RAD-AID International

Improves and optimizes access to medical imaging and radiology in low-resource regions of the world.

Rad-Onc, Radiol

⊕ https://vfmat.ch/537f

RestoringVision

Empowers lives by restoring vision for millions of people in need.

Ophth-Opt

⊕ https://vfmat.ch/e121

Rockefeller Foundation, The

Works to promote the well-being of humanity.

Logist-Op, Nutr, Pub Health

⊕ https://vfmat.ch/5424

Rotary Action Group for Family Health & AIDS Prevention (RFHA)

Works to save and improve the lives of children and families who lack access to preventive healthcare and education.

Dent-OMFS, Infect Dis, OB-GYN, Ophth-Opt, Peds

⊕ https://vfmat.ch/6563

Rotary International

Provides service to others, improves lives, and advances world understanding, goodwill, and peace through its fellowship of business, professional, and community leaders.

ER Med, General, Infect Dis, MF Med, OB-GYN

⊕ https://vfmat.ch/8fb5

Sanofi Espoir Foundation
Contributes to reducing health inequalities among populations that need it most by applying a socially responsible approach focused on fighting childhood cancers in low-income countries, improving maternal and newborn health, and improving access to care.
ER Med, OB-GYN, Peds
⊕ https://vfmat.ch/943b

SCI Foundation
Seeks to prevent and treat neglected infectious diseases, with a focus on eliminating parasitic worm infections through strengthening impactful and comprehensive health programs across Sub-Saharan Africa.
Infect Dis, Pub Health
⊕ https://vfmat.ch/5444

SEE International
Provides sustainable medical, surgical, and educational services through volunteer ophthalmic surgeons, with the objectives of restoring sight and preventing blindness to disadvantaged individuals worldwide.
Ophth-Opt, Surg
⊕ https://vfmat.ch/6e1b

Sightsavers
Works with partners in developing countries to help eliminate avoidable blindness and advocates for equal opportunity for the disabled.
Infect Dis, Ophth-Opt, Surg
⊕ https://vfmat.ch/aa52

SINA Health
Aims to improve the health and educational status of the population in low- and middle-income countries.
General, Logist-Op
⊕ https://vfmat.ch/9ad3

Smile Train, Inc.
Treats children with cleft lip through a sustainable and local model that supports surgery and other forms of essential care.
Logist-Op, Pub Health
⊕ https://vfmat.ch/822c

Solthis
Improves disease prevention and access to quality care by strengthening the health systems and services of the countries served.
General, Infect Dis, Logist-Op, MF Med, Neonat, Path
⊕ https://vfmat.ch/a71d

Sustainable Kidney Care Foundation (SKCF)
Works to provide treatment for kidney injury where none exists, and aims to reduce mortality from treatable acute kidney injury (AKI).
Infect Dis, Medicine, Nephro
⊕ https://vfmat.ch/1926

Task Force for Global Health, The
Consists of programs and focus areas that cover a range of global health issues including neglected tropical diseases, infectious diseases, vaccines, field epidemiology, public health informatics, health workforce development, and global health ethics.
Infect Dis, Logist-Op, Medicine, Ophth-Opt, Peds
⊕ https://vfmat.ch/714c

Tearfund
Responds to crisis and partners with local churches to bring restoration to those living in poverty, inspired by the Christian faith.
ER Med, Logist-Op
⊕ https://vfmat.ch/f6cf

U.S. President's Malaria Initiative (PMI)
Supports low-income countries to help control and eliminate malaria through cost-effective, lifesaving malaria interventions.
Infect Dis, MF Med, OB-GYN
⊕ https://vfmat.ch/dc8b

Union for International Cancer Control (UICC)
Unites and supports the cancer community to reduce the global cancer burden, promote greater equity, and ensure that cancer control continues to be a priority in the world health and development agenda.
Heme-Onc, Pub Health
⊕ https://vfmat.ch/88b1

United Methodist Volunteers in Mission (UMVIM)
Engages in short-term missions each year in ministries as varied as disaster response, community development, pastor training, microenterprise, agriculture, Vacation Bible School, building repair and construction, and medical/dental services.
Dent-OMFS, ER Med, General
⊕ https://vfmat.ch/1ee6

United Nations Children's Fund (UNICEF)
Works in over 190 countries and territories to save children's lives, defend their rights, and help them fulfill their potential, from early childhood through adolescence.
All-Immu, Infect Dis, MF Med, Neonat, Nutr, OB-GYN, Ped Surg, Peds, Pub Health
⊕ https://vfmat.ch/42d7

United Nations High Commissioner for Refugees (UNHCR)
Safeguards the rights and well-being of people who have been forced to flee, ensuring that everybody has the right to seek asylum and find safe refuge in another country, with the goal of seeking lasting solutions.
General, MF Med, Medicine, OB-GYN, Peds, Psych, Pub Health
⊕ https://vfmat.ch/6636

United Nations Population Fund (UNFPA)
Supports reproductive healthcare for women and youth in more than 150 countries, focusing on delivering a world in which every pregnancy is wanted, every childbirth is safe, and every young person's potential is fulfilled.
Infect Dis, MF Med, Neonat, OB-GYN, Peds, Pub Health
⊕ https://vfmat.ch/c969

United States President's Emergency Plan for AIDS Relief (PEPFAR)
The U.S. global HIV/AIDS response works to prevent new HIV infections and accelerate progress to control the global epidemic in more than 50 countries, by partnering with governments to support sustainable, integrated, and country-led responses to HIV/AIDS.
Infect Dis, Pub Health
⊕ https://vfmat.ch/a57c

United Surgeons for Children (USFC)
Pursues greater health and opportunity for children in the most neglected pockets of the world, with a specific focus on and expertise in surgery.
Anesth, CT Surg, Neonat, Neurosurg, OB-GYN, Peds, Radiol, Surg
⊕ https://vfmat.ch/3b4c

University of New Mexico School of Medicine: Project Echo
Seeks to improve health outcomes worldwide through the use of a technology called telementoring, a guided-practice model in which the participating clinician retains responsibility for managing the patient.
General, Infect Dis, MF Med, OB-GYN, Path, Peds
⊕ https://vfmat.ch/6c9a

University of Washington: The International Training and Education Center for Health (I-TECH)
Works with local partners to develop skilled healthcare workers and strong national health systems in resource-limited countries.
Infect Dis, Pub Health
⊕ https://vfmat.ch/642f

USAID: African Strategies for Health
Identifies and advocates for best practices, enhancing technical capacity of African regional institutions, and engaging African stakeholders to address health issues in a sustainable manner.
All-Immu, Infect Dis, OB-GYN, Peds
⊕ https://vfmat.ch/c272

USAID: Global Health Supply Chain Program
Combines 8 complementary projects working globally to achieve stronger, more resilient health supply chains.
Infect Dis, Logist-Op, Pub Health
⊕ https://vfmat.ch/115f

USAID: Health Policy Initiative
Provides field-level programming in health policy development and implementation.
General, Infect Dis, MF Med, OB-GYN, Peds
⊕ https://vfmat.ch/8f84

USAID: Human Resources for Health 2030 (HRH2030)
Helps low- and middle-income countries develop the health workforce needed to prevent maternal and child deaths, support the goals of Family Planning 2020, control the HIV/AIDS epidemic, and protect communities from infectious diseases.
Logist-Op
⊕ https://vfmat.ch/9ea8

USAID: Leadership, Management and Governance Project
Improves leadership, management, and governance practices to strengthen health systems and improve health for all, including vulnerable populations worldwide.
Logist-Op
⊕ https://vfmat.ch/d35e

Vision Outreach International
Advocates for helping the blind in underserved regions of the world and empowers the poor through sight restoration.
Ophth-Opt
⊕ https://vfmat.ch/9721

Vitamin Angels
Helps at-risk populations in need—specifically pregnant women, new mothers, and children under age 5—to gain access to life-changing vitamins and minerals.
General, Nutr
⊕ https://vfmat.ch/7da1

Voices for a Malaria-Free Future
Seeks to expand national movements of private- and public-sector leaders to mobilize political and popular support for malaria control.
Infect Dis, Path
⊕ https://vfmat.ch/4213

West African Health Organization
Aims to attain high standards and protection of health of the people in West Africa through harmonization of policies of the member states to combat health problems.
Infect Dis, MF Med, OB-GYN
⊕ https://vfmat.ch/7363

Wisconsin Medical Project
Provides humanitarian aid, including donated medical equipment and supplies, to hospitals and clinics in areas of great need.
Logist-Op
⊕ https://vfmat.ch/ef3b

World Blind Union (WBU)
Represents those experiencing blindness, speaking to governments and international bodies on issues concerning visual impairments.
Ophth-Opt
⊕ https://vfmat.ch/2bd3

World Federation of Hemophilia (WFH)
Aims to improve and sustain care for people with inherited bleeding disorders by pursuing long-term relationships with individuals and organizations who share the values of WFH's development model.
Heme-Onc
⊕ https://vfmat.ch/5121

World Health Organization, The (WHO)
The United Nations' agency for health provides leadership on global health matters, shapes the health research agenda, sets norms and standards, articulates evidence-based policy options, provides technical support and

monitoring to countries, and assesses health trends.
ER Med, General, Infect Dis, Logist-Op, MF Med, OB-GYN, Peds, Psych, Pub Health
⊕ https://vfmat.ch/c476

World Medical Relief
Facilitates the distribution of surplus medical resources where they are needed.
Logist-Op
⊕ https://vfmat.ch/72dc

Ivory Coast

Healthcare Facilities

Centre Hospitalier Régional d'Abengourou
Abengourou, Comoé, Ivory Coast
⊕ https://vfmat.ch/18c4

Centre Hospitalier Régional d'Odiennê
Odiennê, Denguélé, Ivory Coast
⊕ https://vfmat.ch/de1f

Centre Hospitalier Régional Daloa
Daloa, Sassandra-Marahoué, Ivory Coast
⊕ https://vfmat.ch/155a

Centre Hospitalier Régional de Divo
Dougako, Gôh-Djiboua, Ivory Coast
⊕ https://vfmat.ch/a638

Centre Hospitalier Régional de Gagnoa (CHR)
Barouhio, Gôh-Djiboua, Ivory Coast
⊕ https://vfmat.ch/1b26

Centre Hospitalier Régional de Guiglo
Guiglo, Montagnes, Ivory Coast
⊕ https://vfmat.ch/7311

Centre Hospitalier Régional de Man
Gbapleu, Montagnes, Ivory Coast
⊕ https://vfmat.ch/a72f

Centre Hospitalier Régional de San-Pedro
Poro, Bas-Sassandra, Ivory Coast
⊕ https://vfmat.ch/ab6d

Centre Hospitalier Régional Dimbokro
Dimbokro, Lacs, Ivory Coast
⊕ https://vfmat.ch/46e4

Centre Hospitalier Régional Yamoussoukro
Nzuessi, Yamoussoukro, Ivory Coast
⊕ https://vfmat.ch/d781

Centre Hospitalier Universitaire d'Angré (CHU d'Angré)
Djibi, Abidjan, Ivory Coast
⊕ https://vfmat.ch/6654

Centre Hospitalier Universitaire (CHU de Bouaké)
Kodia Kofikro, Vallée du Bandama, Ivory Coast
⊕ https://vfmat.ch/ae6c

Centre Hospitalier Universitaire de Cocody (CHU de Cocody)
Cocody, Abidjan, Ivory Coast
⊕ https://vfmat.ch/f8ce

Centre Hospitalier Universitaire (CHU de Treichville)
Treichville, Abidjan, Ivory Coast
⊕ https://vfmat.ch/7f66

Centre Hospitalier Universitaire de Yopougon (CHU de Yopougon)
Yopougon, Abidjan, Ivory Coast
⊕ https://vfmat.ch/8672

Clinique Medicale Le Grand Centre
Abidjan, Ivory Coast
https://vfmat.ch/fvqr

Hôpital Général d'Abobo – Nord Houphouet Boigny
Abidjan, Abidjan, Ivory Coast
⊕ https://vfmat.ch/z7g1

Hôpital d'Elibou
Ellibou-Badasso, Ivory Coast
⊕ https://vfmat.ch/6d89

Hôpital de Gbon
Gbon, Savanes, Ivory Coast
⊕ https://vfmat.ch/7dd6

Hôpital de Police du Plateau
Indénie, Abidjan, Ivory Coast
⊕ https://vfmat.ch/9f2c

Hôpital de Pétéyé
Pétéyé, Zanzan, Ivory Coast
⊕ https://vfmat.ch/9e2e

Hôpital des Soeurs Catholique (Don Orion)
Abenan, Abidjan, Ivory Coast
⊕ https://vfmat.ch/d16b

Hôpital Général d'Abobo
Abidjan, Abidjan, Ivory Coast
⊕ https://vfmat.ch/7f8d

Hôpital Général d'Adiaké
Adiaké, Comoé, Ivory Coast
⊕ https://vfmat.ch/6876

Hôpital Général d'Adjamé
Adjamé, Abidjan, Ivory Coast
⊕ https://vfmat.ch/75e9

Hôpital Général d'Agboville
Agboville, Lagunes, Ivory Coast
⊕ https://vfmat.ch/6483

Hôpital Général d'Alépé
Alépé, Lagunes, Ivory Coast
⊕ https://vfmat.ch/17f7

Hôpital Général d'Anyama
Anyama, Abidjan, Ivory Coast
⊕ https://vfmat.ch/e485

Hôpital Général d'Arrah
Arrah, Lacs, Ivory Coast
⊕ https://vfmat.ch/e8a6

Hôpital Général d'Azopé
Biasso, Lagunes, Ivory Coast
⊕ https://vfmat.ch/34e7

Hôpital Général d'Oumé
Gatazra, Gôh-Djiboua, Ivory Coast
⊕ https://vfmat.ch/dafb

Hôpital Général de Bangolo
Bangolo, Montagnes, Ivory Coast
⊕ https://vfmat.ch/679f

Hôpital Général de Bocanda
Bopli, Lacs, Ivory Coast
⊕ https://vfmat.ch/1612

Hôpital Général de Bonoua
Adihao, Comoé, Ivory Coast
⊕ https://vfmat.ch/cbae

Hôpital Général de Boundiali
Boundiali, Savanes, Ivory Coast
⊕ https://vfmat.ch/e969

Hôpital Général de Dabou
Dabou, Lagunes, Ivory Coast
⊕ https://vfmat.ch/ad2b

Hôpital Général de Doropo
Doropo, Ivory Coast
⊕ https://vfmat.ch/cd1b

Hôpital Général de Grand-Bassam
Grand-Bassam, Comoé, Ivory Coast
⊕ https://vfmat.ch/ca9b

Hôpital Général de Guitry
Guitry, Gôh-Djiboua, Ivory Coast
⊕ https://vfmat.ch/2dec

Hôpital Général de Katiola
Katiola, Vallée du Bandama, Ivory Coast
⊕ https://vfmat.ch/fd99

Hôpital Général de Kouibly
Kouibly, Montagnes, Ivory Coast
⊕ https://vfmat.ch/1695

Hôpital Général de Koumassi
Koumassi, Abidjan, Ivory Coast
⊕ https://vfmat.ch/bf32

Hôpital Général de Mankono
Magina, Woroba, Ivory Coast
⊕ https://vfmat.ch/33c4

Hôpital Général de Marcory
Poto-Poto, Abidjan, Ivory Coast
⊕ https://vfmat.ch/ccb8

Hôpital Général de Méagui
Méagui, Soubre, Ivory Coast
⊕ https://vfmat.ch/ad53

Hôpital Général de Port-Bouët
Port-Bouët, Abidjan, Ivory Coast
⊕ https://vfmat.ch/443c

Hôpital Général de Sassandra
Sassandra, Bas-Sassandra, Ivory Coast
⊕ https://vfmat.ch/af28

Hôpital Général de Soubre
Bazabré, Bas-Sassandra, Ivory Coast
⊕ https://vfmat.ch/72c1

Hôpital Général de Taabo
Kokoti-Kouamèkro, Lagunes, Ivory Coast
⊕ https://vfmat.ch/8d4c

Hôpital Général de Tabou
Kablaké, Bas-Sassandra, Ivory Coast
⊕ https://vfmat.ch/cbcd

Hôpital Général de Tiassalé
Niamoué, Lagunes, Ivory Coast
⊕ https://vfmat.ch/ea12

Hôpital Général de Treichville
Marcory, Abidjan, Ivory Coast
⊕ https://vfmat.ch/8bc2

Hôpital Général M'Bahiakro
Trakro, Lacs, Ivory Coast
⊕ https://vfmat.ch/3d51

Hôpital Général Yopougon-Attié
Yopougon, Abidjan, Ivory Coast
⊕ https://vfmat.ch/c94f

Hôpital Henriette Konan Bédié d'Abobo
Abobo, Abidjan, Ivory Coast
⊕ https://vfmat.ch/45cf

Hôpital Islamique de Daloa
Daloa, Sassandra-Marahoué, Ivory Coast
⊕ https://vfmat.ch/8f2d

Hôpital Militaire d'Abidjan (HMA)
Sonitra, Abidjan, Ivory Coast
⊕ https://vfmat.ch/1c8d

Hôpital Municipal de Vridi
Biétri, Abidjan, Ivory Coast
⊕ https://vfmat.ch/a9d6

Hôpital Mère-Enfant de Bingerville
Kouassi Kakou, Abidjan, Ivory Coast
⊕ https://vfmat.ch/cdab

Hôpital Psychiatrique de Bingerville
Kouassi Kakou, Abidjan, Ivory Coast
⊕ https://vfmat.ch/a9b5

Hôpital Psychiatrique de Bouaké
Bouaké, Vallée du Bandama, Ivory Coast
⊕ https://vfmat.ch/e1cd

Hôpital Saint Jean-Baptiste de Bôdô
Boussoukro, Lagunes, Ivory Coast
⊕ https://vfmat.ch/7a3e

Hôpital Saint-Joseph Moscati
Nzuessi, Yamoussoukro, Ivory Coast
⊕ https://vfmat.ch/d829

Hôpital Sainte-Camille
Kodia Kofikro, Vallée du Bandama, Ivory Coast
⊕ https://vfmat.ch/9119

PISAM
Abidjan, Abidjan, Ivory Coast
⊕ https://vfmat.ch/urta

Polyclinique Farah
Abidjan, Abidjan, Ivory Coast
⊕ https://vfmat.ch/pqcj

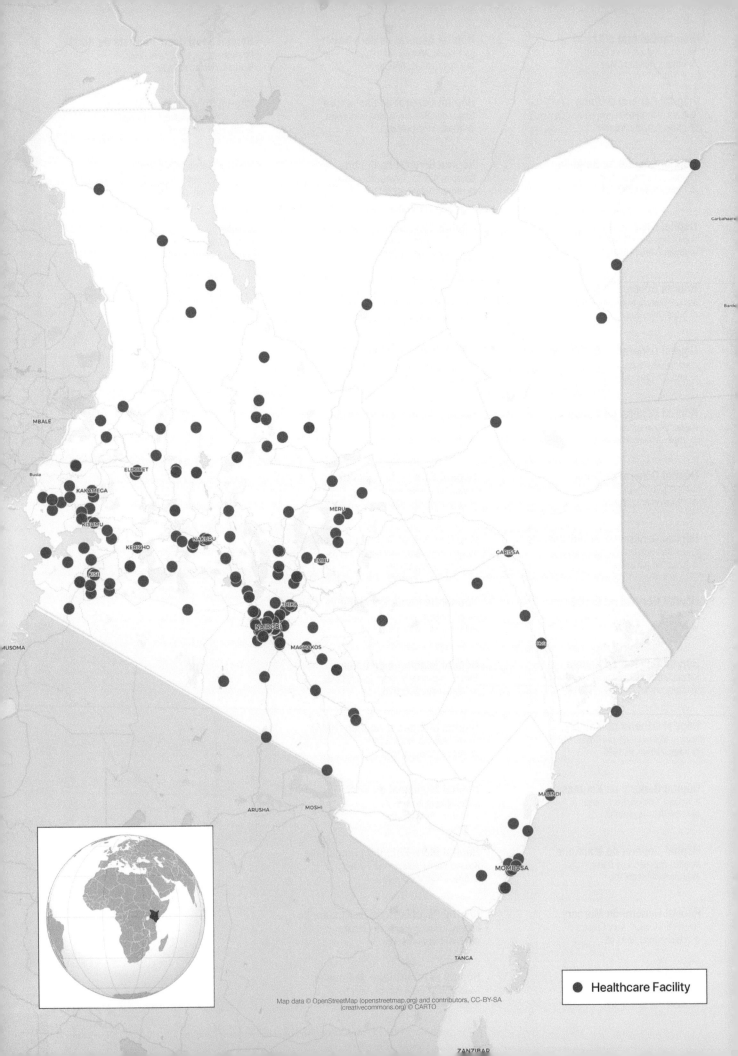

● Healthcare Facility

Kenya

Considered an archeological treasure trove—some of the earliest fossilized human remains were unearthed here along the shores of Lake Rudolf and in the Koobi Fora area—the Republic of Kenya is located in Eastern Africa and bordered by Ethiopia, Somalia, South Sudan, Tanzania, and Uganda. The population of about 54.7 million people is concentrated mostly in the west of the country, near the shores of Lake Victoria, the world's largest tropical lake, and also in the southeast, along the coast of the Indian Ocean. Nairobi, the capital, is home to almost 5 million people, and 28 percent of the population live in urban areas. Kenya is ethnically diverse, with Kikuyu, Luhya, Kalenjin, Luo, Kamba, Somali, Kisii, Mijikenda, Meru, Maasai, and Turkana groups making up the population. English and Kiswahili are the official languages, in addition to several other indigenous languages spoken throughout the country.

Formerly a colony of England, Kenya achieved independence in 1963. It is a major hub of economic activity and transport in Eastern Africa. While the country's economic growth is notable, development has been slowed by corruption and poor governance. As such, Kenya has one of the highest unemployment rates in the world at roughly 40 percent, with about 36 percent of the population living below the poverty line. A lack of infrastructure also precludes efforts to improve unemployment and poverty rates. Agriculture contributes to one-third of the Kenyan GDP, and nearly 75 percent of the Kenyan population is employed by the sector in some capacity.

One of Kenya's biggest health challenges is HIV/AIDS, with some of the highest prevalence rates in the world among adults. While deaths due to HIV/AIDS decreased by over 40 percent between 2009 and 2019, it is still the leading cause of death in the country. Other major causes of death include lower respiratory infections, diarrheal diseases, neonatal disorders, stroke, tuberculosis, ischemic heart disease, cirrhosis, malaria, diabetes, and meningitis. The risk factors that contribute most to death and disability include malnutrition, unsafe sex, insufficient water, sanitation, and hygiene, air pollution, high blood pressure, high body-mass index, high fasting plasma glucose, dietary risks, tobacco, alcohol, and drug use, and intimate partner violence. Of note, there is a very high risk of infectious diseases such as bacterial and protozoal diarrhea, hepatitis A, typhoid fever, malaria, dengue fever, rift valley fever, schistosomiasis, and rabies.

54.7M

Population

$1,838

GDP Per Capita

67 years

Life Expectancy

↑ Improving

16
Doctors/100k

Physician Density

140
Beds/100k

Hospital Bed Density

342
Deaths/100k

Maternal Mortality

Kenya

Nonprofit Organizations

143 LIFE Foundation
Seeks to educate and empower individuals living with malaria, TB, HIV/AIDS, STDs and other health disparities related to sexual health.
Infect Dis, MF Med
⊕ https://vfmat.ch/d59b

2020 MicroClinic Initiative
Aims to improve the health of mothers and their families in medically underserved communities of rural Kenya by improving access to health services, diagnostics and education.
Infect Dis, MF Med, Peds
⊕ https://vfmat.ch/d21e

A Broader View Volunteers
Provides developing countries around the world with significant volunteer programs that aid the neediest communities and forge a lasting bond between those volunteering and those they have helped.
Dent-OMFS, ER Med, Infect Dis, MF Med
⊕ https://vfmat.ch/3bec

Abt Associates
Seeks to improve the quality of life and economic well-being of people worldwide, while striving to meet and exceed the highest professional standards.
General, Logist-Op, MF Med, OB-GYN, Peds
⊕ https://vfmat.ch/cec2

Ace Africa
Aims to enable children and their communities to participate in and take responsibility for their own health, well-being, and development.
Infect Dis, Logist-Op, Nutr, Peds
⊕ https://vfmat.ch/df7f

Aceso Global
Provides strategic healthcare advisory services in low- and middle-income countries to design and deliver highly customized, evidence-based solutions that address the complex nature of healthcare systems, with a goal to strengthen and provide affordable, high-quality care to all.
Logist-Op, Pub Health
⊕ https://vfmat.ch/b3b7

Action Against Hunger
Aims to end life-threatening hunger for good through treating and preventing malnutrition across more than 45 countries.
Nutr
⊕ https://vfmat.ch/2dbc

Action For East African People
Acts on the needs of women and children living in East Africa while promoting the grassroots advancement of the East African community of Bloomington, Minnesota.

Dent-OMFS, General, OB-GYN, Pub Health
⊕ https://vfmat.ch/4db7

Addis Clinic, The
Uses telemedicine to care for people living in medically underserved areas, connects volunteer physicians with global health challenges, and provides support to local partner organizations and frontline health workers.
General, Infect Dis
⊕ https://vfmat.ch/f82f

ADOK – Alzheimers & Dementia Organization Kenya
Aims to create a society in which those living with dementia are supported and accepted, and can live peacefully in their communities without fear or prejudice.
Neuro, Psych, Rehab
⊕ https://vfmat.ch/4d22

Advance Family Planning
Aims to achieve global expansion and access to quality contraceptive information, services, and supplies through financial investment and political commitment.
General, MF Med, Pub Health
⊕ https://vfmat.ch/7478

Adventist Health International
Focuses on upgrading and managing mission hospitals by providing governance, consultation, and technical assistance to a number of affiliated Seventh-Day Adventist hospitals throughout Africa, Asia, and the Americas.
Dent-OMFS, General, Pub Health
⊕ https://vfmat.ch/16aa

Africa CDC
Aims to strengthen the capacity and capability of Africa's public health institutions and partnerships to detect and respond quickly and effectively to disease threats and outbreaks, based on data-driven interventions and programs.
Infect Dis, Logist-Op, Pub Health
⊕ https://vfmat.ch/339c

Africa Health Organisation
Leads collaborative efforts among countries in Africa and other partners to promote health equity, combat disease, and improve quality of life.
Logist-Op, Pub Health
⊕ https://vfmat.ch/b1c5

Africa Humanitarian Action (AHA)
Responds to crises, conflicts, and disasters in Africa, while informing and advising the international community, governments, civil society, and the private sector on humanitarian issues of concern to Africa. Supports institutional and organizational development efforts.
General, Infect Dis, MF Med, Nutr, OB-GYN
⊕ https://vfmat.ch/3ca2

Africa Indoor Residual Spraying Project (AIRS)

Aims to protect millions of people in Africa from malaria by spraying insecticide on walls, ceilings, and other indoor resting places of mosquitoes that transmit malaria.

Infect Dis

⊕ https://vfmat.ch/9bd1

Africa Inland Church (AIC) Litein Hospital

Strives to serve its community by providing quality, affordable, sustainable, and holistic health services, inspired by the Christian faith.

Crit-Care, Dent-OMFS, ENT, Endo, General, Heme-Onc, MF Med, Neonat, Neurosurg, OB-GYN, Ophth-Opt, Ortho, Palliative, Path, Ped Surg, Peds, Radiol, Rehab, Surg, Urol

⊕ https://vfmat.ch/b98c

Africa Inland Mission International

Seeks to establish churches and community development programs including healthcare projects, based in Christian ministry.

Anesth, Dent-OMFS, ER Med, General, MF Med, Medicine, OB-GYN, OB-GYN, Ophth-Opt, Ped Surg, Peds, Rehab

⊕ https://vfmat.ch/f2f6

Africa Relief and Community Development

Provides comprehensive relief and developmental aid to people of the African continent regardless of gender, race, or religion.

Nutr, Pub Health

⊕ https://vfmat.ch/6cd2

African Field Epidemiology Network (AFENET)

Strengthens field epidemiology and public health laboratory capacity to contribute effectively to addressing epidemics and other major public health problems in Africa.

All-Immu, Infect Dis, Path, Pub Health

⊕ https://vfmat.ch/df2e

African Mission Health Foundation

Aims to strengthen African mission hospitals by providing quality, compassionate care for the hurting and forgotten and helping improve Sub-Saharan Africa's health system.

Infect Dis, Neonat, OB-GYN, Peds, Surg

⊕ https://vfmat.ch/5b14

African Neurological Diseases Research Foundation

Operates two clinics in Kibera and Waithaka, two of Kenya's largest slum areas, to clinically assess patients and dispense medication to persons suffering from epilepsy.

Neuro

⊕ https://vfmat.ch/417e

Aga Khan Foundation Canada

Tackles the root causes of poverty, with a special focus on marginalized groups such as women and girls. Programs provide access to education and healthcare, food, and opportunity.

Pub Health

⊕ https://vfmat.ch/7f8b

Against Malaria Foundation

Helps protect people from malaria. Funds anti-malaria nets, specifically long-lasting insecticidal nets (LLINs), and works with distribution partners to ensure they are used. Tracks and reports on net use and malaria case data.

Infect Dis

⊕ https://vfmat.ch/337d

Age International

Helps older people living in some of the world's poorest places to have improved well-being and be treated with dignity through a variety of programs, including emergency relief and cataract surgery.

ER Med, Geri, Logist-Op, Nutr, Ophth-Opt, Palliative, Pub Health

⊕ https://vfmat.ch/c7e2

AIDS Healthcare Foundation

Provides cutting-edge HIV/AIDS medical care and advocacy to over one million people in 43 countries.

Infect Dis

⊕ https://vfmat.ch/b27c

Al Basar International Foundation

Works with local partners to treat preventable blindness, and helps set up sustainable infrastructure so local teams can save sight in their communities.

Ophth-Opt

⊕ https://vfmat.ch/a8b5

Al-Khair Foundation

Provides emergency relief and developmental support in some of the world's most impoverished areas.

Dent-OMFS, General, MF Med, Nutr, Peds

⊕ https://vfmat.ch/921d

Al-Mustafa Welfare Trust

Seeks to alleviate poverty and provides medical and social development assistance to the poor and vulnerable around the world.

General, Ophth-Opt

⊕ https://vfmat.ch/c5f4

Amara Charitable Trust

Seeks to provide clean, well-equipped schools and basic healthcare services for children of rural Kenya.

Pub Health

⊕ https://vfmat.ch/d82d

American Academy of Pediatrics

Seeks to attain optimal physical, mental, and social health and well-being for all infants, children, adolescents, and young adults.

Anesth, Crit-Care, Neonat, Ped Surg

⊕ https://vfmat.ch/9633

American Cancer Society

Saves lives, celebrates lives, and leads the fight for a world without cancer.

Heme-Onc, Logist-Op, Medicine, Rad-Onc, Radiol

⊕ https://vfmat.ch/f996

American Foundation for Children with AIDS

Provides critical comprehensive services to infected and affected HIV-positive children and their caregivers.

Infect Dis, Nutr, Pub Health

⊕ https://vfmat.ch/6258

American Heart Association (AHA)

Fights heart disease and stroke, striving to save and improve lives.

CV Med, Crit-Care, General, Heme-Onc, Medicine, Peds

⊕ https://vfmat.ch/4747

American International Health Alliance (AIHA)

Strengthens health systems and workforce capacity worldwide through locally driven, peer-to-peer institutional partnerships.

CV Med, ER Med, Infect Dis, Medicine, OB-GYN

⊕ https://vfmat.ch/69fd

American Society of Ophthalmic Plastic and Reconstruction Surgery Foundation

Advances training, research and patient care in the fields of aesthetic, plastic and reconstructive surgery specializing in the face, orbits, eyelids, and lacrimal system.

Ophth-Opt, Plast

⊕ https://vfmat.ch/9825

American Stroke Association

Works to prevent, treat, and beat stroke by funding innovative research, fighting for stronger public health policies, and providing lifesaving tools and information.

CV Med, Crit-Care, Heme-Onc, Medicine, Neuro, Pub Health, Pulm-Critic, Vasc Surg

⊕ https://vfmat.ch/746f

Americares

Saves lives and improves health for people affected by poverty or disaster and responds with life-changing medicine, medical supplies, and health programs

including domestic and global medical clinics.
All-Immu, ER Med, General, Infect Dis, MF Med, Nutr
⊕ https://vfmat.ch/e567

Americas Association for the Care of Children (AACC)
Reduces the impact of poverty in marginalized and underserved populations by empowering communities through compassionate and holistic education.
Dent-OMFS, MF Med, OB-GYN, Pub Health
⊕ https://vfmat.ch/19c5

AMREF Flying Doctors
Aims to deliver medical air transport and health services using the latest aviation and medical technology to ensure patients receive unrivaled care.
ER Med, Logist-Op
⊕ https://vfmat.ch/5d5e

Amref Health Africa
Serves millions of people across 35 countries in Sub-Saharan Africa, strengthening health systems, and training African health workers to respond to the continent's most critical health issues.
All-Immu, General, Infect Dis, Logist-Op, MF Med, OB-GYN, Path, Pub Health, Surg
⊕ https://vfmat.ch/6985

AMS – Africa Mission Services
Aims to facilitate community development and relief among the Maasai tribe, including providing healthcare and improving schools by hosting short-term volunteers.
General, MF Med, OB-GYN, Peds
⊕ https://vfmat.ch/eb55

Amsterdam Institute for Global Health and Development (AIGHD)
Provides sustainable solutions to major health problems across our planet by forging synergies among disciplines, healthcare delivery, research, and education.
Infect Dis
⊕ https://vfmat.ch/d73d

Amurtel
Aims to alleviate suffering and provide immediate and long-term relief to women and children in need, and to improve their overall quality of life.
⊕ https://vfmat.ch/2b19

Ananda Marga Universal Relief Team (AMURT) Kenya
Aims to improve the quality of life of poor and marginalized people by improving both the economic status of communities and healthcare through critical health interventions.
Dent-OMFS, ER Med, General, Infect Dis, MF Med, Ophth-Opt, Ortho, Path, Peds, Pub Health, Radiol, Rehab
⊕ https://vfmat.ch/55a7

Answer Africa
Seeks to provide Africa with critical health interventions and aims to eradicate malaria; also partnering to build a maternity wing at the Hearts Afire Mountain Hospital in Eldoret, Kenya.
Infect Dis, Logist-Op
⊕ https://vfmat.ch/57c5

AO Alliance
Builds solutions to lessen the burden of injuries in low- and middle-income countries, while enhancing the care of the injured to reduce human suffering, disability, and poverty.
Ortho, Surg
⊕ https://vfmat.ch/8cd5

Arms Around Africa Foundation
Supports children, empowers women, and helps young people to overcome poverty through talent promotion, education, good health, life skills development, entrepreneurship, and enhanced access to other resources for social and economic development.
General, Infect Dis, OB-GYN, Peds
⊕ https://vfmat.ch/ad98

ASE Foundation
Provides support for education and research to the community of healthcare providers and patients for whom cardiovascular ultrasound is essential.
CT Surg, CV Med, Radiol
⊕ https://vfmat.ch/bb57

Aslan Project, The
Seeks to elevate standards of pediatric cancer care and increase survival rates in limited-resource countries.
Anesth, Heme-Onc, Ped Surg, Peds, Psych, Rad-Onc, Rehab
⊕ https://vfmat.ch/e633

Assist International
Designs and implements humanitarian programs that build capacity, develop opportunities, and save lives around the world.
Infect Dis, Ped Surg, Peds
⊕ https://vfmat.ch/9a3b

Austrian Doctors
Stands for a life in dignity and takes care of the health of disadvantaged people. Helps all people regardless of gender, skin color, religion and sexual orientation.
General, Infect Dis, Medicine
⊕ https://vfmat.ch/e929

Basic Foundations
Supports local projects and organizations that seek to meet the basic human needs of others in their community.
ER Med, General, Peds, Rehab, Surg
⊕ https://vfmat.ch/c4be

Benjamin H. Josephson, MD Fund
Provides healthcare professionals with the financial resources necessary to deliver medical services for those in need throughout the world.
General, OB-GYN
⊕ https://vfmat.ch/6acc

BethanyKids
Transforms the lives of African children with surgical conditions and disabilities through pediatric surgery, rehabilitation, public education, spiritual ministry, and the training of health professionals.
Neurosurg, Nutr, Ortho, Ped Surg, Peds, Rehab, Surg
⊕ https://vfmat.ch/db4e

Beyond Fistula
Aims to help heal and rebuild the lives of women after the severe childbirth injury known as obstetric fistula.
MF Med, OB-GYN
⊕ https://vfmat.ch/c968

BFIRST – British Foundation for International Reconstructive Surgery & Training
Supports projects across the developing world to train surgeons in their local environment to effectively manage devastating injuries.
Anesth, Plast, Surg
⊕ https://vfmat.ch/ad4f

Bill & Melinda Gates Foundation
Focuses on global issues, such as poverty, health, and education, offering the opportunity to dramatically improve the quality of life for billions of people by building partnerships that bring together resources, expertise, and vision to identify issues, find answers, and drive change.
All-Immu, General, Infect Dis, MF Med, Neonat, OB-GYN, Pub Health
⊕ https://vfmat.ch/7cf2

Bless The Children
Aims to help abandoned and impoverished children by empowering them with health, shelter, and nutritional and educational support.
CT Surg, Dent-OMFS, General, Logist-Op, Nutr, Pub Health, Surg
⊕ https://vfmat.ch/f19d

Brain Project Africa
Provides the highest level of medical care, facilitates knowledge transfer, and donates the necessary medical equipment where it's most impactful.

Neuro, Neurosurg, Ortho
⊕ https://vfmat.ch/d4fd

Bread and Water for Africa UK
Aims to create better access to education, nutrition, and healthcare for some of Africa's most vulnerable children and their communities.
General, MF Med, Nutr
⊕ https://vfmat.ch/c855

Breast Cancer Support
Aims to save lives and end breast cancer forever in women and men through education, treatment, emotional assistance, and financial support.
Heme-Onc, Logist-Op, Pub Health, Rad-Onc, Radiol
⊕ https://vfmat.ch/cb78

Bridge of Life
Aims to strengthen healthcare globally through sustainable programs that prevent and treat chronic disease.
Logist-Op, Nephro, OB-GYN, Peds, Surg
⊕ https://vfmat.ch/5b68

Bridge to Health Medical and Dental
Seeks to provide healthcare to those who need it most, based on a philosophy of partnership, education, and community development. Strives to bring solutions to global health issues in underserved communities through clinical outreach and medical and dental training.
Dent-OMFS, General, Infect Dis, MF Med, OB-GYN, Ophth-Opt, Ortho, Pub Health, Radiol
⊕ https://vfmat.ch/bb2c

British Council for Prevention of Blindness (BCPB)
Funds research into blindness prevention and sight restoration in children and adults in low- and lower-middle-income countries.
Ophth-Opt
⊕ https://vfmat.ch/eaf4

BroadReach
Collaborates with governments, multinational health organizations, donors, and private-sector companies to effect healthcare reform and solve the world's biggest health challenges.
Logist-Op
⊕ https://vfmat.ch/7812

Cairdeas International Palliative Care Trust
Promotes and facilitates the provision of high-quality palliative care in the developing world, where such care is limited.
Palliative
⊕ https://vfmat.ch/35c4

Camillian Disaster Service (CADIS) International
Promotes the development of locally based health programs for disaster-stricken communities through compassionate and coordinated interventions.
General, Logist-Op, MF Med
⊕ https://vfmat.ch/5281

Canadian Network for International Surgery, The
Aims to improve maternal health, increase safety, and build local capacity in low-income countries by creating and providing surgical and midwifery courses, training domestically, and transferring skills.
Logist-Op, Surg
⊕ https://vfmat.ch/86ff

Canadian Vision Care
Consists of eye healthcare professionals who donate time and resources to the development of vision care in the developing world.
Ophth-Opt
⊕ https://vfmat.ch/3a38

CARE
Works around the globe to save lives, defeat poverty, and achieve social justice.
ER Med, General
⊕ https://vfmat.ch/7232

Care For a Child's Heart
To facilitate and coordinate medical support programs for marginalized children affected by heart disease, so as to restore health, hope, and happiness.
CT Surg, Logist-Op, Ped Surg
⊕ https://vfmat.ch/221b

Care for AIDS
Aims to empower people to live a life beyond AIDS by carrying out programs centered on physical, social, economic, and spiritual support, based in Christian ministry.
Infect Dis, Pub Health
⊕ https://vfmat.ch/79cf

Care Highway International
Supports children's intellectual, social, and emotional development, while also providing healthcare services such as vaccines, antiparasitics, and dental and vision care.
Dent-OMFS, Dent-OMFS, General, Medicine, Ophth-Opt, Ophth-Opt, Pub Health
⊕ https://vfmat.ch/4357

Care Love Charity Foundation
Works to address poverty by providing programs in education, affordable healthcare, and social economic empowerment to poor and vulnerable communities.
⊕ https://vfmat.ch/d91a

Carolina for Kibera
Offers affordable primary healthcare, educational and work readiness services. and girls' empowerment in Kibera, Nairobi, and other informal settlements globally.
General, Infect Dis, MF Med, Nutr, OB-GYN, Peds
⊕ https://vfmat.ch/ac84

Carter Center, The
Seeks to prevent and resolve conflicts, enhance freedom and democracy, and improve health, while remaining committed to human rights and the alleviation of human suffering.
Infect Dis, MF Med, Ophth-Opt
⊕ https://vfmat.ch/6556

Catholic Medical Mission Board (CMMB)
Works in partnership globally to deliver locally sustainable, quality health solutions to women, children, and their communities.
General, MF Med, Peds
⊕ https://vfmat.ch/9498

Catholic Organization for Relief & Development Aid (CORDAID)
Provides humanitarian assistance and creates opportunities to improve security, healthcare, education, and inclusive economic growth in fragile and conflict-affected areas.
ER Med, Infect Dis, MF Med, OB-GYN, Peds, Psych
⊕ https://vfmat.ch/8ae5

Catholic World Mission
Works to rebuild communities worldwide by helping to alleviate poverty and empower underserved areas, while spreading the message of the Catholic Church.
ER Med, General, Nutr, Peds
⊕ https://vfmat.ch/7b5f

cbm New Zealand
Inspired by the Christian faith, aims to improve the quality of life for those living with the double disadvantage of poverty and disability.
Crit-Care, Infect Dis, Logist-Op, Nutr, OB-GYN, Ophth-Opt, Ortho, Psych, Rehab, Surg
⊕ https://vfmat.ch/c14b

Center for Health and Hope
Supports and advocates for persons infected and affected by HIV/AIDS with programs of education, prevention, care, and treatment.
Pub Health
⊕ https://vfmat.ch/a52e

Center for Private Sector Health Initiatives
Aims to improve the health and well-being of people in developing countries by facilitating partnerships between the public and private sectors.
Infect Dis, Nutr, Peds
⊕ https://vfmat.ch/b198

Centers of Hope Missions International
Sharing the love of Christ through feeding centers, churches, medical mission trips, and orphan care.
General
⊕ https://vfmat.ch/a9ac

CFW Shops (A Project of Healthstore Foundation)
Improves access to essential drugs, basic healthcare, and prevention services for children and families in the developing world.
Logist-Op
⊕ https://vfmat.ch/222d

Chain of Hope
Provides lifesaving heart operations for children around the world and supports the development of cardiac services in numerous developing and war-torn countries.
Anesth, CT Surg, CV Med, Crit-Care, Ped Surg, Peds, Pulm-Critic, Surg
⊕ https://vfmat.ch/1b1b

Challenge Africa
Creates sustainable initiatives that benefit whole communities within rural Africa.
Infect Dis, Logist-Op, Nutr, Peds
⊕ https://vfmat.ch/c8cd

Challenge Initiative, The
Seeks to rapidly and sustainably scale up proven reproductive health solutions among the urban poor.
MF Med, OB-GYN, Peds
⊕ https://vfmat.ch/2f77

Charity Medical Hospital
Offers comprehensive medical, dental, optical, and rehabilitation services as a leading healthcare provider in East and Central Africa.
Crit-Care, Dent-OMFS, MF Med, OB-GYN, Path, Peds, Radiol, Rehab, Surg
⊕ https://vfmat.ch/51f2

CharityVision International
Focuses on restoring curable sight impairment worldwide by empowering local physicians and creating sustainable solutions.
Logist-Op, Ophth-Opt, Surg
⊕ https://vfmat.ch/6231

ChildFund Australia
Works to reduce poverty for children in many of the world's most disadvantaged communities.
ER Med, General, Peds
⊕ https://vfmat.ch/13df

Children & Charity International
Puts people first by providing education, leadership, and nutrition programs along with mentoring and healthcare support services to children, youth, and families.
Nutr, Peds
⊕ https://vfmat.ch/6538

Children of War Foundation
Delivers access to global health and education to communities affected by poverty, war, natural disaster, climate change, and migration challenges.
ER Med, General, Logist-Op, Peds, Surg
⊕ https://vfmat.ch/de51

Children Sickle Cell Foundation Kenya
Provides food, medicine, and support for children and adults with sickle cell disease and their caregivers, and advocates to end prejudice.
Heme-Onc, Peds
⊕ https://vfmat.ch/2e84

Children's Bridge Foundation
Supports health and education programs for orphaned and abandoned children in the developing world.
Infect Dis, Nutr, Peds, Surg
⊕ https://vfmat.ch/6486

Children's of Alabama: Global Surgery Program
Provides the finest pediatric health services to all children in an environment that fosters excellence in research and medical education.
CT Surg, CV Med, Crit-Care, Heme-Onc, Neurosurg, Ortho, Ped Surg, Peds, Surg, Urol
⊕ https://vfmat.ch/ff58

Christian Aid Ministries
Strives to be a trustworthy and efficient channel for Amish, Mennonite, and other conservative Anabaptist groups and individuals to minister to physical and spiritual needs around the world.
CT Surg, ER Med, Logist-Op, Ortho, Pub Health
⊕ https://vfmat.ch/7b33

Christian Blind Mission (CBM)
Aims to improve the quality of life of persons with disabilities in the poorest countries, addressing poverty as a cause and a consequence of disability, and working in partnership to create a society for all.
ENT, General, Infect Dis, OB-GYN, Ophth-Opt, Ortho, Peds, Psych, Rehab, Surg
⊕ https://vfmat.ch/3824

Christian Connections for International Health (CCIH)
Promotes global health and wholeness from a Christian perspective.
All-Immu, General, Infect Dis, MF Med, Neonat, OB-GYN, Psych
⊕ https://vfmat.ch/fa5d

Christian Health Service Corps
Brings Christian doctors, health professionals, and health educators committed to serving the poor to places that otherwise have little or no access to healthcare.
Anesth, Dent-OMFS, General, Medicine, Peds, Surg
⊕ https://vfmat.ch/da57

Christian Medical & Dental Associations
Based in Christian ministry, deploys medical and dental teams to underserved communities to provide vital healthcare.
Anesth, Dent-OMFS, ER Med, General, Medicine, OB-GYN, Ophth-Opt, Peds, Pub Health, Radiol, Rehab, Surg
⊕ https://vfmat.ch/921c

Christian Medical Fellowship of Kenya – CMF-Kenya
Based in Christian ministry, coordinates a network of Christian healthcare professionals and students for missions and outreach to provide medical and dental care.
Dent-OMFS, General, Logist-Op
⊕ https://vfmat.ch/cc76

Clinton Health Access Initiative (CHAI)
Aims to save lives and reduce the burden of disease in low- and middle-income countries. Works with partners to strengthen the capabilities of governments and the private sector to create and sustain high-quality health systems.
General, Heme-Onc, Infect Dis, Logist-Op, MF Med, Medicine, Neonat, Nutr, OB-GYN, Path, Peds, Rad-Onc
⊕ https://vfmat.ch/9ed7

Coast General Teaching And Referral Hospital
Aims to provide highly specialized, quality referral healthcare, research, and training to patients and healthcare staff, reaching the population of seven districts in Coast Province, Kenya.
CT Surg, Crit-Care, Crit-Care, Dent-OMFS, ER Med, ER Med, Heme-Onc, Heme-Onc, Infect Dis, Neuro, Neurosurg, Nutr, Ortho, Palliative, Path, Peds, Plast, Psych, Pub Health, Surg
⊕ https://vfmat.ch/db12

Columbia University: Columbia Office of Global Surgery (COGS)
Helps to increase access to safe and affordable surgical care, as a means to reduce health disparities and the global burden of disease.

Anesth, CT Surg, Crit-Care, Dent-OMFS, ENT, ER Med, Infect Dis, MF Med, Neurosurg, OB-GYN, Ophth-Opt, Ortho, Ped Surg, Plast, Plast, Pub Health, Surg, Urol

⊕ https://vfmat.ch/4349

Columbia University: Global Mental Health Programs

Pioneers research initiatives, promotes mental health, and aims to reduce the burden of mental illness worldwide.

Psych

⊕ https://vfmat.ch/c5cd

Columbia Vagelos College of Physicians and Surgeons Programs in Global Health

Harnesses the expertise of the medical school to improve health worldwide by training global health leaders, building capacity through interdisciplinary education and training programs, and addressing unmet health needs through research and application.

CV Med, Derm, Genetics, Heme-Onc, Infect Dis, Medicine, OB-GYN, Ophth-Opt, Peds, Psych, Pub Health, Pulm-Critic, Surg

⊕ https://vfmat.ch/a9e5

Combat Blindness International

Works to eliminate preventable blindness worldwide by providing sustainable, equitable solutions for sight through partnerships and innovation.

Ophth-Opt

⊕ https://vfmat.ch/28ad

Compassionate Eye

Aims to support the social good by supplying infrastructure and personnel for sanitation, education, medical care, small business, and job training.

General, Infect Dis, MF Med, OB-GYN, Peds

⊕ https://vfmat.ch/1915

Concern Worldwide

Seeks to permanently transform the lives of people living in extreme poverty, tackling its root causes, and building resilience.

Logist-Op, MF Med, Nutr, OB-GYN

⊕ https://vfmat.ch/77e9

Connect with a Child

Provides free medical care, food and shoes, and builds orphanages, schools and wells, inspired by the Christian faith.

General, Infect Dis

⊕ https://vfmat.ch/4817

Core Group

Aims to improve and expand community health practices for underserved populations, especially women and children, through collaborative action and learning.

General, Infect Dis, MF Med, Medicine, OB-GYN, Peds, Pub Health

⊕ https://vfmat.ch/9de3

Covenant Medicine Outreach

Inspired by the Christian faith, provides medical care for those less fortunate.

General

⊕ https://vfmat.ch/769a

COVID-19 Clinical Research Coalition

Advocates and collaborates for the advancement of COVID-19 research driven by the needs of low-resource settings, and works for equitable access to solutions to the pandemic.

All-Immu, Infect-Dis, MF Med, Path, Pub Health

⊕ https://vfmat.ch/d1f4

Cross Catholic Outreach

Mobilizes the global Catholic Church to transform impoverished communities through the provision of food, water, housing, education, orphan support, medical care, microenterprise, and disaster relief.

All-Immu, General, Nutr, OB-GYN, Rehab

⊕ https://vfmat.ch/22f4

Curamericas Global

Partners with communities abroad to save the lives of mothers and children by providing health services and education.

General, Infect Dis, MF Med, OB-GYN, Peds, Pub Health

⊕ https://vfmat.ch/286b

CURE

Operates charitable hospitals and programs in underserved countries worldwide, where patients receive surgical treatment, based in Christian ministry.

Anesth, Neurosurg, Ortho, Ped Surg, Peds, Rehab, Surg

⊕ https://vfmat.ch/aa16

CURE Children's Hospital of Zimbabwe

Heals children living with disabilities such as clubfoot, bowed legs, cleft lips, untreated burns, and hydrocephalus.

ENT, Neurosurg, Ortho, Peds, Plast

⊕ https://vfmat.ch/473c

CureCervicalCancer

Focuses on the early detection and prevention of cervical cancer around the globe for the women who need it most.

Heme-Onc, OB-GYN

⊕ https://vfmat.ch/ace1

DDC Foundation (Dutche Dental Care)

Provides dental care in schools and operates two dental clinics.

Dent-OMFS

⊕ https://vfmat.ch/b7a1

Dentaid

Seeks to treat, equip, train, and educate people in need of dental care.

Dent-OMFS

⊕ https://vfmat.ch/a183

Dental Hope for Children

Seeks to provide dental services to children in underserved areas, based in Christian ministry.

Dent-OMFS

⊕ https://vfmat.ch/1426

Developing Country NGO Delegation: Global Fund to Fight AIDS, TB & Malaria

Works to strengthen the engagement of civil society actors and organizations in developing countries to build a world in which AIDS, TB, and malaria are no longer global, public health, and human rights threats.

Infect Dis, Pub Health

⊕ https://vfmat.ch/3149

Direct Relief

Improves the health and lives of people affected by poverty or emergency situations by mobilizing and providing essential medical resources needed for their care.

ER Med, Logist-Op

⊕ https://vfmat.ch/58e5

Direct Relief of Poverty & Sickness Foundation (DROPS)

This volunteer-led organization uses all donations for direct relief of poverty and illness through initiatives in healthcare education, improving healthcare systems, and providing essential medical help to children and aged people in need.

Dent-OMFS, General, Ophth-Opt

⊕ https://vfmat.ch/af95

DKT INTERNATIONAL INC

Seeks to provide couples with affordable and safe options for family planning and HIV/AIDS prevention through dynamic social marketing.

General, Surg

⊕ https://vfmat.ch/b3a7

Doctors Without Borders/Médecins Sans Frontières (MSF)

Responds to emergencies and provides lifesaving medical care where needed most, including during disasters, conflicts, and epidemics.

Anesth, Crit-Care, ER Med, General, Infect Dis, Nutr, OB-GYN, Ped Surg, Peds, Psych, Pub Health, Surg

⊕ https://vfmat.ch/f363

Dream Sant'Egidio
Seeks to counter HIV/AIDS in Africa by eliminating the transmission of HIV from mother to child, with a focus on women because of the importance of their role in the community.
Infect Dis, MF Med, Neonat, OB-GYN, Path, Peds
⊕ https://vfmat.ch/f466

Drugs for Neglected Diseases Initiative
Develops lifesaving medicines for people with neglected diseases around the world, having developed eight treatments for five deadly diseases and saved millions of lives since 2003.
Infect Dis, Pub Health
⊕ https://vfmat.ch/969c

Duke University: Global Health Institute
Sparks innovation in global health research and education, and brings together knowledge and resources to address the most important global health issues of our time.
All-Immu, Infect Dis, MF Med, OB-GYN, Pub Health
⊕ https://vfmat.ch/c4cd

Eating Stones Fund
Aims to create healthy families and communities, and decrease the prevalence of orphans, in Kenya through the provision of holistic healthcare services.
General, Logist-Op, OB-GYN, Rehab
⊕ https://vfmat.ch/41e2

Edelvale Trust
Provides the community with affordable health services.
Anesth, General, MF Med, OB-GYN, Peds, Surg
⊕ https://vfmat.ch/9c48

Effect: Hope (The Leprosy Mission Canada)
Connects like-minded Canadians to people suffering in isolation from debilitating, neglected tropical diseases such as leprosy, lymphatic filariasis, and Buruli ulcer.
General, Infect Dis
⊕ https://vfmat.ch/f12a

Egmont Trust, The
Works with partner organizations in Sub-Saharan Africa, making grants to help vulnerable children cope with the impact of HIV/AIDS on families and communities.
General, Infect Dis, OB-GYN, Peds
⊕ https://vfmat.ch/57a9

Elizabeth Glaser Pediatric AIDS Foundation
Seeks to end global pediatric HIV/AIDS through prevention and treatment programs, research, and advocacy.
Infect Dis, Nutr, OB-GYN, Peds
⊕ https://vfmat.ch/d6ec

Elton John AIDS Foundation
Seeks to address and overcome the stigma, discrimination, and neglect that prevents ending AIDS by funding local experts to challenge discrimination, prevent infections, and provide treatment.
Infect Dis, Pub Health
⊕ https://vfmat.ch/9d31

END Fund, The
Aims to control and eliminate the most prevalent neglected diseases among the world's poorest and most vulnerable people.
Infect Dis
⊕ https://vfmat.ch/2614

EngenderHealth
Works to implement high-quality, gender-equitable programs that advance sexual and reproductive health and rights.
General, MF Med, OB-GYN, Peds
⊕ https://vfmat.ch/1cb2

Episcopal Relief & Development
Provides relief in times of disaster and promotes sustainable development by identifying and addressing the root causes of suffering.

Infect Dis, MF Med, Neonat, Nutr, Peds
⊕ https://vfmat.ch/7cfa

eRanger
Provides sustainable solutions to transportation and medical provision such as ambulances and mobile clinics in developing countries.
ER Med, General, Logist-Op
⊕ https://vfmat.ch/4c18

Every Infant matters
Focuses on the health of infants, girls, and women, including nutrition, blindness prevention, vaccination, and gender discrimination, in marginalized and poor communities.
Ophth-Opt, Peds, Pub Health
⊕ https://vfmat.ch/4d6a

Evidence Action
Aims to be a world leader in scaling evidence-based and cost-effective programs to reduce the burden of poverty.
General, Infect Dis
⊕ https://vfmat.ch/94b6

Evidence Project, The
Improves family-planning policies, programs, and practices through the strategic generation, translation, and use of evidence.
General, MF Med
⊕ https://vfmat.ch/f9e7

Eye Foundation of America
Works toward a world without childhood blindness.
Ophth-Opt
⊕ https://vfmat.ch/a7eb

Eye Mantra Foundation / Charitable Hospital
Provides affordable eye care and treatment for people living in poverty.
Ophth-Opt, Surg
⊕ https://vfmat.ch/48d2

Faith Aid
Provides support for underserved children, including prevention, testing, treatment, access to care, and wellness programs, inspired by the Christian faith.
General, Infect Dis, Ped Surg, Peds
⊕ https://vfmat.ch/38eb

Faraja Cancer Support
Offers cancer patients and their caregivers information, advice, counseling, and complementary therapies to make their cancer journey more manageable.
Psych
⊕ https://vfmat.ch/37a5

Fertility Education & Medical Management (FEMM)
Aims to make knowledge-based reproductive health accessible to all women and enables them to be informed partners in the choice and delivery of their medical care and services.
MF Med, OB-GYN
⊕ https://vfmat.ch/e8b2

Finn Church Aid
Supports people in the most vulnerable situations within fragile and disaster-affected regions in three thematic priority areas: right to peace, livelihood, and education.
ER Med, Psych, Pub Health
⊕ https://vfmat.ch/9623

Fistula Foundation
Aims to engage the support of people worldwide who are eager to see the day that no woman suffers from obstetric fistula. Raises and directs funds to doctors and hospitals providing life-transforming surgery to women in need.
OB-GYN
⊕ https://vfmat.ch/e958

For Hearts and Souls
Provides medical outreach and care for children through heart-related work, such

as diagnosing heart problems and performing heart-saving surgeries.
Anesth, CT Surg, CV Med, Crit-Care, Peds, Pulm-Critic
⊕ https://vfmat.ch/a162

Forgotten International, The
Develops programs that alleviate poverty and the suffering of impoverished women and children in both the United States and worldwide.
Logist-Op, Nutr, OB-GYN, Peds, Pub Health
⊕ https://vfmat.ch/26f3

Foundation For International Education In Neurological Surgery (FIENS), The
Provides hands-on training and education to neurosurgeons around the world.
Neuro, Neurosurg, Surg
⊕ https://vfmat.ch/bab8

Foundation for Peace
Works with local communities to build schools, medical clinics, water purification facilities, churches, and more.
General, Infect Dis
⊕ https://vfmat.ch/e9f7

Fracarita International
Provides support and services in the fields of mental healthcare, care for people with a disability, and education.
Psych, Rehab
⊕ https://vfmat.ch/8d3c

Fred Hollows Foundation, The
Works toward a world in which no person is needlessly blind or vision impaired.
Ophth-Opt, Pub Health, Surg
⊕ https://vfmat.ch/73e5

Freedom From Fistula
Helps women and girls who are injured and left incontinent following prolonged, obstructed childbirth by providing free surgical repairs for patients already suffering with obstetric fistula, as well as maternity care to prevent these fistulas from happening at all.
MF Med, OB-GYN, Peds
⊕ https://vfmat.ch/6e11

Friends of Maua Methodist Hospital
Assists the Maua Methodist Hospital in providing life-changing medical services and outreach programs.
Dent-OMFS, General, OB-GYN, Ophth-Opt, Peds
⊕ https://vfmat.ch/fcf2

Friends of UNFPA
Promotes the health, dignity, and rights of women and girls around the world by supporting the lifesaving work of UNFPA, the United Nations' reproductive health and rights agency, through education, advocacy, and fundraising.
MF Med, OB-GYN
⊕ https://vfmat.ch/2a3a

Future Health Africa
Strives for sustainable improvement in the health and well-being of people in low- to middle-income countries.
Anesth, ER Med, MF Med, Surg
⊕ https://vfmat.ch/37d2

Gender Violence Recovery Centre
Seeks to ensure quality and comprehensive treatment, recovery, rehabilitation, and reintegration of survivors of sexual and gender-based violence.
General, OB-GYN, Rehab
⊕ https://vfmat.ch/ae39

German Doctors
Conducts voluntary medical work in developing countries and brings help where misery is part of everyday life.
General, Infect Dis, Medicine
⊕ https://vfmat.ch/21ad

Gift of Sight
Works to eradicate preventable blindness by fostering sustainable healthcare delivery in underserved global communities.
Ophth-Opt
⊕ https://vfmat.ch/fdd7

GIVE International
Partners with local organizations on projects that focus on healthcare, child and youth development, education, and sustainable development.
General, Infect Dis, MF Med
⊕ https://vfmat.ch/58d3

Give Us Wings
Supports people in poverty as they transform their lives and become self-sufficient through access to healthcare, education, and economic opportunities.
General, Logist-Op
⊕ https://vfmat.ch/9483

Global Alliance to Prevent Prematurity And Stillbirth (GAPPS)
Seeks to improve birth outcomes worldwide by reducing the burden of premature birth and stillbirth.
All-Immu, Infect Dis, MF Med, Neonat, Neonat, OB-GYN
⊕ https://vfmat.ch/3f74

Global Blood Fund
Delivers grants, equipment, and training to over 50 countries in Africa, Asia, Eastern Europe, the Middle East, Latin America and the Caribbean.
Pub Health
⊕ https://vfmat.ch/6377

Global Civic Sharing
Aims to support our neighbors' self-reliance and realize the sustainable development.
Nutr, Peds, Pub Health
⊕ https://vfmat.ch/d7ab

Global Clubfoot Initiative (GCI)
Promotes and resources the treatment of children with clubfoot in developing countries using the Ponseti technique.
Ortho, Ped Surg
⊕ https://vfmat.ch/f229

Global Dental Relief
Brings free dental care to impoverished children in partnership with local organizations, and delivers treatment and preventive care in dental clinics that serve children in schools and remote villages.
Dent-OMFS
⊕ https://vfmat.ch/29b6

Global Emergency Care Skills
Aims to provide high-quality emergency medical training to healthcare professionals in countries where emergency medicine is a developing specialty.
ER Med
⊕ https://vfmat.ch/1827

Global Eye Mission
Strives to bring hope and healing to the lives of those living in underserved regions of the world by providing high-quality eye care to help the blind see, and improving the quality of life for individuals and entire communities.
Ophth-Opt, Surg
⊕ https://vfmat.ch/197e

Global Medical and Surgical Teams
Provides cleft lip and palate surgery for patients in underserved areas by providing surgical care free of charge to children with cleft lip and palate deformities. Works through medical and surgical missions, education, training, technology, and donor relationships to provide specialized medical and surgical care.
Anesth, Dent-OMFS, ENT, Ped Surg, Plast, Surg
⊕ https://vfmat.ch/6d3e

Global Medical Missions
Organizes medical missions and partners with local medical organizations, usually hospitals or health systems, in fulfilling their mission of reaching their

community's health needs in developing countries by providing needed medical care and screening to those underserved.
General
⊕ https://vfmat.ch/8d73

Global Ministries – The United Methodist Church
As the worldwide mission and development agency of The United Methodist Church, Global Ministries works with more than 300 hospitals and clinics around the world through its Global Health Unit.
Anesth, CT Surg, CV Med, Crit-Care, Dent-OMFS, Derm, ER Med, GI, General, Infect Dis, Logist-Op, MF Med, Medicine, Neonat, Nephro, Nutr, OB-GYN, Ophth-Opt, Ortho, Palliative, Peds, Pod, Psych, Pub Health, Rehab, Rheum, Surg, Urol
⊕ https://vfmat.ch/1723

Global Mission Partners, Inc.
Provides opportunities for short-term global medical mission opportunities, along with evangelism and construction missions, to serve persons who have little or no access to healthcare, adequate housing, and community outreach.
Dent-OMFS, General, Geri, Palliative, Psych
⊕ https://vfmat.ch/7db4

Global Network for Women and Children's Health Research
Aims to improve maternal and child health outcomes and building health research capacity in resource-poor settings by testing cost-effective, sustainable interventions that provide guidance for the practice of evidence-based medicine. Scientists from developing countries, together with peers in the United States, lead teams that address priority research needs through randomized clinical trials and implementation research conducted in low-resource areas.
MF Med, OB-GYN
⊕ https://vfmat.ch/a187

Global Oncology (GO)
Brings the best in cancer care to underserved patients around the world and collaborates across geographic, professional, and academic borders to improve cancer care, research, and education.
Heme-Onc, Path, Rad-Onc
⊕ https://vfmat.ch/fcb8

Global Outreach Doctors
Provides global health medical services in developing countries affected by famine, infant mortality, and chronic health issues.
All-Immu, Anesth, ER Med, General, Infect Dis, MF Med, Peds, Surg
⊕ https://vfmat.ch/8514

Global Polio Eradication Initiative
Aims to eradicate polio worldwide.
All-Immu, Infect-Dis, Logist-Op, Pub Health
⊕ https://vfmat.ch/7e2c

Global Telehealth Network (GTN)
Provides telehealth services with dedicated physician volunteers for people located in medically underserved areas, including low- and medium-resource countries, refugee camps, conflict zones, and disaster areas, and also in the U.S.
ER Med, General, Path, Peds, Psych, Radiol, Surg
⊕ https://vfmat.ch/4345

Global Vision 2020
Provides prescription eyeglasses to people who live in parts of the world lacking necessary infrastructure for obtaining affordable corrective eyewear.
Logist-Op, Ophth-Opt
⊕ https://vfmat.ch/7373

Globus Relief
Aims to improve the delivery of healthcare worldwide by gathering, processing, and distributing surplus medical supplies to charities at home and abroad.
Logist-Op
⊕ https://vfmat.ch/a2b7

GOAL
Works with the most vulnerable communities to help them respond to and recover from humanitarian crises, and to assist them in building transcendent solutions to mitigate poverty and vulnerability.

ER Med, General, Pub Health
⊕ https://vfmat.ch/bbea

Good Shepard International Foundation
Strives to promote inclusive and sustainable development for the most marginalized and vulnerable people, with a special focus on women, girls, and children, inspired by the Christian faith.
ER Med
⊕ https://vfmat.ch/ad9a

Grassroot Soccer
Leverages the power of soccer to educate, inspire, and mobilize at-risk youth in developing countries to overcome their greatest health challenges, live healthier and more productive lives, and be agents for change in their communities.
Infect Dis
⊕ https://vfmat.ch/3521

Great Faith Vision
Partners with like-minded organizations to bring physical and spiritual sight to the communities served, inspired by the Christian faith.
Ophth-Opt
⊕ https://vfmat.ch/21e2

Gynorecare Women's & Fistula Hospital
Provides clinical care for women deprived and excluded by society, by preventing and treating obstetric fistula.
Anesth, Crit-Care, General, Logist-Op, MF Med, OB-GYN, Ortho, Surg, Vasc Surg
⊕ https://vfmat.ch/9a76

Hands Across Oceans
Provides education, medication, medical supplies and development assistance to people in need in Africa.
General, Logist-Op, OB-GYN, Peds, Psych
⊕ https://vfmat.ch/c28e

Hands for Health Foundation
Aims to provide healthcare access and medical supplies to less fortunate people living in the developing world.
General, Nutr, Ophth-Opt
⊕ https://vfmat.ch/776e

Hardcore Help Foundation
Supports healthcare, education, disability, and disaster relief projects in several countries.
General, Logist-Op, Pub Health
⊕ https://vfmat.ch/9ae3

Healing Little Hearts
Sends specialist medical teams to perform free lifesaving heart surgery on babies and children in developing parts of the world.
Anesth, CT Surg, CV Med, Ped Surg, Peds, Surg
⊕ https://vfmat.ch/ffc1

Health Care Volunteers International
Provides direct patient care, capacity building, and educational projects in developing countries, and specializes in leveraging technology in order to provide low-cost solutions, drive better outcomes, and expand care to far more individuals in need around the globe.
General, OB-GYN, Peds, Plast, Rehab
⊕ https://vfmat.ch/69a6

Health Education Africa Resource Team (HEART)
Seeks to empower Africans to survive and overcome the effects of HIV/AIDS through disease prevention, education, and economic development, inspired by the Christian faith.
Logist-Op, Pub Health
⊕ https://vfmat.ch/1989

Health Equity Initiative
Aims to build and sustain a global community that engages across sectors and disciplines to advance health equity.
Pub Health
⊕ https://vfmat.ch/e2e2

Health Poverty Action

Works in partnership with people around the world who are pursuing change in their own communities to demand health justice and challenge power imbalances.

ER Med, General, Infect Dis, Psych, Pub Health

⊕ https://vfmat.ch/ee58

Health[e] Foundation

Supports health professionals and community workers in the world's most vulnerable societies to ensure quality health for everyone in need by providing digital education and information, using e-learning and m-health.

Logist-Op

⊕ https://vfmat.ch/b73b

Healthcare Relief (Health for Africa)

Works toward relief of poverty and sickness, supporting causes including healthcare services, healthy campaigns for those in poverty, and research.

Logist-Op, Pub Health

⊕ https://vfmat.ch/da5a

HealthRight International

Leverages global resources to address local health challenges and create sustainable solutions that empower marginalized communities to live healthy lives.

General, Infect Dis, MF Med, OB-GYN, Psych, Pub Health

⊕ https://vfmat.ch/129d

Hear the World Foundation

Advocates worldwide for equal opportunities and improved quality of life for people in need with hearing loss.

ENT, Peds

⊕ https://vfmat.ch/122c

Hearing Health Foundation

Prevents and cures hearing loss and tinnitus through groundbreaking research and promotes hearing health.

Surg

⊕ https://vfmat.ch/2e71

Heart to Heart International

Strengthens communities through improving health access, providing humanitarian development, and administering crisis relief worldwide. Engages volunteers, collaborates with partners, and deploys resources to achieve this mission.

Anesth, ER Med, General, Logist-Op, Medicine, Path, Path, Peds, Psych, Pub Health, Surg

⊕ https://vfmat.ch/aacb

Heineman Medical Outreach

Provides medical and educational assistance globally to promote sustainable healthcare and enhanced living standards in underserved communities through the International Medical Outreach (IMO) program, a collaborative partnership between Heineman Medical Outreach and Atrium Health.

Anesth, CT Surg, CV Med, ER Med, General, Heme-Onc, Logist-Op, Medicine, Neonat, OB-GYN, Ped Surg, Peds, Surg, Vasc Surg

⊕ https://vfmat.ch/389b

Helen Keller International

Seeks to eliminate preventable vision loss, malnutrition, and diseases of poverty.

Infect Dis, Nutr, OB-GYN, Ophth-Opt, Peds

⊕ https://vfmat.ch/b654

HelpAge International

Works to ensure that people everywhere understand how much older people contribute to society and that they must enjoy their right to healthcare, social services, economic, and physical security.

General, Geri, Infect Dis, Medicine, Pub Health

⊕ https://vfmat.ch/5d91

Hernia International

Aims to provide relief from sickness, and protection and preservation of health, for persons affected by groin and abdominal hernias and residing in low- and middle-income countries.

Surg

⊕ https://vfmat.ch/e98e

Hewatele

Provides medical oxygen at affordable rates to reduce delays in access to emergency healthcare.

Logist-Op, Pub Health

⊕ https://vfmat.ch/4ae7

Hifadhi Africa

Adopt a community-centered approach towards empowerment, transformation, resilience, and support for pastoral communities and slum dwellers for sustainable development.

CV Med, OB-GYN, Pub Health

⊕ https://vfmat.ch/661b

Hope and Healing International

Gives hope and healing to children and families trapped by poverty and disability.

General, Nutr, Ophth-Opt, Peds, Rehab

⊕ https://vfmat.ch/c638

Hope Walks

Frees children, families, and communities from the burden of clubfoot, inspired by the Christian faith.

Ortho, Ped Surg, Peds, Rehab

⊕ https://vfmat.ch/f6d4

Hospice Africa

Aims to provide a holistic and culturally sensitive palliative care service through accurate treatment of pain.

Palliative

⊕ https://vfmat.ch/9f86

Humanity & Inclusion

Works alongside people with disabilities and vulnerable populations, taking action and bearing witness in order to respond to their essential needs, improve their living conditions and health, and promote respect for their dignity and fundamental rights.

General, Infect Dis, MF Med, Medicine, Ortho, Peds, Psych, Pub Health, Rehab

⊕ https://vfmat.ch/16b7

Humanity First

Provides aid and assistance to those in need, offering sustainable development solutions to society while providing and empowering local communities with the resources to help themselves.

ER Med, General, MF Med, Ophth-Opt

⊕ https://vfmat.ch/13cc

Icahn School of Medicine at Mount Sinai Arnhold Institute for Global Health

Specializes in global health systems and implementation research, working toward a world in which vulnerable people in every community have access to healthcare.

CV Med, Endo, General, Infect Dis, Logist-Op, MF Med, Medicine, Neonat, OB-GYN, Ophth-Opt, Peds, Plast, Pub Health

⊕ https://vfmat.ch/a327

ICAP at Columbia University

Serves as global leader in supporting the scale-up of multidisciplinary HIV/AIDS prevention, care, and treatment programs based on a family-focused approach.

General, Infect Dis, MF Med, Medicine, OB-GYN, Pub Health

⊕ https://vfmat.ch/a8ef

IMA World Health

Works to build healthier communities by collaborating with key partners to serve vulnerable people with a focus on health, healing, and well-being for all.

Infect Dis, MF Med, Nutr, OB-GYN, Pub Health

⊕ https://vfmat.ch/8316

Imbaku Public Health

Aims to allay disparities in healthcare, education, and the environment faced by vulnerable populations in Kenya, particularly women and children.

Pub Health

⊕ https://vfmat.ch/9f56

IMPACT Foundation

Works to prevent and alleviate needless disability by restoring sight, mobility, and hearing.

ENT, MF Med, OB-GYN, Ophth-Opt, Ortho, Peds, Surg

⊕ https://vfmat.ch/ba28

International Agency for the Prevention of Blindness (IAPB), The

Leads international efforts in blindness-prevention activities, works toward a world where no one is needlessly visually impaired, and ensures that everyone has access to the best possible standard of eye health.

Infect Dis, Ophth-Opt, Pub Health

⊕ https://vfmat.ch/87a2

International Campaign for Women's Right to Safe Abortion

Works to build an international network and campaign that brings together organizations with an interest in promoting and providing safe abortion to create a shared platform for advocacy, debate, and dialogue and the sharing of skills and experience.

OB-GYN, Pub Health, Surg

⊕ https://vfmat.ch/f341

International Cancer Institute

Aims to prevent and cure cancer through research, to translate new knowledge into better prevention and treatment, and to provide effective and compassionate clinical care.

Heme-Onc, Logist-Op, Path, Rad-Onc

⊕ https://vfmat.ch/ca93

International Council of Ophthalmology

Works with ophthalmologic societies and others to enhance ophthalmic education and improve access to the highest-quality eye care in order to preserve and restore vision for people of the world.

Ophth-Opt

⊕ https://vfmat.ch/ffd2

International Federation of Gynecology and Obstetrics (FIGO)

Implements global projects on specific women's health issues.

MF Med, Medicine, Neonat, OB-GYN, Surg, Urol

⊕ https://vfmat.ch/c4b4

International Federation of Red Cross and Red Crescent Societies (IFRC)

Coordinates and directs international assistance following natural and manmade disasters in nonconflict situations through the world's largest humanitarian and development network. Provides disaster-preparedness programs, healthcare activities, and promotes humanitarian values.

ER Med, General, Infect Dis, Nutr

⊕ https://vfmat.ch/b4ee

International Health Operations Patient Education and Empowerment (IHOPEE)

Aims to provide youth and women empowerment in the USA and Kenya; assist In health, education, and small entrepreneurship; and create a library of literacy programs.

General, MF Med, OB-GYN

⊕ https://vfmat.ch/4c97

International Health Services Group

Aims to improve access to quality health services in underserved areas of the world.

General, OB-GYN, Pub Health

⊕ https://vfmat.ch/d71a

International Hope Missions

Improves local standards of care by enabling complex procedures for women and children and mentoring local medical teams.

General, MF Med, OB-GYN

⊕ https://vfmat.ch/c5c7

International Learning Movement (ILM UK)

Supports some of the world's poorest people in developing countries with core projects in education, safe drinking water, and healthcare.

General, Ophth-Opt

⊕ https://vfmat.ch/b974

International Medical Alliance

Provides access to medical, vision, and dental care in underserved and vulnerable communities around the world, to improve health, wellness, and the quality of life for populations most in need.

Dent-OMFS, General, Infect Dis, OB-GYN, Ophth-Opt, Peds, Surg

⊕ https://vfmat.ch/2e7d

International Medical Relief

Provides sustainable education, training, medical and dental care, and disaster relief and response in vulnerable communities worldwide.

Dent-OMFS, General, Infect Dis, Medicine, OB-GYN

⊕ https://vfmat.ch/b3ed

International Organization for Migration (IOM) – The UN Migration Agency

Promotes evidence-informed policies and holistic, preventive, and curative health programs that are beneficial, accessible, and equitable for vulnerable migrants.

General, Infect Dis, OB-GYN

⊕ https://vfmat.ch/621a

International Planned Parenthood Federation (IPPF)

Leads a locally owned, globally connected civil society movement that provides and enables services and champions sexual and reproductive health and rights for all, especially the underserved.

Infect Dis, MF Med, OB-GYN

⊕ https://vfmat.ch/dc97

International Rescue Committee (IRC)

Responds to the world's worst humanitarian crises and helps people whose lives and livelihoods are shattered by conflict and disaster to survive, recover, and gain control of their future.

ER Med, General, Infect Dis, MF Med, Peds

⊕ https://vfmat.ch/5d24

International Trachoma Initiative (iTi)

Works toward a world free from trachoma, a preventable cause of blindness, and provides comprehensive support to national ministries of health and governmental and nongovernmental organizations to implement a comprehensive approach to fight trachoma.

Infect Dis, Ophth-Opt

⊕ https://vfmat.ch/3278

International Union Against Tuberculosis and Lung Disease

Develops, implements, and assesses anti-tuberculosis, lung health, and noncommunicable disease programs.

Infect Dis, Pub Health, Pulm-Critic

⊕ https://vfmat.ch/3e82

Intersos

Provides emergency medical assistance to victims of armed conflicts, natural disasters, and extreme exclusion, with particular attention to the protection of the most vulnerable people.

ER Med, General, Nutr

⊕ https://vfmat.ch/dbac

IntraHealth International

Improves the performance of health workers and strengthens the systems in which they work.

CV Med, Endo, General, Infect Dis, MF Med, Neonat, Nutr, OB-GYN

⊕ https://vfmat.ch/ddc8

Ipas

Focuses efforts on women and girls who want contraception or abortion, and builds programs around their needs and how best to support them.

OB-GYN

⊕ https://vfmat.ch/8e39

Iris Global

Serves the poor, the destitute, the lost, and the forgotten by providing adoration, outreach, family, education, relief, development, healing, and the arts.

General, Infect Dis, Nutr, Pub Health
⊕ https://vfmat.ch/37f8

Islamic Medical Association of North America
Fosters health promotion, disease prevention, and health maintenance in communities around the world through direct patient care and health programs.
Anesth, Dent-OMFS, ER Med, General, Logist-Op, Ophth-Opt, Peds, Plast, Surg
⊕ https://vfmat.ch/a157

IsraAID
Supports people affected by humanitarian crisis and partners with local communities around the world to provide urgent aid, assist recovery, and reduce the risk of future disasters.
ER Med, Infect Dis, Psych, Rehab
⊕ https://vfmat.ch/de96

IVUmed
Aims to make quality urological care available worldwide by providing medical and surgical education for physicians and nurses, and treatment for thousands of children and adults.
Anesth, OB-GYN, Ped Surg, Surg, Urol
⊕ https://vfmat.ch/e619

Izumi Foundation
Develops and supports programs that improve health and healthcare in neglected regions of Africa and Latin America.

⊕ https://vfmat.ch/f29a

Jacaranda Health
Seeks to improve the quality of care in public hospitals, where the vast majority of low-income women deliver their babies.
MF Med, OB-GYN, Peds
⊕ https://vfmat.ch/1436

Jesus Harvesters Ministries
Reaches communities through medical clinics, dental care, veterinarian outreach, pastor training, and community service, based in Christian ministry.
Dent-OMFS, General, Infect Dis
⊕ https://vfmat.ch/8a23

Jhpiego
Creates and delivers transformative healthcare solutions that save lives, in partnership with national governments, health experts, and local communities.
General, Infect Dis, OB-GYN, Surg
⊕ https://vfmat.ch/45b8

John Snow, Inc. (JSI)
Aims to improve the health and well-being of underserved and vulnerable people and communities throughout the world.
General, Infect Dis, Logist-Op, MF Med, OB-GYN, Peds, Psych, Pub Health
⊕ https://vfmat.ch/ba78

Johns Hopkins Center for Communication Programs
Believes in the power of communication to save lives by empowering people to adopt healthy behaviors for themselves, their families, and their communities.
General, Infect Dis, Logist-Op, OB-GYN, Pub Health
⊕ https://vfmat.ch/1bf9

Johns Hopkins Center for Global Health
Facilitates and focuses the extensive expertise and resources of the Johns Hopkins institutions, together with global collaborators, to effectively address and ameliorate the world's most pressing health issues.
General, Genetics, Logist-Op, MF Med, Peds, Psych, Pub Health, Pulm-Critic
⊕ https://vfmat.ch/54ce

Joint United Nations Programme on HIV/AIDS (UNAIDS)
Aims to place people living with HIV and people affected by the virus at the decision-making table and at the center of designing, delivering, and monitoring the AIDS response.
Infect Dis
⊕ https://vfmat.ch/464a

K2K - Kansas to Kenya
Works with other organizations to achieve the UN's sustainable development goals in Kenya, inspired by the Christian faith.
General, Infect Dis, OB-GYN
⊕ https://vfmat.ch/b1fa

Kageno
Works to transform communities in need into places of hope and opportunity through an integrated model that focuses on healthcare, education, income generation, and conservation.
General, Infect Dis, MF Med, Neonat, Nutr, OB-GYN
⊕ https://vfmat.ch/f5bd

Kaya Responsible Travel
Promotes sustainable social, environmental, and economic development, empowers communities, and cultivates educated, compassionate global citizens through responsible travel.
All-Immu, Crit-Care, Dent-OMFS, ER Med, General, Geri, Infect Dis, MF Med, Medicine, Nutr, OB-GYN, Peds, Psych, Pub Health, Rehab
⊕ https://vfmat.ch/b2cf

Keep a Child Alive
Committed to improving the health and well-being of vulnerable children, young people, adults, and families around the world, with a focus on combating the physical, social, and economic impacts of HIV/AIDS.
Infect Dis, MF Med, Neonat, OB-GYN
⊕ https://vfmat.ch/7f2f

Kenya Aid
Aims to improve the lives of people in Western Kenya by improving the availability and quality of healthcare and education in the region.
General, MF Med, MF Med, OB-GYN, Peds
⊕ https://vfmat.ch/b4d2

Kenya Diabetes Management & Information Center
Strives to eradicate preventable diabetes and enable a long, productive life for those with diabetes.
Endo, General, Nutr
⊕ https://vfmat.ch/786b

Kenya Health
Aims to improve healthcare for those in Kenya through volunteer surgical missions.
General, Infect Dis, OB-GYN, Palliative, Peds, Surg
⊕ https://vfmat.ch/541f

Kenya Medical Mission
Partners with the local church to help meet the medical needs of the people in Kenya, based in Christian ministry.
Dent-OMFS, General, Infect Dis, Peds, Surg
⊕ https://vfmat.ch/9fd3

Kenya Pediatric Association
Seeks to lead in comprehensive child healthcare delivery through best practice standards, training, research, policy formulation, and capacity building.
Dent-OMFS, Neonat, Ped Surg, Peds
⊕ https://vfmat.ch/b96a

Kenya Relief
Aims to rekindle hope for a new generation in Kenya through partnership between communities; operates an orphanage, a school, and a medical clinic in southwestern Kenya; and engages short-term mission teams to provide medical and surgical care.
Anesth, ENT, General, Logist-Op, OB-GYN, Ophth-Opt, Ortho, Path, Ped Surg, Surg
⊕ https://vfmat.ch/64cd

KenyanNetwork of Cancer Organization
Strives, through a network of cancer NGOs, patients groups, and community-based cancer organizations, to promote awareness and provide education, screening, prevention, and patient support in Kenya.
Heme-Onc
⊕ https://vfmat.ch/94d2

Kids Care Everywhere

Seeks to empower physicians in under-resourced environments with multimedia, state-of-the-art medical software, and to inspire young professionals to become future global healthcare leaders.

Logist-Op, Ped Surg, Peds

⊕ https://vfmat.ch/bc23

Kinga Africa

Aims to promote oral health, especially among children in less privileged communities.

Dent-OMFS

⊕ https://vfmat.ch/5652

Kitechild

Aims to empower at-risk children to thrive and reach their potential, whatever their background.

General

⊕ https://vfmat.ch/de1b

Kletjian Foundation

Works toward a world in which all people have access to safe, sustainable, and high-quality medical care, building collaborative networks and supporting entrepreneurial leaders that promote global health equity.

CT Surg, ENT, General, Ortho, Surg

⊕ https://vfmat.ch/12c2

KOHI – Kenya Oral Health Initiative

Aims to provide immediate, comprehensive, and preventive dental services to the general population in Kenya, with special emphasis on the poorest.

Dent-OMFS

⊕ https://vfmat.ch/3552

Kona Hospital Foundation

Seeks to improve Kona Community Hospital by funding medical technology, expanded services and enhanced facilities that would otherwise be unavailable.

Anesth, Heme-Onc, MF Med, OB-GYN, Peds, Surg

⊕ https://vfmat.ch/8a69

Kupenda for the Children

Educates families and communities about the rights of children with disabilities and advocates for their medical care, education, legal rights, and inclusion.

General, Ped Surg, Peds

⊕ https://vfmat.ch/7f33

Land and Life Foundation

Aims to support and design conservation education, community outreach, and conservation initiatives for communities living alongside wildlife in Kenya and Tanzania.

Dent-OMFS, General, Nutr, OB-GYN, Peds

⊕ https://vfmat.ch/8d39

Last Mile Health

Links community health workers with frontline health workers—nurses, doctors, and midwives at community clinics—and supports them to bring lifesaving services to the doorsteps of people living far from care.

General, Logist-Op, OB-GYN, Pub Health

⊕ https://vfmat.ch/37da

Lay Volunteers International Association (LVIA)

Fosters local and global change to help overcome extreme poverty, reinforce equitable and sustainable development, and enhance dialogue between Italian and African communities.

ER Med, Logist-Op, MF Med, Neonat, Nutr, OB-GYN, Peds

⊕ https://vfmat.ch/ecd4

Life for a Child

Supports the provision of the best possible healthcare, given local circumstances, to all children and youth with diabetes in less-resourced countries, through the strengthening of existing diabetes services.

Endo, Medicine, Peds

⊕ https://vfmat.ch/d712

Light for Sight 21

Aims to eliminate severe visual impairment among all children and adolescents with keratoconus.

Ophth-Opt

⊕ https://vfmat.ch/ef55

Light for the World

Contributes to a world in which persons with disabilities fully exercise their rights, and assists persons with disabilities living in poverty.

Ophth-Opt, Rehab

⊕ https://vfmat.ch/3ff6

Lighthouse for Christ Eye Center

Operates a free, modern eye clinic and surgical center in Mombasa and fully equipped satellites in Kilifi, Voi, and Mariakani, inspired by the Christian faith.

Ophth-Opt

⊕ https://vfmat.ch/ce62

Limbs International

Engages communities and transforms lives through affordable, sustainable prosthetic solutions and rehabilitation services in developing countries.

Logist-Op, Ortho, Pod, Rehab

⊕ https://vfmat.ch/dc84

Lions SightFirst Eye Hospital, The

Aims to eliminate preventable and treatable blindness by offering equitable and comprehensive patient care, sight enhancement, and rehabilitation services.

Dent-OMFS, ENT, Ophth-Opt, Surg

⊕ https://vfmat.ch/cefa

Living Goods

Leverages a powerful combination of catalytic technology, high-impact training, and quality treatments that empower government community health workers (CHWs) to deliver quality care to their neighbors' doorsteps.

Infect Dis, Logist-Op, MF Med

⊕ https://vfmat.ch/d6d2

Local Initiatives for Education (L.I.F.E.)

Provides potable water, food, agricultural support, educational resources, and medical care in Africa, while working alongside community leaders to accomplish these goals.

Logist-Op, Pub Health

⊕ https://vfmat.ch/dd91

Lutherans in Medical Missions (LIMM)

Works with local and global partners to promote healing in medically underserved communities.

General, Logist-Op, Pub Health

⊕ https://vfmat.ch/c5aa

M-PESA Foundation

Focuses on community development and sustainable initiatives in areas of health, education, environmental conservation, and integrated livelihoods.

OB-GYN

⊕ https://vfmat.ch/d9ac

MAGNA International

Helps those who are suffering or recovering from conflicts and disasters by reducing the risks of diseases and treating them immediately.

ER Med, General, Infect Dis, Peds, Surg

⊕ https://vfmat.ch/58f4

Maisha Project

Invests in education, health, local entrepreneurs, and infrastructure/community building projects.

General, Infect Dis, Nutr

⊕ https://vfmat.ch/9456

Making A Difference Foundation

Sponsors and organizes medical missions for medical providers to provide care to underserved communities around the world.

CV Med, Dent-OMFS, ER Med, General, Infect Dis, Logist-Op, MF Med, Neonat,

Nutr, OB-GYN, Ophth-Opt, Ortho, Pub Health, Pulm-Critic, Rehab, Surg
⊕ https://vfmat.ch/5556

Management Sciences for Health (MSH)
Works with countries and communities to save lives and improve the health of the world's poorest and most vulnerable people by building strong, resilient, sustainable health systems.
Infect Dis, Logist-Op, Pub Health
⊕ https://vfmat.ch/6aa2

MAP International
Provides medicines and health supplies to those in need around the world so they might experience life to the fullest.
Logist-Op
⊕ https://vfmat.ch/deed

March to the Top Africa
Empowers Kenyan communities through initiatives in health, education, and conservation.
CT Surg, Dent-OMFS, Ophth-Opt, Ortho, Ped Surg, Peds, Pub Health
⊕ https://vfmat.ch/689c

Marie Stopes International
Provides the contraception and safe abortion services that enable women all over the world to choose their own futures.
Infect Dis, MF Med, Neonat, OB-GYN, Pub Health
⊕ https://vfmat.ch/9525

Maryknoll Lay Missioners
Based in Christian ministry, aims to collaborate with poor communities in Africa, Asia, and the Americas in order to respond to basic needs, including heathcare, and to help create a more compassionate world.
Logist-Op, Nutr
⊕ https://vfmat.ch/2ce6

Massachusetts General Hospital Global Surgery Initiative
Aims to improve surgical education and access to advanced surgical care in resource-limited settings around the world by performing surgical operations as visitors, training local surgeons, and sharing medical technology through international partnerships across disciplines.
Anesth, Crit-Care, ER Med, Heme-Onc, Peds, Surg
⊕ https://vfmat.ch/31b1

Mater Misericordiae Hospital
Seeks to deliver exceptional, compassionate healthcare services.
ER Med, General, MF Med, OB-GYN, Path, Peds, Radiol
⊕ https://vfmat.ch/7389

MaterCare International (MCI) (Canada)
Works to improve the lives and health of mothers and babies through programs in healthcare provision, training, research, and advocacy, with the aim to address maternal and perinatal mortality and morbidity in developing countries.
OB-GYN
⊕ https://vfmat.ch/a92e

Maternal Fetal Care International
Helps mothers and children survive and enjoy better health in the poorest regions of the world.
MF Med, Neonat, OB-GYN
⊕ https://vfmat.ch/7e72

Maternity Foundation
Works to ensure safer childbirth for women and newborns everywhere through innovative mobile health solutions such as the Safe Delivery App, a mobile training tool for skilled birth attendants.
MF Med, OB-GYN, Pub Health
⊕ https://vfmat.ch/ff4f

Matibabu Foundation Kenya
Provides tailored health information and services to clients by working with individuals, the community, and government to improve overall health goals.
General, MF Med, Ophth-Opt, Pub Health, Rehab, Surg
⊕ https://vfmat.ch/65bd

Maverick Collective
Aims to build a global community of strategic philanthropists and informed advocates who use their intellectual and financial resources to create change.
Infect Dis, MF Med, OB-GYN
⊕ https://vfmat.ch/ea49

Max Foundation, The
Seeks to increase global access to treatment, care, and support for people living with cancer.
General, Heme-Onc, Pub Health
⊕ https://vfmat.ch/8c7d

McGill University Health Centre: Centre for Global Surgery
Works to reduce the impact of injury by advancing surgical care through research and education in resource-limited settings.
ER Med, Logist-Op, Ped Surg, Surg
⊕ https://vfmat.ch/7246

Med Treks International
Aims to strengthen the global health workforce through education, collaboration, innovation, and empowerment.
General, Infect Dis, MF Med, OB-GYN, Peds, Pub Health
⊕ https://vfmat.ch/8a73

MedHope Africa
Supports relief and development for low-resource communities in Sub-Saharan Africa by addressing dire physical and spiritual needs through medical and vision care, community health interventions, and prayer and Christian evangelism.
General, Logist-Op, Medicine, Ophth-Opt
⊕ https://vfmat.ch/8249

Medical Ambassadors International
Equipping communities through Christ-centered health and development.
Nutr, OB-GYN, Pub Health
⊕ https://vfmat.ch/8e76

Medical Benevolence Foundation (MBF)
Works with partners in developing countries to build sustainable healthcare for those most in need through faith-based global medical missions.
General, Logist-Op, MF Med, OB-GYN, Surg
⊕ https://vfmat.ch/c3e8

Medical Care Development International (MCD International)
Works to strengthen health systems through innovative, sustainable interventions.
Infect Dis, Logist-Op, OB-GYN, Pub Health
⊕ https://vfmat.ch/dc5c

Medical Care Development International
Works to improve the health of vulnerable populations through integrated, sustainable, and locally driven interventions.
Infect Dis, OB-GYN, Peds, Pub Health
⊕ https://vfmat.ch/da87

Medical Mission Trips
Provides medical aid, welfare assistance, and educational opportunities in Brazil, Honduras, Guatemala, Kenya, Burundi, and Ethiopia.
General
⊕ https://vfmat.ch/9117

Medical Missions Abroad Corp
Sponsors missions that provide healthcare, build houses, and care for children.
General, Logist-Op
⊕ https://vfmat.ch/a8ff

Medical Missions Kenya and Hunger Relief (MMK)
Seeks to combat hunger, improve access to healthcare services, and promote health awareness education in underserved Kenyan communities.
General, OB-GYN, Peds
⊕ https://vfmat.ch/e19b

Medical Missions Outreach
Visits developing countries to provide quality, ethical healthcare and outreach to those in need, based in Christian ministry.

Dent-OMFS, Ophth-Opt, Ortho, Surg
⊕ https://vfmat.ch/1197

Medicines for Humanity
Aims to save the lives of vulnerable children by strengthening systems of maternal and child health in the communities served.
Infect Dis, MF Med, OB-GYN
⊕ https://vfmat.ch/8d13

Medicus Mundi Italia
Carries out programs in basic community health, health education, maternal and child health, nutrition, and infectious disease.
General, Infect Dis, Logist-Op, MF Med, Nutr, Peds, Pub Health, Rehab
⊕ https://vfmat.ch/4413

MedSend
Funds qualified healthcare professionals to serve the physical and spiritual needs of people around the world, enabling healthcare providers to work where they have been called.
General
⊕ https://vfmat.ch/661c

MedShare
Aims to improve the quality of life of people, communities, and the planet by sourcing and directly delivering surplus medical supplies and equipment to communities in need around the world.
Logist-Op
⊕ https://vfmat.ch/c8bc

Memusi Foundation
Works with communities and schools in Kenya to provide access to quality education, with the belief that education is the primary route out of poverty for every child.
Dent-OMFS, General, Logist-Op, Nutr, Peds
⊕ https://vfmat.ch/d917

MENTOR Initiative
Saves lives in emergencies through tropical disease control, and helps people recover from crisis with dignity, working side by side with communities, health workers, and health authorities to leave a lasting impact.
ER Med, Infect Dis
⊕ https://vfmat.ch/3bd5

Merck for Mothers
Hopes to create a world where no woman has to die giving life by collaborating with partners to improve the health and well-being of women during pregnancy, childbirth, and the postpartum period.
MF Med, OB-GYN
⊕ https://vfmat.ch/5b51

Mercy and Love Foundation
Aims to provide orphaned and vulnerable children with basic human needs such as food, clothing, and shelter, enabling them to thrive.
General, Peds
⊕ https://vfmat.ch/649a

Mercy Cneter Foundation
Aims to combat disease and poverty in Lare, Kenya, by providing clean water, healthcare, education, and micro-enterprise initiatives.
Dent-OMFS, General, Infect Dis, Logist-Op, MF Med, OB-GYN, Peds
⊕ https://vfmat.ch/31da

MicroResearch: Africa/Asia
Seeks to improve health outcomes in Africa by training, mentoring, and supporting local multidisciplinary health professional researchers.
Infect Dis, Nutr, OB-GYN, Psych
⊕ https://vfmat.ch/13e7

Mildmay
Transforms and empowers lives through the delivery of quality health services, treatment, and care in the UK and Africa.
Infect Dis, MF Med, Neuro, Psych
⊕ https://vfmat.ch/3fd8

Mission Africa
Brings medical care, training, and compassion to underserved communities in Africa, based in Christian ministry.
Dent-OMFS, General, Infect Dis
⊕ https://vfmat.ch/df4d

Mission Bambini
Helps to support children living in poverty and sickness, and lacking education, giving them the opportunity for and hope of a better life.
CT Surg, CV Med, Crit-Care, ER Med, Ped Surg, Peds
⊕ https://vfmat.ch/dc1a

Mission Regan
Collects supplies, medication, and medical equipment and provides them to those who are in desperate need, both locally and globally.
Logist-Op
⊕ https://vfmat.ch/2bc1

Mission to Heal
Aims to heal underserved people and train local practitioners in the most remote areas of the world through global healthcare missions.
Anesth, Infect Dis, OB-GYN, Surg
⊕ https://vfmat.ch/4718

Mission Vision
Seeks to decrease blindness and other eye-related disabilities, and to increase academic performance and general quality of life.
Ophth-Opt
⊕ https://vfmat.ch/83d8

Mission: Restore
Trains medical professionals abroad in complex reconstructive surgery in order to create a sustainable infrastructure in which long-term relationships are forged and permanent change comes to pass.
Plast, Surg
⊕ https://vfmat.ch/3f5f

Molo Medical Missions
Promotes basic healthcare for the community and organizes medical mission trips to provide patient care to the people of Molo, Kenya.
Dent-OMFS, General, Ophth-Opt, Ped Surg, Peds, Surg
⊕ https://vfmat.ch/b4cb

More Than Medicine
Provides ENT head/neck care while supporting local doctors to grow the quality of medicine abroad.
Anesth, ENT, Heme-Onc, Surg
⊕ https://vfmat.ch/c4e8

mothers2mothers (m2m)
Employs and trains local women living with HIV as community health workers called Mentor Mothers to support women, children, and adolescents with vital medical services, education, and support.
Infect Dis, MF Med, OB-GYN, Peds, Pub Health
⊕ https://vfmat.ch/6557

MSD for Mothers
Designs scalable solutions that help end preventable maternal deaths.
MF Med, OB-GYN, Pub Health
⊕ https://vfmat.ch/9f99

MSI Reproductive Choices (Marie Stopes International)
Seeks to deliver quality family planning and reproductive healthcare to women around the world.
MF Med
⊕ https://vfmat.ch/5c82

Multi-Agency International Training and Support (MAITS)
Improves the lives of some of the world's poorest people living with disabilities through better access to quality health and education services and support.
Neuro, Psych, Rehab
⊕ https://vfmat.ch/9dcd

Médecins du Monde/Doctors of the World

Provides care, bears witness, and supports social change worldwide with innovative medical programs and evidence-based advocacy initiatives.

ER Med, General, Infect Dis, MF Med, Neonat, OB-GYN, Peds, Pub Health

⊕ https://vfmat.ch/a43d

Nairobi Hospice

Provides quality palliative care services, caregiver support, and education.

Palliative

⊕ https://vfmat.ch/3154

Nazarene Compassionate Ministries

Partners with local churches around the world to clothe, shelter, feed, heal, educate, and live in solidarity with those in need.

General, Infect Dis, OB-GYN

⊕ https://vfmat.ch/6b4d

Nazareth Hospital Kenya

Seeks to provide accessible, affordable and quality healthcare to the marginalized and needy, inspired by the Christian faith.

All-Immu, Dent-OMFS, ENT, General, Heme-Onc, MF Med, Nephro, Nutr, OB-GYN, Ophth-Opt, Palliative, Peds, Pulm-Critic, Rehab, Surg

⊕ https://vfmat.ch/df91

NCD Alliance

Unites and strengthens civil society to stimulate collaborative advocacy, action, and accountability for NCD (noncommunicable disease) prevention and control.

All-Immu, CV Med, General, Heme-Onc, Medicine, Peds, Psych

⊕ https://vfmat.ch/abdd

NEST 360

Works to ensure that hospitals in Africa can deliver lifesaving care for small and sick newborns, by developing and distributing high-quality technologies and services.

MF Med, Neonat, Peds, Pub Health

⊕ https://vfmat.ch/cea9

Neuroscience Foundation For Africa

Provides opportunities to learn about international healthcare in Africa, treat patients in need of specialized surgical services, and increase awareness for our generation about healthcare needs throughout the world.

Neuro, Neurosurg, Ortho, Surg

⊕ https://vfmat.ch/5a72

New Frontiers Health Force

Supports global medical missions that have included healthcare, disaster relief, and education services in 35 countries.

Crit-Care, General, Infect Dis, MF Med, Neonat, OB-GYN, Path, Peds

⊕ https://vfmat.ch/992a

New Horizons Collaborative

Advances a holistic, integrated approach to high-quality pediatric HIV care and treatment with a specific focus on those in need of advanced treatment.

Infect Dis, Peds, Pub Health

⊕ https://vfmat.ch/a76a

New Life Home Trust UK

Works to rescue and care for abandoned babies in Kenya, some of whom are HIV-positive, and find loving homes for them through adoption.

Infect Dis, Peds

⊕ https://vfmat.ch/c397

NuVasive Spine Foundation (NSF)

Partners with leading spine surgeons, nonprofits, and in-country medical professionals/facilities to bring life-changing spine surgery to under-resourced communities around the world.

Logist-Op, Ortho, Ped Surg, Rehab, Surg

⊕ https://vfmat.ch/6ccc

Ogra Foundation

Seeks to provide disease control and prevention, reproductive health education, emergency preparedness, and maternal and child healthcare.

General, Infect Dis, OB-GYN, Peds

⊕ https://vfmat.ch/72cc

Olalo of Hope Kenya

Aims to help the break the cycle of poverty by providing education, access to urgent medical care, and the skills needed to effect change.

General, Infect Dis

⊕ https://vfmat.ch/bb31

Omni Med

Promotes health volunteerism and provides innovative, cooperative, and sustainable programs with measurable impact.

ER Med, Endo, Medicine, Neuro, OB-GYN, Ophth-Opt, Ortho, Palliative, Peds, Vasc Surg

⊕ https://vfmat.ch/2969

One Good Turn

Provides practical medical education and culturally sensitive medical care to neglected communities worldwide.

Dent-OMFS, General

⊕ https://vfmat.ch/545f

One World One Vision

Aims to reduce vision loss resulting from ocular misalignment and pediatric cataracts.

Anesth, Ophth-Opt, Ped Surg, Surg

⊕ https://vfmat.ch/337b

Operation Eyesight

Works to eliminate blindness in partnership with governments, hospitals, medical professionals, corporations, and community development teams.

Ophth-Opt, Surg

⊕ https://vfmat.ch/b95d

Operation Eyesight Universal

Aims to prevent blindness, restore sight, and eliminate avoidable blindness.

Ophth-Opt

⊕ https://vfmat.ch/f629

Operation International

Offers medical aid to adults and children suffering from lack of quality healthcare in impoverished countries.

Dent-OMFS, ER Med, Heme-Onc, OB-GYN, Ophth-Opt, Ortho, Ped Surg, Plast, Surg

⊕ https://vfmat.ch/b52a

Operation Smile

Treats patients with cleft lip and cleft palate, and creates solutions that deliver safe surgery to people where it's needed most.

Anesth, Dent-OMFS, ENT, Ped Surg, Plast

⊕ https://vfmat.ch/5c29

Operation Walk

Provides the gift of mobility through life-changing joint replacement surgeries, at no cost for those in need in the U.S. and globally.

Anesth, Ortho, Rehab, Surg

⊕ https://vfmat.ch/bafe

Options

Believes in a world in which women and children can access the high-quality health services they need, without financial burden.

Logist-Op, MF Med, Neonat, OB-GYN

⊕ https://vfmat.ch/3a48

Optivest Foundation

Funds strategic opportunities that are holistic and collaborative, inspired by the Christian faith.

General, Nutr

⊕ https://vfmat.ch/f1e6

Optometry Giving Sight

Delivers eye exams and low or no-cost glasses, provides training for local eye care professionals, and establishes optometry schools, vision centers and

optical labs.
Ophth-Opt
⊕ https://vfmat.ch/33ea

Orbis International
Works to prevent and treat blindness through hands-on training and improved access to quality eye care.
Anesth, Ophth-Opt, Surg
⊕ https://vfmat.ch/f2b2

Order of Malta
Supports forgotten or excluded people, especially those living in conflict zones or amid natural disasters, by providing medical assistance, caring for refugees, and distributing medicines and necessities.
ER Med, General, Infect Dis, MF Med, Nephro, OB-GYN, Ortho, Psych
⊕ https://vfmat.ch/1fab

Oromo Relief Association (ORA)
Works for all human beings affected by famine, armed conflicts, and other disasters, man-made or otherwise, without prejudice.
General, Geri
⊕ https://vfmat.ch/bff1

Oxford University Global Surgery Group (OUGSG)
Aims to contribute to the provision of high-quality surgical care globally, particularly in low- and middle-income countries (LMICs), while bringing together students, researchers, and clinicians with an interest in global surgery, anesthesia, and obstetrics and gynecology.
Anesth, MF Med, OB-GYN, Ortho, Surg
⊕ https://vfmat.ch/c624

Pact
Works on the ground to improve the lives of those who are challenged by poverty and marginalization, striving for a world in which all people are heard, capable, and vibrant.
Infect Dis, Logist-Op, MF Med, Pub Health
⊕ https://vfmat.ch/9a6c

Palav
Provides support equipment for newborns with breathing difficulties and trains healthcare providers.
Peds
⊕ https://vfmat.ch/86bd

Pan African Thoracic Society (PATS)
Aims to promote lung health in Africa, the continent most afflicted by morbidity and death from respiratory diseases, by promoting education, research, advocacy, optimal care, and the development of African capacity to address respiratory challenges in the continent.
CV Med, Crit-Care, Pulm-Critic
⊕ https://vfmat.ch/5457

Pan-African Academy of Christian Surgeons (PAACS)
Aims to train and disciple African surgeons and related specialists to become leaders and servants, providing excellent and compassionate care to those most in need, based in Christian ministry.
Anesth, CT Surg, OB-GYN, Ortho, Ped Surg, Plast, Surg
⊕ https://vfmat.ch/b444

Pan-African Academy of Christian Surgeons (PAACS)
Exists to train and support African surgeons to provide excellent, compassionate care to those most in need, inspired by the Christian faith.
Anesth, CT Surg, Neurosurg, OB-GYN, Ortho, Ped Surg, Plast, Surg
⊕ https://vfmat.ch/85ba

PANAHF – Pan Africa Heart Foundation
Targets primary prevention and specialized treatment of cardiovascular disease.
CV Med, Surg
⊕ https://vfmat.ch/8f25

Pastoralist Child Foundation
Advocates against practices that marginalize girls and women and seeks to prevent female genital mutilation (FGM) and forced early marriage. Also provides

scholarships for students.
OB-GYN, Peds
⊕ https://vfmat.ch/b7ab

PATH
Advances health equity through innovation and partnerships so people, communities, and economies can thrive.
All-Immu, CV Med, Endo, Heme-Onc, Infect Dis, MF Med, Neonat, Nutr, OB-GYN, Path, Peds, Pulm-Critic
⊕ https://vfmat.ch/b4db

Pathfinder International
Champions sexual and reproductive health and rights worldwide, mobilizing communities most in need to break through barriers and forge paths to a healthier future.
OB-GYN
⊕ https://vfmat.ch/a7b3

Paul Chester Children's Hope Foundation, The
Aims to improve the health and well-being of children and young adults in developing countries by providing early intervention where services are otherwise unavailable.
Anesth, Dent-OMFS, ENT, General, Logist-Op, Logist-Op, Ophth-Opt, Ped Surg, Peds, Surg
⊕ https://vfmat.ch/83e2

PCEA Kikuyu Hospital
Aims to provide quality, healthcare services, including surgery, dental care, eye care and orthopedic rehabilitation, inspired by the Christian faith.
Dent-OMFS, ENT, ER Med, Endo, General, Medicine, Nephro, Neurosurg, Nutr, OB-GYN, Ophth-Opt, Ortho, Palliative, Path, Peds, Radiol, Rehab, Surg
⊕ https://vfmat.ch/1c2e

Pediatric Universal Life-Saving Effort, Inc. (PULSE)
Aims to increase access to acute- and intensive-care services for children, recognizing that a significant amount of childhood mortality is preventable. Utilizes time, talents, and resources and seeks to persuade others to share their gifts to enrich the lives of children worldwide.
Crit-Care, Logist-Op, Neonat, Ped Surg, Peds
⊕ https://vfmat.ch/f6b9

Pharmacists Without Borders Canada
Provides pharmaceutical and technical assistance in the implementation or improvement of community and hospital pharmacies internationally.
⊕ https://vfmat.ch/7658

Philia Foundation
Seeks to invest sustainably in people and marginalized communities in order to improve health and education in Africa.
Anesth, ER Med, General, Heme-Onc, MF Med, Neurosurg, OB-GYN, Ophth-Opt, Ortho, Pub Health, Surg, Urol
⊕ https://vfmat.ch/a352

Philips Foundation
Aims to reduce healthcare inequality by providing access to quality healthcare for disadvantaged communities.
CV Med, OB-GYN, Ped Surg, Peds, Surg, Urol
⊕ https://vfmat.ch/bacb

Physicians Across Continents
Provides high-quality medical care to people affected by crises and disasters.
CV Med, Dent-OMFS, Heme-Onc, MF Med, Nephro, Nephro, OB-GYN, Ped Surg, Plast, Surg
⊕ https://vfmat.ch/fe5d

Picture of Health Foundation
Provides communities with health education and empowers people to alter unhealthy lifestyles, thus increasing both life expectancy and quality.
General, Pub Health
⊕ https://vfmat.ch/83e3

PINCC Preventing Cervical Cancer
Seeks to prevent female-specific diseases in developing countries by utilizing

low-cost and low-technology methods to create sustainable programs through patient education, medical personnel training, and facility outfitting.
OB-GYN
⊕ https://vfmat.ch/9666

Population Council
Conducts research to address critical health and development issues, helping deliver solutions to improve lives around the world.
Logist-Op, Pub Health
⊕ https://vfmat.ch/1777

Project Concern International (PCI)
Drives innovation from the ground up to enhance health, end hunger, overcome hardship, and advance women and girls—resulting in meaningful and measurable change in people's lives.
Infect Dis, MF Med, Nutr, OB-GYN, Peds
⊕ https://vfmat.ch/5ed7

Project Pacer International
Provides modern cardiac therapy to indigent patients in the developing world.
CT Surg, CV Med
⊕ https://vfmat.ch/f812

Project SOAR
Conducts HIV operations research around the world to identify practical solutions to improve HIV prevention, care, and treatment services.
ER Med, General, MF Med, OB-GYN, Psych
⊕ https://vfmat.ch/1a77

Project Sunshine
Harnesses the power of play to support the psychosocial and developmental needs of children and their families as they face medical challenges in hospitals or at home.
Peds, Psych
⊕ https://vfmat.ch/358b

Project Theia
Provides medical and surgical care to the underserved global community in the areas of oculoplastic, reconstructive, orbital, and facial surgery.
Anesth, General, Ophth-Opt, Plast
⊕ https://vfmat.ch/9d5a

PSI – Population Services International
Aims to improve the health of people in the developing world by focusing on challenges such as a lack of family planning, HIV/AIDS, barriers to maternal health, and the greatest threats to children under the age of 5, including malaria, diarrhea, pneumonia, and malnutrition.
Infect Dis, MF Med, OB-GYN, Peds
⊕ https://vfmat.ch/ffe3

RAD-AID International
Improves and optimizes access to medical imaging and radiology in low-resource regions of the world.
Rad-Onc, Radiol
⊕ https://vfmat.ch/537f

Raising Malawi
Supports community-based organizations that provide Malawi's orphans, vulnerable children, and their caregivers with education, medical care, food and shelter, and psycho-social support.
Crit-Care, General, Infect Dis, Ped Surg, Peds, Pub Health, Surg
⊕ https://vfmat.ch/34c3

Reach
Promotes the health of vulnerable populations through technical support to local, regional, and global efforts to prevent and control rheumatic fever and rheumatic heart disease (RF/RHD).
CV Med, Medicine, Pub Health
⊕ https://vfmat.ch/3f52

Real Medicine Foundation (RMF)
Provides humanitarian support to people living in disaster- and poverty-stricken areas, focusing on the person as a whole by providing medical/physical,

emotional, economic, and social support.
ER Med, General, Infect Dis, Nutr, Peds, Psych
⊕ https://vfmat.ch/d45a

Rescue Hope
Connects medical professionals with opportunities to serve around the world and bring physical and spiritual healing to nations abroad.
ER Med, General
⊕ https://vfmat.ch/1428

RestoringVision
Empowers lives by restoring vision for millions of people in need.
Ophth-Opt
⊕ https://vfmat.ch/e121

Riders for Health International
Aids in the last mile of healthcare delivery, by ensuring that healthcare reaches everyone, everywhere.
ER Med, Infect Dis, Logist-Op, Pub Health
⊕ https://vfmat.ch/85aa

Rockefeller Foundation, The
Works to promote the well-being of humanity.
Logist-Op, Nutr, Pub Health
⊕ https://vfmat.ch/5424

Rotary International
Provides service to others, improves lives, and advances world understanding, goodwill, and peace through its fellowship of business, professional, and community leaders.
ER Med, General, Infect Dis, MF Med, OB-GYN
⊕ https://vfmat.ch/8fb5

ROW Foundation
Works to improve the quality of training for healthcare providers, and the diagnosis and treatment available to people with epilepsy and associated psychiatric disorders in under-resourced areas of the world.
Neuro, Psych
⊕ https://vfmat.ch/25eb

Rutgers New Jersey Medical School
Seeks to support and promote the global health efforts of the faculty, staff, and students in the areas of education, research, and service through the Rutgers New Jersey Medical School's Office of Global Health.
Anesth, CV Med, Crit-Care, Neurosurg, OB-GYN, Psych
⊕ https://vfmat.ch/8e67

Sabatia Eye Hospital
Provides accessible, affordable, and sustainable quality healthcare and training.
Ophth-Opt
⊕ https://vfmat.ch/94c9

Safari Doctors
Provides innovative, community-driven healthcare solutions that promote well-being for marginalized communities.
General, Logist-Op, Pub Health
⊕ https://vfmat.ch/988c

Safe Harbor International
Inspired by the Christian faith, provides people living in poverty with ministry, development, training, and relief services such as medical care.
General
⊕ https://vfmat.ch/3dfe

Salvation Army International, The
Seeks to meet human needs through services in education, healthcare, community support, emergency response, and ministry development, inspired by the Christian faith.
Dent-OMFS, Derm, ER Med, Infect Dis, MF Med, Medicine, Nutr, OB-GYN, Ophth-Opt, Palliative, Psych, Rehab, Surg
⊕ https://vfmat.ch/8eb3

Samaritan's Purse International Disaster Relief

Provides spiritual and physical aid to hurting people around the world, such as victims of war, poverty, natural disasters, disease, and famine, based in Christian ministry.

Anesth, CT Surg, Crit-Care, Dent-OMFS, Derm, ENT, ER Med, Endo, GI, General, Heme-Onc, Infect Dis, MF Med, Neonat, Nephro, Neuro, Neurosurg, Nutr, OB-GYN, Ophth-Opt, Ortho, Path, Ped Surg, Peds, Plast, Psych, Pulm-Critic, Radiol, Rehab, Rheum, Surg, Urol, Vasc Surg

⊕ https://vfmat.ch/87e3

Sanofi Espoir Foundation

Contributes to reducing health inequalities among populations that need it most by applying a socially responsible approach focused on fighting childhood cancers in low-income countries, improving maternal and newborn health, and improving access to care.

ER Med, OB-GYN, Peds

⊕ https://vfmat.ch/943b

Save A Child's Heart

Provides lifesaving cardiac treatment to children in developing countries, and trains healthcare professionals from these countries to deliver quality care in their communities.

CT Surg, CV Med, Crit-Care, Ped Surg, Peds

⊕ https://vfmat.ch/1bef

Save the Children

Gives children around the world a healthy start in life, the opportunity to learn, and protection from harm.

All-Immu, Crit-Care, ER Med, General, Infect Dis, MF Med, Medicine, Neonat, OB-GYN, Peds, Psych, Pub Health

⊕ https://vfmat.ch/2e73

Saving Mothers

Seeks to eradicate preventable maternal deaths and birth-related complications in low-resource settings.

MF Med, Neonat, OB-GYN, Surg

⊕ https://vfmat.ch/ed94

SEE International

Provides sustainable medical, surgical, and educational services through volunteer ophthalmic surgeons, with the objectives of restoring sight and preventing blindness to disadvantaged individuals worldwide.

Ophth-Opt, Surg

⊕ https://vfmat.ch/6e1b

SeeKenya

Aims to transform the provision of eye care in Kenya by ensuring that Kenyans have the opportunity to have access to affordable, local eye care and education in order to improve eyesight and quality of life.

Ophth-Opt

⊕ https://vfmat.ch/f2ca

Serving Others Worldwide

Aims to provide aid to the poor, distressed, and underprivileged by providing healthcare and dental services, and by building schools, orphanages, libraries, and medical clinics in undeveloped countries.

Dent-OMFS, General

⊕ https://vfmat.ch/69cb

SEVA

Delivers vital eye care services to the world's most vulnerable, including women, children, and Indigenous peoples.

Ophth-Opt, Surg

⊕ https://vfmat.ch/1e87

Shamiri Institute

Develops and scales cost-effective interventions that improve the well-being and mental health of Africa's youth while building character strengths and improving academic outcomes.

Psych, Pub Health

⊕ https://vfmat.ch/8a27

Shrimad Rajchandra Love and Care

Serves the underprivileged through holistic community outreach and development programs that provide education, medical and humanitarian care, inspired by a spiritual movement.

Logist-Op, Nutr, Pub Health

⊕ https://vfmat.ch/1e2d

Sightsavers

Works with partners in developing countries to help eliminate avoidable blindness and advocates for equal opportunity for the disabled.

Infect Dis, Ophth-Opt, Surg

⊕ https://vfmat.ch/aa52

SIGN Fracture Care International

Builds orthopedic capacity around the world and provides the injured poor access to fracture surgery by donating orthopedic education and implant systems to surgeons in developing countries.

Ortho, Rehab, Surg

⊕ https://vfmat.ch/123d

Simavi

Strives for a world in which all women and girls are socially and economically empowered and pursue their rights to live a healthy life, free from discrimination, coercion, and violence.

MF Med, OB-GYN

⊕ https://vfmat.ch/b57b

SINA Health

Aims to improve the health and educational status of the population in low- and middle-income countries.

General, Logist-Op

⊕ https://vfmat.ch/9ad3

Sisters of the Immaculate Heart of Mary, Mother of Christ

Based in Chrisitan ministry, seeks to motivate people, especially the poor and the less privileged, to live venerable and dignified lives through credibility-structured programs, education, various medical and humanitarian services, along with self-realization and self-empowerment opportunities.

Infect Dis, Logist-Op, Nutr, Pub Health

⊕ https://vfmat.ch/5774

Smile Train, Inc.

Treats children with cleft lip through a sustainable and local model that supports surgery and other forms of essential care.

Logist-Op, Pub Health

⊕ https://vfmat.ch/822c

SmileStar

Provides free, quality dental care to disadvantaged communities in African countries and India.

Dent-OMFS

⊕ https://vfmat.ch/ade3

Soddo Christian Hospital

Mobilizes volunteers to help transform communities through healthcare and education, based in Christian ministry.

ER Med, General

⊕ https://vfmat.ch/efa4

Sofia Global

Inspired by the Christian faith, promotes an equitable and sustainable society through education, healthcare, pastoral work, and community capacity-building.

General, Heme-Onc, Infect Dis, MF Med, OB-GYN, Peds

⊕ https://vfmat.ch/263c

Sollay Kenyan Foundation

Provides resources to open primary care clinics and to provide primary care medicine to people of Kenya.

General, Logist-Op

⊕ https://vfmat.ch/4db9

SOS Children's Villages International

Supports children through alternative care and family strengthening.

ER Med, Peds
⊕ https://vfmat.ch/aca1

Soteni International
Works in rural Kenya to help prevent and mitigate the effects of diseases, especially HIV/AIDS, through community-based programs.
General, Infect Dis, OB-GYN
⊕ https://vfmat.ch/66fd

Souls International Foundation
Helps orphans, widows, and the poor in their time of need according to the dictates of the Gospel of Jesus Christ, who commanded us to love our neighbors as we love ourselves.
General, Infect Dis
⊕ https://vfmat.ch/52a1

Sri Sathya Sai International Organization
Inspired by spiritual teachings, carries out efforts in global healthcare, education, humanitarian relief, and youth engagement.
Dent-OMFS, General, Logist-Op, Nutr, Ophth-Opt, Pub Health
⊕ https://vfmat.ch/9bda

St Scholastica Uzima Hospital
Provides appropriate and affordable healthcare, available to those who are in need, inspired by the Christian faith.
Dent-OMFS, ER Med, Infect Dis, Neonat, OB-GYN, Path, Radiol, Urol
⊕ https://vfmat.ch/e399

St Theresa Mission Hospital Kiirua
Aims to offer accessible and affordable quality healthcare to all, through motivated caregivers, inspired by the Christian faith.
CV Med, CV Med, Dent-OMFS, Derm, ENT, General, Heme-Onc, OB-GYN, Ophth-Opt, Ortho, Peds, Radiol, Urol, Urol
⊕ https://vfmat.ch/eb13

Still A Mum
Aims to create an all-encompassing quality and inclusive pregnancy and early parenting mental health infrastructure in Africa through a network of support, education, and advocacy.
Psych
⊕ https://vfmat.ch/5ffa

Surgical Hope Children's Fund
Helps children in Kenya receive lifesaving surgical procedures.
Ped Surg
⊕ https://vfmat.ch/641e

Sustainable Medical Missions
Trains and supports Indigenous healthcare and faith leaders in underdeveloped communities to treat neglected tropical diseases (NTDs) and other endemic conditions affecting the poorest community members, by pairing faith-based solutions with best practices.
Infect Dis, Pub Health
⊕ https://vfmat.ch/9165

Swiss Doctors
Aims to improve the health of populations in developing countries through medical-aid projects and training.
General, Infect Dis, Medicine
⊕ https://vfmat.ch/311a

Swiss Tropical and Public Health Institute
Contributes to the improvement of the health of populations internationally, nationally, and locally through excellence in research, education, and services.
Infect Dis, Pub Health
⊕ https://vfmat.ch/2ee4

Task Force for Global Health, The
Consists of programs and focus areas that cover a range of global health issues including neglected tropical diseases, infectious diseases, vaccines, field epidemiology, public health informatics, health workforce development, and global health ethics.

Infect Dis, Logist-Op, Medicine, Ophth-Opt, Peds
⊕ https://vfmat.ch/714c

Team 5 Medical Foundation
Provides medical care in the most overlooked remote areas of the world supported by sponsorships, donations, and the dedication of its volunteers.
ER Med, General, Peds, Plast, Pulm-Critic
⊕ https://vfmat.ch/f267

Team Canada Healing Hands
Provides and develops interdisciplinary rehabilitation treatment, education, and training in areas of need.
ENT, Neuro, Psych, Rehab
⊕ https://vfmat.ch/2eaf

Tearfund
Responds to crisis and partners with local churches to bring restoration to those living in poverty, inspired by the Christian faith.
ER Med, Logist-Op
⊕ https://vfmat.ch/f6cf

Terre des hommes (Tdh) Foundation
Works to improve the daily life of children and their relatives in the areas of health, protection and emergency, in Europe, Africa, Asia, Latin America, and the Near and Middle East.
CT Surg, CV Med, OB-GYN, Ped Surg, Pub Health
⊕ https://vfmat.ch/5c26

Third World Eye Care Society (TWECS)
Collects old, unused eyeglasses and distributes them in conjunction with eye exams given by properly trained individuals.
Logist-Op, Ophth-Opt
⊕ https://vfmat.ch/8618

Tiba Foundation
Partners with local Kenyan healthcare organizations and provides funding, medical volunteers, and strategic guidance to save lives and transform the healthcare landscape for thousands of locals in rural Kenya.
Infect Dis, Medicine, OB-GYN, Peds, Rehab, Surg
⊕ https://vfmat.ch/e1d8

Toto Care Box
Seeks to protect, preserve, and promote the health and well-being of newborns in their first 28 days of life.
Logist-Op, MF Med, OB-GYN, Peds
⊕ https://vfmat.ch/988d

Touching Lives Ministry
Based in Christian ministry, supports communities worldwide through improved healthcare, education, and spiritual and economic development.
General, OB-GYN, Peds, Surg
⊕ https://vfmat.ch/75d3

Tree of Lives
Aims to strengthen the African family in its shared battle against HIV/AIDS and poverty.
General, Infect Dis, Neonat, Peds
⊕ https://vfmat.ch/ebc2

Tumaini International
Seeks to provide humanitarian aid, including programs that focus on care and sponsorship for orphans, medical outreach, healthcare, education, and socioeconomic development.
General, Infect Dis, MF Med, OB-GYN, Peds
⊕ https://vfmat.ch/98b8

Tushinde
Provides care and education to the poorest children and families and helps families stay together by sharing the financial burden.
General, Infect Dis
⊕ https://vfmat.ch/23d6

U.S. President's Malaria Initiative (PMI)
Supports low-income countries to help control and eliminate malaria through cost-effective, lifesaving malaria interventions.
Infect Dis, MF Med, OB-GYN
⊕ https://vfmat.ch/dc8b

Ubuntu Life Foundation
Provides access to essential services and promotes social inclusion for children with special educational and physical needs throughout Kenya.
CV Med, Neurosurg, Ortho, Peds
⊕ https://vfmat.ch/7ed5

Unforgotten Fund, The (UNFF)
Provides lifesaving humanitarian relief to UN Field Operations and projects such as water supply, sanitation and hygiene (WASH), food security, health, and shelter.
ER Med, MF Med, Nutr, OB-GYN, Peds
⊕ https://vfmat.ch/928f

Union for International Cancer Control (UICC)
Unites and supports the cancer community to reduce the global cancer burden, promote greater equity, and ensure that cancer control continues to be a priority in the world health and development agenda.
Heme-Onc, Pub Health
⊕ https://vfmat.ch/88b1

United Hands Relief & Development
Works to funnel efforts toward alleviating and immediately responding to the sufferings of others around the globe, regardless of nationality, race, religion, or social status.
ER Med, General, Infect Dis, Ophth-Opt, Surg
⊕ https://vfmat.ch/2771

United MegaCare
Seeks to deliver high-caliber services and programming across its areas of focus: education, health and wellness, secure families, and disaster resiliency.
ER Med, General, Infect Dis, Nutr, Ophth-Opt, Peds
⊕ https://vfmat.ch/ea18

United Methodist Volunteers in Mission (UMVIM)
Engages in short-term missions each year in ministries as varied as disaster response, community development, pastor training, microenterprise, agriculture, Vacation Bible School, building repair and construction, and medical/dental services.
Dent-OMFS, ER Med, General
⊕ https://vfmat.ch/1ee6

United Nations Children's Fund (UNICEF)
Works in over 190 countries and territories to save children's lives, defend their rights, and help them fulfill their potential, from early childhood through adolescence.
All-Immu, Infect Dis, MF Med, Neonat, Nutr, OB-GYN, Ped Surg, Peds, Pub Health
⊕ https://vfmat.ch/42d7

United Nations Development Programme (UNDP)
Helps countries achieve the simultaneous eradication of extreme poverty and significant reduction of inequalities and exclusion using a sustainable human development approach.
Infect Dis, Logist-Op, Pub Health
⊕ https://vfmat.ch/935c

United Nations High Commissioner for Refugees (UNHCR)
Safeguards the rights and well-being of people who have been forced to flee, ensuring that everybody has the right to seek asylum and find safe refuge in another country, with the goal of seeking lasting solutions.
General, MF Med, Medicine, OB-GYN, Peds, Psych, Pub Health
⊕ https://vfmat.ch/6636

United Nations Population Fund (UNFPA)
Supports reproductive healthcare for women and youth in more than 150 countries, focusing on delivering a world in which every pregnancy is wanted, every childbirth is safe, and every young person's potential is fulfilled.
Infect Dis, MF Med, Neonat, OB-GYN, Peds, Pub Health
⊕ https://vfmat.ch/c969

United States Agency for International Development (USAID)
Promotes and demonstrates democratic values abroad and advances a free, peaceful, and prosperous world. Leads the U.S. government's international development and disaster assistance through partnerships and investments that save lives.
ER Med, Infect Dis, MF Med, OB-GYN, Peds
⊕ https://vfmat.ch/9a99

Universal Care for Africa Foundation (UCAF)
Aims to provide access to healthcare services and resources to people in Africa regardless of age, sex, or demographic area.
Infect Dis, OB-GYN
⊕ https://vfmat.ch/d83e

University of California San Francisco: Institute for Global Health Sciences
Dedicates its efforts to improving health and reducing the burden of disease in the world's most vulnerable populations by integrating expertise in the health, social, and biological sciences, training global health leaders, and developing solutions to the most pressing health challenges.
Infect Dis, OB-GYN, Pub Health
⊕ https://vfmat.ch/6587

University of California, San Francisco: Center for Global Surgery and Health Equity
Leads and supports academic global surgery, while strengthening surgical-care systems in low-resource settings through research and education.
Anesth, OB-GYN, Surg
⊕ https://vfmat.ch/564f

University of California: Global Health Institute
Mobilizes people and resources across the University of California to advance global health research, education, and collaboration.
General, OB-GYN, Pub Health
⊕ https://vfmat.ch/ee7f

University of Colorado: Global Emergency Care Initiative
Strives to sustainably improve emergency care outcomes in low- and middle-income communities worldwide by linking cutting-edge academics with excellent on-the-ground implementation.
ER Med
⊕ https://vfmat.ch/417a

University of New Mexico School of Medicine: Project Echo
Seeks to improve health outcomes worldwide through the use of a technology called telementoring, a guided-practice model in which the participating clinician retains responsibility for managing the patient.
General, Infect Dis, MF Med, OB-GYN, Path, Peds
⊕ https://vfmat.ch/6c9a

University of Pennsylvania Perelman School of Medicine Center for Global Health
Aims to improve health equity worldwide through enhanced public health awareness and access to care, discovery, and outcomes-based research, and comprehensive educational programs grounded in partnership.
Heme-Onc, Infect Dis, OB-GYN
⊕ https://vfmat.ch/cb57

University of Texas at Austin Dell Medical School: Division of Global Health
Revolutionizes how people get and stay healthy by rethinking the role of academic medicine in improving health.
General, Logist-Op, Pub Health, Surg
⊕ https://vfmat.ch/a16b

University of Washington: Department of Global Health
Improves health for all through research, education, training, and service, addresses the causes of disease and health inequities at multiple levels, and collaborates with partners to develop and sustain locally led, quality health systems, programs, and policies.

Infect Dis, Logist-Op, Pub Health
⊕ https://vfmat.ch/f543

University of Washington: The International Training and Education Center for Health (I-TECH)
Works with local partners to develop skilled healthcare workers and strong national health systems in resource-limited countries.
Infect Dis, Pub Health
⊕ https://vfmat.ch/642f

University of Wisconsin-Madison: Department of Surgery
Provides comprehensive educational experiences, groundbreaking research, and superb patient care.
Anesth, ENT, ER Med, Endo, Peds, Plast, Pub Health, Surg
⊕ https://vfmat.ch/64c2

Unstoppable Foundation
Brings sustainable education to children and communities in developing countries.
Pub Health
⊕ https://vfmat.ch/f73c

USA for United Nations High Commissioner for Refugees (UNHCR)
Serves and protects refugees and displaced people through emergency relief, cash assistance, education, resettlement, and the rebuilding of livelihoods.
ER Med, General, Logist-Op, Nutr, Pub Health
⊕ https://vfmat.ch/293c

USAID's Health Research Program
Funds maternal and child health implementation research and translates findings into effective health interventions that can be adapted globally.
Infect Dis, MF Med, OB-GYN, Peds
⊕ https://vfmat.ch/5991

USAID: A2Z The Micronutrient and Child Blindness Project
Aims to increase the use of key micronutrient and blindness interventions to improve child and maternal health.
MF Med, Neonat, Nutr, Ophth-Opt, Surg
⊕ https://vfmat.ch/c5f1

USAID: Health Policy Initiative
Provides field-level programming in health policy development and implementation.
General, Infect Dis, MF Med, OB-GYN, Peds
⊕ https://vfmat.ch/8f84

USAID: Human Resources for Health 2030 (HRH2030)
Helps low- and middle-income countries develop the health workforce needed to prevent maternal and child deaths, support the goals of Family Planning 2020, control the HIV/AIDS epidemic, and protect communities from infectious diseases.
Logist-Op
⊕ https://vfmat.ch/9ea8

USAID: Maternal and Child Health Integrated Program
Works to improve the health of women and their families, including programs for maternal, newborn, and child health, immunization, family planning, nutrition, malaria, and HIV/AIDS.
All-Immu, General, Infect Dis, MF Med
⊕ https://vfmat.ch/4415

USAID: Maternal and Child Survival Program
Works to prevent child and maternal deaths.
Infect Dis, MF Med, Neonat, OB-GYN, Peds
⊕ https://vfmat.ch/6fcf

USAID: TB Care II
Focuses on tuberculosis care and treatment.
Infect Dis
⊕ https://vfmat.ch/57d4

Vanderbilt University Medical Center: Global Surgery
Aims to improve the healthcare of individuals and communities regionally, nationally, and internationally, combining transformative learning programs and compelling discoveries to provide distinctive personalized care.
CT Surg, CV Med, Neurosurg, Ophth-Opt, Ortho, Ped Surg, Surg, Urol
⊕ https://vfmat.ch/ee28

Village HopeCore International
Seeks to promote the alleviation of poverty in Kenya, East Africa, by providing micro loans, business education, health education, and health support with an emphasis on HIV/AIDS, malaria, and mother/child wellness programs.
General, Ophth-Opt, Pub Health
⊕ https://vfmat.ch/74f3

Village Project Africa
Aims to educate children, equip and care for widows, bring hope to villages, and transform lives.
General, Infect Dis
⊕ https://vfmat.ch/2cf7

Vision Care
Restores sight and helps patients get regular treatment at short-term eye camps and long-term base clinics by having doctors, missionaries, volunteers, and sponsors work together.
Ophth-Opt
⊕ https://vfmat.ch/9d7c

Vision Outreach International
Advocates for helping the blind in underserved regions of the world and empowers the poor through sight restoration.
Ophth-Opt
⊕ https://vfmat.ch/9721

Vitamin Angels
Helps at-risk populations in need—specifically pregnant women, new mothers, and children under age 5—to gain access to life-changing vitamins and minerals.
General, Nutr
⊕ https://vfmat.ch/7da1

Voluntary Service Overseas (VSO)
Works with health workers, communities, and governments to improve health services and rights for women, babies, youth, people with disabilities, and prisoners.
General, MF Med, OB-GYN
⊕ https://vfmat.ch/213d

VOSH (Volunteer Optometric Services to Humanity) International
Facilitates the provision and the sustainability of vision care worldwide for people who can neither afford nor obtain such care.
Ophth-Opt
⊕ https://vfmat.ch/a149

Walkabout Foundation
Provides wheelchairs and rehabilitation in the developing world and funds research to find a cure for paralysis.
Logist-Op, Rehab
⊕ https://vfmat.ch/5582

Watsi
Uses technology to make healthcare a reality for those who might not otherwise be able to afford it.
Pub Health, Surg
⊕ https://vfmat.ch/41a3

We Care for Humanity (WCH)
Promotes sustainable social change and the sustainable development goals developed by the United Nations, including: no poverty, good health and well-being, gender equality, human rights, climate action, and strong institutions.
General, Logist-Op, Pub Health
⊕ https://vfmat.ch/8b4e

WF AID
Seeks to build capacity and provide emergency aid, human assistance, and international development, where required in the world.
CT Surg, Dent-OMFS, ENT, ER Med, General, Infect Dis, Logist-Op, Nutr, Ophth-

Opt, Ortho, Path, Radiol, Rehab, Surg
⊕ https://vfmat.ch/ebd7

White Ribbon Alliance, The
Leads a movement for reproductive, maternal, and newborn health and accelerates progress by putting citizens at the center of global, national, and local health efforts.
MF Med, OB-GYN
⊕ https://vfmat.ch/496b

Wisconsin Medical Project
Provides humanitarian aid, including donated medical equipment and supplies, to hospitals and clinics in areas of great need.
Logist-Op
⊕ https://vfmat.ch/ef3b

Women's Refugee Commission
Seeks to improve lives by protecting the rights of women, children, and youth displaced by conflict and crisis through researching their needs, identifying solutions, and advocating for programs and policies to strengthen their resilience.
General, MF Med, Neonat, OB-GYN, Peds, Psych
⊕ https://vfmat.ch/3d8f

World Blind Union (WBU)
Represents those experiencing blindness, speaking to governments and international bodies on issues concerning visual impairments.
Ophth-Opt
⊕ https://vfmat.ch/2bd3

World Child Cancer
Works to improve diagnosis, treatment, and support for children with cancer, and their families, in low- and middle-income parts of the world.
Heme-Onc, Ped Surg, Rad-Onc
⊕ https://vfmat.ch/fbbc

World Children's Fund
Commits to helping children worldwide who are suffering the effects of poverty, disease, natural disaster, famine, abuse, civil strife, and war.
General, Logist-Op, MF Med, Nutr, OB-GYN, Pub Health
⊕ https://vfmat.ch/9cd8

World Council of Optometry
Facilitates the development of optometry worldwide and promotes eye health and vision care through advocacy, education, policy development, and humanitarian outreach.
Ophth-Opt, Pub Health
⊕ https://vfmat.ch/c92e

World Federation of Hemophilia (WFH)
Aims to improve and sustain care for people with inherited bleeding disorders by pursuing long-term relationships with individuals and organizations who share the values of WFH's development model.
Heme-Onc
⊕ https://vfmat.ch/5121

World Health Organization, The (WHO)
The United Nations' agency for health provides leadership on global health matters, shapes the health research agenda, sets norms and standards, articulates evidence-based policy options, provides technical support and monitoring to countries, and assesses health trends.
ER Med, General, Infect Dis, Logist-Op, MF Med, OB-GYN, Peds, Psych, Pub Health
⊕ https://vfmat.ch/c476

World Heart Federation
Leads the global fight against heart disease and stroke, with a focus on low- and middle-income countries.
CV Med, Crit-Care, Heme-Onc, Medicine, Peds
⊕ https://vfmat.ch/ea51

World Medical Relief
Facilitates the distribution of surplus medical resources where they are needed.

Logist-Op
⊕ https://vfmat.ch/72dc

World Relief
Brings sustainable solutions to the world's greatest problems: disasters, extreme poverty, violence, oppression, and mass displacement.
ER Med, Nutr, Psych, Pub Health
⊕ https://vfmat.ch/fbcd

World Vision International
Works with vulnerable communities around the world to overcome poverty and injustice with child-focused programs in disaster management, health, nutrition, economic development, education, clean water, sanitation, and hygiene.
ER Med, General, Infect Dis, MF Med, Nutr, OB-GYN, Peds
⊕ https://vfmat.ch/2642

Worldwide Fistula Fund
Protects and restores the health and dignity of the world's most vulnerable women by preventing and treating devastating childbirth injuries.
OB-GYN
⊕ https://vfmat.ch/8813

Yale School of Medicine: Global Surgery Division
Addresses the rising worldwide surgical disease burden in low-resource settings, both domestically and internationally, by mobilizing a community of surgical leaders to engage in international partnerships and implement quality improvement and training protocols.
ER Med, Infect Dis, Medicine, Peds
⊕ https://vfmat.ch/2bf7

Zana Africa Foundation
Equips adolescent girls in Kenya with the tools they need to safely navigate puberty and leverages reproductive health education for women and girls' empowerment.
OB-GYN
⊕ https://vfmat.ch/b167

Zosseo Overland Support
Seeks to connect essential dental services with the most underserved communities in East Africa.
Dent-OMFS
⊕ https://vfmat.ch/5df2

Kenya

Healthcare Facilities

5th Avenue Medical and Day Surgery Centre
Nairobi, Nairobi Area, Kenya
🌐 https://vfmat.ch/f195

Afrismart Hospital Group Ltd.
Embakasi, Nairobi, Kenya
🌐 https://vfmat.ch/46d2

Aga Khan Hospital, The
Kisumu, Nairobi Area, Kenya
🌐 https://vfmat.ch/2eed

Aga Khan Hospital Kisii
Nyabururu, Kisii, Kenya
🌐 https://vfmat.ch/afb4

Aga Khan University Hospital
Limuru, Nairobi Area, Kenya
🌐 https://vfmat.ch/8116

Aga Khan University Hospital Kitengela
Kitengela, Kajiado, Kenya
🌐 https://vfmat.ch/4b94

Ahero County Hospital
Ahero, Kisumu, Kenya
🌐 https://vfmat.ch/11e5

AIC CURE International Hospital
Nairobi, Nairobi County, Kenya
🌐 https://vfmat.ch/id8v

AIC Kapsowar Hospital
Kapsowar, Elgeyo-Marakwet, Kenya
🌐 https://vfmat.ch/uwpg

AIC Kijabe Hospital
Kijabe, Kiambu, Kenya
🌐 https://vfmat.ch/vghu

AIC Kijabe Naivasha Hospital
Marula Munyu, Nakuru, Kenya
🌐 https://vfmat.ch/5ba9

AIC Litein Hospital
Litein, Kericho, Kenya
🌐 https://vfmat.ch/4bbd

Ambira Sub District Hospital
Ambira, Siaya, Kenya
🌐 https://vfmat.ch/1d2e

Anka General Hospital
Mumias, Nairobi Area, Kenya
🌐 https://vfmat.ch/6318

Avenue Healthcare Hospital
First Parklands Avenue, Nairobi Area, Kenya
🌐 https://vfmat.ch/f536

Avenue Hospital
Mumias, Nairobi Area, Kenya
🌐 https://vfmat.ch/b9c7

Balozi Hospital
Mumias, Nairobi Area, Kenya
🌐 https://vfmat.ch/75ca

Baragoi District Hospital
Baragoi, Samburu, Kenya
🌐 https://vfmat.ch/2f3b

Baringo County Referral Hospital
Kabarnet, Baringo, Kenya
🌐 https://vfmat.ch/119d

Better Living Hospital
Milimani, Nairobi Area, Kenya
🌐 https://vfmat.ch/b86f

Bishop Kioko Catholic Hospital
Kitooni, Machakos, Kenya
🌐 https://vfmat.ch/2fe4

BOMU Hospital
Changamwe, Mombasa, Kenya
🌐 https://vfmat.ch/7cb3

Bristol Park Hospital
Nairobi, Nairobi County, Kenya
🌐 https://vfmat.ch/b5ab

Bristol Park Hospital Utawala
Nairobi, Nairobi, Kenya
🌐 https://vfmat.ch/a857

Bungoma District Hospital
Kanduyi, Bungoma, Kenya
🌐 https://vfmat.ch/12af

Bura Sub-County Hospital
Bura, Garissa, Kenya
🌐 https://vfmat.ch/1cbe

Busia County Referral Hospital
Kenas, Busia, Kenya
🌐 https://vfmat.ch/3eab

Bute District Hospital
Bute, Wajir, Wajir, Kenya
🌐 https://vfmat.ch/bf62

Butere County Hospital
Butere, Kakamega, Kenya
🌐 https://vfmat.ch/2f5d

Care Hospital Ltd.
Mumias, Nairobi Area, Kenya
🌐 https://vfmat.ch/47d2

Chuka County Referral Hospital
Chuka, Tharaka – Nithi, Kenya
🌐 https://vfmat.ch/a6d8

Consolata Hospital Nkubu
Nkubu, Meru County, Kenya
🌐 https://vfmat.ch/47c3

Coptic Hospital
Ngong, Nairobi Area, Kenya
⊕ https://vfmat.ch/ff72

Cottolengo Mission Hospital
Gaitu, Meru, Kenya
⊕ https://vfmat.ch/e48d

Diani Beach Hospital Kwale Clinic
Diani Beach, Kenya
https://vfmat.ch/b48c

Egerton Dispensery
Egerton, Nakuru, Kenya
⊕ https://vfmat.ch/f89d

El Wak Sub-County Referral Hospital
El Wak, Mandera, Kenya
⊕ https://vfmat.ch/8a43

Elburgon Sub-County Hospital
Elburgon, Nakuru, Kenya
⊕ https://vfmat.ch/61d5

Eldama Ravine Sub-County Referral Hospital
Eldama Ravine, Baringo, Kenya
⊕ https://vfmat.ch/2b64

Embu Provincial Hospital
Matakari, Embu, Kenya
⊕ https://vfmat.ch/9fa8

Emuhaya Sub-County Hospital
Emuhaya, Vihiga, Kenya
⊕ https://vfmat.ch/6462

Endebess Sub-County Hospital
Endebess, Trans Nzoia, Kenya
⊕ https://vfmat.ch/4b1c

Fatima Mission Hospital
Ongata Rongai, Kajiado, Kenya
⊕ https://vfmat.ch/ce7a

Garden Specialist Hospital
Kibera, Nairobi Area, Kenya
⊕ https://vfmat.ch/3ada

Garissa County Referral Hospital
Garissa, Garissa County, Kenya
⊕ https://vfmat.ch/58b1

Gatundu Level 4 Hospital
Gatundu, Kiambu County, Kenya
⊕ https://vfmat.ch/d391

Gertrude's Children Hospital Mombasa
Mombasa town, Mombasa, Kenya
⊕ https://vfmat.ch/a8a1

Gertrudes Childrens Hospital-Thika
Nairobi, Kenya
⊕ https://vfmat.ch/4bb8

Gertrude's Children's Hospital Muthaiga
Muthaiga, Nairobi, Kenya
⊕ https://vfmat.ch/61da

Gertrude Childrens Hospital
Muthaiga, Nairobi, Kenya
⊕ https://vfmat.ch/6fb4

Gilgil Sub-County Hospital
Gilgil, Nakuru, Kenya
⊕ https://vfmat.ch/284f

Glory Hospital
Mlango Kubwa, Nairobi Area, Kenya
⊕ https://vfmat.ch/6c92

Great Medical Hospital, The
Air Base, Nairobi Area, Kenya
⊕ https://vfmat.ch/f4ab

Habswein Level IV Hospital
Habaswein, Wajir, Kenya
⊕ https://vfmat.ch/8ae4

Hayat Hospital
Nairobi, Nairobi County, Kenya
⊕ https://vfmat.ch/5738

Health Gate Hospital
Starehe, Nairobi Area, Kenya
⊕ https://vfmat.ch/3a91

Hema Level 5 Hospital
Kisii Town, Kisii County, Kenya
⊕ https://vfmat.ch/49ee

Hola District Hospital
Kibuyu, Galole, Kenya
⊕ https://vfmat.ch/aa37

Homa Bay County Teaching and Referral Hospital
Homa Bay, Nyanza, Kenya
⊕ https://vfmat.ch/c3d9

Inuka Hospital & Maternity Home
North Gem, Siaya, Nyanza, Kenya
⊕ https://vfmat.ch/c74a

Isiolo General Hospital
Garba, Isiolo, Kenya
⊕ https://vfmat.ch/b64c

Iten County Referral Hospital
Iten, Rift Valley, Kenya
⊕ https://vfmat.ch/7bf6

Jamaa Mission Hospital
Air Base, Nairobi Area, Kenya
⊕ https://vfmat.ch/7cdf

Jaramogi Oginga Odinga Teaching & Referral Hospital
Kisumu, Nyanza, Kenya
⊕ https://vfmat.ch/a1e4

Jocham Hospital
Mombasa, Mombasa County, Kenya
⊕ https://vfmat.ch/f1a8

Juja Modern Hospital
Juja, Kiambu, Kenya
⊕ https://vfmat.ch/745f

Kajiado District Hospital
Sajiloni, Kajiado, Kenya
⊕ https://vfmat.ch/2d2f

Kakuma Mission Hospital
Kakuma, Turkana, Kenya
⊕ https://vfmat.ch/3c1b

Kalacha Sub-County Referral Hospital (Chalbi)
Maikona, Marsabit, Kenya
⊕ https://vfmat.ch/cfcb

Kangundo Level 4 Hospital
Kangundo, Machakos, Kenya
⊕ https://vfmat.ch/6e74

Kapenguria Referral Hospital Ward Seven
Kamorow, West Pokot, Kenya
⊕ https://vfmat.ch/1924

Karen Hospital
Langata Road-Karen, Nairobi, Kenya
⊕ https://vfmat.ch/8d6e

Karen Hospital-Nyeri
Nyeri, Kenya
⊕ https://vfmat.ch/bb69

Katito Hospital
Katito, Kisumu, Kenya
⊕ https://vfmat.ch/3d78

Kemrif Hospital
Nairobi, Nairobi County, Kenya
⊕ https://vfmat.ch/d4e4

Kendu Bay District Hospital
Gendia, Homa Bay, Kenya
⊕ https://vfmat.ch/da71

Kenya Defence Forces Memorial Hospital
Kibera, Nairobi Area, Kenya
⊕ https://vfmat.ch/d3cb

Kenyatta National Hospital (KNH)
Nairobi, Kenya
🌐 https://vfmat.ch/7585

Kericho County Referral Hospital
Keongo, Kericho, Kenya
🌐 https://vfmat.ch/d614

Kerugoya County Referral Hospital
Kerugoya, Kirinyaga County, Kenya
🌐 https://vfmat.ch/b259

Khorof Harar Hospital
Khorof Harar, Wajir, Kenya
🌐 https://vfmat.ch/26a7

Kiambu Sub County Level 5 Hospital
Kangoya, Kiambu, Kenya
🌐 https://vfmat.ch/6cdb

Kibera Mental Hospital
Nairobi, Nairobi County, Kenya
🌐 https://vfmat.ch/9964

Kijabe Mission Hospital
Kijabe, Kijabe, Kenya
🌐 https://vfmat.ch/795f

Kilifi County Hospital
Kilifi Creek, Coast Province, Kenya
🌐 https://vfmat.ch/f2fe

Kiminini Cottage Mission Hospital
Kiminini, Trans Nzoia, Kenya
🌐 https://vfmat.ch/ddcc

Kinango Sub-County Hospital
Kinango, Kwale, Kenya
🌐 https://vfmat.ch/b195

King Fahd Lamu District Hospital
Mtambo, Lamu, Kenya
🌐 https://vfmat.ch/a118

Kiria-ini Mission Hospital
Kiriaini, Murang'A, Kenya
🌐 https://vfmat.ch/7459

Kisii Teaching and Referral Hospital
Kisii, Kisii County, Kenya
🌐 https://vfmat.ch/4f7f

Kisumu County Referral
Kanyamedha, Kisumu, Kenya
🌐 https://vfmat.ch/d7da

LifeCare Hospitals Bungoma
Bungoma, Bungoma County, Kenya
🌐 https://vfmat.ch/8419

Lifeline Group of Hospital, The – Wendani
Kahawa Wendani, Nairobi Area, Kenya
🌐 https://vfmat.ch/9396

Likoni Sub-District Hospital
Likoni, Mombasa, Kenya
🌐 https://vfmat.ch/d6c4

Limuru Cottage Hospital
Limuru, Kiambu County, Kenya
🌐 https://vfmat.ch/e6c4

Lions SightFirst Eye Hospital
Nairobi, Nairobi County, Kenya
🌐 https://vfmat.ch/1ea7

Lodwar County Referral Hospital (Lodwar District Hospital)
Lodwar, Turkana, Kenya
🌐 https://vfmat.ch/1947

Loitokitok Sub-County Hospital
Oloitokitok, Kajiado, Kenya
🌐 https://vfmat.ch/519a

Lumumba Hospital
Nyamasaria, Kisumu, Kenya
🌐 https://vfmat.ch/829c

Lumumba Sub-County Hospital
Nyanza, Kisumu, Kenya
🌐 https://vfmat.ch/a6a3

M. P. Shah Hospital
Parklands, Nairobi Area, Kenya
🌐 https://vfmat.ch/2d6a

Machakos Level 5 Hospital
Misakwani, Machakos, Kenya
🌐 https://vfmat.ch/d192

Magadi Hospital
Magadi, Kajiado County, Kenya
🌐 https://vfmat.ch/cddd

Makindu Sub-County Hospital
Makindu, Kibwezi West, Makueni County, Kenya
🌐 https://vfmat.ch/a3de

Makueni County Referral Hospital
Wote, Makueni County, Kenya
🌐 https://vfmat.ch/568f

Malindi Sub-County Hospital
Malindi, Kilifi, Kenya
🌐 https://vfmat.ch/19fc

Mandera County Referral Hospital (Mandera District Hospital)
Mandera, Kenya
🌐 https://vfmat.ch/mjpp

Maragua District Rural Hospital
Maragua, Murang'A, Kenya
🌐 https://vfmat.ch/4377

Maralal District Hospital
Maralal, Samburu, Kenya
🌐 https://vfmat.ch/c1e8

Maria Immaculata Hospital (MCH)
Nairobi, Nairobi, Kenya
🌐 https://vfmat.ch/ff5c

Mariakani Cottage Hospital
Mlolongo, Machakos, Kenya
🌐 https://vfmat.ch/6ac9

Mariakani Hospital
Mumias, Nairobi Area, Kenya
🌐 https://vfmat.ch/3e52

Marigat Hospital
Marigat, Baringo, Kenya
🌐 https://vfmat.ch/ae4a

Marigat Sub-District Hospital
Marigat, Kabarnet, Baringo, Kenya
🌐 https://vfmat.ch/d873

Marsabit County Referral Hospital
Marsabit, Marsabit, Kenya
🌐 https://vfmat.ch/45d5

Masaba District Hospital
Keroka, Kenya
🌐 https://vfmat.ch/8ade

Masaba Hospital
Ngong, Nairobi, Kenya
🌐 https://vfmat.ch/e2db

Masimba Sub-District Hospital
Keroka, Kisii, Kenya
🌐 https://vfmat.ch/1517

Mater Misericordiae Hospital
Nairobi, Nairobi County, Kenya
🌐 https://vfmat.ch/b442

Maua Methodist Hospital
Maua, Meru County, Kenya
🌐 https://vfmat.ch/klfn

Mbagathi District Hospital
Nairobi, Nairobi County, Kenya
🌐 https://vfmat.ch/9355

Mbita Sub-County Hospital
Mbita, Homa Bay, Kenya
🌐 https://vfmat.ch/345e

Mbooni Sub-County Hospital
Mbooni, Makueni, Kenya
🌐 https://vfmat.ch/bd52

Mediheal Group Hospital
Eldoret, Nakuru, Kenya
⊕ https://vfmat.ch/5432

Mediheal Group of Hospitals, Upper Hill
Nairobi, Kenya
⊕ https://vfmat.ch/93ca

Mediheal Hospital, Eastleigh
Nairobi, Nairobi Area, Kenya
⊕ https://vfmat.ch/2dcc

Melchizedek Hospital
Dagoretti, Nairobi Area, Kenya
⊕ https://vfmat.ch/7b99

Mercy Mission Hospital
Eldama Ravine, Baringo County, Kenya
⊕ https://vfmat.ch/7f1a

Mewa Hospital
Sharif Alwikassim Ln, Mombasa, Kenya
⊕ https://vfmat.ch/ba73

Mikindani Hospital
Mombasa, Mombasa County, Kenya
⊕ https://vfmat.ch/37fa

Moi Teaching and Referral Hospital
Nandi Road, Uasin Gishu, Kenya
⊕ https://vfmat.ch/9414

Molo Sub-County Hospital
Molo, Nakuru, Kenya
⊕ https://vfmat.ch/ac5f

Mombasa Hospital
Mombasa, Mombasa County, Kenya
⊕ https://vfmat.ch/be11

Mumias Mission Hospital
Mumias, Kakamega, Kenya
⊕ https://vfmat.ch/ee46

Murang'a Level 5 Hospital
Murang'a, Murang'a, Kenya
⊕ https://vfmat.ch/772f

Mutito Sub County Hospital
Mutitu, Kitui, Kenya
⊕ https://vfmat.ch/6f29

Nairobi Hospital, The
Nairobi, Kenya
⊕ https://vfmat.ch/4da4

Nairobi Spine and Orthopaedic Centre
Nairobi, Kenya
⊕ https://vfmat.ch/fe2e

Nairobi West Hospital, The
Kibera, Nairobi Area, Kenya
⊕ https://vfmat.ch/1c75

Nairobi Women's Hospital, The – Adams
Kilimani, Nairobi Area, Kenya
⊕ https://vfmat.ch/cded

Nairobi Women's Hospital, The – Hurlingham
Nairobi, Kenya
⊕ https://vfmat.ch/ac1d

Nairobi Women's Hospital, The – Ongata Rongai
Ongata Rongai, Kajiado County, Kenya
⊕ https://vfmat.ch/d99d

Nairobi Women's Hospital – Nakuru Hyrax
Nakuru, Rift Valley, Kenya
⊕ https://vfmat.ch/99b9

Naivasha District Hospital
Nakuru, Nakuru County, Kenya
⊕ https://vfmat.ch/6aba

Nakuru Provincial General Hospital
Dawsonville, Nakuru, Kenya
⊕ https://vfmat.ch/93d4

Nakuru War Memorial Hospital
Nakuru, Nakuru, Kenya
⊕ https://vfmat.ch/adc2

Nala Hospital – Kakamega
Kakamega, Kakamega county, Kenya
⊕ https://vfmat.ch/d3bf

Nanyuki Teaching and Referal Hospital
Nanyuki, Laikipia, Kenya
⊕ https://vfmat.ch/2d37

Narok County Referral Hospital
Narok Town, Narok North, Narok County, Kenya
⊕ https://vfmat.ch/1a9b

Neema Hospital
Ruiru, Central Province, Kenya
⊕ https://vfmat.ch/1e8c

New Nyaza Provincial General Hospital
Kisumu, Kenya
⊕ https://vfmat.ch/iwca

New Point Hospital
Njoro, Nakuru, Kenya
⊕ https://vfmat.ch/b6ef

Njoro Sub-County Hospital
Njoro, Nakuru, Kenya
⊕ https://vfmat.ch/58f3

Nyahururu County Referral Hospital
Nyahururu, Laikipia, Kenya
⊕ https://vfmat.ch/ddab

Nyangena Hospital
Suneka, Kisii, Kenya
⊕ https://vfmat.ch/bf9b

Nyasare Province General Hospital, Migori
Migori, Migori, Kenya
⊕ https://vfmat.ch/bbe3

Nyeri Provincial General Hospital (PGH)
Karia, Nyeri, Kenya
⊕ https://vfmat.ch/7ee4

Obama Children's Hospital
Nyamasaria, Kisumu, Kenya
⊕ https://vfmat.ch/ea38

Ogembo Hospital
Ogembo, Kisii, Kenya
⊕ https://vfmat.ch/fd72

Ol Kalou General Hospital
Ol Kalou, Nyandarua, Kenya
⊕ https://vfmat.ch/1457

Olenguruone Sub County Hospital
Olenguruone, Nakuru, Kenya
⊕ https://vfmat.ch/9791

Palm Beach Hospital
Ukunda-Diani, Kwale, Kenya
⊕ https://vfmat.ch/d46a

Pandya Memorial Hospital
Mombasa, Mombasa County, Kenya
⊕ https://vfmat.ch/623c

PCEA Chogoria Hospital
Chogoria, Tharaka-Nithi, Kenya
⊕ https://vfmat.ch/fae9

PCEA Kikuyu Hospital
Kikuyu, Kiambu, Kenya
⊕ https://vfmat.ch/2e8e

Pinnacle Flyover Hospital
Magumu, Nyandarua, Kenya
⊕ https://vfmat.ch/3fef

Plainsview Hospital
Ruiru, Kiambu, Kenya
⊕ https://vfmat.ch/f69e

Premier Hospital
Nyali, Mombasa, Kenya
⊕ https://vfmat.ch/69ae

Racecourse Hospital
Eldoret, Uasin Gishu, Kenya
⊕ https://vfmat.ch/4fbf

Rachuonyo District Hospital
Homa Bay, Homa Bay County, Kenya
⊕ https://vfmat.ch/616e

Radiant Hospital
Kangoya, Kiambu, Kenya
⊕ https://vfmat.ch/e4d9

RAM Hospital
Kisii, Kisii County, Kenya
⊕ https://vfmat.ch/a5f9

Royal Hospital (Level 4)
Rongo, Migori, Kenya
⊕ https://vfmat.ch/9c2e

Ruaraka Uhai Neema Hospital
Ruaraka, Nairobi Area, Kenya
⊕ https://vfmat.ch/37a1

Saint Mary's Hospital
Lang'ata, Nairobi Area, Kenya
⊕ https://vfmat.ch/917f

Shalom Hospital
Misakwani, Machakos, Kenya
⊕ https://vfmat.ch/59d3

Siaya County Referral Hospital
Siaya, Kenya, Kenya
⊕ https://vfmat.ch/3n3c

Siloam Hospital
Kericho, Kericho County, Kenya
⊕ https://vfmat.ch/af2b

Sinai Hospital Rongai
Ongata Rongai, Kajiado, Kenya
⊕ https://vfmat.ch/5597

St. Akidiva Memorial Hospital
Migori, Nyanza, Kenya
⊕ https://vfmat.ch/4a82

St. Elizabeth Hospital Mukumu
Kakamega, Kenya
⊕ https://vfmat.ch/5cc8

St. Francis Community Hospital
Nairobi, Nairobi County, Kenya
⊕ https://vfmat.ch/d47e

St. Jairus Hospital
Nyanza, Kisumu, Kenya
⊕ https://vfmat.ch/d5b1

St. Luke's Orthopaedics & Trauma Hospital
New Hill, Uasin Gishu, Kenya
⊕ https://vfmat.ch/2b4f

St. Mary's Hospital
Embakasi, Nairobi Area, Kenya
⊕ https://vfmat.ch/182b

St. Matia Mulumba Mission Hospital
Makongeni, Nairobi Area, Kenya
⊕ https://vfmat.ch/2483

St. Monica's Hospital
Kisumu, Nyanza, Kenya
⊕ https://vfmat.ch/86f1

St. Scholastica Uzima Hospital
Thika, Nairobi Area, Kenya
⊕ https://vfmat.ch/c9be

St. Teresa Hospital
Kikuyu, Kiambu, Kenya
⊕ https://vfmat.ch/55a3

Star Hospital
Nyamasaria, Kisumu, Kenya
⊕ https://vfmat.ch/19ec

Star Hospital-Malindi
Malindi Town, Kilifi, Kenya
⊕ https://vfmat.ch/b11e

Sultan Hamud Sub District Hospital
Sultan Hamud, Makueni, Kenya
⊕ https://vfmat.ch/eab1

Swiss Cottage Hospital Mtwapa
Mtwapa, Mombasa, Kenya
⊕ https://vfmat.ch/3aff

Tenwek Hospital
Bomet, Bomet County, Kenya
⊕ https://vfmat.ch/55c5

Thika Level 5 Hospital
Thika Town, Kiambu, Kenya
⊕ https://vfmat.ch/e563

Tigoni Level 4 Hospital
Tigoni, Kiambu, Kenya
⊕ https://vfmat.ch/cbd3

Tophill Hospital
Eldoret, Uasin Gishu, Kenya
⊕ https://vfmat.ch/1ef2

Tuungane Hospital
Tom Mboya – Kisumu, Kisumu, Kenya
⊕ https://vfmat.ch/1f7c

Uasin Gishu Memorial Hospital
Eldoret, Uasin Gishu, Kenya
⊕ https://vfmat.ch/96ac

Valley Hospital
Nakuru, Nakuru County, Kenya
⊕ https://vfmat.ch/7957

Vihiga County Referral Hospital
Vihiga, Vihiga County, Kenya
⊕ https://vfmat.ch/2a12

Wamba Catholic Hospital
Wamba, Samburu County, Kenya
⊕ https://vfmat.ch/ddc9

Wamba Hospital
Wamba, Samburu, Kenya
⊕ https://vfmat.ch/61c3

Honolulu•

Majuro•

TOKELAU

SAMOA
AMERICAN
SAMOA

COOK
ISLANDS

NIUE

TONGA

Nuku'alofa•

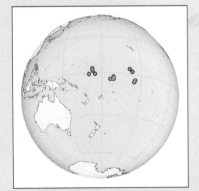

● Healthcare Facility

Kiribati

The Republic of Kiribati is the only country in the world to be located in all four hemispheres. This island nation in the Pacific Ocean consists of 32 atolls (ring-shaped coral reefs) and one raised coral island. The total land area is 811 square kilometers, with islands spread out over 3.5 million square kilometers. The population of 113,000 people is dispersed throughout these islands, with about half of the population residing on the Tarawa Atoll, which is also the capital. The majority of the population identifies as ethnically Kiribati, and speaks both Kiribati and English. Most of the people are Roman Catholic, with smaller portions identifying as Kiribati Uniting Church, Mormon, Baha'i, and Seventh-day Adventist.

Kiribati gained independence from the United Kingdom in 1979. Of the Pacific Island countries, it remains one of the least developed. It has few natural resources, and economic development is limited by Kiribati's lack of skilled labor, poor infrastructure, and distance from international markets. Much of the economic activity involves the public sector: building roads, developing water and hygiene projects, and renovations to infrastructure. Otherwise, fisheries and the export of coconuts and coconut products are the main drivers of economic activity. Because of limited economic opportunities, as much as 31 percent of the population is unemployed.

Kiribati suffers from a variety of health challenges, including one of the highest adult obesity rates in the world. Because about 46 percent of the adult population is considered obese, a litany of non-communicable diseases tops the list of most common causes of death. These include ischemic heart disease, stroke, and diabetes, which all increased substantially between 2009 and 2019. Other leading causes of death include tuberculosis, neonatal disorders, diarrheal diseases, asthma, chronic kidney disease, lower respiratory infections, and self-harm. In addition to high body-mass index, the risk factors that contribute most to death and disability include high fasting plasma glucose, tobacco, high blood pressure, malnutrition, dietary risks, air pollution, high LDL, kidney dysfunction, and insufficient water, sanitation, and hygiene.

0.11M
Population

$1,671
GDP Per Capita

68 years
Life Expectancy
↑ Improving

20
Doctors/100k

Physician Density

186
Beds/100k

Hospital Bed Density

92
Deaths/100k

Maternal Mortality

Kiribati

Nonprofit Organizations

ARC The Australian Respiratory Council
Fosters research to promote respiratory health and works to improve lung health in communities of disadvantaged and Indigenous people.
Infect Dis
🌐 https://vfmat.ch/69f2

Association of Medical Doctors of Asia (AMDA)
Strives to support people affected by disasters and economic distress on their road to recovery, establishing a true partnership with special emphasis on local initiative.
ER Med, Logist-Op, Pub Health
🌐 https://vfmat.ch/e3d4

CharityVision International
Focuses on restoring curable sight impairment worldwide by empowering local physicians and creating sustainable solutions.
Logist-Op, Ophth-Opt, Surg
🌐 https://vfmat.ch/6231

Doctors Assisting In South Pacific Islands (DAISI)
Aims to support and collaborate with its South Pacific neighbors and consists of specialist and nonspecialist doctors, medical students, nurses, allied health professionals, and nonmedical volunteers.
Anesth, Dent-OMFS, OB-GYN, Plast, Surg, Urol
🌐 https://vfmat.ch/2dcd

Global Oncology (GO)
Brings the best in cancer care to underserved patients around the world and collaborates across geographic, professional, and academic borders to improve cancer care, research, and education.
Heme-Onc, Path, Rad-Onc
🌐 https://vfmat.ch/fcb8

Globus Relief
Aims to improve the delivery of healthcare worldwide by gathering, processing, and distributing surplus medical supplies to charities at home and abroad.
Logist-Op
🌐 https://vfmat.ch/a2b7

Hear the World Foundation
Advocates worldwide for equal opportunities and improved quality of life for people in need with hearing loss.
ENT, Peds
🌐 https://vfmat.ch/122c

International Federation of Red Cross and Red Crescent Societies (IFRC)
Coordinates and directs international assistance following natural and manmade disasters in nonconflict situations through the world's largest humanitarian and development network. Provides disaster-preparedness programs, healthcare activities, and promotes humanitarian values.
ER Med, General, Infect Dis, Nutr
🌐 https://vfmat.ch/b4ee

International Planned Parenthood Federation (IPPF)
Leads a locally owned, globally connected civil society movement that provides and enables services and champions sexual and reproductive health and rights for all, especially the underserved.
Infect Dis, MF Med, OB-GYN
🌐 https://vfmat.ch/dc97

International Trachoma Initiative (iTi)
Works toward a world free from trachoma, a preventable cause of blindness, and provides comprehensive support to national ministries of health and governmental and nongovernmental organizations to implement a comprehensive approach to fight trachoma.
Infect Dis, Ophth-Opt
🌐 https://vfmat.ch/3278

Joint United Nations Programme on HIV/AIDS (UNAIDS)
Aims to place people living with HIV and people affected by the virus at the decision-making table and at the center of designing, delivering, and monitoring the AIDS response.
Infect Dis
🌐 https://vfmat.ch/464a

Order of Malta
Supports forgotten or excluded people, especially those living in conflict zones or amid natural disasters, by providing medical assistance, caring for refugees, and distributing medicines and necessities.
ER Med, General, Infect Dis, MF Med, Nephro, OB-GYN, Ortho, Psych
🌐 https://vfmat.ch/1fab

Pacific Leprosy Foundation
Focuses not only on leprosy control but also on the welfare of leprosy patients in the South Pacific.
Derm, Infect Dis, Pub Health
🌐 https://vfmat.ch/781d

Real Medicine Foundation (RMF)
Provides humanitarian support to people living in disaster- and poverty-stricken areas, focusing on the person as a whole by providing medical/physical, emotional, economic, and social support.
ER Med, General, Infect Dis, Nutr, Peds, Psych
🌐 https://vfmat.ch/d45a

RestoringVision
Empowers lives by restoring vision for millions of people in need.
Ophth-Opt
🌐 https://vfmat.ch/e121

Rotary International

Provides service to others, improves lives, and advances world understanding, goodwill, and peace through its fellowship of business, professional, and community leaders.

ER Med, General, Infect Dis, MF Med, OB-GYN

⊕ https://vfmat.ch/8fb5

Task Force for Global Health, The

Consists of programs and focus areas that cover a range of global health issues including neglected tropical diseases, infectious diseases, vaccines, field epidemiology, public health informatics, health workforce development, and global health ethics.

Infect Dis, Logist-Op, Medicine, Ophth-Opt, Peds

⊕ https://vfmat.ch/714c

United Nations Population Fund (UNFPA)

Supports reproductive healthcare for women and youth in more than 150 countries, focusing on delivering a world in which every pregnancy is wanted, every childbirth is safe, and every young person's potential is fulfilled.

Infect Dis, MF Med, Neonat, OB-GYN, Peds, Pub Health

⊕ https://vfmat.ch/c969

World Federation of Hemophilia (WFH)

Aims to improve and sustain care for people with inherited bleeding disorders by pursuing long-term relationships with individuals and organizations who share the values of WFH's development model.

Heme-Onc

⊕ https://vfmat.ch/5121

World Health Organization, The (WHO)

The United Nations' agency for health provides leadership on global health matters, shapes the health research agenda, sets norms and standards, articulates evidence-based policy options, provides technical support and monitoring to countries, and assesses health trends.

ER Med, General, Infect Dis, Logist-Op, MF Med, OB-GYN, Peds, Psych, Pub Health

⊕ https://vfmat.ch/c476

Kiribati

Healthcare Facilities

Betio Hospital
Betio, South Tarawa, Kiribati
⊕ https://vfmat.ch/36rx

London Kiritimati Hospital
London, Kiritimati, Kiribati
⊕ https://vfmat.ch/ymf1

Nawerewere Hospital
Bairiki, South Tarawa, Kiribati
⊕ https://vfmat.ch/wngq

Southern Kiribati Hospital
Utiroa Village, Gilbert Islands, Kiribati
⊕ https://vfmat.ch/177a

Tabiang Hospital
Tabiang Village, Gilbert Islands, Kiribati
⊕ https://vfmat.ch/1cc5

Temakin Clinic
Betio, South Tarawa, Kiribati
https://vfmat.ch/7zuz

Tungaru Central Hospital
Bairiki, South Tarawa, Kiribati
⊕ https://vfmat.ch/svk7

Healthcare Facility

Kyrgyzstan

Known for its mountainous landscape, the Kyrgyz Republic, also referred to as Kirghizia in Russian, is a landlocked country in Central Asia, sharing borders with Kazakhstan, Uzbekistan, Tajikistan, and China. The population of 6 million lives mainly in rural areas, with the most densely inhabited area in the north and in and around the capital of Bishkek, as well as Osh in the western part of the country. About 40 percent of the population lives in urban areas. The majority of the population identifies as ethnically Kyrgyz, with a smaller number identifying as Uzbek and Russian. Kyrgyz and Russian are the official languages, and the overwhelming majority of the population (90 percent) is Sunni Muslim. Several mountain ranges jut throughout its impressive landscape: the Kok Shaal-Tau, Alay, Trans-Alay (Zaalay), and Atbashi ranges. Lowlands account for only one-seventh of the total land area of Kyrgyzstan, and yet this portion of land is home to most of the population.

Kyrgyzstan has a rich and long history, having been a part of the Uyghur Empire and Mongol Empire during the 13th century. After becoming part of the USSR, Kyrgyzstan achieved independence in 1991. The country is rich in natural resources such as hydropower, gold, rare earth metals, coal, oil, natural gas, deposits of nepheline, mercury, bismuth, lead, and zinc. As a result, the economy is focused primarily on the extraction of minerals. Despite a relatively resource-rich economy, the overall well-being of the population is lacking. Though unemployment is low, many people live below the poverty line—as much as 32 percent of the population. Notably, Kyrgyzstan's standard of living as well as its economic and educational attainment levels are some of the lowest among the former Soviet republics.

Kyrgyzstan has many health challenges. High rates of death are caused by ischemic heart disease, stroke, cirrhosis, COPD, neonatal disorders, road injuries, lower respiratory infections, stomach cancer, Alzheimer's disease, and self-harm. While death due to tuberculosis decreased by 38 percent between 2009 and 2019, it is still considered a top cause of death. The risk factors that contribute most to death and disability include dietary risks, high blood pressure, malnutrition, high body-mass index, alcohol and tobacco use, air pollution, high LDL, high fasting plasma glucose, and kidney dysfunction.

6M

Population

$1,174

GDP Per Capita

72 years

Life Expectancy

↑ Improving

22
Doctors/100k

Physician Density

441
Beds/100k

Hospital Bed Density

60
Deaths/100k

Maternal Mortality

Kyrgyzstan

Nonprofit Organizations

Abt Associates
Seeks to improve the quality of life and economic well-being of people worldwide, while striving to meet and exceed the highest professional standards.
General, Logist-Op, MF Med, OB-GYN, Peds
⊕ https://vfmat.ch/cec2

AFEW International
Aims to improve the health of populations in Eastern Europe and Central Asia, strives to increase access to prevention, treatment, and care for HIV, TB, and viral hepatitis, and promotes health and SRHR.
Infect Dis, Pub Health
⊕ https://vfmat.ch/19c6

Aga Khan Foundation Canada
Tackles the root causes of poverty, with a special focus on marginalized groups such as women and girls. Programs provide access to education and healthcare, food, and opportunity.
Pub Health
⊕ https://vfmat.ch/7f8b

Age International
Helps older people living in some of the world's poorest places to have improved well-being and be treated with dignity through a variety of programs, including emergency relief and cataract surgery.
ER Med, Geri, Logist-Op, Nutr, Ophth-Opt, Palliative, Pub Health
⊕ https://vfmat.ch/c7e2

American International Health Alliance (AIHA)
Strengthens health systems and workforce capacity worldwide through locally driven, peer-to-peer institutional partnerships.
CV Med, ER Med, Infect Dis, Medicine, OB-GYN
⊕ https://vfmat.ch/69fd

Americares
Saves lives and improves health for people affected by poverty or disaster and responds with life-changing medicine, medical supplies, and health programs including domestic and global medical clinics.
All-Immu, ER Med, General, Infect Dis, MF Med, Nutr
⊕ https://vfmat.ch/e567

Araketke-Bereket Charitable Foundation
Works with international volunteers and local communities towards improvement in health, education, and development for the people of Kyrgyzstan.
General, OB-GYN, Pub Health
⊕ https://vfmat.ch/b77b

Association of Medical Doctors of Asia (AMDA)
Strives to support people affected by disasters and economic distress on their road to recovery, establishing a true partnership with special emphasis on local initiative.

ER Med, Logist-Op, Pub Health
⊕ https://vfmat.ch/e3d4

Center for Strategic and International Studies (CSIS) Commission on Strengthening America's Health Security
Brings together a distinguished and diverse group of high-level opinion leaders bridging security and health, with the core aim to chart a bold vision for the future of U.S. leadership in global health.
ER Med, Infect Dis, MF Med, Pub Health
⊕ https://vfmat.ch/6d7f

Christian Aid Ministries
Strives to be a trustworthy and efficient channel for Amish, Mennonite, and other conservative Anabaptist groups and individuals to minister to physical and spiritual needs around the world.
CT Surg, ER Med, Logist-Op, Ortho, Pub Health
⊕ https://vfmat.ch/7b33

Developing Country NGO Delegation: Global Fund to Fight AIDS, TB & Malaria
Works to strengthen the engagement of civil society actors and organizations in developing countries to build a world in which AIDS, TB, and malaria are no longer global, public health, and human rights threats.
Infect Dis, Pub Health
⊕ https://vfmat.ch/3149

Doctors Without Borders/Médecins Sans Frontières (MSF)
Responds to emergencies and provides lifesaving medical care where needed most, including during disasters, conflicts, and epidemics.
Anesth, Crit-Care, ER Med, General, Infect Dis, Nutr, OB-GYN, Ped Surg, Peds, Psych, Pub Health, Surg
⊕ https://vfmat.ch/f363

Elton John AIDS Foundation
Seeks to address and overcome the stigma, discrimination, and neglect that prevents ending AIDS by funding local experts to challenge discrimination, prevent infections, and provide treatment.
Infect Dis, Pub Health
⊕ https://vfmat.ch/9d31

Global Ministries – The United Methodist Church
As the worldwide mission and development agency of The United Methodist Church, Global Ministries works with more than 300 hospitals and clinics around the world through its Global Health Unit.
Anesth, CT Surg, CV Med, Crit-Care, Dent-OMFS, Derm, ER Med, GI, General, Infect Dis, Logist-Op, MF Med, Medicine, Neonat, Nephro, Nutr, OB-GYN, Ophth-Opt, Ortho, Palliative, Peds, Pod, Psych, Pub Health, Rehab, Rheum, Surg, Urol
⊕ https://vfmat.ch/1723

Global Oncology (GO)
Brings the best in cancer care to underserved patients around the world and collaborates across geographic, professional, and academic borders to improve cancer care, research, and education.
Heme-Onc, Path, Rad-Onc
⊕ https://vfmat.ch/fcb8

Globus Relief
Aims to improve the delivery of healthcare worldwide by gathering, processing, and distributing surplus medical supplies to charities at home and abroad.
Logist-Op
⊕ https://vfmat.ch/a2b7

Grassroot Soccer
Leverages the power of soccer to educate, inspire, and mobilize at-risk youth in developing countries to overcome their greatest health challenges, live healthier and more productive lives, and are agents for change in their communities.
Infect Dis
⊕ https://vfmat.ch/3521

Health Equity Initiative
Aims to build and sustain a global community that engages across sectors and disciplines to advance health equity.
Pub Health
⊕ https://vfmat.ch/e2e2

HealthProm
Works with local partners to promote health and social care for vulnerable children and their families.
General, MF Med, Peds, Pub Health
⊕ https://vfmat.ch/153d

HealthServe Australia
Develops sustainable health programs that improve health and well-being and partners with community groups to build community capacity to meet health needs.
Infect Dis, Logist-Op, OB-GYN, Psych, Pub Health
⊕ https://vfmat.ch/7276

Healthy DEvelopments
Provides Germany-supported health and social protection programs around the globe in a collaborative knowledge management process.
All-Immu, General, Infect Dis, Logist-Op, MF Med
⊕ https://vfmat.ch/dc31

HelpAge International
Works to ensure that people everywhere understand how much older people contribute to society and that they must enjoy their right to healthcare, social services, economic, and physical security.
General, Geri, Infect Dis, Medicine, Pub Health
⊕ https://vfmat.ch/5d91

ICAP at Columbia University
Serves as global leader in supporting the scale-up of multidisciplinary HIV/AIDS prevention, care, and treatment programs based on a family-focused approach.
General, Infect Dis, MF Med, Medicine, OB-GYN, Pub Health
⊕ https://vfmat.ch/a8ef

International Federation of Gynecology and Obstetrics (FIGO)
Implements global projects on specific women's health issues.
MF Med, Medicine, Neonat, OB-GYN, Surg, Urol
⊕ https://vfmat.ch/c4b4

International Federation of Red Cross and Red Crescent Societies (IFRC)
Coordinates and directs international assistance following natural and manmade disasters in nonconflict situations through the world's largest humanitarian and development network. Provides disaster-preparedness programs, healthcare activities, and promotes humanitarian values.
ER Med, General, Infect Dis, Nutr
⊕ https://vfmat.ch/b4ee

International Insulin Foundation
Aims to prolong the life and promote the health of people with diabetes in developing countries by improving the supply of insulin and education in its use.
Endo, Logist-Op
⊕ https://vfmat.ch/d34f

International Organization for Migration (IOM) – The UN Migration Agency
Promotes evidence-informed policies and holistic, preventive, and curative health programs that are beneficial, accessible, and equitable for vulnerable migrants.
General, Infect Dis, OB-GYN
⊕ https://vfmat.ch/621a

International Planned Parenthood Federation (IPPF)
Leads a locally owned, globally connected civil society movement that provides and enables services and champions sexual and reproductive health and rights for all, especially the underserved.
Infect Dis, MF Med, OB-GYN
⊕ https://vfmat.ch/dc97

John Snow, Inc. (JSI)
Aims to improve the health and well-being of underserved and vulnerable people and communities throughout the world.
General, Infect Dis, Logist-Op, MF Med, OB-GYN, Peds, Psych, Pub Health
⊕ https://vfmat.ch/ba78

Joint United Nations Programme on HIV/AIDS (UNAIDS)
Aims to place people living with HIV and people affected by the virus at the decision-making table and at the center of designing, delivering, and monitoring the AIDS response.
Infect Dis
⊕ https://vfmat.ch/464a

Kyrgystan Red Crescent
Strives to prevent and alleviate the suffering of people in Kyrgyzstan via significant expansion of its activities on health, disaster management, social care, and organizational development.
ER Med, Infect Dis, Ophth-Opt, Palliative, Pub Health, Rehab
⊕ https://vfmat.ch/739c

Light House Medical Missions
Inspired by the Christian faith, provides programs in healthcare provision, nutrition, emergency relief and response, and water, sanitation, and hygiene (WASH).
ER Med, General, Surg
⊕ https://vfmat.ch/cecd

Management Sciences for Health (MSH)
Works with countries and communities to save lives and improve the health of the world's poorest and most vulnerable people by building strong, resilient, sustainable health systems.
Infect Dis, Logist-Op, Pub Health
⊕ https://vfmat.ch/6aa2

MAP International
Provides medicines and health supplies to those in need around the world so they might experience life to the fullest.
Logist-Op
⊕ https://vfmat.ch/deed

Maternity Foundation
Works to ensure safer childbirth for women and newborns everywhere through innovative mobile health solutions such as the Safe Delivery App, a mobile training tool for skilled birth attendants.
MF Med, OB-GYN, Pub Health
⊕ https://vfmat.ch/ff4f

MedShare
Aims to improve the quality of life of people, communities, and the planet by sourcing and directly delivering surplus medical supplies and equipment to communities in need around the world.
Logist-Op
⊕ https://vfmat.ch/c8bc

Operation Mercy

Serves the poor and marginalized through community development and humanitarian aid projects.

General, MF Med, OB-GYN, Peds, Psych, Pub Health, Rehab

🌐 https://vfmat.ch/81c5

RestoringVision

Empowers lives by restoring vision for millions of people in need.

Ophth-Opt

🌐 https://vfmat.ch/e121

Rockefeller Foundation, The

Works to promote the well-being of humanity.

Logist-Op, Nutr, Pub Health

🌐 https://vfmat.ch/5424

Rotary International

Provides service to others, improves lives, and advances world understanding, goodwill, and peace through its fellowship of business, professional, and community leaders.

ER Med, General, Infect Dis, MF Med, OB-GYN

🌐 https://vfmat.ch/8fb5

Scientific Technology and Language Institute (STLI)

Works to build professional relationships with the people of Central Asia and the Middle East through volunteer professionals who utilize their skills for knowledge and skills transfer to the people they serve, in program areas of health, education, agriculture and technology.

Dent-OMFS, General, Rehab

🌐 https://vfmat.ch/fbb7

SINA Health

Aims to improve the health and educational status of the population in low- and middle-income countries.

General, Logist-Op

🌐 https://vfmat.ch/9ad3

SOS Children's Villages International

Supports children through alternative care and family strengthening.

ER Med, Peds

🌐 https://vfmat.ch/aca1

Sri Sathya Sai International Organization

Inspired by spiritual teachings, carries out efforts in global healthcare, education, humanitarian relief, and youth engagement.

Dent-OMFS, General, Logist-Op, Nutr, Ophth-Opt, Pub Health

🌐 https://vfmat.ch/9bda

Task Force for Global Health, The

Consists of programs and focus areas that cover a range of global health issues including neglected tropical diseases, infectious diseases, vaccines, field epidemiology, public health informatics, health workforce development, and global health ethics.

Infect Dis, Logist-Op, Medicine, Ophth-Opt, Peds

🌐 https://vfmat.ch/714c

Union for International Cancer Control (UICC)

Unites and supports the cancer community to reduce the global cancer burden, promote greater equity, and ensure that cancer control continues to be a priority in the world health and development agenda.

Heme-Onc, Pub Health

🌐 https://vfmat.ch/88b1

United Nations Children's Fund (UNICEF)

Works in over 190 countries and territories to save children's lives, defend their rights, and help them fulfill their potential, from early childhood through adolescence.

All-Immu, Infect Dis, MF Med, Neonat, Nutr, OB-GYN, Ped Surg, Peds, Pub Health

🌐 https://vfmat.ch/42d7

United Nations Development Programme (UNDP)

Helps countries achieve the simultaneous eradication of extreme poverty and significant reduction of inequalities and exclusion using a sustainable human development approach.

Infect Dis, Logist-Op, Pub Health

🌐 https://vfmat.ch/935c

United Nations High Commissioner for Refugees (UNHCR)

Safeguards the rights and well-being of people who have been forced to flee, ensuring that everybody has the right to seek asylum and find safe refuge in another country, with the goal of seeking lasting solutions.

General, MF Med, Medicine, OB-GYN, Peds, Psych, Pub Health

🌐 https://vfmat.ch/6636

United Nations Population Fund (UNFPA)

Supports reproductive healthcare for women and youth in more than 150 countries, focusing on delivering a world in which every pregnancy is wanted, every childbirth is safe, and every young person's potential is fulfilled.

Infect Dis, MF Med, Neonat, OB-GYN, Peds, Pub Health

🌐 https://vfmat.ch/c969

University of New Mexico School of Medicine: Project Echo

Seeks to improve health outcomes worldwide through the use of a technology called telementoring, a guided-practice model in which the participating clinician retains responsibility for managing the patient.

General, Infect Dis, MF Med, OB-GYN, Path, Peds

🌐 https://vfmat.ch/6c9a

USAID: Maternal and Child Health Integrated Program

Works to improve the health of women and their families, including programs for maternal, newborn, and child health, immunization, family planning, nutrition, malaria, and HIV/AIDS.

All-Immu, General, Infect Dis, MF Med

🌐 https://vfmat.ch/4415

Vision Care

Restores sight and helps patients get regular treatment at short-term eye camps and long-term base clinics by having doctors, missionaries, volunteers, and sponsors work together.

Ophth-Opt

🌐 https://vfmat.ch/9d7c

World Federation of Hemophilia (WFH)

Aims to improve and sustain care for people with inherited bleeding disorders by pursuing long-term relationships with individuals and organizations who share the values of WFH's development model.

Heme-Onc

🌐 https://vfmat.ch/5121

World Health Organization, The (WHO)

The United Nations' agency for health provides leadership on global health matters, shapes the health research agenda, sets norms and standards, articulates evidence-based policy options, provides technical support and monitoring to countries, and assesses health trends.

ER Med, General, Infect Dis, Logist-Op, MF Med, OB-GYN, Peds, Psych, Pub Health

🌐 https://vfmat.ch/c476

Kyrgyzstan

Healthcare Facilities

Andrology and Urology Center Association
Alamedin, Chüy, Kyrgyzstan
⊕ https://vfmat.ch/df14

Arashan General Practice Center
Tash-Moynok, Chüy, Kyrgyzstan
⊕ https://vfmat.ch/8a71

Aravan District Public Hospital
Aravan, Osh, Kyrgyzstan
⊕ https://vfmat.ch/5b62

At-Bashy Regional Hospital
Ak-Dzhar, Naryn, Kyrgyzstan
⊕ https://vfmat.ch/42af

Azmi Hospital (Asian Medical Institute)
Bishkek, Kyrgyzstan
⊕ https://vfmat.ch/u4bp

Batken Regional Hospital
Bazar-Bashy, Batken, Kyrgyzstan
⊕ https://vfmat.ch/c41e

Batken United Hospital
Kyzyl-Jol, Batken, Kyrgyzstan
⊕ https://vfmat.ch/hdp4

Bishkek City Family Medicine Center #1
Prigorodnoye, Chüy, Kyrgyzstan
⊕ https://vfmat.ch/7aeb

Bishkek City Family Medicine Center #17
Orto-Say, Bishkek, Kyrgyzstan
⊕ https://vfmat.ch/464b

Bishkek City Family Medicine Center #3
Bishkek, Kyrgyzstan
⊕ https://vfmat.ch/b66a

Center for Medical Advisory Services and Sports Medicine
Bishkek, Kyrgyzstan
⊕ https://vfmat.ch/7935

Chui Province General Hospital
Ak-Beshim, Chüy, Kyrgyzstan
⊕ https://vfmat.ch/e99e

Chui Regional United Hospital
Alamedin, Chüy, Kyrgyzstan
⊕ https://vfmat.ch/ad3e

Cortex Neurological Medical Center
Chong-Aryk, Bishkek, Kyrgyzstan
⊕ https://vfmat.ch/56a9

Dolon Village Hospital
Dolon, Issyk Kul, Kyrgyzstan
⊕ https://vfmat.ch/bcfd

Ear Nose and Throat Department of Uzgen Territorial Hospital
Uzgen, Osh, Kyrgyzstan
⊕ https://vfmat.ch/9ff7

Eldik Family Medicine Clinic
Bishkek, Kyrgystan
https://vfmat.ch/niuk

Family Medicine Center of Naryn District
Karabulundun, Naryn, Kyrgyzstan
⊕ https://vfmat.ch/a8c9

First Central Hospital of Bishkek
Bishkek, Chüy, Kyrgyzstan
⊕ https://vfmat.ch/9169

First Maternity Hospital of Bishkek
Bishkek, Kyrgyzstan
⊕ https://vfmat.ch/f569

Infectious Disease Hospital Chaek
Chaek, Kyrgyzstan
⊕ https://vfmat.ch/6bd4

Infectious Disease Hospital Tokmok
Tokmok, Kyrgyzstan
⊕ https://vfmat.ch/afd2

Isfana Regional Hospital
Imeni Gagarina, Batken, Kyrgyzstan
⊕ https://vfmat.ch/cc9c

Issyk-Ata Territorial Hospital
Issyk-Ata, Ivanovka, Chüy, Kyrgyzstan
⊕ https://vfmat.ch/ef74

Issyk-Kul Regional Hospital
Issyk-Kul, Kyrgyzstan
⊕ https://vfmat.ch/e61a

Jalal-Abad City Hospital
Jalal-Abad, Kyrgyzstan
⊕ https://vfmat.ch/1636

Jalal-Abad Maternity Hospital
Khazret-Ayub, Kyrgyzstan
⊕ https://vfmat.ch/8b97

Jalal-Abad Regional Hospital
Kyzyl-Tuu, Jalal-Abad, Kyrgyzstan
⊕ https://vfmat.ch/a3dd

Kara-Buura Territorial Hospital K. Subanbaev
Kara-Buurin District, Kyzyl-Adyr, Talass Region, Kyrgyzstan
⊕ https://vfmat.ch/19f6

Karakulja Regional Hospital
Imeni Tel'mana, Osh, Kyrgyzstan
⊕ https://vfmat.ch/1246

Karasuu Territorial Hospital
Imeni Tel'mana, Osh, Kyrgyzstan
⊕ https://vfmat.ch/3222

Kemin Regional Hospital
Kyzyl-Oktyabr, Chüy, Kyrgyzstan
⊕ https://vfmat.ch/bd8c

Kochkor Rural District Hospital
Kara-Too, Naryn, Kyrgyzstan
⊕ https://vfmat.ch/9d98

Kochkor-Atinskaya Territorial Hospital
Kochkor-Ata, Jalal-Abad, Kyrgyzstan
⊕ https://vfmat.ch/8fd5

Kyrgystan Republican Narcology Center
Bishkek, Kyrgyzstan
⊕ https://vfmat.ch/9a31

M. Alieva's Osh Cardio Medical Center
Osh, Kyrgystan
https://vfmat.ch/1f9a

Mamakeev's National Surgical Center
Bishkek, Kyrgyzstan
⊕ https://vfmat.ch/37c6

Maternity Hospital #4 of Bishkek
Bishkek, Kyrgyzstan
⊕ https://vfmat.ch/dc5e

Naryn Regional United Hospital
Karabulundun, Naryn, Kyrgyzstan
⊕ https://vfmat.ch/1185

National Center of Cardiology and Internal Medicine
Mirakhinov, Kyrgystan
https://vfmat.ch/3aju

National Center for Cardiology and Therapy
Bishkek, Kyrgyzstan
⊕ https://vfmat.ch/2a4a

National Center for Maternal and Child Health
Archa-Beshkik, Kyrgyzstan
⊕ https://vfmat.ch/ad9d

National Hospital of the Republic of Kyrgyzstan
Bishkek, Kyrgyzstan
⊕ https://vfmat.ch/7325

Neomed Clinic
Bishkek, Kyrgyzstan
⊕ https://vfmat.ch/u9qi

Oncology Center of Osh
Yuqori Uvam, Osh, Kyrgyzstan
⊕ https://vfmat.ch/838e

Orlovka General Practice Center
Orlovka, Chüy, Kyrgyzstan
⊕ https://vfmat.ch/f959

Osh City Children's Hospital
Osh, Osh, Kyrgyzstan
⊕ https://vfmat.ch/6bb6

Osh City Maternity Hospital
Tëlëyken, Osh, Kyrgyzstan
⊕ https://vfmat.ch/ee9b

Osh City Millitary Hospital
Dyykan-Kyshtak, Osh, Kyrgyzstan
⊕ https://vfmat.ch/36dc

Osh City Rehabilitation Center
Dyykan-Kyshtak, Osh, Kyrgyzstan
⊕ https://vfmat.ch/8e3c

Osh City Tuberculosis Hospital of Children
Tëlëyken, Osh, Kyrgyzstan
⊕ https://vfmat.ch/9431

Osh Oblast Maternity Hospital
Dyykan-Kyshtak, Osh City, Kyrgyzstan
⊕ https://vfmat.ch/85fc

Osh Regional Hospital
Yuqori Uvam, Osh City, Kyrgyzstan
⊕ https://vfmat.ch/263a

Panfilov District General Hospital
Panfilovskoye, Chüy, Kyrgyzstan
⊕ https://vfmat.ch/3d39

Private Cardio Center in Bishkek
Bishkek, Kyrgyzstan
⊕ https://vfmat.ch/3a5e

Republican Psychiatric Hospital
Chim-Korgon, Chüy, Kyrgyzstan
⊕ https://vfmat.ch/f1c8

Second General Hospital of Taldy-Suu
Taldysu, Naryn, Kyrgyzstan
⊕ https://vfmat.ch/43bc

Skin Diseases Center
Dzhiydalik, Osh, Kyrgyzstan
⊕ https://vfmat.ch/d31a

Sokuluk Territorial Hospital
Romanovka, Chüy, Kyrgyzstan
⊕ https://vfmat.ch/a4ae

State Hospital #3
Vinogradnoye, Chüy, Kyrgyzstan
⊕ https://vfmat.ch/836d

State Hospital #6 Jalal-Abad
Jany-Abad, Jalal-Abad, Kyrgyzstan
⊕ https://vfmat.ch/3194

State Hospital #8
Grigor'yevka, Issyk-Kul, Kyrgyzstan
⊕ https://vfmat.ch/16e6

Talas Regional Hospital
Kök-Oy, Talas, Kyrgyzstan
⊕ https://vfmat.ch/13ba

Tash-Kumyr Family Medicine Center
Dardasan, Jalal-Abad, Kyrgyzstan
⊕ https://vfmat.ch/e58a

TB Hospital of Tyup District
Birlik, Issyk-Kul, Kyrgyzstan
⊕ https://vfmat.ch/f1e5

Territorial Hospital at Ulitsa Lenina
Ulitsa Lenina, Belovodskoe, Kyrgyzstan
⊕ https://vfmat.ch/4a9f

Territorial Hospital of Tash-Kumyr
Dardasan, Jalal-Abad, Kyrgyzstan
⊕ https://vfmat.ch/24d1

Naryn Infectious Diseases Center, The
Orto-Saz, Naryn, Kyrgyzstan
⊕ https://vfmat.ch/8877

Naryn Therapy Center, The
Karabulundun, Naryn, Kyrgyzstan
⊕ https://vfmat.ch/2b86

Third Children Hospital in Bishkek
Chong-Aryk, Bishkek, Kyrgyzstan
⊕ https://vfmat.ch/fd8e

Tokmok Territorial General Hospital
Vinogradnoye, Chüy, Kyrgyzstan
⊕ https://vfmat.ch/8e13

Tokmok Territorial Hospital
Vinogradnoye, Chüy, Kyrgyzstan
⊕ https://vfmat.ch/672c

Uzgen Territorial Hospital
Uzgen, Osh, Kyrgyzstan
⊕ https://vfmat.ch/3991

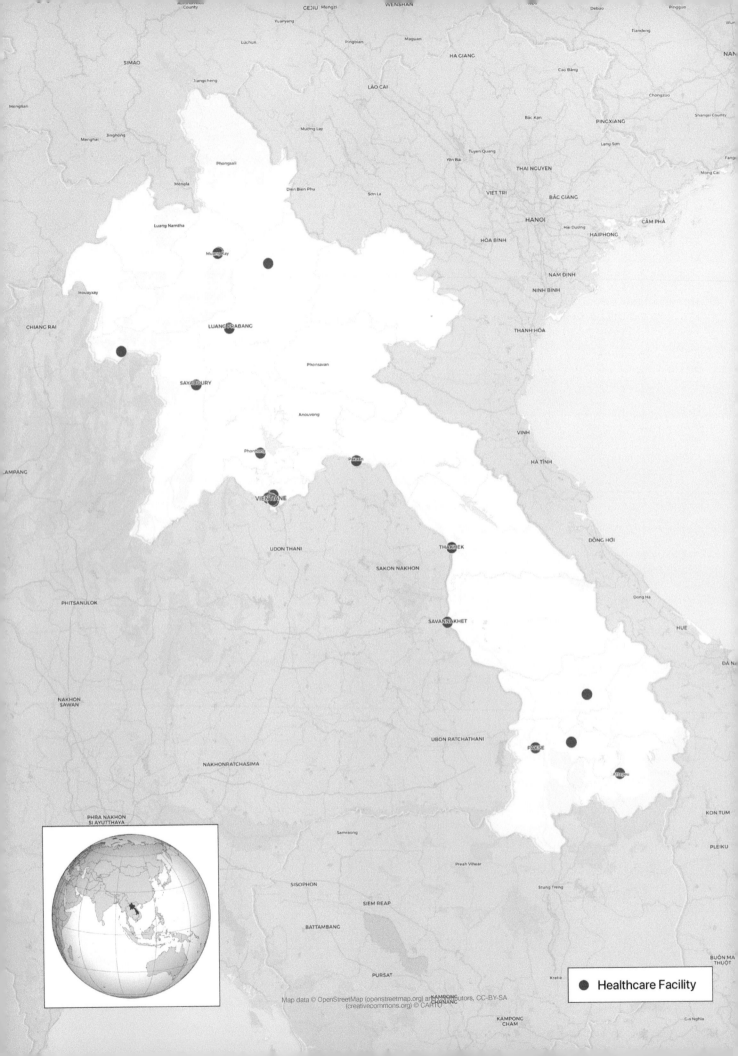

Healthcare Facility

Laos

The Lao People's Democratic Republic, in Southeast Asia, is landlocked by Myanmar, China, Vietnam, Cambodia, and Thailand. The population of 7.6 million people is diverse, with 49 ethnic groups formally recognized by the government. However, as many as 200 different ethnic groups exist overall. The majority of the population identifies as ethnically Lao, with smaller portions identifying as Khmou, Hmong, Phouthay, Tai, Makong, Katong, Lue, and Akha. Languages spoken include the official language, Lao, as well as French, English, and a variety of local ethnic languages. The majority of the population practices Buddhism. About 37 percent of the population lives in urban areas, such as Vientiane, the capital, and some larger settlements along the Mekong River and the southwestern border.

In 1975, Laos emerged from the Vietnam War as a communist state, and remains a one-party socialist republic. It is often criticized for lacking in civil liberties and human rights by the international community. Nonetheless, Laos is one of the fastest-growing economies in Southeast Asia and the Pacific. Since 2009 it has grown on average 7.4 percent a year. This has resulted in improving development indicators like reduced poverty and malnutrition, and better education. However, there is still room for progress on all of these fronts, as education attainment and quality of learning are still lacking. A child in Laos who goes to school for 10.8 years will receive only about 6.4 years of actual learning.

While the economy in Laos continues to rapidly grow, health problems persist and negatively impact the population. Malnutrition continues to cause stunting, afflicting over 30 percent of children under five years of age. In addition, maternal mortality remains high, with 185 deaths per 100,000 births. Other leading causes of death in Laos include stroke, ischemic heart disease, lower respiratory infections, neonatal disorders, tuberculosis, COPD, chronic kidney disease, diabetes, cirrhosis, diarrheal diseases, road injuries, and congenital defects. The risk factors that contribute most to death and disability include malnutrition, air pollution, high blood pressure, high fasting plasma glucose, dietary risks, high body-mass index, alcohol and tobacco use, kidney dysfunction, occupational risks, and insufficient water, sanitation, and hygiene.

7.6M

Population

$2,630

GDP Per Capita

68 years

Life Expectancy

↑ Improving

37
Doctors/100k

Physician Density

150
Beds/100k

Hospital Bed Density

185
Deaths/100k

Maternal Mortality

Laos

Nonprofit Organizations

A Broader View Volunteers
Provides developing countries around the world with significant volunteer programs that aid the neediest communities and forge a lasting bond between those volunteering and those they have helped.
Dent-OMFS, ER Med, Infect Dis, MF Med
⊕ https://vfmat.ch/3bec

A Leg To Stand On (ALTSO)
Provides free, high-quality prosthetic limbs, orthotic devices, and wheelchairs to children with untreated limb disabilities in the developing world.
Logist-Op, Ortho
⊕ https://vfmat.ch/a48d

Abt Associates
Seeks to improve the quality of life and economic well-being of people worldwide, while striving to meet and exceed the highest professional standards.
General, Logist-Op, MF Med, OB-GYN, Peds
⊕ https://vfmat.ch/cec2

Aceso Global
Provides strategic healthcare advisory services in low- and middle-income countries to design and deliver highly customized, evidence-based solutions that address the complex nature of healthcare systems, with a goal to strengthen and provide affordable, high-quality care to all.
Logist-Op, Pub Health
⊕ https://vfmat.ch/b3b7

AIDS Healthcare Foundation
Provides cutting-edge HIV/AIDS medical care and advocacy to over one million people in 43 countries.
Infect Dis
⊕ https://vfmat.ch/b27c

Aloha Medical Mission
Brings hope and changes the lives of people; serves overseas and in Hawai'i.
Anesth, Crit-Care, Dent-OMFS, ENT, ER Med, General, Medicine, OB-GYN, Ophth-Opt, Ortho, Ped Surg, Peds, Plast, Surg, Urol
⊕ https://vfmat.ch/72ac

AO Alliance
Builds solutions to lessen the burden of injuries in low- and middle-income countries, while enhancing the care of the injured to reduce human suffering, disability, and poverty.
Ortho, Surg
⊕ https://vfmat.ch/8cd5

ASAP Ministries
Provides education and healthcare to refugees and the poor, based in Christian ministry.

Dent-OMFS, General
⊕ https://vfmat.ch/266e

Boston Children's Hospital: Global Health Program
Helps solve pediatric global healthcare challenges by transferring expertise through long-term partnerships with scalable impact, while working in the field to strengthen healthcare systems, advocate, research, and provide care delivery or education as a way of sustainably improving the health of children worldwide.
Anesth, CV Med, Crit-Care, ER Med, Heme-Onc, Infect Dis, Medicine, Nutr, Palliative, Ped Surg, Peds
⊕ https://vfmat.ch/f9f8

Bureau of International Health Cooperation
Seeks to improve healthcare around the world, including developing countries, using expertise, and contribute to healthier lives of Japanese people by bringing these experiences back to Japan.
ER Med, Heme-Onc, Infect Dis, Peds, Pub Health
⊕ https://vfmat.ch/947d

Camillian Disaster Service (CADIS) International
Promotes the development of locally based health programs for disaster-stricken communities through compassionate and coordinated interventions.
General, Logist-Op, MF Med
⊕ https://vfmat.ch/5281

CARE
Works around the globe to save lives, defeat poverty, and achieve social justice.
ER Med, General
⊕ https://vfmat.ch/7232

cbm New Zealand
Inspired by the Christian faith, aims to improve the quality of life for those living with the double disadvantage of poverty and disability.
Crit-Care, Infect Dis, Logist-Op, Nutr, OB-GYN, Ophth-Opt, Ortho, Psych, Rehab, Surg
⊕ https://vfmat.ch/c14b

Chain of Hope (La Chaîne de l'Espoir)
Helps underprivileged children around the world by providing them with access to healthcare.
Anesth, CT Surg, Crit-Care, ER Med, Neurosurg, Ortho, Ped Surg, Surg, Vasc Surg
⊕ https://vfmat.ch/e871

ChildFund Australia
Works to reduce poverty for children in many of the world's most disadvantaged communities.
ER Med, General, Peds
⊕ https://vfmat.ch/13df

ChildFund Laos
Focuses on children's rights, improving access to education, child nutrition, sexual and reproductive health and rights, media literacy, and job readiness.
MF Med, Nutr, Pub Health
⊕ https://vfmat.ch/2883

Children's Lifeline International
Provides medical teams and surgical assistance to underprivileged children in developing countries through missions in partnership with local hospitals.
CV Med, Dent-OMFS, General, MF Med, Neurosurg, Peds, Rehab
⊕ https://vfmat.ch/6fea

Christian Blind Mission (CBM)
Aims to improve the quality of life of persons with disabilities in the poorest countries, addressing poverty as a cause and a consequence of disability, and working in partnership to create a society for all.
ENT, General, Infect Dis, OB-GYN, Ophth-Opt, Ortho, Peds, Psych, Rehab, Surg
⊕ https://vfmat.ch/3824

CleanBirth.org
Aims to make birth safer in Salavan Province, Laos, by providing birthing supplies, training for nurses, and funding for nurses to train CleanBirth Village Volunteers.
MF Med, OB-GYN
⊕ https://vfmat.ch/1eed

Clinton Health Access Initiative (CHAI)
Aims to save lives and reduce the burden of disease in low- and middle-income countries. Works with partners to strengthen the capabilities of governments and the private sector to create and sustain high-quality health systems.
General, Heme-Onc, Infect Dis, Logist-Op, MF Med, Medicine, Neonat, Nutr, OB-GYN, Path, Peds, Rad-Onc
⊕ https://vfmat.ch/9ed7

Direct Relief
Improves the health and lives of people affected by poverty or emergency situations by mobilizing and providing essential medical resources needed for their care.
ER Med, Logist-Op
⊕ https://vfmat.ch/58e5

Duke University: Global Health Institute
Sparks innovation in global health research and education, and brings together knowledge and resources to address the most important global health issues of our time.
All-Immu, Infect Dis, MF Med, OB-GYN, Pub Health
⊕ https://vfmat.ch/c4cd

Eye Care Foundation
Helps prevent and cure avoidable blindness and visual impairment in low-income countries.
Ophth-Opt, Surg
⊕ https://vfmat.ch/c8f9

Firefly Mission
Organizes humanitarian missions to help people in less fortunate situations while serving as a vehicle for the spiritual development of members and the beneficiaries of its missions.
Logist-Op, Ophth-Opt, Pub Health
⊕ https://vfmat.ch/d215

Fred Hollows Foundation, The
Works toward a world in which no person is needlessly blind or vision impaired.
Ophth-Opt, Pub Health, Surg
⊕ https://vfmat.ch/73e5

Friends Without A Border
Provides free, high-quality healthcare to children of areas of dire need in Southeast Asia, by developing infrastructure, providing care, creating health education programs, and training local healthcare professionals at Lao Friends Hospital for Children, Angkor Hospital for Children, and The Lake Clinic in Cambodia.
Anesth, ER Med, Infect Dis, Logist-Op, Neonat, Nutr, Ortho, Ped Surg, Peds,

Radiol, Surg
⊕ https://vfmat.ch/58b9

Global Blood Fund
Delivers grants, equipment, and training to over 50 countries in Africa, Asia, Eastern Europe, the Middle East, Latin America and the Caribbean.
Pub Health
⊕ https://vfmat.ch/6377

Global Clubfoot Initiative (GCI)
Promotes and resources the treatment of children with clubfoot in developing countries using the Ponseti technique.
Ortho, Ped Surg
⊕ https://vfmat.ch/f229

Global Medical Volunteers
Aims to advance medical services and education in developing nations around the world.
GI, Surg, Urol
⊕ https://vfmat.ch/dfec

Global Ministries – The United Methodist Church
As the worldwide mission and development agency of The United Methodist Church, Global Ministries works with more than 300 hospitals and clinics around the world through its Global Health Unit.
Anesth, CT Surg, CV Med, Crit-Care, Dent-OMFS, Derm, ER Med, GI, General, Infect Dis, Logist-Op, MF Med, Medicine, Neonat, Nephro, Nutr, OB-GYN, Ophth-Opt, Ortho, Palliative, Peds, Pod, Psych, Pub Health, Rehab, Rheum, Surg, Urol
⊕ https://vfmat.ch/1723

Global Oncology (GO)
Brings the best in cancer care to underserved patients around the world and collaborates across geographic, professional, and academic borders to improve cancer care, research, and education.
Heme-Onc, Path, Rad-Onc
⊕ https://vfmat.ch/fcb8

Global Primary Care
Aims to promote and support individuals and organizations that increase access to primary care through sustainable efforts for people living in the poorest places of the world.
General, Logist-Op, Medicine
⊕ https://vfmat.ch/742b

Globus Relief
Aims to improve the delivery of healthcare worldwide by gathering, processing, and distributing surplus medical supplies to charities at home and abroad.
Logist-Op
⊕ https://vfmat.ch/a2b7

Handa Foundation, The
Builds hospitals and schools in Southeast Asia.
Anesth, Infect Dis, Psych, Surg
⊕ https://vfmat.ch/eacf

Health Frontiers
Provides volunteer support to international health and child development efforts.
ER Med, Medicine, Peds
⊕ https://vfmat.ch/aa14

Health Poverty Action
Works in partnership with people around the world who are pursuing change in their own communities to demand health justice and challenge power imbalances.
ER Med, General, Infect Dis, Psych, Pub Health
⊕ https://vfmat.ch/ee58

Health Volunteers Overseas (HVO)
Improves the availability and quality of healthcare through the education, training, and professional development of the health workforce in resource-scarce countries.
All-Immu, Anesth, CV Med, Dent-OMFS, Derm, ENT, Endo, GI, Heme-Onc, Infect Dis, Medicine, Medicine, Nephro, Neuro, OB-GYN, Ophth-Opt, Ortho,

Peds, Plast, Psych, Pulm-Critic, Rehab, Rheum, Surg
⊕ https://vfmat.ch/42b2

HumaniTerra
Helps countries and populations emerging from economic and human crisis to rebuild their healthcare system in a sustainable way. Committed to three fundamental and complementary actions: operating, training, and rebuilding.
Anesth, ENT, ER Med, MF Med, OB-GYN, Ortho, Plast, Surg
⊕ https://vfmat.ch/b371

Humanity & Inclusion
Works alongside people with disabilities and vulnerable populations, taking action and bearing witness in order to respond to their essential needs, improve their living conditions and health, and promote respect for their dignity and fundamental rights.
General, Infect Dis, MF Med, Medicine, Ortho, Peds, Psych, Pub Health, Rehab
⊕ https://vfmat.ch/16b7

Institute of Applied Dermatology
Aims to alleviate difficult-to-treat skin ailments by combining biomedicine with Ayurveda, homeopathy, yoga, and other traditional Indian medicine.
All-Immu, Derm, Infect Dis, Nutr, Pod, Pub Health
⊕ https://vfmat.ch/c6eb

International Council of Ophthalmology
Works with ophthalmologic societies and others to enhance ophthalmic education and improve access to the highest-quality eye care in order to preserve and restore vision for people of the world.
Ophth-Opt
⊕ https://vfmat.ch/ffd2

International Federation of Red Cross and Red Crescent Societies (IFRC)
Coordinates and directs international assistance following natural and manmade disasters in nonconflict situations through the world's largest humanitarian and development network. Provides disaster-preparedness programs, healthcare activities, and promotes humanitarian values.
ER Med, General, Infect Dis, Nutr
⊕ https://vfmat.ch/b4ee

International Organization for Migration (IOM) – The UN Migration Agency
Promotes evidence-informed policies and holistic, preventive, and curative health programs that are beneficial, accessible, and equitable for vulnerable migrants.
General, Infect Dis, OB-GYN
⊕ https://vfmat.ch/621a

IntraHealth International
Improves the performance of health workers and strengthens the systems in which they work.
CV Med, Endo, General, Infect Dis, MF Med, Neonat, Nutr, OB-GYN
⊕ https://vfmat.ch/ddc8

Japan Heart
Provides medical care in areas where it is currently out of reach, wherever that may be.
Heme-Onc, Medicine, OB-GYN, Ped Surg, Peds, Plast, Surg
⊕ https://vfmat.ch/1cd3

John Snow, Inc. (JSI)
Aims to improve the health and well-being of underserved and vulnerable people and communities throughout the world.
General, Infect Dis, Logist-Op, MF Med, OB-GYN, Peds, Psych, Pub Health
⊕ https://vfmat.ch/ba78

Joint United Nations Programme on HIV/AIDS (UNAIDS)
Aims to place people living with HIV and people affected by the virus at the decision-making table and at the center of designing, delivering, and monitoring the AIDS response.
Infect Dis
⊕ https://vfmat.ch/464a

Kids Care Everywhere
Seeks to empower physicians in under-resourced environments with multimedia, state-of-the-art medical software, and to inspire young professionals to become future global healthcare leaders.
Logist-Op, Ped Surg, Peds
⊕ https://vfmat.ch/bc23

Lao Health Initiative
Ensures that the people of Northern Laos have comprehensive healthcare.
Logist-Op
⊕ https://vfmat.ch/847c

Limbs International
Engages communities and transforms lives through affordable, sustainable prosthetic solutions and rehabilitation services in developing countries.
Logist-Op, Ortho, Pod, Rehab
⊕ https://vfmat.ch/dc84

Maternity Foundation
Works to ensure safer childbirth for women and newborns everywhere through innovative mobile health solutions such as the Safe Delivery App, a mobile training tool for skilled birth attendants.
MF Med, OB-GYN, Pub Health
⊕ https://vfmat.ch/ff4f

MedShare
Aims to improve the quality of life of people, communities, and the planet by sourcing and directly delivering surplus medical supplies and equipment to communities in need around the world.
Logist-Op
⊕ https://vfmat.ch/c8bc

Mission Plasticos
Provides reconstructive plastic surgical care to those in need, and generates sustainable outcomes through training, education, and research.
Plast
⊕ https://vfmat.ch/97cb

Médecins du Monde/Doctors of the World
Provides care, bears witness, and supports social change worldwide with innovative medical programs and evidence-based advocacy initiatives.
ER Med, General, Infect Dis, MF Med, Neonat, OB-GYN, Peds, Pub Health
⊕ https://vfmat.ch/a43d

Mérieux Foundation
Committed to fighting infectious diseases that affect developing countries by capacity building, particularly in clinical laboratories, and focusing on diagnosis.
Logist-Op, Path
⊕ https://vfmat.ch/a23a

Norwegian People's Aid
Aims to improve living conditions, to create a democratic, just, and safe society.
ER Med, Logist-Op
⊕ https://vfmat.ch/2d8e

Nursing Beyond Borders
Provides healthcare and education to children and communities, and focuses as well on disease prevention by providing nurses to serve in orphanages, shelters, schools, and clinics.
Logist-Op, MF Med, Peds
⊕ https://vfmat.ch/71e6

Options
Believes in a world in which women and children can access the high-quality health services they need, without financial burden.
Logist-Op, MF Med, Neonat, OB-GYN
⊕ https://vfmat.ch/3a48

Pact
Works on the ground to improve the lives of those who are challenged by poverty and marginalization, striving for a world in which all people are heard, capable, and vibrant.

Infect Dis, Logist-Op, MF Med, Pub Health
⊕ https://vfmat.ch/9a6c

Partners for Development (PfD)
Works to improve quality of life for vulnerable people in underserved communities through local and international partnerships.
Infect Dis, MF Med, Neonat, Peds
⊕ https://vfmat.ch/d2f6

PSI – Population Services International
Aims to improve the health of people in the developing world by focusing on challenges such as a lack of family planning, HIV/AIDS, barriers to maternal health, and the greatest threats to children under the age of 5, including malaria, diarrhea, pneumonia, and malnutrition.
Infect Dis, MF Med, OB-GYN, Peds
⊕ https://vfmat.ch/ffe3

RAD-AID International
Improves and optimizes access to medical imaging and radiology in low-resource regions of the world.
Rad-Onc, Radiol
⊕ https://vfmat.ch/537f

Resource Exchange International
Provides holistic education and training to improve knowledge and skills and build human capacity within communities in emerging nations.
Derm, ENT, Ortho
⊕ https://vfmat.ch/6d49

Resource Exchange International
Sends long-term staff and short-term professionals in areas of education, medicine, and business to train leaders in emerging nations so that they can train others.
General
⊕ https://vfmat.ch/6863

RestoringVision
Empowers lives by restoring vision for millions of people in need.
Ophth-Opt
⊕ https://vfmat.ch/e121

Rotary International
Provides service to others, improves lives, and advances world understanding, goodwill, and peace through its fellowship of business, professional, and community leaders.
ER Med, General, Infect Dis, MF Med, OB-GYN
⊕ https://vfmat.ch/8fb5

SEE International
Provides sustainable medical, surgical, and educational services through volunteer ophthalmic surgeons, with the objectives of restoring sight and preventing blindness to disadvantaged individuals worldwide.
Ophth-Opt, Surg
⊕ https://vfmat.ch/6e1b

Seeing is Believing
Provides vision screening and eyeglasses to underprivileged people throughout the world.
Logist-Op, OB-GYN, Ophth-Opt
⊕ https://vfmat.ch/b6be

Sight for All
Empowers communities to deliver comprehensive, evidence-based, high-quality eye healthcare through the provision of research, education, and equipment.
Logist-Op, Ophth-Opt, Surg
⊕ https://vfmat.ch/e34b

SIGN Fracture Care International
Builds orthopedic capacity around the world and provides the injured poor access to fracture surgery by donating orthopedic education and implant systems to surgeons in developing countries.
Ortho, Rehab, Surg
⊕ https://vfmat.ch/123d

SINA Health
Aims to improve the health and educational status of the population in low- and middle-income countries.
General, Logist-Op
⊕ https://vfmat.ch/9ad3

Smile Asia
Delivers free surgical care, through medical missions and outreach centers, to children with facial deformities such as cleft lip and cleft palate, and aims to raise standards of medical care by creating opportunities for collaborative learning and exchange of best practices.
Anesth, Dent-OMFS, Ped Surg, Peds, Plast
⊕ https://vfmat.ch/d674

Smile Train, Inc.
Treats children with cleft lip through a sustainable and local model that supports surgery and other forms of essential care.
Logist-Op, Pub Health
⊕ https://vfmat.ch/822c

Sri Sathya Sai International Organization
Inspired by spiritual teachings, carries out efforts in global healthcare, education, humanitarian relief, and youth engagement.
Dent-OMFS, General, Logist-Op, Nutr, Ophth-Opt, Pub Health
⊕ https://vfmat.ch/9bda

Swiss Tropical and Public Health Institute
Contributes to the improvement of the health of populations internationally, nationally, and locally through excellence in research, education, and services.
Infect Dis, Pub Health
⊕ https://vfmat.ch/2ee4

Task Force for Global Health, The
Consists of programs and focus areas that cover a range of global health issues including neglected tropical diseases, infectious diseases, vaccines, field epidemiology, public health informatics, health workforce development, and global health ethics.
Infect Dis, Logist-Op, Medicine, Ophth-Opt, Peds
⊕ https://vfmat.ch/714c

Tearfund
Responds to crisis and partners with local churches to bring restoration to those living in poverty, inspired by the Christian faith.
ER Med, Logist-Op
⊕ https://vfmat.ch/f6cf

Transparent Fish Fund
Inspires others to join in alleviating poverty in East Asia by empowering small but high-impact NGOs to be sustainable and transparent in their programs.
CV Med, General, MF Med, Nutr, Peds
⊕ https://vfmat.ch/7714

Union for International Cancer Control (UICC)
Unites and supports the cancer community to reduce the global cancer burden, promote greater equity, and ensure that cancer control continues to be a priority in the world health and development agenda.
Heme-Onc, Pub Health
⊕ https://vfmat.ch/88b1

United Nations Children's Fund (UNICEF)
Works in over 190 countries and territories to save children's lives, defend their rights, and help them fulfill their potential, from early childhood through adolescence.
All-Immu, Infect Dis, MF Med, Neonat, Nutr, OB-GYN, Ped Surg, Peds, Pub Health
⊕ https://vfmat.ch/42d7

United Nations Development Programme (UNDP)
Helps countries achieve the simultaneous eradication of extreme poverty and significant reduction of inequalities and exclusion using a sustainable human development approach.
Infect Dis, Logist-Op, Pub Health
⊕ https://vfmat.ch/935c

United Nations High Commissioner for Refugees (UNHCR)
Safeguards the rights and well-being of people who have been forced to flee, ensuring that everybody has the right to seek asylum and find safe refuge in another country, with the goal of seeking lasting solutions.
General, MF Med, Medicine, OB-GYN, Peds, Psych, Pub Health
⊕ https://vfmat.ch/6636

United Nations Population Fund (UNFPA)
Supports reproductive healthcare for women and youth in more than 150 countries, focusing on delivering a world in which every pregnancy is wanted, every childbirth is safe, and every young person's potential is fulfilled.
Infect Dis, MF Med, Neonat, OB-GYN, Peds, Pub Health
⊕ https://vfmat.ch/c969

United States Agency for International Development (USAID)
Promotes and demonstrates democratic values abroad and advances a free, peaceful, and prosperous world. Leads the U.S. government's international development and disaster assistance through partnerships and investments that save lives.
ER Med, Infect Dis, MF Med, OB-GYN, Peds
⊕ https://vfmat.ch/9a99

United Surgeons for Children (USFC)
Pursues greater health and opportunity for children in the most neglected pockets of the world, with a specific focus on and expertise in surgery.
Anesth, CT Surg, Neonat, Neurosurg, OB-GYN, Peds, Radiol, Surg
⊕ https://vfmat.ch/3b4c

University of Virginia: Anesthesiology Department Global Health Initiatives
Educates and trains physicians to help people achieve healthy productive lives, and advances knowledge in the medical sciences.
Anesth, Pub Health
⊕ https://vfmat.ch/1b8b

USAID: Leadership, Management and Governance Project
Improves leadership, management, and governance practices to strengthen health systems and improve health for all, including vulnerable populations worldwide.
Logist-Op
⊕ https://vfmat.ch/d35e

USAID: Maternal and Child Survival Program
Works to prevent child and maternal deaths.
Infect Dis, MF Med, Neonat, OB-GYN, Peds
⊕ https://vfmat.ch/6fcf

Vision Care
Restores sight and helps patients get regular treatment at short-term eye camps and long-term base clinics by having doctors, missionaries, volunteers, and sponsors work together.
Ophth-Opt
⊕ https://vfmat.ch/9d7c

Vitamin Angels
Helps at-risk populations in need—specifically pregnant women, new mothers, and children under age 5—to gain access to life-changing vitamins and minerals.
General, Nutr
⊕ https://vfmat.ch/7da1

World Federation of Hemophilia (WFH)
Aims to improve and sustain care for people with inherited bleeding disorders by pursuing long-term relationships with individuals and organizations who share the values of WFH's development model.
Heme-Onc
⊕ https://vfmat.ch/5121

World Health Organization, The (WHO)
The United Nations' agency for health provides leadership on global health matters, shapes the health research agenda, sets norms and standards, articulates evidence-based policy options, provides technical support and monitoring to countries, and assesses health trends.
ER Med, General, Infect Dis, Logist-Op, MF Med, OB-GYN, Peds, Psych, Pub

Health
⊕ https://vfmat.ch/c476

World Medical Relief
Facilitates the distribution of surplus medical resources where they are needed.
Logist-Op
⊕ https://vfmat.ch/72dc

World Vision International
Works with vulnerable communities around the world to overcome poverty and injustice with child-focused programs in disaster management, health, nutrition, economic development, education, clean water, sanitation, and hygiene.
ER Med, General, Infect Dis, MF Med, Nutr, OB-GYN, Peds
⊕ https://vfmat.ch/2642

York County Medical Foundation
Provides medical care and humanitarian relief to the poor, the distressed, and the underprivileged, both locally and internationally.
OB-GYN, Plast, Surg
⊕ https://vfmat.ch/a55d

Laos

Healthcare Facilities

Alliance International Medical Center
Ban Wattayyaithong, Vientiane Capital, Laos
⊕ https://vfmat.ch/lvus

Attapeu Province Hospital
Samakkhixay District, Attepeu, Laos
⊕ https://vfmat.ch/blnf

Bolikhamxay Province Hospital
Paksan District, Bolikhamxay, Laos
⊕ https://vfmat.ch/9vcs

Champasak Province Hospital
Pakse District, Champasak Province, Laos
⊕ https://vfmat.ch/uzxw

French Medical Center
Vientiane, Laos
⊕ https://vfmat.ch/t8ss

Ha Noi-Vientiane Hospital
Chommany, Vientiane Prefecture, Laos
⊕ https://vfmat.ch/648e

Lao Friends Hospital for Children
Luang Prabang, Laos
⊕ https://vfmat.ch/ujpc

Lao Military Hospital 103
Ban Donnôkkhoum, Vientiane Prefecture, Laos
⊕ https://vfmat.ch/1fa9

Lao-Korea National Children's Hospital
Vientiane, Laos
⊕ https://vfmat.ch/wmds

Lao-Viet Hospital
Vientiane, Laos
⊕ https://vfmat.ch/dgjj

Luang Prabang Provincial Hospital
Luang Prabang, Laos
⊕ https://vfmat.ch/wxct

Mahosot Hospital
Ban Sithan Nua, Vientiane, Laos
⊕ https://vfmat.ch/81f6

Maria Theresa Hospital
Phonemy, Laos
⊕ https://vfmat.ch/byf8

Mittaphab (Friendship) Hospital
Vientiane, Laos
⊕ https://vfmat.ch/dy9w

Oudomxay Province Hospital
Ban Donkèo, Oudômxai, Laos
⊕ https://vfmat.ch/7b6a

Paksong Hospital
Ban Lak Si Sip Pèt, Champasak, Laos
⊕ https://vfmat.ch/58dc

Saimangkorn International Hospital
Muang Xay, Laos
⊕ https://vfmat.ch/zzut

Salavan Provincial Hospital
Phonekeo Village, Salavan, Laos
⊕ https://vfmat.ch/i8yf

Savannakhet Hospital
Savannakhet, Laos
⊕ https://vfmat.ch/dfbx

Sayaboury Province Hospital
Ban Toun, Xiagnabouli, Laos
⊕ https://vfmat.ch/c1cf

Setthathirath Hospital
Donkoi Village, Vientiane, Laos
⊕ https://vfmat.ch/857e

Thakek Hospital
Ban Lao, Khammouan, Laos
⊕ https://vfmat.ch/7erd

Xianghon hospital
Ban Kouk, Xiagnabouli, Laos
⊕ https://vfmat.ch/93b6

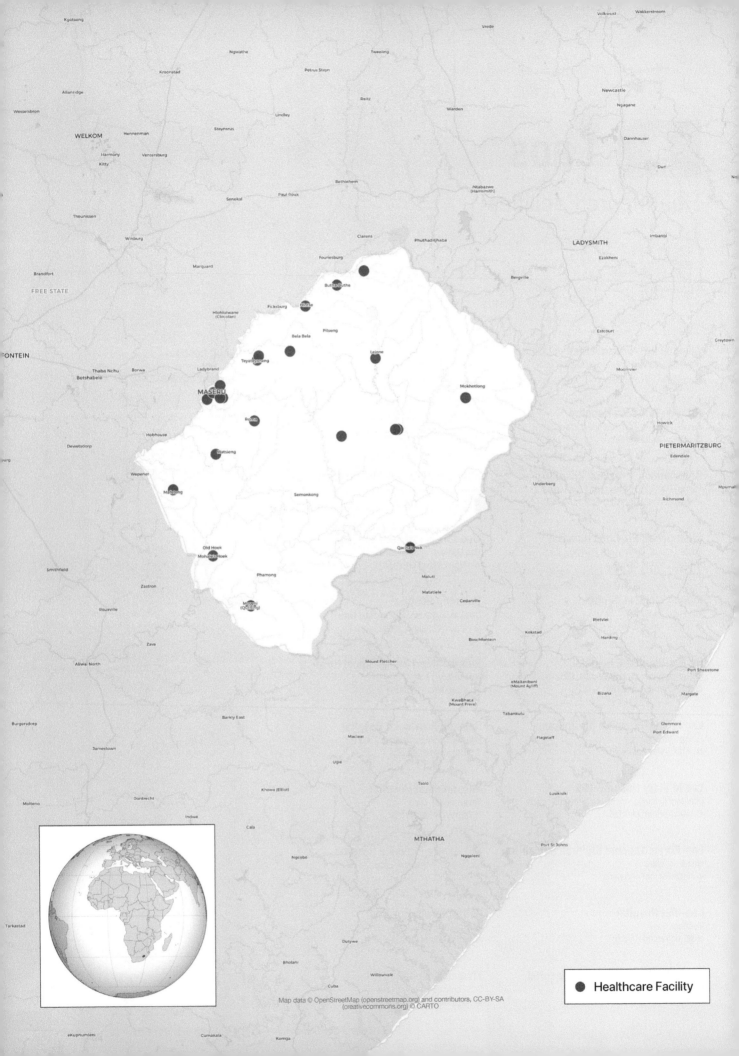

Healthcare Facility

Lesotho

Boasting one of the highest adult literacy rates in Africa, the Kingdom of Lesotho is a small country bordered entirely by South Africa. The population of about 2.2 million resides in an area of about 30,000 square kilometers. Most people live in the western half of the country, and around a few major urban areas, such as Maseru, the capital, home to 202,000 residents. The overwhelming majority of the population consider themselves ethnically Sotho, and speak Sesotho, English, Zulu, and Xhosa. The country is predominantly Christian, with most people identifying as Protestant, Roman Catholic, and other denominations. About two-thirds of Lesotho consists of mountains, with its lowest point 1,400 meters above sea level. Tall mountain ranges form a natural barrier with South Africa. Lesotho is also the source of two of South Africa's largest rivers: the Tugela River and the Orange River. With no other shared borders, Lesotho must depend heavily on a good relationship with South Africa.

Since gaining independence from Britain in 1966, Lesotho has been transformed and modernized, yet not without some initial growing pains. A number of rebellions, military coups, and contentious elections have plagued the country. Lesotho has also struggled with high levels of poverty: More than half the population lives below the poverty line. There are few natural resources, and the country is susceptible to food insecurity and shortages. Many people cross the border to work in South Africa, as opportunities are lacking in Lesotho. Remittances account for 17 percent of the country's GDP, highlighting the scope of the problem. Despite these challenges, Lesotho has made great progress in the area of education and is on track to achieve universal primary education.

Lesotho has the second highest HIV/AIDS rate in the world—25 percent of the adult population is HIV positive—and it is the leading cause of death in the country. Other causes of death include tuberculosis, lower respiratory infections, stroke, diarrheal diseases, ischemic heart disease, diabetes, neonatal disorders, road injuries, interpersonal violence, and COPD. The risk factors that contribute most to death and disability include unsafe sex, malnutrition, air pollution, alcohol and tobacco use, high fasting plasma glucose, high body-mass index, high blood pressure, intimate partner violence, and insufficient water, sanitation, and hygiene. In addition, rates of maternal and infant mortality have remained high over the past decade.

2.2M

Population

$861

GDP Per Capita

54 years

Life Expectancy

↑ Improving

7
Doctors/100k

Physician Density

130
Beds/100k

Hospital Bed Density

544
Deaths/100k

Maternal Mortality

Lesotho

Nonprofit Organizations

Adventist Health International
Focuses on upgrading and managing mission hospitals by providing governance, consultation, and technical assistance to a number of affiliated Seventh-Day Adventist hospitals throughout Africa, Asia, and the Americas.
Dent-OMFS, General, Pub Health
🌐 https://vfmat.ch/16aa

Africa CDC
Aims to strengthen the capacity and capability of Africa's public health institutions and partnerships to detect and respond quickly and effectively to disease threats and outbreaks, based on data-driven interventions and programs.
Infect Dis, Logist-Op, Pub Health
🌐 https://vfmat.ch/339c

Africa Health Organisation
Leads collaborative efforts among countries in Africa and other partners to promote health equity, combat disease, and improve quality of life.
Logist-Op, Pub Health
🌐 https://vfmat.ch/b1c5

Africa Inland Mission International
Seeks to establish churches and community development programs including healthcare projects, based in Christian ministry.
Anesth, Dent-OMFS, ER Med, General, MF Med, Medicine, OB-GYN, OB-GYN, Ophth-Opt, Ped Surg, Peds, Rehab
🌐 https://vfmat.ch/f2f6

Africa Relief and Community Development
Provides comprehensive relief and developmental aid to people of the African continent regardless of gender, race, or religion.
Nutr, Pub Health
🌐 https://vfmat.ch/6cd2

AIDS Healthcare Foundation
Provides cutting-edge HIV/AIDS medical care and advocacy to over one million people in 43 countries.
Infect Dis
🌐 https://vfmat.ch/b27c

AIDS Orphan Care
Provides African children orphaned by HIV/AIDS with food, clothing, a warm bed, an education, healthcare, and the knowledge that somebody cares.
General, Peds, Pub Health
🌐 https://vfmat.ch/6126

Amref Health Africa
Serves millions of people across 35 countries in Sub-Saharan Africa, strengthening health systems, and training African health workers to respond to the continent's most critical health issues.

All-Immu, General, Infect Dis, Logist-Op, MF Med, OB-GYN, Path, Pub Health, Surg
🌐 https://vfmat.ch/6985

Aurum Institute, The
Seeks to impact global health by designing and delivering high-quality care and treatment to people in developing countries.
Infect Dis, Pub Health
🌐 https://vfmat.ch/ae2a

Avert
Works to ensure widespread understanding of HIV/AIDS in order to reduce new infections and improve the lives of those affected.
Infect Dis, Path
🌐 https://vfmat.ch/312d

Baylor International Pediatric AIDS Initiative (BIPAI) at Texas Children's Hospital
Provides high-quality, high-impact, highly ethical pediatric and family-centered healthcare, health professional training, and clinical research focused on HIV/AIDS, tuberculosis, malaria, malnutrition, and other conditions impacting the health of children worldwide.
Infect Dis, Medicine, OB-GYN, Peds, Pub Health, Surg
🌐 https://vfmat.ch/e6ba

Brigham and Women's Hospital Global Health Hub
Cares for patients in underserved settings, provides education to staff who work in those areas to create sustainable change, and conducts research designed to improve health in such settings.
General, Infect Dis
🌐 https://vfmat.ch/a8a3

CARE
Works around the globe to save lives, defeat poverty, and achieve social justice.
ER Med, General
🌐 https://vfmat.ch/7232

Center for Strategic and International Studies (CSIS) Commission on Strengthening America's Health Security
Brings together a distinguished and diverse group of high-level opinion leaders bridging security and health, with the core aim to chart a bold vision for the future of U.S. leadership in global health.
ER Med, Infect Dis, MF Med, Pub Health
🌐 https://vfmat.ch/6d7f

Christian Connections for International Health (CCIH)
Promotes global health and wholeness from a Christian perspective.
All-Immu, General, Infect Dis, MF Med, Neonat, OB-GYN, Psych
🌐 https://vfmat.ch/fa5d

Christian Health Association of Lesotho

Based in Christian ministry, provides about 40% of the healthcare in Lesotho through the association of 6 CHAL member churches, which own 8 hospitals and 71 health centers throughout Lesotho.

General, Infect Dis, Logist-Op, Medicine, OB-GYN, Peds, Surg

⊕ https://vfmat.ch/fbcf

Clinton Health Access Initiative (CHAI)

Aims to save lives and reduce the burden of disease in low- and middle-income countries. Works with partners to strengthen the capabilities of governments and the private sector to create and sustain high-quality health systems.

General, Heme-Onc, Infect Dis, Logist-Op, MF Med, Medicine, Neonat, Nutr, OB-GYN, Path, Peds, Rad-Onc

⊕ https://vfmat.ch/9ed7

Columbia University: Global Mental Health Programs

Pioneers research initiatives, promotes mental health, and aims to reduce the burden of mental illness worldwide.

Psych

⊕ https://vfmat.ch/c5cd

Columbia Vagelos College of Physicians and Surgeons Programs in Global Health

Harnesses the expertise of the medical school to improve health worldwide by training global health leaders, building capacity through interdisciplinary education and training programs, and addressing unmet health needs through research and application.

CV Med, Derm, Genetics, Heme-Onc, Infect Dis, Medicine, OB-GYN, Ophth-Opt, Peds, Psych, Pub Health, Pulm-Critic, Surg

⊕ https://vfmat.ch/a9e5

Developing Country NGO Delegation: Global Fund to Fight AIDS, TB & Malaria

Works to strengthen the engagement of civil society actors and organizations in developing countries to build a world in which AIDS, TB, and malaria are no longer global, public health, and human rights threats.

Infect Dis, Pub Health

⊕ https://vfmat.ch/3149

Direct Relief

Improves the health and lives of people affected by poverty or emergency situations by mobilizing and providing essential medical resources needed for their care.

ER Med, Logist-Op

⊕ https://vfmat.ch/58e5

Elizabeth Glaser Pediatric AIDS Foundation

Seeks to end global pediatric HIV/AIDS through prevention and treatment programs, research, and advocacy.

Infect Dis, Nutr, OB-GYN, Peds

⊕ https://vfmat.ch/d6ec

Global Blood Fund

Delivers grants, equipment, and training to over 50 countries in Africa, Asia, Eastern Europe, the Middle East, Latin America and the Caribbean.

Pub Health

⊕ https://vfmat.ch/6377

Global Oncology (GO)

Brings the best in cancer care to underserved patients around the world and collaborates across geographic, professional, and academic borders to improve cancer care, research, and education.

Heme-Onc, Path, Rad-Onc

⊕ https://vfmat.ch/fcb8

Global Primary Care

Aims to promote and support individuals and organizations that increase access to primary care through sustainable efforts for people living in the poorest places of the world.

General, Logist-Op, Medicine

⊕ https://vfmat.ch/742b

GOAL

Works with the most vulnerable communities to help them respond to and recover from humanitarian crises, and to assist them in building transcendent solutions to mitigate poverty and vulnerability.

ER Med, General, Pub Health

⊕ https://vfmat.ch/bbea

Grassroot Soccer

Leverages the power of soccer to educate, inspire, and mobilize at-risk youth in developing countries to overcome their greatest health challenges, live healthier and more productive lives, and be agents for change in their communities.

Infect Dis

⊕ https://vfmat.ch/3521

Handa Foundation, The

Builds hospitals and schools in Southeast Asia.

Anesth, Infect Dis, Psych, Surg

⊕ https://vfmat.ch/eacf

Health Equity Initiative

Aims to build and sustain a global community that engages across sectors and disciplines to advance health equity.

Pub Health

⊕ https://vfmat.ch/e2e2

Health Poverty Action

Works in partnership with people around the world who are pursuing change in their own communities to demand health justice and challenge power imbalances.

ER Med, General, Infect Dis, Psych, Pub Health

⊕ https://vfmat.ch/ee58

ICAP at Columbia University

Serves as global leader in supporting the scale-up of multidisciplinary HIV/AIDS prevention, care, and treatment programs based on a family-focused approach.

General, Infect Dis, MF Med, Medicine, OB-GYN, Pub Health

⊕ https://vfmat.ch/a8ef

International Federation of Red Cross and Red Crescent Societies (IFRC)

Coordinates and directs international assistance following natural and manmade disasters in nonconflict situations through the world's largest humanitarian and development network. Provides disaster-preparedness programs, healthcare activities, and promotes humanitarian values.

ER Med, General, Infect Dis, Nutr

⊕ https://vfmat.ch/b4ee

International Organization for Migration (IOM) – The UN Migration Agency

Promotes evidence-informed policies and holistic, preventive, and curative health programs that are beneficial, accessible, and equitable for vulnerable migrants.

General, Infect Dis, OB-GYN

⊕ https://vfmat.ch/621a

International Planned Parenthood Federation (IPPF)

Leads a locally owned, globally connected civil society movement that provides and enables services and champions sexual and reproductive health and rights for all, especially the underserved.

Infect Dis, MF Med, OB-GYN

⊕ https://vfmat.ch/dc97

Izumi Foundation

Develops and supports programs that improve health and healthcare in neglected regions of Africa and Latin America.

⊕ https://vfmat.ch/f29a

Jhpiego

Creates and delivers transformative healthcare solutions that save lives, in partnership with national governments, health experts, and local communities.

General, Infect Dis, OB-GYN, Surg

⊕ https://vfmat.ch/45b8

Joint United Nations Programme on HIV/AIDS (UNAIDS)
Aims to place people living with HIV and people affected by the virus at the decision-making table and at the center of designing, delivering, and monitoring the AIDS response.
Infect Dis
⊕ https://vfmat.ch/464a

Kick4Life
Aims to improve the long-term prospects of vulnerable young people in Lesotho through activities focused on health, education, and support towards sustainable livelihoods.
⊕ https://vfmat.ch/dd13

Management Sciences for Health (MSH)
Works with countries and communities to save lives and improve the health of the world's poorest and most vulnerable people by building strong, resilient, sustainable health systems.
Infect Dis, Logist-Op, Pub Health
⊕ https://vfmat.ch/6aa2

Medical Care Development International (MCD International)
Works to strengthen health systems through innovative, sustainable interventions.
Infect Dis, Logist-Op, OB-GYN, Pub Health
⊕ https://vfmat.ch/dc5c

Medical Care Development International
Works to improve the health of vulnerable populations through integrated, sustainable, and locally driven interventions.
Infect Dis, OB-GYN, Peds, Pub Health
⊕ https://vfmat.ch/da87

MedShare
Aims to improve the quality of life of people, communities, and the planet by sourcing and directly delivering surplus medical supplies and equipment to communities in need around the world.
Logist-Op
⊕ https://vfmat.ch/c8bc

Mercy and Love Foundation
Aims to provide orphaned and vulnerable children with basic human needs such as food, clothing, and shelter, enabling them to thrive.
General, Peds
⊕ https://vfmat.ch/649a

Mophato oa Mants'ase Society, The
Fosters the well-being of children through their families, when possible, and provides residential care for the duration of child placement when it is not.
Infect Dis, Peds
⊕ https://vfmat.ch/1f52

mothers2mothers (m2m)
Employs and trains local women living with HIV as community health workers called Mentor Mothers to support women, children, and adolescents with vital medical services, education, and support.
Infect Dis, MF Med, OB-GYN, Peds, Pub Health
⊕ https://vfmat.ch/6557

New Horizons Collaborative
Advances a holistic, integrated approach to high-quality pediatric HIV care and treatment with a specific focus on those in need of advanced treatment.
Infect Dis, Peds, Pub Health
⊕ https://vfmat.ch/a76a

Pact
Works on the ground to improve the lives of those who are challenged by poverty and marginalization, striving for a world in which all people are heard, capable, and vibrant.
Infect Dis, Logist-Op, MF Med, Pub Health
⊕ https://vfmat.ch/9a6c

Partners in Health
Responds to the moral imperative to provide high-quality healthcare globally to those who need it most, while striving to ease suffering by providing a comprehensive model of care that includes access to food, transportation, housing, and other key components of healing.
CT Surg, General, Heme-Onc, Infect Dis, MF Med, Neurosurg, OB-GYN, Ortho, Plast, Psych, Urol
⊕ https://vfmat.ch/dc9c

Positive Action for Treatment Access (PATA)
Ensures that every individual with an illness or disease, especially women and girls, has access to treatment and literacy skills, and to equitable, humane care and empowerment.
Infect Dis, OB-GYN, Peds, Pub Health
⊕ https://vfmat.ch/46f9

Project SOAR
Conducts HIV operations research around the world to identify practical solutions to improve HIV prevention, care, and treatment services.
ER Med, General, MF Med, OB-GYN, Psych
⊕ https://vfmat.ch/1a77

PSI – Population Services International
Aims to improve the health of people in the developing world by focusing on challenges such as a lack of family planning, HIV/AIDS, barriers to maternal health, and the greatest threats to children under the age of 5, including malaria, diarrhea, pneumonia, and malnutrition.
Infect Dis, MF Med, OB-GYN, Peds
⊕ https://vfmat.ch/ffe3

Riders for Health
Strives to ensure that reliable transport is available for healthcare services.
Logist-Op
⊕ https://vfmat.ch/7353

Riders for Health International
Aids in the last mile of healthcare delivery, by ensuring that healthcare reaches everyone, everywhere.
ER Med, Infect Dis, Logist-Op, Pub Health
⊕ https://vfmat.ch/85aa

Right to Care
Responds to public health needs by supporting and delivering innovative, quality healthcare solutions, based on the latest medical research and established best practices, for the prevention, treatment, and management of infectious and chronic diseases.
ER Med, Infect Dis, Logist-Op
⊕ https://vfmat.ch/3383

Rockefeller Foundation, The
Works to promote the well-being of humanity.
Logist-Op, Nutr, Pub Health
⊕ https://vfmat.ch/5424

Rotary Action Group for Family Health & AIDS Prevention (RFHA)
Works to save and improve the lives of children and families who lack access to preventive healthcare and education.
Dent-OMFS, Infect Dis, OB-GYN, Ophth-Opt, Peds
⊕ https://vfmat.ch/6563

Rotary International
Provides service to others, improves lives, and advances world understanding, goodwill, and peace through its fellowship of business, professional, and community leaders.
ER Med, General, Infect Dis, MF Med, OB-GYN
⊕ https://vfmat.ch/8fb5

Salvation Army International, The
Seeks to meet human needs through services in education, healthcare, community support, emergency response, and ministry development, inspired by the Christian faith.
Dent-OMFS, Derm, ER Med, Infect Dis, MF Med, Medicine, Nutr, OB-GYN, Ophth-Opt, Palliative, Psych, Rehab, Surg
⊕ https://vfmat.ch/8eb3

SINA Health
Aims to improve the health and educational status of the population in low- and middle-income countries.
General, Logist-Op
⊕ https://vfmat.ch/9ad3

SOS Children's Villages International
Supports children through alternative care and family strengthening.
ER Med, Peds
⊕ https://vfmat.ch/aca1

STEPS
Works with partners, donors, doctors and parents towards a clear vision of a sustainable and effective solution to the disability caused by untreated clubfoot.
Logist-Op, Ortho, Pod
⊕ https://vfmat.ch/784d

Task Force for Global Health, The
Consists of programs and focus areas that cover a range of global health issues including neglected tropical diseases, infectious diseases, vaccines, field epidemiology, public health informatics, health workforce development, and global health ethics.
Infect Dis, Logist-Op, Medicine, Ophth-Opt, Peds
⊕ https://vfmat.ch/714c

Texas Children's Global Health
Addresses healthcare needs in resource-limited settings locally and globally by improving maternal and child health through the implementation of innovative, sustainable, in-country programs to train health professionals and build functional healthcare infrastructure.
Anesth, ER Med, Heme-Onc, Infect Dis, MF Med, Nutr, OB-GYN, Peds, Pub Health, Surg
⊕ https://vfmat.ch/4a1d

United Nations Children's Fund (UNICEF)
Works in over 190 countries and territories to save children's lives, defend their rights, and help them fulfill their potential, from early childhood through adolescence.
All-Immu, Infect Dis, MF Med, Neonat, Nutr, OB-GYN, Ped Surg, Peds, Pub Health
⊕ https://vfmat.ch/42d7

United Nations Development Programme (UNDP)
Helps countries achieve the simultaneous eradication of extreme poverty and significant reduction of inequalities and exclusion using a sustainable human development approach.
Infect Dis, Logist-Op, Pub Health
⊕ https://vfmat.ch/935c

United Nations High Commissioner for Refugees (UNHCR)
Safeguards the rights and well-being of people who have been forced to flee, ensuring that everybody has the right to seek asylum and find safe refuge in another country, with the goal of seeking lasting solutions.
General, MF Med, Medicine, OB-GYN, Peds, Psych, Pub Health
⊕ https://vfmat.ch/6636

United Nations Population Fund (UNFPA)
Supports reproductive healthcare for women and youth in more than 150 countries, focusing on delivering a world in which every pregnancy is wanted, every childbirth is safe, and every young person's potential is fulfilled.
Infect Dis, MF Med, Neonat, OB-GYN, Peds, Pub Health
⊕ https://vfmat.ch/c969

United States Agency for International Development (USAID)
Promotes and demonstrates democratic values abroad and advances a free, peaceful, and prosperous world. Leads the U.S. government's international development and disaster assistance through partnerships and investments that save lives.
ER Med, Infect Dis, MF Med, OB-GYN, Peds
⊕ https://vfmat.ch/9a99

USAID: A2Z The Micronutrient and Child Blindness Project
Aims to increase the use of key micronutrient and blindness interventions to improve child and maternal health.
MF Med, Neonat, Nutr, Ophth-Opt, Surg
⊕ https://vfmat.ch/c5f1

USAID: EQUIP Health
Exists as an effective, efficient response mechanism to achieving global HIV epidemic control by delivering the right intervention at the right place and in the right way.
Infect Dis
⊕ https://vfmat.ch/d76a

USAID: Health Finance and Governance Project
Uses research to implement strategies to help countries develop robust governance systems, increase their domestic resources for health, manage those resources more effectively, and make wise purchasing decisions.
Logist-Op
⊕ https://vfmat.ch/8652

USAID: Maternal and Child Health Integrated Program
Works to improve the health of women and their families, including programs for maternal, newborn, and child health, immunization, family planning, nutrition, malaria, and HIV/AIDS.
All-Immu, General, Infect Dis, MF Med
⊕ https://vfmat.ch/4415

USAID: TB Care II
Focuses on tuberculosis care and treatment.
Infect Dis
⊕ https://vfmat.ch/57d4

Vitamin Angels
Helps at-risk populations in need—specifically pregnant women, new mothers, and children under age 5—to gain access to life-changing vitamins and minerals.
General, Nutr
⊕ https://vfmat.ch/7da1

Vodacom Foundation
Brings people together to maximize impact in three key areas: health, education, and safety and security.
Logist-Op
⊕ https://vfmat.ch/f116

Voluntary Service Overseas (VSO)
Works with health workers, communities, and governments to improve health services and rights for women, babies, youth, people with disabilities, and prisoners.
General, MF Med, OB-GYN
⊕ https://vfmat.ch/213d

World Health Organization, The (WHO)
The United Nations' agency for health provides leadership on global health matters, shapes the health research agenda, sets norms and standards, articulates evidence-based policy options, provides technical support and monitoring to countries, and assesses health trends.
ER Med, General, Infect Dis, Logist-Op, MF Med, OB-GYN, Peds, Psych, Pub Health
⊕ https://vfmat.ch/c476

World Vision International
Works with vulnerable communities around the world to overcome poverty and injustice with child-focused programs in disaster management, health, nutrition, economic development, education, clean water, sanitation, and hygiene.
ER Med, General, Infect Dis, MF Med, Nutr, OB-GYN, Peds
⊕ https://vfmat.ch/2642

Lesotho

Healthcare Facilities

Butha Buthe Hospital
Ha Kamoho, Butha-Buthe, Lesotho
⊕ https://vfmat.ch/a78a

Centre for Equal Health Access Lesotho
Ha Motjoka, Berea, Lesotho
⊕ https://vfmat.ch/87b5

Machabeng Hospital
Mpite, Lesotho
⊕ https://vfmat.ch/ab58

Mafeteng Hospital
Matlapaneng, Mafeteng, Lesotho
⊕ https://vfmat.ch/764a

Makoanyane Military Hospital
Ha Keiso, Maseru, Lesotho
⊕ https://vfmat.ch/4a6b

Maluti Adventist Hospital
Mokhathis, Lesotho
⊕ https://vfmat.ch/85d6

Maseru Private Hospital
Ha Tsolo, Maseru, Lesotho
⊕ https://vfmat.ch/d2c7

Mokhotlong Hospital
Mokhotlong, Lesotho
https://vfmat.ch/npd5

Motebang Hospital
Lisemeng 1, Leribe, Lesotho
⊕ https://vfmat.ch/2fb7

Ntsekhe Hospital
Likhutlong, Mohale's Hoek, Lesotho
⊕ https://vfmat.ch/7376

Paray Hospital
Thabong I, Thaba-Tseka, Lesotho
⊕ https://vfmat.ch/9852

Paray Mission Hospital
Thabong I, Thaba-Tseka, Lesotho
⊕ https://vfmat.ch/b2af

Queen Elizabeth II Hospital
Hills View, Maseru, Lesotho
⊕ https://vfmat.ch/8114

Queen M'amohato Memorial Hospital
Ha Keiso, Maseru, Lesotho
⊕ https://vfmat.ch/466e

Quthing Hospital
Ha Sikara, Quthing, Lesotho
⊕ https://vfmat.ch/fdc3

Scott Hospital
Morija, Lesotho
⊕ https://vfmat.ch/6ea3

Seboche Hospital
Khukuhune, Lesotho
⊕ https://vfmat.ch/ef81

St. James Mission Hospital
Mantšonyane, Thaba-Tseka, Lesotho
⊕ https://vfmat.ch/f34e

St. Joseph's Hospital
Roma, Lesotho
⊕ https://vfmat.ch/fb71

Tebellong Hospital
Mpite, Lesotho
⊕ https://vfmat.ch/954c

Wilies Mini Hospital
Mabote, Berea, Lesotho
⊕ https://vfmat.ch/4491

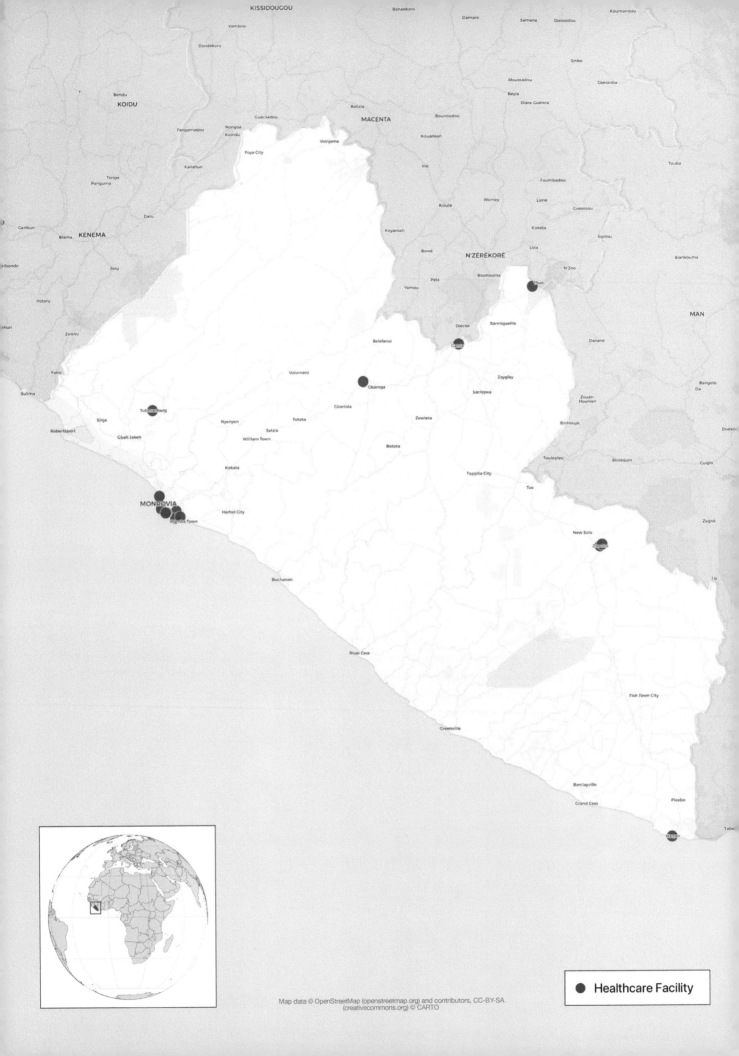

Healthcare Facility

# Liberia

The Republic of Liberia sits on the West African coast, bordered by Sierra Leone, Guinea, and Ivory Coast. The nation has a small majority Christian population of about 5.2 million people, more than half of whom live in or around urban areas and in close proximity to the capital of Monrovia. The ethnically diverse population comprises groups including Kpelle, Bassa, Grebo, Gio, Mano, Kru, Morma, Kissi, Gola, Krahn, Vai, Mandingo, Gbandi, Mednde, and Sapo. As a result, Liberia offers great linguistic diversity, with as many as 30 different languages spoken in addition to English. The history of Liberia is unique; the country was founded by free people of color emigrating from the United States. As a result, Liberia is a country where both traditional and Western-influenced customs coexist.

Liberia is Africa's oldest republic and has never been ruled by a colonial power. The nation has a history of political instability, which has slowly improved over the decades. However, both unemployment and illiteracy are widespread, and around 50 percent of Liberians live below the poverty line.

Liberians face a variety of health challenges. In 2014, a large Ebola outbreak occurred in Guinea and spread to neighboring Sierra Leone and Liberia. The virus infected more than 10,000 and killed nearly 5,000 Liberians. Despite the turmoil caused by Ebola, life expectancy in Liberia continues to improve significantly, having increased from 46 years in 1990 to 64 years in 2019. While overall health may be improving, most deaths in Liberia are caused by malaria, diarrheal disease, neonatal disorders, lower respiratory infections, ischemic heart disease, HIV/AIDS, stroke, tuberculosis, cirrhosis, and maternal disorders.

5.2M
Population

$583
GDP Per Capita

64 years
Life Expectancy
↑ Improving

4
Doctors/100k
Physician Density

80
Beds/100k
Hospital Bed Density

661
Deaths/100k
Maternal Mortality

 **Liberia**

Nonprofit Organizations

143 LIFE Foundation
Seeks to educate and empower individuals living with malaria, TB, HIV/AIDS, STDs and other health disparities related to sexual health.
Infect Dis, MF Med
⊕ https://vfmat.ch/d59b

Abt Associates
Seeks to improve the quality of life and economic well-being of people worldwide, while striving to meet and exceed the highest professional standards.
General, Logist-Op, MF Med, OB-GYN, Peds
⊕ https://vfmat.ch/cec2

Aceso Global
Provides strategic healthcare advisory services in low- and middle-income countries to design and deliver highly customized, evidence-based solutions that address the complex nature of healthcare systems, with a goal to strengthen and provide affordable, high-quality care to all.
Logist-Op, Pub Health
⊕ https://vfmat.ch/b3b7

Action Against Hunger
Aims to end life-threatening hunger for good through treating and preventing malnutrition across more than 45 countries.
Nutr
⊕ https://vfmat.ch/2dbc

Adventist Health International
Focuses on upgrading and managing mission hospitals by providing governance, consultation, and technical assistance to a number of affiliated Seventh-Day Adventist hospitals throughout Africa, Asia, and the Americas.
Dent-OMFS, General, Pub Health
⊕ https://vfmat.ch/16aa

Africa CDC
Aims to strengthen the capacity and capability of Africa's public health institutions and partnerships to detect and respond quickly and effectively to disease threats and outbreaks, based on data-driven interventions and programs.
Infect Dis, Logist-Op, Pub Health
⊕ https://vfmat.ch/339c

Africa Health Organisation
Leads collaborative efforts among countries in Africa and other partners to promote health equity, combat disease, and improve quality of life.
Logist-Op, Pub Health
⊕ https://vfmat.ch/b1c5

Africa Humanitarian Action (AHA)
Responds to crises, conflicts, and disasters in Africa, while informing and advising the international community, governments, civil society, and the private sector on humanitarian issues of concern to Africa. Supports institutional and organizational development efforts.
General, Infect Dis, MF Med, Nutr, OB-GYN
⊕ https://vfmat.ch/3ca2

Africa Indoor Residual Spraying Project (AIRS)
Aims to protect millions of people in Africa from malaria by spraying insecticide on walls, ceilings, and other indoor resting places of mosquitoes that transmit malaria.
Infect Dis
⊕ https://vfmat.ch/9bd1

Africa Relief and Community Development
Provides comprehensive relief and developmental aid to people of the African continent regardless of gender, race, or religion.
Nutr, Pub Health
⊕ https://vfmat.ch/6cd2

African Field Epidemiology Network (AFENET)
Strengthens field epidemiology and public health laboratory capacity to contribute effectively to addressing epidemics and other major public health problems in Africa.
All-Immu, Infect Dis, Path, Pub Health
⊕ https://vfmat.ch/df2e

African Mission Health Foundation
Aims to strengthen African mission hospitals by providing quality, compassionate care for the hurting and forgotten and helping improve Sub-Saharan Africa's health system.
Infect Dis, Neonat, OB-GYN, Peds, Surg
⊕ https://vfmat.ch/5b14

American International Health Alliance (AIHA)
Strengthens health systems and workforce capacity worldwide through locally driven, peer-to-peer institutional partnerships.
CV Med, ER Med, Infect Dis, Medicine, OB-GYN
⊕ https://vfmat.ch/69fd

Americares
Saves lives and improves health for people affected by poverty or disaster and responds with life-changing medicine, medical supplies, and health programs including domestic and global medical clinics.
All-Immu, ER Med, General, Infect Dis, MF Med, Nutr
⊕ https://vfmat.ch/e567

Amref Health Africa
Serves millions of people across 35 countries in Sub-Saharan Africa, strengthening health systems, and training African health workers to respond to the continent's most critical health issues.
All-Immu, General, Infect Dis, Logist-Op, MF Med, OB-GYN, Path, Pub Health, Surg
⊕ https://vfmat.ch/6985

Baylor International Pediatric AIDS Initiative (BIPAI) at Texas Children's Hospital

Provides high-quality, high-impact, highly ethical pediatric and family-centered healthcare, health professional training, and clinical research focused on HIV/AIDS, tuberculosis, malaria, malnutrition, and other conditions impacting the health of children worldwide.

Infect Dis, Medicine, OB-GYN, Peds, Pub Health, Surg
⊕ https://vfmat.ch/e6ba

Bethel SOZO International Surgical Missions

Provides mobile medical clinics and sustainable health education to underserved communities worldwide and offers volunteer opportunities for medical, surgical, and dental professionals and others to provide healthcare, inspired by the Christian faith.

General
⊕ https://vfmat.ch/9d88

Boston Children's Hospital: Global Health Program

Helps solve pediatric global healthcare challenges by transferring expertise through long-term partnerships with scalable impact, while working in the field to strengthen healthcare systems, advocate, research, and provide care delivery or education as a way of sustainably improving the health of children worldwide.

Anesth, CV Med, Crit-Care, ER Med, Heme-Onc, Infect Dis, Medicine, Nutr, Palliative, Ped Surg, Peds
⊕ https://vfmat.ch/f9f8

BRAC USA

Seeks to empower people and communities in situations of poverty, illiteracy, disease, and social injustice. Interventions aim to achieve large-scale, positive changes through economic and social programs that enable everyone to realize their potential.

ER Med, General, Infect Dis, Logist-Op, MF Med, OB-GYN
⊕ https://vfmat.ch/9d9e

Bridges of Hope, Inc.

Focused on bringing hope to Liberians by providing education, clean water, good healthcare, and the gospel of Jesus.

General
⊕ https://vfmat.ch/6b3e

Brigham and Women's Hospital Global Health Hub

Cares for patients in underserved settings, provides education to staff who work in those areas to create sustainable change, and conducts research designed to improve health in such settings.

General, Infect Dis
⊕ https://vfmat.ch/a0a3

BroadReach

Collaborates with governments, multinational health organizations, donors, and private-sector companies to effect healthcare reform and solve the world's biggest health challenges.

Logist-Op
⊕ https://vfmat.ch/7812

Brooks Community Health Center, The (TBCHC)

Delivers high-quality, low-cost, ethical, and sustainable healthcare and healthcare-related educational services to underserved communities in Liberia.

Dent-OMFS, General, Geri, Infect Dis, MF Med, Ophth-Opt
⊕ https://vfmat.ch/7a89

Bureau of International Health Cooperation

Seeks to improve healthcare around the world, including developing countries, using expertise, and contribute to healthier lives of Japanese people by bringing these experiences back to Japan.

ER Med, Heme-Onc, Infect Dis, Peds, Pub Health
⊕ https://vfmat.ch/947d

CARE

Works around the globe to save lives, defeat poverty, and achieve social justice.

ER Med, General
⊕ https://vfmat.ch/7232

Carter Center, The

Seeks to prevent and resolve conflicts, enhance freedom and democracy, and improve health, while remaining committed to human rights and the alleviation of human suffering.

Infect Dis, MF Med, Ophth-Opt
⊕ https://vfmat.ch/6556

Catholic World Mission

Works to rebuild communities worldwide by helping to alleviate poverty and empower underserved areas, while spreading the message of the Catholic Church.

ER Med, General, Nutr, Peds
⊕ https://vfmat.ch/7b5f

CAUSE Canada

Strives to be a catalyst for global justice as a faith-based organization that aims to provide sustainable, integrated community development in rural West Africa and Central America through authentic, collaborative long-term relationships.

General, MF Med, Neonat, OB-GYN, Peds
⊕ https://vfmat.ch/6fc1

Center for Epilepsy and Neurologic Diseases Liberia (CEND-LIB)

Provides neurologic care to people and residents of Liberia, West Africa.

Infect Dis, Neuro
⊕ https://vfmat.ch/c4e9

ChildFund Australia

Works to reduce poverty for children in many of the world's most disadvantaged communities.

ER Med, General, Peds
⊕ https://vfmat.ch/13df

Children & Charity International

Puts people first by providing education, leadership, and nutrition programs along with mentoring and healthcare support services to children, youth, and families.

Nutr, Peds
⊕ https://vfmat.ch/6538

Children of the Nations

Aims to raise children out of poverty and hopelessness so they can become leaders who transform their nations. Emphasizes caring for the whole child—physically, mentally, socially, and spiritually.

Anesth, Dent-OMFS, General, Surg
⊕ https://vfmat.ch/cc52

Children's Surgery International

Provides free medical and surgical services to children in need around the world, and instructs and trains local surgeons and other medical providers such as doctors, anesthesiologists, nurses, and technicians.

Anesth, Dent-OMFS, Ortho, Ped Surg, Peds, Plast, Surg
⊕ https://vfmat.ch/26d3

Christian Aid Ministries

Strives to be a trustworthy and efficient channel for Amish, Mennonite, and other conservative Anabaptist groups and individuals to minister to physical and spiritual needs around the world.

CT Surg, ER Med, Logist-Op, Ortho, Pub Health
⊕ https://vfmat.ch/7b33

Christian Connections for International Health (CCIH)

Promotes global health and wholeness from a Christian perspective.

All-Immu, General, Infect Dis, MF Med, Neonat, OB-GYN, Psych
⊕ https://vfmat.ch/fa5d

Christian Medical & Dental Associations

Based in Christian ministry, deploys medical and dental teams to underserved communities to provide vital healthcare.

Anesth, Dent-OMFS, ER Med, General, Medicine, OB-GYN, Ophth-Opt, Peds, Pub Health, Radiol, Rehab, Surg
⊕ https://vfmat.ch/921c

Clinton Health Access Initiative (CHAI)

Aims to save lives and reduce the burden of disease in low- and middle-income countries. Works with partners to strengthen the capabilities of governments and the private sector to create and sustain high-quality health systems.

General, Heme-Onc, Infect Dis, Logist-Op, MF Med, Medicine, Neonat, Nutr, OB-GYN, Path, Peds, Rad-Onc

⊕ https://vfmat.ch/9ed7

Columbia Vagelos College of Physicians and Surgeons Programs in Global Health

Harnesses the expertise of the medical school to improve health worldwide by training global health leaders, building capacity through interdisciplinary education and training programs, and addressing unmet health needs through research and application.

CV Med, Derm, Genetics, Heme-Onc, Infect Dis, Medicine, OB-GYN, Ophth-Opt, Peds, Psych, Pub Health, Pulm-Critic, Surg

⊕ https://vfmat.ch/a9e5

Concern Worldwide

Seeks to permanently transform the lives of people living in extreme poverty, tackling its root causes, and building resilience.

Logist-Op, MF Med, Nutr, OB-GYN

⊕ https://vfmat.ch/77e9

COVID-19 Clinical Research Coalition

Advocates and collaborates for the advancement of COVID-19 research driven by the needs of low-resource settings, and works for equitable access to solutions to the pandemic.

All-Immu, Infect-Dis, MF Med, Path, Pub Health

⊕ https://vfmat.ch/d1f4

CT Medical Mission

Seeks to minister to the physical needs of the sick and suffering with the help of volunteer Christian physicians, dentists, nurses, and other medical personnel. Also aims to educate and provide healthy foods to people while sharing Christian faith.

Dent-OMFS, ER Med, General, Infect Dis, Surg

⊕ https://vfmat.ch/39de

Curamericas Global

Partners with communities abroad to save the lives of mothers and children by providing health services and education.

General, Infect Dis, MF Med, OB-GYN, Peds, Pub Health

⊕ https://vfmat.ch/286b

DEAR Foundation, The

Provides support for people in need, particularly women and children, by supporting humanitarian projects administered by NGOs, primarily in the areas of health and education.

Dent-OMFS, OB-GYN

⊕ https://vfmat.ch/a747

Dignity: Liberia

Aims to bring restoration and hope to women with obstetric fistula and their communities through healing, education, and prevention.

MF Med, OB-GYN, Surg

⊕ https://vfmat.ch/3732

Direct Relief

Improves the health and lives of people affected by poverty or emergency situations by mobilizing and providing essential medical resources needed for their care.

ER Med, Logist-Op

⊕ https://vfmat.ch/58e5

DKT INTERNATIONAL INC

Seeks to provide couples with affordable and safe options for family planning and HIV/AIDS prevention through dynamic social marketing.

General, Surg

⊕ https://vfmat.ch/b3a7

Doctors Without Borders/Médecins Sans Frontières (MSF)

Responds to emergencies and provides lifesaving medical care where needed most, including during disasters, conflicts, and epidemics.

Anesth, Crit-Care, ER Med, General, Infect Dis, Nutr, OB-GYN, Ped Surg, Peds, Psych, Pub Health, Surg

⊕ https://vfmat.ch/f363

Effect: Hope (The Leprosy Mission Canada)

Connects like-minded Canadians to people suffering in isolation from debilitating, neglected tropical diseases such as leprosy, lymphatic filariasis, and Buruli ulcer.

General, Infect Dis

⊕ https://vfmat.ch/f12a

eHealth Africa

Builds stronger health systems in Africa through the design and implementation of data-driven solutions, responding to local needs and providing underserved communities with the necessary tools to lead healthier lives.

Logist-Op, Path

⊕ https://vfmat.ch/db6a

Episcopal Relief & Development

Provides relief in times of disaster and promotes sustainable development by identifying and addressing the root causes of suffering.

Infect Dis, MF Med, Neonat, Nutr, Peds

⊕ https://vfmat.ch/7cfa

eRanger

Provides sustainable solutions to transportation and medical provision such as ambulances and mobile clinics in developing countries.

ER Med, General, Logist-Op

⊕ https://vfmat.ch/4c18

Finn Church Aid

Supports people in the most vulnerable situations within fragile and disaster-affected regions in three thematic priority areas: right to peace, livelihood, and education.

ER Med, Psych, Pub Health

⊕ https://vfmat.ch/9623

For Hearts and Souls

Provides medical outreach and care for children through heart-related work, such as diagnosing heart problems and performing heart-saving surgeries.

Anesth, CT Surg, CV Med, Crit-Care, Peds, Pulm-Critic

⊕ https://vfmat.ch/a162

Foundation for Special Surgery

Provides high-quality, complex surgical care by increasing surgical expertise in Africa through the participation of surgeons across various specialties to provide premium care and skills transfer/education to benefit patients.

Anesth, CT Surg, ENT, Endo, Neurosurg, Plast, Surg, Urol

⊕ https://vfmat.ch/53db

Friends of Liberia

Seeks to positively affect Liberia and Liberians through education, social, economic, and humanitarian programs and through advocacy efforts.

All-Immu, OB-GYN, Pub Health

⊕ https://vfmat.ch/f4bf

Friends of UNFPA

Promotes the health, dignity, and rights of women and girls around the world by supporting the lifesaving work of UNFPA, the United Nations' reproductive health and rights agency, through education, advocacy, and fundraising.

MF Med, OB-GYN

⊕ https://vfmat.ch/2a3a

Global Aid Network (GAiN) Australia

Inspired by the Christian faith, provides support to people living in crisis through programs in healthcare, humanitarian aid, disaster response, clean water, and sanitation.

Dent-OMFS, Ophth-Opt

⊕ https://vfmat.ch/6cb8

Global Alliance to Prevent Prematurity And Stillbirth (GAPPS)

Seeks to improve birth outcomes worldwide by reducing the burden of premature birth and stillbirth.

All-Immu, Infect Dis, MF Med, Neonat, Neonat, OB-GYN

⊕ https://vfmat.ch/3f74

Global First Responder (GFR)
Acts as a centralized network for individuals and agencies involved in relief work worldwide and organizes and executes mission trips to areas in need, focusing not only on healthcare delivery but also on health education and improvements.
ER Med
⊕ https://vfmat.ch/a3e1

Global Ministries – The United Methodist Church
As the worldwide mission and development agency of The United Methodist Church, Global Ministries works with more than 300 hospitals and clinics around the world through its Global Health Unit.
Anesth, CT Surg, CV Med, Crit-Care, Dent-OMFS, Derm, ER Med, GI, General, Infect Dis, Logist-Op, MF Med, Medicine, Neonat, Nephro, Nutr, OB-GYN, Ophth-Opt, Ortho, Palliative, Peds, Pod, Psych, Pub Health, Rehab, Rheum, Surg, Urol
⊕ https://vfmat.ch/1723

Global Oncology (GO)
Brings the best in cancer care to underserved patients around the world and collaborates across geographic, professional, and academic borders to improve cancer care, research, and education.
Heme-Onc, Path, Rad-Onc
⊕ https://vfmat.ch/fcb8

Global Polio Eradication Initiative
Aims to eradicate polio worldwide.
All-Immu, Infect-Dis, Logist-Op, Pub Health
⊕ https://vfmat.ch/7e2c

Global Strategies
Empowers communities in the most neglected areas of the world to improve the lives of women and children through healthcare.
MF Med, Neonat, OB-GYN, Peds
⊕ https://vfmat.ch/ef92

Global Vision 2020
Provides prescription eyeglasses to people who live in parts of the world lacking necessary infrastructure for obtaining affordable corrective eyewear.
Logist-Op, Ophth-Opt
⊕ https://vfmat.ch/7373

Globus Relief
Aims to improve the delivery of healthcare worldwide by gathering, processing, and distributing surplus medical supplies to charities at home and abroad.
Logist-Op
⊕ https://vfmat.ch/a2b7

GOAL
Works with the most vulnerable communities to help them respond to and recover from humanitarian crises, and to assist them in building transcendent solutions to mitigate poverty and vulnerability.
ER Med, General, Pub Health
⊕ https://vfmat.ch/bbea

Grassroot Soccer
Leverages the power of soccer to educate, inspire, and mobilize at-risk youth in developing countries to overcome their greatest health challenges, live healthier and more productive lives, and be agents for change in their communities.
Infect Dis
⊕ https://vfmat.ch/3521

Headwaters Relief Organization
Addresses public health issues for the most underserved populations of the world, providing psychosocial and medical support along with disaster debris cleanup and rebuilding in partnership with other organizations.
ER Med, Infect Dis, Logist-Op, Psych, Pub Health
⊕ https://vfmat.ch/e511

Healing the Children
Helps underserved children around the world secure the medical care they need to lead more fulfilling lives.
Anesth, Dent-OMFS, ENT, General, Medicine, Ophth-Opt, Ped Surg, Peds, Plast, Surg
⊕ https://vfmat.ch/d4ee

Health Africa Foundation (HAF)
Provides essential medical equipment and supplies to under-resourced healthcare facilities and builds the capacity of Liberian health workers to enhance the delivery of high-quality healthcare services in Liberia.
Anesth, CV Med, Crit-Care, ER Med, Endo, General, Heme-Onc, Infect Dis, MF Med, Medicine, OB-GYN, Path, Peds, Radiol
⊕ https://vfmat.ch/fe3b

Health Education and Relief Through Teaching Foundation (HEARTT Foundation)
Educates and assists local healthcare providers in developing and/or improving the healthcare system and infrastructure.
ER Med, Medicine, OB-GYN, Peds, Psych, Surg
⊕ https://vfmat.ch/ecc3

Health Equity Initiative
Aims to build and sustain a global community that engages across sectors and disciplines to advance health equity.
Pub Health
⊕ https://vfmat.ch/e2e2

Heart to Heart International
Strengthens communities through improving health access, providing humanitarian development, and administering crisis relief worldwide. Engages volunteers, collaborates with partners, and deploys resources to achieve this mission.
Anesth, ER Med, General, Logist-Op, Medicine, Path, Path, Peds, Psych, Pub Health, Surg
⊕ https://vfmat.ch/aacb

Heineman Medical Outreach
Provides medical and educational assistance globally to promote sustainable healthcare and enhanced living standards in underserved communities through the International Medical Outreach (IMO) program, a collaborative partnership between Heineman Medical Outreach and Atrium Health.
Anesth, CT Surg, CV Med, ER Med, General, Heme-Onc, Logist-Op, Medicine, Neonat, OB-GYN, Ped Surg, Peds, Surg, Vasc Surg
⊕ https://vfmat.ch/389b

Hernia International
Aims to provide relief from sickness, and protection and preservation of health, for persons affected by groin and abdominal hernias and residing in low- and middle-income countries.
Surg
⊕ https://vfmat.ch/e98e

HOPE2
Renews hope in the Liberian people through safe water, medical care, education, and training.
ER Med, General, Peds
⊕ https://vfmat.ch/bf5f

Humanity & Inclusion
Works alongside people with disabilities and vulnerable populations, taking action and bearing witness in order to respond to their essential needs, improve their living conditions and health, and promote respect for their dignity and fundamental rights.
General, Infect Dis, MF Med, Medicine, Ortho, Peds, Psych, Pub Health, Rehab
⊕ https://vfmat.ch/16b7

Humanity First
Provides aid and assistance to those in need, offering sustainable development solutions to society while providing and empowering local communities with the resources to help themselves.
ER Med, General, MF Med, Ophth-Opt
⊕ https://vfmat.ch/13cc

HVK Children's Foundation
Works to meet the needs of women, children, and families in Sub-Saharan Africa and Liberia by educating, supporting, and training Liberians to achieve economic self-sufficiency.
All-Immu, Dent-OMFS, Nutr, Ophth-Opt, Peds
⊕ https://vfmat.ch/beb5

ICAP at Columbia University
Serves as global leader in supporting the scale-up of multidisciplinary HIV/AIDS prevention, care, and treatment programs based on a family-focused approach.
General, Infect Dis, MF Med, Medicine, OB-GYN, Pub Health
⊕ https://vfmat.ch/a8ef

International Agency for the Prevention of Blindness (IAPB), The
Leads international efforts in blindness-prevention activities, works toward a world where no one is needlessly visually impaired, and ensures that everyone has access to the best possible standard of eye health.
Infect Dis, Ophth-Opt, Pub Health
⊕ https://vfmat.ch/87a2

International Children's Heart Fund
Aims to promote the international growth and quality of cardiac surgery, particularly in children and young adults.
CT Surg, Ped Surg
⊕ https://vfmat.ch/33fb

International Federation of Red Cross and Red Crescent Societies (IFRC)
Coordinates and directs international assistance following natural and manmade disasters in nonconflict situations through the world's largest humanitarian and development network. Provides disaster-preparedness programs, healthcare activities, and promotes humanitarian values.
ER Med, General, Infect Dis, Nutr
⊕ https://vfmat.ch/b4ee

International Medical Response
Supplements, supports, and enhances healthcare systems in communities across the world that have been incapacitated by natural disaster, extreme poverty, and/or regional conflict by sending a multidisciplinary team of healthcare professionals.
Anesth, General, OB-GYN, Surg
⊕ https://vfmat.ch/9ccd

International Organization for Migration (IOM) – The UN Migration Agency
Promotes evidence-informed policies and holistic, preventive, and curative health programs that are beneficial, accessible, and equitable for vulnerable migrants.
General, Infect Dis, OB-GYN
⊕ https://vfmat.ch/621a

International Planned Parenthood Federation (IPPF)
Leads a locally owned, globally connected civil society movement that provides and enables services and champions sexual and reproductive health and rights for all, especially the underserved.
Infect Dis, MF Med, OB-GYN
⊕ https://vfmat.ch/dc97

International Rescue Committee (IRC)
Responds to the world's worst humanitarian crises and helps people whose lives and livelihoods are shattered by conflict and disaster to survive, recover, and gain control of their future.
ER Med, General, Infect Dis, MF Med, Peds
⊕ https://vfmat.ch/5d24

IntraHealth International
Improves the performance of health workers and strengthens the systems in which they work.
CV Med, Endo, General, Infect Dis, MF Med, Neonat, Nutr, OB-GYN
⊕ https://vfmat.ch/ddc8

Izumi Foundation
Develops and supports programs that improve health and healthcare in neglected regions of Africa and Latin America.
⊕ https://vfmat.ch/f29a

Jhpiego
Creates and delivers transformative healthcare solutions that save lives, in partnership with national governments, health experts, and local communities.
General, Infect Dis, OB-GYN, Surg
⊕ https://vfmat.ch/45b8

John Snow, Inc. (JSI)
Aims to improve the health and well-being of underserved and vulnerable people and communities throughout the world.
General, Infect Dis, Logist-Op, MF Med, OB-GYN, Peds, Psych, Pub Health
⊕ https://vfmat.ch/ba78

Johns Hopkins Center for Communication Programs
Believes in the power of communication to save lives by empowering people to adopt healthy behaviors for themselves, their families, and their communities.
General, Infect Dis, Logist-Op, OB-GYN, Pub Health
⊕ https://vfmat.ch/1bf9

Joint United Nations Programme on HIV/AIDS (UNAIDS)
Aims to place people living with HIV and people affected by the virus at the decision-making table and at the center of designing, delivering, and monitoring the AIDS response.
Infect Dis
⊕ https://vfmat.ch/464a

Kids Against Hunger
Aims to provide nutritious food to impoverished children and families around the world—and around the corner. The organization's goal is for the meals to provide a stable nutritional base from which recipient families can move their families from starvation or food insecurity to self-sufficiency.
General, Nutr
⊕ https://vfmat.ch/993f

Korle-Bu Neuroscience Foundation
Committed to providing medical support for brain and spinal injuries and disease to the people of Ghana and West Africa.
Anesth, Logist-Op, Neuro, Neurosurg, Rehab
⊕ https://vfmat.ch/6695

Last Mile Health
Links community health workers with frontline health workers—nurses, doctors, and midwives at community clinics—and supports them to bring lifesaving services to the doorsteps of people living far from care.
General, Logist-Op, OB-GYN, Pub Health
⊕ https://vfmat.ch/37da

Liberia Medical Mission
Provides free medical, ophthalmic, and mental health services through mission trips to underserved communities in Liberia and other West African countries.
General, Infect Dis, OB-GYN, Ophth-Opt, Ophth-Opt, Palliative, Peds, Psych, Urol
⊕ https://vfmat.ch/8193

Life for a Child
Supports the provision of the best possible healthcare, given local circumstances, to all children and youth with diabetes in less-resourced countries, through the strengthening of existing diabetes services.
Endo, Medicine, Peds
⊕ https://vfmat.ch/d712

Life for African Mothers
Aims to save the lives of pregnant women in Sub-Saharan Africa.
MF Med, Neonat, OB-GYN
⊕ https://vfmat.ch/fce2

Light House Medical Missions
Inspired by the Christian faith, provides programs in healthcare provision, nutrition, emergency relief and response, and water, sanitation, and hygiene (WASH).
ER Med, General, Surg
⊕ https://vfmat.ch/cecd

Limbs International
Engages communities and transforms lives through affordable, sustainable prosthetic solutions and rehabilitation services in developing countries.
Logist-Op, Ortho, Pod, Rehab
⊕ https://vfmat.ch/dc84

Lions Clubs International
Empowers volunteers to serve their communities, meet humanitarian needs,

encourage peace, and promote international understanding through Lions Clubs.
Heme-Onc, Medicine, Nutr, Ophth-Opt
⊕ https://vfmat.ch/7b12

London School of Hygiene & Tropical Medicine: Health in Humanitarian Crises Centre
Advances health and health equity in crisis-affected countries through research, education, and translation of knowledge into policy and practice.
ER Med, Infect Dis, Pub Health
⊕ https://vfmat.ch/96ad

Management Sciences for Health (MSH)
Works with countries and communities to save lives and improve the health of the world's poorest and most vulnerable people by building strong, resilient, sustainable health systems.
Infect Dis, Logist-Op, Pub Health
⊕ https://vfmat.ch/6aa2

MAP International
Provides medicines and health supplies to those in need around the world so they might experience life to the fullest.
Logist-Op
⊕ https://vfmat.ch/deed

Massachusetts General Hospital Global Surgery Initiative
Aims to improve surgical education and access to advanced surgical care in resource-limited settings around the world by performing surgical operations as visitors, training local surgeons, and sharing medical technology through international partnerships across disciplines.
Anesth, Crit-Care, ER Med, Heme-Onc, Peds, Surg
⊕ https://vfmat.ch/31b1

Maternal & Childhealth Advocacy International
Seeks to save and improve the lives of babies, children, and pregnant women in areas of extreme poverty by empowering and enabling in-country partners to strengthen emergency healthcare.
MF Med, Neonat, OB-GYN, Peds
⊕ https://vfmat.ch/ea67

Medical Care Development International
Works to improve the health of vulnerable populations through integrated, sustainable, and locally driven interventions.
Infect Dis, OB-GYN, Peds, Pub Health
⊕ https://vfmat.ch/da87

Medical Equipment Modernization Opportunity (MEMO)
Based in Christian ministry, works with churches and organizations to collect and send hospital equipment and supplies to healthcare facilities in need around the world.
Logist-Op
⊕ https://vfmat.ch/1c78

Medical Missions for Global Health
Seeks to reduce health disparities by providing surgical, medical, and healthcare services and education to underserved communities and developing communities throughout Africa, the Caribbean, Central and South America, and the U.S.
Dent-OMFS, General, Surg
⊕ https://vfmat.ch/cf52

Medical Teams International
Seeks to restore health as the first step to restoring hope, working to bring basic but lifesaving medical care to those in need.
Dent-OMFS, ER Med, General, MF Med, Pub Health
⊕ https://vfmat.ch/8d1c

MedShare
Aims to improve the quality of life of people, communities, and the planet by sourcing and directly delivering surplus medical supplies and equipment to communities in need around the world.
Logist-Op
⊕ https://vfmat.ch/c8bc

MENTOR Initiative
Saves lives in emergencies through tropical disease control, and helps people recover from crisis with dignity, working side by side with communities, health workers, and health authorities to leave a lasting impact.
ER Med, Infect Dis
⊕ https://vfmat.ch/3bd5

Mercy and Love Foundation
Aims to provide orphaned and vulnerable children with basic human needs such as food, clothing, and shelter, enabling them to thrive.
General, Peds
⊕ https://vfmat.ch/649a

Mercy Ships
Operates hospital ships staffed by volunteers to bring hope, healing, and healthcare to underserved communities worldwide.
Anesth, Dent-OMFS, Logist-Op, Neonat, OB-GYN, Ophth-Opt, Ortho, Palliative, Plast, Psych, Surg
⊕ https://vfmat.ch/2e99

MiracleFeet
Brings low-cost treatment to every child on the planet born with clubfoot, a leading cause of physical disability.
Ortho, Peds, Rehab
⊕ https://vfmat.ch/bda8

Mission Regan
Collects supplies, medication, and medical equipment and provides them to those who are in desperate need, both locally and globally.
Logist-Op
⊕ https://vfmat.ch/2bc1

Nazarene Compassionate Ministries
Partners with local churches around the world to clothe, shelter, feed, heal, educate, and live in solidarity with those in need.
General, Infect Dis, OB-GYN
⊕ https://vfmat.ch/6b4d

Newborn, Infant, and Child Health International (NICHE)
Aims to make outstanding care of newborn babies commonplace in poorly resourced areas of the world.
Crit-Care, General, Neonat, Peds
⊕ https://vfmat.ch/8817

One Heart Worldwide
Aims to end preventable deaths related to pregnancy and childbirth worldwide.
MF Med, Neonat, OB-GYN, Pub Health
⊕ https://vfmat.ch/a865

OneSight
Brings eye exams and glasses to people who lack access to vision care.
Ophth-Opt
⊕ https://vfmat.ch/3ecc

Operation Eyesight Universal
Aims to prevent blindness, restore sight, and eliminate avoidable blindness.
Ophth-Opt
⊕ https://vfmat.ch/f629

Operation Fistula
Exists to end obstetric fistula by building models of care that serve every woman, everywhere.
MF Med, OB-GYN, Surg
⊕ https://vfmat.ch/ce8e

Options
Believes in a world in which women and children can access the high-quality health services they need, without financial burden.
Logist-Op, MF Med, Neonat, OB-GYN
⊕ https://vfmat.ch/3a48

Order of Malta
Supports forgotten or excluded people, especially those living in conflict zones or

amid natural disasters, by providing medical assistance, caring for refugees, and distributing medicines and necessities.

ER Med, General, Infect Dis, MF Med, Nephro, OB-GYN, Ortho, Psych

🌐 https://vfmat.ch/1fab

Pact

Works on the ground to improve the lives of those who are challenged by poverty and marginalization, striving for a world in which all people are heard, capable, and vibrant.

Infect Dis, Logist-Op, MF Med, Pub Health

🌐 https://vfmat.ch/9a6c

Partners for Development (PfD)

Works to improve quality of life for vulnerable people in underserved communities through local and international partnerships.

Infect Dis, MF Med, Neonat, Peds

🌐 https://vfmat.ch/d2f6

Partners in Health

Responds to the moral imperative to provide high-quality healthcare globally to those who need it most, while striving to ease suffering by providing a comprehensive model of care that includes access to food, transportation, housing, and other key components of healing.

CT Surg, General, Heme-Onc, Infect Dis, MF Med, Neurosurg, OB-GYN, Ortho, Plast, Psych, Urol

🌐 https://vfmat.ch/dc9c

Picture of Health Foundation

Provides communities with health education and empowers people to alter unhealthy lifestyles, thus increasing both life expectancy and quality.

General, Pub Health

🌐 https://vfmat.ch/83e3

Project Concern International (PCI)

Drives innovation from the ground up to enhance health, end hunger, overcome hardship, and advance women and girls—resulting in meaningful and measurable change in people's lives.

Infect Dis, MF Med, Nutr, OB-GYN, Peds

🌐 https://vfmat.ch/5ed7

PSI – Population Services International

Aims to improve the health of people in the developing world by focusing on challenges such as a lack of family planning, HIV/AIDS, barriers to maternal health, and the greatest threats to children under the age of 5, including malaria, diarrhea, pneumonia, and malnutrition.

Infect Dis, MF Med, OB-GYN, Peds

🌐 https://vfmat.ch/ffe3

RAD-AID International

Improves and optimizes access to medical imaging and radiology in low-resource regions of the world.

Rad-Onc, Radiol

🌐 https://vfmat.ch/537f

RESTORE HOPE: LIBERIA

Aims to provide essential support to vulnerable children, and their caregivers, with timely and sustainable resources and activities that will protect their health and well-being, ensures access to education and economic opportunities beyond school, thus providing a way out of extreme and enduring poverty.

ER Med, General, OB-GYN

🌐 https://vfmat.ch/e2ed

RestoringVision

Empowers lives by restoring vision for millions of people in need.

Ophth-Opt

🌐 https://vfmat.ch/e121

Riders for Health

Strives to ensure that reliable transport is available for healthcare services.

Logist-Op

🌐 https://vfmat.ch/7353

Riders for Health International

Aids in the last mile of healthcare delivery, by ensuring that healthcare reaches everyone, everywhere.

ER Med, Infect Dis, Logist-Op, Pub Health

🌐 https://vfmat.ch/85aa

Rockefeller Foundation, The

Works to promote the well-being of humanity.

Logist-Op, Nutr, Pub Health

🌐 https://vfmat.ch/5424

Rotaplast International

Helps children and families worldwide by eliminating the burden of cleft lip and/or palate, burn scarring, and other deformities by sending medical teams to provide free reconstructive surgery, ancillary treatment, and training.

Anesth, Dent-OMFS, ENT, Ped Surg, Plast, Surg

🌐 https://vfmat.ch/78b3

Rotary International

Provides service to others, improves lives, and advances world understanding, goodwill, and peace through its fellowship of business, professional, and community leaders.

ER Med, General, Infect Dis, MF Med, OB-GYN

🌐 https://vfmat.ch/8fb5

ROW Foundation

Works to improve the quality of training for healthcare providers, and the diagnosis and treatment available to people with epilepsy and associated psychiatric disorders in under-resourced areas of the world.

Neuro, Psych

🌐 https://vfmat.ch/25eb

Saint Joseph's Catholic Hospital

Provides healthcare services to all who need care, without any form of discrimination.

Medicine, OB-GYN, Ortho, Peds, Surg

🌐 https://vfmat.ch/34d2

Salvation Army International, The

Seeks to meet human needs through services in education, healthcare, community support, emergency response, and ministry development, inspired by the Christian faith.

Dent-OMFS, Derm, ER Med, Infect Dis, MF Med, Medicine, Nutr, OB-GYN, Ophth-Opt, Palliative, Psych, Rehab, Surg

🌐 https://vfmat.ch/8eb3

Save the Children

Gives children around the world a healthy start in life, the opportunity to learn, and protection from harm.

All-Immu, Crit-Care, ER Med, General, Infect Dis, MF Med, Medicine, Neonat, OB-GYN, Peds, Psych, Pub Health

🌐 https://vfmat.ch/2e73

SCI Foundation

Seeks to prevent and treat neglected infectious diseases, with a focus on eliminating parasitic worm infections through strengthening impactful and comprehensive health programs across Sub-Saharan Africa.

Infect Dis, Pub Health

🌐 https://vfmat.ch/5444

SEE International

Provides sustainable medical, surgical, and educational services through volunteer ophthalmic surgeons, with the objectives of restoring sight and preventing blindness to disadvantaged individuals worldwide.

Ophth-Opt, Surg

🌐 https://vfmat.ch/6e1b

Seed Global Health

Focuses on human resources for health capacity building at the individual, institutional, and national level through sustained collaborative engagement with partners.

Logist-Op

🌐 https://vfmat.ch/d12e

Set Free Alliance
Works with in-country partners to rescue children, provide clean water, host medical clinics, and plant churches, based in Christian ministry.
General, Peds
⊕ https://vfmat.ch/bdb8

Sightsavers
Works with partners in developing countries to help eliminate avoidable blindness and advocates for equal opportunity for the disabled.
Infect Dis, Ophth-Opt, Surg
⊕ https://vfmat.ch/aa52

SIGN Fracture Care International
Builds orthopedic capacity around the world and provides the injured poor access to fracture surgery by donating orthopedic education and implant systems to surgeons in developing countries.
Ortho, Rehab, Surg
⊕ https://vfmat.ch/123d

SINA Health
Aims to improve the health and educational status of the population in low- and middle-income countries.
General, Logist-Op
⊕ https://vfmat.ch/9ad3

Smile Train, Inc.
Treats children with cleft lip through a sustainable and local model that supports surgery and other forms of essential care.
Logist-Op, Pub Health
⊕ https://vfmat.ch/822c

Sustainable Cardiovascular Health Equity Development Alliance
Fights cardiovascular disease in underserved populations globally via education, training, and increasing interventional capacity.
CV Med, Pub Health, Radiol
⊕ https://vfmat.ch/799c

Swiss Tropical and Public Health Institute
Contributes to the improvement of the health of populations internationally, nationally, and locally through excellence in research, education, and services.
Infect Dis, Pub Health
⊕ https://vfmat.ch/2ee4

Task Force for Global Health, The
Consists of programs and focus areas that cover a range of global health issues including neglected tropical diseases, infectious diseases, vaccines, field epidemiology, public health informatics, health workforce development, and global health ethics.
Infect Dis, Logist-Op, Medicine, Ophth-Opt, Peds
⊕ https://vfmat.ch/714c

Tearfund
Responds to crisis and partners with local churches to bring restoration to those living in poverty, inspired by the Christian faith.
ER Med, Logist-Op
⊕ https://vfmat.ch/f6cf

Turing Foundation
Aims to contribute toward a better world and a better society by focusing on efforts such as health, art, education, and nature.
Infect Dis
⊕ https://vfmat.ch/6bcc

U.S. President's Malaria Initiative (PMI)
Supports low-income countries to help control and eliminate malaria through cost-effective, lifesaving malaria interventions.
Infect Dis, MF Med, OB-GYN
⊕ https://vfmat.ch/dc8b

UNC Health Foundation
Secures resources and supports empathy and expertise in patient care, research, education, and advocacy in underserved communities around the world.

Heme-Onc, Infect Dis, Neuro, Peds, Pub Health
⊕ https://vfmat.ch/7129

United Methodist Volunteers in Mission (UMVIM)
Engages in short-term missions each year in ministries as varied as disaster response, community development, pastor training, microenterprise, agriculture, Vacation Bible School, building repair and construction, and medical/dental services.
Dent-OMFS, ER Med, General
⊕ https://vfmat.ch/1ee6

United Nations Children's Fund (UNICEF)
Works in over 190 countries and territories to save children's lives, defend their rights, and help them fulfill their potential, from early childhood through adolescence.
All-Immu, Infect Dis, MF Med, Neonat, Nutr, OB-GYN, Ped Surg, Peds, Pub Health
⊕ https://vfmat.ch/42d7

United Nations Development Programme (UNDP)
Helps countries achieve the simultaneous eradication of extreme poverty and significant reduction of inequalities and exclusion using a sustainable human development approach.
Infect Dis, Logist-Op, Pub Health
⊕ https://vfmat.ch/935c

United Nations High Commissioner for Refugees (UNHCR)
Safeguards the rights and well-being of people who have been forced to flee, ensuring that everybody has the right to seek asylum and find safe refuge in another country, with the goal of seeking lasting solutions.
General, MF Med, Medicine, OB-GYN, Peds, Psych, Pub Health
⊕ https://vfmat.ch/6636

United Nations Population Fund (UNFPA)
Supports reproductive healthcare for women and youth in more than 150 countries, focusing on delivering a world in which every pregnancy is wanted, every childbirth is safe, and every young person's potential is fulfilled.
Infect Dis, MF Med, Neonat, OB-GYN, Peds, Pub Health
⊕ https://vfmat.ch/c969

United Surgeons for Children (USFC)
Pursues greater health and opportunity for children in the most neglected pockets of the world, with a specific focus on and expertise in surgery.
Anesth, CT Surg, Neonat, Neurosurg, OB-GYN, Peds, Radiol, Surg
⊕ https://vfmat.ch/3b4c

University of California Los Angeles: David Geffen School of Medicine Global Health Program
Catalyzes opportunities to improve health globally by engaging in multi-disciplinary and innovative education programs, research initiatives, and bilateral partnerships that provide opportunities for trainees, faculty, and staff to contribute to sustainable health initiatives and to address health inequities facing the world today.
All-Immu, Infect Dis, Logist-Op, MF Med, Medicine, Neonat, OB-GYN, Ortho, Ped Surg, Peds, Radiol
⊕ https://vfmat.ch/f1a4

University of North Carolina: Institute for Global Health and Infectious Diseases
Harnesses the full resources of UNC and its partners to solve global health problems, reduce the burden of disease, and cultivate the next generation of global health leaders.
Infect Dis, MF Med, OB-GYN, Psych, Surg
⊕ https://vfmat.ch/ed5e

USAID: Deliver Project
Builds a global supply chain to deliver lifesaving health products to people in order to enable countries to provide family planning, protect against malaria, and limit the spread of pandemic threats.
Infect Dis, Logist-Op, MF Med
⊕ https://vfmat.ch/374e

USAID: Leadership, Management and Governance Project
Improves leadership, management, and governance practices to strengthen health

systems and improve health for all, including vulnerable populations worldwide.

Logist-Op

⊕ https://vfmat.ch/d35e

USAID: Maternal and Child Health Integrated Program

Works to improve the health of women and their families, including programs for maternal, newborn, and child health, immunization, family planning, nutrition, malaria, and HIV/AIDS.

All-Immu, General, Infect Dis, MF Med

⊕ https://vfmat.ch/4415

USAID: Maternal and Child Survival Program

Works to prevent child and maternal deaths.

Infect Dis, MF Med, Neonat, OB-GYN, Peds

⊕ https://vfmat.ch/6fcf

Vitamin Angels

Helps at-risk populations in need—specifically pregnant women, new mothers, and children under age 5—to gain access to life-changing vitamins and minerals.

General, Nutr

⊕ https://vfmat.ch/7da1

Voices for a Malaria-Free Future

Seeks to expand national movements of private- and public-sector leaders to mobilize political and popular support for malaria control.

Infect Dis, Path

⊕ https://vfmat.ch/4213

Walkabout Foundation

Provides wheelchairs and rehabilitation in the developing world and funds research to find a cure for paralysis.

Logist-Op, Rehab

⊕ https://vfmat.ch/5582

Women's Refugee Commission

Seeks to improve lives by protecting the rights of women, children, and youth displaced by conflict and crisis through researching their needs, identifying solutions, and advocating for programs and policies to strengthen their resilience.

General, MF Med, Neonat, OB-GYN, Peds, Psych

⊕ https://vfmat.ch/3d8f

World Children's Fund

Commits to helping children worldwide who are suffering the effects of poverty, disease, natural disaster, famine, abuse, civil strife, and war.

General, Logist-Op, MF Med, Nutr, OB-GYN, Pub Health

⊕ https://vfmat.ch/9cd8

World Health Organization, The (WHO)

The United Nations' agency for health provides leadership on global health matters, shapes the health research agenda, sets norms and standards, articulates evidence-based policy options, provides technical support and monitoring to countries, and assesses health trends.

ER Med, General, Infect Dis, Logist-Op, MF Med, OB-GYN, Peds, Psych, Pub Health

⊕ https://vfmat.ch/c476

World Hope International

Empowers the poorest individuals around the world so they can become agents of change within their communities, by offering resources and knowledge.

Infect Dis, Logist-Op, MF Med, OB-GYN, Peds

⊕ https://vfmat.ch/a4b8

World Medical Relief

Facilitates the distribution of surplus medical resources where they are needed.

Logist-Op

⊕ https://vfmat.ch/72dc

World Parkinson's Program

Seeks to improve the quality of life of those affected by Parkinson's disease through education and advocacy, and provides free medication and support services.

Logist-Op, Neuro, Pub Health

⊕ https://vfmat.ch/c96d

Zoe Geh Foundation

Provides financial and logistical assistance to create quality medical facilities and programs in developing countries or other economically challenged areas.

General, Infect Dis, Logist-Op, OB-GYN, Peds, Surg

⊕ https://vfmat.ch/c4d5

 **Liberia**

Healthcare Facilities

Arcelor Mittal Yekepa Hospital
Yekepa, Liberia
⊕ https://vfmat.ch/4e41

Benson Hospital
Tubman Boulevard, Monrovia, Montserrado County,
Liberia
⊕ https://vfmat.ch/e8c8

Bomi Tubmanburg ETU
Tubmanburg, Bomi County, Liberia
⊕ https://vfmat.ch/8183

Catherine Mills Hospital
Dillion Avenue, Monrovia, Montserrado County,
Liberia
⊕ https://vfmat.ch/8a86

Eternal Love Winning Africa Hospital
Monrovia, Liberia
⊕ https://vfmat.ch/cd26

Ganta Methodist Hospital
Ganta, Liberia
⊕ https://vfmat.ch/ee41

J.J. Dossen Hospital
Green Street, Harper, Maryland County, Liberia
⊕ https://vfmat.ch/9b2f

Martha Tubman Memorial Hospital
Breeze Street, Zone 5, Grand Gedeh County, Liberia
⊕ https://vfmat.ch/4bf9

Phebe Hospital & School of Nursing
Phebe, Liberia
⊕ https://vfmat.ch/e4b1

Redemption Hospital
New Kru Town, Liberia
⊕ https://vfmat.ch/ba2e

SDA Cooper Hospital
12th St, Monrovia, Liberia
⊕ https://vfmat.ch/6363

SOS Hospital
Tubman Boulevard, Monrovia, Montserrado County,
Liberia
⊕ https://vfmat.ch/fb2c

St. Joseph's Catholic Hospital
Tubman Boulevard, Monrovia, Montserrado County,
Liberia
⊕ https://vfmat.ch/c7fb

UN Chinese Hospital and UNMIL Base
Towah Street, Zone 2, Grand Gedeh County, Liberia
⊕ https://vfmat.ch/fde5

ANTSIRANANA

MAHAJANGA

Toamasina

MADAGASCAR

ANTANANARIVO

Antsirabe

FIANARANTSOA

TOLIARA

Tolanaro

Mtwara

Moroni

COMOROS

PEMBA

NACALA

NAMPULA

SAINT-DENIS

● Healthcare Facility

Madagascar

The Republic of Madagascar is a large island country located about 400 kilometers off the coast of East Africa, in the Indian Ocean. The population of 27.5 million lives in predominantly rural areas and is made up of various ethnic groups, including Malayo-Indonesian, Cotiers, French, Indian, Creole, and Comoran. Malagasy, French, and English are all spoken, as are local languages. The people practice various forms of Christianity, Islam, and local indigenous religions. The country has diverse animal life, most notably 40 species of indigenous lemurs unique to Madagascar.

Madagascar gained independence from France in 1960 and has since experienced several bouts of political turmoil and instability. A coup in 2009 resulted in a five-year political deadlock; in 2019 the election of a new president ended a decade of political uncertainty. Despite political issues, the country as a whole has made positive economic progress, and the agriculture sector, with crops such as rice, coffee, and vanilla, is the nation's leading employer. Over 70 percent of the young Malagasy population lives in poverty.

Health challenges include chronic malnutrition; nearly half of children under five years of age suffer from stunting. The country also experienced a measles outbreak in 2018 that infected tens of thousands of people. The leading causes of death include diarrheal diseases, lower respiratory infections, neonatal disorders, tuberculosis, malaria, and protein-energy malnutrition. Non-communicable diseases such as stroke, ischemic heart disease, hypertensive heart disease, and cirrhosis have notably increased and are increasingly among the top causes of death in Madagascar.

27.5M

Population

$496

GDP Per Capita

67 years

Life Expectancy

↑ Improving

18
Doctors/100k

Physician Density

20
Beds/100k

Hospital Bed Density

335
Deaths/100k

Maternal Mortality

Madagascar

Nonprofit Organizations

143 LIFE Foundation
Seeks to educate and empower individuals living with malaria, TB, HIV/AIDS, STDs and other health disparities related to sexual health.
Infect Dis, MF Med
🌐 https://vfmat.ch/d59b

Abt Associates
Seeks to improve the quality of life and economic well-being of people worldwide, while striving to meet and exceed the highest professional standards.
General, Logist-Op, MF Med, OB-GYN, Peds
🌐 https://vfmat.ch/cec2

Action Against Hunger
Aims to end life-threatening hunger for good through treating and preventing malnutrition across more than 45 countries.
Nutr
🌐 https://vfmat.ch/2dbc

Advance Family Planning
Aims to achieve global expansion and access to quality contraceptive information, services, and supplies through financial investment and political commitment.
General, MF Med, Pub Health
🌐 https://vfmat.ch/7478

Adventist Health International
Focuses on upgrading and managing mission hospitals by providing governance, consultation, and technical assistance to a number of affiliated Seventh-Day Adventist hospitals throughout Africa, Asia, and the Americas.
Dent-OMFS, General, Pub Health
🌐 https://vfmat.ch/16aa

Africa CDC
Aims to strengthen the capacity and capability of Africa's public health institutions and partnerships to detect and respond quickly and effectively to disease threats and outbreaks, based on data-driven interventions and programs.
Infect Dis, Logist-Op, Pub Health
🌐 https://vfmat.ch/339c

Africa Health Organisation
Leads collaborative efforts among countries in Africa and other partners to promote health equity, combat disease, and improve quality of life.
Logist-Op, Pub Health
🌐 https://vfmat.ch/b1c5

Africa Indoor Residual Spraying Project (AIRS)
Aims to protect millions of people in Africa from malaria by spraying insecticide on walls, ceilings, and other indoor resting places of mosquitoes that transmit malaria.
Infect Dis
🌐 https://vfmat.ch/9bd1

Africa Inland Mission International
Seeks to establish churches and community development programs including healthcare projects, based in Christian ministry.
Anesth, Dent-OMFS, ER Med, General, MF Med, Medicine, OB-GYN, OB-GYN, Ophth-Opt, Ped Surg, Peds, Rehab
🌐 https://vfmat.ch/f2f6

Africa Relief and Community Development
Provides comprehensive relief and developmental aid to people of the African continent regardless of gender, race, or religion.
Nutr, Pub Health
🌐 https://vfmat.ch/6cd2

Aga Khan Foundation Canada
Tackles the root causes of poverty, with a special focus on marginalized groups such as women and girls. Programs provide access to education and healthcare, food, and opportunity.
Pub Health
🌐 https://vfmat.ch/7f8b

Against Malaria Foundation
Helps protect people from malaria. Funds anti-malaria nets, specifically long-lasting insecticidal nets (LLINs), and works with distribution partners to ensure they are used. Tracks and reports on net use and malaria case data.
Infect Dis
🌐 https://vfmat.ch/337d

AISPO
Implements international initiatives in the healthcare sector and remains involved in various projects to combat poverty, social injustice, and disease around the world.
All-Immu, ER Med, GI, General, Infect Dis, Logist-Op, MF Med, Neonat, OB-GYN, Peds, Psych, Pub Health, Radiol
🌐 https://vfmat.ch/c9e6

American Academy of Pediatrics
Seeks to attain optimal physical, mental, and social health and well-being for all infants, children, adolescents, and young adults.
Anesth, Crit-Care, Neonat, Ped Surg
🌐 https://vfmat.ch/9633

Amref Health Africa
Serves millions of people across 35 countries in Sub-Saharan Africa, strengthening health systems, and training African health workers to respond to the continent's most critical health issues.
All-Immu, General, Infect Dis, Logist-Op, MF Med, OB-GYN, Path, Pub Health, Surg
🌐 https://vfmat.ch/6985

Australian Doctors for Africa
Develops healthier environments and builds capacity through the provision of

voluntary medical assistance, while training and teaching doctors, nurses, and allied health workers; improving infrastructure; and providing medical equipment.

Anesth, ENT, GI, Logist-Op, MF Med, OB-GYN, Ortho, Ped Surg, Peds, Urol

⊕ https://vfmat.ch/f769

Basic Foundations
Supports local projects and organizations that seek to meet the basic human needs of others in their community.

ER Med, General, Peds, Rehab, Surg

⊕ https://vfmat.ch/c4be

Beta Humanitarian Help
Provides plastic surgery in underserved areas of the world.

Anesth, Plast

⊕ https://vfmat.ch/7221

BethanyKids
Transforms the lives of African children with surgical conditions and disabilities through pediatric surgery, rehabilitation, public education, spiritual ministry, and the training of health professionals.

Neurosurg, Nutr, Ortho, Ped Surg, Peds, Rehab, Surg

⊕ https://vfmat.ch/db4e

CARE
Works around the globe to save lives, defeat poverty, and achieve social justice.

ER Med, General

⊕ https://vfmat.ch/7232

Carter Center, The
Seeks to prevent and resolve conflicts, enhance freedom and democracy, and improve health, while remaining committed to human rights and the alleviation of human suffering.

Infect Dis, MF Med, Ophth-Opt

⊕ https://vfmat.ch/6556

Chain of Hope (La Chaîne de l'Espoir)
Helps underprivileged children around the world by providing them with access to healthcare.

Anesth, CT Surg, Crit-Care, ER Med, Neurosurg, Ortho, Ped Surg, Surg, Vasc Surg

⊕ https://vfmat.ch/e871

CharityVision International
Focuses on restoring curable sight impairment worldwide by empowering local physicians and creating sustainable solutions.

Logist-Op, Ophth-Opt, Surg

⊕ https://vfmat.ch/6231

Christian Blind Mission (CBM)
Aims to improve the quality of life of persons with disabilities in the poorest countries, addressing poverty as a cause and a consequence of disability, and working in partnership to create a society for all.

ENT, General, Infect Dis, OB-GYN, Ophth-Opt, Ortho, Peds, Psych, Rehab, Surg

⊕ https://vfmat.ch/3824

Core Group
Aims to improve and expand community health practices for underserved populations, especially women and children, through collaborative action and learning.

General, Infect Dis, MF Med, Medicine, OB-GYN, Peds, Pub Health

⊕ https://vfmat.ch/9de3

Direct Relief
Improves the health and lives of people affected by poverty or emergency situations by mobilizing and providing essential medical resources needed for their care.

ER Med, Logist-Op

⊕ https://vfmat.ch/58e5

Direct Relief of Poverty & Sickness Foundation (DROPS)
This volunteer-led organization uses all donations for direct relief of poverty and illness through initiatives in healthcare education, improving healthcare systems, and providing essential medical help to children and aged people in need.

Dent-OMFS, General, Ophth-Opt

⊕ https://vfmat.ch/af95

Doctors for Madagascar
Provides direct medical aid with the goal of improving medical treatment in Madagascar over the long term, focusing particularly on the remote south of the island, one of the poorest regions of the country.

General, Logist-Op, Nutr, OB-GYN

⊕ https://vfmat.ch/12d8

Douleurs Sans Frontières (Pain Without Borders)
Supports local actors in taking charge of the assessment and treatment of pain and suffering, in an integrated manner and adapted to the realities of each country.

Anesth, Palliative, Psych, Rehab

⊕ https://vfmat.ch/324c

Duke University: Global Health Institute
Sparks innovation in global health research and education, and brings together knowledge and resources to address the most important global health issues of our time.

All-Immu, Infect Dis, MF Med, OB-GYN, Pub Health

⊕ https://vfmat.ch/c4cd

END Fund, The
Aims to control and eliminate the most prevalent neglected diseases among the world's poorest and most vulnerable people.

Infect Dis

⊕ https://vfmat.ch/2614

Fistula Foundation
Aims to engage the support of people worldwide who are eager to see the day that no woman suffers from obstetric fistula. Raises and directs funds to doctors and hospitals providing life-transforming surgery to women in need.

OB-GYN

⊕ https://vfmat.ch/e958

Fondation Follereau
Promotes the quality of life of the most vulnerable African communities. Alongside trusted partners, the foundation supports local initiatives in healthcare and education.

General, Infect Dis, OB-GYN

⊕ https://vfmat.ch/bcc7

Freedom From Fistula
Helps women and girls who are injured and left incontinent following prolonged, obstructed childbirth by providing free surgical repairs for patients already suffering with obstetric fistula, as well as maternity care to prevent these fistulas from happening at all.

MF Med, OB-GYN, Peds

⊕ https://vfmat.ch/6e11

Friends of Mandritsara Trust
Supports the work of the Good News Hospital in and around the district of Mandritsara in Northern Madagascar. Based in Christian ministry, aims to meet both the medical and spiritual needs of local communities through medical and surgical services along with church planting.

General, MF Med, OB-GYN, Ophth-Opt, Peds, Pub Health, Surg

⊕ https://vfmat.ch/279f

Global Alliance to Prevent Prematurity And Stillbirth (GAPPS)
Seeks to improve birth outcomes worldwide by reducing the burden of premature birth and stillbirth.

All-Immu, Infect Dis, MF Med, Neonat, Neonat, OB-GYN

⊕ https://vfmat.ch/3f74

Global Clinic
Seeks to ensure that any effort to provide medical services is accompanied by a long-term program to improve the health of residents of its partner communities.

Dent-OMFS, ER Med, General, OB-GYN, OB-GYN, Ophth-Opt, Surg

⊕ https://vfmat.ch/9e48

Global Ministries – The United Methodist Church
As the worldwide mission and development agency of The United Methodist

Church, Global Ministries works with more than 300 hospitals and clinics around the world through its Global Health Unit.

Anesth, CT Surg, CV Med, Crit-Care, Dent-OMFS, Derm, ER Med, GI, General, Infect Dis, Logist-Op, MF Med, Medicine, Neonat, Nephro, Nutr, OB-GYN, Ophth-Opt, Ortho, Palliative, Peds, Pod, Psych, Pub Health, Rehab, Rheum, Surg, Urol

⊕ https://vfmat.ch/1723

Global Oncology (GO)
Brings the best in cancer care to underserved patients around the world and collaborates across geographic, professional, and academic borders to improve cancer care, research, and education.

Heme-Onc, Path, Rad-Onc

⊕ https://vfmat.ch/fcb8

Global Polio Eradication Initiative
Aims to eradicate polio worldwide.

All-Immu, Infect-Dis, Logist-Op, Pub Health

⊕ https://vfmat.ch/7e2c

Global Reconstructive Surgery Outreach
Supports surgeons, doctors, and nurses financially to enable them to provide critically needed plastic and reconstructive surgeries to the poor.

Logist-Op, Surg

⊕ https://vfmat.ch/f262

Globus Relief
Aims to improve the delivery of healthcare worldwide by gathering, processing, and distributing surplus medical supplies to charities at home and abroad.

Logist-Op

⊕ https://vfmat.ch/a2b7

Good Shepard International Foundation
Strives to promote inclusive and sustainable development for the most marginalized and vulnerable people, with a special focus on women, girls, and children, inspired by the Christian faith.

ER Med

⊕ https://vfmat.ch/ad9a

Grace for Impact
Provides high-quality healthcare and education to the rural poor, where it is needed most, in Sub-Saharan Africa and Southeast Asia.

Dent-OMFS, General, Ophth-Opt

⊕ https://vfmat.ch/3ed1

Grassroot Soccer
Leverages the power of soccer to educate, inspire, and mobilize at-risk youth in developing countries to overcome their greatest health challenges, live healthier and more productive lives, and be agents for change in their communities.

Infect Dis

⊕ https://vfmat.ch/3521

Health Equity Initiative
Aims to build and sustain a global community that engages across sectors and disciplines to advance health equity.

Pub Health

⊕ https://vfmat.ch/e2e2

Hear the World (Entendre le Monde)
Aims to operate on as many patients as possible, train surgeons, assess the causes of deafness, and improve the diagnosis and treatment of deafness.

ENT, Peds

⊕ https://vfmat.ch/9c15

HelpMeSee
Trains local cataract specialists in Manual Small Incision Cataract Surgery (MSICS) in significant numbers, to meet the increasing demand for surgical services in the communities most impacted by cataract blindness.

Anesth, Ophth-Opt, Surg

⊕ https://vfmat.ch/973c

HIS Foundation (Holistic Integrated Services Foundation)
Provides free medical services for patients in underserved communities, such as services in orthopedic surgery, plastic surgery, internal medicine, rehabilitation,

and ophthalmology, formed by Christian medical professionals.

Dent-OMFS, Geri, Medicine, Ophth-Opt, Ortho, Plast, Rehab

⊕ https://vfmat.ch/a24b

Humanity & Inclusion
Works alongside people with disabilities and vulnerable populations, taking action and bearing witness in order to respond to their essential needs, improve their living conditions and health, and promote respect for their dignity and fundamental rights.

General, Infect Dis, MF Med, Medicine, Ortho, Peds, Psych, Pub Health, Rehab

⊕ https://vfmat.ch/16b7

International Agency for the Prevention of Blindness (IAPB), The
Leads international efforts in blindness-prevention activities, works toward a world where no one is needlessly visually impaired, and ensures that everyone has access to the best possible standard of eye health.

Infect Dis, Ophth-Opt, Pub Health

⊕ https://vfmat.ch/87a2

International Council of Ophthalmology
Works with ophthalmologic societies and others to enhance ophthalmic education and improve access to the highest-quality eye care in order to preserve and restore vision for people of the world.

Ophth-Opt

⊕ https://vfmat.ch/ffd2

International Medical and Surgical Aid (IMSA)
Aims to save lives and alleviate suffering through education, healthcare, surgical camps, and quality medical programs.

Anesth, General, Ped Surg, Surg

⊕ https://vfmat.ch/2561

International Medical Relief
Provides sustainable education, training, medical and dental care, and disaster relief and response in vulnerable communities worldwide.

Dent-OMFS, General, Infect Dis, Medicine, OB-GYN

⊕ https://vfmat.ch/b3ed

International Organization for Migration (IOM) – The UN Migration Agency
Promotes evidence-informed policies and holistic, preventive, and curative health programs that are beneficial, accessible, and equitable for vulnerable migrants.

General, Infect Dis, OB-GYN

⊕ https://vfmat.ch/621a

International Planned Parenthood Federation (IPPF)
Leads a locally owned, globally connected civil society movement that provides and enables services and champions sexual and reproductive health and rights for all, especially the underserved.

Infect Dis, MF Med, OB-GYN

⊕ https://vfmat.ch/dc97

InterSurgeon
Fosters collaborative partnerships in the field of global surgery that will advance clinical care, teaching, training, research, and the provision and maintenance of medical equipment.

ENT, Neurosurg, Ortho, Ped Surg, Plast, Surg, Urol

⊕ https://vfmat.ch/6f8a

IntraHealth International
Improves the performance of health workers and strengthens the systems in which they work.

CV Med, Endo, General, Infect Dis, MF Med, Neonat, Nutr, OB-GYN

⊕ https://vfmat.ch/ddc8

Iris Global
Serves the poor, the destitute, the lost, and the forgotten by providing adoration, outreach, family, education, relief, development, healing, and the arts.

General, Infect Dis, Nutr, Pub Health

⊕ https://vfmat.ch/37f8

Izumi Foundation
Develops and supports programs that improve health and healthcare in neglected

regions of Africa and Latin America.
⊕ https://vfmat.ch/f29a

Jhpiego
Creates and delivers transformative healthcare solutions that save lives, in partnership with national governments, health experts, and local communities.
General, Infect Dis, OB-GYN, Surg
⊕ https://vfmat.ch/45b8

John Snow, Inc. (JSI)
Aims to improve the health and well-being of underserved and vulnerable people and communities throughout the world.
General, Infect Dis, Logist-Op, MF Med, OB-GYN, Peds, Psych, Pub Health
⊕ https://vfmat.ch/ba78

Johns Hopkins Center for Communication Programs
Believes in the power of communication to save lives by empowering people to adopt healthy behaviors for themselves, their families, and their communities.
General, Infect Dis, Logist-Op, OB-GYN, Pub Health
⊕ https://vfmat.ch/1bf9

Johns Hopkins Center for Global Health
Facilitates and focuses the extensive expertise and resources of the Johns Hopkins institutions, together with global collaborators, to effectively address and ameliorate the world's most pressing health issues.
General, Genetics, Logist-Op, MF Med, Peds, Psych, Pub Health, Pulm-Critic
⊕ https://vfmat.ch/54ce

Joint United Nations Programme on HIV/AIDS (UNAIDS)
Aims to place people living with HIV and people affected by the virus at the decision-making table and at the center of designing, delivering, and monitoring the AIDS response.
Infect Dis
⊕ https://vfmat.ch/464a

Lions Clubs International
Empowers volunteers to serve their communities, meet humanitarian needs, encourage peace, and promote international understanding through Lions Clubs.
Heme-Onc, Medicine, Nutr, Ophth-Opt
⊕ https://vfmat.ch/7b12

Lutherans in Medical Missions (LIMM)
Works with local and global partners to promote healing in medically underserved communities.
General, Logist-Op, Pub Health
⊕ https://vfmat.ch/c5aa

Management Sciences for Health (MSH)
Works with countries and communities to save lives and improve the health of the world's poorest and most vulnerable people by building strong, resilient, sustainable health systems.
Infect Dis, Logist-Op, Pub Health
⊕ https://vfmat.ch/6aa2

MAP International
Provides medicines and health supplies to those in need around the world so they might experience life to the fullest.
Logist-Op
⊕ https://vfmat.ch/deed

Marie Stopes International
Provides the contraception and safe abortion services that enable women all over the world to choose their own futures.
Infect Dis, MF Med, Neonat, OB-GYN, Pub Health
⊕ https://vfmat.ch/9525

Medair
Works to relieve human suffering in some of the world's most remote and devastated places, saving lives in emergencies and helping people in crises survive and recover, inspired by the Christian faith.
ER Med, General, Logist-Op, MF Med, Pub Health
⊕ https://vfmat.ch/5b33

Medical Care Development International (MCD International)
Works to strengthen health systems through innovative, sustainable interventions.
Infect Dis, Logist-Op, OB-GYN, Pub Health
⊕ https://vfmat.ch/dc5c

Medical Care Development International
Works to improve the health of vulnerable populations through integrated, sustainable, and locally driven interventions.
Infect Dis, OB-GYN, Peds, Pub Health
⊕ https://vfmat.ch/da87

MedShare
Aims to improve the quality of life of people, communities, and the planet by sourcing and directly delivering surplus medical supplies and equipment to communities in need around the world.
Logist-Op
⊕ https://vfmat.ch/c8bc

Mercy and Love Foundation
Aims to provide orphaned and vulnerable children with basic human needs such as food, clothing, and shelter, enabling them to thrive.
General, Peds
⊕ https://vfmat.ch/649a

Mercy Ships
Operates hospital ships staffed by volunteers to bring hope, healing, and healthcare to underserved communities worldwide.
Anesth, Dent-OMFS, Logist-Op, Neonat, OB-GYN, Ophth-Opt, Ortho, Palliative, Plast, Psych, Surg
⊕ https://vfmat.ch/2e99

MiracleFeet
Brings low-cost treatment to every child on the planet born with clubfoot, a leading cause of physical disability.
Ortho, Peds, Rehab
⊕ https://vfmat.ch/bda8

Mission Bambini
Helps to support children living in poverty and sickness, and lacking education, giving them the opportunity for and hope of a better life.
CT Surg, CV Med, Crit-Care, ER Med, Ped Surg, Peds
⊕ https://vfmat.ch/dc1a

Mission Vision
Seeks to decrease blindness and other eye-related disabilities, and to increase academic performance and general quality of life.
Ophth-Opt
⊕ https://vfmat.ch/83d8

Modern Dental Care Foundation (MDCF)
Works to give the poorest people of Madagascar access to dental care and prevention in a sustainable and effective manner.
Dent-OMFS
⊕ https://vfmat.ch/5e96

Money for Madagascar
Enables Malagasy people to reduce poverty and protect the environment through sustainable, community-led initiatives.
General
⊕ https://vfmat.ch/3c86

MSI Reproductive Choices (Marie Stopes International)
Seeks to deliver quality family planning and reproductive healthcare to women around the world.
MF Med
⊕ https://vfmat.ch/5c82

Médecins du Monde/Doctors of the World
Provides care, bears witness, and supports social change worldwide with innovative medical programs and evidence-based advocacy initiatives.
ER Med, General, Infect Dis, MF Med, Neonat, OB-GYN, Peds, Pub Health
⊕ https://vfmat.ch/a43d

Mérieux Foundation
Committed to fighting infectious diseases that affect developing countries by capacity building, particularly in clinical laboratories, and focusing on diagnosis.
Logist-Op, Path
⊕ https://vfmat.ch/a23a

NCD Alliance
Unites and strengthens civil society to stimulate collaborative advocacy, action, and accountability for NCD (noncommunicable disease) prevention and control.
All-Immu, CV Med, General, Heme-Onc, Medicine, Peds, Psych
⊕ https://vfmat.ch/abdd

Operation Fistula
Exists to end obstetric fistula by building models of care that serve every woman, everywhere.
MF Med, OB-GYN, Surg
⊕ https://vfmat.ch/ce8e

Operation Smile
Treats patients with cleft lip and cleft palate, and creates solutions that deliver safe surgery to people where it's needed most.
Anesth, Dent-OMFS, ENT, Ped Surg, Plast
⊕ https://vfmat.ch/5c29

Options
Believes in a world in which women and children can access the high-quality health services they need, without financial burden.
Logist-Op, MF Med, Neonat, OB-GYN
⊕ https://vfmat.ch/3a48

Optivest Foundation
Funds strategic opportunities that are holistic and collaborative, inspired by the Christian faith.
General, Nutr
⊕ https://vfmat.ch/f1e6

Order of Malta
Supports forgotten or excluded people, especially those living in conflict zones or amid natural disasters, by providing medical assistance, caring for refugees, and distributing medicines and necessities.
ER Med, General, Infect Dis, MF Med, Nephro, OB-GYN, Ortho, Psych
⊕ https://vfmat.ch/1fab

Organization for the Prevention of Blindness, The (OPC)
Provides research, and treatments and cures for people affected by blindness and blinding diseases in Francophone Africa.
Infect Dis, Ophth-Opt
⊕ https://vfmat.ch/86d6

Pact
Works on the ground to improve the lives of those who are challenged by poverty and marginalization, striving for a world in which all people are heard, capable, and vibrant.
Infect Dis, Logist-Op, MF Med, Pub Health
⊕ https://vfmat.ch/9a6c

Partners in Health
Responds to the moral imperative to provide high-quality healthcare globally to those who need it most, while striving to ease suffering by providing a comprehensive model of care that includes access to food, transportation, housing, and other key components of healing.
CT Surg, General, Heme-Onc, Infect Dis, MF Med, Neurosurg, OB-GYN, Ortho, Plast, Psych, Urol
⊕ https://vfmat.ch/dc9c

Philips Foundation
Aims to reduce healthcare inequality by providing access to quality healthcare for disadvantaged communities.
CV Med, OB-GYN, Ped Surg, Peds, Surg, Urol
⊕ https://vfmat.ch/bacb

PIVOT
Collaborates with the Ministry of Public Health of Madagascar to strengthen the public health system in order to offer quality care to the population of Ifanadiana district.
ER Med, General, Infect Dis, Logist-Op, MF Med, Nutr, OB-GYN, Path, Peds, Pub Health
⊕ https://vfmat.ch/84f2

Project Concern International (PCI)
Drives innovation from the ground up to enhance health, end hunger, overcome hardship, and advance women and girls—resulting in meaningful and measurable change in people's lives.
Infect Dis, MF Med, Nutr, OB-GYN, Peds
⊕ https://vfmat.ch/5ed7

PSI – Population Services International
Aims to improve the health of people in the developing world by focusing on challenges such as a lack of family planning, HIV/AIDS, barriers to maternal health, and the greatest threats to children under the age of 5, including malaria, diarrhea, pneumonia, and malnutrition.
Infect Dis, MF Med, OB-GYN, Peds
⊕ https://vfmat.ch/ffe3

RAD-AID International
Improves and optimizes access to medical imaging and radiology in low-resource regions of the world.
Rad-Onc, Radiol
⊕ https://vfmat.ch/537f

RestoringVision
Empowers lives by restoring vision for millions of people in need.
Ophth-Opt
⊕ https://vfmat.ch/e121

Rockefeller Foundation, The
Works to promote the well-being of humanity.
Logist-Op, Nutr, Pub Health
⊕ https://vfmat.ch/5424

Rose Charities International
Aims to support communities to improve quality of life and reduce the effects of poverty through innovative, self-sustaining projects, and partnerships.
ENT, ER Med, General, Infect Dis, Neonat, OB-GYN, Ophth-Opt, Ped Surg, Peds, Rehab, Urol
⊕ https://vfmat.ch/53df

Rotary International
Provides service to others, improves lives, and advances world understanding, goodwill, and peace through its fellowship of business, professional, and community leaders.
ER Med, General, Infect Dis, MF Med, OB-GYN
⊕ https://vfmat.ch/8fb5

Salvation Army International, The
Seeks to meet human needs through services in education, healthcare, community support, emergency response, and ministry development, inspired by the Christian faith.
Dent-OMFS, Derm, ER Med, Infect Dis, MF Med, Medicine, Nutr, OB-GYN, Ophth-Opt, Palliative, Psych, Rehab, Surg
⊕ https://vfmat.ch/8eb3

Sanofi Espoir Foundation
Contributes to reducing health inequalities among populations that need it most by applying a socially responsible approach focused on fighting childhood cancers in low-income countries, improving maternal and newborn health, and improving access to care.
ER Med, OB-GYN, Peds
⊕ https://vfmat.ch/943b

SCI Foundation
Seeks to prevent and treat neglected infectious diseases, with a focus on eliminating parasitic worm infections through strengthening impactful and comprehensive health programs across Sub-Saharan Africa.
Infect Dis, Pub Health
⊕ https://vfmat.ch/5444

SEVA

Delivers vital eye care services to the world's most vulnerable, including women, children, and Indigenous peoples.

Ophth-Opt, Surg

⊕ https://vfmat.ch/1e87

SIGN Fracture Care International

Builds orthopedic capacity around the world and provides the injured poor access to fracture surgery by donating orthopedic education and implant systems to surgeons in developing countries.

Ortho, Rehab, Surg

⊕ https://vfmat.ch/123d

Smile Train, Inc.

Treats children with cleft lip through a sustainable and local model that supports surgery and other forms of essential care.

Logist-Op, Pub Health

⊕ https://vfmat.ch/822c

Solthis

Improves disease prevention and access to quality care by strengthening the health systems and services of the countries served.

General, Infect Dis, Logist-Op, MF Med, Neonat, Path

⊕ https://vfmat.ch/a71d

SOS Children's Villages International

Supports children through alternative care and family strengthening.

ER Med, Peds

⊕ https://vfmat.ch/aca1

Sri Sathya Sai International Organization

Inspired by spiritual teachings, carries out efforts in global healthcare, education, humanitarian relief, and youth engagement.

Dent-OMFS, General, Logist-Op, Nutr, Ophth-Opt, Pub Health

⊕ https://vfmat.ch/9bda

Students for Kids International Projects (SKIP)

Strives to educate and empower students to initiate and maintain sustainable community projects for the health, welfare, and education of children.

Dent-OMFS, General, Nutr, Peds, Pub Health

⊕ https://vfmat.ch/de4e

Swiss Tropical and Public Health Institute

Contributes to the improvement of the health of populations internationally, nationally, and locally through excellence in research, education, and services.

Infect Dis, Pub Health

⊕ https://vfmat.ch/2ee4

Task Force for Global Health, The

Consists of programs and focus areas that cover a range of global health issues including neglected tropical diseases, infectious diseases, vaccines, field epidemiology, public health informatics, health workforce development, and global health ethics.

Infect Dis, Logist-Op, Medicine, Ophth-Opt, Peds

⊕ https://vfmat.ch/714c

Terre des hommes (Tdh) Foundation

Works to improve the daily life of children and their relatives in the areas of health, protection and emergency, in Europe, Africa, Asia, Latin America, and the Near and Middle East.

CT Surg, CV Med, OB-GYN, Ped Surg, Pub Health

⊕ https://vfmat.ch/5c26

U.S. President's Malaria Initiative (PMI)

Supports low-income countries to help control and eliminate malaria through cost-effective, lifesaving malaria interventions.

Infect Dis, MF Med, OB-GYN

⊕ https://vfmat.ch/dc8b

Union for International Cancer Control (UICC)

Unites and supports the cancer community to reduce the global cancer burden, promote greater equity, and ensure that cancer control continues to be a priority in the world health and development agenda.

Heme-Onc, Pub Health

⊕ https://vfmat.ch/88b1

United Nations Children's Fund (UNICEF)

Works in over 190 countries and territories to save children's lives, defend their rights, and help them fulfill their potential, from early childhood through adolescence.

All-Immu, Infect Dis, MF Med, Neonat, Nutr, OB-GYN, Ped Surg, Peds, Pub Health

⊕ https://vfmat.ch/42d7

United Nations Development Programme (UNDP)

Helps countries achieve the simultaneous eradication of extreme poverty and significant reduction of inequalities and exclusion using a sustainable human development approach.

Infect Dis, Logist-Op, Pub Health

⊕ https://vfmat.ch/935c

United Nations High Commissioner for Refugees (UNHCR)

Safeguards the rights and well-being of people who have been forced to flee, ensuring that everybody has the right to seek asylum and find safe refuge in another country, with the goal of seeking lasting solutions.

General, MF Med, Medicine, OB-GYN, Peds, Psych, Pub Health

⊕ https://vfmat.ch/6636

United Nations Population Fund (UNFPA)

Supports reproductive healthcare for women and youth in more than 150 countries, focusing on delivering a world in which every pregnancy is wanted, every childbirth is safe, and every young person's potential is fulfilled.

Infect Dis, MF Med, Neonat, OB-GYN, Peds, Pub Health

⊕ https://vfmat.ch/c969

United States Agency for International Development (USAID)

Promotes and demonstrates democratic values abroad and advances a free, peaceful, and prosperous world. Leads the U.S. government's international development and disaster assistance through partnerships and investments that save lives.

ER Med, Infect Dis, MF Med, OB-GYN, Peds

⊕ https://vfmat.ch/9a99

United Surgeons for Children (USFC)

Pursues greater health and opportunity for children in the most neglected pockets of the world, with a specific focus on and expertise in surgery.

Anesth, CT Surg, Neonat, Neurosurg, OB-GYN, Peds, Radiol, Surg

⊕ https://vfmat.ch/3b4c

University of California San Francisco: Institute for Global Health Sciences

Dedicates its efforts to improving health and reducing the burden of disease in the world's most vulnerable populations by integrating expertise in the health, social, and biological sciences, training global health leaders, and developing solutions to the most pressing health challenges.

Infect Dis, OB-GYN, Pub Health

⊕ https://vfmat.ch/6587

University of Virginia: Anesthesiology Department Global Health Initiatives

Educates and trains physicians to help people achieve healthy productive lives, and advances knowledge in the medical sciences.

Anesth, Pub Health

⊕ https://vfmat.ch/1b8b

USAID: African Strategies for Health

Identifies and advocates for best practices, enhancing technical capacity of African regional institutions, and engaging African stakeholders to address health issues in a sustainable manner.

All-Immu, Infect Dis, OB-GYN, Peds

⊕ https://vfmat.ch/c272

USAID: Deliver Project

Builds a global supply chain to deliver lifesaving health products to people in order to enable countries to provide family planning, protect against malaria, and limit the spread of pandemic threats.

Infect Dis, Logist-Op, MF Med

⊕ https://vfmat.ch/374e

USAID: Health Policy Initiative

Provides field-level programming in health policy development and implementation.

General, Infect Dis, MF Med, OB-GYN, Peds

⊕ https://vfmat.ch/8f84

USAID: Human Resources for Health 2030 (HRH2030)

Helps low- and middle-income countries develop the health workforce needed to prevent maternal and child deaths, support the goals of Family Planning 2020, control the HIV/AIDS epidemic, and protect communities from infectious diseases.

Logist-Op

⊕ https://vfmat.ch/9ea8

USAID: Leadership, Management and Governance Project

Improves leadership, management, and governance practices to strengthen health systems and improve health for all, including vulnerable populations worldwide.

Logist-Op

⊕ https://vfmat.ch/d35e

USAID: Maternal and Child Health Integrated Program

Works to improve the health of women and their families, including programs for maternal, newborn, and child health, immunization, family planning, nutrition, malaria, and HIV/AIDS.

All-Immu, General, Infect Dis, MF Med

⊕ https://vfmat.ch/4415

USAID: Maternal and Child Survival Program

Works to prevent child and maternal deaths.

Infect Dis, MF Med, Neonat, OB-GYN, Peds

⊕ https://vfmat.ch/6fcf

Vital Strategies

Helps governments strengthen their public health systems to contend with the most important and difficult health challenges, while accelerating progress on the world's most pressing health problems.

CV Med, Infect Dis, Peds

⊕ https://vfmat.ch/fe25

Vitamin Angels

Helps at-risk populations in need—specifically pregnant women, new mothers, and children under age 5—to gain access to life-changing vitamins and minerals.

General, Nutr

⊕ https://vfmat.ch/7da1

VOSH (Volunteer Optometric Services to Humanity) International

Facilitates the provision and the sustainability of vision care worldwide for people who can neither afford nor obtain such care.

Ophth-Opt

⊕ https://vfmat.ch/a149

World Children's Initiative (WCI)

Aims to improve and rebuild the healthcare and educational infrastructure for children in developing areas, both domestic and worldwide.

CV Med, Ped Surg, Surg

⊕ https://vfmat.ch/9ca7

World Federation of Hemophilia (WFH)

Aims to improve and sustain care for people with inherited bleeding disorders by pursuing long-term relationships with individuals and organizations who share the values of WFH's development model.

Heme-Onc

⊕ https://vfmat.ch/5121

World Health Organization, The (WHO)

The United Nations' agency for health provides leadership on global health matters, shapes the health research agenda, sets norms and standards, articulates evidence-based policy options, provides technical support and monitoring to countries, and assesses health trends.

ER Med, General, Infect Dis, Logist-Op, MF Med, OB-GYN, Peds, Psych, Pub Health

⊕ https://vfmat.ch/c476

Madagascar

Healthcare Facilities

Andranomadio Hospital
N 34, Antsirabe, Vakinankaratra, Madagascar
🌐 https://vfmat.ch/b1b1

Centre Hospitalier de Reference Regional (CHRR) Antsohihy
Antsohihy, Madagascar
🌐 https://vfmat.ch/83b6

Centre Hospitalier de Référence Régional de Morondava
Morondava, Madagascar
🌐 https://vfmat.ch/eb4d

Centre Hospitalier de Référence Régionale Ihosy
Ihosy, Madagascar
🌐 https://vfmat.ch/182d

Centre Hospitalier de Soavinandriana
6 bis, Rue du Dr Moss Antananarivo, Madagascar
🌐 https://vfmat.ch/ef5a

Centre Hospitalier Universitaire Zafisaona Gabriel
Rue Marius Barriquand, Mahajanga, Boeny, Madagascar
🌐 https://vfmat.ch/884f

Centre Hospitalier Universitaire Tambohobe
Tambohobe, Fianarantsoa, Madagascar
🌐 https://vfmat.ch/9664

CHD I Mahanoro
Mahanoro, Madagascar
🌐 https://vfmat.ch/2352

CHD II Moramanga
N 2, Moramanga, Alaotra-Mangoro, Madagascar
🌐 https://vfmat.ch/626e

CHRR Manakara
Manakara, Madagascar
🌐 https://vfmat.ch/32c3

CHU Morafeno Toamasina
Route d'Ivoloina, Toamasina, Madagascar
🌐 https://vfmat.ch/3618

Clinique des Soeurs Ankadifotsy
Clinique des Soeurs Ankadifotsy, Antananarivo, Madagascar
🌐 https://vfmat.ch/d12d

CMA
Làlana Nanisana, Antananarivo, Analamanga, Madagascar
🌐 https://vfmat.ch/591f

CSB Farafangana
Farafangana, Madagascar
🌐 https://vfmat.ch/f232

Espace Medical
Antsiranana, Madagascar
🌐 https://vfmat.ch/a947

Hell-Ville Hospital
Avenue Victor Augagneur, Andoany, Diana, Madagascar
🌐 https://vfmat.ch/1a61

Hopitaly Atsimo
Rue Daniel Rakotondrainibe, Antsirabe, Vakinankaratra, Madagascar
🌐 https://vfmat.ch/cc83

Hopitaly Kely
Boulevard de la Libération, Toamasina, Atsinanana, Madagascar
🌐 https://vfmat.ch/b99d

Hopitaly Manarapenitra
Avenue Pasteur, Antsiranana, Diana, Madagascar
🌐 https://vfmat.ch/c82d

Hospital at Ranomafana
Brickaville, Madagascar
🌐 https://vfmat.ch/9c4c

Hospital Chrd Ii Atu
N21, Sainte Marie, Madagascar
🌐 https://vfmat.ch/5fa9

Hospital CSB Ejeda
Ejeda, Madagascar
🌐 https://vfmat.ch/c462

Hospital Loterana Manambaro
Manambaro, Madagascar
🌐 https://vfmat.ch/b986

Hospital Mahajanga
Mahajanga, Madagascar
🌐 https://vfmat.ch/4c5b

Hôpital de Fénérive-Est
N 5, Fenoarivo Atsinanana, Analanjirofo, Madagascar
🌐 https://vfmat.ch/1f67

Hôpital des Enfants
Làlana Andriantsilavo, Antananarivo, Analamanga, Madagascar
🌐 https://vfmat.ch/f664

Hôpital Général de Befelatanana
Làlana Dokotera Ravloud Jacques, Antananarivo, Analamanga, Madagascar
🌐 https://vfmat.ch/b481

Hôpital Itaosy
N 1, Antananarivo, Analamanga, Madagascar
🌐 https://vfmat.ch/83d1

Hôpital Jean Paul II
Mahajanga, Madagascar
🌐 https://vfmat.ch/9c81

Hôpital Joseph Ravoahangy-Andrianavalona
Rue Ravoahangy Andrianavalona, Antananarivo, Analamanga, Madagascar
⊕ https://vfmat.ch/cbd8

Hôpital Luthérien des 67ha
Làlana Agosthino Neto, Antananarivo, Analamanga, Madagascar
⊕ https://vfmat.ch/4a49

Hôpital Mpitsabo Mikambana
Rue Jeneraly Charles de Gaulle, Antananarivo, Madagascar
⊕ https://vfmat.ch/4fc2

Hôpital Municipal de Sandrandahy
Sandrandahy, Madagascar
⊕ https://vfmat.ch/8bde

Hôpital Universitaire Andrainjato
Route de Mahasoabe, Fianarantsoa, Matsiatra Ambony, Madagascar
⊕ https://vfmat.ch/2946

Hôpital Vaovao Mahafaly – The Good News Hospital
Mandritsara, Madagascar
⊕ https://vfmat.ch/5197

Hôpital Vezo
Andavadoaka, Madagascar
⊕ https://vfmat.ch/6952

Joseph Ravoahangy Andrianavalona Hospital
RN 1, Antananarivo 101, Madagascar
⊕ https://vfmat.ch/d266

Lutheran Hospital at Ambohibao
Tobim-pitsaboana Loterana Ambohibao 4
Antananarivo, 105, Madagascar
⊕ https://vfmat.ch/c754

Orthodoxe
Route d'Alasora, Alasora, Analamanga, Madagascar
⊕ https://vfmat.ch/3bf5

OSTIE Anosivavaka
Rue Docteur Joseph Raseta, Antananarivo, Madagascar
⊕ https://vfmat.ch/a5ae

Sampan'asa Loterana Momba ny Fahasalamana Ivory Atsimo
Làlana Pasitera Jessé Rainihifina, Fianarantsoa, Matsiatra Ambony, Madagascar
⊕ https://vfmat.ch/aaa4

Service de Santé de District Mitsinjo
N 19, Antanambao, Boeny, Madagascar
⊕ https://vfmat.ch/2193

Smids
Boulevard Duplex, Antsiranana, Diana, Madagascar
⊕ https://vfmat.ch/352c

Vatomandry
Vatomandry, Madagascar
⊕ https://vfmat.ch/b658

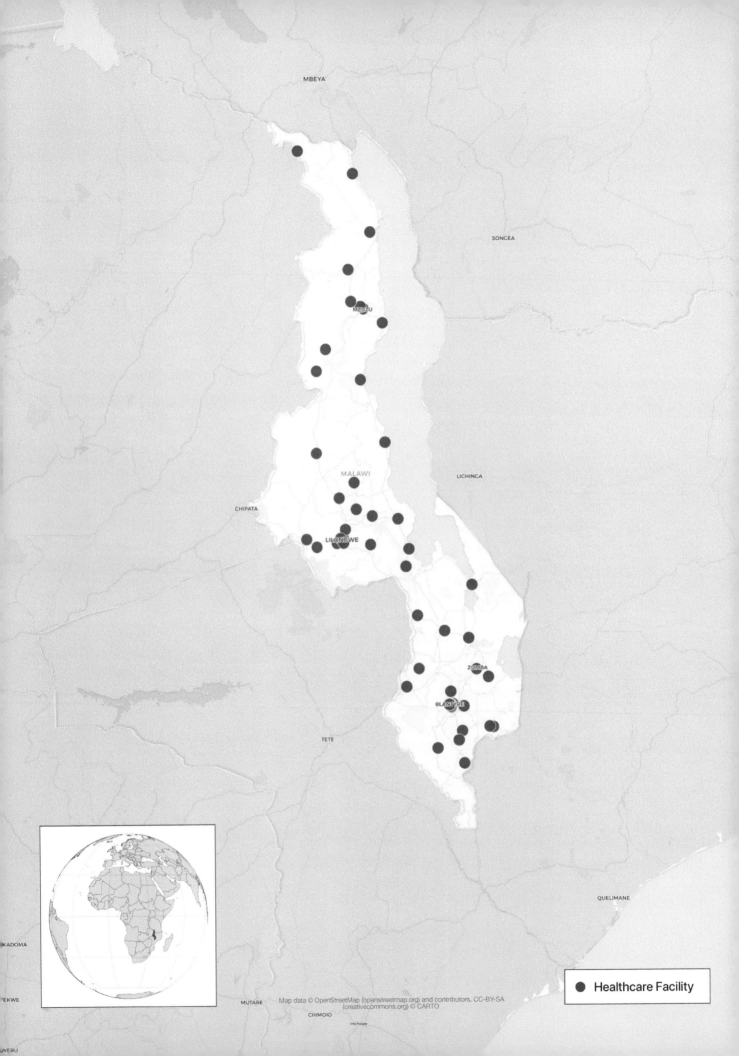

Healthcare Facility

Malawi

The Republic of Malawi, a landlocked country in Southern Africa, shares a border with Tanzania, Mozambique, and Zambia. Lake Nyasa, also known as Lake Malawi, takes up about a third of Malawi's area and is a UNESCO World Heritage Site. The country has a population of 20.3 million people, many of whom live in the highest-density, southern, rural parts of the country and close to Lake Nyasa. Most of the population is Christian and speak the Bantu languages of Chichewa, Chitumbuka, and Chiyao. English is the official language of Malawi.

Formerly a colony of Britain, Malawi is politically stable and has implemented structural and economic reforms to sustain growth. Agriculture is the primary employer for 80 percent of Malawi's people, with tobacco, sugar cane, tea, and corn among the biggest cash crops. Free primary education was made available in the mid-1990s, leading to increased school enrollment. As much as half of the population lives in poverty.

Despite the challenges that poverty presents, there has been an increase in life expectancy, from 40 years to around 64 years between 2000 and 2019. The diseases causing the most deaths in Malawi include HIV/AIDS, neonatal disorders, lower respiratory infections, tuberculosis, diarrheal diseases, and meningitis. Non-communicable diseases have notably increased to cause significant deaths as well, with marked increases in stroke, ischemic heart disease, and cirrhosis. Malawi's healthcare system might not be equipped to face some of these health challenges, as it is susceptible to shortages of supplies, drugs, and health workers. While Malawi initiated the Drug Revolving Funds to supply communities with medications at a discounted cost and has expanded training of health workers, the country is still in need of assistance.

20.3M

Population

$625

GDP Per Capita

64 years

Life Expectancy

↑ Improving

4
Doctors/100k

Physician Density

130
Beds/100k

Hospital Bed Density

349
Deaths/100k

Maternal Mortality

Malawi

Nonprofit Organizations

100X Development Foundation
Empowers children and families for a more hopeful and productive future through the support and care of orphaned children, education and job training for those in need, help for vulnerable youth to escape trafficking, and healthy nutrition and medical care for mothers to enable a safe birth.

ER Med, Infect Dis, OB-GYN, Peds, Psych

🌐 https://vfmat.ch/b629

143 LIFE Foundation
Seeks to educate and empower individuals living with malaria, TB, HIV/AIDS, STDs and other health disparities related to sexual health.

Infect Dis, MF Med

🌐 https://vfmat.ch/d59b

A Broader View Volunteers
Provides developing countries around the world with significant volunteer programs that aid the neediest communities and forge a lasting bond between those volunteering and those they have helped.

Dent-OMFS, ER Med, Infect Dis, MF Med

🌐 https://vfmat.ch/3bec

Access Health Africa
Provides surgical services to Malawi, operating on those who otherwise might not have access to surgical services.

CV Med, Dent-OMFS, Infect Dis, Ped Surg, Pulm-Critic, Surg

🌐 https://vfmat.ch/1b57

Accomplish Children's Trust
Provides education and medical care to children with disabilities. Also addresses the financial implications of caring for a child with disabilities by helping families to earn an income.

Neuro, Peds, Rehab

🌐 https://vfmat.ch/de84

Adventist Health International
Focuses on upgrading and managing mission hospitals by providing governance, consultation, and technical assistance to a number of affiliated Seventh-Day Adventist hospitals throughout Africa, Asia, and the Americas.

Dent-OMFS, General, Pub Health

🌐 https://vfmat.ch/16aa

Africa CDC
Aims to strengthen the capacity and capability of Africa's public health institutions and partnerships to detect and respond quickly and effectively to disease threats and outbreaks, based on data-driven interventions and programs.

Infect Dis, Logist-Op, Pub Health

🌐 https://vfmat.ch/339c

Africa Health Organisation
Leads collaborative efforts among countries in Africa and other partners to promote health equity, combat disease, and improve quality of life.

Logist-Op, Pub Health

🌐 https://vfmat.ch/b1c5

Africa Indoor Residual Spraying Project (AIRS)
Aims to protect millions of people in Africa from malaria by spraying insecticide on walls, ceilings, and other indoor resting places of mosquitoes that transmit malaria.

Infect Dis

🌐 https://vfmat.ch/9bd1

Africa Relief and Community Development
Provides comprehensive relief and developmental aid to people of the African continent regardless of gender, race, or religion.

Nutr, Pub Health

🌐 https://vfmat.ch/6cd2

African Field Epidemiology Network (AFENET)
Strengthens field epidemiology and public health laboratory capacity to contribute effectively to addressing epidemics and other major public health problems in Africa.

All-Immu, Infect Dis, Path, Pub Health

🌐 https://vfmat.ch/df2e

African Mission Health Foundation
Aims to strengthen African mission hospitals by providing quality, compassionate care for the hurting and forgotten and helping improve Sub-Saharan Africa's health system.

Infect Dis, Neonat, OB-GYN, Peds, Surg

🌐 https://vfmat.ch/5b14

African Vision
Strives to help children and vulnerable people of Malawi with the goal of creating a healthy, educated, and self-sufficient community.

Infect Dis, MF Med, Nutr, OB-GYN

🌐 https://vfmat.ch/be7f

Against Malaria Foundation
Helps protect people from malaria. Funds anti-malaria nets, specifically long-lasting insecticidal nets (LLINs), and works with distribution partners to ensure they are used. Tracks and reports on net use and malaria case data.

Infect Dis

🌐 https://vfmat.ch/337d

Age International
Helps older people living in some of the world's poorest places to have improved well-being and be treated with dignity through a variety of programs, including emergency relief and cataract surgery.

ER Med, Geri, Logist-Op, Nutr, Ophth-Opt, Palliative, Pub Health

🌐 https://vfmat.ch/c7e2

Aid Africa's Children
Aims to empower impoverished African children and communities with healthcare, food, clean water, and educational and entrepreneurial opportunities.
ER Med, General, Infect Dis, Nutr, OB-GYN, Palliative, Peds, Pub Health
⊕ https://vfmat.ch/5e2e

AIDS Healthcare Foundation
Provides cutting-edge HIV/AIDS medical care and advocacy to over one million people in 43 countries.
Infect Dis
⊕ https://vfmat.ch/b27c

Al Basar International Foundation
Works with local partners to treat preventable blindness, and helps set up sustainable infrastructure so local teams can save sight in their communities.
Ophth-Opt
⊕ https://vfmat.ch/a8b5

Al-Mustafa Welfare Trust
Seeks to alleviate poverty and provides medical and social development assistance to the poor and vulnerable around the world.
General, Ophth-Opt
⊕ https://vfmat.ch/c5f4

AMARI (African Mental Health Research Initiative)
Seeks to build an Africa-led network of future leaders in mental, neurological, and substance use (MNS) research in Ethiopia, Malawi, South Africa, and Zimbabwe.
Neuro, Psych
⊕ https://vfmat.ch/5e9d

Americares
Saves lives and improves health for people affected by poverty or disaster and responds with life-changing medicine, medical supplies, and health programs including domestic and global medical clinics.
All-Immu, ER Med, General, Infect Dis, MF Med, Nutr
⊕ https://vfmat.ch/e567

AMOR (Aide Mondiale Orphelins Reconfort)
Aims to contribute to significant reductions in global infant and maternal mortality rates by providing medical services to at-risk mothers and appropriate care for orphans.
Infect Dis, MF Med, Neonat, OB-GYN, Ophth-Opt, Ped Surg
⊕ https://vfmat.ch/98a4

Amref Health Africa
Serves millions of people across 35 countries in Sub-Saharan Africa, strengthening health systems, and training African health workers to respond to the continent's most critical health issues.
All-Immu, General, Infect Dis, Logist-Op, MF Med, OB-GYN, Path, Pub Health, Surg
⊕ https://vfmat.ch/6985

AO Alliance
Builds solutions to lessen the burden of injuries in low- and middle-income countries, while enhancing the care of the injured to reduce human suffering, disability, and poverty.
Ortho, Surg
⊕ https://vfmat.ch/8cd5

Aspen Management Partnership for Health (AMP Health)
Works to improve health systems and outcomes by collaborating with governments to strengthen leadership and management capabilities through public-private partnership.
Logist-Op
⊕ https://vfmat.ch/ea78

Avert
Works to ensure widespread understanding of HIV/AIDS in order to reduce new infections and improve the lives of those affected.
Infect Dis, Path
⊕ https://vfmat.ch/312d

Baylor College of Medicine: Global Surgery
Trains leaders in academic global surgery and remains dedicated to advancements in the areas of patient care, biomedical research, and medical education.
ENT, Infect Dis, OB-GYN, Ortho, Ped Surg, Plast, Pub Health, Radiol, Surg, Urol
⊕ https://vfmat.ch/21f5

Baylor International Pediatric AIDS Initiative (BIPAI) at Texas Children's Hospital
Provides high-quality, high-impact, highly ethical pediatric and family-centered healthcare, health professional training, and clinical research focused on HIV/AIDS, tuberculosis, malaria, malnutrition, and other conditions impacting the health of children worldwide.
Infect Dis, Medicine, OB-GYN, Peds, Pub Health, Surg
⊕ https://vfmat.ch/e6ba

Benjamin H. Josephson, MD Fund
Provides healthcare professionals with the financial resources necessary to deliver medical services for those in need throughout the world.
General, OB-GYN
⊕ https://vfmat.ch/6acc

Billy's Malawi Project
Works to improve the overall health status of the village of Cape Maclear (Chembe Village) through the provision of a medical clinic and health center, and also provides educational opportunities and support.
General, OB-GYN, Ophth-Opt, Peds
⊕ https://vfmat.ch/f787

Boston Children's Hospital: Global Health Program
Helps solve pediatric global healthcare challenges by transferring expertise through long-term partnerships with scalable impact, while working in the field to strengthen healthcare systems, advocate, research, and provide care delivery or education as a way of sustainably improving the health of children worldwide.
Anesth, CV Med, Crit-Care, ER Med, Heme-Onc, Infect Dis, Medicine, Nutr, Palliative, Ped Surg, Peds
⊕ https://vfmat.ch/f9f8

Bridges to Malawi
Aims to improve medical care in Malawi by recruiting healthcare specialists, providing supplies and medication, and promoting education.
General, Logist-Op, Pub Health
⊕ https://vfmat.ch/31cd

British Council for Prevention of Blindness (BCPB)
Funds research into blindness prevention and sight restoration in children and adults in low- and lower-middle-income countries.
Ophth-Opt
⊕ https://vfmat.ch/eaf4

Cairdeas International Palliative Care Trust
Promotes and facilitates the provision of high-quality palliative care in the developing world, where such care is limited.
Palliative
⊕ https://vfmat.ch/35c4

Called to go Chiropractic Missions
Provides chiropractic care and education to the people of Malawi.
⊕ https://vfmat.ch/afdb

Canadian Foundation for Women's Health
Seeks to advance the health of women in Canada and around the world through research, education, and advocacy in obstetrics and gynecology.
MF Med, OB-GYN
⊕ https://vfmat.ch/f41e

Canadian Vision Care
Consists of eye healthcare professionals who donate time and resources to the development of vision care in the developing world.
Ophth-Opt
⊕ https://vfmat.ch/3a38

CARE
Works around the globe to save lives, defeat poverty, and achieve social justice.
ER Med, General
⊕ https://vfmat.ch/7232

Caring Hands Worldwide
Inspired by the Christian faith, works to improve dental health of those in need in partner communities in the U.S. and abroad.
Dent-OMFS, Logist-Op
⊕ https://vfmat.ch/62cc

Carter Center, The
Seeks to prevent and resolve conflicts, enhance freedom and democracy, and improve health, while remaining committed to human rights and the alleviation of human suffering.
Infect Dis, MF Med, Ophth-Opt
⊕ https://vfmat.ch/6556

Catholic Health Commission
Implements health programs and provides health/nutrition care services in remote areas of the central region of Malawi. Provides equitable, sustainable, and quality healthcare to all targeted communities regardless of faith.
Anesth, Dent-OMFS, General, General, Infect Dis, MF Med, Medicine, Nutr, OB-GYN, Palliative, Peds, Surg
⊕ https://vfmat.ch/c786

Catholic World Mission
Works to rebuild communities worldwide by helping to alleviate poverty and empower underserved areas, while spreading the message of the Catholic Church.
ER Med, General, Nutr, Peds
⊕ https://vfmat.ch/7b5f

Center for Health and Hope
Supports and advocates for persons infected and affected by HIV/AIDS with programs of education, prevention, care, and treatment.
Pub Health
⊕ https://vfmat.ch/a52e

Center for Strategic and International Studies (CSIS) Commission on Strengthening America's Health Security
Brings together a distinguished and diverse group of high-level opinion leaders bridging security and health, with the core aim to chart a bold vision for the future of U.S. leadership in global health.
ER Med, Infect Dis, MF Med, Pub Health
⊕ https://vfmat.ch/6d7f

Centre for Global Mental Health
Closes the care gap and reduces human rights abuses experienced by people living with mental, neurological, and substance use conditions, particularly in low-resource settings.
Neuro, OB-GYN, Palliative, Peds, Psych
⊕ https://vfmat.ch/a96d

Chain of Hope
Provides lifesaving heart operations for children around the world and supports the development of cardiac services in numerous developing and war-torn countries.
Anesth, CT Surg, CV Med, Crit-Care, Ped Surg, Peds, Pulm-Critic, Surg
⊕ https://vfmat.ch/1b1b

Chikondi Health Foundation
Promotes spiritual and physical health through medical missions at Blessings Hospital in Lumbadzi, Malawi, and through the support of local churches.
Infect Dis, OB-GYN, Surg
⊕ https://vfmat.ch/9125

Child Legacy International
Works in Africa to transform lives by providing opportunities that break the generational cycle of poverty and despair, inspired by the Christian faith.
All-Immu, General, Heme-Onc, Surg
⊕ https://vfmat.ch/a2bd

Children of the Nations
Aims to raise children out of poverty and hopelessness so they can become leaders who transform their nations. Emphasizes caring for the whole child—physically, mentally, socially, and spiritually.
Anesth, Dent-OMFS, General, Surg
⊕ https://vfmat.ch/cc52

Children's Relief International
Inspired by the Christian faith, cares for and educates children, their families, and their communities, including the provision of select healthcare services.
ER Med, General, Nutr
⊕ https://vfmat.ch/8da6

Christian Aid Ministries
Strives to be a trustworthy and efficient channel for Amish, Mennonite, and other conservative Anabaptist groups and individuals to minister to physical and spiritual needs around the world.
CT Surg, ER Med, Logist-Op, Ortho, Pub Health
⊕ https://vfmat.ch/7b33

Christian Blind Mission (CBM)
Aims to improve the quality of life of persons with disabilities in the poorest countries, addressing poverty as a cause and a consequence of disability, and working in partnership to create a society for all.
ENT, General, Infect Dis, OB-GYN, Ophth-Opt, Ortho, Peds, Psych, Rehab, Surg
⊕ https://vfmat.ch/3824

Christian Connections for International Health (CCIH)
Promotes global health and wholeness from a Christian perspective.
All-Immu, General, Infect Dis, MF Med, Neonat, OB-GYN, Psych
⊕ https://vfmat.ch/fa5d

Christian Health Service Corps
Brings Christian doctors, health professionals, and health educators committed to serving the poor to places that otherwise have little or no access to healthcare.
Anesth, Dent-OMFS, General, Medicine, Peds, Surg
⊕ https://vfmat.ch/da57

Christian Medical & Dental Associations
Based in Christian ministry, deploys medical and dental teams to underserved communities to provide vital healthcare.
Anesth, Dent-OMFS, ER Med, General, Medicine, OB-GYN, Ophth-Opt, Peds, Pub Health, Radiol, Rehab, Surg
⊕ https://vfmat.ch/921c

Clinton Health Access Initiative (CHAI)
Aims to save lives and reduce the burden of disease in low- and middle-income countries. Works with partners to strengthen the capabilities of governments and the private sector to create and sustain high-quality health systems.
General, Heme-Onc, Infect Dis, Logist-Op, MF Med, Medicine, Neonat, Nutr, OB-GYN, Path, Peds, Rad-Onc
⊕ https://vfmat.ch/9ed7

Columbia University: Global Mental Health Programs
Pioneers research initiatives, promotes mental health, and aims to reduce the burden of mental illness worldwide.
Psych
⊕ https://vfmat.ch/c5cd

Columbia Vagelos College of Physicians and Surgeons Programs in Global Health
Harnesses the expertise of the medical school to improve health worldwide by training global health leaders, building capacity through interdisciplinary education and training programs, and addressing unmet health needs through research and application.
CV Med, Derm, Genetics, Heme-Onc, Infect Dis, Medicine, OB-GYN, Ophth-Opt, Peds, Psych, Pub Health, Pulm-Critic, Surg
⊕ https://vfmat.ch/a9e5

Concern Worldwide
Seeks to permanently transform the lives of people living in extreme poverty, tackling its root causes, and building resilience.
Logist-Op, MF Med, Nutr, OB-GYN
⊕ https://vfmat.ch/77e9

ConnectMed International
Improves access to sustainable healthcare in resource-limited communities through education, partnership, and research.
Dent-OMFS, Logist-Op, Ped Surg, Plast
🌐 https://vfmat.ch/ce88

Core Group
Aims to improve and expand community health practices for underserved populations, especially women and children, through collaborative action and learning.
General, Infect Dis, MF Med, Medicine, OB-GYN, Peds, Pub Health
🌐 https://vfmat.ch/9de3

COVID-19 Clinical Research Coalition
Advocates and collaborates for the advancement of COVID-19 research driven by the needs of low-resource settings, and works for equitable access to solutions to the pandemic.
All-Immu, Infect-Dis, MF Med, Path, Pub Health
🌐 https://vfmat.ch/d1f4

Cross Catholic Outreach
Mobilizes the global Catholic Church to transform impoverished communities through the provision of food, water, housing, education, orphan support, medical care, microenterprise, and disaster relief.
All-Immu, General, Nutr, OB-GYN, Rehab
🌐 https://vfmat.ch/22f4

CURE
Operates charitable hospitals and programs in underserved countries worldwide, where patients receive surgical treatment, based in Christian ministry.
Anesth, Neurosurg, Ortho, Ped Surg, Peds, Rehab, Surg
🌐 https://vfmat.ch/aa16

CURE Children's Hospital of Zimbabwe
Heals children living with disabilities such as clubfoot, bowed legs, cleft lips, untreated burns, and hydrocephalus.
ENT, Neurosurg, Ortho, Peds, Plast
🌐 https://vfmat.ch/473c

D-tree Digital Global Health
Demonstrates and advocates for the potential of digital technology to transform health systems and improve health and well-being for all.
Logist-Op, MF Med, OB-GYN, Peds, Pub Health
🌐 https://vfmat.ch/1f79

Dentaid
Seeks to treat, equip, train, and educate people in need of dental care.
Dent-OMFS
🌐 https://vfmat.ch/a183

Development Aid From People to People (DAPP)
Strives to promote social and economic development. Through a variety of development models, DAPP complements the government's effort in implementing the Malawi Growth and Development Strategy to achieve the global initiative Vision 2020 for the nation.
Infect Dis, Nutr, Path
🌐 https://vfmat.ch/f8c8

Direct Relief
Improves the health and lives of people affected by poverty or emergency situations by mobilizing and providing essential medical resources needed for their care.
ER Med, Logist-Op
🌐 https://vfmat.ch/58e5

Direct Relief of Poverty & Sickness Foundation (DROPS)
This volunteer-led organization uses all donations for direct relief of poverty and illness through initiatives in healthcare education, improving healthcare systems, and providing essential medical help to children and aged people in need.
Dent-OMFS, General, Ophth-Opt
🌐 https://vfmat.ch/af95

Doctors Without Borders/Médecins Sans Frontières (MSF)
Responds to emergencies and provides lifesaving medical care where needed most, including during disasters, conflicts, and epidemics.
Anesth, Crit-Care, ER Med, General, Infect Dis, Nutr, OB-GYN, Ped Surg, Peds, Psych, Pub Health, Surg
🌐 https://vfmat.ch/f363

Doctors Worldwide
Focuses on health access, health improvement, and health emergencies to serve communities in need so they can build healthier and happier futures.
Dent-OMFS, ER Med, General, MF Med, Palliative, Peds
🌐 https://vfmat.ch/99cd

Dream Sant'Egidio
Seeks to counter HIV/AIDS in Africa by eliminating the transmission of HIV from mother to child, with a focus on women because of the importance of their role in the community.
Infect Dis, MF Med, Neonat, OB-GYN, Path, Peds
🌐 https://vfmat.ch/f466

Drugs for Neglected Diseases Initiative
Develops lifesaving medicines for people with neglected diseases around the world, having developed eight treatments for five deadly diseases and saved millions of lives since 2003.
Infect Dis, Pub Health
🌐 https://vfmat.ch/969c

Egmont Trust, The
Works with partner organizations in Sub-Saharan Africa, making grants to help vulnerable children cope with the impact of HIV/AIDS on families and communities.
General, Infect Dis, OB-GYN, Peds
🌐 https://vfmat.ch/57a9

Elizabeth Glaser Pediatric AIDS Foundation
Seeks to end global pediatric HIV/AIDS through prevention and treatment programs, research, and advocacy.
Infect Dis, Nutr, OB-GYN, Peds
🌐 https://vfmat.ch/d6ec

Embangweni Mission Hospital
Promotes and provides holistic, accessible, and patient-centered care, inspired by the Christian faith. Serves patients from Malawi and Zambia, offering a broad range of services as the main healthcare provider in the Mzimba region of Malawi.
Anesth, Dent-OMFS, General, MF Med, Neonat, Ophth-Opt, Ortho, Path, Peds, Surg
🌐 https://vfmat.ch/b5ae

Episcopal Relief & Development
Provides relief in times of disaster and promotes sustainable development by identifying and addressing the root causes of suffering.
Infect Dis, MF Med, Neonat, Nutr, Peds
🌐 https://vfmat.ch/7cfa

eRanger
Provides sustainable solutions to transportation and medical provision such as ambulances and mobile clinics in developing countries.
ER Med, General, Logist-Op
🌐 https://vfmat.ch/4c18

Evidence Action
Aims to be a world leader in scaling evidence-based and cost-effective programs to reduce the burden of poverty.
General, Infect Dis
🌐 https://vfmat.ch/94b6

Eye Foundation of America
Works toward a world without childhood blindness.
Ophth-Opt
🌐 https://vfmat.ch/a7eb

Feet First Worldwide
Aims to prevent and correct clubfoot in Malawi so that every child is diagnosed

at birth and given access to surgical and other treatment. Also provides care for existing neglected cases, with an emphasis on training local staff in basic surgical techniques and clubfoot management.

Anesth, Ortho, Peds, Radiol, Rehab

⊕ https://vfmat.ch/f119

Freedom From Fistula

Helps women and girls who are injured and left incontinent following prolonged, obstructed childbirth by providing free surgical repairs for patients already suffering with obstetric fistula, as well as maternity care to prevent these fistulas from happening at all.

MF Med, OB-GYN, Peds

⊕ https://vfmat.ch/6e11

Global Alliance to Prevent Prematurity And Stillbirth (GAPPS)

Seeks to improve birth outcomes worldwide by reducing the burden of premature birth and stillbirth.

All-Immu, Infect Dis, MF Med, Neonat, Neonat, OB-GYN

⊕ https://vfmat.ch/3f74

Global Emergency Care Skills

Aims to provide high-quality emergency medical training to healthcare professionals in countries where emergency medicine is a developing specialty.

ER Med

⊕ https://vfmat.ch/1827

Global Health Corps

Mobilizes a diverse community of leaders to build the movement for global health equity, working toward a world in which every person lives a healthy life.

ER Med, General, Pub Health

⊕ https://vfmat.ch/31c6

Global Medical Missions

Organizes medical missions and partners with local medical organizations, usually hospitals or health systems, in fulfilling their mission of reaching their community's health needs in developing countries by providing needed medical care and screening to those underserved.

General

⊕ https://vfmat.ch/8d73

Global Ministries – The United Methodist Church

As the worldwide mission and development agency of The United Methodist Church, Global Ministries works with more than 300 hospitals and clinics around the world through its Global Health Unit.

Anesth, CT Surg, CV Med, Crit-Care, Dent-OMFS, Derm, ER Med, GI, General, Infect Dis, Logist-Op, MF Med, Medicine, Neonat, Nephro, Nutr, OB-GYN, Ophth-Opt, Ortho, Palliative, Peds, Pod, Psych, Pub Health, Rehab, Rheum, Surg, Urol

⊕ https://vfmat.ch/1723

Global Oncology (GO)

Brings the best in cancer care to underserved patients around the world and collaborates across geographic, professional, and academic borders to improve cancer care, research, and education.

Heme-Onc, Path, Rad-Onc

⊕ https://vfmat.ch/fcb8

Global Partners in Care

Works with partner organizations, national associations, and international organizations to enhance access to hospice and palliative care around the world.

Palliative

⊕ https://vfmat.ch/a815

Global Reconstructive Surgery Outreach

Supports surgeons, doctors, and nurses financially to enable them to provide critically needed plastic and reconstructive surgeries to the poor.

Logist-Op, Surg

⊕ https://vfmat.ch/f262

Global Vision 2020

Provides prescription eyeglasses to people who live in parts of the world lacking necessary infrastructure for obtaining affordable corrective eyewear.

Logist-Op, Ophth-Opt

⊕ https://vfmat.ch/7373

GlobalMedic

Provides disaster relief and lifesaving humanitarian aid.

ER Med, Pub Health

⊕ https://vfmat.ch/dfe6

Globus Relief

Aims to improve the delivery of healthcare worldwide by gathering, processing, and distributing surplus medical supplies to charities at home and abroad.

Logist-Op

⊕ https://vfmat.ch/a2b7

GOAL

Works with the most vulnerable communities to help them respond to and recover from humanitarian crises, and to assist them in building transcendent solutions to mitigate poverty and vulnerability.

ER Med, General, Pub Health

⊕ https://vfmat.ch/bbea

Grassroot Soccer

Leverages the power of soccer to educate, inspire, and mobilize at-risk youth in developing countries to overcome their greatest health challenges, live healthier and more productive lives, and be agents for change in their communities.

Infect Dis

⊕ https://vfmat.ch/3521

Hands At Work

Based in Christian ministry, supports those in need through its community intervention model with a focus on food security, education, and basic healthcare.

General, Infect Dis, Nutr, Pub Health

⊕ https://vfmat.ch/7274

Health Equity Initiative

Aims to build and sustain a global community that engages across sectors and disciplines to advance health equity.

Pub Health

⊕ https://vfmat.ch/e2e2

Health Poverty Action

Works in partnership with people around the world who are pursuing change in their own communities to demand health justice and challenge power imbalances.

ER Med, General, Infect Dis, Psych, Pub Health

⊕ https://vfmat.ch/ee58

Health Volunteers Overseas (HVO)

Improves the availability and quality of healthcare through the education, training, and professional development of the health workforce in resource-scarce countries.

All-Immu, Anesth, CV Med, Dent-OMFS, Derm, ENT, ER Med, Endo, GI, Heme-Onc, Infect Dis, Medicine, Medicine, Nephro, Neuro, OB-GYN, Ophth-Opt, Ortho, Peds, Plast, Psych, Pulm-Critic, Rehab, Rheum, Surg

⊕ https://vfmat.ch/42b2

Healthy DEvelopments

Provides Germany-supported health and social protection programs around the globe in a collaborative knowledge management process.

All-Immu, General, Infect Dis, Logist-Op, MF Med

⊕ https://vfmat.ch/dc31

Hear the World Foundation

Advocates worldwide for equal opportunities and improved quality of life for people in need with hearing loss.

ENT, Peds

⊕ https://vfmat.ch/122c

Hearing Health Foundation

Prevents and cures hearing loss and tinnitus through groundbreaking research and promotes hearing health.

Surg

⊕ https://vfmat.ch/2e71

Heart to Heart International

Strengthens communities through improving health access, providing humanitarian development, and administering crisis relief worldwide. Engages volunteers, collaborates with partners, and deploys resources to achieve this mission.

Anesth, ER Med, General, Logist-Op, Medicine, Path, Path, Peds, Psych, Pub Health, Surg

⊕ https://vfmat.ch/aacb

Hernia International
Aims to provide relief from sickness, and protection and preservation of health, for persons affected by groin and abdominal hernias and residing in low- and middle-income countries.

Surg

⊕ https://vfmat.ch/e98e

Hope and Healing International
Gives hope and healing to children and families trapped by poverty and disability.

General, Nutr, Ophth-Opt, Peds, Rehab

⊕ https://vfmat.ch/c638

Hope Walks
Frees children, families, and communities from the burden of clubfoot, inspired by the Christian faith.

Ortho, Ped Surg, Peds, Rehab

⊕ https://vfmat.ch/f6d4

Hospice Africa
Aims to provide a holistic and culturally sensitive palliative care service through accurate treatment of pain.

Palliative

⊕ https://vfmat.ch/9f86

Hunger Project, The
Aims to end hunger and poverty by pioneering sustainable, grassroots, women-centered strategies and advocating for their widespread adoption in countries throughout the world.

Infect Dis, Nutr, OB-GYN, Pub Health

⊕ https://vfmat.ch/3a49

ICAP at Columbia University
Serves as global leader in supporting the scale-up of multidisciplinary HIV/AIDS prevention, care, and treatment programs based on a family-focused approach.

General, Infect Dis, MF Med, Medicine, OB-GYN, Pub Health

⊕ https://vfmat.ch/a8ef

Imaging the World
Develops sustainable models for ultrasound imaging in the world's lowest resource settings and uses a technology-enabled solution to improve healthcare access, integrating lifesaving ultrasound and training programs in rural communities.

Logist-Op, OB-GYN, Radiol

⊕ https://vfmat.ch/59e4

Innovating Health International (IHI)
Treats chronic diseases and addresses women's health issues in Haiti, Somaliland, and Malawi.

ER Med, Heme-Onc, Medicine, OB-GYN, Path, Plast, Pub Health

⊕ https://vfmat.ch/e712

Institute for Healthcare Improvement (IHI)
Aims to improve health and healthcare worldwide by working with health professionals to strengthen systems.

Crit-Care, Infect Dis, MF Med, Medicine, Neonat, OB-GYN, Pub Health

⊕ https://vfmat.ch/ecae

Inter Care Medical and for Africa
Provides targeted medical aid to rural health units in some of the poorest parts of Africa.

Logist-Op

⊕ https://vfmat.ch/64fb

International Agency for the Prevention of Blindness (IAPB), The
Leads international efforts in blindness-prevention activities, works toward a world where no one is needlessly visually impaired, and ensures that everyone has access to the best possible standard of eye health.

Infect Dis, Ophth-Opt, Pub Health

⊕ https://vfmat.ch/87a2

International Campaign for Women's Right to Safe Abortion
Works to build an international network and campaign that brings together organizations with an interest in promoting and providing safe abortion to create a shared platform for advocacy, debate, and dialogue and the sharing of skills and experience.

OB-GYN, Pub Health, Surg

⊕ https://vfmat.ch/f341

International Council of Ophthalmology
Works with ophthalmologic societies and others to enhance ophthalmic education and improve access to the highest-quality eye care in order to preserve and restore vision for people of the world.

Ophth-Opt

⊕ https://vfmat.ch/ffd2

International Eye Foundation (IEF)
Eliminates preventable and treatable blindness by making quality sustainable eye care services accessible and affordable worldwide.

Infect Dis, Logist-Op, Ophth-Opt

⊕ https://vfmat.ch/e839

International Federation of Gynecology and Obstetrics (FIGO)
Implements global projects on specific women's health issues.

MF Med, Medicine, Neonat, OB-GYN, Surg, Urol

⊕ https://vfmat.ch/c4b4

International Federation of Red Cross and Red Crescent Societies (IFRC)
Coordinates and directs international assistance following natural and manmade disasters in nonconflict situations through the world's largest humanitarian and development network. Provides disaster-preparedness programs, healthcare activities, and promotes humanitarian values.

ER Med, General, Infect Dis, Nutr

⊕ https://vfmat.ch/b4ee

International Hearing Foundation
Supports hearing-related service, education, and research.

ENT, Surg

⊕ https://vfmat.ch/3ee2

International Learning Movement (ILM UK)
Supports some of the world's poorest people in developing countries with core projects in education, safe drinking water, and healthcare.

General, Ophth-Opt

⊕ https://vfmat.ch/b974

International Medical Response
Supplements, supports, and enhances healthcare systems in communities across the world that have been incapacitated by natural disaster, extreme poverty, and/or regional conflict by sending a multidisciplinary team of healthcare professionals.

Anesth, General, OB-GYN, Surg

⊕ https://vfmat.ch/9ccd

International Organization for Migration (IOM) – The UN Migration Agency
Promotes evidence-informed policies and holistic, preventive, and curative health programs that are beneficial, accessible, and equitable for vulnerable migrants.

General, Infect Dis, OB-GYN

⊕ https://vfmat.ch/621a

International Pediatric Nephrology Association (IPNA)
Leads global efforts to successfully address the care for all children with kidney disease through advocacy, education, and training.

Medicine, Nephro, Peds

⊕ https://vfmat.ch/b59d

International Planned Parenthood Federation (IPPF)
Leads a locally owned, globally connected civil society movement that provides

and enables services and champions sexual and reproductive health and rights for all, especially the underserved.

Infect Dis, MF Med, OB-GYN

⊕ https://vfmat.ch/dc97

International Relief Teams

Helps families survive and recover after a disaster by delivering timely and effective assistance through programs that improve their health and well-being while also providing a hopeful future for underserved communities.

Dent-OMFS, ER Med, General, Nutr, Ophth-Opt

⊕ https://vfmat.ch/ffd5

International Society of Nephrology

Aims to advance worldwide kidney health.

Nephro

⊕ https://vfmat.ch/1bae

International Trachoma Initiative (iTi)

Works toward a world free from trachoma, a preventable cause of blindness, and provides comprehensive support to national ministries of health and governmental and nongovernmental organizations to implement a comprehensive approach to fight trachoma.

Infect Dis, Ophth-Opt

⊕ https://vfmat.ch/3278

International Union Against Tuberculosis and Lung Disease

Develops, implements, and assesses anti-tuberculosis, lung health, and noncommunicable disease programs.

Infect Dis, Pub Health, Pulm-Critic

⊕ https://vfmat.ch/3e82

InterSurgeon

Fosters collaborative partnerships in the field of global surgery that will advance clinical care, teaching, training, research, and the provision and maintenance of medical equipment.

ENT, Neurosurg, Ortho, Ped Surg, Plast, Surg, Urol

⊕ https://vfmat.ch/6f8a

Ipas

Focuses efforts on women and girls who want contraception or abortion, and builds programs around their needs and how best to support them.

OB-GYN

⊕ https://vfmat.ch/8e39

Iris Global

Serves the poor, the destitute, the lost, and the forgotten by providing adoration, outreach, family, education, relief, development, healing, and the arts.

General, Infect Dis, Nutr, Pub Health

⊕ https://vfmat.ch/37f8

Islamic Medical Association of North America

Fosters health promotion, disease prevention, and health maintenance in communities around the world through direct patient care and health programs.

Anesth, Dent-OMFS, ER Med, General, Logist-Op, Ophth-Opt, Peds, Plast, Surg

⊕ https://vfmat.ch/a157

Izumi Foundation

Develops and supports programs that improve health and healthcare in neglected regions of Africa and Latin America.

⊕ https://vfmat.ch/f29a

Jacaranda Foundation

Provides orphans and vulnerable children in Malawi with education, comprehensive care, and enrichment programs to enable them to become leaders and change agents in their communities.

Nutr, Peds, Rehab

⊕ https://vfmat.ch/acf4

Jhpiego

Creates and delivers transformative healthcare solutions that save lives, in partnership with national governments, health experts, and local communities.

General, Infect Dis, OB-GYN, Surg

⊕ https://vfmat.ch/45b8

John Snow, Inc. (JSI)

Aims to improve the health and well-being of underserved and vulnerable people and communities throughout the world.

General, Infect Dis, Logist-Op, MF Med, OB-GYN, Peds, Psych, Pub Health

⊕ https://vfmat.ch/ba78

Johns Hopkins Center for Communication Programs

Believes in the power of communication to save lives by empowering people to adopt healthy behaviors for themselves, their families, and their communities.

General, Infect Dis, Logist-Op, OB-GYN, Pub Health

⊕ https://vfmat.ch/1bf9

Joint United Nations Programme on HIV/AIDS (UNAIDS)

Aims to place people living with HIV and people affected by the virus at the decision-making table and at the center of designing, delivering, and monitoring the AIDS response.

Infect Dis

⊕ https://vfmat.ch/464a

Kansas University Medical Center: Global Surgery

Improves the lives and communities in Kansas and beyond through innovation in education, research and healthcare.

Neurosurg, Ortho, Ped Surg, Surg, Urol

⊕ https://vfmat.ch/bc97

Last Mile Health

Links community health workers with frontline health workers—nurses, doctors, and midwives at community clinics—and supports them to bring lifesaving services to the doorsteps of people living far from care.

General, Logist-Op, OB-GYN, Pub Health

⊕ https://vfmat.ch/37da

Life Support Foundation

Aims to prevent deaths due to acute, life-threatening conditions in low-income countries through improving the access to, and quality of, basic lifesaving interventions.

Anesth, Crit-Care, ER Med, OB-GYN, Peds

⊕ https://vfmat.ch/799e

LifeCare Malawi Foundation (LCMF)

Inspired by faith, aims to fight for the survival and personal development of Malawi's most vulnerable and disadvantaged citizens, regardless of their tribal, religious, or political affiliation.

General, Infect Dis, MF Med, Nutr

⊕ https://vfmat.ch/839f

LifeNet International

Transforms African healthcare by equipping and empowering existing local health centers to provide quality, sustainable, and lifesaving care to patients.

General, Infect Dis, MF Med, Neonat, OB-GYN, Pub Health

⊕ https://vfmat.ch/e5d2

Lighthouse Trust

Provides improved quality treatment, care, and support services for people living with HIV in Malawi.

General, Infect Dis

⊕ https://vfmat.ch/fbd1

Lions Clubs International

Empowers volunteers to serve their communities, meet humanitarian needs, encourage peace, and promote international understanding through Lions Clubs.

Heme-Onc, Medicine, Nutr, Ophth-Opt

⊕ https://vfmat.ch/7b12

Loma Linda University Health

Faith-based organization that aims to provide a stimulating clinical and research environment for the delivery of healthcare and the education of physicians, nurses, and other health professionals.

All-Immu, Anesth, CT Surg, CV Med, Crit-Care, Dent-OMFS, Derm, ENT, ER Med, Endo, GI, General, Genetics, Geri, Heme-Onc, Infect Dis, Logist-Op, MF Med, Medicine, Neonat, Nephro, Neuro, Neurosurg, Nutr, OB-GYN, Ophth-Opt, Ortho, Palliative, Path, Ped Surg, Peds, Plast, Pod, Psych, Pub Health, Pulm-Critic, Rad-

Onc, Radiol, Rehab, Rheum, Surg, Urol, Vasc Surg
⊕ https://vfmat.ch/f5cb

London School of Hygiene & Tropical Medicine: International Centre for Eye Health
Works to improve eye health and eliminate avoidable visual impairment and blindness with a focus on low-income populations.
Logist-Op, Ophth-Opt, Pub Health
⊕ https://vfmat.ch/6f5f

Love Support Unite
Empowers people to become self-sufficient—with a hand up rather than a handout—and lifts communities out of the cycle of poverty into a cycle of sustainability through community-based projects that integrate education, enterprise, nutrition, and health.
General, Infect Dis, Logist-Op, MF Med, Nutr, Pub Health
⊕ https://vfmat.ch/5378

Luke International (LIN)
Builds bridges between local and international development partners, creates interfaces between health and technology, and advocates and serves where the greatest needs are.
General, Infect Dis, OB-GYN, Peds, Pub Health
⊕ https://vfmat.ch/4681

Malawi AIDS Counseling and Resource Organization (MACRO MW)
Provides high-quality HIV/AIDS treatment and other health-related services to the Malawian population.
Infect Dis, Psych, Pub Health
⊕ https://vfmat.ch/6138

Malawi Children's Initiative
Works to improve the lives of Malawian children through better healthcare, education, and nutrition by building bridges between communities in the United States and Malawi.
General, Logist-Op, Nutr, Peds
⊕ https://vfmat.ch/e9a9

Malawi Healthcare Support UK (MAHECAS UK)
Aims to provide relief and preserve good health among patients in hospitals, health clinics, and other primary healthcare locations across Malawi.
Dent-OMFS, General
⊕ https://vfmat.ch/7b2a

Malawi Stroke Unit
Aims to build and run the first integrated stroke pathway in Malawi, based at Queen Elizabeth Central Hospital, Malawi, and demonstrate substantial improvement in stroke-related mortality and long-term disability while reducing stroke care costs.
CV Med, Neuro, Rehab, Vasc Surg
⊕ https://vfmat.ch/97ba

Malawi Washington Foundation
Aims to improve and strengthen the lives of vulnerable communities through the provision of charitable educational services and support of sustainable programs for the poor, especially women and youth.
Logist-Op
⊕ https://vfmat.ch/7d2a

Maloto
Seeks to transform the lives of vulnerable populations in Malawi living in extreme poverty and provide women and children with the opportunity to reach their full potential in an actively sustainable way.
Nutr
⊕ https://vfmat.ch/f56a

Management Sciences for Health (MSH)
Works with countries and communities to save lives and improve the health of the world's poorest and most vulnerable people by building strong, resilient, sustainable health systems.
Infect Dis, Logist-Op, Pub Health
⊕ https://vfmat.ch/6aa2

MAP International
Provides medicines and health supplies to those in need around the world so they might experience life to the fullest.
Logist-Op
⊕ https://vfmat.ch/deed

Marie Stopes International
Provides the contraception and safe abortion services that enable women all over the world to choose their own futures.
Infect Dis, MF Med, Neonat, OB-GYN, Pub Health
⊕ https://vfmat.ch/9525

Maternity Worldwide
Works with communities and partners to identify and develop appropriate and effective ways to reduce maternal and newborn mortality and morbidity, facilitate communities to access quality skilled maternity care, and support the provision of quality skilled care.
MF Med, OB-GYN
⊕ https://vfmat.ch/822b

Medic Malawi
Provides quality, accessible, sustainable healthcare through partnership with St. Andrew's Hospital and aims to create a safe, loving, supportive, and sustainable environment for the children of Malawi.
Peds
⊕ https://vfmat.ch/1c83

Medical Benevolence Foundation (MBF)
Works with partners in developing countries to build sustainable healthcare for those most in need through faith-based global medical missions.
General, Logist-Op, MF Med, OB-GYN, Surg
⊕ https://vfmat.ch/c3e8

Medical Care Development International
Works to improve the health of vulnerable populations through integrated, sustainable, and locally driven interventions.
Infect Dis, OB-GYN, Peds, Pub Health
⊕ https://vfmat.ch/da87

Medical Ministry International
Provides compassionate healthcare in areas of need, inspired by the Christian faith.
CT Surg, Dent-OMFS, ENT, General, OB-GYN, Ophth-Opt, Ortho, Plast, Rehab, Surg, Urol, Vasc Surg
⊕ https://vfmat.ch/5da6

Medical Servants International
Provides medical care inspired by the Christian faith.
Dent-OMFS, General, OB-GYN, Peds
⊕ https://vfmat.ch/6371

MedSend
Funds qualified healthcare professionals to serve the physical and spiritual needs of people around the world, enabling healthcare providers to work where they have been called.
General
⊕ https://vfmat.ch/661c

MedShare
Aims to improve the quality of life of people, communities, and the planet by sourcing and directly delivering surplus medical supplies and equipment to communities in need around the world.
Logist-Op
⊕ https://vfmat.ch/c8bc

Mercy and Love Foundation
Aims to provide orphaned and vulnerable children with basic human needs such as food, clothing, and shelter, enabling them to thrive.
General, Peds
⊕ https://vfmat.ch/649a

MicroResearch: Africa/Asia
Seeks to improve health outcomes in Africa by training, mentoring, and supporting

local multidisciplinary health professional researchers.
Infect Dis, Nutr, OB-GYN, Psych
⊕ https://vfmat.ch/13e7

Midland International Aid Trust
Provides food, goods, clothing, and equipment to those in financial need or who are suffering as a result of a disaster.
CT Surg, Dent-OMFS, ENT, Logist-Op, OB-GYN, Ophth-Opt, Ortho, Ped Surg, Plast, Pub Health, Rehab
⊕ https://vfmat.ch/7eb2

Miracle for Africa Foundation
Works to end poverty in Malawi by building programs focused on health, education, and agriculture.
Crit-Care, ER Med, General, MF Med, Path, Radiol, Surg
⊕ https://vfmat.ch/b1e3

Mission Doctors Association
Provides life-saving medical care for the poor and training for local healthcare professionals around the world.
CV Med, Dent-OMFS, General, Logist-Op, Medicine, OB-GYN, Ophth-Opt, Peds, Surg
⊕ https://vfmat.ch/6c18

Mission Regan
Collects supplies, medication, and medical equipment and provides them to those who are in desperate need, both locally and globally.
Logist-Op
⊕ https://vfmat.ch/2bc1

Mission Vision
Seeks to decrease blindness and other eye-related disabilities, and to increase academic performance and general quality of life.
Ophth-Opt
⊕ https://vfmat.ch/83d8

mothers2mothers (m2m)
Employs and trains local women living with HIV as community health workers called Mentor Mothers to support women, children, and adolescents with vital medical services, education, and support.
Infect Dis, MF Med, OB-GYN, Peds, Pub Health
⊕ https://vfmat.ch/6557

MSD for Mothers
Designs scalable solutions that help end preventable maternal deaths.
MF Med, OB-GYN, Pub Health
⊕ https://vfmat.ch/9f99

MSI Reproductive Choices (Marie Stopes International)
Seeks to deliver quality family planning and reproductive healthcare to women around the world.
MF Med
⊕ https://vfmat.ch/5c82

Mua Mission Hospital
Works to provide affordable and quality healthcare services to all people in Bwanje Valley and beyond, serving as the principal referral hospital within a poor and remote rural area with a population of more than 130,000 people.
Dent-OMFS, General, Infect Dis, MF Med, Peds, Pub Health, Surg
⊕ https://vfmat.ch/ae41

Mulanje Mission Hospital
Works with a local government hospital to serve a population of 685,000 people in the Mulanje District of southeast Malawi.
General, Infect Dis, MF Med, OB-GYN, Peds, Pub Health, Surg
⊕ https://vfmat.ch/9212

Mustard Seed Communities (MSC)
Inspired by the Christian faith, uplifts the most vulnerable members of society through nutrition, education, community development, child health, and sustainable agriculture programs.
Infect Dis, Logist-Op, Rehab
⊕ https://vfmat.ch/eac5

NCD Alliance
Unites and strengthens civil society to stimulate collaborative advocacy, action, and accountability for NCD (noncommunicable disease) prevention and control.
All-Immu, CV Med, General, Heme-Onc, Medicine, Peds, Psych
⊕ https://vfmat.ch/abdd

Ndi Moyo: The Place Giving Life
Provides patient-centered, home-based palliative care for sick and dying people in Salima, Malawi.
General, Heme-Onc, Palliative
⊕ https://vfmat.ch/745e

NEST 360
Works to ensure that hospitals in Africa can deliver lifesaving care for small and sick newborns, by developing and distributing high-quality technologies and services.
MF Med, Neonat, Peds, Pub Health
⊕ https://vfmat.ch/cea9

Network for Improving Critical Care Systems and Training (NICST)
Provides critical-care training for staff in developing countries.
Crit-Care, General, Pulm-Critic
⊕ https://vfmat.ch/71f8

Nordic Network for Global Surgery and Anesthesia, The
Advocates for universal access to safe, affordable surgical, obstetric, and anesthesia care when needed.
Anesth, OB-GYN, Surg
⊕ https://vfmat.ch/ae66

NYC Medics
Deploys mobile medical teams to remote areas of disaster zones and humanitarian emergencies, providing the highest level of medical care to those who otherwise would not have access to aid and relief efforts.
All-Immu, ER Med, Infect Dis, Surg
⊕ https://vfmat.ch/aeee

OB Foundation
Works in partnership globally to deliver locally sustainable, quality healthcare, health education, and health solutions to medically underserved, rural communities.
General
⊕ https://vfmat.ch/91d7

Operation Medical
Commits efforts to promoting and providing high-quality medical care and education to communities that do not have adequate access.
Anesth, ENT, Logist-Op, OB-GYN, Ped Surg, Plast, Surg, Urol
⊕ https://vfmat.ch/7e1b

Operation Smile
Treats patients with cleft lip and cleft palate, and creates solutions that deliver safe surgery to people where it's needed most.
Anesth, Dent-OMFS, ENT, Ped Surg, Plast
⊕ https://vfmat.ch/5c29

Options
Believes in a world in which women and children can access the high-quality health services they need, without financial burden.
Logist-Op, MF Med, Neonat, OB-GYN
⊕ https://vfmat.ch/3a48

Optivest Foundation
Funds strategic opportunities that are holistic and collaborative, inspired by the Christian faith.
General, Nutr
⊕ https://vfmat.ch/f1e6

Optometry Giving Sight
Delivers eye exams and low or no-cost glasses, provides training for local eye care professionals, and establishes optometry schools, vision centers and optical labs.

Ophth-Opt
⊕ https://vfmat.ch/33ea

Orbis International
Works to prevent and treat blindness through hands-on training and improved access to quality eye care.
Anesth, Ophth-Opt, Surg
⊕ https://vfmat.ch/f2b2

Oxford University Global Surgery Group (OUGSG)
Aims to contribute to the provision of high-quality surgical care globally, particularly in low- and middle-income countries (LMICs), while bringing together students, researchers, and clinicians with an interest in global surgery, anesthesia, and obstetrics and gynecology.
Anesth, MF Med, OB-GYN, Ortho, Surg
⊕ https://vfmat.ch/c624

PACHI Trust (Parent and Child Health Initiative)
Promotes high-quality, sustainable, and cost-effective maternal and child care delivery, capacity building, and research that promotes the health of families in Malawi and beyond.
MF Med, Neonat, OB-GYN, Peds, Pub Health
⊕ https://vfmat.ch/c49c

Pact
Works on the ground to improve the lives of those who are challenged by poverty and marginalization, striving for a world in which all people are heard, capable, and vibrant.
Infect Dis, Logist-Op, MF Med, Pub Health
⊕ https://vfmat.ch/9a6c

Pan African Thoracic Society (PATS)
Aims to promote lung health in Africa, the continent most afflicted by morbidity and death from respiratory diseases, by promoting education, research, advocacy, optimal care, and the development of African capacity to address respiratory challenges in the continent.
CV Med, Crit-Care, Pulm-Critic
⊕ https://vfmat.ch/5457

Pan-African Academy of Christian Surgeons (PAACS)
Aims to train and disciple African surgeons and related specialists to become leaders and servants, providing excellent and compassionate care to those most in need, based in Christian ministry.
Anesth, CT Surg, OB-GYN, Ortho, Ped Surg, Plast, Surg
⊕ https://vfmat.ch/b444

Pan-African Academy of Christian Surgeons (PAACS)
Exists to train and support African surgeons to provide excellent, compassionate care to those most in need, inspired by the Christian faith.
Anesth, CT Surg, Neurosurg, OB-GYN, Ortho, Ped Surg, Plast, Surg
⊕ https://vfmat.ch/85ba

Partners in Health
Responds to the moral imperative to provide high-quality healthcare globally to those who need it most, while striving to ease suffering by providing a comprehensive model of care that includes access to food, transportation, housing, and other key components of healing.
CT Surg, General, Heme-Onc, Infect Dis, MF Med, Neurosurg, OB-GYN, Ortho, Plast, Psych, Urol
⊕ https://vfmat.ch/dc9c

Partners in Hope
Aims to strengthen the capacity of Malawi's healthcare system to deliver quality, equitable, and sustainable services.
ER Med, General, Infect Dis, Nutr, Path, Radiol, Rehab, Surg
⊕ https://vfmat.ch/2a75

PATH
Advances health equity through innovation and partnerships so people, communities, and economies can thrive.
All-Immu, CV Med, Endo, Heme-Onc, Infect Dis, MF Med, Neonat, Nutr, OB-GYN, Path, Peds, Pulm-Critic
⊕ https://vfmat.ch/b4db

Pediatric Health Initiative
Supports the spread of quality pediatric care and its development and progress in low- and middle-income countries.
ER Med, Infect Dis, Neonat, Palliative, Ped Surg, Peds
⊕ https://vfmat.ch/614b

Physicians for Peace
Educates and empowers local providers of surgical care to alleviate suffering and transform lives in under-resourced communities around the world.
Crit-Care, Ped Surg, Plast, Psych, Surg, Urol
⊕ https://vfmat.ch/6a65

PINCC Preventing Cervical Cancer
Seeks to prevent female-specific diseases in developing countries by utilizing low-cost and low-technology methods to create sustainable programs through patient education, medical personnel training, and facility outfitting.
OB-GYN
⊕ https://vfmat.ch/9666

Project Concern International (PCI)
Drives innovation from the ground up to enhance health, end hunger, overcome hardship, and advance women and girls—resulting in meaningful and measurable change in people's lives.
Infect Dis, MF Med, Nutr, OB-GYN, Peds
⊕ https://vfmat.ch/5ed7

Project HOPE
Works on the front lines of the world's health challenges, partnering hand-in-hand with communities, healthcare workers, and public health systems to ensure sustainable change.
CV Med, ER Med, Endo, General, Infect Dis, MF Med, Peds
⊕ https://vfmat.ch/2bd7

Project SOAR
Conducts HIV operations research around the world to identify practical solutions to improve HIV prevention, care, and treatment services.
ER Med, General, MF Med, OB-GYN, Psych
⊕ https://vfmat.ch/1a77

PSI – Population Services International
Aims to improve the health of people in the developing world by focusing on challenges such as a lack of family planning, HIV/AIDS, barriers to maternal health, and the greatest threats to children under the age of 5, including malaria, diarrhea, pneumonia, and malnutrition.
Infect Dis, MF Med, OB-GYN, Peds
⊕ https://vfmat.ch/ffe3

RAD-AID International
Improves and optimizes access to medical imaging and radiology in low-resource regions of the world.
Rad-Onc, Radiol
⊕ https://vfmat.ch/537f

Raising Malawi
Supports community-based organizations that provide Malawi's orphans, vulnerable children, and their caregivers with education, medical care, food and shelter, and psycho-social support.
Crit-Care, General, Infect Dis, Ped Surg, Peds, Pub Health, Surg
⊕ https://vfmat.ch/34c3

RestoringVision
Empowers lives by restoring vision for millions of people in need.
Ophth-Opt
⊕ https://vfmat.ch/e121

Rice 360 Institute for Global Health
Brings together an international group of faculty, students, clinicians, and private- and public-sector partners to design innovative health technologies for low-resource settings, while developing and implementing entrepreneurial approaches that increase access to these technologies around the world.
Crit-Care, Infect Dis, Logist-Op, MF Med, Neonat, Pub Health
⊕ https://vfmat.ch/c82b

Riders for Health
Strives to ensure that reliable transport is available for healthcare services.
Logist-Op
⊕ https://vfmat.ch/7353

Riders for Health International
Aids in the last mile of healthcare delivery, by ensuring that healthcare reaches everyone, everywhere.
ER Med, Infect Dis, Logist-Op, Pub Health
⊕ https://vfmat.ch/85aa

Right to Care
Responds to public health needs by supporting and delivering innovative, quality healthcare solutions, based on the latest medical research and established best practices, for the prevention, treatment, and management of infectious and chronic diseases.
ER Med, Infect Dis, Logist-Op
⊕ https://vfmat.ch/3383

Ripple Africa
Empowers communities to achieve a sustainable future by providing a hand up, not a handout, by developing programs in such areas as the environment, education, and healthcare.
General, Infect Dis, OB-GYN, Ortho, Pub Health, Rehab
⊕ https://vfmat.ch/63bb

Rockefeller Foundation, The
Works to promote the well-being of humanity.
Logist-Op, Nutr, Pub Health
⊕ https://vfmat.ch/5424

Rotary International
Provides service to others, improves lives, and advances world understanding, goodwill, and peace through its fellowship of business, professional, and community leaders.
ER Med, General, Infect Dis, MF Med, OB-GYN
⊕ https://vfmat.ch/8fb5

ROW Foundation
Works to improve the quality of training for healthcare providers, and the diagnosis and treatment available to people with epilepsy and associated psychiatric disorders in under-resourced areas of the world.
Neuro, Psych
⊕ https://vfmat.ch/25eb

Salvation Army International, The
Seeks to meet human needs through services in education, healthcare, community support, emergency response, and ministry development, inspired by the Christian faith.
Dent-OMFS, Derm, ER Med, Infect Dis, MF Med, Medicine, Nutr, OB-GYN, Ophth-Opt, Palliative, Psych, Rehab, Surg
⊕ https://vfmat.ch/8eb3

Samaritan's Purse International Disaster Relief
Provides spiritual and physical aid to hurting people around the world, such as victims of war, poverty, natural disasters, disease, and famine, based in Christian ministry.
Anesth, CT Surg, Crit-Care, Dent-OMFS, Derm, ENT, ER Med, Endo, GI, General, Heme-Onc, Infect Dis, MF Med, Neonat, Nephro, Neuro, Neurosurg, Nutr, OB-GYN, Ophth-Opt, Ortho, Path, Ped Surg, Peds, Plast, Psych, Pulm-Critic, Radiol, Rehab, Rheum, Surg, Urol, Vasc Surg
⊕ https://vfmat.ch/87e3

Sanofi Espoir Foundation
Contributes to reducing health inequalities among populations that need it most by applying a socially responsible approach focused on fighting childhood cancers in low-income countries, improving maternal and newborn health, and improving access to care.
ER Med, OB-GYN, Peds
⊕ https://vfmat.ch/943b

Save A Child's Heart
Provides lifesaving cardiac treatment to children in developing countries, and

trains healthcare professionals from these countries to deliver quality care in their communities.
CT Surg, CV Med, Crit-Care, Ped Surg, Peds
⊕ https://vfmat.ch/1bef

Save the Children
Gives children around the world a healthy start in life, the opportunity to learn, and protection from harm.
All-Immu, Crit-Care, ER Med, General, Infect Dis, MF Med, Medicine, Neonat, OB-GYN, Peds, Psych, Pub Health
⊕ https://vfmat.ch/2e73

SCI Foundation
Seeks to prevent and treat neglected infectious diseases, with a focus on eliminating parasitic worm infections through strengthening impactful and comprehensive health programs across Sub-Saharan Africa.
Infect Dis, Pub Health
⊕ https://vfmat.ch/5444

SEE International
Provides sustainable medical, surgical, and educational services through volunteer ophthalmic surgeons, with the objectives of restoring sight and preventing blindness to disadvantaged individuals worldwide.
Ophth-Opt, Surg
⊕ https://vfmat.ch/6e1b

Seed Global Health
Focuses on human resources for health capacity building at the individual, institutional, and national level through sustained collaborative engagement with partners.
Logist-Op
⊕ https://vfmat.ch/d12e

Sightsavers
Works with partners in developing countries to help eliminate avoidable blindness and advocates for equal opportunity for the disabled.
Infect Dis, Ophth-Opt, Surg
⊕ https://vfmat.ch/aa52

SIGN Fracture Care International
Builds orthopedic capacity around the world and provides the injured poor access to fracture surgery by donating orthopedic education and implant systems to surgeons in developing countries.
Ortho, Rehab, Surg
⊕ https://vfmat.ch/123d

Simavi
Strives for a world in which all women and girls are socially and economically empowered and pursue their rights to live a healthy life, free from discrimination, coercion, and violence.
MF Med, OB-GYN
⊕ https://vfmat.ch/b57b

SINA Health
Aims to improve the health and educational status of the population in low- and middle-income countries.
General, Logist-Op
⊕ https://vfmat.ch/9ad3

Smile Train, Inc.
Treats children with cleft lip through a sustainable and local model that supports surgery and other forms of essential care.
Logist-Op, Pub Health
⊕ https://vfmat.ch/822c

Sound Seekers
Supports people with hearing loss by enabling access to healthcare and education.
ENT
⊕ https://vfmat.ch/ef1c

Sponsel Foundation
Provides resources and services to advance the education, screening, research,

diagnosis, and treatment of ophthalmic diseases and ocular trauma for medically underserved communities, locally and worldwide.
Ophth-Opt, Surg
⊕ https://vfmat.ch/d93e

Sri Sathya Sai International Organization
Inspired by spiritual teachings, carries out efforts in global healthcare, education, humanitarian relief, and youth engagement.
Dent-OMFS, General, Logist-Op, Nutr, Ophth-Opt, Pub Health
⊕ https://vfmat.ch/9bda

Students for Kids International Projects (SKIP)
Strives to educate and empower students to initiate and maintain sustainable community projects for the health, welfare, and education of children.
Dent-OMFS, General, Nutr, Peds, Pub Health
⊕ https://vfmat.ch/de4e

Surgeons OverSeas (SOS)
Works to reduce death and disability from surgically treatable conditions in developing countries.
Anesth, Heme-Onc, Surg
⊕ https://vfmat.ch/5d16

Surgical Healing of Africa's Youth Foundation, The (S.H.A.Y.)
Provides volunteer reconstructive surgery to children in need, including treating congenital anomalies such as cleft lip/palate and general reconstruction.
Anesth, Dent-OMFS, Peds, Plast
⊕ https://vfmat.ch/41a7

Swiss Tropical and Public Health Institute
Contributes to the improvement of the health of populations internationally, nationally, and locally through excellence in research, education, and services.
Infect Dis, Pub Health
⊕ https://vfmat.ch/2ee4

Task Force for Global Health, The
Consists of programs and focus areas that cover a range of global health issues including neglected tropical diseases, infectious diseases, vaccines, field epidemiology, public health informatics, health workforce development, and global health ethics.
Infect Dis, Logist-Op, Medicine, Ophth-Opt, Peds
⊕ https://vfmat.ch/714c

TB Alert
Offers a range of programmatic, advisory, technical, and training services around tuberculosis, and is active in international advocacy initiatives.
Infect Dis, Pub Health, Pulm-Critic
⊕ https://vfmat.ch/1d5e

Tearfund
Responds to crisis and partners with local churches to bring restoration to those living in poverty, inspired by the Christian faith.
ER Med, Logist-Op
⊕ https://vfmat.ch/f6cf

Texas Children's Global Health
Addresses healthcare needs in resource-limited settings locally and globally by improving maternal and child health through the implementation of innovative, sustainable, in-country programs to train health professionals and build functional healthcare infrastructure.
Anesth, ER Med, Heme-Onc, Infect Dis, MF Med, Nutr, OB-GYN, Peds, Pub Health, Surg
⊕ https://vfmat.ch/4a1d

Together! ACT Now
Aims to end the spread of HIV in poor and rural areas of Malawi through theater, education, and access.
Infect Dis, Pub Health
⊕ https://vfmat.ch/2fdc

U.S. President's Malaria Initiative (PMI)
Supports low-income countries to help control and eliminate malaria through cost-effective, lifesaving malaria interventions.

Infect Dis, MF Med, OB-GYN
⊕ https://vfmat.ch/dc8b

UNC Health Foundation
Secures resources and supports empathy and expertise in patient care, research, education, and advocacy in underserved communities around the world.
Heme-Onc, Infect Dis, Neuro, Peds, Pub Health
⊕ https://vfmat.ch/7129

Union for International Cancer Control (UICC)
Unites and supports the cancer community to reduce the global cancer burden, promote greater equity, and ensure that cancer control continues to be a priority in the world health and development agenda.
Heme-Onc, Pub Health
⊕ https://vfmat.ch/88b1

United Nations Children's Fund (UNICEF)
Works in over 190 countries and territories to save children's lives, defend their rights, and help them fulfill their potential, from early childhood through adolescence.
All-Immu, Infect Dis, MF Med, Neonat, Nutr, OB-GYN, Ped Surg, Peds, Pub Health
⊕ https://vfmat.ch/42d7

United Nations Development Programme (UNDP)
Helps countries achieve the simultaneous eradication of extreme poverty and significant reduction of inequalities and exclusion using a sustainable human development approach.
Infect Dis, Logist-Op, Pub Health
⊕ https://vfmat.ch/935c

United Nations High Commissioner for Refugees (UNHCR)
Safeguards the rights and well-being of people who have been forced to flee, ensuring that everybody has the right to seek asylum and find safe refuge in another country, with the goal of seeking lasting solutions.
General, MF Med, Medicine, OB-GYN, Peds, Psych, Pub Health
⊕ https://vfmat.ch/6636

United Nations Population Fund (UNFPA)
Supports reproductive healthcare for women and youth in more than 150 countries, focusing on delivering a world in which every pregnancy is wanted, every childbirth is safe, and every young person's potential is fulfilled.
Infect Dis, MF Med, Neonat, OB-GYN, Peds, Pub Health
⊕ https://vfmat.ch/c969

United States Agency for International Development (USAID)
Promotes and demonstrates democratic values abroad and advances a free, peaceful, and prosperous world. Leads the U.S. government's international development and disaster assistance through partnerships and investments that save lives.
ER Med, Infect Dis, MF Med, OB-GYN, Peds
⊕ https://vfmat.ch/9a99

University of California Los Angeles: David Geffen School of Medicine Global Health Program
Catalyzes opportunities to improve health globally by engaging in multi-disciplinary and innovative education programs, research initiatives, and bilateral partnerships that provide opportunities for trainees, faculty, and staff to contribute to sustainable health initiatives and to address health inequities facing the world today.
All-Immu, Infect Dis, Logist-Op, MF Med, Medicine, Neonat, OB-GYN, Ortho, Ped Surg, Peds, Radiol
⊕ https://vfmat.ch/f1a4

University of California San Francisco: Institute for Global Health Sciences
Dedicates its efforts to improving health and reducing the burden of disease in the world's most vulnerable populations by integrating expertise in the health, social, and biological sciences, training global health leaders, and developing solutions to the most pressing health challenges.
Infect Dis, OB-GYN, Pub Health
⊕ https://vfmat.ch/6587

University of Cincinnati: College of Medicine Global Surgery

Aims to inspire a transformative approach to global health by training the next generation of surgeons, scholars, and leaders.

Plast, Surg

⊕ https://vfmat.ch/13c9

University of New Mexico School of Medicine: Project Echo

Seeks to improve health outcomes worldwide through the use of a technology called telementoring, a guided-practice model in which the participating clinician retains responsibility for managing the patient.

General, Infect Dis, MF Med, OB-GYN, Path, Peds

⊕ https://vfmat.ch/6c9a

University of North Carolina: Institute for Global Health and Infectious Diseases

Harnesses the full resources of UNC and its partners to solve global health problems, reduce the burden of disease, and cultivate the next generation of global health leaders.

Infect Dis, MF Med, OB-GYN, Psych, Surg

⊕ https://vfmat.ch/ed5e

University of Pennsylvania Perelman School of Medicine Center for Global Health

Aims to improve health equity worldwide through enhanced public health awareness and access to care, discovery, and outcomes-based research, and comprehensive educational programs grounded in partnership.

Heme-Onc, Infect Dis, OB-GYN

⊕ https://vfmat.ch/cb57

University of Virginia: Anesthesiology Department Global Health Initiatives

Educates and trains physicians to help people achieve healthy productive lives, and advances knowledge in the medical sciences.

Anesth, Pub Health

⊕ https://vfmat.ch/1b8b

University of Washington: The International Training and Education Center for Health (I-TECH)

Works with local partners to develop skilled healthcare workers and strong national health systems in resource-limited countries.

Infect Dis, Pub Health

⊕ https://vfmat.ch/642f

USA for United Nations High Commissioner for Refugees (UNHCR)

Serves and protects refugees and displaced people through emergency relief, cash assistance, education, resettlement, and the rebuilding of livelihoods.

ER Med, General, Logist-Op, Nutr, Pub Health

⊕ https://vfmat.ch/293c

USAID: A2Z The Micronutrient and Child Blindness Project

Aims to increase the use of key micronutrient and blindness interventions to improve child and maternal health.

MF Med, Neonat, Nutr, Ophth-Opt, Surg

⊕ https://vfmat.ch/c5f1

USAID: African Strategies for Health

Identifies and advocates for best practices, enhancing technical capacity of African regional institutions, and engaging African stakeholders to address health issues in a sustainable manner.

All-Immu, Infect Dis, OB-GYN, Peds

⊕ https://vfmat.ch/c272

USAID: Deliver Project

Builds a global supply chain to deliver lifesaving health products to people in order to enable countries to provide family planning, protect against malaria, and limit the spread of pandemic threats.

Infect Dis, Logist-Op, MF Med

⊕ https://vfmat.ch/374e

USAID: EQUIP Health

Exists as an effective, efficient response mechanism to achieving global HIV epidemic control by delivering the right intervention at the right place and in the right way.

Infect Dis

⊕ https://vfmat.ch/d76a

USAID: Health Policy Initiative

Provides field-level programming in health policy development and implementation.

General, Infect Dis, MF Med, OB-GYN, Peds

⊕ https://vfmat.ch/8f84

USAID: Human Resources for Health 2030 (HRH2030)

Helps low- and middle-income countries develop the health workforce needed to prevent maternal and child deaths, support the goals of Family Planning 2020, control the HIV/AIDS epidemic, and protect communities from infectious diseases.

Logist-Op

⊕ https://vfmat.ch/9ea8

USAID: Maternal and Child Health Integrated Program

Works to improve the health of women and their families, including programs for maternal, newborn, and child health, immunization, family planning, nutrition, malaria, and HIV/AIDS.

All-Immu, General, Infect Dis, MF Med

⊕ https://vfmat.ch/4415

USAID: Maternal and Child Survival Program

Works to prevent child and maternal deaths.

Infect Dis, MF Med, Neonat, OB-GYN, Peds

⊕ https://vfmat.ch/6fcf

USAID: TB Care II

Focuses on tuberculosis care and treatment.

Infect Dis

⊕ https://vfmat.ch/57d4

Ventura Global Health Project (VGHP)

Aims to encourage and facilitate a lifelong interest in global health by providing grants to support local medical professionals providing care to underserved populations.

Dent-OMFS, ER Med, General, Infect Dis, Logist-Op, OB-GYN, Ophth-Opt, Ortho, Peds, Plast, Surg, Urol

⊕ https://vfmat.ch/a746

Virtual Doctors, The

Uses local mobile broadband networks to connect rural clinics with doctors around the world, connecting isolated health centers with volunteer doctors around the world.

Anesth, Derm, ENT, Endo, General, Heme-Onc, Infect Dis, Medicine, Neuro, OB-GYN, Ophth-Opt, Ortho, Palliative, Ped Surg, Peds, Plast, Psych, Surg

⊕ https://vfmat.ch/3d94

Vision Care

Restores sight and helps patients get regular treatment at short-term eye camps and long-term base clinics by having doctors, missionaries, volunteers, and sponsors work together.

Ophth-Opt

⊕ https://vfmat.ch/9d7c

Vitamin Angels

Helps at-risk populations in need—specifically pregnant women, new mothers, and children under age 5—to gain access to life-changing vitamins and minerals.

General, Nutr

⊕ https://vfmat.ch/7da1

Voluntary Service Overseas (VSO)

Works with health workers, communities, and governments to improve health services and rights for women, babies, youth, people with disabilities, and prisoners.

General, MF Med, OB-GYN

⊕ https://vfmat.ch/213d

Walkabout Foundation

Provides wheelchairs and rehabilitation in the developing world and funds research to find a cure for paralysis.

Logist-Op, Rehab
⊕ https://vfmat.ch/5582

Watsi
Uses technology to make healthcare a reality for those who might not otherwise be able to afford it.
Pub Health, Surg
⊕ https://vfmat.ch/41a3

White Ribbon Alliance, The
Leads a movement for reproductive, maternal, and newborn health and accelerates progress by putting citizens at the center of global, national, and local health efforts.
MF Med, OB-GYN
⊕ https://vfmat.ch/496b

Women and Children First
Pioneers approaches that support communities to solve problems themselves.
MF Med, Neonat, OB-GYN, Peds
⊕ https://vfmat.ch/cdc9

World Anaesthesia Society (WAS)
Aims to support anesthesiologists with an interest in working in low-income regions of the world.
Anesth
⊕ https://vfmat.ch/37fe

World Blind Union (WBU)
Represents those experiencing blindness, speaking to governments and international bodies on issues concerning visual impairments.
Ophth-Opt
⊕ https://vfmat.ch/2bd3

World Care Foundation
Encourages humanitarian efforts to help those in need anywhere in the world, regardless of their faith, color, gender, and ethnicity. Projects include orphanages, orphan sponsorship, medical centers, refugee crisis work, and education.
ER Med, General, Pub Health
⊕ https://vfmat.ch/987a

World Child Cancer
Works to improve diagnosis, treatment, and support for children with cancer, and their families, in low- and middle-income parts of the world.
Heme-Onc, Ped Surg, Rad-Onc
⊕ https://vfmat.ch/fbbc

World Children's Fund
Commits to helping children worldwide who are suffering the effects of poverty, disease, natural disaster, famine, abuse, civil strife, and war.
General, Logist-Op, MF Med, Nutr, OB-GYN, Pub Health
⊕ https://vfmat.ch/9cd8

World Compassion Fellowship (WCF)
Serves the global poor and persecuted through relief, medical care, development, and training.
CV Med, ER Med, Endo, GI, General, Infect Dis, Medicine, Nutr, OB-GYN, Ortho, Peds, Psych, Pub Health, Rehab
⊕ https://vfmat.ch/7b97

World Federation of Hemophilia (WFH)
Aims to improve and sustain care for people with inherited bleeding disorders by pursuing long-term relationships with individuals and organizations who share the values of WFH's development model.
Heme-Onc
⊕ https://vfmat.ch/5121

World Health Organization, The (WHO)
The United Nations' agency for health provides leadership on global health matters, shapes the health research agenda, sets norms and standards, articulates evidence-based policy options, provides technical support and monitoring to countries, and assesses health trends.
ER Med, General, Infect Dis, Logist-Op, MF Med, OB-GYN, Peds, Psych, Pub

Health
⊕ https://vfmat.ch/c476

World Medical Fund
Puts an end to children suffering and dying simply because they have no access to medical care.
General, Infect Dis, Peds, Pub Health
⊕ https://vfmat.ch/f74a

World Medical Relief
Facilitates the distribution of surplus medical resources where they are needed.
Logist-Op
⊕ https://vfmat.ch/72dc

World Relief
Brings sustainable solutions to the world's greatest problems: disasters, extreme poverty, violence, oppression, and mass displacement.
ER Med, Nutr, Psych, Pub Health
⊕ https://vfmat.ch/fbcd

World Telehealth Initiative
Provides medical expertise to the world's most vulnerable communities to build local capacity and deliver core health services through a network of volunteer healthcare professionals supported with state-of-the-art technology.
Derm, Infect Dis, MF Med, Medicine, Neuro, OB-GYN, Peds, Pulm-Critic
⊕ https://vfmat.ch/fa91

World Vision International
Works with vulnerable communities around the world to overcome poverty and injustice with child-focused programs in disaster management, health, nutrition, economic development, education, clean water, sanitation, and hygiene.
ER Med, General, Infect Dis, MF Med, Nutr, OB-GYN, Peds
⊕ https://vfmat.ch/2642

Worldwide Radiology
Works to strengthen access to quality diagnostic imaging in underserved areas of low- and middle-income countries, and educates/supports professionals in the use of relevant and appropriate diagnostic imaging equipment and technologies.
Radiol
⊕ https://vfmat.ch/b35b

Yamba Malawi
Uplifts Malawi's most vulnerable children by building local businesses and by enabling investment in children's care.
Nutr, Peds
⊕ https://vfmat.ch/8d5f

Yathu Hospice
Provides hospice palliative care services to individuals with life-limiting conditions and their loved ones, and those who are facing end of life and going through grief and loss.
General, Palliative, Psych
⊕ https://vfmat.ch/ecbb

Malawi

Healthcare Facilities

Balaka District Hospital
Balaka, Malawi
⊕ https://vfmat.ch/9f65

Baylor College of Medicine Children's Foundation Malawi
Mzimba Street, Lilongwe, Lilongwe, Malawi
⊕ https://vfmat.ch/5aab

Beit CURE International Hospital
Chipatala, Blantyre, Malawi
⊕ https://vfmat.ch/e8d9

Blantyre Malaria Project
Ndirande Ring Road, Blantyre, Blantyre, Malawi
⊕ https://vfmat.ch/3d45

Bwaila Hospital
M1, Lilongwe, Lilongwe, Malawi
⊕ https://vfmat.ch/b184

CCAP Embangweni Mission Hospital
S112, Loudon, Malawi
⊕ https://vfmat.ch/f8e1

Child Legacy Hospital
T345, Lilongwe, Lilongwe, Malawi
⊕ https://vfmat.ch/6cbb

Chitawira Private Hospital
Chitawira Road, Limbe, Blantyre, Malawi
⊕ https://vfmat.ch/6718

Chitipa District Hospital
M9, Chitipa, Chitipa, Malawi
⊕ https://vfmat.ch/48f3

Daeyang Luke Hospital
Lilongwe, Malawi
⊕ https://vfmat.ch/86d4

David Gordon Memorial – Livingstonia Hospital
Golodi Road, Livingstonia, Rumphi, Malawi
⊕ https://vfmat.ch/a8dd

District Hospital Mangochi
M3, Mangochi, Mangochi, Malawi
⊕ https://vfmat.ch/b9d2

Dowa District Hospital
M16, Dowa, Dowa, Malawi
⊕ https://vfmat.ch/a85d

Dwambazi Rural Hospital
M5, Dwambazi, Nkhotakota, Malawi
⊕ https://vfmat.ch/f8dd

Ekwendeni Mission Hospital
M1, Ekwendeni, Malawi
⊕ https://vfmat.ch/611d

Kamuzu Central Hospital
Lilongwe, Malawi
⊕ https://vfmat.ch/5efd

Karonga District Hospital
M1, Karonga, Karonga, Malawi
⊕ https://vfmat.ch/43f5

Kasungu District Hospital
M18, Kasungu, Malawi
⊕ https://vfmat.ch/f39c

Lifeline
Salima, Malawi
⊕ https://vfmat.ch/8ff9

Likuni Hospital
S124, Likuni, Lilongwe, Malawi
⊕ https://vfmat.ch/f9b3

Machinga District Hospital
Machinga, Liwonde, Malawi
⊕ https://vfmat.ch/2cb2

Malamulo Rural Hospital
S151, Mangwalala, Thyolo, Malawi
⊕ https://vfmat.ch/e576

Mlambe Hospital
M1, Lunzu, Blantyre, Malawi
⊕ https://vfmat.ch/2123

Mponela Hospital
Mponela, Malawi
⊕ https://vfmat.ch/d8c1

Mua Mission Hospital
M5, Mua, Dedza, Malawi
⊕ https://vfmat.ch/addb

Mulanje District Hospital
M2, Mulanje, Malawi
⊕ https://vfmat.ch/384c

Mulanje Mission Hospital
Mulanje Mission Road, Nkhonya, Mulanje, Malawi
⊕ https://vfmat.ch/5cc1

Mvera Mission Hospital
M14, Mvera Mission, Dowa, Malawi
⊕ https://vfmat.ch/3831

Mwaiwathu Private Hospital
Chileka Road, Blantyre, Blantyre, Malawi
⊕ https://vfmat.ch/a316

Mwanza Hospital
S135, Mwanza, Mwanza, Malawi
⊕ https://vfmat.ch/88cc

Mzimba South District Hospital
M9, Mzimba, Mzimba, Malawi
⊕ https://vfmat.ch/aaad

Mzuzu Central Hospital
M1, Mzuzu, Mzimba, Malawi
⊕ https://vfmat.ch/21ce

Nchalo Baptist Church
M1, Nchalo, Chikwawa, Malawi
⊕ https://vfmat.ch/9972

Neno District Hospital
T397, Neno, Malawi
⊕ https://vfmat.ch/4671

Nguludi Mission Hospital
T411, Nguludi, Chiradzulu, Malawi
⊕ https://vfmat.ch/1d63

Nkhata District Hospital
M5, Nkhata Bay, Nkhata Bay, Malawi
⊕ https://vfmat.ch/187e

Nkhoma Hospital
T374, Gwenembe, Lilongwe, Malawi
⊕ https://vfmat.ch/dee3

Nkhotakota District Hospital
Kasungo Road, Kachuma, Nkhotakota, Malawi
⊕ https://vfmat.ch/c557

Ntcheu District Hospital
M1, Mtandizi, Ntcheu, Malawi
⊕ https://vfmat.ch/32b2

Ntchisi Hospital
T350, Ntchisi, Ntchisi, Malawi
⊕ https://vfmat.ch/276e

Partners in Hope
M1, Lilongwe, Lilongwe, Malawi
⊕ https://vfmat.ch/cfc5

Pirimiti Community Hospital
S144, Thondwe, Zomba, Malawi
⊕ https://vfmat.ch/58fe

Queen Elizabeth Central Hospital
Chipatala Avenue, Blantyre, Blantyre, Malawi
⊕ https://vfmat.ch/d2e7

Rumphi District Hospital
M24, Mputa, Rumphi, Malawi
⊕ https://vfmat.ch/4d77

Salima District Hospital
M5, Salima, Salima, Malawi
⊕ https://vfmat.ch/bdf2

Shifa Hospital
Haile Selassie Avenue, Blantyre, Blantyre, Malawi
⊕ https://vfmat.ch/829b

St. Gabriel Mission Hospital
M12, Namitete, Lilongwe, Malawi
⊕ https://vfmat.ch/3798

St. John's Hospital
Chimaliro Road, Mzuzu, Mzimba, Malawi
⊕ https://vfmat.ch/5955

Surgery Hospital at Blantyre
Sharpe Road, Blantyre, Blantyre, Malawi
⊕ https://vfmat.ch/515e

Thyolo District Hospital
Thyolo Road, Ndalama, Thyolo, Malawi
⊕ https://vfmat.ch/8fbe

Trinity Hospital
S152, Malothi, Nsanje, Malawi
⊕ https://vfmat.ch/c9f5

ZMK Hospital
Queens Road, Lilongwe, Lilongwe, Malawi
⊕ https://vfmat.ch/28c9

Zomba Central Hospital
M3, Matawale, Zomba, Malawi
⊕ https://vfmat.ch/33fc

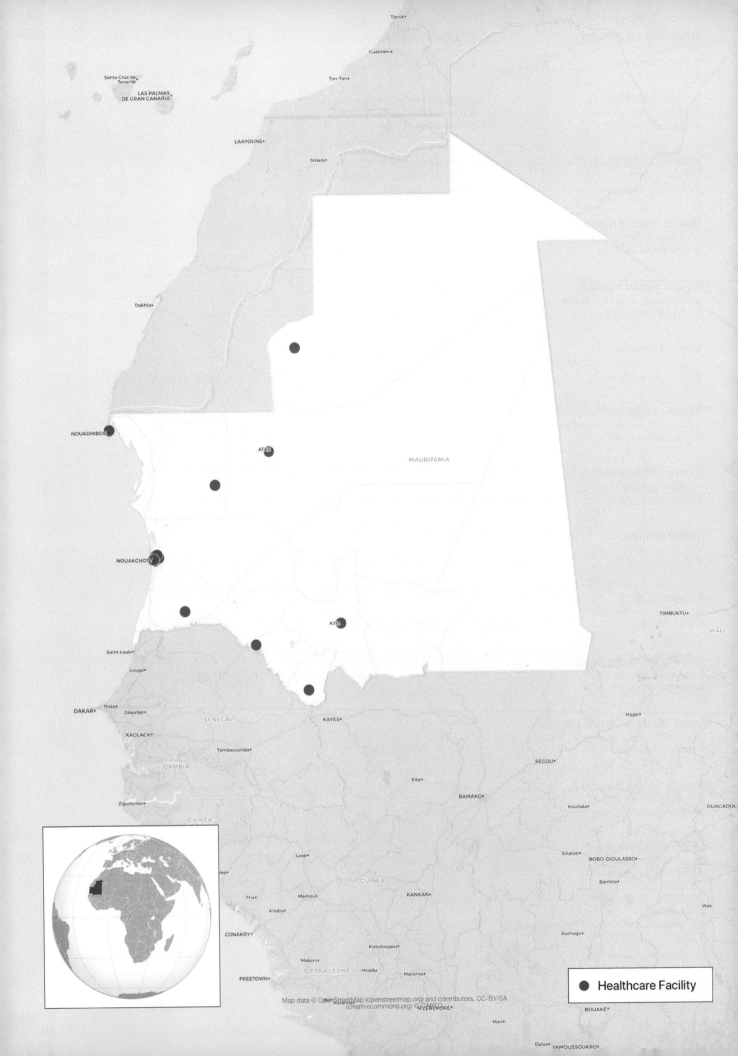

Healthcare Facility

Mauritania

The Islamic Republic of Mauritania is located in the northwest of Africa, bordered by the Atlantic Ocean, Western Sahara, Algeria, Mali, and Senegal. The majority Muslim population of 4.1 million people is ethnically made up of Black and White Moors, Sub-Saharan Mauritanians, Halpulaar, Fulani, Soninke, Wolof, and Bambara ethnic groups. The official language is Arabic—however, French, Pular, Soninke, and Wolof are all widely spoken. About 90 percent of Mauritania's land area is located in the Sahara Desert, and large swaths of the country are completely uninhabited. Most of the population lives in the southern half of the country, with about half the people living near and in the capital, Nouakchott.

Mauritania was a French colony until it gained independence in 1960. A series of coups, periods of authoritarian military rule, and instability followed, and the country has often been criticized for a poor human rights record. There is little arable land in Mauritania but the availability of pastoral land is significant. As such, much of the economy is based on livestock and some agriculture, with other major industries being mining of iron ore, petroleum production, and fishing. The economy is vulnerable to international prices on food and commodities. Other risks include environmental fluctuations, such as drought in an already arid country. Mauritania relies heavily on foreign aid and investment: Approximately 31 percent of the population lives below the poverty line, with 10 percent of the population facing unemployment.

Mauritania has experienced a drastic rise in mortality due to malaria between 2009 and 2019, with the rate of death increasing by over 400 percent. Other leading causes of death include neonatal disorders, ischemic heart disease, lower respiratory infections, diarrheal diseases, stroke, road injuries, diabetes, cirrhosis, chronic kidney disease, maternal disorders, and tuberculosis. The risk factors that contribute most to death and disability include malnutrition, air pollution, high blood pressure, high body-mass index, dietary risks, high fasting plasma glucose, tobacco use, kidney dysfunction, non-optimal temperatures, and a lack of water, sanitation, and hygiene.

4.1M

Population

$1,673

GDP Per Capita

65 years

Life Expectancy

↑ Improving

19
Doctors/100k

Physician Density

40
Beds/100k

Hospital Bed Density

766
Deaths/100k

Maternal Mortality

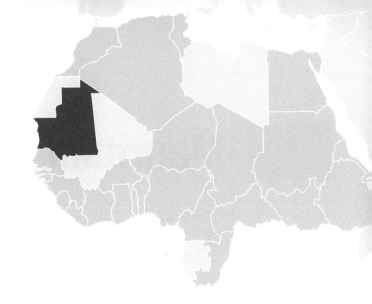

Mauritania

Nonprofit Organizations

Action Against Hunger
Aims to end life-threatening hunger for good through treating and preventing malnutrition across more than 45 countries.
Nutr
🌐 https://vfmat.ch/2dbc

Advance Family Planning
Aims to achieve global expansion and access to quality contraceptive information, services, and supplies through financial investment and political commitment.
General, MF Med, Pub Health
🌐 https://vfmat.ch/7478

Africa CDC
Aims to strengthen the capacity and capability of Africa's public health institutions and partnerships to detect and respond quickly and effectively to disease threats and outbreaks, based on data-driven interventions and programs.
Infect Dis, Logist-Op, Pub Health
🌐 https://vfmat.ch/339c

Africa Health Organisation
Leads collaborative efforts among countries in Africa and other partners to promote health equity, combat disease, and improve quality of life.
Logist-Op, Pub Health
🌐 https://vfmat.ch/b1c5

Africa Relief and Community Development
Provides comprehensive relief and developmental aid to people of the African continent regardless of gender, race, or religion.
Nutr, Pub Health
🌐 https://vfmat.ch/6cd2

African Field Epidemiology Network (AFENET)
Strengthens field epidemiology and public health laboratory capacity to contribute effectively to addressing epidemics and other major public health problems in Africa.
All-Immu, Infect Dis, Path, Pub Health
🌐 https://vfmat.ch/df2e

African Health Now
Promotes and provides information and access to sustainable primary healthcare to women, children, and families living across Sub-Saharan Africa.
Dent-OMFS, Endo, General, Infect Dis, MF Med, OB-GYN
🌐 https://vfmat.ch/c766

Al Basar International Foundation
Works with local partners to treat preventable blindness, and helps set up sustainable infrastructure so local teams can save sight in their communities.
Ophth-Opt
🌐 https://vfmat.ch/a8b5

Alliance for International Medical Action, The (ALIMA)
Provides quality medical care to vulnerable populations, partnering with and developing national medical organizations and conducting medical research to bring innovation to 12 African countries where ALIMA works.
ER Med, General, Infect Dis, Logist-Op, MF Med, OB-GYN, Path, Peds, Psych, Pub Health
🌐 https://vfmat.ch/1c11

Cairdeas International Palliative Care Trust
Promotes and facilitates the provision of high-quality palliative care in the developing world, where such care is limited.
Palliative
🌐 https://vfmat.ch/35c4

Carter Center, The
Seeks to prevent and resolve conflicts, enhance freedom and democracy, and improve health, while remaining committed to human rights and the alleviation of human suffering.
Infect Dis, MF Med, Ophth-Opt
🌐 https://vfmat.ch/6556

COVID-19 Clinical Research Coalition
Advocates and collaborates for the advancement of COVID-19 research driven by the needs of low-resource settings, and works for equitable access to solutions to the pandemic.
All-Immu, Infect-Dis, MF Med, Path, Pub Health
🌐 https://vfmat.ch/d1f4

Developing Country NGO Delegation: Global Fund to Fight AIDS, TB & Malaria
Works to strengthen the engagement of civil society actors and organizations in developing countries to build a world in which AIDS, TB, and malaria are no longer global, public health, and human rights threats.
Infect Dis, Pub Health
🌐 https://vfmat.ch/3149

Direct Relief
Improves the health and lives of people affected by poverty or emergency situations by mobilizing and providing essential medical resources needed for their care.
ER Med, Logist-Op
🌐 https://vfmat.ch/58e5

Doctors Without Borders/Médecins Sans Frontières (MSF)
Responds to emergencies and provides lifesaving medical care where needed most, including during disasters, conflicts, and epidemics.
Anesth, Crit-Care, ER Med, General, Infect Dis, Nutr, OB-GYN, Ped Surg, Peds, Psych, Pub Health, Surg
🌐 https://vfmat.ch/f363

END Fund, The
Aims to control and eliminate the most prevalent neglected diseases among the world's poorest and most vulnerable people.
Infect Dis
⊕ https://vfmat.ch/2614

Fistula Foundation
Aims to engage the support of people worldwide who are eager to see the day that no woman suffers from obstetric fistula. Raises and directs funds to doctors and hospitals providing life-transforming surgery to women in need.
OB-GYN
⊕ https://vfmat.ch/e958

Friends of UNFPA
Promotes the health, dignity, and rights of women and girls around the world by supporting the lifesaving work of UNFPA, the United Nations' reproductive health and rights agency, through education, advocacy, and fundraising.
MF Med, OB-GYN
⊕ https://vfmat.ch/2a3a

Global Oncology (GO)
Brings the best in cancer care to underserved patients around the world and collaborates across geographic, professional, and academic borders to improve cancer care, research, and education.
Heme-Onc, Path, Rad-Onc
⊕ https://vfmat.ch/fcb8

Globus Relief
Aims to improve the delivery of healthcare worldwide by gathering, processing, and distributing surplus medical supplies to charities at home and abroad.
Logist-Op
⊕ https://vfmat.ch/a2b7

Health Equity Initiative
Aims to build and sustain a global community that engages across sectors and disciplines to advance health equity.
Pub Health
⊕ https://vfmat.ch/e2e2

Health Poverty Action
Works in partnership with people around the world who are pursuing change in their own communities to demand health justice and challenge power imbalances.
ER Med, General, Infect Dis, Psych, Pub Health
⊕ https://vfmat.ch/ee58

Heart Fund, The
Aims to save the lives of children suffering from heart disease by developing innovative solutions that revolutionize access to cardiac care in developing countries.
Anesth, CV Med, Ped Surg, Peds, Surg
⊕ https://vfmat.ch/7e67

IMA World Health
Works to build healthier communities by collaborating with key partners to serve vulnerable people with a focus on health, healing, and well-being for all.
Infect Dis, MF Med, Nutr, OB-GYN, Pub Health
⊕ https://vfmat.ch/8316

International Children's Heart Fund
Aims to promote the international growth and quality of cardiac surgery, particularly in children and young adults.
CT Surg, Ped Surg
⊕ https://vfmat.ch/33fb

International Council of Ophthalmology
Works with ophthalmologic societies and others to enhance ophthalmic education and improve access to the highest-quality eye care in order to preserve and restore vision for people of the world.
Ophth-Opt
⊕ https://vfmat.ch/ffd2

International Federation of Red Cross and Red Crescent Societies (IFRC)
Coordinates and directs international assistance following natural and manmade disasters in nonconflict situations through the world's largest humanitarian and development network. Provides disaster-preparedness programs, healthcare activities, and promotes humanitarian values.
ER Med, General, Infect Dis, Nutr
⊕ https://vfmat.ch/b4ee

International Hearing Foundation
Supports hearing-related service, education, and research.
ENT, Surg
⊕ https://vfmat.ch/3ee2

International Organization for Migration (IOM) – The UN Migration Agency
Promotes evidence-informed policies and holistic, preventive, and curative health programs that are beneficial, accessible, and equitable for vulnerable migrants.
General, Infect Dis, OB-GYN
⊕ https://vfmat.ch/621a

International Planned Parenthood Federation (IPPF)
Leads a locally owned, globally connected civil society movement that provides and enables services and champions sexual and reproductive health and rights for all, especially the underserved.
Infect Dis, MF Med, OB-GYN
⊕ https://vfmat.ch/dc97

International Trachoma Initiative (iTi)
Works toward a world free from trachoma, a preventable cause of blindness, and provides comprehensive support to national ministries of health and governmental and nongovernmental organizations to implement a comprehensive approach to fight trachoma.
Infect Dis, Ophth-Opt
⊕ https://vfmat.ch/3278

Joint United Nations Programme on HIV/AIDS (UNAIDS)
Aims to place people living with HIV and people affected by the virus at the decision-making table and at the center of designing, delivering, and monitoring the AIDS response.
Infect Dis
⊕ https://vfmat.ch/464a

Life for a Child
Supports the provision of the best possible healthcare, given local circumstances, to all children and youth with diabetes in less-resourced countries, through the strengthening of existing diabetes services.
Endo, Medicine, Peds
⊕ https://vfmat.ch/d712

Management Sciences for Health (MSH)
Works with countries and communities to save lives and improve the health of the world's poorest and most vulnerable people by building strong, resilient, sustainable health systems.
Infect Dis, Logist-Op, Pub Health
⊕ https://vfmat.ch/6aa2

MedShare
Aims to improve the quality of life of people, communities, and the planet by sourcing and directly delivering surplus medical supplies and equipment to communities in need around the world.
Logist-Op
⊕ https://vfmat.ch/c8bc

Mercy and Love Foundation
Aims to provide orphaned and vulnerable children with basic human needs such as food, clothing, and shelter, enabling them to thrive.
General, Peds
⊕ https://vfmat.ch/649a

Médecins du Monde/Doctors of the World
Provides care, bears witness, and supports social change worldwide with innovative medical programs and evidence-based advocacy initiatives.

ER Med, General, Infect Dis, MF Med, Neonat, OB-GYN, Peds, Pub Health
⊕ https://vfmat.ch/a43d

Operation Mercy
Serves the poor and marginalized through community development and humanitarian aid projects.
General, MF Med, OB-GYN, Peds, Psych, Pub Health, Rehab
⊕ https://vfmat.ch/81c5

Ophtalmo Sans Frontières
Fights against blindness and low vision in French-speaking Africa.
Anesth, Ophth-Opt, Surg
⊕ https://vfmat.ch/7643

Order of Malta
Supports forgotten or excluded people, especially those living in conflict zones or amid natural disasters, by providing medical assistance, caring for refugees, and distributing medicines and necessities.
ER Med, General, Infect Dis, MF Med, Nephro, OB-GYN, Ortho, Psych
⊕ https://vfmat.ch/1fab

Pharmacists Without Borders Canada
Provides pharmaceutical and technical assistance in the implementation or improvement of community and hospital pharmacies internationally.
⊕ https://vfmat.ch/7658

Physicians Across Continents
Provides high-quality medical care to people affected by crises and disasters.
CV Med, Dent-OMFS, Heme-Onc, MF Med, Nephro, Nephro, OB-GYN, Ped Surg, Plast, Surg
⊕ https://vfmat.ch/fe5d

Rockefeller Foundation, The
Works to promote the well-being of humanity.
Logist-Op, Nutr, Pub Health
⊕ https://vfmat.ch/5424

Rotary International
Provides service to others, improves lives, and advances world understanding, goodwill, and peace through its fellowship of business, professional, and community leaders.
ER Med, General, Infect Dis, MF Med, OB-GYN
⊕ https://vfmat.ch/8fb5

Sanofi Espoir Foundation
Contributes to reducing health inequalities among populations that need it most by applying a socially responsible approach focused on fighting childhood cancers in low-income countries, improving maternal and newborn health, and improving access to care.
ER Med, OB-GYN, Peds
⊕ https://vfmat.ch/943b

SCI Foundation
Seeks to prevent and treat neglected infectious diseases, with a focus on eliminating parasitic worm infections through strengthening impactful and comprehensive health programs across Sub-Saharan Africa.
Infect Dis, Pub Health
⊕ https://vfmat.ch/5444

Smile Train, Inc.
Treats children with cleft lip through a sustainable and local model that supports surgery and other forms of essential care.
Logist-Op, Pub Health
⊕ https://vfmat.ch/822c

Solthis
Improves disease prevention and access to quality care by strengthening the health systems and services of the countries served.
General, Infect Dis, Logist-Op, MF Med, Neonat, Path
⊕ https://vfmat.ch/a71d

Task Force for Global Health, The
Consists of programs and focus areas that cover a range of global health

issues including neglected tropical diseases, infectious diseases, vaccines, field epidemiology, public health informatics, health workforce development, and global health ethics.
Infect Dis, Logist-Op, Medicine, Ophth-Opt, Peds
⊕ https://vfmat.ch/714c

Terre des hommes (Tdh) Foundation
Works to improve the daily life of children and their relatives in the areas of health, protection and emergency, in Europe, Africa, Asia, Latin America, and the Near and Middle East.
CT Surg, CV Med, OB-GYN, Ped Surg, Pub Health
⊕ https://vfmat.ch/5c26

Union for International Cancer Control (UICC)
Unites and supports the cancer community to reduce the global cancer burden, promote greater equity, and ensure that cancer control continues to be a priority in the world health and development agenda.
Heme-Onc, Pub Health
⊕ https://vfmat.ch/88b1

United Nations Children's Fund (UNICEF)
Works in over 190 countries and territories to save children's lives, defend their rights, and help them fulfill their potential, from early childhood through adolescence.
All-Immu, Infect Dis, MF Med, Neonat, Nutr, OB-GYN, Ped Surg, Peds, Pub Health
⊕ https://vfmat.ch/42d7

United Nations Development Programme (UNDP)
Helps countries achieve the simultaneous eradication of extreme poverty and significant reduction of inequalities and exclusion using a sustainable human development approach.
Infect Dis, Logist-Op, Pub Health
⊕ https://vfmat.ch/935c

United Nations High Commissioner for Refugees (UNHCR)
Safeguards the rights and well-being of people who have been forced to flee, ensuring that everybody has the right to seek asylum and find safe refuge in another country, with the goal of seeking lasting solutions.
General, MF Med, Medicine, OB-GYN, Peds, Psych, Pub Health
⊕ https://vfmat.ch/6636

United Nations Population Fund (UNFPA)
Supports reproductive healthcare for women and youth in more than 150 countries, focusing on delivering a world in which every pregnancy is wanted, every childbirth is safe, and every young person's potential is fulfilled.
Infect Dis, MF Med, Neonat, OB-GYN, Peds, Pub Health
⊕ https://vfmat.ch/c969

United States Agency for International Development (USAID)
Promotes and demonstrates democratic values abroad and advances a free, peaceful, and prosperous world. Leads the U.S. government's international development and disaster assistance through partnerships and investments that save lives.
ER Med, Infect Dis, MF Med, OB-GYN, Peds
⊕ https://vfmat.ch/9a99

United Surgeons for Children (USFC)
Pursues greater health and opportunity for children in the most neglected pockets of the world, with a specific focus on and expertise in surgery.
Anesth, CT Surg, Neonat, Neurosurg, OB-GYN, Peds, Radiol, Surg
⊕ https://vfmat.ch/3b4c

USA for United Nations High Commissioner for Refugees (UNHCR)
Serves and protects refugees and displaced people through emergency relief, cash assistance, education, resettlement, and the rebuilding of livelihoods.
ER Med, General, Logist-Op, Nutr, Pub Health
⊕ https://vfmat.ch/293c

Vision Care
Restores sight and helps patients get regular treatment at short-term eye camps and long-term base clinics by having doctors, missionaries, volunteers, and sponsors work together.

Ophth-Opt
⊕ https://vfmat.ch/9d7c

World Federation of Hemophilia (WFH)
Aims to improve and sustain care for people with inherited bleeding disorders by pursuing long-term relationships with individuals and organizations who share the values of WFH's development model.
Heme-Onc
⊕ https://vfmat.ch/5121

World Health Organization, The (WHO)
The United Nations' agency for health provides leadership on global health matters, shapes the health research agenda, sets norms and standards, articulates evidence-based policy options, provides technical support and monitoring to countries, and assesses health trends.
ER Med, General, Infect Dis, Logist-Op, MF Med, OB-GYN, Peds, Psych, Pub Health
⊕ https://vfmat.ch/c476

World Vision International
Works with vulnerable communities around the world to overcome poverty and injustice with child-focused programs in disaster management, health, nutrition, economic development, education, clean water, sanitation, and hygiene.
ER Med, General, Infect Dis, MF Med, Nutr, OB-GYN, Peds
⊕ https://vfmat.ch/2642

Mauritania

Healthcare Facilities

Akjoujt Hospital
Akjoujt, Inchiri Region, Mauritania
⊕ https://vfmat.ch/d6av

Al-Saddaaqah Hospital
Nouakchott, Mauritania
⊕ https://vfmat.ch/tnqr

Atar Mauritania Hospital
Atar, Adrar Region, Mauritania
⊕ https://vfmat.ch/kxtn

Boutilimit Hospital
Boutilimit, Trarza Region, Mauritania
⊕ https://vfmat.ch/ftxm

Centre National d'Oncologie
Nouakchott, Mauritania
⊕ https://vfmat.ch/f8fm

Centre Hospitalier Mère-Enfant
Ksar, Nouakchott Ouest, Mauritania
⊕ https://vfmat.ch/a9f4

Centre Hospitalier National de Nouakchott
Nouakchott, Mauritania
⊕ https://vfmat.ch/maia

Centre National de Cardiologie
Ksar, Nouakchott Ouest, Mauritania
⊕ https://vfmat.ch/1f16

Centro Neuro Psychiatrique de Nouakchott
Nouakchott, Mauritania
⊕ https://vfmat.ch/tmvj

Cheikh Zayed Hospital
Ksar, Nouakchott Ouest, Mauritania
⊕ https://vfmat.ch/ba22

Clinique Chiva
Nouakchott, Mauritania
⊕ https://vfmat.ch/p5cg

Clinique El Menar
Nouakchott, Mauritania
⊕ https://vfmat.ch/aahz

Clinique Elihsane
Nouakchott, Mauritania
⊕ https://vfmat.ch/bdmk

Clinique El Inaya
Nouakchott, Mauritania
⊕ https://vfmat.ch/avtg

Clinique Kissi
Ksar, Nouakchott Ouest, Mauritania
⊕ https://vfmat.ch/68d1

Friendship Hospital
Ksar, Nouakchott Ouest, Mauritania
⊕ https://vfmat.ch/e259

General Hospital Nouakchott (Capitol)
Nouakchott, Mauritania
⊕ https://vfmat.ch/rjqn

Hôpital de Kiffa
Koûroudjél, Assaba, Mauritania
⊕ https://vfmat.ch/da1a

Hôpital de Zoueratt
Zoueratt, Tiris Zemmour, Mauritania
⊕ https://vfmat.ch/c5a4

Hôpital Militaire
Riyad, Trarza, Mauritania
⊕ https://vfmat.ch/72c2

Kaédi Regional Hospital
Mollé Wala, Matam, Mauritania
⊕ https://vfmat.ch/a49f

Nouadhibou Regional Hospital
Dakhlet, Nouadhibou Region, Mauritania
⊕ https://vfmat.ch/kjdq

Ophthalmological Hospital
Dâr es Salâm, Hodh El Gharbi, Mauritania
⊕ https://vfmat.ch/6948

Rosso Hospital
Rosso, Trarza Region, Mauritania
⊕ https://vfmat.ch/zsyw

Selibaby Hospital
Selibaby, Guidimaka Region, Mauritania
⊕ https://vfmat.ch/mvcl

Tidjikja Hospital
Tidjikja, Tagant Region, Mauritania
⊕ https://vfmat.ch/vtcb

Zoueirat Hospital
Zoueirat, Tiris Zemmour Region, Mauritania
⊕ https://vfmat.ch/8qav

Jayapura

PAPUA

PAPUA NEW
GUINEA

Lae

Merauke

Port Moresby

Bismarck
Sea

Solomon
Sea

Honiara

SOLOMON
ISLANDS

● Healthcare Facility

Micronesia

The Federated States of Micronesia comprise more than 600 small islands spread throughout the western Pacific, in Oceania. Nearby island neighbors include Indonesia, Papua New Guinea, Guam, the Marianas, Nauru, and several others. The land mass of Micronesia, 271 square miles, is small compared to the amount of ocean it covers: more than 1 million square miles. Micronesia is made up of four major states: Chuuk, Kosrae, Pohnpei, and Yap. The population of 101,675 people lives mostly along the coasts of the larger islands, with about 23 percent in urban areas such as the capital of Palikar. The population is ethnically diverse, including Chuukese, Mortlockese, Pohnpeian, Kosraean, Yapese, and Yap outer islanders. The majority of Micronesians identify as Roman Catholic, with other Christian religions also well represented. English is the official language and it's the language that's most commonly spoken throughout the island nation.

Micronesia was controlled by several countries during the 20th century, including Spain, Germany, Japan, and the United States. The U.S. was the last country to administer Micronesia until 1979, when independence was declared. Ties between the U.S. and Micronesia remain close, both politically and economically. Subsistence farming and fishing are the main sources of income for most people; however, much of the island's food, manufactured goods, and fuel is imported to supplement local resources. Both the service sector and tourism have developed over time, albeit slowly.

Micronesia faces health challenges with both communicable and non-communicable diseases. Obesity is prevalent in the small island nation, with 46 percent of the population considered obese. This has led to an increase in many non-communicable diseases, with ischemic heart disease, diabetes, stroke, chronic kidney disease, COPD, hypertensive heart disease, and cirrhosis as the cause of most deaths. Other major causes of death include lower respiratory infections, self-harm, and road injuries. Of note, death due to HIV/AIDS increased dramatically between 2009 and 2019, growing by over 200 percent. The risk factors that contribute most to death and disability include high body-mass index, high fasting plasma glucose, alcohol and tobacco use, high blood pressure, dietary risks, high LDL, kidney dysfunction, air pollution, unsafe sex, and malnutrition.

0.1M

Population

$3,585

GDP Per Capita

68 years

Life Expectancy

↑ Improving

19

Doctors/100k

Physician Density

88

Deaths/100k

Maternal Mortality

Micronesia

Nonprofit Organizations

Aloha Medical Mission
Brings hope and changes the lives of people; serves overseas and in Hawai'i.
Anesth, Crit-Care, Dent-OMFS, ENT, ER Med, General, Medicine, OB-GYN, Ophth-Opt, Ortho, Ped Surg, Peds, Plast, Surg, Urol
⊕ https://vfmat.ch/72ac

Canvasback Missions
Seeks to bring health and wholeness to Micronesia through diabetes reversal, specialty healthcare, and health education.
CV Med, Dent-OMFS, Derm, ENT, Medicine, OB-GYN, Ophth-Opt, Ortho, Urol
⊕ https://vfmat.ch/b5e9

Caring Hands Worldwide
Inspired by the Christian faith, works to improve dental health of those in need in partner communities in the U.S. and abroad.
Dent-OMFS, Logist-Op
⊕ https://vfmat.ch/62cc

Direct Relief
Improves the health and lives of people affected by poverty or emergency situations by mobilizing and providing essential medical resources needed for their care.
ER Med, Logist-Op
⊕ https://vfmat.ch/58e5

Give Sight Global
Provides vision care to underserved communities around the world by providing treatment for curable blindness and other preventable eye conditions.
Ophth-Opt, Pub Health
⊕ https://vfmat.ch/5c4d

Global Oncology (GO)
Brings the best in cancer care to underserved patients around the world and collaborates across geographic, professional, and academic borders to improve cancer care, research, and education.
Heme-Onc, Path, Rad-Onc
⊕ https://vfmat.ch/fcb8

Globus Relief
Aims to improve the delivery of healthcare worldwide by gathering, processing, and distributing surplus medical supplies to charities at home and abroad.
Logist-Op
⊕ https://vfmat.ch/a2b7

Grace Dental and Medical (GDM) Missions
Sends and supports dental and medical missions based in Christian ministry with the aim of church planting.
Dent-OMFS, ER Med, General
⊕ https://vfmat.ch/bdea

International Federation of Red Cross and Red Crescent Societies (IFRC)
Coordinates and directs international assistance following natural and manmade disasters in nonconflict situations through the world's largest humanitarian and development network. Provides disaster-preparedness programs, healthcare activities, and promotes humanitarian values.
ER Med, General, Infect Dis, Nutr
⊕ https://vfmat.ch/b4ee

International Organization for Migration (IOM) – The UN Migration Agency
Promotes evidence-informed policies and holistic, preventive, and curative health programs that are beneficial, accessible, and equitable for vulnerable migrants.
General, Infect Dis, OB-GYN
⊕ https://vfmat.ch/621a

Joint United Nations Programme on HIV/AIDS (UNAIDS)
Aims to place people living with HIV and people affected by the virus at the decision-making table and at the center of designing, delivering, and monitoring the AIDS response.
Infect Dis
⊕ https://vfmat.ch/464a

MAHI International
Aims to increase quality of life for people in underdeveloped communities of the Pacific Island region.
CV Med, Dent-OMFS, Endo, General, Ophth-Opt
⊕ https://vfmat.ch/8cc3

MedShare
Aims to improve the quality of life of people, communities, and the planet by sourcing and directly delivering surplus medical supplies and equipment to communities in need around the world.
Logist-Op
⊕ https://vfmat.ch/c8bc

Order of Malta
Supports forgotten or excluded people, especially those living in conflict zones or amid natural disasters, by providing medical assistance, caring for refugees, and distributing medicines and necessities.
ER Med, General, Infect Dis, MF Med, Nephro, OB-GYN, Ortho, Psych
⊕ https://vfmat.ch/1fab

RestoringVision
Empowers lives by restoring vision for millions of people in need.
Ophth-Opt
⊕ https://vfmat.ch/e121

Rotary International
Provides service to others, improves lives, and advances world understanding,

goodwill, and peace through its fellowship of business, professional, and community leaders.

ER Med, General, Infect Dis, MF Med, OB-GYN

⊕ https://vfmat.ch/8fb5

Salvation Army International, The

Seeks to meet human needs through services in education, healthcare, community support, emergency response, and ministry development, inspired by the Christian faith.

Dent-OMFS, Derm, ER Med, Infect Dis, MF Med, Medicine, Nutr, OB-GYN, Ophth-Opt, Palliative, Psych, Rehab, Surg

⊕ https://vfmat.ch/8eb3

SEE International

Provides sustainable medical, surgical, and educational services through volunteer ophthalmic surgeons, with the objectives of restoring sight and preventing blindness to disadvantaged individuals worldwide.

Ophth-Opt, Surg

⊕ https://vfmat.ch/6e1b

Task Force for Global Health, The

Consists of programs and focus areas that cover a range of global health issues including neglected tropical diseases, infectious diseases, vaccines, field epidemiology, public health informatics, health workforce development, and global health ethics.

Infect Dis, Logist-Op, Medicine, Ophth-Opt, Peds

⊕ https://vfmat.ch/714c

United Nations Children's Fund (UNICEF)

Works in over 190 countries and territories to save children's lives, defend their rights, and help them fulfill their potential, from early childhood through adolescence.

All-Immu, Infect Dis, MF Med, Neonat, Nutr, OB-GYN, Ped Surg, Peds, Pub Health

⊕ https://vfmat.ch/42d7

United Nations High Commissioner for Refugees (UNHCR)

Safeguards the rights and well-being of people who have been forced to flee, ensuring that everybody has the right to seek asylum and find safe refuge in another country, with the goal of seeking lasting solutions.

General, MF Med, Medicine, OB-GYN, Peds, Psych, Pub Health

⊕ https://vfmat.ch/6636

United Nations Population Fund (UNFPA)

Supports reproductive healthcare for women and youth in more than 150 countries, focusing on delivering a world in which every pregnancy is wanted, every childbirth is safe, and every young person's potential is fulfilled.

Infect Dis, MF Med, Neonat, OB-GYN, Peds, Pub Health

⊕ https://vfmat.ch/c969

United States Agency for International Development (USAID)

Promotes and demonstrates democratic values abroad and advances a free, peaceful, and prosperous world. Leads the U.S. government's international development and disaster assistance through partnerships and investments that save lives.

ER Med, Infect Dis, MF Med, OB-GYN, Peds

⊕ https://vfmat.ch/9a99

World Health Organization, The (WHO)

The United Nations' agency for health provides leadership on global health matters, shapes the health research agenda, sets norms and standards, articulates evidence-based policy options, provides technical support and monitoring to countries, and assesses health trends.

ER Med, General, Infect Dis, Logist-Op, MF Med, OB-GYN, Peds, Psych, Pub Health

⊕ https://vfmat.ch/c476

Micronesia

Healthcare Facilities

Berysin's CHC
Kolonia, Pohnpei, Micronesia
🌐 https://vfmat.ch/hsg1

Chuuk Community Health Clinic
Weno, Chuuk, Micronesia
https://vfmat.ch/nxwq

Chuuk State Hospital
Nepukos, Chuuk, Micronesia
🌐 https://vfmat.ch/f65e

Genesis Hospital
Pohnpei, Kolonia, Micronesia
🌐 https://vfmat.ch/ppwy

Kosrae Hospital
Tofol Village, Kosrae, Micronesia
🌐 https://vfmat.ch/f28a

Medpharm Clinic and Pharmacy
Kolonia, Pohnpei, Micronesia
https://vfmat.ch/ag2c

Pohnpei Family Health Clinic
Kolonia, Pohnpei, Micronesia
https://vfmat.ch/6nnb

Pohnpei State Hospital
Paliais, Pohnpei, Micronesia
🌐 https://vfmat.ch/8eab

Walung Community Health Clinic
Walung, Kosrae, Micronesia
https://vfmat.ch/t8ci

Yap State Memorial Hospital
Colonia, Yap, Micronesia
🌐 https://vfmat.ch/rrba

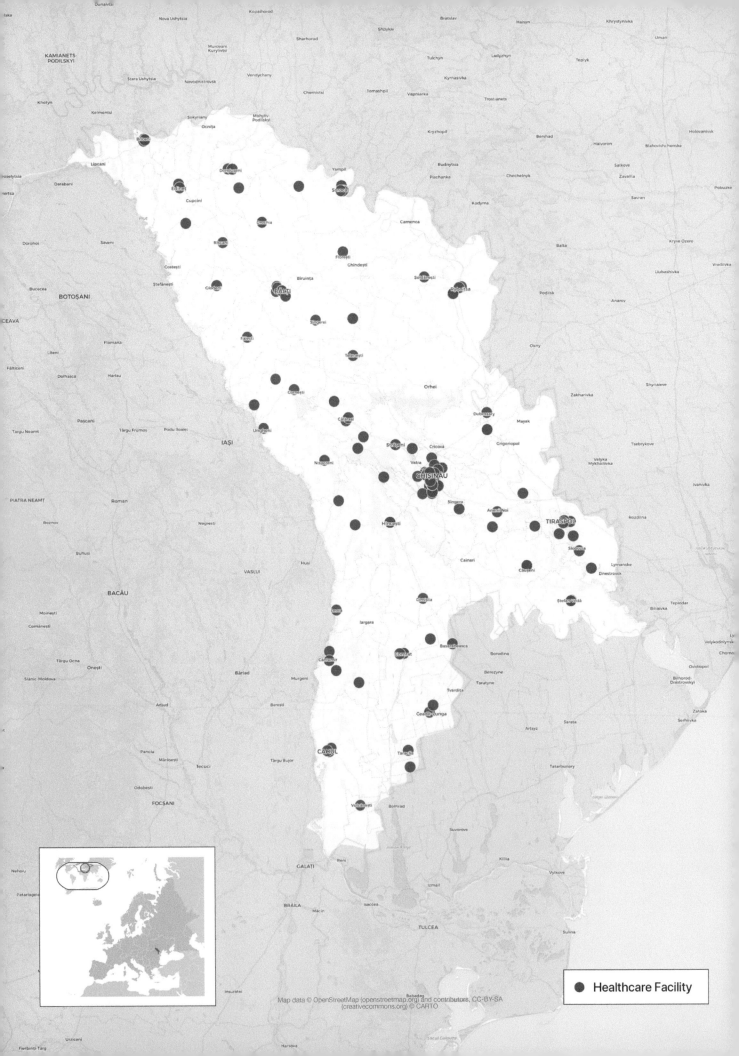

Healthcare Facility

Moldova

The Republic of Moldova is a landlocked country in Eastern Europe. With Chisinau as its largest city and capital, the country is bordered by Romania to the west, and Ukraine to the north, east, and south. Predominantly influenced by the Eastern Orthodox Catholic Church, the Republic of Moldova has a proportionately older population of 3.3 million people, comprising ethnic groups such as Moldovan/ Romanian, Ukrainian, Russian, Gagauz, and Bulgarian. The official language is Moldovan/Romanian, which also serves as the native language of about 82 percent of the population. Available natural resources include lignite, phosphorite, gypsum, limestone, and arable land.

Formerly part of Romania, Moldova was incorporated into the Soviet Union at the close of World War II. Moldova gained independence from the Soviet Union in 1991 and has been working toward successfully integrating into the European Union. Although economic reforms have been slow, largely due to corruption and strong political forces, there has been some market-oriented progress. The country's economy is dependent on agriculture, specifically fruits, vegetables, and tobacco, making it one of the poorest countries in Europe with a small lower-middle-income economy. But Moldova has made significant progress in reducing poverty and promoting inclusive growth, as well as expanding the economy on average by 4.6 percent yearly for the past two decades.

Since independence, Moldova has recorded a steady increase in the rates of both communicable and non-communicable diseases. Life expectancy hovers around 72 years, and the leading causes of death are ischemic heart disease, stroke, cirrhosis, hypertensive heart disease, Alzheimer's disease, lung cancer, colorectal cancer, COPD, lower respiratory infections, and self-harm. Heavy tobacco and alcohol use accounted for a total of 60 percent and 16 percent of male and female deaths respectively in 2010. Mortality due to non-communicable diseases has increased between 2009 and 2019, most notably hypertensive heart disease, which increased by over 95 percent.

3.3M

Population

$4,551

GDP Per Capita

72 years

Life Expectancy

↑ Improving

256
Doctors/100k

Physician Density

566
Beds/100k

Hospital Bed Density

19
Deaths/100k

Maternal Mortality

Moldova

Nonprofit Organizations

100X Development Foundation
Empowers children and families for a more hopeful and productive future through the support and care of orphaned children, education and job training for those in need, help for vulnerable youth to escape trafficking, and healthy nutrition and medical care for mothers to enable a safe birth.
ER Med, Infect Dis, OB-GYN, Peds, Psych
⊕ https://vfmat.ch/b629

Age International
Helps older people living in some of the world's poorest places to have improved well-being and be treated with dignity through a variety of programs, including emergency relief and cataract surgery.
ER Med, Geri, Logist-Op, Nutr, Ophth-Opt, Palliative, Pub Health
⊕ https://vfmat.ch/c7e2

American International Health Alliance (AIHA)
Strengthens health systems and workforce capacity worldwide through locally driven, peer-to-peer institutional partnerships.
CV Med, ER Med, Infect Dis, Medicine, OB-GYN
⊕ https://vfmat.ch/69fd

BroadReach
Collaborates with governments, multinational health organizations, donors, and private-sector companies to effect healthcare reform and solve the world's biggest health challenges.
Logist-Op
⊕ https://vfmat.ch/7812

ChildAid
Aims to support the work of local projects helping disadvantaged children in Eastern Europe, inspired by the Christian faith.
General, Neuro, Peds, Psych, Pub Health, Rehab
⊕ https://vfmat.ch/952a

Children's Emergency Relief International
Works with children, families, communities, and governments to provide a family environment as the first and best option for children to grow in.
General, Pub Health
⊕ https://vfmat.ch/92ae

Christian Aid Ministries
Strives to be a trustworthy and efficient channel for Amish, Mennonite, and other conservative Anabaptist groups and individuals to minister to physical and spiritual needs around the world.
CT Surg, ER Med, Logist-Op, Ortho, Pub Health
⊕ https://vfmat.ch/7b33

Dentaid
Seeks to treat, equip, train, and educate people in need of dental care.

Dent-OMFS
⊕ https://vfmat.ch/a183

Elton John AIDS Foundation
Seeks to address and overcome the stigma, discrimination, and neglect that prevents ending AIDS by funding local experts to challenge discrimination, prevent infections, and provide treatment.
Infect Dis, Pub Health
⊕ https://vfmat.ch/9d31

Friends of UNFPA
Promotes the health, dignity, and rights of women and girls around the world by supporting the lifesaving work of UNFPA, the United Nations' reproductive health and rights agency, through education, advocacy, and fundraising.
MF Med, OB-GYN
⊕ https://vfmat.ch/2a3a

Global Oncology (GO)
Brings the best in cancer care to underserved patients around the world and collaborates across geographic, professional, and academic borders to improve cancer care, research, and education.
Heme-Onc, Path, Rad-Onc
⊕ https://vfmat.ch/fcb8

Globus Relief
Aims to improve the delivery of healthcare worldwide by gathering, processing, and distributing surplus medical supplies to charities at home and abroad.
Logist-Op
⊕ https://vfmat.ch/a2b7

Health Volunteers Overseas (HVO)
Improves the availability and quality of healthcare through the education, training, and professional development of the health workforce in resource-scarce countries.
All-Immu, Anesth, CV Med, Dent-OMFS, Derm, ENT, ER Med, Endo, GI, Heme-Onc, Infect Dis, Medicine, Medicine, Nephro, Neuro, OB-GYN, Ophth-Opt, Ortho, Peds, Plast, Psych, Pulm-Critic, Rehab, Rheum, Surg
⊕ https://vfmat.ch/42b2

HealthProm
Works with local partners to promote health and social care for vulnerable children and their families.
General, MF Med, Peds, Pub Health
⊕ https://vfmat.ch/153d

Hear the World Foundation
Advocates worldwide for equal opportunities and improved quality of life for people in need with hearing loss.
ENT, Peds
⊕ https://vfmat.ch/122c

Heineman Medical Outreach

Provides medical and educational assistance globally to promote sustainable healthcare and enhanced living standards in underserved communities through the International Medical Outreach (IMO) program, a collaborative partnership between Heineman Medical Outreach and Atrium Health.

Anesth, CT Surg, CV Med, ER Med, General, Heme-Onc, Logist-Op, Medicine, Neonat, OB-GYN, Ped Surg, Peds, Surg, Vasc Surg

⊕ https://vfmat.ch/389b

Hernia International

Aims to provide relief from sickness, and protection and preservation of health, for persons affected by groin and abdominal hernias and residing in low- and middle-income countries.

Surg

⊕ https://vfmat.ch/e98e

Hospice Angelus

Provides patients with incurable or life-threatening diseases with free high-quality medical and social services.

Palliative

⊕ https://vfmat.ch/a9d7

Humanitarian Aid Response Team (HART)

Aims to alleviate poverty and injustice in Eastern Europe by working with local leaders, organizations and churches to empower communities, inspired by the Christian faith.

Dent-OMFS, General, Logist-Op, Peds

⊕ https://vfmat.ch/1cdd

International Federation of Gynecology and Obstetrics (FIGO)

Implements global projects on specific women's health issues.

MF Med, Medicine, Neonat, OB-GYN, Surg, Urol

⊕ https://vfmat.ch/c4b4

International Federation of Red Cross and Red Crescent Societies (IFRC)

Coordinates and directs international assistance following natural and manmade disasters in nonconflict situations through the world's largest humanitarian and development network. Provides disaster-preparedness programs, healthcare activities, and promotes humanitarian values.

ER Med, General, Infect Dis, Nutr

⊕ https://vfmat.ch/b4ee

International Organization for Migration (IOM) – The UN Migration Agency

Promotes evidence-informed policies and holistic, preventive, and curative health programs that are beneficial, accessible, and equitable for vulnerable migrants.

General, Infect Dis, OB-GYN

⊕ https://vfmat.ch/621a

Joint United Nations Programme on HIV/AIDS (UNAIDS)

Aims to place people living with HIV and people affected by the virus at the decision-making table and at the center of designing, delivering, and monitoring the AIDS response.

Infect Dis

⊕ https://vfmat.ch/464a

Kybele Incorporated

Aims to create healthcare partnerships across borders to improve childbirth safety.

Anesth, Neonat, OB-GYN, Pub Health

⊕ https://vfmat.ch/5fc9

MAP International

Provides medicines and health supplies to those in need around the world so they might experience life to the fullest.

Logist-Op

⊕ https://vfmat.ch/deed

Optivest Foundation

Funds strategic opportunities that are holistic and collaborative, inspired by the Christian faith.

General, Nutr

⊕ https://vfmat.ch/f1e6

Order of Malta

Supports forgotten or excluded people, especially those living in conflict zones or amid natural disasters, by providing medical assistance, caring for refugees, and distributing medicines and necessities.

ER Med, General, Infect Dis, MF Med, Nephro, OB-GYN, Ortho, Psych

⊕ https://vfmat.ch/1fab

Outreach Moldova

Advocates for and provides medical care and education for abandoned or orphaned children, children with special needs, and terminally ill children in Moldova.

Logist-Op, Nutr, Pub Health

⊕ https://vfmat.ch/f766

Overflowing Hands

Aims to serve children in communities across the U.S. and around the world by providing food, clothing, shelter, and healthcare.

Logist-Op, Pub Health, Radiol

⊕ https://vfmat.ch/8522

Pharmacists Without Borders Canada

Provides pharmaceutical and technical assistance in the implementation or improvement of community and hospital pharmacies internationally.

⊕ https://vfmat.ch/7658

RestoringVision

Empowers lives by restoring vision for millions of people in need.

Ophth-Opt

⊕ https://vfmat.ch/e121

Rotary International

Provides service to others, improves lives, and advances world understanding, goodwill, and peace through its fellowship of business, professional, and community leaders.

ER Med, General, Infect Dis, MF Med, OB-GYN

⊕ https://vfmat.ch/8fb5

Salvation Army International, The

Seeks to meet human needs through services in education, healthcare, community support, emergency response, and ministry development, inspired by the Christian faith.

Dent-OMFS, Derm, ER Med, Infect Dis, MF Med, Medicine, Nutr, OB-GYN, Ophth-Opt, Palliative, Psych, Rehab, Surg

⊕ https://vfmat.ch/8eb3

Sri Sathya Sai International Organization

Inspired by spiritual teachings, carries out efforts in global healthcare, education, humanitarian relief, and youth engagement.

Dent-OMFS, General, Logist-Op, Nutr, Ophth-Opt, Pub Health

⊕ https://vfmat.ch/9bda

Swiss Tropical and Public Health Institute

Contributes to the improvement of the health of populations internationally, nationally, and locally through excellence in research, education, and services.

Infect Dis, Pub Health

⊕ https://vfmat.ch/2ee4

Task Force for Global Health, The

Consists of programs and focus areas that cover a range of global health issues including neglected tropical diseases, infectious diseases, vaccines, field epidemiology, public health informatics, health workforce development, and global health ethics.

Infect Dis, Logist-Op, Medicine, Ophth-Opt, Peds

⊕ https://vfmat.ch/714c

Terre des hommes (Tdh) Foundation

Works to improve the daily life of children and their relatives in the areas of health, protection and emergency, in Europe, Africa, Asia, Latin America, and the Near and Middle East.

CT Surg, CV Med, OB-GYN, Ped Surg, Pub Health

⊕ https://vfmat.ch/5c26

United Nations Children's Fund (UNICEF)

Works in over 190 countries and territories to save children's lives, defend their rights, and help them fulfill their potential, from early childhood through adolescence.

All-Immu, Infect Dis, MF Med, Neonat, Nutr, OB-GYN, Ped Surg, Peds, Pub Health

⊕ https://vfmat.ch/42d7

United Nations Development Programme (UNDP)

Helps countries achieve the simultaneous eradication of extreme poverty and significant reduction of inequalities and exclusion using a sustainable human development approach.

Infect Dis, Logist-Op, Pub Health

⊕ https://vfmat.ch/935c

United Nations High Commissioner for Refugees (UNHCR)

Safeguards the rights and well-being of people who have been forced to flee, ensuring that everybody has the right to seek asylum and find safe refuge in another country, with the goal of seeking lasting solutions.

General, MF Med, Medicine, OB-GYN, Peds, Psych, Pub Health

⊕ https://vfmat.ch/6636

United Nations Population Fund (UNFPA)

Supports reproductive healthcare for women and youth in more than 150 countries, focusing on delivering a world in which every pregnancy is wanted, every childbirth is safe, and every young person's potential is fulfilled.

Infect Dis, MF Med, Neonat, OB-GYN, Peds, Pub Health

⊕ https://vfmat.ch/c969

USAID: Leadership, Management and Governance Project

Improves leadership, management, and governance practices to strengthen health systems and improve health for all, including vulnerable populations worldwide.

Logist-Op

⊕ https://vfmat.ch/d35e

VOSH (Volunteer Optometric Services to Humanity) International

Facilitates the provision and the sustainability of vision care worldwide for people who can neither afford nor obtain such care.

Ophth-Opt

⊕ https://vfmat.ch/a149

World Children's Fund

Commits to helping children worldwide who are suffering the effects of poverty, disease, natural disaster, famine, abuse, civil strife, and war.

General, Logist-Op, MF Med, Nutr, OB-GYN, Pub Health

⊕ https://vfmat.ch/9cd8

World Federation of Hemophilia (WFH)

Aims to improve and sustain care for people with inherited bleeding disorders by pursuing long-term relationships with individuals and organizations who share the values of WFH's development model.

Heme-Onc

⊕ https://vfmat.ch/5121

World Health Organization, The (WHO)

The United Nations' agency for health provides leadership on global health matters, shapes the health research agenda, sets norms and standards, articulates evidence-based policy options, provides technical support and monitoring to countries, and assesses health trends.

ER Med, General, Infect Dis, Logist-Op, MF Med, OB-GYN, Peds, Psych, Pub Health

⊕ https://vfmat.ch/c476

World Medical Relief

Facilitates the distribution of surplus medical resources where they are needed.

Logist-Op

⊕ https://vfmat.ch/72dc

Moldova

Healthcare Facilities

Center for Reproductive Health
Tiraspol, Transnistria, Moldova
⊕ https://vfmat.ch/7283

Centrul Ftiziopneumologic de Reabilitare pentru Copii Cornesti
Cornesti, Ungheni, Moldova
⊕ https://vfmat.ch/jms8

Centrul Republican de Reabilitare pentru Copii
Chisinau, Chisinau, Moldova
⊕ https://vfmat.ch/upbv

Centrul Sanatatii Familiei Galaxia
Chisinau, Moldova
⊕ https://vfmat.ch/6cbd

IMSP Institutul de Cardiologie
Chisinau, Chisinau, Moldova
⊕ https://vfmat.ch/721e

IMSP Institutul de Ftiziopneumologie Chiril Draganiuc
Chisinau, Chisinau, Moldova
⊕ https://vfmat.ch/ewri

IMSP Institutul de Medicina Urgenta
Chisinau, Chisinau, Moldova
⊕ https://vfmat.ch/c83f

IMSP Institutul de Neurologie si Neurochirurgie Diomid Gherman
Chisinau, Chisinau, Moldova
⊕ https://vfmat.ch/11ce

IMSP Institutul Mamei si Copilului
Chisinau, Chisinau, Moldova
⊕ https://vfmat.ch/c6ba

IMSP Institutul Oncologic
Chisinau, Moldova
⊕ https://vfmat.ch/bacf

IMSP Maternitatea Municipala #2
Chisinau, Chisinau, Moldova
⊕ https://vfmat.ch/58b5

IMSP Spitalul de Psihiatrie Balti
Balti, Balti, Moldova
⊕ https://vfmat.ch/19df

IMSP Spitalul de Stat
Chisinau, Chisinau, Moldova
⊕ https://vfmat.ch/1rar

IMSP Spitalul Dermatologie si Maladii Comunicabile
Chisinau, Chisinau, Moldova
⊕ https://vfmat.ch/2276

IMSP Spitalul Raional Anenii Noi
Anenii Noi, Anenii Noi, Moldova
⊕ https://vfmat.ch/5ea7

IMSP Spitalul Raional Basarabeasca
Basarabeasca, Basarabeasca, Moldova
⊕ https://vfmat.ch/vv86

IMSP Spitalul Raional Briceni
Briceni, Briceni, Moldova
⊕ https://vfmat.ch/tjx1

IMSP Spitalul Raional Cahul
Cahul, Cahul, Moldova
⊕ https://vfmat.ch/5245

IMSP Spitalul Raional Calarasi
Calarasi, Calarasi, Moldova
⊕ https://vfmat.ch/lfkb

IMSP Spitalul Raional Cantemir
Cantemir, Cantemir, Moldova
⊕ https://vfmat.ch/5b65

IMSP Spitalul Raional Causeni Ana si Alexandru
Causeni, Causeni, Moldova
⊕ https://vfmat.ch/78a6

IMSP Spitalul Raional Ceadir-Lunga
Ceadir-Lunga, Gagauzia, Moldova
⊕ https://vfmat.ch/8771

IMSP Spitalul Raional Cimislia
Cimislia, Cimislia, Moldova
⊕ https://vfmat.ch/287a

IMSP Spitalul Raional Comrat Isaac Gurfinkel
Comrat, Gagauzia, Moldova
⊕ https://vfmat.ch/ndjn

IMSP Spitalul Raional Criuleni
Criuleni, Criuleni, Moldova
⊕ https://vfmat.ch/df88

IMSP Spitalul Raional Donduseni
Donduseni, Donduseni, Moldova
⊕ https://vfmat.ch/31z2

IMSP Spitalul Raional Drochia Nicolae Testemitanu
Drochia, Drochia, Moldova
⊕ https://vfmat.ch/5684

IMSP Spitalul Raional Edinet
Edinet, Edinet, Moldova
⊕ https://vfmat.ch/176b

IMSP Spitalul Raional Falesti
Falesti, Falesti, Moldova
⊕ https://vfmat.ch/ed6f

IMSP Spitalul Raional Floresti
Floresti, Floresti, Moldova
⊕ https://vfmat.ch/1ab7

IMSP Spitalul Raional Glodeni
Glodeni, Glodeni, Moldova
⊕ https://vfmat.ch/n3z9

IMSP Spitalul Raional Hincesti
Hincesti, Hincesti, Moldova
⊕ https://vfmat.ch/2cbd

IMSP Spitalul Raional Ialoveni
Ialoveni, Chisinau, Moldova
⊕ https://vfmat.ch/26ec

IMSP Spitalul Raional Leova
Leova, Leova, Moldova
⊕ https://vfmat.ch/a142

IMSP Spitalul Raional Rezina
Rezina, Rezina, Moldova
⊕ https://vfmat.ch/3bb7

IMSP Spitalul Raional Riscani
Riscani, Riscani, Moldova
⊕ https://vfmat.ch/6fb9

IMSP Spitalul Raional Singerei
Singerei, Singerei, Moldova
⊕ https://vfmat.ch/7d31

IMSP Spitalul Raional Soldanesti
Soldanesti, Soldanesti, Moldova
⊕ https://vfmat.ch/527f

IMSP Spitalul Raional Soroca A. Prisacari
Soroca, Soroca, Moldova
⊕ https://vfmat.ch/b829

IMSP Spitalul Raional Stefan-Voda
Stefan-Voda, Stefan-Voda, Moldova
⊕ https://vfmat.ch/f24c

IMSP Spitalul Raional Straseni
Straseni, Straseni, Moldova
⊕ https://vfmat.ch/ec33

IMSP Spitalul Raional Taraclia
Taraclia, Taraclia, Moldova
⊕ https://vfmat.ch/6588

IMSP Spitalul Raional Telenesti
Telenesti, Telenesti, Moldova
⊕ https://vfmat.ch/3eb8

IMSP Spitalul Raional Ungheni
Ungheni, Ungheni, Moldova
⊕ https://vfmat.ch/kt3z

IMSP Spitalul Raional Vulcanesti
Vulcanesti, Gagauzia, Moldova
⊕ https://vfmat.ch/b494

IMSP Spitalul Republican al Asociatiei Curativ-Sanatoriale
Chisinau, Chisinau, Moldova
⊕ https://vfmat.ch/54b3

Novamed
Chișinău, Chișinău, Moldova
⊕ https://vfmat.ch/g35b

Physiopneumological Rehabilitation Center for Children Tirnova
Tîrnova, Dondușeni, Moldova
⊕ https://vfmat.ch/5b16

Republican Center of Mother and Child
Sucleia, Tiraspol, Moldova
⊕ https://vfmat.ch/cd72

Sanatoriul Nufarul Alb
Cahul, Moldova
⊕ https://vfmat.ch/6246

Spitalul International Medpark
Chisinau, Chisinau, Moldova
⊕ https://vfmat.ch/256b

Spitalul Raional Central Ribnita IS
Ribnita, Transnistria, Moldova
⊕ https://vfmat.ch/773d

Spitalul Republican al Ministerului Afacerilor Interne
Chisinau, Chisinau, Moldova
⊕ https://vfmat.ch/dfcw

Veteran Hospital Tiraspol
Sucleia, Transnistria, Moldova
⊕ https://vfmat.ch/f1f9

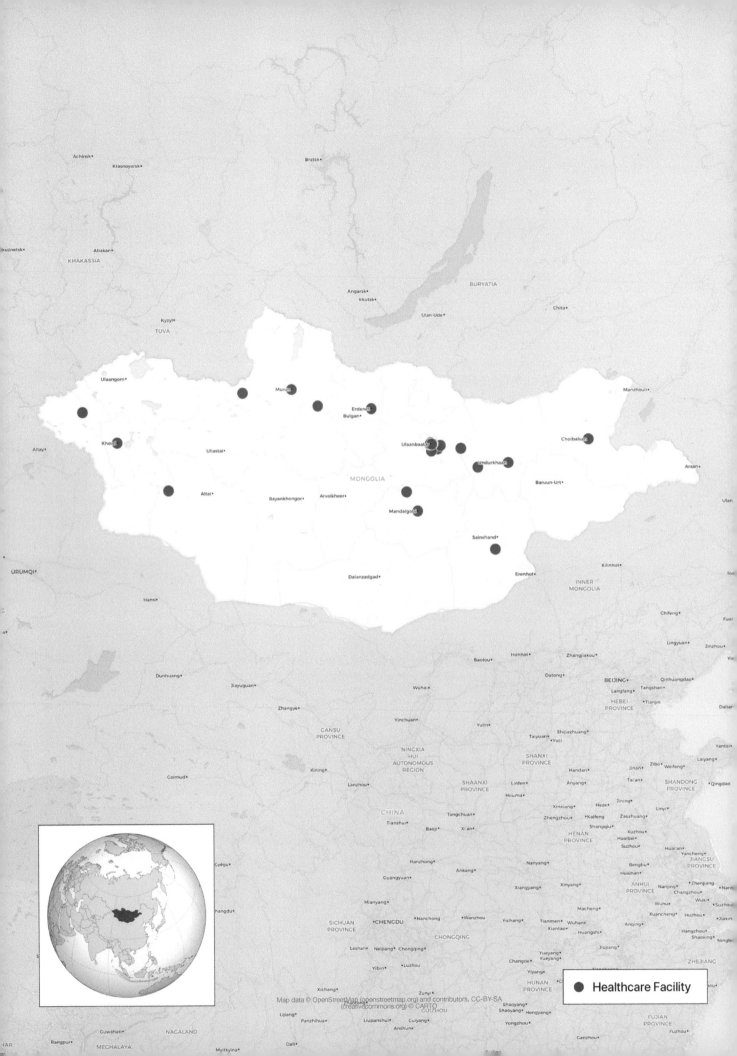

Healthcare Facility

Mongolia

Called the "Land of Blue Sky," with incredible natural features such as mountains in the north and the Gobi Desert in the south, Mongolia is also famous for having more horses than people. It's a landlocked country in East Asia, bordered by Russia to the north and China to the south. While it does not officially border Kazakhstan, it is considered a close neighbor, being only 37 kilometers away in some areas. Mongolia's population of just 3.2 million makes it the world's most sparsely populated country; there are only two people per square kilometer. About half the population lives in the capital city of Ulaanbaatar, while 30 percent of Mongolians remain nomadic and semi-nomadic, with horse culture playing an important role in daily life. Mongolia's ethnic majority is Khalkh, with smaller groups including Kazak, Dorvod, Bayad, Buryat-Gouriates, and Zahkchin. Languages spoken include Mongolian (Khalkha dialect), Turkic, and Russian. About 50 percent of the population is Buddhist, in addition to Muslim, Shamanist, and Christian. Nearly 40 percent of Mongolians do not identify with a specific religion.

Mongolia has an ancient and rich history. The Mongol Empire, led by Genghis Khan, was once the largest empire in the world. Mongolia was absorbed by China but declared independence in 1921. By 1924, it had become a satellite of the Soviet Union. After anti-communist revolutions, a peaceful democratic revolution took place in 1990, and by 1992 Mongolia gained independence. Mongolia is rich in mineral deposits, such as copper, gold, coal, molybdenum, fluorspar, uranium, tin, and tungsten. The extractive industries helped switch the economy from primarily herding and agriculture, and now exports make up 40 percent of the Mongolian GDP. Education in Mongolia has greatly improved since 1921, when the country began building networks of public schools and providing free education. Since then, the networks of schools have expanded, and children are expected to attend school for at least 11 years. As a result, literacy is high, with 98 percent of the population over the age of 15 able to read and write.

Over the past 30 years, Mongolia has made tremendous progress in health indicators. There has been a sharp decline in maternal mortality, which is still improving annually. Child mortality has been decreasing steadily since 1990, while life expectancy has been increasing. Leading causes of death in Mongolia include ischemic heart disease, stroke, liver cancer, cirrhosis, stomach cancer, road injuries, lung cancer, self-harm, alcohol use disorders, neonatal disorders, and lower respiratory infections. The risk factors that contribute most to death and disability include high blood pressure, dietary risks, alcohol and tobacco use, high body-mass index, air pollution, high LDL, malnutrition, kidney dysfunction, and high fasting plasma glucose.

3.2M

Population

$4,007

GDP Per Capita

70 years

Life Expectancy

↑ Improving

385

Doctors/100k

Physician Density

800

Beds/100k

Hospital Bed Density

45

Deaths/100k

Maternal Mortality

Mongolia

Nonprofit Organizations

A Broader View Volunteers
Provides developing countries around the world with significant volunteer programs that aid the neediest communities and forge a lasting bond between those volunteering and those they have helped.

Dent-OMFS, ER Med, Infect Dis, MF Med

⊕ https://vfmat.ch/3bec

Aceso Global
Provides strategic healthcare advisory services in low- and middle-income countries to design and deliver highly customized, evidence-based solutions that address the complex nature of healthcare systems, with a goal to strengthen and provide affordable, high-quality care to all.

Logist-Op, Pub Health

⊕ https://vfmat.ch/b3b7

Americares
Saves lives and improves health for people affected by poverty or disaster and responds with life-changing medicine, medical supplies, and health programs including domestic and global medical clinics.

All-Immu, ER Med, General, Infect Dis, MF Med, Nutr

⊕ https://vfmat.ch/e567

Amurtel
Aims to alleviate suffering and provide immediate and long-term relief to women and children in need, and to improve their overall quality of life.

⊕ https://vfmat.ch/2b19

Assist International
Designs and implements humanitarian programs that build capacity, develop opportunities, and save lives around the world.

Infect Dis, Ped Surg, Peds

⊕ https://vfmat.ch/9a3b

Association of Medical Doctors of Asia (AMDA)
Strives to support people affected by disasters and economic distress on their road to recovery, establishing a true partnership with special emphasis on local initiative.

ER Med, Logist-Op, Pub Health

⊕ https://vfmat.ch/e3d4

Baylor College of Medicine: Global Surgery
Trains leaders in academic global surgery and remains dedicated to advancements in the areas of patient care, biomedical research, and medical education.

ENT, Infect Dis, OB-GYN, Ortho, Ped Surg, Plast, Pub Health, Radiol, Surg, Urol

⊕ https://vfmat.ch/21f5

Bridge of Life
Aims to strengthen healthcare globally through sustainable programs that prevent and treat chronic disease.

Logist-Op, Nephro, OB-GYN, Peds, Surg

⊕ https://vfmat.ch/5b68

British Council for Prevention of Blindness (BCPB)
Funds research into blindness prevention and sight restoration in children and adults in low- and lower-middle-income countries.

Ophth-Opt

⊕ https://vfmat.ch/eaf4

Bureau of International Health Cooperation
Seeks to improve healthcare around the world, including developing countries, using expertise, and contribute to healthier lives of Japanese people by bringing these experiences back to Japan.

ER Med, Heme-Onc, Infect Dis, Peds, Pub Health

⊕ https://vfmat.ch/947d

Caring Hands Worldwide
Inspired by the Christian faith, works to improve dental health of those in need in partner communities in the U.S. and abroad.

Dent-OMFS, Logist-Op

⊕ https://vfmat.ch/62cc

Christian Aid Ministries
Strives to be a trustworthy and efficient channel for Amish, Mennonite, and other conservative Anabaptist groups and individuals to minister to physical and spiritual needs around the world.

CT Surg, ER Med, Logist-Op, Ortho, Pub Health

⊕ https://vfmat.ch/7b33

Columbia University: Global Mental Health Programs
Pioneers research initiatives, promotes mental health, and aims to reduce the burden of mental illness worldwide.

Psych

⊕ https://vfmat.ch/c5cd

Developing Country NGO Delegation: Global Fund to Fight AIDS, TB & Malaria
Works to strengthen the engagement of civil society actors and organizations in developing countries to build a world in which AIDS, TB, and malaria are no longer global, public health, and human rights threats.

Infect Dis, Pub Health

⊕ https://vfmat.ch/3149

Direct Relief
Improves the health and lives of people affected by poverty or emergency situations by mobilizing and providing essential medical resources needed for their care.

ER Med, Logist-Op

⊕ https://vfmat.ch/58e5

Duke University: Global Health Institute
Sparks innovation in global health research and education, and brings together knowledge and resources to address the most important global health issues of our time.
All-Immu, Infect Dis, MF Med, OB-GYN, Pub Health
⊕ https://vfmat.ch/c4cd

Flying Doctors of America
Brings together teams of physicians, dentists, nurses, and other healthcare professionals to care for people who would not otherwise receive medical care.
Dent-OMFS, GI, General, Surg
⊕ https://vfmat.ch/58b6

For Hearts and Souls
Provides medical outreach and care for children through heart-related work, such as diagnosing heart problems and performing heart-saving surgeries.
Anesth, CT Surg, CV Med, Crit-Care, Peds, Pulm-Critic
⊕ https://vfmat.ch/a162

Gift of Life International
Provides lifesaving cardiac treatment to children in developing countries while developing sustainable pediatric cardiac programs by implementing screening, surgical, and training missions.
Anesth, CT Surg, CV Med, Crit-Care, Ped Surg, Peds, Pulm-Critic
⊕ https://vfmat.ch/f2f9

Global Civic Sharing
Aims to support our neighbors' self-reliance and realize the sustainable development.
Nutr, Peds, Pub Health
⊕ https://vfmat.ch/d7ab

Global Foundation For Children With Hearing Loss
Aims to help babies and young children who are deaf or hard of hearing and living in low- and middle-income countries by providing access to early identification, hearing technology, and locally based professional expertise.
Ortho, Peds, Plast
⊕ https://vfmat.ch/d1d1

Global Medical Missions
Organizes medical missions and partners with local medical organizations, usually hospitals or health systems, in fulfilling their mission of reaching their community's health needs in developing countries by providing needed medical care and screening to those underserved.
General
⊕ https://vfmat.ch/8d73

Global Ministries – The United Methodist Church
As the worldwide mission and development agency of The United Methodist Church, Global Ministries works with more than 300 hospitals and clinics around the world through its Global Health Unit.
Anesth, CT Surg, CV Med, Crit-Care, Dent-OMFS, Derm, ER Med, GI, General, Infect Dis, Logist-Op, MF Med, Medicine, Neonat, Nephro, Nutr, OB-GYN, Ophth-Opt, Ortho, Palliative, Peds, Pod, Psych, Pub Health, Rehab, Rheum, Surg, Urol
⊕ https://vfmat.ch/1723

Global Oncology (GO)
Brings the best in cancer care to underserved patients around the world and collaborates across geographic, professional, and academic borders to improve cancer care, research, and education.
Heme-Onc, Path, Rad-Onc
⊕ https://vfmat.ch/fcb8

Globus Relief
Aims to improve the delivery of healthcare worldwide by gathering, processing, and distributing surplus medical supplies to charities at home and abroad.
Logist-Op
⊕ https://vfmat.ch/a2b7

Healing the Children
Helps underserved children around the world secure the medical care they need to lead more fulfilling lives.
Anesth, Dent-OMFS, ENT, General, Medicine, Ophth-Opt, Ped Surg, Peds, Plast, Surg
⊕ https://vfmat.ch/d4ee

HealthProm
Works with local partners to promote health and social care for vulnerable children and their families.
General, MF Med, Peds, Pub Health
⊕ https://vfmat.ch/153d

HealthServe Australia
Develops sustainable health programs that improve health and well-being and partners with community groups to build community capacity to meet health needs.
Infect Dis, Logist-Op, OB-GYN, Psych, Pub Health
⊕ https://vfmat.ch/7276

Hear the World Foundation
Advocates worldwide for equal opportunities and improved quality of life for people in need with hearing loss.
ENT, Peds
⊕ https://vfmat.ch/122c

HelpAge International
Works to ensure that people everywhere understand how much older people contribute to society and that they must enjoy their right to healthcare, social services, economic, and physical security.
General, Geri, Infect Dis, Medicine, Pub Health
⊕ https://vfmat.ch/5d91

Hernia International
Aims to provide relief from sickness, and protection and preservation of health, for persons affected by groin and abdominal hernias and residing in low- and middle-income countries.
Surg
⊕ https://vfmat.ch/e98e

HIS Foundation (Holistic Integrated Services Foundation)
Provides free medical services for patients in underserved communities, such as services in orthopedic surgery, plastic surgery, internal medicine, rehabilitation, and ophthalmology, formed by Christian medical professionals.
Dent-OMFS, Geri, Medicine, Ophth-Opt, Ortho, Plast, Rehab
⊕ https://vfmat.ch/a24b

International Children's Heart Fund
Aims to promote the international growth and quality of cardiac surgery, particularly in children and young adults.
CT Surg, Ped Surg
⊕ https://vfmat.ch/33fb

International Council of Ophthalmology
Works with ophthalmologic societies and others to enhance ophthalmic education and improve access to the highest-quality eye care in order to preserve and restore vision for people of the world.
Ophth-Opt
⊕ https://vfmat.ch/ffd2

International Federation of Gynecology and Obstetrics (FIGO)
Implements global projects on specific women's health issues.
MF Med, Medicine, Neonat, OB-GYN, Surg, Urol
⊕ https://vfmat.ch/c4b4

International Federation of Red Cross and Red Crescent Societies (IFRC)
Coordinates and directs international assistance following natural and manmade disasters in nonconflict situations through the world's largest humanitarian and development network. Provides disaster-preparedness programs, healthcare activities, and promotes humanitarian values.
ER Med, General, Infect Dis, Nutr
⊕ https://vfmat.ch/b4ee

International Organization for Migration (IOM) – The UN Migration Agency
Promotes evidence-informed policies and holistic, preventive, and curative health programs that are beneficial, accessible, and equitable for vulnerable migrants.
General, Infect Dis, OB-GYN
⊕ https://vfmat.ch/621a

International Planned Parenthood Federation (IPPF)
Leads a locally owned, globally connected civil society movement that provides and enables services and champions sexual and reproductive health and rights for all, especially the underserved.
Infect Dis, MF Med, OB-GYN
⊕ https://vfmat.ch/dc97

International Union Against Tuberculosis and Lung Disease
Develops, implements, and assesses anti-tuberculosis, lung health, and noncommunicable disease programs.
Infect Dis, Pub Health, Pulm-Critic
⊕ https://vfmat.ch/3e82

Iris Global
Serves the poor, the destitute, the lost, and the forgotten by providing adoration, outreach, family, education, relief, development, healing, and the arts.
General, Infect Dis, Nutr, Pub Health
⊕ https://vfmat.ch/37f8

IVUmed
Aims to make quality urological care available worldwide by providing medical and surgical education for physicians and nurses, and treatment for thousands of children and adults.
Anesth, OB-GYN, Ped Surg, Surg, Urol
⊕ https://vfmat.ch/e619

Joint United Nations Programme on HIV/AIDS (UNAIDS)
Aims to place people living with HIV and people affected by the virus at the decision-making table and at the center of designing, delivering, and monitoring the AIDS response.
Infect Dis
⊕ https://vfmat.ch/464a

Kids Care Everywhere
Seeks to empower physicians in under-resourced environments with multimedia, state-of-the-art medical software, and to inspire young professionals to become future global healthcare leaders.
Logist-Op, Ped Surg, Peds
⊕ https://vfmat.ch/bc23

Kind Cuts for Kids
Aims to improve medical services for children in developing countries through education, demonstration, and skills transfer to local healthcare professionals.
Anesth, Medicine, Ped Surg, Surg
⊕ https://vfmat.ch/e3d7

Kybele Incorporated
Aims to create healthcare partnerships across borders to improve childbirth safety.
Anesth, Neonat, OB-GYN, Pub Health
⊕ https://vfmat.ch/5fc9

London School of Hygiene & Tropical Medicine: International Centre for Eye Health
Works to improve eye health and eliminate avoidable visual impairment and blindness with a focus on low-income populations.
Logist-Op, Ophth-Opt, Pub Health
⊕ https://vfmat.ch/6f5f

Maitreya Charity
Keeps families together and prevents children from going onto the streets in Mongolia.
General, Logist-Op, Pub Health
⊕ https://vfmat.ch/dfa1

Making A Difference Foundation
Sponsors and organizes medical missions for medical providers to provide care to underserved communities around the world.
CV Med, Dent-OMFS, ER Med, General, Infect Dis, Logist-Op, MF Med, Neonat, Nutr, OB-GYN, Ophth-Opt, Ortho, Pub Health, Pulm-Critic, Rehab, Surg
⊕ https://vfmat.ch/5556

MAP International
Provides medicines and health supplies to those in need around the world so they might experience life to the fullest.
Logist-Op
⊕ https://vfmat.ch/deed

Marie Stopes International
Provides the contraception and safe abortion services that enable women all over the world to choose their own futures.
Infect Dis, MF Med, Neonat, OB-GYN, Pub Health
⊕ https://vfmat.ch/9525

McGill University Health Centre: Centre for Global Surgery
Works to reduce the impact of injury by advancing surgical care through research and education in resource-limited settings.
ER Med, Logist-Op, Ped Surg, Surg
⊕ https://vfmat.ch/7246

MedShare
Aims to improve the quality of life of people, communities, and the planet by sourcing and directly delivering surplus medical supplies and equipment to communities in need around the world.
Logist-Op
⊕ https://vfmat.ch/c8bc

Mercy Ships
Operates hospital ships staffed by volunteers to bring hope, healing, and healthcare to underserved communities worldwide.
Anesth, Dent-OMFS, Logist-Op, Neonat, OB-GYN, Ophth-Opt, Ortho, Palliative, Plast, Psych, Surg
⊕ https://vfmat.ch/2e99

Mission to Heal
Aims to heal underserved people and train local practitioners in the most remote areas of the world through global healthcare missions.
Anesth, Infect Dis, OB-GYN, Surg
⊕ https://vfmat.ch/4718

Mongolian Palliative Care Society
Improves quality and access to palliative care services for Mongolian people through policy, education, drug availability, advocacy, and public awareness.
Palliative
⊕ https://vfmat.ch/1cd6

Mongolian society for Pediatric Nephrology
Promotes care for children with kidney disease through advocacy, education, and disseminating advances in clinical practice and scientific investigation.
Nephro, Ped Surg
⊕ https://vfmat.ch/5a37

Mother Earth (Eejii Yertunts)
Provides palliative care services to terminally ill patients and cancer patients without treatment. Also provides an information center with cancer prevention resources and at-home patient care training.
Nutr, Palliative, Psych
⊕ https://vfmat.ch/b247

MSI Reproductive Choices (Marie Stopes International)
Seeks to deliver quality family planning and reproductive healthcare to women around the world.
MF Med
⊕ https://vfmat.ch/5c82

Médecins du Monde/Doctors of the World
Provides care, bears witness, and supports social change worldwide with innovative medical programs and evidence-based advocacy initiatives.
ER Med, General, Infect Dis, MF Med, Neonat, OB-GYN, Peds, Pub Health
⊕ https://vfmat.ch/a43d

Mérieux Foundation
Committed to fighting infectious diseases that affect developing countries by capacity building, particularly in clinical laboratories, and focusing on diagnosis.

Logist-Op, Path
⊕ https://vfmat.ch/a23a

NuVasive Spine Foundation (NSF)
Partners with leading spine surgeons, nonprofits, and in-country medical professionals/facilities to bring life-changing spine surgery to under-resourced communities around the world.
Logist-Op, Ortho, Ped Surg, Rehab, Surg
⊕ https://vfmat.ch/6ccc

Open Heart International
Provides surgical interventions and best practices to the most disadvantaged communities on the planet.
CT Surg, MF Med, OB-GYN, Ophth-Opt, Plast, Surg
⊕ https://vfmat.ch/dab2

Operation Hernia
Provides high-quality surgery at minimal cost to patients who otherwise would not receive it.
Anesth, Ortho, Surg
⊕ https://vfmat.ch/6e9a

Orbis International
Works to prevent and treat blindness through hands-on training and improved access to quality eye care.
Anesth, Ophth-Opt, Surg
⊕ https://vfmat.ch/f2b2

RestoringVision
Empowers lives by restoring vision for millions of people in need.
Ophth-Opt
⊕ https://vfmat.ch/e121

Rockefeller Foundation, The
Works to promote the well-being of humanity.
Logist-Op, Nutr, Pub Health
⊕ https://vfmat.ch/5424

Rotary International
Provides service to others, improves lives, and advances world understanding, goodwill, and peace through its fellowship of business, professional, and community leaders.
ER Med, General, Infect Dis, MF Med, OB-GYN
⊕ https://vfmat.ch/8fb5

Salvation Army International, The
Seeks to meet human needs through services in education, healthcare, community support, emergency response, and ministry development, inspired by the Christian faith.
Dent-OMFS, Derm, ER Med, Infect Dis, MF Med, Medicine, Nutr, OB-GYN, Ophth-Opt, Palliative, Psych, Rehab, Surg
⊕ https://vfmat.ch/8eb3

Samaritan's Purse International Disaster Relief
Provides spiritual and physical aid to hurting people around the world, such as victims of war, poverty, natural disasters, disease, and famine, based in Christian ministry.
Anesth, CT Surg, Crit-Care, Dent-OMFS, Derm, ENT, ER Med, Endo, GI, General, Heme-Onc, Infect Dis, MF Med, Neonat, Nephro, Neuro, Neurosurg, Nutr, OB-GYN, Ophth-Opt, Ortho, Path, Ped Surg, Peds, Plast, Psych, Pulm-Critic, Radiol, Rehab, Rheum, Surg, Urol, Vasc Surg
⊕ https://vfmat.ch/87e3

Sanofi Espoir Foundation
Contributes to reducing health inequalities among populations that need it most by applying a socially responsible approach focused on fighting childhood cancers in low-income countries, improving maternal and newborn health, and improving access to care.
ER Med, OB-GYN, Peds
⊕ https://vfmat.ch/943b

SEE International
Provides sustainable medical, surgical, and educational services through

volunteer ophthalmic surgeons, with the objectives of restoring sight and preventing blindness to disadvantaged individuals worldwide.
Ophth-Opt, Surg
⊕ https://vfmat.ch/6e1b

SIGN Fracture Care International
Builds orthopedic capacity around the world and provides the injured poor access to fracture surgery by donating orthopedic education and implant systems to surgeons in developing countries.
Ortho, Rehab, Surg
⊕ https://vfmat.ch/123d

Smile Asia
Delivers free surgical care, through medical missions and outreach centers, to children with facial deformities such as cleft lip and cleft palate, and aims to raise standards of medical care by creating opportunities for collaborative learning and exchange of best practices.
Anesth, Dent-OMFS, Ped Surg, Peds, Plast
⊕ https://vfmat.ch/d674

Smile Train, Inc.
Treats children with cleft lip through a sustainable and local model that supports surgery and other forms of essential care.
Logist-Op, Pub Health
⊕ https://vfmat.ch/822c

Spine Care International
Extends spine care to the underprivileged and provides life-changing treatment to those who may otherwise be constrained to living with chronic pain.
Neurosurg, Ortho, Rehab, Surg
⊕ https://vfmat.ch/a867

Stop TB Partnership Korea
Fights against tuberculosis, one of the most dangerous infectious killers in the world.
Infect Dis
⊕ https://vfmat.ch/3e3b

Swiss Tropical and Public Health Institute
Contributes to the improvement of the health of populations internationally, nationally, and locally through excellence in research, education, and services.
Infect Dis, Pub Health
⊕ https://vfmat.ch/2ee4

Task Force for Global Health, The
Consists of programs and focus areas that cover a range of global health issues including neglected tropical diseases, infectious diseases, vaccines, field epidemiology, public health informatics, health workforce development, and global health ethics.
Infect Dis, Logist-Op, Medicine, Ophth-Opt, Peds
⊕ https://vfmat.ch/714c

UC Davis Health: Global Health and Rural Surgery
Aims to train individuals in the art and science of surgery and to develop surgeon leaders in resource-limited environments.
CT Surg, CV Med, Crit-Care, Endo, Heme-Onc, Plast, Surg, Vasc Surg
⊕ https://vfmat.ch/d26e

Union for International Cancer Control (UICC)
Unites and supports the cancer community to reduce the global cancer burden, promote greater equity, and ensure that cancer control continues to be a priority in the world health and development agenda.
Heme-Onc, Pub Health
⊕ https://vfmat.ch/88b1

United Nations Children's Fund (UNICEF)
Works in over 190 countries and territories to save children's lives, defend their rights, and help them fulfill their potential, from early childhood through adolescence.
All-Immu, Infect Dis, MF Med, Neonat, Nutr, OB-GYN, Ped Surg, Peds, Pub Health
⊕ https://vfmat.ch/42d7

United Nations Development Programme (UNDP)

Helps countries achieve the simultaneous eradication of extreme poverty and significant reduction of inequalities and exclusion using a sustainable human development approach.

Infect Dis, Logist-Op, Pub Health

⊕ https://vfmat.ch/935c

United Nations High Commissioner for Refugees (UNHCR)

Safeguards the rights and well-being of people who have been forced to flee, ensuring that everybody has the right to seek asylum and find safe refuge in another country, with the goal of seeking lasting solutions.

General, MF Med, Medicine, OB-GYN, Peds, Psych, Pub Health

⊕ https://vfmat.ch/6636

United Nations Population Fund (UNFPA)

Supports reproductive healthcare for women and youth in more than 150 countries, focusing on delivering a world in which every pregnancy is wanted, every childbirth is safe, and every young person's potential is fulfilled.

Infect Dis, MF Med, Neonat, OB-GYN, Peds, Pub Health

⊕ https://vfmat.ch/c969

University of Utah Global Health

Supports local organizations in their quest to improve quality of life in their communities all over the world.

Anesth, CT Surg, CV Med, Crit-Care, Dent-OMFS, ENT, ER Med, Infect Dis, OB-GYN, Ophth-Opt, Ped Surg, Ped Surg, Peds, Plast, Pub Health, Surg, Urol

⊕ https://vfmat.ch/bacd

University of Utah School of Medicine: Center for Global Surgery

Advocates for improved access to surgery worldwide, creates innovative solutions with measurable impact, and trains leaders to solve the most vexing problems in global health.

CT Surg, CV Med, ENT, ER Med, Plast, Surg, Urol

⊕ https://vfmat.ch/7c88

USAID: Leadership, Management and Governance Project

Improves leadership, management, and governance practices to strengthen health systems and improve health for all, including vulnerable populations worldwide.

Logist-Op

⊕ https://vfmat.ch/d35e

Virtue Foundation

Increases awareness, inspires action and renders assistance through healthcare, education, and empowerment initiatives.

Anesth, Crit-Care, Dent-OMFS, ENT, ER Med, Heme-Onc, Logist-Op, Neurosurg, OB-GYN, Ophth-Opt, Ortho, Path, Ped Surg, Peds, Plast, Radiol, Rehab, Surg

⊕ https://vfmat.ch/6481

Vision Care

Restores sight and helps patients get regular treatment at short-term eye camps and long-term base clinics by having doctors, missionaries, volunteers, and sponsors work together.

Ophth-Opt

⊕ https://vfmat.ch/9d7c

Vital Strategies

Helps governments strengthen their public health systems to contend with the most important and difficult health challenges, while accelerating progress on the world's most pressing health problems.

CV Med, Infect Dis, Peds

⊕ https://vfmat.ch/fe25

Vitamin Angels

Helps at-risk populations in need—specifically pregnant women, new mothers, and children under age 5—to gain access to life-changing vitamins and minerals.

General, Nutr

⊕ https://vfmat.ch/7da1

World Federation of Hemophilia (WFH)

Aims to improve and sustain care for people with inherited bleeding disorders by pursuing long-term relationships with individuals and organizations who share the values of WFH's development model.

Heme-Onc

⊕ https://vfmat.ch/5121

World Health Organization, The (WHO)

The United Nations' agency for health provides leadership on global health matters, shapes the health research agenda, sets norms and standards, articulates evidence-based policy options, provides technical support and monitoring to countries, and assesses health trends.

ER Med, General, Infect Dis, Logist-Op, MF Med, OB-GYN, Peds, Psych, Pub Health

⊕ https://vfmat.ch/c476

World Vision International

Works with vulnerable communities around the world to overcome poverty and injustice with child-focused programs in disaster management, health, nutrition, economic development, education, clean water, sanitation, and hygiene.

ER Med, General, Infect Dis, MF Med, Nutr, OB-GYN, Peds

⊕ https://vfmat.ch/2642

Mongolia

Healthcare Facilities

Achtan Hospital
Ulaanbaatar, Mongolia
🌐 https://vfmat.ch/pzjn

Agape Christian Hospital
Ulaanbaatar, Mongolia
🌐 https://vfmat.ch/9um5

Baganuur District General Hospital
Ulaanbaatar, Mongolia
🌐 https://vfmat.ch/ffec

Bayan-Ulgii City General Hospital
Bugat, Bayan-Ölgiy, Mongolia
🌐 https://vfmat.ch/c7bd

Bayanzurkh District General Hospital
Ulaanbaatar, Mongolia
🌐 https://vfmat.ch/feda

Dornod City General Hospital
Dornod, East Aimak, Mongolia
🌐 https://vfmat.ch/3bde

First Central Hospital
Ulaanbaatar, Mongolia
🌐 https://vfmat.ch/1b9a

Gobi-Altai city General Hospital
Gobi-Altai City, Mongolia
🌐 https://vfmat.ch/32cf

Grandmed Hospital
Ulaanbaatar, Mongolia
🌐 https://vfmat.ch/dkn9

Gurvan Gal Hospital
Ulaanbaatar, Mongolia
🌐 https://vfmat.ch/pxlg

Intermed Hospital
Khan-Uul district, Ulaanbaatar, Mongolia
🌐 https://vfmat.ch/autu

Jargalan Hospital
Murun, Mongolia
🌐 https://vfmat.ch/d174

Khan-Uul district General Hospital
Ulaanbaatar, Mongolia
🌐 https://vfmat.ch/c963

Khentii City General Hospital
Bayan Mönhöiin Shandaiin Örtöö, Hentiy, Mongolia
🌐 https://vfmat.ch/5f46

Khovd City General Hospital
Dund-Us, Hovd, Mongolia
🌐 https://vfmat.ch/8dbd

Khuvsgul City General Hospital
Bandi Gegeenii Hüryee, Hövsgöl, Mongolia
🌐 https://vfmat.ch/2df4

MBG Hospital
Ulaanbaatar, Mongolia
🌐 https://vfmat.ch/83mt

Middle-Gobi City General Hospital
Dundg-Gobi, Middle Gov̌, Mongolia
🌐 https://vfmat.ch/4512

Military Central Hospital
Ulaanbaatar, Mongolia
🌐 https://vfmat.ch/b273

Munkhtenger Hospital
Ulaanbaatar, Sukhbaatar Duureg, Mongolia
🌐 https://vfmat.ch/9936

Nalaikh District General Hospital
Ulaanbaatar, Mongolia
🌐 https://vfmat.ch/8b4a

National Cancer Center
Ulaanbaatar, Mongolia
🌐 https://vfmat.ch/ba9c

National Center for Child and Maternal Health
Ulaanbaatar, Mongolia
🌐 https://vfmat.ch/cbb9

National Orthopaedic Center
Ulaanbaatar, Mongolia
🌐 https://vfmat.ch/d913

National Psychiatric Center in Mongolia
Ulaanbaatar, Mongolia
🌐 https://vfmat.ch/2f16

Nomun Clinic Hospital
Ulaanbaatar, Mongolia
🌐 https://vfmat.ch/wg9z

SOS Medica Mongolia
Ulaanbaatar, Mongolia
🌐 https://vfmat.ch/efzs

Sukhbaatar District General Hospital
Ulaanbaatar, Mongolia
🌐 https://vfmat.ch/4be5

Third State Central Hospital (Shastin Central Hospital)
Ulaanbaatar, Mongolia
🌐 https://vfmat.ch/146f

Tuv City General Hospital
Zuunmod, Mongolia
🌐 https://vfmat.ch/525d

UB Songdo Hospital
Ulaanbaatar, Mongolia
🌐 https://vfmat.ch/6dbt

West-Gobi City General Hospital
Dornogobi, Mongolia
🌐 https://vfmat.ch/f715

Yonsei Friendship Hospital
Ulaanbaatar, Mongolia
🌐 https://vfmat.ch/4ud2

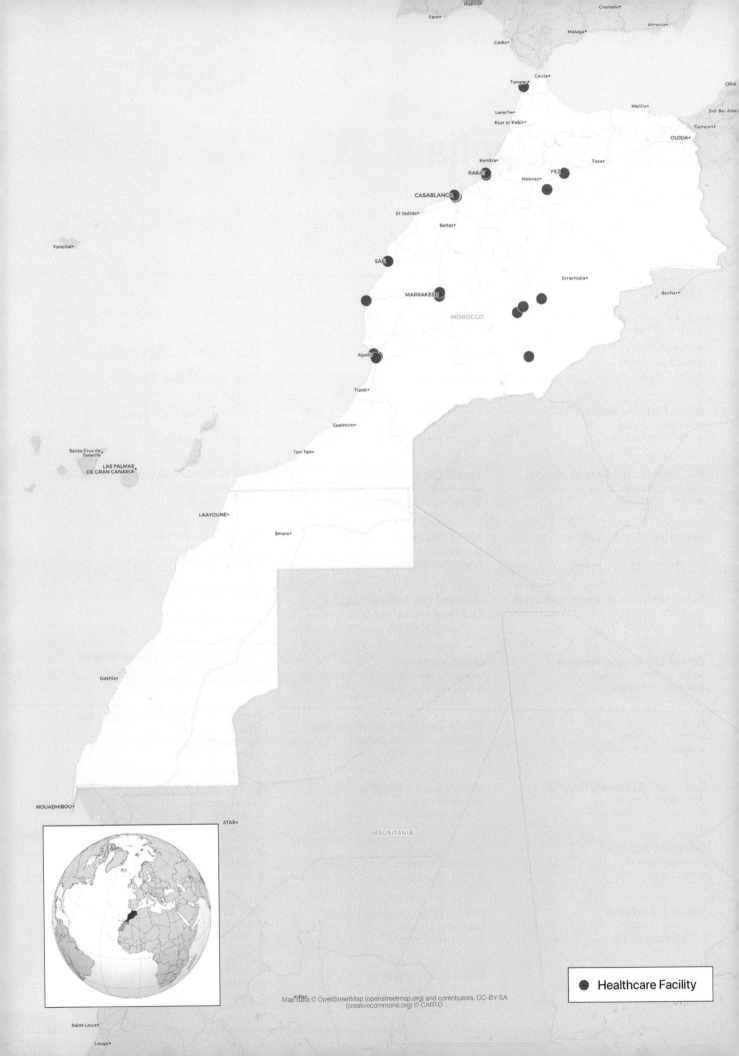

Healthcare Facility

Morocco

The Kingdom of Morocco, in the northwest part of the Maghreb region of North Africa, shares borders with the Mediterranean Sea, the Atlantic Ocean, Algeria, and Western Sahara. The population is about 36.6 million people, including those who live in Western Sahara, which is a disputed territory claimed and occupied primarily by Morocco. Morocco is ethnically homogeneous, with 99 percent of the population identifying as Arab-Berber. The country is also 99 percent Sunni Muslim. The most common languages spoken include the official languages, Arabic and Berber, as well as French, which is often used in business and government. As much as 64 percent of the population lives in urban centers, most densely along the coasts of the Atlantic and the Mediterranean. Casablanca, Rabat (the capital), Fes, Tangier, and Marrakech are some of the most populated cities. At certain points, Morocco is only eight miles away from Europe.

Prior to 1956, Morocco was separated into French and Spanish protectorates. Since achieving independence, Morocco has emerged as a stable and growing country, with the fifth largest economy in Africa. Morocco is rich in resources and arable land. As such, it produces wheat, barley, and corn, and exports fruits and other commercial crops such as cotton, sugarcane, and sunflowers. Manufacturing also plays a major role in the Moroccan economy, accounting for one-sixth of the GDP. This includes food processing, the manufacturing of textiles, and iron and steel manufacturing. While education is mandatory for school-age children, access to schools is more consistent in urban areas. Rural areas have poor school attendance, resulting in lower-than-expected literacy rates across Morocco.

The Moroccan government has emphasized preventive healthcare by establishing networks of health centers around the country. However, rural populations still lack access to health facilities and safe drinking water. Infant mortality rates remain disproportionately high, while one-third of the population suffers from malnutrition. Leading causes of death in Morocco include ischemic heart disease, stroke, hypertensive heart disease, chronic kidney disease, road injuries, diabetes, lower respiratory infection, COPD, lung cancer, neonatal disorders, and tuberculosis. The risk factors that contribute most to death and disability include high blood pressure, high body-mass index, high fasting plasma glucose, dietary risks, high LDL, air pollution, tobacco use, malnutrition, kidney dysfunction, occupational risks, and a lack of water, sanitation, and hygiene.

36.6M

Population

$3,009

GDP Per Capita

77 years

Life Expectancy

↑ Improving

73
Doctors/100k

Physician Density

100
Beds/100k

Hospital Bed Density

70
Deaths/100k

Maternal Mortality

Morocco

Nonprofit Organizations

1040i
Works to provide safe drinking water, medical care, and education to the most vulnerable in West Africa.
Dent-OMFS, General, OB-GYN, Ophth-Opt, Ortho, Surg
⊕ https://vfmat.ch/9bba

Aceso Global
Provides strategic healthcare advisory services in low- and middle-income countries to design and deliver highly customized, evidence-based solutions that address the complex nature of healthcare systems, with a goal to strengthen and provide affordable, high-quality care to all.
Logist-Op, Pub Health
⊕ https://vfmat.ch/b3b7

Africa CDC
Aims to strengthen the capacity and capability of Africa's public health institutions and partnerships to detect and respond quickly and effectively to disease threats and outbreaks, based on data-driven interventions and programs.
Infect Dis, Logist-Op, Pub Health
⊕ https://vfmat.ch/339c

Africa Health Organisation
Leads collaborative efforts among countries in Africa and other partners to promote health equity, combat disease, and improve quality of life.
Logist-Op, Pub Health
⊕ https://vfmat.ch/b1c5

Al Basar International Foundation
Works with local partners to treat preventable blindness, and helps set up sustainable infrastructure so local teams can save sight in their communities.
Ophth-Opt
⊕ https://vfmat.ch/a8b5

Bill & Melinda Gates Foundation
Focuses on global issues, such as poverty, health, and education, offering the opportunity to dramatically improve the quality of life for billions of people by building partnerships that bring together resources, expertise, and vision to identify issues, find answers, and drive change.
All-Immu, General, Infect Dis, MF Med, Neonat, OB-GYN, Pub Health
⊕ https://vfmat.ch/7cf2

BLOOM
Supports Moroccan orphanages with programs targeting early childhood development and mental health, while building a community of support for adoptees living in the United States.
General, Psych
⊕ https://vfmat.ch/de74

Breast Cancer Support
Aims to save lives and end breast cancer forever in women and men through education, treatment, emotional assistance, and financial support.
Heme-Onc, Logist-Op, Pub Health, Rad-Onc, Radiol
⊕ https://vfmat.ch/cb78

CARE
Works around the globe to save lives, defeat poverty, and achieve social justice.
ER Med, General
⊕ https://vfmat.ch/7232

Chain of Hope
Provides lifesaving heart operations for children around the world and supports the development of cardiac services in numerous developing and war-torn countries.
Anesth, CT Surg, CV Med, Crit-Care, Ped Surg, Peds, Pulm-Critic, Surg
⊕ https://vfmat.ch/1b1b

Christian Aid Ministries
Strives to be a trustworthy and efficient channel for Amish, Mennonite, and other conservative Anabaptist groups and individuals to minister to physical and spiritual needs around the world.
CT Surg, ER Med, Logist-Op, Ortho, Pub Health
⊕ https://vfmat.ch/7b33

COVID-19 Clinical Research Coalition
Advocates and collaborates for the advancement of COVID-19 research driven by the needs of low-resource settings, and works for equitable access to solutions to the pandemic.
All-Immu, Infect-Dis, MF Med, Path, Pub Health
⊕ https://vfmat.ch/d1f4

Dentaid
Seeks to treat, equip, train, and educate people in need of dental care.
Dent-OMFS
⊕ https://vfmat.ch/a183

Dental Mavericks (DM)
Makes dental care accessible to vulnerable populations deprived of it, and more broadly, promotes oral hygiene education and practice.
Dent-OMFS
⊕ https://vfmat.ch/d322

Direct Relief
Improves the health and lives of people affected by poverty or emergency situations by mobilizing and providing essential medical resources needed for their care.
ER Med, Logist-Op
⊕ https://vfmat.ch/58e5

Enabel

As the development agency of the Belgian federal government, charged with implementing Belgium's international development policy, carries out public service assignments in Belgium and abroad pursuant to the 2030 Agenda for Sustainable Development.

General, Infect Dis, Logist-Op, MF Med, OB-GYN, Peds, Pub Health

⊕ https://vfmat.ch/5af7

Friends of UNFPA

Promotes the health, dignity, and rights of women and girls around the world by supporting the lifesaving work of UNFPA, the United Nations' reproductive health and rights agency, through education, advocacy, and fundraising.

MF Med, OB-GYN

⊕ https://vfmat.ch/2a3a

Gift of Life International

Provides lifesaving cardiac treatment to children in developing countries while developing sustainable pediatric cardiac programs by implementing screening, surgical, and training missions.

Anesth, CT Surg, CV Med, Crit-Care, Ped Surg, Peds, Pulm-Critic

⊕ https://vfmat.ch/f2f9

Global Oncology (GO)

Brings the best in cancer care to underserved patients around the world and collaborates across geographic, professional, and academic borders to improve cancer care, research, and education.

Heme-Onc, Path, Rad-Onc

⊕ https://vfmat.ch/fcb8

Global Partnership for Zero Leprosy

Facilitates alignment of the leprosy community and accelerates effective collaborative action toward the goal of zero leprosy.

Infect Dis

⊕ https://vfmat.ch/ec7b

Global Vision 2020

Provides prescription eyeglasses to people who live in parts of the world lacking necessary infrastructure for obtaining affordable corrective eyewear.

Logist-Op, Ophth-Opt

⊕ https://vfmat.ch/7373

Globus Relief

Aims to improve the delivery of healthcare worldwide by gathering, processing, and distributing surplus medical supplies to charities at home and abroad.

Logist-Op

⊕ https://vfmat.ch/a2b7

Grassroot Soccer

Leverages the power of soccer to educate, inspire, and mobilize at-risk youth in developing countries to overcome their greatest health challenges, live healthier and more productive lives, and be agents for change in their communities.

Infect Dis

⊕ https://vfmat.ch/3521

Heart Healers International

Brings lifesaving heart diagnostics and treatments to children in Africa with the goal that no child with a treatable heart will be left behind. Works alongside local medical teams in caring for patients, conducting ongoing research, and providing education, including telemedicine.

Anesth, CT Surg, CV Med, Infect Dis, Logist-Op, Ped Surg, Peds

⊕ https://vfmat.ch/f34a

Humanity & Inclusion

Works alongside people with disabilities and vulnerable populations, taking action and bearing witness in order to respond to their essential needs, improve their living conditions and health, and promote respect for their dignity and fundamental rights.

General, Infect Dis, MF Med, Medicine, Ortho, Peds, Psych, Pub Health, Rehab

⊕ https://vfmat.ch/16b7

International Campaign for Women's Right to Safe Abortion

Works to build an international network and campaign that brings together organizations with an interest in promoting and providing safe abortion to create

a shared platform for advocacy, debate, and dialogue and the sharing of skills and experience.

OB-GYN, Pub Health, Surg

⊕ https://vfmat.ch/f341

International Children's Heart Foundation

Provides free surgical care, medical training, and technology to save the lives of children with congenital heart disease in developing countries.

Anesth, CT Surg, CV Med, Crit-Care, Ped Surg, Peds, Pulm-Critic

⊕ https://vfmat.ch/86c1

International Federation of Gynecology and Obstetrics (FIGO)

Implements global projects on specific women's health issues.

MF Med, Medicine, Neonat, OB-GYN, Surg, Urol

⊕ https://vfmat.ch/c4b4

International Federation of Red Cross and Red Crescent Societies (IFRC)

Coordinates and directs international assistance following natural and manmade disasters in nonconflict situations through the world's largest humanitarian and development network. Provides disaster-preparedness programs, healthcare activities, and promotes humanitarian values.

ER Med, General, Infect Dis, Nutr

⊕ https://vfmat.ch/b4ee

International Organization for Migration (IOM) – The UN Migration Agency

Promotes evidence-informed policies and holistic, preventive, and curative health programs that are beneficial, accessible, and equitable for vulnerable migrants.

General, Infect Dis, OB-GYN

⊕ https://vfmat.ch/621a

International Planned Parenthood Federation (IPPF)

Leads a locally owned, globally connected civil society movement that provides and enables services and champions sexual and reproductive health and rights for all, especially the underserved.

Infect Dis, MF Med, OB-GYN

⊕ https://vfmat.ch/dc97

International Trachoma Initiative (iTi)

Works toward a world free from trachoma, a preventable cause of blindness, and provides comprehensive support to national ministries of health and governmental and nongovernmental organizations to implement a comprehensive approach to fight trachoma.

Infect Dis, Ophth-Opt

⊕ https://vfmat.ch/3278

Kaya Responsible Travel

Promotes sustainable social, environmental, and economic development, empowers communities, and cultivates educated, compassionate global citizens through responsible travel.

All-Immu, Crit-Care, Dent-OMFS, ER Med, General, Geri, Infect Dis, MF Med, Medicine, Nutr, OB-GYN, Peds, Psych, Pub Health, Rehab

⊕ https://vfmat.ch/b2cf

Kids Care Everywhere

Seeks to empower physicians in under-resourced environments with multimedia, state-of-the-art medical software, and to inspire young professionals to become future global healthcare leaders.

Logist-Op, Ped Surg, Peds

⊕ https://vfmat.ch/bc23

Light for Sight 21

Aims to eliminate severe visual impairment among all children and adolescents with keratoconus.

Ophth-Opt

⊕ https://vfmat.ch/ef55

Maghreb-American Health Foundation

Promotes education around health equity, the prevention of birth defects, and improvement in quality of life for people of the Maghreb region of North Africa.

Anesth, CV Med, Neurosurg, Ped Surg, Radiol, Surg, Urol

⊕ https://vfmat.ch/b3bd

MedShare
Aims to improve the quality of life of people, communities, and the planet by sourcing and directly delivering surplus medical supplies and equipment to communities in need around the world.
Logist-Op
⊕ https://vfmat.ch/c8bc

MiracleFeet
Brings low-cost treatment to every child on the planet born with clubfoot, a leading cause of physical disability.
Ortho, Peds, Rehab
⊕ https://vfmat.ch/bda8

Médecins du Monde/Doctors of the World
Provides care, bears witness, and supports social change worldwide with innovative medical programs and evidence-based advocacy initiatives.
ER Med, General, Infect Dis, MF Med, Neonat, OB-GYN, Peds, Pub Health
⊕ https://vfmat.ch/a43d

Operation Fistula
Exists to end obstetric fistula by building models of care that serve every woman, everywhere.
MF Med, OB-GYN, Surg
⊕ https://vfmat.ch/ce8e

Operation International
Offers medical aid to adults and children suffering from lack of quality healthcare in impoverished countries.
Dent-OMFS, ER Med, Heme-Onc, OB-GYN, Ophth-Opt, Ortho, Ped Surg, Plast, Surg
⊕ https://vfmat.ch/b52a

Operation Smile
Treats patients with cleft lip and cleft palate, and creates solutions that deliver safe surgery to people where it's needed most.
Anesth, Dent-OMFS, ENT, Ped Surg, Plast
⊕ https://vfmat.ch/5c29

Ophtalmo Sans Frontières
Fights against blindness and low vision in French-speaking Africa.
Anesth, Ophth-Opt, Surg
⊕ https://vfmat.ch/7643

Order of Malta
Supports forgotten or excluded people, especially those living in conflict zones or amid natural disasters, by providing medical assistance, caring for refugees, and distributing medicines and necessities.
ER Med, General, Infect Dis, MF Med, Nephro, OB-GYN, Ortho, Psych
⊕ https://vfmat.ch/1fab

Paul Chester Children's Hope Foundation, The
Aims to improve the health and well-being of children and young adults in developing countries by providing early intervention where services are otherwise unavailable.
Anesth, Dent-OMFS, ENT, General, Logist-Op, Logist-Op, Ophth-Opt, Ped Surg, Peds, Surg
⊕ https://vfmat.ch/83e2

Philia Foundation
Seeks to invest sustainably in people and marginalized communities in order to improve health and education in Africa.
Anesth, ER Med, General, Heme-Onc, MF Med, Neurosurg, OB-GYN, Ophth-Opt, Ortho, Pub Health, Surg, Urol
⊕ https://vfmat.ch/a352

Physicians Across Continents
Provides high-quality medical care to people affected by crises and disasters.
CV Med, Dent-OMFS, Heme-Onc, MF Med, Nephro, Nephro, OB-GYN, Ped Surg, Plast, Surg
⊕ https://vfmat.ch/fe5d

Project Pacer International
Provides modern cardiac therapy to indigent patients in the developing world.

CT Surg, CV Med
⊕ https://vfmat.ch/f812

RAD-AID International
Improves and optimizes access to medical imaging and radiology in low-resource regions of the world.
Rad-Onc, Radiol
⊕ https://vfmat.ch/537f

RestoringVision
Empowers lives by restoring vision for millions of people in need.
Ophth-Opt
⊕ https://vfmat.ch/e121

Rotary International
Provides service to others, improves lives, and advances world understanding, goodwill, and peace through its fellowship of business, professional, and community leaders.
ER Med, General, Infect Dis, MF Med, OB-GYN
⊕ https://vfmat.ch/8fb5

Saham Foundation
Aims to create lasting change among the most vulnerable populations in Morocco and Sub-Saharan Africa through healthcare, youth engagement, and social inclusion.
Anesth, Dent-OMFS, ENT, OB-GYN, Ophth-Opt, Ped Surg, Peds, Pub Health, Radiol, Surg, Urol
⊕ https://vfmat.ch/54d6

SAMU Foundation
Provides medical first response and reconstruction when severe international emergencies occur.
ER Med, Infect Dis, Logist-Op, Psych, Pub Health
⊕ https://vfmat.ch/3196

Sanofi Espoir Foundation
Contributes to reducing health inequalities among populations that need it most by applying a socially responsible approach focused on fighting childhood cancers in low-income countries, improving maternal and newborn health, and improving access to care.
ER Med, OB-GYN, Peds
⊕ https://vfmat.ch/943b

Solthis
Improves disease prevention and access to quality care by strengthening the health systems and services of the countries served.
General, Infect Dis, Logist-Op, MF Med, Neonat, Path
⊕ https://vfmat.ch/a71d

SOS Children's Villages International
Supports children through alternative care and family strengthening.
ER Med, Peds
⊕ https://vfmat.ch/aca1

Sri Sathya Sai International Organization
Inspired by spiritual teachings, carries out efforts in global healthcare, education, humanitarian relief, and youth engagement.
Dent-OMFS, General, Logist-Op, Nutr, Ophth-Opt, Pub Health
⊕ https://vfmat.ch/9bda

Surgical Healing of Africa's Youth Foundation, The (S.H.A.Y.)
Provides volunteer reconstructive surgery to children in need, including treating congenital anomalies such as cleft lip/palate and general reconstruction.
Anesth, Dent-OMFS, Peds, Plast
⊕ https://vfmat.ch/41a7

Swiss Tropical and Public Health Institute
Contributes to the improvement of the health of populations internationally, nationally, and locally through excellence in research, education, and services.
Infect Dis, Pub Health
⊕ https://vfmat.ch/2ee4

Task Force for Global Health, The
Consists of programs and focus areas that cover a range of global health issues including neglected tropical diseases, infectious diseases, vaccines, field epidemiology, public health informatics, health workforce development, and global health ethics.
Infect Dis, Logist-Op, Medicine, Ophth-Opt, Peds
⊕ https://vfmat.ch/714c

Terre des hommes (Tdh) Foundation
Works to improve the daily life of children and their relatives in the areas of health, protection and emergency, in Europe, Africa, Asia, Latin America, and the Near and Middle East.
CT Surg, CV Med, OB-GYN, Ped Surg, Pub Health
⊕ https://vfmat.ch/5c26

Union for International Cancer Control (UICC)
Unites and supports the cancer community to reduce the global cancer burden, promote greater equity, and ensure that cancer control continues to be a priority in the world health and development agenda.
Heme-Onc, Pub Health
⊕ https://vfmat.ch/88b1

Unite 4 Humanity
Aims to provide emergency aid and support for Muslim communities across the world.
General, Nutr, OB-GYN, Ophth-Opt, Plast, Psych, Rehab
⊕ https://vfmat.ch/fbe7

United Nations Children's Fund (UNICEF)
Works in over 190 countries and territories to save children's lives, defend their rights, and help them fulfill their potential, from early childhood through adolescence.
All-Immu, Infect Dis, MF Med, Neonat, Nutr, OB-GYN, Ped Surg, Peds, Pub Health
⊕ https://vfmat.ch/42d7

United Nations Development Programme (UNDP)
Helps countries achieve the simultaneous eradication of extreme poverty and significant reduction of inequalities and exclusion using a sustainable human development approach.
Infect Dis, Logist-Op, Pub Health
⊕ https://vfmat.ch/935c

United Nations High Commissioner for Refugees (UNHCR)
Safeguards the rights and well-being of people who have been forced to flee, ensuring that everybody has the right to seek asylum and find safe refuge in another country, with the goal of seeking lasting solutions.
General, MF Med, Medicine, OB-GYN, Peds, Psych, Pub Health
⊕ https://vfmat.ch/6636

United Nations Population Fund (UNFPA)
Supports reproductive healthcare for women and youth in more than 150 countries, focusing on delivering a world in which every pregnancy is wanted, every childbirth is safe, and every young person's potential is fulfilled.
Infect Dis, MF Med, Neonat, OB-GYN, Peds, Pub Health
⊕ https://vfmat.ch/c969

University of Virginia: Anesthesiology Department Global Health Initiatives
Educates and trains physicians to help people achieve healthy productive lives, and advances knowledge in the medical sciences.
Anesth, Pub Health
⊕ https://vfmat.ch/1b8b

Vision Care
Restores sight and helps patients get regular treatment at short-term eye camps and long-term base clinics by having doctors, missionaries, volunteers, and sponsors work together.
Ophth-Opt
⊕ https://vfmat.ch/9d7c

Volunteer Morocco
Seeks to improve the self-sustainability of underprivileged communities in Morocco with healthcare access, education, farming technologies, and micro-enterprises.
ER Med, General
⊕ https://vfmat.ch/c359

World Federation of Hemophilia (WFH)
Aims to improve and sustain care for people with inherited bleeding disorders by pursuing long-term relationships with individuals and organizations who share the values of WFH's development model.
Heme-Onc
⊕ https://vfmat.ch/5121

World Health Organization, The (WHO)
The United Nations' agency for health provides leadership on global health matters, shapes the health research agenda, sets norms and standards, articulates evidence-based policy options, provides technical support and monitoring to countries, and assesses health trends.
ER Med, General, Infect Dis, Logist-Op, MF Med, OB-GYN, Peds, Psych, Pub Health
⊕ https://vfmat.ch/c476

World Medical Relief
Facilitates the distribution of surplus medical resources where they are needed.
Logist-Op
⊕ https://vfmat.ch/72dc

World Parkinson's Program
Seeks to improve the quality of life of those affected by Parkinson's disease through education and advocacy, and provides free medication and support services.
Logist-Op, Neuro, Pub Health
⊕ https://vfmat.ch/c96d

Morocco

Healthcare Facilities

Agdal Clinic
Rabat, Morocco
https://vfmat.ch/91qc

Centre d'Oncologie
Agadir 80000, Souss-Massa, Morocco
⊕ https://vfmat.ch/6a81

Centre Hospitalier Universitaire Hassan II (CHU Fes)
Fes, Morocco
⊕ https://vfmat.ch/lvpp

Centre Hospitalier Universitaire Mohammed VI
Marrakesh, Morocco
⊕ https://vfmat.ch/f47e

CHU de Tanger-Tétouan-Al Hoceima
Douar Deqadeq, Tanger-Tetouan-Al Hoceima, Morocco
⊕ https://vfmat.ch/12cd

CHU Ibn Rochd
Casablanca, Morocco
⊕ https://vfmat.ch/fweh

CHUIS Hôpital de Moulay Youssef
Rabat, Morocco
⊕ https://vfmat.ch/x6tn

Clinique Internationale de Marrakech
Marrakesh, Morocco
https://vfmat.ch/krre

Hôpital Boumalne-Dades
Boumalne Dades, Morocco
⊕ https://vfmat.ch/4224

Hôpital El Yasmine
Aït Moulay Tahar, Fès-Meknès, Morocco
⊕ https://vfmat.ch/cd2c

Hôpital Kelaat M'gouna
Kelaat M'gouna, Drâa-Tafilalet, Morocco
⊕ https://vfmat.ch/2923

Hôpital Municipal De Tinghir
Tinghir, Drâa-Tafilalet, Morocco
⊕ https://vfmat.ch/13da

Hôpital Privé de Marrakech HPM
Marrakesh, Morocco
⊕ https://vfmat.ch/qqzn

Hôpital Sidi Mohammed Ben Abdellah
Essaouira, Morocco
⊕ https://vfmat.ch/7e82

Hôpital Sidi Othmane
Cité de Bournazel, Casablanca-Settat, Morocco
⊕ https://vfmat.ch/87db

Hôpital Zagora
Zagora, Morocco
⊕ https://vfmat.ch/f928

IBN SINA Rabat University Hospital
Rabat, Morocco
⊕ https://vfmat.ch/871f

Polyclinique Atlas
Casablanca, Morocco
⊕ https://vfmat.ch/ztmp

Private Hospital of Casablanca Aîn Sebaâ
Casablanca, Morocco
https://vfmat.ch/tnik

Rabat Children's Hospital
Rabat, Morocco
⊕ https://vfmat.ch/14c4

Healthcare Facility

Mozambique

Located on the coast of southwest Africa, the Republic of Mozambique is a large country of about 30.9 million people. As much as two-thirds of the Mozambican population live in rural areas and along its long coastline. Maputo, the capital, is located on the shore and is known for being a vibrant and lively tropical city. Nearly 99 percent of the population falls into a few major ethnic groups, including the Makhuwa, Tsonga, Lomwe, and Sena. Portuguese is the official language, but local languages are used as well. Mozambique is also a religiously diverse country, with a population that includes Roman Catholics, Muslims, Zionist Christians, Evangelicals, and Pentecostals.

Ruled by Portugal in the colonial era, Mozambique experienced violent conflict during the latter half of the 20th century. In 1975, a temporary and controversial Marxist government held power. Over the past three decades, Mozambique has seen its economy grow steadily. Yet despite economic and political progress, Mozambique faces an Islamic rebellion in Cabo Delgado, which has contributed to instability. In addition, much of the country's population is vulnerable to natural disasters such as cyclones and tropical storms. These factors, among others, have resulted in endemic poverty rates countrywide.

Mozambique is challenged by a burden of disease that can be largely attributed to high poverty levels. Only 35 percent of the population is within 30 minutes of a health facility. As a result, diseases that cause the most deaths include HIV/AIDS, neonatal disorders, tuberculosis, malaria, lower respiratory infections, diarrheal diseases, and protein-energy malnutrition. Additionally, stroke and ischemic heart disease have risen over time as the non-communicable diseases that contribute to the most deaths in Mozambique. Road injuries have also increased and pose a significant health challenge, becoming a top cause of death in the country.

30.9M

Population

$449

GDP Per Capita

61 years

Life Expectancy

↑ Improving

9	**70**	**289**
Doctors/100k	**Beds**/100k	**Deaths**/100k
Physician Density	Hospital Bed Density	Maternal Mortality

Mozambique

Nonprofit Organizations

143 LIFE Foundation
Seeks to educate and empower individuals living with malaria, TB, HIV/AIDS, STDs and other health disparities related to sexual health.
Infect Dis, MF Med
⊕ https://vfmat.ch/d59b

Abt Associates
Seeks to improve the quality of life and economic well-being of people worldwide, while striving to meet and exceed the highest professional standards.
General, Logist-Op, MF Med, OB-GYN, Peds
⊕ https://vfmat.ch/cec2

Aceso Global
Provides strategic healthcare advisory services in low- and middle-income countries to design and deliver highly customized, evidence-based solutions that address the complex nature of healthcare systems, with a goal to strengthen and provide affordable, high-quality care to all.
Logist-Op, Pub Health
⊕ https://vfmat.ch/b3b7

Adventist Development and Relief Agency (ADRA) Moçambique
Improves lives through emergency relief, community-based projects that target food security, economic development, primary health, and basic education.
General, Infect Dis, Pub Health
⊕ https://vfmat.ch/1d91

Africa CDC
Aims to strengthen the capacity and capability of Africa's public health institutions and partnerships to detect and respond quickly and effectively to disease threats and outbreaks, based on data-driven interventions and programs.
Infect Dis, Logist-Op, Pub Health
⊕ https://vfmat.ch/339c

Africa Health Organisation
Leads collaborative efforts among countries in Africa and other partners to promote health equity, combat disease, and improve quality of life.
Logist-Op, Pub Health
⊕ https://vfmat.ch/b1c5

Africa Indoor Residual Spraying Project (AIRS)
Aims to protect millions of people in Africa from malaria by spraying insecticide on walls, ceilings, and other indoor resting places of mosquitoes that transmit malaria.
Infect Dis
⊕ https://vfmat.ch/9bd1

Africa Inland Mission International
Seeks to establish churches and community development programs including healthcare projects, based in Christian ministry.

Anesth, Dent-OMFS, ER Med, General, MF Med, Medicine, OB-GYN, OB-GYN, Ophth-Opt, Ped Surg, Peds, Rehab
⊕ https://vfmat.ch/f2f6

Africa Relief and Community Development
Provides comprehensive relief and developmental aid to people of the African continent regardless of gender, race, or religion.
Nutr, Pub Health
⊕ https://vfmat.ch/6cd2

African Field Epidemiology Network (AFENET)
Strengthens field epidemiology and public health laboratory capacity to contribute effectively to addressing epidemics and other major public health problems in Africa.
All-Immu, Infect Dis, Path, Pub Health
⊕ https://vfmat.ch/df2e

African Health Now
Promotes and provides information and access to sustainable primary healthcare to women, children, and families living across Sub-Saharan Africa.
Dent-OMFS, Endo, General, Infect Dis, MF Med, OB-GYN
⊕ https://vfmat.ch/c766

Aga Khan Foundation Canada
Tackles the root causes of poverty, with a special focus on marginalized groups such as women and girls. Programs provide access to education and healthcare, food, and opportunity.
Pub Health
⊕ https://vfmat.ch/7f8b

Age International
Helps older people living in some of the world's poorest places to have improved well-being and be treated with dignity through a variety of programs, including emergency relief and cataract surgery.
ER Med, Geri, Logist-Op, Nutr, Ophth-Opt, Palliative, Pub Health
⊕ https://vfmat.ch/c7e2

Aid for the Development of People for People (ADPP) Mozambique
Promotes the social and economic development of the most vulnerable people in society, with special attention to children, orphans, women, and girls.
Infect Dis, Nutr, Pub Health
⊕ https://vfmat.ch/cf53

AIDS Healthcare Foundation
Provides cutting-edge HIV/AIDS medical care and advocacy to over one million people in 43 countries.
Infect Dis
⊕ https://vfmat.ch/b27c

AISPO
Implements international initiatives in the healthcare sector and remains involved in various projects to combat poverty, social injustice, and disease around the world.
All-Immu, ER Med, GI, General, Infect Dis, Logist-Op, MF Med, Neonat, OB-GYN, Peds, Psych, Pub Health, Radiol
⊕ https://vfmat.ch/c9e6

American International Health Alliance (AIHA)
Strengthens health systems and workforce capacity worldwide through locally driven, peer-to-peer institutional partnerships.
CV Med, ER Med, Infect Dis, Medicine, OB-GYN
⊕ https://vfmat.ch/69fd

Americares
Saves lives and improves health for people affected by poverty or disaster and responds with life-changing medicine, medical supplies, and health programs including domestic and global medical clinics.
All-Immu, ER Med, General, Infect Dis, MF Med, Nutr
⊕ https://vfmat.ch/e567

AMOR (Aide Mondiale Orphelins Reconfort)
Aims to contribute to significant reductions in global infant and maternal mortality rates by providing medical services to at-risk mothers and appropriate care for orphans.
Infect Dis, MF Med, Neonat, OB-GYN, Ophth-Opt, Ped Surg
⊕ https://vfmat.ch/98a4

Amref Health Africa
Serves millions of people across 35 countries in Sub-Saharan Africa, strengthening health systems, and training African health workers to respond to the continent's most critical health issues.
All-Immu, General, Infect Dis, Logist-Op, MF Med, OB-GYN, Path, Pub Health, Surg
⊕ https://vfmat.ch/6985

Amsterdam Institute for Global Health and Development (AIGHD)
Provides sustainable solutions to major health problems across our planet by forging synergies among disciplines, healthcare delivery, research, and education.
Infect Dis
⊕ https://vfmat.ch/d73d

Anan Clinica
Focuses on expanding local knowledge on health, while offering basic healthcare, education, agriculture, and water management.
General, Infect Dis, Nutr
⊕ https://vfmat.ch/8281

Aurum Institute, The
Seeks to impact global health by designing and delivering high-quality care and treatment to people in developing countries.
Infect Dis, Pub Health
⊕ https://vfmat.ch/ae2a

Basic Foundations
Supports local projects and organizations that seek to meet the basic human needs of others in their community.
ER Med, General, Peds, Rehab, Surg
⊕ https://vfmat.ch/c4be

CARE
Works around the globe to save lives, defeat poverty, and achieve social justice.
ER Med, General
⊕ https://vfmat.ch/7232

Carter Center, The
Seeks to prevent and resolve conflicts, enhance freedom and democracy, and improve health, while remaining committed to human rights and the alleviation of human suffering.
Infect Dis, MF Med, Ophth-Opt
⊕ https://vfmat.ch/6556

Center for Strategic and International Studies (CSIS) Commission on Strengthening America's Health Security
Brings together a distinguished and diverse group of high-level opinion leaders bridging security and health, with the core aim to chart a bold vision for the future of U.S. leadership in global health.
ER Med, Infect Dis, MF Med, Pub Health
⊕ https://vfmat.ch/6d7f

Centre for Global Mental Health
Closes the care gap and reduces human rights abuses experienced by people living with mental, neurological, and substance use conditions, particularly in low-resource settings.
Neuro, OB-GYN, Palliative, Peds, Psych
⊕ https://vfmat.ch/a96d

Centro de Colaboração em Saúde
Seeks to promote health activities, prevent disease, and improve the quality and equity of access to care and treatment of common diseases in Mozambique, focusing on the health of women, children, and other vulnerable groups.
General, Infect Dis, OB-GYN, Path, Peds
⊕ https://vfmat.ch/6f6c

Chain of Hope
Provides lifesaving heart operations for children around the world and supports the development of cardiac services in numerous developing and war-torn countries.
Anesth, CT Surg, CV Med, Crit-Care, Ped Surg, Peds, Pulm-Critic, Surg
⊕ https://vfmat.ch/1b1b

Chain of Hope (La Chaîne de l'Espoir)
Helps underprivileged children around the world by providing them with access to healthcare.
Anesth, CT Surg, Crit-Care, ER Med, Neurosurg, Ortho, Ped Surg, Surg, Vasc Surg
⊕ https://vfmat.ch/e871

Children's Relief International
Inspired by the Christian faith, cares for and educates children, their families, and their communities, including the provision of select healthcare services.
ER Med, General, Nutr
⊕ https://vfmat.ch/8da6

Christian Aid Ministries
Strives to be a trustworthy and efficient channel for Amish, Mennonite, and other conservative Anabaptist groups and individuals to minister to physical and spiritual needs around the world.
CT Surg, ER Med, Logist-Op, Ortho, Pub Health
⊕ https://vfmat.ch/7b33

Clinton Health Access Initiative (CHAI)
Aims to save lives and reduce the burden of disease in low- and middle-income countries. Works with partners to strengthen the capabilities of governments and the private sector to create and sustain high-quality health systems.
General, Heme-Onc, Infect Dis, Logist-Op, MF Med, Medicine, Neonat, Nutr, OB-GYN, Path, Peds, Rad-Onc
⊕ https://vfmat.ch/9ed7

Columbia University: Global Mental Health Programs
Pioneers research initiatives, promotes mental health, and aims to reduce the burden of mental illness worldwide.
Psych
⊕ https://vfmat.ch/c5cd

Columbia Vagelos College of Physicians and Surgeons Programs in Global Health
Harnesses the expertise of the medical school to improve health worldwide by training global health leaders, building capacity through interdisciplinary education and training programs, and addressing unmet health needs through research and application.
CV Med, Derm, Genetics, Heme-Onc, Infect Dis, Medicine, OB-GYN, Ophth-Opt, Peds, Psych, Pub Health, Pulm-Critic, Surg
⊕ https://vfmat.ch/a9e5

Core Group

Aims to improve and expand community health practices for underserved populations, especially women and children, through collaborative action and learning.

General, Infect Dis, MF Med, Medicine, OB-GYN, Peds, Pub Health

⊕ https://vfmat.ch/9de3

CouldYou?

Seeks to work with African leaders and organizations to develop African solutions to African problems, while helping individuals to find their own unique contribution to impact poverty. It is committed to creating holistic solutions, building a better world for future generations, and doing business with integrity.

All-Immu, General, Nutr, OB-GYN

⊕ https://vfmat.ch/97fb

COVID-19 Clinical Research Coalition

Advocates and collaborates for the advancement of COVID-19 research driven by the needs of low-resource settings, and works for equitable access to solutions to the pandemic.

All-Immu, Infect-Dis, MF Med, Path, Pub Health

⊕ https://vfmat.ch/d1f4

Cross Catholic Outreach

Mobilizes the global Catholic Church to transform impoverished communities through the provision of food, water, housing, education, orphan support, medical care, microenterprise, and disaster relief.

All-Immu, General, Nutr, OB-GYN, Rehab

⊕ https://vfmat.ch/22f4

Developing Country NGO Delegation: Global Fund to Fight AIDS, TB & Malaria

Works to strengthen the engagement of civil society actors and organizations in developing countries to build a world in which AIDS, TB, and malaria are no longer global, public health, and human rights threats.

Infect Dis, Pub Health

⊕ https://vfmat.ch/3149

Direct Relief

Improves the health and lives of people affected by poverty or emergency situations by mobilizing and providing essential medical resources needed for their care.

ER Med, Logist-Op

⊕ https://vfmat.ch/58e5

DKT INTERNATIONAL INC

Seeks to provide couples with affordable and safe options for family planning and HIV/AIDS prevention through dynamic social marketing.

General, Surg

⊕ https://vfmat.ch/b3a7

Doctors with Africa (CUAMM)

Advocates for the universal right to health and promotes the values of international solidarity, justice, and peace. Works to protect and improve the well-being and health of vulnerable communities in Africa with a long-term development perspective.

ER Med, Infect Dis, MF Med, Neonat, OB-GYN, Peds

⊕ https://vfmat.ch/d2fb

Doctors Without Borders/Médecins Sans Frontières (MSF)

Responds to emergencies and provides lifesaving medical care where needed most, including during disasters, conflicts, and epidemics.

Anesth, Crit-Care, ER Med, General, Infect Dis, Nutr, OB-GYN, Ped Surg, Peds, Psych, Pub Health, Surg

⊕ https://vfmat.ch/f363

Douleurs Sans Frontières (Pain Without Borders)

Supports local actors in taking charge of the assessment and treatment of pain and suffering, in an integrated manner and adapted to the realities of each country.

Anesth, Palliative, Psych, Rehab

⊕ https://vfmat.ch/324c

Dream Sant'Egidio

Seeks to counter HIV/AIDS in Africa by eliminating the transmission of HIV from mother to child, with a focus on women because of the importance of their role in the community.

Infect Dis, MF Med, Neonat, OB-GYN, Path, Peds

⊕ https://vfmat.ch/f466

Duke University: Global Health Institute

Sparks innovation in global health research and education, and brings together knowledge and resources to address the most important global health issues of our time.

All-Immu, Infect Dis, MF Med, OB-GYN, Pub Health

⊕ https://vfmat.ch/c4cd

Egmont Trust, The

Works with partner organizations in Sub-Saharan Africa, making grants to help vulnerable children cope with the impact of HIV/AIDS on families and communities.

General, Infect Dis, OB-GYN, Peds

⊕ https://vfmat.ch/57a9

Elizabeth Glaser Pediatric AIDS Foundation

Seeks to end global pediatric HIV/AIDS through prevention and treatment programs, research, and advocacy.

Infect Dis, Nutr, OB-GYN, Peds

⊕ https://vfmat.ch/d6ec

Enabel

As the development agency of the Belgian federal government, charged with implementing Belgium's international development policy, carries out public service assignments in Belgium and abroad pursuant to the 2030 Agenda for Sustainable Development.

General, Infect Dis, Logist-Op, MF Med, OB-GYN, Peds, Pub Health

⊕ https://vfmat.ch/5af7

EngenderHealth

Works to implement high-quality, gender-equitable programs that advance sexual and reproductive health and rights.

General, MF Med, OB-GYN, Peds

⊕ https://vfmat.ch/1cb2

Episcopal Relief & Development

Provides relief in times of disaster and promotes sustainable development by identifying and addressing the root causes of suffering.

Infect Dis, MF Med, Neonat, Nutr, Peds

⊕ https://vfmat.ch/7cfa

eRanger

Provides sustainable solutions to transportation and medical provision such as ambulances and mobile clinics in developing countries.

ER Med, General, Logist-Op

⊕ https://vfmat.ch/4c18

Esperança

Works to improve health and provide hope through disease prevention, education, and medical/surgical treatment.

Anesth, Dent-OMFS, ENT, General, Neurosurg, Nutr, OB-GYN, Ophth-Opt, Ortho, Ped Surg, Peds, Plast, Pub Health, Surg, Urol, Vasc Surg

⊕ https://vfmat.ch/5cf3

Evangelical Alliance Mission, The (TEAM)

Provides services in the areas of church planting, community development, healthcare, social justice, business as mission, and more.

Dent-OMFS, General, Ophth-Opt

⊕ https://vfmat.ch/9faa

Eye Foundation of America

Works toward a world without childhood blindness.

Ophth-Opt

⊕ https://vfmat.ch/a7eb

Friends of UNFPA

Promotes the health, dignity, and rights of women and girls around the world by supporting the lifesaving work of UNFPA, the United Nations' reproductive health and rights agency, through education, advocacy, and fundraising.

MF Med, OB-GYN

🌐 https://vfmat.ch/2a3a

Global Alliance to Prevent Prematurity And Stillbirth (GAPPS)

Seeks to improve birth outcomes worldwide by reducing the burden of premature birth and stillbirth.

All-Immu, Infect Dis, MF Med, Neonat, Neonat, OB-GYN

🌐 https://vfmat.ch/3f74

Global Clubfoot Initiative (GCI)

Promotes and resources the treatment of children with clubfoot in developing countries using the Ponseti technique.

Ortho, Ped Surg

🌐 https://vfmat.ch/f229

Global Ministries – The United Methodist Church

As the worldwide mission and development agency of The United Methodist Church, Global Ministries works with more than 300 hospitals and clinics around the world through its Global Health Unit.

Anesth, CT Surg, CV Med, Crit-Care, Dent-OMFS, Derm, ER Med, GI, General, Infect Dis, Logist-Op, MF Med, Medicine, Neonat, Nephro, Nutr, OB-GYN, Ophth-Opt, Ortho, Palliative, Peds, Pod, Psych, Pub Health, Rehab, Rheum, Surg, Urol

🌐 https://vfmat.ch/1723

Global Oncology (GO)

Brings the best in cancer care to underserved patients around the world and collaborates across geographic, professional, and academic borders to improve cancer care, research, and education.

Heme-Onc, Path, Rad-Onc

🌐 https://vfmat.ch/fcb8

Global Vision 2020

Provides prescription eyeglasses to people who live in parts of the world lacking necessary infrastructure for obtaining affordable corrective eyewear.

Logist-Op, Ophth-Opt

🌐 https://vfmat.ch/7373

GlobalMedic

Provides disaster relief and lifesaving humanitarian aid.

ER Med, Pub Health

🌐 https://vfmat.ch/dfe6

Globus Relief

Aims to improve the delivery of healthcare worldwide by gathering, processing, and distributing surplus medical supplies to charities at home and abroad.

Logist-Op

🌐 https://vfmat.ch/a2b7

Good Shepard International Foundation

Strives to promote inclusive and sustainable development for the most marginalized and vulnerable people, with a special focus on women, girls, and children, inspired by the Christian faith.

ER Med

🌐 https://vfmat.ch/ad9a

Good Shepherd Hospital Eye Clinic

Aims to provide eye care to the people of Eswatini and neighboring countries.

Ophth-Opt, Pub Health, Surg

🌐 https://vfmat.ch/85fe

Grassroot Soccer

Leverages the power of soccer to educate, inspire, and mobilize at-risk youth in developing countries to overcome their greatest health challenges, live healthier and more productive lives, and be agents for change in their communities.

Infect Dis

🌐 https://vfmat.ch/3521

Hands At Work

Based in Christian ministry, supports those in need through its community intervention model with a focus on food security, education, and basic healthcare.

General, Infect Dis, Nutr, Pub Health

🌐 https://vfmat.ch/7274

Health Alliance International

Promotes policies and support programs that strengthen government primary healthcare and foster social, economic, and health equity for all.

General, Infect Dis, Logist-Op, MF Med, Neonat, OB-GYN, Psych

🌐 https://vfmat.ch/6f2d

Health Equity Initiative

Aims to build and sustain a global community that engages across sectors and disciplines to advance health equity.

Pub Health

🌐 https://vfmat.ch/e2e2

Health Poverty Action

Works in partnership with people around the world who are pursuing change in their own communities to demand health justice and challenge power imbalances.

ER Med, General, Infect Dis, Psych, Pub Health

🌐 https://vfmat.ch/ee58

Hearing The Call

Brings quality healthcare to persons with hearing loss locally and globally, helping them connect with education and opportunities.

ENT, Logist-Op

🌐 https://vfmat.ch/d1db

HEART (High-Quality Technical Assistance for Results)

Works to support the use of evidence and expert advice in policymaking in the areas of international development, health, nutrition, education, social protection, and water and sanitation (WASH).

General, Infect Dis, Infect Dis, Logist-Op, MF Med, Medicine, Nutr, OB-GYN, Peds, Psych

🌐 https://vfmat.ch/c491

Helen Keller International

Seeks to eliminate preventable vision loss, malnutrition, and diseases of poverty.

Infect Dis, Nutr, OB-GYN, Ophth-Opt, Peds

🌐 https://vfmat.ch/b654

HELP CODE ITALIA ONLUS

Seeks to improve life conditions of children in the communities where they live, through direct and indirect projects designed to support their well-being, education, and development.

General, Nutr, Pub Health

🌐 https://vfmat.ch/1dd9

HelpAge International

Works to ensure that people everywhere understand how much older people contribute to society and that they must enjoy their right to healthcare, social services, economic, and physical security.

General, Geri, Infect Dis, Medicine, Pub Health

🌐 https://vfmat.ch/5d91

Hernia International

Aims to provide relief from sickness, and protection and preservation of health, for persons affected by groin and abdominal hernias and residing in low- and middle-income countries.

Surg

🌐 https://vfmat.ch/e98e

Hope Walks

Frees children, families, and communities from the burden of clubfoot, inspired by the Christian faith.

Ortho, Ped Surg, Peds, Rehab

🌐 https://vfmat.ch/f6d4

Humanity & Inclusion

Works alongside people with disabilities and vulnerable populations, taking action and bearing witness in order to respond to their essential needs, improve their living conditions and health, and promote respect for their dignity and fundamental rights.

General, Infect Dis, MF Med, Medicine, Ortho, Peds, Psych, Pub Health, Rehab
⊕ https://vfmat.ch/16b7

Hunger Project, The
Aims to end hunger and poverty by pioneering sustainable, grassroots, women-centered strategies and advocating for their widespread adoption in countries throughout the world.
Infect Dis, Nutr, OB-GYN, Pub Health
⊕ https://vfmat.ch/3a49

ICAP at Columbia University
Serves as global leader in supporting the scale-up of multidisciplinary HIV/AIDS prevention, care, and treatment programs based on a family-focused approach.
General, Infect Dis, MF Med, Medicine, OB-GYN, Pub Health
⊕ https://vfmat.ch/a8ef

Imaging the World
Develops sustainable models for ultrasound imaging in the world's lowest resource settings and uses a technology-enabled solution to improve healthcare access, integrating lifesaving ultrasound and training programs in rural communities.
Logist-Op, OB-GYN, Radiol
⊕ https://vfmat.ch/59e4

International Agency for the Prevention of Blindness (IAPB), The
Leads international efforts in blindness-prevention activities, works toward a world where no one is needlessly visually impaired, and ensures that everyone has access to the best possible standard of eye health.
Infect Dis, Ophth-Opt, Pub Health
⊕ https://vfmat.ch/87a2

International Federation of Gynecology and Obstetrics (FIGO)
Implements global projects on specific women's health issues.
MF Med, Medicine, Neonat, OB-GYN, Surg, Urol
⊕ https://vfmat.ch/c4b4

International Federation of Red Cross and Red Crescent Societies (IFRC)
Coordinates and directs international assistance following natural and manmade disasters in nonconflict situations through the world's largest humanitarian and development network. Provides disaster-preparedness programs, healthcare activities, and promotes humanitarian values.
ER Med, General, Infect Dis, Nutr
⊕ https://vfmat.ch/b4ee

International Insulin Foundation
Aims to prolong the life and promote the health of people with diabetes in developing countries by improving the supply of insulin and education in its use.
Endo, Logist-Op
⊕ https://vfmat.ch/d34f

International Organization for Migration (IOM) – The UN Migration Agency
Promotes evidence-informed policies and holistic, preventive, and curative health programs that are beneficial, accessible, and equitable for vulnerable migrants.
General, Infect Dis, OB-GYN
⊕ https://vfmat.ch/621a

International Planned Parenthood Federation (IPPF)
Leads a locally owned, globally connected civil society movement that provides and enables services and champions sexual and reproductive health and rights for all, especially the underserved.
Infect Dis, MF Med, OB-GYN
⊕ https://vfmat.ch/dc97

International Relief Teams
Helps families survive and recover after a disaster by delivering timely and effective assistance through programs that improve their health and well-being while also providing a hopeful future for underserved communities.
Dent-OMFS, ER Med, General, Nutr, Ophth-Opt
⊕ https://vfmat.ch/ffd5

International Trachoma Initiative (iTi)
Works toward a world free from trachoma, a preventable cause of blindness, and provides comprehensive support to national ministries of health and governmental and nongovernmental organizations to implement a comprehensive approach to fight trachoma.
Infect Dis, Ophth-Opt
⊕ https://vfmat.ch/3278

IntraHealth International
Improves the performance of health workers and strengthens the systems in which they work.
CV Med, Endo, General, Infect Dis, MF Med, Neonat, Nutr, OB-GYN
⊕ https://vfmat.ch/ddc8

Ipas
Focuses efforts on women and girls who want contraception or abortion, and builds programs around their needs and how best to support them.
OB-GYN
⊕ https://vfmat.ch/8e39

Iris Global
Serves the poor, the destitute, the lost, and the forgotten by providing adoration, outreach, family, education, relief, development, healing, and the arts.
General, Infect Dis, Nutr, Pub Health
⊕ https://vfmat.ch/37f8

Iris Mundial
Aims to improve the ocular health of underserved people in developing countries by giving them access to high-quality preventive and curative eye care services.
Ophth-Opt
⊕ https://vfmat.ch/4f85

Islamic Medical Association of North America
Fosters health promotion, disease prevention, and health maintenance in communities around the world through direct patient care and health programs.
Anesth, Dent-OMFS, ER Med, General, Logist-Op, Ophth-Opt, Peds, Plast, Surg
⊕ https://vfmat.ch/a157

IsraAID
Supports people affected by humanitarian crisis and partners with local communities around the world to provide urgent aid, assist recovery, and reduce the risk of future disasters.
ER Med, Infect Dis, Psych, Rehab
⊕ https://vfmat.ch/de96

IVUmed
Aims to make quality urological care available worldwide by providing medical and surgical education for physicians and nurses, and treatment for thousands of children and adults.
Anesth, OB-GYN, Ped Surg, Surg, Urol
⊕ https://vfmat.ch/e619

Izumi Foundation
Develops and supports programs that improve health and healthcare in neglected regions of Africa and Latin America.
⊕ https://vfmat.ch/f29a

Jhpiego
Creates and delivers transformative healthcare solutions that save lives, in partnership with national governments, health experts, and local communities.
General, Infect Dis, OB-GYN, Surg
⊕ https://vfmat.ch/45b8

John Snow, Inc. (JSI)
Aims to improve the health and well-being of underserved and vulnerable people and communities throughout the world.
General, Infect Dis, Logist-Op, MF Med, OB-GYN, Peds, Psych, Pub Health
⊕ https://vfmat.ch/ba78

Johns Hopkins Center for Communication Programs
Believes in the power of communication to save lives by empowering people to adopt healthy behaviors for themselves, their families, and their communities.

General, Infect Dis, Logist-Op, OB-GYN, Pub Health
⊕ https://vfmat.ch/1bf9

Joint Aid Management (JAM)
Provides food security, nutrition, water, and sanitation to vulnerable African communities in dignified and sustainable ways.
ER Med, Nutr
⊕ https://vfmat.ch/dcac

Joint Aid Management (JAM) Canada
Strives to provide food security, nutrition, water, and sanitation to vulnerable African communities in dignified and sustainable ways.
Nutr, Pub Health
⊕ https://vfmat.ch/8756

Kaya Responsible Travel
Promotes sustainable social, environmental, and economic development, empowers communities, and cultivates educated, compassionate global citizens through responsible travel.
All-Immu, Crit-Care, Dent-OMFS, ER Med, General, Geri, Infect Dis, MF Med, Medicine, Nutr, OB-GYN, Peds, Psych, Pub Health, Rehab
⊕ https://vfmat.ch/b2cf

La Salle International Foundation
Provides support for educational, health, and human services, along with humanitarian relief to people in developed and underdeveloped areas.
General
⊕ https://vfmat.ch/5891

Lay Volunteers International Association (LVIA)
Fosters local and global change to help overcome extreme poverty, reinforce equitable and sustainable development, and enhance dialogue between Italian and African communities.
ER Med, Logist-Op, MF Med, Neonat, Nutr, OB-GYN, Peds
⊕ https://vfmat.ch/ecd4

Lepra
Works directly with communities in Bangladesh, India, Mozambique, and Zimbabwe to find, treat, and rehabilitate people affected by leprosy.
Infect Dis, Pub Health, Rehab
⊕ https://vfmat.ch/5d1c

Leprosy Mission England and Wales, The
Leads the fight against leprosy by supporting people living with leprosy today and serving future generations by working to end transmission of the disease.
Infect Dis, Pub Health
⊕ https://vfmat.ch/4c67

Leprosy Mission International
Seeks to empower people with leprosy to attain healing, dignity, and life in all its fullness.
Infect Dis
⊕ https://vfmat.ch/95a9

Light for the World
Contributes to a world in which persons with disabilities fully exercise their rights, and assists persons with disabilities living in poverty.
Ophth-Opt, Rehab
⊕ https://vfmat.ch/3ff6

Lions Clubs International
Empowers volunteers to serve their communities, meet humanitarian needs, encourage peace, and promote international understanding through Lions Clubs.
Heme-Onc, Medicine, Nutr, Ophth-Opt
⊕ https://vfmat.ch/7b12

Management Sciences for Health (MSH)
Works with countries and communities to save lives and improve the health of the world's poorest and most vulnerable people by building strong, resilient, sustainable health systems.
Infect Dis, Logist-Op, Pub Health
⊕ https://vfmat.ch/6aa2

MAP International
Provides medicines and health supplies to those in need around the world so they might experience life to the fullest.
Logist-Op
⊕ https://vfmat.ch/deed

Maverick Collective
Aims to build a global community of strategic philanthropists and informed advocates who use their intellectual and financial resources to create change.
Infect Dis, MF Med, OB-GYN
⊕ https://vfmat.ch/ea49

Max Foundation, The
Seeks to increase global access to treatment, care, and support for people living with cancer.
General, Heme-Onc, Pub Health
⊕ https://vfmat.ch/8c7d

Medical Care Development International
Works to improve the health of vulnerable populations through integrated, sustainable, and locally driven interventions.
Infect Dis, OB-GYN, Peds, Pub Health
⊕ https://vfmat.ch/da87

Medicus Mundi Italia
Carries out programs in basic community health, health education, maternal and child health, nutrition, and infectious disease.
General, Infect Dis, Logist-Op, MF Med, Nutr, Peds, Pub Health, Rehab
⊕ https://vfmat.ch/4413

MedShare
Aims to improve the quality of life of people, communities, and the planet by sourcing and directly delivering surplus medical supplies and equipment to communities in need around the world.
Logist-Op
⊕ https://vfmat.ch/c8bc

Mending Kids
Provides free, lifesaving surgical care to sick children worldwide by deploying volunteer medical teams and teaching communities to become medically self-sustaining through the education of local medical staff.
Anesth, CT Surg, ENT, Ortho, Ortho, Ped Surg, Plast, Surg
⊕ https://vfmat.ch/4d61

MENTOR Initiative
Saves lives in emergencies through tropical disease control, and helps people recover from crisis with dignity, working side by side with communities, health workers, and health authorities to leave a lasting impact.
ER Med, Infect Dis
⊕ https://vfmat.ch/3bd5

Mercy and Love Foundation
Aims to provide orphaned and vulnerable children with basic human needs such as food, clothing, and shelter, enabling them to thrive.
General, Peds
⊕ https://vfmat.ch/649a

Mercy Ships
Operates hospital ships staffed by volunteers to bring hope, healing, and healthcare to underserved communities worldwide.
Anesth, Dent-OMFS, Logist-Op, Neonat, OB-GYN, Ophth-Opt, Ortho, Palliative, Plast, Psych, Surg
⊕ https://vfmat.ch/2e99

mothers2mothers (m2m)
Employs and trains local women living with HIV as community health workers called Mentor Mothers to support women, children, and adolescents with vital medical services, education, and support.
Infect Dis, MF Med, OB-GYN, Peds, Pub Health
⊕ https://vfmat.ch/6557

MSD for Mothers
Designs scalable solutions that help end preventable maternal deaths.

MF Med, OB-GYN, Pub Health
⊕ https://vfmat.ch/9f99

Médecins du Monde/Doctors of the World
Provides care, bears witness, and supports social change worldwide with innovative medical programs and evidence-based advocacy initiatives.
ER Med, General, Infect Dis, MF Med, Neonat, OB-GYN, Peds, Pub Health
⊕ https://vfmat.ch/a43d

Nazarene Compassionate Ministries
Partners with local churches around the world to clothe, shelter, feed, heal, educate, and live in solidarity with those in need.
General, Infect Dis, OB-GYN
⊕ https://vfmat.ch/6b4d

NCD Alliance
Unites and strengthens civil society to stimulate collaborative advocacy, action, and accountability for NCD (noncommunicable disease) prevention and control.
All-Immu, CV Med, General, Heme-Onc, Medicine, Peds, Psych
⊕ https://vfmat.ch/abdd

New Hope in Africa
Aims to reach the people of Africa through healthcare, education, and basic necessities such as food and water.
Dent-OMFS, Infect Dis, MF Med, Nutr, OB-GYN, Pub Health
⊕ https://vfmat.ch/b2a8

NLR International
Promotes and supports the prevention and treatment of leprosy, prevention of disabilities, social inclusion, and stigma reduction of people affected by leprosy.
Infect Dis, Pub Health
⊕ https://vfmat.ch/d7bd

Norwegian People's Aid
Aims to improve living conditions, to create a democratic, just, and safe society.
ER Med, Logist-Op
⊕ https://vfmat.ch/2d8e

Ohana One International Surgical Aid & Education
Provides surgical care for the global family through technology and training.
Anesth, Logist-Op, Ped Surg, Peds, Plast, Surg
⊕ https://vfmat.ch/86b8

Operation Fistula
Exists to end obstetric fistula by building models of care that serve every woman, everywhere.
MF Med, OB-GYN, Surg
⊕ https://vfmat.ch/ce8e

Operation Smile
Treats patients with cleft lip and cleft palate, and creates solutions that deliver safe surgery to people where it's needed most.
Anesth, Dent-OMFS, ENT, Ped Surg, Plast
⊕ https://vfmat.ch/5c29

Options
Believes in a world in which women and children can access the high-quality health services they need, without financial burden.
Logist-Op, MF Med, Neonat, OB-GYN
⊕ https://vfmat.ch/3a48

Optometry Giving Sight
Delivers eye exams and low or no-cost glasses, provides training for local eye care professionals, and establishes optometry schools, vision centers and optical labs.
Ophth-Opt
⊕ https://vfmat.ch/33ea

Order of Malta
Supports forgotten or excluded people, especially those living in conflict zones or amid natural disasters, by providing medical assistance, caring for refugees, and distributing medicines and necessities.

ER Med, General, Infect Dis, MF Med, Nephro, OB-GYN, Ortho, Psych
⊕ https://vfmat.ch/1fab

Organization for the Prevention of Blindness, The (OPC)
Provides research, and treatments and cures for people affected by blindness and blinding diseases in Francophone Africa.
Infect Dis, Ophth-Opt
⊕ https://vfmat.ch/86d6

PATH
Advances health equity through innovation and partnerships so people, communities, and economies can thrive.
All-Immu, CV Med, Endo, Heme-Onc, Infect Dis, MF Med, Neonat, Nutr, OB-GYN, Path, Peds, Pulm-Critic
⊕ https://vfmat.ch/b4db

Pathfinder International
Champions sexual and reproductive health and rights worldwide, mobilizing communities most in need to break through barriers and forge paths to a healthier future.
OB-GYN
⊕ https://vfmat.ch/a7b3

PINCC Preventing Cervical Cancer
Seeks to prevent female-specific diseases in developing countries by utilizing low-cost and low-technology methods to create sustainable programs through patient education, medical personnel training, and facility outfitting.
OB-GYN
⊕ https://vfmat.ch/9666

PLeDGE Health
Aims to improve emergency medical care around the world through sustainable partnerships, open-source material development and dissemination, and development of the next generation of educational leaders in low-resource areas.
ER Med, General
⊕ https://vfmat.ch/3a7d

Project Concern International (PCI)
Drives innovation from the ground up to enhance health, end hunger, overcome hardship, and advance women and girls—resulting in meaningful and measurable change in people's lives.
Infect Dis, MF Med, Nutr, OB-GYN, Peds
⊕ https://vfmat.ch/5ed7

Project SOAR
Conducts HIV operations research around the world to identify practical solutions to improve HIV prevention, care, and treatment services.
ER Med, General, MF Med, OB-GYN, Psych
⊕ https://vfmat.ch/1a77

PSI – Population Services International
Aims to improve the health of people in the developing world by focusing on challenges such as a lack of family planning, HIV/AIDS, barriers to maternal health, and the greatest threats to children under the age of 5, including malaria, diarrhea, pneumonia, and malnutrition.
Infect Dis, MF Med, OB-GYN, Peds
⊕ https://vfmat.ch/ffe3

Real Medicine Foundation (RMF)
Provides humanitarian support to people living in disaster- and poverty-stricken areas, focusing on the person as a whole by providing medical/physical, emotional, economic, and social support.
ER Med, General, Infect Dis, Nutr, Peds, Psych
⊕ https://vfmat.ch/d45a

RestoringVision
Empowers lives by restoring vision for millions of people in need.
Ophth-Opt
⊕ https://vfmat.ch/e121

ReSurge International
Provides reconstructive surgical care and builds surgical capacity in developing countries.

Anesth, Dent-OMFS, Ped Surg, Plast, Surg
⊕ https://vfmat.ch/9937

Rockefeller Foundation, The
Works to promote the well-being of humanity.
Logist-Op, Nutr, Pub Health
⊕ https://vfmat.ch/5424

Rotary International
Provides service to others, improves lives, and advances world understanding, goodwill, and peace through its fellowship of business, professional, and community leaders.
ER Med, General, Infect Dis, MF Med, OB-GYN
⊕ https://vfmat.ch/8fb5

Salvation Army International, The
Seeks to meet human needs through services in education, healthcare, community support, emergency response, and ministry development, inspired by the Christian faith.
Dent-OMFS, Derm, ER Med, Infect Dis, MF Med, Medicine, Nutr, OB-GYN, Ophth-Opt, Palliative, Psych, Rehab, Surg
⊕ https://vfmat.ch/8eb3

Samaritan's Purse International Disaster Relief
Provides spiritual and physical aid to hurting people around the world, such as victims of war, poverty, natural disasters, disease, and famine, based in Christian ministry.
Anesth, CT Surg, Crit-Care, Dent-OMFS, Derm, ENT, ER Med, Endo, GI, General, Heme-Onc, Infect Dis, MF Med, Neonat, Nephro, Neuro, Neurosurg, Nutr, OB-GYN, Ophth-Opt, Ortho, Path, Ped Surg, Peds, Plast, Psych, Pulm-Critic, Radiol, Rehab, Rheum, Surg, Urol, Vasc Surg
⊕ https://vfmat.ch/87e3

Save the Children
Gives children around the world a healthy start in life, the opportunity to learn, and protection from harm.
All-Immu, Crit-Care, ER Med, General, Infect Dis, MF Med, Medicine, Neonat, OB-GYN, Peds, Psych, Pub Health
⊕ https://vfmat.ch/2e73

SEVA
Delivers vital eye care services to the world's most vulnerable, including women, children, and Indigenous peoples.
Ophth-Opt, Surg
⊕ https://vfmat.ch/1e87

Sightsavers
Works with partners in developing countries to help eliminate avoidable blindness and advocates for equal opportunity for the disabled.
Infect Dis, Ophth-Opt, Surg
⊕ https://vfmat.ch/aa52

SINA Health
Aims to improve the health and educational status of the population in low- and middle-income countries.
General, Logist-Op
⊕ https://vfmat.ch/9ad3

Smile Train, Inc.
Treats children with cleft lip through a sustainable and local model that supports surgery and other forms of essential care.
Logist-Op, Pub Health
⊕ https://vfmat.ch/822c

SOS Children's Villages International
Supports children through alternative care and family strengthening.
ER Med, Peds
⊕ https://vfmat.ch/aca1

Swiss Tropical and Public Health Institute
Contributes to the improvement of the health of populations internationally, nationally, and locally through excellence in research, education, and services.

Infect Dis, Pub Health
⊕ https://vfmat.ch/2ee4

Task Force for Global Health, The
Consists of programs and focus areas that cover a range of global health issues including neglected tropical diseases, infectious diseases, vaccines, field epidemiology, public health informatics, health workforce development, and global health ethics.
Infect Dis, Logist-Op, Medicine, Ophth-Opt, Peds
⊕ https://vfmat.ch/714c

Tearfund
Responds to crisis and partners with local churches to bring restoration to those living in poverty, inspired by the Christian faith.
ER Med, Logist-Op
⊕ https://vfmat.ch/f6cf

U.S. President's Malaria Initiative (PMI)
Supports low-income countries to help control and eliminate malaria through cost-effective, lifesaving malaria interventions.
Infect Dis, MF Med, OB-GYN
⊕ https://vfmat.ch/dc8b

Union for International Cancer Control (UICC)
Unites and supports the cancer community to reduce the global cancer burden, promote greater equity, and ensure that cancer control continues to be a priority in the world health and development agenda.
Heme-Onc, Pub Health
⊕ https://vfmat.ch/88b1

United Methodist Volunteers in Mission (UMVIM)
Engages in short-term missions each year in ministries as varied as disaster response, community development, pastor training, microenterprise, agriculture, Vacation Bible School, building repair and construction, and medical/dental services.
Dent-OMFS, ER Med, General
⊕ https://vfmat.ch/1ee6

United Nations Children's Fund (UNICEF)
Works in over 190 countries and territories to save children's lives, defend their rights, and help them fulfill their potential, from early childhood through adolescence.
All-Immu, Infect Dis, MF Med, Neonat, Nutr, OB-GYN, Ped Surg, Peds, Pub Health
⊕ https://vfmat.ch/42d7

United Nations Development Programme (UNDP)
Helps countries achieve the simultaneous eradication of extreme poverty and significant reduction of inequalities and exclusion using a sustainable human development approach.
Infect Dis, Logist-Op, Pub Health
⊕ https://vfmat.ch/935c

United Nations High Commissioner for Refugees (UNHCR)
Safeguards the rights and well-being of people who have been forced to flee, ensuring that everybody has the right to seek asylum and find safe refuge in another country, with the goal of seeking lasting solutions.
General, MF Med, Medicine, OB-GYN, Peds, Psych, Pub Health
⊕ https://vfmat.ch/6636

United Nations Population Fund (UNFPA)
Supports reproductive healthcare for women and youth in more than 150 countries, focusing on delivering a world in which every pregnancy is wanted, every childbirth is safe, and every young person's potential is fulfilled.
Infect Dis, MF Med, Neonat, OB-GYN, Peds, Pub Health
⊕ https://vfmat.ch/c969

United States Agency for International Development (USAID)
Promotes and demonstrates democratic values abroad and advances a free, peaceful, and prosperous world. Leads the U.S. government's international development and disaster assistance through partnerships and investments that save lives.

ER Med, Infect Dis, MF Med, OB-GYN, Peds
⊕ https://vfmat.ch/9a99

United States President's Emergency Plan for AIDS Relief (PEPFAR)
The U.S. global HIV/AIDS response works to prevent new HIV infections and accelerate progress to control the global epidemic in more than 50 countries, by partnering with governments to support sustainable, integrated, and country-led responses to HIV/AIDS.
Infect Dis, Pub Health
⊕ https://vfmat.ch/a57c

United Surgeons for Children (USFC)
Pursues greater health and opportunity for children in the most neglected pockets of the world, with a specific focus on and expertise in surgery.
Anesth, CT Surg, Neonat, Neurosurg, OB-GYN, Peds, Radiol, Surg
⊕ https://vfmat.ch/3b4c

University of California Los Angeles: David Geffen School of Medicine Global Health Program
Catalyzes opportunities to improve health globally by engaging in multi-disciplinary and innovative education programs, research initiatives, and bilateral partnerships that provide opportunities for trainees, faculty, and staff to contribute to sustainable health initiatives and to address health inequities facing the world today.
All-Immu, Infect Dis, Logist-Op, MF Med, Medicine, Neonat, OB-GYN, Ortho, Ped Surg, Peds, Radiol
⊕ https://vfmat.ch/f1a4

University of California San Francisco: Institute for Global Health Sciences
Dedicates its efforts to improving health and reducing the burden of disease in the world's most vulnerable populations by integrating expertise in the health, social, and biological sciences, training global health leaders, and developing solutions to the most pressing health challenges.
Infect Dis, OB-GYN, Pub Health
⊕ https://vfmat.ch/6587

University of Washington: The International Training and Education Center for Health (I-TECH)
Works with local partners to develop skilled healthcare workers and strong national health systems in resource-limited countries.
Infect Dis, Pub Health
⊕ https://vfmat.ch/642f

USAID: Deliver Project
Builds a global supply chain to deliver lifesaving health products to people in order to enable countries to provide family planning, protect against malaria, and limit the spread of pandemic threats.
Infect Dis, Logist-Op, MF Med
⊕ https://vfmat.ch/374e

USAID: EQUIP Health
Exists as an effective, efficient response mechanism to achieving global HIV epidemic control by delivering the right intervention at the right place and in the right way.
Infect Dis
⊕ https://vfmat.ch/d76a

USAID: Fistula Care Plus
Builds on, enhances, and expands the work undertaken by the previous Fistula Care project (2007–2013), with attention to prevention, detection, treatment, reintegration and new areas of focus so that obstetric fistula can become a rare event for future generations.
MF Med, OB-GYN, Surg
⊕ https://vfmat.ch/a7cd

USAID: Health Finance and Governance Project
Uses research to implement strategies to help countries develop robust governance systems, increase their domestic resources for health, manage those resources more effectively, and make wise purchasing decisions.
Logist-Op
⊕ https://vfmat.ch/8652

USAID: Health Policy Initiative
Provides field-level programming in health policy development and implementation.
General, Infect Dis, MF Med, OB-GYN, Peds
⊕ https://vfmat.ch/8f84

USAID: Maternal and Child Health Integrated Program
Works to improve the health of women and their families, including programs for maternal, newborn, and child health, immunization, family planning, nutrition, malaria, and HIV/AIDS.
All-Immu, General, Infect Dis, MF Med
⊕ https://vfmat.ch/4415

USAID: Maternal and Child Survival Program
Works to prevent child and maternal deaths.
Infect Dis, MF Med, Neonat, OB-GYN, Peds
⊕ https://vfmat.ch/6fcf

Vision Care
Restores sight and helps patients get regular treatment at short-term eye camps and long-term base clinics by having doctors, missionaries, volunteers, and sponsors work together.
Ophth-Opt
⊕ https://vfmat.ch/9d7c

Vodacom Foundation
Brings people together to maximize impact in three key areas: health, education, and safety and security.
Logist-Op
⊕ https://vfmat.ch/f116

Voluntary Service Overseas (VSO)
Works with health workers, communities, and governments to improve health services and rights for women, babies, youth, people with disabilities, and prisoners.
General, MF Med, OB-GYN
⊕ https://vfmat.ch/213d

World Blind Union (WBU)
Represents those experiencing blindness, speaking to governments and international bodies on issues concerning visual impairments.
Ophth-Opt
⊕ https://vfmat.ch/2bd3

World Children's Fund
Commits to helping children worldwide who are suffering the effects of poverty, disease, natural disaster, famine, abuse, civil strife, and war.
General, Logist-Op, MF Med, Nutr, OB-GYN, Pub Health
⊕ https://vfmat.ch/9cd8

World Federation of Hemophilia (WFH)
Aims to improve and sustain care for people with inherited bleeding disorders by pursuing long-term relationships with individuals and organizations who share the values of WFH's development model.
Heme-Onc
⊕ https://vfmat.ch/5121

World Health Organization, The (WHO)
The United Nations' agency for health provides leadership on global health matters, shapes the health research agenda, sets norms and standards, articulates evidence-based policy options, provides technical support and monitoring to countries, and assesses health trends.
ER Med, General, Infect Dis, Logist-Op, MF Med, OB-GYN, Peds, Psych, Pub Health
⊕ https://vfmat.ch/c476

World Hope International
Empowers the poorest individuals around the world so they can become agents of change within their communities, by offering resources and knowledge.
Infect Dis, Logist-Op, MF Med, OB-GYN, Peds
⊕ https://vfmat.ch/a4b8

World Medical Relief

Facilitates the distribution of surplus medical resources where they are needed.

Logist-Op

🌐 https://vfmat.ch/72dc

World Vision International

Works with vulnerable communities around the world to overcome poverty and injustice with child-focused programs in disaster management, health, nutrition, economic development, education, clean water, sanitation, and hygiene.

ER Med, General, Infect Dis, MF Med, Nutr, OB-GYN, Peds

🌐 https://vfmat.ch/2642

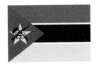

Mozambique

Healthcare Facilities

Central Hospital Nampula
Rua dos Continuadores, Nampula, Nampula, Mozambique
🌐 https://vfmat.ch/c4b9

Distrital Hospital de Marrupa
N360, Marrupa, Niassa, Mozambique
🌐 https://vfmat.ch/ec55

Hospital Antiga da Baixa
N12, Nacala, Nampula, Mozambique
🌐 https://vfmat.ch/3623

Hospital at Inhamizua
Inhamizua, Beira, Mozambique
🌐 https://vfmat.ch/4659

Hospital Central de Maputo
1653 Avenida Eduardo Mondlane, Maputo, Mozambique
🌐 https://vfmat.ch/19b8

Hospital Central de Quelimane
Quelimane, Mozambique
🌐 https://vfmat.ch/5778

Hospital da Ilha
Rua da Solidariedade, Ilha de Mozambique, Nampula, Mozambique
🌐 https://vfmat.ch/242a

Hospital da Salela
N242, Salela, Inhambane, Mozambique
🌐 https://vfmat.ch/153b

Hospital Distrital de Gondola
N6, Gondola, Manica, Mozambique
🌐 https://vfmat.ch/ba9e

Hospital Distrital de Mopeia
R640, Mopeia, Zambézia, Mozambique
🌐 https://vfmat.ch/e2aa

Hospital Distrital de Quissico
N1, Chissibuca, Inhambane, Mozambique
🌐 https://vfmat.ch/f722

Hospital Geral da Machava
Matola, Mozambique
🌐 https://vfmat.ch/e318

Hospital Geral de J. Macamo
Maputo, Mozambique
🌐 https://vfmat.ch/6a3e

Hospital Militar de Maputo
Rua Pêro d'Anaya, Cidade de Maputo, Mozambique
🌐 https://vfmat.ch/ba49

Hospital Polana Caniço A
Rua 3.730, Cidade de Maputo, Mozambique
🌐 https://vfmat.ch/f772

Hospital Privado de Maputo
Rua do Rio Inhamiara, Cidade de Maputo, Mozambique
🌐 https://vfmat.ch/4662

Hospital Provincial de Quelimane
Avenida 7 de Julho, Quelimane, Zambézia, Mozambique
🌐 https://vfmat.ch/8355

Hospital Provincial da Matola
N2, Matola, Maputo, Mozambique
🌐 https://vfmat.ch/d44d

Hospital Provincial de Inhambane
1300 Inhambane, Inhambane, Mozambique
🌐 https://vfmat.ch/d7bb

Hospital Provincial de Manica
Rua do Hospital, Chimoio, Manica, Mozambique
🌐 https://vfmat.ch/7af2

Hospital Provincial de Tete
R1051, Tete, Tete, Mozambique
🌐 https://vfmat.ch/2c1d

Hospital Rural de Angoche
Rua de Parapato, Angoche, Nampula, Mozambique
🌐 https://vfmat.ch/dab6

Hospital Rural de Buzi
Buzi, Sofala, Mozambique
🌐 https://vfmat.ch/75af

Hospital Rural de Chokwe
Avenida 7 de Abril, Chókwè, Gaza, Mozambique
🌐 https://vfmat.ch/32df

Hospital Rural de Cuamba
N13, Cuamba, Niassa, Mozambique
🌐 https://vfmat.ch/b3cf

Hospital Rural de Montepuez
N14, Montepuez, Cabo Delgado, Mozambique
🌐 https://vfmat.ch/5827

Hospital Rural de Vilankulo
N240, Vilankulo, Inhambane, Mozambique
🌐 https://vfmat.ch/f3cc

Hospital Rural do Milange
Rua Joaquim Maquival, Milange, Zambézia, Mozambique
🌐 https://vfmat.ch/6fb2

Instituto do Coração – ICOR
1111 Avenida Kenneth Kaunda, Cidade de Maputo, Mozambique
🌐 https://vfmat.ch/558c

Lenmed Hospital Privado de Maputo
Rua do Rio Inhamiara, 1100 Maputo, Maputo City, Mozambique
🌐 https://vfmat.ch/b34a

Mangungumete Health Home
Maimelane, Mozambique
⊕ https://vfmat.ch/b4b1

Nampula Military Hospital
N104, Nampula, Nampula, Mozambique
⊕ https://vfmat.ch/95fb

Netcare Nhamacunda
N240, Vilankulo, Inhambane, Mozambique
⊕ https://vfmat.ch/e5ac

Rural Hospital of Morrumbala
477, Morrumbala, Zambézia, Mozambique
⊕ https://vfmat.ch/7559

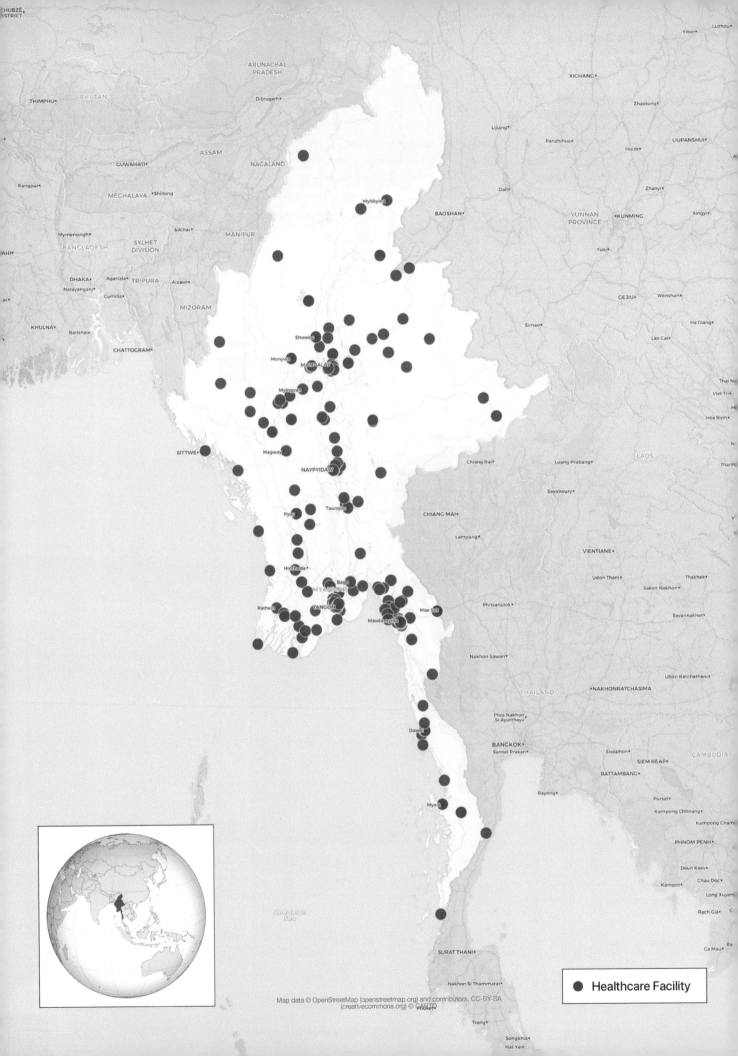

Healthcare Facility

Myanmar

The Republic of the Union of Myanmar (also known as Burma) is located between Bangladesh and Thailand, and bordered by the Andaman Sea and the Bay of Bengal. With an asymmetrically adult population, Myanmar has about 57.1 million people. Myanmar is the largest country by area in Mainland Southeast Asia. The more than 135 officially recognized and distinct ethnic groups are broadly categorized into eight major national groups: Bamar, Chin, Kachin, Kayin, Kayah, Mon, Arakanese, and Shan. Though there are more than 100 languages spoken in Myanmar, two-thirds of the nation's population speak Burmese, the official language. With bustling markets, and numerous parks and lakes, Yangon is the country's largest city, while Naypyidaw, called "the abode of kings," is the capital. The main religions include Buddhism, Christianity, Islam, and Hinduism.

Following Japanese occupation, Myanmar was reconquered by the Allies and granted independence in 1948. The country became a military dictatorship under the Burma Socialist Programme Party in 1962 after a coup d'etat. Since independence, civil wars have become a feature of the country's sociopolitical landscape. Contributing to its vulnerability, Myanmar is prone to persistent and highly destructive natural disasters such as earthquakes, cyclones, flooding, and landslides. With a nominal per capita income of $1,400, unemployment nearing 37 percent, and 26 percent of people living in poverty, Myanmar is one of the poorest countries in Southeast Asia.

The life expectancy of the Burmese people is 67 years, the lowest in Southeast Asia. Despite a steady increase in health expenditures by the government in recent years, the health system is still weak due to decades of neglect. Non-communicable diseases increasingly contribute to the most deaths in the country, including stroke, COPD, ischemic heart disease, diabetes, chronic kidney disease, cirrhosis, and asthma. Other ailments such as lower respiratory infections, neonatal disorders, and diarrheal diseases continue to cause significant numbers of deaths. While incidence of death due to HIV/AIDS and tuberculosis has decreased over time, they still continue to pose a major threat to the country's healthcare system, as well as being a significant cause of death.

57.1M

Population

$1,400

GDP Per Capita

67 years

Life Expectancy

↑ Improving

74
Doctors/100k

Physician Density

104
Beds/100k

Hospital Bed Density

250
Deaths/100k

Maternal Mortality

Myanmar

Nonprofit Organizations

Action Against Hunger
Aims to end life-threatening hunger for good through treating and preventing malnutrition across more than 45 countries.
Nutr
🌐 https://vfmat.ch/2dbc

Age International
Helps older people living in some of the world's poorest places to have improved well-being and be treated with dignity through a variety of programs, including emergency relief and cataract surgery.
ER Med, Geri, Logist-Op, Nutr, Ophth-Opt, Palliative, Pub Health
🌐 https://vfmat.ch/c7e2

AIDS Healthcare Foundation
Provides cutting-edge HIV/AIDS medical care and advocacy to over one million people in 43 countries.
Infect Dis
🌐 https://vfmat.ch/b27c

Al-Khair Foundation
Provides emergency relief and developmental support in some of the world's most impoverished areas.
Dent-OMFS, General, MF Med, Nutr, Peds
🌐 https://vfmat.ch/921d

Al-Mustafa Welfare Trust
Seeks to alleviate poverty and provides medical and social development assistance to the poor and vulnerable around the world.
General, Ophth-Opt
🌐 https://vfmat.ch/c5f4

Alight
Works closely with refugees, trafficked persons, economic migrants, and other displaced persons to co-design solutions that help them build full and fulfilling lives, with healthcare, clean water, shelter protection, and economic opportunity.
ER Med, General, Infect Dis, MF Med, Neonat, Peds
🌐 https://vfmat.ch/5993

Alliance for Smiles
Improves the lives of children and communities impacted by cleft by providing free comprehensive treatment while building local capacity for long-term care.
Dent-OMFS, Ped Surg, Plast, Surg
🌐 https://vfmat.ch/bb32

Aloha Medical Mission
Brings hope and changes the lives of people; serves overseas and in Hawai'i.
Anesth, Crit-Care, Dent-OMFS, ENT, ER Med, General, Medicine, OB-GYN, Ophth-Opt, Ortho, Ped Surg, Peds, Plast, Surg, Urol
🌐 https://vfmat.ch/72ac

Americare Neurosurgery International (AMCANI)
Seeks to increase the level of medical and surgical care in developing countries by providing professional training and development of appropriate resources such as physical therapy, rehabilitation skills, and nursing care.
Surg
🌐 https://vfmat.ch/467b

Americares
Saves lives and improves health for people affected by poverty or disaster and responds with life-changing medicine, medical supplies, and health programs including domestic and global medical clinics.
All-Immu, ER Med, General, Infect Dis, MF Med, Nutr
🌐 https://vfmat.ch/e567

AO Alliance
Builds solutions to lessen the burden of injuries in low- and middle-income countries, while enhancing the care of the injured to reduce human suffering, disability, and poverty.
Ortho, Surg
🌐 https://vfmat.ch/8cd5

ASAP Ministries
Provides education and healthcare to refugees and the poor, based in Christian ministry.
Dent-OMFS, General
🌐 https://vfmat.ch/266e

Association of Medical Doctors of Asia (AMDA)
Strives to support people affected by disasters and economic distress on their road to recovery, establishing a true partnership with special emphasis on local initiative.
ER Med, Logist-Op, Pub Health
🌐 https://vfmat.ch/e3d4

Australian & New Zealand Gastroenterology International Training Association
Aims to improve health in developing Asia Pacific nations by enhancing the standards of practice of gastroenterology and building capacity to treat digestive diseases.
GI
🌐 https://vfmat.ch/5a69

BFIRST – British Foundation for International Reconstructive Surgery & Training
Supports projects across the developing world to train surgeons in their local environment to effectively manage devastating injuries.
Anesth, Plast, Surg
🌐 https://vfmat.ch/ad4f

Blueprints For Pangaea (B4P)

Aims to reallocate unused medical supplies from areas of excess to areas in need.
⊕ https://vfmat.ch/faba

Boston Children's Hospital: Global Health Program

Helps solve pediatric global healthcare challenges by transferring expertise through long-term partnerships with scalable impact, while working in the field to strengthen healthcare systems, advocate, research, and provide care delivery or education as a way of sustainably improving the health of children worldwide.
Anesth, CV Med, Crit-Care, ER Med, Heme-Onc, Infect Dis, Medicine, Nutr, Palliative, Ped Surg, Peds
⊕ https://vfmat.ch/f9f8

BRAC USA

Seeks to empower people and communities in situations of poverty, illiteracy, disease, and social injustice. Interventions aim to achieve large-scale, positive changes through economic and social programs that enable everyone to realize their potential.
ER Med, General, Infect Dis, Logist-Op, MF Med, OB-GYN
⊕ https://vfmat.ch/9d9e

Bureau of International Health Cooperation

Seeks to improve healthcare around the world, including developing countries, using expertise, and contribute to healthier lives of Japanese people by bringing these experiences back to Japan.
ER Med, Heme-Onc, Infect Dis, Peds, Pub Health
⊕ https://vfmat.ch/947d

Burma Humanitarian Mission

Aims to support community-based backpack medics who administer village healthcare services in Burma, grass-roots education projects that empower the youth of Burma, and projects that promote cross-cultural sharing and collaboration for refugees from Burma living in the U.S.
ER Med, Nutr, Palliative, Pub Health
⊕ https://vfmat.ch/51fb

Cambridge Global Health Partnerships (CGHP)

Works in partnership to inspire and enable people to improve healthcare globally.
Crit-Care, Dent-OMFS, ER Med, Heme-Onc, Infect Dis, MF Med, Ophth-Opt, Ortho
⊕ https://vfmat.ch/1599

CardioStart International

Provides free heart surgery and associated medical care to children and adults living in underserved regions of the world, irrespective of political or religious affiliation, through the collective skills of healthcare experts.
Anesth, CT Surg, CV Med, Crit-Care, Pub Health, Pulm-Critic
⊕ https://vfmat.ch/85ef

CARE

Works around the globe to save lives, defeat poverty, and achieve social justice.
ER Med, General
⊕ https://vfmat.ch/7232

Carter Center, The

Seeks to prevent and resolve conflicts, enhance freedom and democracy, and improve health, while remaining committed to human rights and the alleviation of human suffering.
Infect Dis, MF Med, Ophth-Opt
⊕ https://vfmat.ch/6556

Catholic Organization for Relief & Development Aid (CORDAID)

Provides humanitarian assistance and creates opportunities to improve security, healthcare, education, and inclusive economic growth in fragile and conflict-affected areas.
ER Med, Infect Dis, MF Med, OB-GYN, Peds, Psych
⊕ https://vfmat.ch/8ae5

ChildFund Australia

Works to reduce poverty for children in many of the world's most disadvantaged communities.

ER Med, General, Peds
⊕ https://vfmat.ch/13df

Children's Lifeline International

Provides medical teams and surgical assistance to underprivileged children in developing countries through missions in partnership with local hospitals.
CV Med, Dent-OMFS, General, MF Med, Neurosurg, Peds, Rehab
⊕ https://vfmat.ch/6fea

Children's Relief International

Inspired by the Christian faith, cares for and educates children, their families, and their communities, including the provision of select healthcare services.
ER Med, General, Nutr
⊕ https://vfmat.ch/8da6

China California Heart Watch

Seeks to serve the people of Southeast Asia through teaching, improving access to care, and research.
CV Med, Pub Health
⊕ https://vfmat.ch/9955

Christian Aid Ministries

Strives to be a trustworthy and efficient channel for Amish, Mennonite, and other conservative Anabaptist groups and individuals to minister to physical and spiritual needs around the world.
CT Surg, ER Med, Logist-Op, Ortho, Pub Health
⊕ https://vfmat.ch/7b33

Christian Blind Mission (CBM)

Aims to improve the quality of life of persons with disabilities in the poorest countries, addressing poverty as a cause and a consequence of disability, and working in partnership to create a society for all.
ENT, General, Infect Dis, OB-GYN, Ophth-Opt, Ortho, Peds, Psych, Rehab, Surg
⊕ https://vfmat.ch/3824

Christian Connections for International Health (CCIH)

Promotes global health and wholeness from a Christian perspective.
All-Immu, General, Infect Dis, MF Med, Neonat, OB-GYN, Psych
⊕ https://vfmat.ch/fa5d

Clinton Health Access Initiative (CHAI)

Aims to save lives and reduce the burden of disease in low- and middle-income countries. Works with partners to strengthen the capabilities of governments and the private sector to create and sustain high-quality health systems.
General, Heme-Onc, Infect Dis, Logist-Op, MF Med, Medicine, Neonat, Nutr, OB-GYN, Path, Peds, Rad-Onc
⊕ https://vfmat.ch/9ed7

Combat Blindness International

Works to eliminate preventable blindness worldwide by providing sustainable, equitable solutions for sight through partnerships and innovation.
Ophth-Opt
⊕ https://vfmat.ch/28ad

COVID-19 Clinical Research Coalition

Advocates and collaborates for the advancement of COVID-19 research driven by the needs of low-resource settings, and works for equitable access to solutions to the pandemic.
All-Immu, Infect-Dis, MF Med, Path, Pub Health
⊕ https://vfmat.ch/d1f4

Direct Relief

Improves the health and lives of people affected by poverty or emergency situations by mobilizing and providing essential medical resources needed for their care.
ER Med, Logist-Op
⊕ https://vfmat.ch/58e5

DKT INTERNATIONAL INC

Seeks to provide couples with affordable and safe options for family planning and HIV/AIDS prevention through dynamic social marketing.
General, Surg
⊕ https://vfmat.ch/b3a7

Doctors Without Borders/Médecins Sans Frontières (MSF)
Responds to emergencies and provides lifesaving medical care where needed most, including during disasters, conflicts, and epidemics.
Anesth, Crit-Care, ER Med, General, Infect Dis, Nutr, OB-GYN, Ped Surg, Peds, Psych, Pub Health, Surg
⊕ https://vfmat.ch/f363

Drug and Alcohol Recovery and Education
Ensures adequate treatment and prevention services to the people of Myanmar.
Pub Health, Rehab
⊕ https://vfmat.ch/564d

Duke University: Global Health Institute
Sparks innovation in global health research and education, and brings together knowledge and resources to address the most important global health issues of our time.
All-Immu, Infect Dis, MF Med, OB-GYN, Pub Health
⊕ https://vfmat.ch/c4cd

Earth Mission
Empowers healthcare teams with training and knowledge to ensure that all people in Myanmar, especially the Karen ethnic group, have access to high-quality healthcare.
General, OB-GYN, Ophth-Opt, Peds, Pub Health
⊕ https://vfmat.ch/93f3

Episcopal Relief & Development
Provides relief in times of disaster and promotes sustainable development by identifying and addressing the root causes of suffering.
Infect Dis, MF Med, Neonat, Nutr, Peds
⊕ https://vfmat.ch/7cfa

Exceed Worldwide
Supports people with disabilities living in poverty by providing free prosthetic and orthotic services in South and Southeast Asia.
Ortho, Peds
⊕ https://vfmat.ch/dd24

Finn Church Aid
Supports people in the most vulnerable situations within fragile and disaster-affected regions in three thematic priority areas: right to peace, livelihood, and education.
ER Med, Psych, Pub Health
⊕ https://vfmat.ch/9623

Firefly Mission
Organizes humanitarian missions to help people in less fortunate situations while serving as a vehicle for the spiritual development of members and the beneficiaries of its missions.
Logist-Op, Ophth-Opt, Pub Health
⊕ https://vfmat.ch/d215

Foundation For International Education In Neurological Surgery (FIENS), The
Provides hands-on training and education to neurosurgeons around the world.
Neuro, Neurosurg, Surg
⊕ https://vfmat.ch/bab8

Fred Hollows Foundation, The
Works toward a world in which no person is needlessly blind or vision impaired.
Ophth-Opt, Pub Health, Surg
⊕ https://vfmat.ch/73e5

Friends of UNFPA
Promotes the health, dignity, and rights of women and girls around the world by supporting the lifesaving work of UNFPA, the United Nations' reproductive health and rights agency, through education, advocacy, and fundraising.
MF Med, OB-GYN
⊕ https://vfmat.ch/2a3a

GFA World
Based in Christian ministry, sponsors medical camps for the sick, provides disaster relief to vulnerable populations, and empowers impoverished communities with basic necessities such as clean water, vocational training, and education.
General, Infect Dis
⊕ https://vfmat.ch/63ee

Gift of Life International
Provides lifesaving cardiac treatment to children in developing countries while developing sustainable pediatric cardiac programs by implementing screening, surgical, and training missions.
Anesth, CT Surg, CV Med, Crit-Care, Ped Surg, Peds, Pulm-Critic
⊕ https://vfmat.ch/f2f9

Global Alliance to Prevent Prematurity And Stillbirth (GAPPS)
Seeks to improve birth outcomes worldwide by reducing the burden of premature birth and stillbirth.
All-Immu, Infect Dis, MF Med, Neonat, Neonat, OB-GYN
⊕ https://vfmat.ch/3f74

Global Civic Sharing
Aims to support our neighbors' self-reliance and realize the sustainable development.
Nutr, Peds, Pub Health
⊕ https://vfmat.ch/d7ab

Global Clinic
Seeks to ensure that any effort to provide medical services is accompanied by a long-term program to improve the health of residents of its partner communities.
Dent-OMFS, ER Med, General, OB-GYN, OB-GYN, Ophth-Opt, Surg
⊕ https://vfmat.ch/9e48

Global Medical Volunteers
Aims to advance medical services and education in developing nations around the world.
GI, Surg, Urol
⊕ https://vfmat.ch/dfec

Global Ministries – The United Methodist Church
As the worldwide mission and development agency of The United Methodist Church, Global Ministries works with more than 300 hospitals and clinics around the world through its Global Health Unit.
Anesth, CT Surg, CV Med, Crit-Care, Dent-OMFS, Derm, ER Med, GI, General, Infect Dis, Logist-Op, MF Med, Medicine, Neonat, Nephro, Nutr, OB-GYN, Ophth-Opt, Ortho, Palliative, Peds, Pod, Psych, Pub Health, Rehab, Rheum, Surg, Urol
⊕ https://vfmat.ch/1723

Global Oncology (GO)
Brings the best in cancer care to underserved patients around the world and collaborates across geographic, professional, and academic borders to improve cancer care, research, and education.
Heme-Onc, Path, Rad-Onc
⊕ https://vfmat.ch/fcb8

Global Outreach Doctors
Provides global health medical services in developing countries affected by famine, infant mortality, and chronic health issues.
All-Immu, Anesth, ER Med, General, Infect Dis, MF Med, Peds, Surg
⊕ https://vfmat.ch/8514

Global Polio Eradication Initiative
Aims to eradicate polio worldwide.
All-Immu, Infect-Dis, Logist-Op, Pub Health
⊕ https://vfmat.ch/7e2c

Global Primary Care
Aims to promote and support individuals and organizations that increase access to primary care through sustainable efforts for people living in the poorest places of the world.
General, Logist-Op, Medicine
⊕ https://vfmat.ch/742b

Global Vision 2020
Provides prescription eyeglasses to people who live in parts of the world lacking necessary infrastructure for obtaining affordable corrective eyewear.

Logist-Op, Ophth-Opt
⊕ https://vfmat.ch/7373

GlobalMedic
Provides disaster relief and lifesaving humanitarian aid.
ER Med, Pub Health
⊕ https://vfmat.ch/dfe6

Globus Relief
Aims to improve the delivery of healthcare worldwide by gathering, processing, and distributing surplus medical supplies to charities at home and abroad.
Logist-Op
⊕ https://vfmat.ch/a2b7

Good Shepard International Foundation
Strives to promote inclusive and sustainable development for the most marginalized and vulnerable people, with a special focus on women, girls, and children, inspired by the Christian faith.
ER Med
⊕ https://vfmat.ch/ad9a

Health and Hope
Brings hope and development to the poorest people in western Myanmar (Burma), through primary healthcare, education, and food security projects. Our vision is to see lives transformed and communities that are thriving and self-developed.
ER Med, GI, General, Geri, MF Med, Nutr, OB-GYN, Palliative, Peds, Pub Health
⊕ https://vfmat.ch/e3bf

Health Equity Initiative
Aims to build and sustain a global community that engages across sectors and disciplines to advance health equity.
Pub Health
⊕ https://vfmat.ch/e2e2

Health Frontiers
Provides volunteer support to international health and child development efforts.
ER Med, Medicine, Peds
⊕ https://vfmat.ch/aa14

Health Poverty Action
Works in partnership with people around the world who are pursuing change in their own communities to demand health justice and challenge power imbalances.
ER Med, General, Infect Dis, Psych, Pub Health
⊕ https://vfmat.ch/ee58

Health Volunteers Overseas (HVO)
Improves the availability and quality of healthcare through the education, training, and professional development of the health workforce in resource-scarce countries.
All-Immu, Anesth, CV Med, Dent-OMFS, Derm, ENT, ER Med, Endo, GI, Heme-Onc, Infect Dis, Medicine, Medicine, Nephro, Neuro, OB-GYN, Ophth-Opt, Ortho, Peds, Plast, Psych, Pulm-Critic, Rehab, Rheum, Surg
⊕ https://vfmat.ch/42b2

Hear the World Foundation
Advocates worldwide for equal opportunities and improved quality of life for people in need with hearing loss.
ENT, Peds
⊕ https://vfmat.ch/122c

Helen Keller International
Seeks to eliminate preventable vision loss, malnutrition, and diseases of poverty.
Infect Dis, Nutr, OB-GYN, Ophth-Opt, Peds
⊕ https://vfmat.ch/b654

HelpMeSee
Trains local cataract specialists in Manual Small Incision Cataract Surgery (MSICS) in significant numbers, to meet the increasing demand for surgical services in the communities most impacted by cataract blindness.
Anesth, Ophth-Opt, Surg
⊕ https://vfmat.ch/973c

Himalayan Cataract Project
Works to cure needless blindness with the highest quality care at the lowest cost.
Anesth, Ophth-Opt, Surg
⊕ https://vfmat.ch/3b3d

Humanity & Inclusion
Works alongside people with disabilities and vulnerable populations, taking action and bearing witness in order to respond to their essential needs, improve their living conditions and health, and promote respect for their dignity and fundamental rights.
General, Infect Dis, MF Med, Medicine, Ortho, Peds, Psych, Pub Health, Rehab
⊕ https://vfmat.ch/16b7

ICAP at Columbia University
Serves as global leader in supporting the scale-up of multidisciplinary HIV/AIDS prevention, care, and treatment programs based on a family-focused approach.
General, Infect Dis, MF Med, Medicine, OB-GYN, Pub Health
⊕ https://vfmat.ch/a8ef

Institute of Applied Dermatology
Aims to alleviate difficult-to-treat skin ailments by combining biomedicine with Ayurveda, homeopathy, yoga, and other traditional Indian medicine.
All-Immu, Derm, Infect Dis, Nutr, Pod, Pub Health
⊕ https://vfmat.ch/c6eb

International Agency for the Prevention of Blindness (IAPB), The
Leads international efforts in blindness-prevention activities, works toward a world where no one is needlessly visually impaired, and ensures that everyone has access to the best possible standard of eye health.
Infect Dis, Ophth-Opt, Pub Health
⊕ https://vfmat.ch/87a2

International Children's Heart Fund
Aims to promote the international growth and quality of cardiac surgery, particularly in children and young adults.
CT Surg, Ped Surg
⊕ https://vfmat.ch/33fb

International Council of Ophthalmology
Works with ophthalmologic societies and others to enhance ophthalmic education and improve access to the highest-quality eye care in order to preserve and restore vision for people of the world.
Ophth-Opt
⊕ https://vfmat.ch/ffd2

International Federation of Gynecology and Obstetrics (FIGO)
Implements global projects on specific women's health issues.
MF Med, Medicine, Neonat, OB-GYN, Surg, Urol
⊕ https://vfmat.ch/c4b4

International Federation of Red Cross and Red Crescent Societies (IFRC)
Coordinates and directs international assistance following natural and manmade disasters in nonconflict situations through the world's largest humanitarian and development network. Provides disaster-preparedness programs, healthcare activities, and promotes humanitarian values.
ER Med, General, Infect Dis, Nutr
⊕ https://vfmat.ch/b4ee

International Learning Movement (ILM UK)
Supports some of the world's poorest people in developing countries with core projects in education, safe drinking water, and healthcare.
General, Ophth-Opt
⊕ https://vfmat.ch/b974

International Organization for Migration (IOM) – The UN Migration Agency
Promotes evidence-informed policies and holistic, preventive, and curative health programs that are beneficial, accessible, and equitable for vulnerable migrants.
General, Infect Dis, OB-GYN
⊕ https://vfmat.ch/621a

International Pediatric Nephrology Association (IPNA)
Leads global efforts to successfully address the care for all children with kidney disease through advocacy, education, and training.
Medicine, Nephro, Peds
⊕ https://vfmat.ch/b59d

International Rescue Committee (IRC)
Responds to the world's worst humanitarian crises and helps people whose lives and livelihoods are shattered by conflict and disaster to survive, recover, and gain control of their future.
ER Med, General, Infect Dis, MF Med, Peds
⊕ https://vfmat.ch/5d24

International Skills and Training Institute in Health (ISTIH)
Facilitates the appropriate placement of specialist health professionals with international volunteering opportunities.
ER Med
⊕ https://vfmat.ch/fa64

International Union Against Tuberculosis and Lung Disease
Develops, implements, and assesses anti-tuberculosis, lung health, and noncommunicable disease programs.
Infect Dis, Pub Health, Pulm-Critic
⊕ https://vfmat.ch/3e82

InterSurgeon
Fosters collaborative partnerships in the field of global surgery that will advance clinical care, teaching, training, research, and the provision and maintenance of medical equipment.
ENT, Neurosurg, Ortho, Ped Surg, Plast, Surg, Urol
⊕ https://vfmat.ch/6f8a

Ipas
Focuses efforts on women and girls who want contraception or abortion, and builds programs around their needs and how best to support them.
OB-GYN
⊕ https://vfmat.ch/8e39

Iranian Red Crescent
Aims to provide effective relief services in the wake of crises, to alleviate human suffering, and to empower the affected community.
ER Med, General, Infect Dis, Logist-Op, Nutr, OB-GYN, Psych, Rehab
⊕ https://vfmat.ch/c352

iSight Missions
To empower local eye care providers to establish self-supporting eye clinics to offer permanent care to impoverished persons.
Ophth-Opt
⊕ https://vfmat.ch/9739

Islamic Medical Association of North America
Fosters health promotion, disease prevention, and health maintenance in communities around the world through direct patient care and health programs.
Anesth, Dent-OMFS, ER Med, General, Logist-Op, Ophth-Opt, Peds, Plast, Surg
⊕ https://vfmat.ch/a157

Japan Heart
Provides medical care in areas where it is currently out of reach, wherever that may be.
Heme-Onc, Medicine, OB-GYN, Ped Surg, Peds, Plast, Surg
⊕ https://vfmat.ch/1cd3

Jewish World Watch
Brings help and healing to survivors of mass atrocities around the globe and seeks to inspire people of all faiths and cultures to join the ongoing fight against genocide.
ER Med, Logist-Op, OB-GYN, Peds
⊕ https://vfmat.ch/8c92

Jhpiego
Creates and delivers transformative healthcare solutions that save lives, in partnership with national governments, health experts, and local communities.
General, Infect Dis, OB-GYN, Surg
⊕ https://vfmat.ch/45b8

John Snow, Inc. (JSI)
Aims to improve the health and well-being of underserved and vulnerable people and communities throughout the world.
General, Infect Dis, Logist-Op, MF Med, OB-GYN, Peds, Psych, Pub Health
⊕ https://vfmat.ch/ba78

Johns Hopkins Center for Communication Programs
Believes in the power of communication to save lives by empowering people to adopt healthy behaviors for themselves, their families, and their communities.
General, Infect Dis, Logist-Op, OB-GYN, Pub Health
⊕ https://vfmat.ch/1bf9

Joint United Nations Programme on HIV/AIDS (UNAIDS)
Aims to place people living with HIV and people affected by the virus at the decision-making table and at the center of designing, delivering, and monitoring the AIDS response.
Infect Dis
⊕ https://vfmat.ch/464a

KT Care Foundation
Seeks to provide education, health, and emergency preparation and relief services by leveraging local expertise to foster self-empowerment and sustainable development.
Dent-OMFS, General, Ophth-Opt, Plast
⊕ https://vfmat.ch/ef4a

Leprosy Mission England and Wales, The
Leads the fight against leprosy by supporting people living with leprosy today and serving future generations by working to end transmission of the disease.
Infect Dis, Pub Health
⊕ https://vfmat.ch/4c67

Leprosy Mission International
Seeks to empower people with leprosy to attain healing, dignity, and life in all its fullness.
Infect Dis
⊕ https://vfmat.ch/95a9

Limbs International
Engages communities and transforms lives through affordable, sustainable prosthetic solutions and rehabilitation services in developing countries.
Logist-Op, Ortho, Pod, Rehab
⊕ https://vfmat.ch/dc84

Living Goods
Leverages a powerful combination of catalytic technology, high-impact training, and quality treatments that empower government community health workers (CHWs) to deliver quality care to their neighbors' doorsteps.
Infect Dis, Logist-Op, MF Med
⊕ https://vfmat.ch/d6d2

London School of Hygiene & Tropical Medicine: Health in Humanitarian Crises Centre
Advances health and health equity in crisis-affected countries through research, education, and translation of knowledge into policy and practice.
ER Med, Infect Dis, Pub Health
⊕ https://vfmat.ch/96ad

Lutherans in Medical Missions (LIMM)
Works with local and global partners to promote healing in medically underserved communities.
General, Logist-Op, Pub Health
⊕ https://vfmat.ch/c5aa

MAGNA International
Helps those who are suffering or recovering from conflicts and disasters by reducing the risks of diseases and treating them immediately.
ER Med, General, Infect Dis, Peds, Surg
⊕ https://vfmat.ch/58f4

Management Sciences for Health (MSH)
Works with countries and communities to save lives and improve the health of the world's poorest and most vulnerable people by building strong, resilient, sustainable health systems.
Infect Dis, Logist-Op, Pub Health
⊕ https://vfmat.ch/6aa2

MAP International
Provides medicines and health supplies to those in need around the world so they might experience life to the fullest.
Logist-Op
⊕ https://vfmat.ch/deed

Marie Stopes International
Provides the contraception and safe abortion services that enable women all over the world to choose their own futures.
Infect Dis, MF Med, Neonat, OB-GYN, Pub Health
⊕ https://vfmat.ch/9525

Maternity Foundation
Works to ensure safer childbirth for women and newborns everywhere through innovative mobile health solutions such as the Safe Delivery App, a mobile training tool for skilled birth attendants.
MF Med, OB-GYN, Pub Health
⊕ https://vfmat.ch/ff4f

Maverick Collective
Aims to build a global community of strategic philanthropists and informed advocates who use their intellectual and financial resources to create change.
Infect Dis, MF Med, OB-GYN
⊕ https://vfmat.ch/ea49

MedAcross
Focuses on providing free medical care to people in developing countries, with a particular focus on children and teenagers, training medical and paramedical staff on-site in order to develop independent health facilities and create job opportunities for the local population, and supporting humanitarian interventions by cooperating with local associations already at work on the context.
General, Infect Dis, Logist-Op, Peds, Pub Health
⊕ https://vfmat.ch/a526

Medical Care Development International
Works to improve the health of vulnerable populations through integrated, sustainable, and locally driven interventions.
Infect Dis, OB-GYN, Peds, Pub Health
⊕ https://vfmat.ch/da87

Medical Intervention Team eV (MIT)
Seeks to help children in Myanmar with cleft lip and palate through free medical missions.
Dent-OMFS, ENT, Plast
⊕ https://vfmat.ch/3d2b

Medical Mercy Canada
Seeks to improve the quality of life in impoverished areas through humanitarian projects with local participation, and provides funding for orphanages, geriatric and childcare centers, remote health clinics, medical aid centers, hospitals, rural schools, and health programs.
General
⊕ https://vfmat.ch/81dc

Medical Teams International
Seeks to restore health as the first step to restoring hope, working to bring basic but lifesaving medical care to those in need.
Dent-OMFS, ER Med, General, MF Med, Pub Health
⊕ https://vfmat.ch/8d1c

MedShare
Aims to improve the quality of life of people, communities, and the planet by sourcing and directly delivering surplus medical supplies and equipment to communities in need around the world.
Logist-Op
⊕ https://vfmat.ch/c8bc

MiracleFeet
Brings low-cost treatment to every child on the planet born with clubfoot, a leading cause of physical disability.
Ortho, Peds, Rehab
⊕ https://vfmat.ch/bda8

Mission Bambini
Helps to support children living in poverty and sickness, and lacking education, giving them the opportunity for and hope of a better life.
CT Surg, CV Med, Crit-Care, ER Med, Ped Surg, Peds
⊕ https://vfmat.ch/dc1a

Mission: Restore
Trains medical professionals abroad in complex reconstructive surgery in order to create a sustainable infrastructure in which long-term relationships are forged and permanent change comes to pass.
Plast, Surg
⊕ https://vfmat.ch/3f5f

MSD for Mothers
Designs scalable solutions that help end preventable maternal deaths.
MF Med, OB-GYN, Pub Health
⊕ https://vfmat.ch/9f99

MSI Reproductive Choices (Marie Stopes International)
Seeks to deliver quality family planning and reproductive healthcare to women around the world.
MF Med
⊕ https://vfmat.ch/5c82

Muslim Aid
Aims to improve the lives of those in need, and to address the underlying structural and systemic causes of poverty in their communities, inspired by Muslim faith.
ER Med, Infect Dis, MF Med, Nutr
⊕ https://vfmat.ch/a8ed

Muslim Welfare Canada
Serves vulnerable populations by supporting healthcare clinics, food security programs, and other humanitarian projects.
Logist-Op, Nutr
⊕ https://vfmat.ch/a227

Médecins du Monde/Doctors of the World
Provides care, bears witness, and supports social change worldwide with innovative medical programs and evidence-based advocacy initiatives.
ER Med, General, Infect Dis, MF Med, Neonat, OB-GYN, Peds, Pub Health
⊕ https://vfmat.ch/a43d

Mérieux Foundation
Committed to fighting infectious diseases that affect developing countries by capacity building, particularly in clinical laboratories, and focusing on diagnosis.
Logist-Op, Path
⊕ https://vfmat.ch/a23a

NCD Alliance
Unites and strengthens civil society to stimulate collaborative advocacy, action, and accountability for NCD (noncommunicable disease) prevention and control.
All-Immu, CV Med, General, Heme-Onc, Medicine, Peds, Psych
⊕ https://vfmat.ch/abdd

Norwegian People's Aid
Aims to improve living conditions, to create a democratic, just, and safe society.
ER Med, Logist-Op
⊕ https://vfmat.ch/2d8e

Open Heart International
Provides surgical interventions and best practices to the most disadvantaged communities on the planet.
CT Surg, MF Med, OB-GYN, Ophth-Opt, Plast, Surg
⊕ https://vfmat.ch/dab2

Operation Corazón

Offers support to individuals and families in need by delivering humanitarian aid, relief, support services, equipment, clothing, medicine, and food.

General, Nutr

🌐 https://vfmat.ch/5f76

Operation International

Offers medical aid to adults and children suffering from lack of quality healthcare in impoverished countries.

Dent-OMFS, ER Med, Heme-Onc, OB-GYN, Ophth-Opt, Ortho, Ped Surg, Plast, Surg

🌐 https://vfmat.ch/b52a

Operation Smile

Treats patients with cleft lip and cleft palate, and creates solutions that deliver safe surgery to people where it's needed most.

Anesth, Dent-OMFS, ENT, Ped Surg, Plast

🌐 https://vfmat.ch/5c29

Options

Believes in a world in which women and children can access the high-quality health services they need, without financial burden.

Logist-Op, MF Med, Neonat, OB-GYN

🌐 https://vfmat.ch/3a48

Pact

Works on the ground to improve the lives of those who are challenged by poverty and marginalization, striving for a world in which all people are heard, capable, and vibrant.

Infect Dis, Logist-Op, MF Med, Pub Health

🌐 https://vfmat.ch/9a6c

PATH

Advances health equity through innovation and partnerships so people, communities, and economies can thrive.

All-Immu, CV Med, Endo, Heme-Onc, Infect Dis, MF Med, Neonat, Nutr, OB-GYN, Path, Peds, Pulm-Critic

🌐 https://vfmat.ch/b4db

Pathfinder International

Champions sexual and reproductive health and rights worldwide, mobilizing communities most in need to break through barriers and forge paths to a healthier future.

OB-GYN

🌐 https://vfmat.ch/a7b3

Pepal

Brings together NGOs, global corporations, and the public sector to co-create solutions to big social issues, creating immediate and scalable solutions, and developing leaders who are capable of driving change in their communities.

Heme-Onc, Infect Dis, Pub Health

🌐 https://vfmat.ch/6dc5

Première Urgence International

Helps civilians who are marginalized or excluded as a result of natural disasters, war, or economic collapse.

ER Med, General, MF Med, Peds, Psych

🌐 https://vfmat.ch/62ba

PSI – Population Services International

Aims to improve the health of people in the developing world by focusing on challenges such as a lack of family planning, HIV/AIDS, barriers to maternal health, and the greatest threats to children under the age of 5, including malaria, diarrhea, pneumonia, and malnutrition.

Infect Dis, MF Med, OB-GYN, Peds

🌐 https://vfmat.ch/ffe3

Reach Beyond

Aims to reach and impact underserved communities with medical care and community development, based in Christian ministry.

ER Med, General

🌐 https://vfmat.ch/cc5c

Real Medicine Foundation (RMF)

Provides humanitarian support to people living in disaster- and poverty-stricken areas, focusing on the person as a whole by providing medical/physical, emotional, economic, and social support.

ER Med, General, Infect Dis, Nutr, Peds, Psych

🌐 https://vfmat.ch/d45a

Refugee Empowerment International

Funds projects for people displaced by conflict around the world. REI supports projects that provide opportunities for people to lead an independent normal life while staying near to home and their loved ones, projects that enable people to give back to the community and make valuable contributions to the local economy, along with rebuilding their own future.

Crit-Care, OB-GYN, Peds

🌐 https://vfmat.ch/e67d

Relief International

Helps people in fragile settings achieve good health and nutrition by delivering primary healthcare and emergency treatment, and builds local capacity to ensure that communities in vulnerable situations have the access to the quality care they need to live healthy lives.

ER Med, General, MF Med, Neonat, OB-GYN, Peds, Psych

🌐 https://vfmat.ch/1522

RestoringVision

Empowers lives by restoring vision for millions of people in need.

Ophth-Opt

🌐 https://vfmat.ch/e121

ReSurge International

Provides reconstructive surgical care and builds surgical capacity in developing countries.

Anesth, Dent-OMFS, Ped Surg, Plast, Surg

🌐 https://vfmat.ch/9937

Rockefeller Foundation, The

Works to promote the well-being of humanity.

Logist-Op, Nutr, Pub Health

🌐 https://vfmat.ch/5424

Rotaplast International

Helps children and families worldwide by eliminating the burden of cleft lip and/or palate, burn scarring, and other deformities by sending medical teams to provide free reconstructive surgery, ancillary treatment, and training.

Anesth, Dent-OMFS, ENT, Ped Surg, Plast, Surg

🌐 https://vfmat.ch/78b3

Rotary International

Provides service to others, improves lives, and advances world understanding, goodwill, and peace through its fellowship of business, professional, and community leaders.

ER Med, General, Infect Dis, MF Med, OB-GYN

🌐 https://vfmat.ch/8fb5

Saint Lucy Foundation

Seeks to improve eye health by carrying out operations, supplying medicines, and training local staff to prevent and treat eye disease.

Ophth-Opt

🌐 https://vfmat.ch/7583

Salvation Army International, The

Seeks to meet human needs through services in education, healthcare, community support, emergency response, and ministry development, inspired by the Christian faith.

Dent-OMFS, Derm, ER Med, Infect Dis, MF Med, Medicine, Nutr, OB-GYN, Ophth-Opt, Palliative, Psych, Rehab, Surg

🌐 https://vfmat.ch/8eb3

Sanofi Espoir Foundation

Contributes to reducing health inequalities among populations that need it most by applying a socially responsible approach focused on fighting childhood cancers in low-income countries, improving maternal and newborn health, and improving access to care.

ER Med, OB-GYN, Peds
⊕ https://vfmat.ch/943b

Save A Child's Heart
Provides lifesaving cardiac treatment to children in developing countries, and trains healthcare professionals from these countries to deliver quality care in their communities.
CT Surg, CV Med, Crit-Care, Ped Surg, Peds
⊕ https://vfmat.ch/1bef

Save the Children
Gives children around the world a healthy start in life, the opportunity to learn, and protection from harm.
All-Immu, Crit-Care, ER Med, General, Infect Dis, MF Med, Medicine, Neonat, OB-GYN, Peds, Psych, Pub Health
⊕ https://vfmat.ch/2e73

SEE International
Provides sustainable medical, surgical, and educational services through volunteer ophthalmic surgeons, with the objectives of restoring sight and preventing blindness to disadvantaged individuals worldwide.
Ophth-Opt, Surg
⊕ https://vfmat.ch/6e1b

SEVA
Delivers vital eye care services to the world's most vulnerable, including women, children, and Indigenous peoples.
Ophth-Opt, Surg
⊕ https://vfmat.ch/1e87

Shanta Foundation
Aims to build thriving communities through sustainable programs in health, education, leadership, women's empowerment, livelihood and infrastructure, working in partnership with poor rural villages in Myanmar.
Dent-OMFS, MF Med, OB-GYN
⊕ https://vfmat.ch/dbe6

Sight for All
Empowers communities to deliver comprehensive, evidence-based, high-quality eye healthcare through the provision of research, education, and equipment.
Logist-Op, Ophth-Opt, Surg
⊕ https://vfmat.ch/e34b

SIGN Fracture Care International
Builds orthopedic capacity around the world and provides the injured poor access to fracture surgery by donating orthopedic education and implant systems to surgeons in developing countries.
Ortho, Rehab, Surg
⊕ https://vfmat.ch/123d

Singapore Red Cross
Responds to emergencies with a dedication to relieving human suffering and protecting human lives and dignity.
ER Med, General, Logist-Op, Pub Health, Surg
⊕ https://vfmat.ch/4d7c

Smile Asia
Delivers free surgical care, through medical missions and outreach centers, to children with facial deformities such as cleft lip and cleft palate, and aims to raise standards of medical care by creating opportunities for collaborative learning and exchange of best practices.
Anesth, Dent-OMFS, Ped Surg, Peds, Plast
⊕ https://vfmat.ch/d674

Smile Train, Inc.
Treats children with cleft lip through a sustainable and local model that supports surgery and other forms of essential care.
Logist-Op, Pub Health
⊕ https://vfmat.ch/822c

SONNE Social Organization
Aims to create as many opportunities as possible to positively impact and change a child's life, toward a secure, fair and promising livelihood.

ER Med, General, Peds
⊕ https://vfmat.ch/ea6a

Sri Sathya Sai International Organization
Inspired by spiritual teachings, carries out efforts in global healthcare, education, humanitarian relief, and youth engagement.
Dent-OMFS, General, Logist-Op, Nutr, Ophth-Opt, Pub Health
⊕ https://vfmat.ch/9bda

Stand By Me
Helps children facing terrible circumstances and provides the care, love, and attention they need to thrive through children's homes and schools.
Peds
⊕ https://vfmat.ch/a224

Student Action Volunteer Effort - SAVE Myanmar
Organizes medical missions to help underserved populations in Myanmar.
General, Pub Health
⊕ https://vfmat.ch/e4ef

Swiss Tropical and Public Health Institute
Contributes to the improvement of the health of populations internationally, nationally, and locally through excellence in research, education, and services.
Infect Dis, Pub Health
⊕ https://vfmat.ch/2ee4

Task Force for Global Health, The
Consists of programs and focus areas that cover a range of global health issues including neglected tropical diseases, infectious diseases, vaccines, field epidemiology, public health informatics, health workforce development, and global health ethics.
Infect Dis, Logist-Op, Medicine, Ophth-Opt, Peds
⊕ https://vfmat.ch/714c

Tearfund
Responds to crisis and partners with local churches to bring restoration to those living in poverty, inspired by the Christian faith.
ER Med, Logist-Op
⊕ https://vfmat.ch/f6cf

Terre des hommes (Tdh) Foundation
Works to improve the daily life of children and their relatives in the areas of health, protection and emergency, in Europe, Africa, Asia, Latin America, and the Near and Middle East.
CT Surg, CV Med, OB-GYN, Ped Surg, Pub Health
⊕ https://vfmat.ch/5c26

THET Partnerships for Global Health
Trains and educates health workers in Africa and Asia, working in partnership with organizations and volunteers from across the UK.
General
⊕ https://vfmat.ch/f937

Tilganga Institute of Ophthalmology (TIO)
Supports the prevention and control of blindness in Nepal and the region.
Ophth-Opt
⊕ https://vfmat.ch/ff5d

Transparent Fish Fund
Inspires others to join in alleviating poverty in East Asia by empowering small but high-impact NGOs to be sustainable and transparent in their programs.
CV Med, General, MF Med, Nutr, Peds
⊕ https://vfmat.ch/7714

U.S. President's Malaria Initiative (PMI)
Supports low-income countries to help control and eliminate malaria through cost-effective, lifesaving malaria interventions.
Infect Dis, MF Med, OB-GYN
⊕ https://vfmat.ch/dc8b

Union for International Cancer Control (UICC)
Unites and supports the cancer community to reduce the global cancer burden, promote greater equity, and ensure that cancer control continues to be a priority

in the world health and development agenda.
Heme-Onc, Pub Health
🌐 https://vfmat.ch/88b1

Unite 4 Humanity
Aims to provide emergency aid and support for Muslim communities across the world.
General, Nutr, OB-GYN, Ophth-Opt, Plast, Psych, Rehab
🌐 https://vfmat.ch/fbe7

United Nations Children's Fund (UNICEF)
Works in over 190 countries and territories to save children's lives, defend their rights, and help them fulfill their potential, from early childhood through adolescence.
All-Immu, Infect Dis, MF Med, Neonat, Nutr, OB-GYN, Ped Surg, Peds, Pub Health
🌐 https://vfmat.ch/42d7

United Nations Development Programme (UNDP)
Helps countries achieve the simultaneous eradication of extreme poverty and significant reduction of inequalities and exclusion using a sustainable human development approach.
Infect Dis, Logist-Op, Pub Health
🌐 https://vfmat.ch/935c

United Nations High Commissioner for Refugees (UNHCR)
Safeguards the rights and well-being of people who have been forced to flee, ensuring that everybody has the right to seek asylum and find safe refuge in another country, with the goal of seeking lasting solutions.
General, MF Med, Medicine, OB-GYN, Peds, Psych, Pub Health
🌐 https://vfmat.ch/6636

United Nations Office for the Coordination of Humanitarian Affairs (OCHA)
Contributes to principled and effective humanitarian response through coordination, advocacy, policy, information management, and humanitarian financing tools and services, by leveraging functional expertise throughout the organization.
Logist-Op
🌐 https://vfmat.ch/22b8

United Nations Population Fund (UNFPA)
Supports reproductive healthcare for women and youth in more than 150 countries, focusing on delivering a world in which every pregnancy is wanted, every childbirth is safe, and every young person's potential is fulfilled.
Infect Dis, MF Med, Neonat, OB-GYN, Peds, Pub Health
🌐 https://vfmat.ch/c969

University of New Mexico School of Medicine: Project Echo
Seeks to improve health outcomes worldwide through the use of a technology called telementoring, a guided-practice model in which the participating clinician retains responsibility for managing the patient.
General, Infect Dis, MF Med, OB-GYN, Path, Peds
🌐 https://vfmat.ch/6c9a

University of Virginia: Anesthesiology Department Global Health Initiatives
Educates and trains physicians to help people achieve healthy productive lives, and advances knowledge in the medical sciences.
Anesth, Pub Health
🌐 https://vfmat.ch/1b8b

USA for United Nations High Commissioner for Refugees (UNHCR)
Serves and protects refugees and displaced people through emergency relief, cash assistance, education, resettlement, and the rebuilding of livelihoods.
ER Med, General, Logist-Op, Nutr, Pub Health
🌐 https://vfmat.ch/293c

USAID: EQUIP Health
Exists as an effective, efficient response mechanism to achieving global HIV epidemic control by delivering the right intervention at the right place and in the right way.

Infect Dis
🌐 https://vfmat.ch/d76a

USAID: Leadership, Management and Governance Project
Improves leadership, management, and governance practices to strengthen health systems and improve health for all, including vulnerable populations worldwide.
Logist-Op
🌐 https://vfmat.ch/d35e

USAID: Maternal and Child Health Integrated Program
Works to improve the health of women and their families, including programs for maternal, newborn, and child health, immunization, family planning, nutrition, malaria, and HIV/AIDS.
All-Immu, General, Infect Dis, MF Med
🌐 https://vfmat.ch/4415

USAID: Maternal and Child Survival Program
Works to prevent child and maternal deaths.
Infect Dis, MF Med, Neonat, OB-GYN, Peds
🌐 https://vfmat.ch/6fcf

Vision Care
Restores sight and helps patients get regular treatment at short-term eye camps and long-term base clinics by having doctors, missionaries, volunteers, and sponsors work together.
Ophth-Opt
🌐 https://vfmat.ch/9d7c

Visionaries International
Works toward reducing the burden of corneal blindness in the developing world by assessing and addressing what limits corneal surgeons in each locale.
Anesth, Ophth-Opt, Pub Health, Surg
🌐 https://vfmat.ch/3d2e

Vitamin Angels
Helps at-risk populations in need—specifically pregnant women, new mothers, and children under age 5—to gain access to life-changing vitamins and minerals.
General, Nutr
🌐 https://vfmat.ch/7da1

Voluntary Service Overseas (VSO)
Works with health workers, communities, and governments to improve health services and rights for women, babies, youth, people with disabilities, and prisoners.
General, MF Med, OB-GYN
🌐 https://vfmat.ch/213d

Wealth By Health Steps For Change Foundation
Aims to improve the health and well-being of underserved populations by providing accessible resources that support the attainment of greater quality of life.
All-Immu, CV Med, Dent-OMFS, General, Medicine, Ophth-Opt, Palliative, Peds, Pub Health
🌐 https://vfmat.ch/153a

WF AID
Seeks to build capacity and provide emergency aid, human assistance, and international development, where required in the world.
CT Surg, Dent-OMFS, ENT, ER Med, General, Infect Dis, Logist-Op, Nutr, Ophth-Opt, Ortho, Path, Radiol, Rehab, Surg
🌐 https://vfmat.ch/ebd7

Wichita County Medical Alliance
Mobilizes volunteers to assist in public health efforts in the U.S. and abroad, including medical missions and disaster relief.
General, Geri, Nutr, OB-GYN, Pub Health
🌐 https://vfmat.ch/fa55

Women and Children First
Pioneers approaches that support communities to solve problems themselves.
MF Med, Neonat, OB-GYN, Peds
🌐 https://vfmat.ch/cdc9

Women's Refugee Commission

Seeks to improve lives by protecting the rights of women, children, and youth displaced by conflict and crisis through researching their needs, identifying solutions, and advocating for programs and policies to strengthen their resilience.

General, MF Med, Neonat, OB-GYN, Peds, Psych

⊕ https://vfmat.ch/3d8f

World Care Foundation

Encourages humanitarian efforts to help those in need anywhere in the world, regardless of their faith, color, gender, and ethnicity. Projects include orphanages, orphan sponsorship, medical centers, refugee crisis work, and education.

ER Med, General, Pub Health

⊕ https://vfmat.ch/987a

World Child Cancer

Works to improve diagnosis, treatment, and support for children with cancer, and their families, in low- and middle-income parts of the world.

Heme-Onc, Ped Surg, Rad-Onc

⊕ https://vfmat.ch/fbbc

World Children's Fund

Commits to helping children worldwide who are suffering the effects of poverty, disease, natural disaster, famine, abuse, civil strife, and war.

General, Logist-Op, MF Med, Nutr, OB-GYN, Pub Health

⊕ https://vfmat.ch/9cd8

World Federation of Hemophilia (WFH)

Aims to improve and sustain care for people with inherited bleeding disorders by pursuing long-term relationships with individuals and organizations who share the values of WFH's development model.

Heme-Onc

⊕ https://vfmat.ch/5121

World Health Organization, The (WHO)

The United Nations' agency for health provides leadership on global health matters, shapes the health research agenda, sets norms and standards, articulates evidence-based policy options, provides technical support and monitoring to countries, and assesses health trends.

ER Med, General, Infect Dis, Logist-Op, MF Med, OB-GYN, Peds, Psych, Pub Health

⊕ https://vfmat.ch/c476

World Medical Relief

Facilitates the distribution of surplus medical resources where they are needed.

Logist-Op

⊕ https://vfmat.ch/72dc

World Vision International

Works with vulnerable communities around the world to overcome poverty and injustice with child-focused programs in disaster management, health, nutrition, economic development, education, clean water, sanitation, and hygiene.

ER Med, General, Infect Dis, MF Med, Nutr, OB-GYN, Peds

⊕ https://vfmat.ch/2642

Myanmar

Healthcare Facilities

Ahlap District Hospital
Se Ein Su, Mon, Myanmar
⊕ https://vfmat.ch/a135

Ahtaung Station Hospital
Kyonpyaw, Myanmar
⊕ https://vfmat.ch/4ddf

Ar Yaw Jan Hospital
Pyin Oo Lwin, Mandalay, Myanmar
⊕ https://vfmat.ch/e5e6

ARYU International Hospital
Tamwe, Rangoon, Myanmar
⊕ https://vfmat.ch/5e77

Asia Pacific Centre for Medical and Dental Care
Yangon, Myanmar
⊕ https://vfmat.ch/9tdi

Asia Royal Hospital
Yangon, Myanmar
⊕ https://vfmat.ch/5ce5

Aung Myin Myint Mo Hospital
Gyobingauk, Bago Region, Myanmar
⊕ https://vfmat.ch/f46c

Aung Thitsar Hospital
Maymyo, Mandalay, Myanmar
⊕ https://vfmat.ch/4b68

Aung Yadana Hospital
Yangon, Myanmar
⊕ https://vfmat.ch/6f12

Aung Zaw Oo Hospital
Pyay, Bago Region, Myanmar
⊕ https://vfmat.ch/7f22

Aye Chan Tar Hospital
Yenanzu, Mandalay, Myanmar
⊕ https://vfmat.ch/53fc

Aye Thandar Hospital
Mawlamyine, Mon, Myanmar
⊕ https://vfmat.ch/b597

Aye Thu Kha Hospital
Yenanzu, Mandalay, Myanmar
⊕ https://vfmat.ch/9df6

Ayeyarwady Hospital
Pyapon, Pyapon, Myanmar
⊕ https://vfmat.ch/9c43

Ayeyarwady Mental Health Hospital
Yangon, Rangoon, Myanmar
⊕ https://vfmat.ch/4ad2

Ayudana Hospital
TaungYoe Lan Sagaing, Mandalay, Myanmar
⊕ https://vfmat.ch/f8e2

Bago General Hospital
Pegu, Bago, Myanmar
⊕ https://vfmat.ch/22da

Bhamo General Hospital
Bhamo, Kachin, Myanmar
⊕ https://vfmat.ch/4cd1

Bogale Township Hospital
Pyapon, Ayeyarwady, Myanmar
⊕ https://vfmat.ch/d7d3

Central Women's Hospital – Mandalay
Chanayethazan, Mandalay, Myanmar
⊕ https://vfmat.ch/5b2e

Chan Myae Gon Specialist Hospital
Okhpo, Mon, Myanmar
⊕ https://vfmat.ch/b4d7

Chan Myae Hospital – Dawei
Zayit Quarter Dawei, Tanintharyi, Myanmar
⊕ https://vfmat.ch/fb54

Chan Myae Private Hospital
Pakokku, Magway, Myanmar
⊕ https://vfmat.ch/e578

Chan Thar Hospital
North Okkalapa Yangon, Rangoon, Myanmar
⊕ https://vfmat.ch/dcaf

Chanthar Thukha Hospital
Pyin Oo Lwin, Mandalay, Myanmar
⊕ https://vfmat.ch/ca15

Christian Leprosy Specialist Hospital
Mawlamyine, Mon, Myanmar
⊕ https://vfmat.ch/52fb

Cottage Hospital
Paung, Mon, Myanmar
⊕ https://vfmat.ch/c744

Dagon Myothit (North) Hospital
Mada, Rangoon, Myanmar
⊕ https://vfmat.ch/c42b

Datkhina Dipar Hospital
Myeik Township, Thanintharyi Region, Myanmar
⊕ https://vfmat.ch/aba3

Dawei General Hospital
Panthonwa, Tanintharyi, Myanmar
⊕ https://vfmat.ch/2b2d

Defence Services General Hospital
Mingaladon, Yangon, Myanmar
⊕ https://vfmat.ch/1de2

Defence Services Orthopedic Hospital
Mingaladon, Yangon, Myanmar
⊕ https://vfmat.ch/ccea

East West Parami Hospital
North Dagon, Yangon, Myanmar
⊕ https://vfmat.ch/156f

Grand Hantha International Hospital
Kamaryut Township, Yangon, Myanmar
⊕ https://vfmat.ch/38f5

Green Cross Hospital
Lanmadaw, Yangon, Myanmar
⊕ https://vfmat.ch/4933

Hakha General Hospital
Hakha, Chin, Myanmar
⊕ https://vfmat.ch/98db

Hkamti Hospital
Hkamti, Myanmar
⊕ https://vfmat.ch/7bab

Hlaing Thar Yar Hospital
Hlaing Tharyar Township, Yangon, Myanmar
⊕ https://vfmat.ch/81ff

Hlaingbwe Township Hospital
Hlaingbwe, Kayin, Myanmar
⊕ https://vfmat.ch/d8d8

Hlegu Township Hospital
Hlegu, Yangon, Myanmar
⊕ https://vfmat.ch/ead6

Hmattaing Hospital
Hmattaing, Bago, Myanmar
⊕ https://vfmat.ch/a9d8

Hpa Yar Thone Su Hospital
Kawkaraik, Kayin, Myanmar
⊕ https://vfmat.ch/bab7

Hsipaw Township Hospital
Hsipaw, Shan, Myanmar
⊕ https://vfmat.ch/2f97

Htee Saung Eye Hospital
Myinmu, Sagaing, Myanmar
⊕ https://vfmat.ch/2dda

Htoo Foundation Hospital
Hlaingthaya Township, Rangoon, Myanmar
⊕ https://vfmat.ch/d593

HTUN Foundation Hospital
Hlaing Thayar Township, Yangon, Myanmar
⊕ https://vfmat.ch/ce18

Imon Specialist Hospital
Ku Lar Su, Mon, Myanmar
⊕ https://vfmat.ch/c49e

Infectious Disease Hospital – Mandalay
Kangauk, Mandalay, Myanmar
⊕ https://vfmat.ch/8ae2

Insein General Hospital
Insein, Rangoon, Myanmar
⊕ https://vfmat.ch/2759

Jivitadana Sangha Hospital
Pyinmana, Mandalay, Myanmar
⊕ https://vfmat.ch/e1a7

Kala Chaung Gyi District Hospital
Kalagyaunggyi, Bago, Myanmar
⊕ https://vfmat.ch/21c6

Kalein Aung Station Hospital
Dawei, Tanintharyi, Myanmar
⊕ https://vfmat.ch/ce5f

Kanaung Station Hospital
Myanaung, Myanaung, Myanmar
⊕ https://vfmat.ch/b73d

Kant Kaw Hospital
Mandalay, Myanmar
⊕ https://vfmat.ch/2a41

Kawthoung General Hospital
Kawthoung, Tanintharyi, Myanmar
⊕ https://vfmat.ch/feec

Kaytu Hospital
Taungoo, Myanmar
⊕ https://vfmat.ch/13bd

Kehsi Hospital
Ke-hsi Mānsām, Shan State, Myanmar
⊕ https://vfmat.ch/16bf

Kwekabaw Hospital
Insein, Yangon, Myanmar
⊕ https://vfmat.ch/e689

Kyauk Chaung Station Hospital
Kyaukchaung, Ayeyarwady, Myanmar
⊕ https://vfmat.ch/4dc8

Kyauk Htu Station Hospital
Saw, Magway, Myanmar
⊕ https://vfmat.ch/55d3

Kyaukme District Hospital
Kyaukme, Shan, Myanmar
⊕ https://vfmat.ch/88f3

Kyaukpa-Daung Township Hospital
Kyaukpadaung, Mandalay, Myanmar
⊕ https://vfmat.ch/cb2f

Kyun Chaung Hospital
Pakokku, Magway, Myanmar
⊕ https://vfmat.ch/35bb

Lashio General Hospital
Lashio, Shan, Myanmar
⊕ https://vfmat.ch/5c39

Laung she
Peingyaung, Yinye Chaung., Myanmar
⊕ https://vfmat.ch/3ba4

Launglon Township Hospital
Launglon, Tanintharyi, Myanmar
⊕ https://vfmat.ch/e882

Lay Kay Station Hospital
Bilin, Mon, Myanmar
⊕ https://vfmat.ch/87f4

Laymyethnar Township Hospital
Lemyethna, Ayeyarwady Region, Myanmar
⊕ https://vfmat.ch/4797

Loikaw General Hospital
Loikaw, Kayah, Myanmar
⊕ https://vfmat.ch/17ca

Ma Har Myaing Hospital
Sanchaung, Yangon, Myanmar
⊕ https://vfmat.ch/3852

Magway Teaching Hospital
Magway, Magway, Myanmar
⊕ https://vfmat.ch/2fc4

Mandalar Hospital
Chanayethazan, Mandalay, Myanmar
⊕ https://vfmat.ch/8335

Mandalay Children's Hospital
Mandalay, Mandalay, Myanmar
⊕ https://vfmat.ch/6442

Mandalay GEC Hospital
Mandalay, Mandalay, Myanmar
⊕ https://vfmat.ch/6cb3

Mandalay General Hospital
Chanayethazan, Mandalay, Myanmar
⊕ https://vfmat.ch/44aa

Mandalay Orthopaedic Hospital
Boyaywa, Mandalay, Myanmar
⊕ https://vfmat.ch/bec5

Matupi Public Hospital
Matupi, Chin, Myanmar
⊕ https://vfmat.ch/d85a

Maubin Hospital
Maubin, Ayeyarwady, Myanmar
⊕ https://vfmat.ch/1c68

Maw Taung Township Hospital
Ban Nong Thom, Prachuap Khiri Khan, Myanmar
⊕ https://vfmat.ch/d2e6

Mawlamyine Christian Leprosy Hospital (MCLH)
Mawlamyine, Myanmar
⊕ https://vfmat.ch/nagb

Mawlamyine General Hospital
Mawlamyine, Mon, Myanmar
⊕ https://vfmat.ch/67b3

Mawlamyine Traditional Medicine Hospital
Mawlamyine, Mon, Myanmar
⊕ https://vfmat.ch/cd13

Mediland Hospital
Dawei, Tanintharyi, Myanmar
⊕ https://vfmat.ch/2838

Meiktila General Hospital
Meiktila, Mandalay, Myanmar
⊕ https://vfmat.ch/67e9

Military Hospital
Pyin Oo Lwin, Mandalay, Myanmar
⊕ https://vfmat.ch/bdc7

Min Ta Su Station Hospital
Maubin, Ayeyarwady, Myanmar
⊕ https://vfmat.ch/be5d

Minbu General Hospital
Taungoo, Bago, Myanmar
⊕ https://vfmat.ch/b5c6

Mingala-Don HIV Specialist Hospital
Rangoon, Myanmar
⊕ https://vfmat.ch/6947

Moe Myittar Hospital
Kamaryut Township, Yangon, Myanmar
⊕ https://vfmat.ch/9651

Mogaung Township Hospital
Mogaung, Kachin, Myanmar
⊕ https://vfmat.ch/3655

Mogok Hospital
Mogok, Mandalay, Myanmar
⊕ https://vfmat.ch/ec5a

Monywa General Hospital
Monywa, Sagain, Myanmar
⊕ https://vfmat.ch/a42f

Mottama District Hospital
Mee Ya Htar Win, Mon, Myanmar
⊕ https://vfmat.ch/7cac

Muse General Hospital
Muse, Shan, Myanmar
⊕ https://vfmat.ch/6895

Muslim Free Hospital and Medical Relief Society
Yangon, Yangon Region, Myanmar
⊕ https://vfmat.ch/45f4

Myanmar Specialist Hospital
Bago Region, Mandalay, Myanmar
⊕ https://vfmat.ch/49a4

Myat Taw Win Hospital
Shan, Tanintharyi, Myanmar
⊕ https://vfmat.ch/de35

Myat Thitsar Hospital
Taungoo, Bago, Myanmar
⊕ https://vfmat.ch/9ac1

Myat Thu Kha Hospital
Chanayethazan, Mandalay, Myanmar
⊕ https://vfmat.ch/e9bf

Myaungmya General Hospital
Myaungmya, Ayeyarwady, Myanmar
⊕ https://vfmat.ch/ebdb

Myawaddy District Hospital
Myawaddy, Kayin, Myanmar
⊕ https://vfmat.ch/12bb

Myeik General Hospital
Myeik, Tanintharyi, Myanmar
⊕ https://vfmat.ch/4b31

Myeik Traditional Medicine Hospital
Myeik, Tanintharyi, Myanmar
⊕ https://vfmat.ch/ed84

Myene Mandalay District Hospital
Myene, Mandalay, Myanmar
⊕ https://vfmat.ch/2be2

Myingyan General Hospital
Myingyan, Myanmar
⊕ https://vfmat.ch/d447

Myinmu Township Hospital
Myinmu, Sagain, Myanmar
⊕ https://vfmat.ch/b9a6

Myint Mo Oo Hospital
Dawei, Tanintharyi Region, Myanmar
⊕ https://vfmat.ch/fd6b

Myit Chay Hospital
Pakkoku, Magway, Myanmar
⊕ https://vfmat.ch/5763

Myitkyina General Hosipital
Myitkyina, Kachin, Myanmar
⊕ https://vfmat.ch/8463

Myitnge Railway Hospital
Hpyauk Seik Kone, Mandalay, Myanmar
⊕ https://vfmat.ch/983d

Myittar Oo Eye Care Centre
Kamayut Township, Yangon, Myanmar
⊕ https://vfmat.ch/9afd

Myittashin Hospital
Pyigyidagon, Mandalay, Myanmar
⊕ https://vfmat.ch/1aa7

Myo Thu Kha Hospital
Pyay, Myanmar
⊕ https://vfmat.ch/bb64

Nadi Ayar Hospital
Thin Gun Kyun, Rangoon, Myanmar
⊕ https://vfmat.ch/bdaf

Namlan Station Hospital
Hsipaw, Shan, Myanmar
⊕ https://vfmat.ch/965b

Nandaw Palace Hospital
Mandalay, Mandalay, Myanmar
⊕ https://vfmat.ch/3acb

Nay Pyi Taw General Hospital
Kyidaunggan, Nay Pyi Taw, Myanmar
⊕ https://vfmat.ch/4b7d

Nay Pyi Taw Children's Hospital
Thinwindaing, Nay Pyi Taw, Myanmar
⊕ https://vfmat.ch/62be

Nay Pyi Taw Eye, Ear, Nose and Throat Hospital
Thinwindaing, Nay Pyi Taw, Myanmar
⊕ https://vfmat.ch/12e5

Nay Pyi Taw General Hospital
Nay Pyi Taw, Nay Pyi Taw, Myanmar
⊕ https://vfmat.ch/5894

Nay Pyi Taw Orthopedic Hospital
Thinwindaing, Nay Pyi Taw, Myanmar
⊕ https://vfmat.ch/4de2

Neik Ban Station Hospital
Neikban, Bago, Myanmar
⊕ https://vfmat.ch/341d

New Yangon General Hospital
Lanmadaw Tsp., Yangon, Myanmar
⊕ https://vfmat.ch/b19a

Ngapali Hospital
Zibyugôn, Rakhine, Myanmar
⊕ https://vfmat.ch/4a71

Ngwe Moe Hospital
Mawlamyaing, Mon, Myanmar
🌐 https://vfmat.ch/69f7

No. 2 Military Hospital
Wingaba, Rangoon, Myanmar
🌐 https://vfmat.ch/a854

North Okkalapa Teaching & General Hospital
North Okkalapa, Yangon, Myanmar
🌐 https://vfmat.ch/7322

OSC Hospital
North Okkalapa Township, Yangon, Myanmar
🌐 https://vfmat.ch/eab8

Pakokku General Hospital
Pakokku, Magway, Myanmar
🌐 https://vfmat.ch/3693

Palaw Township Hospital
Palaw, Tanintharyi, Myanmar
🌐 https://vfmat.ch/16cf

Panglong Hospital
Togyaunggale, Rangoon, Myanmar
🌐 https://vfmat.ch/5152

Parami General Hospital
Mayangone Township, Yangon, Myanmar
🌐 https://vfmat.ch/56c5

Parami Shin Hospital
Prome, Bago, Myanmar
🌐 https://vfmat.ch/e734

Pathein Hospital
Myoma Ward, Myanmar
🌐 https://vfmat.ch/46a3

Paukkhaung Hospital
Paukkhaung, Myanmar
🌐 https://vfmat.ch/c7e3

Pauktaw Township Hospital
Sittwe, Myanmar
🌐 https://vfmat.ch/7cb2

Paungbyin Township Hospital
Paungbyin, Sagain, Myanmar
🌐 https://vfmat.ch/5c35

Phu Gyi Hospital
Pugyi, Rangoon, Myanmar
🌐 https://vfmat.ch/fa9f

Pinlon Hospital
Togyaunggale, Rangoon, Myanmar
🌐 https://vfmat.ch/7ae5

Pun Hlaing Siloam Hospital
Hlaing Tharyar Township, Yangon, Myanmar
🌐 https://vfmat.ch/347e

Pyi Taw Thar Hospital
Bogon, Rangoon, Myanmar
🌐 https://vfmat.ch/5e18

Pyin Oo Lwin General Hospital
Pyin Oo Lwin, Mandalay, Myanmar
🌐 https://vfmat.ch/75db

Rose Hill ENT & General Hospital
Yangon, Myanmar
🌐 https://vfmat.ch/e4a7

Royal Hospital
Taungoo, Bago, Myanmar
🌐 https://vfmat.ch/673e

Sakura Hospital
Sanchaung Township, Yangon, Myanmar
🌐 https://vfmat.ch/xlj5

Salin Township Hospital
Salin, Magway, Myanmar
🌐 https://vfmat.ch/f34d

San Pya General Hospital
Yangon, Myanmar
🌐 https://vfmat.ch/9443

Sand House District Hospital
Thit Khaung, Mon, Myanmar
🌐 https://vfmat.ch/241a

Sao San Htun Hospital
Taunggyi, Shan, Myanmar
🌐 https://vfmat.ch/149d

Sein General Hospital
Taunggyi, Shan State, Myanmar
🌐 https://vfmat.ch/7726

Sein Thitsar Hospital
Bhamo, Kachin, Myanmar
🌐 https://vfmat.ch/cab4

Shwe Baho Hospital
Tamwe, Yangon, Myanmar
🌐 https://vfmat.ch/f5ca

Shwe Bo General Hospital
Shwebo, Sagain, Myanmar
🌐 https://vfmat.ch/615d

Shwe Indon District Hospital
Shwe In Don, Mon, Myanmar
🌐 https://vfmat.ch/8e99

Shwe La Min Hospital – North Okkalapa
North Okkalapa Township, Yangon, Myanmar
🌐 https://vfmat.ch/a42e

Shwe Pyi Thar Hospital
Ward, Shwe Pyi Thar Tsp., Rangoon, Myanmar
🌐 https://vfmat.ch/2324

Shwe San Pya General Hospital
Shwebo, Sagain, Myanmar
🌐 https://vfmat.ch/27ab

Shwe Taw Win Hospital
Monywa, Yangon, Myanmar
🌐 https://vfmat.ch/16f6

Sinphyukyun Station Hospital
Wayônzu, Magway, Myanmar
🌐 https://vfmat.ch/1429

Sitagu Mawriya Ayupala Tikicchalaya Hospital
Yenanzu, Mandalay, Myanmar
🌐 https://vfmat.ch/a121

South Okkalapa Women & Children Hospital
South Okkalapa, Yangon, Myanmar
🌐 https://vfmat.ch/bb3a

Swan Myittar Hospital
Bamaw, Kachin, Myanmar
🌐 https://vfmat.ch/a757

Taikkyi Township Hospital
Taikkyi, Rangoon, Myanmar
🌐 https://vfmat.ch/44be

Taku District Hospital
Zivita Sangha, Myanmar
🌐 https://vfmat.ch/2e6c

Takundaing District Hospital
Tagundaing, Kayin, Myanmar
🌐 https://vfmat.ch/b172

Tanintharyi Township Hospital
Tanintharyi, Myanmar
🌐 https://vfmat.ch/45d1

Tatkon Township Hospital
Tatkon, Nay Pyi Taw, Myanmar
🌐 https://vfmat.ch/1a62

Taung Kalay Military Hospital
Hpa-an District, Kayin, Myanmar
🌐 https://vfmat.ch/55c1

Taung Sun Station Hospital
Bilin, Mon, Myanmar
🌐 https://vfmat.ch/18f1

Taung Zun Old Hospital
Taung Sun, Mon, Myanmar
🌐 https://vfmat.ch/43cf

Taw Win Hospital
Mawlamyine, Mon, Myanmar
🌐 https://vfmat.ch/b7fe

Tawin Nilar Hospital Pyinmana
Pyinmana, Pyinmana, Myanmar
🌐 https://vfmat.ch/f9e1

Teaching Hospital
Boyaywa, Mandalay, Myanmar
🌐 https://vfmat.ch/6a49

Tet Lan Hospital
Yangon, Rangoon, Myanmar
🌐 https://vfmat.ch/558e

Tha Thi Kho Hospital
Kachaung, Bago, Myanmar
🌐 https://vfmat.ch/3688

Thamine General Hospital
Mayangone Township, Rangoon, Myanmar
🌐 https://vfmat.ch/afcd

Thandaunggyi Township Hospital
Than Daung Gyi, Kayin, Myanmar
🌐 https://vfmat.ch/de13

Thanlyin Military Hospital
Thanlyin, Yangon, Myanmar
🌐 https://vfmat.ch/94df

Thaton District Hospital
Thaton, Mon, Myanmar
🌐 https://vfmat.ch/e988

Thayet Township Hospital
Thayet, Magway, Myanmar
🌐 https://vfmat.ch/9e84

Thellgone General Hospital
Paung, Mon, Myanmar
🌐 https://vfmat.ch/7eac

Thiri Sandar Hospital
Insein, Rangoon, Myanmar
🌐 https://vfmat.ch/46ce

Thiri Thu Kha Specialist Hospital
Pyinmana Township, Nay Pyi Taw, Myanmar
🌐 https://vfmat.ch/5741

Thonze Station Hospital
Thonze, Shan, Myanmar
🌐 https://vfmat.ch/affd

Thukha Htilar Hospital
Meiktila District, Mandalay, Myanmar
🌐 https://vfmat.ch/83a7

Thukha Kwe Hospital
Pweseikkon, Rangoon, Myanmar
🌐 https://vfmat.ch/1fed

Tipitaka Çakkupala Eye Hospital
Tizaung, Sagain, Myanmar
🌐 https://vfmat.ch/c8fd

Traditional Medicine Hospital
Bahan Township, Yangon, Myanmar
🌐 https://vfmat.ch/28fe

Tugyi Station Hospital
Tugyi, Twante, Yangon, Myanmar
🌐 https://vfmat.ch/4d42

University Hospital – Mawlamyine
Mawlamyine, Mon, Myanmar
🌐 https://vfmat.ch/82be

Victoria Hospital
Mayangone Township, Yangon, Myanmar
🌐 https://vfmat.ch/a1ae

Wachat Jivitadana Sanga Hospital
Pyinmana, Myanmar
🌐 https://vfmat.ch/c761

Wachet Jivitadana Sangha Hospital
Wachet, Mandalay, Myanmar
🌐 https://vfmat.ch/d84c

Wai Bar Gi Specialty Hospital
Yangon, Myanmar
🌐 https://vfmat.ch/381c

West Yangon General Hospital
Kyeemyindaing Tsp., Yangon, Myanmar
🌐 https://vfmat.ch/52f8

Wetlet Township Hospital
Wetlet, Sagaing, Myanmar
🌐 https://vfmat.ch/5266

Wetlu Hospital
Mandalay, Mandalay, Myanmar
🌐 https://vfmat.ch/1423

Women and Children Hospital – Mawlamyine
Mawlamyine, Mon, Myanmar
🌐 https://vfmat.ch/d9cc

Wundwin Township Hospital
Wundwin Township, Mandalay, Myanmar
🌐 https://vfmat.ch/b75c

Yadanar Mon Hospital
Mawlamyinc, Mon, Myanmar
🌐 https://vfmat.ch/e157

Yamethin District Hospital
Yamethin, Mandalay, Myanmar
🌐 https://vfmat.ch/aa21

Yangon Central Women's Hospital
Myenigon, Rangoon, Myanmar
🌐 https://vfmat.ch/71fc

Yangon Children Hospital
Myenigon, Rangoon, Myanmar
🌐 https://vfmat.ch/221e

Yangon Ear, Nose and Throat Hospital
Yangon, Myanmar
🌐 https://vfmat.ch/ca28

Yangon East General Hospital
Botahtaung Township, Rangoon, Myanmar
🌐 https://vfmat.ch/12e7

Yangon Eye Hospital
Pyoncho, Rangoon, Myanmar
🌐 https://vfmat.ch/5d6b

Yangon General Hospital
Yangon, Rangoon, Myanmar
🌐 https://vfmat.ch/b9d7

Yangon Workers Hospital
Yangon, Rangoon, Myanmar
🌐 https://vfmat.ch/81b9

Yankin Children's Hospital
Yankin, Yangon, Myanmar
🌐 https://vfmat.ch/4dc1

Yebyu Township Hospital
Yebyu, Tanintharyi, Myanmar
🌐 https://vfmat.ch/5e14

Yedashe General Hospital
Yedashe, Bago, Myanmar
🌐 https://vfmat.ch/9254

Yezin Station Hospital
Yezin, Nay Pyi Taw, Myanmar
🌐 https://vfmat.ch/d2ca

Yin Nyein Station Hospital
Paung, Mon, Myanmar
🌐 https://vfmat.ch/21fa

Yue State Hospital
Ann, Rakhine, Myanmar
🌐 https://vfmat.ch/5318

Zabuthiri Specialist Hospital
Zabuthiri, Nay Pyi Taw Region, Myanmar
🌐 https://vfmat.ch/8b1d

Zarni Bwar Hospital
Mawlamyine, Mon, Myanmar
🌐 https://vfmat.ch/ac89

Zivita Dana Monastic Hospital Mandalay
Than Taik, Tanintharyi, Myanmar
⊕ https://vfmat.ch/2ff8

Zoke Thoke Station Hospital
Bilin, Mon, Myanmar
⊕ https://vfmat.ch/c2aa

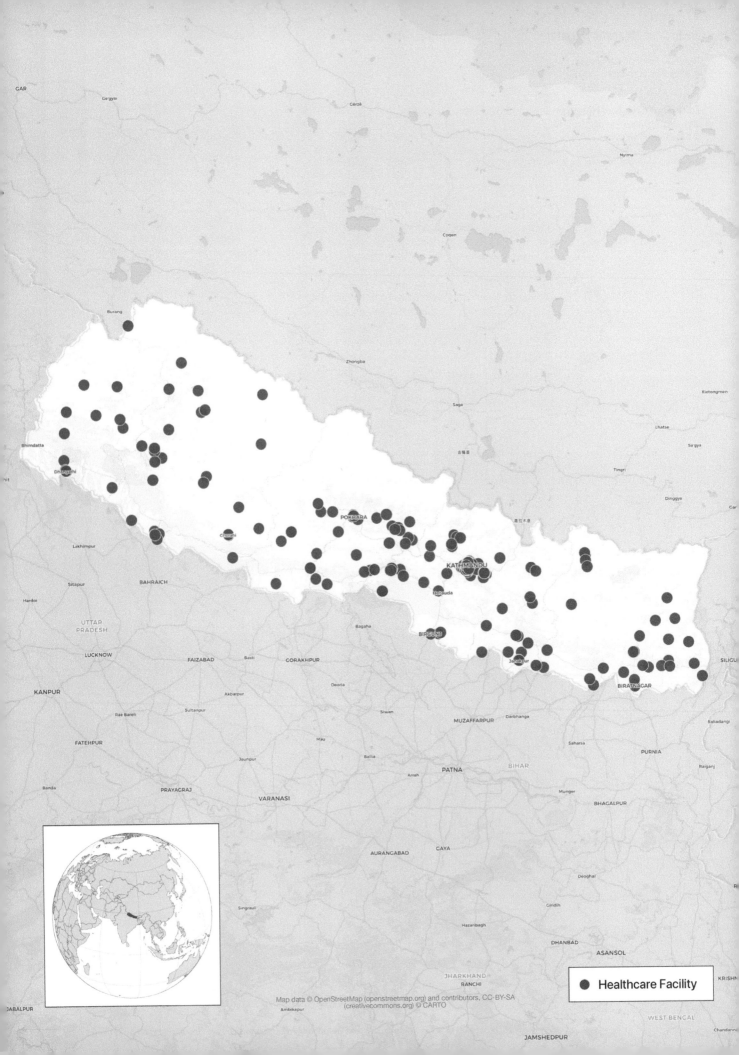

Healthcare Facility

Nepal

The Federal Democratic Republic of Nepal is a landlocked Asian country flanked by China and India. Located in the Himalayas, Nepal is best known for its mountainous terrain, which includes the tallest peak in the world, Mount Everest. The predominantly Hindu nation is home to 30.4 million people, most of whom live in the southern plains region or the hilly central region. Nepal has an incredibly diverse population of 125 different ethnic and caste groups speaking 123 different languages.

For the past several decades, Nepal has experienced periods of turmoil and change, including a Maoist insurgency and the abolition of its monarchy. The creation of a multiparty parliamentary system has resulted in greater political stability as well as opportunities to improve infrastructure and economic conditions. While the poverty rate has largely improved, dropping from 15 percent to 8 percent between 2010 and 2019, around 31 percent of people face significant risk of falling into extreme poverty, and substantial inequities persist in regard to urban-rural areas, gender, and caste.

Free basic health services are available to all citizens, which may have contributed to improving health indicators. The country's life expectancy has increased from 60 years to 71 years since the 1990s. Additionally, Nepal has made significant progress in reducing HIV and TB and is on track to be malaria-free by 2025. Non-communicable diseases increasingly contribute to the most deaths in the country, including COPD, ischemic heart disease, stroke, cirrhosis, asthma, and chronic kidney disease. Ailments such as lower respiratory infections, neonatal disorders, tuberculosis, and diarrheal diseases continue to cause significant deaths, but have decreased over time. Epidemics still occur frequently, leading to high rates of both morbidity and mortality. It should be noted that mental health challenges and depressive disorders also contribute greatly to disability in Nepal, with self-harm being a top cause of death.

30.4M
Population

$1,155
GDP Per Capita

71 years
Life Expectancy
↑ Improving

81
Doctors/100k

Physician Density

30
Beds/100k

Hospital Bed Density

186
Deaths/100k

Maternal Mortality

Nepal

Nonprofit Organizations

1789 Fund, The
Promotes gender equality worldwide through investment in the economic empowerment of women and the health of mothers and newborns.
MF Med, Neonat, OB-GYN
🌐 https://vfmat.ch/7145

A Broader View Volunteers
Provides developing countries around the world with significant volunteer programs that aid the neediest communities and forge a lasting bond between those volunteering and those they have helped.
Dent-OMFS, ER Med, Infect Dis, MF Med
🌐 https://vfmat.ch/3bec

A Leg To Stand On (ALTSO)
Provides free, high-quality prosthetic limbs, orthotic devices, and wheelchairs to children with untreated limb disabilities in the developing world.
Logist-Op, Ortho
🌐 https://vfmat.ch/a48d

A World of Difference
Aids women and children in southeast Asia, with a focus on art education, literacy, and health.
Dent-OMFS
🌐 https://vfmat.ch/8682

Abt Associates
Seeks to improve the quality of life and economic well-being of people worldwide, while striving to meet and exceed the highest professional standards.
General, Logist-Op, MF Med, OB-GYN, Peds
🌐 https://vfmat.ch/cec2

Action Against Hunger
Aims to end life-threatening hunger for good through treating and preventing malnutrition across more than 45 countries.
Nutr
🌐 https://vfmat.ch/2dbc

Adara Group
Seeks to bridge the world of business with people in extreme poverty, and to support vulnerable communities with health, education, and other essential services.
General, MF Med, Neonat, OB-GYN, Ped Surg, Peds
🌐 https://vfmat.ch/c8b4

Advance Family Planning
Aims to achieve global expansion and access to quality contraceptive information, services, and supplies through financial investment and political commitment.
General, MF Med, Pub Health
🌐 https://vfmat.ch/7478

Adventist Health International
Focuses on upgrading and managing mission hospitals by providing governance, consultation, and technical assistance to a number of affiliated Seventh-Day Adventist hospitals throughout Africa, Asia, and the Americas.
Dent-OMFS, General, Pub Health
🌐 https://vfmat.ch/16aa

Against Malaria Foundation
Helps protect people from malaria. Funds anti-malaria nets, specifically long-lasting insecticidal nets (LLINs), and works with distribution partners to ensure they are used. Tracks and reports on net use and malaria case data.
Infect Dis
🌐 https://vfmat.ch/337d

AIDS Healthcare Foundation
Provides cutting-edge HIV/AIDS medical care and advocacy to over one million people in 43 countries.
Infect Dis
🌐 https://vfmat.ch/b27c

Al Basar International Foundation
Works with local partners to treat preventable blindness, and helps set up sustainable infrastructure so local teams can save sight in their communities.
Ophth-Opt
🌐 https://vfmat.ch/a8b5

Aloha Medical Mission
Brings hope and changes the lives of people; serves overseas and in Hawai'i.
Anesth, Crit-Care, Dent-OMFS, ENT, ER Med, General, Medicine, OB-GYN, Ophth-Opt, Ortho, Ped Surg, Peds, Plast, Surg, Urol
🌐 https://vfmat.ch/72ac

America Nepal Medical Foundation
Promotes the advancement of medical training and practice in Nepal and helps strengthen its existing medical capabilities by fostering academic and professional cooperations.
ER Med, General, Surg
🌐 https://vfmat.ch/ec64

American Academy of Pediatrics
Seeks to attain optimal physical, mental, and social health and well-being for all infants, children, adolescents, and young adults.
Anesth, Crit-Care, Neonat, Ped Surg
🌐 https://vfmat.ch/9633

American Heart Association (AHA)
Fights heart disease and stroke, striving to save and improve lives.
CV Med, Crit-Care, General, Heme-Onc, Medicine, Peds
🌐 https://vfmat.ch/4747

American Stroke Association
Works to prevent, treat, and beat stroke by funding innovative research, fighting for stronger public health policies, and providing lifesaving tools and information.
CV Med, Crit-Care, Heme-Onc, Medicine, Neuro, Pub Health, Pulm-Critic, Vasc Surg
⊕ https://vfmat.ch/746f

Americares
Saves lives and improves health for people affected by poverty or disaster and responds with life-changing medicine, medical supplies, and health programs including domestic and global medical clinics.
All-Immu, ER Med, General, Infect Dis, MF Med, Nutr
⊕ https://vfmat.ch/e567

Americas Association for the Care of Children (AACC)
Reduces the impact of poverty in marginalized and underserved populations by empowering communities through compassionate and holistic education.
Dent-OMFS, MF Med, OB-GYN, Pub Health
⊕ https://vfmat.ch/19c5

AO Alliance
Builds solutions to lessen the burden of injuries in low- and middle-income countries, while enhancing the care of the injured to reduce human suffering, disability, and poverty.
Ortho, Surg
⊕ https://vfmat.ch/8cd5

Arbeiter Samariter Bund (Workers' Samaritan Federation)
Engages in areas such as civil protection, rescue services, and social welfare, while operating a network of welcome centers to help refugees.
ER Med, General, Infect Dis, Logist-Op, Rehab
⊕ https://vfmat.ch/8a5b

Association of Medical Doctors of Asia (AMDA)
Strives to support people affected by disasters and economic distress on their road to recovery, establishing a true partnership with special emphasis on local initiative.
ER Med, Logist-Op, Pub Health
⊕ https://vfmat.ch/e3d4

Australian & New Zealand Gastroenterology International Training Association
Aims to improve health in developing Asia Pacific nations by enhancing the standards of practice of gastroenterology and building capacity to treat digestive diseases.
GI
⊕ https://vfmat.ch/5a69

Australian Himalayan Foundation
Works in partnership with people of the remote Himalaya to improve living standards through better education and training, improved health services, and environmental sustainability.
General, MF Med, OB-GYN, Peds
⊕ https://vfmat.ch/3428

Australians for Women's Health
Aims to provide sustainable medical treatment and public health interventions for women in developing countries who are suffering from gynecological or pregnancy-related conditions.
Crit-Care, MF Med, OB-GYN, Surg
⊕ https://vfmat.ch/b4d4

Autism Care Nepal Society
Empowers people with autism to protect and promote their rights and utilize their skills to have a meaningful and effective participation in society.
General, Neuro, Peds, Psych
⊕ https://vfmat.ch/1394

Backpacker Medics
Aims to bring effective medical care to those who need it most through a platform for paramedics and other pre-hospital workers to engage in humanitarian work and travel to remote areas of the world to deliver healthcare, establish healthcare facilities, and provide education.

Crit-Care, ER Med, OB-GYN
⊕ https://vfmat.ch/c4e5

Basic Foundations
Supports local projects and organizations that seek to meet the basic human needs of others in their community.
ER Med, General, Peds, Rehab, Surg
⊕ https://vfmat.ch/c4be

Benjamin H. Josephson, MD Fund
Provides healthcare professionals with the financial resources necessary to deliver medical services for those in need throughout the world.
General, OB-GYN
⊕ https://vfmat.ch/6acc

Beta Humanitarian Help
Provides plastic surgery in underserved areas of the world.
Anesth, Plast
⊕ https://vfmat.ch/7221

Better Vision Foundation Nepal
Aims to provide quality, sustainable, comprehensive, and affordable eye care by identifying and mobilizing resources to eliminate avoidable blindness in Nepal and align with the global initiative of Vision 2020.
Ophth-Opt
⊕ https://vfmat.ch/61a1

BFIRST – British Foundation for International Reconstructive Surgery & Training
Supports projects across the developing world to train surgeons in their local environment to effectively manage devastating injuries.
Anesth, Plast, Surg
⊕ https://vfmat.ch/ad4f

Bicol Clinic Foundation Inc.
Treats patients primarily in the Philippines, Nepal, Haiti, and locally in the USA, while constructing a permanent outpatient clinic in the Bicol region of the Philippines and establishing a disaster-relief fund.
Crit-Care, Derm, ENT, ER Med, Endo, General, Infect Dis, MF Med, Medicine, Nutr, OB-GYN, Ophth-Opt, Pub Health, Surg, Urol
⊕ https://vfmat.ch/3f9e

Birat Nepal Medical Trust (BNMT Nepal)
Ensures equitable access to quality healthcare for socially and economically disadvantaged people.
General, Infect Dis, OB-GYN, Psych
⊕ https://vfmat.ch/6a41

BP Eye Foundation
Empowers people to achieve their full human potential by eliminating barriers of ill health, illiteracy, inequity, and poverty and by employing health as an entry point and education as a door opener for poverty reduction, equity, and social inclusion.
ENT, General, Ophth-Opt, Peds, Pub Health, Rehab
⊕ https://vfmat.ch/c16e

BRAC USA
Seeks to empower people and communities in situations of poverty, illiteracy, disease, and social injustice. Interventions aim to achieve large-scale, positive changes through economic and social programs that enable everyone to realize their potential.
ER Med, General, Infect Dis, Logist-Op, MF Med, OB-GYN
⊕ https://vfmat.ch/9d9e

Breast Cancer Support
Aims to save lives and end breast cancer forever in women and men through education, treatment, emotional assistance, and financial support.
Heme-Onc, Logist-Op, Pub Health, Rad-Onc, Radiol
⊕ https://vfmat.ch/cb78

Bridge of Life
Aims to strengthen healthcare globally through sustainable programs that prevent and treat chronic disease.

Logist-Op, Nephro, OB-GYN, Peds, Surg
⊕ https://vfmat.ch/5b68

Camillian Disaster Service (CADIS) International
Promotes the development of locally based health programs for disaster-stricken communities through compassionate and coordinated interventions.
General, Logist-Op, MF Med
⊕ https://vfmat.ch/5281

Canadian Medical Assistance Teams (CMAT)
Provides relief and medical aid to the victims of natural and man-made disasters around the world.
Anesth, ER Med, Medicine, OB-GYN, Peds, Psych, Rehab, Surg
⊕ https://vfmat.ch/5232

Canadian Reconstructive Surgery Foundation, The
Develops, organizes, and manages, in participation with developing countries, the delivery of reconstructive medical-care programs, technologies, and education to those who cannot otherwise obtain the care they need.
Anesth, Dent-OMFS, Plast
⊕ https://vfmat.ch/15f4

CardioStart International
Provides free heart surgery and associated medical care to children and adults living in underserved regions of the world, irrespective of political or religious affiliation, through the collective skills of healthcare experts.
Anesth, CT Surg, CV Med, Crit-Care, Pub Health, Pulm-Critic
⊕ https://vfmat.ch/85ef

CARE
Works around the globe to save lives, defeat poverty, and achieve social justice.
ER Med, General
⊕ https://vfmat.ch/7232

Care and Development Organization (CDO) Nepal
Works to improve the lives of underprivileged people, children working in brick and carpet factories, internally displaced people, and women in need by providing medical care, raising health awareness, and training.
General, MF Med, Nutr, Ophth-Opt
⊕ https://vfmat.ch/4c98

Carter Center, The
Seeks to prevent and resolve conflicts, enhance freedom and democracy, and improve health, while remaining committed to human rights and the alleviation of human suffering.
Infect Dis, MF Med, Ophth-Opt
⊕ https://vfmat.ch/6556

cbm New Zealand
Inspired by the Christian faith, aims to improve the quality of life for those living with the double disadvantage of poverty and disability.
Crit-Care, Infect Dis, Logist-Op, Nutr, OB-GYN, Ophth-Opt, Ortho, Psych, Rehab, Surg
⊕ https://vfmat.ch/c14b

Center for Private Sector Health Initiatives
Aims to improve the health and well-being of people in developing countries by facilitating partnerships between the public and private sectors.
Infect Dis, Nutr, Peds
⊕ https://vfmat.ch/b198

Chain of Hope (La Chaîne de l'Espoir)
Helps underprivileged children around the world by providing them with access to healthcare.
Anesth, CT Surg, Crit-Care, ER Med, Neurosurg, Ortho, Ped Surg, Surg, Vasc Surg
⊕ https://vfmat.ch/e871

Chance for Nepal
Works closely with established and trusted organizations, schools, and hospitals in Nepal to guarantee aid and support to those families in need and to offer education and training opportunities.

Derm, General, Ped Surg, Peds, Plast
⊕ https://vfmat.ch/f436

CharityVision International
Focuses on restoring curable sight impairment worldwide by empowering local physicians and creating sustainable solutions.
Logist-Op, Ophth-Opt, Surg
⊕ https://vfmat.ch/6231

ChildFund Australia
Works to reduce poverty for children in many of the world's most disadvantaged communities.
ER Med, General, Peds
⊕ https://vfmat.ch/13df

Children's Bridge Foundation
Supports health and education programs for orphaned and abandoned children in the developing world.
Infect Dis, Nutr, Peds, Surg
⊕ https://vfmat.ch/6486

Children's Lifeline International
Provides medical teams and surgical assistance to underprivileged children in developing countries through missions in partnership with local hospitals.
CV Med, Dent-OMFS, General, MF Med, Neurosurg, Peds, Rehab
⊕ https://vfmat.ch/6fea

Christian Aid Ministries
Strives to be a trustworthy and efficient channel for Amish, Mennonite, and other conservative Anabaptist groups and individuals to minister to physical and spiritual needs around the world.
CT Surg, ER Med, Logist-Op, Ortho, Pub Health
⊕ https://vfmat.ch/7b33

Christian Blind Mission (CBM)
Aims to improve the quality of life of persons with disabilities in the poorest countries, addressing poverty as a cause and a consequence of disability, and working in partnership to create a society for all.
ENT, General, Infect Dis, OB-GYN, Ophth-Opt, Ortho, Peds, Psych, Rehab, Surg
⊕ https://vfmat.ch/3824

Christian Medical & Dental Associations
Based in Christian ministry, deploys medical and dental teams to underserved communities to provide vital healthcare.
Anesth, Dent-OMFS, ER Med, General, Medicine, OB-GYN, Ophth-Opt, Peds, Pub Health, Radiol, Rehab, Surg
⊕ https://vfmat.ch/921c

Circle of Health International (COHI)
Aligns with local, community-based organizations led and powered by women to help respond to the needs of the women and children that they serve. Helps with the provision of professional volunteers, capacity training, and procurement of requested and appropriate supplies and equipment. Raises funds for the organizations to provide the services required.
ER Med, Logist-Op, MF Med, Neonat, OB-GYN, Psych
⊕ https://vfmat.ch/8b63

Clinic Nepal
Seeks to help the Meghauli and Daldale communities gain access to education, healthcare, clean water, and sanitary facilities.
ER Med, General, Medicine, Peds, Surg
⊕ https://vfmat.ch/5acd

Columbia University: Global Mental Health Programs
Pioneers research initiatives, promotes mental health, and aims to reduce the burden of mental illness worldwide.
Psych
⊕ https://vfmat.ch/c5cd

Community Action Nepal
Focuses on supporting remote mountain communities and strengthening their resilience by improving healthcare and educational services.

ER Med, General, Pub Health
⊕ https://vfmat.ch/d39a

Compassionate Eye
Aims to support the social good by supplying infrastructure and personnel for sanitation, education, medical care, small business, and job training.
General, Infect Dis, MF Med, OB-GYN, Peds
⊕ https://vfmat.ch/1915

Concern Worldwide
Seeks to permanently transform the lives of people living in extreme poverty, tackling its root causes, and building resilience.
Logist-Op, MF Med, Nutr, OB-GYN
⊕ https://vfmat.ch/77e9

Core Group
Aims to improve and expand community health practices for underserved populations, especially women and children, through collaborative action and learning.
General, Infect Dis, MF Med, Medicine, OB-GYN, Peds, Pub Health
⊕ https://vfmat.ch/9de3

COVID-19 Clinical Research Coalition
Advocates and collaborates for the advancement of COVID-19 research driven by the needs of low-resource settings, and works for equitable access to solutions to the pandemic.
All-Immu, Infect-Dis, MF Med, Path, Pub Health
⊕ https://vfmat.ch/d1f4

Critical Care Disaster Foundation
Seeks to educate in-country healthcare providers from developing countries in disaster and crisis medical management, and to develop an infrastructure of critical care services.
Anesth, Crit-Care, ER Med, Logist-Op, Pulm-Critic
⊕ https://vfmat.ch/a445

Cura for the World
Seeks to heal, nourish, and embrace the neglected by building medical clinics in remote communities in dire need of medical care.
ER Med, General, Peds
⊕ https://vfmat.ch/c55f

Dentaid
Seeks to treat, equip, train, and educate people in need of dental care.
Dent-OMFS
⊕ https://vfmat.ch/a183

Direct Relief
Improves the health and lives of people affected by poverty or emergency situations by mobilizing and providing essential medical resources needed for their care.
ER Med, Logist-Op
⊕ https://vfmat.ch/58e5

Divine Shakti Foundation, The
Provides programs for holistic healthcare and supports research intended for the advancement of women and children's healthcare concerns.
Dent-OMFS, ENT, ER Med, General, OB-GYN, Ophth-Opt, Pub Health, Rehab
⊕ https://vfmat.ch/dc66

Doctors for Nepal
Aims to improve healthcare in rural Nepal through healthcare projects, continuing education for health workers, and sponsoring students from poor rural areas to attend medical, nursing, and midwifery schools in Nepal and, post-graduation, work in these communities.
General
⊕ https://vfmat.ch/f9ff

Dr. GMP Foundation
Aims to promote public health, education, and upbringing of the local population with an emphasis on hygiene and medicine in the Himalayan region, especially India and Nepal.

ER Med, General, Surg
⊕ https://vfmat.ch/aa9b

Duke University: Global Health Institute
Sparks innovation in global health research and education, and brings together knowledge and resources to address the most important global health issues of our time.
All-Immu, Infect Dis, MF Med, OB-GYN, Pub Health
⊕ https://vfmat.ch/c4cd

Ear Aid Nepal
Promotes good ear health by treating and preventing hearing disability in Nepal.
ENT, Surg
⊕ https://vfmat.ch/ef32

Education and Health Nepal
Aims to make a difference by matching volunteers from the growing volunteer movement with placements that support underserved communities.
General, Geri, Medicine, OB-GYN, Peds, Psych, Radiol, Surg
⊕ https://vfmat.ch/fb12

Edwards Lifesciences
Provides innovative solutions for people fighting cardiovascular disease, as a global leader in patient-focused medical innovations for structural heart disease, along with critical care and surgical monitoring.
Anesth, CT Surg, CV Med, Crit-Care, Ped Surg, Peds, Pulm-Critic, Surg, Vasc Surg
⊕ https://vfmat.ch/d671

EngenderHealth
Works to implement high-quality, gender-equitable programs that advance sexual and reproductive health and rights.
General, MF Med, OB-GYN, Peds
⊕ https://vfmat.ch/1cb2

Eye Care Foundation
Helps prevent and cure avoidable blindness and visual impairment in low-income countries.
Ophth-Opt, Surg
⊕ https://vfmat.ch/c8f9

Eye Foundation of America
Works toward a world without childhood blindness.
Ophth-Opt
⊕ https://vfmat.ch/a7eb

Eyes4Everest
Provides primary eye care and prescription eyewear for people of the Everest National Park.
Ophth-Opt
⊕ https://vfmat.ch/436f

FAIRMED Sri Lanka
Aims to improve the circumstances of all people at risk for or affected by leprosy and other neglected tropical diseases in Sri Lanka.
Infect Dis
⊕ https://vfmat.ch/c463

Finn Church Aid
Supports people in the most vulnerable situations within fragile and disaster-affected regions in three thematic priority areas: right to peace, livelihood, and education.
ER Med, Psych, Pub Health
⊕ https://vfmat.ch/9623

Firefly Mission
Organizes humanitarian missions to help people in less fortunate situations while serving as a vehicle for the spiritual development of members and the beneficiaries of its missions.
Logist-Op, Ophth-Opt, Pub Health
⊕ https://vfmat.ch/d215

Fistula Foundation
Aims to engage the support of people worldwide who are eager to see the day that no woman suffers from obstetric fistula. Raises and directs funds to doctors and hospitals providing life-transforming surgery to women in need.
OB-GYN
⊕ https://vfmat.ch/e958

For Hearts and Souls
Provides medical outreach and care for children through heart-related work, such as diagnosing heart problems and performing heart-saving surgeries.
Anesth, CT Surg, CV Med, Crit-Care, Peds, Pulm-Critic
⊕ https://vfmat.ch/a162

Forgotten International, The
Develops programs that alleviate poverty and the suffering of impoverished women and children in both the United States and worldwide.
Logist-Op, Nutr, OB-GYN, Peds, Pub Health
⊕ https://vfmat.ch/26f3

Foundation for International Development Relief (FIDR)
Implements assistance projects in developing countries to improve the living environment of residents, while promoting regional development centered on the welfare of children.
Pub Health
⊕ https://vfmat.ch/7356

Foundation For International Education In Neurological Surgery (FIENS), The
Provides hands-on training and education to neurosurgeons around the world.
Neuro, Neurosurg, Surg
⊕ https://vfmat.ch/bab8

Foundation for International Urogynecological Assistance (FIUGA)
Supports urogynecological education, research, and care around the world.
OB-GYN, Pub Health, Urol
⊕ https://vfmat.ch/f95a

Foundation Human Nature (FHN)
Helps marginalized communities by providing technical, human, and financial resources to sustainably strengthen primary healthcare and public health in Ecuador, Ghana, and Nepal.
ER Med, General, Infect Dis, OB-GYN, Peds, Pub Health
⊕ https://vfmat.ch/6e8c

Fred Hollows Foundation, The
Works toward a world in which no person is needlessly blind or vision impaired.
Ophth-Opt, Pub Health, Surg
⊕ https://vfmat.ch/73e5

Friends for Asia Foundation, The
Develops international volunteer projects that assist local communities in overcoming challenges, and provides volunteers with the experience of contributing to those communities as a valued participant.
General
⊕ https://vfmat.ch/f8a9

Friends of UNFPA
Promotes the health, dignity, and rights of women and girls around the world by supporting the lifesaving work of UNFPA, the United Nations' reproductive health and rights agency, through education, advocacy, and fundraising.
MF Med, OB-GYN
⊕ https://vfmat.ch/2a3a

Gastro & Liver Foundation Nepal
Seeks to raise public awareness of the prevention of liver and gastrointestinal diseases and works to create facilities providing treatment of liver diseases at a low cost or free of charge.
GI, Heme-Onc
⊕ https://vfmat.ch/5b59

GFA World
Based in Christian ministry, sponsors medical camps for the sick, provides

disaster relief to vulnerable populations, and empowers impoverished communities with basic necessities such as clean water, vocational training, and education.
General, Infect Dis
⊕ https://vfmat.ch/63ee

Global Alliance to Prevent Prematurity And Stillbirth (GAPPS)
Seeks to improve birth outcomes worldwide by reducing the burden of premature birth and stillbirth.
All-Immu, Infect Dis, MF Med, Neonat, Neonat, OB-GYN
⊕ https://vfmat.ch/3f74

Global Clinic
Seeks to ensure that any effort to provide medical services is accompanied by a long-term program to improve the health of residents of its partner communities.
Dent-OMFS, ER Med, General, OB-GYN, OB-GYN, Ophth-Opt, Surg
⊕ https://vfmat.ch/9e48

Global Dental Relief
Brings free dental care to impoverished children in partnership with local organizations, and delivers treatment and preventive care in dental clinics that serve children in schools and remote villages.
Dent-OMFS
⊕ https://vfmat.ch/29b6

Global Eye Project
Empowers local communities by building locally managed, sustainable eye clinics through education initiatives and volunteer-run professional training services.
Anesth, Ophth-Opt, Surg
⊕ https://vfmat.ch/cdba

Global First Responder (GFR)
Acts as a centralized network for individuals and agencies involved in relief work worldwide and organizes and executes mission trips to areas in need, focusing not only on healthcare delivery but also on health education and improvements.
ER Med
⊕ https://vfmat.ch/a3e1

Global Force for Healing
Works to end preventable maternal and newborn deaths by supporting the scaling of effective grassroots, community-led, culturally respectful care and education in underserved areas around the globe using the midwifery model of care.
Neonat, OB-GYN
⊕ https://vfmat.ch/deb2

Global Medical Foundation Australia
Provides medical, surgical, dental, and educational welfare to underprivileged communities and gives them access to basics that are often taken for granted.
Dent-OMFS, ER Med, General, OB-GYN, Ortho, Surg
⊕ https://vfmat.ch/fa56

Global Ministries – The United Methodist Church
As the worldwide mission and development agency of The United Methodist Church, Global Ministries works with more than 300 hospitals and clinics around the world through its Global Health Unit.
Anesth, CT Surg, CV Med, Crit-Care, Dent-OMFS, Derm, ER Med, GI, General, Infect Dis, Logist-Op, MF Med, Medicine, Neonat, Nephro, Nutr, OB-GYN, Ophth-Opt, Ortho, Palliative, Peds, Pod, Psych, Pub Health, Rehab, Rheum, Surg, Urol
⊕ https://vfmat.ch/1723

Global Mission Partners, Inc.
Provides opportunities for short-term global medical mission opportunities, along with evangelism and construction missions, to serve persons who have little or no access to healthcare, adequate housing, and community outreach.
Dent-OMFS, General, Geri, Palliative, Psych
⊕ https://vfmat.ch/7db4

Global Offsite Care
Aims to be a catalyst for increased access to specialized healthcare for all, and provides technology platforms to doctors and clinics around the world through Rotary Club-sponsored telemedicine projects.
Crit-Care, ER Med, General, Pulm-Critic
⊕ https://vfmat.ch/61b5

Global Oncology (GO)
Brings the best in cancer care to underserved patients around the world and collaborates across geographic, professional, and academic borders to improve cancer care, research, and education.
Heme-Onc, Path, Rad-Onc
⊕ https://vfmat.ch/fcb8

Global Outreach Doctors
Provides global health medical services in developing countries affected by famine, infant mortality, and chronic health issues.
All-Immu, Anesth, ER Med, General, Infect Dis, MF Med, Peds, Surg
⊕ https://vfmat.ch/8514

Global Partnership for Zero Leprosy
Facilitates alignment of the leprosy community and accelerates effective collaborative action toward the goal of zero leprosy.
Infect Dis
⊕ https://vfmat.ch/ec7b

GlobalMedic
Provides disaster relief and lifesaving humanitarian aid.
ER Med, Pub Health
⊕ https://vfmat.ch/dfe6

Globus Relief
Aims to improve the delivery of healthcare worldwide by gathering, processing, and distributing surplus medical supplies to charities at home and abroad.
Logist-Op
⊕ https://vfmat.ch/a2b7

GOAL
Works with the most vulnerable communities to help them respond to and recover from humanitarian crises, and to assist them in building transcendent solutions to mitigate poverty and vulnerability.
ER Med, General, Pub Health
⊕ https://vfmat.ch/bbea

Good Shepard International Foundation
Strives to promote inclusive and sustainable development for the most marginalized and vulnerable people, with a special focus on women, girls, and children, inspired by the Christian faith.
ER Med
⊕ https://vfmat.ch/ad9a

Hands for Health Foundation
Aims to provide healthcare access and medical supplies to less fortunate people living in the developing world.
General, Nutr, Ophth-Opt
⊕ https://vfmat.ch/776e

Headwaters Relief Organization
Addresses public health issues for the most underserved populations of the world, providing psychosocial and medical support along with disaster debris cleanup and rebuilding in partnership with other organizations.
ER Med, Infect Dis, Logist-Op, Psych, Pub Health
⊕ https://vfmat.ch/e511

Healing the Children
Helps underserved children around the world secure the medical care they need to lead more fulfilling lives.
Anesth, Dent-OMFS, ENT, General, Medicine, Ophth-Opt, Ped Surg, Peds, Plast, Surg
⊕ https://vfmat.ch/d4ee

Health and Development Society Nepal
Aims to provide quality oral health services and integrated general health services, and also engages in development initiatives with a focus on overall health and well-being.
Dent-OMFS, Pub Health
⊕ https://vfmat.ch/71da

Health Equity Initiative
Aims to build and sustain a global community that engages across sectors and disciplines to advance health equity.
Pub Health
⊕ https://vfmat.ch/e2e2

Health Volunteers Overseas (HVO)
Improves the availability and quality of healthcare through the education, training, and professional development of the health workforce in resource-scarce countries.
All-Immu, Anesth, CV Med, Dent-OMFS, Derm, ENT, ER Med, Endo, GI, Heme-Onc, Infect Dis, Medicine, Medicine, Nephro, Neuro, OB-GYN, Ophth-Opt, Ortho, Peds, Plast, Psych, Pulm-Critic, Rehab, Rheum, Surg
⊕ https://vfmat.ch/42b2

Healthcare Nepal
Works to improve healthcare and education in Nepal.
Anesth, Dent-OMFS, MF Med, Neonat, Peds, Plast, Surg
⊕ https://vfmat.ch/3bab

HealthRight International
Leverages global resources to address local health challenges and create sustainable solutions that empower marginalized communities to live healthy lives.
General, Infect Dis, MF Med, OB-GYN, Psych, Pub Health
⊕ https://vfmat.ch/129d

HealthServe Australia
Develops sustainable health programs that improve health and well-being and partners with community groups to build community capacity to meet health needs.
Infect Dis, Logist-Op, OB-GYN, Psych, Pub Health
⊕ https://vfmat.ch/7276

Healthy DEvelopments
Provides Germany-supported health and social protection programs around the globe in a collaborative knowledge management process.
All-Immu, General, Infect Dis, Logist-Op, MF Med
⊕ https://vfmat.ch/dc31

Heart to Heart International
Strengthens communities through improving health access, providing humanitarian development, and administering crisis relief worldwide. Engages volunteers, collaborates with partners, and deploys resources to achieve this mission.
Anesth, ER Med, General, Logist-Op, Medicine, Path, Path, Peds, Psych, Pub Health, Surg
⊕ https://vfmat.ch/aacb

Helen Keller International
Seeks to eliminate preventable vision loss, malnutrition, and diseases of poverty.
Infect Dis, Nutr, OB-GYN, Ophth-Opt, Peds
⊕ https://vfmat.ch/b654

HELP CODE ITALIA ONLUS
Seeks to improve life conditions of children in the communities where they live, through direct and indirect projects designed to support their well-being, education, and development.
General, Nutr, Pub Health
⊕ https://vfmat.ch/1dd9

HelpAge International
Works to ensure that people everywhere understand how much older people contribute to society and that they must enjoy their right to healthcare, social services, economic, and physical security.
General, Geri, Infect Dis, Medicine, Pub Health
⊕ https://vfmat.ch/5d91

Helping Hands Health Education
Provides sustainable health and education services to children and adults throughout the world.
Dent-OMFS, General, Logist-Op, OB-GYN, Ophth-Opt, Peds
⊕ https://vfmat.ch/36da

HelpMeSee

Trains local cataract specialists in Manual Small Incision Cataract Surgery (MSICS) in significant numbers, to meet the increasing demand for surgical services in the communities most impacted by cataract blindness.

Anesth, Ophth-Opt, Surg

⊕ https://vfmat.ch/973c

High Elevation Lives Project

Aims to provide children and adults with healthcare and health education, inspired by faith, compassion, and caring.

General, MF Med, Neonat, Peds

⊕ https://vfmat.ch/91a6

Himalayan Cataract Project

Works to cure needless blindness with the highest quality care at the lowest cost.

Anesth, Ophth-Opt, Surg

⊕ https://vfmat.ch/3b3d

Himalayan Development Foundation

Ensures access to education for all children in the remote Kanchenjunga and Indrawati communities of Nepal.

General, OB-GYN

⊕ https://vfmat.ch/a36b

Himalayan HealthCare

Creates sustainable development programs in remote areas of Nepal that will improve the quality of life for its people by strengthening primary health care, community education, and income-generation opportunities.

ER Med, General, Infect Dis, Medicine, OB-GYN, Ophth-Opt, Peds

⊕ https://vfmat.ch/e6cd

Hospital & Rehabilitation Centre for Disabled Children (HRCD)

Ensures equitable access to quality of life through appropriate interventions and enabling environments for children with physical disabilities.

Ortho, Ped Surg, Peds, Rehab, Surg

⊕ https://vfmat.ch/ea2c

Human Development and Community Services (HDCS)

Aims to provide access and use of affordable, quality health services for poor and marginalized people.

General, MF Med, Peds

⊕ https://vfmat.ch/4568

Humanity & Inclusion

Works alongside people with disabilities and vulnerable populations, taking action and bearing witness in order to respond to their essential needs, improve their living conditions and health, and promote respect for their dignity and fundamental rights.

General, Infect Dis, MF Med, Medicine, Ortho, Peds, Psych, Pub Health, Rehab

⊕ https://vfmat.ch/16b7

Humla Fund

Seeks to strengthen the Bon culture and traditions in the Humla region of Nepal through access to quality education, healthcare, and sustainable economic development.

General, Infect Dis, MF Med, Neuro, Peds

⊕ https://vfmat.ch/2b74

Icahn School of Medicine at Mount Sinai Arnhold Institute for Global Health

Specializes in global health systems and implementation research, working toward a world in which vulnerable people in every community have access to healthcare.

CV Med, Endo, General, Infect Dis, Logist-Op, MF Med, Medicine, Neonat, OB-GYN, Ophth-Opt, Peds, Plast, Pub Health

⊕ https://vfmat.ch/a327

IMA World Health

Works to build healthier communities by collaborating with key partners to serve vulnerable people with a focus on health, healing, and well-being for all.

Infect Dis, MF Med, Nutr, OB-GYN, Pub Health

⊕ https://vfmat.ch/8316

IMPACT Foundation

Works to prevent and alleviate needless disability by restoring sight, mobility, and hearing.

ENT, MF Med, OB-GYN, Ophth-Opt, Ortho, Peds, Surg

⊕ https://vfmat.ch/ba28

International Agency for the Prevention of Blindness (IAPB), The

Leads international efforts in blindness-prevention activities, works toward a world where no one is needlessly visually impaired, and ensures that everyone has access to the best possible standard of eye health.

Infect Dis, Ophth-Opt, Pub Health

⊕ https://vfmat.ch/87a2

International Children's Heart Fund

Aims to promote the international growth and quality of cardiac surgery, particularly in children and young adults.

CT Surg, Ped Surg

⊕ https://vfmat.ch/33fb

International Council of Ophthalmology

Works with ophthalmologic societies and others to enhance ophthalmic education and improve access to the highest-quality eye care in order to preserve and restore vision for people of the world.

Ophth-Opt

⊕ https://vfmat.ch/ffd2

International Federation of Gynecology and Obstetrics (FIGO)

Implements global projects on specific women's health issues.

MF Med, Medicine, Neonat, OB-GYN, Surg, Urol

⊕ https://vfmat.ch/c4b4

International Federation of Red Cross and Red Crescent Societies (IFRC)

Coordinates and directs international assistance following natural and manmade disasters in nonconflict situations through the world's largest humanitarian and development network. Provides disaster-preparedness programs, healthcare activities, and promotes humanitarian values.

ER Med, General, Infect Dis, Nutr

⊕ https://vfmat.ch/b4ee

International Learning Movement (ILM UK)

Supports some of the world's poorest people in developing countries with core projects in education, safe drinking water, and healthcare.

General, Ophth-Opt

⊕ https://vfmat.ch/b974

International Medical Relief

Provides sustainable education, training, medical and dental care, and disaster relief and response in vulnerable communities worldwide.

Dent-OMFS, General, Infect Dis, Medicine, OB-GYN

⊕ https://vfmat.ch/b3ed

International Nepal Fellowship

Helps people affected by leprosy, spinal cord injuries, and other disabilities by facilitating development in some of Nepal's most remote and poorest communities and running medical outreach programs.

ENT, ER Med, MF Med, Nutr, Ortho, Palliative, Rehab, Surg

⊕ https://vfmat.ch/4673

International Nepal Fellowship (INF)

Supports local Nepali communities by providing healthcare services to improve health, reduce poverty, and promote social inclusion.

Derm, ER Med, General, Ortho, Peds, Surg

⊕ https://vfmat.ch/d9ca

International Organization for Migration (IOM) – The UN Migration Agency

Promotes evidence-informed policies and holistic, preventive, and curative health programs that are beneficial, accessible, and equitable for vulnerable migrants.

General, Infect Dis, OB-GYN

⊕ https://vfmat.ch/621a

International Planned Parenthood Federation (IPPF)
Leads a locally owned, globally connected civil society movement that provides and enables services and champions sexual and reproductive health and rights for all, especially the underserved.
Infect Dis, MF Med, OB-GYN
⊕ https://vfmat.ch/dc97

International Skills and Training Institute in Health (ISTIH)
Facilitates the appropriate placement of specialist health professionals with international volunteering opportunities.
ER Med
⊕ https://vfmat.ch/fa64

International Society of Nephrology
Aims to advance worldwide kidney health.
Nephro
⊕ https://vfmat.ch/1bae

International Trachoma Initiative (iTi)
Works toward a world free from trachoma, a preventable cause of blindness, and provides comprehensive support to national ministries of health and governmental and nongovernmental organizations to implement a comprehensive approach to fight trachoma.
Infect Dis, Ophth-Opt
⊕ https://vfmat.ch/3278

International Union Against Tuberculosis and Lung Disease
Develops, implements, and assesses anti-tuberculosis, lung health, and noncommunicable disease programs.
Infect Dis, Pub Health, Pulm-Critic
⊕ https://vfmat.ch/3e82

InterSurgeon
Fosters collaborative partnerships in the field of global surgery that will advance clinical care, teaching, training, research, and the provision and maintenance of medical equipment.
ENT, Neurosurg, Ortho, Ped Surg, Plast, Surg, Urol
⊕ https://vfmat.ch/6f8a

IntraHealth International
Improves the performance of health workers and strengthens the systems in which they work.
CV Med, Endo, General, Infect Dis, MF Med, Neonat, Nutr, OB-GYN
⊕ https://vfmat.ch/ddc8

Ipas
Focuses efforts on women and girls who want contraception or abortion, and builds programs around their needs and how best to support them.
OB-GYN
⊕ https://vfmat.ch/8e39

Iris Global
Serves the poor, the destitute, the lost, and the forgotten by providing adoration, outreach, family, education, relief, development, healing, and the arts.
General, Infect Dis, Nutr, Pub Health
⊕ https://vfmat.ch/37f8

Irish Red Cross
Delivers a wide range of services to some of the most vulnerable people at home and abroad, including heathcare services and relief to those affected by natural disasters and conflict.
ER Med, Infect Dis, Logist-Op, Nutr, Pub Health
⊕ https://vfmat.ch/e35f

Islamic Medical Association of North America
Fosters health promotion, disease prevention, and health maintenance in communities around the world through direct patient care and health programs.
Anesth, Dent-OMFS, ER Med, General, Logist-Op, Ophth-Opt, Peds, Plast, Surg
⊕ https://vfmat.ch/a157

IsraAID
Supports people affected by humanitarian crisis and partners with local communities around the world to provide urgent aid, assist recovery, and reduce the risk of future disasters.
ER Med, Infect Dis, Psych, Rehab
⊕ https://vfmat.ch/de96

Janata Clinic
Aims to improve population health by providing more effective health services, and promotes health as a collaborative service by developing a sustainable model of community-endorsed health programs.
General, OB-GYN, Peds
⊕ https://vfmat.ch/992f

Jeewasha Foundation
Relieves the suffering of kidney patients in Nepal and helps others to avoid kidney failure in their lives.
Medicine, Nephro
⊕ https://vfmat.ch/bc2a

Jericho Road Community Health Center
Provides holistic healthcare for underserved and marginalized communities around the world, inspired by the Christian faith.
Anesth, General, Heme-Onc, Infect Dis, Medicine, OB-GYN, Ped Surg, Peds, Psych, Surg
⊕ https://vfmat.ch/3d6b

Jhpiego
Creates and delivers transformative healthcare solutions that save lives, in partnership with national governments, health experts, and local communities.
General, Infect Dis, OB-GYN, Surg
⊕ https://vfmat.ch/45b8

Jivan Foundation
Aids disabled people around the world in achieving independence in their lives.
Dent-OMFS, General, Heme-Onc, Ophth-Opt, Pub Health
⊕ https://vfmat.ch/cbda

John Snow, Inc. (JSI)
Aims to improve the health and well-being of underserved and vulnerable people and communities throughout the world.
General, Infect Dis, Logist-Op, MF Med, OB-GYN, Peds, Psych, Pub Health
⊕ https://vfmat.ch/ba78

Johns Hopkins Center for Communication Programs
Believes in the power of communication to save lives by empowering people to adopt healthy behaviors for themselves, their families, and their communities.
General, Infect Dis, Logist-Op, OB-GYN, Pub Health
⊕ https://vfmat.ch/1bf9

Johns Hopkins Center for Global Health
Facilitates and focuses the extensive expertise and resources of the Johns Hopkins institutions, together with global collaborators, to effectively address and ameliorate the world's most pressing health issues.
General, Genetics, Logist-Op, MF Med, Peds, Psych, Pub Health, Pulm-Critic
⊕ https://vfmat.ch/54ce

Joint United Nations Programme on HIV/AIDS (UNAIDS)
Aims to place people living with HIV and people affected by the virus at the decision-making table and at the center of designing, delivering, and monitoring the AIDS response.
Infect Dis
⊕ https://vfmat.ch/464a

Kailash Medical Foundation
Aims to improve the health and well-being of those in need around the world by going on missions to developing countries and providing medical, dental, and vision services to the underprivileged.
Dent-OMFS, General, Ophth-Opt
⊕ https://vfmat.ch/db41

Karma Thalo Foundation
Delivers sustainable health programs to the poor in the most remote areas of Nepal, improving quality of life through access to medical care and health education.

Dent-OMFS, General, Geri, MF Med, Ophth-Opt, Peds
⊕ https://vfmat.ch/382b

Karuna Foundation Nepal
Improves the lives of children with disabilities, prevents disabilities, empowers communities, and creates a more inclusive society.
Ortho, Ped Surg, Peds, Rehab
⊕ https://vfmat.ch/1f5f

Kaya Responsible Travel
Promotes sustainable social, environmental, and economic development, empowers communities, and cultivates educated, compassionate global citizens through responsible travel.
All-Immu, Crit-Care, Dent-OMFS, ER Med, General, Geri, Infect Dis, MF Med, Medicine, Nutr, OB-GYN, Peds, Psych, Pub Health, Rehab
⊕ https://vfmat.ch/b2cf

Kids Care Everywhere
Seeks to empower physicians in under-resourced environments with multimedia, state-of-the-art medical software, and to inspire young professionals to become future global healthcare leaders.
Logist-Op, Ped Surg, Peds
⊕ https://vfmat.ch/bc23

Leprosy Mission Australia, The
Provides support to people with leprosy including screening, medical treatment and job opportunities, inspired by the Christian faith.
Infect Dis
⊕ https://vfmat.ch/9e4b

Leprosy Mission England and Wales, The
Leads the fight against leprosy by supporting people living with leprosy today and serving future generations by working to end transmission of the disease.
Infect Dis, Pub Health
⊕ https://vfmat.ch/4c67

Leprosy Mission International
Seeks to empower people with leprosy to attain healing, dignity, and life in all its fullness.
Infect Dis
⊕ https://vfmat.ch/95a9

Leprosy Mission: Northern Ireland, The
Leads the fight against leprosy by supporting people living with leprosy today and serving future generations by working to end the transmission of the disease.
General, Infect Dis
⊕ https://vfmat.ch/e265

Life for a Child
Supports the provision of the best possible healthcare, given local circumstances, to all children and youth with diabetes in less-resourced countries, through the strengthening of existing diabetes services.
Endo, Medicine, Peds
⊕ https://vfmat.ch/d712

Lifebox
Seeks to provide safer surgery and anesthesia in low-resource countries by investing in tools, training, and partnerships for safe surgery.
Anesth, Crit-Care, Surg
⊕ https://vfmat.ch/2d4d

Limbs International
Engages communities and transforms lives through affordable, sustainable prosthetic solutions and rehabilitation services in developing countries.
Logist-Op, Ortho, Pod, Rehab
⊕ https://vfmat.ch/dc84

Lions Clubs International
Empowers volunteers to serve their communities, meet humanitarian needs, encourage peace, and promote international understanding through Lions Clubs.
Heme-Onc, Medicine, Nutr, Ophth-Opt
⊕ https://vfmat.ch/7b12

Little Things, The
Provides vital medical equipment to poorly funded and inadequately equipped hospitals, improving access to healthcare for patients across the globe.

⊕ https://vfmat.ch/2d81

London School of Hygiene & Tropical Medicine: Health in Humanitarian Crises Centre
Advances health and health equity in crisis-affected countries through research, education, and translation of knowledge into policy and practice.
ER Med, Infect Dis, Pub Health
⊕ https://vfmat.ch/96ad

MAGNA International
Helps those who are suffering or recovering from conflicts and disasters by reducing the risks of diseases and treating them immediately.
ER Med, General, Infect Dis, Peds, Surg
⊕ https://vfmat.ch/58f4

Management Sciences for Health (MSH)
Works with countries and communities to save lives and improve the health of the world's poorest and most vulnerable people by building strong, resilient, sustainable health systems.
Infect Dis, Logist-Op, Pub Health
⊕ https://vfmat.ch/6aa2

MAP International
Provides medicines and health supplies to those in need around the world so they might experience life to the fullest.
Logist-Op
⊕ https://vfmat.ch/deed

Marie Stopes International
Provides the contraception and safe abortion services that enable women all over the world to choose their own futures.
Infect Dis, MF Med, Neonat, OB-GYN, Pub Health
⊕ https://vfmat.ch/9525

Massachusetts General Hospital Global Surgery Initiative
Aims to improve surgical education and access to advanced surgical care in resource-limited settings around the world by performing surgical operations as visitors, training local surgeons, and sharing medical technology through international partnerships across disciplines.
Anesth, Crit-Care, ER Med, Heme-Onc, Peds, Surg
⊕ https://vfmat.ch/31b1

Maverick Collective
Aims to build a global community of strategic philanthropists and informed advocates who use their intellectual and financial resources to create change.
Infect Dis, MF Med, OB-GYN
⊕ https://vfmat.ch/ea49

Max Foundation, The
Seeks to increase global access to treatment, care, and support for people living with cancer.
General, Heme-Onc, Pub Health
⊕ https://vfmat.ch/8c7d

McGill University Health Centre: Centre for Global Surgery
Works to reduce the impact of injury by advancing surgical care through research and education in resource-limited settings.
ER Med, Logist-Op, Ped Surg, Surg
⊕ https://vfmat.ch/7246

Medical Mercy Canada
Seeks to improve the quality of life in impoverished areas through humanitarian projects with local participation, and provides funding for orphanages, geriatric and childcare centers, remote health clinics, medical aid centers, hospitals, rural schools, and health programs.
General
⊕ https://vfmat.ch/81dc

Medical Ministry International
Provides compassionate healthcare in areas of need, inspired by the

Christian faith.

CT Surg, Dent-OMFS, ENT, General, OB-GYN, Ophth-Opt, Ortho, Plast, Rehab, Surg, Urol, Vasc Surg

⊕ https://vfmat.ch/5da6

Medical Mission Aid Inc
Advances effective healthcare in disadvantaged communities through medical scholarships, grants for supplies and support for local health initiatives.

Infect Dis, Logist-Op, OB-GYN, Pub Health, Rehab

⊕ https://vfmat.ch/8b83

Medical Teams International
Seeks to restore health as the first step to restoring hope, working to bring basic but lifesaving medical care to those in need.

Dent-OMFS, ER Med, General, MF Med, Pub Health

⊕ https://vfmat.ch/8d1c

MedShare
Aims to improve the quality of life of people, communities, and the planet by sourcing and directly delivering surplus medical supplies and equipment to communities in need around the world.

Logist-Op

⊕ https://vfmat.ch/c8bc

Mercy in Action
Inspired by the Christian faith, carries out programs in maternal and newborn health, primary healthcare for children under 5, and midwifery education.

General, MF Med, Neonat, OB-GYN, Peds, Pub Health

⊕ https://vfmat.ch/cc88

Midland International Aid Trust
Provides food, goods, clothing, and equipment to those in financial need or who are suffering as a result of a disaster.

CT Surg, Dent-OMFS, ENT, Logist-Op, OB-GYN, Ophth-Opt, Ortho, Ped Surg, Plast, Pub Health, Rehab

⊕ https://vfmat.ch/7eb2

Milan Foundation Nepal
Provides access to a good education and good health.

General, Ophth-Opt

⊕ https://vfmat.ch/9e11

MiracleFeet
Brings low-cost treatment to every child on the planet born with clubfoot, a leading cause of physical disability.

Ortho, Peds, Rehab

⊕ https://vfmat.ch/bda8

Mission Bambini
Helps to support children living in poverty and sickness, and lacking education, giving them the opportunity for and hope of a better life.

CT Surg, CV Med, Crit-Care, ER Med, Ped Surg, Peds

⊕ https://vfmat.ch/dc1a

Mission Himalaya
Aims to provide proper education and free healthcare services in the most remote areas of Nepal.

General, Logist-Op, Nutr, Ophth-Opt, Pub Health

⊕ https://vfmat.ch/c112

Mission Plasticos
Provides reconstructive plastic surgical care to those in need, and generates sustainable outcomes through training, education, and research.

Plast

⊕ https://vfmat.ch/97cb

Mission: Restore
Trains medical professionals abroad in complex reconstructive surgery in order to create a sustainable infrastructure in which long-term relationships are forged and permanent change comes to pass.

Plast, Surg

⊕ https://vfmat.ch/3f5f

MSI Reproductive Choices (Marie Stopes International)
Seeks to deliver quality family planning and reproductive healthcare to women around the world.

MF Med

⊕ https://vfmat.ch/5c82

Multi-Agency International Training and Support (MAITS)
Improves the lives of some of the world's poorest people living with disabilities through better access to quality health and education services and support.

Neuro, Psych, Rehab

⊕ https://vfmat.ch/9dcd

Muna Foundation Nepal
Works for the welfare of children, women and girls, and minorities of Nepal to provide shelter, food, clothing, education, and healthcare along with hope, compassion, and love.

General, Infect Dis, Ophth-Opt

⊕ https://vfmat.ch/51d3

Médecins du Monde/Doctors of the World
Provides care, bears witness, and supports social change worldwide with innovative medical programs and evidence-based advocacy initiatives.

ER Med, General, Infect Dis, MF Med, Neonat, OB-GYN, Peds, Pub Health

⊕ https://vfmat.ch/a43d

Namaste Children Nepal
Provides proper shelter, quality education, and healthcare to children without parents.

General, Peds

⊕ https://vfmat.ch/ee74

NCD Alliance
Unites and strengthens civil society to stimulate collaborative advocacy, action, and accountability for NCD (noncommunicable disease) prevention and control.

All-Immu, CV Med, General, Heme-Onc, Medicine, Peds, Psych

⊕ https://vfmat.ch/abdd

Nepal Bharat Maitri Hospital
Delivers high-quality healthcare services that are affordable for and accessible to the general public.

Crit-Care, ER Med, General, OB-GYN, Radiol, Surg

⊕ https://vfmat.ch/adbd

Nepal Eye Hospital
Provides eye care services to the Nepalese community.

Ophth-Opt, Surg

⊕ https://vfmat.ch/e2e3

Nepal Fertility Care Center (NFCC)
Helps to provide available, accessible, and affordable reproductive health for all.

Infect Dis, MF Med, OB-GYN

⊕ https://vfmat.ch/e917

Nepal Healthcare Equipment Development Foundation (NHEDF)
Accepts donated biomedical equipment from government hospitals and health clinics, repurposes it, and tailors its use to the specific needs of Nepalese patients.

ER Med, General, Logist-Op, Psych

⊕ https://vfmat.ch/8399

Nepal Heart Foundation
Promotes awareness among the people to reduce the incidence of heart disease, which has been taking an increased toll of death in the world.

CV Med, Crit-Care, Heme-Onc, Medicine, Peds

⊕ https://vfmat.ch/2c9e

Nepal Leprosy Trust
Aims for the ultimate elimination of leprosy, improved health, and socio-economic development.

Infect Dis, Pub Health

⊕ https://vfmat.ch/37d5

Nepal Netra Jyoti Sangh (NNJS)
Provides high-quality, sustainable, comprehensive, and affordable eye care services by identifying and mobilizing local, national, and international resources.
Infect Dis, Ophth Opt
⊕ https://vfmat.ch/cddc

Nepal Youth Foundation
Brings freedom, health, shelter, and education to Nepal's most impoverished children.
Infect Dis, Nutr, Psych
⊕ https://vfmat.ch/6f8e

Nestling Trust, The (TNT)
Facilitates the construction of village health clinics in collaboration with the Nepal Ministry of Health, equips staff, and ensures sustainability in order to provide basic healthcare in remote areas.
General, OB-GYN, Pub Health
⊕ https://vfmat.ch/498c

NLR International
Promotes and supports the prevention and treatment of leprosy, prevention of disabilities, social inclusion, and stigma reduction of people affected by leprosy.
Infect Dis, Pub Health
⊕ https://vfmat.ch/d7bd

NPI Narayani Samudayik Hospital
Delivers patient-centered care to enhance and contribute to health and well-being in Nepal.
Anesth, CV Med, Dent-OMFS, Derm, ENT, ER Med, General, Heme-Onc, Neuro, OB-GYN, Ortho, Path, Peds, Surg
⊕ https://vfmat.ch/4877

Nyagi
Empowers local healthcare workers in resource-poor areas to diagnose life-threatening health conditions through accelerated, low-cost ultrasound skills training.
Logist-Op, Pub Health
⊕ https://vfmat.ch/5de5

Nyaya Health Nepal
Provides free, quality healthcare for underserved communities in Nepal, through a sustainable model. Works in Achham, a remote district in Far West Province that was disinvested during the decade-long civil war, and Dolakha, in Bagmati Province, an epicenter of the 2015 earthquake.
Anesth, CV Med, ER Med, Endo, General, Infect Dis, Logist-Op, Medicine, OB-GYN, Ortho, Ortho, Path, Peds, Radiol, Surg
⊕ https://vfmat.ch/7825

NYC Medics
Deploys mobile medical teams to remote areas of disaster zones and humanitarian emergencies, providing the highest level of medical care to those who otherwise would not have access to aid and relief efforts.
All-Immu, ER Med, Infect Dis, Surg
⊕ https://vfmat.ch/aeee

Oda Foundation
Develops community-led solutions, helping Nepal's most impoverished and remote communities to thrive.
ER Med, General, OB-GYN
⊕ https://vfmat.ch/9884

One Heart Worldwide
Aims to end preventable deaths related to pregnancy and childbirth worldwide.
MF Med, Neonat, OB-GYN, Pub Health
⊕ https://vfmat.ch/a865

One World One Vision
Aims to reduce vision loss resulting from ocular misalignment and pediatric cataracts.
Anesth, Ophth-Opt, Ped Surg, Surg
⊕ https://vfmat.ch/337b

One World – One Heart Foundation
Seeks to help people and improve the lives of those in need in Nepal.
Dent-OMFS, ER Med, General, Medicine, OB-GYN, Ophth-Opt
⊕ https://vfmat.ch/c3f2

Open Heart International
Provides surgical interventions and best practices to the most disadvantaged communities on the planet.
CT Surg, MF Med, OB-GYN, Ophth-Opt, Plast, Surg
⊕ https://vfmat.ch/dab2

Operation Corazón
Offers support to individuals and families in need by delivering humanitarian aid, relief, support services, equipment, clothing, medicine, and food.
General, Nutr
⊕ https://vfmat.ch/5f76

Operation Eyesight
Works to eliminate blindness in partnership with governments, hospitals, medical professionals, corporations, and community development teams.
Ophth-Opt, Surg
⊕ https://vfmat.ch/b95d

Operation Eyesight Universal
Aims to prevent blindness, restore sight, and eliminate avoidable blindness.
Ophth-Opt
⊕ https://vfmat.ch/f629

Operation International
Offers medical aid to adults and children suffering from lack of quality healthcare in impoverished countries.
Dent-OMFS, ER Med, Heme-Onc, OB-GYN, Ophth-Opt, Ortho, Ped Surg, Plast, Surg
⊕ https://vfmat.ch/b52a

Operation Medical
Commits efforts to promoting and providing high-quality medical care and education to communities that do not have adequate access.
Anesth, ENT, Logist-Op, OB-GYN, Ped Surg, Plast, Surg, Urol
⊕ https://vfmat.ch/7e1b

Operation Walk
Provides the gift of mobility through life-changing joint replacement surgeries, at no cost for those in need in the U.S. and globally.
Anesth, Ortho, Rehab, Surg
⊕ https://vfmat.ch/bafe

Options
Believes in a world in which women and children can access the high-quality health services they need, without financial burden.
Logist-Op, MF Med, Neonat, OB-GYN
⊕ https://vfmat.ch/3a48

Optivest Foundation
Funds strategic opportunities that are holistic and collaborative, inspired by the Christian faith.
General, Nutr
⊕ https://vfmat.ch/f1e6

Optometry Giving Sight
Delivers eye exams and low or no-cost glasses, provides training for local eye care professionals, and establishes optometry schools, vision centers and optical labs.
Ophth-Opt
⊕ https://vfmat.ch/33ea

Orbis International
Works to prevent and treat blindness through hands-on training and improved access to quality eye care.
Anesth, Ophth-Opt, Surg
⊕ https://vfmat.ch/f2b2

Oxford University Global Surgery Group (OUGSG)

Aims to contribute to the provision of high-quality surgical care globally, particularly in low- and middle-income countries (LMICs), while bringing together students, researchers, and clinicians with an interest in global surgery, anesthesia, and obstetrics and gynecology.

Anesth, MF Med, OB-GYN, Ortho, Surg

⊕ https://vfmat.ch/c624

Pact

Works on the ground to improve the lives of those who are challenged by poverty and marginalization, striving for a world in which all people are heard, capable, and vibrant.

Infect Dis, Logist-Op, MF Med, Pub Health

⊕ https://vfmat.ch/9a6c

Partners in Health

Responds to the moral imperative to provide high-quality healthcare globally to those who need it most, while striving to ease suffering by providing a comprehensive model of care that includes access to food, transportation, housing, and other key components of healing.

CT Surg, General, Heme-Onc, Infect Dis, MF Med, Neurosurg, OB-GYN, Ortho, Plast, Psych, Urol

⊕ https://vfmat.ch/dc9c

Partnership for Sustainable Development (PSD) Nepal

Builds capacity in the poorest and most vulnerable communities in Nepal.

General, OB-GYN, Ped Surg, Peds, Psych, Surg

⊕ https://vfmat.ch/1de6

PASHA

Creates opportunities to improve health among vulnerable populations around the world, by bringing together diverse individuals with various areas of expertise and engaging them in solving local and global health challenges.

Derm, Logist-Op, Ophth-Opt, Ortho

⊕ https://vfmat.ch/efbc

PATH

Advances health equity through innovation and partnerships so people, communities, and economies can thrive.

All-Immu, CV Med, Endo, Heme-Onc, Infect Dis, MF Med, Neonat, Nutr, OB-GYN, Path, Peds, Pulm-Critic

⊕ https://vfmat.ch/b4db

Pediatric Universal Life-Saving Effort, Inc. (PULSE)

Aims to increase access to acute- and intensive-care services for children, recognizing that a significant amount of childhood mortality is preventable. Utilizes time, talents, and resources and seeks to persuade others to share their gifts to enrich the lives of children worldwide.

Crit-Care, Logist-Op, Neonat, Ped Surg, Peds

⊕ https://vfmat.ch/f6b9

Phase Worldwide

Empowers isolated communities through integrated and sustainable programs in health, education, and livelihoods.

General, Heme-Onc, MF Med, Medicine, Nutr, OB-GYN, Peds

⊕ https://vfmat.ch/fc74

Philips Foundation

Aims to reduce healthcare inequality by providing access to quality healthcare for disadvantaged communities.

CV Med, OB-GYN, Ped Surg, Peds, Surg, Urol

⊕ https://vfmat.ch/bacb

Phillips Renner Foundation

Works to reduce inequities in nutrition, dental care, and education by delivering high-impact health services and products to children in the poorest communities.

Dent-OMFS, Nutr

⊕ https://vfmat.ch/bce6

PLeDGE Health

Aims to improve emergency medical care around the world through sustainable partnerships, open-source material development and dissemination, and development of the next generation of educational leaders in low-resource areas.

ER Med, General

⊕ https://vfmat.ch/3a7d

Possible / Nyaya Health

Improves healthcare for underserved communities of Nepal and has piloted an integrated care-delivery model that coordinates care from home to facility, using an electronic health record (EHR) that is optimized for low-resource settings.

General, OB-GYN, Peds

⊕ https://vfmat.ch/d949

PSI – Population Services International

Aims to improve the health of people in the developing world by focusing on challenges such as a lack of family planning, HIV/AIDS, barriers to maternal health, and the greatest threats to children under the age of 5, including malaria, diarrhea, pneumonia, and malnutrition.

Infect Dis, MF Med, OB-GYN, Peds

⊕ https://vfmat.ch/ffe3

Public Health Concern Trust Nepal (phect-Nepal)

Advocates for individual rights to healthcare and strives to provide better and affordable healthcare services to people in both urban and rural areas of Nepal.

Crit-Care, Dent-OMFS, ENT, General, MF Med, Medicine, Neurosurg, OB-GYN, Ophth-Opt, Ortho, Ped Surg, Peds, Psych, Pub Health, Radiol, Rehab, Surg

⊕ https://vfmat.ch/26c5

RAD-AID International

Improves and optimizes access to medical imaging and radiology in low-resource regions of the world.

Rad-Onc, Radiol

⊕ https://vfmat.ch/537f

Reach Beyond

Aims to reach and impact underserved communities with medical care and community development, based in Christian ministry.

ER Med, General

⊕ https://vfmat.ch/cc5c

Real Medicine Foundation (RMF)

Provides humanitarian support to people living in disaster- and poverty-stricken areas, focusing on the person as a whole by providing medical/physical, emotional, economic, and social support.

ER Med, General, Infect Dis, Nutr, Peds, Psych

⊕ https://vfmat.ch/d45a

RestoringVision

Empowers lives by restoring vision for millions of people in need.

Ophth-Opt

⊕ https://vfmat.ch/e121

ReSurge International

Provides reconstructive surgical care and builds surgical capacity in developing countries.

Anesth, Dent-OMFS, Ped Surg, Plast, Surg

⊕ https://vfmat.ch/9937

RHD Action

Seeks to reduce the burden of rheumatic heart disease in vulnerable populations throughout the world.

CV Med, Medicine, Pub Health

⊕ https://vfmat.ch/f5d9

Rockefeller Foundation, The

Works to promote the well-being of humanity.

Logist-Op, Nutr, Pub Health

⊕ https://vfmat.ch/5424

Rose Charities International

Aims to support communities to improve quality of life and reduce the effects of poverty through innovative, self-sustaining projects, and partnerships.

ENT, ER Med, General, Infect Dis, Neonat, OB-GYN, Ophth-Opt, Ped Surg, Peds, Rehab, Urol

⊕ https://vfmat.ch/53df

Rotaplast International
Helps children and families worldwide by eliminating the burden of cleft lip and/or palate, burn scarring, and other deformities by sending medical teams to provide free reconstructive surgery, ancillary treatment, and training.
Anesth, Dent-OMFS, ENT, Ped Surg, Plast, Surg
⊕ https://vfmat.ch/78b3

Rotary International
Provides service to others, improves lives, and advances world understanding, goodwill, and peace through its fellowship of business, professional, and community leaders.
ER Med, General, Infect Dis, MF Med, OB-GYN
⊕ https://vfmat.ch/8fb5

Safe Anaesthesia Worldwide
Provides anesthesia to those in need in low-income countries to enable lifesaving surgery.
Anesth, Plast
⊕ https://vfmat.ch/134a

Salvation Army International, The
Seeks to meet human needs through services in education, healthcare, community support, emergency response, and ministry development, inspired by the Christian faith.
Dent-OMFS, Derm, ER Med, Infect Dis, MF Med, Medicine, Nutr, OB-GYN, Ophth-Opt, Palliative, Psych, Rehab, Surg
⊕ https://vfmat.ch/8eb3

SAMU Foundation
Provides medical first response and reconstruction when severe international emergencies occur.
ER Med, Infect Dis, Logist-Op, Psych, Pub Health
⊕ https://vfmat.ch/3196

Save A Child's Heart
Provides lifesaving cardiac treatment to children in developing countries, and trains healthcare professionals from these countries to deliver quality care in their communities.
CT Surg, CV Med, Crit-Care, Ped Surg, Peds
⊕ https://vfmat.ch/1bef

Save the Children
Gives children around the world a healthy start in life, the opportunity to learn, and protection from harm.
All-Immu, Crit-Care, ER Med, General, Infect Dis, MF Med, Medicine, Neonat, OB-GYN, Peds, Psych, Pub Health
⊕ https://vfmat.ch/2e73

Scheer Memorial Adventist Hospital
Provides compassionate, patient-centered care at international standards for all patients.
Anesth, CV Med, Crit-Care, Dent-OMFS, Derm, Endo, OB-GYN, Ortho, Path, Peds, Radiol, Rehab, Surg, Urol
⊕ https://vfmat.ch/fd87

SEE International
Provides sustainable medical, surgical, and educational services through volunteer ophthalmic surgeons, with the objectives of restoring sight and preventing blindness to disadvantaged individuals worldwide.
Ophth-Opt, Surg
⊕ https://vfmat.ch/6e1b

Serving Others Worldwide
Aims to provide aid to the poor, distressed, and underprivileged by providing healthcare and dental services, and by building schools, orphanages, libraries, and medical clinics in undeveloped countries.
Dent-OMFS, General
⊕ https://vfmat.ch/69cb

SEVA
Delivers vital eye care services to the world's most vulnerable, including women, children, and Indigenous peoples.
Ophth-Opt, Surg
⊕ https://vfmat.ch/1e87

Siddhi Memorial Foundation
Seeks to provide quality, accessible healthcare services for women and children through Siddhi Memorial Hospital (SMH), and to serve children, women, and senior citizens in need.
Anesth, Dent-OMFS, ER Med, General, MF Med, Neonat, OB-GYN, Path, Ped Surg, Peds, Surg
⊕ https://vfmat.ch/a52a

Sight for All
Empowers communities to deliver comprehensive, evidence-based, high-quality eye healthcare through the provision of research, education, and equipment.
Logist-Op, Ophth-Opt, Surg
⊕ https://vfmat.ch/e34b

SIGN Fracture Care International
Builds orthopedic capacity around the world and provides the injured poor access to fracture surgery by donating orthopedic education and implant systems to surgeons in developing countries.
Ortho, Rehab, Surg
⊕ https://vfmat.ch/123d

Simavi
Strives for a world in which all women and girls are socially and economically empowered and pursue their rights to live a healthy life, free from discrimination, coercion, and violence.
MF Med, OB-GYN
⊕ https://vfmat.ch/b57b

Small World, The
Seeks to empower communities to realize they are capable of creating lasting solutions using their own skills and abilities.
ER Med, General, Pub Health
⊕ https://vfmat.ch/8d97

Smile Train, Inc.
Treats children with cleft lip through a sustainable and local model that supports surgery and other forms of essential care.
Logist-Op, Pub Health
⊕ https://vfmat.ch/822c

SmileOnU
Empowers dental professionals to help and educate those who may not have adequate dental knowledge and access to oral health services.
Dent-OMFS, Surg
⊕ https://vfmat.ch/cb6d

Social Welfare Association of Nepal (SWAN Nepal)
Strives to support disadvantaged and rural communities in Nepal by providing accessible healthcare and educational opportunities for children, and enabling women to achieve financial independence.
Pub Health
⊕ https://vfmat.ch/a151

SOS Children's Villages International
Supports children through alternative care and family strengthening.
ER Med, Peds
⊕ https://vfmat.ch/aca1

Sri Sathya Sai International Organization
Inspired by spiritual teachings, carries out efforts in global healthcare, education, humanitarian relief, and youth engagement.
Dent-OMFS, General, Logist-Op, Nutr, Ophth-Opt, Pub Health
⊕ https://vfmat.ch/9bda

Stand By Me
Helps children facing terrible circumstances and provides the care, love, and attention they need to thrive through children's homes and schools.
Peds
⊕ https://vfmat.ch/a224

Surgeons OverSeas (SOS)
Works to reduce death and disability from surgically treatable conditions in developing countries.
Anesth, Heme-Onc, Surg
⊕ https://vfmat.ch/5d16

Swasti
Aims to transform the lives of marginalized communities by ensuring their access to quality healthcare and thereby contributing to poverty alleviation.
Pub Health
⊕ https://vfmat.ch/be8b

Swiss Tropical and Public Health Institute
Contributes to the improvement of the health of populations internationally, nationally, and locally through excellence in research, education, and services.
Infect Dis, Pub Health
⊕ https://vfmat.ch/2ee4

Task Force for Global Health, The
Consists of programs and focus areas that cover a range of global health issues including neglected tropical diseases, infectious diseases, vaccines, field epidemiology, public health informatics, health workforce development, and global health ethics.
Infect Dis, Logist-Op, Medicine, Ophth-Opt, Peds
⊕ https://vfmat.ch/714c

Team 5 Medical Foundation
Provides medical care in the most overlooked remote areas of the world supported by sponsorships, donations, and the dedication of its volunteers.
ER Med, General, Peds, Plast, Pulm-Critic
⊕ https://vfmat.ch/f267

Tearfund
Responds to crisis and partners with local churches to bring restoration to those living in poverty, inspired by the Christian faith.
ER Med, Logist-Op
⊕ https://vfmat.ch/f6cf

Terre des hommes (Tdh) Foundation
Works to improve the daily life of children and their relatives in the areas of health, protection and emergency, in Europe, Africa, Asia, Latin America, and the Near and Middle East.
CT Surg, CV Med, OB-GYN, Ped Surg, Pub Health
⊕ https://vfmat.ch/5c26

Third World Eye Care Society (TWECS)
Collects old, unused eyeglasses and distributes them in conjunction with eye exams given by properly trained individuals.
Logist-Op, Ophth-Opt
⊕ https://vfmat.ch/8618

Tilganga Institute of Ophthalmology (TIO)
Supports the prevention and control of blindness in Nepal and the region.
Ophth-Opt
⊕ https://vfmat.ch/ff5d

Touching Lives Ministry
Based in Christian ministry, supports communities worldwide through improved healthcare, education, and spiritual and economic development.
General, OB-GYN, Peds, Surg
⊕ https://vfmat.ch/75d3

Training for Health Equity Network (THEnet)
Contributes to health equity through health workforce education, research, and service, based on principles of social accountability and community engagement.
ER Med, General
⊕ https://vfmat.ch/38c6

Transplant Links Community (TLC)
Provides hands-on training in kidney transplantation for surgeons, doctors, and nurses in low- and middle-income countries.
Nephro, Surg, Urol
⊕ https://vfmat.ch/bb46

Tsering's Fund
Provides assistance through private donations for deserving underprivileged children, young women, and families in Nepal, helping to change lives with educational scholarships, medical care, and basic living assistance.
Dent-OMFS, General
⊕ https://vfmat.ch/39c1

Two Worlds Cancer Collaboration
Collaborates with local care professionals in lesser-resourced countries to help reduce the burden of cancer and other life-limiting illnesses.
Heme-Onc, Palliative, Peds, Pub Health, Rad-Onc
⊕ https://vfmat.ch/fbdd

Union for International Cancer Control (UICC)
Unites and supports the cancer community to reduce the global cancer burden, promote greater equity, and ensure that cancer control continues to be a priority in the world health and development agenda.
Heme-Onc, Pub Health
⊕ https://vfmat.ch/88b1

United Hatzallah
Provides patients with quick response to medical emergencies and professional and appropriate medical aid until an ambulance arrives.
ER Med, General, Logist-Op
⊕ https://vfmat.ch/e581

United Mission Hospital Tansen
Aims to improve the quality of life of people of Palpa District by providing high-quality primary healthcare and to provide training in primary healthcare.
All-Immu, Anesth, Dent-OMFS, Infect Dis, MF Med, Neonat, Psych
⊕ https://vfmat.ch/5811

United Mission to Nepal (UMN)
Strives to address root causes of poverty as it serves the people of Nepal.
ER Med, General, Infect Dis, MF Med, Psych
⊕ https://vfmat.ch/cb26

United Nations Children's Fund (UNICEF)
Works in over 190 countries and territories to save children's lives, defend their rights, and help them fulfill their potential, from early childhood through adolescence.
All-Immu, Infect Dis, MF Med, Neonat, Nutr, OB-GYN, Ped Surg, Peds, Pub Health
⊕ https://vfmat.ch/42d7

United Nations Development Programme (UNDP)
Helps countries achieve the simultaneous eradication of extreme poverty and significant reduction of inequalities and exclusion using a sustainable human development approach.
Infect Dis, Logist-Op, Pub Health
⊕ https://vfmat.ch/935c

United Nations High Commissioner for Refugees (UNHCR)
Safeguards the rights and well-being of people who have been forced to flee, ensuring that everybody has the right to seek asylum and find safe refuge in another country, with the goal of seeking lasting solutions.
General, MF Med, Medicine, OB-GYN, Peds, Psych, Pub Health
⊕ https://vfmat.ch/6636

United Nations Population Fund (UNFPA)
Supports reproductive healthcare for women and youth in more than 150 countries, focusing on delivering a world in which every pregnancy is wanted, every childbirth is safe, and every young person's potential is fulfilled.
Infect Dis, MF Med, Neonat, OB-GYN, Peds, Pub Health
⊕ https://vfmat.ch/c969

United States Agency for International Development (USAID)
Promotes and demonstrates democratic values abroad and advances a free, peaceful, and prosperous world. Leads the U.S. government's international development and disaster assistance through partnerships and investments that save lives.
ER Med, Infect Dis, MF Med, OB-GYN, Peds
⊕ https://vfmat.ch/9a99

United Surgeons for Children (USFC)

Pursues greater health and opportunity for children in the most neglected pockets of the world, with a specific focus on and expertise in surgery.

Anesth, CT Surg, Neonat, Neurosurg, OB-GYN, Peds, Radiol, Surg

⊕ https://vfmat.ch/3b4c

University of California Los Angeles: David Geffen School of Medicine Global Health Program

Catalyzes opportunities to improve health globally by engaging in multi-disciplinary and innovative education programs, research initiatives, and bilateral partnerships that provide opportunities for trainees, faculty, and staff to contribute to sustainable health initiatives and to address health inequities facing the world today.

All-Immu, Infect Dis, Logist-Op, MF Med, Medicine, Neonat, OB-GYN, Ortho, Ped Surg, Peds, Radiol

⊕ https://vfmat.ch/f1a4

University of California San Francisco: Francis I. Proctor Foundation for Ophthalmology

Aims to prevent blindness worldwide through research and teaching focused on infectious and inflammatory eye disease.

Ophth-Opt, Pub Health

⊕ https://vfmat.ch/cf47

University of California San Francisco: Institute for Global Health Sciences

Dedicates its efforts to improving health and reducing the burden of disease in the world's most vulnerable populations by integrating expertise in the health, social, and biological sciences, training global health leaders, and developing solutions to the most pressing health challenges.

Infect Dis, OB-GYN, Pub Health

⊕ https://vfmat.ch/6587

University of Colorado: Global Emergency Care Initiative

Strives to sustainably improve emergency care outcomes in low- and middle-income communities worldwide by linking cutting-edge academics with excellent on-the-ground implementation.

ER Med

⊕ https://vfmat.ch/417a

University of Illinois at Chicago: Center for Global Health

Aims to improve the health of populations around the world and reduce health disparities by collaboratively conducting trans-disciplinary research, training the next generations of global health leaders, and building the capacities of global and local partners.

Pub Health

⊕ https://vfmat.ch/b749

University of Michigan: Department of Surgery Global Health

Improves the health of patients, populations and communities through excellence in education, patient care, community service, research and technology development, and through leadership activities.

Anesth, Ortho, Surg

⊕ https://vfmat.ch/2fd8

University of Pennsylvania Perelman School of Medicine Center for Global Health

Aims to improve health equity worldwide through enhanced public health awareness and access to care, discovery, and outcomes-based research, and comprehensive educational programs grounded in partnership.

Heme-Onc, Infect Dis, OB-GYN

⊕ https://vfmat.ch/cb57

University of Utah Global Health

Supports local organizations in their quest to improve quality of life in their communities all over the world.

Anesth, CT Surg, CV Med, Crit-Care, Dent-OMFS, ENT, ER Med, Infect Dis, OB-GYN, Ophth-Opt, Ped Surg, Ped Surg, Peds, Plast, Pub Health, Surg, Urol

⊕ https://vfmat.ch/bacd

USA for United Nations High Commissioner for Refugees (UNHCR)

Serves and protects refugees and displaced people through emergency relief, cash assistance, education, resettlement, and the rebuilding of livelihoods.

ER Med, General, Logist-Op, Nutr, Pub Health

⊕ https://vfmat.ch/293c

USAID: Maternal and Child Health Integrated Program

Works to improve the health of women and their families, including programs for maternal, newborn, and child health, immunization, family planning, nutrition, malaria, and HIV/AIDS.

All-Immu, General, Infect Dis, MF Med

⊕ https://vfmat.ch/4415

USAID: Maternal and Child Survival Program

Works to prevent child and maternal deaths.

Infect Dis, MF Med, Neonat, OB-GYN, Peds

⊕ https://vfmat.ch/6fcf

Vision Care

Restores sight and helps patients get regular treatment at short-term eye camps and long-term base clinics by having doctors, missionaries, volunteers, and sponsors work together.

Ophth-Opt

⊕ https://vfmat.ch/9d7c

Vision for All Foundation

Implements ophthalmic healthcare projects; aims to create and support ophthalmic centers and existing structures in order to support the training of medical and paramedical personnel in the ophthalmology; and seeks to promote prevention, diagnosis, and treatment of ophthalmic pathologies.

Dent-OMFS, Ophth-Opt, Pub Health

⊕ https://vfmat.ch/dd72

Visionaries International

Works toward reducing the burden of corneal blindness in the developing world by assessing and addressing what limits corneal surgeons in each locale.

Anesth, Ophth-Opt, Pub Health, Surg

⊕ https://vfmat.ch/3d2e

Vitamin Angels

Helps at-risk populations in need—specifically pregnant women, new mothers, and children under age 5—to gain access to life-changing vitamins and minerals.

General, Nutr

⊕ https://vfmat.ch/7da1

Voluntary Service Overseas (VSO)

Works with health workers, communities, and governments to improve health services and rights for women, babies, youth, people with disabilities, and prisoners.

General, MF Med, OB-GYN

⊕ https://vfmat.ch/213d

Volunteers Initiative Nepal (VIN)

Empowers marginalized communities through equitable, inclusive, and holistic development programs in areas such as women's empowerment, children's development, youth empowerment, public health/healthcare, environmental conservation, and DRR.

General, Geri, Medicine, Path, Peds, Pub Health

⊕ https://vfmat.ch/92be

VOSH (Volunteer Optometric Services to Humanity) International

Facilitates the provision and the sustainability of vision care worldwide for people who can neither afford nor obtain such care.

Ophth-Opt

⊕ https://vfmat.ch/a149

Walkabout Foundation

Provides wheelchairs and rehabilitation in the developing world and funds research to find a cure for paralysis.

Logist-Op, Rehab

⊕ https://vfmat.ch/5582

Washington Nepal Health Foundation (WNHF)

Provides reconstructive surgical services and medical/psychological support to underprivileged children with congenital and traumatic deformities such as burn

injuries and cleft lips.
Anesth, Plast
⊕ https://vfmat.ch/4cd3

Watsi
Uses technology to make healthcare a reality for those who might not otherwise be able to afford it.
Pub Health, Surg
⊕ https://vfmat.ch/41a3

We Care for Humanity (WCH)
Promotes sustainable social change and the sustainable development goals developed by the United Nations, including: no poverty, good health and well-being, gender equality, human rights, climate action, and strong institutions.
General, Logist-Op, Pub Health
⊕ https://vfmat.ch/8b4e

White Ribbon Alliance, The
Leads a movement for reproductive, maternal, and newborn health and accelerates progress by putting citizens at the center of global, national, and local health efforts.
MF Med, OB-GYN
⊕ https://vfmat.ch/496b

Women Orthopaedist Global Outreach (WOGO)
Provides free, life-altering orthopedic surgery that eliminates debilitating arthritis and restores disabled joints so that women can reclaim their ability to care for themselves, their families, and their communities.
Anesth, Ortho, Rehab, Surg
⊕ https://vfmat.ch/6386

Women's Foundation Nepal, The
Helps women and children in Nepal who are victims of violence, abuse, and poverty.
Dent-OMFS, Ophth-Opt
⊕ https://vfmat.ch/b251

Women's Refugee Commission
Seeks to improve lives by protecting the rights of women, children, and youth displaced by conflict and crisis through researching their needs, identifying solutions, and advocating for programs and policies to strengthen their resilience.
General, MF Med, Neonat, OB-GYN, Peds, Psych
⊕ https://vfmat.ch/3d8f

World Anaesthesia Society (WAS)
Aims to support anesthesiologists with an interest in working in low-income regions of the world.
Anesth
⊕ https://vfmat.ch/37fe

World Council of Optometry
Facilitates the development of optometry worldwide and promotes eye health and vision care through advocacy, education, policy development, and humanitarian outreach.
Ophth-Opt, Pub Health
⊕ https://vfmat.ch/c92e

World Federation of Hemophilia (WFH)
Aims to improve and sustain care for people with inherited bleeding disorders by pursuing long-term relationships with individuals and organizations who share the values of WFH's development model.
Heme-Onc
⊕ https://vfmat.ch/5121

World Health Organization, The (WHO)
The United Nations' agency for health provides leadership on global health matters, shapes the health research agenda, sets norms and standards, articulates evidence-based policy options, provides technical support and monitoring to countries, and assesses health trends.
ER Med, General, Infect Dis, Logist-Op, MF Med, OB-GYN, Peds, Psych, Pub Health
⊕ https://vfmat.ch/c476

World Medical Relief
Facilitates the distribution of surplus medical resources where they are needed.
Logist-Op
⊕ https://vfmat.ch/72dc

World Parkinson's Program
Seeks to improve the quality of life of those affected by Parkinson's disease through education and advocacy, and provides free medication and support services.
Logist-Op, Neuro, Pub Health
⊕ https://vfmat.ch/c96d

World Vision International
Works with vulnerable communities around the world to overcome poverty and injustice with child-focused programs in disaster management, health, nutrition, economic development, education, clean water, sanitation, and hygiene.
ER Med, General, Infect Dis, MF Med, Nutr, OB-GYN, Peds
⊕ https://vfmat.ch/2642

WorldShare
Connects faith-based groups in the UK with their counterparts in underdeveloped countries to promote community development and holistic support for children.
Dent-OMFS, ER Med, General, Peds, Pub Health, Surg
⊕ https://vfmat.ch/9eae

Worldwide Healing Hands
Works to improve the quality of healthcare for women and children in the most underserved areas of the world and to stop the preventable deaths of mothers.
General, MF Med, Neonat, OB-GYN
⊕ https://vfmat.ch/b331

 # Nepal
Healthcare Facilities

Aama-Baa Hospital Pvt. Ltd.
Abukhaireni-Gorkha Hwy, Gorkha 34000, Nepal
⊕ https://vfmat.ch/487c

Aarogya Swasthya Sadan
Jawalakhel, Patan, वाग्मती प्रदेश, Nepal
⊕ https://vfmat.ch/72a9

Achham District Hospital
69DR017, Mangalsen, Mangalsen, Nepal
⊕ https://vfmat.ch/bb8c

Alive Hospital & Trauma Centre
Bharatpur 44207, Nepal
⊕ https://vfmat.ch/74b1

Alka Hospital Pvt. Ltd.
Lalitpur 44600, Nepal
⊕ https://vfmat.ch/d564

All Nepal Hospital Pvt. Ltd.
Kathmandu 44600, Nepal
⊕ https://vfmat.ch/1e2b

Alpine Medical College Teaching Hospital
Gadhimai 44400, Simara, Nepal
⊕ https://vfmat.ch/cccf

Araddhya Hospital Pvt. Ltd.
Janakpur, Nepal
⊕ https://vfmat.ch/93ee

Asia Medicare Hospital Pvt. Ltd.
Birgunj Busspark, Birgunj, प्रदेश नं. २, Nepal
⊕ https://vfmat.ch/de6f

Ayurveda Hospital
Yogbir Singh Marg, Kathmandu, Bagmati Pradesh, Nepal
⊕ https://vfmat.ch/62c1

Ayurvedic Hospital
Kirtipur Road, Kirtipur, Vagmati Pradesh, Nepal
⊕ https://vfmat.ch/cff7

Ayush Hospital
Suruchi Marga, Kathmandu 44600, Nepal
⊕ https://vfmat.ch/b53d

B.P. Koirala Institute of Health Science
Buddha Road, Dharan 56700, Nepal
⊕ https://vfmat.ch/6794

B.P. Koirala Memorial Cancer Hospital
Madi Thori, Bharatpur Metro, Vagmati Pradesh, Nepal
⊕ https://vfmat.ch/33d6

B.P. Smriti Hospital
Srikanti Marg, Kathmandu 44600, Nepal
⊕ https://vfmat.ch/77e2

Bagmati Health Hub Pvt. Ltd
Sinamangal Marg, Kathmandu, Bagmati Pradesh, Nepal
⊕ https://vfmat.ch/53bc

Bajhang District Hospital
F49, Jaya Prithvi, JayaPrithvi, Nepal
⊕ https://vfmat.ch/6634

Bandipur Hospital
Bandipur 33904, Nepal
⊕ https://vfmat.ch/d9cd

Banepa Hospital and Education Foundation
Banepa 45210, Nepal
⊕ https://vfmat.ch/382d

Bardiya District Hospital
Hospital Road, Gulariya 21800, Nepal
⊕ https://vfmat.ch/879e

Bayalpata Hospital
Madhya Pahaadi Rajmaarga, Sanfebagar 10700, Nepal
⊕ https://vfmat.ch/fe8b

Besisahar Hospital Pvt. Ltd.
Dumre-Besishahar, Besishahar,Gandaki Pradesh, Nepal
⊕ https://vfmat.ch/322f

Bhaktapur Cancer Hospital
Bhaktapur 44800, Nepal
⊕ https://vfmat.ch/37a2

Bhaktapur Hospital Emergency Block
Itachhen, Bhaktapur, Vagmati Pradesh, Nepal
⊕ https://vfmat.ch/54e2

Bharatpur Hospital
Hospital Road, Bharatpur Metro, Vagmati Pradesh, Nepal
⊕ https://vfmat.ch/54ea

Bharosa Hospital Pvt. Ltd.
Devkota Sadak, Kathmandu 44600, Nepal
⊕ https://vfmat.ch/951b

Bheri Zonal Hospital
Nepalgunj 21900, Nepal
⊕ https://vfmat.ch/f2a6

Bijayapur Hospital
Putali line, Dharan 56700, Nepal
⊕ https://vfmat.ch/74d7

Bir Hospital
Aspatal Marg, Kathmandu, Bagmati Pradesh, Nepal
⊕ https://vfmat.ch/b269

Birat Medical and Teaching Hospital
Tankisinuwari 56613, Nepal
⊕ https://vfmat.ch/f2a9

Blue Cross Hospital
Kathmandu, Nepal
⊕ https://vfmat.ch/c2ae

Blue Lotus Hospital
Tripura Marg, Tripureswor 44601, Nepal
⊕ https://vfmat.ch/212b

Bungkot Hospital
36DR036, Bunkot, Gandaki Pradesh, Nepal
⊕ https://vfmat.ch/fcad

Butwal Hospital Pvt. Ltd.
E – W Hwy, Butwal 32907, Nepal
⊕ https://vfmat.ch/b76c

C.P. Hospital Pvt. Ltd.
Bhimdatta Hwy, Dhangadhi 10900, Nepal
⊕ https://vfmat.ch/9981

Charak Hospital
Siddhartha Street, Pokhara 33700, Nepal
⊕ https://vfmat.ch/dd2e

Charak Memorial Hospital
New Bazaar, Pokhara, Gandaki Pradesh, Nepal
⊕ https://vfmat.ch/3832

Chirayu National Hospital & Medical Institute Pvt. Ltd.
रिङ्ग रोड, Kathmandu 44600, Nepal
⊕ https://vfmat.ch/35d5

Chitwan Hospital
Madi-Thori, Madi, Vagmati Pradesh, Nepal
⊕ https://vfmat.ch/daae

Chitwan Hospital Pvt. Ltd.
E – W Hwy, Bharatpur 44207, Nepal
⊕ https://vfmat.ch/26dc

Chitwan Medical College Teaching Hospital
Mahendra Highway, Bharatpur Metro, Vagmati Pradesh, Nepal
⊕ https://vfmat.ch/5866

Chitwan Valley Model Hospital
Doorsanchar Road, Bharatpur Metro, Vagmati Pradesh, Nepal
⊕ https://vfmat.ch/7b75

City Hospital
Siddharthanagar 32900, Nepal
⊕ https://vfmat.ch/198f

Civil Service Hospital
Minbhawan Marg, Kathmandu 44600, Nepal
⊕ https://vfmat.ch/5443

Dadeldhura District Hospital
Hospital Road, Amargadhi, Amargadhi, Nepal
⊕ https://vfmat.ch/1311

Dailekh District Hospital
Dailekh Rajmarg, Narayan Municipality, कर्णाली प्रदेश, Nepal
⊕ https://vfmat.ch/11bb

Dailekh District Hospital
Dailekh Sadak, Narayan Municipality 21600, Nepal
⊕ https://vfmat.ch/46a2

Devchuli Hospital
AH2, Devachuli 33000, Nepal
⊕ https://vfmat.ch/b598

Dhading Hospital
Dhading Besi Marga, Dhading Besi, Vagmati Pradesh, Nilkantha 45100, Nepal
⊕ https://vfmat.ch/33cc

Dhankuta District Hospital
Hulak Tole & Thadobazar Street, Dhankuta 56800, Nepal
⊕ https://vfmat.ch/65c1

Dhaulagiri Zonal Hospital
Darling 33300, Nepal
⊕ https://vfmat.ch/1c98

Dhulikhel Hospital
Dhulikhel 45200, Nepal
⊕ https://vfmat.ch/ef8f

Dullu Hospital
Kal Bhairab Dullu 21600, Nepal
⊕ https://vfmat.ch/cc3d

Dunai District Hospital
F47, Dunai, Karnali Pradesh, Nepal
⊕ https://vfmat.ch/1e5b

Era Hospital
Puspalal Path, Kathmandu 44600, Nepal
⊕ https://vfmat.ch/68a7

Everest Hospital
Madan Bhandari Road, Kathmandu, Nepal
⊕ https://vfmat.ch/8dfb

Fewa City Hospital
Indrapuri Marg, Pokhara, गण्डकी प्रदेश, Nepal
⊕ https://vfmat.ch/c16c

Gadhawa Hospital
Gadhawa 22414, Nepal
⊕ https://vfmat.ch/e147

Gajuri Hospital
Prithvi Rajmarg, Gajuri, Vagmati Pradesh, Nepal
⊕ https://vfmat.ch/49a6

Gandaki Medical College Teaching Hospital & Research Centre Ltd.
New Bazaar, Pokhara, Gandaki Pradesh, Nayabazar Road, Pokhara 33700, Nepal
⊕ https://vfmat.ch/7632

Gauri Shankar Hospital
Charikot – Lamabagar Road, Bhimeshwor Municipality 45500, Nepal
⊕ https://vfmat.ch/5f3a

Gautam Buddha International Cardiac Hospital
Bridge, Ring Road Near Balkumari, Kathmandu 44600, Nepal
⊕ https://vfmat.ch/341f

Ghorahi Hospital Pvt. Ltd.
Tribhuwan Park Road, Ghorahi 22400, Nepal
⊕ https://vfmat.ch/9333

Global Hospital
Ring Road, Patan, वाग्मती प्रदेश, Nepal
⊕ https://vfmat.ch/d8e3

Golden Hospital
Rangeli Road, Biratnagar, प्रदेश नं. १, Nepal
⊕ https://vfmat.ch/86c7

Gorkha District Hospital
Gorkha-Ghyampesal Road, Gorkha, गण्डकी प्रदेश, Nepal
⊕ https://vfmat.ch/836e

Grande City Hospital
Kanti Path, Kathmandu, Bagmati Pradesh, Nepal
⊕ https://vfmat.ch/c947

Grande International Hospital
Tokha Road, Kathmandu 44600, Nepal
⊕ https://vfmat.ch/99ea

Green City Hospital
Ring Road, Kathmandu, Bagmati Pradesh, Nepal
⊕ https://vfmat.ch/2dc9

Hamro Sahayatri Hospital and Birthing Centre
Arniko Raj Marga, Lokanthali, वाग्मती प्रदेश, Nepal
⊕ https://vfmat.ch/33ee

HCH Hospital
Khadichaur – Jiri Highway, Namdu, वाग्मती प्रदेश, Nepal
⊕ https://vfmat.ch/edeb

HDCS Chaurjahari Mission Hospital
Bijayashwari 22000, Nepal
⊕ https://vfmat.ch/6fef

Hillary Hospital
Khumjung, Province No. 1, Nepal
⊕ https://vfmat.ch/997e

Hilsa Hospital
F145, Muchu, Karnali Pradesh, Nepal
⊕ https://vfmat.ch/d513

Himal Hospital
Thirbom Sadak, Chardobato, Gyaneshwor,

Kathmandu, Nepal
⊕ https://vfmat.ch/baf8

Himalaya Sherpa Hospital
Khumjung 56000, Nepal
⊕ https://vfmat.ch/853d

Himalayan Healthcare Inc.
Manbhawan Ekta Galli, Patan, Vagmati Pradesh, Nepal
⊕ https://vfmat.ch/7ce5

Hospital at Bardibas
Bardibas Jaleshwar Highway, Aurahi, प्रदेश नं. २, Nepal
⊕ https://vfmat.ch/4889

Hospital at Bhijer
Bhijer, Nepal
⊕ https://vfmat.ch/badb

Hospital at Bhorle
Bhorle 45000, Nepal
⊕ https://vfmat.ch/d4f8

Hospital at Bidur
Pasang Lhamu Highway, Bidur, वाग्मती प्रदेश, Nepal
⊕ https://vfmat.ch/52a7

Hospital at Biratchok
महेन्द्र राज्मार्ग, Sundar Dulari, प्रदेश नं. १, Nepal
⊕ https://vfmat.ch/cd3b

Hospital at Chakratirtha
37DR042, Chakratirtha, गण्डकी प्रदेश, Nepal
⊕ https://vfmat.ch/e97e

Hospital at Gilunng
37DR013, Gilunng, गण्डकी प्रदेश, Nepal
⊕ https://vfmat.ch/3518

Hospital at Hanspur
36DR012, Hanspur, गण्डकी प्रदेश, Nepal
⊕ https://vfmat.ch/df47

Hospital at Hirmaniya
Hirmaniya Road, Hirminiya, प्रदेश नं. ५, Nepal
⊕ https://vfmat.ch/8fb8

Hospital at Kalikathum
60DR005, Mairi Kalikathum, कर्णाली प्रदेश, Nepal
⊕ https://vfmat.ch/3d6a

Hospital at Khali Puraini Road
Puraini, Nepal
⊕ https://vfmat.ch/56c9

Hospital at Machijhitkaiya
H17, Machijhitkaiya, प्रदेश नं. २, Nepal
⊕ https://vfmat.ch/ba92

Hospital at Marmaparikanda
Marmaparikanda, Nepal
⊕ https://vfmat.ch/5c31

Hospital at Nepalgung Gulariya Road
Nepalgung Gulariya Road, Khajura Khurda, प्रदेश नं. ५, Nepal
⊕ https://vfmat.ch/b8d4

Hospital at Raghunathpur
Raghunathpur, Nepal
⊕ https://vfmat.ch/a268

Hospital at Ramgram
Ramgram, Nepal
⊕ https://vfmat.ch/ea9f

Hospital at Rawatkot
H18, Rawatkot, कर्णाली प्रदेश, Nepal
⊕ https://vfmat.ch/3d99

Hospital at Sandhikharka
Gorusinge-Sandhikharka Rajmarga, Sandhikharka, प्रदेश नं. ५, Nepal
⊕ https://vfmat.ch/d993

Hospital at Santalla
H18, Dailekh, Santalla, Nepal
⊕ https://vfmat.ch/e37b

Hospital at Sukhadhik
Sukhadhik, Nepal
⊕ https://vfmat.ch/c55c

Hospital at Thaha
Tribhuvan Highway, Thaha 44100, Nepal
⊕ https://vfmat.ch/a282

Hospital at Urthu-Ghodsen Road
Urthu-Ghodsen, Patmara, Karnali Pradesh, Nepal
⊕ https://vfmat.ch/f963

Hospital Bakulahat Ratnanagar
35DR012, Ratnanagar, Vagmati Pradesh, Nepal
⊕ https://vfmat.ch/f47b

Hospital Mai Manakamana Hospital Pvt. Ltd.
Manakamana, Nepal
⊕ https://vfmat.ch/4b33

Hospital of Amppipal
Thalipokhari-Amppipal, Palumtar, Gandaki Pradesh, Nepal
⊕ https://vfmat.ch/bc74

Hospital Tamakoshi
Khurkot Manthali Road, Manthali, वाग्मती प्रदेश, Nepal
⊕ https://vfmat.ch/1511

Ilam District Hospital
Ilam, Nepal
⊕ https://vfmat.ch/21d6

Inaruwa Hospital
06DR021, Inaruwa, प्रदेश नं. १, Nepal
⊕ https://vfmat.ch/198e

International Friendship Children's Hospital
Kathmandu 44600, Nepal
⊕ https://vfmat.ch/c7bb

Janaki Medical College and Teaching Hospital
Janaki Medical College-Ramdaiya-Sabaila-paterwa Road, Tarapatti Sirsiya, प्रदेश नं. २, Nepal
⊕ https://vfmat.ch/2487

Janakpur Zonal Hospital
Janakpur 45600, Nepal
⊕ https://vfmat.ch/49c6

Jeevan Jyoti Hospital & Diagnostic Center Pvt. Ltd.
Samsi Bajar Tengar Road, Mahottari, Janakpur, Nepal
⊕ https://vfmat.ch/9854

Jilla Pashusewa Karyalaya Dhangadhi
Main Road, Dhangadi Sub Metropolitan, Dhanhadhi, Nepal
⊕ https://vfmat.ch/4c54

Kalaiya Hospital
Barewa Road, Kalaiya, प्रदेश नं. २, Nepal
⊕ https://vfmat.ch/23e6

Kalika Community Hospital
Siddartha Rajmarg, Darsing Dahathum 33800, Nepal
⊕ https://vfmat.ch/8eff

Kanti Children's Hospital
Kathmandu, Nepal
⊕ https://vfmat.ch/2ac6

Kantipur Hospital
Shree Ganesh Marga, काठमाडौं, वाग्मती प्रदेश, Nepal
⊕ https://vfmat.ch/cbc5

Kantipur Institute of Health Science
Bhakti Marg, Pokhara, गण्डकी प्रदेश, Nepal
⊕ https://vfmat.ch/bc45

Karnali Province Hospital
Ratna Rajmarg, Birendranagar, Karnali Pradesh, Nepal
⊕ https://vfmat.ch/a963

Kaski Model Hospital
Pragati Marg, Pokhara, गण्डकी प्रदेश, Nepal
⊕ https://vfmat.ch/ea62

Kathmandu Hospital
त्रिपुरेश्वर मार्ग, Kathmandu 44600, Nepal
⊕ https://vfmat.ch/47c8

Kathmandu Medical College
Goshwara Marga, काठमाडौँ, वाग्मती प्रदेश, Nepal
⊕ https://vfmat.ch/362c

Kathmandu Medical College Teaching Hospital
Om Nagar Marg, काठमाडौँ, वाग्मती प्रदेश, Nepal
⊕ https://vfmat.ch/e4dd

Kathmandu Military Hospital
King Birendra Marg, Kathmandu, Bagmati Pradesh, Nepal
⊕ https://vfmat.ch/768b

Kathmandu Model Hospital
Red Cross Marga, काठमाडौँ, वाग्मती प्रदेश, Nepal
⊕ https://vfmat.ch/82f2

Kawasoti Ayurvedic Hospital
48DR025, Kawaswoti, गण्डकी प्रदेश, Nepal
⊕ https://vfmat.ch/3d55

Kirtipur Hospital
Kirtipur Ring Road, Kirtipur, वाग्मती प्रदेश, Nepal
⊕ https://vfmat.ch/3aa4

KIST Hospital
Sundar Marga, Patan, वाग्मती प्रदेश, Nepal
⊕ https://vfmat.ch/4782

KIST Medical College Teaching Hospital
Gwarko-Lamatar, Imadol, वाग्मती प्रदेश, Nepal
⊕ https://vfmat.ch/2443

Koshi Hospital
Rangeli Road, Biratnagar 56700, Nepal
⊕ https://vfmat.ch/8c77

Koshi Zonal Hospital
Sahid Marg, Biratnagar, प्रदेश नं. १, Nepal
⊕ https://vfmat.ch/37f5

Krisna Prasad Hospital
Banepa-Panauti-Khopasi Road, Banepa 45210, Nepal
⊕ https://vfmat.ch/3c39

Lake City Hospital and Critical Care
Parshyang – Bagale Tole Marga, Pokhara 33700, Nepal
⊕ https://vfmat.ch/fc12

Lalgadh Leprosy Hospital & Services Centre
Ward 10, East – West Highway, Mithila, Dhanusha 45600, Nepal
⊕ https://vfmat.ch/effe

Lalgadh Model Hospital Pvt. Ltd.
E – W Hwy, Mithila 45600, Nepal
⊕ https://vfmat.ch/77d9

Laxmimarga-Dangihat Hospital
34 Laxmimarga-Dangihat Road, Dangihat, प्रदेश नं.

१, Nepal
⊕ https://vfmat.ch/1994

Lekhnath City Hospital
Prithvi Highway, Pokhara, गण्डकी प्रदेश, Nepal
⊕ https://vfmat.ch/ada5

Life Care Hospital at Bharatpur
Mahendra Highway, Bharatpur Metro, वाग्मती प्रदेश, Nepal
⊕ https://vfmat.ch/d894

Life Care Hospital at Kathmandu
Bagdurbar Marg, काठमाडौँ, वाग्मती प्रदेश, Nepal
⊕ https://vfmat.ch/3f5e

Lifeguard Hospital
Bargachhi Chowk, Biratnagar, Eastern Region, Chandani Marg, Biratnagar 56613, Nepal
⊕ https://vfmat.ch/889c

Lukla Hospital
Chaurikharka, प्रदेश नं. १, Nepal
⊕ https://vfmat.ch/6aa4

Lumbini City Hospital
Sarvan Path, Butwal 32907, Nepal
⊕ https://vfmat.ch/6679

Lumbini Medical College
H 10, Tansen 32500, Nepal
⊕ https://vfmat.ch/afcc

Madhyapur Hospital
Araniko Highway, Madhyapur Thimi, Nepal
⊕ https://vfmat.ch/cf2e

Madi Samudayik Hospital Pvt. Ltd.
Madi-Thori, Madi, वाग्मती प्रदेश, Nepal
⊕ https://vfmat.ch/79a7

Mahendra Narayan Nidhi Memorial Hospital
Shreekanti Marg, Kathmandu 44600, Nepal
⊕ https://vfmat.ch/fbfd

Makawanpur Sahakari Hospital
Bhintuna Marg, Hetauda 44107, Nepal
⊕ https://vfmat.ch/8d2f

Manahari Hospital
Manahari 44100, Nepal
⊕ https://vfmat.ch/fe1b

Mangalbare Hospital Urlabari
Urlabari 56600, Nepal
⊕ https://vfmat.ch/4f8c

Manmohan Memorial Hospital
Thamel Marg, Kathmandu 44600, Nepal
⊕ https://vfmat.ch/41b4

Marie Stopes Nepal
Ring Road 44600, Lalitpur 44700, Nepal
⊕ https://vfmat.ch/f7b8

Maruti Children Hospital
Shree Kanti Marg, Kathmandu, Bagmati Pradesh, Nepal
⊕ https://vfmat.ch/f6df

Maya Metro Hospital
H14, Dhangadi Sub Metropolitan, Dhanhadhi, Nepal
⊕ https://vfmat.ch/b572

Mechi Zonal Hospital
Bhadra Purjhapa Mechi Highway, Bhadrapur, Province No. 1, Nepal
⊕ https://vfmat.ch/d7be

Medical House
Shanischare-Milldanda, Shani-Arjun, Province No. 1, Nepal
⊕ https://vfmat.ch/c3af

Metro City Hospital
Srijana Chowk, Pokhara 33700, Nepal
⊕ https://vfmat.ch/4dc3

Mid City Hospital
Arniko Raj Marga, Lokanthali, Vagmati Pradesh, Nepal
⊕ https://vfmat.ch/2bb6

Midat Hospital
Thaina-Prayagpokhari Road, Patan, Bagmati Pradesh, Nepal
⊕ https://vfmat.ch/386f

Mirchaiya Hospital
F52, Mirchaiya, प्रदेश नं. २, Nepal
⊕ https://vfmat.ch/deeb

Mission Hospital Simikot
Simikot 21000, Nepal
⊕ https://vfmat.ch/3dc7

Mountain Medical Institute, The
Namche 56000, Nepal
⊕ https://vfmat.ch/8468

Myagdi Hospital
Beni – Jomsom Road, Arthunge, गण्डकी प्रदेश, Nepal
⊕ https://vfmat.ch/aca7

Namaste Public Hospital
E – W Hwy, Damak 57217, Nepal
⊕ https://vfmat.ch/7b9d

National Tuberculosis Control Center
Araniko Highway, Madhyapur Thimi 44600, Nepal
⊕ https://vfmat.ch/9181

Natural Health Hospital
Prayag Marg, काठमाडौँ, वाग्मती प्रदेश, Nepal
⊕ https://vfmat.ch/a999

Navajeevan Hospital
Main Road, Dhangadi Sub Metropolitan, Dhanhadhi,
Nepal
⊕ https://vfmat.ch/61ef

Nepal Armed Police Force Hospital
Tribhuvan Rajpath, Naya Naikap, वाग्मती प्रदेश, Nepal
⊕ https://vfmat.ch/bd99

Nepal Bharat Maitri Hospital
Ring Road, काठमाडौँ, वाग्मती प्रदेश, Nepal
⊕ https://vfmat.ch/e5ea

**Nepal Cancer Hospital and Research
Centre**
सातदोबाटो – गोदावरी रोड, Lalitpur 44700, Nepal
⊕ https://vfmat.ch/72e7

Nepal Korea Friendship Hospital
Purano Thimi- Naya Thimi, थिमि, वाग्मती प्रदेश,
Nepal
⊕ https://vfmat.ch/3ed4

**Nepal Medical College and Teaching
Hospital**
Gokarneshwar, Nepal
⊕ https://vfmat.ch/d131

Nepal Mediciti Hospital
Bhaisepati Lalitpur, Nepal
⊕ https://vfmat.ch/ca1f

Nepal National Hospital
Ring Road, काठमाडौँ, वाग्मती प्रदेश, Nepal
⊕ https://vfmat.ch/c367

Nepal Orthopaedic Hospital
Way to Pashupati, Kathmandu, वाग्मती प्रदेश, Nepal
⊕ https://vfmat.ch/9fba

Nepal Skin Hospital
Madan Bhandari Path, काठमाडौँ, वाग्मती प्रदेश, Nepal
⊕ https://vfmat.ch/c334

Nepalgunj Medical College
Kasturi Marg, Nepalgunj Sub Metropolitan City, प्रदेश
नं. ५, Nepal
⊕ https://vfmat.ch/47ee

New Amda Hospital
New Amda Road, Damak 57217, Nepal
⊕ https://vfmat.ch/2788

New Life Health Care Pvt. Ltd.
Tushal Marga, काठमाडौँ, वाग्मती प्रदेश, Nepal
⊕ https://vfmat.ch/e63c

New Padma Hospital
Mahakali Highway, Chhatiwan, Jorayal, Nepal
⊕ https://vfmat.ch/adc3

Nidan Hospital
Pulchowk Marg, Patan, वाग्मती प्रदेश, Nepal
⊕ https://vfmat.ch/66e4

Nobel Hospital
Sinamangal Marg, काठमाडौँ, वाग्मती प्रदेश, Nepal
⊕ https://vfmat.ch/49a1

**Nobel Medical College Teaching
Hospital**
Kanchanbari, Biratnagar Metropolitan City– 5,
Biratnagar 56700, Nepal
⊕ https://vfmat.ch/21a7

North Point Hospital
Golfutar Main Road, Tokha, वाग्मती प्रदेश, Nepal
⊕ https://vfmat.ch/a7aa

Okhaldhunga Community Hospital
Siddhicharan 56100, Nepal
⊕ https://vfmat.ch/338d

Om Hospital
Hospital Road, Bharatpur Metro, वाग्मती प्रदेश, Nepal
⊕ https://vfmat.ch/67ab

Padma Hospital Pvt. Ltd.
Attaria Chowk, Attariya 10900, Nepal
⊕ https://vfmat.ch/d832

Panchamukhi Nagarik Hospital Pvt. Ltd.
Yagyabhumi, Dharapani – Kunaghat marga,
Dhanusadham 33000, Nepal
⊕ https://vfmat.ch/75ab

Panchthar Hospital
मेची राजमार्ग, Phidim, प्रदेश नं. १, Nepal
⊕ https://vfmat.ch/939b

Parkland Hospital
Amar Sing Chowk 10, Pokhara 33700, Nepal
⊕ https://vfmat.ch/6dca

Patan Hospital
Mahalaxmisthan Road, Patan, वाग्मती प्रदेश, Nepal
⊕ https://vfmat.ch/f435

Pina Hospital
Pina, कर्णाली प्रदेश, Nepal
⊕ https://vfmat.ch/89df

Pokhara Regional Hospital Pvt. Ltd.
Pokhara Baglung Rajmarg, Pokhara, गण्डकी प्रदेश,
Nepal
⊕ https://vfmat.ch/14ed

**Pulse Health Care & Diagnostics Pvt.
Ltd.**
Kathmandu 44600, Nepal
⊕ https://vfmat.ch/b7ad

Punarjiban Hospital
Ring Road, Patan, वाग्मती प्रदेश, Nepal
⊕ https://vfmat.ch/8c32

Pyuthan Hospital
F14, Pyuthan, प्रदेश नं. ५, Nepal
⊕ https://vfmat.ch/ad21

Rajhar Ayurved Aushadhalaya
Mahendra Highway, Rajahar, गण्डकी प्रदेश, Nepal
⊕ https://vfmat.ch/5945

Ramechhap District Hospital
21DR033, Ramechhap, वाग्मती प्रदेश, Nepal
⊕ https://vfmat.ch/b28d

Rapti Sub-Regional Hospital
F179, घोराही, प्रदेश नं. ५, Nepal
⊕ https://vfmat.ch/3cf9

Red Cross – Patan
Patan, वाग्मती प्रदेश, Nepal
⊕ https://vfmat.ch/7998

Red Cross – Panauti
Malpi Road, Panauti, वाग्मती प्रदेश, Nepal
⊕ https://vfmat.ch/c643

Resunga Hospital
Purano Bazar Road, Tamghas, प्रदेश नं. ५, Nepal
⊕ https://vfmat.ch/ac83

Rolpa District Hospital
F13, Liwang, प्रदेश नं. ५, Nepal
⊕ https://vfmat.ch/dde5

Sagarmatha Zonal Hospital
8 Kunauli Road, Rajbiraj, प्रदेश नं. २, Nepal
⊕ https://vfmat.ch/5423

Sahara Hospital
Pokhara, गण्डकी प्रदेश, Nepal
⊕ https://vfmat.ch/e51f

Sahodar Hospital
Dhamilikuwa 33600, Nepal
⊕ https://vfmat.ch/fac2

Sai Archana Hospital
Hospital Marg, Pokhara, गण्डकी प्रदेश, Nepal
⊕ https://vfmat.ch/787f

Saptari Model Hospital
Kushaha 56400, Nepal
⊕ https://vfmat.ch/ac1a

Sarbodhaya Sewa Ashram
Tarkughat, Nepal
⊕ https://vfmat.ch/e39b

Sarvanga Hospital
Kupondol Marg, Patan, वाग्मती प्रदेश, Nepal
⊕ https://vfmat.ch/62df

Satya Sai Hospital
Araniko Highway, Banepa, वाग्मती प्रदेश, Nepal
⊕ https://vfmat.ch/adc7

Scheer Memorial Adventist Hospital
Banepa 45210, Nepal
⊕ https://vfmat.ch/cafb

Seti Zonal Hospital, Dhangadhi
Main Road, Dhangadhi Sub Metropolitan, Dhangadhi, Nepal
⊕ https://vfmat.ch/e7bd

Shankarapur Hospital
Jorpati Main Road, Kathmandu, वाग्मती प्रदेश, Nepal
⊕ https://vfmat.ch/b782

Shanti Sewa Griha
Tilaganga B marga, काठमाडौँ, वाग्मती प्रदेश, Nepal
⊕ https://vfmat.ch/3c71

Shree Birendra Hospital
Chhauni Hospital Road, Kathmandu 44600, Nepal
⊕ https://vfmat.ch/3e34

Shree Memorial Hospital
Chandeshwori Marga, Banepa, वाग्मती प्रदेश, Nepal
⊕ https://vfmat.ch/b13d

Shree Tribhuwan Chandra Sainik Hospital
New Road, काठमाडौँ, वाग्मती प्रदेश, Nepal
⊕ https://vfmat.ch/761f

Shuvatara Hospital
Mahalaxmisthan Road, Patan, Bagmati Pradesh, Nepal
⊕ https://vfmat.ch/deb7

Siddhi Memorial Hospital
Hanumante, Bhaktapur, Vagmati Pradesh Nepal
⊕ https://vfmat.ch/7511

Sindhupalchok District Hospital
Chautara-Nawalpur Road, Chautara 45301 Nepal
⊕ https://vfmat.ch/82e7

Siraha District Hospital
Madar – Siraha – Choharwa, Siraha, State No. 2, Nepal
⊕ https://vfmat.ch/ca43

Skin Hospital, The
Lazimpat Road, Kathmandu, Bagmati Pradesh, Nepal
⊕ https://vfmat.ch/d774

Spark B and D Hospital
Jalpa Road, Pokhara, Gandaki Pradesh Nepal
⊕ https://vfmat.ch/544e

Sri Tribhubana Chandra Military Hospital
New Road, Kathmandu 44600, Nepal
⊕ https://vfmat.ch/942f

Star Hospital
Ring Road, Patan, Bagmati Pradesh, Nepal
⊕ https://vfmat.ch/e99a

Sumeru City Hospital
Patan, Bagmati Pradesh, Nepal
⊕ https://vfmat.ch/2738

Sumeru Hospital
F102, Dhapakhel, Vagmati Pradesh, Nepal
⊕ https://vfmat.ch/4b98

Summit Hospital
Tikathali-Lokanthali Road, Lokanthali, Vagmati Pradesh, Nepal
⊕ https://vfmat.ch/6d8b

Surkhet Hospital Pvt. Ltd.
Birendranagar 21700, Nepal
⊕ https://vfmat.ch/26e5

Susma Koirala Memorial Hospital
Sankhu Road, Shankharapur, Vagmati Pradesh, Nepal
⊕ https://vfmat.ch/e92d

Suvechhya Hospital
F75, Kathmandu, Bagmati Pradesh, Nepal
⊕ https://vfmat.ch/8f5c

Swabhiman Hospital Pvt. Ltd.
Hariwon-11, Hariyon, Nepal
⊕ https://vfmat.ch/2e38

T. U. Teaching Hospital
Kathepul Parsa Road, Khairahani, Bagmati Pradesh, Nepal
⊕ https://vfmat.ch/a9fb

Tamghas Hospital
Resunga 32600, Nepal
⊕ https://vfmat.ch/63e7

Taplejung District Hospital
Taplejung 57500, Nepal
⊕ https://vfmat.ch/4dcd

Taulihawa District Hospital
Kapilvastu, Nepal
⊕ https://vfmat.ch/2d25

Teaching Hospital, Karnali Academy of Health Sciences
Hospital Route, Chandannath 21200, Nepal
⊕ https://vfmat.ch/71a8

Terhathum District Hospital
Myanglung 57100, Nepal
⊕ https://vfmat.ch/78d7

Tikapur Hospital
Tikapur Hospital Road, Tikapur, Tikapur, Nepal
⊕ https://vfmat.ch/c48d

Tilahar Old Hospital
Tilahar Sadak, Tilahar 33400, Nepal
⊕ https://vfmat.ch/7d62

Tilottama Hospital
Butwal 32907, Nepal
⊕ https://vfmat.ch/f294

Trishuli Hospital
28DR008, Bidur, Bagmati Pradesh, Nepal
⊕ https://vfmat.ch/5899

TU Teaching Hospital
Maharajgunj, Kathmandu, Nepal
⊕ https://vfmat.ch/a5c7

United Mission Hospital Tansen
Tansen, Nepal
⊕ https://vfmat.ch/f35f

Vayodha Hospital
Ring Road, Kathmandu, Vagmati Pradesh, Nepal
⊕ https://vfmat.ch/f81b

Venus International Hospital
Puja Pratisthan Marga, Kathmandu, Vagmati Pradesh, Nepal
⊕ https://vfmat.ch/3777

Wellness Hospital Pvt. Ltd.
Bansbari Road, Kathmandu, Vagmati Pradesh, Nepal
⊕ https://vfmat.ch/8e52

Western Hospital
Charbahini Road 10, Nepalgunj 21900, Nepal
⊕ https://vfmat.ch/91fe

Western Regional Hospital
Hospital Marg, Pokhara, Gandaki Region, Nepal
⊕ https://vfmat.ch/214f

Yeti Hospital
Ring Road, Kathmandu, Vagmati Pradesh, Nepal
⊕ https://vfmat.ch/293a

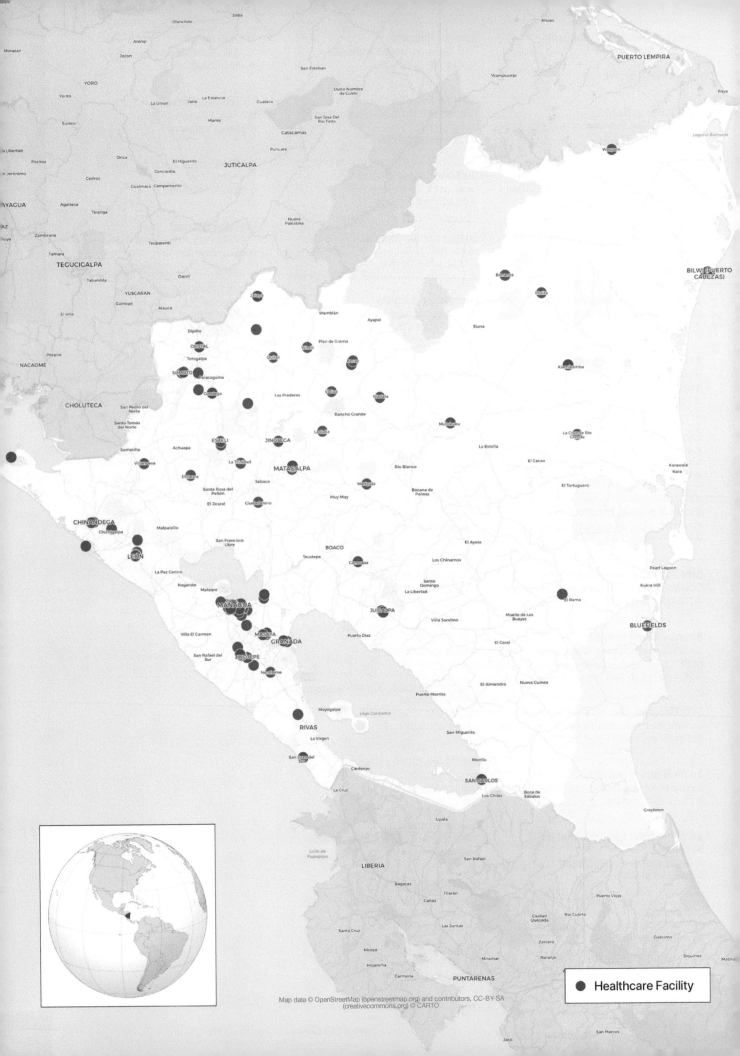

Healthcare Facility

Nicaragua

The Republic of Nicaragua, in Central America, between the Pacific Ocean and the Caribbean Sea, is bordered by Honduras to the northwest, the Caribbean to the east, Costa Rica to the south, and the Pacific Ocean to the southwest. Known for its dramatic terrain of lakes, volcanoes, and beaches, the country has a population of a little over 6.2 million people, with 74 percent age 15 and above. Nicaragua has a multiracial population comprising Africans, indigenous Europeans, and people of Asian heritage. Spanish is the official language. Managua is the country's largest city and capital. Nicaragua's constitution guarantees and promotes religious freedom and tolerance. Though Christianity is the dominant religion, the country has no official religion.

The Republic of Nicaragua gained independence from Spain in 1821 and subsequently became an autonomous territory in 1860. Since independence, the country has faced the challenges of political instability, dictatorship, occupation, fiscal crises, riots such as the Nicaraguan Revolution of the 1960s and 1970s, and the Contra war of the 1980s. Nicaragua has one of the most constricted and challenged economies in the Americas. According to the United Nations Development Programme, 48 percent of the Nicaraguan population lives below the poverty line, with 79.9 percent living on less than $2 per day. With poverty and under-employment on the rise, Nicaragua remains the poorest country in Central America.

The Nicaraguan population faces many challenges as a result of pervasive poverty and poor economic development, including challenges in health. Life expectancy in Nicaragua is 74 years. Despite some improvements in health indicators, the main contributors to death in the country are predominantly non-communicable diseases, including ischemic heart disease, chronic kidney disease, stroke, diabetes, cirrhosis, COPD, Alzheimer's disease, hypertensive heart disease, and congenital defects. Additionally, lower respiratory infections, road injuries, and neonatal disorders are significant causes of death.

6.2M

Population

$1,905

GDP Per Capita

74 years

Life Expectancy

↑ Improving

167
Doctors/100k

Physician Density

93
Beds/100k

Hospital Bed Density

98
Deaths/100k

Maternal Mortality

Nicaragua

Nonprofit Organizations

A Broader View Volunteers
Provides developing countries around the world with significant volunteer programs that aid the neediest communities and forge a lasting bond between those volunteering and those they have helped.
Dent-OMFS, ER Med, Infect Dis, MF Med
⊕ https://vfmat.ch/3bec

A Reason to Smile (ARTS)
Empowers communities without access to dental professionals to achieve and maintain a higher level of oral health by providing hygiene education, direct treatment, and dental supplies.
Dent-OMFS
⊕ https://vfmat.ch/3bae

Action Against Hunger
Aims to end life-threatening hunger for good through treating and preventing malnutrition across more than 45 countries.
Nutr
⊕ https://vfmat.ch/2dbc

Adventist Health International
Focuses on upgrading and managing mission hospitals by providing governance, consultation, and technical assistance to a number of affiliated Seventh-Day Adventist hospitals throughout Africa, Asia, and the Americas.
Dent-OMFS, General, Pub Health
⊕ https://vfmat.ch/16aa

AID FOR AIDS International
Aims to empower communities at risk of HIV and the population at large with comprehensive prevention through treatment, advocacy, education, and training.
Infect Dis, Logist-Op, Nutr, Psych, Pub Health
⊕ https://vfmat.ch/c43e

Aloha Medical Mission
Brings hope and changes the lives of people; serves overseas and in Hawai'i.
Anesth, Crit-Care, Dent-OMFS, ENT, ER Med, General, Medicine, OB-GYN, Ophth-Opt, Ortho, Ped Surg, Peds, Plast, Surg, Urol
⊕ https://vfmat.ch/72ac

American Academy of Pediatrics
Seeks to attain optimal physical, mental, and social health and well-being for all infants, children, adolescents, and young adults.
Anesth, Crit-Care, Neonat, Ped Surg
⊕ https://vfmat.ch/9633

American Nicaraguan Foundation (ANF)
Works to reduce the impact of poverty on the most vulnerable communities in Nicaragua through efforts in housing, health, nutrition, education, water and sanitation, agriculture, and humanitarian aid.

Logist-Op, Nutr, Pub Health
⊕ https://vfmat.ch/174a

Americares
Saves lives and improves health for people affected by poverty or disaster and responds with life-changing medicine, medical supplies, and health programs including domestic and global medical clinics.
All-Immu, ER Med, General, Infect Dis, MF Med, Nutr
⊕ https://vfmat.ch/e567

Americas Association for the Care of Children (AACC)
Reduces the impact of poverty in marginalized and underserved populations by empowering communities through compassionate and holistic education.
Dent-OMFS, MF Med, OB-GYN, Pub Health
⊕ https://vfmat.ch/19c5

Amsterdam Institute for Global Health and Development (AIGHD)
Provides sustainable solutions to major health problems across our planet by forging synergies among disciplines, healthcare delivery, research, and education.
Infect Dis
⊕ https://vfmat.ch/d73d

Amurtel
Aims to alleviate suffering and provide immediate and long-term relief to women and children in need, and to improve their overall quality of life.

⊕ https://vfmat.ch/2b19

Arbeiter Samariter Bund (Workers' Samaritan Federation)
Engages in areas such as civil protection, rescue services, and social welfare, while operating a network of welcome centers to help refugees.
ER Med, General, Infect Dis, Logist-Op, Rehab
⊕ https://vfmat.ch/8a5b

Ascenta Foundation
Provides urgent medical, dental, optometric, and surgical services, along with health education, to medically underserved communities.
Dent-OMFS, General, Ophth-Opt, Pub Health, Surg
⊕ https://vfmat.ch/418f

Austin Samaritans
Seeks to support the people of Nicaragua in three key areas: education, healthcare, and support for the vulnerable.
Dent-OMFS, General, OB-GYN, Pub Health
⊕ https://vfmat.ch/9e3e

Benjamin H. Josephson, MD Fund
Provides healthcare professionals with the financial resources necessary to

deliver medical services for those in need throughout the world.
General, OB-GYN
⊕ https://vfmat.ch/6acc

Bless Back Worldwide
Collaborates with local partners in communities in Haiti and Nicaragua to enhance healthcare, empower businesses and enrich education.
Dent-OMFS, General, Logist-Op, OB-GYN, Peds, Pub Health
⊕ https://vfmat.ch/763d

Bless The Children
Aims to help abandoned and impoverished children by empowering them with health, shelter, and nutritional and educational support.
CT Surg, Dent-OMFS, General, Logist-Op, Nutr, Pub Health, Surg
⊕ https://vfmat.ch/f19d

Bridge of Life
Aims to strengthen healthcare globally through sustainable programs that prevent and treat chronic disease.
Logist-Op, Nephro, OB-GYN, Peds, Surg
⊕ https://vfmat.ch/5b68

CARE
Works around the globe to save lives, defeat poverty, and achieve social justice.
ER Med, General
⊕ https://vfmat.ch/7232

Carter Center, The
Seeks to prevent and resolve conflicts, enhance freedom and democracy, and improve health, while remaining committed to human rights and the alleviation of human suffering.
Infect Dis, MF Med, Ophth-Opt
⊕ https://vfmat.ch/6556

Centers of Hope Missions International
Sharing the love of Christ through feeding centers, churches, medical mission trips, and orphan care.
General
⊕ https://vfmat.ch/a9ac

ChildFund Australia
Works to reduce poverty for children in many of the world's most disadvantaged communities.
ER Med, General, Peds
⊕ https://vfmat.ch/13df

Children of War Foundation
Delivers access to global health and education to communities affected by poverty, war, natural disaster, climate change, and migration challenges.
ER Med, General, Logist-Op, Peds, Surg
⊕ https://vfmat.ch/de51

Children Without Worms
Enhances the health and development of children by reducing intestinal worm infections.
Infect Dis, Pub Health
⊕ https://vfmat.ch/6bee

Christian Aid Ministries
Strives to be a trustworthy and efficient channel for Amish, Mennonite, and other conservative Anabaptist groups and individuals to minister to physical and spiritual needs around the world.
CT Surg, ER Med, Logist-Op, Ortho, Pub Health
⊕ https://vfmat.ch/7b33

Christian Blind Mission (CBM)
Aims to improve the quality of life of persons with disabilities in the poorest countries, addressing poverty as a cause and a consequence of disability, and working in partnership to create a society for all.
ENT, General, Infect Dis, OB-GYN, Ophth-Opt, Ortho, Peds, Psych, Rehab, Surg
⊕ https://vfmat.ch/3824

Christian Connections for International Health (CCIH)
Promotes global health and wholeness from a Christian perspective.
All-Immu, General, Infect Dis, MF Med, Neonat, OB-GYN, Psych
⊕ https://vfmat.ch/fa5d

Christian Medical & Dental Associations
Based in Christian ministry, deploys medical and dental teams to underserved communities to provide vital healthcare.
Anesth, Dent-OMFS, ER Med, General, Medicine, OB-GYN, Ophth-Opt, Peds, Pub Health, Radiol, Rehab, Surg
⊕ https://vfmat.ch/921c

Christian Ophthalmic Surgery Expedition Network (ChOSEN)
Inspired by the Christian faith, seeks to restore the sight of impoverished people through ophthalmic surgery.
Logist-Op, Ophth-Opt
⊕ https://vfmat.ch/1d9b

Circle of Empowerment
Inspired by the Christian faith, works in health, education, and economics to promote an improved quality of life for the people of Aposentillo, Nicaragua.
Dent-OMFS, General, Logist-Op, Neuro, Ortho, Pub Health, Rehab
⊕ https://vfmat.ch/1cd2

Circle of Health International (COHI)
Aligns with local, community-based organizations led and powered by women to help respond to the needs of the women and children that they serve. Helps with the provision of professional volunteers, capacity training, and procurement of requested and appropriate supplies and equipment. Raises funds for the organizations to provide the services required.
ER Med, Logist-Op, MF Med, Neonat, OB-GYN, Psych
⊕ https://vfmat.ch/8b63

Clinica Verde
Provides community-based healthcare and hands-on health education for women and their families in rural Nicaragua, through a preventive approach.
Dent-OMFS, Geri, Infect Dis, Nutr, OB-GYN, Ophth-Opt, Path, Peds, Psych, Radiol
⊕ https://vfmat.ch/6c23

Compassion Med International
Supports medical relief missions worldwide, inspired by the Christian faith.
ER Med, General
⊕ https://vfmat.ch/2615

Connecticut Quest for Peace
Provides humanitarian aid to impoverished communities in Nicaragua through education, microfinance, healthcare, and the provision of supplies.
Dent-OMFS, Ophth-Opt
⊕ https://vfmat.ch/c861

Cross Catholic Outreach
Mobilizes the global Catholic Church to transform impoverished communities through the provision of food, water, housing, education, orphan support, medical care, microenterprise, and disaster relief.
All-Immu, General, Nutr, OB-GYN, Rehab
⊕ https://vfmat.ch/22f4

Dentistry For All
Donates time and services toward dental education, prevention, and corrective treatment to those who cannot otherwise access care.
Dent-OMFS
⊕ https://vfmat.ch/f3e2

Dianova
Works in prevention and treatment of addiction, while promoting social progress in international forums.
Psych, Pub Health
⊕ https://vfmat.ch/1998

Direct Relief
Improves the health and lives of people affected by poverty or emergency situations by mobilizing and providing essential medical resources needed for

their care.
ER Med, Logist-Op
⊕ https://vfmat.ch/58e5

Doctors Without Borders/Médecins Sans Frontières (MSF)
Responds to emergencies and provides lifesaving medical care where needed most, including during disasters, conflicts, and epidemics.
Anesth, Crit-Care, ER Med, General, Infect Dis, Nutr, OB-GYN, Ped Surg, Peds, Psych, Pub Health, Surg
⊕ https://vfmat.ch/f363

Duke University: Global Health Institute
Sparks innovation in global health research and education, and brings together knowledge and resources to address the most important global health issues of our time.
All-Immu, Infect Dis, MF Med, OB-GYN, Pub Health
⊕ https://vfmat.ch/c4cd

El Ayudante, Inc.
Dedicates efforts to partnering with the Nicaraguan people to transform their communities through housing, education, nutrition, and proper medical care.
General, Ortho, Rehab
⊕ https://vfmat.ch/b743

Episcopal Relief & Development
Provides relief in times of disaster and promotes sustainable development by identifying and addressing the root causes of suffering.
Infect Dis, MF Med, Neonat, Nutr, Peds
⊕ https://vfmat.ch/7cfa

Esperança
Works to improve health and provide hope through disease prevention, education, and medical/surgical treatment.
Anesth, Dent-OMFS, ENT, General, Neurosurg, Nutr, OB-GYN, Ophth-Opt, Ortho, Ped Surg, Peds, Plast, Pub Health, Surg, Urol, Vasc Surg
⊕ https://vfmat.ch/5cf3

For The Ninos
Inspired by the Christian faith, helps meet the medical, educational, and spiritual needs of Nicaraguans through medical teams, infrastructure support, education, and financial generosity.
Dent-OMFS, General, Infect Dis, OB-GYN, Rheum
⊕ https://vfmat.ch/2e79

Foundation For International Education In Neurological Surgery (FIENS), The
Provides hands-on training and education to neurosurgeons around the world.
Neuro, Neurosurg, Surg
⊕ https://vfmat.ch/bab8

Foundation for International Medical Relief of Children (FIMRC)
Provides access to healthcare for low-resource and medically underserved families around the world.
General, Infect Dis, Peds, Pub Health
⊕ https://vfmat.ch/78b9

Fracarita International
Provides support and services in the fields of mental healthcare, care for people with a disability, and education.
Psych, Rehab
⊕ https://vfmat.ch/8d3c

Friends of Hope International
Works with vulnerable and at-risk youth in Latin America and the Caribbean by providing food assistance, creating self-sustainable animal husbandry, agriculture and technical projects, and empowering communities towards self-sufficiency.
General, Nutr
⊕ https://vfmat.ch/6e9f

Friends of Rudy (FOR) Nicaraguan Health, Inc.
Brings medical aid to impoverished people of Nicaragua who have limited access to healthcare, sharing medical techniques with FOR's local counterparts.

CV Med, Dent-OMFS, GI, General, Ophth-Opt, Peds, Pub Health
⊕ https://vfmat.ch/9a73

Gift of Life International
Provides lifesaving cardiac treatment to children in developing countries while developing sustainable pediatric cardiac programs by implementing screening, surgical, and training missions.
Anesth, CT Surg, CV Med, Crit-Care, Ped Surg, Peds, Pulm-Critic
⊕ https://vfmat.ch/f2f9

GivingMore
Provides free healthcare and resources such as medical supplies and medications, while providing education in first aid, CPR, basic life support, nutrition, and preventive healthcare.
Dent-OMFS, ER Med, General, Infect Dis, Pub Health
⊕ https://vfmat.ch/923a

Global Brigades
Aims to inspire, mobilize, and collaborate with communities to implement their own healthcare and economic goals.
Dent-OMFS, General, Medicine, OB-GYN, Peds
⊕ https://vfmat.ch/78b2

Global Health Partners (GHP)
Aims to improve the health of children in Latin America through medical treatment, resources and education to create self-sustaining healthcare delivery systems.
Logist-Op, Pub Health, Rehab
⊕ https://vfmat.ch/235a

Global Medical Training
Provides free medical and dental services to communities in Central America, and allows medical students, professionals, and others to expand their medical and cultural awareness.
Dent-OMFS, General, Logist-Op, Pub Health
⊕ https://vfmat.ch/3449

Global Ministries – The United Methodist Church
As the worldwide mission and development agency of The United Methodist Church, Global Ministries works with more than 300 hospitals and clinics around the world through its Global Health Unit.
Anesth, CT Surg, CV Med, Crit-Care, Dent-OMFS, Derm, ER Med, GI, General, Infect Dis, Logist-Op, MF Med, Medicine, Neonat, Nephro, Nutr, OB-GYN, Ophth-Opt, Ortho, Palliative, Peds, Pod, Psych, Pub Health, Rehab, Rheum, Surg, Urol
⊕ https://vfmat.ch/1723

Global Oncology (GO)
Brings the best in cancer care to underserved patients around the world and collaborates across geographic, professional, and academic borders to improve cancer care, research, and education.
Heme-Onc, Path, Rad-Onc
⊕ https://vfmat.ch/fcb8

Global Vision 2020
Provides prescription eyeglasses to people who live in parts of the world lacking necessary infrastructure for obtaining affordable corrective eyewear.
Logist-Op, Ophth-Opt
⊕ https://vfmat.ch/7373

Globus Relief
Aims to improve the delivery of healthcare worldwide by gathering, processing, and distributing surplus medical supplies to charities at home and abroad.
Logist-Op
⊕ https://vfmat.ch/a2b7

Good Shepard International Foundation
Strives to promote inclusive and sustainable development for the most marginalized and vulnerable people, with a special focus on women, girls, and children, inspired by the Christian faith.
ER Med
⊕ https://vfmat.ch/ad9a

Grassroot Soccer

Leverages the power of soccer to educate, inspire, and mobilize at-risk youth in developing countries to overcome their greatest health challenges, live healthier and more productive lives, and be agents for change in their communities.
Infect Dis
⊕ https://vfmat.ch/3521

Hand Help, Inc.

Provides volunteer surgical expeditions to developing nations to perform hand surgery for people who otherwise might not be helped.
Ortho, Plast
⊕ https://vfmat.ch/9c2f

Hand in Hand Ministries

Works hand in hand with individuals and communities and responds to expressed needs through cultural immersion, education, housing, and healthcare.
Infect Dis, Logist-Op, Pub Health
⊕ https://vfmat.ch/da2b

Healing the Children

Helps underserved children around the world secure the medical care they need to lead more fulfilling lives.
Anesth, Dent-OMFS, ENT, General, Medicine, Ophth-Opt, Ped Surg, Peds, Plast, Surg
⊕ https://vfmat.ch/d4ee

Health Care Volunteers International

Provides direct patient care, capacity building, and educational projects in developing countries, and specializes in leveraging technology in order to provide low-cost solutions, drive better outcomes, and expand care to far more individuals in need around the globe.
General, OB-GYN, Peds, Plast, Rehab
⊕ https://vfmat.ch/69a6

Health Talents International (HTI)

Inspired by the Christian faith, seeks to provide teaching and healing services, including surgical mission trips in areas of dentistry, ophthalmology, general surgery, OB/GYN, and otolaryngology.
Dent-OMFS, General, OB-GYN, Ophth-Opt, Plast, Surg, Urol
⊕ https://vfmat.ch/9aa2

Health Volunteers Overseas (HVO)

Improves the availability and quality of healthcare through the education, training, and professional development of the health workforce in resource-scarce countries.
All-Immu, Anesth, CV Med, Dent-OMFS, Derm, ENT, ER Med, Endo, GI, Heme-Onc, Infect Dis, Medicine, Medicine, Nephro, Neuro, OB-GYN, Ophth-Opt, Ortho, Peds, Plast, Psych, Pulm-Critic, Rehab, Rheum, Surg
⊕ https://vfmat.ch/42b2

Health&Help

Treats people living in places where it is otherwise difficult or impossible to get medical care.
Derm, ENT, Endo, General, Infect Dis, Logist-Op, OB-GYN, Peds
⊕ https://vfmat.ch/913e

HealthWorks Collaborative

Focuses on providing public healthcare including surgery, clean water, and improved sanitation, safe cooking methods, health education, and disease prevention to underserved populations.
Logist-Op, Ped Surg, Pub Health
⊕ https://vfmat.ch/e492

Hear the World Foundation

Advocates worldwide for equal opportunities and improved quality of life for people in need with hearing loss.
ENT, Peds
⊕ https://vfmat.ch/122c

Hearts Touching Hearts Foundation

Inspired by theChristian faith, aims to break the cycle of poverty and reduce the number of families living in critical economic conditions by creating multifaceted programs such as those in humanitarian aid, nutrition, and health.

General, Logist-Op, Nutr, Peds
⊕ https://vfmat.ch/fa1a

Heineman Medical Outreach

Provides medical and educational assistance globally to promote sustainable healthcare and enhanced living standards in underserved communities through the International Medical Outreach (IMO) program, a collaborative partnership between Heineman Medical Outreach and Atrium Health.
Anesth, CT Surg, CV Med, ER Med, General, Heme-Onc, Logist-Op, Medicine, Neonat, OB-GYN, Ped Surg, Peds, Surg, Vasc Surg
⊕ https://vfmat.ch/389b

Helping Hands Health Education

Provides sustainable health and education services to children and adults throughout the world.
Dent-OMFS, General, Logist-Op, OB-GYN, Ophth-Opt, Peds
⊕ https://vfmat.ch/36da

Hope Worldwide

Changes lives through the compassion and commitment of dedicated staff and volunteers delivering sustainable, high-impact, community-based services to the poor and underserved.
Dent-OMFS, General, OB-GYN, Ophth-Opt, Peds
⊕ https://vfmat.ch/89b3

Hopeful Ways

Provides medical and humanitarian services and educational opportunities to the people of Nicaragua, to improve quality of life for the impoverished.
ENT, Ophth-Opt, Pub Health
⊕ https://vfmat.ch/f225

House of Hope International

Inspired by the Christian faith, provides rehabilitation for women and children leaving the world of prostitution and human trafficking and helps integrate them into society.
Dent-OMFS, General, OB-GYN
⊕ https://vfmat.ch/2dbb

Humanity & Inclusion

Works alongside people with disabilities and vulnerable populations, taking action and bearing witness in order to respond to their essential needs, improve their living conditions and health, and promote respect for their dignity and fundamental rights.
General, Infect Dis, MF Med, Medicine, Ortho, Peds, Psych, Pub Health, Rehab
⊕ https://vfmat.ch/16b7

IMA World Health

Works to build healthier communities by collaborating with key partners to serve vulnerable people with a focus on health, healing, and well-being for all.
Infect Dis, MF Med, Nutr, OB-GYN, Pub Health
⊕ https://vfmat.ch/8316

IMAHelps

Organizes medical humanitarian missions that provide some of the world's most underserved people with everything from general medical and dental care to life-changing surgeries, prosthetics, and other specialized services that reflect the expertise of our volunteers.
Anesth, CV Med, Dent-OMFS, Neuro, OB-GYN, Ophth-Opt, Ortho, Ped Surg, Peds, Plast, Rehab, Surg
⊕ https://vfmat.ch/d56b

Interfaith Service to Latin America (ISLA)

Aims to improve the quality of life for communities in Latin America, especially Jalapa, Nicaragua, by carrying out programs in healthcare, education, and infrastructure.
General, OB-GYN, Pub Health, Vasc Surg
⊕ https://vfmat.ch/975a

International Children's Heart Foundation

Provides free surgical care, medical training, and technology to save the lives of children with congenital heart disease in developing countries.
Anesth, CT Surg, CV Med, Crit-Care, Ped Surg, Peds, Pulm-Critic
⊕ https://vfmat.ch/86c1

International Eye Foundation (IEF)
Eliminates preventable and treatable blindness by making quality sustainable eye care services accessible and affordable worldwide.
Infect Dis, Logist-Op, Ophth-Opt
⊕ https://vfmat.ch/e839

International Eye Institute, Inc.
Provides adult and pediatric medical and surgical eye care to people with little access to these services.
Ophth-Opt
⊕ https://vfmat.ch/6242

International Federation of Gynecology and Obstetrics (FIGO)
Implements global projects on specific women's health issues.
MF Med, Medicine, Neonat, OB-GYN, Surg, Urol
⊕ https://vfmat.ch/c4b4

International Federation of Red Cross and Red Crescent Societies (IFRC)
Coordinates and directs international assistance following natural and manmade disasters in nonconflict situations through the world's largest humanitarian and development network. Provides disaster-preparedness programs, healthcare activities, and promotes humanitarian values.
ER Med, General, Infect Dis, Nutr
⊕ https://vfmat.ch/b4ee

International Insulin Foundation
Aims to prolong the life and promote the health of people with diabetes in developing countries by improving the supply of insulin and education in its use.
Endo, Logist-Op
⊕ https://vfmat.ch/d34f

International Organization for Migration (IOM) – The UN Migration Agency
Promotes evidence-informed policies and holistic, preventive, and curative health programs that are beneficial, accessible, and equitable for vulnerable migrants.
General, Infect Dis, OB-GYN
⊕ https://vfmat.ch/621a

InterSurgeon
Fosters collaborative partnerships in the field of global surgery that will advance clinical care, teaching, training, research, and the provision and maintenance of medical equipment.
ENT, Neurosurg, Ortho, Ped Surg, Plast, Surg, Urol
⊕ https://vfmat.ch/6f8a

Ipas
Focuses efforts on women and girls who want contraception or abortion, and builds programs around their needs and how best to support them.
OB-GYN
⊕ https://vfmat.ch/8e39

Iris Global
Serves the poor, the destitute, the lost, and the forgotten by providing adoration, outreach, family, education, relief, development, healing, and the arts.
General, Infect Dis, Nutr, Pub Health
⊕ https://vfmat.ch/37f8

Izumi Foundation
Develops and supports programs that improve health and healthcare in neglected regions of Africa and Latin America.

⊕ https://vfmat.ch/f29a

John Snow, Inc. (JSI)
Aims to improve the health and well-being of underserved and vulnerable people and communities throughout the world.
General, Infect Dis, Logist-Op, MF Med, OB-GYN, Peds, Psych, Pub Health
⊕ https://vfmat.ch/ba78

Johns Hopkins Center for Global Health
Facilitates and focuses the extensive expertise and resources of the Johns Hopkins institutions, together with global collaborators, to effectively address and ameliorate the world's most pressing health issues.
General, Genetics, Logist-Op, MF Med, Peds, Psych, Pub Health, Pulm-Critic
⊕ https://vfmat.ch/54ce

Joint United Nations Programme on HIV/AIDS (UNAIDS)
Aims to place people living with HIV and people affected by the virus at the decision-making table and at the center of designing, delivering, and monitoring the AIDS response.
Infect Dis
⊕ https://vfmat.ch/464a

Leadership in Medicine for the Underserved Program at MSU, The
Provides medical students the knowledge and skills necessary to address the varied medical needs of urban, rural, and international underserved populations.
Dent-OMFS, ER Med, Medicine, Nutr, OB-GYN, Peds, Pub Health, Radiol, Surg
⊕ https://vfmat.ch/84f1

Lifebox
Seeks to provide safer surgery and anesthesia in low-resource countries by investing in tools, training, and partnerships for safe surgery.
Anesth, Crit-Care, Surg
⊕ https://vfmat.ch/2d4d

Lily Project, The
Aims to create healthier futures for women and girls in Nicaragua through a women-driven model of development and care.
Logist-Op, OB-GYN, Pub Health, Pub Health
⊕ https://vfmat.ch/99b5

MAGNA International
Helps those who are suffering or recovering from conflicts and disasters by reducing the risks of diseases and treating them immediately.
ER Med, General, Infect Dis, Peds, Surg
⊕ https://vfmat.ch/58f4

Management Sciences for Health (MSH)
Works with countries and communities to save lives and improve the health of the world's poorest and most vulnerable people by building strong, resilient, sustainable health systems.
Infect Dis, Logist-Op, Pub Health
⊕ https://vfmat.ch/6aa2

MAP International
Provides medicines and health supplies to those in need around the world so they might experience life to the fullest.
Logist-Op
⊕ https://vfmat.ch/deed

Maverick Collective
Aims to build a global community of strategic philanthropists and informed advocates who use their intellectual and financial resources to create change.
Infect Dis, MF Med, OB-GYN
⊕ https://vfmat.ch/ea49

Medical Ambassadors International
Equipping communities through Christ-centered health and development.
Nutr, OB-GYN, Pub Health
⊕ https://vfmat.ch/8e76

Medical Equipment Modernization Opportunity (MEMO)
Based in Christian ministry, works with churches and organizations to collect and send hospital equipment and supplies to healthcare facilities in need around the world.
Logist-Op
⊕ https://vfmat.ch/1c78

Medical Missions Outreach
Visits developing countries to provide quality, ethical healthcare and outreach to those in need, based in Christian ministry.
Dent-OMFS, Ophth-Opt, Ortho, Surg
⊕ https://vfmat.ch/1197

Medical Relief Foundation
Provides quality education and comprehensive healthcare partnerships that are responsive to the needs of the patients, the host country, and the community.
CT Surg, ER Med, General, Infect Dis, Vasc Surg
⊕ https://vfmat.ch/9add

MEDLIFE Movement
Partners with low-income communities in Latin America and Africa to improve access to medicine, education, and community development projects.
Dent-OMFS, General, Peds, Pub Health
⊕ https://vfmat.ch/de87

MedShare
Aims to improve the quality of life of people, communities, and the planet by sourcing and directly delivering surplus medical supplies and equipment to communities in need around the world.
Logist-Op
⊕ https://vfmat.ch/c8bc

Mercy Kids, The
Brings hope and healing to children experiencing disability in Nicaragua.
Dent-OMFS, General, Logist-Op, Neuro, Nutr, Ortho, Rehab
⊕ https://vfmat.ch/e535

MiracleFeet
Brings low-cost treatment to every child on the planet born with clubfoot, a leading cause of physical disability.
Ortho, Peds, Rehab
⊕ https://vfmat.ch/bda8

Mission Regan
Collects supplies, medication, and medical equipment and provides them to those who are in desperate need, both locally and globally.
Logist-Op
⊕ https://vfmat.ch/2bc1

Missions of Grace
Inspired by the Christian faith, aims to bring medical aid, disaster relief, and a better quality of life to impoverished peoples of the world.
General, Logist-Op, MF Med, Pub Health, Radiol
⊕ https://vfmat.ch/7d14

Mustard Seed Communities (MSC)
Inspired by the Christian faith, uplifts the most vulnerable members of society through nutrition, education, community development, child health, and sustainable agriculture programs.
Infect Dis, Logist-Op, Rehab
⊕ https://vfmat.ch/eac5

Médecins du Monde/Doctors of the World
Provides care, bears witness, and supports social change worldwide with innovative medical programs and evidence-based advocacy initiatives.
ER Med, General, Infect Dis, MF Med, Neonat, OB-GYN, Peds, Pub Health
⊕ https://vfmat.ch/a43d

New Orleans Medical Mission Services, Inc.
Provides free medical treatment, consultation, education, equipment, and supplies to needy people in foreign countries.
Dent-OMFS, Ophth-Opt, Rehab, Surg
⊕ https://vfmat.ch/e342

Nicaragua Global Health Project
Provides sustainable solutions that empower providers to make interventions that positively impact health outcomes within their communities.
Crit-Care, ER Med, General, Medicine, OB-GYN, Ophth-Opt, Peds, Pub Health, Radiol
⊕ https://vfmat.ch/ac8c

Nicaragua-Projekt e.V.
Supports medical and social projects in northern Nicaragua.
General, Logist-Op, Medicine, Peds
⊕ https://vfmat.ch/389a

Nicaraguan Medical Mission
Provides quality medical and dental services to the indigent population of Nicaragua.
Dent-OMFS, General, General, MF Med, OB-GYN, Ophth-Opt
⊕ https://vfmat.ch/12ee

Northeast VOSH
Provides quality healthcare to those with limited means or access, both internationally and abroad.
Dent-OMFS, General, Nutr, Ophth-Opt, Rehab
⊕ https://vfmat.ch/f7b3

Nuestros Pequeños Hermanos (NPH)
Strives to create a loving and safe family environment for vulnerable children living in extreme conditions.
Psych, Rehab
⊕ https://vfmat.ch/57c4

Nuestros Pequeños Hermanos (Our Little Brothers and Sisters) New Zealand
Helps vulnerable children and families break the cycle of poverty with assistance through its pediatric hospital, healthcare clinics, day care centers, and scholarship programs.
CT Surg, Heme-Onc, Infect Dis, Nutr, OB-GYN, Peds, Rehab
⊕ https://vfmat.ch/e9cc

Nyagi
Empowers local healthcare workers in resource-poor areas to diagnose life-threatening health conditions through accelerated, low-cost ultrasound skills training.
Logist-Op, Pub Health
⊕ https://vfmat.ch/5de5

Olive Tree Inc.
Aims to provide medical services to those in need, teaches communities about health, and provides medications to those who cannot afford to purchase them.
General, OB-GYN, Ophth-Opt, Pub Health
⊕ https://vfmat.ch/ea98

One Good Turn
Provides practical medical education and culturally sensitive medical care to neglected communities worldwide.
Dent-OMFS, General
⊕ https://vfmat.ch/545f

One World Brigades
Assists international communities with dental care and education.
Dent-OMFS, General
⊕ https://vfmat.ch/7933

OneSight
Brings eye exams and glasses to people who lack access to vision care.
Ophth-Opt
⊕ https://vfmat.ch/3ecc

OneWorld Health
Provides quality, affordable healthcare to communities in need and empowers them to achieve long-term improvements in health and quality of life.
Dent-OMFS, General, Infect Dis, Ortho, Peds, Rehab, Surg
⊕ https://vfmat.ch/71d7

Operation Endeavor M99+
Provides direct support for public health and safety, EMS system development, and disaster response in developing and underserved regions, both domestic and abroad, while providing training in rescue, emergency medicine, and trauma care.
Dent-OMFS, ER Med, Infect Dis, Logist-Op, OB-GYN, Peds, Surg
⊕ https://vfmat.ch/d83a

Operation International
Offers medical aid to adults and children suffering from lack of quality healthcare in impoverished countries.
Dent-OMFS, ER Med, Heme-Onc, OB-GYN, Ophth-Opt, Ortho, Ped Surg, Plast,

Surg
⊕ https://vfmat.ch/b52a

Operation Rainbow

Performs free orthopedic surgery, in developing countries, for children and young adults who do not otherwise have access to related medical procedures or equipment.
Anesth, Ortho, Ped Surg, Peds, Rehab, Surg
⊕ https://vfmat.ch/5dad

Operation Smile

Treats patients with cleft lip and cleft palate, and creates solutions that deliver safe surgery to people where it's needed most.
Anesth, Dent-OMFS, ENT, Ped Surg, Plast
⊕ https://vfmat.ch/5c29

Operation Walk

Provides the gift of mobility through life-changing joint replacement surgeries, at no cost for those in need in the U.S. and globally.
Anesth, Ortho, Rehab, Surg
⊕ https://vfmat.ch/bafe

Order of Malta

Supports forgotten or excluded people, especially those living in conflict zones or amid natural disasters, by providing medical assistance, caring for refugees, and distributing medicines and necessities.
ER Med, General, Infect Dis, MF Med, Nephro, OB-GYN, Ortho, Psych
⊕ https://vfmat.ch/1fab

Overflowing Hands

Aims to serve children in communities across the U.S. and around the world by providing food, clothing, shelter, and healthcare.
Logist-Op, Pub Health, Radiol
⊕ https://vfmat.ch/8522

PATH

Advances health equity through innovation and partnerships so people, communities, and economies can thrive.
All-Immu, CV Med, Endo, Heme-Onc, Infect Dis, MF Med, Neonat, Nutr, OB-GYN, Path, Peds, Pulm-Critic
⊕ https://vfmat.ch/b4db

Peace and Hope Trust

Aims to make a positive difference in the lives of the poor in Nicaragua.
Dent-OMFS, Pub Health
⊕ https://vfmat.ch/19c2

Peterborough Paramedics & Beyond (PPAB)

Provides opportunities for healthcare professionals and lay people to offer hands-on, sustainable medical and humanitarian services in impoverished communities.
General, Logist-Op
⊕ https://vfmat.ch/3ba6

Physicians for Peace

Educates and empowers local providers of surgical care to alleviate suffering and transform lives in under-resourced communities around the world.
Crit-Care, Ped Surg, Plast, Psych, Surg, Urol
⊕ https://vfmat.ch/6a65

Project Concern International (PCI)

Drives innovation from the ground up to enhance health, end hunger, overcome hardship, and advance women and girls—resulting in meaningful and measurable change in people's lives.
Infect Dis, MF Med, Nutr, OB-GYN, Peds
⊕ https://vfmat.ch/5ed7

Project El Crucero

Inspired by the Christian faith, serves the people of El Crucero, Nicaragua, and the surrounding communities.
Dent-OMFS, General
⊕ https://vfmat.ch/4848

Project H.O.P.E., Inc.

Mobilizes volunteers to serve in Nicaragua and Haiti, building homes and conducting medical clinics, inspired by the Christian faith.
Dent-OMFS, General, Nutr, Ophth-Opt
⊕ https://vfmat.ch/99af

Project Health for León

Improves medical care for the people of Nicaragua through education, the acquisition of technology, and direct patient consultation and care.
CT Surg, CV Med, Ortho, Peds, Surg, Vasc Surg
⊕ https://vfmat.ch/bfe6

PSI – Population Services International

Aims to improve the health of people in the developing world by focusing on challenges such as a lack of family planning, HIV/AIDS, barriers to maternal health, and the greatest threats to children under the age of 5, including malaria, diarrhea, pneumonia, and malnutrition.
Infect Dis, MF Med, OB-GYN, Peds
⊕ https://vfmat.ch/ffe3

Purpose Medical Mission

Strives to achieve long-term and self-sustaining healthy communities where extreme poverty and lack of basic healthcare and education are a problem.
General, Logist-Op, Medicine, Pub Health, Surg
⊕ https://vfmat.ch/3fe7

RAD-AID International

Improves and optimizes access to medical imaging and radiology in low-resource regions of the world.
Rad-Onc, Radiol
⊕ https://vfmat.ch/537f

RestoringVision

Empowers lives by restoring vision for millions of people in need.
Ophth-Opt
⊕ https://vfmat.ch/e121

ReSurge International

Provides reconstructive surgical care and builds surgical capacity in developing countries.
Anesth, Dent-OMFS, Ped Surg, Plast, Surg
⊕ https://vfmat.ch/9937

Right to Sight and Health

Seeks to reduce the prevalence of blindness and visual impairment, especially among low-income communities in Northern Ghana.
Ophth-Opt
⊕ https://vfmat.ch/7ff1

Robert Clemente Health Clinic, The

Provides affordable access to high-quality healthcare and wellness programs in the Tola coastal communities of Nicaragua.
Dent-OMFS, ER Med, Endo, General, Path, Peds, Pub Health, Radiol
⊕ https://vfmat.ch/1e9c

Rotary International

Provides service to others, improves lives, and advances world understanding, goodwill, and peace through its fellowship of business, professional, and community leaders.
ER Med, General, Infect Dis, MF Med, OB-GYN
⊕ https://vfmat.ch/8fb5

Rutgers New Jersey Medical School

Seeks to support and promote the global health efforts of the faculty, staff, and students in the areas of education, research, and service through the Rutgers New Jersey Medical School's Office of Global Health.
Anesth, CV Med, Crit-Care, Neurosurg, OB-GYN, Psych
⊕ https://vfmat.ch/8e67

Saint Francis International Medical Mission

Brings first-class medical services to those in need.
Anesth, Derm, OB-GYN, Ophth-Opt, Peds, Surg
⊕ https://vfmat.ch/6335

Salvation Army International, The
Seeks to meet human needs through services in education, healthcare, community support, emergency response, and ministry development, inspired by the Christian faith.
Dent-OMFS, Derm, ER Med, Infect Dis, MF Med, Medicine, Nutr, OB-GYN, Ophth-Opt, Palliative, Psych, Rehab, Surg
⊕ https://vfmat.ch/8eb3

San Juan Rio Relief
Acquires and distributes medicine, medical supplies, equipment, and health services to the people of San Juan, Nicaragua, and the surrounding area.
Dent-OMFS, General, Ophth-Opt, Ortho, Peds, Pub Health
⊕ https://vfmat.ch/c81d

Save the Children
Gives children around the world a healthy start in life, the opportunity to learn, and protection from harm.
All-Immu, Crit-Care, ER Med, General, Infect Dis, MF Med, Medicine, Neonat, OB-GYN, Peds, Psych, Pub Health
⊕ https://vfmat.ch/2e73

Saving Little Hearts of Nicaragua (SLHON)
Provides education and support to the children of Nicaragua who suffer from untreated strep throat infections, resulting in rheumatic fever and heart disease.
CT Surg, CV Med, Logist-Op
⊕ https://vfmat.ch/8234

SEE International
Provides sustainable medical, surgical, and educational services through volunteer ophthalmic surgeons, with the objectives of restoring sight and preventing blindness to disadvantaged individuals worldwide.
Ophth-Opt, Surg
⊕ https://vfmat.ch/6e1b

SIGN Fracture Care International
Builds orthopedic capacity around the world and provides the injured poor access to fracture surgery by donating orthopedic education and implant systems to surgeons in developing countries.
Ortho, Rehab, Surg
⊕ https://vfmat.ch/123d

Smile Train, Inc.
Treats children with cleft lip through a sustainable and local model that supports surgery and other forms of essential care.
Logist-Op, Pub Health
⊕ https://vfmat.ch/822c

SOS Children's Villages International
Supports children through alternative care and family strengthening.
ER Med, Peds
⊕ https://vfmat.ch/aca1

Sri Sathya Sai International Organization
Inspired by spiritual teachings, carries out efforts in global healthcare, education, humanitarian relief, and youth engagement.
Dent-OMFS, General, Logist-Op, Nutr, Ophth-Opt, Pub Health
⊕ https://vfmat.ch/9bda

Superemos Foundation
Works to promote health and education in northern Nicaragua, with an emphasis on female empowerment.
Crit-Care, Dent-OMFS, General, OB-GYN, Ophth-Opt, Peds, Pub Health
⊕ https://vfmat.ch/f6f9

Swiss Tropical and Public Health Institute
Contributes to the improvement of the health of populations internationally, nationally, and locally through excellence in research, education, and services.
Infect Dis, Pub Health
⊕ https://vfmat.ch/2ee4

Task Force for Global Health, The
Consists of programs and focus areas that cover a range of global health issues including neglected tropical diseases, infectious diseases, vaccines, field epidemiology, public health informatics, health workforce development, and global health ethics.
Infect Dis, Logist-Op, Medicine, Ophth-Opt, Peds
⊕ https://vfmat.ch/714c

Team Broken Earth
Brings medical relief and education to those who need it most by sending volunteer teams of healthcare professionals to areas of wide-ranging relief response.
Medicine, OB-GYN, Ophth-Opt, Rehab, Surg
⊕ https://vfmat.ch/bfcd

Tearfund
Responds to crisis and partners with local churches to bring restoration to those living in poverty, inspired by the Christian faith.
ER Med, Logist-Op
⊕ https://vfmat.ch/f6cf

Terre des hommes (Tdh) Foundation
Works to improve the daily life of children and their relatives in the areas of health, protection and emergency, in Europe, Africa, Asia, Latin America, and the Near and Middle East.
CT Surg, CV Med, OB-GYN, Ped Surg, Pub Health
⊕ https://vfmat.ch/5c26

Third World Eye Care Society (TWECS)
Collects old, unused eyeglasses and distributes them in conjunction with eye exams given by properly trained individuals.
Logist-Op, Ophth-Opt
⊕ https://vfmat.ch/8618

Threefold Ministries
Inspired by the Christian faith, engages, equips, empowers, energizes, and encourages people to build up strong local communities in Nicaragua.
Dent-OMFS, ER Med, General, OB-GYN
⊕ https://vfmat.ch/2cc4

UNC Health Foundation
Secures resources and supports empathy and expertise in patient care, research, education, and advocacy in underserved communities around the world.
Heme-Onc, Infect Dis, Neuro, Peds, Pub Health
⊕ https://vfmat.ch/7129

Union for International Cancer Control (UICC)
Unites and supports the cancer community to reduce the global cancer burden, promote greater equity, and ensure that cancer control continues to be a priority in the world health and development agenda.
Heme-Onc, Pub Health
⊕ https://vfmat.ch/88b1

United Methodist Volunteers in Mission (UMVIM)
Engages in short-term missions each year in ministries as varied as disaster response, community development, pastor training, microenterprise, agriculture, Vacation Bible School, building repair and construction, and medical/dental services.
Dent-OMFS, ER Med, General
⊕ https://vfmat.ch/1ee6

United Nations Children's Fund (UNICEF)
Works in over 190 countries and territories to save children's lives, defend their rights, and help them fulfill their potential, from early childhood through adolescence.
All-Immu, Infect Dis, MF Med, Neonat, Nutr, OB-GYN, Ped Surg, Peds, Pub Health
⊕ https://vfmat.ch/42d7

United Nations Development Programme (UNDP)
Helps countries achieve the simultaneous eradication of extreme poverty and significant reduction of inequalities and exclusion using a sustainable human development approach.
Infect Dis, Logist-Op, Pub Health
⊕ https://vfmat.ch/935c

United Nations High Commissioner for Refugees (UNHCR)
Safeguards the rights and well-being of people who have been forced to flee, ensuring that everybody has the right to seek asylum and find safe refuge in another country, with the goal of seeking lasting solutions.
General, MF Med, Medicine, OB-GYN, Peds, Psych, Pub Health
⊕ https://vfmat.ch/6636

United Nations Population Fund (UNFPA)
Supports reproductive healthcare for women and youth in more than 150 countries, focusing on delivering a world in which every pregnancy is wanted, every childbirth is safe, and every young person's potential is fulfilled.
Infect Dis, MF Med, Neonat, OB-GYN, Peds, Pub Health
⊕ https://vfmat.ch/c969

University of Florida College of Medicine (Global Health Education Program)
Strives to improve individual and community health through discovery and clinical and translational science, and through technology, education, and patient-centered healthcare.
Anesth, Dent-OMFS, General, Ophth-Opt, Pub Health, Surg
⊕ https://vfmat.ch/aee1

University of North Carolina: Institute for Global Health and Infectious Diseases
Harnesses the full resources of UNC and its partners to solve global health problems, reduce the burden of disease, and cultivate the next generation of global health leaders.
Infect Dis, MF Med, OB-GYN, Psych, Surg
⊕ https://vfmat.ch/ed5e

University of Virginia: Anesthesiology Department Global Health Initiatives
Educates and trains physicians to help people achieve healthy productive lives, and advances knowledge in the medical sciences.
Anesth, Pub Health
⊕ https://vfmat.ch/1b8b

University of Wisconsin-Madison: Department of Surgery
Provides comprehensive educational experiences, groundbreaking research, and superb patient care.
Anesth, ENT, ER Med, Endo, Peds, Plast, Pub Health, Surg
⊕ https://vfmat.ch/64c2

USAID: Deliver Project
Builds a global supply chain to deliver lifesaving health products to people in order to enable countries to provide family planning, protect against malaria, and limit the spread of pandemic threats.
Infect Dis, Logist-Op, MF Med
⊕ https://vfmat.ch/374e

USAID: Leadership, Management and Governance Project
Improves leadership, management, and governance practices to strengthen health systems and improve health for all, including vulnerable populations worldwide.
Logist-Op
⊕ https://vfmat.ch/d35e

Vision for the Poor
Reduces human suffering and improves quality of life through the recovery of sight by building sustainable eye hospitals in developing countries, empowering local eye specialists, funding essential ophthalmic infrastructure, and partnering with like-minded agencies.
Ophth-Opt
⊕ https://vfmat.ch/528e

Vision Health International
Brings high-quality eye care to underserved communities around the world.
Ophth-Opt
⊕ https://vfmat.ch/e97f

Vision Outreach International
Advocates for helping the blind in underserved regions of the world and empowers the poor through sight restoration.

Ophth-Opt
⊕ https://vfmat.ch/9721

Vitamin Angels
Helps at-risk populations in need—specifically pregnant women, new mothers, and children under age 5—to gain access to life-changing vitamins and minerals.
General, Nutr
⊕ https://vfmat.ch/7da1

VOSH (Volunteer Optometric Services to Humanity) International
Facilitates the provision and the sustainability of vision care worldwide for people who can neither afford nor obtain such care.
Ophth-Opt
⊕ https://vfmat.ch/a149

Walk Nicaragua
Aims to transform communities by improving the quality of accessible healthcare through a model of empowerment and sustainability.
Ortho
⊕ https://vfmat.ch/f169

Wichita County Medical Alliance
Mobilizes volunteers to assist in public health efforts in the U.S. and abroad, including medical missions and disaster relief.
General, Geri, Nutr, OB-GYN, Pub Health
⊕ https://vfmat.ch/fa55

Women and Children First
Pioneers approaches that support communities to solve problems themselves.
MF Med, Neonat, OB-GYN, Peds
⊕ https://vfmat.ch/cdc9

Women's Refugee Commission
Seeks to improve lives by protecting the rights of women, children, and youth displaced by conflict and crisis through researching their needs, identifying solutions, and advocating for programs and policies to strengthen their resilience.
General, MF Med, Neonat, OB-GYN, Peds, Psych
⊕ https://vfmat.ch/3d8f

World Compassion Fellowship (WCF)
Serves the global poor and persecuted through relief, medical care, development, and training.
CV Med, ER Med, Endo, GI, General, Infect Dis, Medicine, Nutr, OB-GYN, Ortho, Peds, Psych, Pub Health, Rehab
⊕ https://vfmat.ch/7b97

World Federation of Hemophilia (WFH)
Aims to improve and sustain care for people with inherited bleeding disorders by pursuing long-term relationships with individuals and organizations who share the values of WFH's development model.
Heme-Onc
⊕ https://vfmat.ch/5121

World Health Organization, The (WHO)
The United Nations' agency for health provides leadership on global health matters, shapes the health research agenda, sets norms and standards, articulates evidence-based policy options, provides technical support and monitoring to countries, and assesses health trends.
ER Med, General, Infect Dis, Logist-Op, MF Med, OB-GYN, Peds, Psych, Pub Health
⊕ https://vfmat.ch/c476

World Hope International
Empowers the poorest individuals around the world so they can become agents of change within their communities, by offering resources and knowledge.
Infect Dis, Logist-Op, MF Med, OB-GYN, Peds
⊕ https://vfmat.ch/a4b8

World Medical Relief
Facilitates the distribution of surplus medical resources where they are needed.
Logist-Op
⊕ https://vfmat.ch/72dc

World Missions Outreach

Based in Christian ministry, aims to equip the people of Nicaragua with the right tools to combat the roots of poverty through education and nutrition.

Dent-OMFS, General

⊕ https://vfmat.ch/3cb9

World Missions Possible

Provides EMS capacity-building, along with medical and vision care, to under-developed and rural areas.

ER Med, General, Heme-Onc, Neonat, Ophth-Opt, Surg

⊕ https://vfmat.ch/d6a5

World Vision International

Works with vulnerable communities around the world to overcome poverty and injustice with child-focused programs in disaster management, health, nutrition, economic development, education, clean water, sanitation, and hygiene.

ER Med, General, Infect Dis, MF Med, Nutr, OB-GYN, Peds

⊕ https://vfmat.ch/2642

Worldwide Child Relief Foundation

Helps impoverished communities become economically self-sustaining by providing education, business development, health services, and infrastructure.

Pub Health

⊕ https://vfmat.ch/bc85

Nicaragua

Healthcare Facilities

Bodega de Hospital Monte España
La Argentina, Managua, Nicaragua
⊕ https://vfmat.ch/4fac

Centro Nacional de Dermatología
Colonia Molina, Managua, Nicaragua
⊕ https://vfmat.ch/91bb

Centro Nacional de Oftalmológico Dr. Emilio Alvarez Montalvan
Managua, Managua, Nicaragua
⊕ https://vfmat.ch/eb69

Centro Nacional De Radiologia
Barrio Tierra Prometida, Managua, Nicaragua
⊕ https://vfmat.ch/e328

Centro Oncológico de Quimioterapia y Cuidados Paliativos Dr. Clemente Guido
Managua, Managua, Nicaragua
⊕ https://vfmat.ch/995a

Complejo Nacional Dra. Concepción Palacios – Ministerio de Salud
Mangua, Managua, Nicaragua
⊕ https://vfmat.ch/ab9f

Hospital Alamikamba Prinzu Pawanka
Prinzapolka, North Caribbean Coast, Nicaragua
⊕ https://vfmat.ch/9374

Hospital Alfonso Moncada Guillén
Ocotal, Nueva Segovia, Nicaragua
⊕ https://vfmat.ch/18c1

Hospital Ambrosio Mogorrón
San Jose de Bocay, Jinotega, Nicaragua
⊕ https://vfmat.ch/d254

Hospital Amistad Japón – Nicaragua
Granada, Granada, Nicaragua
⊕ https://vfmat.ch/841f

Hospital Amistad México – Nicaragua
San Jorge, Managua, Nicaragua
⊕ https://vfmat.ch/ca3e

Hospital Bautista
Largaespada, Managua, Nicaragua
⊕ https://vfmat.ch/7d18

Hospital Bello Amanecer
Quilalí, Nueva Segovia, Nicaragua
⊕ https://vfmat.ch/a661

Hospital Bertha Calderón Roque
Managua, Managua, Nicaragua
⊕ https://vfmat.ch/f447

Hospital Blanca Aráuz
Llano de La Tejera, Jinotega, Nicaragua
⊕ https://vfmat.ch/a997

Hospital Carlos Fonseca Amador
Mulukukú, North Caribbean Coast, Nicaragua
⊕ https://vfmat.ch/9db3

Hospital Carlos Roberto Huembes
Colonia Molina, Managua, Nicaragua
⊕ https://vfmat.ch/939a

Hospital Carlos Roberto Huembes filial El Carmen
Colonia Molina, Managua, Nicaragua
⊕ https://vfmat.ch/3ee6

Hospital Carolina Osejo
Villanueva, Chinandega, Nicaragua
⊕ https://vfmat.ch/8681

Hospital Central De Managua Dr. César Amador Kühl
Managua, Managua, Nicaragua
⊕ https://vfmat.ch/11e3

Hospital Consultorio El Verbo
Bilwi, North Caribbean Coast, Nicaragua
⊕ https://vfmat.ch/98cd

Hospital El Maestro
Santa Cecilia, Carazo, Nicaragua
⊕ https://vfmat.ch/f6ec

Hospital EMCSA
Jinotepe, Carazo, Nicaragua
⊕ https://vfmat.ch/fd3c

Hospital Escuela Antonio Lenin Fonseca Martínez
Managua, Managua, Nicaragua
⊕ https://vfmat.ch/18a2

Hospital Escuela Carlos Amador Molina HECAM
Colonia Ruben Dario, Matagalpa, Nicaragua
⊕ https://vfmat.ch/1d98

Hospital Escuela Cesar Amador Molina
Colonia Ruben Dario, Matagalpa, Nicaragua
⊕ https://vfmat.ch/133a

Hospital Escuela Manolo Morales
La Argentina, Managua, Nicaragua
⊕ https://vfmat.ch/9d7d

Hospital Escuela Oscar Danilo Rosales
La Granja, León, Nicaragua
⊕ https://vfmat.ch/3def

Hospital Escuela Regional Santiago Jinotepe
Jinotepe, Carazo, Nicaragua
⊕ https://vfmat.ch/7d6d

Hospital España Chinandega
Chinandega, Chinandega, Nicaragua
⊕ https://vfmat.ch/5ad7

Hospital Esteban Jáenz Serrano
El Bosque, North Caribbean Coast, Nicaragua
⊕ https://vfmat.ch/cecf

Hospital Gaspar García Laviana
San Juan del Sur, Rivas, Nicaragua
⊕ https://vfmat.ch/f4f2

Hospital Hilario Sánchez
Pacayita, Masaya, Nicaragua
⊕ https://vfmat.ch/26ed

Hospital Infantil La Mascota
La Argentina, Managua, Nicaragua
⊕ https://vfmat.ch/ce16

Hospital Iraní
Santa Rosa, Managua, Nicaragua
⊕ https://vfmat.ch/1ceb

Hospital Juan Antonio Brenes
Valle Santa Isabel, Madriz, Nicaragua
⊕ https://vfmat.ch/8ce6

Hospital La Fraternidad
Santa María, León, Nicaragua
⊕ https://vfmat.ch/eb2a

Hospital La Fraternidad – Filial La Recolección
La Granja, León, Nicaragua
⊕ https://vfmat.ch/aa41

Hospital Luis Felipe Moncada
San Antonio, Alajuela, Nicaragua
⊕ https://vfmat.ch/b5b3

Hospital Militar Escuela Dr. Alejandro Dávila Bolaños
Managua, Managua, Nicaragua
⊕ https://vfmat.ch/d3a5

Hospital Monte Carmelo
El Congo, Carazo, Nicaragua
⊕ https://vfmat.ch/c8c2

Hospital Monte España Tipitapa
Tipitapa, Managua, Nicaragua
⊕ https://vfmat.ch/82ba

Hospital Nuevo Amanecer
Bilwi, North Caribbean Coast, Nicaragua
⊕ https://vfmat.ch/7139

Hospital Occidental de Managua Dr. Fernando Velez Paiz
Managua, Managua, Nicaragua
⊕ https://vfmat.ch/711d

Hospital Pastor Jiménez
Jalapa, Nueva Segovia, Nicaragua
⊕ https://vfmat.ch/b1eb

Hospital Pedro Altamirano
La Trinidad, Estelí, Nicaragua
⊕ https://vfmat.ch/3f94

Hospital Primario Ada María López
Condega, Estelí, Nicaragua
⊕ https://vfmat.ch/123c

Hospital Primario Comandante Tomás Borge Martínez
Chichigalpa, Chinandega, Nicaragua
⊕ https://vfmat.ch/2ba5

Hospital Primario de Telica
Telica, León, Nicaragua
⊕ https://vfmat.ch/c37e

Hospital Primario El Jícaro
El Jícaro, Nueva Segovia, Nicaragua
⊕ https://vfmat.ch/5f41

Hospital Primario El Sauce
El Sauce, León, Nicaragua
⊕ https://vfmat.ch/71c9

Hospital Primario Ethel Kandler
Little Corn Island, Nicaragua
⊕ https://vfmat.ch/dea1

Hospital Primario Fidel Ventura
Waslala, North Caribbean Coast, Nicaragua
⊕ https://vfmat.ch/655d

Hospital Primario Héroes y Mártires del Cua
El Cuá, Jinotega, Nicaragua
⊕ https://vfmat.ch/37db

Hospital Primario Héroes y Mártires San José de las Mulas
Las Conchitas, Matagalpa, Nicaragua
⊕ https://vfmat.ch/361c

Hospital Primario Jorge Navarro
Wiwilí, Jinotega, Nicaragua
⊕ https://vfmat.ch/fec4

Hospital Primario José Shendell
Corinto, Chinandega, Nicaragua
⊕ https://vfmat.ch/fed9

Hospital Primario Monseñor Julio César Videa
Pueblo Nuevo, Estelí, Nicaragua
⊕ https://vfmat.ch/33ca

Hospital Primario Nilda Patricia Velasco
Bella Cruz, Managua, Nicaragua
⊕ https://vfmat.ch/7fda

Hospital Primario Niños Mártires De Ayapal
San José de Bocay, Jinotega, Nicaragua
⊕ https://vfmat.ch/89dd

Hospital Primario Oswaldo Padilla
Waspam, North Caribbean Coast, Nicaragua
⊕ https://vfmat.ch/812a

Hospital Primario San José
Matiguas, Matagalpa, Nicaragua
⊕ https://vfmat.ch/ee65

Hospital Privado Cruz Azul
Granada, Granada, Nicaragua
⊕ https://vfmat.ch/6545

Hospital Psiquiátrico Nacional
Managua, Managua, Nicaragua
⊕ https://vfmat.ch/ce4d

Hospital Regional Ernesto Sequeira Blanco
Bluefields, South Caribbean Coast, Nicaragua
⊕ https://vfmat.ch/628e

Hospital Regional Escuela Asunción
El Salto, Chontales, Nicaragua
⊕ https://vfmat.ch/5128

Hospital Rosario Pravia
Rosita, North Caribbean Coast, Nicaragua
⊕ https://vfmat.ch/a293

Hospital Salud Integral
Colonia Molina, Managua, Nicaragua
⊕ https://vfmat.ch/cfa3

Hospital San Francisco de Asís
Camoapa, Boaco, Nicaragua
⊕ https://vfmat.ch/c329

Hospital San José
Santa Cecilia, Carazo, Nicaragua
⊕ https://vfmat.ch/3b16

Hospital San Juan De Dios
El Pastoreo, Estelí, Nicaragua
⊕ https://vfmat.ch/15a2

Hospital SERMESA Bolonia
La Argentina, Managua, Nicaragua
⊕ https://vfmat.ch/9a86

Hospital Solidaridad Managua
Managua, Managua, Nicaragua
⊕ https://vfmat.ch/1d4d

Hospital Solidaridad Tipitapa
El Hatillo, Managua, Nicaragua
⊕ https://vfmat.ch/d991

Hospital SUMEDICO
Bolonia Contiguo, Managua, Nicaragua
⊕ https://vfmat.ch/6a7f

Hospital Victoria Motta
Jinotega, Jinotega, Nicaragua
⊕ https://vfmat.ch/f178

Hospital Vivian Pellas
Managua, Managua, Nicaragua
⊕ https://vfmat.ch/256f

Hospital Yolanda Mayorga
Tipitapa, Managua, Nicaragua
⊕ https://vfmat.ch/d1dd

Nicaragua Adventist Hospital
Estelí, Nicaragua
⊕ https://vfmat.ch/9see

Servicios Médicos Especializados SERMESA Hospital Carazo
Jinotepe, Carazo, Nicaragua
⊕ https://vfmat.ch/79a1

Map data © OpenStreetMap (openstreetmap.org) and contributors, CC-BY-SA
(creativecommons.org) © CARTO

● Healthcare Facility

Niger

The Republic of Niger is a landlocked West African country with a population of about 23.6 million mostly living in rural areas. The country's name stems from the presence of the Niger River that winds through the country. The Niger landscape is unique, composed predominantly of desert plains and sand dunes. The terrain is matched by a desert-like climate: hot, dry, and dusty, with extreme heat sometimes reaching 46 degrees Celsius. A predominantly Muslim country, Niger has a variety of linguistic groups, such as Hausa, a name which also refers to its largest ethnic group.

Following its independence from France in 1960, the country experienced several periods of violence and coups. To this day, access to basic rights remains a problem in Niger; slavery was banned only in 2003. About 41 percent of the population live in extreme poverty.

Despite extreme poverty, life expectancy and child mortality rates have been improving over the decades. The leading causes of death include diarrheal diseases, malaria, lower respiratory infections, neonatal disorders, measles, meningitis, tuberculosis, and invasive nontyphoidal salmonella (iNTS). Non-communicable diseases such as stroke, ischemic heart diseases, and congenital defects have also increased to contribute to a significant number of deaths over time. Malnutrition is the main risk factor for death and disability, as 46 percent of children under age five suffer from chronic malnutrition, and about 10 percent suffer from acute malnutrition. Pediatric ailments persist due to a young population, with death from neonatal disorders rising dramatically. Niger has the highest fertility rate in the world, with approximately seven children per woman.

23.6M

Population

$565

GDP Per Capita

62 years

Life Expectancy

↑ Improving

4	**39**	**509**
Doctors/100k	**Beds**/100k	**Deaths**/100k
Physician Density	Hospital Bed Density	Maternal Mortality

Niger

Nonprofit Organizations

Abt Associates
Seeks to improve the quality of life and economic well-being of people worldwide, while striving to meet and exceed the highest professional standards.
General, Logist-Op, MF Med, OB-GYN, Peds
⊕ https://vfmat.ch/cec2

Action Against Hunger
Aims to end life-threatening hunger for good through treating and preventing malnutrition across more than 45 countries.
Nutr
⊕ https://vfmat.ch/2dbc

Advance Family Planning
Aims to achieve global expansion and access to quality contraceptive information, services, and supplies through financial investment and political commitment.
General, MF Med, Pub Health
⊕ https://vfmat.ch/7478

Africa CDC
Aims to strengthen the capacity and capability of Africa's public health institutions and partnerships to detect and respond quickly and effectively to disease threats and outbreaks, based on data-driven interventions and programs.
Infect Dis, Logist-Op, Pub Health
⊕ https://vfmat.ch/339c

Africa Health Organisation
Leads collaborative efforts among countries in Africa and other partners to promote health equity, combat disease, and improve quality of life.
Logist-Op, Pub Health
⊕ https://vfmat.ch/b1c5

Africa Relief and Community Development
Provides comprehensive relief and developmental aid to people of the African continent regardless of gender, race, or religion.
Nutr, Pub Health
⊕ https://vfmat.ch/6cd2

Al Basar International Foundation
Works with local partners to treat preventable blindness, and helps set up sustainable infrastructure so local teams can save sight in their communities.
Ophth-Opt
⊕ https://vfmat.ch/a8b5

Alliance for International Medical Action, The (ALIMA)
Provides quality medical care to vulnerable populations, partnering with and developing national medical organizations and conducting medical research to bring innovation to 12 African countries where ALIMA works.
ER Med, General, Infect Dis, Logist-Op, MF Med, OB-GYN, Path, Peds, Psych, Pub Health
⊕ https://vfmat.ch/1c11

Americares
Saves lives and improves health for people affected by poverty or disaster and responds with life-changing medicine, medical supplies, and health programs including domestic and global medical clinics.
All-Immu, ER Med, General, Infect Dis, MF Med, Nutr
⊕ https://vfmat.ch/e567

AO Alliance
Builds solutions to lessen the burden of injuries in low- and middle-income countries, while enhancing the care of the injured to reduce human suffering, disability, and poverty.
Ortho, Surg
⊕ https://vfmat.ch/8cd5

Arbeiter Samariter Bund (Workers' Samaritan Federation)
Engages in areas such as civil protection, rescue services, and social welfare, while operating a network of welcome centers to help refugees.
ER Med, General, Infect Dis, Logist-Op, Rehab
⊕ https://vfmat.ch/8a5b

Blueprints For Pangaea (B4P)
Aims to reallocate unused medical supplies from areas of excess to areas in need.

⊕ https://vfmat.ch/faba

BroadReach
Collaborates with governments, multinational health organizations, donors, and private-sector companies to effect healthcare reform and solve the world's biggest health challenges.
Logist-Op
⊕ https://vfmat.ch/7812

CARE
Works around the globe to save lives, defeat poverty, and achieve social justice.
ER Med, General
⊕ https://vfmat.ch/7232

Carter Center, The
Seeks to prevent and resolve conflicts, enhance freedom and democracy, and improve health, while remaining committed to human rights and the alleviation of human suffering.
Infect Dis, MF Med, Ophth-Opt
⊕ https://vfmat.ch/6556

Center for Strategic and International Studies (CSIS) Commission on Strengthening America's Health Security
Brings together a distinguished and diverse group of high-level opinion leaders bridging security and health, with the core aim to chart a bold vision for the future of U.S. leadership in global health.

ER Med, Infect Dis, MF Med, Pub Health
⊕ https://vfmat.ch/6d7f

Challenge Initiative, The
Seeks to rapidly and sustainably scale up proven reproductive health solutions among the urban poor.
MF Med, OB-GYN, Peds
⊕ https://vfmat.ch/2f77

Christian Aid Ministries
Strives to be a trustworthy and efficient channel for Amish, Mennonite, and other conservative Anabaptist groups and individuals to minister to physical and spiritual needs around the world.
CT Surg, ER Med, Logist-Op, Ortho, Pub Health
⊕ https://vfmat.ch/7b33

Christian Blind Mission (CBM)
Aims to improve the quality of life of persons with disabilities in the poorest countries, addressing poverty as a cause and a consequence of disability, and working in partnership to create a society for all.
ENT, General, Infect Dis, OB-GYN, Ophth-Opt, Ortho, Peds, Psych, Rehab, Surg
⊕ https://vfmat.ch/3824

Christian Connections for International Health (CCIH)
Promotes global health and wholeness from a Christian perspective.
All-Immu, General, Infect Dis, MF Med, Neonat, OB-GYN, Psych
⊕ https://vfmat.ch/fa5d

Christian Medical & Dental Associations
Based in Christian ministry, deploys medical and dental teams to underserved communities to provide vital healthcare.
Anesth, Dent-OMFS, ER Med, General, Medicine, OB-GYN, Ophth-Opt, Peds, Pub Health, Radiol, Rehab, Surg
⊕ https://vfmat.ch/921c

Concern Worldwide
Seeks to permanently transform the lives of people living in extreme poverty, tackling its root causes, and building resilience.
Logist-Op, MF Med, Nutr, OB-GYN
⊕ https://vfmat.ch/77e9

Core Group
Aims to improve and expand community health practices for underserved populations, especially women and children, through collaborative action and learning.
General, Infect Dis, MF Med, Medicine, OB-GYN, Peds, Pub Health
⊕ https://vfmat.ch/9de3

COVID-19 Clinical Research Coalition
Advocates and collaborates for the advancement of COVID-19 research driven by the needs of low-resource settings, and works for equitable access to solutions to the pandemic.
All-Immu, Infect-Dis, MF Med, Path, Pub Health
⊕ https://vfmat.ch/d1f4

CURE
Operates charitable hospitals and programs in underserved countries worldwide, where patients receive surgical treatment, based in Christian ministry.
Anesth, Neurosurg, Ortho, Ped Surg, Peds, Rehab, Surg
⊕ https://vfmat.ch/aa16

CURE Children's Hospital of Zimbabwe
Heals children living with disabilities such as clubfoot, bowed legs, cleft lips, untreated burns, and hydrocephalus.
ENT, Neurosurg, Ortho, Peds, Plast
⊕ https://vfmat.ch/473c

Developing Country NGO Delegation: Global Fund to Fight AIDS, TB & Malaria
Works to strengthen the engagement of civil society actors and organizations in developing countries to build a world in which AIDS, TB, and malaria are no longer global, public health, and human rights threats.

Infect Dis, Pub Health
⊕ https://vfmat.ch/3149

Direct Relief
Improves the health and lives of people affected by poverty or emergency situations by mobilizing and providing essential medical resources needed for their care.
ER Med, Logist-Op
⊕ https://vfmat.ch/58e5

Doctors Without Borders/Médecins Sans Frontières (MSF)
Responds to emergencies and provides lifesaving medical care where needed most, including during disasters, conflicts, and epidemics.
Anesth, Crit-Care, ER Med, General, Infect Dis, Nutr, OB-GYN, Ped Surg, Peds, Psych, Pub Health, Surg
⊕ https://vfmat.ch/f363

eHealth Africa
Builds stronger health systems in Africa through the design and implementation of data-driven solutions, responding to local needs and providing underserved communities with the necessary tools to lead healthier lives.
Logist-Op, Path
⊕ https://vfmat.ch/db6a

Enabel
As the development agency of the Belgian federal government, charged with implementing Belgium's international development policy, carries out public service assignments in Belgium and abroad pursuant to the 2030 Agenda for Sustainable Development.
General, Infect Dis, Logist-Op, MF Med, OB-GYN, Peds, Pub Health
⊕ https://vfmat.ch/5af7

END Fund, The
Aims to control and eliminate the most prevalent neglected diseases among the world's poorest and most vulnerable people.
Infect Dis
⊕ https://vfmat.ch/2614

EngenderHealth
Works to implement high-quality, gender-equitable programs that advance sexual and reproductive health and rights.
General, MF Med, OB-GYN, Peds
⊕ https://vfmat.ch/1cb2

Eye Foundation of America
Works toward a world without childhood blindness.
Ophth-Opt
⊕ https://vfmat.ch/a7eb

Fistula Foundation
Aims to engage the support of people worldwide who are eager to see the day that no woman suffers from obstetric fistula. Raises and directs funds to doctors and hospitals providing life-transforming surgery to women in need.
OB-GYN
⊕ https://vfmat.ch/e958

Global Clubfoot Initiative (GCI)
Promotes and resources the treatment of children with clubfoot in developing countries using the Ponseti technique.
Ortho, Ped Surg
⊕ https://vfmat.ch/f229

Global Oncology (GO)
Brings the best in cancer care to underserved patients around the world and collaborates across geographic, professional, and academic borders to improve cancer care, research, and education.
Heme-Onc, Path, Rad-Onc
⊕ https://vfmat.ch/fcb8

Globus Relief
Aims to improve the delivery of healthcare worldwide by gathering, processing, and distributing surplus medical supplies to charities at home and abroad.

Logist-Op
⊕ https://vfmat.ch/a2b7

GOAL
Works with the most vulnerable communities to help them respond to and recover from humanitarian crises, and to assist them in building transcendent solutions to mitigate poverty and vulnerability.
ER Med, General, Pub Health
⊕ https://vfmat.ch/bbea

Health Equity Initiative
Aims to build and sustain a global community that engages across sectors and disciplines to advance health equity.
Pub Health
⊕ https://vfmat.ch/e2e2

Helen Keller International
Seeks to eliminate preventable vision loss, malnutrition, and diseases of poverty.
Infect Dis, Nutr, OB-GYN, Ophth-Opt, Peds
⊕ https://vfmat.ch/b654

Hope Walks
Frees children, families, and communities from the burden of clubfoot, inspired by the Christian faith.
Ortho, Ped Surg, Peds, Rehab
⊕ https://vfmat.ch/f6d4

Hospice Africa
Aims to provide a holistic and culturally sensitive palliative care service through accurate treatment of pain.
Palliative
⊕ https://vfmat.ch/9f86

Humanity & Inclusion
Works alongside people with disabilities and vulnerable populations, taking action and bearing witness in order to respond to their essential needs, improve their living conditions and health, and promote respect for their dignity and fundamental rights.
General, Infect Dis, MF Med, Medicine, Ortho, Peds, Psych, Pub Health, Rehab
⊕ https://vfmat.ch/16b7

Humanity First
Provides aid and assistance to those in need, offering sustainable development solutions to society while providing and empowering local communities with the resources to help themselves.
ER Med, General, MF Med, Ophth-Opt
⊕ https://vfmat.ch/13cc

IHSAN Foundation for West Africa
Seeks to improve the social and economic lives of the people of West Africa through educational, humanitarian, and healthcare projects.
Dent-OMFS, ER Med, General, Infect Dis
⊕ https://vfmat.ch/c719

IMA World Health
Works to build healthier communities by collaborating with key partners to serve vulnerable people with a focus on health, healing, and well-being for all.
Infect Dis, MF Med, Nutr, OB-GYN, Pub Health
⊕ https://vfmat.ch/8316

International Agency for the Prevention of Blindness (IAPB), The
Leads international efforts in blindness-prevention activities, works toward a world where no one is needlessly visually impaired, and ensures that everyone has access to the best possible standard of eye health.
Infect Dis, Ophth-Opt, Pub Health
⊕ https://vfmat.ch/87a2

International Federation of Gynecology and Obstetrics (FIGO)
Implements global projects on specific women's health issues.
MF Med, Medicine, Neonat, OB-GYN, Surg, Urol
⊕ https://vfmat.ch/c4b4

International Federation of Red Cross and Red Crescent Societies (IFRC)
Coordinates and directs international assistance following natural and manmade disasters in nonconflict situations through the world's largest humanitarian and development network. Provides disaster-preparedness programs, healthcare activities, and promotes humanitarian values.
ER Med, General, Infect Dis, Nutr
⊕ https://vfmat.ch/b4ee

International Learning Movement (ILM UK)
Supports some of the world's poorest people in developing countries with core projects in education, safe drinking water, and healthcare.
General, Ophth-Opt
⊕ https://vfmat.ch/b974

International Organization for Migration (IOM) – The UN Migration Agency
Promotes evidence-informed policies and holistic, preventive, and curative health programs that are beneficial, accessible, and equitable for vulnerable migrants.
General, Infect Dis, OB-GYN
⊕ https://vfmat.ch/621a

International Organization for Women and Development (IOWD)
Provides underserved women and children in low-income countries with free medical and surgical services and care.
Anesth, MF Med, Neonat, OB-GYN, Ped Surg, Peds, Surg
⊕ https://vfmat.ch/8ecb

International Relief Teams
Helps families survive and recover after a disaster by delivering timely and effective assistance through programs that improve their health and well-being while also providing a hopeful future for underserved communities.
Dent-OMFS, ER Med, General, Nutr, Ophth-Opt
⊕ https://vfmat.ch/ffd5

International Rescue Committee (IRC)
Responds to the world's worst humanitarian crises and helps people whose lives and livelihoods are shattered by conflict and disaster to survive, recover, and gain control of their future.
ER Med, General, Infect Dis, MF Med, Peds
⊕ https://vfmat.ch/5d24

Intersos
Provides emergency medical assistance to victims of armed conflicts, natural disasters, and extreme exclusion, with particular attention to the protection of the most vulnerable people.
ER Med, General, Nutr
⊕ https://vfmat.ch/dbac

InterSurgeon
Fosters collaborative partnerships in the field of global surgery that will advance clinical care, teaching, training, research, and the provision and maintenance of medical equipment.
ENT, Neurosurg, Ortho, Ped Surg, Plast, Surg, Urol
⊕ https://vfmat.ch/6f8a

IntraHealth International
Improves the performance of health workers and strengthens the systems in which they work.
CV Med, Endo, General, Infect Dis, MF Med, Neonat, Nutr, OB-GYN
⊕ https://vfmat.ch/ddc8

Ipas
Focuses efforts on women and girls who want contraception or abortion, and builds programs around their needs and how best to support them.
OB-GYN
⊕ https://vfmat.ch/8e39

Izumi Foundation
Develops and supports programs that improve health and healthcare in neglected regions of Africa and Latin America.
⊕ https://vfmat.ch/f29a

Jhpiego
Creates and delivers transformative healthcare solutions that save lives, in partnership with national governments, health experts, and local communities.
General, Infect Dis, OB-GYN, Surg
⊕ https://vfmat.ch/45b8

John Snow, Inc. (JSI)
Aims to improve the health and well-being of underserved and vulnerable people and communities throughout the world.
General, Infect Dis, Logist-Op, MF Med, OB-GYN, Peds, Psych, Pub Health
⊕ https://vfmat.ch/ba78

Johns Hopkins Center for Communication Programs
Believes in the power of communication to save lives by empowering people to adopt healthy behaviors for themselves, their families, and their communities.
General, Infect Dis, Logist-Op, OB-GYN, Pub Health
⊕ https://vfmat.ch/1bf9

Joint United Nations Programme on HIV/AIDS (UNAIDS)
Aims to place people living with HIV and people affected by the virus at the decision-making table and at the center of designing, delivering, and monitoring the AIDS response.
Infect Dis
⊕ https://vfmat.ch/464a

Leprosy Mission England and Wales, The
Leads the fight against leprosy by supporting people living with leprosy today and serving future generations by working to end transmission of the disease.
Infect Dis, Pub Health
⊕ https://vfmat.ch/4c67

Leprosy Mission International
Seeks to empower people with leprosy to attain healing, dignity, and life in all its fullness.
Infect Dis
⊕ https://vfmat.ch/95a9

Lions Clubs International
Empowers volunteers to serve their communities, meet humanitarian needs, encourage peace, and promote international understanding through Lions Clubs.
Heme-Onc, Medicine, Nutr, Ophth-Opt
⊕ https://vfmat.ch/7b12

London School of Hygiene & Tropical Medicine: Health in Humanitarian Crises Centre
Advances health and health equity in crisis-affected countries through research, education, and translation of knowledge into policy and practice.
ER Med, Infect Dis, Pub Health
⊕ https://vfmat.ch/96ad

MAP International
Provides medicines and health supplies to those in need around the world so they might experience life to the fullest.
Logist-Op
⊕ https://vfmat.ch/deed

Marie Stopes International
Provides the contraception and safe abortion services that enable women all over the world to choose their own futures.
Infect Dis, MF Med, Neonat, OB-GYN, Pub Health
⊕ https://vfmat.ch/9525

Medical Care Development International (MCD International)
Works to strengthen health systems through innovative, sustainable interventions.
Infect Dis, Logist-Op, OB-GYN, Pub Health
⊕ https://vfmat.ch/dc5c

Medical Care Development International
Works to improve the health of vulnerable populations through integrated, sustainable, and locally driven interventions.
Infect Dis, OB-GYN, Peds, Pub Health
⊕ https://vfmat.ch/da87

Medici Per I Diritti Umani (MEDU)
Treats and brings medical aid to the most vulnerable populations, and—starting from medical practice—denounces violations of human rights and, in particular, exclusion from access to treatment.
ER Med, General, Psych, Pub Health
⊕ https://vfmat.ch/5384

MedShare
Aims to improve the quality of life of people, communities, and the planet by sourcing and directly delivering surplus medical supplies and equipment to communities in need around the world.
Logist-Op
⊕ https://vfmat.ch/c8bc

Mercy and Love Foundation
Aims to provide orphaned and vulnerable children with basic human needs such as food, clothing, and shelter, enabling them to thrive.
General, Peds
⊕ https://vfmat.ch/649a

MSI Reproductive Choices (Marie Stopes International)
Seeks to deliver quality family planning and reproductive healthcare to women around the world.
MF Med
⊕ https://vfmat.ch/5c82

Médecins du Monde/Doctors of the World
Provides care, bears witness, and supports social change worldwide with innovative medical programs and evidence-based advocacy initiatives.
ER Med, General, Infect Dis, MF Med, Neonat, OB-GYN, Peds, Pub Health
⊕ https://vfmat.ch/a43d

Mérieux Foundation
Committed to fighting infectious diseases that affect developing countries by capacity building, particularly in clinical laboratories, and focusing on diagnosis.
Logist-Op, Path
⊕ https://vfmat.ch/a23a

NCD Alliance
Unites and strengthens civil society to stimulate collaborative advocacy, action, and accountability for NCD (noncommunicable disease) prevention and control.
All-Immu, CV Med, General, Heme-Onc, Medicine, Peds, Psych
⊕ https://vfmat.ch/abdd

Operation Fistula
Exists to end obstetric fistula by building models of care that serve every woman, everywhere.
MF Med, OB-GYN, Surg
⊕ https://vfmat.ch/ce8e

Order of Malta
Supports forgotten or excluded people, especially those living in conflict zones or amid natural disasters, by providing medical assistance, caring for refugees, and distributing medicines and necessities.
ER Med, General, Infect Dis, MF Med, Nephro, OB-GYN, Ortho, Psych
⊕ https://vfmat.ch/1fab

Organization for the Prevention of Blindness, The (OPC)
Provides research, and treatments and cures for people affected by blindness and blinding diseases in Francophone Africa.
Infect Dis, Ophth-Opt
⊕ https://vfmat.ch/86d6

Pan-African Academy of Christian Surgeons (PAACS)
Aims to train and disciple African surgeons and related specialists to become leaders and servants, providing excellent and compassionate care to those most in need, based in Christian ministry.
Anesth, CT Surg, OB-GYN, Ortho, Ped Surg, Plast, Surg
⊕ https://vfmat.ch/b444

Pan-African Academy of Christian Surgeons (PAACS)
Exists to train and support African surgeons to provide excellent, compassionate care to those most in need, inspired by the Christian faith.

Anesth, CT Surg, Neurosurg, OB-GYN, Ortho, Ped Surg, Plast, Surg

⊕ https://vfmat.ch/85ba

Pathfinder International
Champions sexual and reproductive health and rights worldwide, mobilizing communities most in need to break through barriers and forge paths to a healthier future.

OB-GYN

⊕ https://vfmat.ch/a7b3

Pharmacists Without Borders Canada
Provides pharmaceutical and technical assistance in the implementation or improvement of community and hospital pharmacies internationally.

⊕ https://vfmat.ch/7658

Philia Foundation
Seeks to invest sustainably in people and marginalized communities in order to improve health and education in Africa.

Anesth, ER Med, General, Heme-Onc, MF Med, Neurosurg, OB-GYN, Ophth-Opt, Ortho, Pub Health, Surg, Urol

⊕ https://vfmat.ch/a352

PSI – Population Services International
Aims to improve the health of people in the developing world by focusing on challenges such as a lack of family planning, HIV/AIDS, barriers to maternal health, and the greatest threats to children under the age of 5, including malaria, diarrhea, pneumonia, and malnutrition.

Infect Dis, MF Med, OB-GYN, Peds

⊕ https://vfmat.ch/ffe3

RestoringVision
Empowers lives by restoring vision for millions of people in need.

Ophth-Opt

⊕ https://vfmat.ch/e121

Rockefeller Foundation, The
Works to promote the well-being of humanity.

Logist-Op, Nutr, Pub Health

⊕ https://vfmat.ch/5424

Rotary International
Provides service to others, improves lives, and advances world understanding, goodwill, and peace through its fellowship of business, professional, and community leaders.

ER Med, General, Infect Dis, MF Med, OB-GYN

⊕ https://vfmat.ch/8fb5

Samaritan's Purse International Disaster Relief
Provides spiritual and physical aid to hurting people around the world, such as victims of war, poverty, natural disasters, disease, and famine, based in Christian ministry.

Anesth, CT Surg, Crit-Care, Dent-OMFS, Derm, ENT, ER Med, Endo, GI, General, Heme-Onc, Infect Dis, MF Med, Neonat, Nephro, Neuro, Neurosurg, Nutr, OB-GYN, Ophth-Opt, Ortho, Path, Ped Surg, Peds, Plast, Psych, Pulm-Critic, Radiol, Rehab, Rheum, Surg, Urol, Vasc Surg

⊕ https://vfmat.ch/87e3

Sanofi Espoir Foundation
Contributes to reducing health inequalities among populations that need it most by applying a socially responsible approach focused on fighting childhood cancers in low-income countries, improving maternal and newborn health, and improving access to care.

ER Med, OB-GYN, Peds

⊕ https://vfmat.ch/943b

SATMED
Serves nongovernmental organizations, hospitals, medical universities, and other healthcare providers active in resource-poor areas, by providing open-access e-health services for the health community.

Logist-Op

⊕ https://vfmat.ch/b8d5

Save the Children
Gives children around the world a healthy start in life, the opportunity to learn, and protection from harm.

All-Immu, Crit-Care, ER Med, General, Infect Dis, MF Med, Medicine, Neonat, OB-GYN, Peds, Psych, Pub Health

⊕ https://vfmat.ch/2e73

SCI Foundation
Seeks to prevent and treat neglected infectious diseases, with a focus on eliminating parasitic worm infections through strengthening impactful and comprehensive health programs across Sub-Saharan Africa.

Infect Dis, Pub Health

⊕ https://vfmat.ch/5444

SIGN Fracture Care International
Builds orthopedic capacity around the world and provides the injured poor access to fracture surgery by donating orthopedic education and implant systems to surgeons in developing countries.

Ortho, Rehab, Surg

⊕ https://vfmat.ch/123d

SINA Health
Aims to improve the health and educational status of the population in low- and middle-income countries.

General, Logist-Op

⊕ https://vfmat.ch/9ad3

Smile Train, Inc.
Treats children with cleft lip through a sustainable and local model that supports surgery and other forms of essential care.

Logist-Op, Pub Health

⊕ https://vfmat.ch/822c

Solthis
Improves disease prevention and access to quality care by strengthening the health systems and services of the countries served.

General, Infect Dis, Logist-Op, MF Med, Neonat, Path

⊕ https://vfmat.ch/a71d

Swiss Tropical and Public Health Institute
Contributes to the improvement of the health of populations internationally, nationally, and locally through excellence in research, education, and services.

Infect Dis, Pub Health

⊕ https://vfmat.ch/2ee4

Task Force for Global Health, The
Consists of programs and focus areas that cover a range of global health issues including neglected tropical diseases, infectious diseases, vaccines, field epidemiology, public health informatics, health workforce development, and global health ethics.

Infect Dis, Logist-Op, Medicine, Ophth-Opt, Peds

⊕ https://vfmat.ch/714c

Tearfund
Responds to crisis and partners with local churches to bring restoration to those living in poverty, inspired by the Christian faith.

ER Med, Logist-Op

⊕ https://vfmat.ch/f6cf

Terre des hommes (Tdh) Foundation
Works to improve the daily life of children and their relatives in the areas of health, protection and emergency, in Europe, Africa, Asia, Latin America, and the Near and Middle East.

CT Surg, CV Med, OB-GYN, Ped Surg, Pub Health

⊕ https://vfmat.ch/5c26

Turing Foundation
Aims to contribute toward a better world and a better society by focusing on efforts such as health, art, education, and nature.

Infect Dis

⊕ https://vfmat.ch/6bcc

U.S. President's Malaria Initiative (PMI)

Supports low-income countries to help control and eliminate malaria through cost-effective, lifesaving malaria interventions.

Infect Dis, MF Med, OB-GYN

⊕ https://vfmat.ch/dc8b

Union for International Cancer Control (UICC)

Unites and supports the cancer community to reduce the global cancer burden, promote greater equity, and ensure that cancer control continues to be a priority in the world health and development agenda.

Heme-Onc, Pub Health

⊕ https://vfmat.ch/88b1

United Nations Children's Fund (UNICEF)

Works in over 190 countries and territories to save children's lives, defend their rights, and help them fulfill their potential, from early childhood through adolescence.

All-Immu, Infect Dis, MF Med, Neonat, Nutr, OB-GYN, Ped Surg, Peds, Pub Health

⊕ https://vfmat.ch/42d7

United Nations High Commissioner for Refugees (UNHCR)

Safeguards the rights and well-being of people who have been forced to flee, ensuring that everybody has the right to seek asylum and find safe refuge in another country, with the goal of seeking lasting solutions.

General, MF Med, Medicine, OB-GYN, Peds, Psych, Pub Health

⊕ https://vfmat.ch/6636

United Nations Office for the Coordination of Humanitarian Affairs (OCHA)

Contributes to principled and effective humanitarian response through coordination, advocacy, policy, information management, and humanitarian financing tools and services, by leveraging functional expertise throughout the organization.

Logist-Op

⊕ https://vfmat.ch/22b8

United Nations Population Fund (UNFPA)

Supports reproductive healthcare for women and youth in more than 150 countries, focusing on delivering a world in which every pregnancy is wanted, every childbirth is safe, and every young person's potential is fulfilled.

Infect Dis, MF Med, Neonat, OB-GYN, Peds, Pub Health

⊕ https://vfmat.ch/c969

United States Agency for International Development (USAID)

Promotes and demonstrates democratic values abroad and advances a free, peaceful, and prosperous world. Leads the U.S. government's international development and disaster assistance through partnerships and investments that save lives.

ER Med, Infect Dis, MF Med, OB-GYN, Peds

⊕ https://vfmat.ch/9a99

University of California San Francisco: Francis I. Proctor Foundation for Ophthalmology

Aims to prevent blindness worldwide through research and teaching focused on infectious and inflammatory eye disease.

Ophth-Opt, Pub Health

⊕ https://vfmat.ch/cf47

USA for United Nations High Commissioner for Refugees (UNHCR)

Serves and protects refugees and displaced people through emergency relief, cash assistance, education, resettlement, and the rebuilding of livelihoods.

ER Med, General, Logist-Op, Nutr, Pub Health

⊕ https://vfmat.ch/293c

USAID: Fistula Care Plus

Builds on, enhances, and expands the work undertaken by the previous Fistula Care project (2007–2013), with attention to prevention, detection, treatment, reintegration and new areas of focus so that obstetric fistula can become a rare event for future generations.

MF Med, OB-GYN, Surg

⊕ https://vfmat.ch/a7cd

USAID: Human Resources for Health 2030 (HRH2030)

Helps low- and middle-income countries develop the health workforce needed to prevent maternal and child deaths, support the goals of Family Planning 2020, control the HIV/AIDS epidemic, and protect communities from infectious diseases.

Logist-Op

⊕ https://vfmat.ch/9ea8

Ventura Global Health Project (VGHP)

Aims to encourage and facilitate a lifelong interest in global health by providing grants to support local medical professionals providing care to underserved populations.

Dent-OMFS, ER Med, General, Infect Dis, Logist-Op, OB-GYN, Ophth-Opt, Ortho, Peds, Plast, Surg, Urol

⊕ https://vfmat.ch/a746

Vision Outreach International

Advocates for helping the blind in underserved regions of the world and empowers the poor through sight restoration.

Ophth-Opt

⊕ https://vfmat.ch/9721

Wells Bring Hope

Strives to transform lives by drilling deep-water wells to provide safe, clean water to rural villagers in Niger, West Africa, the poorest country in the world.

Pub Health

⊕ https://vfmat.ch/c74c

West African Health Organization

Aims to attain high standards and protection of health of the people in West Africa through harmonization of policies of the member states to combat health problems.

Infect Dis, MF Med, OB-GYN

⊕ https://vfmat.ch/7363

World Federation of Hemophilia (WFH)

Aims to improve and sustain care for people with inherited bleeding disorders by pursuing long-term relationships with individuals and organizations who share the values of WFH's development model.

Heme-Onc

⊕ https://vfmat.ch/5121

World Health Organization, The (WHO)

The United Nations' agency for health provides leadership on global health matters, shapes the health research agenda, sets norms and standards, articulates evidence-based policy options, provides technical support and monitoring to countries, and assesses health trends.

ER Med, General, Infect Dis, Logist-Op, MF Med, OB-GYN, Peds, Psych, Pub Health

⊕ https://vfmat.ch/c476

World Medical Relief

Facilitates the distribution of surplus medical resources where they are needed.

Logist-Op

⊕ https://vfmat.ch/72dc

World Vision International

Works with vulnerable communities around the world to overcome poverty and injustice with child-focused programs in disaster management, health, nutrition, economic development, education, clean water, sanitation, and hygiene.

ER Med, General, Infect Dis, MF Med, Nutr, OB-GYN, Peds

⊕ https://vfmat.ch/2642

Worldwide Fistula Fund

Protects and restores the health and dignity of the world's most vulnerable women by preventing and treating devastating childbirth injuries.

OB-GYN

⊕ https://vfmat.ch/8813

Niger

Healthcare Facilities

Aguié Public Hospital
Aguié, Niger
⊕ https://vfmat.ch/8485

Centre Hospitalier Régional
Diffa, Niger
⊕ https://vfmat.ch/541e

Centre Hospitalier Régional Agadez
Agadez, Niger
⊕ https://vfmat.ch/6a3d

Centre Mère et Enfant
Zinder, Niger
⊕ https://vfmat.ch/58aa

Centre Pilote Tessaoua pour la Chirurgie Rurale
Tessaoua, Niger
⊕ https://vfmat.ch/4354

CHU de Lamordé
Niamey, Niger
⊕ https://vfmat.ch/ea85

CURE Niger
Boulevard Ibraim Baré Maïnassara, Niamey, Niamey, Niger
⊕ https://vfmat.ch/1224

Galmi Hospital
Madaoua RN 1, Galmi, Niger
⊕ https://vfmat.ch/8a64

Hospital at Madarounfa
Madarounfa, Madarounfa, Niger
⊕ https://vfmat.ch/cb93

Hospital at Say
Say, Niger
⊕ https://vfmat.ch/42b3

Hôpital d'Ayorou
N 1, Ayorou, Tillabéri, Niger
⊕ https://vfmat.ch/8b3c

Hôpital de District Tânout
Tânout, Niger
⊕ https://vfmat.ch/2a86

Hôpital de Gawèye
Rue KI – 10, Niamey, Niger
⊕ https://vfmat.ch/cfd3

Hôpital District Sanitaire de Togone
Dogondoutchi, Niger
⊕ https://vfmat.ch/7eb5

Hôpital Militaire de Niamey
Corniche de Gamkale, Niamey, Niamey, Niger
⊕ https://vfmat.ch/dc6c

Hôpital National de Niamey
Avenue François Mitterrand, Niamey, Niamey, Niger
⊕ https://vfmat.ch/b7bc

Hôpital Regional de Dosso
Dosso, Niger
⊕ https://vfmat.ch/cb4c

Hôpital Regional de Zinder
N 1, Zinder, Mirriah, Niger
⊕ https://vfmat.ch/1bc9

Kirker Hospital, The
Maine-Soroa, Niger
⊕ https://vfmat.ch/5b18

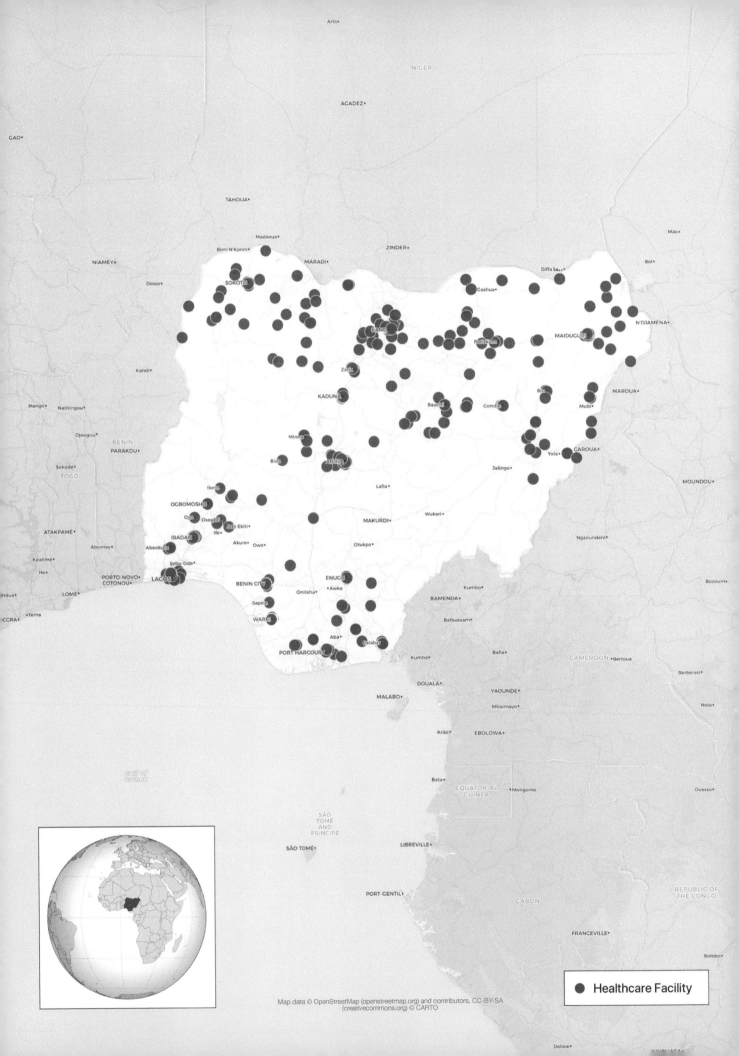

Healthcare Facility

Nigeria

Referred to as the "global giant of Africa," the Federal Republic of Nigeria in West Africa borders Niger in the north, Chad in the northeast, Cameroon in the east, and Benin in the west. The capital is Abuja, while Lagos is the most populous city in the country, as well as one of the largest metropolitan areas in the world. With an estimated 219.5 million people, Nigeria remains the most populous country in Africa and the seventh in the world. With almost 62 percent of the population under the age of 25, Nigeria is also the third largest youth-populated country in the world. Noted for its cultural diversity, the country comprises more than 250 ethnic groups that speak close to 500 different languages. Over 60 percent of the population is linked to the three major ethnic groups: the Yoruba in the west, Hausa-Fulani in the north, and Igbo in the east. English is the official and most widely spoken language. The country is divided nearly in half between Muslims who live predominantly in the north and Christians who live predominantly in the south.

Nigeria gained independence in 1960 and faced post-independence civil unrest from 1970 until 1999, when a stable democracy was finally established. Before the civil war, the country was self-sufficient in food. Since then, the country's agriculture sector has not kept pace with Nigeria's rapid population growth, requiring significant food imports. Nigeria's economy is the 24th largest in the world and the largest economy in Africa, with around $450 billion GDP. Nigeria is considered an emerging lower-middle-income economy, with a gross national income per capita of about $2,097. Religious violence dominated by the Boko Haram insurgency, political instability, income inequality, and ethnic conflict continue to undermine efforts in development. Despite these challenges, the economy continues to grow, significantly reducing poverty levels, and decreasing the number of people living below the poverty line from 61 percent in 2012 to 40 percent in 2020.

Faced with the challenge of "brain drain" due to emigration, Nigeria's healthcare system persistently contends with a scarcity of doctors. As a result, the country faces many health challenges, resulting in an alarmingly low life expectancy of 55 years. The leading causes of death in Nigeria are neonatal disorders, malaria, diarrheal diseases, lower respiratory infections, HIV/AIDS, tuberculosis, congenital defects, and meningitis. Non-communicable diseases such as ischemic heart disease and stroke have increased as major causes of death.

219.5M
Population

$2,097
GDP Per Capita

55 years
Life Expectancy
↑ Improving

38
Doctors/100k
Physician Density

50
Beds/100k
Hospital Bed Density

917
Deaths/100k
Maternal Mortality

Nigeria

Nonprofit Organizations

143 LIFE Foundation
Seeks to educate and empower individuals living with malaria, TB, HIV/AIDS, STDs and other health disparities related to sexual health.
Infect Dis, MF Med
🌐 https://vfmat.ch/d59b

Abt Associates
Seeks to improve the quality of life and economic well-being of people worldwide, while striving to meet and exceed the highest professional standards.
General, Logist-Op, MF Med, OB-GYN, Peds
🌐 https://vfmat.ch/cec2

Aceso Global
Provides strategic healthcare advisory services in low- and middle-income countries to design and deliver highly customized, evidence-based solutions that address the complex nature of healthcare systems, with a goal to strengthen and provide affordable, high-quality care to all.
Logist-Op, Pub Health
🌐 https://vfmat.ch/b3b7

Action Against Hunger
Aims to end life-threatening hunger for good through treating and preventing malnutrition across more than 45 countries.
Nutr
🌐 https://vfmat.ch/2dbc

Adegrange Child Foundation
Addresses the challenges facing children and women in Africa and North America, through strategic interventions and advocacy.
MF Med, OB-GYN, Peds, Pub Health
🌐 https://vfmat.ch/a31c

Advance Family Planning
Aims to achieve global expansion and access to quality contraceptive information, services, and supplies through financial investment and political commitment.
General, MF Med, Pub Health
🌐 https://vfmat.ch/7478

Adventist Health International
Focuses on upgrading and managing mission hospitals by providing governance, consultation, and technical assistance to a number of affiliated Seventh-Day Adventist hospitals throughout Africa, Asia, and the Americas.
Dent-OMFS, General, Pub Health
🌐 https://vfmat.ch/16aa

Africa Cataract and Eye Foundation
Aims to eradicate needless blindness in Africa by reaching out and providing compassionate, quality, affordable, and patient-centered eye care to all.
Ophth-Opt
🌐 https://vfmat.ch/1e33

Africa CDC
Aims to strengthen the capacity and capability of Africa's public health institutions and partnerships to detect and respond quickly and effectively to disease threats and outbreaks, based on data-driven interventions and programs.
Infect Dis, Logist-Op, Pub Health
🌐 https://vfmat.ch/339c

Africa Health Organisation
Leads collaborative efforts among countries in Africa and other partners to promote health equity, combat disease, and improve quality of life.
Logist-Op, Pub Health
🌐 https://vfmat.ch/b1c5

Africa Indoor Residual Spraying Project (AIRS)
Aims to protect millions of people in Africa from malaria by spraying insecticide on walls, ceilings, and other indoor resting places of mosquitoes that transmit malaria.
Infect Dis
🌐 https://vfmat.ch/9bd1

Africa Relief and Community Development
Provides comprehensive relief and developmental aid to people of the African continent regardless of gender, race, or religion.
Nutr, Pub Health
🌐 https://vfmat.ch/6cd2

African Children's Hospitals Foundation, The
Optimizes training, research, and infrastructure development for care in Africa's hospitals dedicated to the well-being of children, while coordinating and integrating these into wider healthcare systems.
MF Med, Peds, Pub Health
🌐 https://vfmat.ch/5838

African Christian Hospitals
Aims to provide excellent healthcare services to all in Nigeria, Ghana, and Tanzania, and equips and empowers African healthcare workers through medical scholarships and investments in hospitals.
General, Surg
🌐 https://vfmat.ch/5ff9

African Field Epidemiology Network (AFENET)
Strengthens field epidemiology and public health laboratory capacity to contribute effectively to addressing epidemics and other major public health problems in Africa.
All-Immu, Infect Dis, Path, Pub Health
🌐 https://vfmat.ch/df2e

African Mission
Aims to fight disease and poverty in Africa by supporting educational and medical projects.

Anesth, General
⊕ https://vfmat.ch/ea31

African Mission Health Foundation
Aims to strengthen African mission hospitals by providing quality, compassionate care for the hurting and forgotten and helping improve Sub-Saharan Africa's health system.
Infect Dis, Neonat, OB-GYN, Peds, Surg
⊕ https://vfmat.ch/5b14

African Primary Healthcare Foundation
Provides free healthcare and healthcare education to indigent persons of Africa and the African diaspora community.
OB-GYN, Ophth-Opt, Surg
⊕ https://vfmat.ch/115d

Against Malaria Foundation
Helps protect people from malaria. Funds anti-malaria nets, specifically long-lasting insecticidal nets (LLINs), and works with distribution partners to ensure they are used. Tracks and reports on net use and malaria case data.
Infect Dis
⊕ https://vfmat.ch/337d

Agatha Foundation, The
Seeks to end poverty and hunger, promote universal education, promote gender equality, reduce child mortality, improve maternal health, and combat HIV/AIDS, malaria, and other diseases.
Infect Dis, Logist-Op, Medicine, OB-GYN, Peds
⊕ https://vfmat.ch/9b26

Aid Africa's Children
Aims to empower impoverished African children and communities with healthcare, food, clean water, and educational and entrepreneurial opportunities.
ER Med, General, Infect Dis, Nutr, OB-GYN, Palliative, Peds, Pub Health
⊕ https://vfmat.ch/5e2e

AIDS Healthcare Foundation
Provides cutting-edge HIV/AIDS medical care and advocacy to over one million people in 43 countries.
Infect Dis
⊕ https://vfmat.ch/b27c

Al Basar International Foundation
Works with local partners to treat preventable blindness, and helps set up sustainable infrastructure so local teams can save sight in their communities.
Ophth-Opt
⊕ https://vfmat.ch/a8b5

Alliance for International Medical Action, The (ALIMA)
Provides quality medical care to vulnerable populations, partnering with and developing national medical organizations and conducting medical research to bring innovation to 12 African countries where ALIMA works.
ER Med, General, Infect Dis, Logist-Op, MF Med, OB-GYN, Path, Peds, Psych, Pub Health
⊕ https://vfmat.ch/1c11

Amazing Care Foundation
Provides healthcare information and sustainable development for women, youth and children in Nigeria, through education and economic and social empowerment.
General, MF Med, Pub Health
⊕ https://vfmat.ch/8e61

American Academy of Ophthalmology
Protects sight and empowers lives by serving as an advocate for patients and the public, leading ophthalmic education, and advancing the profession of ophthalmology.
Ophth-Opt
⊕ https://vfmat.ch/89a2

American Academy of Pediatrics
Seeks to attain optimal physical, mental, and social health and well-being for all infants, children, adolescents, and young adults.

Anesth, Crit-Care, Neonat, Ped Surg
⊕ https://vfmat.ch/9633

American Heart Association (AHA)
Fights heart disease and stroke, striving to save and improve lives.
CV Med, Crit-Care, General, Heme-Onc, Medicine, Peds
⊕ https://vfmat.ch/4747

American International Health Alliance (AIHA)
Strengthens health systems and workforce capacity worldwide through locally driven, peer-to-peer institutional partnerships.
CV Med, ER Med, Infect Dis, Medicine, OB-GYN
⊕ https://vfmat.ch/69fd

American Stroke Association
Works to prevent, treat, and beat stroke by funding innovative research, fighting for stronger public health policies, and providing lifesaving tools and information.
CV Med, Crit-Care, Heme-Onc, Medicine, Neuro, Pub Health, Pulm-Critic, Vasc Surg
⊕ https://vfmat.ch/746f

Americares
Saves lives and improves health for people affected by poverty or disaster and responds with life-changing medicine, medical supplies, and health programs including domestic and global medical clinics.
All-Immu, ER Med, General, Infect Dis, MF Med, Nutr
⊕ https://vfmat.ch/e567

Amref Health Africa
Serves millions of people across 35 countries in Sub-Saharan Africa, strengthening health systems, and training African health workers to respond to the continent's most critical health issues.
All-Immu, General, Infect Dis, Logist-Op, MF Med, OB-GYN, Path, Pub Health, Surg
⊕ https://vfmat.ch/6985

Amsterdam Institute for Global Health and Development (AIGHD)
Provides sustainable solutions to major health problems across our planet by forging synergies among disciplines, healthcare delivery, research, and education.
Infect Dis
⊕ https://vfmat.ch/d73d

Anambra State Association Women in USA, Inc
Develops meaningful projects that sustain and empower women and children in Anambra state, Nigeria, by means such as awareness campaigns, health clinics, and skills acquisition programs.
Heme-Onc, OB-GYN, Pub Health, Rad-Onc, Surg
⊕ https://vfmat.ch/9cad

AO Alliance
Builds solutions to lessen the burden of injuries in low- and middle-income countries, while enhancing the care of the injured to reduce human suffering, disability, and poverty.
Ortho, Surg
⊕ https://vfmat.ch/8cd5

APIN Public Health Initiatives
Provides care and treatment services to patients with HIV/AIDS, tuberculosis, and malaria, while also addressing other significant public health issues such as those concerning reproductive health, family planning, maternal, newborn, and child health, and noncommunicable disease.
General, Infect Dis, MF Med, OB-GYN, Peds, Pub Health
⊕ https://vfmat.ch/4c7e

Ark Outreach
Inspired by the Christian faith, gives hope to the vulnerable by providing them with holistic and loving care so they can embrace this world as contributing members of society.
General, Geri, MF Med, Ophth-Opt, Peds, Psych, Pub Health, Surg
⊕ https://vfmat.ch/7985

Association for Reproductive and Family Health
Collaborates with government and other strategic partners in designing and implementing innovative and high-impact programs for improved health and well-being of individuals, families, and underserved communities in Africa.
Infect Dis, MF Med
⊕ https://vfmat.ch/1f62

Association of Nigerian Physicians in the Americas (ANPA)
Represents the professional interests of physicians, dentists, and allied health professionals of Nigerian descent, and provides a platform for medical dialogue and service on matters of health.
Dent-OMFS, General, Ophth-Opt, Surg
⊕ https://vfmat.ch/83b5

Beatitude Care Foundation
Manages and funds the Beatitude Care Center in Egbelu Nguru, Nigeria, in order to provide healthcare services to women and children in surrounding communities.
MF Med, OB-GYN
⊕ https://vfmat.ch/8fc3

BFIRST – British Foundation for International Reconstructive Surgery & Training
Supports projects across the developing world to train surgeons in their local environment to effectively manage devastating injuries.
Anesth, Plast, Surg
⊕ https://vfmat.ch/ad4f

Bill & Melinda Gates Foundation
Focuses on global issues, such as poverty, health, and education, offering the opportunity to dramatically improve the quality of life for billions of people by building partnerships that bring together resources, expertise, and vision to identify issues, find answers, and drive change.
All-Immu, General, Infect Dis, MF Med, Neonat, OB-GYN, Pub Health
⊕ https://vfmat.ch/7cf2

Brain and Body Foundation
Supports patients living with brain disorders and other chronic diseases through free clinical consultations, education, and research.
Genetics, Heme-Onc
⊕ https://vfmat.ch/c9d3

British Council for Prevention of Blindness (BCPB)
Funds research into blindness prevention and sight restoration in children and adults in low- and lower-middle-income countries.
Ophth-Opt
⊕ https://vfmat.ch/eaf4

BroadReach
Collaborates with governments, multinational health organizations, donors, and private-sector companies to effect healthcare reform and solve the world's biggest health challenges.
Logist-Op
⊕ https://vfmat.ch/7812

Burn Care International
Seeks to improve the lives of burn survivors around the world through effective rehabilitation.
Derm, Nutr, Psych, Surg
⊕ https://vfmat.ch/78d1

Cairdeas International Palliative Care Trust
Promotes and facilitates the provision of high-quality palliative care in the developing world, where such care is limited.
Palliative
⊕ https://vfmat.ch/35c4

Can Obiejemba Foundation, Inc.(CANOFF)
Aims to alleviate extreme poverty, improve health, and support education, vocational training, and agriculture throughout the poorest communities of the world.
General, Ortho, Peds, Psych
⊕ https://vfmat.ch/27c3

Canadian Network for International Surgery, The
Aims to improve maternal health, increase safety, and build local capacity in low-income countries by creating and providing surgical and midwifery courses, training domestically, and transferring skills.
Logist-Op, Surg
⊕ https://vfmat.ch/86ff

CapacityBay Health Initiative
Provides intervention strategies and support to the administration of preventive healthcare services in Nigeria's underprivileged and rural communities.
Anesth, Dent-OMFS, ER Med, OB-GYN, Ophth-Opt, Path, Peds, Radiol, Rehab, Surg
⊕ https://vfmat.ch/fa58

CardioStart International
Provides free heart surgery and associated medical care to children and adults living in underserved regions of the world, irrespective of political or religious affiliation, through the collective skills of healthcare experts.
Anesth, CT Surg, CV Med, Crit-Care, Pub Health, Pulm-Critic
⊕ https://vfmat.ch/85ef

Care Organization Public Enlightenment
Aims to reduce the mortality rate of breast cancer through advocacy, treatment, research, and education.
Heme-Onc
⊕ https://vfmat.ch/c4d2

Careerbridge Foundation
Aims to reduce the mortality rate and alleviate poverty by educating and empowering the poor.
Ophth-Opt
⊕ https://vfmat.ch/57ab

Carter Center, The
Seeks to prevent and resolve conflicts, enhance freedom and democracy, and improve health, while remaining committed to human rights and the alleviation of human suffering.
Infect Dis, MF Med, Ophth-Opt
⊕ https://vfmat.ch/6556

Catholic Organization for Relief & Development Aid (CORDAID)
Provides humanitarian assistance and creates opportunities to improve security, healthcare, education, and inclusive economic growth in fragile and conflict-affected areas.
ER Med, Infect Dis, MF Med, OB-GYN, Peds, Psych
⊕ https://vfmat.ch/8ae5

Catholic World Mission
Works to rebuild communities worldwide by helping to alleviate poverty and empower underserved areas, while spreading the message of the Catholic Church.
ER Med, General, Nutr, Peds
⊕ https://vfmat.ch/7b5f

cbm New Zealand
Inspired by the Christian faith, aims to improve the quality of life for those living with the double disadvantage of poverty and disability.
Crit-Care, Infect Dis, Logist-Op, Nutr, OB-GYN, Ophth-Opt, Ortho, Psych, Rehab, Surg
⊕ https://vfmat.ch/c14b

Center for Clinical Care and Clinical Research
Promotes best practices in healthcare delivery and research using locally adapted, strengthening models of health systems.
Infect Dis, Pub Health
⊕ https://vfmat.ch/1e5d

Center for Private Sector Health Initiatives
Aims to improve the health and well-being of people in developing countries by facilitating partnerships between the public and private sectors.
Infect Dis, Nutr, Peds
⊕ https://vfmat.ch/b198

Center for the Right to Health (CRH)
Provides services and advocates for ethics and human rights in healthcare policies and practices, especially for vulnerable and marginalized groups in Nigeria.
MF Med, Pub Health
⊕ https://vfmat.ch/57ef

Challenge Initiative, The
Seeks to rapidly and sustainably scale up proven reproductive health solutions among the urban poor.
MF Med, OB-GYN, Peds
⊕ https://vfmat.ch/2f77

CharityVision International
Focuses on restoring curable sight impairment worldwide by empowering local physicians and creating sustainable solutions.
Logist-Op, Ophth-Opt, Surg
⊕ https://vfmat.ch/6231

Chief Tony Anenih Geriatric Center
Advances research and education in geriatrics through patient- and family-centered care in a culturally sensitive environment.
Dent-OMFS, Geri, Ophth-Opt, Psych
⊕ https://vfmat.ch/2192

Children & Charity International
Puts people first by providing education, leadership, and nutrition programs along with mentoring and healthcare support services to children, youth, and families.
Nutr, Peds
⊕ https://vfmat.ch/6538

Children's Emergency Relief International
Works with children, families, communities, and governments to provide a family environment as the first and best option for children to grow in.
General, Pub Health
⊕ https://vfmat.ch/92ae

Children's Relief International
Inspired by the Christian faith, cares for and educates children, their families, and their communities, including the provision of select healthcare services.
ER Med, General, Nutr
⊕ https://vfmat.ch/8da6

Christian Aid Ministries
Strives to be a trustworthy and efficient channel for Amish, Mennonite, and other conservative Anabaptist groups and individuals to minister to physical and spiritual needs around the world.
CT Surg, ER Med, Logist-Op, Ortho, Pub Health
⊕ https://vfmat.ch/7b33

Christian Blind Mission (CBM)
Aims to improve the quality of life of persons with disabilities in the poorest countries, addressing poverty as a cause and a consequence of disability, and working in partnership to create a society for all.
ENT, General, Infect Dis, OB-GYN, Ophth-Opt, Ortho, Peds, Psych, Rehab, Surg
⊕ https://vfmat.ch/3824

Christian Connections for International Health (CCIH)
Promotes global health and wholeness from a Christian perspective.
All-Immu, General, Infect Dis, MF Med, Neonat, OB-GYN, Psych
⊕ https://vfmat.ch/fa5d

Class to Care Medical Foundation
Aims to improve healthcare through continuous medical education for practitioners and public health awareness.
ER Med, Pub Health
⊕ https://vfmat.ch/8285

Clear Sight International
Deploys a community-based approach to eye health with the aim of aiding unreached and underserved communities and reducing avoidable blindness.
Logist-Op, Ophth-Opt
⊕ https://vfmat.ch/2ef2

Clinton Health Access Initiative (CHAI)
Aims to save lives and reduce the burden of disease in low- and middle-income countries. Works with partners to strengthen the capabilities of governments and the private sector to create and sustain high-quality health systems.
General, Heme-Onc, Infect Dis, Logist-Op, MF Med, Medicine, Neonat, Nutr, OB-GYN, Path, Peds, Rad-Onc
⊕ https://vfmat.ch/9ed7

Columbia University: Global Mental Health Programs
Pioneers research initiatives, promotes mental health, and aims to reduce the burden of mental illness worldwide.
Psych
⊕ https://vfmat.ch/c5cd

Columbia Vagelos College of Physicians and Surgeons Programs in Global Health
Harnesses the expertise of the medical school to improve health worldwide by training global health leaders, building capacity through interdisciplinary education and training programs, and addressing unmet health needs through research and application.
CV Med, Derm, Genetics, Heme-Onc, Infect Dis, Medicine, OB-GYN, Ophth-Opt, Peds, Psych, Pub Health, Pulm-Critic, Surg
⊕ https://vfmat.ch/a9e5

Combat Blindness International
Works to eliminate preventable blindness worldwide by providing sustainable, equitable solutions for sight through partnerships and innovation.
Ophth-Opt
⊕ https://vfmat.ch/28ad

Community Health Care Network
Eliminates disparities in healthcare quality and access to the most vulnerable and marginalized populations in the region.
CT Surg, MF Med, Ophth-Opt, Peds, Pub Health, Radiol
⊕ https://vfmat.ch/2115

Core Group
Aims to improve and expand community health practices for underserved populations, especially women and children, through collaborative action and learning.
General, Infect Dis, MF Med, Medicine, OB-GYN, Peds, Pub Health
⊕ https://vfmat.ch/9de3

COVID-19 Clinical Research Coalition
Advocates and collaborates for the advancement of COVID-19 research driven by the needs of low-resource settings, and works for equitable access to solutions to the pandemic.
All-Immu, Infect-Dis, MF Med, Path, Pub Health
⊕ https://vfmat.ch/d1f4

CureCervicalCancer
Focuses on the early detection and prevention of cervical cancer around the globe for the women who need it most.
Heme-Onc, OB-GYN
⊕ https://vfmat.ch/ace1

DAGOMO Foundation Nigeria
Focuses interventions on neglected individuals through programs that help address the physical and emotional needs of the elderly population of Nigeria.
General, Geri
⊕ https://vfmat.ch/dc93

Daniel Ogechi Akujobi Memorial Foundation
Supports the provision of education and healthcare services to the less-privileged through viable and sustainable programs, for a better society.
ER Med, General, Logist-Op, Nutr, Ophth-Opt, Pub Health
⊕ https://vfmat.ch/1c8e

Dental Helping Hands
Provides dental health services to underserved communities in developing countries.
Dent-OMFS
⊕ https://vfmat.ch/7ba5

Direct Relief
Improves the health and lives of people affected by poverty or emergency situations by mobilizing and providing essential medical resources needed for their care.
ER Med, Logist-Op
⊕ https://vfmat.ch/58e5

Divine Will Foundation
Funds educational, medical, nutritional, sustainable energy, and water purification projects.
CT Surg, CV Med, Ped Surg, Peds
⊕ https://vfmat.ch/6f1e

DKT INTERNATIONAL INC
Seeks to provide couples with affordable and safe options for family planning and HIV/AIDS prevention through dynamic social marketing.
General, Surg
⊕ https://vfmat.ch/b3a7

Doctors Without Borders/Médecins Sans Frontières (MSF)
Responds to emergencies and provides lifesaving medical care where needed most, including during disasters, conflicts, and epidemics.
Anesth, Crit-Care, ER Med, General, Infect Dis, Nutr, OB-GYN, Ped Surg, Peds, Psych, Pub Health, Surg
⊕ https://vfmat.ch/f363

Dr. Ameyo Stella Adadevoh Health Trust
Works to promote safe water, hygiene, and sanitation; to advance infection prevention and control; and to strengthen emergency preparedness.
Infect Dis, Logist-Op, Pub Health
⊕ https://vfmat.ch/ab23

Dr. Funmi Alakija Foundation
Advocates for improved medical performance and strives to meet the medical needs of disadvantaged people across Nigeria.
Genetics, Logist-Op, Peds
⊕ https://vfmat.ch/27d9

Dream Sant'Egidio
Seeks to counter HIV/AIDS in Africa by eliminating the transmission of HIV from mother to child, with a focus on women because of the importance of their role in the community.
Infect Dis, MF Med, Neonat, OB-GYN, Path, Peds
⊕ https://vfmat.ch/f466

Duke University: Global Health Institute
Sparks innovation in global health research and education, and brings together knowledge and resources to address the most important global health issues of our time.
All-Immu, Infect Dis, MF Med, OB-GYN, Pub Health
⊕ https://vfmat.ch/c4cd

Effect: Hope (The Leprosy Mission Canada)
Connects like-minded Canadians to people suffering in isolation from debilitating, neglected tropical diseases such as leprosy, lymphatic filariasis, and Buruli ulcer.
General, Infect Dis
⊕ https://vfmat.ch/f12a

eHealth Africa
Builds stronger health systems in Africa through the design and implementation of data-driven solutions, responding to local needs and providing underserved communities with the necessary tools to lead healthier lives.
Logist-Op, Path
⊕ https://vfmat.ch/db6a

Elizabeth Glaser Pediatric AIDS Foundation
Seeks to end global pediatric HIV/AIDS through prevention and treatment programs, research, and advocacy.
Infect Dis, Nutr, OB-GYN, Peds
⊕ https://vfmat.ch/d6ec

Elton John AIDS Foundation
Seeks to address and overcome the stigma, discrimination, and neglect that prevents ending AIDS by funding local experts to challenge discrimination, prevent infections, and provide treatment.
Infect Dis, Pub Health
⊕ https://vfmat.ch/9d31

Emmanuel Osemota Foundation
Empowers local communities in Africa, South Florida, and across the world to be self-sustainable through education and high-quality healthcare.
Dent-OMFS, General, Logist-Op, Nutr, Ophth-Opt, Palliative, Pub Health
⊕ https://vfmat.ch/3669

END Fund, The
Aims to control and eliminate the most prevalent neglected diseases among the world's poorest and most vulnerable people.
Infect Dis
⊕ https://vfmat.ch/2614

Ending Eclampsia
Seeks to expand access to proven, underutilized interventions and commodities for the prevention, early detection, and treatment of pre-eclampsia and eclampsia and to strengthen global partnerships.
MF Med, Neonat, OB-GYN
⊕ https://vfmat.ch/8589

EngenderHealth
Works to implement high-quality, gender-equitable programs that advance sexual and reproductive health and rights.
General, MF Med, OB-GYN, Peds
⊕ https://vfmat.ch/1cb2

Equal As One
Aims to alleviate the burdens of poverty by providing healthcare and education to those in need.
General, Ophth-Opt
⊕ https://vfmat.ch/6b52

eRanger
Provides sustainable solutions to transportation and medical provision such as ambulances and mobile clinics in developing countries.
ER Med, General, Logist-Op
⊕ https://vfmat.ch/4c18

Every Infant matters
Focuses on the health of infants, girls, and women, including nutrition, blindness prevention, vaccination, and gender discrimination, in marginalized and poor communities.
Ophth-Opt, Peds, Pub Health
⊕ https://vfmat.ch/4d6a

Evidence Action
Aims to be a world leader in scaling evidence-based and cost-effective programs to reduce the burden of poverty.
General, Infect Dis
⊕ https://vfmat.ch/94b6

Evidence Project, The
Improves family-planning policies, programs, and practices through the strategic generation, translation, and use of evidence.
General, MF Med
⊕ https://vfmat.ch/f9e7

Eye Foundation of America
Works toward a world without childhood blindness.
Ophth-Opt
⊕ https://vfmat.ch/a7eb

Eye Mantra Foundation / Charitable Hospital
Provides affordable eye care and treatment for people living in poverty.
Ophth-Opt, Surg
⊕ https://vfmat.ch/48d2

Faith Alive Foundation - Nigeria
Inspired by the Christian faith, provides compassionate voluntary services and

free holistic healthcare and social serves for improved quality of life.
ER Med, Infect Dis, OB-GYN, Palliative, Path, Radiol, Surg
⊕ https://vfmat.ch/9e9c

Federal Medical Centre, Abeokuta
Provides cost-effective healthcare services, engages in research that improves the health of Nigerians, and contributes to global medical knowledge.
CV Med, Derm, Endo, Heme-Onc, Neonat, Nephro, Neuro, OB-GYN, Ophth-Opt, Ortho, Peds, Psych, Surg, Urol
⊕ https://vfmat.ch/dde4

Fertility Education & Medical Management (FEMM)
Aims to make knowledge-based reproductive health accessible to all women and enables them to be informed partners in the choice and delivery of their medical care and services.
MF Med, OB-GYN
⊕ https://vfmat.ch/e8b2

Fistula Foundation
Aims to engage the support of people worldwide who are eager to see the day that no woman suffers from obstetric fistula. Raises and directs funds to doctors and hospitals providing life-transforming surgery to women in need.
OB-GYN
⊕ https://vfmat.ch/e958

Foundation for Special Surgery
Provides high-quality, complex surgical care by increasing surgical expertise in Africa through the participation of surgeons across various specialties to provide premium care and skills transfer/education to benefit patients.
Anesth, CT Surg, ENT, Endo, Neurosurg, Plast, Surg, Urol
⊕ https://vfmat.ch/53db

Funmi Adewole Foundation, The (FAF)
Provides free basic healthcare to underserved communities across Africa, supports quality education, and promotes cancer awareness initiatives.
Dent-OMFS, General, Heme-Onc, Ophth-Opt
⊕ https://vfmat.ch/685e

GEANCO Foundation, The
Organizes special surgical missions and runs a program to fight anemia and help vulnerable pregnant women safely deliver healthy babies in Nigeria.
MF Med, OB-GYN, Ortho, Surg
⊕ https://vfmat.ch/f7c7

GEMOFITT Public Health Initiative Nigeria
Aims to bridge the gap in affordable quality health for all.
Pub Health
⊕ https://vfmat.ch/12a3

Gift of Life International
Provides lifesaving cardiac treatment to children in developing countries while developing sustainable pediatric cardiac programs by implementing screening, surgical, and training missions.
Anesth, CT Surg, CV Med, Crit-Care, Ped Surg, Peds, Pulm-Critic
⊕ https://vfmat.ch/f2f9

Global Alliance to Prevent Prematurity And Stillbirth (GAPPS)
Seeks to improve birth outcomes worldwide by reducing the burden of premature birth and stillbirth.
All-Immu, Infect Dis, MF Med, Neonat, Neonat, OB-GYN
⊕ https://vfmat.ch/3f74

Global Blood Fund
Delivers grants, equipment, and training to over 50 countries in Africa, Asia, Eastern Europe, the Middle East, Latin America and the Caribbean.
Pub Health
⊕ https://vfmat.ch/6377

Global Image Foundation
Makes a positive impact on communities through healthcare and education initiatives, such as free medical, surgical, and dental missions and workshops in technical skills.
Dent-OMFS, General, OB-GYN, Ophth-Opt, Surg
⊕ https://vfmat.ch/9d7b

Global Kidney Foundation
Aims to reduce the death rate and create awareness about the devastating effects of chronic kidney disease, and to provide food for those in need.
Nephro, Pub Health
⊕ https://vfmat.ch/6df6

Global Ministries – The United Methodist Church
As the worldwide mission and development agency of The United Methodist Church, Global Ministries works with more than 300 hospitals and clinics around the world through its Global Health Unit.
Anesth, CT Surg, CV Med, Crit-Care, Dent-OMFS, Derm, ER Med, GI, General, Infect Dis, Logist-Op, MF Med, Medicine, Neonat, Nephro, Nutr, OB-GYN, Ophth-Opt, Ortho, Palliative, Peds, Pod, Psych, Pub Health, Rehab, Rheum, Surg, Urol
⊕ https://vfmat.ch/1723

Global Offsite Care
Aims to be a catalyst for increased access to specialized healthcare for all, and provides technology platforms to doctors and clinics around the world through Rotary Club-sponsored telemedicine projects.
Crit-Care, ER Med, General, Pulm-Critic
⊕ https://vfmat.ch/61b5

Global Oncology (GO)
Brings the best in cancer care to underserved patients around the world and collaborates across geographic, professional, and academic borders to improve cancer care, research, and education.
Heme-Onc, Path, Rad-Onc
⊕ https://vfmat.ch/fcb8

Global Polio Eradication Initiative
Aims to eradicate polio worldwide.
All-Immu, Infect-Dis, Logist-Op, Pub Health
⊕ https://vfmat.ch/7e2c

Global Strategies
Empowers communities in the most neglected areas of the world to improve the lives of women and children through healthcare.
MF Med, Neonat, OB-GYN, Peds
⊕ https://vfmat.ch/ef92

Globus Relief
Aims to improve the delivery of healthcare worldwide by gathering, processing, and distributing surplus medical supplies to charities at home and abroad.
Logist-Op
⊕ https://vfmat.ch/a2b7

Grace for Impact
Provides high-quality healthcare and education to the rural poor, where it is needed most, in Sub-Saharan Africa and Southeast Asia.
Dent-OMFS, General, Ophth-Opt
⊕ https://vfmat.ch/3ed1

Grassroot Soccer
Leverages the power of soccer to educate, inspire, and mobilize at-risk youth in developing countries to overcome their greatest health challenges, live healthier and more productive lives, and be agents for change in their communities.
Infect Dis
⊕ https://vfmat.ch/3521

Gynea Care Research & Cancer Foundation
Promotes the health and well-being of women in Nigeria by ensuring everyone can access holistic cancer preventive services.
OB-GYN, Rad-Onc
⊕ https://vfmat.ch/79ad

HACEY
Committed to empower and support women, children and young people in Nigeria to live productive and healthy lives through the Innovation, Capacity development, Advocacy, Research, and Education (i.C.A.R.E) approach.
General, OB-GYN
⊕ https://vfmat.ch/ece7

Hands At Work
Based in Christian ministry, supports those in need through its community intervention model with a focus on food security, education, and basic healthcare.
General, Infect Dis, Nutr, Pub Health
⊕ https://vfmat.ch/7274

Healing Little Hearts
Sends specialist medical teams to perform free lifesaving heart surgery on babies and children in developing parts of the world.
Anesth, CT Surg, CV Med, Ped Surg, Peds, Surg
⊕ https://vfmat.ch/ffc1

Healing the Children
Helps underserved children around the world secure the medical care they need to lead more fulfilling lives.
Anesth, Dent-OMFS, ENT, General, Medicine, Ophth-Opt, Ped Surg, Peds, Plast, Surg
⊕ https://vfmat.ch/d4ee

Health Emergency Initiative
Provides emergency medical care to vulnerable people in public hospitals and supports other health-related initiatives, inspired by the Christian faith.
ER Med
⊕ https://vfmat.ch/7b95

Health For Nigeria
Expands access to high-quality primary medical care services to all Nigerians.
General, OB-GYN, Pub Health, Surg
⊕ https://vfmat.ch/7c7b

Health Frontiers
Provides volunteer support to international health and child development efforts.
ER Med, Medicine, Peds
⊕ https://vfmat.ch/aa14

Health Place For Children Initiative
Builds a resilient healthcare system and provides systems to support training in the delivery of adequate care for critically ill children in Nigeria.
General, Peds, Pub Health
⊕ https://vfmat.ch/c7ad

Health[e] Foundation
Supports health professionals and community workers in the world's most vulnerable societies to ensure quality health for everyone in need by providing digital education and information, using e-learning and m-health.
Logist-Op
⊕ https://vfmat.ch/b73b

Healthcare Relief (Health for Africa)
Works toward relief of poverty and sickness, supporting causes including healthcare services, healthy campaigns for those in poverty, and research.
Logist-Op, Pub Health
⊕ https://vfmat.ch/da5a

Healthy DEvelopments
Provides Germany-supported health and social protection programs around the globe in a collaborative knowledge management process.
All-Immu, General, Infect Dis, Logist-Op, MF Med
⊕ https://vfmat.ch/dc31

Heart to Heart International
Strengthens communities through improving health access, providing humanitarian development, and administering crisis relief worldwide. Engages volunteers, collaborates with partners, and deploys resources to achieve this mission.
Anesth, ER Med, General, Logist-Op, Medicine, Path, Path, Peds, Psych, Pub Health, Surg
⊕ https://vfmat.ch/aacb

Helen Keller International
Seeks to eliminate preventable vision loss, malnutrition, and diseases of poverty.
Infect Dis, Nutr, OB-GYN, Ophth-Opt, Peds
⊕ https://vfmat.ch/b654

HelpMum
Aims to eradicate infant and maternal mortality in Nigeria through the distribution of clean birth kits and the training of community birth attendants.
Logist-Op, OB-GYN
⊕ https://vfmat.ch/f156

Hernia International
Aims to provide relief from sickness, and protection and preservation of health, for persons affected by groin and abdominal hernias and residing in low- and middle-income countries.
Surg
⊕ https://vfmat.ch/e98e

Hospice Africa
Aims to provide a holistic and culturally sensitive palliative care service through accurate treatment of pain.
Palliative
⊕ https://vfmat.ch/9f86

Hospitals for Humanity
Works to improve the quality of lives of children who are born with heart defects in countries with limited resources.
Anesth, CT Surg, CV Med, Crit-Care, Ped Surg, Pulm-Critic
⊕ https://vfmat.ch/68b1

Humanity First
Provides aid and assistance to those in need, offering sustainable development solutions to society while providing and empowering local communities with the resources to help themselves.
ER Med, General, MF Med, Ophth-Opt
⊕ https://vfmat.ch/13cc

ICAP at Columbia University
Serves as global leader in supporting the scale-up of multidisciplinary HIV/AIDS prevention, care, and treatment programs based on a family-focused approach.
General, Infect Dis, MF Med, Medicine, OB-GYN, Pub Health
⊕ https://vfmat.ch/a8ef

IHSAN Foundation for West Africa
Seeks to improve the social and economic lives of the people of West Africa through educational, humanitarian, and healthcare projects.
Dent-OMFS, ER Med, General, Infect Dis
⊕ https://vfmat.ch/c719

Institute for Healthcare Improvement (IHI)
Aims to improve health and healthcare worldwide by working with health professionals to strengthen systems.
Crit-Care, Infect Dis, MF Med, Medicine, Neonat, OB-GYN, Pub Health
⊕ https://vfmat.ch/ecae

International Agency for the Prevention of Blindness (IAPB), The
Leads international efforts in blindness-prevention activities, works toward a world where no one is needlessly visually impaired, and ensures that everyone has access to the best possible standard of eye health.
Infect Dis, Ophth-Opt, Pub Health
⊕ https://vfmat.ch/87a2

International Campaign for Women's Right to Safe Abortion
Works to build an international network and campaign that brings together organizations with an interest in promoting and providing safe abortion to create a shared platform for advocacy, debate, and dialogue and the sharing of skills and experience.
OB-GYN, Pub Health, Surg
⊕ https://vfmat.ch/f341

International Children's Heart Foundation
Provides free surgical care, medical training, and technology to save the lives of children with congenital heart disease in developing countries.
Anesth, CT Surg, CV Med, Crit-Care, Ped Surg, Peds, Pulm-Critic
⊕ https://vfmat.ch/86c1

International Council of Ophthalmology

Works with ophthalmologic societies and others to enhance ophthalmic education and improve access to the highest-quality eye care in order to preserve and restore vision for people of the world.

Ophth-Opt

⊕ https://vfmat.ch/ffd2

International Federation of Gynecology and Obstetrics (FIGO)

Implements global projects on specific women's health issues.

MF Med, Medicine, Neonat, OB-GYN, Surg, Urol

⊕ https://vfmat.ch/c4b4

International Federation of Red Cross and Red Crescent Societies (IFRC)

Coordinates and directs international assistance following natural and manmade disasters in nonconflict situations through the world's largest humanitarian and development network. Provides disaster-preparedness programs, healthcare activities, and promotes humanitarian values.

ER Med, General, Infect Dis, Nutr

⊕ https://vfmat.ch/b4ee

International League of Dermatological Socieities

Strives to promote high-quality education, clinical care, research and innovation that will improve skin health globally.

Derm, Infect Dis

⊕ https://vfmat.ch/7388

International Learning Movement (ILM UK)

Supports some of the world's poorest people in developing countries with core projects in education, safe drinking water, and healthcare.

General, Ophth-Opt

⊕ https://vfmat.ch/b974

International Medical Corps

Seeks to improve quality of life through health interventions and related activities that strengthen underserved communities worldwide, with the flexibility to respond rapidly to emergencies and offer medical services and training to people at the highest risk.

ER Med, General, Infect Dis, Nutr, OB-GYN, Peds, Pub Health, Surg

⊕ https://vfmat.ch/a8a5

International Mission Opportunities

Provides medical assistance to as many people as possible.

Dent-OMFS, Ophth-Opt, Pub Health, Surg

⊕ https://vfmat.ch/cc1d

International Organization for Migration (IOM) – The UN Migration Agency

Promotes evidence-informed policies and holistic, preventive, and curative health programs that are beneficial, accessible, and equitable for vulnerable migrants.

General, Infect Dis, OB-GYN

⊕ https://vfmat.ch/621a

International Pediatric Nephrology Association (IPNA)

Leads global efforts to successfully address the care for all children with kidney disease through advocacy, education, and training.

Medicine, Nephro, Peds

⊕ https://vfmat.ch/b59d

International Planned Parenthood Federation (IPPF)

Leads a locally owned, globally connected civil society movement that provides and enables services and champions sexual and reproductive health and rights for all, especially the underserved.

Infect Dis, MF Med, OB-GYN

⊕ https://vfmat.ch/dc97

International Rescue Committee (IRC)

Responds to the world's worst humanitarian crises and helps people whose lives and livelihoods are shattered by conflict and disaster to survive, recover, and gain control of their future.

ER Med, General, Infect Dis, MF Med, Peds

⊕ https://vfmat.ch/5d24

International Trachoma Initiative (iTi)

Works toward a world free from trachoma, a preventable cause of blindness, and provides comprehensive support to national ministries of health and governmental and nongovernmental organizations to implement a comprehensive approach to fight trachoma.

Infect Dis, Ophth-Opt

⊕ https://vfmat.ch/3278

Intersos

Provides emergency medical assistance to victims of armed conflicts, natural disasters, and extreme exclusion, with particular attention to the protection of the most vulnerable people.

ER Med, General, Nutr

⊕ https://vfmat.ch/dbac

InterSurgeon

Fosters collaborative partnerships in the field of global surgery that will advance clinical care, teaching, training, research, and the provision and maintenance of medical equipment.

ENT, Neurosurg, Ortho, Ped Surg, Plast, Surg, Urol

⊕ https://vfmat.ch/6f8a

IntraHealth International

Improves the performance of health workers and strengthens the systems in which they work.

CV Med, Endo, General, Infect Dis, MF Med, Neonat, Nutr, OB-GYN

⊕ https://vfmat.ch/ddc8

Ipas

Focuses efforts on women and girls who want contraception or abortion, and builds programs around their needs and how best to support them.

OB-GYN

⊕ https://vfmat.ch/8e39

IVUmed

Aims to make quality urological care available worldwide by providing medical and surgical education for physicians and nurses, and treatment for thousands of children and adults.

Anesth, OB-GYN, Ped Surg, Surg, Urol

⊕ https://vfmat.ch/e619

Izumi Foundation

Develops and supports programs that improve health and healthcare in neglected regions of Africa and Latin America.

⊕ https://vfmat.ch/f29a

Jhpiego

Creates and delivers transformative healthcare solutions that save lives, in partnership with national governments, health experts, and local communities.

General, Infect Dis, OB-GYN, Surg

⊕ https://vfmat.ch/45b8

John Snow, Inc. (JSI)

Aims to improve the health and well-being of underserved and vulnerable people and communities throughout the world.

General, Infect Dis, Logist-Op, MF Med, OB-GYN, Peds, Psych, Pub Health

⊕ https://vfmat.ch/ba78

Johns Hopkins Center for Communication Programs

Believes in the power of communication to save lives by empowering people to adopt healthy behaviors for themselves, their families, and their communities.

General, Infect Dis, Logist-Op, OB-GYN, Pub Health

⊕ https://vfmat.ch/1bf9

Johns Hopkins Center for Global Health

Facilitates and focuses the extensive expertise and resources of the Johns Hopkins institutions, together with global collaborators, to effectively address and ameliorate the world's most pressing health issues.

General, Genetics, Logist-Op, MF Med, Peds, Psych, Pub Health, Pulm-Critic

⊕ https://vfmat.ch/54ce

Joint United Nations Programme on HIV/AIDS (UNAIDS)

Aims to place people living with HIV and people affected by the virus at the

decision-making table and at the center of designing, delivering, and monitoring the AIDS response.
Infect Dis
⊕ https://vfmat.ch/464a

KNCV Tuberculosis Foundation
Aims to end human suffering through the global elimination of tuberculosis.
Pulm-Critic
⊕ https://vfmat.ch/98bf

Kolawole Interventional Radiology Foundation
Makes life-saving techniques of interventional radiology available to the Nigerian population at large and serves low-resource patients.
Rad-Onc, Radiol
⊕ https://vfmat.ch/f814

Korle-Bu Neuroscience Foundation
Committed to providing medical support for brain and spinal injuries and disease to the people of Ghana and West Africa.
Anesth, Logist-Op, Neuro, Neurosurg, Rehab
⊕ https://vfmat.ch/6695

Labakcare
Aims to improve the health of underserved communities by providing no-cost preventive healthcare services.
General, MF Med, Ophth-Opt
⊕ https://vfmat.ch/1e61

Lady Helen Child Health Foundation
Encourages a culture of informed preventive medical practice and the use of best evidence for managing children's medical needs.
Logist-Op, MF Med, Peds
⊕ https://vfmat.ch/d37e

Lagos State University Teaching Hospital
Provides high-quality healthcare services, advances care through innovative research and education, and improves the health and well-being of diverse communities.
Anesth, Crit-Care, Dent-OMFS, ENT, General, Heme-Onc, Medicine, Nutr, OB-GYN, Ophth-Opt, Path, Peds, Psych, Pub Health, Radiol, Radiol, Rehab, Surg
⊕ https://vfmat.ch/b46b

Lazgrace Charity Foundation
Aims to provide free medical treatment for basics illnesses, along with free secondary education for indigent children.
General
⊕ https://vfmat.ch/788b

Leprosy Mission Australia, The
Provides support to people with leprosy including screening, medical treatment and job opportunities, inspired by the Christian faith.
Infect Dis
⊕ https://vfmat.ch/9e4b

Leprosy Mission England and Wales, The
Leads the fight against leprosy by supporting people living with leprosy today and serving future generations by working to end transmission of the disease.
Infect Dis, Pub Health
⊕ https://vfmat.ch/4c67

Leprosy Mission International
Seeks to empower people with leprosy to attain healing, dignity, and life in all its fullness.
Infect Dis
⊕ https://vfmat.ch/95a9

Leprosy Mission: Northern Ireland, The
Leads the fight against leprosy by supporting people living with leprosy today and serving future generations by working to end the transmission of the disease.
General, Infect Dis
⊕ https://vfmat.ch/e265

Life for a Child
Supports the provision of the best possible healthcare, given local circumstances, to all children and youth with diabetes in less-resourced countries, through the strengthening of existing diabetes services.
Endo, Medicine, Peds
⊕ https://vfmat.ch/d712

Limbs International
Engages communities and transforms lives through affordable, sustainable prosthetic solutions and rehabilitation services in developing countries.
Logist-Op, Ortho, Pod, Rehab
⊕ https://vfmat.ch/dc84

Little Big Souls
Provides necessary support to premature and sick babies in less privileged parts of Africa through equipment donation, medical training, parental support, emergency transportation, and advocacy.
ER Med, Logist-Op, Neonat, Peds
⊕ https://vfmat.ch/2f43

Management Sciences for Health (MSH)
Works with countries and communities to save lives and improve the health of the world's poorest and most vulnerable people by building strong, resilient, sustainable health systems.
Infect Dis, Logist-Op, Pub Health
⊕ https://vfmat.ch/6aa2

MAP International
Provides medicines and health supplies to those in need around the world so they might experience life to the fullest.
Logist-Op
⊕ https://vfmat.ch/deed

Marie Stopes International
Provides the contraception and safe abortion services that enable women all over the world to choose their own futures.
Infect Dis, MF Med, Neonat, OB-GYN, Pub Health
⊕ https://vfmat.ch/9525

Mary Care
Provides access to critical healthcare, nutrition, clean water, and micro-loans to give entrepreneurs the start they need to launch a small business.
Nephro, Neuro
⊕ https://vfmat.ch/bda7

Maternity Worldwide
Works with communities and partners to identify and develop appropriate and effective ways to reduce maternal and newborn mortality and morbidity, facilitate communities to access quality skilled maternity care, and support the provision of quality skilled care.
MF Med, OB-GYN
⊕ https://vfmat.ch/822b

Max Foundation, The
Seeks to increase global access to treatment, care, and support for people living with cancer.
General, Heme-Onc, Pub Health
⊕ https://vfmat.ch/8c7d

Medical Care Development International
Works to improve the health of vulnerable populations through integrated, sustainable, and locally driven interventions.
Infect Dis, OB-GYN, Peds, Pub Health
⊕ https://vfmat.ch/da87

Medical Missions International
Supports Christian medical missions and the development of missionary hospitals to fulfill needs of the people in Nigeria and worldwide. Its Christian outreach mission is conducted through its Christian doctors, dentists, nurses, other healthcare personnel, and ministers.
Anesth, General, Ped Surg, Peds, Surg
⊕ https://vfmat.ch/b252

MedShare

Aims to improve the quality of life of people, communities, and the planet by sourcing and directly delivering surplus medical supplies and equipment to communities in need around the world.

Logist-Op
⊕ https://vfmat.ch/c8bc

MENTOR Initiative

Saves lives in emergencies through tropical disease control, and helps people recover from crisis with dignity, working side by side with communities, health workers, and health authorities to leave a lasting impact.

ER Med, Infect Dis
⊕ https://vfmat.ch/3bd5

Merck for Mothers

Hopes to create a world where no woman has to die giving life by collaborating with partners to improve the health and well-being of women during pregnancy, childbirth, and the postpartum period.

MF Med, OB-GYN
⊕ https://vfmat.ch/5b51

Mercy and Love Foundation

Aims to provide orphaned and vulnerable children with basic human needs such as food, clothing, and shelter, enabling them to thrive.

General, Peds
⊕ https://vfmat.ch/649a

Mercy Hospital, Abak

Restores and promotes the glory of Mercy Hospital.

Ophth-Opt
⊕ https://vfmat.ch/6148

Mercy International Mission

Provides access to basic healthcare services for everyone in Nigeria, especially women, children, and the elderly, regardless of ability to pay.

General, Ophth-Opt, Peds, Surg
⊕ https://vfmat.ch/af49

Mezu International Foundation

Organizes charitable programs for the underserved in the U.S. and Africa in areas of agriculture, community development, healthcare, and education.

All-Immu, General, Infect Dis, Ophth-Opt
⊕ https://vfmat.ch/bf95

Midland International Aid Trust

Provides food, goods, clothing, and equipment to those in financial need or who are suffering as a result of a disaster.

CT Surg, Dent-OMFS, ENT, Logist-Op, OB-GYN, Ophth-Opt, Ortho, Ped Surg, Plast, Pub Health, Rehab
⊕ https://vfmat.ch/7eb2

MiracleFeet

Brings low-cost treatment to every child on the planet born with clubfoot, a leading cause of physical disability.

Ortho, Peds, Rehab
⊕ https://vfmat.ch/bda8

Mission Africa

Brings medical care, training, and compassion to underserved communities in Africa, based in Christian ministry.

Dent-OMFS, General, Infect Dis
⊕ https://vfmat.ch/df4d

Mission Africa US

Engages in self-sustaining projects and programs for the enhancement of vulnerable children's quality of life in three focus areas: education, health and poverty alleviation.

General, Infect Dis, Neuro, Ophth-Opt, Pub Health
⊕ https://vfmat.ch/7ecb

Mission Regan

Collects supplies, medication, and medical equipment and provides them to those who are in desperate need, both locally and globally.

Logist-Op
⊕ https://vfmat.ch/2bc1

Mission Vision

Seeks to decrease blindness and other eye-related disabilities, and to increase academic performance and general quality of life.

Ophth-Opt
⊕ https://vfmat.ch/83d8

Missions Without Walls

Sends volunteers to countries in need of progressive medical care, enhances local practitioners' knowledge, raises resources, and expands projects to other communities in need.

ER Med, General, Logist-Op
⊕ https://vfmat.ch/c7a7

More Than Medicine

Provides ENT head/neck care while supporting local doctors to grow the quality of medicine abroad.

Anesth, ENT, Heme-Onc, Surg
⊕ https://vfmat.ch/c4e8

MSD for Mothers

Designs scalable solutions that help end preventable maternal deaths.

MF Med, OB-GYN, Pub Health
⊕ https://vfmat.ch/9f99

MSI Reproductive Choices (Marie Stopes International)

Seeks to deliver quality family planning and reproductive healthcare to women around the world.

MF Med
⊕ https://vfmat.ch/5c82

Mustard Seed Communities (MSC)

Inspired by the Christian faith, uplifts the most vulnerable members of society through nutrition, education, community development, child health, and sustainable agriculture programs.

Infect Dis, Logist-Op, Rehab
⊕ https://vfmat.ch/eac5

Médecins du Monde/Doctors of the World

Provides care, bears witness, and supports social change worldwide with innovative medical programs and evidence-based advocacy initiatives.

ER Med, General, Infect Dis, MF Med, Neonat, OB-GYN, Peds, Pub Health
⊕ https://vfmat.ch/a43d

NAS Medical Mission

Aims to reach a significant population of indigent Nigerians needing medical help in specifically targeted rural communities.

Dent-OMFS, General, Medicine
⊕ https://vfmat.ch/6cf1

National Ear Care Centre, Kaduna

Seeks to provide quality service through research, training and patient care to the deaf, hearing impaired, and nose and throat patients in Nigeria and Africa as a whole.

ENT, ER Med, Radiol, Surg
⊕ https://vfmat.ch/1c1f

NCD Alliance

Unites and strengthens civil society to stimulate collaborative advocacy, action, and accountability for NCD (noncommunicable disease) prevention and control.

All-Immu, CV Med, General, Heme-Onc, Medicine, Peds, Psych
⊕ https://vfmat.ch/abdd

NEST 360

Works to ensure that hospitals in Africa can deliver lifesaving care for small and sick newborns, by developing and distributing high-quality technologies and services.

MF Med, Neonat, Peds, Pub Health
⊕ https://vfmat.ch/cea9

New Horizons Collaborative

Advances a holistic, integrated approach to high-quality pediatric HIV care and treatment with a specific focus on those in need of advanced treatment.

Infect Dis, Peds, Pub Health

⊕ https://vfmat.ch/a76a

Niola Cancer Care Foundation

Campaigns for wellness and early detection through communication and engagement while leveraging solid partnerships with stakeholders and volunteers.

Heme-Onc, Palliative

⊕ https://vfmat.ch/46d1

Nko Foundation

Provides quality and affordable healthcare to those most in need in Nigeria and Africa in general through varied forms of philanthropy.

ENT, Neurosurg, OB-GYN, Ophth-Opt, Ortho, Surg, Urol

⊕ https://vfmat.ch/c731

Nnadozie Integrated Development Foundation

Promote and advance the rights and well-being of women, girls, and under-served people through economic empowerment and advocacy.

OB-GYN, Peds, Pub Health

⊕ https://vfmat.ch/699d

North American Council of Eastern Nigeria Adventist (NACENA)

Based in Christian ministry, seeks to improve services in hospitals within the Eastern Nigeria Union Conference (ENUC) of Seventh-Day Adventists, with the intent of promoting the delivery of quality, efficient, and patient-centered care.

General, Surg

⊕ https://vfmat.ch/84dd

Oak Rural Health Organization

Provides access to healthcare services, mitigates potential risks to healthy living in rural communities, and engages in programs that consider the community members themselves as stakeholders in proffering solutions to their health needs, so as to make a sustainable impact.

General, Infect Dis, Logist-Op, Nutr, Pub Health

⊕ https://vfmat.ch/7629

OB Foundation

Works in partnership globally to deliver locally sustainable, quality healthcare, health education, and health solutions to medically underserved, rural communities.

General

⊕ https://vfmat.ch/91d7

Operation Healthy Africa

Organizes and participates in medical missions, disease treatment and prevention, vision and hearing care, and other medical services around the world, while also providing medical equipment and other supplies in the areas where it operates.

Dent-OMFS, General, Infect Dis, Logist-Op, MF Med, OB-GYN, Ophth-Opt, Surg

⊕ https://vfmat.ch/c99b

Operation International

Offers medical aid to adults and children suffering from lack of quality healthcare in impoverished countries.

Dent-OMFS, ER Med, Heme-Onc, OB-GYN, Ophth-Opt, Ortho, Ped Surg, Plast, Surg

⊕ https://vfmat.ch/b52a

Options

Believes in a world in which women and children can access the high-quality health services they need, without financial burden.

Logist-Op, MF Med, Neonat, OB-GYN

⊕ https://vfmat.ch/3a48

Optometry Giving Sight

Delivers eye exams and low or no-cost glasses, provides training for local eye care professionals, and establishes optometry schools, vision centers and optical labs.

Ophth-Opt

⊕ https://vfmat.ch/33ea

Order of Malta

Supports forgotten or excluded people, especially those living in conflict zones or amid natural disasters, by providing medical assistance, caring for refugees, and distributing medicines and necessities.

ER Med, General, Infect Dis, MF Med, Nephro, OB-GYN, Ortho, Psych

⊕ https://vfmat.ch/1fab

Osteogenesis Imperfecta Foundation, Nigeria

Creates awareness of the brittle bone condition and equips children in Nigeria with the necessary tools to improve quality of life and be independent.

Endo, Genetics, Peds

⊕ https://vfmat.ch/e879

Pact

Works on the ground to improve the lives of those who are challenged by poverty and marginalization, striving for a world in which all people are heard, capable, and vibrant.

Infect Dis, Logist-Op, MF Med, Pub Health

⊕ https://vfmat.ch/9a6c

Partners for Development (PfD)

Works to improve quality of life for vulnerable people in underserved communities through local and international partnerships.

Infect Dis, MF Med, Neonat, Peds

⊕ https://vfmat.ch/d2f6

PATH

Advances health equity through innovation and partnerships so people, communities, and economies can thrive.

All-Immu, CV Med, Endo, Heme-Onc, Infect Dis, MF Med, Neonat, Nutr, OB-GYN, Path, Peds, Pulm-Critic

⊕ https://vfmat.ch/b4db

Pathfinder International

Champions sexual and reproductive health and rights worldwide, mobilizing communities most in need to break through barriers and forge paths to a healthier future.

OB-GYN

⊕ https://vfmat.ch/a7b3

Physicians Across Continents

Provides high-quality medical care to people affected by crises and disasters.

CV Med, Dent-OMFS, Heme-Onc, MF Med, Nephro, Nephro, OB-GYN, Ped Surg, Plast, Surg

⊕ https://vfmat.ch/fe5d

Picture of Health Foundation

Provides communities with health education and empowers people to alter unhealthy lifestyles, thus increasing both life expectancy and quality.

General, Pub Health

⊕ https://vfmat.ch/83e3

Ponseti International

Provides global leadership in building high-quality, locally directed, and sustainable capacity to deliver the Ponseti clubfoot care pathway at the country level.

Ortho, Ped Surg, Peds, Rehab

⊕ https://vfmat.ch/476b

Population Council

Conducts research to address critical health and development issues, helping deliver solutions to improve lives around the world.

Logist-Op, Pub Health

⊕ https://vfmat.ch/1777

Positive Action for Treatment Access (PATA)

Ensures that every individual with an illness or disease, especially women and girls, has access to treatment and literacy skills, and to equitable, humane care and empowerment.

Infect Dis, OB-GYN, Peds, Pub Health

⊕ https://vfmat.ch/46f9

Première Urgence International

Helps civilians who are marginalized or excluded as a result of natural disasters, war, or economic collapse.

ER Med, General, MF Med, Peds, Psych

⊕ https://vfmat.ch/62ba

Pro-Health International Africa

Provides quality and quantitative healthcare and hope to the poor and less privileged in rural areas of Africa.

Dent-OMFS, ER Med, General, Infect Dis, MF Med, Neonat, OB-GYN, Ophth-Opt, Psych, Surg

⊕ https://vfmat.ch/6b74

Project HOPE

Works on the front lines of the world's health challenges, partnering hand-in-hand with communities, healthcare workers, and public health systems to ensure sustainable change.

CV Med, ER Med, Endo, General, Infect Dis, MF Med, Peds

⊕ https://vfmat.ch/2bd7

Project SOAR

Conducts HIV operations research around the world to identify practical solutions to improve HIV prevention, care, and treatment services.

ER Med, General, MF Med, OB-GYN, Psych

⊕ https://vfmat.ch/1a77

Providence Care Community Initiative

Provides access to free and high-quality healthcare for residents of Amichi, Nigeria.

Dent-OMFS, General, Ophth-Opt, Rehab

⊕ https://vfmat.ch/4b6e

PSI – Population Services International

Aims to improve the health of people in the developing world by focusing on challenges such as a lack of family planning, HIV/AIDS, barriers to maternal health, and the greatest threats to children under the age of 5, including malaria, diarrhea, pneumonia, and malnutrition.

Infect Dis, MF Med, OB-GYN, Peds

⊕ https://vfmat.ch/ffe3

RAD-AID International

Improves and optimizes access to medical imaging and radiology in low-resource regions of the world.

Rad-Onc, Radiol

⊕ https://vfmat.ch/537f

Real Medicine Foundation (RMF)

Provides humanitarian support to people living in disaster- and poverty-stricken areas, focusing on the person as a whole by providing medical/physical, emotional, economic, and social support.

ER Med, General, Infect Dis, Nutr, Peds, Psych

⊕ https://vfmat.ch/d45a

RestoringVision

Empowers lives by restoring vision for millions of people in need.

Ophth-Opt

⊕ https://vfmat.ch/e121

Ret. Pray. Love Foundation

Aims to create a world in which everybody sees better, both physically and spiritually, based in Christian ministry,

Ophth-Opt

⊕ https://vfmat.ch/6e7d

Richgrace Family Healthcare Foundation

Aims to minimize maternal and infant mortality rates in Nigeria, especially in rural communities.

MF Med

⊕ https://vfmat.ch/128c

Riders for Health

Strives to ensure that reliable transport is available for healthcare services.

Logist-Op

⊕ https://vfmat.ch/7353

Riders for Health International

Aids in the last mile of healthcare delivery, by ensuring that healthcare reaches everyone, everywhere.

ER Med, Infect Dis, Logist-Op, Pub Health

⊕ https://vfmat.ch/85aa

Rotary Action Group for Family Health & AIDS Prevention (RFHA)

Works to save and improve the lives of children and families who lack access to preventive healthcare and education.

Dent-OMFS, Infect Dis, OB-GYN, Ophth-Opt, Peds

⊕ https://vfmat.ch/6563

Rotary International

Provides service to others, improves lives, and advances world understanding, goodwill, and peace through its fellowship of business, professional, and community leaders.

ER Med, General, Infect Dis, MF Med, OB-GYN

⊕ https://vfmat.ch/8fb5

ROW Foundation

Works to improve the quality of training for healthcare providers, and the diagnosis and treatment available to people with epilepsy and associated psychiatric disorders in under-resourced areas of the world.

Neuro, Psych

⊕ https://vfmat.ch/25eb

Sakinah Medical outreach

Provides free, quality healthcare services and medical assistance for indigent members of the community.

General, Ophth-Opt

⊕ https://vfmat.ch/8188

Salvation Army International, The

Seeks to meet human needs through services in education, healthcare, community support, emergency response, and ministry development, inspired by the Christian faith.

Dent-OMFS, Derm, ER Med, Infect Dis, MF Med, Medicine, Nutr, OB-GYN, Ophth-Opt, Palliative, Psych, Rehab, Surg

⊕ https://vfmat.ch/8eb3

Samaritan's Purse International Disaster Relief

Provides spiritual and physical aid to hurting people around the world, such as victims of war, poverty, natural disasters, disease, and famine, based in Christian ministry.

Anesth, CT Surg, Crit-Care, Dent-OMFS, Derm, ENT, ER Med, Endo, GI, General, Heme-Onc, Infect Dis, MF Med, Neonat, Nephro, Neuro, Neurosurg, Nutr, OB-GYN, Ophth-Opt, Ortho, Path, Ped Surg, Peds, Plast, Psych, Pulm-Critic, Radiol, Rehab, Rheum, Surg, Urol, Vasc Surg

⊕ https://vfmat.ch/87e3

Sani Bello Foundation

Works to improve the general well-being of Nigerians and aims to achieve the sustainable development goals, including no poverty, good health, and quality education.

General, Pub Health, Surg

⊕ https://vfmat.ch/b671

Save A Child's Heart

Provides lifesaving cardiac treatment to children in developing countries, and trains healthcare professionals from these countries to deliver quality care in their communities.

CT Surg, CV Med, Crit-Care, Ped Surg, Peds

⊕ https://vfmat.ch/1bef

Save the Children

Gives children around the world a healthy start in life, the opportunity to learn, and protection from harm.

All-Immu, Crit-Care, ER Med, General, Infect Dis, MF Med, Medicine, Neonat,

OB-GYN, Peds, Psych, Pub Health
⊕ https://vfmat.ch/2e73

Sebeccly Cancer Care
Helps Nigerian breast cancer patients fulfill their survivorship potential through education, research, advocacy, and delivery of high-quality care.
Heme-Onc, Palliative, Rad-Onc
⊕ https://vfmat.ch/2266

Second Chance Smile Global Dental Outreach Foundation
Provides acute dental care with regular follow-ups and training for local oral health educators, and advocates for sustainable government oral health policy.
Dent-OMFS, Infect Dis, Logist-Op
⊕ https://vfmat.ch/daaf

SEE International
Provides sustainable medical, surgical, and educational services through volunteer ophthalmic surgeons, with the objectives of restoring sight and preventing blindness to disadvantaged individuals worldwide.
Ophth-Opt, Surg
⊕ https://vfmat.ch/6e1b

Sickle Cell Foundation Nigeria
Aims to develop a world-class national sickle cell center for the problems associated with sickle cell and related disorders in Nigeria and beyond.
Heme-Onc, Peds
⊕ https://vfmat.ch/89d1

Sightsavers
Works with partners in developing countries to help eliminate avoidable blindness and advocates for equal opportunity for the disabled.
Infect Dis, Ophth-Opt, Surg
⊕ https://vfmat.ch/aa52

SIGN Fracture Care International
Builds orthopedic capacity around the world and provides the injured poor access to fracture surgery by donating orthopedic education and implant systems to surgeons in developing countries.
Ortho, Rehab, Surg
⊕ https://vfmat.ch/123d

SINA Health
Aims to improve the health and educational status of the population in low- and middle-income countries.
General, Logist-Op
⊕ https://vfmat.ch/9ad3

Sisters of the Immaculate Heart of Mary, Mother of Christ
Based in Chrisitan ministry, seeks to motivate people, especially the poor and the less privileged, to live venerable and dignified lives through credibility-structured programs, education, various medical and humanitarian services, along with self-realization and self-empowerment opportunities.
Infect Dis, Logist-Op, Nutr, Pub Health
⊕ https://vfmat.ch/5774

Smile Train, Inc.
Treats children with cleft lip through a sustainable and local model that supports surgery and other forms of essential care.
Logist-Op, Pub Health
⊕ https://vfmat.ch/822c

SOS Children's Villages International
Supports children through alternative care and family strengthening.
ER Med, Peds
⊕ https://vfmat.ch/aca1

Spem Quia Filii Foundation
Aims to build a sustainable pediatric cardiology service that benefits every Nigerian child and works with hospitals to provide pediatric cardiac surgery.
CT Surg, CV Med, Logist-Op
⊕ https://vfmat.ch/17bc

Sri Sathya Sai International Organization
Inspired by spiritual teachings, carries out efforts in global healthcare, education, humanitarian relief, and youth engagement.
Dent-OMFS, General, Logist-Op, Nutr, Ophth-Opt, Pub Health
⊕ https://vfmat.ch/9bda

St. Joseph's Eye Hospital
Inspired by the Christian faith, aims to provide high-quality and specialty medical care to restore visual impairments.
Ophth-Opt
⊕ https://vfmat.ch/f71d

Suleiman Hearing and Educational Foundation
Provides the gift of hearing and free education to Nigerian children and adults living with disabled hearing.
ENT
⊕ https://vfmat.ch/2581

Suleiman Zuntu Foundation
Aims to impact the lives of people by providing them with basic social and developmental services.
General, Surg
⊕ https://vfmat.ch/9683

Surgeons for Smiles
Brings first-class medical and dental care to those in need, in developing countries around the world.
Anesth, Dent-OMFS, OB-GYN, Ped Surg, Plast, Surg
⊕ https://vfmat.ch/3427

Surgeons OverSeas (SOS)
Works to reduce death and disability from surgically treatable conditions in developing countries.
Anesth, Heme-Onc, Surg
⊕ https://vfmat.ch/5d16

Sustainable Kidney Care Foundation (SKCF)
Works to provide treatment for kidney injury where none exists, and aims to reduce mortality from treatable acute kidney injury (AKI).
Infect Dis, Medicine, Nephro
⊕ https://vfmat.ch/1926

Swasti
Aims to transform the lives of marginalized communities by ensuring their access to quality healthcare and thereby contributing to poverty alleviation.
Pub Health
⊕ https://vfmat.ch/be8b

Swiss Tropical and Public Health Institute
Contributes to the improvement of the health of populations internationally, nationally, and locally through excellence in research, education, and services.
Infect Dis, Pub Health
⊕ https://vfmat.ch/2ee4

Task Force for Global Health, The
Consists of programs and focus areas that cover a range of global health issues including neglected tropical diseases, infectious diseases, vaccines, field epidemiology, public health informatics, health workforce development, and global health ethics.
Infect Dis, Logist-Op, Medicine, Ophth-Opt, Peds
⊕ https://vfmat.ch/714c

Tearfund
Responds to crisis and partners with local churches to bring restoration to those living in poverty, inspired by the Christian faith.
ER Med, Logist-Op
⊕ https://vfmat.ch/f6cf

Terre des hommes (Tdh) Foundation
Works to improve the daily life of children and their relatives in the areas of health, protection and emergency, in Europe, Africa, Asia, Latin America, and the Near and Middle East.

CT Surg, CV Med, OB-GYN, Ped Surg, Pub Health
⊕ https://vfmat.ch/5c26

Timmy Global Health
Expands access to healthcare and empowers volunteers to tackle today's most pressing global health challenges, sending medical teams to support the work of international partners and channel financial, medical, and human resources to community-based health and development.
Endo, General, Logist-Op, Medicine, Pub Health
⊕ https://vfmat.ch/563e

Transplant Links Community (TLC)
Provides hands-on training in kidney transplantation for surgeons, doctors, and nurses in low- and middle-income countries.
Nephro, Surg, Urol
⊕ https://vfmat.ch/bb46

Tulsi Chanrai foundation
Aims to establish high-quality sustainable and replicable models in primary healthcare, provision of safe drinking water, and eye care.
General, Infect Dis, MF Med, Nutr, OB-GYN, Ophth-Opt, Peds
⊕ https://vfmat.ch/3cc2

U.S. President's Malaria Initiative (PMI)
Supports low-income countries to help control and eliminate malaria through cost-effective, lifesaving malaria interventions.
Infect Dis, MF Med, OB-GYN
⊕ https://vfmat.ch/dc8b

Ukala Medical Foundation
Provides free medical and philanthropic outreach to communities in Jamaica, and also to the people of Mbiri community in Nigeria's northeast region of Ika.
Medicine, Pub Health
⊕ https://vfmat.ch/4b9e

Union for International Cancer Control (UICC)
Unites and supports the cancer community to reduce the global cancer burden, promote greater equity, and ensure that cancer control continues to be a priority in the world health and development agenda.
Heme-Onc, Pub Health
⊕ https://vfmat.ch/88b1

Unite 4 Humanity
Aims to provide emergency aid and support for Muslim communities across the world.
General, Nutr, OB-GYN, Ophth-Opt, Plast, Psych, Rehab
⊕ https://vfmat.ch/fbe7

United Nations Children's Fund (UNICEF)
Works in over 190 countries and territories to save children's lives, defend their rights, and help them fulfill their potential, from early childhood through adolescence.
All-Immu, Infect Dis, MF Med, Neonat, Nutr, OB-GYN, Ped Surg, Peds, Pub Health
⊕ https://vfmat.ch/42d7

United Nations Development Programme (UNDP)
Helps countries achieve the simultaneous eradication of extreme poverty and significant reduction of inequalities and exclusion using a sustainable human development approach.
Infect Dis, Logist-Op, Pub Health
⊕ https://vfmat.ch/935c

United Nations High Commissioner for Refugees (UNHCR)
Safeguards the rights and well-being of people who have been forced to flee, ensuring that everybody has the right to seek asylum and find safe refuge in another country, with the goal of seeking lasting solutions.
General, MF Med, Medicine, OB-GYN, Peds, Psych, Pub Health
⊕ https://vfmat.ch/6636

United Nations Office for the Coordination of Humanitarian Affairs (OCHA)
Contributes to principled and effective humanitarian response through

coordination, advocacy, policy, information management, and humanitarian financing tools and services, by leveraging functional expertise throughout the organization.
Logist-Op
⊕ https://vfmat.ch/22b8

United Nations Population Fund (UNFPA)
Supports reproductive healthcare for women and youth in more than 150 countries, focusing on delivering a world in which every pregnancy is wanted, every childbirth is safe, and every young person's potential is fulfilled.
Infect Dis, MF Med, Neonat, OB-GYN, Peds, Pub Health
⊕ https://vfmat.ch/c969

United States Agency for International Development (USAID)
Promotes and demonstrates democratic values abroad and advances a free, peaceful, and prosperous world. Leads the U.S. government's international development and disaster assistance through partnerships and investments that save lives.
ER Med, Infect Dis, MF Med, OB-GYN, Peds
⊕ https://vfmat.ch/9a99

University of California, Berkeley: Bixby Center for Population, Health & Sustainability
Aims to help manage population growth, improve maternal health, and address the unmet need for family planning within a human rights framework.
OB-GYN
⊕ https://vfmat.ch/ff2b

University of Chicago: Center for Global Health
Collaborates with communities locally and globally to democratize education, increase service learning opportunities, and advance sustainable solutions to improve health and well-being while reducing global health inequities.
Genetics, MF Med, Peds, Pub Health
⊕ https://vfmat.ch/4f8f

University of New Mexico School of Medicine: Project Echo
Seeks to improve health outcomes worldwide through the use of a technology called telementoring, a guided-practice model in which the participating clinician retains responsibility for managing the patient.
General, Infect Dis, MF Med, OB-GYN, Path, Peds
⊕ https://vfmat.ch/6c9a

University of Pennsylvania Perelman School of Medicine Center for Global Health
Aims to improve health equity worldwide through enhanced public health awareness and access to care, discovery, and outcomes-based research, and comprehensive educational programs grounded in partnership.
Heme-Onc, Infect Dis, OB-GYN
⊕ https://vfmat.ch/cb57

USAID: Deliver Project
Builds a global supply chain to deliver lifesaving health products to people in order to enable countries to provide family planning, protect against malaria, and limit the spread of pandemic threats.
Infect Dis, Logist-Op, MF Med
⊕ https://vfmat.ch/374e

USAID: EQUIP Health
Exists as an effective, efficient response mechanism to achieving global HIV epidemic control by delivering the right intervention at the right place and in the right way.
Infect Dis
⊕ https://vfmat.ch/d76a

USAID: Fistula Care Plus
Builds on, enhances, and expands the work undertaken by the previous Fistula Care project (2007–2013), with attention to prevention, detection, treatment, reintegration and new areas of focus so that obstetric fistula can become a rare event for future generations.
MF Med, OB-GYN, Surg
⊕ https://vfmat.ch/a7cd

USAID: Health Finance and Governance Project
Uses research to implement strategies to help countries develop robust

governance systems, increase their domestic resources for health, manage those resources more effectively, and make wise purchasing decisions.
Logist-Op
⊕ https://vfmat.ch/8652

USAID: Human Resources for Health 2030 (HRH2030)
Helps low- and middle-income countries develop the health workforce needed to prevent maternal and child deaths, support the goals of Family Planning 2020, control the HIV/AIDS epidemic, and protect communities from infectious diseases.
Logist-Op
⊕ https://vfmat.ch/9ea8

USAID: Leadership, Management and Governance Project
Improves leadership, management, and governance practices to strengthen health systems and improve health for all, including vulnerable populations worldwide.
Logist-Op
⊕ https://vfmat.ch/d35e

USAID: Maternal and Child Health Integrated Program
Works to improve the health of women and their families, including programs for maternal, newborn, and child health, immunization, family planning, nutrition, malaria, and HIV/AIDS.
All-Immu, General, Infect Dis, MF Med
⊕ https://vfmat.ch/4415

USAID: Maternal and Child Survival Program
Works to prevent child and maternal deaths.
Infect Dis, MF Med, Neonat, OB-GYN, Peds
⊕ https://vfmat.ch/6fcf

Uwakah Memorial Medical Foundation
Collaborates with clinics in rural parts of Nigeria and other African countries to reduce infant and maternal deaths.
General, Logist-Op, MF Med, OB-GYN
⊕ https://vfmat.ch/493b

Variety – The Children's Charity International
Funds and delivers programs that focus on multiple unmet needs of children who are sick or disadvantaged, or live with disabilities and other special needs. Works at a local, national and international level, including the delivery of critical healthcare and medical equipment.
General, Infect Dis, Logist-Op
⊕ https://vfmat.ch/41f5

Vision Care
Restores sight and helps patients get regular treatment at short-term eye camps and long-term base clinics by having doctors, missionaries, volunteers, and sponsors work together.
Ophth-Opt
⊕ https://vfmat.ch/9d7c

Vision for the Poor
Reduces human suffering and improves quality of life through the recovery of sight by building sustainable eye hospitals in developing countries, empowering local eye specialists, funding essential ophthalmic infrastructure, and partnering with like-minded agencies.
Ophth-Opt
⊕ https://vfmat.ch/528e

Vision Outreach International
Advocates for helping the blind in underserved regions of the world and empowers the poor through sight restoration.
Ophth-Opt
⊕ https://vfmat.ch/9721

Vital Strategies
Helps governments strengthen their public health systems to contend with the most important and difficult health challenges, while accelerating progress on the world's most pressing health problems.
CV Med, Infect Dis, Peds
⊕ https://vfmat.ch/fe25

Vitamin Angels
Helps at-risk populations in need—specifically pregnant women, new mothers, and children under age 5—to gain access to life-changing vitamins and minerals.
General, Nutr
⊕ https://vfmat.ch/7da1

Vodacom Foundation
Brings people together to maximize impact in three key areas: health, education, and safety and security.
Logist-Op
⊕ https://vfmat.ch/f116

Voices for a Malaria-Free Future
Seeks to expand national movements of private- and public-sector leaders to mobilize political and popular support for malaria control.
Infect Dis, Path
⊕ https://vfmat.ch/4213

Voluntary Service Overseas (VSO)
Works with health workers, communities, and governments to improve health services and rights for women, babies, youth, people with disabilities, and prisoners.
General, MF Med, OB-GYN
⊕ https://vfmat.ch/213d

Watsi
Uses technology to make healthcare a reality for those who might not otherwise be able to afford it.
Pub Health, Surg
⊕ https://vfmat.ch/41a3

We Care Missions, Inc.
Provides free quality medical care to the poor and underprivileged in rural areas of Nigeria who could not otherwise afford it.
Dent-OMFS, Ophth-Opt, Surg
⊕ https://vfmat.ch/a7c9

Wellbeing Foundation Africa
Improves health outcomes for women, infants, and children.
General, MF Med, OB-GYN, Peds
⊕ https://vfmat.ch/8f8a

White Ribbon Alliance, The
Leads a movement for reproductive, maternal, and newborn health and accelerates progress by putting citizens at the center of global, national, and local health efforts.
MF Med, OB-GYN
⊕ https://vfmat.ch/496b

Women for Women International
Supports the most marginalized women to earn and save money, improve health and well-being, influence decisions in their home and community, and connect to networks for support.
MF Med, OB-GYN
⊕ https://vfmat.ch/768c

Women's Health and Action Research Center
Works to improve the reproductive health and social well-being of women and adolescents in Africa so they can lead productive, fulfilling lives and provide a healthy future for their children.
Logist-Op, MF Med, OB-GYN, Pub Health
⊕ https://vfmat.ch/64d3

Women's Refugee Commission
Seeks to improve lives by protecting the rights of women, children, and youth displaced by conflict and crisis through researching their needs, identifying solutions, and advocating for programs and policies to strengthen their resilience.
General, MF Med, Neonat, OB-GYN, Peds, Psych
⊕ https://vfmat.ch/3d8f

World Anaesthesia Society (WAS)
Aims to support anesthesiologists with an interest in working in low-income regions of the world.

Anesth
⊕ https://vfmat.ch/37fe

World Blind Union (WBU)
Represents those experiencing blindness, speaking to governments and international bodies on issues concerning visual impairments.
Ophth-Opt
⊕ https://vfmat.ch/2bd3

World Children's Fund
Commits to helping children worldwide who are suffering the effects of poverty, disease, natural disaster, famine, abuse, civil strife, and war.
General, Logist-Op, MF Med, Nutr, OB-GYN, Pub Health
⊕ https://vfmat.ch/9cd8

World Council of Optometry
Facilitates the development of optometry worldwide and promotes eye health and vision care through advocacy, education, policy development, and humanitarian outreach.
Ophth-Opt, Pub Health
⊕ https://vfmat.ch/c92e

World Federation of Hemophilia (WFH)
Aims to improve and sustain care for people with inherited bleeding disorders by pursuing long-term relationships with individuals and organizations who share the values of WFH's development model.
Heme-Onc
⊕ https://vfmat.ch/5121

World Health Organization, The (WHO)
The United Nations' agency for health provides leadership on global health matters, shapes the health research agenda, sets norms and standards, articulates evidence-based policy options, provides technical support and monitoring to countries, and assesses health trends.
ER Med, General, Infect Dis, Logist-Op, MF Med, OB-GYN, Peds, Psych, Pub Health
⊕ https://vfmat.ch/c476

World Heart Federation
Leads the global fight against heart disease and stroke, with a focus on low- and middle-income countries.
CV Med, Crit-Care, Heme-Onc, Medicine, Peds
⊕ https://vfmat.ch/ea51

World Medical Relief
Facilitates the distribution of surplus medical resources where they are needed.
Logist-Op
⊕ https://vfmat.ch/72dc

World Parkinson's Program
Seeks to improve the quality of life of those affected by Parkinson's disease through education and advocacy, and provides free medication and support services.
Logist-Op, Neuro, Pub Health
⊕ https://vfmat.ch/c96d

World Surgical Foundation
Provides charitable surgical healthcare to the world's poor and underserved in developing nations.
Ped Surg, Surg
⊕ https://vfmat.ch/c162

YORGHAS Foundation
Supports mothers, pregnant women, infants, people with disabilities, and those suffering from humanitarian crises, poverty, or social inequalities, with particular emphasis on women's and children's rights.
MF Med, Neonat
⊕ https://vfmat.ch/9e44

Nigeria

Healthcare Facilities

1 Division Hospital
Rafin Kura, Kaduna, Nigeria
🌐 https://vfmat.ch/acdf

44 Nigerian Army Reference Hospital Kaduna
Badiko, Kaduna, Nigeria
🌐 https://vfmat.ch/u99h

Abdullahi Muhammad Wase Specialist Hospital
Kano, Kano, Nigeria
🌐 https://vfmat.ch/f815

Abia State Specialist Hospital & Diagnostic Centre
Umuahia, Abia State, Nigeria
🌐 https://vfmat.ch/3ggs

Abia State University Teaching Hospital
Aba, Abia, Nigeria
🌐 https://vfmat.ch/f5sh

ABU Teaching Hospital
Tudun Wada, Kaduna, Nigeria
🌐 https://vfmat.ch/f615

Abubakar Tafawa Balewa Teaching Hospital
Bauchi, Bauchi, Nigeria
🌐 https://vfmat.ch/fc8d

Adamawa State Specialist Hospital
Yola, Adamawa State, Nigeria
🌐 https://vfmat.ch/h1mx

Adeoyo State Hospital
Hyperia bts, Oyo, Nigeria
🌐 https://vfmat.ch/f443

Afe Babalola University Multi-System Hospital, Ado-Ekiti
Ado-Ekiti, Ekiti, Nigeria
🌐 https://vfmat.ch/bqhd

Ahmadu Bello University Teaching Hospital (ABUTH)
Zaria, Kaduna, Nigeria
🌐 https://vfmat.ch/44fc

Aisha Muhammadu Buhari General Hospital
Jega, Kebbi, Nigeria
🌐 https://vfmat.ch/2c7f

Ajeromi General Hospital, Ajegunle
Ajegunle, Lagos, Nigeria
🌐 https://vfmat.ch/573d

Al-Noury Specialist Hospital
Kano, Kano, Nigeria
🌐 https://vfmat.ch/b522

Alex Ekwueme Federal University Teaching Hospital Abakaliki
Abakaliki, Ebonyi, Nigeria
🌐 https://vfmat.ch/384f

Aliero General Hospital
Aliero, Kebbi, Nigeria
🌐 https://vfmat.ch/7c36

Alimosho General Hospital Igando
Igando, Lagos, Nigeria
🌐 https://vfmat.ch/56f5

Alkaleri General Hospital
Kasachia, Bauchi, Nigeria
🌐 https://vfmat.ch/c5bd

Allah bamu Lafiya Hospital
Gabas 2, Katsina, Nigeria
🌐 https://vfmat.ch/daec

Alliance Hospital
Garki, Abuja, Nigeria
🌐 https://vfmat.ch/tcdk

Alpha Specialist Hospital
New Haven, Enugu, Nigeria
🌐 https://vfmat.ch/66b5

Aminu Kano Teaching Hospital Kano
Tudun Wada, Kano, Nigeria
🌐 https://vfmat.ch/ac48

Amuwo Odofin Maternal & Childcare Centre
Alapako, Lagos, Nigeria
🌐 https://vfmat.ch/d6b7

Anka General Hospital
Anka, Zamfara, Nigeria
🌐 https://vfmat.ch/823f

Arkilla PHC
Nasarawa, Sokoto, Nigeria
🌐 https://vfmat.ch/9ffe

Asokoro District Hospital
Asokoro, Abuja, Nigeria
🌐 https://vfmat.ch/dc3d

Assumption Catholic Church Hospital
Warri, Delta, Nigeria
🌐 https://vfmat.ch/d545

Avenue Specialist Hospital
Warri, Delta, Nigeria
🌐 https://vfmat.ch/865a

Azare Federal Medical Centre
Azare, Bauchi, Nigeria
🌐 https://vfmat.ch/mmvd

Azuwa Hospital
Benin City, Edo, Nigeria
🌐 https://vfmat.ch/d55a

Barau Dikko
Ungwan Rimi, Kaduna, Nigeria
⊕ https://vfmat.ch/2d2d

Bauchi Emergency Operations Center
Gwalgafuran, Bauchi, Nigeria
⊕ https://vfmat.ch/63b2

Bauchi State Specialist Hospital
Shadowanka, Bauchi, Nigeria
⊕ https://vfmat.ch/bdfe

Bebeji General Hospital
Mai Dakin Alkali, Kano, Nigeria
⊕ https://vfmat.ch/8abc

Belmont Specialist Hospital
Ungwan Bado, Kaduna, Nigeria
⊕ https://vfmat.ch/5f8c

Benue State University Teaching Hospital
Makurdi, Benue, Nigeria
⊕ https://vfmat.ch/qmne

Bichi General Hospital
Bichi, Kano, Nigeria
⊕ https://vfmat.ch/eb61

Birnin Kudu Federal Medical Centre
Birnin Kudu, Jigawa State, Nigeria
⊕ https://vfmat.ch/2vb6

Biu Isolation Centre
Biu, Borno, Nigeria
⊕ https://vfmat.ch/ecdd

Borno State Specialist Hospital Maiduguri
Maiduguri, Borno, Nigeria
⊕ https://vfmat.ch/2313

Bowen University Teaching Hospital (BUTH)
Ogbomoso, Oyo, Nigeria
⊕ https://vfmat.ch/a835

Bryants Hospital
Igbudu, Delta, Nigeria
⊕ https://vfmat.ch/5bdc

Bulumkutu General Hospital
Kalari, Borno, Nigeria
⊕ https://vfmat.ch/47bc

Buni-Yadi General Hospital
Buni-Yadi, Yobe, Nigeria
⊕ https://vfmat.ch/4ab9

CedarCrest Abuja Hospital
Apo, FCT, Nigeria
⊕ https://vfmat.ch/817e

Center for Research and Preventive Health Care
Iguasa, Edo, Nigeria
⊕ https://vfmat.ch/7429

Central Hospital Benin
Benin City, Edo, Nigeria
⊕ https://vfmat.ch/2952

Central Hospital Sapele
Warri, Delta, Nigeria
⊕ https://vfmat.ch/f2ba

Central Hospital Warri
Warri, Delta, Nigeria
⊕ https://vfmat.ch/ea89

Chasel Hospital, The
Ungwan Kanawa, Kaduna, Nigeria
⊕ https://vfmat.ch/b9ff

Children Specialist Hospital, Kaduna
Kabala, Kaduna, Nigeria
⊕ https://vfmat.ch/8d18

Christ The King Hospital
Abakaliki, Ebonyi, Nigeria
⊕ https://vfmat.ch/64ae

Chukwuemeka Odumegwu Ojukwu University Teaching Hospital
Awka, Anambra, Nigeria
⊕ https://vfmat.ch/ldqy

College of Health Sciences, FGC Warri
Ugbo-Wunagweh, Delta, Nigeria
⊕ https://vfmat.ch/69b4

Cottage Hospital Guyuk
Purokayo, Adamawa, Nigeria
⊕ https://vfmat.ch/bb2b

Cottage Hospital Omupo
Omupo, Kwara, Nigeria
⊕ https://vfmat.ch/39d5

Cottage Hospital Wuro Ali
Wuro Ali, Adamawa, Nigeria
⊕ https://vfmat.ch/7fef

Dala National Orthophedic Hospital, Kano
Dala, Kano, Nigeria
⊕ https://vfmat.ch/f6ff

Dalhatu Araf Specialist Hospital (DASH)
Lafia, Nasarawa, Nigeria
⊕ https://vfmat.ch/3eak

Damagum General Hospital
Alhaji, Yobe, Nigeria
⊕ https://vfmat.ch/ff93

Danbatta General Hospital
Jigba, Kano, Nigeria
⊕ https://vfmat.ch/95fe

Daula Hospital and Maternity Home, Gusau
Gusau, Zamfara, Nigeria
⊕ https://vfmat.ch/4417

Dawaki General Hospital
Dawaki, Kano, Nigeria
⊕ https://vfmat.ch/55aa

Dawakin Tofa General Hospital
Tsarkakiya, Kano, Nigeria
⊕ https://vfmat.ch/b5e7

Dawanau Psychiatric Hospital
Dawanau, Kano, Nigeria
⊕ https://vfmat.ch/82ih

Delta State University Teaching Hospital, Oghara
Oghara, Delta, Nigeria
⊕ https://vfmat.ch/ct9e

DIFF Hospital
Abuja, FCT, Nigeria
⊕ https://vfmat.ch/8bba

Dikwa General Hospital
Dikwa, Borno, Nigeria
⊕ https://vfmat.ch/ffd1

Doguwa General Hospital
Dutsen Giginia, Kaduna, Nigeria
⊕ https://vfmat.ch/eeba

Doma Hospital Gombe
Pantame, Gombe, Nigeria
⊕ https://vfmat.ch/28ff

Doren Specialist Hospital
Aja, Lekki, Nigeria
⊕ https://vfmat.ch/7e48

Ebonyi State University Teaching Hospital
Abakaliki, Ebonyi, Nigeria
⊕ https://vfmat.ch/7l6f

Ecwa Hospital Egbe
Egbe, Kogi, Nigeria
⊕ https://vfmat.ch/ud2a

Edi International Hospital
Benin City, Edo, Nigeria
⊕ https://vfmat.ch/2f4b

Ekiti State University Teaching Hospital
Ado Ekiti, Ekiti, Nigeria
⊕ https://vfmat.ch/uvs5

Eko Hospital
Ikeja, Lagos, Nigeria
⊕ https://vfmat.ch/de59

Elele Alimini General Hospital
Elele Alimini, Rivers, Nigeria
⊕ https://vfmat.ch/6137

Emel Hospital
Festac Town, Lagos, Nigeria
⊕ https://vfmat.ch/831c

Emergency Operations Center – Sokoto
Gandu, Sokoto, Nigeria
⊕ https://vfmat.ch/f485

Enugu State Medical Diagnostic Centre
New Haven, Enugu, Nigeria
⊕ https://vfmat.ch/be28

Enugu State University Teaching Hospital (ESUTH), Park Lane
Park Lane, Enugu, Nigeria
⊕ https://vfmat.ch/utzu

Epsilon Specialist Hospital
Kaduna South, Kaduna, Nigeria
⊕ https://vfmat.ch/6ff8

Estate Specialist Hospital
Warri, Delta, Nigeria
⊕ https://vfmat.ch/3295

Eye Foundation Hospital Group, The
Lagos, Nigeria
⊕ https://vfmat.ch/mnip

Fagwalawa Cottage General Hospital
Fagwalawa, Kano, Nigeria
⊕ https://vfmat.ch/98ca

Fairview Hospital
Warri, Delta, Nigeria
⊕ https://vfmat.ch/8c31

Faithcity Hospital Ajao, Lagos
Isolo, Nigeria
⊕ https://vfmat.ch/pqs2

Farida Hospital
Gusau, Zamfara, Nigeria
⊕ https://vfmat.ch/ccc5

Federal Medical Center (FMC) Gusau
Gusau, Zamfara, Nigeria
⊕ https://vfmat.ch/1155

Federal Medical Center Keffi
Keffi, Nasarawa, Nigeria
⊕ https://vfmat.ch/a9jw

Federal Medical Centre (FMC) Owerri
Owerri, Imo, Nigeria
⊕ https://vfmat.ch/h7d2

Federal Medical Centre Abuja
Jabi, Abuja, Nigeria
⊕ https://vfmat.ch/6usd

Federal Medical Centre Asaba
Asaba, Delta, Nigeria
⊕ https://vfmat.ch/qxar

Federal Medical Centre Bida
Bida, Niger, Nigeria
⊕ https://vfmat.ch/nird

Federal Medical Centre Birnin Kebbi
Birnin-Kebbi, Kebbi, Nigeria
⊕ https://vfmat.ch/vywy

Federal Medical Centre Jalingo
Jalingo, Taraba, Nigeria
⊕ https://vfmat.ch/mizp

Federal Medical Centre Owo
Owo, Ondo State, Nigeria
⊕ https://vfmat.ch/tzbk

Federal Medical Centre Umuahia
Umuahia, Abia, Nigeria
⊕ https://vfmat.ch/lmjb

Federal Medical Centre Yenagoa
Yenagoa, Bayelsa, Nigeria
⊕ https://vfmat.ch/mx5f

Federal Medical Centre Yola
Yola, Adamawa, Nigeria
⊕ https://vfmat.ch/jyqr

Federal Medical Centre, Abeokuta
Abeokuta, Ogun, Nigeria
⊕ https://vfmat.ch/uiuc

Federal Medical Centre, Nguru
Nguru, Yobe, Nigeria
⊕ https://vfmat.ch/c2a4

Federal Neuro Psychiatric Hospital, Kware
Kware, Sokoto, Nigeria
⊕ https://vfmat.ch/3z8j

Federal Neuro-Psychiatric Hospital (FNPH) Benin
Benin City, Edo, Nigeria
⊕ https://vfmat.ch/7e44

Federal Neuro-Psychiatric Hospital Kaduna
Kakuri, Kaduna, Nigeria
⊕ https://vfmat.ch/sae1

Federal Neuro-Psychiatric Hospital, Calabar
Calabar, Cross River, Nigeria
⊕ https://vfmat.ch/42tu

Federal Neuro-Psychiatric Hospital, Maiduguri
Maiduguri, Borno, Nigeria
⊕ https://vfmat.ch/gwum

Federal Neuro-Psychiatric Hospital, Enugu
Enugu, Enugu, Nigeria
⊕ https://vfmat.ch/3jtq

Federal Teaching Hospital Gombe
Tempure, Gombe, Nigeria
⊕ https://vfmat.ch/f44f

Federal Teaching Hospital, Ido Ekiti
Ido Ekiti, Ekiti, Nigeria
⊕ https://vfmat.ch/jcjz

FMC Makurdi
Makurdi, Benue, Nigeria
⊕ https://vfmat.ch/xikz

Fountain of Life Hospital
Yenegoa, Bayelsa, Nigeria
⊕ https://vfmat.ch/15ac

Foxglove Multispeciality Hospital
Abuja, Abuja, Nigeria
⊕ https://vfmat.ch/3awd

Fufore Cottage Hospital
Yola, Adamawa, Nigeria
⊕ https://vfmat.ch/99e9

Gajiram General Hospital
Maiduguri, Borno, Nigeria
⊕ https://vfmat.ch/494c

Galway Skane Hospital
Warri, Delta, Nigeria
⊕ https://vfmat.ch/4be4

Garden City Specialist Hospital
Ungwan Rimi, Kaduna, Nigeria
⊕ https://vfmat.ch/63bd

Garki Hospital
Garki, FCT, Nigeria
⊕ https://vfmat.ch/9ea5

Garkuwa Specialist Hospital
Ungwan Sariki, Kaduna, Nigeria
⊕ https://vfmat.ch/bc5e

Gbagada General Hospital
Gbagada, Lagos, Nigeria
⊕ https://vfmat.ch/36a4

General Hospital Argungu
Tasumbuke, Kebbi, Nigeria
⊕ https://vfmat.ch/e13d

General Hospital Azare
Katagum, Bauchi, Nigeria
⊕ https://vfmat.ch/b623

General Hospital Bakura
Dampo, Sokoto, Nigeria
⊕ https://vfmat.ch/e559

General Hospital Bama
Bama, Borno, Nigeria
⊕ https://vfmat.ch/71be

General Hospital Bena
Bena, Kebbi, Nigeria
⊕ https://vfmat.ch/51cf

General Hospital Binji
Toidi Zaidi, Sokoto, Nigeria
⊕ https://vfmat.ch/ab71

General Hospital Biu
Maiduguri, Maiduguri, Borno, Nigeria
⊕ https://vfmat.ch/c8a8

General Hospital Bogoro
Bogoro, Bauchi, Nigeria
⊕ https://vfmat.ch/79b5

General Hospital Bungudu
Guidan Uban Dawaki, Zamfara, Nigeria
⊕ https://vfmat.ch/2293

General Hospital Burra
Burra, Bauchi, Nigeria
⊕ https://vfmat.ch/7a34

General Hospital Calabar
Calabar Municipal, Cross River, Nigeria
⊕ https://vfmat.ch/1e55

General Hospital Dambam
Kaigamari, Bauchi, Nigeria
⊕ https://vfmat.ch/961e

General Hospital Dansadau
Ungwan Rimi, Zamfara, Nigeria
⊕ https://vfmat.ch/51ef

General Hospital Darazo
Darazo, Bauchi, Nigeria
⊕ https://vfmat.ch/6ee3

General Hospital Dogondaji
Dogondaji, Sokoto, Nigeria
⊕ https://vfmat.ch/2b6d

General Hospital Ekpan
Tori, Delta, Nigeria
⊕ https://vfmat.ch/baed

General Hospital Gada
Masuki, Sokoto, Nigeria
⊕ https://vfmat.ch/8f93

General Hospital Gamawa
Gamawa, Bauchi, Nigeria
⊕ https://vfmat.ch/f6bf

General Hospital Gummi
Gummi, Zamfara, Nigeria
⊕ https://vfmat.ch/c12b

General Hospital Ijede
Ikorodu, Lagos, Nigeria
⊕ https://vfmat.ch/b182

General Hospital Ikono
Uyo, Akwa Ibom, Nigeria
⊕ https://vfmat.ch/6716

General Hospital Ikorodu
Ikorodu, Lagos, Nigeria
⊕ https://vfmat.ch/4467

General Hospital Isa
Isa, Sokoto, Nigeria
⊕ https://vfmat.ch/31dc

General Hospital Jama're
Yangamaku, Bauchi, Nigeria
⊕ https://vfmat.ch/1a6c

General Hospital Kafin
Kafin, Niger, Nigeria
⊕ https://vfmat.ch/8cab

General Hospital Kamba
Birnin, Kebbi, Nigeria
⊕ https://vfmat.ch/78ba

General Hospital Kangiwa
Kamba, Kebbi, Nigeria
⊕ https://vfmat.ch/ea1a

General Hospital Katagum
Katagum, Bauchi, Nigeria
⊕ https://vfmat.ch/21e5

General Hospital Kaura Namoda
Kogi, Zamfara, Nigeria
⊕ https://vfmat.ch/6f5d

General Hospital Kukawa
Kukawa, Borno, Nigeria
⊕ https://vfmat.ch/7893

General Hospital Mafa
Mafa, Borno, Nigeria
⊕ https://vfmat.ch/d9be

General Hospital Magami
Gusau, Zamfara, Nigeria
⊕ https://vfmat.ch/9594

General Hospital Maiduguri
Maiduguri, Borno, Nigeria
⊕ https://vfmat.ch/e16a

General Hospital Marama
Marama, Borno, Nigeria
⊕ https://vfmat.ch/2cca

General Hospital Minna
Minna, Niger, Nigeria
⊕ https://vfmat.ch/25c1

General Hospital Monguno
Kuwiya, Borno, Nigeria
⊕ https://vfmat.ch/fabc

General Hospital of Tangaza
Tangaza, Sokoto, Nigeria
⊕ https://vfmat.ch/2879

General Hospital Potiskum
Degubi, Yobe, Nigeria
⊕ https://vfmat.ch/ad97

General Hospital Rabah
Rabah, Sokoto, Nigeria
⊕ https://vfmat.ch/77ed

General Hospital Uba
Uba, Borno, Nigeria
⊕ https://vfmat.ch/2214

General Hospital Wasagu
Wasagu, Kebbi, Nigeria
⊕ https://vfmat.ch/595e

General Hospital Zurmi
Zurmi, Zamfara, Nigeria
⊕ https://vfmat.ch/781f

General Hospital, Aboh Mbaise
Oboama, Imo, Nigeria
⊕ https://vfmat.ch/68fd

Gezawa General Hospital
Gezawa, Kano, Nigeria
⊕ https://vfmat.ch/7946

Giwa Hospital
Ungwar Shanu Ward, Kaduna, Nigeria
⊕ https://vfmat.ch/1b4c

Glen Eagles Hospital
Victoria Island, Lagos, Nigeria
⊕ https://vfmat.ch/ebff

Gold Cross Hospital – Bourdillon
Lagos Island, Lagos, Nigeria
⊕ https://vfmat.ch/98c5

Good Shepherd Specialist Hospital
Nsukka, Enugu, Nigeria
⊕ https://vfmat.ch/bc37

Government Chest Hospital
Ibadan, Oyo, Nigeria
⊕ https://vfmat.ch/5a11

Government Hospital Near Abia State University
Aro, Abia, Nigeria
⊕ https://vfmat.ch/93e6

Gurin Pbf Health Facilities
Gurin, Adamawa, Nigeria
⊕ https://vfmat.ch/822e

Gwaram General Hospital
Gwaram, Bauchi, Nigeria
⊕ https://vfmat.ch/cb97

Gwarzo General Hospital
Gwarzo, Kano, Nigeria
⊕ https://vfmat.ch/3456

Health Solutions Specialist Hospital
New Haven, Enugu, Nigeria
⊕ https://vfmat.ch/e54a

Hospital Yaba
Lagos, Nigeria
⊕ https://vfmat.ch/257b

Humanity Hospital
Enerhe, Delta, Nigeria
⊕ https://vfmat.ch/3931

Ibom Multi-Specialty Hospital
Uyo, Nigeria
⊕ https://vfmat.ch/cefk

Igbinedion University Teaching Hospital, Okada
Okada, Edo, Nigeria
⊕ https://vfmat.ch/glqz

Imo State University Teaching Hospital, Orlu
Orlu, Imo, Nigeria
⊕ https://vfmat.ch/ykcd

Irrua Specialist Teaching Hospital (ISTH)
Irrua, Edo, Nigeria
⊕ https://vfmat.ch/dt9f

Isolo General Hospital
Ewu, Lagos, Nigeria
⊕ https://vfmat.ch/3489

Isuikwuato General Hospital
Amaidi, Imo, Nigeria
⊕ https://vfmat.ch/724c

Jolamade Hospital
Ibadan, Oyo, Nigeria
⊕ https://vfmat.ch/c9e8

Jos University Teaching Hospital (JUTH)
Gwafan, Plateau, Nigeria
⊕ https://vfmat.ch/a647

Kabo Cottage General Hospital
Kabo, Kano, Nigeria
⊕ https://vfmat.ch/dae7

Kaduna Emergency Operations Center
Rimi, Kaduna, Nigeria
⊕ https://vfmat.ch/6979

Kagara General Hospital
Kagara, Zamfara, Nigeria
⊕ https://vfmat.ch/72e4

Kawo General Hospital
Kawo, Kaduna, Nigeria
⊕ https://vfmat.ch/f5e4

Khadija Memorial Hospital
Toro, Bauchi, Nigeria
⊕ https://vfmat.ch/d8ad

King Fahad Hospital
Guidan Damo, Zamfara, Nigeria
⊕ https://vfmat.ch/27e9

Kir Maternal And Child Health Care
Kir, Bauchi, Nigeria
⊕ https://vfmat.ch/145a

Kiru General Hospital
Kiru, Kano, Nigeria
⊕ https://vfmat.ch/9257

Kogi State Specialist Hospital, Lokoja
Lokoja, Kogi, Nigeria
⊕ https://vfmat.ch/9fea

Kogi State University Teaching Hospital
Anyigba, Kogi State, Nigeria
⊕ https://vfmat.ch/glrs

Konduga General Hospital
Yaleri Kurnawa, Borno, Nigeria
⊕ https://vfmat.ch/ce7d

Kowa Hospital
Lafia, Nasarawa, Nigeria
⊕ https://vfmat.ch/dce3

Kubwa General Hospital
Usuma, FCT, Nigeria
⊕ https://vfmat.ch/a59d

Kukuri Maternal and Child Health Care
Kukuri, Yobe, Nigeria
⊕ https://vfmat.ch/6459

Ladoke Akintola University of Technology (LAUTECH) Teaching Hospital, Ogbomoso
Ogbomoso, Oyo, Nigeria
⊕ https://vfmat.ch/rxdr

Lagos Emergency Operations Center
Tinubu, Lagos, Nigeria
⊕ https://vfmat.ch/9db9

Lagos Island General Hospital
Lagos Island, Lagos, Nigeria
⊕ https://vfmat.ch/4151

Lagos State University Teaching Hospital
Ikeja, Lagos, Nigeria
⊕ https://vfmat.ch/7e35

Lagos University Teaching Hospital
Mushin, Lagos, Nigeria
⊕ https://vfmat.ch/f3b2

Lamurde Primary Heath Center
Gomoti, Adamawa, Nigeria
⊕ https://vfmat.ch/3aa8

Lantoro Catholic Hospital
Lapawo, Ogun, Nigeria
⊕ https://vfmat.ch/6387

Lassa General Hospital
Maiduguri, Borno, Nigeria
⊕ https://vfmat.ch/5299

Lella Specialist Hospital
Idunmwunivdiode, Edo, Nigeria
⊕ https://vfmat.ch/2398

Liberty Hospital
Suleja, Niger, Nigeria
⊕ https://vfmat.ch/d365

Lily Hospital
Benin City, Edo, Nigeria
⊕ https://vfmat.ch/bd95

Manek's Hospital
Kaduna South, Kaduna, Nigeria
⊕ https://vfmat.ch/1afc

Maraba Gumai Yamma
Mallemadigo, Bauchi, Nigeria
⊕ https://vfmat.ch/9547

Marte General Hospital
Ajiwa, Borno, Nigeria
⊕ https://vfmat.ch/ae7d

Massey Street Children Hospital
Mekunwen, Lagos, Nigeria
⊕ https://vfmat.ch/7312

Maternal And Child Health Care Old Airport
Dutsen Kura, Niger, Nigeria
🌐 https://vfmat.ch/11de

Maviscope Hospital & Fertility Centre
Ekae, Edo, Nigeria
🌐 https://vfmat.ch/af64

Mbanefo Hospital
New Haven, Enugu, Nigeria
🌐 https://vfmat.ch/1659

Medison Specialist Women's Hospital
Ilado, Lagos, Nigeria
🌐 https://vfmat.ch/3fee

Metro Hospital
Gabukka, Gombe, Nigeria
🌐 https://vfmat.ch/db68

Military Hospital Benin
Benin City, Edo, Nigeria
🌐 https://vfmat.ch/57a4

Military Hospital Port Harcourt
Port Harcourt, Rivers, Nigeria
🌐 https://vfmat.ch/9d85

Minjibir General Hospital
Galawanga, Kano, Nigeria
🌐 https://vfmat.ch/965e

Monarch Specialist Hospital
Rimi, Kaduna, Nigeria
🌐 https://vfmat.ch/bcf5

Mother Of Christ Specialist Hospital
Uwani, Enugu, Nigeria
🌐 https://vfmat.ch/f313

Muhammad Buhari Specialist Hospital
Nasarawa, Kano, Nigeria
🌐 https://vfmat.ch/gyvu

Murtala Muhammad Specialist Hospital, Kano
Kano, Kano, Nigeria
🌐 https://vfmat.ch/76wn

Muslim Hospital, The
Apinrin, Osun, Nigeria
🌐 https://vfmat.ch/ace5

Nakowa Specialist Hospital
Maiduguri, Borno, Nigeria
🌐 https://vfmat.ch/1c81

National Eye Centre Kaduna
Mando, Kaduna, Nigeria
🌐 https://vfmat.ch/clmp

National Hospital Abuja
Kukwaba, FCT, Nigeria
🌐 https://vfmat.ch/bc89

National Obstetrics Fistula Centre
Abakaliki, Ebonyi, Nigeria
🌐 https://vfmat.ch/hih9

National Orthopaedic Hospital Igbobi – Lagos
Tinubu, Lagos, Nigeria
🌐 https://vfmat.ch/e8f6

National Orthopaedic Hospital, Enugu
Enugu, Enugu, Nigeria
🌐 https://vfmat.ch/9xbr

Neo Hospital
New Haven, Enugu, Nigeria
🌐 https://vfmat.ch/eb99

Neuro-Psychiatric Specialist Hospital Akure
Akure, Ondo, Nigeria
🌐 https://vfmat.ch/kvrv

Neuro-Psychiatric Hospital Aro Abeokuta
Aro, Ogun, Nigeria
🌐 https://vfmat.ch/2a5f

Ni'ima Consultant Hospital Bauchi
Bauchi, Bauchi, Nigeria
🌐 https://vfmat.ch/f7fc

Niger Delta University Teaching Hospital, Okolobiri
Okolobiri, Bayelsa, Nigeria
🌐 https://vfmat.ch/2gpi

Niger Foundation Hospital & Diagnostic Center
New Haven, Enugu, Nigeria
🌐 https://vfmat.ch/a458

Nigeria Air Force Base Referral Hospital Daura
Daura, Katsina, Nigeria
🌐 https://vfmat.ch/cmck

Nigerian Air Force (NAF) Hospital
Abuja, FCT, Nigeria
🌐 https://vfmat.ch/33f6

Nigerian Navy Reference Hospital Calabar
Ikot Ansa, Cross River, Nigeria
🌐 https://vfmat.ch/56b6

Nigerian Police Hospital – Falomo
Falomo, Lagos, Nigeria
🌐 https://vfmat.ch/34de

Nizamiye Hospital
Abuja, FCT, Nigeria
🌐 https://vfmat.ch/2349

Nnamdi Azikiwe University Teaching Hospital Nnewi
Nnewi, Nigeria
🌐 https://vfmat.ch/4d94

NOBSAMS Hospital
Port Harcourt, Rivers, Nigeria
🌐 https://vfmat.ch/e321

Noma Children Hospital Sokoto
Abattoir, Sokoto, Nigeria
🌐 https://vfmat.ch/6e38

Obafemi Awolowo University Teaching Hospital
Ile-Ife, Osun, Nigeria
🌐 https://vfmat.ch/nq5b

Obio Cottage Hospital
Port Harcourt, Rivers, Nigeria
🌐 https://vfmat.ch/c4c9

Ogu General Hospital
Ogu Bolo, Rivers, Nigeria
🌐 https://vfmat.ch/29c9

Olabisi Onabanjo University Teaching Hospital, Sagamu
Sagamu, Ogun, Nigeria
🌐 https://vfmat.ch/pnfb

Our Lady of Fatima Hospital Osun
Oshogbo, Osun, Nigeria
🌐 https://vfmat.ch/ec17

Our Lady's Health of the Sick Hospital
Nkpogu, Port Harcourt, Nigeria
🌐 https://vfmat.ch/141d

Pamo Clinics And Hospitals
Port Harcourt, Rivers, Nigeria
🌐 https://vfmat.ch/e2e7

Peerless Hospital
Tori, Delta, Nigeria
🌐 https://vfmat.ch/9249

Piccola Opera Specialist Hospital
Enugu, Nigeria
🌐 https://vfmat.ch/dc15

Plateau State Specialist Hospital
Dogon Karfi, Plateau, Nigeria
🌐 https://vfmat.ch/41c6

Primary Health Care Center, Ibadan North East LG
Asi, Oyo, Nigeria
🌐 https://vfmat.ch/c252

Psychiatric Hospital, Nawfia
Nawfia, Anambra, Nigeria
⊕ https://vfmat.ch/gux1

Randle General Hospital
New Lagos, Lagos, Nigeria
⊕ https://vfmat.ch/ea61

Rano General Hospital
Sabon Gari (RAN), Kano, Nigeria
⊕ https://vfmat.ch/1414

Rasheed Shekoni Specialist Hospital
Dutse, Jigawa, Nigeria
⊕ https://vfmat.ch/b4be

Reemee Medicare Nig. Ltd
Langtang, Bauchi, Nigeria
⊕ https://vfmat.ch/b676

Regal Hospital
Tori, Delta, Nigeria
⊕ https://vfmat.ch/fe92

Rivers State University Hospital (RUST)
Port Harcourt, Rivers, Nigeria
⊕ https://vfmat.ch/4e73

Rogo General Hospital
Ungwan Liman, Kano, Nigeria
⊕ https://vfmat.ch/b4c9

Roman Catholic Health Mission
Sara, Bauchi, Nigeria
⊕ https://vfmat.ch/6d7c

Rose of Sharon Mediplex
Benin City, Edo, Nigeria
⊕ https://vfmat.ch/aac6

S.C.P.U
Yamma 2, Katsina, Nigeria
⊕ https://vfmat.ch/52ea

Sabakuwa Yamma
Sabakwa, Bauchi, Nigeria
⊕ https://vfmat.ch/7d23

Saidu Dange Railway Hospital
Zaria, Kaduna, Nigeria
⊕ https://vfmat.ch/df86

Sick Bay, PH City Council
Orogbum, Rivers, Nigeria
⊕ https://vfmat.ch/78d9

Sir Muhammed Sunusi General Hospital
Hotoro North, Kano, Nigeria
⊕ https://vfmat.ch/66e6

Specialist Hospital Gombe
Gabukka, Gombe, Nigeria
⊕ https://vfmat.ch/afa3

Specialist Hospital Sokoto
Gandu, Sokoto, Nigeria
⊕ https://vfmat.ch/8d5b

St. Gabriel's Specialist Hospital
New Haven, Enugu, Nigeria
⊕ https://vfmat.ch/2179

St. Gerards Catholic Hospital
Kaduna South, Kaduna, Nigeria
⊕ https://vfmat.ch/1d54

St. Nicholas Hospital
Mekunwen, Lagos, Nigeria
⊕ https://vfmat.ch/b49b

St. Raphael Divine Mercy Specialist Hospital
Parafa, Lagos, Nigeria
⊕ https://vfmat.ch/61ec

St. Catherine Specialist Hospital
Ogidigba, Rivers, Nigeria
⊕ https://vfmat.ch/e89c

State Hospital Abeokuta
Abeokuta, Ogun, Nigeria
⊕ https://vfmat.ch/rt5w

State Hospital Oyo
Awe, Oyo, Nigeria
⊕ https://vfmat.ch/8f22

State Isolation Centre
Faria, Borno, Nigeria
⊕ https://vfmat.ch/731c

Sule Galadima Garo General Hospital
Garo, Kano, Nigeria
⊕ https://vfmat.ch/8feb

Suleja Hospital, Niger
Suleja, Niger, Nigeria
⊕ https://vfmat.ch/6bbe

Sunnah Hospital
Gombe, Gombe, Nigeria
⊕ https://vfmat.ch/9787

Symbol Hospital
Uwani, Enugu, Nigeria
⊕ https://vfmat.ch/831e

Taraba State Specialist Hospital, Jalingo
Jalingo, Taraba, Nigeria
⊕ https://vfmat.ch/3nkj

TB Leprosy Referral Hospital
Sabongari, Niger, Nigeria
⊕ https://vfmat.ch/cc46

Tito Asibiti
Larmurde, Adamawa, Nigeria
⊕ https://vfmat.ch/5575

Toro General Hospital
Toro, Bauchi, Nigeria
⊕ https://vfmat.ch/416c

Tulsi Chanrai Foundation Eye Hospital
Kukwaba, Abuja, Nigeria
⊕ https://vfmat.ch/effc

Uba Phc
Uba, Borno, Nigeria
⊕ https://vfmat.ch/b777

Ugep General Hospital
Nkankpo, Cross River, Nigeria
⊕ https://vfmat.ch/4d4e

Umaru Shehu Ultramodern Hospital, Bulumkutu
Kalari, Borno, Nigeria
⊕ https://vfmat.ch/9ff3

UNIOSUN Teaching Hospital, Osogbo
Osogbo, Osun, Nigeria
⊕ https://vfmat.ch/ugxs

Universal Specialist Hospital
Albasa, Kano, Nigeria
⊕ https://vfmat.ch/c4a4

University College Hospital (UCH)
Sango, Oyo, Nigeria
⊕ https://vfmat.ch/fbd4

University Health Services Fed University Of Technology Minna
Bosso, Niger, Nigeria
⊕ https://vfmat.ch/64dc

University of Abuja Teaching Hospital
Gunrafia, FCT, Nigeria
⊕ https://vfmat.ch/9832

University Of Benin Teaching Hospital
Benin City, Edo, Nigeria
⊕ https://vfmat.ch/69d5

University of Calabar Teaching Hospital
Calabar, Cross River, Nigeria
⊕ https://vfmat.ch/6196

University Of Ilorin Teaching Hospital
Yemoja, Kwara, Nigeria
⊕ https://vfmat.ch/81d8

University of Maiduguri Teaching Hospital UMTH
Mai Musari, Borno, Nigeria
⊕ https://vfmat.ch/fc23

University of Nigeria Teaching Hospital, Enugu
Ituku/Ozalla, Enugu, Nigeria
⊕ https://vfmat.ch/mpxb

University of Port Harcourt Teaching Hospital (UPTH)
Port Harcourt, Rivers, Nigeria
⊕ https://vfmat.ch/f4ud

University of Uyo Teaching Hospital
Uyo, Akwa Ibom State, Nigeria
⊕ https://vfmat.ch/e944

Usman Aisha Memorial Hospital
Bida, Niger, Nigeria
⊕ https://vfmat.ch/355d

Usmanu Danfodiyo University Teaching Hospital, Sokoto
Sokoto, Nigeria
⊕ https://vfmat.ch/bfv6

Waziri Shehu Gidado Hospital
Rijiyar Lemo, Kano, Nigeria
⊕ https://vfmat.ch/bdac

Welfare Hospital
Akinfenwa, Oyo, Nigeria
⊕ https://vfmat.ch/7e46

Wellness Hospitals And Diagnostics Limited
Port Harcourt, Rivers, Nigeria
⊕ https://vfmat.ch/61ce

Wesley Guild Hospital, Ilesa
Ilesa, Osun, Nigeria
⊕ https://vfmat.ch/9856

Wudil General Hospital
Utai, Kano, Nigeria
⊕ https://vfmat.ch/5c6f

Wuro Alhaji Hospital
Wuro Alim, Adamawa, Nigeria
⊕ https://vfmat.ch/9d43

Wuse General Hospital
Abuja, FCT, Nigeria
⊕ https://vfmat.ch/fe21

Yadakunya Leprosy General Hospital
Yadakunya, Kano, Nigeria
⊕ https://vfmat.ch/8233

Yariman Bakura Specialist Hospital
Gusau, Zamfara, Nigeria
⊕ https://vfmat.ch/jqwc

Yenagoa Hospital And Maternity
Yenagoa, Bayelsa, Nigeria
⊕ https://vfmat.ch/fa34

Yusuf Dantsoho Memorial Hospital
Tudun Wada, Kaduna, Nigeria
⊕ https://vfmat.ch/7ec5

Yusufari Maternal And Child Health Care
Yusufari, Yobe, Nigeria
⊕ https://vfmat.ch/d619

Zonal Hospital, Bori
Bori, Gokana, Rivers, Nigeria
⊕ https://vfmat.ch/7663

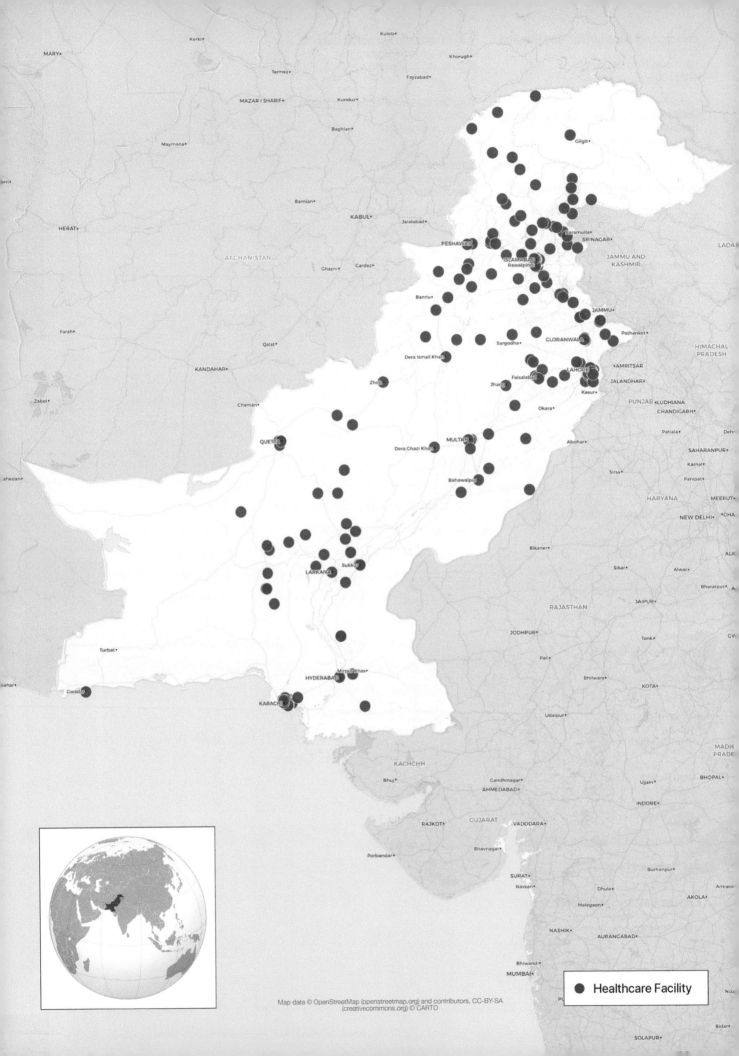

Healthcare Facility

# Pakistan

The Islamic Republic of Pakistan, in South Asia, borders the Arabian Sea and sits between India to the east, Iran and Afghanistan to the west, and China to the north. Besides being the 33rd largest country by area, Pakistan is also the world's fifth most populous country, with nearly 238.2 million people. Noted for its diverse ancient cultures, Pakistan has the second largest Muslim population in the world, with 96 percent of its people practicing Islam. Islamabad is the nation's capital. The country is linguistically and ethnically diverse, with Punjabis, Pashtuns, Sindhis, Saraikis, and Muhajirs as the major ethnic groups. Over 60 languages are spoken, but Urdu and English are the official languages. Natural resources include limestone, arable land, extensive natural gas reserves, limited petroleum, coal, iron ore, copper, and salt.

Pakistan gained independence in 1947 after the partition of the British Indian Empire. Noted for its nuclear power, Pakistan has the sixth-largest standing military in the world. The country is considered a strong emerging and growth-leading economy, due to its large and growing middle class. Despite this growth, Pakistan is faced with challenges such as illiteracy, corruption, and poverty.

Pakistan has experienced a steady increase in both communicable and non-communicable diseases. The major infectious diseases include hepatitis A and E, bacterial diarrhea, typhoid fever, dengue fever, malaria, and rabies. The leading causes of death include neonatal disorders, ischemic heart disease, stroke, diarrheal diseases, lower respiratory infections, tuberculosis, COPD, diabetes, chronic kidney disease, and cirrhosis. Pakistan has one of the highest rates of hepatitis C virus infection in the world, with about 4 percent to 5 percent of its population infected.

238.2M

Population

$1,194

GDP Per Capita

67 years

Life Expectancy

↑ Improving

112
Doctors/100k

Physician Density

63
Beds/100k

Hospital Bed Density

140
Deaths/100k

Maternal Mortality

Pakistan

Nonprofit Organizations

A Leg To Stand On (ALTSO)
Provides free, high-quality prosthetic limbs, orthotic devices, and wheelchairs to children with untreated limb disabilities in the developing world.
Logist-Op, Ortho
⊕ https://vfmat.ch/a48d

Action Against Hunger
Aims to end life-threatening hunger for good through treating and preventing malnutrition across more than 45 countries.
Nutr
⊕ https://vfmat.ch/2dbc

Afghan Institute of Learning
Provides education, training, and health services to vulnerable Afghans in order to foster self-reliance, critical thinking skills, and community participation.
General, Logist-Op, Nutr, OB-GYN, Peds, Pub Health
⊕ https://vfmat.ch/12e9

Afzaal Memorial Thalassemia Foundation
Aims to develop an institute for benign hematology with well-built research where quality clinical care is provided to all patients.
CV Med, Crit-Care, ER Med, Heme-Onc, Neuro, Ophth-Opt, Ortho, Path, Peds, Psych, Radiol
⊕ https://vfmat.ch/2532

Aga Khan Foundation Canada
Tackles the root causes of poverty, with a special focus on marginalized groups such as women and girls. Programs provide access to education and healthcare, food, and opportunity.
Pub Health
⊕ https://vfmat.ch/7f8b

Age International
Helps older people living in some of the world's poorest places to have improved well-being and be treated with dignity through a variety of programs, including emergency relief and cataract surgery.
ER Med, Geri, Logist-Op, Nutr, Ophth-Opt, Palliative, Pub Health
⊕ https://vfmat.ch/c7e2

Al Basar International Foundation
Works with local partners to treat preventable blindness, and helps set up sustainable infrastructure so local teams can save sight in their communities.
Ophth-Opt
⊕ https://vfmat.ch/a8b5

Al-Ain International
Provides financial and material support to hospitals, free medical camps, clinics and other organizations in developing countries.
General, Ophth-Opt
⊕ https://vfmat.ch/c8ca

Al-Khair Foundation
Provides emergency relief and developmental support in some of the world's most impoverished areas.
Dent-OMFS, General, MF Med, Nutr, Peds
⊕ https://vfmat.ch/921d

Al-Mustafa Welfare Trust
Seeks to alleviate poverty and provides medical and social development assistance to the poor and vulnerable around the world.
General, Ophth-Opt
⊕ https://vfmat.ch/c5f4

Al-Shifa Trust Eye Hospital
Aims to prevent and treat blindness by providing sustainable eye care services that all can access and afford.
Ophth-Opt
⊕ https://vfmat.ch/d2fc

Alight
Works closely with refugees, trafficked persons, economic migrants, and other displaced persons to co-design solutions that help them build full and fulfilling lives, with healthcare, clean water, shelter protection, and economic opportunity.
ER Med, General, Infect Dis, MF Med, Neonat, Peds
⊕ https://vfmat.ch/5993

Alkhidmat Foundation Pakistan
Provides relief services of all scopes, including care for orphans, disaster relief, affordable healthcare, and clean water.
ER Med, General, Logist-Op, Pub Health
⊕ https://vfmat.ch/3fb1

American Academy of Pediatrics
Seeks to attain optimal physical, mental, and social health and well-being for all infants, children, adolescents, and young adults.
Anesth, Crit-Care, Neonat, Ped Surg
⊕ https://vfmat.ch/9633

American Heart Association (AHA)
Fights heart disease and stroke, striving to save and improve lives.
CV Med, Crit-Care, General, Heme-Onc, Medicine, Peds
⊕ https://vfmat.ch/4747

American Stroke Association
Works to prevent, treat, and beat stroke by funding innovative research, fighting for stronger public health policies, and providing lifesaving tools and information.
CV Med, Crit-Care, Heme-Onc, Medicine, Neuro, Pub Health, Pulm-Critic, Vasc Surg
⊕ https://vfmat.ch/746f

Americares

Saves lives and improves health for people affected by poverty or disaster and responds with life-changing medicine, medical supplies, and health programs including domestic and global medical clinics.

All-Immu, ER Med, General, Infect Dis, MF Med, Nutr

⊕ https://vfmat.ch/e567

Amsterdam Institute for Global Health and Development (AIGHD)

Provides sustainable solutions to major health problems across our planet by forging synergies among disciplines, healthcare delivery, research, and education.

Infect Dis

⊕ https://vfmat.ch/d73d

Association of Medical Doctors of Asia (AMDA)

Strives to support people affected by disasters and economic distress on their road to recovery, establishing a true partnership with special emphasis on local initiative.

ER Med, Logist-Op, Pub Health

⊕ https://vfmat.ch/e3d4

BFIRST – British Foundation for International Reconstructive Surgery & Training

Supports projects across the developing world to train surgeons in their local environment to effectively manage devastating injuries.

Anesth, Plast, Surg

⊕ https://vfmat.ch/ad4f

Big Heart Foundation

Aims to safeguard the rights and improve the lives of vulnerable children and families worldwide, particularly in the Arab region, through advocacy, humanitarian, and development efforts.

ER Med, Nutr, Ophth-Opt, Plast, Rad-Onc

⊕ https://vfmat.ch/fff4

Boston Children's Hospital: Global Health Program

Helps solve pediatric global healthcare challenges by transferring expertise through long-term partnerships with scalable impact, while working in the field to strengthen healthcare systems, advocate, research, and provide care delivery or education as a way of sustainably improving the health of children worldwide.

Anesth, CV Med, Crit-Care, ER Med, Heme-Onc, Infect Dis, Medicine, Nutr, Palliative, Ped Surg, Peds

⊕ https://vfmat.ch/f9f8

Breast Cancer Support

Aims to save lives and end breast cancer forever in women and men through education, treatment, emotional assistance, and financial support.

Heme-Onc, Logist-Op, Pub Health, Rad-Onc, Radiol

⊕ https://vfmat.ch/cb78

Bridge of Life

Aims to strengthen healthcare globally through sustainable programs that prevent and treat chronic disease.

Logist-Op, Nephro, OB-GYN, Peds, Surg

⊕ https://vfmat.ch/5b68

British Council for Prevention of Blindness (BCPB)

Funds research into blindness prevention and sight restoration in children and adults in low- and lower-middle-income countries.

Ophth-Opt

⊕ https://vfmat.ch/eaf4

Bureau of International Health Cooperation

Seeks to improve healthcare around the world, including developing countries, using expertise, and contribute to healthier lives of Japanese people by bringing these experiences back to Japan.

ER Med, Heme-Onc, Infect Dis, Peds, Pub Health

⊕ https://vfmat.ch/947d

Camillian Disaster Service (CADIS) International

Promotes the development of locally based health programs for disaster-stricken communities through compassionate and coordinated interventions.

General, Logist-Op, MF Med

⊕ https://vfmat.ch/5281

Canadian Medical Assistance Teams (CMAT)

Provides relief and medical aid to the victims of natural and man-made disasters around the world.

Anesth, ER Med, Medicine, OB-GYN, Peds, Psych, Rehab, Surg

⊕ https://vfmat.ch/5232

Cancer Care Hospital and Research Center

Provides free comprehensive cancer treatment while meeting patients' physical, economic, and spiritual needs and teaching medical professionals the latest developments in oncology.

Heme-Onc

⊕ https://vfmat.ch/de8d

Cardiovascular Foundation, The (TCVF)

Aims to address the critical challenge of heart disease in Pakistan by helping to provide timely and quality healthcare and cardiac treatment.

Logist-Op

⊕ https://vfmat.ch/7618

CARE

Works around the globe to save lives, defeat poverty, and achieve social justice.

ER Med, General

⊕ https://vfmat.ch/7232

Care Channels International

We engage communities through a variety of education, health, and livelihood programs.

Dent-OMFS, General, Surg

⊕ https://vfmat.ch/fc48

Caritas Pro Vitae Gradu Charitable Trust

Supports Catholic charitable projects with social and humanitarian efforts, and aims to assist people in need including children, the elderly, sick, and disabled through healthcare, poverty relief, and education.

ER Med, General, Logist-Op, Medicine, OB-GYN, Ophth-Opt, Path, Peds, Pub Health, Radiol, Rehab, Surg

⊕ https://vfmat.ch/b2ca

Carter Center, The

Seeks to prevent and resolve conflicts, enhance freedom and democracy, and improve health, while remaining committed to human rights and the alleviation of human suffering.

Infect Dis, MF Med, Ophth-Opt

⊕ https://vfmat.ch/6556

Central Park Teaching Hospital

Delivers consultation, diagnosis, and treatment services to every patient regardless of ability to pay.

Anesth, CV Med, Crit-Care, Dent-OMFS, Derm, ENT, ER Med, Medicine, OB-GYN, Ophth-Opt, Ortho, Path, Peds, Psych, Radiol, Rehab, Surg, Urol

⊕ https://vfmat.ch/3e79

Chain of Hope

Provides lifesaving heart operations for children around the world and supports the development of cardiac services in numerous developing and war-torn countries.

Anesth, CT Surg, CV Med, Crit-Care, Ped Surg, Peds, Pulm-Critic, Surg

⊕ https://vfmat.ch/1b1b

Charity Right Pakistan

Ensures food is available to the most vulnerable and isolated communities, while working to help children and families in need to become self-sufficient through regular meals.

Logist-Op, Nutr

⊕ https://vfmat.ch/8f38

CharityVision International

Focuses on restoring curable sight impairment worldwide by empowering local physicians and creating sustainable solutions.

Logist-Op, Ophth-Opt, Surg
⊕ https://vfmat.ch/6231

Child Care Foundation of Pakistan

Undertakes programs for community development, grassroots education, health and vocational training to alleviate poverty, empower women, and eliminate child labor.
General
⊕ https://vfmat.ch/e1e8

ChildLife Foundation

Treats pediatric patients through its network of emergency rooms, primary care clinics, and preventive care programs.
ER Med, Neonat, Ped Surg, Peds
⊕ https://vfmat.ch/c62b

Christian Aid Ministries

Strives to be a trustworthy and efficient channel for Amish, Mennonite, and other conservative Anabaptist groups and individuals to minister to physical and spiritual needs around the world.
CT Surg, ER Med, Logist-Op, Ortho, Pub Health
⊕ https://vfmat.ch/7b33

Christian Blind Mission (CBM)

Aims to improve the quality of life of persons with disabilities in the poorest countries, addressing poverty as a cause and a consequence of disability, and working in partnership to create a society for all.
ENT, General, Infect Dis, OB-GYN, Ophth-Opt, Ortho, Peds, Psych, Rehab, Surg
⊕ https://vfmat.ch/3824

Christian Connections for International Health (CCIH)

Promotes global health and wholeness from a Christian perspective.
All-Immu, General, Infect Dis, MF Med, Neonat, OB-GYN, Psych
⊕ https://vfmat.ch/fa5d

Christian Health Service Corps

Brings Christian doctors, health professionals, and health educators committed to serving the poor to places that otherwise have little or no access to healthcare.
Anesth, Dent-OMFS, General, Medicine, Peds, Surg
⊕ https://vfmat.ch/da57

Concern Worldwide

Seeks to permanently transform the lives of people living in extreme poverty, tackling its root causes, and building resilience.
Logist-Op, MF Med, Nutr, OB-GYN
⊕ https://vfmat.ch/77e9

COVID-19 Clinical Research Coalition

Advocates and collaborates for the advancement of COVID-19 research driven by the needs of low-resource settings, and works for equitable access to solutions to the pandemic.
All-Immu, Infect-Dis, MF Med, Path, Pub Health
⊕ https://vfmat.ch/d1f4

Diabetes Centre, The (TDC)

Seeks to ensure effective diagnosis, treatment, management, and education of patients with diabetes types 1 and 2, endocrine disorders and associated risks of diabetes.
CV Med, ER Med, Endo, Nephro, Nutr, OB-GYN, Ophth-Opt, Pod, Pub Health
⊕ https://vfmat.ch/6e14

Diabetic Association of Pakistan (DAP)

Provides specialized medical care, rehabilitation, and education to individuals with diabetes, regardless of gender and economic or social status.
Endo, Nutr, Ophth-Opt, Ortho
⊕ https://vfmat.ch/9bb3

Dianova

Works in prevention and treatment of addiction, while promoting social progress in international forums.
Psych, Pub Health
⊕ https://vfmat.ch/1998

Direct Relief

Improves the health and lives of people affected by poverty or emergency situations by mobilizing and providing essential medical resources needed for their care.
ER Med, Logist-Op
⊕ https://vfmat.ch/58e5

DKT INTERNATIONAL INC

Seeks to provide couples with affordable and safe options for family planning and HIV/AIDS prevention through dynamic social marketing.
General, Surg
⊕ https://vfmat.ch/b3a7

Doctors on Mission

Provides sustainable medical healthcare to needy countries, including those having experienced recent disasters and areas where minority groups are persecuted.
General, Logist-Op, Medicine, Nutr
⊕ https://vfmat.ch/5244

Doctors Without Borders/Médecins Sans Frontières (MSF)

Responds to emergencies and provides lifesaving medical care where needed most, including during disasters, conflicts, and epidemics.
Anesth, Crit-Care, ER Med, General, Infect Dis, Nutr, OB-GYN, Ped Surg, Peds, Psych, Pub Health, Surg
⊕ https://vfmat.ch/f363

Doctors Worldwide

Focuses on health access, health improvement, and health emergencies to serve communities in need so they can build healthier and happier futures.
Dent-OMFS, ER Med, General, MF Med, Palliative, Peds
⊕ https://vfmat.ch/99cd

Dua Foundation

Provides sustainable healthcare through health and hygiene training for the rural population in the province of Sindh, Pakistan.
ER Med, General, Pub Health
⊕ https://vfmat.ch/3bc2

Duke University: Global Health Institute

Sparks innovation in global health research and education, and brings together knowledge and resources to address the most important global health issues of our time.
All-Immu, Infect Dis, MF Med, OB-GYN, Pub Health
⊕ https://vfmat.ch/c4cd

Earth Mission

Empowers healthcare teams with training and knowledge to ensure that all people in Myanmar, especially the Karen ethnic group, have access to high-quality healthcare.
General, OB-GYN, Ophth-Opt, Peds, Pub Health
⊕ https://vfmat.ch/93f3

Emergency Response Team Search And Rescue, The (ERTSAR)

Provides technical rescue and medical response in the immediate aftermath of a disaster while providing strategic, smart, and sustainable solutions.
ER Med, Logist-Op
⊕ https://vfmat.ch/c599

Ending Eclampsia

Seeks to expand access to proven, underutilized interventions and commodities for the prevention, early detection, and treatment of pre-eclampsia and eclampsia and to strengthen global partnerships.
MF Med, Neonat, OB-GYN
⊕ https://vfmat.ch/8589

Evangelical Alliance Mission, The (TEAM)

Provides services in the areas of church planting, community development, healthcare, social justice, business as mission, and more.
Dent-OMFS, General, Ophth-Opt
⊕ https://vfmat.ch/9faa

Evidence Action
Aims to be a world leader in scaling evidence-based and cost-effective programs to reduce the burden of poverty.
General, Infect Dis
⊕ https://vfmat.ch/94b6

Evidence Project, The
Improves family-planning policies, programs, and practices through the strategic generation, translation, and use of evidence.
General, MF Med
⊕ https://vfmat.ch/f9e7

Eye Foundation of America
Works toward a world without childhood blindness.
Ophth-Opt
⊕ https://vfmat.ch/a7eb

Fistula Foundation
Aims to engage the support of people worldwide who are eager to see the day that no woman suffers from obstetric fistula. Raises and directs funds to doctors and hospitals providing life-transforming surgery to women in need.
OB-GYN
⊕ https://vfmat.ch/e958

Fracarita International
Provides support and services in the fields of mental healthcare, care for people with a disability, and education.
Psych, Rehab
⊕ https://vfmat.ch/8d3c

Fred Hollows Foundation, The
Works toward a world in which no person is needlessly blind or vision impaired.
Ophth-Opt, Pub Health, Surg
⊕ https://vfmat.ch/73e5

Gift of Life International
Provides lifesaving cardiac treatment to children in developing countries while developing sustainable pediatric cardiac programs by implementing screening, surgical, and training missions.
Anesth, CT Surg, CV Med, Crit-Care, Ped Surg, Peds, Pulm-Critic
⊕ https://vfmat.ch/f2f9

Global Alliance to Prevent Prematurity And Stillbirth (GAPPS)
Seeks to improve birth outcomes worldwide by reducing the burden of premature birth and stillbirth.
All-Immu, Infect Dis, MF Med, Neonat, Neonat, OB-GYN
⊕ https://vfmat.ch/3f74

Global Ministries – The United Methodist Church
As the worldwide mission and development agency of The United Methodist Church, Global Ministries works with more than 300 hospitals and clinics around the world through its Global Health Unit.
Anesth, CT Surg, CV Med, Crit-Care, Dent-OMFS, Derm, ER Med, GI, General, Infect Dis, Logist-Op, MF Med, Medicine, Neonat, Nephro, Nutr, OB-GYN, Ophth-Opt, Ortho, Palliative, Peds, Pod, Psych, Pub Health, Rehab, Rheum, Surg, Urol
⊕ https://vfmat.ch/1723

Global Network for Women and Children's Health Research
Aims to improve maternal and child health outcomes and building health research capacity in resource-poor settings by testing cost-effective, sustainable interventions that provide guidance for the practice of evidence-based medicine. Scientists from developing countries, together with peers in the United States, lead teams that address priority research needs through randomized clinical trials and implementation research conducted in low-resource areas.
MF Med, OB-GYN
⊕ https://vfmat.ch/a187

Global Oncology (GO)
Brings the best in cancer care to underserved patients around the world and collaborates across geographic, professional, and academic borders to improve cancer care, research, and education.
Heme-Onc, Path, Rad-Onc
⊕ https://vfmat.ch/fcb8

Global Polio Eradication Initiative
Aims to eradicate polio worldwide.
All-Immu, Infect-Dis, Logist-Op, Pub Health
⊕ https://vfmat.ch/7e2c

Globus Relief
Aims to improve the delivery of healthcare worldwide by gathering, processing, and distributing surplus medical supplies to charities at home and abroad.
Logist-Op
⊕ https://vfmat.ch/a2b7

Graham Layton Trust
Aims to treat curable blindness and visual impairment by providing free eye surgery and ophthalmic care for the poor and underprivileged of Pakistan.
Ophth-Opt
⊕ https://vfmat.ch/1aae

Healing Little Hearts
Sends specialist medical teams to perform free lifesaving heart surgery on babies and children in developing parts of the world.
Anesth, CT Surg, CV Med, Ped Surg, Peds, Surg
⊕ https://vfmat.ch/ffc1

Health Equity Initiative
Aims to build and sustain a global community that engages across sectors and disciplines to advance health equity.
Pub Health
⊕ https://vfmat.ch/e2e2

Health Foundation, The
Aims to create awareness and promote healthy practices for management of various diseases with an initial focus on hepatitis B and C.
GI, Infect Dis
⊕ https://vfmat.ch/eb52

Health Frontiers
Provides volunteer support to international health and child development efforts.
ER Med, Medicine, Peds
⊕ https://vfmat.ch/aa14

Health, Education & Literacy Programme (HELP)
Works to design and implement replicable models of health promotion, health delivery, and education for women and children.
General, MF Med
⊕ https://vfmat.ch/c31a

HealthServe Australia
Develops sustainable health programs that improve health and well-being and partners with community groups to build community capacity to meet health needs.
Infect Dis, Logist-Op, OB-GYN, Psych, Pub Health
⊕ https://vfmat.ch/7276

Healthy DEvelopments
Provides Germany-supported health and social protection programs around the globe in a collaborative knowledge management process.
All-Immu, General, Infect Dis, Logist-Op, MF Med
⊕ https://vfmat.ch/dc31

HelpAge International
Works to ensure that people everywhere understand how much older people contribute to society and that they must enjoy their right to healthcare, social services, economic, and physical security.
General, Geri, Infect Dis, Medicine, Pub Health
⊕ https://vfmat.ch/5d91

Hernia International
Aims to provide relief from sickness, and protection and preservation of health, for persons affected by groin and abdominal hernias and residing in low- and middle-income countries.
Surg
⊕ https://vfmat.ch/e98e

Hope and Healing International
Gives hope and healing to children and families trapped by poverty and disability.
General, Nutr, Ophth-Opt, Peds, Rehab
⊕ https://vfmat.ch/c638

Human Development Foundation (HDF)
Aims to facilitate social change and community empowerment through literacy, improved education, universal primary healthcare, and grassroots economic development via social projects.
Logist-Op, MF Med, Nutr, OB-GYN, Path
⊕ https://vfmat.ch/c9fd

Humanity & Inclusion
Works alongside people with disabilities and vulnerable populations, taking action and bearing witness in order to respond to their essential needs, improve their living conditions and health, and promote respect for their dignity and fundamental rights.
General, Infect Dis, MF Med, Medicine, Ortho, Peds, Psych, Pub Health, Rehab
⊕ https://vfmat.ch/16b7

Humanity First
Provides aid and assistance to those in need, offering sustainable development solutions to society while providing and empowering local communities with the resources to help themselves.
ER Med, General, MF Med, Ophth-Opt
⊕ https://vfmat.ch/13cc

Imamia Medics International
Provides health education and healthcare services to underserved populations around the world, while giving Muslim health and science professionals an opportunity for career development.
Logist-Op, Medicine
⊕ https://vfmat.ch/dc22

IMPACT Foundation
Works to prevent and alleviate needless disability by restoring sight, mobility, and hearing.
ENT, MF Med, OB-GYN, Ophth-Opt, Ortho, Peds, Surg
⊕ https://vfmat.ch/ba28

Imran Khan Cancer Appeal
Helps some of the world's poorest individuals beat cancer by offering comprehensive cancer care free of charge in facilities that provide all necessary diagnostic and therapeutic services.
Heme-Onc, Rad-Onc
⊕ https://vfmat.ch/6af9

Incentive Care Foundation
Aims to improve the welfare of people and children in Pakistan by providing shelter, education, healthcare, food, youth training programs, and women's empowerment.
Heme-Onc, Logist-Op
⊕ https://vfmat.ch/b2d8

International Agency for the Prevention of Blindness (IAPB), The
Leads international efforts in blindness-prevention activities, works toward a world where no one is needlessly visually impaired, and ensures that everyone has access to the best possible standard of eye health.
Infect Dis, Ophth-Opt, Pub Health
⊕ https://vfmat.ch/87a2

International Campaign for Women's Right to Safe Abortion
Works to build an international network and campaign that brings together organizations with an interest in promoting and providing safe abortion to create a shared platform for advocacy, debate, and dialogue and the sharing of skills and experience.
OB-GYN, Pub Health, Surg
⊕ https://vfmat.ch/f341

International Children's Heart Foundation
Provides free surgical care, medical training, and technology to save the lives of children with congenital heart disease in developing countries.
Anesth, CT Surg, CV Med, Crit-Care, Ped Surg, Peds, Pulm-Critic
⊕ https://vfmat.ch/86c1

International Council of Ophthalmology
Works with ophthalmologic societies and others to enhance ophthalmic education and improve access to the highest-quality eye care in order to preserve and restore vision for people of the world.
Ophth-Opt
⊕ https://vfmat.ch/ffd2

International Federation of Gynecology and Obstetrics (FIGO)
Implements global projects on specific women's health issues.
MF Med, Medicine, Neonat, OB-GYN, Surg, Urol
⊕ https://vfmat.ch/c4b4

International Federation of Red Cross and Red Crescent Societies (IFRC)
Coordinates and directs international assistance following natural and manmade disasters in nonconflict situations through the world's largest humanitarian and development network. Provides disaster-preparedness programs, healthcare activities, and promotes humanitarian values.
ER Med, General, Infect Dis, Nutr
⊕ https://vfmat.ch/b4ee

International Learning Movement (ILM UK)
Supports some of the world's poorest people in developing countries with core projects in education, safe drinking water, and healthcare.
General, Ophth-Opt
⊕ https://vfmat.ch/b974

International Medical Corps
Seeks to improve quality of life through health interventions and related activities that strengthen underserved communities worldwide, with the flexibility to respond rapidly to emergencies and offer medical services and training to people at the highest risk.
ER Med, General, Infect Dis, Nutr, OB-GYN, Peds, Pub Health, Surg
⊕ https://vfmat.ch/a8a5

International Organization for Migration (IOM) – The UN Migration Agency
Promotes evidence-informed policies and holistic, preventive, and curative health programs that are beneficial, accessible, and equitable for vulnerable migrants.
General, Infect Dis, OB-GYN
⊕ https://vfmat.ch/621a

International Pediatric Nephrology Association (IPNA)
Leads global efforts to successfully address the care for all children with kidney disease through advocacy, education, and training.
Medicine, Nephro, Peds
⊕ https://vfmat.ch/b59d

International Planned Parenthood Federation (IPPF)
Leads a locally owned, globally connected civil society movement that provides and enables services and champions sexual and reproductive health and rights for all, especially the underserved.
Infect Dis, MF Med, OB-GYN
⊕ https://vfmat.ch/dc97

International Rescue Committee (IRC)
Responds to the world's worst humanitarian crises and helps people whose lives and livelihoods are shattered by conflict and disaster to survive, recover, and gain control of their future.
ER Med, General, Infect Dis, MF Med, Peds
⊕ https://vfmat.ch/5d24

International Trachoma Initiative (iTi)
Works toward a world free from trachoma, a preventable cause of blindness, and provides comprehensive support to national ministries of health and governmental and nongovernmental organizations to implement a comprehensive approach to fight trachoma.
Infect Dis, Ophth-Opt
⊕ https://vfmat.ch/3278

International Union Against Tuberculosis and Lung Disease
Develops, implements, and assesses anti-tuberculosis, lung health, and noncommunicable disease programs.

Infect Dis, Pub Health, Pulm-Critic
⊕ https://vfmat.ch/3e82

InterSurgeon
Fosters collaborative partnerships in the field of global surgery that will advance clinical care, teaching, training, research, and the provision and maintenance of medical equipment.
ENT, Neurosurg, Ortho, Ped Surg, Plast, Surg, Urol
⊕ https://vfmat.ch/6f8a

IOF – International Osteoporosis Foundation
Aims to fight against osteoporosis and promote bone and musculoskeletal health worldwide.
Endo, OB-GYN, Ortho
⊕ https://vfmat.ch/89d8

Ipas
Focuses efforts on women and girls who want contraception or abortion, and builds programs around their needs and how best to support them.
OB-GYN
⊕ https://vfmat.ch/8e39

iQra International
Provides medical aid to disabled people globally, and raises awareness of the neglect and discrimination they face in developing countries.
General, Logist-Op, Ophth-Opt
⊕ https://vfmat.ch/9282

Iranian Red Crescent
Aims to provide effective relief services in the wake of crises, to alleviate human suffering, and to empower the affected community.
ER Med, General, Infect Dis, Logist-Op, Nutr, OB-GYN, Psych, Rehab
⊕ https://vfmat.ch/c352

Islamic Medical Association of North America
Fosters health promotion, disease prevention, and health maintenance in communities around the world through direct patient care and health programs.
Anesth, Dent-OMFS, ER Med, General, Logist-Op, Ophth-Opt, Peds, Plast, Surg
⊕ https://vfmat.ch/a157

Jhpiego
Creates and delivers transformative healthcare solutions that save lives, in partnership with national governments, health experts, and local communities.
General, Infect Dis, OB-GYN, Surg
⊕ https://vfmat.ch/45b8

John Snow, Inc. (JSI)
Aims to improve the health and well-being of underserved and vulnerable people and communities throughout the world.
General, Infect Dis, Logist-Op, MF Med, OB-GYN, Peds, Psych, Pub Health
⊕ https://vfmat.ch/ba78

Johns Hopkins Center for Communication Programs
Believes in the power of communication to save lives by empowering people to adopt healthy behaviors for themselves, their families, and their communities.
General, Infect Dis, Logist-Op, OB-GYN, Pub Health
⊕ https://vfmat.ch/1bf9

Johns Hopkins Center for Global Health
Facilitates and focuses the extensive expertise and resources of the Johns Hopkins institutions, together with global collaborators, to effectively address and ameliorate the world's most pressing health issues.
General, Genetics, Logist-Op, MF Med, Peds, Psych, Pub Health, Pulm-Critic
⊕ https://vfmat.ch/54ce

Joint United Nations Programme on HIV/AIDS (UNAIDS)
Aims to place people living with HIV and people affected by the virus at the decision-making table and at the center of designing, delivering, and monitoring the AIDS response.
Infect Dis
⊕ https://vfmat.ch/464a

Kharadar General Hospital
Provides ethical and high-quality medical and social services at affordable rates.
Anesth, CV Med, Crit-Care, Derm, ENT, ER Med, Endo, GI, Heme-Onc, MF Med, Medicine, Neonat, Neuro, Neurosurg, OB-GYN, Ophth-Opt, Ortho, Path, Ped Surg, Peds, Psych, Pulm-Critic, Radiol, Rehab, Surg, Urol
⊕ https://vfmat.ch/51d7

Kletjian Foundation
Works toward a world in which all people have access to safe, sustainable, and high-quality medical care, building collaborative networks and supporting entrepreneurial leaders that promote global health equity.
CT Surg, ENT, General, Ortho, Surg
⊕ https://vfmat.ch/12c2

Lady Dufferin Hospital
Provides obstetric, gynecological, and neonatal pediatric services at little or no cost.
MF Med, Neonat, OB-GYN
⊕ https://vfmat.ch/ab29

Layton Rahmatulla Benevolent Trust (LRBT)
Aiims to create a better Pakistan by preventing the suffering caused by blindness and other eye ailments.
Ophth-Opt
⊕ https://vfmat.ch/d2be

Life for a Child
Supports the provision of the best possible healthcare, given local circumstances, to all children and youth with diabetes in less-resourced countries, through the strengthening of existing diabetes services.
Endo, Medicine, Peds
⊕ https://vfmat.ch/d712

Limbs International
Engages communities and transforms lives through affordable, sustainable prosthetic solutions and rehabilitation services in developing countries.
Logist-Op, Ortho, Pod, Rehab
⊕ https://vfmat.ch/dc84

London School of Hygiene & Tropical Medicine: International Centre for Eye Health
Works to improve eye health and eliminate avoidable visual impairment and blindness with a focus on low-income populations.
Logist-Op, Ophth-Opt, Pub Health
⊕ https://vfmat.ch/6f5f

Mahvash & Jahangir Siddiqui Foundation
Aims to provide healthcare, education and social enterprise through sustainable development to the underprivileged, with a special focus on women, minorities, children, and the disabled.
Derm, Logist-Op, OB-GYN, Ophth-Opt
⊕ https://vfmat.ch/c373

MAP International
Provides medicines and health supplies to those in need around the world so they might experience life to the fullest.
Logist-Op
⊕ https://vfmat.ch/deed

Marie Stopes International
Provides the contraception and safe abortion services that enable women all over the world to choose their own futures.
Infect Dis, MF Med, Neonat, OB-GYN, Pub Health
⊕ https://vfmat.ch/9525

Maternity Worldwide
Works with communities and partners to identify and develop appropriate and effective ways to reduce maternal and newborn mortality and morbidity, facilitate communities to access quality skilled maternity care, and support the provision of quality skilled care.
MF Med, OB-GYN
⊕ https://vfmat.ch/822b

Medical Aid Pakistan

Provides emergency relief, healthcare projects, and individual funding for medical training in Pakistan.

Infect Dis, Psych, Pub Health

⊕ https://vfmat.ch/efe1

Medical Mission Aid Inc

Advances effective healthcare in disadvantaged communities through medical scholarships, grants for supplies and support for local health initiatives.

Infect Dis, Logist-Op, OB-GYN, Pub Health, Rehab

⊕ https://vfmat.ch/8b83

MedShare

Aims to improve the quality of life of people, communities, and the planet by sourcing and directly delivering surplus medical supplies and equipment to communities in need around the world.

Logist-Op

⊕ https://vfmat.ch/c8bc

Memon Medical Institute Hospital (MMI Hospital)

Provides accessible, affordable, quality healthcare and education to all with empathy, dignity, and respect, regardless of caste, creed, color, religion, or ability to pay.

CV Med, Dent-OMFS, Derm, ENT, Endo, GI, General, Heme-Onc, Nephro, Neuro, Neurosurg, Nutr, OB-GYN, Ophth-Opt, Ortho, Ped Surg, Peds, Plast, Pulm-Critic, Surg, Urol

⊕ https://vfmat.ch/97d7

Mercy Without Limits

Educates and empowers women and children by enabling them to have an effective and positive role in constructing a better society.

ER Med

⊕ https://vfmat.ch/c3b6

Mian Muhammad Bukhsh Trust

Empowers marginalized and vulnerable segments of society through sustainable development programs.

General, MF Med, Neonat, Nutr

⊕ https://vfmat.ch/98a9

Midland International Aid Trust

Provides food, goods, clothing, and equipment to those in financial need or who are suffering as a result of a disaster.

CT Surg, Dent-OMFS, ENT, Logist-Op, OB-GYN, Ophth-Opt, Ortho, Ped Surg, Plast, Pub Health, Rehab

⊕ https://vfmat.ch/7eb2

MSI Reproductive Choices (Marie Stopes International)

Seeks to deliver quality family planning and reproductive healthcare to women around the world.

MF Med

⊕ https://vfmat.ch/5c82

Mukhtar A. Sheikh Hospital

Aims to provide exceptional healthcare services to all patients through a variety of medical specialties.

Derm, ENT, GI, General, Medicine, Nephro, Neuro, Neurosurg, OB-GYN, Ortho, Peds, Psych, Rehab, Surg, Urol

⊕ https://vfmat.ch/d3ef

Multi-Agency International Training and Support (MAITS)

Improves the lives of some of the world's poorest people living with disabilities through better access to quality health and education services and support.

Neuro, Psych, Rehab

⊕ https://vfmat.ch/9dcd

Muslim Aid

Aims to improve the lives of those in need, and to address the underlying structural and systemic causes of poverty in their communities, inspired by Muslim faith.

ER Med, Infect Dis, MF Med, Nutr

⊕ https://vfmat.ch/a8ed

Muslim Global Relief

Aims to eliminate poverty and economic exclusion among the hardest-to-reach communities through social enterprise, grassroots empowerment, and sustainability.

General

⊕ https://vfmat.ch/e58e

Muslim Welfare Canada

Serves vulnerable populations by supporting healthcare clinics, food security programs, and other humanitarian projects.

Logist-Op, Nutr

⊕ https://vfmat.ch/a227

Muwakhat Foundation

Aims to bring economic and social stability to women, children, the elderly, and disabled, by providing education, food, healthcare, and legal support.

Nutr, OB-GYN

⊕ https://vfmat.ch/8ca7

Médecins du Monde/Doctors of the World

Provides care, bears witness, and supports social change worldwide with innovative medical programs and evidence-based advocacy initiatives.

ER Med, General, Infect Dis, MF Med, Neonat, OB-GYN, Peds, Pub Health

⊕ https://vfmat.ch/a43d

National Institute of Blood Diseases

Aims to provide comprehensive diagnosis and management of patients suffering from blood disorders.

Genetics, Heme-Onc

⊕ https://vfmat.ch/a852

Network for Improving Critical Care Systems and Training (NICST)

Provides critical-care training for staff in developing countries.

Crit-Care, General, Pulm-Critic

⊕ https://vfmat.ch/71f8

Noor Foundation, The

Works to establish free kidney dialysis centers and provides free kidney dialysis treatment to impoverished individuals.

Logist-Op

⊕ https://vfmat.ch/3bff

NYC Medics

Deploys mobile medical teams to remote areas of disaster zones and humanitarian emergencies, providing the highest level of medical care to those who otherwise would not have access to aid and relief efforts.

All-Immu, ER Med, Infect Dis, Surg

⊕ https://vfmat.ch/aeee

Omeed Ki Kiran Foundation

Seeks to provide free health services, including thalassaemia treatment and OB/GYN care, for poor and vulnerable individuals.

Heme-Onc, OB-GYN

⊕ https://vfmat.ch/246e

One Hope Foundation

Aims to feed, clothe, and shelter the poor, homeless, orphans and refugees, provide clean water, and fund operations for cataracts and cleft lip.

ENT, Ophth-Opt

⊕ https://vfmat.ch/98fa

Operation Corazón

Offers support to individuals and families in need by delivering humanitarian aid, relief, support services, equipment, clothing, medicine, and food.

General, Nutr

⊕ https://vfmat.ch/5f76

Operation Fistula

Exists to end obstetric fistula by building models of care that serve every woman, everywhere.

MF Med, OB-GYN, Surg

⊕ https://vfmat.ch/ce8e

Options

Believes in a world in which women and children can access the high-quality health services they need, without financial burden.

Logist-Op, MF Med, Neonat, OB-GYN

⊕ https://vfmat.ch/3a48

Optometry Giving Sight

Delivers eye exams and low or no-cost glasses, provides training for local eye care professionals, and establishes optometry schools, vision centers and optical labs.

Ophth-Opt

⊕ https://vfmat.ch/33ea

Paani Project

Provides long-term water relief, and strives to combine evidence-based initiatives with cultural competency to empower the community.

Logist-Op, Pub Health

⊕ https://vfmat.ch/42fa

Pak Medical Centre

Facilitates the diagnosis and treatment of impoverished hepatitis patients through a world-class pathology laboratory and highly qualified healthcare providers.

Dent-OMFS, GI, General, OB-GYN, OB-GYN, Path

⊕ https://vfmat.ch/1936

Pak Mission Society

Implements and promotes holistic development to strengthen people's capacities, resilience, and self-reliance.

General, MF Med, Neonat, Peds

⊕ https://vfmat.ch/d94a

Pakistan Children's Heart Foundation (PCHF)

Provides care for children with heart disease, regardless of financial means, trains healthcare professionals, and promotes research into congenital heart disease.

CT Surg, Logist-Op, Ped Surg, Peds

⊕ https://vfmat.ch/aa27

Pakistan Kidney Patients Association

Spreads awareness of renal health issues and provides kidney treatment and dialysis free or at low cost.

General, Logist-Op, Nephro

⊕ https://vfmat.ch/d9bc

PARSA Trust

Seeks to diagnose, treat, and prevent hepatitis, and raise public awareness.

Infect Dis

⊕ https://vfmat.ch/2984

Pathfinder International

Champions sexual and reproductive health and rights worldwide, mobilizing communities most in need to break through barriers and forge paths to a healthier future.

OB-GYN

⊕ https://vfmat.ch/a7b3

Patient Welfare Society Denmark Pakistan [Anjuman-e-Behbood-e-Mareezan Denmark Pakistan (ABMDP)]

Provides sight-saving surgery, eyeglasses, medicine, and other eye care services to thousands of people in underserved communities of Punjab, Pakistan.

Ophth-Opt

⊕ https://vfmat.ch/15ef

Patients Welfare Foundation: PWF Pakistan

Aims to provide welfare services and free medical treatment to the patients of Creek General Hospital.

All-Immu, CV Med, Crit-Care, ENT, Endo, GI, General, Medicine, Neuro, OB-GYN, Peds, Psych, Pulm-Critic, Surg, Urol

⊕ https://vfmat.ch/5fdc

Ponseti International

Provides global leadership in building high-quality, locally directed, and sustainable capacity to deliver the Ponseti clubfoot care pathway at the country level.

Ortho, Ped Surg, Peds, Rehab

⊕ https://vfmat.ch/476b

Population Council

Conducts research to address critical health and development issues, helping deliver solutions to improve lives around the world.

Logist-Op, Pub Health

⊕ https://vfmat.ch/1777

PSI – Population Services International

Aims to improve the health of people in the developing world by focusing on challenges such as a lack of family planning, HIV/AIDS, barriers to maternal health, and the greatest threats to children under the age of 5, including malaria, diarrhea, pneumonia, and malnutrition.

Infect Dis, MF Med, OB-GYN, Peds

⊕ https://vfmat.ch/ffe3

RAD-AID International

Improves and optimizes access to medical imaging and radiology in low-resource regions of the world.

Rad-Onc, Radiol

⊕ https://vfmat.ch/537f

Rahbar Trust

Strives to help communities break the poverty cycle, through service for basic health needs, empowerment of refugees and women, and financial support to achieve self-reliance.

All-Immu, CV Med, Ophth-Opt, Peds

⊕ https://vfmat.ch/5617

RAM Foundation

Provides medical and nutritional service, legal aid, and safe shelter to families who are freed from enslavement and to women who have escaped abusive relationships.

General, Nutr, OB-GYN, Peds

⊕ https://vfmat.ch/79bf

Rawalpindi Eye Donors Organization

Seeks to transform lives through eye donations.

Dent-OMFS, General, Nephro, Ophth-Opt

⊕ https://vfmat.ch/c758

Real Medicine Foundation (RMF)

Provides humanitarian support to people living in disaster- and poverty-stricken areas, focusing on the person as a whole by providing medical/physical, emotional, economic, and social support.

ER Med, General, Infect Dis, Nutr, Peds, Psych

⊕ https://vfmat.ch/d45a

Reconstructing Women International

Treats patients in their local communities through groups of international volunteers made up of female plastic surgeons using local medical facilities, in cooperation with local medical professionals.

Anesth, Plast, Rehab, Surg

⊕ https://vfmat.ch/924a

Relief International

Helps people in fragile settings achieve good health and nutrition by delivering primary healthcare and emergency treatment, and builds local capacity to ensure that communities in vulnerable situations have the access to the quality care they need to live healthy lives.

ER Med, General, MF Med, Neonat, OB-GYN, Peds, Psych

⊕ https://vfmat.ch/1522

RestoringVision

Empowers lives by restoring vision for millions of people in need.

Ophth-Opt

⊕ https://vfmat.ch/e121

Rockefeller Foundation, The

Works to promote the well-being of humanity.

Logist-Op, Nutr, Pub Health

⊕ https://vfmat.ch/5424

Rotary International

Provides service to others, improves lives, and advances world understanding, goodwill, and peace through its fellowship of business, professional, and community leaders.

ER Med, General, Infect Dis, MF Med, OB-GYN

⊕ https://vfmat.ch/8fb5

Rukhsana Foundation

Provides medical and educational facilities and services to the segments of society who, due to poverty or other reasons, are unable to provide such basic necessities to their families.

Derm, General, OB-GYN, Path, Peds

⊕ https://vfmat.ch/6757

Rutgers New Jersey Medical School

Seeks to support and promote the global health efforts of the faculty, staff, and students in the areas of education, research, and service through the Rutgers New Jersey Medical School's Office of Global Health.

Anesth, CV Med, Crit-Care, Neurosurg, OB-GYN, Psych

⊕ https://vfmat.ch/8e67

Salvation Army International, The

Seeks to meet human needs through services in education, healthcare, community support, emergency response, and ministry development, inspired by the Christian faith.

Dent-OMFS, Derm, ER Med, Infect Dis, MF Med, Medicine, Nutr, OB-GYN, Ophth-Opt, Palliative, Psych, Rehab, Surg

⊕ https://vfmat.ch/8eb3

Sanofi Espoir Foundation

Contributes to reducing health inequalities among populations that need it most by applying a socially responsible approach focused on fighting childhood cancers in low-income countries, improving maternal and newborn health, and improving access to care.

ER Med, OB-GYN, Peds

⊕ https://vfmat.ch/943b

Sarwar Foundation

Provides access to quality healthcare and clean drinking water, and tackles poverty by educating children, empowering women, and helping those in need.

ER Med, General, Infect Dis, Nutr, OB-GYN, Ophth-Opt, Surg

⊕ https://vfmat.ch/dea4

Save an orphan

Transforms the lives of children by providing them with medical aid, education, shelter, employment opportunities, and the means for a better tomorrow.

General, Infect Dis, MF Med

⊕ https://vfmat.ch/5742

Save our lives

Aims to deliver state-of-the-art medical care without discrimination, starting with the treatment of kidney diseases, while fostering prevention, research, and medical education.

General, Heme-Onc, Nephro, Surg

⊕ https://vfmat.ch/dace

Save the Children

Gives children around the world a healthy start in life, the opportunity to learn, and protection from harm.

All-Immu, Crit-Care, ER Med, General, Infect Dis, MF Med, Medicine, Neonat, OB-GYN, Peds, Psych, Pub Health

⊕ https://vfmat.ch/2e73

SEE International

Provides sustainable medical, surgical, and educational services through volunteer ophthalmic surgeons, with the objectives of restoring sight and preventing blindness to disadvantaged individuals worldwide.

Ophth-Opt, Surg

⊕ https://vfmat.ch/6e1b

Serve Humanity Foundation (SHF)

Provides education, job training, community creation, and empowerment, and access to medical care to underserved and underprivileged communities.

General

⊕ https://vfmat.ch/d2f5

Serving Others Worldwide

Aims to provide aid to the poor, distressed, and underprivileged by providing healthcare and dental services, and by building schools, orphanages, libraries, and medical clinics in undeveloped countries.

Dent-OMFS, General

⊕ https://vfmat.ch/69cb

SEVA

Delivers vital eye care services to the world's most vulnerable, including women, children, and Indigenous peoples.

Ophth-Opt, Surg

⊕ https://vfmat.ch/1e87

Shaheen Palliative Care Project

Aims to develop a training and service-oriented program to provide compassionate palliative care for patients living with a life-limiting or terminal illness and their families.

Palliative

⊕ https://vfmat.ch/ca89

Shahid Afridi Foundation

Seeks to enable access to education, healthcare services, and water supplies across Pakistan.

General, OB-GYN

⊕ https://vfmat.ch/7ed2

Shaukat Physicians Memorial Cancer Hospital and Research Centre, Lahore

Offers modern curative and palliative therapies for cancer patients, irrespective of their ability to pay, educates health-care professionals and the public; also does cancer research.

Anesth, Heme-Onc, Medicine, Palliative, Path, Peds, Rad-Onc, Radiol

⊕ https://vfmat.ch/774b

Shifa Foundation

Aims to shape the future of underprivileged communities by promoting health and development.

General, MF Med, Nutr, Psych, Pub Health

⊕ https://vfmat.ch/c48b

SHINE Humanity

Provides sustainable healthcare and related services for underprivileged communities.

General, MF Med, OB-GYN

⊕ https://vfmat.ch/3dcd

Sight for Life Trust

Works to eliminate blindness and other sight-related difficulties among some of the world's poorest people.

Ophth-Opt, Pub Health

⊕ https://vfmat.ch/ed76

Sightsavers

Works with partners in developing countries to help eliminate avoidable blindness and advocates for equal opportunity for the disabled.

Infect Dis, Ophth-Opt, Surg

⊕ https://vfmat.ch/aa52

SIGN Fracture Care International

Builds orthopedic capacity around the world and provides the injured poor access to fracture surgery by donating orthopedic education and implant systems to surgeons in developing countries.

Ortho, Rehab, Surg

⊕ https://vfmat.ch/123d

Sindh Institute of Urology and Transplantation (SIUT)

Aims to provide the best healthcare without discrimination, with the goal that healthcare should be of the highest quality and be provided free of cost, with respect and dignity.

Anesth, Crit-Care, ER Med, GI, Heme-Onc, Nephro, Nutr, Ophth-Opt, Path, Peds,

Radiol, Rehab, Surg, Urol
⊕ https://vfmat.ch/8572

Smile Train, Inc.
Treats children with cleft lip through a sustainable and local model that supports surgery and other forms of essential care.
Logist-Op, Pub Health
⊕ https://vfmat.ch/822c

SOS Children's Villages International
Supports children through alternative care and family strengthening.
ER Med, Peds
⊕ https://vfmat.ch/aca1

SSWAB Trust Kidney Care & Dialysis Center
Serves patients who suffer from hypertension, diabetes, and kidney disease, while promoting early diagnosis and awareness of these diseases.
CV Med, ER Med, Endo, Logist-Op, Nephro
⊕ https://vfmat.ch/6ed1

Supporting Health & Education deserving fellows
Seeks to eradicate illiteracy and promote good health in the most marginalized and poor communities.
CV Med, Dent-OMFS, MF Med, Nephro, OB-GYN, Psych
⊕ https://vfmat.ch/2967

Swasti
Aims to transform the lives of marginalized communities by ensuring their access to quality healthcare and thereby contributing to poverty alleviation.
Pub Health
⊕ https://vfmat.ch/be8b

Swiss Tropical and Public Health Institute
Contributes to the improvement of the health of populations internationally, nationally, and locally through excellence in research, education, and services.
Infect Dis, Pub Health
⊕ https://vfmat.ch/2ee4

Syrian American Medical Society (SAMS)
Provides medical professionals with continued training, networking, and opportunities to participate in humanitarian efforts affecting conflict-impacted populations.
CT Surg, CV Med, Crit-Care, Dent-OMFS, Endo, GI, General, Logist-Op, Medicine, Nephro, OB-GYN, Ophth-Opt, Path, Peds, Plast, Psych, Pulm-Critic, Radiol, Rehab, Surg, Urol
⊕ https://vfmat.ch/5dbf

Tabba Kidney Institute
Aims to provide comprehensive care to patients with kidney disease, while creating awareness about kidney disease and its prevention.
ER Med, Nephro, Radiol
⊕ https://vfmat.ch/415c

Task Force for Global Health, The
Consists of programs and focus areas that cover a range of global health issues including neglected tropical diseases, infectious diseases, vaccines, field epidemiology, public health informatics, health workforce development, and global health ethics.
Infect Dis, Logist-Op, Medicine, Ophth-Opt, Peds
⊕ https://vfmat.ch/714c

Team 5 Medical Foundation
Provides medical care in the most overlooked remote areas of the world supported by sponsorships, donations, and the dedication of its volunteers.
ER Med, General, Peds, Plast, Pulm-Critic
⊕ https://vfmat.ch/f267

Tearfund
Responds to crisis and partners with local churches to bring restoration to those living in poverty, inspired by the Christian faith.
ER Med, Logist-Op
⊕ https://vfmat.ch/f6cf

Telha Foundation
Relieves human suffering in the Khyber Pakhtunkhwa (KPK) Province of Pakistan through improvements in quality and accessibility of healthcare.
General, Infect Dis, Medicine, Nephro, OB-GYN
⊕ https://vfmat.ch/ee59

Terre des hommes (Tdh) Foundation
Works to improve the daily life of children and their relatives in the areas of health, protection and emergency, in Europe, Africa, Asia, Latin America, and the Near and Middle East.
CT Surg, CV Med, OB-GYN, Ped Surg, Pub Health
⊕ https://vfmat.ch/5c26

Training for Health Equity Network (THEnet)
Contributes to health equity through health workforce education, research, and service, based on principles of social accountability and community engagement.
ER Med, General
⊕ https://vfmat.ch/38c6

Ummah Charity International
Tackles poverty through innovative and sustainable solutions that enable individuals and their communities to live with dignity.
ER Med, Logist-Op, Nutr, Ophth-Opt
⊕ https://vfmat.ch/29b2

Union for International Cancer Control (UICC)
Unites and supports the cancer community to reduce the global cancer burden, promote greater equity, and ensure that cancer control continues to be a priority in the world health and development agenda.
Heme-Onc, Pub Health
⊕ https://vfmat.ch/88b1

Unite 4 Humanity
Aims to provide emergency aid and support for Muslim communities across the world.
General, Nutr, OB-GYN, Ophth-Opt, Plast, Psych, Rehab
⊕ https://vfmat.ch/fbe7

United Hands Relief & Development
Works to funnel efforts toward alleviating and immediately responding to the sufferings of others around the globe, regardless of nationality, race, religion, or social status.
ER Med, General, Infect Dis, Ophth-Opt, Surg
⊕ https://vfmat.ch/2771

United Nations Children's Fund (UNICEF)
Works in over 190 countries and territories to save children's lives, defend their rights, and help them fulfill their potential, from early childhood through adolescence.
All-Immu, Infect Dis, MF Med, Neonat, Nutr, OB-GYN, Ped Surg, Peds, Pub Health
⊕ https://vfmat.ch/42d7

United Nations Development Programme (UNDP)
Helps countries achieve the simultaneous eradication of extreme poverty and significant reduction of inequalities and exclusion using a sustainable human development approach.
Infect Dis, Logist-Op, Pub Health
⊕ https://vfmat.ch/935c

United Nations High Commissioner for Refugees (UNHCR)
Safeguards the rights and well-being of people who have been forced to flee, ensuring that everybody has the right to seek asylum and find safe refuge in another country, with the goal of seeking lasting solutions.
General, MF Med, Medicine, OB-GYN, Peds, Psych, Pub Health
⊕ https://vfmat.ch/6636

United Nations Population Fund (UNFPA)
Supports reproductive healthcare for women and youth in more than 150 countries, focusing on delivering a world in which every pregnancy is wanted, every childbirth is safe, and every young person's potential is fulfilled.
Infect Dis, MF Med, Neonat, OB-GYN, Peds, Pub Health
⊕ https://vfmat.ch/c969

United States Agency for International Development (USAID)
Promotes and demonstrates democratic values abroad and advances a free, peaceful, and prosperous world. Leads the U.S. government's international development and disaster assistance through partnerships and investments that save lives.
ER Med, Infect Dis, MF Med, OB-GYN, Peds
⊕ https://vfmat.ch/9a99

University of California Los Angeles: David Geffen School of Medicine Global Health Program
Catalyzes opportunities to improve health globally by engaging in multi-disciplinary and innovative education programs, research initiatives, and bilateral partnerships that provide opportunities for trainees, faculty, and staff to contribute to sustainable health initiatives and to address health inequities facing the world today.
All-Immu, Infect Dis, Logist-Op, MF Med, Medicine, Neonat, OB-GYN, Ortho, Ped Surg, Peds, Radiol
⊕ https://vfmat.ch/f1a4

University of New Mexico School of Medicine: Project Echo
Seeks to improve health outcomes worldwide through the use of a technology called telementoring, a guided-practice model in which the participating clinician retains responsibility for managing the patient.
General, Infect Dis, MF Med, OB-GYN, Path, Peds
⊕ https://vfmat.ch/6c9a

University of Pennsylvania Perelman School of Medicine Center for Global Health
Aims to improve health equity worldwide through enhanced public health awareness and access to care, discovery, and outcomes-based research, and comprehensive educational programs grounded in partnership.
Heme-Onc, Infect Dis, OB-GYN
⊕ https://vfmat.ch/cb57

University of Utah Global Health
Supports local organizations in their quest to improve quality of life in their communities all over the world.
Anesth, CT Surg, CV Med, Crit-Care, Dent-OMFS, ENT, ER Med, Infect Dis, OB-GYN, Ophth-Opt, Ped Surg, Ped Surg, Peds, Plast, Pub Health, Surg, Urol
⊕ https://vfmat.ch/bacd

USAID: Deliver Project
Builds a global supply chain to deliver lifesaving health products to people in order to enable countries to provide family planning, protect against malaria, and limit the spread of pandemic threats.
Infect Dis, Logist-Op, MF Med
⊕ https://vfmat.ch/374e

USAID: Leadership, Management and Governance Project
Improves leadership, management, and governance practices to strengthen health systems and improve health for all, including vulnerable populations worldwide.
Logist-Op
⊕ https://vfmat.ch/d35e

USAID: Maternal and Child Health Integrated Program
Works to improve the health of women and their families, including programs for maternal, newborn, and child health, immunization, family planning, nutrition, malaria, and HIV/AIDS.
All-Immu, General, Infect Dis, MF Med
⊕ https://vfmat.ch/4415

USAID: Maternal and Child Survival Program
Works to prevent child and maternal deaths.
Infect Dis, MF Med, Neonat, OB-GYN, Peds
⊕ https://vfmat.ch/6fcf

Vision Care
Restores sight and helps patients get regular treatment at short-term eye camps and long-term base clinics by having doctors, missionaries, volunteers, and sponsors work together.
Ophth-Opt
⊕ https://vfmat.ch/9d7c

Vital Pakistan
Aims to save lives and improve health of mothers and children in Pakistan.
MF Med, Neonat, Nutr, OB-GYN, Peds
⊕ https://vfmat.ch/9d41

Voluntary Service Overseas (VSO)
Works with health workers, communities, and governments to improve health services and rights for women, babies, youth, people with disabilities, and prisoners.
General, MF Med, OB-GYN
⊕ https://vfmat.ch/213d

Walkabout Foundation
Provides wheelchairs and rehabilitation in the developing world and funds research to find a cure for paralysis.
Logist-Op, Rehab
⊕ https://vfmat.ch/5582

We Care for Humanity (WCH)
Promotes sustainable social change and the sustainable development goals developed by the United Nations, including: no poverty, good health and well-being, gender equality, human rights, climate action, and strong institutions.
General, Logist-Op, Pub Health
⊕ https://vfmat.ch/8b4e

WF AID
Seeks to build capacity and provide emergency aid, human assistance, and international development, where required in the world.
CT Surg, Dent-OMFS, ENT, ER Med, General, Infect Dis, Logist-Op, Nutr, Ophth-Opt, Ortho, Path, Radiol, Rehab, Surg
⊕ https://vfmat.ch/ebd7

White Ribbon Alliance, The
Leads a movement for reproductive, maternal, and newborn health and accelerates progress by putting citizens at the center of global, national, and local health efforts.
MF Med, OB-GYN
⊕ https://vfmat.ch/496b

Wichita County Medical Alliance
Mobilizes volunteers to assist in public health efforts in the U.S. and abroad, including medical missions and disaster relief.
General, Geri, Nutr, OB-GYN, Pub Health
⊕ https://vfmat.ch/fa55

Women's Refugee Commission
Seeks to improve lives by protecting the rights of women, children, and youth displaced by conflict and crisis through researching their needs, identifying solutions, and advocating for programs and policies to strengthen their resilience.
General, MF Med, Neonat, OB-GYN, Peds, Psych
⊕ https://vfmat.ch/3d8f

World Care Foundation
Encourages humanitarian efforts to help those in need anywhere in the world, regardless of their faith, color, gender, and ethnicity. Projects include orphanages, orphan sponsorship, medical centers, refugee crisis work, and education.
ER Med, General, Pub Health
⊕ https://vfmat.ch/987a

World Children's Fund
Commits to helping children worldwide who are suffering the effects of poverty, disease, natural disaster, famine, abuse, civil strife, and war.
General, Logist-Op, MF Med, Nutr, OB-GYN, Pub Health
⊕ https://vfmat.ch/9cd8

World Compassion Fellowship (WCF)
Serves the global poor and persecuted through relief, medical care, development, and training.
CV Med, ER Med, Endo, GI, General, Infect Dis, Medicine, Nutr, OB-GYN, Ortho, Peds, Psych, Pub Health, Rehab
⊕ https://vfmat.ch/7b97

World Federation of Hemophilia (WFH)
Aims to improve and sustain care for people with inherited bleeding disorders by pursuing long-term relationships with individuals and organizations who share the values of WFH's development model.
Heme-Onc
⊕ https://vfmat.ch/5121

World Health Organization, The (WHO)
The United Nations' agency for health provides leadership on global health matters, shapes the health research agenda, sets norms and standards, articulates evidence-based policy options, provides technical support and monitoring to countries, and assesses health trends.
ER Med, General, Infect Dis, Logist-Op, MF Med, OB-GYN, Peds, Psych, Pub Health
⊕ https://vfmat.ch/c476

World Heart Federation
Leads the global fight against heart disease and stroke, with a focus on low- and middle-income countries.
CV Med, Crit-Care, Heme-Onc, Medicine, Peds
⊕ https://vfmat.ch/ea51

World Hope International
Empowers the poorest individuals around the world so they can become agents of change within their communities, by offering resources and knowledge.
Infect Dis, Logist-Op, MF Med, OB-GYN, Peds
⊕ https://vfmat.ch/a4b8

World Medical Relief
Facilitates the distribution of surplus medical resources where they are needed.
Logist-Op
⊕ https://vfmat.ch/72dc

World Parkinson's Program
Seeks to improve the quality of life of those affected by Parkinson's disease through education and advocacy, and provides free medication and support services.
Logist-Op, Neuro, Pub Health
⊕ https://vfmat.ch/c96d

World Rehabilitation Fund
Enables individuals around the world with functional limitations and participation restrictions to achieve community and social integration through physical and socioeconomic rehabilitation and advocacy.
Ortho, Rehab
⊕ https://vfmat.ch/a5bc

World Relief
Brings sustainable solutions to the world's greatest problems: disasters, extreme poverty, violence, oppression, and mass displacement.
ER Med, Nutr, Psych, Pub Health
⊕ https://vfmat.ch/fbcd

WorldShare
Connects faith-based groups in the UK with their counterparts in underdeveloped countries to promote community development and holistic support for children.
Dent-OMFS, ER Med, General, Peds, Pub Health, Surg
⊕ https://vfmat.ch/9eae

YORGHAS Foundation
Supports mothers, pregnant women, infants, people with disabilities, and those suffering from humanitarian crises, poverty, or social inequalities, with particular emphasis on women's and children's rights.
MF Med, Neonat
⊕ https://vfmat.ch/9e44

ZMT Primary Healthcare Network
Seeks to strengthen and empower a comprehensive primary healthcare network across Pakistan.
General, OB-GYN, Ophth-Opt, Path, Peds, Psych, Rehab
⊕ https://vfmat.ch/91ae

Pakistan

Healthcare Facilities

Abbasi Shaheed Hospital
Karachi, Karachi City, Sindh, Pakistan
⊕ https://vfmat.ch/e765

Abid Hospital
Islamabad, Islamabad Capital Territory, Pakistan
⊕ https://vfmat.ch/2e47

Afzaal Memorial Thalassemia Foundation
Karachi City, Sindh, Pakistan
⊕ https://vfmat.ch/nlfe

Aga Khan Hospital for Women
Goth Kesari, Sindh, Pakistan
⊕ https://vfmat.ch/9927

Aga Khan University Hospital
Karachi, Pakistan
https://vfmat.ch/5uji

Ahmed Medical Complex
Rawalpindi, Punjab, Pakistan
⊕ https://vfmat.ch/8b71

Al Murtaza Hospital
Karachi, Karachi City, Sindh, Pakistan
⊕ https://vfmat.ch/81db

Al Noor Hospital
Lahore, Punjab, Pakistan
⊕ https://vfmat.ch/e38e

Al Noor Hospital, Pasrur
Pasrur, Sialkot, Punjab, Pakistan
⊕ https://vfmat.ch/9136

Al Razi Hospital
Lahore, Punjab, Pakistan
⊕ https://vfmat.ch/d4a7

Al Sadiq-Saad Shaheed Hospital
Rawalpindi, Punjab, Pakistan
⊕ https://vfmat.ch/bb73

Al-Ibrahim Eye Hospital
Karachi City, Sindh, Pakistan
⊕ https://vfmat.ch/6324

Al-Khidmat Hospital Orangi Town
Orangi Town, Karachi, Sindh, Pakistan
⊕ https://vfmat.ch/26cc

Al-Mustafa Eye Hospital
Lahore, Punjab, Pakistan
⊕ https://vfmat.ch/gtzr

Al-Noor Mother Care Center
Lahore, Punjab, Pakistan
⊕ https://vfmat.ch/a85f

Al-Raee Hospital Gujranwala
Gujranwala, Punjab, Pakistan
⊕ https://vfmat.ch/m2kf

Al-Rehman Hospital Faisalabad
Faisalabad, Punjab, Pakistan
⊕ https://vfmat.ch/aa55

Al-Rehman Hospital Lahore
Lahore, Punjab, Pakistan
⊕ https://vfmat.ch/c1ba

Al-Shifa Trust Eye Hospital Chakwal
Chakwal, Punjab, Pakistan
⊕ https://vfmat.ch/t3p8

Al-Shifa Trust Eye Hospital Kohat
Kohat, Khyber Pakhtunkhwa, Pakistan
⊕ https://vfmat.ch/dtg7

Al-Shifa Trust Eye Hospital Muzaffrabad
Muzaffarabad, Azad Jammu & Kashmir, Pakistan
⊕ https://vfmat.ch/pjvl

Al-Shifa Trust Eye Hospital Rawalpindi
Rawalpindi, Punjab, Pakistan
⊕ https://vfmat.ch/eqen

Al-Shifa Trust Eye Hospital Sukkur
Sukkur, Sindh, Pakistan
⊕ https://vfmat.ch/usk5

Alam Family Hospital
Rawalpindi, Punjab, Pakistan
⊕ https://vfmat.ch/48ff

Ali Children Hospital
Gujrat, Punjab, Pakistan
⊕ https://vfmat.ch/a24c

Ali Hospital
Nankana Sahib, Punjab, Pakistan
⊕ https://vfmat.ch/6994

Ali Medical Centre
Islamabad, Islamabad Capital Territory, Pakistan
⊕ https://vfmat.ch/2adf

Allied Hospital Faisalabad
Faisalabad, Punjab, Pakistan
⊕ https://vfmat.ch/b798

Ammar Medical Complex
Lahore, Punjab, Pakistan
⊕ https://vfmat.ch/496c

Asfandyar Bukhari Civil Hospital DHQ Attock
Attock, Punjab, Pakistan
⊕ https://vfmat.ch/a2ee

Ashfaq Memorial Hospital
Karachi, Karachi City, Sindh, Pakistan
⊕ https://vfmat.ch/b6ce

Azam Majeed Medical Complex
Paka Mari, Punjab, Pakistan
🌐 https://vfmat.ch/fcd9

Aziz Fatimah Hospital
Faisalabad, Punjab, Pakistan
🌐 https://vfmat.ch/5c9d

Bagh-e-Halar General Hospital
Karachi, Karachi City, Sindh, Pakistan
🌐 https://vfmat.ch/1dd5

Bahawal Victoria Hospital, Bahawalpur
Bahawalpur, Punjab, Pakistan
🌐 https://vfmat.ch/61be

Baksh Hospital
Ahmadpur East, Punjab, Pakistan
🌐 https://vfmat.ch/ffeb

Baqai Institute of Oncology
Nazimabad, Karachi, Sindh, Pakistan
🌐 https://vfmat.ch/7165

Baqai University Hospital, Nazimabad
Karachi, Karachi City, Sindh, Pakistan
🌐 https://vfmat.ch/1c9f

Basharat Hospital
Rawalpindi, Punjab, Pakistan
🌐 https://vfmat.ch/cb66

Bashir Hospital Sialkot
Sialkot, Punjab, Pakistan
🌐 https://vfmat.ch/ec32

Begum Zubaida Bani Wing
Chenab Nagar, Punjab, Pakistan
🌐 https://vfmat.ch/2146

Bhatti Child Care Hospital
Golimar Colony, Sindh, Pakistan
🌐 https://vfmat.ch/bf27

Bhitai Hospital Hyderabad
Hyderabad, Sindh, Pakistan
🌐 https://vfmat.ch/vqzd

Bilqis Naz Children Cancer Hospital
Karachi, Sindh, Pakistan
🌐 https://vfmat.ch/lsv2

Bori Khel Hospital
Mianwali, Punjab, Pakistan
🌐 https://vfmat.ch/bdf4

Bukhsh Hospital
Jhelum, Punjab, Pakistan
🌐 https://vfmat.ch/nn36

Cantonment General Hospital Rawalpindi
Rawalpindi, Punjab, Pakistan
🌐 https://vfmat.ch/d5b2

Central Park Teaching Hospital
Lahore, Punjab, Pakistan
🌐 https://vfmat.ch/kyfy

Chandka Medical College Hospital – Larkana
Larkana, Sindh, Pakistan
🌐 https://vfmat.ch/jk3h

Chaudhry Rehmat Ali Memorial Trust Teaching Hospital
Lahore, Punjab, Pakistan
🌐 https://vfmat.ch/a144

Children Emergency Room, Abbasi Shaheed Hospital
Shahrah-e-Quaideen, Karachi, Pakistan
🌐 https://vfmat.ch/ft52

Children Emergency Room, Civil Hospital – Quetta
Quetta, Balochistan, Pakistan
🌐 https://vfmat.ch/79mc

Children Emergency Room, Ghulam Muhammad Mahar Medical College Hospital – Sukkur
Sukkur, Sindh, Pakistan
🌐 https://vfmat.ch/nlh5

Children Emergency Room, Lyari General Hospital
Karachi, Sindh, Pakistan
🌐 https://vfmat.ch/tmze

Children Emergency Room, Peoples Medical College Hospital – Nawabshah
Nawabshah, Sindh, Pakistan
🌐 https://vfmat.ch/tddb

Children Emergency Room, Sindh Government Hospital Korangi – 5
Karachi, Sindh, Pakistan
🌐 https://vfmat.ch/lawm

Children's Hospital & The Institute of Child Health, Lahore, The
Lahore, Punjab, Pakistan
🌐 https://vfmat.ch/ab4b

Chiniot General Hospital
Karachi, Punjab, Pakistan
🌐 https://vfmat.ch/72be

Christian Hospital Tank
Garah Shahbaz, Khyber Pakhtunkhwa, Pakistan
🌐 https://vfmat.ch/sb11

City Children Hospital, Dr.Jai Krishan
Islamabad, Islamabad Capital Territory, Pakistan
🌐 https://vfmat.ch/7766

Civil Hospital – Karachi
Karachi City, Sindh, Pakistan
🌐 https://vfmat.ch/5123

Civil Hospital – Quetta
Quetta, Balochistan, Pakistan
🌐 https://vfmat.ch/aa63

Civil Hospital Gwadar
Gwadar, Balochistan, Pakistan
🌐 https://vfmat.ch/3a99

Civil Hospital Haripur
Pandak, Khyber Pakhtunkhwa, Pakistan
🌐 https://vfmat.ch/38af

Civil Hospital Qazi Ahmed
Qazi Ahmed, Shaheed Benazirabad, Sindh, Pakistan
🌐 https://vfmat.ch/b1c9

Civil Hospital, Killa Saifullah
Kili Jahangir, Balochistan, Pakistan
🌐 https://vfmat.ch/1191

CLAPP Hospital
Faisal Town, Lahore, Punjab, Pakistan
🌐 https://vfmat.ch/xiya

CMH Combined Military Hospital Rawalpindi
Rawalpindi, Punjab, Pakistan
🌐 https://vfmat.ch/a4dd

Combined Military Hospital Dera Ismail Khan
Dera Ismail Khan, North West Frontier, Pakistan
🌐 https://vfmat.ch/c16d

Combined Military Hospital Hyderabad
Hyderabad, Sindh, Pakistan
🌐 https://vfmat.ch/9f72

Combined Military Hospital Lahore
Lahore, Punjab, Pakistan
🌐 https://vfmat.ch/f734

Combined Military Hospital Mardan
Mardan, Khyber Pakhtunkhwa, Pakistan
🌐 https://vfmat.ch/3258

Combined Military Hospital Multan
Dera Ismail Khan, Khyber Pakhtunkhwa, Pakistan
🌐 https://vfmat.ch/8a51

Combined Military Hospital Murree
Murree, Rawalpindi, Khyber Pakhtunkhwa, Pakistan
🌐 https://vfmat.ch/fcfa

Combined Military Hospital Muzaffarabad
Muzaffarabad, Azad Jammu and Kashmir, Pakistan
⊕ https://vfmat.ch/6623

Combined Military Hospital Nowshera
Nowshera, Khyber Pakhtunkhwa, Pakistan
⊕ https://vfmat.ch/264d

Combined Military Hospital Zhob
Zhob, Balochistan, Pakistan
⊕ https://vfmat.ch/76e5

Combined Military Hospital Sialkot
Sialkot,Sialkot Cantonment, Punjab, Pakistan
⊕ https://vfmat.ch/ed35

Creek General Hospital
Karachi, Sindh, Pakistan
⊕ https://vfmat.ch/x4b1

DHQ Hospital Bagh
Bagh, Azad Kashmir, Pakistan
⊕ https://vfmat.ch/1213

DHQ Hospital Jhang
Jhang, Punjab, Pakistan
⊕ https://vfmat.ch/78de

DHQ Hospital Khanewal
Khanewal, Punjab, Pakistan
⊕ https://vfmat.ch/6197

DHQ Hospital Mardan
Mardan, Khyber Pakhtunkhwa, Pakistan
⊕ https://vfmat.ch/378b

DHQ Hospital Nowshera
Nowshera, Khyber Pakhtunkhwa, Pakistan
⊕ https://vfmat.ch/2ba8

DHQ Hospital Sheikhupura
Sheikhupura, Punjab, Pakistan
⊕ https://vfmat.ch/23d3

DHQ/ Teaching Hospital, Gujranwala
Gujranwala, Punjab, Pakistan
⊕ https://vfmat.ch/b896

District Headquarter Hospital Shikarpur
Brohi Mohalla, Shikarpur, Sindh, Pakistan
⊕ https://vfmat.ch/4da3

Dr. Bhura Lal Memorial Hospital
Tando Allahyar, Sindh, Pakistan
⊕ https://vfmat.ch/dadc

Dr. A. Q. Khan Hospital
Lahore, Punjab, Pakistan
⊕ https://vfmat.ch/fa4t

Dr. Ruth K.M. Pfau Civil Hospital
Karachi City, Sindh, Pakistan
⊕ https://vfmat.ch/5eb8

Faisal Hospital Faisalabad
Faisalabad, Punjab, Pakistan
⊕ https://vfmat.ch/85d5

Farooq Hospital Allama Iqbal Town, Lahore
Lahore, Punjab, Pakistan
⊕ https://vfmat.ch/5394

Farooq-e-Azam Medical Hospital
Karachi, Sindh, Pakistan
⊕ https://vfmat.ch/d934

Fatima Jinnah General & Chest Hospital
Quetta, Balochistan, Pakistan
⊕ https://vfmat.ch/f4e8

Fatimiyah Hospital Karachi
Karachi, Sindh, Pakistan
⊕ https://vfmat.ch/gdk6

Fazl-e-Omar Hospital
Chenab Nagar, Chiniot, Punjab, Pakistan
⊕ https://vfmat.ch/675c

Ghani Hospital
Qasimabad, Hyderabad, Sindh, Pakistan
⊕ https://vfmat.ch/d876

Ghaziabad Government Hospital Lahore
Lahore, Punjab, Pakistan
⊕ https://vfmat.ch/a2a5

Gilgit Eye Hospital
Konu Das, Gilgit-Baltistan, Pakistan
⊕ https://vfmat.ch/3d13

Government Mother and Childcare Hospital
Multan, Punjab, Pakistan
⊕ https://vfmat.ch/e865

Government Mozang Teaching Hospital
Lahore, Punjab, Pakistan
⊕ https://vfmat.ch/9eb4

Govt. Vaccination Center
Karachi, Karachi City, Sindh, Pakistan
⊕ https://vfmat.ch/65d9

Govt. General Hospital
Faisalabad, Punjab, Pakistan
⊕ https://vfmat.ch/1eee

Govt. Sardar Begum Teaching Hospital Sialkot
Rehmat Pura Sialkot, Punjab, Pakistan
⊕ https://vfmat.ch/dcc3

Hamdard University Hospital
Karachi, Karachi City, Sindh, Pakistan
⊕ https://vfmat.ch/2764

Hameed Latif Hospital, Misri Shah Branch, Lahore
Lahore, Punjab, Pakistan
⊕ https://vfmat.ch/e723

Hashim Welfare Hospital
Kharian, Pakistan
⊕ https://vfmat.ch/js2s

Hayatabad Medical Complex Peshawar
Peshawar, Khyber Pakhtunkhwa, Pakistan
⊕ https://vfmat.ch/3246

Hijaz Hospital
Lahore, Punjab, Pakistan
⊕ https://vfmat.ch/d52f

Hill Park General Hospital
Karachi, Karachi City, Sindh, Pakistan
⊕ https://vfmat.ch/83ba

Hope Hospital
Chakwal, Punjab, Pakistan
⊕ https://vfmat.ch/nqus

Hospital Chowk
Dera Ghazi Khan, Punjab, Pakistan
⊕ https://vfmat.ch/5f57

Hussain Memorial Hospital
Lahore, Punjab, Pakistan
⊕ https://vfmat.ch/b6c3

IHS Children & Family Hospital
Islamabad, Islamabad Capital Territory, Pakistan
⊕ https://vfmat.ch/292d

Ihsan Mumtaz Hospital
Lahore, Punjab, Pakistan
⊕ https://vfmat.ch/2a95

Independent University Hospital
Faisalabad, Punjab, Pakistan
⊕ https://vfmat.ch/9a83

Institute Of Kidney Diseases
Zakat Colony, Khyber Pakhtunkhwa, Pakistan
⊕ https://vfmat.ch/2fcc

Ittefaq Hospital (Trust) Lahore
Lahore, Punjab, Pakistan
⊕ https://vfmat.ch/7795

Jannat Aziz Eye Hospital
Tehsil Burewala, District Vehari, Punjab, Pakistan
⊕ https://vfmat.ch/1yht

Jinnah Hospital, Lahore
Lahore, Punjab, Pakistan
⊕ https://vfmat.ch/5216

Karachi Adventist Hospital 7th Day
Karachi, Karachi City, Sindh, Pakistan
⊕ https://vfmat.ch/4492

Khursheed Qadir Hospital
Jalalpur Jattan, Punjab, Pakistan
⊕ https://vfmat.ch/6e29

Koohi Goth Hospital
Karachi, Pakistan
⊕ https://vfmat.ch/1c38

Kuwait Teaching Hospital
Peshawar, Khyber Pakhtunkhwa, Pakistan
⊕ https://vfmat.ch/56e1

Lady Dufferin Hospital
Karachi, Sindh, Pakistan
⊕ https://vfmat.ch/j9pn

Lady Willingdon Hospital
Lahore, Punjab, Pakistan
⊕ https://vfmat.ch/3b9a

Lahore General Hospital
Lahore, Punjab, Pakistan
⊕ https://vfmat.ch/ppw9

Lahore Health Care
Lahore, Punjab, Pakistan
⊕ https://vfmat.ch/ghn1

Lahore Medical Complex & The Heart Hospital
Gulberg III, Lahore, Punjab, Pakistan
⊕ https://vfmat.ch/adhu

Liaqat Hospital
Lahore, Punjab, Pakistan
⊕ https://vfmat.ch/c54f

Liaquat National Hospital
Karachi, Pakistan
⊕ https://vfmat.ch/8zxx

Liaquat University Hospital – Hyderabad
Hyderabad, Sindh, Pakistan
⊕ https://vfmat.ch/6ng1

LRBT Chiniot – Free Eye Hospital
Chiniot, Punjab, Pakistan
⊕ https://vfmat.ch/4wmj

LRBT Eye Hospital – Kalakalay
Kalakalay,Tehsil Kabal, Khyber Pakhtoon Khawa, Pakistan
⊕ https://vfmat.ch/8uxe

LRBT Free Secondary Eye Hospital – Shahpur
Shahpur Saddar, Punjab, Pakistan
⊕ https://vfmat.ch/u9zq

LRBT Secondary Eye Hospital – Akora Khattak
Akora Khattak, Nowshera, Khyber Pakhtoon Khawa, Pakistan
⊕ https://vfmat.ch/r3jm

LRBT Secondary Eye Hospital – Arifwala
Ārifwāla, Pakpattan, Punjab, Pakistan
⊕ https://vfmat.ch/xmqn

LRBT Secondary Eye Hospital – Gambat
Gambat, Khairpur, Sindh, Pakistan
⊕ https://vfmat.ch/y3hy

LRBT Secondary Eye Hospital – Khanewal
Khanewal, Punjab, Pakistan
⊕ https://vfmat.ch/53yw

LRBT Secondary Eye Hospital – Lar Multan
Lar Multan, Punjab, Pakistan
⊕ https://vfmat.ch/prul

LRBT Secondary Eye Hospital – Mandra
Mandra, Rawalpindi, Punjab, Pakistan
⊕ https://vfmat.ch/8iev

LRBT Secondary Eye Hospital – Mansehra
Mansehra, Khyber Pakhtoon, Pakistan
⊕ https://vfmat.ch/5uwy

LRBT Secondary Eye Hospital – North Karachi
North Karachi, Karachi, Sindh, Pakistan
⊕ https://vfmat.ch/btwd

LRBT Secondary Eye Hospital – Odigram
Odigram, Swat, Swat, Khyber Pakhtoon Khawa, Pakistan
⊕ https://vfmat.ch/qnvh

LRBT Secondary Eye Hospital – Pasrur
Tehsil Pasrur, Sialkot, Punjab, Pakistan
⊕ https://vfmat.ch/iya8

LRBT Secondary Eye Hospital – Quetta
Quetta, Balochistan, Pakistan
⊕ https://vfmat.ch/bmd3

LRBT Secondary Eye Hospital – Rashidabad
Tando Allahyar, Sindh, Pakistan
⊕ https://vfmat.ch/u5yq

LRBT Secondary Eye Hospital – Tando Bago
Badin, Sindh, Pakistan
⊕ https://vfmat.ch/6vz8

LRBT Tertiary Teaching Eye Hospital – Korangi
Korangi, Karachi, Sindh, Pakistan
⊕ https://vfmat.ch/lyd5

LRBT Tertiary Teaching Eye Hospital – Lahore
Lahore, Punjab, Pakistan
⊕ https://vfmat.ch/sj7e

LRBT Tertiary Teaching Eye Hospital – Lahore (Multan Road)
Lahore, Punjab, Pakistan
⊕ https://vfmat.ch/44uu

Mansoorah Hospital
Lahore, Punjab, Pakistan
⊕ https://vfmat.ch/dw1h

Masroor Hospital
Karachi, Sindh, Pakistan
⊕ https://vfmat.ch/c38a

Mayo Hospital Lahore
Lahore, Punjab, Pakistan
⊕ https://vfmat.ch/c3c6

Mehboob Charity Vision Eye Hospital
Mansehra, Khyber Pakhtunkhwa, Pakistan
⊕ https://vfmat.ch/mmaj

Memon Medical Institute Hospital
Karachi, Sindh, Pakistan
⊕ https://vfmat.ch/e2ee

Memorial Christian Hospital
Sialkot, Punjab, Pakistan
⊕ https://vfmat.ch/julb

Mian Muhammad Trust Hospital
Faisalabad, Punjab, Pakistan
⊕ https://vfmat.ch/438e

Mid City Hospital
Rawari, Punjab, Pakistan
⊕ https://vfmat.ch/96ec

Midland Doctors Medical Institute
Muzaffarabad, Azad Jammu & Kashmir, Pakistan
⊕ https://vfmat.ch/fi4c

Mission Hospital Peshawar
Peshawar, Khyber Pakhtunkhwa, Pakistan
⊕ https://vfmat.ch/b883

Mission Hospital Sialkot
Sialkot, Punjab, Pakistan
⊕ https://vfmat.ch/b2c4

MMC General Hospital
Peshawar, Khyber Pakhtunkhwa, Pakistan
⊕ https://vfmat.ch/679b

Mother & Child Hospital
Rawalpindi, Punjab, Pakistan
⊕ https://vfmat.ch/9692

Mother and Child Healthcare Center
Pattan, Kohistan, Khyber Pakhtunkhwa, Pakistan
⊕ https://vfmat.ch/hggx

Muhammad Hospital Faisalabad
Faisalabad, Punjab, Pakistan
⊕ https://vfmat.ch/173e

Mumtaz Bakhtawar Memorial Trust Hospital Wahdat Road Branch
Lahore, Punjab, Pakistan
⊕ https://vfmat.ch/f598

Muslim Khatri Charitable Hospital
Goth Firoz Khan, Sindh, Pakistan
⊕ https://vfmat.ch/2623

National Institute of Blood Disease & Bone Marrow Transplantation
Karachi, Sindh, Pakistan
⊕ https://vfmat.ch/4ufl

National Institute of Cardiovascular Diseases
Karachi City, Sindh, Pakistan
⊕ https://vfmat.ch/837a

National Institute of Child Health
Karachi, Sindh, Pakistan
⊕ https://vfmat.ch/k2tn

Nawaz Sharif Social Security Hospital
Lahore, Punjab, Pakistan
⊕ https://vfmat.ch/6ce8

Niaz Memorial Hospital
Gujranwala, Punjab, Pakistan
⊕ https://vfmat.ch/dcd3

Niazi Hospital
Lahore, Punjab, Pakistan
⊕ https://vfmat.ch/da23

Nishtar Hospital
Vasalwala, Punjab, Pakistan
⊕ https://vfmat.ch/87b2

Noori Hospital
Rawalpindi, Punjab, Pakistan
⊕ https://vfmat.ch/7ea2

Noreen Nishat Welfare Hospital
Khanewal, Punjab, Pakistan
⊕ https://vfmat.ch/76da

Orthopaedic Medical Complex (OMC) Hospital
Lahore, Punjab, Pakistan
⊕ https://vfmat.ch/1e1d

PAEC General Hospital
Islamabad, Islamabad Capital, Pakistan
⊕ https://vfmat.ch/1dfe

PAF Hospital Islamabad Unit 2
Islamabad, Islamabad Capital Territory, Pakistan
⊕ https://vfmat.ch/ai3t

Pakistan Eye Bank Society (PEBS) Eye & General Hospital
Shadman Town, North Karachi, Karachi, Sindh, Pakistan
⊕ https://vfmat.ch/imha

Pakistan Institute for Medical Sciences
Islamabad, Islamabad Capital Territory, Pakistan
⊕ https://vfmat.ch/b3f7

Pearl International Hospital
Lahore, Punjab, Pakistan
⊕ https://vfmat.ch/4f3b

Peoples Medical College Hospital – Nawabshah
Nawabshah, Shaheed Benazirabad, Sindh, Pakistan
⊕ https://vfmat.ch/nkxi

PINUM Cancer Hospital
Faisalabad, Punjab, Pakistan
⊕ https://vfmat.ch/b271

PNS Hafeez – Naval Hospital
Islamabad, Islamabad Capital Territory, Pakistan
⊕ https://vfmat.ch/bdfa

PNS Rahat
Karachi, Sindh, Pakistan
⊕ https://vfmat.ch/fbec

Prime Care Hospital
Lahore, Punjab, Pakistan
⊕ https://vfmat.ch/9d2e

Punjab Hospital
Multan, Punjab, Pakistan
⊕ https://vfmat.ch/9ca6

Punjab Social Security Hospital
Dharamsalwala, Punjab, Pakistan
⊕ https://vfmat.ch/65e6

Quaid-e-Azam Complex, Hyderabad
Hyderabad, Sindh, Pakistan
⊕ https://vfmat.ch/da81

Rafiq Anwar Memorial Trust Hospital, Gujranwala
Gujranwala, Punjab, Pakistan
⊕ https://vfmat.ch/efd1

Rai Ali Nawaz Foundation Hospital
Chichawatni, Punjab, Pakistan
⊕ https://vfmat.ch/nd2k

Railway Hospital
Dhok Mangtal, Punjab, Pakistan
⊕ https://vfmat.ch/297c

Ravi Hospital
Jaranwala, Punjab, Pakistan
⊕ https://vfmat.ch/f8b1

Rawalpindi Institute of Cardiology
Rawalpindi, Punjab, Pakistan
⊕ https://vfmat.ch/a656

Sahibzada Fazal Rehman Charity Hospital
Kohat, Khyber Pakhtunkhwa, Pakistan
⊕ https://vfmat.ch/d3pi

Said Mittha Hospital
Lahore, Punjab, Pakistan
⊕ https://vfmat.ch/fef4

Saira Memorial Hospital
Lahore, Punjab, Pakistan
⊕ https://vfmat.ch/efa2

Sarwar Foundation Hospital Rajana
Toba Tek Singh District, Rajana, Punjab, Pakistan
⊕ https://vfmat.ch/gwzz

Shaikh Zayed Hospital
Lahore, Punjab, Pakistan
⊕ https://vfmat.ch/qpnr

Shakir Surgical Hospital and Fatima Medical Center
Sheikhupura, Punjab, Pakistan
⊕ https://vfmat.ch/67fc

Sharif Medical City Hospital
Lahore, Punjab, Pakistan
⊕ https://vfmat.ch/a93f

Shaukat Khanum Memorial Cancer Hospital and Research Centre, Lahore
M.A. Johar Town, Lahore, Punjab, Pakistan
⊕ https://vfmat.ch/9591

Shaukat Khanum Memorial Cancer Hospital and Research Centre, Peshawar
Peshawar, Khyber Pakhtunkhwa, Pakistan
⊕ https://vfmat.ch/pcmw

Shaukat Omar Memorial Hospital
Karachi, Sindh, Pakistan
⊕ https://vfmat.ch/a98e

SHED Hospital North Karachi
Karachi, Sindh, Pakistan
⊕ https://vfmat.ch/2zb1

Sheikh Muhammad Saeed Memorial Hospital
Goth Abdul Qadir, Sindh, Pakistan
⊕ https://vfmat.ch/e4c5

Shifa International Hospitals Ltd.
Islamabad, Pakistan
⊕ https://vfmat.ch/c284

Sindh Government Hospital Korangi 5
Landhi Town, Karachi, Sindh, Pakistan
⊕ https://vfmat.ch/r3wx

Sindh Government Lyari General Hospital
Karachi, Karachi City, Sindh, Pakistan
⊕ https://vfmat.ch/n6v5

Sindh Institute of Urology and Transplantation (SIUT)
Karachi, Karachi City, Sindh, Pakistan
⊕ https://vfmat.ch/syiz

Sir Ganga Ram Hospital
Lahore, Punjab, Pakistan
⊕ https://vfmat.ch/bce2

Sir Syed Hospital
Karachi, Sindh, Pakistan
⊕ https://vfmat.ch/7158

SIUT Chablani Medical Centre
Sukkur, Sindh, Pakistan
⊕ https://vfmat.ch/ncjd

SIUT Mehrunnisa Medical Centre
Korangi, Karachi City, Sindh, Pakistan
⊕ https://vfmat.ch/ncyw

Social Security Hospital, Gujranwala
Gujranwala, Punjab, Pakistan
⊕ https://vfmat.ch/1662

Social Security Hospital, Sheikhupura
Sheikhupura, Punjab, Pakistan
⊕ https://vfmat.ch/85d1

Sub District Hospital
Uri, Jammu and Kashmir, Pakistan
⊕ https://vfmat.ch/982c

Sub District Hospital Tangdar
Tangdhār, Jammu and Kashmir, Pakistan
⊕ https://vfmat.ch/39ba

Sughra Shafi Medical Complex
Narowal, Punjab, Pakistan
⊕ https://vfmat.ch/f7de

Surgimed Hospital
Lahore, Punjab, Pakistan
⊕ https://vfmat.ch/2577

Tahir Heart Institute
Jhang, Punjab, Pakistan
⊕ https://vfmat.ch/b93a

Tahira Jamshed Medical Complex
Bahawalpur, Punjab, Pakistan
⊕ https://vfmat.ch/dc5f

Tariq Hospital
Ahāta Thānadār, Punjab, Pakistan
⊕ https://vfmat.ch/11a5

TDC Islamabad
Islamabad, Pakistan
⊕ https://vfmat.ch/dh2e

Telha Foundation Hospital Karak
Karak, Khyber Pakhtunkhwa, Pakistan
⊕ https://vfmat.ch/xtmc

The Indus Hospital – QFNST Campus, Lahore
Lahore, Punjab, Pakistan
⊕ https://vfmat.ch/d954

The Indus Hospital, Korangi Campus
Karachi, Sindh, Pakistan
⊕ https://vfmat.ch/e813

THQ Hospital
Jand, Punjab, Pakistan
⊕ https://vfmat.ch/515a

THQ Hospital Chak Jhumra
Chak Jhumra, Punjab, Pakistan
⊕ https://vfmat.ch/4bef

THQ Hospital Gujar Khan
Tehsil Gujar Khan, District Rawalpindi, Punjab, Pakistan
⊕ https://vfmat.ch/539b

THQ Hospital Kel
Kel, Azad Kashmir, Pakistan
⊕ https://vfmat.ch/4de1

THQ Hospital, Fort Abbas
Bahawalnagar, Punjab, Pakistan
⊕ https://vfmat.ch/82fa

United Christian Hospital
Davisābād, Punjab, Pakistan
⊕ https://vfmat.ch/5695

United Hospital
Karachi, Sindh, Pakistan
⊕ https://vfmat.ch/5788

Victoria Memorial Hospital
Multan, Punjab, Pakistan
⊕ https://vfmat.ch/3916

Wapda Hospital
Lahore, Punjab, Pakistan
⊕ https://vfmat.ch/9497

Wapda Hospital Gujranwala
Gujranwala, Punjab, Pakistan
⊕ https://vfmat.ch/1e74

WAPDA Teaching Hospital Complex
Lahore, Punjab, Pakistan
⊕ https://vfmat.ch/b244

Zanana Joubli Hospital
Bahawalpur, Punjab, Pakistan
⊕ https://vfmat.ch/8cba

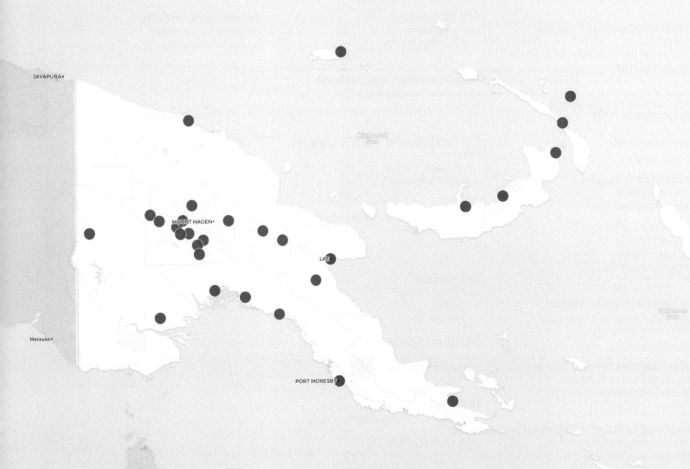

JAYAPURA•

MOUNT HAGEN•

LAE•

PORT MORESBY•

Merauke•

CAIRNS•

TOWNSVILLE•

● Healthcare Facility

Papua New Guinea

Papua New Guinea, formally known as the Independent State of Papua New Guinea and located in Oceania, is the third largest island country in the world. It is made up of the eastern half of New Guinea and several islands throughout Melanesia. The population of 7.4 million is believed to be one of the world's most culturally diverse and socially complex, with ethnic groups including Melanesian, Papuan, Negrito, Micronesian, and Polynesian. Papua New Guinea is home to 839 different indigenous languages, with English and Tok Pisin as the official languages. Only 14 percent of the population lives in urban areas, making Papua New Guinea one of the most rural countries in the world. Much of the population continues to live a traditional lifestyle, in varied settlement patterns.

Papua New Guinea achieved independence from Australia in 1975; since then it has had difficulty governing its culturally diverse population, which is divided by customs, language, and traditions. The majority of the population is employed in the agricultural, forestry, and fishing industries, many of them at a subsistence level. Another major sector includes mineral and energy-resource extraction. Because the economy is resource-dominated, there are few opportunities for young people to pursue formal jobs.

Papua New Guinea faces many health challenges. Residents have a high risk of major infectious diseases such as hepatitis A, typhoid fever, dengue and malaria. In addition, 28 percent of children under age five are underweight, one of the highest rates in the world. As such, life expectancy in Papua New Guinea is one of the lowest in the world, at 65 years. Between 2009 and 2019, the incidence of death due to diabetes increased substantially, by over 51 percent. Other leading causes of death include ischemic heart disease, lower respiratory infection, stroke, COPD, neonatal disorders, HIV/AIDS, diarrheal diseases, road injuries, and congenital defects. Malaria continues to be a leading cause of death, although the total number of deaths due to malaria has decreased by nearly 60 percent since 2009. The risk factors that contribute most to death and disability include malnutrition, air pollution, high fasting plasma glucose, tobacco use, lack of sanitation and clean water, dietary risks, high blood pressure, high body-mass index, unsafe sex, and high LDL.

7.4M

Population

$2,637

GDP Per Capita

65 years

Life Expectancy

↑ Improving

7

Doctors/100k

Physician Density

145

Deaths/100k

Maternal Mortality

Papua New Guinea

Nonprofit Organizations

Abt Associates
Seeks to improve the quality of life and economic well-being of people worldwide, while striving to meet and exceed the highest professional standards.
General, Logist-Op, MF Med, OB-GYN, Peds
🌐 https://vfmat.ch/cec2

Against Malaria Foundation
Helps protect people from malaria. Funds anti-malaria nets, specifically long-lasting insecticidal nets (LLINs), and works with distribution partners to ensure they are used. Tracks and reports on net use and malaria case data.
Infect Dis
🌐 https://vfmat.ch/337d

Aloha Medical Mission
Brings hope and changes the lives of people; serves overseas and in Hawai'i.
Anesth, Crit-Care, Dent-OMFS, ENT, ER Med, General, Medicine, OB-GYN, Ophth-Opt, Ortho, Ped Surg, Peds, Plast, Surg, Urol
🌐 https://vfmat.ch/72ac

Association of Medical Doctors of Asia (AMDA)
Strives to support people affected by disasters and economic distress on their road to recovery, establishing a true partnership with special emphasis on local initiative.
ER Med, Logist-Op, Pub Health
🌐 https://vfmat.ch/e3d4

Australian & New Zealand Gastroenterology International Training Association
Aims to improve health in developing Asia Pacific nations by enhancing the standards of practice of gastroenterology and building capacity to treat digestive diseases.
GI
🌐 https://vfmat.ch/5a69

Australian Doctors International (ADI)
Recruits and deploys volunteer health professionals and implements health projects to provide essential health services in remote Papua New Guinea.
Crit-Care, General, Infect Dis, Logist-Op, MF Med, OB-GYN, Ophth-Opt, Path, Pub Health, Rehab
🌐 https://vfmat.ch/f637

Baylor International Pediatric AIDS Initiative (BIPAI) at Texas Children's Hospital
Provides high-quality, high-impact, highly ethical pediatric and family-centered healthcare, health professional training, and clinical research focused on HIV/AIDS, tuberculosis, malaria, malnutrition, and other conditions impacting the health of children worldwide.
Infect Dis, Medicine, OB-GYN, Peds, Pub Health, Surg
🌐 https://vfmat.ch/e6ba

CARE
Works around the globe to save lives, defeat poverty, and achieve social justice.
ER Med, General
🌐 https://vfmat.ch/7232

cbm New Zealand
Inspired by the Christian faith, aims to improve the quality of life for those living with the double disadvantage of poverty and disability.
Crit-Care, Infect Dis, Logist-Op, Nutr, OB-GYN, Ophth-Opt, Ortho, Psych, Rehab, Surg
🌐 https://vfmat.ch/c14b

ChildFund Australia
Works to reduce poverty for children in many of the world's most disadvantaged communities.
ER Med, General, Peds
🌐 https://vfmat.ch/13df

Christian Blind Mission (CBM)
Aims to improve the quality of life of persons with disabilities in the poorest countries, addressing poverty as a cause and a consequence of disability, and working in partnership to create a society for all.
ENT, General, Infect Dis, OB-GYN, Ophth-Opt, Ortho, Peds, Psych, Rehab, Surg
🌐 https://vfmat.ch/3824

Christian Medical & Dental Associations
Based in Christian ministry, deploys medical and dental teams to underserved communities to provide vital healthcare.
Anesth, Dent-OMFS, ER Med, General, Medicine, OB-GYN, Ophth-Opt, Peds, Pub Health, Radiol, Rehab, Surg
🌐 https://vfmat.ch/921c

Clinton Health Access Initiative (CHAI)
Aims to save lives and reduce the burden of disease in low- and middle-income countries. Works with partners to strengthen the capabilities of governments and the private sector to create and sustain high-quality health systems.
General, Heme-Onc, Infect Dis, Logist-Op, MF Med, Medicine, Neonat, Nutr, OB-GYN, Path, Peds, Rad-Onc
🌐 https://vfmat.ch/9ed7

Direct Relief
Improves the health and lives of people affected by poverty or emergency situations by mobilizing and providing essential medical resources needed for their care.
ER Med, Logist-Op
🌐 https://vfmat.ch/58e5

Doctors Assisting In South Pacific Islands (DAISI)
Aims to support and collaborate with its South Pacific neighbors and consists of specialist and nonspecialist doctors, medical students, nurses, allied health

professionals, and nonmedical volunteers.

Anesth, Dent-OMFS, OB-GYN, Plast, Surg, Urol

⊕ https://vfmat.ch/2dcd

Doctors Without Borders/Médecins Sans Frontières (MSF)
Responds to emergencies and provides lifesaving medical care where needed most, including during disasters, conflicts, and epidemics.

Anesth, Crit-Care, ER Med, General, Infect Dis, Nutr, OB-GYN, Ped Surg, Peds, Psych, Pub Health, Surg

⊕ https://vfmat.ch/f363

EBC Health Services
Provides holistic care and strives to empower individuals, families and communities to improve their health through changes in attitude and behavior, inspired by the Christian faith.

Infect Dis, Logist-Op, Neonat, Nutr, OB-GYN, Pub Health

⊕ https://vfmat.ch/d4fb

For Hearts and Souls
Provides medical outreach and care for children through heart-related work, such as diagnosing heart problems and performing heart-saving surgeries.

Anesth, CT Surg, CV Med, Crit-Care, Peds, Pulm-Critic

⊕ https://vfmat.ch/a162

Global Oncology (GO)
Brings the best in cancer care to underserved patients around the world and collaborates across geographic, professional, and academic borders to improve cancer care, research, and education.

Heme-Onc, Path, Rad-Onc

⊕ https://vfmat.ch/fcb8

Globus Relief
Aims to improve the delivery of healthcare worldwide by gathering, processing, and distributing surplus medical supplies to charities at home and abroad.

Logist-Op

⊕ https://vfmat.ch/a2b7

HealthServe Australia
Develops sustainable health programs that improve health and well-being and partners with community groups to build community capacity to meet health needs.

Infect Dis, Logist-Op, OB-GYN, Psych, Pub Health

⊕ https://vfmat.ch/7276

Heart to Heart International
Strengthens communities through improving health access, providing humanitarian development, and administering crisis relief worldwide. Engages volunteers, collaborates with partners, and deploys resources to achieve this mission.

Anesth, ER Med, General, Logist-Op, Medicine, Path, Path, Peds, Psych, Pub Health, Surg

⊕ https://vfmat.ch/aacb

Highlands Foundation, The
Aims to strengthen existing healthcare facilities in Papua New Guinea with the aim of decreasing the infant and maternal mortality and morbidity rates.

Logist-Op, MF Med

⊕ https://vfmat.ch/2af5

International Federation of Gynecology and Obstetrics (FIGO)
Implements global projects on specific women's health issues.

MF Med, Medicine, Neonat, OB-GYN, Surg, Urol

⊕ https://vfmat.ch/c4b4

International Federation of Red Cross and Red Crescent Societies (IFRC)
Coordinates and directs international assistance following natural and manmade disasters in nonconflict situations through the world's largest humanitarian and development network. Provides disaster-preparedness programs, healthcare activities, and promotes humanitarian values.

ER Med, General, Infect Dis, Nutr

⊕ https://vfmat.ch/b4ee

International Organization for Migration (IOM) – The UN Migration Agency
Promotes evidence-informed policies and holistic, preventive, and curative health programs that are beneficial, accessible, and equitable for vulnerable migrants.

General, Infect Dis, OB-GYN

⊕ https://vfmat.ch/621a

Joint United Nations Programme on HIV/AIDS (UNAIDS)
Aims to place people living with HIV and people affected by the virus at the decision-making table and at the center of designing, delivering, and monitoring the AIDS response.

Infect Dis

⊕ https://vfmat.ch/464a

Kind Cuts for Kids
Aims to improve medical services for children in developing countries through education, demonstration, and skills transfer to local healthcare professionals.

Anesth, Medicine, Ped Surg, Surg

⊕ https://vfmat.ch/e3d7

Kokoda Track Foundation (KTF)
Gives remote and rural communities of Papua New Guinea access to quality primary healthcare, including immunizations for babies and children, pre- and postnatal care for mothers and their babies, and lifesaving medicines for all who need it.

General, Logist-Op, MF Med, OB-GYN, Ophth-Opt, Pub Health

⊕ https://vfmat.ch/6931

Leprosy Mission Australia, The
Provides support to people with leprosy including screening, medical treatment and job opportunities, inspired by the Christian faith.

Infect Dis

⊕ https://vfmat.ch/9e4b

Leprosy Mission International
Seeks to empower people with leprosy to attain healing, dignity, and life in all its fullness.

Infect Dis

⊕ https://vfmat.ch/95a9

Light for the World
Contributes to a world in which persons with disabilities fully exercise their rights, and assists persons with disabilities living in poverty.

Ophth-Opt, Rehab

⊕ https://vfmat.ch/3ff6

MAP International
Provides medicines and health supplies to those in need around the world so they might experience life to the fullest.

Logist-Op

⊕ https://vfmat.ch/deed

Marie Stopes International
Provides the contraception and safe abortion services that enable women all over the world to choose their own futures.

Infect Dis, MF Med, Neonat, OB-GYN, Pub Health

⊕ https://vfmat.ch/9525

Medical Mission Aid Inc
Advances effective healthcare in disadvantaged communities through medical scholarships, grants for supplies and support for local health initiatives.

Infect Dis, Logist-Op, OB-GYN, Pub Health, Rehab

⊕ https://vfmat.ch/8b83

MedSend
Funds qualified healthcare professionals to serve the physical and spiritual needs of people around the world, enabling healthcare providers to work where they have been called.

General

⊕ https://vfmat.ch/661c

MedShare
Aims to improve the quality of life of people, communities, and the planet by

sourcing and directly delivering surplus medical supplies and equipment to communities in need around the world.

Logist-Op

⊕ https://vfmat.ch/c8bc

Mission Doctors Association

Provides life-saving medical care for the poor and training for local healthcare professionals around the world.

CV Med, Dent-OMFS, General, Logist-Op, Medicine, OB-GYN, Ophth-Opt, Peds, Surg

⊕ https://vfmat.ch/6c18

Mission Regan

Collects supplies, medication, and medical equipment and provides them to those who are in desperate need, both locally and globally.

Logist-Op

⊕ https://vfmat.ch/2bc1

MSI Reproductive Choices (Marie Stopes International)

Seeks to deliver quality family planning and reproductive healthcare to women around the world.

MF Med

⊕ https://vfmat.ch/5c82

Open Heart International

Provides surgical interventions and best practices to the most disadvantaged communities on the planet.

CT Surg, MF Med, OB-GYN, Ophth-Opt, Plast, Surg

⊕ https://vfmat.ch/dab2

Options

Believes in a world in which women and children can access the high-quality health services they need, without financial burden.

Logist-Op, MF Med, Neonat, OB-GYN

⊕ https://vfmat.ch/3a48

Optometry Giving Sight

Delivers eye exams and low or no-cost glasses, provides training for local eye care professionals, and establishes optometry schools, vision centers and optical labs.

Ophth-Opt

⊕ https://vfmat.ch/33ea

PAPUA NEW GUINEA TRIBAL FOUNDATION

Works to bring about significant and sustainable development for the people of Papua New Guinea.

Infect Dis, Logist-Op, MF Med

⊕ https://vfmat.ch/52b8

PNG Foundation

Aims to provide access to basic primary healthcare, education and infrastructure to the Kamea community of Papau New Guinea.

Infect Dis, Nutr, OB-GYN, Peds, Pub Health

⊕ https://vfmat.ch/8363

PNG Health Project

Aims to address an ongoing gap in health literacy and make a difference through knowledge and empowerment.

Logist-Op, Pub Health

⊕ https://vfmat.ch/c22d

PSI – Population Services International

Aims to improve the health of people in the developing world by focusing on challenges such as a lack of family planning, HIV/AIDS, barriers to maternal health, and the greatest threats to children under the age of 5, including malaria, diarrhea, pneumonia, and malnutrition.

Infect Dis, MF Med, OB-GYN, Peds

⊕ https://vfmat.ch/ffe3

RestoringVision

Empowers lives by restoring vision for millions of people in need.

Ophth-Opt

⊕ https://vfmat.ch/e121

Rotary International

Provides service to others, improves lives, and advances world understanding, goodwill, and peace through its fellowship of business, professional, and community leaders.

ER Med, General, Infect Dis, MF Med, OB-GYN

⊕ https://vfmat.ch/8fb5

Salvation Army International, The

Seeks to meet human needs through services in education, healthcare, community support, emergency response, and ministry development, inspired by the Christian faith.

Dent-OMFS, Derm, ER Med, Infect Dis, MF Med, Medicine, Nutr, OB-GYN, Ophth-Opt, Palliative, Psych, Rehab, Surg

⊕ https://vfmat.ch/8eb3

Samaritan's Purse International Disaster Relief

Provides spiritual and physical aid to hurting people around the world, such as victims of war, poverty, natural disasters, disease, and famine, based in Christian ministry.

Anesth, CT Surg, Crit-Care, Dent-OMFS, Derm, ENT, ER Med, Endo, GI, General, Heme-Onc, Infect Dis, MF Med, Neonat, Nephro, Neuro, Neurosurg, Nutr, OB-GYN, Ophth-Opt, Ortho, Path, Ped Surg, Peds, Plast, Psych, Pulm-Critic, Radiol, Rehab, Rheum, Surg, Urol, Vasc Surg

⊕ https://vfmat.ch/87e3

SIGN Fracture Care International

Builds orthopedic capacity around the world and provides the injured poor access to fracture surgery by donating orthopedic education and implant systems to surgeons in developing countries.

Ortho, Rehab, Surg

⊕ https://vfmat.ch/123d

Soddo Christian Hospital

Mobilizes volunteers to help transform communities through healthcare and education, based in Christian ministry.

ER Med, General

⊕ https://vfmat.ch/efa4

South Pacific Medical Projects

Aims to advance and support medical projects in developing countries of the South Pacific and other regions in a sustainable manner, in consideration of existing structures.

Logist-Op, Ortho, Rehab, Surg

⊕ https://vfmat.ch/d64e

Sri Sathya Sai International Organization

Inspired by spiritual teachings, carries out efforts in global healthcare, education, humanitarian relief, and youth engagement.

Dent-OMFS, General, Logist-Op, Nutr, Ophth-Opt, Pub Health

⊕ https://vfmat.ch/9bda

Surgical Healing of Africa's Youth Foundation, The (S.H.A.Y.)

Provides volunteer reconstructive surgery to children in need, including treating congenital anomalies such as cleft lip/palate and general reconstruction.

Anesth, Dent-OMFS, Peds, Plast

⊕ https://vfmat.ch/41a7

Sustainable Cardiovascular Health Equity Development Alliance

Fights cardiovascular disease in underserved populations globally via education, training, and increasing interventional capacity.

CV Med, Pub Health, Radiol

⊕ https://vfmat.ch/799c

Swasti

Aims to transform the lives of marginalized communities by ensuring their access to quality healthcare and thereby contributing to poverty alleviation.

Pub Health

⊕ https://vfmat.ch/be8b

Swiss Tropical and Public Health Institute

Contributes to the improvement of the health of populations internationally, nationally, and locally through excellence in research, education, and services.

Infect Dis, Pub Health
⊕ https://vfmat.ch/2ee4

Task Force for Global Health, The
Consists of programs and focus areas that cover a range of global health issues including neglected tropical diseases, infectious diseases, vaccines, field epidemiology, public health informatics, health workforce development, and global health ethics.
Infect Dis, Logist-Op, Medicine, Ophth-Opt, Peds
⊕ https://vfmat.ch/714c

Texas Children's Global Health
Addresses healthcare needs in resource-limited settings locally and globally by improving maternal and child health through the implementation of innovative, sustainable, in-country programs to train health professionals and build functional healthcare infrastructure.
Anesth, ER Med, Heme-Onc, Infect Dis, MF Med, Nutr, OB-GYN, Peds, Pub Health, Surg
⊕ https://vfmat.ch/4a1d

Transplant Links Community (TLC)
Provides hands-on training in kidney transplantation for surgeons, doctors, and nurses in low- and middle-income countries.
Nephro, Surg, Urol
⊕ https://vfmat.ch/bb46

Union for International Cancer Control (UICC)
Unites and supports the cancer community to reduce the global cancer burden, promote greater equity, and ensure that cancer control continues to be a priority in the world health and development agenda.
Heme-Onc, Pub Health
⊕ https://vfmat.ch/88b1

United Nations Children's Fund (UNICEF)
Works in over 190 countries and territories to save children's lives, defend their rights, and help them fulfill their potential, from early childhood through adolescence.
All-Immu, Infect Dis, MF Med, Neonat, Nutr, OB-GYN, Ped Surg, Peds, Pub Health
⊕ https://vfmat.ch/42d7

United Nations Development Programme (UNDP)
Helps countries achieve the simultaneous eradication of extreme poverty and significant reduction of inequalities and exclusion using a sustainable human development approach.
Infect Dis, Logist-Op, Pub Health
⊕ https://vfmat.ch/935c

United Nations High Commissioner for Refugees (UNHCR)
Safeguards the rights and well-being of people who have been forced to flee, ensuring that everybody has the right to seek asylum and find safe refuge in another country, with the goal of seeking lasting solutions.
General, MF Med, Medicine, OB-GYN, Peds, Psych, Pub Health
⊕ https://vfmat.ch/6636

United Nations Population Fund (UNFPA)
Supports reproductive healthcare for women and youth in more than 150 countries, focusing on delivering a world in which every pregnancy is wanted, every childbirth is safe, and every young person's potential is fulfilled.
Infect Dis, MF Med, Neonat, OB-GYN, Peds, Pub Health
⊕ https://vfmat.ch/c969

United States Agency for International Development (USAID)
Promotes and demonstrates democratic values abroad and advances a free, peaceful, and prosperous world. Leads the U.S. government's international development and disaster assistance through partnerships and investments that save lives.
ER Med, Infect Dis, MF Med, OB-GYN, Peds
⊕ https://vfmat.ch/9a99

University of Utah Global Health
Supports local organizations in their quest to improve quality of life in their communities all over the world.
Anesth, CT Surg, CV Med, Crit-Care, Dent-OMFS, ENT, ER Med, Infect Dis, OB-

GYN, Ophth-Opt, Ped Surg, Ped Surg, Peds, Plast, Pub Health, Surg, Urol
⊕ https://vfmat.ch/bacd

Vision Outreach International
Advocates for helping the blind in underserved regions of the world and empowers the poor through sight restoration.
Ophth-Opt
⊕ https://vfmat.ch/9721

Vitamin Angels
Helps at-risk populations in need—specifically pregnant women, new mothers, and children under age 5—to gain access to life-changing vitamins and minerals.
General, Nutr
⊕ https://vfmat.ch/7da1

Voluntary Service Overseas (VSO)
Works with health workers, communities, and governments to improve health services and rights for women, babies, youth, people with disabilities, and prisoners.
General, MF Med, OB-GYN
⊕ https://vfmat.ch/213d

WeCARe! Foundation
Aims to connect with, inspire, motivate, and empower communities to support vulnerable women and children in Papau New Guinea.
Logist-Op, Nutr, OB-GYN, Peds
⊕ https://vfmat.ch/7788

World Health Organization, The (WHO)
The United Nations' agency for health provides leadership on global health matters, shapes the health research agenda, sets norms and standards, articulates evidence-based policy options, provides technical support and monitoring to countries, and assesses health trends.
ER Med, General, Infect Dis, Logist-Op, MF Med, OB-GYN, Peds, Psych, Pub Health
⊕ https://vfmat.ch/c476

World Hope International
Empowers the poorest individuals around the world so they can become agents of change within their communities, by offering resources and knowledge.
Infect Dis, Logist-Op, MF Med, OB-GYN, Peds
⊕ https://vfmat.ch/a4b8

World Medical Relief
Facilitates the distribution of surplus medical resources where they are needed.
Logist-Op
⊕ https://vfmat.ch/72dc

World Vision International
Works with vulnerable communities around the world to overcome poverty and injustice with child-focused programs in disaster management, health, nutrition, economic development, education, clean water, sanitation, and hygiene.
ER Med, General, Infect Dis, MF Med, Nutr, OB-GYN, Peds
⊕ https://vfmat.ch/2642

YWAM Medical Ships
Works in partnership with relevant national and provincial health authorities around a shared vision: healthy villages, and a healthy Papua New Guinea.
Crit-Care, Dent-OMFS, General, Infect Dis, Logist-Op, MF Med, Ophth-Opt, Palliative, Path, Pulm-Critic, Rehab
⊕ https://vfmat.ch/ff44

Papua New Guinea

Healthcare Facilities

2K Medical Centre
Port Moresby, National Capital District, Papua New
Guinea
⊕ https://vfmat.ch/ae28

Alotau General Hospital
Alotau, Milne Bay Province, Papua New Guinea
⊕ https://vfmat.ch/xw5i

Angau General Hospital
Lae, Lae, Papua New Guinea
⊕ https://vfmat.ch/qzga

Angau Memorial Hospital
Lae, Morobe, Papua New Guinea
⊕ https://vfmat.ch/2ba1

Balimo Hospital
Balimo, Western, Papua New Guinea
⊕ https://vfmat.ch/5ab7

Boram General Hospital
Wewak, East Sepik, Papua New Guinea
⊕ https://vfmat.ch/4fbe

Bulolo General Hospital
Bulolo, Morobe, Papua New Guinea
⊕ https://vfmat.ch/2ff7

Daru General Hospital
Daru, Port Moresby, Papua New Guinea
⊕ https://vfmat.ch/pev9

Erave Hospital
Erave, Southern Highlands, Papua New Guinea
⊕ https://vfmat.ch/4fc4

Gerehu General Hospital
Port Moresby, Papua New Guinea
⊕ https://vfmat.ch/apt8

GM Flores Hospital
Morobe, Morobe, Papua New Guinea
⊕ https://vfmat.ch/6bdi

Goroka General Hospital
Goroka, Eastern Highlands, Papua New Guinea
⊕ https://vfmat.ch/f3e8

Goroka Provincial Hospital
Goroka, Goroka, Papua New Guinea
⊕ https://vfmat.ch/z9dq

Ialibu District Hospital
Ialibu, Southern Highlands, Papua New Guinea
⊕ https://vfmat.ch/d566

Kainantu Rural Hospital
Kainantu, Eastern Highlands, Papua New Guinea
⊕ https://vfmat.ch/a931

Kandep District Hospital
Kandep, Enga, Papua New Guinea
⊕ https://vfmat.ch/4eed

Kapuna Hospital
Kapuna, Gulf, Papua New Guinea
⊕ https://vfmat.ch/6237

Kavieng General Hospital
Kavieng, Papua New Guinea
⊕ https://vfmat.ch/tiha

Kerema General Hospital
Kerema, Gulf, Papua New Guinea
⊕ https://vfmat.ch/e3cb

Kikori Hospital
Kikori, Gulf, Papua New Guinea
⊕ https://vfmat.ch/bad9

Kimbe General Hospital
Kimbe, West New Britain, Papua New Guinea
⊕ https://vfmat.ch/12b7

Kiunga District Hospital
Kiunga, Western, Papua New Guinea
⊕ https://vfmat.ch/e45c

Koroba District Hospital
Koroba, Hela, Papua New Guinea
⊕ https://vfmat.ch/971d

Kudjip Nazarene Hospital
Mount Hagen, Western Highlands, Papua New Guinea
⊕ https://vfmat.ch/e9te

Lae International Hospital
Lae, Morobe, Papua New Guinea
⊕ https://vfmat.ch/e739

Lihir Medical Centre
Londolovit, New Ireland, Papua New Guinea
⊕ https://vfmat.ch/26cd

Lorengau General Hospital
Lorengau, Manus, Papua New Guinea
⊕ https://vfmat.ch/93ad

Magarima District Hospital
Magarima, Hela, Papua New Guinea
⊕ https://vfmat.ch/4a53

Mendi Provincial Hospital
Mendi, Southern Highlands, Papua New Guinea
⊕ https://vfmat.ch/53ed

Mount Hagen General Hospital
Mount Hagen, Papua New Guinea
⊕ https://vfmat.ch/t42w

Namatanai District Hospital
Namatanai, New Ireland, Papua New Guinea
⊕ https://vfmat.ch/871d

Nipa District Hospital
Nipa, Southern Highlands, Papua New Guinea
⊕ https://vfmat.ch/f37b

Pacific International Hospital
Port Moresby, National Capital District, Papua New Guinea
⊕ https://vfmat.ch/a95b

Paradise Private Hospital
Port Moresby, Papua New Guinea
https://vfmat.ch/eerb

Popondetta General Hospital
Popondetta, Papua New Guinea
⊕ https://vfmat.ch/xq1j

Port Moresby General Hospital
Port Moresby, National Capital District, Papua New Guinea
⊕ https://vfmat.ch/1d9a

Rabaraba Hospital
Rabaraba, Milne Bay, Papua New Guinea
⊕ https://vfmat.ch/6926

SJNM Kundiawa General Hospital
Kundiawa, Kundiawa, Papua New Guinea
⊕ https://vfmat.ch/ahx4

St. Mary's Hospital
Kokopo, East New Britain, Papua New Guinea
⊕ https://vfmat.ch/ad76

Tari Hospital
Tari, Hela, Papua New Guinea
⊕ https://vfmat.ch/445c

Wabag General Hospital
Wabag, Enga, Papua New Guinea
⊕ https://vfmat.ch/2f64

HEN·
HONG KONG

LAOAC

Vigan   Tuguegarao

BAGUIO
Dagupan

Cabanatuan
Angeles
Olongapo
MANILA Quezon City
San Pablo
Batangas City

PHILIPPINES

Naga

Legazpi

Calbayog

Roxas City   Tacloban
          Cadiz   Ormoc
          Bacolod
ILOILO CITY
          San Carlos
          CEBU CITY

                              Surigao City

                    Bohol
                    Sea
Puerto Princesa   Butuan
                              Gingoog
                    Cagayan de
                    Oro
              Ozamiz Iligan
Pagadian

              Cotabato City   DAVAO CITY
ZAMBOANGA   Tagum
CITY

          GENERAL SANTOS

South
China
Sea

Sulu
Sea

Kota Kinabalu·

          Sandakan·

BANDAR SERI
BEGAWAN
Miri· BRUNEI
          Tawau·

                    Manado·

          NORTH
          SULAWESI   TERNATE· NORTH
GORONTALO   MALUKU

Map data © OpenStreetMap (openstreetmap.org) and contributors, CC-BY-SA
(creativecommons.org) © CARTO

● Healthcare Facility

Samarinda·

BALIKPAPAN·   Palu·   Sorong·

Philippines

The Republic of the Philippines is an archipelago consisting of 7,640 islands in the western Pacific Ocean. It spans an area of 120,000 square miles, with maritime borders including the South China Sea, Philippine Sea, and Celebes Sea. It is located in what is called the "Ring of Fire," making it susceptible to natural disasters such as earthquakes and typhoons. With a population of 110.8 million, it is the 13th most populous country in the world. Manila, the capital and one of the most densely populated cities in the world, is home to 14.6 million people. The Philippines is ethnically diverse: Tagalog, Bisaya/Binisaya, Cebuano, Ilocano, Hiligaynon/Ilonggo, Bikol, and Waray are the predominant ethnic groups. Languages spoken include the official languages of Filipino and English, in addition to eight other common dialects: Tagalog, Cebuano, Ilocano, Hiligaynon or Ilonggo, Bicol, Waray, Pampango, and Pangasinan. The majority of the Filipino population is Roman Catholic, in contrast to many of its Southeast Asian neighbors, which practice Buddhism.

A former colony of Spain, the Philippines achieved independence in 1946. Since then, it has been identified as an emerging economy that is rapidly growing. The country is largely agricultural and is one of the largest producers of coconuts and coconut products in the world. Other major crops include sugarcane, rice, bananas, corn, and pineapples. However, the Philippines is moving toward becoming a strong industrial and manufacturing power. With greater emphasis on education at the end of the 20th century, the Philippines established reputable public school and university systems. As a result, the country has some of the highest literacy rates in Asia. The Philippines is also supported by one of the largest emigrant populations in the world: over 2.2 million people whose remittances make up a significant portion of the economy.

Despite being on a path toward development, the Philippines has many health challenges. Top causes of death include ischemic heart disease, stroke, lower respiratory infections, chronic kidney disease, tuberculosis, diabetes, neonatal disorders, hypertensive heart disease, COPD, and interpersonal violence. Mortality caused by non-communicable diseases has increased between 2009 and 2019, particularly chronic kidney disease, diabetes, and hypertensive heart disease. The risk factors that contribute most to death and disability include high blood pressure, malnutrition, dietary risks, air pollution, high fasting plasma glucose, high body-mass index, kidney dysfunction, alcohol and tobacco use, and high LDL.

110.8M

Population

$3,299

GDP Per Capita

71 years

Life Expectancy

↑ Improving

60
Doctors/100k

Physician Density

99
Beds/100k

Hospital Bed Density

121
Deaths/100k

Maternal Mortality

Philippines

Nonprofit Organizations

Abt Associates
Seeks to improve the quality of life and economic well-being of people worldwide, while striving to meet and exceed the highest professional standards.
General, Logist-Op, MF Med, OB-GYN, Peds
⊕ https://vfmat.ch/cec2

ACCESS Health International
Aims to improve access to high-quality and affordable healthcare for people everywhere, no matter what their age, in low-, middle- and high-income countries.
Logist-Op
⊕ https://vfmat.ch/6613

Aceso Global
Provides strategic healthcare advisory services in low- and middle-income countries to design and deliver highly customized, evidence-based solutions that address the complex nature of healthcare systems, with a goal to strengthen and provide affordable, high-quality care to all.
Logist-Op, Pub Health
⊕ https://vfmat.ch/b3b7

Action Against Hunger
Aims to end life-threatening hunger for good through treating and preventing malnutrition across more than 45 countries.
Nutr
⊕ https://vfmat.ch/2dbc

Advance Family Planning
Aims to achieve global expansion and access to quality contraceptive information, services, and supplies through financial investment and political commitment.
General, MF Med, Pub Health
⊕ https://vfmat.ch/7478

Adventist Health International
Focuses on upgrading and managing mission hospitals by providing governance, consultation, and technical assistance to a number of affiliated Seventh-Day Adventist hospitals throughout Africa, Asia, and the Americas.
Dent-OMFS, General, Pub Health
⊕ https://vfmat.ch/16aa

Age International
Helps older people living in some of the world's poorest places to have improved well-being and be treated with dignity through a variety of programs, including emergency relief and cataract surgery.
ER Med, Geri, Logist-Op, Nutr, Ophth-Opt, Palliative, Pub Health
⊕ https://vfmat.ch/c7e2

AIDS Healthcare Foundation
Provides cutting-edge HIV/AIDS medical care and advocacy to over one million people in 43 countries.

Infect Dis
⊕ https://vfmat.ch/b27c

AIDS Society Of The Philippines
Facilitates information and resource exchange in Philippine communities to reduce HIV infection through knowledge management, resource mobilization, and advocacy.
Crit-Care, General, OB-GYN
⊕ https://vfmat.ch/871a

Al Basar International Foundation
Works with local partners to treat preventable blindness, and helps set up sustainable infrastructure so local teams can save sight in their communities.
Ophth-Opt
⊕ https://vfmat.ch/a8b5

Aloha Medical Mission
Brings hope and changes the lives of people; serves overseas and in Hawai'i.
Anesth, Crit-Care, Dent-OMFS, ENT, ER Med, General, Medicine, OB-GYN, Ophth-Opt, Ortho, Ped Surg, Peds, Plast, Surg, Urol
⊕ https://vfmat.ch/72ac

American Academy of Pediatrics
Seeks to attain optimal physical, mental, and social health and well-being for all infants, children, adolescents, and young adults.
Anesth, Crit-Care, Neonat, Ped Surg
⊕ https://vfmat.ch/9633

American Cancer Society
Saves lives, celebrates lives, and leads the fight for a world without cancer.
Heme-Onc, Logist-Op, Medicine, Rad-Onc, Radiol
⊕ https://vfmat.ch/f996

American International Health Alliance (AIHA)
Strengthens health systems and workforce capacity worldwide through locally driven, peer-to-peer institutional partnerships.
CV Med, ER Med, Infect Dis, Medicine, OB-GYN
⊕ https://vfmat.ch/69fd

Americares
Saves lives and improves health for people affected by poverty or disaster and responds with life-changing medicine, medical supplies, and health programs including domestic and global medical clinics.
All-Immu, ER Med, General, Infect Dis, MF Med, Nutr
⊕ https://vfmat.ch/e567

Amsterdam Institute for Global Health and Development (AIGHD)
Provides sustainable solutions to major health problems across our planet by forging synergies among disciplines, healthcare delivery, research, and education.

Infect Dis
- ⊕ https://vfmat.ch/d73d

Arbeiter Samariter Bund (Workers' Samaritan Federation)
Engages in areas such as civil protection, rescue services, and social welfare, while operating a network of welcome centers to help refugees.
ER Med, General, Infect Dis, Logist-Op, Rehab
- ⊕ https://vfmat.ch/8a5b

Arnel Pineda Foundation, Inc.
Provides underprivileged children with the quality education, health services, and medical attention they require.
Dent-OMFS, General, Geri, Infect Dis, Medicine, Nutr, OB-GYN, Peds, Pub Health
- ⊕ https://vfmat.ch/5537

Ascenta Foundation
Provides urgent medical, dental, optometric, and surgical services, along with health education, to medically underserved communities.
Dent-OMFS, General, Ophth-Opt, Pub Health, Surg
- ⊕ https://vfmat.ch/418f

ASE Foundation
Provides support for education and research to the community of healthcare providers and patients for whom cardiovascular ultrasound is essential.
CT Surg, CV Med, Radiol
- ⊕ https://vfmat.ch/bb57

Association of Medical Doctors of Asia (AMDA)
Strives to support people affected by disasters and economic distress on their road to recovery, establishing a true partnership with special emphasis on local initiative.
ER Med, Logist-Op, Pub Health
- ⊕ https://vfmat.ch/e3d4

Austrian Doctors
Stands for a life in dignity and takes care of the health of disadvantaged people. Helps all people regardless of gender, skin color, religion and sexual orientation.
General, Infect Dis, Medicine
- ⊕ https://vfmat.ch/e929

Bicol Clinic Foundation Inc.
Treats patients primarily in the Philippines, Nepal, Haiti, and locally in the USA, while constructing a permanent outpatient clinic in the Bicol region of the Philippines and establishing a disaster-relief fund.
Crit-Care, Derm, ENT, ER Med, Endo, General, Infect Dis, MF Med, Medicine, Nutr, OB-GYN, Ophth-Opt, Pub Health, Surg, Urol
- ⊕ https://vfmat.ch/3f9e

Boston Children's Hospital: Global Health Program
Helps solve pediatric global healthcare challenges by transferring expertise through long-term partnerships with scalable impact, while working in the field to strengthen healthcare systems, advocate, research, and provide care delivery or education as a way of sustainably improving the health of children worldwide.
Anesth, CV Med, Crit-Care, ER Med, Heme-Onc, Infect Dis, Medicine, Nutr, Palliative, Ped Surg, Peds
- ⊕ https://vfmat.ch/f9f8

BRAC USA
Seeks to empower people and communities in situations of poverty, illiteracy, disease, and social injustice. Interventions aim to achieve large-scale, positive changes through economic and social programs that enable everyone to realize their potential.
ER Med, General, Infect Dis, Logist-Op, MF Med, OB-GYN
- ⊕ https://vfmat.ch/9d9e

Breast Cancer Support
Aims to save lives and end breast cancer forever in women and men through education, treatment, emotional assistance, and financial support.
Heme-Onc, Logist-Op, Pub Health, Rad-Onc, Radiol
- ⊕ https://vfmat.ch/cb78

Bridge of Life
Aims to strengthen healthcare globally through sustainable programs that prevent and treat chronic disease.
Logist-Op, Nephro, OB-GYN, Peds, Surg
- ⊕ https://vfmat.ch/5b68

Bridges Global Missions
Deploys medical teams to Haiti and the Philippines in the aftermath of disasters to address prevailing needs and manage healthcare issues.
Dent-OMFS, ER Med, General, Infect Dis, Logist-Op, Medicine, Nutr, Nutr, Peds, Pub Health
- ⊕ https://vfmat.ch/c8d5

Bureau of International Health Cooperation
Seeks to improve healthcare around the world, including developing countries, using expertise, and contribute to healthier lives of Japanese people by bringing these experiences back to Japan.
ER Med, Heme-Onc, Infect Dis, Peds, Pub Health
- ⊕ https://vfmat.ch/947d

Camillian Disaster Service (CADIS) International
Promotes the development of locally based health programs for disaster-stricken communities through compassionate and coordinated interventions.
General, Logist-Op, MF Med
- ⊕ https://vfmat.ch/5281

Canadian Medical Assistance Teams (CMAT)
Provides relief and medical aid to the victims of natural and man-made disasters around the world.
Anesth, ER Med, Medicine, OB-GYN, Peds, Psych, Rehab, Surg
- ⊕ https://vfmat.ch/5232

Canadian Vision Care
Consists of eye healthcare professionals who donate time and resources to the development of vision care in the developing world.
Ophth-Opt
- ⊕ https://vfmat.ch/3a38

CARE
Works around the globe to save lives, defeat poverty, and achieve social justice.
ER Med, General
- ⊕ https://vfmat.ch/7232

Care Channels International
We engage communities through a variety of education, health, and livelihood programs.
Dent-OMFS, General, Surg
- ⊕ https://vfmat.ch/fc48

Carewell Community
Provides support, education, and, most importantly, hope at no cost to persons with cancer and their loved ones.
Heme-Onc, Infect Dis
- ⊕ https://vfmat.ch/98bc

Carter Center, The
Seeks to prevent and resolve conflicts, enhance freedom and democracy, and improve health, while remaining committed to human rights and the alleviation of human suffering.
Infect Dis, MF Med, Ophth-Opt
- ⊕ https://vfmat.ch/6556

Catholic Organization for Relief & Development Aid (CORDAID)
Provides humanitarian assistance and creates opportunities to improve security, healthcare, education, and inclusive economic growth in fragile and conflict-affected areas.
ER Med, Infect Dis, MF Med, OB-GYN, Peds, Psych
- ⊕ https://vfmat.ch/8ae5

Catholic World Mission
Works to rebuild communities worldwide by helping to alleviate poverty and empower underserved areas, while spreading the message of the Catholic Church.

ER Med, General, Nutr, Peds
⊕ https://vfmat.ch/7b5f

cbm New Zealand
Inspired by the Christian faith, aims to improve the quality of life for those living with the double disadvantage of poverty and disability.
Crit-Care, Infect Dis, Logist-Op, Nutr, OB-GYN, Ophth-Opt, Ortho, Psych, Rehab, Surg
⊕ https://vfmat.ch/c14b

Centro Escolar University Dental Alumni Association
Seeks to help impoverished communities through medical, dental, and relief missions, and to raise awareness of the importance of dental health.
Dent-OMFS
⊕ https://vfmat.ch/ebfd

Charities for Surgery
Offers surgical care to the underprivileged.
Logist-Op, Surg
⊕ https://vfmat.ch/9da2

CharityVision International
Focuses on restoring curable sight impairment worldwide by empowering local physicians and creating sustainable solutions.
Logist-Op, Ophth-Opt, Surg
⊕ https://vfmat.ch/6231

Child Family Health International (CFHI)
Connects students with local health professionals and community leaders transforming perspectives about self, global health, and healing.
General, Infect Dis, OB-GYN, Ophth-Opt, Palliative, Peds
⊕ https://vfmat.ch/729e

ChildFund Australia
Works to reduce poverty for children in many of the world's most disadvantaged communities.
ER Med, General, Peds
⊕ https://vfmat.ch/13df

Children of War Foundation
Delivers access to global health and education to communities affected by poverty, war, natural disaster, climate change, and migration challenges.
ER Med, General, Logist-Op, Peds, Surg
⊕ https://vfmat.ch/de51

Christian Blind Mission (CBM)
Aims to improve the quality of life of persons with disabilities in the poorest countries, addressing poverty as a cause and a consequence of disability, and working in partnership to create a society for all.
ENT, General, Infect Dis, OB-GYN, Ophth-Opt, Ortho, Peds, Psych, Rehab, Surg
⊕ https://vfmat.ch/3824

Christian Connections for International Health (CCIH)
Promotes global health and wholeness from a Christian perspective.
All-Immu, General, Infect Dis, MF Med, Neonat, OB-GYN, Psych
⊕ https://vfmat.ch/fa5d

Circle of Health International (COHI)
Aligns with local, community-based organizations led and powered by women to help respond to the needs of the women and children that they serve. Helps with the provision of professional volunteers, capacity training, and procurement of requested and appropriate supplies and equipment. Raises funds for the organizations to provide the services required.
ER Med, Logist-Op, MF Med, Neonat, OB-GYN, Psych
⊕ https://vfmat.ch/8b63

Columbia University: Global Mental Health Programs
Pioneers research initiatives, promotes mental health, and aims to reduce the burden of mental illness worldwide.
Psych
⊕ https://vfmat.ch/c5cd

Combat Blindness International
Works to eliminate preventable blindness worldwide by providing sustainable, equitable solutions for sight through partnerships and innovation.
Ophth-Opt
⊕ https://vfmat.ch/28ad

COVID-19 Clinical Research Coalition
Advocates and collaborates for the advancement of COVID-19 research driven by the needs of low-resource settings, and works for equitable access to solutions to the pandemic.
All-Immu, Infect-Dis, MF Med, Path, Pub Health
⊕ https://vfmat.ch/d1f4

Cross Catholic Outreach
Mobilizes the global Catholic Church to transform impoverished communities through the provision of food, water, housing, education, orphan support, medical care, microenterprise, and disaster relief.
All-Immu, General, Nutr, OB-GYN, Rehab
⊕ https://vfmat.ch/22f4

CURE
Operates charitable hospitals and programs in underserved countries worldwide, where patients receive surgical treatment, based in Christian ministry.
Anesth, Neurosurg, Ortho, Ped Surg, Peds, Rehab, Surg
⊕ https://vfmat.ch/aa16

CURE Children's Hospital of Zimbabwe
Heals children living with disabilities such as clubfoot, bowed legs, cleft lips, untreated burns, and hydrocephalus.
ENT, Neurosurg, Ortho, Peds, Plast
⊕ https://vfmat.ch/473c

Dentistry For All
Donates time and services toward dental education, prevention, and corrective treatment to those who cannot otherwise access care.
Dent-OMFS
⊕ https://vfmat.ch/f3e2

Direct Relief
Improves the health and lives of people affected by poverty or emergency situations by mobilizing and providing essential medical resources needed for their care.
ER Med, Logist-Op
⊕ https://vfmat.ch/58e5

DKT INTERNATIONAL INC
Seeks to provide couples with affordable and safe options for family planning and HIV/AIDS prevention through dynamic social marketing.
General, Surg
⊕ https://vfmat.ch/b3a7

Doctors Without Borders/Médecins Sans Frontières (MSF)
Responds to emergencies and provides lifesaving medical care where needed most, including during disasters, conflicts, and epidemics.
Anesth, Crit-Care, ER Med, General, Infect Dis, Nutr, OB-GYN, Ped Surg, Peds, Psych, Pub Health, Surg
⊕ https://vfmat.ch/f363

Duke University: Global Health Institute
Sparks innovation in global health research and education, and brings together knowledge and resources to address the most important global health issues of our time.
All-Immu, Infect Dis, MF Med, OB-GYN, Pub Health
⊕ https://vfmat.ch/c4cd

Episcopal Relief & Development
Provides relief in times of disaster and promotes sustainable development by identifying and addressing the root causes of suffering.
Infect Dis, MF Med, Neonat, Nutr, Peds
⊕ https://vfmat.ch/7cfa

Evangelical Alliance Mission, The (TEAM)
Provides services in the areas of church planting, community development,

healthcare, social justice, business as mission, and more.
Dent-OMFS, General, Ophth-Opt
⊕ https://vfmat.ch/9faa

Exceed Worldwide
Supports people with disabilities living in poverty by providing free prosthetic and orthotic services in South and Southeast Asia.
Ortho, Peds
⊕ https://vfmat.ch/dd24

Eye Foundation of America
Works toward a world without childhood blindness.
Ophth-Opt
⊕ https://vfmat.ch/a7eb

Foundation for International Medical Relief of Children (FIMRC)
Provides access to healthcare for low-resource and medically underserved families around the world.
General, Infect Dis, Peds, Pub Health
⊕ https://vfmat.ch/78b9

Fracarita International
Provides support and services in the fields of mental healthcare, care for people with a disability, and education.
Psych, Rehab
⊕ https://vfmat.ch/8d3c

Fred Hollows Foundation, The
Works toward a world in which no person is needlessly blind or vision impaired.
Ophth-Opt, Pub Health, Surg
⊕ https://vfmat.ch/73e5

Free to Smile Foundation
Serves impoverished and underserved children suffering from cleft lip/palate deformities around the world.
Anesth, Dent-OMFS, ENT, Ped Surg, Plast
⊕ https://vfmat.ch/218b

Friends Who Care LLC
Provides specialty surgical and medical care free of charge to indigent patients in the Philippines.
ENT, ER Med, General, Geri, Logist-Op, Ped Surg, Plast, Pub Health, Surg
⊕ https://vfmat.ch/d4f6

German Doctors
Conducts voluntary medical work in developing countries and brings help where misery is part of everyday life.
General, Infect Dis, Medicine
⊕ https://vfmat.ch/21ad

Gift of Life International
Provides lifesaving cardiac treatment to children in developing countries while developing sustainable pediatric cardiac programs by implementing screening, surgical, and training missions.
Anesth, CT Surg, CV Med, Crit-Care, Ped Surg, Peds, Pulm-Critic
⊕ https://vfmat.ch/f2f9

Gift of Sight
Works to eradicate preventable blindness by fostering sustainable healthcare delivery in underserved global communities.
Ophth-Opt
⊕ https://vfmat.ch/fdd7

Giving Tree Medical Charity
Organizes and provides medical services to underserved communities in the U.S., Mexico, China, Vietnam, and the Philippines.
CV Med, Derm, General, Medicine, Nutr, Peds, Psych, Pub Health
⊕ https://vfmat.ch/2d3c

Global Aid Network (GAiN) Australia
Inspired by the Christian faith, provides support to people living in crisis through programs in healthcare, humanitarian aid, disaster response, clean water,

and sanitation.
Dent-OMFS, Ophth-Opt
⊕ https://vfmat.ch/6cb8

Global Clinic
Seeks to ensure that any effort to provide medical services is accompanied by a long-term program to improve the health of residents of its partner communities.
Dent-OMFS, ER Med, General, OB-GYN, OB-GYN, Ophth-Opt, Surg
⊕ https://vfmat.ch/9e48

Global Force for Healing
Works to end preventable maternal and newborn deaths by supporting the scaling of effective grassroots, community-led, culturally respectful care and education in underserved areas around the globe using the midwifery model of care.
Neonat, OB-GYN
⊕ https://vfmat.ch/deb2

Global Legacy
Supports and initiates projects with a high impact on health, education, and the advancement of women in rural communities.
Ophth-Opt
⊕ https://vfmat.ch/ff92

Global Medical Foundation Australia
Provides medical, surgical, dental, and educational welfare to underprivileged communities and gives them access to basics that are often taken for granted.
Dent-OMFS, ER Med, General, OB-GYN, Ortho, Surg
⊕ https://vfmat.ch/fa56

Global Ministries – The United Methodist Church
As the worldwide mission and development agency of The United Methodist Church, Global Ministries works with more than 300 hospitals and clinics around the world through its Global Health Unit.
Anesth, CT Surg, CV Med, Crit-Care, Dent-OMFS, Derm, ER Med, GI, General, Infect Dis, Logist-Op, MF Med, Medicine, Neonat, Nephro, Nutr, OB-GYN, Ophth-Opt, Ortho, Palliative, Peds, Pod, Psych, Pub Health, Rehab, Rheum, Surg, Urol
⊕ https://vfmat.ch/1723

Global Oncology (GO)
Brings the best in cancer care to underserved patients around the world and collaborates across geographic, professional, and academic borders to improve cancer care, research, and education.
Heme-Onc, Path, Rad-Onc
⊕ https://vfmat.ch/fcb8

Global Polio Eradication Initiative
Aims to eradicate polio worldwide.
All-Immu, Infect-Dis, Logist-Op, Pub Health
⊕ https://vfmat.ch/7e2c

Global Vision 2020
Provides prescription eyeglasses to people who live in parts of the world lacking necessary infrastructure for obtaining affordable corrective eyewear.
Logist-Op, Ophth-Opt
⊕ https://vfmat.ch/7373

GlobalMedic
Provides disaster relief and lifesaving humanitarian aid.
ER Med, Pub Health
⊕ https://vfmat.ch/dfe6

Globus Relief
Aims to improve the delivery of healthcare worldwide by gathering, processing, and distributing surplus medical supplies to charities at home and abroad.
Logist-Op
⊕ https://vfmat.ch/a2b7

Good Shepard International Foundation
Strives to promote inclusive and sustainable development for the most marginalized and vulnerable people, with a special focus on women, girls, and children, inspired by the Christian faith.
ER Med
⊕ https://vfmat.ch/ad9a

Grace Dental and Medical (GDM) Missions
Sends and supports dental and medical missions based in Christian ministry with the aim of church planting.
Dent-OMFS, ER Med, General
⊕ https://vfmat.ch/bdea

HAND-Philippines
Works to close gaps in public healthcare and access for impoverished Filipino villages affected by natural disasters.
Dent-OMFS, General, Geri, Infect Dis, Medicine, Nutr, OB-GYN, Peds, Psych, Pub Health
⊕ https://vfmat.ch/de16

Headwaters Relief Organization
Addresses public health issues for the most underserved populations of the world, providing psychosocial and medical support along with disaster debris cleanup and rebuilding in partnership with other organizations.
ER Med, Infect Dis, Logist-Op, Psych, Pub Health
⊕ https://vfmat.ch/e511

Healing Hands Foundation, The
Provides high-quality surgical procedures, medical treatment, dental care, and educational support in under-resourced areas worldwide.
Anesth, Dent-OMFS, General, Ped Surg, Peds, Surg
⊕ https://vfmat.ch/4bfc

Health Futures Foundation
Empowers marginalized families and local governments in achieving access, quality, and equity in health and social development through communities of wellness.
General, Geri, Nutr, OB-GYN, Peds, Pub Health
⊕ https://vfmat.ch/fc39

Health Volunteers Overseas (HVO)
Improves the availability and quality of healthcare through the education, training, and professional development of the health workforce in resource-scarce countries.
All-Immu, Anesth, CV Med, Dent-OMFS, Derm, ENT, ER Med, Endo, GI, Heme-Onc, Infect Dis, Medicine, Medicine, Nephro, Neuro, OB-GYN, Ophth-Opt, Ortho, Peds, Plast, Psych, Pulm-Critic, Rehab, Rheum, Surg
⊕ https://vfmat.ch/42b2

Heartbeat International
Saves lives globally by providing cardiovascular implantable devices to needy people of the world.
CV Med
⊕ https://vfmat.ch/eb38

Heineman Medical Outreach
Provides medical and educational assistance globally to promote sustainable healthcare and enhanced living standards in underserved communities through the International Medical Outreach (IMO) program, a collaborative partnership between Heineman Medical Outreach and Atrium Health.
Anesth, CT Surg, CV Med, ER Med, General, Heme-Onc, Logist-Op, Medicine, Neonat, OB-GYN, Ped Surg, Peds, Surg, Vasc Surg
⊕ https://vfmat.ch/389b

Helen Keller International
Seeks to eliminate preventable vision loss, malnutrition, and diseases of poverty.
Infect Dis, Nutr, OB-GYN, Ophth-Opt, Peds
⊕ https://vfmat.ch/b654

HelpAge International
Works to ensure that people everywhere understand how much older people contribute to society and that they must enjoy their right to healthcare, social services, economic, and physical security.
General, Geri, Infect Dis, Medicine, Pub Health
⊕ https://vfmat.ch/5d91

Helping Hands Medical Missions
Delivers compassionate healthcare by hosting medical missions and treating patients in underserved communities around the world, based in Christian ministry.

Anesth, Dent-OMFS, ER Med, General, OB-GYN, Ophth-Opt, Surg
⊕ https://vfmat.ch/8efd

His Healing Hands
Seeks to provide disease treatment and prevention in partnership with indigenous evangelical Christian organizations that help guide activities.
General
⊕ https://vfmat.ch/ce38

Hope and Healing International
Gives hope and healing to children and families trapped by poverty and disability.
General, Nutr, Ophth-Opt, Peds, Rehab
⊕ https://vfmat.ch/c638

Humanity & Inclusion
Works alongside people with disabilities and vulnerable populations, taking action and bearing witness in order to respond to their essential needs, improve their living conditions and health, and promote respect for their dignity and fundamental rights.
General, Infect Dis, MF Med, Medicine, Ortho, Peds, Psych, Pub Health, Rehab
⊕ https://vfmat.ch/16b7

Humanity First
Provides aid and assistance to those in need, offering sustainable development solutions to society while providing and empowering local communities with the resources to help themselves.
ER Med, General, MF Med, Ophth-Opt
⊕ https://vfmat.ch/13cc

ICAP at Columbia University
Serves as global leader in supporting the scale-up of multidisciplinary HIV/AIDS prevention, care, and treatment programs based on a family-focused approach.
General, Infect Dis, MF Med, Medicine, OB-GYN, Pub Health
⊕ https://vfmat.ch/a8ef

IMA World Health
Works to build healthier communities by collaborating with key partners to serve vulnerable people with a focus on health, healing, and well-being for all.
Infect Dis, MF Med, Nutr, OB-GYN, Pub Health
⊕ https://vfmat.ch/8316

Institute of Applied Dermatology
Aims to alleviate difficult-to-treat skin ailments by combining biomedicine with Ayurveda, homeopathy, yoga, and other traditional Indian medicine.
All-Immu, Derm, Infect Dis, Nutr, Pod, Pub Health
⊕ https://vfmat.ch/c6eb

International Agency for the Prevention of Blindness (IAPB), The
Leads international efforts in blindness-prevention activities, works toward a world where no one is needlessly visually impaired, and ensures that everyone has access to the best possible standard of eye health.
Infect Dis, Ophth-Opt, Pub Health
⊕ https://vfmat.ch/87a2

International Children's Heart Foundation
Provides free surgical care, medical training, and technology to save the lives of children with congenital heart disease in developing countries.
Anesth, CT Surg, CV Med, Crit-Care, Ped Surg, Peds, Pulm-Critic
⊕ https://vfmat.ch/86c1

International Council of Ophthalmology
Works with ophthalmologic societies and others to enhance ophthalmic education and improve access to the highest-quality eye care in order to preserve and restore vision for people of the world.
Ophth-Opt
⊕ https://vfmat.ch/ffd2

International Federation of Gynecology and Obstetrics (FIGO)
Implements global projects on specific women's health issues.
MF Med, Medicine, Neonat, OB-GYN, Surg, Urol
⊕ https://vfmat.ch/c4b4

International Federation of Red Cross and Red Crescent Societies (IFRC)

Coordinates and directs international assistance following natural and manmade disasters in nonconflict situations through the world's largest humanitarian and development network. Provides disaster-preparedness programs, healthcare activities, and promotes humanitarian values.

ER Med, General, Infect Dis, Nutr
⊕ https://vfmat.ch/b4ee

International League of Dermatological Socieities

Strives to promote high-quality education, clinical care, research and innovation that will improve skin health globally.

Derm, Infect Dis
⊕ https://vfmat.ch/7388

International Learning Movement (ILM UK)

Supports some of the world's poorest people in developing countries with core projects in education, safe drinking water, and healthcare.

General, Ophth-Opt
⊕ https://vfmat.ch/b974

International Medical Corps

Seeks to improve quality of life through health interventions and related activities that strengthen underserved communities worldwide, with the flexibility to respond rapidly to emergencies and offer medical services and training to people at the highest risk.

ER Med, General, Infect Dis, Nutr, OB-GYN, Peds, Pub Health, Surg
⊕ https://vfmat.ch/a8a5

International Medical Response

Supplements, supports, and enhances healthcare systems in communities across the world that have been incapacitated by natural disaster, extreme poverty, and/or regional conflict by sending a multidisciplinary team of healthcare professionals.

Anesth, General, OB-GYN, Surg
⊕ https://vfmat.ch/9ccd

International Organization for Migration (IOM) – The UN Migration Agency

Promotes evidence-informed policies and holistic, preventive, and curative health programs that are beneficial, accessible, and equitable for vulnerable migrants.

General, Infect Dis, OB-GYN
⊕ https://vfmat.ch/621a

International Planned Parenthood Federation (IPPF)

Leads a locally owned, globally connected civil society movement that provides and enables services and champions sexual and reproductive health and rights for all, especially the underserved.

Infect Dis, MF Med, OB-GYN
⊕ https://vfmat.ch/dc97

International Union Against Tuberculosis and Lung Disease

Develops, implements, and assesses anti-tuberculosis, lung health, and noncommunicable disease programs.

Infect Dis, Pub Health, Pulm-Critic
⊕ https://vfmat.ch/3e82

InterSurgeon

Fosters collaborative partnerships in the field of global surgery that will advance clinical care, teaching, training, research, and the provision and maintenance of medical equipment.

ENT, Neurosurg, Ortho, Ped Surg, Plast, Surg, Urol
⊕ https://vfmat.ch/6f8a

IOF – International Osteoporosis Foundation

Aims to fight against osteoporosis and promote bone and musculoskeletal health worldwide.

Endo, OB-GYN, Ortho
⊕ https://vfmat.ch/89d8

Iris Global

Serves the poor, the destitute, the lost, and the forgotten by providing adoration, outreach, family, education, relief, development, healing, and the arts.

General, Infect Dis, Nutr, Pub Health
⊕ https://vfmat.ch/37f8

Islamic Medical Association of North America

Fosters health promotion, disease prevention, and health maintenance in communities around the world through direct patient care and health programs.

Anesth, Dent-OMFS, ER Med, General, Logist-Op, Ophth-Opt, Peds, Plast, Surg
⊕ https://vfmat.ch/a157

iVolunteer Philippines

Provides volunteers an easy way to find opportunities that match their skills, interest, and advocacy, while also using the same platform to help organizations find volunteers that match their needs.

Dent-OMFS, General, Geri, Logist-Op, Medicine, Medicine, Peds, Pub Health, Pulm-Critic
⊕ https://vfmat.ch/cf83

Jhpiego

Creates and delivers transformative healthcare solutions that save lives, in partnership with national governments, health experts, and local communities.

General, Infect Dis, OB-GYN, Surg
⊕ https://vfmat.ch/45b8

John Snow, Inc. (JSI)

Aims to improve the health and well-being of underserved and vulnerable people and communities throughout the world.

General, Infect Dis, Logist-Op, MF Med, OB-GYN, Peds, Psych, Pub Health
⊕ https://vfmat.ch/ba78

Joint United Nations Programme on HIV/AIDS (UNAIDS)

Aims to place people living with HIV and people affected by the virus at the decision-making table and at the center of designing, delivering, and monitoring the AIDS response.

Infect Dis
⊕ https://vfmat.ch/464a

Kailash Medical Foundation

Aims to improve the health and well-being of those in need around the world by going on missions to developing countries and providing medical, dental, and vision services to the underprivileged.

Dent-OMFS, General, Ophth-Opt
⊕ https://vfmat.ch/db41

Kalipay Negrense Foundation

Provides fun, healthy, loving homes and support communities where children are empowered and their needs and rights are protected.

General, Ophth-Opt
⊕ https://vfmat.ch/6fa2

Kamanggagawa Foundation Inc.

Seeks to improve the quality of life of indigenous groups, especially the elderly, disabled, orphaned children, and the ill, through programs in housing, health and nutrition, and social services.

Dent-OMFS, Derm, OB-GYN, Ophth-Opt, Peds
⊕ https://vfmat.ch/13c4

Kasusong Pinay

Creates pathways to improve access to information and resources for the comprehensive and integrated care of breast cancer patients.

OB-GYN
⊕ https://vfmat.ch/2ecb

Kaya Responsible Travel

Promotes sustainable social, environmental, and economic development, empowers communities, and cultivates educated, compassionate global citizens through responsible travel.

All-Immu, Crit-Care, Dent-OMFS, ER Med, General, Geri, Infect Dis, MF Med, Medicine, Nutr, OB-GYN, Peds, Psych, Pub Health, Rehab
⊕ https://vfmat.ch/b2cf

La Salle International Foundation

Provides support for educational, health, and human services, along with humanitarian relief to people in developed and underdeveloped areas.

General
🌐 https://vfmat.ch/5891

Let's Save The Brain
Provides support for quality neurological health and services for indigent Filipino patients at the Department of Neurosciences of the University of the Philippines.
Neuro, Neurosurg
🌐 https://vfmat.ch/e3ca

Life for a Child
Supports the provision of the best possible healthcare, given local circumstances, to all children and youth with diabetes in less-resourced countries, through the strengthening of existing diabetes services.
Endo, Medicine, Peds
🌐 https://vfmat.ch/d712

LIG Global Foundation
Supplies medical care, medical training, and a variety of social programs to some of the world's most underserved populations.
CT Surg, CV Med, Logist-Op, Neonat, OB-GYN, Plast, Surg, Urol
🌐 https://vfmat.ch/67aa

Light House Medical Missions
Inspired by the Christian faith, provides programs in healthcare provision, nutrition, emergency relief and response, and water, sanitation, and hygiene (WASH).
ER Med, General, Surg
🌐 https://vfmat.ch/cecd

Limbs International
Engages communities and transforms lives through affordable, sustainable prosthetic solutions and rehabilitation services in developing countries.
Logist-Op, Ortho, Pod, Rehab
🌐 https://vfmat.ch/dc84

Mabuhay Deseret Foundation
Screens for patients, maintains recovery houses, and partners with local doctors and hospitals to facilitate life-changing eye, cleft, and clubfoot surgeries.
Ophth-Opt, Ortho, Plast, Surg
🌐 https://vfmat.ch/1481

Magandang Buhay Foundation
Ensures that every child receives a proper education, health assistance, and nutritional care in the Philippines.
General, Nutr, Pub Health
🌐 https://vfmat.ch/2582

MAGNA International
Helps those who are suffering or recovering from conflicts and disasters by reducing the risks of diseases and treating them immediately.
ER Med, General, Infect Dis, Peds, Surg
🌐 https://vfmat.ch/58f4

Management Sciences for Health (MSH)
Works with countries and communities to save lives and improve the health of the world's poorest and most vulnerable people by building strong, resilient, sustainable health systems.
Infect Dis, Logist-Op, Pub Health
🌐 https://vfmat.ch/6aa2

MAP International
Provides medicines and health supplies to those in need around the world so they might experience life to the fullest.
Logist-Op
🌐 https://vfmat.ch/deed

Massachusetts General Hospital Global Surgery Initiative
Aims to improve surgical education and access to advanced surgical care in resource-limited settings around the world by performing surgical operations as visitors, training local surgeons, and sharing medical technology through international partnerships across disciplines.
Anesth, Crit-Care, ER Med, Heme-Onc, Peds, Surg
🌐 https://vfmat.ch/31b1

Max Foundation, The
Seeks to increase global access to treatment, care, and support for people living with cancer.
General, Heme-Onc, Pub Health
🌐 https://vfmat.ch/8c7d

Medical Evacuation Disaster Intervention Corps (Medic Corps)
Provides emergency response and medical care during times of catastrophic disaster, based in Christian ministry.
ER Med
🌐 https://vfmat.ch/c8cf

Medical Ministry International
Provides compassionate healthcare in areas of need, inspired by the Christian faith.
CT Surg, Dent-OMFS, ENT, General, OB-GYN, Ophth-Opt, Ortho, Plast, Rehab, Surg, Urol, Vasc Surg
🌐 https://vfmat.ch/5da6

Medical Missions for Children (MMFC)
Provides quality surgical and dental services to poor and underprivileged children and young adults in various countries throughout the world, and facilitates the transfer of education, knowledge, and recent innovations to the local medical communities.
Dent-OMFS, ENT, Endo, Ortho, Ped Surg, Peds, Plast
🌐 https://vfmat.ch/1631

Medical Missions Foundation
Provides surgical and medical care in underserved communities throughout the world and hopes to positively impact the lives of children and their families.
Anesth, Ped Surg, Surg
🌐 https://vfmat.ch/f385

Medical Missions Outreach
Visits developing countries to provide quality, ethical healthcare and outreach to those in need, based in Christian ministry.
Dent-OMFS, Ophth-Opt, Ortho, Surg
🌐 https://vfmat.ch/1197

Medical Relief International
Exists to provide dental, medical, humanitarian aid, and other services deemed necessary for the benefit of people in need.
Dent-OMFS, General
🌐 https://vfmat.ch/192b

MedShare
Aims to improve the quality of life of people, communities, and the planet by sourcing and directly delivering surplus medical supplies and equipment to communities in need around the world.
Logist-Op
🌐 https://vfmat.ch/c8bc

Meeting TENTS
Improves the quality of life in communities by promoting public health; works toward a world in which communities ensure people have access to care and the opportunity to thrive.
Pub Health
🌐 https://vfmat.ch/b694

Mending Faces
Restores hope and provides a brighter future to those whose lives are burdened by cleft lip, cleft palate, and other deformities.
Dent-OMFS, General, Nutr, Ped Surg, Peds
🌐 https://vfmat.ch/41a9

Mercy in Action
Inspired by the Christian faith, carries out programs in maternal and newborn health, primary healthcare for children under 5, and midwifery education.
General, MF Med, Neonat, OB-GYN, Peds, Pub Health
🌐 https://vfmat.ch/cc88

Mercy Malaysia

Provides medical relief, sustainable health-related development, and risk reduction activities for vulnerable communities, in both crisis and non-crisis situations.

ER Med, General, OB-GYN, Peds

⊕ https://vfmat.ch/f678

MiracleFeet

Brings low-cost treatment to every child on the planet born with clubfoot, a leading cause of physical disability.

Ortho, Peds, Rehab

⊕ https://vfmat.ch/bda8

Mission Bambini

Helps to support children living in poverty and sickness, and lacking education, giving them the opportunity for and hope of a better life.

CT Surg, CV Med, Crit-Care, ER Med, Ped Surg, Peds

⊕ https://vfmat.ch/dc1a

Mission Regan

Collects supplies, medication, and medical equipment and provides them to those who are in desperate need, both locally and globally.

Logist-Op

⊕ https://vfmat.ch/2bc1

Mission to Heal

Aims to heal underserved people and train local practitioners in the most remote areas of the world through global healthcare missions.

Anesth, Infect Dis, OB-GYN, Surg

⊕ https://vfmat.ch/4718

Mission Vision

Seeks to decrease blindness and other eye-related disabilities, and to increase academic performance and general quality of life.

Ophth-Opt

⊕ https://vfmat.ch/83d8

MSD for Mothers

Designs scalable solutions that help end preventable maternal deaths.

MF Med, OB-GYN, Pub Health

⊕ https://vfmat.ch/9f99

Multi-Agency International Training and Support (MAITS)

Improves the lives of some of the world's poorest people living with disabilities through better access to quality health and education services and support.

Neuro, Psych, Rehab

⊕ https://vfmat.ch/9dcd

Médecins du Monde/Doctors of the World

Provides care, bears witness, and supports social change worldwide with innovative medical programs and evidence-based advocacy initiatives.

ER Med, General, Infect Dis, MF Med, Neonat, OB-GYN, Peds, Pub Health

⊕ https://vfmat.ch/a43d

National Association of Filipino Dentists in America

Provides continuing education, advocacy, and public information for dentists to promote good dental health in their home communities and while serving abroad.

Dent-OMFS, ENT, Ped Surg

⊕ https://vfmat.ch/8cfa

Nurses on world mission

Aims to foster a spirit of service to promote health and wellness of the communities in need around the world, through education and medical missions.

General

⊕ https://vfmat.ch/de3b

Nursing Beyond Borders

Provides healthcare and education to children and communities, and focuses as well on disease prevention by providing nurses to serve in orphanages, shelters, schools, and clinics.

Logist-Op, MF Med, Peds

⊕ https://vfmat.ch/71e6

NYC Medics

Deploys mobile medical teams to remote areas of disaster zones and humanitarian emergencies, providing the highest level of medical care to those who otherwise would not have access to aid and relief efforts.

All-Immu, ER Med, Infect Dis, Surg

⊕ https://vfmat.ch/aeee

Open Heart International

Provides surgical interventions and best practices to the most disadvantaged communities on the planet.

CT Surg, MF Med, OB-GYN, Ophth-Opt, Plast, Surg

⊕ https://vfmat.ch/dab2

Operation International

Offers medical aid to adults and children suffering from lack of quality healthcare in impoverished countries.

Dent-OMFS, ER Med, Heme-Onc, OB-GYN, Ophth-Opt, Ortho, Ped Surg, Plast, Surg

⊕ https://vfmat.ch/b52a

Operation Rainbow

Performs free orthopedic surgery, in developing countries, for children and young adults who do not otherwise have access to related medical procedures or equipment.

Anesth, Ortho, Ped Surg, Peds, Rehab, Surg

⊕ https://vfmat.ch/5dad

Operation Rainbow Canada

Provides free reconstructive surgery and related healthcare for cleft lip and cleft palate deformities to impoverished children and young adults in developing countries.

Surg

⊕ https://vfmat.ch/7f25

Operation Restore Hope

Provides impoverished children in the Philippines with surgical services to treat cleft lip, cleft palate, and other birth defects.

Anesth, Ped Surg, Plast

⊕ https://vfmat.ch/71f5

Operation Smile

Treats patients with cleft lip and cleft palate, and creates solutions that deliver safe surgery to people where it's needed most.

Anesth, Dent-OMFS, ENT, Ped Surg, Plast

⊕ https://vfmat.ch/5c29

Operation Walk

Provides the gift of mobility through life-changing joint replacement surgeries, at no cost for those in need in the U.S. and globally.

Anesth, Ortho, Rehab, Surg

⊕ https://vfmat.ch/bafe

Order of Malta

Supports forgotten or excluded people, especially those living in conflict zones or amid natural disasters, by providing medical assistance, caring for refugees, and distributing medicines and necessities.

ER Med, General, Infect Dis, MF Med, Nephro, OB-GYN, Ortho, Psych

⊕ https://vfmat.ch/1fab

Orphan Life Foundation

Advocates for orphaned children in Burkina Faso by providing educational, health, and foster home and shelter services, while facilitating adoption processes.

Infect Dis, Logist-Op, Nutr, Pub Health

⊕ https://vfmat.ch/14ea

Philippine Leprosy Mission, Inc.

Based in Christian ministry, dedicates services to persons with leprosy, and helps patients and their children stay in school or learn vocational skills.

Derm, ENT, General, Geri, Infect Dis, Medicine, Ped Surg, Peds, Pub Health, Rehab

⊕ https://vfmat.ch/73a2

Philippine Medical Association of New England

Strives to engage Filipino-American healthcare leaders in advancing the health and well-being of communities in New England and abroad by conducting educational, scientific, healthcare, and philanthropic activities.

All-Immu, All-Immu, Anesth, CV Med, Crit-Care, Dent-OMFS, ER Med, Endo, GI, General, Geri, Infect Dis, MF Med, Medicine, Nephro, Neuro, OB-GYN, Ophth-Opt, Ortho, Peds, Pub Health, Pulm-Critic, Surg, Urol

⊕ https://vfmat.ch/fff8

Phoenix International Foundation, Inc.

Aims to improve quality of life by providing medical care to underserved populations, inspired by the Christian faith.

General, Ophth-Opt

⊕ https://vfmat.ch/b464

Project HOPE

Works on the front lines of the world's health challenges, partnering hand-in-hand with communities, healthcare workers, and public health systems to ensure sustainable change.

CV Med, ER Med, Endo, General, Infect Dis, MF Med, Peds

⊕ https://vfmat.ch/2bd7

Project PEARLS

Helps impoverished children to have a better life through education, empowerment, nutrition, nourishment, and healthcare.

Dent-OMFS, General, Peds

⊕ https://vfmat.ch/39bc

Project Red Ribbon Care Management Foundation, Inc.

Improves the quality of life of persons living with HIV through awareness, resources, treatment, care, and support.

Infect Dis

⊕ https://vfmat.ch/dccd

Reach

Promotes the health of vulnerable populations through technical support to local, regional, and global efforts to prevent and control rheumatic fever and rheumatic heart disease (RF/RHD).

CV Med, Medicine, Pub Health

⊕ https://vfmat.ch/3f52

Real Medicine Foundation (RMF)

Provides humanitarian support to people living in disaster- and poverty-stricken areas, focusing on the person as a whole by providing medical/physical, emotional, economic, and social support.

ER Med, General, Infect Dis, Nutr, Peds, Psych

⊕ https://vfmat.ch/d45a

Relief International

Helps people in fragile settings achieve good health and nutrition by delivering primary healthcare and emergency treatment, and builds local capacity to ensure that communities in vulnerable situations have the access to the quality care they need to live healthy lives.

ER Med, General, MF Med, Neonat, OB-GYN, Peds, Psych

⊕ https://vfmat.ch/1522

Remote Area Medical Volunteer Corps

Brings free high-quality medical, vision, dental, and veterinary care to those in need.

Dent-OMFS, ER Med, General, Heme-Onc, MF Med, OB-GYN, Ophth-Opt

⊕ https://vfmat.ch/7669

RestoringVision

Empowers lives by restoring vision for millions of people in need.

Ophth-Opt

⊕ https://vfmat.ch/e121

ReSurge International

Provides reconstructive surgical care and builds surgical capacity in developing countries.

Anesth, Dent-OMFS, Ped Surg, Plast, Surg

⊕ https://vfmat.ch/9937

Right to Sight and Health

Seeks to reduce the prevalence of blindness and visual impairment, especially among low-income communities in Northern Ghana.

Ophth-Opt

⊕ https://vfmat.ch/7ff1

Risen Savior Missions

Inspired by the Christian faith, provides food, spiritual development, educational classes, and livelihood skills for children and families; supports medical mission teams.

General, Nutr, Peds

⊕ https://vfmat.ch/d536

Rose Charities International

Aims to support communities to improve quality of life and reduce the effects of poverty through innovative, self-sustaining projects, and partnerships.

ENT, ER Med, General, Infect Dis, Neonat, OB-GYN, Ophth-Opt, Ped Surg, Peds, Rehab, Urol

⊕ https://vfmat.ch/53df

Rotaplast International

Helps children and families worldwide by eliminating the burden of cleft lip and/or palate, burn scarring, and other deformities by sending medical teams to provide free reconstructive surgery, ancillary treatment, and training.

Anesth, Dent-OMFS, ENT, Ped Surg, Plast, Surg

⊕ https://vfmat.ch/78b3

Rotary International

Provides service to others, improves lives, and advances world understanding, goodwill, and peace through its fellowship of business, professional, and community leaders.

ER Med, General, Infect Dis, MF Med, OB-GYN

⊕ https://vfmat.ch/8fb5

Ruel Foundation

Provides impoverished children with treatable medical conditions with free surgery, medical care, and education, inspired by the Christian faith.

ER Med, General, Logist-Op, Medicine, Nutr, Ped Surg, Peds, Plast, Pub Health, Surg

⊕ https://vfmat.ch/4a14

Rutgers New Jersey Medical School

Seeks to support and promote the global health efforts of the faculty, staff, and students in the areas of education, research, and service through the Rutgers New Jersey Medical School's Office of Global Health.

Anesth, CV Med, Crit-Care, Neurosurg, OB-GYN, Psych

⊕ https://vfmat.ch/8e67

Ruth Foundation, The

Enhances the quality of life for those facing illness and age through compassionate palliative and hospice care, education, and advocacy in the Philippines.

General, Palliative, Pub Health

⊕ https://vfmat.ch/cfdb

Salvation Army International, The

Seeks to meet human needs through services in education, healthcare, community support, emergency response, and ministry development, inspired by the Christian faith.

Dent-OMFS, Derm, ER Med, Infect Dis, MF Med, Medicine, Nutr, OB-GYN, Ophth-Opt, Palliative, Psych, Rehab, Surg

⊕ https://vfmat.ch/8eb3

SAMU Foundation

Provides medical first response and reconstruction when severe international emergencies occur.

ER Med, Infect Dis, Logist-Op, Psych, Pub Health

⊕ https://vfmat.ch/3196

SATMED

Serves nongovernmental organizations, hospitals, medical universities, and other healthcare providers active in resource-poor areas, by providing open-access e-health services for the health community.

Logist-Op
⊕ https://vfmat.ch/b8d5

Save the Children
Gives children around the world a healthy start in life, the opportunity to learn, and protection from harm.
All-Immu, Crit-Care, ER Med, General, Infect Dis, MF Med, Medicine, Neonat, OB-GYN, Peds, Psych, Pub Health
⊕ https://vfmat.ch/2e73

SEE International
Provides sustainable medical, surgical, and educational services through volunteer ophthalmic surgeons, with the objectives of restoring sight and preventing blindness to disadvantaged individuals worldwide.
Ophth-Opt, Surg
⊕ https://vfmat.ch/6e1b

Sight Ministries International
Provides eye care to those in need, inspired by the Christian faith.
Ophth-Opt
⊕ https://vfmat.ch/32fa

SIGN Fracture Care International
Builds orthopedic capacity around the world and provides the injured poor access to fracture surgery by donating orthopedic education and implant systems to surgeons in developing countries.
Ortho, Rehab, Surg
⊕ https://vfmat.ch/123d

Smile Asia
Delivers free surgical care, through medical missions and outreach centers, to children with facial deformities such as cleft lip and cleft palate, and aims to raise standards of medical care by creating opportunities for collaborative learning and exchange of best practices.
Anesth, Dent-OMFS, Ped Surg, Peds, Plast
⊕ https://vfmat.ch/d674

Smile for Me
Helps improve the lives of children in the Philippines born with cleft lip and cleft palate deformities.
Ped Surg, Plast
⊕ https://vfmat.ch/b44c

Smile Train, Inc.
Treats children with cleft lip through a sustainable and local model that supports surgery and other forms of essential care.
Logist-Op, Pub Health
⊕ https://vfmat.ch/822c

SOS Children's Villages International
Supports children through alternative care and family strengthening.
ER Med, Peds
⊕ https://vfmat.ch/aca1

Sri Sathya Sai International Organization
Inspired by spiritual teachings, carries out efforts in global healthcare, education, humanitarian relief, and youth engagement.
Dent-OMFS, General, Logist-Op, Nutr, Ophth-Opt, Pub Health
⊕ https://vfmat.ch/9bda

St. Luke's Medical Center Foundation
Allows greater access to healthcare and information to low-income families, and creates equal opportunities for underprivileged students to enter medical school.
General, Peds, Pub Health
⊕ https://vfmat.ch/3821

Sunshine Care Foundation Inc.
Promotes research and dedicates resources to finding the cure for X-linked dystonia parkinsonism, and provides care for patients and their families with XDP.
General, Geri, Neuro, Pub Health
⊕ https://vfmat.ch/2228

Surgeons for Smiles
Brings first-class medical and dental care to those in need, in developing countries around the world.
Anesth, Dent-OMFS, OB-GYN, Ped Surg, Plast, Surg
⊕ https://vfmat.ch/3427

Sustained Health Initiatives of the Philippines
Bridges gaps in HIV response by strengthening the continuum of care through innovation, partnerships, and capacity-building.
Infect Dis, Medicine, Pub Health
⊕ https://vfmat.ch/9e72

Swiss Doctors
Aims to improve the health of populations in developing countries through medical-aid projects and training.
General, Infect Dis, Medicine
⊕ https://vfmat.ch/311a

Swiss Tropical and Public Health Institute
Contributes to the improvement of the health of populations internationally, nationally, and locally through excellence in research, education, and services.
Infect Dis, Pub Health
⊕ https://vfmat.ch/2ee4

Task Force for Global Health, The
Consists of programs and focus areas that cover a range of global health issues including neglected tropical diseases, infectious diseases, vaccines, field epidemiology, public health informatics, health workforce development, and global health ethics.
Infect Dis, Logist-Op, Medicine, Ophth-Opt, Peds
⊕ https://vfmat.ch/714c

Team Philippines
Aims to provide healthcare and long-term community-led projects to a developing village in the Philippines and to improve the long-term health of the population.
General, Geri, MF Med, Medicine, Nutr, Nutr, OB-GYN, Ophth-Opt, Peds, Pub Health
⊕ https://vfmat.ch/9c44

Tearfund
Responds to crisis and partners with local churches to bring restoration to those living in poverty, inspired by the Christian faith.
ER Med, Logist-Op
⊕ https://vfmat.ch/f6cf

Texas Children's Global Health
Addresses healthcare needs in resource-limited settings locally and globally by improving maternal and child health through the implementation of innovative, sustainable, in-country programs to train health professionals and build functional healthcare infrastructure.
Anesth, ER Med, Heme-Onc, Infect Dis, MF Med, Nutr, OB-GYN, Peds, Pub Health, Surg
⊕ https://vfmat.ch/4a1d

Third World Eye Care Society (TWECS)
Collects old, unused eyeglasses and distributes them in conjunction with eye exams given by properly trained individuals.
Logist-Op, Ophth-Opt
⊕ https://vfmat.ch/8618

Thyroid Cancer Survivors' Association, Inc. (ThyCa)
Provides education, support, handbooks, videos, and resources for patients and healthcare providers about thyroid cancer.
ENT, Endo, Path, Peds, Pub Health, Radiol, Surg
⊕ https://vfmat.ch/6247

Training for Health Equity Network (THEnet)
Contributes to health equity through health workforce education, research, and service, based on principles of social accountability and community engagement.
ER Med, General
⊕ https://vfmat.ch/38c6

UC Davis Health: Global Health and Rural Surgery
Aims to train individuals in the art and science of surgery and to develop surgeon leaders in resource-limited environments.
CT Surg, CV Med, Crit-Care, Endo, Heme-Onc, Plast, Surg, Vasc Surg
⊕ https://vfmat.ch/d26e

UNICEF Philippines
Works across 190 countries and territories, including the Philippines, to help children fulfill their potential, from early childhood through adolescence.
All-Immu, General, Neuro, Nutr, OB-GYN, Peds, Pub Health
⊕ https://vfmat.ch/afe5

Union for International Cancer Control (UICC)
Unites and supports the cancer community to reduce the global cancer burden, promote greater equity, and ensure that cancer control continues to be a priority in the world health and development agenda.
Heme-Onc, Pub Health
⊕ https://vfmat.ch/88b1

United Methodist Volunteers in Mission (UMVIM)
Engages in short-term missions each year in ministries as varied as disaster response, community development, pastor training, microenterprise, agriculture, Vacation Bible School, building repair and construction, and medical/dental services.
Dent-OMFS, ER Med, General
⊕ https://vfmat.ch/1ee6

United Nations Children's Fund (UNICEF)
Works in over 190 countries and territories to save children's lives, defend their rights, and help them fulfill their potential, from early childhood through adolescence.
All-Immu, Infect Dis, MF Med, Neonat, Nutr, OB-GYN, Ped Surg, Peds, Pub Health
⊕ https://vfmat.ch/42d7

United Nations Development Programme (UNDP)
Helps countries achieve the simultaneous eradication of extreme poverty and significant reduction of inequalities and exclusion using a sustainable human development approach.
Infect Dis, Logist-Op, Pub Health
⊕ https://vfmat.ch/935c

United Nations High Commissioner for Refugees (UNHCR)
Safeguards the rights and well-being of people who have been forced to flee, ensuring that everybody has the right to seek asylum and find safe refuge in another country, with the goal of seeking lasting solutions.
General, MF Med, Medicine, OB-GYN, Peds, Psych, Pub Health
⊕ https://vfmat.ch/6636

United Nations Office for the Coordination of Humanitarian Affairs (OCHA)
Contributes to principled and effective humanitarian response through coordination, advocacy, policy, information management, and humanitarian financing tools and services, by leveraging functional expertise throughout the organization.
Logist-Op
⊕ https://vfmat.ch/22b8

United Nations Population Fund (UNFPA)
Supports reproductive healthcare for women and youth in more than 150 countries, focusing on delivering a world in which every pregnancy is wanted, every childbirth is safe, and every young person's potential is fulfilled.
Infect Dis, MF Med, Neonat, OB-GYN, Peds, Pub Health
⊕ https://vfmat.ch/c969

United States Agency for International Development (USAID)
Promotes and demonstrates democratic values abroad and advances a free, peaceful, and prosperous world. Leads the U.S. government's international development and disaster assistance through partnerships and investments that save lives.
ER Med, Infect Dis, MF Med, OB-GYN, Peds
⊕ https://vfmat.ch/9a99

United Way
Aims to improve lives by mobilizing the caring power of communities around the world to advance the common good by fighting for the health, education, and financial stability of every person.
General, Infect Dis, Pub Health
⊕ https://vfmat.ch/c812

University of California Los Angeles: David Geffen School of Medicine Global Health Program
Catalyzes opportunities to improve health globally by engaging in multi-disciplinary and innovative education programs, research initiatives, and bilateral partnerships that provide opportunities for trainees, faculty, and staff to contribute to sustainable health initiatives and to address health inequities facing the world today.
All-Immu, Infect Dis, Logist-Op, MF Med, Medicine, Neonat, OB-GYN, Ortho, Ped Surg, Peds, Radiol
⊕ https://vfmat.ch/f1a4

University of California San Francisco: Institute for Global Health Sciences
Dedicates its efforts to improving health and reducing the burden of disease in the world's most vulnerable populations by integrating expertise in the health, social, and biological sciences, training global health leaders, and developing solutions to the most pressing health challenges.
Infect Dis, OB-GYN, Pub Health
⊕ https://vfmat.ch/6587

University of Toledo: Global Health Program
Aims to be a transformative force in medical education, biomedical research, and healthcare delivery.
CV Med, CV Med, ER Med, Infect Dis, Medicine, Neuro, Neurosurg, OB-GYN, Ophth-Opt, Ortho, Peds, Plast, Psych, Surg
⊕ https://vfmat.ch/71f2

USA for United Nations High Commissioner for Refugees (UNHCR)
Serves and protects refugees and displaced people through emergency relief, cash assistance, education, resettlement, and the rebuilding of livelihoods.
ER Med, General, Logist-Op, Nutr, Pub Health
⊕ https://vfmat.ch/293c

USAID: A2Z The Micronutrient and Child Blindness Project
Aims to increase the use of key micronutrient and blindness interventions to improve child and maternal health.
MF Med, Neonat, Nutr, Ophth-Opt, Surg
⊕ https://vfmat.ch/c5f1

USAID: Human Resources for Health 2030 (HRH2030)
Helps low- and middle-income countries develop the health workforce needed to prevent maternal and child deaths, support the goals of Family Planning 2020, control the HIV/AIDS epidemic, and protect communities from infectious diseases.
Logist-Op
⊕ https://vfmat.ch/9ea8

USAID: Leadership, Management and Governance Project
Improves leadership, management, and governance practices to strengthen health systems and improve health for all, including vulnerable populations worldwide.
Logist-Op
⊕ https://vfmat.ch/d35e

USAID: Maternal and Child Health Integrated Program
Works to improve the health of women and their families, including programs for maternal, newborn, and child health, immunization, family planning, nutrition, malaria, and HIV/AIDS.
All-Immu, General, Infect Dis, MF Med
⊕ https://vfmat.ch/4415

USAID: TB Care II
Focuses on tuberculosis care and treatment.
Infect Dis
⊕ https://vfmat.ch/57d4

Visionaries International
Works toward reducing the burden of corneal blindness in the developing world by assessing and addressing what limits corneal surgeons in each locale.
Anesth, Ophth-Opt, Pub Health, Surg
⊕ https://vfmat.ch/3d2e

Vital Strategies
Helps governments strengthen their public health systems to contend with the most important and difficult health challenges, while accelerating progress on the world's most pressing health problems.
CV Med, Infect Dis, Peds
⊕ https://vfmat.ch/fe25

Vitamin Angels
Helps at-risk populations in need—specifically pregnant women, new mothers, and children under age 5—to gain access to life-changing vitamins and minerals.
General, Nutr
⊕ https://vfmat.ch/7da1

Voluntary Service Overseas (VSO)
Works with health workers, communities, and governments to improve health services and rights for women, babies, youth, people with disabilities, and prisoners.
General, MF Med, OB-GYN
⊕ https://vfmat.ch/213d

Watsi
Uses technology to make healthcare a reality for those who might not otherwise be able to afford it.
Pub Health, Surg
⊕ https://vfmat.ch/41a3

We Care for Humanity (WCH)
Promotes sustainable social change and the sustainable development goals developed by the United Nations, including: no poverty, good health and well-being, gender equality, human rights, climate action, and strong institutions.
General, Logist-Op, Pub Health
⊕ https://vfmat.ch/8b4e

Wichita County Medical Alliance
Mobilizes volunteers to assist in public health efforts in the U.S. and abroad, including medical missions and disaster relief.
General, Geri, Nutr, OB-GYN, Pub Health
⊕ https://vfmat.ch/fa55

Women's Refugee Commission
Seeks to improve lives by protecting the rights of women, children, and youth displaced by conflict and crisis through researching their needs, identifying solutions, and advocating for programs and policies to strengthen their resilience.
General, MF Med, Neonat, OB-GYN, Peds, Psych
⊕ https://vfmat.ch/3d8f

World CF
Helps provide access to innovative surgical care for children and adults with abnormalities of the head and/or face.
Dent-OMFS, Neurosurg, Ped Surg, Plast, Surg
⊕ https://vfmat.ch/3df1

World Child Cancer
Works to improve diagnosis, treatment, and support for children with cancer, and their families, in low- and middle-income parts of the world.
Heme-Onc, Ped Surg, Rad-Onc
⊕ https://vfmat.ch/fbbc

World Children's Fund
Commits to helping children worldwide who are suffering the effects of poverty, disease, natural disaster, famine, abuse, civil strife, and war.
General, Logist-Op, MF Med, Nutr, OB-GYN, Pub Health
⊕ https://vfmat.ch/9cd8

World Compassion Fellowship (WCF)
Serves the global poor and persecuted through relief, medical care, development, and training.

CV Med, ER Med, Endo, GI, General, Infect Dis, Medicine, Nutr, OB-GYN, Ortho, Peds, Psych, Pub Health, Rehab
⊕ https://vfmat.ch/7b97

World Council of Optometry
Facilitates the development of optometry worldwide and promotes eye health and vision care through advocacy, education, policy development, and humanitarian outreach.
Ophth-Opt, Pub Health
⊕ https://vfmat.ch/c92e

World Federation of Hemophilia (WFH)
Aims to improve and sustain care for people with inherited bleeding disorders by pursuing long-term relationships with individuals and organizations who share the values of WFH's development model.
Heme-Onc
⊕ https://vfmat.ch/5121

World Health Organization, The (WHO)
The United Nations' agency for health provides leadership on global health matters, shapes the health research agenda, sets norms and standards, articulates evidence-based policy options, provides technical support and monitoring to countries, and assesses health trends.
ER Med, General, Infect Dis, Logist-Op, MF Med, OB-GYN, Peds, Psych, Pub Health
⊕ https://vfmat.ch/c476

World Hope International
Empowers the poorest individuals around the world so they can become agents of change within their communities, by offering resources and knowledge.
Infect Dis, Logist-Op, MF Med, OB-GYN, Peds
⊕ https://vfmat.ch/a4b8

World Medical Relief
Facilitates the distribution of surplus medical resources where they are needed.
Logist-Op
⊕ https://vfmat.ch/72dc

World Rehabilitation Fund
Enables individuals around the world with functional limitations and participation restrictions to achieve community and social integration through physical and socioeconomic rehabilitation and advocacy.
Ortho, Rehab
⊕ https://vfmat.ch/a5bc

World Surgical Foundation
Provides charitable surgical healthcare to the world's poor and underserved in developing nations.
Ped Surg, Surg
⊕ https://vfmat.ch/c162

World Vision International
Works with vulnerable communities around the world to overcome poverty and injustice with child-focused programs in disaster management, health, nutrition, economic development, education, clean water, sanitation, and hygiene.
ER Med, General, Infect Dis, MF Med, Nutr, OB-GYN, Peds
⊕ https://vfmat.ch/2642

Philippines

Healthcare Facilities

A.U.P. Health Service
Silang, Laguna, Philippines
⊕ https://vfmat.ch/7449

Abandoned Andres-Maria Rios Memorial
San Isidro Ilawod, Albay, Philippines
⊕ https://vfmat.ch/87a8

Abella Midway Hospital
Valencia City, Bukidnon, Philippines
⊕ https://vfmat.ch/33f3

Aborlan Medicare Hospital
Aborlan, Palawan, Philippines
⊕ https://vfmat.ch/4437

Abra Provincial Hospital
Bangued, Abra, Philippines
⊕ https://vfmat.ch/cf61

Adventist Hospital Santiago City
Santiago, Isabela, Philippines
⊕ https://vfmat.ch/61f3

Adventist Hospital – Cebu
Cebu City, Central Visayas, Philippines
⊕ https://vfmat.ch/3f9b

Adventist Medical Center
Pasay, Metro Manila, Philippines
⊕ https://vfmat.ch/nkqe

Ago Medical and Educational Center
Legazpi, Albay, Philippines
⊕ https://vfmat.ch/36a8

Aguinaldo People's Hospital
Aguinaldo, Ifugao, Philippines
⊕ https://vfmat.ch/29a9

Agusan del Norte Provincial Hospital
Butuan City, Agusan del Norte, Philippines
⊕ https://vfmat.ch/d86c

Aisah Medical Hospital
Pagadian City, Zamboanga del Sur, Philippines
⊕ https://vfmat.ch/56a8

Aklan Baptist Hospital
Malay, Aklan, Philippines
⊕ https://vfmat.ch/appe

Albino M. Duran Memorial Hospital
Balangiga, Eastern Samar, Philippines
⊕ https://vfmat.ch/ba39

Albor District Hospital
Libjo, Dinagat Islands, Philippines
⊕ https://vfmat.ch/6cf8

Aleosan District Hospital (ADH)
Alimodian, Iloilo, Philippines
⊕ https://vfmat.ch/5ef7

Alfonso Ponce Enrile Memorial District Hospital
Gonzaga, Cagayan, Philippines
⊕ https://vfmat.ch/45c8

Alfonso Specialist Hospital
Pasig, Metro Manila, Philippines
⊕ https://vfmat.ch/da12

Alfredo E. Marañon, Sr. Memorial District Hospital
Sagay City, Negros Occidental, Philippines
⊕ https://vfmat.ch/8bb3

Allah Valley Medical Specialists' Center, Inc. Hospital
Koronadal City, South Cotabato, Philippines
⊕ https://vfmat.ch/6222

Allegiant Regional Care Hospitals
Lapu-Lapu, Cebu, Philippines
⊕ https://vfmat.ch/cf4a

Allen District Hospital
Allen, Northern Samar, Philippines
⊕ https://vfmat.ch/1443

AM Yumena General Hospital, Inc.
Roxas, Isabela, Philippines
⊕ https://vfmat.ch/11ec

AMOSUP Seamen's Hospital – Intramuros, Manila
Manila, National Capital Region, Philippines
⊕ https://vfmat.ch/8642

AMOSUP Seamen's Hospital – Mandaue City, Cebu
Mandaue, Cebu, Philippines
⊕ https://vfmat.ch/232e

AMOSUP Seamen's Hospital – Iloilo
Iloilo City, Iloilo, Philippines
⊕ https://vfmat.ch/e4ac

Andres Soriano Memorial Hospital Cooperative
Bislig, Surigao del Sur, Philippines
⊕ https://vfmat.ch/7212

Angel Salazar Memorial General Hospital
San Jose de Buenavista, Antique, Philippines
⊕ https://vfmat.ch/8871

Angeles University Foundation Medical Center
Angeles, Pampanga, Philippines
⊕ https://vfmat.ch/bztr

Angono Medics Hospital
Angono, Rizal, Philippines
⊕ https://vfmat.ch/1954

Antipolo City Hospital System Annex 4
Antipolo, Rizal, Philippines
⊕ https://vfmat.ch/8cf1

Antique Medical Center
San Jose, Antique, Philippines
⊕ https://vfmat.ch/3476

Aquino Medical Specialists Hospital Inc.
Tagum, Davao del Norte, Philippines
⊕ https://vfmat.ch/69c5

Army Station Hospital
Tanay, Rizal, Philippines
⊕ https://vfmat.ch/6dfe

Assumption Specialty Hospital and Medical Center
Antipolo, Rizal, Philippines
⊕ https://vfmat.ch/86c9

Atok District Hospital
Atok, Benguet, Philippines
⊕ https://vfmat.ch/c669

Aurora Memorial Hospital
Baler, Aurora, Philippines
⊕ https://vfmat.ch/3c2d

B A Hospital
Meycauan, Bulacan, Philippines
⊕ https://vfmat.ch/2bde

Bacnotan District Hospital
Bacnotan, La Union, Philippines
⊕ https://vfmat.ch/3343

Bacolod Queen of Mercy Hospital
Bacolod, Western Visayas, Philippines
⊕ https://vfmat.ch/5969

Bailan District Hospital
Panitan, Capiz, Philippines
⊕ https://vfmat.ch/aeeb

Ballesteros District Hospital
Ballesteros, Cagayan Valley, Philippines
⊕ https://vfmat.ch/2bf9

Bangui District Hospital
Bangui, Ilocos Norte, Philippines
⊕ https://vfmat.ch/a853

Basa Air Base Hospital
Floridablanca, Pampanga, Philippines
⊕ https://vfmat.ch/77d1

Basilan General Hospital
Isabela., Basilan, Philippines
⊕ https://vfmat.ch/f55c

Bataan Peninsula Medical Center
Dinalupihan, Bataan, Philippines
⊕ https://vfmat.ch/x8tm

Bataan Women's Hospital
Balanga, Bataan, Philippines
⊕ https://vfmat.ch/wf2n

Batanes General Hospital
Basco, Batanes, Philippines
⊕ https://vfmat.ch/e4b2

Batangas Healthcare Hospital – Jesus of Nazareth
Batangas City, Batangas, Philippines
⊕ https://vfmat.ch/e49e

Batangas Medical Center
Batangas City, Batangas, Philippines
⊕ https://vfmat.ch/c789

Bauan General Hospital
Bauan, Batangas, Philippines
⊕ https://vfmat.ch/a9b6

Bautista Hospital Medical Arts Building
Cavite City, Cavite, Philippines
⊕ https://vfmat.ch/b68f

Benguet General Hospital
La Trinidad, Benguet, Philippines
⊕ https://vfmat.ch/cad2

Bermudez Polymedic Hospital
Caloocan, National Capital Region, Philippines
⊕ https://vfmat.ch/7798

Besao District Hospital
Besao, Mountain Province, Philippines
⊕ https://vfmat.ch/4843

Bethany Hospital
San Fernando, La Union, Philippines
⊕ https://vfmat.ch/1111

Bethel Baptist Hospital
Malaybalay, Bukidnon, Philippines
⊕ https://vfmat.ch/f4c5

Bicol Region General Hospital and Geriatric Medical Center
Cabusao, Camarines Sur, Philippines
⊕ https://vfmat.ch/flvn

Bicol Regional Training and Teaching Hospital
Legazpi City, Albay, Philippines
⊕ https://vfmat.ch/8ec1

BICOL Regional Training and Teaching Hospital (BRTTH)
Legazpi City, Albay, Philippines
⊕ https://vfmat.ch/gmvt

Biliran Provincial Hospital
Naval, Biliran, Philippines
⊕ https://vfmat.ch/4988

Bishop Joseph Regan Memorial Hospital
Tagum, Davao del Norte, Philippines
⊕ https://vfmat.ch/8361

Black Nazarene Hospital, Inc, The
San Nicolas, Ilocos Norte, Philippines
⊕ https://vfmat.ch/83c7

Blessed Trinity Hospital
Antipolo, Rizal, Philippines
⊕ https://vfmat.ch/fd5e

Bogo-Medellin Medical Center
Medellin, Cebu, Philippines
⊕ https://vfmat.ch/angc

Bongabon District Hospital
Bongabon, Nueva Ecija, Philippines
⊕ https://vfmat.ch/3767

Bontoc General Hospital
Bontoc, Mountain Province, Philippines
⊕ https://vfmat.ch/e29c

Borbon General Hospital Inc.
Pagadian City, Zamboanga del Sur, Philippines
⊕ https://vfmat.ch/d381

Borja Family Hospital Corporation
Tagbilaran City, Bohol, Philippines
⊕ https://vfmat.ch/vfsp

Bucag Medical Hospital
Cauayan City, Isabela, Philippines
⊕ https://vfmat.ch/b418

Buenavista Emergency Hospital
Buenavista, Guimaras, Philippines
⊕ https://vfmat.ch/2235

Bugallon General Hospital and Dialysis Center
Bugallon, Pangasinan, Philippines
⊕ https://vfmat.ch/43c8

Bukidnon Provincial Hospital
Manolo Fortich, Bukidnon, Philippines
⊕ https://vfmat.ch/a755

Bukidnon Provincial Hospital – Maramag
Maramag, Bukidnon, Philippines
⊕ https://vfmat.ch/9z8y

Bukidnon Provincial Hospital – Talakag
Talakag, Bukidnon, Philippines
⊕ https://vfmat.ch/89bf

Bukidnon Provincial Hospital Malitbog
Malitbog, Bukidnon, Philippines
⊕ https://vfmat.ch/a2b2

Bukidnon Provincial Medical Center
Malaybalay, Bukidnon, Philippines
⊕ https://vfmat.ch/36h8

Bungabong-Sanico Medical Clinic & Maternity Hospital
Santo Tomas, Davao del Norte, Philippines
⊕ https://vfmat.ch/279d

Buruanga Medicare Community Hospital
Buruanga, Aklan, Philippines
⊕ https://vfmat.ch/e92b

C.P. Reyes Hospital
Tanauan, Batangas, Philippines
⊕ https://vfmat.ch/d662

Cabiao General Hospital
Cabiao, Nueva Ecija, Philippines
⊕ https://vfmat.ch/47a1

Cabredo Hospital
Tabaco, Albay, Philippines
⊕ https://vfmat.ch/a67e

Cabuyao City Hospital
Cabuyao, Laguna, Philippines
⊕ https://vfmat.ch/8ec3

Cadiz District Hospital
Cadiz, Western Visayas, Philippines
⊕ https://vfmat.ch/64b5

Cagayan de Oro City Hospital – Tablon
Cagayan de Oro City, Misamis Oriental, Philippines
⊕ https://vfmat.ch/6924

Cagayan De Oro Medical Center Oncology/Cancer Center
Cagayan de Oro, Misamis Oriental, Philippines
⊕ https://vfmat.ch/c7e7

Cagayan de Oro Polymedic General Hospital
Cagayan de Oro, Oriental Mindoro, Philippines
⊕ https://vfmat.ch/t9zv

Cagayan Valley Medical Center
Tuguegarao City, Cagayan, Philippines
⊕ https://vfmat.ch/9f83

Cainglet Medical Hospital, Inc.
Panabo, Davao del Norte, Philippines
⊕ https://vfmat.ch/9448

Cainta Municipal Hospital
Cainta, Rizal, Philippines
⊕ https://vfmat.ch/4962

Calalang General Hospital
Valenzuela City, Metro Manila, Philippines
⊕ https://vfmat.ch/f517

Calauag St. Peter General Hospital
Calauag, Quezon, Philippines
⊕ https://vfmat.ch/e9c6

Calbayog District Hospital
Calbayog, Samar, Philippines
⊕ https://vfmat.ch/7c39

Calumpit District Hospital
Calumpit, Bulacan, Philippines
⊕ https://vfmat.ch/62ae

Camiguin General Hospital
Mambajao, Camiguin, Philippines
⊕ https://vfmat.ch/4fcb

Camp Evangelista Station Hospital, Philippine Army
Cagayan de Oro, Misamis Oriental, Philippines
⊕ https://vfmat.ch/64b7

Camp General Artemio Ricarte Station Hospital, WESCOM, Puerto Princesa
Puerto Princesa, Palawan, Philippines
⊕ https://vfmat.ch/993a

Camp General Emilio Aguinaldo Station Hospital
Quezon City, Metro Manila, Philippines
⊕ https://vfmat.ch/32ac

Camp Navarro General Hospital
Zamboanga City, Zamboanga del Sur, Philippines
⊕ https://vfmat.ch/7d21

Candelaria District Hospital
Candelaria, Zambales, Philippines
⊕ https://vfmat.ch/4e78

Candon General Hospital
Candon, Ilocos Sur, Philippines
⊕ https://vfmat.ch/58c4

Capitol University Medical Center
Cagayan de Oro, Misamis Oriental, Philippines
⊕ https://vfmat.ch/gfd7

Caraga Regional Hospital
Surigao, Surigao del Norte, Philippines
⊕ https://vfmat.ch/6ac3

Caramoan Municipal Hospital
Caramoan, Camarines Sur, Philippines
⊕ https://vfmat.ch/aa2a

Carmelite Hospital
Panabo, Davao del Norte, Philippines
⊕ https://vfmat.ch/26c7

Carmen Copper Corporation Hospital
Toledo City, Cebu, Philippines
⊕ https://vfmat.ch/4572

Cataingan District Hospital
Cataingan, Bicol, Philippines
⊕ https://vfmat.ch/8c3a

Cateel District Hospital
Cateel, Davao Oriental, Philippines
⊕ https://vfmat.ch/8889

Cauayan Medical Specialists Hospital
Cauayan, Isabela, Philippines
⊕ https://vfmat.ch/84ee

Cavite Naval Hospital
Fort San Felipe, Cavite, Philippines
⊕ https://vfmat.ch/36f4

Cebu Doctors' University Hospital
Cebu, Cebu, Philippines
⊕ https://vfmat.ch/d4ae

Cebu North General Hospital
Cebu City, Cebu, Philippines
⊕ https://vfmat.ch/49d6

Cebu Provincial Hospital – Carcar City
Carcar, Cebu, Philippines
⊕ https://vfmat.ch/12c9

Cebu South Medical Center
Talisay, Cebu, Philippines
⊕ https://vfmat.ch/7db8

Cebu Velez General Hospital
Cebu City, Cebu, Philippines
⊕ https://vfmat.ch/wzk7

Cerezo General Hospital
Bani, Pangasinan, Philippines
⊕ https://vfmat.ch/5bbd

Charles W. Selby Memorial Hospital
Aparri, Cagayan, Philippines
⊕ https://vfmat.ch/3318

Chong Hua Hospital – Cebu City
Cebu City, Cebu, Philippines
⊕ https://vfmat.ch/e276

Chong Hua Hospital – Mandaue City
Mandaue City, Cebu, Philippines
⊕ https://vfmat.ch/285e

Christ the King Medical Center Unihealth Las Pinas
Las Pinas City, Metro Manila, Philippines
⊕ https://vfmat.ch/d3e4

Christ the Saviour General Hospital, Inc.
Rosario, Batangas, Philippines
⊕ https://vfmat.ch/a684

Christian General Hospital
Pagsanjan, Laguna, Philippines
⊕ https://vfmat.ch/e8ee

Cicosat Hospital
San Fernando, La Union, Philippines
⊕ https://vfmat.ch/17c7

City of Candon Hospital
Candon, Ilocos Sur, Philippines
⊕ https://vfmat.ch/f11f

Claro M. Recto Memorial Hospital
Infanta, Quezon Province, Philippines
⊕ https://vfmat.ch/ab74

Community Health & Development Cooperative Hospital
Davao City, Davao del Sur, Philippines
⊕ https://vfmat.ch/aurw

Concepcion District Hospital
Concepcion, Tarlac, Philippines
⊕ https://vfmat.ch/52ca

Cong. Lamberto L. Macias Memorial Hospital
Siaton, Negros Oriental, Philippines
⊕ https://vfmat.ch/b5c3

Cong. Simeon G. Toribio Memorial Hospital
Carmen, Bohol, Philippines
⊕ https://vfmat.ch/1e8d

Congressman Enrique M. Cojuangco Memorial District Hospital
Moncada, Tarlac, Philippines
⊕ https://vfmat.ch/245e

Conner District Hospital
Conner, Apayao, Philippines
⊕ https://vfmat.ch/38a3

Corazon Locsin Montelibano Memorial Hospital
Bacolod, Negros Occidental, Philippines
⊕ https://vfmat.ch/acae

Cordillera Hospital of the Divine Grace
La Trinidad, Benguet, Philippines
⊕ https://vfmat.ch/e772

Coron District Hospital
Coron, Palawan, Philippines
⊕ https://vfmat.ch/621e

Cotabato Medical Specialist Hospital
Cotabato City, Maguindanao, Philippines
⊕ https://vfmat.ch/d91b

Cotabato Sanitarium
Sultan Kudarat, Maguindanao, Philippines
⊕ https://vfmat.ch/26f6

Crisostomo General Hospital
Bacoor, Cavite, Philippines
⊕ https://vfmat.ch/e9c9

Cristino M. Paragas Memorial Community Hospital
Zamboanga City, Zamboanga, Philippines
⊕ https://vfmat.ch/48f9

Cruz-Dalida Hospital
Quezon City, Metro Manila, Philippines
⊕ https://vfmat.ch/f4af

Cruz-Rabe Hospital
Taguig, Metro Manila, Philippines
⊕ https://vfmat.ch/e2f1

Culion Sanitarium and General Hospital
Culion, Palawan, Philippines
⊕ https://vfmat.ch/6vnn

Cuyo District Hospital
Cuyo, Palawan, Philippines
⊕ https://vfmat.ch/5b37

Daanbantayan District Hospital
Daanbantayan, Cebu, Philippines
⊕ https://vfmat.ch/35ba

DAET Doctors Hospital Incorporated
Daet, Camarines Norte, Philippines
⊕ https://vfmat.ch/2b69

Dagupan Orthopedic Center
Dagupan, Pangasinan, Philippines
⊕ https://vfmat.ch/b31d

Datu Halun Sakilan Memorial Hospital
Bongao, Tawi-Tawi, Philippines
⊕ https://vfmat.ch/623e

Davao del Sur Provincial Hospital
Digos City, Davao del Sur, Philippines
⊕ https://vfmat.ch/d342

Davao Doctors Hospital
Davao City, Davao del Sur, Philippines
⊕ https://vfmat.ch/a57p

Davao Oriental Provincial Hospital – Manay
Manay, Davao, Philippines
⊕ https://vfmat.ch/d965

De Jesus General Hospital
Baliuag, Bulacan, Philippines
⊕ https://vfmat.ch/c2e5

De La Salle University Medical Center
Dasmariñas, Cavite, Philippines
⊕ https://vfmat.ch/41iu

De La Salle University Poblete Memorial Hospital
Alfonso, Cavite, Philippines
⊕ https://vfmat.ch/4be1

De Los Santos Medical Center
Quezon City, Metro Manila, Philippines
⊕ https://vfmat.ch/izfx

Decena General Hospital
Dagupan, Pangasinan, Philippines
⊕ https://vfmat.ch/5e21

Del Carmen Medical Clinic and Hospital Inc.
Rosales, Pangasinan, Philippines
⊕ https://vfmat.ch/b134

Delfin Albano Memorial Hospital
Delfin Albano, Isabela, Philippines
⊕ https://vfmat.ch/9a26

Dignum Foundation Hospital
Oroquieta City, Misamis Occidental, Philippines
⊕ https://vfmat.ch/b1bf

Dinalupihan District Hospital
Dinalupihan, Bataan, Philippines
⊕ https://vfmat.ch/ee32

Diosdado P. Macapagal Memorial Hospital
Guagua, Pampanga, Philippines
⊕ https://vfmat.ch/4248

Divine Love Medical Center
Lipa, Batangas, Philippines
⊕ https://vfmat.ch/cd2e

Divine Mercy Hospital Bamban
Bamban, Tarlac, Philippines
⊕ https://vfmat.ch/b9a4

Divine Mercy Hospital San Pedro
San Pedro, Laguna, Philippines
⊕ https://vfmat.ch/cd5e

Divine Word Hospital – St. Paul's Hospital
Tacloban City, Leyte, Philippines
⊕ https://vfmat.ch/3f41

Divine Word Hospital Hagonoy
Hagonoy, Bulacan, Philippines
⊕ https://vfmat.ch/9f2d

Domingo Tamondong Memorial Hospital
Esperanza, Sultan Kudarat, Philippines
⊕ https://vfmat.ch/f321

Dominican Hospital
Digos, Davao del Sur, Philippines
⊕ https://vfmat.ch/bd6f

Don Emilio Del Valle Memorial Hospital
Ubay, Bohol, Philippines
⊕ https://vfmat.ch/b28b

Don Salvador Benedicto Memorial District Hospital
La Carlota City, Negros Occidental, Philippines
⊕ https://vfmat.ch/1981

Doña Josefa Edralin Marcos District Hospital
Marcos, Ilocos Norte, Philippines
⊕ https://vfmat.ch/5839

Dr. A.P. Zantua Memorial Hospital
Virac, Catanduanes, Philippines
⊕ https://vfmat.ch/e2eb

Dr. Abdullah Hospital
Marawi City, Lanao del Sur, Philippines
⊕ https://vfmat.ch/354f

Dr. Amado B. Diaz Foundation Provincial Hospital
Midsayap, North Cotabato, Philippines
⊕ https://vfmat.ch/5682

Dr. Amando L Garcia Medical Center, Inc
Angeles City, Philippines
⊕ https://vfmat.ch/4fe6

Dr. Andres J. Luciano District Hospital
Magalang, Pampanga, Philippines
⊕ https://vfmat.ch/12ec

Dr. Apollo Duque Memorial Hospital
Cabiao, Nueva Ecija, Philippines
⊕ https://vfmat.ch/48b6

Dr. Catalino Gallego Nava Provincial Hospital
Jordan, Guimaras, Philippines
⊕ https://vfmat.ch/7a1c

Dr. Damian Reyes Provincial Hospital
Boac, Marinduque, Philippines
⊕ https://vfmat.ch/e8cc

Dr. Domingo B. Tamondong Memorial Hospital and College Foundation, Inc.
Banga, South Cotabato, Philippines
⊕ https://vfmat.ch/9cf9

Dr. Eduardo V. Roquero Memorial Hospital
San Jose del Monte City, Bulacan, Philippines
⊕ https://vfmat.ch/2669

Dr. Emigdio C Cruz Sr. Memorial Hospital
Arayat, Pampanga, Philippines
⊕ https://vfmat.ch/4211

Dr. Ester R. Garcia Medical Center
Cauayan City, Cagayan Valley, Philippines
⊕ https://vfmat.ch/23cb

Dr. Fernando B. Duran Sr. Memorial Hospital
Sorsogon City, Sorsogon, Philippines
⊕ https://vfmat.ch/32a7

Dr. Gloria D. Lacson General Hospital
San Leonardo, Nueva Ecija, Philippines
⊕ https://vfmat.ch/6d77

Dr. Ildefonso Alcantara Memorial Hospital
Dalaguete, Cebu, Philippines
⊕ https://vfmat.ch/cd45

Dr. Jorge P. Royeca Hospital
General Santos City, South Cotabato, Philippines
⊕ https://vfmat.ch/89e7

Dr. Jose Fabella Memorial Hospital
Manila, National Capital Region, Philippines
⊕ https://vfmat.ch/6c7b

Dr. Jose N. Rodriguez Memorial Hospital and Sanitarium
Caloocan, Metro Manila, Philippines
⊕ https://vfmat.ch/5258

Dr. Jose Rizal District Hospital
Rizal, Palawan, Philippines
⊕ https://vfmat.ch/4a78

Dr. Jose Rizal Memorial Hospital
Dapitan City, Zamboanga del Norte, Philippines
⊕ https://vfmat.ch/3a67

Dr. Lito De Luna Belarmino Medical Hospital
Dimasalang, Masbate, Philippines
⊕ https://vfmat.ch/f9a3

Dr. Montano G. Ramos General Hospital
Quezon City, Metro Manila, Philippines
⊕ https://vfmat.ch/f7f8

Dr. Nilo O. Roa Memorial Foundation Hospital
Naga City, Camarines Sur, Philippines
⊕ https://vfmat.ch/ba48

Dr. Peralta Hospital
Plaridel, Bulacan, Philippines
⊕ https://vfmat.ch/8c81

Dr. R. Rosales Memorial Medical Hospital. Inc.
Padre Garcia, Batangas, Philippines
⊕ https://vfmat.ch/633b

Dr. Rafael S. Tumbokon Memorial Hospital
Kalibo, Aklan, Philippines
⊕ https://vfmat.ch/88a6

Dr. Ricardo Y. Ladrido Memorial District Hospital
Lambunao, Iloilo, Philippines
⊕ https://vfmat.ch/3524

Dr. Robosa Hospital
Baao, Camarines Sur, Philippines
⊕ https://vfmat.ch/b6d8

Dr. Romeo Isana Rosales General Hospital
Batangas, Batangas, Philippines
⊕ https://vfmat.ch/7244

Dr. Tomas L. Nolasco Sr. Memorial Hospital
Gattaran, Cagayan, Philippines
⊕ https://vfmat.ch/825d

Dr. Uy Hospital, Inc.
Iligan City, Lanao del Norte, Philippines
⊕ https://vfmat.ch/c89a

Dr. Wilfredo G. Cortez Hospital
Arayat, Pampanga, Philippines
⊕ https://vfmat.ch/e69c

Dr. Yanga General Hospital
Bocaue, Bulacan, Philippines
⊕ https://vfmat.ch/d723

Dulag Rural Health Unit And Municipal Infirmary
Dulag, Leyte, Philippines
⊕ https://vfmat.ch/fba7

Dumlao Hospital
Roxas, Isabela, Philippines
⊕ https://vfmat.ch/9545

Dupax District Hospital DDH
Dupax del Norte, Nueva Vizcaya, Philippines
⊕ https://vfmat.ch/c6c8

Duque General Hospital
San Juan, Batangas, Philippines
⊕ https://vfmat.ch/38bf

E.R Elumba Clinic
La Castellana, Negros Occidental, Philippines
⊕ https://vfmat.ch/cc69

East Avenue Medical Center
Quezon City, Metro Manila, Philippines
⊕ https://vfmat.ch/ntfu

Eastern Laguna Medical Hospital
Famy, Laguna, Philippines
⊕ https://vfmat.ch/db93

Eastern Pangasinan District Hospital
Tayug, Pangasinan, Philippines
⊕ https://vfmat.ch/5371

Eastern Visayas Regional Medical Center (EVRMC)
Tacloban City, Leyte, Philippines
⊕ https://vfmat.ch/f827

Eduardo L. Joson Memorial Hospital
Cabanatuan, Nueva Ecija, Philippines
⊕ https://vfmat.ch/6f26

Edwin Andrews Air Base Hospital
Zamboanga, Zamboanga del Sur, Philippines
⊕ https://vfmat.ch/a3bd

Eleuterio T. Decena Memorial Hospital
Hinoba-an, Negros Occidental, Philippines
⊕ https://vfmat.ch/61a2

Elguira General Hospital
San Carlos City, Pangasinan, Philippines
⊕ https://vfmat.ch/7d72

Emergency Hospital Lamitan City Basin
Lamitan City, Basilan, Philippines
⊕ https://vfmat.ch/eda7

Emilio G. Perez Memorial District Hospital
Hagonoy, Bulacan, Philippines
⊕ https://vfmat.ch/d49d

Emmanuel Hospital
San Miguel, Bulacan, Philippines
⊕ https://vfmat.ch/88fd

Englewood Hospital
Tagbilaran City, Bohol, Philippines
⊕ https://vfmat.ch/86b5

Escolastica Romero District Hospital
Lubao, Pampanga, Philippines
⊕ https://vfmat.ch/81a8

Esperanza Medicare Community Hospital
Esperanza, Agusan del Sur, Philippines
⊕ https://vfmat.ch/9df8

Estevez Memorial Hospital
Legazpi City, Albay, Philippines
⊕ https://vfmat.ch/hrwb

Estrella Hospital
Silang, Cavite, Philippines
⊕ https://vfmat.ch/3ff8

Fatima University Medical Center
Valenzuela, Metro Manila, Philippines
⊕ https://vfmat.ch/zfas

Federico Ramon Tirador Sr. Memorial District Hospital
Jibolo, Iloilo, Philippines
⊕ https://vfmat.ch/8f7c

Fernando Air Base Hospital
Lipa City, Batangas, Philippines
⊕ https://vfmat.ch/e329

Flora District Hospital
Flora, Apayao, Philippines
⊕ https://vfmat.ch/1769

Fort Bonifacio General Hospital Philippine Army
Taguig City, Metro Manila, Philippines
⊕ https://vfmat.ch/fa61

Fort Del Pilar Station Hospital
Baguio, Benguet, Philippines
⊕ https://vfmat.ch/7365

Gabriela Silang General Hospital
Vigan, Ilocos, Philippines
⊕ https://vfmat.ch/e8c9

Gamez Hospital
Calamba, Laguna, Philippines
⊕ https://vfmat.ch/5ce2

Gaoat General Hospital
Batac City, Ilocos Norte, Philippines
⊕ https://vfmat.ch/d378

Gapan District Hospital
Gapan City, Nueva Ecija, Philippines
⊕ https://vfmat.ch/a139

Garcia General Hospital
Marikina City, Metro Manila, Philippines
⊕ https://vfmat.ch/377e

Gen. J. Cailles Memorial District Hospital
Pakil, Laguna, Philippines
⊕ https://vfmat.ch/2dc6

General Emilio Aguinaldo Memorial Hospital
Trece Martires, Cavite, Philippines
⊕ https://vfmat.ch/3ca7

General Malvar Hospital
Quezon City, Metro Manila, Philippines
⊕ https://vfmat.ch/ebeb

Gerona Hospital of the Sacred Heart
Gerona, Tarlac, Philippines
⊕ https://vfmat.ch/6da5

Gigaquit District Hospital
Gigaquit, Surigao del Norte, Philippines
⊕ https://vfmat.ch/f7f6

God's Will Medical Hospital
Cauayan City, Isabela, Philippines
⊕ https://vfmat.ch/d52a

Gonzales General Hospital
San Leonardo, Nueva Ecija, Philippines
⊕ https://vfmat.ch/3b5f

Gonzales-Maranan Memorial Hospital
Digos City, Davao del Sur, Philippines
⊕ https://vfmat.ch/2fa4

Good News Clinic And Hospital
Banaue, Ifugao, Philippines
⊕ https://vfmat.ch/38c5

GoodSam Medical Center
Cabanatuan, Nueva Ecija, Philippines
⊕ https://vfmat.ch/25df

Gov. Faustino M. Dy Sr. Memorial Hospital
Ilagan, Isabela, Philippines
⊕ https://vfmat.ch/a4c4

Gov. Valeriano M. Gatuslao Memorial Hospital
Himamaylan, Negros Occidental, Philippines
⊕ https://vfmat.ch/4f4d

Governor Celestino Gallares Memorial Hospital
Tagbilaran, Bohol, Philippines
⊕ https://vfmat.ch/8586

Governor Roque B. Ablan Sr. Memorial Hospital
Laoag City, Ilocos Norte, Philippines
⊕ https://vfmat.ch/9b6b

Governor William Billy V. Villegas Memorial Hospital
Guihulngan, Negros Oriental, Philippines
⊕ https://vfmat.ch/26de

Grace General Hospital
San Jose del Monte City, Bulacan, Philippines
⊕ https://vfmat.ch/298a

Grace Mission Hospital
Socorro, Oriental Mindoro, Philippines
⊕ https://vfmat.ch/27f4

Gregorio del Pilar District Hospital
Bulakan, Bulacan, Philippines
⊕ https://vfmat.ch/99e3

Guimba District Hospital
Guimba, Nueva Ecija, Philippines
⊕ https://vfmat.ch/5978

Gumaca District Hospital
Gumaca, Quezon, Philippines
⊕ https://vfmat.ch/9465

H Vill Hospital
Managgahan Rodriguez, Rizal, Philippines
⊕ https://vfmat.ch/2c51

Health Centrum Hospital, The
Roxas, Capiz, Philippines
⊕ https://vfmat.ch/e358

Heart of Jesus Hospital
San Jose, Nueva Ecija, Philippines
⊕ https://vfmat.ch/559c

Hilongos District Hospital
Hilongos, Leyte, Philippines
⊕ https://vfmat.ch/479e

Hinatuan District Hospital
Hinatuan, Surigao del Sur, Philippines
⊕ https://vfmat.ch/8d3e

Holy Child Hospital
Dumaguete, Negros Oriental, Philippines
⊕ https://vfmat.ch/d626

Holy Infant Hospital
Tuguegarao, Cagayan, Philippines
⊕ https://vfmat.ch/54b8

Holy Rosary of Cabuyao Hospital
Cabuyao, Laguna, Philippines
⊕ https://vfmat.ch/5288

Holy Spirit Community Hospital of Davao, Inc.
Davao City, Davao, Philippines
⊕ https://vfmat.ch/94a9

Holy Trinity General Hospital
Arayat, Pampanga, Philippines
⊕ https://vfmat.ch/8e65

Hospital de Zamboanga
Zamboanga, Zamboanga del Sur, Philippines
⊕ https://vfmat.ch/2b49

Howard Hubbard Memorial Hospital
Polomolok, South Cotabato, Philippines
⊕ https://vfmat.ch/9d39

Ibajay District Hospital
Ibajay, Aklan, Philippines
⊕ https://vfmat.ch/2563

Ilocos Sur District Hospital – Magsingal
Magsingal, Ilocos Sur, Philippines
⊕ https://vfmat.ch/8ca5

Iloilo Mission Hospital
Iloilo City, Iloilo, Philippines
⊕ https://vfmat.ch/4177

Iloilo Provincial Hospital
Pototan, Iloilo, Philippines
⊕ https://vfmat.ch/963b

Immaculate Heart Of Mary Hospital
Virac, Catanduanes, Philippines
⊕ https://vfmat.ch/87d7

Infante Hospital
Isabela City, Basilan, Philippines
⊕ https://vfmat.ch/b4ff

Irosin District Hospital
Irosin, Sorsogon, Philippines
⊕ https://vfmat.ch/58e7

Isabela South Specialists Hospital Inc.
Echague, Isabela, Philippines
⊕ https://vfmat.ch/47aa

Isidro C. Kintanar Memorial Hospital
Argao, Cebu, Philippines
⊕ https://vfmat.ch/4f3f

Itogon District Hospital
Itogon, Benguet, Philippines
⊕ https://vfmat.ch/e874

J. P. Sioson General Hospital & Colleges, Inc.
Quezon City, Metro Manila, Philippines
⊕ https://vfmat.ch/7cc1

J.R. Borja General Hospital
Cagayan de Oro, Misamis Oriental, Philippines
⊕ https://vfmat.ch/56b9

Jaime B. Berces Memorial Hospital
Tabaco, Albay, Philippines
⊕ https://vfmat.ch/ff71

James L. Gordon Memorial Hospital
Olongapo City, Zambales, Philippines
⊕ https://vfmat.ch/1136

Jane County Hospital, Inc.
Pagbilao, Quezon, Philippines
⊕ https://vfmat.ch/2bd4

Jesus Nazarene General Hospital
Lingayen, Pangasinan, Philippines
⊕ https://vfmat.ch/54c1

Jesus the Good Shepherd Hospital
Pulilan, Bulacan, Philippines
⊕ https://vfmat.ch/95cb

Jesus The Saviour Hospital Inc.
Santa Cruz, Laguna, Philippines
⊕ https://vfmat.ch/a1a5

Jose B. Lingad Memorial Regional Hospital
San Fernando, San Fernando, Philippines
⊕ https://vfmat.ch/952d

Jose J. Golingay General Hospital Inc.
Malalag, Davao del Sur, Philippines
⊕ https://vfmat.ch/2948

Jose S. Lapid District Hospital
Porac, Pampanga, Philippines
⊕ https://vfmat.ch/121b

Josefina Belmonte Duran Memorial Hospital
Ligao, Albay, Philippines
⊕ https://vfmat.ch/1a6d

Juan S. Alano Hospital
Isabela City, Basilan, Philippines
⊕ https://vfmat.ch/25ad

Judge Celestino Guerrero Memorial Hospital
Santa Maria, Ilocos Sur, Philippines
⊕ https://vfmat.ch/9626

Julio Cardinal Rosales Hospital
Dalaguete, Cebu, Philippines
⊕ https://vfmat.ch/54de

Justice Calixto O. Zaldivar Memorial Hospital (formerly Gov. Leandro Fullon District Hospital)
Antique, Western Visayas, Philippines
⊕ https://vfmat.ch/eeff

Justice Jose Abad Santos General Hospital
Manila, Metro Manila, Philippines
⊕ https://vfmat.ch/f2cf

Kalinga Provincial Hospital-KPH
Kalinga, Cordillera, Philippines
⊕ https://vfmat.ch/ce71

Kapalong District Hospital
Kapalong, Davao del Norte, Philippines
⊕ https://vfmat.ch/693c

Kauswagan Provincial Hospital
Kauswagan, Lanao del Norte, Philippines
⊕ https://vfmat.ch/82fc

Kawit Kalayaan Hospital
Kawit, Cavite, Philippines
🌐 https://vfmat.ch/5cb5

Kidapawan City Hospital
Kidapawan, North Cotabato, Philippines
🌐 https://vfmat.ch/6c34

Kidapawan Medical Specialist Center, Inc.
Kidapawan, Cotabato, Philippines
🌐 https://vfmat.ch/a214

Kolambugan Provincial Hospital
Kolambugan, Lanao del Norte, Philippines
🌐 https://vfmat.ch/1231

La Consolacion University General Hospital
Plaridel, Bulacan, Philippines
🌐 https://vfmat.ch/f26e

La Union Medical Diagnostic Center & Hospital
San Fernando, La Union, Philippines
🌐 https://vfmat.ch/212d

Labason District Hospital
Labason, Zamboanga del Norte, Philippines
🌐 https://vfmat.ch/9383

Labo District Hospital
Talobatib, Camarines Norte, Philippines
🌐 https://vfmat.ch/114c

Lahoz Clinic and Hospital
Vigan City, Ilocos Sur, Philippines
🌐 https://vfmat.ch/925b

Lanao del Norte Provincial Hospital
Baroy, Lanao del Norte, Philippines
🌐 https://vfmat.ch/e185

Languyan Municipal Hospital
Languyan, Tawi Tawi, Philippines
🌐 https://vfmat.ch/b14f

Laoag City General Hospital
Laoag City, Ilocos Norte, Philippines
🌐 https://vfmat.ch/b3eb

Laoag Pediatric Hospital
Laoag City, Ilocos Norte, Philippines
🌐 https://vfmat.ch/2daf

Las Nieves Municipal Hospital
Las Nieves, Agusan del Norte, Philippines
🌐 https://vfmat.ch/5c65

Las Piñas City Medical Center
Las Pinas, Metro Manila, Philippines
🌐 https://vfmat.ch/u4f6

Las Piñas General Hospital & Satellite Trauma Center
Manila, Calabarzon, Philippines
🌐 https://vfmat.ch/8ebe

Laurel Memorial District Hospital
Tanauan, Batangas, Philippines
🌐 https://vfmat.ch/fd32

Leona O. Lim Memorial Hospital
Valencia, Bohol, Philippines
🌐 https://vfmat.ch/9e51

Leonardo B Manabat Sr. Hospital, Inc.
Santo Tomas, Pampanga, Philippines
🌐 https://vfmat.ch/6445

Leyte Baptist Hospital
Hilongos, Northern Leyte, Philippines
🌐 https://vfmat.ch/29ul

Leyte Provincial Hospital
Palo, Leyte, Philippines
🌐 https://vfmat.ch/7c83

Lipa City District Hospital
Lipa City, Batangas, Philippines
🌐 https://vfmat.ch/5717

Lipa Hospital
Lipa, Batangas, Philippines
🌐 https://vfmat.ch/2bfa

Living Hope Hospital
Maasin, Southern Leyte, Philippines
🌐 https://vfmat.ch/bd75

Llorente Municipal Hospital
Llorente, Eastern Samar, Philippines
🌐 https://vfmat.ch/974b

Lord's Hospital, The
Meycauayan, Bulacan, Philippines
🌐 https://vfmat.ch/ab92

Lorenzo D Zayco District Hospital
Kabankalan, Negros Occidental, Philippines
🌐 https://vfmat.ch/b4ac

Lourdes Hospital
Iriga City, Camarines Sur, Philippines
🌐 https://vfmat.ch/dd84

Loving Mother General Hospital and Diagnostic Center
Tarlac City, Tarlac, Philippines
🌐 https://vfmat.ch/e2d6

Lucas-Paguila Medical Hospital, Inc.
Alicia, Isabela, Philippines
🌐 https://vfmat.ch/aa92

Lucban MMG Hospital
Lucban, Quezon Province, Philippines
🌐 https://vfmat.ch/6eb7

Lucena MMG General Hospital
Lucena, Quezon, Philippines
🌐 https://vfmat.ch/e711

Luis Hora Memorial Hospital
Bauko, Mountain Province, Philippines
🌐 https://vfmat.ch/b8c1

Lyceum of Aparri Hospital
Aparri, Cagayan, Philippines
🌐 https://vfmat.ch/9b87

M. Napeñas Multi-Specialty Hospital
Concepcion, Tarlac, Philippines
🌐 https://vfmat.ch/35eb

Maasim Municipal Hospital
Maasim, Sarangani, Philippines
🌐 https://vfmat.ch/cf36

Maasin Maternity and Children Hospital
Maasin City, Southern Leyte, Philippines
🌐 https://vfmat.ch/da3d

Mabalacat District Hospital
Mabalacat, Pampanga, Philippines
🌐 https://vfmat.ch/2cc2

Mabini Community Hospital
Mabini, Batangas, Philippines
🌐 https://vfmat.ch/16c2

Macabebe District Hospital
Macabebe, Pampanga, Philippines
🌐 https://vfmat.ch/6fc2

Madalag Hospital
Madalag, Western Visayas, Philippines
🌐 https://vfmat.ch/1286

Madonna and Child Hospital
Cagayan de Oro, Misamis Oriental, Philippines
🌐 https://vfmat.ch/7cdd

Madonna General Hospital
Kidapawan, North Cotabato, Philippines
🌐 https://vfmat.ch/8c5e

Maguindanao Provincial Hospital
Shariff Aguak, Maguindanao, Philippines
🌐 https://vfmat.ch/46c5

Maitum Municipal Hospital
Maitum, Sarangani, Philippines
🌐 https://vfmat.ch/d376

Makilala Midway Hospital
Makilala, North Cotabato, Philippines
🌐 https://vfmat.ch/a598

Malaybalay Medical Hospital Care
Malaybalay, Bukidnon, Philippines
⊕ https://vfmat.ch/64fe

Malaybalay Polymedic General Hospital Incorporated
Malaybalay, Bukidnon, Philippines
⊕ https://vfmat.ch/a392

Malolos EENT Hospital
Bulacan, Central Luzon, Philippines
⊕ https://vfmat.ch/3797

Malolos San Vicente Hospital
Caniogan, Malolos, Philippines
⊕ https://vfmat.ch/a353

Malungon Municipal Hospital
Malungon, Sarangani, Philippines
⊕ https://vfmat.ch/af2c

Mama Rachel Hospital of Mercy Inc.
General Trias, Cavite, Philippines
⊕ https://vfmat.ch/7386

Mambusao District Hospital
Mambusao, Capiz, Philippines
⊕ https://vfmat.ch/2d3b

Mandaue City Hospital
Mandaue, Central Visayas, Philippines
⊕ https://vfmat.ch/f193

Manila Central University (MCU) Hospital – Filemon D. Tanchoco Sr. Medical Foundation
Caloocan, National Capital Region, Philippines
⊕ https://vfmat.ch/ebea

Manito Municipal Hospital
Manito, Albay, Philippines
⊕ https://vfmat.ch/e973

Manuel A. Roxas District Hospital
Roxas, Isabela, Philippines
⊕ https://vfmat.ch/eaef

Manuel Hospital
Kidapawan City, Cotabato, Philippines
⊕ https://vfmat.ch/255d

Manuel J. Santos Hospital
Butuan City, Agusan del Norte, Philippines
⊕ https://vfmat.ch/fffc

Manuel V. Gallego Cabanatuan City General Hospital
Cabanatuan City, Nueva Ecija, Philippines
⊕ https://vfmat.ch/db53

Marcelo – Padilla Hospital
Plaridel, Bulacan, Philippines
⊕ https://vfmat.ch/478e

Marcelo Hospital of Baliwag, Inc.
Baliuag, Bulacan, Philippines
⊕ https://vfmat.ch/5aa7

Margosatubig Regional Hospital
Margosatubig, Zamboanga del Sur, Philippines
⊕ https://vfmat.ch/9e6b

Maria Estrella General Hospital
Calapan, Oriental Mindoro, Philippines
⊕ https://vfmat.ch/2dcf

Maria L. Eleazar Memorial General Hospital
Tagkawayan, Quezon, Philippines
⊕ https://vfmat.ch/817a

Maria Reyna Hospital
Cagayan de Oro, Northern Mindanao, Philippines
⊕ https://vfmat.ch/5cc3

Marian Hospital of Sta. Rosa, Inc.
Sta. Rosa, Laguna, Philippines
⊕ https://vfmat.ch/767f

Marilao Saint Michael Family Hospital, Inc.
Marilao, Bulacan, Philippines
⊕ https://vfmat.ch/781b

Marilog District Hospital
Davao, Davao del Sur, Philippines
⊕ https://vfmat.ch/3e9d

Mariveles District Hospital
Mariveles, Bataan, Philippines
⊕ https://vfmat.ch/825c

Martinez Memorial Hospital
Caloocan, Metro Manila, Philippines
⊕ https://vfmat.ch/99a8

Mary Johnston Hospital
Manila, National Capital Region, Philippines
⊕ https://vfmat.ch/61df

Mary Mediatrix Medical Center
Lipa, Batangas, Philippines
⊕ https://vfmat.ch/kz2y

Marymount Hospital
Meycauayan, Bulacan, Philippines
⊕ https://vfmat.ch/7dcc

Mateo-Mabborang General Hospital
Hagonoy, Bulacan, Philippines
⊕ https://vfmat.ch/455d

Matilde A. Olivas District Hospital
Camalaniugan, Cagayan Valley, Philippines
⊕ https://vfmat.ch/aa75

Mayor Hilarion A. Ramiro Sr. Medical Center – MHARSMC
Ozamiz City, Misamis Occidental, Philippines
⊕ https://vfmat.ch/b9ea

Mayoyao District Hospital
Mayoyao, Ifugao, Philippines
⊕ https://vfmat.ch/1df3

MCU Hospital Dr. Filemon D. Tanchoco, Sr. Medical Foundation Inc.
Caloocan, Metro Manila, Philippines
⊕ https://vfmat.ch/2b93

Medical Center IMUS
Imus, Cavite, Philippines
⊕ https://vfmat.ch/31ad

Medical City, The
Pasig, Metro Manila, Philippines
⊕ https://vfmat.ch/7f99

Medical City Clark, The – Ambulatory Surgical Center
Clark Freeport Zone, Pampanga, Philippines
⊕ https://vfmat.ch/19d1

Medical City Clark, The – Hospital
Clark, Pampanga, Philippines
⊕ https://vfmat.ch/31a5

Medical City, The – Iloilo
Iloilo, Iloilo, Philippines
⊕ https://vfmat.ch/9fa2

Medical City, The – Pangasinan
Dagupan, Pangasinan, Philippines
⊕ https://vfmat.ch/aeca

Medical City, The – South Luzon
L United Blvd, Don Jose, Laguna, Philippines
⊕ https://vfmat.ch/a47e

Medical Mission Group Hospital
Davao City, Davao del Sur, Philippines
⊕ https://vfmat.ch/ab13

Medical Mission Group Hospital & Health Services Cooperative of Bohol
Tagbilaran, Bohol, Philippines
⊕ https://vfmat.ch/9e25

Medical Mission Group Hospital & Health Services Cooperative of Tacurong
Tacurong City, Sultan Kudarat, Philippines
⊕ https://vfmat.ch/1def

Medina General Hospital
Ozamis City, Misamis Occidental, Philippines
⊕ https://vfmat.ch/2ea1

Mendero Medical Center
Consolacion, Cebu, Philippines
⊕ https://vfmat.ch/bpdw

Metro Antipolo Hospital and Medical Center
Antipolo, Rizal, Philippines
⊕ https://vfmat.ch/72fe

Metro Vigan Cooperative Hospital
Bantay, Ilocos Sur, Philippines
⊕ https://vfmat.ch/6b37

Mindanao Medical Center Inc.
General Santos City, Philippines
⊕ https://vfmat.ch/23mm

Mindanao Sanitarium Hospital
Iligan City, Lanao del Norte, Philippines
⊕ https://vfmat.ch/f25a

Misamis Oriental Provincial Hospital – Initao
Initao, Misamis Oriental, Philippines
⊕ https://vfmat.ch/eeda

Misamis Oriental Provincial Hospital- Gingoog
Gingoog City, Misamis Oriental, Philippines
⊕ https://vfmat.ch/2fed

Mission Hospital
Pasig, Metro Manila, Philippines
⊕ https://vfmat.ch/1c24

MMG-PPC Cooperative Hospital
Puerto Princesa, Palawan, Philippines
⊕ https://vfmat.ch/dbe2

MMH Thyroid Center
T'boli, South Cotabato, Philippines
⊕ https://vfmat.ch/1e3e

Moorehouse Mission Hospital (formerly Tboli Evangelical Clinic and Hospital)
T'Boli, South Cotabato, Philippines
⊕ https://vfmat.ch/9emu

Mother and Child General Hospital
Olongapo, Zambales, Philippines
⊕ https://vfmat.ch/7d34

Mt. Carmel Medical Center
Bocaue, Bulacan, Philippines
⊕ https://vfmat.ch/195e

MVM Sto. Rosario District Hospital
Rosario, Batangas, Philippines
⊕ https://vfmat.ch/a933

Naga City Hospital
Naga City, Camarines Sur, Philippines
⊕ https://vfmat.ch/7882

Nagcarlan District Hospital
Nagcarlan, Laguna, Philippines
⊕ https://vfmat.ch/a9b3

Naguilian District Hospital
Naguilian, La Union, Philippines
⊕ https://vfmat.ch/4f72

National Kidney and Transplant Institute
Quezon City, Metro Manila, Philippines
⊕ https://vfmat.ch/d287

Navotas City Hospital
Navotas City, Metro Manila, Philippines
⊕ https://vfmat.ch/c7e8

Nazarenus College and Hospital Foundation Inc.
Meycauayan, Bulacan, Philippines
⊕ https://vfmat.ch/cb89

Nazareth General Hospital
Dagupan, Pangasinan, Philippines
⊕ https://vfmat.ch/7399

Negros Oriental Provincial Hospital
Dumaguete City, Negros Oriental, Philippines
⊕ https://vfmat.ch/2aef

Neopolitan General Hospital
Quezon City, Metro Manila, Philippines
⊕ https://vfmat.ch/5734

New Bayugan Medical Hospital
Bayugan, Agusan del Sur, Philippines
⊕ https://vfmat.ch/d3d4

New Era General Hospital
Quezon City, Metro Manila, Philippines
⊕ https://vfmat.ch/ece2

New Sinai MDI Hospital
Sta. Rosa, Laguna, Philippines
⊕ https://vfmat.ch/c635

New Sultan Kudarat Provincial Hospital
Isulan, Sultan Kudarat, Philippines
⊕ https://vfmat.ch/136d

NLAH – Northern Luzon Adventist Hospital
Sison, Pangasinan, Philippines
⊕ https://vfmat.ch/54aa

Nodado General Hospital
Caloocan, Metro Manila, Philippines
⊕ https://vfmat.ch/55ed

Northern Benguet District Hospital
Buguias, Benguet, Philippines
⊕ https://vfmat.ch/2424

Northern Mindanao Medical Center
Cagayan de Oro, Misamis Oriental, Philippines
⊕ https://vfmat.ch/6upe

Northern Palawan Provincial Hospital
Taytay, Palawan, Philippines
⊕ https://vfmat.ch/7cb8

Northern Samar Provincial Hospital
Catamaran, Nothern Samar, Philippines
⊕ https://vfmat.ch/f1cb

Notre Dame Hospital
Cotabato City, Maguindanao, Philippines
⊕ https://vfmat.ch/7df1

Nuestra Señora de Piat District Hospital
Piat, Cagayan, Philippines
⊕ https://vfmat.ch/a856

Nueva Vizcaya Medical Mission Group Hospital, Inc.
Solano, Nueva Vizcaya, Philippines
⊕ https://vfmat.ch/19b6

Nueva Vizcaya Provincial Hospital
Bambang, Nueva Vizcaya, Philippines
⊕ https://vfmat.ch/c35c

Olegario General Hospital
Clarin, Misamis Occidental, Philippines
⊕ https://vfmat.ch/a7fb

Olivarez General Hospital
Parañaque City, Metro Manila, Philippines
⊕ https://vfmat.ch/fba4

Orani District Hospital
Orani, Bataan, Philippines
⊕ https://vfmat.ch/4cc7

Ordoñez Medical Hospital
Villasis, Pangasinan, Philippines
⊕ https://vfmat.ch/2411

Oriental Mindoro Provincial Hospital
Calapan, Oriental Mindoro, Philippines
⊕ https://vfmat.ch/5c8d

Ospital ng Baras
Baras, Rizal, Philippines
⊕ https://vfmat.ch/5e58

Ospital ng Calaca
Calaca, Batangas, Philippines
⊕ https://vfmat.ch/641b

Ospital Ng Guiguinto
Guiguinto, Bulacan, Philippines
⊕ https://vfmat.ch/ec9d

Ospital ng Imus
Imus, Cavite, Philippines
⊕ https://vfmat.ch/a99b

Ospital ng Kabataan ng DIpolog, Inc.
Dipolog City, Zamboanga del Norte, Philippines
⊕ https://vfmat.ch/9461

Ospital ng Lungsod ng San Jose del Monte (OLSJDM) (also known as San Jose Del Monte General Hospital)
San Jose del Monte City, Bulacan, Philippines
⊕ https://vfmat.ch/565a

Ospital ng Makati
Makati, Metro Manila, Philippines
⊕ https://vfmat.ch/ab9b

Ospital ng Malabon
Malabon, Metro Manila, Philippines
⊕ https://vfmat.ch/349b

Ospital ng Maynila Medical Center
Manila, Metro Manila, Philippines
⊕ https://vfmat.ch/cd52

Ospital ng Muntinlupa
Muntinlupa, Metro Manila, Philippines
⊕ https://vfmat.ch/efe8

Ospital ng Palawan
Puerto Princesa, Palawan, Philippines
⊕ https://vfmat.ch/312c

Ospital ng Parañaque – District II
Parañaque, Metro Manila, Philippines
⊕ https://vfmat.ch/31c1

Ospital ng Sampaloc
Manila, National Capital Region, Philippines
⊕ https://vfmat.ch/ec8e

Ospital ng Tagaytay
Tagaytay, Cavite, Philippines
⊕ https://vfmat.ch/6f4f

Ospital ng Tondo
Tondo, Metro Manila, Philippines
⊕ https://vfmat.ch/2646

Ospital Ning Capas
Capas, Tarlac, Philippines
⊕ https://vfmat.ch/5e47

Our Lady Mediatrix Hospital
Iriga City, Camarines Sur, Philippines
⊕ https://vfmat.ch/71c5

Our Lady of Lourdes Hospital
Manila, Metro Manila, Philippines
⊕ https://vfmat.ch/6f7a

Our Lady of Mt. Carmel Medical Center
San Fernando, Pampanga, Philippines
⊕ https://vfmat.ch/ef87

Our Lady of Porziuncola Hospital, Inc – OLPHI
Calbayog City, Samar, Philippines
⊕ https://vfmat.ch/d664

Paete General Hospital
Paete, Laguna, Philippines
⊕ https://vfmat.ch/f196

Pag-asa Hospital
Binangonan, Rizal, Philippines
⊕ https://vfmat.ch/a2f8

Pagadian City Medical Center (Mendero Hospital)
Pagadian, Zamboanga del Sur, Philippines
⊕ https://vfmat.ch/54a1

Pagamutan ng Dasmariñas
Dasmariñas, Cavite, Philippines
⊕ https://vfmat.ch/db5e

Pagamutang Bayan Ng Malabon
Malabon, Metro Manila, Philippines
⊕ https://vfmat.ch/4e95

Pagamutang Pangmasa ng Laguna
Maitim, Calabarzon, Philippines
⊕ https://vfmat.ch/374c

Palanan Station Hospital
Palanan, Isabela, Philippines
⊕ https://vfmat.ch/fcde

Palawan Baptist Hospital
Roxas, Palawan, Philippines
⊕ https://vfmat.ch/xkhu

Palawan Medical City
Puerto Princesa, Palawan, Philippines
⊕ https://vfmat.ch/d1cd

Palayan City Hospital
Palayan City, Nueza Ecija, Philippines
⊕ https://vfmat.ch/2e8c

Pampanga Medical Specialist Hospital
Guagua, Pampanga, Philippines
⊕ https://vfmat.ch/6fe3

Panabo Polymedic Hospital
Panabo, Davao, Philippines
⊕ https://vfmat.ch/4542

Panay Health Care Multi-Purpose Cooperative Hospital
Kalibo, Aklan, Philippines
⊕ https://vfmat.ch/8f2b

Pandan District Hospital
Pandan, Catanduanes, Philippines
⊕ https://vfmat.ch/824c

Pangasinan Provincial Hospital
San Carlos City, Pangasinan, Philippines
⊕ https://vfmat.ch/1e9f

Paniqui General Hospital
Paniqui, Tarlac, Philippines
⊕ https://vfmat.ch/29f7

Panopdopan District Hospital
Lamut, Ifugao, Philippines
⊕ https://vfmat.ch/aa6e

Paracelis District Hospital
Paracelis, Mountain Province, Philippines
⊕ https://vfmat.ch/5758

Pasay City General Hospital
Pasay, National Capital Region, Philippines
⊕ https://vfmat.ch/f5a2

Pascual General Hospital
Quezon City, Metro Manila, Philippines
⊕ https://vfmat.ch/797c

Pasig City Children's Hospital
Pasig, Metro Manila, Philippines
⊕ https://vfmat.ch/368a

Pasig City General Hospital
Pasig, Metro Manila, Philippines
⊕ https://vfmat.ch/636d

Paulino Hospital
Digos, Davao del Sur, Philippines
⊕ https://vfmat.ch/f597

Pedro L. Gindap Municipal Hospital
Barbaza, Antique, Philippines
⊕ https://vfmat.ch/7a4f

PEEDO Davao del Norte Hospital – Igacos Zone (formerly Samal District Hospital)
Samal, Davao del Norte, Philippines
⊕ https://vfmat.ch/9187

Perpetual Help Hospital
Las Pinas City, Metro Manila, Philippines
⊕ https://vfmat.ch/159b

Perpetual Succor Hospital
Manila, Metro Manila, Philippines
⊕ https://vfmat.ch/khdp

Perpetual Succour Hospital
Cebu City, Cebu, Philippines
⊕ https://vfmat.ch/hqds

Philippine Children's Medical Center
Quezon City, Metro Manila, Philippines
⊕ https://vfmat.ch/tcym

Philippine General Hospital (PGH)
Manila, National Capital Region, Philippines
⊕ https://vfmat.ch/586a

Philippine Heart Center
Quezon City, Metro Manila, Philippines
⊕ https://vfmat.ch/14fd

Philippine National Police (PNP) General Hospital
Quezon City, Metro Manila, Philippines
⊕ https://vfmat.ch/52b6

Philippine Orthopedic Center
Quezon City, Metro Manila, Philippines
⊕ https://vfmat.ch/krxr

Pioduran District Hospital
Pio Duran, Pio Duran, Philippines
⊕ https://vfmat.ch/16c4

Plaridel County Hospital
Plaridel, Bulacan, Philippines
⊕ https://vfmat.ch/e86d

PNP Hospital RO13
Butuan City, Agusan del Norte, Philippines
⊕ https://vfmat.ch/4d2d

PNR General Hospital
Caloocan, Metro Manila, Philippines
⊕ https://vfmat.ch/3b18

Polillo Medicare Hospital
Polillo, Quezon, Philippines
⊕ https://vfmat.ch/57d7

Polomolok Municipal Hospital
Polomolok, South Cotabato, Philippines
⊕ https://vfmat.ch/e8e7

Potia District Hospital
Santa Maria, Ifugao, Philippines
⊕ https://vfmat.ch/tf87

Premiere Medical Center
Cabanatuan City, Nueva Ecija, Philippines
⊕ https://vfmat.ch/4af1

President Diosdado Macapagal District Hospital
Tobias Fornier, Antique, Philippines
⊕ https://vfmat.ch/8e38

President Ramon Magsaysay Memorial Hospital
Iba, Zambales, Philippines
⊕ https://vfmat.ch/7694

Presidential Security Group Station Hospital
Manila, Metro Manila, Philippines
⊕ https://vfmat.ch/cbab

Prieto Diaz Municipal Hospital
Prieto Diaz, Sorsogon, Philippines
⊕ https://vfmat.ch/c55d

Providence Hospital
Quezon City, Metro Manila, Philippines
⊕ https://vfmat.ch/da39

QualiMed Hospital – San Jose Del Monte
San Jose del Monte, Bulacan, Philippines
⊕ https://vfmat.ch/ebbc

Quezon City General Hospital
Quezon City, Metro Manila, Philippines
⊕ https://vfmat.ch/3dcf

Quezon Institute
Quezon City, Metro Manila, Philippines
⊕ https://vfmat.ch/a8e8

Quezon Medicare Hospital
Quezon, Palawan, Philippines
⊕ https://vfmat.ch/584b

Quirino Memorial Medical Center
Quezon City, Metro Manila, Philippines
⊕ https://vfmat.ch/c81b

R.O. Diagan Cooperative Hospital
General Santos City, South Cotabato, Philippines
⊕ https://vfmat.ch/ejrm

Ramirez Bautista Memorial Hospital
Binmaley, Pangasinan, Philippines
⊕ https://vfmat.ch/cc4c

Ramon D. Duremdes District-Hospital (Dumangas District Hospital)
Dumangas, Iloilo, Philippines
⊕ https://vfmat.ch/44a2

Ramon Maza Sr. Memorial District Hospital
Sibalom, Antique, Philippines
⊕ https://vfmat.ch/54f5

Ramos General Hospital
Tarlac City, Central Luzon, Philippines
⊕ https://vfmat.ch/c5f8

Ranada General Hospital
Laoag, Ilocos Norte, Philippines
⊕ https://vfmat.ch/7e51

Rayos-Valentin Hospital INC
Paniqui, Tarlac, Philippines
⊕ https://vfmat.ch/c1b5

Recuenco General Hospital
Taguig, Metro Manila, Philippines
⊕ https://vfmat.ch/4ce3

Region II Trauma and Medical Center (R2TMC)
Bayombong, Nueva Vizcaya, Philippines
⊕ https://vfmat.ch/d9e7

Remedios Trinidad Romualdez Hospital
Tacloban, Leyte, Philippines
⊕ https://vfmat.ch/a56b

Rep. Pedro G. Trono Memorial Hospital
Guimbal, Iloilo, Philippines
⊕ https://vfmat.ch/5c3d

Research Institute for Tropical Medicine
Alabang, Muntinlupa, Metro Manila, Philippines
⊕ https://vfmat.ch/811f

Ricardo Limso Medical Center – Surgery and Pediatrics Clinic
Davao City, Davao del Sur, Philippines
⊕ https://vfmat.ch/7ae8

Ricardo P. Rodriguez Memorial Hospital
San Fernando, Pampanga, Philippines
⊕ https://vfmat.ch/5fb9

Rico Hospital
Tacaco City, Albay, Philippines
⊕ https://vfmat.ch/b297

Ridon's St. Jude Medical Center
Olongapo City, Zambales, Philippines
⊕ https://vfmat.ch/11b7

Riverside Medical Center
Bacolod City, Negros Occidental, Philippines
⊕ https://vfmat.ch/76bf

Rizal Provincial Hospital
Morong, Calabarzon, Philippines
⊕ https://vfmat.ch/349e

Rizal Provincial Hospital System
Antipolo, Rizal, Philippines
⊕ https://vfmat.ch/ab3f

Rizal Provincial Hospital System Angono Annex
Angono, Rizal, Philippines
⊕ https://vfmat.ch/48ef

Roel I. Senador M.D. Memorial Hospital
Tupi, South Cotabato, Philippines
⊕ https://vfmat.ch/fab7

Rogaciano M. Mercado Memorial Hospital
Sta. Maria, Bulacan, Philippines
⊕ https://vfmat.ch/49db

Rogelio M. Garcia Memorial Hospital
Tupi, Timog Cotabato, Philippines
⊕ https://vfmat.ch/d8fa

Romana Pangan District Hospital
Floridablanca, Pampanga, Philippines
⊕ https://vfmat.ch/b24c

Rosales Chua Pun Memorial Hospital
Carmay East, Ilocos, Philippines
⊕ https://vfmat.ch/f5a9

Rosario District Hospital
Rosario, La Union, Philippines
⊕ https://vfmat.ch/3845

Rosario Maclang Bautista General Hospital
Quezon City, Metro Manila, Philippines
⊕ https://vfmat.ch/1eb1

Rosario Memorial Hospital of Guagua, Inc.
Guagua, Pampanga, Philippines
⊕ https://vfmat.ch/42dd

Roxas Medicare Hospital
Roxas, Palawan, Philippines
⊕ https://vfmat.ch/e32b

Roxas Memorial Provincial Hospital
Roxas, Capiz, Philippines
⊕ https://vfmat.ch/e9b9

Rural Health Unit – RHU TBOLI
Camanhagay, South Cotabato, Philippines
⊕ https://vfmat.ch/236b

Sacred Heart Hospital
Cebu City, Central Visayas, Philippines
⊕ https://vfmat.ch/7efa

Sacred Heart Hospital of Malolos, Inc.
Malolos, Bulacan, Philippines
⊕ https://vfmat.ch/75bd

Saint Anthony College Hospital
Roxas City, Capiz, Philippines
⊕ https://vfmat.ch/19e2

Saint Anthony Mother and Child Hospital
Cebu City, Cebu, Philippines
⊕ https://vfmat.ch/de58

Saint Catherine of Alexandria Medical Arts Building
Angeles City, Pampanga, Philippines
⊕ https://vfmat.ch/a115

Saint Elizabeth Hospital
General Santos City, South Cotabato, Philippines
⊕ https://vfmat.ch/7ee3

Saint Felix Medical Hospital
Davao City, Davao del Sur, Philippines
⊕ https://vfmat.ch/6cd6

Saint Gerard General Hospital
Rosario, Batangas, Philippines
⊕ https://vfmat.ch/1ade

Saint Lawrence Hospital
Poblacion III, Victoria, Philippines
⊕ https://vfmat.ch/9b32

Saint Louis University Inc., Hospital of the Sacred Heart, Baguio City
Baguio City, Benguet, Philippines
⊕ https://vfmat.ch/73ef

Saint Martin Mission Hospital
Sablayan, Mimaropa, Philippines
⊕ https://vfmat.ch/ede9

Saint Pio Hospital
Candaba, Pampanga, Philippines
⊕ https://vfmat.ch/9c1f

Saints Francis and Paul General Hospital
San Pablo, Laguna, Philippines
⊕ https://vfmat.ch/b998

Salvacion Oppus Yñiguez Memorial Provincial Hospital
Maasin, Southern Leyte, Philippines
⊕ https://vfmat.ch/af69

Salve Regina General Hospital, Inc.
Pasig, Metro Manila, Philippines
⊕ https://vfmat.ch/1af9

Samar Provincial Hospital
Catbalogan City, Samar, Philippines
⊕ https://vfmat.ch/cfaf

San Antonio District Hospital
San Antonio, Nueva Ecija, Philippines
⊕ https://vfmat.ch/6753

San Antonio Medical Center of Lipa, Inc.
Lipa, Batangas, Philippines
⊕ https://vfmat.ch/jqit

San Diego de Alcala Hospital
Gumaca, Calabarzon, Philippines
⊕ https://vfmat.ch/eaae

San Fernandiño Hospital
San Fernando, Pampanga, Philippines
⊕ https://vfmat.ch/acfe

San Isidro Hospital
Angono, Rizal, Philippines
⊕ https://vfmat.ch/c386

San Joaquin Mother and Child Hospital
San Joaquin, Iloilo, Philippines
⊕ https://vfmat.ch/3b46

San Juan District Hospital
San Juan, Batangas, Philippines
⊕ https://vfmat.ch/fc89

San Lazaro Hospital
Manila, Metro Manila, Philippines
⊕ https://vfmat.ch/2425

San Lorenzo Hospital
Quezon City, Metro Manila, Philippines
⊕ https://vfmat.ch/1ba1

San Lorenzo Ruiz Hospital
Naic, Cavite, Philippines
⊕ https://vfmat.ch/edc5

San Luis District Hospital
San Luis, Pampanga, Philippines
⊕ https://vfmat.ch/71bc

San Marcelino District Hospital
San Marcelino, Zambales, Philippines
⊕ https://vfmat.ch/adc4

San Mateo Medical Center
San Mateo, Rizal, Philippines
⊕ https://vfmat.ch/e9ff

San Miguel District Hospital
San Miguel, Bulacan, Philippines
⊕ https://vfmat.ch/c244

San Pablo City District Hospital
San Pablo City, Laguna, Philippines
⊕ https://vfmat.ch/ddc3

San Pablo City General Hospital
San Pablo City, Laguna, Philippines
⊕ https://vfmat.ch/677a

San Pascual Baylon Maternity And General Hospital
Paombong, Bulacan, Philippines
⊕ https://vfmat.ch/9371

San Pedro Hospital of Davao City, Inc.
Davao City, Davao del Sur, Philippines
⊕ https://vfmat.ch/5a98

San Pedro Jose L. Amante Sr. Emergency Hospital
San Pedro, Laguna, Philippines
⊕ https://vfmat.ch/c85d

San Ramon Hospital
Marikina City, National Capital Region, Philippines
⊕ https://vfmat.ch/3638

San Roque Hospital
Malolos, Bulacan, Philippines
⊕ https://vfmat.ch/7361

Santa Ana Hospital
Santa Ana Manila, Metro Manila, Philippines
⊕ https://vfmat.ch/6a44

Santa Cruz Laguna Polymedic Hospital
Santa Cruz, Laguna, Philippines
⊕ https://vfmat.ch/eeaf

Santisima Trinidad Hospital
Malolos, Bulacan, Philippines
⊕ https://vfmat.ch/5fab

Santo Domingo District Hospital
Santo Domingo, Nueva Ecija, Philippines
⊕ https://vfmat.ch/1b46

Santo Niño Hospital
Bustos, Bulacan, Philippines
⊕ https://vfmat.ch/d3b2

Santo Tomas General Hospital
Sto. Tomas, Batangas, Philippines
⊕ https://vfmat.ch/7463

Santos General Hospital
Malolos, Bulacan, Philippines
⊕ https://vfmat.ch/4e1d

Sara District Hospital
Sara, Iloilo, Philippines
⊕ https://vfmat.ch/29c8

Saroma Hospital
Malalag, Davao del Sur, Philippines
⊕ https://vfmat.ch/ec7f

Schistosomiasis Hospital
Palo, Leyte, Philippines
⊕ https://vfmat.ch/d12c

Severo Verallo Memorial District Hospital
Bogo City, Cebu, Philippines
⊕ https://vfmat.ch/2234

Señor Santo Niño Hospital
Camiling, Tarlac, Philippines
⊕ https://vfmat.ch/7fc8

Shelter Of Goodwill Health Services
Magalang, Pampanga, Philippines
⊕ https://vfmat.ch/a175

Sibuyan District Hospital
Cajidiocan, Romblon, Philippines
⊕ https://vfmat.ch/d717

Simbulan Sto. Niño General Hospital
Don Carlos, Bukidnon, Philippines
⊕ https://vfmat.ch/4e2b

Sindangan District Hospital
Sindangan, Zamboanga del Norte, Philippines
⊕ https://vfmat.ch/14ba

Siniloan Pioneer General Hospital
Siniloan, Laguna, Philippines
⊕ https://vfmat.ch/c43a

Soccomedics Cooperative Hospital
Koronadal City, South Cotabato, Philippines
⊕ https://vfmat.ch/m23i

Socsargen County Hospital
General Santos City, South Cotabato, Philippines
⊕ https://vfmat.ch/t4bs

Sogod District Hospital
Sogod, Southern Leyte, Philippines
⊕ https://vfmat.ch/d2f7

Sorsogon Medical Mission Group Hospital and Health Services Cooperative
Sorsogon City, Sorsogon, Philippines
⊕ https://vfmat.ch/c517

South Cotabato Provincial Hospital
Koronadal City, South Cotabato, Philippines
⊕ https://vfmat.ch/7758

South Davao Medical Specialist Hospital Inc.
Padada, Davao del Sur, Philippines
⊕ https://vfmat.ch/ktmw

Southern Isabela Medical Center
Santiago, Isabela, Philippines
⊕ https://vfmat.ch/arhs

Southern Leyte Provincial Hospital
Maasin City, Southern Leyte, Philippines
⊕ https://vfmat.ch/58db

Southern Palawan Provincial Hospital
Brooke's Point, Palawan, Philippines
⊕ https://vfmat.ch/4eb9

Southern Philippines Medical Center
Davao City, Davao del Sur, Philippines
⊕ https://vfmat.ch/gska

Southern Tagalog Regional Hospital
Bacoor, Cavite, Philippines
⊕ https://vfmat.ch/e5cd

Specialist Group Hospital & Trauma Center
Dagupan, Pangasinan, Philippines
⊕ https://vfmat.ch/936f

St Therese MTCC Hospital
Iloilo City, Iloilo, Philippines
⊕ https://vfmat.ch/b831

St. Benedict Hospital of Davao del Sur, Inc.
Matanao, Davao del Sur, Philippines
⊕ https://vfmat.ch/d2ee

St. Camillus Hospital of Calbayog
Calbayog City, Samar, Philippines
⊕ https://vfmat.ch/3754

St. Camillus Medical Center
Pasig, National Capital Region, Philippines
⊕ https://vfmat.ch/x1ts

St. Clare's Medical Center, Inc.
Makati, Metro Manila, Philippines
⊕ https://vfmat.ch/e751

St. Frances Cabrini Medical Center
Santo Tomas, Batangas, Philippines
⊕ https://vfmat.ch/sc5p

St. James Hospital
Santa Rosa City, Laguna, Philippines
⊕ https://vfmat.ch/7c62

St. John Hospital
Naga City, Camarines Sur, Philippines
⊕ https://vfmat.ch/2ddb

St. Joseph Hospital
Delfin Albano, Isabela, Philippines
⊕ https://vfmat.ch/58ee

St. Joseph Hospital of Remedios
Lubao, Pampanga, Philippines
⊕ https://vfmat.ch/b495

St. Joseph Southern Bukidnon Hospital
Maramag, Bukidnon, Philippines
⊕ https://vfmat.ch/ci5m

St. Jude General Hospital and Medical Center
Manila, Metro Manila, Philippines
⊕ https://vfmat.ch/6561

St. Jude Thaddeus General Hospital
Malaybalay, Bukidnon, Philippines
⊕ https://vfmat.ch/xzv6

St. Luke's Medical Center
Quezon City, Metro Manila, Philippines
⊕ https://vfmat.ch/vahx

St. Magdalene Hospital
San Jose, Occidental Mindoro, Philippines
⊕ https://vfmat.ch/afd6

St. Martin de Porres Charity Hospital
San Juan, Metro Manila, Philippines
⊕ https://vfmat.ch/5fc3

St. Mary's Maternity and Children's Hospital, Inc.
Iligan City, Lanao del Norte, Philippines
⊕ https://vfmat.ch/ef9e

St. Mattheus Medical Hospital
San Mateo, Rizal, Philippines
⊕ https://vfmat.ch/c3d7

St. Paul Hospital
Dasmariñas, Cavite, Philippines
⊕ https://vfmat.ch/2219

St. Paul's Hospital of Iloilo, Inc.
Iloilo City, Iloilo, Philippines
⊕ https://vfmat.ch/f83e

St. Therese – MTCC Hospital
Iloilo City, Western Visayas, Philippines
⊕ https://vfmat.ch/bb4f

St. Therese De Lima Medical Hospital
Teresa, Rizal, Philippines
⊕ https://vfmat.ch/9b29

Sta. Cruz Multispecialty Hospital, Inc.
Calumpit, Bulacan, Philippines
⊕ https://vfmat.ch/f64b

Sta. Marcela District Hospital
Sta. Marcela, Apayao, Philippines
⊕ https://vfmat.ch/2f8c

Sta. Maria Josefa Hospital Foundation, Inc.
Iriga City, Camarines Sur, Philippines
⊕ https://vfmat.ch/64e2

Sto. Domingo – Bemonc Facility
Bansud, Mimaropa, Philippines
⊕ https://vfmat.ch/bddb

Sto. Nino Hospital
Bustos, Bulacan, Philippines
⊕ https://vfmat.ch/fb32

Sto. Rosario Hospital
Rosario, Batangas, Philippines
⊕ https://vfmat.ch/f9de

Sultan Naga Dimaporo Provincial Hospital
Sultan Naga Dimaporo, Lanao del Norte, Philippines
⊕ https://vfmat.ch/4929

Surigao del Norte Provincial Hospital
Placer, Surigao del Norte, Philippines
⊕ https://vfmat.ch/2b52

Surigao Medical Center
Surigao City, Surigao del Norte, Philippines
⊕ https://vfmat.ch/pnmn

Tacloban City Hospital
Tacloban City, Leyte, Philippines
⊕ https://vfmat.ch/9b72

Tacloban Doctors' Medical Center
Tacloban City, Leyte, Philippines
⊕ https://vfmat.ch/69ba

Taguig-Pateros District Hospital
Taguig City, National Capital Region, Philippines
⊕ https://vfmat.ch/74aa

Talavera General Hospital
Talavera, Nueva Ecija, Philippines
⊕ https://vfmat.ch/6f22

Talon General Hospital
Tarlac City, Tarlac, Philippines
⊕ https://vfmat.ch/a584

Tamparan Medical Foundation Inc. Hospital
Tamparan, Lanao del Sur, ARMM, Philippines
⊕ https://vfmat.ch/bff4

Tanay General Hospital
Tanay, Rizal, Philippines
⊕ https://vfmat.ch/1741

Tarlac Provincial Hospital
Tarlac, Tarlac, Philippines
⊕ https://vfmat.ch/9348

Taytay Emergency Hospital
Taytay, Rizal, Philippines
⊕ https://vfmat.ch/eae8

Tebow CURE Hospital
Davao City, Davao del Sur, Philippines
⊕ https://vfmat.ch/cbsc

Teresita Lopez Jalandoni Provincial Hospital
Silay City, Negros Occidental, Philippines
⊕ https://vfmat.ch/8a32

Toledo City General Hospital
Toledo City, Cebu, Philippines
⊕ https://vfmat.ch/aec9

Trinity Woman and Child Hospital
Manila, Metro Manila, Philippines
⊕ https://vfmat.ch/cb3c

Tuburan District Hospital
Poblacion, Tuburan, Philippines
⊕ https://vfmat.ch/17f5

Tuguegarao People's General Hospital
Tuguegarao, Cagayan, Philippines
⊕ https://vfmat.ch/a357

UERM Memorial Medical Center
Quezon City, Metro Manila, Philippines
⊕ https://vfmat.ch/b7fq

Unciano General Hospital
Mandaluyong, Metro Manila, Philippines
⊕ https://vfmat.ch/ac96

University of Cebu Medical Center (UC Med)
Mandaue City, Cebu, Philippines
⊕ https://vfmat.ch/fubu

University of Santo Tomas – Legazpi Hospital
Legazpi, Albay, Philippines
⊕ https://vfmat.ch/e518

University of Santo Tomas Hospital
Manila, Metro Manila, Philippines
⊕ https://vfmat.ch/85e4

University of Southern Mindanao (USM) Hospital
Kabacan, North Cotabato, Philippines
⊕ https://vfmat.ch/8b6c

UPLB University Health Service
Los Baños, Laguna, Philippines
⊕ https://vfmat.ch/3794

Urdaneta District Hospital
Urdaneta City, Pangasinan, Philippines
⊕ https://vfmat.ch/9bb1

Urdaneta Sacred Heart Hospital
Urdaneta, Pangasinan, Philippines
⊕ https://vfmat.ch/41d3

USI Mother Seton Hospital
Naga City, Camarines Sur, Philippines
⊕ https://vfmat.ch/95e4

V.L. Makabali Memorial Hospital Inc.
San Fernando, Pampanga, Philippines
⊕ https://vfmat.ch/ddfe

Valderrama Municipal Hospital
Valderrama, Western Visayas, Philippines
⊕ https://vfmat.ch/4a98

Valencia Medical Hospital
Valencia City, Bukidnon, Philippines
⊕ https://vfmat.ch/888e

Valencia Polymedic General Hospital
Valencia City, Bukidnon, Philippines
⊕ https://vfmat.ch/3595

Valenzuela Citicare Medical Center
Valenzuela, Metro Manila, Philippines
🌐 https://vfmat.ch/vswl

Valenzuela City Emergency Hospital
Valenzuela, Metro Manila, Philippines
🌐 https://vfmat.ch/b7cc

Veterans Memorial Medical Center Hospital
Quezon City, Metro Manila, Philippines
🌐 https://vfmat.ch/39w4

Vicente Gullas Memorial Hospital
Mandaue City, Cebu, Philippines
🌐 https://vfmat.ch/64a2

Vicente L. Peralta Memorial District Hospital
Castilla, Sorsogon, Philippines
🌐 https://vfmat.ch/8c22

Vicente Sotto Memorial Medical Center
Cebu City, Cebu, Philippines
🌐 https://vfmat.ch/rkzn

Villasis Polymedic Hospital
Villasis, Pangasinan, Philippines
🌐 https://vfmat.ch/5a9d

Virgen Milagrosa Medical Center
San Carlos, Pangasinan, Philippines
🌐 https://vfmat.ch/a9dd

Visayas Community Medical Center
Cebu City, Cebu, Philippines
🌐 https://vfmat.ch/jlnr

Wao District Hospital
Wao, Lanao del Sur, Philippines
🌐 https://vfmat.ch/dc29

Western Kalinga District Hospital
Balbalan, Kalinga, Philippines
🌐 https://vfmat.ch/296f

Western Leyte Provincial Hospital
Baybay City, Leyte, Philippines
🌐 https://vfmat.ch/e371

Western Pangasinan District Hospital
Alaminos, Pangasinan, Philippines
🌐 https://vfmat.ch/659f

Word of Hope General Hospital Foundation Inc.
Quezon City, Metro Manila, Philippines
🌐 https://vfmat.ch/5f3d

Zamboanga Puericulture Center Maternity Lying-in Hospital
Zamboanga City, Zamboanga del Sur, Philippines
🌐 https://vfmat.ch/7752

Ziga Memorial District Hospital
Tabaco, Albay, Philippines
🌐 https://vfmat.ch/a3c5

Zigzag Hospital
Mabini, Batangas, Philippines
🌐 https://vfmat.ch/411e

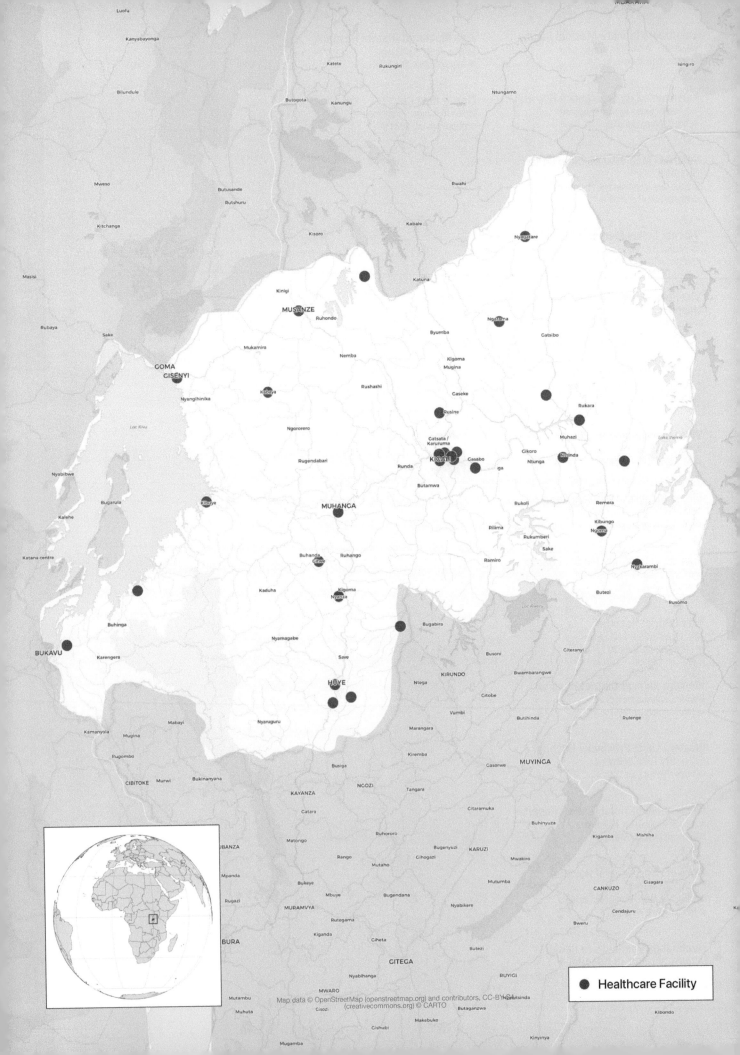

Healthcare Facility

Rwanda

The Republic of Rwanda is a landlocked country just south of the equator in East-Central Africa. While small geographically, the country is home to 12.9 million people, making it one of Africa's most densely populated countries. Rwanda has been highly influenced by Christianity. Its three official languages are Kinyarwanda, English, and French. Rwanda, also called "the land of a thousand hills," is widely known for its nature and wildlife, especially the protected gorillas of Volcanoes National Park.

Rwanda's history has been marked by tension between the Hutu and Tutsi ethnic groups and the brutal genocide of the 1990s. Since the end of the genocide, Rwanda has undergone a period of reconstruction and worked to turn a new chapter, having greatly improved its political stability and economic conditions. This primarily agricultural country has significantly reduced its poverty rate from 77 percent to 55 percent between 2001 and 2017. Rwanda has also made improvements in its social policies, such as near-universal primary school enrollment. At its current rate, the country strives to reach middle-income status by 2035 and high-income status by 2050.

For both males and females, life expectancy has steadily increased. Similarly, child mortality rates have declined by over two-thirds. While some health indicators have improved, the population experiences high levels of death caused by lower respiratory infections, neonatal disorders, tuberculosis, diarrheal diseases, malaria, and HIV/AIDS. Nearly 100 percent of the country is at risk of contracting malaria. Death due to non-communicable diseases is also significant, with congenital defects, stroke, ischemic heart disease, and cirrhosis causing substantial mortality. Rates of cirrhosis, which may be caused by excessive alcohol consumption, are significantly higher than those of other countries in the region. Road injuries also cause significant numbers of deaths in Rwanda.

12.9M
Population

$798
GDP Per Capita

69 years
Life Expectancy
↑ Improving

12
Doctors/100k

Physician Density

160
Beds/100k

Hospital Bed Density

248
Deaths/100k

Maternal Mortality

Rwanda

Nonprofit Organizations

143 LIFE Foundation
Seeks to educate and empower individuals living with malaria, TB, HIV/AIDS, STDs and other health disparities related to sexual health.
Infect Dis, MF Med
🌐 https://vfmat.ch/d59b

A Broader View Volunteers
Provides developing countries around the world with significant volunteer programs that aid the neediest communities and forge a lasting bond between those volunteering and those they have helped.
Dent-OMFS, ER Med, Infect Dis, MF Med
🌐 https://vfmat.ch/3bec

Abt Associates
Seeks to improve the quality of life and economic well-being of people worldwide, while striving to meet and exceed the highest professional standards.
General, Logist-Op, MF Med, OB-GYN, Peds
🌐 https://vfmat.ch/cec2

Aceso Global
Provides strategic healthcare advisory services in low- and middle-income countries to design and deliver highly customized, evidence-based solutions that address the complex nature of healthcare systems, with a goal to strengthen and provide affordable, high-quality care to all.
Logist-Op, Pub Health
🌐 https://vfmat.ch/b3b7

Action Kibogora
Works to redevelop and rebuild the maternity and neonatology wards at Kibogora Hospital, Rwanda.
Logist-Op, MF Med, Neonat, Peds
🌐 https://vfmat.ch/29f9

Adventist Health International
Focuses on upgrading and managing mission hospitals by providing governance, consultation, and technical assistance to a number of affiliated Seventh-Day Adventist hospitals throughout Africa, Asia, and the Americas.
Dent-OMFS, General, Pub Health
🌐 https://vfmat.ch/16aa

Africa CDC
Aims to strengthen the capacity and capability of Africa's public health institutions and partnerships to detect and respond quickly and effectively to disease threats and outbreaks, based on data-driven interventions and programs.
Infect Dis, Logist-Op, Pub Health
🌐 https://vfmat.ch/339c

Africa Health Organisation
Leads collaborative efforts among countries in Africa and other partners to promote health equity, combat disease, and improve quality of life.

Logist-Op, Pub Health
🌐 https://vfmat.ch/b1c5

Africa Humanitarian Action (AHA)
Responds to crises, conflicts, and disasters in Africa, while informing and advising the international community, governments, civil society, and the private sector on humanitarian issues of concern to Africa. Supports institutional and organizational development efforts.
General, Infect Dis, MF Med, Nutr, OB-GYN
🌐 https://vfmat.ch/3ca2

Africa Indoor Residual Spraying Project (AIRS)
Aims to protect millions of people in Africa from malaria by spraying insecticide on walls, ceilings, and other indoor resting places of mosquitoes that transmit malaria.
Infect Dis
🌐 https://vfmat.ch/9bd1

Africa Inland Mission International
Seeks to establish churches and community development programs including healthcare projects, based in Christian ministry.
Anesth, Dent-OMFS, ER Med, General, MF Med, Medicine, OB-GYN, OB-GYN, Ophth-Opt, Ped Surg, Peds, Rehab
🌐 https://vfmat.ch/f2f6

Africa Relief and Community Development
Provides comprehensive relief and developmental aid to people of the African continent regardless of gender, race, or religion.
Nutr, Pub Health
🌐 https://vfmat.ch/6cd2

African Field Epidemiology Network (AFENET)
Strengthens field epidemiology and public health laboratory capacity to contribute effectively to addressing epidemics and other major public health problems in Africa.
All-Immu, Infect Dis, Path, Pub Health
🌐 https://vfmat.ch/df2e

Against Malaria Foundation
Helps protect people from malaria. Funds anti-malaria nets, specifically long-lasting insecticidal nets (LLINs), and works with distribution partners to ensure they are used. Tracks and reports on net use and malaria case data.
Infect Dis
🌐 https://vfmat.ch/337d

AIDS Healthcare Foundation
Provides cutting-edge HIV/AIDS medical care and advocacy to over one million people in 43 countries.
Infect Dis
🌐 https://vfmat.ch/b27c

Al Basar International Foundation
Works with local partners to treat preventable blindness, and helps set up sustainable infrastructure so local teams can save sight in their communities.
Ophth-Opt
⊕ https://vfmat.ch/a8b5

Alight
Works closely with refugees, trafficked persons, economic migrants, and other displaced persons to co-design solutions that help them build full and fulfilling lives, with healthcare, clean water, shelter protection, and economic opportunity.
ER Med, General, Infect Dis, MF Med, Neonat, Peds
⊕ https://vfmat.ch/5993

AMREF Flying Doctors
Aims to deliver medical air transport and health services using the latest aviation and medical technology to ensure patients receive unrivaled care.
ER Med, Logist-Op
⊕ https://vfmat.ch/5d5e

Amref Health Africa
Serves millions of people across 35 countries in Sub-Saharan Africa, strengthening health systems, and training African health workers to respond to the continent's most critical health issues.
All-Immu, General, Infect Dis, Logist-Op, MF Med, OB-GYN, Path, Pub Health, Surg
⊕ https://vfmat.ch/6985

AO Alliance
Builds solutions to lessen the burden of injuries in low- and middle-income countries, while enhancing the care of the injured to reduce human suffering, disability, and poverty.
Ortho, Surg
⊕ https://vfmat.ch/8cd5

Association of Medical Doctors of Asia (AMDA)
Strives to support people affected by disasters and economic distress on their road to recovery, establishing a true partnership with special emphasis on local initiative.
ER Med, Logist-Op, Pub Health
⊕ https://vfmat.ch/e3d4

Avinta Care
Offers quality healthcare while providing a full suite of services from diagnosis to treatment, specializing in fertility and dermatology.
Derm, MF Med, OB-GYN, Path
⊕ https://vfmat.ch/52a6

Benjamin H. Josephson, MD Fund
Provides healthcare professionals with the financial resources necessary to deliver medical services for those in need throughout the world.
General, OB-GYN
⊕ https://vfmat.ch/6acc

Bill & Melinda Gates Foundation
Focuses on global issues, such as poverty, health, and education, offering the opportunity to dramatically improve the quality of life for billions of people by building partnerships that bring together resources, expertise, and vision to identify issues, find answers, and drive change.
All-Immu, General, Infect Dis, MF Med, Neonat, OB-GYN, Pub Health
⊕ https://vfmat.ch/7cf2

Boston Cardiac Foundation, The
Provides advanced medical technologies and cardiac care, such as pacemaker implantation, to patients around the world who would otherwise have no access to these services.
Anesth, CT Surg, CV Med, Crit-Care
⊕ https://vfmat.ch/8fd3

Boston Children's Hospital: Global Health Program
Helps solve pediatric global healthcare challenges by transferring expertise through long-term partnerships with scalable impact, while working in the field to strengthen healthcare systems, advocate, research, and provide care delivery or education as a way of sustainably improving the health of children worldwide.
Anesth, CV Med, Crit-Care, ER Med, Heme-Onc, Infect Dis, Medicine, Nutr, Palliative, Ped Surg, Peds
⊕ https://vfmat.ch/f9f8

Bread and Water for Africa UK
Aims to create better access to education, nutrition, and healthcare for some of Africa's most vulnerable children and their communities.
General, MF Med, Nutr
⊕ https://vfmat.ch/c855

Breast Cancer Initiative East Africa Inc. (BCIEA)
Seeks to ensure that through advocacy, awareness, education, empowerment, access to treatment support, and research, patients do not face breast cancer feeling afraid or helplessly alone.
OB-GYN
⊕ https://vfmat.ch/6c82

Bridge to Health Medical and Dental
Seeks to provide healthcare to those who need it most, based on a philosophy of partnership, education, and community development. Strives to bring solutions to global health issues in underserved communities through clinical outreach and medical and dental training.
Dent-OMFS, General, Infect Dis, MF Med, OB-GYN, Ophth-Opt, Ortho, Pub Health, Radiol
⊕ https://vfmat.ch/bb2c

Brigham and Women's Center for Surgery and Public Health
Advances the science of surgical care delivery by studying effectiveness, quality, equity, and value at the population level, and develops surgeon-scientists committed to excellence in these areas.
Anesth, ER Med, Infect Dis, Pub Health, Surg
⊕ https://vfmat.ch/5d64

Brigham and Women's Hospital Global Health Hub
Cares for patients in underserved settings, provides education to staff who work in those areas to create sustainable change, and conducts research designed to improve health in such settings.
General, Infect Dis
⊕ https://vfmat.ch/a8a3

Canadian Network for International Surgery, The
Aims to improve maternal health, increase safety, and build local capacity in low-income countries by creating and providing surgical and midwifery courses, training domestically, and transferring skills.
Logist-Op, Surg
⊕ https://vfmat.ch/86ff

CARE
Works around the globe to save lives, defeat poverty, and achieve social justice.
ER Med, General
⊕ https://vfmat.ch/7232

CareMe E-Clinic
Uses digital technology, partners with healthcare providers, raises awareness around noncommunicable diseases, and provides healthcare to patients with chronic ailments from underserved communities across Rwanda.
CV Med, Pub Health
⊕ https://vfmat.ch/85c5

Carter Center, The
Seeks to prevent and resolve conflicts, enhance freedom and democracy, and improve health, while remaining committed to human rights and the alleviation of human suffering.
Infect Dis, MF Med, Ophth-Opt
⊕ https://vfmat.ch/6556

cbm New Zealand
Inspired by the Christian faith, aims to improve the quality of life for those living with the double disadvantage of poverty and disability.
Crit-Care, Infect Dis, Logist-Op, Nutr, OB-GYN, Ophth-Opt, Ortho, Psych, Rehab, Surg
⊕ https://vfmat.ch/c14b

Center for Health and Hope

Supports and advocates for persons infected and affected by HIV/AIDS with programs of education, prevention, care, and treatment.

Pub Health

⊕ https://vfmat.ch/a52e

Centre de Chirurgie Orthopédique Pédiatrique et de Réhabilitation Sainte Marie de Rilima

Works to promote health and rehabilitative assistance of children with disabilities, and to promote awareness about disability.

Anesth, General, Medicine, Ortho, Path, Ped Surg, Rehab

⊕ https://vfmat.ch/567b

Centre Marembo

Supports homeless girls in Kigali, Rwanda, providing shelter, education, counseling, and skills training.

General, Infect Dis, OB-GYN, Path, Peds

⊕ https://vfmat.ch/e8e4

Chain of Hope

Provides lifesaving heart operations for children around the world and supports the development of cardiac services in numerous developing and war-torn countries.

Anesth, CT Surg, CV Med, Crit-Care, Ped Surg, Peds, Pulm-Critic, Surg

⊕ https://vfmat.ch/1b1b

Christian Blind Mission (CBM)

Aims to improve the quality of life of persons with disabilities in the poorest countries, addressing poverty as a cause and a consequence of disability, and working in partnership to create a society for all.

ENT, General, Infect Dis, OB-GYN, Ophth-Opt, Ortho, Peds, Psych, Rehab, Surg

⊕ https://vfmat.ch/3824

Christian Connections for International Health (CCIH)

Promotes global health and wholeness from a Christian perspective.

All-Immu, General, Infect Dis, MF Med, Neonat, OB-GYN, Psych

⊕ https://vfmat.ch/fa5d

Christian Health Service Corps

Brings Christian doctors, health professionals, and health educators committed to serving the poor to places that otherwise have little or no access to healthcare.

Anesth, Dent-OMFS, General, Medicine, Peds, Surg

⊕ https://vfmat.ch/da57

Cleft Africa

Strives to provide underserved Africans with cleft lips and palates with access to the best possible treatment for their condition, so that they can live a life free of the health problems caused by cleft.

Anesth, Dent-OMFS, Ped Surg, Surg

⊕ https://vfmat.ch/8298

Clinton Health Access Initiative (CHAI)

Aims to save lives and reduce the burden of disease in low- and middle-income countries. Works with partners to strengthen the capabilities of governments and the private sector to create and sustain high-quality health systems.

General, Heme-Onc, Infect Dis, Logist-Op, MF Med, Medicine, Neonat, Nutr, OB-GYN, Path, Peds, Rad-Onc

⊕ https://vfmat.ch/9ed7

Columbia Vagelos College of Physicians and Surgeons Programs in Global Health

Harnesses the expertise of the medical school to improve health worldwide by training global health leaders, building capacity through interdisciplinary education and training programs, and addressing unmet health needs through research and application.

CV Med, Derm, Genetics, Heme-Onc, Infect Dis, Medicine, OB-GYN, Ophth-Opt, Peds, Psych, Pub Health, Pulm-Critic, Surg

⊕ https://vfmat.ch/a9e5

Concern Worldwide

Seeks to permanently transform the lives of people living in extreme poverty, tackling its root causes, and building resilience.

Logist-Op, MF Med, Nutr, OB-GYN

⊕ https://vfmat.ch/77e9

Cornerstone Education and Research

Seeks to provide the local and global community with medical research and education in orthopedic care, expand medical research in the development of innovative technologies, and provide physician and community education.

Ortho

⊕ https://vfmat.ch/f549

COVID-19 Clinical Research Coalition

Advocates and collaborates for the advancement of COVID-19 research driven by the needs of low-resource settings, and works for equitable access to solutions to the pandemic.

All-Immu, Infect-Dis, MF Med, Path, Pub Health

⊕ https://vfmat.ch/d1f4

Creighton University School of Medicine: Global Surgery Fellowship

Aims to significantly impact the absence of acute surgical care in developing countries by providing free surgery to underserved patients and surgical training for developing country trainees.

Anesth, Ped Surg, Surg

⊕ https://vfmat.ch/777f

Developing Country NGO Delegation: Global Fund to Fight AIDS, TB & Malaria

Works to strengthen the engagement of civil society actors and organizations in developing countries to build a world in which AIDS, TB, and malaria are no longer global, public health, and human rights threats.

Infect Dis, Pub Health

⊕ https://vfmat.ch/3149

Direct Relief

Improves the health and lives of people affected by poverty or emergency situations by mobilizing and providing essential medical resources needed for their care.

ER Med, Logist-Op

⊕ https://vfmat.ch/58e5

Doctors Worldwide

Focuses on health access, health improvement, and health emergencies to serve communities in need so they can build healthier and happier futures.

Dent-OMFS, ER Med, General, MF Med, Palliative, Peds

⊕ https://vfmat.ch/99cd

Duke University: Global Health Institute

Sparks innovation in global health research and education, and brings together knowledge and resources to address the most important global health issues of our time.

All-Immu, Infect Dis, MF Med, OB-GYN, Pub Health

⊕ https://vfmat.ch/c4cd

Edwards Lifesciences

Provides innovative solutions for people fighting cardiovascular disease, as a global leader in patient-focused medical innovations for structural heart disease, along with critical care and surgical monitoring.

Anesth, CT Surg, CV Med, Crit-Care, Ped Surg, Peds, Pulm-Critic, Surg, Vasc Surg

⊕ https://vfmat.ch/d671

Elizabeth Glaser Pediatric AIDS Foundation

Seeks to end global pediatric HIV/AIDS through prevention and treatment programs, research, and advocacy.

Infect Dis, Nutr, OB-GYN, Peds

⊕ https://vfmat.ch/d6ec

Enabel

As the development agency of the Belgian federal government, charged with implementing Belgium's international development policy, carries out public service assignments in Belgium and abroad pursuant to the 2030 Agenda for Sustainable Development.

General, Infect Dis, Logist-Op, MF Med, OB-GYN, Peds, Pub Health
⊕ https://vfmat.ch/5af7

END Fund, The
Aims to control and eliminate the most prevalent neglected diseases among the world's poorest and most vulnerable people.
Infect Dis
⊕ https://vfmat.ch/2614

Eugène Gasana Jr. Foundation
Provides the opportunity for compassionate and quality cancer care for children in developing nations.
Anesth, Heme-Onc, Ped Surg, Peds
⊕ https://vfmat.ch/27cb

Eye Care Foundation
Helps prevent and cure avoidable blindness and visual impairment in low-income countries.
Ophth-Opt, Surg
⊕ https://vfmat.ch/c8f9

Fondation d'Harcourt
Promotes national and international projects and partnerships in the fields of mental health and psychosocial support; provides grants to organizations with specific expertise in mental health or psychosocial support to implement projects; and provides direct services.
Psych, Pub Health
⊕ https://vfmat.ch/4a8a

Foundation for Special Surgery
Provides high-quality, complex surgical care by increasing surgical expertise in Africa through the participation of surgeons across various specialties to provide premium care and skills transfer/education to benefit patients.
Anesth, CT Surg, ENT, Endo, Neurosurg, Plast, Surg, Urol
⊕ https://vfmat.ch/53db

Fracarita International
Provides support and services in the fields of mental healthcare, care for people with a disability, and education.
Psych, Rehab
⊕ https://vfmat.ch/8d3c

Fred Hollows Foundation, The
Works toward a world in which no person is needlessly blind or vision impaired.
Ophth-Opt, Pub Health, Surg
⊕ https://vfmat.ch/73e5

Glo Good Foundation
Committed to building oral-health initiatives in underserved populations globally by educating families on the importance of taking care of their oral health and training local dentists to facilitate the delivery of care when needed.
Dent-OMFS, Nutr
⊕ https://vfmat.ch/38bd

Global Alliance to Prevent Prematurity And Stillbirth (GAPPS)
Seeks to improve birth outcomes worldwide by reducing the burden of premature birth and stillbirth.
All-Immu, Infect Dis, MF Med, Neonat, Neonat, OB-GYN
⊕ https://vfmat.ch/3f74

Global Blood Fund
Delivers grants, equipment, and training to over 50 countries in Africa, Asia, Eastern Europe, the Middle East, Latin America and the Caribbean.
Pub Health
⊕ https://vfmat.ch/6377

Global Civic Sharing
Aims to support our neighbors' self-reliance and realize the sustainable development.
Nutr, Peds, Pub Health
⊕ https://vfmat.ch/d7ab

Global Clubfoot Initiative (GCI)
Promotes and resources the treatment of children with clubfoot in developing countries using the Ponseti technique.
Ortho, Ped Surg
⊕ https://vfmat.ch/f229

Global Health Corps
Mobilizes a diverse community of leaders to build the movement for global health equity, working toward a world in which every person lives a healthy life.
ER Med, General, Pub Health
⊕ https://vfmat.ch/31c6

Global Ministries – The United Methodist Church
As the worldwide mission and development agency of The United Methodist Church, Global Ministries works with more than 300 hospitals and clinics around the world through its Global Health Unit.
Anesth, CT Surg, CV Med, Crit-Care, Dent-OMFS, Derm, ER Med, GI, General, Infect Dis, Logist-Op, MF Med, Medicine, Neonat, Nephro, Nutr, OB-GYN, Ophth-Opt, Ortho, Palliative, Peds, Pod, Psych, Pub Health, Rehab, Rheum, Surg, Urol
⊕ https://vfmat.ch/1723

Global Offsite Care
Aims to be a catalyst for increased access to specialized healthcare for all, and provides technology platforms to doctors and clinics around the world through Rotary Club-sponsored telemedicine projects.
Crit-Care, ER Med, General, Pulm-Critic
⊕ https://vfmat.ch/61b5

Global Oncology (GO)
Brings the best in cancer care to underserved patients around the world and collaborates across geographic, professional, and academic borders to improve cancer care, research, and education.
Heme-Onc, Path, Rad-Onc
⊕ https://vfmat.ch/fcb8

Globus Relief
Aims to improve the delivery of healthcare worldwide by gathering, processing, and distributing surplus medical supplies to charities at home and abroad.
Logist-Op
⊕ https://vfmat.ch/a2b7

HEAL Africa
Compassionately serves vulnerable people and communities in the Democratic Republic of the Congo through a holistic approach to healthcare, education, community action, and leadership development in response to changing needs.
Medicine, OB-GYN, Ortho, Peds, Surg
⊕ https://vfmat.ch/cf5d

Health Builders
Strengthens management, improves clinical care, and builds healthcare infrastructure in Rwanda so every person has access to high-quality healthcare, allowing them to live dignified, healthy, and prosperous lives.
General, Logist-Op, MF Med, Medicine, Neonat, Nutr, OB-GYN, Path, Peds
⊕ https://vfmat.ch/571f

Health Equity Initiative
Aims to build and sustain a global community that engages across sectors and disciplines to advance health equity.
Pub Health
⊕ https://vfmat.ch/e2e2

Health Poverty Action
Works in partnership with people around the world who are pursuing change in their own communities to demand health justice and challenge power imbalances.
ER Med, General, Infect Dis, Psych, Pub Health
⊕ https://vfmat.ch/ee58

Health Volunteers Overseas (HVO)
Improves the availability and quality of healthcare through the education, training, and professional development of the health workforce in resource-scarce countries.
All-Immu, Anesth, CV Med, Dent-OMFS, Derm, ENT, ER Med, Endo, GI, Heme-

Onc, Infect Dis, Medicine, Medicine, Nephro, Neuro, OB-GYN, Ophth-Opt, Ortho, Peds, Plast, Psych, Pulm-Critic, Rehab, Rheum, Surg
⊕ https://vfmat.ch/42b2

Health[e] Foundation
Supports health professionals and community workers in the world's most vulnerable societies to ensure quality health for everyone in need by providing digital education and information, using e-learning and m-health.
Logist-Op
⊕ https://vfmat.ch/b73b

Heart to Heart International
Strengthens communities through improving health access, providing humanitarian development, and administering crisis relief worldwide. Engages volunteers, collaborates with partners, and deploys resources to achieve this mission.
Anesth, ER Med, General, Logist-Op, Medicine, Path, Path, Peds, Psych, Pub Health, Surg
⊕ https://vfmat.ch/aacb

Helping Hands for Rwanda (HHFR)
Brings quality education and healthcare to the Rwandese people.
Anesth, CT Surg, CV Med, Crit-Care, General, Medicine
⊕ https://vfmat.ch/b981

Himalayan Cataract Project
Works to cure needless blindness with the highest quality care at the lowest cost.
Anesth, Ophth-Opt, Surg
⊕ https://vfmat.ch/3b3d

His Hands on Africa
Brings hope and healing to underserved communities in Africa by mobilizing Christian dentists to provide communities with dental care, based in Christian ministry.
Dent-OMFS
⊕ https://vfmat.ch/228c

Home de la Vierge des Pauvres (HVP) Gatagara
Provides high-quality and sustainable education along with orthopedic and rehabilitation services to persons with physical disabilities, in partnership with other stakeholders.
Anesth, Ortho, Psych, Radiol, Rehab
⊕ https://vfmat.ch/9a3f

Hope Walks
Frees children, families, and communities from the burden of clubfoot, inspired by the Christian faith.
Ortho, Ped Surg, Peds, Rehab
⊕ https://vfmat.ch/f6d4

Hospice Africa
Aims to provide a holistic and culturally sensitive palliative care service through accurate treatment of pain.
Palliative
⊕ https://vfmat.ch/9f86

Hospice Without Borders
Improves access to palliative care and hospice programs that preferentially serve marginalized, traumatized, and vulnerable populations both in the U.S. and in Rwanda.
Anesth, Palliative
⊕ https://vfmat.ch/bdb6

Humanity & Inclusion
Works alongside people with disabilities and vulnerable populations, taking action and bearing witness in order to respond to their essential needs, improve their living conditions and health, and promote respect for their dignity and fundamental rights.
General, Infect Dis, MF Med, Medicine, Ortho, Peds, Psych, Pub Health, Rehab
⊕ https://vfmat.ch/16b7

ICAP at Columbia University
Serves as global leader in supporting the scale-up of multidisciplinary HIV/AIDS prevention, care, and treatment programs based on a family-focused approach.
General, Infect Dis, MF Med, Medicine, OB-GYN, Pub Health
⊕ https://vfmat.ch/a8ef

International Agency for the Prevention of Blindness (IAPB), The
Leads international efforts in blindness-prevention activities, works toward a world where no one is needlessly visually impaired, and ensures that everyone has access to the best possible standard of eye health.
Infect Dis, Ophth-Opt, Pub Health
⊕ https://vfmat.ch/87a2

International Council of Ophthalmology
Works with ophthalmologic societies and others to enhance ophthalmic education and improve access to the highest-quality eye care in order to preserve and restore vision for people of the world.
Ophth-Opt
⊕ https://vfmat.ch/ffd2

International Federation of Gynecology and Obstetrics (FIGO)
Implements global projects on specific women's health issues.
MF Med, Medicine, Neonat, OB-GYN, Surg, Urol
⊕ https://vfmat.ch/c4b4

International Federation of Red Cross and Red Crescent Societies (IFRC)
Coordinates and directs international assistance following natural and manmade disasters in nonconflict situations through the world's largest humanitarian and development network. Provides disaster-preparedness programs, healthcare activities, and promotes humanitarian values.
ER Med, General, Infect Dis, Nutr
⊕ https://vfmat.ch/b4ee

International Medical Relief
Provides sustainable education, training, medical and dental care, and disaster relief and response in vulnerable communities worldwide.
Dent-OMFS, General, Infect Dis, Medicine, OB-GYN
⊕ https://vfmat.ch/b3ed

International Medical Response
Supplements, supports, and enhances healthcare systems in communities across the world that have been incapacitated by natural disaster, extreme poverty, and/or regional conflict by sending a multidisciplinary team of healthcare professionals.
Anesth, General, OB-GYN, Surg
⊕ https://vfmat.ch/9ccd

International Organization for Migration (IOM) – The UN Migration Agency
Promotes evidence-informed policies and holistic, preventive, and curative health programs that are beneficial, accessible, and equitable for vulnerable migrants.
General, Infect Dis, OB-GYN
⊕ https://vfmat.ch/621a

International Organization for Women and Development (IOWD)
Provides underserved women and children in low-income countries with free medical and surgical services and care.
Anesth, MF Med, Neonat, OB-GYN, Ped Surg, Peds, Surg
⊕ https://vfmat.ch/8ecb

IntraHealth International
Improves the performance of health workers and strengthens the systems in which they work.
CV Med, Endo, General, Infect Dis, MF Med, Neonat, Nutr, OB-GYN
⊕ https://vfmat.ch/ddc8

Iris Global
Serves the poor, the destitute, the lost, and the forgotten by providing adoration, outreach, family, education, relief, development, healing, and the arts.
General, Infect Dis, Nutr, Pub Health
⊕ https://vfmat.ch/37f8

IVUmed
Aims to make quality urological care available worldwide by providing medical and surgical education for physicians and nurses, and treatment for thousands of children and adults.
Anesth, OB-GYN, Ped Surg, Surg, Urol
⊕ https://vfmat.ch/e619

Izumi Foundation
Develops and supports programs that improve health and healthcare in neglected regions of Africa and Latin America.

⊕ https://vfmat.ch/f29a

Jhpiego
Creates and delivers transformative healthcare solutions that save lives, in partnership with national governments, health experts, and local communities.
General, Infect Dis, OB-GYN, Surg
⊕ https://vfmat.ch/45b8

John Snow, Inc. (JSI)
Aims to improve the health and well-being of underserved and vulnerable people and communities throughout the world.
General, Infect Dis, Logist-Op, MF Med, OB-GYN, Peds, Psych, Pub Health
⊕ https://vfmat.ch/ba78

Johns Hopkins Center for Communication Programs
Believes in the power of communication to save lives by empowering people to adopt healthy behaviors for themselves, their families, and their communities.
General, Infect Dis, Logist-Op, OB-GYN, Pub Health
⊕ https://vfmat.ch/1bf9

Johns Hopkins Center for Global Health
Facilitates and focuses the extensive expertise and resources of the Johns Hopkins institutions, together with global collaborators, to effectively address and ameliorate the world's most pressing health issues.
General, Genetics, Logist-Op, MF Med, Peds, Psych, Pub Health, Pulm-Critic
⊕ https://vfmat.ch/54ce

Joint Aid Management (JAM)
Provides food security, nutrition, water, and sanitation to vulnerable African communities in dignified and sustainable ways.
ER Med, Nutr
⊕ https://vfmat.ch/dcac

Joint Aid Management (JAM) Canada
Strives to provide food security, nutrition, water, and sanitation to vulnerable African communities in dignified and sustainable ways.
Nutr, Pub Health
⊕ https://vfmat.ch/8756

Joint United Nations Programme on HIV/AIDS (UNAIDS)
Aims to place people living with HIV and people affected by the virus at the decision-making table and at the center of designing, delivering, and monitoring the AIDS response.
Infect Dis
⊕ https://vfmat.ch/464a

Kageno
Works to transform communities in need into places of hope and opportunity through an integrated model that focuses on healthcare, education, income generation, and conservation.
General, Infect Dis, MF Med, Neonat, Nutr, OB-GYN
⊕ https://vfmat.ch/f5bd

Keep a Child Alive
Committed to improving the health and well-being of vulnerable children, young people, adults, and families around the world, with a focus on combating the physical, social, and economic impacts of HIV/AIDS.
Infect Dis, MF Med, Neonat, OB-GYN
⊕ https://vfmat.ch/7f2f

Life for a Child
Supports the provision of the best possible healthcare, given local circumstances,

to all children and youth with diabetes in less-resourced countries, through the strengthening of existing diabetes services.
Endo, Medicine, Peds
⊕ https://vfmat.ch/d712

Light for the World
Contributes to a world in which persons with disabilities fully exercise their rights, and assists persons with disabilities living in poverty.
Ophth-Opt, Rehab
⊕ https://vfmat.ch/3ff6

Lions Clubs International
Empowers volunteers to serve their communities, meet humanitarian needs, encourage peace, and promote international understanding through Lions Clubs.
Heme-Onc, Medicine, Nutr, Ophth-Opt
⊕ https://vfmat.ch/7b12

London School of Hygiene & Tropical Medicine: Health in Humanitarian Crises Centre
Advances health and health equity in crisis-affected countries through research, education, and translation of knowledge into policy and practice.
ER Med, Infect Dis, Pub Health
⊕ https://vfmat.ch/96ad

Management Sciences for Health (MSH)
Works with countries and communities to save lives and improve the health of the world's poorest and most vulnerable people by building strong, resilient, sustainable health systems.
Infect Dis, Logist-Op, Pub Health
⊕ https://vfmat.ch/6aa2

MAP International
Provides medicines and health supplies to those in need around the world so they might experience life to the fullest.
Logist-Op
⊕ https://vfmat.ch/deed

Massachusetts General Hospital Global Surgery Initiative
Aims to improve surgical education and access to advanced surgical care in resource-limited settings around the world by performing surgical operations as visitors, training local surgeons, and sharing medical technology through international partnerships across disciplines.
Anesth, Crit-Care, ER Med, Heme-Onc, Peds, Surg
⊕ https://vfmat.ch/31b1

McGill University Health Centre: Centre for Global Surgery
Works to reduce the impact of injury by advancing surgical care through research and education in resource-limited settings.
ER Med, Logist-Op, Ped Surg, Surg
⊕ https://vfmat.ch/7246

MCW Global
Works to address communities' pressing needs by empowering current leaders and readying leaders of tomorrow.
Dent-OMFS
⊕ https://vfmat.ch/1547

Medical Ministry International
Provides compassionate healthcare in areas of need, inspired by the Christian faith.
CT Surg, Dent-OMFS, ENT, General, OB-GYN, Ophth-Opt, Ortho, Plast, Rehab, Surg, Urol, Vasc Surg
⊕ https://vfmat.ch/5da6

Medical Missions for Children (MMFC)
Provides quality surgical and dental services to poor and underprivileged children and young adults in various countries throughout the world, and facilitates the transfer of education, knowledge, and recent innovations to the local medical communities.
Dent-OMFS, ENT, Endo, Ortho, Ped Surg, Peds, Plast
⊕ https://vfmat.ch/1631

MedShare

Aims to improve the quality of life of people, communities, and the planet by sourcing and directly delivering surplus medical supplies and equipment to communities in need around the world.

Logist-Op

⊕ https://vfmat.ch/c8bc

Mercy and Love Foundation

Aims to provide orphaned and vulnerable children with basic human needs such as food, clothing, and shelter, enabling them to thrive.

General, Peds

⊕ https://vfmat.ch/649a

MicroResearch: Africa/Asia

Seeks to improve health outcomes in Africa by training, mentoring, and supporting local multidisciplinary health professional researchers.

Infect Dis, Nutr, OB-GYN, Psych

⊕ https://vfmat.ch/13e7

Mission Regan

Collects supplies, medication, and medical equipment and provides them to those who are in desperate need, both locally and globally.

Logist-Op

⊕ https://vfmat.ch/2bc1

MSD for Mothers

Designs scalable solutions that help end preventable maternal deaths.

MF Med, OB-GYN, Pub Health

⊕ https://vfmat.ch/9f99

Multi-Agency International Training and Support (MAITS)

Improves the lives of some of the world's poorest people living with disabilities through better access to quality health and education services and support.

Neuro, Psych, Rehab

⊕ https://vfmat.ch/9dcd

NCD Alliance

Unites and strengthens civil society to stimulate collaborative advocacy, action, and accountability for NCD (noncommunicable disease) prevention and control.

All-Immu, CV Med, General, Heme-Onc, Medicine, Peds, Psych

⊕ https://vfmat.ch/abdd

Ndengera Polyclinic

Provides quality care and health education to the population, and conducts research to better the quality of health services provided.

Dent-OMFS, General, Medicine, OB-GYN, Peds

⊕ https://vfmat.ch/89cd

New Horizons Collaborative

Advances a holistic, integrated approach to high-quality pediatric HIV care and treatment with a specific focus on those in need of advanced treatment.

Infect Dis, Peds, Pub Health

⊕ https://vfmat.ch/a76a

Northwestern University Feinberg School of Medicine: Institute for Global Health

Aims to improve access to essential surgical care by addressing the barriers to care, with multidisciplinary and bidirectional partnerships, through innovation, research, education, policy, and advocacy. Goals also include training of the next generation of global health leaders, and building sustainable capacity in regions with health inequities.

Anesth, ER Med, Heme-Onc, Logist-Op, MF Med, OB-GYN, Ped Surg, Surg

⊕ https://vfmat.ch/24f3

Norwegian People's Aid

Aims to improve living conditions, to create a democratic, just, and safe society.

ER Med, Logist-Op

⊕ https://vfmat.ch/2d8e

One Family Health

Improves access to quality essential medicines and basic healthcare services in isolated communities of Rwanda, using a sustainable business model to help underserved communities build health as an asset.

General, Logist-Op, Pub Health

⊕ https://vfmat.ch/3259

OneSight

Brings eye exams and glasses to people who lack access to vision care.

Ophth-Opt

⊕ https://vfmat.ch/3ecc

Open Heart International

Provides surgical interventions and best practices to the most disadvantaged communities on the planet.

CT Surg, MF Med, OB-GYN, Ophth-Opt, Plast, Surg

⊕ https://vfmat.ch/dab2

Operation Hernia

Provides high-quality surgery at minimal cost to patients who otherwise would not receive it.

Anesth, Ortho, Surg

⊕ https://vfmat.ch/6e9a

Operation Medical

Commits efforts to promoting and providing high-quality medical care and education to communities that do not have adequate access.

Anesth, ENT, Logist-Op, OB-GYN, Ped Surg, Plast, Surg, Urol

⊕ https://vfmat.ch/7e1b

Operation Smile

Treats patients with cleft lip and cleft palate, and creates solutions that deliver safe surgery to people where it's needed most.

Anesth, Dent-OMFS, ENT, Ped Surg, Plast

⊕ https://vfmat.ch/5c29

Options

Believes in a world in which women and children can access the high-quality health services they need, without financial burden.

Logist-Op, MF Med, Neonat, OB-GYN

⊕ https://vfmat.ch/3a48

Optivest Foundation

Funds strategic opportunities that are holistic and collaborative, inspired by the Christian faith.

General, Nutr

⊕ https://vfmat.ch/f1e6

Orbis International

Works to prevent and treat blindness through hands-on training and improved access to quality eye care.

Anesth, Ophth-Opt, Surg

⊕ https://vfmat.ch/f2b2

Pact

Works on the ground to improve the lives of those who are challenged by poverty and marginalization, striving for a world in which all people are heard, capable, and vibrant.

Infect Dis, Logist-Op, MF Med, Pub Health

⊕ https://vfmat.ch/9a6c

Pan-African Academy of Christian Surgeons (PAACS)

Exists to train and support African surgeons to provide excellent, compassionate care to those most in need, inspired by the Christian faith.

Anesth, CT Surg, Neurosurg, OB-GYN, Ortho, Ped Surg, Plast, Surg

⊕ https://vfmat.ch/85ba

Partners for World Health

Sorts, evaluates, repackages, and prepares supplies and equipment for distribution to individuals, communities, and healthcare facilities in need, both locally and internationally.

ER Med, General, Logist-Op

⊕ https://vfmat.ch/982e

Partners in Health

Responds to the moral imperative to provide high-quality healthcare globally to those who need it most, while striving to ease suffering by providing a

comprehensive model of care that includes access to food, transportation, housing, and other key components of healing.
CT Surg, General, Heme-Onc, Infect Dis, MF Med, Neurosurg, OB-GYN, Ortho, Plast, Psych, Urol
⊕ https://vfmat.ch/dc9c

Pfalzklinikum
Aims to establish community-psychiatry structures in Rwanda and institute the practice of exchanging knowledge in daily medical-psychological and nursing routines.
Psych
⊕ https://vfmat.ch/2da8

Physicians Across Continents
Provides high-quality medical care to people affected by crises and disasters.
CV Med, Dent-OMFS, Heme-Onc, MF Med, Nephro, Nephro, OB-GYN, Ped Surg, Plast, Surg
⊕ https://vfmat.ch/fe5d

PINCC Preventing Cervical Cancer
Seeks to prevent female-specific diseases in developing countries by utilizing low-cost and low-technology methods to create sustainable programs through patient education, medical personnel training, and facility outfitting.
OB-GYN
⊕ https://vfmat.ch/9666

Project SOAR
Conducts HIV operations research around the world to identify practical solutions to improve HIV prevention, care, and treatment services.
ER Med, General, MF Med, OB-GYN, Psych
⊕ https://vfmat.ch/1a77

PSI – Population Services International
Aims to improve the health of people in the developing world by focusing on challenges such as a lack of family planning, HIV/AIDS, barriers to maternal health, and the greatest threats to children under the age of 5, including malaria, diarrhea, pneumonia, and malnutrition.
Infect Dis, MF Med, OB-GYN, Peds
⊕ https://vfmat.ch/ffe3

RAD-AID International
Improves and optimizes access to medical imaging and radiology in low-resource regions of the world.
Rad-Onc, Radiol
⊕ https://vfmat.ch/537f

RD Rwanda
Promotes social welfare through research on disease control and prevention, education and health programs, and economic development initiatives.
Genetics, Infect Dis, Logist-Op, Medicine, Nutr, OB-GYN, Path, Peds, Pub Health
⊕ https://vfmat.ch/eafd

RestoringVision
Empowers lives by restoring vision for millions of people in need.
Ophth-Opt
⊕ https://vfmat.ch/e121

Rockefeller Foundation, The
Works to promote the well-being of humanity.
Logist-Op, Nutr, Pub Health
⊕ https://vfmat.ch/5424

Rotary International
Provides service to others, improves lives, and advances world understanding, goodwill, and peace through its fellowship of business, professional, and community leaders.
ER Med, General, Infect Dis, MF Med, OB-GYN
⊕ https://vfmat.ch/8fb5

Rutgers New Jersey Medical School
Seeks to support and promote the global health efforts of the faculty, staff, and students in the areas of education, research, and service through the Rutgers New Jersey Medical School's Office of Global Health.

Anesth, CV Med, Crit-Care, Neurosurg, OB-GYN, Psych
⊕ https://vfmat.ch/8e67

Rwanda Children
Seeks to provide housing, food, family, and hope to at-risk Rwandan children, inspired by the Christian faith.
General, Peds
⊕ https://vfmat.ch/a132

Rwanda Diabetes Association
Prevents and treats diabetes and its complications, raises awareness for diabetes in Rwanda, researches and promotes the welfare of people living with diabetes, and partners with the local government and other national/international organizations to fight diabetes.
Endo, General
⊕ https://vfmat.ch/4438

Rwanda Legacy of Hope
Supports social welfare programs aimed at improving living conditions in Rwanda, and at providing better education, training opportunities, and health.
ENT, Ortho, Plast, Rehab, Surg
⊕ https://vfmat.ch/ea35

Safe Harbor International
Inspired by the Christian faith, provides people living in poverty with ministry, development, training, and relief services such as medical care.
General
⊕ https://vfmat.ch/3dfe

Salvation Army International, The
Seeks to meet human needs through services in education, healthcare, community support, emergency response, and ministry development, inspired by the Christian faith.
Dent-OMFS, Derm, ER Med, Infect Dis, MF Med, Medicine, Nutr, OB-GYN, Ophth-Opt, Palliative, Psych, Rehab, Surg
⊕ https://vfmat.ch/8eb3

Samaritan's Purse International Disaster Relief
Provides spiritual and physical aid to hurting people around the world, such as victims of war, poverty, natural disasters, disease, and famine, based in Christian ministry.
Anesth, CT Surg, Crit-Care, Dent-OMFS, Derm, ENT, ER Med, Endo, GI, General, Heme-Onc, Infect Dis, MF Med, Neonat, Nephro, Neuro, Neurosurg, Nutr, OB-GYN, Ophth-Opt, Ortho, Path, Ped Surg, Peds, Plast, Psych, Pulm-Critic, Radiol, Rehab, Rheum, Surg, Urol, Vasc Surg
⊕ https://vfmat.ch/87e3

Sanofi Espoir Foundation
Contributes to reducing health inequalities among populations that need it most by applying a socially responsible approach focused on fighting childhood cancers in low-income countries, improving maternal and newborn health, and improving access to care.
ER Med, OB-GYN, Peds
⊕ https://vfmat.ch/943b

Save A Child's Heart
Provides lifesaving cardiac treatment to children in developing countries, and trains healthcare professionals from these countries to deliver quality care in their communities.
CT Surg, CV Med, Crit-Care, Ped Surg, Peds
⊕ https://vfmat.ch/1bef

Save the Children
Gives children around the world a healthy start in life, the opportunity to learn, and protection from harm.
All-Immu, Crit-Care, ER Med, General, Infect Dis, MF Med, Medicine, Neonat, OB-GYN, Peds, Psych, Pub Health
⊕ https://vfmat.ch/2e73

SIGN Fracture Care International
Builds orthopedic capacity around the world and provides the injured poor access to fracture surgery by donating orthopedic education and implant systems to surgeons in developing countries.

Ortho, Rehab, Surg
⊕ https://vfmat.ch/123d

SINA Health
Aims to improve the health and educational status of the population in low- and middle-income countries.
General, Logist-Op
⊕ https://vfmat.ch/9ad3

Smile Train, Inc.
Treats children with cleft lip through a sustainable and local model that supports surgery and other forms of essential care.
Logist-Op, Pub Health
⊕ https://vfmat.ch/822c

Society for Family Health Rwanda
Provides health promotion interventions using evidence-based social and behavior change communication and social marketing to empower Rwandans in choosing healthier lives.
Infect Dis, Logist-Op, MF Med, Nutr
⊕ https://vfmat.ch/455e

Solace Ministries
Meets the needs of widows and orphans by supporting them with health, educational, and psychological services, helping to improve their livelihoods.
General, OB-GYN, Psych
⊕ https://vfmat.ch/d691

SOS Children's Villages International
Supports children through alternative care and family strengthening.
ER Med, Peds
⊕ https://vfmat.ch/aca1

Surgeons OverSeas (SOS)
Works to reduce death and disability from surgically treatable conditions in developing countries.
Anesth, Heme-Onc, Surg
⊕ https://vfmat.ch/5d16

Sustainable Medical Missions
Trains and supports Indigenous healthcare and faith leaders in underdeveloped communities to treat neglected tropical diseases (NTDs) and other endemic conditions affecting the poorest community members, by pairing faith-based solutions with best practices.
Infect Dis, Pub Health
⊕ https://vfmat.ch/9165

Swasti
Aims to transform the lives of marginalized communities by ensuring their access to quality healthcare and thereby contributing to poverty alleviation.
Pub Health
⊕ https://vfmat.ch/be8b

Swiss Tropical and Public Health Institute
Contributes to the improvement of the health of populations internationally, nationally, and locally through excellence in research, education, and services.
Infect Dis, Pub Health
⊕ https://vfmat.ch/2ee4

Task Force for Global Health, The
Consists of programs and focus areas that cover a range of global health issues including neglected tropical diseases, infectious diseases, vaccines, field epidemiology, public health informatics, health workforce development, and global health ethics.
Infect Dis, Logist-Op, Medicine, Ophth-Opt, Peds
⊕ https://vfmat.ch/714c

Team Heart
Addresses the burden of cardiovascular disease in Rwanda by increasing access to specialized, lifesaving cardiac care.
Anesth, CT Surg, CV Med, Crit-Care, Ped Surg, Peds, Surg
⊕ https://vfmat.ch/798e

Tearfund
Responds to crisis and partners with local churches to bring restoration to those living in poverty, inspired by the Christian faith.
ER Med, Logist-Op
⊕ https://vfmat.ch/f6cf

TIP Global Health
Empowers Rwandan communities to develop integrated approaches to complex health challenges by increasing access to overall healthcare, improving healthcare quality, and fostering long-term success through economic development.
Crit-Care, General, Infect Dis, MF Med, Neonat, OB-GYN
⊕ https://vfmat.ch/e7bc

U.S. President's Malaria Initiative (PMI)
Supports low-income countries to help control and eliminate malaria through cost-effective, lifesaving malaria interventions.
Infect Dis, MF Med, OB-GYN
⊕ https://vfmat.ch/dc8b

Union for International Cancer Control (UICC)
Unites and supports the cancer community to reduce the global cancer burden, promote greater equity, and ensure that cancer control continues to be a priority in the world health and development agenda.
Heme-Onc, Pub Health
⊕ https://vfmat.ch/88b1

United Nations Children's Fund (UNICEF)
Works in over 190 countries and territories to save children's lives, defend their rights, and help them fulfill their potential, from early childhood through adolescence.
All-Immu, Infect Dis, MF Med, Neonat, Nutr, OB-GYN, Ped Surg, Peds, Pub Health
⊕ https://vfmat.ch/42d7

United Nations Development Programme (UNDP)
Helps countries achieve the simultaneous eradication of extreme poverty and significant reduction of inequalities and exclusion using a sustainable human development approach.
Infect Dis, Logist-Op, Pub Health
⊕ https://vfmat.ch/935c

United Nations High Commissioner for Refugees (UNHCR)
Safeguards the rights and well-being of people who have been forced to flee, ensuring that everybody has the right to seek asylum and find safe refuge in another country, with the goal of seeking lasting solutions.
General, MF Med, Medicine, OB-GYN, Peds, Psych, Pub Health
⊕ https://vfmat.ch/6636

United Nations Population Fund (UNFPA)
Supports reproductive healthcare for women and youth in more than 150 countries, focusing on delivering a world in which every pregnancy is wanted, every childbirth is safe, and every young person's potential is fulfilled.
Infect Dis, MF Med, Neonat, OB-GYN, Peds, Pub Health
⊕ https://vfmat.ch/c969

United States Agency for International Development (USAID)
Promotes and demonstrates democratic values abroad and advances a free, peaceful, and prosperous world. Leads the U.S. government's international development and disaster assistance through partnerships and investments that save lives.
ER Med, Infect Dis, MF Med, OB-GYN, Peds
⊕ https://vfmat.ch/9a99

United States President's Emergency Plan for AIDS Relief (PEPFAR)
The U.S. global HIV/AIDS response works to prevent new HIV infections and accelerate progress to control the global epidemic in more than 50 countries, by partnering with governments to support sustainable, integrated, and country-led responses to HIV/AIDS.
Infect Dis, Pub Health
⊕ https://vfmat.ch/a57c

University of California, Berkeley: Bixby Center for Population, Health & Sustainability

Aims to help manage population growth, improve maternal health, and address the unmet need for family planning within a human rights framework.

OB-GYN

⊕ https://vfmat.ch/ff2b

University of California: Global Health Institute

Mobilizes people and resources across the University of California to advance global health research, education, and collaboration.

General, OB-GYN, Pub Health

⊕ https://vfmat.ch/ee7f

University of Minnesota: Global Surgery & Disparities Program

Works to understand and improve surgical, anesthesia, and OB/GYN care in underserved areas through partnerships with local providers, while training the next generation of academic global surgery leaders.

All-Immu, Dent-OMFS, ER Med, Heme-Onc, MF Med, Neurosurg, OB-GYN, Ophth-Opt, Path, Ped Surg, Plast, Surg, Urol

⊕ https://vfmat.ch/e59a

University of Utah Global Health

Supports local organizations in their quest to improve quality of life in their communities all over the world.

Anesth, CT Surg, CV Med, Crit-Care, Dent-OMFS, ENT, ER Med, Infect Dis, OB-GYN, Ophth-Opt, Ped Surg, Ped Surg, Peds, Plast, Pub Health, Surg, Urol

⊕ https://vfmat.ch/bacd

University of Virginia: Anesthesiology Department Global Health Initiatives

Educates and trains physicians to help people achieve healthy productive lives, and advances knowledge in the medical sciences.

Anesth, Pub Health

⊕ https://vfmat.ch/1b8b

USA for United Nations High Commissioner for Refugees (UNHCR)

Serves and protects refugees and displaced people through emergency relief, cash assistance, education, resettlement, and the rebuilding of livelihoods.

ER Med, General, Logist-Op, Nutr, Pub Health

⊕ https://vfmat.ch/293c

USAID: Deliver Project

Builds a global supply chain to deliver lifesaving health products to people in order to enable countries to provide family planning, protect against malaria, and limit the spread of pandemic threats.

Infect Dis, Logist-Op, MF Med

⊕ https://vfmat.ch/374e

USAID: Health Policy Initiative

Provides field-level programming in health policy development and implementation.

General, Infect Dis, MF Med, OB-GYN, Peds

⊕ https://vfmat.ch/8f84

USAID: Leadership, Management and Governance Project

Improves leadership, management, and governance practices to strengthen health systems and improve health for all, including vulnerable populations worldwide.

Logist-Op

⊕ https://vfmat.ch/d35e

USAID: Maternal and Child Survival Program

Works to prevent child and maternal deaths.

Infect Dis, MF Med, Neonat, OB-GYN, Peds

⊕ https://vfmat.ch/6fcf

Vision for a Nation

Makes eye care accessible and aims to unlock economic growth and human potential in the world's poorest communities.

Ophth-Opt

⊕ https://vfmat.ch/9c2c

Vision for the Poor

Reduces human suffering and improves quality of life through the recovery of sight by building sustainable eye hospitals in developing countries, empowering local eye specialists, funding essential ophthalmic infrastructure, and partnering with like-minded agencies.

Ophth-Opt

⊕ https://vfmat.ch/528e

Voluntary Service Overseas (VSO)

Works with health workers, communities, and governments to improve health services and rights for women, babies, youth, people with disabilities, and prisoners.

General, MF Med, OB-GYN

⊕ https://vfmat.ch/213d

Walkabout Foundation

Provides wheelchairs and rehabilitation in the developing world and funds research to find a cure for paralysis.

Logist-Op, Rehab

⊕ https://vfmat.ch/5582

Wings of Hope for Africa Foundation

Aims to support family welfare, empowers communities, and develops self-sufficiency programs to end poverty in Burundi and Rwanda, East Africa, and in Calgary, Canada.

Infect Dis, Medicine, Peds

⊕ https://vfmat.ch/8d4e

Women for Women International

Supports the most marginalized women to earn and save money, improve health and well-being, influence decisions in their home and community, and connect to networks for support.

MF Med, OB-GYN

⊕ https://vfmat.ch/768c

Women's Equity in Access to Care & Treatment (WE-ACT)

Increases women's and children's access to primary healthcare and treatment in resource-limited settings at the grassroots level, while remaining committed to a locally driven, collaborative model of primary healthcare and treatment provision.

General, Infect Dis, Psych, Pub Health

⊕ https://vfmat.ch/2654

Women's Refugee Commission

Seeks to improve lives by protecting the rights of women, children, and youth displaced by conflict and crisis through researching their needs, identifying solutions, and advocating for programs and policies to strengthen their resilience.

General, MF Med, Neonat, OB-GYN, Peds, Psych

⊕ https://vfmat.ch/3d8f

World Blind Union (WBU)

Represents those experiencing blindness, speaking to governments and international bodies on issues concerning visual impairments.

Ophth-Opt

⊕ https://vfmat.ch/2bd3

World Compassion Fellowship (WCF)

Serves the global poor and persecuted through relief, medical care, development, and training.

CV Med, ER Med, Endo, GI, General, Infect Dis, Medicine, Nutr, OB-GYN, Ortho, Peds, Psych, Pub Health, Rehab

⊕ https://vfmat.ch/7b97

World Health Organization, The (WHO)

The United Nations' agency for health provides leadership on global health matters, shapes the health research agenda, sets norms and standards, articulates evidence-based policy options, provides technical support and monitoring to countries, and assesses health trends.

ER Med, General, Infect Dis, Logist-Op, MF Med, OB-GYN, Peds, Psych, Pub Health

⊕ https://vfmat.ch/c476

World Relief

Brings sustainable solutions to the world's greatest problems: disasters, extreme

poverty, violence, oppression, and mass displacement.
ER Med, Nutr, Psych, Pub Health
⊕ https://vfmat.ch/fbcd

World Vision International
Works with vulnerable communities around the world to overcome poverty and injustice with child-focused programs in disaster management, health, nutrition, economic development, education, clean water, sanitation, and hygiene.
ER Med, General, Infect Dis, MF Med, Nutr, OB-GYN, Peds
⊕ https://vfmat.ch/2642

Rwanda

Healthcare Facilities

Baho International Hospital
KG 9 Avenue 42, Kigali, Kigali, Rwanda
⊕ https://vfmat.ch/f628

Butaro Hospital
NR21, Butaro, Majyaruguru, Rwanda
⊕ https://vfmat.ch/f85b

Gahini Hospital
NR24, Urugarama, Iburasirasuba, Rwanda
⊕ https://vfmat.ch/57ba

Gakoma
DR90, Mamba, Amajvepfo, Rwanda
⊕ https://vfmat.ch/f2b1

Gihundwe District Hospital
Cyangugu, Rwanda
⊕ https://vfmat.ch/36f2

Gisenyi District Hospital
Gisenyi, Rwanda
⊕ https://vfmat.ch/e48b

Gitwe Hospital
NR6, Bwerama, Amajvepfo, Rwanda
⊕ https://vfmat.ch/e2c9

HVP Gatagara
Kigali, Rwanda
⊕ https://vfmat.ch/ce4b

Hôpital La Croix du Sud
KG 201 St, Kigali, Rwanda
⊕ https://vfmat.ch/3b84

Kabaya Hospital
Kabaya, Rwanda
⊕ https://vfmat.ch/b4bd

Kabgayi District Hospital
Kabgayi – Cyakabiri, Gitarama, Rwanda
⊕ https://vfmat.ch/f3a2

Karongi Hospital
NR11, Bwishyura, Iburengerazuba, Rwanda
⊕ https://vfmat.ch/f59c

Kibagabaga Hospital
KG 265 Street, Kinyinya, Umujyi wa Kigali, Rwanda
⊕ https://vfmat.ch/a2d3

Kibilizi
DR107, Kibilizi, Amajvepfo, Rwanda
⊕ https://vfmat.ch/acdb

Kibogora Hospital
NR11, Kanjongo, Iburengerazuba, Rwanda
⊕ https://vfmat.ch/dcd8

King Faisal Hospital
KG 544 St, Kigali, Rwanda
⊕ https://vfmat.ch/c1c3

Kirehe District Hospital
NR4, Mukarange, Iburasirasuba, Rwanda
⊕ https://vfmat.ch/cd7c

Kiziguro Hospital
NR24, Nyakayaga, Iburasirasuba, Rwanda
⊕ https://vfmat.ch/f88c

Muhima Hospital
Kigali, Rwanda
⊕ https://vfmat.ch/8a12

Mukura Hospital
Mukura, Rwanda
⊕ https://vfmat.ch/2462

Musanze Hospital
Ruhengeri – Gisenyi Road, Muhoza, Majyaruguru,
Rwanda
⊕ https://vfmat.ch/1cfa

Ngarama Hospital
Nyagahita – Ngarama Road, Ngarama, Rwanda
⊕ https://vfmat.ch/6c45

Nyagatare Hospital
Nyagatare, Rwanda
⊕ https://vfmat.ch/d15c

Nyanza District Hospital
Nyanza, Busasamana, Rwanda
⊕ https://vfmat.ch/9d3c

Nyanza Hospital
NR6, Busasamana, Amajvepfo, Rwanda
⊕ https://vfmat.ch/5452

Rwamagana Hospital
Rwamagana-Kayonza Road, Kigabiro, Iburasirasuba,
Rwanda
⊕ https://vfmat.ch/3399

Rwanda Military Hospital
Street KK739ST Kanombe, Kicukiro District, Kigali,
Rwanda
⊕ https://vfmat.ch/8253

Rwanda Red Cross
KG 15 Avenue, Kigali, Rwanda
⊕ https://vfmat.ch/ef3a

Rwinkwavu Hospital
Rwinkwavu, Rwanda
⊕ https://vfmat.ch/2ad6

University Teaching Hospital of Butare
Avenue de l'Universite, Ngoma, Amajvepfo, Rwanda
⊕ https://vfmat.ch/e5b8

University Teaching Hospital of Kigali
KN 4 Avenue, Kigali, Rwanda
⊕ https://vfmat.ch/4a8b

São Tomé and Príncipe

Healthcare Facilities

Santo António

SÃO TOMÉ AND
PRÍNCIPE

Neves

Guadalupe

SÃO TOMÉ

Santana

São João dos
Angolares

● Healthcare Facility

São Tomé and Príncipe

One of Africa's most stable and democratic countries, the Democratic Republic of São Tomé and Príncipe is located in the Gulf of Guinea, off the western equatorial coast of Central Africa. The people of this island country are predominantly Christian with a Catholic majority. The population is young, with 61 percent of São Tomé and Príncipe's 213,948 people under the age of 25. About 98 percent of residents of Sao Tome and Principe speak Portuguese, the official and de facto national language. With a population comprising descendants of immigrant Europeans and African slaves, São Tomé and Príncipe has Mesticos, Angolares, Forros, Servicias, Tongas, Europeans, and Asians as its major ethnic groups.

São Tomé and Príncipe gained independence in 1975. The country has a relatively small economy and is dependent on the export of cocoa beans, which in recent times has substantially declined due to drought and mismanagement. The country is import-dependent, with real GDP growth of 3.9 percent, dropping from 4.2 percent in 2016. Per capita GDP is $2,158. The country has considerable potential for developing tourism and petroleum resources, but these are yet to be explored. Close to 66 percent of the São Toméan population lives below the poverty line. Despite this fact, 97 percent of the population has access to clean drinking water.

The population of São Tomé and Príncipe faces many challenges as a result of high poverty rates, including challenges in health. Non-communicable and communicable diseases such as ischemic heart disease, lower respiratory infections, stroke, chronic kidney disease, cirrhosis, COPD, neonatal disorders, asthma, road injuries, tuberculosis, malaria, and diarrheal diseases are the cause of most deaths in São Tomé and Príncipe. While some communicable diseases have decreased on average, particularly malaria and diarrheal diseases, they continue to be significant contributors to deaths in the country.

0.21M
Population

$2,158
GDP Per Capita

70 years
Life Expectancy
↑ Improving

32
Doctors/100k
Physician Density

290
Beds/100k
Hospital Bed Density

130
Deaths/100k
Maternal Mortality

São Tomé and Príncipe

Nonprofit Organizations

Africa Health Organisation
Leads collaborative efforts among countries in Africa and other partners to promote health equity, combat disease, and improve quality of life.
Logist-Op, Pub Health
⊕ https://vfmat.ch/b1c5

Globus Relief
Aims to improve the delivery of healthcare worldwide by gathering, processing, and distributing surplus medical supplies to charities at home and abroad.
Logist-Op
⊕ https://vfmat.ch/a2b7

Humanity First
Provides aid and assistance to those in need, offering sustainable development solutions to society while providing and empowering local communities with the resources to help themselves.
ER Med, General, MF Med, Ophth-Opt
⊕ https://vfmat.ch/13cc

Medical Care Development International (MCD International)
Works to strengthen health systems through innovative, sustainable interventions.
Infect Dis, Logist-Op, OB-GYN, Pub Health
⊕ https://vfmat.ch/dc5c

Mercy and Love Foundation
Aims to provide orphaned and vulnerable children with basic human needs such as food, clothing, and shelter, enabling them to thrive.
General, Peds
⊕ https://vfmat.ch/649a

Organization for the Prevention of Blindness, The (OPC)
Provides research, and treatments and cures for people affected by blindness and blinding diseases in Francophone Africa.
Infect Dis, Ophth-Opt
⊕ https://vfmat.ch/86d6

Rotary International
Provides service to others, improves lives, and advances world understanding, goodwill, and peace through its fellowship of business, professional, and community leaders.
ER Med, General, Infect Dis, MF Med, OB-GYN
⊕ https://vfmat.ch/8fb5

United Nations Children's Fund (UNICEF)
Works in over 190 countries and territories to save children's lives, defend their rights, and help them fulfill their potential, from early childhood through adolescence.
All-Immu, Infect Dis, MF Med, Neonat, Nutr, OB-GYN, Ped Surg, Peds, Pub Health
⊕ https://vfmat.ch/42d7

United Nations Development Programme (UNDP)
Helps countries achieve the simultaneous eradication of extreme poverty and significant reduction of inequalities and exclusion using a sustainable human development approach.
Infect Dis, Logist-Op, Pub Health
⊕ https://vfmat.ch/935c

United Nations High Commissioner for Refugees (UNHCR)
Safeguards the rights and well-being of people who have been forced to flee, ensuring that everybody has the right to seek asylum and find safe refuge in another country, with the goal of seeking lasting solutions.
General, MF Med, Medicine, OB-GYN, Peds, Psych, Pub Health
⊕ https://vfmat.ch/6636

United Nations Population Fund (UNFPA)
Supports reproductive healthcare for women and youth in more than 150 countries, focusing on delivering a world in which every pregnancy is wanted, every childbirth is safe, and every young person's potential is fulfilled.
Infect Dis, MF Med, Neonat, OB-GYN, Peds, Pub Health
⊕ https://vfmat.ch/c969

World Health Organization, The (WHO)
The United Nations' agency for health provides leadership on global health matters, shapes the health research agenda, sets norms and standards, articulates evidence-based policy options, provides technical support and monitoring to countries, and assesses health trends.
ER Med, General, Infect Dis, Logist-Op, MF Med, OB-GYN, Peds, Psych, Pub Health
⊕ https://vfmat.ch/c476

São Tomé and Príncipe

Healthcare Facilities

Centre de Saúde Cidade da Trindade
Cidade da Trindade, São Tomé, São Tomé and Príncipe
⊕ https://vfmat.ch/xkis

Delegacia de Saúde de São Tomé
São Tomé, São Tomé, São Tomé and Príncipe
⊕ https://vfmat.ch/8tyy

Hospital Agostinho Neto
Agostinho Neto, Lobata District, São Tomé and Príncipe
⊕ https://vfmat.ch/smim

Hospital Ayres de Menezes (Hospital Central de São Tomé)
Nazaré, São Tomé Island, São Tomé and Príncipe
⊕ https://vfmat.ch/4334

Hospital de Cantagalo
Ubabudo, São Tomé Island, São Tomé and Príncipe
⊕ https://vfmat.ch/54e6

Hospital de Santa Margarida
São Francisco, São Tomé Island, São Tomé and Príncipe
⊕ https://vfmat.ch/1a81

Hospital de Água Izé
São Tomé, São Tomé, São Tomé and Príncipe
⊕ https://vfmat.ch/x2tn

Hospital Dr. Manuel Quaresma Dias da Graça
Santo António, Príncipe, São Tomé and Príncipe
⊕ https://vfmat.ch/7fbb

Príncipe Hospital San António
San Antonio, Príncipe, São Tomé and Príncipe
⊕ https://vfmat.ch/ai2v

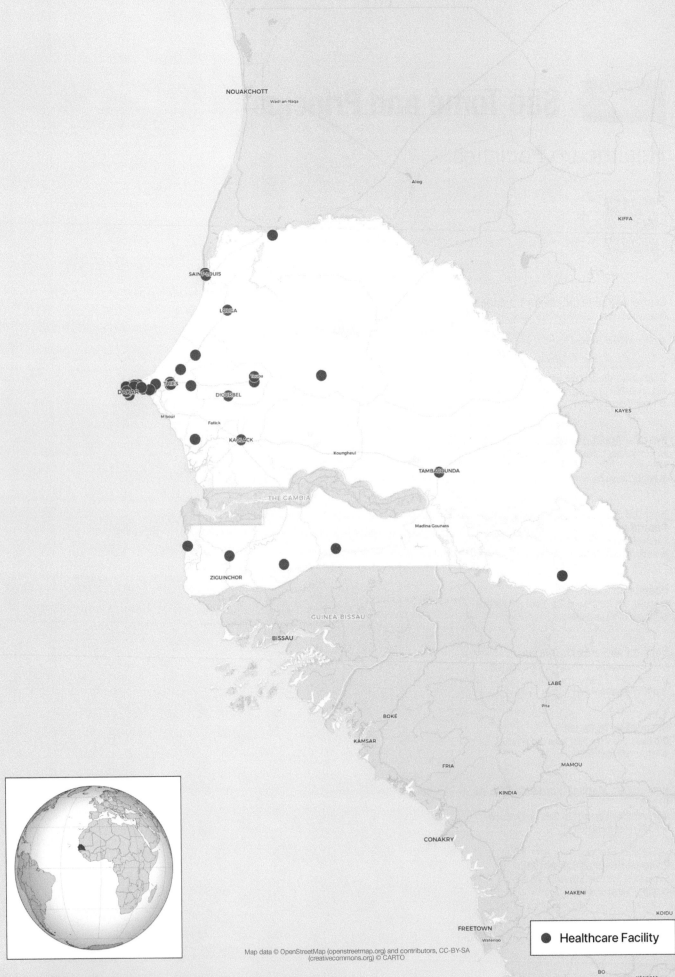

Healthcare Facility

Senegal

The Republic of Senegal, in West Africa, is bordered by Mauritania in the north, Mali to the east, Guinea to the southeast, and Guinea-Bissau to the southwest. Senegal nearly surrounds The Gambia. Mostly Muslim, Senegal has a young population of 16.1 million people, with about 61 percent age 24 or younger. The country comprises diverse ethnic and linguistic communities, the largest being the Wolof, Fula, Serer, Mandinka, Jola, and Soninka, who speak their namesake languages as well as the country's official language, French. Dakar is the capital, home to 3.2 million people.

Senegal gained independence from France in 1960. It is one of the most stable democracies in the world and represents one of the more successful post-colonial democratic transitions in Africa. The country has a long history of participating in international peacekeeping and regional mediation. The main sources of employment and the driving forces of Senegal's economy are mining, construction, tourism, fishing, and agriculture. Despite an economic growth rate of 7.2 percent, the high cost of electricity, an inefficient justice system, corruption, cumbersome bureaucratic systems, and a failing education sector present significant obstacles to Senegal's economic development. Based on 2011 estimates, 47 percent of the population lives below the poverty line. Senegal is classified as a heavily indebted poor country, with a relatively low human development index.

Despite its high poverty rates and low human development indicators, life expectancy continues to rise, nearing 68 years. Communicable and non-communicable diseases contribute the most to death in the country, including neonatal disorders, ischemic heart disease, lower respiratory infections, malaria, diarrheal diseases, stroke, tuberculosis, diabetes, chronic kidney disease, cirrhosis, congenital defects, HIV/AIDS, and meningitis. Between 2009 and 2019, mortality due to non-communicable diseases has increased on average, while mortality due to communicable diseases has decreased. The risk factors that contribute most to death and disability include malnutrition, air pollution, insufficient water and sanitation, high blood pressure, high fasting plasma glucose, high body-mass index, dietary risks, tobacco use, kidney dysfunction, and unsafe sex.

16.1M

Population

$1,488

GDP Per Capita

68 years

Life Expectancy

↑ Improving

9
Doctors/100k

Physician Density

30
Beds/100k

Hospital Bed Density

315
Deaths/100k

Maternal Mortality

Senegal

Nonprofit Organizations

143 LIFE Foundation
Seeks to educate and empower individuals living with malaria, TB, HIV/AIDS, STDs and other health disparities related to sexual health.
Infect Dis, MF Med
⊕ https://vfmat.ch/d59b

A Reason to Smile (ARTS)
Empowers communities without access to dental professionals to achieve and maintain a higher level of oral health by providing hygiene education, direct treatment, and dental supplies.
Dent-OMFS
⊕ https://vfmat.ch/3bae

Abt Associates
Seeks to improve the quality of life and economic well-being of people worldwide, while striving to meet and exceed the highest professional standards.
General, Logist-Op, MF Med, OB-GYN, Peds
⊕ https://vfmat.ch/cec2

Aceso Global
Provides strategic healthcare advisory services in low- and middle-income countries to design and deliver highly customized, evidence-based solutions that address the complex nature of healthcare systems, with a goal to strengthen and provide affordable, high-quality care to all.
Logist-Op, Pub Health
⊕ https://vfmat.ch/b3b7

Action Against Hunger
Aims to end life-threatening hunger for good through treating and preventing malnutrition across more than 45 countries.
Nutr
⊕ https://vfmat.ch/2dbc

Advance Family Planning
Aims to achieve global expansion and access to quality contraceptive information, services, and supplies through financial investment and political commitment.
General, MF Med, Pub Health
⊕ https://vfmat.ch/7478

Africa CDC
Aims to strengthen the capacity and capability of Africa's public health institutions and partnerships to detect and respond quickly and effectively to disease threats and outbreaks, based on data-driven interventions and programs.
Infect Dis, Logist-Op, Pub Health
⊕ https://vfmat.ch/339c

Africa Health Organisation
Leads collaborative efforts among countries in Africa and other partners to promote health equity, combat disease, and improve quality of life.

Logist-Op, Pub Health
⊕ https://vfmat.ch/b1c5

Africa Indoor Residual Spraying Project (AIRS)
Aims to protect millions of people in Africa from malaria by spraying insecticide on walls, ceilings, and other indoor resting places of mosquitoes that transmit malaria.
Infect Dis
⊕ https://vfmat.ch/9bd1

Africa Relief and Community Development
Provides comprehensive relief and developmental aid to people of the African continent regardless of gender, race, or religion.
Nutr, Pub Health
⊕ https://vfmat.ch/6cd2

African Aid International
Works to improve the lives of those most in need in practical and sustainable ways.
Dent-OMFS, Logist-Op
⊕ https://vfmat.ch/9372

African Cultural Exchange, Inc., The
Enriches lives through humanitarian programs in culture, development, education, and healthcare.
General
⊕ https://vfmat.ch/f238

African Field Epidemiology Network (AFENET)
Strengthens field epidemiology and public health laboratory capacity to contribute effectively to addressing epidemics and other major public health problems in Africa.
All-Immu, Infect Dis, Path, Pub Health
⊕ https://vfmat.ch/df2e

African Revival Ministries – Senegal
Based in Christian ministry, aims to improve and develop Senegalese communities through programs in healthcare, nutrition and education, and to provide services to orphan children.
General, Pub Health
⊕ https://vfmat.ch/e85d

Against Malaria Foundation
Helps protect people from malaria. Funds anti-malaria nets, specifically long-lasting insecticidal nets (LLINs), and works with distribution partners to ensure they are used. Tracks and reports on net use and malaria case data.
Infect Dis
⊕ https://vfmat.ch/337d

Al Basar International Foundation

Works with local partners to treat preventable blindness, and helps set up sustainable infrastructure so local teams can save sight in their communities.

Ophth-Opt

⊕ https://vfmat.ch/a8b5

Alliance for International Medical Action, The (ALIMA)

Provides quality medical care to vulnerable populations, partnering with and developing national medical organizations and conducting medical research to bring innovation to 12 African countries where ALIMA works.

ER Med, General, Infect Dis, Logist-Op, MF Med, OB-GYN, Path, Peds, Psych, Pub Health

⊕ https://vfmat.ch/1c11

Americares

Saves lives and improves health for people affected by poverty or disaster and responds with life-changing medicine, medical supplies, and health programs including domestic and global medical clinics.

All-Immu, ER Med, General, Infect Dis, MF Med, Nutr

⊕ https://vfmat.ch/e567

AMREF Flying Doctors

Aims to deliver medical air transport and health services using the latest aviation and medical technology to ensure patients receive unrivaled care.

ER Med, Logist-Op

⊕ https://vfmat.ch/5d5e

Amref Health Africa

Serves millions of people across 35 countries in Sub-Saharan Africa, strengthening health systems, and training African health workers to respond to the continent's most critical health issues.

All-Immu, General, Infect Dis, Logist-Op, MF Med, OB-GYN, Path, Pub Health, Surg

⊕ https://vfmat.ch/6985

Amsterdam Institute for Global Health and Development (AIGHD)

Provides sustainable solutions to major health problems across our planet by forging synergies among disciplines, healthcare delivery, research, and education.

Infect Dis

⊕ https://vfmat.ch/d73d

AO Alliance

Builds solutions to lessen the burden of injuries in low- and middle-income countries, while enhancing the care of the injured to reduce human suffering, disability, and poverty.

Ortho, Surg

⊕ https://vfmat.ch/8cd5

Brain Project Africa

Provides the highest level of medical care, facilitates knowledge transfer, and donates the necessary medical equipment where it's most impactful.

Neuro, Neurosurg, Ortho

⊕ https://vfmat.ch/d4fd

Bridge of Life

Aims to strengthen healthcare globally through sustainable programs that prevent and treat chronic disease.

Logist-Op, Nephro, OB-GYN, Peds, Surg

⊕ https://vfmat.ch/5b68

Brigham and Women's Hospital Global Health Hub

Cares for patients in underserved settings, provides education to staff who work in those areas to create sustainable change, and conducts research designed to improve health in such settings.

General, Infect Dis

⊕ https://vfmat.ch/a8a3

BroadReach

Collaborates with governments, multinational health organizations, donors, and private-sector companies to effect healthcare reform and solve the world's biggest health challenges.

Logist-Op

⊕ https://vfmat.ch/7812

Bureau of International Health Cooperation

Seeks to improve healthcare around the world, including developing countries, using expertise, and contribute to healthier lives of Japanese people by bringing these experiences back to Japan.

ER Med, Heme-Onc, Infect Dis, Peds, Pub Health

⊕ https://vfmat.ch/947d

Carter Center, The

Seeks to prevent and resolve conflicts, enhance freedom and democracy, and improve health, while remaining committed to human rights and the alleviation of human suffering.

Infect Dis, MF Med, Ophth-Opt

⊕ https://vfmat.ch/6556

Chain of Hope

Provides lifesaving heart operations for children around the world and supports the development of cardiac services in numerous developing and war-torn countries.

Anesth, CT Surg, CV Med, Crit-Care, Ped Surg, Peds, Pulm-Critic, Surg

⊕ https://vfmat.ch/1b1b

Chain of Hope (La Chaîne de l'Espoir)

Helps underprivileged children around the world by providing them with access to healthcare.

Anesth, CT Surg, Crit-Care, ER Med, Neurosurg, Ortho, Ped Surg, Surg, Vasc Surg

⊕ https://vfmat.ch/e871

Challenge Initiative, The

Seeks to rapidly and sustainably scale up proven reproductive health solutions among the urban poor.

MF Med, OB-GYN, Peds

⊕ https://vfmat.ch/2f77

Child Aid Gambia

Alleviates poverty among children and their families living in The Gambia and Senegal, and works to improve quality of life for children through specific projects for nutrition, education, and health.

Logist-Op, Nutr, OB-GYN, Peds

⊕ https://vfmat.ch/77a1

ChildFund Australia

Works to reduce poverty for children in many of the world's most disadvantaged communities.

ER Med, General, Peds

⊕ https://vfmat.ch/13df

Clinton Health Access Initiative (CHAI)

Aims to save lives and reduce the burden of disease in low- and middle-income countries. Works with partners to strengthen the capabilities of governments and the private sector to create and sustain high-quality health systems.

General, Heme-Onc, Infect Dis, Logist-Op, MF Med, Medicine, Neonat, Nutr, OB-GYN, Path, Peds, Rad-Onc

⊕ https://vfmat.ch/9ed7

COVID-19 Clinical Research Coalition

Advocates and collaborates for the advancement of COVID-19 research driven by the needs of low-resource settings, and works for equitable access to solutions to the pandemic.

All-Immu, Infect-Dis, MF Med, Path, Pub Health

⊕ https://vfmat.ch/d1f4

Developing Country NGO Delegation: Global Fund to Fight AIDS, TB & Malaria

Works to strengthen the engagement of civil society actors and organizations in developing countries to build a world in which AIDS, TB, and malaria are no longer global, public health, and human rights threats.

Infect Dis, Pub Health

⊕ https://vfmat.ch/3149

Direct Relief
Improves the health and lives of people affected by poverty or emergency situations by mobilizing and providing essential medical resources needed for their care.
ER Med, Logist-Op
🌐 https://vfmat.ch/58e5

DKT INTERNATIONAL INC
Seeks to provide couples with affordable and safe options for family planning and HIV/AIDS prevention through dynamic social marketing.
General, Surg
🌐 https://vfmat.ch/b3a7

Enabel
As the development agency of the Belgian federal government, charged with implementing Belgium's international development policy, carries out public service assignments in Belgium and abroad pursuant to the 2030 Agenda for Sustainable Development.
General, Infect Dis, Logist-Op, MF Med, OB-GYN, Peds, Pub Health
🌐 https://vfmat.ch/5af7

END Fund, The
Aims to control and eliminate the most prevalent neglected diseases among the world's poorest and most vulnerable people.
Infect Dis
🌐 https://vfmat.ch/2614

EngenderHealth
Works to implement high-quality, gender-equitable programs that advance sexual and reproductive health and rights.
General, MF Med, OB-GYN, Peds
🌐 https://vfmat.ch/1cb2

eRanger
Provides sustainable solutions to transportation and medical provision such as ambulances and mobile clinics in developing countries.
ER Med, General, Logist-Op
🌐 https://vfmat.ch/4c18

Evidence Project, The
Improves family-planning policies, programs, and practices through the strategic generation, translation, and use of evidence.
General, MF Med
🌐 https://vfmat.ch/f9e7

Foundation for a Healthier Senegal
Aims to improve health outcomes in rural Senegalese communities.
MF Med, Peds
🌐 https://vfmat.ch/b5db

Global Alliance to Prevent Prematurity And Stillbirth (GAPPS)
Seeks to improve birth outcomes worldwide by reducing the burden of premature birth and stillbirth.
All-Immu, Infect Dis, MF Med, Neonat, Neonat, OB-GYN
🌐 https://vfmat.ch/3f74

Global Ministries – The United Methodist Church
As the worldwide mission and development agency of The United Methodist Church, Global Ministries works with more than 300 hospitals and clinics around the world through its Global Health Unit.
Anesth, CT Surg, CV Med, Crit-Care, Dent-OMFS, Derm, ER Med, GI, General, Infect Dis, Logist-Op, MF Med, Medicine, Neonat, Nephro, Nutr, OB-GYN, Ophth-Opt, Ortho, Palliative, Peds, Pod, Psych, Pub Health, Rehab, Rheum, Surg, Urol
🌐 https://vfmat.ch/1723

Global Oncology (GO)
Brings the best in cancer care to underserved patients around the world and collaborates across geographic, professional, and academic borders to improve cancer care, research, and education.
Heme-Onc, Path, Rad-Onc
🌐 https://vfmat.ch/fcb8

Global Reconstructive Surgery Outreach
Supports surgeons, doctors, and nurses financially to enable them to provide critically needed plastic and reconstructive surgeries to the poor.
Logist-Op, Surg
🌐 https://vfmat.ch/f262

Globus Relief
Aims to improve the delivery of healthcare worldwide by gathering, processing, and distributing surplus medical supplies to charities at home and abroad.
Logist-Op
🌐 https://vfmat.ch/a2b7

GOAL
Works with the most vulnerable communities to help them respond to and recover from humanitarian crises, and to assist them in building transcendent solutions to mitigate poverty and vulnerability.
ER Med, General, Pub Health
🌐 https://vfmat.ch/bbea

Good Shepard International Foundation
Strives to promote inclusive and sustainable development for the most marginalized and vulnerable people, with a special focus on women, girls, and children, inspired by the Christian faith.
ER Med
🌐 https://vfmat.ch/ad9a

Grassroot Soccer
Leverages the power of soccer to educate, inspire, and mobilize at-risk youth in developing countries to overcome their greatest health challenges, live healthier and more productive lives, and be agents for change in their communities.
Infect Dis
🌐 https://vfmat.ch/3521

Health Equity Initiative
Aims to build and sustain a global community that engages across sectors and disciplines to advance health equity.
Pub Health
🌐 https://vfmat.ch/e2e2

Heart to Heart International
Strengthens communities through improving health access, providing humanitarian development, and administering crisis relief worldwide. Engages volunteers, collaborates with partners, and deploys resources to achieve this mission.
Anesth, ER Med, General, Logist-Op, Medicine, Path, Path, Peds, Psych, Pub Health, Surg
🌐 https://vfmat.ch/aacb

Helen Keller International
Seeks to eliminate preventable vision loss, malnutrition, and diseases of poverty.
Infect Dis, Nutr, OB-GYN, Ophth-Opt, Peds
🌐 https://vfmat.ch/b654

Hernia International
Aims to provide relief from sickness, and protection and preservation of health, for persons affected by groin and abdominal hernias and residing in low- and middle-income countries.
Surg
🌐 https://vfmat.ch/e98e

Hospice Africa
Aims to provide a holistic and culturally sensitive palliative care service through accurate treatment of pain.
Palliative
🌐 https://vfmat.ch/9f86

Humanity & Inclusion
Works alongside people with disabilities and vulnerable populations, taking action and bearing witness in order to respond to their essential needs, improve their living conditions and health, and promote respect for their dignity and fundamental rights.
General, Infect Dis, MF Med, Medicine, Ortho, Peds, Psych, Pub Health, Rehab
🌐 https://vfmat.ch/16b7

Humanity First
Provides aid and assistance to those in need, offering sustainable development solutions to society while providing and empowering local communities with the resources to help themselves.
ER Med, General, MF Med, Ophth-Opt
⊕ https://vfmat.ch/13cc

Hunger Project, The
Aims to end hunger and poverty by pioneering sustainable, grassroots, women-centered strategies and advocating for their widespread adoption in countries throughout the world.
Infect Dis, Nutr, OB-GYN, Pub Health
⊕ https://vfmat.ch/3a49

International Children's Heart Fund
Aims to promote the international growth and quality of cardiac surgery, particularly in children and young adults.
CT Surg, Ped Surg
⊕ https://vfmat.ch/33fb

International Council of Ophthalmology
Works with ophthalmologic societies and others to enhance ophthalmic education and improve access to the highest-quality eye care in order to preserve and restore vision for people of the world.
Ophth-Opt
⊕ https://vfmat.ch/ffd2

International Federation of Gynecology and Obstetrics (FIGO)
Implements global projects on specific women's health issues.
MF Med, Medicine, Neonat, OB-GYN, Surg, Urol
⊕ https://vfmat.ch/c4b4

International Federation of Red Cross and Red Crescent Societies (IFRC)
Coordinates and directs international assistance following natural and manmade disasters in nonconflict situations through the world's largest humanitarian and development network. Provides disaster-preparedness programs, healthcare activities, and promotes humanitarian values.
ER Med, General, Infect Dis, Nutr
⊕ https://vfmat.ch/b4ee

International Hearing Foundation
Supports hearing-related service, education, and research.
ENT, Surg
⊕ https://vfmat.ch/3ee2

International Medical Relief
Provides sustainable education, training, medical and dental care, and disaster relief and response in vulnerable communities worldwide.
Dent-OMFS, General, Infect Dis, Medicine, OB-GYN
⊕ https://vfmat.ch/b3ed

International Organization for Migration (IOM) – The UN Migration Agency
Promotes evidence-informed policies and holistic, preventive, and curative health programs that are beneficial, accessible, and equitable for vulnerable migrants.
General, Infect Dis, OB-GYN
⊕ https://vfmat.ch/621a

International Planned Parenthood Federation (IPPF)
Leads a locally owned, globally connected civil society movement that provides and enables services and champions sexual and reproductive health and rights for all, especially the underserved.
Infect Dis, MF Med, OB-GYN
⊕ https://vfmat.ch/dc97

International Trachoma Initiative (iTi)
Works toward a world free from trachoma, a preventable cause of blindness, and provides comprehensive support to national ministries of health and governmental and nongovernmental organizations to implement a comprehensive approach to fight trachoma.
Infect Dis, Ophth-Opt
⊕ https://vfmat.ch/3278

InterSurgeon
Fosters collaborative partnerships in the field of global surgery that will advance clinical care, teaching, training, research, and the provision and maintenance of medical equipment.
ENT, Neurosurg, Ortho, Ped Surg, Plast, Surg, Urol
⊕ https://vfmat.ch/6f8a

IntraHealth International
Improves the performance of health workers and strengthens the systems in which they work.
CV Med, Endo, General, Infect Dis, MF Med, Neonat, Nutr, OB-GYN
⊕ https://vfmat.ch/ddc8

Iris Global
Serves the poor, the destitute, the lost, and the forgotten by providing adoration, outreach, family, education, relief, development, healing, and the arts.
General, Infect Dis, Nutr, Pub Health
⊕ https://vfmat.ch/37f8

Iris Mundial
Aims to improve the ocular health of underserved people in developing countries by giving them access to high-quality preventive and curative eye care services.
Ophth-Opt
⊕ https://vfmat.ch/4f85

IVUmed
Aims to make quality urological care available worldwide by providing medical and surgical education for physicians and nurses, and treatment for thousands of children and adults.
Anesth, OB-GYN, Ped Surg, Surg, Urol
⊕ https://vfmat.ch/e619

Izumi Foundation
Develops and supports programs that improve health and healthcare in neglected regions of Africa and Latin America.
⊕ https://vfmat.ch/f29a

John Snow, Inc. (JSI)
Aims to improve the health and well-being of underserved and vulnerable people and communities throughout the world.
General, Infect Dis, Logist-Op, MF Med, OB-GYN, Peds, Psych, Pub Health
⊕ https://vfmat.ch/ba78

Johns Hopkins Center for Communication Programs
Believes in the power of communication to save lives by empowering people to adopt healthy behaviors for themselves, their families, and their communities.
General, Infect Dis, Logist-Op, OB-GYN, Pub Health
⊕ https://vfmat.ch/1bf9

Johns Hopkins Center for Global Health
Facilitates and focuses the extensive expertise and resources of the Johns Hopkins institutions, together with global collaborators, to effectively address and ameliorate the world's most pressing health issues.
General, Genetics, Logist-Op, MF Med, Peds, Psych, Pub Health, Pulm-Critic
⊕ https://vfmat.ch/54ce

Joint United Nations Programme on HIV/AIDS (UNAIDS)
Aims to place people living with HIV and people affected by the virus at the decision-making table and at the center of designing, delivering, and monitoring the AIDS response.
Infect Dis
⊕ https://vfmat.ch/464a

Kids Care Everywhere
Seeks to empower physicians in under-resourced environments with multimedia, state-of-the-art medical software, and to inspire young professionals to become future global healthcare leaders.
Logist-Op, Ped Surg, Peds
⊕ https://vfmat.ch/bc23

Lay Volunteers International Association (LVIA)
Fosters local and global change to help overcome extreme poverty, reinforce equitable and sustainable development, and enhance dialogue between Italian

and African communities.
ER Med, Logist-Op, MF Med, Neonat, Nutr, OB-GYN, Peds
⊕ https://vfmat.ch/ecd4

Le Korsa
Works to improve the conditions of health, education, culture, and agriculture in southeast Senegal, specifically in the region of Tambacounda.
Dent-OMFS, Derm, General, OB-GYN, Ophth-Opt
⊕ https://vfmat.ch/7d3e

Limbs International
Engages communities and transforms lives through affordable, sustainable prosthetic solutions and rehabilitation services in developing countries.
Logist-Op, Ortho, Pod, Rehab
⊕ https://vfmat.ch/dc84

Management Sciences for Health (MSH)
Works with countries and communities to save lives and improve the health of the world's poorest and most vulnerable people by building strong, resilient, sustainable health systems.
Infect Dis, Logist-Op, Pub Health
⊕ https://vfmat.ch/6aa2

MAP International
Provides medicines and health supplies to those in need around the world so they might experience life to the fullest.
Logist-Op
⊕ https://vfmat.ch/deed

Marie Stopes International
Provides the contraception and safe abortion services that enable women all over the world to choose their own futures.
Infect Dis, MF Med, Neonat, OB-GYN, Pub Health
⊕ https://vfmat.ch/9525

Massachusetts General Hospital Global Surgery Initiative
Aims to improve surgical education and access to advanced surgical care in resource-limited settings around the world by performing surgical operations as visitors, training local surgeons, and sharing medical technology through international partnerships across disciplines.
Anesth, Crit-Care, ER Med, Heme-Onc, Peds, Surg
⊕ https://vfmat.ch/31b1

Maverick Collective
Aims to build a global community of strategic philanthropists and informed advocates who use their intellectual and financial resources to create change.
Infect Dis, MF Med, OB-GYN
⊕ https://vfmat.ch/ea49

Max Foundation, The
Seeks to increase global access to treatment, care, and support for people living with cancer.
General, Heme-Onc, Pub Health
⊕ https://vfmat.ch/8c7d

Medical Ambassadors International
Equipping communities through Christ-centered health and development.
Nutr, OB-GYN, Pub Health
⊕ https://vfmat.ch/8e76

Medical Care Development International (MCD International)
Works to strengthen health systems through innovative, sustainable interventions.
Infect Dis, Logist-Op, OB-GYN, Pub Health
⊕ https://vfmat.ch/dc5c

Medical Care Development International
Works to improve the health of vulnerable populations through integrated, sustainable, and locally driven interventions.
Infect Dis, OB-GYN, Peds, Pub Health
⊕ https://vfmat.ch/da87

MedShare
Aims to improve the quality of life of people, communities, and the planet by

sourcing and directly delivering surplus medical supplies and equipment to communities in need around the world.
Logist-Op
⊕ https://vfmat.ch/c8bc

Merck for Mothers
Hopes to create a world where no woman has to die giving life by collaborating with partners to improve the health and well-being of women during pregnancy, childbirth, and the postpartum period.
MF Med, OB-GYN
⊕ https://vfmat.ch/5b51

Mercy and Love Foundation
Aims to provide orphaned and vulnerable children with basic human needs such as food, clothing, and shelter, enabling them to thrive.
General, Peds
⊕ https://vfmat.ch/649a

Mercy Ships
Operates hospital ships staffed by volunteers to bring hope, healing, and healthcare to underserved communities worldwide.
Anesth, Dent-OMFS, Logist-Op, Neonat, OB-GYN, Ophth-Opt, Ortho, Palliative, Plast, Psych, Surg
⊕ https://vfmat.ch/2e99

MiracleFeet
Brings low-cost treatment to every child on the planet born with clubfoot, a leading cause of physical disability.
Ortho, Peds, Rehab
⊕ https://vfmat.ch/bda8

Mission Bambini
Helps to support children living in poverty and sickness, and lacking education, giving them the opportunity for and hope of a better life.
CT Surg, CV Med, Crit-Care, ER Med, Ped Surg, Peds
⊕ https://vfmat.ch/dc1a

Mobility Outreach International
Enables mobility for children and adults in under-resourced areas of the world, and creates a sustainable orthopedic surgery model using local resources.
Ortho, Rehab
⊕ https://vfmat.ch/9376

MSD for Mothers
Designs scalable solutions that help end preventable maternal deaths.
MF Med, OB-GYN, Pub Health
⊕ https://vfmat.ch/9f99

MSI Reproductive Choices (Marie Stopes International)
Seeks to deliver quality family planning and reproductive healthcare to women around the world.
MF Med
⊕ https://vfmat.ch/5c82

Médecins du Monde/Doctors of the World
Provides care, bears witness, and supports social change worldwide with innovative medical programs and evidence-based advocacy initiatives.
ER Med, General, Infect Dis, MF Med, Neonat, OB-GYN, Peds, Pub Health
⊕ https://vfmat.ch/a43d

Mérieux Foundation
Committed to fighting infectious diseases that affect developing countries by capacity building, particularly in clinical laboratories, and focusing on diagnosis.
Logist-Op, Path
⊕ https://vfmat.ch/a23a

Options
Believes in a world in which women and children can access the high-quality health services they need, without financial burden.
Logist-Op, MF Med, Neonat, OB-GYN
⊕ https://vfmat.ch/3a48

Order of Malta

Supports forgotten or excluded people, especially those living in conflict zones or amid natural disasters, by providing medical assistance, caring for refugees, and distributing medicines and necessities.

ER Med, General, Infect Dis, MF Med, Nephro, OB-GYN, Ortho, Psych

⊕ https://vfmat.ch/1fab

Organization for the Prevention of Blindness, The (OPC)

Provides research, and treatments and cures for people affected by blindness and blinding diseases in Francophone Africa.

Infect Dis, Ophth-Opt

⊕ https://vfmat.ch/86d6

Partners for World Health

Sorts, evaluates, repackages, and prepares supplies and equipment for distribution to individuals, communities, and healthcare facilities in need, both locally and internationally.

ER Med, General, Logist-Op

⊕ https://vfmat.ch/982e

PATH

Advances health equity through innovation and partnerships so people, communities, and economies can thrive.

All-Immu, CV Med, Endo, Heme-Onc, Infect Dis, MF Med, Neonat, Nutr, OB-GYN, Path, Peds, Pulm-Critic

⊕ https://vfmat.ch/b4db

People for Change

Helps to eliminate the scarcity of access to basic healthcare, improve children's educational prospects in underdeveloped areas, and improve communities' sustainable access to wholesome food.

General, Infect Dis, Nutr, Peds

⊕ https://vfmat.ch/7499

Philia Foundation

Seeks to invest sustainably in people and marginalized communities in order to improve health and education in Africa.

Anesth, ER Med, General, Heme-Onc, MF Med, Neurosurg, OB-GYN, Ophth-Opt, Ortho, Pub Health, Surg, Urol

⊕ https://vfmat.ch/a352

Philips Foundation

Aims to reduce healthcare inequality by providing access to quality healthcare for disadvantaged communities.

CV Med, OB-GYN, Ped Surg, Peds, Surg, Urol

⊕ https://vfmat.ch/bacb

Picture of Health Foundation

Provides communities with health education and empowers people to alter unhealthy lifestyles, thus increasing both life expectancy and quality.

General, Pub Health

⊕ https://vfmat.ch/83e3

Population Council

Conducts research to address critical health and development issues, helping deliver solutions to improve lives around the world.

Logist-Op, Pub Health

⊕ https://vfmat.ch/1777

Praesens

Provides solutions that improve surveillance and rapid deployment in case of disease outbreaks in areas regularly affected by epidemic and endemic diseases, while driving change and making countries safe from epidemics by working for and with local partners.

Logist-Op, Path, Pub Health

⊕ https://vfmat.ch/ab96

Première Urgence International

Helps civilians who are marginalized or excluded as a result of natural disasters, war, or economic collapse.

ER Med, General, MF Med, Peds, Psych

⊕ https://vfmat.ch/62ba

Project SOAR

Conducts HIV operations research around the world to identify practical solutions to improve HIV prevention, care, and treatment services.

ER Med, General, MF Med, OB-GYN, Psych

⊕ https://vfmat.ch/1a77

PSI – Population Services International

Aims to improve the health of people in the developing world by focusing on challenges such as a lack of family planning, HIV/AIDS, barriers to maternal health, and the greatest threats to children under the age of 5, including malaria, diarrhea, pneumonia, and malnutrition.

Infect Dis, MF Med, OB-GYN, Peds

⊕ https://vfmat.ch/ffe3

Queen Sheba Village

Focuses on the well-being of women and girls in rural Senegal, West Africa.

MF Med, Pub Health

⊕ https://vfmat.ch/9dac

RestoringVision

Empowers lives by restoring vision for millions of people in need.

Ophth-Opt

⊕ https://vfmat.ch/e121

Right to Sight and Health

Seeks to reduce the prevalence of blindness and visual impairment, especially among low-income communities in Northern Ghana.

Ophth-Opt

⊕ https://vfmat.ch/7ff1

Rockefeller Foundation, The

Works to promote the well-being of humanity.

Logist-Op, Nutr, Pub Health

⊕ https://vfmat.ch/5424

Rotary International

Provides service to others, improves lives, and advances world understanding, goodwill, and peace through its fellowship of business, professional, and community leaders.

ER Med, General, Infect Dis, MF Med, OB-GYN

⊕ https://vfmat.ch/8fb5

Saham Foundation

Aims to create lasting change among the most vulnerable populations in Morocco and Sub-Saharan Africa through healthcare, youth engagement, and social inclusion.

Anesth, Dent-OMFS, ENT, OB-GYN, Ophth-Opt, Ped Surg, Peds, Pub Health, Radiol, Surg, Urol

⊕ https://vfmat.ch/54d6

Sanofi Espoir Foundation

Contributes to reducing health inequalities among populations that need it most by applying a socially responsible approach focused on fighting childhood cancers in low-income countries, improving maternal and newborn health, and improving access to care.

ER Med, OB-GYN, Peds

⊕ https://vfmat.ch/943b

Santé Diabète

Addresses the lack of access to care for people with diabetes in Africa, with the mission of saving lives through disease prevention and management and improving quality of life through care delivery.

Endo, Medicine, Vasc Surg

⊕ https://vfmat.ch/7652

Save A Child's Heart

Provides lifesaving cardiac treatment to children in developing countries, and trains healthcare professionals from these countries to deliver quality care in their communities.

CT Surg, CV Med, Crit-Care, Ped Surg, Peds

⊕ https://vfmat.ch/1bef

Sightsavers
Works with partners in developing countries to help eliminate avoidable blindness and advocates for equal opportunity for the disabled.
Infect Dis, Ophth-Opt, Surg
⊕ https://vfmat.ch/aa52

SINA Health
Aims to improve the health and educational status of the population in low- and middle-income countries.
General, Logist-Op
⊕ https://vfmat.ch/9ad3

Smile Train, Inc.
Treats children with cleft lip through a sustainable and local model that supports surgery and other forms of essential care.
Logist-Op, Pub Health
⊕ https://vfmat.ch/822c

Solthis
Improves disease prevention and access to quality care by strengthening the health systems and services of the countries served.
General, Infect Dis, Logist-Op, MF Med, Neonat, Path
⊕ https://vfmat.ch/a71d

SOS Children's Villages International
Supports children through alternative care and family strengthening.
ER Med, Peds
⊕ https://vfmat.ch/aca1

Soutoura
Supports vulnerable communities in Senegal by facilitating their access to healthcare and basic education.
CV Med, General, Heme-Onc, Logist-Op, Ortho, Radiol, Surg
⊕ https://vfmat.ch/e5e2

Swiss Tropical and Public Health Institute
Contributes to the improvement of the health of populations internationally, nationally, and locally through excellence in research, education, and services.
Infect Dis, Pub Health
⊕ https://vfmat.ch/2ee4

Task Force for Global Health, The
Consists of programs and focus areas that cover a range of global health issues including neglected tropical diseases, infectious diseases, vaccines, field epidemiology, public health informatics, health workforce development, and global health ethics.
Infect Dis, Logist-Op, Medicine, Ophth-Opt, Peds
⊕ https://vfmat.ch/714c

Terre des hommes (Tdh) Foundation
Works to improve the daily life of children and their relatives in the areas of health, protection and emergency, in Europe, Africa, Asia, Latin America, and the Near and Middle East.
CT Surg, CV Med, OB-GYN, Ped Surg, Pub Health
⊕ https://vfmat.ch/5c26

U.S. President's Malaria Initiative (PMI)
Supports low-income countries to help control and eliminate malaria through cost-effective, lifesaving malaria interventions.
Infect Dis, MF Med, OB-GYN
⊕ https://vfmat.ch/dc8b

Union for International Cancer Control (UICC)
Unites and supports the cancer community to reduce the global cancer burden, promote greater equity, and ensure that cancer control continues to be a priority in the world health and development agenda.
Heme-Onc, Pub Health
⊕ https://vfmat.ch/88b1

United Methodist Volunteers in Mission (UMVIM)
Engages in short-term missions each year in ministries as varied as disaster response, community development, pastor training, microenterprise, agriculture, Vacation Bible School, building repair and construction, and medical/

dental services.
Dent-OMFS, ER Med, General
⊕ https://vfmat.ch/1ee6

United Nations Children's Fund (UNICEF)
Works in over 190 countries and territories to save children's lives, defend their rights, and help them fulfill their potential, from early childhood through adolescence.
All-Immu, Infect Dis, MF Med, Neonat, Nutr, OB-GYN, Ped Surg, Peds, Pub Health
⊕ https://vfmat.ch/42d7

United Nations Development Programme (UNDP)
Helps countries achieve the simultaneous eradication of extreme poverty and significant reduction of inequalities and exclusion using a sustainable human development approach.
Infect Dis, Logist-Op, Pub Health
⊕ https://vfmat.ch/935c

United Nations High Commissioner for Refugees (UNHCR)
Safeguards the rights and well-being of people who have been forced to flee, ensuring that everybody has the right to seek asylum and find safe refuge in another country, with the goal of seeking lasting solutions.
General, MF Med, Medicine, OB-GYN, Peds, Psych, Pub Health
⊕ https://vfmat.ch/6636

United Nations Population Fund (UNFPA)
Supports reproductive healthcare for women and youth in more than 150 countries, focusing on delivering a world in which every pregnancy is wanted, every childbirth is safe, and every young person's potential is fulfilled.
Infect Dis, MF Med, Neonat, OB-GYN, Peds, Pub Health
⊕ https://vfmat.ch/c969

United States Agency for International Development (USAID)
Promotes and demonstrates democratic values abroad and advances a free, peaceful, and prosperous world. Leads the U.S. government's international development and disaster assistance through partnerships and investments that save lives.
ER Med, Infect Dis, MF Med, OB-GYN, Peds
⊕ https://vfmat.ch/9a99

United Surgeons for Children (USFC)
Pursues greater health and opportunity for children in the most neglected pockets of the world, with a specific focus on and expertise in surgery.
Anesth, CT Surg, Neonat, Neurosurg, OB-GYN, Peds, Radiol, Surg
⊕ https://vfmat.ch/3b4c

University of California, Berkeley: Bixby Center for Population, Health & Sustainability
Aims to help manage population growth, improve maternal health, and address the unmet need for family planning within a human rights framework.
OB-GYN
⊕ https://vfmat.ch/ff2b

USAID: Health Policy Initiative
Provides field-level programming in health policy development and implementation.
General, Infect Dis, MF Med, OB-GYN, Peds
⊕ https://vfmat.ch/8f84

USAID: Human Resources for Health 2030 (HRH2030)
Helps low- and middle-income countries develop the health workforce needed to prevent maternal and child deaths, support the goals of Family Planning 2020, control the HIV/AIDS epidemic, and protect communities from infectious diseases.
Logist-Op
⊕ https://vfmat.ch/9ea8

Vitamin Angels
Helps at-risk populations in need—specifically pregnant women, new mothers, and children under age 5—to gain access to life-changing vitamins and minerals.
General, Nutr
⊕ https://vfmat.ch/7da1

VOSH (Volunteer Optometric Services to Humanity) International
Facilitates the provision and the sustainability of vision care worldwide for people who can neither afford nor obtain such care.
Ophth-Opt
⊕ https://vfmat.ch/a149

Wisconsin Medical Project
Provides humanitarian aid, including donated medical equipment and supplies, to hospitals and clinics in areas of great need.
Logist-Op
⊕ https://vfmat.ch/ef3b

World Anaesthesia Society (WAS)
Aims to support anesthesiologists with an interest in working in low-income regions of the world.
Anesth
⊕ https://vfmat.ch/37fe

World Federation of Hemophilia (WFH)
Aims to improve and sustain care for people with inherited bleeding disorders by pursuing long-term relationships with individuals and organizations who share the values of WFH's development model.
Heme-Onc
⊕ https://vfmat.ch/5121

World Health Organization, The (WHO)
The United Nations' agency for health provides leadership on global health matters, shapes the health research agenda, sets norms and standards, articulates evidence-based policy options, provides technical support and monitoring to countries, and assesses health trends.
ER Med, General, Infect Dis, Logist-Op, MF Med, OB-GYN, Peds, Psych, Pub Health
⊕ https://vfmat.ch/c476

World Medical Relief
Facilitates the distribution of surplus medical resources where they are needed.
Logist-Op
⊕ https://vfmat.ch/72dc

World Vision International
Works with vulnerable communities around the world to overcome poverty and injustice with child-focused programs in disaster management, health, nutrition, economic development, education, clean water, sanitation, and hygiene.
ER Med, General, Infect Dis, MF Med, Nutr, OB-GYN, Peds
⊕ https://vfmat.ch/2642

Senegal

Healthcare Facilities

Centre Elisabeth Diouf Gueule Tapee
Dakar, Senegal
⊕ https://vfmat.ch/h7zn

Centre Hospitalier Abass Ndao
Dakar, Senegal
⊕ https://vfmat.ch/ssnc

Centre Hospitalier National Dalal Jamm
Guédiawaye, Dakar, Senegal
⊕ https://vfmat.ch/92f5

Centre Hospitalier National de Pikine
Dakar, Senegal
⊕ https://vfmat.ch/a5d9

Centre Hospitalier National Mathlaboul Fawzaini de Touba
Touba, Senegal
⊕ https://vfmat.ch/32b4

Centre Hospitalier National Universitaire de Fann
Dakar, Senegal
⊕ https://vfmat.ch/ace4

Centre Hospitalier Régional Amadou Sakhir Mbaye Louga
Dagaït, Louga, Senegal
⊕ https://vfmat.ch/1f68

Centre Hospitalier Régional de Kolda
Kolda, Senegal
⊕ https://vfmat.ch/11a4

Centre Hospitalier Régional de Saint-Louis
Saint-Louis, Senegal
⊕ https://vfmat.ch/2169

Centre National d'Enfants Albert Royer
Dakar, Senegal
⊕ https://vfmat.ch/268b

Centre de Santé Philippe Maguilène Senghor
Dakar, Senegal
https://vfmat.ch/3ca9

Entrée Hôpital Régional de Thiès
Thiès Nones, Thiès, Senegal
⊕ https://vfmat.ch/d84f

Hospital Center Regional de Fatick
Fatick, Fatick Region, Senegal
⊕ https://vfmat.ch/mvnn

Hospital Regional
Ziguinchor, Ziguinchor Region, Senegal
⊕ https://vfmat.ch/qju1

Hôpital Abdoul Aziz Sy Dabakh
Sintiou Pir, Thiès, Senegal
⊕ https://vfmat.ch/d211

Hôpital Aristide Le Dantec
Dakar, Senegal
⊕ https://vfmat.ch/e49f

Hôpital Barthimée
Thiès, Senegal
⊕ https://vfmat.ch/eaaf

Hôpital de Mbacké
Mbaké, Diourbel, Senegal
⊕ https://vfmat.ch/1ae1

Hôpital des Enfants de Diamniadio
Diamniadio, Senegal
⊕ https://vfmat.ch/424c

Hôpital El Hadji Ibrahima Niass
Kaolack, Kaolack region, Senegal
⊕ https://vfmat.ch/888f

Hôpital Général de Grand Yoff
Dakar, Dakar, Senegal
⊕ https://vfmat.ch/2fa3

Hôpital Militaire de Ouakam
Dakar, Senegal
⊕ https://vfmat.ch/1efb

Hôpital Ousmane Ngom
Saint-Louis, Senegal
⊕ https://vfmat.ch/8c42

Hôpital Principal de Dakar
Dakar, Senegal
⊕ https://vfmat.ch/2fc7

Hôpital Psychiatrique de Thiaroye
Dakar, Senegal
⊕ https://vfmat.ch/cb35

Hôpital Roi Baudouin
Dakar, Senegal
⊕ https://vfmat.ch/1dcc

Hôpital Régional de Diourbel
Diourbel, Senegal
⊕ https://vfmat.ch/a9ce

Hôpital Régional de Kolda
Kolda, Senegal
⊕ https://vfmat.ch/6eca

Hôpital Régional de Tambacounda
Tambacounda, Senegal
⊕ https://vfmat.ch/9459

Hôpital Régional El Hadji Ahmadou Sakhir Ndieguene de Thiès
Thies, Senegal
⊕ https://vfmat.ch/412e

Hôpital Saint-Jean de Dieu
Darou Ramane, Thiès, Senegal
⊕ https://vfmat.ch/7da3

Hôpital SAMU Municipal de Grande Yoff
Dakar, Senegal
⊕ https://vfmat.ch/3e3d

Hôpital Soeurs Keur
Sam-Notaire, Guediawaye, Senegal
⊕ https://vfmat.ch/f8da

Hôpital Traditionnel de Keur Massar
Keur Massar, Dakar Region, Senegal
⊕ https://vfmat.ch/7b79

Hôpital Youssou Mbargane Diop
Dakar, Senegal
⊕ https://vfmat.ch/ff16

Masroor Humanity First Hospital Senegal
Dakar, Senegal
⊕ https://vfmat.ch/mbeq

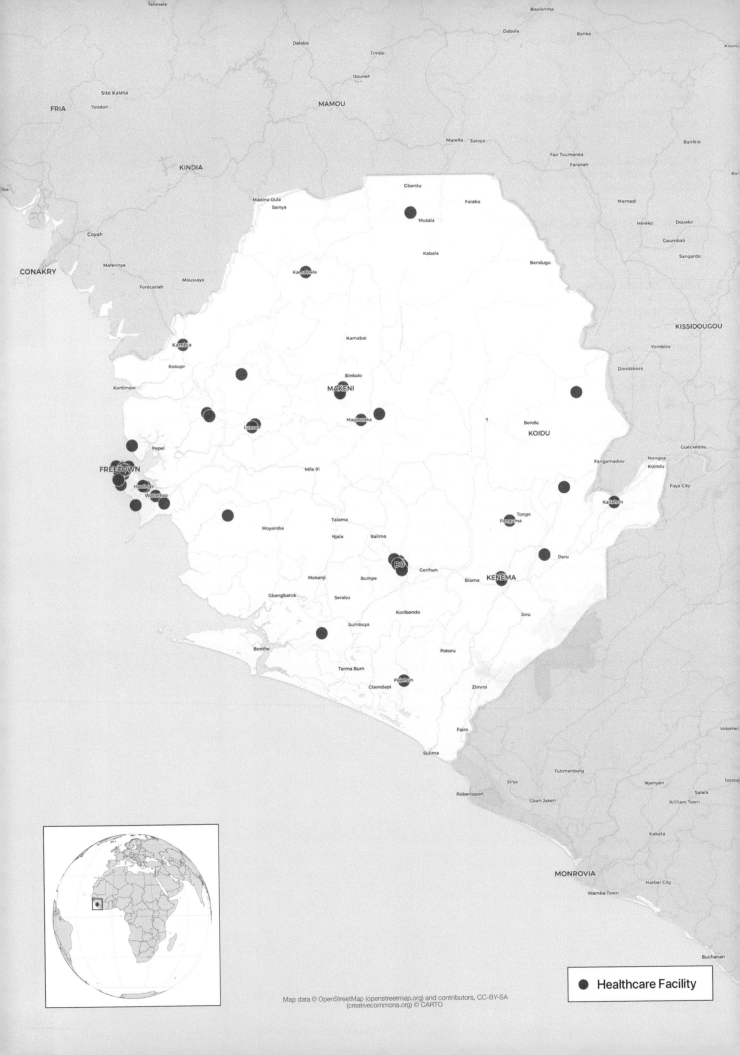

Healthcare Facility

Sierra Leone

Located on West Africa's coast, the Republic of Sierra Leone has a population of about 6.8 million people. The Portuguese origins of the country's name translates to "Lion Mountains," referencing the hills that surround the capital of Freetown, one the largest natural harbors in the world. The primarily agricultural country has deposits of gold, diamonds, bauxite, and rutile. Large ethnic groups include the Mende and the Temne; English and Krio are the nation's official languages.

The country continues to recover from a devastating civil war that ended in 2002. Since then, Sierra Leone has had significant and impressive economic growth and was on track to reach middle-income status by 2035. However, progress was hindered by an Ebola outbreak in 2014 that infected more than 14,000 and killed nearly 4,000 people. The country is still recovering from this crisis.

While life expectancy continues to increase in Sierra Leone, it is still one of the lowest in the world at around 55 years. Likewise, although child mortality continues to decrease, the maternal mortality rate remains one of the highest in the world. The country has significantly higher rates of malaria than other countries in the same region. While some progress has been made to address illness and disease, the impact of the civil war left the country with a debilitated health system, tens of thousands of war amputees, and shortages of equipment, supplies, and doctors. Both communicable and non-communicable diseases such as malaria, lower respiratory infections, neonatal disorders, ischemic heart disease, diarrheal diseases, stroke, HIV/AIDS, congenital defects, tuberculosis, and meningitis cause the most deaths in Sierra Leone.

6.8M
Population

$485
GDP Per Capita

55 years
Life Expectancy
↑ Improving

7	**40**	**1,120**
Doctors/100k	**Beds**/100k	**Deaths**/100k
Physician Density	Hospital Bed Density	Maternal Mortality

Sierra Leone

Nonprofit Organizations

143 LIFE Foundation
Seeks to educate and empower individuals living with malaria, TB, HIV/AIDS, STDs and other health disparities related to sexual health.
Infect Dis, MF Med
⊕ https://vfmat.ch/d59b

Abt Associates
Seeks to improve the quality of life and economic well-being of people worldwide, while striving to meet and exceed the highest professional standards.
General, Logist-Op, MF Med, OB-GYN, Peds
⊕ https://vfmat.ch/cec2

Action Against Hunger
Aims to end life-threatening hunger for good through treating and preventing malnutrition across more than 45 countries.
Nutr
⊕ https://vfmat.ch/2dbc

Advance Family Planning
Aims to achieve global expansion and access to quality contraceptive information, services, and supplies through financial investment and political commitment.
General, MF Med, Pub Health
⊕ https://vfmat.ch/7478

Adventist Health International
Focuses on upgrading and managing mission hospitals by providing governance, consultation, and technical assistance to a number of affiliated Seventh-Day Adventist hospitals throughout Africa, Asia, and the Americas.
Dent-OMFS, General, Pub Health
⊕ https://vfmat.ch/16aa

Africa CDC
Aims to strengthen the capacity and capability of Africa's public health institutions and partnerships to detect and respond quickly and effectively to disease threats and outbreaks, based on data-driven interventions and programs.
Infect Dis, Logist-Op, Pub Health
⊕ https://vfmat.ch/339c

Africa Health Organisation
Leads collaborative efforts among countries in Africa and other partners to promote health equity, combat disease, and improve quality of life.
Logist-Op, Pub Health
⊕ https://vfmat.ch/b1c5

Africa Humanitarian Action (AHA)
Responds to crises, conflicts, and disasters in Africa, while informing and advising the international community, governments, civil society, and the private sector on humanitarian issues of concern to Africa. Supports institutional and organizational development efforts.

General, Infect Dis, MF Med, Nutr, OB-GYN
⊕ https://vfmat.ch/3ca2

Africa Relief and Community Development
Provides comprehensive relief and developmental aid to people of the African continent regardless of gender, race, or religion.
Nutr, Pub Health
⊕ https://vfmat.ch/6cd2

Africa Uplifted
Seeks to enrich the lives of the people of Sierra Leone by promoting basic wellness, removing barriers to education, satisfying essential physical needs, and nurturing spiritual development.
General
⊕ https://vfmat.ch/ba33

African Cultural Exchange, Inc., The
Enriches lives through humanitarian programs in culture, development, education, and healthcare.
General
⊕ https://vfmat.ch/f238

Against Malaria Foundation
Helps protect people from malaria. Funds anti-malaria nets, specifically long-lasting insecticidal nets (LLINs), and works with distribution partners to ensure they are used. Tracks and reports on net use and malaria case data.
Infect Dis
⊕ https://vfmat.ch/337d

Agatha Foundation, The
Seeks to end poverty and hunger, promote universal education, promote gender equality, reduce child mortality, improve maternal health, and combat HIV/AIDS, malaria, and other diseases.
Infect Dis, Logist-Op, Medicine, OB-GYN, Peds
⊕ https://vfmat.ch/9b26

AIDS Healthcare Foundation
Provides cutting-edge HIV/AIDS medical care and advocacy to over one million people in 43 countries.
Infect Dis
⊕ https://vfmat.ch/b27c

AISPO
Implements international initiatives in the healthcare sector and remains involved in various projects to combat poverty, social injustice, and disease around the world.
All-Immu, ER Med, GI, General, Infect Dis, Logist-Op, MF Med, Neonat, OB-GYN, Peds, Psych, Pub Health, Radiol
⊕ https://vfmat.ch/c9e6

Al Basar International Foundation
Works with local partners to treat preventable blindness, and helps set up sustainable infrastructure so local teams can save sight in their communities.
Ophth-Opt
⊕ https://vfmat.ch/a8b5

Americares
Saves lives and improves health for people affected by poverty or disaster and responds with life-changing medicine, medical supplies, and health programs including domestic and global medical clinics.
All-Immu, ER Med, General, Infect Dis, MF Med, Nutr
⊕ https://vfmat.ch/e567

Aminata Maternal Foundation
Aims to improve maternal mortality outcomes for women and girls in Sierra Leone.
MF Med, Neonat, OB-GYN
⊕ https://vfmat.ch/a9f2

Amref Health Africa
Serves millions of people across 35 countries in Sub-Saharan Africa, strengthening health systems, and training African health workers to respond to the continent's most critical health issues.
All-Immu, General, Infect Dis, Logist-Op, MF Med, OB-GYN, Path, Pub Health, Surg
⊕ https://vfmat.ch/6985

Aspen Management Partnership for Health (AMP Health)
Works to improve health systems and outcomes by collaborating with governments to strengthen leadership and management capabilities through public-private partnership.
Logist-Op
⊕ https://vfmat.ch/ea78

Association of Sierra Leonean Health Professionals in the US, The (TASHPUS)
Works to improve the standard of health for the people of Sierra Leone through educating, partnering with and empowering communities, and strengthening health systems.
General, Infect Dis, Logist-Op, Peds, Surg
⊕ https://vfmat.ch/fcba

Austrian Doctors
Stands for a life in dignity and takes care of the health of disadvantaged people. Helps all people regardless of gender, skin color, religion and sexual orientation.
General, Infect Dis, Medicine
⊕ https://vfmat.ch/e929

BethanyKids
Transforms the lives of African children with surgical conditions and disabilities through pediatric surgery, rehabilitation, public education, spiritual ministry, and the training of health professionals.
Neurosurg, Nutr, Ortho, Ped Surg, Peds, Rehab, Surg
⊕ https://vfmat.ch/db4e

Bo Children's Hospital
Cares for sick children and provides health education for families in Sierra Leone.
All-Immu, Anesth, Infect Dis, MF Med, Neonat, Nutr, Peds
⊕ https://vfmat.ch/6f11

BRAC USA
Seeks to empower people and communities in situations of poverty, illiteracy, disease, and social injustice. Interventions aim to achieve large-scale, positive changes through economic and social programs that enable everyone to realize their potential.
ER Med, General, Infect Dis, Logist-Op, MF Med, OB-GYN
⊕ https://vfmat.ch/9d9e

Bread and Water for Africa UK
Aims to create better access to education, nutrition, and healthcare for some of Africa's most vulnerable children and their communities.
General, MF Med, Nutr
⊕ https://vfmat.ch/c855

BroadReach
Collaborates with governments, multinational health organizations, donors, and private-sector companies to effect healthcare reform and solve the world's biggest health challenges.
Logist-Op
⊕ https://vfmat.ch/7812

Bureau of International Health Cooperation
Seeks to improve healthcare around the world, including developing countries, using expertise, and contribute to healthier lives of Japanese people by bringing these experiences back to Japan.
ER Med, Heme-Onc, Infect Dis, Peds, Pub Health
⊕ https://vfmat.ch/947d

Camillian Disaster Service (CADIS) International
Promotes the development of locally based health programs for disaster-stricken communities through compassionate and coordinated interventions.
General, Logist-Op, MF Med
⊕ https://vfmat.ch/5281

Carter Center, The
Seeks to prevent and resolve conflicts, enhance freedom and democracy, and improve health, while remaining committed to human rights and the alleviation of human suffering.
Infect Dis, MF Med, Ophth-Opt
⊕ https://vfmat.ch/6556

Catholic Organization for Relief & Development Aid (CORDAID)
Provides humanitarian assistance and creates opportunities to improve security, healthcare, education, and inclusive economic growth in fragile and conflict-affected areas.
ER Med, Infect Dis, MF Med, OB-GYN, Peds, Psych
⊕ https://vfmat.ch/8ae5

CAUSE Canada
Strives to be a catalyst for global justice as a faith-based organization that aims to provide sustainable, integrated community development in rural West Africa and Central America through authentic, collaborative long-term relationships.
General, MF Med, Neonat, OB-GYN, Peds
⊕ https://vfmat.ch/6fc1

Centre for Global Mental Health
Closes the care gap and reduces human rights abuses experienced by people living with mental, neurological, and substance use conditions, particularly in low-resource settings.
Neuro, OB-GYN, Palliative, Peds, Psych
⊕ https://vfmat.ch/a96d

Chain of Hope
Provides lifesaving heart operations for children around the world and supports the development of cardiac services in numerous developing and war-torn countries.
Anesth, CT Surg, CV Med, Crit-Care, Ped Surg, Peds, Pulm-Critic, Surg
⊕ https://vfmat.ch/1b1b

ChildFund Australia
Works to reduce poverty for children in many of the world's most disadvantaged communities.
ER Med, General, Peds
⊕ https://vfmat.ch/13df

Children & Charity International
Puts people first by providing education, leadership, and nutrition programs along with mentoring and healthcare support services to children, youth, and families.
Nutr, Peds
⊕ https://vfmat.ch/6538

Children of the Nations
Aims to raise children out of poverty and hopelessness so they can become leaders who transform their nations. Emphasizes caring for the whole child—physically, mentally, socially, and spiritually.

Anesth, Dent-OMFS, General, Surg
⊕ https://vfmat.ch/cc52

Children Without Worms
Enhances the health and development of children by reducing intestinal worm infections.
Infect Dis, Pub Health
⊕ https://vfmat.ch/6bee

Children's Lifeline International
Provides medical teams and surgical assistance to underprivileged children in developing countries through missions in partnership with local hospitals.
CV Med, Dent-OMFS, General, MF Med, Neurosurg, Peds, Rehab
⊕ https://vfmat.ch/6fea

Childspring International
Provides life-changing surgeries for children from developing countries and transforms communities.
CT Surg, Medicine, Ophth-Opt, Ortho, Ped Surg, Peds, Surg
⊕ https://vfmat.ch/f939

Christian Aid Ministries
Strives to be a trustworthy and efficient channel for Amish, Mennonite, and other conservative Anabaptist groups and individuals to minister to physical and spiritual needs around the world.
CT Surg, ER Med, Logist-Op, Ortho, Pub Health
⊕ https://vfmat.ch/7b33

Christian Blind Mission (CBM)
Aims to improve the quality of life of persons with disabilities in the poorest countries, addressing poverty as a cause and a consequence of disability, and working in partnership to create a society for all.
ENT, General, Infect Dis, OB-GYN, Ophth-Opt, Ortho, Peds, Psych, Rehab, Surg
⊕ https://vfmat.ch/3824

Christian Connections for International Health (CCIH)
Promotes global health and wholeness from a Christian perspective.
All-Immu, General, Infect Dis, MF Med, Neonat, OB-GYN, Psych
⊕ https://vfmat.ch/fa5d

Circle of Health International (COHI)
Aligns with local, community-based organizations led and powered by women to help respond to the needs of the women and children that they serve. Helps with the provision of professional volunteers, capacity training, and procurement of requested and appropriate supplies and equipment. Raises funds for the organizations to provide the services required.
ER Med, Logist-Op, MF Med, Neonat, OB-GYN, Psych
⊕ https://vfmat.ch/8b63

City Garden Clinic
Works to provide quality patient care with attention to clinical excellence and patient safety.
Crit-Care, General, Infect Dis, OB-GYN, Ortho, Surg, Urol
⊕ https://vfmat.ch/dbeb

Clinton Health Access Initiative (CHAI)
Aims to save lives and reduce the burden of disease in low- and middle-income countries. Works with partners to strengthen the capabilities of governments and the private sector to create and sustain high-quality health systems.
General, Heme-Onc, Infect Dis, Logist-Op, MF Med, Medicine, Neonat, Nutr, OB-GYN, Path, Peds, Rad-Onc
⊕ https://vfmat.ch/9ed7

Columbia Vagelos College of Physicians and Surgeons Programs in Global Health
Harnesses the expertise of the medical school to improve health worldwide by training global health leaders, building capacity through interdisciplinary education and training programs, and addressing unmet health needs through research and application.
CV Med, Derm, Genetics, Heme-Onc, Infect Dis, Medicine, OB-GYN, Ophth-Opt, Peds, Psych, Pub Health, Pulm-Critic, Surg
⊕ https://vfmat.ch/a9e5

Compassion Med International
Supports medical relief missions worldwide, inspired by the Christian faith.
ER Med, General
⊕ https://vfmat.ch/2615

Compassionate Eye
Aims to support the social good by supplying infrastructure and personnel for sanitation, education, medical care, small business, and job training.
General, Infect Dis, MF Med, OB-GYN, Peds
⊕ https://vfmat.ch/1915

Concern Worldwide
Seeks to permanently transform the lives of people living in extreme poverty, tackling its root causes, and building resilience.
Logist-Op, MF Med, Nutr, OB-GYN
⊕ https://vfmat.ch/77e9

COVID-19 Clinical Research Coalition
Advocates and collaborates for the advancement of COVID-19 research driven by the needs of low-resource settings, and works for equitable access to solutions to the pandemic.
All-Immu, Infect-Dis, MF Med, Path, Pub Health
⊕ https://vfmat.ch/d1f4

Curamericas Global
Partners with communities abroad to save the lives of mothers and children by providing health services and education.
General, Infect Dis, MF Med, OB-GYN, Peds, Pub Health
⊕ https://vfmat.ch/286b

Dentaid
Seeks to treat, equip, train, and educate people in need of dental care.
Dent-OMFS
⊕ https://vfmat.ch/a183

Direct Relief
Improves the health and lives of people affected by poverty or emergency situations by mobilizing and providing essential medical resources needed for their care.
ER Med, Logist-Op
⊕ https://vfmat.ch/58e5

DKT INTERNATIONAL INC
Seeks to provide couples with affordable and safe options for family planning and HIV/AIDS prevention through dynamic social marketing.
General, Surg
⊕ https://vfmat.ch/b3a7

Doctors with Africa (CUAMM)
Advocates for the universal right to health and promotes the values of international solidarity, justice, and peace. Works to protect and improve the well-being and health of vulnerable communities in Africa with a long-term development perspective.
ER Med, Infect Dis, MF Med, Neonat, OB-GYN, Peds
⊕ https://vfmat.ch/d2fb

Doctors Without Borders/Médecins Sans Frontières (MSF)
Responds to emergencies and provides lifesaving medical care where needed most, including during disasters, conflicts, and epidemics.
Anesth, Crit-Care, ER Med, General, Infect Dis, Nutr, OB-GYN, Ped Surg, Peds, Psych, Pub Health, Surg
⊕ https://vfmat.ch/f363

eHealth Africa
Builds stronger health systems in Africa through the design and implementation of data-driven solutions, responding to local needs and providing underserved communities with the necessary tools to lead healthier lives.
Logist-Op, Path
⊕ https://vfmat.ch/db6a

EMERGENCY
Provides free, high-quality healthcare to victims of war, poverty, and landmines. Also builds hospitals and trains local staff, while pursuing medicine based on

human rights.
ER Med, Neonat, OB-GYN, Ophth-Opt, Ped Surg
⊕ https://vfmat.ch/c361

Engage Now Africa
Works to heal, rescue, and lift vulnerable individuals, families and communities of Africa out of extreme poverty and into self-reliance.
General, Ophth-Opt, Peds, Pub Health
⊕ https://vfmat.ch/16cd

Episcopal Relief & Development
Provides relief in times of disaster and promotes sustainable development by identifying and addressing the root causes of suffering.
Infect Dis, MF Med, Neonat, Nutr, Peds
⊕ https://vfmat.ch/7cfa

eRanger
Provides sustainable solutions to transportation and medical provision such as ambulances and mobile clinics in developing countries.
ER Med, General, Logist-Op
⊕ https://vfmat.ch/4c18

Footprints Missions
Serves the needs of people around the world in a variety of ways to the glory of God.
General, Logist-Op
⊕ https://vfmat.ch/ddef

Freedom From Fistula
Helps women and girls who are injured and left incontinent following prolonged, obstructed childbirth by providing free surgical repairs for patients already suffering with obstetric fistula, as well as maternity care to prevent these fistulas from happening at all.
MF Med, OB-GYN, Peds
⊕ https://vfmat.ch/6e11

Friends of Nixon Memorial Hospital
Supports the Nixon Memorial Hospital in providing inpatient and outpatient care to the town of Segbwema and surrounding rural villages in Sierra Leone.
General, Logist-Op, OB-GYN, Path, Peds
⊕ https://vfmat.ch/545b

German Doctors
Conducts voluntary medical work in developing countries and brings help where misery is part of everyday life.
General, Infect Dis, Medicine
⊕ https://vfmat.ch/21ad

Global Alliance to Prevent Prematurity And Stillbirth (GAPPS)
Seeks to improve birth outcomes worldwide by reducing the burden of premature birth and stillbirth.
All-Immu, Infect Dis, MF Med, Neonat, Neonat, OB-GYN
⊕ https://vfmat.ch/3f74

Global Ministries – The United Methodist Church
As the worldwide mission and development agency of The United Methodist Church, Global Ministries works with more than 300 hospitals and clinics around the world through its Global Health Unit.
Anesth, CT Surg, CV Med, Crit-Care, Dent-OMFS, Derm, ER Med, GI, General, Infect Dis, Logist-Op, MF Med, Medicine, Neonat, Nephro, Nutr, OB-GYN, Ophth-Opt, Ortho, Palliative, Peds, Pod, Psych, Pub Health, Rehab, Rheum, Surg, Urol
⊕ https://vfmat.ch/1723

Global Oncology (GO)
Brings the best in cancer care to underserved patients around the world and collaborates across geographic, professional, and academic borders to improve cancer care, research, and education.
Heme-Onc, Path, Rad-Onc
⊕ https://vfmat.ch/fcb8

Global Polio Eradication Initiative
Aims to eradicate polio worldwide.

All-Immu, Infect-Dis, Logist-Op, Pub Health
⊕ https://vfmat.ch/7e2c

Globus Relief
Aims to improve the delivery of healthcare worldwide by gathering, processing, and distributing surplus medical supplies to charities at home and abroad.
Logist-Op
⊕ https://vfmat.ch/a2b7

GOAL
Works with the most vulnerable communities to help them respond to and recover from humanitarian crises, and to assist them in building transcendent solutions to mitigate poverty and vulnerability.
ER Med, General, Pub Health
⊕ https://vfmat.ch/bbea

Hands for Africa
Provides innocent civil war victims in Africa with tools that enable them to become self-reliant, such as immediate needs such as food, water, clothing, and shelter, while developing and implementing successful programs that foster self-reliance.
Ortho, Rehab
⊕ https://vfmat.ch/19a3

Healing Hands Foundation, The
Provides high-quality surgical procedures, medical treatment, dental care, and educational support in under-resourced areas worldwide.
Anesth, Dent-OMFS, General, Ped Surg, Peds, Surg
⊕ https://vfmat.ch/4bfc

Health Equity Initiative
Aims to build and sustain a global community that engages across sectors and disciplines to advance health equity.
Pub Health
⊕ https://vfmat.ch/e2e2

Health For All Mission
Promotes health and wellness in the following areas: healthcare, education, economic development, and the environment.
Dent-OMFS, General, Pub Health
⊕ https://vfmat.ch/fe1a

Health Poverty Action
Works in partnership with people around the world who are pursuing change in their own communities to demand health justice and challenge power imbalances.
ER Med, General, Infect Dis, Psych, Pub Health
⊕ https://vfmat.ch/ee58

Heart to Heart International
Strengthens communities through improving health access, providing humanitarian development, and administering crisis relief worldwide. Engages volunteers, collaborates with partners, and deploys resources to achieve this mission.
Anesth, ER Med, General, Logist-Op, Medicine, Path, Path, Peds, Psych, Pub Health, Surg
⊕ https://vfmat.ch/aacb

Heineman Medical Outreach
Provides medical and educational assistance globally to promote sustainable healthcare and enhanced living standards in underserved communities through the International Medical Outreach (IMO) program, a collaborative partnership between Heineman Medical Outreach and Atrium Health.
Anesth, CT Surg, CV Med, ER Med, General, Heme-Onc, Logist-Op, Medicine, Neonat, OB-GYN, Ped Surg, Peds, Surg, Vasc Surg
⊕ https://vfmat.ch/389b

Helen Keller International
Seeks to eliminate preventable vision loss, malnutrition, and diseases of poverty.
Infect Dis, Nutr, OB-GYN, Ophth-Opt, Peds
⊕ https://vfmat.ch/b654

Help Madina
Envisions a world in which every citizen of Sierra Leone is healthy and has

the opportunity to contribute meaningfully to society. Works hand in hand with those living in the Madina district and other locations in Sierra Leone to improve people's health and well-being.

Endo, General, Geri, Infect Dis, Nutr, Ophth-Opt, Peds, Pub Health

⊕ https://vfmat.ch/86c8

Helping Children Worldwide

Supports programs that provide vulnerable children and their families with education, healthcare, and spiritual mentoring, in order to help transform communities and create sustainable futures, inspired by the Christian faith.

Heme-Onc, Infect Dis, Nutr, OB-GYN, Ped Surg, Peds

⊕ https://vfmat.ch/c3c1

HelpMeSee

Trains local cataract specialists in Manual Small Incision Cataract Surgery (MSICS) in significant numbers, to meet the increasing demand for surgical services in the communities most impacted by cataract blindness.

Anesth, Ophth-Opt, Surg

⊕ https://vfmat.ch/973c

Hernia International

Aims to provide relief from sickness, and protection and preservation of health, for persons affected by groin and abdominal hernias and residing in low- and middle-income countries.

Surg

⊕ https://vfmat.ch/e98e

Hospice Africa

Aims to provide a holistic and culturally sensitive palliative care service through accurate treatment of pain.

Palliative

⊕ https://vfmat.ch/9f86

Humanity & Inclusion

Works alongside people with disabilities and vulnerable populations, taking action and bearing witness in order to respond to their essential needs, improve their living conditions and health, and promote respect for their dignity and fundamental rights.

General, Infect Dis, MF Med, Medicine, Ortho, Peds, Psych, Pub Health, Rehab

⊕ https://vfmat.ch/16b7

Humanity First

Provides aid and assistance to those in need, offering sustainable development solutions to society while providing and empowering local communities with the resources to help themselves.

ER Med, General, MF Med, Ophth-Opt

⊕ https://vfmat.ch/13cc

ICAP at Columbia University

Serves as global leader in supporting the scale-up of multidisciplinary HIV/AIDS prevention, care, and treatment programs based on a family-focused approach.

General, Infect Dis, MF Med, Medicine, OB-GYN, Pub Health

⊕ https://vfmat.ch/a8ef

IHSAN Foundation for West Africa

Seeks to improve the social and economic lives of the people of West Africa through educational, humanitarian, and healthcare projects.

Dent-OMFS, ER Med, General, Infect Dis

⊕ https://vfmat.ch/c719

Inter Care Medical and for Africa

Provides targeted medical aid to rural health units in some of the poorest parts of Africa.

Logist-Op

⊕ https://vfmat.ch/64fb

International Agency for the Prevention of Blindness (IAPB), The

Leads international efforts in blindness-prevention activities, works toward a world where no one is needlessly visually impaired, and ensures that everyone has access to the best possible standard of eye health.

Infect Dis, Ophth-Opt, Pub Health

⊕ https://vfmat.ch/87a2

International Federation of Gynecology and Obstetrics (FIGO)

Implements global projects on specific women's health issues.

MF Med, Medicine, Neonat, OB-GYN, Surg, Urol

⊕ https://vfmat.ch/c4b4

International Federation of Red Cross and Red Crescent Societies (IFRC)

Coordinates and directs international assistance following natural and manmade disasters in nonconflict situations through the world's largest humanitarian and development network. Provides disaster-preparedness programs, healthcare activities, and promotes humanitarian values.

ER Med, General, Infect Dis, Nutr

⊕ https://vfmat.ch/b4ee

International HELP

Works alongside churches, organizations, and community groups to help educate and empower local people in sustainable and effective ways for the improvement of health, while also providing health education and health services related to first aid, nutrition, water, sanitation, and hygiene.

General, MF Med

⊕ https://vfmat.ch/ccf5

International Learning Movement (ILM UK)

Supports some of the world's poorest people in developing countries with core projects in education, safe drinking water, and healthcare.

General, Ophth-Opt

⊕ https://vfmat.ch/b974

International Organization for Migration (IOM) – The UN Migration Agency

Promotes evidence-informed policies and holistic, preventive, and curative health programs that are beneficial, accessible, and equitable for vulnerable migrants.

General, Infect Dis, OB-GYN

⊕ https://vfmat.ch/621a

International Planned Parenthood Federation (IPPF)

Leads a locally owned, globally connected civil society movement that provides and enables services and champions sexual and reproductive health and rights for all, especially the underserved.

Infect Dis, MF Med, OB-GYN

⊕ https://vfmat.ch/dc97

International Rescue Committee (IRC)

Responds to the world's worst humanitarian crises and helps people whose lives and livelihoods are shattered by conflict and disaster to survive, recover, and gain control of their future.

ER Med, General, Infect Dis, MF Med, Peds

⊕ https://vfmat.ch/5d24

International Surgical Health Initiative (ISHI)

Provides free surgical care to underserved communities worldwide, regardless of race, religion, politics, geography, or financial considerations.

Anesth, ER Med, Logist-Op, Ped Surg, Surg, Urol

⊕ https://vfmat.ch/2374

InterSurgeon

Fosters collaborative partnerships in the field of global surgery that will advance clinical care, teaching, training, research, and the provision and maintenance of medical equipment.

ENT, Neurosurg, Ortho, Ped Surg, Plast, Surg, Urol

⊕ https://vfmat.ch/6f8a

IntraHealth International

Improves the performance of health workers and strengthens the systems in which they work.

CV Med, Endo, General, Infect Dis, MF Med, Neonat, Nutr, OB-GYN

⊕ https://vfmat.ch/ddc8

Iris Global

Serves the poor, the destitute, the lost, and the forgotten by providing adoration, outreach, family, education, relief, development, healing, and the arts.

General, Infect Dis, Nutr, Pub Health

⊕ https://vfmat.ch/37f8

IsraAID
Supports people affected by humanitarian crisis and partners with local communities around the world to provide urgent aid, assist recovery, and reduce the risk of future disasters.
ER Med, Infect Dis, Psych, Rehab
⊕ https://vfmat.ch/de96

IVUmed
Aims to make quality urological care available worldwide by providing medical and surgical education for physicians and nurses, and treatment for thousands of children and adults.
Anesth, OB-GYN, Ped Surg, Surg, Urol
⊕ https://vfmat.ch/e619

Izumi Foundation
Develops and supports programs that improve health and healthcare in neglected regions of Africa and Latin America.

⊕ https://vfmat.ch/f29a

John Snow, Inc. (JSI)
Aims to improve the health and well-being of underserved and vulnerable people and communities throughout the world.
General, Infect Dis, Logist-Op, MF Med, OB-GYN, Peds, Psych, Pub Health
⊕ https://vfmat.ch/ba78

Johns Hopkins Center for Communication Programs
Believes in the power of communication to save lives by empowering people to adopt healthy behaviors for themselves, their families, and their communities.
General, Infect Dis, Logist-Op, OB-GYN, Pub Health
⊕ https://vfmat.ch/1bf9

Joint Aid Management (JAM)
Provides food security, nutrition, water, and sanitation to vulnerable African communities in dignified and sustainable ways.
ER Med, Nutr
⊕ https://vfmat.ch/dcac

Joint Aid Management (JAM) Canada
Strives to provide food security, nutrition, water, and sanitation to vulnerable African communities in dignified and sustainable ways.
Nutr, Pub Health
⊕ https://vfmat.ch/8756

Joint United Nations Programme on HIV/AIDS (UNAIDS)
Aims to place people living with HIV and people affected by the virus at the decision-making table and at the center of designing, delivering, and monitoring the AIDS response.
Infect Dis
⊕ https://vfmat.ch/464a

Kambia Appeal, The
Works in collaboration with the key groups in the Kambia District to support and strengthen existing health facilities owned and managed by the government of Sierra Leone to improve maternal and child health.
General, MF Med, Neonat, OB-GYN
⊕ https://vfmat.ch/b128

King's Sierra Leone Partnership
Aims to build a strong and resilient health system in Sierra Leone.
Crit-Care, Dent-OMFS, ER Med, Infect Dis, Medicine, Path, Psych, Rehab, Surg
⊕ https://vfmat.ch/e4f1

Korle-Bu Neuroscience Foundation
Committed to providing medical support for brain and spinal injuries and disease to the people of Ghana and West Africa.
Anesth, Logist-Op, Neuro, Neurosurg, Rehab
⊕ https://vfmat.ch/6695

Life for African Mothers
Aims to save the lives of pregnant women in Sub-Saharan Africa.
MF Med, Neonat, OB-GYN
⊕ https://vfmat.ch/fce2

Light House Medical Missions
Inspired by the Christian faith, provides programs in healthcare provision, nutrition, emergency relief and response, and water, sanitation, and hygiene (WASH).
ER Med, General, Surg
⊕ https://vfmat.ch/cecd

Limbs International
Engages communities and transforms lives through affordable, sustainable prosthetic solutions and rehabilitation services in developing countries.
Logist-Op, Ortho, Pod, Rehab
⊕ https://vfmat.ch/dc84

Lions Clubs International
Empowers volunteers to serve their communities, meet humanitarian needs, encourage peace, and promote international understanding through Lions Clubs.
Heme-Onc, Medicine, Nutr, Ophth-Opt
⊕ https://vfmat.ch/7b12

London School of Hygiene & Tropical Medicine: Health in Humanitarian Crises Centre
Advances health and health equity in crisis-affected countries through research, education, and translation of knowledge into policy and practice.
ER Med, Infect Dis, Pub Health
⊕ https://vfmat.ch/96ad

London School of Hygiene & Tropical Medicine: International Centre for Eye Health
Works to improve eye health and eliminate avoidable visual impairment and blindness with a focus on low-income populations.
Logist-Op, Ophth-Opt, Pub Health
⊕ https://vfmat.ch/6f5f

Lutherans in Medical Missions (LIMM)
Works with local and global partners to promote healing in medically underserved communities.
General, Logist-Op, Pub Health
⊕ https://vfmat.ch/c5aa

Mama-Pikin Foundation
Helps enhance, improve, and otherwise positively contribute to the health and well-being of mothers, children, and families in Sierra Leone, West Africa.
General, MF Med, Neonat, Nutr, OB-GYN
⊕ https://vfmat.ch/4aa6

Management Sciences for Health (MSH)
Works with countries and communities to save lives and improve the health of the world's poorest and most vulnerable people by building strong, resilient, sustainable health systems.
Infect Dis, Logist-Op, Pub Health
⊕ https://vfmat.ch/6aa2

MAP International
Provides medicines and health supplies to those in need around the world so they might experience life to the fullest.
Logist-Op
⊕ https://vfmat.ch/deed

Marie Stopes International
Provides the contraception and safe abortion services that enable women all over the world to choose their own futures.
Infect Dis, MF Med, Neonat, OB-GYN, Pub Health
⊕ https://vfmat.ch/9525

Massachusetts General Hospital Global Surgery Initiative
Aims to improve surgical education and access to advanced surgical care in resource-limited settings around the world by performing surgical operations as visitors, training local surgeons, and sharing medical technology through international partnerships across disciplines.
Anesth, Crit-Care, ER Med, Heme-Onc, Peds, Surg
⊕ https://vfmat.ch/31b1

Maternal Fetal Care International

Helps mothers and children survive and enjoy better health in the poorest regions of the world.

MF Med, Neonat, OB-GYN

⊕ https://vfmat.ch/7e72

Maternity Foundation

Works to ensure safer childbirth for women and newborns everywhere through innovative mobile health solutions such as the Safe Delivery App, a mobile training tool for skilled birth attendants.

MF Med, OB-GYN, Pub Health

⊕ https://vfmat.ch/ff4f

Maternity Worldwide

Works with communities and partners to identify and develop appropriate and effective ways to reduce maternal and newborn mortality and morbidity, facilitate communities to access quality skilled maternity care, and support the provision of quality skilled care.

MF Med, OB-GYN

⊕ https://vfmat.ch/822b

Medical Assistance Sierra Leone

Supports access to healthcare and urgent medical treatment for communities and individuals in Sierra Leone.

General, Neuro

⊕ https://vfmat.ch/3925

Medical Care Development International (MCD International)

Works to strengthen health systems through innovative, sustainable interventions.

Infect Dis, Logist-Op, OB-GYN, Pub Health

⊕ https://vfmat.ch/dc5c

Medical Care Development International

Works to improve the health of vulnerable populations through integrated, sustainable, and locally driven interventions.

Infect Dis, OB-GYN, Peds, Pub Health

⊕ https://vfmat.ch/da87

MedShare

Aims to improve the quality of life of people, communities, and the planet by sourcing and directly delivering surplus medical supplies and equipment to communities in need around the world.

Logist-Op

⊕ https://vfmat.ch/c8bc

MENTOR Initiative

Saves lives in emergencies through tropical disease control, and helps people recover from crisis with dignity, working side by side with communities, health workers, and health authorities to leave a lasting impact.

ER Med, Infect Dis

⊕ https://vfmat.ch/3bd5

Mercy and Love Foundation

Aims to provide orphaned and vulnerable children with basic human needs such as food, clothing, and shelter, enabling them to thrive.

General, Peds

⊕ https://vfmat.ch/649a

Mercy Ships

Operates hospital ships staffed by volunteers to bring hope, healing, and healthcare to underserved communities worldwide.

Anesth, Dent-OMFS, Logist-Op, Neonat, OB-GYN, Ophth-Opt, Ortho, Palliative, Plast, Psych, Surg

⊕ https://vfmat.ch/2e99

Mercy Without Limits

Educates and empowers women and children by enabling them to have an effective and positive role in constructing a better society.

ER Med

⊕ https://vfmat.ch/c3b6

MiracleFeet

Brings low-cost treatment to every child on the planet born with clubfoot, a leading cause of physical disability.

Ortho, Peds, Rehab

⊕ https://vfmat.ch/bda8

Mission Doctors Association

Provides life-saving medical care for the poor and training for local healthcare professionals around the world.

CV Med, Dent-OMFS, General, Logist-Op, Medicine, OB-GYN, Ophth-Opt, Peds, Surg

⊕ https://vfmat.ch/6c18

Mission Regan

Collects supplies, medication, and medical equipment and provides them to those who are in desperate need, both locally and globally.

Logist-Op

⊕ https://vfmat.ch/2bc1

Mobility Outreach International

Enables mobility for children and adults in under-resourced areas of the world, and creates a sustainable orthopedic surgery model using local resources.

Ortho, Rehab

⊕ https://vfmat.ch/9376

MSI Reproductive Choices (Marie Stopes International)

Seeks to deliver quality family planning and reproductive healthcare to women around the world.

MF Med

⊕ https://vfmat.ch/5c82

Médecins du Monde/Doctors of the World

Provides care, bears witness, and supports social change worldwide with innovative medical programs and evidence-based advocacy initiatives.

ER Med, General, Infect Dis, MF Med, Neonat, OB-GYN, Peds, Pub Health

⊕ https://vfmat.ch/a43d

Nazarene Compassionate Ministries

Partners with local churches around the world to clothe, shelter, feed, heal, educate, and live in solidarity with those in need.

General, Infect Dis, OB-GYN

⊕ https://vfmat.ch/6b4d

Operation Fistula

Exists to end obstetric fistula by building models of care that serve every woman, everywhere.

MF Med, OB-GYN, Surg

⊕ https://vfmat.ch/ce8e

Options

Believes in a world in which women and children can access the high-quality health services they need, without financial burden.

Logist-Op, MF Med, Neonat, OB-GYN

⊕ https://vfmat.ch/3a48

Order of Malta

Supports forgotten or excluded people, especially those living in conflict zones or amid natural disasters, by providing medical assistance, caring for refugees, and distributing medicines and necessities.

ER Med, General, Infect Dis, MF Med, Nephro, OB-GYN, Ortho, Psych

⊕ https://vfmat.ch/1fab

Pact

Works on the ground to improve the lives of those who are challenged by poverty and marginalization, striving for a world in which all people are heard, capable, and vibrant.

Infect Dis, Logist-Op, MF Med, Pub Health

⊕ https://vfmat.ch/9a6c

Partners for World Health

Sorts, evaluates, repackages, and prepares supplies and equipment for distribution to individuals, communities, and healthcare facilities in need, both locally and internationally.

ER Med, General, Logist-Op

⊕ https://vfmat.ch/982e

Partners in Health
Responds to the moral imperative to provide high-quality healthcare globally to those who need it most, while striving to ease suffering by providing a comprehensive model of care that includes access to food, transportation, housing, and other key components of healing.
CT Surg, General, Heme-Onc, Infect Dis, MF Med, Neurosurg, OB-GYN, Ortho, Plast, Psych, Urol
⊕ https://vfmat.ch/dc9c

Patcha Foundation
Aims to support and provide the latest and most innovative approaches to diagnosis and treatment of cancer and other chronic diseases in limited-resource settings in Africa.
ER Med, General, Logist-Op, Nutr, Palliative, Peds, Surg
⊕ https://vfmat.ch/ea4a

Practical Tools Initiative
Provides or assists in the provision of education, training, healthcare projects, and all the necessary support designed to enable individuals to generate a sustainable income.
General, Logist-Op, MF Med
⊕ https://vfmat.ch/16b6

Project HOPE
Works on the front lines of the world's health challenges, partnering hand-in-hand with communities, healthcare workers, and public health systems to ensure sustainable change.
CV Med, ER Med, Endo, General, Infect Dis, MF Med, Peds
⊕ https://vfmat.ch/2bd7

PSI – Population Services International
Aims to improve the health of people in the developing world by focusing on challenges such as a lack of family planning, HIV/AIDS, barriers to maternal health, and the greatest threats to children under the age of 5, including malaria, diarrhea, pneumonia, and malnutrition.
Infect Dis, MF Med, OB-GYN, Peds
⊕ https://vfmat.ch/ffe3

RAD-AID International
Improves and optimizes access to medical imaging and radiology in low-resource regions of the world.
Rad-Onc, Radiol
⊕ https://vfmat.ch/537f

RestoringVision
Empowers lives by restoring vision for millions of people in need.
Ophth-Opt
⊕ https://vfmat.ch/e121

Rockefeller Foundation, The
Works to promote the well-being of humanity.
Logist-Op, Nutr, Pub Health
⊕ https://vfmat.ch/5424

Rotary International
Provides service to others, improves lives, and advances world understanding, goodwill, and peace through its fellowship of business, professional, and community leaders.
ER Med, General, Infect Dis, MF Med, OB-GYN
⊕ https://vfmat.ch/8fb5

ROW Foundation
Works to improve the quality of training for healthcare providers, and the diagnosis and treatment available to people with epilepsy and associated psychiatric disorders in under-resourced areas of the world.
Neuro, Psych
⊕ https://vfmat.ch/25eb

Rutgers New Jersey Medical School
Seeks to support and promote the global health efforts of the faculty, staff, and students in the areas of education, research, and service through the Rutgers New Jersey Medical School's Office of Global Health.

Anesth, CV Med, Crit-Care, Neurosurg, OB-GYN, Psych
⊕ https://vfmat.ch/8e67

Salvation Army International, The
Seeks to meet human needs through services in education, healthcare, community support, emergency response, and ministry development, inspired by the Christian faith.
Dent-OMFS, Derm, ER Med, Infect Dis, MF Med, Medicine, Nutr, OB-GYN, Ophth-Opt, Palliative, Psych, Rehab, Surg
⊕ https://vfmat.ch/8eb3

Sanofi Espoir Foundation
Contributes to reducing health inequalities among populations that need it most by applying a socially responsible approach focused on fighting childhood cancers in low-income countries, improving maternal and newborn health, and improving access to care.
ER Med, OB-GYN, Peds
⊕ https://vfmat.ch/943b

SATMED
Serves nongovernmental organizations, hospitals, medical universities, and other healthcare providers active in resource-poor areas, by providing open-access e-health services for the health community.
Logist-Op
⊕ https://vfmat.ch/b8d5

Save the Children
Gives children around the world a healthy start in life, the opportunity to learn, and protection from harm.
All-Immu, Crit-Care, ER Med, General, Infect Dis, MF Med, Medicine, Neonat, OB-GYN, Peds, Psych, Pub Health
⊕ https://vfmat.ch/2e73

SEE International
Provides sustainable medical, surgical, and educational services through volunteer ophthalmic surgeons, with the objectives of restoring sight and preventing blindness to disadvantaged individuals worldwide.
Ophth-Opt, Surg
⊕ https://vfmat.ch/6e1b

Set Free Alliance
Works with in-country partners to rescue children, provide clean water, host medical clinics, and plant churches, based in Christian ministry.
General, Peds
⊕ https://vfmat.ch/bdb8

Shepherd's Hospice Sierra Leone, The
Promotes competent, compassionate care of patients and families of patients with life-limiting illnesses.
Palliative
⊕ https://vfmat.ch/5831

Sierra Leone Missions and Development
Brings hope, help, and healing to Sierra Leone though agriculture, education, leadership training, healthcare missions, and disaster relief programs.
ER Med, General, Peds
⊕ https://vfmat.ch/e6f5

Sightsavers
Works with partners in developing countries to help eliminate avoidable blindness and advocates for equal opportunity for the disabled.
Infect Dis, Ophth-Opt, Surg
⊕ https://vfmat.ch/aa52

SIGN Fracture Care International
Builds orthopedic capacity around the world and provides the injured poor access to fracture surgery by donating orthopedic education and implant systems to surgeons in developing countries.
Ortho, Rehab, Surg
⊕ https://vfmat.ch/123d

SINA Health
Aims to improve the health and educational status of the population in low- and

middle-income countries.
General, Logist-Op
🌐 https://vfmat.ch/9ad3

Sisters of the Immaculate Heart of Mary, Mother of Christ
Based in Chrisitan ministry, seeks to motivate people, especially the poor and the less privileged, to live venerable and dignified lives through credibility-structured programs, education, various medical and humanitarian services, along with self-realization and self-empowerment opportunities.
Infect Dis, Logist-Op, Nutr, Pub Health
🌐 https://vfmat.ch/5774

Smile Train, Inc.
Treats children with cleft lip through a sustainable and local model that supports surgery and other forms of essential care.
Logist-Op, Pub Health
🌐 https://vfmat.ch/822c

Solthis
Improves disease prevention and access to quality care by strengthening the health systems and services of the countries served.
General, Infect Dis, Logist-Op, MF Med, Neonat, Path
🌐 https://vfmat.ch/a71d

Sound Seekers
Supports people with hearing loss by enabling access to healthcare and education.
ENT
🌐 https://vfmat.ch/ef1c

Stepping Forward
Aims to be a practical and creative hub of information, support, and strategies for people affected by disability.
Rehab
🌐 https://vfmat.ch/97de

Surg+ Restore
Creates pathways to sustainable health infrastructure to those living in nations where opportunities are lacking, through professional education, training of medical professionals, and purchasing of medical equipment.
Anesth, Dent-OMFS, ENT, Infect Dis, Logist-Op, Plast, Surg
🌐 https://vfmat.ch/39cc

Surgeons OverSeas (SOS)
Works to reduce death and disability from surgically treatable conditions in developing countries.
Anesth, Heme-Onc, Surg
🌐 https://vfmat.ch/5d16

Sustainable Cardiovascular Health Equity Development Alliance
Fights cardiovascular disease in underserved populations globally via education, training, and increasing interventional capacity.
CV Med, Pub Health, Radiol
🌐 https://vfmat.ch/799c

Swiss Doctors
Aims to improve the health of populations in developing countries through medical-aid projects and training.
General, Infect Dis, Medicine
🌐 https://vfmat.ch/311a

Swiss Sierra Leone Development Foundation
Provides long- and short-term support to communities in Northern Sierra Leone, such as health, education, and community development, with the continuing aim of self-sustainability.
Infect Dis, MF Med, Neonat
🌐 https://vfmat.ch/fea7

Swiss Tropical and Public Health Institute
Contributes to the improvement of the health of populations internationally, nationally, and locally through excellence in research, education, and services.

Infect Dis, Pub Health
🌐 https://vfmat.ch/2ee4

Task Force for Global Health, The
Consists of programs and focus areas that cover a range of global health issues including neglected tropical diseases, infectious diseases, vaccines, field epidemiology, public health informatics, health workforce development, and global health ethics.
Infect Dis, Logist-Op, Medicine, Ophth-Opt, Peds
🌐 https://vfmat.ch/714c

Tearfund
Responds to crisis and partners with local churches to bring restoration to those living in poverty, inspired by the Christian faith.
ER Med, Logist-Op
🌐 https://vfmat.ch/f6cf

Touch of Grace
Provides world-class healthcare services, education, and research with compassion and grace to underserved communities and regions.
General
🌐 https://vfmat.ch/dad7

Turing Foundation
Aims to contribute toward a better world and a better society by focusing on efforts such as health, art, education, and nature.
Infect Dis
🌐 https://vfmat.ch/6bcc

U.S. President's Malaria Initiative (PMI)
Supports low-income countries to help control and eliminate malaria through cost-effective, lifesaving malaria interventions.
Infect Dis, MF Med, OB-GYN
🌐 https://vfmat.ch/dc8b

Unforgotten Fund, The (UNFF)
Provides lifesaving humanitarian relief to UN Field Operations and projects such as water supply, sanitation and hygiene (WASH), food security, health, and shelter.
ER Med, MF Med, Nutr, OB-GYN, Peds
🌐 https://vfmat.ch/928f

Union for International Cancer Control (UICC)
Unites and supports the cancer community to reduce the global cancer burden, promote greater equity, and ensure that cancer control continues to be a priority in the world health and development agenda.
Heme-Onc, Pub Health
🌐 https://vfmat.ch/88b1

Unite 4 Humanity
Aims to provide emergency aid and support for Muslim communities across the world.
General, Nutr, OB-GYN, Ophth-Opt, Plast, Psych, Rehab
🌐 https://vfmat.ch/fbe7

United Methodist Volunteers in Mission (UMVIM)
Engages in short-term missions each year in ministries as varied as disaster response, community development, pastor training, microenterprise, agriculture, Vacation Bible School, building repair and construction, and medical/dental services.
Dent-OMFS, ER Med, General
🌐 https://vfmat.ch/1ee6

United Nations Children's Fund (UNICEF)
Works in over 190 countries and territories to save children's lives, defend their rights, and help them fulfill their potential, from early childhood through adolescence.
All-Immu, Infect Dis, MF Med, Neonat, Nutr, OB-GYN, Ped Surg, Peds, Pub Health
🌐 https://vfmat.ch/42d7

United Nations Development Programme (UNDP)
Helps countries achieve the simultaneous eradication of extreme poverty and significant reduction of inequalities and exclusion using a sustainable human

development approach.
Infect Dis, Logist-Op, Pub Health
⊕ https://vfmat.ch/935c

United Nations High Commissioner for Refugees (UNHCR)
Safeguards the rights and well-being of people who have been forced to flee, ensuring that everybody has the right to seek asylum and find safe refuge in another country, with the goal of seeking lasting solutions.
General, MF Med, Medicine, OB-GYN, Peds, Psych, Pub Health
⊕ https://vfmat.ch/6636

United Nations Population Fund (UNFPA)
Supports reproductive healthcare for women and youth in more than 150 countries, focusing on delivering a world in which every pregnancy is wanted, every childbirth is safe, and every young person's potential is fulfilled.
Infect Dis, MF Med, Neonat, OB-GYN, Peds, Pub Health
⊕ https://vfmat.ch/c969

USAID: A2Z The Micronutrient and Child Blindness Project
Aims to increase the use of key micronutrient and blindness interventions to improve child and maternal health.
MF Med, Neonat, Nutr, Ophth-Opt, Surg
⊕ https://vfmat.ch/c5f1

USAID: Human Resources for Health 2030 (HRH2030)
Helps low- and middle-income countries develop the health workforce needed to prevent maternal and child deaths, support the goals of Family Planning 2020, control the HIV/AIDS epidemic, and protect communities from infectious diseases.
Logist-Op
⊕ https://vfmat.ch/9ea8

USAID: Leadership, Management and Governance Project
Improves leadership, management, and governance practices to strengthen health systems and improve health for all, including vulnerable populations worldwide.
Logist-Op
⊕ https://vfmat.ch/d35e

Village Medical Project for Sierra Leone
Provides free medical treatment to local community members in Sierra Leone.
General, OB-GYN, Peds
⊕ https://vfmat.ch/61f8

Vision Aid Overseas
Enables people living in poverty to access affordable glasses and eye care.
Ophth-Opt
⊕ https://vfmat.ch/c695

Vision Outreach International
Advocates for helping the blind in underserved regions of the world and empowers the poor through sight restoration.
Ophth-Opt
⊕ https://vfmat.ch/9721

Vitamin Angels
Helps at-risk populations in need—specifically pregnant women, new mothers, and children under age 5—to gain access to life-changing vitamins and minerals.
General, Nutr
⊕ https://vfmat.ch/7da1

Voluntary Service Overseas (VSO)
Works with health workers, communities, and governments to improve health services and rights for women, babies, youth, people with disabilities, and prisoners.
General, MF Med, OB-GYN
⊕ https://vfmat.ch/213d

Walkabout Foundation
Provides wheelchairs and rehabilitation in the developing world and funds research to find a cure for paralysis.
Logist-Op, Rehab
⊕ https://vfmat.ch/5582

Watsi
Uses technology to make healthcare a reality for those who might not otherwise be able to afford it.
Pub Health, Surg
⊕ https://vfmat.ch/41a3

West Africa Fistula Foundation (WAFF)
Works to bring value back to the lives of the women of Sierra Leone by providing them with access to education and resources to help reduce the number of new obstetric fistulas and to surgically remedy those that already exist.
Anesth, MF Med, OB-GYN
⊕ https://vfmat.ch/a2ed

West African Education and Medical Mission (WAEMM)
Works to help people access healthcare in Sierra Leone and oversees 14 hospitals and 40 clinics across the country, helping to support the ongoing problem of medical supply shortages.
General, MF Med, Nutr, Ophth-Opt
⊕ https://vfmat.ch/13f3

Willing and Abel
Seeks to provide connections between children in developing nations and specialist centers, helping with visas, passports, transportation, and finances.
Anesth, Dent-OMFS, Ped Surg
⊕ https://vfmat.ch/9dc7

Wisconsin Medical Project
Provides humanitarian aid, including donated medical equipment and supplies, to hospitals and clinics in areas of great need.
Logist-Op
⊕ https://vfmat.ch/ef3b

Women and Children First
Pioneers approaches that support communities to solve problems themselves.
MF Med, Neonat, OB-GYN, Peds
⊕ https://vfmat.ch/cdc9

Women's Refugee Commission
Seeks to improve lives by protecting the rights of women, children, and youth displaced by conflict and crisis through researching their needs, identifying solutions, and advocating for programs and policies to strengthen their resilience.
General, MF Med, Neonat, OB-GYN, Peds, Psych
⊕ https://vfmat.ch/3d8f

World Changing Centre
Aims to provide children and young people in Sierra Leone with a better quality of life and improve standards of living in the community through education, healthcare, and sanitation activities.
General, Peds
⊕ https://vfmat.ch/28bb

World Children's Fund
Commits to helping children worldwide who are suffering the effects of poverty, disease, natural disaster, famine, abuse, civil strife, and war.
General, Logist-Op, MF Med, Nutr, OB-GYN, Pub Health
⊕ https://vfmat.ch/9cd8

World Federation of Hemophilia (WFH)
Aims to improve and sustain care for people with inherited bleeding disorders by pursuing long-term relationships with individuals and organizations who share the values of WFH's development model.
Heme-Onc
⊕ https://vfmat.ch/5121

World Health Organization, The (WHO)
The United Nations' agency for health provides leadership on global health matters, shapes the health research agenda, sets norms and standards, articulates evidence-based policy options, provides technical support and monitoring to countries, and assesses health trends.
ER Med, General, Infect Dis, Logist-Op, MF Med, OB-GYN, Peds, Psych, Pub Health
⊕ https://vfmat.ch/c476

World Hope International
Empowers the poorest individuals around the world so they can become agents of change within their communities, by offering resources and knowledge.
Infect Dis, Logist-Op, MF Med, OB-GYN, Peds
⊕ https://vfmat.ch/a4b8

World Medical Relief
Facilitates the distribution of surplus medical resources where they are needed.
Logist-Op
⊕ https://vfmat.ch/72dc

World Missions Possible
Provides EMS capacity-building, along with medical and vision care, to under-developed and rural areas.
ER Med, General, Heme-Onc, Neonat, Ophth-Opt, Surg
⊕ https://vfmat.ch/d6a5

World Vision International
Works with vulnerable communities around the world to overcome poverty and injustice with child-focused programs in disaster management, health, nutrition, economic development, education, clean water, sanitation, and hygiene.
ER Med, General, Infect Dis, MF Med, Nutr, OB-GYN, Peds
⊕ https://vfmat.ch/2642

Worldwide Healing Hands
Works to improve the quality of healthcare for women and children in the most underserved areas of the world and to stop the preventable deaths of mothers.
General, MF Med, Neonat, OB-GYN
⊕ https://vfmat.ch/b331

Sierra Leone

Healthcare Facilities

34 Military Hospital
Regent Road, Freetown, Western Area, Sierra Leone
🌐 https://vfmat.ch/2737

Ahmadiyya Hospital
Hanga Road, Kenema, Sierra Leone
🌐 https://vfmat.ch/de2d

AHS – Waterloo Hospital
New Main Motor Road, Rokel, Western Area, Sierra Leone
🌐 https://vfmat.ch/77fa

ARAB Hospital
Magburaka Highway, Makeni, Bombali District, Sierra Leone
🌐 https://vfmat.ch/44a5

Aspen Medical Sierra Leone Private Hospital
Bass Street, Freetown, Western Area, Sierra Leone
🌐 https://vfmat.ch/9bca

Blue Shield Hospital
Ascension Town Road, Freetown, Western Area, Sierra Leone
🌐 https://vfmat.ch/1c57

Bo Children's Hospital
Bo-Tiama Highway, Bo, Southern Province, Sierra Leone
🌐 https://vfmat.ch/5984

Brookfields
Maboikandoh Road, Waterloo, Western Area, Sierra Leone
🌐 https://vfmat.ch/f26d

China-SL Friendship Hospital, Jui
New Main Motor Road, Jui, Western Area, Sierra Leone
🌐 https://vfmat.ch/b15c

Choithram Memorial Hospital
Damaya Drive, Freetown, Western Area, Sierra Leone
🌐 https://vfmat.ch/b258

Connaught Hospital
Bathurst Street, Freetown, Western Area, Sierra Leone
🌐 https://vfmat.ch/bb17

Curney Barnes Hospital
Cannon Street, Freetown, Western Area, Sierra Leone
🌐 https://vfmat.ch/d284

EDC Unit
Moriaw Lane, Bo, Southern Province, Sierra Leone
🌐 https://vfmat.ch/7c13

Emergency Hospital
Sugarland Drive, Adonkia Village, Western Area, Sierra Leone
🌐 https://vfmat.ch/afaf

Gandorhun CHC
Koidu, Eastern Province, Sierra Leone
🌐 https://vfmat.ch/f7f4

Goderich ETC
MMCET Road, Freetown, Western Area, Sierra Leone
🌐 https://vfmat.ch/17de

Holy Mary Hospital
Holy Mary Drive, Bo, Southern Province, Sierra Leone
🌐 https://vfmat.ch/28bf

Holy Spirit Hospital
Wallace Johnson Street, Makeni, Bombali District, Sierra Leone
🌐 https://vfmat.ch/379a

Kailahun Government Hospital
Kailahun, Eastern Province, Sierra Leone
🌐 https://vfmat.ch/bc46

Kamakwie Wesleyan Hospital
Kamakwie Makeni Road, Bombali, Sierra Leone
🌐 https://vfmat.ch/1b62

Kambia General Hospital
TAH 7, Kambia, North Western Province, Sierra Leone
🌐 https://vfmat.ch/a952

Kenema Government Hospital
Combema Road, Kenema, Eastern Province, Sierra Leone
🌐 https://vfmat.ch/dd2c

Kindoya Hospital
Prince Williams Street, Bo, Sierra Leone
🌐 https://vfmat.ch/dd99

Kingharman Maternal and Child Health Hospital
King Harman Road, Freetown, Sierra Leone
🌐 https://vfmat.ch/91e7

Lakka Hospital ETU
St. Micheal Drive, Angola Town, Western Area, Sierra Leone
🌐 https://vfmat.ch/6c83

Maforki ETU
TAH 7, Port Loko, Port Loko District, Sierra Leone
🌐 https://vfmat.ch/174e

Magburaka Hospital
Police Roundabout, Magburaka, Northern Province, Sierra Leone
🌐 https://vfmat.ch/2b6c

Mahera Hospital
Mahera Hospital Road, Mahera, Port Loko District, Sierra Leone
🌐 https://vfmat.ch/f3ea

Makeni Regional Hospital
Aggienold Road, Makeni, Bombali District, Sierra Leone
⊕ https://vfmat.ch/5bb6

Malema
Malema, Eastern Province, Sierra Leone
⊕ https://vfmat.ch/f521

Mamudia MCHP
Mamudia, Koinadugu District, Sierra Leone
⊕ https://vfmat.ch/685f

Masanga Hospital
Ms Road, Masanga, Northern Province, Sierra Leone
⊕ https://vfmat.ch/77b4

Mattru General Hospital
Momaligie Road, Mattru Jong, Southern Province, Sierra Leone
⊕ https://vfmat.ch/39ee

Mercy Hospital
Mahei Boima Road, Bo, Southern Province, Sierra Leone
⊕ https://vfmat.ch/a84c

Morning Star
73 Old Railway Line, Bo, Southern Province, Sierra Leone
⊕ https://vfmat.ch/7c9d

National Emergency Medical Service (NEMS)
Freetown, Sierra Leone
⊕ https://vfmat.ch/b43e

Ola During Children's Hospital
Fourah Bay Road, Freetown, Western Area, Sierra Leone
⊕ https://vfmat.ch/c1bf

Panguma Hospital
Minor Road, Panguma, Eastern Province, Sierra Leone
⊕ https://vfmat.ch/9c77

Police Training Sch-Hastings 1 ETC
Leigh Road, Hastings, Western Area, Sierra Leone
⊕ https://vfmat.ch/2c2c

Port Loko Hospital
Kandebaleh Street, Port Loko, Port Loko District, Sierra Leone
⊕ https://vfmat.ch/f1f8

Pujehun Government Hospital
Gobaru, Southern Province, Sierra Leone
⊕ https://vfmat.ch/bf6e

Segbwema Nixon Memorial Hospital
Male Bridge, Masahun, Eastern Province, Sierra Leone
⊕ https://vfmat.ch/1969

Shuman Hospital
Tower Hill, Freetown, Sierra Leone
⊕ https://vfmat.ch/1d48

Sierra Leone Police Hospital
Battery Street, Freetown, Sierra Leone
⊕ https://vfmat.ch/867a

St. John of God Hospital Sierra Leone
Gbinti, Sierra Leone
⊕ https://vfmat.ch/d787

St. John-of-God Catholic Hospital
Lunsar-Makeni Highway, Lunsar, Port Loko District, Sierra Leone
⊕ https://vfmat.ch/c2cf

St. Mary Hospital
Lunsar Makeni Hwy, Port Loko, Sierra Leone
⊕ https://vfmat.ch/b3dd

Towama Old Town Hospital
Torwama Village, Kailey Street, Bo, Sierra Leone
⊕ https://vfmat.ch/c1fe

United Methodist Hatfield Archer Memorial Hospital
Rotifunk, Southern Province, Sierra Leone
⊕ https://vfmat.ch/6b6f

York Hospital
Black Street, York, Western Area, Sierra Leone
⊕ https://vfmat.ch/5fe8

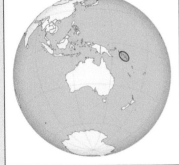

● Healthcare Facility

Solomon Islands

Solomon Islands is a sovereign state in the Melanesia subregion of Oceania in the Western Pacific Ocean. It comprises six major islands and over 900 smaller islands largely located to the east of Papua New Guinea. Honiara, the capital, is situated on Guadalcanal, the largest island, and its bustling central market showcases the islands' produce and traditional handicrafts. The other principal urban centers include Gizo, Auki, and Kirakira. The population is young: 53 percent of Solomon Islands' 690,598 people are under 24. There are over 80 spoken local languages and dialects in Solomon Islands, with English designated as the official language and Melanesian pidgin as the lingua franca. Solomon Islanders are predominantly Christians of various denominations, with about 5 percent of the population maintaining traditional beliefs.

Solomon Islands gained self-government in 1976, and two years later attained independence. Having endured a five-year ethnic conflict on Guadalcanal, spanning 1999 to 2003, coupled with frequent natural disasters such as cyclones and earthquakes, the country has faced serious economic, political, and environmental challenges. While efforts are being made to improve economic conditions, the situation remains unstable. Over 75 percent of Solomon Islanders work in agriculture and engage in subsistence farming and fishing. The nation, however, is rich in underdeveloped mineral resources such as lead, zinc, nickel, and gold.

There are only two fully trained doctors for every 10,000 people in Solomon Islands, and a lack of other properly trained healthcare workers, including nurses. Non-communicable diseases account for 60 percent of total deaths, while communicable diseases are responsible for about 35 percent of deaths. The most common diseases that contribute most substantially to mortality are ischemic heart disease, stroke, lower respiratory infections, diabetes, diarrheal diseases, COPD, road injuries, breast cancer, self-harm, cirrhosis, neonatal disorders, and malaria.

0.69M

Population

$2,258

GDP Per Capita

73 years

Life Expectancy

↑ Improving

19
Doctors/100k

Physician Density

140
Beds/100k

Hospital Bed Density

104
Deaths/100k

Maternal Mortality

Solomon Islands

Nonprofit Organizations

Aloha Medical Mission
Brings hope and changes the lives of people; serves overseas and in Hawai'i.
Anesth, Crit-Care, Dent-OMFS, ENT, ER Med, General, Medicine, OB-GYN, Ophth-Opt, Ortho, Ped Surg, Peds, Plast, Surg, Urol
⊕ https://vfmat.ch/72ac

AO Alliance
Builds solutions to lessen the burden of injuries in low- and middle-income countries, while enhancing the care of the injured to reduce human suffering, disability, and poverty.
Ortho, Surg
⊕ https://vfmat.ch/8cd5

ARC The Australian Respiratory Council
Fosters research to promote respiratory health and works to improve lung health in communities of disadvantaged and Indigenous people.
Infect Dis
⊕ https://vfmat.ch/69f2

Australian & New Zealand Gastroenterology International Training Association
Aims to improve health in developing Asia Pacific nations by enhancing the standards of practice of gastroenterology and building capacity to treat digestive diseases.
GI
⊕ https://vfmat.ch/5a69

Direct Relief
Improves the health and lives of people affected by poverty or emergency situations by mobilizing and providing essential medical resources needed for their care.
ER Med, Logist-Op
⊕ https://vfmat.ch/58e5

Doctors Assisting In South Pacific Islands (DAISI)
Aims to support and collaborate with its South Pacific neighbors and consists of specialist and nonspecialist doctors, medical students, nurses, allied health professionals, and nonmedical volunteers.
Anesth, Dent-OMFS, OB-GYN, Plast, Surg, Urol
⊕ https://vfmat.ch/2dcd

Episcopal Relief & Development
Provides relief in times of disaster and promotes sustainable development by identifying and addressing the root causes of suffering.
Infect Dis, MF Med, Neonat, Nutr, Peds
⊕ https://vfmat.ch/7cfa

Global Oncology (GO)
Brings the best in cancer care to underserved patients around the world and collaborates across geographic, professional, and academic borders to improve cancer care, research, and education.
Heme-Onc, Path, Rad-Onc
⊕ https://vfmat.ch/fcb8

Globus Relief
Aims to improve the delivery of healthcare worldwide by gathering, processing, and distributing surplus medical supplies to charities at home and abroad.
Logist-Op
⊕ https://vfmat.ch/a2b7

Health Education Development Solutions (HEDS) Solomon Islands
Focuses on relieving poverty and providing health and educational relief programs in the Marovo Lagoon.
Anesth, ER Med, Endo, GI, General, Heme-Onc, OB-GYN, Ped Surg, Rheum, Surg, Urol
⊕ https://vfmat.ch/8f3d

International Federation of Red Cross and Red Crescent Societies (IFRC)
Coordinates and directs international assistance following natural and manmade disasters in nonconflict situations through the world's largest humanitarian and development network. Provides disaster-preparedness programs, healthcare activities, and promotes humanitarian values.
ER Med, General, Infect Dis, Nutr
⊕ https://vfmat.ch/b4ee

International Organization for Migration (IOM) – The UN Migration Agency
Promotes evidence-informed policies and holistic, preventive, and curative health programs that are beneficial, accessible, and equitable for vulnerable migrants.
General, Infect Dis, OB-GYN
⊕ https://vfmat.ch/621a

International Planned Parenthood Federation (IPPF)
Leads a locally owned, globally connected civil society movement that provides and enables services and champions sexual and reproductive health and rights for all, especially the underserved.
Infect Dis, MF Med, OB-GYN
⊕ https://vfmat.ch/dc97

International Skills and Training Institute in Health (ISTIH)
Facilitates the appropriate placement of specialist health professionals with international volunteering opportunities.
ER Med
⊕ https://vfmat.ch/fa64

International Trachoma Initiative (iTi)
Works toward a world free from trachoma, a preventable cause of blindness, and provides comprehensive support to national ministries of health and governmental and nongovernmental organizations to implement a comprehensive approach to fight trachoma.
Infect Dis, Ophth-Opt
⊕ https://vfmat.ch/3278

Joint United Nations Programme on HIV/AIDS (UNAIDS)
Aims to place people living with HIV and people affected by the virus at the decision-making table and at the center of designing, delivering, and monitoring the AIDS response.
Infect Dis
⊕ https://vfmat.ch/464a

Kind Cuts for Kids
Aims to improve medical services for children in developing countries through education, demonstration, and skills transfer to local healthcare professionals.
Anesth, Medicine, Ped Surg, Surg
⊕ https://vfmat.ch/e3d7

Marovo Medical Foundaiton
Seeks to expand the limited healthcare options currently available to the 20,000 people of the Marovo Lagoon, New Georgia Islands.
Dent-OMFS, General, Peds
⊕ https://vfmat.ch/7953

Medical Mission Trips
Provides medical aid, welfare assistance, and educational opportunities in Brazil, Honduras, Guatemala, Kenya, Burundi, and Ethiopia.
General
⊕ https://vfmat.ch/9117

Norwegian People's Aid
Aims to improve living conditions, to create a democratic, just, and safe society.
ER Med, Logist-Op
⊕ https://vfmat.ch/2d8e

Open Heart International
Provides surgical interventions and best practices to the most disadvantaged communities on the planet.
CT Surg, MF Med, OB-GYN, Ophth-Opt, Plast, Surg
⊕ https://vfmat.ch/dab2

Pacific Leprosy Foundation
Focuses not only on leprosy control but also on the welfare of leprosy patients in the South Pacific.
Derm, Infect Dis, Pub Health
⊕ https://vfmat.ch/781d

RestoringVision
Empowers lives by restoring vision for millions of people in need.
Ophth-Opt
⊕ https://vfmat.ch/e121

Rotary International
Provides service to others, improves lives, and advances world understanding, goodwill, and peace through its fellowship of business, professional, and community leaders.
ER Med, General, Infect Dis, MF Med, OB-GYN
⊕ https://vfmat.ch/8fb5

Salvation Army International, The
Seeks to meet human needs through services in education, healthcare, community support, emergency response, and ministry development, inspired by the Christian faith.
Dent-OMFS, Derm, ER Med, Infect Dis, MF Med, Medicine, Nutr, OB-GYN, Ophth-Opt, Palliative, Psych, Rehab, Surg
⊕ https://vfmat.ch/8eb3

Save A Child's Heart
Provides lifesaving cardiac treatment to children in developing countries, and trains healthcare professionals from these countries to deliver quality care in their communities.
CT Surg, CV Med, Crit-Care, Ped Surg, Peds
⊕ https://vfmat.ch/1bef

SIGN Fracture Care International
Builds orthopedic capacity around the world and provides the injured poor access to fracture surgery by donating orthopedic education and implant systems to surgeons in developing countries.

Ortho, Rehab, Surg
⊕ https://vfmat.ch/123d

Solomon Islands Foundation, The
Aims to build capacity in the Solomon Islands healthcare system and supports educational initiatives for young people.
CT Surg, CV Med, General, Peds
⊕ https://vfmat.ch/b9d9

South Pacific Medical Projects
Aims to advance and support medical projects in developing countries of the South Pacific and other regions in a sustainable manner, in consideration of existing structures.
Logist-Op, Ortho, Rehab, Surg
⊕ https://vfmat.ch/d64e

Task Force for Global Health, The
Consists of programs and focus areas that cover a range of global health issues including neglected tropical diseases, infectious diseases, vaccines, field epidemiology, public health informatics, health workforce development, and global health ethics.
Infect Dis, Logist-Op, Medicine, Ophth-Opt, Peds
⊕ https://vfmat.ch/714c

United Nations Children's Fund (UNICEF)
Works in over 190 countries and territories to save children's lives, defend their rights, and help them fulfill their potential, from early childhood through adolescence.
All-Immu, Infect Dis, MF Med, Neonat, Nutr, OB-GYN, Ped Surg, Peds, Pub Health
⊕ https://vfmat.ch/42d7

United Nations Population Fund (UNFPA)
Supports reproductive healthcare for women and youth in more than 150 countries, focusing on delivering a world in which every pregnancy is wanted, every childbirth is safe, and every young person's potential is fulfilled.
Infect Dis, MF Med, Neonat, OB-GYN, Peds, Pub Health
⊕ https://vfmat.ch/c969

United States Agency for International Development (USAID)
Promotes and demonstrates democratic values abroad and advances a free, peaceful, and prosperous world. Leads the U.S. government's international development and disaster assistance through partnerships and investments that save lives.
ER Med, Infect Dis, MF Med, OB-GYN, Peds
⊕ https://vfmat.ch/9a99

UnitingCare
Provides aged care, disability support, healthcare, and crisis response to improve the health and well-being of individuals, families, and communities.
CT Surg, CV Med, Crit-Care, Dent-OMFS, Derm, ENT, ER Med, Endo, General, Geri, Heme-Onc, Logist-Op, MF Med, Medicine, Neonat, Nephro, Neuro, Nutr, OB-GYN, Ophth-Opt, Ortho, Palliative, Path, Ped Surg, Peds, Plast, Psych, Radiol, Rehab, Surg, Urol, Vasc Surg
⊕ https://vfmat.ch/1c9e

World Health Organization, The (WHO)
The United Nations' agency for health provides leadership on global health matters, shapes the health research agenda, sets norms and standards, articulates evidence-based policy options, provides technical support and monitoring to countries, and assesses health trends.
ER Med, General, Infect Dis, Logist-Op, MF Med, OB-GYN, Peds, Psych, Pub Health
⊕ https://vfmat.ch/c476

World Vision International
Works with vulnerable communities around the world to overcome poverty and injustice with child-focused programs in disaster management, health, nutrition, economic development, education, clean water, sanitation, and hygiene.
ER Med, General, Infect Dis, MF Med, Nutr, OB-GYN, Peds
⊕ https://vfmat.ch/2642

Solomon Islands

Healthcare Facilities

Atoifi Adventist Hospital
Atoifi, Malaita Province, Solomon Islands
🌐 https://vfmat.ch/6pdz

Buala Hospital
Buala, Isabel Province, Solomon Islands
🌐 https://vfmat.ch/qpta

Gizo Hospital
Gizo, Western Province, Solomon Islands
🌐 https://vfmat.ch/slba

Good Samaritan Hospital (GSH)
Tetere, Guadalcanal Province, Solomon Islands
🌐 https://vfmat.ch/r9np

Helena Goldie Hospital (HGH)
Munda, Western Province, Solomon Islands
🌐 https://vfmat.ch/g5xt

Kilu 'ufi Hospital
Aimela, Malaita Province, Solomon Islands
🌐 https://vfmat.ch/zbm3

Kirakira Hospital
Kirakira, Makira-Ulawa Province, Solomon Islands
🌐 https://vfmat.ch/5c92

Lata Hospital
Lata, Temotu Province, Solomon Islands
🌐 https://vfmat.ch/e9eb

Namuga Hospital
Namuga, Makira-Ulawa Province, Solomon Islands
🌐 https://vfmat.ch/6h1c

National Referral Hospital (NGH)
Honiara, Guadalcanal Province, Solomon Islands
🌐 https://vfmat.ch/ab91

Sasamunga Hospital
Sasamunga, Choiseul Province, Solomon Islands
🌐 https://vfmat.ch/lxly

Taro Hospital
Taro, Choiseul Province, Solomon Islands
🌐 https://vfmat.ch/xrue

Tulagi Hospital
Tulagi, Central Province, Solomon Islands
🌐 https://vfmat.ch/2z1p

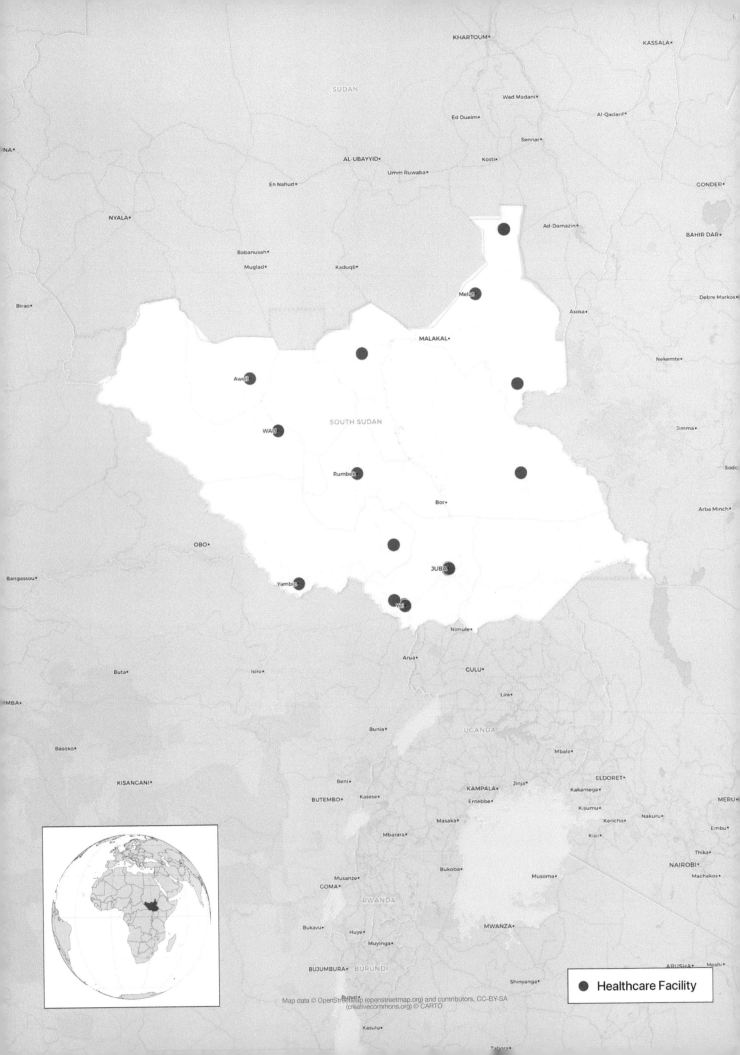

Healthcare Facility

South Sudan

The Republic of South Sudan is a landlocked nation in East-Central Africa whose bordering neighbors are Sudan, Ethiopia, Kenya, the Democratic Republic of the Congo, Uganda, and the Central African Republic. South Sudan is one of the most culturally diverse countries in sub-Saharan Africa, with a population of about 11 million people and more than 60 different major ethnic groups. About 20 percent of the population lives in urban areas, including Juba, the capital. South Sudan is also home to the second largest animal migration in the world: a significant movement of antelopes, specifically the tiang and white-eared kob.

South Sudan is also Africa's newest country, a distinction achieved after it won independence from Sudan in July 2011. The country's newfound nationhood followed an agreement that ended Africa's longest-running civil war. Yet the violent conflict did not stop: In 2013, another civil war broke out, leading to large-scale conflict that devastated the economy. During the war, more than a third of the population was forced to leave their homes, resulting in a poverty rate that rose from 51 percent to 82 percent between 2009 and 2016.

The ongoing instability has affected health in South Sudan. Severe acute food insecurity is pervasive, and more than half the population requires some form of humanitarian assistance. The average life expectancy is only 58 years, and the under-five mortality rate is about 91 deaths per 1,000 live births. Diseases contributing to the most deaths in South Sudan include neonatal disorders, lower respiratory infections, diarrheal diseases, malaria, HIV/AIDS, tuberculosis, protein-energy malnutrition, and meningitis. Non-communicable diseases such as congenital defects, stroke, and ischemic heart disease have also increased, causing significant deaths in the country. Overall, the healthcare system suffers from an extreme shortage of professionals, forcing the country at times to rely on inadequately trained or low-skilled health workers. The country's hospital infrastructure remains insufficiently developed.

11M

Population

$1,120

GDP Per Capita

58 years

Life Expectancy

↑ Improving

2

Doctors/100k

Physician Density

1,150

Deaths/100k

Maternal Mortality

South Sudan

Nonprofit Organizations

143 LIFE Foundation
Seeks to educate and empower individuals living with malaria, TB, HIV/AIDS, STDs and other health disparities related to sexual health.
Infect Dis, MF Med
⊕ https://vfmat.ch/d59b

Abt Associates
Seeks to improve the quality of life and economic well-being of people worldwide, while striving to meet and exceed the highest professional standards.
General, Logist-Op, MF Med, OB-GYN, Peds
⊕ https://vfmat.ch/cec2

Action Against Hunger
Aims to end life-threatening hunger for good through treating and preventing malnutrition across more than 45 countries.
Nutr
⊕ https://vfmat.ch/2dbc

Advance Family Planning
Aims to achieve global expansion and access to quality contraceptive information, services, and supplies through financial investment and political commitment.
General, MF Med, Pub Health
⊕ https://vfmat.ch/7478

Africa CDC
Aims to strengthen the capacity and capability of Africa's public health institutions and partnerships to detect and respond quickly and effectively to disease threats and outbreaks, based on data-driven interventions and programs.
Infect Dis, Logist-Op, Pub Health
⊕ https://vfmat.ch/339c

Africa Health Organisation
Leads collaborative efforts among countries in Africa and other partners to promote health equity, combat disease, and improve quality of life.
Logist-Op, Pub Health
⊕ https://vfmat.ch/b1c5

Africa Humanitarian Action (AHA)
Responds to crises, conflicts, and disasters in Africa, while informing and advising the international community, governments, civil society, and the private sector on humanitarian issues of concern to Africa. Supports institutional and organizational development efforts.
General, Infect Dis, MF Med, Nutr, OB-GYN
⊕ https://vfmat.ch/3ca2

Africa Inland Mission International
Seeks to establish churches and community development programs including healthcare projects, based in Christian ministry.
Anesth, Dent-OMFS, ER Med, General, MF Med, Medicine, OB-GYN, OB-GYN,

Ophth-Opt, Ped Surg, Peds, Rehab
⊕ https://vfmat.ch/f2f6

African Field Epidemiology Network (AFENET)
Strengthens field epidemiology and public health laboratory capacity to contribute effectively to addressing epidemics and other major public health problems in Africa.
All-Immu, Infect Dis, Path, Pub Health
⊕ https://vfmat.ch/df2e

African Mission Health Foundation
Aims to strengthen African mission hospitals by providing quality, compassionate care for the hurting and forgotten and helping improve Sub-Saharan Africa's health system.
Infect Dis, Neonat, OB-GYN, Peds, Surg
⊕ https://vfmat.ch/5b14

Age International
Helps older people living in some of the world's poorest places to have improved well-being and be treated with dignity through a variety of programs, including emergency relief and cataract surgery.
ER Med, Geri, Logist-Op, Nutr, Ophth-Opt, Palliative, Pub Health
⊕ https://vfmat.ch/c7e2

AISPO
Implements international initiatives in the healthcare sector and remains involved in various projects to combat poverty, social injustice, and disease around the world.
All-Immu, ER Med, GI, General, Infect Dis, Logist-Op, MF Med, Neonat, OB-GYN, Peds, Psych, Pub Health, Radiol
⊕ https://vfmat.ch/c9e6

Al-Mustafa Welfare Trust
Seeks to alleviate poverty and provides medical and social development assistance to the poor and vulnerable around the world.
General, Ophth-Opt
⊕ https://vfmat.ch/c5f4

Alaska Sudan Medical Project
Works to provide vital humanitarian aid to a remote, isolated region in South Sudan with the mission of saving lives through health, water, and agriculture.
Crit-Care, ER Med, General, Infect Dis, Medicine, Nutr, Surg
⊕ https://vfmat.ch/7c19

Alight
Works closely with refugees, trafficked persons, economic migrants, and other displaced persons to co-design solutions that help them build full and fulfilling lives, with healthcare, clean water, shelter protection, and economic opportunity.
ER Med, General, Infect Dis, MF Med, Neonat, Peds
⊕ https://vfmat.ch/5993

Alliance for International Medical Action, The (ALIMA)
Provides quality medical care to vulnerable populations, partnering with and developing national medical organizations and conducting medical research to bring innovation to 12 African countries where ALIMA works.
ER Med, General, Infect Dis, Logist-Op, MF Med, OB-GYN, Path, Peds, Psych, Pub Health
⊕ https://vfmat.ch/1c11

Americares
Saves lives and improves health for people affected by poverty or disaster and responds with life-changing medicine, medical supplies, and health programs including domestic and global medical clinics.
All-Immu, ER Med, General, Infect Dis, MF Med, Nutr
⊕ https://vfmat.ch/e567

AMREF Flying Doctors
Aims to deliver medical air transport and health services using the latest aviation and medical technology to ensure patients receive unrivaled care.
ER Med, Logist-Op
⊕ https://vfmat.ch/5d5e

Amref Health Africa
Serves millions of people across 35 countries in Sub-Saharan Africa, strengthening health systems, and training African health workers to respond to the continent's most critical health issues.
All-Immu, General, Infect Dis, Logist-Op, MF Med, OB-GYN, Path, Pub Health, Surg
⊕ https://vfmat.ch/6985

BRAC USA
Seeks to empower people and communities in situations of poverty, illiteracy, disease, and social injustice. Interventions aim to achieve large-scale, positive changes through economic and social programs that enable everyone to realize their potential.
ER Med, General, Infect Dis, Logist-Op, MF Med, OB-GYN
⊕ https://vfmat.ch/9d9e

BroadReach
Collaborates with governments, multinational health organizations, donors, and private-sector companies to effect healthcare reform and solve the world's biggest health challenges.
Logist-Op
⊕ https://vfmat.ch/7812

Buckeye Clinic in South Sudan
Improves the health of persons living in Piol, Twic East County, South Sudan, and surrounding villages, with a primary focus on maternal and child health.
General, MF Med, OB-GYN, Peds
⊕ https://vfmat.ch/6ef2

Canadian Network for International Surgery, The
Aims to improve maternal health, increase safety, and build local capacity in low-income countries by creating and providing surgical and midwifery courses, training domestically, and transferring skills.
Logist-Op, Surg
⊕ https://vfmat.ch/86ff

CARE
Works around the globe to save lives, defeat poverty, and achieve social justice.
ER Med, General
⊕ https://vfmat.ch/7232

Caritas Pro Vitae Gradu Charitable Trust
Supports Catholic charitable projects with social and humanitarian efforts, and aims to assist people in need including children, the elderly, sick, and disabled through healthcare, poverty relief, and education.
ER Med, General, Logist-Op, Medicine, OB-GYN, Ophth-Opt, Path, Peds, Pub Health, Radiol, Rehab, Surg
⊕ https://vfmat.ch/b2ca

Carter Center, The
Seeks to prevent and resolve conflicts, enhance freedom and democracy, and improve health, while remaining committed to human rights and the alleviation of human suffering.
Infect Dis, MF Med, Ophth-Opt
⊕ https://vfmat.ch/6556

Catholic Medical Mission Board (CMMB)
Works in partnership globally to deliver locally sustainable, quality health solutions to women, children, and their communities.
General, MF Med, Peds
⊕ https://vfmat.ch/9498

Catholic Organization for Relief & Development Aid (CORDAID)
Provides humanitarian assistance and creates opportunities to improve security, healthcare, education, and inclusive economic growth in fragile and conflict-affected areas.
ER Med, Infect Dis, MF Med, OB-GYN, Peds, Psych
⊕ https://vfmat.ch/8ae5

Children of War Foundation
Delivers access to global health and education to communities affected by poverty, war, natural disaster, climate change, and migration challenges.
ER Med, General, Logist-Op, Peds, Surg
⊕ https://vfmat.ch/de51

Christian Aid Ministries
Strives to be a trustworthy and efficient channel for Amish, Mennonite, and other conservative Anabaptist groups and individuals to minister to physical and spiritual needs around the world.
CT Surg, ER Med, Logist-Op, Ortho, Pub Health
⊕ https://vfmat.ch/7b33

Christian Blind Mission (CBM)
Aims to improve the quality of life of persons with disabilities in the poorest countries, addressing poverty as a cause and a consequence of disability, and working in partnership to create a society for all.
ENT, General, Infect Dis, OB-GYN, Ophth-Opt, Ortho, Peds, Psych, Rehab, Surg
⊕ https://vfmat.ch/3824

Comitato Collaborazione Medica (CCM)
Supports development processes that safeguard and promote the right to health with a global approach, working on health needs and influencing socio-economic factors, identifying poverty as the main cause for the lack of health.
All-Immu, General, Infect Dis, MF Med, OB-GYN
⊕ https://vfmat.ch/4272

Concern Worldwide
Seeks to permanently transform the lives of people living in extreme poverty, tackling its root causes, and building resilience.
Logist-Op, MF Med, Nutr, OB-GYN
⊕ https://vfmat.ch/77e9

Confident Children Out of Conflict
Provides vulnerable children with a safe space to sleep, eat, learn, and play to help them develop into young adults, fulfilling their potential, and supports households to develop a protective environment for safe reintegration of these children into communities.
All-Immu, General, Peds, Psych
⊕ https://vfmat.ch/daf7

Core Group
Aims to improve and expand community health practices for underserved populations, especially women and children, through collaborative action and learning.
General, Infect Dis, MF Med, Medicine, OB-GYN, Peds, Pub Health
⊕ https://vfmat.ch/9de3

COVID-19 Clinical Research Coalition
Advocates and collaborates for the advancement of COVID-19 research driven by the needs of low-resource settings, and works for equitable access to solutions to the pandemic.
All-Immu, Infect-Dis, MF Med, Path, Pub Health
⊕ https://vfmat.ch/d1f4

Deng Foundation

Strives to provide the children of Aweil East, South Sudan, with access to clean water, basic healthcare, and the proper educational infrastructure to have a better childhood. Also works to fight malaria in South Sudan.

General, Peds, Pub Health

⊕ https://vfmat.ch/d89c

Direct Relief

Improves the health and lives of people affected by poverty or emergency situations by mobilizing and providing essential medical resources needed for their care.

ER Med, Logist-Op

⊕ https://vfmat.ch/58e5

Doctors with Africa (CUAMM)

Advocates for the universal right to health and promotes the values of international solidarity, justice, and peace. Works to protect and improve the well-being and health of vulnerable communities in Africa with a long-term development perspective.

ER Med, Infect Dis, MF Med, Neonat, OB-GYN, Peds

⊕ https://vfmat.ch/d2fb

Doctors Without Borders/Médecins Sans Frontières (MSF)

Responds to emergencies and provides lifesaving medical care where needed most, including during disasters, conflicts, and epidemics.

Anesth, Crit-Care, ER Med, General, Infect Dis, Nutr, OB-GYN, Ped Surg, Peds, Psych, Pub Health, Surg

⊕ https://vfmat.ch/f363

END Fund, The

Aims to control and eliminate the most prevalent neglected diseases among the world's poorest and most vulnerable people.

Infect Dis

⊕ https://vfmat.ch/2614

Episcopal Relief & Development

Provides relief in times of disaster and promotes sustainable development by identifying and addressing the root causes of suffering.

Infect Dis, MF Med, Neonat, Nutr, Peds

⊕ https://vfmat.ch/7cfa

Finn Church Aid

Supports people in the most vulnerable situations within fragile and disaster-affected regions in three thematic priority areas: right to peace, livelihood, and education.

ER Med, Psych, Pub Health

⊕ https://vfmat.ch/9623

Fistula Foundation

Aims to engage the support of people worldwide who are eager to see the day that no woman suffers from obstetric fistula. Raises and directs funds to doctors and hospitals providing life-transforming surgery to women in need.

OB-GYN

⊕ https://vfmat.ch/e958

Friends of UNFPA

Promotes the health, dignity, and rights of women and girls around the world by supporting the lifesaving work of UNFPA, the United Nations' reproductive health and rights agency, through education, advocacy, and fundraising.

MF Med, OB-GYN

⊕ https://vfmat.ch/2a3a

Global Alliance to Prevent Prematurity And Stillbirth (GAPPS)

Seeks to improve birth outcomes worldwide by reducing the burden of premature birth and stillbirth.

All-Immu, Infect Dis, MF Med, Neonat, Neonat, OB-GYN

⊕ https://vfmat.ch/3f74

Global Ministries – The United Methodist Church

As the worldwide mission and development agency of The United Methodist Church, Global Ministries works with more than 300 hospitals and clinics around the world through its Global Health Unit.

Anesth, CT Surg, CV Med, Crit-Care, Dent-OMFS, Derm, ER Med, GI, General,

Infect Dis, Logist-Op, MF Med, Medicine, Neonat, Nephro, Nutr, OB-GYN, Ophth-Opt, Ortho, Palliative, Peds, Pod, Psych, Pub Health, Rehab, Rheum, Surg, Urol

⊕ https://vfmat.ch/1723

Global Oncology (GO)

Brings the best in cancer care to underserved patients around the world and collaborates across geographic, professional, and academic borders to improve cancer care, research, and education.

Heme-Onc, Path, Rad-Onc

⊕ https://vfmat.ch/fcb8

Global Polio Eradication Initiative

Aims to eradicate polio worldwide.

All-Immu, Infect-Dis, Logist-Op, Pub Health

⊕ https://vfmat.ch/7e2c

Globus Relief

Aims to improve the delivery of healthcare worldwide by gathering, processing, and distributing surplus medical supplies to charities at home and abroad.

Logist-Op

⊕ https://vfmat.ch/a2b7

GOAL

Works with the most vulnerable communities to help them respond to and recover from humanitarian crises, and to assist them in building transcendent solutions to mitigate poverty and vulnerability.

ER Med, General, Pub Health

⊕ https://vfmat.ch/bbea

Good Shepard International Foundation

Strives to promote inclusive and sustainable development for the most marginalized and vulnerable people, with a special focus on women, girls, and children, inspired by the Christian faith.

ER Med

⊕ https://vfmat.ch/ad9a

Grassroot Soccer

Leverages the power of soccer to educate, inspire, and mobilize at-risk youth in developing countries to overcome their greatest health challenges, live healthier and more productive lives, and be agents for change in their communities.

Infect Dis

⊕ https://vfmat.ch/3521

Healing Kadi Foundation

Works with the people of South Sudan and Uganda to provide sustainable high-quality healthcare, education for local healthcare providers, and psychological and spiritual counseling.

All-Immu, Dent-OMFS, General, Infect Dis, MF Med, Neonat, OB-GYN, Peds, Psych

⊕ https://vfmat.ch/a7f1

Health Link South Sudan

Contributes toward the reduction and elimination of absolute poverty and social inequalities by promoting social justice, equity, and the dignity of the human person.

General, Infect Dis, Medicine, OB-GYN, Peds, Psych

⊕ https://vfmat.ch/38fd

Health Outreach to the Middle East (H.O.M.E.)

Offers physical and Christian-inspired spiritual healing to people in need in the Middle East, providing medical care and education.

Anesth, Dent-OMFS, ER Med, General, Geri, Infect Dis, MF Med, Medicine, OB-GYN, Path, Peds, Psych, Surg

⊕ https://vfmat.ch/134e

HealthNet TPO

Aims to facilitate and strengthen communities and help them to regain control and maintain their health and well-being, believing that even the most vulnerable people have the inner strength to build a better future for themselves.

Crit-Care, General, Infect Dis, Logist-Op, Medicine, OB-GYN, Ophth-Opt, Peds, Psych, Pub Health, Surg

⊕ https://vfmat.ch/67d6

HealthServe Australia
Develops sustainable health programs that improve health and well-being and partners with community groups to build community capacity to meet health needs.
Infect Dis, Logist-Op, OB-GYN, Psych, Pub Health
⊕ https://vfmat.ch/7276

HEART (High-Quality Technical Assistance for Results)
Works to support the use of evidence and expert advice in policymaking in the areas of international development, health, nutrition, education, social protection, and water and sanitation (WASH).
General, Infect Dis, Infect Dis, Logist-Op, MF Med, Medicine, Nutr, OB-GYN, Peds, Psych
⊕ https://vfmat.ch/c491

HelpAge International
Works to ensure that people everywhere understand how much older people contribute to society and that they must enjoy their right to healthcare, social services, economic, and physical security.
General, Geri, Infect Dis, Medicine, Pub Health
⊕ https://vfmat.ch/5d91

Hope and Healing International
Gives hope and healing to children and families trapped by poverty and disability.
General, Nutr, Ophth-Opt, Peds, Rehab
⊕ https://vfmat.ch/c638

Hope Health Action
Facilitates sustainable, lifesaving health, and disability care for the world's most vulnerable, without any discrimination.
ER Med, MF Med, Neonat, Nutr, OB-GYN, Peds, Rehab
⊕ https://vfmat.ch/86f7

ICAP at Columbia University
Serves as global leader in supporting the scale-up of multidisciplinary HIV/AIDS prevention, care, and treatment programs based on a family-focused approach.
General, Infect Dis, MF Med, Medicine, OB-GYN, Pub Health
⊕ https://vfmat.ch/a8ef

IMA World Health
Works to build healthier communities by collaborating with key partners to serve vulnerable people with a focus on health, healing, and well-being for all.
Infect Dis, MF Med, Nutr, OB-GYN, Pub Health
⊕ https://vfmat.ch/8316

In Deed and Truth Ministries
Serves the community of Tonj, South Sudan, through medical care, pastoral training, and discipleship.
All-Immu, ER Med, General, OB-GYN
⊕ https://vfmat.ch/f9ce

International Council of Ophthalmology
Works with ophthalmologic societies and others to enhance ophthalmic education and improve access to the highest-quality eye care in order to preserve and restore vision for people of the world.
Ophth-Opt
⊕ https://vfmat.ch/ffd2

International Federation of Red Cross and Red Crescent Societies (IFRC)
Coordinates and directs international assistance following natural and manmade disasters in nonconflict situations through the world's largest humanitarian and development network. Provides disaster-preparedness programs, healthcare activities, and promotes humanitarian values.
ER Med, General, Infect Dis, Nutr
⊕ https://vfmat.ch/b4ee

International Medical Corps
Seeks to improve quality of life through health interventions and related activities that strengthen underserved communities worldwide, with the flexibility to respond rapidly to emergencies and offer medical services and training to people at the highest risk.

ER Med, General, Infect Dis, Nutr, OB-GYN, Peds, Pub Health, Surg
⊕ https://vfmat.ch/a8a5

International Organization for Migration (IOM) – The UN Migration Agency
Promotes evidence-informed policies and holistic, preventive, and curative health programs that are beneficial, accessible, and equitable for vulnerable migrants.
General, Infect Dis, OB-GYN
⊕ https://vfmat.ch/621a

International Rescue Committee (IRC)
Responds to the world's worst humanitarian crises and helps people whose lives and livelihoods are shattered by conflict and disaster to survive, recover, and gain control of their future.
ER Med, General, Infect Dis, MF Med, Peds
⊕ https://vfmat.ch/5d24

International Trachoma Initiative (iTi)
Works toward a world free from trachoma, a preventable cause of blindness, and provides comprehensive support to national ministries of health and governmental and nongovernmental organizations to implement a comprehensive approach to fight trachoma.
Infect Dis, Ophth-Opt
⊕ https://vfmat.ch/3278

Intersos
Provides emergency medical assistance to victims of armed conflicts, natural disasters, and extreme exclusion, with particular attention to the protection of the most vulnerable people.
ER Med, General, Nutr
⊕ https://vfmat.ch/dbac

InterSurgeon
Fosters collaborative partnerships in the field of global surgery that will advance clinical care, teaching, training, research, and the provision and maintenance of medical equipment.
ENT, Neurosurg, Ortho, Ped Surg, Plast, Surg, Urol
⊕ https://vfmat.ch/6f8a

IntraHealth International
Improves the performance of health workers and strengthens the systems in which they work.
CV Med, Endo, General, Infect Dis, MF Med, Neonat, Nutr, OB-GYN
⊕ https://vfmat.ch/ddc8

IsraAID
Supports people affected by humanitarian crisis and partners with local communities around the world to provide urgent aid, assist recovery, and reduce the risk of future disasters.
ER Med, Infect Dis, Psych, Rehab
⊕ https://vfmat.ch/de96

Jesus Harvesters Ministries
Reaches communities through medical clinics, dental care, veterinarian outreach, pastor training, and community service, based in Christian ministry.
Dent-OMFS, General, Infect Dis
⊕ https://vfmat.ch/8a23

Jewish World Watch
Brings help and healing to survivors of mass atrocities around the globe and seeks to inspire people of all faiths and cultures to join the ongoing fight against genocide.
ER Med, Logist-Op, OB-GYN, Peds
⊕ https://vfmat.ch/8c92

Jhpiego
Creates and delivers transformative healthcare solutions that save lives, in partnership with national governments, health experts, and local communities.
General, Infect Dis, OB-GYN, Surg
⊕ https://vfmat.ch/45b8

John Snow, Inc. (JSI)
Aims to improve the health and well-being of underserved and vulnerable people

and communities throughout the world.
General, Infect Dis, Logist-Op, MF Med, OB-GYN, Peds, Psych, Pub Health
🌐 https://vfmat.ch/ba78

Joint Aid Management (JAM)
Provides food security, nutrition, water, and sanitation to vulnerable African communities in dignified and sustainable ways.
ER Med, Nutr
🌐 https://vfmat.ch/dcac

Joint Aid Management (JAM) Canada
Strives to provide food security, nutrition, water, and sanitation to vulnerable African communities in dignified and sustainable ways.
Nutr, Pub Health
🌐 https://vfmat.ch/8756

Joint United Nations Programme on HIV/AIDS (UNAIDS)
Aims to place people living with HIV and people affected by the virus at the decision-making table and at the center of designing, delivering, and monitoring the AIDS response.
Infect Dis
🌐 https://vfmat.ch/464a

Kajo Keji Health Training Institute (KKHTI)
Addresses the severe shortage of medical personnel in South Sudan by training quality healthcare workers.
General, Infect Dis, MF Med
🌐 https://vfmat.ch/ff59

La Salle International Foundation
Provides support for educational, health, and human services, along with humanitarian relief to people in developed and underdeveloped areas.
General
🌐 https://vfmat.ch/5891

Light for the World
Contributes to a world in which persons with disabilities fully exercise their rights, and assists persons with disabilities living in poverty.
Ophth-Opt, Rehab
🌐 https://vfmat.ch/3ff6

Lions Clubs International
Empowers volunteers to serve their communities, meet humanitarian needs, encourage peace, and promote international understanding through Lions Clubs.
Heme-Onc, Medicine, Nutr, Ophth-Opt
🌐 https://vfmat.ch/7b12

London School of Hygiene & Tropical Medicine: Health in Humanitarian Crises Centre
Advances health and health equity in crisis-affected countries through research, education, and translation of knowledge into policy and practice.
ER Med, Infect Dis, Pub Health
🌐 https://vfmat.ch/96ad

MAGNA International
Helps those who are suffering or recovering from conflicts and disasters by reducing the risks of diseases and treating them immediately.
ER Med, General, Infect Dis, Peds, Surg
🌐 https://vfmat.ch/58f4

Management Sciences for Health (MSH)
Works with countries and communities to save lives and improve the health of the world's poorest and most vulnerable people by building strong, resilient, sustainable health systems.
Infect Dis, Logist-Op, Pub Health
🌐 https://vfmat.ch/6aa2

MAP International
Provides medicines and health supplies to those in need around the world so they might experience life to the fullest.
Logist-Op
🌐 https://vfmat.ch/deed

Maryknoll Lay Missioners
Based in Christian ministry, aims to collaborate with poor communities in Africa, Asia, and the Americas in order to respond to basic needs, including heathcare, and to help create a more compassionate world.
Logist-Op, Nutr
🌐 https://vfmat.ch/2ce6

Medair
Works to relieve human suffering in some of the world's most remote and devastated places, saving lives in emergencies and helping people in crises survive and recover, inspired by the Christian faith.
ER Med, General, Logist-Op, MF Med, Pub Health
🌐 https://vfmat.ch/5b33

MedHope Africa
Supports relief and development for low-resource communities in Sub-Saharan Africa by addressing dire physical and spiritual needs through medical and vision care, community health interventions, and prayer and Christian evangelism.
General, Logist-Op, Medicine, Ophth-Opt
🌐 https://vfmat.ch/8249

Medical Mission Aid Inc
Advances effective healthcare in disadvantaged communities through medical scholarships, grants for supplies and support for local health initiatives.
Infect Dis, Logist-Op, OB-GYN, Pub Health, Rehab
🌐 https://vfmat.ch/8b83

MedShare
Aims to improve the quality of life of people, communities, and the planet by sourcing and directly delivering surplus medical supplies and equipment to communities in need around the world.
Logist-Op
🌐 https://vfmat.ch/c8bc

MENTOR Initiative
Saves lives in emergencies through tropical disease control, and helps people recover from crisis with dignity, working side by side with communities, health workers, and health authorities to leave a lasting impact.
ER Med, Infect Dis
🌐 https://vfmat.ch/3bd5

Mercy and Love Foundation
Aims to provide orphaned and vulnerable children with basic human needs such as food, clothing, and shelter, enabling them to thrive.
General, Peds
🌐 https://vfmat.ch/649a

Mercy Ships
Operates hospital ships staffed by volunteers to bring hope, healing, and healthcare to underserved communities worldwide.
Anesth, Dent-OMFS, Logist-Op, Neonat, OB-GYN, Ophth-Opt, Ortho, Palliative, Plast, Psych, Surg
🌐 https://vfmat.ch/2e99

MiracleFeet
Brings low-cost treatment to every child on the planet born with clubfoot, a leading cause of physical disability.
Ortho, Peds, Rehab
🌐 https://vfmat.ch/bda8

Mission Regan
Collects supplies, medication, and medical equipment and provides them to those who are in desperate need, both locally and globally.
Logist-Op
🌐 https://vfmat.ch/2bc1

Médecins du Monde/Doctors of the World
Provides care, bears witness, and supports social change worldwide with innovative medical programs and evidence-based advocacy initiatives.
ER Med, General, Infect Dis, MF Med, Neonat, OB-GYN, Peds, Pub Health
🌐 https://vfmat.ch/a43d

Norwegian People's Aid
Aims to improve living conditions, to create a democratic, just, and safe society.
ER Med, Logist-Op
🌐 https://vfmat.ch/2d8e

Options
Believes in a world in which women and children can access the high-quality health services they need, without financial burden.
Logist-Op, MF Med, Neonat, OB-GYN
🌐 https://vfmat.ch/3a48

Order of Malta
Supports forgotten or excluded people, especially those living in conflict zones or amid natural disasters, by providing medical assistance, caring for refugees, and distributing medicines and necessities.
ER Med, General, Infect Dis, MF Med, Nephro, OB-GYN, Ortho, Psych
🌐 https://vfmat.ch/1fab

Pact
Works on the ground to improve the lives of those who are challenged by poverty and marginalization, striving for a world in which all people are heard, capable, and vibrant.
Infect Dis, Logist-Op, MF Med, Pub Health
🌐 https://vfmat.ch/9a6c

Partners in Compassionate Care
Works to provide hope, medical care, and healing to the people of South Sudan, based in Christian ministry.
General, Ophth-Opt
🌐 https://vfmat.ch/74e2

Pharmacists Without Borders Canada
Provides pharmaceutical and technical assistance in the implementation or improvement of community and hospital pharmacies internationally.

🌐 https://vfmat.ch/7658

Poole Africa Link
Provides a link of training for doctors, nurses, midwives, and student nurses between Poole Hospital NHS Foundation Trust and Wau Hospital in South Sudan.
Logist-Op, OB-GYN
🌐 https://vfmat.ch/1f6f

Première Urgence International
Helps civilians who are marginalized or excluded as a result of natural disasters, war, or economic collapse.
ER Med, General, MF Med, Peds, Psych
🌐 https://vfmat.ch/62ba

Real Medicine Foundation (RMF)
Provides humanitarian support to people living in disaster- and poverty-stricken areas, focusing on the person as a whole by providing medical/physical, emotional, economic, and social support.
ER Med, General, Infect Dis, Nutr, Peds, Psych
🌐 https://vfmat.ch/d45a

Relief International
Helps people in fragile settings achieve good health and nutrition by delivering primary healthcare and emergency treatment, and builds local capacity to ensure that communities in vulnerable situations have the access to the quality care they need to live healthy lives.
ER Med, General, MF Med, Neonat, OB-GYN, Peds, Psych
🌐 https://vfmat.ch/1522

RestoringVision
Empowers lives by restoring vision for millions of people in need.
Ophth-Opt
🌐 https://vfmat.ch/e121

Rotary International
Provides service to others, improves lives, and advances world understanding, goodwill, and peace through its fellowship of business, professional, and community leaders.

ER Med, General, Infect Dis, MF Med, OB-GYN
🌐 https://vfmat.ch/8fb5

Safe Harbor International
Inspired by the Christian faith, provides people living in poverty with ministry, development, training, and relief services such as medical care.
General
🌐 https://vfmat.ch/3dfe

Sanofi Espoir Foundation
Contributes to reducing health inequalities among populations that need it most by applying a socially responsible approach focused on fighting childhood cancers in low-income countries, improving maternal and newborn health, and improving access to care.
ER Med, OB-GYN, Peds
🌐 https://vfmat.ch/943b

Save Lives Initiative
Moves to save and improve the lives of people less privileged in the Republic of South Sudan, through participation and empowerment.
General, OB-GYN
🌐 https://vfmat.ch/23c4

Save the Children
Gives children around the world a healthy start in life, the opportunity to learn, and protection from harm.
All-Immu, Crit-Care, ER Med, General, Infect Dis, MF Med, Medicine, Neonat, OB-GYN, Peds, Psych, Pub Health
🌐 https://vfmat.ch/2e73

Sightsavers
Works with partners in developing countries to help eliminate avoidable blindness and advocates for equal opportunity for the disabled.
Infect Dis, Ophth-Opt, Surg
🌐 https://vfmat.ch/aa52

SIGN Fracture Care International
Builds orthopedic capacity around the world and provides the injured poor access to fracture surgery by donating orthopedic education and implant systems to surgeons in developing countries.
Ortho, Rehab, Surg
🌐 https://vfmat.ch/123d

SINA Health
Aims to improve the health and educational status of the population in low- and middle-income countries.
General, Logist-Op
🌐 https://vfmat.ch/9ad3

Soddo Christian Hospital
Mobilizes volunteers to help transform communities through healthcare and education, based in Christian ministry.
ER Med, General
🌐 https://vfmat.ch/efa4

South Sudan Medical Relief
Provides the best possible healthcare in a remote area of South Sudan, primarily offering clinical services and ongoing training, and striving for increased equity in healthcare access across many areas of primary and consultant healthcare.
General, Infect Dis, OB-GYN, Peds
🌐 https://vfmat.ch/c475

South Sudan Villages Clinic, Inc.
Aims to provide curative and preventive care to people in the county of Korok East and surrounding villages in South Sudan.
Dent-OMFS, General, Infect Dis, OB-GYN, Ophth-Opt, Peds, Pub Health
🌐 https://vfmat.ch/4554

Southern Sudan Healthcare Organization
Provides healthcare services, medical supplies, and education to lift up the people of South Sudan and bring hope where it is lost.
General, MF Med, Neonat, OB-GYN, Peds
🌐 https://vfmat.ch/cd91

Sudan Relief Fund
Brings aid in the form of food, clothing, shelter, and medical attention to people of South Sudan.
ER Med, General, Nutr
⊕ https://vfmat.ch/542a

Task Force for Global Health, The
Consists of programs and focus areas that cover a range of global health issues including neglected tropical diseases, infectious diseases, vaccines, field epidemiology, public health informatics, health workforce development, and global health ethics.
Infect Dis, Logist-Op, Medicine, Ophth-Opt, Peds
⊕ https://vfmat.ch/714c

Tearfund
Responds to crisis and partners with local churches to bring restoration to those living in poverty, inspired by the Christian faith.
ER Med, Logist-Op
⊕ https://vfmat.ch/f6cf

Terre des hommes (Tdh) Foundation
Works to improve the daily life of children and their relatives in the areas of health, protection and emergency, in Europe, Africa, Asia, Latin America, and the Near and Middle East.
CT Surg, CV Med, OB-GYN, Ped Surg, Pub Health
⊕ https://vfmat.ch/5c26

Unforgotten Fund, The (UNFF)
Provides lifesaving humanitarian relief to UN Field Operations and projects such as water supply, sanitation and hygiene (WASH), food security, health, and shelter.
ER Med, MF Med, Nutr, OB-GYN, Peds
⊕ https://vfmat.ch/928f

United Nations Children's Fund (UNICEF)
Works in over 190 countries and territories to save children's lives, defend their rights, and help them fulfill their potential, from early childhood through adolescence.
All-Immu, Infect Dis, MF Med, Neonat, Nutr, OB-GYN, Ped Surg, Peds, Pub Health
⊕ https://vfmat.ch/42d7

United Nations Development Programme (UNDP)
Helps countries achieve the simultaneous eradication of extreme poverty and significant reduction of inequalities and exclusion using a sustainable human development approach.
Infect Dis, Logist-Op, Pub Health
⊕ https://vfmat.ch/935c

United Nations High Commissioner for Refugees (UNHCR)
Safeguards the rights and well-being of people who have been forced to flee, ensuring that everybody has the right to seek asylum and find safe refuge in another country, with the goal of seeking lasting solutions.
General, MF Med, Medicine, OB-GYN, Peds, Psych, Pub Health
⊕ https://vfmat.ch/6636

United Nations Office for the Coordination of Humanitarian Affairs (OCHA)
Contributes to principled and effective humanitarian response through coordination, advocacy, policy, information management, and humanitarian financing tools and services, by leveraging functional expertise throughout the organization.
Logist-Op
⊕ https://vfmat.ch/22b8

United Nations Population Fund (UNFPA)
Supports reproductive healthcare for women and youth in more than 150 countries, focusing on delivering a world in which every pregnancy is wanted, every childbirth is safe, and every young person's potential is fulfilled.
Infect Dis, MF Med, Neonat, OB-GYN, Peds, Pub Health
⊕ https://vfmat.ch/c969

United States Agency for International Development (USAID)
Promotes and demonstrates democratic values abroad and advances a free, peaceful, and prosperous world. Leads the U.S. government's international development and disaster assistance through partnerships and investments that save lives.
ER Med, Infect Dis, MF Med, OB-GYN, Peds
⊕ https://vfmat.ch/9a99

United States President's Emergency Plan for AIDS Relief (PEPFAR)
The U.S. global HIV/AIDS response works to prevent new HIV infections and accelerate progress to control the global epidemic in more than 50 countries, by partnering with governments to support sustainable, integrated, and country-led responses to HIV/AIDS.
Infect Dis, Pub Health
⊕ https://vfmat.ch/a57c

University of British Columbia – Faculty of Medicine: Branch for International Surgical Care
Aims to advance sustainable improvements in the delivery of surgical care in the world's most underserved countries, by building capacity within the field of surgery through the provision of care in low-resource settings.
Anesth, ER Med, Neurosurg, Surg, Urol
⊕ https://vfmat.ch/4164

USA for United Nations High Commissioner for Refugees (UNHCR)
Serves and protects refugees and displaced people through emergency relief, cash assistance, education, resettlement, and the rebuilding of livelihoods.
ER Med, General, Logist-Op, Nutr, Pub Health
⊕ https://vfmat.ch/293c

USAID: A2Z The Micronutrient and Child Blindness Project
Aims to increase the use of key micronutrient and blindness interventions to improve child and maternal health.
MF Med, Neonat, Nutr, Ophth-Opt, Surg
⊕ https://vfmat.ch/c5f1

USAID: Deliver Project
Builds a global supply chain to deliver lifesaving health products to people in order to enable countries to provide family planning, protect against malaria, and limit the spread of pandemic threats.
Infect Dis, Logist-Op, MF Med
⊕ https://vfmat.ch/374e

USAID: Maternal and Child Health Integrated Program
Works to improve the health of women and their families, including programs for maternal, newborn, and child health, immunization, family planning, nutrition, malaria, and HIV/AIDS.
All-Immu, General, Infect Dis, MF Med
⊕ https://vfmat.ch/4415

Village Help for South Sudan
Delivers education, opportunity, healthcare, and sanitation to remote areas of South Sudan.
General, Neonat, OB-GYN
⊕ https://vfmat.ch/41c2

Vitamin Angels
Helps at-risk populations in need—specifically pregnant women, new mothers, and children under age 5—to gain access to life-changing vitamins and minerals.
General, Nutr
⊕ https://vfmat.ch/7da1

Watsi
Uses technology to make healthcare a reality for those who might not otherwise be able to afford it.
Pub Health, Surg
⊕ https://vfmat.ch/41a3

Women for Women International
Supports the most marginalized women to earn and save money, improve health and well-being, influence decisions in their home and community, and connect to networks for support.

MF Med, OB-GYN
⊕ https://vfmat.ch/768c

Women's Refugee Commission
Seeks to improve lives by protecting the rights of women, children, and youth
displaced by conflict and crisis through researching their needs, identifying
solutions, and advocating for programs and policies to strengthen their resilience.
General, MF Med, Neonat, OB-GYN, Peds, Psych
⊕ https://vfmat.ch/3d8f

World Children's Fund
Commits to helping children worldwide who are suffering the effects of poverty,
disease, natural disaster, famine, abuse, civil strife, and war.
General, Logist-Op, MF Med, Nutr, OB-GYN, Pub Health
⊕ https://vfmat.ch/9cd8

World Federation of Hemophilia (WFH)
Aims to improve and sustain care for people with inherited bleeding disorders by
pursuing long-term relationships with individuals and organizations who share the
values of WFH's development model.
Heme-Onc
⊕ https://vfmat.ch/5121

World Health Organization, The (WHO)
The United Nations' agency for health provides leadership on global health
matters, shapes the health research agenda, sets norms and standards,
articulates evidence-based policy options, provides technical support and
monitoring to countries, and assesses health trends.
*ER Med, General, Infect Dis, Logist-Op, MF Med, OB-GYN, Peds, Psych, Pub
Health*
⊕ https://vfmat.ch/c476

World Relief
Brings sustainable solutions to the world's greatest problems: disasters, extreme
poverty, violence, oppression, and mass displacement.
ER Med, Nutr, Psych, Pub Health
⊕ https://vfmat.ch/fbcd

World Vision International
Works with vulnerable communities around the world to overcome poverty and
injustice with child-focused programs in disaster management, health, nutrition,
economic development, education, clean water, sanitation, and hygiene.
ER Med, General, Infect Dis, MF Med, Nutr, OB-GYN, Peds
⊕ https://vfmat.ch/2642

South Sudan

Healthcare Facilities

Al Amin Hospital
Juba, South Sudan
⊕ https://vfmat.ch/4fb2

Al Sabbah Children's Hospital
Gombura Street, Juba, Central Equatoria, South
Sudan
⊕ https://vfmat.ch/9adb

Aweil Civil Hospital
Wau-Aweil, Aweil, Northern Bahr el Ghazal, South
Sudan
⊕ https://vfmat.ch/bc8e

Bentiu Hospital
Bentiu-Leer, Mir Mir, Unity, South Sudan
⊕ https://vfmat.ch/229e

Comboni Hospital
Wau-Raja, Wau, Western Bahr el Ghazal, South
Sudan
⊕ https://vfmat.ch/a2a6

Goli Hospital
Yei Maridi, Goli, Central Equatoria, South Sudan
⊕ https://vfmat.ch/b1fc

Government Hospital at Naseer
Nasser-Ethiopia, Jikmir, Upper Nile, South Sudan
⊕ https://vfmat.ch/ef7a

His House of Hope Hospital
Yei Maridi, Yei, Central Equatoria, South Sudan
⊕ https://vfmat.ch/dcdb

Hospital Yambio
Yambio, South Sudan
⊕ https://vfmat.ch/6953

Juba Teaching Hospital
Unity Avenue, Juba, Central Equatoria, South Sudan
⊕ https://vfmat.ch/6856

Juba Military Hospital
Hamia Road, Juba, Central Equatoria, South Sudan
⊕ https://vfmat.ch/a6b4

Lakes State Hospital
Rumbek, South Sudan
⊕ https://vfmat.ch/4b47

Lui Hospital
Juba-Mundri, Lui, Western Equatoria, South Sudan
⊕ https://vfmat.ch/6fe7

Melut Hospital
Melut – Mabek Track, Melut, Upper Nile, South Sudan
⊕ https://vfmat.ch/8693

MSF Hospital
Boma-Pibor, Pibor, Jonglei, South Sudan
⊕ https://vfmat.ch/65a5

Police Hospital
Juba University Road, Juba, Central Equatoria, South
Sudan
⊕ https://vfmat.ch/e6df

Renk Civil Hospital
Renk-Kosti, Renk, Upper Nile, South Sudan
⊕ https://vfmat.ch/8218

Renk Military Hospital
Renk-Kosti, Renk, Upper Nile, South Sudan
⊕ https://vfmat.ch/cd86

UNMISS Hospital
Juba, Central Equatoria, South Sudan
⊕ https://vfmat.ch/eac7

Usratuna PHCC
Usratuna Road, Juba, Central Equatoria, South Sudan
⊕ https://vfmat.ch/f89c

Wau Teaching Hospital
Wau, South Sudan
⊕ https://vfmat.ch/1f35

Yei Civil Hospital
Congo Road, Yei, Central Equatoria, South Sudan
⊕ https://vfmat.ch/77b1

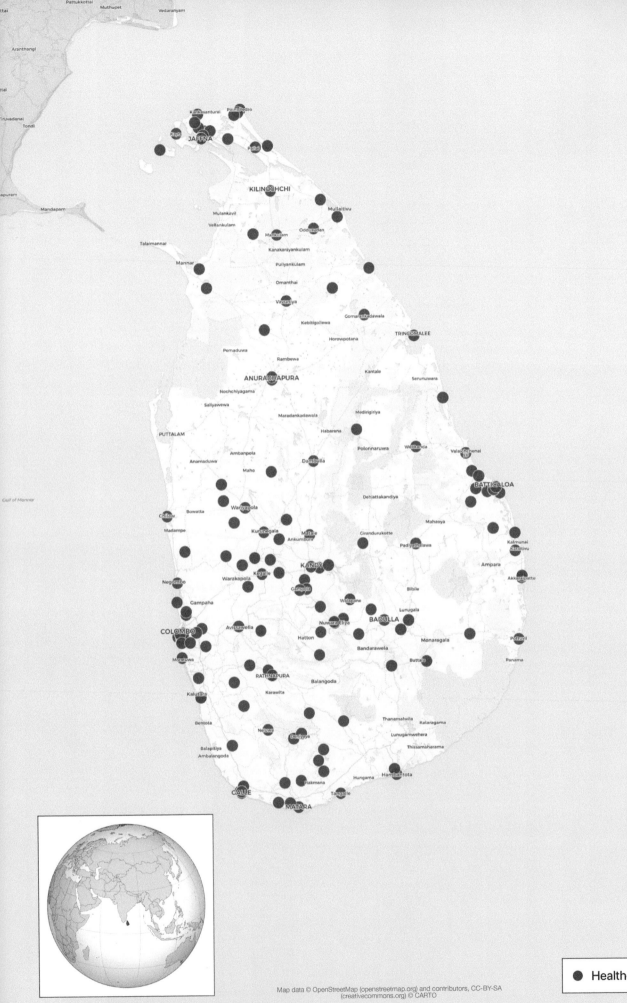

Healthcare Facility

Sri Lanka

Formerly known as Ceylon, the Democratic Socialist Republic of Sri Lanka is a South Asian island nation located in the Indian Ocean. Because of its unique location off the southern coast of India, it has been nicknamed the "Teardrop of India." The population of 23 million people is distributed around the island, with larger concentrations in the southwest, in metropolitan areas along the eastern coast, and in the north. Colombo, the capital, is home to 619,000 people. The population is ethnically diverse, with the majority being Sinhalese. Other ethnic groups include Sri Lankan Tamil, Sri Lankan Moor, and Indian Tamil. The official languages of Sri Lanka are Sinhala and Tamil, while English is also spoken as a secondary language. As much as 70 percent of the population identifies as Buddhist, while smaller portions are Hindu, Muslim, Roman Catholic, and Christian. Sri Lanka is home to the oldest tree ever planted by a human, the 2,300-year-old Sri Maha Bodhi tree.

Sri Lanka gained independence from British rule in 1948. It remained part of the British Commonwealth until 1972. A 26-year civil war ended in 2009. Since then, Sri Lanka has become a leader in Asia, with one of the highest ratings on the human development index among South Asian countries. The education system in Sri Lanka is well established, providing free universal primary and secondary education. As much as 85 percent of the population is literate. The main economic sectors include tourism, clothing production, and the agricultural production of crops such as rice. Sri Lanka is known for its tea, and it is the world's largest tea exporter.

Sri Lanka's government-sponsored health system is well established and free. Because of the extensive network of hospitals throughout the country, overall health conditions in Sri Lanka have greatly improved, and life expectancy is 10 percent higher than the world average. Non-communicable diseases contribute to the most deaths, including ischemic heart disease, stroke, diabetes, asthma, chronic kidney disease, COPD, cirrhosis, and Alzheimer's disease. Lower respiratory infections, self-harm, and conflict also continue to be leading causes of death. The risk factors that contribute most to death and disability include high fasting plasma glucose, high blood pressure, high body-mass index, dietary risks, alcohol and tobacco use, air pollution, high LDL, kidney dysfunction, and malnutrition. Notably, Sri Lanka has the highest number of deaths in Asia due to suicide.

23M
Population

$3,682
GDP Per Capita

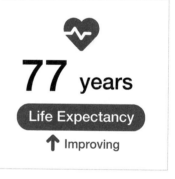

77 years
Life Expectancy
↑ Improving

115
Doctors/100k
Physician Density

415
Beds/100k
Hospital Bed Density

36
Deaths/100k
Maternal Mortality

Sri Lanka

Nonprofit Organizations

A Broader View Volunteers
Provides developing countries around the world with significant volunteer programs that aid the neediest communities and forge a lasting bond between those volunteering and those they have helped.
Dent-OMFS, ER Med, Infect Dis, MF Med
⊕ https://vfmat.ch/3bec

Age International
Helps older people living in some of the world's poorest places to have improved well-being and be treated with dignity through a variety of programs, including emergency relief and cataract surgery.
ER Med, Geri, Logist-Op, Nutr, Ophth-Opt, Palliative, Pub Health
⊕ https://vfmat.ch/c7e2

AIDS Foundation of Sri Lanka
Provides comprehensive care for those afflicted and affected by AIDS in Sri Lanka, together with prevention and awareness programs.
All-Immu
⊕ https://vfmat.ch/ada3

Al Basar International Foundation
Works with local partners to treat preventable blindness, and helps set up sustainable infrastructure so local teams can save sight in their communities.
Ophth-Opt
⊕ https://vfmat.ch/a8b5

Al-Mustafa Welfare Trust
Seeks to alleviate poverty and provides medical and social development assistance to the poor and vulnerable around the world.
General, Ophth-Opt
⊕ https://vfmat.ch/c5f4

Americares
Saves lives and improves health for people affected by poverty or disaster and responds with life-changing medicine, medical supplies, and health programs including domestic and global medical clinics.
All-Immu, ER Med, General, Infect Dis, MF Med, Nutr
⊕ https://vfmat.ch/e567

AO Alliance
Builds solutions to lessen the burden of injuries in low- and middle-income countries, while enhancing the care of the injured to reduce human suffering, disability, and poverty.
Ortho, Surg
⊕ https://vfmat.ch/8cd5

Association of Medical Doctors of Asia (AMDA)
Strives to support people affected by disasters and economic distress on their road to recovery, establishing a true partnership with special emphasis on local initiative.

ER Med, Logist-Op, Pub Health
⊕ https://vfmat.ch/e3d4

Australia Sri Lanka Medical Aid Team
Works towards providing improved access to quality healthcare, with a strong focus on sustainability and education.
General
⊕ https://vfmat.ch/2877

BFIRST – British Foundation for International Reconstructive Surgery & Training
Supports projects across the developing world to train surgeons in their local environment to effectively manage devastating injuries.
Anesth, Plast, Surg
⊕ https://vfmat.ch/ad4f

Buddhist Tzu Chi Medical Foundation
Provides healthcare to the poor, operates six hospitals in Taiwan and mobile medical and dental clinics in the U.S., manages a bone marrow bank, and organizes over 8,600 physicians who provide free medical services to more than 2 million people globally.
Crit-Care, Dent-OMFS, ER Med, General
⊕ https://vfmat.ch/ff61

Bureau of International Health Cooperation
Seeks to improve healthcare around the world, including developing countries, using expertise, and contribute to healthier lives of Japanese people by bringing these experiences back to Japan.
ER Med, Heme-Onc, Infect Dis, Peds, Pub Health
⊕ https://vfmat.ch/947d

CARE
Works around the globe to save lives, defeat poverty, and achieve social justice.
ER Med, General
⊕ https://vfmat.ch/7232

Carter Center, The
Seeks to prevent and resolve conflicts, enhance freedom and democracy, and improve health, while remaining committed to human rights and the alleviation of human suffering.
Infect Dis, MF Med, Ophth-Opt
⊕ https://vfmat.ch/6556

Catholic World Mission
Works to rebuild communities worldwide by helping to alleviate poverty and empower underserved areas, while spreading the message of the Catholic Church.
ER Med, General, Nutr, Peds
⊕ https://vfmat.ch/7b5f

Child Action Lanka

Provides education, health, and nutrition to disadvantaged children and promotes their needs, rights, and interests to empower them, their families, and communities.

Nutr, Peds

⊕ https://vfmat.ch/89aa

ChildFund Australia

Works to reduce poverty for children in many of the world's most disadvantaged communities.

ER Med, General, Peds

⊕ https://vfmat.ch/13df

Children's Emergency Relief International

Works with children, families, communities, and governments to provide a family environment as the first and best option for children to grow in.

General, Pub Health

⊕ https://vfmat.ch/92ae

Christian Blind Mission (CBM)

Aims to improve the quality of life of persons with disabilities in the poorest countries, addressing poverty as a cause and a consequence of disability, and working in partnership to create a society for all.

ENT, General, Infect Dis, OB-GYN, Ophth-Opt, Ortho, Peds, Psych, Rehab, Surg

⊕ https://vfmat.ch/3824

Circle of Health International (COHI)

Aligns with local, community-based organizations led and powered by women to help respond to the needs of the women and children that they serve. Helps with the provision of professional volunteers, capacity training, and procurement of requested and appropriate supplies and equipment. Raises funds for the organizations to provide the services required.

ER Med, Logist-Op, MF Med, Neonat, OB-GYN, Psych

⊕ https://vfmat.ch/8b63

COVID-19 Clinical Research Coalition

Advocates and collaborates for the advancement of COVID-19 research driven by the needs of low-resource settings, and works for equitable access to solutions to the pandemic.

All-Immu, Infect-Dis, MF Med, Path, Pub Health

⊕ https://vfmat.ch/d1f4

Dentaid

Seeks to treat, equip, train, and educate people in need of dental care.

Dent-OMFS

⊕ https://vfmat.ch/a183

Direct Relief

Improves the health and lives of people affected by poverty or emergency situations by mobilizing and providing essential medical resources needed for their care.

ER Med, Logist-Op

⊕ https://vfmat.ch/58e5

Direct Relief of Poverty & Sickness Foundation (DROPS)

This volunteer-led organization uses all donations for direct relief of poverty and illness through initiatives in healthcare education, improving healthcare systems, and providing essential medical help to children and aged people in need.

Dent-OMFS, General, Ophth-Opt

⊕ https://vfmat.ch/af95

Divine Will Foundation

Funds educational, medical, nutritional, sustainable energy, and water purification projects.

CT Surg, CV Med, Ped Surg, Peds

⊕ https://vfmat.ch/6f1e

Duke University: Global Health Institute

Sparks innovation in global health research and education, and brings together knowledge and resources to address the most important global health issues of our time.

All-Immu, Infect Dis, MF Med, OB-GYN, Pub Health

⊕ https://vfmat.ch/c4cd

Emergency Response Team Search And Rescue, The (ERTSAR)

Provides technical rescue and medical response in the immediate aftermath of a disaster while providing strategic, smart, and sustainable solutions.

ER Med, Logist-Op

⊕ https://vfmat.ch/c599

Episcopal Relief & Development

Provides relief in times of disaster and promotes sustainable development by identifying and addressing the root causes of suffering.

Infect Dis, MF Med, Neonat, Nutr, Peds

⊕ https://vfmat.ch/7cfa

Exceed Worldwide

Supports people with disabilities living in poverty by providing free prosthetic and orthotic services in South and Southeast Asia.

Ortho, Peds

⊕ https://vfmat.ch/dd24

Eye Foundation of America

Works toward a world without childhood blindness.

Ophth-Opt

⊕ https://vfmat.ch/a7eb

FAIRMED Sri Lanka

Aims to improve the circumstances of all people at risk for or affected by leprosy and other neglected tropical diseases in Sri Lanka.

Infect Dis

⊕ https://vfmat.ch/c463

Firefly Mission

Organizes humanitarian missions to help people in less fortunate situations while serving as a vehicle for the spiritual development of members and the beneficiaries of its missions.

Logist-Op, Ophth-Opt, Pub Health

⊕ https://vfmat.ch/d215

Fracarita International

Provides support and services in the fields of mental healthcare, care for people with a disability, and education.

Psych, Rehab

⊕ https://vfmat.ch/8d3c

GFA World

Based in Christian ministry, sponsors medical camps for the sick, provides disaster relief to vulnerable populations, and empowers impoverished communities with basic necessities such as clean water, vocational training, and education.

General, Infect Dis

⊕ https://vfmat.ch/63ee

Global Ministries – The United Methodist Church

As the worldwide mission and development agency of The United Methodist Church, Global Ministries works with more than 300 hospitals and clinics around the world through its Global Health Unit.

Anesth, CT Surg, CV Med, Crit-Care, Dent-OMFS, Derm, ER Med, GI, General, Infect Dis, Logist-Op, MF Med, Medicine, Neonat, Nephro, Nutr, OB-GYN, Ophth-Opt, Ortho, Palliative, Peds, Pod, Psych, Pub Health, Rehab, Rheum, Surg, Urol

⊕ https://vfmat.ch/1723

Global Oncology (GO)

Brings the best in cancer care to underserved patients around the world and collaborates across geographic, professional, and academic borders to improve cancer care, research, and education.

Heme-Onc, Path, Rad-Onc

⊕ https://vfmat.ch/fcb8

Globus Relief

Aims to improve the delivery of healthcare worldwide by gathering, processing, and distributing surplus medical supplies to charities at home and abroad.

Logist-Op

⊕ https://vfmat.ch/a2b7

Good Shepard International Foundation

Strives to promote inclusive and sustainable development for the most marginalized and vulnerable people, with a special focus on women, girls, and children, inspired by the Christian faith.

ER Med

⊕ https://vfmat.ch/ad9a

Grace for Impact

Provides high-quality healthcare and education to the rural poor, where it is needed most, in Sub-Saharan Africa and Southeast Asia.

Dent-OMFS, General, Ophth-Opt

⊕ https://vfmat.ch/3ed1

Hadassah International

Works with medical institutions around the world to establish hospitals and research facilities, and to pioneer advances in healthcare.

Anesth, CV Med, Crit-Care, ER Med, General, Heme-Onc, Medicine, Neuro, OB-GYN, Ophth-Opt, Peds, Urol

⊕ https://vfmat.ch/56c7

Heart Reach Australia

Brings programs, medical facilities, education, and assistance to those living in substandard conditions largely related to poverty.

ER Med, General, Nephro, Ophth-Opt, Peds

⊕ https://vfmat.ch/fac5

HelpAge International

Works to ensure that people everywhere understand how much older people contribute to society and that they must enjoy their right to healthcare, social services, economic, and physical security.

General, Geri, Infect Dis, Medicine, Pub Health

⊕ https://vfmat.ch/5d91

Humanity & Inclusion

Works alongside people with disabilities and vulnerable populations, taking action and bearing witness in order to respond to their essential needs, improve their living conditions and health, and promote respect for their dignity and fundamental rights.

General, Infect Dis, MF Med, Medicine, Ortho, Peds, Psych, Pub Health, Rehab

⊕ https://vfmat.ch/16b7

IMPACT Foundation

Works to prevent and alleviate needless disability by restoring sight, mobility, and hearing.

ENT, MF Med, OB-GYN, Ophth-Opt, Ortho, Peds, Surg

⊕ https://vfmat.ch/ba28

International Campaign for Women's Right to Safe Abortion

Works to build an international network and campaign that brings together organizations with an interest in promoting and providing safe abortion to create a shared platform for advocacy, debate, and dialogue and the sharing of skills and experience.

OB-GYN, Pub Health, Surg

⊕ https://vfmat.ch/f341

International Council of Ophthalmology

Works with ophthalmologic societies and others to enhance ophthalmic education and improve access to the highest-quality eye care in order to preserve and restore vision for people of the world.

Ophth-Opt

⊕ https://vfmat.ch/ffd2

International Federation of Gynecology and Obstetrics (FIGO)

Implements global projects on specific women's health issues.

MF Med, Medicine, Neonat, OB-GYN, Surg, Urol

⊕ https://vfmat.ch/c4b4

International Federation of Red Cross and Red Crescent Societies (IFRC)

Coordinates and directs international assistance following natural and manmade disasters in nonconflict situations through the world's largest humanitarian and development network. Provides disaster-preparedness programs, healthcare activities, and promotes humanitarian values.

ER Med, General, Infect Dis, Nutr

⊕ https://vfmat.ch/b4ee

International Learning Movement (ILM UK)

Supports some of the world's poorest people in developing countries with core projects in education, safe drinking water, and healthcare.

General, Ophth-Opt

⊕ https://vfmat.ch/b974

International Organization for Migration (IOM) – The UN Migration Agency

Promotes evidence-informed policies and holistic, preventive, and curative health programs that are beneficial, accessible, and equitable for vulnerable migrants.

General, Infect Dis, OB-GYN

⊕ https://vfmat.ch/621a

International Planned Parenthood Federation (IPPF)

Leads a locally owned, globally connected civil society movement that provides and enables services and champions sexual and reproductive health and rights for all, especially the underserved.

Infect Dis, MF Med, OB-GYN

⊕ https://vfmat.ch/dc97

International Union Against Tuberculosis and Lung Disease

Develops, implements, and assesses anti-tuberculosis, lung health, and noncommunicable disease programs.

Infect Dis, Pub Health, Pulm-Critic

⊕ https://vfmat.ch/3e82

Islamic Medical Association of North America

Fosters health promotion, disease prevention, and health maintenance in communities around the world through direct patient care and health programs.

Anesth, Dent-OMFS, ER Med, General, Logist-Op, Ophth-Opt, Peds, Plast, Surg

⊕ https://vfmat.ch/a157

Johns Hopkins Center for Communication Programs

Believes in the power of communication to save lives by empowering people to adopt healthy behaviors for themselves, their families, and their communities.

General, Infect Dis, Logist-Op, OB-GYN, Pub Health

⊕ https://vfmat.ch/1bf9

Joint United Nations Programme on HIV/AIDS (UNAIDS)

Aims to place people living with HIV and people affected by the virus at the decision-making table and at the center of designing, delivering, and monitoring the AIDS response.

Infect Dis

⊕ https://vfmat.ch/464a

Kaya Responsible Travel

Promotes sustainable social, environmental, and economic development, empowers communities, and cultivates educated, compassionate global citizens through responsible travel.

All-Immu, Crit-Care, Dent-OMFS, ER Med, General, Geri, Infect Dis, MF Med, Medicine, Nutr, OB-GYN, Peds, Psych, Pub Health, Rehab

⊕ https://vfmat.ch/b2cf

Kind Cuts for Kids

Aims to improve medical services for children in developing countries through education, demonstration, and skills transfer to local healthcare professionals.

Anesth, Medicine, Ped Surg, Surg

⊕ https://vfmat.ch/e3d7

Leprosy Mission England and Wales, The

Leads the fight against leprosy by supporting people living with leprosy today and serving future generations by working to end transmission of the disease.

Infect Dis, Pub Health

⊕ https://vfmat.ch/4c67

Leprosy Mission International

Seeks to empower people with leprosy to attain healing, dignity, and life in all its fullness.

Infect Dis

⊕ https://vfmat.ch/95a9

Life for a Child
Supports the provision of the best possible healthcare, given local circumstances, to all children and youth with diabetes in less-resourced countries, through the strengthening of existing diabetes services.
Endo, Medicine, Peds
⊕ https://vfmat.ch/d712

Limbs International
Engages communities and transforms lives through affordable, sustainable prosthetic solutions and rehabilitation services in developing countries.
Logist-Op, Ortho, Pod, Rehab
⊕ https://vfmat.ch/dc84

Little Things, The
Provides vital medical equipment to poorly funded and inadequately equipped hospitals, improving access to healthcare for patients across the globe.
⊕ https://vfmat.ch/2d81

London School of Hygiene & Tropical Medicine: Health in Humanitarian Crises Centre
Advances health and health equity in crisis-affected countries through research, education, and translation of knowledge into policy and practice.
ER Med, Infect Dis, Pub Health
⊕ https://vfmat.ch/96ad

Marie Stopes International
Provides the contraception and safe abortion services that enable women all over the world to choose their own futures.
Infect Dis, MF Med, Neonat, OB-GYN, Pub Health
⊕ https://vfmat.ch/9525

MiracleFeet
Brings low-cost treatment to every child on the planet born with clubfoot, a leading cause of physical disability.
Ortho, Peds, Rehab
⊕ https://vfmat.ch/bda8

MSI Reproductive Choices (Marie Stopes International)
Seeks to deliver quality family planning and reproductive healthcare to women around the world.
MF Med
⊕ https://vfmat.ch/5c82

Multi-Agency International Training and Support (MAITS)
Improves the lives of some of the world's poorest people living with disabilities through better access to quality health and education services and support.
Neuro, Psych, Rehab
⊕ https://vfmat.ch/9dcd

Muslim Aid
Aims to improve the lives of those in need, and to address the underlying structural and systemic causes of poverty in their communities, inspired by Muslim faith.
ER Med, Infect Dis, MF Med, Nutr
⊕ https://vfmat.ch/a8ed

Muslim Welfare Canada
Serves vulnerable populations by supporting healthcare clinics, food security programs, and other humanitarian projects.
Logist-Op, Nutr
⊕ https://vfmat.ch/a227

Médecins du Monde/Doctors of the World
Provides care, bears witness, and supports social change worldwide with innovative medical programs and evidence-based advocacy initiatives.
ER Med, General, Infect Dis, MF Med, Neonat, OB-GYN, Peds, Pub Health
⊕ https://vfmat.ch/a43d

Nazarene Compassionate Ministries
Partners with local churches around the world to clothe, shelter, feed, heal, educate, and live in solidarity with those in need.
General, Infect Dis, OB-GYN
⊕ https://vfmat.ch/6b4d

NCD Alliance
Unites and strengthens civil society to stimulate collaborative advocacy, action, and accountability for NCD (noncommunicable disease) prevention and control.
All-Immu, CV Med, General, Heme-Onc, Medicine, Peds, Psych
⊕ https://vfmat.ch/abdd

Network for Improving Critical Care Systems and Training (NICST)
Provides critical-care training for staff in developing countries.
Crit-Care, General, Pulm-Critic
⊕ https://vfmat.ch/71f8

Oxford University Global Surgery Group (OUGSG)
Aims to contribute to the provision of high-quality surgical care globally, particularly in low- and middle-income countries (LMICs), while bringing together students, researchers, and clinicians with an interest in global surgery, anesthesia, and obstetrics and gynecology.
Anesth, MF Med, OB-GYN, Ortho, Surg
⊕ https://vfmat.ch/c624

Palav
Provides support equipment for newborns with breathing difficulties and trains healthcare providers.
Peds
⊕ https://vfmat.ch/86bd

Reach Beyond
Aims to reach and impact underserved communities with medical care and community development, based in Christian ministry.
ER Med, General
⊕ https://vfmat.ch/cc5c

Real Medicine Foundation (RMF)
Provides humanitarian support to people living in disaster- and poverty-stricken areas, focusing on the person as a whole by providing medical/physical, emotional, economic, and social support.
ER Med, General, Infect Dis, Nutr, Peds, Psych
⊕ https://vfmat.ch/d45a

RestoringVision
Empowers lives by restoring vision for millions of people in need.
Ophth-Opt
⊕ https://vfmat.ch/e121

Rose Charities International
Aims to support communities to improve quality of life and reduce the effects of poverty through innovative, self-sustaining projects, and partnerships.
ENT, ER Med, General, Infect Dis, Neonat, OB-GYN, Ophth-Opt, Ped Surg, Peds, Rehab, Urol
⊕ https://vfmat.ch/53df

Rotary International
Provides service to others, improves lives, and advances world understanding, goodwill, and peace through its fellowship of business, professional, and community leaders.
ER Med, General, Infect Dis, MF Med, OB-GYN
⊕ https://vfmat.ch/8fb5

Salvation Army International, The
Seeks to meet human needs through services in education, healthcare, community support, emergency response, and ministry development, inspired by the Christian faith.
Dent-OMFS, Derm, ER Med, Infect Dis, MF Med, Medicine, Nutr, OB-GYN, Ophth-Opt, Palliative, Psych, Rehab, Surg
⊕ https://vfmat.ch/8eb3

SAMU Foundation
Provides medical first response and reconstruction when severe international emergencies occur.
ER Med, Infect Dis, Logist-Op, Psych, Pub Health
⊕ https://vfmat.ch/3196

Serve Humanity Foundation (SHF)
Provides education, job training, community creation, and empowerment, and access to medical care to underserved and underprivileged communities.
General
🌐 https://vfmat.ch/d2f5

Sight for All
Empowers communities to deliver comprehensive, evidence-based, high-quality eye healthcare through the provision of research, education, and equipment.
Logist-Op, Ophth-Opt, Surg
🌐 https://vfmat.ch/e34b

Singapore Red Cross
Responds to emergencies with a dedication to relieving human suffering and protecting human lives and dignity.
ER Med, General, Logist-Op, Pub Health, Surg
🌐 https://vfmat.ch/4d7c

SLK Foundation
Provides dialysis units, erythropoietin injections, and day-to-day comfort to patients while raising awareness of renal disease in Sri Lanka.
Nephro, Pub Health
🌐 https://vfmat.ch/56a6

Smile Train, Inc.
Treats children with cleft lip through a sustainable and local model that supports surgery and other forms of essential care.
Logist-Op, Pub Health
🌐 https://vfmat.ch/822c

SOS Children's Villages International
Supports children through alternative care and family strengthening.
ER Med, Peds
🌐 https://vfmat.ch/aca1

Sri Lanka Medical Association of North America Western Region, Inc., The
Aims to bring together professionals and students for humanitarian service including disease prevention and the care and treatment of the sick, injured, afflicted, infirm, disabled, and destitute.
General, Nutr, Peds, Pub Health
🌐 https://vfmat.ch/71cb

Sri Lanka Red Cross Society
Strives to enhance volunteer actions, maximize capacities, and mobilize resources to build community resilience and create a safer environment for those exposed to disasters, emergencies, and social exclusion.
Dent-OMFS, General, Infect Dis, Nutr, Ophth-Opt, Peds, Pub Health
🌐 https://vfmat.ch/9ce4

Sri Sathya Sai International Organization
Inspired by spiritual teachings, carries out efforts in global healthcare, education, humanitarian relief, and youth engagement.
Dent-OMFS, General, Logist-Op, Nutr, Ophth-Opt, Pub Health
🌐 https://vfmat.ch/9bda

Students for Kids International Projects (SKIP)
Strives to educate and empower students to initiate and maintain sustainable community projects for the health, welfare, and education of children.
Dent-OMFS, General, Nutr, Peds, Pub Health
🌐 https://vfmat.ch/de4e

Swasti
Aims to transform the lives of marginalized communities by ensuring their access to quality healthcare and thereby contributing to poverty alleviation.
Pub Health
🌐 https://vfmat.ch/be8b

Task Force for Global Health, The
Consists of programs and focus areas that cover a range of global health issues including neglected tropical diseases, infectious diseases, vaccines, field epidemiology, public health informatics, health workforce development, and global health ethics.

Infect Dis, Logist-Op, Medicine, Ophth-Opt, Peds
🌐 https://vfmat.ch/714c

Two Worlds Cancer Collaboration
Collaborates with local care professionals in lesser-resourced countries to help reduce the burden of cancer and other life-limiting illnesses.
Heme-Onc, Palliative, Peds, Pub Health, Rad-Onc
🌐 https://vfmat.ch/fbdd

Union for International Cancer Control (UICC)
Unites and supports the cancer community to reduce the global cancer burden, promote greater equity, and ensure that cancer control continues to be a priority in the world health and development agenda.
Heme-Onc, Pub Health
🌐 https://vfmat.ch/88b1

United Nations Children's Fund (UNICEF)
Works in over 190 countries and territories to save children's lives, defend their rights, and help them fulfill their potential, from early childhood through adolescence.
All-Immu, Infect Dis, MF Med, Neonat, Nutr, OB-GYN, Ped Surg, Peds, Pub Health
🌐 https://vfmat.ch/42d7

United Nations Development Programme (UNDP)
Helps countries achieve the simultaneous eradication of extreme poverty and significant reduction of inequalities and exclusion using a sustainable human development approach.
Infect Dis, Logist-Op, Pub Health
🌐 https://vfmat.ch/935c

United Nations High Commissioner for Refugees (UNHCR)
Safeguards the rights and well-being of people who have been forced to flee, ensuring that everybody has the right to seek asylum and find safe refuge in another country, with the goal of seeking lasting solutions.
General, MF Med, Medicine, OB-GYN, Peds, Psych, Pub Health
🌐 https://vfmat.ch/6636

United Nations Population Fund (UNFPA)
Supports reproductive healthcare for women and youth in more than 150 countries, focusing on delivering a world in which every pregnancy is wanted, every childbirth is safe, and every young person's potential is fulfilled.
Infect Dis, MF Med, Neonat, OB-GYN, Peds, Pub Health
🌐 https://vfmat.ch/c969

University of California San Francisco: Institute for Global Health Sciences
Dedicates its efforts to improving health and reducing the burden of disease in the world's most vulnerable populations by integrating expertise in the health, social, and biological sciences, training global health leaders, and developing solutions to the most pressing health challenges.
Infect Dis, OB-GYN, Pub Health
🌐 https://vfmat.ch/6587

USAID: Leadership, Management and Governance Project
Improves leadership, management, and governance practices to strengthen health systems and improve health for all, including vulnerable populations worldwide.
Logist-Op
🌐 https://vfmat.ch/d35e

Vision Care
Restores sight and helps patients get regular treatment at short-term eye camps and long-term base clinics by having doctors, missionaries, volunteers, and sponsors work together.
Ophth-Opt
🌐 https://vfmat.ch/9d7c

Vision of Love
Aims to help the poorest of the poor in getting their vision back on track by funding cataract operations carried out in Sri Lanka.
Ophth-Opt
🌐 https://vfmat.ch/d896

We Care for Humanity (WCH)

Promotes sustainable social change and the sustainable development goals developed by the United Nations, including: no poverty, good health and well-being, gender equality, human rights, climate action, and strong institutions.
General, Logist-Op, Pub Health
⊕ https://vfmat.ch/8b4e

Women's Refugee Commission

Seeks to improve lives by protecting the rights of women, children, and youth displaced by conflict and crisis through researching their needs, identifying solutions, and advocating for programs and policies to strengthen their resilience.
General, MF Med, Neonat, OB-GYN, Peds, Psych
⊕ https://vfmat.ch/3d8f

World Children's Fund

Commits to helping children worldwide who are suffering the effects of poverty, disease, natural disaster, famine, abuse, civil strife, and war.
General, Logist-Op, MF Med, Nutr, OB-GYN, Pub Health
⊕ https://vfmat.ch/9cd8

World Children's Initiative (WCI)

Aims to improve and rebuild the healthcare and educational infrastructure for children in developing areas, both domestic and worldwide.
CV Med, Ped Surg, Surg
⊕ https://vfmat.ch/9ca7

World Council of Optometry

Facilitates the development of optometry worldwide and promotes eye health and vision care through advocacy, education, policy development, and humanitarian outreach.
Ophth-Opt, Pub Health
⊕ https://vfmat.ch/c92e

World Federation of Hemophilia (WFH)

Aims to improve and sustain care for people with inherited bleeding disorders by pursuing long-term relationships with individuals and organizations who share the values of WFH's development model.
Heme-Onc
⊕ https://vfmat.ch/5121

World Health Organization, The (WHO)

The United Nations' agency for health provides leadership on global health matters, shapes the health research agenda, sets norms and standards, articulates evidence-based policy options, provides technical support and monitoring to countries, and assesses health trends.
ER Med, General, Infect Dis, Logist-Op, MF Med, OB-GYN, Peds, Psych, Pub Health
⊕ https://vfmat.ch/c476

World Hope International

Empowers the poorest individuals around the world so they can become agents of change within their communities, by offering resources and knowledge.
Infect Dis, Logist-Op, MF Med, OB-GYN, Peds
⊕ https://vfmat.ch/a4b8

World Vision International

Works with vulnerable communities around the world to overcome poverty and injustice with child-focused programs in disaster management, health, nutrition, economic development, education, clean water, sanitation, and hygiene.
ER Med, General, Infect Dis, MF Med, Nutr, OB-GYN, Peds
⊕ https://vfmat.ch/2642

York County Medical Foundation

Provides medical care and humanitarian relief to the poor, the distressed, and the underprivileged, both locally and internationally.
OB-GYN, Plast, Surg
⊕ https://vfmat.ch/a55d

 # Sri Lanka

Healthcare Facilities

34 Military Hospital
Hill Station, Western Area, Sri Lanka
⊕ https://vfmat.ch/2737

Ahmadiyya Hospital
Tosu, Eastern Province, Sri Lanka
⊕ https://vfmat.ch/de2d

AHS – Waterloo Hospital
Waterloo, Western Area, Sri Lanka
⊕ https://vfmat.ch/77fa

ARAB Hospital
Mabain, Northern Province, Sri Lanka
⊕ https://vfmat.ch/44a5

Aspen Medical Sierra Leone Private Hospital
Madongo Town, Western Area, Sri Lanka
⊕ https://vfmat.ch/9bca

Blue Shield Hospital
Kingtom, Western Area, Sri Lanka
⊕ https://vfmat.ch/1c57

Bo Children's Hospital
Geoma, Southern Province, Sri Lanka
⊕ https://vfmat.ch/5984

Bonthe Governmental Hospital
Bonthe, Sri Lanka
⊕ https://vfmat.ch/vz18

Brookfields
Mafonike, Western Area, Sri Lanka
⊕ https://vfmat.ch/f26d

China-SL Friendship Hospital, Jui
Kosso Town, Western Area, Sri Lanka
⊕ https://vfmat.ch/b15c

Choithram Memorial Hospital
Mirimboe, Western Area, Sri Lanka
⊕ https://vfmat.ch/b258

Connaught Hospital
Tower Hill, Western Area, Sri Lanka
⊕ https://vfmat.ch/bb17

Curney Barnes Hospital
Tower Hill, Western Area, Sri Lanka
⊕ https://vfmat.ch/d284

EDC Unit
Gbomboma, Southern Province, Sri Lanka
⊕ https://vfmat.ch/7c13

Emergency Hospital
Adonkia, Western Area, Sri Lanka
⊕ https://vfmat.ch/afaf

Gandorhun CHC
Konelo, Eastern Province, Sri Lanka
⊕ https://vfmat.ch/f7f4

Goderich ETC
Fonima, Western Area, Sri Lanka
⊕ https://vfmat.ch/17de

Holy Mary Hospital
Gbewobu, Southern Province, Sri Lanka
⊕ https://vfmat.ch/28bf

Holy Spirit Hospital
Mankane, Northern Province, Sri Lanka
⊕ https://vfmat.ch/379a

Kailahun Government Hospital
Kailahun, Eastern Province, Sri Lanka
⊕ https://vfmat.ch/bc46

Kamakwie Wesleyan Hospital
Kamakwie, Northern Province, Sri Lanka
⊕ https://vfmat.ch/1b62

Kambia General Hospital
Kambia, Northern Province, Sri Lanka
⊕ https://vfmat.ch/a952

Kenema Government Hospital
Kijehun, Eastern Province, Sri Lanka
⊕ https://vfmat.ch/dd2c

Kindoya Hospital
Mendewa, Southern Province, Sri Lanka
⊕ https://vfmat.ch/dd99

Kingharman Maternal and Child Health Hospital
Aberdeen, Western Area, Sri Lanka
⊕ https://vfmat.ch/91e7

Lakka Hospital ETU
Lakka, Western Area, Sri Lanka
⊕ https://vfmat.ch/6c83

Maforki ETU
Magbali Lol, Northern Province, Sri Lanka
⊕ https://vfmat.ch/174e

Magburaka Hospital
Magbass, Northern Province, Sri Lanka
⊕ https://vfmat.ch/2b6c

Mahera Hospital
Mahera, Northern Province, Sri Lanka
⊕ https://vfmat.ch/f3ea

Makeni Regional Hospital
Petifu, Northern Province, Sri Lanka
⊕ https://vfmat.ch/5bb6

Malema
Malema, Eastern Province, Sri Lanka
⊕ https://vfmat.ch/f521

Mamudia MCHP
Mamudia, Northern Province, Sri Lanka
⊕ https://vfmat.ch/685f

Masanga Hospital
Makolo, Northern Province, Sri Lanka
⊕ https://vfmat.ch/77b4

Mattru General Hospital
Gbangiyema, Southern Province, Sri Lanka
⊕ https://vfmat.ch/39ee

Mercy Hospital
Tongima, Southern Province, Sri Lanka
⊕ https://vfmat.ch/a84c

Morning Star
Mendewa, Southern Province, Sri Lanka
⊕ https://vfmat.ch/7c9d

National Emergency Medical Service (NEMS)
Lumley, Western Area, Sri Lanka
⊕ https://vfmat.ch/b43e

Ola During Children's Hospital
Mount Aureol, Western Area, Sri Lanka
⊕ https://vfmat.ch/c1bf

Panguma Hospital
Panguma, Eastern Province, Sri Lanka
⊕ https://vfmat.ch/9c77

Police Training Sch-Hastings 1 ETC
Hastings, Western Area, Sri Lanka
⊕ https://vfmat.ch/2c2c

Port Loko Hospital
Masiaka, Northern Province, Sri Lanka
⊕ hllps://vfmat.ch/f1f8

Pujehun Government Hospital
Pujehun, Southern Province, Sri Lanka
⊕ https://vfmat.ch/bf6e

Segbwema Nixon Memorial Hospital
Lago, Eastern Province, Sri Lanka
⊕ https://vfmat.ch/1969

Shuman Hospital
Tower Hill, Western Area, Sri Lanka
⊕ https://vfmat.ch/1d48

Sierra Leone Police Hospital
Kingtom, Western Area, Sri Lanka
⊕ https://vfmat.ch/867a

St John of God Hospital Sierra Leone
Gbinti, Northern Province, Sri Lanka
⊕ https://vfmat.ch/d787

St John-of-God Catholic Hospital
Mabesene, Northern Province, Sri Lanka
⊕ https://vfmat.ch/c2cf

St. Mary Hospital
Lunsar, Northern Province, Sri Lanka
⊕ https://vfmat.ch/b3dd

Towama Old Town Hospital
Nyaiagoehun, Southern Province, Sri Lanka
⊕ https://vfmat.ch/c1fe

United Methodist Hatfield Archer Memorial Hospital
Rotifunk, Southern Province, Sri Lanka
⊕ https://vfmat.ch/6b6f

York Hospital
York, Western Area, Sri Lanka
⊕ https://vfmat.ch/5fe8

Healthcare Facility

Sudan

The Republic of the Sudan is a country located in Northeast Africa, bordered by Egypt, Libya, Chad, Central African Republic, South Sudan, Ethiopia, Eritrea, and the Red Sea. It is the third largest country by area in Africa. The population of 46.8 million people lives mostly in the southern half of the country, with about 36 percent of the population living in urban areas such as the capital of Khartoum. The population is predominantly ethnically Sudanese Arab, in addition to Fur, Beja, Nuba, and Fallata. The majority of the Sudanese population identifies as Sunni Muslim, with a small unspecified Christian minority. Arabic and English are the official languages and are most commonly spoken throughout the country, in addition to Nubian, Ta Bedawie, and Fur. While neighboring Egypt is more famous for its pyramids, Sudan is home to the world's largest number of pyramids in a single country: around 200–250 structures.

Sudan became an independent country in 1956, and has since experienced decades of conflict and political unrest. A long, deadly civil war between the north and south of the country carried on from 1955–1972, pausing for a few short years before resuming again from 1983 until 2005. In 2005, the conflict ceased, the southern part of the country was granted autonomy, and a referendum in support of South Sudan's independence came into effect in 2011. As a result of this long history of conflict and Southern secession, Sudan has experienced significant economic instability and inflation. In addition, Sudan is home to large groups of refugees and internally displaced persons, putting more pressure on an already strained country.

Sudan's history of conflict has also impacted the health of the population. Life expectancy is low, at 65 years. Other challenges include one of the highest maternal mortality rates in the world. Leading causes of death include both communicable and non-communicable diseases, including ischemic heart disease, neonatal disorders, stroke, congenital defects, road injuries, hypertensive heart disease, lower respiratory infections, diarrheal diseases, HIV/AIDS, chronic kidney disease, and COPD. The risk factors that contribute most to death and disability include malnutrition, high blood pressure, air pollution, high body-mass index, dietary risks, high fasting plasma glucose, insufficient clean water and sanitation, tobacco use, high LDL, and kidney dysfunction.

46.8M
Population

$596
GDP Per Capita

65 years
Life Expectancy
↑ Improving

26	74	295
Doctors/100k	**Beds**/100k	**Deaths**/100k
Physician Density	Hospital Bed Density	Maternal Mortality

 # Sudan

Nonprofit Organizations

Aceso Global
Provides strategic healthcare advisory services in low- and middle-income countries to design and deliver highly customized, evidence-based solutions that address the complex nature of healthcare systems, with a goal to strengthen and provide affordable, high-quality care to all.
Logist-Op, Pub Health
⊕ https://vfmat.ch/b3b7

Africa CDC
Aims to strengthen the capacity and capability of Africa's public health institutions and partnerships to detect and respond quickly and effectively to disease threats and outbreaks, based on data-driven interventions and programs.
Infect Dis, Logist-Op, Pub Health
⊕ https://vfmat.ch/339c

Africa Health Organisation
Leads collaborative efforts among countries in Africa and other partners to promote health equity, combat disease, and improve quality of life.
Logist-Op, Pub Health
⊕ https://vfmat.ch/b1c5

Africa Humanitarian Action (AHA)
Responds to crises, conflicts, and disasters in Africa, while informing and advising the international community, governments, civil society, and the private sector on humanitarian issues of concern to Africa. Supports institutional and organizational development efforts.
General, Infect Dis, MF Med, Nutr, OB-GYN
⊕ https://vfmat.ch/3ca2

African Mission Health Foundation
Aims to strengthen African mission hospitals by providing quality, compassionate care for the hurting and forgotten and helping improve Sub-Saharan Africa's health system.
Infect Dis, Neonat, OB-GYN, Peds, Surg
⊕ https://vfmat.ch/5b14

Against Malaria Foundation
Helps protect people from malaria. Funds anti-malaria nets, specifically long-lasting insecticidal nets (LLINs), and works with distribution partners to ensure they are used. Tracks and reports on net use and malaria case data.
Infect Dis
⊕ https://vfmat.ch/337d

AISPO
Implements international initiatives in the healthcare sector and remains involved in various projects to combat poverty, social injustice, and disease around the world.
All-Immu, ER Med, GI, General, Infect Dis, Logist-Op, MF Med, Neonat, OB-GYN, Peds, Psych, Pub Health, Radiol
⊕ https://vfmat.ch/c9e6

Al Basar International Foundation
Works with local partners to treat preventable blindness, and helps set up sustainable infrastructure so local teams can save sight in their communities.
Ophth-Opt
⊕ https://vfmat.ch/a8b5

Alight
Works closely with refugees, trafficked persons, economic migrants, and other displaced persons to co-design solutions that help them build full and fulfilling lives, with healthcare, clean water, shelter protection, and economic opportunity.
ER Med, General, Infect Dis, MF Med, Neonat, Peds
⊕ https://vfmat.ch/5993

Americares
Saves lives and improves health for people affected by poverty or disaster and responds with life-changing medicine, medical supplies, and health programs including domestic and global medical clinics.
All-Immu, ER Med, General, Infect Dis, MF Med, Nutr
⊕ https://vfmat.ch/e567

Amref Health Africa
Serves millions of people across 35 countries in Sub-Saharan Africa, strengthening health systems, and training African health workers to respond to the continent's most critical health issues.
All-Immu, General, Infect Dis, Logist-Op, MF Med, OB-GYN, Path, Pub Health, Surg
⊕ https://vfmat.ch/6985

Anba Abraam Charity
Aims to improve the lives of underprivileged and vulnerable people with a focus on funding healthcare and surgical programs, programs for the physically and mentally disabled, and support for people without speech, inspired by the Christian faith.
Dent-OMFS, Logist-Op, Nutr, Rehab
⊕ https://vfmat.ch/b62d

Association for Aid and Relief, Japan (AAR JAPAN)
Provides assistance to those affected by hardships such as conflicts, natural disasters and poverty.
Infect Dis
⊕ https://vfmat.ch/pmiq

Association of Medical Doctors of Asia (AMDA)
Strives to support people affected by disasters and economic distress on their road to recovery, establishing a true partnership with special emphasis on local initiative.
ER Med, Logist-Op, Pub Health
⊕ https://vfmat.ch/e3d4

Associazione la Nostra Famiglia

Protects the dignity and improves the quality of life—through specific rehabilitation interventions—for people with disabilities, especially children and young people.

General

⊕ https://vfmat.ch/f6pi

BFIRST – British Foundation for International Reconstructive Surgery & Training

Supports projects across the developing world to train surgeons in their local environment to effectively manage devastating injuries.

Anesth, Plast, Surg

⊕ https://vfmat.ch/ad4f

Bill & Melinda Gates Foundation

Focuses on global issues, such as poverty, health, and education, offering the opportunity to dramatically improve the quality of life for billions of people by building partnerships that bring together resources, expertise, and vision to identify issues, find answers, and drive change.

All-Immu, General, Infect Dis, MF Med, Neonat, OB-GYN, Pub Health

⊕ https://vfmat.ch/7cf2

Brigham and Women's Hospital Global Health Hub

Cares for patients in underserved settings, provides education to staff who work in those areas to create sustainable change, and conducts research designed to improve health in such settings.

General, Infect Dis

⊕ https://vfmat.ch/a8a3

BroadReach

Collaborates with governments, multinational health organizations, donors, and private-sector companies to effect healthcare reform and solve the world's biggest health challenges.

Logist-Op

⊕ https://vfmat.ch/7812

Cairdeas International Palliative Care Trust

Promotes and facilitates the provision of high-quality palliative care in the developing world, where such care is limited.

Palliative

⊕ https://vfmat.ch/35c4

CARE

Works around the globe to save lives, defeat poverty, and achieve social justice.

ER Med, General

⊕ https://vfmat.ch/7232

Carter Center, The

Seeks to prevent and resolve conflicts, enhance freedom and democracy, and improve health, while remaining committed to human rights and the alleviation of human suffering.

Infect Dis, MF Med, Ophth-Opt

⊕ https://vfmat.ch/6556

Chain of Hope

Provides lifesaving heart operations for children around the world and supports the development of cardiac services in numerous developing and war-torn countries.

Anesth, CT Surg, CV Med, Crit-Care, Ped Surg, Peds, Pulm-Critic, Surg

⊕ https://vfmat.ch/1b1b

Children of War Foundation

Delivers access to global health and education to communities affected by poverty, war, natural disaster, climate change, and migration challenges.

ER Med, General, Logist-Op, Peds, Surg

⊕ https://vfmat.ch/de51

Christian Aid Ministries

Strives to be a trustworthy and efficient channel for Amish, Mennonite, and other conservative Anabaptist groups and individuals to minister to physical and spiritual needs around the world.

CT Surg, ER Med, Logist-Op, Ortho, Pub Health

⊕ https://vfmat.ch/7b33

Christian Medical & Dental Associations

Based in Christian ministry, deploys medical and dental teams to underserved communities to provide vital healthcare.

Anesth, Dent-OMFS, ER Med, General, Medicine, OB-GYN, Ophth-Opt, Peds, Pub Health, Radiol, Rehab, Surg

⊕ https://vfmat.ch/921c

Circle of Health International (COHI)

Aligns with local, community-based organizations led and powered by women to help respond to the needs of the women and children that they serve. Helps with the provision of professional volunteers, capacity training, and procurement of requested and appropriate supplies and equipment. Raises funds for the organizations to provide the services required.

ER Med, Logist-Op, MF Med, Neonat, OB-GYN, Psych

⊕ https://vfmat.ch/8b63

Concern Worldwide

Seeks to permanently transform the lives of people living in extreme poverty, tackling its root causes, and building resilience.

Logist-Op, MF Med, Nutr, OB-GYN

⊕ https://vfmat.ch/77e9

COVID-19 Clinical Research Coalition

Advocates and collaborates for the advancement of COVID-19 research driven by the needs of low-resource settings, and works for equitable access to solutions to the pandemic.

All-Immu, Infect-Dis, MF Med, Path, Pub Health

⊕ https://vfmat.ch/d1f4

Dental Helping Hands

Provides dental health services to underserved communities in developing countries.

Dent-OMFS

⊕ https://vfmat.ch/7ba5

Direct Relief

Improves the health and lives of people affected by poverty or emergency situations by mobilizing and providing essential medical resources needed for their care.

ER Med, Logist-Op

⊕ https://vfmat.ch/58e5

DKT INTERNATIONAL INC

Seeks to provide couples with affordable and safe options for family planning and HIV/AIDS prevention through dynamic social marketing.

General, Surg

⊕ https://vfmat.ch/b3a7

Doctors Without Borders/Médecins Sans Frontières (MSF)

Responds to emergencies and provides lifesaving medical care where needed most, including during disasters, conflicts, and epidemics.

Anesth, Crit-Care, ER Med, General, Infect Dis, Nutr, OB-GYN, Ped Surg, Peds, Psych, Pub Health, Surg

⊕ https://vfmat.ch/f363

Drugs for Neglected Diseases Initiative

Develops lifesaving medicines for people with neglected diseases around the world, having developed eight treatments for five deadly diseases and saved millions of lives since 2003.

Infect Dis, Pub Health

⊕ https://vfmat.ch/969c

EMERGENCY

Provides free, high-quality healthcare to victims of war, poverty, and landmines. Also builds hospitals and trains local staff, while pursuing medicine based on human rights.

ER Med, Neonat, OB-GYN, Ophth-Opt, Ped Surg

⊕ https://vfmat.ch/c361

END Fund, The

Aims to control and eliminate the most prevalent neglected diseases among the world's poorest and most vulnerable people.

Infect Dis
⊕ https://vfmat.ch/2614

Episcopal Relief & Development
Provides relief in times of disaster and promotes sustainable development by identifying and addressing the root causes of suffering.
Infect Dis, MF Med, Neonat, Nutr, Peds
⊕ https://vfmat.ch/7cfa

eRanger
Provides sustainable solutions to transportation and medical provision such as ambulances and mobile clinics in developing countries.
ER Med, General, Logist-Op
⊕ https://vfmat.ch/4c18

For Hearts and Souls
Provides medical outreach and care for children through heart-related work, such as diagnosing heart problems and performing heart-saving surgeries.
Anesth, CT Surg, CV Med, Crit-Care, Peds, Pulm-Critic
⊕ https://vfmat.ch/a162

Global Ministries – The United Methodist Church
As the worldwide mission and development agency of The United Methodist Church, Global Ministries works with more than 300 hospitals and clinics around the world through its Global Health Unit.
Anesth, CT Surg, CV Med, Crit-Care, Dent-OMFS, Derm, ER Med, GI, General, Infect Dis, Logist-Op, MF Med, Medicine, Neonat, Nephro, Nutr, OB-GYN, Ophth-Opt, Ortho, Palliative, Peds, Pod, Psych, Pub Health, Rehab, Rheum, Surg, Urol
⊕ https://vfmat.ch/1723

Global Oncology (GO)
Brings the best in cancer care to underserved patients around the world and collaborates across geographic, professional, and academic borders to improve cancer care, research, and education.
Heme-Onc, Path, Rad-Onc
⊕ https://vfmat.ch/fcb8

Globus Relief
Aims to improve the delivery of healthcare worldwide by gathering, processing, and distributing surplus medical supplies to charities at home and abroad.
Logist-Op
⊕ https://vfmat.ch/a2b7

GOAL
Works with the most vulnerable communities to help them respond to and recover from humanitarian crises, and to assist them in building transcendent solutions to mitigate poverty and vulnerability.
ER Med, General, Pub Health
⊕ https://vfmat.ch/bbea

Health Outreach to the Middle East (H.O.M.E.)
Offers physical and Christian-inspired spiritual healing to people in need in the Middle East, providing medical care and education.
Anesth, Dent-OMFS, ER Med, General, Geri, Infect Dis, MF Med, Medicine, OB-GYN, Path, Peds, Psych, Surg
⊕ https://vfmat.ch/134e

Hope Walks
Frees children, families, and communities from the burden of clubfoot, inspired by the Christian faith.
Ortho, Ped Surg, Peds, Rehab
⊕ https://vfmat.ch/f6d4

Hospice Africa
Aims to provide a holistic and culturally sensitive palliative care service through accurate treatment of pain.
Palliative
⊕ https://vfmat.ch/9f86

Humanitarian Aid Relief Trust (HART)
Serves those suffering from oppression and persecution, combining aid and advocacy; providing resources for humanitarian aid; and serving as advocates for those unable to communicate with the wider world.

General
⊕ https://vfmat.ch/jlxv

Humedica
Engages in emergency and disaster relief, supply assistance and long-term development cooperation.
ER Med
⊕ https://vfmat.ch/7m5m

International Children's Heart Foundation
Provides free surgical care, medical training, and technology to save the lives of children with congenital heart disease in developing countries.
Anesth, CT Surg, CV Med, Crit-Care, Ped Surg, Peds, Pulm-Critic
⊕ https://vfmat.ch/86c1

International Federation of Gynecology and Obstetrics (FIGO)
Implements global projects on specific women's health issues.
MF Med, Medicine, Neonat, OB-GYN, Surg, Urol
⊕ https://vfmat.ch/c4b4

International Federation of Red Cross and Red Crescent Societies (IFRC)
Coordinates and directs international assistance following natural and manmade disasters in nonconflict situations through the world's largest humanitarian and development network. Provides disaster-preparedness programs, healthcare activities, and promotes humanitarian values.
ER Med, General, Infect Dis, Nutr
⊕ https://vfmat.ch/b4ee

International Learning Movement (ILM UK)
Supports some of the world's poorest people in developing countries with core projects in education, safe drinking water, and healthcare.
General, Ophth-Opt
⊕ https://vfmat.ch/b974

International Medical Corps
Seeks to improve quality of life through health interventions and related activities that strengthen underserved communities worldwide, with the flexibility to respond rapidly to emergencies and offer medical services and training to people at the highest risk.
ER Med, General, Infect Dis, Nutr, OB-GYN, Peds, Pub Health, Surg
⊕ https://vfmat.ch/a8a5

International Organization for Migration (IOM) – The UN Migration Agency
Promotes evidence-informed policies and holistic, preventive, and curative health programs that are beneficial, accessible, and equitable for vulnerable migrants.
General, Infect Dis, OB-GYN
⊕ https://vfmat.ch/621a

International Planned Parenthood Federation (IPPF)
Leads a locally owned, globally connected civil society movement that provides and enables services and champions sexual and reproductive health and rights for all, especially the underserved.
Infect Dis, MF Med, OB-GYN
⊕ https://vfmat.ch/dc97

International Trachoma Initiative (iTi)
Works toward a world free from trachoma, a preventable cause of blindness, and provides comprehensive support to national ministries of health and governmental and nongovernmental organizations to implement a comprehensive approach to fight trachoma.
Infect Dis, Ophth-Opt
⊕ https://vfmat.ch/3278

International Union Against Tuberculosis and Lung Disease
Develops, implements, and assesses anti-tuberculosis, lung health, and noncommunicable disease programs.
Infect Dis, Pub Health, Pulm-Critic
⊕ https://vfmat.ch/3e82

InterSurgeon
Fosters collaborative partnerships in the field of global surgery that will advance

clinical care, teaching, training, research, and the provision and maintenance of medical equipment.
ENT, Neurosurg, Ortho, Ped Surg, Plast, Surg, Urol
⊕ https://vfmat.ch/6f8a

Islamic Medical Association of North America
Fosters health promotion, disease prevention, and health maintenance in communities around the world through direct patient care and health programs.
Anesth, Dent-OMFS, ER Med, General, Logist-Op, Ophth-Opt, Peds, Plast, Surg
⊕ https://vfmat.ch/a157

IVUmed
Aims to make quality urological care available worldwide by providing medical and surgical education for physicians and nurses, and treatment for thousands of children and adults.
Anesth, OB-GYN, Ped Surg, Surg, Urol
⊕ https://vfmat.ch/e619

Jewish World Watch
Brings help and healing to survivors of mass atrocities around the globe and seeks to inspire people of all faiths and cultures to join the ongoing fight against genocide.
ER Med, Logist-Op, OB-GYN, Peds
⊕ https://vfmat.ch/8c92

Kafel Aid
Works with partners to ensure that poverty is eradicated from the lives of the most vulnerable, while empowering them to create their own destinies.
General, Ophth-Opt
⊕ https://vfmat.ch/ea4d

Kids for Kids
Adopts remote villages in Darfur, where children are living in intolerable poverty. Projects are tailored to each village, with input from the villagers, to empower local people and train them to run the projects themselves.
General, Pub Health
⊕ https://vfmat.ch/8fuw

Leprosy Mission England and Wales, The
Leads the fight against leprosy by supporting people living with leprosy today and serving future generations by working to end transmission of the disease.
Infect Dis, Pub Health
⊕ https://vfmat.ch/4c67

Leprosy Mission International
Seeks to empower people with leprosy to attain healing, dignity, and life in all its fullness.
Infect Dis
⊕ https://vfmat.ch/95a9

Life for a Child
Supports the provision of the best possible healthcare, given local circumstances, to all children and youth with diabetes in less-resourced countries, through the strengthening of existing diabetes services.
Endo, Medicine, Peds
⊕ https://vfmat.ch/d712

Limbs International
Engages communities and transforms lives through affordable, sustainable prosthetic solutions and rehabilitation services in developing countries.
Logist-Op, Ortho, Pod, Rehab
⊕ https://vfmat.ch/dc84

London School of Hygiene & Tropical Medicine: Health in Humanitarian Crises Centre
Advances health and health equity in crisis-affected countries through research, education, and translation of knowledge into policy and practice.
ER Med, Infect Dis, Pub Health
⊕ https://vfmat.ch/96ad

London School of Hygiene & Tropical Medicine: International Centre for Eye Health
Works to improve eye health and eliminate avoidable visual impairment and

blindness with a focus on low-income populations.
Logist-Op, Ophth-Opt, Pub Health
⊕ https://vfmat.ch/6f5f

McGill University Health Centre: Centre for Global Surgery
Works to reduce the impact of injury by advancing surgical care through research and education in resource-limited settings.
ER Med, Logist-Op, Ped Surg, Surg
⊕ https://vfmat.ch/7246

Medical Care Development International
Works to improve the health of vulnerable populations through integrated, sustainable, and locally driven interventions.
Infect Dis, OB-GYN, Peds, Pub Health
⊕ https://vfmat.ch/da87

Medical Teams International
Seeks to restore health as the first step to restoring hope, working to bring basic but lifesaving medical care to those in need.
Dent-OMFS, ER Med, General, MF Med, Pub Health
⊕ https://vfmat.ch/8d1c

Medicines for Humanity
Aims to save the lives of vulnerable children by strengthening systems of maternal and child health in the communities served.
Infect Dis, MF Med, OB-GYN
⊕ https://vfmat.ch/8d13

MedShare
Aims to improve the quality of life of people, communities, and the planet by sourcing and directly delivering surplus medical supplies and equipment to communities in need around the world.
Logist-Op
⊕ https://vfmat.ch/c8bc

Mercy and Love Foundation
Aims to provide orphaned and vulnerable children with basic human needs such as food, clothing, and shelter, enabling them to thrive.
General, Peds
⊕ https://vfmat.ch/649a

Muslim Aid
Aims to improve the lives of those in need, and to address the underlying structural and systemic causes of poverty in their communities, inspired by Muslim faith.
ER Med, Infect Dis, MF Med, Nutr
⊕ https://vfmat.ch/a8ed

Options
Believes in a world in which women and children can access the high-quality health services they need, without financial burden.
Logist-Op, MF Med, Neonat, OB-GYN
⊕ https://vfmat.ch/3a48

Order of Malta
Supports forgotten or excluded people, especially those living in conflict zones or amid natural disasters, by providing medical assistance, caring for refugees, and distributing medicines and necessities.
ER Med, General, Infect Dis, MF Med, Nephro, OB-GYN, Ortho, Psych
⊕ https://vfmat.ch/1fab

Patients Helping Fund, The
Works to provide healthcare through hospitals and health centers in Sudan and beyond.
General, Pub Health
⊕ https://vfmat.ch/y4l9

Physicians Across Continents
Provides high-quality medical care to people affected by crises and disasters.
CV Med, Dent-OMFS, Heme-Onc, MF Med, Nephro, Nephro, OB-GYN, Ped Surg, Plast, Surg
⊕ https://vfmat.ch/fe5d

Qatar Red Crescent Society

To improve the lives of the weak by activating the energies of humanity inside and outside Qatar, under the umbrella of the Basic Principles of International Humanitarian Action.

Anesth, CV Med, Crit-Care, Dent-OMFS, ER Med, General, Geri, Medicine, OB-GYN, Ophth-Opt, Path, Peds, Pub Health, Radiol, Surg

⊕ https://vfmat.ch/4c5d

RAD-AID International

Improves and optimizes access to medical imaging and radiology in low-resource regions of the world.

Rad-Onc, Radiol

⊕ https://vfmat.ch/537f

Relief International

Helps people in fragile settings achieve good health and nutrition by delivering primary healthcare and emergency treatment, and builds local capacity to ensure that communities in vulnerable situations have the access to the quality care they need to live healthy lives.

ER Med, General, MF Med, Neonat, OB-GYN, Peds, Psych

⊕ https://vfmat.ch/1522

RestoringVision

Empowers lives by restoring vision for millions of people in need.

Ophth-Opt

⊕ https://vfmat.ch/e121

Rotary International

Provides service to others, improves lives, and advances world understanding, goodwill, and peace through its fellowship of business, professional, and community leaders.

ER Med, General, Infect Dis, MF Med, OB-GYN

⊕ https://vfmat.ch/8fb5

ROW Foundation

Works to improve the quality of training for healthcare providers, and the diagnosis and treatment available to people with epilepsy and associated psychiatric disorders in under-resourced areas of the world.

Neuro, Psych

⊕ https://vfmat.ch/25eb

Safe Harbor International

Inspired by the Christian faith, provides people living in poverty with ministry, development, training, and relief services such as medical care.

General

⊕ https://vfmat.ch/3dfe

SAMU Foundation

Provides medical first response and reconstruction when severe international emergencies occur.

ER Med, Infect Dis, Logist-Op, Psych, Pub Health

⊕ https://vfmat.ch/3196

Save the Children

Gives children around the world a healthy start in life, the opportunity to learn, and protection from harm.

All-Immu, Crit-Care, ER Med, General, Infect Dis, MF Med, Medicine, Neonat, OB-GYN, Peds, Psych, Pub Health

⊕ https://vfmat.ch/2e73

SCI Foundation

Seeks to prevent and treat neglected infectious diseases, with a focus on eliminating parasitic worm infections through strengthening impactful and comprehensive health programs across Sub-Saharan Africa.

Infect Dis, Pub Health

⊕ https://vfmat.ch/5444

Sightsavers

Works with partners in developing countries to help eliminate avoidable blindness and advocates for equal opportunity for the disabled.

Infect Dis, Ophth-Opt, Surg

⊕ https://vfmat.ch/aa52

Sudan Doctors Union UK

Takes a leading role in the development of health services and medical training in the Sudan.

General

⊕ https://vfmat.ch/pq7s

Sudanense American Medical Association (SAMA)

Contributes to the medical profession in Sudan by supporting continuing medical education and enhancing of the medical knowledge of physicians.

CV Med, Dent-OMFS, OB-GYN, Plast, Surg

⊕ https://vfmat.ch/5a96

Sudanese and London Association Medical Aids Trust (SALAMAT)

Engages Sudanese British, their network and other UK-based organizations in charitable giving and capacity-building initiatives in Sudan.

General

⊕ https://vfmat.ch/mrqh

Swiss Tropical and Public Health Institute

Contributes to the improvement of the health of populations internationally, nationally, and locally through excellence in research, education, and services.

Infect Dis, Pub Health

⊕ https://vfmat.ch/2ee4

Task Force for Global Health, The

Consists of programs and focus areas that cover a range of global health issues including neglected tropical diseases, infectious diseases, vaccines, field epidemiology, public health informatics, health workforce development, and global health ethics.

Infect Dis, Logist-Op, Medicine, Ophth-Opt, Peds

⊕ https://vfmat.ch/714c

Training for Health Equity Network (THEnet)

Contributes to health equity through health workforce education, research, and service, based on principles of social accountability and community engagement.

ER Med, General

⊕ https://vfmat.ch/38c6

Union for International Cancer Control (UICC)

Unites and supports the cancer community to reduce the global cancer burden, promote greater equity, and ensure that cancer control continues to be a priority in the world health and development agenda.

Heme-Onc, Pub Health

⊕ https://vfmat.ch/88b1

United Nations Children's Fund (UNICEF)

Works in over 190 countries and territories to save children's lives, defend their rights, and help them fulfill their potential, from early childhood through adolescence.

All-Immu, Infect Dis, MF Med, Neonat, Nutr, OB-GYN, Ped Surg, Peds, Pub Health

⊕ https://vfmat.ch/42d7

United Nations Development Programme (UNDP)

Helps countries achieve the simultaneous eradication of extreme poverty and significant reduction of inequalities and exclusion using a sustainable human development approach.

Infect Dis, Logist-Op, Pub Health

⊕ https://vfmat.ch/935c

United Nations High Commissioner for Refugees (UNHCR)

Safeguards the rights and well-being of people who have been forced to flee, ensuring that everybody has the right to seek asylum and find safe refuge in another country, with the goal of seeking lasting solutions.

General, MF Med, Medicine, OB-GYN, Peds, Psych, Pub Health

⊕ https://vfmat.ch/6636

United Nations Office for the Coordination of Humanitarian Affairs (OCHA)

Contributes to principled and effective humanitarian response through coordination, advocacy, policy, information management, and humanitarian financing tools and services, by leveraging functional expertise throughout

the organization.
Logist-Op
⊕ https://vfmat.ch/22b8

United Nations Population Fund (UNFPA)
Supports reproductive healthcare for women and youth in more than 150 countries, focusing on delivering a world in which every pregnancy is wanted, every childbirth is safe, and every young person's potential is fulfilled.
Infect Dis, MF Med, Neonat, OB-GYN, Peds, Pub Health
⊕ https://vfmat.ch/c969

United States Agency for International Development (USAID)
Promotes and demonstrates democratic values abroad and advances a free, peaceful, and prosperous world. Leads the U.S. government's international development and disaster assistance through partnerships and investments that save lives.
ER Med, Infect Dis, MF Med, OB-GYN, Peds
⊕ https://vfmat.ch/9a99

University of California: Global Health Institute
Mobilizes people and resources across the University of California to advance global health research, education, and collaboration.
General, OB-GYN, Pub Health
⊕ https://vfmat.ch/ee7f

University of Pennsylvania Perelman School of Medicine Center for Global Health
Aims to improve health equity worldwide through enhanced public health awareness and access to care, discovery, and outcomes-based research, and comprehensive educational programs grounded in partnership.
Heme-Onc, Infect Dis, OB-GYN
⊕ https://vfmat.ch/cb57

USA for United Nations High Commissioner for Refugees (UNHCR)
Serves and protects refugees and displaced people through emergency relief, cash assistance, education, resettlement, and the rebuilding of livelihoods.
ER Med, General, Logist-Op, Nutr, Pub Health
⊕ https://vfmat.ch/293c

USAID: Leadership, Management and Governance Project
Improves leadership, management, and governance practices to strengthen health systems and improve health for all, including vulnerable populations worldwide.
Logist-Op
⊕ https://vfmat.ch/d35e

Visionaries International
Works toward reducing the burden of corneal blindness in the developing world by assessing and addressing what limits corneal surgeons in each locale.
Anesth, Ophth-Opt, Pub Health, Surg
⊕ https://vfmat.ch/3d2e

Walkabout Foundation
Provides wheelchairs and rehabilitation in the developing world and funds research to find a cure for paralysis.
Logist-Op, Rehab
⊕ https://vfmat.ch/5582

Women's Refugee Commission
Seeks to improve lives by protecting the rights of women, children, and youth displaced by conflict and crisis through researching their needs, identifying solutions, and advocating for programs and policies to strengthen their resilience.
General, MF Med, Neonat, OB-GYN, Peds, Psych
⊕ https://vfmat.ch/3d8f

World Children's Fund
Commits to helping children worldwide who are suffering the effects of poverty, disease, natural disaster, famine, abuse, civil strife, and war.
General, Logist-Op, MF Med, Nutr, OB-GYN, Pub Health
⊕ https://vfmat.ch/9cd8

World Federation of Hemophilia (WFH)
Aims to improve and sustain care for people with inherited bleeding disorders by

pursuing long-term relationships with individuals and organizations who share the values of WFH's development model.
Heme-Onc
⊕ https://vfmat.ch/5121

World Health Organization, The (WHO)
The United Nations' agency for health provides leadership on global health matters, shapes the health research agenda, sets norms and standards, articulates evidence-based policy options, provides technical support and monitoring to countries, and assesses health trends.
ER Med, General, Infect Dis, Logist-Op, MF Med, OB-GYN, Peds, Psych, Pub Health
⊕ https://vfmat.ch/c476

World Heart Federation
Leads the global fight against heart disease and stroke, with a focus on low- and middle-income countries.
CV Med, Crit-Care, Heme-Onc, Medicine, Peds
⊕ https://vfmat.ch/ea51

World Medical Relief
Facilitates the distribution of surplus medical resources where they are needed.
Logist-Op
⊕ https://vfmat.ch/72dc

World Relief
Brings sustainable solutions to the world's greatest problems: disasters, extreme poverty, violence, oppression, and mass displacement.
ER Med, Nutr, Psych, Pub Health
⊕ https://vfmat.ch/fbcd

World Vision International
Works with vulnerable communities around the world to overcome poverty and injustice with child-focused programs in disaster management, health, nutrition, economic development, education, clean water, sanitation, and hygiene.
ER Med, General, Infect Dis, MF Med, Nutr, OB-GYN, Peds
⊕ https://vfmat.ch/2642

Sudan

Healthcare Facilities

Abu Anga Hospital
Omdurman, Khartoum, Sudan
⊕ https://vfmat.ch/61km

Africa Medical Center
Khartoum, Khartoum, Sudan
⊕ https://vfmat.ch/nt9f

Al Amal National Hospital Khartoum 2
Khartoum, Khartoum, Sudan
⊕ https://vfmat.ch/rez7

Al Amal Specialized Hospital
Khartoum, Khartoum, Sudan
⊕ https://vfmat.ch/evls

Al Faisal Specialized Hospital
Khartoum, Khartoum, Sudan
⊕ https://vfmat.ch/xfrv

Al Mawada Hospital
Khartoum, Khartoum, Sudan
⊕ https://vfmat.ch/kn2w

Al Rawda Hospital
Omdurman, Khartoum, Sudan
⊕ https://vfmat.ch/g67v

Al Saha Specialized Hospital
Khartoum, Khartoum, Sudan
⊕ https://vfmat.ch/qgbd

Al Sharif Specialist Hospital
Khartoum, Khartoum, Sudan
⊕ https://vfmat.ch/jj5n

Al Shifa Specialized Hospital
Khartoum, Khartoum, Sudan
⊕ https://vfmat.ch/ittf

Al-injaz Sudanese German Specialized Hospital
Khartoum, Khartoum, Sudan
⊕ https://vfmat.ch/gwkp

Al-Tigany Al-Mahy Mental Health Hospital
Omdurman, Khartoum, Sudan
⊕ https://vfmat.ch/rbm7

Al-Widad hospital
Omdurman, Khartoum, Sudan
⊕ https://vfmat.ch/dchk

AlFouad Hospital
Khartoum, Khartoum, Sudan
⊕ https://vfmat.ch/qhfv

Aljawda Hospital
Khartoum, Khartoum, Sudan
⊕ https://vfmat.ch/zs6l

AlNau Hospital
Omdurman, Khartoum, Sudan
⊕ https://vfmat.ch/cyus

Alqima Specialized Hospital
Khartoum, Khartoum, Sudan
⊕ https://vfmat.ch/jm7y

Alzaytouna Specialised Hospital
Khartoum, Khartoum, Sudan
⊕ https://vfmat.ch/hyuf

Anfal Hospital
Ombada, Khartoum, Sudan
⊕ https://vfmat.ch/fncm

Antalya Medical Center
Khartoum, Khartoum, Sudan
⊕ https://vfmat.ch/wvt2

Arabic Center For Physiotherapy and Rehabilitation
Khartoum North, Khartoum, Sudan
⊕ https://vfmat.ch/xa6i

Asia Hospital
Omdurman, Khartoum, Sudan
⊕ https://vfmat.ch/syd7

Awtad Prosthetics Hospital
Khartoum, Khartoum, Sudan
⊕ https://vfmat.ch/45tc

Baraha Medical City
Khartoum North, Khartoum, Sudan
⊕ https://vfmat.ch/ypln

Bashair Teaching Hospital
Khartoum, Khartoum, Sudan
⊕ https://vfmat.ch/yypr

Best Care Hospital
Khartoum, Khartoum, Sudan
⊕ https://vfmat.ch/vgwh

Blue Nile Hospital
Omdurman, Khartoum, Sudan
⊕ https://vfmat.ch/r4gy

Chinese Friendship Hospital
Omdurman, Khartoum, Sudan
⊕ https://vfmat.ch/jbru

Cima Alkhairy Eye Hospital
Khartoum North, Khartoum, Sudan
⊕ https://vfmat.ch/mvjg

Dar Al Elaj Hospital
Khartoum, Khartoum, Sudan
⊕ https://vfmat.ch/rfqn

Delmon Private Hospital
Khartoum, Khartoum, Sudan
⊕ https://vfmat.ch/amfl

Dr. Nageeb Specialized Hospital
Omdurman, Khartoum, Sudan
⊕ https://vfmat.ch/7l1d

Dream Specialized Hospital
Khartoum, Khartoum, Sudan
⊕ https://vfmat.ch/4jmd

East Nile Hospital
Khartoum, Khartoum, Sudan
⊕ https://vfmat.ch/l93g

El Obeid Teaching Hospital
El Obeid, Samal Kurdufan, Sudan
⊕ https://vfmat.ch/ivwt

El-Ban Jadeed Hospital
Khartoum North, Khartoum, Sudan
⊕ https://vfmat.ch/whzj

El-Sheikh Hospital
Khartoum, Khartoum, Sudan
⊕ https://vfmat.ch/byl2

ElDesoki Specialist Hospital
Omdurman, Khartoum, Sudan
⊕ https://vfmat.ch/bl3y

Elrazi University's Educational Hospital
Khartoum, Khartoum, Sudan
⊕ https://vfmat.ch/xgts

Elswedy Charity Hospital
Khartoum, Khartoum, Sudan
⊕ https://vfmat.ch/4wkh

Eye Hospital (Abdul-Fadil Almaz)
Khartoum, Khartoum, Sudan
⊕ https://vfmat.ch/e76j

Fatima Diage Hospital
Kassala, Kassala, Sudan
⊕ https://vfmat.ch/2hbd

Fedail Hospital
Khartoum, Khartoum, Sudan
⊕ https://vfmat.ch/t7sy

General Omer Sawi's Hospital
Khartoum, Khartoum, Sudan
⊕ https://vfmat.ch/ldr4

Haj El-Safi Teaching Hospital
Khartoum North, Khartoum, Sudan
⊕ https://vfmat.ch/34jf

Health Care Hospital
Khartoum, Khartoum, Sudan
⊕ https://vfmat.ch/tivk

Hira Hospital
Khartoum, Khartoum, Sudan
⊕ https://vfmat.ch/liuh

Ibn Al Haitham Specialized Center
Khartoum, Khartoum, Sudan
⊕ https://vfmat.ch/igkr

Ibn Sina Specialized Hospital
Khartoum, Khartoum, Sudan
⊕ https://vfmat.ch/bbh1

Ibrahim Malik Teaching Hospital
Khartoum, Khartoum, Sudan
⊕ https://vfmat.ch/fhim

Imperial Hospital
Khartoum, Khartoum, Sudan
⊕ https://vfmat.ch/br6b

Jabir Abu Eliz Diabetic Center (JADC)
Khartoum, Khartoum, Sudan
⊕ https://vfmat.ch/svbb

Jarash International Specialized Hospital
Khartoum, Khartoum, Sudan
⊕ https://vfmat.ch/56tz

Jebel Aulia Hospital
Jebel Aulia, Khartoum, Sudan
⊕ https://vfmat.ch/t4xf

Kalid Hamiday Hospital
Khartoum, Khartoum, Sudan
⊕ https://vfmat.ch/qtv7

Khartoum Bahri Teaching Hospital
Khartoum North, Khartoum, Sudan
⊕ https://vfmat.ch/hvwk

Khartoum Breast Care Centre
Khartoum, Khartoum, Sudan
⊕ https://vfmat.ch/hsvf

Khartoum Teaching Hospital
Khartoum, Khartoum, Sudan
⊕ https://vfmat.ch/ei9v

Libya Specialist Hospital
Omdurman, Khartoum, Sudan
⊕ https://vfmat.ch/8zm1

Mahira Specialized Hospital
Khartoum, Khartoum, Sudan
⊕ https://vfmat.ch/dpfu

Martyr Al-Moez Al-Abadi Hospital
Khartoum, Khartoum, Sudan
⊕ https://vfmat.ch/y8uc

Mecca Eye Hospital
Omdurman, Khartoum, Sudan
⊕ https://vfmat.ch/rr2d

Mecca Ophthalmology Hospital Al-kalakla
Al-kalakla, Khartoum, Sudan
⊕ https://vfmat.ch/iIgj

Military Hospital Bahri
Khartoum North, Khartoum, Sudan
⊕ https://vfmat.ch/g8bj

Military Hospital Helipad
Omdurman, Khartoum, Sudan
⊕ https://vfmat.ch/7j5t

Mncot Hospital
Kassala, Kassala, Sudan
⊕ https://vfmat.ch/gqxs

Mohammed Al-Amin Hamed Children's Hospital
Omdurman, Khartoum, Sudan
⊕ https://vfmat.ch/qk5c

Muqrin University Hospital
Khartoum, Khartoum, Sudan
⊕ https://vfmat.ch/jt7p

Nyala Turkish Hospital
Nyala, South Darfur, Sudan
⊕ https://vfmat.ch/x8hu

Ombada Hospital
Omdurman, Khartoum, Sudan
⊕ https://vfmat.ch/drfz

Omdurman Maternity Hospital
Omdurman, Khartoum, Sudan
⊕ https://vfmat.ch/yan3

Omdurman Teaching Hospital
Omdurman, Khartoum, Sudan
⊕ https://vfmat.ch/7zrq

Othman Digna Hospital
Port Sudan, Red Sea, Sudan
⊕ https://vfmat.ch/i1df

People's Hospital
Khartoum, Khartoum, Sudan
⊕ https://vfmat.ch/iIac

Queen Specialist Hospital
Khartoum, Khartoum, Sudan
⊕ https://vfmat.ch/jdhn

Radiation and Isotopes Centre Khartoum – Amal Tower
Khartoum, Khartoum, Sudan
⊕ https://vfmat.ch/4t9n

Rama Specialist Hospital
Kassala, Kassala, Sudan
⊕ https://vfmat.ch/44bq

Ribat University Hospital
Khartoum, Khartoum, Sudan
⊕ https://vfmat.ch/vmlv

Royal Care International Hospital
Khartoum, Khartoum, Sudan
⊕ https://vfmat.ch/gs3s

Saudi Hospital
Omdurman, Khartoum, Sudan
⊕ https://vfmat.ch/lduh

Soba University Hospital
Khartoum, Khartoum, Sudan
⊕ https://vfmat.ch/swic

Specialist Hospital Yamamah
Kosti, White Nile, Sudan
⊕ https://vfmat.ch/mday

St Mary's Maternity Hospital
Khartoum, Khartoum, Sudan
⊕ https://vfmat.ch/vs3g

Sudan Heart Center
Khartoum, Khartoum, Sudan
⊕ https://vfmat.ch/uuus

Sudanese Center for Physical Therapy
Omdurman, Khartoum, Sudan
⊕ https://vfmat.ch/dtvn

Tabarak Children's Hospital
Omdurman, Khartoum, Sudan
⊕ https://vfmat.ch/ec7v

Taha Baashar Psychiatric Hospital
Khartoum, Khartoum, Sudan
⊕ https://vfmat.ch/9j1z

Taiba Hospital
Omdurman, Khartoum, Sudan
⊕ https://vfmat.ch/ewxr

The Salam Centre for Cardiac Surgery
Khartoum, Sudan
⊕ https://vfmat.ch/kq7t

The Tropical Disease Hospital Omdurman
Omdurman, Khartoum, Sudan
⊕ https://vfmat.ch/lizu

Trauma and Emergency Silah Tebbi
Omdurman, Khartoum, Sudan
⊕ https://vfmat.ch/jtby

Turkish Hospital
Khartoum, Khartoum, Sudan
⊕ https://vfmat.ch/ng8n

Universal Hospital Sudan UHS
Khartoum North, Khartoum, Sudan
⊕ https://vfmat.ch/dmp6

Waad Specialist Hospital
Omdurman, Khartoum, Sudan
⊕ https://vfmat.ch/udj5

Yastabshiron Hospital
Khartoum, Khartoum, Sudan
⊕ https://vfmat.ch/vskc

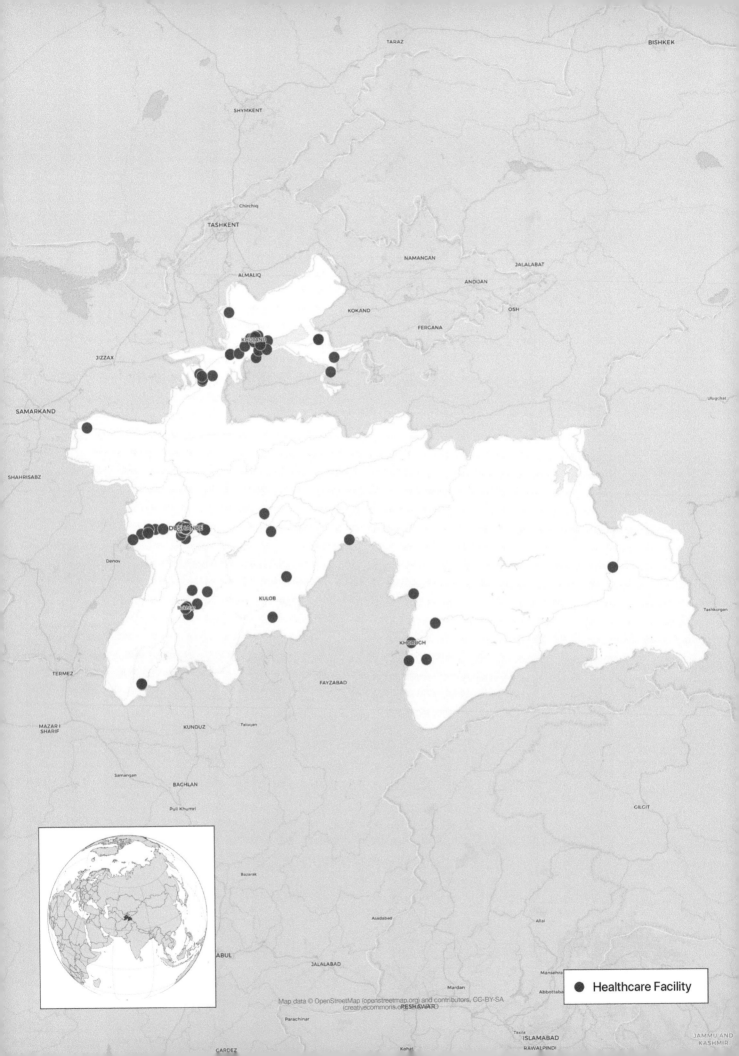

Map data © OpenStreetMap (openstreetmap.org) and contributors, CC-BY-SA
(creativecommons.org)

● Healthcare Facility

Tajikistan

The Republic of Tajikistan is a mountainous, landlocked country in Central Asia. The country's history is ancient: The Silk Road once passed through Tajikistan. In a population of 9 million people, 90 percent live in lower elevations, predominantly in settlements called qishlaqs, with population density increasing from east to west. The population is overwhelmingly of the Tajik ethnicity, and the majority of Tajikistanis are Muslim. The nation is rich in mineral resources such as iron, lead, zinc, salt, fluorite, and precious stones.

The country is relatively young, having broken off from the Soviet Union in 1991. Shortly after independence, anti-government demonstrations sparked a five-year civil war ending in 1997. Despite the turmoil, Tajikistan has since increased its political stability and made significant economic progress. Over two decades, from 2000 to 2018, the country dramatically decreased poverty rates from 83 percent to 27 percent.

Tajikistan must still work to repair its healthcare system after infrastructure damage from the civil war and decades of underinvestment. The country continues to have the lowest health expenditure in the WHO European Region. Since its civil war, Tajikistan has made gains in life expectancy, hitting a plateau of around 71 years. Likewise, the under-five mortality rate has improved, dropping from over 90 deaths per 1,000 live births in the early 1990s to under 50 deaths per 1,000 live births in 2019. Lower respiratory infections, neonatal disorders, and diarrheal diseases continue to cause a significant number of deaths, but have improved over time. Significantly, non-communicable diseases contribute most to death in Tajikistan, with ischemic heart disease, stroke, cirrhosis, congenital defects, diabetes, hypertensive heart disease, stomach cancer, and COPD causing the most deaths.

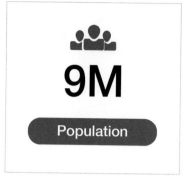

9M
Population

$859
GDP Per Capita

71 years
Life Expectancy
↑ Improving

172
Doctors/100k

Physician Density

467
Beds/100k

Hospital Bed Density

17
Deaths/100k

Maternal Mortality

Tajikistan

Nonprofit Organizations

Abt Associates
Seeks to improve the quality of life and economic well-being of people worldwide, while striving to meet and exceed the highest professional standards.
General, Logist-Op, MF Med, OB-GYN, Peds
⊕ https://vfmat.ch/cec2

AFEW International
Aims to improve the health of populations in Eastern Europe and Central Asia, strives to increase access to prevention, treatment, and care for HIV, TB, and viral hepatitis, and promotes health and SRHR.
Infect Dis, Pub Health
⊕ https://vfmat.ch/19c6

Aga Khan Foundation Canada
Tackles the root causes of poverty, with a special focus on marginalized groups such as women and girls. Programs provide access to education and healthcare, food, and opportunity.
Pub Health
⊕ https://vfmat.ch/7f8b

American International Health Alliance (AIHA)
Strengthens health systems and workforce capacity worldwide through locally driven, peer-to-peer institutional partnerships.
CV Med, ER Med, Infect Dis, Medicine, OB-GYN
⊕ https://vfmat.ch/69fd

Center for Strategic and International Studies (CSIS) Commission on Strengthening America's Health Security
Brings together a distinguished and diverse group of high-level opinion leaders bridging security and health, with the core aim to chart a bold vision for the future of U.S. leadership in global health.
ER Med, Infect Dis, MF Med, Pub Health
⊕ https://vfmat.ch/6d7f

Christian Aid Ministries
Strives to be a trustworthy and efficient channel for Amish, Mennonite, and other conservative Anabaptist groups and individuals to minister to physical and spiritual needs around the world.
CT Surg, ER Med, Logist-Op, Ortho, Pub Health
⊕ https://vfmat.ch/7b33

Developing Country NGO Delegation: Global Fund to Fight AIDS, TB & Malaria
Works to strengthen the engagement of civil society actors and organizations in developing countries to build a world in which AIDS, TB, and malaria are no longer global, public health, and human rights threats.
Infect Dis, Pub Health
⊕ https://vfmat.ch/3149

Direct Relief
Improves the health and lives of people affected by poverty or emergency situations by mobilizing and providing essential medical resources needed for their care.
ER Med, Logist-Op
⊕ https://vfmat.ch/58e5

Doctors Without Borders/Médecins Sans Frontières (MSF)
Responds to emergencies and provides lifesaving medical care where needed most, including during disasters, conflicts, and epidemics.
Anesth, Crit-Care, ER Med, General, Infect Dis, Nutr, OB-GYN, Ped Surg, Peds, Psych, Pub Health, Surg
⊕ https://vfmat.ch/f363

Elton John AIDS Foundation
Seeks to address and overcome the stigma, discrimination, and neglect that prevents ending AIDS by funding local experts to challenge discrimination, prevent infections, and provide treatment.
Infect Dis, Pub Health
⊕ https://vfmat.ch/9d31

Gift of Life International
Provides lifesaving cardiac treatment to children in developing countries while developing sustainable pediatric cardiac programs by implementing screening, surgical, and training missions.
Anesth, CT Surg, CV Med, Crit-Care, Ped Surg, Peds, Pulm-Critic
⊕ https://vfmat.ch/f2f9

Global Oncology (GO)
Brings the best in cancer care to underserved patients around the world and collaborates across geographic, professional, and academic borders to improve cancer care, research, and education.
Heme-Onc, Path, Rad-Onc
⊕ https://vfmat.ch/fcb8

Health Equity Initiative
Aims to build and sustain a global community that engages across sectors and disciplines to advance health equity.
Pub Health
⊕ https://vfmat.ch/e2e2

HealthProm
Works with local partners to promote health and social care for vulnerable children and their families.
General, MF Med, Peds, Pub Health
⊕ https://vfmat.ch/153d

Healthy DEvelopments
Provides Germany-supported health and social protection programs around the globe in a collaborative knowledge management process.

All-Immu, General, Infect Dis, Logist-Op, MF Med
⊕ https://vfmat.ch/dc31

ICAP at Columbia University
Serves as global leader in supporting the scale-up of multidisciplinary HIV/AIDS prevention, care, and treatment programs based on a family-focused approach.
General, Infect Dis, MF Med, Medicine, OB-GYN, Pub Health
⊕ https://vfmat.ch/a8ef

International Federation of Red Cross and Red Crescent Societies (IFRC)
Coordinates and directs international assistance following natural and manmade disasters in nonconflict situations through the world's largest humanitarian and development network. Provides disaster-preparedness programs, healthcare activities, and promotes humanitarian values.
ER Med, General, Infect Dis, Nutr
⊕ https://vfmat.ch/b4ee

International Organization for Migration (IOM) – The UN Migration Agency
Promotes evidence-informed policies and holistic, preventive, and curative health programs that are beneficial, accessible, and equitable for vulnerable migrants.
General, Infect Dis, OB-GYN
⊕ https://vfmat.ch/621a

International Planned Parenthood Federation (IPPF)
Leads a locally owned, globally connected civil society movement that provides and enables services and champions sexual and reproductive health and rights for all, especially the underserved.
Infect Dis, MF Med, OB-GYN
⊕ https://vfmat.ch/dc97

IntraHealth International
Improves the performance of health workers and strengthens the systems in which they work.
CV Med, Endo, General, Infect Dis, MF Med, Neonat, Nutr, OB-GYN
⊕ https://vfmat.ch/ddc8

John Snow, Inc. (JSI)
Aims to improve the health and well-being of underserved and vulnerable people and communities throughout the world.
General, Infect Dis, Logist-Op, MF Med, OB-GYN, Peds, Psych, Pub Health
⊕ https://vfmat.ch/ba78

Joint United Nations Programme on HIV/AIDS (UNAIDS)
Aims to place people living with HIV and people affected by the virus at the decision-making table and at the center of designing, delivering, and monitoring the AIDS response.
Infect Dis
⊕ https://vfmat.ch/464a

Life for a Child
Supports the provision of the best possible healthcare, given local circumstances, to all children and youth with diabetes in less-resourced countries, through the strengthening of existing diabetes services.
Endo, Medicine, Peds
⊕ https://vfmat.ch/d712

Lions Clubs International
Empowers volunteers to serve their communities, meet humanitarian needs, encourage peace, and promote international understanding through Lions Clubs.
Heme-Onc, Medicine, Nutr, Ophth-Opt
⊕ https://vfmat.ch/7b12

Management Sciences for Health (MSH)
Works with countries and communities to save lives and improve the health of the world's poorest and most vulnerable people by building strong, resilient, sustainable health systems.
Infect Dis, Logist-Op, Pub Health
⊕ https://vfmat.ch/6aa2

MedShare
Aims to improve the quality of life of people, communities, and the planet by sourcing and directly delivering surplus medical supplies and equipment to communities in need around the world.
Logist-Op
⊕ https://vfmat.ch/c8bc

Norwegian People's Aid
Aims to improve living conditions, to create a democratic, just, and safe society.
ER Med, Logist-Op
⊕ https://vfmat.ch/2d8e

Operation Fistula
Exists to end obstetric fistula by building models of care that serve every woman, everywhere.
MF Med, OB-GYN, Surg
⊕ https://vfmat.ch/ce8e

Operation Mercy
Serves the poor and marginalized through community development and humanitarian aid projects.
General, MF Med, OB-GYN, Peds, Psych, Pub Health, Rehab
⊕ https://vfmat.ch/81c5

Order of Malta
Supports forgotten or excluded people, especially those living in conflict zones or amid natural disasters, by providing medical assistance, caring for refugees, and distributing medicines and necessities.
ER Med, General, Infect Dis, MF Med, Nephro, OB-GYN, Ortho, Psych
⊕ https://vfmat.ch/1fab

PASHA
Creates opportunities to improve health among vulnerable populations around the world, by bringing together diverse individuals with various areas of expertise and engaging them in solving local and global health challenges.
Derm, Logist-Op, Ophth-Opt, Ortho
⊕ https://vfmat.ch/efbc

Pharmacists Without Borders Canada
Provides pharmaceutical and technical assistance in the implementation or improvement of community and hospital pharmacies internationally.

⊕ https://vfmat.ch/7658

RestoringVision
Empowers lives by restoring vision for millions of people in need.
Ophth-Opt
⊕ https://vfmat.ch/e121

Rockefeller Foundation, The
Works to promote the well-being of humanity.
Logist-Op, Nutr, Pub Health
⊕ https://vfmat.ch/5424

Rotary International
Provides service to others, improves lives, and advances world understanding, goodwill, and peace through its fellowship of business, professional, and community leaders.
ER Med, General, Infect Dis, MF Med, OB-GYN
⊕ https://vfmat.ch/8fb5

Save A Child's Heart
Provides lifesaving cardiac treatment to children in developing countries, and trains healthcare professionals from these countries to deliver quality care in their communities.
CT Surg, CV Med, Crit-Care, Ped Surg, Peds
⊕ https://vfmat.ch/1bef

Save the Children
Gives children around the world a healthy start in life, the opportunity to learn, and protection from harm.
All-Immu, Crit-Care, ER Med, General, Infect Dis, MF Med, Medicine, Neonat, OB-GYN, Peds, Psych, Pub Health
⊕ https://vfmat.ch/2e73

Task Force for Global Health, The

Consists of programs and focus areas that cover a range of global health issues including neglected tropical diseases, infectious diseases, vaccines, field epidemiology, public health informatics, health workforce development, and global health ethics.

Infect Dis, Logist-Op, Medicine, Ophth-Opt, Peds

⊕ https://vfmat.ch/714c

Union for International Cancer Control (UICC)

Unites and supports the cancer community to reduce the global cancer burden, promote greater equity, and ensure that cancer control continues to be a priority in the world health and development agenda.

Heme-Onc, Pub Health

⊕ https://vfmat.ch/88b1

United Nations Children's Fund (UNICEF)

Works in over 190 countries and territories to save children's lives, defend their rights, and help them fulfill their potential, from early childhood through adolescence.

All-Immu, Infect Dis, MF Med, Neonat, Nutr, OB-GYN, Ped Surg, Peds, Pub Health

⊕ https://vfmat.ch/42d7

United Nations Development Programme (UNDP)

Helps countries achieve the simultaneous eradication of extreme poverty and significant reduction of inequalities and exclusion using a sustainable human development approach.

Infect Dis, Logist-Op, Pub Health

⊕ https://vfmat.ch/935c

United Nations High Commissioner for Refugees (UNHCR)

Safeguards the rights and well-being of people who have been forced to flee, ensuring that everybody has the right to seek asylum and find safe refuge in another country, with the goal of seeking lasting solutions.

General, MF Med, Medicine, OB-GYN, Peds, Psych, Pub Health

⊕ https://vfmat.ch/6636

United Nations Population Fund (UNFPA)

Supports reproductive healthcare for women and youth in more than 150 countries, focusing on delivering a world in which every pregnancy is wanted, every childbirth is safe, and every young person's potential is fulfilled.

Infect Dis, MF Med, Neonat, OB-GYN, Peds, Pub Health

⊕ https://vfmat.ch/c969

University of Illinois at Chicago: Center for Global Health

Aims to improve the health of populations around the world and reduce health disparities by collaboratively conducting trans-disciplinary research, training the next generations of global health leaders, and building the capacities of global and local partners.

Pub Health

⊕ https://vfmat.ch/b749

USAID: Leadership, Management and Governance Project

Improves leadership, management, and governance practices to strengthen health systems and improve health for all, including vulnerable populations worldwide.

Logist-Op

⊕ https://vfmat.ch/d35e

USAID: Maternal and Child Health Integrated Program

Works to improve the health of women and their families, including programs for maternal, newborn, and child health, immunization, family planning, nutrition, malaria, and HIV/AIDS.

All-Immu, General, Infect Dis, MF Med

⊕ https://vfmat.ch/4415

USAID: TB Care II

Focuses on tuberculosis care and treatment.

Infect Dis

⊕ https://vfmat.ch/57d4

Vision Care

Restores sight and helps patients get regular treatment at short-term eye camps and long-term base clinics by having doctors, missionaries, volunteers, and

sponsors work together.

Ophth-Opt

⊕ https://vfmat.ch/9d7c

World Federation of Hemophilia (WFH)

Aims to improve and sustain care for people with inherited bleeding disorders by pursuing long-term relationships with individuals and organizations who share the values of WFH's development model.

Heme-Onc

⊕ https://vfmat.ch/5121

World Health Organization, The (WHO)

The United Nations' agency for health provides leadership on global health matters, shapes the health research agenda, sets norms and standards, articulates evidence-based policy options, provides technical support and monitoring to countries, and assesses health trends.

ER Med, General, Infect Dis, Logist-Op, MF Med, OB-GYN, Peds, Psych, Pub Health

⊕ https://vfmat.ch/c476

World Medical Relief

Facilitates the distribution of surplus medical resources where they are needed.

Logist-Op

⊕ https://vfmat.ch/72dc

Tajikistan

Healthcare Facilities

Abu Ibn Sino Hospital
Street Foteh Niyozi 34, Dushanbe, Tajikistan
⊕ https://vfmat.ch/ccc3

Avis Hospital
Budyonniy Street, Istaravshan, Sughd Region,
Tajikistan
⊕ https://vfmat.ch/d8fe

Avis Siti
M34, Rugund, Sughd Province, Tajikistan
⊕ https://vfmat.ch/3759

Bactria Hospital
Sina Street, Ismoili Somoni, Khatlon Province,
Tajikistan
⊕ https://vfmat.ch/15b5

**Bemorkhonai Kariyai Bolo Maternity
Hospital**
Borbad Street, Tursunzoda, Districts of Republican
Subordination, Tajikistan
⊕ https://vfmat.ch/fa8d

Cardiac Hospital Khujand
Avenue Rahmon Nabieva, Khujand, Sughd Province,
Tajikistan
⊕ https://vfmat.ch/b517

Central District Hospital Munimabad
RJ033, Muminabad, Khatlon Province, Tajikistan
⊕ https://vfmat.ch/1af8

Central Hospital
20th Anniversary of Independence Street, Vahdat,
Districts of Republican Subordination, Tajikistan
⊕ https://vfmat.ch/5391

Central Hospital at Vahdat
20-Solagii Istiglaliyyat Str 39, Vahdat 735400,
Tajikistan
⊕ https://vfmat.ch/7efb

Central Hospital of Gonchi District
Ghonchi, Sughd Province, Tajikistan
⊕ https://vfmat.ch/fecb

Central Hospital of Rogun
Gidrostroiteley Avenue, Rogun, Districts of
Republican Subordination, Tajikistan
⊕ https://vfmat.ch/d64f

Central Hospital of Sharinav
Otdel Street, Shahrinav, Districts of Republican
Subordination, Tajikistan
⊕ https://vfmat.ch/82b9

CGB
Istiqlol Street, Guliston, Sughd, Tajikistan
⊕ https://vfmat.ch/3121

Children's Clinical Hospital of Khujand
S. Khofiz Street, Khujand, Sughd Region, Tajikistan
⊕ https://vfmat.ch/dc4e

Children's Hospital of Bokhtar
86 Ayni Street, Bokhtar, Khatlon Province, Tajikistan
⊕ https://vfmat.ch/ab3b

Children's Hospital of Panjakent
Tereshkova Street, Panjakent, Sughd Region,
Tajikistan
⊕ https://vfmat.ch/a998

**Children's Infectious Disease Clinical
Hospital**
Sheroz Street, Dushanbe, Dushanbe, Tajikistan
⊕ https://vfmat.ch/4d89

Children's Surgery Hospital
Jalal Ikromi Street, Dushanbe, Dushanbe, Tajikistan
⊕ https://vfmat.ch/5c2c

Chinor Hospital
Frunze Street, Khistevarz, Sughd Region, Tajikistan
⊕ https://vfmat.ch/99db

Chorku Hospital
Chorku, Sughd Province, Tajikistan
⊕ https://vfmat.ch/3c53

**City Center for Skin and Venereal
Diseases**
Rahmon Nabiev Street, Dushanbe, Dushanbe,
Tajikistan
⊕ https://vfmat.ch/11c4

City Clinical Hospital #5
Samadi Ghani Street, Dushanbe, Dushanbe,
Tajikistan
⊕ https://vfmat.ch/8fb1

City Hospital
Academics Rajabov Street, Dushanbe, Tajikistan
⊕ https://vfmat.ch/82e9

City Hospital
Mir Street, D.C. Olimov, Sughd Province, Tajikistan
⊕ https://vfmat.ch/6ac5

City Hospital #1
Gagarin Street, Khujand, Tajikistan
⊕ https://vfmat.ch/ce81

City Hospital #2 of Khujand
Rahbara Kasymova Street, Khujand, Sughd Region,
Tajikistan
⊕ https://vfmat.ch/9c1e

City Hospital #7
Abay Street, Dushanbe, Dushanbe, Tajikistan
⊕ https://vfmat.ch/3775

City Maternity Hospital
1 Kucha, Khujand, Sughd, Tajikistan
⊕ https://vfmat.ch/28f5

CRCB
M34, Istaravshan, Sughd, Tajikistan
⊕ https://vfmat.ch/9222

Davo Hospital
Ayni Street, Bokhtar, Khatlon Province, Tajikistan
⊕ https://vfmat.ch/75f5

District Central Hospital of Bustan
RB14, Bustan, Sughd Province, Tajikistan
⊕ https://vfmat.ch/ea96

Gafurov District Hospital
Gafurov Avenue, Khujand, Sughd Province, Tajikistan
⊕ https://vfmat.ch/97fc

Murghab District Hospital
RB 05, Murgab, Gorno-Badakhshan Autonomous
Oblast, Tajikistan
⊕ https://vfmat.ch/3a22

**Dushanbe Municipal Emergency Clinic
Hospital**
Sadriddin Aini Street, Dushanbe, Dushanbe, Tajikistan
⊕ https://vfmat.ch/e7a2

Emergency Station
M. Tanburi Street, Khujand, Viloyati Sughd, Tajikistan
⊕ https://vfmat.ch/5fdb

Eshdavlat Doctor
Teshiktosh, Viloyati Khatlon, Tajikistan
⊕ https://vfmat.ch/671c

Eye Hospital of Bokhtar
N. Huvaydulloev Street, Bokhtar, Khatlon Province,
Tajikistan
⊕ https://vfmat.ch/fd37

Gastroenterology Center
Ismoili Somoni Street, Dushanbe, Dushanbe,
Tajikistan
⊕ https://vfmat.ch/3975

**Gorodskaya Bolnitsa Chkalovska
Hospital**
Hospital Patrice Lumumby Street, Bostan, Sughd
Province, Tajikistan
⊕ https://vfmat.ch/d6c6

**GU Republican Scientific and Clinical
Center of Urology**
Dushanbe, Tajikistan
⊕ https://vfmat.ch/dd9a

Gulakandoz Hospital
Davron Samadov, Gulakandoz, Sughd Province,
Tajikistan
⊕ https://vfmat.ch/961f

Hospital at Ispechak
Alisher Navoi Street, Dushanbe, Dushanbe, Tajikistan
⊕ https://vfmat.ch/f724

Hospital at Istaravshan
Budyonniy Street, Istaravshan, Sughd Region,
Tajikistan
⊕ https://vfmat.ch/b9b8

Hospital at Kazanguzar
Zagertut-Zagerti, Khatlon Province, Tajikistan
⊕ https://vfmat.ch/4e9e

Hospital at Kuliev
RJ04, Navabad, Gorno-Badakhshan Autonomous
Oblast, Tajikistan
⊕ https://vfmat.ch/83c1

Hospital at Machiton
RB01, Rugund, Sughd Province, Tajikistan
⊕ https://vfmat.ch/4f88

Hospital at Ozodii-Shark
Ozodii-Shark, Khatlon Province, Tajikistan
⊕ https://vfmat.ch/2feb

Hospital at Qurgonteppa
2 Sino Street, Bokhtar, Khatlon Province, Tajikistan
⊕ https://vfmat.ch/84e7

Hospital at Rasulov
Zhdanov Street, Ghafurov, Sughd Region, Tajikistan
⊕ https://vfmat.ch/5473

Hospital at Rŭshan
Rŭshan, Tajikistan
⊕ https://vfmat.ch/1798

Hospital at Shakhrinaw
Otdel Street, Shahrinav, Districts of Republican
Subordination, Tajikistan
⊕ https://vfmat.ch/486b

Hospital at Shichozg
Karamshoev Street, Pish, Gorno-Badakhshan
Autonomous Oblast, Tajikistan
⊕ https://vfmat.ch/49ef

Hospital at Stakhanov
PJ042, Dushanbe, Dushanbe, Tajikistan
⊕ https://vfmat.ch/5cbb

Hospital at Teshiktosh
Teshiktosh, Khatlon Province, Tajikistan
⊕ https://vfmat.ch/2213

Hospital at Yogodka
32 MKR, Khujand, Sughd Province, Tajikistan
⊕ https://vfmat.ch/cc2d

Hospital for Infectious Disease
2th Makhalla, Khujand, Sughd Province, Tajikistan
⊕ https://vfmat.ch/cb54

Hospital of Infectious Diseases
M34, Rugund, Sughd Province, Tajikistan
⊕ https://vfmat.ch/fd4e

Hospital of Mirza-ali
RJ036, Sari Chashma Jamoat, Khatlon Province,
Tajikistan
⊕ https://vfmat.ch/f2cd

Hospital of Sarband
RJ057, Levakant, Khatlon Province, Tajikistan
⊕ https://vfmat.ch/c1a2

Hospital Sugh Region
84 Sharq Street, Khujand, Sughd Region, Tajikistan
⊕ https://vfmat.ch/7f77

**Infectious Disease Clinical Hospital of
Dushanbe**
Ismoili Somoni Avenue, Dushanbe, Dushanbe,
Tajikistan
⊕ https://vfmat.ch/13c5

Infectious Diseases Children's Hospital
20 Sheroz Street, 734025, Dushanbe, Tajikistan
⊕ https://vfmat.ch/619e

Isfara Hospital
RB16, Isfara, Sughd Province, Tajikistan
⊕ https://vfmat.ch/9943

Isham Hospital
PB02, Otkanoq, Districts of Republican
Subordination, Tajikistan
⊕ https://vfmat.ch/78c6

Istiklol Hospital
6A Nemat Karaboev Avenue, Dushanbe, Dushanbe,
Tajikistan
⊕ https://vfmat.ch/ede8

Khatlon Medical Center
Ayni Street, Bokhtar, Khatlon Province, Tajikistan
⊕ https://vfmat.ch/9c93

Kulundinskaya Gorodskaya Bol'nitsa
Интернационал, Кыргызстан, Tajikistan
⊕ https://vfmat.ch/86e3

Maternity Hospital #2
Husseinzoda Street 5, Dushanbe, Tajikistan
⊕ https://vfmat.ch/1d27

Military Hospital
Rudaki Avenue, Dushanbe, Dushanbe, Tajikistan
⊕ https://vfmat.ch/8fbf

Military Medical
Dushanbe, Tajikistan
⊕ https://vfmat.ch/15a7

National Medical Center
Sharaf Street, Dushanbe, Dushanbe, Tajikistan
⊕ https://vfmat.ch/ae8f

Nov Maternity Hospital
Lenin Street, Nov, Sughd, Tajikistan
⊕ https://vfmat.ch/ac7b

Oncology Hospital
Narrow Street N. Huvaydulloev, Bokhtar, Khatlon
Region, Tajikistan
⊕ https://vfmat.ch/dab7

Pakhtaobod Hospital
RJ02, Zarbdor, Districts of Republican Subordination, Tajikistan
⊕ https://vfmat.ch/88f4

Paradise Hospital
Lenin Street, Nov, Sughd Region, Tajikistan
⊕ https://vfmat.ch/2222

Physiotherapeutic Hospital of Khujand
Avenue Rahmon Nabieva, Khujand, Sughd Province, Tajikistan
⊕ https://vfmat.ch/8ee6

Psychiatric Hospital of Khujand
Lunacharsky Street, Khujand, Sughd Region, Tajikistan
⊕ https://vfmat.ch/b5af

Qal'ai Khumb Hospital
Shohmansur Street, Kalai Khumb, Gorno-Badakhshan Autonomous Oblast, Tajikistan
⊕ https://vfmat.ch/afd5

Regional Hospital Karabollo
Vahdat Street 1, Bokhtar, Khatlon Province, Tajikistan
⊕ https://vfmat.ch/bc3f

Regional Maternity Hospital
Nabiev Street, Khujand, Sughd, Tajikistan
⊕ https://vfmat.ch/da3e

Regional Psychiatric Hospital
Roshtqala Road, Barjangal, Gorno-Badakhshan Autonomous Oblast, Tajikistan
⊕ https://vfmat.ch/9129

Roddom Hospital
Istaravshan, Tajikistan
⊕ https://vfmat.ch/96c9

Roddom Regional Hospital
Lenin Street, Khorog, Gorno-Badakhshan Autonomous Oblast, Tajikistan
⊕ https://vfmat.ch/1fa4

Russian Military Hospital
126 Khanzhin Street, Dushanbe, Dushanbe, Tajikistan
⊕ https://vfmat.ch/5777

Shaydon Hospital
Sari Khosor, Sari Khosor – Shahidon, Вилояти Хатлон, Tajikistan
⊕ https://vfmat.ch/e31d

SHIFO Medical Center
Druzhba Narodov Street, Dushanbe, Dushanbe, Tajikistan
⊕ https://vfmat.ch/a2b4

Skin Hospital
Saida Valiyeva Street, Khujand, Sughd Region, Tajikistan
⊕ https://vfmat.ch/a5a4

Solim Med
Omar Khayam Street, Dushanbe, Tajikistan
⊕ https://vfmat.ch/ab43

State Epidemiological Service of the Republic of Tajikistan
Saida Valiyeva Street, Khujand, Sughd, Tajikistan
⊕ https://vfmat.ch/8bf7

State Unitary Enterprise Tajik Railway Hospital
Moensho Nazarshoev Street, Dushanbe, Dushanbe, Tajikistan
⊕ https://vfmat.ch/bf99

Sughd Regional Hospital Khujand
Severnaya Street, Khujand, Sughd Region, Tajikistan
⊕ https://vfmat.ch/4373

Tadzhikskiy Gosudarstvennyy Meditsinskiy Universitet
Shamsi Street, Dushanbe, Dushanbe, Tajikistan
⊕ https://vfmat.ch/4414

Tuberculosis Hospital
RB 13, Khujand, Sughd, Tajikistan
⊕ https://vfmat.ch/5bb7

Vodnik Hospital
Bahor Street, Khujand, Sughd Region, Tajikistan
⊕ https://vfmat.ch/d679

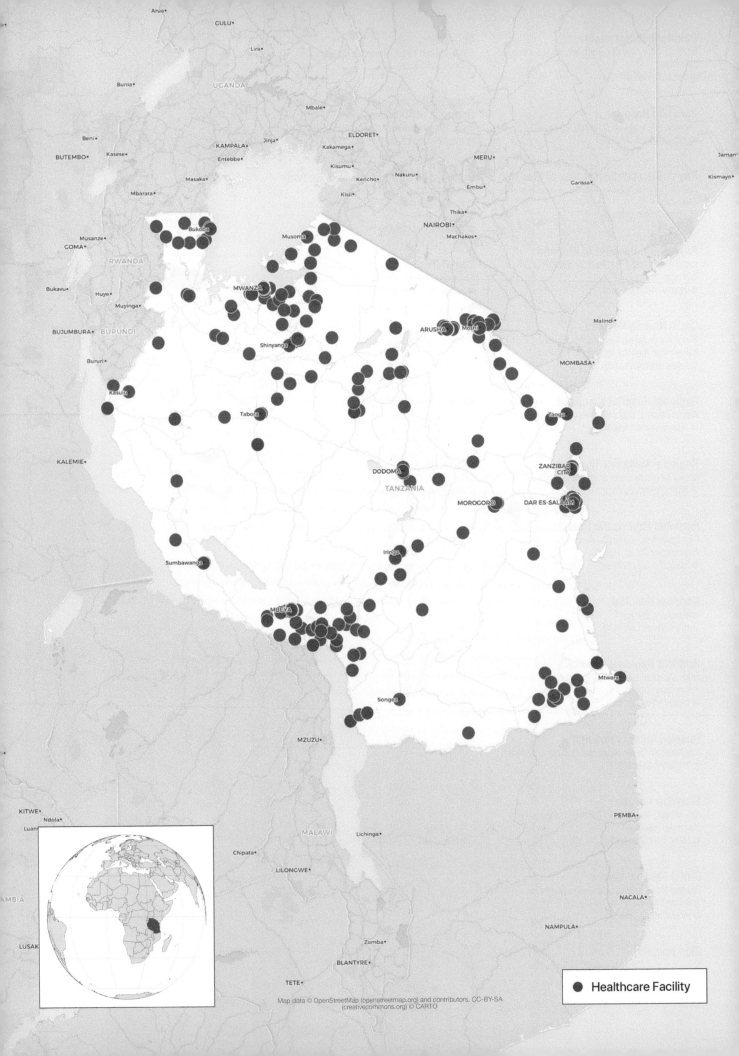

Healthcare Facility

Tanzania

Located on the coast of East Africa, the United Republic of Tanzania is home to 62.1 million people representing more than 120 local indigenous groups. Formerly two separate nations, Tanganyika and Zanzibar unified in 1964 to become modern-day Tanzania, where English and Swahili are the country's official languages. Most of Tanzania's diverse population can be found living in the rural part of the country, while approximately 34 percent are in urban centers. The country's incredible natural features include Mount Kilimanjaro, diverse wildlife, and several UNESCO World Heritage Sites. Tanzania's rich history dates back 1.75 million years, with Olduvai Gorge being the site of some of the oldest-known human ancestor remains.

Since its formation, the country has seen improvements in its economic conditions and political stability. Tanzania still faces a variety of development challenges such as poor infrastructure, low education levels, and disparities in population health. Additionally, there exist significant social and economic inequities between urban and rural populations regarding access to opportunity and basic services, such as access to clean water.

The Tanzanian government is both the major provider and financier of health services in the country. The national Tanzanian health system supports local village-based health centers, while larger, more advanced hospitals are located in urban areas. Health indicators such as life expectancy and under-five and under-one mortality rates have improved over time, but challenges to health in the region persist. Diseases among the top causes of death in Tanzania include neonatal disorders, lower respiratory infections, HIV/AIDS, tuberculosis, malaria, diarrheal diseases, and protein-energy malnutrition. Increasingly, non-communicable diseases such as congenital defects, stroke, ischemic heart diseases, and cirrhosis have increased over time to also contribute substantially as top causes of death in Tanzania. To address major health challenges in the country, national health policies have focused on preventive medicine and health.

62.1M
Population

$1,077
GDP Per Capita

65 years
Life Expectancy
↑ Improving

6
Doctors/100k
Physician Density

70
Beds/100k
Hospital Bed Density

524
Deaths/100k
Maternal Mortality

Tanzania

Nonprofit Organizations

143 LIFE Foundation
Seeks to educate and empower individuals living with malaria, TB, HIV/AIDS, STDs and other health disparities related to sexual health.
Infect Dis, MF Med
⊕ https://vfmat.ch/d59b

A Broader View Volunteers
Provides developing countries around the world with significant volunteer programs that aid the neediest communities and forge a lasting bond between those volunteering and those they have helped.
Dent-OMFS, ER Med, Infect Dis, MF Med
⊕ https://vfmat.ch/3bec

Abt Associates
Seeks to improve the quality of life and economic well-being of people worldwide, while striving to meet and exceed the highest professional standards.
General, Logist-Op, MF Med, OB-GYN, Peds
⊕ https://vfmat.ch/cec2

Ace Africa
Aims to enable children and their communities to participate in and take responsibility for their own health, well-being, and development.
Infect Dis, Logist-Op, Nutr, Peds
⊕ https://vfmat.ch/df7f

Action Against Hunger
Aims to end life-threatening hunger for good through treating and preventing malnutrition across more than 45 countries.
Nutr
⊕ https://vfmat.ch/2dbc

Addis Clinic, The
Uses telemedicine to care for people living in medically underserved areas, connects volunteer physicians with global health challenges, and provides support to local partner organizations and frontline health workers.
General, Infect Dis
⊕ https://vfmat.ch/f82f

Advance Family Planning
Aims to achieve global expansion and access to quality contraceptive information, services, and supplies through financial investment and political commitment.
General, MF Med, Pub Health
⊕ https://vfmat.ch/7478

Africa CDC
Aims to strengthen the capacity and capability of Africa's public health institutions and partnerships to detect and respond quickly and effectively to disease threats and outbreaks, based on data-driven interventions and programs.
Infect Dis, Logist-Op, Pub Health
⊕ https://vfmat.ch/339c

Africa Health Organisation
Leads collaborative efforts among countries in Africa and other partners to promote health equity, combat disease, and improve quality of life.
Logist-Op, Pub Health
⊕ https://vfmat.ch/b1c5

Africa Indoor Residual Spraying Project (AIRS)
Aims to protect millions of people in Africa from malaria by spraying insecticide on walls, ceilings, and other indoor resting places of mosquitoes that transmit malaria.
Infect Dis
⊕ https://vfmat.ch/9bd1

Africa Inland Mission International
Seeks to establish churches and community development programs including healthcare projects, based in Christian ministry.
Anesth, Dent-OMFS, ER Med, General, MF Med, Medicine, OB-GYN, OB-GYN, Ophth-Opt, Ped Surg, Peds, Rehab
⊕ https://vfmat.ch/f2f6

Africa Relief and Community Development
Provides comprehensive relief and developmental aid to people of the African continent regardless of gender, race, or religion.
Nutr, Pub Health
⊕ https://vfmat.ch/6cd2

African Christian Hospitals
Aims to provide excellent healthcare services to all in Nigeria, Ghana, and Tanzania, and equips and empowers African healthcare workers through medical scholarships and investments in hospitals.
General, Surg
⊕ https://vfmat.ch/5ff9

African Field Epidemiology Network (AFENET)
Strengthens field epidemiology and public health laboratory capacity to contribute effectively to addressing epidemics and other major public health problems in Africa.
All-Immu, Infect Dis, Path, Pub Health
⊕ https://vfmat.ch/df2e

African Mission
Aims to fight disease and poverty in Africa by supporting educational and medical projects.
Anesth, General
⊕ https://vfmat.ch/ea31

African Mission Health Foundation
Aims to strengthen African mission hospitals by providing quality, compassionate care for the hurting and forgotten and helping improve Sub-Saharan Africa's health system.

Infect Dis, Neonat, OB-GYN, Peds, Surg
⊕ https://vfmat.ch/5b14

Aga Khan Foundation Canada
Tackles the root causes of poverty, with a special focus on marginalized groups such as women and girls. Programs provide access to education and healthcare, food, and opportunity.
Pub Health
⊕ https://vfmat.ch/7f8b

Age International
Helps older people living in some of the world's poorest places to have improved well-being and be treated with dignity through a variety of programs, including emergency relief and cataract surgery.
ER Med, Geri, Logist-Op, Nutr, Ophth-Opt, Palliative, Pub Health
⊕ https://vfmat.ch/c7e2

Aid Africa's Children
Aims to empower impoverished African children and communities with healthcare, food, clean water, and educational and entrepreneurial opportunities.
ER Med, General, Infect Dis, Nutr, OB-GYN, Palliative, Peds, Pub Health
⊕ https://vfmat.ch/5e2e

Al Basar International Foundation
Works with local partners to treat preventable blindness, and helps set up sustainable infrastructure so local teams can save sight in their communities.
Ophth-Opt
⊕ https://vfmat.ch/a8b5

Al-Mustafa Welfare Trust
Seeks to alleviate poverty and provides medical and social development assistance to the poor and vulnerable around the world.
General, Ophth-Opt
⊕ https://vfmat.ch/c5f4

Aloha Medical Mission
Brings hope and changes the lives of people; serves overseas and in Hawai'i.
Anesth, Crit-Care, Dent-OMFS, ENT, ER Med, General, Medicine, OB-GYN, Ophth-Opt, Ortho, Ped Surg, Peds, Plast, Surg, Urol
⊕ https://vfmat.ch/72ac

Alshifa Ltd.
Seeks to provide those with end-stage renal disease with dialysis services at minimum cost, with free services for the low-income community.
Dent-OMFS, Derm, ENT, General, Heme-Onc, Heme-Onc, Nephro, Path, Peds
⊕ https://vfmat.ch/3f97

American Academy of Pediatrics
Seeks to attain optimal physical, mental, and social health and well-being for all infants, children, adolescents, and young adults.
Anesth, Crit-Care, Neonat, Ped Surg
⊕ https://vfmat.ch/9633

American Heart Association (AHA)
Fights heart disease and stroke, striving to save and improve lives.
CV Med, Crit-Care, General, Heme-Onc, Medicine, Peds
⊕ https://vfmat.ch/4747

American International Health Alliance (AIHA)
Strengthens health systems and workforce capacity worldwide through locally driven, peer-to-peer institutional partnerships.
CV Med, ER Med, Infect Dis, Medicine, OB-GYN
⊕ https://vfmat.ch/69fd

American Stroke Association
Works to prevent, treat, and beat stroke by funding innovative research, fighting for stronger public health policies, and providing lifesaving tools and information.
CV Med, Crit-Care, Heme-Onc, Medicine, Neuro, Pub Health, Pulm-Critic, Vasc Surg
⊕ https://vfmat.ch/746f

Americares
Saves lives and improves health for people affected by poverty or disaster and

responds with life-changing medicine, medical supplies, and health programs including domestic and global medical clinics.
All-Immu, ER Med, General, Infect Dis, MF Med, Nutr
⊕ https://vfmat.ch/e567

AMREF Flying Doctors
Aims to deliver medical air transport and health services using the latest aviation and medical technology to ensure patients receive unrivaled care.
ER Med, Logist-Op
⊕ https://vfmat.ch/5d5e

Amref Health Africa
Serves millions of people across 35 countries in Sub-Saharan Africa, strengthening health systems, and training African health workers to respond to the continent's most critical health issues.
All-Immu, General, Infect Dis, Logist-Op, MF Med, OB-GYN, Path, Pub Health, Surg
⊕ https://vfmat.ch/6985

Amsterdam Institute for Global Health and Development (AIGHD)
Provides sustainable solutions to major health problems across our planet by forging synergies among disciplines, healthcare delivery, research, and education.
Infect Dis
⊕ https://vfmat.ch/d73d

AO Alliance
Builds solutions to lessen the burden of injuries in low- and middle-income countries, while enhancing the care of the injured to reduce human suffering, disability, and poverty.
Ortho, Surg
⊕ https://vfmat.ch/8cd5

Arms Around Africa Foundation
Supports children, empowers women, and helps young people to overcome poverty through talent promotion, education, good health, life skills development, entrepreneurship, and enhanced access to other resources for social and economic development.
General, Infect Dis, OB-GYN, Peds
⊕ https://vfmat.ch/ad98

Assist International
Designs and implements humanitarian programs that build capacity, develop opportunities, and save lives around the world.
Infect Dis, Ped Surg, Peds
⊕ https://vfmat.ch/9a3b

Avinta Care
Offers quality healthcare while providing a full suite of services from diagnosis to treatment, specializing in fertility and dermatology.
Derm, MF Med, OB-GYN, Path
⊕ https://vfmat.ch/52a6

Baylor College of Medicine: Global Surgery
Trains leaders in academic global surgery and remains dedicated to advancements in the areas of patient care, biomedical research, and medical education.
ENT, Infect Dis, OB-GYN, Ortho, Ped Surg, Plast, Pub Health, Radiol, Surg, Urol
⊕ https://vfmat.ch/21f5

Baylor International Pediatric AIDS Initiative (BIPAI) at Texas Children's Hospital
Provides high-quality, high-impact, highly ethical pediatric and family-centered healthcare, health professional training, and clinical research focused on HIV/AIDS, tuberculosis, malaria, malnutrition, and other conditions impacting the health of children worldwide.
Infect Dis, Medicine, OB-GYN, Peds, Pub Health, Surg
⊕ https://vfmat.ch/e6ba

BFIRST – British Foundation for International Reconstructive Surgery & Training
Supports projects across the developing world to train surgeons in their local environment to effectively manage devastating injuries.

Anesth, Plast, Surg
🌐 https://vfmat.ch/ad4f

Boston Children's Hospital: Global Health Program
Helps solve pediatric global healthcare challenges by transferring expertise through long-term partnerships with scalable impact, while working in the field to strengthen healthcare systems, advocate, research, and provide care delivery or education as a way of sustainably improving the health of children worldwide.
Anesth, CV Med, Crit-Care, ER Med, Heme-Onc, Infect Dis, Medicine, Nutr, Palliative, Ped Surg, Peds
🌐 https://vfmat.ch/f9f8

BRAC USA
Seeks to empower people and communities in situations of poverty, illiteracy, disease, and social injustice. Interventions aim to achieve large-scale, positive changes through economic and social programs that enable everyone to realize their potential.
ER Med, General, Infect Dis, Logist-Op, MF Med, OB-GYN
🌐 https://vfmat.ch/9d9e

Breast Cancer Support
Aims to save lives and end breast cancer forever in women and men through education, treatment, emotional assistance, and financial support.
Heme-Onc, Logist-Op, Pub Health, Rad-Onc, Radiol
🌐 https://vfmat.ch/cb78

Bridge of Life
Aims to strengthen healthcare globally through sustainable programs that prevent and treat chronic disease.
Logist-Op, Nephro, OB-GYN, Peds, Surg
🌐 https://vfmat.ch/5b68

Bridge2Aid
Provides access to simple, safe, emergency dental treatment.
Dent-OMFS
🌐 https://vfmat.ch/e682

British Council for Prevention of Blindness (BCPB)
Funds research into blindness prevention and sight restoration in children and adults in low- and lower-middle-income countries.
Ophth-Opt
🌐 https://vfmat.ch/eaf4

Burn Care International
Seeks to improve the lives of burn survivors around the world through effective rehabilitation.
Derm, Nutr, Psych, Surg
🌐 https://vfmat.ch/78d1

Cairdeas International Palliative Care Trust
Promotes and facilitates the provision of high-quality palliative care in the developing world, where such care is limited.
Palliative
🌐 https://vfmat.ch/35c4

Canada-Africa Community Health Alliance
Sends Canadian volunteer teams on two- to three-week missions to African communities to work hand-in-hand with local partners.
General, Infect Dis, MF Med, OB-GYN, Peds, Surg
🌐 https://vfmat.ch/4c94

Canadian Foundation for Women's Health
Seeks to advance the health of women in Canada and around the world through research, education, and advocacy in obstetrics and gynecology.
MF Med, OB-GYN
🌐 https://vfmat.ch/f41e

Canadian Network for International Surgery, The
Aims to improve maternal health, increase safety, and build local capacity in low-income countries by creating and providing surgical and midwifery courses, training domestically, and transferring skills.
Logist-Op, Surg
🌐 https://vfmat.ch/86ff

CardioStart International
Provides free heart surgery and associated medical care to children and adults living in underserved regions of the world, irrespective of political or religious affiliation, through the collective skills of healthcare experts.
Anesth, CT Surg, CV Med, Crit-Care, Pub Health, Pulm-Critic
🌐 https://vfmat.ch/85ef

CARE
Works around the globe to save lives, defeat poverty, and achieve social justice.
ER Med, General
🌐 https://vfmat.ch/7232

Care for Africa
Seeks to empower communities with sustainable access to healthcare through its Rural School Health Clinic. Works with counterparts in Tanzania's Tarime region to share resources and knowledge and build capacity.
ER Med, General, Infect Dis, Ortho, Ped Surg, Peds, Rehab, Surg
🌐 https://vfmat.ch/bd21

Care for AIDS
Aims to empower people to live a life beyond AIDS by carrying out programs centered on physical, social, economic, and spiritual support, based in Christian ministry.
Infect Dis, Pub Health
🌐 https://vfmat.ch/79cf

Caritas Pro Vitae Gradu Charitable Trust
Supports Catholic charitable projects with social and humanitarian efforts, and aims to assist people in need including children, the elderly, sick, and disabled through healthcare, poverty relief, and education.
ER Med, General, Logist-Op, Medicine, OB-GYN, Ophth-Opt, Path, Peds, Pub Health, Radiol, Rehab, Surg
🌐 https://vfmat.ch/b2ca

Carter Center, The
Seeks to prevent and resolve conflicts, enhance freedom and democracy, and improve health, while remaining committed to human rights and the alleviation of human suffering.
Infect Dis, MF Med, Ophth-Opt
🌐 https://vfmat.ch/6556

Catholic World Mission
Works to rebuild communities worldwide by helping to alleviate poverty and empower underserved areas, while spreading the message of the Catholic Church.
ER Med, General, Nutr, Peds
🌐 https://vfmat.ch/7b5f

Center for Private Sector Health Initiatives
Aims to improve the health and well-being of people in developing countries by facilitating partnerships between the public and private sectors.
Infect Dis, Nutr, Peds
🌐 https://vfmat.ch/b198

Chain of Hope
Provides lifesaving heart operations for children around the world and supports the development of cardiac services in numerous developing and war-torn countries.
Anesth, CT Surg, CV Med, Crit-Care, Ped Surg, Peds, Pulm-Critic, Surg
🌐 https://vfmat.ch/1b1b

Challenge Initiative, The
Seeks to rapidly and sustainably scale up proven reproductive health solutions among the urban poor.
MF Med, OB-GYN, Peds
🌐 https://vfmat.ch/2f77

CharityVision International
Focuses on restoring curable sight impairment worldwide by empowering local physicians and creating sustainable solutions.
Logist-Op, Ophth-Opt, Surg
🌐 https://vfmat.ch/6231

Child Family Health International (CFHI)
Connects students with local health professionals and community leaders transforming perspectives about self, global health, and healing.
General, Infect Dis, OB-GYN, Ophth-Opt, Palliative, Peds
⊕ https://vfmat.ch/729e

Children Without Worms
Enhances the health and development of children by reducing intestinal worm infections.
Infect Dis, Pub Health
⊕ https://vfmat.ch/6bee

Christian Aid Ministries
Strives to be a trustworthy and efficient channel for Amish, Mennonite, and other conservative Anabaptist groups and individuals to minister to physical and spiritual needs around the world.
CT Surg, ER Med, Logist-Op, Ortho, Pub Health
⊕ https://vfmat.ch/7b33

Christian Blind Mission (CBM)
Aims to improve the quality of life of persons with disabilities in the poorest countries, addressing poverty as a cause and a consequence of disability, and working in partnership to create a society for all.
ENT, General, Infect Dis, OB-GYN, Ophth-Opt, Ortho, Peds, Psych, Rehab, Surg
⊕ https://vfmat.ch/3824

Christian Connections for International Health (CCIH)
Promotes global health and wholeness from a Christian perspective.
All-Immu, General, Infect Dis, MF Med, Neonat, OB-GYN, Psych
⊕ https://vfmat.ch/fa5d

Christian Medical & Dental Associations
Based in Christian ministry, deploys medical and dental teams to underserved communities to provide vital healthcare.
Anesth, Dent-OMFS, ER Med, General, Medicine, OB-GYN, Ophth-Opt, Peds, Pub Health, Radiol, Rehab, Surg
⊕ https://vfmat.ch/921c

Circle of Health International (COHI)
Aligns with local, community-based organizations led and powered by women to help respond to the needs of the women and children that they serve. Helps with the provision of professional volunteers, capacity training, and procurement of requested and appropriate supplies and equipment. Raises funds for the organizations to provide the services required.
ER Med, Logist-Op, MF Med, Neonat, OB-GYN, Psych
⊕ https://vfmat.ch/8b63

Cleft Africa
Strives to provide underserved Africans with cleft lips and palates with access to the best possible treatment for their condition, so that they can live a life free of the health problems caused by cleft.
Anesth, Dent-OMFS, Ped Surg, Surg
⊕ https://vfmat.ch/8298

Clinton Health Access Initiative (CHAI)
Aims to save lives and reduce the burden of disease in low- and middle-income countries. Works with partners to strengthen the capabilities of governments and the private sector to create and sustain high-quality health systems.
General, Heme-Onc, Infect Dis, Logist-Op, MF Med, Medicine, Neonat, Nutr, OB-GYN, Path, Peds, Rad-Onc
⊕ https://vfmat.ch/9ed7

Columbia Vagelos College of Physicians and Surgeons Programs in Global Health
Harnesses the expertise of the medical school to improve health worldwide by training global health leaders, building capacity through interdisciplinary education and training programs, and addressing unmet health needs through research and application.
CV Med, Derm, Genetics, Heme-Onc, Infect Dis, Medicine, OB-GYN, Ophth-Opt, Peds, Psych, Pub Health, Pulm-Critic, Surg
⊕ https://vfmat.ch/a9e5

Comprehensive Community Based Rehabilitation in Tanzania (CCBRT)
Aims to become a healthcare social enterprise serving the community and the most vulnerable with accessible, specialized services and development programs.
General, MF Med, Neonat, OB-GYN
⊕ https://vfmat.ch/be24

Core Group
Aims to improve and expand community health practices for underserved populations, especially women and children, through collaborative action and learning.
General, Infect Dis, MF Med, Medicine, OB-GYN, Peds, Pub Health
⊕ https://vfmat.ch/9de3

COVID-19 Clinical Research Coalition
Advocates and collaborates for the advancement of COVID-19 research driven by the needs of low-resource settings, and works for equitable access to solutions to the pandemic.
All-Immu, Infect-Dis, MF Med, Path, Pub Health
⊕ https://vfmat.ch/d1f4

Creighton University School of Medicine: Global Surgery Fellowship
Aims to significantly impact the absence of acute surgical care in developing countries by providing free surgery to underserved patients and surgical training for developing country trainees.
Anesth, Ped Surg, Surg
⊕ https://vfmat.ch/777f

Cross Catholic Outreach
Mobilizes the global Catholic Church to transform impoverished communities through the provision of food, water, housing, education, orphan support, medical care, microenterprise, and disaster relief.
All-Immu, General, Nutr, OB-GYN, Rehab
⊕ https://vfmat.ch/22f4

Cura for the World
Seeks to heal, nourish, and embrace the neglected by building medical clinics in remote communities in dire need of medical care.
ER Med, General, Peds
⊕ https://vfmat.ch/c55f

CURE
Operates charitable hospitals and programs in underserved countries worldwide, where patients receive surgical treatment, based in Christian ministry.
Anesth, Neurosurg, Ortho, Ped Surg, Peds, Rehab, Surg
⊕ https://vfmat.ch/aa16

CureCervicalCancer
Focuses on the early detection and prevention of cervical cancer around the globe for the women who need it most.
Heme-Onc, OB-GYN
⊕ https://vfmat.ch/ace1

D-tree Digital Global Health
Demonstrates and advocates for the potential of digital technology to transform health systems and improve health and well-being for all.
Logist-Op, MF Med, OB-GYN, Peds, Pub Health
⊕ https://vfmat.ch/1f79

DEAR Foundation, The
Provides support for people in need, particularly women and children, by supporting humanitarian projects administered by NGOs, primarily in the areas of health and education.
Dent-OMFS, OB-GYN
⊕ https://vfmat.ch/a747

Dental Helping Hands
Provides dental health services to underserved communities in developing countries.
Dent-OMFS
⊕ https://vfmat.ch/7ba5

Direct Relief

Improves the health and lives of people affected by poverty or emergency situations by mobilizing and providing essential medical resources needed for their care.

ER Med, Logist-Op

⊕ https://vfmat.ch/58e5

DKT INTERNATIONAL INC

Seeks to provide couples with affordable and safe options for family planning and HIV/AIDS prevention through dynamic social marketing.

General, Surg

⊕ https://vfmat.ch/b3a7

Doctors with Africa (CUAMM)

Advocates for the universal right to health and promotes the values of international solidarity, justice, and peace. Works to protect and improve the well-being and health of vulnerable communities in Africa with a long-term development perspective.

ER Med, Infect Dis, MF Med, Neonat, OB-GYN, Peds

⊕ https://vfmat.ch/d2fb

Doctors Without Borders/Médecins Sans Frontières (MSF)

Responds to emergencies and provides lifesaving medical care where needed most, including during disasters, conflicts, and epidemics.

Anesth, Crit-Care, ER Med, General, Infect Dis, Nutr, OB-GYN, Ped Surg, Peds, Psych, Pub Health, Surg

⊕ https://vfmat.ch/f363

Dodoma Christian Medical Centre Trust (DCMCT)

Works to bring health and hope to the people of central Tanzania and beyond.

CV Med, Crit-Care, Dent-OMFS, General, Infect Dis, OB-GYN, Path, Peds, Radiol, Surg

⊕ https://vfmat.ch/f9cc

Dodoma Tanzania Health Development

Aims to ensure high-quality, compassionate, Tanzanian-led healthcare for the people of Central Tanzania by developing the capacity and sustainability of Dodoma Christian Medical Center.

Anesth, Crit-Care, Dent-OMFS, General, Infect Dis, MF Med, Medicine, OB-GYN, Ophth-Opt, Path, Ped Surg, Peds, Radiol, Rehab, Surg

⊕ https://vfmat.ch/c33a

Dream Sant'Egidio

Seeks to counter HIV/AIDS in Africa by eliminating the transmission of HIV from mother to child, with a focus on women because of the importance of their role in the community.

Infect Dis, MF Med, Neonat, OB-GYN, Path, Peds

⊕ https://vfmat.ch/f466

Drugs for Neglected Diseases Initiative

Develops lifesaving medicines for people with neglected diseases around the world, having developed eight treatments for five deadly diseases and saved millions of lives since 2003.

Infect Dis, Pub Health

⊕ https://vfmat.ch/969c

Duke University: Global Health Institute

Sparks innovation in global health research and education, and brings together knowledge and resources to address the most important global health issues of our time.

All-Immu, Infect Dis, MF Med, OB-GYN, Pub Health

⊕ https://vfmat.ch/c4cd

East Africa Children's Healthcare Foundation

Provides healthcare insurance for children in order to treat disease more quickly, thereby opening up more opportunities for them to further their education and become successful adults in the Tanzanian community.

Peds

⊕ https://vfmat.ch/ff32

East Africa Medical Assistance Foundation

To improve radiological services and related medical care in East Africa.

Pub Health, Pulm-Critic, Radiol

⊕ https://vfmat.ch/4b27

Egmont Trust, The

Works with partner organizations in Sub-Saharan Africa, making grants to help vulnerable children cope with the impact of HIV/AIDS on families and communities.

General, Infect Dis, OB-GYN, Peds

⊕ https://vfmat.ch/57a9

Elizabeth Glaser Pediatric AIDS Foundation

Seeks to end global pediatric HIV/AIDS through prevention and treatment programs, research, and advocacy.

Infect Dis, Nutr, OB-GYN, Peds

⊕ https://vfmat.ch/d6ec

Elton John AIDS Foundation

Seeks to address and overcome the stigma, discrimination, and neglect that prevents ending AIDS by funding local experts to challenge discrimination, prevent infections, and provide treatment.

Infect Dis, Pub Health

⊕ https://vfmat.ch/9d31

Empower Tanzania

Works in partnership with Tanzanians to develop models that sustainably improve the quality of life and resilience of rural areas through health improvements, education, and economic empowerment.

General, Infect Dis, MF Med, OB-GYN, Palliative

⊕ https://vfmat.ch/ba24

Enabel

As the development agency of the Belgian federal government, charged with implementing Belgium's international development policy, carries out public service assignments in Belgium and abroad pursuant to the 2030 Agenda for Sustainable Development.

General, Infect Dis, Logist-Op, MF Med, OB-GYN, Peds, Pub Health

⊕ https://vfmat.ch/5af7

END Fund, The

Aims to control and eliminate the most prevalent neglected diseases among the world's poorest and most vulnerable people.

Infect Dis

⊕ https://vfmat.ch/2614

EngenderHealth

Works to implement high-quality, gender-equitable programs that advance sexual and reproductive health and rights.

General, MF Med, OB-GYN, Peds

⊕ https://vfmat.ch/1cb2

Episcopal Relief & Development

Provides relief in times of disaster and promotes sustainable development by identifying and addressing the root causes of suffering.

Infect Dis, MF Med, Neonat, Nutr, Peds

⊕ https://vfmat.ch/7cfa

eRanger

Provides sustainable solutions to transportation and medical provision such as ambulances and mobile clinics in developing countries.

ER Med, General, Logist-Op

⊕ https://vfmat.ch/4c18

Evidence Project, The

Improves family-planning policies, programs, and practices through the strategic generation, translation, and use of evidence.

General, MF Med

⊕ https://vfmat.ch/f9e7

Eye Care Foundation

Helps prevent and cure avoidable blindness and visual impairment in low-income countries.

Ophth-Opt, Surg

⊕ https://vfmat.ch/c8f9

Eye Mantra Foundation / Charitable Hospital

Provides affordable eye care and treatment for people living in poverty.

Ophth-Opt, Surg

⊕ https://vfmat.ch/48d2

Fertility Education & Medical Management (FEMM)

Aims to make knowledge-based reproductive health accessible to all women and enables them to be informed partners in the choice and delivery of their medical care and services.

MF Med, OB-GYN

⊕ https://vfmat.ch/e8b2

Fistula Foundation

Aims to engage the support of people worldwide who are eager to see the day that no woman suffers from obstetric fistula. Raises and directs funds to doctors and hospitals providing life-transforming surgery to women in need.

OB-GYN

⊕ https://vfmat.ch/e958

Forever Projects

Aims to empower women and their families with self-sustainability and build a brighter future for themselves.

Nutr

⊕ https://vfmat.ch/5ea5

Foundation for African Medicine & Education (FAME)

Improves access and advances patient-centered care for under-resourced communities in rural Tanzania.

General, Infect Dis, Logist-Op, MF Med, OB-GYN, Peds, Surg

⊕ https://vfmat.ch/cb82

Foundation For International Education In Neurological Surgery (FIENS), The

Provides hands-on training and education to neurosurgeons around the world.

Neuro, Neurosurg, Surg

⊕ https://vfmat.ch/bab8

Fracarita International

Provides support and services in the fields of mental healthcare, care for people with a disability, and education.

Psych, Rehab

⊕ https://vfmat.ch/8d3c

Friends of UNFPA

Promotes the health, dignity, and rights of women and girls around the world by supporting the lifesaving work of UNFPA, the United Nations' reproductive health and rights agency, through education, advocacy, and fundraising.

MF Med, OB-GYN

⊕ https://vfmat.ch/2a3a

Gift of Life International

Provides lifesaving cardiac treatment to children in developing countries while developing sustainable pediatric cardiac programs by implementing screening, surgical, and training missions.

Anesth, CT Surg, CV Med, Crit-Care, Ped Surg, Peds, Pulm-Critic

⊕ https://vfmat.ch/f2f9

GIVE International

Partners with local organizations on projects that focus on healthcare, child and youth development, education, and sustainable development.

General, Infect Dis, MF Med

⊕ https://vfmat.ch/58d3

Give Sight Global

Provides vision care to underserved communities around the world by providing treatment for curable blindness and other preventable eye conditions.

Ophth-Opt, Pub Health

⊕ https://vfmat.ch/5c4d

Global Alliance to Prevent Prematurity And Stillbirth (GAPPS)

Seeks to improve birth outcomes worldwide by reducing the burden of premature birth and stillbirth.

All-Immu, Infect Dis, MF Med, Neonat, Neonat, OB-GYN

⊕ https://vfmat.ch/3f74

Global Blood Fund

Delivers grants, equipment, and training to over 50 countries in Africa, Asia, Eastern Europe, the Middle East, Latin America and the Caribbean.

Pub Health

⊕ https://vfmat.ch/6377

Global Emergency Care Skills

Aims to provide high-quality emergency medical training to healthcare professionals in countries where emergency medicine is a developing specialty.

ER Med

⊕ https://vfmat.ch/1827

Global Eye Mission

Strives to bring hope and healing to the lives of those living in underserved regions of the world by providing high-quality eye care to help the blind see, and improving the quality of life for individuals and entire communities.

Ophth-Opt, Surg

⊕ https://vfmat.ch/197e

Global Eye Project

Empowers local communities by building locally managed, sustainable eye clinics through education initiatives and volunteer-run professional training services.

Anesth, Ophth-Opt, Surg

⊕ https://vfmat.ch/cdba

Global Ministries – The United Methodist Church

As the worldwide mission and development agency of The United Methodist Church, Global Ministries works with more than 300 hospitals and clinics around the world through its Global Health Unit.

Anesth, CT Surg, CV Med, Crit-Care, Dent-OMFS, Derm, ER Med, GI, General, Infect Dis, Logist-Op, MF Med, Medicine, Neonat, Nephro, Nutr, OB-GYN, Ophth-Opt, Ortho, Palliative, Peds, Pod, Psych, Pub Health, Rehab, Rheum, Surg, Urol

⊕ https://vfmat.ch/1723

Global Oncology (GO)

Brings the best in cancer care to underserved patients around the world and collaborates across geographic, professional, and academic borders to improve cancer care, research, and education.

Heme-Onc, Path, Rad-Onc

⊕ https://vfmat.ch/fcb8

Global Surgical Access Foundation

Partners with underserved communities to provide competent, safe, and sustainable surgical care.

Anesth, Surg

⊕ https://vfmat.ch/ea5f

Global Telehealth Network (GTN)

Provides telehealth services with dedicated physician volunteers for people located in medically underserved areas, including low- and medium-resource countries, refugee camps, conflict zones, and disaster areas, and also in the U.S.

ER Med, General, Path, Peds, Psych, Radiol, Surg

⊕ https://vfmat.ch/4345

Global Vision 2020

Provides prescription eyeglasses to people who live in parts of the world lacking necessary infrastructure for obtaining affordable corrective eyewear.

Logist-Op, Ophth-Opt

⊕ https://vfmat.ch/7373

Globus Relief

Aims to improve the delivery of healthcare worldwide by gathering, processing, and distributing surplus medical supplies to charities at home and abroad.

Logist-Op

⊕ https://vfmat.ch/a2b7

Grassroot Soccer

Leverages the power of soccer to educate, inspire, and mobilize at-risk youth in developing countries to overcome their greatest health challenges, live healthier and more productive lives, and be agents for change in their communities.

Infect Dis
⊕ https://vfmat.ch/3521

Harvard Global Health Institute
Devoted to improving global health and pioneering the next generation of global health research, education, policy, and practice, with an evidence-based, innovative, integrative, and collaborative approach, harnessing the unique breadth of excellence within Harvard.
General, Infect Dis, Logist-Op
⊕ https://vfmat.ch/5867

HEAL International
Provides health education, micro grants for women, and health-related support to resource-limited communities.
Pub Health
⊕ https://vfmat.ch/3f4d

Healing Little Hearts
Sends specialist medical teams to perform free lifesaving heart surgery on babies and children in developing parts of the world.
Anesth, CT Surg, CV Med, Ped Surg, Peds, Surg
⊕ https://vfmat.ch/ffc1

Health Amplifier
Transforms the lives of people living in extreme poverty by providing quality healthcare and community development.
Dent-OMFS, General, Infect Dis, MF Med, Pub Health
⊕ https://vfmat.ch/e51a

Health Equity Initiative
Aims to build and sustain a global community that engages across sectors and disciplines to advance health equity.
Pub Health
⊕ https://vfmat.ch/e2e2

Health Improvement Project Zanzibar
Works with the government and communities of Zanzibar toward the goal of achieving universal health coverage, while managing two hospitals, training local staff, and running a progressive mental health program.
ER Med, General, Logist-Op, Medicine, Neonat, Nutr, OB-GYN, Peds, Psych, Surg
⊕ https://vfmat.ch/33ad

Health Tanzania
Seeks to improve the health and education of underserved Tanzanians, with the help of its partners. Inspired by the Christian faith, it works to provide outpatient and inpatient care, community health and prevention programs, and primary education.
All-Immu, Anesth, General, Infect Dis, MF Med, OB-GYN, Peds, Psych, Pub Health
⊕ https://vfmat.ch/8141

Health Volunteers Overseas (HVO)
Improves the availability and quality of healthcare through the education, training, and professional development of the health workforce in resource-scarce countries.
All-Immu, Anesth, CV Med, Dent-OMFS, Derm, ENT, ER Med, Endo, GI, Heme-Onc, Infect Dis, Medicine, Medicine, Nephro, Neuro, OB-GYN, Ophth-Opt, Ortho, Peds, Plast, Psych, Pulm-Critic, Rehab, Rheum, Surg
⊕ https://vfmat.ch/42b2

Health[e] Foundation
Supports health professionals and community workers in the world's most vulnerable societies to ensure quality health for everyone in need by providing digital education and information, using e-learning and m-health.
Logist-Op
⊕ https://vfmat.ch/b73b

Healthy Child Uganda
Supports medical training and clinical care and initiates a community-based education project targeting child health.
Logist-Op, Peds
⊕ https://vfmat.ch/ebc5

Healthy DEvelopments
Provides Germany-supported health and social protection programs around the globe in a collaborative knowledge management process.
All-Immu, General, Infect Dis, Logist-Op, MF Med
⊕ https://vfmat.ch/dc31

Heart to Heart International
Strengthens communities through improving health access, providing humanitarian development, and administering crisis relief worldwide. Engages volunteers, collaborates with partners, and deploys resources to achieve this mission.
Anesth, ER Med, General, Logist-Op, Medicine, Path, Path, Peds, Psych, Pub Health, Surg
⊕ https://vfmat.ch/aacb

Heineman Medical Outreach
Provides medical and educational assistance globally to promote sustainable healthcare and enhanced living standards in underserved communities through the International Medical Outreach (IMO) program, a collaborative partnership between Heineman Medical Outreach and Atrium Health.
Anesth, CT Surg, CV Med, ER Med, General, Heme-Onc, Logist-Op, Medicine, Neonat, OB-GYN, Ped Surg, Peds, Surg, Vasc Surg
⊕ https://vfmat.ch/389b

Helen Keller International
Seeks to eliminate preventable vision loss, malnutrition, and diseases of poverty.
Infect Dis, Nutr, OB-GYN, Ophth-Opt, Peds
⊕ https://vfmat.ch/b654

HelpAge International
Works to ensure that people everywhere understand how much older people contribute to society and that they must enjoy their right to healthcare, social services, economic, and physical security.
General, Geri, Infect Dis, Medicine, Pub Health
⊕ https://vfmat.ch/5d91

Hernia International
Aims to provide relief from sickness, and protection and preservation of health, for persons affected by groin and abdominal hernias and residing in low- and middle-income countries.
Surg
⊕ https://vfmat.ch/e98e

Hope and Healing International
Gives hope and healing to children and families trapped by poverty and disability.
General, Nutr, Ophth-Opt, Peds, Rehab
⊕ https://vfmat.ch/c638

Hospice Africa
Aims to provide a holistic and culturally sensitive palliative care service through accurate treatment of pain.
Palliative
⊕ https://vfmat.ch/9f86

Humanity First
Provides aid and assistance to those in need, offering sustainable development solutions to society while providing and empowering local communities with the resources to help themselves.
ER Med, General, MF Med, Ophth-Opt
⊕ https://vfmat.ch/13cc

ICAP at Columbia University
Serves as global leader in supporting the scale-up of multidisciplinary HIV/AIDS prevention, care, and treatment programs based on a family-focused approach.
General, Infect Dis, MF Med, Medicine, OB-GYN, Pub Health
⊕ https://vfmat.ch/a8ef

IMA World Health
Works to build healthier communities by collaborating with key partners to serve vulnerable people with a focus on health, healing, and well-being for all.
Infect Dis, MF Med, Nutr, OB-GYN, Pub Health
⊕ https://vfmat.ch/8316

Imamia Medics International

Provides health education and healthcare services to underserved populations around the world, while giving Muslim health and science professionals an opportunity for career development.

Logist-Op, Medicine

🌐 https://vfmat.ch/dc22

IMPACT Foundation

Works to prevent and alleviate needless disability by restoring sight, mobility, and hearing.

ENT, MF Med, OB-GYN, Ophth-Opt, Ortho, Peds, Surg

🌐 https://vfmat.ch/ba28

Inter Care Medical and for Africa

Provides targeted medical aid to rural health units in some of the poorest parts of Africa.

Logist-Op

🌐 https://vfmat.ch/64fb

International Agency for the Prevention of Blindness (IAPB), The

Leads international efforts in blindness-prevention activities, works toward a world where no one is needlessly visually impaired, and ensures that everyone has access to the best possible standard of eye health.

Infect Dis, Ophth-Opt, Pub Health

🌐 https://vfmat.ch/87a2

International Campaign for Women's Right to Safe Abortion

Works to build an international network and campaign that brings together organizations with an interest in promoting and providing safe abortion to create a shared platform for advocacy, debate, and dialogue and the sharing of skills and experience.

OB-GYN, Pub Health, Surg

🌐 https://vfmat.ch/f341

International Children's Heart Fund

Aims to promote the international growth and quality of cardiac surgery, particularly in children and young adults.

CT Surg, Ped Surg

🌐 https://vfmat.ch/33fb

International Council of Ophthalmology

Works with ophthalmologic societies and others to enhance ophthalmic education and improve access to the highest-quality eye care in order to preserve and restore vision for people of the world.

Ophth-Opt

🌐 https://vfmat.ch/ffd2

International Eye Foundation (IEF)

Eliminates preventable and treatable blindness by making quality sustainable eye care services accessible and affordable worldwide.

Infect Dis, Logist-Op, Ophth-Opt

🌐 https://vfmat.ch/e839

International Federation of Gynecology and Obstetrics (FIGO)

Implements global projects on specific women's health issues.

MF Med, Medicine, Neonat, OB-GYN, Surg, Urol

🌐 https://vfmat.ch/c4b4

International Federation of Red Cross and Red Crescent Societies (IFRC)

Coordinates and directs international assistance following natural and manmade disasters in nonconflict situations through the world's largest humanitarian and development network. Provides disaster-preparedness programs, healthcare activities, and promotes humanitarian values.

ER Med, General, Infect Dis, Nutr

🌐 https://vfmat.ch/b4ee

International Health Partners – U.S. Inc.

Seeks to improve healthcare for the people of Tanzania by integrating medical knowledge, techniques, and best practices within the East African culture.

Derm, General, Infect Dis, MF Med, Medicine, Path, Peds

🌐 https://vfmat.ch/d4dd

International Hope Missions

Improves local standards of care by enabling complex procedures for women and children and mentoring local medical teams.

General, MF Med, OB-GYN

🌐 https://vfmat.ch/c5c7

International Medical and Surgical Aid (IMSA)

Aims to save lives and alleviate suffering through education, healthcare, surgical camps, and quality medical programs.

Anesth, General, Ped Surg, Surg

🌐 https://vfmat.ch/2561

International Medical Relief

Provides sustainable education, training, medical and dental care, and disaster relief and response in vulnerable communities worldwide.

Dent-OMFS, General, Infect Dis, Medicine, OB-GYN

🌐 https://vfmat.ch/b3ed

International Organization for Migration (IOM) – The UN Migration Agency

Promotes evidence-informed policies and holistic, preventive, and curative health programs that are beneficial, accessible, and equitable for vulnerable migrants.

General, Infect Dis, OB-GYN

🌐 https://vfmat.ch/621a

International Pediatric Nephrology Association (IPNA)

Leads global efforts to successfully address the care for all children with kidney disease through advocacy, education, and training.

Medicine, Nephro, Peds

🌐 https://vfmat.ch/b59d

International Planned Parenthood Federation (IPPF)

Leads a locally owned, globally connected civil society movement that provides and enables services and champions sexual and reproductive health and rights for all, especially the underserved.

Infect Dis, MF Med, OB-GYN

🌐 https://vfmat.ch/dc97

International Rescue Committee (IRC)

Responds to the world's worst humanitarian crises and helps people whose lives and livelihoods are shattered by conflict and disaster to survive, recover, and gain control of their future.

ER Med, General, Infect Dis, MF Med, Peds

🌐 https://vfmat.ch/5d24

International Smile Power

Partners with people to improve and sustain dental health and build bridges of friendship around the world.

Dent-OMFS

🌐 https://vfmat.ch/ba69

International Trachoma Initiative (iTi)

Works toward a world free from trachoma, a preventable cause of blindness, and provides comprehensive support to national ministries of health and governmental and nongovernmental organizations to implement a comprehensive approach to fight trachoma.

Infect Dis, Ophth-Opt

🌐 https://vfmat.ch/3278

International Union Against Tuberculosis and Lung Disease

Develops, implements, and assesses anti-tuberculosis, lung health, and noncommunicable disease programs.

Infect Dis, Pub Health, Pulm-Critic

🌐 https://vfmat.ch/3e82

IntraHealth International

Improves the performance of health workers and strengthens the systems in which they work.

CV Med, Endo, General, Infect Dis, MF Med, Neonat, Nutr, OB-GYN

🌐 https://vfmat.ch/ddc8

IVUmed
Aims to make quality urological care available worldwide by providing medical and surgical education for physicians and nurses, and treatment for thousands of children and adults.
Anesth, OB-GYN, Ped Surg, Surg, Urol
⊕ https://vfmat.ch/e619

Izumi Foundation
Develops and supports programs that improve health and healthcare in neglected regions of Africa and Latin America.
⊕ https://vfmat.ch/f29a

Jakaya Kikwete Cardiac Institute
Provides high-quality affordable cardiovascular care for patients and facilitates sustainable delivery of tertiary cardiovascular care services, while providing specialized and super-specialized postgraduate courses in the field of cardiovascular medicine.
Anesth, CV Med, Crit-Care, Surg
⊕ https://vfmat.ch/bb41

Jesus Harvesters Ministries
Reaches communities through medical clinics, dental care, veterinarian outreach, pastor training, and community service, based in Christian ministry.
Dent-OMFS, General, Infect Dis
⊕ https://vfmat.ch/8a23

Jhpiego
Creates and delivers transformative healthcare solutions that save lives, in partnership with national governments, health experts, and local communities.
General, Infect Dis, OB-GYN, Surg
⊕ https://vfmat.ch/45b8

John Snow, Inc. (JSI)
Aims to improve the health and well-being of underserved and vulnerable people and communities throughout the world.
General, Infect Dis, Logist-Op, MF Med, OB-GYN, Peds, Psych, Pub Health
⊕ https://vfmat.ch/ba78

Johns Hopkins Center for Communication Programs
Believes in the power of communication to save lives by empowering people to adopt healthy behaviors for themselves, their families, and their communities.
General, Infect Dis, Logist-Op, OB-GYN, Pub Health
⊕ https://vfmat.ch/1bf9

Johns Hopkins Center for Global Health
Facilitates and focuses the extensive expertise and resources of the Johns Hopkins institutions, together with global collaborators, to effectively address and ameliorate the world's most pressing health issues.
General, Genetics, Logist-Op, MF Med, Peds, Psych, Pub Health, Pulm-Critic
⊕ https://vfmat.ch/54ce

Joint United Nations Programme on HIV/AIDS (UNAIDS)
Aims to place people living with HIV and people affected by the virus at the decision-making table and at the center of designing, delivering, and monitoring the AIDS response.
Infect Dis
⊕ https://vfmat.ch/464a

Kagondo St. Joseph Hospital Foundation
Improves the accessibility of services for orthopedic care, treatment of trauma, skin grafting, birth defect correction, and artificial limbs, and supplies orthopedic implants and other necessary equipment for people in Tanzania.
Endo, Ortho, Ped Surg, Peds, Surg
⊕ https://vfmat.ch/2848

Kaya Responsible Travel
Promotes sustainable social, environmental, and economic development, empowers communities, and cultivates educated, compassionate global citizens through responsible travel.
All-Immu, Crit-Care, Dent-OMFS, ER Med, General, Geri, Infect Dis, MF Med, Medicine, Nutr, OB-GYN, Peds, Psych, Pub Health, Rehab
⊕ https://vfmat.ch/b2cf

Kids Care Everywhere
Seeks to empower physicians in under-resourced environments with multimedia, state-of-the-art medical software, and to inspire young professionals to become future global healthcare leaders.
Logist-Op, Ped Surg, Peds
⊕ https://vfmat.ch/bc23

KidzCare Tanzania
Provides underprivileged children and orphans with education, nutrition, and medical programs.
Dent-OMFS, Nutr, Ortho, Ped Surg, Peds
⊕ https://vfmat.ch/5a57

Kilimanjaro Centre Community Ophthalmology
Works with local partners across Africa to design, implement and evaluate eye health programs to prevent and cure blindness.
Ophth-Opt
⊕ https://vfmat.ch/2dcb

Kilimanjaro Christian Medical Center
Excels in quality service, training, and research, providing accessible and quality healthcare services as a key referral hospital.
Dent-OMFS, ENT, ER Med, Endo, General, General, Heme-Onc, Medicine, Medicine, OB-GYN, Ophth-Opt, Ortho, Path, Peds, Psych, Radiol, Rehab, Urol
⊕ https://vfmat.ch/bbc5

Kletjian Foundation
Works toward a world in which all people have access to safe, sustainable, and high-quality medical care, building collaborative networks and supporting entrepreneurial leaders that promote global health equity.
CT Surg, ENT, General, Ortho, Surg
⊕ https://vfmat.ch/12c2

KNCV Tuberculosis Foundation
Aims to end human suffering through the global elimination of tuberculosis.
Pulm-Critic
⊕ https://vfmat.ch/98bf

Kupona Foundation
Works to prevent disability and maternal and neonatal mortality and morbidity, and to provide equitable access to affordable, quality medical rehabilitative services.
MF Med, Neonat, OB-GYN, Rehab
⊕ https://vfmat.ch/4198

Land and Life Foundation
Aims to support and design conservation education, community outreach, and conservation initiatives for communities living alongside wildlife in Kenya and Tanzania.
Dent-OMFS, General, Nutr, OB-GYN, Peds
⊕ https://vfmat.ch/8d39

Lay Volunteers International Association (LVIA)
Fosters local and global change to help overcome extreme poverty, reinforce equitable and sustainable development, and enhance dialogue between Italian and African communities.
ER Med, Logist-Op, MF Med, Neonat, Nutr, OB-GYN, Peds
⊕ https://vfmat.ch/ecd4

Leprosy Mission International
Seeks to empower people with leprosy to attain healing, dignity, and life in all its fullness.
Infect Dis
⊕ https://vfmat.ch/95a9

Leprosy Mission: Northern Ireland, The
Leads the fight against leprosy by supporting people living with leprosy today and serving future generations by working to end the transmission of the disease.
General, Infect Dis
⊕ https://vfmat.ch/e265

Life for a Child
Supports the provision of the best possible healthcare, given local circumstances,

to all children and youth with diabetes in less-resourced countries, through the strengthening of existing diabetes services.

Endo, Medicine, Peds

⊕ https://vfmat.ch/d712

Life Support Foundation
Aims to prevent deaths due to acute, life-threatening conditions in low-income countries through improving the access to, and quality of, basic lifesaving interventions.

Anesth, Crit-Care, ER Med, OB-GYN, Peds

⊕ https://vfmat.ch/799e

Lifebox
Seeks to provide safer surgery and anesthesia in low-resource countries by investing in tools, training, and partnerships for safe surgery.

Anesth, Crit-Care, Surg

⊕ https://vfmat.ch/2d4d

Light for the World
Contributes to a world in which persons with disabilities fully exercise their rights, and assists persons with disabilities living in poverty.

Ophth-Opt, Rehab

⊕ https://vfmat.ch/3ff6

Light House Medical Missions
Inspired by the Christian faith, provides programs in healthcare provision, nutrition, emergency relief and response, and water, sanitation, and hygiene (WASH).

ER Med, General, Surg

⊕ https://vfmat.ch/cecd

Limbs International
Engages communities and transforms lives through affordable, sustainable prosthetic solutions and rehabilitation services in developing countries.

Logist-Op, Ortho, Pod, Rehab

⊕ https://vfmat.ch/dc84

Lions Clubs International
Empowers volunteers to serve their communities, meet humanitarian needs, encourage peace, and promote international understanding through Lions Clubs.

Heme-Onc, Medicine, Nutr, Ophth-Opt

⊕ https://vfmat.ch/7b12

Little Things, The
Provides vital medical equipment to poorly funded and inadequately equipped hospitals, improving access to healthcare for patients across the globe.

⊕ https://vfmat.ch/2d81

London School of Hygiene & Tropical Medicine: International Centre for Eye Health
Works to improve eye health and eliminate avoidable visual impairment and blindness with a focus on low-income populations.

Logist-Op, Ophth-Opt, Pub Health

⊕ https://vfmat.ch/6f5f

Lutherans in Medical Missions (LIMM)
Works with local and global partners to promote healing in medically underserved communities.

General, Logist-Op, Pub Health

⊕ https://vfmat.ch/c5aa

Maasai Women Development Organization (MWEDO)
Aims to empower Maasai women economically and socially through improved access to education, health services, and economic opportunities.

General, Infect Dis, MF Med, Nutr, OB-GYN, Peds, Surg

⊕ https://vfmat.ch/2a9a

Madaktari Africa
Aims to advance medical expertise and care in Sub-Saharan Africa through the training and education of local medical personnel.

CT Surg, CV Med, ER Med, Nephro, Neurosurg

⊕ https://vfmat.ch/7856

Making A Difference Foundation
Sponsors and organizes medical missions for medical providers to provide care to underserved communities around the world.

CV Med, Dent-OMFS, ER Med, General, Infect Dis, Logist-Op, MF Med, Neonat, Nutr, OB-GYN, Ophth-Opt, Ortho, Pub Health, Pulm-Critic, Rehab, Surg

⊕ https://vfmat.ch/5556

Mama na Mtoto (Mother and Child)
Strives to improve maternal, newborn, and child health in rural Tanzania.

Logist-Op, MF Med, OB-GYN, Peds

⊕ https://vfmat.ch/2551

Management Sciences for Health (MSH)
Works with countries and communities to save lives and improve the health of the world's poorest and most vulnerable people by building strong, resilient, sustainable health systems.

Infect Dis, Logist-Op, Pub Health

⊕ https://vfmat.ch/6aa2

MAP International
Provides medicines and health supplies to those in need around the world so they might experience life to the fullest.

Logist-Op

⊕ https://vfmat.ch/deed

Marie Stopes International
Provides the contraception and safe abortion services that enable women all over the world to choose their own futures.

Infect Dis, MF Med, Neonat, OB-GYN, Pub Health

⊕ https://vfmat.ch/9525

Maryknoll Lay Missioners
Based in Christian ministry, aims to collaborate with poor communities in Africa, Asia, and the Americas in order to respond to basic needs, including heathcare, and to help create a more compassionate world.

Logist-Op, Nutr

⊕ https://vfmat.ch/2ce6

Maternity Foundation
Works to ensure safer childbirth for women and newborns everywhere through innovative mobile health solutions such as the Safe Delivery App, a mobile training tool for skilled birth attendants.

MF Med, OB-GYN, Pub Health

⊕ https://vfmat.ch/ff4f

Maternity Worldwide
Works with communities and partners to identify and develop appropriate and effective ways to reduce maternal and newborn mortality and morbidity, facilitate communities to access quality skilled maternity care, and support the provision of quality skilled care.

MF Med, OB-GYN

⊕ https://vfmat.ch/822b

McGill University Health Centre: Centre for Global Surgery
Works to reduce the impact of injury by advancing surgical care through research and education in resource-limited settings.

ER Med, Logist-Op, Ped Surg, Surg

⊕ https://vfmat.ch/7246

MCW Global
Works to address communities' pressing needs by empowering current leaders and readying leaders of tomorrow.

Dent-OMFS

⊕ https://vfmat.ch/1547

Medical Care Development International
Works to improve the health of vulnerable populations through integrated, sustainable, and locally driven interventions.

Infect Dis, OB-GYN, Peds, Pub Health

⊕ https://vfmat.ch/da87

Medical Mission Aid Inc
Advances effective healthcare in disadvantaged communities through medical

scholarships, grants for supplies and support for local health initiatives.
Infect Dis, Logist-Op, OB-GYN, Pub Health, Rehab
⊕ https://vfmat.ch/8b83

Medical Missions for Children (MMFC)
Provides quality surgical and dental services to poor and underprivileged children and young adults in various countries throughout the world, and facilitates the transfer of education, knowledge, and recent innovations to the local medical communities.
Dent-OMFS, ENT, Endo, Ortho, Ped Surg, Peds, Plast
⊕ https://vfmat.ch/1631

Medical Missions for Global Health
Seeks to reduce health disparities by providing surgical, medical, and healthcare services and education to underserved communities and developing communities throughout Africa, the Caribbean, Central and South America, and the U.S.
Dent-OMFS, General, Surg
⊕ https://vfmat.ch/cf52

Medical Missions Outreach
Visits developing countries to provide quality, ethical healthcare and outreach to those in need, based in Christian ministry.
Dent-OMFS, Ophth-Opt, Ortho, Surg
⊕ https://vfmat.ch/1197

Medical Relief Foundation
Provides quality education and comprehensive healthcare partnerships that are responsive to the needs of the patients, the host country, and the community.
CT Surg, ER Med, General, Infect Dis, Vasc Surg
⊕ https://vfmat.ch/9add

Medical Relief International
Exists to provide dental, medical, humanitarian aid, and other services deemed necessary for the benefit of people in need.
Dent-OMFS, General
⊕ https://vfmat.ch/192b

Medical Teams International
Seeks to restore health as the first step to restoring hope, working to bring basic but lifesaving medical care to those in need.
Dent-OMFS, ER Med, General, MF Med, Pub Health
⊕ https://vfmat.ch/8d1c

MEDLIFE Movement
Partners with low-income communities in Latin America and Africa to improve access to medicine, education, and community development projects.
Dent-OMFS, General, Peds, Pub Health
⊕ https://vfmat.ch/de87

MedSend
Funds qualified healthcare professionals to serve the physical and spiritual needs of people around the world, enabling healthcare providers to work where they have been called.
General
⊕ https://vfmat.ch/661c

MedShare
Aims to improve the quality of life of people, communities, and the planet by sourcing and directly delivering surplus medical supplies and equipment to communities in need around the world.
Logist-Op
⊕ https://vfmat.ch/c8bc

Mending Kids
Provides free, lifesaving surgical care to sick children worldwide by deploying volunteer medical teams and teaching communities to become medically self-sustaining through the education of local medical staff.
Anesth, CT Surg, ENT, Ortho, Ortho, Ped Surg, Plast, Surg
⊕ https://vfmat.ch/4d61

Mercy and Love Foundation
Aims to provide orphaned and vulnerable children with basic human needs such as food, clothing, and shelter, enabling them to thrive.

General, Peds
⊕ https://vfmat.ch/649a

MHS-Massana Hospital
Promotes the health and well-being of the local population in Mbezi Beach Area and from all over the city of Dar es Salaam and Tanzania at large.
Endo, General, MF Med, Medicine, OB-GYN, Ophth-Opt, Peds, Radiol
⊕ https://vfmat.ch/8df5

Midwife Vision
Promotes maternal and child health through education, global community participation, and the provision of resources for the nursing and midwifery force.
MF Med, Neonat, OB-GYN
⊕ https://vfmat.ch/21d7

Miga Solutions Foundation
Improves global healthcare through the donations of medical equipment to underserved communities in the U.S. and around the world.
Logist-Op
⊕ https://vfmat.ch/2bf2

Millen Magese Foundation
Empowers women and girls in Tanzania to promote gender equality through access to education and reproductive health, by building schools, securing education supplies, and providing access to health services.
MF Med, OB-GYN
⊕ https://vfmat.ch/3eae

MiracleFeet
Brings low-cost treatment to every child on the planet born with clubfoot, a leading cause of physical disability.
Ortho, Peds, Rehab
⊕ https://vfmat.ch/bda8

Mission Doctors Association
Provides life-saving medical care for the poor and training for local healthcare professionals around the world.
CV Med, Dent-OMFS, General, Logist-Op, Medicine, OB-GYN, Ophth-Opt, Peds, Surg
⊕ https://vfmat.ch/6c18

Mission: Restore
Trains medical professionals abroad in complex reconstructive surgery in order to create a sustainable infrastructure in which long-term relationships are forged and permanent change comes to pass.
Plast, Surg
⊕ https://vfmat.ch/3f5f

Missions for Humanity
Inspired by the Christian faith, aims to break the cycle of poverty and reduce the number of families living in critical economic conditions by creating multifaceted programs such as those in humanitarian aid, nutrition, and health.
Dent-OMFS, General, Ophth-Opt
⊕ https://vfmat.ch/5bca

mothers2mothers (m2m)
Employs and trains local women living with HIV as community health workers called Mentor Mothers to support women, children, and adolescents with vital medical services, education, and support.
Infect Dis, MF Med, OB-GYN, Peds, Pub Health
⊕ https://vfmat.ch/6557

MSD for Mothers
Designs scalable solutions that help end preventable maternal deaths.
MF Med, OB-GYN, Pub Health
⊕ https://vfmat.ch/9f99

MSI Reproductive Choices (Marie Stopes International)
Seeks to deliver quality family planning and reproductive healthcare to women around the world.
MF Med
⊕ https://vfmat.ch/5c82

Mufindi Orphans
Provides educational opportunities and health access for vulnerable children and families in Tanzania.
General, Infect Dis, Nutr, Peds
⊕ https://vfmat.ch/976e

Médecins du Monde/Doctors of the World
Provides care, bears witness, and supports social change worldwide with innovative medical programs and evidence-based advocacy initiatives.
ER Med, General, Infect Dis, MF Med, Neonat, OB-GYN, Peds, Pub Health
⊕ https://vfmat.ch/a43d

NEST 360
Works to ensure that hospitals in Africa can deliver lifesaving care for small and sick newborns, by developing and distributing high-quality technologies and services.
MF Med, Neonat, Peds, Pub Health
⊕ https://vfmat.ch/cea9

Nyagi
Empowers local healthcare workers in resource-poor areas to diagnose life-threatening health conditions through accelerated, low-cost ultrasound skills training.
Logist-Op, Pub Health
⊕ https://vfmat.ch/5de5

Okoa Project, The / Moving Health
Designs motorcycle ambulances, creates jobs, and saves lives one ride at a time.
ER Med, Logist-Op
⊕ https://vfmat.ch/1f6c

Olmoti Clinic/Our One Community
Provides comprehensive medical care and transformative education as a foundation for a sustainable Maasai community in Tanzania.
General, Infect Dis, MF Med, OB-GYN, Ophth-Opt, Surg
⊕ https://vfmat.ch/911e

OneSight
Brings eye exams and glasses to people who lack access to vision care.
Ophth-Opt
⊕ https://vfmat.ch/3ecc

Open Heart International
Provides surgical interventions and best practices to the most disadvantaged communities on the planet.
CT Surg, MF Med, OB-GYN, Ophth-Opt, Plast, Surg
⊕ https://vfmat.ch/dab2

Operation Fistula
Exists to end obstetric fistula by building models of care that serve every woman, everywhere.
MF Med, OB-GYN, Surg
⊕ https://vfmat.ch/ce8e

Operation International
Offers medical aid to adults and children suffering from lack of quality healthcare in impoverished countries.
Dent-OMFS, ER Med, Heme-Onc, OB-GYN, Ophth-Opt, Ortho, Ped Surg, Plast, Surg
⊕ https://vfmat.ch/b52a

Operation Walk
Provides the gift of mobility through life-changing joint replacement surgeries, at no cost for those in need in the U.S. and globally.
Anesth, Ortho, Rehab, Surg
⊕ https://vfmat.ch/bafe

Options
Believes in a world in which women and children can access the high-quality health services they need, without financial burden.
Logist-Op, MF Med, Neonat, OB-GYN
⊕ https://vfmat.ch/3a48

Optivest Foundation
Funds strategic opportunities that are holistic and collaborative, inspired by the Christian faith.
General, Nutr
⊕ https://vfmat.ch/f1e6

Optometry Giving Sight
Delivers eye exams and low or no-cost glasses, provides training for local eye care professionals, and establishes optometry schools, vision centers and optical labs.
Ophth-Opt
⊕ https://vfmat.ch/33ea

Orbis International
Works to prevent and treat blindness through hands-on training and improved access to quality eye care.
Anesth, Ophth-Opt, Surg
⊕ https://vfmat.ch/f2b2

Oregon Health Sciences University: Global Health Advocacy Program in Surgery
Contributes to the care of patients across the globe and advances OHSU's strategic plan to become an international leader in health and science.
General, Medicine, Peds, Pub Health, Surg
⊕ https://vfmat.ch/77a4

Orthopedic Surgery For Africa Kühn Foundation
Aim to improve the situation in African clinics as much as possible.
Ortho
⊕ https://vfmat.ch/f5ed

Oxford University Global Surgery Group (OUGSG)
Aims to contribute to the provision of high-quality surgical care globally, particularly in low- and middle-income countries (LMICs), while bringing together students, researchers, and clinicians with an interest in global surgery, anesthesia, and obstetrics and gynecology.
Anesth, MF Med, OB-GYN, Ortho, Surg
⊕ https://vfmat.ch/c624

Pact
Works on the ground to improve the lives of those who are challenged by poverty and marginalization, striving for a world in which all people are heard, capable, and vibrant.
Infect Dis, Logist-Op, MF Med, Pub Health
⊕ https://vfmat.ch/9a6c

Pan African Thoracic Society (PATS)
Aims to promote lung health in Africa, the continent most afflicted by morbidity and death from respiratory diseases, by promoting education, research, advocacy, optimal care, and the development of African capacity to address respiratory challenges in the continent.
CV Med, Crit-Care, Pulm-Critic
⊕ https://vfmat.ch/5457

Pan-African Academy of Christian Surgeons (PAACS)
Aims to train and disciple African surgeons and related specialists to become leaders and servants, providing excellent and compassionate care to those most in need, based in Christian ministry.
Anesth, CT Surg, OB-GYN, Ortho, Ped Surg, Plast, Surg
⊕ https://vfmat.ch/b444

Pan-African Academy of Christian Surgeons (PAACS)
Exists to train and support African surgeons to provide excellent, compassionate care to those most in need, inspired by the Christian faith.
Anesth, CT Surg, Neurosurg, OB-GYN, Ortho, Ped Surg, Plast, Surg
⊕ https://vfmat.ch/85ba

Partners for Development (PfD)
Works to improve quality of life for vulnerable people in underserved communities through local and international partnerships.
Infect Dis, MF Med, Neonat, Peds
⊕ https://vfmat.ch/d2f6

Partners for World Health

Sorts, evaluates, repackages, and prepares supplies and equipment for distribution to individuals, communities, and healthcare facilities in need, both locally and internationally.

ER Med, General, Logist-Op

⊕ https://vfmat.ch/982e

PATH

Advances health equity through innovation and partnerships so people, communities, and economies can thrive.

All-Immu, CV Med, Endo, Heme-Onc, Infect Dis, MF Med, Neonat, Nutr, OB-GYN, Path, Peds, Pulm-Critic

⊕ https://vfmat.ch/b4db

Pathfinder International

Champions sexual and reproductive health and rights worldwide, mobilizing communities most in need to break through barriers and forge paths to a healthier future.

OB-GYN

⊕ https://vfmat.ch/a7b3

Pediatric Health Initiative

Supports the spread of quality pediatric care and its development and progress in low- and middle-income countries.

ER Med, Infect Dis, Neonat, Palliative, Ped Surg, Peds

⊕ https://vfmat.ch/614b

Pepal

Brings together NGOs, global corporations, and the public sector to co-create solutions to big social issues, creating immediate and scalable solutions, and developing leaders who are capable of driving change in their communities.

Heme-Onc, Infect Dis, Pub Health

⊕ https://vfmat.ch/6dc5

Phil Simon Clinic: Tanzania Project

Provides medical, surgical, and psychosocial support in Tanzania.

General, Infect Dis

⊕ https://vfmat.ch/8a68

PINCC Preventing Cervical Cancer

Seeks to prevent female-specific diseases in developing countries by utilizing low-cost and low-technology methods to create sustainable programs through patient education, medical personnel training, and facility outfitting.

OB-GYN

⊕ https://vfmat.ch/9666

Plaster House, The

Provides low-cost surgical rehabilitation to Tanzanian children living with treatable congenital and traumatic disabilities.

Dent-OMFS, Logist-Op, Ortho, Ped Surg, Plast, Pub Health, Rehab

⊕ https://vfmat.ch/7ab9

Project Concern International (PCI)

Drives innovation from the ground up to enhance health, end hunger, overcome hardship, and advance women and girls—resulting in meaningful and measurable change in people's lives.

Infect Dis, MF Med, Nutr, OB-GYN, Peds

⊕ https://vfmat.ch/5ed7

Project SOAR

Conducts HIV operations research around the world to identify practical solutions to improve HIV prevention, care, and treatment services.

ER Med, General, MF Med, OB-GYN, Psych

⊕ https://vfmat.ch/1a77

Provision Charitable Foundation

Improves the lives of Tanzanian people suffering from epilepsy and seizures through education, healthcare, and opportunities.

Dent-OMFS, MF Med, Neonat, Neuro

⊕ https://vfmat.ch/af24

PSI – Population Services International

Aims to improve the health of people in the developing world by focusing on

challenges such as a lack of family planning, HIV/AIDS, barriers to maternal health, and the greatest threats to children under the age of 5, including malaria, diarrhea, pneumonia, and malnutrition.

Infect Dis, MF Med, OB-GYN, Peds

⊕ https://vfmat.ch/ffe3

RAD-AID International

Improves and optimizes access to medical imaging and radiology in low-resource regions of the world.

Rad-Onc, Radiol

⊕ https://vfmat.ch/537f

REACH Shirati

Works in partnership with local communities in rural Tanzania to enhance education, improve healthcare, and promote community development.

General, Infect Dis, OB-GYN, Peds, Pub Health, Surg

⊕ https://vfmat.ch/a3ff

Reconstructing Women International

Treats patients in their local communities through groups of international volunteers made up of female plastic surgeons using local medical facilities, in cooperation with local medical professionals.

Anesth, Plast, Rehab, Surg

⊕ https://vfmat.ch/924a

RestoringVision

Empowers lives by restoring vision for millions of people in need.

Ophth-Opt

⊕ https://vfmat.ch/e121

ReSurge International

Provides reconstructive surgical care and builds surgical capacity in developing countries.

Anesth, Dent-OMFS, Ped Surg, Plast, Surg

⊕ https://vfmat.ch/9937

RHD Action

Seeks to reduce the burden of rheumatic heart disease in vulnerable populations throughout the world.

CV Med, Medicine, Pub Health

⊕ https://vfmat.ch/f5d9

Rockefeller Foundation, The

Works to promote the well-being of humanity.

Logist-Op, Nutr, Pub Health

⊕ https://vfmat.ch/5424

Rotaplast International

Helps children and families worldwide by eliminating the burden of cleft lip and/or palate, burn scarring, and other deformities by sending medical teams to provide free reconstructive surgery, ancillary treatment, and training.

Anesth, Dent-OMFS, ENT, Ped Surg, Plast, Surg

⊕ https://vfmat.ch/78b3

Rotary International

Provides service to others, improves lives, and advances world understanding, goodwill, and peace through its fellowship of business, professional, and community leaders.

ER Med, General, Infect Dis, MF Med, OB-GYN

⊕ https://vfmat.ch/8fb5

ROW Foundation

Works to improve the quality of training for healthcare providers, and the diagnosis and treatment available to people with epilepsy and associated psychiatric disorders in under-resourced areas of the world.

Neuro, Psych

⊕ https://vfmat.ch/25eb

Safe Anaesthesia Worldwide

Provides anesthesia to those in need in low-income countries to enable lifesaving surgery.

Anesth, Plast

⊕ https://vfmat.ch/134a

Saint Lucy Foundation

Seeks to improve eye health by carrying out operations, supplying medicines, and training local staff to prevent and treat eye disease.

Ophth-Opt

⊕ https://vfmat.ch/7583

Salvation Army International, The

Seeks to meet human needs through services in education, healthcare, community support, emergency response, and ministry development, inspired by the Christian faith.

Dent-OMFS, Derm, ER Med, Infect Dis, MF Med, Medicine, Nutr, OB-GYN, Ophth-Opt, Palliative, Psych, Rehab, Surg

⊕ https://vfmat.ch/8eb3

Sanofi Espoir Foundation

Contributes to reducing health inequalities among populations that need it most by applying a socially responsible approach focused on fighting childhood cancers in low-income countries, improving maternal and newborn health, and improving access to care.

ER Med, OB-GYN, Peds

⊕ https://vfmat.ch/943b

Save A Child's Heart

Provides lifesaving cardiac treatment to children in developing countries, and trains healthcare professionals from these countries to deliver quality care in their communities.

CT Surg, CV Med, Crit-Care, Ped Surg, Peds

⊕ https://vfmat.ch/1bef

Save the Children

Gives children around the world a healthy start in life, the opportunity to learn, and protection from harm.

All-Immu, Crit-Care, ER Med, General, Infect Dis, MF Med, Medicine, Neonat, OB-GYN, Peds, Psych, Pub Health

⊕ https://vfmat.ch/2e73

SCI Foundation

Seeks to prevent and treat neglected infectious diseases, with a focus on eliminating parasitic worm infections through strengthening impactful and comprehensive health programs across Sub-Saharan Africa.

Infect Dis, Pub Health

⊕ https://vfmat.ch/5444

SEE International

Provides sustainable medical, surgical, and educational services through volunteer ophthalmic surgeons, with the objectives of restoring sight and preventing blindness to disadvantaged individuals worldwide.

Ophth-Opt, Surg

⊕ https://vfmat.ch/6e1b

SEVA

Delivers vital eye care services to the world's most vulnerable, including women, children, and Indigenous peoples.

Ophth-Opt, Surg

⊕ https://vfmat.ch/1e87

Shirati Health, Education, and Development (SHED) Foundation

Provides healthcare, education, and development services to underserved communities in Tanzania.

General, Heme-Onc, Infect Dis, OB-GYN, Ped Surg, Peds

⊕ https://vfmat.ch/1e1b

Sightsavers

Works with partners in developing countries to help eliminate avoidable blindness and advocates for equal opportunity for the disabled.

Infect Dis, Ophth-Opt, Surg

⊕ https://vfmat.ch/aa52

SIGN Fracture Care International

Builds orthopedic capacity around the world and provides the injured poor access to fracture surgery by donating orthopedic education and implant systems to surgeons in developing countries.

Ortho, Rehab, Surg

⊕ https://vfmat.ch/123d

Simavi

Strives for a world in which all women and girls are socially and economically empowered and pursue their rights to live a healthy life, free from discrimination, coercion, and violence.

MF Med, OB-GYN

⊕ https://vfmat.ch/b57b

SINA Health

Aims to improve the health and educational status of the population in low- and middle-income countries.

General, Logist-Op

⊕ https://vfmat.ch/9ad3

Singapore Red Cross

Responds to emergencies with a dedication to relieving human suffering and protecting human lives and dignity.

ER Med, General, Logist-Op, Pub Health, Surg

⊕ https://vfmat.ch/4d7c

Sisters of the Immaculate Heart of Mary, Mother of Christ

Based in Chrisitan ministry, seeks to motivate people, especially the poor and the less privileged, to live venerable and dignified lives through credibility-structured programs, education, various medical and humanitarian services, along with self-realization and self-empowerment opportunities.

Infect Dis, Logist-Op, Nutr, Pub Health

⊕ https://vfmat.ch/5774

Smile Train, Inc.

Treats children with cleft lip through a sustainable and local model that supports surgery and other forms of essential care.

Logist-Op, Pub Health

⊕ https://vfmat.ch/822c

SmileStar

Provides free, quality dental care to disadvantaged communities in African countries and India.

Dent-OMFS

⊕ https://vfmat.ch/ade3

Sofia Global

Inspired by the Christian faith, promotes an equitable and sustainable society through education, healthcare, pastoral work, and community capacity-building.

General, Heme-Onc, Infect Dis, MF Med, OB-GYN, Peds

⊕ https://vfmat.ch/263c

SOS Children's Villages International

Supports children through alternative care and family strengthening.

ER Med, Peds

⊕ https://vfmat.ch/aca1

Souls International Foundation

Helps orphans, widows, and the poor in their time of need according to the dictates of the Gospel of Jesus Christ, who commanded us to love our neighbors as we love ourselves.

General, Infect Dis

⊕ https://vfmat.ch/52a1

Sri Sathya Sai International Organization

Inspired by spiritual teachings, carries out efforts in global healthcare, education, humanitarian relief, and youth engagement.

Dent-OMFS, General, Logist-Op, Nutr, Ophth-Opt, Pub Health

⊕ https://vfmat.ch/9bda

St. Benedict Ndanda Referral Hospital

Provides quality healthcare services to all patients, irrespective of faith and socio-economic status.

Dent-OMFS, ER Med, Endo, Nephro, OB-GYN, Ophth-Opt, Peds, Radiol, Rehab, Surg

⊕ https://vfmat.ch/4656

STEPS

Works with partners, donors, doctors and parents towards a clear vision of a sustainable and effective solution to the disability caused by untreated clubfoot.

Logist-Op, Ortho, Pod

⊕ https://vfmat.ch/784d

Students for Kids International Projects (SKIP)

Strives to educate and empower students to initiate and maintain sustainable community projects for the health, welfare, and education of children.

Dent-OMFS, General, Nutr, Peds, Pub Health

⊕ https://vfmat.ch/de4e

Sustainable Kidney Care Foundation (SKCF)

Works to provide treatment for kidney injury where none exists, and aims to reduce mortality from treatable acute kidney injury (AKI).

Infect Dis, Medicine, Nephro

⊕ https://vfmat.ch/1926

Swiss Tropical and Public Health Institute

Contributes to the improvement of the health of populations internationally, nationally, and locally through excellence in research, education, and services.

Infect Dis, Pub Health

⊕ https://vfmat.ch/2ee4

Tanzanian Cardiac Hospital Foundation, Inc. (TCHF)

Seeks to build and sustain a Catholic cardiac hospital in Tanzania and provide cardiac services to the Tanzanian community.

CT Surg, CV Med, Crit-Care, General, MF Med, Surg

⊕ https://vfmat.ch/3f3c

Task Force for Global Health, The

Consists of programs and focus areas that cover a range of global health issues including neglected tropical diseases, infectious diseases, vaccines, field epidemiology, public health informatics, health workforce development, and global health ethics.

Infect Dis, Logist-Op, Medicine, Ophth-Opt, Peds

⊕ https://vfmat.ch/714c

Tearfund

Responds to crisis and partners with local churches to bring restoration to those living in poverty, inspired by the Christian faith.

ER Med, Logist-Op

⊕ https://vfmat.ch/f6cf

Texas Children's Global Health

Addresses healthcare needs in resource-limited settings locally and globally by improving maternal and child health through the implementation of innovative, sustainable, in-country programs to train health professionals and build functional healthcare infrastructure.

Anesth, ER Med, Heme-Onc, Infect Dis, MF Med, Nutr, OB-GYN, Peds, Pub Health, Surg

⊕ https://vfmat.ch/4a1d

THET Partnerships for Global Health

Trains and educates health workers in Africa and Asia, working in partnership with organizations and volunteers from across the UK.

General

⊕ https://vfmat.ch/f937

Third World Eye Care Society (TWECS)

Collects old, unused eyeglasses and distributes them in conjunction with eye exams given by properly trained individuals.

Logist-Op, Ophth-Opt

⊕ https://vfmat.ch/8618

Total Health Africa

Aims to increase the capacity of local healthcare providers to deliver quality healthcare to underserved communities through training and providing resources.

General, Infect Dis, OB-GYN, Peds

⊕ https://vfmat.ch/9f62

Touch Foundation

Seeks to save lives and relieve human suffering by strengthening healthcare in Sub-Saharan Africa, providing better access to care, and improving the quality of local health systems.

General, MF Med, Neonat, OB-GYN

⊕ https://vfmat.ch/fdbb

U.S. President's Malaria Initiative (PMI)

Supports low-income countries to help control and eliminate malaria through cost-effective, lifesaving malaria interventions.

Infect Dis, MF Med, OB-GYN

⊕ https://vfmat.ch/dc8b

Umoja

Provides education and welfare support to the most vulnerable children and young people in Tanzania, empowering them to develop the knowledge and skills needed to create positive change for themselves and the wider community.

General, Peds, Psych

⊕ https://vfmat.ch/c978

UNC Health Foundation

Secures resources and supports empathy and expertise in patient care, research, education, and advocacy in underserved communities around the world.

Heme-Onc, Infect Dis, Neuro, Peds, Pub Health

⊕ https://vfmat.ch/7129

Union for International Cancer Control (UICC)

Unites and supports the cancer community to reduce the global cancer burden, promote greater equity, and ensure that cancer control continues to be a priority in the world health and development agenda.

Heme-Onc, Pub Health

⊕ https://vfmat.ch/88b1

United Hands Relief & Development

Works to funnel efforts toward alleviating and immediately responding to the sufferings of others around the globe, regardless of nationality, race, religion, or social status.

ER Med, General, Infect Dis, Ophth-Opt, Surg

⊕ https://vfmat.ch/2771

United Methodist Volunteers in Mission (UMVIM)

Engages in short-term missions each year in ministries as varied as disaster response, community development, pastor training, microenterprise, agriculture, Vacation Bible School, building repair and construction, and medical/dental services.

Dent-OMFS, ER Med, General

⊕ https://vfmat.ch/1ee6

United Nations Children's Fund (UNICEF)

Works in over 190 countries and territories to save children's lives, defend their rights, and help them fulfill their potential, from early childhood through adolescence.

All-Immu, Infect Dis, MF Med, Neonat, Nutr, OB-GYN, Ped Surg, Peds, Pub Health

⊕ https://vfmat.ch/42d7

United Nations Development Programme (UNDP)

Helps countries achieve the simultaneous eradication of extreme poverty and significant reduction of inequalities and exclusion using a sustainable human development approach.

Infect Dis, Logist-Op, Pub Health

⊕ https://vfmat.ch/935c

United Nations High Commissioner for Refugees (UNHCR)

Safeguards the rights and well-being of people who have been forced to flee, ensuring that everybody has the right to seek asylum and find safe refuge in another country, with the goal of seeking lasting solutions.

General, MF Med, Medicine, OB-GYN, Peds, Psych, Pub Health

⊕ https://vfmat.ch/6636

United Nations Population Fund (UNFPA)

Supports reproductive healthcare for women and youth in more than 150 countries, focusing on delivering a world in which every pregnancy is wanted, every childbirth is safe, and every young person's potential is fulfilled.

Infect Dis, MF Med, Neonat, OB-GYN, Peds, Pub Health
⊕ https://vfmat.ch/c969

United States President's Emergency Plan for AIDS Relief (PEPFAR)
The U.S. global HIV/AIDS response works to prevent new HIV infections and accelerate progress to control the global epidemic in more than 50 countries, by partnering with governments to support sustainable, integrated, and country-led responses to HIV/AIDS.
Infect Dis, Pub Health
⊕ https://vfmat.ch/a57c

University of California San Francisco: Institute for Global Health Sciences
Dedicates its efforts to improving health and reducing the burden of disease in the world's most vulnerable populations by integrating expertise in the health, social, and biological sciences, training global health leaders, and developing solutions to the most pressing health challenges.
Infect Dis, OB-GYN, Pub Health
⊕ https://vfmat.ch/6587

University of California, Berkeley: Bixby Center for Population, Health & Sustainability
Aims to help manage population growth, improve maternal health, and address the unmet need for family planning within a human rights framework.
OB-GYN
⊕ https://vfmat.ch/ff2b

University of Chicago: Center for Global Health
Collaborates with communities locally and globally to democratize education, increase service learning opportunities, and advance sustainable solutions to improve health and well-being while reducing global health inequities.
Genetics, MF Med, Peds, Pub Health
⊕ https://vfmat.ch/4f8f

University of Colorado: Global Emergency Care Initiative
Strives to sustainably improve emergency care outcomes in low- and middle-income communities worldwide by linking cutting-edge academics with excellent on-the-ground implementation.
ER Med
⊕ https://vfmat.ch/417a

University of New Mexico School of Medicine: Project Echo
Seeks to improve health outcomes worldwide through the use of a technology called telementoring, a guided-practice model in which the participating clinician retains responsibility for managing the patient.
General, Infect Dis, MF Med, OB-GYN, Path, Peds
⊕ https://vfmat.ch/6c9a

University of Virginia: Anesthesiology Department Global Health Initiatives
Educates and trains physicians to help people achieve healthy productive lives, and advances knowledge in the medical sciences.
Anesth, Pub Health
⊕ https://vfmat.ch/1b8b

University of Washington: Department of Global Health
Improves health for all through research, education, training, and service, addresses the causes of disease and health inequities at multiple levels, and collaborates with partners to develop and sustain locally led, quality health systems, programs, and policies.
Infect Dis, Logist-Op, Pub Health
⊕ https://vfmat.ch/f543

University of Washington: The International Training and Education Center for Health (I-TECH)
Works with local partners to develop skilled healthcare workers and strong national health systems in resource-limited countries.
Infect Dis, Pub Health
⊕ https://vfmat.ch/642f

USA for United Nations High Commissioner for Refugees (UNHCR)
Serves and protects refugees and displaced people through emergency relief,

cash assistance, education, resettlement, and the rebuilding of livelihoods.
ER Med, General, Logist-Op, Nutr, Pub Health
⊕ https://vfmat.ch/293c

USAID: A2Z The Micronutrient and Child Blindness Project
Aims to increase the use of key micronutrient and blindness interventions to improve child and maternal health.
MF Med, Neonat, Nutr, Ophth-Opt, Surg
⊕ https://vfmat.ch/c5f1

USAID: Deliver Project
Builds a global supply chain to deliver lifesaving health products to people in order to enable countries to provide family planning, protect against malaria, and limit the spread of pandemic threats.
Infect Dis, Logist-Op, MF Med
⊕ https://vfmat.ch/374e

USAID: EQUIP Health
Exists as an effective, efficient response mechanism to achieving global HIV epidemic control by delivering the right intervention at the right place and in the right way.
Infect Dis
⊕ https://vfmat.ch/d76a

USAID: Global Health Supply Chain Program
Combines 8 complementary projects working globally to achieve stronger, more resilient health supply chains.
Infect Dis, Logist-Op, Pub Health
⊕ https://vfmat.ch/115f

USAID: Health Finance and Governance Project
Uses research to implement strategies to help countries develop robust governance systems, increase their domestic resources for health, manage those resources more effectively, and make wise purchasing decisions.
Logist-Op
⊕ https://vfmat.ch/8652

USAID: Health Policy Initiative
Provides field-level programming in health policy development and implementation.
General, Infect Dis, MF Med, OB-GYN, Peds
⊕ https://vfmat.ch/8f84

USAID: Human Resources for Health 2030 (HRH2030)
Helps low- and middle-income countries develop the health workforce needed to prevent maternal and child deaths, support the goals of Family Planning 2020, control the HIV/AIDS epidemic, and protect communities from infectious diseases.
Logist-Op
⊕ https://vfmat.ch/9ea8

USAID: Leadership, Management and Governance Project
Improves leadership, management, and governance practices to strengthen health systems and improve health for all, including vulnerable populations worldwide.
Logist-Op
⊕ https://vfmat.ch/d35e

USAID: Maternal and Child Health Integrated Program
Works to improve the health of women and their families, including programs for maternal, newborn, and child health, immunization, family planning, nutrition, malaria, and HIV/AIDS.
All-Immu, General, Infect Dis, MF Med
⊕ https://vfmat.ch/4415

USAID: Maternal and Child Survival Program
Works to prevent child and maternal deaths.
Infect Dis, MF Med, Neonat, OB-GYN, Peds
⊕ https://vfmat.ch/6fcf

Vision Care
Restores sight and helps patients get regular treatment at short-term eye camps and long-term base clinics by having doctors, missionaries, volunteers, and sponsors work together.

Ophth-Opt
⊕ https://vfmat.ch/9d7c

Vision Health International
Brings high-quality eye care to underserved communities around the world.
Ophth-Opt
⊕ https://vfmat.ch/e97f

Vision Outreach International
Advocates for helping the blind in underserved regions of the world and empowers the poor through sight restoration.
Ophth-Opt
⊕ https://vfmat.ch/9721

Vital Strategies
Helps governments strengthen their public health systems to contend with the most important and difficult health challenges, while accelerating progress on the world's most pressing health problems.
CV Med, Infect Dis, Peds
⊕ https://vfmat.ch/fe25

Vitamin Angels
Helps at-risk populations in need—specifically pregnant women, new mothers, and children under age 5—to gain access to life-changing vitamins and minerals.
General, Nutr
⊕ https://vfmat.ch/7da1

Vodacom Foundation
Brings people together to maximize impact in three key areas: health, education, and safety and security.
Logist-Op
⊕ https://vfmat.ch/f116

Voices for a Malaria-Free Future
Seeks to expand national movements of private- and public-sector leaders to mobilize political and popular support for malaria control.
Infect Dis, Path
⊕ https://vfmat.ch/4213

Voluntary Service Overseas (VSO)
Works with health workers, communities, and governments to improve health services and rights for women, babies, youth, people with disabilities, and prisoners.
General, MF Med, OB-GYN
⊕ https://vfmat.ch/213d

VOSH (Volunteer Optometric Services to Humanity) International
Facilitates the provision and the sustainability of vision care worldwide for people who can neither afford nor obtain such care.
Ophth-Opt
⊕ https://vfmat.ch/a149

Wajamama Wellness Center
Empowers women, children, and communities in Zanzibar through health promotion and disease prevention.
General, OB-GYN, Peds
⊕ https://vfmat.ch/5349

Walkabout Foundation
Provides wheelchairs and rehabilitation in the developing world and funds research to find a cure for paralysis.
Logist-Op, Rehab
⊕ https://vfmat.ch/5582

Watsi
Uses technology to make healthcare a reality for those who might not otherwise be able to afford it.
Pub Health, Surg
⊕ https://vfmat.ch/41a3

Weill Cornell Medicine: Center for Global Health
Collaborates with international partners to improve the health of people in

resource-poor countries through research, training, and service.
General, Infect Dis, OB-GYN
⊕ https://vfmat.ch/1813

WellShare International
Partners with diverse communities to promote health and well-being, and to achieve equitable healthcare and resources where all individuals are able to live healthy and fulfilling lives.
Geri, MF Med, Nutr, Pulm-Critic
⊕ https://vfmat.ch/2e9c

WF AID
Seeks to build capacity and provide emergency aid, human assistance, and international development, where required in the world.
CT Surg, Dent-OMFS, ENT, ER Med, General, Infect Dis, Logist-Op, Nutr, Ophth-Opt, Ortho, Path, Radiol, Rehab, Surg
⊕ https://vfmat.ch/ebd7

White Ribbon Alliance, The
Leads a movement for reproductive, maternal, and newborn health and accelerates progress by putting citizens at the center of global, national, and local health efforts.
MF Med, OB-GYN
⊕ https://vfmat.ch/496b

Women Orthopaedist Global Outreach (WOGO)
Provides free, life-altering orthopedic surgery that eliminates debilitating arthritis and restores disabled joints so that women can reclaim their ability to care for themselves, their families, and their communities.
Anesth, Ortho, Rehab, Surg
⊕ https://vfmat.ch/6386

Women's Refugee Commission
Seeks to improve lives by protecting the rights of women, children, and youth displaced by conflict and crisis through researching their needs, identifying solutions, and advocating for programs and policies to strengthen their resilience.
General, MF Med, Neonat, OB-GYN, Peds, Psych
⊕ https://vfmat.ch/3d8f

World Anaesthesia Society (WAS)
Aims to support anesthesiologists with an interest in working in low-income regions of the world.
Anesth
⊕ https://vfmat.ch/37fe

World Blind Union (WBU)
Represents those experiencing blindness, speaking to governments and international bodies on issues concerning visual impairments.
Ophth-Opt
⊕ https://vfmat.ch/2bd3

World Children's Fund
Commits to helping children worldwide who are suffering the effects of poverty, disease, natural disaster, famine, abuse, civil strife, and war.
General, Logist-Op, MF Med, Nutr, OB-GYN, Pub Health
⊕ https://vfmat.ch/9cd8

World Federation of Hemophilia (WFH)
Aims to improve and sustain care for people with inherited bleeding disorders by pursuing long-term relationships with individuals and organizations who share the values of WFH's development model.
Heme-Onc
⊕ https://vfmat.ch/5121

World Health Organization, The (WHO)
The United Nations' agency for health provides leadership on global health matters, shapes the health research agenda, sets norms and standards, articulates evidence-based policy options, provides technical support and monitoring to countries, and assesses health trends.
ER Med, General, Infect Dis, Logist-Op, MF Med, OB-GYN, Peds, Psych, Pub Health
⊕ https://vfmat.ch/c476

World Heart Federation

Leads the global fight against heart disease and stroke, with a focus on low- and middle-income countries.

CV Med, Crit-Care, Heme-Onc, Medicine, Peds

⊕ https://vfmat.ch/ea51

World Medical Relief

Facilitates the distribution of surplus medical resources where they are needed.

Logist-Op

⊕ https://vfmat.ch/72dc

World Vision International

Works with vulnerable communities around the world to overcome poverty and injustice with child-focused programs in disaster management, health, nutrition, economic development, education, clean water, sanitation, and hygiene.

ER Med, General, Infect Dis, MF Med, Nutr, OB-GYN, Peds

⊕ https://vfmat.ch/2642

Worldwide Healing Hands

Works to improve the quality of healthcare for women and children in the most underserved areas of the world and to stop the preventable deaths of mothers.

General, MF Med, Neonat, OB-GYN

⊕ https://vfmat.ch/b331

YORGHAS Foundation

Supports mothers, pregnant women, infants, people with disabilities, and those suffering from humanitarian crises, poverty, or social inequalities, with particular emphasis on women's and children's rights.

MF Med, Neonat

⊕ https://vfmat.ch/9e44

Zanzibar Outreach Program

Aims to improve the community's access to healthcare, clean water, and education.

Dent-OMFS, ENT, General, Geri, OB-GYN, Ophth-Opt, Ortho, Pub Health, Surg

⊕ https://vfmat.ch/7e96

Tanzania

Healthcare Facilities

Aga Khan Hospital, Dar es Salaam
Seaview Road, Dar es Salaam, Coastal Zone,
Tanzania
⊕ https://vfmat.ch/8aac

Aga Khan University Hospital, The
Seth Benjamin Street, Arusha, Arusha, Tanzania
⊕ https://vfmat.ch/4219

AICC Hospital
Nyerere Road, Arusha, Arusha, Tanzania
⊕ https://vfmat.ch/f8fe

AL Ijumaa Hospital
Lumumba, Mwanza, Mwanza, Tanzania
⊕ https://vfmat.ch/9f78

Amana Referral Hospital
Dar es Salaam, Tanzania
⊕ https://vfmat.ch/46dc

Arusha Hospital
T5, Kwa Idd, Arusha, Tanzania
⊕ https://vfmat.ch/bbee

Arusha Lutheran Medical Centre
Wachaga Street, Arusha, Arusha, Tanzania
⊕ https://vfmat.ch/b763

Bagamoyo District Hospital
Bagamoyo Road, Bagamoyo, Pwani, Tanzania
⊕ https://vfmat.ch/6ec3

Bahama Hospital
Balewa Road, Mwanza, Mwanza, Tanzania
⊕ https://vfmat.ch/7537

Bariadi Hospital
Bariadi, Shinyanga Region, Tanzania
⊕ https://vfmat.ch/8315

Besha Hospital
Tanga, Tanzania
⊕ https://vfmat.ch/a845

**Biharamulo Designated District
Hospital**
Biharamulo Road, Biharamulo, Kagera, Tanzania
⊕ https://vfmat.ch/255c

Bochi Hospital Limited
Dar es Salaam, Tanzania
⊕ https://vfmat.ch/8ad9

Bombo Hospital
Bombo Road, Tanga, Tanzania
⊕ https://vfmat.ch/73d4

Bombo Regional Referral Hospital
Makongoro Road, Tanga, Tanzania
⊕ https://vfmat.ch/851b

Bugando Medical Center
Mwanza, Tanzania
⊕ https://vfmat.ch/7b67

Buguruni Hospital
Mnyamani Road, Dar es Salaam, Coastal Zone,
Tanzania
⊕ https://vfmat.ch/a91b

Bukombe
Rwanda Road, Bukombe, Geita, Tanzania
⊕ https://vfmat.ch/728d

Bukombe District Hospital
Bukombe, Tanzania
⊕ https://vfmat.ch/8ffe

Bukumbi Hospital
T4, Kigongo, Mwanza, Tanzania
⊕ https://vfmat.ch/99fe

Bulongwa Lutheran Hospital
Church Road, Iniho, Njombe, Tanzania
⊕ https://vfmat.ch/61c9

Bunda DDH Hospital
T4, Balili, Mara, Tanzania
⊕ https://vfmat.ch/ab3c

Busekwa
Bujora Minor Road, Bujora, Mwanza, Tanzania
⊕ https://vfmat.ch/f86d

Butiama Hospital
R193, Butiama, Mara, Tanzania
⊕ https://vfmat.ch/5422

Cardinal Rugambwa Hospital
R759, Dar es Salaam, Coastal Zone, Tanzania
⊕ https://vfmat.ch/3685

Catholic Mission Hospital
Usokami, Iringa, Tanzania
⊕ https://vfmat.ch/ef88

CCBRT Hospital
Ali Bin Said Road, Dar es Salaam, Coastal Zone,
Tanzania
⊕ https://vfmat.ch/82ee

CF Hospital
Station Road, Mwanza, Mwanza, Tanzania
⊕ https://vfmat.ch/f3f2

Chake Chake Hospital
Tibirinzi Street, Chake Chake, Kusini Pemba, Tanzania
⊕ https://vfmat.ch/8e19

Chambala
Kinampanda, Shinyanga, Tanzania
⊕ https://vfmat.ch/37b5

Chikunja
R853, Naipanga, Masasi, Tanzania
⊕ https://vfmat.ch/8efe

Children's Ward
Sengerema, Tanzania
⊕ https://vfmat.ch/7875

Chimala Mission Hospital
S.L.P. 724, Mbeya, Tanzania
⊕ https://vfmat.ch/5abe

Chingulungulu
Masasi, Tanzania
⊕ https://vfmat.ch/8f4d

Chingungwe
Tandahimba, Tanzania
⊕ https://vfmat.ch/bbd9

Chipuputa
T42, Mangaka, Masasi, Tanzania
⊕ https://vfmat.ch/a437

Chisegu
T6, Masasi, Masasi, Tanzania
⊕ https://vfmat.ch/42e4

Chiwonga
R875, Kitangari, Mtwara, Tanzania
⊕ https://vfmat.ch/86ed

Consolata Hospital Ikonda
Ikonda, Njombe, Tanzania
⊕ https://vfmat.ch/ad22

Coptic Hospital
T17, Musoma, Mara, Tanzania
⊕ https://vfmat.ch/9921

Dareda Mission Hospital
Seloto, Manyara, Tanzania
⊕ https://vfmat.ch/b175

Dodoma Hospital
Dodoma, Tanzania
⊕ https://vfmat.ch/7331

Dr. Atiman Kristu Mfalme Hospital
T9, Sumbawanga, Rukwa, Tanzania
⊕ https://vfmat.ch/dccf

Dr. Jakaya M. Kikwete District Hospital
Kishapu, Tanzania
⊕ https://vfmat.ch/8221

Edward Michaud Hospital
Dar es Salaam, Tanzania
⊕ https://vfmat.ch/8457

Ekenywa Hospital
Usimulizi Street, Dar es Salaam, Coastal Zone,

Tanzania
⊕ https://vfmat.ch/9c67

Emergency Hospital
Senga Road, Dar es Salaam, Coastal Zone, Tanzania
⊕ https://vfmat.ch/c7cb

First Health Hospital
Rindi Lane, Moshi, Kilimanjaro, Tanzania
⊕ https://vfmat.ch/6df2

First Hospital
R151, Nyamizeze, Mwanza, Tanzania
⊕ https://vfmat.ch/963e

Frelimo District Hospital
R622, Ndiuka, Iringa, Tanzania
⊕ https://vfmat.ch/39e5

Geita Hospital
T4, Nyanza, Geita, Tanzania
⊕ https://vfmat.ch/4322

Gonja Lutheran Hospital
Mkomazi-Ndungu Road, Maore, Kilimanjaro, Tanzania
⊕ https://vfmat.ch/44b3

Hai District Hospital
Hai, Tanzania
⊕ https://vfmat.ch/ce7b

Haydom Lutheran Hospital
Mbulu, Tanzania
⊕ https://vfmat.ch/c897

Heri Adventist Hospital
Buhigwe, Tanzania
⊕ https://vfmat.ch/74ff

Hospital ya Wahind
NKOMO, Mwanza, Mwanza, Tanzania
⊕ https://vfmat.ch/5c99

Hospitali Teule ya Wilaya Nkansi
Namanyere, Tanzania
⊕ https://vfmat.ch/ef72

Hospitali ya Masista
Tanzania to Zambia Road, Mafinga, Iringa, Tanzania
⊕ https://vfmat.ch/3447

Hospitali ya Mkoa Mbeya
Regional Hospital Road, Mbeya, Mbeya, Tanzania
⊕ https://vfmat.ch/8bfe

Hospitali ya Wilaya
T28, Kyela, Mbeya, Tanzania
⊕ https://vfmat.ch/4cc3

Hospitali ya Wilaya ya Nachingwea
R857, Nachingwea, Lindi, Tanzania
⊕ https://vfmat.ch/f738

Huruma District Hospital
T21, Mkuu, Kilimanjaro, Tanzania
⊕ https://vfmat.ch/3ebd

Iambi Lutheran Hospital
Mkalama, Tanzania
⊕ https://vfmat.ch/2c8d

Idende
Makete, Tanzania
⊕ https://vfmat.ch/defd

Idunda
Njombe, Tanzania
⊕ https://vfmat.ch/594f

Igodivaha
Wanging'Ombe, Tanzania
⊕ https://vfmat.ch/7a4c

Igogwe Hospital
T10, Kiwira, Mbeya, Tanzania
⊕ https://vfmat.ch/3423

Igumbilo
Igumbilo, Njombe, Tanzania
⊕ https://vfmat.ch/ffa5

Igunga Hospital
T3, Igunga, Tabora, Tanzania
⊕ https://vfmat.ch/4ac2

Igwachanya Hospital
R646, Igwachanya, Njombe, Tanzania
⊕ https://vfmat.ch/7347

Ihanga
Iwawa, Njombe, Tanzania
⊕ https://vfmat.ch/6c96

Ilembula Lutheran Hospital
T1, Wanging'ombe, Njombe, Tanzania
⊕ https://vfmat.ch/5d3c

Ilininda
Ilininda, Njombe, Tanzania
⊕ https://vfmat.ch/da4a

Ilula Mission Hospital
Iringa Road, Kimamba, Iringa, Tanzania
⊕ https://vfmat.ch/2534

Ilungu
Ludilu, Njombe, Tanzania
⊕ https://vfmat.ch/b661

Imalilo
Wanging'ombe, Tanzania
⊕ https://vfmat.ch/ac64

Imecc
A104, Iringa, Tanzania
⊕ https://vfmat.ch/e431

IMTU Hospital
Dar es Salaam, Coastal Zone, Tanzania
⊕ https://vfmat.ch/9343

Iniho
Church Road, Iniho, Njombe, Tanzania
⊕ https://vfmat.ch/6f34

International Eye Hospital
New Bagamoyo Road, Dar es Salaam, Coastal Zone, Tanzania
⊕ https://vfmat.ch/f58c

Ipamba Hospital
Tanzania to Zambia Road, Mafinga, Iringa, Tanzania
⊕ https://vfmat.ch/ccff

Ipelele
Ipelele, Mbeya, Tanzania
⊕ https://vfmat.ch/1bd8

Iringa
Sokoni Street, Ndiuka, Iringa, Tanzania
⊕ https://vfmat.ch/b3ec

Isapulano
Makete, Tanzania
⊕ https://vfmat.ch/3175

Iseresere Hospital
Nyamongo Road, Busawe Village, Mara, Tanzania
⊕ https://vfmat.ch/4bbe

Isingilo Hospital
R101, Rugasha, Kagera, Tanzania
⊕ https://vfmat.ch/1566

Isoko Hospital
R599, Ndembo, Mbeya, Tanzania
⊕ https://vfmat.ch/c5eb

Itete Lutheran Hospital
R600, Mbambo, Mbeya, Tanzania
⊕ https://vfmat.ch/2b53

Ithna-Asheri Hospital
Mt. Karakana, Arusha, Arusha, Tanzania
⊕ https://vfmat.ch/c686

Itumba Hospital
Ileje, Mbeya, Tanzania
⊕ https://vfmat.ch/1376

Jaffery Charitable Medical Services
Ghala Road, Moshi, Tanzania
⊕ https://vfmat.ch/b9dd

Kagera Regional Hospital
Uganda Road, Bukoba, Kagera, Tanzania
⊕ https://vfmat.ch/4813

Kagera Sugar Hospital
Missenyi, Tanzania
⊕ https://vfmat.ch/8ed6

Kagondo Hospital
T4, Muhutwe, Kagera, Tanzania
⊕ https://vfmat.ch/ec88

Kahama Hospital
Ngaya Road, Kahama, Shinyanga, Tanzania
⊕ https://vfmat.ch/3722

Kairuki University
Hubert Kairuki Street, Dar es Salaam, Coastal Zone, Tanzania
⊕ https://vfmat.ch/9e16

Kamanga
T4, Mwanza, Mwanza, Tanzania
⊕ https://vfmat.ch/22c3

Karatu Lutheran Hospital
B144, Karatu, Arusha, Tanzania
⊕ https://vfmat.ch/68be

Kasulu District Hospital
R326, Kisodji, Kigoma, Tanzania
⊕ https://vfmat.ch/8c97

Katavi Regional Referral Hospital
216 Two Way, Mpanda, Katavi, Tanzania
⊕ https://vfmat.ch/c5e2

Kibena Regional Hospital
T6, Ilunda, Njombe, Tanzania
⊕ https://vfmat.ch/cb3f

Kibondo
T9, Kibondo, Kigoma, Tanzania
⊕ https://vfmat.ch/99d9

Kibosho Hospital
Kibosho Road, Kibosho, Kilimanjaro, Tanzania
⊕ https://vfmat.ch/c79e

Kigoma Baptist Hospital
Katubuka, Kigoma, Tanzania
⊕ https://vfmat.ch/5a64

Kilimanjaro Christian Medical Centre at Moshi
Moshi, Tanzania
⊕ https://vfmat.ch/c42e

Kilimanjaro Christian Medical Centre at Same
Same, Tanzania
⊕ https://vfmat.ch/2d69

Kilindi CDH
Kilindi, Tanzania
⊕ https://vfmat.ch/c3b3

Kilosa District Hospital
Kilosa, Tanzania
⊕ https://vfmat.ch/c6f6

Kimamba Hospital
Gairo, Tanzania
⊕ https://vfmat.ch/bd46

Kinondoni Hospital
Mahakamani Road, Dar es Salaam, Coastal Zone, Tanzania
⊕ https://vfmat.ch/92f8

Kinyonga Hospital
Kilwa-Nangurukuru Road, Kilwa Masoko, Lindi, Tanzania
⊕ https://vfmat.ch/4d2f

Kipatimu Mission Hospital
Kipatimu – Utete Road, Kipatimu, Lindi, Tanzania
⊕ https://vfmat.ch/8ddc

Kisarawe Hospital
Kisarawe, Tanzania
⊕ https://vfmat.ch/882f

Kitete Regional Hospital
T8, Tabora, Tabora, Tanzania
⊕ https://vfmat.ch/38d5

Kiungani Street Hospital
Kiungani Street, Dar es Salaam, Tanzania
⊕ https://vfmat.ch/f682

Kiwanja Mpaka
Independence Avenue, Mbeya, Mbeya, Tanzania
⊕ https://vfmat.ch/89a9

KMKM Hospital
Malawi Road, Zanzibar City زنجبار مدينة, Unguja Mjini Magharibi, Tanzania
⊕ https://vfmat.ch/9a29

KOICA Mbagala Rangi Tatu Hospital
Hospitali Street, Dar es Salaam, Coastal Zone, Tanzania
⊕ https://vfmat.ch/49e6

Kolandoto Hospital
T8, Ibadakuli, Shinyanga, Tanzania
⊕ https://vfmat.ch/d94e

Kondoa Hospital
R462, Kondoa, Dodoma, Tanzania
⊕ https://vfmat.ch/8e78

Kowak Regional Hospital
Kowaki, Tanzania
⊕ https://vfmat.ch/bd3c

Kusini Hospital
Kusini, Tanzania
⊕ https://vfmat.ch/ee26

Kyela District Hospital
Kyela, Tanzania
⊕ https://vfmat.ch/538a

Lancet Hospital
Barabara ya Vumbi Dawasco, Dar es Salaam, Coastal Zone, Tanzania
⊕ https://vfmat.ch/88bd

Ligula Hospital
T6, Mtwara, Mtwara, Tanzania
⊕ https://vfmat.ch/cb1b

Likawage Hospital
Likawage, Lindi, Tanzania
⊕ https://vfmat.ch/7b5e

Litembo Hospital
Litembo, Ruvuma, Tanzania
⊕ https://vfmat.ch/e364

Liuli Hospital
Liuli, Ruvuma, Tanzania
⊕ https://vfmat.ch/e869

Lubaga
Old Shinyanga Road, Lubaga Farm, Shinyanga, Tanzania
⊕ https://vfmat.ch/a2e9

Ludewa District Hospital
T31, Ludewa, Njombe, Tanzania
⊕ https://vfmat.ch/665a

Lugala Hospital
R675, Malinyi, Morogoro, Tanzania
⊕ https://vfmat.ch/8fb4

Lugulu
T36, Lugulu kijiji, Simiyu, Tanzania
⊕ https://vfmat.ch/989b

Lumumba Hospital
Zanzibar, Tanzania
⊕ https://vfmat.ch/c2ac

Lushoto Hospital
Lushoto, Tanzania
⊕ https://vfmat.ch/2a54

Lutindi Mental Hospital
Korogwe, Tanzania
⊕ https://vfmat.ch/65a3

Machame Hospital
Nkwarungo Road, Machame, Kilimanjaro, Tanzania
⊕ https://vfmat.ch/db9d

Mafiga Hospital
Barabara ya Chamwino, Morogoro, Morogoro, Tanzania
⊕ https://vfmat.ch/be67

Mafinga District Hospital
Tanzania to Zambia Road, Mafinga, Iringa, Tanzania
⊕ https://vfmat.ch/18b8

Magomeni Hospital
Minaki Road, Dar es Salaam, Coastal Zone, Tanzania
⊕ https://vfmat.ch/9779

Magu Hospital
Magu Circle, Isandula, Mwanza, Tanzania
⊕ https://vfmat.ch/971f

Makambako Hospital
Makambako, Tanzania
⊕ https://vfmat.ch/5f73

Makandana Hospital
T10, Katumba, Mbeya, Tanzania
⊕ https://vfmat.ch/8138

Makiungu Hospital
Mungaa, Singida, Tanzania
⊕ https://vfmat.ch/b825

Makole Hospital
Hospital Road, Dodoma, Dodoma, Tanzania
⊕ https://vfmat.ch/3789

Malya
R160, Mwandu, Simiyu, Tanzania
⊕ https://vfmat.ch/fda1

Mama Ngoma Health Service
12 Kilwa Street, Dar es Salaam, Coastal Zone, Tanzania
⊕ https://vfmat.ch/6885

Manyara Regional Referral Hospital
T14, Singu, Manyara, Tanzania
⊕ https://vfmat.ch/e445

Marangu Hospital
T21, Marangu, Kilimanjaro, Tanzania
⊕ https://vfmat.ch/d6a8

Masoko Hospital
Kilwa-Nangurukuru Road, Kilwa Masoko, Lindi, Tanzania
⊕ https://vfmat.ch/826c

Massana Hospital
Peace Street, Dar es Salaam, Coastal Zone, Tanzania
⊕ https://vfmat.ch/d448

Maswa District Hospital
T36, Zanzui, Simiyu, Tanzania
⊕ https://vfmat.ch/acaa

Matema Lutheran Hospital
Matema Road, Matema, Mbeya, Tanzania
⊕ https://vfmat.ch/3eed

Maweni Hospital
Burega Street, Lutale, Kigoma, Tanzania
⊕ https://vfmat.ch/f17e

Mawenzi Hospital
Maendeleo Street, Dar es Salaam, Coastal Zone, Tanzania
⊕ https://vfmat.ch/debb

Mawimbini Medical Centre
Kaskazini A, Tanzania
⊕ https://vfmat.ch/bedf

Mbalizi Hospital
A104, Mbeya, Tanzania
⊕ https://vfmat.ch/be9d

Mbesa Mission Hospital
Tunduru, Tanzania
⊕ https://vfmat.ch/263f

Mbeya Consultant Hospital
Chunya Street, Mbeya, Mbeya, Tanzania
⊕ https://vfmat.ch/926f

Mbeya Hospital
Mbeya, Tanzania
⊕ https://vfmat.ch/bf59

Mbeya Referral Hospital
Independence Avenue, Mbeya, Mbeya, Tanzania
⊕ https://vfmat.ch/9d5f

Mbinga District Hospital
T12, Mbinga, Ruvuma, Tanzania
⊕ https://vfmat.ch/6912

Mbozi Mission Hospital
Mlowo, Mbeya, Tanzania
⊕ https://vfmat.ch/69bb

Mbulu Hospital
Mbulu, Tanzania
⊕ https://vfmat.ch/b17b

Meatu Hospital
T37, Mwanhuzi, Simiyu, Tanzania
⊕ https://vfmat.ch/9e8e

Meru Hospital
T2, Tengeru, Arusha, Tanzania
⊕ https://vfmat.ch/ff46

Mirembe Hospital
T5, Dodoma, Dodoma, Tanzania
⊕ https://vfmat.ch/3e47

Misungwi Hospital
T8, Iteja, Mwanza, Tanzania
⊕ https://vfmat.ch/9ce2

Mkomaindo District Hospital
Tunduru Road, Mlasi, Masasi, Tanzania
⊕ https://vfmat.ch/9438

Mkula Hospital
T36, Mkula, Simiyu, Tanzania
⊕ https://vfmat.ch/b51d

Mnazi Mmoja Hospital Dar es Salaam
Bibi Titi Mohamed Road, Dar es Salaam, Coastal
Zone, Tanzania
⊕ https://vfmat.ch/4ab8

Mnazi Mmoja Hospital Zanzibar
Zanzibar, Tanzania
⊕ https://vfmat.ch/fb78

Mnero Hospital
R853, Nachingwea, Lindi, Tanzania
⊕ https://vfmat.ch/f87e

Moravian Leprosy Hospital
T8, Sikonge, Tabora, Tanzania
⊕ https://vfmat.ch/931e

Morogoro Hospital
Morogoro, Tanzania
⊕ https://vfmat.ch/376f

Morogoro Regional Hospital
Old Dar es Salaam Road, Morogoro, Morogoro,
Tanzania
⊕ https://vfmat.ch/1a4b

Mount Meru Regional Hospital
Barabara ya Afrika Mashariki, Arusha, Arusha,
Tanzania
⊕ https://vfmat.ch/5eef

Moyo Hospital
Kinondoni Shamba Road, Dar es Salaam, Coastal
Zone, Tanzania
⊕ https://vfmat.ch/a72a

Moyo Safi Wa Maria Health Care
Msewe Street, Dar es Salaam, Coastal Zone,
Tanzania
⊕ https://vfmat.ch/f8a3

Mpwapwa District Hospital
Road to Kibakwe, Mpwapwa, Dodoma, Tanzania
⊕ https://vfmat.ch/65c5

Mrara Hospital
Gorowa Road, Babati, Manyara, Tanzania
⊕ https://vfmat.ch/8961

Mugana Designated District Hospital
Kantare, Kagera, Tanzania
⊕ https://vfmat.ch/bd29

Muheza DDH
T13, Muheza, Tanga, Tanzania
⊕ https://vfmat.ch/f943

Muhimbili National Hospital
Dar es Salaam, Tanzania
⊕ https://vfmat.ch/7f95

Murangi
R186, Lyasembe, Mara, Tanzania
⊕ https://vfmat.ch/bd49

Mvumi Mission Hospital
Dodoma, Tanzania
⊕ https://vfmat.ch/f2e1

Mwadui Hospital
T8, Maganzo, Shinyanga, Tanzania
⊕ https://vfmat.ch/d975

Mwananchi Hospital
Temple Street, Mwanza, Mwanza, Tanzania
⊕ https://vfmat.ch/95da

Mwananyamala Hospital
Minazini Street, Dar es Salaam, Coastal Zone, Tanzania
⊕ https://vfmat.ch/a477

Mwanekeyi
Mwanekeyi, Mwanza, Tanzania
⊕ https://vfmat.ch/2482

Mwembeladu Hospital
Zanzibar, Tanzania
⊕ https://vfmat.ch/ab4c

Mzinga Hospital
Morogoro, Tanzania
⊕ https://vfmat.ch/5ef8

Ndolage Hospital
R109, Ndolage, Kagera, Tanzania
⊕ https://vfmat.ch/6add

Ngoyoni Hospital
Lower Road, Shimbi Mashariki, Kilimanjaro, Tanzania
⊕ https://vfmat.ch/fdb7

Ngudu Hospital
R159, Ngudu, Mwanza, Tanzania
⊕ https://vfmat.ch/68dd

Ngulyati H/C
R365, Ngulyati, Simiyu, Tanzania
⊕ https://vfmat.ch/bd4a

Nguruka Hospital
Urundin Road, Nguruka, Kigoma, Tanzania
⊕ https://vfmat.ch/e556

Nkinga Hospital
R390, Nkinga, Tabora, Tanzania
⊕ https://vfmat.ch/7c8a

Nkoaranga Hospital
T2, Tengeru, Arusha, Tanzania
⊕ https://vfmat.ch/47ad

Nkwenda
R101, Kagenyi, Kagera, Tanzania
⊕ https://vfmat.ch/9b5e

Nshambya Hospital
Kashozi Road, Bukoba, Kagera, Tanzania
⊕ https://vfmat.ch/b755

Nyakahanga Designated District Hospital
T38, Bisheshe, Kagera, Tanzania
⊕ https://vfmat.ch/2729

Nyalwanzaja
R161, Buyagu, Geita, Tanzania
⊕ https://vfmat.ch/c518

Nyamagana Hospital
T4, Mwanza, Mwanza, Tanzania
⊕ https://vfmat.ch/a466

Nyamiaga Hospital
Ngara-Rusumo Road, Murukulazo, Kagera, Tanzania
⊕ https://vfmat.ch/95b2

Nzega Government Hospital
R393, Bukooba, Shinyanga, Tanzania
⊕ https://vfmat.ch/64b2

Ocean Road Hospital
Luthuli Street, Dar es Salaam, Coastal Zone, Tanzania
⊕ https://vfmat.ch/f37f

Oltrument Hospital
TPRI Road, Ngaramtoni, Arusha, Tanzania
⊕ https://vfmat.ch/3ac3

Omubweya Bukoba Rural in Tanzania
Kibirizi, Kagera, Tanzania
⊕ https://vfmat.ch/6788

Pasua Hospital
Mill Road, Moshi, Kilimanjaro, Tanzania
⊕ https://vfmat.ch/daef

Police Hospital
Mchinga Road, Lindi, Lindi, Tanzania
⊕ https://vfmat.ch/2415

Puge Hospital
R390, Puge, Tabora, Tanzania
⊕ https://vfmat.ch/86bf

Puma Mission Hospital
T3, Mkiwa village, Singida, Tanzania
⊕ https://vfmat.ch/cc64

Queen of Universe Hospital
T3, Mkiwa village, Singida, Tanzania
⊕ https://vfmat.ch/b157

Red Cross Hospital
Balewa Road, Mwanza, Tanzania
⊕ https://vfmat.ch/6cdf

Regency Hospital
Allykhan Road, Dar es Salaam, Coastal Zone,
Tanzania
⊕ https://vfmat.ch/877f

Ruvuma Regional Hospital
Sokoine Road, Songea, Ruvuma, Tanzania
⊕ https://vfmat.ch/2dd8

Sabasaba Hospital
Kingo Street, Morogoro, Morogoro, Tanzania
⊕ https://vfmat.ch/49f4

Saidia Watoto
Makongoro Road, Medical Research, Mwanza,
Tanzania
⊕ https://vfmat.ch/7467

Salaaman Hospital
Kiongi Road, Dar es Salaam, Coastal Zone, Tanzania
⊕ https://vfmat.ch/52e9

Sali Hospital
Yacht Club Road, Dar es Salaam, Coastal Zone,
Tanzania
⊕ https://vfmat.ch/8789

Sanitas Hospital
168 Mwai Kibaki Road, Dar es Salaam, Tanzania
⊕ https://vfmat.ch/df73

Sekou-Toure Hospital
Machemba Street, Isamilo Kaskazini, Mwanza,
Tanzania
⊕ https://vfmat.ch/23b1

Selian Lutheran Hospital Ngaramtoni
T2, Arusha, Arusha, Tanzania
⊕ https://vfmat.ch/db74

Sengerema District Hospital
R149, Mission, Mwanza, Tanzania
⊕ https://vfmat.ch/ffcb

Sengerema Hospital
Sengerema, Tanzania
⊕ https://vfmat.ch/2657

Serengeti International Hospital
Serengeti, Tanzania
⊕ https://vfmat.ch/8637

Shinyanga Government Hospital
Old Shinyanga Road, Shinyanga, Shinyanga, Tanzania
⊕ https://vfmat.ch/7862

Shree Hindu Hospital
Pandit Street, Arusha, Arusha, Tanzania
⊕ https://vfmat.ch/89bb

Shree Hindu Mandal Hospital
Wurzburg Road, Mwanza, Mwanza, Tanzania
⊕ https://vfmat.ch/fcac

Siha Hospital
R262, Engarenairobi, Kilimanjaro, Tanzania
⊕ https://vfmat.ch/59b1

Sikonge District Hospital
T8, Sikonge, Tabora, Tanzania
⊕ https://vfmat.ch/d5da

Singida Regional Hospital
T14, Singida, Singida, Tanzania
⊕ https://vfmat.ch/9db5

Sinza Hospital
Palestina Hospital Road, Dar es Salaam, Coastal
Zone, Tanzania
⊕ https://vfmat.ch/dafe

Sokoine Hospital
Mtanda Street, Lindi, Lindi, Tanzania
⊕ https://vfmat.ch/fa5a

Somanda District Hospital
Bariadi, Shinyanga Region, Tanzania
⊕ https://vfmat.ch/8ae3

Songwe
T1, Ivugula, Mbeya, Tanzania
⊕ https://vfmat.ch/ed3f

St. Benedict Hospital
Dar es Salaam, Tanzania
⊕ https://vfmat.ch/4645

St. Carolus
Singida, Tanzania
⊕ https://vfmat.ch/feae

St. Gemma Hospital
T5, Dodoma, Dodoma, Tanzania
⊕ https://vfmat.ch/a7ea

St. Anna Mission Hospital
T8, Tabora, Tabora, Tanzania
⊕ https://vfmat.ch/524e

St. Anne's Hospital
Nyasa, Tanzania
⊕ https://vfmat.ch/5746

St. Benedict Hospital
St. Benedict Road, Dar es Salaam, Coastal Zone,
Tanzania
⊕ https://vfmat.ch/2ed2

St. Benedict's Hospital
Masasi, Tanzania
⊕ https://vfmat.ch/2bb5

St. Elizabeth Hospital
Kigoma Street, Arusha, Arusha, Tanzania
⊕ https://vfmat.ch/132e

St. John's Hospital
Lugarawa, Njombe, Tanzania
⊕ https://vfmat.ch/d6b2

St. Joseph Hospital
Mailimoja Road, Soweto, Kilimanjaro, Tanzania
⊕ https://vfmat.ch/79b6

St. Otto Hospital
T4, Kikomakoma, Kagera, Tanzania
⊕ https://vfmat.ch/4f31

St. Walburgs Hospital
Nyangao, Tanzania
⊕ https://vfmat.ch/23a6

Sumbawanga Regional Hospital
Sokoine Street, Sumbawanga, Rukwa, Tanzania
⊕ https://vfmat.ch/5ad8

Sumve DDH Hospital
R160, Koromije, Mwanza, Tanzania
⊕ https://vfmat.ch/e5fc

Sumve District Designated Hospital
Kwimba, Tanzania
⊕ https://vfmat.ch/375c

Swaya
Halengo Road, Mbeya, Mbeya, Tanzania
⊕ https://vfmat.ch/d4c6

Tandale Hospital
Sokoni Road, Dar es Salaam, Coastal Zone, Tanzania
⊕ https://vfmat.ch/6617

Tanzania Charitable Hospital
Zimbili Road, Dar es Salaam, Coastal Zone, Tanzania
⊕ https://vfmat.ch/21da

Tanzania Occupational Health Service
Dar es Salaam, Tanzania
⊕ https://vfmat.ch/5151

Tarime District Hospital
R194, Tarime, Mara, Tanzania
⊕ https://vfmat.ch/f1b6

Temeke District Referral Hospital
Temeke Road, Dar es Salaam, Coastal Zone, Tanzania
⊕ https://vfmat.ch/7a27

Teule
T13, Muheza, Tanga, Tanzania
⊕ https://vfmat.ch/1462

TMJ Hospital
Old Bagamoyo Road, Dar es Salaam, Coastal Zone,

Tanzania
⊕ https://vfmat.ch/c971

TPC Hospital
Newvillage Road, Arusha Chini, Manyara, Tanzania
⊕ https://vfmat.ch/9831

Tumaini Hospital
Magore Street, Dar es Salaam, Tanzania
⊕ https://vfmat.ch/f1cf

Uhuru Hospital
Rufiji, Tanzania
⊕ https://vfmat.ch/29db

Ukerewe Hospital
R141, Bukongo, Mwanza, Tanzania
⊕ https://vfmat.ch/f885

Urambo Hospital
T18, Urambo, Tabora, Tanzania
⊕ https://vfmat.ch/65e9

Usalama Hospital
Senga Road, Dar es Salaam, Coastal Zone, Tanzania
⊕ https://vfmat.ch/fd46

Usangi Hospital
Usangi, Kilimanjaro, Tanzania
⊕ https://vfmat.ch/2575

Uvinza Hospital
Uvinza, Tanzania
⊕ https://vfmat.ch/9868

Uyole Hospital
3344 T10, Uyole, Mbeya, Tanzania
⊕ https://vfmat.ch/24c3

Vingunguti Hospital
Mzambarauni Street, Dar es Salaam, Coastal Zone,
Tanzania
⊕ https://vfmat.ch/69c2

Vwawa District Hospital
Vwawa, Tanzania
⊕ https://vfmat.ch/1e6b

Wasso Hospital
Wasso, Arusha, Tanzania
⊕ https://vfmat.ch/83d4

Healthcare Facility

Timor-Leste

The Democratic Republic of Timor-Leste (also known as East Timor), in Southeast Asia, is made up of several islands, including the eastern half of Timor, Atauro, and Jaco. Australia is Timor-Leste's neighbor to the south, separated by the Timor Sea. Timor-Leste's predominantly mountainous terrain is home to 1.4 million people, with most living in the western portion of the country in or around the capital of Dili. The Timorese population is ethnically diverse, including groups such as Austronesian, Melanesia-Pauan, Bunak, Fataluku, Bakasai, Tetun, Mambai, Tokodede, Galoli, Kemak, and Baikeno. Because of this diversity, the population speaks a variety of languages including the official languages of Tetun and Portuguese alongside English, Indonesian, and 32 other indigenous languages. The vast majority of the population, as much as 98 percent, identifies as Roman Catholic.

East Timor was at one time colonized by Portugal and was called Portuguese Timor. It gained independence in 1975, only to be invaded by Indonesia shortly thereafter. The Indonesian occupation lasted for several violent decades, as East Timor struggled for true independence. In 1999, Indonesia relinquished control of East Timor, and Timor-Leste was named a sovereign state in 2002. Despite being a relatively new country with an impoverished population, progress has been made on Timorese living standards. Overall poverty levels decreased from 50 percent to 42 percent between 2007 and 2014. Agriculture is a major component of the Timorese economy, and employs a majority of the population. However, in terms of value, offshore natural gas deposits and hydrocarbon production make up the largest portion of the economy.

Timor-Leste is characterized by a high population growth rate, about 2.2 percent annually. This has resulted in a young population, with 40 percent of Timorese under the age of 15. Average life expectancy has increased to 69 by 2019. Most common causes of death include stroke, ischemic heart disease, lower respiratory infection, neonatal disorders, COPD, tuberculosis, HIV/AIDS, diarrheal diseases, chronic kidney disease, cirrhosis, congenital defects, and malaria. The risk factors that contribute most to death and disability include malnutrition, air pollution, high blood pressure, dietary risks, high fasting plasma glucose, kidney dysfunction, insufficient sanitation and clean water, high LDL, alcohol and tobacco use, unsafe sex, and occupational risks.

1.4M

Population

$1,381

GDP Per Capita

69 years

Life Expectancy

↑ Improving

77
Doctors/100k

Physician Density

590
Beds/100k

Hospital Bed Density

142
Deaths/100k

Maternal Mortality

Timor-Leste

Nonprofit Organizations

Abt Associates
Seeks to improve the quality of life and economic well-being of people worldwide, while striving to meet and exceed the highest professional standards.
General, Logist-Op, MF Med, OB-GYN, Peds
🌐 https://vfmat.ch/cec2

Aloha Medical Mission
Brings hope and changes the lives of people; serves overseas and in Hawaiʻi.
Anesth, Crit-Care, Dent-OMFS, ENT, ER Med, General, Medicine, OB-GYN, Ophth-Opt, Ortho, Ped Surg, Peds, Plast, Surg, Urol
🌐 https://vfmat.ch/72ac

ARC The Australian Respiratory Council
Fosters research to promote respiratory health and works to improve lung health in communities of disadvantaged and Indigenous people.
Infect Dis
🌐 https://vfmat.ch/69f2

Australian & New Zealand Gastroenterology International Training Association
Aims to improve health in developing Asia Pacific nations by enhancing the standards of practice of gastroenterology and building capacity to treat digestive diseases.
GI
🌐 https://vfmat.ch/5a69

CARE
Works around the globe to save lives, defeat poverty, and achieve social justice.
ER Med, General
🌐 https://vfmat.ch/7232

Care Channels International
We engage communities through a variety of education, health, and livelihood programs.
Dent-OMFS, General, Surg
🌐 https://vfmat.ch/fc48

Carter Center, The
Seeks to prevent and resolve conflicts, enhance freedom and democracy, and improve health, while remaining committed to human rights and the alleviation of human suffering.
Infect Dis, MF Med, Ophth-Opt
🌐 https://vfmat.ch/6556

ChildFund Australia
Works to reduce poverty for children in many of the world's most disadvantaged communities.
ER Med, General, Peds
🌐 https://vfmat.ch/13df

East Timor Hearts Fund
Aims to reduce death and disability from rheumatic and other heart disease in Timor-Leste through excellence in research, prevention, treatment, and capacity building.
CT Surg, CV Med
🌐 https://vfmat.ch/df5f

Fred Hollows Foundation, The
Works toward a world in which no person is needlessly blind or vision impaired.
Ophth-Opt, Pub Health, Surg
🌐 https://vfmat.ch/73e5

Fundação Lafaek Diak (The Good Crocodile Foundation)
Aims to develop integrated agriculture that respects the environment, provides community-based healthcare, education, and training, and supports small business development.
General, MF Med, Path
🌐 https://vfmat.ch/3391

Gift of Life International
Provides lifesaving cardiac treatment to children in developing countries while developing sustainable pediatric cardiac programs by implementing screening, surgical, and training missions.
Anesth, CT Surg, CV Med, Crit-Care, Ped Surg, Peds, Pulm-Critic
🌐 https://vfmat.ch/f2f9

Global Civic Sharing
Aims to support our neighbors' self-reliance and realize the sustainable development.
Nutr, Peds, Pub Health
🌐 https://vfmat.ch/d7ab

Global Oncology (GO)
Brings the best in cancer care to underserved patients around the world and collaborates across geographic, professional, and academic borders to improve cancer care, research, and education.
Heme-Onc, Path, Rad-Onc
🌐 https://vfmat.ch/fcb8

Health Alliance International
Promotes policies and support programs that strengthen government primary healthcare and foster social, economic, and health equity for all.
General, Infect Dis, Logist-Op, MF Med, Neonat, OB-GYN, Psych
🌐 https://vfmat.ch/6f2d

Institute of Applied Dermatology
Aims to alleviate difficult-to-treat skin ailments by combining biomedicine with Ayurveda, homeopathy, yoga, and other traditional Indian medicine.
All-Immu, Derm, Infect Dis, Nutr, Pod, Pub Health
🌐 https://vfmat.ch/c6eb

International Federation of Red Cross and Red Crescent Societies (IFRC)
Coordinates and directs international assistance following natural and manmade disasters in nonconflict situations through the world's largest humanitarian and development network. Provides disaster-preparedness programs, healthcare activities, and promotes humanitarian values.
ER Med, General, Infect Dis, Nutr
⊕ https://vfmat.ch/b4ee

International Organization for Migration (IOM) – The UN Migration Agency
Promotes evidence-informed policies and holistic, preventive, and curative health programs that are beneficial, accessible, and equitable for vulnerable migrants.
General, Infect Dis, OB-GYN
⊕ https://vfmat.ch/621a

John Snow, Inc. (JSI)
Aims to improve the health and well-being of underserved and vulnerable people and communities throughout the world.
General, Infect Dis, Logist-Op, MF Med, OB-GYN, Peds, Psych, Pub Health
⊕ https://vfmat.ch/ba78

Joint United Nations Programme on HIV/AIDS (UNAIDS)
Aims to place people living with HIV and people affected by the virus at the decision-making table and at the center of designing, delivering, and monitoring the AIDS response.
Infect Dis
⊕ https://vfmat.ch/464a

Leprosy Mission Australia, The
Provides support to people with leprosy including screening, medical treatment and job opportunities, inspired by the Christian faith.
Infect Dis
⊕ https://vfmat.ch/9e4b

Leprosy Mission International
Seeks to empower people with leprosy to attain healing, dignity, and life in all its fullness.
Infect Dis
⊕ https://vfmat.ch/95a9

Maluk Timor
Advances primary healthcare in Timor-Leste and helps to fill unmet needs for health services by providing care in tuberculosis, HIV, malnutrition, rheumatic heart disease, and other disorders.
CV Med, Dent-OMFS, Infect Dis, Nutr, OB-GYN
⊕ https://vfmat.ch/bab2

Marie Stopes International
Provides the contraception and safe abortion services that enable women all over the world to choose their own futures.
Infect Dis, MF Med, Neonat, OB-GYN, Pub Health
⊕ https://vfmat.ch/9525

MSI Reproductive Choices (Marie Stopes International)
Seeks to deliver quality family planning and reproductive healthcare to women around the world.
MF Med
⊕ https://vfmat.ch/5c82

One-2-One Charitable Trust
Aims to support dental, medical, educational, vocational, and physical needs, regardless of ethnicity, gender, and religion.
Dent-OMFS, General, Logist-Op, MF Med, Nutr
⊕ https://vfmat.ch/6aaf

OneSight
Brings eye exams and glasses to people who lack access to vision care.
Ophth-Opt
⊕ https://vfmat.ch/3ecc

Operation Fistula
Exists to end obstetric fistula by building models of care that serve every

woman, everywhere.
MF Med, OB-GYN, Surg
⊕ https://vfmat.ch/ce8e

Order of Malta
Supports forgotten or excluded people, especially those living in conflict zones or amid natural disasters, by providing medical assistance, caring for refugees, and distributing medicines and necessities.
ER Med, General, Infect Dis, MF Med, Nephro, OB-GYN, Ortho, Psych
⊕ https://vfmat.ch/1fab

Reach
Promotes the health of vulnerable populations through technical support to local, regional, and global efforts to prevent and control rheumatic fever and rheumatic heart disease (RF/RHD).
CV Med, Medicine, Pub Health
⊕ https://vfmat.ch/3f52

Rotary International
Provides service to others, improves lives, and advances world understanding, goodwill, and peace through its fellowship of business, professional, and community leaders.
ER Med, General, Infect Dis, MF Med, OB-GYN
⊕ https://vfmat.ch/8fb5

Smile Asia
Delivers free surgical care, through medical missions and outreach centers, to children with facial deformities such as cleft lip and cleft palate, and aims to raise standards of medical care by creating opportunities for collaborative learning and exchange of best practices.
Anesth, Dent-OMFS, Ped Surg, Peds, Plast
⊕ https://vfmat.ch/d674

Timor Children's Foundation
Seeks to empower the future leaders of Timor-Leste by providing opportunities through education, improving health and nutrition, offering scholarships, and providing infrastructure.
Dent-OMFS
⊕ https://vfmat.ch/c4f1

Union for International Cancer Control (UICC)
Unites and supports the cancer community to reduce the global cancer burden, promote greater equity, and ensure that cancer control continues to be a priority in the world health and development agenda.
Heme-Onc, Pub Health
⊕ https://vfmat.ch/88b1

United Nations Children's Fund (UNICEF)
Works in over 190 countries and territories to save children's lives, defend their rights, and help them fulfill their potential, from early childhood through adolescence.
All-Immu, Infect Dis, MF Med, Neonat, Nutr, OB-GYN, Ped Surg, Peds, Pub Health
⊕ https://vfmat.ch/42d7

United Nations Development Programme (UNDP)
Helps countries achieve the simultaneous eradication of extreme poverty and significant reduction of inequalities and exclusion using a sustainable human development approach.
Infect Dis, Logist-Op, Pub Health
⊕ https://vfmat.ch/935c

United Nations High Commissioner for Refugees (UNHCR)
Safeguards the rights and well-being of people who have been forced to flee, ensuring that everybody has the right to seek asylum and find safe refuge in another country, with the goal of seeking lasting solutions.
General, MF Med, Medicine, OB-GYN, Peds, Psych, Pub Health
⊕ https://vfmat.ch/6636

United Nations Population Fund (UNFPA)
Supports reproductive healthcare for women and youth in more than 150 countries, focusing on delivering a world in which every pregnancy is wanted, every childbirth is safe, and every young person's potential is fulfilled.

Infect Dis, MF Med, Neonat, OB-GYN, Peds, Pub Health
⊕ https://vfmat.ch/c969

USAID: Maternal and Child Health Integrated Program
Works to improve the health of women and their families, including programs for maternal, newborn, and child health, immunization, family planning, nutrition, malaria, and HIV/AIDS.
All-Immu, General, Infect Dis, MF Med
⊕ https://vfmat.ch/4415

Variety – The Children's Charity International
Funds and delivers programs that focus on multiple unmet needs of children who are sick or disadvantaged, or live with disabilities and other special needs. Works at a local, national and international level, including the delivery of critical healthcare and medical equipment.
General, Infect Dis, Logist-Op
⊕ https://vfmat.ch/41f5

Vision Care
Restores sight and helps patients get regular treatment at short-term eye camps and long-term base clinics by having doctors, missionaries, volunteers, and sponsors work together.
Ophth-Opt
⊕ https://vfmat.ch/9d7c

World Health Organization, The (WHO)
The United Nations' agency for health provides leadership on global health matters, shapes the health research agenda, sets norms and standards, articulates evidence-based policy options, provides technical support and monitoring to countries, and assesses health trends.
ER Med, General, Infect Dis, Logist-Op, MF Med, OB-GYN, Peds, Psych, Pub Health
⊕ https://vfmat.ch/c476

World Vision International
Works with vulnerable communities around the world to overcome poverty and injustice with child-focused programs in disaster management, health, nutrition, economic development, education, clean water, sanitation, and hygiene.
ER Med, General, Infect Dis, MF Med, Nutr, OB-GYN, Peds
⊕ https://vfmat.ch/2642

 # Timor-Leste

Healthcare Facilities

Ermera Hospital
Fatubessi, Ermera, Timor-Leste
⊕ https://vfmat.ch/8115

Guido Valadares National Hospital
Díli, Timor-Leste
⊕ https://vfmat.ch/am3w

Hospital Dato Rua
Forohem, Timor-Leste
⊕ https://vfmat.ch/tkgp

Hospital Referal de Lospalos
Rua São Paulo, Lospalos, Timor-Leste
⊕ https://vfmat.ch/b9zs

Kids Ark Medical Clinic
Dili, Timor-Leste
https://vfmat.ch/tdnt

Maliana Referral Hospitals
Maliana, Timor-Leste
⊕ https://vfmat.ch/kxu2

Manatuto Hospital
Travessa HahiRain, Manatuto, Timor-Leste
⊕ https://vfmat.ch/ywsx

Maubisse Referral Hospital
Maubisse, Timor-Leste
⊕ https://vfmat.ch/kerf

New Referral Hospital of Baucau
Baucau, Timor-Leste
⊕ https://vfmat.ch/zchn

Stamford Medical
Díli, Timor-Leste
⊕ https://vfmat.ch/1s7u

Viqueque Hospital
Mamulak, Viqueque, Timor-Leste
⊕ https://vfmat.ch/de63

Healthcare Facility

Map data © OpenStreetMap (openstreetmap.org) and contributors, CC-BY-SA
(creativecommons.org) © CARTO

Togo

Sandwiched between Ghana and Benin in West Africa, the Togolese Republic (Togo) is one of the smallest countries on the continent. It boasts a rapidly increasing population of 8.3 million people representing at least 37 different ethnic groups. While many people speak one of the four major Togolese languages, French is the official language of the country. Togo boasts a wide array of natural landscapes, including beaches, forests, hills, and savannas.

Since gaining independence in 1960—after control by German, French, and British governments—Togo has struggled to maintain consistent economic and political stability and experiences occasional demonstrations, strikes, and marches. And while poverty has decreased by several percentage points over the past two decades, it is still widespread, especially in rural areas, where about 70 percent of households live below the poverty line. Togo's economy is based mainly on agriculture, with nearly 60 percent of the workforce employed in the subsistence and commercial farming of crops such as coffee, cocoa, cotton, yams, cassava, corn, beans, rice, millet, and sorghum. Togo is also a mining nation with large quantities of phosphate.

Life expectancy in Togo has increased significantly, from age 53 to 61, between 2000 and 2018. Similarly, under-five mortality rates decreased from 141 to 63 deaths per 1,000 live births between 1990 and 2019. While these are overall improvements, the population is still vulnerable to poor health. Currently, leading causes of death in Togo include diseases such as diarrheal diseases, malaria, neonatal disorders, lower respiratory infections, HIV/AIDS, and tuberculosis. However, non-communicable diseases have also increased substantially in recent years, and top causes of death now include ischemic heart disease, stroke, and cirrhosis. Trauma and mortality from road injuries are also significant.

8.3M

Population

$915

GDP Per Capita

61 years

Life Expectancy

↑ Improving

8
Doctors/100k

Physician Density

70
Beds/100k

Hospital Bed Density

396
Deaths/100k

Maternal Mortality

Togo

Nonprofit Organizations

Advance Family Planning
Aims to achieve global expansion and access to quality contraceptive information, services, and supplies through financial investment and political commitment.
General, MF Med, Pub Health
⊕ https://vfmat.ch/7478

Africa Health Organisation
Leads collaborative efforts among countries in Africa and other partners to promote health equity, combat disease, and improve quality of life.
Logist-Op, Pub Health
⊕ https://vfmat.ch/b1c5

Africa Relief and Community Development
Provides comprehensive relief and developmental aid to people of the African continent regardless of gender, race, or religion.
Nutr, Pub Health
⊕ https://vfmat.ch/6cd2

African Health Now
Promotes and provides information and access to sustainable primary healthcare to women, children, and families living across Sub-Saharan Africa.
Dent-OMFS, Endo, General, Infect Dis, MF Med, OB-GYN
⊕ https://vfmat.ch/c766

Against Malaria Foundation
Helps protect people from malaria. Funds anti-malaria nets, specifically long-lasting insecticidal nets (LLINs), and works with distribution partners to ensure they are used. Tracks and reports on net use and malaria case data.
Infect Dis
⊕ https://vfmat.ch/337d

Al Basar International Foundation
Works with local partners to treat preventable blindness, and helps set up sustainable infrastructure so local teams can save sight in their communities.
Ophth-Opt
⊕ https://vfmat.ch/a8b5

Al-Khair Foundation
Provides emergency relief and developmental support in some of the world's most impoverished areas.
Dent-OMFS, General, MF Med, Nutr, Peds
⊕ https://vfmat.ch/921d

AO Alliance
Builds solutions to lessen the burden of injuries in low- and middle-income countries, while enhancing the care of the injured to reduce human suffering, disability, and poverty.
Ortho, Surg
⊕ https://vfmat.ch/8cd5

Assist Africa
Believes that through education, entrepreneurial support, and access to healthcare, quality of life for many people can be improved dramatically and that sustainable economic growth and overall well-being are attainable through a focus on these three cornerstones.
Dent-OMFS, General, Surg
⊕ https://vfmat.ch/37fd

Beta Humanitarian Help
Provides plastic surgery in underserved areas of the world.
Anesth, Plast
⊕ https://vfmat.ch/7221

BroadReach
Collaborates with governments, multinational health organizations, donors, and private-sector companies to effect healthcare reform and solve the world's biggest health challenges.
Logist-Op
⊕ https://vfmat.ch/7812

CARE
Works around the globe to save lives, defeat poverty, and achieve social justice.
ER Med, General
⊕ https://vfmat.ch/7232

Carter Center, The
Seeks to prevent and resolve conflicts, enhance freedom and democracy, and improve health, while remaining committed to human rights and the alleviation of human suffering.
Infect Dis, MF Med, Ophth-Opt
⊕ https://vfmat.ch/6556

Center for Strategic and International Studies (CSIS) Commission on Strengthening America's Health Security
Brings together a distinguished and diverse group of high-level opinion leaders bridging security and health, with the core aim to chart a bold vision for the future of U.S. leadership in global health.
ER Med, Infect Dis, MF Med, Pub Health
⊕ https://vfmat.ch/6d7f

Chain of Hope (La Chaîne de l'Espoir)
Helps underprivileged children around the world by providing them with access to healthcare.
Anesth, CT Surg, Crit-Care, ER Med, Neurosurg, Ortho, Ped Surg, Surg, Vasc Surg
⊕ https://vfmat.ch/e871

Christian Blind Mission (CBM)
Aims to improve the quality of life of persons with disabilities in the poorest countries, addressing poverty as a cause and a consequence of disability, and

working in partnership to create a society for all.

ENT, General, Infect Dis, OB-GYN, Ophth-Opt, Ortho, Peds, Psych, Rehab, Surg

⊕ https://vfmat.ch/3824

Christian Medical & Dental Associations
Based in Christian ministry, deploys medical and dental teams to underserved communities to provide vital healthcare.

Anesth, Dent-OMFS, ER Med, General, Medicine, OB-GYN, Ophth-Opt, Peds, Pub Health, Radiol, Rehab, Surg

⊕ https://vfmat.ch/921c

COVID-19 Clinical Research Coalition
Advocates and collaborates for the advancement of COVID-19 research driven by the needs of low-resource settings, and works for equitable access to solutions to the pandemic.

All-Immu, Infect-Dis, MF Med, Path, Pub Health

⊕ https://vfmat.ch/d1f4

Developing Country NGO Delegation: Global Fund to Fight AIDS, TB & Malaria
Works to strengthen the engagement of civil society actors and organizations in developing countries to build a world in which AIDS, TB, and malaria are no longer global, public health, and human rights threats.

Infect Dis, Pub Health

⊕ https://vfmat.ch/3149

Dianova
Works in prevention and treatment of addiction, while promoting social progress in international forums.

Psych, Pub Health

⊕ https://vfmat.ch/1998

Direct Relief
Improves the health and lives of people affected by poverty or emergency situations by mobilizing and providing essential medical resources needed for their care.

ER Med, Logist-Op

⊕ https://vfmat.ch/58e5

Duke University: Global Health Institute
Sparks innovation in global health research and education, and brings together knowledge and resources to address the most important global health issues of our time.

All-Immu, Infect Dis, MF Med, OB-GYN, Pub Health

⊕ https://vfmat.ch/c4cd

EngenderHealth
Works to implement high-quality, gender-equitable programs that advance sexual and reproductive health and rights.

General, MF Med, OB-GYN, Peds

⊕ https://vfmat.ch/1cb2

eRanger
Provides sustainable solutions to transportation and medical provision such as ambulances and mobile clinics in developing countries.

ER Med, General, Logist-Op

⊕ https://vfmat.ch/4c18

Fondation Follereau
Promotes the quality of life of the most vulnerable African communities. Alongside trusted partners, the foundation supports local initiatives in healthcare and education.

General, Infect Dis, OB-GYN

⊕ https://vfmat.ch/bcc7

Foundation for Healthcare for Humanity
Provide assistance in the development and implementation of medical programs in the United States, Africa, South America, Eastern Europe, and the Caribbean.

General

⊕ https://vfmat.ch/ba7f

Global Blood Fund
Delivers grants, equipment, and training to over 50 countries in Africa, Asia,

Eastern Europe, the Middle East, Latin America and the Caribbean.

Pub Health

⊕ https://vfmat.ch/6377

Global Clubfoot Initiative (GCI)
Promotes and resources the treatment of children with clubfoot in developing countries using the Ponseti technique.

Ortho, Ped Surg

⊕ https://vfmat.ch/f229

Global Ministries – The United Methodist Church
As the worldwide mission and development agency of The United Methodist Church, Global Ministries works with more than 300 hospitals and clinics around the world through its Global Health Unit.

Anesth, CT Surg, CV Med, Crit-Care, Dent-OMFS, Derm, ER Med, GI, General, Infect Dis, Logist-Op, MF Med, Medicine, Neonat, Nephro, Nutr, OB-GYN, Ophth-Opt, Ortho, Palliative, Peds, Pod, Psych, Pub Health, Rehab, Rheum, Surg, Urol

⊕ https://vfmat.ch/1723

Global Oncology (GO)
Brings the best in cancer care to underserved patients around the world and collaborates across geographic, professional, and academic borders to improve cancer care, research, and education.

Heme-Onc, Path, Rad-Onc

⊕ https://vfmat.ch/fcb8

Global Vision 2020
Provides prescription eyeglasses to people who live in parts of the world lacking necessary infrastructure for obtaining affordable corrective eyewear.

Logist-Op, Ophth-Opt

⊕ https://vfmat.ch/7373

Globus Relief
Aims to improve the delivery of healthcare worldwide by gathering, processing, and distributing surplus medical supplies to charities at home and abroad.

Logist-Op

⊕ https://vfmat.ch/a2b7

Grassroot Soccer
Leverages the power of soccer to educate, inspire, and mobilize at-risk youth in developing countries to overcome their greatest health challenges, live healthier and more productive lives, and be agents for change in their communities.

Infect Dis

⊕ https://vfmat.ch/3521

Health & Development International (HDI)
Aims to prevent obstetric fistula and deaths from obstructed labor, preventing postpartum hemorrhage, and eradicating Guinea worm disease and lymphatic filariasis in Africa and elsewhere. Goal is to advance world public health, human dignity, and socioeconomics.

Infect Dis, OB-GYN

⊕ https://vfmat.ch/25cd

Healthy DEvelopments
Provides Germany-supported health and social protection programs around the globe in a collaborative knowledge management process.

All-Immu, General, Infect Dis, Logist-Op, MF Med

⊕ https://vfmat.ch/dc31

Heart to Heart International
Strengthens communities through improving health access, providing humanitarian development, and administering crisis relief worldwide. Engages volunteers, collaborates with partners, and deploys resources to achieve this mission.

Anesth, ER Med, General, Logist-Op, Medicine, Path, Path, Peds, Psych, Pub Health, Surg

⊕ https://vfmat.ch/aacb

HelpMeSee
Trains local cataract specialists in Manual Small Incision Cataract Surgery (MSICS) in significant numbers, to meet the increasing demand for surgical services in the communities most impacted by cataract blindness.

Anesth, Ophth-Opt, Surg

⊕ https://vfmat.ch/973c

Hope Walks

Frees children, families, and communities from the burden of clubfoot, inspired by the Christian faith.

Ortho, Ped Surg, Peds, Rehab

⊕ https://vfmat.ch/f6d4

Hospice Africa

Aims to provide a holistic and culturally sensitive palliative care service through accurate treatment of pain.

Palliative

⊕ https://vfmat.ch/9f86

Hospital of Hope

Works to meet patients' physical, emotional, and spiritual needs and offers an outpatient clinic with 11 consultation rooms including OB, surgery, and medicine.

Dent-OMFS, General, Infect Dis, Neonat, OB-GYN, Peds, Radiol, Surg

⊕ https://vfmat.ch/c623

Humanity & Inclusion

Works alongside people with disabilities and vulnerable populations, taking action and bearing witness in order to respond to their essential needs, improve their living conditions and health, and promote respect for their dignity and fundamental rights.

General, Infect Dis, MF Med, Medicine, Ortho, Peds, Psych, Pub Health, Rehab

⊕ https://vfmat.ch/16b7

Humanity First

Provides aid and assistance to those in need, offering sustainable development solutions to society while providing and empowering local communities with the resources to help themselves.

ER Med, General, MF Med, Ophth-Opt

⊕ https://vfmat.ch/13cc

International Agency for the Prevention of Blindness (IAPB), The

Leads international efforts in blindness-prevention activities, works toward a world where no one is needlessly visually impaired, and ensures that everyone has access to the best possible standard of eye health.

Infect Dis, Ophth-Opt, Pub Health

⊕ https://vfmat.ch/87a2

International Council of Ophthalmology

Works with ophthalmologic societies and others to enhance ophthalmic education and improve access to the highest-quality eye care in order to preserve and restore vision for people of the world.

Ophth-Opt

⊕ https://vfmat.ch/ffd2

International Federation of Red Cross and Red Crescent Societies (IFRC)

Coordinates and directs international assistance following natural and manmade disasters in nonconflict situations through the world's largest humanitarian and development network. Provides disaster-preparedness programs, healthcare activities, and promotes humanitarian values.

ER Med, General, Infect Dis, Nutr

⊕ https://vfmat.ch/b4ee

International Medical Relief

Provides sustainable education, training, medical and dental care, and disaster relief and response in vulnerable communities worldwide.

Dent-OMFS, General, Infect Dis, Medicine, OB-GYN

⊕ https://vfmat.ch/b3ed

International Organization for Migration (IOM) – The UN Migration Agency

Promotes evidence-informed policies and holistic, preventive, and curative health programs that are beneficial, accessible, and equitable for vulnerable migrants.

General, Infect Dis, OB-GYN

⊕ https://vfmat.ch/621a

International Planned Parenthood Federation (IPPF)

Leads a locally owned, globally connected civil society movement that provides and enables services and champions sexual and reproductive health and rights for all, especially the underserved.

Infect Dis, MF Med, OB-GYN

⊕ https://vfmat.ch/dc97

IntraHealth International

Improves the performance of health workers and strengthens the systems in which they work.

CV Med, Endo, General, Infect Dis, MF Med, Neonat, Nutr, OB-GYN

⊕ https://vfmat.ch/ddc8

Ipas

Focuses efforts on women and girls who want contraception or abortion, and builds programs around their needs and how best to support them.

OB-GYN

⊕ https://vfmat.ch/8e39

Jhpiego

Creates and delivers transformative healthcare solutions that save lives, in partnership with national governments, health experts, and local communities.

General, Infect Dis, OB-GYN, Surg

⊕ https://vfmat.ch/45b8

Johns Hopkins Center for Communication Programs

Believes in the power of communication to save lives by empowering people to adopt healthy behaviors for themselves, their families, and their communities.

General, Infect Dis, Logist-Op, OB-GYN, Pub Health

⊕ https://vfmat.ch/1bf9

Joint United Nations Programme on HIV/AIDS (UNAIDS)

Aims to place people living with HIV and people affected by the virus at the decision-making table and at the center of designing, delivering, and monitoring the AIDS response.

Infect Dis

⊕ https://vfmat.ch/464a

Life for a Child

Supports the provision of the best possible healthcare, given local circumstances, to all children and youth with diabetes in less-resourced countries, through the strengthening of existing diabetes services.

Endo, Medicine, Peds

⊕ https://vfmat.ch/d712

Light in the World Development Foundation

Enhances the dignity and quality of life in underserved areas of Africa by ensuring access to clean water, quality education, and affordable healthcare.

General, Infect Dis, MF Med

⊕ https://vfmat.ch/e1d6

Lions Clubs International

Empowers volunteers to serve their communities, meet humanitarian needs, encourage peace, and promote international understanding through Lions Clubs.

Heme-Onc, Medicine, Nutr, Ophth-Opt

⊕ https://vfmat.ch/7b12

Lutherans in Medical Missions (LIMM)

Works with local and global partners to promote healing in medically underserved communities.

General, Logist-Op, Pub Health

⊕ https://vfmat.ch/c5aa

Management Sciences for Health (MSH)

Works with countries and communities to save lives and improve the health of the world's poorest and most vulnerable people by building strong, resilient, sustainable health systems.

Infect Dis, Logist-Op, Pub Health

⊕ https://vfmat.ch/6aa2

MAP International

Provides medicines and health supplies to those in need around the world so they might experience life to the fullest.

Logist-Op
⊕ https://vfmat.ch/deed

Maternity Foundation
Works to ensure safer childbirth for women and newborns everywhere through innovative mobile health solutions such as the Safe Delivery App, a mobile training tool for skilled birth attendants.
MF Med, OB-GYN, Pub Health
⊕ https://vfmat.ch/ff4f

Medical Care Development International
Works to improve the health of vulnerable populations through integrated, sustainable, and locally driven interventions.
Infect Dis, OB-GYN, Peds, Pub Health
⊕ https://vfmat.ch/da87

MedSend
Funds qualified healthcare professionals to serve the physical and spiritual needs of people around the world, enabling healthcare providers to work where they have been called.
General
⊕ https://vfmat.ch/661c

MedShare
Aims to improve the quality of life of people, communities, and the planet by sourcing and directly delivering surplus medical supplies and equipment to communities in need around the world.
Logist-Op
⊕ https://vfmat.ch/c8bc

Mercy and Love Foundation
Aims to provide orphaned and vulnerable children with basic human needs such as food, clothing, and shelter, enabling them to thrive.
General, Peds
⊕ https://vfmat.ch/649a

Mercy Ships
Operates hospital ships staffed by volunteers to bring hope, healing, and healthcare to underserved communities worldwide.
Anesth, Dent-OMFS, Logist-Op, Neonat, OB-GYN, Ophth-Opt, Ortho, Palliative, Plast, Psych, Surg
⊕ https://vfmat.ch/2e99

Mission Regan
Collects supplies, medication, and medical equipment and provides them to those who are in desperate need, both locally and globally.
Logist-Op
⊕ https://vfmat.ch/2bc1

Médecins du Monde/Doctors of the World
Provides care, bears witness, and supports social change worldwide with innovative medical programs and evidence-based advocacy initiatives.
ER Med, General, Infect Dis, MF Med, Neonat, OB-GYN, Peds, Pub Health
⊕ https://vfmat.ch/a43d

Mérieux Foundation
Committed to fighting infectious diseases that affect developing countries by capacity building, particularly in clinical laboratories, and focusing on diagnosis.
Logist-Op, Path
⊕ https://vfmat.ch/a23a

Order of Malta
Supports forgotten or excluded people, especially those living in conflict zones or amid natural disasters, by providing medical assistance, caring for refugees, and distributing medicines and necessities.
ER Med, General, Infect Dis, MF Med, Nephro, OB-GYN, Ortho, Psych
⊕ https://vfmat.ch/1fab

Pathfinder International
Champions sexual and reproductive health and rights worldwide, mobilizing communities most in need to break through barriers and forge paths to a healthier future.

OB-GYN
⊕ https://vfmat.ch/a7b3

Philips Foundation
Aims to reduce healthcare inequality by providing access to quality healthcare for disadvantaged communities.
CV Med, OB-GYN, Ped Surg, Peds, Surg, Urol
⊕ https://vfmat.ch/bacb

RestoringVision
Empowers lives by restoring vision for millions of people in need.
Ophth-Opt
⊕ https://vfmat.ch/e121

Rockefeller Foundation, The
Works to promote the well-being of humanity.
Logist-Op, Nutr, Pub Health
⊕ https://vfmat.ch/5424

Rotaplast International
Helps children and families worldwide by eliminating the burden of cleft lip and/or palate, burn scarring, and other deformities by sending medical teams to provide free reconstructive surgery, ancillary treatment, and training.
Anesth, Dent-OMFS, ENT, Ped Surg, Plast, Surg
⊕ https://vfmat.ch/78b3

Rotary Action Group for Family Health & AIDS Prevention (RFHA)
Works to save and improve the lives of children and families who lack access to preventive healthcare and education.
Dent-OMFS, Infect Dis, OB-GYN, Ophth-Opt, Peds
⊕ https://vfmat.ch/6563

Rotary International
Provides service to others, improves lives, and advances world understanding, goodwill, and peace through its fellowship of business, professional, and community leaders.
ER Med, General, Infect Dis, MF Med, OB-GYN
⊕ https://vfmat.ch/8fb5

Salvation Army International, The
Seeks to meet human needs through services in education, healthcare, community support, emergency response, and ministry development, inspired by the Christian faith.
Dent-OMFS, Derm, ER Med, Infect Dis, MF Med, Medicine, Nutr, OB-GYN, Ophth-Opt, Palliative, Psych, Rehab, Surg
⊕ https://vfmat.ch/8eb3

Samaritan's Purse International Disaster Relief
Provides spiritual and physical aid to hurting people around the world, such as victims of war, poverty, natural disasters, disease, and famine, based in Christian ministry.
Anesth, CT Surg, Crit-Care, Dent-OMFS, Derm, ENT, ER Med, Endo, GI, General, Heme-Onc, Infect Dis, MF Med, Neonat, Nephro, Neuro, Neurosurg, Nutr, OB-GYN, Ophth-Opt, Ortho, Path, Ped Surg, Peds, Plast, Psych, Pulm-Critic, Radiol, Rehab, Rheum, Surg, Urol, Vasc Surg
⊕ https://vfmat.ch/87e3

Sanofi Espoir Foundation
Contributes to reducing health inequalities among populations that need it most by applying a socially responsible approach focused on fighting childhood cancers in low-income countries, improving maternal and newborn health, and improving access to care.
ER Med, OB-GYN, Peds
⊕ https://vfmat.ch/943b

Santé Diabète
Addresses the lack of access to care for people with diabetes in Africa, with the mission of saving lives through disease prevention and management and improving quality of life through care delivery.
Endo, Medicine, Vasc Surg
⊕ https://vfmat.ch/7652

Save A Child's Heart

Provides lifesaving cardiac treatment to children in developing countries, and trains healthcare professionals from these countries to deliver quality care in their communities.

CT Surg, CV Med, Crit-Care, Ped Surg, Peds

⊕ https://vfmat.ch/1bef

SEE International

Provides sustainable medical, surgical, and educational services through volunteer ophthalmic surgeons, with the objectives of restoring sight and preventing blindness to disadvantaged individuals worldwide.

Ophth-Opt, Surg

⊕ https://vfmat.ch/6e1b

Sight.org

Proclaims the gospel to the most unserved regions of Africa by combating blindness through surgery and prevention.

Ophth-Opt, Pub Health

⊕ https://vfmat.ch/2be7

Sightsavers

Works with partners in developing countries to help eliminate avoidable blindness and advocates for equal opportunity for the disabled.

Infect Dis, Ophth-Opt, Surg

⊕ https://vfmat.ch/aa52

SIGN Fracture Care International

Builds orthopedic capacity around the world and provides the injured poor access to fracture surgery by donating orthopedic education and implant systems to surgeons in developing countries.

Ortho, Rehab, Surg

⊕ https://vfmat.ch/123d

SINA Health

Aims to improve the health and educational status of the population in low- and middle-income countries.

General, Logist-Op

⊕ https://vfmat.ch/9ad3

Smile Train, Inc.

Treats children with cleft lip through a sustainable and local model that supports surgery and other forms of essential care.

Logist-Op, Pub Health

⊕ https://vfmat.ch/822c

Swiss Tropical and Public Health Institute

Contributes to the improvement of the health of populations internationally, nationally, and locally through excellence in research, education, and services.

Infect Dis, Pub Health

⊕ https://vfmat.ch/2ee4

Task Force for Global Health, The

Consists of programs and focus areas that cover a range of global health issues including neglected tropical diseases, infectious diseases, vaccines, field epidemiology, public health informatics, health workforce development, and global health ethics.

Infect Dis, Logist-Op, Medicine, Ophth-Opt, Peds

⊕ https://vfmat.ch/714c

Terre des hommes (Tdh) Foundation

Works to improve the daily life of children and their relatives in the areas of health, protection and emergency, in Europe, Africa, Asia, Latin America, and the Near and Middle East.

CT Surg, CV Med, OB-GYN, Ped Surg, Pub Health

⊕ https://vfmat.ch/5c26

Turing Foundation

Aims to contribute toward a better world and a better society by focusing on efforts such as health, art, education, and nature.

Infect Dis

⊕ https://vfmat.ch/6bcc

Union for International Cancer Control (UICC)

Unites and supports the cancer community to reduce the global cancer burden, promote greater equity, and ensure that cancer control continues to be a priority in the world health and development agenda.

Heme-Onc, Pub Health

⊕ https://vfmat.ch/88b1

United Nations Development Programme (UNDP)

Helps countries achieve the simultaneous eradication of extreme poverty and significant reduction of inequalities and exclusion using a sustainable human development approach.

Infect Dis, Logist-Op, Pub Health

⊕ https://vfmat.ch/935c

United Nations High Commissioner for Refugees (UNHCR)

Safeguards the rights and well-being of people who have been forced to flee, ensuring that everybody has the right to seek asylum and find safe refuge in another country, with the goal of seeking lasting solutions.

General, MF Med, Medicine, OB-GYN, Peds, Psych, Pub Health

⊕ https://vfmat.ch/6636

United Nations Population Fund (UNFPA)

Supports reproductive healthcare for women and youth in more than 150 countries, focusing on delivering a world in which every pregnancy is wanted, every childbirth is safe, and every young person's potential is fulfilled.

Infect Dis, MF Med, Neonat, OB-GYN, Peds, Pub Health

⊕ https://vfmat.ch/c969

United Surgeons for Children (USFC)

Pursues greater health and opportunity for children in the most neglected pockets of the world, with a specific focus on and expertise in surgery.

Anesth, CT Surg, Neonat, Neurosurg, OB-GYN, Peds, Radiol, Surg

⊕ https://vfmat.ch/3b4c

USAID: African Strategies for Health

Identifies and advocates for best practices, enhancing technical capacity of African regional institutions, and engaging African stakeholders to address health issues in a sustainable manner.

All-Immu, Infect Dis, OB-GYN, Peds

⊕ https://vfmat.ch/c272

USAID: Human Resources for Health 2030 (HRH2030)

Helps low- and middle-income countries develop the health workforce needed to prevent maternal and child deaths, support the goals of Family Planning 2020, control the HIV/AIDS epidemic, and protect communities from infectious diseases.

Logist-Op

⊕ https://vfmat.ch/9ea8

Vision for All Foundation

Implements ophthalmic healthcare projects; aims to create and support ophthalmic centers and existing structures in order to support the training of medical and paramedical personnel in the ophthalmology; and seeks to promote prevention, diagnosis, and treatment of ophthalmic pathologies.

Dent-OMFS, Ophth-Opt, Pub Health

⊕ https://vfmat.ch/dd72

Vision Outreach International

Advocates for helping the blind in underserved regions of the world and empowers the poor through sight restoration.

Ophth-Opt

⊕ https://vfmat.ch/9721

Vitamin Angels

Helps at-risk populations in need—specifically pregnant women, new mothers, and children under age 5—to gain access to life-changing vitamins and minerals.

General, Nutr

⊕ https://vfmat.ch/7da1

World Blind Union (WBU)

Represents those experiencing blindness, speaking to governments and international bodies on issues concerning visual impairments.

Ophth-Opt

⊕ https://vfmat.ch/2bd3

World Federation of Hemophilia (WFH)
Aims to improve and sustain care for people with inherited bleeding disorders by pursuing long-term relationships with individuals and organizations who share the values of WFH's development model.
Heme-Onc
⊕ https://vfmat.ch/5121

World Health Organization, The (WHO)
The United Nations' agency for health provides leadership on global health matters, shapes the health research agenda, sets norms and standards, articulates evidence-based policy options, provides technical support and monitoring to countries, and assesses health trends.
ER Med, General, Infect Dis, Logist-Op, MF Med, OB-GYN, Peds, Psych, Pub Health
⊕ https://vfmat.ch/c476

World Medical Relief
Facilitates the distribution of surplus medical resources where they are needed.
Logist-Op
⊕ https://vfmat.ch/72dc

World Missions Possible
Provides EMS capacity-building, along with medical and vision care, to under-developed and rural areas.
ER Med, General, Heme-Onc, Neonat, Ophth-Opt, Surg
⊕ https://vfmat.ch/d6a5

Togo

Healthcare Facilities

Aneho Psychiatric Hospital
N36, Aného, Région Maritime, Togo
🌐 https://vfmat.ch/d4cd

Association Espoir Pour Demain (AED)
Rue Wakada, Kara, Région de la Kara, Togo
🌐 https://vfmat.ch/f998

CHP Bassar
N17, Bassar, Région de la Kara, Togo
🌐 https://vfmat.ch/cf66

CHR de Sokodé
Sokodé – Bassar, Sokodé, Région Centrale, Togo
🌐 https://vfmat.ch/66c6

CHU du Campus
N1, Lomé, Togo
🌐 https://vfmat.ch/9198

CHU Kara
Kara, Togo
🌐 https://vfmat.ch/d1df

CHU Tokoin
Avenue de la Victoire, Lomé, Togo
🌐 https://vfmat.ch/ee4c

Croix-Rouge at Kara
Avenue Maman N'Danida, Kara, Région de la Kara,
Togo
🌐 https://vfmat.ch/c2d7

Hospital of Hope
Lomé – Ouagadougou, Mango, Région des Savanes,
Togo
🌐 https://vfmat.ch/5ba1

Hôpital Baptiste Biblique
Tsiko, Togo
🌐 https://vfmat.ch/9668

Hôpital Bethesda
Kloto, Togo
🌐 https://vfmat.ch/7414

Hôpital Bon Sécours de Kegué
Route de la Nouvelle Présidence, Lomé, Togo
🌐 https://vfmat.ch/873e

Hôpital de Blitta
Lomé – Cinkassé, Blitta, Région Centrale, Togo
🌐 https://vfmat.ch/3f84

Hôpital de Sotouboua
Sotouboua, Togo
🌐 https://vfmat.ch/56de

Hôpital Mère et Enfants SOS
Avenue Maman N'Danida, Kara, Région de la Kara,
Togo
🌐 https://vfmat.ch/8fe7

Hôpital Préfectoral de Vogan
Route Lomé – Vogan, Vogan, Région Maritime, Togo
🌐 https://vfmat.ch/fed4

USP
Rue Wakada, Kara, Région de la Kara, Togo
🌐 https://vfmat.ch/f4b5

USP de Lama-Kpédah
Rue Bakali, Poudè, Région de la Kara, Togo
🌐 https://vfmat.ch/2611

Healthcare Facility

Tunisia

The Republic of Tunisia, in North Africa, is bordered by Algeria, Libya, and the Mediterranean Sea. Geographically diverse, Tunisia is home to part of the Atlas Mountain range as well as the Sahara Desert. The city of Cape Angela is located on the coast and is the northernmost point on the African continent, while Tunis is its largest city and also the capital. The population of 11.8 million people is predominantly ethnically Arab and identifies as Sunni Muslim. Arabic is the official language, while French and Berber are also spoken widely throughout the country. As much as 70 percent of the population lives in urban areas, specifically in the northern half of the country. The southern half remains sparsely populated.

Tunisia was a French colony from 1881 until it declared independence in 1957. In 2011, the Tunisian Revolution took place in reaction to the lack of freedom and democracy under the prolonged rule of President Zine El Abidine Ben Ali—an event that ignited the Arab Spring across the region. Despite this political turmoil, Tunisia is one of the few countries in Africa ranking high on the human development index, and has one of the highest GDPs per capita on the African continent. Education is free and mandatory for school-aged children.

Tunisia's national health system provides nearly the entire population with access to quality medical care. Hospitals and clinics contribute to rising health indicators, such as one of the lowest infant mortality rates in Africa. Life expectancy has increased substantially as well and is projected to continue rising. While most people in Tunisia enjoy relatively good health, non-communicable diseases cause the majority of deaths in the country. Leading causes of death include ischemic heart disease, stroke, hypertensive heart disease, chronic kidney disease, Alzheimer's disease, lung cancer, road injuries, lower respiratory infections, COPD, diabetes, and neonatal disorders. The risk factors that contribute most to death and disability include high blood pressure, high body-mass index, high fasting plasma glucose, tobacco use, dietary risks, high LDL, air pollution, kidney dysfunction, malnutrition, non-optimal temperature, and occupational risks.

11.8M

Population

$3,320

GDP Per Capita

77 years

Life Expectancy

↑ Improving

130.3
Doctors/100k

Physician Density

218
Beds/100k

Hospital Bed Density

43
Deaths/100k

Maternal Mortality

Tunisia

Nonprofit Organizations

Africa CDC
Aims to strengthen the capacity and capability of Africa's public health institutions and partnerships to detect and respond quickly and effectively to disease threats and outbreaks, based on data-driven interventions and programs.
Infect Dis, Logist-Op, Pub Health
⊕ https://vfmat.ch/339c

Africa Health Organisation
Leads collaborative efforts among countries in Africa and other partners to promote health equity, combat disease, and improve quality of life.
Logist-Op, Pub Health
⊕ https://vfmat.ch/b1c5

Bill & Melinda Gates Foundation
Focuses on global issues, such as poverty, health, and education, offering the opportunity to dramatically improve the quality of life for billions of people by building partnerships that bring together resources, expertise, and vision to identify issues, find answers, and drive change.
All-Immu, General, Infect Dis, MF Med, Neonat, OB-GYN, Pub Health
⊕ https://vfmat.ch/7cf2

Breast Cancer Support
Aims to save lives and end breast cancer forever in women and men through education, treatment, emotional assistance, and financial support.
Heme-Onc, Logist-Op, Pub Health, Rad-Onc, Radiol
⊕ https://vfmat.ch/cb78

Cairdeas International Palliative Care Trust
Promotes and facilitates the provision of high-quality palliative care in the developing world, where such care is limited.
Palliative
⊕ https://vfmat.ch/35c4

Carter Center, The
Seeks to prevent and resolve conflicts, enhance freedom and democracy, and improve health, while remaining committed to human rights and the alleviation of human suffering.
Infect Dis, MF Med, Ophth-Opt
⊕ https://vfmat.ch/6556

Children of War Foundation
Delivers access to global health and education to communities affected by poverty, war, natural disaster, climate change, and migration challenges.
ER Med, General, Logist-Op, Peds, Surg
⊕ https://vfmat.ch/de51

Children's Surgery International
Provides free medical and surgical services to children in need around the world, and instructs and trains local surgeons and other medical providers such as doctors, anesthesiologists, nurses, and technicians.

Anesth, Dent-OMFS, Ortho, Ped Surg, Peds, Plast, Surg
⊕ https://vfmat.ch/26d3

Christian Aid Ministries
Strives to be a trustworthy and efficient channel for Amish, Mennonite, and other conservative Anabaptist groups and individuals to minister to physical and spiritual needs around the world.
CT Surg, ER Med, Logist-Op, Ortho, Pub Health
⊕ https://vfmat.ch/7b33

Direct Relief
Improves the health and lives of people affected by poverty or emergency situations by mobilizing and providing essential medical resources needed for their care.
ER Med, Logist-Op
⊕ https://vfmat.ch/58e5

Global Ministries – The United Methodist Church
As the worldwide mission and development agency of The United Methodist Church, Global Ministries works with more than 300 hospitals and clinics around the world through its Global Health Unit.
Anesth, CT Surg, CV Med, Crit-Care, Dent-OMFS, Derm, ER Med, GI, General, Infect Dis, Logist-Op, MF Med, Medicine, Neonat, Nephro, Nutr, OB-GYN, Ophth-Opt, Ortho, Palliative, Peds, Pod, Psych, Pub Health, Rehab, Rheum, Surg, Urol
⊕ https://vfmat.ch/1723

Global Oncology (GO)
Brings the best in cancer care to underserved patients around the world and collaborates across geographic, professional, and academic borders to improve cancer care, research, and education.
Heme-Onc, Path, Rad-Onc
⊕ https://vfmat.ch/fcb8

Hospice Africa
Aims to provide a holistic and culturally sensitive palliative care service through accurate treatment of pain.
Palliative
⊕ https://vfmat.ch/9f86

HumaniTerra
Helps countries and populations emerging from economic and human crisis to rebuild their healthcare system in a sustainable way. Committed to three fundamental and complementary actions: operating, training, and rebuilding.
Anesth, ENT, ER Med, MF Med, OB-GYN, Ortho, Plast, Surg
⊕ https://vfmat.ch/b371

Humanity & Inclusion
Works alongside people with disabilities and vulnerable populations, taking action and bearing witness in order to respond to their essential needs, improve their living conditions and health, and promote respect for their dignity and

fundamental rights.
General, Infect Dis, MF Med, Medicine, Ortho, Peds, Psych, Pub Health, Rehab
⊕ https://vfmat.ch/16b7

Humanity First
Provides aid and assistance to those in need, offering sustainable development solutions to society while providing and empowering local communities with the resources to help themselves.
ER Med, General, MF Med, Ophth-Opt
⊕ https://vfmat.ch/13cc

International Federation of Gynecology and Obstetrics (FIGO)
Implements global projects on specific women's health issues.
MF Med, Medicine, Neonat, OB-GYN, Surg, Urol
⊕ https://vfmat.ch/c4b4

International Federation of Red Cross and Red Crescent Societies (IFRC)
Coordinates and directs international assistance following natural and manmade disasters in nonconflict situations through the world's largest humanitarian and development network. Provides disaster-preparedness programs, healthcare activities, and promotes humanitarian values.
ER Med, General, Infect Dis, Nutr
⊕ https://vfmat.ch/b4ee

International Organization for Migration (IOM) – The UN Migration Agency
Promotes evidence-informed policies and holistic, preventive, and curative health programs that are beneficial, accessible, and equitable for vulnerable migrants.
General, Infect Dis, OB-GYN
⊕ https://vfmat.ch/621a

International Planned Parenthood Federation (IPPF)
Leads a locally owned, globally connected civil society movement that provides and enables services and champions sexual and reproductive health and rights for all, especially the underserved.
Infect Dis, MF Med, OB-GYN
⊕ https://vfmat.ch/dc97

Maghreb-American Health Foundation
Promotes education around health equity, the prevention of birth defects, and improvement in quality of life for people of the Maghreb region of North Africa.
Anesth, CV Med, Neurosurg, Ped Surg, Radiol, Surg, Urol
⊕ https://vfmat.ch/b3bd

Medical Care Development International
Works to improve the health of vulnerable populations through integrated, sustainable, and locally driven interventions.
Infect Dis, OB-GYN, Peds, Pub Health
⊕ https://vfmat.ch/da87

Médecins du Monde/Doctors of the World
Provides care, bears witness, and supports social change worldwide with innovative medical programs and evidence-based advocacy initiatives.
ER Med, General, Infect Dis, MF Med, Neonat, OB-GYN, Peds, Pub Health
⊕ https://vfmat.ch/a43d

Physicians Across Continents
Provides high-quality medical care to people affected by crises and disasters.
CV Med, Dent-OMFS, Heme-Onc, MF Med, Nephro, Nephro, OB-GYN, Ped Surg, Plast, Surg
⊕ https://vfmat.ch/fe5d

Rotary International
Provides service to others, improves lives, and advances world understanding, goodwill, and peace through its fellowship of business, professional, and community leaders.
ER Med, General, Infect Dis, MF Med, OB-GYN
⊕ https://vfmat.ch/8fb5

Sanofi Espoir Foundation
Contributes to reducing health inequalities among populations that need it most by applying a socially responsible approach focused on fighting childhood cancers

in low-income countries, improving maternal and newborn health, and improving access to care.
ER Med, OB-GYN, Peds
⊕ https://vfmat.ch/943b

Solthis
Improves disease prevention and access to quality care by strengthening the health systems and services of the countries served.
General, Infect Dis, Logist-Op, MF Med, Neonat, Path
⊕ https://vfmat.ch/a71d

SOS Children's Villages International
Supports children through alternative care and family strengthening.
ER Med, Peds
⊕ https://vfmat.ch/aca1

Task Force for Global Health, The
Consists of programs and focus areas that cover a range of global health issues including neglected tropical diseases, infectious diseases, vaccines, field epidemiology, public health informatics, health workforce development, and global health ethics.
Infect Dis, Logist-Op, Medicine, Ophth-Opt, Peds
⊕ https://vfmat.ch/714c

Terre des hommes (Tdh) Foundation
Works to improve the daily life of children and their relatives in the areas of health, protection and emergency, in Europe, Africa, Asia, Latin America, and the Near and Middle East.
CT Surg, CV Med, OB-GYN, Ped Surg, Pub Health
⊕ https://vfmat.ch/5c26

Union for International Cancer Control (UICC)
Unites and supports the cancer community to reduce the global cancer burden, promote greater equity, and ensure that cancer control continues to be a priority in the world health and development agenda.
Heme-Onc, Pub Health
⊕ https://vfmat.ch/88b1

United Nations Children's Fund (UNICEF)
Works in over 190 countries and territories to save children's lives, defend their rights, and help them fulfill their potential, from early childhood through adolescence.
All-Immu, Infect Dis, MF Med, Neonat, Nutr, OB-GYN, Ped Surg, Peds, Pub Health
⊕ https://vfmat.ch/42d7

United Nations Development Programme (UNDP)
Helps countries achieve the simultaneous eradication of extreme poverty and significant reduction of inequalities and exclusion using a sustainable human development approach.
Infect Dis, Logist-Op, Pub Health
⊕ https://vfmat.ch/935c

United Nations High Commissioner for Refugees (UNHCR)
Safeguards the rights and well-being of people who have been forced to flee, ensuring that everybody has the right to seek asylum and find safe refuge in another country, with the goal of seeking lasting solutions.
General, MF Med, Medicine, OB-GYN, Peds, Psych, Pub Health
⊕ https://vfmat.ch/6636

United Nations Population Fund (UNFPA)
Supports reproductive healthcare for women and youth in more than 150 countries, focusing on delivering a world in which every pregnancy is wanted, every childbirth is safe, and every young person's potential is fulfilled.
Infect Dis, MF Med, Neonat, OB-GYN, Peds, Pub Health
⊕ https://vfmat.ch/c969

We Care for Humanity (WCH)
Promotes sustainable social change and the sustainable development goals developed by the United Nations, including: no poverty, good health and well-being, gender equality, human rights, climate action, and strong institutions.
General, Logist-Op, Pub Health
⊕ https://vfmat.ch/8b4e

World Federation of Hemophilia (WFH)
Aims to improve and sustain care for people with inherited bleeding disorders by pursuing long-term relationships with individuals and organizations who share the values of WFH's development model.
Heme-Onc
⊕ https://vfmat.ch/5121

World Health Organization, The (WHO)
The United Nations' agency for health provides leadership on global health matters, shapes the health research agenda, sets norms and standards, articulates evidence-based policy options, provides technical support and monitoring to countries, and assesses health trends.
ER Med, General, Infect Dis, Logist-Op, MF Med, OB-GYN, Peds, Psych, Pub Health
⊕ https://vfmat.ch/c476

World Medical Relief
Facilitates the distribution of surplus medical resources where they are needed.
Logist-Op
⊕ https://vfmat.ch/72dc

Tunisia

Healthcare Facilities

Bou Salem Hospital
Bou Salem, Jendouba, Tunisia
⊕ https://vfmat.ch/26a9

Centre d'Enfants Bourguiba
Tunis, Tunis, Tunisia
⊕ https://vfmat.ch/c2bd

Centre International Carthage Médical
Monastir, Monastir, Tunisia
⊕ https://vfmat.ch/kabt

Clinique Amen Bizerte
Bizerte, Tunisia
⊕ https://vfmat.ch/zbdc

Clinique Amen Nabeul
Nabuel, Tunisia
⊕ https://vfmat.ch/5naa

Clinique Soukra
Ariana, Tunisia
https://vfmat.ch/bl8s

El Manar Clinic
Tunis, Tunisia
https://vfmat.ch/ttkd

Hannibal International Clinic
Tunis, Tunisia
https://vfmat.ch/ampr

Hedi Raies d'institut de Tunis is Ophtalmologie
Bir Atig, Tūnis, Tunisia
⊕ https://vfmat.ch/1844

Hospital des Forces de Securité Interieures (F.S.I)
Ben Achour, Tūnis, Tunisia
⊕ https://vfmat.ch/1fd8

Hospital Habib Bourguiba De Sfax
Sfax, Ṣafāqis, Tunisia
⊕ https://vfmat.ch/9dc2

Hospital Rabta
Tunis, Tunis, Tunisia
⊕ https://vfmat.ch/a13c

Hôpital Charles Nicolle
Bir Atig, Tūnis, Tunisia
⊕ https://vfmat.ch/1975

Hôpital Circonscription Fattouma Limam – Menzel Bouzelfa
Mennzel Bou Zelfa, Nābul, Tunisia
⊕ https://vfmat.ch/8be5

Hôpital d'Enfants Regueb
Regueb, Sidi Bou Zid, Tunisia
⊕ https://vfmat.ch/86e1

Hôpital de Korba
Korba, Nābul, Tunisia
⊕ https://vfmat.ch/12e2

Hôpital De Mareth
Mareth, Qābis, Tunisia
⊕ https://vfmat.ch/f496

Hôpital Habib Thameur
Tunis, Tunisia
⊕ https://vfmat.ch/13c8

Hôpital Hédi Chaker
Sfax, Sfax, Tunisia
⊕ https://vfmat.ch/446c

Hôpital Infantil Bèchir Hamza
Bir Atig, Tūnis, Tunisia
⊕ https://vfmat.ch/fe26

Hôpital Maternité Bizerte
Bizerte, Bizerte, Tunisia
⊕ https://vfmat.ch/3e69

Hôpital Midoun
El Mgarsa, Madanīn, Tunisia
⊕ https://vfmat.ch/8d7f

Hôpital Militaire de Gabès
Sidi Boulbaba, Qābis, Tunisia
⊕ https://vfmat.ch/7bc5

Hôpital Mongi Slim
Dar Jeziri, Tūnis, Tunisia
⊕ https://vfmat.ch/7d7e

Hôpital Régional de Ben Arous
Ben Arous, Ben Arous, Tunisia
⊕ https://vfmat.ch/1484

Hôpital Régional de Degache
Degache, Tawzar, Tunisia
⊕ https://vfmat.ch/b641

Hôpital Régional de Kheireddine
Kheireddine, Tūnis, Tunisia
⊕ https://vfmat.ch/aded

Hôpital Régional de Medjez el Bab
Medjez el Bab, Béja, Tunisia
⊕ https://vfmat.ch/71b7

Hôpital Régional de Metlaoui
Metlaoui, Gafsa, Tunisia
⊕ https://vfmat.ch/f274

Hôpital Régional de Tataouine
Ksar Chouline, Tataouine, Tunisia
⊕ https://vfmat.ch/886d

Hôpital Régional Dr. Mohamed Ben Salah
Moknine, Al Munastīr, Tunisia
⊕ https://vfmat.ch/9492

Hôpital Universitaire Sahloul
Sousse, Sousse, Tunisia
⊕ https://vfmat.ch/12d4

Institut National de Neurologie Mongi-Ben Hamida
Tunis, Tunis, Tunisia
⊕ https://vfmat.ch/45c9

La Clinique Méditerranéenne
Tunis, Tunisia
⊕ https://vfmat.ch/4lmw

Polyclinique Jasmine
Tunis, Tunisia
https://vfmat.ch/7fma

University Hospital Tahar Sfar
Mahdia, Tunisia
⊕ https://vfmat.ch/wpcb

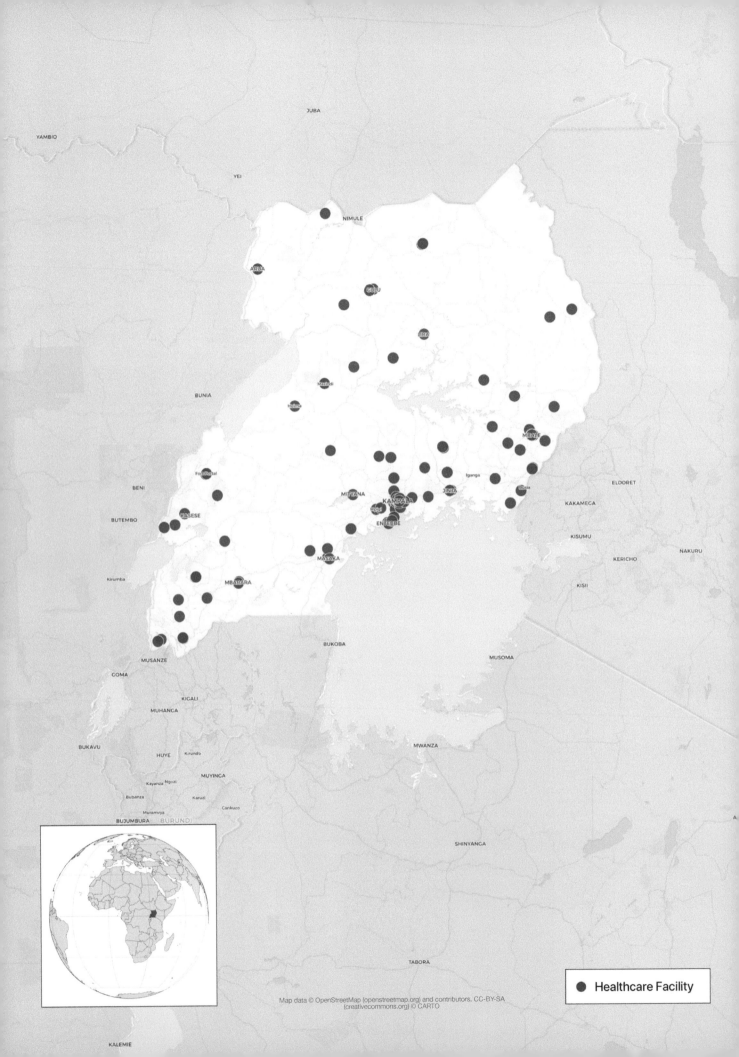

Map data © OpenStreetMap (openstreetmap.org) and contributors, CC-BY-SA
(creativecommons.org) © CARTO

● Healthcare Facility

Uganda

The Republic of Uganda, landlocked in East-Central Africa, has a large and burgeoning population of about 44.7 million people. The population density of Uganda is high relative to other African countries, and many people live in the capital city of Kampala, in the central and southern regions, and along the shorelines of Lake Albert and Lake Victoria. English is the official language, with Swahili also widely spoken. This scenic nation is known for Lake Victoria, the largest lake in Africa.

After the country won its independence from Britain in 1962, Uganda experienced a period of political instability and violence, but things have improved significantly since the 1980s. Poverty was reduced by half between 1992 and 2013, mainly due to the growth and development of the agriculture sector, which now employs as much as 70 percent of Ugandans. The country's population is one of the youngest and most rapidly increasing in the world. This is fueled by a high fertility rate—5.8 children per woman. However, Uganda faces specific challenges when it comes to its economy, education, livelihood, and especially health.

Uganda has some of the highest maternal mortality rates in the world, and one-third of children under five are stunted due to malnutrition. However, the Ugandan government has significantly improved the country's health infrastructure, supplies, and training. The result: A decrease in the under-five mortality rate—from about 162 deaths down to 58 deaths per 1,000 live births between 1990 and 2019—and an overall improvement in life expectancy. While improvements have been made to health, diseases such as neonatal disorders, malaria, HIV/AIDS, lower respiratory infections, tuberculosis, stroke, diarrheal diseases, ischemic heart disease, congenital defects, and meningitis cause the most deaths in the country. Notably, sexually transmitted infections are also a top cause of death in Uganda, and have increased over time.

44.7M

Population

$817

GDP Per Capita

63 years

Life Expectancy

↑ Improving

17
Doctors/100k

Physician Density

50
Beds/100k

Hospital Bed Density

375
Deaths/100k

Maternal Mortality

Uganda

Nonprofit Organizations

100X Development Foundation
Empowers children and families for a more hopeful and productive future through the support and care of orphaned children, education and job training for those in need, help for vulnerable youth to escape trafficking, and healthy nutrition and medical care for mothers to enable a safe birth.
ER Med, Infect Dis, OB-GYN, Peds, Psych
⊕ https://vfmat.ch/b629

143 LIFE Foundation
Seeks to educate and empower individuals living with malaria, TB, HIV/AIDS, STDs and other health disparities related to sexual health.
Infect Dis, MF Med
⊕ https://vfmat.ch/d59b

1789 Fund, The
Promotes gender equality worldwide through investment in the economic empowerment of women and the health of mothers and newborns.
MF Med, Neonat, OB-GYN
⊕ https://vfmat.ch/7145

A Broader View Volunteers
Provides developing countries around the world with significant volunteer programs that aid the neediest communities and forge a lasting bond between those volunteering and those they have helped.
Dent-OMFS, ER Med, Infect Dis, MF Med
⊕ https://vfmat.ch/3bec

A Leg To Stand On (ALTSO)
Provides free, high-quality prosthetic limbs, orthotic devices, and wheelchairs to children with untreated limb disabilities in the developing world.
Logist-Op, Ortho
⊕ https://vfmat.ch/a48d

A Reason to Smile (ARTS)
Empowers communities without access to dental professionals to achieve and maintain a higher level of oral health by providing hygiene education, direct treatment, and dental supplies.
Dent-OMFS
⊕ https://vfmat.ch/3bae

A Stitch in Time
Seeks to address socially crippling but readily treatable conditions, such as genital prolapse in women who lack access, by providing technically advanced pelvic reconstructive surgery, free of charge, to restore women's bodies in geographically or access remote areas of the world.
Anesth, OB-GYN
⊕ https://vfmat.ch/6474

Abaana Community Outreach- Africa
Creates sustainable socioeconomic changes capable of generating lasting

impacts on communities affected by deprivation, with women and children as key target groups.
Infect Dis, Pub Health
⊕ https://vfmat.ch/fb55

Abalon Trust
Provides ophthalmic eye services in developing countries.
Ophth-Opt
⊕ https://vfmat.ch/d7ed

Abt Associates
Seeks to improve the quality of life and economic well-being of people worldwide, while striving to meet and exceed the highest professional standards.
General, Logist-Op, MF Med, OB-GYN, Peds
⊕ https://vfmat.ch/cec2

Accomplish Children's Trust
Provides education and medical care to children with disabilities. Also addresses the financial implications of caring for a child with disabilities by helping families to earn an income.
Neuro, Peds, Rehab
⊕ https://vfmat.ch/de84

Action Against Hunger
Aims to end life-threatening hunger for good through treating and preventing malnutrition across more than 45 countries.
Nutr
⊕ https://vfmat.ch/2dbc

Adara Group
Seeks to bridge the world of business with people in extreme poverty, and to support vulnerable communities with health, education, and other essential services.
General, MF Med, Neonat, OB-GYN, Ped Surg, Peds
⊕ https://vfmat.ch/c8b4

Advance Family Planning
Aims to achieve global expansion and access to quality contraceptive information, services, and supplies through financial investment and political commitment.
General, MF Med, Pub Health
⊕ https://vfmat.ch/7478

Africa CDC
Aims to strengthen the capacity and capability of Africa's public health institutions and partnerships to detect and respond quickly and effectively to disease threats and outbreaks, based on data-driven interventions and programs.
Infect Dis, Logist-Op, Pub Health
⊕ https://vfmat.ch/339c

Africa Health Organisation

Leads collaborative efforts among countries in Africa and other partners to promote health equity, combat disease, and improve quality of life.

Logist-Op, Pub Health

⊕ https://vfmat.ch/b1c5

Africa Humanitarian Action (AHA)

Responds to crises, conflicts, and disasters in Africa, while informing and advising the international community, governments, civil society, and the private sector on humanitarian issues of concern to Africa. Supports institutional and organizational development efforts.

General, Infect Dis, MF Med, Nutr, OB-GYN

⊕ https://vfmat.ch/3ca2

Africa Inland Mission International

Seeks to establish churches and community development programs including healthcare projects, based in Christian ministry.

Anesth, Dent-OMFS, ER Med, General, MF Med, Medicine, OB-GYN, OB-GYN, Ophth-Opt, Ped Surg, Peds, Rehab

⊕ https://vfmat.ch/f2f6

Africa Relief and Community Development

Provides comprehensive relief and developmental aid to people of the African continent regardless of gender, race, or religion.

Nutr, Pub Health

⊕ https://vfmat.ch/6cd2

African Community Center for Social Sustainability (ACCESS)

Works with vulnerable people in resource-limited settings by providing medical care, education, and economic empowerment to create long-lasting change that entire communities own.

General, Infect Dis, MF Med, Neonat, Peds

⊕ https://vfmat.ch/f9cf

African Field Epidemiology Network (AFENET)

Strengthens field epidemiology and public health laboratory capacity to contribute effectively to addressing epidemics and other major public health problems in Africa.

All-Immu, Infect Dis, Path, Pub Health

⊕ https://vfmat.ch/df2e

African Mission

Aims to fight disease and poverty in Africa by supporting educational and medical projects.

Anesth, General

⊕ https://vfmat.ch/ea31

African Mission Health Foundation

Aims to strengthen African mission hospitals by providing quality, compassionate care for the hurting and forgotten and helping improve Sub-Saharan Africa's health system.

Infect Dis, Neonat, OB-GYN, Peds, Surg

⊕ https://vfmat.ch/5b14

Aga Khan Foundation Canada

Tackles the root causes of poverty, with a special focus on marginalized groups such as women and girls. Programs provide access to education and healthcare, food, and opportunity.

Pub Health

⊕ https://vfmat.ch/7f8b

Against Malaria Foundation

Helps protect people from malaria. Funds anti-malaria nets, specifically long-lasting insecticidal nets (LLINs), and works with distribution partners to ensure they are used. Tracks and reports on net use and malaria case data.

Infect Dis

⊕ https://vfmat.ch/337d

Agatha Foundation, The

Seeks to end poverty and hunger, promote universal education, promote gender equality, reduce child mortality, improve maternal health, and combat HIV/AIDS, malaria, and other diseases.

Infect Dis, Logist-Op, Medicine, OB-GYN, Peds

⊕ https://vfmat.ch/9b26

Age International

Helps older people living in some of the world's poorest places to have improved well-being and be treated with dignity through a variety of programs, including emergency relief and cataract surgery.

ER Med, Geri, Logist-Op, Nutr, Ophth-Opt, Palliative, Pub Health

⊕ https://vfmat.ch/c7e2

AIDS Healthcare Foundation

Provides cutting-edge HIV/AIDS medical care and advocacy to over one million people in 43 countries.

Infect Dis

⊕ https://vfmat.ch/b27c

AIDS Information Centre – Uganda

Provides sustainable, collaborative, and integrated HIV/AIDS and other related health services in Uganda.

Infect Dis, Logist-Op, Pub Health

⊕ https://vfmat.ch/672f

AISPO

Implements international initiatives in the healthcare sector and remains involved in various projects to combat poverty, social injustice, and disease around the world.

All-Immu, ER Med, GI, General, Infect Dis, Logist-Op, MF Med, Neonat, OB-GYN, Peds, Psych, Pub Health, Radiol

⊕ https://vfmat.ch/c9e6

Al Basar International Foundation

Works with local partners to treat preventable blindness, and helps set up sustainable infrastructure so local teams can save sight in their communities.

Ophth-Opt

⊕ https://vfmat.ch/a8b5

Alight

Works closely with refugees, trafficked persons, economic migrants, and other displaced persons to co-design solutions that help them build full and fulfilling lives, with healthcare, clean water, shelter protection, and economic opportunity.

ER Med, General, Infect Dis, MF Med, Neonat, Peds

⊕ https://vfmat.ch/5993

American Academy of Pediatrics

Seeks to attain optimal physical, mental, and social health and well-being for all infants, children, adolescents, and young adults.

Anesth, Crit-Care, Neonat, Ped Surg

⊕ https://vfmat.ch/9633

American Foundation for Children with AIDS

Provides critical comprehensive services to infected and affected HIV-positive children and their caregivers.

Infect Dis, Nutr, Pub Health

⊕ https://vfmat.ch/6258

American International Health Alliance (AIHA)

Strengthens health systems and workforce capacity worldwide through locally driven, peer-to-peer institutional partnerships.

CV Med, ER Med, Infect Dis, Medicine, OB-GYN

⊕ https://vfmat.ch/69fd

Americares

Saves lives and improves health for people affected by poverty or disaster and responds with life-changing medicine, medical supplies, and health programs including domestic and global medical clinics.

All-Immu, ER Med, General, Infect Dis, MF Med, Nutr

⊕ https://vfmat.ch/e567

AMG International

Inspired by theChristian faith, provides children with both food and care in youth development centers and medical help in hospitals, clinics and leprosy centers.

General, Geri, Medicine, Nutr, OB-GYN, Peds, Pub Health

⊕ https://vfmat.ch/cf71

AMREF Flying Doctors
Aims to deliver medical air transport and health services using the latest aviation and medical technology to ensure patients receive unrivaled care.
ER Med, Logist-Op
⊕ https://vfmat.ch/5d5e

Amref Health Africa
Serves millions of people across 35 countries in Sub-Saharan Africa, strengthening health systems, and training African health workers to respond to the continent's most critical health issues.
All-Immu, General, Infect Dis, Logist-Op, MF Med, OB-GYN, Path, Pub Health, Surg
⊕ https://vfmat.ch/6985

Amsterdam Institute for Global Health and Development (AIGHD)
Provides sustainable solutions to major health problems across our planet by forging synergies among disciplines, healthcare delivery, research, and education.
Infect Dis
⊕ https://vfmat.ch/d73d

AO Alliance
Builds solutions to lessen the burden of injuries in low- and middle-income countries, while enhancing the care of the injured to reduce human suffering, disability, and poverty.
Ortho, Surg
⊕ https://vfmat.ch/8cd5

Arms Around Africa Foundation
Supports children, empowers women, and helps young people to overcome poverty through talent promotion, education, good health, life skills development, entrepreneurship, and enhanced access to other resources for social and economic development.
General, Infect Dis, OB-GYN, Peds
⊕ https://vfmat.ch/ad98

Assist International
Designs and implements humanitarian programs that build capacity, develop opportunities, and save lives around the world.
Infect Dis, Ped Surg, Peds
⊕ https://vfmat.ch/9a3b

AYINET – African Youth Initiative Network
Mobilizes and empowers youth and communities in promoting a healthy, peaceful, and just society.
Infect Dis, Psych, Pub Health, Rehab, Surg
⊕ https://vfmat.ch/9bac

Baylor College of Medicine: Global Surgery
Trains leaders in academic global surgery and remains dedicated to advancements in the areas of patient care, biomedical research, and medical education.
ENT, Infect Dis, OB-GYN, Ortho, Ped Surg, Plast, Pub Health, Radiol, Surg, Urol
⊕ https://vfmat.ch/21f5

Baylor International Pediatric AIDS Initiative (BIPAI) at Texas Children's Hospital
Provides high-quality, high-impact, highly ethical pediatric and family-centered healthcare, health professional training, and clinical research focused on HIV/AIDS, tuberculosis, malaria, malnutrition, and other conditions impacting the health of children worldwide.
Infect Dis, Medicine, OB-GYN, Peds, Pub Health, Surg
⊕ https://vfmat.ch/e6ba

Bega Kwa Bega Uganda
Enables communities in Uganda to support their orphans and vulnerable children so they may live in their own homes and on land with their basic needs ensured—and, through education, gain the knowledge and skills needed to become self-sufficient.
General, Infect Dis, Nutr, OB-GYN, Peds, Pub Health
⊕ https://vfmat.ch/a373

Benjamin H. Josephson, MD Fund
Provides healthcare professionals with the financial resources necessary to deliver medical services for those in need throughout the world.
General, OB-GYN
⊕ https://vfmat.ch/6acc

Beta Humanitarian Help
Provides plastic surgery in underserved areas of the world.
Anesth, Plast
⊕ https://vfmat.ch/7221

BethanyKids
Transforms the lives of African children with surgical conditions and disabilities through pediatric surgery, rehabilitation, public education, spiritual ministry, and the training of health professionals.
Neurosurg, Nutr, Ortho, Ped Surg, Peds, Rehab, Surg
⊕ https://vfmat.ch/db4e

Bill & Melinda Gates Foundation
Focuses on global issues, such as poverty, health, and education, offering the opportunity to dramatically improve the quality of life for billions of people by building partnerships that bring together resources, expertise, and vision to identify issues, find answers, and drive change.
All-Immu, General, Infect Dis, MF Med, Neonat, OB-GYN, Pub Health
⊕ https://vfmat.ch/7cf2

Birth With Dignity
Seeks to educate, support, and equip nurses and midwives of Uganda to improve care for patients and families with high-risk perinatal needs, with the goal of decreasing maternal and neonatal deaths, and to care for families with perinatal loss.
MF Med
⊕ https://vfmat.ch/7696

Bless The Children
Aims to help abandoned and impoverished children by empowering them with health, shelter, and nutritional and educational support.
CT Surg, Dent-OMFS, General, Logist-Op, Nutr, Pub Health, Surg
⊕ https://vfmat.ch/f19d

Blessing Foundation, The
Mobilizes resources that promote education, create employment, and enhance healthy living for the underserved and disadvantaged population in Africa.
General, Infect Dis, MF Med, Ophth-Opt
⊕ https://vfmat.ch/89af

Boston Children's Hospital: Global Health Program
Helps solve pediatric global healthcare challenges by transferring expertise through long-term partnerships with scalable impact, while working in the field to strengthen healthcare systems, advocate, research, and provide care delivery or education as a way of sustainably improving the health of children worldwide.
Anesth, CV Med, Crit-Care, ER Med, Heme-Onc, Infect Dis, Medicine, Nutr, Palliative, Ped Surg, Peds
⊕ https://vfmat.ch/f9f8

BRAC USA
Seeks to empower people and communities in situations of poverty, illiteracy, disease, and social injustice. Interventions aim to achieve large-scale, positive changes through economic and social programs that enable everyone to realize their potential.
ER Med, General, Infect Dis, Logist-Op, MF Med, OB-GYN
⊕ https://vfmat.ch/9d9e

Braveheart
Aims to inspire hope and improve the quality of life for people coping with illness, the loss of a loved one, or emotional trauma through ongoing peer-to-peer support.
Dent-OMFS, Infect Dis, Nutr, Peds, Pod
⊕ https://vfmat.ch/8aeb

Brick by Brick
Creates partnerships to improve education, health, and economic opportunity in East Africa.

Neonat, OB-GYN, Peds
⊕ https://vfmat.ch/71c3

Bridge to Health Medical and Dental
Seeks to provide healthcare to those who need it most, based on a philosophy of partnership, education, and community development. Strives to bring solutions to global health issues in underserved communities through clinical outreach and medical and dental training.
Dent-OMFS, General, Infect Dis, MF Med, OB-GYN, Ophth-Opt, Ortho, Pub Health, Radiol
⊕ https://vfmat.ch/bb2c

Brigham and Women's Center for Surgery and Public Health
Advances the science of surgical care delivery by studying effectiveness, quality, equity, and value at the population level, and develops surgeon-scientists committed to excellence in these areas.
Anesth, ER Med, Infect Dis, Pub Health, Surg
⊕ https://vfmat.ch/5d64

Brigham and Women's Hospital Global Health Hub
Cares for patients in underserved settings, provides education to staff who work in those areas to create sustainable change, and conducts research designed to improve health in such settings.
General, Infect Dis
⊕ https://vfmat.ch/a8a3

Bright Eyes Uganda
Cares for the underserved populations of Uganda, specifically children, by improving the infrastructure of rural villages, and providing clean water, nutritional food, accessible healthcare, and quality education.
General, Infect Dis, Nutr, Peds
⊕ https://vfmat.ch/146e

BroadReach
Collaborates with governments, multinational health organizations, donors, and private-sector companies to effect healthcare reform and solve the world's biggest health challenges.
Logist-Op
⊕ https://vfmat.ch/7812

Bulamu Healthcare
Strives to improve the well-being of rural Ugandans by providing affordable access to primary healthcare and related services.
Dent-OMFS, General, Infect Dis, OB-GYN, Ophth-Opt, Ped Surg, Peds
⊕ https://vfmat.ch/df64

Cairdeas International Palliative Care Trust
Promotes and facilitates the provision of high-quality palliative care in the developing world, where such care is limited.
Palliative
⊕ https://vfmat.ch/35c4

Cambridge Global Health Partnerships (CGHP)
Works in partnership to inspire and enable people to improve healthcare globally.
Crit-Care, Dent-OMFS, ER Med, Heme-Onc, Infect Dis, MF Med, Ophth-Opt, Ortho
⊕ https://vfmat.ch/1599

Canada-Africa Community Health Alliance
Sends Canadian volunteer teams on two- to three-week missions to African communities to work hand-in-hand with local partners.
General, Infect Dis, MF Med, OB-GYN, Peds, Surg
⊕ https://vfmat.ch/4c94

Canadian Network for International Surgery, The
Aims to improve maternal health, increase safety, and build local capacity in low-income countries by creating and providing surgical and midwifery courses, training domestically, and transferring skills.
Logist-Op, Surg
⊕ https://vfmat.ch/86ff

CardioStart International
Provides free heart surgery and associated medical care to children and adults

living in underserved regions of the world, irrespective of political or religious affiliation, through the collective skills of healthcare experts.
Anesth, CT Surg, CV Med, Crit-Care, Pub Health, Pulm-Critic
⊕ https://vfmat.ch/85ef

CARE
Works around the globe to save lives, defeat poverty, and achieve social justice.
ER Med, General
⊕ https://vfmat.ch/7232

Care for AIDS
Aims to empower people to live a life beyond AIDS by carrying out programs centered on physical, social, economic, and spiritual support, based in Christian ministry.
Infect Dis, Pub Health
⊕ https://vfmat.ch/79cf

Care for Uganda
Works in Uganda to achieve the United Nations' Sustainable Development Goals by 2030.
Logist-Op, MF Med, Nutr, Surg
⊕ https://vfmat.ch/44e6

Care Old Age & Child Foundation
Works toward empowering orphans and vulnerable children under the direct care of elderly-headed households in the Ssese Islands of Uganda by providing healthcare services and economic education and support.
General, General, Geri, Infect Dis, Palliative, Peds
⊕ https://vfmat.ch/8d36

Caritas Pro Vitae Gradu Charitable Trust
Supports Catholic charitable projects with social and humanitarian efforts, and aims to assist people in need including children, the elderly, sick, and disabled through healthcare, poverty relief, and education.
ER Med, General, Logist-Op, Medicine, OB-GYN, Ophth-Opt, Path, Peds, Pub Health, Radiol, Rehab, Surg
⊕ https://vfmat.ch/b2ca

Carter Center, The
Seeks to prevent and resolve conflicts, enhance freedom and democracy, and improve health, while remaining committed to human rights and the alleviation of human suffering.
Infect Dis, MF Med, Ophth-Opt
⊕ https://vfmat.ch/6556

Catholic Organization for Relief & Development Aid (CORDAID)
Provides humanitarian assistance and creates opportunities to improve security, healthcare, education, and inclusive economic growth in fragile and conflict-affected areas.
ER Med, Infect Dis, MF Med, OB-GYN, Peds, Psych
⊕ https://vfmat.ch/8ae5

Catholic World Mission
Works to rebuild communities worldwide by helping to alleviate poverty and empower underserved areas, while spreading the message of the Catholic Church.
ER Med, General, Nutr, Peds
⊕ https://vfmat.ch/7b5f

Chain of Hope
Provides lifesaving heart operations for children around the world and supports the development of cardiac services in numerous developing and war-torn countries.
Anesth, CT Surg, CV Med, Crit-Care, Ped Surg, Peds, Pulm-Critic, Surg
⊕ https://vfmat.ch/1b1b

Challenge Initiative, The
Seeks to rapidly and sustainably scale up proven reproductive health solutions among the urban poor.
MF Med, OB-GYN, Peds
⊕ https://vfmat.ch/2f77

Cherish Uganda

Focuses on helping Ugandan children with HIV/AIDS by providing healing, hope, and a future.

General, Infect Dis, Logist-Op, MF Med, Peds, Pub Health

⊕ https://vfmat.ch/232c

Child Care Africa

Aims to support vulnerable children in Africa with access to education, healthcare, safety, and counseling.

Ped Surg, Peds

⊕ https://vfmat.ch/9974

Child Care And Youth Empowerment Foundation

Improves the well-being of vulnerable children and youth through education, socio-economic interventions, nutrition, WASH (water, sanitation and hygiene), and primary healthcare.

General, Nutr, OB-GYN, Peds

⊕ https://vfmat.ch/bd62

Child Family Health International (CFHI)

Connects students with local health professionals and community leaders transforming perspectives about self, global health, and healing.

General, Infect Dis, OB-GYN, Ophth-Opt, Palliative, Peds

⊕ https://vfmat.ch/729e

ChildFund Australia

Works to reduce poverty for children in many of the world's most disadvantaged communities.

ER Med, General, Peds

⊕ https://vfmat.ch/13df

Children & Charity International

Puts people first by providing education, leadership, and nutrition programs along with mentoring and healthcare support services to children, youth, and families.

Nutr, Peds

⊕ https://vfmat.ch/6538

Children Care Uganda (CCU)

Provides vulnerable children; disabled children; poor young, single mothers; and jobless youths with hope for a brighter future, encouragement, and support in any medical or educational issue in their daily lives.

General, Infect Dis, Peds

⊕ https://vfmat.ch/a3f8

Children of the Nations

Aims to raise children out of poverty and hopelessness so they can become leaders who transform their nations. Emphasizes caring for the whole child—physically, mentally, socially, and spiritually.

Anesth, Dent-OMFS, General, Surg

⊕ https://vfmat.ch/cc52

Children of Uganda (UK)

Provides educational, vocational, and welfare support, along with infrastructure programs to enhance the health and well-being of children and village communities in Uganda.

General, Peds

⊕ https://vfmat.ch/c341

Children of War Foundation

Delivers access to global health and education to communities affected by poverty, war, natural disaster, climate change, and migration challenges.

ER Med, General, Logist-Op, Peds, Surg

⊕ https://vfmat.ch/de51

Children's Lifeline International

Provides medical teams and surgical assistance to underprivileged children in developing countries through missions in partnership with local hospitals.

CV Med, Dent-OMFS, General, MF Med, Neurosurg, Peds, Rehab

⊕ https://vfmat.ch/6fea

Children's Relief International

Inspired by the Christian faith, cares for and educates children, their families, and their communities, including the provision of select healthcare services.

ER Med, General, Nutr

⊕ https://vfmat.ch/8da6

Christian Aid Ministries

Strives to be a trustworthy and efficient channel for Amish, Mennonite, and other conservative Anabaptist groups and individuals to minister to physical and spiritual needs around the world.

CT Surg, ER Med, Logist-Op, Ortho, Pub Health

⊕ https://vfmat.ch/7b33

Christian Blind Mission (CBM)

Aims to improve the quality of life of persons with disabilities in the poorest countries, addressing poverty as a cause and a consequence of disability, and working in partnership to create a society for all.

ENT, General, Infect Dis, OB-GYN, Ophth-Opt, Ortho, Peds, Psych, Rehab, Surg

⊕ https://vfmat.ch/3824

Christian Connections for International Health (CCIH)

Promotes global health and wholeness from a Christian perspective.

All-Immu, General, Infect Dis, MF Med, Neonat, OB-GYN, Psych

⊕ https://vfmat.ch/fa5d

Christian Health Service Corps

Brings Christian doctors, health professionals, and health educators committed to serving the poor to places that otherwise have little or no access to healthcare.

Anesth, Dent-OMFS, General, Medicine, Peds, Surg

⊕ https://vfmat.ch/da57

Cleft Africa

Strives to provide underserved Africans with cleft lips and palates with access to the best possible treatment for their condition, so that they can live a life free of the health problems caused by cleft.

Anesth, Dent-OMFS, Ped Surg, Surg

⊕ https://vfmat.ch/8298

Clinton Health Access Initiative (CHAI)

Aims to save lives and reduce the burden of disease in low- and middle-income countries. Works with partners to strengthen the capabilities of governments and the private sector to create and sustain high-quality health systems.

General, Heme-Onc, Infect Dis, Logist-Op, MF Med, Medicine, Neonat, Nutr, OB-GYN, Path, Peds, Rad-Onc

⊕ https://vfmat.ch/9ed7

Columbia University: Global Mental Health Programs

Pioneers research initiatives, promotes mental health, and aims to reduce the burden of mental illness worldwide.

Psych

⊕ https://vfmat.ch/c5cd

Columbia Vagelos College of Physicians and Surgeons Programs in Global Health

Harnesses the expertise of the medical school to improve health worldwide by training global health leaders, building capacity through interdisciplinary education and training programs, and addressing unmet health needs through research and application.

CV Med, Derm, Genetics, Heme-Onc, Infect Dis, Medicine, OB-GYN, Ophth-Opt, Peds, Psych, Pub Health, Pulm-Critic, Surg

⊕ https://vfmat.ch/a9e5

Comitato Collaborazione Medica (CCM)

Supports development processes that safeguard and promote the right to health with a global approach, working on health needs and influencing socio-economic factors, identifying poverty as the main cause for the lack of health.

All-Immu, General, Infect Dis, MF Med, OB-GYN

⊕ https://vfmat.ch/4272

Confident Children Out of Conflict

Provides vulnerable children with a safe space to sleep, eat, learn, and play to help them develop into young adults, fulfilling their potential, and supports households to develop a protective environment for safe reintegration of these children into communities.

All-Immu, General, Peds, Psych

⊕ https://vfmat.ch/daf7

ConnectMed International
Improves access to sustainable healthcare in resource-limited communities through education, partnership, and research.
Dent-OMFS, Logist-Op, Ped Surg, Plast
⊕ https://vfmat.ch/ce88

Core Group
Aims to improve and expand community health practices for underserved populations, especially women and children, through collaborative action and learning.
General, Infect Dis, MF Med, Medicine, OB-GYN, Peds, Pub Health
⊕ https://vfmat.ch/9de3

Cornerstone Education and Research
Seeks to provide the local and global community with medical research and education in orthopedic care, expand medical research in the development of innovative technologies, and provide physician and community education.
Ortho
⊕ https://vfmat.ch/f549

COVID-19 Clinical Research Coalition
Advocates and collaborates for the advancement of COVID-19 research driven by the needs of low-resource settings, and works for equitable access to solutions to the pandemic.
All-Immu, Infect-Dis, MF Med, Path, Pub Health
⊕ https://vfmat.ch/d1f4

Cross Catholic Outreach
Mobilizes the global Catholic Church to transform impoverished communities through the provision of food, water, housing, education, orphan support, medical care, microenterprise, and disaster relief.
All-Immu, General, Nutr, OB-GYN, Rehab
⊕ https://vfmat.ch/22f4

Cura for the World
Seeks to heal, nourish, and embrace the neglected by building medical clinics in remote communities in dire need of medical care.
ER Med, General, Peds
⊕ https://vfmat.ch/c55f

CURE
Operates charitable hospitals and programs in underserved countries worldwide, where patients receive surgical treatment, based in Christian ministry.
Anesth, Neurosurg, Ortho, Ped Surg, Peds, Rehab, Surg
⊕ https://vfmat.ch/aa16

CURE Children's Hospital of Zimbabwe
Heals children living with disabilities such as clubfoot, bowed legs, cleft lips, untreated burns, and hydrocephalus.
ENT, Neurosurg, Ortho, Peds, Plast
⊕ https://vfmat.ch/473c

Delight Children's Health Rights Initiative
Seeks to ensure that children born with congenital disorders survive and live a meaningful life; supports families, communities, and rural healthcare facilities and professionals.
Nutr, OB-GYN, Peds
⊕ https://vfmat.ch/bb71

Dentaid
Seeks to treat, equip, train, and educate people in need of dental care.
Dent-OMFS
⊕ https://vfmat.ch/a183

Dental Hope for Children
Seeks to provide dental services to children in underserved areas, based in Christian ministry.
Dent-OMFS
⊕ https://vfmat.ch/1426

Direct Relief
Improves the health and lives of people affected by poverty or emergency situations by mobilizing and providing essential medical resources needed for their care.
ER Med, Logist-Op
⊕ https://vfmat.ch/58e5

Direct Relief of Poverty & Sickness Foundation (DROPS)
This volunteer-led organization uses all donations for direct relief of poverty and illness through initiatives in healthcare education, improving healthcare systems, and providing essential medical help to children and aged people in need.
Dent-OMFS, General, Ophth-Opt
⊕ https://vfmat.ch/af95

DKT INTERNATIONAL INC
Seeks to provide couples with affordable and safe options for family planning and HIV/AIDS prevention through dynamic social marketing.
General, Surg
⊕ https://vfmat.ch/b3a7

Doctors with Africa (CUAMM)
Advocates for the universal right to health and promotes the values of international solidarity, justice, and peace. Works to protect and improve the well-being and health of vulnerable communities in Africa with a long-term development perspective.
ER Med, Infect Dis, MF Med, Neonat, OB-GYN, Peds
⊕ https://vfmat.ch/d2fb

Doctors Without Borders/Médecins Sans Frontières (MSF)
Responds to emergencies and provides lifesaving medical care where needed most, including during disasters, conflicts, and epidemics.
Anesth, Crit-Care, ER Med, General, Infect Dis, Nutr, OB-GYN, Ped Surg, Peds, Psych, Pub Health, Surg
⊕ https://vfmat.ch/f363

Drugs for Neglected Diseases Initiative
Develops lifesaving medicines for people with neglected diseases around the world, having developed eight treatments for five deadly diseases and saved millions of lives since 2003.
Infect Dis, Pub Health
⊕ https://vfmat.ch/969c

Duke Health: Global Neurosurgery and Neurology
Promotes health in low- and middle-income countries through a multi-faceted, evidence-based, and collaborative approach to improve patient access to care and health outcomes, strengthen health systems, and inform policy.
Anesth, Neuro, Neurosurg
⊕ https://vfmat.ch/d9d4

Duke University School of Medicine: Global Pediatric Surgery
Engages in active partnerships in Guatemala and Uganda that include capacity building, research, and service initiatives to address global surgical needs.
Anesth, Heme-Onc, Logist-Op, Ped Surg, Peds
⊕ https://vfmat.ch/2d75

Duke University: Global Health Institute
Sparks innovation in global health research and education, and brings together knowledge and resources to address the most important global health issues of our time.
All-Immu, Infect Dis, MF Med, OB-GYN, Pub Health
⊕ https://vfmat.ch/c4cd

Elizabeth Glaser Pediatric AIDS Foundation
Seeks to end global pediatric HIV/AIDS through prevention and treatment programs, research, and advocacy.
Infect Dis, Nutr, OB-GYN, Peds
⊕ https://vfmat.ch/d6ec

Elton John AIDS Foundation
Seeks to address and overcome the stigma, discrimination, and neglect that prevents ending AIDS by funding local experts to challenge discrimination, prevent infections, and provide treatment.
Infect Dis, Pub Health
⊕ https://vfmat.ch/9d31

EMERGENCY

Provides free, high-quality healthcare to victims of war, poverty, and landmines. Also builds hospitals and trains local staff, while pursuing medicine based on human rights.

ER Med, Neonat, OB-GYN, Ophth-Opt, Ped Surg

⊕ https://vfmat.ch/c361

Empower Through Health

Aims to improve healthcare access to the world's most vulnerable by providing direct evidence-based medical care, helping build local healthcare capacity and addressing root causes of poor health outcomes with the full participation of communities.

GI, General, Infect Dis, OB-GYN, Path, Peds, Pub Health, Radiol

⊕ https://vfmat.ch/68ff

Enabel

As the development agency of the Belgian federal government, charged with implementing Belgium's international development policy, carries out public service assignments in Belgium and abroad pursuant to the 2030 Agenda for Sustainable Development.

General, Infect Dis, Logist-Op, MF Med, OB-GYN, Peds, Pub Health

⊕ https://vfmat.ch/5af7

Engage Now Africa

Works to heal, rescue, and lift vulnerable individuals, families and communities of Africa out of extreme poverty and into self-reliance.

General, Ophth-Opt, Peds, Pub Health

⊕ https://vfmat.ch/16cd

EngenderHealth

Works to implement high-quality, gender-equitable programs that advance sexual and reproductive health and rights.

General, MF Med, OB-GYN, Peds

⊕ https://vfmat.ch/1cb2

Engeye

Empowers the people of Ddegeya Village in rural Uganda by supporting healthcare, education, and community development initiatives.

General, MF Med, Neonat, OB-GYN, Peds

⊕ https://vfmat.ch/6b8d

eRanger

Provides sustainable solutions to transportation and medical provision such as ambulances and mobile clinics in developing countries.

ER Med, General, Logist-Op

⊕ https://vfmat.ch/4c18

Evidence Action

Aims to be a world leader in scaling evidence-based and cost-effective programs to reduce the burden of poverty.

General, Infect Dis

⊕ https://vfmat.ch/94b6

Evidence Project, The

Improves family-planning policies, programs, and practices through the strategic generation, translation, and use of evidence.

General, MF Med

⊕ https://vfmat.ch/f9e7

Eye Health Uganda

Provides and supports quality eye healthcare services to mitigate preventable blindness as a means to empower individuals and communities.

Ophth-Opt

⊕ https://vfmat.ch/8cfc

Fertility Education & Medical Management (FEMM)

Aims to make knowledge-based reproductive health accessible to all women and enables them to be informed partners in the choice and delivery of their medical care and services.

MF Med, OB-GYN

⊕ https://vfmat.ch/e8b2

Finn Church Aid

Supports people in the most vulnerable situations within fragile and disaster-affected regions in three thematic priority areas: right to peace, livelihood, and education.

ER Med, Psych, Pub Health

⊕ https://vfmat.ch/9623

Fistula Foundation

Aims to engage the support of people worldwide who are eager to see the day that no woman suffers from obstetric fistula. Raises and directs funds to doctors and hospitals providing life-transforming surgery to women in need.

OB-GYN

⊕ https://vfmat.ch/e958

Fondation d'Harcourt

Promotes national and international projects and partnerships in the fields of mental health and psychosocial support; provides grants to organizations with specific expertise in mental health or psychosocial support to implement projects; and provides direct services.

Psych, Pub Health

⊕ https://vfmat.ch/4a8a

Fondazione Corti Onlus

Provides medical screening for children with congenital heart defects and helps establish pediatric cardiac care wherever there is need, inspired by the Christian faith.

All-Immu, Anesth, General, Infect Dis, Ortho, Peds, Surg

⊕ https://vfmat.ch/4a3b

Forgotten International, The

Develops programs that alleviate poverty and the suffering of impoverished women and children in both the United States and worldwide.

Logist-Op, Nutr, OB-GYN, Peds, Pub Health

⊕ https://vfmat.ch/26f3

Foundation for International Medical Relief of Children (FIMRC)

Provides access to healthcare for low-resource and medically underserved families around the world.

General, Infect Dis, Peds, Pub Health

⊕ https://vfmat.ch/78b9

Friends of East Africa Foundation

Provides high-quality, comprehensive, and affordable medical services to all who need them by funding the Ruth Gaylord Hospital Maganjo in Kampala, Uganda.

Dent-OMFS, Infect Dis, MF Med, Neonat, OB-GYN, Ophth-Opt, Peds, Surg

⊕ https://vfmat.ch/9315

Gift of Life International

Provides lifesaving cardiac treatment to children in developing countries while developing sustainable pediatric cardiac programs by implementing screening, surgical, and training missions.

Anesth, CT Surg, CV Med, Crit-Care, Ped Surg, Peds, Pulm-Critic

⊕ https://vfmat.ch/f2f9

GIVE International

Partners with local organizations on projects that focus on healthcare, child and youth development, education, and sustainable development.

General, Infect Dis, MF Med

⊕ https://vfmat.ch/58d3

Give Us Wings

Supports people in poverty as they transform their lives and become self-sufficient through access to healthcare, education, and economic opportunities.

General, Logist-Op

⊕ https://vfmat.ch/9483

Global Alliance to Prevent Prematurity And Stillbirth (GAPPS)

Seeks to improve birth outcomes worldwide by reducing the burden of premature birth and stillbirth.

All-Immu, Infect Dis, MF Med, Neonat, Neonat, OB-GYN

⊕ https://vfmat.ch/3f74

Global Blood Fund
Delivers grants, equipment, and training to over 50 countries in Africa, Asia, Eastern Europe, the Middle East, Latin America and the Caribbean.
Pub Health
⊕ https://vfmat.ch/6377

Global Emergency Care
Aims to make lifesaving medical care available to all by training nonphysician clinicians in emergency medicine to increase the availability of highly trained providers in areas where there are none.
ER Med, General, Radiol
⊕ https://vfmat.ch/1fad

Global Force for Healing
Works to end preventable maternal and newborn deaths by supporting the scaling of effective grassroots, community-led, culturally respectful care and education in underserved areas around the globe using the midwifery model of care.
Neonat, OB-GYN
⊕ https://vfmat.ch/deb2

Global Health Corps
Mobilizes a diverse community of leaders to build the movement for global health equity, working toward a world in which every person lives a healthy life.
ER Med, General, Pub Health
⊕ https://vfmat.ch/31c6

Global Health Network
Promotes, protects, and preserves the health of all Ugandans through good leadership, public-private partnerships, innovation, and concerted action in primary healthcare and reproductive health.
General, Infect Dis, MF Med, OB-GYN, Peds
⊕ https://vfmat.ch/f84c

Global Medical and Surgical Teams
Provides cleft lip and palate surgery for patients in underserved areas by providing surgical care free of charge to children with cleft lip and palate deformities. Works through medical and surgical missions, education, training, technology, and donor relationships to provide specialized medical and surgical care.
Anesth, Dent-OMFS, ENT, Ped Surg, Plast, Surg
⊕ https://vfmat.ch/6d3e

Global Ministries – The United Methodist Church
As the worldwide mission and development agency of The United Methodist Church, Global Ministries works with more than 300 hospitals and clinics around the world through its Global Health Unit.
Anesth, CT Surg, CV Med, Crit-Carc, Dent-OMFS, Derm, ER Med, GI, General, Infect Dis, Logist-Op, MF Med, Medicine, Neonat, Nephro, Nutr, OB-GYN, Ophth-Opt, Ortho, Palliative, Peds, Pod, Psych, Pub Health, Rehab, Rheum, Surg, Urol
⊕ https://vfmat.ch/1723

Global Oncology (GO)
Brings the best in cancer care to underserved patients around the world and collaborates across geographic, professional, and academic borders to improve cancer care, research, and education.
Heme-Onc, Path, Rad-Onc
⊕ https://vfmat.ch/fcb8

Global Strategies
Empowers communities in the most neglected areas of the world to improve the lives of women and children through healthcare.
MF Med, Neonat, OB-GYN, Peds
⊕ https://vfmat.ch/ef92

Global Telehealth Network (GTN)
Provides telehealth services with dedicated physician volunteers for people located in medically underserved areas, including low- and medium-resource countries, refugee camps, conflict zones, and disaster areas, and also in the U.S.
ER Med, General, Path, Peds, Psych, Radiol, Surg
⊕ https://vfmat.ch/4345

Globus Relief
Aims to improve the delivery of healthcare worldwide by gathering, processing, and distributing surplus medical supplies to charities at home and abroad.

Logist-Op
⊕ https://vfmat.ch/a2b7

GOAL
Works with the most vulnerable communities to help them respond to and recover from humanitarian crises, and to assist them in building transcendent solutions to mitigate poverty and vulnerability.
ER Med, General, Pub Health
⊕ https://vfmat.ch/bbea

Grassroot Soccer
Leverages the power of soccer to educate, inspire, and mobilize at-risk youth in developing countries to overcome their greatest health challenges, live healthier and more productive lives, and be agents for change in their communities.
Infect Dis
⊕ https://vfmat.ch/3521

Harpenden Spotlight on Africa
Creates links between communities in the UK and Africa through charitable projects relating to education, health, clean water, and economic development.
General, MF Med, Medicine, Neonat, OB-GYN
⊕ https://vfmat.ch/27aa

Harvard Global Health Institute
Devoted to improving global health and pioneering the next generation of global health research, education, policy, and practice, with an evidence-based, innovative, integrative, and collaborative approach, harnessing the unique breadth of excellence within Harvard.
General, Infect Dis, Logist-Op
⊕ https://vfmat.ch/5867

Head and Neck Outreach
Seeks to improve healthcare in developing countries through sustainable education, research, and surgical programs. Aims to develop sustainable healthcare programs to improve head and neck care.
Anesth, ENT, Surg
⊕ https://vfmat.ch/f7b1

Healing Kadi Foundation
Works with the people of South Sudan and Uganda to provide sustainable high-quality healthcare, education for local healthcare providers, and psychological and spiritual counseling.
All-Immu, Dent-OMFS, General, Infect Dis, MF Med, Neonat, OB-GYN, Peds, Psych
⊕ https://vfmat.ch/a7f1

Healing the Children
Helps underserved children around the world secure the medical care they need to lead more fulfilling lives.
Anesth, Dent-OMFS, ENT, General, Medicine, Ophth-Opt, Ped Surg, Peds, Plast, Surg
⊕ https://vfmat.ch/d4ee

Health Equity Initiative
Aims to build and sustain a global community that engages across sectors and disciplines to advance health equity.
Pub Health
⊕ https://vfmat.ch/e2e2

Health Poverty Action
Works in partnership with people around the world who are pursuing change in their own communities to demand health justice and challenge power imbalances.
ER Med, General, Infect Dis, Psych, Pub Health
⊕ https://vfmat.ch/ee58

Health Volunteers Overseas (HVO)
Improves the availability and quality of healthcare through the education, training, and professional development of the health workforce in resource-scarce countries.
All-Immu, Anesth, CV Med, Dent-OMFS, Derm, ENT, ER Med, Endo, GI, Heme-Onc, Infect Dis, Medicine, Medicine, Nephro, Neuro, OB-GYN, Ophth-Opt, Ortho, Peds, Plast, Psych, Pulm-Critic, Rehab, Rheum, Surg
⊕ https://vfmat.ch/42b2

Health[e] Foundation

Supports health professionals and community workers in the world's most vulnerable societies to ensure quality health for everyone in need by providing digital education and information, using e-learning and m-health.

Logist-Op

🌐 https://vfmat.ch/b73b

HealthRight International

Leverages global resources to address local health challenges and create sustainable solutions that empower marginalized communities to live healthy lives.

General, Infect Dis, MF Med, OB-GYN, Psych, Pub Health

🌐 https://vfmat.ch/129d

HealthServe Australia

Develops sustainable health programs that improve health and well-being and partners with community groups to build community capacity to meet health needs.

Infect Dis, Logist-Op, OB-GYN, Psych, Pub Health

🌐 https://vfmat.ch/7276

Healthy Child Uganda

Supports medical training and clinical care and initiates a community-based education project targeting child health.

Logist-Op, Peds

🌐 https://vfmat.ch/ebc5

Heart Healers International

Brings lifesaving heart diagnostics and treatments to children in Africa with the goal that no child with a treatable heart will be left behind. Works alongside local medical teams in caring for patients, conducting ongoing research, and providing education, including telemedicine.

Anesth, CT Surg, CV Med, Infect Dis, Logist-Op, Ped Surg, Peds

🌐 https://vfmat.ch/f34a

Heart to Heart International

Strengthens communities through improving health access, providing humanitarian development, and administering crisis relief worldwide. Engages volunteers, collaborates with partners, and deploys resources to achieve this mission.

Anesth, ER Med, General, Logist-Op, Medicine, Path, Path, Peds, Psych, Pub Health, Surg

🌐 https://vfmat.ch/aacb

Heineman Medical Outreach

Provides medical and educational assistance globally to promote sustainable healthcare and enhanced living standards in underserved communities through the International Medical Outreach (IMO) program, a collaborative partnership between Heineman Medical Outreach and Atrium Health.

Anesth, CT Surg, CV Med, ER Med, General, Heme-Onc, Logist-Op, Medicine, Neonat, OB-GYN, Ped Surg, Peds, Surg, Vasc Surg

🌐 https://vfmat.ch/389b

HelpAge International

Works to ensure that people everywhere understand how much older people contribute to society and that they must enjoy their right to healthcare, social services, economic, and physical security.

General, Geri, Infect Dis, Medicine, Pub Health

🌐 https://vfmat.ch/5d91

Helping Hands Medical Missions

Delivers compassionate healthcare by hosting medical missions and treating patients in underserved communities around the world, based in Christian ministry.

Anesth, Dent-OMFS, ER Med, General, OB-GYN, Ophth-Opt, Surg

🌐 https://vfmat.ch/8efd

Hernia International

Aims to provide relief from sickness, and protection and preservation of health, for persons affected by groin and abdominal hernias and residing in low- and middle-income countries.

Surg

🌐 https://vfmat.ch/e98e

Holy Innocents Children's Hospital Uganda

Works to bring better health to all children of Mbarara, Uganda, and its surrounding villages through better medical care and prevention.

Ped Surg, Peds

🌐 https://vfmat.ch/4964

Hope and Healing International

Gives hope and healing to children and families trapped by poverty and disability.

General, Nutr, Ophth-Opt, Peds, Rehab

🌐 https://vfmat.ch/c638

Hope Health Action

Facilitates sustainable, lifesaving health, and disability care for the world's most vulnerable, without any discrimination.

ER Med, MF Med, Neonat, Nutr, OB-GYN, Peds, Rehab

🌐 https://vfmat.ch/86f7

Hope Line Organisation

Builds schools to provide free basic education to young children, supports women's community development, and provides healthcare outreach in Buikwe District in Central Uganda.

Dent-OMFS, General, Infect Dis, Peds

🌐 https://vfmat.ch/5426

Hope Smiles

Develops and empowers healthcare leaders to restore hope and transform lives by mobilizing and equipping sustainable dental teams in unreached communities.

Dent-OMFS, Pub Health, Surg

🌐 https://vfmat.ch/8a76

Hospice Africa

Aims to provide a holistic and culturally sensitive palliative care service through accurate treatment of pain.

Palliative

🌐 https://vfmat.ch/9f86

Humanity & Inclusion

Works alongside people with disabilities and vulnerable populations, taking action and bearing witness in order to respond to their essential needs, improve their living conditions and health, and promote respect for their dignity and fundamental rights.

General, Infect Dis, MF Med, Medicine, Ortho, Peds, Psych, Pub Health, Rehab

🌐 https://vfmat.ch/16b7

Humanity First

Provides aid and assistance to those in need, offering sustainable development solutions to society while providing and empowering local communities with the resources to help themselves.

ER Med, General, MF Med, Ophth-Opt

🌐 https://vfmat.ch/13cc

Hunger Project, The

Aims to end hunger and poverty by pioneering sustainable, grassroots, women-centered strategies and advocating for their widespread adoption in countries throughout the world.

Infect Dis, Nutr, OB-GYN, Pub Health

🌐 https://vfmat.ch/3a49

ICAP at Columbia University

Serves as global leader in supporting the scale-up of multidisciplinary HIV/AIDS prevention, care, and treatment programs based on a family-focused approach.

General, Infect Dis, MF Med, Medicine, OB-GYN, Pub Health

🌐 https://vfmat.ch/a8ef

IMA World Health

Works to build healthier communities by collaborating with key partners to serve vulnerable people with a focus on health, healing, and well-being for all.

Infect Dis, MF Med, Nutr, OB-GYN, Pub Health

🌐 https://vfmat.ch/8316

Imaging the World

Develops sustainable models for ultrasound imaging in the world's lowest resource settings and uses a technology-enabled solution to improve

healthcare access, integrating lifesaving ultrasound and training programs in rural communities.
Logist-Op, OB-GYN, Radiol
⊕ https://vfmat.ch/59e4

Infectious Diseases Institute: College of Health Sciences, Makerere University
Works to strengthen health systems in Africa, with a strong emphasis on infectious diseases, through research and capacity development.
General, Infect Dis, Logist-Op, Pub Health
⊕ https://vfmat.ch/9fc3

Interface Uganda
Aims to provide essential reconstructive surgery and to equip and train local specialists in Uganda and surrounding areas.
Anesth, Dent-OMFS, Ped Surg, Plast, Surg
⊕ https://vfmat.ch/837b

International Agency for the Prevention of Blindness (IAPB), The
Leads international efforts in blindness-prevention activities, works toward a world where no one is needlessly visually impaired, and ensures that everyone has access to the best possible standard of eye health.
Infect Dis, Ophth-Opt, Pub Health
⊕ https://vfmat.ch/87a2

International Campaign for Women's Right to Safe Abortion
Works to build an international network and campaign that brings together organizations with an interest in promoting and providing safe abortion to create a shared platform for advocacy, debate, and dialogue and the sharing of skills and experience.
OB-GYN, Pub Health, Surg
⊕ https://vfmat.ch/f341

International Children's Heart Fund
Aims to promote the international growth and quality of cardiac surgery, particularly in children and young adults.
CT Surg, Ped Surg
⊕ https://vfmat.ch/33fb

International Federation of Gynecology and Obstetrics (FIGO)
Implements global projects on specific women's health issues.
MF Med, Medicine, Neonat, OB-GYN, Surg, Urol
⊕ https://vfmat.ch/c4b4

International Federation of Red Cross and Red Crescent Societies (IFRC)
Coordinates and directs international assistance following natural and manmade disasters in nonconflict situations through the world's largest humanitarian and development network. Provides disaster-preparedness programs, healthcare activities, and promotes humanitarian values.
ER Med, General, Infect Dis, Nutr
⊕ https://vfmat.ch/b4ee

International Learning Movement (ILM UK)
Supports some of the world's poorest people in developing countries with core projects in education, safe drinking water, and healthcare.
General, Ophth-Opt
⊕ https://vfmat.ch/b974

International Medical Professionals Initiative Inc.
Works to improve healthcare in developing nations.
General, Nutr
⊕ https://vfmat.ch/514a

International Medical Relief
Provides sustainable education, training, medical and dental care, and disaster relief and response in vulnerable communities worldwide.
Dent-OMFS, General, Infect Dis, Medicine, OB-GYN
⊕ https://vfmat.ch/b3ed

International Organization for Migration (IOM) – The UN Migration Agency
Promotes evidence-informed policies and holistic, preventive, and curative health programs that are beneficial, accessible, and equitable for vulnerable migrants.
General, Infect Dis, OB-GYN
⊕ https://vfmat.ch/621a

International Outreach Program of St. Joseph's Health System
Works to save lives in developing countries by training doctors through partnerships with universities, medical schools, and teaching hospitals in countries that need more doctors.
Logist-Op
⊕ https://vfmat.ch/a751

International Pediatric Nephrology Association (IPNA)
Leads global efforts to successfully address the care for all children with kidney disease through advocacy, education, and training.
Medicine, Nephro, Peds
⊕ https://vfmat.ch/b59d

International Planned Parenthood Federation (IPPF)
Leads a locally owned, globally connected civil society movement that provides and enables services and champions sexual and reproductive health and rights for all, especially the underserved.
Infect Dis, MF Med, OB-GYN
⊕ https://vfmat.ch/dc97

International Rescue Committee (IRC)
Responds to the world's worst humanitarian crises and helps people whose lives and livelihoods are shattered by conflict and disaster to survive, recover, and gain control of their future.
ER Med, General, Infect Dis, MF Med, Peds
⊕ https://vfmat.ch/5d24

International Smile Power
Partners with people to improve and sustain dental health and build bridges of friendship around the world.
Dent-OMFS
⊕ https://vfmat.ch/ba69

International Trachoma Initiative (iTi)
Works toward a world free from trachoma, a preventable cause of blindness, and provides comprehensive support to national ministries of health and governmental and nongovernmental organizations to implement a comprehensive approach to fight trachoma.
Infect Dis, Ophth-Opt
⊕ https://vfmat.ch/3278

International Union Against Tuberculosis and Lung Disease
Develops, implements, and assesses anti-tuberculosis, lung health, and noncommunicable disease programs.
Infect Dis, Pub Health, Pulm-Critic
⊕ https://vfmat.ch/3e82

InterSurgeon
Fosters collaborative partnerships in the field of global surgery that will advance clinical care, teaching, training, research, and the provision and maintenance of medical equipment.
ENT, Neurosurg, Ortho, Ped Surg, Plast, Surg, Urol
⊕ https://vfmat.ch/6f8a

IntraHealth International
Improves the performance of health workers and strengthens the systems in which they work.
CV Med, Endo, General, Infect Dis, MF Med, Neonat, Nutr, OB-GYN
⊕ https://vfmat.ch/ddc8

Ipas
Focuses efforts on women and girls who want contraception or abortion, and builds programs around their needs and how best to support them.
OB-GYN
⊕ https://vfmat.ch/8e39

Iris Global
Serves the poor, the destitute, the lost, and the forgotten by providing adoration, outreach, family, education, relief, development, healing, and the arts.
General, Infect Dis, Nutr, Pub Health
⊕ https://vfmat.ch/37f8

Islamic Medical Association of North America
Fosters health promotion, disease prevention, and health maintenance in communities around the world through direct patient care and health programs.
Anesth, Dent-OMFS, ER Med, General, Logist-Op, Ophth-Opt, Peds, Plast, Surg
⊕ https://vfmat.ch/a157

Island Mission Uganda
Aims to improve the lives of people living with HIV/AIDS, especially children, and integrates primary healthcare services in the remote island communities of Lake Victoria.
Infect Dis, Peds
⊕ https://vfmat.ch/a778

IsraAID
Supports people affected by humanitarian crisis and partners with local communities around the world to provide urgent aid, assist recovery, and reduce the risk of future disasters.
ER Med, Infect Dis, Psych, Rehab
⊕ https://vfmat.ch/de96

IVUmed
Aims to make quality urological care available worldwide by providing medical and surgical education for physicians and nurses, and treatment for thousands of children and adults.
Anesth, OB-GYN, Ped Surg, Surg, Urol
⊕ https://vfmat.ch/e619

Izumi Foundation
Develops and supports programs that improve health and healthcare in neglected regions of Africa and Latin America.
⊕ https://vfmat.ch/f29a

Jesus Harvesters Ministries
Reaches communities through medical clinics, dental care, veterinarian outreach, pastor training, and community service, based in Christian ministry.
Dent-OMFS, General, Infect Dis
⊕ https://vfmat.ch/8a23

Jhpiego
Creates and delivers transformative healthcare solutions that save lives, in partnership with national governments, health experts, and local communities.
General, Infect Dis, OB-GYN, Surg
⊕ https://vfmat.ch/45b8

John Snow, Inc. (JSI)
Aims to improve the health and well-being of underserved and vulnerable people and communities throughout the world.
General, Infect Dis, Logist-Op, MF Med, OB-GYN, Peds, Psych, Pub Health
⊕ https://vfmat.ch/ba78

Johns Hopkins Center for Communication Programs
Believes in the power of communication to save lives by empowering people to adopt healthy behaviors for themselves, their families, and their communities.
General, Infect Dis, Logist-Op, OB-GYN, Pub Health
⊕ https://vfmat.ch/1bf9

Johns Hopkins Center for Global Health
Facilitates and focuses the extensive expertise and resources of the Johns Hopkins institutions, together with global collaborators, to effectively address and ameliorate the world's most pressing health issues.
General, Genetics, Logist-Op, MF Med, Peds, Psych, Pub Health, Pulm-Critic
⊕ https://vfmat.ch/54ce

Joint Aid Management (JAM)
Provides food security, nutrition, water, and sanitation to vulnerable African communities in dignified and sustainable ways.

ER Med, Nutr
⊕ https://vfmat.ch/dcac

Joint Aid Management (JAM) Canada
Strives to provide food security, nutrition, water, and sanitation to vulnerable African communities in dignified and sustainable ways.
Nutr, Pub Health
⊕ https://vfmat.ch/8756

Joint United Nations Programme on HIV/AIDS (UNAIDS)
Aims to place people living with HIV and people affected by the virus at the decision-making table and at the center of designing, delivering, and monitoring the AIDS response.
Infect Dis
⊕ https://vfmat.ch/464a

Kagando Rural Development Center (KARUDEC)
Provides integrated community programs and holistic care through Kagando Hospital, along with microfinance projects, farms, community outreach for palliative care, mental health, water supply, and entrepreneurship programs.
Crit-Care, Dent-OMFS, Ophth-Opt, Path, Psych, Radiol, Rehab
⊕ https://vfmat.ch/997d

Kajo Keji Health Training Institute (KKHTI)
Addresses the severe shortage of medical personnel in South Sudan by training quality healthcare workers.
General, Infect Dis, MF Med
⊕ https://vfmat.ch/ff59

Kamuli Friends
Organizes support to Kamuli Mission Hospital in the form of building projects, medical equipment, and international volunteers in response to the needs of the hospital.
General, Medicine, OB-GYN, Peds, Surg
⊕ https://vfmat.ch/1e99

Karin Community Initiatives Uganda (KCIU)
Seeks to transform lives and heal communities by providing quality healthcare services, inspired by the Christian faith.
General, Infect Dis, MF Med, OB-GYN, Peds
⊕ https://vfmat.ch/31ed

Katalemwa Cheshire Home
Provides holistic rehabilitation services, such as quality medical care, social economic support, and orthopedic appliances to children and young persons with disabilities.
Ortho, Peds, Rehab
⊕ https://vfmat.ch/1edd

Kaya Responsible Travel
Promotes sustainable social, environmental, and economic development, empowers communities, and cultivates educated, compassionate global citizens through responsible travel.
All-Immu, Crit-Care, Dent-OMFS, ER Med, General, Geri, Infect Dis, MF Med, Medicine, Nutr, OB-GYN, Peds, Psych, Pub Health, Rehab
⊕ https://vfmat.ch/b2cf

Kellermann Foundation, The
To provide resources and health, education, spiritual outreach, and economic empowerment to the Batwa pygmies and adjacent communities.
General, Neonat, Peds, Pub Health, Surg
⊕ https://vfmat.ch/1e79

Kimbra Foundation
Provides opportunity to African children in need.
General, Nutr, Peds
⊕ https://vfmat.ch/f11d

Kletjian Foundation
Works toward a world in which all people have access to safe, sustainable, and high-quality medical care, building collaborative networks and supporting entrepreneurial leaders that promote global health equity.

CT Surg, ENT, General, Ortho, Surg
⊕ https://vfmat.ch/12c2

Knowledge 4 Change
Improve the standard of healthcare and education provision for the poorest members of society in low- and middle-income countries (LMICs).
OB-GYN, Pub Health
⊕ https://vfmat.ch/3f8b

Kumi Hospital Uganda
Provides holistic, preventive, curative, and rehabilitative services, based in Christian ministry.
All-Immu, General, Infect Dis, OB-GYN, Ortho, Peds, Surg
⊕ https://vfmat.ch/4942

Last Mile Health
Links community health workers with frontline health workers—nurses, doctors, and midwives at community clinics—and supports them to bring lifesaving services to the doorsteps of people living far from care.
General, Logist-Op, OB-GYN, Pub Health
⊕ https://vfmat.ch/37da

Leadership in Medicine for the Underserved Program at MSU, The
Provides medical students the knowledge and skills necessary to address the varied medical needs of urban, rural, and international underserved populations.
Dent-OMFS, ER Med, Medicine, Nutr, OB-GYN, Peds, Pub Health, Radiol, Surg
⊕ https://vfmat.ch/84f1

Life for a Child
Supports the provision of the best possible healthcare, given local circumstances, to all children and youth with diabetes in less-resourced countries, through the strengthening of existing diabetes services.
Endo, Medicine, Peds
⊕ https://vfmat.ch/d712

LifeNet International
Transforms African healthcare by equipping and empowering existing local health centers to provide quality, sustainable, and lifesaving care to patients.
General, Infect Dis, MF Med, Neonat, OB-GYN, Pub Health
⊕ https://vfmat.ch/e5d2

Light for the World
Contributes to a world in which persons with disabilities fully exercise their rights, and assists persons with disabilities living in poverty.
Ophth Opt, Rehab
⊕ https://vfmat.ch/3ff6

Light House Medical Missions
Inspired by the Christian faith, provides programs in healthcare provision, nutrition, emergency relief and response, and water, sanitation, and hygiene (WASH).
ER Med, General, Surg
⊕ https://vfmat.ch/cecd

Limbs International
Engages communities and transforms lives through affordable, sustainable prosthetic solutions and rehabilitation services in developing countries.
Logist-Op, Ortho, Pod, Rehab
⊕ https://vfmat.ch/dc84

Lions Clubs International
Empowers volunteers to serve their communities, meet humanitarian needs, encourage peace, and promote international understanding through Lions Clubs.
Heme-Onc, Medicine, Nutr, Ophth-Opt
⊕ https://vfmat.ch/7b12

Little Things, The
Provides vital medical equipment to poorly funded and inadequately equipped hospitals, improving access to healthcare for patients across the globe.
⊕ https://vfmat.ch/2d81

Living Goods
Leverages a powerful combination of catalytic technology, high-impact training, and quality treatments that empower government community health workers (CHWs) to deliver quality care to their neighbors' doorsteps.
Infect Dis, Logist-Op, MF Med
⊕ https://vfmat.ch/d6d2

London School of Hygiene & Tropical Medicine
Seeks to improve health and health equity in the UK and worldwide, working in partnership to achieve excellence in public and global health research, education, and translation of knowledge into policy and practice.
Infect Dis, Pub Health
⊕ https://vfmat.ch/349a

London School of Hygiene & Tropical Medicine: Health in Humanitarian Crises Centre
Advances health and health equity in crisis-affected countries through research, education, and translation of knowledge into policy and practice.
ER Med, Infect Dis, Pub Health
⊕ https://vfmat.ch/96ad

Love One International
Ensures the children of Uganda receive the emergency healthcare and rehabilitative services they need.
General, Infect Dis, Peds
⊕ https://vfmat.ch/ef2e

Love Without Boundaries
Provides healing, education, and refuge to vulnerable children worldwide.
CT Surg, Dent-OMFS, Nutr, Ortho, Ped Surg, Peds, Rehab, Surg
⊕ https://vfmat.ch/d1fc

Lámha Suas
Aims to improve the lives of young women in Uganda by supporting the education and healthcare of girls.
General, Nutr, OB-GYN, Rehab
⊕ https://vfmat.ch/a489

Making A Difference Foundation
Sponsors and organizes medical missions for medical providers to provide care to underserved communities around the world.
CV Med, Dent-OMFS, ER Med, General, Infect Dis, Logist-Op, MF Med, Neonat, Nutr, OB-GYN, Ophth-Opt, Ortho, Pub Health, Pulm-Critic, Rehab, Surg
⊕ https://vfmat.ch/5556

Mama na Mtoto (Mother and Child)
Strives to improve maternal, newborn, and child health in rural Tanzania.
Logist-Op, MF Med, OB-GYN, Peds
⊕ https://vfmat.ch/2551

Management Sciences for Health (MSH)
Works with countries and communities to save lives and improve the health of the world's poorest and most vulnerable people by building strong, resilient, sustainable health systems.
Infect Dis, Logist-Op, Pub Health
⊕ https://vfmat.ch/6aa2

MAP International
Provides medicines and health supplies to those in need around the world so they might experience life to the fullest.
Logist-Op
⊕ https://vfmat.ch/deed

Maranatha Health
Works to improve health outcomes, empower the poor, and make positive, lasting change in Uganda by collaborating with local communities in rural Western Uganda, namely Kamwenge and Kabarole Districts, to improve health, inspired by the Christian faith.
Anesth, ENT, Infect Dis, Neonat, Nutr, OB-GYN, Ophth-Opt, Ped Surg, Peds, Radiol, Surg
⊕ https://vfmat.ch/c4a9

Marie Stopes International
Provides the contraception and safe abortion services that enable women all over the world to choose their own futures.
Infect Dis, MF Med, Neonat, OB-GYN, Pub Health
⊕ https://vfmat.ch/9525

Mary Mission Incorporated
Restores hope and dignity in a peaceful and safe environment by providing for the needs of the poor and vulnerable with education, food, clothing, healthcare, and shelter.
General
⊕ https://vfmat.ch/3ec5

Massachusetts General Hospital Global Surgery Initiative
Aims to improve surgical education and access to advanced surgical care in resource-limited settings around the world by performing surgical operations as visitors, training local surgeons, and sharing medical technology through international partnerships across disciplines.
Anesth, Crit-Care, ER Med, Heme-Onc, Peds, Surg
⊕ https://vfmat.ch/31b1

MaterCare International (MCI) (Canada)
Works to improve the lives and health of mothers and babies through programs in healthcare provision, training, research, and advocacy, with the aim to address maternal and perinatal mortality and morbidity in developing countries.
OB-GYN
⊕ https://vfmat.ch/a92e

Maternity Worldwide
Works with communities and partners to identify and develop appropriate and effective ways to reduce maternal and newborn mortality and morbidity, facilitate communities to access quality skilled maternity care, and support the provision of quality skilled care.
MF Med, OB-GYN
⊕ https://vfmat.ch/822b

Maverick Collective
Aims to build a global community of strategic philanthropists and informed advocates who use their intellectual and financial resources to create change.
Infect Dis, MF Med, OB-GYN
⊕ https://vfmat.ch/ea49

McGill University Health Centre: Centre for Global Surgery
Works to reduce the impact of injury by advancing surgical care through research and education in resource-limited settings.
ER Med, Logist-Op, Ped Surg, Surg
⊕ https://vfmat.ch/7246

MedAid United Kingdom
Strives to save and improve the lives of disadvantaged families in rural communities in Africa, through healthcare and education.
Dent-OMFS, General, Infect Dis, MF Med
⊕ https://vfmat.ch/52e7

MedHope Africa
Supports relief and development for low-resource communities in Sub-Saharan Africa by addressing dire physical and spiritual needs through medical and vision care, community health interventions, and prayer and Christian evangelism.
General, Logist-Op, Medicine, Ophth-Opt
⊕ https://vfmat.ch/8249

Medical Care Development International
Works to improve the health of vulnerable populations through integrated, sustainable, and locally driven interventions.
Infect Dis, OB-GYN, Peds, Pub Health
⊕ https://vfmat.ch/da87

Medical Missions Foundation
Provides surgical and medical care in underserved communities throughout the world and hopes to positively impact the lives of children and their families.
Anesth, Ped Surg, Surg
⊕ https://vfmat.ch/f385

Medical Teams International
Seeks to restore health as the first step to restoring hope, working to bring basic but lifesaving medical care to those in need.
Dent-OMFS, ER Med, General, MF Med, Pub Health
⊕ https://vfmat.ch/8d1c

MedShare
Aims to improve the quality of life of people, communities, and the planet by sourcing and directly delivering surplus medical supplies and equipment to communities in need around the world.
Logist-Op
⊕ https://vfmat.ch/c8bc

MENTOR Initiative
Saves lives in emergencies through tropical disease control, and helps people recover from crisis with dignity, working side by side with communities, health workers, and health authorities to leave a lasting impact.
ER Med, Infect Dis
⊕ https://vfmat.ch/3bd5

Merck for Mothers
Hopes to create a world where no woman has to die giving life by collaborating with partners to improve the health and well-being of women during pregnancy, childbirth, and the postpartum period.
MF Med, OB-GYN
⊕ https://vfmat.ch/5b51

Mercy and Love Foundation
Aims to provide orphaned and vulnerable children with basic human needs such as food, clothing, and shelter, enabling them to thrive.
General, Peds
⊕ https://vfmat.ch/649a

Mercy Ships
Operates hospital ships staffed by volunteers to bring hope, healing, and healthcare to underserved communities worldwide.
Anesth, Dent-OMFS, Logist-Op, Neonat, OB-GYN, Ophth-Opt, Ortho, Palliative, Plast, Psych, Surg
⊕ https://vfmat.ch/2e99

MicroResearch: Africa/Asia
Seeks to improve health outcomes in Africa by training, mentoring, and supporting local multidisciplinary health professional researchers.
Infect Dis, Nutr, OB-GYN, Psych
⊕ https://vfmat.ch/13e7

Mildmay
Transforms and empowers lives through the delivery of quality health services, treatment, and care in the UK and Africa.
Infect Dis, MF Med, Neuro, Psych
⊕ https://vfmat.ch/3fd8

MiracleFeet
Brings low-cost treatment to every child on the planet born with clubfoot, a leading cause of physical disability.
Ortho, Peds, Rehab
⊕ https://vfmat.ch/bda8

Mission Bambini
Helps to support children living in poverty and sickness, and lacking education, giving them the opportunity for and hope of a better life.
CT Surg, CV Med, Crit-Care, ER Med, Ped Surg, Peds
⊕ https://vfmat.ch/dc1a

Mission Doctors Association
Provides life-saving medical care for the poor and training for local healthcare professionals around the world.
CV Med, Dent-OMFS, General, Logist-Op, Medicine, OB-GYN, Ophth-Opt, Peds, Surg
⊕ https://vfmat.ch/6c18

Mission Regan
Collects supplies, medication, and medical equipment and provides them to those

who are in desperate need, both locally and globally.
Logist-Op
⊕ https://vfmat.ch/2bc1

Mission to Heal
Aims to heal underserved people and train local practitioners in the most remote areas of the world through global healthcare missions.
Anesth, Infect Dis, OB-GYN, Surg
⊕ https://vfmat.ch/4718

Mission Vision
Seeks to decrease blindness and other eye-related disabilities, and to increase academic performance and general quality of life.
Ophth-Opt
⊕ https://vfmat.ch/83d8

More Than Medicine
Provides ENT head/neck care while supporting local doctors to grow the quality of medicine abroad.
Anesth, ENT, Heme-Onc, Surg
⊕ https://vfmat.ch/c4e8

Mothers and Children Support International
Provides education and health services in rural Uganda, focusing on orphans, mothers, and children.
General, Infect Dis, Pub Health
⊕ https://vfmat.ch/fd5f

mothers2mothers (m2m)
Employs and trains local women living with HIV as community health workers called Mentor Mothers to support women, children, and adolescents with vital medical services, education, and support.
Infect Dis, MF Med, OB-GYN, Peds, Pub Health
⊕ https://vfmat.ch/6557

MPACT for Mankind
Transforms communities by improving health outcomes, enhancing knowledge, and providing hope while promoting sustainable growth.
ER Med, General
⊕ https://vfmat.ch/1c61

MSD for Mothers
Designs scalable solutions that help end preventable maternal deaths.
MF Med, OB-GYN, Pub Health
⊕ https://vfmat.ch/9f99

MSI Reproductive Choices (Marie Stopes International)
Seeks to deliver quality family planning and reproductive healthcare to women around the world.
MF Med
⊕ https://vfmat.ch/5c82

Multi-Agency International Training and Support (MAITS)
Improves the lives of some of the world's poorest people living with disabilities through better access to quality health and education services and support.
Neuro, Psych, Rehab
⊕ https://vfmat.ch/9dcd

NCD Alliance
Unites and strengthens civil society to stimulate collaborative advocacy, action, and accountability for NCD (noncommunicable disease) prevention and control.
All-Immu, CV Med, General, Heme-Onc, Medicine, Peds, Psych
⊕ https://vfmat.ch/abdd

New Horizons Collaborative
Advances a holistic, integrated approach to high-quality pediatric HIV care and treatment with a specific focus on those in need of advanced treatment.
Infect Dis, Peds, Pub Health
⊕ https://vfmat.ch/a76a

Nurture Africa
Provides access to healthcare, education, and economic empowerment for vulnerable families in Uganda.

General, MF Med, Medicine, Peds, Rehab
⊕ https://vfmat.ch/95f8

NuVasive Spine Foundation (NSF)
Partners with leading spine surgeons, nonprofits, and in-country medical professionals/facilities to bring life-changing spine surgery to under-resourced communities around the world.
Logist-Op, Ortho, Ped Surg, Rehab, Surg
⊕ https://vfmat.ch/6ccc

Omni Med
Promotes health volunteerism and provides innovative, cooperative, and sustainable programs with measurable impact.
ER Med, Endo, Medicine, Neuro, OB-GYN, Ophth-Opt, Ortho, Palliative, Peds, Vasc Surg
⊕ https://vfmat.ch/2969

One World Brigades
Assists international communities with dental care and education.
Dent-OMFS, General
⊕ https://vfmat.ch/7933

OneWorld Health
Provides quality, affordable healthcare to communities in need and empowers them to achieve long-term improvements in health and quality of life.
Dent-OMFS, General, Infect Dis, Ortho, Peds, Rehab, Surg
⊕ https://vfmat.ch/71d7

Operation Fistula
Exists to end obstetric fistula by building models of care that serve every woman, everywhere.
MF Med, OB-GYN, Surg
⊕ https://vfmat.ch/ce8e

Operation Healthy Africa
Organizes and participates in medical missions, disease treatment and prevention, vision and hearing care, and other medical services around the world, while also providing medical equipment and other supplies in the areas where it operates.
Dent-OMFS, General, Infect Dis, Logist-Op, MF Med, OB-GYN, Ophth-Opt, Surg
⊕ https://vfmat.ch/c99b

Operation Hernia
Provides high-quality surgery at minimal cost to patients who otherwise would not receive it.
Anesth, Ortho, Surg
⊕ https://vfmat.ch/6e9a

Operation International
Offers medical aid to adults and children suffering from lack of quality healthcare in impoverished countries.
Dent-OMFS, ER Med, Heme-Onc, OB-GYN, Ophth-Opt, Ortho, Ped Surg, Plast, Surg
⊕ https://vfmat.ch/b52a

Options
Believes in a world in which women and children can access the high-quality health services they need, without financial burden.
Logist-Op, MF Med, Neonat, OB-GYN
⊕ https://vfmat.ch/3a48

Optometry Giving Sight
Delivers eye exams and low or no-cost glasses, provides training for local eye care professionals, and establishes optometry schools, vision centers and optical labs.
Ophth-Opt
⊕ https://vfmat.ch/33ea

Orbis International
Works to prevent and treat blindness through hands-on training and improved access to quality eye care.
Anesth, Ophth-Opt, Surg
⊕ https://vfmat.ch/f2b2

Oregon Health Sciences University: Global Health Advocacy Program in Surgery

Contributes to the care of patients across the globe and advances OHSU's strategic plan to become an international leader in health and science.

General, Medicine, Peds, Pub Health, Surg

🌐 https://vfmat.ch/77a4

Ostomates Uganda

Brings attention to the suffering of ostomates, lobbies for support, provides education opportunities, and provides psychosocial support for the ostomates and their families.

GI, Psych

🌐 https://vfmat.ch/ad24

Oxford University Global Surgery Group (OUGSG)

Aims to contribute to the provision of high-quality surgical care globally, particularly in low- and middle-income countries (LMICs), while bringing together students, researchers, and clinicians with an interest in global surgery, anesthesia, and obstetrics and gynecology.

Anesth, MF Med, OB-GYN, Ortho, Surg

🌐 https://vfmat.ch/c624

Pact

Works on the ground to improve the lives of those who are challenged by poverty and marginalization, striving for a world in which all people are heard, capable, and vibrant.

Infect Dis, Logist-Op, MF Med, Pub Health

🌐 https://vfmat.ch/9a6c

Partners for World Health

Sorts, evaluates, repackages, and prepares supplies and equipment for distribution to individuals, communities, and healthcare facilities in need, both locally and internationally.

ER Med, General, Logist-Op

🌐 https://vfmat.ch/982e

PATH

Advances health equity through innovation and partnerships so people, communities, and economies can thrive.

All-Immu, CV Med, Endo, Heme-Onc, Infect Dis, MF Med, Neonat, Nutr, OB-GYN, Path, Peds, Pulm-Critic

🌐 https://vfmat.ch/b4db

Pathfinder International

Champions sexual and reproductive health and rights worldwide, mobilizing communities most in need to break through barriers and forge paths to a healthier future.

OB-GYN

🌐 https://vfmat.ch/a7b3

Pearl of Africa Child Care

Aims to break the cycle of poverty for Ugandan children by investing in education, health, water, and sustainable food programs, in consultation with our Ugandan partners.

General, Logist-Op

🌐 https://vfmat.ch/abba

Pediatric Health Initiative

Supports the spread of quality pediatric care and its development and progress in low- and middle-income countries.

ER Med, Infect Dis, Neonat, Palliative, Ped Surg, Peds

🌐 https://vfmat.ch/614b

Pepal

Brings together NGOs, global corporations, and the public sector to co-create solutions to big social issues, creating immediate and scalable solutions, and developing leaders who are capable of driving change in their communities.

Heme-Onc, Infect Dis, Pub Health

🌐 https://vfmat.ch/6dc5

Perspective for Children

Supports HIV/AIDS affected and disabled children and adolescents in Uganda.

General, Infect Dis, MF Med, OB-GYN

🌐 https://vfmat.ch/efd6

Physicians Across Continents

Provides high-quality medical care to people affected by crises and disasters.

CV Med, Dent-OMFS, Heme-Onc, MF Med, Nephro, Nephro, OB-GYN, Ped Surg, Plast, Surg

🌐 https://vfmat.ch/fe5d

Poole Africa Link

Provides a link of training for doctors, nurses, midwives, and student nurses between Poole Hospital NHS Foundation Trust and Wau Hospital in South Sudan.

Logist-Op, OB-GYN

🌐 https://vfmat.ch/1f6f

Positive Action for Treatment Access (PATA)

Ensures that every individual with an illness or disease, especially women and girls, has access to treatment and literacy skills, and to equitable, humane care and empowerment.

Infect Dis, OB-GYN, Peds, Pub Health

🌐 https://vfmat.ch/46f9

Programme for Nutrition and Eye Care (PRONEC)

Champions access to affordable eye care, nutrition education, and services, including HIV/AIDS education, among the rural poor in Uganda.

General, Infect Dis, Nutr, Ophth-Opt

🌐 https://vfmat.ch/ac8b

Project Concern International (PCI)

Drives innovation from the ground up to enhance health, end hunger, overcome hardship, and advance women and girls—resulting in meaningful and measurable change in people's lives.

Infect Dis, MF Med, Nutr, OB-GYN, Peds

🌐 https://vfmat.ch/5ed7

Project SOAR

Conducts HIV operations research around the world to identify practical solutions to improve HIV prevention, care, and treatment services.

ER Med, General, MF Med, OB-GYN, Psych

🌐 https://vfmat.ch/1a77

Project Turquoise

Raises awareness and supports the needs of displaced families and provides humanitarian support locally and abroad.

Dent-OMFS, ER Med

🌐 https://vfmat.ch/88bf

RAD-AID International

Improves and optimizes access to medical imaging and radiology in low-resource regions of the world.

Rad-Onc, Radiol

🌐 https://vfmat.ch/537f

Rakai Health Sciences Program

Conducts innovative and relevant health research in infectious diseases, communicable and noncommunicable diseases, and reproductive health, and provides health-related services in order to improve public health and inform policy.

GI, Infect Dis, Neuro, Path, Pub Health

🌐 https://vfmat.ch/ee73

Rays of Hope Hospice Jinja

Provides palliative care and improves the quality of life for all people with life-limiting illnesses and their families in the Busoga Region and neighboring districts.

🌐 https://vfmat.ch/9816

Real Medicine Foundation (RMF)

Provides humanitarian support to people living in disaster- and poverty-stricken areas, focusing on the person as a whole by providing medical/physical, emotional, economic, and social support.

ER Med, General, Infect Dis, Nutr, Peds, Psych

🌐 https://vfmat.ch/d45a

Rescue Hope
Connects medical professionals with opportunities to serve around the world and bring physical and spiritual healing to nations abroad.
ER Med, General
🌐 https://vfmat.ch/1428

RestoringVision
Empowers lives by restoring vision for millions of people in need.
Ophth-Opt
🌐 https://vfmat.ch/e121

RHD Action
Seeks to reduce the burden of rheumatic heart disease in vulnerable populations throughout the world.
CV Med, Medicine, Pub Health
🌐 https://vfmat.ch/f5d9

Rockefeller Foundation, The
Works to promote the well-being of humanity.
Logist-Op, Nutr, Pub Health
🌐 https://vfmat.ch/5424

Rose Charities International
Aims to support communities to improve quality of life and reduce the effects of poverty through innovative, self-sustaining projects, and partnerships.
ENT, ER Med, General, Infect Dis, Neonat, OB-GYN, Ophth-Opt, Ped Surg, Peds, Rehab, Urol
🌐 https://vfmat.ch/53df

Rotary Action Group for Family Health & AIDS Prevention (RFHA)
Works to save and improve the lives of children and families who lack access to preventive healthcare and education.
Dent-OMFS, Infect Dis, OB-GYN, Ophth-Opt, Peds
🌐 https://vfmat.ch/6563

Rotary International
Provides service to others, improves lives, and advances world understanding, goodwill, and peace through its fellowship of business, professional, and community leaders.
ER Med, General, Infect Dis, MF Med, OB-GYN
🌐 https://vfmat.ch/8fb5

ROW Foundation
Works to improve the quality of training for healthcare providers, and the diagnosis and treatment available to people with epilepsy and associated psychiatric disorders in under-resourced areas of the world.
Neuro, Psych
🌐 https://vfmat.ch/25eb

Rukundo International
Empowers the most vulnerable populations through educational and economic opportunities that create pathways to self-sustaining communities.
Dent-OMFS, General
🌐 https://vfmat.ch/f45a

Rural Health Care Foundation Uganda
Works to make a difference in local communities by providing basic healthcare and programs supporting people with HIV/AIDS; access to clean, safe water; education on sustainable hygiene and sanitation practices; and treating opportunistic infections.
General, Infect Dis, Nutr, OB-GYN, Peds, Urol
🌐 https://vfmat.ch/d65d

Ruth Gaylord Hospital Maganjo
Provides self-sustaining, affordable, and equitable community-based healthcare services through a dedicated and professional workforce.
Crit-Care, Infect Dis, OB-GYN, Ophth-Opt
🌐 https://vfmat.ch/2d7e

Safe Anaesthesia Worldwide
Provides anesthesia to those in need in low-income countries to enable lifesaving surgery.

Anesth, Plast
🌐 https://vfmat.ch/134a

Safe Harbor International
Inspired by the Christian faith, provides people living in poverty with ministry, development, training, and relief services such as medical care.
General
🌐 https://vfmat.ch/3dfe

Safe Places Uganda Foundation
Works to improve the mental health and well-being of people in Uganda and seeks to build an inclusive society that values mental health, respects the rights of persons with mental illnesses, and is free of any related stigma.
General, Peds, Psych
🌐 https://vfmat.ch/b3fc

Salvation Army International, The
Seeks to meet human needs through services in education, healthcare, community support, emergency response, and ministry development, inspired by the Christian faith.
Dent-OMFS, Derm, ER Med, Infect Dis, MF Med, Medicine, Nutr, OB-GYN, Ophth-Opt, Palliative, Psych, Rehab, Surg
🌐 https://vfmat.ch/8eb3

Samaritan's Purse International Disaster Relief
Provides spiritual and physical aid to hurting people around the world, such as victims of war, poverty, natural disasters, disease, and famine, based in Christian ministry.
Anesth, CT Surg, Crit-Care, Dent-OMFS, Derm, ENT, ER Med, Endo, GI, General, Heme-Onc, Infect Dis, MF Med, Neonat, Nephro, Neuro, Neurosurg, Nutr, OB-GYN, Ophth-Opt, Ortho, Path, Ped Surg, Peds, Plast, Psych, Pulm-Critic, Radiol, Rehab, Rheum, Surg, Urol, Vasc Surg
🌐 https://vfmat.ch/87e3

Sanofi Espoir Foundation
Contributes to reducing health inequalities among populations that need it most by applying a socially responsible approach focused on fighting childhood cancers in low-income countries, improving maternal and newborn health, and improving access to care.
ER Med, OB-GYN, Peds
🌐 https://vfmat.ch/943b

Save A Child's Heart
Provides lifesaving cardiac treatment to children in developing countries, and trains healthcare professionals from these countries to deliver quality care in their communities.
CT Surg, CV Med, Crit-Care, Ped Surg, Peds
🌐 https://vfmat.ch/1bef

Save the Children
Gives children around the world a healthy start in life, the opportunity to learn, and protection from harm.
All-Immu, Crit-Care, ER Med, General, Infect Dis, MF Med, Medicine, Neonat, OB-GYN, Peds, Psych, Pub Health
🌐 https://vfmat.ch/2e73

Save the Mothers
Promotes maternal health in developing countries through education, public awareness, and advocacy.
General, MF Med, Neonat, OB-GYN, Peds
🌐 https://vfmat.ch/498f

Saving Mothers
Seeks to eradicate preventable maternal deaths and birth-related complications in low-resource settings.
MF Med, Neonat, OB-GYN, Surg
🌐 https://vfmat.ch/ed94

SCI Foundation
Seeks to prevent and treat neglected infectious diseases, with a focus on eliminating parasitic worm infections through strengthening impactful and comprehensive health programs across Sub-Saharan Africa.

Infect Dis, Pub Health

⊕ https://vfmat.ch/5444

SEE International

Provides sustainable medical, surgical, and educational services through volunteer ophthalmic surgeons, with the objectives of restoring sight and preventing blindness to disadvantaged individuals worldwide.

Ophth-Opt, Surg

⊕ https://vfmat.ch/6e1b

Seed Global Health

Focuses on human resources for health capacity building at the individual, institutional, and national level through sustained collaborative engagement with partners.

Logist-Op

⊕ https://vfmat.ch/d12e

Senior Citizens Agecare Foundation Uganda (SCACFU)

Fights isolation, loneliness, neglect, abuse, and poverty to ensure senior citizens live self-fulfilled lives by encouraging active aging and the goal of retiring gracefully with dignity.

Geri

⊕ https://vfmat.ch/1c4c

SEVA

Delivers vital eye care services to the world's most vulnerable, including women, children, and Indigenous peoples.

Ophth-Opt, Surg

⊕ https://vfmat.ch/1e87

Share Uganda

Focuses on providing quality and sustainable health services, supporting the education of local healthcare professionals, and developing collaborative solutions to local healthcare challenges.

General, Infect Dis, Neonat, OB-GYN, Pub Health

⊕ https://vfmat.ch/c6e6

Shines Children's Foundation

Aims to protect the rights of children and provide them access to education, healthcare, and shelter.

General, Infect Dis, Nutr, Pub Health

⊕ https://vfmat.ch/da64

Sightsavers

Works with partners in developing countries to help eliminate avoidable blindness and advocates for equal opportunity for the disabled.

Infect Dis, Ophth-Opt, Surg

⊕ https://vfmat.ch/aa52

SIGN Fracture Care International

Builds orthopedic capacity around the world and provides the injured poor access to fracture surgery by donating orthopedic education and implant systems to surgeons in developing countries.

Ortho, Rehab, Surg

⊕ https://vfmat.ch/123d

Simavi

Strives for a world in which all women and girls are socially and economically empowered and pursue their rights to live a healthy life, free from discrimination, coercion, and violence.

MF Med, OB-GYN

⊕ https://vfmat.ch/b57b

SINA Health

Aims to improve the health and educational status of the population in low- and middle-income countries.

General, Logist-Op

⊕ https://vfmat.ch/9ad3

SladeChild Foundation

Provides food, clothing, shelter, education, and medical care to some of the world's most impoverished children.

Dent-OMFS, General, Logist-Op, Ophth-Opt

⊕ https://vfmat.ch/14c5

Smile Train, Inc.

Treats children with cleft lip through a sustainable and local model that supports surgery and other forms of essential care.

Logist-Op, Pub Health

⊕ https://vfmat.ch/822c

SmileStar

Provides free, quality dental care to disadvantaged communities in African countries and India.

Dent-OMFS

⊕ https://vfmat.ch/ade3

Soddo Christian Hospital

Mobilizes volunteers to help transform communities through healthcare and education, based in Christian ministry.

ER Med, General

⊕ https://vfmat.ch/efa4

Soft Power Health

Provides primary healthcare, health education and prevention, and health-promoting activities for people in need.

General, Infect Dis, MF Med, Nutr, Pub Health

⊕ https://vfmat.ch/e587

SOS Children's Villages International

Supports children through alternative care and family strengthening.

ER Med, Peds

⊕ https://vfmat.ch/aca1

Sovereign Wings of Hope Ministries (SWOH)

Renders medical, spiritual, and humanitarian services to enrich communities in Uganda.

Palliative

⊕ https://vfmat.ch/937d

Sri Sathya Sai International Organization

Inspired by spiritual teachings, carries out efforts in global healthcare, education, humanitarian relief, and youth engagement.

Dent-OMFS, General, Logist-Op, Nutr, Ophth-Opt, Pub Health

⊕ https://vfmat.ch/9bda

St. Francis Hospital Nsambya

Provides sustainable quality healthcare, training, and research, while supporting economically disadvantaged communities.

Dent-OMFS, Heme-Onc, Medicine, Neonat, Path, Peds, Radiol, Surg

⊕ https://vfmat.ch/d9f8

St. Mary's Hospital Lacor

Provides healthcare to those in need and helps to fight disease and poverty.

Anesth, ER Med, General, Infect Dis, MF Med, OB-GYN, Peds, Surg

⊕ https://vfmat.ch/ecc1

Stanford Global Health Neurosurgery Initiative

Shares knowledge and expertise in areas where neurosurgeons are few and access to neurosurgical treatment is lacking, sending nurses, residents, and surgeons to different parts of the world to provide clinical care and conduct research.

Anesth, Neuro, Neurosurg, Ortho, Rehab, Surg

⊕ https://vfmat.ch/f4d4

Sustainable Cardiovascular Health Equity Development Alliance

Fights cardiovascular disease in underserved populations globally via education, training, and increasing interventional capacity.

CV Med, Pub Health, Radiol

⊕ https://vfmat.ch/799c

Sustainable Kidney Care Foundation (SKCF)

Works to provide treatment for kidney injury where none exists, and aims to reduce mortality from treatable acute kidney injury (AKI).

Infect Dis, Medicine, Nephro
⊕ https://vfmat.ch/1926

Sustainable Medical Missions
Trains and supports Indigenous healthcare and faith leaders in underdeveloped communities to treat neglected tropical diseases (NTDs) and other endemic conditions affecting the poorest community members, by pairing faith-based solutions with best practices.
Infect Dis, Pub Health
⊕ https://vfmat.ch/9165

Swedish Organization for Global Health
Aims to improve the quality and accessibility of healthcare and health promotion through local and international partnerships.
Logist-Op, OB-GYN, Pub Health
⊕ https://vfmat.ch/a5b1

Swiss Tropical and Public Health Institute
Contributes to the improvement of the health of populations internationally, nationally, and locally through excellence in research, education, and services.
Infect Dis, Pub Health
⊕ https://vfmat.ch/2ee4

Task Force for Global Health, The
Consists of programs and focus areas that cover a range of global health issues including neglected tropical diseases, infectious diseases, vaccines, field epidemiology, public health informatics, health workforce development, and global health ethics.
Infect Dis, Logist-Op, Medicine, Ophth-Opt, Peds
⊕ https://vfmat.ch/714c

Team Canada Healing Hands
Provides and develops interdisciplinary rehabilitation treatment, education, and training in areas of need.
ENT, Neuro, Psych, Rehab
⊕ https://vfmat.ch/2eaf

Tearfund
Responds to crisis and partners with local churches to bring restoration to those living in poverty, inspired by the Christian faith.
ER Med, Logist-Op
⊕ https://vfmat.ch/f6cf

Teasdale-Corti Foundation/St. Mary's Hospital Lacor
Guarantees affordable medical services, especially to those most in need, and ensures the continuity of healthcare, training, and growth of Lacor Hospital in Uganda.
CV Med, Crit-Care, General, Infect Dis, MF Med, OB-GYN, Ped Surg, Peds
⊕ https://vfmat.ch/f1da

Terrewode Women's Fund
Supports quality surgical treatment and social reintegration to thousands of Ugandan women suffering from obstetric fistula.
MF Med, OB-GYN, Surg
⊕ https://vfmat.ch/1d12

Texas Children's Global Health
Addresses healthcare needs in resource-limited settings locally and globally by improving maternal and child health through the implementation of innovative, sustainable, in-country programs to train health professionals and build functional healthcare infrastructure.
Anesth, ER Med, Heme-Onc, Infect Dis, MF Med, Nutr, OB-GYN, Peds, Pub Health, Surg
⊕ https://vfmat.ch/4a1d

THET Partnerships for Global Health
Trains and educates health workers in Africa and Asia, working in partnership with organizations and volunteers from across the UK.
General
⊕ https://vfmat.ch/f937

Think Humanity
Saves lives and provides hope for refugees and underdeveloped communities in

Africa by improving provisions for healthcare, clean water, education, and socio-economic development.
General, Infect Dis, Peds
⊕ https://vfmat.ch/e537

U.S. President's Malaria Initiative (PMI)
Supports low-income countries to help control and eliminate malaria through cost-effective, lifesaving malaria interventions.
Infect Dis, MF Med, OB-GYN
⊕ https://vfmat.ch/dc8b

Uganda Child Cancer Foundation
Supports children and young persons with cancer in Uganda through direct support, advocacy, and awareness about cancer.
Heme-Onc, Ped Surg, Peds
⊕ https://vfmat.ch/ea73

Uganda Kidney Foundation
Works in the prevention and management of kidney disease through awareness, education, and research.
Nephro
⊕ https://vfmat.ch/5848

Uganda Rural Fund
Empowers orphans, underprivileged youth, and women to fight poverty in Uganda's rural communities through the creation of educational and sustainable development opportunities.
General, Infect Dis, Pub Health
⊕ https://vfmat.ch/6657

Uganda Spine Surgery Mission
Provides the best possible spine care to Ugandan patients afflicted by infectious, degenerative, traumatic, and congenital spinal ailments.
Ortho, Surg
⊕ https://vfmat.ch/b413

Uganda Village Project
Facilitates community health and well-being in rural Uganda through improved access, education, and prevention.
General, Infect Dis, MF Med, OB-GYN, Surg
⊕ https://vfmat.ch/76ac

UNC Health Foundation
Secures resources and supports empathy and expertise in patient care, research, education, and advocacy in underserved communities around the world.
Heme-Onc, Infect Dis, Neuro, Peds, Pub Health
⊕ https://vfmat.ch/7129

Union for International Cancer Control (UICC)
Unites and supports the cancer community to reduce the global cancer burden, promote greater equity, and ensure that cancer control continues to be a priority in the world health and development agenda.
Heme-Onc, Pub Health
⊕ https://vfmat.ch/88b1

Unite 4 Humanity
Aims to provide emergency aid and support for Muslim communities across the world.
General, Nutr, OB-GYN, Ophth-Opt, Plast, Psych, Rehab
⊕ https://vfmat.ch/fbe7

United Hands Relief & Development
Works to funnel efforts toward alleviating and immediately responding to the sufferings of others around the globe, regardless of nationality, race, religion, or social status.
ER Med, General, Infect Dis, Ophth-Opt, Surg
⊕ https://vfmat.ch/2771

United Hatzallah
Provides patients with quick response to medical emergencies and professional and appropriate medical aid until an ambulance arrives.
ER Med, General, Logist-Op
⊕ https://vfmat.ch/e581

United MegaCare
Seeks to deliver high-caliber services and programming across its areas of focus: education, health and wellness, secure families, and disaster resiliency.
ER Med, General, Infect Dis, Nutr, Ophth-Opt, Peds
⊕ https://vfmat.ch/ea18

United Methodist Volunteers in Mission (UMVIM)
Engages in short-term missions each year in ministries as varied as disaster response, community development, pastor training, microenterprise, agriculture, Vacation Bible School, building repair and construction, and medical/dental services.
Dent-OMFS, ER Med, General
⊕ https://vfmat.ch/1ee6

United Nations Children's Fund (UNICEF)
Works in over 190 countries and territories to save children's lives, defend their rights, and help them fulfill their potential, from early childhood through adolescence.
All-Immu, Infect Dis, MF Med, Neonat, Nutr, OB-GYN, Ped Surg, Peds, Pub Health
⊕ https://vfmat.ch/42d7

United Nations Development Programme (UNDP)
Helps countries achieve the simultaneous eradication of extreme poverty and significant reduction of inequalities and exclusion using a sustainable human development approach.
Infect Dis, Logist-Op, Pub Health
⊕ https://vfmat.ch/935c

United Nations High Commissioner for Refugees (UNHCR)
Safeguards the rights and well-being of people who have been forced to flee, ensuring that everybody has the right to seek asylum and find safe refuge in another country, with the goal of seeking lasting solutions.
General, MF Med, Medicine, OB-GYN, Peds, Psych, Pub Health
⊕ https://vfmat.ch/6636

United Nations Population Fund (UNFPA)
Supports reproductive healthcare for women and youth in more than 150 countries, focusing on delivering a world in which every pregnancy is wanted, every childbirth is safe, and every young person's potential is fulfilled.
Infect Dis, MF Med, Neonat, OB-GYN, Peds, Pub Health
⊕ https://vfmat.ch/c969

United States Agency for International Development (USAID)
Promotes and demonstrates democratic values abroad and advances a free, peaceful, and prosperous world. Leads the U.S. government's international development and disaster assistance through partnerships and investments that save lives.
ER Med, Infect Dis, MF Med, OB-GYN, Peds
⊕ https://vfmat.ch/9a99

United States President's Emergency Plan for AIDS Relief (PEPFAR)
The U.S. global HIV/AIDS response works to prevent new HIV infections and accelerate progress to control the global epidemic in more than 50 countries, by partnering with governments to support sustainable, integrated, and country-led responses to HIV/AIDS.
Infect Dis, Pub Health
⊕ https://vfmat.ch/a57c

United Way
Aims to improve lives by mobilizing the caring power of communities around the world to advance the common good by fighting for the health, education, and financial stability of every person.
General, Infect Dis, Pub Health
⊕ https://vfmat.ch/c812

University of California Los Angeles: David Geffen School of Medicine Global Health Program
Catalyzes opportunities to improve health globally by engaging in multi-disciplinary and innovative education programs, research initiatives, and bilateral partnerships that provide opportunities for trainees, faculty, and staff to contribute to sustainable health initiatives and to address health inequities facing the world today.

All-Immu, Infect Dis, Logist-Op, MF Med, Medicine, Neonat, OB-GYN, Ortho, Ped Surg, Peds, Radiol
⊕ https://vfmat.ch/f1a4

University of California San Francisco: Institute for Global Health Sciences
Dedicates its efforts to improving health and reducing the burden of disease in the world's most vulnerable populations by integrating expertise in the health, social, and biological sciences, training global health leaders, and developing solutions to the most pressing health challenges.
Infect Dis, OB-GYN, Pub Health
⊕ https://vfmat.ch/6587

University of California, San Francisco: Center for Global Surgery and Health Equity
Leads and supports academic global surgery, while strengthening surgical-care systems in low-resource settings through research and education.
Anesth, OB-GYN, Surg
⊕ https://vfmat.ch/564f

University of Colorado: Global Emergency Care Initiative
Strives to sustainably improve emergency care outcomes in low- and middle-income communities worldwide by linking cutting-edge academics with excellent on-the-ground implementation.
ER Med
⊕ https://vfmat.ch/417a

University of Michigan Medical School Global REACH
Aims to facilitate health research, education, and collaboration among Michigan Medicine learners and faculty with our global partners to reduce health disparities for the benefit of communities worldwide.
ENT, General, Ophth-Opt, Peds, Psych, Pub Health, Urol
⊕ https://vfmat.ch/5f19

University of Minnesota: Global Surgery & Disparities Program
Works to understand and improve surgical, anesthesia, and OB/GYN care in underserved areas through partnerships with local providers, while training the next generation of academic global surgery leaders.
All-Immu, Dent-OMFS, ER Med, Heme-Onc, MF Med, Neurosurg, OB-GYN, Ophth-Opt, Path, Ped Surg, Plast, Surg, Urol
⊕ https://vfmat.ch/e59a

University of New Mexico School of Medicine: Project Echo
Seeks to improve health outcomes worldwide through the use of a technology called telementoring, a guided-practice model in which the participating clinician retains responsibility for managing the patient.
General, Infect Dis, MF Med, OB-GYN, Path, Peds
⊕ https://vfmat.ch/6c9a

University of Virginia: Anesthesiology Department Global Health Initiatives
Educates and trains physicians to help people achieve healthy productive lives, and advances knowledge in the medical sciences.
Anesth, Pub Health
⊕ https://vfmat.ch/1b8b

University of Washington: Department of Global Health
Improves health for all through research, education, training, and service, addresses the causes of disease and health inequities at multiple levels, and collaborates with partners to develop and sustain locally led, quality health systems, programs, and policies.
Infect Dis, Logist-Op, Pub Health
⊕ https://vfmat.ch/f543

USA for United Nations High Commissioner for Refugees (UNHCR)
Serves and protects refugees and displaced people through emergency relief, cash assistance, education, resettlement, and the rebuilding of livelihoods.
ER Med, General, Logist-Op, Nutr, Pub Health
⊕ https://vfmat.ch/293c

USAID's Health Research Program
Funds maternal and child health implementation research and translates findings

into effective health interventions that can be adapted globally.
Infect Dis, MF Med, OB-GYN, Peds
⊕ https://vfmat.ch/5991

USAID: A2Z The Micronutrient and Child Blindness Project
Aims to increase the use of key micronutrient and blindness interventions to improve child and maternal health.
MF Med, Neonat, Nutr, Ophth-Opt, Surg
⊕ https://vfmat.ch/c5f1

USAID: EQUIP Health
Exists as an effective, efficient response mechanism to achieving global HIV epidemic control by delivering the right intervention at the right place and in the right way.
Infect Dis
⊕ https://vfmat.ch/d76a

USAID: Fistula Care Plus
Builds on, enhances, and expands the work undertaken by the previous Fistula Care project (2007–2013), with attention to prevention, detection, treatment, reintegration and new areas of focus so that obstetric fistula can become a rare event for future generations.
MF Med, OB-GYN, Surg
⊕ https://vfmat.ch/a7cd

USAID: Human Resources for Health 2030 (HRH2030)
Helps low- and middle-income countries develop the health workforce needed to prevent maternal and child deaths, support the goals of Family Planning 2020, control the HIV/AIDS epidemic, and protect communities from infectious diseases.
Logist-Op
⊕ https://vfmat.ch/9ea8

USAID: Leadership, Management and Governance Project
Improves leadership, management, and governance practices to strengthen health systems and improve health for all, including vulnerable populations worldwide.
Logist-Op
⊕ https://vfmat.ch/d35e

USAID: Maternal and Child Health Integrated Program
Works to improve the health of women and their families, including programs for maternal, newborn, and child health, immunization, family planning, nutrition, malaria, and HIV/AIDS.
All-Immu, General, Infect Dis, MF Med
⊕ https://vfmat.ch/4415

USAID: Maternal and Child Survival Program
Works to prevent child and maternal deaths.
Infect Dis, MF Med, Neonat, OB-GYN, Peds
⊕ https://vfmat.ch/6fcf

Vision Care
Restores sight and helps patients get regular treatment at short-term eye camps and long-term base clinics by having doctors, missionaries, volunteers, and sponsors work together.
Ophth-Opt
⊕ https://vfmat.ch/9d7c

Vision for the Poor
Reduces human suffering and improves quality of life through the recovery of sight by building sustainable eye hospitals in developing countries, empowering local eye specialists, funding essential ophthalmic infrastructure, and partnering with like-minded agencies.
Ophth-Opt
⊕ https://vfmat.ch/528e

Vital Strategies
Helps governments strengthen their public health systems to contend with the most important and difficult health challenges, while accelerating progress on the world's most pressing health problems.
CV Med, Infect Dis, Peds
⊕ https://vfmat.ch/fe25

Vitamin Angels
Helps at-risk populations in need—specifically pregnant women, new mothers, and children under age 5—to gain access to life-changing vitamins and minerals.
General, Nutr
⊕ https://vfmat.ch/7da1

Voices for a Malaria-Free Future
Seeks to expand national movements of private- and public-sector leaders to mobilize political and popular support for malaria control.
Infect Dis, Path
⊕ https://vfmat.ch/4213

Voluntary Service Overseas (VSO)
Works with health workers, communities, and governments to improve health services and rights for women, babies, youth, people with disabilities, and prisoners.
General, MF Med, OB-GYN
⊕ https://vfmat.ch/213d

Volunteering in Uganda
Constructs volunteer programs with purpose and focus on community development, education, healthcare, and childcare.
General, Peds
⊕ https://vfmat.ch/8414

VOSH (Volunteer Optometric Services to Humanity) International
Facilitates the provision and the sustainability of vision care worldwide for people who can neither afford nor obtain such care.
Ophth-Opt
⊕ https://vfmat.ch/a149

Walkabout Foundation
Provides wheelchairs and rehabilitation in the developing world and funds research to find a cure for paralysis.
Logist-Op, Rehab
⊕ https://vfmat.ch/5582

Watsi
Uses technology to make healthcare a reality for those who might not otherwise be able to afford it.
Pub Health, Surg
⊕ https://vfmat.ch/41a3

Waves of Health, The
Supports the primary healthcare needs of underserved communities and educates others about the medical challenges in the developing world.
ER Med, Infect Dis, Medicine
⊕ https://vfmat.ch/63ff

We Care for Humanity (WCH)
Promotes sustainable social change and the sustainable development goals developed by the United Nations, including: no poverty, good health and well-being, gender equality, human rights, climate action, and strong institutions.
General, Logist-Op, Pub Health
⊕ https://vfmat.ch/8b4e

WellShare International
Partners with diverse communities to promote health and well-being, and to achieve equitable healthcare and resources where all individuals are able to live healthy and fulfilling lives.
Geri, MF Med, Nutr, Pulm-Critic
⊕ https://vfmat.ch/2e9c

WF AID
Seeks to build capacity and provide emergency aid, human assistance, and international development, where required in the world.
CT Surg, Dent-OMFS, ENT, ER Med, General, Infect Dis, Logist-Op, Nutr, Ophth-Opt, Ortho, Path, Radiol, Rehab, Surg
⊕ https://vfmat.ch/ebd7

White Ribbon Alliance, The

Leads a movement for reproductive, maternal, and newborn health and accelerates progress by putting citizens at the center of global, national, and local health efforts.

MF Med, OB-GYN

⊕ https://vfmat.ch/496b

Willing and Abel

Seeks to provide connections between children in developing nations and specialist centers, helping with visas, passports, transportation, and finances.

Anesth, Dent-OMFS, Ped Surg

⊕ https://vfmat.ch/9dc7

Women and Children First

Pioneers approaches that support communities to solve problems themselves.

MF Med, Neonat, OB-GYN, Peds

⊕ https://vfmat.ch/cdc9

Women's Refugee Commission

Seeks to improve lives by protecting the rights of women, children, and youth displaced by conflict and crisis through researching their needs, identifying solutions, and advocating for programs and policies to strengthen their resilience.

General, MF Med, Neonat, OB-GYN, Peds, Psych

⊕ https://vfmat.ch/3d8f

World Blind Union (WBU)

Represents those experiencing blindness, speaking to governments and international bodies on issues concerning visual impairments.

Ophth-Opt

⊕ https://vfmat.ch/2bd3

World Care Foundation

Encourages humanitarian efforts to help those in need anywhere in the world, regardless of their faith, color, gender, and ethnicity. Projects include orphanages, orphan sponsorship, medical centers, refugee crisis work, and education.

ER Med, General, Pub Health

⊕ https://vfmat.ch/987a

World Children's Fund

Commits to helping children worldwide who are suffering the effects of poverty, disease, natural disaster, famine, abuse, civil strife, and war.

General, Logist-Op, MF Med, Nutr, OB-GYN, Pub Health

⊕ https://vfmat.ch/9cd8

World Children's Initiative (WCI)

Aims to improve and rebuild the healthcare and educational infrastructure for children in developing areas, both domestic and worldwide.

CV Med, Ped Surg, Surg

⊕ https://vfmat.ch/9ca7

World Compassion Fellowship (WCF)

Serves the global poor and persecuted through relief, medical care, development, and training.

CV Med, ER Med, Endo, GI, General, Infect Dis, Medicine, Nutr, OB-GYN, Ortho, Peds, Psych, Pub Health, Rehab

⊕ https://vfmat.ch/7b97

World Council of Optometry

Facilitates the development of optometry worldwide and promotes eye health and vision care through advocacy, education, policy development, and humanitarian outreach.

Ophth-Opt, Pub Health

⊕ https://vfmat.ch/c92e

World Federation of Hemophilia (WFH)

Aims to improve and sustain care for people with inherited bleeding disorders by pursuing long-term relationships with individuals and organizations who share the values of WFH's development model.

Heme-Onc

⊕ https://vfmat.ch/5121

World Health Organization, The (WHO)

The United Nations' agency for health provides leadership on global health matters, shapes the health research agenda, sets norms and standards, articulates evidence-based policy options, provides technical support and monitoring to countries, and assesses health trends.

ER Med, General, Infect Dis, Logist-Op, MF Med, OB-GYN, Peds, Psych, Pub Health

⊕ https://vfmat.ch/c476

World Medical Relief

Facilitates the distribution of surplus medical resources where they are needed.

Logist-Op

⊕ https://vfmat.ch/72dc

World Missions Possible

Provides EMS capacity-building, along with medical and vision care, to under-developed and rural areas.

ER Med, General, Heme-Onc, Neonat, Ophth-Opt, Surg

⊕ https://vfmat.ch/d6a5

World Parkinson's Program

Seeks to improve the quality of life of those affected by Parkinson's disease through education and advocacy, and provides free medication and support services.

Logist-Op, Neuro, Pub Health

⊕ https://vfmat.ch/c96d

World Vision International

Works with vulnerable communities around the world to overcome poverty and injustice with child-focused programs in disaster management, health, nutrition, economic development, education, clean water, sanitation, and hygiene.

ER Med, General, Infect Dis, MF Med, Nutr, OB-GYN, Peds

⊕ https://vfmat.ch/2642

Worldwide Fistula Fund

Protects and restores the health and dignity of the world's most vulnerable women by preventing and treating devastating childbirth injuries.

OB-GYN

⊕ https://vfmat.ch/8813

Worldwide Healing Hands

Works to improve the quality of healthcare for women and children in the most underserved areas of the world and to stop the preventable deaths of mothers.

General, MF Med, Neonat, OB-GYN

⊕ https://vfmat.ch/b331

Yale School of Medicine: Global Surgery Division

Addresses the rising worldwide surgical disease burden in low-resource settings, both domestically and internationally, by mobilizing a community of surgical leaders to engage in international partnerships and implement quality improvement and training protocols.

ER Med, Infect Dis, Medicine, Peds

⊕ https://vfmat.ch/2bf7

YORGHAS Foundation

Supports mothers, pregnant women, infants, people with disabilities, and those suffering from humanitarian crises, poverty, or social inequalities, with particular emphasis on women's and children's rights.

MF Med, Neonat

⊕ https://vfmat.ch/9e44

Uganda

Healthcare Facilities

Anaka Hospital
Anaka, Nwoya, Uganda
⊕ https://vfmat.ch/3f66

Apac General Hospital
Olelpek Road, Apac, Apac, Uganda
⊕ https://vfmat.ch/bb13

Arua Regional Referral Hospital
Hospital Road, River Oli, Arua, Uganda
⊕ https://vfmat.ch/69fe

Baylor
Kampala, Uganda
⊕ https://vfmat.ch/c763

Bishop Caesar Asili Hospital
Gulu – Kampala Road, Luweero, Uganda
⊕ https://vfmat.ch/befb

Bombo Military Hospital
Gulu – Kampala Road, Bombo, Luweero, Uganda
⊕ https://vfmat.ch/5218

Bududa Hospital
Bududa Ring, Namaitsu, Bududa, Uganda
⊕ https://vfmat.ch/b5f2

Bugiri Main Hospital
Bugiri, Uganda
⊕ https://vfmat.ch/9abc

Buhinga Fort Portal Regional Referral Hospital
Mugurusi Road, Fort Portal, Kabarole, Uganda
⊕ https://vfmat.ch/6256

Butabika Hospital
Butabika Road, Kampala, Central Region, Uganda
⊕ https://vfmat.ch/be9e

Buwenge Hospital
Jinja Kamuli Road, Kasambira, Kamuli, Uganda
⊕ https://vfmat.ch/d1a2

Bwera Hospital
Kaserengethe II, Kasese, Uganda
⊕ https://vfmat.ch/e5af

Bwindi Community Hospital
Kanungu, Uganda
⊕ https://vfmat.ch/831f

China-Uganda Friendship Hospital
Shoprite Road, Kampala, Central Region, Uganda
⊕ https://vfmat.ch/e6f6

CoRSU Hospital
Kawuku, Entebbe Road, Uganda
⊕ https://vfmat.ch/47f6

Cure Children's Hospital at Uganda
Mbale, Uganda
⊕ https://vfmat.ch/9dae

Dabani Hospital
B1, Bumulimba, Busia, Uganda
⊕ https://vfmat.ch/9393

Eggwonero Life Saving Hospital
Kawempe I 2482, Kampala, Central Region, Uganda
⊕ https://vfmat.ch/d647

Entebbe Hospital
Kampala Road, Entebbe, Wakiso, Uganda
⊕ https://vfmat.ch/b383

Gulu Hospital
Awere Road, Gulu, Uganda
⊕ https://vfmat.ch/2c91

Hoima Regional Referral Hospital
Main Street, Hoima, Uganda
⊕ https://vfmat.ch/66e2

Hope and Faith
Kibuye Natete Road, Kampala, Central Region, Uganda
⊕ https://vfmat.ch/f3db

International Hospital Kampala
4686 St. Barnabas Road, Kampala, Central Region, Uganda
⊕ https://vfmat.ch/6a87

Ishaka Adventist Hospital
Nungamo – Katunguru Road, Kashenyi, Bushenyi, Uganda
⊕ https://vfmat.ch/dfd5

Islamic Hospital
Gulu – Kampala Road, Matugga, Wakiso, Uganda
⊕ https://vfmat.ch/3b2b

Itojo Hospital
Itojo, Uganda
⊕ https://vfmat.ch/3d37

Jinja Hospital
Naranbhai Road, Jinja, Uganda
⊕ https://vfmat.ch/4e48

Jinja Main Hospital
Nile Avenue, Jinja, Uganda
⊕ https://vfmat.ch/28e3

Kabale Regional Hospital
Corryndon Road, Kabale, Kabale, Uganda
⊕ https://vfmat.ch/fbd2

Kabarole Hospital
Fort Portal – Kasese Road, Kasusu, Kabarole, Uganda
⊕ https://vfmat.ch/d7e8

Kadic Hospital
Kiira Road, Kampala, Central Region, Uganda
⊕ https://vfmat.ch/3e9a

Kagando Hospital
Kagando, Kasese, Uganda
⊕ https://vfmat.ch/f8ff

Kampala Hospital
Plot 6C Makindu Close, Kampala, Central Region,
Uganda
⊕ https://vfmat.ch/3271

Kampala Medical Chambers Hospital
Buganda, Kampala, Uganda
⊕ https://vfmat.ch/9b36

Kamu Medical Centre
Wakoli, Jinja, Uganda
⊕ https://vfmat.ch/6941

Kamuli General Hospital
Kamuli, Uganda
⊕ https://vfmat.ch/b14d

Kamuli Mission Hospital
Gabula Road, Kamuli, Kamuli, Uganda
⊕ https://vfmat.ch/23b5

Kapchorwa Hospital
Mbale-Sironko-Kapchorwa Highway, Kapchorwa,
Kapchorwa, Uganda
⊕ https://vfmat.ch/e2ab

Katabi UPDAF Hospital
Katabi, Uganda
⊕ https://vfmat.ch/5626

Katimba Parish Hospital
Kabingo Road, Katimba, Sembabule, Uganda
⊕ https://vfmat.ch/8495

Kawolo Hospital
Jinja – Kampala Road, Najjembe, Buikwe, Uganda
⊕ https://vfmat.ch/dada

Kayunga Hospital
Busaana Road, Kaazi, Kayunga, Uganda
⊕ https://vfmat.ch/ce34

Kiboga Hospital
Hoima – Kampala Road, Munsambya, Kyankwanzi,
Uganda
⊕ https://vfmat.ch/d435

Kibuli Muslim Hospital
Prince Badru Kakungulu Road, Kampala, Central
Region, Uganda
⊕ https://vfmat.ch/1358

Kilembe Hospital
Kilembe Road, Chanjojo, Kasese, Uganda
⊕ https://vfmat.ch/6e57

Kiruddu General Referral Hospital
Salaama Road, Kampala, Central Region, Uganda
⊕ https://vfmat.ch/38c1

Kiryandongo Hospital
Gulu – Kampala Road, Kigumba, Kiryandongo,
Uganda
⊕ https://vfmat.ch/dc13

Kisiizi Hospital
Rukungiri, Uganda
⊕ https://vfmat.ch/4ef6

Kisoro Hospital
Kisoro – Bunagana Road, Bunagana Trading Centre,
Kisoro, Uganda
⊕ https://vfmat.ch/299f

Kisubi Hospital
Road to White House Sister's Residence, Kisubi,
Wakiso, Uganda
⊕ https://vfmat.ch/c524

Kitara Medical Center
Hoima Road, Masindi, Uganda
⊕ https://vfmat.ch/9796

Kitgum Hospital
Gulu-Kitgum Road, Acholibur, Pader, Uganda
⊕ https://vfmat.ch/732a

Kitovu General Hospital
Senyange Road, Masaka, Masaka, Uganda
⊕ https://vfmat.ch/f272

KIU Teaching Hospital
Kabirisi Road, Ishaka, Bushenyi, Uganda
⊕ https://vfmat.ch/fcc1

Kiwoko Hospital
Kiwoko Road, Kiwoko, Nakaseke, Uganda
⊕ https://vfmat.ch/d72a

Kololo Hospital Kampala Ltd.
16 Kawalya Kaggwa Close, Kampala, Central Region,
Uganda
⊕ https://vfmat.ch/e412

Kumi Hospital
Ongino Road, Kumi, Uganda
⊕ https://vfmat.ch/96fa

Lira Regional Referral Hospital
Plot 9/19, 21-41 Ngetta Road Police Road, Lira,
Uganda
⊕ https://vfmat.ch/c5fa

Makerere University Hospital
Kagugube Semuliki Walk, Kampala, Central Region,
Uganda
⊕ https://vfmat.ch/edb7

Masaka Referral Hospital
Alex Ssebowa Road, Masaka, Masaka, Uganda
⊕ https://vfmat.ch/ad2e

Masindi District Hospital
Kijunjubwa Road, Masindi, Uganda
⊕ https://vfmat.ch/1bce

Mayanja Memorial Hospital
Mbarara, Uganda
⊕ https://vfmat.ch/562d

Mbale General Hospital
Lira – Mbale Road, Mbale, Uganda
⊕ https://vfmat.ch/c5b6

Mbale Regional Referral Hospital
Lira – Mbale Road, Mbale, Uganda
⊕ https://vfmat.ch/645e

**Mbarara District Regional Referral
Hospital**
Hospital Road, Mbarara, Mbarara, Uganda
⊕ https://vfmat.ch/22cc

Medik Hospital
Bombo Road, Kampala, Central Region, Uganda
⊕ https://vfmat.ch/a336

Mengo Hospital
Catherdral Hill Road, Kampala, Central Region,
Uganda
⊕ https://vfmat.ch/8ff1

MGH
Ggaba Road, Kampala, Central Region, Uganda
⊕ https://vfmat.ch/c391

**Middle East Hospital & Diagnostic
Centre**
Spring Road, Kampala, Uganda
⊕ https://vfmat.ch/51b2

Mildmay Uganda
Entebbe Road, Lubowa, Wakiso, Uganda
⊕ https://vfmat.ch/586e

Mityana Hospital
Fort Portal – Kampala Road, Zigoti, Mityana, Uganda
⊕ https://vfmat.ch/7977

Moroto Regional Referral Hospital
Moroto Highway and Mainstreet, Moroto, Uganda
⊕ https://vfmat.ch/895d

Mount Sinai Kyabirwa Surgical Facility
Jinja, Uganda
⊕ https://vfmat.ch/7vsb

Moyo Hospital
Okudi Road, Moyo, Moyo, Uganda
⊕ https://vfmat.ch/efcd

Mpigi Hospital
Mpigi Kabasanda Road, Mpigi, Uganda
⊕ https://vfmat.ch/cb33

MRC/UVRI & LSHTM Uganda Research Unit
Nakiwogo Road, Entebbe, Uganda
⊕ https://vfmat.ch/8362

Mount Elgon Hospital
Cathedral Avenue, Mbale, Uganda
⊕ https://vfmat.ch/4125

Mukesh Madhvani Children's Hospital
Clive Road, Jinja, Uganda
⊕ https://vfmat.ch/9fc7

Mukono Church of Uganda Hospital
Jinja – Kampala Road, Mukono, Mukono, Uganda
⊕ https://vfmat.ch/4146

Mulago National Referral Hospital
Upper Mulago Hill Road, Kampala, Central Region, Uganda
⊕ https://vfmat.ch/83da

Mundindi
Busia, Busia, Uganda
⊕ https://vfmat.ch/3ab9

Mutolere Hospital
Mutolere Road, Mutolere, Kisoro, Uganda
⊕ https://vfmat.ch/c652

Nakasero Hospital
Nakasero Hill, Kampala, Uganda
⊕ https://vfmat.ch/5f4d

Nansanga Hospital
Nansanga, Uganda
⊕ https://vfmat.ch/3355

Nile International Hospital
Kyabazinga Road, Jinja, Uganda
⊕ https://vfmat.ch/7495

Nkozl Hospital
Nkozi, Mpigi, Uganda
⊕ https://vfmat.ch/68bb

Norvik Hospital
Bombo Road, Kampala, Central Region, Uganda
⊕ https://vfmat.ch/16b2

Nyakibale Hospital
Kambuga – Ntungamo, Rukungiri, Uganda
⊕ https://vfmat.ch/944a

Pallisa Hospital
Kanyumu Road, Pallisa, Uganda
⊕ https://vfmat.ch/c97b

Paragon Hospital
6A/7A Luthuli Avenue, Kampala, Central Region, Uganda
⊕ https://vfmat.ch/ed72

Rubaga Hospital
Muteesa Road, Kampala, Central Region, Uganda
⊕ https://vfmat.ch/47e2

Rugarama Hospital
Rugarama Road, Rugarama, Kabale, Uganda
⊕ https://vfmat.ch/b3c1

Rushere Community Hospital
Rushere, Kiruhura District, Western Region, Uganda
⊕ https://vfmat.ch/b619

Ruth Gaylord Hospital Maganjo
Bombo Road, Kampala, Central Region, Uganda
⊕ https://vfmat.ch/78fe

Saint Catherine's Hospital
Buganda, Kampala, Uganda
⊕ https://vfmat.ch/fac1

Salem Hospital
Nakaloke-Kabwangasi, Nakaloke, Mbale, Uganda
⊕ https://vfmat.ch/36be

Soroti Regional Referral Hospital
A104, Opuyo, Soroti, Uganda
⊕ https://vfmat.ch/3bb4

Spontaneous Healing Center, The
Mbale-Nkokonjeru, Mbale, Uganda
⊕ https://vfmat.ch/9916

St. Joseph's Hospital
Gulu-Kitgum Road, Acholibur, Pader, Uganda
⊕ https://vfmat.ch/c4fc

St. Monica Katende HC III
Kampala – Masaka Road, Katende, Mpigi, Uganda
⊕ https://vfmat.ch/dbd1

St. Anthony's Hospital
Busia Road, Tororo, Uganda
⊕ https://vfmat.ch/adc9

St. Francis Hospital Nsambya
Nsambya Road, Kampala, Central Region, Uganda
⊕ https://vfmat.ch/afae

St. Kizito Hospital
Matany, Napak, Uganda
⊕ https://vfmat.ch/7275

St. Mary's Hospital Lacor
Nimule – Gulu Road, Aciak, Amuru, Uganda
⊕ https://vfmat.ch/e14f

Taso
Italy Road, Mbale, Uganda
⊕ https://vfmat.ch/9a39

Tororo Hospital
Station Road, Railway Village, Tororo, Uganda
⊕ https://vfmat.ch/9e69

Uganda Cancer Institute
Upper Mulago Hill Road, Kampala, Uganda
⊕ https://vfmat.ch/c41a

Uganda Children's Hospital
Jinja – Mbale Road, Mbale, Uganda
⊕ https://vfmat.ch/d3b3

Uganda Martyrs Ibanda Hospital
Ibanda, Uganda
⊕ https://vfmat.ch/37e4

Uganda Red Cross
Maluku, Mbale, Uganda
⊕ https://vfmat.ch/a212

Victoria Hospital
Kira Road, Kampala, Central Region, Uganda
⊕ https://vfmat.ch/e281

Villa Maria Hospital
Weaver Bird Road, Masaka, Uganda
⊕ https://vfmat.ch/fc59

Whisper's Magical Children's Hospital
32 Madhvani Road, Jinja, Uganda
⊕ https://vfmat.ch/25b3

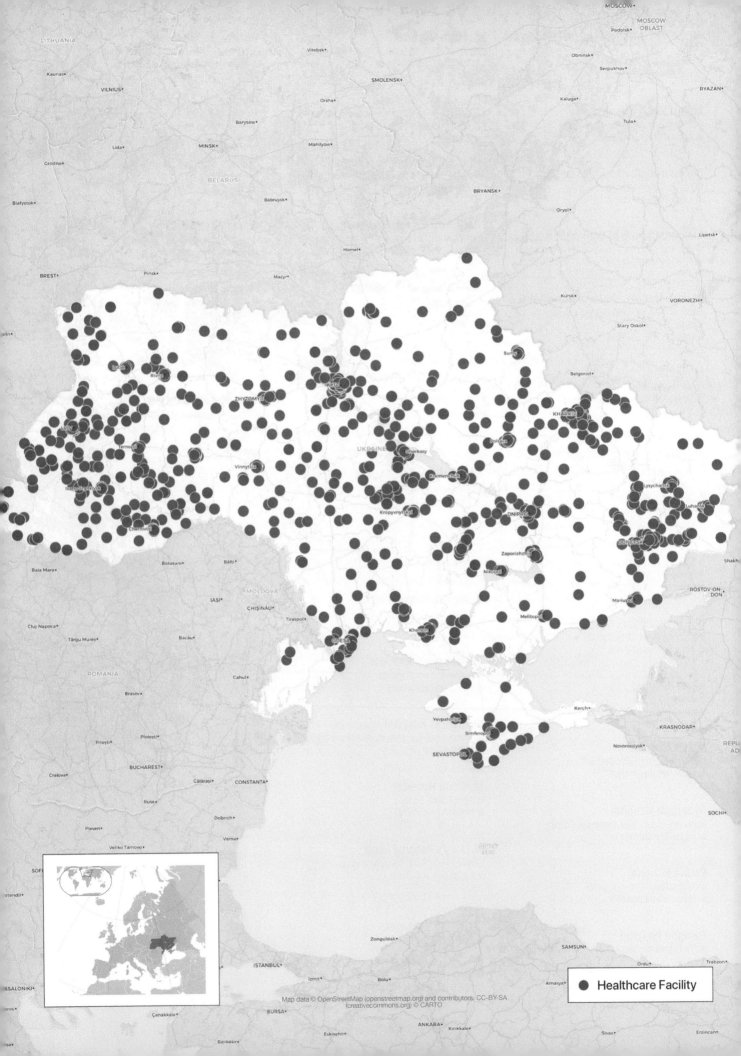

Healthcare Facility

Ukraine

Ukraine is the second largest country in Europe, bordered by Russia, Belarus, Poland, Slovakia, Hungary, Romania, Moldova, the Sea of Azov, and the Black Sea. Home to seven World Heritage Sites, and also the presumed geographical center of the European continent, Ukraine has the eighth highest population in Europe, with approximately 43.7 million people. About 70 percent of the population lives in urban areas, including major metropolitan centers such as Kharkiv, Odessa, Dnipropetrovsk, Donetsk, and the capital, Kyiv. The majority of the population is ethnically Ukrainian, but other groups include Russian, Belarusian, Moldovan, Crimean Tata, Bulgarian, Hungarian, Romanian, Polish, and Jewish. The country is majority Christian, with two-thirds identifying as Orthodox. Languages spoken include Ukrainian, the official language, and Russian.

Ukraine became independent from the Soviet Union in 1991. Since the early 1990s, the country has experienced volatile growth but also had a significant economic downturn in 2009. Russia's occupation of Crimea, and conflict in the eastern end of Ukraine, have contributed to Ukraine's economic struggles. It is considered to be the poorest country in Europe, with high rates of poverty and corruption. Ukraine is one of the world's largest exporters of grain, with other major crops including potatoes, sugar beets, and sunflower oil.

The Ukrainian population suffers from heavy alcohol consumption, one of the highest per capita rates in the world. As a result, cirrhosis is a top cause of death. Other leading causes of death include ischemic heart disease, stroke, lung cancer, Alzheimer's disease, cardiomyopathy, colorectal cancer, COPD, and stomach cancer. The risk factors that contribute to the most death and disability include high blood pressure, dietary risks, high LDL, high body-mass index, alcohol and tobacco use, high fasting plasma glucose, air pollution, kidney dysfunction, and non-optimal temperature.

43.7M

Population

$3,727

GDP Per Capita

72 years

Life Expectancy

↑ Improving

299
Doctors/100k

Physician Density

746
Beds/100k

Hospital Bed Density

19
Deaths/100k

Maternal Mortality

Ukraine

Nonprofit Organizations

Abt Associates
Seeks to improve the quality of life and economic well-being of people worldwide, while striving to meet and exceed the highest professional standards.
General, Logist-Op, MF Med, OB-GYN, Peds
🌐 https://vfmat.ch/cec2

Adventist Health International
Focuses on upgrading and managing mission hospitals by providing governance, consultation, and technical assistance to a number of affiliated Seventh-Day Adventist hospitals throughout Africa, Asia, and the Americas.
Dent-OMFS, General, Pub Health
🌐 https://vfmat.ch/16aa

AFEW International
Aims to improve the health of populations in Eastern Europe and Central Asia, strives to increase access to prevention, treatment, and care for HIV, TB, and viral hepatitis, and promotes health and SRHR.
Infect Dis, Pub Health
🌐 https://vfmat.ch/19c6

Age International
Helps older people living in some of the world's poorest places to have improved well-being and be treated with dignity through a variety of programs, including emergency relief and cataract surgery.
ER Med, Geri, Logist-Op, Nutr, Ophth-Opt, Palliative, Pub Health
🌐 https://vfmat.ch/c7e2

AIDS Healthcare Foundation
Provides cutting-edge HIV/AIDS medical care and advocacy to over one million people in 43 countries.
Infect Dis
🌐 https://vfmat.ch/b27c

American International Health Alliance (AIHA)
Strengthens health systems and workforce capacity worldwide through locally driven, peer-to-peer institutional partnerships.
CV Med, ER Med, Infect Dis, Medicine, OB-GYN
🌐 https://vfmat.ch/69fd

Arbeiter Samariter Bund (Workers' Samaritan Federation)
Engages in areas such as civil protection, rescue services, and social welfare, while operating a network of welcome centers to help refugees.
ER Med, General, Infect Dis, Logist-Op, Rehab
🌐 https://vfmat.ch/8a5b

Arlene Campbell Humanitarian Foundation
Provides medical supplies for hospitals in Kyiv, Ukraine, and helps facilitate physician training and research programs for U.S. and Ukrainian doctors.
CV Med, Logist-Op
🌐 https://vfmat.ch/4174

Bright Kids Charity
Provides underprivileged children with the support they need through the provision of education, medical treatment, rehabilitation, and recreational activities.
Logist-Op
🌐 https://vfmat.ch/8318

Chernobyl Children International
Gives support and hope to children living in the aftermath of the Chernobyl nuclear disaster, by providing services in housing and community reintegration.
Ped Surg, Radiol
🌐 https://vfmat.ch/b2eb

ChildAid
Aims to support the work of local projects helping disadvantaged children in Eastern Europe, inspired by the Christian faith.
General, Neuro, Peds, Psych, Pub Health, Rehab
🌐 https://vfmat.ch/952a

Children's Lifeline International
Provides medical teams and surgical assistance to underprivileged children in developing countries through missions in partnership with local hospitals.
CV Med, Dent-OMFS, General, MF Med, Neurosurg, Peds, Rehab
🌐 https://vfmat.ch/6fea

Christian Aid Ministries
Strives to be a trustworthy and efficient channel for Amish, Mennonite, and other conservative Anabaptist groups and individuals to minister to physical and spiritual needs around the world.
CT Surg, ER Med, Logist-Op, Ortho, Pub Health
🌐 https://vfmat.ch/7b33

Christian Health Service Corps
Brings Christian doctors, health professionals, and health educators committed to serving the poor to places that otherwise have little or no access to healthcare.
Anesth, Dent-OMFS, General, Medicine, Peds, Surg
🌐 https://vfmat.ch/da57

Christian Medical & Dental Associations
Based in Christian ministry, deploys medical and dental teams to underserved communities to provide vital healthcare.
Anesth, Dent-OMFS, ER Med, General, Medicine, OB-GYN, Ophth-Opt, Peds, Pub Health, Radiol, Rehab, Surg
🌐 https://vfmat.ch/921c

Christian Mobile Medical Team, The
Provides healthcare via a mobile clinic, inspired by the Christian faith.
Dent-OMFS, General, OB-GYN, Ophth-Opt, Ortho, Peds, Surg
🌐 https://vfmat.ch/718f

Clean Future Fund
Seeks to support communities affected by industrial accidents by raising awareness and providing education, healthcare, and safe work environments.
Logist-Op, Radiol
⊕ https://vfmat.ch/9234

Core Group
Aims to improve and expand community health practices for underserved populations, especially women and children, through collaborative action and learning.
General, Infect Dis, MF Med, Medicine, OB-GYN, Peds, Pub Health
⊕ https://vfmat.ch/9de3

Direct Relief
Improves the health and lives of people affected by poverty or emergency situations by mobilizing and providing essential medical resources needed for their care.
ER Med, Logist-Op
⊕ https://vfmat.ch/58e5

Doctors Without Borders/Médecins Sans Frontières (MSF)
Responds to emergencies and provides lifesaving medical care where needed most, including during disasters, conflicts, and epidemics.
Anesth, Crit-Care, ER Med, General, Infect Dis, Nutr, OB-GYN, Ped Surg, Peds, Psych, Pub Health, Surg
⊕ https://vfmat.ch/f363

Elton John AIDS Foundation
Seeks to address and overcome the stigma, discrimination, and neglect that prevents ending AIDS by funding local experts to challenge discrimination, prevent infections, and provide treatment.
Infect Dis, Pub Health
⊕ https://vfmat.ch/9d31

Evangelical Alliance Mission, The (TEAM)
Provides services in the areas of church planting, community development, healthcare, social justice, business as mission, and more.
Dent-OMFS, General, Ophth-Opt
⊕ https://vfmat.ch/9faa

Foundation for Healthcare for Humanity
Provide assistance in the development and implementation of medical programs in the United States, Africa, South America, Eastern Europe, and the Caribbean.
General
⊕ https://vfmat.ch/ba7f

Gift of Life International
Provides lifesaving cardiac treatment to children in developing countries while developing sustainable pediatric cardiac programs by implementing screening, surgical, and training missions.
Anesth, CT Surg, CV Med, Crit-Care, Ped Surg, Peds, Pulm-Critic
⊕ https://vfmat.ch/f2f9

Global ENT Outreach
Saves lives and prevents avoidable deafness from ear disease for those affected by poverty and lack of care so they can reach their full human potential.
ENT, Surg
⊕ https://vfmat.ch/ef5c

Global Ministries – The United Methodist Church
As the worldwide mission and development agency of The United Methodist Church, Global Ministries works with more than 300 hospitals and clinics around the world through its Global Health Unit.
Anesth, CT Surg, CV Med, Crit-Care, Dent-OMFS, Derm, ER Med, GI, General, Infect Dis, Logist-Op, MF Med, Medicine, Neonat, Nephro, Nutr, OB-GYN, Ophth-Opt, Ortho, Palliative, Peds, Pod, Psych, Pub Health, Rehab, Rheum, Surg, Urol
⊕ https://vfmat.ch/1723

Global Oncology (GO)
Brings the best in cancer care to underserved patients around the world and collaborates across geographic, professional, and academic borders to improve cancer care, research, and education.

Heme-Onc, Path, Rad-Onc
⊕ https://vfmat.ch/fcb8

Global Polio Eradication Initiative
Aims to eradicate polio worldwide.
All-Immu, Infect-Dis, Logist-Op, Pub Health
⊕ https://vfmat.ch/7e2c

GlobalMedic
Provides disaster relief and lifesaving humanitarian aid.
ER Med, Pub Health
⊕ https://vfmat.ch/dfe6

Globus Relief
Aims to improve the delivery of healthcare worldwide by gathering, processing, and distributing surplus medical supplies to charities at home and abroad.
Logist-Op
⊕ https://vfmat.ch/a2b7

Grassroot Soccer
Leverages the power of soccer to educate, inspire, and mobilize at-risk youth in developing countries to overcome their greatest health challenges, live healthier and more productive lives, and be agents for change in their communities.
Infect Dis
⊕ https://vfmat.ch/3521

HealthProm
Works with local partners to promote health and social care for vulnerable children and their families.
General, MF Med, Peds, Pub Health
⊕ https://vfmat.ch/153d

HealthRight International
Leverages global resources to address local health challenges and create sustainable solutions that empower marginalized communities to live healthy lives.
General, Infect Dis, MF Med, OB-GYN, Psych, Pub Health
⊕ https://vfmat.ch/129d

Healthy DEvelopments
Provides Germany-supported health and social protection programs around the globe in a collaborative knowledge management process.
All-Immu, General, Infect Dis, Logist-Op, MF Med
⊕ https://vfmat.ch/dc31

Hear the World Foundation
Advocates worldwide for equal opportunities and improved quality of life for people in need with hearing loss.
ENT, Peds
⊕ https://vfmat.ch/122c

Hearing Health Foundation
Prevents and cures hearing loss and tinnitus through groundbreaking research and promotes hearing health.
Surg
⊕ https://vfmat.ch/2e71

Heart to Heart International
Strengthens communities through improving health access, providing humanitarian development, and administering crisis relief worldwide. Engages volunteers, collaborates with partners, and deploys resources to achieve this mission.
Anesth, ER Med, General, Logist-Op, Medicine, Path, Path, Peds, Psych, Pub Health, Surg
⊕ https://vfmat.ch/aacb

Help The Children
Seeks to promote the welfare of children in need, including children with physical disabilities and/or life-threatening diseases.
Logist-Op, Ped Surg, Peds, Radiol
⊕ https://vfmat.ch/ce9b

HelpAge Canada
Works in partnerships to improve and maintain the quality of life of vulnerable older persons and their communities in Canada and around the world.
ER Med, Geri
⊕ https://vfmat.ch/9945

HelpAge International
Works to ensure that people everywhere understand how much older people contribute to society and that they must enjoy their right to healthcare, social services, economic, and physical security.
General, Geri, Infect Dis, Medicine, Pub Health
⊕ https://vfmat.ch/5d91

Humanitarian Aid Response Team (HART)
Aims to alleviate poverty and injustice in Eastern Europe by working with local leaders, organizations and churches to empower communities, inspired by the Christian faith.
Dent-OMFS, General, Logist-Op, Peds
⊕ https://vfmat.ch/1cdd

ICAP at Columbia University
Serves as global leader in supporting the scale-up of multidisciplinary HIV/AIDS prevention, care, and treatment programs based on a family-focused approach.
General, Infect Dis, MF Med, Medicine, OB-GYN, Pub Health
⊕ https://vfmat.ch/a8ef

IMA World Health
Works to build healthier communities by collaborating with key partners to serve vulnerable people with a focus on health, healing, and well-being for all.
Infect Dis, MF Med, Nutr, OB-GYN, Pub Health
⊕ https://vfmat.ch/8316

International Children's Heart Foundation
Provides free surgical care, medical training, and technology to save the lives of children with congenital heart disease in developing countries.
Anesth, CT Surg, CV Med, Crit-Care, Ped Surg, Peds, Pulm-Critic
⊕ https://vfmat.ch/86c1

International Federation of Gynecology and Obstetrics (FIGO)
Implements global projects on specific women's health issues.
MF Med, Medicine, Neonat, OB-GYN, Surg, Urol
⊕ https://vfmat.ch/c4b4

International Federation of Red Cross and Red Crescent Societies (IFRC)
Coordinates and directs international assistance following natural and manmade disasters in nonconflict situations through the world's largest humanitarian and development network. Provides disaster-preparedness programs, healthcare activities, and promotes humanitarian values.
ER Med, General, Infect Dis, Nutr
⊕ https://vfmat.ch/b4ee

International Medical Corps
Seeks to improve quality of life through health interventions and related activities that strengthen underserved communities worldwide, with the flexibility to respond rapidly to emergencies and offer medical services and training to people at the highest risk.
ER Med, General, Infect Dis, Nutr, OB-GYN, Peds, Pub Health, Surg
⊕ https://vfmat.ch/a8a5

International Organization for Migration (IOM) – The UN Migration Agency
Promotes evidence-informed policies and holistic, preventive, and curative health programs that are beneficial, accessible, and equitable for vulnerable migrants.
General, Infect Dis, OB-GYN
⊕ https://vfmat.ch/621a

International Planned Parenthood Federation (IPPF)
Leads a locally owned, globally connected civil society movement that provides and enables services and champions sexual and reproductive health and rights for all, especially the underserved.
Infect Dis, MF Med, OB-GYN
⊕ https://vfmat.ch/dc97

InterSurgeon
Fosters collaborative partnerships in the field of global surgery that will advance clinical care, teaching, training, research, and the provision and maintenance of medical equipment.
ENT, Neurosurg, Ortho, Ped Surg, Plast, Surg, Urol
⊕ https://vfmat.ch/6f8a

John Snow, Inc. (JSI)
Aims to improve the health and well-being of underserved and vulnerable people and communities throughout the world.
General, Infect Dis, Logist-Op, MF Med, OB-GYN, Peds, Psych, Pub Health
⊕ https://vfmat.ch/ba78

Joint United Nations Programme on HIV/AIDS (UNAIDS)
Aims to place people living with HIV and people affected by the virus at the decision-making table and at the center of designing, delivering, and monitoring the AIDS response.
Infect Dis
⊕ https://vfmat.ch/464a

Kybele Incorporated
Aims to create healthcare partnerships across borders to improve childbirth safety.
Anesth, Neonat, OB-GYN, Pub Health
⊕ https://vfmat.ch/5fc9

Lifebox
Seeks to provide safer surgery and anesthesia in low-resource countries by investing in tools, training, and partnerships for safe surgery.
Anesth, Crit-Care, Surg
⊕ https://vfmat.ch/2d4d

Limbs International
Engages communities and transforms lives through affordable, sustainable prosthetic solutions and rehabilitation services in developing countries.
Logist-Op, Ortho, Pod, Rehab
⊕ https://vfmat.ch/dc84

Management Sciences for Health (MSH)
Works with countries and communities to save lives and improve the health of the world's poorest and most vulnerable people by building strong, resilient, sustainable health systems.
Infect Dis, Logist-Op, Pub Health
⊕ https://vfmat.ch/6aa2

MAP International
Provides medicines and health supplies to those in need around the world so they might experience life to the fullest.
Logist-Op
⊕ https://vfmat.ch/deed

Medical Mercy Canada
Seeks to improve the quality of life in impoverished areas through humanitarian projects with local participation, and provides funding for orphanages, geriatric and childcare centers, remote health clinics, medical aid centers, hospitals, rural schools, and health programs.
General
⊕ https://vfmat.ch/81dc

Medical Ministry International
Provides compassionate healthcare in areas of need, inspired by the Christian faith.
CT Surg, Dent-OMFS, ENT, General, OB-GYN, Ophth-Opt, Ortho, Plast, Rehab, Surg, Urol, Vasc Surg
⊕ https://vfmat.ch/5da6

Medical Relief Foundation
Provides quality education and comprehensive healthcare partnerships that are responsive to the needs of the patients, the host country, and the community.
CT Surg, ER Med, General, Infect Dis, Vasc Surg
⊕ https://vfmat.ch/9add

MedShare
Aims to improve the quality of life of people, communities, and the planet by sourcing and directly delivering surplus medical supplies and equipment to communities in need around the world.
Logist-Op
⊕ https://vfmat.ch/c8bc

Mission Eurasia
Based in Christian ministry, trains, equips, and mobilizes individuals to be leaders in their communities and serve in areas of evangelism, refugee assistance, and humanitarian response.
General, Logist-Op, Ophth-Opt
⊕ https://vfmat.ch/d21f

Mission Regan
Collects supplies, medication, and medical equipment and provides them to those who are in desperate need, both locally and globally.
Logist-Op
⊕ https://vfmat.ch/2bc1

Mission to Ukraine
Provides services including education and medical care for special-needs children, and medical care and support for pregnant women and new mothers, inspired by the Christian faith.
Dent-OMFS, General, Psych
⊕ https://vfmat.ch/36a3

MSD for Mothers
Designs scalable solutions that help end preventable maternal deaths.
MF Med, OB-GYN, Pub Health
⊕ https://vfmat.ch/9f99

Médecins du Monde/Doctors of the World
Provides care, bears witness, and supports social change worldwide with innovative medical programs and evidence-based advocacy initiatives.
ER Med, General, Infect Dis, MF Med, Neonat, OB-GYN, Peds, Pub Health
⊕ https://vfmat.ch/a43d

Mérieux Foundation
Committed to fighting infectious diseases that affect developing countries by capacity building, particularly in clinical laboratories, and focusing on diagnosis.
Logist-Op, Path
⊕ https://vfmat.ch/a23a

Nova Ukraine
Provides humanitarian assistance to vulnerable groups in Ukraine, and strives to build a strong civil society, reform the education system, and eliminate corruption.
Logist-Op
⊕ https://vfmat.ch/bdcd

Novick Cardiac Alliance
Committed to bringing sustainable healthcare solutions to children with cardiac disease in the developing world.
Anesth, CT Surg, CV Med, Crit-Care, Ped Surg, Peds
⊕ https://vfmat.ch/72db

Operation Rainbow Canada
Provides free reconstructive surgery and related healthcare for cleft lip and cleft palate deformities to impoverished children and young adults in developing countries.
Surg
⊕ https://vfmat.ch/7f25

Order of Malta
Supports forgotten or excluded people, especially those living in conflict zones or amid natural disasters, by providing medical assistance, caring for refugees, and distributing medicines and necessities.
ER Med, General, Infect Dis, MF Med, Nephro, OB-GYN, Ortho, Psych
⊕ https://vfmat.ch/1fab

Orphan World Relief
Helps children in crisis, including orphans and refugees, by providing committed and compassionate support for their needs.

Logist-Op, Nutr
⊕ https://vfmat.ch/b841

Orphans' Aid Society (OAS)
Provides material and moral support for Ukrainian orphans up to age 18.
Logist-Op, Ophth-Opt
⊕ https://vfmat.ch/82dd

Overflowing Hands
Aims to serve children in communities across the U.S. and around the world by providing food, clothing, shelter, and healthcare.
Logist-Op, Pub Health, Radiol
⊕ https://vfmat.ch/8522

Pact
Works on the ground to improve the lives of those who are challenged by poverty and marginalization, striving for a world in which all people are heard, capable, and vibrant.
Infect Dis, Logist-Op, MF Med, Pub Health
⊕ https://vfmat.ch/9a6c

PATH
Advances health equity through innovation and partnerships so people, communities, and economies can thrive.
All-Immu, CV Med, Endo, Heme-Onc, Infect Dis, MF Med, Neonat, Nutr, OB-GYN, Path, Peds, Pulm-Critic
⊕ https://vfmat.ch/b4db

Première Urgence International
Helps civilians who are marginalized or excluded as a result of natural disasters, war, or economic collapse.
ER Med, General, MF Med, Peds, Psych
⊕ https://vfmat.ch/62ba

RestoringVision
Empowers lives by restoring vision for millions of people in need.
Ophth-Opt
⊕ https://vfmat.ch/e121

Rinat Akhmetov Foundation
Supports public health efforts such as providing ambulances and medical equipment, along with tuberculosis and cancer awareness and prevention.
General, Heme-Onc, Infect Dis, Logist-Op, Ped Surg
⊕ https://vfmat.ch/e13f

Rotary International
Provides service to others, improves lives, and advances world understanding, goodwill, and peace through its fellowship of business, professional, and community leaders.
ER Med, General, Infect Dis, MF Med, OB-GYN
⊕ https://vfmat.ch/8fb5

Salvation Army International, The
Seeks to meet human needs through services in education, healthcare, community support, emergency response, and ministry development, inspired by the Christian faith.
Dent-OMFS, Derm, ER Med, Infect Dis, MF Med, Medicine, Nutr, OB-GYN, Ophth-Opt, Palliative, Psych, Rehab, Surg
⊕ https://vfmat.ch/8eb3

Sanofi Espoir Foundation
Contributes to reducing health inequalities among populations that need it most by applying a socially responsible approach focused on fighting childhood cancers in low-income countries, improving maternal and newborn health, and improving access to care.
ER Med, OB-GYN, Peds
⊕ https://vfmat.ch/943b

Serving Others Worldwide
Aims to provide aid to the poor, distressed, and underprivileged by providing healthcare and dental services, and by building schools, orphanages, libraries, and medical clinics in undeveloped countries.

Dent-OMFS, General
⊕ https://vfmat.ch/69cb

Sheptytsky Hospital Charitable Fund
Provides medical care for the most vulnerable segments of the population.
ER Med, General, Logist-Op, Palliative, Path
⊕ https://vfmat.ch/11b9

SladeChild Foundation
Provides food, clothing, shelter, education, and medical care to some of the world's most impoverished children.
Dent-OMFS, General, Logist-Op, Ophth-Opt
⊕ https://vfmat.ch/14c5

Smile Train, Inc.
Treats children with cleft lip through a sustainable and local model that supports surgery and other forms of essential care.
Logist-Op, Pub Health
⊕ https://vfmat.ch/822c

SOS Children's Villages International
Supports children through alternative care and family strengthening.
ER Med, Peds
⊕ https://vfmat.ch/aca1

Splashes of Hope
Aims to facilitate healing through art, by bringing murals and other artistic projects to medical and social service facilities around the globe.
Logist-Op
⊕ https://vfmat.ch/c633

Sri Sathya Sai International Organization
Inspired by spiritual teachings, carries out efforts in global healthcare, education, humanitarian relief, and youth engagement.
Dent-OMFS, General, Logist-Op, Nutr, Ophth-Opt, Pub Health
⊕ https://vfmat.ch/9bda

Swiss Tropical and Public Health Institute
Contributes to the improvement of the health of populations internationally, nationally, and locally through excellence in research, education, and services.
Infect Dis, Pub Health
⊕ https://vfmat.ch/2ee4

Task Force for Global Health, The
Consists of programs and focus areas that cover a range of global health issues including neglected tropical diseases, infectious diseases, vaccines, field epidemiology, public health informatics, health workforce development, and global health ethics.
Infect Dis, Logist-Op, Medicine, Ophth-Opt, Peds
⊕ https://vfmat.ch/714c

Terre des hommes (Tdh) Foundation
Works to improve the daily life of children and their relatives in the areas of health, protection and emergency, in Europe, Africa, Asia, Latin America, and the Near and Middle East.
CT Surg, CV Med, OB-GYN, Ped Surg, Pub Health
⊕ https://vfmat.ch/5c26

Trans-Atlantic Relief Medical Foundation
Reaches out to the disenfranchised and facilitates improvement in healthcare through education, prevention, and availability of resources.
Infect Dis, Neonat, OB-GYN
⊕ https://vfmat.ch/465b

Union for International Cancer Control (UICC)
Unites and supports the cancer community to reduce the global cancer burden, promote greater equity, and ensure that cancer control continues to be a priority in the world health and development agenda.
Heme-Onc, Pub Health
⊕ https://vfmat.ch/88b1

United Hatzallah
Provides patients with quick response to medical emergencies and professional

and appropriate medical aid until an ambulance arrives.
ER Med, General, Logist-Op
⊕ https://vfmat.ch/e581

United Nations Children's Fund (UNICEF)
Works in over 190 countries and territories to save children's lives, defend their rights, and help them fulfill their potential, from early childhood through adolescence.
All-Immu, Infect Dis, MF Med, Neonat, Nutr, OB-GYN, Ped Surg, Peds, Pub Health
⊕ https://vfmat.ch/42d7

United Nations Development Programme (UNDP)
Helps countries achieve the simultaneous eradication of extreme poverty and significant reduction of inequalities and exclusion using a sustainable human development approach.
Infect Dis, Logist-Op, Pub Health
⊕ https://vfmat.ch/935c

United Nations High Commissioner for Refugees (UNHCR)
Safeguards the rights and well-being of people who have been forced to flee, ensuring that everybody has the right to seek asylum and find safe refuge in another country, with the goal of seeking lasting solutions.
General, MF Med, Medicine, OB-GYN, Peds, Psych, Pub Health
⊕ https://vfmat.ch/6636

United Nations Office for the Coordination of Humanitarian Affairs (OCHA)
Contributes to principled and effective humanitarian response through coordination, advocacy, policy, information management, and humanitarian financing tools and services, by leveraging functional expertise throughout the organization.
Logist-Op
⊕ https://vfmat.ch/22b8

United Nations Population Fund (UNFPA)
Supports reproductive healthcare for women and youth in more than 150 countries, focusing on delivering a world in which every pregnancy is wanted, every childbirth is safe, and every young person's potential is fulfilled.
Infect Dis, MF Med, Neonat, OB-GYN, Peds, Pub Health
⊕ https://vfmat.ch/c969

United States Agency for International Development (USAID)
Promotes and demonstrates democratic values abroad and advances a free, peaceful, and prosperous world. Leads the U.S. government's international development and disaster assistance through partnerships and investments that save lives.
ER Med, Infect Dis, MF Med, OB-GYN, Peds
⊕ https://vfmat.ch/9a99

Universal Aid for Children of Ukraine
Strives to provide direct humanitarian aid including nutrition, healthcare, psychological counseling, and educational programs to thousands of orphaned and displaced children.
Crit-Care, Dent-OMFS, General, Nutr, Ophth-Opt, Ortho, Plast, Psych
⊕ https://vfmat.ch/a41f

University of California Los Angeles: David Geffen School of Medicine Global Health Program
Catalyzes opportunities to improve health globally by engaging in multi-disciplinary and innovative education programs, research initiatives, and bilateral partnerships that provide opportunities for trainees, faculty, and staff to contribute to sustainable health initiatives and to address health inequities facing the world today.
All-Immu, Infect Dis, Logist-Op, MF Med, Medicine, Neonat, OB-GYN, Ortho, Ped Surg, Peds, Radiol
⊕ https://vfmat.ch/f1a4

University of Illinois at Chicago: Center for Global Health
Aims to improve the health of populations around the world and reduce health disparities by collaboratively conducting trans-disciplinary research, training the next generations of global health leaders, and building the capacities of global and local partners.

Pub Health
⊕ https://vfmat.ch/b749

University of Michigan: Department of Surgery Global Health
Improves the health of patients, populations and communities through excellence in education, patient care, community service, research and technology development, and through leadership activities.
Anesth, Ortho, Surg
⊕ https://vfmat.ch/2fd8

University of Toronto: Global Surgery
Focuses on excellent clinical care, outstanding research productivity, and the delivery of state-of-the-art educational programs.
Surg
⊕ https://vfmat.ch/1ad5

University of Washington: The International Training and Education Center for Health (I-TECH)
Works with local partners to develop skilled healthcare workers and strong national health systems in resource-limited countries.
Infect Dis, Pub Health
⊕ https://vfmat.ch/642f

USA for United Nations High Commissioner for Refugees (UNHCR)
Serves and protects refugees and displaced people through emergency relief, cash assistance, education, resettlement, and the rebuilding of livelihoods.
ER Med, General, Logist-Op, Nutr, Pub Health
⊕ https://vfmat.ch/293c

USAID: EQUIP Health
Exists as an effective, efficient response mechanism to achieving global HIV epidemic control by delivering the right intervention at the right place and in the right way.
Infect Dis
⊕ https://vfmat.ch/d76a

USAID: Health Finance and Governance Project
Uses research to implement strategies to help countries develop robust governance systems, increase their domestic resources for health, manage those resources more effectively, and make wise purchasing decisions.
Logist-Op
⊕ https://vfmat.ch/8652

USAID: Health Policy Initiative
Provides field-level programming in health policy development and implementation.
General, Infect Dis, MF Med, OB-GYN, Peds
⊕ https://vfmat.ch/8f84

USAID: Leadership, Management and Governance Project
Improves leadership, management, and governance practices to strengthen health systems and improve health for all, including vulnerable populations worldwide.
Logist-Op
⊕ https://vfmat.ch/d35e

USAID: Maternal and Child Health Integrated Program
Works to improve the health of women and their families, including programs for maternal, newborn, and child health, immunization, family planning, nutrition, malaria, and HIV/AIDS.
All-Immu, General, Infect Dis, MF Med
⊕ https://vfmat.ch/4415

Variety – The Children's Charity International
Funds and delivers programs that focus on multiple unmet needs of children who are sick or disadvantaged, or live with disabilities and other special needs. Works at a local, national and international level, including the delivery of critical healthcare and medical equipment.
General, Infect Dis, Logist-Op
⊕ https://vfmat.ch/41f5

Vitamin Angels
Helps at-risk populations in need—specifically pregnant women, new mothers, and children under age 5—to gain access to life-changing vitamins and minerals.
General, Nutr
⊕ https://vfmat.ch/7da1

World Federation of Hemophilia (WFH)
Aims to improve and sustain care for people with inherited bleeding disorders by pursuing long-term relationships with individuals and organizations who share the values of WFH's development model.
Heme-Onc
⊕ https://vfmat.ch/5121

World Health Organization, The (WHO)
The United Nations' agency for health provides leadership on global health matters, shapes the health research agenda, sets norms and standards, articulates evidence-based policy options, provides technical support and monitoring to countries, and assesses health trends.
ER Med, General, Infect Dis, Logist-Op, MF Med, OB-GYN, Peds, Psych, Pub Health
⊕ https://vfmat.ch/c476

World Medical Relief
Facilitates the distribution of surplus medical resources where they are needed.
Logist-Op
⊕ https://vfmat.ch/72dc

World Rehabilitation Fund
Enables individuals around the world with functional limitations and participation restrictions to achieve community and social integration through physical and socioeconomic rehabilitation and advocacy.
Ortho, Rehab
⊕ https://vfmat.ch/a5bc

Ukraine

Healthcare Facilities

4-A City Hospital
Topoli, Sumy, Ukraine
⊕ https://vfmat.ch/f135

5-A City Children's Neurological Hospital
Kharkiv, Ukraine
⊕ https://vfmat.ch/8e3d

Aibolit Medical Transportation
Cherkasy, Cherkasy Region, Ukraine
⊕ https://vfmat.ch/bccd

Alchevs'k, Central City Hospital
Alchevs'k, Luhansk, Ukraine
⊕ https://vfmat.ch/42d2

Alexandria Central City Hospital
Alexandria, Kirovohrad Oblast, Ukraine
⊕ https://vfmat.ch/e642

Alushta Central City Hospital
Alushta, Crimea, Ukraine
⊕ https://vfmat.ch/291e

Ambulance and Inpatient Treatment, Ternivka
Ternivka, Vinnytsya Oblast, Ukraine
⊕ https://vfmat.ch/1639

Ambulance Station
Sharovechka, Khmelnytskyy Oblast, Ukraine
⊕ https://vfmat.ch/1f29

Andriyivs'ka Tsentral'na Rayonna Likarnya
Andreyevka, Zaporozhye, Ukraine
⊕ https://vfmat.ch/d851

Andrushivka Central District Hospital
Andrushivka, Zhytomyrska Oblast, Ukraine
⊕ https://vfmat.ch/e7ca

Apostolov Central District Hospital
Apostolove, Apostolovsky District, Dnipropetrovska Oblast, Ukraine
⊕ https://vfmat.ch/23fb

Audiyiv Central City Hospital
Avdiivka, Donetsk, Ukraine
⊕ https://vfmat.ch/6741

Bakhchisarai Central District Hospital
Bakhchisarai, Crimea, Ukraine
⊕ https://vfmat.ch/81ef

Bakhmut Children's Hospital
Bakhmut, Donetsk, Ukraine
⊕ https://vfmat.ch/22dc

Bakhmut Multidisciplinary Intensive Care Hospital
Bakhmut, Donetsk, Ukraine
⊕ https://vfmat.ch/5411

Balakley Central Clinical District Hospital
Balakliya, Kharkiv, Ukraine
⊕ https://vfmat.ch/73dd

Baltic Central District Hospital
Myrony, Odessa, Ukraine
⊕ https://vfmat.ch/2b8a

Bar City Hospital
Balky, Vinnytsya Oblast, Ukraine
⊕ https://vfmat.ch/d5d9

Baryshivka Central District Hospital
Baryshivka, Kiev, Ukraine
⊕ https://vfmat.ch/d88c

Belgorod-Dnistrovsk Central District Hospital
Belgorod-Dniester, Odessa, Ukraine
⊕ https://vfmat.ch/f7a8

Berdyansk City Hospital
Berdyansk, Zaporozhye Region, Ukraine
⊕ https://vfmat.ch/3f2c

Berdychiv Hospital for War Veterans
Berdychiv, Zhytomyr, Ukraine
⊕ https://vfmat.ch/2c99

Berehovo Central District Hospital
Berehovo, Zakarpattia Region, Ukraine
⊕ https://vfmat.ch/a3e4

Berestechkivsk District Hospital
Berestechko, Volynska Oblast, Ukraine
⊕ https://vfmat.ch/d11c

Berezivka Central District Hospital
Berezivka, Odessa, Ukraine
⊕ https://vfmat.ch/8e7a

Bershad Central District Hospital
Bershad, Vinnytska Oblast, Ukraine
⊕ https://vfmat.ch/7448

Bila Tserkva City Hospital #1
Aleksandriya, Kiev, Ukraine
⊕ https://vfmat.ch/d9d2

Bila Tserkva City Hospital #2
Bila Tserkva, Kyiv Region, Ukraine
⊕ https://vfmat.ch/2f18

Bila Tserkva City Hospital #3
Bila Tserkva, Kiev Oblast, Ukraine
⊕ https://vfmat.ch/b816

Bila Tserkva Military Hospital
Bila Tserkva, Kiev, Ukraine
⊕ https://vfmat.ch/824e

Bila Tserkva Regional Oncology Center
Bila Tserkva, Kiev, Ukraine
⊕ https://vfmat.ch/1f36

Bilohirsk Central District Hospital
Bilohirsk, Crimea, Ukraine
⊕ https://vfmat.ch/e78d

Bilokurakyne Central District Hospital
Bilokurakyne, Luhansk Region, Ukraine
⊕ https://vfmat.ch/ef8c

Bilokurakynsky District Center of Primary Health Care
Bilokurakyne, Luhansk, Ukraine
⊕ https://vfmat.ch/7ea6

Bilopol Primary Medical Care Center
Bilopillya, Sumy, Ukraine
⊕ https://vfmat.ch/b3c2

Bilovodsk Central District Hospital
Bilovodsk, Luhansk, Ukraine
⊕ https://vfmat.ch/be52

Bilyaiv Central District Hospital
Bilyaevka, Odesska Oblast, Ukraine
⊕ https://vfmat.ch/6a53

Bilytske City Hospital
Belitskoye, Donetsk, Ukraine
⊕ https://vfmat.ch/7959

Bobrovytsia District Hospital
Bobrovytsia, Chernihiv Oblast, Ukraine
⊕ https://vfmat.ch/5111

Bohodukhiv District Hospital
Bohodukhiv, Kharkiv, Ukraine
⊕ https://vfmat.ch/4ab7

Bohodukhiv Hospital
Bogodukhovka, Cherkasy Oblast, Ukraine
⊕ https://vfmat.ch/7e5e

Bolekhiv Central City Hospital
Bolekhiv, Ivano-Frankivsk Oblast, Ukraine
⊕ https://vfmat.ch/a62f

Borodyanka Central District Hospital
Borodyanka Township, Kyivska Oblast, Ukraine
⊕ https://vfmat.ch/2871

Boromlya Village Hospital
Boromlya, Sumy, Ukraine
⊕ https://vfmat.ch/bc5b

Borshchiv Central District Clinical Hospital
Borshchiv, Ternopil Oblast, Ukraine
⊕ https://vfmat.ch/bd65

Borynska Municipal City Hospital
Shtukovets, Lviv Oblast, Ukraine
⊕ https://vfmat.ch/d931

Boryslav Central City Hospital
Boryslav, Lvivska Oblast, Ukraine
⊕ https://vfmat.ch/444a

Boryslav City Maternity Hospital
Boryslav, Lviv, Ukraine
⊕ https://vfmat.ch/b4c1

Boryspil Central District Hospital
Boryspil, Kiev Region, Ukraine
⊕ https://vfmat.ch/2321

Bozhedarivsky Center of Primary Medical Care
Shchorsk, Dnipropetrovsk Oblast, Ukraine
⊕ https://vfmat.ch/fabe

Brody Central District Hospital
Brody, Lviv, Ukraine
⊕ https://vfmat.ch/25ff

Broshniv City Hospital
Broshniv-Osada, Ivano-Frankivsk Oblast, Ukraine
⊕ https://vfmat.ch/aa73

Brotherly Central District Hospital of Brotherland District Council of Mykolaiv Region
Bratske Urban-Type Settlement, Mykolayiv Oblast, Ukraine
⊕ https://vfmat.ch/7c6b

Brzezany Central District Clinical Hospital
Berezhany, Ternopil Region, Ukraine
⊕ https://vfmat.ch/131d

Bucha Center for Primary Health Care
Yablon'ki, Kiev, Ukraine
⊕ https://vfmat.ch/c136

Budaniv Regional Psychoneurological Hospital
Budaniv, Ternopil Oblast, Ukraine
⊕ https://vfmat.ch/e3e8

Burshtyn Central City Hospital
Burshtyn, Ivano-Frankivsk Oblast, Ukraine
⊕ https://vfmat.ch/afef

Busk Central District Hospital
Busk, Lviv Region, Ukraine
⊕ https://vfmat.ch/a4a6

Center for Allergic Diseases of the Upper Respiratory Tract
Kyiv, Ukraine
⊕ https://vfmat.ch/51d2

Center for Innovative Medicine and Laser Surgery
Chernivtsi, Chernivetska Oblast, Ukraine
⊕ https://vfmat.ch/8369

Center of Primary Medical and Sanitary Care of Pulinsk Village Council
Pulyny, Zhytomyr, Ukraine
⊕ https://vfmat.ch/9713

Central Children's City Hospital
Zhytomyr, Zhytomyr Oblast, Ukraine
⊕ https://vfmat.ch/543d

Central City Clinical Hospital #1 Donetsk
Donetsk, Donetsk Oblast, Ukraine
⊕ https://vfmat.ch/137d

Central City Clinical Hospital #3
Donetsk, Donetsk Oblast, Ukraine
⊕ https://vfmat.ch/9cde

Central City Hospital in New Kakhovka
Nova Kakhovka, Kherson Oblast, Ukraine
⊕ https://vfmat.ch/ae91

Central City Hospital Khartsyzsk
Khartsyzsk, Donetsk, Ukraine
⊕ https://vfmat.ch/1f2c

Central City Hospital M. Boryslav
Boryslav, Lviv, Ukraine
⊕ https://vfmat.ch/bf38

Central City Hospital of Chervonohrad City Council
Chervonohrad, Lviv Region, Ukraine
⊕ https://vfmat.ch/c7db

Central City Hospital of Novogrodiv City Council
Novogrodovka, Donetsk, Ukraine
⊕ https://vfmat.ch/c12d

Central City Hospital of the Pokrovsky City Council
Pokrov, Dnipropetrovska Oblast, Ukraine
⊕ https://vfmat.ch/9cb1

Central City Hospital Snizhne
Snizhne, Donetsk, Ukraine
⊕ https://vfmat.ch/2688

Central City Hospital Titova
Lisichansk, Luhansk, Ukraine
⊕ https://vfmat.ch/8722

Central District Hospital Kamin-Kashirsky
Kamin-Kashirsky, Volyn Region, Ukraine
⊕ https://vfmat.ch/b86a

Central District Hospital Krolevets
Krolevets, Sumy, Ukraine
⊕ https://vfmat.ch/b412

Central District Hospital Luhansk
Village of Luhansk, Luhansk Region, Ukraine
⊕ https://vfmat.ch/f5e7

Central District Hospital of Berdychiv District
Berdychiv, Zhytomyr Region, Ukraine
⊕ https://vfmat.ch/198b

Central District Hospital of Rozdilna
Rozdilna, Odessa, Ukraine
⊕ https://vfmat.ch/29ce

Central District Hospital Verkhn'odniprovs'k
Verkhn'odniprovs'k, Dnipropetrovsk Oblast, Ukraine
⊕ https://vfmat.ch/4f74

Central Military Hospital at Odessa
Odessa, Odessa Region, Ukraine
⊕ https://vfmat.ch/3ad7

Chasovoyarsk City Hospital #3
Chasiv Yar, Donetsk, Ukraine
⊕ https://vfmat.ch/a939

Chemerovetsk Multiprofile Hospital
Chemerivtsi, Khmelnytskyy Oblast, Ukraine
⊕ https://vfmat.ch/1549

Cherkasy Central District Hospital
Chervona Sloboda, Cherkasy Oblast, Ukraine
⊕ https://vfmat.ch/6bcd

Cherkasy City Children's Hospital
Cherkasy, Cherkasy Oblast, Ukraine
⊕ https://vfmat.ch/fb7b

Cherkasy City Hospital #1, The
Heronymivka, Cherkasy Oblast, Ukraine
⊕ https://vfmat.ch/23db

Cherkasy District Hospital of S. Moshny
Moshny, Cherkasy Oblast, Ukraine
⊕ https://vfmat.ch/bcd2

Cherkasy Regional Children's Hospital
Cherkasy, Cherkasy Oblast, Ukraine
⊕ https://vfmat.ch/b679

Cherkasy Regional Hospital for War Invalids
Khutory, Cherkasy Oblast, Ukraine
⊕ https://vfmat.ch/7942

Cherkasy Regional Psychiatric Hospital
Smila, Cherkasy Region, Ukraine
⊕ https://vfmat.ch/e784

Chernigiv City Hospital #3
Chernihiv, Chernihiv Region, Ukraine
⊕ https://vfmat.ch/c3a3

Chernihiv Central District Hospital
Chernihiv, Chernihiv, Ukraine
⊕ https://vfmat.ch/22c5

Chernihiv City Hospital #2
Pavlivka, Chernihiv, Ukraine
⊕ https://vfmat.ch/c387

Chernihiv District Hospital
Tokmachansk, Zaporizhzhya Oblast, Ukraine
⊕ https://vfmat.ch/3c5c

Chernihiv Regional Medical Center for Socially Significant and Dangerous Diseases
Novyy Bilous Village, Chernihivska Oblast, Ukraine
⊕ https://vfmat.ch/4cc1

Chernivtsi City Hospital #4
Chernivtsi, Chernivtsi Oblast, Ukraine
⊕ https://vfmat.ch/fd8d

Chernivtsi District Hospital of Chernivtsi Village Council
Chernivtsi, Vinnytsya Oblast, Ukraine
⊕ https://vfmat.ch/4c96

Chernivtsi Maternity Building #2
Hodyliv, Chernivtsi Oblast, Ukraine
⊕ https://vfmat.ch/34f2

Chernivtsi Regional Hospital for Invalids of the Patriotic War
Buda, Chernivtsi Oblast, Ukraine
⊕ https://vfmat.ch/a887

Cherniakhiv Central Hospital
Cherniakhiv, Zhytomyr Region, Ukraine
⊕ https://vfmat.ch/7c5e

Children's District Hospital
Dolyna, Ivano-Frankivsk Oblast, Ukraine
⊕ https://vfmat.ch/8cce

Children's Clinical Hospital #5 Sviatoshynskyi District
Kyiv, Ukraine
⊕ https://vfmat.ch/db7e

Children's Clinical Hospital #7 of Pechersk District
Telychka, Kyiv City, Ukraine
⊕ https://vfmat.ch/6177

Children's Hospital
Kropyvnytskyi, Kirovohrad Oblast, Ukraine
⊕ https://vfmat.ch/fa72

Children's Hospital #1
Makeyevka, Donetsk, Ukraine
⊕ https://vfmat.ch/d7d7

Children's Hospital #2, Zaporizhia
Zaporizhia, Zaporizhzhya Oblast, Ukraine
⊕ https://vfmat.ch/2b1e

Children's Hospital – Makeyevka
Makeyevka, Donetska Oblast, Ukraine
⊕ https://vfmat.ch/7be9

Children's Regional Hospital, Kropyvnytskyi
Kropyvnytskyi, Kirovohrad Oblast, Ukraine
⊕ https://vfmat.ch/62e6

Children's Tuberculosis Sanatorium
Kryvyi Rih, Dnipropetrovsk Oblast, Ukraine
⊕ https://vfmat.ch/ab79

Children's City Hospital
Alexandria, Kirovohrad Oblast, Ukraine
⊕ https://vfmat.ch/2d3f

Chop City Hospital
Chop, Zakarpattia Region, Ukraine
⊕ https://vfmat.ch/2699

Chutivska District Hospital
Chutove, Poltava Oblast, Ukraine
⊕ https://vfmat.ch/b2f1

Chyhyryn Multiprofile Hospital
Chyhyryn, Cherkasy Oblast, Ukraine
⊕ https://vfmat.ch/789e

CI InterRegional Center for Medical Genetics and Prenatal Diagnostics
Kryvyi Rih, Dnipropetrovsk Oblast, Ukraine
⊕ https://vfmat.ch/ca23

City Ambulance Hospital
Mykolaiv, Mykolayivska Oblast, Ukraine
⊕ https://vfmat.ch/6471

City Children's Clinical Hospital
Chernivtsi, Chernivetska Oblast, Ukraine
⊕ https://vfmat.ch/13c1

City Children's Clinical Hospital #3
Donetsk, Donetsk Oblast, Ukraine
⊕ https://vfmat.ch/3ec9

City Children's Clinical Hospital #5 Dnipro
Dnipro, Dnipropetrovsk Oblast, Ukraine
⊕ https://vfmat.ch/d7ff

City Children's Clinical Hospital #5 Donetsk
Donetsk, Donetsk Region, Ukraine
⊕ https://vfmat.ch/2d17

City Children's Hospital #2, Nikolaev City
Karavelove, Mykolayiv Oblast, Ukraine
⊕ https://vfmat.ch/589b

City Children's Hospital #3 of Rivne City Council
Rivne, Rivne Region, Ukraine
🌐 https://vfmat.ch/6e9d

City Children's Hospital #4
Donetsk, Donetska Oblast, Ukraine
🌐 https://vfmat.ch/77bc

City Children's Clinical Hospital #2 Of Dniprovsk City Council
Lomovka, Dnipropetrovsk Oblast, Ukraine
🌐 https://vfmat.ch/de64

City Children's Clinical Hospital #24 Kharkiv City Council
Kotlyary, Kharkiv, Ukraine
🌐 https://vfmat.ch/369b

City Children's Clinical Hospital #6 of Dniprovsk City Council
Dnipro, Dnipropetrovsk Oblast, Ukraine
🌐 https://vfmat.ch/3bad

City Children's Hospital #2 Donetska
Snizhne, Donetsk, Ukraine
🌐 https://vfmat.ch/edfc

City Clinical Hospital #3 of Poltava City Council
Makukhivka, Poltava Oblast, Ukraine
🌐 https://vfmat.ch/eb7a

City Clinical Hospital #4 of Poltava City Council
Poltava, Poltava Oblast, Ukraine
🌐 https://vfmat.ch/588b

City Clinical Hospital #1
Poltava, Poltava Oblast, Ukraine
🌐 https://vfmat.ch/87e1

City Clinical Hospital #1 Kharkiv
Kharkiv, Kharkiv Oblast, Ukraine
🌐 https://vfmat.ch/c563

City Clinical Hospital #1 of Odessa City Council
Odessa, Odessa Region, Ukraine
🌐 https://vfmat.ch/f236

City Clinical Hospital #10
Cheremushky, Odessa, Ukraine
🌐 https://vfmat.ch/42ea

City Clinical Hospital #11
Krivaya Balka, Odessa, Ukraine
🌐 https://vfmat.ch/6c36

City Clinical Hospital #2 Enerhetyk
Donetsk, Donetska Oblast, Ukraine
🌐 https://vfmat.ch/2684

City Clinical Hospital #2 Prof. O.O. Shalimov
Kharkiv, Kharkiv Region, Ukraine
🌐 https://vfmat.ch/17c2

City Clinical Hospital #20 Donetsk
Donetsk, Donetsk Region, Ukraine
🌐 https://vfmat.ch/cd77

City Clinical Hospital #21
Donetsk Region, Ukraine
🌐 https://vfmat.ch/cc8f

City Clinical Hospital #3
Chernivtsi, Chernivtsi Oblast, Ukraine
🌐 https://vfmat.ch/4dee

City Clinical Hospital #4 Lviv
Lviv, Lvivska Oblast, Ukraine
🌐 https://vfmat.ch/877b

City Clinical Hospital #5 Poltava
Poltava, Poltava Oblast, Ukraine
🌐 https://vfmat.ch/e5e4

City Clinical Hospital #7
Donetsk, Donetska Oblast, Ukraine
🌐 https://vfmat.ch/ccbb

City Clinical Hospital for Emergency and Emergency Medical Care Prof. Meschaninova
Ryzhiy, Kharkiv, Ukraine
🌐 https://vfmat.ch/7945

City Clinical Hospital #24
Donetsk, Donetsk Oblast, Ukraine
🌐 https://vfmat.ch/db6c

City Clinical Infectious Hospital
Odessa, Odessa Region, Ukraine
🌐 https://vfmat.ch/6a55

City Clinical Maternity Hospital #7
Losevo, Kharkiv, Ukraine
🌐 https://vfmat.ch/129a

City Clinical Maternity Hospital of Poltava City Council
Poltava, Poltava Oblast, Ukraine
🌐 https://vfmat.ch/6fad

City Clinical Multidisciplinary Hospital #25
Kharkiv, Ukraine
🌐 https://vfmat.ch/db5c

City Hospital #2
Heronymivka, Cherkasy Oblast, Ukraine
🌐 https://vfmat.ch/3547

City Hospital #2 (East)
Makeyevka, Donetsk, Ukraine
🌐 https://vfmat.ch/8cef

City Hospital #2 Cities of Yenakiev
Yenakiieve, Donetsk, Ukraine
🌐 https://vfmat.ch/4b44

City Hospital #2 Lugansk
Lugansk, Luhansk, Ukraine
🌐 https://vfmat.ch/abec

City Hospital #2 Rivne City Council
Rivne, Rivne Region, Ukraine
🌐 https://vfmat.ch/c7dc

City Hospital #3
Petrikov, Ternopil Oblast, Ukraine
🌐 https://vfmat.ch/cdbc

City Hospital #3 (North)
Novochaykino, Donetsk Oblast, Ukraine
🌐 https://vfmat.ch/e4be

City Hospital #3 Oleksandriysk City Council
Oktyabr'skoye, Kirovohrad Oblast, Ukraine
🌐 https://vfmat.ch/253f

City Hospital #3 Zaporizhia City Council
Zaporizhia, Zaporizhzhya Oblast, Ukraine
🌐 https://vfmat.ch/f9f5

City Hospital #3 Horlivka
Horlivka, Donetsk Oblast, Ukraine
🌐 https://vfmat.ch/eb54

City Hospital #6 Zaporizhia
Zaporizhia, Zaporizhzhya Oblast, Ukraine
🌐 https://vfmat.ch/4188

City Hospital #7 Zaporizhia City Council
Zaporizhia, Zaporizhzhya Oblast, Ukraine
🌐 https://vfmat.ch/13ec

City Hospital #8
Odessa, Odessa Oblast, Ukraine
🌐 https://vfmat.ch/1e7f

City Hospital #9 Hydrotherapy
Novochaykino, Donetsk, Ukraine
🌐 https://vfmat.ch/f2f3

City Hospital #9 Sonyachne
Sonyachne, Zaporizhzhya Oblast, Ukraine
🌐 https://vfmat.ch/4938

City Hospital (Svitlovodsk)
Svitlovodsk, Kirovohrad Oblast, Ukraine
🌐 https://vfmat.ch/46e2

City Hospital, Olenovka (Volnovakha District)
Olenovka, Elenovsky Village Council, Donetsk, Ukraine
🌐 https://vfmat.ch/babd

City Maternity Hospital #6
Kharkiv, Kharkivska, Ukraine
⊕ https://vfmat.ch/7fd7

City Multidisciplinary Hospital #18 Kharkiv City Council
Kharkiv, Kharkivska, Ukraine
⊕ https://vfmat.ch/7aa2

City Polyclinic #8
Kharkiv, Kharkivska, Ukraine
⊕ https://vfmat.ch/b67f

Clinical Hospital #4 Prof. L. L. Girschmana
Nova Olekciyivka, Kharkiv, Ukraine
⊕ https://vfmat.ch/35c5

Clinical Hospital #5
Sumy, Sumska Oblast, Ukraine
⊕ https://vfmat.ch/335f

Clinical Hospital for War Veterans
Simferopol, Crimea, Ukraine
⊕ https://vfmat.ch/fa7d

Clinical Hospital of the Oil Refining Industry of Ukraine
Kyiv, Kyivska Oblast, Ukraine
⊕ https://vfmat.ch/7199

Communal Municipal Clinical Hospital #5
Lviv, Lviv Oblast, Ukraine
⊕ https://vfmat.ch/48a7

D-Plus Medical Center
Ana-Yurt, Crimea, Ukraine
⊕ https://vfmat.ch/5986

Demidiv Central District Hospital
Demydivka, Rivne Region, Ukraine
⊕ https://vfmat.ch/c6e1

Department of Health Hospital of the Ministry of Internal Affairs Odessa Region
Odessa, Odessa Oblast, Ukraine
⊕ https://vfmat.ch/c2f5

Dimitrov Central Hospital
Myrnograd, Donetsk, Ukraine
⊕ https://vfmat.ch/62b8

Diomedes
Chernivts, Chernivtsi Oblast, Ukraine
⊕ https://vfmat.ch/9286

District Hospital Kamianka
Kamianka, Cherkasy Oblast, Ukraine
⊕ https://vfmat.ch/9555

District Hospital, Petrivka-Romenska
Petrivka-Romenska, Poltava Oblast, Ukraine
⊕ https://vfmat.ch/2943

Dnipro City Clinical Hospital #6
Dnipro, Dnipropetrovska Oblast, Ukraine
⊕ https://vfmat.ch/24ce

Dnipro Regional Clinical Oncology Center
Dnipro, Dnipropetrovsk Oblast, Ukraine
⊕ https://vfmat.ch/8aca

Dnipropetrovsk City Clinical Hospital #9
Dnipro, Dnipropetrovsk Oblast, Ukraine
⊕ https://vfmat.ch/cffd

Dnipropetrovsk City Hospital #5
Dnipro, Dnipropetrovsk Oblast, Ukraine
⊕ https://vfmat.ch/c5e4

Dnipropetrovsk Regional Clinical Center of Cardiology and Cardiac Surgery
Lomovka, Dnipropetrovsk Oblast, Ukraine
⊕ https://vfmat.ch/82a6

Dnipropetrovsk Regional Hospital for War Veterans
Dnipro, Dnipropetrovsk Oblast, Ukraine
⊕ https://vfmat.ch/4253

Dnipropetrovsk Regional Medical Center for Communicable Diseases
Dnipro, Dnipropetrovsk Oblast, Ukraine
⊕ https://vfmat.ch/f48c

Dnipropetrovsk Regional Perinatal Hospital Center
Dnipro, Dnipropetrovsk Oblast, Ukraine
⊕ https://vfmat.ch/2ddf

Dniprovsk Center of Primary Medical and Sanitary Care #10 Dniprovsk City Council
Dnipro, Dnipropetrovsk Oblast, Ukraine
⊕ https://vfmat.ch/f47f

Dniprovsk City Clinical Hospital #11
Dnipro City, Dnipropetrovsk Oblast, Ukraine
⊕ https://vfmat.ch/7fba

Dniprovsk City Maternity Building #1
Dnipro, Dnipropetrovsk Oblast, Ukraine
⊕ https://vfmat.ch/3b8f

Dobromil District Hospital
Dobromil, Lvivska Oblast, Ukraine
⊕ https://vfmat.ch/65da

Dobroslav Multiprofile Hospital for Intensive Treatment
Zorynove, Odessa, Ukraine
⊕ https://vfmat.ch/519d

Dobrotvir City Hospital
Dobrotvir, Lviv, Ukraine
⊕ https://vfmat.ch/d4fc

Dobrovelichkivska Hospital
Dobrovelychkivka, Kirovohrad Oblast, Ukraine
⊕ https://vfmat.ch/9144

Dolynsk Central Hospital of Dolynsk City Council
Dolynska, Kirovohrad Oblast, Ukraine
⊕ https://vfmat.ch/ceef

Donetsk City Children's Clinical Hospital #1
Donetsk, Donetsk, Ukraine
⊕ https://vfmat.ch/f6a4

Donetsk City Clinical Hospital #9
Donetsk, Donetsk, Ukraine
⊕ https://vfmat.ch/31e4

Donetsk City Hospital #4
Mariupol, Donetsk Region, Ukraine
⊕ https://vfmat.ch/b5a8

Donetsk Clinical Hospital #14
Donetsk, Donetsk Region, Ukraine
⊕ https://vfmat.ch/7e8c

Donetsk Clinical Hospital #6
Donetsk, Donetsk Region, Ukraine
⊕ https://vfmat.ch/fb31

Donetsk Clinical Territorial Medical Association
Donetsk, Donetsk Oblast, Ukraine
⊕ https://vfmat.ch/ea9a

Donetsk Regional Children's Clinical Center for Neurorehabilitation
Novochaykino, Donetsk, Ukraine
⊕ https://vfmat.ch/f5ae

Donetsk Regional Clinical Trauma Hospital
Donetsk, Donetsk, Ukraine
⊕ https://vfmat.ch/72f7

Dovzhansk Central City General Hospital
Dovzhansk, Luhanska Oblast, Ukraine
⊕ https://vfmat.ch/cd47

Drohobych City Children's Hospital
Stare Selo, Lviv, Ukraine
⊕ https://vfmat.ch/f39e

Drohobych City Maternity Hospital
Drohobych, Lviv, Ukraine
⊕ https://vfmat.ch/a8b9

Drohobych District Hospital #4
Drohobytskyi Rayon, Noviy Kropivnyk, Lviv Region, Ukraine
⊕ https://vfmat.ch/2145

Druzhkivka City Clinical Hospital #1
Druzhkivka, Donetsk Region, Ukraine
⊕ https://vfmat.ch/6216

DU TMO of the Ministry of Internal Affairs of Ukraine
Chernivtsi, Chernivtsi Oblast, Ukraine
⊕ https://vfmat.ch/e2cf

Dubensk City Hospital
Dubno, Rivne Region, Ukraine
⊕ https://vfmat.ch/4489

Dunayevets Central District Hospital
Dunaivtsi, Khmelnytskyy Oblast, Ukraine
⊕ https://vfmat.ch/aa8b

Dykansky Hospital of Planned Treatment
Dykanka, Poltava Oblast, Ukraine
⊕ https://vfmat.ch/2f46

Dymer District Hospital
Dymer, Vyshhorod District, Kyivska Oblast, Ukraine
⊕ https://vfmat.ch/cd2f

Effect Medical Center
Ivano-Frankivsk, Ivano-Frankivsk Oblast, Ukraine
⊕ https://vfmat.ch/9649

Embryotek Medical Center
Belichi, Kyiv City, Ukraine
⊕ https://vfmat.ch/ab46

ENT Center Chernivtsi Regional Clinical Hospital
Chernivtsi, Chernivtsi Oblast, Ukraine
⊕ https://vfmat.ch/71dc

Family Medicine Hospital
Slovyansk, Donetsk Oblast, Ukraine
⊕ https://vfmat.ch/18ed

Family Medicine Hospital Medical Center
Horlivka, Donetsk Oblast, Ukraine
⊕ https://vfmat.ch/a81d

FAP, Znob-Novgorod Village
Znob Trubchevska, Sumy, Ukraine
⊕ https://vfmat.ch/6d67

Fastiv Central District Hospital
Fastiv, Kyivska Oblast, Ukraine
⊕ https://vfmat.ch/f9ca

Feldsher-Obstetric Station, Velikodolinskaya Settlement
Velykodolynske, Odessa, Ukraine
⊕ https://vfmat.ch/431e

Feodosiya City Children's Hospital
Feodosiya, Crimea, Ukraine
⊕ https://vfmat.ch/15a8

Genichesk Central District Hospital
Genichesk, Kherson Region, Ukraine
⊕ https://vfmat.ch/bb5a

Goschan Multiprofile Hospital
Goshcha, Rivne, Ukraine
⊕ https://vfmat.ch/341e

Government Hospital in Lviv – Ministry of Internal Affairs
Lviv, Lviv Region, Ukraine
⊕ https://vfmat.ch/b8f7

Heikivska Regional Psychoneurological Hospital
Kryvyi Rih, Dnipropetrovsk Oblast, Ukraine
⊕ https://vfmat.ch/ca75

Helmyaziv District Hospital
Hel'myaziv, Cherkasy Oblast, Ukraine
⊕ https://vfmat.ch/83f9

Hematology Building
Spartak, Donetsk, Ukraine
⊕ https://vfmat.ch/4f3a

Holovanivsk Central District Hospital
Golovanovsk, Kirovograd Region, Ukraine
⊕ https://vfmat.ch/fd48

Horlivka City Hospital #2
Horlivka, Donetsk, Ukraine
⊕ https://vfmat.ch/3173

Horodenka Central District Hospital
Horodenka, Ivano-Frankivsk Oblast, Ukraine
⊕ https://vfmat.ch/42fe

Hospital #6 Artëmovskiy
Artëmovskiy Rayon, Luhansk, Ukraine
⊕ https://vfmat.ch/cd58

Hospital at Simferopol
Simferopol, Crimea, Ukraine
⊕ https://vfmat.ch/1918

Hospital of the Ministry of Internal Affairs
Vinnytsia, Vinnytsya Oblast, Ukraine
⊕ https://vfmat.ch/bbf9

Husyatyn District Hospital
Husyatyn, Ternopil Oblast, Ukraine
⊕ https://vfmat.ch/a9ca

Hvizdetska District Hospital #2
Hvizdets, Ivano-Frankivsk Oblast, Ukraine
⊕ https://vfmat.ch/8837

Ichnya Central District Hospital
Ichnya, Chernihiv, Ukraine
⊕ https://vfmat.ch/afc5

Infectious Diseases Department – Sarny Central Regional Hospital
Novoselitsa, Transcarpathia, Ukraine
⊕ https://vfmat.ch/1261

Infectious Diseases Hospital #3 Lviv
Lviv, Lviv Region, Ukraine
⊕ https://vfmat.ch/f246

Institute of Neurology, Psychiatry and Addiction of the National Academy of Medical Sciences of Ukraine
Kharkiv, Kharkivska Oblast, Ukraine
⊕ https://vfmat.ch/3f88

Inter LDC, Mammology Center
Artëmovskiy Rayon, Luhansk, Ukraine
⊕ https://vfmat.ch/6992

Interdistrict Specialized Oncological MSEC
Rivne, Rivne Oblast, Ukraine
⊕ https://vfmat.ch/f1f1

Interdistrict Specialized Psychoneurological MSEC
Yaseninichi, Rivne, Ukraine
⊕ https://vfmat.ch/b7f4

Irpin Children's City Hospital
Irpin, Kiev, Ukraine
⊕ https://vfmat.ch/89de

Irpin Military Hospital of the Ministry of Defense of Ukraine
Irpin, Kiev, Ukraine
⊕ https://vfmat.ch/774d

Ivankivska Central District Hospital
Ivankiv, Kiev, Ukraine
⊕ https://vfmat.ch/bfa4

Ivano-Frankivsk Central Clinical Hospital
Ivano-Frankivsk, Ivano-Frankivsk Oblast, Ukraine
⊕ https://vfmat.ch/5d18

Ivano-Frankivsk City Children's Clinical Hospital
Leonuvka, Ivano-Frankivsk Oblast, Ukraine
⊕ https://vfmat.ch/f621

Ivano-Frankivsk City Clinical Maternity Hospital
Ivano-Frankivsk, Ivano-Frankivsk Oblast, Ukraine
⊕ https://vfmat.ch/21f4

Ivano-Frankivsk Hospital
Ivanopil, Zhytomyr, Ukraine
⊕ https://vfmat.ch/a2b6

Ivano-Frankivsk Regional Clinical Hospital
Ivano-Frankivsk, Ivano-Frankivsk Oblast, Ukraine
⊕ https://vfmat.ch/957b

Ivano-Frankivsk Regional Phthisiopulmonology Center
Ivano-Frankivsk, Ivano-Frankivsk Oblast, Ukraine
⊕ https://vfmat.ch/118b

Ivanovo Central District Hospital
Ivanivka, Odessa, Ukraine
⊕ https://vfmat.ch/ac23

Jezupil City Hospital
Yezupil, Ivano-Frankivsk Oblast, Ukraine
⊕ https://vfmat.ch/13fa

Kagarlitsk Multiprofile Hospital
Kagarlyk, Kiev, Ukraine
⊕ https://vfmat.ch/e299

Kakhovka District Hospital
Kakhovka, Kherson Oblast, Ukraine
⊕ https://vfmat.ch/ab3a

Kalinin Regional Clinical Hospital
Novochaykino, Donetsk, Ukraine
⊕ https://vfmat.ch/864f

Kamianets-Podilskyi City Maternity Hospital
Kamianets-Podilskyi, Khmelnytska Oblast, Ukraine
⊕ https://vfmat.ch/8118

Kamianka-Buzka Central District Hospital
Kamianka-Buzka, Lvivska Oblast, Ukraine
⊕ https://vfmat.ch/629a

Kaniv Multidisciplinary Hospital
Kaniv, Cherkasy Oblast, Ukraine
⊕ https://vfmat.ch/fd91

Kapitanivka District Hospital
Kapitanivka, Kirovohrad Oblast, Ukraine
⊕ https://vfmat.ch/564e

Karlivka Central District Hospital
Karlivka, Poltava Oblast, Ukraine
⊕ https://vfmat.ch/df6a

Kharkiv City Children's Clinical Hospital #19
Kharkiv, Kharkiv Oblast, Ukraine
⊕ https://vfmat.ch/7dae

Kharkiv City Children's Clinical Hospital #24
Kharkiv, Kharkiv Oblast, Ukraine
⊕ https://vfmat.ch/51ba

Kharkiv City Clinical Hospital #31
Zalyutino, Kharkiv, Ukraine
⊕ https://vfmat.ch/bbf6

Kharkiv City Hospital #3
Kharkiv, Kharkiv Region, Ukraine
⊕ https://vfmat.ch/6d91

Kharkiv Clinical Hospital on Railway Transport #1 Radiation Diagnostics Center
Kharkiv, Kharkiv, Ukraine
⊕ https://vfmat.ch/c6ed

Kharkiv Military Medical Clinical Center of the Northern Region
Nova Olekciyivka, Kharkiv, Ukraine
⊕ https://vfmat.ch/e3da

Kharkiv Regional Children's Clinical Hospital #1
Kharkiv, Kharkiv, Ukraine
⊕ https://vfmat.ch/b1cf

Khartsyzsk City Hospital
Khartsyzsk, Donetsk, Ukraine
⊕ https://vfmat.ch/f39d

Kherson Children's Regional Clinical Hospital
Kherson, Kherson Oblast, Ukraine
⊕ https://vfmat.ch/21ff

Kherson Railway Station Surgery Hospital
Kherson, Kherson Oblast, Ukraine
⊕ https://vfmat.ch/b44e

Kherson Regional Hospital
Zymivnyk, Kherson Oblast, Ukraine
⊕ https://vfmat.ch/73ea

Kherson Regional Hospital Hospice
Kherson, Khersonska Oblast, Ukraine
⊕ https://vfmat.ch/e2bb

Kherson Regional Infectious Hospital Gorbatchevski
Kherson, Kherson Oblast, Ukraine
⊕ https://vfmat.ch/f4a8

Khmelnytski Infectious Diseases Hospital
Khmelnytskyi, Khmelnytska Oblast, Ukraine
⊕ https://vfmat.ch/29de

Khmelnytski Regional Hospital
Khmelnytskyi, Khmelnytska Oblast, Ukraine
⊕ https://vfmat.ch/3553

Khmelnytski Regional Hospital for War Veterans
Ruzhychanka, Khmelnytskyy Oblast, Ukraine
⊕ https://vfmat.ch/648b

Khmelnytski Regional Physiotherapy Hospital
Khmilnyk, Vinnytsia Region, Ukraine
⊕ https://vfmat.ch/5c8f

Khmelnytskyi Central District Hospital
Khmelnytskyi, Khmelnytskyi Oblast, Ukraine
⊕ https://vfmat.ch/53ec

Khmelnytskyi City Children's Hospital
Sharovechka, Khmelnytski Oblast, Ukraine
⊕ https://vfmat.ch/2757

Khmelnytskyi Regional Clinical Hospital, Housing #4
Khmelnytskyi, Khmelnytskyi Oblast, Ukraine
⊕ https://vfmat.ch/8a7b

Khmelnytskyi Regional Clinical Hospital, Housing #7
Khmelnytsky, Khmelnytski Region, Ukraine
⊕ https://vfmat.ch/f489

Khotyn Central District Hospital
Khotyn, Chernivtsi Region, Ukraine
⊕ https://vfmat.ch/a532

Khyriv City Hospital
Khyriv, Lvivska Oblast, Ukraine
⊕ https://vfmat.ch/5274

Kiev City Clinical Hospital #18
Bohatyrivka, Zaporizhzhya Oblast, Ukraine
⊕ https://vfmat.ch/7cb5

Kirovohrad City Hospital #3
Kropyvnytskyi, Kirovohrad Oblast, Ukraine
⊕ https://vfmat.ch/b7f8

Kirovohrad Regional Hospital
Kropyvnytskyi, Kirovohrad Oblast, Ukraine
⊕ https://vfmat.ch/125d

Kirovohrad Regional Psychiatric Hospital
Kropyvnytskyi, Kirovohrad Oblast, Ukraine
⊕ https://vfmat.ch/e3ac

Kitsman District Hospital
Kitsman, Chernivetska Oblast, Ukraine
⊕ https://vfmat.ch/7ab5

KNP Brovarska Multidisciplinary Clinical Hospital
Brovary, Kiev, Ukraine
⊕ https://vfmat.ch/f921

KNP City Clinical Hospital #21 Prof. EG Popkova
Dnipro, Dnipropetrovsk Oblast, Ukraine
⊕ https://vfmat.ch/e5cf

KNP Kosmatsky District Hospital
Pancheve, Kirovohrad Oblast, Ukraine
⊕ https://vfmat.ch/d633

Knyagininskaya City Hospital
Khrustalnyi, Luhansk Oblast, Ukraine
⊕ https://vfmat.ch/b647

Kolomatsk District Hospital
Kolomak, Kharkiv Region, Ukraine
⊕ https://vfmat.ch/9dee

Kolomyia Central District Hospital
Kolomyia, Ivano-Frankivsk Oblast, Ukraine
⊕ https://vfmat.ch/75c3

Komyshansk Rural District Hospital
Gukov, Khmelnytskyi Oblast, Ukraine
⊕ https://vfmat.ch/5358

Kopichinetsk Municipal Hospital
Kopychyntsi, Ternopil Oblast, Ukraine
⊕ https://vfmat.ch/7918

Korosten Central District Hospital
Korosten, Zhytomyrska Oblast, Ukraine
⊕ https://vfmat.ch/7a17

Korosten City Hospital
Korosten, Zhytomyrska Oblast, Ukraine
⊕ https://vfmat.ch/726a

Korostyshiv Central District Hospital Dr. Potekhin of Korostyshiv City Council
Korostyshiv, Zhytomyr Region, Ukraine
⊕ https://vfmat.ch/bb21

Korsun-Shevchenkivska Central District Hospital
Korsun-Shevchenkivskyi, Cherkaska Oblast, Ukraine
⊕ https://vfmat.ch/3c7d

Kovel City District Territorial Medical Association
Kovel, Volyn, Ukraine
⊕ https://vfmat.ch/995b

Kovel City Hospital
Verbka, Volyn, Ukraine
⊕ https://vfmat.ch/3429

Kovel Maternity Hospital
Kovel, Volyn, Ukraine
⊕ https://vfmat.ch/c2ec

Kozeletsk Central District Hospital
Oleksiivshchyna, Chernihiv, Ukraine
⊕ https://vfmat.ch/6a7b

Kozelskaya Central Hospital
Kozelskinskaya Village Community, Poltava Oblast, Ukraine
⊕ https://vfmat.ch/4e8a

Koziv Central District Municipal Hospital
Kozova, Ternopilska Oblast, Ukraine
⊕ https://vfmat.ch/fefe

Kramatorsk City Hospital #1
Kramatorsk, Donetska Oblast, Ukraine
⊕ https://vfmat.ch/8ef2

Krasnograd Central District Hospital
Krasnograd, Krasnograd District, Kharkivska Oblast, Ukraine
⊕ https://vfmat.ch/e29e

Krasnoyarsk City Hospital
Krasne, Lviv, Ukraine
⊕ https://vfmat.ch/e69d

Krasyliv Central Regional Hospital
Krasyliv, Khmelnytskyi Oblast, Ukraine
⊕ https://vfmat.ch/4b8d

Kremenchuk City Hospital Righside
Kremenchuk, Poltava Oblast, Ukraine
⊕ https://vfmat.ch/36b1

Kremenchuk City Maternity Hospital
Kremenchuk, Poltava Oblast, Ukraine
⊕ https://vfmat.ch/3c27

Kremenchuk Regional Hospital for War Veterans
Kremenchuk, Poltava Oblast, Ukraine
⊕ https://vfmat.ch/c6b4

Kremenchuk Hospital #4
Kremenchuk, Poltava Oblast, Ukraine
⊕ https://vfmat.ch/4a3d

Kropyvnytskyi City Hospital #4
Kropyvnytskyi, Kirovohrad Oblast, Ukraine
⊕ https://vfmat.ch/4f47

Kropyvnytskyi City Maternity Hospital
Kropyvnytskyi, Kirovohrad Region, Ukraine
⊕ https://vfmat.ch/499b

Krynychansk Central District Hospital
Krynychky Township, Krynychanskyi District, Dnipropetrovska Oblast, Ukraine
⊕ https://vfmat.ch/e2f9

Kryvoriz'ka Infectious Diseases Hospital #1
Kryvyi Rih, Dnipropetrovsk Oblast, Ukraine
⊕ https://vfmat.ch/333d

Kryvyi Rih AIDS Prevention and Treatment Centre
Dolgintsevo, Dnipropetrovsk Oblast, Ukraine
⊕ https://vfmat.ch/7b21

Kryvyi Rih Central District Hospital of Dnipropetrovsk Regional Council
Novopillya, Dnipropetrovsk Oblast, Ukraine
⊕ https://vfmat.ch/7475

Kryvyi Rih City Children's Hospital #1
Kryvyi Rih, Dnipropetrovsk Oblast, Ukraine
⊕ https://vfmat.ch/8754

Kryvyi Rih City Children's Hospital #4
Kryvyi Rih, Dnipropetrovsk Oblast, Ukraine
⊕ https://vfmat.ch/8ba8

Kryvyi Rih City Children's Hospital #2
Kryvyi Rih, Dnipropetrovsk Oblast, Ukraine
⊕ https://vfmat.ch/53c9

Kryvyi Rih City Clinical Hospital #2
Kryvyi Rih, Dnipropetrovsk Oblast, Ukraine
⊕ https://vfmat.ch/bece

Kryvyi Rih City Clinical Hospital #8
Kryvyi Rih, Dnipropetrovska Oblast, Ukraine
⊕ https://vfmat.ch/ce17

Kryvyi Rih City Clinical Maternity Hospital #1
Kryvyi Rih, Dnipropetrovsk Oblast, Ukraine
⊕ https://vfmat.ch/2bce

Kryvyi Rih City Hospital #11
Kryvyi Rih, Dnipropetrovsk Oblast, Ukraine
⊕ https://vfmat.ch/c9b4

Kryvyi Rih City Hospital #16
Kryvyi Rih, Dnipropetrovsk Oblast, Ukraine
⊕ https://vfmat.ch/7b7a

Kryvyi Rih City Hospital #3
Novo-Ukrainka, Dnipropetrovsk Oblast, Ukraine
⊕ https://vfmat.ch/5da2

Kryvyi Rih City Hospital #5
Shmakovo, Dnipropetrovsk Oblast, Ukraine
⊕ https://vfmat.ch/5166

Kryvyi Rih City Hospital #7
Kryvyi Rih, Dnipropetrovsk Oblast, Ukraine
⊕ https://vfmat.ch/1dad

Kryvyi Rih City Hospital #9
Kryvyi Rih, Dnipropetrovsk Oblast, Ukraine
⊕ https://vfmat.ch/e2ce

Kulykivka Central District Hospital
Kulykivka, Chernihivska Oblast, Ukraine
⊕ https://vfmat.ch/8624

Kupyansk Central City Hospital
Kupyansk, Kharkiv Region, Ukraine
⊕ https://vfmat.ch/a358

Kurakhiv City Hospital
Kurakhove, Donetsk, Ukraine
⊕ https://vfmat.ch/f656

Kuzeminsk Rural District Hospital
Kuzemin, Sumy, Ukraine
⊕ https://vfmat.ch/1c67

Kyiv City Children Clinical Hospital # 1
Peredmistna Slobidka, Kyiv City, Ukraine
⊕ https://vfmat.ch/4e36

Kyiv City Children's Clinical Hospital #1 Kyiv
Kyiv, Ukraine
⊕ https://vfmat.ch/1d42

Kyiv City Children's Clinical Hospital #2
Kyiv, Ukraine
⊕ https://vfmat.ch/e155

Kyiv City Children's Clinical Infectious Diseases Hospital
Obolon, Kyiv City, Ukraine
⊕ https://vfmat.ch/a59a

Kyiv City Children's Clinical Tuberculosis Hospital
Kyiv, Ukraine
⊕ https://vfmat.ch/7457

Kyiv City Clinical Ambulance Hospital
Kyiv, Ukraine
⊕ https://vfmat.ch/4f6f

Kyiv City Clinical Dermatological and Venereological Hospital
Kyiv, Kyivska Oblast, Ukraine
⊕ https://vfmat.ch/7982

Kyiv City Clinical Hospital #8
Rostushche, Zaporizhzhya Oblast, Ukraine
⊕ https://vfmat.ch/2ecf

Kyiv City Clinical Hospital #1
Bortnychi, Kyiv City, Ukraine
⊕ https://vfmat.ch/b7cd

Kyiv City Clinical Hospital #10
Kyiv, Ukraine
⊕ https://vfmat.ch/75ce

Kyiv City Clinical Hospital #12
Kyiv, Ukraine
⊕ https://vfmat.ch/bdc6

Kyiv City Clinical Hospital #17
Peredmistna Slobidka, Kyiv City, Ukraine
⊕ https://vfmat.ch/1285

Kyiv City Clinical Hospital #18
Kyiv, Ukraine
⊕ https://vfmat.ch/7f67

Kyiv City Clinical Hospital #2
Kyiv, Ukraine
⊕ https://vfmat.ch/5593

Kyiv City Clinical Hospital #3
Bykovnia, Kyiv City, Ukraine
⊕ https://vfmat.ch/a2cc

Kyiv City Clinical Hospital #7 Traumatology and Orthopedics
Kyiv, Ukraine
⊕ https://vfmat.ch/1b76

Kyiv City Clinical Hospital #8
Kyiv, Kyivska Oblast, Ukraine
⊕ https://vfmat.ch/4f19

Kyiv City Clinical Hospital #9
Belichi, Kyiv City, Ukraine
⊕ https://vfmat.ch/bc77

Kyiv City Clinical Hospital for War Veterans
Kyiv, Ukraine
⊕ https://vfmat.ch/3575

Kyiv City Clinical Oncology Center
Kyiv, Kyivska Oblast, Ukraine
⊕ https://vfmat.ch/c9c4

Kyiv City Maternity Hospital #1
Kyiv, Ukraine
⊕ https://vfmat.ch/f8ed

Kyiv City Maternity Hospital #1 Peredmistna Slobidka
Peredmistna Slobidka, Kyiv City, Ukraine
⊕ https://vfmat.ch/e862

Kyiv City Narcological Clinical Hospital Sociotherapy
Telychka, Kyiv City, Ukraine
⊕ https://vfmat.ch/2d89

Kyiv City Psychiatric Hospital I. Pavlov
Kyiv, Kyivska Oblast, Ukraine
⊕ https://vfmat.ch/3729

Kyiv City Tuberculosis Hospital #1 DV
Kyiv, Ukraine
⊕ https://vfmat.ch/34f4

Kyiv Regional Children's Hospital #2
Bila Tserkva, Kyiv Region, Ukraine
⊕ https://vfmat.ch/b887

Kyiv Regional Psychoneurological Hospital #2
Vorzel, Kyivska Oblast, Ukraine
⊕ https://vfmat.ch/ee5f

Kyiv Regional Tuberculosis Hospital #2
Klavdiyevo-Tarasovo, Kyiv Region, Ukraine
⊕ https://vfmat.ch/38d8

Lincon Medical Center
Vulka, Lviv, Ukraine
⊕ https://vfmat.ch/b3af

Lipetsk Hospital
Liptsy, Kharkiv, Ukraine
⊕ https://vfmat.ch/88a3

Lypovets Central District Hospital
Lypovets, Vinnytska Oblast, Ukraine
⊕ https://vfmat.ch/9a68

LISOD-Israel Hospital of Modern Cancer Care
Plyuty, Kiev Region, Ukraine
⊕ https://vfmat.ch/1b82

Lubensk Central City Hospital
Lubny, Poltava Oblast, Ukraine
⊕ https://vfmat.ch/c363

Lubny Regional Hospital for War Veterans of Poltava Regional Council
Lubny, Poltava Region, Ukraine
⊕ https://vfmat.ch/ff2f

Liuboml Central District Hospital
Liuboml, Volyn, Ukraine
⊕ https://vfmat.ch/16cb

Luhansk Central City Hospital
Khrustalnyi, Luhansk, Ukraine
⊕ https://vfmat.ch/a1b5

Luhansk City Multidisciplinary Hospital #1
Vasil'yevka, Luhansk, Ukraine
⊕ https://vfmat.ch/77a7

Luhansk City Multidisciplinary Hospital #3
Razdolinovka, Luhansk, Ukraine
⊕ https://vfmat.ch/22e3

Luhansk City Multiprofile Hospital #15
Yubileynoye, Luhansk Region, Ukraine
⊕ https://vfmat.ch/9ead

Luhansk City Multiprofile Hospital #4
Artëmovskiy Rayon, Luhansk, Ukraine
⊕ https://vfmat.ch/cb69

Luhansk Regional Children's Clinical Hospital
Lysychans'k, Luhansk Oblast, Ukraine
⊕ https://vfmat.ch/432a

Lutsk Central District Hospital
Lypyny, Volyn, Ukraine
⊕ https://vfmat.ch/2ac4

Lutuhyne District Territorial Medical Association
Lutuhyne, Luhanska Oblast, Ukraine
⊕ https://vfmat.ch/c2a7

Lviv City Clinical Hospital Prince Leo
Lviv, Lviv Region, Ukraine
⊕ https://vfmat.ch/a9ff

Lviv City Hospital #1
Lviv, Lviv Region, Ukraine
⊕ https://vfmat.ch/2918

Lviv Clinical Hospital of the State Border Guard Service of Ukraine
Lviv, Lviv Region, Ukraine
🌐 https://vfmat.ch/2da9

Lviv Regional Children's Clinical Hospital Okhmatdyt
Lviv, Lviv Region, Ukraine
🌐 https://vfmat.ch/985f

Lviv Regional Hospital for Extrapulmonary Tuberculosis
Lviv, Lviv Region, Ukraine
🌐 https://vfmat.ch/9c9a

Lviv Regional Infectious Clinical Hospital
Vulka, Lviv Region, Ukraine
🌐 https://vfmat.ch/b4cf

Lviv Regional Phthisiopulmonology Center
Sykhiv, Lviv, Ukraine
🌐 https://vfmat.ch/65bf

Lviv State Regional Clinical Perinatal Center
Lviv, Lviv Region, Ukraine
🌐 https://vfmat.ch/4c39

Lysetska Central District Hospital
Lysets, Ivano-Frankivsk Oblast, Ukraine
🌐 https://vfmat.ch/b9fb

Lyubotyn Central City Hospital
Lyubotyn, Kharkiv, Ukraine
🌐 https://vfmat.ch/6951

Magdalynivsk Village Council of Dnipropetrovsk Region
Magdalinivka, Dnipropetrovsk Oblast, Ukraine
🌐 https://vfmat.ch/bcaa

Main Military Clinical Hospital
Kyiv, Ukraine
🌐 https://vfmat.ch/4586

Makiivka City Hospital #4
Makiivka, Donetsk Oblast, Ukraine
🌐 https://vfmat.ch/d792

Makiivka City Hospital #7
Makiivka, Donetsk Oblast, Ukraine
🌐 https://vfmat.ch/d57d

Makiivka City Clinical Hospital #5
Makiivka, Donetska Oblast, Ukraine
🌐 https://vfmat.ch/1a13

Malovyskiv Hospital
Mala Vyska, Malovyskiv District, Kirovohradska Oblast, Ukraine
🌐 https://vfmat.ch/3f3b

Mankiv Central District Hospital
Mala Man'kivka, Cherkasy Oblast, Ukraine
🌐 https://vfmat.ch/344f

Mariupol City Hospital #1
Aerodrom, Donetsk, Ukraine
🌐 https://vfmat.ch/cd65

Mariupol City Hospital #9
Mariupol, Donetsk, Ukraine
🌐 https://vfmat.ch/b8e1

Mariupol City Hospital of Emergency Medical Care
Mariupol, Donetsk, Ukraine
🌐 https://vfmat.ch/5994

Mariupol Regional Intensive Care Hospital
Mariupol, Donetsk, Ukraine
🌐 https://vfmat.ch/df3d

Marquine Central District Hospital
Krasnogorovka, Donetsk, Ukraine
🌐 https://vfmat.ch/1658

Marriott Medical Center
Truskavets, Lviv, Ukraine
🌐 https://vfmat.ch/85a3

Maternity (Ternopil Regional Perinatal Center for Mother and Child)
Ternopil, Ternopil Oblast, Ukraine
🌐 https://vfmat.ch/6227

Maternity Building #2 Of Odessa City Council
Odessa, Odessa, Ukraine
🌐 https://vfmat.ch/42b7

Maternity Home of Rivne City Council
Rivne, Rivne Region, Ukraine
🌐 https://vfmat.ch/bf9d

Maternity Hospital
Podolsk, Odesska Oblast, Ukraine
🌐 https://vfmat.ch/55b8

Maternity Hospital #1
Arkadiya, Odessa, Ukraine
🌐 https://vfmat.ch/1b5e

Maternity Hospital #1 Khutory
Khutory, Cherkasy Oblast, Ukraine
🌐 https://vfmat.ch/f8df

Maternity Hospital #4 Sonyachne
Sonyachne, Zaporizhzhya Oblast, Ukraine
🌐 https://vfmat.ch/93e2

Maternity Hospital #5 Odessa
Odessa, Odessa Region, Ukraine
🌐 https://vfmat.ch/d8cf

Maternity Hospital #7 Cheremushky
Cheremushky, Odessa Region, Ukraine
🌐 https://vfmat.ch/d554

Maternity Hospital of Chernihiv City Council
Chernihiv, Chernihiv Oblast, Ukraine
🌐 https://vfmat.ch/6466

Maternity Hospital of the City Clinical Hospital #3
Lviv, Lviv Oblast, Ukraine
🌐 https://vfmat.ch/9241

Medical and Obstetric Point
Velyka Kalynka, Lviv Oblast, Ukraine
🌐 https://vfmat.ch/faa5

Medical Center
Bokiima, Rivnens'ka Oblast, Ukraine
🌐 https://vfmat.ch/47ae

Medical Service of Dobropole
Dobropol'ye, Donetsk, Ukraine
🌐 https://vfmat.ch/3a71

Medicine Krivbas
Kryvyi Rih, Dnipropetrovsk Oblast, Ukraine
🌐 https://vfmat.ch/d6cf

Meditsinskiy Tsentr Starlab
Smferopol, Simferopol, Ukraine
🌐 https://vfmat.ch/b228

Melitopol City Children's Hospital
Melitopol, Zaporizhzhya Oblast, Ukraine
🌐 https://vfmat.ch/f97c

Melitopol City Hospital #2
Melitopol, Zaporizhzhya Oblast, Ukraine
🌐 https://vfmat.ch/a83e

Melitopol City Hospital #1
Kostiantynivka, Zaporizhzhya Oblast, Ukraine
🌐 https://vfmat.ch/9fc5

Melitopol District Hospital
Melitopol, Zaporizhzhya Oblast, Ukraine
🌐 https://vfmat.ch/881c

Mikolayiv Military Hospital, The
Mykolayiv, Mykolayiv Oblast, Ukraine
🌐 https://vfmat.ch/8f74

Military and Medical Department of the Security Service of Ukraine
Kyiv, Ukraine
🌐 https://vfmat.ch/446f

Military Hospital at Simferopol
Simferopol, Crimea, Ukraine
🌐 https://vfmat.ch/c668

Military Hospital at Zhytomyr
Zhytomyr, Zhytomyr Oblast, Ukraine
⊕ https://vfmat.ch/25c2

Military Medical Center of the Air Force of Ukraine
Sobariv, Vinnytsya Oblast, Ukraine
⊕ https://vfmat.ch/467f

Military Medical Clinical Center of the Eastern Region
Dnipro, Dnipropetrovsk Region, Ukraine
⊕ https://vfmat.ch/da38

Military Medical Clinical Center of the Western Region
Lviv, Lviv Region, Ukraine
⊕ https://vfmat.ch/f32b

Morshyn Lviv City Hospital
Morshyn, Lviv Oblast, Ukraine
⊕ https://vfmat.ch/e5ab

Mother and Child Center Maternity Hospital Base #2
Cherkasy, Cherkasy Oblast, Ukraine
⊕ https://vfmat.ch/4c2e

Mukachevo Central District Hospital
Mukachevo, Zakarpattia Oblast, Ukraine
⊕ https://vfmat.ch/494e

Multidisciplinary Hospital #3 Razdolinovka
Razdolinovka, Luhansk, Ukraine
⊕ https://vfmat.ch/9fc6

Multidisciplinary Hospital of St. Catherine's Clinic
Odesa, Odessa Oblast, Ukraine
⊕ https://vfmat.ch/fe28

Multiprofile Central District Hospital
Kamyanets-Podilsky, Khmelnytskyy Oblast, Ukraine
⊕ https://vfmat.ch/3a96

Municipal City Clinical Hospital #3 of Lviv
Lviv, Lvivska Oblast, Ukraine
⊕ https://vfmat.ch/4a59

Municipal City Clinical Hospital #8 of Lviv
Sykhiv, Lviv, Ukraine
⊕ https://vfmat.ch/d8d6

Municipal City Clinical Hospital of Ambulance of Lviv
Lviv, Lviv Region, Ukraine
⊕ https://vfmat.ch/ad2d

Municipal Clinical Maternity Hospital #1
Chernivtsi, Chernivtsi Oblast, Ukraine
⊕ https://vfmat.ch/6abd

Municipal Institution Staroosotsky Children's Regional Anti-Tuberculosis Sanatorium
Poselianivka, Kirovohrad Oblast, Ukraine
⊕ https://vfmat.ch/7193

Mykolaev Regional Blood Transfusion Station, The
Mykolayiv, Mykolayiv Oblast, Ukraine
⊕ https://vfmat.ch/3a4f

Mykolaiv City Hospital #5
Mykolaiv, Ukraine
⊕ https://vfmat.ch/7a6b

Mykolaiv Regional Center for Emergency Care and Disaster Medicine
Radisnyy Sad, Mykolayiv Oblast, Ukraine
⊕ https://vfmat.ch/9789

Mykolaiv Regional Center of Treatment of Infectious Diseases
Mykolaiv, Mykolayiv Oblast, Ukraine
⊕ https://vfmat.ch/f63b

Mykolaivska Central District Hospital
Mykolaiv, Mykolayivska Oblast, Ukraine
⊕ https://vfmat.ch/f5b4

Mykolayivka Medical and Obstetric Point
Mykolaivka, Kirovohrad Oblast, Ukraine
⊕ https://vfmat.ch/849c

Mykulynets Regional Rehabilitation Hospital
Mykulyntsi, Ternopil Oblast, Ukraine
⊕ https://vfmat.ch/4f6d

Myrnograd City Infectious Hospital
Mirnograd, Donetsk Region, Ukraine
⊕ https://vfmat.ch/d25a

Nadvirna Central District Hospital
Nadvirna, Ivano-Frankivsk Oblast, Ukraine
⊕ https://vfmat.ch/847b

Narkolohichnyy Dyspanser
Ivano-Frankivsk, Ivano-Frankivsk Oblast, Ukraine
⊕ https://vfmat.ch/6b38

Narodytska Hospital
Narodychi, Zhytomyr, Ukraine
⊕ https://vfmat.ch/ee6b

National Institute of Cardiovascular Surgery M.M. Amosov
Kyiv, Kyivska Oblast, Ukraine
⊕ https://vfmat.ch/45af

National Scientific Center M.D. Strazhesko Institute of Cardiology
Kiev, Ukraine
⊕ https://vfmat.ch/97d4

Neboleyka Children's Treatment and Prevention Center
Kharkiv, Ukraine
⊕ https://vfmat.ch/52ee

Nedrigailiv Central District Hospital
Terni, Sumy Region, Ukraine
⊕ https://vfmat.ch/b656

Nikolaev Regional Hospital, The
Peremoha, Odessa, Ukraine
⊕ https://vfmat.ch/22ec

Nikopol City Hospital #1
Nikopol, Dnipropetrovska Oblast, Ukraine
⊕ https://vfmat.ch/cebf

Nikopol City Hospital #3
Nikopol, Dnipropetrovska Oblast, Ukraine
⊕ https://vfmat.ch/3c9d

Nizhnosirogozka Central District Hospital
Novodmytrivka Persha, Kherson Oblast, Ukraine
⊕ https://vfmat.ch/787b

Nizhyn Central City Hospital M. Halytsky
Nizhyn, Chernihivska Oblast, Ukraine
⊕ https://vfmat.ch/cd88

Novolodolazka Central Hospital
Nova Vodolaha, Kharkiv, Ukraine
⊕ https://vfmat.ch/16af

Novomoskovsk Central City Hospital
Novomoskovsk, Dnipropetrovsk Oblast, Ukraine
⊕ https://vfmat.ch/d6b5

Novomoskovsk Central District Hospital
Novomoskovsk, Dnipropetrovsk Region, Ukraine
⊕ https://vfmat.ch/a716

Novomykolayiv Tuberculosis Hospital
Novomykolayivka, Dnipropetrovsk Oblast, Ukraine
⊕ https://vfmat.ch/eb3c

Novorozdil City Hospital
Novyi Rozdil, Lviv, Ukraine
⊕ https://vfmat.ch/82cf

Novosanzharsk Central District Hospital
Novi Sanzhary, Poltava Oblast, Ukraine
⊕ https://vfmat.ch/ac4f

Novoselytsia Central District Hospital
Marshyntsi, Chernivtsi Oblast, Ukraine
⊕ https://vfmat.ch/7b18

Novotroitsk Tuberculosis Hospital
Novotroitsk, Khersonska Oblast, Ukraine
⊕ https://vfmat.ch/7dda

Novoukrainian City Hospital
Novoukrainka, Kirovograd Region, Ukraine
⊕ https://vfmat.ch/cd41

Novoushinsk Central District Hospital
Nova Ushytsia Township, Khmelnytska Oblast, Ukraine
⊕ https://vfmat.ch/84f6

Novoyarychiv District Hospital
Novyi Yarychiv, Lviv, Ukraine
⊕ https://vfmat.ch/5952

Novoyavorivsk District Hospital #1
Novoyavorovske, Lviv Oblast, Ukraine
⊕ https://vfmat.ch/e488

Oblast Hospital for Veterans of World War II
Deribasovka, Odessa, Ukraine
⊕ https://vfmat.ch/41d5

Obukhiv Central District Hospital
Obukhiv, Kyivska Oblast, Ukraine
⊕ https://vfmat.ch/5ff7

Odessa City Clinical Hospital #3 Prof. Lyaleynikova
Odessa, Odessa Region, Ukraine
⊕ https://vfmat.ch/3edf

Odessa City Clinical Hospital #9
Krivaya Balka, Odessa, Ukraine
⊕ https://vfmat.ch/df16

Odessa City Hospital
Yuzhne, Odessa Oblast, Ukraine
⊕ https://vfmat.ch/6edc

Odessa Regional Children's Clinical Hospital
Odessa, Odessa Oblast, Ukraine
⊕ https://vfmat.ch/ee54

Odessa Regional Children's Dermatological and Venereological Hospital
Odessa, Odessa Oblast, Ukraine
⊕ https://vfmat.ch/f515

Odessa Regional Clinical Hospital
Odessa, Ukraine
⊕ https://vfmat.ch/9e29

Odessa Regional Clinical Medical Center
Odessa, Ukraine
⊕ https://vfmat.ch/7fdb

Odessa Regional Medical Center for Mental Health
Odessa, Odessa Region, Ukraine
⊕ https://vfmat.ch/7858

Odessa Regional Tuberculosis Clinical Hospital
Krivaya Balka, Odessa, Ukraine
⊕ https://vfmat.ch/9e4f

Oleksandrivsk Central District Hospital
Oleksandrivka, Kirovohradska Oblast, Ukraine
⊕ https://vfmat.ch/1784

Olevsk Central District Hospital
Olevsk, Zhytomyrska Oblast, Ukraine
⊕ https://vfmat.ch/2116

Ophthalmological Clinic, Hirschman
Nova Olekciyivka, Kharkiv, Ukraine
⊕ https://vfmat.ch/9bf6

Opishnyan District Hospital
Opishnya, Poltava Oblast, Ukraine
⊕ https://vfmat.ch/4b13

Opishnyan Tuberculosis Regional Hospital of Poltava Regional Council
Opishnya, Poltava Oblast, Ukraine
⊕ https://vfmat.ch/e16b

Orativ Central District Hospital
Orativ, Vinnytsia Region, Vinnytska Oblast, Ukraine
⊕ https://vfmat.ch/8ca4

Orzhytsya Central District Hospital
Orzhytsia, Poltavska Oblast, Ukraine
⊕ https://vfmat.ch/37ac

Osterska District Hospital
Ostër, Chernihiv, Ukraine
⊕ https://vfmat.ch/362e

Otyniya District Hospital #1
Otyniya, Ivano-Frankivsk Oblast, Ukraine
⊕ https://vfmat.ch/4b8e

Ovidiopol Central District Hospital
Moldava, Odessa, Ukraine
⊕ https://vfmat.ch/6d46

Pavlograd Central District Hospital
Pavlograd, Dnipropetrovsk Oblast, Ukraine
⊕ https://vfmat.ch/51c2

Pavlograd City Hospital #4
Pavlograd, Dnipropetrovsk Oblast, Ukraine
⊕ https://vfmat.ch/fe6a

Pavlohrad City Hospital #1
Pavlohrad, Ukraine
⊕ https://vfmat.ch/5bfc

Pecheneg CRH
Pechenegi, Kharkiv, Ukraine
⊕ https://vfmat.ch/e421

Perehinskaya Hospital #2 Perehinskaya Village Council
Perehinske, Ivano-Frankivsk Oblast, Ukraine
⊕ https://vfmat.ch/647e

Pereschepin District Hospital #2 of Dnipropetrovsk Regional Council
Pereshchepyne, Dnipropetrovsk Oblast, Ukraine
⊕ https://vfmat.ch/88c8

Perinatal Center of Kyiv, The
Telychka, Kyiv City, Ukraine
⊕ https://vfmat.ch/8efc

Perinatal Center of Mariupol
Mariupol, Donetsk Region, Ukraine
⊕ https://vfmat.ch/cb76

Pervomaisk Multidisciplinary City Hospital
Pervomaysk, Luhansk, Ukraine
⊕ https://vfmat.ch/6a6f

Pervomaysk Central District Hospital
Pervomaysk, Mykolayiv Oblast, Ukraine
⊕ https://vfmat.ch/e3db

Petrykivska Central District Hospital
Mala Petrykivka, Dnipropetrovsk Oblast, Ukraine
⊕ https://vfmat.ch/82cd

Pidbuzka District Hospital
Pidbuzh, Lviv, Ukraine
⊕ https://vfmat.ch/e59c

Pidkaminska City Hospital
Pidkamin, Lviv Oblast, Ukraine
⊕ https://vfmat.ch/f5ac

Pishchan District Hospital
Paliyove, Vinnytsia Oblast, Ukraine
⊕ https://vfmat.ch/cad5

Podilsk Central District Hospital
Podolsk, Odessa, Ukraine
⊕ https://vfmat.ch/bd82

Podolsk City Hospital, Infectious Diseases Department
Kuyalnyk, Odessa, Ukraine
⊕ https://vfmat.ch/f377

Podolsk Regional Oncology Center
Vinnytsia, Vinnytsya Oblast, Ukraine
⊕ https://vfmat.ch/45ba

Pohrebyshche Central District Hospital
Pohrebyshche, Vinnytsia Region, Vinnytska Oblast, Ukraine
⊕ https://vfmat.ch/d13f

Pokrovskaya Central District Hospital
Pokrovsk, Donetsk Region, Ukraine
⊕ https://vfmat.ch/8c38

Pologiv Railway Hospital
Pologi, Zaporizhia Region, Ukraine
⊕ https://vfmat.ch/f88e

Polonsk Central District Hospital
Novo-Polonnoye, Khmelnytsky Region, Ukraine
⊕ https://vfmat.ch/387a

Poltava Regional Center of Addiction Therapy of Poltava Regional Council
Poltava, Poltava Oblast, Ukraine
⊕ https://vfmat.ch/5a5a

Poltava Regional Center of Emergency Medical Care and Medicine Disasters of Poltava Regional Council
Shmyhli, Poltava Oblast, Ukraine
⊕ https://vfmat.ch/ea11

Poltava Regional Clinical Hospital M.V. Sklifosovsky
Poltava, Poltava Region, Ukraine
⊕ https://vfmat.ch/b5a6

Ppo Klpu Regional Clinical Tuberculosis Hospital
Donetsk, Donetsk Oblast, Ukraine
⊕ https://vfmat.ch/c248

Priazovskaya Central District Hospital
Priazovske, Zaporizhzhya Oblast, Ukraine
⊕ https://vfmat.ch/3a64

Primary Health Care Center #10
Zaporizhia, Zaporizhzhya Oblast, Ukraine
⊕ https://vfmat.ch/7ca7

Primary Health Care Center #2
Mishkovo-Pohorilove, Mykolayiv Oblast, Ukraine
⊕ https://vfmat.ch/a8a2

Primorsky Central District Hospital
Primorsk, Zaporizhia Region, Ukraine
⊕ https://vfmat.ch/8d82

Prydniprovska Hospital
Kremenchuk, Poltava Oblast, Ukraine
⊕ https://vfmat.ch/c412

Psychiatric Hospital #1
Krinichnaya, Donetsk, Ukraine
⊕ https://vfmat.ch/665e

Psychiatric Hospital #3
Petrenkov, Kharkiv, Ukraine
⊕ https://vfmat.ch/3cf6

Putivl' Central District Hospital
Putyvl', Sumy, Ukraine
⊕ https://vfmat.ch/2859

Pyatikhat Central City Hospital
Pyatihatki, Dnipropetrovsk Oblast, Ukraine
⊕ https://vfmat.ch/1cc1

Pyriatyn Hospital of the Pyriatyn City Council
Pyriatyn, Poltava Region, Ukraine
⊕ https://vfmat.ch/6a97

Radyvyliv Central District Hospital
Radyvyliv, Rivne Region, Ukraine
⊕ https://vfmat.ch/d744

Railway Hospital
Khrystynivka, Cherkasy Oblast, Ukraine
⊕ https://vfmat.ch/e84b

Razdolne District Hospital
Razdolne District, Crimea, Ukraine
⊕ https://vfmat.ch/a382

Regional Allergy Hospital
Solotvyno, Zakarpattia Oblast, Ukraine
⊕ https://vfmat.ch/63ba

Regional Children's Clinical Hospital
Artëmovskiy Rayon, Luhansk, Ukraine
⊕ https://vfmat.ch/fb93

Regional Children's Hospital M. Slovyansk
Slavyansk, Donetsk, Ukraine
⊕ https://vfmat.ch/dad5

Regional Clinical and Diagnostic Laboratory
Ruzhychna, Khmelnytskyy Oblast, Ukraine
⊕ https://vfmat.ch/1eb7

Regional Clinical Hospital for Rehabilitation and Diagnostics
Poltava, Poltavska Oblast, Ukraine
⊕ https://vfmat.ch/b45f

Regional Clinical Psychoneurological Hospital
Donetsk, Donetska Oblast, Ukraine
⊕ https://vfmat.ch/5aef

Regional Hospital for Disabled Veterans
Cherkasy, Cherkasy Oblast, Ukraine
⊕ https://vfmat.ch/1f4f

Regional Infectious Diseases Hospital
Zaporizhia, Zaporizhzhya Oblast, Ukraine
⊕ https://vfmat.ch/1157

Regional Interdistrict Diagnostic Center in Korosten
Korosten, Zhytomyr Region, Ukraine
⊕ https://vfmat.ch/5f35

Regional Medical Center for Human Reproduction
Baburka, Zaporizhzhya Oblast, Ukraine
⊕ https://vfmat.ch/1e5a

Regional Medical Consulting and Diagnostic Center of the Zhytomyr Regional Council
Zarichany, Zhytomyr, Ukraine
⊕ https://vfmat.ch/15e9

Regional Municipal Institution Chernivtsi Oblast Clinical Hospital
Chernivtsi, Chernivtsi Oblast, Ukraine
⊕ https://vfmat.ch/bdca

Regional Ophthalmological Hospital
Mykolayivske, Mykolayiv Oblast, Ukraine
⊕ https://vfmat.ch/3dad

Regional Psychiatric Hospital Village Orlivka
Orlivka, Rivne, Ukraine
⊕ https://vfmat.ch/cc87

Regional Specialized Children's Sanatorium Pulmonological
Onokivtsi, Zakarpattia Oblast, Ukraine
⊕ https://vfmat.ch/74bc

Rehabilitation Center Elite
Vulka, Lviv, Ukraine
⊕ https://vfmat.ch/8c62

Republican Clinical Hospital of the Ministry of Health of Ukraine
Kyiv, Ukraine
⊕ https://vfmat.ch/ebf5

Reshetyliv Central Hospital of Reshetyliv City Council of Poltava Region
Reshetylivka, Poltava Oblast, Ukraine
⊕ https://vfmat.ch/213a

Rivne Central City Hospital
Rivne, Rivnenska Oblast, Ukraine
⊕ https://vfmat.ch/d6f3

Rivne City Hospital
Rivne, Ukraine
⊕ https://vfmat.ch/e47a

Rivne Regional Hospital for War Invalids
Klevan, Rivne Region, Ukraine
⊕ https://vfmat.ch/cf6d

Rivne Regional Perinatal Center
Rivne, Rivnenska Oblast, Ukraine
⊕ https://vfmat.ch/9b91

Road Clinical Hospital
Dnipro, Dnipropetrovsk Oblast, Ukraine
⊕ https://vfmat.ch/7f74

Road Clinical Hospital, Donetsk Station
Donetsk, Donetska Oblast, Ukraine
⊕ https://vfmat.ch/64fd

Rohatyn Central District Hospital
Rohatyn, Ivano-Frankivsk Oblast, Ukraine
⊕ https://vfmat.ch/2299

Rokytnivsky Multiprofile Hospital for Intensive Treatment
Rokytne, Rivne, Ukraine
⊕ https://vfmat.ch/4b55

Romanivsk Central District Hospital
Romaniv, Zhytomyr, Ukraine
⊕ https://vfmat.ch/e22d

Romenskaya Central District Hospital
Romny, Sumy Region, Ukraine
⊕ https://vfmat.ch/587f

Rozhnyativ District Hospital
Nyzhnii Strutyn, Ivano-Frankivsk Oblast, Ukraine
⊕ https://vfmat.ch/91c9

RRC Hospital
Donetsk, Donetsk Oblast, Ukraine
⊕ https://vfmat.ch/d7a8

Ruzhyn District Hospital
Ruzhyn, Zhytomyr Oblast, Ukraine
⊕ https://vfmat.ch/8417

Sakhnovshchynsk Central District Hospital
Sakhnovshchyna, Kharkivska Oblast, Ukraine
⊕ https://vfmat.ch/c2c9

Sambir Central District Hospital
Sambir, Lviv Region, Ukraine
⊕ https://vfmat.ch/1365

Sambir City Children's Hospital
Sambir, Lviv, Ukraine
⊕ https://vfmat.ch/332a

Sarny Central District Hospital
Sarny, Rivne Region, Ukraine
⊕ https://vfmat.ch/395e

Severodonetsk City Multidisciplinary Hospital Severodonetsk City Council
Severodonetsk, Luhansk Region, Ukraine
⊕ https://vfmat.ch/ccef

Shatsk District Hospital
Shatsk, Volynska Oblast, Ukraine
⊕ https://vfmat.ch/1c25

Shepetivka Central District Hospital
Shepetivka, Khmelnytskyy Oblast, Ukraine
⊕ https://vfmat.ch/f8ac

Shevchenkivska Central District Hospital
Shevchenkove, Kharkiv, Ukraine
⊕ https://vfmat.ch/b7b2

Shishak Central District Hospital
Shishaky, Poltava Region, Ukraine
⊕ https://vfmat.ch/e372

Simferopol Central District Clinical Hospital
Simferopol, Ukraine
⊕ https://vfmat.ch/1ec6

Sinevo Medical Laboratory
Vinnytsia, Vinnytsya Oblast, Ukraine
⊕ https://vfmat.ch/9332

Skeliv Infectious Hospital
Starosambirskyi District, village Skelivka, Lviv, Ukraine
⊕ https://vfmat.ch/6e65

Sloviansk City Hospital #1
Sloviansk, Donetsk, Ukraine
⊕ https://vfmat.ch/d653

Smilyansk Central District Hospital
Zalevky, Cherkasy Oblast, Ukraine
⊕ https://vfmat.ch/a4da

Sniatyn Central District Hospital
Sorochanka, Ivano-Frankivsk Oblast, Ukraine
⊕ https://vfmat.ch/bcc4

Sokal Central District Hospital
Sokal, Lviv, Ukraine
⊕ https://vfmat.ch/9c8b

Solonyanska Multidisciplinary Hospital
Novoselivka, Dnipropetrovsk Oblast, Ukraine
⊕ https://vfmat.ch/39d4

Solotvyno Regional Allergy Hospital
Solotvyno, Zakarpattia Region, Ukraine
⊕ https://vfmat.ch/7f28

Sosnytsia District Hospital
Sosnytsia, Chernihiv, Ukraine
⊕ https://vfmat.ch/daf1

Specialized Medical Part #4
Netishyn, Khmelnytskyy Oblast, Ukraine
⊕ https://vfmat.ch/c99c

St. Luke's Hospital
Kropyvnytskyi, Kirovohradska Oblast, Ukraine
⊕ https://vfmat.ch/28eb

St. Paraskeva Medical Center
Lviv, Lviv Oblast, Ukraine
⊕ https://vfmat.ch/487b

Starokostiantyniv Military Hospital
Sloboda Novomeyskaya, Khmelnytskyy Oblast, Ukraine
⊕ https://vfmat.ch/cb7f

Staroushytska District Hospital #3
Stara Ushytsya, Khmelnytskyy Oblast, Ukraine
⊕ https://vfmat.ch/ae38

Starovyzhiv Central District Hospital
Stara Vyzhivka, Volyn, Ukraine
⊕ https://vfmat.ch/1ae7

State Hospital of the Ministry of Internal Affairs of Ukraine in the City of Kryvyi Rih
Kryvyi Rih, Dnipropetrovsk Oblast, Ukraine
⊕ https://vfmat.ch/97ef

Stryi Central City Hospital
Stryi, Lvivska Oblast, Ukraine
⊕ https://vfmat.ch/f451

Stryi Central District Hospital
Stryi, Lvivska Oblast, Ukraine
⊕ https://vfmat.ch/cfff

Stryi City Children's Hospital
Stryi, Lvivska Oblast, Ukraine
⊕ https://vfmat.ch/3c78

Sudak City Hospital
Sudak, Crimea, Ukraine
⊕ https://vfmat.ch/a4ad

Sudovyshnyanskiy City Hospital
Sudova Vyshnya, Lvivska Oblast, Ukraine
⊕ https://vfmat.ch/7e28

Sumy City Children's Clinical Hospital St. Zinaida
Sumy, Ukraine
⊕ https://vfmat.ch/ad45

Sumy City Clinical Hospital #4
Sumy, Sumska Oblast, Ukraine
⊕ https://vfmat.ch/1cb3

Sumy City Clinical Maternity Hospital of the Holy Virgin Mary
Zamost'ye, Sumy, Ukraine
⊕ https://vfmat.ch/4e9a

Sumy District Central Clinical Hospital
Sumy, Sumska Oblast, Ukraine
⊕ https://vfmat.ch/226a

Sumy Regional Children's Clinical Hospital
Sumy, Sumy Region, Ukraine
⊕ https://vfmat.ch/425f

Sumy Regional Children's Clinical Hospital
Pryshyb, Sumy, Ukraine
⊕ https://vfmat.ch/f144

Sverdlovsk Central City Hospital #1
Dovzhansk city, Lugansk Region, Ukraine
⊕ https://vfmat.ch/4f26

Svitlovodsk Central District Hospital
Svitlovodsk, Kirovohradska Oblast, Ukraine
⊕ https://vfmat.ch/f9ba

Talnivska Central District Hospital
Hordashivka, Cherkasy Oblast, Ukraine
⊕ https://vfmat.ch/81c9

Tarutyn Central District Hospital
Maloyaroslavets Druhyy, Odessa, Ukraine
⊕ https://vfmat.ch/3482

Teplodar Central City Hospital
Teplodar, Odessa, Ukraine
⊕ https://vfmat.ch/f633

Terebovlya City Hospital
Terebovlia, Ternopilska Oblast, Ukraine
⊕ https://vfmat.ch/5211

Ternopil Central District Hospital
Ternopil, Ternopil Oblast, Ukraine
⊕ https://vfmat.ch/28a8

Ternopil City Children's Municipal Hospital
Ternopil, Ternopilska Oblast, Ukraine
⊕ https://vfmat.ch/8922

Ternopil City Municipal Ambulance Hospital
Petrikov, Ternopil Oblast, Ukraine
⊕ https://vfmat.ch/984d

Ternopil Municipal City Hospital #2
Ternopil, Ternopilska Oblast, Ukraine
⊕ https://vfmat.ch/2559

Ternopil Regional Children's Clinical Hospital
Ternopil, Ternopilska Oblast, Ukraine
⊕ https://vfmat.ch/35f1

Ternopil Regional Communal Clinical Psychoneurological Hospital
Ternopil, Ternopilska Oblast, Ukraine
⊕ https://vfmat.ch/58ae

Ternopil University Hospital
Ternopil, Ternopilska Oblast, Ukraine
⊕ https://vfmat.ch/1938

Territorial Medical Association of the Ministry of Internal Affairs of Ukraine in the Dnipropetrovska Oblast
Dnipro, Dnipropetrovsk Oblast, Ukraine
⊕ https://vfmat.ch/1ab2

Territorial Medical Association of the Ministry of Internal Affairs of Ukraine in Kyiv Region
Obolon, Kyiv City, Ukraine
⊕ https://vfmat.ch/3988

Tetiiv Central District Hospital
Tetiiv, Kiev, Ukraine
⊕ https://vfmat.ch/1aec

Therapeutic Building of the Sarny CDH
Yaroslav, Ukraine
⊕ https://vfmat.ch/dc67

Third Cherkasy City Ambulance Hospital
Khutory, Cherkasy Region, Ukraine
⊕ https://vfmat.ch/119b

Tkachenko Cardiology, cardiology and ultrasound diagnostics
Kharkiv, Kharkiv Region, Ukraine
⊕ https://vfmat.ch/8d3b

Tores Central City Hospital
Torez, Donetsk, Ukraine
⊕ https://vfmat.ch/f3ed

Trauma Center of Khmelnytsky Branch
Khmelnytskyi, Khmelnytskyy Oblast, Ukraine
⊕ https://vfmat.ch/7b54

Trostyanets Central District Hospital
Trostyanets, Vinnytska Oblast, Ukraine
⊕ https://vfmat.ch/1ac1

Truskavets City Hospital
Truskavets, Lvivska Oblast, Ukraine
⊕ https://vfmat.ch/8556

Tuberculosis Hospital #1
Odessa, Ukraine
⊕ https://vfmat.ch/b439

Tulchyn Central District Hospital
Tulchyn, Vinnytsya Oblast, Ukraine
⊕ https://vfmat.ch/d347

Turia Central District Hospital
Turiisk, Volyn, Ukraine
⊕ https://vfmat.ch/63c9

Tyachiv District Hospital #1
Tyachiv, Zakarpattia Oblast, Ukraine
⊕ https://vfmat.ch/84b9

Tyvrivsk Central District Hospital
Tyvriv, Vinnytsia Region, Ukraine
⊕ https://vfmat.ch/93be

Ukrainian Scientific and Practical Center for Endocrine Surgery, Transplantation of Endocrine Organs and Tissues of the Ministry of Health of Ukraine
Kyiv, Kyivska Oblast, Ukraine
⊕ https://vfmat.ch/cf75

Ukrainian State Medical and Social Center for War Veterans
Tsybli, Kiev, Ukraine
⊕ https://vfmat.ch/cad9

Uman Central District Hospital
Umanskyi District, Rodnykivka Village, Cherkasy Oblast, Ukraine
⊕ https://vfmat.ch/af3d

Uman City Children's Hospital
Uman, Cherkaska Oblast, Ukraine
⊕ https://vfmat.ch/d865

Uman Maternity Hospital
Uman, Cherkaska Oblast, Ukraine
⊕ https://vfmat.ch/fce1

Ustiluz City Hospital
Ustyluh, Volyn, Ukraine
⊕ https://vfmat.ch/3ca5

Ustya District hospital
Ustia, Vinnytsya Oblast, Ukraine
⊕ https://vfmat.ch/33bc

Valkiv Central District Hospital
Valky, Kharkiv Region, Ukraine
⊕ https://vfmat.ch/3c4b

Vasyliv Central District Hospital
Vasilievka, Zaporizhzhya Oblast, Ukraine
⊕ https://vfmat.ch/763e

Vasylkiv Maternity Hospital
Vasylkiv, Kyivska Oblast, Ukraine
⊕ https://vfmat.ch/b937

Vasylkivsk Central District Hospital
Vasylkiv, Kyivska Oblast, Ukraine
⊕ https://vfmat.ch/8b8b

Vatutine City Hospital
Vatutine, Cherkasy Oblast, Ukraine
⊕ https://vfmat.ch/831d

Velikoburlutsk Central Hospital
Velykoburlutskyi District, Urban-Type Settlement Velykyi Burluk, Kharkiv Region, Ukraine
⊕ https://vfmat.ch/9ecd

Velykobagachanska Central District Hospital
Velyka Bagachka, Poltava Oblast, Ukraine
⊕ https://vfmat.ch/1cc3

Velykobereznyanska Central District Hospital
Velykyy Bereznyy, Transcarpathia, Ukraine
⊕ https://vfmat.ch/feb2

Velykobereznyanska District Hospital
Velykyi Bereznyi, Zakarpatska Oblast, Ukraine
⊕ https://vfmat.ch/57b1

Velykomostivska City Hospital
Velyki Mosty, Lviv, Ukraine
⊕ https://vfmat.ch/7ca1

Velykosoltanivska Hospital
Velyka Soltanivka, Kiev, Ukraine
⊕ https://vfmat.ch/2aa8

Verkhivtsev City Hospital
Verkhivtseve, Dnipropetrovsk Oblast, Ukraine
⊕ https://vfmat.ch/8e8d

Verkhnovysotsk District Hospital
Verkhnie Vysotske, Lviv, Ukraine
⊕ https://vfmat.ch/f6e3

Verkhovyna District Hospital
Verhovyna District, Ivano-Frankivsk Oblast, Ukraine
⊕ https://vfmat.ch/63df

Vesele City Hospital #17
Vesele, Donetsk, Ukraine
⊕ https://vfmat.ch/6e13

Veselinovskaya Central District Hospital
Veselinovo, Nikolaev area, Ukraine
⊕ https://vfmat.ch/61a8

Viiskova Mobile Hospital #66
Pokrovsk, Donetsk, Ukraine
⊕ https://vfmat.ch/38e9

Vik Zdorov'ya
Lviv, Lviv Oblast, Ukraine
⊕ https://vfmat.ch/8cbf

Vilnogorsk Central City Hospital of Dnipropetrovsk Regional Council
Krynychky, Dnipropetrovsk Oblast, Ukraine
⊕ https://vfmat.ch/6d52

Vilshansk District Hospital
Vilshana, Cherkasy Oblast, Ukraine
⊕ https://vfmat.ch/bb6c

Vinnitsa Central District Clinical Hospital
Vinnytsia, Vinnytsia Region, Ukraine
⊕ https://vfmat.ch/dffa

Vinnitsa City Clinical Hospital #2
Vinnytsia, Vinnytsya Oblast, Ukraine
⊕ https://vfmat.ch/7c3f

Vinnitsa City Clinical Maternity Hospital #2
Malyye Khutora, Vinnytsya Oblast, Ukraine
⊕ https://vfmat.ch/af81

Vinnitsa Regional Clinical Highly Specialized Endocrinological Center
Pirogovo, Vinnytsya Oblast, Ukraine
⊕ https://vfmat.ch/ae72

Vinnitsa Regional Clinical Hospital of War Veterans of Vinnitsa Regional Council
Vinnytsia, Vinnytsia Region, Ukraine
⊕ https://vfmat.ch/7f11

Vinnytsia City Clinical Hospital #3, Center of Primary Health Medicine #4
Sobariv, Vinnytsya Oblast, Ukraine
⊕ https://vfmat.ch/79ae

Vinnytsia District Sanitary and Epidemiological Station
Vinnytsya, Vinnytsya Oblast, Ukraine
⊕ https://vfmat.ch/dd7d

Vinnytsia Regional Children's Clinical Hospital
Vinnytsia, Ukraine
⊕ https://vfmat.ch/bde4

Vinnytsia Regional Pirogov Clinical Hospital
Vinnytsya, Ukraine
⊕ https://vfmat.ch/ed3e

Volodar Central District Hospital
Volodarka, Kyiv Region, Ukraine
⊕ https://vfmat.ch/d95d

Volyn Regional Blood Transfusion Station M.Volodymyr-Volynsky
Volodymyr-Volynsky, Volyn, Ukraine
⊕ https://vfmat.ch/b6b4

Volyn Regional Hospital for War Invalids
Lutsk, Volynska Oblast, Ukraine
⊕ https://vfmat.ch/1a85

Volyn Regional Medical Oncology Centre
Gnidava, Volyn, Ukraine
⊕ https://vfmat.ch/2693

Vovchansk Central District Hospital
Kharkiv, Kharkiv, Ukraine
⊕ https://vfmat.ch/cf1a

Voznesenska District Hospital
Voznesenka, Zaporizhzhya Oblast, Ukraine
⊕ https://vfmat.ch/c6c4

VP Komissarenko Institute of Endocrinology and Metabolism of the National Academy of Medical Sciences of Ukraine
Shevchenka, Kyiv City, Ukraine
⊕ https://vfmat.ch/f168

Vynohradiv District Hospital
Vynohradiv, Zakarpats'ka, Ukraine
⊕ https://vfmat.ch/8271

Vyshniv City Hospital
Vyshneve, Kiev, Ukraine
⊕ https://vfmat.ch/c77b

Vyzlova Hospital #1 of Darnytsia Station
Kyiv, Ukraine
⊕ https://vfmat.ch/82ef

Western Ukrainian Specialized Children's Medical Center
Lviv, Lviv Region, Ukraine
⊕ https://vfmat.ch/5328

Women's Consultation of the City Clinical Maternity Hospital #1
Chernivtsi, Chernivtsi Oblast, Ukraine
⊕ https://vfmat.ch/188e

Yahotyn District Hospital
Yahotyn, Kiev Region, Ukraine
⊕ https://vfmat.ch/7fcc

Yalta Maternity Hospital, Gynecology
Yalta, Crimea, Ukraine
⊕ https://vfmat.ch/df2d

Yampil' Central District Hospital
Yampil', Sumy Region, Ukraine
⊕ https://vfmat.ch/733c

Yaremchan Central City Hospital
Yaremche, Ivano-Frankivsk Oblast, Ukraine
⊕ https://vfmat.ch/164d

Yarmolynets Central District Hospital
Yarmolyntsi, Khmelnytskyy Oblast, Ukraine
⊕ https://vfmat.ch/7434

Yasynuvata Central District Hospital
Yasynuvata, Donetska Oblast, Ukraine
⊕ https://vfmat.ch/e336

Yelanets Central District Hospital
Velidarivka, Mykolaiv Region, Ukraine
⊕ https://vfmat.ch/49bf

Yenakiieve City Hospital #7
Yenakiieve, Donetska Oblast, Ukraine
⊕ https://vfmat.ch/5d51

Zaporizhia City Clinical Hospital #10
Baburka, Zaporizhzhya Oblast, Ukraine
⊕ https://vfmat.ch/cb9f

Zaporizhia City Hospital #6
Zaporizhia, Ukraine
⊕ https://vfmat.ch/d547

Zaporozhye City Clinical Hospital #2
Zaporizhia, Zaporizhzhya Oblast, Ukraine
⊕ https://vfmat.ch/78d6

Zarichne Multiprofile Hospital
Zarichne, Rivne, Ukraine
⊕ https://vfmat.ch/d59a

Zbarazh Central District Clinical Hospital
Zbarazh, Ternopil Region, Ukraine
⊕ https://vfmat.ch/afba

Zboriv Central District Clinical Hospital
Zboriv, Ternopil Oblast, Ukraine
⊕ https://vfmat.ch/bc9a

Zelenodolsk City Hospital
Mala Kostromka, Dnipropetrovsk Oblast, Ukraine
⊕ https://vfmat.ch/c263

Zhashkiv Central District Hospital
Lytvynivka, Cherkasy Oblast, Ukraine
⊕ https://vfmat.ch/f588

Zhmerynka Central District Hospital
Zhmerynka, Vinnytska Oblast, Ukraine
⊕ https://vfmat.ch/b5d6

Zhmerynka Railway Hospital
Zhmerynka, Vinnytsya Oblast, Ukraine
⊕ https://vfmat.ch/c9ab

Zhovkiv Central District Hospital
Zhovkva, Lviv, Ukraine
⊕ https://vfmat.ch/b22a

Zhovtneva Central District Hospital
Mykolaiv, Mykolayiv Oblast, Ukraine
⊕ https://vfmat.ch/6578

Zhovtovodsk City Hospital
Zhovti Vody, Dnipropetrovska Oblast, Ukraine
⊕ https://vfmat.ch/4e47

Zhuravnivska City Hospital
Zhuravno, Lviv Region, Ukraine
⊕ https://vfmat.ch/4653

Zhvanets Village Council Hospital
Zhvanets, Khmelnytskyy Oblast, Ukraine
⊕ https://vfmat.ch/43d3

Zhydachiv Central District Hospital
Zhydachiv, Lvivska Oblast, Ukraine
⊕ https://vfmat.ch/8e34

Zhytomyr Central City Hospital #1
Zhytomyr, Zhytomyr Region, Ukraine
⊕ https://vfmat.ch/dbfe

Zhytomyr City Council Hospital #2 V.P. Pavlusenko
Boguniya, Zhytomyr, Ukraine
⊕ https://vfmat.ch/3b35

Zhytomyr Multidisciplinary Hospital of Novoguyvynsk Village Council
Stanyshivka village, Zhytomyrska Oblast, Ukraine
⊕ https://vfmat.ch/7d94

Zhytomyr Regional Clinical Hospital of Gerbachevsky
Zarichany, Zhytomyr, Ukraine
⊕ https://vfmat.ch/da63

Zinkiv City Central Hospital
Zinkiv, Poltava Oblast, Ukraine
⊕ https://vfmat.ch/cd55

Zmiiv Central District Hospital
Zmiyiv, Kharkiv, Ukraine
⊕ https://vfmat.ch/24f4

Znamyansk Regional Balneological Hospital
Znamyanka, Kirovohrad Region, Ukraine
⊕ https://vfmat.ch/faad

Zolochiv Central District Hospital
Zolochiv, Lviv Region, Ukraine
⊕ https://vfmat.ch/2f45

Zolotonosha Central District Hospital
Zolotonosha, Cherkasy Region, Ukraine
⊕ https://vfmat.ch/7b2c

Zolotonosha Children's District Hospital
Zolotonosha, Cherkasy Oblast, Ukraine
⊕ https://vfmat.ch/96ef

Zuya District Hospital
Zuya,Belogorsky District, Crimea, Ukraine
⊕ https://vfmat.ch/3118

Healthcare Facility

Uzbekistan

The Republic of Uzbekistan, in Central Asia, is bordered by Kazakhstan to the north, Kyrgyzstan to the northeast, Tajikistan to the southeast, Afghanistan to the south, and Turkmenistan to the southwest. A former Soviet republic, Uzbekistan is known for its mosques, mausoleums, and other sites linked to the Silk Road, the ancient trade route between China and the Mediterranean. Its capital is Tashkent. Though there are recognized regional languages such as Karakalpak, the official language is Uzbek. Uzbekistan's population of 30.8 million people is 50 percent urban and 50 percent rural. Islam is the predominant religion; 92 percent of the population is Muslim. Uzbekistan is a significant producer of gold and has the largest open-pit gold mine in the world, in addition to substantial deposits of silver, strategic minerals, gas, and oil.

The country broke from the Soviet Union in 1991. As a sovereign state, Uzbekistan is a secular, unitary constitutional republic. Since independence, Uzbekistan has been slow to transform to a market economy. Its restrictive trade regime and generally interventionist policies continue to have a negative effect on the economy. The nation's GDP declined during the first years of transition and then recovered after 1995 due to a considerable reduction of inflation and budget deficit. The economy showed robust growth, rising by 4 percent per year between 1998 and 2003; in 2011, growth rose to 9 percent. The total number of people employed also rose from 8.5 million in 1995 to 13.5 million in 2011. Despite this achievement, unemployment increased to 5.5 percent in 2019.

Uzbekistan boasts a large network of rural medical facilities. However, the healthcare system, and particularly its infrastructure, could benefit from more investment. Uzbekistan's life expectancy has improved over time, and is roughly 72 years. The under-five mortality rate has also improved, dropping from over 62 deaths per 1,000 live births in 2000, to 17 deaths per 1,000 live births in 2019. Among the most common diseases are those associated with polluted drinking water, such as typhoid, hepatitis, dysentery, and cholera. That aside, the leading causes of death are ischemic heart disease, stroke, cirrhosis, lower respiratory infections, diabetes, neonatal disorders, road injuries, chronic kidney disease, self-harm, hypertensive heart disease, and tuberculosis. Recent records show that there were 892 diet-related deaths per 100,000 people a year when reported in 2019, the highest in the world.

30.8M

Population

$1,686

GDP Per Capita

72 years

Life Expectancy

↑ Improving

237
Doctors/100k

Physician Density

398
Beds/100k

Hospital Bed Density

29
Deaths/100k

Maternal Mortality

Uzbekistan

Nonprofit Organizations

Abt Associates
Seeks to improve the quality of life and economic well-being of people worldwide, while striving to meet and exceed the highest professional standards.
General, Logist-Op, MF Med, OB-GYN, Peds
🌐 https://vfmat.ch/cec2

American International Health Alliance (AIHA)
Strengthens health systems and workforce capacity worldwide through locally driven, peer-to-peer institutional partnerships.
CV Med, ER Med, Infect Dis, Medicine, OB-GYN
🌐 https://vfmat.ch/69fd

Americares
Saves lives and improves health for people affected by poverty or disaster and responds with life-changing medicine, medical supplies, and health programs including domestic and global medical clinics.
All-Immu, ER Med, General, Infect Dis, MF Med, Nutr
🌐 https://vfmat.ch/e567

Center for Strategic and International Studies (CSIS) Commission on Strengthening America's Health Security
Brings together a distinguished and diverse group of high-level opinion leaders bridging security and health, with the core aim to chart a bold vision for the future of U.S. leadership in global health.
ER Med, Infect Dis, MF Med, Pub Health
🌐 https://vfmat.ch/6d7f

Chain of Hope (La Chaîne de l'Espoir)
Helps underprivileged children around the world by providing them with access to healthcare.
Anesth, CT Surg, Crit-Care, ER Med, Neurosurg, Ortho, Ped Surg, Surg, Vasc Surg
🌐 https://vfmat.ch/e871

Christian Aid Ministries
Strives to be a trustworthy and efficient channel for Amish, Mennonite, and other conservative Anabaptist groups and individuals to minister to physical and spiritual needs around the world.
CT Surg, ER Med, Logist-Op, Ortho, Pub Health
🌐 https://vfmat.ch/7b33

Developing Country NGO Delegation: Global Fund to Fight AIDS, TB & Malaria
Works to strengthen the engagement of civil society actors and organizations in developing countries to build a world in which AIDS, TB, and malaria are no longer global, public health, and human rights threats.
Infect Dis, Pub Health
🌐 https://vfmat.ch/3149

Doctors Without Borders/Médecins Sans Frontières (MSF)
Responds to emergencies and provides lifesaving medical care where needed most, including during disasters, conflicts, and epidemics.
Anesth, Crit-Care, ER Med, General, Infect Dis, Nutr, OB-GYN, Ped Surg, Peds, Psych, Pub Health, Surg
🌐 https://vfmat.ch/f363

Elton John AIDS Foundation
Seeks to address and overcome the stigma, discrimination, and neglect that prevents ending AIDS by funding local experts to challenge discrimination, prevent infections, and provide treatment.
Infect Dis, Pub Health
🌐 https://vfmat.ch/9d31

For Hearts and Souls
Provides medical outreach and care for children through heart-related work, such as diagnosing heart problems and performing heart-saving surgeries.
Anesth, CT Surg, CV Med, Crit-Care, Peds, Pulm-Critic
🌐 https://vfmat.ch/a162

Gift of Life International
Provides lifesaving cardiac treatment to children in developing countries while developing sustainable pediatric cardiac programs by implementing screening, surgical, and training missions.
Anesth, CT Surg, CV Med, Crit-Care, Ped Surg, Peds, Pulm-Critic
🌐 https://vfmat.ch/f2f9

Global Oncology (GO)
Brings the best in cancer care to underserved patients around the world and collaborates across geographic, professional, and academic borders to improve cancer care, research, and education.
Heme-Onc, Path, Rad-Onc
🌐 https://vfmat.ch/fcb8

Globus Relief
Aims to improve the delivery of healthcare worldwide by gathering, processing, and distributing surplus medical supplies to charities at home and abroad.
Logist-Op
🌐 https://vfmat.ch/a2b7

Health Equity Initiative
Aims to build and sustain a global community that engages across sectors and disciplines to advance health equity.
Pub Health
🌐 https://vfmat.ch/e2e2

Healthy DEvelopments
Provides Germany-supported health and social protection programs around the globe in a collaborative knowledge management process.

All-Immu, General, Infect Dis, Logist-Op, MF Med
⊕ https://vfmat.ch/dc31

International Children's Heart Foundation
Provides free surgical care, medical training, and technology to save the lives of children with congenital heart disease in developing countries.
Anesth, CT Surg, CV Med, Crit-Care, Ped Surg, Peds, Pulm-Critic
⊕ https://vfmat.ch/86c1

International Council of Ophthalmology
Works with ophthalmologic societies and others to enhance ophthalmic education and improve access to the highest-quality eye care in order to preserve and restore vision for people of the world.
Ophth-Opt
⊕ https://vfmat.ch/ffd2

International Federation of Gynecology and Obstetrics (FIGO)
Implements global projects on specific women's health issues.
MF Med, Medicine, Neonat, OB-GYN, Surg, Urol
⊕ https://vfmat.ch/c4b4

International Federation of Red Cross and Red Crescent Societies (IFRC)
Coordinates and directs international assistance following natural and manmade disasters in nonconflict situations through the world's largest humanitarian and development network. Provides disaster-preparedness programs, healthcare activities, and promotes humanitarian values.
ER Med, General, Infect Dis, Nutr
⊕ https://vfmat.ch/b4ee

International Organization for Migration (IOM) – The UN Migration Agency
Promotes evidence-informed policies and holistic, preventive, and curative health programs that are beneficial, accessible, and equitable for vulnerable migrants.
General, Infect Dis, OB-GYN
⊕ https://vfmat.ch/621a

Joint United Nations Programme on HIV/AIDS (UNAIDS)
Aims to place people living with HIV and people affected by the virus at the decision-making table and at the center of designing, delivering, and monitoring the AIDS response.
Infect Dis
⊕ https://vfmat.ch/464a

Life for a Child
Supports the provision of the best possible healthcare, given local circumstances, to all children and youth with diabetes in less-resourced countries, through the strengthening of existing diabetes services.
Endo, Medicine, Peds
⊕ https://vfmat.ch/d712

Management Sciences for Health (MSH)
Works with countries and communities to save lives and improve the health of the world's poorest and most vulnerable people by building strong, resilient, sustainable health systems.
Infect Dis, Logist-Op, Pub Health
⊕ https://vfmat.ch/6aa2

Max Foundation, The
Seeks to increase global access to treatment, care, and support for people living with cancer.
General, Heme-Onc, Pub Health
⊕ https://vfmat.ch/8c7d

MedShare
Aims to improve the quality of life of people, communities, and the planet by sourcing and directly delivering surplus medical supplies and equipment to communities in need around the world.
Logist-Op
⊕ https://vfmat.ch/c8bc

RestoringVision
Empowers lives by restoring vision for millions of people in need.

Ophth-Opt
⊕ https://vfmat.ch/e121

Rockefeller Foundation, The
Works to promote the well-being of humanity.
Logist-Op, Nutr, Pub Health
⊕ https://vfmat.ch/5424

Rotary International
Provides service to others, improves lives, and advances world understanding, goodwill, and peace through its fellowship of business, professional, and community leaders.
ER Med, General, Infect Dis, MF Med, OB-GYN
⊕ https://vfmat.ch/8fb5

Save A Child's Heart
Provides lifesaving cardiac treatment to children in developing countries, and trains healthcare professionals from these countries to deliver quality care in their communities.
CT Surg, CV Med, Crit-Care, Ped Surg, Peds
⊕ https://vfmat.ch/1bef

Smile Asia
Delivers free surgical care, through medical missions and outreach centers, to children with facial deformities such as cleft lip and cleft palate, and aims to raise standards of medical care by creating opportunities for collaborative learning and exchange of best practices.
Anesth, Dent-OMFS, Ped Surg, Peds, Plast
⊕ https://vfmat.ch/d674

Smile Train, Inc.
Treats children with cleft lip through a sustainable and local model that supports surgery and other forms of essential care.
Logist-Op, Pub Health
⊕ https://vfmat.ch/822c

SOS Children's Villages International
Supports children through alternative care and family strengthening.
ER Med, Peds
⊕ https://vfmat.ch/aca1

Sri Sathya Sai International Organization
Inspired by spiritual teachings, carries out efforts in global healthcare, education, humanitarian relief, and youth engagement.
Dent-OMFS, General, Logist-Op, Nutr, Ophth-Opt, Pub Health
⊕ https://vfmat.ch/9bda

Swiss Tropical and Public Health Institute
Contributes to the improvement of the health of populations internationally, nationally, and locally through excellence in research, education, and services.
Infect Dis, Pub Health
⊕ https://vfmat.ch/2ee4

Task Force for Global Health, The
Consists of programs and focus areas that cover a range of global health issues including neglected tropical diseases, infectious diseases, vaccines, field epidemiology, public health informatics, health workforce development, and global health ethics.
Infect Dis, Logist-Op, Medicine, Ophth-Opt, Peds
⊕ https://vfmat.ch/714c

United Nations Children's Fund (UNICEF)
Works in over 190 countries and territories to save children's lives, defend their rights, and help them fulfill their potential, from early childhood through adolescence.
All-Immu, Infect Dis, MF Med, Neonat, Nutr, OB-GYN, Ped Surg, Peds, Pub Health
⊕ https://vfmat.ch/42d7

United Nations Development Programme (UNDP)
Helps countries achieve the simultaneous eradication of extreme poverty and significant reduction of inequalities and exclusion using a sustainable human development approach.

Infect Dis, Logist-Op, Pub Health
⊕ https://vfmat.ch/935c

United Nations High Commissioner for Refugees (UNHCR)
Safeguards the rights and well-being of people who have been forced to flee, ensuring that everybody has the right to seek asylum and find safe refuge in another country, with the goal of seeking lasting solutions.
General, MF Med, Medicine, OB-GYN, Peds, Psych, Pub Health
⊕ https://vfmat.ch/6636

United Nations Population Fund (UNFPA)
Supports reproductive healthcare for women and youth in more than 150 countries, focusing on delivering a world in which every pregnancy is wanted, every childbirth is safe, and every young person's potential is fulfilled.
Infect Dis, MF Med, Neonat, OB-GYN, Peds, Pub Health
⊕ https://vfmat.ch/c969

United States Agency for International Development (USAID)
Promotes and demonstrates democratic values abroad and advances a free, peaceful, and prosperous world. Leads the U.S. government's international development and disaster assistance through partnerships and investments that save lives.
ER Med, Infect Dis, MF Med, OB-GYN, Peds
⊕ https://vfmat.ch/9a99

United Surgeons for Children (USFC)
Pursues greater health and opportunity for children in the most neglected pockets of the world, with a specific focus on and expertise in surgery.
Anesth, CT Surg, Neonat, Neurosurg, OB-GYN, Peds, Radiol, Surg
⊕ https://vfmat.ch/3b4c

Vision Care
Restores sight and helps patients get regular treatment at short-term eye camps and long-term base clinics by having doctors, missionaries, volunteers, and sponsors work together.
Ophth-Opt
⊕ https://vfmat.ch/9d7c

World Federation of Hemophilia (WFH)
Aims to improve and sustain care for people with inherited bleeding disorders by pursuing long-term relationships with individuals and organizations who share the values of WFH's development model.
Heme-Onc
⊕ https://vfmat.ch/5121

World Health Organization, The (WHO)
The United Nations' agency for health provides leadership on global health matters, shapes the health research agenda, sets norms and standards, articulates evidence-based policy options, provides technical support and monitoring to countries, and assesses health trends.
ER Med, General, Infect Dis, Logist-Op, MF Med, OB-GYN, Peds, Psych, Pub Health
⊕ https://vfmat.ch/c476

World Medical Relief
Facilitates the distribution of surplus medical resources where they are needed.
Logist-Op
⊕ https://vfmat.ch/72dc

Uzbekistan

Healthcare Facilities

Azimed Hospital
Bukhara, Uzbekistan
⊕ https://vfmat.ch/akya

Azizbek Shifo Servis
Bukhara, Uzbekistan
⊕ https://vfmat.ch/qahn

Bratsk District Hospital
Beshbo'ynoq, Andijon, Uzbekistan
⊕ https://vfmat.ch/95de

Buka Regional Hospital
Buka, Tashkent, Uzbekistan
⊕ https://vfmat.ch/816a

Bukhara City Medical Association
Bukhara, Bukhara region, Uzbekistan
⊕ https://vfmat.ch/5a8a

Bukhara Regional Oncological Dispensary
Bukhara, Bukhara, Uzbekistan
⊕ https://vfmat.ch/c31d

Bukhara Regional Children's Infectious Hospital
Tsyplan, Uzbekistan
⊕ https://vfmat.ch/ffda

Byrkguzar City Perinatal Center #1
Byrkguzar, Tashkent, Uzbekistan
⊕ https://vfmat.ch/e8ac

Central Clinical Hospital #2, Tashkent
Tashkent, Mirzo-Ulugbekskyst, Uzbekistan
⊕ https://vfmat.ch/d78f

Central Clinical Hospital of JSC "Uzbekiston Temir Yullari," Tashkent
Tashkent, Uzbekistan
⊕ https://vfmat.ch/2ae6

Central Hospital of Balykchy Region
Kattabuloq, Andijon, Uzbekistan
⊕ https://vfmat.ch/7d8c

Central Hospital of Shakhrisabz District
Chorshanbe, Kashkadarya region, Uzbekistan
⊕ https://vfmat.ch/b8fb

Central Hospital of the Ministry of Internal Affairs of the Republic of Uzbekistan
Olmazor, Tashkent, Uzbekistan
⊕ https://vfmat.ch/a736

Central Hospital, Bagdan (Central Hospital of Forish Disctrict)
Bagdan, Uzbekistan
⊕ https://vfmat.ch/2295

Central Military Hospital
Tashkent, Almazar, Uzbekistan
⊕ https://vfmat.ch/25a7

Children's Clinical Hospital
Evalak, Toshkent, Uzbekistan
⊕ https://vfmat.ch/4d41

Children's Hospital Jizzakh
Jizzakh, Uzbekistan
⊕ https://vfmat.ch/92a6

Children's Hospital Khojayli
Khojayli, Uzbekistan
⊕ https://vfmat.ch/8c28

Children's Infectious Diseases Hospital #4 Tashkent
Koshkurgan, Tashkent, Uzbekistan
⊕ https://vfmat.ch/7725

Children's Hospital, Namangan
Namangan, Uzbekistan
⊕ https://vfmat.ch/7525

Chirchik City Central Hospital
Chirchik, Tashkent Region, Uzbekistan
⊕ https://vfmat.ch/ccda

Chust District Hospital
Hisorak, Namangan, Uzbekistan
⊕ https://vfmat.ch/3f27

City Clinical Infectious Disease Hospital #1
Tashkent, Uzbekistan
⊕ https://vfmat.ch/6ff1

City Clinical Infectious Diseases Hospital
Kokand, Fergana, Uzbekistan
⊕ https://vfmat.ch/542e

City Infectious Diseases Hospital #5
Tashkent, Uzbekistan
⊕ https://vfmat.ch/6848

Derma Venerological Dispensary, Yunusabad district
Tashkent, Uzbekistan
⊕ https://vfmat.ch/6b22

Dr. Maks Kardio Clinic
Bukhara, Uzbekistan
⊕ https://vfmat.ch/qwid

Dustlik District Center for Sanitary and Epidemiological Surveillance
Bog'zor, Jizzax, Uzbekistan
⊕ https://vfmat.ch/3f4a

Eye Diseases Hospital
Toshkent, Uzbekistan
⊕ https://vfmat.ch/ed2f

Faculty and Hospital Therapy #2
Burdzhar, Toshkent, Uzbekistan
⊕ https://vfmat.ch/55c2

Himchan Bukhara Hospital
Tsyplan, Uzbekistan
⊕ https://vfmat.ch/cee7

Horev Medical Center
Tashkent, Uzbekistan
⊕ https://vfmat.ch/vqfh

Infectious Diseases Hospital #3
Khonobod, Toshkent, Uzbekistan
⊕ https://vfmat.ch/9b33

Jizak Regional Children's Tuberculosis Hospital
Jizak, Uzbekistan
⊕ https://vfmat.ch/56cb

Kagan City Hospital
Kagan, Bukhara, Uzbekistan
⊕ https://vfmat.ch/a9ba

Khorezm Regional Hospital
Urgench, Uzbekistan
⊕ https://vfmat.ch/a8fc

Kungrad Railway Hospital
Qŭnghirot, Karakalpakstan, Uzbekistan
⊕ https://vfmat.ch/1d24

MDS-Service
Tashkent, Tashkent, Uzbekistan
⊕ https://vfmat.ch/e7d2

Medical Center Shifokor
Samarkand, Uzbekistan
⊕ https://vfmat.ch/ca3c

Military Hospital Fergana
Ulitsa Khudzhant, Fergana, Uzbekistan
⊕ https://vfmat.ch/fe8f

MRT Diagnostika
Bukhara, Uzbekistan
⊕ https://vfmat.ch/m2vk

Multidisciplinary Children's Hospital
Samarkand, Samarkand, Uzbekistan
⊕ https://vfmat.ch/fd88

Multipurpose Medical Center
Yangiariq, Navoiy, Uzbekistan
⊕ https://vfmat.ch/b367

Namangan Central Perinatal Center #1
Namangan, Uzbekistan
⊕ https://vfmat.ch/fc56

National Children's Medical Center
Yalanghoch, Toshkent, Uzbekistan
⊕ https://vfmat.ch/a692

Perinatal Center of Navoi Region
Yangiariq, Navoiy, Uzbekistan
⊕ https://vfmat.ch/f84d

Pop Central Hospital
Pop, Namangan, Uzbekistan
⊕ https://vfmat.ch/5a4c

Qibray Hospital
Dŭrmon, Toshkent, Uzbekistan
⊕ https://vfmat.ch/a5b2

Railway Hospital Qarshi City
Karshi, Kashkadarya Region, Uzbekistan
⊕ https://vfmat.ch/bcdf

Regional Adult Multidisciplinary Medical Center, Termez
Barinchi-Garma, Uzbekistan
⊕ https://vfmat.ch/e49b

Republican AIDS Center of Uzbekistan
Tashkent, Karakalpakstan, Uzbekistan
⊕ https://vfmat.ch/634f

Republican Clinical Hospital #1
Koshkurgan, Tashkent, Uzbekistan
⊕ https://vfmat.ch/3ad1

Republican Clinical Ophthalmological Hospital
Olmazor, Tashkent, Uzbekistan
⊕ https://vfmat.ch/774f

Republican Dermatovenerologic Dispensary
Tashkent, Uzbekistan
⊕ https://vfmat.ch/fac4

Republican Research Center of Neurosurgery
Salor, Toshkent, Uzbekistan
⊕ https://vfmat.ch/b756

Republican Scientific Center for Emergency Medical Aid
Toshkent, Uzbekistan
⊕ https://vfmat.ch/d348

Republican Scientific Center for Emergency Medical Aid, Termez
Termez, Surkhandarya region, Uzbekistan
⊕ https://vfmat.ch/5b82

Republican Specialized Scientific and Practical Medical Center for Dermatovenereology and Cosmetology
Tashkent, Uzbekistan
⊕ https://vfmat.ch/2a52

Republican Specialized Scientific and Practical Medical Center of Pediatrics
Olmazor, Tashkent, Uzbekistan
⊕ https://vfmat.ch/57cd

Research Institute of Hematology and Blood Transfusion
Byrkguzar, Tashkent, Uzbekistan
⊕ https://vfmat.ch/cde4

Samarkand City Hospital #1
Samarkand, Uzbekistan
⊕ https://vfmat.ch/c63a

Samarkand Regional Cardiology Hospital
Bukharikishlak, Uzbekistan
⊕ https://vfmat.ch/4d66

Samarkand Regional Hospital
Samarkand, Samarkand, Uzbekistan
⊕ https://vfmat.ch/cee4

Samarqand Viloyat Nogironlar Reabilitasiya Markazi
Samarqand, Uzbekistan
⊕ https://vfmat.ch/2c79

Shahrixon Central Hospital
Shahrixon, Andijan, Uzbekistan
⊕ https://vfmat.ch/a7df

Specialized Infectious Diseases Hospital
Burdzhar, Toshkent, Uzbekistan
⊕ https://vfmat.ch/55df

Substation Of Emergency And Emergency Care #9
Toshkent, Uzbekistan
⊕ https://vfmat.ch/e8a5

Tashkent City Children's Clinical Hospital #3
Tashkent, Uzbekistan
⊕ https://vfmat.ch/1581

Tashkent City Clinical Emergency Hospital
Tashkent, Uzbekistan
⊕ https://vfmat.ch/eaa6

Tashkent City Clinical Hospital #5
Yalanghoch, Toshkent, Uzbekistan
⊕ https://vfmat.ch/d24f

Tashkent International Clinic
Byrkguzar, Tashkent, Uzbekistan
⊕ https://vfmat.ch/ce41

Tashkent Urban Teenage Dispensary
Tashkent, Uzbekistan
⊕ https://vfmat.ch/8487

Tashkentskaya City Clinical Tuberculosis Hospital #1
Psikhiotricheskaya Bol'nitsa, Toshkent, Uzbekistan
⊕ https://vfmat.ch/a17a

Ulugbek Ultramed
Bukhara, Uzbekistan
⊕ https://vfmat.ch/sz1r

Viloyat Regional Dermatovenous Dispensary
Aral, Qashqadaryo, Uzbekistan
⊕ https://vfmat.ch/9ce8

Viloyat Regional Perinatal Center
Barinchi-Garma, Uzbekistan
⊕ https://vfmat.ch/34bc

Yangiyul District Central Hospital
Yangiyul, Tashkent Region, Uzbekistan
⊕ https://vfmat.ch/6719

LUGANVILLE

VANUATU

PORT VILA

Lenakel

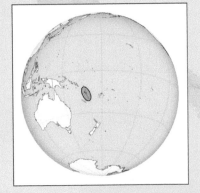

● Healthcare Facility

Vanuatu

The Republic of Vanuatu, an archipelago in the South Pacific Ocean, consists of 13 main islands and many more smaller ones. Distant neighbors include Australia, New Caledonia, New Guinea, Solomon Islands, and Fiji. Vanuatu is home to active volcanoes, including Yasur, one of the most active volcanoes in the world. The population of about 300,000 is majority ethnic Melanesian, and they speak more than 100 local languages, in addition to Bislama, English, and French. As much as 70 percent of the population identifies as Protestant, with a smaller proportion of Roman Catholics. Over two-thirds of Vanuatu's population lives in rural areas; urban dwellers reside in the capital of Port Vila and in Luganville.

During its colonial history, Vanuatu was colonized and governed by Spain in the 1600s, and later France and the United Kingdom. However, a movement for independence started in the 1970s, and by 1980 the Republic of Vanuatu was established. Since then the economy has remained grounded in small-scale and subsistence agriculture, with a few larger commodities such as kava, beef, copra, timber, and cocoa. However, because of climate instability and fluctuations in commodity prices, the country is diversifying its economy with manufacturing, service-sector businesses, and tourism.

Residents and visitors to Vanuatu face a high risk of infectious diseases, such as malaria and bacterial diarrhea. These have decreased over time, but continue to contribute to the leading causes of death in the country. In addition, non-communicable diseases have increased substantially over time as causes of the most deaths in Vanuatu. These include ischemic heart disease, stroke, diabetes, COPD, and chronic kidney disease. The risk factors that contribute most to death and disability include high blood pressure, air pollution, high fasting plasma glucose, high body-mass index, dietary risks, malnutrition, tobacco use, high LDL levels, kidney dysfunction, and insufficient sanitation and clean water.

0.3M

Population

$2,783

GDP Per Capita

70 years

Life Expectancy

↑ Improving

17
Doctors/100k

Physician Density

72
Deaths/100k

Maternal Mortality

# Vanuatu

Nonprofit Organizations

Aloha Medical Mission
Brings hope and changes the lives of people; serves overseas and in Hawai'i.
Anesth, Crit-Care, Dent-OMFS, ENT, ER Med, General, Medicine, OB-GYN, Ophth-Opt, Ortho, Ped Surg, Peds, Plast, Surg, Urol
⊕ https://vfmat.ch/72ac

Bridging Health Inc.
Works to improve healthcare in underdeveloped countries, beginning with Tanna Island, Vanuatu.
Peds
⊕ https://vfmat.ch/715c

CARE
Works around the globe to save lives, defeat poverty, and achieve social justice.
ER Med, General
⊕ https://vfmat.ch/7232

ChildFund Australia
Works to reduce poverty for children in many of the world's most disadvantaged communities.
ER Med, General, Peds
⊕ https://vfmat.ch/13df

Churches of Christ Medical Santo (Medical Santo)
Aims to build the capacity of local medical staff, meet human needs both physical and spiritual, and work for a lasting change in the lives of all, inspired by the Christian faith.
Dent-OMFS, ER Med, General, Geri, Logist-Op, Nutr, OB-GYN, Pub Health
⊕ https://vfmat.ch/a627

Dentaid
Seeks to treat, equip, train, and educate people in need of dental care.
Dent-OMFS
⊕ https://vfmat.ch/a183

Direct Relief
Improves the health and lives of people affected by poverty or emergency situations by mobilizing and providing essential medical resources needed for their care.
ER Med, Logist-Op
⊕ https://vfmat.ch/58e5

Doctors Assisting In South Pacific Islands (DAISI)
Aims to support and collaborate with its South Pacific neighbors and consists of specialist and nonspecialist doctors, medical students, nurses, allied health professionals, and nonmedical volunteers.
Anesth, Dent-OMFS, OB-GYN, Plast, Surg, Urol
⊕ https://vfmat.ch/2dcd

Episcopal Relief & Development
Provides relief in times of disaster and promotes sustainable development by identifying and addressing the root causes of suffering.
Infect Dis, MF Med, Neonat, Nutr, Peds
⊕ https://vfmat.ch/7cfa

Family Care Centre Charitable Trust
Provides medical and dental care, skills-based education, and community development projects in Vanuatu, inspired by the Christian faith.
Dent-OMFS, General, Geri, Infect Dis, Logist-Op, MF Med, Nutr, OB-GYN, Ophth-Opt, Path, Peds, Pub Health, Rehab, Surg
⊕ https://vfmat.ch/87e5

Global Blood Fund
Delivers grants, equipment, and training to over 50 countries in Africa, Asia, Eastern Europe, the Middle East, Latin America and the Caribbean.
Pub Health
⊕ https://vfmat.ch/6377

Global Oncology (GO)
Brings the best in cancer care to underserved patients around the world and collaborates across geographic, professional, and academic borders to improve cancer care, research, and education.
Heme-Onc, Path, Rad-Onc
⊕ https://vfmat.ch/fcb8

Globus Relief
Aims to improve the delivery of healthcare worldwide by gathering, processing, and distributing surplus medical supplies to charities at home and abroad.
Logist-Op
⊕ https://vfmat.ch/a2b7

Grassroot Soccer
Leverages the power of soccer to educate, inspire, and mobilize at-risk youth in developing countries to overcome their greatest health challenges, live healthier and more productive lives, and be agents for change in their communities.
Infect Dis
⊕ https://vfmat.ch/3521

International Federation of Red Cross and Red Crescent Societies (IFRC)
Coordinates and directs international assistance following natural and manmade disasters in nonconflict situations through the world's largest humanitarian and development network. Provides disaster-preparedness programs, healthcare activities, and promotes humanitarian values.
ER Med, General, Infect Dis, Nutr
⊕ https://vfmat.ch/b4ee

International Organization for Migration (IOM) – The UN Migration Agency
Promotes evidence-informed policies and holistic, preventive, and curative health programs that are beneficial, accessible, and equitable for vulnerable migrants.
General, Infect Dis, OB-GYN
⊕ https://vfmat.ch/621a

International Planned Parenthood Federation (IPPF)
Leads a locally owned, globally connected civil society movement that provides and enables services and champions sexual and reproductive health and rights for all, especially the underserved.
Infect Dis, MF Med, OB-GYN
⊕ https://vfmat.ch/dc97

International Trachoma Initiative (iTi)
Works toward a world free from trachoma, a preventable cause of blindness, and provides comprehensive support to national ministries of health and governmental and nongovernmental organizations to implement a comprehensive approach to fight trachoma.
Infect Dis, Ophth-Opt
⊕ https://vfmat.ch/3278

IsraAID
Supports people affected by humanitarian crisis and partners with local communities around the world to provide urgent aid, assist recovery, and reduce the risk of future disasters.
ER Med, Infect Dis, Psych, Rehab
⊕ https://vfmat.ch/de96

Joint Therapy Outreach Incorporated
Aims to provide health and therapy support/services to people with disabilities and health challenges in impoverished circumstances.
General, Neuro, Ortho, Peds, Rehab
⊕ https://vfmat.ch/f7a5

Joint United Nations Programme on HIV/AIDS (UNAIDS)
Aims to place people living with HIV and people affected by the virus at the decision-making table and at the center of designing, delivering, and monitoring the AIDS response.
Infect Dis
⊕ https://vfmat.ch/464a

Kids Care Everywhere
Seeks to empower physicians in under-resourced environments with multimedia, state-of-the-art medical software, and to inspire young professionals to become future global healthcare leaders.
Logist-Op, Ped Surg, Peds
⊕ https://vfmat.ch/bc23

Medical and Educational Sustainable Community Help (MESCH)
Seeks to develop health and well-being and safer, more resilient communities in developing countries and also provide sustainable aid through education and training.
Anesth, Dent-OMFS, ENT, ER Med, General, Ophth-Opt, Ortho, Pub Health, Surg
⊕ https://vfmat.ch/24c2

Melanie Jewson Foundation
Develops partnerships and supports efforts in health and education in Vanuatu.
CV Med, MF Med, Medicine, Ophth-Opt, Peds, Rehab, Surg
⊕ https://vfmat.ch/9b53

NYC Medics
Deploys mobile medical teams to remote areas of disaster zones and humanitarian emergencies, providing the highest level of medical care to those who otherwise would not have access to aid and relief efforts.
All-Immu, ER Med, Infect Dis, Surg
⊕ https://vfmat.ch/aeee

Open Heart International
Provides surgical interventions and best practices to the most disadvantaged communities on the planet.

CT Surg, MF Med, OB-GYN, Ophth-Opt, Plast, Surg
⊕ https://vfmat.ch/dab2

Pacific Islands Health and Education Limited (PIHEL)
Provides health and education services to proactively enhance the physical, emotional, and spiritual well-being of people in need in the Pacific Islands.
Dent-OMFS, General, Geri, Logist-Op, OB-GYN, Path, Pub Health
⊕ https://vfmat.ch/922c

Pacific Leprosy Foundation
Focuses not only on leprosy control but also on the welfare of leprosy patients in the South Pacific.
Derm, Infect Dis, Pub Health
⊕ https://vfmat.ch/781d

RestoringVision
Empowers lives by restoring vision for millions of people in need.
Ophth-Opt
⊕ https://vfmat.ch/e121

Rotary International
Provides service to others, improves lives, and advances world understanding, goodwill, and peace through its fellowship of business, professional, and community leaders.
ER Med, General, Infect Dis, MF Med, OB-GYN
⊕ https://vfmat.ch/8fb5

Save the Children
Gives children around the world a healthy start in life, the opportunity to learn, and protection from harm.
All-Immu, Crit-Care, ER Med, General, Infect Dis, MF Med, Medicine, Neonat, OB-GYN, Peds, Psych, Pub Health
⊕ https://vfmat.ch/2e73

SEE International
Provides sustainable medical, surgical, and educational services through volunteer ophthalmic surgeons, with the objectives of restoring sight and preventing blindness to disadvantaged individuals worldwide.
Ophth-Opt, Surg
⊕ https://vfmat.ch/6e1b

Task Force for Global Health, The
Consists of programs and focus areas that cover a range of global health issues including neglected tropical diseases, infectious diseases, vaccines, field epidemiology, public health informatics, health workforce development, and global health ethics.
Infect Dis, Logist-Op, Medicine, Ophth-Opt, Peds
⊕ https://vfmat.ch/714c

United Nations Children's Fund (UNICEF)
Works in over 190 countries and territories to save children's lives, defend their rights, and help them fulfill their potential, from early childhood through adolescence.
All-Immu, Infect Dis, MF Med, Neonat, Nutr, OB-GYN, Ped Surg, Peds, Pub Health
⊕ https://vfmat.ch/42d7

United Nations High Commissioner for Refugees (UNHCR)
Safeguards the rights and well-being of people who have been forced to flee, ensuring that everybody has the right to seek asylum and find safe refuge in another country, with the goal of seeking lasting solutions.
General, MF Med, Medicine, OB-GYN, Peds, Psych, Pub Health
⊕ https://vfmat.ch/6636

United Nations Population Fund (UNFPA)
Supports reproductive healthcare for women and youth in more than 150 countries, focusing on delivering a world in which every pregnancy is wanted, every childbirth is safe, and every young person's potential is fulfilled.
Infect Dis, MF Med, Neonat, OB-GYN, Peds, Pub Health
⊕ https://vfmat.ch/c969

United States Agency for International Development (USAID)
Promotes and demonstrates democratic values abroad and advances a free,

peaceful, and prosperous world. Leads the U.S. government's international development and disaster assistance through partnerships and investments that save lives.
ER Med, Infect Dis, MF Med, OB-GYN, Peds
⊕ https://vfmat.ch/9a99

USAID: Leadership, Management and Governance Project
Improves leadership, management, and governance practices to strengthen health systems and improve health for all, including vulnerable populations worldwide.
Logist-Op
⊕ https://vfmat.ch/d35e

Wichita County Medical Alliance
Mobilizes volunteers to assist in public health efforts in the U.S. and abroad, including medical missions and disaster relief.
General, Geri, Nutr, OB-GYN, Pub Health
⊕ https://vfmat.ch/fa55

World Health Organization, The (WHO)
The United Nations' agency for health provides leadership on global health matters, shapes the health research agenda, sets norms and standards, articulates evidence-based policy options, provides technical support and monitoring to countries, and assesses health trends.
ER Med, General, Infect Dis, Logist-Op, MF Med, OB-GYN, Peds, Psych, Pub Health
⊕ https://vfmat.ch/c476

World Vision International
Works with vulnerable communities around the world to overcome poverty and injustice with child-focused programs in disaster management, health, nutrition, economic development, education, clean water, sanitation, and hygiene.
ER Med, General, Infect Dis, MF Med, Nutr, OB-GYN, Peds
⊕ https://vfmat.ch/2642

 # Vanuatu

Healthcare Facilities

Barereo Hospital
Parereo, Vanuatu
⊕ https://vfmat.ch/87ej

Lenakel Hospital
Lenakel, Tanna Island, Tafea Province, Vanuatu
⊕ https://vfmat.ch/3yyd

Lolowai Godden Memorial Hospital
Lowaluieuru, Lolopuepue, Lolowaï, Ambae Island,
Penama Province, Vanuatu
⊕ https://vfmat.ch/e824

Mauna Hospital
Abwatuntora, Pentacost Island, Vanuatu
⊕ https://vfmat.ch/wkma

Norsup Hospital
Norsup, Malekula Island, Malampa Province, Vanuatu
⊕ https://vfmat.ch/6a62

Northern District Hospital
Luganville, Espiritu Santo Island, Sanma Province,
Vanuatu
⊕ https://vfmat.ch/6f45

Port Vila Central Hospital
Port Vila, Les Lagunes, Efate Island, Shefa Province,
Vanuatu
⊕ https://vfmat.ch/3454

Vanuatu Private Hospital
Port Vila, Vanuatu
⊕ https://vfmat.ch/wrzx

Vanuatu ProMedical
Les Lagunes, Shefa, Vanuatu
⊕ https://vfmat.ch/a8b2

● Healthcare Facility

Vietnam

The Socialist Republic of Vietnam, in Southeast Asia, is on the eastern edge of the Indo-Chinese Peninsula. Vietnam is bordered by China, Laos, and Cambodia. It is the sixteenth most populous country in the world, with 102.8 million people. About 38 percent of the population lives in urban areas, such as Ho Chi Minh City, Hai Phong, and Hanoi, the capital. Major ethnic groups include Kinh (Viet), with smaller groups being Tay, Thai, Muong, Khmer, Mong, Nung, and Hoa. About 80 percent of the population does not identify with any particular religion, but small portions do identify as Buddhist, Catholic, Hoa Hao, Cao Dai, and Protestant. English and Vietnamese are the most commonly spoken languages. Vietnam is known for intriguing geographical features; at its narrowest point, the country is only 50 kilometers wide. It is also home to the world's largest cave.

North and South Vietnam unified after the Vietnam War in 1975, and the country has since grown substantially, with one of the fastest-growing economies in the world. Tourism, manufacturing, and exports have led to increasing per capita GDP. Poverty rates have decreased from over 70 percent to around 6 percent since political and economic reforms were launched in 1986. Improvements have been made across many sectors, including education and health. Literacy rates are high due to the strong network of public schools, while life expectancy has also steadily increased. However, corruption runs rampant and continues to be a persistent issue.

Alongside progress in poverty reduction, Vietnam has made tremendous gains in addressing major health issues. Rates of malaria have decreased substantially, and illness due to poor sanitation has also decreased as more people gain access to clean water. In addition, tuberculosis remains a persistent health concern and a leading cause of death. Other leading causes of death include stroke, ischemic heart disease, diabetes, COPD, lung cancer, road injuries, cirrhosis, chronic kidney disease, lower respiratory infections, Alzheimer's disease, and hypertensive heart disease. The risk factors that contribute most to death and disability include high blood pressure, high fasting plasma glucose, dietary risks, air pollution, alcohol and tobacco use, high body-mass index, kidney dysfunction, occupational risks, high LDL, and malnutrition.

102.8M
Population

$2,786
GDP Per Capita

75 years
Life Expectancy
↑ Improving

83
Doctors/100k
Physician Density

318
Beds/100k
Hospital Bed Density

43
Deaths/100k
Maternal Mortality

Vietnam

Nonprofit Organizations

A Broader View Volunteers
Provides developing countries around the world with significant volunteer programs that aid the neediest communities and forge a lasting bond between those volunteering and those they have helped.
Dent-OMFS, ER Med, Infect Dis, MF Med
🌐 https://vfmat.ch/3bec

Abt Associates
Seeks to improve the quality of life and economic well-being of people worldwide, while striving to meet and exceed the highest professional standards.
General, Logist-Op, MF Med, OB-GYN, Peds
🌐 https://vfmat.ch/cec2

Aceso Global
Provides strategic healthcare advisory services in low- and middle-income countries to design and deliver highly customized, evidence-based solutions that address the complex nature of healthcare systems, with a goal to strengthen and provide affordable, high-quality care to all.
Logist-Op, Pub Health
🌐 https://vfmat.ch/b3b7

Age International
Helps older people living in some of the world's poorest places to have improved well-being and be treated with dignity through a variety of programs, including emergency relief and cataract surgery.
ER Med, Geri, Logist-Op, Nutr, Ophth-Opt, Palliative, Pub Health
🌐 https://vfmat.ch/c7e2

AIDS Healthcare Foundation
Provides cutting-edge HIV/AIDS medical care and advocacy to over one million people in 43 countries.
Infect Dis
🌐 https://vfmat.ch/b27c

AISPO
Implements international initiatives in the healthcare sector and remains involved in various projects to combat poverty, social injustice, and disease around the world.
All-Immu, ER Med, GI, General, Infect Dis, Logist-Op, MF Med, Neonat, OB-GYN, Peds, Psych, Pub Health, Radiol
🌐 https://vfmat.ch/c9e6

Alliance for Children Foundation
Seeks to improve the lives of orphaned and at-risk children and their families ,where the need is greatest worldwide, by working with local partners to provide food, shelter, medical care, and educational programs.
General, Nutr, Ped Surg, Peds
🌐 https://vfmat.ch/7acb

Aloha Medical Mission
Brings hope and changes the lives of people; serves overseas and in Hawai'i.
Anesth, Crit-Care, Dent-OMFS, ENT, ER Med, General, Medicine, OB-GYN, Ophth-Opt, Ortho, Ped Surg, Peds, Plast, Surg, Urol
🌐 https://vfmat.ch/72ac

Americare Neurosurgery International (AMCANI)
Seeks to increase the level of medical and surgical care in developing countries by providing professional training and development of appropriate resources such as physical therapy, rehabilitation skills, and nursing care.
Surg
🌐 https://vfmat.ch/467b

Americares
Saves lives and improves health for people affected by poverty or disaster and responds with life-changing medicine, medical supplies, and health programs including domestic and global medical clinics.
All-Immu, ER Med, General, Infect Dis, MF Med, Nutr
🌐 https://vfmat.ch/e567

Amsterdam Institute for Global Health and Development (AIGHD)
Provides sustainable solutions to major health problems across our planet by forging synergies among disciplines, healthcare delivery, research, and education.
Infect Dis
🌐 https://vfmat.ch/d73d

AO Alliance
Builds solutions to lessen the burden of injuries in low- and middle-income countries, while enhancing the care of the injured to reduce human suffering, disability, and poverty.
Ortho, Surg
🌐 https://vfmat.ch/8cd5

ARC The Australian Respiratory Council
Fosters research to promote respiratory health and works to improve lung health in communities of disadvantaged and Indigenous people.
Infect Dis
🌐 https://vfmat.ch/69f2

ASAP Ministries
Provides education and healthcare to refugees and the poor, based in Christian ministry.
Dent-OMFS, General
🌐 https://vfmat.ch/266e

ASE Foundation
Provides support for education and research to the community of healthcare providers and patients for whom cardiovascular ultrasound is essential.

CT Surg, CV Med, Radiol
🌐 https://vfmat.ch/bb57

Association of Medical Doctors of Asia (AMDA)
Strives to support people affected by disasters and economic distress on their road to recovery, establishing a true partnership with special emphasis on local initiative.
ER Med, Logist-Op, Pub Health
🌐 https://vfmat.ch/e3d4

Australian Health Humanitarian Aid (AHHA)
Provides free eye surgery, eye care, and medical and dental treatment to the underprivileged, along with training to local students and doctors.
Dent-OMFS, Ophth-Opt, Surg
🌐 https://vfmat.ch/dffc

AusViet Charity Foundation Limited
Provides free direct health services and humanitarian aid to those in need, especially those in disadvantaged and remote areas of Vietnam.
Dent-OMFS, General, Pub Health
🌐 https://vfmat.ch/c481

Baylor College of Medicine: Global Surgery
Trains leaders in academic global surgery and remains dedicated to advancements in the areas of patient care, biomedical research, and medical education.
ENT, Infect Dis, OB-GYN, Ortho, Ped Surg, Plast, Pub Health, Radiol, Surg, Urol
🌐 https://vfmat.ch/21f5

BFIRST – British Foundation for International Reconstructive Surgery & Training
Supports projects across the developing world to train surgeons in their local environment to effectively manage devastating injuries.
Anesth, Plast, Surg
🌐 https://vfmat.ch/ad4f

Bless The Children
Aims to help abandoned and impoverished children by empowering them with health, shelter, and nutritional and educational support.
CT Surg, Dent-OMFS, General, Logist-Op, Nutr, Pub Health, Surg
🌐 https://vfmat.ch/f19d

Breast Cancer Support
Aims to save lives and end breast cancer forever in women and men through education, treatment, emotional assistance, and financial support.
Heme-Onc, Logist-Op, Pub Health, Rad-Onc, Radiol
🌐 https://vfmat.ch/cb78

Bridge of Life
Aims to strengthen healthcare globally through sustainable programs that prevent and treat chronic disease.
Logist-Op, Nephro, OB-GYN, Peds, Surg
🌐 https://vfmat.ch/5b68

Brigham and Women's Hospital Global Health Hub
Cares for patients in underserved settings, provides education to staff who work in those areas to create sustainable change, and conducts research designed to improve health in such settings.
General, Infect Dis
🌐 https://vfmat.ch/a8a3

Bureau of International Health Cooperation
Seeks to improve healthcare around the world, including developing countries, using expertise, and contribute to healthier lives of Japanese people by bringing these experiences back to Japan.
ER Med, Heme-Onc, Infect Dis, Peds, Pub Health
🌐 https://vfmat.ch/947d

CardioStart International
Provides free heart surgery and associated medical care to children and adults living in underserved regions of the world, irrespective of political or religious affiliation, through the collective skills of healthcare experts.

Anesth, CT Surg, CV Med, Crit-Care, Pub Health, Pulm-Critic
🌐 https://vfmat.ch/85ef

CARE
Works around the globe to save lives, defeat poverty, and achieve social justice.
ER Med, General
🌐 https://vfmat.ch/7232

Center for Strategic and International Studies (CSIS) Commission on Strengthening America's Health Security
Brings together a distinguished and diverse group of high-level opinion leaders bridging security and health, with the core aim to chart a bold vision for the future of U.S. leadership in global health.
ER Med, Infect Dis, MF Med, Pub Health
🌐 https://vfmat.ch/6d7f

Chain of Hope
Provides lifesaving heart operations for children around the world and supports the development of cardiac services in numerous developing and war-torn countries.
Anesth, CT Surg, CV Med, Crit-Care, Ped Surg, Peds, Pulm-Critic, Surg
🌐 https://vfmat.ch/1b1b

ChildFund Australia
Works to reduce poverty for children in many of the world's most disadvantaged communities.
ER Med, General, Peds
🌐 https://vfmat.ch/13df

Children's Bridge Foundation
Supports health and education programs for orphaned and abandoned children in the developing world.
Infect Dis, Nutr, Peds, Surg
🌐 https://vfmat.ch/6486

Children's HeartLink
Aims to save children's lives by transforming pediatric cardiac care in underserved parts of the world through long-term educational partnerships and robust monitoring.
🌐 https://vfmat.ch/24b3

Children's of Alabama: Global Surgery Program
Provides the finest pediatric health services to all children in an environment that fosters excellence in research and medical education.
CT Surg, CV Med, Crit-Care, Heme-Onc, Neurosurg, Ortho, Ped Surg, Peds, Surg, Urol
🌐 https://vfmat.ch/ff58

Children's Surgery International
Provides free medical and surgical services to children in need around the world, and instructs and trains local surgeons and other medical providers such as doctors, anesthesiologists, nurses, and technicians.
Anesth, Dent-OMFS, Ortho, Ped Surg, Peds, Plast, Surg
🌐 https://vfmat.ch/26d3

Christian Aid Ministries
Strives to be a trustworthy and efficient channel for Amish, Mennonite, and other conservative Anabaptist groups and individuals to minister to physical and spiritual needs around the world.
CT Surg, ER Med, Logist-Op, Ortho, Pub Health
🌐 https://vfmat.ch/7b33

Christian Blind Mission (CBM)
Aims to improve the quality of life of persons with disabilities in the poorest countries, addressing poverty as a cause and a consequence of disability, and working in partnership to create a society for all.
ENT, General, Infect Dis, OB-GYN, Ophth-Opt, Ortho, Peds, Psych, Rehab, Surg
🌐 https://vfmat.ch/3824

Clinton Health Access Initiative (CHAI)
Aims to save lives and reduce the burden of disease in low- and middle-income countries. Works with partners to strengthen the capabilities of governments and the private sector to create and sustain high-quality health systems.

General, Heme-Onc, Infect Dis, Logist-Op, MF Med, Medicine, Neonat, Nutr, OB-GYN, Path, Peds, Rad-Onc
⊕ https://vfmat.ch/9ed7

Combat Blindness International
Works to eliminate preventable blindness worldwide by providing sustainable, equitable solutions for sight through partnerships and innovation.
Ophth-Opt
⊕ https://vfmat.ch/28ad

ConnectMed International
Improves access to sustainable healthcare in resource-limited communities through education, partnership, and research.
Dent-OMFS, Logist-Op, Ped Surg, Plast
⊕ https://vfmat.ch/ce88

COVID-19 Clinical Research Coalition
Advocates and collaborates for the advancement of COVID-19 research driven by the needs of low-resource settings, and works for equitable access to solutions to the pandemic.
All-Immu, Infect-Dis, MF Med, Path, Pub Health
⊕ https://vfmat.ch/d1f4

Cross Catholic Outreach
Mobilizes the global Catholic Church to transform impoverished communities through the provision of food, water, housing, education, orphan support, medical care, microenterprise, and disaster relief.
All-Immu, General, Nutr, OB-GYN, Rehab
⊕ https://vfmat.ch/22f4

CURE
Operates charitable hospitals and programs in underserved countries worldwide, where patients receive surgical treatment, based in Christian ministry.
Anesth, Neurosurg, Ortho, Ped Surg, Peds, Rehab, Surg
⊕ https://vfmat.ch/aa16

CureCervicalCancer
Focuses on the early detection and prevention of cervical cancer around the globe for the women who need it most.
Heme-Onc, OB-GYN
⊕ https://vfmat.ch/ace1

Direct Relief
Improves the health and lives of people affected by poverty or emergency situations by mobilizing and providing essential medical resources needed for their care.
ER Med, Logist-Op
⊕ https://vfmat.ch/58e5

DKT INTERNATIONAL INC
Seeks to provide couples with affordable and safe options for family planning and HIV/AIDS prevention through dynamic social marketing.
General, Surg
⊕ https://vfmat.ch/b3a7

Duke University: Global Health Institute
Sparks innovation in global health research and education, and brings together knowledge and resources to address the most important global health issues of our time.
All-Immu, Infect Dis, MF Med, OB-GYN, Pub Health
⊕ https://vfmat.ch/c4cd

Eye Care Foundation
Helps prevent and cure avoidable blindness and visual impairment in low-income countries.
Ophth-Opt, Surg
⊕ https://vfmat.ch/c8f9

Facing the World
Pioneers a bold new approach to sustainable healthcare, resulting in self-run centers of excellence in the countries where we work, that are able to provide crucial surgery to children born with disabling facial differences, and that can be replicated.

Anesth, Crit-Care, Dent-OMFS, ENT, Neurosurg, Ophth-Opt, Ped Surg, Plast
⊕ https://vfmat.ch/e9fa

Flying Doctors of America
Brings together teams of physicians, dentists, nurses, and other healthcare professionals to care for people who would not otherwise receive medical care.
Dent-OMFS, GI, General, Surg
⊕ https://vfmat.ch/58b6

Foundation for International Development Relief (FIDR)
Implements assistance projects in developing countries to improve the living environment of residents, while promoting regional development centered on the welfare of children.
Pub Health
⊕ https://vfmat.ch/7356

Foundation for Special Surgery
Provides high-quality, complex surgical care by increasing surgical expertise in Africa through the participation of surgeons across various specialties to provide premium care and skills transfer/education to benefit patients.
Anesth, CT Surg, ENT, Endo, Neurosurg, Plast, Surg, Urol
⊕ https://vfmat.ch/53db

Fracarita International
Provides support and services in the fields of mental healthcare, care for people with a disability, and education.
Psych, Rehab
⊕ https://vfmat.ch/8d3c

Fred Hollows Foundation, The
Works toward a world in which no person is needlessly blind or vision impaired.
Ophth-Opt, Pub Health, Surg
⊕ https://vfmat.ch/73e5

Friends for Asia Foundation, The
Develops international volunteer projects that assist local communities in overcoming challenges, and provides volunteers with the experience of contributing to those communities as a valued participant.
General
⊕ https://vfmat.ch/f8a9

Friends of Hue Foundation
Provides educational and social outreach to underserved and marginalized groups, and builds better community by bridging cultural gaps while improving access to healthcare and social services.
ER Med, General, Peds, Pub Health
⊕ https://vfmat.ch/e5ca

Gift of Life International
Provides lifesaving cardiac treatment to children in developing countries while developing sustainable pediatric cardiac programs by implementing screening, surgical, and training missions.
Anesth, CT Surg, CV Med, Crit-Care, Ped Surg, Peds, Pulm-Critic
⊕ https://vfmat.ch/f2f9

Gift of Sight
Works to eradicate preventable blindness by fostering sustainable healthcare delivery in underserved global communities.
Ophth-Opt
⊕ https://vfmat.ch/fdd7

Giving Tree Medical Charity
Organizes and provides medical services to underserved communities in the U.S., Mexico, China, Vietnam, and the Philippines.
CV Med, Derm, General, Medicine, Nutr, Peds, Psych, Pub Health
⊕ https://vfmat.ch/2d3c

Global Civic Sharing
Aims to support our neighbors' self-reliance and realize the sustainable development.
Nutr, Peds, Pub Health
⊕ https://vfmat.ch/d7ab

Global Foundation For Children With Hearing Loss
Aims to help babies and young children who are deaf or hard of hearing and living in low- and middle-income countries by providing access to early identification, hearing technology, and locally based professional expertise.
Ortho, Peds, Plast
⊕ https://vfmat.ch/d1d1

Global Healing
Improves access to high-quality healthcare in underserved countries by training medical professionals across the globe to improve pediatric healthcare using sustainable resources.
ER Med, General, Heme-Onc, Path
⊕ https://vfmat.ch/a787

Global Medical Volunteers
Aims to advance medical services and education in developing nations around the world.
GI, Surg, Urol
⊕ https://vfmat.ch/dfec

Global Ministries – The United Methodist Church
As the worldwide mission and development agency of The United Methodist Church, Global Ministries works with more than 300 hospitals and clinics around the world through its Global Health Unit.
Anesth, CT Surg, CV Med, Crit-Care, Dent-OMFS, Derm, ER Med, GI, General, Infect Dis, Logist-Op, MF Med, Medicine, Neonat, Nephro, Nutr, OB-GYN, Ophth-Opt, Ortho, Palliative, Peds, Pod, Psych, Pub Health, Rehab, Rheum, Surg, Urol
⊕ https://vfmat.ch/1723

Global Oncology (GO)
Brings the best in cancer care to underserved patients around the world and collaborates across geographic, professional, and academic borders to improve cancer care, research, and education.
Heme-Onc, Path, Rad-Onc
⊕ https://vfmat.ch/fcb8

Global Primary Care
Aims to promote and support individuals and organizations that increase access to primary care through sustainable efforts for people living in the poorest places of the world.
General, Logist-Op, Medicine
⊕ https://vfmat.ch/742b

Global Vision 2020
Provides prescription eyeglasses to people who live in parts of the world lacking necessary infrastructure for obtaining affordable corrective eyewear.
Logist-Op, Ophth-Opt
⊕ https://vfmat.ch/7373

Globus Relief
Aims to improve the delivery of healthcare worldwide by gathering, processing, and distributing surplus medical supplies to charities at home and abroad.
Logist-Op
⊕ https://vfmat.ch/a2b7

Good Samaritan Medical Dental Ministry
Since 2000, the Primary Care Team has traveled throughout the three regions of Vietnam, providing medical, surgical, dental, vision, pharmacy, and full diagnostic services to the poor.
Anesth, CV Med, ENT, General, OB-GYN, Ophth-Opt, Ortho
⊕ https://vfmat.ch/328c

Good Shepard International Foundation
Strives to promote inclusive and sustainable development for the most marginalized and vulnerable people, with a special focus on women, girls, and children, inspired by the Christian faith.
ER Med
⊕ https://vfmat.ch/ad9a

Hands for Hope
Reduces poverty in Vietnam by providing disadvantaged children with access to quality education and medical services.

Ped Surg, Peds, Surg
⊕ https://vfmat.ch/a265

Healing Hearts Vietnam
Provides financial assistance to make life-saving cardiac surgeries available for needy Vietnamese families.
CT Surg, CV Med
⊕ https://vfmat.ch/9a5d

Health Equity Initiative
Aims to build and sustain a global community that engages across sectors and disciplines to advance health equity.
Pub Health
⊕ https://vfmat.ch/e2e2

Health Poverty Action
Works in partnership with people around the world who are pursuing change in their own communities to demand health justice and challenge power imbalances.
ER Med, General, Infect Dis, Psych, Pub Health
⊕ https://vfmat.ch/ee58

Health Volunteers Overseas (HVO)
Improves the availability and quality of healthcare through the education, training, and professional development of the health workforce in resource-scarce countries.
All-Immu, Anesth, CV Med, Dent-OMFS, Derm, ENT, ER Med, Endo, GI, Heme-Onc, Infect Dis, Medicine, Medicine, Nephro, Neuro, OB-GYN, Ophth-Opt, Ortho, Peds, Plast, Psych, Pulm-Critic, Rehab, Rheum, Surg
⊕ https://vfmat.ch/42b2

HealthRight International
Leverages global resources to address local health challenges and create sustainable solutions that empower marginalized communities to live healthy lives.
General, Infect Dis, MF Med, OB-GYN, Psych, Pub Health
⊕ https://vfmat.ch/129d

Hear the World Foundation
Advocates worldwide for equal opportunities and improved quality of life for people in need with hearing loss.
ENT, Peds
⊕ https://vfmat.ch/122c

Hearing Health Foundation
Prevents and cures hearing loss and tinnitus through groundbreaking research and promotes hearing health.
Surg
⊕ https://vfmat.ch/2e71

Heart Reach Australia
Brings programs, medical facilities, education, and assistance to those living in substandard conditions largely related to poverty.
ER Med, General, Nephro, Ophth-Opt, Peds
⊕ https://vfmat.ch/fac5

Heart to Heart International
Strengthens communities through improving health access, providing humanitarian development, and administering crisis relief worldwide. Engages volunteers, collaborates with partners, and deploys resources to achieve this mission.
Anesth, ER Med, General, Logist-Op, Medicine, Path, Path, Peds, Psych, Pub Health, Surg
⊕ https://vfmat.ch/aacb

Helen Keller International
Seeks to eliminate preventable vision loss, malnutrition, and diseases of poverty.
Infect Dis, Nutr, OB-GYN, Ophth-Opt, Peds
⊕ https://vfmat.ch/b654

HelpAge International
Works to ensure that people everywhere understand how much older people contribute to society and that they must enjoy their right to healthcare, social

services, economic, and physical security.
General, Geri, Infect Dis, Medicine, Pub Health
⊕ https://vfmat.ch/5d91

HelpMeSee
Trains local cataract specialists in Manual Small Incision Cataract Surgery (MSICS) in significant numbers, to meet the increasing demand for surgical services in the communities most impacted by cataract blindness.
Anesth, Ophth-Opt, Surg
⊕ https://vfmat.ch/973c

HIS Foundation (Holistic Integrated Services Foundation)
Provides free medical services for patients in underserved communities, such as services in orthopedic surgery, plastic surgery, internal medicine, rehabilitation, and ophthalmology, formed by Christian medical professionals.
Dent-OMFS, Geri, Medicine, Ophth-Opt, Ortho, Plast, Rehab
⊕ https://vfmat.ch/a24b

Humanity & Inclusion
Works alongside people with disabilities and vulnerable populations, taking action and bearing witness in order to respond to their essential needs, improve their living conditions and health, and promote respect for their dignity and fundamental rights.
General, Infect Dis, MF Med, Medicine, Ortho, Peds, Psych, Pub Health, Rehab
⊕ https://vfmat.ch/16b7

Institute of Applied Dermatology
Aims to alleviate difficult-to-treat skin ailments by combining biomedicine with Ayurveda, homeopathy, yoga, and other traditional Indian medicine.
All-Immu, Derm, Infect Dis, Nutr, Pod, Pub Health
⊕ https://vfmat.ch/c6eb

International Agency for the Prevention of Blindness (IAPB), The
Leads international efforts in blindness-prevention activities, works toward a world where no one is needlessly visually impaired, and ensures that everyone has access to the best possible standard of eye health.
Infect Dis, Ophth-Opt, Pub Health
⊕ https://vfmat.ch/87a2

International Children's Heart Fund
Aims to promote the international growth and quality of cardiac surgery, particularly in children and young adults.
CT Surg, Ped Surg
⊕ https://vfmat.ch/33fb

International Community Initiatives
Supports the charity and development projects of underserved communities by engaging volunteers, professionals and students in collaborative work with our partnering organizations.
ER Med, Peds, Pub Health
⊕ https://vfmat.ch/d54d

International Council of Ophthalmology
Works with ophthalmologic societies and others to enhance ophthalmic education and improve access to the highest-quality eye care in order to preserve and restore vision for people of the world.
Ophth-Opt
⊕ https://vfmat.ch/ffd2

International Federation of Gynecology and Obstetrics (FIGO)
Implements global projects on specific women's health issues.
MF Med, Medicine, Neonat, OB-GYN, Surg, Urol
⊕ https://vfmat.ch/c4b4

International Federation of Red Cross and Red Crescent Societies (IFRC)
Coordinates and directs international assistance following natural and manmade disasters in nonconflict situations through the world's largest humanitarian and development network. Provides disaster-preparedness programs, healthcare activities, and promotes humanitarian values.
ER Med, General, Infect Dis, Nutr
⊕ https://vfmat.ch/b4ee

International Insulin Foundation
Aims to prolong the life and promote the health of people with diabetes in developing countries by improving the supply of insulin and education in its use.
Endo, Logist-Op
⊕ https://vfmat.ch/d34f

International Medical Relief
Provides sustainable education, training, medical and dental care, and disaster relief and response in vulnerable communities worldwide.
Dent-OMFS, General, Infect Dis, Medicine, OB-GYN
⊕ https://vfmat.ch/b3ed

International Organization for Migration (IOM) – The UN Migration Agency
Promotes evidence-informed policies and holistic, preventive, and curative health programs that are beneficial, accessible, and equitable for vulnerable migrants.
General, Infect Dis, OB-GYN
⊕ https://vfmat.ch/621a

International Organization for Women and Development (IOWD)
Provides underserved women and children in low-income countries with free medical and surgical services and care.
Anesth, MF Med, Neonat, OB-GYN, Ped Surg, Peds, Surg
⊕ https://vfmat.ch/8ecb

International Planned Parenthood Federation (IPPF)
Leads a locally owned, globally connected civil society movement that provides and enables services and champions sexual and reproductive health and rights for all, especially the underserved.
Infect Dis, MF Med, OB-GYN
⊕ https://vfmat.ch/dc97

International Trachoma Initiative (iTi)
Works toward a world free from trachoma, a preventable cause of blindness, and provides comprehensive support to national ministries of health and governmental and nongovernmental organizations to implement a comprehensive approach to fight trachoma.
Infect Dis, Ophth-Opt
⊕ https://vfmat.ch/3278

International Union Against Tuberculosis and Lung Disease
Develops, implements, and assesses anti-tuberculosis, lung health, and noncommunicable disease programs.
Infect Dis, Pub Health, Pulm-Critic
⊕ https://vfmat.ch/3e82

InterSurgeon
Fosters collaborative partnerships in the field of global surgery that will advance clinical care, teaching, training, research, and the provision and maintenance of medical equipment.
ENT, Neurosurg, Ortho, Ped Surg, Plast, Surg, Urol
⊕ https://vfmat.ch/6f8a

IVUmed
Aims to make quality urological care available worldwide by providing medical and surgical education for physicians and nurses, and treatment for thousands of children and adults.
Anesth, OB-GYN, Ped Surg, Surg, Urol
⊕ https://vfmat.ch/e619

John Snow, Inc. (JSI)
Aims to improve the health and well-being of underserved and vulnerable people and communities throughout the world.
General, Infect Dis, Logist-Op, MF Med, OB-GYN, Peds, Psych, Pub Health
⊕ https://vfmat.ch/ba78

Johns Hopkins Center for Communication Programs
Believes in the power of communication to save lives by empowering people to adopt healthy behaviors for themselves, their families, and their communities.
General, Infect Dis, Logist-Op, OB-GYN, Pub Health
⊕ https://vfmat.ch/1bf9

Joint United Nations Programme on HIV/AIDS (UNAIDS)
Aims to place people living with HIV and people affected by the virus at the decision-making table and at the center of designing, delivering, and monitoring the AIDS response.
Infect Dis
⊕ https://vfmat.ch/464a

Kaya Responsible Travel
Promotes sustainable social, environmental, and economic development, empowers communities, and cultivates educated, compassionate global citizens through responsible travel.
All-Immu, Crit-Care, Dent-OMFS, ER Med, General, Geri, Infect Dis, MF Med, Medicine, Nutr, OB-GYN, Peds, Psych, Pub Health, Rehab
⊕ https://vfmat.ch/b2cf

Kids Care Everywhere
Seeks to empower physicians in under-resourced environments with multimedia, state-of-the-art medical software, and to inspire young professionals to become future global healthcare leaders.
Logist-Op, Ped Surg, Peds
⊕ https://vfmat.ch/bc23

Kind Cuts for Kids
Aims to improve medical services for children in developing countries through education, demonstration, and skills transfer to local healthcare professionals.
Anesth, Medicine, Ped Surg, Surg
⊕ https://vfmat.ch/e3d7

Kybele Incorporated
Aims to create healthcare partnerships across borders to improve childbirth safety.
Anesth, Neonat, OB-GYN, Pub Health
⊕ https://vfmat.ch/5fc9

Life for a Child
Supports the provision of the best possible healthcare, given local circumstances, to all children and youth with diabetes in less-resourced countries, through the strengthening of existing diabetes services.
Endo, Medicine, Peds
⊕ https://vfmat.ch/d712

Limbs International
Engages communities and transforms lives through affordable, sustainable prosthetic solutions and rehabilitation services in developing countries.
Logist-Op, Ortho, Pod, Rehab
⊕ https://vfmat.ch/dc84

Little Feather Foundation
Provides palliative and end-of-life care for infants and young children living with life-limiting and life-threatening conditions throughout Vietnam.
Palliative, Peds, Pub Health
⊕ https://vfmat.ch/cc61

MAGNA International
Helps those who are suffering or recovering from conflicts and disasters by reducing the risks of diseases and treating them immediately.
ER Med, General, Infect Dis, Peds, Surg
⊕ https://vfmat.ch/58f4

Making A Difference Foundation
Sponsors and organizes medical missions for medical providers to provide care to underserved communities around the world.
CV Med, Dent-OMFS, ER Med, General, Infect Dis, Logist-Op, MF Med, Neonat, Nutr, OB-GYN, Ophth-Opt, Ortho, Pub Health, Pulm-Critic, Rehab, Surg
⊕ https://vfmat.ch/5556

Management Sciences for Health (MSH)
Works with countries and communities to save lives and improve the health of the world's poorest and most vulnerable people by building strong, resilient, sustainable health systems.
Infect Dis, Logist-Op, Pub Health
⊕ https://vfmat.ch/6aa2

MAP International
Provides medicines and health supplies to those in need around the world so they might experience life to the fullest.
Logist-Op
⊕ https://vfmat.ch/deed

Marie Stopes International
Provides the contraception and safe abortion services that enable women all over the world to choose their own futures.
Infect Dis, MF Med, Neonat, OB-GYN, Pub Health
⊕ https://vfmat.ch/9525

Maverick Collective
Aims to build a global community of strategic philanthropists and informed advocates who use their intellectual and financial resources to create change.
Infect Dis, MF Med, OB-GYN
⊕ https://vfmat.ch/ea49

Max Foundation, The
Seeks to increase global access to treatment, care, and support for people living with cancer.
General, Heme-Onc, Pub Health
⊕ https://vfmat.ch/8c7d

Medical and Educational Sustainable Community Help (MESCH)
Seeks to develop health and well-being and safer, more resilient communities in developing countries and also provide sustainable aid through education and training.
Anesth, Dent-OMFS, ENT, ER Med, General, Ophth-Opt, Ortho, Pub Health, Surg
⊕ https://vfmat.ch/24c2

Medical, Educational Missions and Outreach
Provides medical care and educational opportunities to impoverished villagers in Vietnam.
CT Surg, Dent-OMFS, General, Nutr, Pub Health
⊕ https://vfmat.ch/1d8a

MEDRIX
Saves lives and improves the quality of life in Southeast Asia by providing medical resources, international health education, child heart surgeries, and safe water development.
CT Surg, General, Peds
⊕ https://vfmat.ch/1719

MedShare
Aims to improve the quality of life of people, communities, and the planet by sourcing and directly delivering surplus medical supplies and equipment to communities in need around the world.
Logist-Op
⊕ https://vfmat.ch/c8bc

Mercy Ships
Operates hospital ships staffed by volunteers to bring hope, healing, and healthcare to underserved communities worldwide.
Anesth, Dent-OMFS, Logist-Op, Neonat, OB-GYN, Ophth-Opt, Ortho, Palliative, Plast, Psych, Surg
⊕ https://vfmat.ch/2e99

Mission Vision
Seeks to decrease blindness and other eye-related disabilities, and to increase academic performance and general quality of life.
Ophth-Opt
⊕ https://vfmat.ch/83d8

Mitral Foundation
Committed to advancing the care of patients with mitral valve disease on a global scale.
CT Surg, CV Med, Crit-Care
⊕ https://vfmat.ch/a421

Mobility Outreach International
Enables mobility for children and adults in under-resourced areas of the world,

and creates a sustainable orthopedic surgery model using local resources.
Ortho, Rehab
🌐 https://vfmat.ch/9376

MSD for Mothers
Designs scalable solutions that help end preventable maternal deaths.
MF Med, OB-GYN, Pub Health
🌐 https://vfmat.ch/9f99

MSI Reproductive Choices (Marie Stopes International)
Seeks to deliver quality family planning and reproductive healthcare to women around the world.
MF Med
🌐 https://vfmat.ch/5c82

NCD Alliance
Unites and strengthens civil society to stimulate collaborative advocacy, action, and accountability for NCD (noncommunicable disease) prevention and control.
All-Immu, CV Med, General, Heme-Onc, Medicine, Peds, Psych
🌐 https://vfmat.ch/abdd

Norwegian People's Aid
Aims to improve living conditions, to create a democratic, just, and safe society.
ER Med, Logist-Op
🌐 https://vfmat.ch/2d8e

OneSight
Brings eye exams and glasses to people who lack access to vision care.
Ophth-Opt
🌐 https://vfmat.ch/3ecc

Open Eyes Beyond Border
Brings positive impact, direct care, and support to underserved children and provides the greatest possible degree of transparency to the public.
ER Med, Ophth-Opt, Pub Health
🌐 https://vfmat.ch/74bb

Open Heart International
Provides surgical interventions and best practices to the most disadvantaged communities on the planet.
CT Surg, MF Med, OB-GYN, Ophth-Opt, Plast, Surg
🌐 https://vfmat.ch/dab2

Operation International
Offers medical aid to adults and children suffering from lack of quality healthcare in impoverished countries.
Dent-OMFS, ER Med, Heme-Onc, OB-GYN, Ophth-Opt, Ortho, Ped Surg, Plast, Surg
🌐 https://vfmat.ch/b52a

Operation Smile
Treats patients with cleft lip and cleft palate, and creates solutions that deliver safe surgery to people where it's needed most.
Anesth, Dent-OMFS, ENT, Ped Surg, Plast
🌐 https://vfmat.ch/5c29

Operation Walk
Provides the gift of mobility through life-changing joint replacement surgeries, at no cost for those in need in the U.S. and globally.
Anesth, Ortho, Rehab, Surg
🌐 https://vfmat.ch/bafe

Optometry Giving Sight
Delivers eye exams and low or no-cost glasses, provides training for local eye care professionals, and establishes optometry schools, vision centers and optical labs.
Ophth-Opt
🌐 https://vfmat.ch/33ea

Orbis International
Works to prevent and treat blindness through hands-on training and improved access to quality eye care.

Anesth, Ophth-Opt, Surg
🌐 https://vfmat.ch/f2b2

Pact
Works on the ground to improve the lives of those who are challenged by poverty and marginalization, striving for a world in which all people are heard, capable, and vibrant.
Infect Dis, Logist-Op, MF Med, Pub Health
🌐 https://vfmat.ch/9a6c

PATH
Advances health equity through innovation and partnerships so people, communities, and economies can thrive.
All-Immu, CV Med, Endo, Heme-Onc, Infect Dis, MF Med, Neonat, Nutr, OB-GYN, Path, Peds, Pulm-Critic
🌐 https://vfmat.ch/b4db

PLeDGE Health
Aims to improve emergency medical care around the world through sustainable partnerships, open-source material development and dissemination, and development of the next generation of educational leaders in low-resource areas.
ER Med, General
🌐 https://vfmat.ch/3a7d

Ponseti International
Provides global leadership in building high-quality, locally directed, and sustainable capacity to deliver the Ponseti clubfoot care pathway at the country level.
Ortho, Ped Surg, Peds, Rehab
🌐 https://vfmat.ch/476b

RAD-AID International
Improves and optimizes access to medical imaging and radiology in low-resource regions of the world.
Rad-Onc, Radiol
🌐 https://vfmat.ch/537f

Resource Exchange International
Provides holistic education and training to improve knowledge and skills and build human capacity within communities in emerging nations.
Derm, ENT, Ortho
🌐 https://vfmat.ch/6d49

Resource Exchange International
Sends long-term staff and short-term professionals in areas of education, medicine, and business to train leaders in emerging nations so that they can train others.
General
🌐 https://vfmat.ch/6863

RestoringVision
Empowers lives by restoring vision for millions of people in need.
Ophth-Opt
🌐 https://vfmat.ch/e121

ReSurge International
Provides reconstructive surgical care and builds surgical capacity in developing countries.
Anesth, Dent-OMFS, Ped Surg, Plast, Surg
🌐 https://vfmat.ch/9937

Rockefeller Foundation, The
Works to promote the well-being of humanity.
Logist-Op, Nutr, Pub Health
🌐 https://vfmat.ch/5424

Rose Charities International
Aims to support communities to improve quality of life and reduce the effects of poverty through innovative, self-sustaining projects, and partnerships.
ENT, ER Med, General, Infect Dis, Neonat, OB-GYN, Ophth-Opt, Ped Surg, Peds, Rehab, Urol
🌐 https://vfmat.ch/53df

Rotaplast International
Helps children and families worldwide by eliminating the burden of cleft lip and/or palate, burn scarring, and other deformities by sending medical teams to provide free reconstructive surgery, ancillary treatment, and training.
Anesth, Dent-OMFS, ENT, Ped Surg, Plast, Surg
⊕ https://vfmat.ch/78b3

Rotary International
Provides service to others, improves lives, and advances world understanding, goodwill, and peace through its fellowship of business, professional, and community leaders.
ER Med, General, Infect Dis, MF Med, OB-GYN
⊕ https://vfmat.ch/8fb5

Save the Children
Gives children around the world a healthy start in life, the opportunity to learn, and protection from harm.
All-Immu, Crit-Care, ER Med, General, Infect Dis, MF Med, Medicine, Neonat, OB-GYN, Peds, Psych, Pub Health
⊕ https://vfmat.ch/2e73

SEVA
Delivers vital eye care services to the world's most vulnerable, including women, children, and Indigenous peoples.
Ophth-Opt, Surg
⊕ https://vfmat.ch/1e87

Sight for All
Empowers communities to deliver comprehensive, evidence-based, high-quality eye healthcare through the provision of research, education, and equipment.
Logist-Op, Ophth-Opt, Surg
⊕ https://vfmat.ch/e34b

SIGN Fracture Care International
Builds orthopedic capacity around the world and provides the injured poor access to fracture surgery by donating orthopedic education and implant systems to surgeons in developing countries.
Ortho, Rehab, Surg
⊕ https://vfmat.ch/123d

Smile Outreach Foundation
Brings volunteers together to deliver free world-class medical services to underserved or disadvantaged populations around the world.
Dent-OMFS, Pub Health
⊕ https://vfmat.ch/338a

Smile Train, Inc.
Treats children with cleft lip through a sustainable and local model that supports surgery and other forms of essential care.
Logist-Op, Pub Health
⊕ https://vfmat.ch/822c

Social Assistance Program for Vietnam
Improves the quality of life for the poor and the disabled in Vietnam and locally, with services mainly in healthcare, education, and social welfare.
CT Surg, Dent-OMFS, Nutr, Ophth-Opt, Ped Surg, Pub Health, Surg
⊕ https://vfmat.ch/9de4

SOS Children's Villages International
Supports children through alternative care and family strengthening.
ER Med, Peds
⊕ https://vfmat.ch/aca1

Sri Sathya Sai International Organization
Inspired by spiritual teachings, carries out efforts in global healthcare, education, humanitarian relief, and youth engagement.
Dent-OMFS, General, Logist-Op, Nutr, Ophth-Opt, Pub Health
⊕ https://vfmat.ch/9bda

Swasti
Aims to transform the lives of marginalized communities by ensuring their access to quality healthcare and thereby contributing to poverty alleviation.

Pub Health
⊕ https://vfmat.ch/be8b

Swiss Tropical and Public Health Institute
Contributes to the improvement of the health of populations internationally, nationally, and locally through excellence in research, education, and services.
Infect Dis, Pub Health
⊕ https://vfmat.ch/2ee4

Task Force for Global Health, The
Consists of programs and focus areas that cover a range of global health issues including neglected tropical diseases, infectious diseases, vaccines, field epidemiology, public health informatics, health workforce development, and global health ethics.
Infect Dis, Logist-Op, Medicine, Ophth-Opt, Peds
⊕ https://vfmat.ch/714c

Third World Eye Care Society (TWECS)
Collects old, unused eyeglasses and distributes them in conjunction with eye exams given by properly trained individuals.
Logist-Op, Ophth-Opt
⊕ https://vfmat.ch/8618

Transparent Fish Fund
Inspires others to join in alleviating poverty in East Asia by empowering small but high-impact NGOs to be sustainable and transparent in their programs.
CV Med, General, MF Med, Nutr, Peds
⊕ https://vfmat.ch/7714

Trinh Foundation Australia
Provides ongoing clinical training to health professionals across Vietnam about aspects of speech-language therapy and works to establish speech therapy as a profession in the country.
Path, Pub Health, Rehab
⊕ https://vfmat.ch/5c7c

UNC Health Foundation
Secures resources and supports empathy and expertise in patient care, research, education, and advocacy in underserved communities around the world.
Heme-Onc, Infect Dis, Neuro, Peds, Pub Health
⊕ https://vfmat.ch/7129

Union for International Cancer Control (UICC)
Unites and supports the cancer community to reduce the global cancer burden, promote greater equity, and ensure that cancer control continues to be a priority in the world health and development agenda.
Heme-Onc, Pub Health
⊕ https://vfmat.ch/88b1

United Nations Children's Fund (UNICEF)
Works in over 190 countries and territories to save children's lives, defend their rights, and help them fulfill their potential, from early childhood through adolescence.
All-Immu, Infect Dis, MF Med, Neonat, Nutr, OB-GYN, Ped Surg, Peds, Pub Health
⊕ https://vfmat.ch/42d7

United Nations Development Programme (UNDP)
Helps countries achieve the simultaneous eradication of extreme poverty and significant reduction of inequalities and exclusion using a sustainable human development approach.
Infect Dis, Logist-Op, Pub Health
⊕ https://vfmat.ch/935c

United Nations High Commissioner for Refugees (UNHCR)
Safeguards the rights and well-being of people who have been forced to flee, ensuring that everybody has the right to seek asylum and find safe refuge in another country, with the goal of seeking lasting solutions.
General, MF Med, Medicine, OB-GYN, Peds, Psych, Pub Health
⊕ https://vfmat.ch/6636

United Nations Population Fund (UNFPA)
Supports reproductive healthcare for women and youth in more than 150

countries, focusing on delivering a world in which every pregnancy is wanted, every childbirth is safe, and every young person's potential is fulfilled.

Infect Dis, MF Med, Neonat, OB-GYN, Peds, Pub Health

⊕ https://vfmat.ch/c969

United States Agency for International Development (USAID)
Promotes and demonstrates democratic values abroad and advances a free, peaceful, and prosperous world. Leads the U.S. government's international development and disaster assistance through partnerships and investments that save lives.

ER Med, Infect Dis, MF Med, OB-GYN, Peds

⊕ https://vfmat.ch/9a99

University of California Los Angeles: David Geffen School of Medicine Global Health Program
Catalyzes opportunities to improve health globally by engaging in multi-disciplinary and innovative education programs, research initiatives, and bilateral partnerships that provide opportunities for trainees, faculty, and staff to contribute to sustainable health initiatives and to address health inequities facing the world today.

All-Immu, Infect Dis, Logist-Op, MF Med, Medicine, Neonat, OB-GYN, Ortho, Ped Surg, Peds, Radiol

⊕ https://vfmat.ch/f1a4

University of New Mexico School of Medicine: Project Echo
Seeks to improve health outcomes worldwide through the use of a technology called telementoring, a guided-practice model in which the participating clinician retains responsibility for managing the patient.

General, Infect Dis, MF Med, OB-GYN, Path, Peds

⊕ https://vfmat.ch/6c9a

University of North Carolina: Institute for Global Health and Infectious Diseases
Harnesses the full resources of UNC and its partners to solve global health problems, reduce the burden of disease, and cultivate the next generation of global health leaders.

Infect Dis, MF Med, OB-GYN, Psych, Surg

⊕ https://vfmat.ch/ed5e

University of Pennsylvania Perelman School of Medicine Center for Global Health
Aims to improve health equity worldwide through enhanced public health awareness and access to care, discovery, and outcomes-based research, and comprehensive educational programs grounded in partnership.

Heme-Onc, Infect Dis, OB-GYN

⊕ https://vfmat.ch/cb57

University of Utah Global Health
Supports local organizations in their quest to improve quality of life in their communities all over the world.

Anesth, CT Surg, CV Med, Crit-Care, Dent-OMFS, ENT, ER Med, Infect Dis, OB-GYN, Ophth-Opt, Ped Surg, Ped Surg, Peds, Plast, Pub Health, Surg, Urol

⊕ https://vfmat.ch/bacd

University of Washington: Department of Global Health
Improves health for all through research, education, training, and service, addresses the causes of disease and health inequities at multiple levels, and collaborates with partners to develop and sustain locally led, quality health systems, programs, and policies.

Infect Dis, Logist-Op, Pub Health

⊕ https://vfmat.ch/f543

University of Washington: The International Training and Education Center for Health (I-TECH)
Works with local partners to develop skilled healthcare workers and strong national health systems in resource-limited countries.

Infect Dis, Pub Health

⊕ https://vfmat.ch/642f

USAID: Health Finance and Governance Project
Uses research to implement strategies to help countries develop robust governance systems, increase their domestic resources for health, manage those resources more effectively, and make wise purchasing decisions.

Logist-Op

⊕ https://vfmat.ch/8652

USAID: Health Policy Initiative
Provides field-level programming in health policy development and implementation.

General, Infect Dis, MF Med, OB-GYN, Peds

⊕ https://vfmat.ch/8f84

USAID: Leadership, Management and Governance Project
Improves leadership, management, and governance practices to strengthen health systems and improve health for all, including vulnerable populations worldwide.

Logist-Op

⊕ https://vfmat.ch/d35e

USAID: Maternal and Child Health Integrated Program
Works to improve the health of women and their families, including programs for maternal, newborn, and child health, immunization, family planning, nutrition, malaria, and HIV/AIDS.

All-Immu, General, Infect Dis, MF Med

⊕ https://vfmat.ch/4415

USAID: TB Care II
Focuses on tuberculosis care and treatment.

Infect Dis

⊕ https://vfmat.ch/57d4

Viet Duc University Hospital
Educates and trains doctors, technicians, and nurses to provide comprehensive patient care using the newest technology and procedures.

CT Surg, Dent-OMFS, GI, Heme-Onc, Neuro, Neurosurg, Ortho, Ped Surg, Plast, Surg, Urol

⊕ https://vfmat.ch/7d46

VietMD Clinic
Provides help to Vietnamese doctors and patients in the U.S. and Vietnam through direct healthcare services and support of continued medical education.

Derm, Derm, General, Medicine, Path

⊕ https://vfmat.ch/ab59

Vietnam Health Clinic
Improves access to healthcare for under-resourced communities in Vietnam.

Dent-OMFS, General, Ophth-Opt, Pub Health, Rehab

⊕ https://vfmat.ch/dc94

Vision Care
Restores sight and helps patients get regular treatment at short-term eye camps and long-term base clinics by having doctors, missionaries, volunteers, and sponsors work together.

Ophth-Opt

⊕ https://vfmat.ch/9d7c

Vision Outreach International
Advocates for helping the blind in underserved regions of the world and empowers the poor through sight restoration.

Ophth-Opt

⊕ https://vfmat.ch/9721

Visionaries International
Works toward reducing the burden of corneal blindness in the developing world by assessing and addressing what limits corneal surgeons in each locale.

Anesth, Ophth-Opt, Pub Health, Surg

⊕ https://vfmat.ch/3d2e

Vitamin Angels
Helps at-risk populations in need—specifically pregnant women, new mothers, and children under age 5—to gain access to life-changing vitamins and minerals.

General, Nutr

⊕ https://vfmat.ch/7da1

VnHOPE Alliance
Provides much-needed care to those in Vietnam who are unable to access services due to financial, transportation, or social reasons, including gynecologic,

dental, and optometric care to the rural underserved.

Crit-Care, General, MF Med, OB-GYN, Ophth-Opt, Peds, Pub Health, Rehab

⊕ https://vfmat.ch/97e9

World Children's Fund
Commits to helping children worldwide who are suffering the effects of poverty, disease, natural disaster, famine, abuse, civil strife, and war.

General, Logist-Op, MF Med, Nutr, OB-GYN, Pub Health

⊕ https://vfmat.ch/9cd8

World Council of Optometry
Facilitates the development of optometry worldwide and promotes eye health and vision care through advocacy, education, policy development, and humanitarian outreach.

Ophth-Opt, Pub Health

⊕ https://vfmat.ch/c92e

World Federation of Hemophilia (WFH)
Aims to improve and sustain care for people with inherited bleeding disorders by pursuing long-term relationships with individuals and organizations who share the values of WFH's development model.

Heme-Onc

⊕ https://vfmat.ch/5121

World Health Organization, The (WHO)
The United Nations' agency for health provides leadership on global health matters, shapes the health research agenda, sets norms and standards, articulates evidence-based policy options, provides technical support and monitoring to countries, and assesses health trends.

ER Med, General, Infect Dis, Logist-Op, MF Med, OB-GYN, Peds, Psych, Pub Health

⊕ https://vfmat.ch/c476

World Heart Federation
Leads the global fight against heart disease and stroke, with a focus on low- and middle-income countries.

CV Med, Crit-Care, Heme-Onc, Medicine, Peds

⊕ https://vfmat.ch/ea51

World Medical Relief
Facilitates the distribution of surplus medical resources where they are needed.

Logist-Op

⊕ https://vfmat.ch/72dc

World Missions Possible
Provides EMS capacity-building, along with medical and vision care, to under-developed and rural areas.

ER Med, General, Heme-Onc, Neonat, Ophth-Opt, Surg

⊕ https://vfmat.ch/d6a5

World Telehealth Initiative
Provides medical expertise to the world's most vulnerable communities to build local capacity and deliver core health services through a network of volunteer healthcare professionals supported with state-of-the-art technology.

Derm, Infect Dis, MF Med, Medicine, Neuro, OB-GYN, Peds, Pulm-Critic

⊕ https://vfmat.ch/fa91

World Vision International
Works with vulnerable communities around the world to overcome poverty and injustice with child-focused programs in disaster management, health, nutrition, economic development, education, clean water, sanitation, and hygiene.

ER Med, General, Infect Dis, MF Med, Nutr, OB-GYN, Peds

⊕ https://vfmat.ch/2642

WorldWide Orphans (WWO)
Seeks to transform the lives of vulnerable children, families, and communities through trauma-informed, evidence-based programming.

General, Peds, Pub Health

⊕ https://vfmat.ch/2538

Yale School of Medicine: Global Surgery Division
Addresses the rising worldwide surgical disease burden in low-resource settings, both domestically and internationally, by mobilizing a community of surgical leaders to engage in international partnerships and implement quality improvement and training protocols.

ER Med, Infect Dis, Medicine, Peds

⊕ https://vfmat.ch/2bf7

Vietnam

Healthcare Facilities

105 Military Hospital
Son Tay, Hanoi, Vietnam
⊕ https://vfmat.ch/effa

108 Military Central Hospital
Hai Ba Trung, Hanoi, Vietnam
⊕ https://vfmat.ch/e53e

121 Military Hospital
Ninh Kieu District, Can Tho City, Vietnam
⊕ https://vfmat.ch/aa51

24 Ngõ 168 Tựu Liệt
Van Thôn, Hanoi, Vietnam
⊕ https://vfmat.ch/9d8f

354 Military Hospital
Ba Dinh, Hanoi, Vietnam
⊕ https://vfmat.ch/ca85

7A Military Hospital
District 5, Ho Chi Minh, Vietnam
⊕ https://vfmat.ch/3cd7

7B Military Medical Hospital
Tan Tien, City, Đồng Nai, Vietnam
⊕ https://vfmat.ch/3d96

91 Military Medical Hospital
Pho Yen, Thai Nguyen, Vietnam
⊕ https://vfmat.ch/73fc

An Binh Hospital
Chợ Rẫy, Ho Chi Minh, Vietnam
⊕ https://vfmat.ch/6253

An Duc Obstetrics and Gynecology Hospital
Thai Binh City, Thái Bình, Vietnam
⊕ https://vfmat.ch/6f4e

An Nhon Hospital
An Nhon, Binh Dinh, Vietnam
⊕ https://vfmat.ch/2f9e

An Phước
Ấp Tân An, Bình Thuận, Vietnam
⊕ https://vfmat.ch/4852

An Sinh Hospital
Chí Hòa, Ho Chi Minh, Vietnam
⊕ https://vfmat.ch/97bc

An Ward Medical Station
Cao Lanh, Da Nang, Vietnam
⊕ https://vfmat.ch/4fce

April 30 Hospital, Ministry of Public Security
District 5, Ho Chi Minh, Vietnam
⊕ https://vfmat.ch/de3f

Ba Ria
Ấp Tây, Bà Rịa-Vũng Tàu, Vietnam
⊕ https://vfmat.ch/dfcf

Ba Ria Vung Tau Eye Hospital
Ấp Long Kiên I, Bà Rịa-Vũng Tàu, Vietnam
⊕ https://vfmat.ch/25c4

Ba Vi General Hospital
Đồng Bảng, Hanoi, Vietnam
⊕ https://vfmat.ch/1c59

Bac Ha Hospital
Long Bien, Hanoi, Vietnam
⊕ https://vfmat.ch/7294

Bac Lieu Province General Hospital
Vinh Lợi, Bạc Liêu, Vietnam
⊕ https://vfmat.ch/2d9f

Bac Ninh General Hospital
Vo Cuong Ward, Bắc Ninh, Vietnam
⊕ https://vfmat.ch/845a

Bach Mai Hospital
Hanoi, Vietnam
⊕ https://vfmat.ch/a64v

Bai Chay Hospital
Hạ Long, Quảng Ninh, Vietnam
⊕ https://vfmat.ch/3fae

Ben Luc General Hospital
Bến Lức, Long An, Vietnam
⊕ https://vfmat.ch/927b

Ben Vien Răng Hàm Mặt
District 1, City, Ho Chi Minh, Vietnam
⊕ https://vfmat.ch/ae2c

Benh Vien A
Yên Lãng, Hanoi, Vietnam
⊕ https://vfmat.ch/fce8

Benh Vien Da Khoa Binh Dan
Phương Xuân Hòa, Da Nang, Vietnam
⊕ https://vfmat.ch/4ee5

Benh Vien Da Khoa Vinh Toan
An Hải, Da Nang, Vietnam
⊕ https://vfmat.ch/2bfb

Benh Vien Gtvt 5
Lien Chieu, Da Nang, Vietnam
⊕ https://vfmat.ch/bcb5

Benh Vien Phu Nu Tp Da Nang
Ấp Ba, Da Nang, Vietnam
⊕ https://vfmat.ch/a7f5

Bien Vien Le Ngoc Tung
Ấp Thái Thông (1), Tây Ninh Province, Vietnam
⊕ https://vfmat.ch/f4ae

Binh An Commune Health Station
Di An Town, Binh Duong, Vietnam
🌐 https://vfmat.ch/7dbf

Binh An Hospital
Rach Gia City, Kiến Giang, Vietnam
🌐 https://vfmat.ch/124d

Binh Chanh District Hospital
Chợ Đệm, Ho Chi Minh, Vietnam
🌐 https://vfmat.ch/a7f9

Binh Dinh Eye Hospital
Qui Nhon City, Bình Định, Vietnam
🌐 https://vfmat.ch/4b7e

Binh Duong Commune Medical Station
Binh Son, Quang Ngai, Vietnam
🌐 https://vfmat.ch/b524

Binh Phuc Traditional Medical Hospital
Dong Xoai, Binh Phuoc, Vietnam
🌐 https://vfmat.ch/5a39

Binh Thanh Hospital
Cầu Bông, Ho Chi Minh, Vietnam
🌐 https://vfmat.ch/73f6

Binh Thanh Medical Station
Binh Thanh District, An Giang, Vietnam
🌐 https://vfmat.ch/4a41

Bình Chánh
Bình Điền, Ho Chi Minh, Vietnam
🌐 https://vfmat.ch/d459

Biệnh Viện 19-8 Bộ Công An
Cầu Giấy, Hà Nội, Vietnam
🌐 https://vfmat.ch/4262

Buon Ma Thuot City Hospital
Thành phố Buôn Ma Thuột, Đắk Lắk, Vietnam
🌐 https://vfmat.ch/6e44

BV Anh Đức
My Tho City, Tiền Giang, Vietnam
🌐 https://vfmat.ch/2a6a

BV Bình Thuan
Ấp Đại Tài, Bình Thuận, Vietnam
🌐 https://vfmat.ch/1421

BV gò công (Phượng)
Ấp Nhì, Tiền Giang, Vietnam
🌐 https://vfmat.ch/c2b9

BV Răng-Hàm-Mặt
Ấp An Mỹ, Long An, Vietnam
🌐 https://vfmat.ch/e7cd

BV Tai Mũi Họng Sài Gòn
Xóm Chiếu, Ho Chi Minh, Vietnam
🌐 https://vfmat.ch/8d9a

BV Thu Duc
Phú Châu, Ho Chi Minh, Vietnam
🌐 https://vfmat.ch/15c1

BV Đa Khoa Bình Minh
Đông Bình A, Vĩnh Long, Vietnam
🌐 https://vfmat.ch/bf39

BV Đa khoa Hồng Ngự
Hồng Ngự, Đồng Tháp, Vietnam
🌐 https://vfmat.ch/d127

BV Đa khoa quận Ô Môn
Thới Hòa E, Can Tho, Vietnam
🌐 https://vfmat.ch/66b4

BV Đa khoa Thạnh Hóa
Khóm Bốn, Long An, Vietnam
🌐 https://vfmat.ch/5b22

BV Đa khoa Đức Huệ
Ấp Ba, Long An, Vietnam
🌐 https://vfmat.ch/9495

BVĐK Bình Thuận – khu vực Phía Bắc
Phan Lý, Bình Thuận, Vietnam
🌐 https://vfmat.ch/ed1b

Bãi Đậu Xe
Hoi An, Quảng Nam, Vietnam
🌐 https://vfmat.ch/3b82

Bênh Viện Phụ Sản Hải Phòng
Thượng Lý, Haiphong, Vietnam
🌐 https://vfmat.ch/4347

Bệnh Viện Mắt Và Da Liễu Hải Dương
Thành phố Hải Dương, Hải Dương, Vietnam
🌐 https://vfmat.ch/cd81

Bệnh Viện Đường Sắt
Long Biên, Hanoi, Vietnam
🌐 https://vfmat.ch/fedf

Bệnh Viên Tp Vinh
Yên Dung, Thua Thien-Hue, Vietnam
🌐 https://vfmat.ch/8779

Bệnh Viện 175
Gò Vấp, Ho Chi Minh, Vietnam
🌐 https://vfmat.ch/accd

Bệnh Viện 211 Tây Nguyên
Plei Kếp, Gia Lai, Vietnam
🌐 https://vfmat.ch/f391

Bệnh Viện 22/12
Thôn Điền Hạ, Khánh Hòa, Vietnam
🌐 https://vfmat.ch/ab25

Bệnh Viện A Thái Nguyên
Thịnh Đán, Thái Nguyên, Vietnam
🌐 https://vfmat.ch/d48c

Bệnh Viện An Giang
Đông Thịnh B, An Giang, Vietnam
🌐 https://vfmat.ch/3e1b

Bệnh Viện B
Sầm Sơn, Thanh Hóa, Vietnam
🌐 https://vfmat.ch/69de

Bệnh viện Bà Rịa
Ấp Tây, Bà Rịa-Vũng Tàu, Vietnam
🌐 https://vfmat.ch/9e68

Bệnh Viện Bình Dân
Khóm Bốn, An Giang, Vietnam
🌐 https://vfmat.ch/f6dd

Bệnh viện Bình Tân (Binh Tan District Hospital)
Bình Trị Đông, Ho Chi Minh, Vietnam
🌐 https://vfmat.ch/743f

Bệnh Viện Bạch Mai
Hà Nội, Vietnam
🌐 https://vfmat.ch/7727

Bệnh Viện Bảo Lâm
Minrong Sekang, Lâm Đồng, Vietnam
🌐 https://vfmat.ch/444f

Bệnh viện Bệnh Nhiệt đới Trung Ương
Trung Phụng, Hanoi, Vietnam
🌐 https://vfmat.ch/1ffc

Bệnh Viện Cao Văn Chí
Phú Khương, Tây Ninh Province, Vietnam
🌐 https://vfmat.ch/a866

Bệnh Viện Châu Phú
Cồn Nhỏ, An Giang, Vietnam
🌐 https://vfmat.ch/381b

Bệnh viện Chấn Thương Chỉnh Hình
Xóm Ông Đội, Ho Chi Minh, Vietnam
🌐 https://vfmat.ch/e4f4

Bệnh Viện Chỉnh Hình – Phục Hồi Chức Năng
Tay Phuong, Bình Định, Vietnam
🌐 https://vfmat.ch/67ef

Bệnh Viện Công An Thành Phố Hà Nội
Hà Đông, Hà Nội, Vietnam
🌐 https://vfmat.ch/9bcb

Bệnh Viện Cấp Cứu Trưng Vương
Chợ Rẫy, Ho Chi Minh, Vietnam
🌐 https://vfmat.ch/4844

Bệnh Viện Da Khoa Kinh Bắc
Xóm Năm, Bắc Ninh, Vietnam
🌐 https://vfmat.ch/977e

Bệnh Viện Da Khoa Tràng An
Đống Đa, Hà Nội, Vietnam
⊕ https://vfmat.ch/6432

Bệnh Viện Da liễu Hà Nội
Hữu Tiếp, Hanoi, Vietnam
⊕ https://vfmat.ch/de15

Bệnh viện Da Liễu Thành Phố Đà Nẵng (Da Nang City Dermatology Hospital)
Thanh Khe, Da Nang, Vietnam
⊕ https://vfmat.ch/248f

Bệnh viện Da Liễu TPHCM
Xóm Chiếu, Ho Chi Minh, Vietnam
⊕ https://vfmat.ch/eef9

Bệnh Viện E
Cầu Giấy, Hà Nội, Vietnam
⊕ https://vfmat.ch/1b64

Bệnh Viện Gia Định
Cầu Bông, Ho Chi Minh, Vietnam
⊕ https://vfmat.ch/c2ff

Bệnh Viện giao thông hải phòng
Lãm Hạ, Haiphong, Vietnam
⊕ https://vfmat.ch/c9df

Bệnh viện Giao thông Vận tải Trung ương
Dich Vong Trung, Hanoi, Vietnam
⊕ https://vfmat.ch/95c2

Bệnh Viện Hoàn Mỹ Cửu Long
Ấp Năm, Can Tho, Vietnam
⊕ https://vfmat.ch/c4ea

Bệnh viện Huyết học Truyền máu
Thới Nhựt, Can Tho, Vietnam
⊕ https://vfmat.ch/be42

Bệnh Viện Huyện Bến Cầu
Bến Cầu, Tây Ninh, Vietnam
⊕ https://vfmat.ch/2739

Bệnh viện huyện Kiến Thụy
Xuan La, Haiphong, Vietnam
⊕ https://vfmat.ch/b51c

Bệnh Viện Huyện Nghi Xuân
Tiền Điền, Thua Thien-Hue, Vietnam
⊕ https://vfmat.ch/f9a1

Bệnh Viện Huyện Tuy Phước
Mỹ Điền, Bình Định, Vietnam
⊕ https://vfmat.ch/7c72

Bệnh Viện Huyện Đăk Rlap
Quang Duc, Đắk Nông, Vietnam
⊕ https://vfmat.ch/9c5c

Bệnh Viện Hòa Vang
Thạch Nhơn, Da Nang, Vietnam
⊕ https://vfmat.ch/bf65

Bệnh Viện Hồng Ngọc
Xóm Pho, Hanoi, Vietnam
⊕ https://vfmat.ch/b9b4

Bệnh Viện Hội an
Hoi An, Quảng Nam, Vietnam
⊕ https://vfmat.ch/589e

Bệnh Viện Hữu Nghị Việt Tiệp
Thượng Lý, Haiphong, Vietnam
⊕ https://vfmat.ch/269b

Bệnh Viện K
Hoan Kiem, Hanoi, Vietnam
⊕ https://vfmat.ch/181b

Bệnh Viện K120
Bình Tạo, Tiền Giang, Vietnam
⊕ https://vfmat.ch/93cf

Bệnh viện Lao phổi Hải Dương
Thanh Cương, Hải Dương, Vietnam
⊕ https://vfmat.ch/1781

Bệnh Viện Lao Phổi Thành Phố Buôn Ma Thuộc
Khối Năm, Đắk Lắk, Vietnam
⊕ https://vfmat.ch/faff

Bệnh viện Lão khoa Trung Ương (Central Geriatric Hospital)
Trung Phụng, Hanoi, Vietnam
⊕ https://vfmat.ch/cd95

Bệnh viện Mắt Hà Nội
Xóm Trong, Hanoi, Vietnam
⊕ https://vfmat.ch/c813

Bệnh Viện Mắt Phú Yên
Ninh Tịnh, Phú Yên, Vietnam
⊕ https://vfmat.ch/a94e

Bệnh viện mắt Sài Gòn
Xóm Chiếu, Ho Chi Minh, Vietnam
⊕ https://vfmat.ch/2c78

Bệnh Viện Mắt Thái Nguyên
Cầu The, Thái Nguyên, Vietnam
⊕ https://vfmat.ch/d42f

Bệnh Viện Mới Huyện Cần Giờ
Cần Giờ, Thành phố Ho Chi Minh, Vietnam
⊕ https://vfmat.ch/6f1b

Bệnh Viện Mỹ Đức
Ấp Nhì, Ho Chi Minh, Vietnam
⊕ https://vfmat.ch/4bfe

Bệnh viện Ngọc Phú
Xóm Chuối, Ho Chi Minh, Vietnam
⊕ https://vfmat.ch/9897

Bệnh Viện Nhi Trung Ương
Nhà ở, Hà Tây, Vietnam
⊕ https://vfmat.ch/9ec9

Bệnh Viện Nhi Tỉnh Nam Định
Nang Tinh, Nam Định, Vietnam
⊕ https://vfmat.ch/1738

Bệnh viện Nhi đồng Thành phố
Mỹ Phú, Ho Chi Minh, Vietnam
⊕ https://vfmat.ch/d444

Bệnh viện Nhi đồng TP Cần Thơ
Lợi Dũ B, Can Tho, Vietnam
⊕ https://vfmat.ch/46cf

Bệnh viện Nhiệt Đới
Xóm Ông Đội, Ho Chi Minh, Vietnam
⊕ https://vfmat.ch/8653

Bệnh Viện Nhân dân Gia Định
Cầu Bông, Ho Chi Minh, Vietnam
⊕ https://vfmat.ch/a165

Bệnh Viện Nhật Tân
Châu Long 4, An Giang, Vietnam
⊕ https://vfmat.ch/16b5

Bệnh viện Phan Thiết
Ấp Tân An, Bình Thuận, Vietnam
⊕ https://vfmat.ch/7885

Bệnh Viện Phù Cát
An Hành, Bình Định, Vietnam
⊕ https://vfmat.ch/34fc

Bệnh Viện Phạm Ngọc Thạch
Chợ Rẫy, Ho Chi Minh, Vietnam
⊕ https://vfmat.ch/9a3a

Bệnh Viện Phổ Yên
Cốt Ngạnh, Thái Nguyên, Vietnam
⊕ https://vfmat.ch/bfa6

Bệnh Viện Phổi Phạm Hữu Chí
Xã An Nhứt, Bà Rịa-Vũng Tàu, Vietnam
⊕ https://vfmat.ch/d199

Bệnh Viện Phụ Sản – Nhi Tỉnh Quảng Nam
Phường Hòa, Quảng Nam, Vietnam
⊕ https://vfmat.ch/592c

Bệnh Viện Phụ Sản Quốc Tế Phương Châu
Thới Nhựt, Can Tho, Vietnam
⊕ https://vfmat.ch/a56f

Bệnh Viện Phụ Sản Tiền Giang
Tân Thuận, Tiền Giang, Vietnam
⊕ https://vfmat.ch/76ba

Bệnh Viện Phụ Sản Tp Cần Thơ
Thới Nhật, Can Tho, Vietnam
⊕ https://vfmat.ch/dff3

Bệnh Viện Phụ Sản Trung ương
Xóm Pho, Hanoi, Vietnam
⊕ https://vfmat.ch/d972

Bệnh Viện Phụ Sản Vuông Tròn
Thành phố Long Xuyên, An Giang, Vietnam
⊕ https://vfmat.ch/5db7

Bệnh Viện Phụ Sản Âu Cơ
Hố Nai, Đồng Nai, Vietnam
⊕ https://vfmat.ch/b8ea

Bệnh Viện Phục Hồi Chức Năng
Tân Lập, Lào Cai, Vietnam
⊕ https://vfmat.ch/956b

Bệnh Viện Quân Dân Y 16
Đôn Luân, Bình Phước, Vietnam
⊕ https://vfmat.ch/fb3a

Bệnh Viện Quân Dân Y Tỉnh Sóc Trăng
Châu Thành, Sóc Trăng, Vietnam
⊕ https://vfmat.ch/3461

Bệnh Viện Quân Dân Ya
District 9, Hồ Chí Minh, Vietnam
⊕ https://vfmat.ch/b95f

Bệnh Viện Quân Y 103
Hà Đông, Hanoi, Vietnam
⊕ https://vfmat.ch/eb5b

Bệnh Viện Quân Y 211
Plei Kếp, Gia Lai, Vietnam
⊕ https://vfmat.ch/a1e9

Bệnh Viện Quận 1
Cầu Bông, Ho Chi Minh, Vietnam
⊕ https://vfmat.ch/7357

Bệnh viện Quận 10
Chí Hòa, Ho Chi Minh, Vietnam
⊕ https://vfmat.ch/f2ce

Bệnh Viện Quận 5
Thành phố, Hồ Chí Minh, Vietnam
⊕ https://vfmat.ch/17d6

Bệnh viện quận 9
Tăng Nhơn Phú, Ho Chi Minh, Vietnam
⊕ https://vfmat.ch/bd1b

Bệnh viện Quận Gò Vấp
Xóm Nhà Thờ, Ho Chi Minh, Vietnam
⊕ https://vfmat.ch/a625

Bệnh viện quận Phú Nhuận
Chí Hòa, Ho Chi Minh, Vietnam
⊕ https://vfmat.ch/4eec

Bệnh viện Quận Tân Phú
Phú Trung, Ho Chi Minh, Vietnam
⊕ https://vfmat.ch/8aab

Bệnh viện Quốc tế Hạ Long
Cây Quéo, Quảng Ninh, Vietnam
⊕ https://vfmat.ch/bb55

Bệnh Viện Quốc tế Hạnh Phúc
Bình Phước, Ho Chi Minh, Vietnam
⊕ https://vfmat.ch/255b

Bệnh Viện Quốc Tế Trung Ương Huế
Thôn Kim Long, Thừa Thiên-Huế, Vietnam
⊕ https://vfmat.ch/bb66

Bệnh Viện Quốc Tế Vinmec
Ấp Ba, Da Nang, Vietnam
⊕ https://vfmat.ch/c9db

Bệnh Viện Quốc tế Đồng Nai
Đức Tu, Đồng Nai, Vietnam
⊕ https://vfmat.ch/88b6

Bệnh Viện Sơn Tây
Thiều Xuân, Ha Tay, Vietnam
⊕ https://vfmat.ch/38d3

Bệnh Viện Sản Nhi
Ấp Chánh, Cà Mau, Vietnam
⊕ https://vfmat.ch/e911

Bệnh Viện Sản Nhi Hậu Giang (mới)
Ấp Nàng Chăng, Hậu Giang, Vietnam
⊕ https://vfmat.ch/5fd4

Bệnh Viện Sản Nhi Sóc Trăng
Nhâm Lăng, Sóc Trăng, Vietnam
⊕ https://vfmat.ch/2ca8

Bệnh viện Tai – Mũi – Họng Trung Ương
Trung Phụng, Hanoi, Vietnam
⊕ https://vfmat.ch/dc5b

Bệnh Viện Tai – Mũi-Họng TP. Cần Thơ
Thới Nhật, Can Tho, Vietnam
⊕ https://vfmat.ch/ebe2

Bệnh Viện Thanh Khê
Thanh Khê, Da Nang, Vietnam
⊕ https://vfmat.ch/ce23

Bệnh Viện Thành Phố BMT
Khối Một, Đắk Lắk, Vietnam
⊕ https://vfmat.ch/6713

Bệnh Viện Thượng Lý
Thượng Lý, Haiphong, Vietnam
⊕ https://vfmat.ch/faeb

Bệnh Viện Thị xã La Gi
Tân Tạo, Bình Thuận, Vietnam
⊕ https://vfmat.ch/9766

Bệnh Viện Thốt Nốt
Tràng Thọ Hai, Can Tho, Vietnam
⊕ https://vfmat.ch/2ea9

Bệnh Viện Tim Mạch An Giang
Bình Long Hai, An Giang, Vietnam
⊕ https://vfmat.ch/c44f

Bệnh Viện Tim Tâm Đức
Tân Thuận, Ho Chi Minh, Vietnam
⊕ https://vfmat.ch/dbcd

Bệnh viện Tiên Yên
Khê Tư, Quảng Ninh, Vietnam
⊕ https://vfmat.ch/71cd

Bệnh Viện TP Long Xuyên
Khóm Bốn, An Giang, Vietnam
⊕ https://vfmat.ch/b7cb

Bệnh viện Trung ương Huế
Thôn Kim Long, Thừa Thiên-Huế, Vietnam
⊕ https://vfmat.ch/b6dd

Bệnh Viện Truyền Máu Huyết Học
Chợ Rẫy, Ho Chi Minh, Vietnam
⊕ https://vfmat.ch/2a9f

Bệnh Viện Trường Đại học Tây Nguyên
Thành phố Buôn Ma Thuột, Đắk Lắk, Vietnam
⊕ https://vfmat.ch/8a39

Bệnh Viện Tâm Hồng Phước
Ấp Thành, Đồng Nai, Vietnam
⊕ https://vfmat.ch/c32f

Bệnh viện Tâm Thần Bà Rịa
Ấp Sáu, Bà Rịa-Vũng Tàu, Vietnam
⊕ https://vfmat.ch/698f

Bệnh Viện Tâm Thần HN
Tram Thon, Hanoi, Vietnam
⊕ https://vfmat.ch/8e23

Bệnh viện Tâm thần Long An
Ấp Nhơn Hòa, Long An, Vietnam
⊕ https://vfmat.ch/65cd

Bệnh Viện Tâm Thần tp. Cần thơ
Lợi Nguyên B, Can Tho, Vietnam
⊕ https://vfmat.ch/67a4

Bệnh viện Tâm thần Tỉnh Bà Rịa – Vũng Tàu
La Sơn, Bà Rịa-Vũng Tàu, Vietnam
🌐 https://vfmat.ch/d218

Bệnh Viện Tâm Thần Tỉnh Đắk Lắk
Khối Năm, Đắk Lắk, Vietnam
🌐 https://vfmat.ch/7ac3

Bệnh Viện Tâm Thần Đông Khê
Đông Khê, Haiphong, Vietnam
🌐 https://vfmat.ch/7cc7

Bệnh Viện Tân Trụ
Tân Trụ, Long An, Vietnam
🌐 https://vfmat.ch/59c3

Bệnh Viện Từ Dũ
Xóm Chiếu, Ho Chi Minh, Vietnam
🌐 https://vfmat.ch/4d78

Bệnh viện Ung Bướu cơ sở 2
Long Hữu, Ho Chi Minh, Vietnam
🌐 https://vfmat.ch/e15d

Bệnh Viện Ung bướu Hà Nội
Xóm Trong, Hanoi, Vietnam
🌐 https://vfmat.ch/db4f

Bệnh Viện Ung Bứu Thành Phố Cần Thơ Cơ Sở 2
Ấp An Mỹ, Long An, Vietnam
🌐 https://vfmat.ch/577b

Bệnh Viện Việt Đức
Xóm Pho, Hanoi, Vietnam
🌐 https://vfmat.ch/54ef

Bệnh viện Văn Giang
Lai Ốc, Hưng Yên, Vietnam
🌐 https://vfmat.ch/2de5

Bệnh viện Vạn Hạnh
Chí Hòa, Ho Chi Minh, Vietnam
🌐 https://vfmat.ch/856a

Bệnh viện Vạn Phúc 2 (Van Phuc 2 General Hospital)
Bình Phước Khu Bốn, Bình Dương, Vietnam
🌐 https://vfmat.ch/9642

Bệnh viện Xóm Củi
Chợ Rẫy, Ho Chi Minh, Vietnam
🌐 https://vfmat.ch/7c1d

Bệnh Viện Y Cổ Truyền
Xã Tân Phát, Lâm Đồng, Vietnam
🌐 https://vfmat.ch/6e4c

Bệnh Viện Y Học Cổ Truyền Bộ Công An
Trung Văn, Hanoi, Vietnam
🌐 https://vfmat.ch/7486

Bệnh Viện Y Học Cổ Truyền Cần Thơ
Lợi Nguyên B, Can Tho, Vietnam
🌐 https://vfmat.ch/16e3

Bệnh Viện Y Học Cổ Truyền Khối Bốn
Khối Bốn, Đắk Lắk, Vietnam
🌐 https://vfmat.ch/3ff1

Bệnh Viện Y Học Cổ Truyền Thành Phố
Thành phố, Ho Chi Minh, Vietnam
🌐 https://vfmat.ch/49e3

Bệnh Viện Y Học Cổ Truyền Trung Ương
Xóm Trong, Hanoi, Vietnam
🌐 https://vfmat.ch/b79e

Bệnh viện Y dược cổ truyền và phục hồi chức năng
Dữu Lâu, Phú Thọ, Vietnam
🌐 https://vfmat.ch/cc44

Bệnh Viện Đa Khoa Bù Đốp
Bù Đốp, Bình Phước, Vietnam
🌐 https://vfmat.ch/7296

Bệnh Viện Đa Khoa Bồng Sơn
Khối Một, Bình Định, Vietnam
🌐 https://vfmat.ch/37c3

Bệnh Viện Đa khoa Châu Thành
Châu Thành, Kiến Giang, Vietnam
🌐 https://vfmat.ch/7ed1

Bệnh viện Đa Khoa Cái Răng
Ấp Yên Thượng, Can Tho, Vietnam
🌐 https://vfmat.ch/23de

Bệnh Viện đa Khoa Gia Phước
Thới Nhật, Can Tho, Vietnam
🌐 https://vfmat.ch/12eb

Bệnh Viện đa Khoa H.Châu Thành
Hòa Phú Một, An Giang, Vietnam
🌐 https://vfmat.ch/fa51

Bệnh Viện Đa khoa Hoàn Hảo Medic Cần Thơ
Thới Nhật, Can Tho, Vietnam
🌐 https://vfmat.ch/e73a

Bệnh Viện Đa Khoa Hoàn Mỹ Đà Lạt
Ấp Đa Lợi, Lâm Đồng, Vietnam
🌐 https://vfmat.ch/48d6

Bệnh Viện Đa Khoa Huyện Ba Tri
Ấp Vĩnh An, Bến Tre, Vietnam
🌐 https://vfmat.ch/1fca

Bệnh Viện Đa Khoa Huyện Cẩm Mỹ
Ấp Suối Cả, Đồng Nai, Vietnam
🌐 https://vfmat.ch/d555

Bệnh Viện Đa Khoa Huyện Hương Sơn
Hương Sơn, Hà Tĩnh, Vietnam
🌐 https://vfmat.ch/6a38

Bệnh viện Đa khoa huyện Mỹ Lộc
Vạn Đồn, Nam Định, Vietnam
🌐 https://vfmat.ch/e451

Bệnh Viện Đa Khoa Huyện Nhơn Trạch
Xóm Bàu Cá, Đồng Nai, Vietnam
🌐 https://vfmat.ch/99df

Bệnh Viện Đa Khoa Huyện Phù Cát
An Hành, Bình Định, Vietnam
🌐 https://vfmat.ch/c559

Bệnh Viện Đa Khoa Huyện Vĩnh Thạnh
Ấp Qui, Can Tho, Vietnam
🌐 https://vfmat.ch/29c6

Bệnh viện Đa khoa Huyện Đồng Văn
Làng Xao Vang, Hà Giang, Vietnam
🌐 https://vfmat.ch/885f

Bệnh Viện Đa Khoa Hưng Thịnh
Chính Cường, Lào Cai, Vietnam
🌐 https://vfmat.ch/aae9

Bệnh Viện Đa Khoa Hồng Phát
Hai Bà Trưng, Hà Nội, Vietnam
🌐 https://vfmat.ch/a463

Bệnh Viện Đa Khoa Hội An
Hoi An, Quảng Nam, Vietnam
🌐 https://vfmat.ch/e46a

Bệnh Viện Đa Khoa II Lâm Đồng
Ấp Thiện Lập, Lâm Đồng, Vietnam
🌐 https://vfmat.ch/29fe

Bệnh Viện Đa Khoa Khu Vực Quảng Nam
Điện Bàn, Quảng Nam, Vietnam
🌐 https://vfmat.ch/7863

Bệnh Viện Đa khoa Khu Vực Yên Minh
Yen Minh, Hà Giang, Vietnam
🌐 https://vfmat.ch/ed86

Bệnh Viện Đa Khoa Kiên Giang
Rach Gia, Kiến Giang, Vietnam
🌐 https://vfmat.ch/5472

Bệnh viện Đa khoa Lai Châu
Pan Linh, Lai Châu, Vietnam
🌐 https://vfmat.ch/1d17

Bệnh viện Đa khoa Long An
Ấp Nhơn Hòa, Long An, Vietnam
🌐 https://vfmat.ch/2c6b

Bệnh Viện Đa Khoa Long An – Khoa Nội A1
Ấp Bình Phú, Long An, Vietnam
⊕ https://vfmat.ch/f19c

Bệnh Viện Đa Khoa Long Thành
Khu Mười Hai, Đồng Nai, Vietnam
⊕ https://vfmat.ch/c882

Bệnh Viện Đa Khoa Lâm Đồng
Thành phố Đà Lạt, Lâm Đồng, Vietnam
⊕ https://vfmat.ch/f6d8

Bệnh Viện đa Khoa Lê Chân II
Trang Quan, Haiphong, Vietnam
⊕ https://vfmat.ch/3d9e

Bệnh Viện Đa khoa Lạng Sơn
Kỳ Lừa, Lạng Sơn, Vietnam
⊕ https://vfmat.ch/bb7d

Bệnh Viện Đa Khoa Lệ Thủy
Xuân Lai, Quảng Bình, Vietnam
⊕ https://vfmat.ch/d6c1

Bệnh viện Đa khoa Móng Cái
Chuc Tchia, Quảng Ninh, Vietnam
⊕ https://vfmat.ch/e921

Bệnh Viện Đa Khoa Ngũ Hành Sơn
Ngũ Hành Sơn, Đà Nẵng, Vietnam
⊕ https://vfmat.ch/61ca

Bệnh Viện Đa khoa Phù Mỹ
Trà Quang, Bình Định, Vietnam
⊕ https://vfmat.ch/23cc

Bệnh Viện Đa khoa Phú Giáo
Phuoc Vinh, Bình Dương, Vietnam
⊕ https://vfmat.ch/e18f

Bệnh Viện Đa Khoa Phương Đông
Cao Đình, Hanoi, Vietnam
⊕ https://vfmat.ch/36ec

Bệnh Viện Đa Khoa Quận Hải An
Hải An, Haiphong, Vietnam
⊕ https://vfmat.ch/5588

Bệnh Viện Đa khoa Quận Hải Châu
Cô Mân, Da Nang, Vietnam
⊕ https://vfmat.ch/f951

Bệnh Viện Đa Khoa Quốc tế Thu Cúc
Thụy Khuê, Hanoi, Vietnam
⊕ https://vfmat.ch/2fad

Bệnh Viện Đa khoa Thiện Hạnh
Khối Sáu, Đắk Lắk, Vietnam
⊕ https://vfmat.ch/9776

Bệnh Viện Đa Khoa Thành An – Thăng Long
Hòa Đình, Bắc Ninh, Vietnam
⊕ https://vfmat.ch/b9ec

Bệnh Viện Đa Khoa Thành Phố Pleiku
Plei Jut, Gia Lai, Vietnam
⊕ https://vfmat.ch/db84

Bệnh Viện đa Khoa Thành Phố Thanh Hoá
Tinh Xa, Thanh Hóa, Vietnam
⊕ https://vfmat.ch/9ca8

Bệnh Viện Đa Khoa Thăng Long
Giáp Nh, Hanoi, Vietnam
⊕ https://vfmat.ch/9259

Bệnh Viện Đa Khoa Thị Xã Bình Long
Bình Long, Bình Phước, Vietnam
⊕ https://vfmat.ch/a993

Bệnh Viện Đa Khoa Thị Xã Mường Lay
Mường Lay, Điện Biên, Vietnam
⊕ https://vfmat.ch/6724

Bệnh viện đa khoa Thị xã Sa Đéc
Tân Hưng, Đồng Tháp, Vietnam
⊕ https://vfmat.ch/3ae3

Bệnh Viện Đa khoa Thị xã Thuận An
Ấp Bình Thạnh, Binh Dinh, Vietnam
⊕ https://vfmat.ch/bf17

Bệnh Viện Đa Khoa Thị Xã Từ Sơn
Cẩm Giang, Bắc Ninh, Vietnam
⊕ https://vfmat.ch/da6e

Bệnh Viện Đa khoa Thủ Thừa
Ấp Đạo, Long An, Vietnam
⊕ https://vfmat.ch/89d7

Bệnh Viện Đa Khoa Tinh Sóc Trăng
Nhâm Lăng, Sóc Trăng, Vietnam
⊕ https://vfmat.ch/5417

Bệnh Viện Đa Khoa Tiền Giang
Tân Thuận, Tiền Giang, Vietnam
⊕ https://vfmat.ch/2797

Bệnh Viện đa Khoa TP. Cần Thơ
Ấp An Mỹ, Long An, Vietnam
⊕ https://vfmat.ch/8fcf

Bệnh viện đa khoa Tri Tôn
Sốc Chi Ca Eng, An Giang, Vietnam
⊕ https://vfmat.ch/35c7

Bệnh Viện Đa Khoa Trung Tâm An Giang
Bình Long Ba, An Giang, Vietnam
⊕ https://vfmat.ch/dfbd

Bệnh viện Đa khoa Trung Ương Thái Nguyên
Go La, Thái Nguyên, Vietnam
⊕ https://vfmat.ch/e8c5

Bệnh Viện Đa Khoa Tâm Anh
Xóm Ngoai, Hanoi, Vietnam
⊕ https://vfmat.ch/3296

Bệnh viện Đa khoa Tâm Trí Đà Nẵng
Tuyên Hóa, Da Nang, Vietnam
⊕ https://vfmat.ch/38e5

Bệnh Viện Đa Khoa Tân Thạnh
Xóm Thang, Long An, Vietnam
⊕ https://vfmat.ch/b48d

Bệnh Viện Đa Khoa Tây Ninh
Ấp Bình Trung, Tây Ninh Province, Vietnam
⊕ https://vfmat.ch/8896

Bệnh Viện Đa Khoa Tư Nhân Mỹ Phước
Mỹ Phước, Gia Lai, Vietnam
⊕ https://vfmat.ch/a5aa

Bệnh viện đa khoa tỉnh Bình Dương
Khu Phố Năm, Bình Dương, Vietnam
⊕ https://vfmat.ch/9481

Bệnh Viện Đa Khoa Tỉnh Bình Phước
Ấp Một, Bình Phước, Vietnam
⊕ https://vfmat.ch/3bd1

Bệnh Viện Đa khoa Tỉnh Bình Định
Tay Phuong, Bình Định, Vietnam
⊕ https://vfmat.ch/7b83

Bệnh Viện đa Khoa Tỉnh Hòa Bình
Tiến sơn, Vietnam
⊕ https://vfmat.ch/78e3

Bệnh Viện Đa Khoa Tỉnh Khánh Hòa
Thôn Điền Hạ, Khánh Hòa, Vietnam
⊕ https://vfmat.ch/fb6d

Bệnh viện Đa khoa tỉnh Kon Tum
Xã Phường Quy, Kon Tum, Vietnam
⊕ https://vfmat.ch/e181

Bệnh Viện Đa Khoa Tỉnh Lào Cai
Làng Giàng, Lào Cai, Vietnam
⊕ https://vfmat.ch/5e1c

Bệnh Viện Đa Khoa Tỉnh Ninh Bình
Kỳ Vĩ, Ninh Bình, Vietnam
⊕ https://vfmat.ch/cc72

Bệnh viện Đa khoa tỉnh Quảng Ninh
Cột La, Quảng Ninh, Vietnam
⊕ https://vfmat.ch/e22e

Bệnh Viện Đa Khoa tỉnh Quảng Trị
Đại Độ, Quảng Trị, Vietnam
⊕ https://vfmat.ch/e316

Bệnh Viện Đa Khoa Vinmec Hạ Long
Vạ Chai, Quảng Ninh, Vietnam
⊕ https://vfmat.ch/3bcc

Bệnh Viện Đa Khoa Vùng Tây Nguyên
Khối Bảy, Đắk Lắk, Vietnam
⊕ https://vfmat.ch/2782

Bệnh Viện Đa khoa Vĩnh Long
Phước Ngươn A, Vĩnh Long, Vietnam
⊕ https://vfmat.ch/6c57

Bệnh viện Đa khoa Vĩnh Phúc
Xóm Tram, Vĩnh Phúc, Vietnam
⊕ https://vfmat.ch/3b39

Bệnh Viện Đa Khoa Vạn Hạnh
Chí Hòa, Ho Chi Minh, Vietnam
⊕ https://vfmat.ch/97bf

Bệnh Viện Đa khoa Xanh Pôn
Hữu Tiệp, Hanoi, Vietnam
⊕ https://vfmat.ch/5ae1

Bệnh Viện Đa Khoa Y Học Cổ Truyền
Mai Dich, Hanoi, Vietnam
⊕ https://vfmat.ch/9429

Bệnh Viện đa Khoa Yên Bình
Thị Trấn Ba Hàng, Thái Nguyên, Vietnam
⊕ https://vfmat.ch/be5b

Bệnh Viện Đa khoa Đại An
Trà Sơn Thượng, Thanh Hóa, Vietnam
⊕ https://vfmat.ch/cb88

Bệnh Viện Đa Khoa Đồng Nai
Đức Tu, Đồng Nai, Vietnam
⊕ https://vfmat.ch/cdb8

Bệnh Viện Đa Khoa Đồng Phú
Đồng Phú, Bình Phước, Vietnam
⊕ https://vfmat.ch/b171

Bệnh Viện Điều Dưỡng
Tân Chánh, Ho Chi Minh, Vietnam
⊕ https://vfmat.ch/15b6

Bệnh viện ĐK Phố Nối
Phú Đa, Hưng Yên, Vietnam
⊕ https://vfmat.ch/f541

Bệnh Viện ĐK Đôn Lương
Hòa Hy, Haiphong, Vietnam
⊕ https://vfmat.ch/2f4f

Bệnh Viện Đông Y Hà Tĩnh
Vân Hòa, Hà Tĩnh, Vietnam
⊕ https://vfmat.ch/3e25

Bệnh Viện Đông Đô
Làng Mie, Hanoi, Vietnam
⊕ https://vfmat.ch/9561

Bệnh viện Đại học Quốc gia Hà Nội
Kim Lũ, Hanoi, Vietnam
⊕ https://vfmat.ch/f4e1

Bệnh Viện Đại Học Y Dược (Cơ sở 2)
Chợ Rẫy, Ho Chi Minh, Vietnam
⊕ https://vfmat.ch/79d3

Bệnh Viện Đại Học Y Dược Shingmark Đồng Nai
Long Bình, Binh Thuan, Vietnam
⊕ https://vfmat.ch/a718

Bệnh Viện Đại Học Y Dược TP. Hồ Chí Minh
Thành phố Hồ Chí Minh, Vietnam
⊕ https://vfmat.ch/448f

Bệnh viện Đống Đa
Làng Mie, Hanoi, Vietnam
⊕ https://vfmat.ch/6467

C17 Military Hospital
Hai Chau, Da Nang, Vietnam
⊕ https://vfmat.ch/394c

Cai Khe Ward Medical Station
Ninh Kieu, Can Tho, Vietnam
⊕ https://vfmat.ch/e2b8

Cam Pha General Hospital
Cam Thanh, Cam Pha, Vietnam
⊕ https://vfmat.ch/5ff4

Can Tho Central General Hospital
An Khanh Ward, Ninh Kieu, Vietnam
⊕ https://vfmat.ch/5a43

Can Tho City Cancer Hospital
Ấp An Mỹ, Long An, Vietnam
⊕ https://vfmat.ch/c2f8

Can Tho Dermatology Hospital
Lợi Nguyên B, Can Tho, Vietnam
⊕ https://vfmat.ch/6551

Center for Preventive Medicine in District 6
District 6, City, Ho Chi Minh, Vietnam
⊕ https://vfmat.ch/4a8d

Central Acupuncture Hospital
Xóm Tren, Hanoi, Vietnam
⊕ https://vfmat.ch/ec39

Central Hospital of Traditional Medicine, The
Ấp Vĩnh Lạc, Kiến Giang, Vietnam
⊕ https://vfmat.ch/3358

Central Lung Hospital (Bệnh viện Phổi Trung ương)
Thụy Khuê, Hanoi, Vietnam
⊕ https://vfmat.ch/af6c

Central Mental Hospital 2
Bien Hoa City, Đồng Nai, Vietnam
⊕ https://vfmat.ch/5c59

Chau Thanh District Hospital
Chau Thanh District, Dong Thap, Vietnam
⊕ https://vfmat.ch/ba9f

Children's Hospital 1
District 10, Ho Chi Minh, Vietnam
⊕ https://vfmat.ch/ec13

Children's Hospital 2
Thành phố, Ho Chi Minh, Vietnam
⊕ https://vfmat.ch/61fe

Children's Maternity Hospital
Thu Dau Mot, Binh Dinh, Vietnam
⊕ https://vfmat.ch/11b8

Cho Ray Hospital
District 5, City, Hồ Chí Minh, Vietnam
⊕ https://vfmat.ch/9efa

City Children's Hospital
Bình Chánh, Ho Chi Minh City, Vietnam
⊕ https://vfmat.ch/ej9t

City Heart Institute
District 10, Ho Chi Minh, Vietnam
⊕ https://vfmat.ch/e7ac

City Hospital Chau Doc
Châu Long 4, An Giang, Vietnam
⊕ https://vfmat.ch/385a

City International Hospital
Mỹ Trung, Ho Chi Minh, Vietnam
⊕ https://vfmat.ch/131e

City Medical Center Vung Tau
Ba Ria City, Bà Rịa-Vũng Tàu, Vietnam
⊕ https://vfmat.ch/ade8

Columbia Asia
Cầu Bông, Ho Chi Minh, Vietnam
⊕ https://vfmat.ch/6a27

Columbia Asia Hospital
Búng, Binh Dinh, Vietnam
⊕ https://vfmat.ch/bebe

Columbia Asia Saigon
Xóm Chiếu, Ho Chi Minh, Vietnam
⊕ https://vfmat.ch/b88b

Cu Ba Dông Hôi
Động Hỏi, Quảng Bình, Vietnam
⊕ https://vfmat.ch/abc5

Căng Tin Bệnh Viện
Hoang Xa, Hanoi, Vietnam
⊕ https://vfmat.ch/3eff

Cổng Bảo vệ Hướng Hẻm 10/6 Trần Đại Nghĩa
Bình Kỳ, Quang Nam-Da Nang, Vietnam
⊕ https://vfmat.ch/47b6

Cổng Bảo vệ Hướng Nam Kỳ Khởi Nghĩa
Bình Kỳ, Quang Nam-Da Nang, Vietnam
⊕ https://vfmat.ch/fe53

Cục Hậu Cần Quân Khu 3 – Bệnh Viện 5
Kỳ Vĩ, Ninh Bình, Vietnam
⊕ https://vfmat.ch/5f52

Da Nang Eye Hospital
Hai Chau, Da Nang, Vietnam
⊕ https://vfmat.ch/da45

Da Nang General Hospital
Da Nang City, Da Nang, Vietnam
⊕ https://vfmat.ch/f3ce

Da Nang Hospital C
Hai Chau District, Da Nang, Vietnam
⊕ https://vfmat.ch/e494

Da Nang Hospital for Women and Children
Ngu Hanh Son, Da Nang, Vietnam
⊕ https://vfmat.ch/dcab

Danang Traditional Medicine Hospital, The
Hai Chau, Da Nang, Vietnam
⊕ https://vfmat.ch/86fe

Dak Glong General Hospital
Thôn Hai, Đắk Nông, Vietnam
⊕ https://vfmat.ch/fcc8

Dak Nong Provincial General Hospital
Gia Nghia, Đắk Nông, Vietnam
⊕ https://vfmat.ch/ff1a

Dak R'Lap District General Hospital
Dak R'Lap, Đắk Nông, Vietnam
⊕ https://vfmat.ch/7dd1

Dat Do District Medical Center
Ba Ria city, Bà Rịa-Vũng Tàu, Vietnam
⊕ https://vfmat.ch/48b7

Dau Giay General Hospital
Thong Nhat, Đồng Nai, Vietnam
⊕ https://vfmat.ch/fc15

District 12 Hospital
District 12, City, Ho Chi Minh, Vietnam
⊕ https://vfmat.ch/dbe1

District 2 Hospital
District 2, Ho Chi Minh, Vietnam
⊕ https://vfmat.ch/8165

District 6 Hospital
District 6, Ho Chi Minh, Vietnam
⊕ https://vfmat.ch/26b1

District 8 Preventive Medicine Center
Chợ Rẫy, Ho Chi Minh, Vietnam
⊕ https://vfmat.ch/3f3e

District 9 Preventive Medicine Center
Tang Nhon Phu B, District 9, Ho Chi Minh, Vietnam
⊕ https://vfmat.ch/6e7a

Dong Hy District General Hospital
Dong Hy, Thai Nguyen, Vietnam
⊕ https://vfmat.ch/9c7d

Dong Hy District Health Center
Tam Tài, Thái Nguyên, Vietnam
⊕ https://vfmat.ch/da41

Dong Nai Children's Hospital
Quarter 5 City, Đồng Nai, Vietnam
⊕ https://vfmat.ch/18bb

Dong Quang Commune Health Station
Quoc Oai, Bình Định, Vietnam
⊕ https://vfmat.ch/b7c3

Dong Thap Military Hospital
Cao Lanh City, Đồng Tháp, Vietnam
⊕ https://vfmat.ch/5768

Dong Thap Rehabilitation Hospital
Lanh, Dong, Đồng Tháp, Vietnam
⊕ https://vfmat.ch/3138

Duong Hoa Medical Station
Kien Luong, Kiến Giang, Vietnam
⊕ https://vfmat.ch/fa3a

Duyen Hai General Hospital
Duyen Hai Town, Trà Vinh, Vietnam
⊕ https://vfmat.ch/f118

Endocrine Central Hospital
Giáp Nh, Hanoi, Vietnam
⊕ https://vfmat.ch/c134

Eurasian Aesthetic Hospital
District 1, City, Ho Chi Minh, Vietnam
⊕ https://vfmat.ch/ca39

Eye Hospital of Ho Chi Minh City
District 3, Ho Chi Minh, Vietnam
⊕ https://vfmat.ch/fe18

France-Vietnam Hospital
Ho Chi Minh City, Vietnam
⊕ https://vfmat.ch/3a45

FV Hospital
Tân Thuận, Ho Chi Minh, Vietnam
⊕ https://vfmat.ch/f359

General Hospital in Binh Thuan Province
Phan Thiet City, Bình Thuận, Vietnam
⊕ https://vfmat.ch/de23

General Hospital of Hau Nghia
Duc Hoa, Long An, Vietnam
⊕ https://vfmat.ch/743a

Gia Lam Hospital
Gia Lam, Hanoi, Vietnam
⊕ https://vfmat.ch/5dd9

Ha Dong General Hospital
Ha Dong District, Hanoi, Vietnam
⊕ https://vfmat.ch/5796

Ha Tinh City Hospital
Tổ Chín, Hà Tĩnh, Vietnam
⊕ https://vfmat.ch/3888

Ha Tinh Eye Hospital
Ha Tinh City, Hà Tĩnh, Vietnam
⊕ https://vfmat.ch/82bf

Ha Tinh General Hospital
Ha Tinh City, Hà Tĩnh, Vietnam
⊕ https://vfmat.ch/2b6f

Hai Duong City General Hospital
Thanh Cương, Hải Dương, Vietnam
⊕ https://vfmat.ch/b411

Hai Phong International Hospital
Cựu Đôi, Haiphong, Vietnam
⊕ https://vfmat.ch/27cd

Hai Thanh Ward Medical Station
Dương Kinh, Haiphong, Vietnam
⊕ https://vfmat.ch/f162

Hanh Phuc An Giang General Hospital
Long Xuyen City, An Giang, Vietnam
⊕ https://vfmat.ch/864a

Hanoi Central Odonto-Stomatology Hospital
Hoan Kiem, Hanoi, Vietnam
⊕ https://vfmat.ch/36cf

Hanoi Heart Hospital
Hoan Kiem District, Hanoi, Vietnam
⊕ https://vfmat.ch/54c2

Hanoi Lung Hospital
Ba Trung, Hanoi, Vietnam
🌐 https://vfmat.ch/b21d

Hanoi Maternity Hospital
Đống Đa, Hanoi, Vietnam
🌐 https://vfmat.ch/ded4

Heart and Virtue Hospital
Tân Thuận, Ho Chi Minh, Vietnam
🌐 https://vfmat.ch/a62a

Heart Hospitals of An Giang
Long Xuyên, An Giang, Vietnam
🌐 https://vfmat.ch/b748

Hieu Phung Commune Medical Station
Hieu Phung, Vung Liem, Vietnam
🌐 https://vfmat.ch/1ea8

Highland Hospital
Buon Ma Thuot, Đắk Lắk, Vietnam
🌐 https://vfmat.ch/2914

Ho Chi Minh City Oncology Hospital
Binh Thanh District, City, Ho Chi Minh, Vietnam
🌐 https://vfmat.ch/29bf

Ho Chi Minh City Police Hospital
District 5, Ho Chi Minh City, Vietnam
🌐 https://vfmat.ch/d8b8

Hoan My Saigon Hospital
Phu Nhuan, Ho Chi Minh, Vietnam
🌐 https://vfmat.ch/93b5

Hong Duc Hospital
District 12, City, Ho Chi Minh, Vietnam
🌐 https://vfmat.ch/f6e5

Hong Ha General Hospital
Dong Da, Hanoi, Vietnam
🌐 https://vfmat.ch/83b3

Hong Ngoc General Hospital
Hanoi, Vietnam
🌐 https://vfmat.ch/ah4h

Hong Ngu District General Hospital
Hồng Ngự, Đồng Tháp, Vietnam
🌐 https://vfmat.ch/aeaf

Hop Luc General Hospital
Đông Tac, Thanh Hóa, Vietnam
🌐 https://vfmat.ch/8b89

Hospital 199
Son Tra, Da Nang, Vietnam
🌐 https://vfmat.ch/2ab9

Hospital 22-12
Tan Lap, Nha Trang City, Khánh Hòa, Vietnam
🌐 https://vfmat.ch/1c74

Hospital District 11
District 11, Ho Chi Minh, Vietnam
🌐 https://vfmat.ch/ef21

Hospital District 4
District 4, Ho Chi Minh, Vietnam
🌐 https://vfmat.ch/4c1b

Hospital District 8
District 8 City, Ho Chi Minh, Vietnam
🌐 https://vfmat.ch/f3f8

Hospital Duong Minh Chau
TT. Duong Minh Chau, Tây Ninh Province, Vietnam
🌐 https://vfmat.ch/83e4

Hospital Haiphong Medical University
Ngo Quyen, Haiphong, Vietnam
🌐 https://vfmat.ch/9ed5

Hospital Hoa Thanh district
Hoa Thanh, Tây Ninh Province, Vietnam
🌐 https://vfmat.ch/8a56

Hospital Nam Truc
Nam Trực, Nam Định, Vietnam
🌐 https://vfmat.ch/b188

Hospital Number Ten
Chau Thanh A, Hau Giang, Vietnam
🌐 https://vfmat.ch/a8c8

Hospital of District 7
District 7, City, Ho Chi Minh, Vietnam
🌐 https://vfmat.ch/6312

Hospital of Ea Kar District
Ea Kar, Đắk Lắk, Vietnam
🌐 https://vfmat.ch/57f8

Hospital of Giong Rieng District (Bệnh viện Đa khoa Huyện Giồng Riềng)
Ấp Kinh Xáng, Kiến Giang, Vietnam
🌐 https://vfmat.ch/6e54

Hospital of Traditional Medicine Ho Chi Minh City
District 3, Ho Chi Minh City, Vietnam
🌐 https://vfmat.ch/b773

Hospital Orthopedics and Rehabilitation HCMC
Tan Binh District, Ho Chi Minh, Vietnam
🌐 https://vfmat.ch/ee87

Hospital Saigon – Nam Dinh
Loc Vuong, Nam Định, Vietnam
🌐 https://vfmat.ch/eac9

Hospital Vi Xuyen
Xuyen district, Hà Giang, Vietnam
🌐 https://vfmat.ch/f24f

Hospital VINMEC
Thôn Trường Tây, Khánh Hòa, Vietnam
🌐 https://vfmat.ch/5881

Hue Central Hospital
Thôn Kim Long, Thừa Thiên-Huế, Vietnam
🌐 https://vfmat.ch/2ad7

Hue University Hospital
Hue, Hu, Thừa Thiên-Huế, Vietnam
🌐 https://vfmat.ch/54f3

Hung Loi Ward Medical Station
Hung Loi Ninh Kieu, Can Tho, Vietnam
🌐 https://vfmat.ch/c944

Hung Vuong Hospital
District 5, Ho Chi Minh, Vietnam
🌐 https://vfmat.ch/7d87

Hữu Nghị Clinic
Xóm Đình, Ho Chi Minh, Vietnam
🌐 https://vfmat.ch/6d51

Hồ Chí Minh City Hospital of Hematology and Blood Transfusion
District 1, City, Can Tho, Vietnam
🌐 https://vfmat.ch/946f

Hội Đông Y
Ấp An Mỹ, Long An, Vietnam
🌐 https://vfmat.ch/3b85

Institute of Ethnic Medicine and Pharmacy
Phu Nhuan District, Ho Chi Minh, Vietnam
🌐 https://vfmat.ch/a7d6

K Tan Trieu Hospital
Tan Trieu, Thanh Tri, Vietnam
🌐 https://vfmat.ch/b513

Khu Điều Trị
Nà Phia, Cao Bằng, Vietnam
🌐 https://vfmat.ch/3e26

Kim Son District General Hospital
Kim Son, Ninh Bình, Vietnam
🌐 https://vfmat.ch/87b7

Krong Nang District General Hospital
Krong Nang, Đắk Lắk, Vietnam
🌐 https://vfmat.ch/cb87

Lai Chau Provincial Hospital
Lai Chau Town, Lai Châu, Vietnam
🌐 https://vfmat.ch/e697

Lao Cai Endocrinology Hospital
Chính Cường, Lào Cai, Vietnam
🌐 https://vfmat.ch/16c5

Lao Cai Obstetrics and Children's Hospital
Lao Cai City, Lào Cai, Vietnam
⊕ https://vfmat.ch/229c

Le Loi Hospital
Ba Ria City, Vung Tau Province, Vietnam
⊕ https://vfmat.ch/25a5

Le Ngoc Tung General Hospital
Tay Ninh, Tây Ninh Province, Vietnam
⊕ https://vfmat.ch/ee3d

Long An General Hospital
Tan An, Long An, Vietnam
⊕ https://vfmat.ch/d7d9

Long Thanh District Medical Center
Long Thành, Dong Nai, Vietnam
⊕ https://vfmat.ch/828b

MeKong Obstetrics and Gynecology Hospital
Binh District, Ho Chi Minh, Vietnam
⊕ https://vfmat.ch/747a

Military Hospital 175
District, City, Ho Chi Minh, Vietnam
⊕ https://vfmat.ch/8bbf

Military Medical Academy 7
Thượng Lý, Haiphong, Vietnam
⊕ https://vfmat.ch/1b81

Minh Anh Hospital
District Binh Tan, City., Ho Chi Minh, Vietnam
⊕ https://vfmat.ch/b7d6

My Phuoc Hospital
My Phuoc Ward, Binh Duong, Vietnam
⊕ https://vfmat.ch/f817

My Phuoc Medical Station
Long Xuyen City, An Giang, Vietnam
⊕ https://vfmat.ch/8f1c

My Thoi Ward Medical Station
Long Xuyen City, An Giang, Vietnam
⊕ https://vfmat.ch/9c1a

Nam Tu Liem District Medical Center
Nam Tu Liem District, Hanoi, Vietnam
⊕ https://vfmat.ch/7e88

National Hospital of Dermatology
Trung Phụng, Hanoi, Vietnam
⊕ https://vfmat.ch/7242

National Hospital of Endocrinology
Lang Ha, Hanoi, Vietnam
⊕ https://vfmat.ch/5622

National Hospital of Ophthalmology
Hai Ba Trung District, Hanoi, Vietnam
⊕ https://vfmat.ch/36b9

National Lung Hospital
Ba Dinh, Hanoi, Vietnam
⊕ https://vfmat.ch/2f3e

Navy Medical Institute
Duong Kinh, Haiphong, Vietnam
⊕ https://vfmat.ch/1792

Nga Bay City General Hospital
Nga Bay City, Hậu Giang, Vietnam
⊕ https://vfmat.ch/34d8

Nga Nam Town General Hospital
Nga Nam, Sóc Trăng, Vietnam
⊕ https://vfmat.ch/a8df

Ngo Quyen General Hospital
Ngo Quyen, Haiphong, Vietnam
⊕ https://vfmat.ch/b942

Ngoc Hien District Medical Center
Ngoc Hien District, Cà Mau, Vietnam
⊕ https://vfmat.ch/ba87

Nguyen Tri Phuong Hospital
Chợ Rẫy, Ho Chi Minh, Vietnam
⊕ https://vfmat.ch/bf14

Nguyễn Trãi Hospital
Ward 8, District 5, Ho Chi Minh, Vietnam
⊕ https://vfmat.ch/1da7

Ngọc Linh
Gò Vấp, Ho Chi Minh, Vietnam
⊕ https://vfmat.ch/ca14

Nha Khoa
Phúc Lễ, Hanoi, Vietnam
⊕ https://vfmat.ch/3cfe

Nhà hộ Sinh A
Xóm Trong, Hanoi, Vietnam
⊕ https://vfmat.ch/a6a8

Ninh Binh Obstetrics and Pediatrics Hospital
Nam Thanh Ward, Ninh Binh City, Vietnam
⊕ https://vfmat.ch/5f9c

Ninh Hoa Town Hospital
Ninh Hoa, Khánh Hòa, Vietnam
⊕ https://vfmat.ch/ad12

On-Demand Treatment
My Tho City, Tiền Giang, Vietnam
⊕ https://vfmat.ch/a1b7

Pacific Hospital Hoi An
Hoi An, Quảng Nam, Vietnam
⊕ https://vfmat.ch/6c9c

Pacific Hospital Tam Kỳ
Tam Kỳ, Quảng Nam, Vietnam
⊕ https://vfmat.ch/36d9

People's Hospital 115
District 10, Ho Chi Minh, Vietnam
⊕ https://vfmat.ch/2232

Phong Dien General Hospital
Nhơn Thọ Hai, Can Tho, Vietnam
⊕ https://vfmat.ch/e5d7

Phòng Khám YHCT Gia Đức
Ninh Kieu, Can Tho, Vietnam
⊕ https://vfmat.ch/1773

Phu Nhuan District Hospital
Ward 8, Ho Chi Minh, Vietnam
⊕ https://vfmat.ch/97d6

Phu Phong General Hospital
Hai Bà Trưng, Hà Nội, Vietnam
⊕ https://vfmat.ch/1d53

Phu Tho Provincial General Hospital
Viet Tri City, Phú Thọ, Vietnam
⊕ https://vfmat.ch/9e5b

Phung Chau Medical Station
Chuong My District, Phung Chau, Hanoi, Vietnam
⊕ https://vfmat.ch/d3ad

Phung Hiep District Medical Center
Phung Hiep, Hậu Giang, Vietnam
⊕ https://vfmat.ch/e8d6

Phuoc Binh Medical Station
Phước Long Xã, Ho Chi Minh, Vietnam
⊕ https://vfmat.ch/936a

Phuoc Long-Bac Lieu District Hospital
Phuoc Long District, Bac Lieu, Vietnam
⊕ https://vfmat.ch/1a4f

Phuong Chau International Hospital
District, Ninh Kieu, City, Can Tho, Vietnam
⊕ https://vfmat.ch/e446

Phòng khám ACC Đà Nẵng
An Hải, Da Nang, Vietnam
⊕ https://vfmat.ch/6bce

Phòng Khám BS Phước
Vũng Tàu, Bà Rịa-Vũng Tàu, Vietnam
⊕ https://vfmat.ch/afa8

Phòng Khám Đa Khoa
Nam Pháp, Haiphong, Vietnam
⊕ https://vfmat.ch/b8fd

Phòng Khám Đa Khoa An Phúc
Chợ Rẫy, Ho Chi Minh, Vietnam
🌐 https://vfmat.ch/9ddb

Phòng khám đa khoa khu vực Tân Thành
Thị Trấn Tân Thành, Đồng Tháp, Vietnam
🌐 https://vfmat.ch/e88c

Phòng Khám Đa KHoa Quốc Tế Hà Nội – Y Tế Quốc Tế Việt
Làng Mie, Hanoi, Vietnam
🌐 https://vfmat.ch/8c25

Phòng trực cấp cứu
Hòa Hy, Haiphong, Vietnam
🌐 https://vfmat.ch/e9c5

Preventive Medicine Center Long An
Ấp Vĩnh Phú, An Giang, Vietnam
🌐 https://vfmat.ch/238a

Provincial General Hospital
P. Minh Khai, Hà Giang, Vietnam
🌐 https://vfmat.ch/de68

Public Health Institute
District 8, Ho Chi Minh, Vietnam
🌐 https://vfmat.ch/72b2

Quang Khoi General Hospital
Di Ward, Nghệ An, Vietnam
🌐 https://vfmat.ch/5a5c

Quang Nam Provincial General Hospital
Ấp Thiện Lập, Lâm Đồng, Vietnam
🌐 https://vfmat.ch/6f36

Quang Ngai City Hospital
Nghia Chanh Bac, City., Quảng Ngãi Province, Vietnam
🌐 https://vfmat.ch/26fc

Quang Ninh Traditional Hospital
Hong Ha Ward, Ha Long City, Vietnam
🌐 https://vfmat.ch/6fe4

Quy Hoa Central Dermatology Hospital
Qui Nhon City, Bình Định, Vietnam
🌐 https://vfmat.ch/28ed

Quy Nhon City Hospital
Qui Nhon City, Bình Định, Vietnam
🌐 https://vfmat.ch/9226

Rehabilitation Hospital of Quang Ninh
Quan Hanh, Quảng Ninh, Vietnam
🌐 https://vfmat.ch/9b39

Sa Dec Hospital
Ward 2, City. Sa Dec, Đồng Tháp, Vietnam
🌐 https://vfmat.ch/4966

Saigon Can Tho Eye Hospital
Ninh Kieu District, Can Tho City, Vietnam
🌐 https://vfmat.ch/a33y

Saigon General Hospital
District 1, Ho Chi Minh, Vietnam
🌐 https://vfmat.ch/6586

Saigon International Obstetrics and Gynecology Hospital
Pham Ngu Lao Ward, District 1, Ho Chi Minh City, Vietnam
🌐 https://vfmat.ch/bd76

Saigon Pharmaceutical and Medical School Hospital
Ho Chi Minh City, Vietnam
🌐 https://vfmat.ch/lqjc

Saint Paul Hospital
Hai Duong, Vietnam
🌐 https://vfmat.ch/piyv

Son Tra Hospital
Son Tra, Da Nang, Vietnam
🌐 https://vfmat.ch/f23f

Sân Bệnh Viện Y Tế Công Cộng
Thụy Phương, Hanoi, Vietnam
🌐 https://vfmat.ch/14d4

Tai Mũi Họng Thành phố Hồ Chí Minh
Cầu Bông, Ho Chi Minh, Vietnam
🌐 https://vfmat.ch/ce84

Tam Duong District Hospital
Tam Duong, Vinh Phuc, Vietnam
🌐 https://vfmat.ch/b272

Tam Tri Hospital
Long Ward, City, Nha Trang, Vietnam
🌐 https://vfmat.ch/c7be

Tan An City Medical Center
Tan An, Long An, Vietnam
🌐 https://vfmat.ch/3752

Tan Bien Ward Clinics
Bien Hoa City, Tây Ninh Province, Vietnam
🌐 https://vfmat.ch/5f51

Tan Binh District Hospital
Tân Bình, Thành phố, Ho Chi Minh, Vietnam
🌐 https://vfmat.ch/87cb

Tan Hiep District Hospital
Tan Hiep District, Kiến Giang, Vietnam
🌐 https://vfmat.ch/3d72

Tan Hung Medical Station
Ba Ria, Can Tho, Vietnam
🌐 https://vfmat.ch/af5e

Tay Giang District Hospital
Tay Giang, Quảng Nam, Vietnam
🌐 https://vfmat.ch/1489

Tay Ninh City Hospital
Ward 2, City, Tây Ninh Province, Vietnam
🌐 https://vfmat.ch/8b2d

Thai Hoa Hospital
Cao Lanh, Đồng Tháp, Vietnam
🌐 https://vfmat.ch/4383

Thai Nguyen C Hospital
Pho Co Ward, Thái Nguyên, Vietnam
🌐 https://vfmat.ch/af55

Thanh Binh Hospital
Thanh Bình, Đồng Tháp, Vietnam
🌐 https://vfmat.ch/7bd8

Thanh Ha General Hospital
Thanh Hoa City, Hải Dương, Vietnam
🌐 https://vfmat.ch/2e4b

Thanh My Commune Health Station
Tay, Hanoi, Can Tho, Vietnam
🌐 https://vfmat.ch/57d5

Thanh Nhan Hospital
Hai Ba Trung, Hanoi, Vietnam
🌐 https://vfmat.ch/78b5

Thanh Vu Medic Bac Lieu General Hospital
Bac Lieu City, Bạc Liêu, Vietnam
🌐 https://vfmat.ch/f33a

The Hospital of Traditional Medicine – Rehabilitation of Binh Thuan Province
Ấp Bình Hưng, Bình Thuận, Vietnam
🌐 https://vfmat.ch/374b

Thien Nhan Hospital
Hai Chau, Da Nang, Vietnam
🌐 https://vfmat.ch/a45f

Thoi Lai District Hospital
Thới Hòa A, Can Tho, Vietnam
🌐 https://vfmat.ch/353b

Thong Nhat Dong Nai Hospital
Bien Hoa, Đồng Nai, Vietnam
🌐 https://vfmat.ch/97db

Thong Nhat Hospital
Tan Binh, City, Ho Chi Minh, Vietnam
🌐 https://vfmat.ch/6c1f

Thot Not Hospital
Phụng Thạnh Hai, Can Tho, Vietnam
🌐 https://vfmat.ch/79d9

Thu Duc City Hospital
Thu Duc city, Ho Chi Minh, Vietnam
⊕ https://vfmat.ch/9491

Thái Bình Hospital
Thái Bình, Vietnam
⊕ https://vfmat.ch/d9cb

Thẩm mỹ viện Hoàn Mỹ Cần Thơ
Đông Phú, Long An, Vietnam
⊕ https://vfmat.ch/22fe

TRA General Hospital
Mỹ Hòa, Vĩnh Long, Vietnam
⊕ https://vfmat.ch/5835

Tra Vinh City General Hospital
Tra Vinh City, Trà Vinh, Vietnam
⊕ https://vfmat.ch/f5b6

Traditional Medicine Hospital
Thượng Lý, Haiphong, Vietnam
⊕ https://vfmat.ch/f66f

Traditional Medicine Hospital of Phu Yen Province
Ninh Tịnh, Phú Yên, Vietnam
⊕ https://vfmat.ch/87e4

Traditional Medicine Pham Ngoc Thach
Da Lat City, Lâm Đồng, Vietnam
⊕ https://vfmat.ch/575e

Trieu An Hospital
Binh Tan, Ho Chi Minh, Vietnam
⊕ https://vfmat.ch/dc87

Trung Tam Bac Si Gia Dinh Da Nang
Ấp Ba, Da Nang, Vietnam
⊕ https://vfmat.ch/c19c

Trung Tâm Chăm Sóc Sức Khỏe Sinh Sản Tỉnh Bình Thuận
Ấp Tân An, Bình Thuận, Vietnam
⊕ https://vfmat.ch/1dfb

Trung Tâm Chẩn Đoán Y Khoa Medic (Hòa Hảo)
Chợ Rẫy, Ho Chi Minh, Vietnam
⊕ https://vfmat.ch/564b

Trung Tâm Dân Quân Y Côn Đảo
Côn Đảo, Bà Rịa – Vũng Tàu, Vietnam
⊕ https://vfmat.ch/e767

Trung Tâm Giám Định Pháp Y
Tân Thuận, Tiền Giang, Vietnam
⊕ https://vfmat.ch/4e7b

Trung Tâm Sức Khỏe Sinh Sản Hải Phòng
Trang Quan, Haiphong, Vietnam
⊕ https://vfmat.ch/324a

Trung Tâm Y Tế Công Ty Cao Su Phú Riềng
Phú Riềng, Bình Phước, Vietnam
⊕ https://vfmat.ch/ac87

Trung Tâm Y Tế Dự Phòng – Phòng Khám Tiêm Phòng
Xóm Chiếu, Ho Chi Minh, Vietnam
⊕ https://vfmat.ch/7db5

Trung Tâm Y Tế dự Phòng Cần Thơ
Thới Nhật, Can Tho, Vietnam
⊕ https://vfmat.ch/68d5

Trung Tâm Y Tế Dự Phòng Tỉnh
Thành Phố Hải Dương, Hải Dương, Vietnam
⊕ https://vfmat.ch/fc43

Trung Tâm Y Tế huyện
Quang Duc, Đắk Nông, Vietnam
⊕ https://vfmat.ch/3b38

Trung Tâm Y Tế Huyện Cao Lộc
Cao Lộc, Lạng Sơn, Vietnam
⊕ https://vfmat.ch/ed4e

Trung Tâm Y Tế Huyện Kon Lông
Kon Plông, Kon Tum, Vietnam
⊕ https://vfmat.ch/8744

Trung Tâm Y Tế Huyện Lai Vung
Khóm 3, Đồng Tháp, Vietnam
⊕ https://vfmat.ch/8238

Trung tâm Y tế Huyện Long Điền
Ấp Chô Bên, Bà Rịa-Vũng Tàu, Vietnam
⊕ https://vfmat.ch/67a9

Trung Tâm Y Tế Huyện Lấp Vò
Lấp Vò, Đồng Tháp, Vietnam
⊕ https://vfmat.ch/479f

Trung Tâm Y Tế Huyện Mỹ Tú
Mỹ Tú, Sóc Trăng, Vietnam
⊕ https://vfmat.ch/7eb9

Trung Tâm Y tế Huyện Phong Thổ
Pa So, Lai Châu, Vietnam
⊕ https://vfmat.ch/ed1e

Trung Tâm Y Tế Huyện Tân Hồng
Tân Hồng, Đồng Tháp, Vietnam
⊕ https://vfmat.ch/5add

Trung Tâm Y tế Huyện Vĩnh Thạnh
Định Bình, Bình Định, Vietnam
⊕ https://vfmat.ch/39f4

Trung tâm Y tế huyện Đông Giang
Mê Ra, Quảng Nam, Vietnam
⊕ https://vfmat.ch/35dc

Trung tâm Y tế Nậm Tăm
Phiềng Chá, Lai Châu, Vietnam
⊕ https://vfmat.ch/1bf6

Trung Tâm Y tế Quận Hoàn Kiếm
Xóm Pho, Hanoi, Vietnam
⊕ https://vfmat.ch/8715

Trung Tâm Y Tế Thị Xã Từ Sơn
Phù Lưu, Bắc Ninh, Vietnam
⊕ https://vfmat.ch/6dc9

Trung Tâm Điều Dưỡng Người Bệnh Tâm Thần Thủ Đức
Tam Hải, Ho Chi Minh, Vietnam
⊕ https://vfmat.ch/af6d

Trung Yâm y tế Thành Phố Chí Linh
Mật Sơn, Hải Dương, Vietnam
⊕ https://vfmat.ch/ce12

Trạm Bảo Hành Kangaroo
Bảo Châu, Hưng Yên, Vietnam
⊕ https://vfmat.ch/51e8

Trạm Xá
Ninh Tịnh, Phú Yên, Vietnam
⊕ https://vfmat.ch/4b36

Trạm xá xã Đa Tốn (Da Ton commune clinic)
Thuận Tốn, Ha Tay, Vietnam
⊕ https://vfmat.ch/fc5a

Trạm y Tế
Trùm Thuật, Cà Mau, Vietnam
⊕ https://vfmat.ch/7ea5

Trạm Y tế Hòa Thuận
Ấp Hòa Lạc, Đồng Tháp, Vietnam
⊕ https://vfmat.ch/3e73

Trạm Y tế P. Xuân Khánh
Ấp An Mỹ, Long An, Vietnam
⊕ https://vfmat.ch/efce

Trạm Y Tế Phường 7 Quận Phú Nhuận
District 1, Hồ Chí Minh, Vietnam
⊕ https://vfmat.ch/15aa

Trạm Y Tế Phường An Phú
An Phu, District 2, City, Ho Chi Minh, Vietnam
⊕ https://vfmat.ch/bc27

Trạm Y Tế Phường Phúc Đồng
Long Biên, Hà Nội, Vietnam
⊕ https://vfmat.ch/cfe3

Trạm Y Tế Xã Mỹ Khánh
Ấp Mỹ Phước, Can Tho, Vietnam
⊕ https://vfmat.ch/4e23

Trạm Y tế Xã Nghĩa Hương
Lập Tuyết, Hanoi, Vietnam
⊕ https://vfmat.ch/fa3b

TT Nha khoa Mỹ Thuật Cao
Thới Nhật, Can Tho, Vietnam
⊕ https://vfmat.ch/259e

TT Y tế dự Phòng Đăk Lăk
Khối Sáu, Đắk Lắk, Vietnam
⊕ https://vfmat.ch/6d75

Tuberculosis and Lung Can Tho Hospital
Thới Nhật, Can Tho, Vietnam
⊕ https://vfmat.ch/2e5d

Tuệ Tĩnh
Kim Lũ, Hanoi, Vietnam
⊕ https://vfmat.ch/3dc1

Tây Nguyên Optometry
Khối Bốn, Đắk Lắk, Vietnam
⊕ https://vfmat.ch/f683

University Medical Center
District 5, Ho Chi Minh, Vietnam
⊕ https://vfmat.ch/eda6

Van Canh Medical Station
Nhỗn, Hanoi, Vietnam
⊕ https://vfmat.ch/e298

Van Cao Private General Hospital
Van Cao, Haiphong, Vietnam
⊕ https://vfmat.ch/ddcb

Van Don District Medical Center
Thị Trấn Cái Rồng, Quảng Ninh, Vietnam
⊕ https://vfmat.ch/38f9

Viet Duc University Hospital
Hanoi, Vietnam
⊕ https://vfmat.ch/ltxa

Viet Xo Friendship Hospital
Hai Ba Trung, Hanoi, Vietnam
⊕ https://vfmat.ch/33e3

Vietnam – Cuba Hospital
Xóm Trong, Hanoi, Vietnam
⊕ https://vfmat.ch/ac88

Vietnam – Russia International Eye Hospital
District 10, Ho Chi Minh, Vietnam
⊕ https://vfmat.ch/85ed

Vietnam – Sweden Hospital
Uong Bi City, Quảng Ninh, Vietnam
⊕ https://vfmat.ch/b1b5

Vietnam Cuba Friendship Hospital
Hanoi, Vietnam
⊕ https://vfmat.ch/ycmg

Vietnam Heart Institute
Trung Phụng, Hanoi, Vietnam
⊕ https://vfmat.ch/49d1

Vietnam National Children's Hospital
Hanoi, Vietnam
⊕ https://vfmat.ch/xmne

Vietnam Sport Hospital
Tu Liem, Hanoi, Vietnam
⊕ https://vfmat.ch/972f

Vietsovpetro Medical Center
Ward 7 City., Vung Tau, Vietnam
⊕ https://vfmat.ch/7a55

Vinh Chau District General Hospital
Giồng Trà Mâu, Sóc Trăng, Vietnam
⊕ https://vfmat.ch/c537

Vinh Phuc General Hospital
Vinh Yen City, Vĩnh Phúc, Vietnam
⊕ https://vfmat.ch/fff1

Vinh Tuong Hospital
Vĩnh Tường, Vĩnh Phúc, Vietnam
⊕ https://vfmat.ch/8e51

Vinmec Healthcare System
Cẩm Lệ District, Da Nang, Vietnam
⊕ https://vfmat.ch/a18c

Vinmec International General Hospital
Ho Chi Minh City, Vietnam
⊕ https://vfmat.ch/a831

Viện 69
Ba Dinh, Hà Tây, Vietnam
⊕ https://vfmat.ch/7cc3

Viện Bỏng Quốc Gia
Hà Đông, Hanoi, Vietnam
⊕ https://vfmat.ch/b238

Viện Huyết học – Truyền máu Trung ương
Mễ Trì, Hanoi, Vietnam
⊕ https://vfmat.ch/9bfe

Viện Pasteur
Cầu Bông, Ho Chi Minh, Vietnam
⊕ https://vfmat.ch/f62a

Viện Pasteur HCM
Cầu Bông, Ho Chi Minh, Vietnam
⊕ https://vfmat.ch/1e95

Viện Quân Y 7
Thượng Lý, Haiphong, Vietnam
⊕ https://vfmat.ch/49d2

Viện Y Học Cổ Truyền Quân Đội
Hoàng Mai, Hà Nội, Vietnam
⊕ https://vfmat.ch/f184

Viện Y Học Phòng Không – Không Quân
Trung Phụng, Hanoi, Vietnam
⊕ https://vfmat.ch/42f9

VK Hospital
Nha Trang, Vietnam
⊕ https://vfmat.ch/f97f

Xuan Canh Medical Station
Dong Anh, Hanoi, Vietnam
⊕ https://vfmat.ch/d9ef

Xuyen A General Hospital
Cu Chi District, City, Ho Chi Minh, Vietnam
⊕ https://vfmat.ch/916a

Y Te Du Phong
Chí Hòa, Ho Chi Minh, Vietnam
⊕ https://vfmat.ch/1bd2

Yên Hòa Medical Clinic
Cau Giay, Hanoi, Vietnam
⊕ https://vfmat.ch/7ac6

Đa Khoa Thành phố Cần Thơ
Ấp An Mỹ, Long An, Vietnam
⊕ https://vfmat.ch/7e89

Đa Khoa Thế Giới
Xóm Ông Đội, Ho Chi Minh, Vietnam
⊕ https://vfmat.ch/4791

Healthcare Facility

Zambia

Formerly known as Northern Rhodesia, Zambia became a republic upon gaining independence from Britain in 1964. Located in Southern Africa, Zambia features rugged terrain, diverse wildlife, parks, and safari areas. It is a landlocked nation that shares borders with eight countries, including Angola, Botswana, Democratic Republic of Congo, Malawi, Mozambique, Namibia, Tanzania, and Zimbabwe. Located at its border with Zimbabwe is Victoria Falls, locally called Mosi-Oa-Tunya, and one of Africa's most famous natural features and tourist destinations. Lusaka is Zambia's capital and largest city and one of the fastest developing cities in the Southern African Development Community. The country's 19.1 million people, all of them members of the Bantu family, speak several major indigenous languages, while also using English as the official language.

Boasting a relatively stable democracy since 1991, Zambia's government has peacefully transferred among three political parties: UNIP, MMD, and PF. The Economist Intelligence Unit (EIU) has consistently put Zambia among the top 10 most democratic African countries. Zambia attained middle-income status in 2011 and was regarded as one of the fastest-growing economies in Africa. However, in recent times, declining copper prices, significant fiscal deficits, and energy shortages have stalled Zambia's economic performance. Unemployment and under-employment are major issues and Zambia's per capita GDP stands at $1,051 as of 2020. In 2000, the agriculture sector represented 20 percent of Zambia's GDP and accounted for 85 percent of its employment.

Zambia's life expectancy of 64 years shows a continuous improvement. But communicable and non-communicable diseases continue to present a challenge to the health of the country, contributing to significant death and disability. Major causes of death include HIV/AIDS, neonatal disorders, stroke, lower respiratory infections, diarrheal diseases, tuberculosis, ischemic heart disease, malaria, cirrhosis, hypertensive heart disease, and meningitis. Deaths due to non-communicable diseases have increased substantially between 2009 and 2019, particularly stroke and hypertensive heart disease, which both rose by over 50 percent.

19.1M
Population

$1,051
GDP Per Capita

64 years
Life Expectancy
↑ Improving

9
Doctors/100k
Physician Density

200
Beds/100k
Hospital Bed Density

213
Deaths/100k
Maternal Mortality

Zambia

Nonprofit Organizations

143 LIFE Foundation
Seeks to educate and empower individuals living with malaria, TB, HIV/AIDS, STDs and other health disparities related to sexual health.
Infect Dis, MF Med
⊕ https://vfmat.ch/d59b

A Broader View Volunteers
Provides developing countries around the world with significant volunteer programs that aid the neediest communities and forge a lasting bond between those volunteering and those they have helped.
Dent-OMFS, ER Med, Infect Dis, MF Med
⊕ https://vfmat.ch/3bec

Abt Associates
Seeks to improve the quality of life and economic well-being of people worldwide, while striving to meet and exceed the highest professional standards.
General, Logist-Op, MF Med, OB-GYN, Peds
⊕ https://vfmat.ch/cec2

Advance Family Planning
Aims to achieve global expansion and access to quality contraceptive information, services, and supplies through financial investment and political commitment.
General, MF Med, Pub Health
⊕ https://vfmat.ch/7478

Africa CDC
Aims to strengthen the capacity and capability of Africa's public health institutions and partnerships to detect and respond quickly and effectively to disease threats and outbreaks, based on data-driven interventions and programs.
Infect Dis, Logist-Op, Pub Health
⊕ https://vfmat.ch/339c

Africa Health Organisation
Leads collaborative efforts among countries in Africa and other partners to promote health equity, combat disease, and improve quality of life.
Logist-Op, Pub Health
⊕ https://vfmat.ch/b1c5

Africa Humanitarian Action (AHA)
Responds to crises, conflicts, and disasters in Africa, while informing and advising the international community, governments, civil society, and the private sector on humanitarian issues of concern to Africa. Supports institutional and organizational development efforts.
General, Infect Dis, MF Med, Nutr, OB-GYN
⊕ https://vfmat.ch/3ca2

Africa Indoor Residual Spraying Project (AIRS)
Aims to protect millions of people in Africa from malaria by spraying insecticide on walls, ceilings, and other indoor resting places of mosquitoes that transmit malaria.

Infect Dis
⊕ https://vfmat.ch/9bd1

Africa Relief and Community Development
Provides comprehensive relief and developmental aid to people of the African continent regardless of gender, race, or religion.
Nutr, Pub Health
⊕ https://vfmat.ch/6cd2

Against Malaria Foundation
Helps protect people from malaria. Funds anti-malaria nets, specifically long-lasting insecticidal nets (LLINs), and works with distribution partners to ensure they are used. Tracks and reports on net use and malaria case data.
Infect Dis
⊕ https://vfmat.ch/337d

Aid Africa's Children
Aims to empower impoverished African children and communities with healthcare, food, clean water, and educational and entrepreneurial opportunities.
ER Med, General, Infect Dis, Nutr, OB-GYN, Palliative, Peds, Pub Health
⊕ https://vfmat.ch/5e2e

AIDS Healthcare Foundation
Provides cutting-edge HIV/AIDS medical care and advocacy to over one million people in 43 countries.
Infect Dis
⊕ https://vfmat.ch/b27c

Albinism Foundation of Zambia
Works to promote the welfare of people with albinism in Zambia through initiatives in education, advocacy, healthcare, and empowerment.
Pub Health
⊕ https://vfmat.ch/1fa7

American Academy of Pediatrics
Seeks to attain optimal physical, mental, and social health and well-being for all infants, children, adolescents, and young adults.
Anesth, Crit-Care, Neonat, Ped Surg
⊕ https://vfmat.ch/9633

American Cancer Society
Saves lives, celebrates lives, and leads the fight for a world without cancer.
Heme-Onc, Logist-Op, Medicine, Rad-Onc, Radiol
⊕ https://vfmat.ch/f996

American International Health Alliance (AIHA)
Strengthens health systems and workforce capacity worldwide through locally driven, peer-to-peer institutional partnerships.

CV Med, ER Med, Infect Dis, Medicine, OB-GYN
⊕ https://vfmat.ch/69fd

AMREF Flying Doctors
Aims to deliver medical air transport and health services using the latest aviation and medical technology to ensure patients receive unrivaled care.
ER Med, Logist-Op
⊕ https://vfmat.ch/5d5e

Amref Health Africa
Serves millions of people across 35 countries in Sub-Saharan Africa, strengthening health systems, and training African health workers to respond to the continent's most critical health issues.
All-Immu, General, Infect Dis, Logist-Op, MF Med, OB-GYN, Path, Pub Health, Surg
⊕ https://vfmat.ch/6985

Amsterdam Institute for Global Health and Development (AIGHD)
Provides sustainable solutions to major health problems across our planet by forging synergies among disciplines, healthcare delivery, research, and education.
Infect Dis
⊕ https://vfmat.ch/d73d

AO Alliance
Builds solutions to lessen the burden of injuries in low- and middle-income countries, while enhancing the care of the injured to reduce human suffering, disability, and poverty.
Ortho, Surg
⊕ https://vfmat.ch/8cd5

Aspen Management Partnership for Health (AMP Health)
Works to improve health systems and outcomes by collaborating with governments to strengthen leadership and management capabilities through public-private partnership.
Logist-Op
⊕ https://vfmat.ch/ea78

Avert
Works to ensure widespread understanding of HIV/AIDS in order to reduce new infections and improve the lives of those affected.
Infect Dis, Path
⊕ https://vfmat.ch/312d

Avinta Care
Offers quality healthcare while providing a full suite of services from diagnosis to treatment, specializing in fertility and dermatology.
Derm, MF Med, OB-GYN, Path
⊕ https://vfmat.ch/52a6

Boston Children's Hospital: Global Health Program
Helps solve pediatric global healthcare challenges by transferring expertise through long-term partnerships with scalable impact, while working in the field to strengthen healthcare systems, advocate, research, and provide care delivery or education as a way of sustainably improving the health of children worldwide.
Anesth, CV Med, Crit-Care, ER Med, Heme-Onc, Infect Dis, Medicine, Nutr, Palliative, Ped Surg, Peds
⊕ https://vfmat.ch/f9f8

Bridge Trust Ltd., The
Engages in relief, education, training, and development in India and Zambia, along with the U.K. and other developed nations.
General, Infect Dis, OB-GYN
⊕ https://vfmat.ch/e463

Brigham and Women's Hospital Global Health Hub
Cares for patients in underserved settings, provides education to staff who work in those areas to create sustainable change, and conducts research designed to improve health in such settings.
General, Infect Dis
⊕ https://vfmat.ch/a8a3

Bureau of International Health Cooperation
Seeks to improve healthcare around the world, including developing countries, using expertise, and contribute to healthier lives of Japanese people by bringing these experiences back to Japan.
ER Med, Heme-Onc, Infect Dis, Peds, Pub Health
⊕ https://vfmat.ch/947d

Cairdeas International Palliative Care Trust
Promotes and facilitates the provision of high-quality palliative care in the developing world, where such care is limited.
Palliative
⊕ https://vfmat.ch/35c4

CARE
Works around the globe to save lives, defeat poverty, and achieve social justice.
ER Med, General
⊕ https://vfmat.ch/7232

Caring Hands Worldwide
Inspired by the Christian faith, works to improve dental health of those in need in partner communities in the U.S. and abroad.
Dent-OMFS, Logist-Op
⊕ https://vfmat.ch/62cc

Carter Center, The
Seeks to prevent and resolve conflicts, enhance freedom and democracy, and improve health, while remaining committed to human rights and the alleviation of human suffering.
Infect Dis, MF Med, Ophth-Opt
⊕ https://vfmat.ch/6556

Catholic Medical Mission Board (CMMB)
Works in partnership globally to deliver locally sustainable, quality health solutions to women, children, and their communities.
General, MF Med, Peds
⊕ https://vfmat.ch/9498

ChildFund Australia
Works to reduce poverty for children in many of the world's most disadvantaged communities.
ER Med, General, Peds
⊕ https://vfmat.ch/13df

Children's Bridge Foundation
Supports health and education programs for orphaned and abandoned children in the developing world.
Infect Dis, Nutr, Peds, Surg
⊕ https://vfmat.ch/6486

Children's Lifeline International
Provides medical teams and surgical assistance to underprivileged children in developing countries through missions in partnership with local hospitals.
CV Med, Dent-OMFS, General, MF Med, Neurosurg, Peds, Rehab
⊕ https://vfmat.ch/6fea

Christian Blind Mission (CBM)
Aims to improve the quality of life of persons with disabilities in the poorest countries, addressing poverty as a cause and a consequence of disability, and working in partnership to create a society for all.
ENT, General, Infect Dis, OB-GYN, Ophth-Opt, Ortho, Peds, Psych, Rehab, Surg
⊕ https://vfmat.ch/3824

Christian Connections for International Health (CCIH)
Promotes global health and wholeness from a Christian perspective.
All-Immu, General, Infect Dis, MF Med, Neonat, OB-GYN, Psych
⊕ https://vfmat.ch/fa5d

Christian Health Service Corps
Brings Christian doctors, health professionals, and health educators committed to serving the poor to places that otherwise have little or no access to healthcare.
Anesth, Dent-OMFS, General, Medicine, Peds, Surg
⊕ https://vfmat.ch/da57

Christian Medical & Dental Associations

Based in Christian ministry, deploys medical and dental teams to underserved communities to provide vital healthcare.

Anesth, Dent-OMFS, ER Med, General, Medicine, OB-GYN, Ophth-Opt, Peds, Pub Health, Radiol, Rehab, Surg

🌐 https://vfmat.ch/921c

Church of Central Africa Presbyterian (CCAP) synod of Zambia

Based in Christian ministry, seeks to provide health services, education, HIV/AIDS care, clean water, and sustainable farming practices.

General, Infect Dis

🌐 https://vfmat.ch/9fec

Clinton Health Access Initiative (CHAI)

Aims to save lives and reduce the burden of disease in low- and middle-income countries. Works with partners to strengthen the capabilities of governments and the private sector to create and sustain high-quality health systems.

General, Heme-Onc, Infect Dis, Logist-Op, MF Med, Medicine, Neonat, Nutr, OB-GYN, Path, Peds, Rad-Onc

🌐 https://vfmat.ch/9ed7

Columbia University: Global Mental Health Programs

Pioneers research initiatives, promotes mental health, and aims to reduce the burden of mental illness worldwide.

Psych

🌐 https://vfmat.ch/c5cd

Columbia Vagelos College of Physicians and Surgeons Programs in Global Health

Harnesses the expertise of the medical school to improve health worldwide by training global health leaders, building capacity through interdisciplinary education and training programs, and addressing unmet health needs through research and application.

CV Med, Derm, Genetics, Heme-Onc, Infect Dis, Medicine, OB-GYN, Ophth-Opt, Peds, Psych, Pub Health, Pulm-Critic, Surg

🌐 https://vfmat.ch/a9e5

Communities Without Borders

Aims to enable a better future for orphans and vulnerable children in Zambia through access to education and related care.

All-Immu, General, Nutr, Ophth-Opt

🌐 https://vfmat.ch/95db

COVID-19 Clinical Research Coalition

Advocates and collaborates for the advancement of COVID-19 research driven by the needs of low-resource settings, and works for equitable access to solutions to the pandemic.

All-Immu, Infect-Dis, MF Med, Path, Pub Health

🌐 https://vfmat.ch/d1f4

Cross Catholic Outreach

Mobilizes the global Catholic Church to transform impoverished communities through the provision of food, water, housing, education, orphan support, medical care, microenterprise, and disaster relief.

All-Immu, General, Nutr, OB-GYN, Rehab

🌐 https://vfmat.ch/22f4

CURE

Operates charitable hospitals and programs in underserved countries worldwide, where patients receive surgical treatment, based in Christian ministry.

Anesth, Neurosurg, Ortho, Ped Surg, Peds, Rehab, Surg

🌐 https://vfmat.ch/aa16

CURE Children's Hospital of Zimbabwe

Heals children living with disabilities such as clubfoot, bowed legs, cleft lips, untreated burns, and hydrocephalus.

ENT, Neurosurg, Ortho, Peds, Plast

🌐 https://vfmat.ch/473c

D-tree Digital Global Health

Demonstrates and advocates for the potential of digital technology to transform health systems and improve health and well-being for all.

Logist-Op, MF Med, OB-GYN, Peds, Pub Health

🌐 https://vfmat.ch/1f79

Developing Country NGO Delegation: Global Fund to Fight AIDS, TB & Malaria

Works to strengthen the engagement of civil society actors and organizations in developing countries to build a world in which AIDS, TB, and malaria are no longer global, public health, and human rights threats.

Infect Dis, Pub Health

🌐 https://vfmat.ch/3149

Doctors Without Borders/Médecins Sans Frontières (MSF)

Responds to emergencies and provides lifesaving medical care where needed most, including during disasters, conflicts, and epidemics.

Anesth, Crit-Care, ER Med, General, Infect Dis, Nutr, OB-GYN, Ped Surg, Peds, Psych, Pub Health, Surg

🌐 https://vfmat.ch/f363

Doors of Hope Zambia

Addresses social, economic, educational, and medical issues, especially among children and the elderly, by providing services including healthcare, food, and clean water, inspired by the Christian faith.

General, Infect Dis

🌐 https://vfmat.ch/a61f

Egmont Trust, The

Works with partner organizations in Sub-Saharan Africa, making grants to help vulnerable children cope with the impact of HIV/AIDS on families and communities.

General, Infect Dis, OB-GYN, Peds

🌐 https://vfmat.ch/57a9

Elizabeth Glaser Pediatric AIDS Foundation

Seeks to end global pediatric HIV/AIDS through prevention and treatment programs, research, and advocacy.

Infect Dis, Nutr, OB-GYN, Peds

🌐 https://vfmat.ch/d6ec

Elton John AIDS Foundation

Seeks to address and overcome the stigma, discrimination, and neglect that prevents ending AIDS by funding local experts to challenge discrimination, prevent infections, and provide treatment.

Infect Dis, Pub Health

🌐 https://vfmat.ch/9d31

Episcopal Relief & Development

Provides relief in times of disaster and promotes sustainable development by identifying and addressing the root causes of suffering.

Infect Dis, MF Med, Neonat, Nutr, Peds

🌐 https://vfmat.ch/7cfa

eRanger

Provides sustainable solutions to transportation and medical provision such as ambulances and mobile clinics in developing countries.

ER Med, General, Logist-Op

🌐 https://vfmat.ch/4c18

Evidence Project, The

Improves family-planning policies, programs, and practices through the strategic generation, translation, and use of evidence.

General, MF Med

🌐 https://vfmat.ch/f9e7

Eye Care Foundation

Helps prevent and cure avoidable blindness and visual impairment in low-income countries.

Ophth-Opt, Surg

🌐 https://vfmat.ch/c8f9

Fistula Foundation

Aims to engage the support of people worldwide who are eager to see the day that no woman suffers from obstetric fistula. Raises and directs funds to doctors and hospitals providing life-transforming surgery to women in need.

OB-GYN
⊕ https://vfmat.ch/e958

FlySpec
Provides free orthopedic, plastic and reconstructive surgery, along with prosthetic and orthotic services, to individuals with disabilities in the most remote areas of Zambia.
Ortho
⊕ https://vfmat.ch/c772

For Hearts and Souls
Provides medical outreach and care for children through heart-related work, such as diagnosing heart problems and performing heart-saving surgeries.
Anesth, CT Surg, CV Med, Crit-Care, Peds, Pulm-Critic
⊕ https://vfmat.ch/a162

Gift of Life International
Provides lifesaving cardiac treatment to children in developing countries while developing sustainable pediatric cardiac programs by implementing screening, surgical, and training missions.
Anesth, CT Surg, CV Med, Crit-Care, Ped Surg, Peds, Pulm-Critic
⊕ https://vfmat.ch/f2f9

Global Alliance to Prevent Prematurity And Stillbirth (GAPPS)
Seeks to improve birth outcomes worldwide by reducing the burden of premature birth and stillbirth.
All-Immu, Infect Dis, MF Med, Neonat, Neonat, OB-GYN
⊕ https://vfmat.ch/3f74

Global Clinic
Seeks to ensure that any effort to provide medical services is accompanied by a long-term program to improve the health of residents of its partner communities.
Dent-OMFS, ER Med, General, OB-GYN, OB-GYN, Ophth-Opt, Surg
⊕ https://vfmat.ch/9e48

Global Emergency Care Skills
Aims to provide high-quality emergency medical training to healthcare professionals in countries where emergency medicine is a developing specialty.
ER Med
⊕ https://vfmat.ch/1827

Global Health Corps
Mobilizes a diverse community of leaders to build the movement for global health equity, working toward a world in which every person lives a healthy life.
ER Med, General, Pub Health
⊕ https://vfmat.ch/31c6

Global Ministries – The United Methodist Church
As the worldwide mission and development agency of The United Methodist Church, Global Ministries works with more than 300 hospitals and clinics around the world through its Global Health Unit.
Anesth, CT Surg, CV Med, Crit-Care, Dent-OMFS, Derm, ER Med, GI, General, Infect Dis, Logist-Op, MF Med, Medicine, Neonat, Nephro, Nutr, OB-GYN, Ophth-Opt, Ortho, Palliative, Peds, Pod, Psych, Pub Health, Rehab, Rheum, Surg, Urol
⊕ https://vfmat.ch/1723

Global Network for Women and Children's Health Research
Aims to improve maternal and child health outcomes and building health research capacity in resource-poor settings by testing cost-effective, sustainable interventions that provide guidance for the practice of evidence-based medicine. Scientists from developing countries, together with peers in the United States, lead teams that address priority research needs through randomized clinical trials and implementation research conducted in low-resource areas.
MF Med, OB-GYN
⊕ https://vfmat.ch/a187

Global Oncology (GO)
Brings the best in cancer care to underserved patients around the world and collaborates across geographic, professional, and academic borders to improve cancer care, research, and education.
Heme-Onc, Path, Rad-Onc
⊕ https://vfmat.ch/fcb8

Global Reconstructive Surgery Outreach
Supports surgeons, doctors, and nurses financially to enable them to provide critically needed plastic and reconstructive surgeries to the poor.
Logist-Op, Surg
⊕ https://vfmat.ch/f262

Globalinks Medical Foundation
Provides free medical and midwifery care to those who would otherwise have no access to health services in isolated communities around the world.
General, MF Med, OB-GYN, Ophth-Opt, Peds, Pub Health
⊕ https://vfmat.ch/936c

Globus Relief
Aims to improve the delivery of healthcare worldwide by gathering, processing, and distributing surplus medical supplies to charities at home and abroad.
Logist-Op
⊕ https://vfmat.ch/a2b7

Grassroot Soccer
Leverages the power of soccer to educate, inspire, and mobilize at-risk youth in developing countries to overcome their greatest health challenges, live healthier and more productive lives, and be agents for change in their communities.
Infect Dis
⊕ https://vfmat.ch/3521

Hands At Work
Based in Christian ministry, supports those in need through its community intervention model with a focus on food security, education, and basic healthcare.
General, Infect Dis, Nutr, Pub Health
⊕ https://vfmat.ch/7274

Health Equity Initiative
Aims to build and sustain a global community that engages across sectors and disciplines to advance health equity.
Pub Health
⊕ https://vfmat.ch/e2e2

Healthy DEvelopments
Provides Germany-supported health and social protection programs around the globe in a collaborative knowledge management process.
All-Immu, General, Infect Dis, Logist-Op, MF Med
⊕ https://vfmat.ch/dc31

Healthy Learners
Aims to improve the health of school-aged children in Zambia through school-based community health.
General
⊕ https://vfmat.ch/8bda

Healthy Smiles Society
Seeks to provide and promote mobile dental services in rural developing countries.
Dent-OMFS
⊕ https://vfmat.ch/5d8e

Hear the World Foundation
Advocates worldwide for equal opportunities and improved quality of life for people in need with hearing loss.
ENT, Peds
⊕ https://vfmat.ch/122c

Hearing The Call
Brings quality healthcare to persons with hearing loss locally and globally, helping them connect with education and opportunities.
ENT, Logist-Op
⊕ https://vfmat.ch/d1db

Heart to Heart International
Strengthens communities through improving health access, providing humanitarian development, and administering crisis relief worldwide. Engages volunteers, collaborates with partners, and deploys resources to achieve this mission.
Anesth, ER Med, General, Logist-Op, Medicine, Path, Path, Peds, Psych, Pub

Health, Surg
⊕ https://vfmat.ch/aacb

Heineman Medical Outreach
Provides medical and educational assistance globally to promote sustainable healthcare and enhanced living standards in underserved communities through the International Medical Outreach (IMO) program, a collaborative partnership between Heineman Medical Outreach and Atrium Health.
Anesth, CT Surg, CV Med, ER Med, General, Heme-Onc, Logist-Op, Medicine, Neonat, OB-GYN, Ped Surg, Peds, Surg, Vasc Surg
⊕ https://vfmat.ch/389b

Hope and Healing International
Gives hope and healing to children and families trapped by poverty and disability.
General, Nutr, Ophth-Opt, Peds, Rehab
⊕ https://vfmat.ch/c638

Hope Walks
Frees children, families, and communities from the burden of clubfoot, inspired by the Christian faith.
Ortho, Ped Surg, Peds, Rehab
⊕ https://vfmat.ch/f6d4

Hospice Africa
Aims to provide a holistic and culturally sensitive palliative care service through accurate treatment of pain.
Palliative
⊕ https://vfmat.ch/9f86

Hunger Project, The
Aims to end hunger and poverty by pioneering sustainable, grassroots, women-centered strategies and advocating for their widespread adoption in countries throughout the world.
Infect Dis, Nutr, OB-GYN, Pub Health
⊕ https://vfmat.ch/3a49

ICAP at Columbia University
Serves as global leader in supporting the scale-up of multidisciplinary HIV/AIDS prevention, care, and treatment programs based on a family-focused approach.
General, Infect Dis, MF Med, Medicine, OB-GYN, Pub Health
⊕ https://vfmat.ch/a8ef

Immunisation 4 Life (i4Life)
Seeks to achieve a sustainable and healthy future for children under 5 by reducing disease and malnutrition in low-resource countries.
All-Immu, Nutr, Peds
⊕ https://vfmat.ch/cf9d

Inter Care Medical and for Africa
Provides targeted medical aid to rural health units in some of the poorest parts of Africa.
Logist-Op
⊕ https://vfmat.ch/64fb

International Agency for the Prevention of Blindness (IAPB), The
Leads international efforts in blindness-prevention activities, works toward a world where no one is needlessly visually impaired, and ensures that everyone has access to the best possible standard of eye health.
Infect Dis, Ophth-Opt, Pub Health
⊕ https://vfmat.ch/87a2

International Council of Ophthalmology
Works with ophthalmologic societies and others to enhance ophthalmic education and improve access to the highest-quality eye care in order to preserve and restore vision for people of the world.
Ophth-Opt
⊕ https://vfmat.ch/ffd2

International Eye Foundation (IEF)
Eliminates preventable and treatable blindness by making quality sustainable eye care services accessible and affordable worldwide.
Infect Dis, Logist-Op, Ophth-Opt
⊕ https://vfmat.ch/e839

International Federation of Gynecology and Obstetrics (FIGO)
Implements global projects on specific women's health issues.
MF Med, Medicine, Neonat, OB-GYN, Surg, Urol
⊕ https://vfmat.ch/c4b4

International Federation of Red Cross and Red Crescent Societies (IFRC)
Coordinates and directs international assistance following natural and manmade disasters in nonconflict situations through the world's largest humanitarian and development network. Provides disaster-preparedness programs, healthcare activities, and promotes humanitarian values.
ER Med, General, Infect Dis, Nutr
⊕ https://vfmat.ch/b4ee

International Insulin Foundation
Aims to prolong the life and promote the health of people with diabetes in developing countries by improving the supply of insulin and education in its use.
Endo, Logist-Op
⊕ https://vfmat.ch/d34f

International Organization for Migration (IOM) – The UN Migration Agency
Promotes evidence-informed policies and holistic, preventive, and curative health programs that are beneficial, accessible, and equitable for vulnerable migrants.
General, Infect Dis, OB-GYN
⊕ https://vfmat.ch/621a

International Planned Parenthood Federation (IPPF)
Leads a locally owned, globally connected civil society movement that provides and enables services and champions sexual and reproductive health and rights for all, especially the underserved.
Infect Dis, MF Med, OB-GYN
⊕ https://vfmat.ch/dc97

International Trachoma Initiative (iTi)
Works toward a world free from trachoma, a preventable cause of blindness, and provides comprehensive support to national ministries of health and governmental and nongovernmental organizations to implement a comprehensive approach to fight trachoma.
Infect Dis, Ophth-Opt
⊕ https://vfmat.ch/3278

International Vision Volunteers USA
Seeks to bring sight and eye care to adults and children in Africa.
Ophth-Opt
⊕ https://vfmat.ch/43f9

InterSurgeon
Fosters collaborative partnerships in the field of global surgery that will advance clinical care, teaching, training, research, and the provision and maintenance of medical equipment.
ENT, Neurosurg, Ortho, Ped Surg, Plast, Surg, Urol
⊕ https://vfmat.ch/6f8a

IntraHealth International
Improves the performance of health workers and strengthens the systems in which they work.
CV Med, Endo, General, Infect Dis, MF Med, Neonat, Nutr, OB-GYN
⊕ https://vfmat.ch/ddc8

Ipas
Focuses efforts on women and girls who want contraception or abortion, and builds programs around their needs and how best to support them.
OB-GYN
⊕ https://vfmat.ch/8e39

Iris Global
Serves the poor, the destitute, the lost, and the forgotten by providing adoration, outreach, family, education, relief, development, healing, and the arts.
General, Infect Dis, Nutr, Pub Health
⊕ https://vfmat.ch/37f8

Islamic Medical Association of North America

Fosters health promotion, disease prevention, and health maintenance in communities around the world through direct patient care and health programs.

Anesth, Dent-OMFS, ER Med, General, Logist-Op, Ophth-Opt, Peds, Plast, Surg

⊕ https://vfmat.ch/a157

IVUmed

Aims to make quality urological care available worldwide by providing medical and surgical education for physicians and nurses, and treatment for thousands of children and adults.

Anesth, OB-GYN, Ped Surg, Surg, Urol

⊕ https://vfmat.ch/e619

Izumi Foundation

Develops and supports programs that improve health and healthcare in neglected regions of Africa and Latin America.

⊕ https://vfmat.ch/f29a

Jhpiego

Creates and delivers transformative healthcare solutions that save lives, in partnership with national governments, health experts, and local communities.

General, Infect Dis, OB-GYN, Surg

⊕ https://vfmat.ch/45b8

John Snow, Inc. (JSI)

Aims to improve the health and well-being of underserved and vulnerable people and communities throughout the world.

General, Infect Dis, Logist-Op, MF Med, OB-GYN, Peds, Psych, Pub Health

⊕ https://vfmat.ch/ba78

Johns Hopkins Center for Communication Programs

Believes in the power of communication to save lives by empowering people to adopt healthy behaviors for themselves, their families, and their communities.

General, Infect Dis, Logist-Op, OB-GYN, Pub Health

⊕ https://vfmat.ch/1bf9

Johns Hopkins Center for Global Health

Facilitates and focuses the extensive expertise and resources of the Johns Hopkins institutions, together with global collaborators, to effectively address and ameliorate the world's most pressing health issues.

General, Genetics, Logist-Op, MF Med, Peds, Psych, Pub Health, Pulm-Critic

⊕ https://vfmat.ch/54ce

Joint United Nations Programme on HIV/AIDS (UNAIDS)

Aims to place people living with HIV and people affected by the virus at the decision-making table and at the center of designing, delivering, and monitoring the AIDS response.

Infect Dis

⊕ https://vfmat.ch/464a

Kailash Medical Foundation

Aims to improve the health and well-being of those in need around the world by going on missions to developing countries and providing medical, dental, and vision services to the underprivileged.

Dent-OMFS, General, Ophth-Opt

⊕ https://vfmat.ch/db41

Kaya Responsible Travel

Promotes sustainable social, environmental, and economic development, empowers communities, and cultivates educated, compassionate global citizens through responsible travel.

All-Immu, Crit-Care, Dent-OMFS, ER Med, General, Geri, Infect Dis, MF Med, Medicine, Nutr, OB-GYN, Peds, Psych, Pub Health, Rehab

⊕ https://vfmat.ch/b2cf

Kids Care Everywhere

Seeks to empower physicians in under-resourced environments with multimedia, state-of-the-art medical software, and to inspire young professionals to become future global healthcare leaders.

Logist-Op, Ped Surg, Peds

⊕ https://vfmat.ch/bc23

Kletjian Foundation

Works toward a world in which all people have access to safe, sustainable, and high-quality medical care, building collaborative networks and supporting entrepreneurial leaders that promote global health equity.

CT Surg, ENT, General, Ortho, Surg

⊕ https://vfmat.ch/12c2

KNCV Tuberculosis Foundation

Aims to end human suffering through the global elimination of tuberculosis.

Pulm-Critic

⊕ https://vfmat.ch/98bf

Lifebox

Seeks to provide safer surgery and anesthesia in low-resource countries by investing in tools, training, and partnerships for safe surgery.

Anesth, Crit-Care, Surg

⊕ https://vfmat.ch/2d4d

Limbs International

Engages communities and transforms lives through affordable, sustainable prosthetic solutions and rehabilitation services in developing countries.

Logist-Op, Ortho, Pod, Rehab

⊕ https://vfmat.ch/dc84

Management Sciences for Health (MSH)

Works with countries and communities to save lives and improve the health of the world's poorest and most vulnerable people by building strong, resilient, sustainable health systems.

Infect Dis, Logist-Op, Pub Health

⊕ https://vfmat.ch/6aa2

MAP International

Provides medicines and health supplies to those in need around the world so they might experience life to the fullest.

Logist-Op

⊕ https://vfmat.ch/deed

Marie Stopes International

Provides the contraception and safe abortion services that enable women all over the world to choose their own futures.

Infect Dis, MF Med, Neonat, OB-GYN, Pub Health

⊕ https://vfmat.ch/9525

Mary Begg Community Clinic

Provides quality healthcare for the Zambian community by working with the public health sector and the private sector in national health programs, including mother-child health, HIV management, and nursing care training.

Dent-OMFS, Derm, General, OB-GYN, Path, Peds, Surg, Urol

⊕ https://vfmat.ch/3511

Maternity Foundation

Works to ensure safer childbirth for women and newborns everywhere through innovative mobile health solutions such as the Safe Delivery App, a mobile training tool for skilled birth attendants.

MF Med, OB-GYN, Pub Health

⊕ https://vfmat.ch/ff4f

Maternity Worldwide

Works with communities and partners to identify and develop appropriate and effective ways to reduce maternal and newborn mortality and morbidity, facilitate communities to access quality skilled maternity care, and support the provision of quality skilled care.

MF Med, OB-GYN

⊕ https://vfmat.ch/822b

MCW Global

Works to address communities' pressing needs by empowering current leaders and readying leaders of tomorrow.

Dent-OMFS

⊕ https://vfmat.ch/1547

Medical Care Development International (MCD International)

Works to strengthen health systems through innovative, sustainable interventions.

Infect Dis, Logist-Op, OB-GYN, Pub Health
⊕ https://vfmat.ch/dc5c

Medical Care Development International
Works to improve the health of vulnerable populations through integrated, sustainable, and locally driven interventions.
Infect Dis, OB-GYN, Peds, Pub Health
⊕ https://vfmat.ch/da87

Medical Care for the Nations (MCN)
Provides medical care in poor and underserved areas and strives to educate local residents about basic healthcare, first aid, and disease prevention.
General, Logist-Op
⊕ https://vfmat.ch/2881

Medical Ministry International
Provides compassionate healthcare in areas of need, inspired by the Christian faith.
CT Surg, Dent-OMFS, ENT, General, OB-GYN, Ophth-Opt, Ortho, Plast, Rehab, Surg, Urol, Vasc Surg
⊕ https://vfmat.ch/5da6

Medical Mission of Hope to Zambia
Provides medical, dental, educational, and social services to the people of Feira in Zambia, inspired by the Christian faith.
Dent-OMFS, General, Logist-Op
⊕ https://vfmat.ch/9cdb

Medical Missions Outreach
Visits developing countries to provide quality, ethical healthcare and outreach to those in need, based in Christian ministry.
Dent-OMFS, Ophth-Opt, Ortho, Surg
⊕ https://vfmat.ch/1197

Medicines for Humanity
Aims to save the lives of vulnerable children by strengthening systems of maternal and child health in the communities served.
Infect Dis, MF Med, OB-GYN
⊕ https://vfmat.ch/8d13

MedSend
Funds qualified healthcare professionals to serve the physical and spiritual needs of people around the world, enabling healthcare providers to work where they have been called.
General
⊕ https://vfmat.ch/661c

MedShare
Aims to improve the quality of life of people, communities, and the planet by sourcing and directly delivering surplus medical supplies and equipment to communities in need around the world.
Logist-Op
⊕ https://vfmat.ch/c8bc

MENTOR Initiative
Saves lives in emergencies through tropical disease control, and helps people recover from crisis with dignity, working side by side with communities, health workers, and health authorities to leave a lasting impact.
ER Med, Infect Dis
⊕ https://vfmat.ch/3bd5

Mercy and Love Foundation
Aims to provide orphaned and vulnerable children with basic human needs such as food, clothing, and shelter, enabling them to thrive.
General, Peds
⊕ https://vfmat.ch/649a

Mission Bambini
Helps to support children living in poverty and sickness, and lacking education, giving them the opportunity for and hope of a better life.
CT Surg, CV Med, Crit-Care, ER Med, Ped Surg, Peds
⊕ https://vfmat.ch/dc1a

Mission Regan
Collects supplies, medication, and medical equipment and provides them to those who are in desperate need, both locally and globally.
Logist-Op
⊕ https://vfmat.ch/2bc1

mothers2mothers (m2m)
Employs and trains local women living with HIV as community health workers called Mentor Mothers to support women, children, and adolescents with vital medical services, education, and support.
Infect Dis, MF Med, OB-GYN, Peds, Pub Health
⊕ https://vfmat.ch/6557

MSD for Mothers
Designs scalable solutions that help end preventable maternal deaths.
MF Med, OB-GYN, Pub Health
⊕ https://vfmat.ch/9f99

MSI Reproductive Choices (Marie Stopes International)
Seeks to deliver quality family planning and reproductive healthcare to women around the world.
MF Med
⊕ https://vfmat.ch/5c82

Multi-Agency International Training and Support (MAITS)
Improves the lives of some of the world's poorest people living with disabilities through better access to quality health and education services and support.
Neuro, Psych, Rehab
⊕ https://vfmat.ch/9dcd

NCD Alliance
Unites and strengthens civil society to stimulate collaborative advocacy, action, and accountability for NCD (noncommunicable disease) prevention and control.
All-Immu, CV Med, General, Heme-Onc, Medicine, Peds, Psych
⊕ https://vfmat.ch/abdd

New Horizons Collaborative
Advances a holistic, integrated approach to high-quality pediatric HIV care and treatment with a specific focus on those in need of advanced treatment.
Infect Dis, Peds, Pub Health
⊕ https://vfmat.ch/a76a

On Call Africa
Improves access to healthcare in rural Zambia by strengthening local systems to sustain improved health outcomes.
General, Pub Health
⊕ https://vfmat.ch/cccb

OneSight
Brings eye exams and glasses to people who lack access to vision care.
Ophth-Opt
⊕ https://vfmat.ch/3ecc

Operation Eyesight
Works to eliminate blindness in partnership with governments, hospitals, medical professionals, corporations, and community development teams.
Ophth-Opt, Surg
⊕ https://vfmat.ch/b95d

Operation Eyesight Universal
Aims to prevent blindness, restore sight, and eliminate avoidable blindness.
Ophth-Opt
⊕ https://vfmat.ch/f629

Operation Fistula
Exists to end obstetric fistula by building models of care that serve every woman, everywhere.
MF Med, OB-GYN, Surg
⊕ https://vfmat.ch/ce8e

Operation International
Offers medical aid to adults and children suffering from lack of quality healthcare in impoverished countries.

Dent-OMFS, ER Med, Heme-Onc, OB-GYN, Ophth-Opt, Ortho, Ped Surg, Plast, Surg
⊕ https://vfmat.ch/b52a

Options
Believes in a world in which women and children can access the high-quality health services they need, without financial burden.
Logist-Op, MF Med, Neonat, OB-GYN
⊕ https://vfmat.ch/3a48

Optivest Foundation
Funds strategic opportunities that are holistic and collaborative, inspired by the Christian faith.
General, Nutr
⊕ https://vfmat.ch/f1e6

Optometry Giving Sight
Delivers eye exams and low or no-cost glasses, provides training for local eye care professionals, and establishes optometry schools, vision centers and optical labs.
Ophth-Opt
⊕ https://vfmat.ch/33ea

Orbis International
Works to prevent and treat blindness through hands-on training and improved access to quality eye care.
Anesth, Ophth-Opt, Surg
⊕ https://vfmat.ch/f2b2

Oxford University Global Surgery Group (OUGSG)
Aims to contribute to the provision of high-quality surgical care globally, particularly in low- and middle-income countries (LMICs), while bringing together students, researchers, and clinicians with an interest in global surgery, anesthesia, and obstetrics and gynecology.
Anesth, MF Med, OB-GYN, Ortho, Surg
⊕ https://vfmat.ch/c624

Pact
Works on the ground to improve the lives of those who are challenged by poverty and marginalization, striving for a world in which all people are heard, capable, and vibrant.
Infect Dis, Logist-Op, MF Med, Pub Health
⊕ https://vfmat.ch/9a6c

PATH
Advances health equity through innovation and partnerships so people, communities, and economies can thrive.
All-Immu, CV Med, Endo, Heme-Onc, Infect Dis, MF Med, Neonat, Nutr, OB-GYN, Path, Peds, Pulm-Critic
⊕ https://vfmat.ch/b4db

Penn State College of Medicine: Global Health Center
An interdisciplinary center that provides organization and oversight for the medical center's educational, service, community research, and clinical care activities in global health.
CV Med, General, Pub Health, Surg
⊕ https://vfmat.ch/6f37

Phillips Renner Foundation
Works to reduce inequities in nutrition, dental care, and education by delivering high-impact health services and products to children in the poorest communities.
Dent-OMFS, Nutr
⊕ https://vfmat.ch/bce6

Population Council
Conducts research to address critical health and development issues, helping deliver solutions to improve lives around the world.
Logist-Op, Pub Health
⊕ https://vfmat.ch/1777

Power of Love Foundation
Aims to build strong and vibrant communities by ensuring that no child is born with HIV and to care for HIV-positive infants and children.

Infect Dis, Peds
⊕ https://vfmat.ch/72c6

Project Concern International (PCI)
Drives innovation from the ground up to enhance health, end hunger, overcome hardship, and advance women and girls—resulting in meaningful and measurable change in people's lives.
Infect Dis, MF Med, Nutr, OB-GYN, Peds
⊕ https://vfmat.ch/5ed7

Project SOAR
Conducts HIV operations research around the world to identify practical solutions to improve HIV prevention, care, and treatment services.
ER Med, General, MF Med, OB-GYN, Psych
⊕ https://vfmat.ch/1a77

PSI – Population Services International
Aims to improve the health of people in the developing world by focusing on challenges such as a lack of family planning, HIV/AIDS, barriers to maternal health, and the greatest threats to children under the age of 5, including malaria, diarrhea, pneumonia, and malnutrition.
Infect Dis, MF Med, OB-GYN, Peds
⊕ https://vfmat.ch/ffe3

RAD-AID International
Improves and optimizes access to medical imaging and radiology in low-resource regions of the world.
Rad-Onc, Radiol
⊕ https://vfmat.ch/537f

RestoringVision
Empowers lives by restoring vision for millions of people in need.
Ophth-Opt
⊕ https://vfmat.ch/e121

ReSurge International
Provides reconstructive surgical care and builds surgical capacity in developing countries.
Anesth, Dent-OMFS, Ped Surg, Plast, Surg
⊕ https://vfmat.ch/9937

Riders for Health International
Aids in the last mile of healthcare delivery, by ensuring that healthcare reaches everyone, everywhere.
ER Med, Infect Dis, Logist-Op, Pub Health
⊕ https://vfmat.ch/85aa

Right to Care
Responds to public health needs by supporting and delivering innovative, quality healthcare solutions, based on the latest medical research and established best practices, for the prevention, treatment, and management of infectious and chronic diseases.
ER Med, Infect Dis, Logist-Op
⊕ https://vfmat.ch/3383

Rockefeller Foundation, The
Works to promote the well-being of humanity.
Logist-Op, Nutr, Pub Health
⊕ https://vfmat.ch/5424

Rose Charities International
Aims to support communities to improve quality of life and reduce the effects of poverty through innovative, self-sustaining projects, and partnerships.
ENT, ER Med, General, Infect Dis, Neonat, OB-GYN, Ophth-Opt, Ped Surg, Peds, Rehab, Urol
⊕ https://vfmat.ch/53df

Rotary International
Provides service to others, improves lives, and advances world understanding, goodwill, and peace through its fellowship of business, professional, and community leaders.
ER Med, General, Infect Dis, MF Med, OB-GYN
⊕ https://vfmat.ch/8fb5

ROW Foundation

Works to improve the quality of training for healthcare providers, and the diagnosis and treatment available to people with epilepsy and associated psychiatric disorders in under-resourced areas of the world.

Neuro, Psych

⊕ https://vfmat.ch/25eb

Salvation Army International, The

Seeks to meet human needs through services in education, healthcare, community support, emergency response, and ministry development, inspired by the Christian faith.

Dent-OMFS, Derm, ER Med, Infect Dis, MF Med, Medicine, Nutr, OB-GYN, Ophth-Opt, Palliative, Psych, Rehab, Surg

⊕ https://vfmat.ch/8eb3

Samaritan's Purse International Disaster Relief

Provides spiritual and physical aid to hurting people around the world, such as victims of war, poverty, natural disasters, disease, and famine, based in Christian ministry.

Anesth, CT Surg, Crit-Care, Dent-OMFS, Derm, ENT, ER Med, Endo, GI, General, Heme-Onc, Infect Dis, MF Med, Neonat, Nephro, Neuro, Neurosurg, Nutr, OB-GYN, Ophth-Opt, Ortho, Path, Ped Surg, Peds, Plast, Psych, Pulm-Critic, Radiol, Rehab, Rheum, Surg, Urol, Vasc Surg

⊕ https://vfmat.ch/87e3

Sanofi Espoir Foundation

Contributes to reducing health inequalities among populations that need it most by applying a socially responsible approach focused on fighting childhood cancers in low-income countries, improving maternal and newborn health, and improving access to care.

ER Med, OB-GYN, Peds

⊕ https://vfmat.ch/943b

Save A Child's Heart

Provides lifesaving cardiac treatment to children in developing countries, and trains healthcare professionals from these countries to deliver quality care in their communities.

CT Surg, CV Med, Crit-Care, Ped Surg, Peds

⊕ https://vfmat.ch/1bef

Save the Children

Gives children around the world a healthy start in life, the opportunity to learn, and protection from harm.

All-Immu, Crit-Care, ER Med, General, Infect Dis, MF Med, Medicine, Neonat, OB-GYN, Peds, Psych, Pub Health

⊕ https://vfmat.ch/2e73

SEE International

Provides sustainable medical, surgical, and educational services through volunteer ophthalmic surgeons, with the objectives of restoring sight and preventing blindness to disadvantaged individuals worldwide.

Ophth-Opt, Surg

⊕ https://vfmat.ch/6e1b

Seed Global Health

Focuses on human resources for health capacity building at the individual, institutional, and national level through sustained collaborative engagement with partners.

Logist-Op

⊕ https://vfmat.ch/d12e

Sightsavers

Works with partners in developing countries to help eliminate avoidable blindness and advocates for equal opportunity for the disabled.

Infect Dis, Ophth-Opt, Surg

⊕ https://vfmat.ch/aa52

SIGN Fracture Care International

Builds orthopedic capacity around the world and provides the injured poor access to fracture surgery by donating orthopedic education and implant systems to surgeons in developing countries.

Ortho, Rehab, Surg

⊕ https://vfmat.ch/123d

SINA Health

Aims to improve the health and educational status of the population in low- and middle-income countries.

General, Logist-Op

⊕ https://vfmat.ch/9ad3

Smile Train, Inc.

Treats children with cleft lip through a sustainable and local model that supports surgery and other forms of essential care.

Logist-Op, Pub Health

⊕ https://vfmat.ch/822c

SOS Children's Villages International

Supports children through alternative care and family strengthening.

ER Med, Peds

⊕ https://vfmat.ch/aca1

Sound Seekers

Supports people with hearing loss by enabling access to healthcare and education.

ENT

⊕ https://vfmat.ch/ef1c

Sri Sathya Sai International Organization

Inspired by spiritual teachings, carries out efforts in global healthcare, education, humanitarian relief, and youth engagement.

Dent-OMFS, General, Logist-Op, Nutr, Ophth-Opt, Pub Health

⊕ https://vfmat.ch/9bda

Students for Kids International Projects (SKIP)

Strives to educate and empower students to initiate and maintain sustainable community projects for the health, welfare, and education of children.

Dent-OMFS, General, Nutr, Peds, Pub Health

⊕ https://vfmat.ch/de4e

Swiss Tropical and Public Health Institute

Contributes to the improvement of the health of populations internationally, nationally, and locally through excellence in research, education, and services.

Infect Dis, Pub Health

⊕ https://vfmat.ch/2ee4

Task Force for Global Health, The

Consists of programs and focus areas that cover a range of global health issues including neglected tropical diseases, infectious diseases, vaccines, field epidemiology, public health informatics, health workforce development, and global health ethics.

Infect Dis, Logist-Op, Medicine, Ophth-Opt, Peds

⊕ https://vfmat.ch/714c

TB Alert

Offers a range of programmatic, advisory, technical, and training services around tuberculosis, and is active in international advocacy initiatives.

Infect Dis, Pub Health, Pulm-Critic

⊕ https://vfmat.ch/1d5e

Tearfund

Responds to crisis and partners with local churches to bring restoration to those living in poverty, inspired by the Christian faith.

ER Med, Logist-Op

⊕ https://vfmat.ch/f6cf

THET Partnerships for Global Health

Trains and educates health workers in Africa and Asia, working in partnership with organizations and volunteers from across the UK.

General

⊕ https://vfmat.ch/f937

Tiny Tim and Friends

Works towards zero transmission of HIV by providing free treatment, care and support to HIV+ children, adolescents, and pregnant women in Zambia.

Infect Dis

⊕ https://vfmat.ch/c5af

U.S. President's Malaria Initiative (PMI)
Supports low-income countries to help control and eliminate malaria through cost-effective, lifesaving malaria interventions.
Infect Dis, MF Med, OB-GYN
⊕ https://vfmat.ch/dc8b

UNC Health Foundation
Secures resources and supports empathy and expertise in patient care, research, education, and advocacy in underserved communities around the world.
Heme-Onc, Infect Dis, Neuro, Peds, Pub Health
⊕ https://vfmat.ch/7129

Unforgotten Fund, The (UNFF)
Provides lifesaving humanitarian relief to UN Field Operations and projects such as water supply, sanitation and hygiene (WASH), food security, health, and shelter.
ER Med, MF Med, Nutr, OB-GYN, Peds
⊕ https://vfmat.ch/928f

Union for International Cancer Control (UICC)
Unites and supports the cancer community to reduce the global cancer burden, promote greater equity, and ensure that cancer control continues to be a priority in the world health and development agenda.
Heme-Onc, Pub Health
⊕ https://vfmat.ch/88b1

United MegaCare
Seeks to deliver high-caliber services and programming across its areas of focus: education, health and wellness, secure families, and disaster resiliency.
ER Med, General, Infect Dis, Nutr, Ophth-Opt, Peds
⊕ https://vfmat.ch/ea18

United Nations Children's Fund (UNICEF)
Works in over 190 countries and territories to save children's lives, defend their rights, and help them fulfill their potential, from early childhood through adolescence.
All-Immu, Infect Dis, MF Med, Neonat, Nutr, OB-GYN, Ped Surg, Peds, Pub Health
⊕ https://vfmat.ch/42d7

United Nations Development Programme (UNDP)
Helps countries achieve the simultaneous eradication of extreme poverty and significant reduction of inequalities and exclusion using a sustainable human development approach.
Infect Dis, Logist-Op, Pub Health
⊕ https://vfmat.ch/935c

United Nations High Commissioner for Refugees (UNHCR)
Safeguards the rights and well-being of people who have been forced to flee, ensuring that everybody has the right to seek asylum and find safe refuge in another country, with the goal of seeking lasting solutions.
General, MF Med, Medicine, OB-GYN, Peds, Psych, Pub Health
⊕ https://vfmat.ch/6636

United Nations Population Fund (UNFPA)
Supports reproductive healthcare for women and youth in more than 150 countries, focusing on delivering a world in which every pregnancy is wanted, every childbirth is safe, and every young person's potential is fulfilled.
Infect Dis, MF Med, Neonat, OB-GYN, Peds, Pub Health
⊕ https://vfmat.ch/c969

United States Agency for International Development (USAID)
Promotes and demonstrates democratic values abroad and advances a free, peaceful, and prosperous world. Leads the U.S. government's international development and disaster assistance through partnerships and investments that save lives.
ER Med, Infect Dis, MF Med, OB-GYN, Peds
⊕ https://vfmat.ch/9a99

United States President's Emergency Plan for AIDS Relief (PEPFAR)
The U.S. global HIV/AIDS response works to prevent new HIV infections and accelerate progress to control the global epidemic in more than 50 countries, by partnering with governments to support sustainable, integrated, and country-led responses to HIV/AIDS.
Infect Dis, Pub Health
⊕ https://vfmat.ch/a57c

University of California San Francisco: Institute for Global Health Sciences
Dedicates its efforts to improving health and reducing the burden of disease in the world's most vulnerable populations by integrating expertise in the health, social, and biological sciences, training global health leaders, and developing solutions to the most pressing health challenges.
Infect Dis, OB-GYN, Pub Health
⊕ https://vfmat.ch/6587

University of Colorado: Global Emergency Care Initiative
Strives to sustainably improve emergency care outcomes in low- and middle-income communities worldwide by linking cutting-edge academics with excellent on-the-ground implementation.
ER Med
⊕ https://vfmat.ch/417a

University of New Mexico School of Medicine: Project Echo
Seeks to improve health outcomes worldwide through the use of a technology called telementoring, a guided-practice model in which the participating clinician retains responsibility for managing the patient.
General, Infect Dis, MF Med, OB-GYN, Path, Peds
⊕ https://vfmat.ch/6c9a

University of North Carolina: Institute for Global Health and Infectious Diseases
Harnesses the full resources of UNC and its partners to solve global health problems, reduce the burden of disease, and cultivate the next generation of global health leaders.
Infect Dis, MF Med, OB-GYN, Psych, Surg
⊕ https://vfmat.ch/ed5e

University of Pennsylvania Perelman School of Medicine Center for Global Health
Aims to improve health equity worldwide through enhanced public health awareness and access to care, discovery, and outcomes-based research, and comprehensive educational programs grounded in partnership.
Heme-Onc, Infect Dis, OB-GYN
⊕ https://vfmat.ch/cb57

USAID's Health Research Program
Funds maternal and child health implementation research and translates findings into effective health interventions that can be adapted globally.
Infect Dis, MF Med, OB-GYN, Peds
⊕ https://vfmat.ch/5991

USAID: A2Z The Micronutrient and Child Blindness Project
Aims to increase the use of key micronutrient and blindness interventions to improve child and maternal health.
MF Med, Neonat, Nutr, Ophth-Opt, Surg
⊕ https://vfmat.ch/c5f1

USAID: Deliver Project
Builds a global supply chain to deliver lifesaving health products to people in order to enable countries to provide family planning, protect against malaria, and limit the spread of pandemic threats.
Infect Dis, Logist-Op, MF Med
⊕ https://vfmat.ch/374e

USAID: EQUIP Health
Exists as an effective, efficient response mechanism to achieving global HIV epidemic control by delivering the right intervention at the right place and in the right way.
Infect Dis
⊕ https://vfmat.ch/d76a

USAID: Human Resources for Health 2030 (HRH2030)
Helps low- and middle-income countries develop the health workforce needed to prevent maternal and child deaths, support the goals of Family Planning 2020, control the HIV/AIDS epidemic, and protect communities from infectious diseases.

Logist-Op
⊕ https://vfmat.ch/9ea8

USAID: Maternal and Child Health Integrated Program
Works to improve the health of women and their families, including programs for maternal, newborn, and child health, immunization, family planning, nutrition, malaria, and HIV/AIDS.
All-Immu, General, Infect Dis, MF Med
⊕ https://vfmat.ch/4415

USAID: Maternal and Child Survival Program
Works to prevent child and maternal deaths.
Infect Dis, MF Med, Neonat, OB-GYN, Peds
⊕ https://vfmat.ch/6fcf

USAID: TB Care II
Focuses on tuberculosis care and treatment.
Infect Dis
⊕ https://vfmat.ch/57d4

Virtual Doctors, The
Uses local mobile broadband networks to connect rural clinics with doctors around the world, connecting isolated health centers with volunteer doctors around the world.
Anesth, Derm, ENT, Endo, General, Heme-Onc, Infect Dis, Medicine, Neuro, OB-GYN, Ophth-Opt, Ortho, Palliative, Ped Surg, Peds, Plast, Psych, Surg
⊕ https://vfmat.ch/3d94

Vision Aid Overseas
Enables people living in poverty to access affordable glasses and eye care.
Ophth-Opt
⊕ https://vfmat.ch/c695

Vision Care
Restores sight and helps patients get regular treatment at short-term eye camps and long-term base clinics by having doctors, missionaries, volunteers, and sponsors work together.
Ophth-Opt
⊕ https://vfmat.ch/9d7c

Vision Outreach International
Advocates for helping the blind in underserved regions of the world and empowers the poor through sight restoration.
Ophth-Opt
⊕ https://vfmat.ch/9721

Vitamin Angels
Helps at-risk populations in need—specifically pregnant women, new mothers, and children under age 5—to gain access to life-changing vitamins and minerals.
General, Nutr
⊕ https://vfmat.ch/7da1

Voluntary Service Overseas (VSO)
Works with health workers, communities, and governments to improve health services and rights for women, babies, youth, people with disabilities, and prisoners.
General, MF Med, OB-GYN
⊕ https://vfmat.ch/213d

Watsi
Uses technology to make healthcare a reality for those who might not otherwise be able to afford it.
Pub Health, Surg
⊕ https://vfmat.ch/41a3

Women's Refugee Commission
Seeks to improve lives by protecting the rights of women, children, and youth displaced by conflict and crisis through researching their needs, identifying solutions, and advocating for programs and policies to strengthen their resilience.
General, MF Med, Neonat, OB-GYN, Peds, Psych
⊕ https://vfmat.ch/3d8f

World Blind Union (WBU)
Represents those experiencing blindness, speaking to governments and international bodies on issues concerning visual impairments.
Ophth-Opt
⊕ https://vfmat.ch/2bd3

World Children's Fund
Commits to helping children worldwide who are suffering the effects of poverty, disease, natural disaster, famine, abuse, civil strife, and war.
General, Logist-Op, MF Med, Nutr, OB-GYN, Pub Health
⊕ https://vfmat.ch/9cd8

World Federation of Hemophilia (WFH)
Aims to improve and sustain care for people with inherited bleeding disorders by pursuing long-term relationships with individuals and organizations who share the values of WFH's development model.
Heme-Onc
⊕ https://vfmat.ch/5121

World Health Organization, The (WHO)
The United Nations' agency for health provides leadership on global health matters, shapes the health research agenda, sets norms and standards, articulates evidence-based policy options, provides technical support and monitoring to countries, and assesses health trends.
ER Med, General, Infect Dis, Logist-Op, MF Med, OB-GYN, Peds, Psych, Pub Health
⊕ https://vfmat.ch/c476

World Hope International
Empowers the poorest individuals around the world so they can become agents of change within their communities, by offering resources and knowledge.
Infect Dis, Logist-Op, MF Med, OB-GYN, Peds
⊕ https://vfmat.ch/a4b8

World Medical Relief
Facilitates the distribution of surplus medical resources where they are needed.
Logist-Op
⊕ https://vfmat.ch/72dc

World Missions Possible
Provides EMS capacity-building, along with medical and vision care, to under-developed and rural areas.
ER Med, General, Heme-Onc, Neonat, Ophth-Opt, Surg
⊕ https://vfmat.ch/d6a5

World Parkinson's Program
Seeks to improve the quality of life of those affected by Parkinson's disease through education and advocacy, and provides free medication and support services.
Logist-Op, Neuro, Pub Health
⊕ https://vfmat.ch/c96d

World Vision International
Works with vulnerable communities around the world to overcome poverty and injustice with child-focused programs in disaster management, health, nutrition, economic development, education, clean water, sanitation, and hygiene.
ER Med, General, Infect Dis, MF Med, Nutr, OB-GYN, Peds
⊕ https://vfmat.ch/2642

Zambia

Healthcare Facilities

Arthur Davidson Children's Hospital
Ndola, Copperbelt, Zambia
⊕ https://vfmat.ch/17e1

Beit CURE Hospital of Zambia
Lusaka, Zambia
⊕ https://vfmat.ch/itwu

Care For Business Medical Centre
Lusaka, Lusaka, Zambia
⊕ https://vfmat.ch/3d54

Chawama First Level Hospital
Lusaka, Lusaka Region, Zambia
⊕ https://vfmat.ch/wjys

Chikuni Mission Hospital
Monze, Southern Province, Zambia
⊕ https://vfmat.ch/a7dc

Chilenje Level 1 Hospital
Kabulonga, Lusaka, Zambia
⊕ https://vfmat.ch/e165

Chipata Central Hospital
Chipata, Eastern Province, Zambia
⊕ https://vfmat.ch/56c1

Chitokoloki Mission Hospital
Zambezi, Zambia
⊕ https://vfmat.ch/uezk

Chongwe District Hospital
Lusaka, Lusaka, Zambia
⊕ https://vfmat.ch/7e56

Coptic Hospital – Zambia
Lusaka, Lusaka, Zambia
⊕ https://vfmat.ch/bf74

CURE Children's Hospital of Zambia, The
Lusaka, Lusaka, Zambia
⊕ https://vfmat.ch/8qbj

Fairview Hospital
Lusaka, Zambia
⊕ https://vfmat.ch/cbxe

Hilltop Hospital Lusaka
Lusaka, Lusaka, Zambia
⊕ https://vfmat.ch/64b4

Hilltop Hospital Ndola
Ndola, Copperbelt, Zambia
⊕ https://vfmat.ch/7f26

Itezhi-Tezhi District Hospital
Itezhi-Tezhi, Southern Province, Zambia
⊕ https://vfmat.ch/c64c

Kabwe Women, Newborn and Children's Hospital
Kabwe, Central Province, Zambia
⊕ https://vfmat.ch/ff8a

Kalene Mission Hospital
Ikelenge, North-Western Province, Zambia
⊕ https://vfmat.ch/d984

Kalomo District Hospital
Kalomo, Southern Province, Zambia
⊕ https://vfmat.ch/2397

Kalulushi Hospital
Kalulushi, Copperbelt, Zambia
⊕ https://vfmat.ch/c3a5

Kitwe Central Hospital
Kitwe, Copperbelt, Zambia
⊕ https://vfmat.ch/5933

Lewanika General Hospital
Mongu, Western Province, Zambia
⊕ https://vfmat.ch/2b56

Livingstone General Hospital
Livingstone, Southern, Zambia
⊕ https://vfmat.ch/49ac

Lundazi District Hospital
Lundazi, Eastern Province, Zambia
⊕ https://vfmat.ch/2f67

Lusaka Trust Hospital
Lusaka, Lusaka, Zambia
⊕ https://vfmat.ch/89d3

Luwingu District Hospital
Luwingu, Zambia
⊕ https://vfmat.ch/1vk8

Macha Mission Hospital
Choma, Zambia
⊕ https://vfmat.ch/l1g9

Maina Soko Military Hospital
Lusaka, Lusaka, Zambia
⊕ https://vfmat.ch/241e

Mansa General Hospital
Mansa, Luapula, Zambia
⊕ https://vfmat.ch/8568

Mary Begg Kansanshi Mine Hospital
Solwezi, North-Western Province, Zambia
⊕ https://vfmat.ch/22cf

Matero Level 1 Hospital
Lusaka, Lusaka, Zambia
⊕ https://vfmat.ch/edc7

Mazabuka General Hospital
Mazabuka, Southern Province, Zambia
⊕ https://vfmat.ch/9cb4

Medcross Hospital
Lusaka, Lusaka, Zambia
⊕ https://vfmat.ch/c767

Medland Health Services
Lusaka, Lusaka Region, Zambia
⊕ https://vfmat.ch/3z7q

Minga Mission Hospital
Petauke, Eastern Province, Zambia
⊕ https://vfmat.ch/7d53

MKP TMS Hospital
Lusaka, Lusaka, Zambia
⊕ https://vfmat.ch/b5b7

Monze Mission Hospital
Monze, Southern Province, Zambia
⊕ https://vfmat.ch/53fa

Mukinge Mission Hospital
Kasempa, North-Western Province, Zambia
⊕ https://vfmat.ch/eivp

Mumbwa General Hospital
Mumbwa, Central Province, Zambia
⊕ https://vfmat.ch/539f

Ndola Teaching Hospital
Ndola, Copperbelt, Zambia
⊕ https://vfmat.ch/578e

Northern Command Military Hospital
Ndola, Copperbelt, Zambia
⊕ https://vfmat.ch/2468

Pearl of Health Hospital
Lusaka, Zambia
⊕ https://vfmat.ch/eqxg

Progress Medical Centre
Kitwe, Copperbelt, Zambia
⊕ https://vfmat.ch/43ai

Siavonga District Hospital
Siavonga, Lusaka, Zambia
⊕ https://vfmat.ch/cb92

Sinozam Friendship Hospital
Kitwe, Copperbelt, Zambia
⊕ https://vfmat.ch/8c8b

Solwezi General Hospital
Solwezi, North-Western Province, Zambia
⊕ https://vfmat.ch/ef7c

St Francis' Mission Hospital
Katete, Eastern Province, Zambia
⊕ https://vfmat.ch/f4f1

St. Pauls Mission Hospital
Kashikishi, Luapula, Zambia
⊕ https://vfmat.ch/e39e

University Teaching Hospital (UTH)
Lusaka, Zambia
⊕ https://vfmat.ch/a8a9

Victoria Hospital at Lusaka
Lusaka, Zambia
⊕ https://vfmat.ch/b93f

Victoria Hospital at Mazabuka
Mazabuka, Southern, Zambia
⊕ https://vfmat.ch/e2c6

Viva Med Hospital
Lusaka, Lusaka Region, Zambia
⊕ https://vfmat.ch/cmez

Zambezi Hospital
Zambezi, North-Western Province, Zambia
⊕ https://vfmat.ch/5a74

Zambian – Italian Orthopaedic Hospital
Lusaka, Lusaka, Zambia
⊕ https://vfmat.ch/7fac

Zimba Mission Hospital
ZImba, Southern Province, Zambia
⊕ https://vfmat.ch/9be6

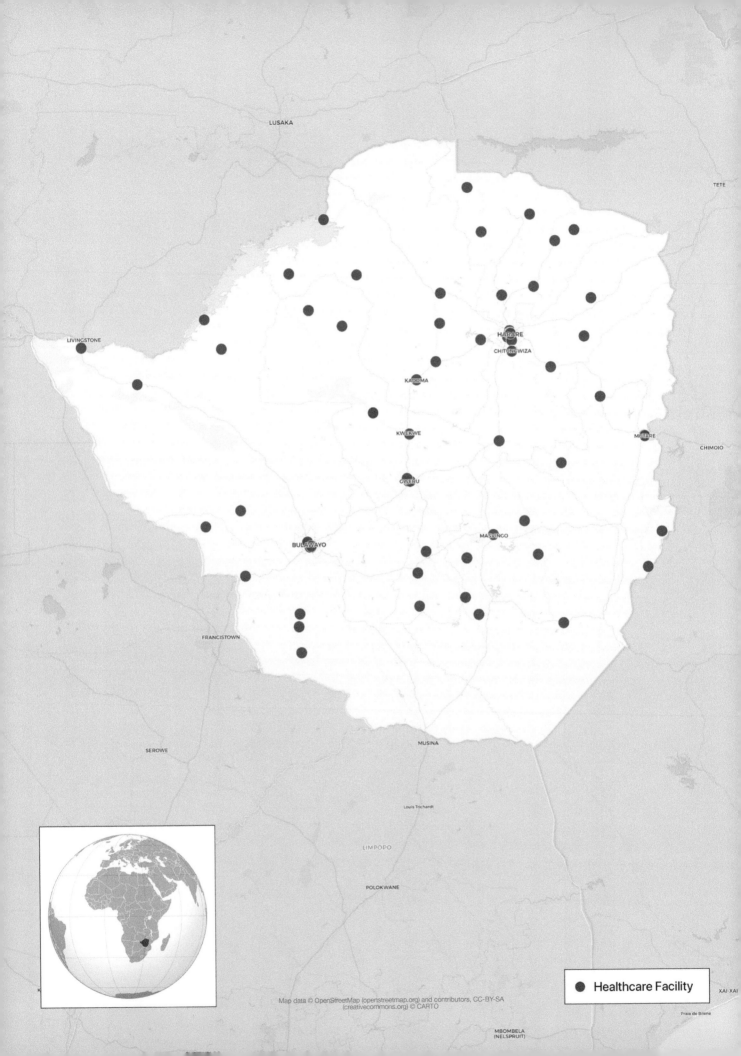

● Healthcare Facility

Zimbabwe

With dramatic landscapes and diverse wildlife filling its parks and reserves, Zimbabwe is known for its stunning natural beauty. Prior to its independence in 1980, the country had been known by several names: Rhodesia, Southern Rhodesia, and Zimbabwe Rhodesia. Officially referred to as the Republic of Zimbabwe, this landlocked country is located in Southern Africa, between the Zambezi and Limpopo Rivers. The country has reserves of metallurgical-grade chromite and other commercial mineral deposits such as coal, asbestos, copper, nickel, gold, platinum, and iron ore. Zimbabwe has a population of about 14.8 million people, with an estimated 3 million people residing in its capital, Harare. This culturally diverse country has 16 official languages, with up to 76 percent of the population speaking Bantu languages and Ndebele (18 percent).

Agriculture and mining are the main export-driving forces, making Zimbabwe one of the fastest-growing economies in the world. These successes represent a recovery from negative growth between 1998 and 2008, which is largely blamed on land reform policy and corruption. The country has adequate internal transportation and an electric power network, but maintenance has been neglected over the years. Poorly paved roads link the major urban and industrial centers, and rail lines managed by the National Railways of Zimbabwe tie into an extensive Central African Railroad Network. In recent years, there have been widespread violations of human rights. Elections have been marked by political violence and intimidation, along with the politicization of the judiciary, military, police force, and public services.

Zimbabwe faces many challenges as a result of underdevelopment, including challenges in health. Zimbabwe has a life expectancy of 61 years as of 2019. The common causes of death include lower respiratory infections, tuberculosis, ischemic heart disease, neonatal disorders, stroke, diarrheal diseases, diabetes, road injuries, and protein-energy malnutrition. Deaths due to communicable diseases have decreased substantially between 2009 and 2019, particularly HIV/AIDS and malaria, which both decreased by 70 percent and 50 percent respectively. However, they still remain top causes of death, indicating that there is still much improvement to be made in addressing these two diseases.

14.8M
Population

$1,128
GDP Per Capita

61 years
Life Expectancy
↑ Improving

21
Doctors/100k
Physician Density

170
Beds/100k
Hospital Bed Density

458
Deaths/100k
Maternal Mortality

Zimbabwe

Nonprofit Organizations

143 LIFE Foundation
Seeks to educate and empower individuals living with malaria, TB, HIV/AIDS, STDs and other health disparities related to sexual health.
Infect Dis, MF Med
⊕ https://vfmat.ch/d59b

A Light For Zimbabwe
Provides sponsorships for school fees, establishes sustainable projects for rural villages, and offers healthcare in remote areas.
Infect Dis, Logist-Op, Ped Surg, Peds
⊕ https://vfmat.ch/c28a

Abalon Trust
Provides ophthalmic eye services in developing countries.
Ophth-Opt
⊕ https://vfmat.ch/d7ed

Abt Associates
Seeks to improve the quality of life and economic well-being of people worldwide, while striving to meet and exceed the highest professional standards.
General, Logist-Op, MF Med, OB-GYN, Peds
⊕ https://vfmat.ch/cec2

Action Against Hunger
Aims to end life-threatening hunger for good through treating and preventing malnutrition across more than 45 countries.
Nutr
⊕ https://vfmat.ch/2dbc

Advance Family Planning
Aims to achieve global expansion and access to quality contraceptive information, services, and supplies through financial investment and political commitment.
General, MF Med, Pub Health
⊕ https://vfmat.ch/7478

Adventist Health International
Focuses on upgrading and managing mission hospitals by providing governance, consultation, and technical assistance to a number of affiliated Seventh-Day Adventist hospitals throughout Africa, Asia, and the Americas.
Dent-OMFS, General, Pub Health
⊕ https://vfmat.ch/16aa

Africa CDC
Aims to strengthen the capacity and capability of Africa's public health institutions and partnerships to detect and respond quickly and effectively to disease threats and outbreaks, based on data-driven interventions and programs.
Infect Dis, Logist-Op, Pub Health
⊕ https://vfmat.ch/339c

Africa Health Organisation
Leads collaborative efforts among countries in Africa and other partners to promote health equity, combat disease, and improve quality of life.
Logist-Op, Pub Health
⊕ https://vfmat.ch/b1c5

Africa Indoor Residual Spraying Project (AIRS)
Aims to protect millions of people in Africa from malaria by spraying insecticide on walls, ceilings, and other indoor resting places of mosquitoes that transmit malaria.
Infect Dis
⊕ https://vfmat.ch/9bd1

Africa Relief and Community Development
Provides comprehensive relief and developmental aid to people of the African continent regardless of gender, race, or religion.
Nutr, Pub Health
⊕ https://vfmat.ch/6cd2

African Field Epidemiology Network (AFENET)
Strengthens field epidemiology and public health laboratory capacity to contribute effectively to addressing epidemics and other major public health problems in Africa.
All-Immu, Infect Dis, Path, Pub Health
⊕ https://vfmat.ch/df2e

African Mission
Aims to fight disease and poverty in Africa by supporting educational and medical projects.
Anesth, General
⊕ https://vfmat.ch/ea31

Against Malaria Foundation
Helps protect people from malaria. Funds anti-malaria nets, specifically long-lasting insecticidal nets (LLINs), and works with distribution partners to ensure they are used. Tracks and reports on net use and malaria case data.
Infect Dis
⊕ https://vfmat.ch/337d

Age International
Helps older people living in some of the world's poorest places to have improved well-being and be treated with dignity through a variety of programs, including emergency relief and cataract surgery.
ER Med, Geri, Logist-Op, Nutr, Ophth-Opt, Palliative, Pub Health
⊕ https://vfmat.ch/c7e2

AIDS Healthcare Foundation
Provides cutting-edge HIV/AIDS medical care and advocacy to over one million people in 43 countries.

Infect Dis
⊕ https://vfmat.ch/b27c

Al Basar International Foundation
Works with local partners to treat preventable blindness, and helps set up sustainable infrastructure so local teams can save sight in their communities.
Ophth-Opt
⊕ https://vfmat.ch/a8b5

AMARI (African Mental Health Research Initiative)
Seeks to build an Africa-led network of future leaders in mental, neurological, and substance use (MNS) research in Ethiopia, Malawi, South Africa, and Zimbabwe.
Neuro, Psych
⊕ https://vfmat.ch/5e9d

American Cancer Society
Saves lives, celebrates lives, and leads the fight for a world without cancer.
Heme-Onc, Logist-Op, Medicine, Rad-Onc, Radiol
⊕ https://vfmat.ch/f996

American Foundation for Children with AIDS
Provides critical comprehensive services to infected and affected HIV-positive children and their caregivers.
Infect Dis, Nutr, Pub Health
⊕ https://vfmat.ch/6258

Americares
Saves lives and improves health for people affected by poverty or disaster and responds with life-changing medicine, medical supplies, and health programs including domestic and global medical clinics.
All-Immu, ER Med, General, Infect Dis, MF Med, Nutr
⊕ https://vfmat.ch/e567

Amref Health Africa
Serves millions of people across 35 countries in Sub-Saharan Africa, strengthening health systems, and training African health workers to respond to the continent's most critical health issues.
All-Immu, General, Infect Dis, Logist-Op, MF Med, OB-GYN, Path, Pub Health, Surg
⊕ https://vfmat.ch/6985

Amsterdam Institute for Global Health and Development (AIGHD)
Provides sustainable solutions to major health problems across our planet by forging synergies among disciplines, healthcare delivery, research, and education.
Infcct Dis
⊕ https://vfmat.ch/d73d

Angels Foundation
Inspired by the Christian faith, aims to provide services and assist the most vulnerable and elderly populations through programs in community development, healthcare, disaster relief, and disability aid.
Dent-OMFS, General
⊕ https://vfmat.ch/e683

AO Alliance
Builds solutions to lessen the burden of injuries in low- and middle-income countries, while enhancing the care of the injured to reduce human suffering, disability, and poverty.
Ortho, Surg
⊕ https://vfmat.ch/8cd5

Avert
Works to ensure widespread understanding of HIV/AIDS in order to reduce new infections and improve the lives of those affected.
Infect Dis, Path
⊕ https://vfmat.ch/312d

Better Healthcare for Africa (BHA)
Improves healthcare in Africa with a focus on reducing suffering from cancer, improving maternal health, and helping hospitals meet critical needs.
Crit-Care, Heme-Onc, Infect Dis, MF Med, OB-GYN
⊕ https://vfmat.ch/5b6f

BFIRST – British Foundation for International Reconstructive Surgery & Training
Supports projects across the developing world to train surgeons in their local environment to effectively manage devastating injuries.
Anesth, Plast, Surg
⊕ https://vfmat.ch/ad4f

Bread and Water for Africa UK
Aims to create better access to education, nutrition, and healthcare for some of Africa's most vulnerable children and their communities.
General, MF Med, Nutr
⊕ https://vfmat.ch/c855

Buy A Brick Foundation
Aims to help create self-sustaining, thriving communities in Zimbabwe and nourish the holistic needs of its people.
ER Med, General, Infect Dis, Logist-Op
⊕ https://vfmat.ch/f35b

CARE
Works around the globe to save lives, defeat poverty, and achieve social justice.
ER Med, General
⊕ https://vfmat.ch/7232

Catholic Organization for Relief & Development Aid (CORDAID)
Provides humanitarian assistance and creates opportunities to improve security, healthcare, education, and inclusive economic growth in fragile and conflict-affected areas.
ER Med, Infect Dis, MF Med, OB-GYN, Peds, Psych
⊕ https://vfmat.ch/8ae5

Center for Strategic and International Studies (CSIS) Commission on Strengthening America's Health Security
Brings together a distinguished and diverse group of high-level opinion leaders bridging security and health, with the core aim to chart a bold vision for the future of U.S. leadership in global health.
ER Med, Infect Dis, MF Med, Pub Health
⊕ https://vfmat.ch/6d7f

Centre for Global Mental Health
Closes the care gap and reduces human rights abuses experienced by people living with mental, neurological, and substance use conditions, particularly in low-resource settings.
Neuro, OB-GYN, Palliative, Peds, Psych
⊕ https://vfmat.ch/a96d

Chain of Hope
Provides lifesaving heart operations for children around the world and supports the development of cardiac services in numerous developing and war-torn countries.
Anesth, CT Surg, CV Med, Crit-Care, Ped Surg, Peds, Pulm-Critic, Surg
⊕ https://vfmat.ch/1b1b

CharityVision International
Focuses on restoring curable sight impairment worldwide by empowering local physicians and creating sustainable solutions.
Logist-Op, Ophth-Opt, Surg
⊕ https://vfmat.ch/6231

Child Legacy International
Works in Africa to transform lives by providing opportunities that break the generational cycle of poverty and despair, inspired by the Christian faith.
All-Immu, General, Heme-Onc, Surg
⊕ https://vfmat.ch/a2bd

Christian Blind Mission (CBM)
Aims to improve the quality of life of persons with disabilities in the poorest countries, addressing poverty as a cause and a consequence of disability, and working in partnership to create a society for all.
ENT, General, Infect Dis, OB-GYN, Ophth-Opt, Ortho, Peds, Psych, Rehab, Surg
⊕ https://vfmat.ch/3824

Christian Connections for International Health (CCIH)
Promotes global health and wholeness from a Christian perspective.
All-Immu, General, Infect Dis, MF Med, Neonat, OB-GYN, Psych
⊕ https://vfmat.ch/fa5d

Clinton Health Access Initiative (CHAI)
Aims to save lives and reduce the burden of disease in low- and middle-income countries. Works with partners to strengthen the capabilities of governments and the private sector to create and sustain high-quality health systems.
General, Heme-Onc, Infect Dis, Logist-Op, MF Med, Medicine, Neonat, Nutr, OB-GYN, Path, Peds, Rad-Onc
⊕ https://vfmat.ch/9ed7

Columbia Vagelos College of Physicians and Surgeons Programs in Global Health
Harnesses the expertise of the medical school to improve health worldwide by training global health leaders, building capacity through interdisciplinary education and training programs, and addressing unmet health needs through research and application.
CV Med, Derm, Genetics, Heme-Onc, Infect Dis, Medicine, OB-GYN, Ophth-Opt, Peds, Psych, Pub Health, Pulm-Critic, Surg
⊕ https://vfmat.ch/a9e5

COVID-19 Clinical Research Coalition
Advocates and collaborates for the advancement of COVID-19 research driven by the needs of low-resource settings, and works for equitable access to solutions to the pandemic.
All-Immu, Infect-Dis, MF Med, Path, Pub Health
⊕ https://vfmat.ch/d1f4

CURE Children's Hospital of Zimbabwe
Heals children living with disabilities such as clubfoot, bowed legs, cleft lips, untreated burns, and hydrocephalus.
ENT, Neurosurg, Ortho, Peds, Plast
⊕ https://vfmat.ch/473c

Delta Philanthropies
Invests in four strategic pillars to implement projects in areas critical for human capital development, including education, health, rural transformation and sustainable livelihoods, and disaster preparedness and relief.
General, Infect Dis, Pub Health
⊕ https://vfmat.ch/1362

Direct Relief
Improves the health and lives of people affected by poverty or emergency situations by mobilizing and providing essential medical resources needed for their care.
ER Med, Logist-Op
⊕ https://vfmat.ch/58e5

Doctors Without Borders/Médecins Sans Frontières (MSF)
Responds to emergencies and provides lifesaving medical care where needed most, including during disasters, conflicts, and epidemics.
Anesth, Crit-Care, ER Med, General, Infect Dis, Nutr, OB-GYN, Ped Surg, Peds, Psych, Pub Health, Surg
⊕ https://vfmat.ch/f363

Duke University: Global Health Institute
Sparks innovation in global health research and education, and brings together knowledge and resources to address the most important global health issues of our time.
All-Immu, Infect Dis, MF Med, OB-GYN, Pub Health
⊕ https://vfmat.ch/c4cd

Egmont Trust, The
Works with partner organizations in Sub-Saharan Africa, making grants to help vulnerable children cope with the impact of HIV/AIDS on families and communities.
General, Infect Dis, OB-GYN, Peds
⊕ https://vfmat.ch/57a9

Elizabeth Glaser Pediatric AIDS Foundation
Seeks to end global pediatric HIV/AIDS through prevention and treatment programs, research, and advocacy.
Infect Dis, Nutr, OB-GYN, Peds
⊕ https://vfmat.ch/d6ec

Elton John AIDS Foundation
Seeks to address and overcome the stigma, discrimination, and neglect that prevents ending AIDS by funding local experts to challenge discrimination, prevent infections, and provide treatment.
Infect Dis, Pub Health
⊕ https://vfmat.ch/9d31

END Fund, The
Aims to control and eliminate the most prevalent neglected diseases among the world's poorest and most vulnerable people.
Infect Dis
⊕ https://vfmat.ch/2614

Episcopal Relief & Development
Provides relief in times of disaster and promotes sustainable development by identifying and addressing the root causes of suffering.
Infect Dis, MF Med, Neonat, Nutr, Peds
⊕ https://vfmat.ch/7cfa

eRanger
Provides sustainable solutions to transportation and medical provision such as ambulances and mobile clinics in developing countries.
ER Med, General, Logist-Op
⊕ https://vfmat.ch/4c18

Evangelical Alliance Mission, The (TEAM)
Provides services in the areas of church planting, community development, healthcare, social justice, business as mission, and more.
Dent-OMFS, General, Ophth-Opt
⊕ https://vfmat.ch/9faa

Eye Foundation of America
Works toward a world without childhood blindness.
Ophth-Opt
⊕ https://vfmat.ch/a7eb

Fistula Foundation
Aims to engage the support of people worldwide who are eager to see the day that no woman suffers from obstetric fistula. Raises and directs funds to doctors and hospitals providing life-transforming surgery to women in need.
OB-GYN
⊕ https://vfmat.ch/e958

Foundation For International Education In Neurological Surgery (FIENS), The
Provides hands-on training and education to neurosurgeons around the world.
Neuro, Neurosurg, Surg
⊕ https://vfmat.ch/bab8

Friends of Murambinda Hospital
Works to improve the health of the people of Buhera, Zimbabwe, by partnering with Murambinda Mission Hospital to treat the local population and provide medical and social services to nearby communities.
General, Logist-Op
⊕ https://vfmat.ch/f881

Gift of Life International
Provides lifesaving cardiac treatment to children in developing countries while developing sustainable pediatric cardiac programs by implementing screening, surgical, and training missions.
Anesth, CT Surg, CV Med, Crit-Care, Ped Surg, Peds, Pulm-Critic
⊕ https://vfmat.ch/f2f9

Global Aid Missions
Offers counselling, health, education, advocacy, employment networks, and protection against abuse for people with albinism.
Genetics
⊕ https://vfmat.ch/dcf3

Global Blood Fund
Delivers grants, equipment, and training to over 50 countries in Africa, Asia, Eastern Europe, the Middle East, Latin America and the Caribbean.
Pub Health
⊕ https://vfmat.ch/6377

Global First Responder (GFR)
Acts as a centralized network for individuals and agencies involved in relief work worldwide and organizes and executes mission trips to areas in need, focusing not only on healthcare delivery but also on health education and improvements.
ER Med
⊕ https://vfmat.ch/a3e1

Global Medical Missions
Organizes medical missions and partners with local medical organizations, usually hospitals or health systems, in fulfilling their mission of reaching their community's health needs in developing countries by providing needed medical care and screening to those underserved.
General
⊕ https://vfmat.ch/8d73

Global Ministries – The United Methodist Church
As the worldwide mission and development agency of The United Methodist Church, Global Ministries works with more than 300 hospitals and clinics around the world through its Global Health Unit.
Anesth, CT Surg, CV Med, Crit-Care, Dent-OMFS, Derm, ER Med, GI, General, Infect Dis, Logist-Op, MF Med, Medicine, Neonat, Nephro, Nutr, OB-GYN, Ophth-Opt, Ortho, Palliative, Peds, Pod, Psych, Pub Health, Rehab, Rheum, Surg, Urol
⊕ https://vfmat.ch/1723

Global Offsite Care
Aims to be a catalyst for increased access to specialized healthcare for all, and provides technology platforms to doctors and clinics around the world through Rotary Club-sponsored telemedicine projects.
Crit-Care, ER Med, General, Pulm-Critic
⊕ https://vfmat.ch/61b5

Global Oncology (GO)
Brings the best in cancer care to underserved patients around the world and collaborates across geographic, professional, and academic borders to improve cancer care, research, and education.
Heme-Onc, Path, Rad-Onc
⊕ https://vfmat.ch/fcb8

GlobalMedic
Provides disaster relief and lifesaving humanitarian aid.
ER Med, Pub Health
⊕ https://vfmat.ch/dfe6

Globus Relief
Aims to improve the delivery of healthcare worldwide by gathering, processing, and distributing surplus medical supplies to charities at home and abroad.
Logist-Op
⊕ https://vfmat.ch/a2b7

GOAL
Works with the most vulnerable communities to help them respond to and recover from humanitarian crises, and to assist them in building transcendent solutions to mitigate poverty and vulnerability.
ER Med, General, Pub Health
⊕ https://vfmat.ch/bbea

Grassroot Soccer
Leverages the power of soccer to educate, inspire, and mobilize at-risk youth in developing countries to overcome their greatest health challenges, live healthier and more productive lives, and be agents for change in their communities.
Infect Dis
⊕ https://vfmat.ch/3521

Hands At Work
Based in Christian ministry, supports those in need through its community intervention model with a focus on food security, education, and basic healthcare.

General, Infect Dis, Nutr, Pub Health
⊕ https://vfmat.ch/7274

Health Care Advocates International (HCAI)
Seeks to end HIV as a global health crisis, and reduce morbidity and mortality from HIV/AIDS (and its associated co-morbidities) and other sexually transmitted diseases.
General, Infect Dis, Plast, Psych
⊕ https://vfmat.ch/16ca

Health Poverty Action
Works in partnership with people around the world who are pursuing change in their own communities to demand health justice and challenge power imbalances.
ER Med, General, Infect Dis, Psych, Pub Health
⊕ https://vfmat.ch/ee58

Healthy Smiles Society
Seeks to provide and promote mobile dental services in rural developing countries.
Dent-OMFS
⊕ https://vfmat.ch/5d8e

Heineman Medical Outreach
Provides medical and educational assistance globally to promote sustainable healthcare and enhanced living standards in underserved communities through the International Medical Outreach (IMO) program, a collaborative partnership between Heineman Medical Outreach and Atrium Health.
Anesth, CT Surg, CV Med, ER Med, General, Heme-Onc, Logist-Op, Medicine, Neonat, OB-GYN, Ped Surg, Peds, Surg, Vasc Surg
⊕ https://vfmat.ch/389b

Hernia International
Aims to provide relief from sickness, and protection and preservation of health, for persons affected by groin and abdominal hernias and residing in low- and middle-income countries.
Surg
⊕ https://vfmat.ch/e98e

Hope and Healing International
Gives hope and healing to children and families trapped by poverty and disability.
General, Nutr, Ophth-Opt, Peds, Rehab
⊕ https://vfmat.ch/c638

Hospice Africa
Aims to provide a holistic and culturally sensitive palliative care service through accurate treatment of pain.
Palliative
⊕ https://vfmat.ch/9f86

Hospice and Palliative Care Association of Zimbabwe (HOSPAZ)
Promotes and supports palliative care for all in Zimbabwe through capacity development, coordination, and advocacy.
Palliative, Peds
⊕ https://vfmat.ch/decd

ICAP at Columbia University
Serves as global leader in supporting the scale-up of multidisciplinary HIV/AIDS prevention, care, and treatment programs based on a family-focused approach.
General, Infect Dis, MF Med, Medicine, OB-GYN, Pub Health
⊕ https://vfmat.ch/a8ef

International Agency for the Prevention of Blindness (IAPB), The
Leads international efforts in blindness-prevention activities, works toward a world where no one is needlessly visually impaired, and ensures that everyone has access to the best possible standard of eye health.
Infect Dis, Ophth-Opt, Pub Health
⊕ https://vfmat.ch/87a2

International Campaign for Women's Right to Safe Abortion
Works to build an international network and campaign that brings together

organizations with an interest in promoting and providing safe abortion to create a shared platform for advocacy, debate, and dialogue and the sharing of skills and experience.

OB-GYN, Pub Health, Surg

⊕ https://vfmat.ch/f341

International Council of Ophthalmology
Works with ophthalmologic societies and others to enhance ophthalmic education and improve access to the highest-quality eye care in order to preserve and restore vision for people of the world.

Ophth-Opt

⊕ https://vfmat.ch/ffd2

International Federation of Gynecology and Obstetrics (FIGO)
Implements global projects on specific women's health issues.

MF Med, Medicine, Neonat, OB-GYN, Surg, Urol

⊕ https://vfmat.ch/c4b4

International Federation of Red Cross and Red Crescent Societies (IFRC)
Coordinates and directs international assistance following natural and manmade disasters in nonconflict situations through the world's largest humanitarian and development network. Provides disaster-preparedness programs, healthcare activities, and promotes humanitarian values.

ER Med, General, Infect Dis, Nutr

⊕ https://vfmat.ch/b4ee

International Medical Corps
Seeks to improve quality of life through health interventions and related activities that strengthen underserved communities worldwide, with the flexibility to respond rapidly to emergencies and offer medical services and training to people at the highest risk.

ER Med, General, Infect Dis, Nutr, OB-GYN, Peds, Pub Health, Surg

⊕ https://vfmat.ch/a8a5

International Organization for Migration (IOM) – The UN Migration Agency
Promotes evidence-informed policies and holistic, preventive, and curative health programs that are beneficial, accessible, and equitable for vulnerable migrants.

General, Infect Dis, OB-GYN

⊕ https://vfmat.ch/621a

International Rescue Committee (IRC)
Responds to the world's worst humanitarian crises and helps people whose lives and livelihoods are shattered by conflict and disaster to survive, recover, and gain control of their future.

ER Med, General, Infect Dis, MF Med, Peds

⊕ https://vfmat.ch/5d24

International Trachoma Initiative (iTi)
Works toward a world free from trachoma, a preventable cause of blindness, and provides comprehensive support to national ministries of health and governmental and nongovernmental organizations to implement a comprehensive approach to fight trachoma.

Infect Dis, Ophth-Opt

⊕ https://vfmat.ch/3278

InterSurgeon
Fosters collaborative partnerships in the field of global surgery that will advance clinical care, teaching, training, research, and the provision and maintenance of medical equipment.

ENT, Neurosurg, Ortho, Ped Surg, Plast, Surg, Urol

⊕ https://vfmat.ch/6f8a

IntraHealth International
Improves the performance of health workers and strengthens the systems in which they work.

CV Med, Endo, General, Infect Dis, MF Med, Neonat, Nutr, OB-GYN

⊕ https://vfmat.ch/ddc8

iQra International
Provides medical aid to disabled people globally, and raises awareness of the neglect and discrimination they face in developing countries.

General, Logist-Op, Ophth-Opt

⊕ https://vfmat.ch/9282

Iris Global
Serves the poor, the destitute, the lost, and the forgotten by providing adoration, outreach, family, education, relief, development, healing, and the arts.

General, Infect Dis, Nutr, Pub Health

⊕ https://vfmat.ch/37f8

Islamic Medical Association of North America
Fosters health promotion, disease prevention, and health maintenance in communities around the world through direct patient care and health programs.

Anesth, Dent-OMFS, ER Med, General, Logist-Op, Ophth-Opt, Peds, Plast, Surg

⊕ https://vfmat.ch/a157

Island Hospice
Provides home-based palliative care and a compassionate bereavement service.

Infect Dis, Palliative, Peds

⊕ https://vfmat.ch/b1e1

IVUmed
Aims to make quality urological care available worldwide by providing medical and surgical education for physicians and nurses, and treatment for thousands of children and adults.

Anesth, OB-GYN, Ped Surg, Surg, Urol

⊕ https://vfmat.ch/e619

Jhpiego
Creates and delivers transformative healthcare solutions that save lives, in partnership with national governments, health experts, and local communities.

General, Infect Dis, OB-GYN, Surg

⊕ https://vfmat.ch/45b8

John Snow, Inc. (JSI)
Aims to improve the health and well-being of underserved and vulnerable people and communities throughout the world.

General, Infect Dis, Logist-Op, MF Med, OB-GYN, Peds, Psych, Pub Health

⊕ https://vfmat.ch/ba78

Johns Hopkins Center for Communication Programs
Believes in the power of communication to save lives by empowering people to adopt healthy behaviors for themselves, their families, and their communities.

General, Infect Dis, Logist-Op, OB-GYN, Pub Health

⊕ https://vfmat.ch/1bf9

Joint United Nations Programme on HIV/AIDS (UNAIDS)
Aims to place people living with HIV and people affected by the virus at the decision-making table and at the center of designing, delivering, and monitoring the AIDS response.

Infect Dis

⊕ https://vfmat.ch/464a

Kaya Responsible Travel
Promotes sustainable social, environmental, and economic development, empowers communities, and cultivates educated, compassionate global citizens through responsible travel.

All-Immu, Crit-Care, Dent-OMFS, ER Med, General, Geri, Infect Dis, MF Med, Medicine, Nutr, OB-GYN, Peds, Psych, Pub Health, Rehab

⊕ https://vfmat.ch/b2cf

Kind Cuts for Kids
Aims to improve medical services for children in developing countries through education, demonstration, and skills transfer to local healthcare professionals.

Anesth, Medicine, Ped Surg, Surg

⊕ https://vfmat.ch/e3d7

LEAP Global Missions
Provides specialized surgical services to underserved populations around the world.

Anesth, Dent-OMFS, ENT, Ped Surg, Peds, Plast, Surg

⊕ https://vfmat.ch/b447

Lepra

Works directly with communities in Bangladesh, India, Mozambique, and Zimbabwe to find, treat, and rehabilitate people affected by leprosy.

Infect Dis, Pub Health, Rehab

⊕ https://vfmat.ch/5d1c

Life for a Child

Supports the provision of the best possible healthcare, given local circumstances, to all children and youth with diabetes in less-resourced countries, through the strengthening of existing diabetes services.

Endo, Medicine, Peds

⊕ https://vfmat.ch/d712

Lifebox

Seeks to provide safer surgery and anesthesia in low-resource countries by investing in tools, training, and partnerships for safe surgery.

Anesth, Crit-Care, Surg

⊕ https://vfmat.ch/2d4d

Management Sciences for Health (MSH)

Works with countries and communities to save lives and improve the health of the world's poorest and most vulnerable people by building strong, resilient, sustainable health systems.

Infect Dis, Logist-Op, Pub Health

⊕ https://vfmat.ch/6aa2

MAP International

Provides medicines and health supplies to those in need around the world so they might experience life to the fullest.

Logist-Op

⊕ https://vfmat.ch/deed

Marie Stopes International

Provides the contraception and safe abortion services that enable women all over the world to choose their own futures.

Infect Dis, MF Med, Neonat, OB-GYN, Pub Health

⊕ https://vfmat.ch/9525

Mashoko Christian Hospital

Based in Christian ministry, provides healthcare services and community support to those in need.

Infect Dis, Neonat, OB-GYN

⊕ https://vfmat.ch/1c9c

Maternity Worldwide

Works with communities and partners to identify and develop appropriate and effective ways to reduce maternal and newborn mortality and morbidity, facilitate communities to access quality skilled maternity care, and support the provision of quality skilled care.

MF Med, OB-GYN

⊕ https://vfmat.ch/822b

Maverick Collective

Aims to build a global community of strategic philanthropists and informed advocates who use their intellectual and financial resources to create change.

Infect Dis, MF Med, OB-GYN

⊕ https://vfmat.ch/ea49

Medical Equipment Modernization Opportunity (MEMO)

Based in Christian ministry, works with churches and organizations to collect and send hospital equipment and supplies to healthcare facilities in need around the world.

Logist-Op

⊕ https://vfmat.ch/1c78

MedShare

Aims to improve the quality of life of people, communities, and the planet by sourcing and directly delivering surplus medical supplies and equipment to communities in need around the world.

Logist-Op

⊕ https://vfmat.ch/c8bc

Meikles Foundation, The

Creates a roadmap for business by empowering partnerships that create value through social, moral, strategic, and environmental corporate social responsibility initiatives in Zimbabwe.

Dent-OMFS, General

⊕ https://vfmat.ch/cfbc

Mercy and Love Foundation

Aims to provide orphaned and vulnerable children with basic human needs such as food, clothing, and shelter, enabling them to thrive.

General, Peds

⊕ https://vfmat.ch/649a

MiracleFeet

Brings low-cost treatment to every child on the planet born with clubfoot, a leading cause of physical disability.

Ortho, Peds, Rehab

⊕ https://vfmat.ch/bda8

Mission Bambini

Helps to support children living in poverty and sickness, and lacking education, giving them the opportunity for and hope of a better life.

CT Surg, CV Med, Crit-Care, ER Med, Ped Surg, Peds

⊕ https://vfmat.ch/dc1a

Mission Doctors Association

Provides life-saving medical care for the poor and training for local healthcare professionals around the world.

CV Med, Dent-OMFS, General, Logist-Op, Medicine, OB-GYN, Ophth-Opt, Peds, Surg

⊕ https://vfmat.ch/6c18

Mission Vision

Seeks to decrease blindness and other eye-related disabilities, and to increase academic performance and general quality of life.

Ophth-Opt

⊕ https://vfmat.ch/83d8

MSI Reproductive Choices (Marie Stopes International)

Seeks to deliver quality family planning and reproductive healthcare to women around the world.

MF Med

⊕ https://vfmat.ch/5c82

Mugwagwa Elderly Foundation Trust

Improves the health and welfare of the elderly population below the poverty line in Zimbabwe.

Logist-Op, Palliative

⊕ https://vfmat.ch/be7b

Mustard Seed Communities (MSC)

Inspired by the Christian faith, uplifts the most vulnerable members of society through nutrition, education, community development, child health, and sustainable agriculture programs.

Infect Dis, Logist-Op, Rehab

⊕ https://vfmat.ch/eac5

New Horizons Collaborative

Advances a holistic, integrated approach to high-quality pediatric HIV care and treatment with a specific focus on those in need of advanced treatment.

Infect Dis, Peds, Pub Health

⊕ https://vfmat.ch/a76a

Newstart Children's Home, The

Provides shelter, medical and dental services, education, and basic necessities to children experiencing homelessness.

Peds

⊕ https://vfmat.ch/a419

Nhaka Foundation

Educates, feeds, and improves the health of orphans and vulnerable children of Africa.

Peds, Pub Health
⊕ https://vfmat.ch/2d86

Nhowe Mission
Provides for the physical, spiritual, and emotional needs of those in rural Zimbabwe.
Infect Dis, OB-GYN, Surg
⊕ https://vfmat.ch/521d

Norwegian People's Aid
Aims to improve living conditions, to create a democratic, just, and safe society.
ER Med, Logist-Op
⊕ https://vfmat.ch/2d8e

Novick Cardiac Alliance
Committed to bringing sustainable healthcare solutions to children with cardiac disease in the developing world.
Anesth, CT Surg, CV Med, Crit-Care, Ped Surg, Peds
⊕ https://vfmat.ch/72db

Operation of Hope
Provides free, life-changing surgery and healthcare for children in desperate need and creates a self-sustaining program of hope through education.
Dent-OMFS, ENT, Neonat, Ortho, Ped Surg, Plast
⊕ https://vfmat.ch/e26b

Options
Believes in a world in which women and children can access the high-quality health services they need, without financial burden.
Logist-Op, MF Med, Neonat, OB-GYN
⊕ https://vfmat.ch/3a48

Pact
Works on the ground to improve the lives of those who are challenged by poverty and marginalization, striving for a world in which all people are heard, capable, and vibrant.
Infect Dis, Logist-Op, MF Med, Pub Health
⊕ https://vfmat.ch/9a6c

Pangaea Zimbabwe Aids Trust (PZAT)
Strives to transform the lives of people living with and affected by HIV, and to ensure the delivery of comprehensive HIV and sexual health services in safe and supportive environments.
Infect Dis, Pub Health
⊕ https://vfmat.ch/5f3c

PLeDGE Health
Aims to improve emergency medical care around the world through sustainable partnerships, open-source material development and dissemination, and development of the next generation of educational leaders in low-resource areas.
ER Med, General
⊕ https://vfmat.ch/3a7d

Positive Action for Treatment Access (PATA)
Ensures that every individual with an illness or disease, especially women and girls, has access to treatment and literacy skills, and to equitable, humane care and empowerment.
Infect Dis, OB-GYN, Peds, Pub Health
⊕ https://vfmat.ch/46f9

Project SOAR
Conducts HIV operations research around the world to identify practical solutions to improve HIV prevention, care, and treatment services.
ER Med, General, MF Med, OB-GYN, Psych
⊕ https://vfmat.ch/1a77

RestoringVision
Empowers lives by restoring vision for millions of people in need.
Ophth-Opt
⊕ https://vfmat.ch/e121

ReSurge International
Provides reconstructive surgical care and builds surgical capacity in

developing countries.
Anesth, Dent-OMFS, Ped Surg, Plast, Surg
⊕ https://vfmat.ch/9937

Riders for Health International
Aids in the last mile of healthcare delivery, by ensuring that healthcare reaches everyone, everywhere.
ER Med, Infect Dis, Logist-Op, Pub Health
⊕ https://vfmat.ch/85aa

Rockefeller Foundation, The
Works to promote the well-being of humanity.
Logist-Op, Nutr, Pub Health
⊕ https://vfmat.ch/5424

Rotary International
Provides service to others, improves lives, and advances world understanding, goodwill, and peace through its fellowship of business, professional, and community leaders.
ER Med, General, Infect Dis, MF Med, OB-GYN
⊕ https://vfmat.ch/8fb5

ROW Foundation
Works to improve the quality of training for healthcare providers, and the diagnosis and treatment available to people with epilepsy and associated psychiatric disorders in under-resourced areas of the world.
Neuro, Psych
⊕ https://vfmat.ch/25eb

Rutgers New Jersey Medical School
Seeks to support and promote the global health efforts of the faculty, staff, and students in the areas of education, research, and service through the Rutgers New Jersey Medical School's Office of Global Health.
Anesth, CV Med, Crit-Care, Neurosurg, OB-GYN, Psych
⊕ https://vfmat.ch/8e67

Salvation Army International, The
Seeks to meet human needs through services in education, healthcare, community support, emergency response, and ministry development, inspired by the Christian faith.
Dent-OMFS, Derm, ER Med, Infect Dis, MF Med, Medicine, Nutr, OB-GYN, Ophth-Opt, Palliative, Psych, Rehab, Surg
⊕ https://vfmat.ch/8eb3

Samaritan's Purse International Disaster Relief
Provides spiritual and physical aid to hurting people around the world, such as victims of war, poverty, natural disasters, disease, and famine, based in Christian ministry.
Anesth, CT Surg, Crit-Care, Dent-OMFS, Derm, ENT, ER Med, Endo, GI, General, Heme-Onc, Infect Dis, MF Med, Neonat, Nephro, Neuro, Neurosurg, Nutr, OB-GYN, Ophth-Opt, Ortho, Path, Ped Surg, Peds, Plast, Psych, Pulm-Critic, Radiol, Rehab, Rheum, Surg, Urol, Vasc Surg
⊕ https://vfmat.ch/87e3

Save the Children
Gives children around the world a healthy start in life, the opportunity to learn, and protection from harm.
All-Immu, Crit-Care, ER Med, General, Infect Dis, MF Med, Medicine, Neonat, OB-GYN, Peds, Psych, Pub Health
⊕ https://vfmat.ch/2e73

Sightsavers
Works with partners in developing countries to help eliminate avoidable blindness and advocates for equal opportunity for the disabled.
Infect Dis, Ophth-Opt, Surg
⊕ https://vfmat.ch/aa52

SIGN Fracture Care International
Builds orthopedic capacity around the world and provides the injured poor access to fracture surgery by donating orthopedic education and implant systems to surgeons in developing countries.
Ortho, Rehab, Surg
⊕ https://vfmat.ch/123d

SINA Health
Aims to improve the health and educational status of the population in low- and middle-income countries.
General, Logist-Op
⊕ https://vfmat.ch/9ad3

Smile Train, Inc.
Treats children with cleft lip through a sustainable and local model that supports surgery and other forms of essential care.
Logist-Op, Pub Health
⊕ https://vfmat.ch/822c

Sri Sathya Sai International Organization
Inspired by spiritual teachings, carries out efforts in global healthcare, education, humanitarian relief, and youth engagement.
Dent-OMFS, General, Logist-Op, Nutr, Ophth-Opt, Pub Health
⊕ https://vfmat.ch/9bda

Surgical Healing of Africa's Youth Foundation, The (S.H.A.Y.)
Provides volunteer reconstructive surgery to children in need, including treating congenital anomalies such as cleft lip/palate and general reconstruction.
Anesth, Dent-OMFS, Peds, Plast
⊕ https://vfmat.ch/41a7

Sustainable Cardiovascular Health Equity Development Alliance
Fights cardiovascular disease in underserved populations globally via education, training, and increasing interventional capacity.
CV Med, Pub Health, Radiol
⊕ https://vfmat.ch/799c

Swiss Tropical and Public Health Institute
Contributes to the improvement of the health of populations internationally, nationally, and locally through excellence in research, education, and services.
Infect Dis, Pub Health
⊕ https://vfmat.ch/2ee4

Task Force for Global Health, The
Consists of programs and focus areas that cover a range of global health issues including neglected tropical diseases, infectious diseases, vaccines, field epidemiology, public health informatics, health workforce development, and global health ethics.
Infect Dis, Logist-Op, Medicine, Ophth-Opt, Peds
⊕ https://vfmat.ch/714c

TB Alert
Offers a range of programmatic, advisory, technical, and training services around tuberculosis, and is active in international advocacy initiatives.
Infect Dis, Pub Health, Pulm-Critic
⊕ https://vfmat.ch/1d5e

Tearfund
Responds to crisis and partners with local churches to bring restoration to those living in poverty, inspired by the Christian faith.
ER Med, Logist-Op
⊕ https://vfmat.ch/f6cf

Tekeshe Foundation, The
Provides and promotes economic empowerment, advocates for literacy and higher education, and assists HIV/AIDS patients and their families with social-economic help in the Chipinge district of Zimbabwe.
ER Med, General, Infect Dis, Logist-Op, Nutr
⊕ https://vfmat.ch/eda9

Transplant Links Community (TLC)
Provides hands-on training in kidney transplantation for surgeons, doctors, and nurses in low- and middle-income countries.
Nephro, Surg, Urol
⊕ https://vfmat.ch/bb46

U.S. President's Malaria Initiative (PMI)
Supports low-income countries to help control and eliminate malaria through cost-effective, lifesaving malaria interventions.

Infect Dis, MF Med, OB-GYN
⊕ https://vfmat.ch/dc8b

Union for International Cancer Control (UICC)
Unites and supports the cancer community to reduce the global cancer burden, promote greater equity, and ensure that cancer control continues to be a priority in the world health and development agenda.
Heme-Onc, Pub Health
⊕ https://vfmat.ch/88b1

United Nations Children's Fund (UNICEF)
Works in over 190 countries and territories to save children's lives, defend their rights, and help them fulfill their potential, from early childhood through adolescence.
All-Immu, Infect Dis, MF Med, Neonat, Nutr, OB-GYN, Ped Surg, Peds, Pub Health
⊕ https://vfmat.ch/42d7

United Nations Development Programme (UNDP)
Helps countries achieve the simultaneous eradication of extreme poverty and significant reduction of inequalities and exclusion using a sustainable human development approach.
Infect Dis, Logist-Op, Pub Health
⊕ https://vfmat.ch/935c

United Nations High Commissioner for Refugees (UNHCR)
Safeguards the rights and well-being of people who have been forced to flee, ensuring that everybody has the right to seek asylum and find safe refuge in another country, with the goal of seeking lasting solutions.
General, MF Med, Medicine, OB-GYN, Peds, Psych, Pub Health
⊕ https://vfmat.ch/6636

United Nations Population Fund (UNFPA)
Supports reproductive healthcare for women and youth in more than 150 countries, focusing on delivering a world in which every pregnancy is wanted, every childbirth is safe, and every young person's potential is fulfilled.
Infect Dis, MF Med, Neonat, OB-GYN, Peds, Pub Health
⊕ https://vfmat.ch/c969

United States Agency for International Development (USAID)
Promotes and demonstrates democratic values abroad and advances a free, peaceful, and prosperous world. Leads the U.S. government's international development and disaster assistance through partnerships and investments that save lives.
ER Med, Infect Dis, MF Med, OB-GYN, Peds
⊕ https://vfmat.ch/9a99

United States President's Emergency Plan for AIDS Relief (PEPFAR)
The U.S. global HIV/AIDS response works to prevent new HIV infections and accelerate progress to control the global epidemic in more than 50 countries, by partnering with governments to support sustainable, integrated, and country-led responses to HIV/AIDS.
Infect Dis, Pub Health
⊕ https://vfmat.ch/a57c

University of Colorado: Global Emergency Care Initiative
Strives to sustainably improve emergency care outcomes in low- and middle-income communities worldwide by linking cutting-edge academics with excellent on-the-ground implementation.
ER Med
⊕ https://vfmat.ch/417a

University of New Mexico School of Medicine: Project Echo
Seeks to improve health outcomes worldwide through the use of a technology called telementoring, a guided-practice model in which the participating clinician retains responsibility for managing the patient.
General, Infect Dis, MF Med, OB-GYN, Path, Peds
⊕ https://vfmat.ch/6c9a

University of Pennsylvania Perelman School of Medicine Center for Global Health
Aims to improve health equity worldwide through enhanced public health awareness and access to care, discovery, and outcomes-based research, and

comprehensive educational programs grounded in partnership.
Heme-Onc, Infect Dis, OB-GYN
⊕ https://vfmat.ch/cb57

University of Washington: The International Training and Education Center for Health (I-TECH)
Works with local partners to develop skilled healthcare workers and strong national health systems in resource-limited countries.
Infect Dis, Pub Health
⊕ https://vfmat.ch/642f

USAID: A2Z The Micronutrient and Child Blindness Project
Aims to increase the use of key micronutrient and blindness interventions to improve child and maternal health.
MF Med, Neonat, Nutr, Ophth-Opt, Surg
⊕ https://vfmat.ch/c5f1

USAID: Deliver Project
Builds a global supply chain to deliver lifesaving health products to people in order to enable countries to provide family planning, protect against malaria, and limit the spread of pandemic threats.
Infect Dis, Logist-Op, MF Med
⊕ https://vfmat.ch/374e

USAID: EQUIP Health
Exists as an effective, efficient response mechanism to achieving global HIV epidemic control by delivering the right intervention at the right place and in the right way.
Infect Dis
⊕ https://vfmat.ch/d76a

USAID: Leadership, Management and Governance Project
Improves leadership, management, and governance practices to strengthen health systems and improve health for all, including vulnerable populations worldwide.
Logist-Op
⊕ https://vfmat.ch/d35e

USAID: Maternal and Child Health Integrated Program
Works to improve the health of women and their families, including programs for maternal, newborn, and child health, immunization, family planning, nutrition, malaria, and HIV/AIDS.
All-Immu, General, Infect Dis, MF Med
⊕ https://vfmat.ch/4415

USAID: TB Care II
Focuses on tuberculosis care and treatment.
Infect Dis
⊕ https://vfmat.ch/57d4

Virginia Commonwealth University: Family Medicine & Epidemiology Global Health Program
Aims to build relationships with communities, develop sustainable medical services, and better appreciate the importance of health disparities and barriers to care.
General, MF Med, Medicine, Nutr, OB-GYN, Peds, Pub Health, Surg
⊕ https://vfmat.ch/a591

Vision Care
Restores sight and helps patients get regular treatment at short-term eye camps and long-term base clinics by having doctors, missionaries, volunteers, and sponsors work together.
Ophth-Opt
⊕ https://vfmat.ch/9d7c

Vision Outreach International
Advocates for helping the blind in underserved regions of the world and empowers the poor through sight restoration.
Ophth-Opt
⊕ https://vfmat.ch/9721

Vitamin Angels
Helps at-risk populations in need—specifically pregnant women, new mothers, and children under age 5—to gain access to life-changing vitamins and minerals.

General, Nutr
⊕ https://vfmat.ch/7da1

Voluntary Service Overseas (VSO)
Works with health workers, communities, and governments to improve health services and rights for women, babies, youth, people with disabilities, and prisoners.
General, MF Med, OB-GYN
⊕ https://vfmat.ch/213d

White Ribbon Alliance, The
Leads a movement for reproductive, maternal, and newborn health and accelerates progress by putting citizens at the center of global, national, and local health efforts.
MF Med, OB-GYN
⊕ https://vfmat.ch/496b

World Blind Union (WBU)
Represents those experiencing blindness, speaking to governments and international bodies on issues concerning visual impairments.
Ophth-Opt
⊕ https://vfmat.ch/2bd3

World Children's Fund
Commits to helping children worldwide who are suffering the effects of poverty, disease, natural disaster, famine, abuse, civil strife, and war.
General, Logist-Op, MF Med, Nutr, OB-GYN, Pub Health
⊕ https://vfmat.ch/9cd8

World Council of Optometry
Facilitates the development of optometry worldwide and promotes eye health and vision care through advocacy, education, policy development, and humanitarian outreach.
Ophth-Opt, Pub Health
⊕ https://vfmat.ch/c92e

World Federation of Hemophilia (WFH)
Aims to improve and sustain care for people with inherited bleeding disorders by pursuing long-term relationships with individuals and organizations who share the values of WFH's development model.
Heme-Onc
⊕ https://vfmat.ch/5121

World Health Organization, The (WHO)
The United Nations' agency for health provides leadership on global health matters, shapes the health research agenda, sets norms and standards, articulates evidence-based policy options, provides technical support and monitoring to countries, and assesses health trends.
ER Med, General, Infect Dis, Logist-Op, MF Med, OB-GYN, Peds, Psych, Pub Health
⊕ https://vfmat.ch/c476

World Medical Relief
Facilitates the distribution of surplus medical resources where they are needed.
Logist-Op
⊕ https://vfmat.ch/72dc

World Missions Possible
Provides EMS capacity-building, along with medical and vision care, to under-developed and rural areas.
ER Med, General, Heme-Onc, Neonat, Ophth-Opt, Surg
⊕ https://vfmat.ch/d6a5

World Parkinson's Program
Seeks to improve the quality of life of those affected by Parkinson's disease through education and advocacy, and provides free medication and support services.
Logist-Op, Neuro, Pub Health
⊕ https://vfmat.ch/c96d

World Vision International
Works with vulnerable communities around the world to overcome poverty and injustice with child-focused programs in disaster management, health, nutrition,

economic development, education, clean water, sanitation, and hygiene.
ER Med, General, Infect Dis, MF Med, Nutr, OB-GYN, Peds
⊕ https://vfmat.ch/2642

YORGHAS Foundation
Supports mothers, pregnant women, infants, people with disabilities, and those suffering from humanitarian crises, poverty, or social inequalities, with particular emphasis on women's and children's rights.
MF Med, Neonat
⊕ https://vfmat.ch/9e44

Zimbabwe Council for the Blind (ZCfB)
Seeks to prevent blindness, educate, and rehabilitate the blind, and supply low-cost eyeglasses.
Logist-Op, Ophth-Opt
⊕ https://vfmat.ch/baf9

Zimbabwe Gecko Society, The
Aims to break the cycle of poverty in Zimbabwe by creating long-term and sustainable health, focusing efforts on one community at a time.
Logist-Op, Peds, Pub Health
⊕ https://vfmat.ch/ce2a

Zimbabwe Health Interventions (ZHI)
Develops and delivers innovative and sustainable high-impact, integrated health interventions to the communities served, while working with and strengthening existing institutions.
Crit-Care, Infect Dis
⊕ https://vfmat.ch/e793

Zimbabwe Medical Project
Strives to eradicate preventable and curable blindness through cataract surgery and vitamin A distribution, educate and train medical staff, and support urgent local needs.
Ophth-Opt
⊕ https://vfmat.ch/4ead

Zimbabwe Mission Partnership (ZMP)
Provides a venue for participating churches and the wider community to work together to enhance the habitation, nutrition, public health, education, and spiritual development of the orphans of Zimbabwe.
Infect Dis, Peds, Pub Health
⊕ https://vfmat.ch/7783

 # Zimbabwe

Healthcare Facilities

Antelope Mine Hospital
Antelope Mine, Matabeleland South, Zimbabwe
⊕ https://vfmat.ch/9296

Baines Avenue Clinic
Harare, Harare Region, Zimbabwe
https://vfmat.ch/nrgv

Bindura General Hospital
Bindura, Mashonaland Central, Zimbabwe
⊕ https://vfmat.ch/cf56

Binga District Hospital
Binga, Matabeleland North, Zimbabwe
⊕ https://vfmat.ch/ec77

Chegutu District Hospital
Chegutu, Mashonaland West, Zimbabwe
⊕ https://vfmat.ch/8ebf

Chidamoyo Hospital
Karoi., Mashonaland West, Zimbabwe
⊕ https://vfmat.ch/5118

Chinhoyi Provincial Hospital
Chinhoyi, Mashonaland West, Zimbabwe
⊕ https://vfmat.ch/4da7

Chiredzi General Hospital
Chiredzi, Masvingo, Zimbabwe
⊕ https://vfmat.ch/68b4

Chireya Mission Hospital
Gokwe, Midlands, Zimbabwe
⊕ https://vfmat.ch/62b1

Chitando District Hospital
Chief Makore, Masvingo, Zimbabwe
⊕ https://vfmat.ch/c1f7

Chitungwiza Central Hospital
Kaseke, Harare, Zimbabwe
⊕ https://vfmat.ch/d1e9

Chivhu General Hospital
Chivhu, Mashonaland East, Zimbabwe
⊕ https://vfmat.ch/a28d

Chivi District Hospital
Chivi, Masvingo, Zimbabwe
⊕ https://vfmat.ch/8b81

Citimed Chitungwiza Hospital
Chitungwiza, Harare, Zimbabwe
⊕ https://vfmat.ch/6575

Concession District Hospital
Concession, Mashonaland Central, Zimbabwe
⊕ https://vfmat.ch/5b42

Gokwe North District Hospital
Nembudziya, Midlands, Zimbabwe
⊕ https://vfmat.ch/f3d9

Guruve District Hospital
Chiporiro, Mashonaland Central, Zimbabwe
⊕ https://vfmat.ch/cdea

Gweru General Hospital
Gweru, Midlands, Zimbabwe
⊕ https://vfmat.ch/7746

Harare Central Hospital
Harare, Mashonaland East, Zimbabwe
⊕ https://vfmat.ch/3bfa

Hwange Colliery Hospital
Hwange, Matabeleland North, Zimbabwe
⊕ https://vfmat.ch/b4cd

Jeka Rural Hospital
Mberengwa, Midlands, Zimbabwe
⊕ https://vfmat.ch/6ba4

Kadoma General Hospital
Kadoma, Mashonaland West, Zimbabwe
⊕ https://vfmat.ch/f9fb

Karanda Mission Hospital
Marlborough, Harare, Zimbabwe
⊕ https://vfmat.ch/55c3

Kariba District Hospital
Kariba, Mashonaland West, Zimbabwe
⊕ https://vfmat.ch/88cf

Kariyangwe Mission Hospital
Kariyangwe, Matabeleland North, Zimbabwe
⊕ https://vfmat.ch/ff3f

Kezi Rural District Hospital
Kezi, Matabeleland South, Zimbabwe
⊕ https://vfmat.ch/5da5

Kwekwe General Hospital
Kwekwe, Midlands, Zimbabwe
⊕ https://vfmat.ch/7d25

Lundi Rural Hospital
Lundi, Masvingo, Zimbabwe
⊕ https://vfmat.ch/47f3

Marondera Provincial Hospital
Marondera, Mashonaland East, Zimbabwe
⊕ https://vfmat.ch/dc4c

Masvingo General Hospital
Mucheke Township, Masvingo, Zimbabwe
⊕ https://vfmat.ch/cb9c

Mater Dei Hospital
Bulawayo, Bulawayo, Zimbabwe
⊕ https://vfmat.ch/54dd

Matibi Mission Hospital
Matibi, Masvingo, Zimbabwe
⊕ https://vfmat.ch/cfc7

Mberengwa District Hospital
Belingwe, Midlands, Zimbabwe
⊕ https://vfmat.ch/c422

Mbire District Hospital
Chief Chitsungo, Mashonaland Central, Zimbabwe
⊕ https://vfmat.ch/9299

Mbuya Dorcas Hospital
Dunowen, Harare, Zimbabwe
⊕ https://vfmat.ch/6a84

Midlands Private Hospital
Gweru, Midlands, Zimbabwe
⊕ https://vfmat.ch/c5d5

Milton Park Medical Centre
Harare, Harare Region, Zimbabwe
⊕ https://vfmat.ch/nhr6

Mpilo Central Hospital
Glengarry, Bulawayo, Zimbabwe
⊕ https://vfmat.ch/f5c9

Mt. Darwin Hospital
Darwin, Mashonaland Central, Zimbabwe
⊕ https://vfmat.ch/ccc7

Mt. Selinda Hospital
Chief Mapungwana, Manicaland, Zimbabwe
⊕ https://vfmat.ch/fa35

Murambinda Mission Hospital
Murambinda, Manicaland, Zimbabwe
⊕ https://vfmat.ch/a8c7

Mutare Provincial Hospital
Mutare, Manicaland, Zimbabwe
⊕ https://vfmat.ch/87c5

Ndolwane
Ndolwane, Matabeleland South, Zimbabwe
⊕ https://vfmat.ch/11c7

Neshuro District Hospital
Neshuro, Masvingo, Zimbabwe
⊕ https://vfmat.ch/fed3

Nhowe Mission Brian Lemons Memorial Hospital
Chief Mangwende, Mashonaland East, Zimbabwe
⊕ https://vfmat.ch/cc31

Norton Hospital
Norton, Mashonaland West, Zimbabwe
⊕ https://vfmat.ch/935d

Nyadire Mission Hospital
Mutoko, Mashonaland East, Zimbabwe
⊕ https://vfmat.ch/2e87

Parirenyatwa General Hospital
Harare, Harare, Zimbabwe
⊕ https://vfmat.ch/17e3

Plumtree Hospital
Plumtree, Matabeleland South, Zimbabwe
⊕ https://vfmat.ch/d562

Premier Hillside Hospital
Bulawayo, Bulawayo, Zimbabwe
⊕ https://vfmat.ch/97aa

PSMAS Zimbabwe
Yeovil, Manicaland, Zimbabwe
⊕ https://vfmat.ch/c24d

Rusape General Hospital
Rusape, Manicaland, Zimbabwe
⊕ https://vfmat.ch/22e6

Rusitu Mission Hospital
Chimanimani, Manicaland, Zimbabwe
⊕ https://vfmat.ch/1bcf

Saint Anne's Hospital
Avondale, Harare, Zimbabwe
⊕ https://vfmat.ch/c539

Siakobvu District Hospital
Kapoka, Mashonaland West, Zimbabwe
⊕ https://vfmat.ch/b2ce

St. Albert's Mission Hospital
Maclear, Mashonaland Central, Zimbabwe
⊕ https://vfmat.ch/e6e6

Trauma Centre & Hospital Harare
Harare, Zimbabwe
⊕ https://vfmat.ch/cskw

Tshelanyemba Mission Hospital
Legion, Matabeleland South, Zimbabwe
⊕ https://vfmat.ch/8bf6

Tsholotsho District Hospital
Mbute, Matabeleland North, Zimbabwe
⊕ https://vfmat.ch/2a96

United Bulawayo Hospitals
Bulawayo, Bulawayo, Zimbabwe
⊕ https://vfmat.ch/becf

West End Hospital, PSMI
Harare, Mashonaland East, Zimbabwe
⊕ https://vfmat.ch/7e37

Westend Extension
Montagu Centre, Mashonaland East, Zimbabwe
⊕ https://vfmat.ch/ce7c

Wilkins Hospital
Harare, Harare, Zimbabwe
⊕ https://vfmat.ch/de42

Zhombe Mission Hospital
Zhombe, Midlands, Zimbabwe
⊕ https://vfmat.ch/d7e5

Zvimba Rural District Hospital
Murombedzi, Mashonaland West, Zimbabwe
⊕ https://vfmat.ch/8947

Sources of Data for Country Introductions

"10 cool facts about Sri Lanka." The Journal by Intrepid Travel. Intrepid Travel. September 25, 2018. https://www.intrepidtravel.com/adventures/sri-lanka-facts/.

"10 facts you might not know about Honduras." The Journal by Intrepid Travel. Intrepid Travel. September 25, 2018. https://www.intrepidtravel.com/adventures/honduras-facts/.

"10 Most Censored Countries." Committee to Protect Journalists. Committee to Protect Journalists. Accessed September 2, 2021. https://cpj.org/reports/2019/09/10-most-censored-eritrea-north-korea-turkmenistan-journalist/#1.

"12 Interesting Facts About Algeria." Afrikanza. Afrikanza. December 30. 2017. https://afrikanza.com/blogs/culture-history/facts-about-algeria.

"2014–2016 Ebola Outbreak in West Africa." Centers for Disease Control and Prevention. U.S. Department of Health & Human Services. Accessed September 2, 2021. https://www.cdc.gov/vhf/ebola/history/2014-2016-outbreak/index.html.

"51 Interesting Facts About Bolivia." TheFactFile. TheFactFile. Accessed August 23, 2021. https://thefactfile.org/bolivia-facts/.

Adotevi, Stanislas Spero, et al. "Benin." Britannica. Encyclopædia Britannica, Inc. Accessed September 2, 2021. https://www.britannica.com/place/Benin.

"Algeria." The World Factbook. Central Intelligence Agency. Accessed August 18, 2021. https://www.cia.gov/the-world-factbook/countries/algeria/#people-and-society.

"Algeria." Wikipedia. Wikipedia. Accessed August 23, 2021. https://en.wikipedia.org/wiki/Algeria.

Allchin, Frank Raymond, et al. "India." Britannica. Encyclopædia Britannica, Inc. Accessed August 23, 2021. https://www.britannica.com/place/India. "Algeria." IHME (Institute for Health Metrics and Evaluation). University of Washington. Accessed August 23, 2021. http://www.healthdata.org/algeria.

Allworth, Edward, et al. "Kyrgyzstan." Britannica. Encyclopædia Britannica, Inc. Accessed August 15, 2021. https://www.britannica.com/place/Kyrgyzstan.

"An overview of Tanzania's political history." Oxford Business Group. Oxford Business Group. Accessed September 2, 2021. https://oxfordbusinessgroup.com/overview/clearing-hurdles-country-stable-political-ground.

"Angola." The World Factbook. Central Intelligence Agency. Accessed August 18, 2021. https://www.cia.gov/the-world-factbook/countries/angola/.

"Angola." Wikipedia. Wikipedia. Accessed August 24, 2021. https://en.wikipedia.org/wiki/Angola.

"Annex 5. Tanzania." Accessed September 2, 2021. https://www.who.int/workforcealliance/knowledge/resources/MLHWCountryCaseStudies_annex5_Tanzania.pdf.

Arasaratnam, Sinnappam, et al. "Sri Lanka." Britannica. Encyclopædia Britannica, Inc. Accessed August 23. 2021. https://www.britannica.com/place/Sri-Lanka.

"Bangladesh." IHME (Institute for Health Metrics and Evaluation). University of Washington. Accessed August 23, 2021. http://www.healthdata.org/bangladesh.

"Bangladesh." The World Factbook. Central Intelligence Agency. Accessed August 23, 2021. https://www.cia.gov/the-world-factbook/countries/bangladesh/#people-and-society.

Benneh, George et al. "Cameroon." Britannica. Encyclopædia Britannica, Inc. Accessed August 13. 2021. https://www.britannica.com/place/Cameroon.

"Benin." IHME (Institute for Health Metrics and Evaluation). University of Washington. Accessed October 23, 2020. http://www.healthdata.org/benin/.

"Benin." Lonely Planet. Lonely Planet. Accessed October 23, 2020. https://www.lonelyplanet.com/benin.

"Benin." Nations Online. Nationsonline.org. Accessed September 2, 20211. https://www.nationsonline.org/oneworld/benin.htm.

"Benin." The World Bank. World Bank Group. Accessed September 2, 2021. https://data.worldbank.org/country/BJ/.

"Benin." The World Factbook. Central Intelligence Agency. Accessed August 18, 2021. https://www.cia.gov/the-world-factbook/countries/benin/.

"Benin – Airports." iExplore. iExplore. Accessed October 23, 2020. https://www.iexplore.com/articles/travel-guides/africa/benin/airports.

"Benin country profile." BBC. BBC. April 29, 2019. https://www.bbc.com/news/world-africa-13037572.

"Benin – History and Culture." iExplore. iExplore. Accessed October 23, 2020. https://www.iexplore.com/articles/travel-guides/africa/benin/history-and-culture.

"Bhutan." IHME (Institute for Health Metrics and Evaluation). University of Washington. Accessed August 24, 2021. http://www.healthdata.org/bhutan.

"Bhutan." The World Factbook. Central Intelligence Agency. Accessed August 24, 2021. https://www.cia.gov/the-world-factbook/countries/bhutan/.

"Bhutan." Wikipedia. Wikipedia. Accessed August 24, 2021. https://en.wikipedia.org/wiki/Bhutan.

"Bolivia." The World Factbook. Central Intelligence Agency. Accessed August 23, 2021. https://www.cia.gov/the-world-factbook/countries/bolivia/#people-and-society.

"Bolivia." Wikipedia. Wikipedia. Accessed August 23, 2021. https://en.wikipedia.org/wiki/Bolivia#Health.

"Bolivia (Plurinational State of)." IHME (Institute for Health Metrics and Evaluation). University of Washington. Accessed August 23, 2021. http://www.healthdata.org/bolivia.

Borlaza, Gregorio C., et al. "Philippines." Britannica. Encyclopædia Britannica, Inc. August 20. 2021. https://www.britannica.com/place/Philippines.

"Burkina Faso." IHME (Institute for Health Metrics and Evaluation). University of Washington. Accessed September 10, 2021. http://www.healthdata.org/burkina-faso.

"Burkina Faso." The World Factbook. Central Intelligence Agency. Accessed September 10, 2021. https://www.cia.gov/the-world-factbook/countries/burkina-faso/#people-and-society.

"Burkina Faso." Wikipedia. Wikipedia. Accessed September 10, 2021. https://en.wikipedia.org/wiki/Burkina_Faso.

"Burma Socialist Programme Party." Wikipedia. Wikipedia. Accessed August 21, 2021. https://en.wikipedia.org/wiki/Burma_Socialist_Programme_Party.

"Burundi." IHME (Institute for Health Metrics and Evaluation). University of Washington. Accessed September 2, 2021. http://www.healthdata.org/burundi.

"Burundi." The World Factbook. Central Intelligence Agency. Accessed August 15, 2021. https://www.cia.gov/the-world-factbook/countries/burundi/.

"Burundi: Control of corruption." TheGlobalEconomy.com. TheGlobalEconomy.com. Accessed September 2, 2021. https://www.theglobaleconomy.com/Burundi/wb_corruption/.

"Burundi: Political stability." TheGlobalEconomy.com. TheGlobalEconomy.com. Accessed September 2, 2021. https://www.theglobaleconomy.com/Burundi/wb_political_stability/.

"Burundi: Poverty ratio." TheGlobalEconomy.com. TheGlobalEconomy.com. Accessed September 2, 2021. https://www.theglobaleconomy.com/Burundi/poverty_ratio/.

"Cambodia." IHME (Institute for Health Metrics and Evaluation). University of Washington. Accessed August 13, 2021. http://www.healthdata.org/cambodia.

Camera, Mohamed, and Yassima Camara. "The healthcare system in Africa: the case of Guinea." *International Journal of Community Medicine and Public Health* 2, no. 4 (January 2015): 685–689. https://www.researchgate.net/publication/283239841_The_healthcare_system_in_Africa_the_case_of_guinea.

"Cameroon." Wikipedia. Wikipedia. Accessed August 13, 2021. https://en.wikipedia.org/wiki/Cameroon#Geography.

"Cameroon." The World Factbook. Central Intelligence Agency. Accessed August 2021. https://www.cia.gov/the-world-factbook/countries/cameroon/#people-and-society.

"Cabo Verde." IHME (Institute for Health Metrics and Evaluation). University of Washington. Accessed August 24, 2021. http://www.healthdata.org/cape-verde.

"Cabo Verde." The World Factbook. Central Intelligence Agency. Accessed August 18, 2021. https://www.cia.gov/the-world-factbook/countries/cabo-verde/.

"Cape Verde." Wikipedia. Wikipedia. Accessed August 24, 2021. https://en.wikipedia.org/wiki/Cape_Verde

"Case Counts." Centers for Disease Control and Prevention. U.S. Department of Health & Human Services. Accessed September 2, 2021. https://www.cdc.gov/vhf/ebola/history/2014-2016-outbreak/case-counts.html.

"CDC in Benin." Centers for Disease Control and Prevention. U.S. Department of Health and Human Services. Accessed October 23, 2020. https://www.cdc.gov/globalhealth/countries/benin/pdf/Benin_Factsheet.pdf.

"CDC in Zimbabwe." Centers for Disease Control and Prevention. U.S. Department of Health and Human Services. Accessed August 23, 2021. https://www.cdc.gov/globalhealth/countries/zimbabwe/default.htm.

"Central African Republic." International Crisis Group. International Crisis Group. Accessed September 2, 2021. https://www.crisisgroup.org/africa/central-africa/central-african-republic.

"Central African Republic." IHME (Institute for Health Metrics and Evaluation). University of Washington. Accessed September 2, 2021. http://www.healthdata.org/central-african-republic.

"Central African Republic." The World Factbook. Central Intelligence Agency. Accessed August 25, 2021. https://www.cia.gov/the-world-factbook/countries/central-african-republic/.

"Central African Republic." World Health Organization. World Health Organization. Accessed September 2, 2021. https://www.who.int/countries/caf/.

"Central African Republic: Life expectancy." TheGlobalEconomy.com. TheGlobalEconomy.com. Accessed September 2, 2021. https://www.theglobaleconomy.com/Central-African-Republic/Life_expectancy/.

"Chad." Global Health Workforce Alliance. WHO. Accessed September 2, 2021. https://www.who.int/workforcealliance/countries/tcd/en/.

"Chad." IHME (Institute for Health Metrics and Evaluation). University of Washington. Accessed Septemebr 2, 2021. http://www.healthdata.org/chad.

"Chad." UNHCR: The UN Refugee Agency. UNHCR: The UN Refugee Agency. Accessed September 2, 2021. https://reporting.unhcr.org/node/2533#_ga=2.96357343.270408414.1571428048-115620519.1571428048.

"Chad." United Nations World Food Programme. World Food Programme. Accessed September 2, 2021. https://www.wfp.org/countries/chad/.

"Chad." The World Factbook. Central Intelligence Agency. Accessed August 21, 2021. https://www.cia.gov/the-world-factbook/countries/chad/.

"Chad country profile." BBC. BBC. May 8, 2018. https://www.bbc.com/news/world-africa-13164686.

"Chad – History and Culture." iExplore. iExplore. Accessed September 2, 2021. https://www.iexplore.com/articles/travel-guides/africa/chad/history-and-culture.

"Chad travel guide." World Travel Guide. Columbus Travel Media Ltd. Accessed September 2, 2021. https://www.worldtravelguide.net/guides/africa/chad/.

Chandlerli, Abdel Kader, et al. "Algeria." Britannica. Encyclopædia Britannica, Inc. Accessed August 23, 2021. https://www.britannica.com/place/Algeria.

Clay, Daniel, et al. "Rwanda." Britannica. Encyclopædia Britannica, Inc. Accessed September 2, 2021. https://www.britannica.com/place/Rwanda.

"Comoros." IHME (Institute for Health Metrics and Evaluation). University of Washington. Accessed August 13, 2021. http://www.healthdata.org/comoros.

"Comoros." The World Factbook. Central Intelligence Agency. Accessed August 15, 2021. https://www.cia.gov/the-world-factbook/countries/comoros/#geography.

"Comoros." Wikipedia. Wikipedia. Accessed August 13, 2021. https://en.wikipedia.org/wiki/Comoros.

"Congo." IHME (Institute for Health Metrics and Evaluation). University of Washington. Accessed August 13, 2021. http://www.healthdata.org/congo.

"Congo, Dem. Rep." The World Bank. World Bank Group. Accessed September 2, 2021. https://data.worldbank.org/country/congo-dem-rep.

"Congo, Republic of the." The World Factbook. Central Intelligence Agency. Accessed August 28, 2021. https://www.cia.gov/the-world-factbook/countries/congo-republic-of-the/.

Cordell, Dennis D. "Republic of the Congo." Britannica. Encyclopædia Britannica, Inc. Accessed September 2, 2021. https://www.britannica.com/place/Republic-of-the-Congo.

"Côte d'Ivoire." IHME (Institute for Health Metrics and Evaluation). University of Washington. Accessed August 13, 2021. http://www.healthdata.org/cote-divoire.

"Cote d'Ivoire." The World Factbook. Central Intelligence Agency. Accessed August 28, 2021. https://www.cia.gov/the-world-factbook/countries/cote-divoire/#people-and-society.

"Culture." Embassy of the Republic of Malawi in the United States. Embassy of the Republic of Malawi. Accessed September 2, 2021. http://www.malawiembassy-dc.org/page/culture.

Deschamps, Hubert Jules. "Mauritania." Britannica. Encyclopædia Britannica, Inc. Accessed August 15. 2021. https://www.britannica.com/place/Mauritania.

"Democratic Republic of the Congo." The World Factbook. Central Intelligence Agency. Accessed August 28, 2021. https://www.cia.gov/the-world-factbook/countries/congo-democratic-republic-of-the/.

"Democratic Republic of the Congo." IHME (Institute for Health Metrics and Evaluation). University of Washington. Accessed September 2, 2021. http://www.healthdata.org/democratic-republic-congo.

"Democratic Republic of Congo in Detail: Flights & getting there." Lonely Planet. Lonely Planet. Accessed October 22, 2020. https://www.lonelyplanet.com/democratic-republic-of-congo/narratives/practical-information/transport/getting-there-away.

"Demographics of Nigeria." Wikipedia. Wikipedia. Accessed August 21, 2021. https://en.wikipedia.org/wiki/Demographics_of_Nigeria.

"Demographics of Senegal." Wikipedia. Wikipedia. Accessed August 22, 2021. https://en.wikipedia.org/wiki/Demographics_of_Senegal.

"Djibouti." IHME (Institute for Health Metrics and Evaluation). University of Washington. Accessed August 15, 2021. http://www.healthdata.org/djibouti.

"Djibouti." Wikipedia. Wikipedia. Accessed August 15, 2021. https://en.wikipedia.org/wiki/Djibouti. .

"Djibouti." The World Factbook. Central Intelligence Agency. Accessed August 25, 2021. https://www.cia.gov/the-world-factbook/countries/djibouti/#people-and-society.

Dresch, Jean, et al. "Burkina Faso." Britannica. Encyclopædia Britannica, Inc. Accessed September 10, 2021. https://www.britannica.com/place/Burkina-Faso.

"East Timor." Britannica. Encyclopædia Britannica, Inc. Accessed August 24, 2021. https://www.britannica.com/place/East-Timor.

"Ebola virus disease." World Health Organization. World Health Organization. February 10, 2020. https://www.who.int/news-room/fact-sheets/detail/ebola-virus-disease.

Echenberg, Myron. "Togo." Britannica. Encyclopædia Britannica, Inc. Accessed September 2, 2021. https://www.britannica.com/place/Togo.

"Economy of Zambia." Wikipedia. Wikipedia. Accessed August 23, 2021. https://en.wikipedia.org/wiki/Economy_of_Zambia.

Eggers, Ellen Kahan, et al. Britannica. Encyclopædia Britannica, Inc. Accessed September 2, 2021. https://www.britannica.com/place/Burundi.

"Egypt." IHME (Institute for Health Metrics and Evaluation). University of Washington. Accessed August 15, 2021. http://www.healthdata.org/egypt.

"Egypt." Wikipedia. Wikipedia. Accessed August 15, 2021. /https://en.wikipedia.org/wiki/Egypt.

"Egypt." The World Factbook. Central Intelligence Agency. Accessed August 15, 2021. https://www.cia.gov/the-world-factbook/countries/egypt/#people-and-society.

"Egypt Isn't the Country with the most Pyramids" Science Alert. Science Alert. November 27, 2016. https://www.sciencealert.com/sorry-egypt-but-sudan-is-the-pyramid-capital-of-the-world.

"El Salvador." IHME (Institute for Health Metrics and Evaluation). University of Washington. Accessed August 23, 2021. http://www.healthdata.org/el-salvador.

"El Salvador." The World Factbook. Central Intelligence Agency. Accessed August 17, 2021. https://www.cia.gov/the-world-factbook/countries/el-salvador/#people-and-society.

"El Salvador." Wikipedia. Wikipedia. Accessed August 23, 2021. https://en.wikipedia.org/wiki/El_Salvador.

"Eritrea." Global Health Workforce Alliance. WHO. Accessed October 22, 2020. https://www.who.int/workforcealliance/countries/eri/en/.

"Eritrea." IHME (Institute for Health Metrics and Evaluation). University of Washington. Accessed September 2, 2021. http://www.healthdata.org/eritrea.

"Eritrea." Lonely Planet. Lonely Planet. Accessed October 22, 2020. https://www.lonelyplanet.com/eritrea.

"Eritrea." The World Factbook. Central Intelligence Agency. Accessed September 2, 2021. https://www.cia.gov/the-world-factbook/countries/eritrea/.

"Eritrea country profile." BBC. BBC. November 15, 2018. https://www.bbc.com/news/world-africa-13349078.

"Eritrea profile - Timeline." BBC. BBC. November 15, 2018. https://www.bbc.com/news/world-africa-13349395.

"Eswatini." IHME (Institute for Health Metrics and Evaluation). University of

Washington. Accessed September 7, 2021. http://www.healthdata.org/swaziland.

"Eswatini." The World Factbook. Central Intelligence Agency. Accessed September 2, 2021. https://www.cia.gov/the-world-factbook/countries/eswatini/.

"Eswatini." Wikipedia. Wikipedia. Accessed September 7, 2021. https://en.wikipedia.org/wiki/Eswatini.

"Ethiopia." IHME (Institute for Health Metrics and Evaluation). University of Washington. Accessed September 2, 2021. http://www.healthdata.org/ethiopia.

"Ethiopia." World Health Organization. WHO. Accessed October 22, 2020. https://www.who.int/hac/donorinfo/callsformobilisation/eth/en/.

"Ethnic groups in Pakistan." Wikipedia. Wikipedia. Accessed August 21, 2021. https://en.wikipedia.org/wiki/Ethnic_groups_in_Pakistan.

"Federal Capital Territory, Nigeria." Wikipedia. Wikipedia. Accessed August 21, 2021. https://en.wikipedia.org/wiki/Federal_Capital_Territory,_Nigeria.

"Field Listing: Population." The World Factbook. Central Intelligence Agency. Accessed September 2, 2021. https://www.cia.gov/the-world-factbook/countries/gambia-the/

Flemion, Philip F., et al. "El Salvador." Britannica. Encyclopædia Britannica, Inc. Accessed August 23, 2021. https://www.britannica.com/place/El-Salvador.

Foster, Sophie, et al. "Vanuatu." Britannica. Encyclopædia Britannica, Inc. Accessed August 24, 2021. https://www.britannica.com/place/Vanuatu.

Fuglestad, Finn, et al. "Niger." Britannica. Encyclopædia Britannica, Inc. Accessed September 2, 2021. https://www.britannica.com/place/Niger.

Gailey, Harry A., et al. "The Gambia." Britannica. Encyclopædia Britannica, Inc. Accessed September 2, 2021. https://www.britannica.com/place/The-Gambia.

Galli, Rosemary Elizabeth, et al. "Guinea-Bissau." Britannica. Encyclopædia Britannica, Inc. September 2, 2021. https://www.britannica.com/place/Guinea-Bissau.

"Gambia." IHME (Institute for Health Metrics and Evaluation). University of Washington. Accessed September 2, 2021. http://www.healthdata.org/gambia. "Gambia." United Nations World Food Programme. World Food Programme. Accessed September 2, 2021. https://www.wfp.org/countries/gambia#:~:text=The%20Gambia's%20poverty%20rate%20remains,leading%20a%20food%20security%20emergency.

"Gambia: Political stability." TheGlobalEconomy.com. TheGlobalEconomy.com. Accessed September 2, 2021. https://www.theglobaleconomy.com/Gambia/wb_political_stability/.

"Gambia, The." The World Bank. World Bank Group. Accessed September 2, 2021. https://data.worldbank.org/country/gambia-the.

"Getting Around Benin." World Travel Guide. Columbus Travel Media Ltd. Accessed October 23, 2020. https://www.worldtravelguide.net/guides/africa/benin/getting-around/.

"GDP per capita (current US$)." The World Bank. The World Bank Group. Accessed October 25, 2020. https://data.worldbank.org/indicator/NY.GDP.PCAP.CD.

"GDP per capita (current US$) - Solomon Islands." The World Bank. The World Bank Group. Accessed August 23, 2021. https://data.worldbank.org/indicator/NY.GDP.PCAP.CD?locations=SB.

"GDP per capita (current US$) - Zambia." The World Bank. The World Bank Group. Accessed August 23, 2021. https://data.worldbank.org/indicator/NY.GDP.PCAP.CD?locations=ZM.

"Getting Around Burundi." World Travel Guide. Columbus Travel Media Ltd. Accessed October 23, 2020. https://www.worldtravelguide.net/guides/africa/burundi/getting-around/

"Getting Around." Malawi: The Warm Heart of Africa. Malawi Travel Marketing Consortium. Accessed October 22, 2020. https://malawitourism.com/getting-around/.

"Getting Around Chad." World Travel Guide. Columbus Travel Media Ltd. Accessed October 22, 2020. https://www.worldtravelguide.net/guides/africa/chad/getting-around/.

"Getting Around Eritrea." World Travel Guide. Columbus Travel Media Ltd. Accessed October 22, 2020. https://www.worldtravelguide.net/guides/africa/eritrea/getting-around/.

"Getting Around Haiti." World Travel Guide. Columbus Travel Media Ltd. Accessed October 22, 2020. https://www.worldtravelguide.net/guides/caribbean/haiti/getting-around/.

"Getting Around Uganda." World Travel Guide. Columbus Travel Media Ltd. Accessed October 23, 2020. https://www.worldtravelguide.net/guides/africa/uganda/getting-around/.

"Getting There." Malawi: The Warm Heart of Africa. Malawi Travel Marketing Consortium. Accessed October 22, 2020. https://www.malawitourism.com/getting-there/.

"Ghana." IHME (Institute for Health Metrics and Evaluation). University of Washington. Accessed August 24, 2021. http://www.healthdata.org/ghana.

"Global Health." USAID. USAID. Accessed October 23, 2020. https://www.usaid.gov/burundi/global-health#:~:text=Burundi's%20health%20system%20suffers%20from,health%2C%20and%20strengthen%20health%20systems.

"Global Health – Guinea." Centers for Disease Control and Prevention. U.S. Department of Health & Human Services. June 4, 2019.

"Global Health – Liberia." Centers for Disease Control and Prevention. U.S. Department of Health & Human Services. Accessed October 22, 2020. https://www.cdc.gov/globalhealth/countries/liberia/default.htm.

"Gold Coast (British colony)." Wikipedia. Wikipedia. Accessed August 21, 2021. https://en.wikipedia.org/wiki/Gold_Coast_(British_colony).

"Gross National Happiness." Wikipedia. Wikipedia. Accessed August 24, 2021. https://en.wikipedia.org/wiki/Gross_National_Happiness.

Grove, Alfred Thomas, et al. "Chad." Britannica. Encyclopædia Britannica, Inc. Accessed September 2, 2021. https://www.britannica.com/place/Chad.

Guerreiro, Cátia Sá, Augusto Paulo Silva, Tomé Cá, and Paulo Ferrinho. "Strategic planning in Guiné-Bissau's health sector: evolution, influences and process." Anais do IHMT. An Inst Hig MedTrop 2017, 16 (Supl. 1): S55–S68. https://research.unl.pt/ws/portalfiles/portal/4168743/Planeamento_estrat_gico_no_setor_da_sa_de.pdf.

"Guinea." IHME (Institute for Health Metrics and Evaluation). University of Washington. Accessed November 6, 2020. http://www.healthdata.org/guinea.

"Guinea." World Health Organization. World Health Organization. Accessed October 22, 2020. https://www.who.int/countries/gin/.

"Guinea-Bissau." IHME (Institute for Health Metrics and Evaluation). University of Washington. Accessed September 2, 2021. http://www.healthdata.org/guinea-bissau.

"Guinea-Bissau." The World Bank. The World Bank Group. Accessed September 2, 2021 https://data.worldbank.org/country/guinea-bissau.

"Guinea History, Language and Culture." World Travel Guide. Columbus Travel Media Ltd. Accessed September 2, 2021. https://www.worldtravelguide.net/guides/africa/guinea/history-language-culture/.

"Guinea: Poverty ratio." TheGlobalEconomy.com. TheGlobalEconomy.com. Accessed September 2, 2021. https://www.theglobaleconomy.com/Guinea/poverty_ratio/.

"Guinea profile – Timeline." BBC. BBC. May 14, 2018. https://www.bbc.com/news/world-africa-13443183.

"Gunneweg – TheHealthFactory." Gunneweg@TheHealthFactory. THE HEALTH FACTORY: Health System Strengthening & Governance and Decentralised Health Management. Accessed October 23, 2020. https://www.gunneweg-thehealthfactory.nl/.

Habtom, Gebremichael Kibreab. "Designing innovative pro-poor healthcare financing system in sub-Saharan Africa: The case of Eritrea." *Journal of Public Administration and Policy Research* 9, no. 4 (May 18, 2017): 51–67. https://academicjournals.org/journal/JPAPR/article-full-text-pdf/9B68E9D65935.

Hajda, Lubomyr A., et al. "Ukraine." Britannica. Encyclopædia Britannica, Inc. Accessed August 23, 2021. https://www.britannica.com/place/Ukraine.

"Haiti." Health in the Americas. Pan American Health Organization. Accessed September 2, 2021. https://www.paho.org/salud-en-las-americas-2017/?p=4110#:~:text=The%20health%20care%20delivery%20system,specialized%20centers%20provide%20tertiary%20care.

"Haiti." IHME (Institute for Health Metrics and Evaluation). University of Washington. Accessed September 2, 2021. http://www.healthdata.org/haiti. "Haiti country profile." BBC. BBC. July 7, 2021. https://www.bbc.com/news/world-latin-america-19548810.

"Haiti: Country profile." World Health Organization. World Health Organization. Accessed October 22, 2020. https://www.who.int/hac/crises/hti/background/profile/en/.

Harris, Chauncy D., et al. Britannica. Encyclopædia Britannica, Inc. Accessed August 23, 2021. https://en.wikipedia.org/wiki/Mongolia.

"Health expenditure as share of GDP in Nigeria from 2006 to 2018." Statista. Statista. https://www.statista.com/statistics/1126455/health-expenditure-as-share-of-gdp-in-nigeria/.

Hezel, Francis X.. et al.Britannica. Encyclopædia Britannica, Inc. Accessed September 7, 2021. "Micronesia." https://www.britannica.com/place/Micronesia-republic-Pacific-Ocean#ref54001.

Hibbett, Kristen. "Addressing the Barriers to Proper Health Care in Ethiopia." The

Borgen Project. The Borgen Project. June 1, 2018. https://borgenproject.org/addressing-the-barriers-to-proper-health-care-in-ethiopia/.

Hickey, Gerald C., et al. "Vietnam." Britannica. Encyclopædia Britannica, Inc. Accessed August 23, 2021. https://www.britannica.com/place/Vietnam.

"History of Nicaragua." Wikipedia. Wikipedia. Accessed August 21, 2021. https://en.wikipedia.org/wiki/History_of_Nicaragua.

"History of Senegal." Wikipedia. Wikipedia. Accessed August 22, 2021. https://en.wikipedia.org/wiki/History_of_Senegal.

"History of Zambia." Wikipedia. Wikipedia. Accessed August 23, 2021. https://en.wikipedia.org/wiki/History_of_Zambia.

"Honduras." IHME (Institute for Health Metrics and Evaluation). University of Washington. Accessed August 24, 2021. http://www.healthdata.org/honduras.

"Honduras." The World Factbook. Central Intelligence Agency. Accessed August 24, 2021. https://www.cia.gov/the-world-factbook/countries/honduras/#people-and-society.

"Honduras." Wikipedia. Wikipedia. Accessed August 24, 2021. https://en.wikipedia.org/wiki/Honduras.

Hopwood, Derek, et al. "Egypt." Britannica. Encyclopædia Britannica, Inc. Accessed August 15, 2021. https://www.britannica.com/place/Egypt.

"Hospital beds (per 10 000 population)." World Health Organization. World Health Organization. Accessed October 25, 2020. https://www.who.int/data/gho/data/indicators/indicator-details/GHO/hospital-beds-(per-10-000-population).

"Human Capital Index and Components, 2018." The World Bank. The World Bank Group. October 18, 2018. https://www.worldbank.org/en/data/interactive/2018/10/18/human-capital-index-and-components-2018. "Human Development Reports." United Nations Development Programme. United Nations Development Programme. Accessed October 22, 2020. http://hdr.undp.org/en/composite/HDI.

Husain, Syed Sajjad, et al. "Bangladesh." Encyclopædia Britannica, Inc. Accessed August 23, 2021. https://www.britannica.com/place/Bangladesh.

"Independence Day (Myanmar)." Wikipedia. Wikipedia. Accessed August 21, 2021. https://en.wikipedia.org/wiki/Independence_Day_(Myanmar).

"India." The World Factbook. Central Intelligence Agency. Accessed August 23, 2021. https://www.cia.gov/the-world-factbook/countries/india/#people-and-society.

"India." Wikipedia. Wikipedia. Accessed August 23, 2021. https://en.wikipedia.org/wiki/India.

Ingham, Kenneth. "Malawi." Encyclopædia Britannica, Inc. Accessed October 22, 2020. https://www.britannica.com/place/Malawi.

"Interesting Facts About Bangladesh." Once in a Lifetime Journey. Once in a Lifetime Journey. Accessed August 23, 2021. https://www.onceinalifetimejourney.com/inspiration/interesting-facts-about-bangladesh/.

"Ivory Coast." Wikipedia. Wikipedia. Accessed August 13, 2021. https://en.wikipedia.org/wiki/Ivory_Coast.

Jackson, Richard T., et al. "Papua New Guinea." Encyclopædia Britannica, Inc. Accessed August 23, 2021. https://www.britannica.com/place/Papua-New-Guinea.

Jones, Abeodu Bowen, et al. "Liberia." Encyclopædia Britannica, Inc. Accessed Septmeber 2, 2021. https://www.britannica.com/place/Liberia.

"Kenya." IHME (Institute for Health Metrics and Evaluation). University of Washington. Accessed August 15, 2021. http://www.healthdata.org/kenya.

"Kenya." Wikipedia. Wikipedia. Accessed August 15, 2021. https://en.wikipedia.org/wiki/Kenya/

"Kenya." The World Factbook. Central Intelligence Agency. Accessed August 13, 2021. https://www.cia.gov/the-world-factbook/countries/kenya/#people-and-society.

"Kiribati." IHME (Institute for Health Metrics and Evaluation). University of Washington. Accessed August 15, 2021. http://www.healthdata.org/kiribati.

"Kiribati." Wikipedia. Wikipedia. Accessed August 15, 2021. https://en.wikipedia.org/wiki/Kiribati.

"Kiribati." The World Factbook. Central Intelligence Agency. Accessed August 14, 2021. https://www.cia.gov/the-world-factbook/countries/kiribati/#people-and-society.

"Kyrgyzstan." IHME (Institute for Health Metrics and Evaluation). University of Washington. Accessed August 15, 2021. http://www.healthdata.org/kyrgyzstan.

"Kyrgyzstan." Wikipedia. Wikipedia. Accessed August 15, 2021. https://en.wikipedia.org/wiki/Kyrgyzstan.

"Kyrgyzstan." The World Factbook. Central Intelligence Agency. Accessed August 14, 2021. https://www.cia.gov/the-world-factbook/countries/kyrgyzstan/.

Lobban, Richard Andrew, et al. "Cabo Verde." Encyclopædia Britannica, Inc. Accessed August 24, 2021. https://www.britannica.com/place/Cabo-Verde.

"Land reform in Zimbabwe." Wikipedia. Wikipedia. Accessed August 23, 2021. https://en.wikipedia.org/wiki/Land_reform_in_Zimbabwe.

"Languages of Moldova." Wikipedia. Wikipedia. Accessed August 22, 2021. https://en.wikipedia.org/wiki/Languages_of_Moldova.

"Languages of Sao Tomé and Príncipe." Wikipedia. Wikipedia. Accessed August 22, 2021. https://en.wikipedia.org/wiki/Languages_of_São_Tomé_and_Pr%C3%ADncipe.

"Languages of Senegal." Wikipedia. Wikipedia. Accessed August 22, 2021. https://en.wikipedia.org/wiki/Languages_of_Senegal.

"Lagos." Wikipedia. Wikipedia. Accessed August 21, 2021. https://en.wikipedia.org/wiki/Lagos.

"Lao People's Democratic Republic." IHME (Institute for Health Metrics and Evaluation). University of Washington. Accessed August 23, 2021. http://www.healthdata.org/laos.

"Laos." The World Factbook. Central Intelligence Agency. Accessed August 13, 2021. https://www.cia.gov/the-world-factbook/countries/laos/#people-and-society.

"Laos." Wikipedia. Wikipedia. Accessed August 21, 2021. https://en.wikipedia.org/wiki/Laos.

Lawler, Nancy Ellen. "Côte d'Ivoire." Britannica. Encyclopædia Britannica, Inc. Accessed August 13, 2021. https://www.britannica.com/place/Cote-dIvoire.

Lawless, Robert, et al. "Haiti." Britannica. Encyclopædia Britannica, Inc. Accessed September 2, 2021. https://www.britannica.com/place/Haiti.

"Least Developed Country Category: Niger Profile." United Nations: Department of Economic and Social Affairs. United Nations. 2018. Accessed October 23, 2020. https://www.un.org/development/desa/dpad/least-developed-country-category-niger.html.

Legum, Colin. "Lesotho." Britannica. Encyclopædia Britannica, Inc. Accessed August 13, 2021. https://www.britannica.com/place/Lesotho.

"Lesotho." IHME (Institute for Health Metrics and Evaluation). University of Washington. Accessed August 15, 2021. http://www.healthdata.org/lesotho.

"Lesotho." The World Factbook. Central Intelligence Agency. Accessed August 15, 2021. https://www.cia.gov/the-world-factbook/countries/lesotho/#people-and-society.

"Liberia." IHME (Institute for Health Metrics and Evaluation). University of Washington. Accessed September 2, 2021. http://www.healthdata.org/liberia.

"Liberia." Travel.State.Gov. U.S. Department of State. Accessed October 22, 2020. https://travel.state.gov/content/travel/en/international-travel/International-Travel-Country-Information-Pages/Liberia.html.

"Liberia country profile." BBC. BBC. January 22, 2018. https://www.bbc.com/news/world-africa-13729504.

"Liberia: Life Expectancy." TheGlobalEconomy.com. TheGlobalEconomy.com. Accessed September 2, 2021. https://www.theglobaleconomy.com/Liberia/Life_expectancy/.

"Liberia: Political stability." TheGlobalEconomy.com. TheGlobalEconomy.com. Accessed September 2, 2021. https://www.theglobaleconomy.com/Liberia/wb_political_stability/#:~:text=Liberia%3A%20Political%20stability%20index%20(%2D2.5%20weak%3B%202.5%20strong)&text=For%20comparison%2C%20the%20world%20average,195%20countries%20is%20%2D0.05%20points.&text=The%20index%20is%20an%20average,Political%20Risk%20Services%2C%20among%20others.

"Liberia: Poverty ratio." TheGlobalEconomy.com. TheGlobalEconomy.com. Accessed October 22, 2020. https://www.theglobaleconomy.com/Liberia/poverty_ratio/.

"Liberia profile – Timeline." BBC. BBC. January 22, 2018. https://www.bbc.com/news/world-africa-13732188.

"Liberia." The World Factbook. Central Intelligence Agency. Accessed October 15, 2020. https://www.cia.gov/the-world-factbook/countries/liberia/.

"Life expectancy at birth, total (years)." The World Bank. The World Bank Group. Accessed September 2, 2021. https://data.worldbank.org/indicator/SP.DYN.LE00.IN.

"Life expectancy at birth, total (years) – Ghana." The World Bank. The World Bank Group. Accessed August 24, 2021. https://data.worldbank.org/indicator/SP.DYN.LE00.IN?locations=GH.

"Life expectancy at birth, total (years) – Moldova." The World Bank. The World Bank Group. Accessed August 22, 2021. https://data.worldbank.org/indicator/SP.DYN.LE00.IN?locations=MD.

"Life expectancy at birth, total (years) – Myanmar." The World Bank. The World

Bank Group. Accessed August 21, 2021. https://data.worldbank.org/indicator/SP.DYN.LE00.IN?locations=MM.

"Life expectancy at birth, total (years) – Nicaragua." The World Bank. The World Bank Group. Accessed August 21, 2021.https://data.worldbank.org/indicator/SP.DYN.LE00.IN?locations=NI.

"Life expectancy at birth, total (years) – Rwanda." The World Bank. The World Bank Group. Accessed September 2, 2021. https://data.worldbank.org/indicator/SP.DYN.LE00.IN?locations=RW.

"Life expectancy at birth, total (years) – Togo." The World Bank. The World Bank Group. Accessed September 2, 2021. https://data.worldbank.org/indicator/SP.DYN.LE00.IN?locations=TG.

"Life expectancy at birth, total (years) – Uganda." The World Bank. The World Bank Group. Accessed September 2, 2021. https://data.worldbank.org/indicator/SP.DYN.LE00.IN?locations=UG.

"Life expectancy at birth, total (years) – Uzbekistan." The World Bank. The World Bank Group. Accessed August 23, 2021. https://data.worldbank.org/indicator/SP.DYN.LE00.IN?locations=UZ.

"Life Expectancy of the World Population." Worldometer. Worldometer. Accessed September 2, 22. https://www.worldometers.info/demographics/life-expectancy/.

"List of cities proper by population density." Wikipedia. Wikipedia. Accessed August 23, 2021. https://en.wikipedia.org/wiki/List_of_cities_proper_by_population_density.

"List of volcanoes in El Salvador." Wikipedia. Wikipedia. Accessed August 23, 2021. https://en.wikipedia.org/wiki/List_of_volcanoes_in_El_Salvador.

Lyons, Maryinez. "Uganda." Britannica. Encyclopædia Britannica, Inc. September 2, 2021. https://www.britannica.com/place/Uganda.

Mackenzie, Lindsay. "WHO warns against potential Ebola spread in DR Congo and beyond." UN News. United Nations. September 11, 2020. https://news.un.org/en/story/2020/09/1072152/.

"Madagascar." IHME (Institute for Health Metrics and Evaluation). University of Washington. Accessed September 2, 2021. http://www.healthdata.org/madagascar.

"Madagascar." The World Bank. The World Bank Group. Accessed October 22, 2020. https://data.worldbank.org/country/madagascar.

"Madagascar country profile." BBC. BBC. November 15, 2019. https://www.bbc.com/news/world-africa-13861843.

"Madagascar: GDP, constant dollars." TheGlobalEconomy.com. TheGlobalEconomy.com. Accessed October 22, 2020. https://www.theglobaleconomy.com/Madagascar/GDP_constant_dollars/.

"Madagascar: Poverty ratio." TheGlobalEconomy.com. TheGlobalEconomy.com. Accessed September 2, 2021. https://www.theglobaleconomy.com/Madagascar/poverty_ratio/.

"Malawi." IHME (Institute for Health Metrics and Evaluation). University of Washington. Accessed September 2, 2021. http://www.healthdata.org/malawi.

"Malawi Government." Malawi Government. Government of the Republic of Malawi. 2013. Accessed October 22, 2020. https://www.malawi.gov.mw/.

"Malawi: Life expectancy." TheGlobalEconomy.com. TheGlobalEconomy.com. Accessed September 2, 2021. https://www.theglobaleconomy.com/Malawi/Life_expectancy/.

"Malawi: Political stability." TheGlobalEconomy.com. TheGlobalEconomy.com. Accessed September 2, 2021. https://www.theglobaleconomy.com/Malawi/wb_political_stability/.

"Malawi: Poverty ratio." TheGlobalEconomy.com. TheGlobalEconomy.com. Accessed September 2, 2021. https://www.theglobaleconomy.com/Malawi/poverty_ratio/.

"Malawi." The World Factbook. Central Intelligence Agency. Accessed September 2, 2021. https://www.cia.gov/the-world-factbook/countries/malawi/.

Markakis, John, et al. "Eritrea." Britannica. Encyclopædia Britannica, Inc. September 2, 2021. https://www.britannica.com/place/Eritrea. Mascarenhas, Adolfo C., et al. "Tanzania." Britannica. Encyclopædia Britannica, Inc. September 2, 2021. https://www.britannica.com/place/Tanzania.

Masson, John Richard, et al. "Eswatini." Britannica. Encyclopædia Britannica, Inc. July 19, 2021. https://www.britannica.com/place/Eswatini#ref44099.

"Maternal mortality ratio (modeled estimate, per 100,000 live births) – Benin." The World Bank. The World Bank Group. Accessed October 25, 2020. https://data.worldbank.org/indicator/SH.STA.MMRT?locations=BJ.

"Mauritania." IHME (Institute for Health Metrics and Evaluation). University of Washington. Accessed August 15, 2021. http://www.healthdata.org/mauritania.

"Mauritania." Wikipedia. Wikipedia. Accessed August 15, 2021. https://en.wikipedia.org/wiki/Mauritania.

"Mauritania." The World Factbook. Central Intelligence Agency. Accessed August 23, 2021. https://www.cia.gov/the-world-factbook/countries/mauritania/#people-and-society.

"Measles – Madagascar." World Health Organization. World Health Organization. January 17, 2019.https://www.who.int/emergencies/disease-outbreak-news/item/17-january-2019-measles-madagascar-en.

"Medical doctors (per 10 000 population)." World Health Organization. World Health Organization. Accessed October 25, 2020. https://www.who.int/data/gho/data/indicators/indicator-details/GHO/medical-doctors-(per-10-000-population).

"Micronesia." Nations Encyclopedia. Advameg, Inc. Accessed September 7, 2021. https://www.nationsencyclopedia.com/economies/Asia-and-the-Pacific/Micronesia.html.

"Micronesia (Federated States of)." IHME (Institute for Health Metrics and Evaluation). University of Washington. Accessed September 7, 2021. http://www.healthdata.org/federated-states-micronesia.

"Micronesia, Federated States of." The World Factbook. Central Intelligence Agency. Accessed September 7, 2021. https://www.cia.gov/the-world-factbook/countries/micronesia-federated-states-of/.

"Mining industry of Zimbabwe." Wikipedia. Wikipedia. Accessed August 23, 2021. https://en.wikipedia.org/wiki/Mining_industry_of_Zimbabwe.

Moncada R, J. Roberto, et al. "Honduras." Britannica. Encyclopædia Britannica, Inc. Accessed August 24, 2021. https://www.britannica.com/place/Honduras.

"Mongolia." IHME (Institute for Health Metrics and Evaluation). University of Washington. Accessed August 23, 2021. http://www.healthdata.org/mongolia.

"Mongolia." The World Factbook. Central Intelligence Agency. Accessed August 23, 2021. https://www.cia.gov/the-world-factbook/countries/mongolia/#people-and-society.

"Mongolia." Wikipedia. Wikipedia. Accessed August 23. 2021. https://en.wikipedia.org/wiki/Mongolia.

"Moldovan language." Wikipedia. Wikipedia. Accessed August 21, 2021. https://en.wikipedia.org/wiki/Moldovan_language.

"Morocco." IHME (Institute for Health Metrics and Evaluation). University of Washington. Accessed August 23, 2021. http://www.healthdata.org/morocco.

"Morocco." The World Factbook. Central Intelligence Agency. Accessed August 23, 2021. https://www.cia.gov/the-world-factbook/countries/morocco/#people-and-society.

"Morocco." Wikipedia. Wikipedia. Accessed August 21, 2021. https://en.wikipedia.org/wiki/Morocco#Health.

Morris, Hugh. "25 facts you didn't know about Ukraine, the heart of Europe." The Telegraph. The Telegraph. https://www.telegraph.co.uk/travel/destinations/europe/ukraine/articles/amazing-fact-you-probably-didnt-know-about-ukraine/.

"Mortality rate, under-5 (per 1,000 live births) - Ghana." The World Bank. The World Bank Group. Accessed August 24, 2021. https://data.worldbank.org/indicator/SH.DYN.MORT?locations=GH.

"Mortality rate, under-5 (per 1,000 live births) - Uzbekistan." The World Bank. The World Bank Group. Accessed August 23, 2021. https://data.worldbank.org/indicator/SH.DYN.MORT?locations=UZ.

"Mozambique." IHME (Institute for Health Metrics and Evaluation). University of Washington. Accessed September 2, 2021. http://www.healthdata.org/mozambique.

"Mozambique." The World Bank. The World Bank Group. Accessed October 22, 2020. https://data.worldbank.org/country/mozambique.

"Mozambique." World Health Organization. World Health Organization. Accessed October 22, 2020. https://www.who.int/countries/moz/.

"Mozambique: GDP, constant dollars." TheGlobalEconomy.com. TheGlobalEconomy.com. Accessed September 2, 2021. https://www.theglobaleconomy.com/Mozambique/GDP_constant_dollars/.

"Mozambique: Is Cabo Delgado the latest Islamic State outpost?" BBC. BBC. May 4. Accessed September 2, 2021. https://www.bbc.com/news/world-africa-52532741.

Mudge, Lewis. "Central African Republic Events of 2019." Human Rights Watch. Human Rights Watch. 2019 https://www.hrw.org/world-report/2019/country-chapters/central-african-republic#.

"Nepal." IHME (Institute for Health Metrics and Evaluation). University of Washington. Accessed September 2, 2021. http://www.healthdata.org/nepal.

"Nicaragua." The World Factbook. Central Intelligence Agency. Accessed August 21,

2021. https://www.cia.gov/the-world-factbook/countries/nicaragua/.

"Nicaraguan Revolution." Wikipedia. Wikipedia. Accessed August 21, 2021. https://en.wikipedia.org/wiki/Nicaraguan_Revolution.

"Niger." IHME (Institute for Health Metrics and Evaluation). University of Washington. Accessed September 2, 2021. http://www.healthdata.org/niger.

"Niger." The World Factbook. Central Intelligence Agency. Accessed October 16, 2020. https://www.cia.gov/the-world-factbook/countries/niger/.

"Niger." UNESCO. UNESCO Institute of Statistics. Accessed October 23, 2020. http://uis.unesco.org/en/country/ne.

"Niger country profile." BBC. BBC. April 12, 2021. https://www.bbc.com/news/world-africa-13943662.

"Niger: Nutrition Profile." USAID. USAID. February 2018. Accessed September 2, 2021.

https://www.usaid.gov/global-health/health-areas/nutrition/countries/niger-nutrition-profile.

"Niger slavery: Background." The Guardian. Guardian News & Media Limited. October 27, 2008. https://www.theguardian.com/world/2008/oct/27/humanrights1.

"Niger 2020 Crime & Safety Report." OSAC. Overseas Security Advisory Council, Bureau of Diplomatic Security, U.S. Department of State. April 16, 2020. https://www.osac.gov/Country/Niger/Content/Detail/Report/bfb3f35d-08e2-4008-ab52-18760b02138a.

"Nigeria." Wikipedia. Wikipedia. Accessed August 21, 2021. https://en.wikipedia.org/wiki/Nigeria.

Norbu, Dawa, et al. "Bhutan." Britannica. Encyclopædia Britannica, Inc. Accessed August 24, 2021. https://www.britannica.com/place/Bhutan.

"Northern Rhodesia." Wikipedia. Wikipedia. Accessed August 23, 2021. https://en.wikipedia.org/wiki/Northern_Rhodesia.

Ntarangwi, Mwenda. "Kenya." Britannica. Encyclopædia Britannica, Inc. August 15, 2021. https://www.britannica.com/place/Kenya.

Ntembwa, Hyppolite Kalambay and Wim Van Lerberghe. "Improving Health System Efficiency: Democratic Republic of the Congo improving aid coordination in the health sector." Health Systems Governance & Financing. World Health Organization. 2015. https://apps.who.int/iris/bitstream/handle/10665/186673/WHO_HIS_HGF_CaseStudy_15.4_eng.pdf?sequence=1.

O'Toole, Thomas E. "Guinea." Britannica. Encyclopædia Britannica, Inc. September 2, 2021. https://www.britannica.com/place/Guinea.

Ottenheimer, Harriet Joseph. "Comoros." Britannica. Encyclopædia Britannica, Inc. August 13, 2021. https://www.britannica.com/place/Comoros.

"Pakistan." IHME (Institute for Health Metrics and Evaluation). University of Washington. Accessed August 21. 2021. http://www.healthdata.org/pakistan.

"Pakistan." The World Bank. The World Bank Group. Accessed August 21, 2021. https://data.worldbank.org/country/pakistan.

"Pakistan." The World Factbook. Central Intelligence Agency. Accessed August 21, 2021. https://www.cia.gov/the-world-factbook/countries/pakistan/.

"Pakistan." Wikipedia. Wikipedia. Accessed August 21, 2021. https://en.wikipedia.org/wiki/Pakistan.

Pape, Utz and Arden Finn. "How conflict and economic crises exacerbate poverty in South Sudan." World Bank Blogs. World Bank Group. April 23, 2019. https://blogs.worldbank.org/africacan/how-conflict-and-economic-crises-exacerbate-poverty-in-south-sudan.

"Papua New Guinea." IHME (Institute for Health Metrics and Evaluation). University of Washington. Accessed August 24, 2021. http://www.healthdata.org/papua-new-guinea.

"Papua New Guinea." The World Factbook. Central Intelligence Agency. Accessed August 24, 2021. https://www.cia.gov/the-world-factbook/countries/papua-new-guinea/

"Papua New Guinea." Wikipedia. Wikipedia. Accessed August 24, 2021. https://en.wikipedia.org/wiki/Papua_New_Guinea.

Payanzo, Ntsomo, et al. "Democratic Republic of the Congo." Britannica. Encyclopædia Britannica, Inc. Accessed September 2, 2021. https://www.britannica.com/place/Democratic-Republic-of-the-Congo.

"Philippines." Wikipedia. Wikipedia. Accessed August 23, 2021. https://en.wikipedia.org/wiki/Philippines.

"Philippines." IHME (Institute for Health Metrics and Evaluation). University of Washington. Accessed August 23, 2021. http://www.healthdata.org/Philippines.

"Philippines." The World Factbook. Central Intelligence Agency. Accessed August 23, 2021. https://www.cia.gov/the-world-factbook/countries/philippines/#people-and-society.

"Politics of Senegal." Wikipedia. Wikipedia. Accessed August 22, 2021. https://en.wikipedia.org/wiki/Politics_of_Senegal.

"Population below poverty line." The World Factbook. Central Intelligence Agency. Accessed August 22, 2021. https://www.cia.gov/the-world-factbook/field/population-below-poverty-line/.

"Population total - Ghana." The World Bank. The World Bank Group. Accessed August 24 2021. https://data.worldbank.org/indicator/SP.POP.TOTL?locations=GH.

"Population, total - Moldova" The World Bank. The World Bank Group. Accessed August 21, 2021. https://data.worldbank.org/indicator/SP.POP.TOTL?locations=MD.

"Population, total - Myanmar." The World Bank. The World Bank Group. Accessed August 21, 2021. https://data.worldbank.org/indicator/SP.POP.TOTL?locations=MM.

"Population, total - Nicaragua." The World Bank. The World Bank Group. Accessed August 21, 2021. https://data.worldbank.org/indicator/SP.POP.TOTL?locations=NI.

"Population, total - Sao Tome and Principe." The World Bank. The World Bank Group. Accessed August 23, 2021. https://data.worldbank.org/indicator/SP.POP.TOTL?locations=ST.

"Population, total - Solomon Islands." The World Bank. The World Bank Group. Accessed August 22, 2021. https://data.worldbank.org/indicator/SP.POP.TOTL?locations=SB.

"Population, total – Tanzania." The World Bank. The World Bank Group. Accessed October 23, 2020. https://data.worldbank.org/indicator/SP.POP.TOTL?locations=TZ.

"Population, total – Zambia." The World Bank. The World Bank Group. AccessedAugust 23, 2021. https://data.worldbank.org/indicator/SP.POP.TOTL?locations=TZ.

"Republic of the Congo." Wikipedia. Wikipedia. Accessed August 23, 2021. https://en.wikipedia.org/wiki/Republic_of_the_Congo.

"Republic of Moldova: Profile of Health and Well-being." World Health Organization Regional Office for Europe. World Health Organization. Accessed August 22, 2021. https://www.euro.who.int/__data/assets/pdf_file/0005/323258/Profile-health-well-being-Rep-Moldova.pdf.

Roser, Max, Esteban Ortiz-Ospina, and Hannah Ritchie. "Life Expectancy." Our World in Data. Global Change Data Lab. October 2019. Accessed October 23, 2020. https://ourworldindata.org/life-expectancy#:~:text=The%20inequality%20of%20life%20expectancy,expectancy%20is%2030%20years%20longer.

"Rwanda." IHME (Institute for Health Metrics and Evaluation). University of Washington. Accessed September 2, 2021. http://www.healthdata.org/rwanda.

"Rwanda." PMI: President's Malaria Initiative Fighting Malaria and Saving Lives. U.S. President's Malaria Initiative. 2018. Accessed September 2, 2021. https://www.pmi.gov/where-we-work/rwanda/.

"Rwanda." The World Factbook. Central Intelligence Agency. Accessed September 2, 2021. https://www.cia.gov/the-world-factbook/countries/rwanda/.

"Rwanda: Political stability." TheGlobalEconomy.com. TheGlobalEconomy.com. Accessed September 2, 2021. https://www.theglobaleconomy.com/Rwanda/wb_political_stability/.

"Rwanda travel guide." World Travel Guide. Columbus Travel Media Ltd. Accessed September 2, 2021. https://www.worldtravelguide.net/guides/africa/rwanda/.

"Sao Tome and Principe." The World Factbook. Central Intelligence Agency. Accessed August 22, 2021. https://www.cia.gov/the-world-factbook/countries/sao-tome-and-principe/.

"Sao Tomé and Príncipe." Wikipedia. Wikipedia. Accessed August 22, 2021. https://en.wikipedia.org/wiki/São_Tomé_and_Pr%C3%ADncipe.

Schraeder, Peter J. "Djibouti." Britannica. Encyclopædia Britannica, Inc. Accessed August 15, 2021. https://www.britannica.com/place/Djibouti.

Schriever, Norm. "20 Incredible Facts About The Philippines." Huffpost Travel. Huffpost. February 21, 2017. https://www.huffpost.com/entry/20-incredible-facts-about-the-philippines_b_58a80363e4b026a89a7a2b80.

Sesay, Shekou M., et al. "Sierra Leone." Britannica. Encyclopædia Britannica, Inc. Accessed September 2, 2021. https://www.britannica.com/place/Sierra-Leone.

"Senegal." The World Bank. World Bank Group. Accessed August 23, 2021. https://data.worldbank.org/country/SN.

"Senegal." The World Factbook. Central Intelligence Agency. Accessed August 22, 2021. https://www.cia.gov/the-world-factbook/countries/senegal/.

Sheldon, Kathleen Eddy, et al. "Mozambique." Britannica. Encyclopædia Britannica, Inc. Accessed September 2, 2021. https://www.britannica.com/

place/Mozambique.

"Sierra Leone." IHME (Institute for Health Metrics and Evaluation). University of Washington. Accessed September 2, 2021. http://www.healthdata.org/sierra-leone.

"Sierra Leone." The World Factbook. Central Intelligence Agency. Accessed September 2, 2021. https://www.cia.gov/the-world-factbook/countries/sierra-leone/.

"Sierra Leone." World Health Organization. World Health Organization. Accessed October 23, 2020. https://www.who.int/countries/sle/.

"Sierra Leone country profile." BBC. BBC. April 5, 2018. https://www.bbc.com/news/world-africa-14094194.

"Sierra Leone: Economic growth." TheGlobalEconomy.com. TheGlobalEconomy.com. Accessed September 2, 2021. https://www.theglobaleconomy.com/Sierra-Leone/Economic_growth/.

"Sierra Leone: Life expectancy." TheGlobalEconomy.com. TheGlobalEconomy.com. Accessed September 2, 2021. https://www.theglobaleconomy.com/Sierra-Leone/Life_expectancy/.

"Solomon Islands." The World Factbook. Central Intelligence Agency. Accessed August 23, 2021. https://www.cia.gov/the-world-factbook/countries/solomon-islands/.

"Southeast Asia." Wikipedia. Wikipedia. Accessed August 17, 2021. https://en.wikipedia.org/wiki/Southeast_Asia.

"South Sudan." Global Health Workforce Alliance. WHO. Accessed September 2, 2021. https://www.who.int/workforcealliance/countries/ssd/en/.

"South Sudan." IHME (Institute for Health Metrics and Evaluation). University of Washington. Accessed September 2, 2021. http://www.healthdata.org/south-sudan.

"South Sudan." World Health Organization. World Health Organization. Accessed October 23, 2020. https://www.who.int/countries/ssd/.

"South Sudan country profile." BBC. BBC. August 6, 2018. https://www.bbc.com/news/world-africa-14069082.

Southall, Aidan William, et al. "Madagascar." Britannica. Encyclopædia Britannica, Inc. September 2, 2021. https://www.britannica.com/place/Madagascar.

Spaulding, Jay L., et al. "South Sudan." Britannica. Encyclopædia

Britannica, Inc. Accessed October 23, 2020. https://www.britannica.com/place/South-Sudan.

Spaulding, Jay L., et al. "Sudan." Britannica. Encyclopædia Britannica, Inc. Accessed September 10, 2021. https://www.britannica.com/place/Sudan.

"Sri Lanka." IHME (Institute for Health Metrics and Evaluation). University of Washington. Accessed August 23, 2021. http://www.healthdata.org/sri-lanka.

"Sri Lanka." The World Factbook. Central Intelligence Agency. Accessed August 23, 2021. https://www.cia.gov/the-world-factbook/countries/sri-lanka/.

"Sri Lanka." Wikipedia. Wikipedia. Accessed August 23, 2021. https://en.wikipedia.org/wiki/Sri_Lanka#Health.

"Sri Lanka - Fun Facts." Goway. Goway Travel. Accessed August 23, 2021. https://www.goway.com/travel-information/asia/sri-lanka/sri-lanka-fun-facts/.

"Sri Lankan independence movement." Wikipedia. Wikipedia. Accessed August 23, 2021. https://en.wikipedia.org/wiki/Sri_Lankan_independence_movement.

"Strengthening Maternal and Child Health Service Delivery in Guinea-Bissau." The World Bank. The World Bank. June 13, 2017. 1–13. http://documents1.worldbank.org/curated/pt/753341512739828724/pdf/Concept-Project-Information-Document-Integrated-Safeguards-Data-Sheet.pdf.

"Sudan." IHME (Institute for Health Metrics and Evaluation). University of Washington. Accessed September 10, 2021. http://www.healthdata.org/sudan.

"Sudan." The World Factbook. Central Intelligence Agency. Accessed September 10, 2021. https://www.cia.gov/the-world-factbook/countries/sudan/#government.

"Sudan." Wikipedia. Wikipedia. Accessed September 10, 2021. https://en.wikipedia.org/wiki/Sudan.

Swearingen, Will D., et al. "Morocco." Britannica. Encyclopædia

Britannica, Inc. Accessed August 23, 2021. https://www.britannica.com/place/Morocco.

"Tajikistan." IHME (Institute for Health Metrics and Evaluation). University of Washington. Accessed September 2, 2021. http://www.healthdata.org/tajikistan.

"Tajikistan profile – Timeline." BBC. BBC. July 31, 2018. https://www.bbc.com/news/world-asia-16201087.

"Tanzania." IHME (Institute for Health Metrics and Evaluation). University of Washington. Accessed September 2, 2021. http://www.healthdata.org/tanzania.

"The 1 largest airports and airlines in Burundi." WorldData.info. WorldData.info. Accessed October 23, 2020. https://www.worlddata.info/africa/burundi/airports.php.

"The biggest airports in Liberia." WorldData.info. WorldData.info. Accessed October 22, 2020. https://www.worlddata.info/africa/liberia/airports.php.

"The Gambia." Lonely Planet. Lonely Planet. Accessed October 22, 2020. https://www.lonelyplanet.com/the-gambia.

"The Land of the Blue Sky." Discover Mongolia. Discover Mongolia Travel Co. March 4, 2015. https://www.discovermongolia.mn/blogs/discover-mongolia-land-of-the-blue-sky.

"The World Bank In Bangladesh." The World Bank. World Bank Group. Accessed August 23, 2021.https://www.worldbank.org/en/country/bangladesh/overview.

"The World Bank In Benin." The World Bank. World Bank Group. Accessed September 2, 2021. https://www.worldbank.org/en/country/benin/overview.

"The World Bank in Bhutan." The World Bank. World Bank Group. Accessed August 24, 2021. https://www.worldbank.org/en/country/bhutan/overview.

"The World Bank in Burkina Faso." The World Bank. World Bank Group. Accessed September 10, 2021. https://www.worldbank.org/en/country/burkinafaso/overview.

"The World Bank In Burundi." The World Bank. World Bank Group. Accessed September 2, 2021. https://www.worldbank.org/en/country/burundi/overview.

"The World Bank In Cabo Verde." The World Bank. World Bank Group. Accessed August 24, 2021. https://www.worldbank.org/en/country/caboverde.

"The World Bank In Cambodia." The World Bank. World Bank Group. Accessed August 13, 2021. https://www.worldbank.org/en/country/cambodia/overview

"The World Bank in Central African Republic." The World Bank. World Bank Group. Accessed September 2, 2021. https://www.worldbank.org/en/country/centralafricanrepublic/overview.

"The World Bank in Chad." The World Bank. World Bank Group. Accessed September 2, 2021. https://www.worldbank.org/en/country/chad/overview.

"The World Bank in Côte d'Ivoire." The World Bank. World Bank Group. Accessed August 13, 2021. https://www.worldbank.org/en/country/cotedivoire/overview.

"The World Bank in DRC." The World Bank. World Bank Group. Accessed September 2, 2021. https://www.worldbank.org/en/country/drc/overview.

"The World Bank in El Salvador." The World Bank. World Bank Group. Accessed August 23, 2021. https://www.worldbank.org/en/country/elsalvador/overview,

"The World Bank in Eritrea." The World Bank. World Bank Group. Accessed September 2, 2021. https://www.worldbank.org/en/country/eritrea/overview.

"The World Bank in Eswatini." The World Bank. World Bank Group. Accessed September 7, 2021. https://www.worldbank.org/en/country/eswatini/overview.

"The World Bank in The Gambia." The World Bank. World Bank Group. Accessed October 22, 2020. https://www.worldbank.org/en/country/gambia/overview.

"The World Bank in Guinea. The World Bank. World Bank Group. Accessed September 2, 2021.. https://www.worldbank.org/en/country/guinea/overview.

"The World Bank in Guinea-Bissau." The World Bank. World Bank Group. Accessed October 22, 2020. https://www.worldbank.org/en/country/guineabissau/overview.

"The World Bank in Haiti." The World Bank. World Bank Group. Accessed September 2, 2021. https://www.worldbank.org/en/country/haiti/overview.

"The World Bank in Honduras." The World Bank. World Bank Group. Accessed August 24, 2021. https://www.worldbank.org/en/country/honduras/overview.

"The World Bank in India." The World Bank. World Bank Group. Accessed August 23, 2021. https://www.worldbank.org/en/country/india/overview.

"The World Bank in Lao PDR." The World Bank. World Bank Group. Accessed August 23, 2021. https://www.worldbank.org/en/country/lao/overview.

"The World Bank in Lesotho." The World Bank. World Bank Group. Accessed August 15, 2021. https://www.worldbank.org/en/country/lesotho/overview.

"The World Bank in Madagascar." The World Bank. World Bank Group. Accessed September 2, 2021. https://www.worldbank.org/en/country/madagascar/overview.

"The World Bank in Malawi." The World Bank. World Bank Group. Accessed September 2, 20210. https://www.worldbank.org/en/country/malawi/overview.

"The World Bank in Mauritania." The World Bank. World Bank Group. Accessed August 15, 2021. https://www.worldbank.org/en/country/mauritania/overview.

"The World Bank in Moldova." The World Bank. World Bank Group. Accessed August 22, 2021. https://www.worldbank.org/en/country/moldova/overview.

"The World Bank in Mozambique." The World Bank. World Bank Group. Accessed September 2, 2021.. https://www.worldbank.org/en/country/mozambique/

overview#1.

"The World Bank in Niger." The World Bank. World Bank Group. Accessed October 23, 2020. https://www.worldbank.org/en/country/niger/overview.

"The World Bank in Papua New Guinea." The World Bank. World Bank Group. Accessed August 24, 2021. https://www.worldbank.org/en/country/png/overview.

"The World Bank in the Republic of Congo." The World Bank. World Bank Group. Accessed August 13, 2020. https://www.worldbank.org/en/country/congo/overview.

"The World Bank in Rwanda." The World Bank. World Bank Group. Accessed September 2. 2021. https://www.worldbank.org/en/country/rwanda/overview.

"The World Bank in Sierra Leone." The World Bank. World Bank Group. Accessed September 2021. https://www.worldbank.org/en/country/sierraleone/overview.

"The World Bank in South Sudan." The World Bank. World Bank Group. Accessed September 2, 2021. https://www.worldbank.org/en/country/southsudan/overview.

"The World Bank in Sudan." The World Bank. World Bank Group. Accessed September 10, 2021. https://www.worldbank.org/en/country/sudan/overview.

"The World Bank in Tajikistan." The World Bank. World Bank Group. Accessed September 2, 2021. https://www.worldbank.org/en/country/tajikistan/overview#1.

"The World Bank in Timor-Leste." The World Bank. World Bank Group. Accessed August 24, 2021. https://www.worldbank.org/en/country/timor-leste/overview.

"The World Bank in Togo." The World Bank. World Bank Group. Accessed September 2 2021. https://www.worldbank.org/en/country/togo/overview.

"The World Bank in Uganda." The World Bank. World Bank Group. Accessed September 2, 2021. https://www.worldbank.org/en/country/uganda/overview.

"The World Bank in Vietnam." The World Bank. World Bank Group. Accessed August 23, 2021. https://www.worldbank.org/en/country/vietnam/overview.

Thornton, John Kelly, et al. Britannica. Encyclopædia Britannica, Inc. Accessed August 24, 2021. https://www.britannica.com/place/Angola.

"Timor-Leste." IHME (Institute for Health Metrics and Evaluation). University of Washington. Accessed August 24, 2021. http://www.healthdata.org/timor-leste.

"Timor-Leste." The World Factbook. Central Intelligence Agency. Accessed August 24, 2021. https://www.cia.gov/the-world-factbook/countries/timor-leste/#people-and-society.

"Togo country profile." BBC. BBC. February 24. Accessed September 2, 2021. https://www.bbc.com/news/world-africa-14106781.

"Togo 2020 Crime & Safety Report." OSAC. Overseas Security Advisory Council, Bureau of Diplomatic Security, U.S. Department of State. April 9, 2020. https://www.osac.gov/Country/Togo/Content/Detail/Report/1afba1d9-f4a6-414b-b1e1-1867c0edd3f3.

"Togo." IHME (Institute for Health Metrics and Evaluation). University of Washington. Accessed September 2, 2021. http://www.healthdata.org/togo.

"Togo." Britannica. Encyclopædia Britannica, Inc. Accessed September 2, 2021. https://www.britannica.com/place/Togo.

Togo." The World Factbook. Central Intelligence Agency. Accessed September 2, 2021. https://www.cia.gov/the-world-factbook/countries/togo/.

"Travel to Haiti." World Travel Guide. Columbus Travel Media Ltd. Accessed October 22, 2020. https://www.worldtravelguide.net/guides/caribbean/haiti/travel-by/.

"Travel to Mozambique." World Travel Guide. Columbus Travel Media Ltd. Accessed October 22, 2020. https://www.worldtravelguide.net/guides/africa/mozambique/travel-by/.

"Travel to Niger." World Travel Guide. Columbus Travel Media Ltd. Accessed October 23, 2020. https://www.worldtravelguide.net/guides/africa/niger/travel-by/.

"Travel to Uganda." World Travel Guide. Columbus Travel Media Ltd. Accessed October 23, 2020. https://www.worldtravelguide.net/guides/africa/uganda/travel-by/.

"Tunisia." IHME (Institute for Health Metrics and Evaluation). University of Washington. Accessed August 23, 2021. http://www.healthdata.org/tunisia.

"Tunisia." The World Factbook. Central Intelligence Agency. Accessed August 23, 2021. https://www.cia.gov/the-world-factbook/countries/tunisia/#people-and-society.

"Tunisia." Wikipedia. Wikipedia. Accessed August 23, 2021. https://en.wikipedia.org/wiki/Tunisia.

"Uganda." IHME (Institute for Health Metrics and Evaluation). University of Washington. Accessed September 2, 2021. http://www.healthdata.org/uganda.

"Uganda." The World Factbook. Central Intelligence Agency. Accessed October 19, 2020. https://www.cia.gov/the-world-factbook/countries/uganda/.

"Uganda country profile." BBC. BBC. May 10, 2018. https://www.bbc.com/news/world-africa-14107906.

"Ukraine." IHME (Institute for Health Metrics and Evaluation). University of Washington. Accessed August 23, 2021. http://www.healthdata.org/ukraine.

"Ukraine." The World Factbook. Central Intelligence Agency. Accessed August 23, 2021. https://www.cia.gov/the-world-factbook/countries/ukraine/#people-and-society.

"Ukraine." Wikipedia. Wikipedia. Accessed August 23, 2021. https://en.wikipedia.org/wiki/Ukraine.

"UN list of Least Developed Countries." UNCTAD. United Nations Conference on Trade and Development. Accessed September 2, 2021. https://unctad.org/topic/least-developed-countries/list. "UNICEF Sierra Leone." UNICEF Sierra Leone. UNICEF. Accessed September 2, 2021. https://www.unicef.org/sierraleone/#:~:text=With%201%2C360%20mothers%20dying%20per,of%20death%20associated%20to%20childbirth.

"United Republic of Tanzania." IHME (Institute for Health Metrics and Evaluation). University of Washington. Accessed September 2, 2021. http://www.healthdata.org/tanzania. "Uzbekistan Population." Worldometer. Worldometer. Accessed August 23, 2021. https://www.worldometers.info/world-population/uzbekistan-population/.

Van Hoogstraten, Jan S.F, et al. "Central African Republic." Britannica. Encyclopædia Britannica, Inc. Accessed October 15, 2020. https://www.britannica.com/place/Central-African-Republic.

"Vanuatu." IHME (Institute for Health Metrics and Evaluation). University of Washington. Accessed August 25, 2021. http://www.healthdata.org/vanuatu.

"Vanuatu." The World Factbook. Central Intelligence Agency. Accessed August 24, 2021. https://www.cia.gov/the-world-factbook/countries/vanuatu.

"Vanuatu." Wikipedia. Wikipedia. Accessed August 24, 2021. https://en.wikipedia.org/wiki/Vanuatu.

"Vietnam." The World Factbook. Central Intelligence Agency. Accessed August 23, 2021. https://www.cia.gov/the-world-factbook/countries/vietnam/#people-and-society.

"Vietnam." Wikipedia. Wikipedia. Accessed August 23, 2021. https://en.wikipedia.org/wiki/Vietnam#Health.

"Welcome to Rwanda." Republic of Rwanda. Republic of Rwanda. Accessed September 2, 2021. https://www.gov.rw/.

"WHO called to return to the Declaration of Alma-Ata." World Health Organization. World Health Organization. Accessed August 23, 2021. https://www.who.int/teams/social-determinants-of-health/declaration-of-alma-ata.

"Zimbabwe: 16 Official Languages and Counting." Listen & Learn Blog. Language Courses and Language Services Australia & New Zealand. Accessed August 23, 2021. https://www.listenandlearnaustralia.com.au/blog/zimbabwe-16-official-languages-and-counting/.

"Zimbabwe Life Expectancy 1950-2021." Macrotrends. Macrotrends LLC. Accessed August 23, 2021. https://www.macrotrends.net/countries/ZWE/zimbabwe/life-expectancy.

"Zimbabwe Population." Worldometer. Worldometer. Accessed August 23, 2021. https://www.worldometers.info/world-population/zimbabwe-population/.

Index

Ahmadu Bello University Teaching Hospital
  (ABUTH) 608
Ahmed Galal Military Hospital 192
Ahmed Maher Teaching Hospital 192
Ahmed Medical Complex 630
Ahmed Ouroua 8
AHOPE for Children 227
AHS – Waterloo 717, 746
Ahtaung Station Hospital 534
Ahwene Memorial Hospital 271
Aibolit Medical Transportation 854
AICC Hospital 788
AIC CURE International Hospital 393
AIC Kapsowar Hospital 393
AIC Kijabe Hospital 393
AIC Kijabe Naivasha Hospital 393
AIC Litein Hospital 393
Aid Africa's Children 455
Aid Africa's Children 593
Aid Africa's Children 771
Aid Africa's Children 914
AID FOR AIDS International 200, 294, 318, 566
Aid for Haiti 294
Aid for the Development of People for People (ADPP)
  Mozambique 510
AIDS Foundation of Sri Lanka 740
AIDS Healthcare Foundation 102, 200, 218, 227,
  294, 335, 371, 414, 422, 455, 510, 524, 542, 593,
  646, 676, 706, 823, 848, 888, 914, 930
AIDS Information Centre – Uganda 823
AIDS Orphan Care 422
AIDS Society Of The Philippines 646
AIMS Hospital Ltd. 35
Aïn Naadja Military Hospital 8
Air Force Hospital (Aviation Hospital) 192
Aisah Medical Hospital 658
Aisha Muhammadu Buhari General Hospital 608
AISPO 162, 186, 442, 511, 706, 728, 750, 823, 888
AITAM Hospital-Adabar 35
Ajeromi General Hospital, Ajegunle 608
Akim Oda Government Hospital 271
Akjoujt Hospital 476
Aklan Baptist Hospital 658
Akomaa Memorial Aventist Hospital 271
Āk'ordat Hospital 215
Āksum K'idist Maryam Hospital 242
Akuse Government Hospital 271
Al Agouza Hospital 192
Al-Ain International 618
Al Amal Hospital 192
Al Amal National Hospital Khartoum 2 756
Al Amal Specialized Hospital 756
Alam Family Hospital 630
Al Amin Dental College And General Hospital 35
Al Amin Hospital 736
Alaska Sudan Medical Project 728
Al Azhar Clinic 8
Al Azhar University Hospital 192
Al Bank Al Ahly Hospital 192
Al Basar International Foundation 22, 46, 74, 102,
  118, 132, 140, 150, 156, 163, 212, 227, 248, 257,
  278, 288, 335, 371, 455, 472, 502, 542, 582, 593,
  618, 646, 677, 694, 706, 740, 750, 771, 804,
  823, 931
Albert Schweitzer Hospital 294
Albinism Foundation of Zambia 914
Albino M. Duran Memorial Hospital 658
Albor District Hospital 658
Alchevs'k, Central City Hospital 854
Al Delta Hospital 192
A Leg To Stand On (ALTSO) 22, 102, 334, 414, 542,
  618, 822
Aleosan District Hospital (ADH) 658
Alert Hospital 242
Alexandria Central City Hospital 854
Alexandria International Hospital 192
Alexandria Pediatric Oncology Charity 186

Alexandria University Hospital For Students 192
Alex Ekwueme Federal University Teaching Hospital
  Abakaliki 608
Al Faisal Specialized Hospital 756
Al Fath Islamic Hospital 192
Alfonso Ponce Enrile Memorial District Hospital 658
Alfonso Specialist Hospital 658
AlFouad Hospital 756
Alfredo E. Marañon, Sr. Memorial District
  Hospital 658
Al Hayat Hospital 192
Al Helal Hospital 192
Al-Helal Specialized Hospital Limited 35
Al-Ibrahim Eye Hospital 630
Ali Children Hospital 630
Aliero General Hospital 608
Alight 163, 200, 524, 618, 677, 728, 750, 823
A Light For Zimbabwe 930
Ali Hospital 630
Al-Ihsan Foundation 227
AL Ijumaa Hospital 788
Ali Medical Centre 630
Alimosho General Hospital Igando 608
Al-injaz Sudanese German Specialized Hospital 756
Alive Hospital & Trauma Centre 558
Aljawda Hospital 756
Alka Hospital Pvt. Ltd. 558
Alkaleri General Hospital 608
Al-Khair Foundation 22, 371, 524, 618, 804
Alkhidmat Foundation Pakistan 618
Al-Khidmat Hospital Orangi Town 630
Allah bamu Lafiya Hospital 608
Allah Valley Medical Specialists' Center, Inc.
  Hospital 658
Allegiant Regional Care Hospitals 658
Allen District Hospital 658
Alliance for Children Foundation 294, 888
Alliance for International Medical Action, The
  (ALIMA) 74, 118, 132, 140, 163, 278, 472, 582,
  593, 695, 728, 22
Alliance for Smiles 163, 186, 318, 524
Alliance Hospital 608
Alliance International Medical Center 419
Allied Hospital Faisalabad 630
All Nepal Hospital Pvt. Ltd. 558
Alma Mater 313
Al-Manar Hospital Ltd. 35
Al Mawada Hospital 756
Al Murtaza Hospital 630
Al-Mustafa Eye Hospital 630
Al-Mustafa Welfare Trust 22, 248, 371, 455, 524,
  618, 728, 740, 771
Al Nas Hospital 192
AlNau Hospital 756
Al Noor Hospital 630
Al Noor Hospital, Pasrur 630
Al-Noor Mother Care Center 630
Al-Noury Specialist Hospital 608
Aloha Medical Mission 22, 102, 318, 335, 414, 480,
  524, 542, 566, 638, 646, 722, 771, 798, 882, 888
Alotau General Hospital 642
Alpha Specialist Hospital 608
Alpine Medical College Teaching Hospital 558
Alqima Specialized Hospital 756
Al-Quds District Hospital Public Corporation 8
Al-Raee Hospital Gujranwala 630
Al Rahma Hospital 182
Al-Raji Hospital 35
Al Rawda Hospital 192, 756
Al Razi Hospital 630
Al-Rehman Hospital Faisalabad 630
Al-Rehman Hospital Lahore 630
Al Sabbah Children's Hospital 736
Al-Saddaaqah Hospital 476
Al Sadiq-Saad Shaheed Hospital 630
Al Safwa Hospital 192
Al Saha Specialized Hospital 756

Al Salam Eye Hospital 192
Al Salam Hospital 192
Alsalam Hospital – El Mohandessin 192
Al Sharif Specialist Hospital 756
Alshifa Ltd. 771
Al Shifa Specialized Hospital 756
Al-Shifa Trust Eye Hospital 618
Al-Shifa Trust Eye Hospital Chakwal 630
Al-Shifa Trust Eye Hospital Kohat 630
Al-Shifa Trust Eye Hospital Muzaffrabad 630
Al-Shifa Trust Eye Hospital Rawalpindi 630
Al-Shifa Trust Eye Hospital Sukkur 630
Al Shorouk Hospital 192
Al-Tigany Al-Mahy Mental Health Hospital 756
Aluma 91
Alushta Central City Hospital 854
Al Wadi Hospital 192
Al Watany Eye Hospital (WEH) 192
Al-Widad hospital 756
Alzaytouna Specialised Hospital 756
Amal Foundation 22
Amana Referral Hospital 788
Amanuel Hospital 242
Amara Charitable Trust 371
Amar Gandhi Foundation (AGF) 335
AMARI (African Mental Health Research
  Initiative) 227, 455, 931
Amazing Care Foundation 593
Ambia Memorial Hospital 35
Ambira Sub District Hospital 393
Ambulance and Inpatient Treatment, Ternivka 854
Ambulance Station 854
Amdework Hospital 242
America Australia Bangladesh Friendship
  Hospital 35
American Academy of Ophthalmology 84, 218, 227,
  257, 294, 335, 593
American Academy of Pediatrics 74, 132, 163, 200,
  227, 294, 318, 360, 371, 442, 542, 566, 593, 618,
  646, 771, 823, 914
American Cancer Society 318, 335, 371, 646, 914,
  931
America Nepal Medical Foundation 542
American Foundation for Children with AIDS 163,
  371, 823, 931
American Heart Association (AHA) 23, 186, 257, 335,
  371, 542, 593, 618, 771
American International Health Alliance (AIHA) 102,
  227, 360, 371, 406, 430, 486, 511, 593, 646, 762,
  771, 823, 848, 874, 914
American Nicaraguan Foundation (ANF) 566
Americans Caring Teaching Serving (ACTS)
  Honduras 318
American Society of Ophthalmic Plastic and
  Reconstruction Surgery Foundation 371
American Stroke Association 23, 186, 257, 335, 371,
  543, 593, 618, 771
American Tamil Medical Association (ATMA) 335
Americare Neurosurgery International (AMCANI) 524,
  888
Americares 23, 62, 102, 140, 163, 200, 212, 227,
  257, 294, 318, 335, 371, 406, 430, 455, 494, 511,
  524, 543, 566, 582, 593, 619, 646, 695, 707, 729,
  740, 750, 771, 823, 874, 888, 931
Americas Association for the Care of Children
  (AACC) 56, 294, 335, 372, 543, 566
AMG International 294, 335, 823
Amicus Onlus 257
Aminata Maternal Foundation 707
Amin General Hospital 242
Aminu Kano Teaching Hospital Kano 608
Ammar Medical Complex 630
Amoah Memorial Hospital 271
AMOR (Aide Mondiale Orphelins Reconfort) 455, 511
AMOSUP Seamen's Hospital – Iloilo 658
AMOSUP Seamen's Hospital – Intramuros,
  Manila 658

AMOSUP Seamen's Hospital – Mandaue City, Cebu 658
AMREF Flying Doctors 227, 372, 677, 695, 729, 771, 823, 915
Amref Health Africa 12, 46, 84, 118, 156, 163, 212, 218, 227, 257, 278, 360, 372, 422, 430, 442, 455, 511, 593, 677, 695, 707, 729, 750, 771, 824, 915, 931
Amrita Hospital 335
AMS – Africa Mission Services 372
Amsterdam Institute for Global Health and Development (AIGHD) 23, 119, 227, 257, 335, 372, 511, 566, 593, 619, 646, 695, 771, 824, 888, 915, 931
Amtali Upazila Health Complex 35
Amurtel 295, 335, 372, 494, 566
Amuwo Odofin Maternal & Childcare Centre 608
AM Yumena General Hospital, Inc. 658
Anaka Hospital 843
Anambra State Association Women in USA, Inc 593
Anan Clinica 511
Ananda Marga Universal Relief Team (AMURT) Kenya 372
Anania Mothers and Children Specialized Medical Center 227
Anba Abraam Charity 62, 186
Anba Abraam Charity 750
An Binh Hospital 898
Ancien Hôpital de Goré 145
Andalusia Hospital Maadi 192
Andean Medical Mission 62
Andranomadio Hospital 449
Andres Soriano Memorial Hospital Cooperative 658
Andriyivs'ka Tsentral'na Rayonna Likarnya 854
Andrology and Urology Center Association 409
Andrushivka Central District Hospital 854
An Duc Obstetrics and Gynecology Hospital 898
Aneho Psychiatric Hospital 810
Anfal Hospital 756
Angau General Hospital 642
Angau Memorial Hospital 642
Angeles University Foundation Medical Center 658
Angel of Mercy 119
Angel Salazar Memorial General Hospital 658
Angels Foundation 931
Angel Wings International 295
Angkor Chum Referral Hospital 113
Angkor Hospital for Children 113
AngloGold Ashanti Hospital 271
Angono Medics Hospital 658
Ang Snoul Referral Hospital 113
Anka General Hospital 393
Anka General Hospital 608
An Nhon Hospital 898
An Phước 898
Anse Rouge Hospital Anse Rouge (AFME) 313
An Sinh Hospital 898
Answer Africa 372
Antalya Medical Center 756
Antelope Mine Hospital 940
Antipolo City Hospital System Annex 4 659
Antique Medical Center 659
An Ward Medical Station 898
AO Alliance 23, 46, 74, 84, 102, 119, 140, 156, 163, 227, 248, 257, 278, 360, 372, 414, 455, 524, 543, 582, 593, 677, 695, 722, 740, 771, 804, 824, 888, 915, 931
Apac General Hospital 843
APIN Public Health Initiatives 593
Apnalaya: Empowering the Urban Poor 335
Apostolov Central District Hospital 854
April 30 Hospital, Ministry of Public Security 898
Aquino Medical Specialists Hospital Inc. 659
Arab Contractors Medical Center 193
ARAB Hospital 717, 746
Arabic Center For Physiotherapy and Rehabilitation 756
Araddhya Hospital Pvt. Ltd. 558

Araketke-Bereket Charitable Foundation 406
Arashan General Practice Center 409
Aravan District Public Hospital 409
Aravind Eye Foundation 335
Arba Minch Hospital 242
Arbeiter Samariter Bund (Workers' Samaritan Federation) 248, 295, 543, 566, 582, 647, 848
Arcahaie Hospital Saint Joseph de Galilée 313
Arcelor Mittal Yekepa Hospital 439
Arch Bishop Dery Memorial Hospital 271
ARC The Australian Respiratory Council 23, 102, 400, 722, 798, 888
A Reason to Smile (ARTS) 566, 694, 822
Ark Hospital Limited 35
Arkilla PHC 608
Ark Outreach 593
Arlene Campbell Humanitarian Foundation 848
Armed Forces Hospital Kobry El Kobba 193
Arms Around Africa Foundation 218, 372, 771, 824
Army Station Hospital 659
Arnel Pineda Foundation, Inc. 647
Arogya World 335
Art Hospital 242
Arthritis Foundation of Asia 335
Arthur Davidson Children's Hospital 925
Arua Regional Referral Hospital 843
Arunodaya Charitable Trust 335
Arusha Hospital 788
Arusha Lutheran Medical Centre 788
Ar Yaw Jan Hospital 534
ARYU International Hospital 534
Asaita Referral Hospital 242
Asamang SDA Hospital 257
Asamankese Government Hospital 271
ASAP Foundation 74
ASAP Ministries 102, 414, 524, 888
Asare Odei Hospital 271
Ascenta Foundation 566, 647
Asclepius Snakebite Foundation 46, 278
ASE Foundation 335, 372, 647, 888
Asella Hospital 242
Asesewa Government Hospital 271
Asfandyar Bukhari Civil Hospital DHQ Attock 630
Asgar Ali Hospital 35
Ashfaq Memorial Hospital 630
ASHIC Foundation 23
Ashraya Initiative for Children 336
Ashuganj Upazila Health Complex 35
Asia Hospital 756
Asia Medicare Hospital Pvt. Ltd. 558
Asia Pacific Centre for Medical and Dental Care 534
Asia Royal Hospital 534
Aslan Project, The 227, 372
Asokoro District Hospital 608
Aspen Management Partnership for Health (AMP Health) 257, 455, 707, 915
Aspen Medical Sierra Leone Private Hospital 717, 746
Assab Hospital 215
As-Salam International Hospital 193
Assemblies of God Hospital Saboba 271
Assist Africa 257
Assist Africa 804
Assist International 102, 227, 372, 494, 771, 824
Association Espoir Pour Demain (AED) 810
Association for Aid and Relief, Japan (AAR JAPAN) 750
Association for Reproductive and Family Health 594
Association for the Promotion of Human Health (APSH), Burundi 84
Association Haïtienne de Développement Humain (AHDH) 295
Association of Baptists - AOB 23
Association of Haitian Physicians Abroad (AMHE) 295
Association of Medical Doctors of Asia (AMDA) 6, 23, 56, 62, 103, 163, 180, 295, 318, 336, 400, 406, 494, 524, 543, 619, 638, 647, 677, 740, 750, 889

Association of Nigerian Physicians in the Americas (ANPA) 594
Association of Sierra Leonean Health Professionals in the US, The (TASHPUS) 707
Associazione la Nostra Famiglia 751
Assosa Hospital 242
Assumption Catholic Church Hospital 608
Assumption Specialty Hospital and Medical Center 659
A Stitch in Time 22, 822
Aswan Chest Diseases Hospital 193
Aswan Military Hospital 193
Asyut University Hospital 193
Atar Mauritania Hospital 476
Atasomanso Hospital 271
At-Bashy Regional Hospital 409
Atebubu Government Hospital 271
Atibie Government Hospital 271
Atoifi Adventist Hospital 724
Atok District Hospital 659
Atpara Upazila Health Complex 35
Atsbi Hospital 242
Atsyor Hospital Complex 271
Attapeu Province Hospital 419
Attat Hospital 242
Atua Government Hospital 271
Atwari Upazila Health Complex 35
Audiyiv Central City Hospital 854
Aung Myin Myint Mo Hospital 534
Aung Thitsar Hospital 534
Aung Yadana Hospital 534
Aung Zaw Oo Hospital 534
A.U.P. Health Service 658
Aurora Memorial Hospital 659
Aurum Institute, The 257, 422, 511
Austin Samaritans 566
Australian Doctors for Africa 150, 227, 442
Australian Doctors International (ADI) 638
Australian Health Humanitarian Aid (AHHA) 103, 889
Australian Himalayan Foundation 56, 336, 543
Australian & New Zealand Gastroenterology International Training Association 524, 543, 638, 722, 798
Australians for Women's Health 543
Australia Sri Lanka Medical Aid Team 740
Austrian Doctors 23, 336, 372, 647, 707
AusViet Charity Foundation Limited 889
Autism Care Nepal Society 543
Avenue Healthcare Hospital 393
Avenue Hospital 393
Avenue Specialist Hospital 608
Avert 422, 455, 915, 931
Avicenna Hospital 35
Avinta Care 677, 771, 915
Avis Hospital 765
Avis Siti 765
AVSI 313
Aweil Civil Hospital 736
A World of Difference 102, 334, 542
Awtad Prosthetics Hospital 756
Aya Project 360
Ayder Referral Hospital 242
Aye Chan Tar Hospital 534
Aye Thandar Hospital 534
Aye Thu Kha Hospital 534
Ayeyarwady Hospital 534
Ayeyarwady Mental Health Hospital 534
AYINET – African Youth Initiative Network 824
Aysha Memorial Specialised Hospital (Pvt.) Ltd. 35
Ayudana Hospital 534
Ayurveda Hospital 558
Ayurvedic Hospital 558
Ayush Hospital 558
Azam Majeed Medical Complex 631
Azare Federal Medical Centre 608
Azimed Hospital 877
Aziza's Place 103

Bulolo General Hospital 642
Bulongwa Lutheran Hospital 788
Bulumkutu General Hospital 609
Bumerec 91
Bunda DDH Hospital 788
Bungabong-Sanico Medical Clinic & Maternity Hospital 660
Bungkot Hospital 559
Bungoma District Hospital 393
Buni-Yadi General Hospital 609
Buon Ma Thuot City Hospital 899
Bura Sub-County Hospital 393
Bureau of International Health Cooperation 103, 163, 258, 295, 414, 431, 494, 525, 619, 647, 695, 707, 740, 889, 915
Burkina Health Foundation 75
Burma Humanitarian Mission 525
Burn Advocates 296
Burn Advocates 337
Burn Care International 62, 228, 594, 772
Burshtyn Central City Hospital 855
Buruanga Medicare Community Hospital 660
Busekwa 788
Busia County Referral Hospital 393
Busk Central District Hospital 855
Butabika Hospital 843
Butajira General Hospital 243
Butaro Hospital 687
Bute District Hospital 393
Butere County Hospital 393
Butha Buthe Hospital 426
Butiama Hospital 788
Butwal Hospital Pvt. Ltd. 559
Buwenge Hospital 843
Buy A Brick Foundation 931
BV Anh Đức 899
BV Binh Thuan 899
BV Đa Khoa Bình Minh 899
BV Đa khoa Đức Huệ 899
BV Đa khoa Hồng Ngự 899
BV Đa khoa quận Ô Môn 899
BV Đa khoa Thanh Hóa 899
BVĐK Bình Thuận – khu vực Phía Bắc 899
BV gò công (Phượng) 899
BV Răng-Hàm-Mặt 899
BV Tai Mũi Họng Sài Gòn 899
BV Thu Duc 899
Bwaila Hospital 468
Bwera Hospital 843
Bwiam General Hospital 253
Bwindi Community Hospital 843
Byrkguzar City Perinatal Center #1 877
C17 Military Hospital 904
Cabara 91
Cabiao General Hospital 660
Cabredo Hospital 660
Cabrini Ministries Swaziland 218
Cabuyao City Hospital 660
Cadiz District Hospital 660
Cagayan de Oro City Hospital – Tablon 660
Cagayan De Oro Medical Center Oncology/Cancer Center 660
Cagayan de Oro Polymedic General Hospital 660
Cagayan Valley Medical Center 660
Cai Khe Ward Medical Station 904
Cainglet Medical Hospital, Inc. 660
Cainta Municipal Hospital 660
Caiquo Hospital 272
Cairdeas International Palliative Care Trust 258, 337, 373, 455, 472, 594, 751, 772, 814, 825, 915
Cairo University Hospitals 193
Calalang General Hospital 660
Calauag St. Peter General Hospital 660
Calbayog District Hospital 660
Cal de Madian 313
CAL de Mont Organise 313
Called to go Chiropractic Missions 455

Calmette Hospital 113
Calumpit District Hospital 660
Cambodia-China Friendship Preah Kossamak Hospital 113
Cambodia-Dutch Foundation, The 103
Cambodian Buddhism Association for Vulnerable Children 103
Cambodian Diabetes Association Siem Reap 103
Cambodian Health Professionals Association of America 103
Cambodia Vision Foundation 103
Cambodia World Family 103
Cambridge Global Health Partnerships (CGHP) 200, 525, 825
Cameroon Baptist Convention (CBC) Health Services 119
Cameroon Oncology Center 127
Camiguin General Hospital 660
Camillian Disaster Service (CADIS) International 296, 337, 373, 414, 544, 619, 647, 707
Camp Evangelista Station Hospital, Philippine Army 660
Camp General Artemio Ricarte Station Hospital, WESCOM, Puerto Princesa 660
Camp General Emilio Aguinaldo Station Hospital 660
Cam Pha General Hospital 904
Camp Navarro General Hospital 660
Canada-Africa Community Health Alliance 46, 163, 772, 825
Canadian Dental Relief International 62
Canadian Foundation for Women's Health 85, 163, 455, 772
Canadian Medical Assistance Teams (CMAT) 24, 296, 544, 619, 647
Canadian Network for International Surgery, The 228, 373, 594, 677, 729, 772, 825
Canadian Reconstructive Surgery Foundation, The 24, 62, 337, 544
Canadian Vision Care 103, 373, 455, 647
Cancer Care Ethiopia 228
Cancer Care Hospital and Research Center 619
Candelaria District Hospital 660
Candon General Hospital 660
Căng Tin Bệnh Viện 905
CanKids KidsCan 337
Cankuzo Hospital 91
Can Obiejemba Foundation, Inc.(CANOFF) 594
Can Protect Foundation 337
Can Tho Central General Hospital 904
Can Tho City Cancer Hospital 904
Can Tho Dermatology Hospital 904
Cantonment General Hospital 36
Cantonment General Hospital Rawalpindi 631
Canvasback Missions 480
Canwinn Foundation 337
CapacityBay Health Initiative 594
Cape CARES Central American Relief Efforts 319
Cape Coast Teaching Hospital 272
Cap Haitien Dental Institute 296
Capitol University Medical Center 660
CapraCare 296
Caraga Regional Hospital 660
Caramoan Municipal Hospital 660
Cardiac Center Shisong-Kumbo 127
Cardiac Hospital Khujand 765
Cardinal Rugambwa Hospital 788
CardioStart International 258, 296, 319, 337, 525, 544, 594, 772, 825, 889
Cardiovascular Foundation, The (TCVF) 619
CARE 12, 24, 46, 62, 85, 103, 119, 140, 163, 180, 187, 200, 228, 258, 296, 319, 337, 360, 373, 414, 422, 431, 443, 456, 502, 511, 525, 544, 567, 582, 619, 638, 647, 677, 729, 740, 751, 772, 798, 804, 825, 882, 889, 915, 931
Care 2 Communities (C2C) 296
Care and Development Organization (CDO) Nepal 544
CARE Bihar 337

Care Channels International 24, 619, 647, 798
Careerbridge Foundation 594
Care For a Child's Heart 373
Care for Africa 772, 373, 772, 825
Care For Business Medical Centre 925
Care for Uganda 825
Care Highway International 373
Care Hospital Ltd. 393
Care Love Charity Foundation 373
CARe Medical College Hospital 36
CARe Medical College Hospital Ltd 36
CareMe E-Clinic 677
Care Old Age & Child Foundation 825
Care Organization Public Enlightenment 594
Care SOS France 313
Carewell Community 647
Caring Hands Worldwide 456, 480, 494, 915
Caring Souls Foundation (CASOF) 337
Caritas Hospital & Institute of Health Sciences 337
Caritas Pro Vitae Gradu Charitable Trust 12, 46, 212, 228, 619, 729, 772, 825
Carmelite Hospital 660
Carmen Copper Corporation Hospital 660
Carolina for Kibera 373
Carrefour Joute 313
Carter Center, The 6, 12, 24, 47, 62, 75, 85, 119, 132, 140, 163, 187, 200, 212, 228, 258, 278, 296, 319, 337, 361, 373, 431, 443, 456, 472, 511, 525, 544, 567, 582, 594, 619, 647, 677, 695, 707, 729, 740, 751, 772, 798, 804, 814, 825, 915
Cataingan District Hospital 660
Cateel District Hospital 660
Catherine Hamlin Fistula Foundation 228
Catherine Mills Hospital 439
Catholic Health Association of India 337
Catholic Healthcare Association of Southern Africa, The 218
Catholic Health Commission 456
Catholic Medical Mission Board (CMMB) 296, 373, 729, 915
Catholic Mission Hospital 788
Catholic Organization for Relief & Development Aid (CORDAID) 85, 119, 132, 163, 228, 373, 525, 594, 647, 707, 729, 825, 931
Catholic World Mission 24, 119, 163, 200, 258, 296, 319, 337, 373, 431, 456, 594, 647, 740, 772, 825
Cauayan Medical Specialists Hospital 660
CAUSE Canada 319, 431, 707
Cavite Naval Hospital 660
cbm New Zealand 24, 75, 228, 337, 373, 414, 544, 594, 638, 648, 677
CBP St. Raphael 313
CCAP Embangweni Mission Hospital 468
CCBRT Hospital 788
CDC Cottage Hospital 127
Cebu Doctors' University Hospital 660
Cebu North General Hospital 660
Cebu Provincial Hospital – Carcar City 660
Cebu South Medical Center 660
Cebu Velez General Hospital 660
CedarCrest Abuja Hospital 609
Cemadif 91
CEML Hospital (Centro Evangelico de Medicina do Lubango) 17
Center for Allergic Diseases of the Upper Respiratory Tract 855
Center for Clinical Care and Clinical Research 594
Center for Epilepsy and Neurologic Diseases Liberia (CEND-LIB) 431
Center for Health and Hope 337, 373, 456, 678
Center for Innovative Medicine and Laser Surgery 855
Center for Medical Advisory Services and Sports Medicine 409
Center for Preventive Medicine in District 6 904
Center for Private Sector Health Initiatives 337, 374, 544, 594, 772

Center for Reproductive Health 489
Center for Research and Preventive Health Care 609
Center for Specialized Care & Research (CSCR) Hospital & Diagnostic Center 36
Center for Strategic and International Studies (CSIS) Commission on Strengthening America's Health Security 85, 150, 163, 212, 248, 288, 319, 406, 422, 456, 511, 582, 762, 804, 884, 889, 931
Center for the Right to Health (CRH) 595
Center of Primary Medical and Sanitary Care of Pulinsk Village Council 855
Centers of Hope Missions International 374, 567
Central Acupuncture Hospital 904
Central American Eye Clinics (CAEC) 200, 319
Central American Medical Outreach (CAMO) Nutrition Program 319
Central American Relief Efforts 319
Central Bashabo General Hospital 36
Central Children's City Hospital 855
Central City Clinical Hospital #1 Donetsk 855
Central City Clinical Hospital #3 855
Central City Hospital in New Kakhova 855
Central City Hospital Khartsyzsk 855
Central City Hospital M. Boryslav 855
Central City Hospital of Chervonohrad City Council 855
Central City Hospital of Novogrodiv City Council 855
Central City Hospital of the Pokrovsky City Council 855
Central City Hospital Snizhne 855
Central City Hospital Titova 855
Central Clinical Hospital #2, Tashkent 877
Central Clinical Hospital of JSC "Uzbekiston Temir Yullari," Tashkent 877
Central Congo Partnership 163
Central District Hospital Kamin-Kashirsky 855
Central District Hospital Krolevets 855
Central District Hospital Luhansk 856
Central District Hospital Munimabad 765
Central District Hospital of Berdychiv District 856
Central District Hospital of Rozdilna 856
Central District Hospital Verkhn'odniprovs'k 856
Central Hospital 765
Central Hospital at Vahdat 765
Central Hospital, Bagdan (Central Hospital of Forish Disctrict) 877
Central Hospital Benin 609
Central Hospital Cox's Bazar 36
Central Hospital Dhaka 36
Central Hospital Nampula 520
Central Hospital of Balykchy Region 877
Central Hospital of Gonchi District 765
Central Hospital of Rogun 765
Central Hospital of Shakhrisabz District 877
Central Hospital of Sharinav 765
Central Hospital of the Ministry of Internal Affairs of the Republic of Uzbekistan 877
Central Hospital of Traditional Medicine, The 904
Central Hospital Phnom Penh 113
Central Hospital Sapele 609
Central Hospital Sylhet 36
Central Hospital Warri 609
Central Lung Hospital (Bệnh viện Phổi Trung ương) 904
Central Mental Hospital 2 904
Central Military Hospital 877
Central Military Hospital at Odessa 856
Central Park Teaching Hospital 619, 631
Central Regional Referral Hospital, Gelephu 59
Central Women's Hospital – Mandalay 534
Centre Abel Sanou 80
Centre Ambulancier National 313
Centre de Chirurgie Orthopédique Pédiatrique et de Réhabilitation Sainte Marie de Rilima 678
Centre d'Enfants Bourguiba 817
Centre de Santé de Tika 52
Centre de Santé Oganla de Ketou 52
Centre de Santé Philippe Maguilène Senghor 702

Centre de Sante Roi Fayca 145
Centre de Saúde Cidade da Trindade 691
Centre d'Imagerie Médicale 152
Centre d'Oncologie 506
Centre Elisabeth Diouf Gueule Tapee 702
Centre for Equal Health Access Lesotho 426
Centre for Global Mental Health 228, 456, 511, 707, 931
Centre for HIV-AIDS Prevention Studies, The (CHAPS) 218
Centre for the Rehabilitation of the Paralysed - CRP 24, 36
Centre Hospitalier Abass Ndao 702
Centre Hospitalier Christian Martinez 313
Centre Hospitalier de Fomboni 152
Centre Hospitalier de Lamardelle 313
Centre Hospitalier Départemental de Borgou-Alibori 52
Centre Hospitalier Départemental de Mono 52
Centre Hospitalier Départemental de Natitingou (CHD) 52
Centre Hospitalier de Recherche et d'Application en Chirurgie Endoscopique et Reproduction Humaine 127
Centre Hospitalier de Reference Regional (CHRR) Antsohihy 449
Centre Hospitalier de Référence Régional de Morondava 449
Centre Hospitalier de Référence Régionale Ihosy 449
Centre Hospitalier de Soavinandriana 449
Centre Hospitalier Fontaine 313
Centre Hospitalier Mère-Enfant 476
Centre Hospitalier National Dalal Jamm 702
Centre Hospitalier National de Nouakchott 476
Centre Hospitalier National de Pikine 702
Centre Hospitalier National El Maarouf 152
Centre Hospitalier National Mathlaboul Fawzaini de Touba 702
Centre Hospitalier National Universitaire de Fann 702
Centre Hospitalier Régional 588
Centre Hospitalier Régional Agadez 588
Centre Hospitalier Régional Amadou Sakhir Mbaye Louga 702
Centre Hospitalier Régional d'Abengourou 366
Centre Hospitalier Régional Daloa 366
Centre Hôspitalier Régional de Banfora 80
Centre Hospitalier Régional de Divo 366
Centre Hôspitalier Régional de Dori 80
Centre Hospitalier Régional de Gagnoa (CHR) 366
Centre Hospitalier Régional de Guiglo 366
Centre Hospitalier Régional de Kaya 80
Centre Hospitalier Régional de Kolda 702
Centre Hospitalier régional de Koudougou 80
Centre Hospitalier Régional de Man 366
Centre Hospitalier Régional de Saint-Louis 702
Centre Hospitalier Régional de San-Pedro 366
Centre Hospitalier Régional Dimbokro 366
Centre Hospitalier Régional d'Odiennê 366
Centre Hospitalier Régional Yamoussoukro 366
Centre Hospitalier Universitaire (CHU de Bouaké) 366
Centre Hospitalier Universitaire (CHU de Treichville) 366
Centre Hospitalier Universitaire d'Angré (CHU d'Angré) 366
Centre Hospitalier Universitaire de Brazzaville (CHU-BZV) 159
Centre Hospitalier Universitaire de Cocody (CHU de Cocody) 366
Centre Hospitalier Universitaire de Ouahigouya 80
Centre Hospitalier Universitaire Départemental de l'Ouémé-Plateau 52
Centre Hospitalier Universitaire de Tingandogo 80
Centre Hospitalier Universitaire de Yopougon (CHU de Yopougon) 366
Centre Hospitalier Universitaire Hassan II (CHU Fes) 506

Centre Hospitalier Universitaire Mohammed VI 506
Centre Hospitalier Universitaire Tambohobe 449
Centre Hospitalier Universitaire Yalgado Ouédraogo 80
Centre Hospitalier Universitaire Zafisaona Gabriel 449
Centre International Carthage Médical 817
Centre Marembo 678
Centre Médical Béraca (CMB) 296
Centre Médical de Nagrin 80
Centre Médical de Nouna 80
Centre Médical de TYO-Ville 127
Centre Médical Paul VI 80
Centre Medico Chirurgical de Kinindo (CMCK) 91
Centre Médico-technique de Ngozi 91
Centre Mère et Enfant 588
Centre National de Cardiologie 476
Centre National d'Enfants Albert Royer 702
Centre National de Sécurité Sociale 159
Centre National d'Oncologie 476
Centre Pilote Tessaoua pour la Chirurgie Rurale 588
Centre Point Hospital Limited 36
Centre Yonis Toussaint Hospital 182
Centro Auditivo Internacional de Angola (CAINA) 17
Centro de Colaboração em Saúde 511
Centro de Saúde da Boa Vista 98
Centro de Saúde de Tarrafal de São Nicolau 98
Centro de Saude do Machiqueira 17
Centro de Trauma Hospital Corazón de Jesús 69
Centro Escolar University Dental Alumni Association 648
Centro Evangelico de Medicina do Lubango (CEML) 12
Centro Medico Susan Hou 62
Centro Nacional de Dermatología 576
Centro Nacional de Oftalmológico Dr. Emilio Alvarez Montalvan 576
Centro Nacional De Radiologia 576
Centro Neuro Psychiatrique de Nouakchott 476
Centro Oncológico de Quimioterapia y Cuidados Paliativos Dr. Clemente Guido 576
Centrul Ftiziopneumologic de Reabilitare pentru Copii Cornesti 489
Centrul Republican de Reabilitare pentru Copii 489
Centrul Sanatatii Familiei Galaxia 489
Cerezo General Hospital 660
CF Hospital 788
CFW Shops (A Project of Healthstore Foundation) 374
CGB 765
Chain of Hope 62, 85, 119, 187, 200, 212, 228, 249, 296, 374, 456, 502, 511, 619, 678, 695, 707, 751, 772, 825, 889, 931
Chain of Hope (La Chaîne de l'Espoir) 24, 47, 75, 103, 163, 296, 337, 361, 414, 443, 511, 544, 695, 804, 874
Chake Chake Hospital 788
Challenge Africa 374
Challenge Initiative, The 47, 75, 338, 361, 374, 583, 595, 695, 772, 825
Challenge Ministries Swaziland 218
Chambala 788
Chamkor Morn Referral Hospital 113
Champasak Province Hospital 419
Chance for Nepal 544
Chances for Children 296
Chandina General Hospital 36
Chandina Upazila Health Complex 36
Chandka Medical College Hospital – Larkana 631
Chandpur General Hospital 36
Changing Lives Together 258
Chan Myae Gon Specialist Hospital 534
Chan Myae Hospital – Dawei 534
Chan Myae Private Hospital 534
Chan Thar Hospital 534
Chanthar Thukha Hospital 534
CH Anuarite 173

Chapai Nawabganj Abhunik Sadar Hospital 36
Charak Hospital 559
Charak Memorial Hospital 559
Charghat Upazila Health Complex 37
Charities for Surgery 648
Charity Hospital 272
Charity Medical Hospital 374
Charity Right Pakistan 619
CharityVision International 62, 103, 187, 201, 228, 296,
  338, 374, 400, 443, 544, 595, 619, 648, 772, 931
Charles W. Selby Memorial Hospital 660
Char Rajibpur Upazila Health Complex 36
Chasel Hospital, The 609
Chasovoyarsk City Hospital #3 856
Chatkhil Upazila Health Complex 37
Chattogram Maa-O-Shishu Hospital 37
Chattogram Port Authority Hospital 37
Chaudhry Rehmat Ali Memorial Trust Teaching
  Hospital 631
Chau Thanh District Hospital 904
Chawama First Level Hospital 925
CH Baraka 173
CH Butuhe 173
CH Cbca 173
CH Cemebu 173
CHD Centre Hospitalier du Zou 52
CH de Gloria 173
CH Dieu Merci 173
CHD II Moramanga 449
CHD I Mahanoro 449
CH Don Beni 173
Checkup Diagnostic Center 37
Cheerful Heart Mission 296
Cheerful Hearts Foundation 258
Chegutu District Hospital 940
Cheikh Zayed Hospital 476
Chemerovetsk Multiprofile Hospital 856
Chencha Hospital 243
Chennai Liver Foundation 338
Cherish Uganda 825
Cherkasy Central District Hospital 856
Cherkasy City Children's Hospital 856
Cherkasy City Hospital #1, The 856
Cherkasy District Hospital of S. Moshny 856
Cherkasy Regional Children's Hospital 856
Cherkasy Regional Hospital for War Invalids 856
Cherkasy Regional Psychiatric Hospital 856
Chcrniakhiv Central Hospital 856
Chernigiv City Hospital #3 856
Chernihiv Central District Hospital 856
Chernihiv City Hospital #2 856
Chernihiv District Hospital 856
Chernihiv Regional Medical Center for Socially
  Significant and Dangerous Diseases 856
Chernivtsi City Hospital #4 856
Chernivtsi District Hospital of Chernivtsi Village
  Council 856
Chernivtsi Maternity Building #2 856
Chernivtsi Regional Hospital for Invalids of the
  Patriotic War 856
Chernobyl Children International 848
Cheung Prey Referral Hospital 113
Ch Fepsi 173
Chhlat Health 103
Chidamoyo Hospital 940
Chief Tony Anenih Geriatric Center 595
Chikondi Health Foundation 456
Chikuni Mission Hospital 925
Chikunja 789
Child Action Lanka 741
ChildAid 486
ChildAid 848
Child Aid Gambia 249, 695
Child Care Africa 826
Child Care And Youth Empowerment Foundation 826
Child Care Foundation of Pakistan 620
ChildCare Hospital 37

Child Family Health International (CFHI) 63, 258,
  338, 648, 773, 826
ChildFund Australia 63, 103, 228, 279, 338, 374,
  414, 431, 525, 544, 567, 638, 648, 695, 707, 741,
  798, 826, 882, 889, 915
ChildFund Laos 415
Child Health Awareness Foundation (CHAF) 24
Child Help Foundation 338
Child in Need Institute (CINI) 338
Child Legacy Hospital 468
Child Legacy International 456, 931
ChildLife Foundation 620
Children Care Uganda (CCU) 826
Children & Charity International 258, 296, 374, 431,
  595, 707, 826
Children Emergency Room, Abbasi Shaheed
  Hospital 631
Children Emergency Room, Civil Hospital –
  Quetta 631
Children Emergency Room, Ghulam Muhammad
  Mahar Medical College Hospital – Sukkur 631
Children Emergency Room, Lyari General
  Hospital 631
Children Emergency Room, Peoples Medical College
  Hospital – Nawabshah 631
Children Emergency Room, Sindh Government
  Hospital Korangi – 5 631
Children of the Nations 296, 431, 456, 707, 826
Children of Uganda (UK) 826
Children of War Foundation 103, 140, 187, 258, 296,
  338, 374, 567, 648, 729, 751, 814, 826
Children's Bridge Foundation 228, 374, 544, 889, 915
Children's Cancer Hospital Egypt 57357 193
Children's Cancer Hospital Foundation Egypt 187
Children's Cardiac Foundation of Africa, The 258
Children's City Hospital 856
Children's Clinical Hospital 877
Children's Clinical Hospital #5 Sviatoshynskyi
  District 856
Children's Clinical Hospital #7 of Pechersk
  District 856
Children's Clinical Hospital of Khujand 765
Children's District Hospital 856
Children's Emergency Relief International 132, 338,
  486, 595, 741
Children's Health Ministries 296
Children's HeartLink 338, 889
Children's Hope India 338
Children's Hospital 856
Children's Hospital #1 856
Children's Hospital 1 904
Children's Hospital 2 904
Children's Hospital #2, Zaporizhia 856
Children's Hospital Jizzakh 877
Children's Hospital Khojayli 877
Children's Hospital – Makeyevka 856
Children's Hospital, Namangan 877
Children's Hospital of Bokhtar 765
Children's Hospital of Panjakent 765
Children's Hospital & The Institute of Child Health,
  Lahore, The 631
Children Sickle Cell Foundation Kenya 374
Children's Infectious Disease Clinical Hospital 765
Children's Infectious Diseases Hospital #4
  Tashkent 877
Children's Lifeline International 47, 75, 103, 187,
  228, 249, 258, 296, 319, 338, 415, 525, 544, 708,
  826, 848, 915
Children's Maternity Hospital 904
Children's of Alabama: Global Surgery Program 258,
  374, 889
Children Specialist Hospital, Kaduna 609
Children's Regional Hospital, Kropyvnytskyi 856
Children's Relief International 456, 511, 525, 595, 826
Children's Surgery Hospital 765
Children's Surgery International 24, 228, 258, 296,
  431, 814, 889

Children's Tuberculosis Sanatorium 856
Children's Ward 789
Children Without Worms 24, 63, 96, 103, 119, 567,
  708, 773
Childspring International 201, 297, 319, 338, 708
Chilenje Level 1 Hospital 925
Chimala Mission Hospital 789
China California Heart Watch 525
China-SL Friendship Hospital, Jui 717, 746
China-Uganda Friendship Hospital 843
Chinese Friendship Hospital 756
Chingulungulu 789
Chingungwe 789
Chinhoyi Provincial Hospital 940
Chiniot General Hospital 631
Chinior Hospital 765
Chipata Central Hospital 925
Chipuputa 789
Chirayu National Hospital & Medical Institute Pvt.
  Ltd. 559
Chirchik City Central Hospital 877
Chiredzi General Hospital 940
Chireya Mission Hospital 940
Chisegu 789
Chitalmari Upazila Health Complex 37
Chitando District Hospital 940
Chitawira Private Hospital 468
Chitipa District Hospital 468
Chitokoloki Mission Hospital 925
Chittagong General Hospital 37
Chittagong Medical College Hospital 37
Chittagong Metropolitan Hospital Limited 37
Chitungwiza Central Hospital 940
Chitwan Hospital 559
Chitwan Hospital Pvt. Ltd. 559
Chitwan Medical College Teaching Hospital 559
Chitwan Valley Model Hospital 559
Chivhu General Hospital 940
Chivi District Hospital 940
Chiwonga 789
CH Kasinga 173
CH Maboya 173
CH Mahamba 173
CH Makasi 173
CH Mama Muyisa 173
CH Matanda 173
CH Muchanga 173
CH Mukongo 173
CH Mukuna 173
Choithram Memorial Hospital 717
Choithram Memorial Hospital 746
Chong Hua Hospital – Cebu City 660
Chong Hua Hospital – Mandaue City 660
Chongwe District Hospital 925
Chop City Hospital 856
Cho Ray Hospital 904
Cho Ray Phnom Penh Hospital 113
Chorku Hospital 765
CHP Bassar 810
CHR de Sokodé 810
CHR de Ziniaré 80
CHR Fada 80
Christian Aid Ministries 6, 24, 63, 103, 140, 187, 201,
  212, 228, 258, 297, 319, 338, 374, 406, 431, 456,
  486, 494, 502, 511, 525, 544, 567, 583, 595, 620,
  708, 729, 751, 762, 773, 814, 826, 848, 874, 889
Christian Blind Mission (CBM) 24, 47, 63, 75, 85,
  119, 141, 163, 229, 258, 279, 297, 319, 338, 361,
  374, 415, 443, 456, 525, 544, 567, 583, 595, 620,
  638, 648, 678, 708, 729, 741, 773, 804, 826, 889,
  915, 931
Christian Connections for International Health
  (CCIH) 24, 47, 75, 103, 119, 141, 163, 258, 338,
  374, 422, 431, 456, 525, 567, 583, 595, 620, 648,
  678, 708, 773, 826, 915, 932
Christian Eye Ministry 258, 319
Christian General Hospital 661

Christian Health Association of Ghana (CHAG) 259
Christian Health Association of Lesotho 422
Christian Health Service Corps 13, 103, 141, 164, 229, 259, 297, 319, 361, 374, 456, 620, 678, 826, 848, 915
Christian Hospital Tank 631
Christian Leprosy Specialist Hospital 534
Christian Medical & Dental Associations 13, 24, 63, 119, 132, 156, 201, 229, 259, 279, 297, 319, 374, 431, 456, 544, 567, 583, 638, 751, 773, 805, 848, 916
Christian Medical Fellowship of Kenya – CMF-Kenya 374
Christian Medical Ministry to Cambodia/Jeremiah's Hope 104
Christian Mobile Medical Team, The 848
Christian Ophthalmic Surgery Expedition Network (ChOSEN) 567
Christie's Heart Samaritan Care Foundation 297
Christ The King Hospital 609
Christ the King Medical Center Unihealth Las Pinas 660
Christ the Saviour General Hospital, Inc. 661
Chronic Care International 297
CHRR Manakara 449
CH Rughenda 173
CH Rwenzori 173
CH Sainte Famille 173
CH Sainte Stella 173
CH Saint Luc 173
CH Tumaini 173
CHU Annaba Ibn Rochd University Hospital 8
CHU Béjaïa, Khelil Amrane Hospital 8
CHU de Donka 284
CHU de Lamordé 588
CHU de Mbandaka 174
CHU de Ruwenzori 174
CHU de Tanger-Tétouan-Al Hoceima 506
CHU du Campus 810
CHU/EPSP Zéralda Belkacemi Tayeb 8
CHU Ibn Rochd 506
CHU Ignace Deen 284
Chui Province General Hospital 409
Chui Regional United Hospital 409
CHUIS Hôpital de Moulay Youssef 506
Chuka County Referral Hospital 393
CHU Kara 810
Chukwuemeka Odumegwu Ojukwu University Teaching Hospital 609
CHU Morafeno Toamasina 449
CH Uor 173
Churches of Christ Medical Santo (Medical Santo) 882
Church of Central Africa Presbyterian (CCAP) synod of Zambia 916
Chust District Hospital 877
Chutivska District Hospital 856
CHU Tokoin 810
Chuuk Community Health Clinic 482
Chuuk State Hospital 482
CH Vighole 174
Chyhyryn Multiprofile Hospital 856
Cibitoke District Hospital 91
Cicosat Hospital 661
CI InterRegional Center for Medical Genetics and Prenatal Diagnostics 856
Cima Alkhairy Eye Hospital 756
Cipla Foundation 338
Circle of Empowerment 567
Circle of Health International (COHI) 297, 319, 544, 567, 648, 708, 741, 751, 773
Citimed Chitungwiza Hospital 940
City Ambulance Hospital 856
City Center for Skin and Venereal Diseases 765
City Children Hospital, Dr.Jai Krishan 631
City Children's Clinical Hospital 856
City Children's Clinical Hospital #2 Of Dniprovsk City Council 857

City Children's Clinical Hospital #3 856
City Children's Clinical Hospital #5 Dnipro 856
City Children's Clinical Hospital #5 Donetsk 856
City Children's Clinical Hospital #6 of Dniprovsk City Council 857
City Children's Clinical Hospital #24 Kharkiv City Council 857
City Children's Hospital 904
City Children's Hospital #2 Donetska 857
City Children's Hospital #2, Nikolaev City 856
City Children's Hospital #3 of Rivne City Council 857
City Children's Hospital #4 857
City Clinical Hospital #1 857
City Clinical Hospital #1 Kharkiv 857
City Clinical Hospital #1 of Odessa City Council 857
City Clinical Hospital #2 Enerhetyk 857
City Clinical Hospital #2 Prof. O.O. Shalimov 857
City Clinical Hospital #3 857
City Clinical Hospital #3 of Poltava City Council 857
City Clinical Hospital #4 Lviv 857
City Clinical Hospital #4 of Poltava City Council 857
City Clinical Hospital #5 765
City Clinical Hospital #5 Poltava 857
City Clinical Hospital #7 857
City Clinical Hospital #10 857
City Clinical Hospital #11 857
City Clinical Hospital #20 Donetsk 857
City Clinical Hospital #21 857
City Clinical Hospital #24 857
City Clinical Hospital for Emergency and Emergency Medical Care Prof. Meschaninova 857
City Clinical Infectious Disease Hospital #1 877
City Clinical Infectious Diseases Hospital 877
City Clinical Infectious Hospital 857
City Clinical Maternity Hospital #7 857
City Clinical Maternity Hospital of Poltava City Council 857
City Clinical Multidisciplinary Hospital #25 857
City Corporation General Hospital 37
City Garden Clinic 708
City Heart Institute 904
City Hospital 272, 559, 765, 765
City Hospital #1 765
City Hospital #2 857
City Hospital #2 Cities of Yenakiev 857
City Hospital #2 (East) 857
City Hospital #2 Lugansk 857
City Hospital #2 of Khujand 765
City Hospital #2 Rivne City Council 857
City Hospital #3 857
City Hospital #3 Horlivka 857
City Hospital #3 (North) 857
City Hospital #3 Oleksandriysk City Council 857
City Hospital #3 Zaporizhia City Council 857
City Hospital #6 Zaporizhia 857
City Hospital #7 765
City Hospital #7 Zaporizhia City Council 857
City Hospital #8 857
City Hospital #9 Hydrotherapy 857
City Hospital #9 Sonyachne 857
City Hospital Chau Doc 904
City Hospital, Jashore 37
City Hospital Ltd. 37
City Hospital, Olenovka (Volnovakha District) 857
City Hospital (Svitlovodsk) 857
City Infectious Diseases Hospital #5 877
City International Hospital 904
City Maternity Hospital 765
City Maternity Hospital #6 858
City Medical Center Vung Tau 904
City Multidisciplinary Hospital #18 Kharkiv City Council 858
City of Candon Hospital 661
City Polyclinic #8 858
Civil Hospital Gwadar 631
Civil Hospital Haripur 631
Civil Hospital – Karachi 631

Civil Hospital, Killa Saifullah 631
Civil Hospital Qazi Ahmed 631
Civil Hospital – Quetta 631
Civil Service Hospital 559
CLAPP Hospital 631
Claro M. Recto Memorial Hospital 661
Class to Care Medical Foundation 595
CleanBirth.org 415
Clean Future Fund 849
Clear Sight International 595
Cleft Africa 85, 678, 773, 826
Cleopatra Hospitals – Nile Badrawi Hospital 193
Clinica de Especialidades Salud Integral 329
Clínica do Hospital Municipal do Namacunde 17
Clinical El Fateh Suka 80
Clinical Hospital #4 Prof. L. L. Girschmana 858
Clinical Hospital #5 858
Clinical Hospital for War Veterans 858
Clinical Hospital of the Oil Refining Industry of Ukraine 858
Clinical Louise Michel 159
Clinical Medico-Chirurgicale Cogemo 159
Clínica Multiperfil 17
Clinica Saint Jude 69
Clinica Verde 567
Clinic Nepal 544
Clinique Amen Bizerte 817
Clinique Amen Nabeul 817
Clinique Chiva 476
Clinique des Soeurs Ankadifotsy 449
Clinique Elihsane 476
Clinique El Inaya 476
Clinique El Menar 476
Clinique Internationale de Marrakech 506
Clinique Kissi 476
Clinique La Grace Marie 80
Clinique Medicale Le Grand Centre 366
Clinique Ngaliema 174
Clinique Securex 159
Clinique Soukra 817
Clinitur 98
Clinton Health Access Initiative (CHAI) 104, 119, 164, 219, 229, 297, 320, 338, 374, 415, 423, 432, 456, 511, 525, 595, 638, 678, 695, 708, 773, 826, 889, 916, 932
Cloud Foundation 297
Clubfoot India Initiative Trust 338
CM1 (Hospital) de Tougan 80
CMA 449
CMA de Batié 80
CMA de Boromo 80
CMA de Gourcy 80
CMA de Ouargaye 80
CMA de Pissy 80
CMA de Sabou 80
CMA de Sanogho 80
CMC Bernard Kouchner de Coronthie 284
CMC Mitsamiouli 152
CMH Combined Military Hospital Rawalpindi 631
CNHU Centre National Hospitalier Universitaire 52
COAR Peace Mission 201
Coast General Teaching And Referral Hospital 374
Coimbatore Cancer Foundation (CCF) 338
College of Health Sciences, FGC Warri 609
Columbia Asia 904
Columbia Asia Hospital 904
Columbia Asia Saigon 904
Columbia University: Columbia Office of Global Surgery (COGS) 229, 297, 338, 374
Columbia University: Global Mental Health Programs 24, 63, 229, 297, 338, 375, 423, 456, 494, 511, 544, 595, 648, 826, 916
Columbia Vagelos College of Physicians and Surgeons Programs in Global Health 119, 187, 201, 229, 259, 297, 338, 375, 423, 432, 456, 511, 595, 678, 708, 773, 826, 916, 932
Combat Blindness International 297, 339, 375, 525,

Hôpital Général d'Alépé 366
Hôpital Général d'Anyama 366
Hôpital Général d'Arrah 366
Hôpital Général d'Azopé 367
Hôpital Général de Bangolo 367
Hôpital Général de Befelatanana 449
Hôpital Général de Bikoro 175
Hôpital Général de Bocanda 367
Hôpital Général de Bonoua 367
Hôpital Général de Boundiali 367
Hôpital Général de Dabou 367
Hôpital Général de Dipumba 175
Hôpital Général de Doba 146
Hôpital Général de Dolisie 159
Hôpital Général de Doropo 367
Hôpital Général de Douala 128
Hôpital Général de Fizi 175
Hôpital Général de Grand-Bassam 367
Hôpital Général de Grand Yoff 702
Hôpital Général de Guitry 367
Hôpital Général de Katiola 367
Hôpital Général de Kouibly 367
Hôpital Général de Koumassi 367
Hôpital Général de Mandima 175
Hôpital Général de Mankono 367
Hôpital Général de Marcory 367
Hôpital Général de Méagui 367
Hôpital Général de Mpanda 92
Hôpital Général de Nia-Nia 175
Hôpital Général de Nkombo 159
Hôpital Général de Patra 159
Hôpital Général de Port-Bouët 367
Hôpital Général de Référence 175
Hôpital General de Référence de Bafwasende 174
Hôpital Général de Référence de Geti 175
Hôpital General de Référence de Kalemie 174
Hôpital Général de Référence de Kikwit 175
Hôpital Général de Référence de Kindu/HGR 175
Hôpital General de Reference de Lubutu 174
Hôpital Général de Référence de Mbandaka 175
Hôpital Général de Référence de Monkoto 175
Hôpital Général de Référence de Mushie 175
Hôpital Général de Référence de Mutwanga 175
Hôpital Général de Référence de Nundu 175
Hôpital Général de Référence de Panzi 175
Hôpital Général de Référence de Sia 175
Hôpital Général de Référence de Tshikapa 175
Hôpital Général de Référence d'Oshwe 175
Hôpital Général de Référence du Nord Kivu 175
Hôpital Général de Référence d'Uvira 175
Hôpital Général de Référence Tunda 175
Hôpital Général de Référence Wangata 175
Hôpital Général de Référence Yalimbongo 175
Hôpital Général de Sassandra 367
Hôpital Général de Shabunda 174
Hôpital Général de Soubre 367
Hôpital Général de Taabo 367
Hôpital Général de Tabou 367
Hôpital Général de Tiassalé 367
Hôpital Général de Treichville 367
Hôpital Général de Yaoundé 128
Hôpital Général de Yumbi 175
Hôpital Général d'Oumé 367
Hôpital Général du Cinquantenaire 175
Hôpital Général Edith Lucie Bongo Ondimba 159
Hôpital Général M'Bahiakro 367
Hôpital Général Yopougon-Attié 367
Hôpital Genyco Obstetrique de Douala (HGOPED)
    (Hôpital Gynéco-Obstétrique et Pédiatrique de
    Douala (HGOPED)) 128
Hôpital Géréral de Référence de Panzi 175
Hôpital Glacis Courreaux 314
Hôpital Habib Thameur 817
Hôpital Hédi Chaker 817
Hôpital Henriette Konan Bédié d'Abobo 367
Hôpital Immaculée Conception 314
Hôpital Indo Guinéen 284

Hôpital Infantil Bèchir Hamza 817
Hôpital Islamique de Daloa 367
Hôpital Itaosy 449
Hôpital Jean-Paul 2 284
Hôpital Jean Paul II 449
Hôpital Jésus Sauve et Guérit Full Gospel
    Mission 128
Hôpital Joseph Ravoahangy-Andrianavalona 450
Hôpital Justinien 314
Hôpital Karakoro 284
Hôpital Kelaat M'gouna 506
Hôpital Kibumbu 92
Hôpital Kimbanguiste 175
Hôpital La Croix de Zinvié 53
Hôpital La Croix du Sud 687
Hôpital La Providence des Gonaives 314
Hôpital Laquintinie 128
Hôpital L'Eglise de Dieu Réformé 314
Hôpital Leproserie de la Dibamba 128
Hôpital Luthérien des 67ha 450
Hôpital Mabayi 92
Hôpital Maternité Bizerte 817
Hôpital Mère-Enfant Blanche Gomez 159
Hôpital Mère-Enfant de Bingerville 367
Hôpital Mère et Enfant 146
Hôpital Mère et Enfants SOS 810
Hôpital Midoun 817
Hôpital Militaire 476
Hôpital Militaire d'Abidjan (HMA) 367
Hôpital Militaire de Buea 128
Hôpital Militaire de Camp Yeyap 2 129
Hôpital Militaire de Dolisie 159
Hôpital Militaire de Douala 129
Hôpital Militaire de Gabès 817
Hôpital Militaire de Garoua 129
Hôpital Militaire de Kamenge 92
Hôpital Militaire de Niamey 588
Hôpital Militaire de Ouakam 702
Hôpital Militaire de Yaounde 129
Hôpital Militaire Djibouti-Soudan 182
Hôpital Militaire Régional de Kinshasa Camp
    Kokolo 175
Hôpital Militaire Up Station Bamenda 129
Hôpital Moderne – Lopitálo ya motindo mwa sika 175
Hôpital Mohamed Boudiaf 8
Hôpital Mongi Slim 817
Hôpital Monkole 3 175
Hôpital Mpitsabo Mikambana 450
Hôpital MSF de l'Arche 92
Hôpital Muea 129
Hôpital Municipal de Sandrandahy 450
Hôpital Municipal De Tinghir 506
Hôpital Municipal de Vridi 367
Hôpital Mutombo 175
Hôpital National de Niamey 588
Hôpital Notre Dame 314
Hôpital Notre Dame de La Paix de Jean-Rabel 314
Hôpital Notre Dame des Palmistes 314
Hôpital Nyanzalac 92
Hôpital Ousmane Ngom 702
Hôpital Padre Pio N'Dali 53
Hôpital Palia 129
Hôpital Pédiatrique de Kalembelembe 175
Hôpital PNC/Camp Soyo 175
Hôpital Pneumo-Phtisiologique Chakib Saad
    Omar 182
Hôpital Préfectoral 136
Hôpital Préfectoral de Kaga-Bandoro 136
Hôpital Préfectoral de Koubia 284
Hôpital Préfectoral de Mandiana 284
Hôpital Préfectoral de Siguiri 284
Hôpital Préfectoral de Vogan 810
Hôpital Préfectorale de Coyah 284
Hôpital Prince Régent Charles (HPRC) 92
Hôpital Principal de Dakar 702
Hôpital Privé de Marrakech HPM 506
Hôpital Privé Islamique de Bamaré 129

Hôpital Protestant Bonaberi CEBEC 129
Hôpital Protestant Cité Sic 129
Hôpital Protestant Mbouo 129
Hôpital Provincial de Moussoro 146
Hôpital Provincial Général de Reférence de
    Bukavu 175
Hôpital Provincial Général de Référence de
    Kinshasa 175
Hôpital Psychiatrique de Bingerville 367
Hôpital Psychiatrique de Bouaké 367
Hôpital Psychiatrique de Thiaroye 702
Hôpital Radem 175
Hôpital Référence de Sangmelima 129
Hôpital Régional Alpha Oumar Diallo 284
Hôpital Régional d'Abéché 146
Hôpital Regional D'Ali Sabieh Dr. Ahmed Absieh
    Warsama 182
Hôpital Régional de Bafoussam 129
Hôpital Régional de Bamenda 129
Hôpital Régional de Ben Arous 817
Hôpital Régional de Berbérati 136
Hôpital Régional de Bertoua 129
Hôpital Régional de Boké 284
Hôpital Régional de Bol 146
Hôpital Régional de Bongor 146
Hôpital Régional de Bria 136
Hôpital Régional de Buea 129
Hôpital Régional de Degache 817
Hôpital Régional de Diourbel 702
Hôpital Regional de Dosso 588
Hôpital Régional de Ebolowa 129
Hôpital Régional de Garoua 129
Hôpital Régional de Gitega 92
Hôpital Régional de Goz Beida 146
Hôpital Régional de Kankan 284
Hôpital Régional de Kheireddine 817
Hôpital Régional de Kolda 702
Hôpital Régional de Labé 284
Hôpital Régional de Limbe 129
Hôpital Régional de Medjez el Bab 817
Hôpital Régional de Metlaoui 817
Hôpital Régional de Ngaoundéré 129
Hôpital Régional de Nkongsamba 129
Hôpital Régional des Armées de Pointe-Noire 159
Hôpital Régional de Tambacounda 702
Hôpital Régional de Tataouine 817
Hôpital Régional de Yagoua 129
Hôpital Regional de Zinder 588
Hôpital Régional Dr. Mohamed Ben Salah 818
Hôpital Régional El Hadji Ahmadou Sakhir Ndieguene
    de Thiès 702
Hôpital Roi Baudouin 702
Hôpital Roi Khaled 92
Hôpital Saadaoui Mokhtar 8
Hôpital Saint Antoine 314
Hôpital Saint Boniface 314
Hôpital Saint Camille de Nanoro 80
Hôpital Saint Camille de Ouagadougou 80
Hôpital Sainte-Anne 315
Hôpital Sainte Bakhita 53
Hôpital Sainte-Camille 367
Hôpital Sainte Catherine 314
Hôpital Sainte Croix 315
Hôpital Sainte Jeanne-Antide Thouret 129
Hôpital Sainte Marie Etoile de Mer 315
Hôpital Sainte Thérèse de Hinche 315
Hôpital Sainte Thérèse de Miragoâne 315
Hôpital Saint Jean-Baptiste de Bôdô 367
Hôpital Saint-Jean-Baptiste de Bonzola 175
Hôpital Saint-Jean de Dieu 703
Hôpital Saint Jean de Dieu Tanguiéta 53
Hôpital Saint-Jean de Limbé 314
Hôpital Saint Joseph 146
Hôpital Saint-Joseph Moscati 367
Hôpital Saint Landy 314
Hôpital Saint-Luc 129
Hôpital Saint Luc de Cotonou 53

Hôpital Saint Luc de Kisantu 175
Hôpital Saint-Martin à Papané 53
Hôpital Saint Nicolas 314
Hôpital Saint-Pierre 314
Hôpital Saint-Rosaire 129
Hôpital SAMU Municipal de Grande Yoff 703
Hôpital Sanitaire de N'Dali 53
Hôpital Santa Helena PK11 129
Hôpital Sidi Mohammed Ben Abdellah 506
Hôpital Sidi Othmane 506
Hôpital Sino-Congolaise de Mfilou 159
Hôpital SNCC/KINDU 175
Hôpital Soeurs Keur 703
Hôpital SS Mabanga 176
Hôpital St. Martin de Porres 129
Hôpital St.Thérèse de Nomayos 129
Hôpital St Vincent de Paul 129
Hôpital Sunon Séro 53
Hôpital Traditionnel de Keur Massar 703
Hôpital Tshiamala 176
Hôpital Universitaire Andrainjato 450
Hôpital Universitaire de la Paix 315
Hôpital Universitaire de Mirebalais 315
Hôpital Universitaire Régional de Bambari 136
Hôpital Universitaire Sahloul 818
Hôpital Vaovao Mahafaly – The Good News
    Hospital 450
Hôpital Vezo 450
Hopitaly Atsimo 449
Hopitaly Kely 449
Hopitaly Manarapenitra 449
Hôpital Youssou Mbargane Diop 703
Hôpital Zagora 506
Hop Luc General Hospital 906
Horev Medical Center 878
Horizon 91
Horizons Trust UK 249
Horlivka City Hospital #2 859
Horn of Africa Neonatal Development Services
    (HANDS) 232
Horodenka Central District Hospital 859
Hospice Africa 48, 76, 86, 121, 165, 232, 261, 280,
    362, 379, 459, 584, 598, 680, 696, 710, 752, 776,
    806, 814, 830, 918, 933
Hospice and Palliative Care Association of Zimbabwe
    (HOSPAZ) 933
Hospice Angelus 487
Hospice Egypt 188
Hospice Without Borders 680
Hospital 3 de Agosto 291
Hospital #6 Artëmovskiy 859
Hospital 22-12 906
Hospital 199 906
Hospital Adventista 329
Hospital Agostinho Neto 691
Hospital Agramont 69
Hospital Alamikamba Prinzu Pawanka 576
Hospital Alfonso Moncada Guillén 576
Hospital Alima 145
Hospital Alivio del Sufrimiento 329
Hospital Amatepec 207
Hospital Ambrosio Mogorrón 576
Hospital Américo Boavida (HAB) 17
Hospital Amistad Japón – Nicaragua 576
Hospital Amistad México – Nicaragua 576
Hospital and Clinic Ferraro 329
Hospital Anibal Murillo Escobar 329
Hospital Antiga da Baixa 520
Hospital Arco Iris 69
Hospital Area Bembérékè-Sinendé 52
Hospital at Abéché 145
Hospital at Bahir Dar 243
Hospital at Bardibas 560
Hospital at Batangafo 136
Hospital at Beni 174
Hospital at Bhijer 560
Hospital at Bhorle 560

Hospital at Bidur 560
Hospital at Biratchok 560
Hospital at Bisoro 91
Hospital at Bubera 91
Hospital at Buta 91
Hospital at Bwatemba 91
Hospital at Chakratirtha 560
Hospital at Dédougou 80
Hospital at Denan 243
Hospital at Dohiya 136
Hospital at Dourbali 145
Hospital at Edaga Hamus Town 243
Hospital at Gashirwe 91
Hospital at Gatabo 91
Hospital at Gatakazi 91
Hospital at Gihanga 91
Hospital at Gilunng 560
Hospital at Gishiha 91
Hospital at Hanspur 560
Hospital at Hawassa 243
Hospital at Hirmaniya 560
Hospital at Inhamizua 520
Hospital at Ispechak 766
Hospital at Istaravshan 766
Hospital at Jinka 243
Hospital at Kalikathum 560
Hospital at Kanyosha 91
Hospital at Kazanguzar 766
Hospital at Kella Moelle 136
Hospital at Kembolcha 243
Hospital at Kemse 244
Hospital at Khali Puraini Road 560
Hospital at Kigwena 91
Hospital at Kochan 145
Hospital at Kokol 136
Hospital at Kounpala 136
Hospital at Kounpo 136
Hospital at Kuliev 766
Hospital at Machijhitkaiya 560
Hospital at Machiton 766
Hospital at Madarounfa 588
Hospital at Makamba 91
Hospital at Marmaparikanda 560
Hospital at Matara 91
Hospital at Matongo 91
Hospital at Mekele 244
Hospital at Metu 244
Hospital at Monkole 174
Hospital at Mugeni 92
Hospital at Muhama 92
Hospital at Munini 92
Hospital at Muramvya 92
Hospital at Musenyi 92
Hospital at Nazret 244
Hospital at Nepalgung Gulariya Road 560
Hospital at Nyabihanga 92
Hospital at Nyakararo 92
Hospital at Nyakuguma 92
Hospital at Nyarurama 92
Hospital at Ozodii-Shark 766
Hospital at Qurgonteppa 766
Hospital at Raghunathpur 560
Hospital at Ramgram 560
Hospital at Ranomafana 449
Hospital at Rasulov 766
Hospital at Rawatkot 560
Hospital at Rorero 92
Hospital at Rukago 92
Hospital at Rŭshan 766
Hospital at Sandhikharka 560
Hospital at Sanja 244
Hospital at Santalla 560
Hospital at Say 588
Hospital at Shakhrinaw 766
Hospital at Shashamene 244
Hospital at Shichozg 766
Hospital at Shoa Robit 244

Hospital at Simferopol 859
Hospital at Stakhanov 766
Hospital at Sukhadhik 560
Hospital at Teshiktosh 766
Hospital at Thaha 560
Hospital at Tigray 244
Hospital at Timberi 145
Hospital at Urthu-Ghodsen Road 560
Hospital at Weldiya 244
Hospital at Wukro Maray 244
Hospital at Yelewa 136
Hospital at Yogodka 766
Hospital Aurelio Melean 69
Hospital Ayres de Menezes (Hospital Central de São
    Tomé) 691
Hospital Bakulahat Ratnanagar 560
Hospital Bautista 576
Hospital Bautista BMDMI Guaimaca 329
Hospital Bautista de El Salvador 207
Hospital Belga 69
Hospital Bello Amanecer 576
Hospital Bendaña 329
Hospital Bertha Calderón Roque 576
Hospital Bethel Fonds-des-Nègres/Armée du
    Salut 313
Hospital Blanca Aráuz 576
Hospital Bokoro 145
Hospital Boliviano Canadiense Santa Maria
    Magdalena 69
Hospital Boliviano Espanol de Patacamaya 69
Hospital Bonneau St. Joseph 314
Hospital Bwiza Jabe 92
Hospital Cader 207
Hospital Carlos Fonseca Amador 576
Hospital Carlos Roberto Huembes 576
Hospital Carlos Roberto Huembes filial El
    Carmen 576
Hospital Carolina Osejo 576
Hospital Católico San Pío de Pietrelcina 329
Hospital CEMESA 329
Hospital Center Regional de Fatick 702
Hospital Central De Managua Dr. César Amador
    Kühl 576
Hospital Central de Maputo 520
Hospital Central de Quelimane 520
Hospital Central do Lobito 17
Hospital Central do Lubango 17
Hospital Central Ivirgarzama 69
Hospital Central Privado San Salvador 207
Hospital Centro de Diagnóstico Colonia Medical 207
Hospital Centro Ginecológico 207
Hospital Centro Pediátrico 207
Hospital Chowk 632
Hospital Chrd Ii Atu 449
Hospital Climesa 207
Hospital Climosal 207
Hospital Clinico Viedma 69
Hospital Cochabamba 69
Hospital COMBASE (Comision Boliviana de Accion
    Social Evangelica) 69
Hospital Comunitario Valle Hermoso 69
Hospital Consultorio El Verbo 576
Hospital COSSMIL (La Paz) 69
Hospital COSSMIL (Tarija) 69
Hospital Cristo de las Americas 69
Hospital CSB Ejeda 449
Hospital Cubano Chacaltaya 69
Hospital Cutelo de Acucar 98
Hospital da Ilha 520
Hospital da Missão Católica do Chiulo 17
Hospital Daniel Bracamonte 69
Hospital das 500 Casas 17
Hospital da Salela 520
Hospital Dato Rua 801
Hospital de Água Izé 691
Hospital de Cantagalo 691
Hospital de Capinota 69

Hospital de Diagnostico 207
Hospital de Emergencias 207
Hospital de Especialidades Metropol 207
Hospital de Especialidades Nuestra Señora de la Paz 207
Hospital de Especialidades San Felipe 329
Hospital de Especialidades Santa Rosa de Lima 207
Hospital de Hombo 152
Hospital de Huachacalla 69
Hospital de Kalukembe 17
Hospital de la Mujer 69
Hospital de la Mujer 207
Hospital de la Republica de Iran 69
Hospital del Caribe 329
Hospital del Niño Manuel Ascencio Villarroel 69
Hospital del Norte (Cochabamba) 70
Hospital del Norte (El Alto) 70
Hospital del Sud 70
Hospital del Valle 329
Hospital de Maternidad la Divina Providencia in Texacuangos 207
Hospital de Menongue 17
Hospital de Niños 69
Hospital de Niños René Balderas Lopez 69
Hospital de Occidente 329
Hospital de Oncología 207
Hospital de Oriente Gabriela Alvarado 329
Hospital de Psiquiatría 69
Hospital de Puerto Cortés 329
Hospital de Reyes 69
Hospital de Ribeira Brava 98
Hospital de Santa Bárbara 69
Hospital de Santa Margarida 691
Hospital de São Domingos 98
Hospital des Forces de Securité Interieures (F.S.I) 817
Hospital de Tiquipaya 69
Hospital de Vacas 69
Hospital de Zamboanga 664
Hospital DIME 329
Hospital District 4 906
Hospital District 8 906
Hospital District 11 906
Hospital District de Massakory 145
Hospital Distrital de Gondola 520
Hospital Distrital de Mopeia 520
Hospital Distrital de Quissico 520
Hospital Divina Providencia 207
Hospital do Caminho de Ferro 17
Hospital Dogbo 52
Hospital do Maio 98
Hospital do Prenda 17
Hospital do Sal 98
Hospital dos Cajueiros 17
Hospital do Sumbe 17
Hospital Dr. Agostinho Neto 98
Hospital Dr. Baptista de Sousa 98
Hospital Dr. Enrique Aguilar Cerrato 329
Hospital Dr. Juan Manuel Galvez 329
Hospital Dr. Manuel Quaresma Dias da Graça 691
Hospital Duong Minh Chau 906
Hospital Edgar Montano 70
Hospital El Alto Sur 70
Hospital El Carmen 329
Hospital Elizabeth Seton 70
Hospital El Maestro 576
Hospital El Salvador 207
Hospital EMCSA 576
Hospital Emmanuel Cathedrale of Robe 244
Hospital Escuela 329
Hospital Escuela Antonio Lenin Fonseca Martínez 576
Hospital Escuela Carlos Amador Molina HECAM 576
Hospital Escuela Cesar Amador Molina 576
Hospital Escuela Manolo Morales 576
Hospital Escuela Oscar Danilo Rosales 576
Hospital Escuela Regional Santiago Jinotepe 576

Hospital España Chinandega 576
Hospital Esteban Jáenz Serrano 577
Hospital Evangélico 329
Hospital Ferguson 329
Hospital Finca 314
Hospital Florida 70
Hospital for Infectious Disease 766
Hospital Fosref/Lakay Saint Marc 314
Hospital Gaheta 92
Hospital Gahombo 92
Hospital Gaspar García Laviana 577
Hospital Gecamines Kambove 174
Hospital General Atlántida 329
Hospital General da Barra do Dande 17
Hospital General de Benguela 17
Hospital General del ISSS 207
Hospital General de Mukongola 174
Hospital General Peltier 182
Hospital General San Juan de Dios 70
Hospital Geral 17 de Setembro 17
Hospital Geral da Machava 520
Hospital Geral de J. Macamo 520
Hospital Geral de Luanda 17
Hospital Gineco Obstetrico y Neonatal Dr. Jaime Sanchez Porcel 70
Hospital Habib Bourguiba De Sfax 817
Hospital Haiphong Medical University 906
Hospital Harry Williams 70
Hospital Hermano Pedro 329
Hospital Hilario Sánchez 577
Hospital Hoa Thanh district 906
Hospital Honduras Medical Center 329
Hospital Infantil La Mascota 577
Hospital Inmaculada Concepcion 70
Hospital in São Martinho Ribeira Grande de Santiago 98
Hospital in Sidi Khaled 8
Hospital Instituto del Cáncer 207
Hospital Integrado Santa Bárbara 329
Hospital Iraní 577
Hospitali Teule ya Wilaya Nkansi 789
Hospitali ya Masista 789
Hospitali ya Mkoa Mbeya 789
Hospitali ya Wilaya 789
Hospitali ya Wilaya ya Nachingwea 789
Hospital Jacobo Abularach 70
Hospital Jaime Mendoza 70
Hospital Japonés 70
Hospital Josefino Vilaseca 207
Hospital Josina Machel 17
Hospital Juan Antonio Brenes 577
Hospital Juan XXIII 70
Hospital Kankima 92
Hospital Karehe 92
Hospital Kolping 70
Hospital Kouga 145
Hospital La Ceiba 207
Hospital La Fraternidad 577
Hospital La Fraternidad – Filial La Recolección 577
Hospital La Merced 70
Hospital La Paz 70
Hospital La Policlínica 329
Hospital La Sainte Famille 314
Hospital Leonardo Martinez 329
Hospital Loma de Luz 330
Hospital Loterana Manambaro 449
Hospital Luis Espinal 70
Hospital Luis Felipe Moncada 577
Hospital Luis Uria de la Oliva 70
Hospital Madre Teresa de Calcuta 70
Hospital Mahajanga 449
Hospital Mai Manakamana Hospital Pvt. Ltd. 560
Hospital Makour Hamou 8
Hospital Malanville Karimama 52
Hospital Mamerto Eguez 70
Hospital Manuel de Jesús Subirana 330
Hospital Marcelino Banca 291

Hospital María Especialidades Pediátricas 330
Hospital Médico Quirúrgico del Instituto Salvadoreño Del Seguro Social 207
Hospital Médico Quirúrgico Sonsonate 207
Hospital Merliot 207
Hospital Metodista 70
Hospital Militar 207, 330
Hospital Militar Aviação 17
Hospital Militar Central 17
Hospital Militar da Catumbela 17
Hospital Militar de Bissau 291
Hospital Militar de Maputo 520
Hospital Militar do Lubango 17
Hospital Militar e Civil 291
Hospital Militar Escuela Dr. Alejandro Dávila Bolaños 577
Hospital Monte Carmelo 577
Hospital Montecillos 330
Hospital Monte España Tipitapa 577
Hospital Moussoro 145
Hospital Mtaa Wa Kivu Kusini 174
Hospital Municipal 3 De Noviembre 70
Hospital Municipal Achacachi Capitán Juan Uriona 70
Hospital Municipal Alfonso Gumucio R. 70
Hospital Municipal Andres Cuschieri 70
Hospital Municipal Bajío del Oriente 70
Hospital Municipal Barrios Mineros 70
Hospital Municipal Bernardino Gil Julio 70
Hospital Municipal Boliviano Holandes 70
Hospital Municipal Camiri 70
Hospital Municipal Carmen Lopez 70
Hospital Municipal Cotahuma 70
Hospital Municipal Cuatro Canadas 70
Hospital Municipal de Ascensión de Guarayos 70
Hospital Municipal de Cacuaco 17
Hospital Municipal de Caranavi 70
Hospital Municipal de Chipindo 17
Hospital Municipal de Viana Kapalanga 17
Hospital Municipal Distrital Pampa de la Isla 70
Hospital Municipal DM7 El Tatu 70
Hospital Municipal do Sambizanga 17
Hospital Municipal El Torno 70
Hospital Municipal Francés 70
Hospital Municipal Los Andes 70
Hospital Municipal Los Negros 70
Hospital Municipal Los Pinos 70
Hospital Municipal Modelo Corea 70
Hospital Municipal Nuestra Señora del Rosario 71
Hospital Municipal Principe de Paz 71
Hospital Municipal Señor de Malta 71
Hospital Municipal Viacha 71
Hospital Municipal Virgen de Cotoca 71
Hospital Muramvya 92
Hospital Mutaho 92
Hospital Nacional de Chalchuapa 207
Hospital Nacional de Ciudad Barrios Monseñor Oscar Arnulfo Romero 207
Hospital Nacional de Ilobasco 208
Hospital Nacional de la Unión 208
Hospital Nacional de Metapán 208
Hospital Nacional de Ninos Benjamin Bloom 208
Hospital Nacional de Nueva Concepción 208
Hospital Nacional de San Francisco Gotera 208
Hospital Nacional de Sensuntepeque 208
Hospital Nacional Dr. Jorge Arturo Mena 208
Hospital Nacional Dr. Jorge Mazzini Villacorte Sonsonate 208
Hospital Nacional Dr. Juan José Fernández Zacamil 208
Hospital Nacional Dr. Luis Edmundo Vásquez 208
Hospital Nacional General 208
Hospital Nacional General Francisco Menéndez 208
Hospital Nacional Nor-Occidental Dr. Mario Catarino Rivas 330
Hospital Nacional Psiquiátrico 208
Hospital Nacional Rosales 208

Hospital Nacional San Bartolo 208
Hospital Nacional San Juan de Dios 208
Hospital Nacional San Rafael 208
Hospital Nacional Santa Gertrudis 208
Hospital Nacional Santa Rosa de Lima 208
Hospital Nacional Santa Teresa 208
Hospital Nacional Santiago de María 208
Hospital Nacional Simão Mendes 291
Hospital Nam Truc 906
Hospital National San Pedro Usulutan 208
Hospital Neuropsiquiátrico Mario Mendoza 330
Hospital Neves Bendinha 17
Hospital Nossa Senhora da Paz 17
Hospital Nuevo Amanecer 577
Hospital Number Ten 906
Hospital Obrero No.1 (La Paz) 71
Hospital Obrero No.4 (Oruro) 71
Hospital Obrero No.6 Dr. Jaime Mendoza (Sucre) 71
Hospital Obrero No.7 (Tarija) 71
Hospital Obrero No.8 (Trinidad) 71
Hospital Obrero Villa 1 de Mayo (Santa Cruz) 71
Hospital Occidental de Managua Dr. Fernando Velez
  Paiz 577
Hospital of Amppipal 560
Hospital of District 7 906
Hospital of Ea Kar District 906
Hospital of Giong Rieng District (Bệnh viện Đa khoa
  Huyện Giồng Riềng) 906
Hospital of Hope 806, 810
Hospital of Infectious Diseases 766
Hospital of Mirza-ali 766
Hospital of Sarband 766
Hospital Oftálmologico Ponce 330
Hospital of the Ministry of Internal Affairs 859
Hospital of Traditional Medicine Ho Chi Minh
  City 906
Hospital Orthopedics and Rehabilitation HCMC 906
Hospital Oruro-Corea 71
Hospital Otorrino-Oftalmologico 71
Hospital Padilla Dr. Marco Rojas Zurita 71
Hospital Paravida 208
Hospital Pastor Jiménez 577
Hospital Pediatrico David Bernardino 17
Hospital Pediátrico Pioneiro Zeca 18
Hospital Pedro Altamirano 577
Hospital Polana Caniço A 520
Hospital Prefectural de Dalaba 284
Hospital Primario Ada María López 577
Hospital Primario Comandante Tomás Borge
  Martínez 577
Hospital Primario de Telica 577
Hospital Primario El Jícaro 577
Hospital Primario El Sauce 577
Hospital Primario Ethel Kandler 577
Hospital Primario Fidel Ventura 577
Hospital Primario Héroes y Mártires del Cua 577
Hospital Primario Héroes y Mártires San José de las
  Mulas 577
Hospital Primario Jorge Navarro 577
Hospital Primario José Shendell 577
Hospital Primario Monseñor Julio César Videa 577
Hospital Primario Nilda Patricia Velasco 577
Hospital Primario Niños Mártires De Ayapal 577
Hospital Primario Oswaldo Padilla 577
Hospital Primario San José 577
Hospital Primero de Mayo ISSS 208
Hospital Privado Cruz Azul 577
Hospital Privado de Maputo 520
Hospital Provincial da Matola 520
Hospital Provincial de Inhambane 520
Hospital Provincial de Manica 520
Hospital Provincial de Quelimane 520
Hospital Provincial de Tete 520
Hospital Provincial do Cunene 18
Hospital Provincial do Uíge 18
Hospital Provincial Ngola Kimbanda 18
Hospital Psiquiátrico de Luanda 18

Hospital Psiquiátrico Nacional 577
Hospital Psiquiatrico San Benito Menni 71
Hospital Puerto Lempira 330
Hospital Raboteau 314
Hospital Rabta 817
Hospital Raoul Follereau 291
Hospital Referal de Lospalos 801
Hospital Regional 702
Hospital Regional Atlantida 330
Hospital Regional del Sur 330
Hospital Regional de Sonsonate 208
Hospital Regional do Huambo 18
Hospital Regional Dr. João Morais 98
Hospital Regional Ernesto Sequeira Blanco 577
Hospital Regional Escuela Asunción 577
Hospital Regional San Juan de Dios 71
Hospital Regional Santiago Norte 98
Hospital & Rehabilitation Centre for Disabled
  Children (HRCD) 548
Hospital Renato Castro 71
Hospital Roatán 330
Hospital Roberto Suazo Córdova 330
Hospital Rosario Pravia 577
Hospital Rural de Angoche 520
Hospital Rural de Buzi 520
Hospital Rural de Chokwe 520
Hospital Rural de Cuamba 520
Hospital Rural de Montepuez 520
Hospital Rural de Vilankulo 520
Hospital Rural do Milange 520
Hospital Saigon – Nam Dinh 906
Hospital Saint Joseph 174
Hospital Salud Integral 577
Hospital Sanatório de Luanda 18
Hospital San Felipe 330
Hospital San Francisco de Asís 71
Hospital San Francisco de Asís 577
Hospital San Francisco El Salvador 208
Hospital San Gabriel 71
Hospital San José 577
Hospital San Juan De Dios 577
Hospital San Juan de Dios (Camargo) 71
Hospital San Juan de Dios (Cliza) 71
Hospital San Juan de Dios Santa Ana 208
Hospital San Juan de Dios (Santa Cruz) 71
Hospital San Lorenzo 330
Hospital San Martin de Porres (Huanuni) 71
Hospital San Martin de Porres (Tiraque) 71
Hospital San Mateo 208
Hospital San Pedro Claver 71
Hospital San Roque Padcaya 71
Hospital Santa Maria 71
Hospital Santo Hermano Pedro 330
Hospital Seguro Social Universitario (Cobija) 71
Hospital Seguro Social Universitario
  (Cochabamba) 71
Hospital Seguro Social Universitario (La Paz) 71
Hospital Seguro Social Universitario (Potosí) 71
Hospital Seguro Social Universitario (Sucre) 71
Hospital SERMESA Bolonia 577
Hospitals for Humanity 598
Hospital Sheik Hussein 244
Hospital Solidaridad Managua 577
Hospital Solidaridad Tipitapa 577
Hospital Solidariedade de Bolama 291
Hospital Solomon Klein Sacaba 71
Hospital Sugh Region 766
Hospital Sula Socorro de lo Alto 330
Hospital SUMEDICO 577
Hospital Tamakoshi 560
Hospital Tela Integrado 330
Hospital Trinidad 71
Hospital Univalle 71
Hospital Univalle de Norte 71
Hospital Universitario Hernández Vera 71
Hospital Universitario Nuestra Señora de La Paz 71
Hospital Universitario San Franciso Xavier 71

Hospital Vicente D'Antoni 330
Hospital Victoria Motta 578
Hospital Villa Yunguyo 71
Hospital VINMEC 906
Hospital Virgen de las Angustias 71
Hospital Virgen Milagrosa 71
Hospital Vivian Pellas 578
Hospital Vi Xuyen 906
Hospital Vladimir Bejarano 71
Hospital Wacha 244
Hospital Yaba 612
Hospital Yambio 736
Hospital ya Wahind 789
Hospital Yolanda Mayorga 578
Hospital Zone de Kandi 52
Hospital Zone de Tchaourou 52
Hossainpur Upazila Health Complex 38
Houari Boumediene Kasr El Hiran Public Hospital 8
House of Hope International 64, 322, 569
Houston Shoulder to Shoulder Foundation 322
Howard Hubbard Memorial Hospital 664
Hpa Yar Thone Su Hospital 535
Hsipaw Township Hospital 535
Htee Saung Eye Hospital 535
Htoo Foundation Hospital 535
HTUN Foundation Hospital 535
Hue Central Hospital 906
Hue University Hospital 906
Hulsehet Referral Hospital 244
Human Development and Community Services
  (HDCS) 548
Human Development Foundation (HDF) 622
Humanitarian Aid Relief Trust (HART) 752
Humanitarian Aid Response Team (HART) 487, 850
Humanita 262
HumaniTerra 26, 76, 106, 121, 133, 303, 343, 416, 814
Humanity First 26, 48, 76, 121, 141, 166, 249, 262,
  280, 288, 343, 362, 379, 433, 584, 598, 622, 650,
  690, 696, 710, 776, 806, 815, 830
Humanity Hospital 612
Humanity & Inclusion 6, 48, 64, 76, 96, 106, 141,
  188, 232, 288, 303, 343, 379, 416, 433, 444, 503,
  513, 527, 548, 569, 584, 622, 650, 680, 696, 710,
  742, 806, 814, 830, 892
Humedica 752
Humla Fund 548
Hunger Project, The 27, 48, 76, 232, 262, 343, 459,
  514, 697, 830, 918
Hunger Relief International 303
Hung Loi Ward Medical Station 906
Hung Vuong Hospital 906
Hunt Foundation, The 232
Hurghada Fever Hospital 194
Hurghada General Hospital 194
Hurghada Military Hospital 194
Huruma District Hospital 789
Hussain Memorial Hospital 632
Husyatyn District Hospital 859
Hữu Nghị Clinic 906
H Vill Hospital 664
Hvizdetska District Hospital #2 859
HVK Children's Foundation 433
HVP Gatagara 687
Hwange Colliery Hospital 940
HZ Allada 52
HZ Saint-Jean de Dieu Parakou 52
Ialibu District Hospital 642
Iambi Lutheran Hospital 789
Ibajay District Hospital 664
Ibex Hospital 244
Ibitalo ya Butezi 92
Ibn Al Haitham Specialized Center 757
Ibn Sina Hospital 8, 194
Ibn Sina Hospital Sylhet Limited 38
Ibn Sina Medical College Hospital 39
IBN SINA Rabat University Hospital 506
Ibn Sina Specialized Hospital 757

Ibn Sina Specialized Hospital, Dhanmondi 39
Ibom Multi-Specialty Hospital 612
Ibrahim Cardiac Hospital & Research Institute 39
Ibrahim General Hospital 39
Ibrahim Iqbal Memorial Hospital 39
Ibrahim Malik Teaching Hospital 757, 262
Icahn School of Medicine at Mount Sinai Arnhold
    Institute for Global Health 379, 548
ICAP at Columbia University 13, 86, 121, 166, 219, 232,
    303, 362, 379, 407, 423, 434, 459, 514, 527, 598,
    650, 680, 710, 731, 763, 776, 830, 850, 918, 933
I Care International 322
Ichnya Central District Hospital 859
ICMC Hospital 244
Idende 789
Idunda 789
Igbinedion University Teaching Hospital, Okada 612
Igodivaha 789
Igogwe Hospital 789
Igumbilo 789
Igunga Hospital 789
Igwachanya Hospital 789
Ihanga 789
IHSAN Foundation for West Africa 121, 133, 262,
    280, 584, 598, 710
Ihsan Mumtaz Hospital 632
IHS Children & Family Hospital 632
I-India 343
Ilam District Hospital 560
Ilembula Lutheran Hospital 789
Ilininda 789
Ilocos Sur District Hospital – Magsingal 664
Iloilo Mission Hospital 664
Iloilo Provincial Hospital 664
Ilula Mission Hospital 789
Ilungu 789
Imaging the World 166, 219, 459, 514, 830
IMAHelps 202, 343, 569
Imalilo 789
Imamia Medics International 343, 622, 777
IMA World Health 13, 76, 166, 180, 202, 303, 322, 343,
    379, 473, 548, 569, 584, 650, 731, 776, 830, 850
Imbaku Public Health 379
Imecc 789
IME Loko 176
Immaculate Heart Of Mary Hospital 664
Immunisation 4 Life (i4Life) 918
Imon Specialist Hospital 535
Imo State University Teaching Hospital, Orlu 612
ImPaCCT Foundation 343
IMPACT Foundation 27, 106, 344, 380, 548, 622,
    742, 777
Impact India Foundation 344
Imperial Hospital 757
Imperial Hospital Limited 39
Impulse Hospital 39
Imran Khan Cancer Appeal 622
IMSP Institutul de Cardiologie 489
IMSP Institutul de Ftiziopneumologie Chiril
    Draganiuc 489
IMSP Institutul de Medicina Urgenta 489
IMSP Institutul de Neurologie si Neurochirurgie
    Diomid Gherman 489
IMSP Institutul Mamei si Copilului 489
IMSP Institutul Oncologic 489
IMSP Maternitatea Municipala #2 489
IMSP Spitalul de Psihiatrie Balti 489
IMSP Spitalul Dermatologie si Maladii
    Comunicabile 489
IMSP Spitalul de Stat 489
IMSP Spitalul Raional Anenii Noi 489
IMSP Spitalul Raional Basarabeasca 489
IMSP Spitalul Raional Briceni 489
IMSP Spitalul Raional Cahul 489
IMSP Spitalul Raional Calarasi 489
IMSP Spitalul Raional Cantemir 489
IMSP Spitalul Raional Causeni Ana si Alexandru 489

IMSP Spitalul Raional Ceadir-Lunga 489
IMSP Spitalul Raional Cimislia 489
IMSP Spitalul Raional Comrat Isaac Gurfinkel 489
IMSP Spitalul Raional Criuleni 489
IMSP Spitalul Raional Donduseni 489
IMSP Spitalul Raional Drochia Nicolae Testemitanu 489
IMSP Spitalul Raional Edinet 489
IMSP Spitalul Raional Falesti 489
IMSP Spitalul Raional Floresti 489
IMSP Spitalul Raional Glodeni 490
IMSP Spitalul Raional Hincesti 490
IMSP Spitalul Raional Ialoveni 490
IMSP Spitalul Raional Leova 490
IMSP Spitalul Raional Rezina 490
IMSP Spitalul Raional Riscani 490
IMSP Spitalul Raional Singerei 490
IMSP Spitalul Raional Soldanesti 490
IMSP Spitalul Raional Soroca A. Prisacari 490
IMSP Spitalul Raional Stefan-Voda 490
IMSP Spitalul Raional Straseni 490
IMSP Spitalul Raional Taraclia 490
IMSP Spitalul Raional Telenesti 490
IMSP Spitalul Raional Ungheni 490
IMSP Spitalul Raional Vulcanesti 490
IMSP Spitalul Republican al Asociatiei Curativ-
    Sanatoriale 490
Imtrat Hospital 59
IMTU Hospital 790
Inani Union Sub Center 39
Inaruwa Hospital 560
Incentive Care Foundation 622
In Deed and Truth Ministries 731
Independent University Hospital 632
India Gospel League 344
Indian Cancer Society 344
Indian Renal Foundation (IRF) 344
India Tribal Care Trust (ITCT) 344
India Vision Institute (IVI) 344
Infante Hospital 664
Infectious Disease Clinical Hospital of
    Dushanbe 766
Infectious Disease Hospital Chaek 409
Infectious Disease Hospital – Mandalay 535
Infectious Disease Hospital Tokmok 409
Infectious Diseases Children's Hospital 766
Infectious Diseases Department – Sarny Central
    Regional Hospital 859
Infectious Diseases Hospital #3 878
Infectious Diseases Hospital #3 Lviv 859
Infectious Diseases Institute: College of Health
    Sciences, Makerere University 831
Inga Health Foundation 344
Iniho 790
Innovating Health International (IHI) 303, 459
Insein General Hospital 535
Insolafrica 129
Institute for Healthcare Improvement (IHI) 27, 188,
    232, 262, 344, 459, 598
Institute of Applied Dermatology 106, 416, 527, 650,
    798, 892
Institute of Ethnic Medicine and Pharmacy 906
Institute Of Kidney Diseases 632
Institute of Neurology, Psychiatry and Addiction of
    the National Academy of Medical Sciences of
    Ukraine 859
Institute Pasteur du Cambodge 113
Institut Fame Pereo 315
Institut Médico Psycho Educatif 81
Institut National de Neurologie Mongi-Ben
    Hamida 818
Instituto de Gastroenterología Boliviano-Japonés 71
Instituto do Coração – ICOR 520
InterAmerican Restoration Corporation, The 322
Inter Care Medical and for Africa 262, 459, 710,
    777, 918
Interdistrict Specialized Oncological MSEC 859
Interdistrict Specialized Psychoneurological

MSEC 859
Interface Uganda 831
Interfaith Service to Latin America (ISLA) 569
Inter LDC, Mammology Center 859
Intermed Hospital 499
Internal Medicine Hospital Kasr Alainy 194
International Agency for the Prevention of Blindness
    (IAPB), The 27, 48, 86, 106, 121, 133, 141, 166,
    213, 232, 249, 262, 280, 288, 344, 362, 380, 434,
    444, 459, 514, 527, 548, 584, 598, 622, 650, 680,
    710, 777, 806, 831, 892, 918, 933
International Allied Missions (IAM), Haiti 303
International Campaign for Women's Right to Safe
    Abortion 27, 64, 322, 344, 380, 459, 503, 598,
    622, 742, 777, 831, 933
International Cancer Institute 380
International Children's Heart Foundation 64, 188,
    232, 303, 322, 344, 503, 569, 598, 622, 650, 752,
    850, 875
International Children's Heart Fund 233, 303, 344,
    434, 473, 495, 527, 548, 697, 777, 831, 892
International Community Initiatives 303, 892
International Council of Ophthalmology 6, 27, 48, 64,
    86, 106, 121, 166, 188, 233, 262, 303, 322, 344,
    362, 380, 416, 444, 459, 473, 495, 527, 548, 599,
    622, 650, 680, 697, 731, 742, 777, 806, 875, 892,
    918, 934
International Eye Foundation (IEF) 27, 188, 202, 233,
    262, 303, 322, 344, 459, 570, 777, 918
International Eye Hospital 790
International Eye Institute, Inc. 322, 570
International Federation of Gynecology and
    Obstetrics (FIGO) 6, 27, 48, 64, 76, 106, 121, 188,
    202, 213, 233, 262, 280, 303, 322, 344, 380, 407,
    459, 487, 495, 503, 514, 527, 548, 570, 584, 599,
    622, 639, 650, 680, 697, 710, 742, 752, 777, 815,
    831, 850, 875, 892, 918, 934
International Federation of Red Cross and Red
    Crescent Societies (IFRC) 6, 14, 27, 48, 56, 64,
    76, 86, 96, 106, 121, 133, 141, 150, 156, 166,
    180, 188, 202, 213, 219, 233, 249, 262, 280, 289,
    303, 322, 344, 362, 380, 400, 407, 416, 423, 434,
    459, 473, 480, 487, 495, 503, 514, 527, 548, 570,
    584, 599, 622, 639, 651, 680, 697, 710, 722, 731,
    742, 752, 763, 777, 799, 806, 815, 831, 850, 875,
    882, 892, 918, 934
International Friendship Children's Hospital 560
International Health & Development Network
    (IHDN) 262
International Health Operations Patient Education
    and Empowerment (IHOPEE) 380
International Health Partners – U.S. Inc. 777
International Health Services Group 322, 380
International Hearing Foundation 106, 233, 459,
    473, 697
International HELP 202, 303, 322, 710
International Hope Missions 380, 777
International Hospital Kampala 843
International Insulin Foundation 407, 514, 570, 892,
    918
International League of Dermatological
    Socieities 106, 233, 599, 651
International Learning Movement (ILM UK) 27, 188,
    233, 249, 303, 344, 380, 459, 527, 548, 584, 599,
    622, 651, 710, 742, 752, 831
International Medical Alliance 303
International Medical Alliance 380
International Medical and Surgical Aid (IMSA) 86,
    141, 150, 233, 444, 777
International Medical Assistance Foundation 322
International Medical Corps 86, 121, 133, 166, 233,
    599, 622, 651, 731, 752, 850, 934
International Medical Professionals Initiative
    Inc. 831
International Medical Relief 64, 106, 249, 303, 322,
    344, 380, 444, 548, 680, 697, 777, 806, 831, 892
International Medical Response 303, 434, 459, 651,

711, 732, 832
Joint Therapy Outreach Incorporated 883
Joint United Nations Programme on HIV/AIDS (UNAIDS) 14, 28, 49, 57, 65, 77, 86, 96, 107, 122, 134, 142, 150, 167, 203, 213, 234, 280, 289, 304, 323, 345, 363, 381, 400, 407, 416, 423, 434, 445, 460, 473, 480, 487, 496, 528, 549, 570, 585, 599, 623, 639, 651, 681, 697, 711, 723, 732, 742, 763, 778, 799, 806, 832, 850, 875, 883, 893, 919, 934
Jolamade Hospital 612
Jose B. Lingad Memorial Regional Hospital 664
Josefina Belmonte Duran Memorial Hospital 664
Jose J. Golingay General Hospital Inc. 664
Joseph Ravoahangy Andrianavalona Hospital 450
Jose S. Lapid District Hospital 664
Jos University Teaching Hospital (JUTH) 612
J. P. Sioson General Hospital & Colleges, Inc. 664
J.R. Borja General Hospital 664
Juaben Government Hospital 273
Juan S. Alano Hospital 664
Juaso District Hospital 273
Jubail Specialist Hospital 273
Juba Military Hospital 736
Juba Teaching Hospital 736
Judge Celestino Guerrero Memorial Hospital 664
Jugal Hospital 244
Juja Modern Hospital 394
Jukayi 176
Julio Cardinal Rosales Hospital 664
Justice Calixto O. Zaldivar Memorial Hospital (formerly Gov. Leandro Fullon District Hospital) 664
Justice Jose Abad Santos General Hospital 664
K2K - Kansas to Kenya 381
Kabale Regional Hospital 843
Kabarole Hospital 843
Kabaya Hospital 687
Kabgayi District Hospital 687
Kabo Cottage General Hospital 612
Kabwe Women, Newborn and Children's Hospital 925
Kachua Upazila Health Complex 39
Kadic Hospital 843
Kadisco General Hospital 244
Kadoma General Hospital 940
Kaduna Emergency Operations Center 612
Kaédi Regional Hospital 476
Kafel Aid 753
Kagan City Hospital 878
Kagando Hospital 844
Kagando Rural Development Center (KARUDEC) 832
Kagara General Hospital 612
Kagarlitsk Multiprofile Hospital 860
Kageno 381, 681
Kagera Regional Hospital 790
Kagera Sugar Hospital 790
Kagondo Hospital 790
Kagondo St. Joseph Hospital Foundation 778
Kahama Hospital 790
Kailahun Government Hospital 717, 746
Kailash Medical Foundation 345, 549, 651, 919
Kainantu Rural Hospital 642
Kairuki University 790
Kajiado District Hospital 394
Kajo Keji Health Training Institute (KKHTI) 732, 832
Kakhovka District Hospital 860
Kakuma Mission Hospital 394
Kalacha Sub-County Referral Hospital (Chalbi) 394
Kala Chaung Gyi District Hospital 535
Kalaiya Hospital 560
Kalaroa Upazila Health Complex 39
Kalein Aung Station Hospital 535
Kalene Mission Hospital 925
Kalid Hamiday Hospital 757
Kaliganj Upazila Health Complex 39
Kalihati Upazila Health Complex 39
Kalika Community Hospital 560

Kalinga Provincial Hospital-KPH 664
Kalinin Regional Clinical Hospital 860
Kalipay Negrense Foundation 651
Kalkini Upazila Health Complex 39
Kalmakanda Upazila Health Complex 39
Kalomo District Hospital 925
Kalulushi Hospital 925
Kamakwie Wesleyan Hospital 717, 746
Kamanga 790
Kamanggagawa Foundation Inc. 651
Kambia Appeal, The 711
Kambia General Hospital 717, 746
Kamchaymear Referral Hospital 113
Kamianets-Podilskyi City Maternity Hospital 860
Kamianka-Buzka Central District Hospital 860
Kampala Hospital 844
Kampala Medical Chambers Hospital 844
Kampong Cham Provincial Hospital 113
Kampong Chhnang Hospital 113
Kampong Speu Referral Hospital 113
Kampong Thom Provincial Hospital 113
Kampong Trach Referral Hospital 113
Kampot Referral Hospital 113
Kamrangirchar Hospital 39
Kamuli Friends 832
Kamuli General Hospital 844
Kamuli Mission Hospital 844
Kamu Medical Centre 844
Kamuzu Central Hospital 468
Kanaighat Upazila Health Complex 39
Kanaung Station Hospital 535
Kandep District Hospital 642
Kangundo Level 4 Hospital 394
Kaniv Multidisciplinary Hospital 860
Kansas University Medical Center: Global Surgery 460
Kantha Bopha IV Children's Hospital 113
Kantha Bopha Jayavarmann VII Hospital 113
Kanti Children's Hospital 560
Kantipur Hospital 560
Kantipur Institute of Health Science 560
Kant Kaw Hospital 535
Kapalong District Hospital 664
Kapchorwa Hospital 844
Kapenguria Referral Hospital Ward Seven 394
Kapitanivka District Hospital 860
Kapuna Hospital 642
Kara-Buura Territorial Hospital K. Subanbaev 409
Karachi Adventist Hospital 7th Day 633
Karakulja Regional Hospital 409
Karamara General Hospital 244
Karanda Mission Hospital 940
Karasuu Territorial Hospital 410
Karatu Lutheran Hospital 790
Karen Hospital 394
Karen Hospital-Nyeri 394
Kariba District Hospital 940
Karikari Brobbery Hospital 273
Karin Community Initiatives Uganda (KCIU) 832
Kariyangwe Mission Hospital 940
Karlivka Central District Hospital 860
Karma Thalo Foundation 549
Karnali Province Hospital 560
Karonga District Hospital 468
Karongi Hospital 687
Karuna Foundation Nepal 550
Kashipur Al-Habib Hospital 39
Kaski Model Hospital 560
Kasulu District Hospital 790
Kasungu District Hospital 468
Kasusong Pinay 651
Katabi UPDAF Hospital 844
Katalemwa Cheshire Home 832
Katavi Regional Referral Hospital 790
Katha Bopha I Children's Hospital 113
Katha Bopha II Children's Hospital 113
Kathmandu Hospital 560

Kathmandu Medical College 561
Kathmandu Medical College Teaching Hospital 561
Kathmandu Military Hospital 561
Kathmandu Model Hospital 561
Katimba Parish Hospital 844
Katito Hospital 394
Kaukhali Upazila Health Complex 39
Kauswagan Provincial Hospital 664
Kavieng General Hospital 642
Kawasoti Ayurvedic Hospital 561
Kawembe General Referral Hospital 176
Kawit Kalayaan Hospital 665
Kawo General Hospital 612
Kawolo Hospital 844
Kawthoung General Hospital 535
Kaya Responsible Travel 65, 107, 220, 263, 345, 381, 503, 515, 550, 651, 742, 778, 832, 893, 919, 934
Kay Mackenson Clinic for Children with Chronic Diseases 304
Kayogoro 92
Kay Sante Pa' W 315
Kaytu Hospital 535
Kayunga Hospital 844
KC Hospital & Diagnostic Center 39
Keep a Child Alive 346, 381, 681
Keffam Hospital 273
Kehsi Hospital 535
Kellermann Foundation, The 832
KEM Hospital Pune 346
Kemin Regional Hospital 410
Kemrif Hospital 394
Kendua Upazila Health Complex 39
Kendu Bay District Hospital 394
Kenema Government Hospital 717, 746
Kenya Aid 381
Kenya Defence Forces Memorial Hospital 394
Kenya Diabetes Management & Information Center 381
Kenya Health 381
Kenya Medical Mission 381
KenyanNetwork of Cancer Organization 381
Kenya Pediatric Association 381
Kenya Relief 381
Kenyatta National Hospital (KNH) 395
Keraniganj Upazila Health Complex 39
Kerema General Hospital 642
Keren Hospital 215
Kericho County Referral Hospital 395
Kerugoya County Referral Hospital 395
Keshabpur Upazila Health Complex 39
Kezi Rural District Hospital 940
Khadija Memorial Hospital 612
Khambhati Charity International 346
Khamis Specialized Hospital 194
Khan-Uul district General Hospital 499
Kharadar General Hospital 623
Kharkiv City Children's Clinical Hospital #19 860
Kharkiv City Children's Clinical Hospital #24 860
Kharkiv City Clinical Hospital #31 860
Kharkiv City Hospital #3 860
Kharkiv Clinical Hospital on Railway Transport #1 Radiation Diagnostics Center 860
Kharkiv Military Medical Clinical Center of the Northern Region 860
Kharkiv Regional Children's Clinical Hospital #1 860
Khartoum Bahri Teaching Hospital 757
Khartoum Breast Care Centre 757
Khartoum Teaching Hospital 757
Khartsyzsk City Hospital 860
Khatlon Medical Center 766
Khentii City General Hospital 499
Kherson Children's Regional Clinical Hospital 860
Kherson Railway Station Surgery Hospital 860
Kherson Regional Hospital 860
Kherson Regional Hospital Hospice 860
Kherson Regional Infectious Hospital

Kumasi South Hospital 273
Kumi Hospital 844
Kumi Hospital Uganda 833
Kumorji Hospital 273
Kumudini Hospital 40
Kungrad Railway Hospital 878
Kuntenase Government Hospital 273
Kupenda for the Children 382
Kupona Foundation 778
Kupyansk Central City Hospital 861
Kurakhiv City Hospital 861
Kurmitola General Hospital 40
Kushtia General Hospital 40
Kusini Hospital 790
Kutupalong Hospital 40
Kuwait Bangladesh Friendship Government
    Hospital 40
Kuwait Teaching Hospital 633
Kuyi Hospital 244
Kuzeminsk Rural District Hospital 861
Kwabre District Hospital 273
Kwahu Government Hospital 273
Kwante 244
Kwekabaw Hospital 535
Kwekwe General Hospital 940
Kyauk Chaung Station Hospital 535
Kyauk Htu Station Hospital 535
Kyaukme District Hospital 535
Kyaukpa-Daung Township Hospital 535
Kybele Incorporated 65, 188, 263, 487, 496, 850,
    893
Kyebi Government Hospital 273
Kyei Memorial Hospital 273
Kyela District Hospital 791
Kyiv City Children Clinical Hospital # 1 861
Kyiv City Children's Clinical Hospital #1 Kyiv 862
Kyiv City Children's Clinical Hospital #2 862
Kyiv City Children's Clinical Infectious Diseases
    Hospital 862
Kyiv City Children's Clinical Tuberculosis
    Hospital 862
Kyiv City Clinical Ambulance Hospital 862
Kyiv City Clinical Dermatological and Venereological
    Hospital 862
Kyiv City Clinical Hospital #1 862
Kyiv City Clinical Hospital #2 862
Kyiv City Clinical Hospital #3 862
Kyiv City Clinical Hospital #7 Traumatology and
    Orthopedics 862
Kyiv City Clinical Hospital #8 862
Kyiv City Clinical Hospital #8 862
Kyiv City Clinical Hospital #9 862
Kyiv City Clinical Hospital #10 862
Kyiv City Clinical Hospital #12 862
Kyiv City Clinical Hospital #17 862
Kyiv City Clinical Hospital #18 862
Kyiv City Clinical Hospital for War Veterans 862
Kyiv City Clinical Oncology Center 862
Kyiv City Maternity Hospital #1 862
Kyiv City Maternity Hospital #1 Peredmistna
    Slobidka 862
Kyiv City Narcological Clinical Hospital
    Sociotherapy 862
Kyiv City Psychiatric Hospital I. Pavlov 862
Kyiv City Tuberculosis Hospital #1 DV 862
Kyiv Regional Children's Hospital #2 862
Kyiv Regional Psychoneurological Hospital #2 862
Kyiv Regional Tuberculosis Hospital #2 862
Kyrgystan Red Crescent 407
Kyrgystan Republican Narcology Center 410
Kyun Chaung Hospital 535
LABAID Diagnostic Chattogram 40
Labaid Specialized Hospital 40
LABAID Specialized Hospital 40
Labaid Specialized Hospital – Malibag 40
Labakcare 304, 600
Labason District Hospital 665

Labo District Hospital 665
Lab One Diagnostic Center 40
La Charité 92
La Clinique Méditerranéenne 818
La Consolacion University General Hospital 665
Ladakh Heart Foundation 346
Ladoke Akintola University of Technology (LAUTECH)
    Teaching Hospital, Ogbomoso 612
Lady Dufferin Hospital 623, 633
Lady Helen Child Health Foundation 600
Lady Willingdon Hospital 633
Lae International Hospital 642
La General Hospital 273
Lagos Emergency Operations Center 612
Lagos Island General Hospital 612
Lagos State University Teaching Hospital 600, 612
Lagos University Teaching Hospital 612
Lahore General Hospital 633
Lahore Health Care 633
Lahore Medical Complex & The Heart Hospital 633
Lahoz Clinic and Hospital 665
Lai Chau Provincial Hospital 906
Lake City Hospital and Critical Care 561
Lakes State Hospital 736
Lakka Hospital ETU 717, 746
Laksham Upazila Health Complex 40
Lakshmipur Sadar Hospital 40
Lalgadh Leprosy Hospital & Services Centre 561
Lalgadh Model Hospital Pvt. Ltd. 561
Lalibela Hospital 244
Lalon Shah Diagnostic Center & Hospital 40
LAMB 28
LAMB Hospital 40
Lámha Suas 833
Lamp for Haiti 304
Lamurde Primary Heath Center 612
Lanao del Norte Provincial Hospital 665
Lancet Hospital 791
Land and Life Foundation 382, 778
Land Mark Hospital 244
Languyan Municipal Hospital 665
Lantoro Catholic Hospital 612
Laoag City General Hospital 665
Laoag Pediatric Hospital 665
Lao Cai Endocrinology Hospital 906
Lao Cai Obstetrics and Children's Hospital 907
Lao Friends Hospital for Children 419
Lao Health Initiative 416
Lao-Korea National Children's Hospital 419
Lao Military Hospital 103 419
Lao-Viet Hospital 419
La Salle International Foundation 188, 234, 304,
    363, 515, 651, 732
Lashio General Hospital 535
Las Nieves Municipal Hospital 665
Las Piñas City Medical Center 665
Las Piñas General Hospital & Satellite Trauma
    Center 665
Lassa General Hospital 612
Last Mile Health 28, 167, 234, 304, 382, 434, 460,
    833
Lata Hospital 724
Launglon Township Hospital 535
Laung she 535
La Union Medical Diagnostic Center & Hospital 665
Laurel Memorial District Hospital 665
Lavi Project 305
Laxmimarga-Dangihat Hospital 561
Lay Kay Station Hospital 535
Laymyethnar Township Hospital 535
Layton Rahmatulla Benevolent Trust (LRBT) 623
Lay Volunteers International Association (LVIA) 77,
    87, 234, 280, 289, 382, 515, 697, 778
Lazgrace Charity Foundation 600
Leadership in Medicine for the Underserved Program
    at MSU, The 203, 346, 570, 833
LEAP Global Missions 305, 346, 934

Le Bon Samaritain Hospital 146
Leja Bulela 167
Lekhnath City Hospital 561
Le Korsa 698
Leland Dental Charities (LDC) 203
Lella Specialist Hospital 612
Le Loi Hospital 907
Le Mete Ghana 263
Lena Carl Hospital 244
Lenakel Hospital 885
Le Ngoc Tung General Hospital 907
Lenmed Hospital Privado de Maputo 520
Leona O. Lim Memorial Hospital 665
Leonardo B Manabat Sr. Hospital, Inc. 665
Lepra 28, 346, 515, 935
Leprosy Mission Australia, The 346, 550, 600, 639, 799
Leprosy Mission England and Wales, The 28, 234,
    346, 515, 528, 550, 585, 600, 742, 753
Leprosy Mission International 28, 142, 167, 234,
    346, 515, 528, 550, 585, 600, 639, 742, 753,
    778, 799
Leprosy Mission: Northern Ireland, The 28, 234, 346,
    550, 600, 778
Les Aiglons 176
Lespwa Lavi 305
Less Privileged Ghana Foundation 263
Let's Save The Brain 652
Lewanika General Hospital 925
Leyte Baptist Hospital 665
Leyte Provincial Hospital 665
Liaqat Hospital 633
Liaquat National Hospital 633
Liaquat University Hospital – Hyderabad 633
Liberia Medical Mission 434
Liberty Hospital 612
Libya Specialist Hospital 757
Lifebox 28, 203, 234, 280, 323, 346, 550, 570, 779,
    850, 919, 935
Life Care Hospital at Bharatpur 561
Life Care Hospital at Kathmandu 561
LifeCare Hospitals Bungoma 395
LifeCare Malawi Foundation (LCMF) 460
Life for a Child 28, 77, 87, 134, 157, 167, 213, 234,
    263, 305, 346, 382, 434, 473, 550, 600, 623, 652,
    681, 743, 753, 763, 778, 806, 833, 875, 893, 935
Life for African Mothers 122, 434, 711
Lifeguard Hospital 561
Lifeline 468
Lifeline Group of Hospital, The – Wendani 395
Life Line Hospital and Cardiac Center 40
LifeNet International 87, 167, 460, 833
Life Support Foundation 460, 779
LIG Global Foundation 652
Light for Sight 21 189, 346, 382, 503
Light for the World 28, 65, 77, 107, 167, 234, 280,
    346, 382, 515, 639, 681, 732, 779, 833
Lighthouse for Christ Eye Center 382
Light House Medical Missions 49, 77, 87, 167, 250,
    289, 407, 434, 652, 711, 779, 833
Lighthouse Trust 460
Light in the World Development Foundation 806
Ligula Hospital 791
Lihir Medical Centre 642
Likawage Hospital 791
Likoni Sub-District Hospital 395
Likuni Hospital 468
Lily Hospital 612
Lily Project, The 570
Limbs International 28, 65, 87, 107, 167, 189, 203, 234,
    263, 305, 346, 382, 416, 434, 528, 550, 600, 623,
    652, 698, 711, 743, 753, 779, 833, 850, 893, 919
Limuru Cottage Hospital 395
Lincon Medical Center 862
Lions Clubs International 49, 87, 134, 142, 234, 250,
    280, 289, 305, 346, 434, 445, 460, 515, 550, 585,
    681, 711, 732, 763, 779, 806, 833
Lions SightFirst Eye Hospital 395

Maloto 461
Malovyskiv Hospital 863
Maluk Timor 799
Malungon Municipal Hospital 666
Maluti Adventist Hospital 426
Malya 791
Mamakeev's National Surgical Center 410
Mama na Mtoto (Mother and Child) 779, 833
Mama Ngoma Health Service 791
Mama-Pikin Foundation 711
Mama Rachel Hospital of Mercy Inc. 666
Mambusao District Hospital 666
Ma-Moni Hospital 40
Mampong District Hospital 273
Mamudia MCHP 718
Mamudia MCHP 747
Mamun Private Hospital 40
Management Sciences for Health (MSH) 7, 14, 28, 49, 65, 77, 87, 122, 142, 150, 167, 189, 203, 220, 234, 250, 263, 281, 305, 323, 363, 383, 407, 424, 435, 445, 461, 473, 515, 529, 550, 570, 600, 652, 681, 698, 711, 732, 763, 779, 806, 833, 850, 875, 893, 919, 935
Manahari Hospital 561
Manatuto Hospital 801
Manav Sadhna 347
Mandalar Hospital 535
Mandalay Children's Hospital 535
Mandalay GEC Hospital 535
Mandalay General Hospital 535
Mandalay Orthopaedic Hospital 535
Mandaue City Hospital 666
Mandera County Referral Hospital (Mandera District Hospital) 395
Manek's Hospital 612
Mangalbare Hospital Urlabari 561
Mangungumete Health Home 521
Manhyia Hospital 273
Manikchari Upazila Health Complex 40
Manikganj District Hospital 40
Manila Central University (MCU) Hospital – Filemon D. Tanchoco Sr. Medical Foundation 666
Manirampur Upazila Health Complex 40
Manito Municipal Hospital 666
Mankayane Government Hospital 222
Mankiv Central District Hospital 863
Mankranso Government Hospital 273
Manmohan Memorial Hospital 561
Manna Mission Hospital 273
Manpura Upazila Health Complex 40
Mansa General Hospital 925
Mansheyet El Bakry General Hospital 195
Mansoorah Hospital 633
Mansoura International Hospital 195
Mansoura Military Hospital 195
Mansoura University Hospital 195
Manthan Eye Healthcare Foundation 347
Manuel A. Roxas District Hospital 666
Manuel Hospital 666
Manuel J. Santos Hospital 666
Manuel V. Gallego Cabanatuan City General Hospital 666
Manyara Regional Referral Hospital 791
MAP International 14, 28, 49, 57, 65, 87, 107, 122, 134, 142, 167, 189, 203, 220, 235, 250, 264, 281, 323, 347, 363, 383, 407, 435, 445, 461, 487, 496, 515, 529, 550, 570, 585, 600, 623, 639, 652, 681, 698, 711, 732, 779, 806, 833, 850, 893, 919, 935
Maraba Gumai Yamma 612
Maragua District Rural Hospital 395
Maralal District Hospital 395
Maranatha Health 833
Marangu Hospital 791
Marcelo Hospital of Baliwag, Inc. 666
Marcelo – Padilla Hospital 666
March to the Top Africa 383
Margosatubig Regional Hospital 666

Maria Estrella General Hospital 666
Maria Hospital, Pediatric Specialties 330
Maria Immaculata Hospital (MCH) 395
Mariakani Cottage Hospital 395
Mariakani Hospital 395
Maria L. Eleazar Memorial General Hospital 666
Marian Hospital of Sta. Rosa, Inc. 666
Maria Reyna Hospital 666
Maria Theresa Hospital 419
Marie Stopes Bangladesh 40, 28, 65, 77, 107, 167, 235, 264, 347, 383, 445, 461, 496, 529, 550, 585, 600, 623, 639, 698, 711, 743, 779, 799, 833, 893, 919, 935
Marie Stopes Nepal 561
Marigat Hospital 395
Marigat Sub-District Hospital 395
Marilao Saint Michael Family Hospital, Inc. 666
Marilog District Hospital 666
Mariupol City Hospital #1 863
Mariupol City Hospital #9 863
Mariupol City Hospital of Emergency Medical Care 863
Mariupol Regional Intensive Care Hospital 863
Mariveles District Hospital 666
Markos Hospital 244
MARKS Medical College & Hospital 40
Marondera Provincial Hospital 940
Marovo Medical Foundaiton 723
Marquine Central District Hospital 863
Marriott Medical Center 863
Marsabit County Referral Hospital 395
Marte General Hospital 612
Martha Tubman Memorial Hospital 439
Martinez Memorial Hospital 666
Martin Memorial Hospital 273
Martyr Al-Moez Al-Abadi Hospital 757
Maruti Children Hospital 561
Mary Begg Community Clinic 919
Mary Begg Kansanshi Mine Hospital 925
Mary Care 600
Mary Health of Africa General Hospital 129
Mary Johnston Hospital 666
Maryknoll Lay Missioners 65, 107, 203, 305, 383, 732, 779
Mary Mediatrix Medical Center 666
Mary Mission Incorporated 834
Marymount Hospital 666
Masaba District Hospital 395
Masaba Hospital 395
Masaka Referral Hospital 844
Masanga Hospital 718, 747
Maseru Private Hospital 426
Mashoko Christian Hospital 935
Masimba Sub-District Hospital 395
Masindi District Hospital 844
Masoko Hospital 791
Masroor Hospital 633
Masroor Humanity First Hospital Senegal 703
Massachusetts Eye and Ear: Operation Airway 203
Massachusetts General Hospital Global Surgery Initiative 28, 65, 122, 134, 203, 235, 264, 305, 323, 383, 435, 550, 652, 681, 698, 711, 834
Massana Hospital 791
Massawa Hospital 215
Massey Street Children Hospital 612
Masvingo General Hospital 940
Maswa District Hospital 791
Matema Lutheran Hospital 791
Mateo-Mabborang General Hospital 666
MaterCare International (MCI) (Canada) 264, 305, 383, 834
Mater Dei Hospital 940
Mater Misericordiae Hospital 383, 395
Maternal And Child Health Care Old Airport 613
Maternal and Child Health Hospital 273
Maternal and Child Health Training Institute 40
Maternal & Childhealth Advocacy International 250,

435
Maternal Fetal Care International 213, 264, 347, 383, 712
Maternal Rights Ghana 264
Maternidade Augusto N'Gangula 18
Maternity Building #2 Of Odessa City Council 863
Maternity Foundation 28, 49, 235, 264, 305, 347, 383, 407, 416, 529, 712, 779, 807, 919
Maternity Home of Rivne City Council 863
Maternity Hospital 863
Maternity Hospital #1 863
Maternity Hospital #1 Khutory 863
Maternity Hospital #2 766
Maternity Hospital #4 of Bishkek 410
Maternity Hospital #4 Sonyachne 863
Maternity Hospital #5 Odessa 863
Maternity Hospital #7 Cheremushky 863
Maternity Hospital of Chernihiv City Council 863
Maternity Hospital of the City Clinical Hospital #3 863
Maternity (Ternopil Regional Perinatal Center for Mother and Child) 863
Maternity Worldwide 235, 250, 305, 461, 600, 623, 712, 779, 834, 919, 935
Matero Level 1 Hospital 925
Mathangeni Clinic 222
Mathbaria Upazila Health Complex 40
Mathias Hospital 273
Matibabu Foundation Kenya 383
Matibi Mission Hospital 940
Matilde A. Olivas District Hospital 666
Matiranga Upazila Health Complex 40
Matlab Upazila Health Complex 40
Matrouh General Hospital 195
Mattru General Hospital 718, 747
Matupi Public Hospital 535
Maua Methodist Hospital 395
Maubin Hospital 535
Maubisse Referral Hospital 801
Maula Buksh Sardar Datobbo Chokkhu Hospital 40
Mauna Hospital 885
Maverick Collective 203, 235, 305, 323, 347, 363, 383, 515, 529, 550, 570, 698, 834, 893, 935
Maviscope Hospital & Fertility Centre 613
Maweni Hospital 791
Mawenzi Hospital 791
Mawimbini Medical Centre 791
Mawlamyine Christian Leprosy Hospital (MCLH) 536
Mawlamyine General Hospital 536
Mawlamyine Traditional Medicine Hospital 536
Maw Taung Township Hospital 535
Max Foundation, The 235, 347, 383, 515, 550, 600, 652, 698, 875, 893
Max Hospital & Diagnostic Ltd. 40
Maya Metro Hospital 561
Mayanja Memorial Hospital 844
Mayo Hospital Lahore 633
Mayor Hilarion A. Ramiro Sr. Medical Center – MHARSMC 666
Mayoyao District Hospital 666
Mazabuka General Hospital 925
Mbabane Clinic 222
Mbabane Government Hospital 222
Mbagathi District Hospital 395
Mbale General Hospital 844
Mbale Regional Referral Hospital 844
Mbalizi Hospital 791
Mbanefo Hospital 613
Mbanza-Ngungu Hospital 176
Mbarara District Regional Referral Hospital 844
Mberengwa District Hospital 940
Mbesa Mission Hospital 791
Mbeya Consultant Hospital 791
Mbeya Hospital 791
Mbeya Referral Hospital 791
MBG Hospital 499
Mbinga District Hospital 791

Mbingo Baptist Hospital 122, 129
Mbire District Hospital 941
Mbita Sub-County Hospital 395
Mbooni Sub-County Hospital 395
Mboppi Baptist Hospital 129
Mbozi Mission Hospital 791
Mbrom Hospital 273
Mbulu Hospital 791
Mbuya Dorcas Hospital 941
McGill University Health Centre: Centre for Global
    Surgery 235, 264, 305, 383, 496, 550, 681, 753,
    779, 834
MCM 244
MCM General Hospital 235
MCU Hospital Dr. Filemon D. Tanchoco, Sr. Medical
    Foundation Inc. 666
MCW Global 681, 779, 919
MDS-Service 878
Mean Chey Referral Hospital 114
Meatu Hospital 791
Mecca Eye Hospital 757
Mecca Ophthalmology Hospital Al-kalakla 757
Mechi Zonal Hospital 561
MedAcross 529
MedAid United Kingdom 834
Medair 29, 167, 445, 732
Medcross Hospital 926
Médecins d'Afrique 53
Médecins du Monde/Doctors of the World 7, 14, 29,
    49, 66, 77, 108, 123, 134, 168, 189, 204, 236,
    307, 324, 363, 385, 416, 445, 473, 496, 504, 516,
    529, 551, 571, 585, 601, 624, 653, 698, 712, 732,
    743, 781, 807, 815, 851
Medecins Sans Frontieres (MSF) Hospital IPD 40
MedHope Africa 383, 732, 834
Medical Aid Pakistan 624
Medical Aid to Haiti (MATH) 305
Medical Ambassadors International 305, 383, 570,
    698
Medical and Educational Sustainable Community
    Help (MESCH) 883, 893
Medical and Obstetric Point 863
Medical Assistance Sierra Leone 712
Medical Benevolence Foundation (MBF) 167, 306,
    383, 461
Medical Care Development International 289, 424
Medical Care Development International (MCD
    International) 49, 122, 167, 203, 264, 281, 363,
    383, 424, 445, 585, 690, 698, 712, 919
Medical Care Development International 14, 49, 65,
    77, 87, 122, 134, 142, 157, 168, 181, 203, 220,
    235, 250, 264, 281, 306, 363, 383, 435, 445, 461,
    515, 529, 585, 600, 698, 712, 753, 779, 807, 815,
    834, 920
Medical Care for the Nations (MCN) 920
Medical Center 863
Medical Center IMUS 666
Medical Center Le Jourdain 129
Medical Center Shifokor 878
Medical City Clark, The – Ambulatory Surgical
    Center 666
Medical City Clark, The – Hospital 666
Medical City, The 666
Medical City, The – Iloilo 666
Medical City, The – Pangasinan 666
Medical City, The – South Luzon 666
Medical, Educational Missions and Outreach 893
Medical Equipment Modernization Opportunity
    (MEMO) 203, 435, 570, 935
Medical Evacuation Disaster Intervention Corps
    (Medic Corps) 306, 652
Medical House 561
Medical Intervention Team eV (MIT) 529
Medical Mercy Canada 347, 529, 550, 850
Medical Ministry International 65, 107, 203, 235,
    264, 306, 323, 347, 461, 550, 652, 681, 850, 920
Medical Mission Aid Inc 168, 189, 551, 624, 639,

732, 779
Medical Missionaries 306
Medical Mission Exchange (MMEX) 306, 323
Medical Mission Group Hospital 666
Medical Mission Group Hospital & Health Services
    Cooperative of Bohol 666
Medical Mission Group Hospital & Health Services
    Cooperative of Tacurong 666
Medical Mission of Hope to Zambia 920
Medical Missions Abroad Corp 264, 383
Medical Missions for Children (MMFC) 107, 323,
    347, 652, 681, 780
Medical Missions for Global Health 435, 780
Medical Missions Foundation 347, 652, 834
Medical Missions International 600
Medical Missions Kenya and Hunger Relief
    (MMK) 383
Medical Missions Outreach 203, 235, 323, 383, 570,
    652, 780, 920
Medical Mission Trips 87, 235, 306, 323, 383, 723
Medical Relief for India 347
Medical Relief Foundation 235, 571, 780, 850
Medical Relief International 108, 306, 652, 780
Medical Research Council 253
Medical Servants International 461
Medical Service of Dobropole 863
Medical Teams International 29, 108, 203, 235, 306,
    435, 529, 551, 753, 780, 834
Medicas Hospital 273
Medicine Krivbas 863
Medicines for Humanity 122, 306, 384, 753, 920
Medici Per I Diritti Umani (MEDU) 189, 585
Medic Malawi 461
Medics for Humanity 250
Medicus Mundi Italia 65, 77, 87, 347, 384, 515
Medifem Hospital 273
Mediheal Group Hospital 396
Mediheal Group of Hospitals, Upper Hill 396
Mediheal Hospital, Eastleigh 396
Medik Hospital 844
Mediland Hospital 536
Medimax Hospital 315
Medina General Hospital 666
Medison Specialist Women's Hospital 613
Meditsinskiy Tsentr Starlab 863
Medland Health Services 926
MEDLIFE Movement 571, 780
Medpharm Clinic and Pharmacy 482
MEDRIX 893
MedSend 65, 264, 384, 461, 639, 780, 807, 920
MedShare 14, 29, 49, 57, 66, 77, 87, 96, 108, 122,
    168, 189, 203, 213, 220, 235, 250, 264, 281, 289,
    306, 323, 347, 363, 384, 407, 416, 424, 435, 445,
    461, 473, 480, 496, 504, 515, 529, 551, 571, 585,
    601, 624, 639, 652, 682, 698, 712, 732, 753, 763,
    780, 807, 834, 851, 875, 893, 920, 935
Med Treks International 383
Meeting TENTS 652
Mehboob Charity Vision Eye Hospital 633
Meherpur General Hospital 40
Meikles Foundation, The 935
Meiktila General Hospital 536
Mekane Hiwot Hospital 215
Mekelle Hospital 244
MeKong Obstetrics and Gynecology Hospital 907
Melanie Jewson Foundation 883
Melchizedek Hospital 396
Meles Zenawi Memorial Referral Hospital 244
Melitopol City Children's Hospital 863
Melitopol City Hospital #1 863
Melitopol City Hospital #2 863
Melitopol District Hospital 863
Melut Hospital 736
Memon Medical Institute Hospital 633
Memon Medical Institute Hospital (MMI
    Hospital) 624
Memorial Christian Hospital 40, 633

Memusi Foundation 384
Mendefera Referral Hospital 215
Mendero Medical Center 667
Mending Faces 204, 652
Mending Kids 66, 323, 348, 515, 780
Mendi Provincial Hospital 642
Menelik II Referral Hospital 244
Mengo Hospital 844
Menjong Diagnostic Centre Private Limited 59
MENTOR Initiative 14, 122, 134, 142, 168, 281, 363,
    384, 435, 515, 601, 712, 732, 834, 920
Merck for Mothers 348, 384, 601, 698, 834
Mercy and Love Foundation 14, 49, 77, 87, 96, 122, 134,
    142, 150, 157, 168, 213, 235, 250, 281, 289, 363,
    384, 424, 435, 445, 461, 473, 515, 585, 601, 682,
    690, 698, 712, 732, 753, 780, 807, 834, 920, 935
Mercy Cneter Foundation 384
Mercy Hospital 718, 747
Mercy Hospital, Abak 601
Mercy in Action 108, 348, 551, 652
Mercy International Mission 601
Mercy Kids, The 571
Mercy Malaysia 29, 653
Mercy Medical Center Cambodia 108
Mercy Mission Hospital 396
Mercy Ships 49, 66, 87, 122, 134, 151, 168, 213,
    250, 281, 289, 323, 435, 445, 496, 515, 698, 712,
    732, 807, 834, 893
Mercy Without Limits 29, 264, 624, 712
Mérieux Foundation 29, 49, 77, 108, 123, 281, 307,
    348, 416, 446, 496, 529, 585, 698, 807, 851
Meru Hospital 791
Methodist Faith Healing Hospital 273
Methodist Faith Healing Hospital Ankaase 264
Metro Antipolo Hospital and Medical Center 667
Metro City Hospital 561
Metro Diagnostic Center Ltd. 40
Metro Hospital 613
Metro Vigan Cooperative Hospital 667
Mewa Hospital 396
Mezu International Foundation 601
MGH 844
MGM Eye Institute 348
MHS-Massana Hospital 780
Mian Muhammad Bukhsh Trust 624
Mian Muhammad Trust Hospital 633
Micro Hospital Gran Paititi 71
MicroResearch: Africa/Asia 235, 384, 461, 682, 834
Midat Hospital 561
Mid City Hospital 561, 633
Middle East Hospital & Diagnostic Centre 844
Middle-Gobi City General Hospital 499
Middle Ground 306
Midland Doctors Medical Institute 633
Midland International Aid Trust 29, 348, 462, 551,
    601, 624
Midlands Private Hospital 941
Midwife Vision 780
Midwives for Haiti 306
Miga Solutions Foundation 780
Mikindani Hospital 396
Mikolayiv Military Hospital, The 863
Milan Foundation Nepal 551
Mildmay 384, 834
Mildmay Uganda 844
Military and Medical Department of the Security
    Service of Ukraine 863
Military Central Hospital 499
Military Hospital 114, 536, 766
Military Hospital 175 907
Military Hospital at Simferopol 863
Military Hospital at Zhytomyr 864
Military Hospital Bahri 757
Military Hospital Benin 613
Military Hospital Fergana 878
Military Hospital Helipad 757
Military Hospital Port Harcourt 613

Military Medical 766
Military Medical Academy 7 907
Military Medical Center of the Air Force of Ukraine 864
Military Medical Clinical Center of the Eastern Region 864
Military Medical Clinical Center of the Western Region 864
Military Region II Hospital 114
Millen Magese Foundation 780
Milton Park Medical Centre 941
Minbu General Hospital 536
Mindanao Medical Center Inc. 667
Mindanao Sanitarium Hospital 667
Mingala-Don HIV Specialist Hospital 536
Minga Mission Hospital 926
Minh Anh Hospital 907
Mini Hospital 215
Mini Molars Cambodia 108
Minjibir General Hospital 613
Min Ta Su Station Hospital 536
Minya General Hospital 195
Minya University Hospital 195
MiracleFeet 29, 66, 108, 168, 250, 281, 348, 435, 445, 504, 529, 551, 571, 601, 653, 698, 712, 732, 743, 780, 834, 935
Miracle for Africa Foundation 462
Miragoane District Hospital 315
Miragoane Hospital Paillant 315
Mirchaiya Hospital 561
Mirembe Hospital 791
Mirpur Adhunik Hospital & Diagnostic Center 40
Mirror Hospital 40
Mirzaganj Upazila Health Complex 41
Misamis Oriental Provincial Hospital- Gingoog 667
Misamis Oriental Provincial Hospital – Initao 667
Misericorde 92
Misr Al Gadida Military Hospital 195
Misr International Hospital (Dokki Branch) 195
Mission Africa 77, 142, 384, 601
Mission Africa US 601
Mission Bambini 29, 66, 108, 122, 168, 204, 213, 235, 289, 348, 384, 445, 529, 551, 653, 698, 834, 920, 935
Mission Doctors Association 123, 264, 324, 462, 640, 712, 780, 834, 935
Mission Eurasia 851
Mission-Haiti 306
Mission: Haiti 306
Mission Himalaya 551
Mission Hospital 667
Mission Hospital Peshawar 633
Mission Hospital Sialkot 633
Mission Hospital Simikot 561
Mission of Hope 306
Mission of Love 306, 324
Mission Partners for Christ 49, 87
Mission Plasticos 108, 416, 551
Mission Regan 57, 66, 77, 168, 235, 264, 306, 324, 384, 435, 462, 571, 601, 640, 653, 682, 712, 732, 807, 834, 851, 920
Mission: Restore 306, 348, 384, 529, 551, 780
Missions for Humanity 324, 780
Missions Honduras 324
Missions Medical Relief 264
Missions of Grace 571
Missions Without Walls 601
Mission to Heal 264, 384, 496, 653, 834
Mission to Ukraine 851
Mission UpReach 324
Mission Vision 235, 264, 306, 324, 384, 445, 462, 601, 653, 835, 893, 935
Missoula Medical Aid 324
Misungwi Hospital 791
Mitral Foundation 324, 893
Mittaphab (Friendship) Hospital 419
Mityana Hospital 844

MIVO Foundation 306
Mizan-Aman Teaching Hospital 244
Mkazi Hospital 152
Mkhiwa Clinic 222
Mkomaindo District Hospital 792
MKP TMS Hospital 926
Mkula Hospital 792
Mlambe Hospital 468
MMC General Hospital 634
MMG-PPC Cooperative Hospital 667
MMH Thyroid Center 667
M. Napeñas Multi-Specialty Hospital 665
Mnazi Mmoja Hospital Dar es Salaam 792
Mnazi Mmoja Hospital Zanzibar 792
Mncot Hospital 757
Mnero Hospital 792
Mobayi Mbongo General Reference Hospital 176
Mobility Outreach International 306, 698, 712, 893
Modern Dental Care Foundation (MDCF) 445
Moe Myittar Hospital 536
Mogaung Township Hospital 536
Mogok Hospital 536
Mohammed Al-Amin Hamed Children's Hospital 757
Mohanpur Upazila Health Complex 41
Moi Teaching and Referral Hospital 396
Mokattam Specialized Hospital 195
Mokhotlong Hospital 426
Mollahat Upazila Health Complex 41
Molo Medical Missions 384
Molo Sub-County Hospital 396
Mombasa Hospital 396
Mombin Crochu Hospital 315
Momtaz Uddin General Hospital 41
Monarch Specialist Hospital 613
Money for Madagascar 445
Mongolian Palliative Care Society 496
Mongolian society for Pediatric Nephrology 496
Monowara Hospital 41
Montanha 98
Mont Organisé Hospital 315
Monu Miya Hospital 41
Monywa General Hospital 536
Monze Mission Hospital 926
Moon Hospital 41
Moorehouse Mission Hospital (formerly Tboli Evangelical Clinic and Hospital) 667
Mophato oa Mants'ase Society, The 424
Moravian Leprosy Hospital 792
Morbidity Management and Disability Prevention Project (MMPD) 77, 123, 235
More Than Medicine 306, 384, 601, 835
Morning Star 718, 747
Morogoro Hospital 792
Morogoro Regional Hospital 792
Moroto Regional Referral Hospital 844
Morshyn Lviv City Hospital 864
Mossy Foot Project, The 235
Mostafa Kamel Hospital for Armed Forces 195
Motebang Hospital 426
Motech Life-UK 264
Mother and Child Center Maternity Hospital Base #2 864
Mother and Child General Hospital 667
Mother and Child Healthcare Center 634
Mother Care Hospital 41
Mother & Child Hospital 634
Mother Earth (Eejii Yertunts) 496
Mother Of Christ Specialist Hospital 613
mothers2mothers (m2m) 14, 264, 384, 424, 462, 515, 780, 835, 920
Mothers and Children Support International 835
Mother Teresa Foundation 348
Mottama District Hospital 536
Mount Adora Hospital – Akhalia 41
Mountain Medical Institute, The 561
Mount Elgon Hospital 845
Mount Hagen General Hospital 642

Mount Meru Regional Hospital 792
Mount Sinai Kyabirwa Surgical Facility 844
Moyo Hospital 792, 844
Moyo Safi Wa Maria Health Care 792
MPACT for Mankind 168, 307, 835
M-PESA Foundation 382
Mpigi Hospital 844
Mpilo Central Hospital 941
M. P. Shah Hospital 395
Mpwapwa District Hospital 792
Mrara Hospital 792
MRC/UVRI & LSHTM Uganda Research Unit 845
MRT Diagnostika 878
MSD for Mothers 108, 168, 189, 236, 307, 348, 384, 462, 515, 529, 601, 653, 682, 698, 780, 835, 851, 894, 920
MSF – Bon Marché 176
MSF Hospital 736
MSI Reproductive Choices (Marie Stopes International) 29, 66, 77, 108, 168, 236, 265, 348, 384, 445, 462, 496, 529, 551, 585, 601, 624, 640, 698, 712, 743, 780, 799, 835, 894, 920, 935
Mt. Carmel Medical Center 667
Mt. Darwin Hospital 941
Mt. Selinda Hospital 941
Mua Mission Hospital 462, 468
Muberure 92
Mufindi Orphans 781
Mugana Designated District Hospital 792
Mugda Medical College and Hospital 41
Mugendo 92
Mugwagwa Elderly Foundation Trust 935
Muhammad Buhari Specialist Hospital 613
Muhammad Hospital Faisalabad 634
Muheza DDH 792
Muhima Hospital 687
Muhimbili National Hospital 792
Muhweza 92
Mukachevo Central District Hospital 864
Mukesh Madhvani Children's Hospital 845
Mukhtar A. Sheikh Hospital 624
Mukinge Mission Hospital 926
Mukono Church of Uganda Hospital 845
Mukura Hospital 687
Mulago National Referral Hospital 845
Mulanje District Hospital 468
Mulanje Mission Hospital 462, 468
Multi-Agency International Training and Support (MAITS) 29, 108, 236, 265, 348, 384, 551, 624, 653, 682, 743, 835, 920
Multidisciplinary Children's Hospital 878
Multidisciplinary Hospital #3 Razdolinovka 864
Multidisciplinary Hospital of St. Catherine's Clinic 864
Multiprofile Central District Hospital 864
Multipurpose Medical Center 878
Mumbai Cancer Care 348
Mumbwa General Hospital 926
Mumias Mission Hospital 396
Mumtaz Bakhtawar Memorial Trust Hospital Wahdat Road Branch 634
Muna Foundation Nepal 551
Mundindi 845
Municipal City Clinical Hospital #3 of Lviv 864
Municipal City Clinical Hospital #8 of Lviv 864
Municipal City Clinical Hospital of Ambulance of Lviv 864
Municipal Clinical Maternity Hospital #1 864
Municipal Institution Staroosotsky Children's Regional Anti-Tuberculosis Sanatorium 864
Munkhtenger Hospital 499
Munshiganj District Hospital 41
Muqrin University Hospital 757
Muradnagar Upazila Health Complex 41
Murambinda Mission Hospital 941
Murang'a Level 5 Hospital 396

Nepal Cancer Hospital and Research Centre 562
Nepal Eye Hospital 551
Nepal Fertility Care Center (NFCC) 551
Nepalgunj Medical College 562
Nepal Healthcare Equipment Development
    Foundation (NHEDF) 551
Nepal Heart Foundation 551
Nepal Korea Friendship Hospital 562
Nepal Leprosy Trust 551
Nepal Medical College and Teaching Hospital 562
Nepal Mediciti Hospital 562
Nepal National Hospital 562
Nepal Netra Jyoti Sangh (NNJS) 552
Nepal Orthopaedic Hospital 562
Nepal Skin Hospital 562
Nepal Youth Foundation 552
Neshuro District Hospital 941
NEST 360 385, 462, 601, 781
Nestling Trust, The (TNT) 552
Netcare Nhamacunda 521
Netra Jyoti Charitable Trust 348
Netrakona Ideal Hospital Private, Ltd. 41
Netrokona District Hospital 41
Network for Improving Critical Care Systems and
    Training (NICST) 29, 462, 624, 743
Neuro-Psychiatric Hospital Aro Abeokuta 613
Neuro-Psychiatric Specialist Hospital Akure 613
Neuroscience Foundation For Africa 385
New Amda Hospital 562
New Bayugan Medical Hospital 667
Newborn, Infant, and Child Health International
    (NICHE) 123, 435
New Delhi Children's Hospital & Research Centre
    (NDCHRC) 348
New Edubiase Government Hospital 273
New Era General Hospital 667
New Frontiers Health Force 385
New Hope in Africa 516
New Horizons Collaborative 123, 168, 220, 236,
    385, 424, 602, 682, 835, 920, 935
New Hospital of Bordj Badji Mokhtar, The 8
New Life Health Care Pvt. Ltd. 562
New Life Home Trust UK 385
Newlife Hospital 273
New National Hospital Guadalupe 208
New Nyaza Provincial General Hospital 396
New Orleans Medical Mission Services, Inc. 32, 571
New Padrna Hospital 562
New Point Hospital 396
New Referral Hospital of Baucau 801
New Sight Eye Care 157
New Sinai MDI Hospital 667
Newstart Children's Home, The 935
New Sultan Kudarat Provincial Hospital 667
New Town Hospital 273
New University Hospital 195
New Wa Regional Hospital 273
New Yangon General Hospital 536
NextSteps Cambodia 108
Nga Bay City General Hospital 907
Nga Nam Town General Hospital 907
Ngapali Hospital 536
Ngarama Hospital 687
Ngoc Hien District Medical Center 907
Ngọc Linh 907
Ngo Quyen General Hospital 907
Ngoyoni Hospital 792
Ngudu Hospital 792
Nguludi Mission Hospital 469
Ngulyati H/C 792
Nguruka Hospital 792
Nguyễn Trãi Hospital 907
Nguyen Tri Phuong Hospital 907
Ngwe Moe Hospital 537
Nhà hộ Sinh A 907
Nhaka Foundation 935
Nha Khoa 907

Nhowe Mission 936
Nhowe Mission Brian Lemons Memorial
    Hospital 941
Niazi Hospital 634
Niaz Memorial Hospital 634
Nibedita Shishu Hospital Ltd. 41
Nicaragua Adventist Hospital 578
Nicaragua Global Health Project 571
Nicaraguan Medical Mission 571
Nicaragua-Projekt e.V. 571
Nidan Hospital 562
Nidhi Foundation 348
Niger Delta University Teaching Hospital,
    Okolobiri 613
Niger Foundation Hospital & Diagnostic Center 613
Nigeria Air Force Base Referral Hospital Daura 613
Nigerian Air Force (NAF) Hospital 613
Nigerian Navy Reference Hospital Calabar 613
Nigerian Police Hospital – Falomo 613
Ni'ima Consultant Hospital Bauchi 613
Nikki-Hospital 53
Nikolaev Regional Hospital, The 864
Nikopol City Hospital #1 864
Nikopol City Hospital #3 864
Nile Health Insurance Hospital 195
Nile Hospital 195
Nile International Hospital 845
Ninh Binh Obstetrics and Pediatrics Hospital 907
Ninh Hoa Town Hospital 907
Niola Cancer Care Foundation 602
Nipa District Hospital 642
Nishtar Hospital 634
Nizamiye Hospital 613
Nizhnosirogozka Central District Hospital 864
Nizhyn Central City Hospital M. Halytsky 864
Njoro Sub-County Hospital 396
Nkawie-Toase Government Hospital 273
Nkawkaw Holy Family Hospital 273
Nkenkaasu District Government Hospital 273
Nkhata District Hospital 469
Nkhoma Hospital 469
Nkhotakota District Hospital 469
Nkinga Hospital 792
Nkoaranga Hospital 792
Nko Foundation 602
Nkozi Hospital 845
Nkwabeng Hospital 273
Nkwenda 792
NLAH – Northern Luzon Adventist Hospital 667
NLR International 348, 516, 552
Nnadozie Integrated Development Foundation 602
Nnamdi Azikiwe University Teaching Hospital
    Nnewi 613
No. 2 Military Hospital 537
Nobel Hospital 562
Nobel Medical College Teaching Hospital 562
NOBSAMS Hospital 613
Nodado General Hospital 667
Nokor Tep Foundation 108
Nokor Tep Women's Hospital 114
Noma Children Hospital Sokoto 613
Noma Fund 123
Nomun Clinic Hospital 499
Noor Foundation, The 624
Noori Hospital 634
Noor Mohammadi Specialist Hospital 195
Nordic Medical Centre (NMC) 236
Nordic Network for Global Surgery and Anesthesia,
    The 462
Noreen Nishat Welfare Hospital 634
Norsup Hospital 885
North American Council of Eastern Nigeria Adventist
    (NACENA) 602
Northeast Hope for Haiti 307
North East Medical College & Hospital 41
Northeast VOSH 204, 324, 571
Northern Benguet District Hospital 667

Northern Command Military Hospital 926
Northern Community Eye Hospital 274
Northern District Hospital 885
Northern Medical College & Hospital 41
Northern Mindanao Medical Center 667
Northern Palawan Provincial Hospital 667
Northern Samar Provincial Hospital 667
North Legon Hospital 273
North Okkalapa Teaching & General Hospital 537
North Point Hospital 562
Northwestern University Feinberg School of
    Medicine: Institute for Global Health 66, 108, 682
Northwest Haiti Christian Mission (NWHCM) 307
Northwest Medical Volunteers 108
Norton Hospital 941
Norvik Hospital 845
Norwegian People's Aid 14, 66, 108, 168, 204, 324,
    416, 516, 529, 682, 723, 733, 763, 894, 936
Notre Dame des Pins d'Orianie 315
Notre Dame Hospital 667
Nouadhibou Regional Hospital 476
Novamed 490
Nova Ukraine 851
Novick Cardiac Alliance 851, 936
Nov Maternity Hospital 766
Novolodolazka Central Hospital 864
Novomoskovsk Central City Hospital 864
Novomoskovsk Central District Hospital 864
Novomykolayiv Tuberculosis Hospital 864
Novorozdil City Hospital 864
Novosanzharsk Central District Hospital 864
Novoselytsia Central District Hospital 864
Novotroitsk Tuberculosis Hospital 864
Novoukrainian City Hospital 865
Novoushinsk Central District Hospital 865
Novoyarychiv District Hospital 865
Novoyavorivsk District Hospital #1 865
NPI Narayani Samudayik Hospital 552
NRI SEVA Foundation 349
Nsawam Hospital 274
Nshambya Hospital 792
NSIF Hospital 129
Ntcheu District Hospital 469
Ntchisi Hospital 469
NTD Advocacy Learning Action (NALA) 236
Ntsekhe Hospital 426
Nuestra Señora de Piat District Hospital 667
Nuestros Pequeños Hermanos (NPH) 66, 204, 307,
    324, 571
Nuestros Pequeños Hermanos (Our Little Brothers
    and Sisters) New Zealand 66, 204, 307, 324, 571
Nueva Vizcaya Medical Mission Group Hospital, Inc. 667
Nueva Vizcaya Provincial Hospital 667
Number One Health Station 244
Nurse on a Mission 324
Nurses on world mission 653
Nurses with Purpose 168
Nursing Beyond Borders 108, 265, 416, 653
Nurture Africa 835
NuVasive Spine Foundation (NSF) 236, 324, 385,
    497, 835
Nyabiraba 93
Nyadire Mission Hospital 941
Nyagatare Hospital 687
Nyagi 307, 552, 571, 781
Nyahururu County Referral Hospital 396
Nyakahanga Designated District Hospital 792
Nyakaraye 93
Nyakibale Hospital 845
Nyala Turkish Hospital 757
Nyalwanzaja 792
Nyamagana Hospital 792
Nyamiaga Hospital 792
Nyangena Hospital 396
Nyanza District Hospital 687
Nyanza Hospital 687
Nyarko Cleft Care 265

Pakhtaobod Hospital 767
Pakistan Children's Heart Foundation (PCHF) 625
Pakistan Eye Bank Society (PEBS) Eye & General Hospital 634
Pakistan Institute for Medical Sciences 634
Pakistan Kidney Patients Association 625
Pak Medical Centre 625
Pak Mission Society 625
Pakokku General Hospital 537
Paksong Hospital 419
Palanan Station Hospital 668
Palav 265, 350, 386, 743
Palawan Baptist Hospital 668
Palawan Medical City 668
Palaw Township Hospital 537
Palayan City Hospital 668
Palcare: The Jimmy S Bilimoria Foundation 350
Palestine Hospital 195
Pallisa Hospital 845
Pallium India 350
Palm Beach Hospital 396
Palms Care foundation 350
Pamo Clinics And Hospitals 613
Pampanga Medical Specialist Hospital 668
Panabo Polymedic Hospital 668
Pan-African Academy of Christian Surgeons (PAACS) 87, 123, 123, 189, 189, 236, 236, 386, 386, 463, 463, 585, 585, 682, 781, 781
Pan African Thoracic Society (PATS) 123, 386, 463, 781
PANAHF – Pan Africa Heart Foundation 265, 386
Panay Health Care Multi-Purpose Cooperative Hospital 668
Panchagarh General Hospital 41
Panchamukhi Nagarik Hospital Pvt. Ltd. 562
Panchbibi Upazila Health Complex 42
Panchthar Hospital 562
Pandan District Hospital 668
Pandya Memorial Hospital 396
Panfilov District General Hospital 410
Pangaea Zimbabwe Aids Trust (PZAT) 936
Pangasinan Provincial Hospital 668
Panglong Hospital 537
Pangsha Upazila Health Complex 42
Panguma Hospital 718, 747
Paniqui General Hospital 668
Panopdopan District Hospital 668
Pan Pacific Hospital, Training & Research Institute Ltd. 41
Pantang Hospital 274
Panzi Hospital 176
Panzi Hospital and Foundations 168
PAPUA NEW GUINEA TRIBAL FOUNDATION 640
Parable 93
Paracelis District Hospital 668
Paradise Hospital 767
Paradise Private Hospital 643
Paragon Hospital 845
Parami General Hospital 537
Parami Shin Hospital 537
Paray Hospital 426
Paray Mission Hospital 426
Parirenyatwa General Hospital 941
Parkland Hospital 562
Paro District Hospital 59
PARSA Trust 625
Partners for Development (PfD) 14, 49, 109, 157, 417, 436, 602, 781
Partners for Visual Health 204
Partners for World Health 30, 109, 123, 682, 699, 712, 782, 836
Partnership for Sustainable Development (PSD) Nepal 553
Partners in Compassionate Care 733
Partners in Health 87, 308, 424, 436, 446, 463, 553, 682, 713
Partners in Hope 463, 469
Pasay City General Hospital 668

Pascual General Hospital 668
PASHA 553, 763
Pasig City Children's Hospital 668
Pasig City General Hospital 668
Pastoralist Child Foundation 386
Pasua Hospital 792
Patan Hospital 562
Patcha Foundation 123, 713
Patenga Naval Hospital 42
PATH 78, 109, 169, 204, 236, 251, 265, 325, 350, 386, 463, 516, 530, 553, 572, 602, 699, 782, 836, 851, 894, 921
Pathein Hospital 537
Pathfinder International 30, 78, 87, 169, 189, 236, 350, 363, 386, 516, 530, 586, 602, 625, 782, 807, 836
Patients Helping Fund, The 753
Patients Welfare Foundation: PWF Pakistan 625
Patient Welfare Society Denmark Pakistan [Anjuman-e-Behbood-e-Mareezan Denmark Pakistan (ABMDP)] 625
Patuakhali Medical College Hospital 42
Patuakhali Sadar Hospital 42
Paukkhaung Hospital 537
Pauktaw Township Hospital 537
Paul Carlson Partnership 169
Paul Chester Children's Hope Foundation, The 308, 386, 504
Paulino Hospital 668
Paungbyin Township Hospital 537
Pavlograd Central District Hospital 865
Pavlograd City Hospital #4 865
Pavlohrad City Hospital #1 865
PCEA Chogoria Hospital 396
PCEA Kikuyu Hospital 386
PCEA Kikuyu Hospital 396
P. D. Hinduja Hospital and Medical Research Centre 349
PEACE 189
Peace and Hope Trust 572
Peace and Love Hospital 274
Pearl International Hospital 634
Pearl of Africa Child Care 836
Pearl of Health Hospital 926
Pecheneg CRH 865
Pediatric Health Initiative 463, 782, 836
Pediatric Universal Life-Saving Effort, Inc. (PULSE) 308, 325, 386, 553
Pedro L. Gindap Municipal Hospital 668
PEDSI Global Health 30
Peedh Parai International 350
PEEDO Davao del Norte Hospital – Igacos Zone (formerly Samal District Hospital) 668
Peerless Hospital 613
Pella Area Teams to Honduras (PATTH) 325
Penn State College of Medicine: Global Health Center 265
Penn State College of Medicine: Global Health Center 921
People for Change 251, 699
People's Hospital 757
People's Hospital 115 907
People's Hospital Ltd., Chattogram 42
Peoples Medical College Hospital – Nawabshah 634
People to People 237
People to People Canada (P2P) 213, 237
Pepal 350, 530, 782, 836
Perehinskaya Hospital #2 Perehinskaya Village Council 865
Perescrepin District Hospital #2 of Dnipropetrovsk Regional Council 865
Perinatal Center of Kyiv, The 865
Perinatal Center of Mariupol 865
Perinatal Center of Navoi Region 878
Perpetual Help Hospital 668
Perpetual Succor Hospital 668
Perpetual Succour Hospital 668

Perspective for Children 836
Pervomaisk Multidisciplinary City Hospital 865
Pervomaysk Central District Hospital 865
Peterborough Paramedics & Beyond (PPAB) 308, 572
Petroleum Gas – Petrogas Hospital 195
Petroleum Hospital 195
Petrykivska Central District Hospital 865
Pfalzklinikum 683
Pharmacists Without Borders Canada 78, 109, 308, 325, 386, 474, 487, 586, 733, 763
Phase Worldwide 553
Phebe Hospital & School of Nursing 439
Philani Maswati Charity 220
Philia Foundation 134, 157, 386, 504, 586, 699
Philippine Children's Medical Center 669
Philippine General Hospital (PGH) 669
Philippine Heart Center 669
Philippine Leprosy Mission, Inc. 653
Philippine Medical Association of New England 654
Philippine National Police (PNP) General Hospital 669
Philippine Orthopedic Center 669
Philips Foundation 169, 181, 265, 350, 386, 446, 553, 699, 807
Phillips Renner Foundation 350, 553, 921
Phil Simon Clinic: Tanzania Project 782
Phnom Penh Referral Hospital 114
Phoenix International Foundation, Inc. 109, 654
Phoenix Rising for Haiti 308
Phong Dien General Hospital 907
Phòng khám ACC Đà Nẵng 907
Phòng Khám BS Phước 907
Phòng Khám Đa Khoa 907
Phòng Khám Đa Khoa An Phúc 908
Phòng khám đa khoa khu vực Tân Thành 908
Phòng Khám Đa KHoa Quốc Tế Hà Nội – Y Tế Quốc Tế Việt 908
Phòng Khám YHCT Gia Đức 907
Phòng trực cấp cứu 908
Phu Gyi Hospital 537
Phulpur Upazila Health Complex 42
Phung Chau Medical Station 907
Phung Hiep District Medical Center 907
Phu Nhuan District Hospital 907
Phuntsholing Hospital 59
Phuoc Binh Medical Station 907
Phuoc Long-Bac Lieu District Hospital 907
Phuong Chau International Hospital 907
Phu Phong General Hospital 907
Phu Tho Provincial General Hospital 907
Physicians Across Continents 30, 109, 157, 386, 474, 504, 602, 683, 753, 815, 836
Physicians for Peace 204, 325, 463, 572
Physiopneumological Rehabilitation Center for Children Tirnova 490
Physiotherapeutic Hospital of Khujand 767
Piccola Opera Specialist Hospital 613
Picture of Health Foundation 308, 386, 436, 602, 699
Pidbuzka District Hospital 865
Pidkaminska City Hospital 865
Piggs Peak Government Hospital 222
Pina Hospital 562
PINCC Preventing Cervical Cancer 49, 88, 109, 265, 325, 350, 386, 463, 516, 683, 782
Pinlon Hospital 537
Pinnacle Flyover Hospital 396
PINUM Cancer Hospital 634
Pioduran District Hospital 669
Pioneer Christian Hospital 157, 159
Pioneer Hospital and Diagnostic Center Ltd. 42
Pirimiti Community Hospital 469
PISAM 367
Pishchan District Hospital 865
PIVOT 446
Plainsview Hospital 396

Radiant Hospital 397
Radiation and Isotopes Centre Khartoum – Amal
  Tower 757
Radyvyliv Central District Hospital 866
Rafatullah Community Hospital 42
Rafiq Anwar Memorial Trust Hospital,
  Gujranwala 634
Rahbar Foundation 351
Rahbar Trust 625
Rai Ali Nawaz Foundation Hospital 634
Railroad Hospital 176
Railway General Hospital 42
Railway Hospital 634, 866
Railway Hospital Qarshi City 878
Rainbow Humanitarian Caretaker Foundation 237
Raindrops Children's Foundation 351
Raipur Upazila Health Complex 42
Raise and Support The Poor (RSP) 109
Raising Malawi 387, 463
Rajapur Upazila Health Complex 42
Rajhar Ayurved Aushadhalaya 562
Rajiv Gandhi Mahila Vikas Pariyojana (RGMVP) 351
Rajoir Upazila Health Complex 42
Rajshahi Cancer Hospital and Research Center
  Trust 42
Rajshahi Eye Hospital 42
Rajshahi Shishu Hospital 42
Rakai Health Sciences Program 836
Raleigh Fitkin Memorial Hospital 222
Rama Specialist Hospital 758
Ramechhap District Hospital 562
RAM Foundation 625
RAM Hospital 397
Ramirez Bautista Memorial Hospital 669
Ramon D. Duremdes District-Hospital (Dumangas
  District Hospital) 669
Ramon Maza Sr. Memorial District Hospital 669
Ramos General Hospital 669
Ranada General Hospital 669
Randle General Hospital 614
Rangamati General Hospital 42
Rangpur Medical College Hospital 42
Rano General Hospital 614
Rapid Response 351
Rapti Sub-Regional Hospital 562
Rare Disease Ghana Initiative 266
Ras Desta Hospital 244
Ras El Bar Central Hospital 195
Rasheed Shekoni Specialist Hospital 614
Ras Sidr General Hospital 195
Ratanakiri Provincial Referral Hospital 114
Ratna Nidhi Charitable Trust 351
Ravi Hospital 634
Rawalpindi Eye Donors Organization 625
Rawalpindi Institute of Cardiology 634
Rayos-Valentin Hospital INC 669
Rays of Hope Hospice Jinja 836
Razdolne District Hospital 866
RD Rwanda 683
Reach 190, 387, 654, 799
Reach Beyond 30, 530, 553, 743
REACH Shirati 782
Real Love Ministries International 308
Real Medicine Foundation (RMF) 190, 308, 351, 387,
  400, 516, 530, 553, 603, 625, 654, 733, 743, 836
Rebecca Foundation, The 266
Reconstructing Women International 30, 308, 351,
  625, 782
Recuenco General Hospital 669
Red Cross Hospital 793
Red Cross – Panauti 562
Red Cross – Patan 562
Red Descentralizada de Salud La Unión La
  Iguala 330
Redemption Hospital 439
Reemee Medicare Nig. Ltd 614
Refugee Empowerment International 530

Refuge Egypt 190
Regal Hospital 614
Regency Hospital 793
Regent Hospital Ltd. 42
Regional Adult Multidisciplinary Medical Center,
  Termez 878
Regional Allergy Hospital 866
Regional Children's Clinical Hospital 866
Regional Children's Hospital M. Slovyansk 866
Regional Clinical and Diagnostic Laboratory 866
Regional Clinical Hospital for Rehabilitation and
  Diagnostics 866
Regional Clinical Psychoneurological Hospital 866
Regional Hospital at Nzérékoré 284
Regional Hospital for Disabled Veterans 866
Regional Hospital Karabollo 767
Regional Infectious Diseases Hospital 866
Regional Interdistrict Diagnostic Center in
  Korosten 866
Regional Maternity Hospital 767
Regional Medical Center for Human
  Reproduction 866
Regional Medical Consulting and Diagnostic Center
  of the Zhytomyr Regional Council 866
Regional Municipal Institution Chernivtsi Oblast
  Clinical Hospital 866
Regional Ophthalmological Hospital 866
Regional Psychiatric Hospital 767
Regional Psychiatric Hospital Village Orlivka 866
Regional Specialized Children's Sanatorium
  Pulmonological 866
Region II Trauma and Medical Center (R2TMC) 669
Rehabilitation Center Elite 866
Rehabilitation Hospital of Quang Ninh 908
Reliance Foundation 351
Relief International 30, 266, 530, 625, 654, 733, 754
REMA 93
Remedios Trinidad Romualdez Hospital 669
Remote Area Medical Volunteer Corps 308, 654
RENEW 57
Renk Civil Hospital 736
Renk Military Hospital 736
Rep. Pedro G. Trono Memorial Hospital 669
Republican AIDS Center of Uzbekistan 878
Republican Center of Mother and Child 490
Republican Clinical Hospital #1 878
Republican Clinical Hospital of the Ministry of Health
  of Ukraine 866
Republican Clinical Ophthalmological Hospital 878
Republican Dermatovenerologic Dispensary 878
Republican Psychiatric Hospital 410
Republican Research Center of Neurosurgery 878
Republican Scientific Center for Emergency Medical
  Aid 878
Republican Scientific Center for Emergency Medical
  Aid, Termez 878
Republican Specialized Scientific and Practical
  Medical Center for Dermatovenereology and
  Cosmetology 878
Republican Specialized Scientific and Practical
  Medical Center of Pediatrics 878
Rescue Hope 325, 387, 836
Research Institute for Tropical Medicine 669
Research Institute of Hematology and Blood
  Transfusion 878
Research Institute of Ophthalmology 195
Reshetyliv Central Hospital of Reshetyliv City Council
  of Poltava Region 866
Resolute Health Outreach 237
Resource Exchange International 181, 181, 190,
  190, 417, 417, 894, 894
RESTORE HOPE: LIBERIA 436
Restore Sight 204, 325
RestoringVision 30, 50, 57, 66, 78, 88, 109, 123,
  134, 142, 151, 157, 169, 181, 190, 204, 213, 220,
  237, 251, 266, 281, 308, 325, 351, 363, 387, 400,
  408, 417, 436, 446, 463, 480, 487, 497, 504, 516,

  530, 553, 572, 586, 603, 625, 640, 654, 683, 699,
  713, 723, 733, 743, 754, 763, 782, 807, 837, 851,
  875, 883, 894, 921, 936
Resunga Hospital 562
ReSurge International 30, 57, 66, 109, 220, 325,
  351, 516, 530, 553, 572, 654, 782, 894, 921, 936
Ret. Pray. Love Foundation 603
Rezaul Haque Trust Hospital 42
RHD Action 351, 553, 782, 837
Rheumatology for All 237
Ribat University Hospital 758
Ricardo Limso Medical Center – Surgery and
  Pediatrics Clinic 669
Ricardo P. Rodriguez Memorial Hospital 669
Rice 360 Institute for Global Health 463
Rice Foundation 325
Richgrace Family Healthcare Foundation 603
Rico Hospital 669
Riddhi Siddhi Charitable Trust 351
Riders for Health 251, 424, 436, 464, 603
Riders for Health International 251, 387, 424, 436,
  464, 603, 921, 936
Ridge Hospital 274
Ridon's St. Jude Medical Center 669
Right to Care 424, 464, 921
Right to Sight and Health 109, 123, 266, 308, 572,
  654, 699
Rim and Men's Hospital 244
Rinat Akhmetov Foundation 851
Ripple Africa 464
Risen Savior Missions 654
Rising Star Outreach 351
Riverside Hospital 42
Riverside Medical Center 669
Rivers State University Hospital (RUST) 614
Rivne Central City Hospital 866
Rivne City Hospital 866
Rivne Regional Hospital for War Invalids 866
Rivne Regional Perinatal Center 866
Rizal Provincial Hospital 669
Rizal Provincial Hospital System 669
Rizal Provincial Hospital System Angono Annex 669
Road Clinical Hospital 866
Road Clinical Hospital, Donetsk Station 866
Robert Clemente Health Clinic, The 572
Rockefeller Foundation, The 50, 66, 78, 88, 109,
  124, 142, 151, 169, 213, 237, 251, 281, 289, 325,
  363, 387, 408, 424, 436, 446, 464, 474, 497, 517,
  530, 553, 586, 625, 683, 699, 713, 763, 782, 807,
  837, 875, 894, 921, 936
Roddom Hospital 767
Roddom Regional Hospital 767
R.O. Diagan Cooperative Hospital 669
Roel I. Senador M.D. Memorial Hospital 669
Rogaciano M. Mercado Memorial Hospital 669
Rogelio M. Garcia Memorial Hospital 670
Rogo General Hospital 614
Rohatyn Central District Hospital 867
Rokytnivsky Multiprofile Hospital for Intensive
  Treatment 867
Rolpa District Hospital 562
Romana Pangan District Hospital 670
Roman Catholic Health Mission 614
Romanivsk Central District Hospital 867
Romenskaya Central District Hospital 867
Rophi Hospital 274
Rosales Chua Pun Memorial Hospital 670
Rosario District Hospital 670
Rosario Maclang Bautista General Hospital 670
Rosario Memorial Hospital of Guagua, Inc. 670
Rosa Vera Fund, The 67
Rose Charities International 109, 237, 309, 446,
  553, 654, 743, 837, 894, 921
Rose Hill ENT & General Hospital 537
Rose of Sharon Mediplex 614
Rosso Hospital 476, 30
Rotaplast International 190, 204, 237, 351, 436,

530, 554, 654, 782, 807, 895

Rotary Action Group for Family Health & AIDS Prevention (RFHA) 30, 50, 266, 351, 363, 424, 603, 807, 837

Rotary International 7, 14, 30, 50, 57, 67, 78, 88, 97, 109, 124, 134, 142, 151, 157, 169, 181, 190, 204, 214, 220, 237, 251, 266, 281, 289, 309, 326, 351, 363, 387, 401, 408, 417, 424, 436, 446, 464, 474, 480, 487, 497, 504, 517, 530, 554, 572, 586, 603, 626, 640, 654, 683, 690, 699, 713, 723, 733, 743, 754, 763, 782, 799, 807, 815, 837, 851, 875, 883, 895, 921, 936

ROW Foundation 67, 169, 237, 281, 309, 351, 387, 436, 464, 603, 713, 754, 782, 837, 922, 936

Roxas Medicare Hospital 670
Roxas Memorial Provincial Hospital 670
Royal Angkor International Hospital 114
Royal Ash Hospital 274
Royal Bhutan Army Hospital 59
Royal Care and Surgical Hospital 42
Royal Care International Hospital 758
Royal Hospital 195, 537
Royal Hospital (Level 4) 397
Royal Hospital Limited 42
Royal Hospital – Phnom Penh 114
Rozhnyativ District Hospital 867
RRC Hospital 867
Ruaraka Uhai Neema Hospital 397
Rubaga Hospital 845
Ruel Foundation 654
Rugarama Hospital 845
Rukhsana Foundation 626
Rukundo International 837
Rumphi District Hospital 469
Rural Development Trust 351
Rural Health Care Foundation Uganda 837
Rural Health Unit – RHU TBOLI 670
Rural Hospital of Morrumbala 521
Rusape General Hospital 941
Rushere Community Hospital 845
Rusitu Mission Hospital 941
Russian Military Hospital 767
Rutgers New Jersey Medical School 30, 67, 110, 237, 266, 309, 351, 387, 572, 626, 654, 683, 713, 936
Ruth Foundation, The 654
Ruth Gaylord Hospital Maganjo 837, 845
Ruth Paz Foundation 326
Ruvuma Regional Hospital 793
Ruzhyn District Hospital 867
Rwamagana Hospital 687
Rwanda Children 683
Rwanda Diabetes Association 683
Rwanda Legacy of Hope 683
Rwanda Military Hospital 687
Rwanda Red Cross 687
Rwinkwavu Hospital 687
SAAR Foundation 352
Sabakuwa Yamma 614
Sabasaba Hospital 793
Sabatia Eye Hospital 387
Sabs Hospital 274
Sacred Heart Hospital 670
Sacred Heart Hospital of Malolos, Inc. 670
Sa Dec Hospital 908
Sadr Esna Hospital 195
Saej Yahya Public Facility 8
Safari Doctors 387
Safe Anaesthesia Worldwide 251, 554, 782, 837
Safe Harbor International 387, 683, 733, 754, 837
Safe Places Uganda Foundation 837
Safwat Al Golf Hospital 195
Sagarmatha Zonal Hospital 562
Saghatta Upazila Health Complex 42
Saham Foundation 14, 504, 699
Sahara Hospital 562
Sahibzada Fazal Rehman Charity Hospital 634

Sahla Hospital 196
Sahodar Hospital 562
Sahyog Foundation 352
Sai Archana Hospital 562
Saidia Watoto 793
Said Mittha Hospital 634
Saidu Dange Railway Hospital 614
Saigon Can Tho Eye Hospital 908
Saigon General Hospital 908
Saigon International Obstetrics and Gynecology Hospital 908
Saigon Pharmaceutical and Medical School Hospital 908
Saimangkorn International Hospital 419
Saint Anne's Hospital 941
Saint Anthony College Hospital 670
Saint Anthony Mother and Child Hospital 670
Saint Catherine Hospital 196
Saint Catherine of Alexandria Medical Arts Building 670
Saint Catherine's Hospital 845
Saint David 93
Sainte Claire de Corail 315
Saint Elizabeth Hospital 670
Saint Felix Medical Hospital 670
Saint Francis International Medical Mission 326, 572
Saint Gerard General Hospital 670
Saint Joseph Hospital 81
Saint Joseph's Catholic Hospital 436
Saint Lawrence Hospital 670
Saint Louis University Inc., Hospital of the Sacred Heart, Baguio City 670
Saint Lucy Foundation 530, 783
Saint Luke Hospital Croix de Bouquets 315
Saint Martin Mission Hospital 670
Saint Mary's Hospital 397
Saint Paul Hospital 908
Saint Pio Hospital 670
Saint Rock Haiti Foundation 309
Saint Sauveur 93
Saints Francis and Paul General Hospital 670
Saira Memorial Hospital 634
SAJIDA Foundation 30
Sakhnovshchynsk Central District Hospital 867
Sakinah Medical outreach 603
Sakura Hospital 537
Salaaman Hospital 793
Salaam Baalak Trust 352
Salaga Hospital 274
Salauddin Specialized Hospital 42
Salavan Provincial Hospital 419
Salem Hospital 845
Sali Hospital 793
Salima District Hospital 469
Salin Township Hospital 537
Salvacion Oppus Yñiguez Memorial Provincial Hospital 670
Salvation Army International, The 15, 30, 67, 78, 88, 110, 157, 169, 204, 220, 266, 309, 326, 352, 387, 424, 436, 446, 464, 481, 487, 497, 517, 530, 554, 573, 603, 626, 640, 654, 683, 713, 723, 743, 783, 807, 837, 851, 922, 936
Salve Regina General Hospital, Inc. 670
Samaritan's Purse International Disaster Relief 30, 67, 88, 204, 237, 266, 326, 388, 464, 497, 517, 586, 603, 640, 683, 807, 837, 922, 936
Samarkand City Hospital #1 878
Samarkand Regional Cardiology Hospital 878
Samarkand Regional Hospital 878
Samar Provincial Hospital 670
Samarqand Viloyat Nogironlar Reabilitasiya Markazi 878
Sambir Central District Hospital 867
Sambir City Children's Hospital 867
Samdech Ov Referral Hospital 114
Samdrup Jongkhar General Hospital 59
SAM Hospital 53

Samorita Hospital Limited 42
Sampa Hospital 274
Sampan'asa Loterana Momba ny Fahasalamana Ivory Atsimo 450
SAMU Foundation 309, 504, 554, 654, 743, 754
Sanafi Hospital 215
San Antonio District Hospital 670
San Antonio Medical Center of Lipa, Inc. 670
Sanatoriul Nufarul Alb 490
Sân Bệnh Viện Y Tế Công Cộng 908
Sandema Hospital 274
Sand House District Hospital 537
San Diego de Alcala Hospital 670
Sandoub Health Insurance Hospital 196
San Fernandiño Hospital 670
Sanguere Lim 136
Sani Bello Foundation 603
San Isidro Hospital 670
Sanitas Hospital 793
Sanjeevani 352
San Joaquin Mother and Child Hospital 670
San Juan District Hospital 670
San Juan Rio Relief 573
Sankar Foundation Eye Institute 352
San Lazaro Hospital 670
San Lorenzo Hospital 670
San Lorenzo Ruiz Hospital 670
San Luis District Hospital 670
Sanman 352
San Marcelino District Hospital 670
San Mateo Medical Center 670
San Miguel District Hospital 670
Sanofi Espoir Foundation 7, 31, 50, 78, 124, 134, 151, 169, 220, 281, 326, 352, 364, 388, 446, 464, 474, 497, 504, 530, 586, 626, 683, 699, 713, 733, 783, 807, 815, 837, 851, 922
San Pablo City District Hospital 670
San Pablo City General Hospital 670
San Pascual Baylon Maternity And General Hospital 670
San Pedro Hospital of Davao City, Inc. 670
San Pedro Jose L. Amante Sr. Emergency Hospital 670
San Pya General Hospital 537
San Ramon Hospital 670
San Roque Hospital 671
Santa Ana Hospital 671
Santa Cruz Laguna Polymedic Hospital 671
Santé Communauté Développement 88
Santé Diabète 78, 151, 699, 807
Sante Haiti 309
Santé Pour Tous 93, 315
Santisima Trinidad Hospital 671
Santo Domingo District Hospital 671
Santo Niño Hospital 671
Santos General Hospital 671
Santo Tomas General Hospital 671
Sao San Htun Hospital 537
Sape Agbo Memorial Hospital 274
Saptari Model Hospital 562
Sara District Hospital 671
Sarail Upazila Health Complex 42
Sarbodhaya Sewa Ashram 562
Sariakandi Upazila Health Complex 42
Sarishabari Upazila Health Complex 42
Sarkari Karmachari Hospital 42
Sarny Central District Hospital 867
Saroma Hospital 671
Sarpang Hospital 59
Sarvanga Hospital 562
Sarwar Foundation 626
Sarwar Foundation Hospital Rajana 634
Sasamunga Hospital 724
Sathitun Nesa Eye Hospital 42
Satkhira District Hospital 42
Satkhira Medical College Hospital 42
SATMED 31, 50, 214, 586, 654, 713

St. Martin's Hospital 274
St. Martins Hospital 274
St. Mary Hospital 718, 747
St. Mary's Hospital 274, 397, 643
St. Mary's Hospital Lacor 838, 845
St. Mary's Maternity and Children's Hospital,
    Inc. 672
St Mary's Maternity Hospital 758
St. Mary's Psychiatric Hospital Sembel 215
St. Matia Mulumba Mission Hospital 397
St. Mattheus Medical Hospital 672
St. Michael's Hospital – Pramso 274
St. Monica Katende HC III 845
St. Monica's Hospital 397
St. Nicholas Hospital 274, 614
Sto. Domingo – Bemonc Facility 672
Sto. Nino Hospital 672
Stop TB Partnership Korea 110, 497
Sto. Rosario Hospital 672
St. Otto Hospital 793
St. Paraskeva Medical Center 867
St. Patricks Hospital 275
St. Paul Hospital 672
St. Paul's Hospital 245
St. Paul's Hospital of Iloilo, Inc. 672
St. Pauls Mission Hospital 926
St. Peter's Hospital 275
St. Petros Specialized TB Hospital 245
St. Raphael Divine Mercy Specialist Hospital 614
Stryi Central City Hospital 867
Stryi Central District Hospital 867
Stryi City Children's Hospital 867
St Scholastica Uzima Hospital 389
St. Scholastica Uzima Hospital 397
St. Teresa Hospital 397
St Theresa Mission Hospital Kiirua 389
St. Theresa's Hospital 275
St. Therese De Lima Medical Hospital 672
St Therese MTCC Hospital 671
St. Therese – MTCC Hospital 672
Student Action Volunteer Effort - SAVE Myanmar 531
Students for Kids International Projects (SKIP) 110,
    251, 353, 447, 465, 744, 784, 922
Stung Treng Referral Hospital 114
St. Walburgs Hospital 793
St. Yared Hospital 245
Sub District Hospital 635
Sub District Hospital Tangdar 635
Substation Of Emergency And Emergency Care
    #9 878
Sudak City Hospital 867
Sudan Doctors Union UK 754
Sudanense American Medical Association
    (SAMA) 754
Sudanese and London Association Medical Aids Trust
    (SALAMAT) 754
Sudanese Center for Physical Therapy 758
Sudan Heart Center 758
Sudan Relief Fund 734
Sudovyshnyanskiy City Hospital 867
Suez Canal Authority Hospital 196
Sughd Regional Hospital Khujand 767
Sughra Shafi Medical Complex 635
Suhul Referral Hospital 245
Suhum Government Hospital 275
Sukhbaatar District General Hospital 499
Sule Galadima Garo General Hospital 614
Suleiman Hearing and Educational Foundation 604
Suleiman Zuntu Foundation 604
Suleja Hospital, Niger 614
Sulemana Memorial Hospital Ltd 275
Sultan Hamud Sub District Hospital 397
Sultan Naga Dimaporo Provincial Hospital 672
Sumbawanga Regional Hospital 793
Sumeru City Hospital 563
Sumeru Hospital 563
Summit Hospital 563

Summit in Honduras 326
Sumve DDH Hospital 793
Sumve District Designated Hospital 793
Sumy City Children's Clinical Hospital St.
    Zinaida 867
Sumy City Clinical Hospital #4 867
Sumy City Clinical Maternity Hospital of the Holy
    Virgin Mary 867
Sumy District Central Clinical Hospital 867
Sumy Regional Children's Clinical Hospital 867
Sunamganj Sadar Hospital 43
Sundaram Medical Foundation 353
Sundarganj Upazila Health Complex 43
Sunnah Hospital 614
Sunrise Japan Hospital – Phnom Penh 114
Sunshine Care Foundation Inc. 655
Suntreso Government Hospital 275
Sunyani Municipal Hospital 275
Sunyani Regional Hospital 275
Super Care Hospital 275
Superemos Foundation 573
Supporting Health & Education deserving
    fellows 627
Suraj Eye Institute 353
Surg+ Restore 714
Surgeons for Smiles 31, 214, 604, 655
Surgeons of Service 205, 326
Surgeons OverSeas (SOS) 465, 555, 604, 684, 714
Surgery Hospital at Blantyre 469
Surgical Friends Foundation 67, 111, 310
Surgical Healing of Africa's Youth Foundation,
    The (S.H.A.Y.) 170, 465, 504, 640, 937
Surgical Hope Children's Fund 389
Surgimed Hospital 635
Surgiscope Hospital – Unit 1 43
Surgiscope Hospital – Unit 2 43
Surigao del Norte Provincial Hospital 672
Surigao Medical Center 672
Surkhet Hospital Pvt. Ltd. 563
Susma Koirala Memorial Hospital 563
Sustainabililty for Agriculture, Health, Education and
    Environment (Sahee) 220
Sustainable Cardiovascular Health Equity
    Development Alliance 170, 238, 251, 289, 437,
    640, 714, 838, 937
Sustainable Health Empowerment (SHE) 111
Sustainable Kidney Care Foundation (SKCF) 50, 111,
    124, 170, 238, 267, 310, 364, 604, 784, 838
Sustainable Medical Missions 170, 267, 353, 389,
    684, 839
Sustainable Therapy And New Development (STAND):
    The Haiti Project 310
Sustained Health Initiatives of the Philippines 655
Suvechhya Hospital 563
Svay Rieng Provincial Referral Hospital 114
Sverdlovsk Central City Hospital #1 868
SVG Africa (Salormey Volunteers Group) 267
Svitlovodsk Central District Hospital 868
Swaa-Burundi 93
Swabhiman Hospital Pvt. Ltd. 563
Swadhar Institute for Development of Women and
    Children (Swadhar IDWC) 353
Swan Myittar Hospital 537
Swasti 31, 57, 111, 220, 238, 353, 555, 604, 627,
    640, 684, 744, 895
Swaya 793
Swedish Organization for Global Health 839
Swiss Cottage Hospital Mtwapa 397
Swiss Doctors 31, 353, 389, 655, 714
Swiss Sierra Leone Development Foundation 714
Swiss Tropical and Public Health Institute 7, 15, 31,
    50, 67, 78, 88, 111, 124, 134, 143, 170, 205, 238,
    251, 267, 282, 289, 326, 353, 389, 417, 437, 447,
    465, 487, 497, 504, 517, 531, 555, 573, 586, 604,
    627, 640, 655, 684, 700, 714, 754, 784, 808, 839,
    852, 875, 895, 922, 937
Sylhet MAG Osmani Medical College Hospital 43

Sylhet Women's Medical College Hospital 43
Symbiosis 31
Symbol Hospital 614
Syrian American Medical Society (SAMS) 31, 190,
    627
T1International 170, 251
Tabarak Children's Hospital 758
Tabarak Maternity and Children Hospital (Golf Ground
    Branch) 196
Tabarak Maternity and Children Hospital (New Cairo
    Branch) 196
Tabba Kidney Institute 627
Tabiang Hospital 402
Tacloban City Hospital 672
Tacloban Doctors' Medical Center 672
Tadzhikskiy Gosudarstvennyy Meditsinskiy
    Universitet 767
Tafo Government Hospital 275
Tafo Hospital 275
Taguig-Pateros District Hospital 672
Taha Baashar Psychiatric Hospital 758
Tahira Jamshed Medical Complex 635
Tahir Heart Institute 635
Tahirpur Upazila Health Complex 43
Tahta General Hospital 196
Taiba Hospital 758
Taikkyi Township Hospital 537
Tai Mũi Họng Thành phố Hồ Chí Minh 908
Takeo Referral Hospital 114
Taku District Hospital 537
Takundaing District Hospital 537
Talas Regional Hospital 410
Talavera General Hospital 672
Talnivska Central District Hospital 868
Talon General Hospital 672
Tamale Central Hospital 275
Tamale Teaching Hospital 275
Tamale West Hospital 275
Tam Duong District Hospital 908
Tamghas Hospital 563
Tamil Nadu Foundation 353
Tamparan Medical Foundation Inc. Hospital 672
Tam Tri Hospital 908
Tan An City Medical Center 908
Tanay General Hospital 672
Tan Bien Ward Clinics 908
Tan Binh District Hospital 908
Tandale Hospital 793
Tan Hiep District Hospital 908
Tan Hung Medical Station 908
Tania Specialist Hospital 275
Tanintharyi Township Hospital 537
Tanzania Charitable Hospital 793
Tanzanian Cardiac Hospital Foundation, Inc.
    (TCHF) 784
Tanzania Occupational Health Service 793
Taplejung District Hospital 563
Taraba State Specialist Hospital, Jalingo 614
Tara Foundation 353
Tarail Upazila Health Complex 43
Tarash Eye Hospital 43
Tari Hospital 643
Tarime District Hospital 793
Tariq Hospital 635
Tarlac Provincial Hospital 672
Taro Hospital 724
Tarutyn Central District Hospital 868
Tashkent City Children's Clinical Hospital #3 878
Tashkent City Clinical Emergency Hospital 878
Tashkent City Clinical Hospital #5 878
Tashkent International Clinic 878
Tashkentskaya City Clinical Tuberculosis Hospital
    #1 878
Tashkent Urban Teenage Dispensary 878
Tash-Kumyr Family Medicine Center 410
Task Force for Global Health, The 15, 32, 50, 57, 67,
    78, 88, 97, 111, 124, 134, 143, 157, 170, 190,

205, 214, 220, 238, 252, 267, 282, 289, 310, 326, 353, 364, 389, 401, 408, 417, 425, 437, 447, 465, 474, 481, 487, 497, 505, 517, 531, 555, 573, 586, 604, 627, 641, 655, 684, 700, 714, 723, 734, 744, 754, 764, 784, 808, 815, 839, 852, 875, 883, 895, 922, 937

Taso 845

Tatkon Township Hospital 537

Taulihawa District Hospital 563

Taung Kalay Military Hospital 537

Taung Sun Station Hospital 537

Taung Zun Old Hospital 537

Tawin Nilar Hospital Pyinmana 538

Taw Win Hospital 538

Tay Giang District Hospital 908

Tây Nguyên Optometry 910

Tay Ninh City Hospital 908

Taytay Emergency Hospital 672

TB Alert 354, 465, 922, 937

TB Hospital 43

T.B. Hospital Jessore 43

TB Hospital of Tyup District 410

TB Leprosy Referral Hospital 614

TDC Islamabad 635

Teachers Hospital 196, 538

Teaching Hospital, Karnali Academy of Health Sciences 563

Team 5 Medical Foundation 111, 190, 389, 555, 627

Team Broken Earth 32, 310, 573

Team Canada Healing Hands 310, 389, 839

Team Heart 684

Team Nuestra Familia 205

Team Philippines 655

Tearfund 15, 32, 67, 78, 88, 111, 135, 143, 170, 190, 238, 310, 326, 354, 364, 389, 417, 437, 465, 517, 531, 555, 573, 586, 604, 627, 655, 684, 714, 734, 784, 839, 922, 937

Teasdale-Corti Foundation/St. Mary's Hospital Lacor 839

Tebellong Hospital 426

Tebow CURE Hospital 672

Tefera Hailu Memorial Hospital 245

Tekelehaymanot Hospital 245

Tekeshe Foundation, The 937

Teknaf Upazila Health Complex 43

Telha Foundation 627

Telha Foundation Hospital Karak 635

Tema General Hospital 275

Temakin Clinic 402

Tema Women's Hospital 275

Temeke District Referral Hospital 793

Tenwek Hospital 397

Tepa District Hospital 275

Tepi General Hospital 245

Teplodar Central City Hospital 868

Terebovlya City Hospital 868

Teresita Lopez Jalandoni Provincial Hospital 672

Terhathum District Hospital 563

Ternopil Central District Hospital 868

Ternopil City Children's Municipal Hospital 868

Ternopil City Municipal Ambulance Hospital 868

Ternopil Municipal City Hospital #2 868

Ternopil Regional Children's Clinical Hospital 868

Ternopil Regional Communal Clinical Psychoneurological Hospital 868

Ternopil University Hospital 868

Terokhada Upazila Health Complex 43

Terre des hommes (Tdh) Foundation 32, 50, 78, 88, 190, 282, 310, 354, 389, 447, 474, 487, 505, 531, 555, 573, 586, 604, 627, 700, 734, 808, 815, 852

Terrewode Women's Fund 839

Territorial Hospital at Ulitsa Lenina 410

Territorial Hospital of Tash-Kumyr 410

Territorial Medical Association of the Ministry of Internal Affairs of Ukraine in Kyiv Region 868

Territorial Medical Association of the Ministry of Internal Affairs of Ukraine in the Dnipropetrovska

Oblast 868

Tessenei Hospital 215

Tetiiv Central District Hospital 868

Tet Lan Hospital 538

Tetteh Quarshie Memorial Hospital 275

Teule 793

Texas Children's Global Health 15, 221, 354, 425, 465, 641, 655, 784, 839

Tezena 245

Thái Bình Hospital 909

Thai Hoa Hospital 908

Thai Nguyen C Hospital 908

Thakek Hospital 419

Thakurgaon District Hospital 43

Thakurgoan BGB Hospital 43

Thamine General Hospital 538

Thẩm mỹ viện Hoàn Mỹ Cần Thơ 909

Thandaunggyi Township Hospital 538

Thanh Binh Hospital 908

Thanh Ha General Hospital 908

Thanh My Commune Health Station 908

Thanh Nhan Hospital 908

Thanh Vu Medic Bac Lieu General Hospital 908

Thanlyin Military Hospital 538

Tha Thi Kho Hospital 538

Thaton District Hospital 538

Thayet Township Hospital 538

The Bank Hospital 275

The Hospital of Traditional Medicine – Rehabilitation of Binh Thuan Province 908

The Indus Hospital, Korangi Campus 635

The Indus Hospital – QFNST Campus, Lahore 635

Thellgone General Hospital 538

Therapeutic Building of the Sarny CDH 868

The Rock Hospital 275

The Salam Centre for Cardiac Surgery 758

THET Partnerships for Global Health 238, 531, 784, 839, 922

The Tropical Disease Hospital Omdurman 758

The Trust Hospital (SSNIT) 275

Thien Nhan Hospital 908

Thika Level 5 Hospital 397

Think Humanity 839

Third Cherkasy City Ambulance Hospital 868

Third Children Hospital in Bishkek 410

Third State Central Hospital (Shastin Central Hospital) 499

Third World Eye Care Society (TWECS) 238, 354, 389, 555, 573, 655, 784, 895

Thiri Sandar Hospital 538

Thiri Thu Kha Specialist Hospital 538

Thirumalai Charity Trust - TCT 354

Thmor Koul District Referral Hospital 114

Thoi Lai District Hospital 908

Thong Nhat Dong Nai Hospital 908

Thong Nhat Hospital 908

Thonze Station Hospital 538

Thot Not Hospital 908

THQ Hospital 635

THQ Hospital Chak Jhumra 635

THQ Hospital, Fort Abbas 635

THQ Hospital Gujar Khan 635

THQ Hospital Kel 635

Threefold Ministries 573

Three Roots International 238

Thu Duc City Hospital 909

Thukha Htilar Hospital 538

Thukha Kwe Hospital 538

Thyolo District Hospital 469

Thyroid Cancer Survivors' Association, Inc. (ThyCa) 655

Thyroid Ghana Foundation 267

Tiba Foundation 389

Tibati Baptist Health Center 129

Tidjikja Hospital 476

Tienschinecam 129

Tigoni Level 4 Hospital 397

Tikapur Hospital 563

Tikur Anbass General Specialized Hospital 245

Tilahar Old Hospital 563

Tilganga Institute of Ophthalmology (TIO) 32, 57, 239, 267, 354, 531, 555

Tilottama Hospital 563

Timmy Global Health 605

Timor Children's Foundation 799

Tiny Tim and Friends 922

TIP Global Health 684

Tipitaka Çakkupala Eye Hospital 538

Tirunesh Dibaba Hospital 245

Tito Asibiti 614

Tkachenko Cardiology, cardiology and ultrasound diagnostics 868

TMJ Hospital 793

Together! ACT Now 465

Together for Ghana 267

Tokmok Territorial General Hospital 410

Tokmok Territorial Hospital 410

Toledo City General Hospital 672

Tomorrow Come Foundation 239

Tongibari Upazila Health Complex 43

Tophill Hospital 397

Tores Central City Hospital 868

Tor Hailoch 245

Toro General Hospital 614

Tororo Hospital 845

Total Health Africa 784

Toto Care Box 389

Touch Foundation 784

Touching Lives Ministry 389, 555

Touch of Grace 714

Towama Old Town Hospital 718, 747

TPC Hospital 794

Traditional Medicine Hospital 538, 909

Traditional Medicine Hospital of Phu Yen Province 909

Traditional Medicine Pham Ngoc Thach 909

TRA General Hospital 909

Training for Health Equity Network (THEnet) 555, 627, 655, 754

Trạm Bảo Hành Kangaroo 909

Trạm Xá 909

Trạm xá xã Đa Tốn (Da Ton commune clinic) 909

Trạm y tế 909

Trạm Y tế Hòa Thuận 909

Trạm Y Tế Phường 7 Quận Phú Nhuận 909

Trạm Y Tế Phường An Phú 909

Trạm Y Tế Phường Phúc Đồng 909

Trạm Y tế P. Xuân Khánh 909

Trạm Y tế Xã Mỹ Khánh 909

Trạm Y tế Xã Nghĩa Hương 910

Trans-Atlantic Relief Medical Foundation 852

Transparent Fish Fund 111, 417, 531, 895

Transplant Links Community (TLC) 190, 267, 555, 605, 641, 937

Trauma and Emergency Silah Tebbi 758

Trauma Center of Khmelnytsky Branch 868

Trauma Centre & Hospital Harare 941

Tra Vinh City General Hospital 909

Tree of Lives 389

Trieu An Hospital 909

Trinh Foundation Australia 895

Trinity Hospital 469

Trinity Woman and Child Hospital 672

Trishuli Hospital 563

Trostyanets Central District Hospital 868

Trung Tam Bac Si Gia Dinh Da Nang 909

Trung Tâm Chăm Sóc Sức Khỏe Sinh Sản Tỉnh Bình Thuận 909

Trung Tâm Chẩn Đoán Y Khoa Medic (Hòa Hảo) 909

Trung Tâm Dân Quân Y Côn Đảo 909

Trung Tâm Điều Dưỡng Người Bệnh Tâm Thần Thủ Đức 909

Trung Tâm Giám Định Pháp Y 909

Trung Tâm Sức Khỏe Sinh Sản Hải Phòng 909

Vinnitsa Central District Clinical Hospital 869
Vinnitsa City Clinical Hospital #2 869
Vinnitsa City Clinical Maternity Hospital #2 869
Vinnitsa Regional Clinical Highly Specialized
   Endocrinological Center 869
Vinnitsa Regional Clinical Hospital of War Veterans of
   Vinnitsa Regional Council 869
Vinnytsia City Clinical Hospital #3, Center of Primary
   Health Medicine #4 869
Vinnytsia District Sanitary and Epidemiological
   Station 869
Vinnytsia Regional Children's Clinical Hospital 869
Vinnytsia Regional Pirogov Clinical Hospital 869
Viqueque Hospital 801
Virgen Milagrosa Medical Center 673
Virginia Commonwealth University: Family Medicine
   & Epidemiology Global Health Program 327, 938
Virginia Hospital Center Medical Brigade 327
Virtual Doctors, The 466, 924
Virtue Foundation 112, 269, 327, 498
Visayas Community Medical Center 673
Vision Aid Overseas 240, 269, 715, 924
Visionaries International 191, 240, 356, 532, 556,
   657, 755, 896
Vision Care 33, 68, 112, 191, 205, 221, 252, 269,
   311, 356, 391, 408, 418, 466, 474, 498, 505, 518,
   532, 556, 606, 628, 744, 764, 785, 800, 841, 876,
   896, 924, 938
Vision for All Foundation 125, 171, 191, 356, 556,
   808
Vision for a Nation 269, 685
Vision for the Poor 89, 269, 311, 574, 606, 685, 841
Vision Health International 328, 574, 786
Vision of Love 744
Vision Outreach International 68, 89, 191, 221, 240,
   269, 311, 328, 356, 365, 391, 574, 587, 606, 641,
   715, 786, 808, 896, 924, 938
Visitation Hospital Foundation 311
Vital Pakistan 628
Vital Strategies 33, 240, 448, 498, 606, 657, 786,
   841
Vitamin Angels 15, 33, 68, 79, 89, 112, 125, 135,
   171, 206, 240, 252, 269, 282, 311, 328, 356, 365,
   391, 418, 425, 438, 448, 466, 498, 532, 556, 574,
   606, 641, 657, 700, 715, 734, 786, 808, 841, 853,
   896, 924, 938
Viva Med Hospital 926
VK Hospital 910
V.L. Makabali Memorial Hospital Inc. 672
VnHOPE Alliance 896
Vodacom Foundation 171, 425, 518, 606, 786
Vodnik Hospital 767
Voices for a Malaria-Free Future 269, 365, 438, 606,
   786, 841
Volodar Central District Hospital 869
Volta Regional Hospital (Ho Teaching Hospital) 275
Voluntary Health Services (VHS) 356
Voluntary Service Overseas (VSO) 33, 112, 221, 240,
   269, 356, 391, 425, 466, 518, 532, 556, 606, 628,
   641, 657, 685, 715, 786, 841, 924, 938
Volunteering in Uganda 841
Volunteer Morocco 505
Volunteers Initiative Nepal (VIN) 556
Volunteers in Medical Missions (VIMM) 328
Volyn Regional Blood Transfusion Station
   M.Volodymyr-Volynsky 869
Volyn Regional Hospital for War Invalids 869
Volyn Regional Medical Oncology Centre 869
VOSH (Volunteer Optometric Services to Humanity)
   International 112, 206, 269, 312, 328, 391, 448,
   488, 556, 574, 701, 786, 841
Vovchansk Central District Hospital 869
Voznesenska District Hospital 869
VP Komissarenko Institute of Endocrinology and
   Metabolism of the National Academy of Medical
   Sciences of Ukraine 869
VRA Hospital 275

VT SEVA: Volunteering Together for Service 356
Vwawa District Hospital 794
Vynohradiv District Hospital 869
Vyshniv City Hospital 869
Vyzlova Hospital #1 of Darnytsia Station 869
Waad Specialist Hospital 758
Wabag General Hospital 643
Wachat Jivitadana Sanga Hospital 538
Wachet Jivitadana Sangha Hospital 538
Wai Bar Gi Specialty Hospital 538
Wajamama Wellness Center 786
Walewale Hospital 275
Walkabout Foundation 206, 269, 282, 312, 356, 391,
   438, 466, 557, 628, 685, 715, 755, 786, 841
Walk for Life 33
Walk Nicaragua 574
Walung Community Health Clinic 482
Wamba Catholic Hospital 397
Wamba Hospital 397
Wa Municipal Hospital 275
Wangdicholing Hospital 59
Wanted Life Hospital 245
Wao District Hospital 673
Wapda Hospital 635
Wapda Hospital Gujranwala 635
WAPDA Teaching Hospital Complex 635
War Memorial Hospital 275
Washie Hospital 275
Washington Nepal Health Foundation (WNHF) 556
Wasso Hospital 794
Water and Healthcare Foundation (WAH) 112
Watsi 112, 126, 171, 240, 269, 312, 391, 467, 557,
   606, 657, 715, 734, 786, 841, 924
Wau Teaching Hospital 736
Waves of Health, The 841
Wax and Gold 240
Waziri Shehu Gidado Hospital 615
Wealth By Health Steps For Change Foundation 112,
   356, 532
We Care for Humanity (WCH) 33, 191, 391, 557,
   628, 657, 745, 815, 841
WeCARe! Foundation 641
We Care Missions, Inc. 606
WEEMA International 240
Weill Cornell Medicine: Center for Global Health 312,
   356, 786
Welcare Hospital Limited 43
Welfare Hospital 615
Wellbeing Foundation Africa 606
Wellness Hospital Pvt. Ltd. 563
Wellness Hospitals And Diagnostics Limited 615
Wells Bring Hope 587
WellShare International 786, 841
Wenchi Methodist Hospital 275
Wesleyan Hospital 315
Wesley Guild Hospital, Ilesa 615
West Africa Fistula Foundation (WAFF) 715
West African AIDS Foundation 269
West African Education and Medical Mission
   (WAEMM) 715
West African Health Organization 79
West African Health Organization 365, 587
West Bengal Charity Foundation 357
Westend Extension 941
West End Hospital, PSMI 941
Western Hospital 563
Western Kalinga District Hospital 673
Western Leyte Provincial Hospital 673
Western Pangasinan District Hospital 673
Western Regional Hospital 563
Western Ukrainian Specialized Children's Medical
   Center 869
West-Gobi City General Hospital 499
Westphalian Hospital Complex 275
West Yangon General Hospital 538
Wetlet Township Hospital 538
Wetlu Hospital 538

WF AID 33, 357, 391, 532, 628, 786, 841
Whisper's Magical Children's Hospital 845
White Ribbon Alliance, The 33, 357, 392, 467, 557,
   606, 628, 786, 842, 938
Wichita County Medical Alliance 312, 533, 574, 628,
   657, 884
Wilies Mini Hospital 426
Wilkins Hospital 941
Willing and Abel 79, 126, 269, 282, 715, 842
Wings of Healing 191, 240
Wings of Hope for Africa Foundation 89, 685
Wipe-Away Foundation 269
Wisconsin Medical Project 252, 269, 282, 365, 392,
   701, 715
Wisdom Hospital 275
Wolayita Sodo University Hospital 245
Women and Children First 33, 206, 240, 328, 467,
   532, 574, 715, 842
Women and Children Hospital – Mawlamyine 538
Women and Children's Hospital 222
Women for Women International 171, 606, 685, 734
Women Orthopaedist Global Outreach (WOGO) 68,
   171, 557, 786
Women's Consultation of the City Clinical Maternity
   Hospital #1 869
Women's Equity in Access to Care & Treatment
   (WE-ACT) 685
Women's Foundation Nepal, The 557
Women's Health and Action Research Center 606
Women's Health to Wealth (WHW) 269
Women's Refugee Commission 16, 33, 89, 143, 171,
   181, 206, 214, 241, 312, 328, 357, 392, 438, 533,
   557, 574, 606, 628, 657, 685, 715, 735, 745, 755,
   786, 842, 924
Word of Hope General Hospital Foundation Inc. 673
World Anaesthesia Society (WAS) 89, 143, 241, 283,
   357, 467, 557, 606, 701, 786
World Blind Union (WBU) 16, 33, 51, 241, 365, 392,
   467, 518, 607, 685, 786, 808, 842, 924, 938
World Cancer Care Charitable Society 357
World Care Foundation 33, 357, 467, 533, 628, 842
World CF 357, 657
World Changing Centre 715
World Child Cancer 33, 126, 269, 392, 467, 533,
   657
World Children's Fund 79, 171, 241, 312, 357, 392,
   438, 467, 488, 518, 533, 607, 628, 657, 715, 735,
   745, 755, 786, 842, 897, 924, 938
World Children's Initiative (WCI) 448, 745, 842
World Compassion Fellowship (WCF) 312, 357, 467,
   574, 628, 657, 685, 842
World Council of Optometry 33, 68, 126, 241, 269,
   312, 357, 392, 557, 607, 657, 745, 842, 897, 938
World Federation of Hemophilia (WFH) 7, 16, 33, 51,
   68, 79, 112, 126, 158, 172, 181, 191, 206, 214,
   221, 241, 270, 328, 357, 365, 392, 401, 408, 418,
   448, 467, 475, 488, 498, 505, 518, 533, 557, 574,
   587, 607, 629, 657, 701, 715, 735, 745, 755, 764,
   786, 809, 816, 842, 853, 876, 897, 924, 938
World Health Organization, The (WHO) 7, 16, 33, 51,
   58, 68, 79, 89, 97, 112, 126, 135, 144, 151, 158,
   172, 181, 191, 206, 214, 221, 241, 252, 270, 283,
   290, 312, 328, 357, 365, 392, 401, 408, 418, 425,
   438, 448, 467, 475, 481, 488, 498, 505, 518, 533,
   557, 574, 587, 607, 629, 641, 657, 685, 690, 701,
   715, 723, 735, 745, 755, 764, 786, 800, 809, 816,
   842, 853, 876, 884, 897, 924, 938
World Health Partnerships 312
World Heart Federation 126, 270, 357, 392, 607,
   629, 755, 787, 897
World Hope International 79, 112, 172, 270, 312,
   328, 357, 438, 518, 574, 629, 641, 657, 716,
   745, 924
World Mate Emergency Hospital 114
World Medical Fund 467
World Medical Relief 16, 33, 51, 68, 79, 112,
   158, 191, 206, 241, 252, 270, 312, 328,